P9-BYC-407

The New York Times

GUIDE TO ESSENTIAL KNOWLEDGE

A DESK REFERENCE FOR THE **CURIOUS MIND**

ST MARTIN'S PRESS NEW YORK

www.stmartins.com

ISBN 0-312-31367-5
EAN 978-0312-31367-8

First U.S. Edition: October 2004

10 9 8 7 6 5 4 3 2 1

For The New York Times:

Administration: Thomas K. Carley, President, News Services; Nancy Lee, Vice President, Business Development; Alex Ward, Editorial Director, Book Development; Mitchel Levitas, Executive Associate.

Featured Writers: Natalie Angier, Sandra Blakeslee, William J. Broad, Jane E. Brody, James Glanz, Linda Greenhouse, Michiko Kakutani, Michael Kimmelman, Stephen Kinzer, Anna Kisselgoff, Steve Lohr, Dennis Overbye, Andrew Revkin, Sara Robinson, Will Shortz, Louis Uchitelle, Hal Varian, Nicholas Wade, John Noble Wilford.

Contributors:

This book was assembled and edited by the staff of Elizabeth Publishing and by a group of academic and professional writers.

Elizabeth Publishing:

General Editor: John W. Wright
Executive Editor: Alan Joyce
Designer: Virginia Norey

Senior Writers and Editors:

Herb Addison (Architecture, Business, Economics); Grant Flowers (Advertising, Print Media, Sports); Colleen Hamilton (Literature); John Major, Ph.D. (Art, World History, Languages); David Major, Ph.D. (Chemistry, Economics, Geography, Religion); Michael Miller (Classical Music, Computers, Photography, Science); Robert Murphy (Literature; Biographies); Lincoln Paine (Geography, History, Biographies); Johanna Stoberock, M.F.A. (Literature, Biographies); Jenny Tesar (Biochemistry, Biology, Medicine, Nutrition).

Principal Contributors:

Christopher Anderson, Ph.D., Indiana University (Radio and Television); Bryan Bunch (Math, Physics); Richard Carlin (Popular Music, Dance); T. Susan Chang (Food); Michael Coffey (Baseball); Susan Doll (Film); Abigail Elbow (Photography); Alice Finer (Mythology, Biographies); Pete Fornatale (Sports); Kurt Hettler (Wine); Michael Kaufmann, Ph.D., San Jose State University (Astronomy); Christine Leahy (Art, Biographies); Gregory Morris (Finance); Edward O'Donnell, Ph.D., Holy Cross College (American History); Robert Sharp (Major Wars); Michael Signer, Ph.D., J.D. (Law); David Sobel (Geology); Murray Sperber, Ph.D., Indiana University (College Sports); Karen Tolchin, Ph.D., Florida Atlantic University (American Literature); Harvey Wiener, Ph.D., formerly of City University of New York and Adelphi University (Writer's Guide).

Contributing Editors: Dianne Condon, Terry Golway, Jeff Hacker, Peter Harper, Elizabeth McCabe, James McCaffrey, Lisa Renaud, Elda Rotor, John Rosenthal, Laura Stickney, Brian Tarcy, Randy Te Velde, Joseph Wiener, Saul Wiener.

Senior Copy Editors: Jerold Kappes, Susan Gamer

Data Entry, Indexing, Proofreading: James Garver, Fred Riccardi, Patti Sonntag

The New York Times
Guide to Essential Knowledge

TABLE OF CONTENTS

Introduction: In Praise of Facts
By John Leonard vi

The Arts

Architecture 2
A Brief History of Western Architecture 2
Non-Western Architecture 12
Glossary of Architectural Terms 14

Dance 17
Ballet 17
Modern Dance 18
Social Dance 19
Times Focus: Balanchine: The Radical in Classical Garb *By Anna Kisselgoff* 21

Film 22
History of Film 22
International Film 30
Glossary of Film Terms 37

Music 40
History of Western Classical Music 40
Musical Forms 53
History of American Popular Music 61
Times Focus: The Man Who Made Jazz Hot: Jelly Roll Morton *By Stephen Kinzer* 70
World Music 78
Musical Instruments 79
Glossary of Musical Terms 81
Music Symbols and Notation 84

Painting and Sculpture 88
History of Art in the Western Tradition 88

Photography 104
A Technical History of Photography 104
Times Focus: Back to the Kodak Moment When Light Was Captured *By Michael Kimmelman* 106
Digital Photography 111
An Art History of Photography 113
Glossary of Photographic Terms 116

Economics, Business and Finance

Economics 120
Economic History 120
Microeconomics 121
Macroeconomics 124
Times Focus: A Way to Break the Cycle of Servitude *By Louis Uchitelle* 127
Development Economics 130
International Economics 132
Times Focus: Why Currency Exchange Rates Matter *By Hal Varian* 133
Glossary of Economic Terms 135

Business 138
A Brief History of Business 138
Advertising 151
Glossary of Business Terms 154

Finance 158
A Brief History of Finance 158
Stock Markets 163
Mutual Funds 166
Glossary of Finance Terms 168

Geography 171
Physical Geography 172
The Continents 174
The United States 185
World Population 188
Oceans 190
Major Seas, Gulfs, and Straits of the World 190
Rivers and Canals of the World 194
Islands and Archipelagos of the World 198
Mountain Ranges 204
Glossary of Geographical Terms 207

History 209
World History 210
Major Wars in World History 253
Times Focus: Is War Our Biological Destiny? *By Natalie Angier* 271
American History 272

Law **293**
A Brief History of Law 294
The American Constitutional System 297
Criminal Law and Civil Law 299
Other Legal Systems 302
Important Supreme Court Decisions 303
Times Focus: The Supreme Court: Federalism After 9-11 *By Linda Greenhouse* 305
Glossary of Legal Terms 308
The Constitution of the United States: An Annotated Guide 313

Literature and Drama **337**
World Literature 338
English Poetry 348
The English Novel 354
American Literature 358
Times Focus: New Wave of Writers Reinvents Literature *By Michiko Kakutani* 366
Popular Literature 368
History of Western Drama 374
World Theater 384
Glossary of Literary Terms 384

Mathematics **389**
History of Mathematics 390
Branches of Mathematics 392
Mathematical Formulas 393
Numbers and Number Systems 396
Probability 398
Glossary of Mathematical Terms 398

Media **404**
Electronic Media 404
Print Media 430

Medicine **435**
A Brief History of Medicine 436
Disease 442
Times Focus: Success Stories Abound in Efforts to Prevent and Control Cancer *By Jane E. Brody* 448
Times Focus: The Hard Facts of Hypertension *By Jane E. Brody* 452
Diagnostic Tests 462
Medications 466

Mythology **469**
Classical Mythology 470
Mesopotamian Mythology 479
Egyptian Mythology 480
Norse Mythology 481

Philosophy **483**
History of Western Philosophy 484

Religion **495**
Judaism 496
Christianity 498
Islam 506
Hinduism 508
Buddhism 511
Other World Religions 513
Glossary of Religious Terms 518
The Bible 519

SCIENCE AND TECHNOLOGY

Astronomy **529**
History of Astronomy 530
Techniques of Astronomy 532
Contents of the Universe 534
Glossary of Astronomical Terms 545
Times Focus: "Dark Energy" May Be Splitting the Universe *By Dennis Overbye* 547

Biology **548**
History of Biology 548
Times Focus: How Did Life Begin? *By Nicholas Wade* 550
Taxonomy 551
Basic Life Processes 551
Cell Biology 552
The Human Body 556
Times Focus: How Does the Brain Work? *By Sandra Blakeslee* 562
Evolution 565
Genetics 567
Times Focus: The End of Evolution? *By Nicholas Wade* 568
Ecology 570
Times Focus: Managing Planet Earth: Environmental Challenges Lie Ahead *by Andrew Revkin* 572
Biochemistry 576

Chemistry **577**
History of Chemistry 577
The Elements 579
Glossary of Chemistry Terms 591

Geology **593**
History of Geology 593
Historical Geology 594

Physical Geology 597
Structural Geology 598
The Earth in Upheaval 600
Paleontology 602
Times Focus: Seven Million Year Old Fossil Pushes Back Human Origins *By John Noble Wilford* 604
Physics 605
History of Physics 605
Times Focus: What Happened Before the Big Bang? *By Dennis Overbye* 607
Times Focus: Demolition Derby of Physics Jars Loose Clues on Subatomic Glue *By James Glanz* *612*
Basic Laws of Physics 613
Subatomic Particles 617
Glossary of Physics Terms 619
Times Focus: Zillions of Universes? Or Did Ours Get Lucky? *By Dennis Overbye* 623
Psychology 625
Areas of Psychological Research 625
A Brief History of Psychology 625
Disorders 628
Common Treatments 631
Technology 633
History of Significant Technologies 633
Times Focus: Human or Computer? Take This Test *By Sara Robinson* 645
History of Computing 646
Times Focus: Teaching Computers to Work in Unison *By Steve Lohr* 657
Glossary of Computer and Internet Terms 659
History of Home Video Games 666
Times Focus: Does Science Matter? *by William J. Broad and James Glanz* 668
Sports 671
Baseball 672
Basketball 686
Football 697
Ice Hockey 710
Golf 717
Tennis 725
Soccer 734
Horse Racing 739
Olympic Games 745
Times Focus: When the Games Began: Olympic Archaeology *by John Noble Wilford* 752
Track and Field 753
Boxing 756
Swimming 760
Auto Racing 763

A Reference Library

A Writer's Guide 768
Languages 801
Crossword Puzzles 805
How to Solve the *New York Times* Crossword Puzzle *By Will Shortz* 805
Concise Crossword Dictionary *By Will Shortz* 806
Nations of the World 813
U.S. States and Cities 861
Awards & Prizes 883
Weights and Measures 921
A Dictionary of Food 925
Wine: A Primer 940
Guide to Nutrition 948
Biographical Dictionary 955
Index 1073

INTRODUCTION: IN PRAISE OF FACTS

BY JOHN LEONARD

"I grow daily to honor facts more and more," wrote Thomas Carlyle to Ralph Waldo Emerson in 1836, "and theory less and less. A fact, it seems to me, is a great thing—a sentence printed, if not by God, then at least by the devil." Twenty-four years later, T.H. Huxley wrote to Charles Kingsley in a similar frame of tactile-mindedness: "Sit down before fact as a little child, be prepared to give up every preconceived notion, follow humbly wherever and to whatever abyss nature leads, or you shall learn nothing."

Indeed. Every theory is a seedless grape, whereas even the humblest fact is still a thumbtack, pinning something down. Theory melts away like the morning mist. Fact, like a dog, is always there when you want a wag. Many years ago, I dragged my then-small children to the opening of a brand-new museum in Manhattan, the Guinness World Records Exhibit Hall in the concourse of the Empire State Building, whose simple purpose was to celebrate nothing but raw fact—the quiddity pure and self-contained, its own essence and subtlety, what-ness and is-ness in perfect accord, standing in no relation to anything else, not even wisdom and goodness; simply true.

And I loved all of it just as much as the kids did: the replicas of the tallest, fattest, longest, and smallest; the closed-circuit TV screens for every sports feat known to mammals; representations of the costliest canine (Shar-pei, the Chinese fighting dog at $10,000 per all four legs) and the now-extinct $100,000 bill (with Woodrow Wilson on it like a wanted-poster mugshot); a brief account of a 30-minute war between Zanzibar and Great Britain, a park ranger's hat and shoes struck five times by lightning, a swarm of locusts almost the size of the state of Delaware, and a button to push that activated an X-ray of the esophagus of a sword-swallower.

To be sure, even back then, they had commercialized this quiddity with a gift shop ready to take orders for Dixie cups, T-shirts, parlor games, and crossword puzzles, not to mention mink-lined golf shoes with ruby-tipped gold spikes, at $6,500 a pair. But the gift shop seemed a small price to pay for learning that the approximate number of different chess games was astronomically higher than the number of atoms in the observable universe. That the annual defense budget of Andorra was $5. That "the lowest nightclub in the world" was the Minus 206 in Tiberias, Israel, on the shores of the Sea of Galilee, 676 feet (206 meters) below sea level. That 33.1 per 100,000 Hungarians had committed suicide in 1971 versus 0.04 Jordanians per 100,000 in 1970. That the record for stone-skipping on a water surface was 21, including plinkers and pitty-pats, and that the longest-living rodent was the Indian crested porcupine, with a life expectancy of 22 years.

Well yes, W.S. Gilbert did remind us in *The Mikado* that "Her taste exact/ For faultless fact/ Amounts to a disease." But not as many innocent people seem to perish of this disease as they have on the ramparts and in the trenches of theory and faith. While most of us would agree with Salman Rushdie in *Haroun and the Sea of Stories* that the world is full of things we haven't seen in person but nevertheless believe in, like Africa, submarines, kangaroos, pagodas, Mt. Fuji, and the North Pole, as well as the past ("did it happen?") and the future ("will it come?"), we are also asked to believe in the ferocious existence of such specters as the Invisible Hand, the Laffer Curve, and sperm-sucking alien invaders. "A thing is not necessarily true because a man dies for it," said Oscar Wilde, who was not necessarily wrong because he was Oscar Wilde.

"Buy the truth, and sell it not," Proverbs XXVIII 23 reminded us back in 350 BC. Far from making fun of odd and sticky facts, I cherish them. In a tawdry time of blue meanies and nameless dread, it is a comfort rather than a casus belli to know the world's records for pole-sitting, plate-spinning, pogostick-jumping, chicken-plucking, and fastest psychiatrist in the West (50 patients a day); to meet a seven-foot earthworm, a 90-pound (predried) wool sponge, and a Brown Swiss cow named Ivetta who gave her owner 13,607 pounds of butterfat in 4,515 days; to be told that the longest serious novel ever written was *Men of Good Will* by Jules Romains (27 volumes in French), the longest serious poem the *Mahabharata* (three million words in Sanskrit), and the longest word in literature lopadotenachoselachogaleokranioleipsanodrimpotrimatosilphioparomelitokatakechymenokichlepikossyphophattoperisteralektryonoptekephalliokigklopleiolagoiosiraiobaphetraganopterygon (from Aristophanes's *The Ecclesiazusae*—a fricassee of 17 sweet and sour ingredients including mullet, brains, honey, vinegar, pickles, marrow, and ouzo).

You won't find any of this information in the book you are about to browse, because that would be cheating. What will you find? If I had my absolute preference for a book of knowledge, I'd like the one everybody in Neal Stephanson's 1995 science-fiction novel *The Diamond Age* ran around trying to steal. Called *A Young Lady's Illustrated Primer*, this "propaedeutic enchiridion" came with its own power pack, a voice-recognition interface, "smart paper" computer pages, "nanoreceptors" to measure the reader's pulse, and a database of epic poems, fairy-tale quests, myths and legends that amounted to "a catalogue of the collective unconscious." Until you could read it on your own, it told you stories in a lovely contralto, even while you slept, about what you dreamt. Designed to grow up alongside feisty four-year-old girls, it encouraged heroic behavior and subversive thinking.

Not possible, not yet. Alternatively, there is the ancient but forceful means of communication and instruction mentioned by the Soviet turncoat Victor Sheymov, in his memoir *Tower of Secrets*. Sheymov's KGB instructor explained "one of the earliest techniques for concealing a message. First, the sender had to write the message on the freshly shaved head of the messenger. Then, after his hair grew long enough to cover the message, the messenger was dispatched to his destination. Having arrived, his head was shaven again, chopped off for extra security, and delivered to the addressee on a silver platter." While such labor-intensive invisible writing is probably authorized by some spymaster somewhere, it would waste an awful lot of messengers.

The editors of *The Times* have done the next best thing to nanotechnology and decapitation. What you will find here, first of all—unspoken but corporeal, a kind of timbered housing—is the firm conviction that the world we live in can be seen, heard, touched, tasted, measured, and inscribed, including "did it happen?" and "will it come?" That, no matter what we are told by deconstructed agnostics about reality itself, there is genuine blood out there among the problematics—authentic dirt, deep time, secret police, footprints and bone deposits, prayer mats and astrolabes, bare ruined choirs and human genomes. The men and women gathered by *The Times* to canvass what we know about ourselves actually believe they can tell us stories in which intelligent action and moral purpose are made coherent.

This is a welcome surprise. It is still fashionable among our higher faculties to suspect that everything in the data drizzle and the magnetic flash is equally weightless or trivial, that all books, films, ads, television shows, baseball cards and music videos are socially constructed compost heaps of previous texts, at best unwilling stooges and at worst bad-faith purveyors of the usual dominant discourse, and that each of us, Chicken Little or Tiny Tim, is the helpless vector of forces we can't even locate, much less modify. And it is still obligatory for the poster boys of postmodernism in the unreadable quarterlies and in the blogosphere to put on warpaint, a terrorist ski mask or a social-bandit game face before hang-gliding off on toots of vandalism, bricolage, and mediascape pastiche. Over and over, these Geronimos of consumer violence have explained that the little narratives of causality and continuity, of gunpowder and the fork, are a hoax; that the master narratives of class struggle, scientific progress, the sorrow songs, and the Oedipus complex are bankrupt; and that all meaning is lost in cyberspace, in those digit havens of the matrix where everything is virtual and everything is contingent and there is no gravity and there is no grace.

Against such strut and fret, *The Times* proposes a work of reference that needs no batteries, a wireless box of words organized according to principles as old and obvious as the first almanacs (Poor Richard's, Farmer's, de Gotha), atlases (Titans and maps), and Books of the Dead (Egyptian, Tibetan); as orderly as alphabets, with more of a nod to such stalwarts as the concordance, the encyclopedia, the glossary, the grammar, the incunabulum, the opuscule, the syllabus, the thesaurus, and the vademecum than any obeisance to remote control of the TV set or double-clicking the World Wide Web; and so old-fashioned as to have checked these facts before their publication, although whether the "Astronomy" section has caught up with Stephen Hawking's change of heart on black holes, I can't tell you. "Dictionaries are like watches," Samuel Johnson once explained; "the worst is better than none, and the best cannot be expected to be quite true." If we didn't think we could learn from and improve on the past, we wouldn't bother to get up in the morning and make breakfast for our children.

This is a book guilty of association with rational comment, abstract ideas, compound sentences, the history of human thought, the library of human feelings, home truths and collective memory. So what if, no longer privileged at the display terminal or the plasma screen, you aren't looking down as if from elephants or zeppelins on a discourse of jingles and insults, grunts and ogles, slogans and cliches, brand names and bumper stickers, with multiple views of Paris Hilton in intimate focus or broad scan, and an IV feed of lewd data? At least you won't lose an afternoon and your sanity fighting your way past a site map, a search engine flameout, an atomic clock, a Smithsonian link, a Thought for the Day, a Current Event Topic, a Potpourri and the Quick Find, before dumping your question. Nor will anybody try to sell you a car by promising adventure or to sell you a beer by promising friendship. *The New York Times Guide to Essential Knowledge* is not a game show.

Rather, it endeavors to explain what we know about whatever—Japanese movies, sociobiology, surplus value, mass migration, or Erasmus—as clearly and quickly as possible, with glossaries instead of footnotes. (That is, thumbnail definitions of such key terms as Kuiper Belt and Oort cloud, jump cut and neorealism, habitus and praxis.) It is, on the one hand, what the anthropologists call "thick description," like the 27 volumes of Pliny's first-century AD *Naturalis historia*. But, on the other equally important hand, it is also sort of tool drawer, with a hammer and a chisel, scissors and stapler, wrench and drill, saw and trowel, pliers, screws, extension cord and aspirin tablet—most of what we can imagine needing to fix up the holes in our heads.

THE ARTS

Architecture

A Brief History of Western Architecture 2
Non-Western Architecture 12
Glossary of Architectural Terms 14

Dance

Ballet 17
Modern Dance 18
Social Dance 19
Times Focus: *Balanchine: The Radical in Classical Garb By Anna Kisselgoff* 21

Film

History of Film 22
International Film 30
Glossary of Film Terms 37
The Production Crew 39

Music

History of Western Classical Music 40
Musical Forms 53
History of American Popular Music 61
Times Focus: *The Who Made Jazz Hot: Jelly Roll Morton By Stephen Kinzer* 70
World Music 78
Musical Instruments 79
Glossary of Musical Terms 81
Music Symbols and Notation 84

Painting and Sculpture

History of Art in the Western Tradition 88
Ancient Art 88
Gothic Art 91
Renaissance Art (1400–1600) 92
Baroque Art (1600–1750) 94
Neoclassicism and Romanticism (1750–1850) 95
Realism, Impressionism, and Post-Impressionism (1850–1900) 97
Modernism (1900–1950) 99
Postmodernism (1950–) 102

Photography

A Technical History of Photography ..104
Times Focus: *Back to the Kodak Moment When Light Was Captured By Michael Kimmelman* 106
Digital Photography 111
An Art History of Photography 113
Glossary of Photographic Terms 116

ARCHITECTURE

A Brief History of Architecture

A noted architectural historian stated: "Architecture, in the end, is nothing more, and nothing less than the gift of making places for some human purpose" (Kostoff, 1985, 1995). This almost deceptively simple definition captures the essence of what we call architecture. The definition is broad enough to include the Paleolithic caves inhabited by early humans, the great Gothic cathedrals, and modern Levittowns of hundreds of nearly identical suburban houses.

The characteristics of individual works of architecture reflect this definition and derive from the interplay of three elements that are inseparable from one another: *purpose*, the reason for the building to exist; *design*, the shape that a building takes in response to its perceived purpose; and *structure*, the way the building is put together out of its constituent parts.

Paleolithic Architecture

The earliest known humans who left evidence of their dwelling places were hunters who followed migratory game herds and did not establish permanent living places. They did, however, stay in some locations long enough to seek shelter in caves and build huts to which they regularly returned. These primitive dwellings were the earliest beginnings of architecture.

Caves Beginning around 40,000 years ago in Europe, the modern humans who displaced the earlier Neanderthals began to create domestic and ceremonial spaces in caves that were often elaborately decorated with wall paintings. A typical example is the cave at Lascaux in southwestern France, which was inhabited between 10,000 and 20,000 years ago. Not only does it contain evidence of daily life, but its walls are painted with pictures of animals and humans of exquisite sensitivity; these paintings are assumed to have had religious or magical significance.

Structures The earliest known structures built by archaic humans (*Homo erectus*) are at Terra Amata in southern France, dating to about 380,000 years ago. The site consists of some 20 huts built of branches held in place by large stones arrayed in oval rings. Small groups of people occupied the encampment regularly each late spring, leaving it abandoned until the following spring.

Ice-age huts built of mammoth bones that would have been covered by hides have been found in many sites in eastern Europe, including a famous example at Mezhirich (Ukraine), dating to about 15,000 years ago.

Neolithic Architecture

A warming climate about 12,000–10,000 years ago brought about the end of the last ice age. Improved techniques of managing game herds and harvesting wild plants led to an increase in population, which in turn required more intensive development of food sources. As people began growing crops and domesticating animals they began to form permanent, settled communities.

Dwellings Neolithic people in many parts of the world built small houses of woven tree limbs, pitched roofs, roof beams held up by supporting posts, and walls filled in with mud. In some places the houses were large enough to accommodate numbers of families, and in other places groups of houses were ringed by stones with paths between them defined by rows of stones.

Monuments In parts of western Europe from the Neolithic period through the Bronze Age and into the Iron Age, people built circular or linear arrays of stone (megaliths) of surprising size and complexity. Many of these ceremonial monuments still exist, the most famous of which is Stonehenge, in southwest England. There, from about 2750 to 1500 B.C., successive builders erected enormous stones in circular formations. There are many theories to explain the purpose of Stonehenge. The inner circles open toward a stone over which the sun rises on the summer solstice. The prodigious effort of construction and the elaborate layout of the stones suggest that Stonehenge must have been a ceremonial place central to the builders' culture.

Western Asian Architecture

In the area of the Tigris and Euphrates Rivers in western Asia, Neolithic settlements became larger, wealthier, and socially more complex. With the rise of civilization beginning about 7500 B.C., people gathered together in cities and produced a profusion of impressive architecture.

Western Asian builders invented construction methods that were as important as their architectural forms. An absence of large stones for building—especially for long beams between columns—forced builders to find other ways of covering wide enclosed spaces. These included the round arch built of voussoirs (wedge-shaped stones or bricks) and the dome. In later times arches and domes would become central to some of the great works of architecture.

Towns and Cities The earliest surviving evidence of a town is Jericho on the Jordan River, where settlement began around 7500 B.C. Built largely of mud bricks in successive waves of construction, the settlement already showed traits that would characterize later cities: a population much larger than prehistoric villages, a perimeter wall to defend against enemies, and public buildings set among private dwellings.

Temples and Ziggurats With the growth of cities, organized, state-sponsored religions appeared, and temples became a key element in the urban fabric. From small shrines in prehistoric villages, temples evolved into one of the most striking forms in architecture, the ziggurat. In its classic form, the ziggurat was a stepped pyramid set on a platform with stairs leading to the summit—a place nearest to heaven—where the supreme god was worshipped. The ziggurat of Ur-Nammu in Ur, built around 2000 B.C., is a well-known example.

In the first millennium B.C., temples of the Assyrian Empire (in present-day Iraq) were elaborately decorated with free-standing stone sculptures and narrative sculptural reliefs. One of the finest monuments of late Mesopotamian architecture, the Ishtar Gate of the Babylonian Empire (ca. 575 B.C., now at the Staatliche Museum, Berlin) is made of blue-glazed brick and decorated with reliefs of bulls and other sacred animals.

Palaces As the social order became more complex, the ruler became dominant and palaces began to overshadow ziggurats. Huge palaces were built by the Assyrian kings. Rock-cut tombs and cities of the eastern Mediterranean, such as the city of Petra (in present-day Jordan) show Greek influence, as do the buildings of the Persian Empire, rivals of the Greeks. The palaces of Persepolis (in what is now west-central Iran) are an example of the sophistication and imagination achieved by the Persian architects. Built by Darius (ca.550–486 B.C.) and his son Xerxes (519–465 B.C.), the complex includes both Greek-influenced hypostyle (having roofs supported by columns) temples and palaces and Mesopotamian-style narrative sculptural reliefs.

Egyptian Architecture

At the same time that literate city-states were forming in western Asia, people along the Nile River in northern Africa were also developing an advanced civilization. In contrast to western Asia, there was an abundance of sandstone, limestone, and granite with which to build. This civilization produced architecture of great beauty and power.

Tombs and Pyramids Early Egyptian kings were considered gods, and their tombs reflect the importance of perpetuating their life after death. One of the first architects of record was Imhotep, who designed the pyramid complex at Saqqara in 2680 B.C. as King Zoser's tomb. Equally famous are the three pyramids at Gizeh, built about 2570–2500 B.C. The largest and oldest of these, the pyramid of Cheops, was originally 482 feet high and 760 feet square, and occupies about 13 acres. The manipulation of the huge stones used to build these structures required both the large-scale mobilization of labor and the invention of ingenious engineering techniques.

Temples Later pharaohs were buried in more modest tombs, furnished with sculptures and painted pictorial reliefs. For example, the tombs of Mentuhotep, about 2050 B.C., and Queen Hatshepsut, about 1500 B.C., at Deir el-Bahri, are considerably smaller than the pyramids at Gizeh. The temple replaced the tomb as Egypt's dominant architectural work. The temple of Karnak—dedicated to the sun god Amon—was built in stages over a period from about 1525 B.C. to about 1350 B.C.; Karnak's hypostyle hall is one of the great works of ancient architecture.

Greek Architecture

The architectural building types and orders developed in Greece began a long evolution in European, and eventually American, architecture that continued well into the 20th century. Early Greek building was influenced by the monumentality of Egyptian buildings and the use of columns to achieve a powerful visual effect. But Greek architects brought the hypostyle building to an unprecedented level of beauty and refinement. An abundance of fine-grained native marble provided them with an excellent building material.

Temples The most important and influential Greek building was the temple. Greeks believed in a pantheon of gods, and temples were dedicated to individual gods. The temple form began evolving in the 11th and 12th centuries B.C., took its characteristic form during the period beginning in 700 B.C., and reached a high point of refinement after 400 B.C.

Temples in their final form were set on a stylobate, a rectangular platform of three steps. A peristyle, a row of columns, was placed at the periphery. The columns supported a horizontal entablature. At the short ends a triangular pediment closed the ends of the pitched roof. Within the peristyle was a cella, or naos, a structure that housed a statue of the dedicated god or goddess and associated treasures.

Architectural Orders Greek architects also developed architectural orders called Doric, Ionic, and Corinthian. Each is easily distinguished by its fluted columns.

The Doric order was the first developed, and its column has a simple capital between the shaft and the entablature. The proportion of the width to height is less than in later orders; the effect of a Doric temple is of superbly proportioned solidity. The best known Doric temple is the Parthenon on the Acropolis in Athens (447–432 B.C.), dedicated to the goddess Athena and designed by the architects Callicrates and Iktinos.

The Ionic order denotes a style of columns that have a capital with scroll-like volutes that spread the load where the column meets the entablature. The column is more slender than the Doric, giving Ionic temples a graceful appearance. The Erechtheion (421-405 B.C.) on the Acropolis in Athens, is an example that also includes a porch with carayatids, draped female figures, taking the place of columns that support a roof structure.

The Corinthian order, though not often employed by the Greeks, is distinguished by column capitals with acanthus leaves. The columns are tall and graceful like the Ionic and support Doric or Ionic entablatures interchangeably. One of the few examples is the Olympieion in Athens designed by the Greeks but built by the Romans.

Other Building Types Though the Greek temple became a seminal icon for future architects, the Greeks developed other building types that provided models for Western architecture. The open-air theater, usually carved from a hillside, consisted of an orchestra, stage, and auditorium. The stadion, an athletic arena, was long and narrow, straight at one end and circular at the other, with tiered rows of seats on three sides. Greek democracy was reflected in the agora, an open-air forum where citizens gathered to hear speeches, discuss issues, shop, and socialize. And sometimes adjoining the agora was the stoa, a simple structure, usually long and narrow, with a flat or pitched roof that housed court sessions, shops, banquets, and public gatherings in general.

Roman Architecture

The Romans were great empire builders and equally great architectural builders. As they conquered societies from western Asia to the Atlantic Ocean, they created daring new structures as they shaped their architecture in the service of an imperial society. Roman ideas about architecture are known from the writings of the architect and theorist Marcus Vitruvius Pollio (46–30 B.C.), whose *Ten Books on Architecture* remains one of the most important works ever written on the subject.

Roman architects copied the true arch, using voussior stones, from Etruscan buildings in the north. The arch and its expanded variants were crucial to the prodigious achievements of Roman architects. Extend an arch in a single direction and the result is a barrel vault; a barrel vault intersected by another barrel vault is a groin vault; an arch rotated through 180° becomes a dome. These structural elements are ubiquitous in Roman buildings.

The Italian peninsula provided a variety of building materials, including travertine, tufa, peperino, lava, and marble, as well as sand and gravel. The latter were basic to the Roman invention of concrete, which allowed them to create unprecedented new building forms. Sand mixed with lime and water became very hard and, when shaped by wooden forms, liberated Roman architecture from the limitations of post-and-lintel structures.

Forums The evolution of Roman forums reflects the changes in Roman governance. When Rome became a republic in about 500 B.C., nominally governed by elected representatives, Roman architects adapted the Greek agora for their forums. The Roman Forum in the heart of the city of Rome is the most important of its kind, and its ruins today give a sense of its scope.

As the empire grew through conquest and political power passed from the people to the emperor, later forums were constructed more to impress the populace with the majesty of the emperor than as democratic meeting places. Adjacent to the Roman Forum are the more impressive imperial forums of the Emperors Vespian, Augustus, and Trajan.

Temples Roman temples began by imitating the Greek peristyle, but with columns that engaged the *cella* instead of standing free. Roman architects freely used the Doric, Ionic, and Corinthian orders, even mixing them on the same building. To the three Greek orders, Roman architects added the Tuscan and Composite orders. Tuscan columns had a plain capital similar to Doric, but were not fluted. Composite capitals blended Ionic volutes with Corinthian acanthus leaves.

The Romans were not bound by past examples, however, and created new architectural forms for worship. The Pantheon in Rome is a round structure with a portico and crowned by a magnificent dome that is just over 142 feet across and 142 feet high. The rotunda was constructed in A.D. 120–127 and, though the building has undergone changes over the years, it is in good condition and preserves the impressive feeling of the great space under the dome.

Baths The Romans were fond of bathing, and public baths were important elements of civic architecture throughout the empire. Some were enormous and architecturally complex. The buildings enclosed three main rooms visited sequentially by the bathers—the warm room (Tepidarium), the hot room (Calidarium), and the cool room (Frigidarium). Wide barrel-vaulted ceilings covered many of the rooms, and beneath the floor were systems of ducts that brought hot air from nearby furnaces to heat the rooms.

Theaters and Amphitheaters Other places of diversions for citizens of the Roman Empire were theaters and amphitheaters. Roman theaters were similar to Greek theaters except for the decreasing size of the orchestra between the auditorium and the stage. Roman builders also built free-standing theaters instead of carving them out of convenient hills, as with the Theater of Marcellus in Rome, built in 23–13 B.C.

The amphitheater, either round or oval, with seating surrounding the arena, was a Roman invention. The Colosseum in Rome, completed in A.D. 80, seated 50,000 spectators and is a structure of great complexity, including stairs and aisles to the seats, and a labyrinthine system of rooms and passages under the arena for animals, workers, and machinery.

Aqueducts and Bridges Roman engineers understood hydrodynamics and built large arched aqueducts to carry water across rivers and ravines to large cities throughout their empire. The Aqua Claudio aqueduct (A.D. 38–52) serving Rome is a well-preserved example, as are the Pont du Garde (ca. 19 B.C.) in Nimes, France, and the Segovia aqueduct (ca. A.D. 100) in Spain, in use until the late 19th century. Roman bridges were arched structures similar to aqueducts.

Basilicas Adjacent to most forums were basilicas, which contained law courts and commercial activities. Basilicas were often rectangular, with the length twice as long as the width, and featured a central nave, two or four lower side aisles, and a circular apse at one or both ends with seating and an altar for sacrifices before ceremonies. Two rows of columns supported the nave ceiling, and with four aisles two more rows of columns supported the two-aisle ceiling. Often clerestory windows in the nave walls above the aisles admitted light into the interior. The ceilings were either timber trusses or barrel vaults.

Early Christian and Byzantine Architecture

In the centuries following the death of Jesus of Nazareth the fabric of the Roman Empire began to weaken. As the populace began to convert to Christianity, they needed new places of public worship.

Basilican Churches In contrast to Greek and Roman temples that enclosed statues of the deities while worshipers gathered outside, Christians brought worshipers indoors. For this they developed the rectangular basilican church, a building creatively adapted from the Roman model.

Romans entered basilicas on the long side, but Christians entered their churches through an atrium, an open colonnaded court at the end. Crossing the atrium, worshipers entered the church proper through a narthex vestibule, into a central nave covered by a timber roof where they heard the services. At the far end was a half-domed apse derived from the Roman apse. In front of the apse was an ambo, or pulpit, for Bible reading and services. Early churches were oriented with the apse facing west while the priest faced east toward the congregation. The basilican church became the basis for Christian churches for centuries thereafter.

Byzantine Architecture In A.D. 330, the Christian emperor Constantine I moved the capital of the empire to Byzantium (later called Constantinople, now Istanbul), on the Bosporus Strait. Byzantium offered no good building stones, which forced builders to import marble and other fine stones; it also fostered the use of concrete, which made possible bold new interior spaces.

Byzantine architects found a new expression for Christian worship beyond the rectangular early Christian churches. Borrowing the western Asian dome, they created interiors of soaring spaces. They solved the problem of placing a circular dome over a square space by inventing the pendentive, a triangular piece in the corners to provide the transition between the square and the dome. The outward thrust of the dome was transferred to half-domes at the sides, or to buttresses. Inside, the architects enhanced the effect of the space with glittering mosaics. The supreme example of Byzantine ecclesiastical design is Hagia Sophia, the Church of the Holy Wisdom, in Constantinople; it was designed by the architects Anthemios of Tralles and Isidoros of Miletus, and built in 532–537.

Romanesque Architecture

After the fall of Rome in A.D. 476, the early Christian basilican church underwent gradual changes. Eventually this gave rise to a new form, called Romanesque, that spread rapidly beginning in the 11th century. There was no pure form of Romanesque; each country presented a different culture, available building materials, and climate, that shaped its version of the Romanesque church.

Italy The spatial organization of Italian Romanesque churches is different from early Christian churches, though they continue a basic basilican plan. The atrium is abandoned in favor of a decorative treatment of the western façade leading directly to the narthex. The transept, an intersecting structure at 90° to the axis of the nave, forms a Latin cross with the nave; the chancel is extended beyond the transept, with the apse terminating the central interior space in the east. Rounded arches and wood-trussed ceilings are carried over from early Christian churches, but barrel vaults now frequently replace timber ceilings. Towers are added either attached or separate from the church.

Italian Romanesque churches, with the availability of fine stones such as marble, were often faced in contrasting colorful marbles and had small windows to filter the bright sunlight. A striking example is Pisa Cathedral, built in 1063–1092. The exterior is faced with alternating bands of red and white marble, and the west façade is enlivened with rows of arcades.

France In the south, French Romanesque churches often had only a nave with no aisles, while in the north there were aisles and a nave. Windows were narrow, especially in the sunny south. Saint Sernin in Toulouse, built in 1080–96, is a well-preserved example of southern French Romanesque; the Abbaye-aux-Hommes in Caen, also known as Saint Etienne, built in 1066–77, is a splendid example of northern Romanesque.

Germany German Romanesque churches differ from Italian and French by including more towers, transepts, and apses at both east and west ends. Windows are larger and roofs steeper to shed winter snow. The availability of suitable stone varied with region and resulted in stone construction in some places and brick in others. A fine example of German Romanesque is Worms Cathedral, built in 1110–81.

Gothic Architecture

In the 12th century, political and religious competition played a major role in the development of a new kind of architecture that came to be called Gothic. While Gothic builders produced many important halls and castles, their supreme achievement was in the equipoise of the elements of architecture—purpose, design, and structure—in Gothic cathedrals.

France Gothic architecture began in France. The kings of France sought to consolidate their power over the monasteries that owed their allegiance to the pope, and they wanted an architectural expression different from the Romanesque monasteries. Just north of Paris, Abbé Suger responded by creating the first Gothic choir at Saint-Denis, begun in 1144.

Three structural elements are at the heart of Gothic cathedrals: the pointed arch, the ribbed vault, and the flying buttress. Gothic builders created an entirely new ecclesiastical expression with these structural elements. Walls, freed from having to support heavy vaults, could be much lighter and pierced by large clerestory windows that could rise to the vaults themselves. The ribbed vaulting and flying buttresses allowed the height of the nave to be made higher and higher. The exteriors of Gothic cathedrals were carved in a delicate profusion of statues, windows, and arcades that often combined with towers on the western end to give a sense of verticality to the whole.

The unique power of the Gothic cathedrals, however, was the result both of their structure and of the interior that the structure created. The great height of the naves, with the pointed vaults and clerestory windows, drew the eyes of worshipers upward toward heaven. Multicolored light filtering through the stained glass windows created a feeling of reverence that was enhanced by the biblical scenes in the windows that served to instruct worshipers.

The choir at Saint-Denis was almost immediately emulated as cities in the Île-de-France, the area surrounding Paris, competed to erect higher and more elegant Gothic cathedrals. First was Chartres (1140–1260), followed by Notre Dame in Paris (1163–1235), Rheims (1212–1300), Amiens (1220–1280), and others.

Germany French Gothic soon spread across Europe, and in Germany this often took the form of the "hall church," in which the aisles were the same height as the nave. The Frauenkirche in Nuremberg (1354–61) is an example, as is Cologne cathedral (1248–1880).

Spain Spain enthusiastically embraced Gothic architecture. The result was a number of fine cathedrals and churches in major cities, including Toledo (1226–1493), Burgos (1220–1500), and Seville (1401–1520)—the largest medieval cathedral in Europe.

Italy With a few exceptions, Italy seemed inhibited by its classical heritage and never caught the spirit of French Gothic, beyond employing pointed vaulting and windows. For example, Siena cathedral (1245–1380), with its thick walls without flying buttresses, lacks the Gothic verticality found elsewhere in Europe. Milan cathedral (1385–1485) in the north (closer to the influence of France and Germany) is a notable exception, with its delicate pinnacles, flying buttresses, and high stained glass windows.

England After the Norman conquest in 1066, England began importing ideas, words, and architecture from France. The first Gothic cathedral was erected at Canterbury (1174–1400), designed initially by William of Sens (d. ca. 1180) from France. Many Gothic cathedrals and churches followed, among which are Salisbury (1220–58), Westminster Abbey in London (1245–1740), and York Minster (1261–1324). With their lower vaults, extended choirs, and square apses, English Gothic cathedrals have their own character in the canon of Gothic architecture.

Renaissance Architecture

In the late Middle Ages, scholars began to rediscover the classical writings of ancient philosophers and scientists, and there was a growing humanistic rejection of the medieval world, including Gothic architecture. Architects, now considered artists rather than simply master builders like their medieval predecessors, became individually identified with their buildings; many drew inspiration from the classical models of Greece and Rome, and included rounded arches in their designs.

Italy The problem facing Renaissance architects was to adapt classical models to buildings that did not exist in ancient times. A competition held in 1418 to design a dome to complete the cathedral of Florence that had been begun in 1296 during the Gothic era was won by Filippo Brunelleschi (1377–1446). His design is a masterpiece of blending a Renaissance dome with an Italian Gothic cathedral.

In Rome, St. Peter's Church was begun in 1506 by Donato Bramante (1444–1514). After his death, a succession of architects changed the design several times until Michelangelo Buonarroti (1475–1564) was brought in at the age of 72 to redesign the structure, including the dome.

The Renaissance architect with the longest-lasting influence was Andrea Palladio (1508–1580), who worked in Venice and Vicenza. A number of his villas, including the Villa Capra (1560's)—also known as the Rotonda—set the design for centuries of domestic and public architecture. His influence was also spread by his *Four Books on Architecture*, a theoretical work of idealized buildings that ranks among the most important written works about architecture. In it he implicitly rejected the Gothic style while paying tribute to the Romans—who, he said, "in building well, vastly excelled all those who have [lived] since their time."

France In France Italian Renaissance architecture became the model for a number of châteaux and palaces, including the Palais de Fountainebleau (1528), designed by Gilles Le Breton (1506?–1558). But the transition from Gothic was not always smooth; Saint Eustache in Paris (1532–89), begun as a Gothic church, was finished in Renaissance details, including round arches.

Germany Renaissance architecture came slowly to Germany and had a limited impact there. Heidelberg Castle (1513–1612) had many additions over time that reflect different periods of German Renaissance architecture. Political and religious turmoil in Germany inhibited the building of significant new churches during the 16th and 17th centuries, limiting the influence of the Renaissance style.

Spain Spain's wealth and power rose to its zenith during the Renaissance, and its architects had ample opportunities for major works. King Philip II built the imposing palace of San Lorenzo de El Escorial (1559–84) near Madrid, begun by Juan Bautista de Toledo (?–1567) and finished by Juan de Herrera (1530?–1597). Granada cathedral (1529), designed by Diego de Siloe (1495?–1563), is a fine example of a Spanish Renaissance church.

England Renaissance architecture came last to England, and was practiced while the Continent was entering the Baroque period. Inigo Jones (1573–1652) studied in Italy, especially Palladio's buildings, and his subsequent work strongly influenced English Renaissance design. Jones's Banqueting House in London (1619–21) is a famous example of his work. The Great London fire of 1666 provided Christopher Wren (1632–1723) the opportunity to design many parish churches of ingeniously differing designs, as well as Saint Paul's Cathedral (1675–1710), with its monumental western façade, splendid dome, and barrel-vaulted interior.

Baroque Architecture

The term *Baroque* (possibly from the Portuguese word *barroco*, an irregularly shaped pearl) was originally used to mean grotesque, excessive, or bizarre. Baroque architecture created palaces and churches characterized by elaborate and often fanciful decorative elements.

Churches The great Baroque Catholic churches were designed and built after the Counter-Reformation. Giovanni Lorenzo Bernini (1598–1680), one of the great Baroque architects, asserted that churches should "reach out to Catholics in order to reaffirm their faith, to heretics to reunite them with the church, and to agnostics to enlighten them with the true faith." (Varriano, 1986). Bernini is best known for the magnificent colonnade (1629–62) that forms the piazza in front of the entrance façade of Saint Peter's.

Baroque architects manipulated interior spaces to be more plastic and flowing than ordered Renaissance spaces. Using stucco, an inexpensive and infinitely malleable material, they created free-flowing surfaces and elaborate decorations that would have been too expensive to carve in marble and other fine stonework.

Francesco Boromini (1599–1667) was one of the most daring in manipulating spaces. His church of San Carlo alle Quattro Fontane (1638–41) in Rome, with its oval plan, curvilinear walls, and dome that flows up from the walls, is a superb example of Baroque architecture.

Palaces and Gardens French Baroque architecture was expressed most characteristically in palaces and their associated gardens. Until the late 17th century, the Louvre in Paris was the king's official residence, and successive kings enlarged it, joined it to the Tuileries palace, and extended an elaborately planned garden, designed by André Le Notre (1613–1700), along the banks of the Seine. The buildings themselves were restrained and classic—hardly the Baroque of Italian churches—but their relationship to the extended garden created a new sense of transition between the city and the palace.

When King Louis XIV decided to move his main residence to Versailles in 1677, he greatly enlarged the existing palace into the largest in Europe. He also engaged Le Notre to lay out the gardens. The palace and gardens, with their enormous scope and subtle symmetry, became the model for palaces throughout Europe, such as the Hermitage and other palaces along the Neva River in Peter the Great's new Russian capital of St. Petersburg.

The Baroque was succeeded by the Rococo style, even more refined and decorative and often incorporating chinoiserie and other exotic elements. A noted example is Frederick the Great's summer palace, Sans-Souci (1745–47), at Potsdam.

18th- and 19th-Century Architecture

The Age of Enlightenment—led by philosophers and who relied on the power of reason to challenge accepted values and beliefs—had a profound and lasting impact on architecture. No longer were architects and their patrons certain about the immutable models of the Greek, Roman, Gothic, or Baroque builders. Architects of the Enlightenment created a welter of movements, revival styles, and schools that vied with one another for supremacy.

One such movement was neoclassicism, which stripped excess ornament from Baroque forms to reveal their basic geometric power. A related movement in Great Britain was the 18th-century Georgian style of domestic architecture, championed by the brothers James Adam

(1728–92) and Robert Adam (1730–94); notable examples are the terraced houses at Bath and the New Town district of Edinburgh. The first half of the 19th century also saw a Gothic revival, given legitimacy in the English Houses of Parliament (1835–70) by Charles Barry (1795–1860) and Augustus Welby Northmore Pugin (1812–52). In Germany the Gothic revival resulted in the scrupulous completion of Cologne cathedral in the 19th century from medieval designs.

Classicism was not dead during this period, but it took new forms. An important impetus to rethinking classicism was the École des Beaux-Arts in Paris, formed after the French revolution in 1789; it taught that classical forms could be adapted to new kinds of buildings, such as bridges and office buildings. Its students, who came from a number of countries, returned home to produce new buildings in the classical manner. Examples are found virtually everywhere in Europe.

Technology Until the 19th century, most large buildings were constructed of stone, masonry, and wood. The Industrial Revolution yielded two new materials of great importance to architects: inexpensive iron, and glass produced on a large scale. When iron became cheaper than masonry, some 19th-century architects recognized its expressive potential. For example, Pierre-François-Henri Labrouste (1801–75) designed the library of Sainte-Geneviève (1838–50) and the Bibliothèque Nationale (1854–75) in Paris using classical Roman forms, but with iron construction and ample glass fenestration.

Probably the most striking iron and glass building of its time was the Crystal Palace in London, designed by Joseph Paxton (1803–65) for the Great Exhibition of 1851. Assembled entirely of cast iron members, standard sheets of glass, and wooden supports, the transparent building showed the world that new kinds of architectural experiences were possible using industrial technology.

The Skyscraper As land prices rose steadily in the heart of rapidly growing cities, there was a need to make maximum use of a given lot. The answer was to build vertically, and the industrial age had provided the means: the development of steel as a construction material, and the invention of the elevator.

The type of building that became known as the skyscraper was born in Chicago, where two visionary architects grappled with the esthetics of tall building design. William Le Baron Jenney (1832–1907) and Louis Henri Sullivan (1856–1924) pushed their buildings up to new heights and clothed them in ways that plainly celebrated their verticality. Sullivan's Wainright Building in St. Louis (1890–91) epitomizes his famous statement that a tall building "must be every inch a proud and soaring thing" (Mumford 1931). The maxim that "form follows function" —that is, the look of a building must be subordinate to its purpose—is also attributed to Sullivan, and was later taken up by 20th-century architects.

Modern Architecture

Architecture at the dawn of the 20th century underwent a seismic change as significant as any in the history of architecture. An American architect and a small group of European architects broke free from historical models and created a new architecture called "modern." This new architecture was enabled by a new material, reinforced concrete, that combined the compressive strength of concrete with the tensile strength of steel and could be shaped into structures that were previously impossible.

Frank Lloyd Wright A seminal modern architect, Frank Lloyd Wright (1867–1959) paradoxically influenced but stood apart from nearly all of his modernist contemporaries. After serving an apprenticeship with Louis Sullivan, Wright opened his own office in 1893 and began designing houses in the Chicago suburbs. By the early 1900's, he had developed his distinctive Prairie houses with their open plans arranged around large central fireplaces, and hovering hipped roofs parallel to the ground. The Robie House (1906–10) in Chicago is a masterpiece of Prairie design. Wright also produced two major large works that had a lasting impact on European architects, Unity Temple (1904) in the suburb of Oak Park, and the Larkin Company Administration Building (1903–06, demolished) in Buffalo.

Some of Wright's greatest works—which were at odds with orthodox modernism—came after he turned 60 years old. In the 1930's he surprised the architectural world with Fallingwater (1936–38), a country residence in western Pennsylvania with cantilevered reinforced concrete terraces built over a stream, as well as the curvilinear brick Johnson Wax Building (1936–37) in Racine, Wisconsin. His Solomon R. Guggenheim Museum (1956–59) in New York City, with its spiral exhibition ramp, is a major work realized in his last years.

But Wright's Usonian houses, designed in the 1930's to be affordable to middle-class owners, were perhaps his most important achievement. The Herbert Jacobs House

(1936) in Madison, Wisconsin, was an early example of his method of conserving of space by allowing the living room-dining room-kitchen to flow into one another without walls. Countless tract homes, including the post-World War II Levittowns, later mirrored his conservation of interior space.

Early European Modernists In 1910–11 the German publisher Wasmuth brought out two illustrated volumes of Wright's work that caught the imagination of his European contemporaries. European architects quickly grasped the spirit of Wright's rejection of historical models, his free flow of interior spaces, and the beauty of the sensitively proportioned plain exterior surfaces.

Five significant European architects developed a functional approach to design, using modern materials primarily in large commercial buildings: Peter Behrens (1868–1940), who designed a notable turbine factory in Berlin (1908–09); Otto Wagner (1841–1918), who designed Vienna's Post Office Savings Bank (1904–06); Adolf Loos (1878–1933), who designed Vienna's starkly geometric Steiner House (1910); Hendrik Petrus Berlage (1856–1934), who designed the Amsterdam Stock Exchange (1898–1903); and Auguste Perret (1874–1954), who designed the church of Notre Dame in Le Raincy (1922–24).

Bauhaus and the International Style One of Peter Behrens's young assistants, Georg Walter Adolf Gropius (1883–1969), went on to surpass his mentor in his contribution to modern architecture. His major influence began in 1919, when he founded the Bauhaus in Weimar, Germany, a school that combined craftsmanship with design and brought together artisans, painters, sculptors, and architects.

In 1926 Gropius moved the Bauhaus to Dessau, into a radical new building complex he had designed that was laid out on a pinwheel plan and constructed of concrete, steel, and glass. It became an icon of what came to be called the International Style. The interconnecting buildings were designed to foster the interaction of designers and craftspeople to create mass-produced furniture, utilitarian household objects, and low-cost housing. The ideal of inexpensive mass-produced items was never achieved, but some Bauhaus designs, especially furniture, have ironically become widely sold as luxury items.

The last director of the Bauhaus (appointed in 1930) was Ludwig Mies van der Rohe (1886–1969), born Ludwig Mies. Mies's stature does not rest on his association with the Bauhaus, however, but with his many buildings based on an intense study of new building materials, their esthetic potential, and the plasticity of architectural space. He developed his ideas in a series of houses built over a 10-year period, culminating in the Tugendhat House (1928–1930) in Brno, Czech Republic. The house stands on a sloping site, constructed of concrete and steel, with carefully defined interpenetrating living spaces, and a glass wall facing the view, part of which retracted to open the interior to the air.

In 1938 Mies became director of the architectural department at Illinois Institute of Technology. There he tested his ideas on the simplification of architectural elements that he summed up in his famous phrase, "less is more." The design idiom he developed at IIT and in later buildings, particularly his bronze Seagram Building (1954–58) on Park Avenue in New York City, influenced building design in hundreds of cities in America and Europe.

Le Corbusier Born Charles-Edouard Jeanneret-Gris, Le Corbusier (1887–1965) traveled widely and met many early modern architects. He sought to reconcile his deeply felt responses to their work with the historical works he studied in his travels, particularly Greek temples.

In the 1920's, Le Corbusier found a vocabulary for domestic architecture that resulted in one of the great works of modern architecture, the Villa Savoye in Poissy, France (1928–30). Standing alone in a field, the pristine white house is supported on pilotis, slender concrete columns that carry the load of the floors and free the interior to be developed into flowing horizontal and vertical spaces. In a seminal book, *Towards a New Architecture* (1923), he delivered his notorious dictum, "The house is a machine for living in," but his houses were elegant, with hints of classicism, and far from machinelike.

The New Modernists Classicism and historicism slowly lost the struggle with modernism, and the International Style became synonymous with modernism. After World War II, modern architecture—broadly defined—was the new orthodoxy.

Building on the works of the old masters, a new generation of architects found a wide range of expression within the modern idiom. These architects include Finnish Hugo Alvar Hendrik Aalto (1898–1976), who began in a strict International Style but later softened his work, as demonstrated by the Baker House dormitory (1947–49) at the Massachusetts Institute of Technology; Eero Saarinen

(1910–61), who moved creatively between International Style–inspired designs such as the elegant rectilinear General Motors Technical Center (1948–56) in Warren, Michigan, and the sculptural, birdlike concrete TWA Terminal (1956–62) at Kennedy Airport in New York; Philip Cortelyou Johnson (b. 1906), who worked with Mies on the Seagram Building and established his own modernist credentials with the Glass House (1949) in New Canaan, Connecticut; Minoru Yamasaki (1912–86), who is best known for the twin towers of New York's World Trade Center (1966–73, destroyed); and I.M. Pei (b. 1917), born in China, who practiced in America and found new expressive forms in modernism.

Probably the purest of the new modernists is Richard Alan Meier (b. 1934). Early in his career he established a vocabulary of impeccably white buildings, composed mostly of abstract rectilinear forms, like the Smith House (1965) on Long Island, New York. His Getty Center complex (1989–97) in Los Angeles is the latter-day International Style writ large in a major work.

Beyond Modern Architecture

If modernism, and especially the International Style, had become an orthodoxy following World War II, it was never universally accepted. Though widely practiced in commercial and public buildings, modernism had never caught on in domestic building. Only a few, and usually wealthy, clients could both afford and want to live in the iconic concrete, steel, and glass houses epitomized by Le Corbusier's Villa Savoye and Mies's Farnsworth House. Frank Lloyd Wright, alone among the early giants of modern architecture, continued to produce his sheltering Usonian houses for less affluent clients.

Postmodernism By the 1960's the sense that something important in modernism was missing was captured by Robert Venturi (b. 1925) in his highly influential book, *Complexity and Contradiction in Architecture* (1966). His argument is suggested in his criticism of the esthetic purity of late modernism: "Less is a bore." Lacking, he said, were elements of the ambiguity found in much of historical building, and this lack risked "separating architecture from the experience of life and the needs of society." His book, together with his designs—including his early Guild House (1960–63) in Philadelphia and the Vanna Venturi House (1963) in Chestnut Hill, Pennsylvania— were a catalyst for the movement that came to be called postmodern.

Postmodernism is characterized by often outsized fragments of historical orders (such as arches, broken pediments, and keystones) and other incongruous elements appearing on otherwise plain buildings, creating the kind of complexity and contradiction Venturi admired. Good examples of Postmodernism include Philip Johnson's AT&T building (1979) in New York City, with its Chippendale top above a traditional skyscraper design, and Michael Graves's (b. 1934) Team Disney Corporate Headquarters (1986) in Burbank, California, with Disney's Seven Dwarfs serving as enormous caryatids on the entrance façade.

Skyscrapers The skyscraper continued to evolve during the 20th century, mostly in America, but not in the radical new International Style. Many American architects adopted the Art Deco style—an eclectic combination of Egyptian, Aztec, and other exotic elements—to decorate tall buildings. The Chrysler Building (1928–30) by William van Alen (1882–1954) and the Empire State Building (1930–31) by the firm of Shreve, Lamb & Harmon, both in New York, are conspicuous examples. Rockefeller Center (1929-39) in New York is an arrangement of slablike buildings in restrained Art Deco, designed by a group of leading architects and laid out in a superb urban plan.

In the last decades of the 20th century, skyscrapers began to appear in many cities outside the United States, and the competition was on to build the highest in the world. Currently the tallest skyscrapers are the twin Petronas Towers (1992–97) in Kuala Lumpur by Cesar Pelli (b. 1926), designed to reflect the diverse elements of Malaysian culture. But a number of cities, including Shanghai, Tokyo, and New York, are building, or have plans to build, even taller buildings.

Non-Western Architecture

The non-Western world includes a number of architectural traditions that developed largely independently of one another and, until recent times, of European influence. Major religions, particularly Buddhism and Islam, created distinctive architectural styles that transcend national boundaries.

East Asian Architecture

Beginning in the second millennium B.C., China developed a distinctive form of architecture for palaces and other signficant structures. A raised platform was constructed of compacted earth, on which wooden pillars were erected to support a bracket-work roof shingled with tile. The spaces between the pillars were filled in with brick, stucco, or other materials, but the entire load of the building was carried by its pillars. Palaces and temples built in this style were generally laid out on a north-south axis, with doorways facing southward.

The Forbidden City, a palace complex in the center of Beijing, is the best-preserved group of ancient buildings in China. The great beauty of the individual buildings, the relationships of the buildings to one another, the open spaces between them, and the subtle changes in level both outside and inside the buildings, create one of the greatest of all architectural complexes. It was built during the Ming period (1368–1644), although most existing buildings were built or reconstructed early in the Qing period (1644-1911).

Chinese-style pillar-and-bracket architecture reached Japan in the sixth century, with the spread of Buddhism to Japan via Korea. The world's oldest surviving wooden buildings (seventh century), at the Horyuji near Nara, exemplify this style. The Phoenix Hall of the Fujiwara family mansion at Uji is the world's only surviving example of a palace in Tang Dynasty (618–907) Chinese style.

Architecture in the Chinese style coexisted in Japan with an older native style, in which rectangular buildings, often with thatched roofs, are raised above ground level on stiltlike pillars; this style survives principally in Shinto shrines. The characteristic Japanese wooden house, with straw-mat floors and internal dividing walls of paper, is a late development, dating from the 14th century. The 17th-century Imperial Villa at Katsura, near Kyoto, is regarded as the epitome of Japanese domestic architecture.

Japan's military heritage is expressed in castle architecture. Rising above the modern city of Himeji is the handsome Shirasagijo (Castle of the White Heron), a fortress built, and rebuilt, from 1333 to 1618. Several moats protect the outer perimeter, while narrow and twisting alleys—exposing invaders to fire from above—lead to the heart of the complex. The Daitenshu (Main Tower) has five exterior levels but seven stories in the interior.

South Asian Architecture

South Asian architecture began with the great Indus Valley cities such as Harappa and Mohenjo-Daro (2500–1500 B.C.). The evolution of religious belief and associated cultural expression, from ancient and elite Brahmanism to later and more popular Hinduism, gave rise to numerous local forms of Hindu temples devoted to various gods; these characteristically are built from stone or brick and have a tall tower above the main entrance gate. In many parts of India, temples, complete with pillars supporting interior ceilings, have been hewn from solid stone; well-known examples (seventh century) are at Mahabalipuram, in the southeastern Indian state of Tamil Nadu.

As Hinduism spread to Southeast Asia from India, it led to the creation of many monumental works of architecture, such as the temple at Prambanan (ca. 900), in central Java (Indonesia). The finest architectural expression of Hinduism in Southeast Asia is the Temple of Angkor vat in what is now Cambodia. Constructed of sandstone by King Suryavarman II from 1113 to 1150, though not completed during his reign, Angkor vat was dedicated to the Hindu god Vishnu and its central stepped pyramid represented the cosmic mountain Meru. In the 15th century, Angkor fell to invaders and its temples were abandoned.

The coming of Islam to South Asia, and especially the establishment of the Moghul Dynasty in 1526, added an overlay of international Islamic architecture to the older indigenous forms. (See Islamic Architecture.)

Buddhist Architecture

Buddhist architecture originated in South Asia, but developed largely outside the Indian peninsula. Its basic form is the stupa, originally a domed temple topped by a narrow spire; this underwent many transformations as Buddhism spread throughout central, eastern, and southeastern Asia.

The domed stupa is substantially preserved in Buddhist architecture in Southeast Asia, for example the bell-shaped shrines atop the mandala-mountain of Borobudur (central Java, Indonesia, ca. 800). The most spectacular example is the great bell-shaped dome, covered with tons of gold leaf, of Shwe Dagon Temple, on a hilltop dominating the city of Yan'gon (formerly Rangoon), capital of Myanmar (formerly Burma).

In Central Asia and East Asia, the dome of the stupa shrank, and the spire became enlarged, producing the characteristic building known as a pagoda. The Chinese city of Xi'an, once the eastern terminus of the Silk Road, is home to the Daya ta, the Great Wild Goose Pagoda. Originally constructed during the Tang Dynasty in A.D. 652 as a square, five-storied pagoda, it was later rebuilt to seven stories. It is 240 feet tall, constructed of brick, and was built to house Buddhist sutras (scriptures) brought from India by the monk Xuanzang.

Islamic Architecture

The characteristic Islamic building is the mosque, designed to enclose a large space to hold large numbers of people for communal prayers. The usual design, inherited from Byzantine church architecture, is a square building surmounted by a dome. A mihrab (arched niche) indicates the direction of Mecca, toward which worshipers face while praying. Adjacent to the mosque may be a minaret, a tall tower from which the call to prayer is chanted five times daily. Mosques of this basic design (but with local variations of style) followed the spread of Islam across North Africa to Spain, and across Asia to India, China, Indonesia, and beyond.

The first major surviving Islamic building is the Qubbat al-Sakhra (Dome of the Rock) in Jerusalem. It was originally built by the caliph Abd al-Malik in A.D. 692. Octagonal in shape and surmounted by a dome, it is a transitional building between contemporaneous Byzantine architecture and later pure forms of Islamic architecture, and was partly modeled on the Holy Sepulchre in Jerusalem (328–336) built by Emperor Constantine I.

After the fall of Constantinople to the Ottoman Turks in 1453, many important Islamic buildings were built in what is now Istanbul, including the Süleymaniye Mosque (1550–57). Commissioned by the sultan Süleyman I (ca. 1494–1566), the mosque was designed by the court architect Sinan (1489–1578), and is a part of a complex that included theological colleges, schools, a hospital, an alms-kitchen, a bath, and the tombs of its founder and his wife. It is a masterpiece of design, engineering, and construction, and the account books that have survived make it the best documented of the great Ottoman buildings.

In India, the Jami' Masjid (Friday Mosque) in Old Delhi is the largest of the many mosques that were built by its Mughal emperors after successive Islamic invasions and migrations. The emperor Shah Jahan (1592–1666), who also built the Taj Mahal, supervised the construction from 1650–1656 and regularly attended Friday prayers there during his reign. It can accommodate more than 20,000 worshippers for communal prayers. Also in India, at the center of the city of Jaipur, is the City Palace (1727), which combines elements of Mughal and traditional Rajasthan architecture. It is constructed of pink-colored sandstone and matches the rest of the central buildings in this "pink city." Today the Chandra Mahal (Moon Palace) in the City Palace is still the residence of the Maharaja of Jaipur.

African Architecture

The meaning of the word *zimbabwe* has changed over the years, but came to be used to designate the "ruler's court" or "house"; the largest of all was Great Zimbabwe in what is now the country of Zimbabwe. Though first settled by A.D. 500, the great stone walls and mud buildings by which the site is best known were built in the 14th and 15th centuries and had an estimated population of over 10,000. Scholars believe the stone walls were not for defense but were symbols of the ruler's power. Beginning in the 15th century Great Zimbabwe declined and was eventually abandoned.

In Ghana the remaining Ashanti (or Asanti) traditional buildings are the last examples of the once great Ashanti civilization. The Ashanti reached their height in the 18th century and in the 19th century fought the British colonizers in battles that largely destroyed their villages. Made of earth, wood and straw, the remaining buildings near the city of Kumasi are vulnerable to the elements.

Indigenous American Architecture

At its height in the sixth century A.D., the city of Teotihuacán, near present-day Mexico City, had an estimated population of 200,000 and was the sixth most populous city in the world. It was laid out on a grand scale along the north-south Avenue of the Dead with the Pyramid of the Moon at the north end and the Temple of Quetzalcóatl at the south end. East of the Avenue of the Dead, and just north of the intersection of the East and West Avenues, is the largest structure, the Pyramid of the Sun, which faces west toward the setting sun. The city collapsed in the seventh or eighth century and its population apparently dispersed.

The city of Uxmal in northern Yucatán, Mexico, is considered by many scholars to be the finest work of Mayan architecture. It is in the Puuk region and flourished from about A.D. 800 to 1000. The conquering Spanish gave its buildings names that do not correspond to their use in Mayan times. Notable among these are the Pyramid of the Magician, the Nunnery, the Governor's Palace, and a ball court. The complex was laid out to emphasize sight lines between the buildings and to align with astronomical phenomena, including the setting sun on the summer solstice. The Mayans abandoned the site following the Spanish conquest in the 16th century.

Set in a spectacular site in the southern mountains of Peru, Machu Picchu was built by the Inca in the 14th and 15th centuries. Scholars differ on the exact purpose of the site, but its size and the sophistication of its construction indicate its importance in Inca civilization. The inhabitants were supported by agriculture on a series of terraces irrigated by an intricate system of channels and canals to direct rainwater to the fields. After the Spanish conquest in the 16th century the city was abandoned, but was rediscovered and excavated in the 20th century.

In southwestern Colorado, most of the cliff dwellings at Mesa Verde were built by the Anasazi ("ancient enemies") culture from A.D. 1230 to 1240, though they had been living in the area for 500 to 1000 years. They built multiroomed living structures in the eroded cliff sides below a mesa and cultivated the land on the mesa. Their cliff dwellings and structures elsewhere on canyon floors are considered the most elaborate and sophisticated Native American architecture. In the late 13th century the Anasazi abandoned the site for reasons that are still not understood.

The Acoma pueblo in northwestern New Mexico is one of the oldest continuously occupied villages in the United States. It sits atop a mesa and is believed to have been inhabited for a thousand years. In 1598 its original buildings were destroyed by Spanish invaders, but were rebuilt in the early 17th century. Today it is inhabited by families who pass the right to live in individual dwellings down through their youngest daughters.

Glossary of Architectural Terms

agora open area for assemblies, meetings, and markets in ancient Greece.

aisle division of the main structure of Roman basilicas and Christian churches into lateral areas adjacent to, and on both sides of, the nave.

akropolis group of main temples on an elevated section, or hill, in ancient Greek cities.

ambo pulpit or stand in Early Christian or Byzantine churches used for readings.

amphitheater outdoor theater, either round or semicircular, with tiered seats for the audience.

apse semicircular, polygonal, or square end of a Roman basilica or Christian church.

aqueduct means of channeling or carrying water; arched Roman aqueducts carried water over rivers and valleys.

arch curved structure that spans an opening and is usually formed by voussoirs; see *corbeled arch*.

arcade series of arches carried on columns; can be attached to a wall or freestanding.

atrium court with open roof; in Roman houses it included a basin to catch rainwater; in Early Christian churches, a forecourt with colonnade leading to the church entrance; in modern times often a glass-covered interior.

auditorium in an amphitheater, the circular or semicircular area of tiered seats for the audience.

barrel vault continuous semicircular ceiling.

basilica Roman meeting hall with high central nave, clerestory windows, apse, and often side aisles, used for law courts, meetings, and other assemblies; adapted in Early Christian churches; see *basilican church*.

basilican church early Christian church based on the basilica with central nave and clerestory windows, two or four side aisles, an apse at one end, and covered with a timber roof; the basilica remained a basic Christian church building type until modern times.

broken pediment pediment that has a gap where the apex would be.

buttress heavy structure against a wall that carries the outward thrust of a vault or dome down to a lower support or the ground.

cantilever beam or other structural member that projects past its support at one end and is free at the other.

caryatid sculpture of a figure, usually a draped female, used in place of a column.

cathedral church where the bishop presides; other churches in the bishop's area of authority are subordinate.

capital highest part of a column where it meets the entablature; design reflects different architectural orders.

cella room in a classical temple that houses the statue of the god of that temple; same as the Greek naos.

chancel extension of a Christian church, usually beyond the transept, that includes the choir and apse.

choir area in the chancel, usually immediately beyond the transept, in which the choir is seated; can also mean the entire chancel.

Classical architecture architecture of ancient Greece and Rome; also applied to later buildings based on Greek and Roman forms.

clerestory windows windows in the walls of a nave that rise above the roofs of the side aisles.

cloister covered and often colonnaded structure in monasteries, with open courtyard in the center, that is reserved for monks or nuns.

colonnade row of columns supporting a beam, entablature, or roof structure.

column cylindrical vertical support member; see *post*.

composite order combination of Corinthian and Ionic orders; the capital combines acanthus leaves and scroll volutes.

concrete structural material composed of cement, water, and aggregate, that can be cast in a multitude of shapes; see *reinforced concrete*.

corbeled arch arch constructed of horizontal stone layers in which each layer projects beyond the one below until they meet at the top of the arch.

Corinthian order Greek order with slim fluted columns and capitals decorated with acanthus leaves.

crossing space created in a basilican church where the nave is intersected by the transept.

cupola small dome, sometimes on a top of a larger dome.

dome circular convex structure that covers an interior space; sometimes mounted on a drum; semicircular domes often cover apses and can also act as buttresses.

Doric order Greek order with sturdy fluted columns and plain capitals.

drum circular or polygonal wall that supports a dome or cupola.

elevation projection of a building from one side onto a vertical plane showing the arrangement of windows, roof, etc.; see *plan* and *section*.

entablature horizontal structure supported by columns in classical architecture.

entasis slight convex swelling of the sides of classical columns to counteract the optical illusion that a column with straight sides is slightly thinner in the center than at the top and bottom.

fenestration windows.

fluting vertical grooving of columns and pilasters.

flying buttress detached vertical structure adjacent to vaulting that arches over to the main structure at the point of outward thrust from the vault and carries the thrust down to a lower support; a feature of Gothic cathedrals that permits thin walls and large clerestory windows; see *buttress*.

forum open square in ancient Rome used for assemblies, meetings, and business; often surrounded by a colonnade with adjacent basilica and temple.

groin vault ceiling structure that is formed when one barrel vault intersects another.

hall church church in which the side aisles are as high, or nearly as high, as the nave.

hypostyle room with roof supported by rows of columns.

Ionic order Greek order with slim fluted columns and capitals decorated with scrolls, or volutes.

lintel horizontal beam supported by columns, as in post and lintel construction.

mosaic small, usually rectangular pieces of colored glass or stone set into walls by plaster or mortar and arranged in designs or pictures.

mosque Muslim holy building.

narthex anteroom or vestibule spanning the full width of the building at the entrance to an Early Christian church.

nave in Roman basilicas the central section higher than the side aisles and illuminated by clerestory windows; in Christian churches the central section from the entrance to the transept that is usually higher than the side aisles and illuminated by clerestory windows.

naos Greek name for the room in a classical temple that houses the statue of the god of that temple and other treasures; same as the cella.

Neolithic the "New Stone" Age beginning in about 8000 B.C., when polished stone tools appeared, settled agricultural communities were formed, and animals were domesticated.

orchestra in ancient Greek and Roman theaters the circular or semicircular area in front of the stage; often used for singing and dancing that accompanied performances on the stage.

orders in classical architecture, the design of columns and entablature according to defined models. See *Doric, Ionic, Corinthian, Composite,* and *Tuscan* orders.

Paleolithic the "Old Stone" Age that began when the first crude stone tools appeared about 750,000 years ago.

pediment originally the triangular structure closing the end of a pitched roof of a classical temple; later used to describe any crowning structure over a door or window; see *broken pediment*.

pendentive curved triangular piece in the corners of a square or rectangular space that forms the transition to a circular drum or dome.

peristyle row of columns that surrounds the outside of a structure such as a temple or the inside of a courtyard.

piazza open paved area in a city surrounded by buildings or other structures.

pilaster flat column attached to a wall, usually for decorative purposes.

pilotis columns that support the main structure of a building above the ground, with the ground level left open; often used by Le Corbusier.

plan projection of a building or other area onto a horizontal plane showing the arrangement of rooms, walls, doors, etc.; see *elevation* and *section*.

portico covered entrance supported by columns.

post vertical support member like a column; see *post and lintel*.

post and lintel construction system consisting of columns supporting beams.

refectory dining hall in a religious or secular building.

ribbed vault vaulting that is supported by a system of ribs that support the ceiling between the ribs.

reinforced concrete concrete with steel bars cast in the places where external loads force the concrete to be in tension; the bars absorb the tension, which concrete cannot; elsewhere the concrete absorbs the compression resulting from external loads.

section view, or projection, of a building as if it were cut by a plane vertically or horizontally, showing interior spaces and structure.

stage raised structure in a theater behind the orchestra on which the performance takes place.

stoa roofed portico in ancient Greece with columns in the front and a wall at the back.

stucco plaster material that can be molded into a multitude of shapes; important in Baroque and Rococo buildings.

stylobate raised platform, usually the top step, of a temple or other structure on which the columns are placed.

transept structure that crosses the long axis of a church at 90°; on one side of the crossing is the nave and on the other the chancel.

truss rigid structure made of interlocking triangular members used to span open spaces; early trusses were of timber while later trusses were of iron, steel and other metals.

Tuscan order Roman order with slender columns and plain capitals, without fluting.

vault elongated arch that forms a ceiling or roof.

volute scroll-like form used in the Ionic order.

voussoir wedge or triangular shaped stones that form arches or vaults; see *corbeled arch*.

ziggurat stepped pyramid in ancient western Asia set on a platform with stairs leading to the summit where the supreme god was worshipped.

DANCE

Dance is one of humankind's earliest forms of expression. Early dance was associated with religious ritual, and we also know that the Greeks and Romans included dance in their theatrical presentations. World dance is a vast subject, covering everything from theatrical traditions to "folk" dances of various cultures. This overview will focus on the history of dance performance from the 18th century to today.

Ballet

Webster's Dictionary defines ballet as "an artistic dance form based on an elaborate formal technique, characterized by gestures and movements of grace, precision, and fluidity." Ballet dates back to the 16th-century French courts. In 1581 Catherine de Medici brought a group of Italian dancers to the court to provide entertainment for a wedding; the spectacle was called *Le Ballet Comique de la Reine* (The Comic Ballet of the Queen). Based on the kind of performances given in Italy since the Renaissance, ballet caught on as a favorite court entertainment in France. For its first 100 years ballet was performed by male courtiers as an amateur entertainment.

In 1661 French king Louis XIV—a major supporter of ballet—established an Academie de Danse to train professional ballet dancers, appointing Jean-Baptiste Lully (1632–87) its first director; women also entered the profession at this time. In 1588 Thoinot Arbeau's book *Orchésographie* was published, the first French book on ballet technique, and in 1725 Pierre Rameau's *Dancing Master* outlined the "five positions," the basics of ballet technique. The last great 18th-century book on ballet, *Letters on the Dance* by Jean-Georges Noverre, appeared in 1760, emphasizing the importance of dramatic movement. In 1786 choreographer Jean Dauberval created *La Fille Mal Gardée*, the first ballet with a plot drawn from "peasant" life, and the oldest ballet still in the repertoire.

Meanwhile, news of the development was spreading through Europe. After making a tour of Europe in the late 17th century, Czar Peter the Great returned to Russia and began a process of introducing the contemporary arts to his homeland. French ballet teacher Jean Baptiste Lande came to Russia, and in 1738 established the first school there, the Imperial Theatre School in St. Petersburg. Several French masters followed in his wake, and the seeds of the great age of Russian ballet were planted.

The nascent United States did not miss out on the craze for ballet. As early as 1735, ballet troupes performed in the American colonies. The first ballet produced in the U.S. was staged by Alexander Placide and his wife in Charleston, South Carolina, in 1791, followed a year later by an entire season presented by them in New York. The first American professional dancer, John Durang, said to be George Washington's favorite, appeared in this production.

The 19th century was the heyday of the Romantic ballet. Dance technique had matured to the point where truly expressive, plot-driven works could be created. These techniques were summarized in Carlo Blasis's landmark 1820 work, *An Elementary Treatise Upon the Theory and Practice of the Art of Dancing*, which was published in Milan. Blasis taught in Italy, France, and England, spreading the technique. In 1832 Italian choreographer/dancer Fillipo Taglioni's ballet *La Sylphide* appeared, generally accepted as the first Romantic ballet. It featured his daughter, Marie, in the lead, establishing the importance of the prima ballerina as the "star." Marie popularized dancing on point (some credit her as the originator of the technique). It was followed by a second great Romantic work, *Giselle*, in 1841, starring another great Italian ballerina, Carlotta Grissi.

The Romantic ballet dancer Fanny Elssler spread the new style far and wide. In 1840 she toured the United States, making the bold (for the time) choice of partnering with an American dancer, George Washington Smith; the tour helped build an audience for dance in America. Eight years later, she traveled to Russia with dancer Jules Perrot, and they were an immediate sensation. Perrot remained in Russia, where he would head the Maryinsky Ballet for a decade. He was succeeded by another Frenchman, Arthur Saint-Leon, who remained in Russia from 1858 to 1870, and then returned to France, where he created the last great

Romantic ballet, *Coppélia*. That same year, Marius Petipa traveled to Russia to head the Maryinsky Ballet; there, in 1892, he created *The Nutcracker*, by far the most popular ballet in the world today.

By the early 20th century, the great patrons of the Romantic ballet—the courts of France, Russia, and Italy—were no longer able to sponsor lavish productions and the associated schools. Meanwhile, changes in the art world were bringing new ideas to dance makers, who were rejecting the artifice of the 19th-century plots and the highly stylized dancing that accompanied them. Key to the new movement was a Russian ballet producer named Sergei Diaghilev (1872–1929). In 1911, he brought his company, Les Ballets Russes, to Paris, and a revolutionary new style was born. Diaghilev sought out the greatest modern artists to create sets and costumes for his dances—including Leon Bakst, Pablo Picasso, and Henri Matisse—and contemporary musicians—Igor Stravinsky, Sergei Prokofiev, Maurice Ravel, Claude Debussy, and Erik Satie—to create dynamic new scores. He also nurtured the careers of great dancers and choreographers, including the troubled dancer Vaslav Nijinsky (1890–1950), his sister Bronislava Nijinska, and master dance makers Mikhail Fokine, Leonide Massine, and George Balanchine. Diaghliev's production of *The Rite of Spring* (*Sacre du Printemps*; choreography by Nijinsky, music by Stravinsky) famously inspired riots on its premiere in Paris in 1913.

Modern ballet in America has its roots in the vision and persistence of one man: dance critic and promoter Lincoln Kirstein (1907–96). While still a student at Harvard in the early 1930's, Kirstein began dreaming of creating an American ballet company. In 1933 he first engaged Russian émigré choreographer George Balanchine to open the School of American Ballet, followed a year later by establishing a related company. Others had similar ideas, and new companies sprang up through this period, notably in San Francisco (in 1933), Chicago (The Littlefield Ballet, a year later), and New York (American Ballet Theatre, in 1937). After several false starts, Kirstein and Balanchine established the New York City Ballet in 1948, still one of the world's great ballet companies. Balanchine would create many notable dances for the troupe. New York became a center for dance-making in the post–World War II years. In 1954 the Joffrey Ballet gave its first performance, and in 1971 the Dance Theatre of Harlem—directed by ex-New York City Ballet dancer Arthur Mitchell–premiered.

By the end of the 20th and beginning of the 21st centuries, ballet was facing new challenges and absorbing new techniques. Most notably, ballet and modern dance—after a century of being pitted against each other as rivals—were moving closer together, in both spirit and actual productions. The work of modern dance maverick Merce Cunningham (b. 1919)—once shunned even by progressive audiences—was staged by companies such as American Ballet Theatre, an acknowledgment of the similarities between Cunningham and the ballet masters. Younger choreographers such as Mark Morris freely combine the influences of world dance, modern, and ballet, and do not feel inhibited by any of these categories.

Modern Dance

In the early years of the 20th century, in a reaction to the sentimental plots and exaggerated movement style of ballet, a few dancers, primarily in America and Germany, began experimenting with more "natural" movement styles. In America Isadora Duncan championed a return to a pseudo-classical dance style, featuring free-flowing tunics, bare feet, and movements based on what she imagined Greco-Roman dance to have been. Like Duncan, Ruth St. Denis created exotic dances based on her ideas of what world dances styles—notably Egyptian dance in her famous solo, "Incense." A third dancer, Loie Fuller, experimented with oversized costumes, bathing herself in dramatic stage lighting; she became a favorite among French audiences in the teens and 20's, inspiring Art Deco artists to create "Loie Fuller lamps" and other objects.

In Germany choreographer-dancer Mary Wigman (1886–1973) pioneered a dance style that mirrored the Expressionist movement in theater and the arts. Her angular, dramatic poses expressed deep-seated emotions. The powerful theatricality of her style would be passed on by her students, most notably Hanya Holm, who became a leading choreographer in the 1930's after she moved to the United States

Ruth St. Denis had the longest-lasting impact on modern dance because, along with dancer/husband Ted Shawn, she formed a dance company and school, known as Denishawn, in the mid-teens. Two of their most talented students became the leading choreographers of the next generation: Martha Graham (1894–1991) and Doris Humphrey (1895–1958). Graham is better remembered today, but both Graham and Humphrey were leaders in the modern dance world in the late 20's and 30's. Graham was a dramatic dancer who absorbed the psychological interests of Wigman in dances like her "Primitive Mysteries" (1935), featuring a set by sculptor Isamu Noguchi. Her 1944 work "Appalachian Spring" (with music by Aaron Copland) is recognized as one of the masterpieces of modern dance. Humphrey, with her dance partner Charles Weidman, explored everything from movements drawn from nature ("Life of a Bee") to the dangers of fascism ("With My Red Fires").

Humphrey's legacy was continued after World War II by her student José Limón (1908–72), while Graham continued to actively perform and choreograph through the mid-60's. Graham also nurtured the careers of dancer/choreographers Erick Hawkins (1909–94), Merce Cunningham, and Paul Taylor (b. 1930), all of whom led major companies beginning in the 1950's. Carrying on the legacy of Hanya Holm was Alwin Nikolais (1910–93), who began staging his artfully theatrical dancers—featuring music scores, costumes (often with elaborate masks and body extensions), and sets by the choreographer—in the 1950s. His lead dancer, Murray Louis (b. 1926), also became a leading choreographer. But it was Cunningham—along with his partner, composer John Cage—who had the strongest impact on successive generations of dancers. In the early 1960's, a group of dancers in New York, primarily working out of the Judson Church, carried Cunningham's vision further to encompass even freer, more naturalistic movement. Among these young choreographer/dancers were Twyla Tharp (b. 1941), Yvonne Rainer (b. 1934), Meredith Monk (b. 1942), and Steve Paxton (b. 1939).

Beginning in the mid-70's, ballet and modern dance began moving closer together. George Balanchine shared many of the same concerns as the modern choreographers, and the divisions that seemed to exist between the two techniques began to fade. Twyla Tharp began choreographing for American Ballet Theatre, and that same company also staged some of Cunningham's landmark works, notably "Summerspace." American choreographer William Forsythe began a two-decade-long association with the now defunct Frankfurt Ballet in the 80's, but his work was very modern in style and concerns, despite this association.

Social Dance

Social dance in America goes back to the square dances, jigs, and reels that were imported by the European colonists. In the mid-19th century, French quadrilles became popular—elaborate series of dances that were always performed in a fixed order. Similarly, the craze for Eastern European polkas and waltzes was imported to America beginning in the mid-19th century through succeeding generations of immigrants.

However, truly indigenous American dance styles—like most great American art forms—were mainly derived through the wedding of European and African-American traditions. The first true American dance style was probably clog dancing, which evolved from Irish step dancing and African-American dance styles that imitated animal movements. By the minstrel era of the 1850's, dances like the buck-and-wing were adopted by blackface performers, probably based largely on dances performed by slaves. Later in the 1880's and 90's, the craze for the cakewalk—based on plantation dances by slaves imitating (and satirizing) the dances of their European masters—was another unique American style born of this cross-cultural interchange.

However, like many originally African-American art forms, it took a pair of white dancers—British-born Vernon Castle and his American-born wife, Irene—to popularize African-flavored dances in the early 20th century. They developed a dance called the fox-trot, with music provided by their (African-American) bandleader, James Reese Europe, which launched the craze for "animal" dances in the later teens and 1920's: the turkey trot, bunny hug, and countless others. The Charleston, with its syncopated 4/4 rhythm, became the most popular dance craze of the jazz age 1920's

Meanwhile, black vaudevillians had developed clog dancing into a new style, which became tap dancing. In the teens and 1920's, virtuosic dance teams developed many elaborate forms of tap, each trying to top the moves of the others. Perhaps most famous and inventive were the Nicholas Brothers, who developed a highly athletic dance style featuring incredible splits, leaps, and slides. Bill "Bojangles" Robinson (1878–1949) was the other leading tap dancer of the day. White tap dancers—most notably Fred Astaire—brought the style to Broadway and eventually to films.

Popular dance reached a height of athleticism in the 30's with the craze for big band jazz and the development of swing dancing, notably the Lindy Hop (named for Charles Lindbergh). Large ballrooms catering to dance enthusiasts sprang up in major cities, and the competition was intense for couples to develop the most intricate movements. The Lindy Hop and jitter bug incorporated precision moves between the male and female performers, demanding a high level of skill.

Latin or Latin-flavored dances were also extremely popular from the early 20th century on. The Argentinian tango was among the first to inspire a wide following, originally in Paris and then—thanks again to Vernon and Irene Castle—in the U.S. in the teens and 20's. Movie star Rudolf Valentino got his start performing his own version of the dance, which established him as a major sex symbol. In the 30's the tango was supplanted by the Cuban rumba, propelled by several popular Cuban-American performers, as well as the popularity of Havana as a playground for the American elite. The 40's brought the samba, popularized by film star (and fruit-behatted) Carmen Miranda.

During the post–World War II era, a new generation of dancers arose. While the older dancers continued to perform the social dances of their youth, albeit in more sedate versions, teenagers—influenced by the growth of rock 'n' roll—adapted more free-form versions of dance expression. Notable dance crazes spawned by the rock revolution included Chubby Checker's landmark "Twist" (with its many variants) in the late 50's and early 60's; followed by a number of even less structured dances, including the frug, watusi, swim, and dozens more. The message was that anyone could dance, and that—on the dance floor—anything goes.

As a backlash against the free-form 60's, the 70's saw a return to more formal and difficult-to-perform dance styles, notably the many versions of disco dances. Dances like the hustle showed strong influence from the ballroom styles of the 50's and 60's, notably the Latin mambo and cha-cha (an American adaptation incorporating several Latin-flavored moves). Arising in the black and gay communities, disco demanded precision movement, athletic capability, and intense dedication. Clubs arose to serve the new dance population, and—again—the dance moved into the mainstream thanks to a white performer, John Travolta, in the landmark film *Saturday Night Fever* (1975).

Meanwhile, African-American youth moved on to an even higher level of precision dancing, in the many styles that began to blossom with the growth of rap/hip hop music. Mobile DJs had their own "crews," including "b-boys" who danced during the musical breaks, giving the new style its name, break dancing. Some dancers developed incredible body control, mimicking the look of strobe lighting on the dance floor in such moves as the Moonwalk (popularized by singer Michael Jackson in the mid-80's). Highly athletic moves—such as performing head spins and "pop locking," in which joints and muscles are manipulated in unnatural ways—became part of the necessary skills for break-dancers.

In reaction to the precision of break dancing, the punk rock movement and its spinoffs (including grunge and garage rock) spawned "dance" forms that involved little or no training. Stage diving–literally jumping offstage into the crowd—epitomized this self-made dance style. The free form ethos of 60's rock dance was carried to its logical extreme in these dance styles.

Many popular singers have made dance an integral part of their presentation, whether onstage or in music videos. Madonna took various club dance styles of the 80's and helped popularize them, notably "voguing," in which dancers "strike a pose" emulating the exaggerated stances of fashion models. Paula Abdul and Jennifer Lopez both began their careers as dancers, and each parlayed her dance skills into a successful singing career. Almost all contemporary rap videos feature at least rhythmic movement, much of it highly sexually suggestive. Again, white stars like Britney Spears have adapted these moves for a broader audience. Spears draws from a variety of sources, paying homage to Michael Jackson in one routine and then moving into the frenetic, video-game-influenced style of contemporary African-American dance in another.

Balanchine: The Radical in Classical Garb

by ANNA KISSELGOFF

"I don't want my ballets laughed at 50 years from now." So said George Balanchine when I asked him if he wanted his works to survive him.

What did he mean? That over time ballets are distorted or modified by dancers and choreographers when their creators are gone? Yes, but more certainly he meant that tastes change, that dancing changes and that, since he choreographed for his time, even if his ballets were preserved in amber, they would not speak to another age.

Very likely Balanchine will be proved wrong. It has been 20 years since he died, and his ballets are performed more widely than ever. Balanchine was one of the greatest choreographers in the history of ballet and one of the 20th century's most innovative artists. To know Balanchine in depth is to know him through his work. His monumental achievement remains relevant for all time.

Moving past Serge Diaghilev's definition of ballet as a synthesis of painting, music and dance, Balanchine insisted that dance was primary. Like an abstract painter concerned with paint, he created nonillusionist art. It was art focused on its own essence. In a typical Balanchine ballet, the material of dance is dance.

To anyone familiar with Balanchine, such concepts are basic truths. More than anyone, he raised choreography in ballet to an independent art. He introduced speed, energy, attack and startling compositional patterns that pushed dance into the space age.

When *Agon*, the milestone Balanchine-Stravinsky collaboration, had its premiere in 1957, the choreographer and Lincoln Kirstein, City Ballet's founders, compared the work in a program note to an I.B.M. computer. (How many people in 1957 knew what a computer was?) Yet in the seminal *Agon* Balanchine also remained loyal to the 350-year-old idiom of classical ballet. He transformed it and extended it into a contemporary language but respected it as a grammar of movement. Unlike Isadora Duncan, Martha Graham, and Merce Cunningham, he rejected the idea of a personalized dance idiom.

Tradition was the springboard for his innovation. That he used toe shoes and a centuries-old vocabulary did not make him old fashioned. Even today his focus on pure dance, steps and structure, is too rigorous for those who demand dance-drama or movement that expresses specific emotion.

It is worth repeating the significant statement Balanchine made upon his arrival in New York in 1933. "Classicism is enduring because it is impersonal." The dance idiom he chose was classical (codified) and impersonal. If Balanchine will indeed remain relevant in other times, it is precisely because he uses this classical vocabulary as both form and content. It is, in fact, enduring.

Can anyone date two of his signature works by looking at them? *Concerto Barocco*, created in 1941 to Bach's Double Violin Concerto, has undergone a series of costume changes. Now stripped of its overdone designs and danced in white tunics for the women and black tights for its sole male dancer, it is arguably Balanchine's greatest and most spiritual work. Streamlined in its clear design but complex in its interplay between music and dance, between soloists and ensemble, it looks freshly choreographed. By contrast *Symphony in C* is a grand tutu ballet. But its partnering and technique are contemporary. It is not, as might seem, one of Balanchine's tributes to the Russian Imperial Ballet.

Balanchine became Balanchine as we know him today in the 1940's. That is, he arrived at his signature style after initial, more rebellious experiments. Tradition, however, was in his training. His family encouraged him to study both music and dance in the Russian academies. After entering the school of the Maryinsky Ballet in St. Petersburg, he was virtually abandoned, when his parents, brother and sister moved to Tbilisi in 1918.

The myth is that Balanchine, as a Maryinsky student, was part of the czar's household. The reality is that his formative years were spent in the maelstrom following the czar's overthrow in 1917. Life was hard but exciting. He lived through the artistic ferment of Russia in the 1920's and choreographed ballets for Diaghilev, for the Royal Danish Ballet, and for English music halls. He had been asked to be ballet master at the Paris Opera Ballet. But in New York he was initially treated as a talented unknown by all but his patron, Lincoln Kirstein. When Balanchine said, "Classicism is enduring," most in the dance audience didn't know what he was talking about in 1933. Now they do.

FILM

History of Film

As popular entertainment, the origins of cinema lie in the magic lantern and shadow puppet shows that had been around as early as the 17th century. Scientifically, its history begins with Joseph Plateau's (1801–83) theories of the persistence of vision (1829) and the stroboscopic effect (1836), which he demonstrated with a device he called a Phenakistocope, an illustrated wheel that when spun gave the illusion of motion. A similar device, the Zoetrope ("Wheel of Life") was invented by William George Horner (1786–1837) in 1834. By the 1870's Eadweard Muybridge (1830–1904) was using banks of as many as 40 still cameras to photograph motion studies of animals. In 1880 he exhibited some of these photographic series with a sort of projecting Phenakistocope that he called a Zoopraxiscope.

The Dawn of Film (1888–1908)

Although several inventors from America, Britain, France, and Germany were working on the idea simultaneously, credit for the invention of the motion picture camera is most often given to the Thomas Edison laboratories. By 1889, Edison's assistant, William Kennedy Laurie Dickson (1860–1937), had synthesized Edison's ideas into a workable motion picture camera, which he called a Kinetograph. He followed the Kinetograph with a device for viewing his short films called the Kinetoscope, a peep-show box with a scope on top. One person at a time looked into the scope to watch the films, which were looped through the machine in 50-foot strips. Powered by a huge electric motor, the kinetograph was large, bulky, and therefore stationary. Many celebrities such as boxer "Gentleman" Jim Corbett and vaudeville performer Annabella the Serpentine Dancer made the journey to the Edison labs in New Jersey to be photographed in a 30-second film.

The Lumières and Film Projection Edison did not believe motion pictures would grow beyond a parlor amusement, so he did not bother to pay the extra $150 for an international patent to prevent European inventors from developing their own versions of the Kinetograph or Kinetoscope. Two such entrepreneurs were the Lumière brothers, Auguste (1862–1954) and Louis (1864–1948), from Lyons, France, who invented their own version of the motion picture camera around 1895. Instead of being powered by electricity, the Lumières' Cinématographe was hand-cranked and weighed only 16 pounds. It was not only a camera; it was also a printer and a projector all in one machine. On December 28, 1895, they held the first paid public showing of projected motion pictures in the Salon Indien in the basement of the Grand Café in Paris. Projection quickly became the format of choice for commercial showings of motion pictures around the world; the obvious advantage was that many viewers could watch the same films at the same time.

The portability of the Cinématographe broadened the content of the Lumière films. They recorded the happenings of life—workers at their jobs, parades in the park, children at play—using simple titles that telegraphed the subject of their 30-second films, such as *Workers Leaving the Lumière Factory*, *Baby's Lunch*, or *Train Arriving at a Station*.

Storytelling on Film Like Dickson, the Lumières simply recorded whatever unfolded in front of the camera, without attempting to tell a story. That step was taken by Georges Méliès (1861–1938), who was already in show business when he began making motion pictures in 1896. He owned the Théatre Robert-Houdin, which specialized in showcasing magicians and mounting plays with supernatural or fantastic narratives. Méliès—ever the showman—discovered simple visual effects such as dissolves, superimpositions, fast and slow motion, and stop-motion animation, then constructed increasingly complicated stories to exploit them. Most of his films were fairy tales or fantasy stories, such as his 1902 adventure *A Trip to the Moon*, in which a group of stuffy scientists journey to the moon. In expanding the storytelling possibilities of the new medium, Méliès gradually increased the average length of a film to one reel—a little less than 1,000 feet, or 12–14 minutes at 16 feet per second (fps)—the standard length until the mid-1910's.

The movies soon outgrew vaudeville houses and one-night traveling shows. The first permanent movie theater in America was Thomas H. Tally's Electric Theater, which opened in Los Angeles in 1902. The Nickelodeon, whose name became generic for these early storefront theaters, opened in Pittsburgh in 1905. The first important American director was Edwin S. Porter (1870–1941), who, while working for the Edison Company, stumbled across the fundamentals of editing when he made *Life of an American Fireman* in 1903. He combined stock footage of a fire engine racing to a fire with staged shots of a mother and child trapped in a burning house, cutting back and forth between the two scenes in such a way as to suggest they were happening simultaneously, a technique later called parallel editing. Later that year, Porter made his masterwork, *The Great Train Robbery*, which contained simple but effective cinematic techniques, including cutting on motion, moving the camera to keep the action centered in the frame, and using diagonal compositions to exploit the depth that only the cinema offers.

D.W. Griffith and the Language of Film (1908–15)

David Wark Griffith (1875–1948) was introduced to filmmaking in 1907, when he acted in Porter's *Rescued from an Eagle's Nest*. He soon left the Edison Company for Biograph, for whom he acted and supplied story ideas. In 1908 he directed his first film, *The Adventures of Dollie*. Between 1908 and 1913, Griffith made hundreds of one-reelers for Biograph in which he developed and mastered the techniques that became the language of film. While Griffith did not invent many of these techniques, he had an instinct for exploiting them to advance the narrative, create drama, and evoke emotion in the viewer.

Innovations in Editing Griffith varied his shots in terms of distance from the camera, carefully dividing his scenes into long, medium, and close-up shots. Each type of shot had a specific function, with close-ups carrying the most emotional weight because they could suggest what a character was thinking or feeling. In addition, Griffith added a deliberate rhythm to the editing of his shots, increasing or decreasing the pacing depending on the content of the scene. Although Porter had been the first to use parallel editing, Griffith became such a master at using it to add excitement to his conclusions that the technique became known as "the Griffith last-minute rescue." He also used a range of optical effects for transitions between shots, including the cut, the dissolve, the fade, and the iris, and he gave each effect a consistently specific function. Ably assisted by the first great cameraman, Billy Bitzer (1872–1944), Griffith innovated techniques and practices still in use today. Collectively, the techniques that Griffith pioneered are known as the classic narrative style, or the classical style.

New Acting Styles Moving the camera closer to the actors necessitated a more realistic style of acting than what was found in most one-reelers at the time. Together with his stable of actors at Biograph, including Dorothy and Lillian Gish, Henry B. Walthall, Lionel Barrymore, and Mary Pickford, Griffith developed a style of acting for film that was more natural and less broad than stage acting.

The Feature-Length Film Inspired by the spectacular historical epics of early Italian directors, including *Quo Vadis* (Enrico Guazzoni, 1912) and *Cabiria* (Giovanni Pastrone, 1914), Griffith began pushing Biograph to let him direct longer films with complex and meaningful stories. When Biograph resisted, he left and joined the Mutual Film Company in Hollywood. In 1915 he directed *The Birth of a Nation*, a three-hour historical epic about the Civil War and Reconstruction that was the culmination of his innovations in film. It was an exciting, artistic use of his techniques, representing his complete control of the medium on a grand scale. Unfortunately, the script was an adaptation of two racist pieces of literature by Thomas Dixon. Griffith's film offered indefensible stereotypes of African Americans while depicting the Ku Klux Klan as the heroic saviors of a defeated South.

The Rise of the American Film Industry (1915–30)

Hollywood European moviemaking was severely curtailed by World War I, and the American film industry soon dominated the world market. The first commercial production companies, such as American Biograph, Vitagraph, and Selig, had been established in New York, New Jersey, and Chicago. Led by Edison, who by now was putting as much energy into patent litigation as he used to put into laboratory experiments, the nine most powerful of these companies attempted to monopolize the production, distribution, and exhibition of motion pictures by forming a trust, the Motion Picture Patents Company (MPPC), in 1909. To escape the MPPC's oppressive business tactics, independent filmmakers moved west as early as 1911. Most of them settled in a sleepy community just outside Los Angeles called Hollywood.

The Studio System The move coincided with the development of more organized business practices, including the studio system, which was started by independent producer Thomas Ince (1882–1924) in 1912. Ince's studio, dubbed "Inceville," was much larger than the production companies based in New York and included administrative offices, shooting stages, permanent outdoor sets, photo labs, and wardrobe warehouses—a method of operation that facilitated the efficient mass production of movies. Instead of writing, directing, and editing himself, Ince hired others who were talented in these areas to execute these tasks. He then oversaw the production of their films, retaining financial and creative control. He also instituted the practices of shooting out of sequence to save time and adhering to strict budgets and schedules. These practices were soon adopted by other independents who established their own studios and became powerful figures by the end of World War I, including Carl Laemmle at Universal Studios and Adolph Zukor at Famous Players-Lasky (Paramount).

New Genres, New Directors Many genres emerged in this period, including the western, the action-adventure film, the romantic melodrama, and the historical/biblical epic. These genres share a sense of scale, larger-than-life romance, and fantasy that were well suited to the silent film—an art form dependent on images, action, and imagination. From these, the western can be singled out because of its cultural significance as America's foundation myth, but also because of its rapid evolution during the silent era. Launched by *The Great Train Robbery* in 1903, the genre at first consisted of cheap shorts shown primarily in small-town theaters. But during the teen years, cowboy star William S. Hart appeared in a series of gritty, serious films that added prestige to the genre. In western epics such as *The Iron Horse* (1924), directed by John Ford, and *The Covered Wagon* (1925), directed by James Cruze, the western developed during the 1920's with mature and substantive narratives.

Mack Sennett (1880–1960), head of the Keystone Studio and producer-director of hundreds of slapstick comedies, developed a style of physical humor that was fast-paced and action-oriented but also character-driven, establishing a tradition of American screen comedy that still survives. Directly or indirectly, he passed this style on to a pantheon of comedians who epitomize the best of the silent era, including Fatty Arbuckle, Harold Lloyd, and Harry Langdon, as well as two others who must be counted among the greatest film artists of all time—Charles Chaplin (1889–1977) and Buster Keaton (1895–1966).

Though specific directors are associated with certain genres, such as Ford with the western, Cecil B. DeMille with the biblical epic, and Erich von Stroheim with the historical drama, many directors were adept in any genre, including Allan Dwan (1885–1981) and King Vidor (1894–1982). Many survived the coming of sound, becoming the veterans who helped the industry bridge the gap between the two eras.

The Star System Despite the great directors of the silent era, films were rarely promoted based on who was behind the camera. Instead, they were sold based on the personalities who appeared in them, an industry practice known as the star system, which had begun in 1909, when the "Biograph Girl" was publicized under her real name, Florence Lawrence. A star's image was a consistent persona or archetype that an actor played repeatedly until the audience associated the actor with it. The stars were under contract to the studios, who used publicity and promotion to showcase the actors' images to attract audiences to their films. Stars provided a way to differentiate films for audiences and a way to boost sales for studios. The star system became so successful that often a film's narrative, camerawork, lighting, and editing were designed around its stars. The great stars of the 1920's included swashbuckling adventurer Douglas Fairbanks, Sr., Latin lover Rudolph Valentino, America's sweetheart, Mary Pickford, and sophisticated lady Gloria Swanson.

Censorship and the Hays Office Civic and religious pressure groups attempted to censor the movies as far back as the 1890's, when some of the vaudeville acts recorded by W.K.L. Dickson featured women in skin-baring costumes. Through the early 1920's, local and state authorities attempted to protect their individual jurisdictions, using censorship systems that were inconsistent, haphazard, and often unworkable. As the film industry grew larger and movies became more popular, religious and civic pressure groups called for governmental censorship at the federal level. Fearful of federal interference of any kind, the film industry embraced self-regulation. The major studio heads established the Motion Picture Producers and Distributors of America (MPPDA) in 1922, and made former postmaster-general Will H. Hays (1879–1954) its president. Hays proved to be an artful speaker and a persuasive public relations man; because of his high profile, the censorship arm of the MPPDA was nicknamed the Hays Office. He temporarily appeased the pressure groups with the Purity Code (1927), known as the "Don'ts and Be Carefuls," for filmmakers to follow.

In 1930 Hays adopted a strict, extensive set of guidelines to regulate onscreen content—the Motion Picture Production Code, coauthored by Father Daniel Lord, a Jesuit priest, and Martin Quigley, a prominent Catholic layman. The code detailed specific suggestions and prohibitions for such topics as crime, sex, profanity, religion, and race. At first, following the code was voluntary for studios, but in 1934, at Hays's urging and under increased pressure from the Catholic Church and other watchdog groups, the MPPDA voted to make the code mandatory for all films from all studios. Hays created the Production Code Administration (PCA), to be headed by Joseph Breen (1890–1965), whose sole purpose was to administer the code.

The Academy of Motion Picture Arts and Sciences

As a trade organization, the MPPDA worked behind the scenes to support and aid the film industry, but the Academy of Motion Pictures Arts and Sciences (AMPAS) chose a more public profile with its stated goal of advancing the cultural, educational, and technical standards of American movies. Initially organized in 1927 to combat the rise of trade unions in Hollywood, the Academy soon settled into its main function, which was the annual presentation of awards for distinguished film achievement. Presented in 1929, the first Academy Awards (also called Oscars) went to *Wings* (William Wyler) as outstanding picture, and *Sunrise* (F. W. Murnau) as best artistic achievement. Emil Jannings was the first to win the best actor award, while Janet Gaynor was named best actress.

Oscar Micheaux and Independent Black Cinema

The history of Hollywood is not necessarily the history of the entire American cinema. Movies produced and directed by African Americans during the silent era provided an alternative to the limited and often racist portrayal of blacks in Hollywood films. Using all-black casts, these films were exhibited through a small circuit of theaters across the South and northern industrial centers that catered specifically to African-Americans. These films and filmmakers operated outside the production, distribution, and exhibition outlets of Hollywood, making them pioneers in the arena of independent filmmaking.

The most enduring independent African-American filmmaker was Oscar Micheaux (1884–1951). His films explored issues of concern to black audiences, including lynching, interracial marriage, and the effects of racism on the black community. Of the 30 or so films attributed to Micheaux, *Within Our Gates* (1920), which featured controversial rape and lynching scenes, and *Body and Soul* (1924), which starred Paul Robeson, are the most acclaimed. While most black-operated production companies folded because of the coming of sound, Micheaux managed to come back from bankruptcy to make *The Exile*, the first synch sound film directed by an African American.

The Coming of Sound (1927–1934)

The Hollywood industry was the first to successfully add synchronized sound to film. Warner Brothers studio produced several synch-sound musical shorts in the mid-1920's before adding a soundtrack to a feature-length film titled *Don Juan* in 1926, consisting of sound effects and orchestrated music but no spoken dialogue. The next step taken by Warner Brothers was to add musical performances to a feature film, which they did for *The Jazz Singer* (1927), starring Al Jolson. For the studio, the focus was on the six songs performed by Jolson; the rest of the film was shot in the silent format. However, for the audience, the attraction was the few hundred unscripted words ad-libbed by Jolson during a scene in which his character jokes with his mother. It was soon apparent that silent films and sound films could not coexist; audiences were simply riveted by spoken dialogue. By 1930, Hollywood was producing only sound movies. Chaplin alone successfully resisted; *City Lights* (1931) and *Modern Times* (1936) contain synchronized sound effects but no dialogue. When Chaplin finally did speak, it was to ridicule Hitler in *The Great Dictator* (1940).

The change from silent to sound films was not easy to accomplish. The expense of changing equipment for the studios and for the theaters was enormous, but other short-term problems also existed: few Hollywood personnel were trained to make sound films; each studio had a backlog of silent movies rendered obsolete by sound; some silent stars with heavy accents could not make the adjustment to talking films; and some foreign markets were lost because they were not interested in films in which the characters spoke English. The biggest problem proved to be the limitations imposed by the poor and cumbersome synch-sound equipment, resulting in talky, static-looking films.

By the early 1930's, these problems were resolved, but the coming of sound had permanently changed production practices from the scriptwriting stage through post-production. Production moved inside the studio for the majority of films, the method and manner of directing actors on the set changed, and dialogue necessitated a different style of acting. No longer entirely dependent on visual techniques to depict the narrative, sound films generally used fewer close-ups and required less editing. While some critics mourned the loss of visual artistry, sound brought an immediacy and spontaneity to the movies that made them more exciting and appealing for audiences.

The Golden Age of Hollywood (1934–1948)

The Studio Era After the problems related to the introduction of sound were resolved, eight studios emerged to dominate the Hollywood film industry. The key to their domination was the vertical control the studios had over the industry, meaning they controlled the means of production, distribution, and exhibition. The five major studios, Paramount, MGM, Warner Brothers, RKO, and Twentieth Century Fox, not only owned their own production facility but also a distribution company and a chain of theaters in the large urban centers. Universal, Columbia, and United Artists, known as the minors, did not own any theaters, but they did produce and distribute their films. Together, these eight studios produced around 80 percent of the feature films released during the 1930's and 1940's, and they took in roughly 85 percent of the total rental income. Each studio produced about 50 feature films per year, a rate of production possible only because of the effectiveness of the studio system.

Producers, Directors, Stars During this period, the average moviegoer was more likely to identify the style of a film with its studio than with its director or even its star. A studio head, such as Louis B. Mayer of MGM or Harry Cohn of Columbia, had ultimate creative and financial control of all films, but the day-to-day management of filmmaking was in the hands of producers. Producers answered directly to the studio head for the slate of films under their control. In general, they oversaw the writing of scripts, assigned directors and stars to films, supervised editing, and kept the process on schedule and under budget. This industrial, hierarchal organization gave each studio its own standardized, corporate identity. MGM, for whom Irving Thalberg (1899–1936) produced such films as *The Crowd* (1928), *Mutiny on the Bounty* (1935), and *The Good Earth* (1937), was known for prestige, glamour, and "more stars than there are in Heaven." Later on, Arthur Freed (1894–1973) produced MGM's glossy Technicolor musicals, including *On the Town* (1949), *An American in Paris* (1951), and *Singin' in the Rain* (1952), all starring Gene Kelly. Val Lewton (1904–51) of RKO oversaw a series of low-budget but acclaimed horror films in the 1940's, including *Cat People* (1942) and *The Body Snatcher* (1945). Warner Brothers was known for gangster films starring James Cagney and Edward G. Robinson, as well as social problem films such as *I Am a Fugitive from a Chain Gang* (1932), while Universal was famous for horror films starring Boris Karloff and Bela Lugosi.

In this producer-dominated system, several directors adapted well enough to the studio system to add distinctive touches to their films, making their work identifiable as their own. John Ford (1895–1973) shaped the conventions of the western into a personal chronicle of American history (*Stagecoach*, 1939); Frank Capra (1897–1991) encapsulated the virtue of the common man and idealized small-town values in his social comedies (*Mr. Smith Goes to Washington*, 1939); Alfred Hitchcock (1899–1980) depicted moral ambiguity in his sharply crafted mystery thrillers (*Notorious*, 1946). Other important directors of the period included Howard Hawks (1896–1977), Preston Sturges (1898–1959), Joseph Von Sternberg (1894–1969), and Dorothy Arzner (1897–1979).

The star system reached its zenith during the studio era, and some stars became icons of the era: John Wayne (1907–79) was the ultimate cowboy hero; James Cagney (1899–1986) the urban gangster; Jean Harlow (1911–37) the blonde bombshell; James Stewart (1908–97) the morally upright everyman; Humphrey Bogart (1899–1957) the hard-boiled private eye; Katharine Hepburn (1907–2003) the independent woman.

Despite the dependence on systems, standards, conventions, and formulas—and perhaps because of them—this period produced a variety of genres. Such diverse films as *It Happened One Night* (1934), *Gone With the Wind* (1939), *The Philadelphia Story* (1940), and *Casablanca* (1942) epitomize the glamour, craft, and appeal of Hollywood. Unfortunately, the system that perfected generic formulae discouraged formal experimentation. An exception is *Citizen Kane* (1941), cowritten (with Herman J. Mankiewicz) and directed by the iconoclastic Orson Welles (1915–85). With its deep-focus photography (by Gregg Toland), chiaroscuro lighting, and expressive camera angles, *Citizen Kane* looked decidedly unlike any other film. Eschewing the linear plot, Welles offered a dark, complex fable of American capitalism and enterprise that featured no big stars and no happy ending. The film failed at the box office and garnered little support from the industry, save an Academy Award for best original screenplay. The very reasons for its failure—not following the systems and practices of the era—are now part of the reason for its reputation as arguably the greatest American film ever made.

Hollywood in Transition (1948–1962)

Fall of the Studio System In 1948 the Supreme Court ruled that certain business practices favorable to the eight major studios, including vertical control and block booking, violated American antitrust laws. Often referred to as the Paramount decree or the antitrust decree, the Court's ruling forced the studios to sell their theaters and to halt block booking (a practice in which the distributor coerced exhibitors into renting additional films in order to get the desired hits). The ruling made filmmaking riskier for the major studios, because they no longer had a guaranteed outlet for every film. As a result, studios began making fewer films and cutting costs.

They stopped financing expensive publicity tours or extensive buildups for new starlets and leading men, dropped many stars from their contracts, and reduced the average length of a contract from seven years to three years. Some stars, such as Burt Lancaster, Kirk Douglas, and Marilyn Monroe, took control of their own images and careers by forming their own production companies.

The Independent Production System The studios also let go of directors and producers, some of whom formed independent production companies, which were not under long-term contract to a studio nor directly involved with distribution. An independent producer or director found a book, play, or story to turn into a script, and then looked for interested stars, thereby putting the project and star together into one deal. He then took the deal to a major studio, which partially financed the film and distributed it after completion. This package-unit system, or independent production system, dominated Hollywood production by the mid-1950's, replacing the studio system of the Golden Age. The major studios were still a force in the industry, but their role became that of financiers and distributors rather than producers.

Freed from the contractual binds of the studios, several producers and directors took advantage of the package-unit system to make their best films. Though visually conventional, the films of Stanley Kramer (1913–2003) are notable for their social content, particularly because the major studios had shied away from controversial topics. *The Defiant Ones* (1958) offered a portrait of race relations while cementing the stardom of African-American actor Sidney Poitier (b. 1927). Poitier's Academy Award nomination as best actor paved the way for other black actors and actresses to secure roles that broke free from the hideous stereotypes of the Golden Age. The dark comic genius of Billy Wilder (1906–2001) peaked during this era in *Sunset Boulevard* (1950), with its masterly written script (by Wilder and Charles Brackett), and in *The Seven Year Itch* (1955) and *Some Like It Hot* (1959), two sex farces starring Marilyn Monroe.

The Impact of Television The television industry expanded rapidly after World War II, and by 1949 the film industry began to lose a large percentage of its audience to television. That year theater attendance dropped to 70 million, down from 90 million the year before. The decline would continue throughout the 1950's, accelerated by the suburbanization of America. Young couples and families began moving to the outskirts of urban centers, where the dominant leisure activities were television, listening to recorded music, children's sports, and bowling. By 1957 the film industry's profits had dropped 74 percent. The film industry eventually made peace with television. Some studios established subsidiaries to produce filmed programming for television; others rented their backlots to television production companies and sold or rented their libraries of film titles to television.

New Film and Projection Technology Color (in the form of hand-tinted prints) and wide-screen technologies, such as the three-screen-wide presentation of Abel Gance's *Napoleon* (1927), had been around since the silent era, but were mainly used for experiments, curiosities, and blockbusters like *Gone With the Wind* and *The Wizard of Oz* (both 1939). Now, in order to draw spectators back into the theaters, Hollywood embraced technology that offered visual experiences audiences could not get on the small black-and-white television screens. For example, color filmmaking increased rapidly at this time, particularly after the introduction of film stocks that were cheaper and easier to use than the standard three-strip Technicolor process. In the Golden Age, 20 percent of films were in color; during the 1950's, 50 percent were in color.

The screen size became bigger and changed shape between 1952 and 1955, when wide-screen processes were adopted by the studios. Cinerama, a wide-screen system that required three electronically synchronized cameras, was introduced in 1952 with the novelty film *This Is Cinerama*. Over the next decade, a handful of feature films were made in Cinerama, but its multicamera setup for production and three-projector system for exhibition proved too expensive and too cumbersome for widespread use. CinemaScope, introduced in 1953 with *The Robe*, became the wide-screen process of choice because it used conventional 35mm film and required only a change in lens. The anamorphic lens squeezed the image onto 35mm film stock during production; then a special projector lens widened the image during projection. Panavision, another anamorphic process, replaced CinemaScope in the early 1960's. Most wide-screen films were recorded in stereo, so the increase in image size was complemented by sound with depth. Ironically, although wide-screen is still the norm, most films today are composed with everything happening in the center of the frame, so that the image can fit easily onto a standard TV screen.

Color, wide-screen, and stereo became permanent changes to the film image, but the studios tinkered with a few technological wonders that were not successful in the long term. A stereoscopic, or 3-D, projection system was introduced in 1952 in *Bwana Devil*, but by mid-1954 the public's interest in 3-D had greatly diminished, largely because the process had been reduced to a gimmick. Also, the awkward glasses that patrons had to wear to make the illusion work were a nuisance and gave some people headaches.

The New Movie Audience Television and suburbanization altered the nature of the movie audience, at least indirectly. Because families and mature adults routinely spent their leisure time at home or in their communities, young adults and teens became the most consistent audience for movies in theaters. In 1956 young adults and teens bought seven-eighths of all movie tickets. For the first time, the industry began to seriously target the youth market, instead of focusing all of their attention on the mainstream market. In the landmark *Burstyn vs. Wilson* case of 1952, the Supreme Court ruled that films were protected by the First Amendment. This decision, along with the demise of the old studio heads, severely weakened the authority of the industry's self-regulated censorship system. In addition, producers and directors no longer under contract to the studios were far less concerned with following the rigid guidelines of the old Production Code, while exhibitors were no longer obligated to show only films with a code seal. As for the new youth audience, if they noticed a subtle change in the content of films during this period, they did not seem to mind.

Hollywood in the 1960's and 1970's

During the 1960's movie attendance continued to decline, and studios released fewer films per year. Senior producers in the studios floundered in the changing industry, and some of them steered their studios toward big-budget, large-scale ventures that seemed out of date compared to the modern styles of European films. By the end of the decade, every studio faced financial difficulties. Many were absorbed by larger, healthier conglomerates, leading the industry to accept and even embrace a corporate mentality. Universal was acquired by MCA in 1962, Paramount was absorbed into Gulf and Western in 1966, and Warner Brothers was bought by Seven Arts in 1967. The studios no longer had a system to foster new talent, increasing the uncertainty over their future.

The American "New Wave" As it turned out, the next generation of writers and directors came from unexpected sources: some, such as Francis Ford Coppola, Martin Scorsese, Brian DePalma, Steven Spielberg, and George Lucas, had attended university film programs; others, such as Robert Altman, Woody Allen, Mel Brooks, Sidney Lumet, and Arthur Penn, had learned how to write or direct by working in live television during the 1950's; and, a few, such as Peter Bogdanovich and Paul Schrader, had written film criticism. Many had been exposed to the new waves and new directions that were part of European and Asian film.

The unique training, artistic predilections, and exposure to world cinema gave this generation a kind of media literacy. They were well versed in the history of film, understood the techniques of the medium, and realized the impact of those techniques on the audience in ways the old studio directors had not. At first dubbed the "New Hollywood," and then disparagingly called "the movie brats," this group of directors has since been labeled the "Film School Generation."

Hollywood's dire financial situation made it open to new ideas, particularly after the release of three films in 1967: *Bonnie and Clyde*, *The Graduate*, and *Cool Hand Luke*. The critical and financial success of these films signaled the arrival of a "new wave" of American filmmakers. In *Bonnie and Clyde*, director Arthur Penn (b. 1922) used several editing techniques generally not associated with continuity editing. His combination of slow-motion photography and montage editing in the climactic shoot-out became a standard technique for the depiction of onscreen violence. In *The Graduate*, director Mike Nichols (b. 1931) used pop songs by Simon and Garfunkel played over wordless scenes to comment on the state of mind of the main character, a use of music that became a staple for this generation of directors. Finally, *Cool Hand Luke*, directed by Stuart Rosenberg (b. 1927), showcased Paul Newman (b. 1925) in the title role as a rebel who is alienated from the social institutions and common goals of mainstream society.

End of the Production Code By the 1960's, enforcement of the Motion Picture Production Code was impractical, and many directors paid little attention to it. Jack Valenti (b. 1921), who became head of the Motion Pictures Association of America in 1966, replaced the code with a letter-ratings system two years later. The ratings system used a series of letters to represent the degree of graphic or adult content in films: G (suggested for general audiences); M (suggested for mature audiences); R (children under 17 not admitted without adult guardian); and X (children under 17 not admitted). The system was designed to alert viewers to the nature of a film's content, rather than prevent them from seeing certain types of material. In theory, the system freed directors to pursue explicit imagery and adult ideas.

New American Classics The Film School Generation produced many outstanding films, such as *In the Heat of the Night* (1967), *Easy Rider* (1969), *The Godfather* (1972), *Dog Day Afternoon*, *One Flew Over the Cuckoo's Nest* (both 1975), *Taxi Driver* (1976), and *Days of Heaven* (1978). They were innovative, entertaining, and daring in form and/or content. Most directors experienced minimal interference from the studios when making their films. They approved the mixing of the soundtracks, inserted all optical effects, determined that all necessary shots and scenes had been included, and approved the final sound mix.

The era of the Film School Generation came to an end because the business side of Hollywood could not endure chaos indefinitely. By the close of the 1970's, many filmmakers were guilty of self-indulgence, driving the budgets and schedules of their films higher and higher in pursuit of their artistic visions. Initially, these directors had gained creative control and power because of the large returns on their low-budget films, but their later films followed the inverse equation, prompting the studios to step in. In 1980 the budget overruns on the western *Heaven's Gate* almost destroyed United Artists, and the industry blamed the situation on the excesses of director Michael Cimino. The film was a financial flop; consequently, executives at all studios became more closely involved with creative decisions. The policy of allowing directors substantial creative control quickly fell out of favor.

The Blockbuster Era (1975–)

Birth of the Blockbuster Many of the industry practices that define the contemporary cinema began with *Jaws* (1975), directed by Steven Spielberg, and were cemented with *Star Wars* (1977), directed by George Lucas. Both films were action-driven narratives fueled by mechanical and special effects, which became blockbusters that attracted youth audiences and set box-office records. Released in July, *Jaws* established summer as the season of action blockbusters. Both *Jaws* and *Star Wars* benefitted from product tie-ins, including T-shirts, mugs and cups, and action figures.

Contemporary Hollywood In the 1980's and 1990's the studios reclaimed their control over the industry. While the studios continued to solicit films from small production companies and produce films in conjunction with them, they exerted more creative control over script preparation, casting, and editing. Studios continued to be absorbed into large corporations: Columbia Pictures was purchased by Sony Corporation; Universal became part of Seagram. Only the Disney Company remained a free-standing, independent entity, though their other holdings (amusement parts, television networks) turned them into a corporate giant as well.

A corporate mentality, in which films are dubbed "products" and series of films are called "franchises," pervades contemporary Hollywood. Unlike the movie moguls of the Golden Age, who had experienced firsthand the many facets of the movie business, contemporary studio executives are recruited from talent agencies, the television industry, or business and marketing programs. They prefer the familiar stories of formulaic genres or projects that showcase popular stars, because those films appeal to mass audiences and inspire repeated viewings. The studios have moved the commercial Hollywood cinema away from the artistic inclinations of the Film School Generation as a way to secure box-office success.

The costs for producing films rapidly increased during this period, due to the high salaries and participation percentages of stars and emphasis on special effects and computer-generated imagery. The marketing and promotion of major studio films also expanded, with marketing costs sometimes equaling and even exceeding the film's initial budget.

To handle the costs of large-scale films that are heavy on action and dependent on special effects, the big studios sometimes cofinance with companies related to the industry, or seek product tie-in deals with toy and fast-food companies.

Independent Filmmakers The emergence of a large independent filmmaking community has become the main source of artistically driven films in the United States. Independent filmmakers generally find the funding for their low-budget, no-frills productions on their own to avoid studio interference. After the film is completed, it is showcased at large and small film festivals in the hopes that a studio or distributor will pick it up for release. Film festivals such as those at the Sundance Institute in Park City, Utah, which was established by actor Robert Redford, and Telluride, Colorado, have become important outlets for new talent.

The success of some independent filmmakers has allowed them to straddle both worlds. Some talented directors, such as Quentin Tarantino (*Pulp Fiction*, 1994), the Coen Brothers (*Fargo*, 1996; *O Brother Where Art Thou?*, 2000), Spike Lee (*Do the Right Thing*, 1989) and Steven Soderbergh (*Traffic*, 2000), began as independents and then gradually moved to big Hollywood studios, where they enjoy more creative control than most directors. Others, including John Sayles (*Lone Star*, 1996) and Jim Jarmusch (*Ghost Dog*, 2000), prefer to make their films completely outside the studios.

International Film

France

Following the pioneering efforts of Méliès and the Lumières, France took the lead in film production during the years before World War I. The stage-bound *Films d'art* were popular around the world. The most important figure in early French film was Louis Feuillade, whose crime serials (*Les Vampires*, 1915) were admired by the Surrealists and the New Wave cineastes for their naturalistic surfaces, dreamlike logic, and subtle eroticism.

During the 1920's, Surrealist and Dadaist artists such as Man Ray and Salvador Dali experimented with the possibilities of film to manipulate time and space or to depict dream states (as in the 1929 Surrealist masterpiece, Luis Buñuel's *Un Chien Andalou*). Simultaneously, a loosely knit group of avant-garde filmmakers gathered around author-editor Louis Delluc (1890–1924) to expand upon the ideas of the various artistic movements centered in Paris. Known as the Impressionists, these filmmakers—Germaine Dulac, Jean Epstein, Marcel L'Herbier, and Abel Gance—were seeking a poetic cinema in which content or story were subordinate to the imagery, or an expressive cinema in which visual techniques were used to depict interior states.

Their work influenced subsequent filmmakers such as Jean Cocteau, René Clair, Jean Vigo, and Marcel Carné to be expressive and distinctive in their styles and themes. Cocteau (1889–1963), for example, was an artist, poet, playwright, and filmmaker who knew some of the surrealist artists and writers. That he was heavily influenced by them is evident in most of his films—from the personal symbolism of *Le Sang d'un Poète* (1930) to the imaginative set design of *La Belle et la Bête* (1946).

Though various artistic movements inspired specific French filmmakers, the style known as poetic realism defined French film of the 1930's. The term implied a skillful integration of two seemingly contradictory ideas—the settings and characters of everyday life combined with a lyrical, expressive visual style designed to evoke a heavy atmosphere of fate and longing. The darkest of the poetic realists was Marcel Carné (1909–96), who collaborated with the surrealist poet Jacques Prévert (1900–77) to produce the most haunting films of the era, *Quai des Brumes* (1938) and *Le Jour se Lève* (1939). Both films showcase legendary French screen star Jean Gabin (1904–76) as a decent man irreversibly trapped by fate, and both favor the low-key lighting and emphasis on mise-en-scène associated with poetic realism.

Jean Renoir (1874–1979), the son of the famous Impressionist painter, became the most celebrated director to emerge from the era. Marginally connected to poetic realism because of the social commentary in his films, Renoir preferred stories that examined class differences or skewered the lifestyle of the bourgeois, as in *Boudu Sauve des Eaux* (1932). As Renoir's commitment to social causes grew, themes involving class issues and politics pervaded his work, including his two masterpieces, *La Grande Illusion* (1937) and *La Règle du Jeu* (*The Rules of the Game*,

1939). During the war, he worked in Hollywood on several films, most notably *The Southerner* (1945). He returned to France in 1954 to experiment with color and motion in his later films. A filmmaker with a strong personal vision and lengthy career, Renoir represented a pinnacle of French filmmaking in the era between the wars.

The French New Wave In the mid-1950's, the directors who made up the new generation of French filmmakers began as film critics, protégés of the great critic André Bazin, and centered on the film journal *Cahiers du cinema*. The group taught themselves world cinema by viewing the whole of its history at Henri Langlois's Cinémathèque Français. In their writings, they tended to attack the French film establishment while championing the films of older master directors such as Renoir and Cocteau. They also appreciated and admired mainstream Hollywood films, singling out films by directors who transcended the constraints of the studio system to forge their own style or vision. By the end of the decade, the Cahiers group had begun to make their own films. They released three award-winning films in 1959: *Les Quatre Cents Coups* (*The 400 Blows*) by François Truffaut won the director's award at the Cannes International Film Festival; *Hiroshima, Mon Amour* by Alain Resnais won the critics prize at Cannes; and *A Bout de Souffle* (*Breathless*) by Jean-Luc Godard won the director's award at the Berlin International Film Festival. The acclaim bestowed on these young directors focused attention on them as a group, prompting the press to dub them *la nouvelle vague* (the New Wave).

Visually, the New Wave sought to achieve the opposite effect of the seamless and invisible classic narrative style. Their films often looked rough, casual, even sloppy. They were shot on location with hand-held cameras, using natural lighting and direct sound. They purposefully played with the possibilities of editing, camera movement, sound, and mise-en-scène. The characteristic most associated with the New Wave was the use of *hommage*, or "quoting" from the films and directors that influenced them. Other important New Wave directors include Claude Chabrol, Jacques Rivette, Eric Rohmer, Jacques Demy, Agnès Varda, and Louis Malle.

More recent French film has seen a return to more conventional narratives and production values, while retaining youthful themes and expressive techniques of the New Wave. Andre Téchiné, Claude Sautet, Claire Denis, Léos Carax, and Olivier Assayas have all managed to impress a personal style onto their provocative films.

Germany

German Expressionism While Hollywood edged closer to a domination of the international motion picture market after World War I, Germany pushed film to a higher level of artistry. The German filmmakers offered a more sophisticated use of mise-en-scène while pursuing a dark subject matter with psychological undertones.

Three types of film dominated German production during the 1920's. Historical/mythological films, such as Ernst Lubitsch's *Passion Madame du Barry* (1919) and Fritz Lang's *Die Niebelungen* (1924), used stylized architectural settings, elaborate costuming, and the calculated blocking of massive crowds to portray history and mythology in spectacular fashion. The opposite of the historical/mythological films, at least in scope, were the "street films," which were intimate studies of working-class life, often set in an entertainment or underworld milieu. Concerned primarily with the personal disintegration of individuals, street films depicted the dark psychological states of the characters. More significant, they made a fuller use of the moving camera. *The Last Laugh* (1924), directed by F.W. Murnau and photographed by Karl Freund, used the moving camera as a narrative tool to introduce the setting and to scrutinize the central character.

Best known were the Expressionist films, which dealt with fantastic or supernatural subjects rendered in low-key and high-contrast lighting styles, obtuse camera angles, and fantastic set designs. A part of the art movement known as German Expressionism, these films attempted to visually depict inner feelings or states of mind. *The Cabinet of Dr. Caligari* (1919), directed by Robert Weine, presents an exaggerated, distorted mise-en-scène to represent the tortured mind of its insane protagonist. *Metropolis* (1924), directed by Fritz Lang, is a futuristic tale of the oppressed working class that uses low-key lighting to create an atmosphere of despair and massive sets to suggest the subjugation of the masses.

Many great German directors, actors, and cameramen were lured to Hollywood, either by money or to escape the increasing control of the Nazis. Expressionist techniques, such as distorted lighting styles and camerawork, were easily absorbed into the classic narrative style. Nowhere is the Expressionist influence more realized than in the American horror genre, which was born at Universal Studios in the early 1930's, just after the arrival of the German émigrés.

Aside from the horribly effective propaganda films of Leni Riefenstahl, Nazi Germany produced no notable cinema. In fact, it took more than 20 years for the German film industry to recover from the war. In the 1970's a new generation of iconoclastic directors turned on the conformism and bad faith of the Adenauer years with a vengeance. R. W. Fassbinder, Wim Wenders, and Werner Herzog made intense, formally inventive films about wanderers, drug addicts, and seemingly every kind of physical and mental defective. Herzog's *Aguirre, the Wrath of God* (1972), about Spanish conquistadors in the Amazon, ends with the title character, alone, dreaming of fathering a new race of supermen upon his daughter, while his corpse-covered raft is overrun by marmosets.

Great Britain

The Brighton School At the turn of the 20th century, the filmmakers of the "Brighton School" drew upon the work of the French while in some ways anticipating Porter and Griffith. Cecil Hepworth's *Rescued by Rover* (1905), presented entirely without titles, showed how to keep an audience oriented to a swiftly moving narrative by carefully repeating sets and shots.

The Documentary Influence Britain's finest achievements in film prior to World War II were in documentaries. John Grierson (1898–1972) launched a documentary movement in Great Britain in the late 1920's that produced films related to public needs and national interest. *Drifters* (1929) detailed the hard work of the Scottish herring fisherman; *Night Mail* (1936) told the story of the dedicated mail train that transported letters and packages across the British Empire.

When war began in 1939, a series of semi-documentary films were released that drew on Grierson's ideas about the capacity for documentary to fulfill a public service. The narratives were fictional but the subject matter and characters were authentic. *Target For Tonight* (1941), directed by Harry Watt, followed the activities of Royal Air Force (R.A.F.) fliers on a fictional bombing mission over Germany. Starring actual R.A.F. pilots, the film informed the public about the R.A.F., while rallying support and bolstering national confidence.

Although the semi-documentary film disappeared after the war, Grierson's documentary tradition exerted a strong influence over feature filmmaking in Great Britain. The Ealing Studios hired several of the documentarians to direct their feature films, including a series known as the Ealing comedies. Postwar bureaucratic entanglements were tackled in Henry Cornelius's *Passport to Pimlico* (1949); the hostilities of the Scottish for the British were exposed in Alexander MacKendrick's *Whiskey Galore* (aka, *Tight Little Island*, 1949); and the eccentricities of the British middle class were showcased in Charles Crichton's *The Lavender Hill Mob* (1951). These films introduced the world to the comic genius of the likes of Alec Guinness and Peter Sellers.

In the late 1950's the British documentary tradition was revived and reworked in the films of the Free Cinema movement. According to filmmakers Lindsay Anderson, Karel Reisz, and Tony Richardson, "free" meant free from serving a sponsor's purpose and free from pandering to the tastes of the box office. Their documentaries, such as Anderson's *O Dreamland* (1954) and Reisz's *Momma Don't Allow* (1955), revealed a class consciousness and a social commitment. The themes and rough style of Free Cinema fit the working-class narratives of the Angry Young Men, giving birth to a social realist type of filmmaking in Jack Clayton's *Room at the Top* and Richardson's *Look Back in Anger* (both 1959).

Aside from the Free Cinema, British cinema has been, like British art in general, more of a collection of eccentric individual talents than a series of movements or schools. That is especially true today, when Ken Russell's hysterical expressionism, Mike Leigh's proletarian comedies, Ken Loach's politically committed tales, Peter Greenaway's super-baroque art films, and the eloquent lunacy of Monty Python all remain resolutely sui generis.

The Soviet Union

Silent Filmmakers Unlike the capitalist-based film industries of the United States and Europe, the Soviet film industry was rooted in socialist economics. Film production had existed in Russia prior to 1917, but the Bolshevik Revolution of that year sparked a full-fledged industry financially supported by the state and characterized by formal experimentation. The Bolsheviks, led by V.I. Lenin (1870–1924), believed film to be the most effective means to indoctrinate the masses to their new form of government.

The newsreels of Dziga Vertov (b. Denis Kaufman, 1896–1954) explored the possibilities of editing through the specific juxtaposition of images in order to create a meaning. In 1922 he launched a monthly newsreel called

Kino Pravda, the ultimate goal of which was to support the tenets of the revolution. For instance, when Vertov combined one shot of the former czar sternly reviewing his troops with another of the shirtsleeved Lenin with a group of workers, he made an effective and persuasive political statement.

Theory of Montage Instrumental in advancing the art of editing was teacher-theorist-director Lev Kuleshov (1899–1970), who conducted editing experiments in his capacity as an instructor at the Vsesoyuznyi Gosudarstvenyi Institut Kinematografia (VGIK), Moscow's state film school. His experiments ultimately concluded that each shot in a film acquired meaning from its immediate context, which is the shot that comes before it and the shot that follows it. This discovery became the foundation of montage editing, which focuses on the impact created by the juxtaposition of one or more shots. Russian montage is dynamic and often discontinuous in comparison to Hollywood's continuity editing, which offers the illusion of continuous action from shot to shot.

Sergei Eisenstein (1898–1948) used what is called "intellectual montage," which was the juxtaposition of two or more shots to create a metaphor or idea not inherent in any one of the shots themselves. In *Battleship Potemkin* (1925), about a real-life mutiny in the Russian Navy in 1905, Eisenstein juxtaposes a close-up of an officer's sword with a close-up of a priest's cross to suggest that both are instruments of oppression to keep the masses in their place. In addition to intellectual montage, *Potemkin* uses other editing tactics, including the juxtaposition of opposing shots, such as light shots with dark ones, static shots with movement, and close-ups with long shots.

Not all Russian directors held the same views regarding editing. Vsevolod I. Pudovkin (1893–1953) was the most conventional of the Russian filmmakers of the 1920's, preferring a less radical style of editing and a more traditional approach to filmmaking. To Pudovkin, editing had to work in conjunction with a message-driven story and credible acting in order to produce a powerful film, such as his heart-wrenching drama *Mother* (1926). Alexander Dovzhenko (1894–1956) stood apart from those experimenting with editing and form. A regionalist, Dovzhenko celebrated the agricultural lifestyle of his native Ukraine in such poetic films as *Earth*, which stressed imagery over form and mood over pacing.

The era of the great Russian silent filmmakers drew to a close with the consolidation of the Soviet government under Josef Stalin during the early 1930's and the coming of sound. Stalin, who was as provincial as Lenin had been intellectual, disliked the esoteric nature of montage-driven films and demanded Soviet movies be simple stories readily understandable to all audiences. The 50's and 60's saw brief glimmers of hope for a resurgence of Soviet cinema in the regional films of Sergei Paradjanov and the literary adaptations of Grigori Kozintsev. The U.S.S.R. finally gave the world one last cinematic artist, Andrei Tarkovsky, just before its collapse in the 1990's.

Eastern Europe

The film industries of the Soviet Union and satellite countries of Czechoslovakia, Poland, Yugoslavia, and Hungary were under the supervision of the Communist Party until the fall of Soviet-style communism in 1989. The Party favored socialist realism, which consisted of simple, uplifting stories of communist heroes whose lives had meaning for the revolution, or ideologically correct stories in which everyday people enacted or embodied the tenets of communism. National film schools trained directors, actors, and technicians who went on to work for studios controlled and funded by the state. Despite this rigid control, a few great films and filmmakers emerged from Eastern Europe.

After Josef Stalin died in 1953, the Eastern bloc film industries enjoyed a relaxation of internal controls and a growing expression of national sentiment known as the Great Thaw. In Poland in 1956, the Poznan uprising protested Soviet control, which resulted in loosened censorship over the arts. Director Andrzej Wajda (b. 1926) led a resurgence of Polish production in the late 1950's, which included his films *Kanal* (1956) and *Ashes and Diamonds* (1958). Combined with an earlier work, *A Generation* (1954), the films explored Poland's sad history during the German occupation of World War II.

Agnieszka Holland (b. 1948) was part of Poland's "cinema of moral concern," also known as the "cinema of moral unrest." Most of this generation of film directors had attended the film school in Lodz, Poland, during the 1970's, and were united by an interest in personal moral issues, or in the struggles of the individual to do what's right in a corrupt system. In addition to Holland, the group included Krysztof Zanussi (b. 1939) and Krysztof Kieslowski (1941–96).

In Czechoslovakia the political climate loosened sufficiently during the 1960's to allow a greater degree of experimentation in the arts, including film. A young generation of filmmakers educated at FAMU, the national film academy in Prague, produced a cinema of wry social commentary, acutely observed comedy, and formal experimentation. Dubbed the "Czech New Wave," these directors include Milos Forman, Vera Chytilova, Jan Nemec, Ivan Passer, Jiri Menzel, and Jaromil Jires. Milos Forman's (b. 1932) award-winning Czech films, *Black Peter* (1964), *Loves of a Blonde* (1965), and *The Fireman's Ball* (1967), are characterized by an acute observation of ordinary people, a documentary-like visual style influenced by the French New Wave, and excellent performances by nonprofessionals. The most unconventional filmmaker of the Czech New Wave is Vera Chytilova (b. 1929), whose formal experimentation and surreal imagery in her best-known feature, *Daisies* (1966), tested the patience of the political tastemakers. Like Forman, Ivan Passer (b. 1933) and Jiri Menzel (b. 1938) directed films in which close observations of ordinary people produced wry comedies about contemporary life. Menzel's best-known film is the Academy Award–winning *Closely Watched Trains* (1966), a coming-of-age story about a shy train station attendant. Passer, who cowrote Forman's *Fireman's Ball*, directed *Intimate Lighting* (1966), about the reunion of two old musicians whose lives have gone in different directions.

Important filmmakers have also come from other countries behind the Iron Curtain. Hungary gave filmgoers the swooping camera and intricate compositions of Miklos Janczo and the historical dramas of Istvan Szabo. Before it disintegrated into civil war, Yugoslavia produced the anarchic comedies of Dusan Makevejev. Since the fall of communism, the former Eastern bloc countries have struggled to keep their film industries afloat in a free-enterprise system. With the distribution of Hollywood films in Eastern Europe, fewer and fewer native filmmakers find their films on the big screens.

Italy

After World War I, the Italian film industry that had produced the great silent superspectacles quickly declined into mediocrity. Despite the construction of the massive state-funded Cinecittà studio complex, fascist Italy produced nothing more notable than "white telephone" movies, named after the instruments into which the characters in these films were seen interminably speaking.

Italian Neorealism Perhaps the most influential postwar movement, Italian neorealism strove to capture the dignity of ordinary people in everyday life in a stripped-down documentary style. Neorealism actually began while the war was still raging. *Ossessione*, directed by Luchino Visconti (1906–76), considered to be the blueprint for neorealism, was released in 1943, and *Open City*, directed by Roberto Rossellini (1906–77), the first neorealist film to reach other countries, was shot in 1944 and released the following year. *Open City* was a loosely structured story based on actual events that occurred just as the Allies were approaching Rome. It used documentary-like techniques that became associated with the movement, including on-location shooting, the use of nonprofessional actors, a focus on the daily lives of ordinary people, and references to recent history. *The Bicycle Thief* (1949), directed by Vittorio de Sica, is considered the undisputed masterpiece of the movement.

Neorealism as a movement ended during the early 1950's, but it remained a strong influence on Italian filmmaking for many decades. The postwar generation of Italian directors, such as Federico Fellini and Michelangelo Antonioni, adopted such neorealistic characteristics as location shooting, long shots in long takes, and nonprofessional actors, but they used them to shape their own individual styles.

Italian filmmakers of the 1960's, dubbed the New Italian Cinema, returned to films with sociopolitical content and themes. Bernardo Bertolucci and Ermanno Olmi mixed their neorealist roots with a pronounced French New Wave influence.

Spain

Thanks to the Franco regime, Spain's greatest filmmaker, Luis Buñuel (1900–83), made very few films in Spain. After a few odd jobs in the United States, he divided his directorial career between Mexico and France, where he applied Surrealist poetics and antifascist politics to narratives a shade more conventional than *Un Chien Andalou*. After the death of Franco, a national cinema finally emerged, led by Carlos Saura and Victor Erice, while the work of Pedro Almodovar happily walks back and forth across the line that separates art from camp.

Scandinavia

In the 1910's and 1920's Denmark boasted the directorial talents of Holger Madsen, Carl-Theodor Dreyer, and Benjamin Christensen, while Danish superstar Asta Nielsen enjoyed international popularity. In Sweden Charles Magnusson guided the Svensk Filmindustri into a leading force in film production, while directors Victor Sjostrom and Mauritz Stiller achieved a unique national expression. Because Sweden remained neutral during World War I, their film industry continued to thrive into the 1920's. Thereafter, the Swedish film industry often teetered financially, but it managed to retain its national identity. After World War II, Ingmar Bergman (b. 1918) emerged to become an eminent filmmaker around the world. Bergman began his directorial career in 1945, but *Smiles of a Summer Night* (1955), *The Seventh Seal* (1957), and *Wild Strawberries* (1957) announced him as an international force.

The Danish film industry struggled to continue after World War II. Its recovery has been steady but slow. From the 1960's through the 1980's, the films of such directors as Henning Carlson and Bille August turned attention toward Denmark periodically, while the simplified practices and stripped-down style of iconoclast Lars Von Trier (*Zentropa*) grabbed the spotlight in the 1990's. Other noteworthy contemporary Scandinavian filmmakers include Jan Troell (*Hamsun*), the unclassifiable Aki Kaurismaki, and Lucas Moodysson (*Togetherness*).

India

In 1956 at the Cannes International Film festival, director Satyajit Ray's *Pather Panchali* garnered critical acclaim as well as a jury prize for being "the best human document." Ray (1921–93) followed *Pather Panchali* with *Aparajito* (1956) and *The World of Apu* (1958); together, these films form a trilogy about the lives of a Bengali family in the 1920's and 1930's. Strongly influenced by Italian neorealism, Ray's films are humanist and naturalist, focusing on small subjects, scenes of everyday life, and ordinary people. His other major films included *The Music Room* (1963) and *Distant Thunder* (1973).

Ray's films stood apart from most of the Indian film industry, a highly commercial enterprise that still produces more films per year than any other film industry. The center of production for the popular Hindi cinema is Bombay, nicknamed "Bollywood" because of its focus on producing slick, big-budget genre films for the masses.

Ray made films outside the styles and confines of Bollywood, and his work influenced other politically minded directors. Around 1969 the New Indian Cinema, or Parallel Cinema, was founded by directors Ritwak Ghatak and Mrinal Sen (b. 1923) and financed in part by the government. Ghatak and Sen, both Marxists, made films about social problems and serious issues. Sen's biggest success was *Bhuvan Shome* (1969), about a railroad executive who is transformed by a trip to rural India. Perhaps the best known member of the New Cinema is Shyam Benegal (b. 1934), whose critically acclaimed and widely successful films include *Manthan* (1976) and *Bhumika* (1977).

During the late 1980's and 1990's, several Indian directors gained attention by directing for the film industries of other countries. Mira Nair, whose films include *Salaam Bombay!* (1988) and *Mississippi Masala* (1991), moved to Hollywood; Deepa Mehta, who directed *Fire* (1996), is based in Canada. After scoring an international success with *The Bandit Queen* (1994), Shakhar Kapur relocated to Great Britain to direct *Elizabeth* (1999), before ending up in Hollywood to make *The Four Feathers* (2001).

China

The history of filmmaking in China is a tale of three cinemas—those of the People's Republic of China, Hong Kong, and Taiwan.

The film industry in the People's Republic, or mainland China, produced films primarily for indoctrination until 1978, when constraints on the state-supported studios were lifted by the government. At that point, the studios began to make films for entertainment. Most of the filmmakers who initially rose to prominence had graduated from the Beijing Film Academy, which prompted critics to group them together, referring to them as the "Fifth Generation." Success at high-profile film festivals brought this group of directors international attention, beginning in the mid-1980's with Chen Kaige and his beautifully photographed *Yellow Earth* (1984). While each director of the Fifth Generation worked toward a personal style, they all shared a sophisticated pictorial sense. Most celebrated is Zhang Yimou (b. 1950), who had been the cinematographer on *Yellow Earth*. When he turned to directing in 1988, his films became renowned for their stunning visuals, radiant color, and precise compositions. Thematically, Yimou's films, including *Ju Dou* (1990), *Raise the Red Lantern* (1991), and *Shanghai Triad* (1996), are notable for their focus on the oppression of women.

Hong Kong has always benefitted from a capitalist-based film industry, in which films are produced fast and furiously. In the 1970's its movies were known for choppy editing, laughably out-of-synch overdubbing, and the Kung Fu legend of Bruce Lee. Even after Hong Kong was returned to China in 1997, the film industry was left alone to operate as it always had. Unlike the artistic aspirations of mainland China's film industry, Hong Kong prefers the formulaic narratives of popular genres—gangster films, martial-arts films, and comedies. Characterized by a dynamic editing style, energetic camerawork, elaborate stunts, and stylized violence, Hong Kong films appealed to American audiences, prompting Hollywood to lure away such major directors and actors as John Woo, Chow Yun-Fat, and Jackie Chan.

Filmmaking in Taiwan became possible after martial law ended in 1987. Taiwanese films are less known than those of mainland China or Hong Kong, probably because they emphasize the country's history and traditional Chinese formal techniques, making them less accessible to Western audiences. Taiwan's first internationally acclaimed feature was *City of Sadness* (1988), which launched director Hou Hsiao-hsien's career (b. 1947). Hou's films, including *The Puppetmaster* (1993) and *Flowers of Shanghai* (1995), are contemplative essays on his country's history and culture. His work contrasts with that of fellow Taiwanese director Ang Lee, whose films (*The Wedding Banquet*, 1993) have been influenced by the West. In the late 1990's, Lee was absorbed into the Hollywood system, where he has worked on large-scale commercial films for the major studios, including *Sense and Sensibility* (1995) and *The Hulk* (2003). In 2000 he directed an award-winning independent feature, *Crouching Tiger, Hidden Dragon*, a martial-arts fairy tale designed to appeal to Western audiences.

Japan

The Japanese film industry was launched in 1904–05, when the first film studios were constructed. Similar to Hollywood, the industry was dominated by a handful of studios, which also controlled distribution and exhibition. Most Japanese films fell into two central types: the *jidai-geki*, which were period dramas set in the in past, and the *gendai-geki*, modern-era stories set in urban centers.

In 1951 Japanese film was internationally celebrated for the first time when *Rashomon*, directed by Akira Kurosawa (1910–98), won the Golden Lion at the Venice Film Festival. *Rashomon's* fragmented, nonlinear narrative structure established Kurosawa as a master filmmaker. His loose adaptations of Shakespeare's plays and his action-filled samurai films, including *Yojimbo* (1961) and *Sanjuro* (1962), made his work accessible to Western audiences. Kurosawa's films set in the contemporary era, such as *Ikiru* (1952), eschewed the action and sensory appeal of his samurai films to focus on subtle, complex characters, and modern social problems. Kurosawa's key collaborator in his films was actor Toshiro Mifune (1920–97), who interpreted the director's central characters with charisma and intensity.

Other Japanese directors who drew attention to Japanese cinema during this period were Kenji Mizoguchi (1898–1956) and Yasujiro Ozu (1903–63). Mizoguchi, whose style and subjects were more traditionally Japanese than Kurosawa's, favored historical films that focused on the plight of women. *Street of Shame* (1956) and *Women of the Night* (1957) dealt with prostitution; *Princess Yang Kwei Fei* (1955) focused on the false importance placed on the appearance of women. His masterpiece, *Ugetsu Monogatari* (1953), dealt with the effect of war on humanity. The films of Ozu are unique in their austerity: most take place in interiors, feature little camera movement, and consist largely of conversations. The most recognizable stylistic characteristic of Ozu's films is the position of his camera, which generally present the point of view of a person seated on a tatami mat. The rigid formal style seemed appropriate for his key theme, which contrasted traditional Japanese ways with contemporary changes. His best-known films, *Late Autumn* (1960), *Early Summer* (1951), and *Late Spring* (1949), have titles that recall the cyclical nature of life.

In the 1960's a group of young Japanese directors began their careers with the help of the Arts Theater Guild, which financed and showcased more daring films than the studios were willing to support. Shohei Imamura (*The Pornographers*, 1966), Nagisa Oshima (*In the Realm of the Senses*, 1976), and Masahiro Shinoda (*Pale Flower*, 1964) made films that were more modernist than their predecessors, resulting in the label "Japanese New Wave."

By the mid-1970's, the golden age of Japanese cinema had ended. In 1972 the continued decline of the Japanese cinema induced the government to create a fund for quality productions. In the 1980's and 1990's a new generation of filmmakers, including Yoshimitsu Morita and Juzo Itami, emerged to breathe life into the Japanese industry.

Latin America

The films of many Latin American directors feature strong sociopolitical content, reflecting the backlash against the various military regimes, ruling elites, and colonialist policies that have dominated this part of the world. Their work attempts to raise social awareness in the hopes of improving conditions, especially among the peasantry and urban poor. Added to the political commitment are influences from the traditions and aesthetics of Latin American painting, music, and literature, including a predilection for allegory, vivid color, and powerful music, a style generally referred to as "tropicalism."

Cuba's modern film industry began in 1959, when the new revolutionary government centralized the film industry to regulate all production, distribution, and exhibition. At first, newsreels and documentaries were produced to meet the needs of the people as determined by the new government. Narrative filmmaking often captured the immediacy and naturalism of documentary, while focusing on content involving the issues and problems of the new revolutionary culture. Tomas Gutierrez Alea (1928–96) became the best-known Cuban director when his *Memories of Underdevelopment* (1968) garnered international recognition. Alea continued to explore problems in Cuban society till the end of his life when he directed *Strawberry and Chocolate* (1993), an exploration of gay sexuality in a machismo-based culture.

Elsewhere in Latin America, filmmakers struggled to find funding for indigenous films. In some countries cooperatives were formed, which united filmmakers economically and politically. In Brazil directors Ruy Guerra, Glauber Rocha, and Nelson Pereira dos Santos formed the Cinema Novo cooperative and secured funding from a state-supported agency. Cinema Novo was dedicated to films that focused on the impoverished and the disenfranchised. In these films serious political allegories were depicted in a tropicalist style. Rocha led Cinema Novo, becoming an internationally known director with *Black God, White Devil* (1964) and *Antonio das Mortes* (1969). The generation after Cinema Novo, led by Hector Babenco (*Kiss of the Spider Woman*, 1985) has been more prolific, producing both political and commercial films.

A group of political directors in Argentina also established a cooperative to facilitate filmmaking in their country. The Grupo Cine Liberacion (GCL) were more politically driven than Cinema Novo, advocating filmmaking that was, according to their manifesto, "militant in politics and experimental in language." To the GCL, part of the filmic experience should be active audience involvement in the form of political discussion and debate inspired by the films. Their most inspired achievement to that end was Fernando Solanas and Octavio Getino's *The Hour of the Furnaces* (1968), a three-part documentary in which the second and third sections were developed from audience reaction to the first section. More recent Argentinean directors who have used film for sociopolitical criticism include Eliseo Subiola (*Man Facing Southeast*, 1986) and Maria Luisa Bemberg (*Camila*, 1984).

Africa

While indigenous filmmaking in Africa has been limited, largely due to poverty and the ever-changing political scene, some important directors have emerged since the 1970's. Because distribution is controlled through American, European, and East Indian systems, African filmmakers experience difficulty obtaining funding and getting exposure and recognition. The type of films associated with Africa are frequently described as belonging to traditions of folklore, particularly those of oral storytelling. Political criticism and anticolonial sentiment are sometimes intertwined with folkloric structures to form powerful narratives, as in the films of novelist and filmmaker Ousmane Sembene (b. 1923) of Senegal. Sembene burst onto the international scene in 1966 with his first film, *Black Girl*, an attack on the racism endured by blacks at the hands of French colonists. Dedicated if not prolific, Sembene continued to make films into the millennium (*Faat Kine*, 2000), earning his nickname as the father of black African film. Other important African directors include Souleymane Cissé (b. 1940), of Mali (*Yeelen*, 1987) and Idrissa Ouedraogo (b. 1954) from Burkina Faso (*Yaaba*, 1989).

Glossary of Film Terms

angle *normal angle* (or eye level) is the standard camera position in which the camera is placed straight on to the subject at approximate eye level. When the camera deviates from that position, a connotation or idea is suggested. In a *high-angle* shot, the camera is placed above the subject, suggesting the subject is weak or vulnerable. In a *low-angle* shot, the camera is placed below the subject to suggest importance or power. In a *bird's-eye view*, or *God's-eye view*, the camera is in an extremely high angle to suggest fate or God looking down upon the subject. A *dutch*, or *oblique*, angle occurs when the camera is tilted, suggesting that something about the subject is wrong or off-kilter.

classic narrative style standard style used by the Hollywood industry to depict a story on film. Also called the classical style or the invisible style, it strives for a subtlety or unobtrusiveness so that the audience is unaware of its impact on them. It consists of a consistent approach to camera work, editing, and lighting and a consistent depiction of plot and character.

continuity editing standard style of editing by the Hollywood industry. It offers the illusion of continuous action from shot to shot by moving the action forward in time in a smooth, fluid, and logical way.

cut editing transition accomplished by splicing one shot to another shot. It suggests an instantaneous passage of time. Also called an edit.

dissolve editing transition accomplished by the slow fading out of one shot and the gradual fading in of the next shot. At one point, both images are superimposed. It suggests the slow passage of time.

fade editing transition in which the image gradually appears from an all-black screen, or gradually disappears to an all-black screen. Fades *from* black are used to open a film, while fades *to* black conclude a film. When used within the body of a film, fades suggest a complete break in time or place.

freeze frame shot frozen on screen for a desired length of time to resemble a still photograph.

genre type or category of story, such as westerns, horror films, or musicals.

hand-held camera work footage shot by a cameraman who is holding the camera instead of using a tripod or dolly. The resulting footage appears shaky or unsteady, suggesting the action is unfolding instantaneously and spontaneously as though the viewer is there witnessing it.

lighting Most films utilize *high-key lighting*, in which the lighting is bright and even, with few discernible shadows. To deviate from high-key adds a suggestion or connotation to a shot or scene. *Low-key lighting*, which implies that something is hidden, mysterious, or evil, consists of an overall dark look, with dark, diffused shadows dominating the set. *High-contrast lighting*, which tends to intensify mood or emotion, consists of harsh contrast between light and dark in the same shot.

intertitles titles between shots in a silent film to help explain the action or provide dialogue or commentary for the scene.

iris transition to open a scene in which the image is brought into view by starting with a circle at center screen and expanding the circle until the entire image is on screen, or to close a scene by gradually shrinking the image in circular form until the screen is black. A partial iris occurs when the screen closes in on a character or object via a circular shape, leaving the rest of the screen black.

jump cut edit between two shots that are so similar that a jarring or abrupt effect is created. In continuity editing, jump cuts are errors because they disrupt the smooth flow of images, but the French New Wave used them deliberately to disorient and disturb the viewer.

mise-en-scène all of the visual elements that go into composing a shot, including camera angle, lighting style, set design, props, position of the character in the frame, and costumes and makeup.

montage style of editing developed by the Russian filmmakers of the 1920's in which a collection of shots are edited together to form an impression, emotion, or idea. The impression or effect is created through the accumulation, frequency, and the juxtaposition of shots. *Intellectual montage* is a specific technique of montage in which two unrelated shots are edited together to suggest a metaphor or concept not inherent in either shot by itself.

package-unit system system of organization for the production of films in the Hollywood industry begun after the decline of the studios in the 1950's. In this system independent production companies or producers find a book, play, or story to turn into a script, and then seek interested stars, putting the project and star together into one deal. The deal is taken to a major studio, which partially finances the film and distributes it after completion. Also called the *independent production system*.

pan rotation of the camera around its vertical axis, creating a panoramic effect.

parallel editing cutting back and forth between two or more scenes to create the illusion of simultaneous action.

persistence of vision theory on which the motion picture camera was developed. It involves the capacity of the eye to maintain an image on the retina for a brief instant after the image disappears, thus giving continuity to a succession of still images and creating the illusion of movement.

production phase of filmmaking in which the shooting occurs and the raw footage is produced. The action is shot, the principal sound recorded, and the entire crew is put to full use. This phase comes after preproduction, in which the script is written and prepared, the actors hired, and the director does required preparation. It comes before postproduction, in which the film is edited, the sound is assembled in its final form, and special effects are added.

scene segment of film consisting of related shots.

shot basic unit of film construction. A single piece of film without any breaks in the action; an unedited, uncut strip of film. Different types of shots have different functions in a scene. The purpose of a *close-up*, in which the camera is closest to the subject, is to show the emotion of the character or elicit emotion from the audience. A *medium shot* best shows the interrelationship among characters, and the *long shot*, in which the camera is farthest from the subject, establishes the setting. In a *zoom shot*, the magnification of objects by the camera's lenses is increased (zoom in) or decreased (zoom out/back). A *two-shot* is a medium close-up shot of two subjects, usually framed from the chest up. A *point of view shot* (or *POV*) is a brief shot from the perspective of a specific character so the viewer sees what that character sees from his or her angle of vision. (see also *angle, subjective camera movement*)

shot sequence segment of film composed of related scenes, leading to a climax or resolution of some sort.

star system method or manner of exploiting movie stars to market films and lure audiences into the theater.

studio system system for organizing the major studios in the Hollywood industry that began in the 1910's and lasted until the 1950's. In the studio system, the head of the studio had creative and financial control, which he delegated through his producers. They in turn oversaw the work of the writers, directors, actors, and editors, who were all under contract to the studio and were assigned to films by the producers.

subjective camera movement shot in which the camera takes on the viewpoint of a specific character for a deliberate amount of time, so that the camera moves about the set as though it were that character. The viewer sees what that character sees from his or her angle of vision.

synchronized sound sound that seems to emanate directly from its source on the screen, as when spoken dialogue is heard at the exact moment it is seen being spoken.

tilt rotation of the camera around its horizontal axis.

tracking moving the camera alongside, above, beneath, behind, or ahead of the subject, generally following the movement of the subject. Movement is accomplished via a wheeled support, such as a dolly on a small track.

vertical control term applied to the major studios' ownership of production, distribution, and exhibition during the silent era and the Golden Age.

wide-screen any film employing an aspect ratio wider than 4:3 or 1.33:1, giving the screen a rectangular shape. Wide-screen processes were adopted by the industry during the 1950's to combat the popularity of television. From the silent era to the 1950's the screen had been standardized at a ratio of 1.33:1, which was almost square.

wipe transition device in which the image moves diagonally across the screen to reveal the next image. A wipe signifies a complete change in time and/or locale. (see also *iris*)

The Production Crew

art director person responsible for the design of the film's sets or locations; also responsible for their construction.

best boy assistant to the gaffer; sometimes the assistant to the head grip.

cinematographer (director of photography) person responsible for photographing the images for the film. Cinematography involves technical knowledge about cameras, lenses, film stock, and lighting in addition to an aesthetic sense involving camera placement, angle, the interplay of light and shadow, and movement.

director person responsible for translating the script, which is the written word, into a film, which is a visual and performance-based medium.

editor person responsible for assembling the film's footage into its final form.

foley artist specialist in sound effects that are dubbed onto the visuals.

gaffer chief electrician in a film production, responsible for lighting the set.

grip jack-of-all-trades responsible for a variety of tasks on the set, including the transportation and movement of equipment and scenery, laying down dolly track, and pushing the dolly along the track. The *key grip* is the person in charge of a group of grips.

producer person in charge of the financial and administrative duties for a film, including securing the rights to a book, story, or script, monitoring scriptwriting, and keeping the film on schedule and on budget. Sometimes the producer is involved in casting, raising finances for the film, and monitoring the editing. The *executive producer* usually deals with business and legal affairs.

screenwriter person who writes the script, either adapting it from another source or creating an original story. Often, several scriptwriters are employed to create and polish a single script.

MUSIC

History of Western Classical Music

The history of Western music is the history of both standardization and increasing sophistication. Over the centuries, composers have learned to combine the 12 pitches of the Western tonal system in increasingly complex ways. Where music from earlier eras was limited to the naturally occurring (*diatonic*) notes of the major or minor scales, modern music is free to incorporate notes and harmonies from outside the natural scale. This approach, known as *chromaticism*, has extended the boundaries of traditional Western tonality—and resulted in new musical forms that challenge musicians and listeners alike.

Early Music (4000 B.C.–A.D. 400)

Archeological findings of ancient instruments demonstrate that humans have made music from the earliest times. While we don't know how this early music sounded, it's clear that Western music, as we know it, evolved from ancient Near Eastern culture.

Ancient Egyptian society regarded music as a gift from the gods. The appearance and the sound of early musical instruments had symbolic significance in Egyptian culture, where music played an important role in religious practice.

Some of the earliest-known instruments were stringed harps and lutes, known to be played in Egypt as early as 4000 B.C.; lyres and double clarinets were played as early as 3500 B.C. and percussion instruments were added to Egyptian orchestral music ca. 2000 B.C., while the tambourine was known to be used by the Hittites ca. 1500 B.C., along with the guitar, lyre, and trumpet.

All ancient Mesopotamian societies—including the kingdoms of Akkadia, Assyria, Babylonia, Chaldea, and Sumeria—made music central to their religious rites and festivals. Starting around 1800 B.C., Babylonian liturgical services were known to include a variety of psalms and hymns. The musical style was *antiphonal*, with two different voices alternating in chant. Instruments of the time included harps, flutes, drums, and lyres.

The earliest-known written music dates to Sumeria, ca. 800 B.C., in the form of a hymn written in cuneiform on a stone tablet. The first-known musical scales, incorporating five and seven tones per octave, began to appear in Babylonian music during the same period.

The central role of music in Hebrew society is documented in the pages of the Bible. Music was known to be a part of both secular and nonsecular Jewish life; the Old Testament tells of trumpet signals in war, of victories celebrated with women's choirs, and of music played in religious festivals. During this period, the Levites were appointed to perform both instrumental and vocal music in the church—using stringed instruments, harps, and cymbals, according to the First Book of Chronicles. Music of this era was primarily *monophonic*, meaning that it contained a single melody line with no harmonic accompaniment.

Greece and Rome The first European music is that of the ancient Greeks and Romans, dating from roughly 500 B.C. to A.D. 300. Fewer than a dozen examples of Greek music from this period, written in an alphabetical notation, survive. Ancient Greek philosophers believed that music originated from the god Apollo, as well as from the mythological musician Orpheus and other divinities. They also believed that music reflected in microcosm the laws of harmony that rule the universe, and that music influenced human thought and actions.

The Greek philosopher Pythagoras (ca. 580 B.C.–ca. 500 B.C.) discovered the mathematical relationships between specific frequencies and *musical intervals*, using a single-string instrument (called a monochord) to produce the various intervals. For example, two notes whose frequencies form a ratio of 2:1 sound one *octave* apart; a ratio of 3:2 forms an interval of a *fifth*, and a ratio of 4:3 forms a *fourth*. These basic intervals combine to create the modes and scales on which all Western melodies and harmony are based.

Aristotle (384 B.C.–322 B.C.), in his treatise *The Politics*, noted that different musical melodies, modes, and rhythms have different effects on the listener. He argued that since music has the power of forming character, it should be an important part of the education of the young. His student, Aristoxenus of Tarentum (364 B.C.–304 B.C.), in his *Elements of Harmony*, formalized the Greek scheme of *modes*, which utilize a limited series of pitches defined by set intervals. These modes, such as the Dorian, Ionian, Lydian, and Phrygian, predated the modern major and minor scales that came to prominence in the 16th and 17th centuries.

Greek music was primarily *monophonic*, without complex harmonies or chords. In song, the music duplicated the rhythms of the text; in instrumental pieces, the melody followed the rhythmic patterns of the various poetic feet. The internal structure of Greek music was based on a system of modes, similar to that used in Arab and Indian music today.

The musical principles and ideas developed by the Greeks were preserved by the Romans throughout their history. Roman music was also influenced by the music of the many kingdoms conquered by the Roman Empire. From 27 B.C. to A.D. 192, slave musicians and dancers were recruited throughout the Empire, musical theater flourished, and both Greek and Roman musicians had their own professional organizations.

The Middle Ages (ca. 500–1400)

In the period following the fall of the Roman Empire in 476, the newly emerged Christian Church came to dominate European societies and culture by providing stabilizing institutions and charitable services to the populace. By A.D. 800 the church wielded political as well as spiritual power and as the era's most important institution eventually dictated the destiny of art, literature, and music.

Since the Christian Church exerted such control over all artistic fields, most professional musicians were employed by the church, and most medieval music was created in monasteries. The church was opposed to the paganism associated with ancient Greece and Rome, which led to the decline of Greek and Roman music and the rise of new sacred musical forms, based on the so-called church modes. Both sacred and secular music of the period incorporated both voices and a wide variety of instruments, including the lyre, medieval fiddle (viele), organ, small drums, and bells.

Early Medieval Music and Gregorian Chant In the early medieval period music was almost exclusively monophonic. The unaccompanied chant called *plainsong* or *plainchant* was performed by ancient monks in the services of the early Christian Church. This chant consisted of Latin words derived from the Roman Catholic mass, set to a simple unharmonized *modal* melody. This style of medieval music was known as *ars nova*. Plainsong eventually evolved into *Gregorian chant*, after Pope Gregory I (b. Italy, ca. 540; d. 604), who encouraged a ritualized use of music by the church. Gregory first ordered the organization and compilation of church chants, titled "antiphonar."

Troubadours and Other Secular Music By the turn of the second millennium, sacred musical forms were supplemented by a developing folk music tradition. This music typically took the form of poetry set to music, performed on simple string instruments.

Sometime prior to the 11th century, a form of secular music sprang forth in southern France. This music was played and sung by roving poet-minstrels, called *troubadours*, who went from castle to castle, singing songs, telling stories, and otherwise entertaining the lords and ladies of the upper class.

These troubadours introduced the idea of *fin' amours* ("pure love") into Western culture. Their music, still monophonic, was simpler in design than that produced in the church of the time. The secular songs of the troubadours were often faster than sacred songs, used the common language of the people (instead of Latin), and were accompanied by string and percussion instruments such as the lyre, fiddle, and drums.

The influence of the troubadours spread northward throughout the Middle Ages, giving rise to their successors, the *trouvères* of France and the *minnesingers* of Germany.

By the dawn of the 14th century a greater range of song forms began to emerge. Many of these forms, such as the *rondeau* and *virelai*, were based on peasant dances. Perhaps the most prolific songwriter of the late Middle Ages was Guillaume de Machaut (ca. 1300–77). Machaut not only composed some 100 songs, he was also one of the first known composers to explore polyphonic forms.

The Rise of Polyphony Western music remained monophonic through approximately A.D. 900. At that time many musicians felt the need for music more elaborate than an unadorned melody. The later Middle Ages gave rise to *polyphony*, in the form of additional melodic lines sung simultaneously with the original melody.

The first polyphonic musical form was known as *organum*, which added an extra voice part sung in tandem with sections of the basic Gregorian chant. In early organum the voice part was sung a fourth or a fifth above (and parallel to) the chant melody. Later variations featured the second voice singing an independent countermelody; by the early 12th century, organum incorporated three and four separate voices.

Another type of composition developed alongside organum in the south of France. *Conductus* was similar to organum, but with newly composed texts, often secular in nature. What truly set conductus apart from organum, however, was speed; in conductus, the words were declaimed at a rapid rate, compared to organum's slower pace. The conductus eventually evolved into the *motet*.

Ars Nova Style During the 14th century a major stylistic change occurred. Dubbed *Ars Nova* (Latin for "new art"), this was a more sophisticated music, incorporating a new rhythmic complexity. Composers of Ars Nova created rhythmic patterns of a dozen or more notes, then repeated those patterns over and over in multiple voices. By layering other melodies over these *isorhythmic* voice parts, composers created intricate polyphonic designs. In these pieces the foundation voice (known as the *cantus firmus*) was typically borrowed from Gregorian chant.

The concepts of Ars Nova and isorhythm led to the development of the *motet*, a polyphonic form, originally for two voices, in which the ornate upper voice (called the *tenor*) is given a different text from the chant melody. In this respect a motet is like a song accompanied by a tenor. Motets of the medieval period were typically based on sacred texts. The form was expanded late in the 13th century, when three- and four-voice motets were introduced.

The Roman Catholic Mass Polyphony also found its way into the Roman Catholic mass, which had incorporated music—in the form of plainchant—since at least the fourth century. During the early Middle Ages, ceremonial music was limited to the *Proper* of the mass. The first known mass cycle was Machaut's *Messe de Nostre Dame*, written in the early 1360's, which set all movements of the mass in four-part scoring.

During the late 14th century composers began to create mass settings in which the movements were musically related to one another. In England, Lionel Power (d. 1445) and John Dunstable (ca. 1390–1453) unified the mass by basing all the movements on the same plainchant *cantus firmus*. By the end of the medieval period these English masses became available in northern Italy; their impact helped to launch the fully unified mass cycle that reigned through the end of the 17th century, and to establish the polyphonic mass as the most serious of musical forms of that period.

Music Notation The rise of polyphony in the late Middle Ages contributed to the development of the modern system of music notation; musicians had to be able to read and perform several different parts simultaneously, hence the need for a precise system of pitch and rhythmic notation. The 11th-century Benedictine monk Guido d'Arezzo (995–ca. 1033) thus conceived of a five-line staff, with each line and space representing a specific pitch; individual notes were represented as square symbols called *neumes*. A system of rhythmic notation was similarly introduced in the late 13th century by German theorist Franco of Cologne (ca. 1240–ca. 1280).

The Renaissance (1420–1600)

Music, like all the arts, flourished during the Renaissance. With the rise of the middle class, more people moved to cities and spent their leisure time attending plays, concerts, and other entertainment. Music became part of the common education, and—thanks to the invention of the printing press (ca. 1450)—sheet music and method books (for lute, recorder, and guitar) were made available to the populace.

The music of the Renaissance, while building on the polyphonic developments of the late Middle Ages, also reflected a reaction against the complexities of Ars Nova. This took the form of simpler, smoother-flowing melodies and harmonies, with less emphasis on highly structured counterpoint. In addition, many new instruments came to prominence during the Renaissance. These included the viol (predecessor to the modern violin), guitar, harp, recorder, sackbut (predecessor to the trombone), harpsichord, and clavichord.

Renaissance Polyphony Polyphony in the Renaissance period evolved from the independent counterpoint of the early 1400's into a more harmonious form of melody and accompaniment. Renaissance polyphony is characterized by the equal participation of voices in an exchange of motifs and phrases. The contrapuntal music of the Renaissance evolved to rely heavily on a style called "statement and imitation," where the additional voices successfully restate parts of the original melodic idea. When one part imitates another consistently for a relatively long time span, the two voices form what is called a *canon*. One of the foremost proponents of polyphonic music was Josquin Després (1440–1521), who was one of the first to use repetition or imitation of melodies within a composition. He distinguished himself by writing 18 masses, nearly 100 motets, and more than 70 chansons and other secular works.

Church Music Church music in the Renaissance reflected the growing influence of secular music—despite the attempts of Catholic authorities in Italy and Spain to curb what they viewed as the seductive and profane excesses of music. Also key was the impact of the Reformation, and Martin Luther's desire to break with tradition and use songs that could be sung by the whole congregation, not just the choir.

The Latin Mass Perhaps the most important musical form of the Renaissance was the Latin mass, typically composed of five related passages. Many Renaissance composers employed a cantus firmus based on chansons or other secular melodies to unify all five sections; this is in contrast to masses in the Middle Ages, which typically used Gregorian chant for the cantus firmus.

The Renaissance-era mass also became more elaborate as composers used more voices and instruments, and added more and more ornamentation to the music. Thus the mass became a work of epic proportions, comparable in scope to the symphonies of the 19th century. The master of the Renaissance-era mass was Giovanni Pierluigi da Palestrina (1525–94). His 104 masses are considered the epitome of the Renaissance mass style. Other notable composers of the period include Guillaume Du Fay (1397–1474) and Tomás Luis de Victoria (1548–1611).

Motet At the beginning of the Renaissance, the motet was a relatively small-scale sacred form, as defined during the late Middle Ages. But as the mass form developed in the 15th and 16th centuries, composers turned to the motet as a vehicle of experimentation. These later motets were full of contrasts, with passages for all voices paired with passages for just two or three voices, or sections in *duple* time (two beats per measure) followed by sections in triple time (three beats per measure). This more sophisticated motet form is best represented by the works of Orlande de Lassus (1532–94), who also emphasized the depiction of individual words in the text, incorporating techniques developed earlier in the madrigal form.

Chorale The rise of the various Protestant sects in the 1500's created a new musical tradition, less rigid than that of the Catholic Church. Martin Luther commissioned a new catalogue of songs with easy-to-sing melodies, based on familiar folk songs, for unison singing by the entire congregation. This new style of sacred song—dubbed the *chorale*—was the basis for many of the Lutheran hymns that are still sung today, and presaged the more elaborate chorales of J. S. Bach and his contemporaries in the Baroque era.

Renaissance Secular Music Secular music in the Renaissance took the form of various types of song. Early song forms were monophonic; later they incorporated various degrees of polyphony and counterpoint, with two or more lines played in contrast to each other.

Chanson The Ars Nova movement of the late Middle Ages, while initially embraced by sacred composers, was also incorporated into the secular music of the early Renaissance period. In particular, the unharmonized melodies sung by 13th-century troubadours evolved during the early 14th century into two- and three-voice pieces called *chansons* (French for "songs"). The type of line repetition used determined the overall form of the music; the most commonly used schemes were the rondeau, the virelai, the ballade, the caccia, and the ballata. Notable early chanson composers included Du Fay and Gilles de Bins dit Binchois (ca. 1400–60). By the 16th century, the chanson evolved from its simple beginnings to include elaborate contrapuntal melodies and musical allusions to birdcalls, the cries of street vendors, and so forth. Masters of this later form of chanson included Claude de Sermisy (1490–1562) and Clément Janequin (1485–1558).

Madrigal A further song form inspired by the *ars nova* movement was the *madrigal*, which set secular poetic text in a polyphonic arrangement for four to six voices. The first madrigals were sung in Italy at the end of the 13th century; by the 16th century, the form had become more complex in its polyphony, and had spread across Europe to England. Key madrigal composers include Palestrina, Lassus, and, in England, Thomas Morley (1557–1602).

The Baroque Period (1600–1750)

The Baroque period was all about drama and ornamentation, and the music of the Baroque echoed the dramatic styles of the period's fashions and architecture. Simple melodies evolved into flamboyant airs, full of trills and turns and other ornamentation. Elaborate melodies were layered on top of one another, and the concept of chordal accompaniment—with three or more notes played simultaneously under the melody—gained favor. New musical forms came into prominence, incorporating more and different combinations of instruments—and, in the case of opera, encouraging the interplay of voices and instruments.

With the rise of these new genres, the basic concepts of musical structure were transformed. Instead of writing pieces in which all voices participated equally in the musical activity, Baroque composers often concentrated on the soprano and bass parts, filling in the middle parts of the musical space with chords. To many composers the exact spacing of the chords was unimportant, and keyboard players were often allowed to create their own parts—marking some of the first instances of musical improvisation.

The early Baroque period saw a clear break with the music of the Renaissance; twelve-tone tonality and harmony replaced the limited modality of sacred chants, and composers explored new musical resources such as *chromaticism* (the inclusion of notes outside the natural scale) and *dissonance* (the jarring quality of two close pitches played simultaneously). By the mid-1600's these new resources had become fully integrated into the musical firmament, and in the late Baroque period composers took firm control over the complex forces of tonality by establishing a single emotional quality (called an *affect*) through the course of a piece. During this period the dominant musical forms reached an almost excessive degree of elaborateness, and musical expression became formalized, if not somewhat mechanical in its construction.

Composers While Palestrina and Claudio Monteverdi (1567–1643) bridged the Renaissance and Baroque eras, the most influential Baroque composers were those of the later period—notably Johann Sebastian Bach (1685–1750) and George Frideric Handel (1685–1759), both of whom created music that was virtuosic in its mastery of harmony and tonality. Other outstanding composers of the Baroque period included Henry Purcell (1659–95), Alessandro Scarlatti (1660–1725) and his son Domenico (1685–1757), Heinrich Schütz (1585–1672), and Antonio Vivaldi (1678–1741).

Composers of the Baroque era were often employed by the wealthy ruling class as part of what was called the patronage system. As such, the patron paid the composer for each work, and usually decided what kind of piece the composer should write. Even the major composers partook of this patronage; Bach spent several years as Kapellmeister (music director) to Prince Leopold of Anhalt-Cöthen; Handel wrote various works for the duke of Chandos; and Domenico Scarlatti was in the employ of Princess Maria Barbara of Portugal (later queen of Spain) for most of his career.

Musical forms favored by patrons—in essence, the popular music of this era—included dances, preludes, and suites. While writing within these genres could be creatively limiting, the best of the Baroque composers were able to thoroughly explore, and in some cases expand, these and other Baroque-era forms.

Opera Europe in the 17th century was host to a great rise in dramatic theater. In England this dramatic revival was led by the works of William Shakespeare and Christopher Marlowe; in France, by Pierre Corneille and Jean Racine. In Italy, however, this movement was not in the spoken word, but rather in a new form that combined drama with music—opera.

The very first opera is generally considered to be *Daphne*, composed in 1597 by Jacopo Peri (1561–1633); his contemporaries in early opera included Giulio Caccini (ca. 1545–1618) and Emilio del Cavalieri (ca. 1550–1602). These early operas were referred to as *drama per musica* (drama through music), and their plots were typically based on myth, much like their inspiration, the classic dramas of ancient Greece and Rome; later operas most often concerned themselves with historical figures.

These first operas did not yet fully integrate music and drama. Half-sung passages, called *recitatives*, alternated with orchestral interludes and choruses that commented on the dramatic events. Improvisation was discouraged; all ornamentation and other expressive details were carefully written out, and the *continuo* (a type of bass accompaniment played in the lower register of the organ) was carefully paced to match the rhythms of the singer's words.

Claudio Monteverdi (1567–1643) contributed more to the development of the opera form in the 17th century than anyone else. He established the fully sung *aria* (in place of the earlier recitative) and used a larger and richer-sounding orchestra. Monteverdi's work became a model for the operatic composers who followed and helped to bring opera to the masses, first in Venice and then throughout Europe

By the 18th century opera had become the most widely cultivated musical form, with most major composers contributing to the repertory. The later Baroque period saw the creation of several different operatic styles, including *opera seria* ("serious opera"), *opera buffa* ("comic opera"), and the French *opèra-ballet*, which merged opera with narrative dance.

In France Jean-Baptiste Lully (1632–87) developed the *tragèdie lyrique* style, with its greater emphasis on the recitative, its prominent roles for choir and orchestra (and, often, dancers), and its use of shorter *airs* in place of the more elaborate Italian *arias*. Also notable during this period were Handel's nearly 50 powerful operas, including *Rinaldo*, *Guilio Cesare* (Julius Caesar), and *Orlando*.

Vocal and Church Works Other genres of vocal music developed during the Baroque era. Most of these vocal forms were sacred in nature.

Grand Motet The motet continued to be a integral part of the Roman Catholic tradition throughout the Baroque era. In France, however, the motet evolved into the *grand motet*, which contrasted solo voices (accompanied by continuo instruments, such as bass viol or harpsichord) with a larger chorus. In Germany the grand motet was characterized by antiphonal exchanges between choirs and instruments.

Anthem In England the main feature of the Anglican choral service became the *anthem*, in which verses for solo voices (with organ accompaniment) alternated with verses sung by the full choir. In contrast to the Roman Catholic mass, anthems were sung in English, not Latin.

Oratorio The oratorio form flourished throughout 17th-century Italy, then spread throughout the rest of Europe. Essentially an unstaged opera with sacred text, in oratorio vocal soloists are accompanied by orchestra or instrumental ensemble; singing can be in either recitative or aria style. The first known oratorio, Cavalieri's *Rappresentatione di Anima et di Corpo*, debuted in 1600 in Rome. Notable oratorios were composed by Schütz, Bach, Georg Philipp Telemann (1681–1767), Giacomo Carissimi (1605–74), and Handel.

Cantata Derived from the Italian word *cantare*, "to sing," the cantata emerged in Italy early in the Baroque era, having evolved from the madrigal. Originally a short work for one or two voices and continuo, it evolved into a more substantial series of recitatives and arias with orchestral accompaniment—in essence, a small, unstaged, secular opera.

A chief proponent of the form was Alessandro Scarlatti, who wrote 600 or so cantatas, primarily for solo voice. Scarlatti bridged recitatives and arias with passages sung midway between the two styles, called *arioso*. Also notable are the cantatas of Handel and Bach; while he was *Kantor* in Leipzeig, Bach provided a new cantata every Sunday, close to 300 in all.

Instrumental Works During the late Baroque period, orchestral music gained popular status in the public concerts that proliferated in many European cities. During this era many of the "modern" orchestral instruments still in use today were first developed. Wind instruments that came to prominence during the Baroque period included the flute, clarinet, oboe, bassoon, trumpet, and French horn. In addition, the entire string family that we know today was developed during the Baroque period—including the violin, viola, cello, and double bass.

The rise of instrumental music served to diminish the importance of sacred musical forms. Before 1600 the church had been the center of musical development, with vocal music dominating. After 1600 the influence of church music began to wane; secular forms such as the sonata and the concerto gained prominence. Composers began to write music for a specific instrument, such as the violin, rather than music that could be sung or played by any combination of voices or instruments, as had been the case in previous eras.

Ricercare One of the earliest Baroque instrumental forms was the *ricercare*, which was first developed as a literal transcription of an existing vocal work for keyboard or other instruments. By the mid-Baroque period the ricercare had evolved into an independent instrumental form, primarily contrapuntal in nature. The mature ricercare was a single-movement form, with no clear-cut division of sections.

Sonata Even more notable was the development of a competing type of instrumental piece, composed of contrasting sections, called the *sonata*. During the early Baroque era, the sonata took the form of a piece for two melody instruments and continuo—typically two violins with cello or harpsichord—called the *trio sonata*. By the late Baroque, this had evolved into the *solo sonata*, for solo instrument and continuo. The Baroque-era sonata was typically in four movements (slow-fast-slow-fast), with the third and fourth movements based on popular dances, such as the *sarabande* and *gigue*.

During the Baroque period the violin was the most popular sonata instrument, although sonatas were written for all variety of instruments, including the oboe, flute, and cello—as well as for solo keyboard. Domenico Scarlatti, for example, wrote more than 500 sonatas for harpsichord, all in single-movement form.

Suite Contrast was important in the Baroque era, which led to the development of longer instrumental forms that incorporated multiple contrasting sections. Most notable was the *suite*, which was constructed from individual dance movements, often in the same key. In the early Baroque the suite consisted of four core movements (*allemande*, *courante*, *sarabande*, and *gigue*); by the late Baroque composers had gained the freedom to supplement these four movements with additional dances.

Handel wrote several well-known suites, primarily for keyboard, but also including the orchestral *Water Music* and *Music for the Royal Fireworks*. Also notable are the suites by Bach and Jean-Philippe Rameau (1683–1764).

Concerto The early 18th century saw the rise of the *concerto* form, with its emphasis on solo virtuosity. As developed by Vivaldi, Bach, and their counterparts, the concerto focused on one or more solo instruments supported by the larger orchestra. Vivaldi alone wrote close to 350 concertos, mainly for violin, but also for flute, oboe, and other instruments. An earlier influence was Tomaso Albinoni (1671–1751), who was the first composer to write concertos in three movements.

The *concerto grosso* became popular during the late Baroque era. This form alternated sections for orchestra with sections for a small ensemble within the larger orchestra, called the *concertino*. This form reached maturity in the works of Bach and Vivaldi, most notably those in Vivaldi's first published collection of concertos, titled *L'estro armonico*. Also notable were the works of Handel, especially his 12 *Concerti Grossi* op. 6, for strings and optional woodwinds.

Interestingly, many famous composers of the Baroque era were also noted instrumentalists who used the concerto form to showcase their instrumental skills. Bach, for example, was a highly accomplished keyboardist, and Vivaldi was a virtuoso violinist.

The Music of Johann Sebastian Bach The music of the late Baroque era is best represented by the numerous works of Johann Sebastian Bach. He produced an astounding variety of chamber and orchestral works (including the "Brandenburg" Concertos), as well as a large number of organ and keyboard works (such as *The Well-Tempered Clavier* and *The Art of Fugue*). His choral works included a variety of sacred and secular cantatas, motets and other large choral pieces (including *St. Matthew Passion* and *Christmas Oratorio*), and chorales and sacred songs. What makes Bach unique is his absolute mastery of the strict compositional techniques of his day. His innate talent enabled him to combine expressive melodies with the rigorous intricacy of counterpoint and the fugal form—most notably in his suites for solo violin and solo cello, as well as in much of his harpsichord music.

The Classical Period (1750–1820)

Each new period in Western music is marked by a revolt against the conventions of the previous period. This was especially true for the Classical period, in which younger musicians rebelled against the heavy ornamentation and perceived restrictions of Baroque-era counterpoint, as well as the emotionally constraining constructions of Bach and Handel. The musical revolution of the Classical period mirrored the cultural and political revolutions taking place in the last half of the 18th century. This period was host to the American Revolution, the French Revolution, and the Napoleonic Wars; writers such as Voltaire, Rousseau, and Paine challenged conventional political thought, while the Enlightenment helped to diminish the dominance of church on Western society.

Equally significant was the musical revolution of the Classical period. The patronage system of the Baroque era died out and was replaced by public concerts and a newfound freedom of choice in terms of compositional inspiration and form. Polyphony gave way to harmony, counterpoint gave way to melody, and ornamentation gave way to simplicity—and emotional detachment gave way to a more spontaneous and emotional musical expression.

The Classical Style In the early Classical period, this expression took different forms in different countries. In France the new style was called *rococo* or *gallant* ("courtly"), and bridged the Baroque and the Classical eras by blending a gracefully ornamented melody with chordal accompaniment. In Germany the new style was known as *empfindsamer Stil* ("sensitive style"), and resulted in longer compositions and the development of large orchestral forms, such as the concerto, sonata, and symphony. Italians did not have a name for their new style, although they were also important contributors to the development of the symphony and other new genres.

The later Classical period saw the development of a more lyrical style, and a focus on structural clarity rather than textural intricacy. Composers began to exploit the web of harmonic relationships among separate tones and chords within a key, and among several keys. The dominant approach was that of obbligato harmony rather than structured polyphony, with each voice playing an essential role in the texture and harmony of the music; graceful melodies with a light accompaniment replaced the heavy counterpoint of the Baroque period.

The Viennese School The Classical period is widely recognized as an exceptional period in terms of musical achievement. The climax of the era's musical development came at the end of the 18th century, with a group of musicians known collectively as the Viennese classical school.

By the mid-1700's, the city of Vienna had become a magnet to musicians from all of Europe, thanks in part to an abundance of wealthy patrons. This confluence of talent resulted in convergence of musical styles and a melting pot of ideas, out of which emerged the Classical style.

This new style was primarily forged by the three greatest composers living in Vienna at the time: Franz Joseph

Haydn (1732–1809), Wolfgang Amadeus Mozart (1756–91), and Ludwig van Beethoven (1770–1827). These three musical geniuses created a body of work—consisting of majestic sonatas, string quartets, symphonies, and operas—that has for generations defined the term *classical music*.

Instrumental Works During the Classical period, instrumental music finally became more important than vocal music. This was due in part to the improved technical quality of instruments that was achieved during this period, as well as to the development of several new and more expressive instruments.

The Piano and the Classical Orchestra Chief among these new instruments was the *pianoforte* (Italian for "soft-loud"), known simply as the piano. While the first piano was created ca. 1700, it was during the late 1700's that the instrument developed into the form we know today. The piano supplanted previous keyboard instruments such as the harpsichord and clavichord, and was capable of a wider range of dynamics than those earlier instruments could reproduce.

The Classical period also saw the development of the modern orchestra. During the Baroque period the orchestra was dominated by the string section, with wind instruments used only for doubling, reinforcing, and filling in harmonies. By the late 18th century, however, wind instruments were being used for more important and more independent material. The wind instruments were now regarded as equal to the strings in terms of playing the melody, as well as supplying harmony.

Haydn and Mozart helped to standardize the instrumental makeup of the orchestra—pairs of flutes, oboes, clarinets, bassoons, horns, and trumpet, along with the standard first and second violins, violas, cellos, double basses, and timpani. In the Classical orchestra, strings and winds were self-contained, melodically and harmonically independent of each other.

String Quartet Chamber music gained popularity in the Classical period, with works for small instrumental ensembles designed to be played in private residences. The most popular form of chamber music was the string quartet, with its extremely versatile grouping of two violins, viola, and cello.

The string quartet as we know it was primarily the invention of Haydn. Haydn's quartets consisted of four movements: fast, slow, minuet (a triple-time dance), and fast, with the first, second, and final movements in sonata form.

Later, Mozart built on Haydn's themes, adding a more sophisticated four-part texture and chromatic effects. It was also during this later Classical period that the string quartet moved from the private salon to the concert hall, firmly establishing the form in musical history.

Sonata In the Baroque period, sonatas were characterized by a light, dance-music style. In the Classical era, the Viennese composers injected drama and complexity into the sonata, creating a substantially new form with richer textures, more varied accompaniments, and a broader harmonic vocabulary. Notable in this regard is Haydn's Sonata in C Minor no. 36, which is rightly said to mark the introduction of the Viennese Classical style.

Many Classical composers embraced the newest instrument of the period, the piano, with its capacity for dynamic contrast and dramatic effects. This resulted in many notable piano sonatas, including Beethoven's "Pathètique" and "Moonlight" sonatas.

Key to the development of the Classical sonata was the *sonata form*, with its three-part structure of *exposition*, *development*, and *recapitulation*. This form was not only used in sonata pieces; it pervades nearly all the music of the Classical era, especially in regard to its treatment of tonality and theme.

Concerto The concerto form continued forward from the Baroque period. Haydn's early concertos were heavily influenced by the earlier work of J.S. and C.P.E. Bach (1714–88), while Mozart tended to write more in the Italian style. Mozart later wrote many concertos for piano and orchestra, with the orchestra sharing some of the melodic themes in addition to providing accompaniment. Mozart also introduced the *cadenza*, a virtuoso solo passage designed to display the technical skills of the soloist.

Symphony The symphony has its roots in the Italian *overture* of the late 17th century, but came to maturity in the Classical era. The Viennese composers introduced a richer, more developed orchestral style, and standardized on a three-movement form with well-defined contrasts of theme and color.

Haydn is popularly known as the "father of the symphony," for both his mastery of the form and his prodigious output. Haydn composed 104 symphonies; his final dozen symphonies, composed in London between 1791 and 1795, were his most notable works. Mozart was also a prolific symphonic composer, with 41 works to his name.

It was Beethoven, however, who decisively established the symphonic form in the musical firmament. Each of Beethoven's nine symphonies is highly individual, while at the same time retaining many traditional elements. Building on Haydn's example, Beethoven confirmed the symphony as a grand, unified structure, the apex of instrumental composition and arrangement.

Vocal Works Even though the emphasis of the Classical period was on new, longer instrumental works, the great composers continued to create both secular and sacred vocal works—in particular, masses and oratorios.

Mass The mass, as a musical style, continued to flourish in the Classical period, even as it took on more modern stylings. The Viennese composers introduced a more integrated structure to the mass, often merging the *Gloria* and *Credo* into a single section. Haydn employed symphonic techniques alongside more traditional practices, as did Mozart; Mozart's Coronation Mass contains many symphonic devices, as well as an almost-operatic intensity in the solo voices.

Oratorio and Cantata Sacred and secular cantatas declined in importance during the Classical period. The oratorio, however, increased in popularity. In Italy the most popular type of oratorio was the *oratorio volgare*, a two-part form with Italian (rather than Latin) lyrics. There were two primary types of oratorio in Germany: a dramatic form with biblical themes, and a contemplative form that emphasized sentimental expression. The most notable oratorios of the late Classical period were composed by Haydn. His oratorios—in particular, *Die Schöpfung* ("The Creation") and *Die Jahreszeiten* ("The Seasons")—are poetic celebrations of faith and nature, in a mature symphonic style.

Opera Opera underwent many important changes in the Classical era. By the late Baroque period, Italian opera had become a series of overly wrought arias designed to display the talents of superstar singers. As a reaction to this perceived vocal excess, Classical composers cut back on the ornamentation, reintroduced instrumental interludes and accompaniments between arias, and made greater use of choral singing. They also sought to combine groups of recitatives, arias, duets, choruses, and instrumental sections into unified scenes.

The Classical period also saw the decline of serious Italian opera (*opera seria*) and the rise of lighter forms, such as *opera buffa* and *opéra comique*. These new forms used more realistic spoken dialogue interspersed with songs; the music was also of a simpler style.

The most important reformer during the Classical era was Christoph Willibald von Gluck (1714–87). In his works—including *Orfeo ed Eurodice* and *Iphigénie en Tauride*—the music served the drama, without interruption by unnecessary orchestral passages or florid singing.

The reformation movement climaxed in the stage works of Mozart, in which every aspect of the vocal and instrumental portions contributed to the overall plot development and characterization. In Mozart's operas, such as *Le Nozze di Figaro* (The Marriage of Figaro), the music for each character is distinct in tone and style from the other characters, and the action is reflected in the structure of the work.

The Romantic Period (1820–1900)

Beginning in the early 19th century, composers began to extend the Classical style in new and unique ways. Instead of adhering to the formal guidelines set forth in the Classical period, Romantic composers followed the inspiration of literary, historical, pictorial, and other nonmusical sources. The emphasis, then, was on the personal expression of emotion and the freedom of form; there were no restrictions on the length of a piece, the number of movements, or the types of instruments or voices used.

This new movement resulted not in revolution, but in evolution—in both the expansion of established musical forms and the creation of new and related forms, such as the *symphonic poem* and German art song (*lieder*). The expansion of expression was seen in the use of unusual chord progressions, sophisticated harmonies and chromaticism, and unexpected modulations. While Romantic music was more complex than anything that came before—and ultimately brought about a disintegration of tonality—it was also infused by grand, sweeping, truly romantic melodies.

Instrumental Works The Romantic period saw the final evolution of most of the musical instruments used in symphonic orchestras today. Many of these developments—the use of valves on brass instruments, new key systems on woodwinds, and so on—made the instruments much easier to play, which encouraged their greater use in Romantic-era compositions.

Symphony In many ways the Romantic symphony is an expanded version of the Classical symphony. This is best seen in the later symphonies of Beethoven, which bridged the Classical and Romantic periods. Beethoven's Ninth Symphony, for example, is twice the length of his earlier symphonic works, and adds a large choir to the normal orchestral instrumentation.

While symphonic music of the Romantic era remained faithful to the concept of the Classical symphony, it also responded to the grandeur suggested in Beethoven's later works. Romantic-era symphonies tend to use larger orchestras than in the Classical period, and often incorporate more than four movements.

Key symphonic composers of the Romantic period included Felix Mendelssohn (1809–47), Robert Schumann (1810–56), Anton Bruckner (1824–96), and Antonín Dvorák (1841–1904). Bruckner was especially influential; his nine symphonies were on a monumental scale comparable to those of Beethoven, complete with soaring melodies and rich chromatic harmony.

Programme Music and the Symphonic Poem The late Romantic period saw the development of *programme music*—an instrumental work that is associated with an extramusical image or narrative text. Programme music doesn't attempt a literal musical interpretation of the chosen text, but rather provides an impression that the listener can use as a starting point to grasp the poetic idea of the subject. The best-known type of programme music is the *symphonic poem*, an extended orchestral piece in a single movement. Franz Liszt (1811–86) was the most visible proponent of this new genre; other sympathetic composers include Richard Strauss (1864–1949) and Hector Berlioz (1803–69). Notable symphonic poems include Liszt's *Tasso: Lamento e Trionfo* and *Héroïde funèbre*, along with Strauss's *Don Juan*.

Concerto The concerto also was expanded in the Romantic period. Starting with Beethoven, composers elevated the orchestra beyond mere accompaniment to more of an equal role to the soloist. In this respect Romantic concertos began to take on symphonic qualities. The Romantic period also saw an increase in popularity for the piano concerto. Mendelssohn, Schumann, and other composers created works that emphasized sustained dialogues between the piano and the orchestra, weaving both parts together into a dramatic whole.

Sonata Just as Romantic-era concertos emphasized an equality between soloist and accompanying instruments, sonatas of the period increased the importance of the piano accompaniment in regard to the solo instrument. Romantic sonatas were as much piano works as solo vehicles, and often demanded a new level of technical dexterity of the keyboardist.

Later in the Romantic period, some composers began to add to the traditional three- or four-movement sonata form. Schumann, for example, created sonatas that more closely resembled fantasias; Liszt used a programmatic approach to unify the sonata's sections. Most representative of this newer approach is Liszt's Piano Sonata in B Minor, written in three thematically unified movements that are designed to be played without a break.

Vocal Works Vocal music in the Romantic period explored the same boundaries as the instrumental music of the period—with both shorter, more intimate works and longer, more epic works joining the repertory.

Lieder Music based on poetry was the basis for another new Romantic musical form, the German art song, otherwise known as *lieder* (plural of *lied*, or "song"). In these art songs, composers attempted to portray with music the imagery and moods of the texts—typically 18th- and 19th-century poems. The most popular lieder of the Romantic era were composed by Schumann, Richard Strauss, Johannes Brahms (1833–97), Franz Schubert (1797–1828), and Hugo Wolf (1860–1903).

Sacred Music By the start of the 19th century, new masses were being written largely to celebrate state occasions. These new works—such as Berlioz' *Grande messe des morts*—were typically conceived on a large scale, complete with orchestra and brass bands. In addition, the oratorio gained new prominence, along with similarly epic form, as typified by Mendelssohn's *Elijah* and Berlioz's *L'enfance du Christ*.

Dramatic Music Some of the most significant innovations in style and form during the Romantic period were in musical drama—most notably the spectacular operas of France, Italy, and Germany.

Opera Even with the introduction of new instrumental forms, opera remained the most popular music of the 19th century. During the Romantic period, the art of opera reached its zenith, producing grand spectacles and offering numerous showcases for spectacular singing. In every way, Romantic operas were longer, bigger, and more majestic than their Classical-era counterparts.

Characteristic of the new Romantic opera was the French *grand opéra*. This type of work—such as Berlioz's epic *Les Troyens*—was not only longer in duration than previous French opera, but also employed more musicians, more artists, more technicians, and more stagehands. This style was supplemented by *drame lyrique*, a more lyrical and sentimental style typified by Charles-François Gounod's (1818–93) *Faust*.

In Italy Gioacchino Antonio Rossini (1792–1868) introduced a new style known as *bel canto* (literally, "beautiful singing"). This new style of opera featured complex and ornate melodic lines (which vocalists could ornament at will), simple harmonic structure, and musical numbers that combined to make composite scenes. Later in the 19th century, Rossini's countryman Guiseppe Verdi (1813–1901) introduced a new realism and intensity of expression to the form; his operas—such as *Rigoletto* and *La Traviata*—combined rhythmic vitality with superbly crafted melodies to great popular acclaim.

In Germany Richard Wagner (1813–83) advanced the majestic *music drama*, which combined elements from Greek tragedy and the symphonies of Beethoven into a dramatic whole that was referred to as *Gesamtkunstwerk* ("Complete Artwork"). Wagner's operas—most notably *Tristan und Isolde* and the four-opera cycle *Der Ring des Nibelungen*—pushed the boundaries of traditional tonality and impelled the art form to a larger scale. His groundbreaking work changed the nature of opera and influenced virtually all musical forms for decades to come.

Operetta In stark contrast to Wagner's imposing dramatic operas, was the debut of a new, less ponderous musical form called *operetta*. Rooted in the song and dance music of the late 19th century, the operetta was a form of light entertainment that, as practiced by Jacques Offenbach (1819–80) and Johann Strauss (1825–99), was a definite contrast to the often self-consciously "heavy" music of the times. While this form was often dismissed as inconsequential and predictable, it proved phenomenally popular among audiences of the time.

Ballet Prior to the Romantic period, music for the ballet was typically a mix of existing compositions and piecework by staff composers. Beginning with Beethoven's score for *Die Geschöpfe des Prometheus*, however, choreographers began to commission original music for their productions. This trend was particularly notable in Russia, where Pyotr Tchaikovsky (1840–93) set new standards for the role of music in classical ballet. His most enduring works include *Swan Lake*, *The Sleeping Beauty*, and *The Nutcracker*.

The Twentieth Century (1900–2000)

If the Romantic period represented an evolution from the Classical period, the 20th century witnessed a full-fledged musical revolution. The high value placed on individuality and personal expression in the late 1800's grew even more pronounced in the 1900's, with the very fabric of tonality being ripped apart in the search for new and unique musical forms. The defining feature of 20th-century music, then, is the lack of any central defining feature. Composers represent an enormous range of tastes, skills, and styles; what the general public continues to call "classical music" has splintered into a virtual plethora of competing styles and genres.

Musical Forms Twentieth-century composers continued to work in the mature musical forms of the Romantic period as well as new forms unique to the modern era.

Symphony Most major composers of the 20th century used and expanded upon the symphonic form. The modern symphony, however, was likely to incorporate extreme dissonances and jagged rhythms; many composers abandoned traditional tonality to embrace the various experimental styles typical of other 20th-century music.

Representative of the modern symphonic form are the later works of Gustav Mahler (1860–1911) and the symphonies of Jean Sibelius (1865–1957). Mahler composed lengthy works for large orchestras, some augmented by vocal soloists and massed choirs. Sibelius's compositions, in contrast, were shorter works for more traditional orchestras; he viewed the form as an abstract drama with a tight internal logic.

Other important symphonic composers of the 20th century include Sergey Rachmaninov (1873–1953), Sergey Prokofiev (1891–1953), and Dmitry Shostakovich (1906–75).

Opera Opera in the first half of the 20th century continued to be influenced by the works of the Romantic era. Richard Strauss, who bridged the Romantic and modern eras, composed intense works that reflected the tremendous influence of Wagner; Giacomo Puccini (1858–1924), with works such as *Tosca* and *Turandot*, continued the Italian grand opera tradition of Verdi and Rossini.

World War II proved to be a turning point for 20th-century opera, with postwar composers seeking to revitalize the form that had apparently come to a conclusion with the outbreak of hostilities in Europe. These newer composers, led by Benjamin Britten (1913–76), breathed new life into opera by judiciously integrating other 20th-century movements into the established art form.

Britten himself often worked outside opera's conventional boundaries, writing operas for children, for the church, and even for television. Later composers, such as Krzysztof Penderecki (b. 1933) and Karlheinz Stockhausen (b. 1928), further pushed opera's musical boundaries, while Virgil Thomson (1896–1989) and Douglas Moore

(1893–1969) injected American musical styles into the form. At the dawn of the new millennium, composers such as Philip Glass (b. 1937) and John Adams (b. 1947) continued to change the face of opera, introducing multimedia elements, political commentary, rock music and other unconventional elements.

Ballet Ballet in the early 20th century continued the late 19th-century practice of using specially written music by noted composers, such as Claude Debussy (1862–1918), Igor Stravinsky (1882–1971), Maurice Ravel (1746–1810), and R. Strauss. Perhaps the most notable—or notorious—of these new ballets was Stravinsky's *The Rite of Spring*. With music by Stravinsky and choreography by Vaclav Nijinsky (1889–1950), this 1913 work shocked audiences of the time; its Parisian premiere resulted in a near-riot among concertgoers. Stravinsky's score was revolutionary, full of violent rhythms and harsh harmonies, its dissonant melodies masterly yet unsettling. While the original audiences were overwhelmed by the work's unconventionality, critics recognized its genius, and *The Rite of Spring* has become one of the best-known and most influential pieces in the 20th-century repertory.

The second half of the century saw many ballet companies return to the historic practice of staging new ballets to existing compositions. There were several notable exceptions to this practice, however, including *Billy the Kid* and *Rodeo*, both by Aaron Copland (1900–90); *Undine* by Hans Werner Henze (b. 1926); and Britten's *The Prince of the Pagodas*.

Musical Theater The art form known as *musical theater* evolved from the operettas of the Romantic era and from the American vaudeville and European music hall traditions. During the last half of the 20th century many serious composers were drawn to the form, creating works that were very much in debt to traditional opera. Most notable were Leonard Bernstein (1918–90) and Steven Sondheim (b. 1930); their operatic-like works, together and apart, include *Candide*, *West Side Story*, and *Sweeney Todd*.

Film Music The newly developed cinematic art form of the 20th century presented another new venue for serious musical development, in the form of film soundtracks. The most innovative film composers—including Elmer Bernstein (b.1922), Bernard Herrman (1911–1975), Max Steiner (1888–1971), and Dmitri Tiomkin (1894–1979)—used all manner of modern musical conventions, and many of the 20th century's leading "classical" composers also made contributions to the genre or had their works adapted for the screen.

Musical Styles Composers in the 20th century experimented with all manner of musical styles, expanding on the sophisticated harmonies of the late Romantic period with increasingly radical explorations of chromaticism and non-traditional tonalities.

Impressionism Early in the 20th century, Claude Debussy became fascinated by Eastern music and the whole-tone scale. He helped create a style of music named after the style of painting known as *impressionism*, in which solo and orchestral music is created from subtle blends of sound similar to the blends of color in the paintings of Monet and Renoir. Other composers working in the form include Ravel and Karol Szymanowski (1882–1937); representative works include Debussy's *La mer* (The Sea) and *Prélude à l'aprés-midi d'un faune* (Prelude to the Afternoon of a Faun).

Chromaticism and the Twelve-Tone Method The Romantic concept of chromaticism continued to evolve in the modern era. The most extreme expression of chromaticism was *atonality*, as forwarded by the 12-tone music of Arnold Schoenberg (1874–1951). In Schoenberg's hands, the 12 tones of the octave are played in a predetermined order, creating an almost mechanical tonality with little or no relationship to the traditional tonalities of previous eras.

Microtonality and Polytonality Twelve-tone music led to the development of several similar musical styles, including *microtonality* and *polytonality*. Microtonal music uses the same serial approach as 12-tone, but divides the octave into more and smaller harmonic intervals; polytonality uses more than one tonality simultaneously.

Serialism *Serialism* is another style that evolved from the 12-tone method. In this method, pitches, rhythms, and dynamics are presented in a pre-determined fashion; the result is often called *total serialism*, in contrast to the 12-tone method's limited serialism. The most influential serial composers of the 20th century include Stockhausen, Milton Babbitt (b. 1916), and Pierre Boulez (b. 1925).

Interdeterminancy While serialism is highly programmed, later composers believed that some aspects of their music should be left to chance—letting the performer choose which notes to play, or basing some sound choices on the outcome of a random event, such as the rolling of dice. In some cases, proponents of *indeterminancy* use colors and symbols in place of traditional music notation. Composers within this genre include John Cage (1912–92) and Earle Brown (b. 1926).

Minimalism The style known as *minimalism* arose in response to the increasing complexity of both "classical" and popular music forms, including the highly sophisticated type of jazz known as bebop. Minimalism is hypnotic in its repetition, characterized by relatively simple melodies and rhythms employed with diatonic harmony and long pedal points. Chief among the minimalists of the late 20th century are Philip Glass (b. 1937) and Steve Reich (b. 1936), who have both had success with traditional and popular applications of this style.

Musique Concrète In 1948 the engineer and composer Pierre Schaeffer (1910–95) began to use the newly developed magnetic tape recorder to record various everyday sounds, and then combine those sounds in various ways. The result was dubbed *musique concrète* (French, "concrete music"), as it consisted of "real-world" sounds, rather than the "artificial" sounds of musical instruments.

Electronic Music *Musique concrète* marked the beginning of what we now call electronic music. In this new and developing genre, electronic equipment—including but not limited to computers and synthesizers—is used to generate, modify, and combine all manner of sounds. Early composers of electronic music included Cage, Stockhausen, and Herbert Eimert (1897–1972); this style became more prevalent (and integrated into other musical forms) as newer types of electronic instruments were developed in the later years of the 20th century.

Neo-Classicism In a world of increasingly experimental and eclectic compositions, the style known as *Neo-Classicism* offered a welcome respite from oppressively progressive musical approaches. The neoclassical style marked a return to the classic concept that all elements of a composition should contribute to the overall structure of the piece; it blended formal schemes from the Baroque and Classical eras with a modified sense of tonality that embraced chromaticism and other elements of the Romantic and modern eras.

The foremost proponent of the Neo-Classical style was Igor Stravinsky. Retreating from the experimentation of his earlier works, Stravinsky began, in the early 1920's, to embrace the musical forms and instrumentation of earlier periods. He abandoned the dense chords and shifting meters characteristic of *The Rite of Spring* and other controversial works, substituting a more traditional tonality—although still filtered through modern harmonic sensibilities.

Other composers using the Neo-Classical style included the Europeans Prokofiev, Shostakovich, and Paul Hindemith (1895–1963), along with American composers Thomson and Elliott Carter (b. 1908). Representative works include Stravinsky's *The Symphony of Psalms* and *Oedipus Rex*.

Nationalism and Folk Music *Nationalism* describes serious musical forms that embrace elements of *folk music* native to specific countries. In the 20th century, composers such as Copland and Charles Ives (1874–1954) introduced themes from American folk and religious music into classical forms, similar to the way Dvorák integrated folk melodies into his music of the late Romantic period. Other modern composers also worked with the folk music of their native countries; notable examples include Béla Bartók (1881–1945), Leos Janáçek (1854–1928), and Ralph Vaughan Williams (1872–1958). Representative works in this style include Copland's *Appalachian Spring* and Vaughan Williams's *A London Symphony*.

American Music and Third Stream While Copland helped to define American "classical" music in the 20th century, other composers further wedded native musical forms (such as blues and jazz) to create an even more complete American musical language. Chief among these architects were George Gershwin (1898–1937) and Gunther Schuller (b. 1925), who coined the term *third stream* for the new musical styles that combined jazz and concert works.

Musical Forms

Church Music

From the earliest times, music has been associated with religious worship. Many vocal forms have their roots in the music of the Catholic and Protestant Churches.

Anthem The *anthem* is the Protestant Church's version of the Latin motet. In most instances the choir is accompanied by organ; many anthems include passages for vocal soloists, either individually or in combination. Major composers of this form include Henry Purcell and John Blow (1649–1708).

Chorale The *chorale* (in German, *choral*) is a type of unison hymn characteristic of the German Reformed Church. This sacred form resulted from Martin Luther's desire to restore the congregation's role in church services. Most chorales feature simple devotional words set to familiar tunes—either folk songs or the traditional ecclesiastical melodies known as plainsong—intended for singing by the congregation. (This is in contrast to the more formal Catholic mass, which is sung by a separate choir.)

Early Lutheran chorales had much of the free rhythm of plainsong, often mixing duple and triple time. Later chorales employed a more rigid metric scheme. The melody of early chorales was often placed in the tenor voice. During the 17th century the melody moved to the treble voice, and four-part chorales became popular during the 17th and 18th centuries.

One of the most prolific composers for the chorale was J. S. Bach, during the Baroque era. Bach composed some 30 chorales, and reharmonized 400 others. He also used several chorale melodies in his *St. John Passion* and *St. Matthew Passion*.

Conductus A *conductus* is a metrical Latin song, either sacred or secular, for two or three voices. The conductus originated in France during the 12th century, and was superseded by the motet.

Lauda The *lauda* is a religious song not based on liturgical texts, typically performed in either Italian or Latin. This form was popular during the 13th, 15th, and 16th centuries.

Mass The Roman Catholic *Mass* has inspired many great vocal works. The five passages of the Mass that are frequently set for choir or for choir and vocal soloists include the *Kyrie* ("Lord have mercy"), *Gloria in excelsis Deo* ("Glory be to God on high"), *Credo* ("I believe"), *Sanctus* ("Holy, holy"), and *Agnus Dei* ("O Lamb of God"). In some later Masses these five sections are subdivided even further; for example, J. S. Bach divided the *Kyrie* into three parts: *Kyrie eleison* ("Lord have mercy"), *Christe eleison* ("Christ, have mercy"), and a second *Kyrie eleison*.

The earliest polyphonic masses were set in the 14th century, by Machaut. In the 15th century secular tunes were introduced to the Mass as a *cantus firmus*, courtesy of Du Fay and his 15th-century contemporaries. By the end of the 16th century the Mass had evolved into an unaccompanied contrapuntal style, as practiced by Palestrina, Victoria, and William Byrd (1542–1623).

In the 17th and 18th centuries the mass welcomed an increase in solo singing and then, moving into the 19th century, evolved into more of an oratorio style. Examples of this mature style include Bach's Mass in B Minor and Beethoven's Mass in D.

Motet The *motet* is a short unaccompanied choral work, derived from the earlier *conductus*, popular from the 13th through the 16th centuries. The early motet was exclusively a sacred form, based on pre-existing melodies; other words and melodies were added in counterpoint. In the 15th century Du Fay introduced secular melodies as part of the motet's cantus firmus. Other notable motet composers include Palestrina, Victoria, Byrd, and J. S. Bach. The secular counterpart of the motet is the madrigal.

Grand Motet This musical form is a motet for large ensembles of voices and instruments, contrasting solo voices with the larger chorus. The grand motet was originally performed in the liturgies of the court chapel of Louis XIV, and later performed as concert pieces throughout 18th-century France and Germany.

Oratorio An *oratorio* is a dramatic musical setting of a religious libretto, for solo singers, choir, and orchestra. An oratorio is like a nonsecular opera, but without the scenery or costumes; oratorios are typically performed in concert halls or churches. The oratorio originated in plays given in the Oratory of St. Philip Neri in 16th-century Rome; the musical form developed ca. 1600. Emilio del Cavalieri's (ca. 1550–1602) *La rappresentazione di anima e di corpo* (The Representation of Soul and Body) is generally recognized as the first oratorio. Later oratorios were written by A. Scarlatti, Schütz, Haydn, Beethoven, Mendelssohn, and Handel; Handel's *Messiah* is perhaps the most recognized of all oratorios.

Some secular works, such as Handel's *Semele* and Stravinsky's *Oedipus Rex*, are also considered oratorios—or, in some cases, *opera-oratorios*. Certain biblical oratorios, such as Shütz's *The Christmas History*, are called *historia*.

Plainsong *Plainsong*, also known as *plainchant*, is the large body of traditional ritual melody of the Western Christian Church. A plainsong is a chant composed of a single line of vocal melody, typically unaccompanied and performed in a free rhythm. The rhythm of plainsong is the free rhythm of speech.

Plainsong developed during the early centuries of Christianity. The form matured during the sixth century, at the request of Pope Gregory I, and was subsequently known as *Gregorian chant*.

Plainsong has its own system of notation, using a four-line staff (in contrast to the modern five-line staff) and no bar lines. There are two primary types of plainsong: *responsorial* (developed from the recitation of psalms) and *antiphonal* (developed as pure melody).

Other religions, including the Greek Orthodox and Jewish churches, have similar types of ritual songs, although they are not included in the definition of plainsong.

Voluntary A *voluntary* is an organ piece played before or after a service of the Anglican Church. The voluntary is often, but not always, extemporized.

Vocal Music

Western vocal music evolved from both sacred forms and secular folk songs. Vocal forms can incorporate either solo vocals (either *a cappella* or with instrumental accompaniment) or group (choral) vocals.

Aria As developed in Italy during the 18th century, an *aria* is a lengthy and involved solo vocal piece in A-B-A form. The aria is an integral part of the operatic form.

There are eight primary types of arias: *aria cantabile*, slow and smooth; *aria di portamento*, dignified in a legato style; *aria di mezzo carattere*, passionate and with elaborate orchestral accompaniment; *aria parlante*, declamatory; *aria di bravura*, requiring great vocal control; *aria all'unisono*, with accompaniment in unison or octaves with the vocal part; *aria d'imitazione*, imitative of bird songs or other natural sounds; and *aria concertata*, with elaborate instrumental accompaniment.

Arietta The *arietta* is a shorter and simpler aria, typically without the middle (B) section.

Caccia The *caccia* is a 14th-century Italian form in which two vocalists "chase" each other in strict canon. The word *caccia* means "chase" or "hunt" in Italian, and the text often deals with hunting.

Cantata The term *cantata* has described different musical forms over the centuries. The earliest form, as practiced in the 17th century, referred to a dramatic madrigal sung by a solo vocalist or vocalists, accompanied by lute or basso continuo. There were two variations of this cantata form, the secular *cantata da camera* ("chamber cantata") and nonsecular *cantata da chiesa* ("church cantata"). A. Scarlatti was one of the chief proponents of this form, writing more than 600 pieces.

During the 18th century the cantata became longer and more complex, typically containing recitatives and arias—much like a short, unstaged opera. This type of cantata typically was written for soloist with organ or orchestral accompaniment. Composers in this style included Bach (who wrote close to 300 church cantatas), Handel, Schütz, and Telemann. Representative cantatas of this period include Bach's *Coffee Cantata* and *Peasant Cantata*.

By the 19th century the cantata evolved into a form resembling a short oratorio, on both sacred and secular themes. In the 20th century the term defines vocal music of various forms, although still loosely defined as vocal solo with instrumental accompaniment.

Canzona The *canzona* is a song form, similar to the madrigal, originally practiced by troubadours of the 16th century. The canzona evolved from a literal transcription of French chanson into Italian, and has a characteristic A-A-B form.

In the late 16th and 17th centuries, the vocal canzona was translated into lute and keyboard compositions that foreshadowed the later sonata and fugue forms. Primary practitioners of the keyboard canzona included J. S. Bach, Girolamo Frescobaldi (1583–1643), and Andrea Gabrieli (1510–86).

Chanson *Chanson* is, literally, French for "song." The representative chanson is a song with repeating verses; the form originated in France and northern Italy in the 14th century, surviving until the late 16th century.

Early chansons were written for a solo voice or small group of voices, with instrumental accompaniment. Later chansons became more elaborate, incorporating contrapuntal techniques and vocal effects that mimicked bird calls and the like. Notable chanson composers include Du Fay, Binchois, Sermisy, and Janequin.

Concert Aria The *concert aria* is a virtuoso solo song, with accompaniment, based on the Italian operatic aria.

Lieder The word *lieder* is the plural of *lied*—German for "song." In popular usage, lieder refer to a distinctive type of German vocal composition of the Romantic period.

The traditional lieder is a nonoperatic art song with lyrics based on a dramatic poem; in performance, the vocal and the piano accompaniment are of equal importance.

There are two types of lieder. *Strophic song* is similar to a hymn, with each stanza receiving the same melody; *through-composed* song provides different music for every stanza. Brahms, Schubert, Schumann, Mahler, and Strauss were all noted for their lieder; representative examples include Schubert's "Gretchen am Spinnrade" and Brahms's extended cycle of solo songs, the *Magelone* Romances, Op. 33.

Madrigal The *madrigal* is a secular vocal composition that originated in Italy during the 13th century. The typical madrigal is a polyphonic composition for four to six voices, typically unaccompanied, based on a poem or other secular text. Early composers in the madrigal form included Lassus, Palestrina, and A. Gabrieli; chief among the later Italian madrigal composers was Monteverdi, who created several madrigals based on sacred text.

The madrigal was introduced to England in the late 16th century, most notably by Nicholas Yonge's (d. 1619) 1588 publication of *Musica Transalpina*, a collection of Italian madrigals with English words. Several English composers embraced the madrigal form, notably Morley, William Byrd (1543–1623), and Thomas Weelkes (ca. 1576–1623).

The madrigal survived another hundred years, but was superseded by the cantata by the early 17th century.

Ode An ode is a ceremonial vocal work, typically with orchestral accompaniment. Examples include Purcell's *Ode for St. Cecilia's Day* and Sir Edward Elgar's (1857–1934) *Coronation Ode*.

Serenata A *serenata* is a type of serenade performed outdoors in the evening.

Instrumental Music

Instrumental music developed later than vocal music, as it was dependent on the evolving musical instrument technology over the ages. Many instrumental forms are based on types of local dance; others evolved from earlier sacred and vocal forms.

Allemande As derived from German and Swiss peasant dance, the *allemande* is a dance in 4/4 or duple time, popular in the 17th and early 18th centuries. The allemande was often the first movement of a suite, or the first movement after the prelude. It has a serious character and moderate tempo.

Chaconne A *chaconne*, also known as a *passacaglia*, is a dance in triple time with a repeating bass line (known as *ground bass*). Many operas of the Baroque era—by Lully, Rameau, and others—ended with a chaconne movement. Some of the best-known chaconnes include the solo violin section at the end of Bach's 2nd Partita in D Minor; Purcell's aria *"When I am laid in earth,"* from *Dido* and *Aeneas*; Beethoven's 21 Variations in C minor for piano; and the finale of Brahms's Symphony no. 4.

Chamber Music *Chamber music* is music for a small group of solo instruments, originally designed for performance in houses and small halls—not intended for the church, theater, or large concert hall.

Chamber music is easiest understood as what it is not; it is not music for a vocal or instrumental soloist, nor is it music for an orchestra or chorus. Instead, most chamber music is written for two (duet), three (trio), four (quartet), five (quintet), six (sextet), seven (septet), or eight (octet) instruments, with all the parts being relatively equal in importance—that is, the music is not intended for a soloist with accompaniment.

Chamber music can be written for string or wind instruments. Perhaps the most popular form is the *string quartet*, composed of two violins, one viola, and one cello.

Haydn could be considered the father of modern chamber music. Before Haydn, most music of this type was supplied with a figured bass, extemporized on harpsichord. Haydn introduced the concept of four (or more) equal parts, precisely arranged without room for extemporization. Subsequently, most major composers have contributed in some way to the modern chamber music repertory.

Choral Symphony A *choral symphony* is a symphony that incorporates a choir. The most notable example of this form is Beethoven's Symphony no. 9 in D Minor, in which the choir joins the orchestra in the final movement, an adaptation of Schiller's *Ode to Joy*.

Chorale Prelude The *chorale prelude* (also known as the *choral prelude*) is a solo keyboard piece that grew out of the custom of playing organ preludes and interludes to the vocal chorale in the services of the Protestant Church. There are two types of chorale preludes. The first is based on an imaginative treatment of the chorale melody, often with elaborate counterpoint; the second suggests rather than reproduces the chorale melody, by means of elaboration on the first few notes of the theme.

Composers who helped to developed the form included Jan Pieterszoon Sweelinck (1562–1621), Samuel Scheidt

(1587–1654), and Johann Pachelbel (1653–1706). Chief among the practitioners of the mature form were J. S. Bach and Henry Purcell.

Concertino As developed in the 19th century, a *concertino* is a short concerto for orchestra and one or more soloists. (The term *concertino* can also refer to a small instrumental ensemble within a larger orchestra.)

Concerto A *concerto* is an instrumental work in which one or more solo instruments are contrasted with a larger orchestra. While the first known concertos date back to the late 16th century, the form came to prominence in the late Baroque era with Vivaldi's violin concertos (notably his programmatic "Four Seasons"), Handel's organ concertos, and Bach's harpsichord concertos; also notable are Bach's orchestral "Brandenburg" Concertos.

The modern concerto was established by Mozart, who composed nearly 50 works for various combinations of instruments. Most modern concertos are in three movements. While early concertos featured a *cadenza* where the soloist would display his virtuoso skills via improvisation, modern composers are more likely to write out the cadenza beforehand, dispensing with the improvisation.

Many different types of concertos were composed during the Baroque era. A concerto designed for performance in a secular venue was called *concerto da camera*, or chamber concerto. A concerto designed for performance in church was called *concerto da chiesa*, or church concerto. A concerto with a small group of soloists (called a *concertino*), in addition to the traditional orchestra or string ensemble, was called *concerto grosso*, or great concerto.

In the 20th century the term *concerto for orchestra* was used to describe a concerto-like work that did not have a specific soloist (although individual members of the orchestra might be called upon to perform solo passages). Composers in this form include Bartók, Zoltán Kodály (1882–1967), and Sir Michael Tippett (1905–98).

Courante The *courante* is a French dance in rapid time, popular in the 17th century. Some variations combine simple triple time with compound duple rhythms; Bach, especially, favored this variation, representing the conflicting rhythms in the right and left hands of his keyboard pieces. The courante was typically the second movement of the suite.

Divertimento A *divertimento* is an 18th-century Italian suite of light entertaining music, typically written for a small number of instruments. Mozart wrote 25 of these pieces; they are sometimes referred to as serenades or cassations. The French version of divertimento is *divertissement*; these are sometimes inserted into ballet, opera, or other stage spectacles.

Fantasia A *fantasia* is an instrumental composition that avoids conventional forms and structures; form is of secondary importance. As developed in 16th century Italy, early fantasias strictly imitated vocal motets; early English fantasias (called *fancy*) were primarily contrapuntal in construction and in several sections with a common theme, thus representing an early version of theme and variation. Later organ fantasias by Sweelinck and Bach suggested more of an improvisational character and the play of free fancy.

In the 19th century several composers used the term *fantasia* to describe their short mood pieces; most notable of these pieces is Schumann's *Fantasie-stücke*. The term can also describe a composition comprising a string of tunes from an opera. The English equivalent of the fantasia is the *fancy*; the French is *fantaisie*; and the German, *fantasie*.

Fugue The *fugue* is a particularly strict type of contrapuntal composition, usually for instruments but occasionally for choir. In a fugue, the first "voice" states a short melody or phrase (known as the *subject*); additional voices enter successively in imitation. Bach wrote a number of organ and other instrumental fugues. Also notable is Beethoven's *Grosse fuge* for string quartet, op. 133. A shortened type of fugue is sometimes called a *fughetta*. A passage in fugal style from another musical form is called *fugato*.

Gavotte The *gavotte* is a French dance in common time, popularized in the court of Louis XIV by Lully and other composers.

Intermezzo As originally conceived in the 16th century, an *intermezzo* was an instrumental piece played between sections of more serious fare. In this context, an intermezzo might be a song or madrigal performed between the acts of a play.

In the early 18th century, the concept of the intermezzo had evolved to describe the separate plots introduced by secondary, comic characters recently introduced into opera seria. (This development eventually became the new form called opera buffa.) By the 19th century, the word *intermezzo* was applied to any short instrumental interlude inserted into an opera to denote a passage of time. The word *intermezzo* also describes a short piano piece with no set form, such as Brahms's eight *Klavierstücke*, Op. 76.

Miniature As established in the Romantic period, a *miniature* is a short piano piece based on a single musical idea. Several different types of works carry this classification, including the *ballade*, *etude*, *impromptu*, and *nocturne*. Frédéric Chopin's (1810–49) *Ballade in G Minor* is an example of a ballade miniature.

Minuet A *minuet* is a dance in triple time, originally as practiced by the court of the 17th century. The minuet originated and was adapted from French rustic dance, and is so-called because of its characteristic small steps. Lully and other Baroque-era composers embraced the form, and it soon became one of the optional movements of the instrumental suite. Bach and Handel incorporated the minuet into their overtures, and in the 18th century the minuet was integrated into symphonies (as the standard third movement) by Haydn, Mozart, and others.

A typical minuet is in A-B-A form. The B section is often a contrasting minuet called the *trio*. (The name comes from the practice of some French composers who wrote this middle section in three-part harmony.)

Overture Not to be confused with the piece of instrumental music played before an opera, oratorio, or play, this type of *overture* (sometimes called a *concert overture*) is an independent single-movement instrumental work, typically used to open a concert. Some overtures are written in sonata form; others are more like symphonic poems. A good example of the later style is Mendelssohn's *The Hebrides*.

Prelude Strictly defined, a *prelude* is a piece of music that precedes something else. Examples would be the first movement of a suite, or an orchestral introduction to an opera. The word *prelude* is also used to describe a short piece for solo piano. Composers contributing to the prelude repertory include Debussy, Chopin, and Rachmaninov.

Programme Music As originally described by Liszt, *programme music* is instrumental music that tells a story, illustrates a literary idea, or evolves a pictorial scene. Primary contributors to the form included Liszt, Berlioz, Tchaikovsky, Strauss, and Modest Petrovich Mussorgsky (1839–81). Notable works include Berlioz' *Symphonie Fantastique*, Strauss's *Also sprach Zarathustra*, and Mussorgsky's *Pictures at an Exhibition*.

Ricercare The *ricercare* was initially a transcription of a vocal work for keyboard or instrumental ensemble; in the 16th and 17th centuries it evolved into an independent instrumental work. There are two types of ricercare: homophonic (with a single melody line) and contrapuntal (with two or more contrasting melody lines). The last style is more common, typically with elaborate fugal or canonic stylings, as witnessed in Bach's *Das musikalische Opfer*.

Sarabande The *sarabande* is a dance form that originated in Latin America. It appeared in Spain in the early 16th century, and traveled to France and England in the early 17th century. The Spanish sarabonde was in a lively triple time, but the French and English preferred a more stately version of the form. It became a standard version of the instrumental suite, as practiced by Purcell, Bach, Handel, and others.

Sonata A *sonata* is a composition for solo piano or another instrument with piano accompaniment; sonatas typically have no more than two performers.

The sonata originated in the 16th century as any piece that was played rather than sung. During the 17th century the term was used to describe instrumental compositions divided into five or more contrasting sections. The Baroque sonata, as practiced by A. Scarlatti, C. P. E. Bach, and others, had from three to six movements, like a suite. During the Classical period, Haydn, Mozart, and Beethoven established the sonata as having three movements, allegro-andante-allegro; this format, dubbed *sonata form*, is also used in other musical forms.

Baroque-era sonatas designed for performance in secular venues are called *sonata da camera* or chamber sonata. Sonatas from the same era designed for performance in church are called *sonata da chiesa* or church sonata. The *trio sonata* is a Baroque-era sonata for voice, violin, and cello, and the *sonatina* ("little sonata") is a short sonata, typically lighter and easier to perform than a regular sonata.

String Quartet The *string quartet* is a particular form of chamber music written for two violins, viola, and cello. In terms of importance, the string quartet is to chamber music as the symphony is to orchestral music; most major composers have contributed to the string quartet repertory.

The first string quartets were written at the beginning of the 18th century, during the closing years of the Baroque era. Early composers for the string quartet included A. Scarlatti and Guiseppe Tartini (1692–1770), but the form reached its zenith with the works of Haydn, Mozart, Beethoven, and Schubert.

Suite As established in the Baroque period, a *suite* is a piece of instrumental music in several movements, usually in dance style. The form was most important in the 17th and 18th centuries.

A typical suite of the Baroque period might commence with an overture and include the following movements: allemande, courante, sarabande, and gigue, all typically in the same key. Additional movements might include bourrée, gavotte, minuet, musette, passepied, and rigaudon. Examples of Baroque-era suites include Handel's *Fireworks Music* and Bach's six cello and four orchestral suites.

In later eras the term was used to describe assemblages of movements from ballet or opera scores, as well as original multimovement compositions. Popular instrumental suites include Ravel's *Daphnis et Chloé*, Tchaikovsky's *Nutcracker Suite*, and Gustav Holst's (1874–1934) *Planets Suite*.

Symphony The *symphony* (in Italian, *sinfonia*) evolved from the overture to late 17th-century operas, as first practiced by A. Scarlatti, and came to prominence in the 18th century. The modern symphony is a large-scale instrumental composition, much like a sonata for orchestra, usually in four movements (although this varies). In the Classical and Romantic periods, the typical symphony opened with an allegro movement, followed by a slow movement, then a minuet or scherzo, ending with an allegro or rondo movement; in some instances the slow movement is moved to the third or fourth position.

The symphonic orchestra of the 18th century typically included strings, woodwinds, horns, and a harpsichord or other continuo instrument. Symphonic composers of this era included C. P. E. Bach, Giovanni-Battista Sammartini (ca. 1700–75), François Gossec (1734–1829), William Boyce (1711–79), and Johann Wenzel Stamitz (1717–57).

It was Haydn who most completely defined the symphonic form. Haydn's 104 symphonic works helped to expand the form, and to break it from its rigid four movement structure. His symphonies drew on a broad variety of source material, including folk songs and music originally written for plays, and he employed all manner of forms and variations.

Haydn thus influenced his contemporary, Mozart, who made his own impressive contributions to the repertory, most notably no. 38 in D (*Prague*) and no. 41 in C (*Jupiter*). Mozart's later symphonies further influenced Haydn's last 12 symphonies (collectively called the *London Symphonies*), especially no. 94 in G (*Surprise*) and no. 102 in B♭ (*London*).

The dawn of the 19th century saw a new artistic peak for the symphonic form. Beethoven introduced a heightened level of emotional expression to the form, accompanied by a boldness of harmony and tonal relationships, beginning with no. 3 in E♭ (*Eroica*). Beethoven's other defining symphonies included No. 6 in F (*Pastoral*) and no. 9 in D minor (*Choral*), which incorporated vocals into the finale in a setting of Schiller's *Ode to Joy*.

The Romantic period saw Mendelssohn and Schumann interject romantic feeling and pictorialism into the classic symphonic form, Liszt adapt the form into symphonic poems, Berlioz introduce programmatic elements (in his *Symphonie Fantastique*), and Brahms uphold the classical design. It is Bruckner's nine symphonies, however, that represent the epitome of the Romantic-era symphony, exploring classical principles on a grand architectural scale.

Symphonic music in the 20th century was subject to the same stylistic schisms that typified other musical forms. Sibelius attempted to compress the symphony into a more essential form, while Mahler expanded the symphony in both theme and instrumentation. Other composers, such as Vaughan Williams, Shostakovich, and Ives, also contributed significant works to the 20th-century symphonic canon.

Symphonic Poem As developed by Liszt, *the symphonic poem*—also called the tone poem—is a single-movement orchestral work on a symphonic scale. The symphonic poem is a type of programme music; Liszt composed 13 symphonic poems that dealt with subjects taken from classical mythology, Romantic literature, and imaginative fantasy, including *Prometheus* and *Les Préludes*. Other proponents of the form include Tchaikovsky, Bedrich Smetana (1824–84), and Camille Saint-Saëns (1835–1921). Richard Strauss composed symphonic poems that he dubbed *Tondichtungen*, or "tone-poems."

Toccata The *toccata* is a short keyboard piece, originally a movement (often a prelude) within a longer instrumental work but later a self-contained solo work. The foremost composer for the toccata form was J. S. Bach, who wrote several toccatas and fugues, as well as harpsichord toccatas in multiple movements.

Dramatic Music

Vocal and instrumental music are often combined with acting or dance to present dramatic stories in a theatrical fashion. The most notable forms of dramatic music include ballet and opera, and, in the 20th century, the musical theater and film soundtracks.

Ballet A *ballet* is an entertainment in which dancers perform to music to tell a story or, in some cases, to express a mood. Over the years music for the ballet has proven as vital in the classical repertory as music for the symphony and the opera; most major composers—including Mozart, Beethoven, Verdi, Wagner, Tchaikovsky, Ravel, and Stravinsky—have composed for the ballet.

The ballet came into being in France and Italy during the 16th and 17th centuries, especially in the court of Louis XIV. The first ballet is generally acknowledged to be *Balet comique de la Royne*, given in Paris in 1581.

Ballets of the Baroque era were quite formal and rigid in structure and theme. In the 18th century J.G. Noverre (1717–1810), collaborating with Gluck, Mozart, and others, helped to breach convention and establish the ballet as a more dramatic form. By the 19th century ballet had become an integral part of opera, and the 20th century saw the introduction of less conventional choreography to the form—and the export of the ballet into more popular art forms, such as the musical theater.

Musically, the ballet reached its zenith in the late 19th century works of Tchaikovsky (*Swan Lake*, *Sleeping Beauty*, *Nutcracker*) and the more progressive works of 20th century composers such as Ravel (*Daphnis et Chloé*), Stravinsky (*Firebird*, *The Rite of Spring*), and Prokofiev (*Cinderella*, *Romeo and Juliet*).

There are many different types of ballet, including: *acte de ballet*, an 18th-century French form, combining opera and ballet in a single act; *ballet d'action*, a dramatic ballet, as established in the late 18th century; *ballet de cour*, a 17th-century ballet of the French court; and *comédie-ballet*, a late 17th-century French combination of opera and ballet.

Film Music Music written to accompany the action in motion pictures is called *film music*. In the days of silent film, live music was provided by a pianist or small orchestra in the movie theater; the first piece of original film music was written by Saint-Saens for the 1908 film *L'Assassinat du Duc de Guise*.

With the advent of sound recording, film music was included as part of the movie soundtrack. While much film music is truly incidental, many notable composers have contributed distinguished scores that could easily survive as stand-alone works. The most accomplished film composers include Max Steiner (*Casablanca*, *Gone With the Wind*), Elmer Bernstein (*The Magnificent Seven*, *The Great Escape*), Bernard Herrman (*Citizen Kane*, *Vertigo*), Dmitri Tiomkin (*High Noon*, *The High and the Mighty*), John Williams (1932–2004) (*Star Wars*, *Raiders of the Lost Ark*), and John Barry (b. 1933) (*Born Free*, *Out of Africa*). In addition, many films have used existing compositions in their scores, most notably Strauss's *Also sprach Zarathustra* in *2001—A Space Oddysey* and Rachmaninov's C minor piano concerto in *Brief Encounter*.

Intermedio The term *intermedio* refers to vocal and instrumental music performed between the acts of a play.

Masque A *masque* is a dramatic entertainment with vocal and instrumental music, popular in 17th century England. The form is derived from the Italian intermedio.

Musical Theater *Musical theater* (also known as *musical comedy* or just *musical*) is a type of light musical entertainment, derived from the earlier operetta, that combines popular song with dramatic acting in service of the plot. The form developed in England in the late 19th century (the first musical is thought to be 1892's *In Town*), but gained enormous popularity in the United States during the first half of the 20th century.

Early musicals tended to be light on plot and heavy on vocal and dance numbers. Many musicals were showcases for the latest songs from the popular composers of the day (Jerome Kern, George Gershwin, Cole Porter, et al.), with the dramatic action coming to a halt with the commencement of each self-contained musical number. Starting with *Oklahoma*! (1943), however, the music and drama became more integrated, with each song serving to advance the plot; later musicals, such as *Phantom of the Opera*, became almost operatic in they way they blended music and drama.

Notable composers of the musical theater form include Richard Rodgers (1902–79) and Oscar Hammerstein II (1895–1960), with *Oklahoma!*, *South Pacific*, and *The Sound of Music*; Frederick Loewe (1901–88) and Alan Jay Lerner (1918–86), with *My Fair Lady* and *Camelot*; Frank Loesser (1910–69), with *Guys and Dolls* and *How to Succeed in Business Without Really Trying*; Leonard Bernstein (1918–90), with *West Side Story* and *Candide*; Stephen Sondheim (b. 1930), with *Company*, *A Little Night Music*, and *Sweeney Todd*; Andrew Lloyd Webber (b. 1948), with *Jesus Christ Superstar*, *Evita*, *Cats*, and *Phantom of the Opera*; and Claude-Michel Shönberg (b. 1944), composer of *Les Miserables* and *Miss Saigon*.

Opera *Opera* (short for *opera in musica*) is a drama set to music. In practice, opera consists of vocals with instrumental accompaniment, with the singers typically in costume in an elaborate theatrical production; while musical passages may be separated by spoken dialogue, the music is an integral part of the opera. (This is in contrast to the later musical theater, where the plot can often exist separate from the music.)

The operatic form originated in Florence, Italy, near the end of the 16th century; it grew out of attempts to re-create the effect of ancient Greek and Roman dramas. The opera's immediate predecessors were the madrigal, madrigal cycle (a type of madrigal comedy), masque, and intermedio.

The earliest known opera was *Daphne*, written in 1597 by Jacopo Peri. Other notable early operas include Peri's *Euridice*; Stefano Landi's (1586–1639) *Sant'Alessio*, which formalized the various sections of the opera; and Monteverdi's *Orfeo* ("Orpheus"), which was one of the first works to combine choruses, dances, madrigals, and duets.

Many of these formative works were only half sung, with vocal passages separated by orchestral interludes. Peri, along with Caccini and Cavalieri, pioneered a new style of solo singing that could be used for dramatic purposes, a blend of spoken recitation and singing called *recitative*. In this style the music was subservient to the words. Also contributing to the development of the recitative was A. Scarlatti, who composed 115 operas and introduced instrumental accompaniment for recitative sections.

By the 1620's, however, a different type of vocal style gained prominence. In contrast to the recitative, the *aria* was more expressive and melodious, with the music more important than the words. The aria was used prominently in the later operas of Monteverdi, especially *Il ritorno d'Ulisse in patria* (Ulysses's Homecoming) and *L'incoronazione di Poppea* (The Coronation of Poppaea). Over time, the aria became a showcase for virtuoso singing.

While opera was born in Venice and Rome, it quickly spread throughout all of Europe; by 1700, Vienna, Paris, Hamburg, and London were all operatic centers. Lully and Rameau pioneered French operas, while Schütz and Reinhard Keiser (1674–1739) established the musical form in Germany. Of greater importance were the operas of Handel, especially those composed in London between 1711 and 1741 (*Radamisto, Orlando, Ariodante, Alcina*); also notable were the later operas of Gluck (*Orfeo ed Euridice, Alceste*), who shortened the aria and emphasized vocal ensembles and the operatic choir.

Handel composed most of his operas in the *opera seria* style; later composers deemphasized this serious style for the lighter *opera buffa*. Mozart brought the orchestra to the forefront of the opera, and moved beyond established *opera seria* and *opera buffa* styles in works such as *Le Nozze di Figaro* (The Marriage of Figaro) and *Don Giovanni*.

The beginning of the 19th century saw the comic operas of Rossini, including *Il Barbiere di Siviglia* (The Barber of Seville) and *Guillaume Tell* (William Tell), as well as the romantic operas of Carl Maria von Weber (1786–1826), such as *Der Freischütz* and *Euryanthe*. The latter part of the century witnessed the grand operas of Wagner (*Tristan und Isolde, Die Meistersinger von Nürnberg, Parsifal*), who converted recitative and aria into a continuous symphonic whole; the more refined, traditional works of Verdi (*Aida, Falstaff*); and the well-crafted, melodic works of Puccini (*La Bohème, Tosca, Madama Butterfly*). In the 20th century notable operas were created by Richard Strauss (*Salome, Der Rosenkavalier*), Benjamin Britten (*Peter Grimes*), and George Gershwin (*Porgy and Bess*).

Throughout the ages there have been various styles of opera:

Bel canto literally, "beautiful singing," a type of Italian opera with complex and ornate melodies.

Drame lyrique a lyrical French opera of the late 19th century.

Grand opera a large-scale French dramatic opera.

Music drama a German form of dramatic opera, typified by Wagner's majestic works.

Opéra-ballet a French stage work of the late 17th century that combines music and dance.

Opera buffa a type of comic opera popular in the 18th century. In France, *opéra bouffe*.

Opéra comique a lighthearted French opera with spoken dialogue.

Opera seria the serious operatic form that dominated the 17th and 18th centuries.

Semi-opera an English drama of the late 17th/early 18th century in which the leading roles are spoken, rather than sung.

Tragédie lyrique a French tragic or epic opera of the late 17th or 18th century.

Verismo an opera of the late Romantic period in which violent or sordid events are realistically portrayed in contemporary settings.

Operetta An *operetta* is, literally, a "little opera." More precisely, it is a play with overture, songs, entr'actes, and dances, a type of light opera or musical comedy. Examples include Offenbach's *La Belle Hélène* and Johann Strauss's *Die Fledermaus*; also notable are the 14 operettas of Sir W. S. Gilbert (1836–1911) and Sir Arthur Sullivan (1842–1900), including *HMS Pinafore, The Pirates of Penzance*, and *The Mikado*.

History of American Popular Music

Music from The Civil War to World War I

The original settlers of the American continent brought their popular musics with them. Prior to the Civil War, much of America's popular music was directly influenced by these sources; fiddle tunes and dance music, mostly derived from British and French roots, along with a rich tradition of folk balladry and songs, were the staples of the popular music repertoire. The first truly "American" songs were topical ones, addressing political campaigns, the hard life faced by the settlers, and military/patriotic songs.

Minstrel Music In the period just prior to the Civil War, a new American musical hybrid came to the fore: the minstrel song. Minstrels were white performers who performed in black face, supposedly presenting "authentic" versions of African-American dance tunes and songs. By the early 1840's minstrel troupes gained popularity, beginning with the famous Virginia Minstrels, featuring Dan Emmett (1815–1904). These troupes toured Europe as well as the United States.

Initial minstrel hits included such perennials as "Old Zip Coon" (later known as "Turkey in the Straw"). The Civil War inspired countless new songs, including Emmett's "Dixie" (which became the official anthem of the Confederacy) and its Northern counterpart, "The Battle Hymn of the Republic." Abolitionist and pro-slavery forces alike developed songs to promote their causes.

Stephen Foster The first great American songwriter was undoubtedly Stephen Foster (1826–64). Foster made his name with minstrel songs, many of which he sold to Edward Christy, leader of Christy Minstrels. His early hits include "Oh! Susanna" from 1848,"De Camptown Races," (1850) "Old Folks at Home" (1851; also known as "Swanee River"), and 1853's "Old Kentucky Home." Later in his career, Foster turned to writing sentimental ballads, most famously "Jeannie With the Light Brown Hair" (1854) and the posthumously published "Beautiful Dreamer."

African-American Composers African-American composers also began to receive recognition during this period. Most notable was James Bland (1854–1911), a performer and songwriter best remembered for his major hits, "Carry Me Back to Ole Virginny" (1873), "In the Evening by the Moonlight," and "Oh, Dem Golden Slippers" (1879). Other prominent African-American composers of the era include Will Marion Cook, Bert Williams (the famous comic performer), and the Johnson Brothers.

Brass Bands The late 19th century was the heyday of the brass band movement and the instrumental march. Perhaps the best-known bandleader/composer of the era was John Philip Sousa (1854–1932), who led the U.S. Marine Band from 1880 to 1892 before forming his own famous outfit. His numerous hits included such classics as "The Washington Post" (1889), "The Liberty Bell" (1893), and "The Stars and Stripes Forever" (1896), among many others.

Ragtime The march form became the format for a new piano instrumental style called ragtime. Scott Joplin (1868–1917) had composed marches himself before syncopating its oom-pah beat to form the "classic" piano rag. Joplin's 1899 "Maple Leaf Rag" was the first instrumental sheet music publication to sell over a million copies, and became the classic model for Joplin's later works and rags by other prominent composers.

Joplin was a master creator of memorable melodies, from the bouncing "The Entertainer" (used as the theme for the 1973 film, *The Sting*) to the lyrical "Wall Street Rag." Joplin influenced many other composers, including James Scott, Arthur Marshall, and white pianist Joseph Lamb.

The great popularity of ragtime spread from rural areas to the major cities, first St. Louis, then Chicago and New York. More than 1,000 rags were published during the genre's heyday from 1900 to 1925.

The Growth of the Music Publishing Industry During the final three decades of the 19th century, the American music industry continued to grow. Smaller publishing houses became "farm teams" for the bigger ones, so that a local hit would eventually be purchased for republication by a larger house, gaining it national exposure. Popular song was basically divided into two main streams: minstrel or "coon" songs, written in a pseudo-African-American style, usually on comic themes; and sentimental or "parlor" ballads, aimed at young ladies to perform at home, usually on themes of romantic love (or loss). Topical songs also continued to enjoy popularity.

Prominent among the hit makers of the final decades of the 19th century was Charles K. Harris (1867–1930), who wrote the classic "After the Ball" in 1893, which eventually sold more than 5 million.

American Popular Song

The term *American popular song* loosely refers to nonclassical music created in the first half of the 20th century. These songs make up what aficionados call the "Great American Songbook"—some 300,000 compositions copyrighted between 1900 and 1950.

The classic American popular song had a characteristic sound and feel. Most American popular songs followed a 32 bar form, typically divided into four sections: two verses, a chorus, and a repeat of the verse—the AABA form. More important than this structural consistency was the way the melodies of these songs were written, so they could be sung by a person with no more than an average vocal range. These melodies were typically harmonized with chords native to the scale, with few unexpected harmonies or dissonant notes.

Tin Pan Alley The lyricists and composers who worked for New York's major music publishers from approximately 1880 to 1940 are remembered for creating some of the most memorable popular songs of the day. The publishing area—centered on 28th Street, between Broadway and Sixth Avenue—came to be known as "Tin Pan Alley"; writer Monroe Rosenfield coined the term, likening the cacophony of so many songwriters pounding on pianos to the sound of beating on tin pans. Many of these songwriters also wrote scores for Broadway shows and, after the movie musical burst on the scene in the late 1920's, had distinguished careers in Hollywood.

Tin Pan Alley song established the verse-chorus format for popular song that is still heard today. An emphasis on upbeat tunes, often romantic lyrics, and hummable melodies made Tin Pan Alley products extremely popular. The songs were popularized through performances in cabarets and clubs, but mostly spread through the publication of sheet music, and then, beginning in the mid-1920's, through radio and recordings. Performers would often be offered a "cut" or percent of the royalties on a song in return for promoting it.

Irving Berlin Although many Tin Pan Alley songs were formulaic at best, a number of composers rose above the crowd to create a distinct body of work. Perhaps the most prolific and successful of all was Irving Berlin (1888–1989), who had a long career creating some of America's best-loved songs. Beginning in 1907 with the pseudo-Italian ditty "Marie from Sunny Italy," Berlin rode the crest of several fads in the musical world. He was responsible for popularizing the idea of syncopated music in his song "Alexander's Ragtime Band," a tremendous hit in 1911. In the 1920's and 1930's, Berlin created jazzy swing in numbers such as "Blue Skies" (1926) and his famous score for the Fred Astaire-Ginger Rogers film, *Top Hat* (1935). In 1938 he captured perfectly a growing sense of patriotism in his song "God Bless America" (which was actually written during World War I).

The Gershwins George (1898–1937) and Ira (1896–1983) Gershwin were two other products of the Alley who created classic American songs. George Gershwin was an innovative composer whose work ranged from pop songs to classical pieces such as "Rhapsody in Blue" (1927). Ira's clever lyrics perfectly matched his brother's innovative compositions in songs such as "Oh, Lady Be Good" (1924), "I Got Rhythm" (1930), and the hits from their jazz opera, 1935's *Porgy and Bess* ("Summertime," "I Got Plenty O Nuttin'," and many others).

Other Tin Pan Alley Songwriters Other Tin Pan Alley songwriters who had great success include Harold Arlen ("Stormy Weather"); the team of Dorothy Fields (words) and Jimmy McHugh (music; "On the Sunny Side of the Street"); lyricist Irving Caesar ("Tea for Two," with music by Vincent Youmans; "Swanee," with music by George Gershwin); Hoagy Carmichael ("Georgia on My Mind," "Lazybones"); the trio team of Buddy DeSylva, Lew Brown, and Ray Henderson ("You're the Cream in My Coffee"); composer Walter Donaldson ("Yes Sir, That's My Baby," with lyrics by Gus Kahn); and lyricist E.Y. "Yip" Harburg (best–remembered for his Depression era song "Brother, Can You Spare A Dime," with music by Jay Gorney, and the score to *The Wizard of Oz*, with music by Harold Arlen).

The End of an Era The golden age of Tin Pan Alley ended after World War II when rock 'n' roll and teen pop began to dominate the charts, and the movie and stage musical began to go into decline. New 45-rpm records ("singles") became the major means of selling songs, and individual performers became more important than the songwriters. During the late 1950's and particularly the 1960's, sheet music sales declined, and it became less common for music publishers to hire their own stables of songwriters.

Broadway Musical The golden age of the Broadway musical stretches from the mid-1920's through the mid-

1960's, and in turn fed a steady stream of successful film musicals from the late 1920's through the mid-1950's. Hit songs from these shows often turned up on the pop charts of the days, forming a core repertory for popular singers on radio and recordings.

1920's and 1930's The so-called book musical—a musical play that tells a coherent story, with the songs tied to the plot—is generally traced to Jerome Kern's hit play *Show Boat*, with book and lyrics by Oscar Hammerstein II (1895–1960), which opened in 1927. *Show Boat's* success was highly influential on other Broadway composers, including the teams of George and Ira Gerhswin and Richard Rodgers (1902–79) and Lorenz Hart (1895–1943). The Gershwins' jazz opera *Porgy and Bess* shows the strong influence of *Show Boat* in its coherent story and theme of racial struggle. Rodgers and Hart's mid-1930's shows, including the classic *On Your Toes* (1936), also reflected a more mature approach to wedding story and music. Another innovator was composer-lyricist Cole Porter (1891–1964), whose urbane wit made his songs instant classics in such well-loved shows as 1934's *Anything Goes* (which made a star of Ethel Merman) and 1948's *Kiss Me, Kate*.

1940's and 1950's In the early 1940's Rodgers formed a new partnership with veteran lyricist Oscar Hammerstein II. The result was the landmark *Oklahoma!* (1943), with its rich book, innovative staging, and classic songs (including the title song; "Oh What A Beautiful Morning"; "People Will Say We're in Love"; and "The Surrey with the Fringe on Top"). *Oklahoma!* became the model for many other book musicals, and Rodgers and Hammerstein had a distinguished career through the late 1950's, creating classic musicals such as *Carousel* (1945), *South Pacific* (1949), *The King and I* (1951), and *The Sound of Music* (1959).

Rodgers and Hammerstein's shows set the model that most other composer-lyricists emulated. The team of Alan J. Lerner and Frederick Loewe created several hit musicals in the late 1950's and early 1960's, notably *My Fair Lady* (1956) and *Camelot* (1960). Classical composer Leonard Bernstein, collaborating with young lyricist Stephen Sondheim and choreographer Jerome Robbins, created 1957's classic *West Side Story*. Based on Shakespeare's *Romeo and Juliet* but set among the street gangs of New York, it created a new standard for realism in musicals.

Another prolific composer of the era was Jule Styne (1905–94), initially working in collaboration with lyricist Sammy Cahn (1913–93). After a successful career as a pop songwriter and some work in Hollywood, he had several major Broadway hits, starting with *High Button Shoes* (1947), and continuing through *Peter Pan* (1954), *Gypsy* (1959; with lyrics by Stephen Sondheim), and *Funny Girl* (1964; with lyrics by Bob Merrill).

1960's, 1970's, and Beyond The 1960's and 1970's saw a further outpouring of musical talent, including such crowd pleasers as Jerry Herman (*Hello, Dolly!*, 1964; *Mame*, 1966) and the more sophisticated works of Stephen Sondheim (*Company*, 1970; *Follies*, 1971; *A Little Night Music*, 1973; *Sweeney Todd*, 1979). Others who enjoyed success during this period include composer-lyricist-librettist Meredith Willson (*The Music Man*, 1957), and the team of Sheldon Harnick (lyrics) and Jerry Bock (music) with the classic *Fiddler on the Roof* (1964).

While Broadway cast albums of the 1950's and 1960's were among the best selling records of their time, the changing landscape of pop music lead to a steady decline of Broadway's impact on the pop charts. Similarly, the aging of Broadway's most creative songwriters and the parallel graying of the Broadway audience—plus the increased expense involved in mounting musicals—led to fewer new musicals appearing on Broadway beginning in the early 1970's.

Blues, R&B, and Rap

African-American culture contributed significantly to the American musical landscape of the 20th century. Beginning with the rural blues, black music evolved into a variety of musical styles, from rhythm & blues to hip hop—and informed virtually all forms of popular music in the second half of the century.

Blues The style commonly called "the blues" is actually an entire family of musical styles, all sharing similar roots although each having a unique development. The blues style dates back at least to the post-Civil War period, when the guitar was introduced to rural black culture. Black guitarists shaped a unique accompaniment style that enabled them to to sing songs using many flattened notes (called "blue notes"), vocal slides, and syncopated rhythms. Blues guitarists were able to "bend" notes when they played the guitar by pushing against the strings with the fingers of their fretting hand; this allowed them to play many quarter and half tones that lie between the notes of the scale.

Blues Form The classic blues structure is called the twelve-bar blues. This form is comprised of three melodic phrases, each four bars long. Another distinguishing feature of the blues is its narrowly defined chord progression. The *blues scale* is different from the normal major scale, using the scale tones 1-*b*3-4-*b*5-5-*b*7.

Blues music is important not only in its own right, but also because it is incorporated into so many other musical genres. Many jazz tunes are based on the blues progression, and many jazz soloists lean heavily on the blues scale. Much of rock is also blues-based, and many lead guitarists rely on a large repertoire of blues licks.

Delta Blues The Mississippi Delta area produced an intense, highly charged style of blues performance. Delta blues guitarists played mostly slow blues tunes, letting the guitar take the place of the vocalist and "sing," and using a metal or glass slide and special tunings to play the melodies. Famous Delta bluesmen include Charley Patton (1887–1934), Robert Johnson (c. 1912–37), and Son House (Edgar James House Jr., 1902–ca. 75).

Ragtime-Blues In the middle South, a more lighthearted blues was performed. This is sometimes called *ragtime-blues*, because of its syncopated melodies. The guitarists picked the strings with their fingers, the thumb establishing a regular bass on the lower strings and the second and third fingers picking a melody that emphasized the offbeats. Famous ragtime blues performers include Blind Boy Fuller (Fulton Allen, 1908–41) and Blind Blake (ca. 1890–ca. 1933).

Religious Blues Another popular blues form joined words about religious experiences with a blues guitar accompaniment. These *religious blues* were related to the spirituals and ring shouts that came before them. The singer often shouted the lyrics, to express his or her deep conviction. Noted religious blues singers include Blind Willie Johnson (1902–49) and Reverend Gary Davis (1894–1972).

Urban Blues The country blues were brought to new audiences as blacks migrated from the country to the city. At the turn of the last century, the song "The Memphis Blues" was a hit, and it made composer W. (William) C. (Christopher) Handy (1873–1958) famous. Handy, a trained musician, made the blues attractive to a city audience by smoothing out its irregularities, and adapting the blues to the dance band format.

Many city blues singers were female, beginning with the great Ma Rainey (Gertrude Malissa Nix Pridgett, 1866–1939), the first blues singer to achieve a major hit recording. She was followed by perhaps the best known of all blues performers, Bessie Smith (1895–1937), known as "The Empress of the Blues." Smith began recording in 1923, and often was accompanied by the great jazz players of the day, including Louis Armstrong. Her use of blue notes, syncopated delivery, rasping vocals, and occasional gospel shouts all became standard jazz techniques, and she inspired many great jazz singers, including Billie Holiday.

Electric Blues After World War II, a new development transformed the blues from a solo guitar tradition. The introduction of the electric guitar enabled bluesmen to perform in noisy bars. A large number of blacks in urban areas, particularly in Chicago, made up a ready audience for this music. The result was *city* or *electric blues*. Famous city bluesmen include Muddy Waters (McKinley Morganfield, 1915–80), Howlin' Wolf (Chester Arthur Burnett, 1910–76), and B.B. King (b. Riley B. King, 1925).

Rhythm & Blues (R&B) From the early days of sound recording, recordings by black artists had been marketed separately from those by whites. World War II pop music was breaking down into distinct categories, reflected by *Billboard's* new charts for mainstream pop, country, and a new genre that was called Rhythm & Blues (quickly shortened to R&B).

Louis Jordan R&B has its roots in the jump jazz ensembles of the late 1940's and early 1950's, notably Louis Jordan's (1908–75) very popular ensemble. With lean instrumentation, heavy beat, and lighthearted lyrics, Jordan's music was ideal for an urban dance audience. In addition, Jordan was one of the first black entertainers to have significant record sales to the white pop audience.

Ray Charles By the mid-1950's, performers such as Ray Charles (1930–2004) and Ruth Brown broke through with their own combination of jazz, blues, and pop. Signing with Atlantic Records in 1955, Charles had his first major R&B hit, "I Got a Woman." Charles's intense vocals—showing the influence of gospel—set the pattern for later hits, notably his 1958 pop crossover, "What'd I Say."

Sam Cooke Charles's main competition among male singers in the later 50's was Sam Cooke (1931–64) who came out of a gospel background. Cooke's first hit, 1956's "You Send Me," showed a mix of gospel-tinged pleading in the vocal similar to Charles's "I Got a Woman," but had more of a pop accompaniment. Cooke continued to cut classic R&B songs such as "Chain Gang," but increasingly sought a broad audience with more pop material and lusher accompaniments.

Motown By the 1960's R&B as a genre began to break down into distinct streams: Motown picked up the teen-pop end of the spectrum, while soul took up the gospel intensity and high energy of the best R&B performers.

The Motown Sound The Motown label and sound is rooted in the vision of two men: Berry Gordy (b. 1929) a onetime boxing promoter and would-be songwriter, and Smokey Robinson, a songwriter, singer, and Gordy's right-hand man through most of the 1960's. Thanks to a talented staff of studio musicians, Motown's recordings had a distinctive sound that set them apart. The label developed a stable of female (Supremes, Martha and the Vandellas) and male (Miracles, Four Tops, Temptations) groups, along with numerous solo stars. The success of Motown showed the potential for black music to cross over onto the traditionally white pop charts, which would have a profound impact on the development of all forms of popular music.

Social Relevance In the early 1970's several Motown artists rebelled against Gordy's formula and were able to achieve independence while still maintaining popular success. Most noteworthy among these was Stevie Wonder (b. 1950), with a string of critically acclaimed early 1970's albums (culminating in the multi disc set, *Songs in the Key of Life*), and Marvin Gaye (1939–84), whose landmark 1971 album, *What's Going On*, provided a black perspective on current events.

Funk and Soul James Brown (b. 1933) created a high-energy, rhythmic style called funk that propelled him to great success in the mid-to-late 60's. In songs like "Papa's Got a Brand New Bag" and "I Got You (I Feel Good)" (1965), "Cold Sweat" (1967), and the anthemic "Say It Loud—I'm Black and I'm Proud (Part 1)" (1968), Brown combined stripped-down harmonies, driving rhythms, and his high-energy vocals to create a compelling musical mix. Brown's message of black pride resonated during the upheavals of the Civil Rights movement.

If Brown was the King of Funk, Aretha Franklin (b. 1942) was Queen of Soul. Franklin had begun her career singing jazz and gospel; producer Jerry Wexler recognized her potential, and sent her to Muscle Shoals's studio to produce her great 1960's hits, including "Respect," "A Natural Woman," and "Chain of Fools," all from 1967.

Urban Contemporary There is a long tradition in R&B—going back to Sam Cooke—of softer, more pop-oriented singers specializing in pop ballads. During the 1960's, Dionne Warwick (b. 1940)—working with producers/songwriters Burt Bacharach (b. 1928) and Hal David (b. 1921)—had a string of hits with pop ballads, including "Walk On By" (1964), "I Say A Little Prayer" (1967), and "I'll Never Fall in Love Again" (1970). Others who achieved success with more mainstream ballad singing included Smokey Robinson, Barry White, Teddy Pendergrass, and Roberta Flack and Donny Hathaway, alone and in duet.

In the 1980's and 1990's, this style of soft soul crooning became known as *urban contemporary*. Many urban contemporary artists, such as Whitney Houston, Luther Vandross, and Kenneth "Babyface" Edmonds, were able to cross over into the pop charts. Other artists, such as Janet Jackson and En Vogue, blended urban contemporary with elements of hip hop.

Rap/Hip Hop Rap music as a genre is over a quarter-century old, and has gone through many changes in its history. Rap is the general term for the musical expression; it is a part of a broader movement, known as *hip hop*, that includes dance, graffiti art, fashion, and political expression. Nonetheless, the two terms are used somewhat interchangeably to refer to a variety of musical styles.

First Generation The first generation of rappers developed alongside the mobile deejay movement, which was first seen in Jamaica and then came to urban neighborhoods in New York and Los Angeles. Deejays outfitted trucks with powerful sound systems that they set up in a local park or playground. They would spin their records, while improvising boasts over the music. Eventually, the role of rapper and deejay separated, with the rapper taking on the job of drawing the crowds, while the deejay focused on manipulating the turntables.

The first commercially successful rap group was New York's Sugarhill Gang, with their 1979 release, "Rapper's Delight." Other important early rappers include Kurtis Blow, with his 1981 single, "The Breaks"; Afrika Bambaaataa, with his 1982 recording, "Planet Rock"; and Grandmaster Flash and The Furious Five, who issued 1982's powerful "The Message," one of the first rap songs to deal with contemporary urban issues.

Second Generation The first second-generation rap group was Run D.M.C., who began issuing records in 1983. The group wed heavy metal rhythms to a tough, urban sensibility, epitomized by their cover of Aerosmith's

"Walk This Way" from 1986, the first rap recording to cross over to popularity among traditional rock fans. Following Run D.M.C. were more popularly oriented rap groups, including the humorous Fat Boys, and the more romantic material popularized by L. L. Cool J.

Gangsta Rap The next innovation in rap came with the so-called *gangsta* style, originating on the West Coast. Rapper Ice-T's 1986 release "6 'N the Mornin'" is considered among the first gangsta rap recordings, but it was N.W.A.'s 1988 album, *Straight Outta Compton*, that was the most influential and controversial work in the new style. The group's violent imagery was deplored by the mainstream press, making them all the more attractive to their core listeners. The group's members included Dr. Dre, Eazy-E, and Ice Cube, all of whom went on to have solo careers.

Later gangsta rappers became so embroiled in the genre's mythology of violence that they fell victim (literally) to their own success. Rappers Tupac Shakur and the Notorious B.I.G. died within six months of each other, each murdered by unknown assailants. This brought more bad publicity to the music, and led some major record labels to disassociate themselves with their rap subsidiaries.

Female Rappers Rap also had its noteworthy female stars, who could be just as macho as their male counterparts. Queen Latifah (b. Dana Owens, 1970) was among the first and most feminist in her message, beginning with her 1989 single, "Ladies First." Salt-n-Pepa were the first all-female crew, and broke through to great popularity in the late 1980's and early 1990's with their mix of frank lyrics and brassy stage presentation.

Other important female rappers include Lil' Kim, Missy "Misdemeanor" Elliott, and Lauryn Hill, who combined rap with R&B, soul, and gospel influences.

Rap Becomes Mainstream As the 1990's wore on, rap became less political and more mainstream. Sean Combs (aka Puff Daddy; P. Diddy) was the major entrepreneur of rap in the later 1990's, as both performer and producer. Elements of rap were heard in all styles of music, and rap stars were regularly featured on MTV and at the top of the pop charts.

Country

Country music is, like the blues, a traditionally simple musical form that lends itself to endless variation. Even though many country songs are built around three chords and a simple melody, these songs can be interpreted in a variety of styles, from the gritty sounds of honky-tonk to the smooth stylings of country pop.

Traditional Country Country music grew out of southern American folk music, including Appalachian folk and rural blues forms. Old-time country music was simple and folksy, often performed with just guitars and fiddles.

First Recordings The first popular country recording, "Turkey in the Straw," was made in 1922, by Texas fiddlers Eck Robinson and Henry Gilliland. The following year, Okeh Records released "The Little Log Cabin in the Lane," by Fiddlin' John Carson, which sold an impressive number of copies. In 1927 Victor Records spent two weeks recording acts in Bristol, Tennessee; included in these legendary "Bristol Sessions" were the first recorded performances of Jimmie Rodgers and the Carter Family.

Jimmie Rodgers Rodgers (1897–1933) brought rural country music to national popularity by streamlining the music and lyrics, thus making the genre a viable commercial property. Known as the "Singing Brakeman," he cut 110 records in just six years, singing in a bluesy style with a trademark high-pitched yodel.

The Grand Ole Opry Country music was the staple of local radio for the mid-20's. One of the most popular of all these programs was the "Grand Ole Opry,' a weekly radio broadcast that defined the world of country music in the 1930's and 1940's.

Western Swing Western Swing is a unique combination of string band music with jazz styles. It was born in the Texas-Oklahoma region in the late 20's. The band credited with creating the Western Swing sound was The Lightcrust Doughboys. This band, popular in 1931–32, featured fiddler Bob Wills and vocalist Milton Brown, who soon formed their own bands. A second wave of Western Swing came in the late 1940's in Southern California, where many Western musicians had settled after the war.

The 1950's and 1960's were lean times for Western Swing, but in the early 1970's new young bands, such as Asleep at the Wheel, began introducing a new generation to the sound. Country superstar Merle Haggard recorded an album in homage to Wills's music, and then brought the star out of retirement for his famous last session in 1973.

Bluegrass Developing at the end of World War II, bluegrass music drew on the earlier string band music and melded it with influences from Western Swing, cowboy, and honky tonk. A typical bluegrass band consists of mandolin, banjo, fiddle, guitar, and bass, with a lead vocalist often complemented on the chorus by tenor and bass singers.

Traditional Bluegrass Bill Monroe (1911–96) is generally called the "father of bluegrass music." His group, the Blue Grass Boys, was named for his home state of Kentucky. In 1946, vocalist/guitarist Lester Flatt and 19-year-old North Carolina-born banjo player Earl Scruggs joined the band and it quickly became the model for others, beginning with Flatt and Scruggs themselves, who left to form their own band in 1948. Virginia's Stanley Brothers were another group to pick up the bluegrass mantle.

Contemporary Bluegrass During the 1950's and 1960's bluegrass's popularity began to spread to several urban centers, with groups like the Country Gentlemen, the Greenbriar Boys, and the Charles River Valley Boys. By the 1970's, jazz, folk, and world music influences all became part of the bluegrass style, as evidenced by eclectic mandolinist David Grisman. The 1980's saw a return to traditional bluegrass styles among younger musicians, and by the mid-1990's, Nashville took a renewed interest in bluegrass music.

Singer/fiddler Alison Krauss was the first new bluegrass artist to break onto the country charts, followed by her protégés, the band Nickel Creek. Ricky Skaggs, whose mainstream country career had slowed in the later 1980's and early 1990's, returned to playing bluegrass, and his band, Kentucky Thunder, brought him renewed popularity. Established country singers, including Dolly Parton, Patty Loveless, and the Dixie Chicks, all recorded bluegrass albums.

Honky-Tonk Music Following World War II, the honky-tonk—a small bar often located on the outskirts of town—became a center of musical creation. In the period from about 1948 to 1955, honky-tonk music—with lyrics about drifting husbands and the subsequent lyin', cheatin', and heartbreak—became the predominant country form.

The foremost honky-tonk performer was Hank Williams (1923–53), whose backup combo of crying steel guitar and scratchy fiddle became the model for thousands of honky-tonk bands. The honky-tonk style reached its apex in Hank Thompson's 1952 recording of "The Wild Side of Life," which inspired the wonderful answer song, "It Wasn't God that Made Honky Tonk Angels," that made a major star out of Kitty Wells.

Country-Pop Following the emergence of rock and roll, country music began to incorporate more pop oriented production techniques, resulting in a smoother sound than was typical with traditional country.

The Nashville Sound In the 1950's RCA Records producer/guitarist Chet Atkins and Owen Bradley combined country and pop music in what became known as the *Nashville Sound*. Atkins surrounded country's traditionally simple melodies and song structures with polished pop-oriented arrangements, creating a lush sound that blended rural sensibility with urban sophistication. The result was increased popularity for the country genre, and a number of pop crossover hits for artists such as Jim Reeves and Patsy Cline.

Countrypolitan By the late 1960's the Nashville Sound had metamorphosed into *countrypolitan*, with an even heavier emphasis on pop production flourishes; most countrypolitan recordings featured multiple layers of keyboards, guitars, strings, and vocals. Producer Billy Sherrill was especially noted for this style which produced numerous crossover hits for George Jones, Tammy Wynette, Charlie Rich, Conway Twitty, and other artists.

Progressive and Alternative Country Progressive country developed in the late 1960's as a reaction to the increasingly polished sound of mainstream country music. This was a songwriter-based genre inspired in parts by the of classic honky-tonk, the hard-driving beat of rock 'n' roll, and the introspective writing of Bob Dylan and other contemporary folk musicians.

Very much anti-Nashville in its sentiments, progressive country was both rootsier and more intellectual than the country-pop of its day. The top progressive artists—including Kris Kristofferson, Willie Nelson, Tom T. Hall, and Jimmie Dale Gilmore—were better known for their songwriting than for their singing skills, and wrote distinctive, individual songs that pushed the boundaries of the country genre. In the 1980's progressive country evolved into *alternative country*, as popularized by Emmylou Harris, Lyle Lovett, k.d. lang, and similar artists.

Country-Folk and Americana During the 1980's and 1990's, several artists blurred the lines between country and folk music, creating a subgenre alternately known as *country-folk* and *Americana*. The most popular country-folk and Americana artists also fall under the singer/songwriter umbrella. The most prominent of these artists include Mary Chapin Carpenter, Steve Earl, Nanci Griffith, John Hiatt, Shelby Lynne, Kathy Mattea, and Lucinda Williams.

Contemporary Country By the late 1980's a new breed of country-pop evolved that was significantly influenced by pop/rock sensibilities, spawning crossover superstars such as Garth Brooks and Billy Ray Cyrus. A wave of male singers—dubbed "hat acts," after their ubiquitous cowboy headwear—dominated the country charts with songs that sounded more like rock than traditional country.

A decade later, the emphasis had shifted to female vocalists, typically bathed in glossy pop productions. These vocalists—most notably Shania Twain, LeAnn Rimes, and Faith Hill—deemphasized traditional country twang and found massive success with a mainstream audience.

Folk Music

American folk music describes everyday events and common people, often in mythic terms. Modern folk music stands alone as its own independent genre, yet also informs many other styles, including rock and country.

Traditional Folk Although there had been collections of dance music, songs, and spirituals through the 19th century, folk music itself was not really prized until the early years of the 20th century. The first music collection to have a major impact was Texas song collector John Lomax's *Cowboy Songs and Other Frontier Ballads*, published in 1910. In 1928 the Library of Congress established its Archive of American Folk Song, to preserve and promote America's traditional music.

Lead Belly In 1933, with the support of the Archive of American Folk Song, John Lomax and his son, Alan, made a collecting trip to southern prisons. There they discovered a 12-string guitar player/singer nicknamed Lead Belly (b. Huddie Ledbetter, 1888–1949) by his fellow prisoners because of his unusual strength and physical stamina. The Lomaxes brought Lead Belly north to perform for urban audiences, where he recorded for various labels through the later 1930's and until his death in 1949.

Woody Guthrie Another important Lomax "discovery" was Woody Guthrie (1912–67). Born in Oklahoma, Guthrie was an itinerant sign painter and guitarist who gained fame as a member of the New York folk community in the 1930's. A banjo player named Pete Seeger (b. 1915) became a close friend, and the two often performed together at union rallies and labor meetings. Guthrie was a prolific songwriter, churning out dozens of songs, including the classics "Pastures of Plenty," "Roll On, Columbia," and "This Land Is Your Land." He continued to record and perform until the early 1950's, when an inherited disease, Huntington's chorea, began to affect his motor skills. He was eventually hospitalized and died in 1967.

The Weavers Pete Seeger was also a member of the influential group The Weavers. In the late 1940's and early 1950's, the group enjoyed mainstream pop hits with Lead Belly's "Irene Goodnight," the African "Wimoweh," and the Israeli "Tzena, Tzena." The Weavers were the model for many of the popular folk groups of the late 1950's and early 1960's, including The Kingston Trio and the Chad Mitchell Trio; after the group's breakup, Seeger continued as a solo perfomer.

1960's Folk Revival A second generation of folk music fans formed the seedbed for the next great folk performers of the late 1950's and early 1960's. Some were oriented toward strict re-creation of earlier folk styles, such as the old-time country stringband The New Lost City Ramblers; others were influenced by Woody Guthrie to take up topical songwriting.

Bob Dylan Perhaps the best and most creative of the Guthrie acolytes was a young Minnesotan who came to New York to visit Guthrie in his hospital room. Taking the name of Bob Dylan (b. Robert Zimmerman, 1940), the young singer soon established the social-protest genre, penning such folk classics as "Blowin' in the Wind" and "The Times They Are A-Changin'." Others who wrote in this style included Phil Ochs, Tom Paxton, Malvina Reynolds, and Buffy Sainte-Marie.

Folk-Pop Although Dylan was a talented performer, his songs were initially popularized by more polished musicians, notably the popular folk trio of Peter, Paul and Mary. They topped the charts with compositions by Dylan and the other "folkniks."

Another important early champion of Dylan's songwriting was Joan Baez (b. 1941), the sweet-voiced singer who began her career covering old ballads and folksongs but soon took on social causes including the Civil Rights and anti-Vietnam War movements.

Contemporary Folk The folk movement of the 1960's splintered into many smaller, more focused movements in the 1970's and 1980's, such as the bluegrass and old-time music revivals; the beginnings of interest in world music; and New Age and "new acoustic" music. Meanwhile, many folk performers had already crossed over into performing either folk-rock or country-rock.

Several new singer/songwriters were promoted as "New Dylans," beginning with Chicago's Steve Goodman (writer of "The City of New Orleans") and the wry Loudon Wainwright. Female singer/songwriters were very successful, ranging from the melancholy Joni Mitchell to the more playful songs of the Canadian sisters Kate and Anna McGarrigle. The Texas "outlaw" movement spawned several talented songwriters, ranging from country's Willie Nelson to the category-bending work of Jerry Jeff Walker ("Mr. Bojangles"), Townes Van Zandt ("Poncho and Lefty"), and Joe Ely.

In the mid-1980's, social conscience songwriting returned in the hands of songwriters such as Suzanne Vega ("Luka") and Tracey Chapman ("Fast Car"). Even rock performers such as Bruce Springsteen and John Cougar Mellencamp showed an interest in folk song; Springsteen consciously emulated Woody Guthrie in the sparse songs he wrote for his albums *Nebraska* (1982) and *The Ghost of Tom Joad* (1995), and Mellencamp put together an all-acoustic band for his 1987 album, *Lonesome Jubilee*.

Jazz

Jazz is America's home-grown classical music. Derived from the blues, it is one of this country's truly indigenous musical styles. For a time, jazz was the country's popular music; as the genre evolved, it became more improvisational and experimental, encouraging group interplay and musical virtuosity.

New Orleans/Dixieland Jazz The style of jazz that developed in the New Orleans region from about 1885 through 1915 is known as *New Orleans, Dixieland,* or just *classic jazz*. New Orleans bands of that era usually had five to seven pieces, led by cornet, clarinet, and trombone on melody, with tuba or string bass, piano, banjo or guitar, and drums on accompaniment. Initially, there were no soloists; the group played all at once, with the melody instruments improvising around one another's parts. The rhythmic accompaniment emphasized a regular, four-beat accent, as a basis for the melodic syncopation.

Buddy Bolden and King Oliver Cornetist Buddy Bolden (b. Charles Joseph Bolden, 1877–1931) is generally considered to be among the first great jazz cornetists. Contemporaries reported that he played with a loud, piercing tone that could be heard over considerable distances. He was said to be a particularly expressive player of the blues.

Bolden served as a model for the next generation of players, beginning with cornet player Joseph "King" Oliver (1885–1938). Oliver was only eight years younger than Bolden, but he nonetheless took Bolden's style to a new level, first in New Orleans, and then on the road in Chicago and Los Angeles. Like Bolden, Oliver specialized in playing slow blues, using a growling style that would influence the "jungle" style of Duke Ellington. In 1919 Oliver took his band to Chicago, where it made its first recordings in April 1923. These records, including "Chime Blues" and "Dippermouth Blues," are considered the first classic New Orleans jazz recordings.

Louis Armstrong One name towers over all others in the history of early jazz: trumpeter and vocalist Louis Armstrong (1901–71). His small ensemble recordings of the mid-1920's, famously known as the Hot Fives and Hot Sevens, revolutionized jazz music and introduced the era of the virtuosic leader/soloist. Armstrong was the "star," and his solo breaks, comic vocals, and overall musical personality dominated. He also greatly expanded the typical band repertory, introducing popular and comic novelty songs, his own compositions, and more contemporary dance numbers through his recordings.

Armstrong's classic recordings of this period include the oft-praised "West End Blues," which features a stunning solo that showed Armstrong's incredible range, power, and imagination as a trumpeter. More breezy vocal numbers such as "You Rascal You" displayed the playful side of Armstrong's performing personality.

Jelly Roll Morton and Jazz Piano Besides small-band jazz, New Orleans was a center for the development of jazz piano. Its famous Storyville district—a legal center for bars and houses of prostitution—created a great demand for pianists who could attract customers. These pianists were called on to accompany the energetic show dances and more sensuous slow drags that the prostitutes performed to bewitch their customers, as well as to provide general entertainment and accompany songs.

The greatest of the New Orleans jazz pianists—and the most influential—was Jelly Roll Morton (b. Ferdinand Joseph La Menthe, or Lamothe, 1890–1941). Morton's piano style melded blues, Spanish dance rhythms, ragtime, and folk and classical influences. Morton's flamboyant originality made his compositions, such as "King Porter Stomp," "The Pearls," and "Milenberg Joys," stand out; melodic, with dramatic contrasts in timbre, rhythm, and volume, they were perhaps the most thoughtfully composed of early jazz compositions.

Swing and Big Band Jazz By the mid-1920's, the center of jazz development had moved from New Orleans

The Man Who Made Jazz Hot: More than 60 Years After His Death, Jelly Roll Morton Gets Respect

By STEPHEN KINZER

When the jazz pioneer Jelly Roll Morton died penniless and alone more than 60 years ago, his reputation was already fading. New musical styles had displaced the hot jazz he helped invent, and a younger generation of players disdained him.

Today, however, Morton is resurgent. New books and recordings, together with changing attitudes among scholars, musicians, and listeners are placing him back at the peak of the jazz pantheon.

Part of Morton's appeal was his picaresque and arrogant style. He wore flashy suits, sported a diamond implanted in one of his front teeth, and often told players who were not from New Orleans that their music was pitifully inadequate. He was a larger-than-life figure.

Northern musicians like Duke Ellington, including those who emerged from big bands to develop the modern bebop style, dismissed him as a braggart who had failed to keep up with the times and was never as great as he imagined.

But the revival of Morton's reputation grew steadily through the 1990's. The musical *Jelly's Last Jam* by George C. Wolfe brought Morton's name and musical style to a new audience, especially in a 1992 Broadway production starring Gregory Hines.

As part of a celebration of his life and work that was part of the 2000 Chicago Humanities Festival, the Chicago Jazz Ensemble played several Morton pieces found in a jazz archive after being lost for decades. About one of these, "Gan-Jam," the jazz critic Howard Reich said, "This is writing that's unbelievably sophisticated. It's like a tone poem, written in classical sonata form. It's just an astonishing piece of music."

Morton enjoyed precisely that kind of acclaim early in his career. Born Ferdinand Lamothe into a New Orleans Creole family in 1890, he grew up in a formal musical environment shaped by players at the city's symphony orchestras and opera companies.

By the time he reached his teens, Morton found his way to Storyville, the city's red-light district, where ragtime musicians played and jazz was beginning to take shape. Whether he actually invented jazz, as he often claimed, will always be debatable. Beyond much doubt, however, he was the first serious jazz composer, the first to write multithemed pieces and develop a distinctive jazz style.

After a lucrative period during which he became recognized as one of the greatest figures in this new kind of music, Morton began traveling the country, to learn what styles were emerging in different areas and to show off his own mastery. In the late 1920's he made a series of recordings at the head the Red Hot Peppers that still form the bedrock of his reputation. The best are available on the Bluebird label under the title "Birth of the Hot."

Morton's later years were heavy with disappointment. Like many musicians of color, he was denied membership in Ascap, the organization that collects royalties for composers. Publishers who distributed Morton's later sheet music, notably the Chicago-based Melrose brothers, also cheated him out of his financial due.

In a final bid to recover his lost reputation and prosperity, Morton moved to Los Angeles. Several film producers apparently expressed interest in featuring him or his music, but he died in July 1941 with those plans unfulfilled. No film clips of him are known to exist.

Today many jazz scholars agree that Morton was a dominant figure in creating this music.

"He's now generally cited as the first great composer in jazz history," Bruce Raeburn, curator of the Hogan Jazz Archives at Tulane University, said. "Morton took a kind of rough communal music based in New Orleans, then polished it and created a coherence that had never been there before. He was extremely flamboyant as a composer and arranger, but it always works. Pieces like 'Black Bottom Stomp' are like Fabergé eggs, full of tricks and layers, with time changes, coloration and texture."

Morton's rehabilitation is beginning to extend beyond academe and concert halls into jazz clubs and popular recordings. When young musicians perform Morton's music, they pay him an homage that is the opposite of the disdain heaped on him by the bebop generation.

to major urban centers, notably Chicago and New York. New Orleans jazz evolved into *swing*, and most jazz groups grew into *big bands*. Big band swing was the popular music of its day, featuring a combination of complex arrangements, innovative improvisation, and smooth vocals by the likes of Bing Crosby and Frank Sinatra.

The swing style marked a basic change in approach to jazz's basic rhythm. The New Orleans jazz bands inherited from ragtime an oom-pah beat, with the heavy emphasis falling on the first and third beats of the four-beat measure. In swing, the emphasis was evened out so that all four beats were lightly accented, making for a much less mechanical feel.

Birth of the Big Band While there had been large bands active since the teens, these early dance bands primarily played in a lightly syncopated manner, and were not true jazz ensembles. The innovation that brought jazz to a larger band format is generally credited to arranger Don Redman, who worked for Fletcher Henderson's orchestra from 1923 to 1927. Redman came up with the idea of dividing the band into two primary voices, the brasses (trumpets, trombones) and the reeds (saxes, clarinets), which would trade riffs back and forth in a call-and-response format. These parts were relatively fixed; improvisation was introduced through the featured soloists, who were brought forward to play one or two choruses.

During the big band era, the bands were further divided by jazz fans into two camps: "hot" versus "sweet" bands. The "sweet" bands focussed on moody ballads and lightly syncopated dance music. The "hot" bands emphasized syncopation and improvised solos over playing popular melodies.

Count Basie The Count Basie (b. William Basien, 1904–84) Orchestra is generally credited as one of the first great swing bands, with its famous rhythm section of piano, guitar, bass, and drums. Basie's light piano accompaniment also helped keep the music flowing and eliminated some of the four-square feeling that a more regular piano accompaniment gave earlier bands. Previously, jazz drummers had kept a steady beat by hitting the bass drum, making a heavy, thudding sound; Basie's drummer, Jo Jones, keep the steady beat on the ride cymbal, creating a lighter, more airy accompaniment.

Benny Goodman Benny Goodman's (1909–86) band was important not only as the first major popularizer of swing music but also for its many great band members. Jazz critic and producer John Hammond took Goodman under his wing early in the clarinetist's career and was responsible for introducing Goodman to Don Redman's innovative new arrangements. He also encouraged him to hire black musicians to create the first integrated jazz band, including pianist Teddy Wilson, vibraphone player Lionel Hampton, and the innovative electric guitarist Charlie Christian.

Duke Ellington One of the most original big bands was led by pianist/composer/arranger Duke Ellington (b. Edward Kennedy Ellington, 1899–1974). Ellington's band predated the official swing era, coming into being in the late 1920's as the house band at New York's Cotton Club. Ellington was an unusually gifted and perceptive arranger, and the long tenure of many of the musicians who played in his band allowed him a unique opportunity to craft his music to reflect their individual personalities.

Ellington's band originally was known for its "jungle" style, featuring often campy effects such as growling trumpets and wailing clarinets, aimed to be immediate audience pleasers. However, by the mid-1930's, Ellington had matured into a unusually sensitive composer, writing a number of classic jazz compositions, ranging from 1932's "It Don't Mean a Thing (if It Ain't Got that Swing)" and "Sophisticated Lady" to 1935's "In a Sentimental Mood" and 1942's "Don't Get Around Much Anymore." Aided by his second-in-command, arranger/composer Billy Strayhorn (who joined the band in 1939), Ellington extended considerably the palette of jazz composition.

Big Band Vocalists With the exception of very popular vocalists such as Bing Crosby (b. Harry Lillis Crosby, 1903–77), nearly every jazz singer of the era was associated with one of the leading bands, sometimes moving from band to band. Artie Shaw broke the color line when he took singer Billie Holiday (b. Eleanora Fagan, 1915–59) on the road with his band, although this arrangement didn't last long due to the difficulties that they encountered. Frank Sinatra (1915–98) began his career singing for the Dorsey Brothers and Harry James bands; Ella Fitzgerald (1917–96) sang with Chick Webb's band (and became the band's de facto leader after Webb's death). It wasn't until after World War II that singers like Sinatra achieved enough personal success that they could strike out on their own.

Bebop Bebop was a new style of jazz music that developed in New York City during the early to mid-1940's, reaching its height immediately after World War II. The typical bebop ensemble was much smaller than the big bands that it replaced. Taking a new approach to melody, rhythm, and harmony, the bop musicians revolutionized jazz, transforming it from a commercial, popular music into a serious art form.

Bebop's story centers on the lives and music of two seminal jazzmen: saxophone player Charlie "Bird" Parker (1920–55) and trumpeter John Birks "Dizzy" Gillespie (1917–93), who began jamming together at after-hours clubs like Minton's in Harlem. Using the basic chord structures of well-known pop songs, the musicians experimented with new melodies, harmonies, and rhythms, often taken at breakneck speed. The bebop musicians emphasized instrumental virtuosity. While jazzmen had always used flatted notes (or "blue notes") and seventh chords, bebop musicians used more unusual chord harmonies, either by "altering" standard chords (by lowering one or two notes in the chord to purposely disrupt the usual harmony), extending chords (by using ninths, elevenths, or thirteenths as harmony notes), or by substituting related chords. The results may have sounded dissonant, but in fact were stretching the boundaries of chord harmony.

The role of the accompanying instruments radically changed in bop. The pianist mostly "comped" in the accompaniment, playing disjointed, fragmentary chords behind the soloist; Thelonious Monk (1917–82) and Bud (Earl) Powell (1924–66) are the two pianists credited with creating this new style. Bebop drummers, led by Kenny Clarke (1914–85) and Max Roach (b. 1925), also were innovators, eliminating the traditional use of the bass drum and snare as timekeepers; instead they kept time lightly on the high-hat cymbal, dropping the occasional "bomb" on the bass.

Cool Jazz On the other side of the spectrum from the high-powered and energetic bebop style was "cool jazz," which came into popularity in the early 1950's. Cool jazz artists took a purposely intellectual approach to jazz, trying to wed white classical music to black soul. There were two branches of cool players, one based on the West Coast and the other in the East; the dominance of the West Coast musicians led to cool sometimes being referred to as "West Coast" jazz. Cool jazz ensembles included the sweetly classical Modern Jazz Quartet, led by pianist John Lewis and vibes player Milt Jackson; the very popular Dave Brubeck Quartet, featuring Brubeck on piano and Paul Desmond on alto sax; and the ultimate cool ensemble, Miles Davis' mid-1950's group that featured John Coltrane or Sonny Rollins on sax and Davis on trumpet. There were even cool soloists, such as the cerebral jazz pianist Bill Evans.

Hard Bop Hard bop was a reaction to both bebop and cool jazz. Bebop certainly had power and energy, but it seemed to lack the deep emotions and the kind of interaction between musicians and audience found in black gospel music. Similarly, jazz didn't need to get closer to white classical music, the hard boppers argued, but rather to its roots in black folk forms. To that end, hard bop was out to infuse bebop's power with the intensity of soul.

A prime mover in hard bop was pianist/group leader Horace Silver (b. 1928), whose familiarity with gospel piano and organ led him to introduce gospel-shaded harmonies and melodic riffs borrowed from gospel song. Another key figure in the growth of hard bop was drummer/bandleader Art Blakey (1919–90), whose group the Jazz Messengers focused on accessible music with a tight, propulsive drive. Also associated with the beginnings of hard bop were tenor saxophone player Sonny Rollins (b. 1929) and alto sax player Nat "Cannonball" Adderly (1928–75).

Soul Jazz Hard bop eventually mutated into a more R&B-oriented form called soul jazz, which became one of the most popular types of jazz in the 1960's. Soul jazz incorporates a more contemporary rock/soul beat, complete with a funky bass line, with hard bop and bebop-type chord progressions. Popular soul jazz musicians include pianists Horace Silver and Ramsey Lewis, organist Jimmy Smith, and saxophonists Eddie Harris and Stanley Turrentine.

Free Jazz Free jazz musicians, led by sax player Ornette Coleman (b. 1930) and pianist/composer Cecil Taylor (b. 1929), felt they should be free to explore all of the tones and textures of their instruments, without adhering to traditional harmonic demands. For this reason, many people associate free jazz with dissonant squawks and squeals produced by frenzied and self-absorbed musicians. In fact, free jazz was based on musicians listening carefully and reacting to one another's playing; the point was to extend the soloist's capabilities, and not be hampered by chord changes and melodic clichés.

Jazz/Rock Fusion By the mid-1960's rock 'n' roll was dominating the airwaves and record charts. The adventuresome avant-garde of jazz was appealing to its own specialized but limited audience. Older jazz figures, such as Miles Davis, were still respected, but their record sales were minuscule compared with rock. It appeared that jazz was going to fizzle out without much public notice—when a group of pioneering musicians decided to blend the rock and jazz idioms in a new jazz/rock, or fusion style.

In reality, the two musics discovered each other. Many progressive rockers were playing improvised melodic parts, and looked to the great jazz players for inspiration. Still others—such as Chicago and Blood, Sweat, and Tears—introduced brass instruments into the rock format and borrowed classic jazz tunes for their hits. Jazz players, meanwhile, were fascinated with the possibilities that electric instruments offered and the special effects that could be generated by wiring acoustic ones for amplification. Many of the young sidemen in jazz sympathized with the rock revolution.

Miles Davis Several tentative jazz/rock outfits cropped up in the mid-1960's, but it took Miles Davis (1926–91) to popularize the style. Tentatively edging toward a more rock-oriented sound, Davis released a series of records that featured steadier, rocklike drumming, occasional electric piano, and funkier melodies. Davis's two major thrusts into rock and roll were the 1969 recordings, *In a Silent Way* and *Bitches Brew*. On these albums, Davis borrowed rock instrumentation, supplemented the drums with exotic percussion instruments, and amplified his own trumpet playing with special effects. Davis also changed his style of playing to fit in with the more aggressive arrangements. No longer coolly laid back as it had been in the 1950's, his playing was now emotional and angry. Although he still played slow ballads, he was usually fiery and outgoing, playing throughout the entire range of the instrument, including the ultra-high register—a legacy of free jazz.

Mahavishnu Orchestra Many of the musicians who played with Davis's first fusion bands would become leaders in the new movement. British jazz/rock guitarist John McLaughlin (b. 1942) played with Davis and then formed his own Mahavishnu Orchestra, which gained rock-level popularity in the early 1970's. McLaughlin's music is an interesting amalgam of the energy of jazz with many of the techniques of rock, often played over complicated odd-time signatures.

Weather Report Perhaps the most successful of all the fusion groups was Weather Report, founded by Austrian pianist/composer Joe Zawinul (b. 1932). Previously, Zawinul had composed "In a Silent Way," the title track of Davis's first jazz-rock album, and also served as arranger for *Bitches Brew*. In 1971 he assembled a group featuring Davis alumnus Wayne Shorter (b. 1933) on saxophone, Miroslav Vitous on bass, and drummer Alphonse Moreira. Zawinul took an orchestral approach in his compositions, using each instrument as an individual voice to construct a coherent and complex whole. The hiring of bassist Jaco Pastorius (1951–87) in 1976 considerably beefed up the Weather Report sound; Pastorius always contributed a virtuoso bass solo to the group's live performances.

Other Fusion Innovators The creative and financial success of these bands led many older, more seasoned hands to embrace fusion music. Some of these musicians, such as Herbie Hancock (b. 1940) and Chick Corea (b. Armando Anthony Corea, 1941), achieved significant popularity with their fusion bands, but also managed to work in the "pure jazz" idiom. For many, the sharp demarcation line between jazz and rock was an artificial one; they failed to see any reason to limit their music. In fact, the 1970's and 1980's saw much more dialogue between jazz and all other types of music, as well as an increased acceptance of jazz as an art form.

Post Bop

In the 1980's and 1990's, there was a resurgence of more traditional jazz, incorporating hard bop harmonies with a variety of swing, rock, and funk beats. This fresh approach to the jazz genre, which incorporates a variety of musical influences, is alternately known as *post bop*, *contemporary*, or *modern mainstream*—terms that describe virtually all serious jazz being played today. The most notable post bop players include saxophonists Kenny Garrett, Joshua Redman, and Wayne Shorter; trumpeter Freddie Hubbard; guitarists Pat Metheny, and John Scofield; and pianists Ahmad Jamal and Keith Jarrett.

Smooth Jazz

While post bop appeals to jazz traditionalists, the most popular form of jazz today is a controversial genre known as *smooth jazz*. Purists deride the genre's slick arrangements and play-it-safe improvisations; fans say that it's a particularly melodic and listenable form of jazz. Mood music or not, smooth jazz *does* feature jazz-inspired improvised solos, and many of its adherents are veterans of the 1970's/1980's fusion scene. And even critics admit that smooth jazz has become the most commercially viable form of jazz since the 1940's, with popular artists such as pianist David Benoit; guitarists George Benson, Larry Carlton, and Lee Ritenour; saxophonist David Sanborn; and the groups Fourplay, Spyro Gyra, and the Yellowjackets.

Rock

The term *rock* has become somewhat generic, referring to a wide range of music popular in the second half of the 20th century. Everything from Chuck Berry's pounding, three-chord rockers to the sweet harmonies of the Beatles to the angry white noise of Sonic Youth has been categorized as rock—and correctly so.

In all its forms, rock is defined by its energy, its driving beat, its simple melodies and catchy hooks, and, above all else, its attitude. From Brill Building pop to heavy metal, from disco to grunge, rock is about youth and rebellion.

The Beginnings of Rock 'n' Roll There is considerable controversy over exactly when rock 'n' roll was born and who can lay claim to being the first artist to record a rock record. Suffice to say, rock developed gradually after World War II out of a convergence of a number of different styles, artists, and influences, crystallizing in the popular imagination around 1954 in recordings by Bill Haley (1925–81) and Elvis Presley (1935–77).

Black and White Musicians Radio formats and record releases were highly segregated in the 1950's, yet no one could control the free interchange of musical ideas once the music was available, on disc or over the air. The greatest 1950's rock stars brought together influences from black and white musical styles; Elvis famously was described by record producer Sam Phillips as a "white man who sounds black."

Despite the segregation practiced by the music industry, many black artists were also successful in the early years of rock 'n' roll. Chuck Berry (b. 1926) was able to craft songs that addressed classic teenage topics—from car hopping to girl chasing—while also developing a clean, jazz-influenced lead guitar style. In New Orleans, Little Richard (b. Richard Pennimann, 1932) combined a gospel fervor with piano-pounding theatrics, while Fats Domino (b. Antoine Domino, 1929) melded a lazy, New Orleans backbeat with pop-flavored material.

Rockabilly Sun Records, the small Memphis label where Elvis first recorded, became the center of a variant of the basic rock style known as rockabilly. A more country-flavored music than mainstream rock, it was one strand of Elvis's initial style, and was built on by several Sun artists, most notably Carl Perkins (1932–98) a talented guitarist and songwriter ("Blue Suede Shoes"). Johnny Cash (1932–2003) initially began his career in the rockabilly mold, although he always had a hard-country edge, which soon became predominant in his music. Jerry Lee Lewis (b. 1935) was the closest to Little Richard-styled R&B in piano playing and performance style; his music was country on overdrive. Texan Buddy Holly (1936–59) created a unique rockabilly sound in hits like "Peggy Sue" (1957) and "Rave On" (1958).

Teen Pop The first era of rock 'n' roll is generally defined as lasting from about 1954 through 1959. At the turn of the decade, Elvis was inducted into the army, Buddy Holly died in a plane crash, Jerry Lee Lewis fell from grace when he married his 13-year-old cousin, and Chuck Berry was imprisoned for violating the Mann Act . But the real death knell for this first-generation rock was the music industry's ability to co-opt the surface appeal of the music by offering up stars who combined teenage good looks, snappy songs, and just enough rebelliousness to please the growing teen audience.

Teen Idols One of the first of the white male "teen idols" was Pat Boone (b. 1934), who offered heavily watered-down covers of R&B hits, ("Ain't That a Shame" became the more grammatically proper—but far less satisfying—"Isn't That a Shame"). However, the most successful purveyor of the new teen pop was businessman/promoter/TV host Dick Clark. His enormously popular *American Bandstand* television program became a launching pad for several singers who came from the program's hometown of Philadelphia. "Teen idol" singers such as Paul Anka, Bobby Dee, and Bobby Darin were soon dominating the charts.

Girl Groups The other major pop music trend of the early 1960's was the popularity of so-called girl groups. Groups of teenage girls—both black and white—recorded songs about romantic love, problems in school, and other youthful topics. Most of their songs were provided by professional songwriting teams such as Barry Mann and Cynthia Weil and Carole King and Gerry Goffin. Popular girl groups included the Shirelles, the Ronettes, and even Motown groups such as the Supremes.

Phil Spector One of the leading teen pop producers was Phil Spector (b. 1940), who aimed to create what he called "teenaged symphonies." Using a stable of professional musicians and singers, he created a dense sonic style that became known as "The Wall of Sound." Spector produced recordings by many of the most popular girl groups, including the Ronettes and the Crystals. Among his most successful productions were the Crystals' "Da Doo Ron Ron" and "You've Lost That Lovin' Feelin'," by the Righteous Brothers.

Brian Wilson One other producer played a key role in the development of 1960's rock: Brian Wilson (b. 1942). Wilson and his two brothers, Carl and Dennis, cousin Mike Love, and friend Al Jardine formed a vocal group in the early 1960's. Latching onto the craze for surfing in Southern California, they took the name the Beach Boys, and enjoyed their initial hits singing about sun, sand, and girls.

Wilson, an untrained but naturally gifted composer and arranger, began experimenting with more intricate accompaniments, vocal harmonies, and song structures. Even though the Beach Boys were celebrated for their upbeat image, Wilson was able to capture a unique feeling of teenage angst in such classics as "In My Room" and "I Just Wasn't Made for These Times." Wilson's greatest achievement was the 1966 album *Pet Sounds*, considered among the best rock albums of all time.

The British Invasion The arrival of the Beatles in America on February 7, 1964, to appear on the Ed Sullivan television show, announced a new force in popular music. Their musical style—a perky blend of American country, R&B, and early rock 'n' roll—enhanced by their boyish good looks made them an immediate sensation.

Suddenly, all things British were the rage, and dozens of groups were marketed as being in the Beatles mold. While the Beatles quickly developed their sound in innovative ways, many of the British Invasion groups that enjoyed initial success—Gerry and the Pacemakers, the Dave Clark Five, Herman's Hermits, and Peter and Gordon—quickly faded.

The Beatles The Beatles had the good fortune to be fronted by two gifted songwriters, John Lennon (1940–80) and Paul McCartney (b. 1942), who also sang most of their hit songs. Guitarist George Harrison (1943–2001) became an able songwriter as he matured, but was overshadowed in the group by his two more talented bandmates. By the mid-1960's, the group began experimenting in the studio, producing unique effects using backwards tape loops, overtracking, vocal processing, and feedback. They also pioneered the "concept album" with 1967's *Sergeant Pepper's Lonely Hearts Club Band*; the creation of a "group within the group" was also a first, which would influence future artists to create musical alter egos.

The Rolling Stones In contrast to the teen-friendly Beatles, the Rolling Stones were cleverly marketed as the "bad boys" of rock n roll. The Stones originally were a blues band, but inspired by the Beatles' success in songwriting, band members Mick Jagger (b. 1943) and Keith Richard (b. 1943) decided to write their own material. The Stones's more aggressive sound and lyrics (in songs such as "Satisfaction," "Let's Spend the Night Together," and "Paint It Black") were influential on other British bands, including the Animals.

Other British Invaders Other British Invasion bands picked up on different aspects of the Beatles and Stones sound. The Kinks combined a fine pop sensibility with an ironic lyric content that often satirized the British class system. The Who also took the pop sound and song format to a new level of sophistication, in songs that expressed the frustrations of a new generation seeking to establish its own fashions, language, and culture.

Folk Rock The mid-1960's folk music revival was a natural seedbed for America's answer to the British Invasion. These performers were used to writing their own material and playing their own instruments, plus they took a more sophisticated approach to lyrics and song structure. They were also very impressed with the Beatles' ability to create a unique, commercial sound.

The most popular folk artist of the day, Bob Dylan, befriended the Beatles and immediately saw the artistic possibilities in performing with electric instruments. But while Dylan's approach was highly idiosyncratic, others were able to quickly adapt the Beatles sound; Roger McGuinn and the Byrds, the Mamas and the Papas, and Buffalo Springfield are just a few of the groups that emerged out of the folk movement who adapted the instrumentation and basic style of the Beatles to their own ends.

From Rock 'n' Roll to Just Rock In the mid-to-late 1960's, rock 'n' roll matured into "rock," which combined influences from folk, country, jazz, pop, and other musical styles. Many of the best-known rock groups came out of the Haight-Ashbury district of San Francisco, where low rents, good weather, and a sympathetic culture attracted many would-be musicians and hangers-on.

The longest-lasting of these groups was the Grateful Dead, which began its life as a communal group living together in a rented house in the neighborhood. The Dead combined elements of blues, jazz, bluegrass, avant-garde classical, and pop into a musical stew that appealed to the burgeoning community of hippies.

Psychedelic Rock Psychedelic rock—an attempt to capture the drug experience by performing music of a looser, more improvisational style—had a brief but powerful influence in this period. It involved experiments with new sounds, created through amplification (particularly feedback), special sound manipulators (the wah-wah pedal for the guitar), and changes in recording techniques (using tape montage, backwards tape, multiple-tracking, and other devices).

Jimi Hendrix (1942–70) was perhaps the greatest live performer in this style, as he was able to create numerous effects on the guitar through different playing methods and creative use of amplification, distortion, and feedback. Going beyond the live performance aspect of the music, groups such as Pink Floyd developed as pure recording bands, creating soundscapes that could not be reproduced live.

Woodstock and Altamont: The End of an Era The 1960's came to a close with two major festivals, each emblematic of its era. Woodstock was the ultimate hippie dream; a three-day gathering of peace, love, and heavy rain and mud, it epitomized the belief that people could live together freely sharing love, drugs, and music. The fact that a half million people gathered peacefully on Max Yasgur's farm in upstate New York was a testament to the power of the hippie movement in its heyday, and there was much memorable music created over the three days that summed up the major movements in rock. The film of Woodstock enabled millions more to participate (vicariously) in the free love and good feelings of the festival.

The Altamont festival, featuring the Rolling Stones, represented the dark underbelly of the 1960's. Held at a desolate race track in Southern California, the festival's "security force" was the notorious Hell's Angels. When a scuffle broke out during the Stones' set, one listener was savagely beaten to death while a horrified crowd witnessed the event. Remarkably, the event was captured on film and even more remarkably the Stones allowed the film to be released; this film had a more sobering impact than the Woodstock documentary.

Pop/Rock in the 1970's Once the innocence of the 1960's was shattered, rock itself could no longer be a unified force. The 1970's were a time of regrouping, of developing new musical strategies. The musical possibilities hinted at by the major 1960's creators—the Beatles, Stones, Bob Dylan—were all extended, parodied, and explored further over the coming decade. And these 1970's styles in turn would form the basis for the following decades of rock's explorations.

Country-Rock In the 1960's many rock acts rediscovered the joys of real country music. Probably the first and most important country-rock LP was the Byrds' 1968 release, *Sweetheart of the Rodeo*, which featured country standards along with compositions by Bob Dylan and new member Gram Parsons, performed by the band along with some of the better, younger Nashville session men. A year later, Bob Dylan gave the movement added legitimacy by releasing *Nashville Skyline*.

In the early 1970's Gram Parsons and Byrds bassman Chris Hillman formed the most influential country-rock band, the Flying Burrito Brothers. Their first two LPs are considered classics today, combining traditional country subject matter and sounds with a decidedly new outlook.

Singer/Songwriters The 1960's-era folk and country rock movements naturally evolved into the singer/songwriter movement of the early 1970's. Artists such as James Taylor, Carly Simon, Carole King, and Joni Mitchell all took the notion of writing their own material away from social protest, and toward self-exploration and autobiography. King's 1971 album, *Tapestry*, was among the decade's most successful; in it she explored her personal growth as a woman of the 1960's. Joni Mitchell became one of the most articulate voices for both the liberation and confusion felt by young women as sexual roles shifted. Even Bob Dylan turned inward, chronicling the collapse of his marriage in the classic album *Blood on the Tracks* (1974).

Heavy Metal At the opposite end of the spectrum from the singer/songwriters, heavy metal emphasized rock's raw power. Heavy metal is loudly aggressive rock, appealing primarily to a male, adolescent audience.

British bands Led Zeppelin and Black Sabbath (with lead singer Ozzy Osbourne b. 1948) are generally cited as among the first metal bands in the early 1970's, taking the earlier blues-rock style and exaggerating its aggressive, loud guitar parts, playing repetitive riffs accompanied by pounding bass and drums. The style first came to America in the work of Alice Cooper, who brought a heightened theatricality to the form, and then in the band Kiss, which combined glam-rock makeup with the metal style.

Metal evolved somewhat in the later 1970's, when newer bands (such as Judas Priest and Iron Maiden) emerged who played more aggressively, faster, and louder than the earlier generation of bands. However, as metal became increasingly popular, a return-to-roots movement was inevitable; new American bands of the 1980's, such as Metallica and Megadeath, pioneered the subgenre of thrash-metal, returning metal to its roots in noise and speed.

Progressive Rock Progressive rock—also known as "prog" or art rock—was popular from the late 1960's through the mid-1970's and featured more ambitious instrumentation, extended compositions, and lyrics influenced by myth, science fiction, and other literary sources. Although there had been some hints of the progressive movement, it was King Crimson's 1969 debut album, *In the Court of the Crimson King*, that is generally viewed as the first great prog-rock album. Through the mid-1970's, several bands carried the progressive-rock banner, including Emerson, Lake and Palmer, Genesis, and Pink Floyd.

Glam-Rock Glam-rock is a gender-bending, highly theatrical form of rock that developed in Britain in the early 1970's. The British group T. Rex, led by flamboyant lead singer Marc Bolan (1948–77), is the epitome of pure glam-rock; the entire focus is on Bolan's unabashed showmanship, with the music taking a secondary role. However, more ambitious musicians were also drawn to glam, notably David Bowie (b. 1947) during his Ziggy Stardust/Spiders from Mars period.

Disco Disco is a mid-1970's dance style emphasizing a heavy, repeated beat, melodic riffs, and simple lyrics. As it developed in the gay dance clubs of New York, the disco style was pioneered by deejays who took to creating remixes of popular songs, particularly soul and funk tracks that emphasized a repetitive beat. By sequencing songs with the same basic rhythm and tempo, they could extend a dance session up to 30 minutes.

Early disco groups, such as KC & the Sunshine Band and Niles Rodgers's (b. 1952) Chic, evolved out of funk bands. Other artists quickly evolved to cater to this new musical style, some with an overtly gay image (such as the Village People), others exploiting heterosexuality (Donna Summer, b. 1948). The disco craze reached its greatest mainstream acceptance thanks to the 1977 film *Saturday Night Fever*, which featured the Bee Gees playing such songs as "Stayin' Alive."

Punk Punk rock was a "back to basics" movement that occurred in the mid-1970's, in reaction to the increasing commercialism and aging of the previous generation of rock stars. Most punk songs were simple to play, as a reaction to the increasing complexity of the music of progressive rock. Punk also tackled topics from homosexuality to radical politics that were not usually addressed by rock songs.

In England, the punk rockers Sex Pistols were purposely poor musicians, emphasizing outrageous clothes and hair styles and an aggressive, in-your-face stage presence; their single "God Save the Queen" was banned on British radio. However, the greatest politically oriented punk band was undoubtedly the Clash, whose 1978 album *London Calling* is recognized as one of the great rock albums of all time.

In New York City, the punk movement centered on a small club in New York's Bowery district, CBGB's. New York punk artists ranged from the Ramones, who specialized in ultra-short, purposely simple, and aggressively loud songs performed at breakneck speeds, to poet Patti Smith (b. 1946).

California Rock One of the most successful groups of the late 1970's-early 1980's was the Eagles, a group that began its life as a country-rock band but developed into a mainstream pop act. Combining a Southern Californian singer/songwriter sensibility, sweet vocal harmonies, and a powerful twin-guitar lead sound, the group had many top ten hits.

Another group that combined confessional songwriting with a rock beat was Fleetwood Mac, which in its 1970's/mid-1980's lineup combined the British rhythm section of John McVie and Mick Fleetwood with the romantic themes of the group's three singer/songwriters, Stevie Nicks, Lindsey Buckingham, and Christine McVie. The soap opera couplings and uncouplings among the group's members also helped sell their records.

Pop/Rock in the 1980's and 1990's While the 1970's saw a splintering of rock's main line into many subgenres, the 1980's and 1990's saw a gradually decreasing presence of rock as a mainstream pop music. It was a time of nostalgic retrenchment, when older groups such as the Who and Rolling Stones were able to sell out major stadiums, but few new groups arose with equal drawing power.

MTV The year 1981 was a watershed year for pop music, thanks to the launch of MTV, the first cable network devoted solely to music. MTV's combination of music videos, youthful video jockeys (VJs), irreverent commentary, and music news resulted in immediate and widespread popularity among youthful viewers. More important, MTV's music videos helped to define the sound—and the look—of popular music throughout the 1980's.

The early format of the network was modeled after Top 40 radio, with popular videos played in heavy rotation. A large number of pop stars were made household names by MTV; artists such as Duran Duran and Madonna gained widespread success based primarily on the popularity of their music videos.

New Wave The New Wave movement of the early 1980's came out of punk, but had a far more commercial edge. Groups such as the Police combined punk attitude with a pure pop sound. Talking Heads began as an art-punk band propelled by the off-center sensibility of lead singer/songwriter David Byrne (b. 1952), but developed into a band that combined elements of commercial pop with world beat and contemporary classical music. And singer/songwriter Elvis Costello (b. Declan MacManus, 1954) adopted some of punk's back-to-basics ethos but wed it to far more sophisticated lyrics and arrangements.

Bruce Springsteen Straight-ahead rock 'n' roll music in the post-punk world was defined by Bruce Springsteen (b. 1949). Springsteen combined in his music elements of Bob Dylan's word-strewn folk-rock; a love for classic 1960's rock styles, from Motown to Stax to garage-rock; and his own Wagnerian sensibilities, enhanced by his primal backup group, the E Street Band. Springsteen's 1985 album, *Born in the USA*, represented his greatest commercial success, producing multiple hit singles and a long-running, financially rewarding world tour of stadiums.

Pop-Rock Pop-rock music in the early 1980's was dominated by the dance-oriented music of Michael Jackson (b. 1958) and Madonna (b. Madonna Louise Ciccone, 1958). Twenty-five-year-old Jackson, former lead singer of the Motown group the Jackson Five, released *Thriller* in 1982; the album became the biggest-selling pop record of all time. Madonna was one of MTV's first video stars; she continuously redefined her sound and image over the course of two decades, beginning with a "boy toy" teen pop phase and then maturing into a plethora of fashion looks and musical styles.

Grunge The early 1990's saw the birth of a new hybrid of punk and heavy metal music, dubbed *grunge*, that was a back-to-basics response to the synthesized pop music of the 1980's. Born out of the Seattle music scene, the first wave of grunge bands—including Green River, Munhoney, and Soundgarden—played music that blended angst-ridden, introspective lyrics with distorted guitars and pounding drums. Grunge's second wave, led by Nirvana and Pearl Jam, achieved widespread popularity with a slightly more melodic sound.

Grunge was history by the mid-1990's, but the grunge sound lived on in more mainstream post-grunge bands, including Creed and Matchbox 20. These bands applied grunge instrumentation and production to more radio-friendly lyrics and melodies.

Teen Pop The late 1990's were notable for its many "manufactured" teen pop artists, from Britain's Spice Girls to America's Backstreet Boys and *NSYNC boy bands to pop Lolitas (and ex-Mouseketeers) Britney Spears (b. 1982) and Christina Aguilera (b. 1980). These artists distinguished themselves more as entertainers than musicians, although their mixture of sugary-sweet pop melodies with heavy hip hop beats proved popular, especially among the pre-teen audience.

World Music

To Western audiences, the term *world music* refers to music that doesn't fall into the North American and Western European pop tradition. World music is indigenous music from a variety of countries, often combined with Western pop sensibilities.

African Music There is no single "African" musical style; as expected of a continent covering more than 50 independent nations, African music varies, evolving out of a multiplicity of cultures and histories. Most African music incorporates complex rhythms, exotic instruments, and call and response singing, as exemplified by the *mbube*, an a cappella choral music of the South African Zulus.

Caribbean Music The Caribbean is primarily known for two indigenous musical forms, *reggae* and *calypso*. Reggae comes from Jamaica, where it evolved from the rhythmic *ska* style that was the island's interpretation of early R&B. Reggae, as interpreted by Bob Marley (1945–81) and other local musicians, has a slower beat with a heavier emphasis on the upbeat. Calypso comes from the island of Trinidad, and incorporates a traditional rhythm section with steel drums and horns. It is typically built around a syncopated bass guitar line and an infectious uptempo dance beat.

Celtic Music Celtic music encompasses the folk music of Ireland and Scotland—both traditional and contemporary. Instrumentation typically includes stringed instruments, fiddles, and pipes; contemporary Celtic music often adds New Age spirituality and production.

Central and Eastern European Music Central European music includes traditional Greek music, as well as gypsy music characterized by exotic rhythms and folk dances. Eastern European music is also home to gypsy music, as well as folk dances such as *polka* and the *mazurka*. The music of Eastern European Jews, known as *klezmer*, has enjoyed a revival since the mid-1970's.

Indian Music Indian music is rhythmically and harmonically complex, compared with popular Western music. Classical Indian compositions are called *ragas*, and are typically played on tabla, sitar, and other native instruments.

Latin Music Latin music describes a number of diverse styles from different regions and countries in Latin America. The best known of these styles include *bossa nova*, a laid-back jazz-influenced dance music; *mambo*, an Afro-Cuban dance with a characteristic quadruple meter rhythmic pattern; *mariachi*, a traditional Mexican music built around an ensemble of trumpets, violins, guitar, and bass guitar; *rumba*, an Afro-Cuban dance in duple or quadruple time; *salsa*, a lively Brazilian dance music; *samba*, a dance built around a pulsating bass drum rhythm; and *Tejano*, a form of contemporary Latin pop.

Middle Eastern Music Middle Eastern music shows the influence of Arabic culture and the Muslim religion. Traditional music from this area is overwhelmingly vocal, often without any instrumental accompaniment. More popular forms include Turkish *Sufi* and Algerian *rai* music, both representative of the high-energy, melismatic fervor of their Muslim heritage.

Worldbeat The term *worldbeat* refers not to a style of music, but rather to the fusion of musical styles in a multicultural approach designed to expose ethnic music to a world audience. This often takes the form of traditional folk music set to a Western dance beat, or Western melodies set to native rhythms. Western proponents include Paul Simon (*Graceland*), Peter Gabriel, and David Byrne.

Selected World Music Styles

bolero Spanish dance in triple time.

bossa nova (1) Brazilian dance, similar to the samba. (2) Brazilian jazz.

fandango lively Spanish dance, believed to be of South American origin, in triple or compound duple time.

gagaku traditional court music of Japan.

gamelan musical ensemble of Java or Bali, comprised of gongs, chimes, drums, and other instruments.

habanera Cuban dance in moderate duple meter.

jarabe traditional Mexican dance form, with multiple sections in contrasting meters and tempos.

jota spanish dance song in a quick triple meter, typically with guitar and castanet accompaniment.

jig vigorous dance in compound meter, developed in Britain and Ireland.

mazurka Polish folk dance in triple meter.

mbube a cappella choral singing style of the South African Zulus, featuring call-and response patterns and close-knit harmonies.

polka lively Bohemian dance.

polonaise national Polish dance, in triple time and of moderate tempo.

raga Indian melodic pattern. There are various raga "systems" that describe different series of pitches, patterns, and ornamentation.

reel dance in rapid quadruple time for two or more couples; popular in Scotland, Ireland, and parts of England.

tango Argentinean dance at a slow walking pace in duple time.

tarantella Neapolitan dance in 6/8 time.

Musical Instruments

String Family

The string family of instruments consists of those that are primarily played with a bow, and those that are primarily plucked with fingers or a pick. Sound is created by the vibration of thin strings of wire or gut, typically amplified by a hollow resonating chamber within the body of the instrument.

Bowed These instruments can be either bowed or plucked, although bowing is more typical of orchestral use. Primary bowed instruments include: **Violin, Viola, Cello, Double bass.**

Plucked These instruments are either plucked one string at a time, or strummed to sound multiple strings simultaneously. Primary plucked instruments include: **Harp, Lute, Guitar, Banjo, Mandolin, Ukulele.**

Brass Family

The brass family consists of wind instruments made of brass or other similar metals. (It does not include instruments formerly made of wood but now sometimes made of metal, such as the flute, or metal instruments with reed mouthpieces, such as the saxophone.) All brass instruments include a cup- or funnel-shaped mouthpiece, which is pressed against the player's lips and then vibrates to produce a tone. The tone is amplified through a long metal tubing, intricately coiled around itself, which culminates in a flared bell. Different pitches are produced by varying the vibration of the lips and by pressing (in most instruments) a series of valves. The notable exception is the trombone, which uses a slide to change the length of the brass tubing, changing the pitch accordingly. Primary brass instruments include: **Trumpet, Piccolo trumpet, Flugelhorn, Bugle, Trombone, French horn, Baritone horn, Tuba.**

Woodwind Family

The woodwind family of instruments consists of wind instruments originally and usually made of wood, either blown directly by mouth or by means of a thin wooden reed. Many woodwind instruments are available in different sizes to produce differing pitch ranges; for example, the clarinet family consists of alto, bass, and contrabass instruments.

Single Reed Single reed instruments incorporate a mouthpiece with a wide and flat single reed. Sound is generated by blowing against the reed, causing it to vibrate. Primary single-reed instruments include: **Clarinet (alto, bass, contrabass), Saxophone (soprano, alto, tenor, baritone, bass, contrabass).**

Double Reed Double-reed instruments incorporate a mouthpiece with two thin and narrow reeds. Sound is reproduced by blowing air between the two reeds, causing them to vibrate against each other. Primary double-reed instruments include: **Oboe, Bassoon, Contrabassoon, English horn.**

Direct Blown Direct-blown woodwind instruments reproduce sound when air is blown across (flute, piccolo) or into (recorder) a small round mouth-hole at one end of the instrument. Different pitches are reproduced by opening and closing a series of finger holes aligned along the length of the instrument. Primary direct-blown woodwind instruments include: **Flute, Piccolo, Recorder.**

Percussion Family

Percussion instruments are those that are played (generally) by striking a resonating surface with the hand, a stick or mallet, or a pedal. Other percussion instruments, such as the tambourine and maracas, are played by shaking or rattling the instrument.

There are two general types of percussion instruments: those that generate a definite pitch, and those that do not.

Definite-Pitched Percussion instruments that reproduce definite pitches include: **Glockenspiel, Xylophone, Marimba, Vibraphone, Chimes (tubular bells), Timpani.**

Indefinite-Pitched Percussion instruments that do not generate a definite pitch include: **Drum, Bongo, Conga, Timbale, Cymbal, Triangle, Tambourine, Maracas.**

Keyboard Instruments

Keyboard instruments are those in which specific pitches are determined by depressing one of a number of keys, typically presented in a continuous sequential arrangement. The actual sound of the keyboard instrument is generated by a related apparatus; for example, the piano generates sound by hitting a string with a small mallet, whereas the organ generates sound by blowing air through a reed or large pipe.

Some experts classify keyboard instruments as part of the string family, even though they are played percussively. Primary keyboard instruments include: **Piano (pianoforte), Harpsichord, Clavier, Organ.**

Electronic Instruments

The late 20th century saw the invention of a new class of instruments called electrophones. These instruments generate sound via any number of nonphysical methods, such as oscillation, electromagnetic, or electrostatic means. (The family of electronic instruments does not include those that simply amplify acoustically generated sounds electronically, such as the electric guitar or electric piano.) Primary electronic instruments include: **Synthesizer, Sequencer.**

Glossary of Musical Terms

a cappella vocal music without instrumental accompaniment.

accent a note played louder or with more emphasis than regular notes.

accompaniment a background performance, typically instrumental, subservient to the main performer.

air (1) a melody. (2) melodious composition.

alto that female voice below the soprano, in much choral music the lowest primary female voice.

antiphonal a singing style characterized by two parts of a choir singing alternately, one answering another.

atonal having no tonal center, and no underlying key. In pure atonal music, the notes of the chromatic scale are used impartially and independently, with no home degree or tonic.

ballad (1) A song to be danced to. (2) Self-contained narrative song, such as Schubert's *Erlkönig*.

ballade a type of piano miniature, typically dramatic or heroic in nature.

ballata a poetic form of secular song in 14th and early 15th century Italy.

band a body of instrumental players. Sometimes defined by the primary instrumental grouping or function, as in "brass band" or "dance band."

baritone a male voice category between bass and tenor voices; not present in all choral music. Sometimes called bass-baritone.

bass (1) the lowest male voice. (2) the lowest pitch of a chord (not necessarily the root).

basso low male bass voice.

basso continuo continuous bass; a bass line in music of the 17th and 18th centuries, played by the organist.

beat any pulsing unit of musical time.

blend (1) the combination of voices in group singing so that individual performers are indistinguishable. (2) Smooth transitions between the registers of the singing voice.

blue note (1) the flatted third, fifth, or seventh tone of the scale, common in blues and jazz. (2) a slight drop of pitch on the third, fifth, or seventh tones; also known as bent pitch.

bourrée lively French dance in duple meter, popular in the Baroque period.

break in jazz, a short improvised solo without accompaniment that "breaks" an ensemble passage or introduces an extended solo.

bridge a short section that links two important sections of a piece of music.

cadenza (1) in opera, a flourish of difficult, fast, high notes sung at the end of an aria, designed to demonstrate the vocal ability of the singer. (2) a virtuosic unaccompanied improvisation, typically free of key or meter.

call and response (1) melodic technique where a phrase is stated in the first part of the melody, and then answered in the second part. (2) performance style with a singing leader who is imitated by a chorus of followers; also called responsorial singing, and commonly heard in spiritual or gospel music.

canon strictest form of contrapuntal imitation. Simple forms of choral canon include the catch and the round.

strict canon canon in which the intervals of the imitating voice are exactly the same as the voice being imitated.

choir a group of singers who perform together, usually in parts, with several singers on each part; often associated with church singing.

chorale a singing group.

chord progression a series of chords over a number of measures.

chorus (1) fairly large group of singers who perform together, usually with several on each part. (2) a choral movement of a large-scale work. (3) in jazz, a single statement of the melodic-harmonic pattern. (4) in popular music, the part of the song (typically following the verse) that recurs at intervals; also known as the B section of a song.

chromatic pitches outside the underlying key or scale. The opposite of diatonic.

chromaticism (1) the use of chromatic intervals, chords, and scales. (2) a style of composing that employs chromatic harmony.

contrapuntal see *counterpoint*.

counterpoint two or more simultaneous, independent lines or voices in a piece of music. The art of counterpoint developed in the ninth century, and reached its zenith in the late 16th and early 17th centuries; some music theorists apply strict rules to the creation of contrapuntal lines.

country blues early guitar-driven blues form, performed primarily on acoustic instruments, complete with elaborate fingerpicking and slide playing. Notable country blues musicians include Lonnie Johnson, Josh White, and Scrapper Blackwell.

cover a performance or recording that remakes a previously recorded song.

crossover a recording or artist that appeals primarily to one audience but also becomes popular with another.

dissonance a combination of tones that sounds discordant and unstable, in need of resolution to a more pleasing and stable harmony. The opposite of consonance.

double indicates that a second voice or instrument is to duplicate a particular line of music, either in unison or an octave above or below.

duet a musical composition for two performers.

electronic music music that employs computers, synthesizers, and other electronic equipment to generate, modify, and combine all manner of sounds.

ensemble literally, "together;" a group of performers singing or playing together at the same time.

entr'acte a musical composition played between acts or scenes of an opera.

exposition (1) in the sonata form, the first section of the composition, in which the principal themes are first presented. (2) in a fugue, the first statement of the subject by all the voices in turn.

falsetto vocal technique whereby men can sing above their normal range, producing a lighter, higher sound.

finale the last song of an act, or the last movement of a multiple-movement work.

folk music (1) traditional songs, generally local or regional in origin. (2) traditional American music, typically consisting of vocals accompanied by guitars and other acoustic instruments.

form the structure or shape of a musical work, based on repetition, contrast, and variation; the organizing principle in music.

frequency a scientific measurement of how fast molecules of air are vibrating; the faster the vibrations, the higher the pitch. Frequency is measured in vibrations per second, or Hertz (Hz).

funk see *groove*.

gigue (1) English Baroque dance type in lively compound meter. (2) A standard movement of the Baroque suite.

gospel 20th century sacred music style associated with the Protestant African-American church.

groove (1) a specific beat. (2) indicating that a song was played at just the right tempo and feel, as in "in the groove." (3) a dance-oriented type of jazz, derived from soul jazz in the late 1970s, with a deep bass line and blues-oriented chord progressions.

ground bass a repeating bass line, typically a short motif over which other parts play changing harmonies.

harmonic interval two notes sounded simultaneously.

harmonization the choice of chords to accompany a melodic line.

harmony (1) the sound of tones in combination. (2) accompanying parts behind the main melody.

head register a vocal adjustment producing light, flute-like tones, conducive to soft and high singing. Also called head tone or head voice.

homophony music composed of melody and accompanying harmony, as distinct from polyphony or monophony.

hook a piece of melody designed to deliberately grab the attention of the listener.

hymn song in praise of God.

improvisation spontaneous creation of a musical composition while it is being performed; a musical performance without a written score.

intonation the act of singing or playing in tune. Intonation can be "good" (in tune) or "bad" (out of tune).

introduction the beginning of a piece of music.

isorhythmic the art of repeating a rhythmic idea over and over, typically in multiple voices.

libretto the text of an opera or oratorio. (Literally, "little book.")

madrigal comedy short drama set to music, as a series of secular vocal pieces.

march a musical style incorporating characteristics of military music, including strongly accented duple meter in simple, repetitive rhythmic patterns.

melisma a group of notes sung to a single syllable, typically including both a primary note and ornamentation.

melodic improvisation the art of creating a continuous new melodic line using a song's existing chords—not just playing chord- or scale-based patterns.

melody the combination of tone and rhythm in a logical sequence.

modulation a change of key. For example, when a piece of music changes from the key of C to the key of G midway through, that piece of music has modulated.

motif a brief melodic or rhythmic idea within a piece of music. Sometimes called a figure or motive.

movement self-contained part within a larger musical work.

new age music musical style characterized by soothing timbres and repetitive forms. First popular in the 1980's.

nocturne a type of piano miniature, of romantic character.

opus (1) a single work or composition. (2) when followed by a number, e.g. Opus 12, used for the numbering of a composer's works.

ornamentation notes that embellish and decorate a melody.

passepied French Baroque court dance; a faster version of the minuet.

pedal point a note sustained below changing harmonies.

phrase within a piece of music, a segment that is unified by rhythms, melodies, or harmonies and that comes to some sort of closure; typically composed in groups of 2, 4, 8, 16, or 32 measures.

pitch the highness or lowness of a tone.

placement a technique of singing guided by sensations of vibrations in the face, behind the teeth, in the nose, etc.; i.e., "forward placement".

portamento a smooth movement from one note to the next.

quarter tone an interval half the distance of a Western half-step; difficult to notate, and impossible to play on a traditional keyboard instrument.

range the distance between the lowest and highest tones of a melody, instrument, or voice. This span is typically described as narrow, medium, or wide.

register (1) the specific area in the range of a voice or an instrument. (2) a series of tones that are produced by similar vocal fold vibration and placement, resulting in similar tone quality (i.e., chest register or head register).

repetition a technique that involves repeating all or part of a motif; typically used in conjunction with variation.

rhapsody a composition, in a single continuous movement, based on popular, national, or folk melodies.

riff a short melodic or rhythmic pattern.

rondeau Medieval and Renaissance fixed poetic form; type of chanson.

rondo a type of instrumental composition in which one section intermittently recurs; the usual form for the last movement of a concerto or sontata.

sacred music religious or spiritual music, for church or devotional use. Also called non-secular music.

score (1) the written depiction of all the individual parts played by each of the instruments in an ensemble. (2) to orchestrate a composition.

shuffle a rhythmic feel based on triplets or a dotted eighth note/sixteenth note pattern.

solo a vocal or instrumental piece or passage performed by one performer, with or without accompaniment.

song short vocal composition.

soprano the highest female voice.

spiritual American folk-hymn, typically of the African-American church tradition.

stanza see *verse*.

string band musical style from the early 1900's that precurses modern bluegrass and country music, characterized by guitars, mandolins, fiddles, and other stringed instruments.

style a characteristic manner of presentation of musical elements such as melody, harmony, rhythm, or dynamics.

subject a motif, phrase, or melody that is a basic element in a musical composition.

syncopation an accent on an unexpected beat, or the lack of an accent on an expected beat.

synthesizer electronic instrument, typically activated via a keyboard, that reproduces a wide variety of sounds via the use of sound generators and modifiers.

tenor the highest male voice.

theme a recurring melodic or rhythmic pattern.

theme and variations musical technique involving the statement of a theme and then the varying of that theme, either in pitch or rhythm. See *variation*.

timbre tone quality or tone color. (Pronounced "tambor.")

tonality the organization of musical notes around a tonic, or home pitch, based on a major or minor scale or mode.

tune (1) melody (2) as a verb, to establish correct intonation of an instrument.

unison (1) two notes of the same pitch. (2) voices or instruments all singing or playing the same pitch.

valve mechanism that alters the pitch of a brass instrument by opening or closing the metal tube, thus increasing or decreasing the length of the tube.

variation a technique in which some aspects of the music are altered but the original is still recognizable. Typically used in conjunction with repetition. See also *theme and variations*.

verse (1) a short division of a musical composition. (2) in popular music, the first or A section of a song, preceding the chorus.

virtuoso performer of extraordinary technical ability.

vocalize to exercise the voice.

voice melodic or harmonic line.

Music Symbols and Notation

Notation

enharmonic different notations of the same pitch. For example, F♯ and G♭ are enharmonic notes.

half step the smallest distance between notes in the Western chromatic scale.

interval the distance between two pitches. Typically measured in half-step or whole steps, or expressed numerically (second, third, fourth, etc.).

ledger lines short lines above or below a musical staff, indicating notes too high or low to appear on the staff itself.

notation the art of writing musical notes on paper.

semitone the interval of a half-step.

staff an assemblage of horizontal lines and spaces that represent different pitches. Also called a stave.

whole step an interval equal to two half steps.

Tempo

backbeat in 4/4 time, beats two and four; in popular music, the backbeat is typically played by the drummer on the snare drum.

bar line vertical line placed on the staff between measures.

bar see *measure*.

coda (1) ending section of a piece of music. (2) a specific music symbol indicating the ending section of a piece of music.

common time the 4/4 time signature. Also known as quadruple meter.

compound time or compound meter time signature in which each beat in a measure consists of a dotted note or its equivalent. For example, 9/8 time can be treated as compound time, by playing three dotted eighth-note beats per measure.

downbeat the major beats in a measure; in 4/4 time, the downbeats are 1, 2, 3, and 4.

measure a group of beats, indicated by the placement of bar lines on the staff.

meter the organization of beats and their divisions.

odd time any non-4/4 time signature, such as 3/4, 5/4, or 9/8.

simple time meter in which each beat has a simple note value. For example, 3/4 and 4/4 are both simple time signatures. Compare to compound time, where each beat has the value of a dotted note.

staccato an articulation that indicates a note is to be played short and clipped.

tie a curved line over or under two or more notes that "ties" the two notes together into one.

time fundamental rhythmical patterns of music.

triple meter metrical pattern with three beats to a measure.

triple time any time signature with three beats per measure. For example, both 3/8 and 3/4 are triple time.

triplet a group of three notes performed in the space of two.

upbeat (1) the last beat of a measure as conducted; a weak beat which anticipates the downbeat (the first beat of the next measure). (2) the eighth-note "and" after the downbeat.

Scales

chromatic scale a scale containing 12 equal divisions of the octave—all the white keys and black keys within an octave.

diatonic notes or chords that are contained in the underlying key or scale. For example, in the key of C Major, the diatonic notes are C, D, E, F, G, A, and B; all other notes are chromatic.

major scale the most common scale, consisting of the following intervals: whole-whole-half-whole-whole-whole-half.

minor scale one of three scales, each with a flatted third of the scale. The natural minor scale is identical to the Aeolian mode. The harmonic minor scale is the same as the natural minor scale, but with a raised seventh. The melodic minor scale used in jazz and popular music is the same as the harmonic minor scale, but with a raised sixth as well; in classical music, this scale contains the raised sixth and seventh when ascending, but when descending lowers the sixth and seventh (making it identical to the natural minor scale).

relative keys keys that share the same key signature, but not the same root. For example, A minor and C Major are relative keys.

scale a sequence of related pitches, arranged in ascending or descending order.

tonic (1) the primary note in a scale or key; the "Do" in Solfeggio. (2) The chord built on a scale's first degree.

whole tone scale a seven-note scale (including the octave) with each degree a whole step part. For example, the C whole tone scale includes the notes C-D-E-F♯-G♯-A♯-C.

Intervals

interval the distance between two pitches. Typically measured in half-step or whole steps, or expressed numerically (second, third, fourth, etc.).

major interval in the major scale, the distances between the tonic and the second, third, sixth, and seventh scale degrees. For example, in the C Major scale, the distance between C and E is a major third interval.

minor interval any major interval lowered by a half step. For example, a minor third interval from the note C is the note E♭.

Chords

chord three or more notes played simultaneously.

major chord a chord with a major third (1-3-5). For example, the C Major chord contains the notes C-E-G.

minor chord a chord with a minor third (1-♭3-5). For example, the C minor chord contains the notes C-E♭-G.

Modes

Aeolian mode a mode starting on the sixth degree of the corresponding major scale, equivalent to the natural minor scale.

Dorian mode a mode starting on the second degree of the corresponding major scale.

Ionian mode a mode starting on the first degree of the corresponding major scale, equivalent to the major scale.

Locrian mode a mode starting on the seventh degree of the corresponding major scale.

Lydian mode a mode starting on the fourth degree of the corresponding major scale.

Mixolydian mode a mode starting on the fifth degree of the corresponding major scale. Also known as the dominant scale.

mode a set of scales, based on centuries-old church music, that preceded today's major and minor scales. The modes are based on and named for the note of the major scale on which they start and stop; these include the Dorian, Phrygian, Lydian, Mixolydian, Ionian, Locrian, and Aeolian modes.

Phrygian mode a mode starting on the third degree of the corresponding major scale.

Embellishments

embellishment melodic decoration, either improvised or indicated through ornamentation signs in the music.

trill melodic ornament consisting of the rapid alternation between one tone and the next above it.

turn a five-note melodic ornament, starting on the original note, then up one scale step, back down to the original note, down one scale step, and then up to the original note again.

Expression

a tempo return to the previous tempo after some sort of deviation; literally, "in time."

accelerando gradually speed up. (Abbreviated as accel.)

adagio (1) tempo marking for moderately slow. (2) A slow movement in a larger work of music.

adante tempo marking for a moderate, walking pace.

agitato agitated or restless.

allegro (1) tempo marking for a fast, cheerful tempo. (2) A fast movement in a larger work of music.

andante slow

cantabile singable or singingly, typically with the melody smoothly articulated. In Italian, "in a singing style."

con amore with love; tenderly.

con fuoco with fire.

con passione with passion.

crescendo gradually louder.

da capo an indication to return to the beginning of a piece. Abbreviated D.C. See *D.C. al Coda* and *D.C. al Fine.*

decrescendo gradually softer.

doice sweetly.

dolente sad; weeping.

doppio movimento play twice as fast.

espressivo expressively.

fin end.

forte loud. (Abbreviated as f.)

fortissimo very loud. (Abbreviated as ff.)

gioioso joyous.

grave tempo marking for a very slow or solemn pace.

lamentoso like a lament.

largo tempo marking for slow and dignified.

legato notes sung or played smoothly together, for the full rhythmic value of each note. (From the Italian, meaning "bound" or "tied.")

lento tempo marking for slow.

maestoso majestic.

meno less.

mesto sad.

mezza voce Italian for "medium voice," an indication to lower the singing volume.

mezzo forte medium loud. (Abbreviated as mf.)

mezzo piano medium soft. (Abbreviated as mp.)

misterioso mysteriously

moderato tempo marking for a moderate pace.

molto very. For example, allegro molto indicates that a piece is to be played very quickly.

non troppo not too much.

obbligato indispensable; an instrumental or vocal part where the part is obligatory, and often special or unusual in effect.

pianissimo very soft. (Abbreviated as pp.)

piano (1) soft. (Abbreviated as p.)

pizzicato notes on a string instrument that are plucked rather than bowed.

poco a little; used to modify tempo and other markings. For example, poco lento means "a little slow."

prestissimo tempo marking for an extremely fast tempo, faster than presto.

presto tempo marking for a very fast tempo.

rallentando gradually slow down. (Abbreviated as rall.)

ritardando gradually slow down. (Abbreviated as rit. or ritard.)

ritenuto hold back the tempo. (Abbreviated as rit. or riten.)

rubato "borrowed time," common in Romantic music, where the performer either hesitates or rushes through certain notes, imparting flexibility to the written note values.

sforzando a sudden stress or accent on a single note or chord.

sostenuto sustained singing; long, rather slow phrases that the singer is capable of singing on one breath. Considered one of the hallmarks of bel canto singing.

sotto voce in a soft voice.

subito suddenly.

tempo a piacere performer designates tempo; "please yourself" as to speed.

tempo comodo play at a convenient or moderate speed.

tempo di ballo play at a dance tempo

tempo di gavotte at gavotte speed.

tempo giusto in exact time; play at the tempo the music demands.

tempo minore moderate speed.

tempo ordinario play in ordinary time; moderate speed.

tempo primo return to the tempo designated at the beginning of a piece. In German, tempo wie vorher.

tempo rubato see *rubato*.

tempo the rate of speed at which beats are played in a song. For example, a tempo of presto is very fast; a tempo of largo is slow. Sometimes expressed in precise beats per minute. Plural is tempi.

tenendo sustaining.

tenero tender.

tutti "all," the opposite of solo.

vivace tempo marking for a lively tempo.

Notes

Whole note	Half note	Quarter note	Eighth note	Sixteenth note

Rests

Whole rest	Half rest	Quarter rest	Eighth rest	Sixteenth rest

Accidentals

Sharp	Flat	Natural
♯	♭	♮

Key Signatures

C Major (A minor)	Db Major (Bb minor)	D Major (B minor)	Eb Major (C minor)	E Major (D minor)
F Major (D minor)	Gb Major (Eb minor)	G Major (E minor)	Ab Major (F minor)	A Major (F# minor)
Bb Major (G minor)	B Major (G# minor)			

PAINTING AND SCULPTURE

History of Art in the Western Tradition

Ancient Art

Egyptian Art Beginning in the Old Kingdom period (early third millennium B.C.), Egyptian tombs often contained not only a mummified body, but also a stone portrait sculpture of the deceased. Egyptian art remained religious, and particularly funerary, over a span of more than two thousand years, gradually becoming more elaborate and refined but essentially stable in purpose. By the New Kingdom dynasties (mid-second millennium B.C.), Egyptian art both influenced and was influenced by Mesopotamian and Minoan art. Monumental statues of pharaohs and gods were produced in great numbers, tombs were often decorated with elaborate mural paintings showing scenes from daily life and the afterlife, and portrait sculptures, though stylized, were often highly expressive of the appearance and character of their subjects; a painted limestone portrait bust of Queen Nefertiti (ca. 1360 B.C.) is a famous example. Egyptian art was subsumed into Hellennic art after the conquest of Egypt by Alexander the Great (331 B.C.), but local features endured. Hundreds of portrait paintings, done in encaustic (pigments in a wax base) on wood and placed inside coffins of wealthy citizens, have been found in the Fayyum region of Egypt; they testify to the continued vigor of Hellenized Egyptian art under Roman rule (first–third centuries A.D.).

Art of Ancient Mesopotamia A succession of great civilizations flourished in the land between the Tigris and Euphrates Rivers and adjacent regions, beginning with the Sumerians (ca. 4000–2300 B.C.). They were followed by the Akkadians (ca. 2350–2180 B.C.), the Hittites (ca. 1900–1200 B.C., whose empire was based in Anatolia, in the northern reaches of Mesopotamia), the Babylonians (ca. 1792–1600 B.C.), and the Assyrians (ca. 1350–612 B.C.). Among the most characteristic expressions of Mesopotamian art are stone sculptures in the round or in high relief showing winged bulls, lions, magnificently bearded warrior-kings, and deities, often in association with temple architecture, and cylinder seals that are masterpieces of miniature sculpture. One of the finest works of Mesopotamian art is the Ishtar Gate of the second Babylonian Empire (612–539 B.C.), a work of blue-glazed faience brick and low-relief sculpture now reconstructed in the State Museum, Berlin. The various cultures of Mesopotamia and adjacent regions were absorbed into the Persian Empire (559–331 B.C.) and influenced its art, an effect seen, for example, in the elaborate relief sculptures of the ceremonial city of Persepolis (ca. 500 B.C.).

Art of Ancient Greece The art of ancient Greece is generally regarded as the foundation of subsequent European art. Greek art itself was derived from the art of the much earlier Minoan civilization of Crete. By the seventh century B.C., Greek artists working in vase painting, wall painting, and stone sculpture had built upon Minoan roots and fully incorporated artistic influences from Egypt and Mesopotamia to create uniquely Greek styles.

Archaic Painting During the Archaic period (ca. 700–480 B.C.), Greek artists were decorating vases with complex narrative scenes from myths, legend, and everyday life. Such scenes were rendered as drawings filled in with flat areas of solid color. In earlier vases, the figures were painted with a black glaze, and rested against an unpainted background, which was the red color of the clay. In later vases, this method was reversed, so that the background spaces were painted with black glaze, and the figures were the red color of the clay.

By the end of the fifth century B.C., artists were concentrating their efforts on wall painting, which was more versatile than the limited palette of vase painting. It allowed them to gradually develop the techniques of modeling, or using changes of tone within a figure to indicate three-dimensional shape, as well as spatial perspective, the ability to indicate distance or depth within the picture space. None of these wall paintings, however, survives—they are known to historians by literary accounts and copies made for Romans in later years.

Archaic Sculpture By 650 B.C., two types of sculpture were being widely produced: the *Kouros*, or standing male youth, and *Kore*, or standing maiden. They are the first known examples of free-standing statues, unattached to an architectural support. The Kouros statues were slim nudes with stylized features and wiglike hair, standing in a tight pose with clenched fists and the left foot forward. Kore were posed and styled similarly, but clothed. Figural sculptures toward the end of the archaic period often featured a placid expression with a closed-mouthed smile, which became known as the archaic smile.

In the Archaic period the Greeks also developed a characteristic style of stone temple with an entablature (roof structure) supported by stone columns. They customarily decorated such temples with figurative sculpture, filling the space of the triangular pediment, and creating horizontal bands of decoration known as a frieze.

Classical Period (480–323 B.C.) During this period (from the great Greek naval victory over the Persians at Salamis to the death of Alexander the Great), sculpture became much more naturalistic and illusionistic, moving away from the rigid stylizations of the Archaic period. While most statues still represented an idealized beauty, they became remarkably lifelike, with anatomically accurate muscles and skeletal structures. Clothed figures wore drapery that mimicked the appearance of real cloth, with creases and folds. Although today the austere purity of white marble is appreciated as one of the beauties of Greek sculpture, in ancient Greece statues were in fact painted in bright colors to imitate naturalistic colors of skin, hair, and clothing.

One of the most important developments in classical scupture was the introduction of the *contrapposto* pose, in which the sculpted figure stands at ease, resting his weight on one leg and giving the body an asymmetrical and relaxed stance. The famous nude *Kritios Boy* (ca. 480 B.C.) is the earliest known sculpture to exhibit this feature. This pose has been copied repeatedly in other sculptural traditions up to the present day, and as far afield as the Buddhist sculpture of Central and East Asia.

Once Greek sculptors had learned to depict the body at rest, they went on to develop techniques for showing it in motion, in the form of charioteers, discus-throwers, and other active figures. To cite a famous example, the ambitiously conceived marble decorations made for the temple of the Parthenon in Athens (448–432 B.C.) depict many deities in a variety of lifelike poses.

Hellenistic Period (323 B.C.–A.D. 31.) Sculptors in this period (from the death of Alexander to the Roman conquest of Alexandria) continued to develop the naturalism of classical art, engaging their figures in increasingly dramatic and action-filled poses. The most famous work from this time, *Nike of Samothrace* (ca. 200–190 B.C.) is a victory monument showing a winged goddess descending on the prow of a ship, with a strong headwind pushing her clothing against her body in sensuous and energetic folds. Another significant piece from this period is the *Laocoön* Group (second century B.C. to first century A.D.), which shows the mythical Laocoön and his two sons being attacked by sea serpents.

Etruscan Art The Etruscan city-states dominated northern and central Italy politically and culturally from the early eighth century B.C. to 510 B.C., when the last Etruscan king of Rome was overthrown. The Etruscans spoke a non-Indo-European language, known from numerous tomb inscriptions but not yet deciphered despite many attempts. Their art was strongly influenced by Greek art of the Archaic period, which the Etruscans knew from the Greek colonies that had been established in southern Italy and Sicily beginning around 750 B.C. Etruscan art was profoundly conservative, characterized by marble and bronze sculptures and painted tomb murals that retained the static poses, archaic smiles, and lack of realistic modeling of Archaic art long after the Greeks themselves had embarked on classical refinements. Akin to Greek art and antecedent to Roman art, the art of the Etruscans remains, like the people who made it, imperfectly understood.

Roman Art The Roman republic was founded ca. 509 B.C., after the overthrow of the Etruscan Tarquinian dynasty; two centuries later, Rome controlled the entire Italian peninsula and had begun its expansion into other lands. The Romans were great builders, and in the ensuing centuries they built cities, complete with temples, palaces, baths, arenas, theaters, and civil engineering works such as aqueducts and roads, from Spain to the Near East, and from North Africa to Britain. Roman art, strongly influenced by Etruscan, classical Greek, and Hellenistic art, was closely allied to architecture; temples were endowed with stone and bronze sculptures of deities, while public and domestic buildings often had pictorial mosaic floors and walls entirely covered with mural paintings. Many fine examples of these from the first century B.C. have been excavated from the ash-buried city of Pompeii. The art of portraiture flourished, especially in the form of bronze and marble sculptural busts. The free-standing equestrian statue, portraying a figure astride a horse, was a Roman innovation; many equestrian portraits of Roman emperors and generals survive. The triumphal arch, embellished with heroic sculpture, was also a Roman innovation. Stone coffins (sarcophagi) with narrative scenes in high relief also provided a medium for the Roman love of sculpture.

The criticism is often made, though somewhat unfairly, that Roman art was produced with consummate technical skill but lacked the aesthetic spirit of the classical Greek and Hellenistic art that the Romans themselves so greatly admired.

Celtic Art The Celtic peoples occupied much of central and western Europe in the early first millennium B.C., with populations extending through Central Asia as far as what is now western China. Early Celtic art, for example of the Hallstatt and La Tène Cultures (eighth–fifth centuries B.C.), has much in common with the art of the Germanic peoples of northern Europe and the Scythians of the steppe lands of Asia; it is characterized by fantastic, intertwining animal and plant designs on bronze, iron, or gold weapons, jewelry, and various utilitarian and decorative objects. In later La Tène art, Greek influence is both pervasive and totally assimilated to the Celtic "animal style."

The Celtic peoples were absorbed or displaced by the expansion of the Roman Empire and the northern Germanic tribes, surviving as intact cultures only in isolated areas of eastern Europe, Anatolia, Iberia, and westernmost Europe including Britain and Ireland. Celtic art re-emerged in importance with the Christian conversion of Britain and Ireland in the fifth century A.D. Metalwork, enamel painting, and manuscript illumination all employed characteristic Celtic intertwining patterns of knotwork, animals, or stylized plants; a particular innovation of Celtic manuscript art was the elaboration of initial capital letters into fantastic compositions of entwined lines. The epitome of Celtic Christian art is the *Book of Kells*, executed on the Scottish island of Iona around A.D. 800 and preserved in Ireland after the Viking destruction of Iona in 807.

Byzantine Art The Roman Empire, already in decline in the third century A.D., became a Christian empire under Constantine (ca. 274–337), who became emperor at Rome in 312 and conquered the empire's eastern provinces in 324. In 330 Constantine founded the city of Constantinople (also known by its older name, Byzantium), which would for many centuries thereafter serve as the principal capital of the Roman Empire. Constantine's patronage of church building and the creation of Christian ecclesiastical regalia marked the beginning of Byzantine art, a style that was to survive and evolve for more than a thousand years.

Released from the bonds of secrecy that had inhibited the early church, Christian art flourished during the fourth century, for example in New Testament scenes on the sarcophagi of wealthy Christians, but in that early phase Christian sculpture followed visual conventions inherited from Hellenistic and Roman art. The earliest murals and mosaics in churches (now lost) also very likely were in the Roman style.

In the fifth century, despite energetic church building that affirmed the primacy of the bishop of Rome (who by then was customarily called the pope), the repeated sacking of Rome by successive waves of barbarians left Constantinople as the political, economic, and, in many ways, spiritual capital of the empire. Thus released from Roman conventions, Byzantine art flourished. Debates about how to depict Christ and the saints were resolved in favor of a vocabulary of symbolism that rejected classical naturalism; the frontal poses, elongated bodies, large eyes, and glowing halos of the mosaics at St. Vitale in Ravenna (547) give clear evidence of this shift. The vast domed structure of the church of Hagia Sophia (532–37) at Constantinople likewise represents a definitive break with Roman architecture, and its lavish mosaics affirm its key place in Byzantine art. With the collapse of the Western Roman Empire and the nearly complete loss of Roman conventions and techniques in art, Byzantine art reigned supreme in much of the Christian world, except for the Celtic fringe, as Orthodoxy also gained primacy in Christian belief and practice.

The most characteristic product of Byzantine and later Orthodox art is the icon, a small, portable image of Christ, the Virgin and Child, or one or more saints. These were produced in increasing quantities for both churches and private chapels beginning in the seventh century and became not merely symbolic depictions, but objects of devotion in themselves, often heavily framed and encrusted with gold and jewels. Icon painting was extremely conservative in style, but there was slow change over the centuries; late examples show the influence of Italian Renaissance modeling and perspective. With the fall of Constantinople to the Ottoman Turks in 1453, the Eastern Roman Empire came to an end. Byzantine art had already, for several centuries, been overshadowed by Islamic art in most of the eastern empire's former territory.

Islamic Art Islam, which dates its founding to A.D. 622 (Year 1 of the Muslim calendar), was quickly spread by conquering Arab armies throughout the Middle East and North Africa. A distinctive Islamic style of architecture and art quickly developed to serve the needs of the faithful. Most important was the mosque, designed to hold large numbers of people for communal worship; the usual form was a square or rectangular building with a dome supported by interior columns or pillars. Mosques were built not only in North Africa, the Middle East, and Central Asia, but also in parts of Europe—most notably in Sicily and in parts of Spain (Cordoba, Seville, Granada), as well as, much later, in the Balkans. Because Islam prohibits the depiction of living creatures, its decorative style in architecture relied on foliate, geometric, or calligraphic designs in stone, stucco, brick, or tile; similar ornamentation was used for ceramic and metalwork objects. Chief among the arts of Islam was calligraphy and the decoration of books; finely embellished copies of the *Koran* influenced the Christian art of illuminated sacred books. Through trade, warfare, and actual incorporation of parts of southern Europe into the world of Islam, Islamic art influenced both Byzantine art and the revived arts of western Europe in the Middle Ages.

Gothic Art

The crowning of Charlemagne as Holy Roman Emperor in 800 presaged a revival of Western Christian art (impeded during the ninth century by Viking raids) that diverged increasingly from Byzantine art, just as the Roman and Orthodox churches diverged increasingly in dogma and practice. Important in both Western art and theology of the time was a renewed emphasis on the Crucifixion and the suffering and redemption of Christ.

The increasing wealth and stability of the feudal monarchies of northern and western Europe led in the 10th century to a vigorous period of church building in the new Romanesque style, which employed rib-vaulting and other engineering innovations to span unprecedentedly large interior spaces. Cathedrals and religious-order chapter houses were often decorated with vigorously lifelike stone sculptures in high relief that depicted biblical stories in a way that was immediately accessible to illiterate pilgrims. A celebrated work of pictorial art from the same period but in another medium is the *Bayeux Tapestry* (late 11th century), not a true (woven) tapestry but rather a work of embroidery, depicting the Norman conquest of England in a semi-naturalistic style.

By the mid-12th century the Romanesque style of cathedral-building had given way to the Gothic, with higher and wider vaults, more slender columns, and larger windows; among many examples are the cathedrals of Canterbury (England), Notre-Dame de Paris and Chartres (France), and Cologne (Germany). These were often profusely ornamented with stone scuptures, elongated vertically to complement the verticality of the buildings themselves; the interiors were illuminated by sunlight filtered through elaborate windows of pictorial stained glass.

The Gothic Style in Italy Italian artists working in the Gothic style were particularly innovative in the fields of sculpture and painting. Giovanni Pisano (fl. 1265–1314) executed sculptures in the round and in high relief that revived the classical *contrapposto* stance, directly anticipating the sculpture of the Renaissance. Italian Gothic painting showed its direct descent from Byzantine art in the work of Duccio di Buoninsegna (fl. 1278–1318), whose richly gilded altarpieces and other religious paintings seem more sculptural than painterly. His near contemporary Giotto di Bondone (ca. 1267–1337), a native of Florence, broke with tradition to place naturalistically conceived figures in architectural or landscape settings. The Sienese painter Ambrogio Lorenzetti (fl. 1319–47) went even further in setting biblical narrative scenes in realistic Tuscan landscapes.

Late Gothic Painting in France and the Netherlands The early 15th century in the Netherlands marks the transition from the last phase of Gothic painting to the first phase of Early Renaissance art. The epitome of the late Gothic style is the *Trés Riches Heures*, an illustrated devotional book created ca. 1413–16 for the Duc de Berry by the Limbourg brothers, Flemish artists working in Burgundy. Their gemlike miniature paintings give an idealized but wholly convincing image of Burgundian life in the High Middle Ages. Another important artist of this transitional period is known as the Master of Flémalle (he may have been Robert Campin, ca. 1378–1444), whose paintings imitated reality with revolutionary precision. His *Merode Altarpiece* (ca. 1425–30) was the first known artwork to place the Annunciation scene in a contemporary domestic interior. While Gothic artists had mixed realistic details with fantastical or celestial settings that often did not convey an accurate sense of three-dimensional space, the Master of Flémalle made his figures appear to exist in the same world as the viewer with unprecedented realism. The Master of Flémalle was the first artist to promote oil painting instead of tempera (pigments in an organic emulsion, such as egg yolk), allowing him to use brilliant colors and re-create the nuanced effects of light, which would have been impossible with the less versatile tempera.

The other great Flemish master of the time, Jan van Eyck (1395–1441), also used oil painting to excellent effect. He is credited with developing atmospheric perspective—a gradual changing of tone used to represent objects farther away in picture space, which was instrumental in conveying distance in a two-dimensional medium.

Renaissance Art (1400–1600)

The Early Renaissance in Italy The Renaissance (literally, "rebirth") looked back past the beginning of the Christian era to Classical Greek ideals in literature, philosophy, science, and art; it was stimulated by the recovery of classical works of philosophy and literature that had been lost in the post-Roman West but preserved in the Islamic world. In Renaissance art, there was a shift in interest away from an idealized afterlife and toward the human world of the here-and-now.

Sculptors and painters in Florence in the early 15th century made a series of achievements that fully established Renaissance ideas and techniques in art. The sculptor Donatello (ca. 1386–1466) built on the Gothic tradition of Pisano to create statues employing the classical *contrapposto* pose; his *St. Mark* (1411-13), for example, leans at ease on one leg, assuming a remarkably graceful and naturalistic stance. Donatello's unclothed bronze statue of a youthful *David* (ca. 1425-30) revived the tradition of the classical nude, which had had no place in the Christian art of the Middle Ages.

Donatello and his teacher Lorenzo Ghiberti (1378–1455) also made important developments in relief sculpture. They created the illusion of three-dimensional depth on a two-dimensional surface by employing the scientific method of linear perspective devised by the architect Filippo Brunelleschi (1377–1466). Brunelleschi's method was central to Renaissance advancements; its mathematical precision allowed artists to represent three-dimensional reality with utter faithfulness.

Brunellesci's approach to perspective was soon taken up by painters. Masaccio (Tommaso Di Giovanni Di Simone Guidi, 1401–28), the first great master of the Early Renaissance, produced lifelike figures that achieved in painting what Donatello achieved in sculpture. His figures seemed to exist in real spaces, not just on backgrounds, because Masaccio was able to master both linear and atmospheric perspective. His use of color, however, lacked the virtuosity of his Flemish contemporaries. Later in the century, the Venetian artist Giovanni Bellini (ca. 1430–1516) adopted the rich colors favored by northern painters, an approach that was kept up by later Venetian painters.

Other important painters of religious themes in the fifteenth century included Guido di Pietro, known as Fra Angelico (ca. 1400–55); Piero della Francisco (ca. 1420–92), a skilled mathematician who contributed to the perfection of perspective painting; and Domenico Ghirlandaio (1449–94). The painting of portraits and other secular subjects began to flourish in the 15th century, as did the weaving of large and elaborate pictorial tapestries. Sandro Botticelli (1445–1510) reunited the newly revived classical realism with classical, pre-Christian subjects; his painting *The Birth of Venus* (ca. 1480), which depicts a nude Venus rising from the water on a seashell, is now one of the world's best known artworks.

The High Renaissance The brief period between about 1495 and 1520 was dominated by revolutionary masters who brought the achievements of the Early Renaissance to new heights. The works they created demonstrate an increasingly harmonious fidelity to nature. The concept of the "artist" itself is a Renaissance idea; individual painters and sculptors rose in status as they came to be regarded as individual geniuses rather than, as in earlier ages, simply skilled craftsmen.

Leonardo da Vinci (1452–1519), the first great master of the period, developed groundbreaking new techniques with oil paint. With his method of *chiaroscuro*, he shaped figures by imitating the effects of light on three-dimensional forms, rather than defining them with outline. Leonardo also developed an effect called *sfumato*, which imitates the quality of a hazy atmosphere. These techniques created the soft, poetic qualities that characterize Leonardo's most famous painting, the thoughtful *Mona Lisa* (1503–05).

Michelangelo (Michelangelo di Lodovico Buonarroti Simoni, 1475–1564) carved monumental statues influenced by Hellenistic sculptures that were recovered archaeologically in his lifetime. He succeeded in endowing his sculpted figures, such as the nude *David* (1501–4), with both an air of calm and an underlying feeling of potential energy. Also a painter, Michelangelo created a brilliant series of frescoes on the ceiling of the Sistine

Chapel in Rome (1508–12), in which biblical scenes are acted out by monumental figures orchestrated in a complex, dramatic composition.

The painter Raphael (Raffaello Sanzio, 1483–1520) was unsurpassed in his technical mastery, and in the degree to which he embodied the Renaissance ideals of harmony and unity. His paintings for the Stanza della Segnatura in the Vatican Palace in Rome (1509–11) are a perfect blend of classical composition and Christian thematic art. Raphael's work is often considered to be the epitome of classic Renaissance style.

Artists of the Venetian school, such as Giorgione (1477–1510), took full advantage of the range of effects made possible by oil paint. Influenced by the northern masters, they were partial to sensuous colors and glowing light. Titian (Tiziano Vecellio, 1488/90-1576), the most famous of the Venetian masters, operated a large and busy studio, where assistants filled in the less important parts of many of his paintings. He painted portraits, religious subjects, and also explored classical themes, such as the *Bacchanal* (ca. 1518), a scene of outdoor revelry. Tintoretto (Jacopo Robusti, 1518–94) trained in Titian's studio and carried on the tradition of Venetian Renaissance art.

The Northern Renaissance The Northern Renaissance was a product of intellectual and artistic influences from the Italian Renaissance, strongly modified by the work of northern intellectuals such as the humanist Desiderius Erasmus (1466–1536) and religious reformers, including Martin Luther (1483–1546) and John Calvin (1509–64). After the turn of the 16th century the influence of Italian painting began to be felt in northern Europe. The German artist Matthais Gothardt Neithardt (often known as Grünewald, ca. 1480–1528) was among the first to combine the bold use of color and sharp attention to detail, championed by earlier Flemish masters, with Italian methods like linear perspective. Albrecht Dürer (1471-1528), the foremost northern artist of his time, traveled to Venice and brought both Italian techniques and a Renaissance sensibility to his art.

Both Grünewald and Dürer painted many religious works, and the distinctive German art of carved wooden altarpieces continued to flourish, but the influence of the Reformation also was strongly felt in the world of art. Luther was indifferent to religious art, which continued to flourish in the Catholic realms of Germany but declined in importance in the Luthern world. Calvin was actively hostile to religious art, so in the Calvinist Netherlands it fell entirely out of demand. Portraiture flourished; Hans Holbein the Younger (1497/8–1543), a German artist working in Switzerland and England, became famous for his monumental, intensely detailed portraits of King Henry VIII and others; Lucas Cranach the Elder (1473–1553) painted several notable portraits of Luther.

Other northern artists turned toward secular subject matter. Pieter Bruegel the Elder (1525/30–69) painted scenes of peasant life that document the daily life of the time but also suggest allegory. His *Hunters in the Snow* (1565), for example, shows empty-handed men and their dogs returning to a wintry town; the painting's mood invites the viewer to consider symbolic meaning. Albrecht Altdorfer (ca. 1480–1538) also painted landscapes that seem to invite allegorical interpretation. These secular works pointed the way for the development of the landscape and genre painting characteristic of northern art of the next century.

Mannerism The period of the Late Renaissance in Italy, spanning roughly the last two-thirds of the 16th century, saw many artists striving for dramatic effects that would go beyond the work of the High Renaissance masters. The term *Mannerism* was initially applied derisively to the work of certain Roman and Florentine artists whose paintings were thought to be artificially mannered, cold, and stiff. More recently, Mannerism has come to be appreciated as a legitimate painting style in its own right. Rosso Fiorentino's (1495–1540) painting, *Descent from the Cross* (1521) abandoned the Renaissance-era preference for balance and harmony, instead evoking the drama of the scene with unharmonious colors and a crowded, dizzying composition. Parmigianino (1503–40), while less aggressively anticlassical, nonetheless departed significantly from the Renaissance emphasis on naturalism. His *Madonna with the Long Neck* (ca. 1535), for example, presents the viewer with other-worldly figures with unnatural, elongated forms of peculiar beauty. Agnolo Bronzino (1503–72), famous for his psychologically penetrating portraits, was also the creator of one of the most famous Mannerist allegorical paintings, *Venus, Cupid, Folly, and Time*, the symbolic complexities of which have not yet been fully deciphered.

Domenicos Theotocopolous, known as El Greco (ca. 1541–1614) is sometimes classified as a Mannerist, but he developed an artistic and emotional vocabulary uniquely his own. His paintings are characterized by vivid Venetian colors and crowded, restless compositions.

Baroque Art (1600–1750)

Known as the "century of genius" for such scientific giants as Galileo, Descartes, and Newton, the 17th century gave rise to a number of movements in the visual arts that had in common an interest in ornament and the play of light. Some, but not all, of these movements are contained within the boundaries of the Baroque movement.

The term *baroque* (possibly from the Portuguese *barroco*, an irregularly shaped pearl) was originally used to mean grotesque, excessive, and bizarre. The Baroque style was characterized by an interest in movement and the dramatic; Baroque artists explored the drama of psychology and emotion, created dramatic decorative flourishes, and made full use of light (contrasted with dark) as a theatrical device.

Italy and the Baroque In Italy Michelangelo Merisi da Caravaggio (1571–1610) developed a new type of realism known as *naturalism*. He insisted upon using common people as models and placing them in ordinary contemporary settings. He is credited with developing the technique of lighting known as *tenebrism*, produced by a single source of light coming into the picture at a sharp angle, used to enhance dramatic gestures and highlight the most important features of the scene; other parts of the picture were thrown into deep, rich shadows. Especially when applied to biblical scenes, Caravaggio's naturalist techniques were considered shocking and unseemly by many of his contemporaries. One of Caravaggio's best-known followers was Artemesia Gentileschi (1593–1652/3), whose bold use of chiaroscuro and tenebristic lighting lent powerful emotional impact to her paintings.

Other Roman artists developed the classically derived style of idealism, derived from the harmonious, idealized aesthetic of Renaissance artists like Raphael. One of the most important advocates of this style, Annibale Carracci (1560–1609), is best known for his ceiling paintings in the Palazzo Farnese, Rome, inspired by Michelangelo's Sistine Chapel frescos. Carracci in turn influenced later generations of artists, notably Giambattista Tiepolo (1696–1770), whose work is a celebration of classically inspired pageantry.

The decorative impulses of Baroque art are found with particular force in Italian sculpture and architecture. Figures are often shown during climactic moments of action, and seem to be fully engaged in the space around them. The work of the ornamentalist Gianlorenzo Bernini (1598–1680) typifies the excesses of Baroque sculpture. Bernini's most famous piece, The *Ecstasy of St. Theresa* (1645–52), shows the saint, whose heart is about to be pierced by an angel's arrow, rising heavenward on wavelike clouds while golden shafts of light come down from above.

The Baroque in Flanders and Holland Peter Paul Rubens (1577–1640) studied in Italy and brought Baroque painting to northern Europe, reuniting northern and southern styles, much as Dürer had during the Renaissance. Rubens painted grand historical and religious scenes that combined Italian qualities, like warm Venetian color, a sensuous, painterly flourish, and active, almost tumbling compositions, with a typically Flemish attention to realistic detail. In a highly successful career, Rubens was not only a painter but also a scholar, a diplomat, and (like Titian) the proprietor of a vast studio staffed by many assistants.

Dutch artists developed a Baroque style through contact with Rubens and Caravaggio. In middle-class Protestant Holland, the biggest art consumers were prosperous citizens rather than church institutions, and artists sold their work in a market system. Artists created still lifes and landscapes of familiar contemporary objects and places, as well as genre scenes of everyday life—a type of image that soon became popular all over Europe.

Dutch painters found that naturalism in the style of Caravaggio fit in well with the secular northern tradition, and they tended to paint with less of the rosy flourish that characterizes Rubens. Some of the most important Dutch artists of the time include Frans Hals (1581/5–1666), who produced genre scenes, and Rembrandt van Rijn (1606–69), often considered the period's greatest master, who was fascinated with Old Testament scenes and the effects of light, producing dramas of unsurpassed emotional and psychological subtlety. Jan Vermeer (1632–75) was a unique genre painter who painted quiet, contemplative images of everyday domesticity that often feature exquisite renderings of daylight.

The Baroque in Spain Like the Dutch, Spanish artists were influenced by Caravaggio and by the Flemish, developing a tenebristic, realistic style. In devoutly Catholic Spain, religious painting retained its popularity well after it had waned in much of Europe. Francisco de Zurbarán, one of the foremost painters of the Spanish Baroque, is known for his quiet, intense devotional images. The most famous Spanish artist of the time was Diego Velázquez (1599–1660), and his masterpiece, *Las Meninas* (1656), has become one of the best-known works in Western art. A large group portrait centered on Spain's young princess, the painting exhibits a typically Baroque fascination with countless variations in the qualities of light.

The Baroque in France and England A Carracci-inspired classicism came to dominate French Baroque painting, mainly because of the influence of painters Nicolas Poussin (1594–1665) and Claude Lorrain (1604/5–1682). Poussin's classical landscapes and scenes from ancient literature are rendered with restraint, austerity, and a seriousness meant to appeal to the mind instead of the senses, while Lorrain became known for idyllic classical landscapes in which the elements of nature are arranged to produce an ideal beauty. Poussin's followers, known as the Poussinistes, emulated his emphasis on design over color, and they were soon opposed by artists known as Rubénistes, who favored the sensuous, rosy qualities typical of Rubens.

Rococo Toward the end of the Baroque period, the Rubénistes became more popular. Three painters in this style, Jean-Antoine Watteau (1684–1721), François Boucher (1703–70) and Jean-Honoré Fragonard (1732–1806), who painted scenes of merrymaking in lush landscapes, typify the Rococo movement, which mainly affected architecture and the decorative arts in southern Germany, Austria, and Central Europe; the aesthetic favored ornate and playful decorative motifs, often based on themes of water, shells, and other organic sources.

A prominent theme in Rococo art was *chinoiserie*, a decorative style based on Chinese art (particularly painted porcelain) but modified to satisfy a European taste for picturesque exotica. Throughout the 18th century, wealthy patrons indulged their fancies for chinoiserie gardens, pavilions, and pagodas, filled with real or faux Chinese porcelain and lacquerware; the movement provided a powerful stimulus to the production of European porcelain and other decorative arts.

The 18th century saw the first internationally important group of English painters since the Middle Ages, all of whom were influenced by the polished hues and idealized detail of the Rococo. They included William Hogarth (1697–1764), famous for painting scenes of biting social commentary, such as *The Rake's Progress*; the portraitist Thomas Gainsborough (1727–88); and the classicist Sir Joshua Reynolds (1723–92).

Neoclassicism and Romanticism (1750–1850)

Neoclassicism The Neoclassical movement was a revival of the popular Renaissance style based on Classical Greek and Roman art. Neoclassicism was linked with the principles of the Enlightenment, which championed reason as the noblest human attribute; the ideal beauty created by classical artists was thought to exemplify natural law and the principles of reason.

Many artists since the Renaissance had embraced classical values, but the Neoclassical movement differed from previous revivals. It was prompted in part by a series of archaeological discoveries that made much more ancient art accessible to contemporary artists. In addition, the American Revolution of 1776 and French Revolution of 1789 questioned established authority in fundamental ways. The Rococo style of the mid-18th century was seen by intellectuals of the revolutionary era as frivolous and aristocratic. Many artists looked instead to the serious historical and mythological paintings of the Baroque classicist painter Poussin for guidance on how the classical style could be adopted to modern times.

Neoclassical sculptors, such as Jean Antoine Houdon (1741–1828) and Antonio Canova (1757–1822), created portraits of important contemporary figures such as Napoleon and the Enlightenment thinker Voltaire. They gave their figures a sense of historical importance by portraying them in the costumes typical of classical gods and rulers.

Neoclassical painters also sometimes used this device, recording scenes from recent history with an emphasis on line and structural composition and with figures that reveal an ideal yet austere beauty. The French painter Jacques Louis David (1748–1825) became famous for his portrait of the freshly murdered revolutionary leader Georges Danton, while the American Benjamin West (1738–1820), working in Europe, staked a claim for the neoclassical heritage of his new nation by painting scenes of American history, such as *The Death of General Wolfe* (1770).

Later in the period, the French painter Jean-Auguste-Dominique Ingres (1780–1867) built on David's style, though his images, which have an obsessive neoclassical attention to detail, are often romantic in subject. His portraits of young women, as well as his many paintings of orientalist themes such as the *Odalisque* (1819), conjure up a romanticized ideal of plump, opulent womanhood.

Romanticism The Romantic movement did not necessarily favor a specific aesthetic; instead, Romanticism is characterized by an approach to art in which emotion is more important than reason. While Neoclassicism and Romanticism seem to follow opposing trends, it could also be argued that Neoclassicism is a romantic revival of the past, and thus simply one phase of Romanticism.

Romanticism began as a trend in literature, and it remained a movement in which the written and visual arts were closely linked, one often serving as inspiration for the other. Romantic artists were attracted to subjects that were thrilling, awe-inspiring, grotesque, and often fanciful. Because Romantic artists believed in the expression of the subjective experiences of the individual, the movement supported any number of styles, including a revival of several older styles. The self-taught English painter William Blake (1757–1827) was strongly influenced by Michelangelo and Dürer; Blake's art reflects a rejection of the Enlightenment ideal of reason in favor of a deeply held mystical vision of God's role in the universe.

Other Romantic artists looked back to the Baroque era for inspiration. Francisco Goya (1746–1828), for example, based his aesthetic on the dramatic lighting and dark palette of Baroque artists Rembrandt and Velázquez. Goya painted gruesome scenes documenting contemporary battles as well as violently thrilling nightmare images. Other important neo-Baroque painters were the French artists Jean-Antoine Gros (1771–1835), Eugène Delacroix (1798–1863), and Théodore Géricault (1791–1834), whose painting *The Raft of the Medusa* depicted shipwrecked sailors in a manner that combined Classical composition with Romantic intensity of emotion.

Romantic Landscape Painting Romantic artists admired nature for its wild, untamed qualities, believing that people connected with the natural world on an emotional, instead of a cerebral, level. While Neoclassical landscape painters had painted idealized visions of nature, Romantic painters, believing in the importance of sincerity, wanted to capture nature as it was, without altering her most essential qualities.

The French painter Camille Corot (1796–1875) was known for executing finished paintings out of doors, unlike the Neoclassicists, who painted out of doors only to make studies. Corot was highly influential to the Barbizon school of painters, who worked on often loosely painted landscapes and country scenes in and near the village of Barbizon, not far from Paris; the school focused on Théodore Rousseau (1812–67) and is also associated with the realist François Millet (1814–75).

In England, John Constable (1776–1837) and J.M.W. Turner (1775–1851) painted landscapes that focused on fleeting qualities of light and atmosphere, evoking the sublime power of nature. Turner, in particular, emphasized the importance of color over line, in a reversal of the Neoclassical preference, and recalling the sensuous hues of Rubens.

Orientalism During the early 19th century, European trade and political involvement in the Middle East, North Africa, India, and other parts of what was vaguely known as "the Orient" led to a fascination with artistic portrayals of those lands. Many of the Romantics pursued Oriental themes. Orientalist art combined careful depiction of exotic objects (buildings, costumes, objects of daily use) with wholly imaginary scenes of life in "Eastern" harems and palaces. The Orient was romanticized as colorful, exotic, erotic, and feminine, a place where female nudity could safely be exposed to the evaluating European gaze. The odalisques and harem scenes of Ingres contributed to the popularity of the Orientalist genre; other prominent Orientalists were Eugène Delacroix and J. L. Gérôme (1824–1904).

The Hudson River School The Hudson River School was the most important art movement in 19th-century America. The founders of the movement, Thomas Cole (1801–48) and Asher Durand (1796–1886) painted many of their works in the Hudson River Valley and nearby regions (the Catskill and Adirondack Mountains, Lake George); prior to the opening of the West, this was the most dramatic scenery to be found in the early United States. Other artists associated with the movement, such as the prolific John Frederick Kensett (1816–72), ranged widely among the rivers and mountains of New England and the Middle Atlantic states, and among the rocks and salt marshes of the seacoast from Maine to Long Island. The characteristic features of Hudson River School paintings include an interplay of sky and water; dramatic lighting; picturesque rocks and trees; and a sense of awe created through a comparison of the grandeur of nature with people and buildings depicted as small and insubstantial.

The Hudson River School painters were among the first professionally trained artists in America (except for a few earlier portraitists, notably Gilbert Stuart), and their paintings, many of which were publicly exhibited, would have been the first professional works of art seen by many Americans. Concentrating on landscape painting and the effects of light, the Hudson River School painters were influenced by European landscape painting of the 17th century and also by contemporary European Romantic landscape artists (Constable, Turner, Friedrich). The Americans generally rejected the concept of Romanticism, believing that they were letting the power of nature and the spiritual qualities of the untamed American wilderness speak for themselves, but in retrospect it is clear that they were idealizing a landscape that was already being transformed by agriculture, industry, and a growing network of canals and railroads.

After the Civil War the movement lost some of its coherence, and a number of artists associated with the Hudson River School went on to address other subjects. As early as the 1830's Thomas Cole himself had painted huge allegorical works, notably the five-canvas *The Course of Empire*. Frederick Edwin Church (1826–1900), one of several painters whose fascination with dramatic lighting is known as Luminism, traveled widely and painted scenes of the Arctic and the Andes Mountains of South America. German-born Albert Bierstadt (1830–1902) was famous for his paintings of the American West, especially the Rocky Mountains. Martin Johnson Heade (1819–1904) began his career as a painter of seascapes and salt marshes but, after a trip to South America, revised his style entirely to concentrate on small, jewel-like paintings of tropical flowers and birds. Nevertheless, during its long heyday the Hudson River School had a profound influence on how Americans viewed their own country.

Academic Painting During the 17th and 18th centuries, academies of painting had been established under royal patronage in all of the major capitals of Europe, including Paris, London, Berlin, and Rome. The academies functioned as a kind of artistic civil service, producing paintings to decorate royal palaces and public buildings and to commemorate important national events. The academies also functioned as schools, training painters, sculptors, and other artists in the demanding techniques required to produce large, polished works of art that combined highly realistic details with heroic grandeur of conception. The academies also functioned to grant a sort of official seal of approval on the work of favored artists, who were invited to submit works to annual exhibitions (such as the Salons of Paris and the Burlington House exhibitions of the Royal Academy in London). During the 19th century the academies became bastions of conservative styles such as Historicism and Orientalism. Academic painters such as the French Paul Delaroche (1797–1856) and the English Lord Frederick Leighton (1830–96) were hugely admired in their own time but regarded as hopelessly old-fashioned by later generations. The experiments of Impressionists, Pointillists, Symbolists, and other avant-garde artists of the later 19th century were undertaken in conscious opposition to academic art.

Realism, Impressionism, and Post-Impressionism (1850–1900)

Realism In the mid-19th century, a group of French painters led by Gustave Courbet (1819–77), reacting against academic tradition, made it their aim to produce objective, unidealized images. Painters such as François Millet (1814–75) and Honoré Daumier (1808–79), chose as their subjects peasants and moments of everyday reality previously considered unworthy of the high art tradition. Another French painter, Edouard Manet (1832–83), created what the poet Charles Baudelaire called "paintings of modern life," with contemporary themes not softened by filters of romanticism or classicism. His 1863 painting *Déjeuner sur l'Herbe* caused a scandal with its enigmatic female nude participant in a sylvan picnic. Manet's loose brushwork and use of flat patches of color reflect the influence of *Japonisme*, a movement that drew inspiration from Japanese woodblock prints, textiles, and other visual and decorative arts. Other artists whose work shows strong Japanese influence include Mary Cassatt, Henri Toulouse-Lautrec, and especially James McNeill Whistler (1834–1903), an American working in England who conceived of his portraits and landscapes as formal compositions of color and shape rather than as "pictures." Whistler was part of the Aesthetic Movement, which stressed abstract, symbolic, and emotional aspects of art more than pure representation.

In the United States, a realistic approach to painting was seen as part of the democratic American tradition. Winslow Homer (1836–1910) and Thomas Eakins (1844–1916) both traveled to Paris and were influenced by the French Realists; Homer painted plain scenes of everyday American life, while Eakins approached his art with scientific precision.

The Pre-Raphaelites In 1848 eight English artists formed the Pre-Raphaelite Brotherhood, a society dedicated to reviving what they considered to be the sincerity and naturalism of the early Renaissance masters, especially those of northern Europe. In eschewing artistic frivolity and adopting a position of moral consciousness in art, they hoped to help reform the ills of modern civilization, and they depicted historical and literary subjects in clear, detailed images that often involved visual symbolism. Members of the original group, including Dante Gabriel Rossetti (1828–82), William Holman Hunt (1827–1910) and John Everett Millais (1829–96) were later joined by other like-minded artists such as William Morris (1834–96) and Edward Burne-Jones (1833–98).

Impressionism In 1863 a group of innovative French artists, inspired by the Realists and frustrated by the conservative standards of the annual Paris Salon, decided to show their work in a *Salon des Refusés*—an exhibition of paintings that had been turned down for exhibition by the official Salon. The "Refusés" included Eduard Manet, Claude Monet (1840–1926), Edgar Degas (1834–1917), Camille Pissarro (1830–1903), and Paul Cézanne (1839–1906), among many others. They were to form the key proponents of the radically new style of painting called Impressionism. The artists had been working since the 1860's toward an aesthetic that could capture the essential qualities of an image, such as the shifting effects of light and atmosphere. The term *Impressionism* itself, coined by a critic, was first used derisively after the artists' group exhibition (1874), referring to Monet's painting, *Impression, Sunrise* (1873). The Impressionists worked in a loose style, often painting out of doors (*en plein air*), using high color values and broken brushwork, and were influenced by Japanese prints.

Typical Impressionist subjects included landscapes, scenes of bourgeois recreation, and urban slices of life. Degas became known especially for his candid depictions of ballet dancers, races horses and jockeys, and other scenes of bourgeois leisure. Auguste Renoir (1841–1919) painted appealing, plump young women and scenes of working-class Parisian life, such as his famous *Dancing at the Moulin de la Galette, Montmartre* (1876). Other important Impressionist painters included the Englishman Alfred Sisley (1840–99) and the Americans Mary Cassatt (1845–1926) and Berthe Morisot (1841–95). Criticized by conservative writers for seeming unfinished, sloppy, and primitive in technique, Impressionism eventually became extremely popular and had a strong influence on many later artistic movements.

Pointillism The French painter Georges Seurat (1859–1891) was inspired by the broken brushstrokes and patterned use of color popularized by the Impressionists. Monet, for example, had done an extensive series of paintings of the facade of Rouen Cathedral, using tiny brushstrokes of many different colors to build up images that imitate the impression of light falling on the facade at different seasons and times of day. Seurat studied optics and color theory, developing a method of painting in small dots of unmixed color, which he called Divisionism (also referred to as Pointillism). Seurat's best-known work, *A Sunday Afternoon on the Island of La Grande Jatte* (1884–85), was a triumphant vindication of his theories. Pissarro became a convert to Pointillism, and the technique was also used by the younger artist Paul Signac (1863–1935). The Pointillists are also sometimes known as Neo-Impressionists.

Post-Impressionism The term *Post-Impressionism* was first used by the English critic Roger Fry to refer to avant-garde artists who were influenced by Impressionism but departed from the movement with their own unique styles. Paul Cézanne (1839–1906), Vincent van Gogh (1853–90), and Paul Gauguin (1848–1903) made use of Impressionist innovations such as a bright palette and broken brushstroke, but were bolder in their distortions of space and their departure from naturalistic hues, making significant developments in the direction of abstraction. European artists at the end of the 19th century were also influenced by the Art Nouveau movement in design, architecture, and the decorative arts. The movement called for a style free of historical precedent that favored curving linear patterns, and its influences can be seen in the garish Parisian nightlife scenes of graphic artist and painter Henri de Toulouse-Lautrec (1864–1901).

Symbolism Paul Gauguin turned from a career in banking to become first an amateur, then a professional painter, an early member of the Impressionist circle. Later he was strongly influenced by Cézanne. In 1891 he sailed for Tahiti, leaving behind France and family, and spent the remainder of his life there, inventing a new visual vocabulary strongly influenced by his Polynesian surroundings. This late work made him a leading figure in the Symbolist movement, which involved both literature and art in the late 19th century. The Symbolists, who included the "naïve" painter Henri Rousseau (1844–1910) and Odilon Redon (1840–1916), whose work often featured fantastic imaginary creatures, opposed rationality and materialism and embraced emotion and spirituality. They were followed by a group that called themselves the Nabis, which is the Hebrew word for prophet; their work stressed outline and the bold, simplified use of color. Leading members of the group included Edouard Vuillard (1868–1940), Pierre Bonnard (1867–1947), and the sculptor Aristide Maillol (1861–1944). Amedeo Modigliani (1884–1920), though of a later generation, shared much of their sensibility.

Symbolism was extremely influential to the emotionally charged Expressionist artists at the turn of the last century, including Edvard Munch (1863–1944), whose now-iconic image *The Scream* (1893) depicts a nightmarish vision of a solitary, cartoonlike figure standing under a feverish sky.

Nineteenth-Century Sculpture The painter Edgar Degas created a scandal when he exhibited his unidealized statue of the *Little Dancer, Aged Fourteen* (1878–81), which included real hair and a ribbon and was considered both ugly and technically bizarre. It nevertheless was a landmark in liberating sculpture from academic formalism. The most influential sculptor of the late 19th century was probably Auguste Rodin (1840–1917). His figures, in unconventional poses and with exaggerated shapes, struck some critics as looking unfinished; this has led some art historians to compare him with the Impressionists, though he was more strongly influenced by the Realists. Rodin's assistant and mistress, Camille Claudel (1864–1943), was also successful at a similarly expressive style.

Modernism (1900–1950)

Many of the trends in art during the first half of the 20th century can be described as part of the modernist movement. Modernism flourished in a period when an avant-garde outlook in all the arts encouraged innovation and experimentation. It was a way of thinking that led to a rapid accumulation of movements that built on and reacted against one another. The fast pace of artistic development mirrored the enormous changes taking place in the modern world; the period saw two world wars, the Depression, the spread of communism, and major advances in technology, communication and transportation. (In cultural history, *modern* is not simply a synonym for *up-to-date*; the modernist era was finite both in its inception and its coming to an end, and it has been succeeded by an era known, for want of a better term, as *postmodern*.)

The movements and styles of the modern era can be characterized by several general trends. Many artists moved away from illusionism and toward abstraction, gradually abandoning representational images in favor of pure line, color, and form. Artists also took a self-conscious interest in the process of artmaking, emphasizing qualities like brushstrokes and chisel marks that call attention to the actions of the artist. Others introduced new and unconventional materials to their art. Alongside abstraction, several strains of realism continued to flourish, particularly in the United States.

The two most important artists of the modernist era, Henri Matisse (1869–1954) and Pablo Picasso (1881–1973), were to some extent identified with particular schools or trends in painting, but they also defined or anticipated a broad range of modernist possibilities in art. Matisse was a mature painter by the beginning of the 20th century, but he helped to forge the modernist sensibility through his vivid sense of color, his skewed use of perspective (influenced by Japonisme), and his bold approach to design. Many of Matisse's best-known paintings explore the play of light in settings in southern France and North Africa.

Picasso was born in Spain but lived his entire adult life in France. A prodigiously gifted painter, he was able to work in a multitude of styles. His "Blue Period" paintings (1903–06) are tinged with a sad and poetic beauty, emotional tones that he overthrew completely and deliberately with his masterpiece *Les Demoiselles d'Avignon* (1907), which was in effect a modernist manifesto. Influenced by African sculpture, Picasso devoted much of his artistic career to exploring the ways in which solid shapes could be broken down visually into sets of planes; one result of this was his initiation of the Cubist movement (see below).

Expressionism European artists at the turn of the century continued to develop the trends set in motion by the Impressionists and Post-Impressionists, many of which were inspired by the aesthetics of African, Oceanic, and pre-Columbian art. Painters were attracted to the simplified shapes and flat patches of color used by artists like Gauguin, believing that a departure from illusionistic accuracy allowed more room for imaginative and emotional expression. Artists working with these concepts developed a number of styles that can be called Expressionist.

The first, and very short-lived, Expressionist movement became known as the *Fauves*, or wild beasts, because their heavy outlining, loud color schemes, and seemingly clumsy shapes gave viewers the impression that the artists were untrained or primitive. Matisse was the movement's leading participant; Georges Rouault (1871–1958), later known for his religious paintings, was another.

Another Expressionist movement, the Vienna Secession, was influenced by the Art Nouveau trend in the decorative arts, which favored organic, asymmetrical linear patterns. The leader of the Vienna Secession, Gustav Klimt (1862–1918), mixed abstract geometric decorative motifs with illusionistic objects and figures in his often erotic images.

The lushness of Klimt's paintings contrasts with the austere and pessimistic canvases of the German Expressionists Emile Nolde (1867–1956) and Ernst Ludwig Kirchner (1880–1938). Allied with a group known as Die Brücke (the Bridge), they stressed the ideal of painting as an expression of inner conviction. The same spirit animates the often anguished work of the Austrian Egon Schiele (1890–1918), who died in the great influenza epidemic of 1918.

Cubism The invention of Cubism by Picasso and Georges Braque (1882–1963) was one of the most important developments in early 20th century art. It is a style of painting in which a picture, usually based on a representational image, is depicted in fragmented planes, rendering it highly abstract. An image of a face, for example, might be shown as four different trapezoidal shapes, each trapezoid acting as a frame through which we see parts of the face from different angles. The shifting perspective is said to represent different moments in time.

The visual and theoretical complexity of Cubism was so unprecedented that at first it met with perplexed reactions, even from avant-garde artists. But it quickly became influential to a number of later movements, including Futurism, in which dynamic fragmented images feature subjects of industrialization, speed, and technology. One of its leading practitioners was the Italian painter and sculptor Umberto Boccioni (1882-1916).

Cubism was closely linked with the genre of collage, a work of art in two dimensions, with scraps of paper, cloth and other materials pasted together in a composition. While forms of collage had been in use for some time, Picasso first introduced it as a high-art technique.

Dada and Surrealism In reaction to the traditional social and political structures they felt were responsible for World War I, a group of artists who called their movement Dada made it their mission to overthrow artistic tradition. Using a variety of experimental artmaking techniques, they relied on chance, intuition, and nonsense instead of reason and rules. One such technique was called *automatism*, in which artists tried to let their unconscious take control of their actions, hoping to produce artwork free of inhibition. Hans (Jean) Arp (1887–1966), for example, created collages by dropping square pieces of paper onto a single sheet of paper, and glued them in the chance arrangements in which they landed. Other Dadaists made collages piecing together photos cut from newspapers and magazines, inventing the technique of photomontage.

Dadaism lasted for only a short time, and many of its artists joined the movement's successor, Surrealism, which was started by the poet André Breton. Surrealist artists, influenced by psychoanalytic theory and interested in the unconscious, used many of the techniques of Dada. Salvador Dali's (1904–89) paintings of imaginary landscapes and strange biomorphic forms have a nonsensical, dreamlike quality that is typical of Surrealist art. Other important Surrealist figures included René Magritte (1898–1967) and Marcel Duchamp (1887–1968).

Realism in the United States European modernism did not immediately affect most artists in the United States until the famous Armory Show of 1913 shocked New York audiences with various Post-Impressionist and modernist styles. American artists at the beginning of the 20th century developed several realist styles, some of which were independent of modernist influence, some of which reacted against modernism, and some of which were influenced by it.

A group of artists known as The Eight or the Ashcan School developed around the artist Robert Henri (1865–1929), painting unglamorous and unadorned scenes of everyday urban life in a loose, painterly fashion that was considered anti-academic. The American Scene Painters worked in a tighter, more detailed style, focusing on images of American life that were meant to be accessible to everyone. A Midwestern contingent of American Scene Painting was known as Regionalism, and one if its leading artists, Grant Wood (1891–1942), is best known for *American Gothic* (1930), his famous portrait of a serious, steadfast man and wife standing in front of a Carpenter Gothic-style farmhouse.

Other important American realists included Edward Hopper (1882–1967), who painted isolated figures in urban settings, and Georgia O'Keeffe (1887–1986), who painted representational subjects in a simplified, slightly abstracted style; she is best known for her series of large, close-up flower images.

Abstraction The semiabstraction of Cubism and Expressionism encouraged a number of modernist European painters to develop abstract styles. The Expressionist Vasily Kandinsky (1866–1944) was associated with the German group Der Blaue Reiter (the Blue Rider), whose paintings, with their emphasis on brushwork and color, were among the first to anticipate pure abstraction. Piet Mondrian (1872–1944) was a leading force in the Dutch group De Stijl (the Style); his simple, gridlike geometric forms, which evolved progressively as simplifications of landscapes, eventually became entirely abstract. These artists believed that by eliminating the representational image, they could evoke the universal emotions produced by pure color, line, and shape.

Abstract Expressionism: The New York School New York became a center of avant-gardism when many European artists moved there to escape World War II, influencing native artists. In the 1940's a group of painters who became known as the New York School, or the Abstract Expressionists, developed new forms of abstraction that incorporated the interest in chance and the unconscious that had been central to the Surrealists. Many of the artists in the group, sometimes called Action Painters, worked in styles that evoke a sense of movement, prompting viewers to consider the act of painting. Jackson Pollock (1912–56), for example, became best known for his drip paintings, in which he poured or flung splashes of paint onto the surface of his canvas, creating dynamic patterns. Another well-known Abstract Expressionist, Willem de Kooning (1904–97), used wild and impulsive-looking brushstrokes that made it seem that his paintings were created in a state of energetic frenzy. Larry Rivers (1923–2002) began his career as a jazz saxophonist before becoming a painter; closely associated with de Kooning, he maintained a more representational style than many of the New York Abstract Expressionists.

The Color Field Painters, who are considered part of the Abstract Expressionist movement, focused on the effects of large, concentrated areas of color. Mark Rothko (1903–70), for example, created pieces that feature hazy rectangles of a single, subtly modulated color.

While some abstract painters, such as Joan Mitchell (1926–92), continued to work with the gesturely, messy brushwork developed by de Kooning, others developed a style that the critic Clement Greenberg called "post-painterly"—a cleaner, simpler, hard-edged approach. Ellsworth Kelly (b. 1923), for example, painted large, flat geometric shapes, with sober, even lines. A group of painters working in similar modes, but who produced much busier geometric patterns, became part of the Op Art movement, known as such because their work was intended to appeal to the optical senses instead of the emotions.

Modern Sculpture Modern sculpture followed many of the same patterns as painting, with artists pursuing abstracted forms. Constantin Brancusi (1876–1957), for example, is famous for his sculptures of simplified bird shapes, while Henry Moore (1898–1986) worked on abstracted human figures, often using large empty spaces or holes within the figure. Other sculptors also explored this use of negative space. Defining empty space with the contours of the sculpture ironically created a sense of shape and volume. This effect mirrored what was happening in painting, for in moving toward abstraction, painters had blurred the distinction between foreground and background.

After the development of Cubism, many sculptors applied the principles of Cubist painting to three dimensions, creating figures and objects that seem to be pieced together in such a way that their planes and contours are jagged or broken. Picasso invented a genre of sculpture called *assemblage*, the equivalent of collage in three dimensions, in which found objects are pieced together into a new shape. The Surrealist Marcel Duchamp (1887–1968) took this genre one step further with his ready-mades—found functional objects, like bicycle wheels and urinals, displayed with little or no alteration in an art setting.

Other important trends in sculpture included the introduction of welded metal as a sculptural medium. Alexander Calder (1898–1976) invented the mobile, or kinetic sculpture, a hanging metal work with components made of simple abstracted shapes that move in response to air currents.

Postmodernism (1950–)

The stylistic pluralism that characterized the first half of the 20th century continued after 1950 to an even greater degree, with the art world placing increasing value on originality and experimentation. By the 1970's many artists and critics claimed that this pluralism was a product of *Postmodernism*, a movement that, they argued, ended the era of Modernism that had started at the beginning of the century. While there has been much debate over the exact meaning of the term *Postmodern*, it is generally agreed to be a way of thinking that questions cultural authority and eschews the notion of an artistic mainstream, instead embracing the existence of simultaneous yet diverse trends in culture and the arts.

Minimalism The post-painterly aesthetic was highly influential to the Minimalist movement, which introduced a form of abstraction that became popular in the 1960's. Minimalist artists created visual objects that were stripped down to the bare essentials; without representation, symbolism, or drama, the work usually consisted of simple geometric forms, producing a calm, impersonal yet grand effect. Painters used limited palettes, while sculptors often worked with basic industrial materials, like Plexiglas. A famous Donald Judd (1928–94) sculpture, *Untitled* (1965), for example, consists of a series of identical boxes made of galvanized iron, attached to a wall in a straight line.

Figurative Styles Many artists have continued to develop a wide range of figurative, or representational, modes of painting and sculpture. After World War II, expressionistic styles were particularly popular in Europe. The French painter Jean Dubuffet (1901–85), for example, was inspired by the impulsive aesthetic he found in the art of children and the insane, while the English painter Francis Bacon (1909–92) painted nightmarish biomorphic forms. In the United States in the late 1970's and early 1980's, Neo-Expressionism became popular with artists such as Jean-Michel Basquiat (1960–88), who was influenced by the rapid urgency of graffiti.

In another trend in figurative art, Photorealism, artists produced highly illusionistic objects. The paintings of Richard Estes (b. 1932) look as detailed and realistic as photographs, and the sculptures of Duane Hanson (1925–96), fiberglass casts made from human models, are at first glance hard to distinguish from real people.

Pop Art Turning to mundane or everyday subjects has been a provocative tactic for artists throughout history, and artists in the 1960's took this tradition in a new direction by examining contemporary pop culture. They portrayed the consumer products that had become much more widely available to Americans and western Europeans after World War II, and they mimicked the production methods and aesthetics popularized by advertising, comic books, and Hollywood. Andy Warhol (1928–87) used the commercial process of silkscreening to mass-produce images of Campbell's soup cans and celebrities such as Marilyn Monroe. Jasper Johns (b. 1930) painted images of targets and the American flag, while Claes Oldenburg (b. 1929) made large sewn and stuffed sculptures of cake slices and household appliances.

Conceptual Art After the "pure" abstraction of such movements as Abstract Expressionism and Minimalism, some artists saw themselves up against a difficult question: if avant-gardism had been moving along a path to abstraction, then what was next? It seemed that all new visual possibilities had been exhausted, and some artists began to think beyond the canvas and the object. Inspired by the theories of Duchamp, who claimed that the most important aspect of an artwork is the idea behind it, not its physical qualities, conceptual artists deemphasized or altogether abandoned the actual art object. Sol LeWitt (b. 1928), for example, created wall drawings that are represented simply by a written set of instructions—anyone, in theory, can execute them. Other artists incorporated unconventional elements, such as sound or the human body, into their work, complicating the distinction between art and nonart.

A type of conceptual art called performance art became popular in the 1960's. By staging visual events, artists created work that could not be bought, sold, or owned. Allan Kaprow (b. 1927) put on live multimedia events known as *happenings*—productions involving actors and props engaged in a sequence of not necessarily narrative events, embracing the quality of nonsense admired by the Surrealists. Another performance artist, Joseph Beuys (b. 1945), produced "actions" based on his own personal mythology. Performance art is usually documented by photographs or written statements.

The work of Jeff Koons (b. 1955) and other later conceptual artists is sometimes called Neo-Conceptual. Koons conceives of works that are fabricated according to his specifications, but never built by the artist himself. His piece, *Rabbit* (1986), looks like a cheap plastic blow-up toy, but is rendered in elegant and costly stainless steel.

Installation In the 1960's and 70's, artwork designed for a specific location or specific type of location, conceived to alter the space itself, became known by the term *installation*. Such pieces can include objects, sound, performance, and any other element, and they can be temporary or permanent. The artist Nam June Paik (b. 1932), for example, creates videos that are displayed on custom-built monitors, arranged in sculptural ensembles suited to specific places. Paik's work can also be described as *video art*, a genre that became popular as video equipment grew inexpensive and readily accessible. Paik's well-known video piece *Global Groove* (1973), which incorporates Korean drummers, Japanese Pepsi commercials, tap dancers, and Allen Ginsberg reading his poetry, is characteristic of the art world's recent interest in multiculturalism.

Postmodern feminist artists have often made pieces that call attention to the lack of recognition traditionally given to female artists, as well as other gender-related issues. Judy Chicago's (b. 1939) installation *The Dinner Party* (1979) features long tables arranged in a triangular shape, with place-settings marked for famous women throughout history.

Public Art and Earthworks Site-specific installations in natural outdoor settings, which often make use of natural materials, are known as earthworks. Robert Smithson (1938–73) is famous for his earthwork *Spiral Jetty* (1969–70), a large stone and earth construction that winds in a spiral shape into Utah's Great Salt Lake.

The term *public art* refers to a work designed for a public space instead of a traditional art setting. David Hammons (b. 1943), for example, built a piece called *Higher Goals* (1982), made of basketball hoops attached to telephone poles that were decorated with bottle caps; he displayed the work in Brooklyn parks and other places because he wanted it to promote discussion in African-American communities, and not just be seen by the elite audiences at galleries and museums.

Christo (b. Christo Javacheff, 1935), born in Bulgaria and trained in Paris, is best known for a fabric-based public art in which buildings, bridges, and other large structures are temporarily wrapped in cloth, or temporary linear sculptures of cloth and other materials are created to form part of a landscape; the ephemeral works are extensively documented in drawings and photographs. One of his best-known works is *Running Fence* (California, 1976).

PHOTOGRAPHY

A Technical History of Photography

The word "photography," from the Greek for "light" and "to draw," was first used by Sir John F.W. Herschel in 1839, a year that also marks the formal beginning of photography as we know it. But the origins of the medium date back long before the word itself was ever used.

First Visions

In the fifth century B.C. in China, the philosopher Mo Ti (ca. 470 B.C.–391 B.C.) made the first recorded observation that light passing through a small hole into a dark chamber created an inverted but exact image of the scene outside the chamber. In the 10th century, an Arabian scholar, Abu 'Ali al-Hasan ibn Al-Haytham (Alhazen) (965–1040), discovered that the image thus seen was made clearer with a smaller hole or aperture. Roger Bacon (ca. 1214–92) in the 13th century and Reinerius Gemma-Frisius (1508–55) in the 16th century made similar observations. The phenomenon these men observed was the basis for the *camera obscura*, formally developed during the Renaissance.

Camera Obscura Initially, a camera obscura (literally "dark room") was an actual room with a tiny opening in one wall that permitted an image of the outside to be projected on the opposite wall. It could then be drawn or traced by the artist standing in the room. A number of 16th-century scholars, including Leonardo da Vinci (1452–1519), Girolamo Cardano (1501–76), Erasmus Reinhold (1511–33) and Gemma-Frisius, all recorded descriptions of camera obscurae; no one knows who first invented the device. By the mid-1550's it was widely familiar to scientists, artists, and magicians; by the 17th century it was a common tool for artists and draftsmen.

Capturing the Image In 1727 Johann Heinrich Schulze (1687–1744) discovered the light-sensitivity of silver salts (especially halides) while experimenting with the production of phosphorous, and called his chalk-silver nitric acid mixture scotophorous ("bringer of darkness"). In the mid-1700's Giacomo Battista Beccaria (1716–81) and Carl Wilhelm Scheele (1742–86) independently discovered the light-sensitivity of silver chloride.

Among the first to use silver salts as an emulsion on an object were Dr. William Lewis and Joseph Priestley (1733–1804), who painted silver nitrate onto bone and recorded the light that hit it. Their work was followed by Josiah Wedgwood (1730–95), the famous British potter, and his son Thomas (1771–1805). Thomas created "sun prints" by putting objects or painted transparencies directly on sensitized paper or leather and exposing them to daylight until the exposed areas darkened. However he had no way to make the images permanent; any further exposure turned the rest of the paper dark.

Niépce and Daguerre Joseph Nicéphore Niépce (1765–1833)—considered one of the two "fathers of photography"—took the next step in recording light. Working with his brother Claude (1763–1828), he used paper sensitized with silver chloride to capture the camera's images. He succeeded in making negative paper images but had no way to make positive prints from them. Soon he discovered a new light-sensitive substance that he called bitumen of Judea (used as a ground when etching copper plates with acid). The bitumen hardened when exposed to light, and Niépce used it to create accurate reproductions of engravings and drawings. The principle Niépce had discovered—differential hardening of a substance on exposure to light—was fundamental to future developments in visual media. Niépce used the process to make positive images from a camera; some consider these heliographs to be the first photographs ever made, but that credit is usually given to Daguerre.

Louis Jacques Mandé Daguerre (1787–1851), a scenic artist, was also working on a way to record the images of a camera obscura, in order to create large and realistic stage sets. Niépce and Daguerre were put in contact by Charles Chevalier (1804–59), Daguerre's lens maker, and between Daguerre's camera design and Niépce's success with light-sensitive chemicals, the two had a productive partnership until Niépce's death.

Daguerre continued working, and by 1837 had made a successful still-life photograph using his new method. He called the finished product a daguerreotype. Daguerreotypes are made beginning with a highly polished silver-plated sheet of copper. The plate is sensitized with iodine to create silver iodide, which is reduced to silver as it is exposed to light. The image is made visible by placing the plate face-down over a box of heated mercury, which combines with the reduced silver to form an image in white mercury tones. The remaining silver iodide is desensitized in a strong solution of sodium chloride (table salt). The finished plates, delicate to the touch, were kept in glass-fronted cases to protect the surface from scratches or smudges.

Talbot In the 1830's an Englishman by the name of William Henry Fox Talbot (1800–77) was simultaneously arriving at his own way of recording a camera's image, but using paper instead of metal plates. He bathed a sheet of paper first in a weak solution of sodium chloride, and then (when dry) in strong silver nitrate, which reacted to form silver chloride. He made negative contact prints of objects such as leaves and lace. Where the sun hit the paper it turned dark; where it was shadowed by the object it remained light. Talbot (imperfectly) preserved the images by washing the prints in strong sodium chloride or potassium iodide.

He then began using a box camera (nicknamed a "mousetrap" by his wife) with various lenses to create negative pictures, the most famous being of a lattice window in Lacock Abbey (August 1835). He presented his "photogenic drawings" to the Royal Society of London early in 1839, and went on to make even more important contributions to the field of photography (see "Calotype").

Fixing the Image Sir John F. W. Herschel (1792–1871), knowing of the work of both Daguerre and Talbot, researched ways to preserve photographic images from further light action. In 1819 he had discovered that hyposulfite of soda (now called sodium thiosulfate, but still referred to by photographers as "hypo") dissolved silver salts. In 1839 he applied his discovery to photographic images, using the substance to wash away the unexposed silver salts. He soon gave his process to both Daguerre and Talbot, who could finally make permanent prints.

Improvements Three major improvements in 1840 made daguerreotype portraiture both practical and economically feasible. Peter Friedrich Voigtländer (1812–78) began marketing a vastly improved lens designed by Josef Max Petzval (1807–91). The new "German lens" let in 20 times more light than the Chevalier lenses that Daguerre had used. Second, daguerreotype plates were made far more light-sensitive by recoating the iodized plates with additional halogens, such as bromine and/or chlorine. John Frederick Goddard (1795–1866) was the first to publish this process, calling the material an "accelerator" or "quickstuff." Finally, gold chloride was used as a toner to darken and stabilize the daguerreotype image, a process invented by Hippolyte Fizeau (1819–96). Together these three improvements brought exposure time down from several minutes to as little as five seconds—little enough time for a person to hold still.

Calotype Calotypes (from the Greek for "beautiful picture," and sometimes called Talbotypes) were patented by Talbot in 1841, and were based on the fundamental principle of development of a latent image—possibly Talbot's most important contribution to photography. Initially, paper negatives had to be exposed until the image was actually visible. But Talbot discovered that if he bathed his already sensitized (but not yet exposed) paper in "gallo-nitrate of silver" (a mixture of gallic acid and silver nitrate), the paper became far more light-sensitive. He could then expose the paper briefly and bring out the unseen image using a second bath in the same solution. The process finally made paper negatives a feasible option.

Gustave Le Gray (1820–82) improved the calotype in 1851 by waxing the negative paper before sensitizing it. This made it possible to adjust the developing time to correct exposure problems. Louis Désiré Blanquart-Evrard (1802–72) developed a variation on the process, called a developing-out paper, whose short exposure times facilitated mass-printing for publications.

Glass Plates Glass had been suggested as a base for emulsions since 1839, but it wasn't until 1847 that a workable system was devised by Claude Félix Abel Niépce de Saint-Victor (1805–70), a relative of Joseph Nicéphore Niépce. He mixed egg white (albumen) with potassium iodide and sodium chloride, coated a glass plate with this mixture and then immersed the plate in silver nitrate to sensitize it. The plates were developed using gallic and pyrogallic acid.

Collodion The use of glass plates succeeded with the development of the collodion or "wet-plate" process, invented in 1850 by Frederick Scott Archer (1813–57). Glass plates were coated with a mixture of collodion and potassium iodide, then bathed in silver nitrate to form silver iodide. However, the plates had to be exposed and developed (in ferrous sulphite) while the collodion was still wet. This meant photographers had to bring a full

Back to the Kodak Moment When Light Was Captured

By MICHAEL KIMMELMAN

Among the earliest photographs William Henry Fox Talbot made was a picture of lace. Talbot placed the lace on a piece of paper he had sensitized with silver salts, then put them both in the sun. After a few minutes he removed the lace. The paper, reacting to the sunlight, retained the impression of the fabric as a silhouette.

Amazing. The image today looks mysterious: a fine, flat, abstract shape, irregular and ghostly. It takes a moment to recognize it. Before that, we assume the intent is art, accustomed as we are to seeing abstract images in museums that way, which was certainly not how Talbot thought about the photograph.

We can only imagine the original magic of it. Vision became a physical object fixed on paper; three dimensions became two not through the intermediary of somebody wrestling with a pencil or brush but directly through nature, and in more detail than anybody, or almost anybody, could match by hand. The famous story is that Talbot, frustrated at his own infelicitous attempts to sketch landscapes while at Lake Como in Italy in 1833, determined to find another way "to cause these natural images to imprint themselves durably."

So photography was born partly as a kind of convenience, a labor-saving alternative to drawing, but also an impersonal machine, dispassionate, unlike the human hand, except that it soon became obvious to Talbot and every other thinking person that photography was still a tool of human manipulation and individual taste.

Nothing can return us to the state of innocence before photography was invented—invented twice, by Talbot and by Louis Jacques Mandé Daguerre, separately, using different techniques. But Talbot's early work can remind us how utterly the world was changed by their invention. Talbot reshaped how people saw their surroundings: photography became, as a visual tool, the threshold between the past and modernity.

Talbot photographed Byronic landscapes and also pensive men sitting in plush armchairs gazing dreamily into the ether. He contrived stagy scenes of laborers, who posed holding saws and hammers or stood beside ladders. Shadowy streets and university buildings, empty (because the photographs required long exposures and so couldn't capture people moving), look ghostly like ruins.

Talbot brought about a world now largely imagined through images people see through a viewfinder, accumulate, hold in their hands. Photographs define the rituals of our lives; they make everyone a potential artist and document reality, while also altering it, because photographs have their own particular truth and integrity. Photographs fragment and dislocate the world, and reduce everything to the same scale.

They also concentrate attention on what the eye might not normally bother to notice, which, when set apart on a sheet of paper, becomes strange, new and beautiful. Talbot made a beautiful photograph of books on shelves, perhaps imitating a still life, perhaps suggesting photography's potential as evidence, legal or otherwise, perhaps implying a self-portrait. Those are Talbot's books, about subjects he studied, and include volumes with articles he wrote in them. We're meant to read the titles on the spines. Do they add up to a diary of a life? The meaning is up to you. Talbot's genius was to raise the different possibilities.

He identified from the start, with what now seems astonishing speed and clarity, photography's implications, which he laid out in *The Pencil of Nature*, the first book illustrated with photographs. This proved a different point: not just that art can be photographed and the photographs dispersed, but that lighting alters the appearance of whatever is in a photograph, as every Hollywood star knows.

Talbot saw the future, in which photography would become an industry. His panorama of the Reading Establishment shows the world's first commercial photographic company to produce prints from calotype paper negatives. He and his associates pose to illustrate photography's potential: a man sits for his portrait; a Velázquez engraving and a maquette of Canova's *Three Graces* await photographers; technicians monitor prints for *The Pencil of Nature*. This is a picture of photographers photographing themselves while preparing the first book of photographs about photography.

Inventions age and are supplanted. Art is constant. Talbot's technique is being replaced by digital technology, but his pictures remain vivid and alluring. The art of his photographs is clearly in the enduring freshness of their wonderment.

traveling darkroom or "dark-tent" wherever they went in order to sensitize and process the plates.

Ambrotypes The collodion process was also used to make direct positives, called Ambrotypes, named in 1854 by Marcus Aurelius Root (1808–88), and patented in the same year by Joseph Ambrose Cutting (1814–67). The process worked on the principle that when camphor and potassium bromide were added to the collodion and a weak negative was made, the exposed areas appeared light in tone; unexposed (and thus empty) areas were dark when the glass plate was held against a black background.

Tintypes Another popular adaptation of the wet-plate process was the tintype (also called melainotype and ferrotype). The process was invented by Hamilton L. Smith (1818–1903), who assigned the patent in 1856 to his student Peter Neff (1827–1903); manufacture began the same year under the Neffs and Victor M. Griswold (1819–72). Tintypes were made using thin sheets of black-enameled iron instead of glass; the plates were easy to make and not nearly so fragile as daguerreotypes or ambrotypes.

Cartes-de-Visite A third use of the collodion process was known as the carte-de-visite, and was patented by André Adolphe-Eugène Disdéri (1819–89) in 1854. He used a special camera with a movable plate and four lenses. This allowed four exposures on each half of the plate, for a total of eight poses. The negative was contact printed onto a single paper, which was then cut into the separate images, each of which was mounted onto a 4-by-2-inch mount—the same size as visiting cards, hence the name. These prints were easily produced using unskilled labor, and greatly increased studio productivity.

Early Printing

Daguerreotypes and other metal plate processes produced positive prints on the plates themselves. Glass plate and paper negatives, however, needed to be printed onto paper to achieve the final photograph. The next improvement needed in photography was a feasible and efficient way to make these prints—not only for creating individual photographs, but also for reproducing multiple (and even mass) quantities of a given image, such as for newspapers.

Albumen Paper Albumen paper, which became the most common printing medium for collodion negatives, was invented in 1850 by Blanquart-Evrard. He mixed potassium bromide and acetic acid with egg white and coated paper with the mixture, then sensitized it in a silver nitrate solution. The paper was exposed to sunlight under a negative, sometimes for several hours, until the image appeared. The prints were then toned and burnished for deeper hues and a glossy surface. Photographers could buy paper with the albumen coating already on it, ready to sensitize, thus contributing to large-scale printing, and massive egg use (more than 60,000 a day in one company alone).

Carbon Printing Both albumen paper and Talbot's salted paper prints were somewhat unstable and prone to fading. In response in 1856 Adolphe Louis Poitevin (1819–82) devised a non-silver carbon process, based on earlier research by Mungo Ponton (1802–80). Particles of carbon were added to a mixture of gelatin and light-sensitive potassium bichromate. The combined substance hardened differentially on exposure to light beneath a negative, and the unexposed emulsion washed out, leaving a stable carbon-pigmented gelatin image.

The carbon process was greatly improved by Sir Joseph Wilson Swan (1828–1914), with his 1864 carbon transfer process. He coated a sheet of tissue paper with the carbon gelatin, sensitizing and exposing it in the same way as Poitevin. Then using a series of water baths and squeegeeing, Swan transferred the carbon image on the tissue to a blank sheet of paper. Soon the tissues were made with a wide variety of pigments, for prints in over 50 different colors.

Photomechanical Reproduction In 1852 photogravure was developed, based on work by Talbot. It worked by etching steel plates using gauze or crosshatched glass to break up continuous tone spaces. In 1855 Poitevin perfected photolithography, which relied on the properties of bichromated colloids on stone and their repulsion (after exposure to light) to greasy ink. Collotypes or albertypes were a similar variation, perfected in 1868 by Josef Albert (1825–86). And woodburytypes, invented in 1866 by Walter Bentley Woodbury (1834–85), used bichromated gelatin (like that in carbon prints) as a relief image to create a lead mold, which could then be inked and printed onto paper.

Each of these printing methods was moderately successful; but the real goal was printing images alongside text for newspapers, for example, and so far no technique could reproduce an image using a text-style printing press. Half-tone printing provided the solution. Talbot's mesh idea was used again, in a complex process involving double exposure, bichromated gelatin and etching of metal plates. The result was a plate with clusters of raised dots that together represented the dark tones of the image, and the whole plate could be mounted alongside typeface and printed on a standard press.

Advances in Equipment

Cameras Sliding box cameras like those used by Daguerre and Talbot were replaced with the first bellows cameras in 1851 by the firm of W. and W.H. Lewis. Their "Lewis Folding Camera" had a sliding rectangular camera box, with an access door, and was connected by a bellows to a fixed front piece fitted with a lens. By the 1860's, cameras were made with rising fronts and swing fronts and backs, allowing adjustments in focus, angle, and perspective.

In 1844 Fredrich von Martens (1809–75) designed the first arc-pivoted camera, which could make panoramics on curved daguerreotype plates. Photographers also used curved glass plates with the collodion process for the same purpose. The "Pantascope camera" was patented in 1862; it rotated the entire camera on a circular base while a collodion plate was pulled past an exposing slot using a system of string and pulleys.

Early Enlargers Throughout the 1800's, most negatives were contact printed—that is, with the negative directly in contact with the printing paper, creating a print the same size as the negative. However enlargements were occasionally made with the use of " solar cameras," or daylight enlargers. The devices were generally large, often rooftop constructions that allowed sunlight in one end, through a glass or paper negative and a set of lenses, and onto a sheet of albumen paper at the back. The enlargers could be turned and angled to follow the sun during the long exposures needed.

Shutters and Multiple Exposures Eadweard Muybridge (1830–1904) invented one of the first camera shutters in 1869, which he perfected for the use of stop-action photography in 1877. His silhouetted images of horses mid-stride were the first views of their true gait, and defied all previous conceptions—a striking example of photography's ability to show us what we cannot see. Muybridge also created what he called a zoetrope—a strip of sequential pictures viewed through slits in a cylindrical drum to give the illusion of motion (a precursor to modern motion pictures). In 1880 he used a similar technique to project pictures onto a screen with a device he called a zoogyroscope or zoopraxiscope.

Dry Plates The cumbersome on-site sensitizing and processing requirements of the collodion wet-plate process led many to search for a better emulsion system. In 1871 Richard Leach Maddox (1816-1902) introduced a gelatin-emulsion dry-plate process, involving a gelatin matrix infused with silver bromide crystals, which was poured onto glass and dried hard. The process was refined over the next decade, especially through a "ripening" technique (keeping the emulsion at 90° F.) that resulted in a more sensitive emulsion.

Celluloid and Film In 1888 the Eastman Company (later Eastman Kodak) began to produce the first roll film, as opposed to single plates. Long enough for 100 exposures, the film's gelatin emulsion initially had to be transferred from its paper backing to glass before processing. However a year later, the company began to use a new backing substance: celluloid. Developed in the 1860's by John Wesley Hyatt (1837–1920), it was a much more flexible backing that could be manufactured to a .01-inch thickness. Celluloid and roll film became mainstays of photography and made possible the development of motion picture photography.

New Printing Papers At the same time that gelatin dry plates came into use, new printing papers, manufactured ready for commercial use, were marketed in two major types. "Printing-out papers" required no chemical developing: the image appeared upon exposure. These used a gelatin-silver-chloride emulsion, and in the United States were sold beginning in 1890 as Aristotype and Solio papers. The other type was called "developing-out paper," and needed chemicals to bring the image to view. This silver-bromide emulsion paper was first introduced in 1873, but was not widely used until the 1880's. Along with the improved printing papers came rapid and vast automation of printing by commercial studios.

A third type of paper, called the platinotype, was invented by William Willis (1841–1923) in 1873, based on the properties of iron salts and platinum when exposed to light. This expensive paper produced a broad and subtle tonal range, and was used by wealthy amateur and "artistically-minded" photographers; its use continues today for high-quality fine-art prints.

Evolving Equipment

Along with the wider range of negative materials of the late 1800's came a new series of evolutions in photography equipment. Cameras became more sophisticated, in their design and in individual components like shutters and lenses. And for the first time, indoor photography became possible with the advent of the flash.

View Cameras In 1895 Frederick H. Sanderson designed a more precise view camera that allowed vertical, horizontal, and swing movement of the front panel. This allowed the photographer to adjust not only focusing distance, but also the angle of the plane of focus, as well as angles of perspective. These design elements continue to be the standard for professional view-cameras today.

Single Lens Reflex and Specialty Cameras In contrast to these large, somewhat cumbersome cameras, smaller reflex cameras were also manufactured, making possible fast exposure, focusing control, and a large image size. First they were built as twin-lens reflex cameras that used two identical lenses: one exposed the plate; the other, directly above, with an angled mirror that bounced the image up to a horizontal ground glass for framing and focusing.

The introduction in 1902 of single-lens reflex cameras, like the well-known Graflex, allowed photographers to see the exact image they were taking through the lens itself; the mirror swung out of the way during exposure. SLR cameras, as they are now known, became widely used and valuable for a variety of photographic situations. They were light and easy to carry in one's hand or on a tripod, and could be used in the natural field, for news and street photography, and for portraiture.

There were also a variety of so-called "detective" cameras marketed in the 1880's. Fairly inconspicuous to operate, they included novelty versions in the forms of walking sticks, revolvers, books, and binoculars. The most popular was the Kodak, invented and manufactured beginning in 1888 by George Eastman (1854–1932) of the Eastman Company of Rochester.

Shutters Shutters initially took the form of string— or pneumatically-controlled flaps, drops, or sliding plates. Focal-plane shutters, situated between the lens and the plate, followed the window-shade form first designed by Muybridge, and even at this point could make very short exposures. Alternately, between-the-lens diaphragm shutters—a set of metal blades that simulate the iris of an eye—were sometimes attached inside the lens barrel itself. Then in 1904 the Zeiss Company manufactured a compound shutter designed by Friedrich Deckel (1871–1948). This blade shutter worked like a diaphragm shutter, but controlled both the length of exposure and the size of the aperture; it became standard equipment on many hand cameras.

Lenses Progress in lens design came in 1866 with the rapid rectilinear lens, designed independently but simultaneously by Hugo Adolph Steinheil (1832–93) and John Henry Dallmeyer (1830–83) to correct both spherical aberration and some astigmatism. The development in 1886 of barium crown glass by the Schott Glass Works in Germany made possible the first true anastigmat lenses: those that correct distortion both vertically and horizontally. Two of the most popular were the Double Anastigmat or Dagor lens (1893), and Zeiss's Tessar lens (1902). Dallmeyer also patented the first telephoto lens in 1860.

Lighting and Flashes The first experiments into artificial lighting used electric batteries, which often required exposures of up to 18 minutes; these were replaced beginning in 1864 by magnesium wire and then powder. Blitzlichtpulver, or "flashlight powder,' as the most common form was called, created harsh light and clouds of smoke, but remained the primary type of artificial light until after the First World War. In 1925 Dr. Paul Vierkötter encased the magnesium inside a glass bulb, which eliminated the acrid smoke and high contrast. Four years later flash bulbs were made to hold aluminum foil; these popular bulbs were soon synchronized to camera shutters.

Electric flash systems, the precursor of today's electronic flashes, were known as early as the 1852 to be capable of extremely short flashes. In 1938 Harold Edgerton (1903–90) invented a xenon-filled tube for use in his groundbreaking stroboscopic work. Multiple strobe (flash) units that could be placed around a room, independently controlled, and synchronized together, were manufactured for studio photography in the 1940's.

Color

From the early days of photography, prints were sometimes hand tinted or toned to achieve color. But there remained no way to photographically record natural colors. After numerous attempts, success finally came out of scientific research into human vision: the discovery that all color comes from combinations of red, green, and blue light, which can either be added together or subtracted (using filters) to create a full range of colors.

First Color Photographs James Clerk Maxwell (1831–79) made one of the first color photographs in 1861.

He photographed a piece of tartan three times, each time through a different filter (a glass filled with either red, green, or blue liquid), and then projected the three images onto a screen through the same filters. The three pictures overlapped and formed a full-color image, in a technique that uses the additive properties of light. Frederic E. Ives (1856–1937) in 1892 invented a more convenient and portable device called a Kromskop, which united the three images without the use of lanterns and liquid filters.

Autochromes The next step was to create a one-piece color transparency. John Joly (1857–1933) accomplished the task by photographing through a screen with microscopic areas of red, green, and blue dye. The same screen was permanently attached to the resulting plate, and the colors mixed in viewing to form a color image. (In effect this was the same as Maxwell's liquid filter system, only with hundreds of tiny filters.) In 1907 the Lumière brothers, Auguste (1865–1954) and Louis (1864–1948), devised the most successful early color system, using the same principle, called autochromes. A plate was coated with starch grains in the three primary colors (orange, green, and violet), dusted with black powder, and then coated with silver bromide panchromatic emulsion. The end product was a single positive transparency. Autochromes were marketed until 1932, at which point subtractive color alternatives were in use.

Film and Printing in the 20th Century

Since the First World War, black and white films have become remarkably faster (perhaps as much as 24 million times faster than the daguerreotypes of 1839), and are now available in ratings from ASA 65 to 3200 or more. (ASA is an international film speed rating system based on work by Kodak in the 1940's.) The larger silver halide crystals of faster films work in low-light situations, but produce grainier negatives and prints. Specialty infrared and color-process black and white films are also currently marketed.

Subtractive Color Until 1925 most color images were produced using the additive theory of color. As early as 1869, a subtractive process was suggested, in separate but simultaneous announcements by Louis Ducos du Hauron (1837–1920), and Charles Cros (1842–88). As in Maxwell's process, three separate photos (called color separation negatives) were taken through red, green and blue filters. This time a black and white transparency was made from each negative, then each slide was dyed or tinted in the complementary color of the filter (cyan, magenta, and yellow). When these three slides were held together, an accurate color image was seen.

Kodachrome These methods eventually developed into more sophisticated color transparency films, the foremost of which was Kodachrome, invented by Leopold Godowsky (1900–83) and Leopold Mannes (1899–1964). It was the first "tripak" film, which meant the film had three layers of emulsion, each with a primary color filter layer (called a " dye-coupler") that would block out the complementary color. The effect was the same as taking separate photos and reassembling them. But Kodak's new film, released first for movies (1935) then in sheet (1938) and roll film (1942), made unique color positive images from a single instantaneous exposure.

Color Prints Kodak and another firm, Ansco, both released tripak films that the photographer could process in the darkroom (instead of sending to the company for processing): Ansco-Color film in 1942 and Ektachrome shortly thereafter. In response to the need for true color-negative film—for making multiple prints instead of a single unique positive—Kodak released Kodacolor film in 1941, and then in 1947 released Ektacolor film which the photographer could process by hand.

Color Film Technology Currently two main systems are used in color films. The dye-destruction (or dye-bleach) system uses film with a complete set of dyes present at exposure; those not needed are removed during processing. Chromogenic techniques add dyes to the film during processing, either by dye-injection or dye-incorporation, in which the dyes, along with the filters, are included in the film's emulsion layers to be activated during processing. This last is the process used in the majority of negative and positive films on the market today.

Modern Cameras

Professional cameras improved and expanded dramatically during the 20th century. Large-format view cameras continued to follow much the same form, but hand-held cameras underwent significant changes. In 1949 the Zeiss-Ikon company introduced the popular Contax-S single-lens reflex camera, the first to use a pentaprism mirror system that allowed eye-level viewing. In 1913 35mm cameras were first designed as a way to use leftover motion picture film. Beginning with the Leica, introduced in 1925, 35mm cameras became the standard of SLR photography. Newer cameras have been further improved by adding features such as: motor drives that advance film and reset the shutter; autofocus lenses; multiple exposure meter settings; auto-bracketing; and a host of electronic features.

The Eastman Brownie camera, introduced in 1900, was a turning point in amateur photography, bringing snapshot photography to the public at large. It evolved by 1963 into the Kodak Instamatic, and in 1973 was adapted as the pocket Instamatic for 16mm film. So-called point-and-shoot 35mm cameras followed, experiencing mass public acceptance and becoming standard items in most American homes. In the 1990's the Advanced Photo System (APS) was released as an alternative. It uses drop-in film cassettes and allows for multiple format options (e.g., panoramic, wide, and standard) on the same roll.

Instant Photography The Polaroid Land Camera, invented by Edwin H. Land (1909–91) and introduced in 1948, was groundbreaking: it processed the film inside the camera itself. The camera used special film containing a pod with processing chemicals, which after exposure was squeezed through rollers along with the negative and paper, generating a final print in less than a minute. At first these were black-and-white prints, but in 1962 Polaroid Polacolor film was introduced. A variety of Polaroid cameras and film systems are now used for amateur snapshots, by professionals to test lighting and exposures setups, as well as in some art photography. As innovative as Polaroid was, the company declared bankruptcy in 2002 , due in part, many suggest, to the revolution of digital photography.

Digital Photography

The History of Digital Photography

In 1969 a new type of semiconductor, called a charge coupled device, or CCD, was developed by George Smith and Willard Boyle of Bell Labs. Roughly a year later, Bell Labs created a solid-state video camera that used this new chip as an image sensor. The original intent was to develop a small, low-powered camera that could be used in a videophone device; by 1975 they were able to demonstrate a CCD camera with image quality sharp enough for broadcast television.

Building on the development of the CCD, in 1972, Texas Instruments patented a film-less electronic camera. The first commercial electronic camera was Sony's Mavica, released in 1981. The Mavica saved images onto a recordable mini disc; the mini disc was then inserted into a video reader that was connected to a television monitor or color printer. Over the next decade Eastman Kodak led the way in developing professional-level cameras, but it took the computer companies to bring them to the consumer.

Consumer-Level Digital Cameras The first digital camera for the consumer market was introduced in 1994 by Apple. The Apple QuickTake 100 camera connected to any Apple personal computer by means of a serial cable.

Other early consumer digital cameras were the Kodak DC40 and Casio QV-11 (both released in 1995), and the Sony Cyber-Shot Digital Still Camera (1996). Kodak was particularly aggressive in promoting digital photography to a mass market, partnering with Microsoft and Kinko's to place digital image-editing workstations and kiosks in all Kinko's locations. These workstations enabled consumers to edit and print digital photographs, as well as create Photo CD discs. Simultaneously, Kodak partnered with IBM to create an Internet-based image exchange, and Hewlett-Packard marketed the first color inkjet printers designed especially for the printing of digital photographs.

How Digital Cameras Work

Digital cameras function much like traditional cameras, with lenses, shutters, and apertures. The main difference between traditional film cameras and digital cameras is how the photographic image is generated. Film cameras generate images on light-sensitive film; a digital camera uses no film, instead utilizing an electronic sensor to generate images.

Sensing the Image Most digital cameras today use CCDs to record images; some cameras use similar sensors that employ complementary metal oxide semiconductor (CMOS) technology. Both CCD and CMOS sensors are made up of a large number of tiny light-sensitive diodes. These diodes, also called photosites, convert photons (light) into electrons (an electrical charge). The brighter the light that hits a photosite, the greater the electrical charge that accumulates at that site.

The analog value of the photosite's electrical charge is read by the CCD or CMOS device, and then converted to a digital value by means of an analog-to-digital converter

(ADC). When the individual photosite values are combined into a single image, a microprocessor is used to interpolate the values between the photosites, and thus create a seamless picture.

Capturing Color A photosite only captures the intensity of light at a given point—not the color of that light. To create a color image, the image sensor employs one of two different schemes. Some high-end cameras use three different image sensors, one for each different primary color. Most consumer-level cameras, however, employ a stationary filter, called a Bayer filter, that "colors" individual pixels red, green or blue. Whatever the capture method, each color is recorded separately then added back together to create the full spectrum of colors in the photographic image.

Resolution The sharpness (or resolution) of a digital image is measured in terms of pixels. One tiny digital image is called a pixel, and the more pixels contained in an image, the sharper the picture. In digital photography, the number of photosites on a sensor is roughly equal to the number of pixels captured. (Not all photosites are used for imaging, which is why this is an inexact calculation.) Thus a sensor that has roughly 2.1 million photosites is said to have 2.1 megapixel resolution (1 million pixels equals 1 megapixel).

Output Options Unlike film photography, which generates hard copy images on paper or transparencies, digital photographs can be output on a wide variety of media. Digital images can be viewed on personal computer or television displays; inserted into Web pages; transmitted via e-mail; or printed on paper or transparency film.

One of the most popular output options is to create photo prints from a special color photo printer. These printers typically use inkjet technology to create photo-quality prints on special photographic paper. All photo printers can be connected to your personal computer, and some allow direct printing (without a PC) from your digital camera's memory card.

Graphics Formats Most digital cameras also let you choose a specific graphics file format for the images you store. Some graphics formats are *lossy*, which compress the image with some degree of degradation, or *lossless*, which are larger in size but nondegrading in nature.

The two most common graphics formats used in digital photography today are TIFF and JPG. TIFF (Tagged Image File Format)is a lossless format preferred for photo prints and other hard copy output; it creates large files unsuited for digital transmission. JPG (Joint Photo Experts Group) is a lossy, compressed format that produces acceptable image quality with small-sized files; it is ideal for use on the Internet

Storage Options Digital images are typically stored on rewritable media connected to or inserted into the digital camera. Most consumer-level digital cameras use some sort of solid-state memory card media, such as CompactFlash, SmartMedia, or Sony's Memory Stick. These storage devices can be removed from the camera and then inserted into a computer or printer to transfer or print the stored images; most digital cameras also enable direct connect to a PC for image transfer.

Lenses and Other Considerations Many low-end digital cameras come with a fixed focal-length lens and fully automatic operation—the digital equivalent of the point-and-shoot film camera. More expensive digital cameras permit manual override of the automatic settings, and feature higher-quality lenses. Many of these better cameras feature zoom lenses (referred to as optical zoom), which enable you to manually vary the focal length of the lens. A zoom lens is not to be confused with digital zoom, featured in many low-end cameras, where the image sensor magnifies a portion of the image to create a low-resolution faux-zoom effect. In all cases, optical zoom is preferable to digital zoom.

Digital Image Editing When an image is captured digitally, it is possible to manipulate the individual pixels in the image and thus created an enhanced or changed version of the original image. While it is possible to perform some slight manipulation of photographic film, digital images enable easier and more extensive image editing—which is one of the appeals of digital photography.

This type of enhancement ranges from simple fixes—removing "red eye," deleting scratches, sharpening or smoothing edges, or brightening dark images—to more elaborate photo manipulations. A dedicated digital editor can make a normal picture look like an aged sepia tone print, crop unwanted items or people out of a photograph, or even insert other items and people into a scene. Today it is rare to see a photograph in a newspaper or magazine that has not been digitally touched up in this manner; even beginning photographers have become adept at "fixing" poorly taken photographs.

An Art History of Photography

Photography initially came about as a means to make drawing, especially portraits, easier. It was a quicker way of accurately recording a scene and ideally would require no artistic skill. Over time, however, the unique advantages of the medium brought it respect and significance for its own sake.

Daguerreotypes When the secret of Daguerreotypes was released in 1839, what the French dubbed "daguérrotypomanie" spread like wildfire throughout Europe, England, and the United States. At first, due to the length of exposure time required, most pictures taken were of landscapes, architecture, and especially foreign places. Publisher N. M. P. Lerebours (1807–73) put out a series called Excursions daguerriennes between 1840 and 1844; a collection of daguerreotypes taken in locations from the Middle East to North Africa to Niagara Falls. This work, along with that of other traveling daguerreotypists, brought to the west views of a world most had little idea of.

Portraiture When improvements in the daguerreotype process made portraits feasible, commercial studios opened up in major cities everywhere. Because of the relatively cheap price, almost anyone could have his or her portrait taken. For example, in Massachusetts in one year, 403,626 daguerreotypes were taken. A studio in New York reported taking up to 1,000 portraits a day.

Generally these portraits were simple, posed, and straightforward. However, a few studio photographers added a creative touch, notably Albert Sands Southworth (1811–94) and Josiah Johnson Hawes (1808–1901). Their well-known portrait of the chief justice of the Massachusetts Supreme Court in 1851 used bright overhead lighting—emphasizing his wild hair and the contours of his weathered face.

Calotypes With the advent of paper calotype negatives came expansion in the uses of photography. David Octavius Hill (1802–70) and Robert Adamson (1821–48) took more than 1,500 photographs of common people across Scotland, including a well-known set of informal portraits of one fishing community. Mostly, however, calotypes continued to be used for landscape and architectural photography.

Folk Portraiture Wet-plate collodion technology brought photography further into the hands of everyday individuals in the 1800's. Tintypes—easy to make and far less fragile than daguerreotypes—were used, for instance, during the Civil War in America, for soldiers to send home pictures of themselves to their families. Cartes-de-visite swept the Western world with "cardomania." Many people had portraits taken of themselves, and for the first time mass-produced prints of famous people and places were sold widely—for example, 70,000 of the Prince Consort in England in the week after his death.

Early Artistry It was not all folk art, however. Many Young Romantics of the Latin Quarter were using collodion plates to work artistically. Perhaps the most famous was Nadar, born Gaspard Félix Tournachon (1820–1910), who created artistic and caricature portraits of well-known Parisians for his Panthéon-Nadar (released beginning in 1854). His studio itself became a sort of salon for liberal thinkers in the city, and Nadar went on to explore both air travel and electric lighting for photography.

Other photographers working at the same time included Étienne Carjat (1828–1906), and Antony Samuel Adam-Salomon (1811–81), whose use of high side light on his sitters is to this day known as "Rembrandt lighting," following the painter's style. Napoleon Sarony (1821–96), working in the 1860's, specialized in theatrical photographs, in which he experimented with elaborate props and backdrops, and especially with the attitude of the sitter—exploring the playful and dramatic side of his actor subjects. Julia Margaret Cameron (1815–79) made headshots of her famous friends in which she attempted to show the spirit and "truth" of the people she photographed.

War Photography's strength of veracity found an outlet in the documentation of war. Roger Fenton (1819–69) in London was one of the first war photographers, working in Crimea. Matthew Brady (1823–96) contributed unique and renowned coverage of the Civil War in America. His photographs provided the public with some of the first views of the destructive and gruesome nature of warfare.

Exploration In the mid-1800's collodion photography was used throughout North America as part of the United States Geological Survey's exploratory expeditions, including Powell's travels along the Colorado River. William Henry Jackson (1843–1942) took photographs of Yellowstone that were instrumental in getting the area designated as the first National Park in 1872; without his images no one believed the area's shooting geysers, steaming sulfur pools and otherworldly landscape truly existed.

Early Social Documentation Jacob A. Riis (1849–1914), a police reporter in New York City, was one of the earliest to use his camera as a documentary tool, which he employed to illustrate the misery of immigrant slum life in New York in a way that his writing never could. However, due to the poor photomechanical techniques available at the time (ca. 1890), his photographic work was not recognized until 1947, when Alexander Alland (1902–89) made prints from Riis's original negatives.

Adam Clark Vroman (1856–1916) and Edward S. Curtis (1868–1952) each took their cameras to Native American reservations, making photographic studies of American Indians. Their work served both as sympathetic portraits (Vroman) and as a substantial record of what was by then a dying culture (Curtis).

Pictorial Photography Starting in 1886 Peter Henry Emerson (1856–1936) led a revolt toward what he called "Naturalistic" or "Pictorial Photography," which paradoxically saw the reproduction of nature as the primary aesthetic goal of photography. He suggested pictures be taken slightly out of focus to mimic the human eye's inability to hold all of a scene in focus at once; critics called these images "fuzzygraphs." In 1891 Emerson reversed his opinions completely, and decided that photography was not in fact art. In an odd twist, he continued to make photographs and publish a photography textbook.

Galleries and Groups At the end of the 19th century, the fight between photography and art was heating up across Europe. Galleries and groups were beginning to hold controversial juried photography exhibitions, with painters and sculptors as the judges. Before this, photographs had generally been assessed for their technical achievements, not their artistic merits.

A London-based group called the Linked Ring formed in 1892 as an art-focused breakaway from the London Photographic society. The group wanted to free photography from the bondage of science and technology. One member, Alfred Stieglitz (1864–1946), spent his remarkable career working to improve and evolve American photography. As part of this effort, Stieglitz established the Camera Club of New York (1896), and its influential publication Camera Notes. The Club held exhibitions featuring work by important new photographers such as Gertrude Käsebier (1852–1934) and Edward Steichen (1879–1973).

In 1902 Stieglitz founded a new group, Photo-Secession, following the German and American avant-garde's mission to separate itself from the academic establishment. The Little Galleries of the Photo-Secession at 291 Fifth Avenue (commonly called "291"), along with the group's publication, *Camera Work*, showcased work by leading photographers, as well as avant-garde artists, including Matisse, Picasso, and O'Keeffe.

Straight Photography A new style of "straight photography"—photographs that did not try to emulate paintings—began to flourish at this time, with Stieglitz among its advocates. His portraits were considered remarkable for portraying depth of soul and character with perfect technique, but with no pretense or artificiality. Paul Strand (1890-1976) and Edward Weston (1886–1958) furthered the trend, emphasizing form and design and the beauty of everyday objects.

A new group formed in 1934 following in the straight photography tradition. They called themselves group "f/64" in reference to the narrow aperture that produces the greatest depth of field and focal sharpness. The founding members included some of the biggest names in photography: Ansel Adams (1902–84), Imogen Cunningham (1883–1976), John Paul Edwards (1883–1958), Sonya Noskowiak (1905–75), Henry Swift (1891–1960), Willard Van Dyke (1906–86), and Edward Weston. The group's code was strict realism, and soon the designation f/64 came to refer to anyone practicing this style of photography.

Ansel Adams is worth noting for several reasons, not only for his conservation work and technical innovations, but for making photography as an art form accessible to the public. In addition, his "zone system" of exposure and processing was one of the most important developments in photography in the 20th century. By breaking down the tones of a scene into values on a scale from zero to IX and exposing and processing his film based on those values, Adams was able to produce prints with the rich tonal range that has made his images renowned.

Alternative Views In the same postwar years, some photographers experimented instead with alternative perspective and abstraction. Alvin Langdon Coburn (1882–1966) and Alexander Rodchenko (1891–1956) created memorable works using novel angles of view, mirrored camera attachments (Coburn) and multiple exposures (Rodchenko). Even further from straight photography's realism were László Moholy-Nagy (1895–1946) and Man Ray (1890–1976). They made true camera-less abstractions called photograms and rayograms, respectively, by placing objects onto light-sensitive paper and exposing to create shadows and shapes. Others found influence in science and motion studies, while followers of the Dada modern painting group and the Bauhaus movement began to create photomontages and photocollages—new work that relied on juxtaposition and contrast to create meaning and messages that were often political or social in nature.

Documentary Photography Early in the 1900's Lewis W. Hine (1874–1940) made what he called "photo-interpretations" or "human documents." These included series on immigrant workers in New York and Red Cross workers in Europe. Hine intended his work to spread knowledge and improve the human condition. Along with Riis's similar photographic style, Hine's photography ushered in the documentary photography movement that was especially strong during the Great Depression. The Farm Security Administration, created as part of Roosevelt's efforts to assist those devastated by the drought, undertook the documentation of the government's aid efforts and life in rural America in general. The two best-known F.S.A. photographers were Walker Evans (1903–75) and Dorothea Lange (1895–1965), whose stark but sympathetic portraits of farmworkers continue to influence aspiring photographers.

Photojournalism The release of fast hand-held cameras permitted the first indoor available-light photography, which meant events and meetings could be covered without the intrusive light and smoke of flash powder. This led to a new trend: documentation of the political and social events that shaped history. The camera's ability to capture decisive moments like the Hindenburg disaster (1937) further pushed the use of photography as a news medium. Photography's place in newspapers and journalism was clinched by the invention of the half-tone printing process, which made it possible to print both text and images using the same press. This new form of photography, photojournalism, was pioneered especially by German photographers like Erich Salomon (1886-1944), Felix H. Man (1893-1985), André Kertész (1894-1985), and Alfred Eisenstaedt (1898-1995).

Magazines also played an important role in the development of photojournalism. The founder of *Time* and *Fortune*, Henry Luce (1898–1967), started Life magazine in 1936 with the specific intention of incorporating photography into the stories. With the help of staff photographers like Margaret Bourke-White (1904–71), Life initiated a new kind of magazine and a new kind of photography, driven by the "mind-guided camera." Instead of capturing a news event that happened to occur, the photographer had a preset assignment; her job was to take all the photographs needed in order to capture the few images that would best tell the story.

Modern Realism Starting in the 1960's, a branch of art photographers began to focus on what was called the "social landscape." Walker Evans and Harry Callahan (1912–99), working in the 1940's, first established this style, characterized by the straightforward depiction of daily life. Robert Frank (b. 1924) and Diane Arbus (1923–71) were exemplary photographers in this vein—Frank with his extensive documentation of America, and Arbus sympathetically portraying outcast groups.

Conceptualism At the same time there emerged a new sense of postmodernism: the idea that the camera could not be an objective or factual viewer. Photographers taking this attitude often used series or juxtapositions of the same object from multiple angles or viewpoints. They also engaged in deliberate manipulations of images, or carried theatrical staging to its limits, to create unreal, bizarre, or simply questioning images. Cindy Sherman (b. 1954), with her disguised self-portraits and mannequin images, is a prime example of a photographer this genre.

With the rise of color and chemical photographic techniques, expressive possibilities expanded even further. The abstract avant-garde styles of the Bauhaus followers grew and flourished in the 1960's and 70's, with techniques whose names hint at their variety: photogenics, crystallography, lightgraphics, luminograms, chemigrams. Together, photographers have drawn on an expanding panoply of methods, all in name of meaningful and conceptual imagemaking.

Glossary of Photographic Terms

35mm standard film type used in hand-held cameras. Measurement reflects the size of the image frame, measured lengthwise (actually 36mm).

additive color the principle that any color can be produced by starting with black (absence of color) and adding proportions of red, green, and blue (RGB) light.

aperture the opening in a camera or camera lens that allows light through, or the size of that opening.

APS (Advanced Photo System) recent type of consumer film, camera, and processing technology that uses drop-in film loading, user-picked picture format, and alternative processing that provides thumbnails, print-format choice, and stores the pictures in the film canister.

ASA a standard system developed by the American Standards Association to rate film speed; higher numbers mean faster films, which require less light. It was replaced by the ISO (International Standards Organization) system which uses the same scale.

autofocus (or AF) a lens designed to set its focus automatically on an object in its view, using sensors. Or a camera equipped to work with AF lenses.

backlight lighting on a subject that comes from behind the subject, often used to create a halo (where the edges of a person's hair are lit) or silhouette effect.

bounce the use of a reflector or reflective surface (such as a ceiling or wall) to bounce an indirect light source onto a subject, resulting in softer, more diffuse lighting.

bracketing the technique of taking a series of pictures of the same image, with a range of exposures around the 'proper' exposure. Used in situations where there is doubt as to the best exposure, or the image has a wider range of light/dark tones than the film can record.

calotype from Greek "beautiful picture," a print type invented by William Henry Fox Talbot, it uses silver nitrate, gallic acid, and acetic acid to sensitize a paper before exposure, and to develop the picture after exposure. Innovative because it used a latent image—the image could not be seen until development, whereas previous techniques all relied on exposing the paper for long periods until the image was visible.

camera obscura a precursor to modern photographic cameras. Initially a dark room with a hole in one wall, causing an image of the outside to be projected (upside-down and reversed) on the opposite wall. Later designed as boxes with a lens, aperture, and access door.

CCD ("Charge Coupled Device") a wafer-thin piece of hardware covered with tens of thousands of capacitors (or diodes or conductors), used in digital photography to capture an image. Exposure to light builds a charge on each receptor cell, converting the light into an electrical signal, which is then transferred to an amplifier and detector.

CMOS ("Complementary Metal Oxide Semiconductor") an alternate form of digital image capture that works essentially the same as a CCD, used in some brands of digital cameras.

CMYK for "cyan," "magenta," "yellow," and "black", the primary colors used in four-color printing to create full color images, with black added for true black. Printing uses additive color, the complement to which is subtractive (light-based) RGB color.

color depth (bit depth) refers to the number of bits (a single on-off choice) used to represent a color in a digital image. 8-bit color (or 1 byte) represents 256 colors (2^8 possible combinations); 24-bit gives approximately 16 million values or colors. Usually refers to a digital image, but also used to show a monitor's capabilities.

composition how a photographer chooses what should be included in an image—including foreground, background, and objects—and where those components are positioned in the frame.

compression a method or format for storing a computer file that reduces its size and may or may not degrade the file (image) quality. Lossy compression degrades the file, while lossless does not.

contact print a photographic print made by putting a negative in direct contact with light-sensitive material, resulting in a print the exact size of the negative.

crop removing sections of a photograph along the edges in order to improve the composition and enlarge it.

Daguerreotype considered the "first" photographs, based on a process devised by Louis Jacques Mandé Daguerre, that used silver-plated copper, iodine, and mercury to form a unique image after exposure to light in a camera.

depth of field the 'depth' or extent of the focal plane of an image—the range of what is in focus. It is determined by the type and focal length of lens used, and the aperture.

digitization the act of converting analog information to digital information; sometimes the word 'input' (verb form) is used by digital imagers to refer to this process.

DPI ("Dots Per Inch") technically the number of dots of ink per inch a printer lays down; a measure of a printer's resolution, or the resolution of a digital image file.

emulsion a light-sensitive chemical substance applied to film, paper, plate, or other backing, that receives light and is processed to produce a negative or positive image.

enlarger a device used to make a (larger) print from a negative, by shining light through the negative and then through a lens, onto light-sensitive material.

exposure the act of allowing light to reach light-sensitive material, or the amount of light that reaches that material, as modified by shutter speed and aperture size.

f/number also called f-stop, the size of the aperture opening, expressed as a numerical designation, e.g. f/2, f/2.8, etc.

fill the use of light, from a flash or other source, to balance or fill in direct ambient light sources, in order to reduce the contrast between brightly lit and shadowed areas.

filter transparent attachment for camera or enlarger lens used to alter the color, range, or other characteristic of light entering the lens. Examples include (red and yellow) B&W contrast filters, polarizing filters, and special effects filters.

fish eye super wide angle lenses, with nearly infinite depth-of-field, whose angle of view can approach 180 degrees. Views through these lenses results in extreme distortion, like that of a door peep-hole.

flash an artificial light source, usually mounted on top of a camera, that provides a short burst of light, timed to match the opening of the camera shutter. Many are now equipped with fast-acting diodes to measure the light that bounces back from the subject and automatically provide the proper exposure. Larger studio models are called 'strobes.'

focal length the distance between the lens and the focal plane, or sharp object in an image. Combined with the film format, it determines the lens angle of view. With 35mm film, lenses with focal length around 50mm are "normal" (they approximate the view without any lens); less than 35mm are wide angle; and greater than 70 are called telephoto lenses.

halftone process used to print continuous tone photographic images by representing tones as a series of black dots (or CMYK dots for color images); the density of the dots, when viewed from a distance, recreates the scale of grey tones in the image. Devised for reproducing photographs on newspaper printing presses.

infrared the electromagnetic radiation above the red end of the light spectrum. Infrared film is sensitive to this wavelength, along with visible light, and results in altered appearance of surfaces that reflect the light—especially foliage.

large format photography using film in single sheets larger ranging in size from 4 x 5 inches up to 20 x 24 inches. Large format cameras generally have bellows and component to allow swing and pitch adjustments and viewing on a ground glass plate.

lens simple lenses consist of a glass or plastic element that is curved on one or both sides. Most photographic lenses are compound, using between three and 20 elements in order to correct aberrations, allow a sharp focus across the entire picture, and aid in focusing and (in zoom lenses) changing focal length.

luminance the brightness of a surface or image, determined by how much light it emits or reflects. In digital photography, it is a value given to each pixel.

macrophotography also called "close up photography," any photography with magnification of the subject greater than 1:1.

megapixel 1 million pixels. Used as a rating for digital cameras' capture and resolution capabilities.

multiple exposure exposing a single frame of film many times, to show motion or for special effects.

negative a print or piece of film whose tonalities are reversed from the natural scene. Light projected through a negative onto light-sensitive material produces a positive image when that material is processed.

optical zoom the use of multiple lens elements in differential motion to enable a lens to move smoothly between different focal lengths.

overexpose too much light when exposing film; results in a washed out or overly light print.

photogravure from French for "photo engraving," a method of etching copper plates by placing photosensitive material on the plate that hardens differentially when exposed to light, then washing away the unhardened material after exposure through a negative, and using acid to etch the exposed copper. The plate is then used to print multiple copies of the photograph, with finer quality than halftone printing. Photogravure was regularly used by Alfred Stieglitz and his followers.

plate generally a glass or metal sheet, coated with a light-sensitive emulsion, which is placed in a camera for exposure and processed to make a negative or positive image.

point and shoot hand-held, usually consumer-level cameras with automatic exposure and focusing, and a separate viewfinder.

positive a print or piece of film whose tonalities match that of the natural scene; produced either directly from the camera (as with positive transparencies or slides) or by printing from a negative.

PPI (pixels per inch) the number of pixels per square inch—more pixels means better resolution, better image quality.

processing in photography, using chemicals to turn an exposed piece of film (latent image) into a stable image.

red eye the effect resulting from light from a flash striking the back of a person's retina and reflecting straight back into the camera, causing the irises to look red. This occurs predominantly in low light situations—where pupils are dilated—when the flash is close to the camera.

resolution the sharpness of an image, based on the number and density of pixels; more pixels result in better detail and a higher resolution. Often expressed in dpi or dots per inch

shutter the mechanical device between a lens and film in a camera that opens to allow light in for a set amount of time. Focal plane shutters are part of the camera body and mimic window shades. Between-the-lens shutters use metal blades and work like the iris/pupil of an eye and adjust not only for time but for the size of the opening.

shutter speed the amount of time a camera shutter stays open to let light onto the film. Expressed in fractions of a second, it ranges in most cameras between 1 (or more) seconds down to 2000 (1/2000th of a second).

SLR (single lens reflex) hand-held cameras in which the viewfinder (what the photographer looks through) shows the actual image through the lens, using a series of mirrors that lift out of the way when the shutter is released. These are the standard cameras for most serious amateur or professional photographers.

speed a rating of the light-sensitivity of film, commonly expressed in ASA ratings.

stereoscope a device used to merge (in viewing) two images of the same scene, taken at slightly different angles, by having each eye view one image, so that together the effect is a three-dimensional view.

stroboscope a special flash unit that fires multiple flashes in rapid succession, used with a moving subject and a long camera exposure, in order to break the motion down into discreet units that are all (usually) recorded on a single frame.

subtractive color the principle that any color can be produced by starting with a white light (all colors present), and using cyan, yellow, and magenta (CMY) filters to remove complementary colors. It is the basis for most modern color photography.

telephoto a lens with a focal length generally greater than 70mm (or longer than the diagonal of the film format). The effect is enlargement of the image and a decreased depth of field.

tintype also called melainotype and ferrotype and popular especially during the Civil War, these direct positives were made by coating black-enameled iron sheets with light-sensitive material. Processing stripped away unexposed areas, and the black backing made the image appear positive. Tintypes are fast and easy to make, and so were extremely popular with the public at large.

transparency processed direct positive film. In 35mm format, this is called "slide" film.

twain a data source manager that operates between a driver and a device; the interface standard for scanners, which come with TWAIN drivers to make them compatible with TWAIN-supporting software.

twin lens reflex a camera with two identical lenses, one to expose the film, and the other above it to focus the camera. The distance between the two lenses makes framing of very close subjects more difficult because of parallax error.

underexpose an image that was exposed with too little light. The result is a dark image.

wide angle lenses with a short focal length, generally smaller than the diagonal of the film format. The result is an increased angle of view (the number of degrees from perpendicular to the film that are included in the image), and increased depth of field. The shorter the focal length, the more distorted the image becomes to accommodate the wide angle.

zoetrope a drum-like device with slits in the sides, used to view a strip of images in quick succession so that the subject appears to move.

zoom a lens with variable focal length, allowing the user to change magnification without altering focus or perspective. Sometimes inappropriately used to refer to any long (telephoto) lens.

ECONOMICS, BUSINESS, AND FINANCE

Economics

Economic History 120
Microeconomics. 121
Macroeconomics 124
Times Focus: *A Way to Break the Cycle of Servitude by Louis Uchitelle*. 127
Development Economics 130
International Economics 132
Times Focus: *Why Currency Exchange Rates Matter by Hal R. Varian* 133
Glossary of Economic Terms. 135

Business

A Brief History of Business. 138
Advertising 151
Glossary of Business Terms 154

Finance

A Brief History of Finance 158
Stock Markets 163
Mutual Funds 166
Glossary of Finance Terms 168

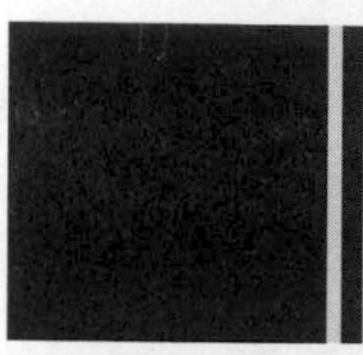

ECONOMICS

Economics (from the Greek, meaning "management of a household") is the study of how human beings coordinate their wants by the efficient production and distribution of goods and services. The four central issues addressed by economics are (1) what to produce; (2) how much to produce; (3) how to produce it; and (4) for whom to produce it.

Economics today deals not only with individuals and households but with cities, regions, nations, and worldwide trade. The principal concerns of economics are markets for good and services, but there are many other aspects of economics—including the distribution of income, labor relations, the welfare of citizens, and the environment.

There are two main branches of economics: *microeconomics*, which deals with individual choices; and *macroeconomics*, which deals with large-scale or general economic factors, usually of nations. Additional specializations include *development economics*, the study of improving the economies of underdeveloped countries; *international economics*, the study of economic issues on a global scale; *labor economics*, the study of wages, workers, and unions; *econometrics*, the application of statistical methods to estimate economic relationships; *urban economics*, the study of cities, infrastructure, and urban populations; *Soviet economics*, the assessment of the command economy of the Soviet Union; and *environmental economics*, the analysis of environmental costs and benefits.

Economic History

Preindustrial Economies

Economies of the preindustrial past included, in the ancient world, agricultural villages, city-states, civilizations based on large irrigation systems, and trading empires such as those of the Phoenicians, the Greeks, and the Carthaginians in the Mediterranean region. In medieval Europe from the ninth to the 15th centuries, the dominant system of political and economic organization was feudalism, which defined the relationship between people of different social statuses. Most numerous were the peasants, who were entitled to farm their lord's land in exchange for rendering homage and service—including a portion of what they grew. In return, lords were obligated to render protection to their vassals. The feudal order was not limited to the relationship between tenants and lords: minor nobles, nobles, and kings stood in a comparable relationship to one another. Feudalism ended as a result of many factors, including a crucial one, the Black Death, which diminished the workforce to such an extent that laborers could demand better terms for their service, and migration to cities.

During the Renaissance (14th–16th centuries), banking systems were developed in Florence and other Italian cities. Joint-stock companies were formed in the 16th and 17th centuries in England and the Netherlands. From the 16th century to the 19th, European economies followed the system of mercantilism. The theory underlying mercantilism was that economic prosperity depended on the acquisition of gold and silver (bullion), which could be secured only by maintaining a positive balance of trade. Mercantilism encouraged foreign trade and the opening of new markets, the encouragement of domestic industry and agriculture to produce goods or crops for sale in those markets, trading companies to control the trade, and protectionist policies to protect domestic markets from competition and to minimize imports. Colonies were desirable both as sources of raw materials and as export markets, and naval power was essential to protecting sea trade and colonies. Mercantilism eventually gave way to more liberal free-trade policies based on more flexible concepts of wealth and economic prosperity.

The Industrial Revolution and Capitalism

About 1750 the Industrial Revolution began in Great Britain, with key technologies such as the steam engine, and initially in the textile industry. Industrial development followed in other countries in the 19th century, including France, Germany, and the United States, and led to the rise of the economic system known as *capitalism*.

As the tools of industrial manufacturing were created, a person with money to invest could seek out the latest leading-edge inventions and develop a more efficient factory, thus stealing market share from now outdated rivals. Instead of slowly amassing wealth over a lifetime, there was now a systematic way to amass wealth relatively quickly. This new method of amassing wealth through investment in capital was called capitalism; a capitalist invests money in an enterprise with the objective of receiving more in return than what was initially invested.

The Industrial Revolution and the growth of capitalism brought unparalleled growth in economic output and in population, but also substantial dislocation of agricultural populations, destruction of natural environments, and very often harsh conditions for workers.

The Rise of Socialism

In response to both the unprecedented productivity of capitalist systems and the ills that they brought about, a variety of socialist and utopian ideas arose in the late 18th century and the 19th century. Among early socialists were F. N. Babeuf (1760–97), proponent of class conflict; the utopian Robert Owen (1771–1858), creator of cooperative communities; and Ferdinand Lassalle (1825–64), a founder of the first workers' party in Germany in 1863.

The principal historical figure in the history of socialism is Karl Marx (1818–83), who, along with Friedrich Engels (1820–95), conceived the theory and tactics of revolutionary proletarian socialism, which became known as Marxism. Marx was primarily concerned with the dynamics of capitalism and the historical laws he believed would cause its replacement, rather than with the structure of a socialist system. His most famous work, cowritten with Engels in 1848, was the *Communist Manifesto*, which outlined a theory of class struggle and the revolutionary role of the proletariat. His greatest work was *Das Kapital*, published in three volumes (1867, 1885, 1894). Marx's doctrines influenced the creation of numerous communist states and their associated command economies, where all economic decisions are dictated by the central government.

The Great Depression

Capitalism continued as the world's primary economic system, and increased trading between countries in the early 20th century helped to create a more connected global economy. The business cycles of local economies began to have worldwide effects, and when the U.S. stock market boom of the 1920's turned bust on October 29, 1929 ("Black Tuesday"), it helped to throw the fragile global economy that was still recovering from World War I into a deep worldwide depression.

At the depths of what came to be called the Great Depression, in 1931, world industrial production was 38 percent less than what it had been in June 1929, and there were an estimated 30 million unemployed people worldwide. This single year saw countries descend into mass unemployment and hunger, the breakdown of international exchange, and the failure of great financial institutions.

The recovery that began in 1932 brought the world economy back to life by 1937, thanks to increased governmental deficit spending and the country-by-country abandonment of the gold standard. But the global economic downturn had lasting effects on all it touched, and helped to sow the seeds of World War II in Europe.

Social Welfare

Partly in response to the mass unemployment of the Great Depression, most advanced nations today have market systems with some form of social safety net. Markets are generally subject to standards of openness and disclosure to ensure competition, and there are prohibitions against unfair labor practices and environmental damage.

Social welfare programs date back at least to Germany in the 19th century; in the United States today these programs include Social Security, Medicare, and Medicaid. The developed European countries almost all have substantially larger social welfare programs than the United States. In addition, many developed economies have government-subsidized agricultural sectors, and some have subsidized banking and industrial enterprises; there is continuing pressure to improve productivity by eliminating such subsidies.

Microeconomics

Microeconomics is a bottom-up view of the economy, focusing on individual households and firms and the allocation of economic resources through supply and demand. It provides answers to the essential questions of which goods and services to produce, how, in what quantities, and for whom.

The economist and philosopher Adam Smith (1723–90) was the first great exponent of the market system, and his work ultimately led to modern microeconomics. He saw that competitive markets, where individuals pursue their own interests, could achieve the objectives of efficient production and economic growth. In his memorable phrase, the market acted as an "invisible hand" that allocated goods and services and made the economy work.

The economist Alfred Marshall (1842–1924), of Cambridge, developed many of the basic tools of microeconomics, such as the *demand curve*. In 1938 the American economist Abram Bergson (1914–2003) showed mathematically that, with certain assumptions, markets yield an optimal allocation of resources. At the same time, the conceptual foundations of economic analysis were further developed by the Nobel prize–winning economist Paul Samuelson (b. 1915).

The Microeconomic System

In the competitive system central to microeconomics, consumers and producers meet in markets in which, through the self-interested actions of many consumers and producers, the prices and amounts produced of each good and service are determined.

Consumers In microeconomic theory, consumers are people who maximize their happiness through the pursuit of their most desired bundle of goods. This is the concept of what is called *economic man*, someone whose concerns are solely devoted to economic values.

Consumers can be individuals or groups of individuals united in a household; the desires of consumers guide the allocation of resources. Each individual or household begins with its income and its preferences for goods and services, and allocates its resources in the present and future among the choices that are available. Individuals compare their budgets and the prices of each alternative good, examining the utility to them of an extra hamburger versus an extra soda; this helps them decide on the final market basket of goods and services they will purchase.

Consumers' bids for goods and services give rise to the *demand curve*. This is a relationship that shows how many units of a good or service will be demanded at each given price point. There is a demand curve for each product by each consumer, and an aggregate demand curve for the market for each good and service.

Producers Producers are responsible for the production of goods and services. They may be individuals or groups of individuals organized as companies. Many or most producers are also consumers, but in microeconomic theory their actions as producers are analyzed separately from their expenditures as consumers. Producers attempt to maximize the profits from their work; left to their own devices, they have an incentive to dominate markets for their own benefit. It is the existence of competition which keeps small groups of producers from taking control of a market, and which helps to ensure that prices will be at free-market levels and that profits will be at competitive rather than monopolistic levels.

Producers act within the constraints that every society faces: fixed supplies of labor, capital, land, and technology. Although these supplies are fixed at any moment, they are changeable over time (labor may increase or decrease, technology improves) and producers adapt to such changes. By bidding for resources in competitive markets and then combining them in production processes, individuals and companies supply products and services.

Generally speaking, increasing the supply of a good at a point in time can be accomplished only with increasing costs (e.g., using more expensive overtime labor). This yields the *supply curve*, which is the relationship describing the amount that will be supplied by producers at each possible price point. In some circumstances larger production can be accomplished at lower unit costs; this is the phenomenon called *increasing returns to scale*, where production is more efficient as the total amount produced increases.

Markets, Pricing, and the Allocation of Resources The key to the allocation of goods and services in the market is the interplay between demand curves and supply curves. These two curves determine the market price of each good, and thus the amounts of each good produced and the quantity that each consumer receives.

An equilibrium of price and quantity in a market is determined by the decentralized actions of many consumers and producers each acting in his or her own interest; this is the "invisible hand" of Adam Smith. If markets function correctly, they provide an allocation mechanism that does not require any central guidance. The operation of the markets for both inputs and outputs in a society as a whole is the *market system*. Given the distribution of income and skills in a society, if the markets operate fairly and without instances of "market failure," the allocation of resources is the right one.

Natural Monopolies occur when a service is provided most efficiently by a single supplier. Utilities and transportation systems typically have elements of natural monopoly.

For example, having more than one set of railroad tracks

between two points might yield an element of competition; but a single shared set of tracks may be most efficient in terms of resource use. The owners of single sets of tracks, left to their own devices, will tend to maximize their own profits, charging higher prices and providing less transportation than would be supplied in a freely competitive market. The government intervenes by regulating the natural monopoly to ensure that consumers are charged a fair price, similar to what would be achieved in a free market. Government intervention in utilities and transportation has been common, but such intervention carries its own problems of administrative efficiency.

Public Goods are products that benefit everyone, even those who do not pay for them; a standard example is a defense system. If an antimissile system is installed to protect a whole country, no one person has an incentive to pay for it individually, since each person is protected whether or not each pays. A public good is therefore unlike a standard good, such as a hamburger, which we cannot consume unless we pay for it. As a practical matter, then, society as a whole must pay for these public goods by the imposition of taxes.

Tools for Social Policy

To forward these and other noneconomic goals, a society can wield three primary microeconomic tools: regulation, deregulation, and price incentives. These tools can be applied by local or federal governments, or by industrial trade organizations.

Regulation involves government control of pricing, production, or practices in an entire industry. A primary example of microeconomic manipulation by regulation can be found in the agricultural markets. Agricultural policies in the United States and many other countries have been designed to regulate free markets to support the agricultural sector and the ideals of small-family farms and rural life. These policies go back many decades and have taken various forms, all of which interfere with the market equilibrium of demand and supply by such methods as supporting prices (and storing, donating, or selling surplus crops overseas); reducing the amount supplied by paying farmers not to produce; and providing subsidized loans to farmers.

Unfortunately, regulation often has unintended side effects. In the example of agricultural regulation, many of these market interventions have proved costly for the government and consumers as a whole, and have tended to benefit mostly large producers rather than small farms. Moreover, subsidized sales to developing countries, by the U.S. and especially by European countries, have had drastic effects on low-income farmers in the developing countries. As the costs of such market interventions become more widely known (it has been estimated that the average European cow enjoys a subsidy of $2 per day), pressures for deregulation of agriculture are likely to increase; such deregulation increases production and lowers prices for consumers, but could also hurt those farmers who have benefited by controlled markets.

Deregulation is the replacement of a government-regulated market with a free market. A good example of deregulation is the U.S. air transport market. Before 1978, the U.S. Civil Aeronautics Board regulated many aspects of air transport, including routes, fares, and schedules, and chose airlines to serve particular routes. This system, designed for the objective of building an efficient national air transport system, became highly cumbersome and was challenged by free market advocates.

Air transport in the United States was deregulated in 1978, and competition resulted in lower fares, the development of new airline companies, the creation of the hub-and-spoke system of service, and newly differentiated service levels. There have also been some negative effects, such as the loss of air service to some small markets and difficult economic conditions for large traditional airlines (which have high-cost structures compared with low-cost startups). However, the deregulation of air transport is generally regarded as a successful use of microeconomic policy making, and has been copied in Europe and elsewhere.

Price incentives are generally regarded by economists as more efficient than regulation. For example, the long-standing beverage container deposit rewards those who collect and return aluminum, plastic, and glass containers for recycling, thus forwarding a pro-environmental agenda and helping to reduce pollution.

Perhaps the most innovative market method for pollution control, however, has been emissions trading. In this approach, a company that reduces its emission of pollutants below the permitted level can sell a "permit to emit" to another company. The social benefit of this is that the second company can avoid the high costs of controlling its excess emissions, but the total emissions stay within the prescribed limits. It is estimated that billions of dollars have been saved in the United States through trading in air-quality emissions permits, with thousands of transactions among companies. This approach has been approved for international trading in emissions under the Kyoto Protocol to reduce greenhouse gas emissions, and also has been used in other sectors in the United States, such as trading in water use reduction permits in California.

Macroeconomics

Macroeconomics is the top-down study of the economy as a whole: output, employment, price levels, and rate of growth. It provides ways to analyze such issues as levels of output, business cycles, inflation and deflation, short- and long-term unemployment, exports, and economic development.

The Development of Modern Macroeconomics

Economists have long been concerned with financial crises and business cycles, but prior to the 1930's there was no satisfactory understanding of the determinants of an economy's output, employment, and price levels. A common view was that economies naturally tended toward full employment with flexible prices and wages, and that crises tended to be caused by events such as financial panics.

However, the idea of "natural" full employment was hard to accept during the Great Depression of the 1930's. It was during that depression that the modern subject of macroeconomics was born. John Maynard Keynes (1883–1946), in his widely influential book *The General Theory of Employment, Interest, and Money* (1936), was the first to develop an effective theory of employment, output, and interest rates, and to explain how monetary and fiscal policies could be used to achieve full employment. His policy recommendations reversed the received wisdom; at the start of the Great Depression, the U.S. government thought that the best course of action was to reduce expenditures, but in fact the opposite was true—bringing an economy out of depression required an increase in government spending to increase aggregate demand for goods and services.

Measuring a Nation's Economic Output

To measure a nation's economic output more accurately, economists developed the system of *national accounts*. These accounts, the work of Simon Kuznets (1901–85) and other economists, focus on the output of an economy over a given time period.

Gross Domestic Product The most comprehensive and widely used measure of an economy's output is the *Gross Domestic Product* (G.D.P.), defined as the sum of consumption of goods and services, gross investment, government purchases of good and services, and net exports produced within a given country in a specified time period (usually one calendar year).

Economists and government policy planners have come to focus more on G.D.P. than an earlier measurement, *Gross National Product* (G.N.P.). G.N.P., in addition to measuring production within a nation's boundaries, also measured net property income flows from overseas.

G.D.P. measures goods and services that are sold to final purchasers. Intermediate goods, such as the metal, plastic, and composites that are used to make an automobile, are not counted separately—their value is included in the final price of the car. Intermediate goods are tracked in another form of economic analysis, the *input-output* system, developed by Wassily Leontief (1905–99).

G.D.P. and other national income aggregates can be measured in current dollars, or the dollars can be made comparable for different years ("constant dollars") by accounting for the effects of year-to-year price changes. In the U.S. economy, the consumption sector of G.D.P. is by far the largest, followed by government and gross investment (which are similar in magnitude), and net exports, which have been negative in recent years.

National Income The output side of the national income accounts, as measured by G.D.P., is matched by an income side. All output flows result in costs and profits, and outputs will be equal to incomes because of the balancing effect of profits (which can be positive or negative).

There are two primary measures of this income—*national income* (N.I.) and *disposable income* (D.I.). N.I., the total income for factors of production, is equal to G.D.P. minus depreciation and indirect taxes. D.I., the total amount available to households for expenditure, is equal to N.I. minus direct taxes (such as income taxes) and net business savings (the amount of business income not distributed to consumers), plus transfer payments from government (such as Social Security).

These national income accounts are not comprehensive, primarily because some outputs, while important, are difficult to measure. For example, the value of homemaking, which is large, is omitted from all calculations. Another issue is gross investment; ideally, net investment would be used, but figures for depreciation are difficult to estimate and so gross investment (before depreciation) is used instead. In any case, the national income accounts provide a reasonable measure of economic output, and are key determinants of social well-being.

Common Macroeconomic Issues

Macroeconomics is concerned with the level of economic output as expressed in the national accounts systems, the level of employment, price stability, business cycles, trade, and long-term economic development, and how each one of these issues affects economic and social welfare. Various fiscal and monetary policies are used to make an impact on these objectives, and to deal with a variety of common issues.

Output and Employment In the macroeconomic system, consumers, investors, the government, and international trading partners all strive to achieve short- and long-term goals. The interaction of these efforts determines levels of output, employment, and prices.

A key insight of macroeconomics is that there is no automatic equilibrating mechanism to ensure that aggregate demand equals full employment output (i.e., total purchases of goods and services do not always equal total output of goods and services at full employment). To understand this, consider the relationships of disposable income, consumption, saving, and investment. Some earlier economists believed that all income was spent as either consumption or investment, and that there was therefore a tendency toward full employment mediated through flexible prices and wages. However, desired savings and investment are not necessarily equal; the people who save are not the same group as the people who invest, and the decisions of the two groups are made on different grounds. Consumers make decisions that result in the consumption component of G.D.P., and businesses make decisions responsible for the gross investment component. If the saved portion of consumers' disposable income that is available to businesses for investment, when the economy is at full employment, exceeds full-employment investment by businesses, their output will exceed aggregate demand, full employment output will not be sold, profits will drop, and production and employment will fall.

Most macroeconomists also believe that the problem of employment is exacerbated by rigidity (resistance to change) in wages and prices, many of which are set under administered conditions (e.g., labor contracts) rather than free-market conditions. Thus the classical assumption of price and wage flexibility cannot be counted on to ensure full employment.

Employment usually tracks the movement of output fairly consistently: "Okun's Law," named after Arthur M. Okun (1928–80), suggests that for every two percent decline in G.N.P., the unemployment rate rises by about one percentage point. Unemployment estimates are derived from careful random sampling of tens of thousands of households each month. The labor force is considered to be composed of those working and those actively looking for work; those who are not looking for work are considered not to be in the labor force.

The Labor Force The *Labor Force Participation Rate* (L.F.P.R.), often referred to simply as the labor force, is the proportion of the population that is either employed or actively seeking employment. It represents the supply of labor available to the economy. The L.F.P.R. is lower for young people because many are in school, and for older people because many have retired. It is highest for married men and for women who are heads of households. In 2002, 66 percent of the U.S. population was in the labor force (144.8 million people), up from 60 percent in 1970. The increase is the result of many more women entering the work force.

Unemployment rate One of the most closely watched labor force statistics is the unemployment rate, which in 1997 fell below 5 percent for the first time in 30 years. It dropped all the way to 3.9 percent in April 2000, before climbing slowly back to over 5 percent in September 2001. Contrary to popular opinion, the unemployment rate is only an indirect measure of the people without jobs, since it measures only the number of active (within the last four weeks) job seekers as a proportion of the total labor force. So the unemployment rate may rise as new job seekers enter the labor force. Every spring, for example, it rises slightly as school graduates enter the labor force and look for jobs. It may also fall as workers retire or otherwise leave the labor force. And when the economy is in a prolonged recession, the unemployment rate may actually drop slightly because some of the job seekers may give up trying to find a job and withdraw from the labor force.

The unemployment rate over time for the United States is a measure associated with identifying periods of expansion and recession. It reached a peak of 9.6 percent during the recession of 1982–83. The relatively high periods of unemployment beginning in the mid-1970's are in part due to the expansion of the labor force as the baby boom generation left school and began looking for work. Unemployment rates for women have paralleled those for men since 1990.

Productivity measures how much output an economy or organization can generate from a given amount of input. Higher levels of productivity suggest greater efficiency—doing more with the same amount of resources, just as an efficient or economical car goes farther on a gallon of gasoline. Increases in productivity, as the result of better tools or improved methods, provide the main mechanism for increasing output in an economy and ultimately for raising standards of living. Productivity is usually measured in terms of labor—output per worker or per hour of labor—not only because labor is the most important resource but also because it is one of the easiest to measure.

Wages vary not only among the different professions but also between sexes and regions of the country. For example, women in year-round, full-time executive, administrative, and managerial positions have a median yearly income of only 61 percent of the median income for men in the same occupation group. This percentage is higher in the field of laborers, precision production, craft, and repair; but for all major occupation groups reported by the U.S. Bureau of the Census, women receive only a fraction of what is received by their male counterparts. This may be due, in part, to the fact that women enter and leave the workforce more times throughout their lives than men do and spend a smaller percentage of their lives economically active.

Another factor influencing the discrepancy between men's and women's wages is the concentration of women in occupations that pay less. Women made up 98 percent of child care workers and 97 percent of receptionists, two low-paying positions.

The first minimum wage in the nation was enacted by the state of Massachusetts in 1912; it covered only women, and was designed to shorten hours and raise pay in the covered industries. The nationwide minimum wage was established in 1938, and since then has grown in both dollar value and the types of employees it covers. Some states may establish minimum wages higher than the federal minimum.

Prices and Inflation Over time, prices in general can rise, fall, or remain stable. An increase in price levels is known as *inflation*, and a decrease is known as *deflation*; the latter has been uncommon in the U.S. for many decades. Stable prices enable businesses and households to make informed decisions, and prevent the unfairness and hardship that occur when, for example, inflation erodes the value of savings.

Price levels are estimated by means of price indexes, which are average prices over time of a selected mix of goods and services. The most commonly used in the United States are the *Consumer Price Index* (based on goods bought by consumers) and the G.D.P. *deflator* (including consumer goods, investment goods, and government purchases of goods).

When an economy is nearing full employment, there are pressures on price levels. Some economists posit a functional relationship between full employment and inflation, such that society must make a choice between accepting some unemployment or accepting some inflation. The best-known version of this idea is the *Phillips curve*, as espoused by the economist A. W. Phillips (1914–75), a graph believed to represent a trade-off that can be modified by long-term developments such as technological change, which can increase productivity without affecting unemployment.

Forecasts and Business Cycles In looking toward the future, economists make forecasts based on *econometric* methods, statistically derived estimated relationships that are used to project changes in macroeconomic variables over time. Although the future is unknowable, such econometric methods give forecasts that, in retrospect, are considerably better than "naive" forecasts based on simple rules such as "G.D.P. will grow next year by the same percentage that it grew this year."

One use of forecasts is to anticipate the rise and fall of G.D.P. and employment. Business cycles have a long history of analysis in economic literature; there have been many theories of business cycles, including financial panics, external shocks, and internal dynamics of boom and bust. At present, while it is generally accepted that the economy will move up and down over time, there is no single accepted business cycle theory. It is believed that many elements enter into business cycles, including changes in consumer demand, business investment (including inventory) decisions, and various overseas events.

International Trade A *closed economy* is one without international trade; conversely, an *open economy* is one with such trade. Open economies have imports and exports that create the net export component of G.D.P. In open economies, considerations of macroeconomic fiscal and monetary policy must be extended to include internation-

A Way To Break The Cycle Of Servitude

By LOUIS UCHITELLE

Let us remember low-wage workers. Twenty percent of the work force—26 million people—earn $8.23 an hour or less. Most of them are not teenagers snagging pocket money, but adults supporting families. With so little income, too many Americans are pushed into poverty, and getting out of this trap is increasingly difficult.

As many studies have shown, rising income inequality has driven people apart. And low-wage workers, occupying the bottom rung in this ruptured society, have descended into what amounts to a servant class. It is not their work that makes them servants. We need factory assemblers, store clerks, child care workers and the telephone operators who field calls to "800" numbers, processing much of the nation's commerce.

What makes them servants is the miserable pay. Measuring status by wage, as many Americans do, no one—the employers of low-wage worker, the public or the low-wage workers themselves seems to value this class of work. Promotion, or higher pay, would be a way out. Unfortunately, neither solution kicks in very often. More than in the past, low-wage workers are stuck in place.

That path has become self-perpetuating. Employers are under constant pressure to cut costs. Hospitals, for example, have to bid for good medical staffs, so they offset this cost by squeezing the wages of unskilled kitchen workers. Or they outsource food preparation to contractors who pay even less. In either case, the result is a constant, dispiriting turnover. But it is tolerated. The low wage more than offsets the cost of one or two days of training for each new hire.

So wages barely rise. Adjusted for inflation, the $8.23 an hour of 2003 is only 9 percent higher than the $7.55 that the workers in the 20th percentile earned 30 years ago, according to the Economic Policy Institute. All of that improvement came in the very tight labor markets of the late 1990's, when even low-wage workers could command higher pay.

The constant turnover of people in these jobs often leaves the impression that low-wage workers are irresponsible and unambitious. But they might have to quit a job because of a personal crisis—a sick child, for example—because low-wage jobs seldom come with time off to deal with such matters.

Training is a way up the wage ladder, but employers of low-wage workers seldom offer it or give those workers time away from daily tasks. Manpower Inc. offers training, but for jobs that pay $9 an hour and up. Most of the more than 180,000 people that Manpower sends out each day earn at least this wage, but 30 percent draw only $8.50 an hour or less. For them, the instruction is less than respectful. Job readiness, it is called.

Far from lifting these workers, the unfettered American marketplace holds them down. They need help, ideally from employers, if only those employers could find their way back to the pre-1970's system of long-term employment in low-skilled jobs that included training, promotions and raises. In some places, unions still force this to happen—at New York City hospitals, for example—and no hospital is at a disadvantage because each is bound by the same wage scale. But in this era of disappearing unions, that is not likely to work.

Raising the minimum wage would be a quicker route, if only Congress and the administration would make that a priority. The minimum wage once went up regularly, peaking in 1968 at the equivalent of $7.08 an hour today, adjusted for inflation. That's nearly $2 above today's actual minimum of $5.15 an hour. Just restoring the minimum to its old value of $7.08 would also push up wages that are just above the minimum.

Suddenly, the bottom 20 percent of the work force would be making up to $10 an hour, instead of $8.23. That might be a large enough raise to justify training and job security, and new respect for the men and women in these jobs—respect as workers, not servants.

al repercussions. For example, an increase in government spending (fiscal policy) will have a smaller effect if there are imports than if there are no imports, since part of the new spending will be for imports rather than domestically produced goods. Of course, the better off other economies are, the more they will import from the United States.

Long-Term Growth Long-term economic growth is a key objective of most societies, because it provides higher living standards for individuals (see *Development Economics*). The four basic inputs to long-term growth are human resources, natural resources, capital, and technology; the first three were traditionally labeled labor, land, and capital. Whereas earlier economists tended to emphasize the growth of the first three components, in recent decades, thanks in part to the work of Robert Solow (b. 1924) of MIT, much more attention has been paid to the effects of technological change, education, and research on long-term growth.

Fiscal Policy

To address these macroeconomic issues, governments can use either *fiscal* or *monetary* policies. Fiscal policy is typically used to manage output, employment, and prices, and has two main instruments: changes in taxes and changes in government expenditure. It uses the relationships in the economy first analyzed by Keynes, and uses the information developed in the national income accounts as inputs to policy making.

Disposable Income A fundamental element in fiscal policy is the behavioral relationship that governs the use of disposable income. Consumers spend some of their income and save another part. When a consumer receives an extra dollar of income, the amount that the consumer will spend, and not save, is called the *marginal propensity to consume*. This measurement helps to determine the impact of fiscal policy.

Multipliers and Accelerators When the government, as part of fiscal policy, either spends more money or reduces taxes, this increases the disposable personal income of individuals. Individuals expend more on goods and services according to their marginal propensities to consume. But this new consumption adds to other people's personal incomes, and this new personal income again gives rise to consumption.

This chain of events is called the *multiplier*, because the initial increase in income from fiscal policy has a multiplied effect on total consumption (and thus production). The multiplier is greater from government expenditure than from tax reduction; government expenditure is an addition to income, but a tax reduction produces more consumption and partly more savings. Textbooks give simple formulas for the multiplier, but in fact the actual effects in a given time period are complex.

In addition, when consumption goes up, businesses tend to invest more in inventories, plant, and equipment. This increase is the *accelerator* theory of investment, i.e., generation of investment by new consumption.

Government Expenditures versus Tax Policy While government expenditure can increase total demand through the multiplier, in practice it is difficult to time government spending to manipulate employment and output. This is because of the time required to design programs, and the complex process of congressional approval that is required. Tax policy is also effective, but tax changes can also take a long time to implement.

In both cases, there are questions of who should get the spending or the tax decrease in order to have the biggest impact on aggregate demand. There are also issues of fairness in the distribution of spending and tax decreases. It would be possible to make fiscal policy more flexible by giving the government standby authority to change tax rates within strictly defined limits; this approach is not used in the United States, and has the disadvantage that a government could use its flexibility for purposes other than countercyclical fiscal policy.

Another issue with fiscal policy is that financing government spending or tax cuts can require a substantial increase in government indebtedness. This causes distortions of investment in later time periods, because of its upward impact on interest rates. A result of these considerations is that though government occasionally uses fiscal measures, they are not routinely used in the United States for countercyclical purposes.

Monetary Policy

Monetary policy, the other principal part of macroeconomic policy, is designed to influence investment, products, employment, and prices by means of planned changes in the money supply and interest rates. Monetary policy is the primary countercyclical macroeconomic policy in the United States; it is loosened when the economy falters, and tightened when inflation threatens.

Federal Reserve System Monetary policy is implemented through the banking system. In the United States the banking system operates through the Federal Reserve System (the "Fed"), a group of 12 regional banks chartered in 1913. It is governed by a seven-member board of governors, appointed by the president with the consent of the Senate. Because of the importance of monetary policy, the chairman of the board of governors is one of the most important economic officials in the country.

Although legally a corporation owned by the commercial banks that are members of the system, in fact the Fed operates as an independent public agency in the United States. It issues currency, against which it holds interest-bearing government securities, is one of the regulators of the banking system, and controls monetary policy.

Fractional Reserves and the Money Supply The banking system in the United States is a fractional reserve system. Banks are not required to hold all their deposits as reserves; the Fed requires only that banks hold a certain proportion of their obligations as reserves, and the rest can be lent out at interest. For example, if a bank has $100 in deposits and the reserve requirement is 10 percent, then the bank is required to hold only $10 in cash; the remaining $90 can be lent out. The total money supply in the system is defined as the checking accounts in banks plus the currency issued by the Fed.

Open Market Transactions There are three primary types of monetary policy: open market transactions, discount rate, and reserve requirements. These operate within the institutional context of the Fed, the fractional reserve system, and also the public's demand for money as opposed to interest-bearing assets.

Open market transactions, the most important part of monetary policy, are the sale or purchase of government securities by the Fed. The Federal Open Market Committee (FOMC) is composed of the seven governors and five of the regional bank presidents. At its regular meetings the FOMC decides whether economic activity should be restrained or promoted. If the FOMC decides that restraint is called for, it orders the Fed to sell securities; these sales are paid for by funds drawn from banks, which causes the banking system to lose reserves. Because the system is a fractional reserve system, total deposits in the banking system fall by a multiple of the amount of securities sales. This contraction of the money supply raises interest rates, and thus acts to restrain interest-sensitive economic activity such as investment and housing starts. The result is to reduce aggregate demand, and thus reduce inflationary pressure on prices.

Discount Rate Changes In discount rate changes, the Fed raises or lowers the interest rate it charges for short-term loans to member banks (to cover temporary shortfalls in their reserves). This has a direct effect on commercial and consumer interest rates. When the Fed lowers its interest rate, consumer interest rates fall; when the Fed raises its interest rate, consumer interest rates rise. Another tool of the Fed is the *federal funds rate*, the interest rate at which banks borrow from one another, usually overnight, to maintain required reserves. The Fed does not set the federal funds rate—which is a floating rate—but it can set target rates and manage the rate by buying and selling securities. The discount rate and federal funds rate are powerful tools the Fed uses as a part of controlling interest rates generally.

Reserve Requirements The third instrument, changes in reserve ratios (within legally set limits), is rarely used. The intended results can be accomplished by open market policy with much less disruption than would be caused by an abrupt change in reserve ratios.

Monetarism Another approach to monetary policy is called *monetarism*. Monetarists, such as Milton Friedman (b. 1912), believe that the best way to ensure long-run growth is to have a constant, steady increase in the money supply—rather than to try to implement monetary policy in a countercyclical manner through open market transactions or changes in discount rates. This approach depends on the relative constancy of the turnover of money (the *velocity of money*), which has become much less stable then before; for this reason, there has been a steady move away from monetarism.

Rational Expectations Still another perspective on monetary policy is the idea of rational expectations. This view is that if people make unbiased full-information forecasts about the future, they can anticipate policy—and thereby make it less effective. The empirical relevance of this view remains uncertain.

Macroeconomic Challenges in the New World Economy

In an increasingly linked world, macroeconomic policy faces new and more complex challenges of stability, employment, balance of trade, and international equity. The trend is for economies to become more and more open, with the continuous reduction of trade barriers. As a result, domestic fiscal and monetary policy in each country must take into account impacts from outside the national economy. The ramifications of these interconnections are not fully understood; thus there is an additional degree of uncertainty in national economic management. In some cases, notably the European Union, there is an attempt to have multinational, coordinated monetary and fiscal policy.

The new international economy poses particular issues for developing countries. As trade barriers fall, especially with respect to primary products, and as farm subsidies drop, as they will over the long term, there are greater opportunities for developing countries to export. To take full advantage of the new willingness of companies in developed countries to outsource work to developing countries (e.g., software development in India, and call centers in many countries), these developing countries will have to achieve more economic and political stability, and better legal systems to protect investments.

Development Economics

As the Industrial Revolution unfolded, classical economists were increasingly concerned with economic growth. Adam Smith described the "progressive state," in which increasing division of labor would lower the costs of output, increase wealth, and extend markets, which in turn would promote further economic growth. Thomas Malthus (1766–1834) took a dimmer view of the future, contrasting the geometric growth of population with the arithmetic growth of agricultural production, leading to forced reductions of population through war, famine, disease, and "moral restraint." David Ricardo (1772–1823) developed his theory of comparative advantage and free trade, and, unlike Smith, considered that diminishing returns in productivity (increasing investment that results in a smaller increase in output) would lead to a steady state rather than unlimited growth.

This long concern with economic growth was heightened in the aftermath of World War II, and the field of development economics was born. War-damaged Western economies were reconstructed, but it was the economic development of former colonies that became the economic counterpart of their political transformation. Most of the newly independent nations (the so-called third world, by contrast to the first world of the Western allies and the second world of the Soviet bloc) were dependent on agriculture, the export of raw materials, and low-tech industries. If economic development would not occur "naturally," how could it be made to happen in these newly independent countries? Development economics, defined at first as growth in per capita output, attempted to provide answers.

Managing Economic Development

One approach was "balanced growth," advocated by Ragnar Nurkse (1907–59), in which there would be a coordinated application of capital to a range of industries. Albert O. Hirschman (b. 1915), on the other hand, advocated "unbalanced growth" to force decision making and take advantage of local resources that are hidden, scattered, and underutilized. W. W. Rostow (1916–2003) codified growth in a series of stages with the metaphor of a "take-off" into sustained growth. Many early development economists were pessimistic about the role of markets and focused on specific structural changes that might be implemented by government central planning, such as developing local industries whose products would substitute for imports.

On the whole, the general theories of the first generation of development economists had limited success. Government central planning, especially in poor countries, was rife with deficiencies relating to corruption, the immaturity of governmental and commercial institutions, and the unequal distribution of the benefits of growth.

Microanalysis versus Central Planning

In the 1970's, economists and aid organizations tended to focus on alleviating poverty and improving the distribution of benefits, rather than on simply increasing total output. There was a new emphasis on rural development as compared with industrialization; "basic needs" such as water and sanitary facilities; women's roles in development; improvements in human capital; and the use of "appropriate technology" rather than simply borrowing technology from advanced countries. There were also institutional changes in development assistance. The Grameen Bank in Bangladesh (1976), for example, focuses on small loans to groups of poor individuals; because no collateral is required, these loans can serve the landless poor.

Overall, there has been a movement toward microanalysis as compared with grand overarching schemes.

The most important shift in development thinking, beginning in the 1980's, has been toward the emphasis in *neoclassical economics* on the importance of markets and away from structuralist approaches and central planning.

Institutions for Economic Development

Most contemporary analyses of the global economy begin with the assumption that the nations of the world are divided into two basic categories, developed and developing. The developed ones are those with the highest G.N.P. figures, and are characterized by high per capita income and low rates of population growth and illiteracy, as well as having a low proportion of their labor force in agriculture or mining or both.

These wealthy nations are at the center of the global economy and are responsible for promoting international trade, helping to finance development in the poorer countries, and maintaining a stable economic world. They attempt to do this through several multilateral and bilateral institutions that give development advice and assistance to poorer nations.

World Bank The most important of these development institutions is the World Bank (the International Bank for Reconstruction and Development). This is one of the group of institutions founded at the conference of 1944 in Bretton Woods, New Hampshire, to restructure the world financial system after the conclusion of World War II. The World Bank, a specialized agency of the United Nations headquartered in Washington, D.C., lends money for approved development projects in many countries; it also has an affiliate, the International Development Association (IDA), that was set up in 1960 to provide loans on advantageous terms aimed at improving the lot of the poorest people in the poorest countries.

To evaluate specific projects, the World Bank uses the technique of *benefit-cost analysis*; the forecast economic benefits of a proposed project are compared with the costs, and the percentage rate of return on the project is calculated. In principle, the best projects are then undertaken with development aid, to be repaid by the recipients. This technique is still central to development lending, although in recent years it has often been applied in modified ways to take into account such issues as environmental impact and the distribution of benefits.

Other Development Institutions Other international institutions involved in economic development include the Group of Eight (G-8), a loosely knit group of the largest economic powers whose representatives meet once a year to discuss and influence global economic policy; the Organization of Economic Cooperation and Development (O.E.C.D.), a 30-member group formed to promote economic growth, employment, and improved standards of living through the coordination of economic policy; and the International Monetary Fund (I.M.F.), a sister organization to the World Bank charged with making loans to nations having trouble with debt.

On a national level, many countries have specific agencies that provide aid for developing countries. In the U.S. this agency is U.S. Agency for International Development (USAID); there are numerous counterparts among European countries and Japan. During the cold war era, the countries of the Soviet bloc also gave direct aid.

The Impact of Economic Development

Much of the earliest development aid, and a great deal today, was in the area of infrastructure: roads, dams, energy, and other sectors designed to provide the framework for economic development. Unfortunately, in many countries this development aid was often affected by governmental and private corruption and by inadequate institutional structures, with the result that many projects had mixed or negative results. Projects often showed inadequate economic returns, resulted in environmental damage, and produced a highly skewed distribution of benefits—that is, income did not necessarily "trickle down" to help the neediest. On the other hand, many projects were beneficial, and many nations were helped by this developmental aid, especially in Asia but also in some countries of Latin America.

East Asia East Asia is a shining example of developmental success, beginning with Japan (a special case of reconstruction after World War II) and the "four tigers": Hong Kong, Singapore, Taiwan, and South Korea. More recently, China, Indonesia, Malaysia, and Thailand have had developmental successes. While all these countries have been recipients of aid projects, the fundamental causes of their success seem to be high levels of domestic capital formation, widespread schooling (investment in human capital), and relatively stable and supportive commercial and financial institutions.

Africa Failures in development and in development aid are particularly prevalent today in sub-Saharan Africa. Target nations are often complex amalgams of disparate peoples and colonial legacies, and in many cases have modest resource endowments in water and soil. The World Bank has reported that the causes of inadequate development in sub-Saharan Africa include low investment, dependence on aid, poor governance, lack of diversification, inadequate health care, and high fertility rates. Its policies now include attempts to remedy these deficiencies.

Development Economics Today

The *World Bank Atlas* lists 207 individual economies in terms of Gross National Income (G.N.I.) per capita in the year 2000. By the bank's standard (less than $755 in per capita income), 63 of these were classified as low-income countries. Most of these countries are in sub-Saharan Africa, Central Asia, and South Asia. Of an estimated total world G.N.I. of $31.3 trillion, these 63 countries had G.N.I. of $1 trillion, or just 3 percent of world G.N.I. At the same time, the low-income countries had a total population of 2.46 billion, or 41 percent of the world total of 6.06 billion.

These numbers highlight the continuing need for global economic development. Great challenges remain, including globalization, technical change, civil strife, and concern with environmental and distributional impacts. At the same time, there are new opportunities, such as the ability to leapfrog technologies (e.g., the use of cell phones rather than expensive land lines).

Development economics has set aside most of its grand theories and can be expected to focus in the coming years on markets, microanalysis, and a concern for issues in addition to per capita income. These key issues include distribution of benefits, the environment, development for human needs (basic nutrition, sanitation, health care), and participation in the new information economy.

International Economics

International trade takes place because some nations have an advantage in producing certain kinds of products, because they have either a comparative wealth of resources (capital, labor, natural resources) or more efficient production techniques. Even an economy with the most efficient technology has a limit on its resources, and rather than using them to produce a wide variety of products, it tends to concentrate its resources on what it makes most efficiently. It then trades those particular goods for other commodities, importing those that it produces least efficiently. As a result, all countries are better off with this type of international trade; specialization results in the expansion of the total supply of goods, and the cost of acquiring them then falls.

Global Movement of Capital The current interaction among rich and poor economies—aided greatly by the technological revolution—has set in motion an unprecedented global movement of capital from the wealthiest nations to developing ones. Because holders of capital always seek greater returns on their investments, they will put their money in economies that show potential growth; if they own or run corporations, they will look for ways to reduce the costs of manufacturing, especially labor costs, so that they realize a greater profit. When they invest in foreign companies or establish their businesses in foreign nations, the power of capital can rapidly transform the economies of poorer nations while rearranging the patterns of daily life for millions.

The total amount of private capital going overseas (net private capital flows) from the United States, Japan, and the European Union nations to developing countries exploded from $43.9 billion in 1990 to $299 billion in 1997. Over 80 percent of this came in two categories: *foreign direct investment* (the investment by private companies of one nation in the territory of another) and *portfolio investment* (investing in the stocks and bonds of foreign nations).

Exchange Rates Because countries have their own currencies, trade between them also involves exchanging or trading currencies. The exchange rate between currencies represents the ratio at which they can be exchanged or the price of one currency in terms of the other. For example, if the exchange rate between the British pound and the U.S. dollar is $1.50, then one British pound can be purchased at that price.

Before World War I, exchange rates for world currencies were artificially fixed by tying them to a certain amount of gold. Central banks would then buy and sell gold in order to equalize supply and demand for the currencies and maintain the fixed exchange rates. For this reason, the central banks maintained enormous gold stockpiles, like the one the United States had at Fort Knox. Long-term changes in trading relationships and in the demand for various currencies eventually made the fixed exchange rates of the gold standard impossible to support; in 1944

Why Currency Exchange Rates Matter

By HAL R. VARIAN

Imagine living in a world where you had to have yen to buy a TV, renminbi to buy toys, and dollars to buy food. Surprise. That's the world we live in.

Most TV's we buy are manufactured in Japan, most toys come from China, and most of our food is produced in the United States. And by and large, the workers who produce those goods want to be paid in their domestic currency.

When you buy an imported TV with dollars, these dollars are exchanged—by currency traders—for yen, somewhere along the way, to pay the Japanese workers who built the TV.

The basic force determining the exchange rate is supply and demand. If the demand for yen exceeds the supply at the current exchange rate, the cost of yen in terms of dollars will rise; and if supply exceeds demand, it will fall.

If the only reason to buy foreign currency was to use it to purchase foreign goods, international exchange would be quite simple. But people also want to acquire foreign currency to make investments. If America's interest rates are higher than Japan's, Japanese investors will want to buy our bonds to take advantage of those higher rates. To do so, they must first sell yen and buy dollars. This is where things get tricky.

Eventually, those Japanese investors will want to end up with yen. So their expected return, denominated in yen, involves both the rate of interest and the likely movement of exchange rates in the future. This means that the demand for yen will depend not only on the current exchange rate, but also on anticipations of future exchange rates.

The demand for currency to support international trade is fairly predictable, since the short-term trade patterns are reasonably predictable. It's the speculative demand that causes most short-term fluctuations; foreign exchange traders have to make guesses—continually being revised—about the future.

Central banks also intervene in foreign exchange markets, for quite different reasons. The Bank of Japan might decide to sell yen on the foreign exchange market. This would push down the value of yen, making Japanese goods cheaper in dollar terms.

This translates into cheaper TV's and Toyotas, which means Americans keep buying those products, and Japanese factories—and employment—keep humming along.

In recent years the United States has had abnormally low interest rates. As a result, demand for dollars has weakened, making yen more costly, thereby raising the price and reducing sales of those imported TV's.

But to avoid increasing domestic unemployment, the Bank of Japan sold yen, keeping the currency lower than it otherwise would have been. The dollars received in exchange were used to buy Treasury bonds, with the Japanese accumulating $577 billion as of the end of January 2004.

Taiwan and China also bought United States Treasury bonds, trying to keep their currencies from appreciating against the dollar.

But the Japanese economy seems to be recovering, and the Chinese economy is overheating. This suggests that these two financial powerhouses will cut back on their purchases of dollars, pushing the value of the dollar down relative to their own currencies.

On the other hand, American interest rates are also increasing. As the economy recovers, the Fed will push rates up, making United States bonds more attractive, which will tend to push the value of the dollar up.

So will the dollar go up or down?

Many experts think the foreign exchange interventions of the last several years have maintained the dollar's value at an unnaturally high level.

Maybe. But by how much? And if it is overvalued, how rapidly will it fall? In one scenario, the dollar has a steady decline against the renminbi and the yen; the Chinese economy has a soft landing; the Japanese recovery persists; and the American economy has a healthy recovery.

In a less rosy scenario, the dollar drops precipitously; prices of imported goods shoot up here, rekindling inflation; the Japanese economy falters; and unemployed Chinese workers riot.

Keep your eye on those exchange rates. They have a lot to do with America's recovery and the health of the world economy.

the Bretton Woods agreement established the U.S. dollar as the world standard.

Today, the exchange rate of a currency rises or appreciates when the demand for it rises or the supply falls, or both. This may happen because foreign buyers want to buy more of a nation's goods or because consumers within the country decide to buy fewer imports. It may also happen because the country reduces its money supply. In addition, the central banks of countries can manipulate their exchange rates slightly by buying and selling their own and other currencies.

Balance of Trade When a country imports goods from another country worth more than the value of its exports to that country, there is said to be a deficit in the balance of trade between the countries. The balance of trade is an important issue because it indicates something about how a nation's economy is changing and, ultimately, about its competitiveness vis-à-vis other countries. A rising balance-of-trade deficit indicates that an economy is not able to sell its goods abroad and that consumers are favoring imports over domestically produced goods.

In the 1990's, when the global economy grew increasingly robust, the U.S. trade deficit climbed from $19.4 billion in 1990 to $164 billion in 1998. The entire U.S. trade deficit is traditionally in the manufactured goods sector; the United States runs a small surplus in the services sector. Its exports of goods have not kept up with imports, in part because the strength of the dollar makes its goods more expensive for foreign nations to buy, while people in the U.S. have more money to spend on cheaper imports.

Tariffs and Quotas One way to protect a country's own producers, especially when they are inefficient compared with the international competition, is with import tariffs—taxes on goods that are produced abroad. Import tariffs raise the price of imports relative to domestic alternatives and discourage demand for the former. If one country is the sole importer or even the main importer of another's exports, it is possible that an import tariff will simply force the exporter to cut its selling price (in order to keep the price to consumers—including the tariff—from rising sharply and cutting off demand). If, on the other hand, the importer badly needs the import and there are few substitutes, raising the tariff simply raises the costs to one's own consumers.

Import quotas attempt to achieve a restriction on imports without the price rises associated with tariffs, by setting direct limits on the number of items imported. So-called trade wars start when one country imposes a tariff on imports from a second country, and the latter responds with tariffs of its own against the first country.

Free Trade The arguments about the benefits of trade have led to efforts to restrict the use of tariffs and maintain free trade, i.e., trade without any restrictions. Economists argue that unrestricted trade will always promote economic growth by forcing domestic prices to reflect world prices, thereby encouraging the efficient allocation of resources.

Over the last 50 years—i.e., since the end of World War II—many of the leading nations have made a strong and continuous effort to lower or eliminate tariffs, first regionally, then around the world. The most successful regional organization has been the European Union, which has encouraged the formation of many other such alliances in all parts of the world. Chief among these alliances are the General Agreement on Tariffs and Trade (GATT) and its successor organization, the World Trade Organization (W.T.O.).

GATT and the W.T.O. The General Agreement on Tariffs and Trade was first established in 1948, in an attempt to regulate world trade. The representatives of 23 leading nations agreed to find ways to lower tariffs, lower quotas, and make free trade their final goal. Over a period of almost 50 years the most important trading nations met regularly to discuss specific trade matters and to continue to remove restrictions from trade; each series of negotiations (called a "round") lasted several years.

By 1975 tariffs on manufactured goods had been reduced from 40 percent to 10 percent and world trade more than tripled. By the 1980's, however, the nature of world trade had changed. In 1986 the so-called Uruguay Round of GATT (now with 92 nations represented) addressed these and other issues over a period of eight years. The results—lowering of tariffs of all kinds, banning quotas, and protecting copyrights and patents—have been projected to add $500 billion annually to the global economy.

The most important accomplishment of the GATT Agreement in 1994 was the establishment of the World Trade Organization, a permanent institution with real power to oversee trade agreements, enforce trade rules, and settle disputes. When it was approved by the U.S. Congress on January 1, 1995, the organization became a reality, with 110 members. By 2004 there were 147 members, including China. The basic principles of the W.T.O. are the encouragement of fair competition and increased access to markets.

Glossary of Economic Terms

accelerator relationship between a change in demand and the subsequent change in investment.

advanced economies as defined by the International Monetary Fund, the seven largest countries by G.D.P., all the other members of the European Union, the four "tigers" of Asia (Singapore, South Korea, Hong Kong, and Taiwan), Australia, New Zealand, and Israel.

aggregate demand total demand for goods and services from consumers, business, government, and international trade in a given time period.

aggregate supply total amount of goods and services that producers willingly produce in a given time period.

business cycles upward and downward movements of an economy's output, incomes, and employment over a period of time, usually several years.

capitalism method of amassing wealth by investment in capital; a capitalist invests money in an enterprise with the objective of receiving more in return than what was initially invested.

cartel combination of producers designed to raise prices and control a market.

closed economy economy without international trade.

command economy economy in which decisions about production and distribution are made by government rather than by markets.

competition the existence of many consumers and producers in a given market, so that no one consumer or producer is able to substantially affect prices.

Consumer Price Index (C.P.I.) estimator of the change in overall prices of goods purchased by consumers; it is an index of price changes for a selected market basket of goods.

consumer's surplus difference between what a consumer in a competitive market pays for a given quantity of goods at the market price and the amount that the consumer would be willing to pay if required to by an all-or-nothing offer from a single supplier.

deflation sustained drop in the general price level in the economy.

demand and supply the two sides of a market, representing desires to purchase and willingness to supply goods and services, that determine the prices and quantities of goods and services.

demand curve relationship that shows the amount of a good or service demanded at each price.

developing countries as defined by the International Monetary Fund, the burgeoning economies of China, India, Brazil, and Chile, as well as the poorest nations of sub-Saharan Africa (Mozambique, Ethiopia, and Niger, for example) and Asia (Bangladesh, Cambodia, Vietnam).

diminishing returns in productivity concept that increasing investment results in smaller increases in output.

disposable income (D.I.) national income (N.I.) minus direct taxes (such as income taxes) and net business savings, plus transfer payments from government.

disposable personal income income after personal tax and nontax payments; this is the income available for spending and saving.

duopoly market in which there are only two suppliers.

Employment Cost Index (E.C.I.) measures the rate of change in total employee compensation (wages, salaries, employer cost for employee benefits) in nonfarm private industry and in state and local governments. Provided quarterly by the Bureau of Labor Statistics, the E.C.I. has become one of the most closely watched indexes because any significant rise could signal an inflationary trend.

exchange rate ratio at which two currencies can be exchanged, or the price of one currency in terms of the other. For example, if the exchange rate between the British pound and the U.S. dollar is $1.50, then one British pound can be purchased at that price.

externalities effects of the actions of consumers and producers that affect others outside of, or external to, markets.

factor prices prices for inputs in the production of a good or service, such as land, labor, and capital.

factors of production inputs to the production process, including land, labor, and capital.

fiscal policy use of government expenditure and taxes to influence output and employment.

foreign direct investment (F.D.I.) investment by private companies of one nation in the territory of another nation. The investment can be in an existing enterprise of the host nation or the building of new facilities for the investing foreign company (which would then be known as a multinational enterprise).

free trade trade between two or more countries unhindered by any governmental restrictions, such as tariffs or quotas.

G.D.P. deflator price index used to convert G.D.P. from

different years into constant dollars. Also called the *implicit price deflator*.

General Agreement on Tariffs and Trade (GATT) as first established in 1948, an attempt to regulate the world's trade by lowering tariffs and quotas, with the goal of establishing global free trade.

gross investment total investment in an economy, not adjusted for depreciation. It is a component of G.D.P. and G.N.P.

Gross Domestic Product (G.D.P.) measure of the output of production attributable to all factors of production (labor and property) physically located within a country. G.D.P. excludes net property income from abroad (such as the earnings of U.S. nationals working overseas), which is included in the G.N.P.

Gross National Product (G.N.P.) total national output of goods and services valued at market prices. G.N.P. measures the output attributable to the factors of production—labor and property—supplied by a country's residents, with allowances for depreciation and for indirect business taxes (sales and property taxes).

Group of Eight (G-8) loosely knit group of the largest economic powers whose representatives meet once a year to discuss policy in what has become a well-publicized media event. Members include Canada, France, Germany, Italy, Japan, Russia, the U.K., and the United States. Originally the Group of Seven (G-7), without Russia.

inflation sustained rise in the general price level in the economy.

input-output table comprehensive system for tracking flows of intermediate and final goods in an economy during a given time period.

International Monetary Fund (I.M.F.) a specialized agency of the United Nations charged with making loans to nations having trouble with debt.

joint stock company company in which investors pool their money and receive profits or dividends in proportion to their investments. Often are limited-liability in that investors are liable only for any debts in the amount of their original investments.

leading economic indicators composite of 10 economic statistics, published by the U.S. Department of Commerce, Bureau of Economic Analysis, that are said to "lead" economic trends because their numbers change months in advance of a change in the general level of economic activity.

liquidity extent to which an asset can be converted quickly to cash, with little loss in value.

M1 the Fed's original and most commonly reported measure of the money supply, which embraces currency and coins, demand deposits, traveler's checks, and other checkable deposits.

M2 as measured by the Fed, M1 plus money-market accounts, and savings and small time-deposits.

M3 as measured by the Fed, M2 plus money-market mutual-fund balances held by financial institutions, term repurchase agreements and term Eurodollars, and large time-deposits.

macroeconomics study of large-scale or general economic factors; a country's total economic activity.

marginal analysis approach, characteristic of microeconomics, of examining the costs and benefits of purchasing and producing increments of inputs and outputs to reach decisions about production and consumption.

marginal propensity to consume the fraction of a dollar of additional income that consumers will spend.

market system economic system in which markets determine the allocation of resources and the goods and services produced.

Marxism economic theory based on the work of Karl Marx that postulated class struggle, the eventual decline of capitalism, and its replacement by rule of the proletariat through a centrally planned economy.

mercantilism economic system prevalent in medieval and early modern times, the result of a concerted effort to establish a centralized economic unity and political control that included protectionism of a nation's businesses.

microeconomics study of economic factors affecting individual consumers and firms.

monetarism doctrine that the best way to ensure long-run economic growth is to have a continual, steady increase in the money supply, rather than to try to implement monetary policy in a countercyclical manner.

monetary policy policy undertaken by the central bank to influence interest rates, investment, and output through open market operations, changes in the discount rate, and changes in reserve requirements.

money income income received before payments for such things as personal income taxes, Social Security, union dues, and Medicare. Money income does not include income in the form of noncash benefits such as food stamps, health benefits, and subsidized housing.

monopoly market in which there is only one supplier.

multiplier total amount by which a given change in government expenditure or taxes will raise or lower total income.

neoclassical economics movement in the late 19th century and early 20th century that relates prices to the allocation of resources and uses advanced mathematics to derive models.

national income (N.I.) G.D.P. minus depreciation and indirect taxes.

national income accounts system of accounts that measures total output and its components per time period.

natural monopoly market condition resulting when a service is provided most efficiently by a single supplier.

net exports difference between total exports and total imports; a component of G.D.P.

North American Free Trade Agreement (NAFTA) as enacted in 1994, an agreement to remove all barriers to trade among the three signatory nations (Canada, Mexico, and the United States).

oligopoly market in which there are only a few suppliers, less than the number required to ensure competition.

open economy economy that engages in trade with other countries.

open market operations purchases and sales of Treasury obligations to influence the money supply and thus interest rates and investment.

personal income current income received by persons from all sources minus their personal contributions for social insurance.

Phillips curve curve showing the relationship between percentage unemployment and percentage rate of inflation.

portfolio investment investing in the stocks and bonds of foreign nations.

poverty level estimate of the income necessary to purchase what society defines as a minimally acceptable standard of living; classification is based on the poverty index originated by the Social Security Administration in 1964 (revised in 1969 and 1980). In 2002 a family of four with income less than $18,100 lived below the poverty level.

present value the value today of an asset; determined by applying an interest (discount) rate to future streams of income and costs to calculate their value at present.

Producer Price Index (P.P.I.) measurement of average changes in prices received by producers of all commodities, at all stages of processing, produced in the United States.

producer's surplus difference between the costs of production of a quantity of a good or service, and the amount actually received in a competitive market by the producer.

production function relationship between combinations of factor inputs and varying levels of output.

socialism economic system that focuses on government or collective ownership of the means of production.

supply curve function showing the amount of a good or service that producers are willing to supply at each price.

trade deficit occurs when a country imports goods from another country worth more than the value of its exports to that other country.

velocity of money speed with which money circulates, defined as G.N.P. in current dollars divided by the supply of money.

World Bank agency of the United Nations charged with encouraging and funding long-term growth and development among poorer nations.

BUSINESS

A Brief History of Business

Most histories of business start out with the premise that business began with the advent of money and the end of the barter system. Many ancient civilizations therefore had a primitive business model with goods and services being sold for what we would call cash. Trade among various cultures was also a feature of the ancient world, dating back as far as the third millennium B.C. in Egypt. The Phoenecians, Greeks, and Carthaginians all created wealthy and powerful trading states during the first millennium B.C.; the Roman Empire built much of its dominance of the Mediterranean world on its continuous contact with other cultures and used its armies to help enforce good trading terms with client states.

With the decline of the empire in the fifth and sixth centuries, barter returned throughout much of Europe until the 12th and 13th centuries, when the city-states of Italy (Venice and Genoa among others) brought about a tremendous resurgence of trade on the Mediterranean. By the time the great age of exploration arrived in the late 15th century, the business of foreign trade, whether founded by monarchies or pools of investors, had been well established.

The seven northern provinces that formed the Dutch Republic were flexible enough to respond to these international market conditions; by the middle of the 17th century the Dutch were the supreme economic power, and Amsterdam was the world's leading financial and commercial center. This balance of power shifted by the beginning of the 18th century, when Britain led the world into an industrial revolution; this is the point when the history of modern business can be truly said to have begun.

The Industrial Revolution

In the late 17th and 18th centuries, economic power grew fastest in Great Britain. It arose from a proliferation of inventions, the availability of capital, a relatively fluid social order, a rising and mobile population, a responsive legal system, a government with power divided between the king and parliament, and an entrepreneurial spirit that was shared by all of the social classes. These factors—collectively called the Industrial Revolution—produced a profound change in the nature of commerce and business.

Inventions Beginning in the 18th century, the pace of invention began to quicken as industrialization created unprecedented opportunities for wealth—and a powerful incentive for invention. The invention of the process of invention during the period of industrialization has been called the most important invention of all.

One of the inventions that drove the Industrial Revolution was the steam engine. Before the 17th century, there were essentially four means of applying power to do work: humans (pushing, lifting, carrying), animals (pulling plows, transporting people), wind (powering sailing ships and windmills), and water (turning water wheels). The steam engine changed all this, providing a reliable source of power that could be used in many of the new industries that were being developed at the time.

The first commercially successful steam engine was developed by Thomas Newcomen (1663–1729) and first used in 1712. Newcomen's primitive engine was improved upon by James Watt (1736–1819), who produced a more efficient engine using rotary mechanics. Thanks to Watt's steam engine, factories were liberated from water wheels and built closer to their sources of supply; ships could move in all directions, no longer dependent on the direction of the wind or the currents. The steam engine also made possible a critical new mode of transportation—the railroad.

Transportation The invention of the steam engine also made possible steam-powered ships that could travel to their destination more directly than sailing ships, reducing the time and costs of voyages. Now goods that moved along the railroads to port cities moved overseas on steamships, creating a vast flow of commerce between trading nations.

One of the reasons that Britain's industrialization moved at the pace it did was the availability of cheap transportation. From the 17th to the 19th centuries, Parliament passed a number of acts that facilitated the construction of roads, canals, and railroads.

In 1829 George Stephenson (1781–1848) and his son Robert (1803–59) successfully demonstrated a steam locomotive that traveled on iron rails. In 1830 it was adopted by the Liverpool and Manchester Railway and immediately put Britain ahead of the rest of the world in a form of transportation that was even cheaper than shipping by canals. Thereafter no country that aspired to industrialization could succeed without a network of railroads to carry the goods.

The Factory System The first important industry to undergo profound changes during the Industrial Revolution was the textile industry, which was transformed by a series of inventions. Prior to 1700, most of the processes used to turn raw cotton or wool into fabrics were performed by hand, often by people working at home. During the 18th century, machines replaced human beings in all of the essential processes. This caused the cost of production to drop over time; merchants were able to sell fabric at lower prices, thus finding a mass market for their products.

The change from small groups of widely dispersed workers to mechanized processes performed under one roof signaled the birth of the modern factory. Factories provided employment to hundreds of thousands of workers who otherwise would have found no employment or means of survival, although conditions in the factories and settlements where the workers lived were often deplorable. And although Britain had a social system based on class, it did not prevent entrepreneurs of the lower classes from rising to become factory supervisors, managers, and owners.

Industrialization Spreads to Europe As Britain was expanding under industrialization, it not only traded with European countries but also was a party—sometimes reluctantly—to the transfer of technologies and ideas to the continent. European countries paid British engineers to help them establish new industrial enterprises; they hired British workers to come and work for them, and—as they imported the goods of British industry—they learned how the goods were manufactured. They even were the beneficiaries of British investment in some of their enterprises. Investors thus had an incentive to transfer ideas and technologies to receptive European countries. The more forward-looking of the continental countries made full use of these advantages.

Germany In 1850 Germany was a politically diverse group of rural and agrarian states. Though it was slow to industrialize, Germany eventually enabled its nobility to engage in commerce, abolished the guilds and other obstacles to industry, and provided trained workers from schools that were the first modern educational system. As Germany's states unified, they formed a tariff union (*Zollverein*) that eliminated tolls and customs and allowed trade to flow freely within its borders. To tie these areas together, the country built a network of railroads similar to the one that played such an important role in Britain's industrialization.

The country was also rich in resources, especially coal; it was also aggressive in developing its iron production capability. Germany was quick to adopt the new refining methods being used elsewhere, and by 1895 its steel output surpassed Britain's. Germany ultimately excelled in industries that were fostered by its many fine universities. It came to dominate the field of chemistry and it made important advances in the production and applications of electricity.

France As early as the late 18th century, France realized that industrialization would play a leading role in economic growth. In 1794, the country established the first institution of higher learning devoted to science and technology, the École Polytechnique. In 1829, a private applied engineering school, École Centrale des Arts et Manufactures, was established. French engineers developed sophisticated weaving machines, notably the Jacquard loom, named for its developer, J. M. Jacquard (1752–1834).

Measured by industrial output against population, France was close to Britain and Germany. But in absolute growth, it lagged behind and never caught up, owing in part to slow population growth, slow urbanization, a succession of wars, a reliance on water power, the small size of its enterprises, and the scarcity of coal. France's weak industrial capability was obvious during World War I.

Industrialization in the United States

In 1800 the United States was a new nation struggling to define itself; by 1900 it had the largest economy in the world and was the world's leading industrial nation. America's extraordinary economic growth during the 19th century is probably the most important business story in history.

The country, even before westward expansion, was vast in comparison with its population. There was abundant fertile land on which to grow food and other useful crops such as cotton. Natural resources were also abundant, in the form of wood, coal, iron and copper ores, and oil.

But America's greatest resource was its people. A high birth rate provided most, but not all, of the rapidly growing population. Added to this were waves of immigrants who were ambitious, energetic, skilled, and entrepreneurial, eager to put their talents to work in the opportunities that the new country afforded. The first United States census in 1790 enumerated fewer than 4 million inhabitants; by 1870 there were almost 40 million inhabitants

This rapidly growing population not only supplied labor to industry but was also a growing pool of customers for the products of that industry. But even with this rapid population growth, there was a constant shortage of workers; agriculture and industry simply grew faster than the population.

The country's chronic labor shortage had two salutary effects on the growth of business and commerce. The first was that wages rose, attracting both native workers and ambitious and talented immigrants. The other was that agriculture and industry compensated for scarce workers by adopting and developing new technologies to increase productivity. By 1830—a surprisingly early date—productivity in the United States exceeded that of Great Britain.

Transportation Constructing roads, canals, and railroads to connect the vast expanses of the North American continent required vast amounts of capital. The federal government did not have the financial resources to pay for transportation projects as public works, so it was up to the states and the private sector—including investors from abroad—to find most of the money. This created opportunities for visionaries to build the arteries of commerce—and, at the same time, create great wealth for themselves.

Canals During the 18th century and the early 19th, water transportation was less expensive than land transportation—especially after the introduction of steam power. The existing rivers were soon supplemented and connected by systems of canals. The longest of these canals, and the one that inspired a wave of imitators, was the Erie Canal. The governor of New York state, DeWitt Clinton (1769–1828), understood the potential of connecting the Eastern seaboard with what was then the interior of the country. He pushed through the state legislature an authorization for $7 million to build a canal from Albany on the upper Hudson River to Buffalo on Lake Erie—a distance of 363 miles. It was one of the great engineering and construction projects of the century. After overcoming many obstacles, the canal opened in 1825 to great success. Soon many states and localities had built their own canals and created a web of water transportation.

Railroads America's canals were soon displaced by an even more economical means of transportation—the railroad. The building of the nation's railroad system required enormous amounts of capital. Fortunes were made by entrepreneurs who could combine building with financing—although it was sometimes difficult to distinguish between the builders and scoundrels. The first great railroad entrepreneur was Cornelius Vanderbilt (1794–1877). He began to invest in the stock of eastern railroad companies in the 1840's; by the time of his death he controlled railroads that stretched from New York City to Chicago.

The watershed achievement of railroad building in the 19th century was the completion of the first transcontinental railroad. As the nation expanded westward it clearly needed a rail connection to California. In 1862, President Abraham Lincoln signed the Pacific Railway Act that authorized the Union Pacific to build west from Omaha and the Central Pacific to build east from Sacramento until they met at a still undetermined location. On May 10, 1869, the two lines celebrated their linking-up in Promontory Point, Utah, northwest of Salt Lake City.

Although Thomas Clark Durant (1820–85) was president of the Union Pacific, Oakes Ames (1804–73) received much of the credit for building the Union Pacific Railroad to meet the Central Pacific. It was Ames and his brother Oliver who invested their money to fund construction of the Union Pacific part of the transcontinental railroad.

On the opposite coast, the Central Pacific was a joint enterprise operated by men who became known as "the Big Four," outsize personalities who collaborated to build the western half of the transcontinental railroad. The key figure was Collis Potter Huntington (1821–1900), who, along with Mark Hopkins (1813–78), Charles Crocker (1822–88) and Leland Stanford (1824–93), incorporated the Central Pacific Railroad. Their construction company was later investigated by the government when it was revealed that it had been paid approximately twice as much as its part of the construction should have cost.

Following that first meeting of the tracks at Promontory Point, several other transcontinental lines were laid, as well as many other trunk and feeder lines. As early as 1840 the total mileage of American railroads was 4,510—exceeding the total mileage of Britain and continental Europe combined.

Inventors Inventions and innovations had been essential to industrialization in Britain and Europe—and it was the same in the United States.

Textiles American manufacturers were eager to learn about advances in technologies in their industries, and offered bounties, high pay, and advancement as inducements to ambitious Europeans willing to emigrate. One of the most influential of these immigrant inventors was Samuel Slater (1768–1835), who had apprenticed in Britain with Jedediah Strutt (1726–97), developer of the first water-powered spinning machine. In 1789 Slater immigrated to the United States, where he engaged in a series of ventures to build water-driven spinning machines. He continued to develop textile manufacturing technology and was a major innovator in the development of the American factory system.

Steamships A number of inventors contributed to the development of a reliable steam-powered shipping industry. The most important was Robert Fulton (1765–1815); in August 1807 his boat, the *Clermont*, made a test run from New York to Albany. Fulton proved the practicality of steamboat travel the following year when his rebuilt boat began weekly trips between the two cities.

The "American System" of Manufacturing A number of inventors working in different industries developed manufacturing processes that, taken together, were more important than the products they manufactured. This came to be known as the "American System"—special-purpose machines and standardized work processes that resulted in repetitive tasks that could be performed rapidly by relatively unskilled workers. This system gave American industry a competitive edge in the growing world economy.

Eli Whitney (1765–1825) is best known for inventing the cotton gin, the machine that separated cotton seeds from cotton fiber. It revolutionized textile production, but it was widely pirated, and Whitney never realized the wealth that should have been his. He also developed a precision process to make uniform parts that could be assembled interchangeably into finished guns—an achievement that was arguably as important as the cotton gin.

Another important contributor to the "American System" was Cyrus Hall McCormick (1809–84) , who developed the grain reaper. This invention not only increased agricultural productivity—releasing surplus farm workers for growing industry—but also refined the efficiency of the manufacturing processes.

Thomas Edison The most prolific inventor of all was Thomas Alva Edison (1847–1931), who differed from earlier inventors by using a sustained and organized invention process. In 1876, he combined his research laboratory with his manufacturing facility. From then until his death in 1931, he worked tirelessly to produce a steady flood of commercially viable products.

General Electric The model for institutionalizing innovation was established by Charles Proteus Steinmetz (1865–1923), who fled Germany for New York in 1889, and obtained employment with an electrical equipment company. He soon founded his own laboratory, which in 1892 was acquired by the General Electric Co.. In 1900 General Electric organized the first modern industrial research laboratory, and the following year it promoted Steinmetz to chief consulting engineer.

Other companies, including DuPont, Corning Glass, Parke-Davis pharmaceuticals, and Eastman Kodak, soon had their own research laboratories, which would be the source of countless new products and processes over the coming years.

Communications If commerce were to flourish in a county as large as the United States, there needed to be not only a large and efficient transportation system but also a way to speed communication between far-flung areas. Initially, mail was conveyed by railroad; the Railway Mail Service was established in 1869 as a separate branch of the Post Office Department. But faster communications were needed—and, during the first half of the 19th century, a number of inventors in Europe and the United States worked on the problem of transmitting messages by means of electricity.

The Telegraph Samuel Finley Breese Morse (1791–1872) believed that the flow of electricity could be made visible and that "intelligence" could be transmitted by wires across distances. He and other experts constructed a machine that transmitted electrical impulses through a wire that then drove another device at the other end to inscribe a series of dots and dashes on a moving strip of paper. Morse devised a code of dots and dashes for the letters of the alphabet. The system thus permitted messages to be sent almost instantaneously between two points.

On May 24, 1844, the message, "What hath God wrought," flashed from the nation's capital to Baltimore and then back again. This was the beginning of the telegraph system and the coding that became known as "Morse Code." Morse's company, the Morse Electromagnetic Telegraphy Co., licensed his patent; the Western Union Telegraph Co. ultimately came to dominate long-distance telegraphic communications.

The Telephone If words could be transmitted by code, inventors soon realized that the voice itself might be transmitted, as well. Alexander Graham Bell (1847–1922) developed a system that converted sound waves to a varying current of electricity. His father-in-law, Gardner Greene Hubbard (1822–1897), submitted Bell's patent application on February 14, 1876. It was granted on March 7, 1876; some have called it the single most valuable patent in history. In 1877 Hubbard headed a group that formed the Bell Telephone Company (later renamed American Bell), although Bell ultimately lost interest in further developing the technology.

The Telephone System In 1880 Theodore Newton Vail (1845–1920) was hired to be the first general manager of American Bell. Vail envisioned linking all of the phones in the United States into one system. He started by persuading a potential competitor, Western Union, not to enter the telephone business, and he then acquired a controlling interest in Western Electric to provide technology and equipment for his countrywide network.

In 1907 as head of American Telephone and Telegraph (a wholly owned subsidiary of American Bell), Vail successfully fought and bought out most of his competitors. He realized, however, that the monopoly he was creating would be vulnerable to government antitrust action. To forestall such action, he proposed a regulatory commission to monitor AT&T's business, ceased acquiring competitors, and agreed to connect his long-distance lines with any local independent operator that wanted to be a part of the system. In return, the government agreed not to bring antitrust actions against the company.

The agreement lasted until 1974, when the U.S. Justice Department filed an antitrust suit against AT&T—"Ma Bell"—which was then the world's largest company. The company split itself into pieces, separating its long-distance and regional phone operations. The breakup launched competition within the telephone industry, and eventually the telecommunications revolution.

Entrepreneurs and Financiers Industrialization and the growth of the American economy in the 19th century created opportunities for many ambitious and talented entrepreneurs to become extraordinarily wealthy. Along with their wealth came power—the power to shape industries, and even the power to affect government.

John Pierpont Morgan (1837–1913) played a central role in shaping the course of American industrialization. He established his own investment bank, J. P. Morgan & Co., in 1861. The railroad boom was on, and railroads required huge amounts of capital that Morgan began to provide. Morgan's investment reach also extended to other industries; he underwrote Edison's incandescent light, invested in Edison's power generation and distribution plants, and in 1892 financed the creation of General Electric. His greatest achievement in industrial finance was the creation of the United Steel Corp., the largest industrial company in the world.

Andrew Carnegie (1835–1919) began investing at the age of 22, and established an iron works company in 1864. He used these early investments to create an empire of iron and steel. He relentlessly sought ways to reduce the costs of production by gaining control of the entire process from mining the ore, transporting it to the plants, buying the coke to convert the ore, and then processing it with the latest technology. At the same time, he bought out competitors and combined them into an ever-larger empire.

In early 1901 Carnegie sold his company to J. P. Morgan for the then unheard-of price of $480 million. Morgan combined Carnegie's company with his own to form the United States Steel Co.

John Davison Rockefeller (1839–1937) entered the refining business in 1863—four years after the first oil well was drilled at Titusville, Pennsylvania, giving birth to the American petroleum industry. Cleveland soon became a major refining center, but Rockefeller disliked the disorderly and fragmented industry and moved to bring order to it. In 1870 he organized the Standard Oil Company; his strategy was to buy smaller companies and combine them into a company large enough to exert control over the market. By the end of 1872 Standard Oil had bought 34 competitors and controlled almost all of the refining companies in Cleveland; by 1879 the company controlled 90 percent of America's refining capacity

In its search for a way of legally organizing its large and diverse business, the company tried a number of organizational structures. In 1882 it created the first modern trust in American history, the Standard Oil Trust in Ohio. But the Ohio attorney general brought suit against the trust, and in 1892 the Ohio Supreme Court annulled the charter. The company then moved the trust to New Jersey and renamed itself Standard Oil (New Jersey). By this time the company owned an estimated three-fourths of all of the petroleum business in the United States.

The passage of the Sherman Antitrust Act of 1890 intensified attention on the giant company, and it was constantly fighting efforts to break it up and limit its power. Court battles with the company continued until a Supreme

Court antitrust decision of May 15, 1911, dissolved Standard Oil Trust and reorganized it into 38 companies.

The Birth of Marketing

Industrialization not only created opportunities for mass production, but also led to the development of mass markets—and mass marketing.

Mass Marketing Before the Industrial Revolution, products were mostly handcrafted and sold on a one-to-one basis to customers. The mass production of consumer goods enabled retailers to sell quantities of similar products to a larger base of customers. Selling to mass markets required companies to communicate to all of their potential customers. Advertising, a small and scattered industry, began transforming itself into a sophisticated group of comparatively large companies.

Retail Merchandisers The 19th century brought the ascendancy of merchandisers that combined distribution with mass marketing. The growing urban population provided a concentrated market for John Wanamaker (1838–1922), who saw an opportunity to create a new kind of store—the department store—that offered a wide variety of wares under a single roof.

Wanamaker opened his first store in 1861. From the beginning he worked to build customer loyalty, and in 1868 he opened a second store and renamed the company John Wanamaker & Co. He wrote and bought advertising that proclaimed his policies: a full guarantee on all merchandise, one price for all, payment in cash, and a cash refund if the customer was not satisfied. The primary brand image was the store, and customers flocked to a store with a name they had come to trust.

A different segment of the market beckoned to Frank Winfield Woolworth (1852–1919). In 1878, Woolworth was working in a store in Watertown, N.Y., when he helped to create a new five-cent counter. He grasped the potential of the idea of eliminating skilled, expensive clerks and replacing them with low-paid women clerks. The following year, 1879, Woolworth tested his idea with his first store in Utica, N.Y., but it failed because of a poor location. That same year he opened a similar store in Lancaster, Pa., that was an immediate success.

Despite early setbacks, Woolworth persevered and continued to expand. Selling many low-priced products, he relentlessly looked for low-cost merchandise, including toys, ornaments, and glass goods from Europe. In 1900 he began to build a strong brand identity by creating a uniform design for his 59 existing stores, and by 1919 there were 1,081 Woolworth stores in the United States and Canada—with even more in Britain, where he had extended his chain in 1909.

Mail Order Merchandisers During a selling trip to small towns in the Midwest, Aaron Montgomery Ward (1844–1913) realized that many rural folks were suspicious of local stores and disliked patronizing them. He saw an opportunity and began a business in 1872 to sell directly to customers through the mail, developing proprietary systems for buying, warehousing, advertising, processing orders, and shipping goods to his rural customers. Ward's catalogs, promising "satisfaction guaranteed—or your money back," were known as "dream books," and enticed farmers to join urban dwellers in the growing consumer culture that mass production had made possible.

What Ward had begun, Richard Warren Sears (1863–1914) improved. In 1891 Sears formed a mail order partnership with Alvah Curtis Roebuck (1864–1948) that became Sears, Roebuck and Company. Sears was a born salesman and risk taker who produced catalogs that promised thousands of items at low prices. Roebuck sold his interest to Sears in 1895, and Sears then had the good fortune to add two new partners, one of whom was Julius Rosenwald (1862–1932), who ran the business side while Sears managed the marketing. Sears offered rebates and sweepstakes, and even offered farmers the opportunity to examine goods before paying for them, with the promise "Send no money." With Sears's marketing flair and Rosenwald's business discipline, the company grew rapidly; by 1900 it had $10 million in sales, surpassing Montgomery Ward.

Product Innovation Industrialization made mass production of traditional products possible, and also led to the development of new kinds of products.

Packaged foods Willie Keith (W. K.) Kellogg (1860–1951) began experimenting with foods based on nuts and grains while he was at his brother's Seventh Day Adventist sanitarium in 1880. The brothers built machinery to produce wheat flakes, and in 1984 created cornflakes and sought to build a national market for W. K.'s packaged breakfast foods. W. K. left his brother's employ in 1902, and in 1906 incorporated the Battle Creek Toasted Corn Flake Co., later changed to the W. K. Kellogg Co. From the beginning W. K. spent heavily on advertising, and by 1909 company sales surpassed 1 million cases.

In 1891 Charles William Post (1854–1914), plagued by stomach ailments, came to Kellogg's sanitarium, hoping for a cure. When he failed to regain his health, he was treated by a local Christian Scientist and soon recovered. Convinced that part of his recovery was the result of a healthy diet, Post began experimenting with a coffee substitute made of wheat, bran, and molasses. In 1895 he launched this product as Postum, a cereal beverage, and in 1896 he incorporated the Postum Cereal Co. The next year Post brought out Grape-Nuts cereal, and in 1904 he began to compete directly with Kellogg in the corn flake cereal market with a product he eventually called Post Toasties. Post, like Kellogg, realized that advertising was the key to success, and by 1899 he was spending $400,000 annually to promote his packaged foods.

Coca-Cola Health claims were also important to the beginnings of another product that is now consumed worldwide. Coca-Cola was concocted in 1886 by a druggist in Atlanta, Dr. John S. Pemberton (1831–88), and touted as a nerve and brain tonic. The drink was not a success, and the druggist sold his ownership in pieces, with one share going to Asa Griggs Candler (1851–1929) in 1888. In 1891 Candler became the sole owner of the product, its formula, and its trademark. Candler was a marketing innovator, and before the end of the 19th century, Coca-Cola was sold in soda fountains in all of the 48 states.

It was a further innovation, however, that multiplied the company's growth. In 1899 two attorneys in Chattanooga, Tennessee, negotiated a contract with Candler for exclusive bottling rights in most of the United States, thus separating the bottling businesses from Candler's company. By the end of the 1920s bottled Coke outsold fountain Coke, and soon the company's trademark was one of the best-known in the world.

Disposable Razors When King Camp Gillette (1855–1932) took a sales job in 1891 with a company making crimped bottle caps, the president advised him to invent a similarly disposable product. Gillette enthusiastically took up the challenge, and in 1895 he conceived of a razor made up of thin disposable blades clamped in a device to hold them rigid while men shaved. He engaged an MIT graduate who developed machinery to sharpen steel ribbons into blades. By 1903, Gillette's small Boston firm was able to produce his new razors and, like other entrepreneurs with a vision, he invested in heavy advertising. By 1908 the company sold 300,000 holders and 14 million blades—and established a legacy of product innovation.

Brand Management The idea that a product or company name could become a marketing focus was not new at the end of the 19th century. Many producers and manufacturers had promoted an awareness among customers of their company or product names as a way of distinguishing them from competitors. The art of "brand management," however, was not perfected until the 20th century.

Procter and Gamble The Procter and Gamble Company, founded in 1837, introduced a cake of white soap that floated on water, taking out its first advertisement for the product in 1881. The company named this product Ivory Soap. Though Procter and Gamble advertised it widely, the company did not establish a clear and consistent theme about its virtues; nevertheless, the soap was very successful and alerted the company—and its competitors—to the possibilities of promoting products to a national market in a coordinated and carefully planned fashion.

When Procter and Gamble launched its next important product in 1912, a vegetable shortening called Crisco, it had its strategy in place. Under its president William Cooper Procter (1862–1934), son of the cofounder, the company had tested and refined the product with women cooks, secured testimonials from scientists and home economists, and persuaded one railroad to use the shortening exclusively in its dining cars. The company tested a variety of different marketing campaigns in different cities, researched how consumers used shortening, and studied how competitors' products were selling and used. Crisco was a huge success—and established the model for brands that were specifically created and marketed. Procter and Gamble became the leader in building a portfolio of branded products; the brand names, not the company name, became king.

Lever Brothers In Britain a similar company was founded in 1885 by William Hesketh Lever (1851–1925) and his brother. Lever Brothers' first product was a packaged soap that they named Sunlight—the world's first packaged and branded laundry soap. Made mostly from vegetable oil, the soap rapidly caught on with the pubic, and by 1911 the company was producing one-third of the soap sold in Britain.

Lever expanded the soap line through acquisitions, and in 1917 he diversified into foods. By 1924 the company had grown to be the largest commercial company of its kind in the world. In 1930 Lever merged the company with a Dutch margarine producer, Margarine Unie, and changed its name to Unilever.

The Growth of the Automobile Industry

Industrialization in the first half of the 20th century produced the largest industry of all, the automobile industry. Most consider Karl Benz (1844–1929) and Gottlieb Daimler (1834–1900), who in 1885 invented the internal combustion engine, the founders of this important new industry—although the industry soon revolved around a few key American automotive companies.

Ford Motor Company Henry Ford (1863–1947) wanted to produce cars he could sell at a low price, and he saw the assembly line as the means of vastly increasing the productivity of his workers—thereby lowering the cost of producing each car. He also saw that the more individual components he could produce internally—instead of buying them from outside suppliers—the more he could control the cost of the completed car. Finally, by paying his workers the unheard-of wage of $5 a day, Ford guaranteed his company a loyal and productive workforce.

Ford's great success, the Model T, was first shipped to dealers in October 1908, after two years of design and development. By the time the last Model T was produced in May 1927, 15 million cars had been sold. Ford had managed to reduce the price of the coupe to $290, and the car had made the American family mobile. It had forced governments to pave dirt roads and to create highways for long-distance travel. It had spawned a host of roadside businesses, including gas stations, restaurants, hotels, and a new kind of lodging, the "motel."

General Motors Ford's primary competitor was General Motors, which was founded by William C. Durant (1861–1947). Durant, however, was an erratic manager, and he gained and lost control of the company several times. By 1920 General Motors was again in financial trouble, and Pierre S. du Pont (1870–1954), whose family company was the second largest shareholder, forced Durant to resign. Whatever Durant's failings as a manager, his vision of mass-marketed cars, along with models of differing styles and prices, was the basis of General Motors' growth. It became the largest auto manufacturer in the United States—and, by 1928, the largest and most profitable industrial company in the world.

The man who realized Durant's vision, Alfred Pritchard Sloan, Jr. (1875–1966), had come into the organization when Durant bought the Hyatt Roller Bearing Company in 1916. From 1920 to 1923, when he became president of General Motors, Sloan began an organizational transformation that was to become the model for several generations of chief executives in widely differing industries.

Under Sloan, GM offered more comfortable cars, more stylishly designed, at every price range, and with a choice of colors. He also understood that buyers at different income levels wanted different kinds of cars; this led him to organize the GM product line by income level corresponding to car price. These lines evolved into Chevrolet at the lowest price level (competing with Ford's Model T), followed in increasing price ranges by Pontiac, Oldsmobile, Buick, and Cadillac. GM also introduced the annual model change, small but noticeable changes in the styling of the cars each year to create a steady demand for new models. Chevrolet remained the auto sales leader for most of the next five decades.

Chrysler Corporation The third large U.S. automobile manufacturer, Chrysler, was created in the early 1920's by Walter P. Chrysler (1875–1940). Chrysler moved through a number of executive positions in different automobile companies, and from 1923 to 1924 he and a team of engineers at Maxwell Motors, where he was president, designed a new moderately priced car with advanced engineering features, which he named the Chrysler. It was an immediate success, and in 1925 Chrysler renamed the company the Chrysler Corp.

In 1928 Chrysler launched the Plymouth, which incorporated advanced engineering features not available on similarly priced cars. The car was an instant success, even though it cost half again as much as comparable Fords and Chevrolets. By increasing manufacturing capacity and reducing costs, Chrysler was able to reduce the price of the Plymouth and move it almost to reasonable price parity with Ford and Chevrolet. Chrysler's basic strategy of producing well-engineered cars at a slightly higher price than competitors proved successful over a long period of time.

Organizing the Corporation

The larger these new companies grew, the more problems executives encountered in managing them. It was not until the 20th century that top executives devised new organizational solutions to the increasing problems of size.

E.I. Du Pont The company that had the widest and longest-lasting influence on corporate structures was E. I. du Pont de Nemours & Company, which in 1900 was a loose collection of companies producing different kinds of explosives, owned and managed by various groups of family members. When the elders of the family considering selling the company in 1902, Pierre S. du Pont and two cousins bought them out to preserve the business within the family. The three cousins organized the firm into a centrally controlled structure with clear lines of responsibility for functional areas. Sales and profits grew faster than they had grown before the changes.

Until the end of World War I, the centralized structure of the firm served the business well. When the war ended, the company expanded into paints, chemicals, and dyestuffs. The company had been accustomed to selling explosives by the ton to a small number of customers; now it had products like paint that were sold in small quantities to innumerable customers through retail outlets. The company's centralized structure did not lend itself to a diverse product line, and in 1921 the board of directors approved a restructuring plan that created autonomous divisions.

These divisions produced and marketed distinct product lines, run by general managers who were responsible and accountable for the performance of their own division. Coordination was through an executive committee that included the president and other senior executives, but none of the operating general managers. Thus a balance was struck between the relative autonomy of the divisions and a central coordinating entity.

General Motors During GM's crisis of 1920, Pierre S. du Pont gave Alfred P. Sloan the opportunity to put into practice his evolving ideas about organization.

The organizational challenge facing Sloan was the opposite of that facing du Pont at that time. Whereas du Pont needed to find an organizing structure to manage its new diversified product lines, GM was a loosely federated group of entities that needed some kind of stronger centralized control. In December 1920 the GM board approved Sloan's plan to create a structure with autonomous divisions under a central office with coordinating control.

Subject only to the executive control of the president and the executive committee, the general manager of each division was expected to know the demands of the market for his product line and to develop it to its fullest potential. He was held responsible for his division's success or failure.

The central coordinating group of the firm was the executive committee, consisting nearly entirely of senior officers who did not have operating responsibilities. Together with the president, the committee governed the firm by setting broad strategic policies and approving major initiatives to accomplish these policies. The finance committee oversaw the company's financial performance.

Word of the GM model's success spread rapidly to other firms that were grappling with many of the same problems of diversification. Sears, Roebuck adopted a similar multidivisional structure after it realized that the United States was becoming increasingly urbanized and that its traditional catalog business would fail to capture customers who now lived in cities. The company's divisions, as eventually structured, were geographic regions rather than product lines. This gave the company an early advantage that its competitor Montgomery Ward was never able to overcome.

Oil companies, led by Standard Oil (New Jersey), responded to the need for vertical integration and crude oil sources spread increasingly all over the world by creating similar regional divisions. As they began to develop new markets for petrochemicals they also created divisions along product lines.

Management Theorists With industrialization and the advent of the factory system, large groups of workers were brought together for the first time to produce goods using machines. Factory owners pushed workers for maximum productivity and this policy resulted in long hours at low pay, frequent injuries from dangerous machines, the use of child labor, and appalling living conditions in factory towns. The idea that treating workers well and organizing their work with careful planning would result in productivity increases was virtually unknown. That would change gradually over more than a century until the new field of "management" was born and its applications spread beyond factories to all kinds of organizations.

Robert Owen The first important thinker to address the question of how to manage factory workers was Robert Owen (1771–1858). Owen's major contribution to management came in 1800, when he and his partners bought the large cotton mills at New Lanark near Glasgow. His past experience in mill management had convinced him that if he treated workers decently and with respect, their productivity would significantly increase. He stopped employing children under the age of 10, built schools for infants and older children, and shortened the working day. He improved workers' housing, paved the streets, and opened a company store with low prices. Owen's reforms enabled the mill to prosper, and its schools became widely known.

Frederick W. Taylor The concept that both owners and workers can prosper under the right conditions was carried forward by Frederick Winslow Taylor (1856–1915), arguably the most influential management thinker in the first half of the 20th century.

As a management consultant, Taylor experimented with ways of speeding up the production of the workers, including the introduction of piecework and the use of a stopwatch to find the best way to coordinate the actions of the workers and their machines. He believed that "there is always one method and one implement which is quicker and better than any of the rest." In 1911 he published the most widely read business book of the first half of the century, *The Principles of Scientific Management*, which helped to spread the gospel of "Taylorism."

George Elton Mayo In 1927 AT&T invited a Harvard business professor, George Elton Mayo (1880–1949), to study workers at the Hawthorne Works of Western Electric in Chicago. AT&T was interested in knowing if the level of illumination in the plant had any effect on workers' productivity—a classic instance of the Taylor approach. Mayo and his team studied a room where five young women were assembling electromagnetic relay switches; over the period of 1928 to 1932 the team varied the working conditions in the room—not only illumination, but rates of pay, periods of rest, and other factors—and collected reams of data on performance. The results at first baffled them. It seemed as if everything they did improved productivity. When they introduced piecework, added rest periods, provided a free meal, and shortened the workday, output increased. But when they took all these elements away and returned the room to its original conditions, output increased to the highest level ever.

Mayo's team realized that the workers had become a dynamic social group and had responded to the attention the researchers were paying them. They concluded that the very fact of their interest in the workers had motivated the women to show the researchers how well they could work—what became known as the "Hawthorne effect." Mayo's theories, which were the beginning of the human relations approach to management, became increasingly important in the second half of the 20th century, eventually displacing the practice of Taylorism.

Chester I. Barnard It took a working executive to fully understand and articulate the realities of managing people in large organizations. Chester Irving Barnard (1886–1961) held a succession of management positions at AT&T, Pennsylvania Bell, and New Jersey Bell, where he was responsible for consolidating a number of smaller companies into each of the larger companies. The lessons he learned in dealing with the human dimension of integrating many diverse personalities into a new whole shaped his thinking on how organizations function, what motivates workers, and how authority flows from top to bottom.

Barnard delivered a series of lectures at the Lowell Institute in Cambridge, Mass., that became a classic of management thought when they were published under the title *The Functions of the Executive* in 1938. He argued that the harmony and cooperation necessary for carrying out the purpose of the organization are achieved only when workers sense that their interests and aspirations are aligned with the organization's goals. Top management achieves this by the exercise of its authority, but workers will accept that authority only if they understand the task at hand, believe the request is consistent with the organization's goals, believe the request is compatible with their own interests, and are able mentally and physically to carry out the task.

Postwar Recovery

At the end of the 1920's a worldwide depression brought widespread business failures and a decade of struggle for the survivors. With the coming of World War II, businesses turned to the challenge of meeting the needs of wartime economies. The end of the war in 1945 created an unprecedented economic boom in the United States, as pent-up consumer demand was finally unleashed. Consumers who were deprived of many goods during the war had bought war bonds and had accumulated money to spend. Young G.I.'s returned home eager to start their lives, so they married and had children right away, helping to create the greatest baby boom in history. They also began a mass exodus out of the nation's cities to the new so-called suburbs.

The late 1940's saw an audacious bet on the future by William Jaird Levitt (1907–94) and his father and brother. They believed that they could profitably build and sell low-priced small houses in suburban areas by using mass production techniques they had learned building civilian and military housing during the war. Their first project, Levittown, was begun in 1947. Levittown consisted of 17,500 two-bedroom Cape Cod houses on Long Island, N.Y. Veteran loans helped new families to pay for the houses, and by 1951 the company began a second Levittown in Bucks County, Pa., comprising 16,000 houses. Later Levittowns appeared in New Jersey and Florida.

The Automobile Market Suburban living demanded flexible transportation, and nothing provided it better than the automobile.

The government had brought Henry Ford II (1917–87) back from military service and installed him at Ford in 1943, fearing that his aging grandfather, Henry Ford, could not manage the company's wartime production. He led the company through several decades of successful new models, to become a strong second to General Motors.

Alfred P. Sloan retired as CEO of General Motors in 1946 and as chairman in 1956. His successors continued his management structure, which proved to be robust as the company continued to lead the U.S. automobile industry.

After some initial postwar success, the Chrysler Corporation had difficulty in finding the right product mix. Although the company pioneered the popular minivan in the 1980's, it remained third behind GM and Ford and merged with the German company Daimler-Benz in 1998.

In the late 1940's, an odd-looking car built in Germany began to appear on European streets and roads. It was noisy, with a rear-mounted, air-cooled engine and a rounded shape that looked like a giant bug. The car had been conceived and designed in the late 1930's by Ferdinand Porsche (1875–1951) to be a low-priced "people's car," or Volkswagen. The "beetle," as it was dubbed by *The New York Times*, eventually became the largest-selling car in history.

Plans to manufacture the car were interrupted by World War II, but following the war production began in Germany under the enlightened leadership of Heinz Nordhoff (1899–1968). He focused on building high-quality cars and creating a large international dealer and service organization.

In 1972 Volkswagen produced the 15,007,034th beetle and announced that it had surpassed the production of Ford's Model T. Customers—often young families—discovered that an inexpensive car could be as well-made as a luxury car. This discovery was to reverberate throughout the automobile market, as Japanese makers began to offer small, inexpensive cars of high quality in the years following. A generation of young buyers became converts to foreign cars before American manufacturers awoke to the consequences of global competition.

The oil shocks of the 1970's accelerated a major shift in the world automobile market. The Organization of Petroleum Exporting Countries (OPEC) created crises in the availability of the world's supply of oil. The steep rise in the price of gasoline that followed made smaller, fuel-efficient cars more desirable than they had been when gas was cheap and plentiful.

Unfortunately, Detroit had left the small car market to foreign producers, most of them Japanese. These foreign cars began to sell as never before, and owners discovered what earlier buyers of the Volkswagen beetle had discovered—the cars were made to high quality standards, were reliable, and were supported by strong dealer and service organizations.

The Quality Movement Prior to World War II, Japan had been known for the poor quality of its export goods. After the war both the government and industry realized that its economic recovery would depend first on its domestic market and later on exports. To compete effectively, Japanese industries had to produce goods of the highest quality. They found inspiration and methods in a surprising source—two Americans, William Edwards Deming (1900–93) and Joseph Moses Juran (b. 1904). Deming and Juran developed a range of quality concepts that found only a limited audience in the United States, but after they were invited to deliver lectures on quality control in Japan, Japanese manufacturers eagerly adopted their ideas.

The basic concept of quality control can be summarized as "Build it right the first time." Conventional mass production relied on a stage at the end of the assembly line to correct any defects that had been built into a product. But it was less expensive not to have built defects into the product as it was being manufactured. That would require an extra effort by production workers to ensure that what they did was free of defects. Japanese manufacturers developed management protocols to achieve this commitment from every worker.

The Toyota Production System Quality became the most important management movement since the end of World War II—the most notable example being the production system of Japan's Toyota Motor Company, which combined mass production and individual craft methods.

Under Kiichiro Toyoda (1894–1952), the company instituted a just-in-time (JIT) inventory system that delivered parts to the assembly line at the time they were needed—creating a more flexible manufacturing system than Fordism enabled. This was just the start of Toyota's much-vaunted production system. In 1950 a young Toyota engineer, Eiji Toyoda (b. 1913), who in 1967 became president of the company, visited Ford's vast Rouge plant to study its production methods. After three months he wrote to headquarters that he "thought there were some possibilities to improve the production system." Under its innovative production engineer, Taiichi Ohno (1912–90), Toyota instituted statistical quality control and continuous improvement (*kaizen*), and further developed its system of just-in-time inventory control (*kanban*). The company worked with its supplier companies to make them a part of its production system. Toyota also adopted its "total quality management" (TQM) system, which became the most visible aspect of its production system.

Japanese Cars on the World Market In the 1970's and 1980's, responding partly to limitations of domestic capacity, Toyota and other Japanese manufacturers opened plants in North America and successfully transplanted their production systems to American workers. They also began to produce larger cars, first family sedans and later luxury cars. Their reputation for high-quality small cars carried over to the larger cars, and now Detroit faced direct competition in its core markets.

In 1989 the Honda Accord family sedan outsold Ford's popular Taurus; Toyota's Camry took over this lead position in 1997. Internationally, by the end of the 1990's, Toyota had sold over 29 million of its compact Corollas—making it the best-selling automobile in history. In addition, Japanese cars forced European manufacturers to confront the challenge of the evolving global marketplace and to examine the source of Japan's success.

Consumer Electronics

Cars were not the only consumer products at which Japanese companies excelled. In 1957 a Japanese company—later renamed Sony—cofounded by Akio Morita (1921–99) released the TR-63, the first commercially successful pocket-sized transistor radio. The success of the TR-63 in world markets was the beginning of a shift of consumer electronics production outside the United States, mainly to Japan. Japanese manufacturers quickly learned the technology of miniaturization and applied it to a number of other products, including television sets, videotape recorders, hand-held calculators, portable cassette tape players, CD and DVD players, and cellular telephones. By combining a creative approach to new product design with high-quality manufacturing, Japanese manufacturers captured the world market for many consumer electronics products.

Business at the Turn of the Century

As the end of the 20th century neared, businesses in Europe, Japan, and the United States began to shift from a primarily manufacturing base to technology- and information-driven organizations. Advances in communications and the spread of capitalism led to globalization, the opening of markets worldwide to competition. The industrial age was at an end, replaced by the new information age. Advances in communications and the spread of capitalism led to globalization, the opening of markets worldwide to competition.

Information Technology

In the post-World War II boom, as companies grew in size and the number of transactions multiplied, they sought economies in converting repetitive tasks requiring increasing numbers of workers into automated processes employing far fewer workers. These economies were realized by the development of the digital computer.

IBM and the Digital Computer The first computers (see *Computers*) were large mainframe machines that automated the billing process and related accounting functions. In 1964 I.B.M., under its CEO Thomas J. Watson, Jr. (1914–93), introduced its System 360 machines—a family of computers graded in size with interchangeable software and peripherals. These relatively smaller, relatively less expensive machines led to the accelerating adoption of computers by major companies, and IBM became the dominant computer manufacturer through the 1970's.

Computer Networks Improved computer technology in the 1960's made possible interconnected computers and greater flexibility for users outside the data processing department. One of the most successful adaptations of networked computers was American Airlines' SABRE computer reservation system. Developed in the early 1960's as a way of keeping track of one airline's sales of seats, SABRE was extended to travel agents' desks in 1976, presenting a choice of seats on many competing airlines. Eventually the system was augmented to include hotel, car, rail, and entertainment reservations; the system ultimately became more profitable for American Airlines than its passenger flights.

The Personal Computer During the 1970's and 1980's the mainframe computer was downsized, and the so-called personal computer (PC) was born. The first inexpensive general-purpose PC was the Altair, introduced by Micro Instrumentation Telementry Systems. The PC enabled workers to run a range of application software—including word processing, spreadsheets, databases, and graphic presentations—on their desktops. It also served as the terminal for access to management information originating in remote server computers.

The Software Industry In the early 1970's, a student at Harvard University, Bill Gates (b. 1955), wrote a version of the computer language BASIC for the Altair. In 1975, along with Paul Allen (b. 1953), he founded Microsoft to sell software products for the new PCs. Microsoft came to dominate the computer industry through its ubiquitous operating system, Windows, which ran on an estimated 95 percent of computers worldwide. Microsoft also successfully sold products ranging from computer games to word processing software. Its aggressive sales tactics and size made it a continual target of competitors' lawsuits and antitrust regulators. At the turn of the century Bill Gates was the world's richest man.

Networked computers developed in the 1960's and 1970's enabled information systems that encompassed all the workings of an organization. The German firm SAP offered company-wide software systems to integrate all aspects of a business, giving workers access to real-time management information. By the beginning of the 21st century SAP was one of the world's largest independent software companies, and an example of the globalization of the marketplace in a software industry long dominated by the United States.

The Internet In the 1990's, the growth of the Internet, a network that linked computers all over the world, created new marketing opportunities for business. Companies opened Web sites from which they marketed their products and services, and used electronic mail (e-mail) to communicate within the office and with other offices around the world.

One of the fastest-growing businesses spawned by the Internet was that of providing Internet access to PC users. The most successful Internet service provider (ISP) was America Online (AOL), founded by Stephen M. Case (b. 1958) in 1985. During the 1990's AOL added subscribers at a much faster rate than competitors, and its market value soared so high that it was able to acquire the Time Warner media conglomerate in 2000. The merger resulted in little real business benefit. By 2003, AOL Time Warner had dropped AOL from its name and was running AOL as one of its many subsidiaries.

The Internet also created a new kind of business, dubbed e-business, in which entrepreneurs hoped to eliminate the need for "bricks and mortar" stores and sell directly to customers. One of the most successful e-businesses was Amazon.com, founded by Jeffrey P. Bezos (b. 1954) in 1995 as an online bookseller. Amazon.com's revenues have grown steadily over succeeding years—aided by the addition of new product lines.

The most successful large Internet firm was eBay, launched in 1995 by Pierre Omidyar (b. 1968). An Internet auction house that brings sellers and buyers together in cyberspace, eBay adapted the auction concept to the Internet and has experienced rapid revenue and profit growth. In the process, it created a trading economy of $20 billion a year.

In what has been called the "dot-com boom" of the 1990's, thousands of entrepreneurs opened Web sites offering a staggering array of goods and services; significant venture capital flowed into these companies, and their stock prices climbed to astronomical heights. Then came the "dot-com bust." The stock prices of most Internet companies collapsed in 2000, as it became apparent to investors that most of the dot-com companies had few actual sales.

Telecommunications Information technology created vast amounts of data; and transmitting these data to the growing world of computer networks required a comparable increase in the means of communication. Local phone companies and long-distance carriers rushed to add capacity and created a boom in business for suppliers of fiber-optic cable and sophisticated switching and routing systems. The added capacity far outstripped demand, however, and many companies, large and small, were caught with heavy capital investments in transmission capacity but no revenues to pay for them. The result, in 2000–01, was a series of severe downsizings of many major companies and bankruptcies at others. The largest casualty was the long-distance giant MCI, which emerged from bankruptcy in 2004 after a two-year reorganization.

Big-Box Retail The continuing suburban expansion of the late 20th century gave retailers a new opportunity to change the basic nature of shopping. With large tracts of land available for building they created "big-box" stores, which earned their profits not through price markups but by sales volume. Big-box stores came to dominate many retail categories, including bookselling (Barnes & Noble), hardware (Home Depot), and electronic goods (Best Buy). They put many traditional mom-and-pop stores out of business and relegated others to niche positions.

Wal-Mart, a low-priced department store, became the biggest big-box chain. Founded in 1962 by Sam Walton (1918–92), Wal-Mart was guided by one overriding principle, efficiency. By simplifying store layout, pressuring suppliers to design products to its specifications, and hastening the pace at which its distributors operated, it squeezed costs out of the retail supply chain and passed on the price savings to customers. At the turn of the century Wal-Mart was the largest private employer in the United States and the world's largest company, with sales of $220 billion in 2001. Its influence was felt throughout the retail economy, as many of its competitors were forced to adopt the same high-speed, low-overhead tactics that Wal-Mart used. Wal-Mart's huge size and market power made it a target for critics who accused it of ruining downtowns across the country and depressing retail wages and benefits industry-wide.

The Biotechnology Industry In 1973 two young biologists, Herbert Wayne Boyer (b. 1936) and Stanley Norman Cohen (b. 1935), genetically engineered molecules in foreign cells to produce predetermined patterns of DNA—called recombinant DNA—and began the modern biotechnology industry, which may become the dominant industry of the 21st century.

Genentech In 1976 Herbert Boyer, along with the venture capitalist Robert Arthur Swanson (1947–99), founded the pioneer biotechnology company Genentech. Within the first three years the fledgling company cloned the first human protein in a microorganism, cloned human insulin, and cloned human growth hormone. In 1982 it marketed the first recombinant DNA drug, human insulin, which it licensed to Eli Lilly and Company. The same year Genentech marketed a growth hormone for children with a growth hormone deficiency, becoming the first biotechnology company to manufacture and market its own recombinant pharmaceutical product.

The Growth of Biotechnology By 1999 more than 1,200 U.S. companies were spending an estimated $11 billion in R&D in the areas of medicine, agriculture, and the environment—even though biotechnology industry revenues totaled only $20 billion. By 2002, the number of biotechnology companies had risen to over 1,400, with revenues of only $28 billion. Along with smaller firms run by scientists and entrepreneurs, the industry also included pharmaceutical giants like U.S.-based Johnson & Johnson and Pfizer, and U.K-based GlaxoSmithKline, which sponsored their own research and made investments in smaller companies.

Biotechnology raises many contentious issues. Food crops genetically engineered in the United States have been banned in Europe. Genetically "improved" livestock are feared by some as possibly harmful and decried by others as destructive of animal rights. Stem cell research looking for cures for Alzheimer's disease and diabetes, among other diseases, is limited by political pressure from some religious groups. Advances in genetic engineering hold the promise of creating human babies with traits ordered up by parents—and the cloning of humans might make possible the re-creation of geniuses into succeeding generations.

The biotechnology industry will have to confront these and many other issues as it looks for new areas of growth in the 21st century. As a global business it faces the probability that a line of research forbidden in one country could be pursued without opposition in another.

Advertising

History

Although rudimentary advertising existed in medieval Europe, it was the advent of the printing press in the 15th century that enabled information to be disseminated quickly and cheaply. Previously, shop owners advertised their products by displaying a pictorial sign—essential in a largely illiterate society—or hand-lettered posters to gain attention.

The first printed advertisement in English—announcing a prayer book for sale—appeared in 1477. Other early advertisements included printed handbills that shop owners passed to their customers or citizens in the street. As the newspaper became commonplace in Europe, advertising quickly became a standard feature. In the 17th century and the early 18th, British newspapers carried small, straightforward items that resemble the classified advertisements of modern newspapers. The *Tatler*, an early 18th-century London periodical, sold advertisement space at a discount to clients who promised to run a specified number of ads in a particular period. This was the first instance of the "frequency rate," a practice still in use in modern advertising.

In American cities in the 18th century, newspapers consisted mostly of advertisements, usually for a shop or a service provider. The technological changes of the Industrial Revolution set the stage for the explosive growth of manufacturing on both sides of the Atlantic, allowing for the mass production of goods at low costs. Improvements in newspaper and magazine production allowed for larger issues that cost less. Manufacturers, with an abundance of goods to sell, needed to build demand for their products by reaching a mass market, and newspapers and magazines could help them do it.

While the advertisements may not have been sophisticated, manufacturers discovered that buying display space in publications was a complicated business. The burgeoning business required a middleman, and hence the advertising agent was born. The earliest known advertising agent in the United States was Volney Palmer of Philadelphia, who operated in the early 1840's. Palmer represented several newspapers and business clients, and when a firm purchased space in a paper, he would pass along the written copy and receive a percentage of the advertisement's revenue. Other advertising agents purchased blocks of space from newspapers at a discount and then broke the space into sections for smaller, slightly marked up advertisements. By the onset of the Civil War, approximately 30 of these primitive agencies existed in the United States, most of them in New York.

The agencies brought standard business practices to advertising, including a transparent "open contract" that told advertisers exactly what their costs were and that the agency would take a 15 percent commission. This system was started in 1869 by the N. W. Ayer Agency and is still the basis for most of today's advertising transactions. As publishers realized the significance of advertising revenues, newspapers and magazines relaxed their advertising guidelines, so that advertisements could be larger and more sophisticated. Illustrations began to appear in advertisements, particularly for those selling typewriters, sewing machines, and patent medicines.

The growth of advertising fueled the demand for many products that originated in the 19th century. Consumers seeing frequent advertising messages began to connect the advertiser with a sense of quality. In 1868 James Walter Thompson (1847–1928) joined a small New York advertising agency. He knew that the popular ladies' magazines and prestige literary magazines were read and reread, and that their prestige would rub off on products advertised within. He demonstrated the power of his idea when he placed ads for asbestos roofing in the women's magazines *Godey's* and *Peterson's*; these ads sold more roofing than the company had ever sold before. Thompson went on to monopolize magazine advertising, buying out the agency's owner in 1878 and renaming the firm for himself. Thompson also pioneered the creation of the account executive position—the liaison between agency and client.

Advertising Agencies By the end of the 19th century, advertising had become an integral part of the business world. Advertising agencies grew in number and enhanced their role in the game of printed salesmanship. They no longer served merely as the middlemen between the client and the media; they now created advertisements on the client's behalf. Around the turn of the century, advertising writers developed new ways to appeal to consumers. One style of advertising, dubbed the "reason-why" style, used extensive logical arguments several paragraphs in length about why a product was better than its competitors. The Chicago-based agency Lord & Thomas was a prominent practicioner of this style in the early 20th century. An executive at Lord & Thomas, Albert Lasker, and the copywriter Claude Hopkins used the "reason-why" approach in illustrated, wordy ads for products like Sunkist oranges or Schlitz beer. In its advertisements for Palmolive soap, Lord & Thomas displayed alongside the text a larger slogan—"Keep That Schoolgirl Complexion"—that the agency created to increase sales to married women. Hopkins called this "salesmanship-on-paper," and he and Lasker went on to create numerous successful advertising campaigns, most notably for Lucky Strike cigarettes with a strategy to convince women that smoking was sophisticated.

Radio and Television With the emergence of radio as a popular source of public entertainment in the 1920's and 1930's, advertising moved into uncharted territory. Initially, the radio program was sponsored by a corporation, and the corporation's advertising agency took on the responsibility for producing the content. Batten Barton Durstine & Osborn (BBDO) coordinated the *Du Pont Cavalcade of America,* and Blackett-Sample-Hummert developed the daytime "soap opera" as showcases for various home products from their clients. (See also "Radio" in the *Media* section.)

The widespread introduction of television following World War II offered advertisers a powerful opportunity, and advertisers fell all over themselves for the chance to present their products simultaneously through visual and aural methods. In television's infancy, as with radio, advertising agencies produced shows on behalf of their clients. The Kudner Agency created a hit with its *Texaco Star Theater*, hosted by Milton Berle, and J. Walter Thompson (JWT) produced *Kraft Television Theater*.

The costs of producing content for television soon became too exorbitant for sponsors to handle. The television networks saw an opportunity to build their business by creating their own content and opening the airwaves to many more advertisers. By 1959 the networks had taken creative control of programming. (See *Media*)

With the combination of print, radio, and television available to spread advertising through several media, advertising grew rapidly in the 1950's. Overall industry expenditures for media placements, not including the cost of producing the ads, doubled from $5.7 billion in 1950 to $12.0 billion in 1960. Film actors, baseball players, and socialites became spokespeople in ads and became associated with the products they pitched. Famous advertising characters were born as well, including such icons as the Jolly Green Giant, the Pillsbury Doughboy, and the Marlboro Man, all created by the famous Leo Burnett agency of Chicago.

In the 1960's the creative departments of advertising agencies released a torrent of ads that reflected the counterculture elements of contemporary society. William Bernbach of Doyle Dane Bernbach (DDB), a New York agency, launched several notable campaigns during this period, including a series of clever print and television spots for the Volkswagen Beetle and Avis Rent-a-Car ("We're Number 2—We Try Harder"). Both print and television advertisements gained sophistication during the period, with print ads prefering photography over illustrations and the copious text copy of earlier times. Boosted by the improvement of editing techniques, the television commercial also came of age.

Mergers and Explosive Growth But the creative eruption of the 1960's gave way in the 1970's to a series of industry mergers that formed gigantic advertising agencies. Interpublic, a holding company formed by Marion Harper of the ad agency McCann-Erickson, added several other advertising agencies to its portfolio, each operating as a separate division.

The wave of mergers continued into the 1980's, with the addition of the decade's infamous and characteristic feature—the hostile takeover. In 1987 the WPP Group, headed by Martin Sorrell, purchased the J. Walter Thompson Company for $566 million. Two years later WPP acquired the Ogilvy Group for $864 million. The holding company Omnicom was formed in 1987 in a move that combined Doyle Dane Bernbach with another agency and also added BBDO. Companies went international, as well, with offices in Europe and elsewhere.

The 1980's were a decade of explosive growth in the American advertising industry. In 1980, domestic expenditures for advertising totaled $54.8 billion. In 1990 advertisers spent approximately $130 billion on advertisements in the United States. Television commercials became famous for their pitches, such as "Where's the beef?"—spoken by an elderly woman in a commercial for the fast-food chain Wendy's—or the pink bunny that pounded a drum in more than 100 spots for Energizer, a household battery.

Advertising Today In the early 21st century, advertising continues to spur the American economy, largely based on mass consumption of mass-produced goods. Advertising dollars also provide the financial underpinnings of every major media outlet. According to industry projections, advertisers will spend approximately $498.3 billion on worldwide advertising buys in 2004, with $266.4 billion of that in the United States alone. And this trend shows no sign of stopping. In 2000, the Super Bowl, the championship game of the National Football League, garnered $2.2 million per 30-second commercial, with many of the spots purchased by Internet-based companies that would hit bottom later in the year. In May 2004 advertisers ponied up more than $2 million for a 30-second advertisement in the final episode of *Friends*, a sitcom on NBC.

The growth of cable television has weakened the powerful advertising position of network television. The preponderance of channels aiming at various demographic categories—such as the youth market served by MTV—was a marketing dream for advertising agencies and clients, who can now theoretically reach a more interested audience for much lower rates. The growth of the Internet since the mid-1990's has provided advertisers with another outlet, although just how effective the ads are and will be remains a mystery.

U.S. Advertising Spending, 2003

Media	Expenditures, in billions
Newspapers	$45.5
Broadcast television	$43.2
Cable television	$14.1
Radio	$19.5
Magazines	$11.8
Internet	$5.6
Direct mail	$49.0
Yellow pages	$13.9
Other	$46.6
TOTAL	**$249.2**

Source: Advertising Age and Universal McCann

Advertising Expenditures in the U.S., 1776–2003 (millions)

Year	Amount	Year	Amount	Year	Amount
1776	$0.2	1900	$450	1990	$128,640
1800	1	1909	1,000	1995	160,930
1820	3	1915	1,100	1999	215,301
1840	7	1940	2,110	2000	243,680
1850	12	1950	5,700	2001	231,300
1860	22	1960	11,960	2002	236,880
1867	40	1970	19,550	2003	249,200
1880	175	1980	54,780		
1890	300	1985	94,750		

Source: Advertising Age. These are estimated figures of the monies spent on placing advertising in all media; the costs of producing the advertising are not included.

Glossary of Business Terms

after-sales service service provided to buyers after a sale; often tied to warranty contracts; in some industries it is more profitable than the sale; maintains contact with the buyer and can increase the probability of repeat sales.

agile manufacturing ability of manufacturing processes to respond to individual customer demands to deliver a semi-customized product without sacrificing quality; its main object is customer satisfaction.

authority power vested in managers to direct the activities of their subordinates; accepted by subordinates because they perceive the legitimacy of that authority.

B2B commerce conducted between two or more businesses by electronic means, usually the Internet; distinguished from business conducted electronically between businesses and individual customers.

brand equity quality of a branded product or service that is recognized by customers favorably; can allow brand owners to charge a premium price over competing products or services.

brand management approach to management that focuses on the successful introduction of new brands and the continuing marketing management of the brand during its commercial life; the intention is to establish the brand in the consumer's mind and to ensure that it achieves as long a commercial life as possible.

centralized management organization of *line management* and *staff management* functions in a central location; distinguished from a *multidivisional organization*.

Chapter 11 chapter of the 1978 Bankruptcy Act that permits debtors to retain control of their businesses; debtors and creditors are given flexibility in working out a plan to keep the business operating while paying off some or all of their debt.

chief executive officer (C.E.O.) most senior executive of a firm, or other organization, who has ultimate responsibility for the whole organization; reports to a board of directors.

chief operating officer (C.O.O.) senior executive who is responsible for the day-to-day operation of the firm or organization; usually reports to the chief executive officer.

conglomerate corporation composed of several companies operating in different industries; in theory, different companies prosper in different market conditions, leveling the performance of the whole; conglomerates have generally fallen out of favor, as many were not able to effectively manage their diverse activities.

continuous improvement (*kaizen*) production process in which workers continually improve their working practices; introduced by the Japanese and a factor in the high quality of Japanese products.

corporate brand reputation a company develops that distinguishes it from its competitors; distinguished from product brand; see *brand equity*.

corporate culture values, beliefs, ethics, and ways of doing things, within an organization; often communicated informally among workers; can be an important adjunct to management but can also be an impediment to change.

corporate governance control of private corporations by top management and boards of directors; can contribute to improving business performance and preventing mismanagement and fraud.

corporate strategy identification of a corporation's long-term goal for success and the organization of its resources to achieve that goal.

corporation business organization legally chartered by a state or the federal government, having its own rights, privileges, and liabilities, and distinct from its owners. Investors own shares and, in *limited liability*, their potential loss in case the business fails is limited to the amount of their investments; see *partnership*.

deindustrialization flight of industry from a region that results from a change in technologies or the economy; frequently caused by foreign competition.

delayering removal of layers of management deemed unnecessary; intended to increase the speed of decision making and improve responsiveness to customers.

diversification strategy that increases the company's number of products or services in order to achieve growth or to lessen the market risk of individual products or services.

e-business commerce conducted electronically between sellers and buyers, usually over the Internet.

economies of scale cost of producing a product or service declines as a firm grows in size; associated unit costs decrease when more products and services are produced.

first mover (advantage) company that first introduces a product or service; can be an advantage in some instances; some companies specialize successfully in being second movers.

Fordism production of inexpensive goods by assembly-line methods; named for Henry Ford's assembly lines that produced the Model T; see *mass production*.

general manager executive of an organization who is vested with the authority and responsibility for all aspects of the organization; in a *multidivisional organization* the general manager may be one of several, each of whom is responsible for a separate division.

globalization opening up of markets in many countries of the world to competition; companies have access to new markets but also face new competitors.

Hawthorne effect often favorable effect that supervisors can have on workers' performance when they pay special attention to the workers; named for the studies conducted by George Elton Mayo (1880-1949) at the Western Electric Hawthorne plant in Chicago from 1928 to 1932; interpretations differ on exactly what the studies showed, but the prevailing view is that the very act of the researchers' closely studying the workers motivated the latter to improve their performance.

horizontal organization organization that has minimized the layers of management between top management and the production process (of goods or services); intended to speed up decision making and responsiveness to customers; often includes reorganizing the management of process flow; see *delayering*.

human capital skills and knowledge acquired by people that improve their productive capacity; results from investment in education, health care, and training.

human resource management (HRM) approach to management that emphasizes the value of individuals and their differences; distinguished from management that applies a single approach to everyone; see *scientific management*.

information technology systems of computers, software, and telecommunications that generate and analyze data from the operation of a firm and communicate it to decision makers.

intellectual capital/property concepts, ideas, computer programs, patents, and other creative products that are definable, measurable, and proprietary; distinguished from tangible assets such as factories and real estate.

just-in-time (*kanban*) production process in which the components of a product are produced and delivered during the final assembly; requires that manufacturers and suppliers coordinate their production schedules; minimizes the cost of idle inventory.

kanban See *just-in-time*.

kaizen See *continuous improvement*.

keiretsu network of Japanese firms linked by mutual obligations; consists of complementary firms that can include banks, manufacturers, suppliers, distributors; allows for sharing of information and resources, coordination of activities, and mutual support.

knowledge industry industry in which the principle asset is the knowledge (education, training, skills, and experience) of those who work in it; distinguished from an industry in which the principal assets are tangible; increasingly firms are realizing that almost any industry depends on the assets of the knowledge of its workers.

lean production system of production introduced by Toyota that combines *total quality management* (TQM); a highly motivated and committed workforce organized in teams; a manufacturing process so flexible that it allows different models of the same car to be built at the same time on the same assembly line in response to shifting market demand; a cooperative supplier network system that delivers high-quality components at exactly the moment they are needed during assembly; and an innumerable number of refinements in work-flow, eliminating all tasks that do not contribute value to the end result.

limited liability principle that investors in a business organization are limited in their potential loss to the amount of their investments in the event that the business fails.

line management managers who have direct responsibility for the production of products or services which generate the firm's revenues; distinguished from *staff management*.

mass customization production process in which the methods of mass production have been modified to allow for limited variation, often based on demand, of individual products; allows low pricing of customized products; see *agile manufacturing*.

mass market market that includes large numbers of consumers.

mass production production of large numbers of a single product; unit costs are minimized allowing competitive pricing.

middle management managers in an organization who are below senior management and above junior management; many organizations have eliminated layers of middle managers deemed unnecessary, in an effort to increase efficiency and responsiveness to customers.

multidivisional organization organization in which a central corporate office administers and coordinates the activities of autonomous divisions responsible for producing products for different markets, or divisions that operate in different geographical areas.

outsourcing procurement of products, or services, outside an organization; in some organizations outsourcing is limited to peripheral items or services; in others it can encompass a wide range of items; see *just-in-time* and *virtual organization*.

partnership nonincorporated business arrangement of two or more investors who agree to share profits and debts; individuals are responsible for the debts of the company if it fails; see *unlimited liability*.

postindustrial society concept that the principal source of value and wealth will come from workers' information and knowledge; argues that the traditional sources of value and wealth, labor and capital, are comparatively less important to society.

price war competition between two or more companies in which each lowers prices to increase market share; can drive some competitors out of business (which may have been the strategy of one or more of the others).

principal agent (problem) relationship between the owners of a firm and the firm's managers (agents); sometimes characterized by a conflict between the interests of shareholders and the managers who run the firm.

productivity measure of the output of goods or services compared with the input required to produce them; higher productivity results in greater profits if prices are stable; also allows for lower pricing if competition requires it.

putting-out gainful small-scale manufacturing work done in the home; a widespread means of production before the age of industrialization.

quality control process of reducing the number of defects in the products and services being produced.

reindustrialization process of restoring a former industrial area; often requires initial government assistance; allows for the introduction of new technologies that can enhance competitiveness; Japan and Germany are examples of successful reindustrialization following World War II.

research and development (R&D) systematic development of new ideas, products, and processes, that can be applied to the benefit of a business organization; grew out of the requirements of industrialization for technological innovation; modeled on early laboratories, including those of Thomas Edison and General Electric.

scientific management comprehensive system of management advocated by Frederick Winslow Taylor (1856–1915). It included detailed cost accounting; meticulous production scheduling; coordinated purchasing, inventory, storage, and maintenance procedures; time studies of workers; and an incentive wage based on piecework; sometimes mistakenly thought to consist only of time and motion studies of workers.

shareholder one who owns equity securities issued by a limited corporation; the shareholder is entitled to attend annual meetings, vote on officers and initiatives presented to shareholders, and receive dividends if the corporation pays them; the shareholder is limited in liability to the amount of the shareholder's investment in the event that the corporation fails; see *limited liability*.

six sigma measure of quality that requires fewer than 3.4 defects per million operations; popularized by General Electric.

skunkworks group, generally outside the main organization, charged with developing a new product or service in a short period of time; the emphasis is on total commitment of members to rapid innovation; term coined at Lockheed during World War II to designate groups charged with developing advanced aircraft, including the P-38 fighter; term derives from the comic strip "Li'l Abner."

staff management executives and workers who advise but do not direct other managers and who are not directly responsible for the production of products or services which generate the firm's revenues; distinguished from *line management*.

strategic alliance agreement between two companies to cooperate on a specific business activity; the intention is to combine complementary strengths to the advantage of each; the combination often has a limited life span.

synergy value that accrues when two or more companies combine, through merger or acquisition, in excess of their total values before combining; complementary strengths reinforce each other when synergy is achieved. This has proved difficult to achieve in practice.

systems analysis application of the concepts of systems to organizations and processes; systems are conceived as elements working together to achieve a common end in which the operation of each element affects one or more of the other elements; no element can be understood apart from its effect on at least one other element, and often on more than one other element.

Taylorism See *scientific management*.

team designated, usually small, group of workers who are charged with a specific task; they are given considerable latitude in they way that they carry out their task.

technology application of science to practical products or processes, especially in industry; technologies before the age of industrialization were mainly mechanical and were invented by trial and error.

total quality management (TQM) approach to management that empowers everyone in an organization to deliver a high-quality product or service to the customer; the customer can be the next stage within the organization or the end buyer; the object is to achieve maximum customer satisfaction at the lowest cost.

Toyota production (manufacturing) system system of production pioneered by Toyota that eliminates all waste from a manufacturing system and at the same time delivers products of highest quality to customers; evolved into *lean production*.

unlimited liability organization in which the principals are all responsible for debts should the organization fail; as distinguished from *limited liability*.

virtual organization organization comprising a network of independent groups that cooperate and coordinate their activities to produce a product or service; uses information technologies to manage the process; requires new management methods to achieve the required coordination and cooperation.

zero defects approach to management in which an organization sets a goal to deliver products or services that are 100 percent free of defects; an important component of *total quality management*.

FINANCE

Finance is the management of money and other assets—often in very large amounts. It includes mainly public finance (the disposition of revenues by government) and corporate finance (the capital required to start and maintain a business).

Ever since the invention of money by the ancients it has been a medium of exchange for goods and services and a means of storing value over time. Without the medium of money, and its management, it is not an exaggeration to say that the economic growth of the world to the beginning of the 21st century would not have been possible. The major means by which money is managed are banking systems and stock markets. The following examines the history of both institutions and describes how they operate today.

A Brief History of Finance

The earliest examples of finance are short-term loans made in civilizations in the Middle East, North America, Asia, and Africa, in cities where money first emerged. The first banks were formed in Europe during the Renaissance, after legal and accounting systems had been designed that could track money. Banks allowed people to pool their money for large-scale transactions. By the 17th century, the first stock markets gave businesses and governments the chance to raise money by selling equity rather than borrowing money. The modern era of finance has been marked by the development of ever more sophisticated and technological vehicles for managing money. Globalization is spreading this Western style of finance around the world.

Money

Money was developed by traders who understood the serious shortcomings of barter, which is the exchange of goods or services. In the barter system, a laborer might keep a share of the crop he helped harvest, or a farm wife could exchange eggs and butter for an ax. Barter works only if each party has goods or services that the other wants. Values have to be renegotiated for every transaction, keeping records is difficult, and proper accounting is impossible.

The use of money brought three big improvements to barter. First, money gives goods and services a stable value, allowing exchanges to occur more efficiently. Stability also allows record keeping and, in advanced economic systems, accounting.

Money also stores value. When goods or services are exchanged for money, the value is stored for long after the goods have been consumed or the work has been done. Over time, value stored in money can build up and become surplus wealth. Surplus wealth, especially when pooled, is called capital, and can be lent to fund the large projects on which cities and nations are built.

Finally, money provides a scale of value. A scale of value makes it possible to compare unlike objects: $10 could buy a book or a shirt; $100,000 could buy a fancy car or a modest house.

Earliest Coins Anywhere that cities arose, money emerged. Precious metals valued by weight became the basis for money in the earliest Mesopotamian civilizations, before 2000 B.C. Gold and silver were ideal because they were rare enough to be valuable, but common enough to be accepted. Precious stones have also served as money, as have cacao seeds in South America, and cowrie shells in Africa, India, and China.

The earliest coins were beads of electrum, an alloy of gold and silver. They were developed in the trading kingdom of Lydia in southwestern Anatolia, today's Turkey. Though little more than nuggets, they were stamped with symbols to show their weight and origin. The electrum beads varied widely in ratio of gold to silver, and were soon replaced with flat, round, all-silver coins. Because the coins were certified by an authority and did not have to be weighed for each transaction, they made trade easier.

Lydian society reached its peak of affluence around 550 B.C. under King Croesus. The vitality of Lydian trade made its merchants and rulers wealthy and widely known. The expression "rich as Croesus" survives to this day.

Inflation In the fifth century B.C., Athens had ample supplies of silver, and city leaders issued more money to foster commerce. They discovered that when the amount of currency in circulation exceeded the needs of trade, the value of money decreased, an effect called inflation.

Athenians also discovered that their coins, drachmae, had a higher value than the content because of their convenience and reliability. That premium, now called seigniorage, discouraged leaders from debasing the currency. It also encouraged them to use taxes to pay for public works, the arts, and defense, rather than causing inflation by issuing too much money.

Rome adopted Greek monetary principles, and a basic silver coin, which was called the denarius. To this day several countries' currency is the "dinar," and "dinero" means money in several languages. As the Roman Empire grew rich through conquest rather than productivity, however, corruption and dissipation undermined the economy. The empire's infrastructure and bureaucracy were expensive, but Roman politicians knew that raising taxes was unpopular. They preferred to issue more money. The government put more gold and silver put into circulation, and adulterated coins by making them smaller or adding base metals. Inflation was a chronic problem for Roman emperors and bureaucrats.

With the rise of Islam after 622, the newly affluent societies at first copied classical coins—the Roman-derived dinar in Africa and the Near East, the Greek-derived dirham in Persia and central Asia—and then developed their own currencies.

China By about A.D. 50 Chinese money had adopted its classic form: round coins symbolizing heaven and square holes representing Earth. Paper money was first used by the Chinese about A.D. 1000. By the 13th century, the powerful Yuan dynasty had established a successful paper currency. Eventually, most societies adopted paper currency, as the need for capital to wage war outstripped supplies of hard currency.

The Renaissance

After the fall of Rome, most of Western Europe reverted to barter. Some Celtic and Germanic cultures used denominated coins, but most precious-metal transactions were by weight of bullion. Money reentered most societies in Europe during the late Middle Ages. In Florence, trade was powered with gold from Africa, and by the mid-13th century, the gold florin was issued, and then the gold ducat.

Large silver deposits were discovered in Tyrolia, in Saxony, and in 1512 in Joachimsthal, Bohemia. The large silver Joachimsthaler coin soon supplanted the florin and the ducat, and the shortened name, thaler, or dollar, became generic. In the 1540's, huge new supplies of gold and silver from sub-Saharan Africa and the New World began to flow into Europe. Large copper deposits entered production in Sweden, making smaller-denomination coins available. At that point even daily transactions began to leave the barter system.

Banking Many of the functions of today's banks developed during the Renaissance as pawnbrokers, goldsmiths, and money changers began to lend at interest and to issue letters of credit. City and state governments in Italy and elsewhere in Europe began raising funds for large civic projects by issuing public debt—borrowing at interest from willing individuals rather than raising compulsory taxes.

Formal banks started when wealthy individuals or small groups put surplus wealth, capital, to use by making loans, building public works, or backing ambitious ventures. What made this possible were legal and accounting systems to record who had the money and where it went. Ironically, it is this "fixing" of the assets that frees the capital. In countries where the legal and accounting systems are weak, people are forced to keep physical ownership of their money, or buy and hoard nonperishable goods. Even a wealthy economy withers for lack of capital.

First banks In 1609 the Wisselbank opened in Amsterdam to provide credit for local and regional governments and for the Dutch trading empires. Its notes—a bank's promises to pay a specific sum to the bearer—circulated widely, and it is considered the first bank in the modern sense. In 1683 it was allowed to do business with individuals.

Sweden's first bank arose out of the country's use of copper, rather than gold or silver, for its currency. For Swedish coins to have value comparable to other nations' coins, the coins had to be big. That was inconvenient, so in 1661 the Stockholm Banco, founded by Johan Palmstruch about five years earlier, got a charter to issue paper money. The temptation to print notes in excess of metal reserves was too great. By 1667 the notes were worthless.

The Bank of England was the first lasting and effective central bank, although it was not founded as one. The "Old Woman of Threadneedle Street" was proposed by William Paterson (1658–1719) as a joint-stock company, in which the capital of several people was pooled. The bank issued the first national notes in 1694. They were backed by a loan of 1.2 million pounds sterling to King William III, formerly William of Orange, who had brought familiarity with banking and paper money from his native Holland.

The notes were accepted readily, and the new liquidity stimulated commerce. Historians credit England's ability to raise capital and spread risk as a primary factor in the small country's rise to empire.

Banking in the United States The first paper currency in North America was issued in 1690 by the Massachusetts Bay Colony to pay soldiers for an expedition against Quebec. Over time, most American colonies issued fiduciary paper money backed by taxes. Though rich in resources, they lacked precious metals that would have enabled them to issue large amounts of hard currency.

American business was conducted in colonial pounds, shillings, and pence. Those were worth about three-quarters of the same denominations in England. However, hardly any British currency circulated in the colonies. The balance of trade favored the mother country, and by law coins could not leave Britain or be minted in the colonies. Instead, Spanish eight-real dollars, or pieces of eight, were the most common coins. A quarter dollar was two reales, or two bits—and is so called even today.

The legacy of the Spanish eight-bit silver coin remained part of the U.S. economy for more than 300 years. Stocks on the New York Stock Exchange traded in halves, quarters, and eighths of dollars until 2000, when the NYSE shifted from fractional prices to decimal trading, thus erasing this vestige of the colonial Spanish eight-bit silver coin upon which the U.S. dollar was originally based.

American Revolution

As other wars had done, the American Revolution created a great need for fast money. Congress met the liquidity crisis with several issues of paper currency, collectively called continentals. They were fiat money. Backed by nothing but their status as legal tender, they were disdained from the start. First issued in 1775, continentals fell to half their face value by the end of that year, and to a low of $200 paper to $1 in gold by the end of the Revolution in 1783.

Under the Articles of Confederation, the federal government had no taxing authority; it could only ask the states for money. The result was economic chaos. Merchants and urban dwellers were hardest hit, while the countryside fell back on barter and self-sufficiency. The crisis came when a former officer, Daniel Shays, led other Massachusetts farmers in a tax revolt in 1786. The next year each state sent delegates to a Constitutional Convention in Philadelphia.

After leading the effort to have the Constitution adopted, Alexander Hamilton of New York, the first secretary of the treasury, proposed that Congress assume the states' outstanding war debt, redeem the debased currency at the rate of 100 continentals to one new dollar, and issue new federal notes. Opposition, led by the Virginians Thomas Jefferson and James Madison, was fierce. Many former soldiers and farmers, paid in continentals, had sold them to speculators at around the prevailing rate, 200:1. Many people thought it was grossly unfair for the speculators to be rewarded at the expense of those who had borne the brunt of the conflict. Hamilton argued they had made the best deal they could at the time, and that it would be impossible to trace the notes to their original owners. Ironically, the demand stimulated by the speculators brought the value of the continentals up to the proposed rate of 100:1 within a few months.

More ominously, states that had paid off their debt, mostly in the south, objected to a plan that would relieve other states, mostly in the north, from their debts. In April 1790 Hamilton struck a bargain over dinner with Jefferson and Madison. In return for Jefferson's support of assumption and a Bank of the United States, Hamilton would support legislation moving the U.S. capital from New York to a spot on the Potomac River that would become Washington, D.C.

The Bank of the United States

The first Bank of the United States received a 20-year charter in 1791. Hamilton's assumption and new currency plan went so well that English banks accumulated most of the new U.S. bonds originally bought by the French and Dutch. In effect Hamilton got the British to pay for the Revolution. But by 1811, when the Bank's charter came up for renewal, sentiment had turned against Europe and hard-money backers in the U.S. Creditors, especially bankers and financiers, favor tight, or hard, money linked to bullion, and low inflation. Borrowers, especially farmers, favor soft money, easy credit, and some inflation, which allows debts to be paid in dollars worth a little less down the road. Agricultural interests from southern and western states opposed the bank's hard-money policies, and the bank was not rechartered.

In 1812 a second war with England broke out. When it ended in 1815, U.S. finances were again a shambles. By 1816 a second Bank of the United States was given a 20-year charter, and again brought financial stability. When that was due for renewal, the same southern and western interests again opposed recharter. The bill passed in 1832, but was vetoed by the populist president Andrew Jackson. This left local banknotes and the meager output from the U.S. Mint, plus foreign coins, as the only currency. Most banks issued sound notes, but many—primarily in the south and west—were undercapitalized and some were simply fraudulent. The period from 1836, when the Bank closed, to 1863, when Abraham Lincoln's administration issued new federal notes, is called the "thirty years in the wilderness."

Greenbacks The Gold Rush of 1849 allowed the banks of Sutters Mill, Calif., to provide liquidity in the decade and a half before the Civil War. For the first time in U.S. history, sufficient hard currency was circulating in most of the nation. However, the gold wasn't enough to finance the Civil War, and in 1862 Congress authorized $450 million in fiat money. In contrast to the colorful and artistic local banknotes of the time, the government printed drab bills, black on the front and green on the back. The greenbacks lost value, as the continentals had, but not nearly as much: They traded at about 70 percent of face value after a Union victory, and as low as 30 percent of face value after a Confederate victory.

The greenbacks were merely an expedient; by the next year, the federal government had come up with a way to get more federal notes into circulation. The National Bank Act of 1863, and amendments the next year, gave the government new taxing powers, including the first income tax, and a 10 percent tax on local banknotes. The tax drove the local banknotes out of circulation. Banks that wanted to issue notes had to get a federal charter requiring them to invest at least a third of their capital in federal bonds. They could then issue federal banknotes, up to the value of 90 percent of their bond holdings.

The Gold Standard After the Civil War, a dispute over whether to use gold or silver to back paper money intensified. Bankers favored gold because it better limited inflation. Debtors, including the recently returned soldiers of the North and South, favored silver to spur growth; vast new mines in the West promised plenty of material.

The country had been operating with a system of bimetallism. Unlimited coinage of silver and gold was authorized. The government bought any bullion brought to it; this policy meant that paper money was backed by gold and silver. When notes were redeemed, the metal entered circulation as coins. The only problem was that the ratio of silver to gold was set at 15:1, which put too much value on silver. Under Gresham's law—bad money drives out good—people hoarded gold and spent silver.

Between 1837 and 1893 four contradictory laws were passed to tinker with the system, generally favoring gold and, thereby, lenders and businesses over borrowers and farmers. Saying to eastern plutocrats, "you shall not crucify mankind upon a cross of gold," William Jennings Bryan (1860–1925) ran for president in 1896 on a populist platform of free coinage of silver. He lost to William McKinley, who signed the Gold Standard Act in 1900.

The U.S. remained on the gold standard for three-quarters of a century, with the exception of a period during Franklin Roosevelt's administration. In 1971 President Richard Nixon took the U.S. off the gold standard for good, because the country's foreign-exchange debt exceeded the country's gold reserves. All U.S. currency, and virtually all money worldwide, is now fiat money.

J. P. Morgan and the Panic of 1907 The American economy emerged after the Civil War as an irresistible force. The transcontinental railroad was completed in 1869, and soon a sprawling network of rails brought the outputs of mines, farms, and grazing lands to eastern cities recently swelled by immigrants. The wealth created by unbridled capitalism led Mark Twain to title his novel of the era *The Gilded Age*.

It was the age of the great industrialists—Vanderbilt, Rockefeller, and others (see *Business*)—but the most powerful of all was John Pierpont Morgan (1837–1913), who established his own stock brokerage in 1862 and emerged after the Civil War as the most powerful financier in the country. His acquisitions consolidated many industries, especially railroads and steel mills. He reorganized General Electric, and his formation of U.S. Steel in 1901 created the first billion-dollar corporation in history.

Morgan put his fortune and prestige on the line to end the Panic of 1907. After several large corporations and stock brokerages went bankrupt, stock prices fell, causing traders to withdraw money from banks to cover their losses. Bank failures and a nationwide recession seemed likely. Morgan, however, assembled a team of businessmen who shored up weak banks and invested in corporations that were sound, but needed help. The strategy worked, and the crisis passed. The bank and brokerage house that bears J. P. Morgan's name is still one of the largest in the world.

The Federal Reserve The grim reality that the federal government had to call upon a private citizen to solve a national financial crisis led to the passage of the Federal Reserve Act in 1913. It created the Federal Reserve Board, which later became the Federal Reserve System, commonly called the Fed. The system, which is one of the most powerful institutions in America, consists of a board of governors and 12 regional reserve banks. The Fed regulates the money supply by buying and selling federal notes. It also sets the discount rate, the interest rate at which it lends money to its commercial bank customers. The discount rate helps decide interest rates that the banks, in turn, charge their customers. Finally, the Fed also helps regulate commercial banks.

Causes of the Great Depression While the European landscape and economy were in ruins after World War I, the U.S. emerged from the conflict relatively unscathed. The postwar strength produced the roaring twenties, a decade in which social exuberance was matched by wild speculations in the credit and stock markets. The optimism was fueled by low interest rates and a prevailing belief that the Fed had firm control of the economy.

Few within the Fed saw the trouble that was coming. One exception was Benjamin Strong (1872–1928), head of the Federal Reserve Bank of New York. He raised interest rates in his district to try to slow the economy, but without the support of other board members, he had only a limited effect. On October 29, 1929, "Black Tuesday," the stock market crashed.

A recession after such a crash was almost inevitable. Three factors turned it into the Great Depression. First, interest rates were left high even after the bubble burst, making it difficult for surviving companies to borrow. Then the administration of Herbert Hoover pushed through a massive tax increase to boost sagging federal revenues. Worst of all, Congress bowed to special interests and passed the protectionist Smoot-Hawley Tariff.

Other countries quickly retaliated, and global trade slowed to a trickle. Similar mismanagement in other countries turned the recession into a global depression. The 1930's were the most traumatic times in U.S. financial history, as industrial output fell to half, unemployment reached 25 percent, and hundreds of banks failed, wiping out family savings across the country.

Economic conditions were worse in Europe, where hyperinflation stalked Germany and helped bring the Nazi Party to power.

The New Deal and Reform Soon after taking office, President Franklin Roosevelt declared a bank holiday to give solvent institutions time to recover. Senator Carter Glass of Virginia (1858–1946) and Representative Henry B. Steagall of Alabama (1873–1943) sponsored the most sweeping banking reform in the country since the days of Hamilton. The Banking Act of 1933 created the Federal Deposit Insurance Corp., ending bank runs at a stroke by establishing an insurance system for depositors' money. The act also separated banking and brokerage. Commercial banks were prohibited from underwriting stocks and bonds; investment banking firms were prohibited from taking deposits. Savings and industrial banks were allowed to join the Fed, and branch banking was allowed.

Under Franklin Roosevelt's "New Deal," massive relief efforts and huge public works projects kept the country from anarchy, but another recession struck in 1937, driven mostly by the failure of cotton crops in the South and the Dust Bowl in the West.

World War II helped to salvage the U.S. economy. All of the major corporations had mobilized to fight the war, and productivity soared. Unemployment declined dramatically and tens of millions of American workers were earning more money than ever before. Wartime restrictions, however, made consumer goods scarce or nonexistent (no new cars, for example, were built in 1942–46). When the war was won, the combination of the capacity and the pent-up demand produced the biggest boom ever. It was stoked by $200 billion in maturing war bonds and an upwardly mobile, college-educated workforce created by the G.I. Bill.

Stagflation The decade of the 1970's was marked by the unprecedented combination of rising prices and slow economic growth. Economists coined a new term for the global phenomenon: stagflation. The factors that led to this malaise included the end of the gold standard in 1971, the Arab oil embargo of 1973, expanded social programs, and the war in Vietnam, which necessitated higher taxes. Inflation was 5–10 percent during every year of the 1970's, reaching a peak of 13.5 percent in 1980.

President Jimmy Carter (b. 1924) got most of the blame for stagflation, but decades of fiscal policy had set the stage. It took harsh treatment to get the economy moving again. Federal Reserve Chairman Paul Volcker (b. 1927) reduced the supply of money in circulation by selling federal bonds. The contraction produced a sharp recession in the early 1980's, but it ended stagflation.

Banking in the United States Today Globalization and the drive for profits during the economic boom of the 1990's pushed the largest banks to consider acquisitions of insurance companies and brokerage houses, both extremely profitable kinds of businesses. In 1998, Travelers Insurance, one of the largest insurance underwriters, was set to merge with Citigroup, one of the largest banks. Such a deal was prohibited under the Glass-Steagall Act, but banking overhauls had been rattling around Congress for many years. On cue, legislators passed the Financial Services Modernization Act of 1999, called Gramm-Leach-Bliley after its sponsors. Banks, brokerages, and insurance firms were allowed to compete with and buy each other, and to do business across state lines.

At the turn of the century, there were about 10,000 commercial banks in the United States, divided into three groups: small local banks, which were rapidly being acquired by larger banks; larger regional banks with networks that covered one or more states; and huge national banks. The largest banks, Citigroup, J. P. Morgan Chase & Co., and Bank of America, competed internationally with similarly huge Japanese, German, and British banks.

Globalization The seeds of globalization were planted at the end of World War II. In 1944, at a summit in Bretton Woods, N.H., a dollar-dominated global economic system was designed. The agreement created the International Monetary Fund to mitigate international currency crises by making short-term loans to countries facing a credit or liquidity crunch. It also created the International Bank for Reconstruction and Development, commonly called the World Bank, to provide long-term credit to poor and underdeveloped countries. The International Monetary Fund and the World Bank provided a measure of global financial stability that made it easier for companies to do business internationally.

By the late 1980's, advances in communications were opening up seemingly endless new opportunities for businesses. The flow of capital from developed nations to developing nations swelled from 43.9 billion in 1990 to an estimated $299 billion in 1997.

The European Union and the Euro In 1952 West Germany, France, the Netherlands, Italy, Belgium, and Luxembourg formed the European Coal and Steel Community. Six years later it expanded into the European Economic Community, often called the Common Market, and then the European Union. Currency trading ranges were established with the goal of a single currency.

The U.K. joined the EU but retained its own currency. It did, however, convert to a decimal system in 1971, with 100 new pence to the pound. The conversion included a mild devaluation, leaving pensioners ever after to mutter about the value of "old money."

In 1988, the Delors Report laid out a four-step plan for a single European currency. In 1998 the European Central Bank was created; before that, the German Bundesbank was the de facto central bank for Europe. In 1999 the euro entered use for electronic transactions, but it was not until 2002 that notes and coins entered circulation. Old currencies were withdrawn six months later.

Stock Markets

Stock markets are systems for raising capital and spreading risk. From the beginnings of civilization until the Renaissance rulers and wealthy families sponsored public works and ambitious ventures. Early in the Renaissance, joint-stock companies were developed under which individuals, families, villages, and trade guilds could pool their capital to underwrite new companies or trading expeditions. Trade guilds, in particular, became very powerful because of their strong organizations and ability to raise large amounts of money relatively quickly.

First Stock Market

Once ownership of a company or the right to the bounty of a trading expedition was in multiple hands, the shares became another valuable commodity that could be sold or traded. The world's first stock market began informal business in 1602 on Damrak Street in Amsterdam, trading shares of the world's first large multinational venture, the Verenidge Oost-Indische Companie (United East-India Co.). The oldest surviving stock certificates, just handwritten notes, are of the VOC from 1606.

Within a year or two futures and options on shares had been developed in Amsterdam. A futures contract represents immediate payment for future delivery of a security or commodity. An option is even more malleable; it is the right to buy or sell a commodity or security at a given price within a specific period. Once a futures contract is agreed upon, the commodity or security will be delivered. An option, however, can be left to expire unexercised.

Other Early Exchanges

The Frankfurt Stock Exchange traces its ancestry to 1585, but what existed then was a currency exchange. Bonds were added 100 years later, and stocks were not added until 1820. The London Stock Exchange traces its history to informal trading in shares in 1698 at Jonathan's Coffee-House, where trading had been going on for some time.

Meanwhile, the English physician, surveyor, and economist Sir William Petty (1623–87) was posted to Ireland, where he quantified an ancient concept that the fair market value of any land is equal to its production—from crops, timber, minerals, or livestock—over 20 years. In essence Petty around 1650 had formalized the most fundamental measure of any commodity or security, its price-to-earnings ratio, an essential value indicator to this day.

Speculators

An investor buys and sells securities for their inherent value. Speculators buy and sell because they want to bet that securities will rise or decline in value. A little speculation helps keeps markets active and provides capital for new ventures. When speculation runs out of control, uninformed people flock to the markets in hopes of a quick profit. The results are invariably a crash and widespread economic distress.

Tulipmania The technology-stock bubble of the late 1990's was the latest in a long line of financial crises dating back to tulipmania, which hit Holland in the 1630's. The normally sober and industrious Netherlanders were overcome by a speculative fever. Fortunes were exchanged for rare tulip bulbs; the few clearheaded critics were ignored. Bubbles always burst when enough people lose their euphoria, and want to sell. The panic buying turns in a moment into panic selling. The tulip bubble burst in 1637, ruining many and bringing on a severe recession.

The South Sea Bubble Less than a hundred years later it all happened again, this time in England. The South Sea Co. was founded in 1711 as a legitimate trading firm. But when granted a monopoly from Parliament, the founders proposed to retire the national debt in exchange for company stock. Stories were planted about fabulous wealth; 50:1 returns were promised. Huge dividends were paid with the money pouring in, turning the company into a pyramid scheme. The house of cards tumbled in 1720, and even some members of Parliament were ruined.

Mississippi Co. Madness also prevailed in France. The Scotsman John Law (1671–1729), a brilliant scoundrel, got a royal charter from the regent of Louis XV to open a bank in 1716. His well-backed notes traded at a premium. He then chartered the Company of the West, commonly called the Mississippi Co., to operate the Louisiana colony. He further offered to sell shares for deeply discounted national paper money. Preposterous dividends were promised, just as for the South Sea Co. Overnight wealth gave birth to the term "millionaire," and inflation soared. The Mississippi Bubble burst about the same time as the South Sea Bubble. The Bourbon dynasty was irreparably damaged, many nobles were ruined, land and tax reforms were abandoned, and the economy was in tatters.

The U.S. Stock Market

The first stock exchange in North America opened in 1790 in Philadelphia, the second-largest city in the British Empire at the time of the Revolution. Markets hate uncertainty, so it is significant that the Philadelphia Bourse opened seven years after the end of the Revolution, the same year the federal government issued $80 million in Treasury bonds to pay off the debts from the Revolution.

NYSE The New York exchange was created on May 17, 1792, when 24 stockbrokers and merchants convened under a buttonwood tree on Wall Street. According to a two-sentence contract signed that day, known as the Buttonwood Agreement, the men would trade stocks and bonds only among themselves, fix commissions (at "one quarter per cent of specie value"), and participate in no auctions other than their own.

Market activity took a quantum leap after the War of 1812, as government debt again sparked heavy trading in federal certificates. In addition, scores of new banks and insurance companies were established in the next few years and were listed on the exchange by 1815; the sale of securities generated much of the venture capital necessary to fund these new enterprises. In March 1817 the original exchange passed a formal constitution with rules of conduct, adopted the name New York Stock & Exchange Board—shortened to New York Stock Exchange (NYSE) in 1863—and moved into a rented room at 40 Wall Street.

AMEX Meanwhile, smaller exchanges in New York and elsewhere competed for business. Among the largest New York rivals was a group known as the Curbstone Brokers, which conducted its trade outdoors, rain or shine, beginning in the early 1800's. Later known as the New York Curb Exchange, the group finally moved indoors at 86 Trinity Place, just west of Wall Street, in 1921. Renamed the American Stock Exchange (AMEX) in 1953, it continues to operate today, emphasizing lower-priced stocks and younger, growing companies, at the same location.

Boom and Bust Cycle Rapid economic growth and westward expansion in the first half of the 19th century brought dramatic increases in trading volume and the number and value of available stocks. Average daily volume on the NYSE hit 8,500 shares in 1830, representing a 50-fold increase in only seven years. The number of publicly traded companies rose from 20 in 1800 to more than 120 by 1835. After the first railroad stock was issued in 1830, the acceleration of track construction caused market growth in the ensuing decades. Railroads remained the nation's largest and most powerful companies throughout the 19th century, with mining, farm equipment, steel, and other manufacturing companies prominent on the exchange by the 1870's.

The financial markets proved volatile. Wall Street's first major "panic" began in 1836, amid wild speculation in federal land and commodity imports. The government responded by issuing a "specie circular" for the purchase of public land (requiring payment in gold or silver), which led to a collapse in prices and the failure of thousands of banks and businesses. Production and employment fell off rapidly, and the nation suffered a six-year depression. Overinvestment in land and railroads produced another wave of panic selling in 1857–58. Gold prices, run up during the attempt of the financiers Jay Gould (1836–92) and James Fisk (1834–72) to corner the supply, dropped precipitously when the federal government released its own gold into the market—causing a financial debacle on September 24, 1869, known as "Black Friday."

The boom that powered the U.S. economy after the Civil War was no bar to instability. The worst financial crisis of the 19th century began in 1873, when heavy speculation in securities and the failure of Jay Cooke's banking house toppled business after business, forced the NYSE to close for 10 days, and triggered a six-year depression. In 1893, a series of railroad bankruptcies caused hundreds of banks to fail, thousands of companies to shut down, and widespread unemployment to persist for the next four years.

Securities regulation

Amid the boom-and-bust cycles, a host of innovations brought tighter regulation and improved efficiency to the securities markets. In 1853 the NYSE began requiring listed companies to file complete statements of outstanding shares and capital resources. In 1868 memberships on the exchange were put up for sale, rather than reserved for life. And the following year, to keep companies from issuing too many stocks ("watering"), the NYSE began requiring them to register shares at a bank or another appropriate institution. Also in 1868, the first ticker tapes were introduced on the trading floor.

The year 1871 began an era of change for the NYSE, as the traditional "call market" (in which an auctioneer called out the name of each stock and brokers shouted their offers to sell or buy) was replaced by today's continuous auction market. By 1899 all listed companies provided regular financial statements both to the NYSE and to stockholders (in 1910 the exchange discontinued trading in unlisted securities).

Dow Jones industrial average The NYSE had its first million-share day in 1886, as heavy industry began to dominate trading. The Dow Jones industrial average, the first stock index devoted exclusively to this sector, became the market bellwether by the mid-1890's. It remains a key indicator today.

The Crash and the New Deal

The NYSE relocated to its current location at 11 Wall Street in 1922, and the move was soon followed by a historic bull run. Beginning in 1923, stock prices and trading volume surged, virtually unchecked, for more than six years. In 1928, single-day share volume on the NYSE broke the 5 million level. The crash of October 29, 1929 ("Black Tuesday") produced a record volume of more than 16 million shares—most of them sales. The Dow Jones average dropped 11 percent in one day.

The Dow hit bottom, down 89 percent from its 1929 peak, in July 1932. The New Deal brought some relief and much reform: the Securities Act of 1933 required full disclosure to investors and prohibited fraud in the sale of securities; the Securities Exchange Act of 1934 established the Securities and Exchange Commission (SEC) to oversee the markets and protect investors against malpractice.

Longest Bull Run in History

Industrial mobilization during World War II restored the economy, and the postwar period brought sustained financial growth. A bull run that began in 1949 was the longest to date, with stock prices rising almost without interruption for the next eight years. The Dow shot past the 500 mark in 1956.

Merrill Lynch Old-line brokers and investment bankers opposed the reforms of the mid-1930's as government interference in private enterprise, but some saw a new horizon opening. In the 1940's Charles E. Merrill (1885–1956) hired hundreds of investment advisers, paid them a salary, and had them solicit business from the burgeoning middle class. Until then most brokers worked largely on commission, and only wealthy clients were worth these brokers' time. Merrill also began to advertise in 1948. By 1960 Merrill Lynch had more than half a million clients and was four times the size of the next-largest brokerage.

First mutual fund Mutual funds also became prominent after the war. The first, the Massachusetts Investors Trust, was launched in 1924. But mutual funds first began to be popular in the 1950's. People of modest means were not willing to invest their small savings until the regulatory reforms of the 1930's took hold and the "mass affluent" had begun to respond to the enticements of Merrill Lynch and its competitors.

With people and money pouring into the market and manufacturing running at capacity, stocks broke the pre-crash levels in 1954, and soared higher. The NYSE had its first billion-share day in 1959. The boom rolled on, but by the late 1960's several factors began to drag at equities. Technology failed to keep up with volume, and markets became victims of their own success. Inflation, domestic unrest, and international troubles also took their toll.

Modern Era

The incorporation of the NYSE and the creation of an inter-dealer, over-the-counter (OTC) market—the National Association of Securities Dealers Automated Quotation system (NASDAQ)—both in 1971, opened the modern era in U.S. securities trading. NASDAQ became the first stock exchange to rely on sophisticated computer and telecommunications systems to trade and monitor millions of securities on a daily basis. Trading was no longer limited to a single location; millions of dealers across the globe now were connected by an electronic network to execute trades and deliver data in real time. NASDAQ's acquisition of the AMEX in 1998 made it the second-largest U.S. stock exchange (after the NYSE). NASDAQ and the AMEX continue to operate as separate entities, with the former emphasizing start-up and established companies in the technology sector.

In the 1970's and 1980's, the spread of regulated, high-tech exchanges in Europe and Asia contributed to an expanding financial base. The abolition of fixed commissions (1975), the popularization of mutual funds and pension funds, and the advent of online brokerage brought tens of millions of new U.S. investors into the market. Single-day share volume on the NYSE hit 100 million in 1982; the Dow passed 1,000 in 1972 and 2,000 in 1987.

Leveraged buyouts In most bull markets there is some new wrinkle, and in the 1980's it was leveraged buyouts. Corporate raiders borrowed against the stock of the company they were planning to acquire. They also raised huge sums with unsecured or "junk" bonds. Separately, well-intentioned efforts to improve the profitability of savings and loan institutions combined with an unprecedented real-estate boom made the S&Ls subject to manipulation and fraud. Both the LBO bubble and the S&L crisis came to a head in 1986. In October 1987 markets experienced one of the worst one-day falls.

However, the expected recession never occurred; the Fed cut interest rates and increased cash in the system, so individual investors did not panic. The market recovered quickly, leaving investors and money managers alike with the mistaken idea that the Fed could prevent any market fall.

Dot-com bubble In place of the LBOs of the 1980's, the new fad of the 1990's was the initial public offering (IPO). Tiny technology companies had their initial public offerings and saw their share prices reach the stratosphere on the first day of trading. The Dow soared from 5,000 in 1995 to 11,000 in 1999 before plummeting to below 9,000 in 2001. "Dot-com" companies, which sold goods and services over the Internet, led the technology boom.

As the frenzy built, some executives took to manipulating their company's financial results to sustain their stock prices. Many big accounting firms were now consultants to the same firms they audited, but denied that there was a conflict of interest. A little shuffling of costs and revenue soon gave way to wholesale fraud at some firms, aided and abetted by their erstwhile auditors. When the bubble burst, and the profits were found to be fake, huge firms went bankrupt and some of their executives were brought to trial. One of the largest and most prestigious accounting firms, Arthur Andersen, collapsed in the midst of the scandals.

Mutual Funds

Mutual funds date back to the 1800's in England and Scotland, but did not become available in the United States until 1924. Their popularity surged in the 1980's, when many companies dropped their traditional pension plans and more Americans became responsible for planning for their own retirement incomes. When the Investment Company Institute, the trade organization of the mutual fund industry, was created in 1940, its members included 68 funds worth a total of $2.1 billion. Today, the ICI counts nearly 9,000 different funds, representing more than 90 million shareholders, and with total assets of more than $6 trillion.

A mutual fund is a type of investment in which

investors pool their money and then collectively invest that money in a variety of stocks, bonds, or other money instruments. Every mutual fund has a particular strategy that determines how much to allocate to each type of investment. For example, a fund seeking higher rewards might invest only in stocks, while a fund seeking very low risk might invest in a variety of bonds. Each mutual fund's strategy, as well its fees and information about how to buy and sell shares, is outlined in the fund prospectus.

The strategy of each mutual fund is determined by the fund manager. The fund manager is a professional investor who monitors the financial markets and continually reallocates the fund's assets to reap the best return. Mutual funds allow investors to diversify their portfolios by making a wide range of investments. Diversification reduces the risk of losing a large amount of money at one time. Like individual securities investments, mutual funds are not guaranteed by the Federal Deposit Insurance Corp. the way bank accounts are, and may lose money.

Kinds of Mutual Funds The earliest mutual funds invested almost entirely in equities, or shares of stock in publicly traded corporations. Today, mutual funds invest in the entire spectrum of money instruments. Broadly speaking, there are four different kinds of mutual funds. Within the four categories are thousands of mutual funds, each with its own goal and strategies for achieving that goal.

Stock funds, or equity funds, are by far the most common type of mutual funds, representing more than half of all funds. These mutual funds are invested entirely in stocks. The similarities among the various kinds of stock funds end here. *Aggressive growth funds* invest in small companies poised for growth. *Growth funds* invest primarily in large well-established companies. *Sector funds* invest only in companies in a certain segment of the economy, for example, health care. *Growth and income funds* invest in large companies with growth potential and a strong record of dividend payouts. *Income-equity funds* are even more concerned with dividend income, and are less interested in growth potential. *Emerging market funds* invest in companies in developing nations. *Regional equity funds* invest only in companies in a certain part of the world. *Global equity funds* invest in equity securities traded internationally, including those of U.S. companies.

Index funds are stock funds whose portfolio mirrors the performance of various stock market indexes, such as Standard and Poor's 500 or the Dow Jones industrial average. Because a computer, rather than a person, manages this portfolio, the management costs of index funds are usually lower than other funds.

Bond funds invest in government- and corporate-issued long-term bonds. They are generally more conservative than stock funds but promise a steadier return. This category of funds can be divided into two subcategories: taxable bond funds and tax-free or municipal bond funds.

Hybrid funds invest in a mix of stocks and bonds. Some hybrid funds have fixed percentages allotted to each type of security; other funds allow the fund manager to change the percentages depending on market conditions.

Money market funds are often called short-term funds because they invest in short-term securities (with an average maturity of 90 days or less), such as Treasury bills, CDs, and commercial paper. Within this category are both taxable funds and tax-exempt funds. Because they are free from federal taxes (and in some cases state and local taxes as well), tax-exempt funds usually provide a lower rate of return than taxable funds.

Key Terms for Mutual Funds

closed-end funds most mutual funds are considered "open-end" funds because they offer new shares to the public at all times, and will buy back shares from shareholders at any time. A closed-end fund has a fixed number of shares, which usually trade on a major stock exchange.

expense ratio cost of managing a mutual fund. The ratio is the total amount that the fund manager charges as a percentage of the fund's total assets. The costs include the fund manager's salary and the administrative costs for keeping records and mailing statements. The average mutual fund has an expense ratio of about 1.5 percent. Index funds have an expense ratio of about 0.25 percent.

load fee or sales charge for purchasing shares of a mutual fund, similar to a commission for purchasing stocks. Mutual funds are generally divided into load funds (those that charge a fee) and no-load funds (those that don't).

net asset value share price for a mutual fund. It is equal to the market value of all the fund's securities (minus expenses), divided by the total number of shares.

Glossary of Finance Terms

American Stock Exchange (ASE) one of the major American stock exchanges; emphasizes lower-priced stocks and younger, growing companies; see *New York Stock Exchange.*

auction market sale in which an item is offered to bidders by an auctioneer who sells the item to the highest bidder.

barter exchange of goods or services of one kind for another without the use of money.

bear market stock market in which traders expect prices to fall; traders sell stocks, driving down prices and fulfilling their expectations; see *bull market.*

Black Tuesday October 29, 1929, the day the stock market produced a record volume of more than 16 million shares—most of them sales—and the Dow Jones industrial average dropped 11 percent in one day; began a prolonged decline in the stock market that was a contributor to the Great Depression.

bond security issued by government or public company promising to repay borrowed money at a set interest rate in a specified period of time; see *junk bond.*

bubble market in which the price of an asset continues to rise because speculators believe it will continue to rise even further, until prices reach a level that is not sustainable; panic selling begins and the price falls precipitously.

bull market stock market in which traders expect prices to rise; traders buy stocks, driving up prices and fulfilling their expectations; see *bear market.*

business cycle tendency for the economy to expand and contract; different theories attribute the cause to government policies, economic shocks (e.g., the rate of technological progress), lags in timing of economic decisionmaking, or a combination of these and other factors.

call see *option*.

central bank A bank that controls the money supply and monetary policy in a country; see *Bank of England* and *Federal Reserve System*.

closed-end fund A mutual fund that has a fixed number of shares which usually trade on a major stock exchange; see open-end fund.

collateralized mortgage obligation (CMO) a security, backed by a pool of mortgages, structured so that there are several classes of bondholders with varying maturities called tranches. The principal payments from the underlying pool of pass-through securities are used to retire the bonds on a priority basis as specified in the prospectus. Also known as mortgage pass-through security.

commercial bank bank that deals with the general public; it accepts interest-paying deposits and lends to a wide variety of households and small businesses; see *investment bank*.

commercial paper short-term unsecured promissory notes issued by a corporation. The maturity of commercial paper is typically less than nine months; the most common maturity range is 30 to 50 days or less.

decimal trading trading in securities priced in hundredths of a unit of money; in the United States decimal trading began at the New York Stock Exchange in 2000; see *fractional trading*.

debenture any debt obligation backed strictly by the borrower's integrity, e.g., an unsecured bond.

debt money borrowed.

debt service interest payments plus repayments of principal to creditors. Investors pay close attention to whether or not a company is making enough money to service its debt.

derivative financial contract whose value is based on, or "derived" from, a traditional security such as a stock or bond, commodity, or market index.

discount rate interest rate charged by the U.S. Federal Reserve for short-term borrowing by member banks.

diversification in investing, holding a variety of assets in order to minimize the risk of losses in any single asset.

dividend portion of a company's profit paid to holders of its common and preferred stocks. A stock selling for $20 with an annual dividend of $1 a share yields the investor a 5 percent dividend.

Dow Jones industrial average An index based on the prices of 30 widely traded United States industrial stocks; often considered a gauge of overall stock market performance.

earnings before interest, taxes, depreciation, and amortization (EBITDA) financial measure defined as revenues less cost of goods sold and selling, general, and administrative expenses. In other words, a company's profit before the deduction of interest, income taxes, depreciation, and amortization expenses. EBITDA became popular in the 1980's when corporate raiders tried to assess what a company's operation generated, not counting interest, taxes, or noncash expenses such as depreciation and amortization that reflect diminished values of a company's assets.

equity ownership interest in a firm or asset. In real estate, dollar difference between what a property could be sold for and debts claimed against it, such as a mortgage. In a brokerage account, equity equals the value of the account's securities minus any money borrowed from a brokerage firm in a margin account. "Equities" is another name for stocks or company shares.

euro (€) unit of currency of the European Union; adopted in 1999, it replaced the currencies of all of the EU countries except the United Kingdom.

Federal Deposit Insurance Corporation (F.D.I.C.) U.S. regulatory body formed by the Banking Act of 1933, it charters banks and insures the deposits (up to a maximum of $100,000 per depositor) in member banks; financed by charges paid by member banks.

federal funds rate interest rate that banks with excess reserves at a Federal Reserve district bank charge other banks that need overnight loans. The fed-funds rate, as it is called, often points to the direction of U.S. interest rates because it is set daily by the market, unlike the prime rate and the discount rate. The Federal Reserve does not have a target for the fed-funds rate, which it moves periodically.

Federal Reserve System created in 1913 by the Federal Reserve Act, it is the U.S. central bank system. It consists of a board of governors and 12 district reserve banks; they fix bank reserve and margin requirements, the discount rate, and manage the federal funds rate; the board manages monetary policy with the intention of minimizing the fluctuations of business cycles.

fiat money money that circulates by command of the state; originally money was coined of valuable metals that corresponded to their face value; but when money was coined of base metals, and paper currency came into use, its value had to be established by the power of the state; modern money is fiat money.

fiduciary money money that is backed by real assets and owes it acceptability to pubic trust and confidence.

fractional trading trading in securities priced in halves, quarters, and eighths of a dollar; in 2000 the New York Stock Exchange converted to decimal trading.

futures market market in which contracts commit two parties to buy and sell commodities, securities, or currencies on a date in the future at a price fixed when the contact is made; if the market price at the time the contract matures is higher than the contract price, the buyer profits; if the market price is lower, the seller profits.

gold standard system of fixing exchange rates to the price of gold in order to facilitate trade between nations.

Gresham's law tendency for people to spend money of low intrinsic value (coins of base metal and paper currency) and hoard money of higher intrinsic value (coins of precious metals) when these forms of money circulate concurrently; often stated as "bad money drives out good"; first articulated by Sir Thomas Gresham (ca. 1519–79), an adviser to Queen Elizabeth I.

hard money money which can be converted into other money or whose price compared with other money is expected to remain stable or to rise; see *soft money*.

hedge fund investment strategy that employs a variety of techniques to enhance returns, such as both buying and shorting stocks.

inflation condition in which prices and wages increase as measured by changes in an appropriate price index such as the Consumer Price Index.

initial public offering (IPO) stock issued for the first time by a public company.

investment bank bank dealing with other firms rather than the general public; see *commercial bank*.

investor buyer and seller of securities who considers their inherent value; see *speculator*.

joint-stock company company in which investors pool their money and receive profits or dividends in proportion to their investments; often are limited liability companies in that investors are liable only for any debts in the amount of their original investments.

junk bond bond issued by companies with low credit ratings that compensate for high risk by paying high interest rates; also called a "high yield bond."

legal tender form of money that a creditor is legally obligated to accept in payment of a debt.

letter of credit letter issued by a bank authorizing the bearer to withdraw a stated amount of money from the issuing bank or its branches and agencies.

leveraged buyout purchase of the equity of a company financed mostly by borrowing against the stock of the target company; during the heyday of leveraged buyouts in the 1980's corporate raiders also raised large sums with unsecured junk bonds.

limited liability company (LLC) company in which investors' potential loss is limited to the amount of their investments in the event that the business fails.

liquid assets assets that can be converted into money rapidly and at a reasonably predictable rate.

liquidity property of assets that allows them to be converted into money rapidly and at a reasonably predictable rate; in a company, having assets that are liquid.

margin the difference between the market value of a stock and the loan a broker makes; allows investors to buy securities by borrowing money from a broker.

money medium of exchange in goods and services and a means of storing value over time.

money market fund pooled fund that invests in short-term loans.

NASDAQ (National Association of Securities Dealers and Automated Quotation system) opened in 1971, NASDAQ was the first stock exchange to rely on sophisticated computer and telecommunications systems to trade and monitor millions of securities on a daily basis. Trading was no longer limited to a single location; millions of dealers across the globe were connected by an electronic network to execute trades and deliver data in real time.

New York Stock Exchange (NYSE) largest U.S. market for trading stocks and bonds based on the specialist system.

price-to-earnings ratio (P/E) ratio obtained by dividing the current market price of a stock by the most recently published earnings for equity per share.

put see *option.*

pyramid scheme illegal, fraudulent scheme in which a con artist persuades victims to invest by promising an extraordinary return; he or she embezzles the funds while using the minimum necessary to pay off any investors who insist on terminating their investment.

ROI (return on investment) generally, income as a proportion of a company's net book value. Also known as profitability ratio.

savings and loan institution (S&L) financial institution that accepts deposits from the public and lends its funds primarily as home mortgages.

Securities and Exchange Commission (SEC) created by the Securities Exchange Act of 1934, it monitors and regulates the sale of corporate securities in the U.S.

seigniorage originally the profit made by a ruler who issues money with a face value exceeding the cost of production; today it refers to the ability of governments to issue new money to pay for goods and services.

selling short (short selling) sale of a stock that is not actually owned. If an investor thinks the price of a stock is going down, the investor borrows the stock from a broker and sells it.

soft money money which cannot be converted into other money or whose price compared with other money is expected to fall; see *hard money.*

speculator buyer and seller of securities betting that they will rise or decline in value; see *investor.*

specialist individual on the floor of a stock exchange who is employed by a specialist firm to match buyers and sellers of stocks of specific companies; obligated to "make a market" in a stock by buying shares when there are no other buyers and to sell shares from the firm's inventory when there are no other sellers.

specie money in the form of coins, not paper currency.

stock capital that a company raises by selling shares that entitle the owner to dividends and other rights of ownership.

stock exchange place where stocks, bonds, and other financial instruments are bought and sold.

stock market stock exchange; also can refer to the overall performance of the prices of stocks and bonds, as in, "The stock market rose today."

tight money money that is difficult to borrow because of high interest rates or limited availability.

traders individuals who take positions in securities and their derivatives with the objective of making profits.

trading buying and selling securities.

Treasury bill (T-bill) debt obligation of the U.S. Treasury that has maturity of one year or less. Maturities for T-bills are usually 91 days, 182 days, or 52 weeks.

Treasury bond debt obligation of the U.S. Treasury that has maturity of two years or more.

venture capital capital invested in new or small businesses, with comparatively high risk, in the hope of making a substantial profit if the businesses prosper.

yield percentage rate of return paid on a stock in the form of dividends, or the effective rate of interest paid on a bond or note.

GEOGRAPHY

Physical Geography 172

The Continents 174

The United States 185

World Population 188

Oceans 190

Major Seas, Gulfs, and Straits of the World 190

Rivers and Canals of the World 194

Islands and Archipelagos of the World 198

Mountain Ranges 204

Glossary of Geographical Terms 207

GEOGRAPHY

Geography, in the broadest sense, is the systematic study of the Earth, its physical makeup (oceans, rivers, continents, islands, climate, etc.), and how those elements affect the way humans organize their societies and live productive lives. More specifically geographers examine human populations and population distribution by region and by urban and rural segmentation; political systems; and economic structures such as agriculture, trade,industry ,and transportation.

This section focuses on physical geography, which is the study of those parts of the Earth that have the greatest impact on human life: the atmosphere (the air, and in particular climate and weather); the hydrosphere (oceans, lakes, and rivers); the lithosphere (the Earth's crust, the surface of which is the land and the ocean floor); and the biosphere (that part of the atmosphere, lithosphere, and hydrosphere inhabited by living things).

Physical Geography

Features of Physical Geography

First-order features of the Earth's geography are the continents and the oceans. Second-order continental features include mountain ranges, valleys, plains, and deserts. Third-order features include mountains and valleys.

The boundaries of continents and oceans are affected by long-term global changes such as glaciation. During an ice age, much of the globe's water is frozen in ice on land, and sea levels drop accordingly. During the last ice age, which ended about 11,500 years ago, the oceans were about 100 meters (328 ft.) lower than they are today. At that time, the now submerged Bering land bridge connected Asia and North America.

Climate and Weather

Climate is generally defined as the characteristic condition of the atmosphere near the Earth's surface in a particular place or region. It includes patterns of temperature, wind, precipitation, cloud cover, and other variables. Earth's climate is ultimately dependent on solar radiation, its distance from the sun (which varies by about 6 million kilometers/3.5 million miles over the course of a year), the orientation of the Earth's axis of spin away from or toward the sun, and other factors. Climate varies from region to region depending on such things as latitude, the topography of the land, ocean water currents and temperature, and atmospheric pressure and wind. It is predictable in terms of the average and variation of temperature, precipitation, and other variables, but it is subject to change due to the long-term cycle of ice ages and human activities.

Winds The world's major wind systems are determined by variations in atmospheric pressure. Broadly speaking, the Earth is covered by seven belts of atmospheric pressure, alternately low and high, starting with a low at the equator and working toward highs at the poles. These pressure systems are themselves regions of relatively light and variable winds: *the equatorial low* (or *intertropical convergence zone*), which straddles the equator between about 10°S and 10°N; *the subtropical highs*, or *horse latitudes*, between 30° and 40°S, and 30° and 40°N; and the *subpolar lows* at about 50°-60°S and 50°-60°N. The poles are capped by *polar high pressure zones*.

The major wind systems are found between these zones of low and high pressure. North and south of the equatorial trough, the *northeast* and *southeast trade winds* blow toward the equator and west in bands about 1,200 miles wide. (Winds are named for the direction *from* which they come.) Between the horse latitudes and the subpolar lows, the winds blow away from the equator and toward the east. In the northern hemisphere, the *westerlies* cross the Atlantic, Eurasia, the Pacific, and North America. The strong westerlies of the Southern Ocean, almost uninterrupted by land, are called the *roaring forties* and *furious fifties*, depending on latitude. Between the subpolar lows and the polar high are the *polar easterlies*.

The *trade winds* do not prevail in the northern Indian Ocean (the Arabian Sea and Bay of Bengal) or the northwest Pacific, including the South China Sea and waters around Japan. Here the general pattern is modified by the seasonal warming and cooling of adjacent land masses that creates areas of low and high pressure respectively. The resulting wind system is called the monsoon (from the Arabic *mawsim*, or season). The *northeast*, or dry, *monsoon* (during which the wind blows from the northeast to the southwest) is strongest between November and March, when the land is cooler than the ocean. (In the Pacific, the northeast monsoon lasts from about September to April.)

Weather is the climate at a place at a particular time. It is predictable in detail over short periods of time (several days), and over somewhat longer periods of time (months) for some purposes. Climatologists have defined climate zones in term of climate variables such as temperature and precipitation; the best-known system is the Köppen-Geiger system, which has five basic categories: tropical rainy climates, dry climates, mild humid climates, snowy-forest climates, and polar climates. These are defined in terms of temperature, except for dry climates, which are defined in terms of ratios of precipitation to evaporation. Geographers have more recently attempted to characterize areas by adding characteristics relating to ecosystems (see below).

Global interrelationships of climate In recent decades there has been sharply increased scientific and popular awareness of the extent to which climate in one part of the world, especially the Pacific, affects climate elsewhere. The *El Niño* and *La Niña* phenomena in the Pacific, and the associated changes of air pressure in the region (the "Southern Oscillation") are known jointly as the *El Niño-Southern Oscillation (ENSO)*. The principal element of El Niño is the presence of large amounts of warm water in the eastern Pacific every three to eight years, and the associated lower barometric pressure over the eastern Pacific and higher pressures over the Western Pacific (Indonesia and Australia). Cold water in the eastern Pacific, and the associated reversal of air pressure, is known as La Niña. The climate effects of ENSO affect weather throughout the globe, including North America Enough is known about ENSO and its effects that some practical forecasts are attainable. For example, it is possible to forecast ENSO effects months in advance to provide guidance to farmers in East Africa on what crops to plant, and when. It was recognized in the early 20th century that the strength of the Asian monsoon was related to atmospheric pressure in the Pacific, but it has been the great increase in data and analytic capability in recent decades that has permitted the analysis of global climate impacts such as that of ENSO.

Deserts are generally defined as areas with less than 10" (25 cm) of precipitation. (Semiarid land is defined as land with annual precipitation of 10" to 20" [25 to 51 cm]). Deserts are located in many latitudes, and their lack of precipitation can be caused by their locations with respect to mountain ranges, wind patterns, air pressure, and temperature. Some deserts are sandy, but others have land surfaces of rocks, pebbles and even mountains. The largest desert in the world is the Sahara in Africa; the second-largest is the desert area of central and western Australia. The Gobi desert in China and Mongolia is a large mid-latitude desert. Other significant desert areas lie in the region from northwestern India through Pakistan, Afghanistan, Iran, Iraq, and Arabia. The United States has deserts in the Southwest; the largest is the Chihuahuan Desert that stretches from Texas, Arizona, and New Mexico into Mexico; the Death Valley Desert in California and Nevada

World Land Area and Population by Selected Region, 2000

	Land Area			Population			
Region	Square miles	Square kilometers	Percent of world total	Total ('000s)	Percent of total	Per square mile	Per square kilometer
World total[1]	57,308,738	148,429,000	100.0%	6,068,511	100.0%	99.5	38.4
Africa	11,608,156	30,065,000	20.3	805,243	13.3	69.4	40.9
Antarctica	5,404,000	14,000,000	9.4	(2)	(2)	(2)	(2)
Asia	17,212,041	44,579,000	30.0	3,688,072	60.8	214.3	82.7
Australia	2,967,966	7,687,000	5.2	19,164	0.3	6.5	2.5
Europe	3,837,082	9,938,000	6.7	728,981	12.0	190.0	73.4
North America	9,365,290	24,256,000	16.3	480,545	8.0	51.3	19.8
South America	6,879,952	17,819,000	12.0	346,504	5.7	50.4	19.4

1. Land only. Includes small islands not shown separately. 2. Antarctica has no indigenous population.

includes the lowest point in the Western Hemisphere (282 feet/86m below sea level).

In addition to areas normally thought of a desert, the lands at the poles are in effect desert, because of low precipitation caused by high air temperatures; these are called "cold" or polar deserts. Warm deserts cover about 1/5 of the Earth's land surface (1/3 if semi-arid lands are included), and "cold deserts" cover about 1/6 of the land surface. Europe is the only continent without deserts, but there is semiarid land by the Black and Caspian seas and in parts of Ukraine and the north Caucasus.

The Continents

Africa

Physical features Africa is the second-largest continent, between Asia and North America, with a land area of 30,065,000 square kilometers (11,608,156 square miles). On the north, the continent is bounded by the Mediterranean Sea, on the west and south by the Atlantic Ocean, and on the east and south by the Indian Ocean. The greatest east-west dimension, in the north, is about 7,400 kilometers (4,600 miles); the greatest north-south dimension is about 8,050 kilometers (5,000 miles.) from Tunisia to Cape Agulhas, South Africa. Africa is connected with Asia across the Sinai Peninsula.

The main islands and island groups around Africa include the Madeiras, the Canary Islands, the Cape Verde Islands, São Tomé and Príncipe, in the Atlantic Ocean, and Socotra, Zanzibar, the Seychelles, the Comoros, and Madagascar in the Indian Ocean.

One of Africa's largest and most dramatic topographical features is the East African Rift System, an extension of a rift system that begins in Jordan in the north and includes the Red Sea, the Danakil Depression of Eritrea and Ethiopia, the East African lake system, and ends on the coast of northern Mozambique—a total distance of about 6,400 kilometers (4,000 miles). Lake Assal, in Djibouti, is the continent's lowest point, 156 meters (512 feet) below sea level. The Danakil Depression is the hottest place on Earth, with an average annual temperature of 35°C (95°F); the world's highest temperature was 58°C (136°F) recorded at Al-'Aziziyah, near Tripoli, Libya, in 1922.

The East African lakes include Victoria (headwaters of the Nile and the world's second-largest freshwater lake), Tanganyika, at 1,435 meters (4,710 feet), the world's deepest, and Nyasa. The East African Rift is bounded on the west by the Ethiopian Highlands, which rise to more than 4,570 meters (15,000 feet) and the Ruwenzori Mountains of Uganda and Congo, more than 4,880 meters high (16,000 feet), and on the east by Mts. Kenya and Kilimanjaro—at 5,895 meters (19,340 feet), the highest on the continent. Other important mountains are the Drakensberg Range in South Africa, the Atlas Mountains of Morocco and Algeria (highest peak 4,167 meters (13,671 feet), the Egypt's Red Sea Mountains, the Nimba Mountains of Guinea, Liberia, and Côte d'Ivoire.

Africa's single-largest geographic feature is the Sahara, the largest desert on Earth and seven times larger than the Gobi Desert, the next biggest. Covering 9,065,000 square kilometers (3.5 million square miles, slightly less than the total area of the United States), the Sahara is bounded on the north by the Atlas Mountains of Morocco and Algeria, and the Mediterranean, on the east by the Red Sea, and on the south by the Nuba Mountains of western Sudan, Lake Chad and its tributaries, and the Niger River. Lake Chad, which borders Chad, Niger, Cameroon, and Nigeria, is one of the world's shallowest, with a maximum depth of only seven meters. The main deserts of southern Africa are the Kalahari of southern Africa (which ranks fifth), and the Namib Desert of coastal Namibia (16th).

Africa has relatively few major rivers that offer navigable access to the interior because they flow through regions of uneven terrain and are characterized by stretches of rapids, cataracts (as on the Nile), and waterfalls (such as Victoria Falls). The world's longest river is the 6,673-kilometer-long Nile, sources of which are in the Ethiopian Highlands (the Blue Nile) and Lake Victoria (the White Nile) and which flows north through Sudan and Egypt to the Mediterranean. Other major rivers include the Senegal, Volta, Niger, Congo (with its tributary the Kasai), and Orange, which flow into the Atlantic, and the Zambezi and Limpopo, which empty into the Indian Ocean. The Okavango River rises in Angola and flows through Namibia before emptying into the wildlife rich Okavango Delta north of the Kalahari Desert.

Climate Africa is the most tropical of the continents, stretching from 37°N to almost 35°S; the climate of its northern and southern halves is broadly symmetrical. The equatorial center of the continent is characterized by lush tropical and subtropical rain forests that extend from the East African lakes region in the east to the Atlantic coast and along the southern coast of West Africa as far as Guinea. There are also rain forests in the southeast (coastal Mozambique and South Africa) and the eastern half of Madagascar.

To the north, east, and south is a zone of savannah and other grasslands, including the semi-arid Sahel region, which borders the Sahara to the north. This zone reaches from the Atlantic to the Horn of Africa in the north, encompasses much of the East African Rift, and south of the equator extends from the Indian Ocean and the Atlantic. A large area of central southern Africa—mostly Zambia and Angola—is characterized by dry forest.

By far the largest uninterrupted climate zone is desert or dry steppe, including the Sahara from the Atlantic to the Red Sea and south in a narrow band along the coast of the Horn of Africa to just below the equator. Another band of desert stretches along the Atlantic coast from central Angola, across Namibia, and into western South Africa.

After Australia, Africa is the driest inhabited continent. Africa has 22 percent of the world's land area, 15 percent of the world's population, but less than 10 percent of the world's renewable water resources. Less than a fifth of the continent experiences sufficient annual moisture for plant growth throughout the whole year.

People Africa is the second-largest continent in population, between Asia and Europe; the estimated 2000 population is 805,243,000. The continent is sparsely populated; however there are many large urban areas, including Lagos, Nigeria (eighth-largest in the world, 13.4 million), and Cairo, Egypt (19th, 10.6 million).

Africa includes 53 nations and some 1,000 linguistic and cultural groups. There are six major language groups: Hamito-Semitic (or Afro-Asiatic, including Arabic), north of a line drawn from southern Somalia to southern Mauritania; Nilo-Saharan, spoken in a broad area around the headwaters of the Nile and northwest of Lake Chad; Niger-Congo, spoken throughout west, central, and southeast Africa; Khoisan, spoken in remote areas of Namibia and Botswana; Indo-European (English and Afrikaans, derived from Dutch), spoken in South Africa south of the Orange River; and Malayo-Polynesian, spoken in Madagascar.

The continent's colonial past is reflected in the fact that 50 nations use Arabic or a European language as an official language. French and English are official languages in 18 countries (in some cases they are both official), Portuguese in five, and Spanish in one. Eighteen countries have two or more official languages, and South Africa has 11—five more than the number of working languages at the United Nations. Nonetheless, indigenous languages are spoken throughout the continent, and in many countries only a minority of the people speaks the official language.

Economy The U.N. classifies 31 countries in Africa as "least developed countries," and all 53 countries on the continent are members of the "Group of 77" developing countries. Of the 26 countries with the lowest per capita income worldwide, all but three are in Africa. Not one of the world's 25 leading merchandise exporters or importers is in Africa, and not one of the world's 50 largest banks or 100 largest industrial companies is headquartered in an African nation.

Although industrial production in Africa is low, the continent has an abundance of mineral wealth. Among the principal mineral resources are iron ore, ferro alloy metals (chrome, chromite, and manganese), copper, bauxite (aluminum ore), cobalt, gold, petroleum, and diamonds. Leading producers of primary energy include South Africa, which ranks sixth for production of coal, Algeria, eighth-largest producer of liquid natural gas, and Nigeria, 11th-largest producer of crude oil. Other oil producers include Angola, Equatorial Guinea, Chad, Gabon, Congo, Cameroon, Democratic Republic of Congo, and Cote d'Ivoire; plentiful reserves have also been found in São Tomé.

The most important regional alliances include: the Organization of African Unity (53 members); the Common Market for Eastern and Southern Africa (20); the Economic Community of West Africa States (16); and the Southern African Development Community (13). Algeria, Libya, and Nigeria are members of OPEC. The 14 countries of the African Financial Community share a common currency, the CFA franc, created in 1945. There are two versions, one used by Benin, Burkina Faso, Côte d'Ivoire, Guinea-Bissau, Mali, Niger, Senegal, and Togo, the other by Cameroon, Central African Republic, Chad, Republic of Congo, Equatorial Guinea, and Gabon.

Africa accounts for only about 10 percent of world exports and 5 percent of world imports, and in consequence has relatively few major ports. The most important include Durban (which ranks 23rd in the world) and Richard's Bay, South Africa; Lagos, Nigeria; and

Alexandria, Egypt. One reason for the relatively low volume of trade and industrial development is that imperial administrators tended to build transportation corridors between colonies in the interior and a seaport but to neglect intercolonial transportation networks. Seven percent of the world's seaborne trade transits the Suez Canal.

The extensive, if diminishing, reserves of big game—including elephants, lions, antelopes, zebras, rhinoceros, and hippopotamus, as well as great apes—are an increasingly important part of the tourist economy in eastern and southern Africa.

Antarctica

Physical features Antarctica is the fifth-largest continent with an area of 14,000,000 square kilometers (5,404,000 square miles). Apart from the tip of the Antarctic Peninsula, the continent lies entirely within the Antarctic Circle (latitude 66°30'S). West Antarctica is a mountainous region that includes the Antarctic Peninsula and is separated from East Antarctica by the Transantarctic Mountains. The continent is covered by an ice sheet with an average thickness of about 2,160 meters—at its thickest the ice is 4,776 meters—which makes Antarctica the world's highest continent. The highest point on the continent is the top of the Vinson Massif (5,140 meters) in the Sentinel Range near the base of the Antarctic Peninsula.

There are two large coastal indentations: the Weddell Sea (about 45°W) faces the Atlantic Ocean, and the Ross Sea (175°W) faces the Pacific. In each of these areas, there are large ice shelves, the Filchner-Ronne ice shelf and the Ross ice shelf, respectively. Fed by glaciers and snow accumulations, they move steadily outward and large bergs break off at the seaward margins. Smaller ice shelves are found around the coast, and the continent is surrounded by the Southern Ocean, a continuous band of ocean in which the strong prevailing winds of the "Roaring Forties" and "Furious Fifties" blow from west to east.

In 2002 the Larsen B ice shelf on the Antarctic Peninsula collapsed due to a regional rise in temperature. The ice shelf was relatively small—3,250 square kilometers and approximately 200 meters thick.

Climate The climate of Antarctica is characterized by extreme cold and high winds. According to some estimates, the conversion of all of Antarctica's ice to water would raise global sea levels by 45 to 60 meters (150–200 feet). Although the ice sheet contains approximately 70 percent of the world's fresh water in a frozen state, because cold air holds little water vapor for precipitation, Antarctica is the driest continent on the planet. The enormous accumulations of snow and ice have taken place over long periods, and most blizzards consist mainly of existing snow blown by high winds. Although some snow falls around the warmer margins of the continent, the average precipitation over interior Antarctica is about 50 millimeters. High altitude, high latitude, and the absence of sunlight in winter combine to make the interior of Antarctica the coldest place on Earth, with mean temperatures around of -57°C (-70°F). The lowest temperature ever recorded on Earth was -88.3°C (-126.9°F) at Vostok, a Russian scientific station located at 78°S, 106°E.

People Antarctica has no indigenous population; the only humans are at research stations, and there are no large land animals. The few species of plant life adapted to the Antarctic environment include mosses, lichens, and algae. On the Antarctic Peninsula there are several species of flowering plants. The birds and seals that spend part of their time on coastal lands depend on the sea for food; Antarctic waters are rich in plankton that is eaten by krill, small shrimplike crustaceans that are the principal food of some species of whales, seals, penguins, and fish.

Although geographers had long postulated the existence of a southern continent, James Cook (England, 1728–79) was the first navigator to cross the Antarctic Circle (1768). Antarctica was first sighted in January 1820, first by the Russian Fabian Gottlieb von Bellingshausen, and independently by the British sealer William Smith sailing as pilot of a Royal Navy ship. Sealers and whalers continued to visit Antarctic waters through the century, but no one stepped foot on the continent until 1895, the same year that the Sixth International Geographical Congress pronounced Antarctica "the greatest piece of geographical exploration still to be undertaken." A Norwegian team of five men led by Roald Amundsen (1872–1928) was the first to reach the South Pole, on December 14, 1911.

Many countries have established research stations on the continent. During the International Geophysical Year (1957–58), 12 nations maintained 65 research stations and operational facilities in Antarctica. The Antarctic Treaty of 1959 prohibited military operations, nuclear explosions, and the disposal of radioactive waste in Antarctica and provides for cooperation in scientific research. A 1991 protocol to the treaty barred for 50 years the exploration of Antarctica for oil or minerals, and contained additional provisions covering wildlife protection, waste disposal, and marine pollution.

Asia

Physical features Asia is the world's largest continent, with a land area of 44,579,000 square kilometers (17,212,041 square miles). Asia is the larger part of the Eurasian land mass, which it shares with Europe. By convention, the boundary between the two continents is defined by the Ural Mountains, the Ural River, the Caspian Sea, and the Caucasus Mountains.

Asia is bounded on the north by the Arctic Ocean and its marginal seas (the Kara, Laptev, and East Siberian Seas), on the east by the Pacific Ocean (the Sea of Japan, East China Sea, and South China Sea), on the south by the Indian Ocean (the Bay of Bengal, the Arabian Sea, the Gulf of Aden, and the Red Sea), and on the east by the Mediterranean, Aegean, and Black Seas and Europe. Asia is connected to Africa by the Sinai Peninsula (the Suez Canal is an artificial divider), and is separated in the extreme northeast from North America by the 90-kilometer (55-mile)-wide Bering Strait. Major islands and island groups include Sakhalin, the Japanese Islands, the Philippines, the islands of Indonesia and Malaysia in the east, the Andaman and Nicobars, the Maldives, and Laccadives in the south, and in the Arctic the Northern Land (Severnaya Zemlya) and New Siberian Islands (Novosibirskiye Ostrova).

Mountains stretch from Asia Minor across northern Southwest Asia and the Caucasus, through Iran and Afghanistan. The Himalayas divide the flat Gangetic Plain of northern India from the Tibetan Highlands, which have an elevation of about 4,570 meters (15,000 feet). Mount Everest is the world's tallest, 8,856 meters (29,035 feet), and all of the world's 50 tallest mountains are in Asia. To the east and southeast, the Himalayas and Tibetan Plateau give way to the Szechuan Basin, South China highlands, and the highlands of mainland Southeast Asia. To the west of the Tibetan Plateau are the Pamir Mountains, and to the north the Taklimakan Desert, beyond Tien Shan and Altai Mountains. The world's lowest point is the Dead Sea, between Jordan and Israel, 408 meters (1,339 feet) below sea level.

In the north are the lowlands of the West Siberian Plain, the Central Siberian Plateau, the Chersky Range, and the mountainous Kamchatka Peninsula. Eastern China is dominated by the North China Plain, south of Beijing. A sequence of plateaus and uplands runs northeast from the Caspian Sea toward Siberia. In India, the Indo-Gangetic Plain runs in a broad crescent from the Arabian Sea, northeast to the base of the Himalayas, and then southwest toward the Bay of Bengal. To the south are the Deccan Plateau and a number of smaller mountain ranges. The principal island groups of Asia also contain mountainous regions, including Sri Lanka, Malaysia, Indonesia, and Japan.

Eighteen of the world's 50 largest rivers are found in Asia, which helps account for the enormous concentrations of people found on the continent. These rivers generally have their sources in the high plateau region and flow through mountain ranges toward broad alluvial lowlands and the sea. The great rivers of ancient civilization included the Tigris and Euphrates of Mesopotamia, which rise in Turkey and flow through Iraq to the Persian Gulf; the Indus River, which descends from the Himalayas through Pakistan to the Arabian Sea; and the Huang Ho (Yellow) River of north China, which enters the East China Sea near Shanghai.

Of equal or greater importance since antiquity are the Ganges (sacred to Hindus), and Brahmaputra, which flow southeast from the Himalayas to the Bay of Bengal; the Mekong, which rises in the Himalayas and flows through Southeast Asia to the South China Sea; and the Yangtze, which rises in the Kunlun Mountains and flows into the East China Sea. Other important rivers of southern Asia are the Salween and Irriwaddy, which enter the Bay of Bengal and the Honghe (Red) River of northern Vietnam. Many of the rivers of northern Asia flow toward the Arctic Sea, among them the Yenisei-Angara, the Ob-Irtysh, the Lena, and the Kolyma in Siberia.

Other water resources of particular importance are the large lakes of northern Asia, including the saltwater Caspian Sea (at 371 million square kilometers, the world's largest lake), the Aral Sea (fourth) and Lake Balkash. Russia's Lake Baikal is the largest freshwater lake in Asia and the eighth largest in the world. Central Asia has large areas of interior drainage, where watercourses form interior lakes or disappear into the ground.

Six of the world's largest deserts are found in Asia: the Gobi (second), Great Arabian Desert, including much of Saudi Arabia, and part of Jordan, Syria, and Iraq (fourth), China's Taklimakan (sixth), Turkmenistan's Kara Kum (eighth), the Thar in India and Pakistan (ninth) and Uzbekistan's Kyzyl Kum (10th).

Climate Asia has a vast range of climate conditions. In the north there is arctic cold. In some areas of northern India and central China there are moderate climates, and in the southeast there are the rains and heat of the monsoon climate. The wettest place on Earth is Mawsynram, Assam, India, with an annual rainfall of 11.9 meters (38.9 feet). There are arid areas with little precipitation, such as parts of the Gobi Desert that receive 50–100 millimeters (2–8 inches) per year.

The Asian landmass also accounts for one of the world's most dramatic climatic features, the monsoons. As the warm air over Asia rises during the summer, it draws cooler air off the water to create the southwest monsoon, which is characterized by hot, moist air with heavy rains and lasts from April to September. In winter, the process is reversed, as the relatively warm air over the ocean draws off the colder and dryer northeast monsoon, which lasts from October to March. The pattern of monsoon winds, which varies in duration, intensity, and direction depending on one's location on the coast of Asia, accounts for the widespread dissemination of trade and culture from East Africa to East Asia over the past 3,000 years.

People Asia accounts for about 30 percent of the world's landmass, but contains 60 percent of the world's population. All or part of 50 countries are in Asia, including six of the 10 most populous nations: China (first, with 1.3 billion people), India (second; 1.1 billion), Indonesia (fourth, 220 million), Pakistan (sixth), Bangladesh (seventh), and Japan (ninth). (Russia ranks eighth, but more than three-quarters of its people live in European Russia. Part of Turkey is also in Europe, and most of Egypt is in Africa.) The nations of Asia are often grouped into regions. The definitions are inexact, but one grouping is as follows: Asia Minor and the South Caucasus (Turkey, Armenia, Azerbaijian, and Georgia); Southwest Asia, also known as the Middle East or Near East (the countries of the Arabian Peninsula, Jordan, Israel, Palestine, Syria, Iraq, and Iran); South Asia (Pakistan, India, Bangladesh, the countries of the Himalayas, Sri Lanka, and the Maldives); Central Asia (Afghanistan, Kazakhstan, Kyrgyzstan, Tajikistan, Turkmenistan, and Uzbekistan); Southeast Asia (Burma, Thailand, Malaysia, Laos, Cambodia, and Vietnam on the mainland) and the islands (chiefly Indonesia, the Philippines, and Singapore); and East Asia (Asiatic Russia, Mongolia, China, the Koreas, and Japan).

Some areas in northern and Central Asia are sparsely populated, but the bulk of Asia's population is distributed in areas of adequate rainfall and fertile soils in the east, southeast, and south. Areas such as the North China Plain, the valley of the Yangzte in China, and the Gangetic Plain of India have especially dense populations. Fourteen of the world's 25 largest urban areas are found in the densely settled areas of the east, southeast, and south: in Japan, Tokyo (first, with 26.4 million people) and Osaka (fourteenth, 11 million); in India, Mumbai (Bombay, third, 18.1 million), Calcutta (ninth, 12.9 million), Delhi (13th, 11.7 million), and Hyderabad (22nd, ca. 9 million); in China, Shanghai (seventh, 12.9 million) and Beijing (15th, 10.8 million) and Tianjin (21st, ca. 9 million); Dhaka, Bangladesh (11th, 12.3 million); Karachi, Pakistan (12th, 11.8 million); Jakarta, Indonesia (16th, 11.0 million); Manila, the Philippines (17th, 10.9 million); and Bangkok, Thailand (23rd, 7.2 million).

More than 30 languages have official status in Asia, and there are scores of other languages in common use. By far the languages with the greatest number of speakers are Chinese (various dialects in China, Taiwan, and Singapore, where it is one of four official languages), Hindi, Malay (various dialects in Indonesia, Malaysia, Singapore, and Brunei), Japanese, and Bengali. Arabic is the official language in most of the countries of Southwest Asia.

Asia is also the most religiously diverse continent, as well as the birthplace of all the world's major religions: Judaism, Christianity, Islam, Hinduism, and Buddhism.

Economy Asia is a continent of great but uneven economic potential. Japan has the second-largest economy in the world, but only four other countries in Asia are considered to have advanced economies: Israel, Singapore, South Korea, and Taiwan. Nine of the countries in the top 25 merchandise exporters and seven of the exporters are in Asia. Six of the world's largest 50 banks are based in Asia—all of them in Japan. Of the world's top 100 industrial companies, 23 are based in Asia, all but three of them in Japan; two are South Korean and one is Chinese. Thirty-seven of the "Group of 77" developing nations are in Asia. The Asian countries of the former Soviet Union are considered transitional economies, while eight Asian states rank among the world's "least developed." Tajikstan, Nepal, Cambodia, and Kyrgyzstan rank in the bottom 25 by per capita income.

The major Asian alliances are the Asia Pacific Economic Cooperation, the Association of South East Asian Nations (ASEAN), the Arab League (22 members, 13 in Asia and 11 in Africa), and the Commonwealth of Independent States (nine Asian members, and three European). Seven of the 11 members of OPEC are located in Asia.

Oil and gas are the pillars of the economy of Southwest Asia, where Saudi Arabia, Iran, and Iraq rank first, fourth, and ninth in crude oil production; Russia and China are the second-and-fifth biggest producers, respectively. Indonesia, and Southwest and Central Asia also have large reserves of natural gas. Five of the world's largest producers of coal are also in Asia: China (first), India (fourth), Russia (fifth), North Korea (ninth), and Indonesia (10th). Among the more important non-fossil-fuel mineral resources include antimony, boron, copper, fluorspar, gemstones, gold, iodine, lead, magnesite, manganese, molybdenum, nickel, rare earths, tin, titanium, tungsten, and zinc.

The "little tigers" (South Korea, Taiwan, Singapore, and Hong Kong) experienced rapid economic growth starting in the 1970's and 1980's, as did Malaysia and Indonesia. More recently, China and India have emerged as engines of economic growth. India has developed a high-tech industry of software production and other services. Asian agriculture is very intensive, especially rice growing; because of the dense populations of many Asian countries, much agricultural production is for the home market. Some areas have developed hydroelectric energy, and the Three Gorges project on the Yangtze in China will be the world's largest.

Transportation networks have not fully kept up with other economic developments. Nonetheless, Asia is home to 15 of the world's 25 largest ports, including Singapore (the world's busiest), Hong Kong, China (second), Kaohsiung, Taiwan (fourth), Busan, South Korea (sixth), and Nagoya, Japan (10th).

Australia

Physical features Australia is the smallest continent, 7,687,000 square kilometers (2,967,966 square miles). It is the only continent that constitutes a single country, and it is the most southerly of the inhabited continents. Lying between the Indian and Pacific Oceans, Australia measures about 3,860 kilometers (2,400 miles) east to west and about 3,220 kilometers (2,000 miles) north to south. It is surrounded by the Indian Ocean to the northwest and west, the Southern Ocean to the south, the Tasman Sea and Coral Sea to the east, and the Gulf of Carpentaria, Arafura Sea, and Timor Sea to the north. Its closest land neighbor is Papua New Guinea, from which the Cape York Peninsula is separated by the 80-mile wide Torres Strait.

Australia is a geologically inert continent. Its highest elevation, Mt. Koskiusko in New South Wales, only 2,228 meters (7,310 feet)—lower than any other continent—and its lowest point, Lake Eyre, in South Australia, is 16 meters (52 feet) below sea level—higher than any other continent. From the narrow western coastal plain the land rises to a rough plateau that occupies the western half of the continent. There is a small area of fertile soil and moist climate in the southwest, but most of the state of Western Australia, which comprises about half the country, is arid. At 1,554,000 square kilometers, the Australian Desert (including the Great Sandy, Gibson, Great Victoria, and Simpson Deserts) is the third-largest in the world. In the north there are areas with tropical temperatures and a winter dry season. On the eastern side of the continent are the mountains of the Great Dividing Range, which parallels the coast from northern Queensland to Melbourne, and the temperate areas of the south and east, the center of settlement in Australia. The longest Australian river system, the Murray River and its tributaries, drains the southern part of the interior basin that lies between the mountains and the great plateau.

The major offshore islands include Tasmania and Kangeroo Island on the south, the Torres Strait Islands on the north, and on the northeast, the Great Barrier Reef, a 2,000-kilometer-long maze of coral reefs and islands that make up the world's largest coral reef along the northeast coast of the continent.

Australia has a number of large, shallow lakes whose surface area varies considerably with the season, including Lake Eyre (maximum depth one meter), Torrens (0.2 meters), and Gairdner (0.2 meters); Eyre and Gairdner are saltwater lakes.

Climate Australia is the driest of the six inhabited continents. Eighty percent of the continent has annual rainfall of less than 600 mm, and this rainfall has high variability. The low rainfall combined with high evaporation, especially in the inland areas, results in low surface water flow. The plant life of the interior areas is adapted to dry conditions, and responds rapidly when rainfall occurs. Temperatures in coastal areas are moderate year-round, but there are occasional frosts inland. Because of its isolation from other continents in recent geologic time, Australia has developed unique ecosystems with many forms of plant and animal life not found elsewhere. Most distinctive are the marsupials such as kangaroos, koalas, wombats, and Tasmanian devils, and the world's only egg-laying mammals, the duck-billed platypus and echidna.

People Humans have populated Australia for some 40,000 years, arriving from Asia, and there are today close to 400,000 descendants of the original indigenous population, now referred to as Aborigines (from the Latin *ab origine* meaning "from the beginning"). The continent may also have been visited by various peoples of the Pacific islands, though without permanent settlement. The first Europeans to visit the continent were the Dutch, who landed in 1606. Captain James Cook claimed the east coast for Britain in 1770, and eight years later the British established a convict settlement at Port Jackson near modern Sydney. Between 1901 (when it gained independence) and 1973, Australia had a "whites only" immigration policy, which meant that the majority of its nonaboriginal population was of European origin or descent. More open immigration has led to a rapid rise in Asian immigration.

Despite its considerable size, Australia has only 19,164,000 people, who make up one of the most urban populations in the world. More than 90 percent of the people live in cities. Brisbane (1.4 million), Sydney (3.7 million), Melbourne (3.2 million), and Adelaide (1.1 million) in the east and southeast are the principal industrial and commercial cities; the capital, Canberra (325,000), is also in the southeast. Perth (1.2 million), the principal city of Western Australia, is considered one of the most remote urban areas on the planet; the closest city is Adelaide, 2,200 kilometers to the east across the Nullarbor (Latin for "no tree") Plain. Darwin, the largest city in the north, has a population of about 104,000.

Most Australians speak English. In the 20th century there were approximately 260 Australian Aboriginal languages. Of these, many are now extinct and only about 20 have a sufficient number of speakers to ensure survival.

Economy Australia has a highly developed economy and ranks 20th in the world in terms of per capita income, and 25th among the world's exporters. The most important exports are from mining—bauxite, copper, gold, iron ore, lead, nickel, silver, titanium, uranium, and zinc—and agriculture, including wool, beef (of which Australia is the world's largest exporter), and mutton, and industrial products. The National Australia Bank ranks 48th worldwide. Australia's major seaports include Melbourne, Sydney, Brisbane, Fremantle, and Newcastle, the largest coal port in the world. Long oriented to British and other western markets, the Australian economy is increasingly dependent on economic ties with Asia and the Pacific Rim.

Europe

Physical features Europe is the sixth-largest continent, between Antarctica and Australia, with an area of 9,938,000 square kilometers (3,837,082 square miles). Europe is not a geographically distinct continent, but rather a large peninsula of Eurasia. By convention, the boundary between Europe and Asia is defined by the Ural Mountains, the Ural River, the Caspian Sea, and the Caucasus Mountains. Europe is bounded on the south by the Black Sea and Mediterranean, including the Aegean and Adriatic Seas, to the west by the Atlantic Ocean, and North Sea, and to the north by the Arctic Ocean.

The British Isles are separated from continent by the 20-mile-wide English Channel, and northern Europe is indented by the Baltic Sea, including the Gulf of Bothnia and Gulf of Finland. Other large islands include Iceland and the Faeroes in the Atlantic, and Spitzbergen, Franz Josef Land, and Novaya Zemlya in the Arctic Ocean.

In the south, along the coast of the Mediterranean, Europe is mountainous and heavily indented. The principal mountain chains are the Pyrenees, between Spain and France, the Alps (France, Switzerland, Italy, Germany, and Austria), the Apennines in Italy, the Julian and Dinaric Alps in the Balkans, and the Pindus Mountains in Greece, and the Carpathians in Ukraine and Romania. To the north is a broad plain that runs from the Atlantic coast of France across Germany and into Russia, where it widens to the north and south before reaching the Urals. Much of this plain, which includes hills and low mountains, is highly fertile. Toward the east are the steppe and forest regions. The long peninsula occupied by Norway and Sweden is mountainous in the west. The highest points are Mt. Elbrus 5,633 meters (18,481 feet) in the Russian Caucasus and Mont Blanc 4,807 meters (15,771 feet) in the French Alps. Europe's lowest point is 28 meters (92 feet) below sea level, on the surface of the Caspian Sea.

Europe is especially favored with a number of long navigable rivers that provide good communication between the coasts and the interior. On the Atlantic and North Sea coasts are the Tagus, Garonne, Loire, Rhine, and Elbe, and in England the Thames. The Baltic receives the Oder, the Vistula; the Danube, Dnieper, and Don (via the Sea of Azov) flow into the Black Sea; and the Volga into the Caspian Sea. The Rhone is the only major river to enter the

Mediterranean. In 1992/93, the last section of the Rhine-Main-Canal was opened, making it possible to ship goods by water diagonally across Europe from the North Sea to the Black Sea.

Climate The climate of Europe varies from warm subtropical climates to polar conditions in the far north. The Mediterranean climate of the south is dry and warm. The western and northwestern parts have a mild, generally humid climate. In central and eastern Europe the climate is more continental, with cooler summers. The deep ocean thermohaline ("heat and salt") circulation of the Gulf Stream brings heat to Europe's North Atlantic coast, which makes northwest Europe considerably warmer than places at the same latitude on the east coasts of North America or Asia. There are no significant desert areas in Europe, although there is concern that areas of European Russia, Portugal, Spain, Italy, and Greece are now threatened with desertification.

People With an estimated 728,981,000 inhabitants, Europe ranks third among the continents in terms of population, between Africa and North America. Except for areas in northern Scandinavia and a few other regions, Europe is the most densely populated of the world's highly developed areas. Two of the continent's cities rank among the world's 25 largest urban areas: Paris is 24th (9.6 million people) and Moscow 25th (9.3 million); London ranks 26th (7.3 million people). However, there are many other major urban throughout the continent.

Europe is home to all or part of some 46 countries (Russia and Turkey are partly in Asia). European nations range from large and influential countries such as Germany, the United Kingdom, and France, to small independent principalities such as Andorra and San Marino. Since World War II, the political situation has been characterized by two broad phases. The cold war division pitted the Western capitalist democracies against the communist countries of Eastern Europe. The collapse of the Soviet Union and related political institutions in the early 1990's was followed by the expansion of Western alliances. Formerly eastern bloc countries Czech Republic, Hungary, and Poland were admitted to NATO (the North Atlantic Treaty Organization, founded in 1949 to maintain European security in the face of perceived Soviet expansion).

With the exception of Finno-Ugric (Finnish and Hungarian) and a few language isolates such as Basque, most European languages are part of the Indo-European language family. These include the Romance, Germanic, Balto-Slavic, and Greek languages, as well as Albanian and Celtic. There are almost as many national languages as there are nations in Europe, and the 15-member European Union has 11 working languages: Danish, Dutch, English, Finnish, French, German, Greek, Italian, Portuguese, Spanish, and Swedish. Enlargement of the EU will probably lead to the addition of a further eight: Estonian, Latvian, Lithuanian, Polish, Czech, Slovak, Hungarian, and Slovene.

Economy Western Europe as a whole is highly developed in the west but less so in the east. The largest economies are Germany, France, the United Kingdom, and Italy. However, the U.N. describes the 14 Eastern European nations that were formerly part of the Soviet Union, members of the Warsaw Pact, part of Yugoslavia, and Albania, as having transitional economies. Only four European nations are members of the "Group of 77" developing nations: Bosnia and Herzegovina, Cyprus, Malta, and Romania.

Among the areas in which Western economies are strong are financial services, heavy industry (including cars, aircraft, and ships), and engineering: 35 of the world's 50 largest banks, and 39 of the top 100 industrial corporations are headquartered in Europe. Tourism is an important industry in many countries. There is also extensive agriculture, much of it heavily subsidized; forestry industries in the far north; and fishing. Mineral resources include coal, copper, mercury, potash, tin, and zinc, and oil and gas in the North Sea and in Eastern Europe. Europe also relies heavily on both hydroelectric and nuclear power generation; 214 of the world's 439 nuclear power plants are located there.

Europe's transportation infrastructure is highly developed, and there are extensive rail, road, water, and air networks. Twelve of the world's 25 biggest importing nations and 12 of the exporting nations are in Europe. Not surprisingly, the continent boasts some of the world's busiest seaports, notably Rotterdam, the Netherlands (third in the world), Antwerp (ninth), Le Havre, France (14th), and Hamburg, Germany (17th).

The European Union has 15 member states. Ten more are scheduled to join in 2004 and three other applications are under review. Since 2002, the euro has been the official currency of 12 countries: Austria, Belgium, France, Germany, Finland, Greece, Ireland, Italy, Luxembourg, the Netherlands, Portugal, and Spain.

North America

Physical features North America is the third-largest continent, between Africa and South America, with a land area of 24,256,000 square kilometers (9,365,290 square miles). North America includes all of the mainland and related offshore islands lying north of the Isthmus of Panama, which connects it with South America, and the Caribbean islands. The continent is bounded on the west by the Pacific Ocean and the Bering Sea, on the north by the Arctic Ocean, and on the east by the Atlantic Ocean and the Gulf of Mexico, and on the south by South America. Geographically, North America stretches from about 9°N to 83°N south to north (Panama to the tip of Ellesmere Island), and about 166°E to 50°W east to west (from the end of the Aleutian Islands to Greenland).

Geographers divide North America into 13 physiographic regions. The northernmost are the narrow Arctic plain of Alaska and northwest Canada, the Canadian or Laurentian Shield, which includes much of Ontario and Nunavut, as well as the island of Greenland, and the islands of the Canadian Arctic Archipelago. The western half of the continent is dominated by mountain ranges: the Western Cordillera, which stretches from the Aleutians and southern Alaska along the west coast as far south as Baja California and the adjacent coast of Mexico. Roughly parallel to this, from west to east, are the Intermontaine Plateaus, the Eastern Cordillera, and the Great Plains, all three of which end at about the U.S.-Mexico border.

The large, irregularly shaped Interior Lowlands dominate the center of the United States and part of south central Canada, and the Appalachian Mountains stretch from Georgia northeast through the Canadian Maritimes and Newfoundland. The Coastal Plains run from the Yucatán Peninsula around the Gulf of Mexico and up the Atlantic coast as far as Long Island, New York.

Central Mexico is dominated by the Mexican Highlands, which run into the Central American Ranges. The Caribbean islands comprise a region known as the Antilles Arc, including a ring of volcanic islands that stretches from Puerto Rico to South America. The highest peak in North America is Denali or Mt. McKinley, 6,194 meters (20,320 feet), in the Alaska Range.

The dominant river system of North America comprises the Missouri-Mississippi River and their tributaries, which drain an area of 3.2 square kilometers (1.2 million square miles). The fifth-largest drainage system in the world includes all or part of 31 of the United States and two Canadian provinces from the Rocky Mountains in the west to the Appalachians in the east, and flows into the Gulf of Mexico in a broad delta below Baton Rouge, Louisiana. From the Gulf to its headwaters in Lake Itasca, Minnesota, the Mississippi measures 3,780 kilometers (2,348 miles). However, a case can be made that the lower Mississippi is an extension of the Missouri River, which meets the upper Mississippi just above St. Louis.

The Missouri River is formed by the confluence of three smaller rivers in Three Forks, Montana, from which it is 3,969 kilometers (2,466 miles) to the Gulf. Other major tributaries of the Mississippi include the Illinois, Ohio, Cumberland, Tennessee, and Yazoo to the east, and the Arkansas and Ouachita to the west. Up until the 1940s, the Red River also flowed into the Mississippi, but it was captured by the Atchafalaya 50 miles above Baton Rouge, Louisiana. Recognizing that without intervention, the Atchafalaya would also capture the Mississippi, the U.S. Army Corps of Engineers created the Old River Control Project to keep this from happening. Were the Mississippi to shift its channel, the current river channel would become a saltwater estuary past Baton Rouge while the Atchafalaya—which now receives 30 percent of the river's flow—would overflow its banks. Such an event would change the geographic, demographic, and economic landscape of southern Louisiana beyond recognition.

Other large or economically important North American rivers include, on the Atlantic seaboard, the St. Lawrence (which forms part of the U.S.-Canada border), Hudson (connected to the Great Lakes via the Erie Canal), and Delaware; the Rio Grande, which forms part of the U.S.-Mexico border and flows into the Gulf of Mexico; the Colorado, which flows into the Gulf of California; the San Joaquin, Sacramento, and Columbia, which flow into the Pacific; the Yukon, which flows from Canada through Alaska to the Bering Sea; the Mackenzie, which flows north into the Arctic Sea, and the Nelson, which flows into Hudson Bay. There are no major rivers in Central America or the Caribbean islands.

Another notable characteristic of North America's hydrographic landscape is the abundance of lakes, including the five interconnected Great Lakes of the United States and Canada, the largest of which is Lake Superior, at 82,414 square kilometers (31,820 square miles), the second largest lake in the world; the others are Huron (fifth), Michigan (sixth), Erie (12th), and Ontario (14th). In addition to these, 10 of the world's 50 largest lakes are found in Canada. The only other large North American lakes south of the Canadian border are the Great Salt Lake (43rd) in Utah, and Lake Nicaragua, or Cocibolca (22nd), which is home to the only freshwater sharks in the world.

Major deserts in North America include the Chihuahan (the world's sixth largest, which covers parts of Mexico, Texas, New Mexico, and Arizona), the Sonoran (Mexico, California, and Arizona), the Mojave (California and Arizona), the Painted Desert (Arizona), and Death Valley (California and Nevada). Death Valley is also the lowest point on the continent, 86 meters (282 feet) below sea level.

The North American mainland is also surrounded by large islands, including Greenland (the world's largest), the Canadian Arctic (which includes four of the world's 25 largest islands); on the Atlantic Ocean, Newfoundland, Long Island, the Outer Banks, and the West Indies, including Cuba (which ranks 14th) and Hispaniola (23rd); and on the Pacific Canada's Queen Charlotte Islands and the Aleutians, which extend 2,700 kilometers almost to Asia. The largest marginal seas around North America are the Caribbean Sea, the Gulf of Mexico, the Gulf of California, the Bering Sea, and Hudson Bay.

Climate North America extends across 74° of latitude, from 9°N to 83°N, and every major climatic type is found there, from permanent ice cap in central Greenland to tropical rain forest in parts of southern Central America. The northernmost reaches of Alaska and Canada have an Arctic and sub-Arctic climate with tundra and, in central Greenland, ice cap. Farther south the climate is mostly temperate—continental in the north, subtropical in the south—with adequate rainfall for a wide variety of crops. West of the Mississippi River, the climate is semi-arid, becoming arid in the desert areas of the southwest and northern Mexico. The climate of southern Florida, the Caribbean islands, southern Mexico, and Central America is tropical.

People The fourth-largest continent in population, between Europe and South America, North America is home to 480,545,000 people. The United States (third) and Mexico (11th) are the only two countries in the North America that rank in the top 20 by population. Although Canada is the second-largest country in the world by area, its population is only about 10 percent larger than that of California. There are very sparsely populated areas in North America, especially in northern Canada, Alaska, and the western mountains and plains of the United States and Canada. The majority of people in United States and Canada live in urban areas, while Mexico and the countries of Central America and the Caribbean are more rural. North America includes three of the world's 25 largest urban areas: Mexico City (second largest, 2000 urban population 18.1 million); New York (fifth, 16.6 million), and Los Angeles (sixth, 13.1 million).

The major cultural regions include Central America, the island nations of the Caribbean, Mexico, the United States, and Canada. The population of Arctic and sub-Arctic regions of Alaska, Canada, and Greenland also make up a unique cultural zone.

There are 23 independent countries in North America, as well as overseas territories of France, Great Britain, the Netherlands, and the United Kingdom. There are a number of international trade organizations, including the North American Free Trade Agreement (NAFTA), composed of the United States, Canada, and Mexico), the Caribbean Community, and the Central American Common Market. In addition, all countries are members of the Organization of American States, together with the nations of South America.

The dominant languages are English (the United States, Canada, Belize, and several Caribbean nations and territories) and Spanish (Mexico, Costa Rica, El Salvador, Guatemala, Honduras, Nicaragua, and Panama, and in the Caribbean, Cuba and the Dominican Republic). About 20 million people in the United States consider Spanish their first language. French is one of two official languages in Canada (with English) and Haiti (Creole). It is estimated that about 300,000 people still speak one of the roughly 200 Native-American languages still extant in North America as far south as Mexico and parts of Central America, and from Greenland in the east to the Aleutian Islands to the west. There are thought to be about 5 million speakers of the 70 Meso-American languages—chiefly Mayan, Uto-Aztecan, and Oto-Manguean—still in use in Central America.

Economy The United States has the world's largest and most diversified economy, and it is a leader in many fields of information technology, industry, and defense technology, although agriculture is an also important part of the economy. Canada mirrors the U.S., though on a smaller scale. The U.S. and Canada rank fifth and eighteenth, respectively, in per capita income. Together, the U.S., Canada, and Mexico produce about a third of the world's measured G.N.P., and all three number among the world's leading importing nations and exporting nations.

(The U.S.ranks first in both categories.). Nonetheless, Mexico's economy is one of 20 North American members of the "Group of 77" developing nations. Of the world's 50 largest banks, eight are headquartered in the United States and one in Canada, while 36 of the world's 100 largest corporations are based in the United States.

The five largest ports in North America are Los Angeles/Long Beach, California (fifth in the world), New Orleans (seventh), Houston (eighth), Port of New York and New Jersey (12th), and San Francisco (13th).

The United States, Canada, and Mexico are leading producers of primary energy, ranking first, second and fourth, respectively, in the production of liquid natural gas. In the production of crude oil, the U.S. ranks third and Mexico sixth; in dry natural gas, the U.S. is 2nd and Mexico eighth; while the U.S. is the world's second largest producer of coal. Canada also produces more energy from hydroelectric power than any other country, while the U.S. ranks fourth, and the U.S. ranks first in production of nuclear-generated electricity, and Canada ranks eighth. North America's abundant mineral wealth includes silver, lead, zinc, aluminum, nickel, and gold. Jamaica accounts for nine percent of the world's bauxite production.

North America has extensive and productive agricultural lands. The continent produces much of the world's corn, meat, cotton, soybeans, and wheat. Farm employment in Mexico, Central America, and the Caribbean is higher than in the U.S. or Canada. Tourism is of particular importance for the countries of the Caribbean. Since 1976 the Eastern Caribbean dollar has been the official currency of six sovereign states—Antigua and Barbuda, Dominica, Grenada, St. Kitts and Nevis, St. Lucia, St. Vincent, and the Grenadines—and the British dependencies of Anguilla and Montserrat.

South America

Physical features South America is the fourth-largest continent, between North America and Antarctica, with an area of 17,819,000 square kilometers (6,880,000 square miles), and the fifth in terms of population (346,500,000), between North America and Australia. The continent extends about 7,640 kilometers (4,750 miles) from Punta Gallinas, Colombia, south to Cape Horn, Chile, in the south. At its broadest point south of the equator, the continent extends 5,300 kilometers (3,300 miles) from east to west. South America is connected to North America by the Isthmus of Panama. It is bordered by the Caribbean Sea to the north, the Atlantic Ocean to the east, the Drake Strait of the Southern Ocean to the south, and the Pacific Ocean to the west.

The principal physical features of the continent include the South American cordillera of the Andes, a high, seismically active mountain range that extends nearly the whole length of the continent on its western side. At 7,265 meters (23,834 feet), Argentina's Aconcagua is the highest point in the Western Hemisphere. There are two main highland areas, the Guiana Highlands to the north and the Brazilian Highlands to the south of the Amazon basin. The only substantial desert is the Atacama Desert, on the Pacific Coast of northern Chile. Roughly 150 kilometers from east to west and about 1,000 kilometers from north to south, the Atacama is the driest place on Earth; in some parts, no rain has ever been recorded.

The continent's three main river systems include Orinoco, which flows north from the Guinea Highlands to the Caribbean; the Amazon, the world's largest river by volume and second-largest by length, which rises in the Peruvian Andes and flows some 6,440 kilometers (4,000 miles) to the Atlantic. Its drainage basin includes the world's largest rain forest. Farther south is the La Plata system, including the Paraguay, Paraná and Uruguay Rivers, which flow out of the Brazilian highlands to the Atlantic. Other major rivers include the Madeira and Purus, which are tributaries of the Andes, and Brazil's São Francisco and Para-Tocatins, which flow into the Atlantic. The three largest lakes are Maracaibo (18th), Patos (19th), and Titicaca (21st). The former two are lagoons, while Titicaca, on the border of Bolivia and Peru, is the highest major lake in the world, at an elevation of 3,810 meters (12,500 feet).

Climate The climate of South America is largely tropical especially in the vast region east of the Andes and extending from the Caribbean to the Tropic of Capricorn, an area dominated by the tropical rain forests of the Amazon and Orinoco drainage basins, and along the coast as far south as Ecuador. The climate of the Andean regions is characterized by cooler highland climate. The narrow lowland along the west coast tends to be dryer, the extreme being found in the Atacama Desert of northern Chile, the driest place on Earth. The south coast of Chile is characterized by a cooler, moister climate. The climate of Paraguay, Uruguay, southern Brazil, and northern Argentina is warm and moist. The climate of southern Argentina becomes drier as one moves south and west.

People South America has 12 independent countries—Argentina, Bolivia, Brazil, Chile, Colombia, Ecuador, Guyana, Paraguay, Peru, Suriname, Uruguay, and Venezuela—while French Guiana is an overseas department of France, and the Falkland Islands (Islas Malvinas) are a dependency of the United Kingdom contested by Argentina. The ethnic composition of South American countries varies widely and reflects the degree to which Europeans and Africans assimilated with or in some cases replaced native populations. At one extreme, the people of Argentina, Chile, and Uruguay are overwhelmingly of European origin. Bolivia's population is 55 percent Indian, 30 percent mestizo, and 15 percent Indian, while Peru's population is 45 percent Indian and 37 percent mestizo, and 95 percent of Paraguayans are classified as mestizo. East Indians comprise half the population of Guyana and nearly a third that of Suriname, where another 15 percent are classified as Javanese. Slightly more than half of Brazilians are white, 38 percent mestizo, and 6 percent black, proportions that belie the heavy influence of African culture on the country.

Although there is substantial rural subsistence farming and many interior areas with few inhabitants, South America is also a heavily urbanized continent. Three of the 25 largest urban areas in the world are São Paulo, Brazil (fourth, 17.8 million), Buenos Aires, Argentina (10th, 14.1 million), and Rio de Janeiro, Brazil (18th, 11.9 million). These and other urban areas combine modern business and cultural districts with outlying districts of immigrants, usually characterized by poverty, high unemployment, and inadequate services such as water, policing, and sewage.

The primary languages of South America are Spanish (Argentina, Bolivia, Chile, Colombia, Ecuador, Paraguay, Peru, Uruguay, Venezuela) and Portuguese (Brazil). American Indian languages are official in Bolivia (Quechua and Aymara), Peru (Quechua), and Paraguay (Guarani). English is the official language of Guyana, and Dutch of Suriname, where Sranang Tongo (Surinamese or Taki-Taki), Hindustani, and Javanese are also widely spoken. An estimated 15 million people still speak the 400 or so indigenous languages still used in South America. Probably three-quarters of these speakers live in the central Andean highlands of Peru, Bolivia, and Ecuador, where the most widely spoken languages are those of the Quechumaran group, including the various Quechuan and Aymaran languages.

Economy The economy of South America is highly varied, but all 12 nations are members of the "Group of 77" developing nations. There are still hunter-gatherer tribes in the interior, and agriculture ranges from widespread subsistence farming to commercial farming and ranching in Argentina, Uruguay, Brazil, and elsewhere. Brazil has a significant industrial sector, and Venezuela, the only member of OPEC in the Americas, is the world's fifth largest exporter of oil and the eighth largest exporter of liquid natural gas; Argentina ranks seventh in the production of dry natural gas. South America's other mineral resources include copper, tin, iron, silver, bauxite, zinc, and gold. Brazil ranks second, after Canada, in the production of hydroelectricity. Major ports include Santos (the biggest in South America) and Rio de Janeiro, Brazil; Buenos Aires, Argentina; Cartagena, Colombia; Callao, Peru; and Curaçao, Venezuela.

The United States

The United States shares the North American continent with Canada, Mexico, and the Central American nations. [See *North America*, above.] It is the third-largest country in the world in land area (3,717,797 sq. mi/6,629,091 km^2, after Russia and Canada) and the third-largest country in population (after China and India). The United States is by far the world's largest and most advanced economy, a leader in many fields of information technology, industry, and defense technology. The 48 conterminous states are bordered on the north by Canada, on the South by Mexico and the Gulf of Mexico, on the east by the Atlantic, and on the West by the Pacific. Alaska is bordered on the east by Canada, on the north by the Arctic Ocean, and on the west by the Pacific. The Hawaiian Islands lie approximately 2,400 southwest of California.

U.S. Census geographic divisions

The United States Bureau of the Census groups the states into four geographic divisions, with nine subdivisions. These are used to define, group, and present demographic and other information.

Northeast The Northeast region includes two subdivisions: New England (Maine, New Hampshire, Vermont, Massachusetts, Rhode Island, Connecticut) and Middle Atlantic (New York, New Jersey, Pennsylvania).

Midwest The Midwest region includes two subdivisions: East North Central (Ohio, Indiana, Illinois, Michigan, Wisconsin) and West North Central (Minnesota, Iowa, Missouri, North Dakota, South Dakota, Nebraska, Kansas).

South The South region includes three divisions: South Atlantic (Delaware, Maryland, District of Columbia, Virginia, West Virginia, North Carolina, South Carolina, Georgia, Florida); East South Central (Kentucky, Tennessee, Alabama, Mississippi); and West South Central (Arkansas, Louisiana, Oklahoma, Texas).

Pacific The Pacific region includes two subdivisions: Mountain (Montana, Idaho, Wyoming, Colorado, New Mexico, Arizona, Utah, Nevada) and Pacific (Washington, Oregon, California, Alaska, Hawaii).

Geographic Distribution of Population The 2000 United States population of 281,421,906 was distributed among the four main census regions as shown in the table below, which also includes total and regional population for 1980 and 1990. This table illustrates the gradual long-term geographic shift of population toward the south and west of the United States.

Urban areas and urbanization Although the parks and great open landscapes of the United States are tourist destinations, and although there are areas in the north central and western U.S. that are uninhabited or very lightly populated, the United States population is largely urban, located mostly in densely settled urban areas or suburban areas. U.S. Census definitions of urban have changed in recent censuses, so that comparison are inexact, but by 1980 the urban population was 73.7 percent of the total, by 1990 75.2 percent.

In 2000, more than 80 percent of the population lived in metropolitan areas, defined as urban counties surrounding a city with a population of at least 50,000. Remote sensing images of the United States paint a clear picture of the urban nature of the country, with dense urban belts in the Northeast Corridor, around Dallas-Fort Worth, Houston, Chicago, Phoenix, Los Angeles, and other areas, and smaller urban areas throughout much of the eastern half of the country, in settled areas in the mountain west, and along the West Coast. The fastest growing urban areas are in the west and southwest.

Geography and Physiographic Regions of the United States The broad geographic outlines of the United States begin with the beaches and lowlands of the Eastern coastal plains and the large cities of the East dating to colonial times. Further inland are the ranges of the Appalachians, important in the nation's history, in industrial development (coal) and for recreation. To the north are the Great Lakes, a key shipping route shared with Canada. The rivers flowing into the Ohio are the eastern boundary of the great Mississippi basin, which includes the fertile interior plains and the Great Plains, with a drainage area stretching all the way to the Rocky Mountains. Beyond the Rockies is the intermountain West reaching to the coastal ranges of the West Coast and the long Pacific coastline of Washington, Oregon, and California. In the Southwest are the arid areas of Arizona, New Mexico, and eastern California. Underlying this broad outline are the seven physiographic regions—the main geological features and landforms—into which the United States is divided.

Atlantic and Gulf Coast Plains These extend from the islands of southern New England, Cape Cod, and Long Island through New Jersey, Delaware, Maryland, Virginia, North Carolina, South Carolina, Georgia, Florida, Alabama, Mississippi, Louisiana, and Texas; it also includes lower Mississippi Valley in Arkansas, Missouri, and Tennessee. The Atlantic plain is narrower in the north and widens toward the south where it meets the Gulf plain.

Appalachian System The Appalachians, a system of old weathered mountains, are divided into five parts:

New England White Mountains (New Hampshire), Green Mountains (Vermont), Champlain Lowland and Hudson Valley (Vermont, New York), Catskill Mountains (New York).

Regional populations and percentages, United States 1980, 1990 and 2000.

Region	1980 pop.	% of total	1990 pop.	% of total	2000 pop.	% of total
Northeast	49,135,283	22	50,809,299	21	53,594,378	19
Midwest	58,865,670	26	59,668,632	24	64,392,776	23
South	75,372,362	33	85,445,930	34	100,236,820	36
West	43,172,490	19	52,786,082	21	63,197,932	22
Total	**226,545,805**	**100**	**248,709,873**	**100**	**281,421,906**	**100**

The Piedmont Pennsylvania, Virginia, North Carolina, South Carolina, Georgia, Alabama.

Great Smoky and Blue Ridge Mountains Pennsylvania (Poconos), Virginia, North Carolina, Georgia.

Ridge and Valley Pennsylvania, West Virginia, Virginia, Kentucky, Tennessee, Alabama.

Appalachian Plateau Pennsylvania, Ohio, West Virginia, Kentucky, Tennessee, Alabama.

Canadian (or Laurentian) Shield This region covers much of eastern Canada and extends into the U.S. in two places: the Adirondack Mountains in New York, and Superior Upland in Upper Michigan, Wisconsin, and Minnesota.

Central Lowland The Central Lowland includes most of the U.S. interior. This area was earlier in geologic time covered by a large inland sea. The Central Lowland is divided into four parts:

Interior Lowlands Ohio, Kentucky, Tennessee.

Mississippi Great Lakes Basin Ohio, Indiana, Illinois, Michigan, Wisconsin, Iowa, North Dakota, South Dakota.

Interior Highlands Ozark Mountains (Missouri, Arkansas, Oklahoma); Ouachita Mountains (Arkansas, Oklahoma).

Great Plains North Dakota, South Dakota, Nebraska, Kansas, Oklahoma, Texas, Montana, Wyoming, Colorado, New Mexico.

Cordilleran Province This province includes the Rocky Mountain states of New Mexico, Colorado, Wyoming, and Montana. The Rocky Mountains are a geologically young range.

Intermontane Region This generally arid area of mountains, river basins, and plateaus is divided into four sections:

Colorado Plateau Colorado, Utah, New Mexico, Arizona (including Grand Canyon).

Basin and Range Plateau Nevada, Utah (including Wasatch Range).

Desert Basin and Range California (including Death Valley), Arizona.

Snake and Columbia River Basins Idaho, Washington, Oregon.

Pacific Coastlands This region is divided into four sections, three oriented north-south, the other east-west:

Cascade Mountains and Sierra Nevada: Washington, Oregon, California, Nevada.

Puget Sound, Willamette Valley, and Central Valley Washington, Oregon, California.

Coast Ranges Washington, Oregon, and California.

Los Angeles Extension Tehachapi Mountains (east west), San Gabriel Mountains, and San Bernardino Mountains.

The National Park System One of the most striking aspects of the physical and bio-geography of the United States is the extensive National Park System. This had its origin in 1872 with the establishment of the Yellowstone National Park in the Territories of Montana and Wyoming, "as a public park or pleasuring-ground for the benefit and enjoyment of the people." This is believed to be the first area in the world designated as a National Park, and it was placed under the secretary of the interior in part because no state governments were in place in the area of the park. Among the other early parks created by Congress were Sequoia, Yosemite, Mount Rainer, Crater Lake, and Glacier.

President Woodrow Wilson created the National Park Service as a bureau within the Department of the Interior in 1916, and charged it with protecting the 35 national parks and monuments then in existence. Through the 1920's the national park system was essentially a western park system, with only Acadia National Park in Maine east of the Mississippi. In 1926 Congress authorized Shenandoah, Great Smoky Mountains, and Mammoth Cave national parks, and in later decades many smaller historical sites in the east became part of the system. The U.S. National Park System now includes nearly comprises 385 areas covering more than 79 million acres (three percent of total U.S. area) in 49 states (there are no areas in Delaware), the District of Columbia, Guam, Puerto Rico, Saipan, and the Virgin Islands. Additions to the National Park System are generally made through acts of Congress, and national parks can be created only through such acts. But under the Antiquities Act of 1906, the president has authority to proclaim national monuments on lands already under federal jurisdiction.

The diversity of the parks managed by the National Park Service (NPS) is reflected in the variety of titles given to them. Although the system is best known for its scenic National Parks, more than half the areas of the National Park System preserve places, and commemorate persons, events, and activities important in the nation's history. The types of holdings in the system include at least 16 categories, from National Battlefield to Wild and Scenic River.

World Population

In 2003 world population reached 6.3 billion, of which 1.2 billion were in developed countries and 5.1 billion were in developing regions. The United Nations Population Fund (U.N.F.P.A.) estimates that world population will reach 8.9 billion by 2050.

World population grew by 77 million in 2003. That's a growth rate of 1.2 percent, down significantly from the all-time high of around 2 percent. Almost all of the increase in world population (95 percent) came in less developed regions of Africa, Asia and Latin America. Six countries were responsible for half of the increase: India (21 percent), China (12 percent), Pakistan (5 percent), Bangladesh (4 percent), Nigeria (4 percent) and the United States (4 percent).

China and India both have more than a billion people (China has 1,304,196,000 people; India has 1,065,462,000). The United States has the third-largest population with

World Births, Deaths, and Population Growth, 2003

Characteristic	World	More Developed	Less Developed
Population	6,302,486,693	1,202,572,059	5,099,914,634
Births	131,903,973	13,216,000	119,563,000
Deaths	55,508,568	12,248,000	1,898,000
Natural increase	73,250,395	968,000	7,665,000
Births per 1,000 population	20.4	11	22.6
Deaths per 1,000 population	8.8	10	8.5
Growth rate (percent)	1.2%	0.11%	1.4%

Source: U.S. Bureau of the Census, International Data Base (2003)

World's Largest Countries, by Population, 2003-50

2003		2015		2025		2050	
Rank, Country	Population	Rank	Population	Rank	Population	Rank	Population
1. China	1,304,196,000	1	1,402,321,000	1	1,445,100,000	2	1,462,100,000
2. India	1,065,462,000	2	1,246,351,000	2	1,369,284,000	1	1,572,100,000
3. United States	294,043,000	3	329,669,000	3	358,030,000	3	397,100,000
4. Indonesia	219,883,000	4	250,428,000	4	270,113,000	5	311,300,000
5. Brazil	178,470,000	6	201,970,000	6	216,372,000	8	247,200,000
6. Pakistan	153,578,000	5	204,465,000	5	249,766,000	4	344,200,000
7. Bangladesh	146,736,000	7	181,428,000	7	208,268,000	7	265,400,000
8. Russia	143,246,000	9	133,429,000	10	124,428,000	16	104,300,000
9. Japan	127,654,000	10	127,224,000	11	123,444,000	15	109,200,000
10. Nigeria	124,009,000	8	161,726,000	8	192,115,000	6	278,800,000
11. Mexico	103,457,000	11	119,618,000	9	129,866,000	10	146,700,000
12. Germany	82,476,000	16	82,497,000	18	81,959,000	19	70,800,000
13. Vietnam	81,377,000	13	94,742,000	14	104,649,000	12	123,800,000
14. Philippines	79,999,000	12	96,338,000	13	108,589,000	11	128,400,000
15. Egypt	71,031,000	15	89,996,000	15	103,165,000	14	113,800,000
16. Turkey	71,325,000	17	82,150,000	17	88,995,000	17	98,800,000
17. Ethiopia	70,678,000	14	93,845,000	12	116,006,000	9	186,500,000
18. Iran	68,920,000	18	81,422,000	16	90,927,000	13	121,400,000
19. Thailand	62,833,000	19	69,585,000	19	73,869,000	18	82,500,000
20. France	60,144,000	20	62,841,000	20	64,165,000	20	61,800,000

Source: United Nations Dept. of Economic and Social Affairs, Population Division

294,043,000 people, followed by Indonesia with 219,883,000, and Brazil with 178,470,000 people.

By 2016, the U.N. estimates that India will have a population of 1.22 billion, which will be larger than all the more developed countries combined, that is, all the countries of Europe, including Russia, Australia, New Zealand, Japan, Canada, and the United States. It is projected that India will have a larger population than China by 2045, with a total of 1.501 billion people (compared to China's 1.496 billion).

Urbanization

According to the United Nations, 47 percent of the world's population resided in urban areas in 2000; 76 percent of the people in developed countries lived in urban areas; and 39.9 percent of the people in developing regions lived in cities. Worldwide, 2.9 billion of the world's 6.1 billion people (or 47.5 percent) lived in urban areas. Urbanites are expected to make up half the world's population by 2007, and by 2030 they are expected to increase to about 60 percent (4.9 billion out of a world population of 8.1 billion). Most of the population increase expected during 2000–30 will take place in less developed countries where urban population will potentially increase from 1.9 billion in 2000 to 3.9 billion in 2030. Latin America and the Caribbean is one of the most highly urbanized developing regions in the world, with 75 percent of the people living in cities in 2000. Asia was 37 percent urbanized and Africa 38 percent in 2000. The U.N. projects that by 2030, Africa and Asia will be 55 and 53 percent urban respectively; Latin America and the Caribbean will be 83 percent urban.

The World's Largest Urban Areas, 1950-2015

2000 Rank, Urban area	Population (millions) 1950	1970	1990	2000	2015	Rank 1950	Rank 2015
1. Tokyo, Japan	6.9	16.5	25.0	26.4	26.4	3	1
2. Mexico City, Mexico	3.1	9.1	15.1	18.1	19.2	13	7
3. Bombay, India	2.9	5.8	12.2	18.1	26.1	15	2
4. São Paulo, Brazil	2.4	8.1	14.8	17.8	20.4	18	5
5. New York, U.S.	12.3	16.2	16.1	16.6	17.4	1	8
6. Lagos, Nigeria	N.A.	N.A.	7.7	13.4	23.2	N.A.	3
7. Los Angeles, U.S.	4.0	8.4	11.5	13.1	14.1	11	14
8. Calcutta, India	4.4	6.9	10.7	12.9	17.3	9	9
9. Shanghai, China	5.3	11.2	13.5	12.9	14.6	6	13
10. Buenos Aires, Argentina	5.0	8.4	10.6	12.6	14.1	7	15
11. Dhaka, Bangladesh	N.A.	N.A.	5.9	12.3	21.1	N.A.	4
12. Karachi, Pakistan	N.A.	N.A.	8.0	11.8	19.2	N.A.	6
13. Delhi, India	N.A.	3.5	8.2	11.7	16.8	N.A.	11
14. Jakarta, Indonesia	N.A.	3.9	9.3	11.0	17.3	N.A.	10
15. Osaka, Japan	4.1	9.4	10.5	11.0	11.0	10	20
16. Metro Manila, Philippines	N.A.	3.5	8.0	10.9	14.8	N.A.	12
17. Beijing, China	3.9	8.1	10.9	10.8	12.3	12	18
18. Rio de Janeiro, Brazil	2.9	7.0	9.5	10.6	11.9	14	19
19. Cairo, Egypt	2.4	5.3	8.6	10.6	13.8	16	16
20. Istanbul, Turkey	N.A.	N.A.	6.5	9.3	12.5	N.A.	17
21. Tianjin, China	2.4	5.2	9.3	N.A.	10.7	17	21
22 Hyderabad, India	N.A.	N.A.	N.A.	N.A.	10.5	N.A.	22
23. Bangkok, Thailand	N.A.	N.A.	5.9	N.A.	10.1	N.A.	23
24. Paris, France	5.4	8.5	9.3	9.6	N.A.	5	N.A.
25. Moscow, Russia	5.4	7.1	9.0	9.3	N.A.	4	N.A.
26. London, U.K.	8.7	8.6	7.3	7.3	N.A.	2	N.A.
27. Chicago, U.S.	4.9	6.7	6.8	7.0	N.A.	8	N.A.

Note: An urban area is a central city or central cities, and the surrounding urbanized areas, also called a metropolitan area.
Source: United Nations Population Division.

Oceans

The water of the world's oceans covers more than 70 percent of the world's surface. While for most of the 20th century the so-called World Ocean was divided into the Pacific, Atlantic, Indian, and Arctic Oceans, a decision by the International Hydrographic Organization in 2000 delimited a fifth ocean, the Southern Ocean, extending from 60 degrees south latitude to the coast of Antarctica.

Arctic Ocean northern polar sea between North America, Asia, and Europe; fifth-largest ocean.

Atlantic Ocean second-largest ocean, between South America, North America, Europe, and Africa.

Indian Ocean third-largest ocean, between Africa, Asia, and Australia.

Pacific Ocean largest ocean, between Australia, Asia, North America, and South America.

Southern Ocean fourth-largest ocean, south of the Antarctic Circle (66°30'S); completely encircles Antarctica.

Second-order submarine features of the oceans include *continental shelves*, *abyssal plains*, *mid-ocean ridges*, and *trenches*. Continental shelves generally slope gently away from the shore to a depth of about 600 feet (183 meters). The seafloor then turns sharply down a continental slope to the abyssal plain, or sea floor. In the middle of the oceans there are typically mid-ocean ridges, which occur where the ocean crust is slowly separating and molten magma seeps to the surface and hardens. The global mid-ocean ridge runs north to south through the Arctic and Atlantic Oceans, the Indian Ocean, the South Pacific, and north to North America. In the Pacific, the western part of the ocean floor includes mountain arcs that rise above sea level as island groups (such as the Solomons and New Zealand). Ocean trenches, the deepest of which are at the outer margins of the western Pacific continental shelf, form where tectonic plates meet and one edge is driven under the other.

Major Seas, Gulfs, and Straits of the World

Other large bodies of water such as the Caribbean Sea, the Gulf of Mexico, Hudson Bay, the Mediterranean and Black Seas, and the South China Sea are termed marginal seas. The International Hydrographic Organization identifies 66 seas, gulfs, bays, bights, straits, channels, and passages, many of which are further subdivided. For instance, the Mediterranean Sea is divided into western and eastern basins, and the western basin is subdivided into the Strait of Gibraltar, Aboran Sea, Balearic Sea, Ligurian Sea, Tyrrhenian Sea, Ionian Sea, Adriatic Sea, and Aegean Sea.

Aden, Gulf of arm of western Indian Ocean between Yemen and Somalia.

Adriatic Sea arm of Mediterranean between Italy, Croatia, Bosnia and Herzegovina, Serbia and Montenegro, and Albania.

Aegean Sea arm of Mediterranean between Greece and Turkey.

Alaska, Gulf of arm of Pacific off southeast coast of Alaska.

Albemarle Sound inlet of Atlantic between North Carolina and Outer Banks.

Amundsen Sea part of Southern Ocean off Marie Byrd Land, Antarctica.

Anadyrskiy Zaliv (Anadyr Gulf) arm of Bering Sea off northeast Russia.

Andaman Sea arm of Indian Ocean between Andaman Islands, Myanmar, Malaysia, and Indonesia.

Aqaba, Gulf of arm of the Red Sea between Egypt, Israel, Jordan, and Saudi Arabia.

Arabian Sea arm of Indian Ocean between Oman, Iran, Pakistan, and India.

Arafura Sea arm of Indian Ocean between East Timor, Indonesia, New Guinea, and Australia.

Aral Sea landlocked Asian sea between Kazakhstan and Uzbekistan.

Azov, Sea of small sea north of Black Sea between Ukraine and Russia.

Bab el Mandeb passage from Red Sea to Indian Ocean (Gulf of Aden) between Djibouti and Yemen.

Baffin Bay arm of Arctic Ocean between Baffin Is. and Greenland.

Bali Sea Indonesian sea between Java and Bali.

Baltic Sea nearly enclosed European sea between Denmark, Sweden, Finland, Russia, Estonia, Latvia, Lithuania, Poland, and Germany.

Banda Sea Indonesian sea between Timor, Celebes, and Seram Islands.

Barents Sea arm of Arctic Ocean between Norway, Spitsbergen, Novaya Zemlya, and Russia.

Bass Strait passage from Indian Ocean to Tasman Sea between Australia and Tasmania.

Beaufort Sea arm of Arctic Ocean off coast of Alaska and Canada.

Belle Isle, Strait of passage from Atlantic to Gulf of St. Lawrence between Labrador and Newfoundland.

Bellingshausen Sea part of Southern Ocean west of Antarctic Peninsula.

Bengal, Bay of arm of Indian Ocean between by India, Bangladesh, Myanmar, and Sri Lanka.

Berau, Gulf of arm of Seram Sea in western New Guinea.

Bering Sea arm of Pacific Ocean between Russia, Alaska, and Aleutian Is.

Bering Strait passage from Pacific to Bering Sea between Russia and Alaska.

Biscay, Bay of arm of Atlantic between Spain and France.

Bismarck Sea arm of Pacific between Bismarck Archipelago, and New Guinea.

Black Sea nearly enclosed sea between Turkey, Bulgaria, Romania, Ukraine, Russia, and Georgia, with outlet to Aegean via Bosporus.

Bo Hai (Gulf of Chihli) arm of Yellow Sea between Shandong and Liadong Peninsulas.

Bosporus Turkish strait from Black Sea and Sea of Marmara.

Bothnia, Gulf of arm of Baltic Sea between Sweden and Finland.

Bristol Channel arm of Celtic Sea in southwest England between England and Wales.

Cabot Strait passage from Atlantic to Gulf of St. Lawrence between Nova Scotia and Newfoundland.

California, Gulf of arm of Pacific in northwest Mexico.

Campeche, Bay of southwest arm of Gulf of Mexico on Mexican coast.

Canso, Strait of passage from Atlantic to Gulf of St. Lawrence between mainland Nova Scotia and Cape Breton Is.

Cape Cod Bay arm of Massachusetts Bay.

Caribbean Sea arm of Atlantic Ocean between Panama, Costa Rica, Nicaragua, Honduras, Guatemala, Mexico, West Indies, Venezuela, and Colombia.

Carpentaria, Gulf of Australian arm of Indian Ocean between Arnhem Land and Cape York Peninsula.

Caspian Sea central Asian sea between Azerbaijan, Russia, Kazakhstan, Turkmenistan, and Iran.

Celebes (Sulawesi) Sea Indonesian sea between Celebes, Kalimantan (Borneo), and Philippines.

Celtic Sea arm of Atlantic south of Ireland and England.

Chesapeake Bay inlet of Atlantic between Maryland and Virginia.

Chukchi Sea arm of Arctic Ocean between Siberia and Alaska.

Cook Strait passage from Pacific to Tasman Sea between North and South Is. of New Zealand.

Coral Sea arm of Pacific between Australia, Papua New Guinea, Solomon Islands, Vanuatu, and New Caledonia.

Dardanelles Turkish strait from Aegean to Sea of Marmara.

Davis Strait passage from Labrador Sea to Baffin Bay between Baffin Is. and Greenland.

Delaware Bay inlet of Atlantic between New Jersey and Delaware.

Denmark Strait passage from Atlantic to Norwegian Sea between Greenland and Iceland.

Dover, Strait of passage from English Channel to North Sea between Great Britain and France.

Drake Passage broad passage from Atlantic to Pacific south of South America.

East China Sea (Dong Hai) arm of Pacific between Taiwan, China, South Korea, and Japan.

East Sea (Sea of Japan) sea between South and North Korea, China, Russia, and Japan.

East Siberian Sea arm of Arctic Ocean between Siberia and New Siberian Islands.

English Channel arm of Atlantic between England and France

Finland, Gulf of arm of Baltic between Finland, Russia, Lithuania, Latvia, and Estonia.

Flores Sea Indonesian sea between Flores and Celebes.

Florida, Straits of passage from Gulf of Mexico to Atlantic between Florida and Cuba.

Foxe Basin arm of Hudson Bay between Nunavut and Baffin Is.

Fundy, Bay of arm of Atlantic between Maine, New Brunswick, and Nova Scotia; has greatest tidal ranges (16 m/53 ft.) in the world.

Galveston Bay inlet of Gulf of Mexico on coast of Texas.

Gibraltar, Strait of passage from Atlantic to Mediterranean between Morocco and Spain.

Great Australian Bight arm of Indian Ocean, off south coast of Western Australia.

Greenland Sea arm of Arctic Ocean between Greenland and Spitsbergen.

Guayaquil, Gulf of arm of Pacific off coast of Ecuador.

Guinea, Gulf of arm of Atlantic between Ghana, Togo, Benin, Nigeria, Cameroon, Equatorial Guinea, and Gabon.

Hecate Strait passage between Queen Charlotte Is. and British Columbia.

Hormuz, Strait of passage from Persian Gulf to Gulf of Oman between Oman and Iran.

Huang Hai (Yellow Sea) arm of East China Sea between China and Korean Peninsula.

Hudson Bay Canadian Bay between Ontario, Manitoba, Nunavut, and Quebec.

Hudson Strait passage from Labrador Sea to Hudson Bay.

Inland Sea (Seto Naikai) Japanese sea between Kyushu, Honshu, and Shikoku Is.

Ionian Sea arm of Mediterranean between Italy and Greece.

Irish Sea arm of Atlantic between Ireland and England.

James Bay arm of Hudson Bay between Ontario and Quebec.

Japan, Sea of see *East Sea*.

Java Sea arm of South China Sea between Sumatra, Borneo, and Java.

Juan de Fuca Strait passage from Pacific to Puget Sound between Washington and Vancouver Is.

Kara Sea arm of Arctic Ocean between Russia, Novaya Zemlya, and Severnaya Zemlya.

Kattegat passage from Skagerak and Baltic to Denmark and Sweden.

Korea Strait (Strait of Tsushima) passage from East China to East Seas between South Korea and Japan.

La Perouse Strait passage from Sea of Okhotsk to East Sea between Hokkaido and Sakhalin Is.

Labrador Sea arm of Atlantic between Labrador, Baffin Island, and Greenland.

Laguna Madre inlet of Gulf of Mexico between Texas and Padre Is.

Laptev Sea arm of Arctic Ocean west of Novosibirskiye Ostrova (New Siberian Is.).

Leyte Gulf Philippines gulf between Samar and Leyte.

Liaodong Wan (Gulf) arm of Bo Hai.

Ligurian Sea arm of Mediterranean between Corsica, France, and Italy.

Lincoln Sea arm of Arctic Ocean between Ellesmere Is. and Greenland.

Lion, Gulf of arm of Mediterranean off southern France.

Lombok Strait passage from Indian Ocean to Java Sea between Bali and Lombok Is.

Long Island Sound passage from Atlantic to New York Harbor between Connecticut, Rhode Island, and Long Is.

Luzon Strait broad passage from Pacific to South China Sea between Taiwan and Philippines.

Magellan, Strait of passage from Atlantic to Pacific between Chile and Tierra del Fuego.

Maine, Gulf of arm of Atlantic between Massachusetts, New Hampshire, Maine, New Brunswick, and Nova Scotia.

Makassar Strait Indonesian strait between Java and Celebes Seas between Kalimantan (Borneo) and Celebes.

Malacca, Strait of main passage from Indian Ocean to South China Sea between Indonesia (Sumatra), Malaysia, and Singapore.

Mannar, Gulf of arm of Indian Ocean between India and Sri Lanka.

Marmara, Sea of nearly enclosed Turkish sea, with outlets to Aegean via Dardanelles and Black Sea via Bosporus.

Massachusetts Bay arm of Atlantic off Massachusetts.

Matagorda Bay inlet of Gulf of Mexico on Texas coast.

Mediterranean Sea marginal sea of the Atlantic between Africa, Europe and Asia, with outlets to Atlantic via Strait of Gibraltar, Black Sea via Bosporus, and Red Sea via Suez Canal.

Melaku (Halmahera) Sea Indonesian arm of Pacific between Celebes and Halmahera.

Mexico, Gulf of arm of Atlantic Ocean between Mexico,

Texas, Louisiana, Mississippi, Alabama, Florida, and Cuba.

Mobile Bay inlet of Gulf of Mexico in Alabama.

Mona Passage passage from Atlantic to Caribbean between Puerto Rico and Dominican Republic.

Mozambique Channel Indian Ocean passage between Mozambique, Comoros, and Madagascar.

Nantucket Sound arm of Atlantic between Nantucket, Martha's Vineyard, and Cape Cod.

Nares Strait Arctic passage from Baffin Bay and Lincoln Sea.

New Georgia Sound Solomon Is. arm of the Pacific west of Guadalcanal; also known as "The Slot" and "Ironbottom Sound."

North Sea arm of the Atlantic between Great Britain, Norway, Denmark, Germany, Netherland, and Belgium.

Northern Sea Route east-west Arctic passage between Atlantic and Pacific across top of Norway and Russia; first west-east transit, 1878–79.

Northumberland Strait Gulf of St. Lawrence Passage from Nova Scotia and Prince Edward Is.

Northwest Passage east-west Arctic passage between Atlantic to Pacific across top of Canada and U.S.; first east-west transit 1904–1906; first west-east transit, 1941–42.

Norwegian Sea arm of Atlantic and Arctic Oceans between Norway and Iceland.

Okhotsk, Sea of arm of northwest Pacific between Sakhalin Is., Siberia, Kamchatka Peninsula, and Kurile Is.

Oman, Gulf of arm of Indian Ocean bordered by Oman, United Arab Emirates, and Iran.

Oresund passage from Kattegat to Baltic between Denmark and Sweden.

Palk Strait passage from Bay of Bengal to Gulf of Mannar between India and Sri Lanka; maximum draft is 4 meters.

Pamlico Sound inlet of Atlantic between North Carolina and Outer Banks.

Panama, Gulf of arm of Pacific on south coast of Panama.

Persian Gulf arm of Indian Ocean between United Arab Emirates, Saudi Arabia, Qatar, Bahrain, Kuwait, Iraq, and Iran.

Philippine Sea arm of Pacific between Philippines, Northern Marianas, Micronesia (Caroline Islands), and Palau.

Plata, Rio de la arm of the Atlantic between Argentina and Uruguay.

Red Sea arm of Indian Ocean between Djibouti, Eritrea, Sudan, Egypt, Israel, Jordan, Saudi Arabia, and Yemen.

Ross Sea arm of Southern Ocean off Ross Ice Shelf, Antarctica.

St. Georges Channel passage from Celtic Sea and Irish Sea.

St. Lawrence, Gulf of Canadian arm of the Atlantic between New Brunswick, Quebec, Newfoundland, Nova Scotia, and Prince Edward Is.

Sakhalinskiy Zaliv arm of Sea of Okhotsk between Russia and Sakhalin Is.

San Bernardino Strait Philippines passage between Luzon and Samar.

San Jorge, Golfo arm of Atlantic off southern Argentina.

San Matias, Golfo arm of Atlantic off southern Argentina.

Savu Sea (Sawu Sea) Indonesian sea between Sumba, Flores, and Timor.

Scotia Sea arm of Southern Ocean east of Drake Passage between South Georgia, South Sandwich, and South Orkney Is.

Seram (Ceram) Sea Indonesian sea between Seram, Halmahera, and New Guinea.

Shelikhova, Zaliv (Shelikhova Bay) arm of Sea of Okhotsk between Siberia and Kamchatka Peninsula.

Sibuyan Sea Philippine sea between Panay, Mindoro, and Luzon.

Sicily, Strait of east-west Mediterranean passage between Sicily and Tunisia.

Singapore Strait passage from Malacca Strait to South China Sea between Malay Peninsula and Singapore.

Skaggerak strait between North and Baltic Seas between Denmark and Norway.

Solomon Sea arm of Pacific between Papua New Guinea and Solomon Islands.

South China Sea (Nan Hai) arm of Pacific between China, Philippines, Malaysia, Brunei, Indonesia, Singapore, Thailand, Cambodia, and Vietnam.

Spencer Gulf inlet of Indian Ocean between South Australia and Kangaroo Is.

Suez Canal Egyptian canal between Mediterranean Sea and Red Sea.

Suez, Gulf of arm of Red Sea bounded entirely by Egypt, with access to Mediterranean via Suez Canal.

Sulu Sea nearly enclosed sea between Borneo (Malaysia) and Philippine islands of Palawan, Panay, Negros, Mindanao, and Sulu Archipelago.

Sunda Strait passage from Indian Ocean to Java Sea between Sumatra and Java.

Surigao Strait Philippines passage from Pacific to Sulu Sea between Leyte and Mindanao.

Taiwan (Formosa) Strait passage from South China to East China Sea between China and Taiwan.

Tasman Sea arm of Pacific between Australia and New Zealand.

Tatarskiy Proliv (Tatar Strait) passage from East Sea to Sea of Okhotsk between Russia and Sakhalin Is.

Teluk Bone (Gulf of Bone) arm of Banda Sea in southern Celebes.

Teluk Tomini (Gulf of Tomini) arm of Melaku Sea in northern Celebes.

Thailand, Gulf of arm of South China Sea between Thailand and Cambodia.

Timor Sea arm of Indian Ocean between East Timor and Australia.

Tongking, Gulf of arm of South China Sea between Vietnam and Hainan Island, China.

Torres Strait passage from Pacific Ocean to Arafura Sea between Papua New Guinea and Australia.

Tsushima, Strait of see *Korea Strait*.

Tyrrhenian Sea part of Mediterranean between Sardinia, Corsica, Italy, and Sicily.

Venezuela, Gulf of arm of Caribbean in western Venezuela.

Weddell Sea part of Southern Ocean east of Antarctic Peninsula.

White Sea arm of Arctic Ocean in northwest Russia.

Windward Passage passage from Atlantic to Caribbean between Cuba and Haiti.

Yellow Sea see *Huang Hai*.

Yucatán Channel passage from Caribbean to Gulf of Mexico between Mexico and Cuba.

Rivers and Canals of the World

Amazon 4,007 mi. (6,448 km). World's largest river by volume and second-largest in length rises in Peruvian Andes as Marañón River and flows through Brazil to Atlantic.

Amu Darya (Oxus) 1,578 mi. (2,541 km). Rises in Tajikistan and flows through or borders Afghanistan, Turkmenistan, and Uzbekistan to Aral Sea.

Amur (Heilong Jiang) 2,705 mi. (4,355 km). Formed by confluence of Silka and Argun Rivers on Chinese/Russian border, flows through Russia to the Tatar Strait.

Apalachicola 90 mi. (145 km). Flows from Lake Seminole through Florida to Gulf of Mexico.

Arkansas 1,450 mi. (2,335 km). Rises in the Colorado Rockies and flows through Kansas, Oklahoma, and Arkansas (Little Rock) to Mississippi. McClellan-Kerr Arkansas River System (455 mi./733 km) is combination of natural and artificial waterways—including sections of Verdigris, Arkansas and White Rivers—from Catoosa, Okla. (near Tulsa) and junction of White and Mississippi Rivers.

Arno 150 mi. (242 km). Rises in Apennines and flows via Florence to Ligurian Sea.

Atchafalaya 220 mi. (354 km). Flows from confluence of Mississippi and Red Rivers through Louisiana via Morgan City to Gulf of Mexico.

Baltic-White Sea Canal 141 mi. (227 km). Complex of natural and manmade Russian waterways connecting Baltic and White Seas.

Black Warrior 217 mi. (350 km). Rises in Alabama and flows into the Tombigbee.

Brahmaputra 1,770 mi. (2,850 km). Rises in Tibet and flows through China, India and Bangladesh (Dhaka) to the Ganges-Brahmaputra Delta and Bay of Bengal.

Cape Cod Canal 17 mi. (27 km). Canal between Massachusetts Bay and Buzzards Bay built in 1914.

Cape Fear 202 mi. (325 km). Rises in North Carolina and flows to Atlantic.

Chao Phraya (Me Nam) 227 mi. (365 km). Rises in Thailand and flows via Bangkok to Gulf of Thailand.

Chattahoochee 436 mi. (702 km). Rises in Georgia. Dammed to create Lake Seminole (on Alabama border) from which flows the Apalachicola.

Chesapeake and Delaware Canal 14 mi. (23 km). Canal between Delaware Bay (Delaware) and Chesapeake Bay (Maryland) built in 1824–29.

Colorado 1,450 mi. (2,335 km). Rises in Colorado Rockies, flows through Utah, Arizona (Grand Canyon), Nevada, California, Baja California Norte, and Sonora to the Gulf of California.

Columbia 1,243 mi. (2,001 km). Rises in British Columbia and flows through Washington and Oregon (Portland) to the Pacific.

Congo (Zaire) 2,900 mi. (4,669 km). Rises in Zaire and flows along border with Congo via Kinshasa and Brazzaville to Atlantic.

Connecticut 407 mi. (655 km). Rises in New Hampshire and flows through Vermont, Massachusetts, and Connecticut (Hartford) to Long Island Sound.

Cumberland 694 mi. (1,117 km). Rises in Kentucky and flows through Tennessee to the Ohio.

Danube (Donau) 1,776 mi. (2,859 km). Rises in Germany and flows through and/or forms border of Austria (Vienna), Hungary (Budapest), Croatia, Yugoslavia (Belgrade), Bulgaria, Ukraine and Romania, where it enters Black Sea. Part of Rhine-Main-Danube Waterway.

Delaware 367 mi. (590 km). Rises in New York and borders New York, New Jersey (Trenton), Pennsylvania (Philadelphia), and Delaware (Wilmington) en route to Delaware Bay.

Dnieper 1,420 mi. (2,286 km). Rises in Russia and flows through Belarus and Ukraine (Kiev and Dnepropetrovsk) to Black Sea.

Dniester 877 mi. (1,412 km). Rises in Ukraine and flows along Moldova border to Black Sea.

Don (Tanais) 1,224 mi. (1,970 km). Russian river that flows to Black Sea via Voronezh and Rostov.

Douro (Duero) 556 mi. (895 km). Rises in Spain and flows through Portugal (Oporto) to Atlantic.

Elbe 724 mi. (1,165 km). Rises in Czech Republic and flows through Germany (Hamburg) to North Sea.

Erie Canal 363 mi. (584 km). Main artery of New York State Barge Canal, built 1817–25 between Hudson River (Albany) and Lake Erie (Buffalo).

Euphrates 1,510 mi. (2,431 km). Rises in Turkey and flows through Syria and Iraq to join the Tigris and form the Shatt-al-Arab.

Ganges (Ganga) 1,560 mi. (2,512 km). Rises in India and flows through Bangladesh to the Ganges-Brahmaputra Delta and Bay of Bengal.

Garonne 357 mi. (575 km). French river that forms, with the Dordogne, Gironde Estuary on the Atlantic below Bordeaux.

Grand Canal (Da Yunhe) 1,114 mi. (1,795 km). Inland canal in China between Beijing and Hangzhou. First stage between Yangtze River (Chiang Jiang) and Yellow River (Huang He) built in 5th century B.C.; extended south to Hangzhou on East China Sea, A.D. 618, and north to Beijing, 1292.

Green 360 mi. (580 km). Rises in Kentucky and flows into Ohio River.

Guadalquivir 408 mi. (657 km). Spanish river that flows via Córdoba and Seville to Atlantic.

Houston Ship Channel 57 mi. (92 km). Waterway cut through Buffalo Bayou between Houston and Galveston, Texas, in 1914.

Hudson 306 mi. (493 km). New York river that flows via Albany and New York City to Atlantic.

Illinois Waterway 327 mi. (526 km). Natural and man-made waterways connecting Lake Michigan and Mississippi and comprising Chicago River, Chicago Sanitary and Ship Canal (1900), Des Plaines River, and Illinois River.

Indus 1,800 mi. (2,898 km). Rises in Tibet and flows through China, Jammu & Kashmir and Pakistan to Arabian Sea.

Intracoastal Waterway Improved channels, both natural and man-made, authorized by U.S. Congress in 1919 to provide sheltered navigation from Massachusetts to Texas. A trans-Florida section was never built, and it is divided into the Atlantic Intracoastal Waterway (1,800 mi./2,900 km) from Cape Cod to Miami, and the Gulf Intracoastal Waterway (1,100 mi./1,770 km) from Apalachee Bay, Fla., to Brownsville, Tex.

Irrawaddy 1,300 mi. (2,093 km). Rises in Myanmar and flows into Bay of Bengal

Irtysh River 2,760 mi. (4,444 km). Rises in China and flows through Kazakhstan and Russia (Novosibirsk) to Ob. Combined length of Lower Ob and Irtysh is 3,360 mi./5,410 km.

James 340 mi. (547 km). Rises in Virginia and flows via Richmond and Hampton Roads to Chesapeake Bay.

Jordan 200 mi. (322 km). Rises in Syria and flows through or borders Lebanon, Israel, and Jordan to the Dead Sea via Sea of Galilee.

Kanawha 97 mi. (156 km). Rises in West Virginia and flows into Ohio River.

Kasai 1,338 mi. (2,154 km). Rises in Angola and flows through Zaire and Congo to the Congo.

Kentucky 259 mi. (417 km). Rises in Kentucky and flows into the Ohio.

Kiel Canal (Nord-Ostsee Kanal) 53 mi. (86 km). German canal built in 1887-95 between Baltic (Kiel) and North Sea (mouth of the Elbe).

Kwai (Khwae) Noi Western Thailand river across which infamous railway "bridge on the River Kwai" at Kanchanaburi was built during World War II, at the cost of more than 60,000 lives.

Lena 2,730 mi. (4,395 km). Russian river that flows via Yakutsk to Laptev Sea.

Liffey 50 mi. (80 km). Irish River that flows into Irish Sea at Dublin.

Limpopo (Crocodile) 1,600 mi. (2,575 km). Rises in South Africa and borders and/or flows through Botswana, Zimbabwe and Mozambique to Indian Ocean.

Loire 634 mi. (1,020 km). French river that flows via Orléans and St. Nazaire to Bay of Biscay.

Mackenzie 2,635 mi. (4,242 km). Rises in British Columbia and flows through Alberta and Northwest Terr. to Beaufort Sea. Length includes Peace River above Great Slave Lake, and Finlay River above Williston Lake.

Madeira 2,013 mi. (3,241 km). Formed by confluence of Mamoré and Beni Rivers at Bolivian border and flows through Brazil to the Amazon.

Marne 326 mi. (525 km). French river that flows to the Seine.

Mekong 2,600 mi. (4,186 km). Rises in China and flows through or borders Laos (Vientaine), Myanmar, Thailand, Cambodia (Phnom Penh), and Vietnam to South China Sea.

Mississippi 2,348 mi. (3,780). Rises in Minnesota (Minneapolis/St. Paul) and forms all or part of eastern border of Iowa, Missouri (St. Louis), Arkansas and Louisiana, and western border of Wisconsin, Illinois, Kentucky, Tennessee (Memphis) and Mississippi; flows through Louisiana (Baton Rouge and New Orleans) to Gulf of Mexico. Measured from head of the Missouri, total length is 3,740 mi./6,021 km (not including Upper Mississippi.

Missouri 2,315 mi. (3,725 km). Rises in Montana and flows through and/or borders North Dakota (Bismarck), South Dakota (Pierre), Iowa (Sioux City), Nebraska (Omaha), Kansas and Missouri (Kansas City), en route to the Mississippi..

Mobile 45 mi. (72 km). Alabama river that flows via Mobile to Mobile Bay.

Monongahela 129 mi. (208 km). Rises in West Virginia and flows through Pennsylvania to the Ohio.

Moscow Canal 80 mi. (129 km). Canal built in 1937 to link Russian capital to the Volga.

Murray-Darling 2,330 mi. (3,751 km). Rises in the Great Dividing Range and flows to Indian Ocean.

Nelson 1,600 mi. (2,576 km). Rises in Alberta and flows through Saskatchewan and Manitoba to Hudson Bay; length includes Saskatchewan River above Lake Winnipeg and Bow River near Calgary.

New York State Barge Canal 353 mi. (568 km). Network of waterways between Hudson River and Lake Erie including Erie Canal, Champlain Canal (to Lake Champlain), and Oswego Canal (to Lake Ontario).

Niagara 35 mi. (56 km). Forms border between New York and Ontario and flows from Lake Erie to Ontario; unnavigable because of the 170-ft.-high (52-m) Niagara Falls. See *Welland Canal*.

Niger 2,600 mi. (4,186 km). Rises in Guinea and flows through Mali (Bamako and Tombouctou), Niger (Niamey), Benin and Nigeria to Gulf of Guinea.

Nile 4,145 mi. (6,673 km). World's longest river rises in Uganda and flows through Sudan (Khartoum) and Egypt (Cairo, Alexandria, and Rosetta) to Mediterranean. Passes through Lakes Victoria, Kyoga, and Albert. Known as White Nile in Sudan; at Khartoum merges with Blue Nile (850 mi./1,370 km), which rises in Ethiopia.

Ob River 2,287 mi. (3,682 km). Russian river that flows via Tobolsk to Gulf of Ob (Kara Sea). With Irtysh River, 3,360 mi. (5,410 km).

Oder 567 mi. (912 km). Rises in Czech Republic and flows through Poland via German border and Szczecin to Baltic.

Ohio 981 mi. (1,580 km). Formed by confluence of the Monongahela and Allegheny at Pittsburgh, Pennsylvania, and flows through Ohio (Cincinnati), West Virginia,

Indiana, Kentucky, and Illinois to the Mississippi.

Orange 1,300 mi. (2,093 km). Rises in Lesotho and flows through South Africa and along Namibian border to Atlantic.

Orinoco 1,600 mi. (2,576 km). Rises in Venezuela and flows to Caribbean; forms part of border with Colombia.

Ouachita 605 mi. (974 km). Rises in Arkansas, and flows through Louisiana to the Mississippi. Lower 57 mi. (92 km) known as Black River.

Panama Canal 50 mi. (80 km). Panamanian waterway built 1904–14 between Atlantic (Colón) and Pacific (Panamá).

Paraguay 1,610 mi. (2,592 km). Rises in Brazil and flows through Paraguay (Asunción) and Argentina to the Paraná.

Paraná 1,827 mi. (2,941 km). Rises in Brazil and flows through and/or borders Paraguay and Argentina en route to La Plata.

Pará-Tocantins 1,710 mi. (2,753 km). Brazilian river that flows to the Amazon via Pará. The Pará River is southern branch of the Amazon at its mouth.

Plata (Plate) 123 mi. (198 km). Estuary of Paraná and Uruguay Rivers that flows to Atlantic and washes Buenos Aires and Montevideo.

Po 405 mi. (652 km). Italian river that flows via Turin to Adriatic.

Potomac 287 mi. (462 km). Rises in West Virginia and flows through and/or borders Maryland, Virginia, and Washington, D.C., to Chesapeake Bay.

Purus 1,860 mi. (2,995 km). Rises in Peru and flows through Brazil to the Amazon above Manaus.

Red 1,018 mi. (1,639 km). Rises in New Mexico and flows through and/or borders Texas, Oklahoma, Arkansas, and Louisiana (Shreveport) to Mississippi.

Rhine 820 mi. (1,320 km). Rises in Switzerland (Basel) and flows through and/or borders Liechtenstein, Austria, Germany (Köln), France (Strasbourg), and the Netherlands (Rotterdam) to North Sea.

Rhine-Main-Danube Waterway 2,173 mi. (3,505 km) Trans-Europe canal linking North and Black Seas: Rhine River from North Sea to Mainz (334 mi./539 km); Main River to Bamberg (238 mi./384 km); Main-Danube Canal (106 mi./171 km); Danube River to Black Sea (1,495 mi./2,411 km). Waterway completed in 1992—1,199 years after Charlemagne first attempted to link Rhine and Danube.

Rhone 300 mi. (485 km). Rises in Switzerland and France and flows via Marseilles to Mediterranean.

Rio Grande (Río Bravo, Río Bravo del Norte) 1,885 mi. (3,035 km). Rises in New Mexico and forms border between Texas (El Paso, Brownsville) and Mexican states of Chihuahua (Ciudad Juarez), Coahuila, Nuevo León, and Tamaulipas (Matamoros) to Gulf of Mexico.

Roanoke 410 mi. (660 km). Rises in Virginia and flows through North Carolina to Albemarle Sound.

Sacramento 374 mi. (602 km). California river that flows via Sacramento to San Francisco Bay.

Saint Johns 285 mi. (459 km). Florida river that flows via Jacksonville to Atlantic.

St. Lawrence 800 mi. (1,288 km). Rises in Ontario and flows through Quebec (Montreal and Quebec) and New York to Gulf of St. Lawrence. The St. Lawrence Seaway—2,340 mi. (3,766 km)—is a U.S./Canadian navigational project (1954–59) that allows ocean-going ships to ascend St. Lawrence and cross the Great Lakes to Duluth, Minn., and includes Welland Canal and Sault Ste. Marie Canals.

Salween 1,750 mi. (2,818 km). Rises in China, flows through Myanmar, forms part of border with Thailand, and enters Bay of Bengal at Moulmein, Myanmar.

San Joaquin 340 mi. (547 km). California river that flows to the Sacramento.

São Francisco 1,988 mi. (3,201 km). Brazilian river that flows to Atlantic Ocean.

Sault Ste. Marie (Soo) Canals 1.6 mi. (2.6 km). Built to overcome 12 ft. (3.7 m) drop between Lakes Superior and Huron; first built 1895. Part of St. Lawrence Seaway.

Savannah 314 mi. (506 km). Rises in South Carolina and flows through Georgia (Savannah) to the Atlantic.

Seine 482 mi. (776 km). French river that flows via Paris and Le Havre to English Channel.

Shannon 270 mi. (370 km). Irish river that flows via Limerick to Atlantic.

Shatt-al-Arab 120 mi. (193 km). Waterway between confluence of Tigris and Euphrates and the Persian Gulf; forms part of Iran/Iraq border. Major cities include Basra, Abadan, and Khorramshar.

Snake 1,083 mi. (1,744 km). Rises in Wyoming and flows through Idaho, Oregon, and Washington to the Columbia.

Somme 152 mi. (245 km). French river that flows via Amiens to English Channel. Scene of World War I battle, July–November 1916.

Suez Canal 101 mi. (163 km). Egyptian canal, built 1859–69, between Mediterranean (Port Said) and Red Sea (Suez).

Syr Darya 1,370 mi. (2,206 km). Rises in Uzbekistan and flows through Kazakhstan to Aral Sea.

Tagus 675 mi. (1,007 km). Rises in Spain and flows through Portugal to Atlantic at Lisbon.

Tennessee 652 mi. (1,050 km). Rises in Tennessee (Chattanooga) and flows through Alabama, Mississippi, and Kentucky to the Ohio.

Tennessee-Tombigbee Waterway 253 mi. (407 km). Manmade waterway, completed 1985, between the Tennessee in Mississippi and the Tombigbee in Alabama.

Thames 210 mi. (338 km). English river that flows via London to North Sea.

Tiber 252 mi. (406 km). Italian river that flows via Rome to Tyrrhenian Sea.

Tigris 1,180 mi. (1,900 km). Rises in Turkey and flows through Iraq (Mosul, Baghdad) and joins the Euphrates to form the Shatt-al-Arab above Persian Gulf.

Tombigbee 362 mi. (583 km). Rises in Mississippi and flows through Alabama to the Mobile.

Tunguska, Lower 1,860 mi. (2,995 km). Russian river that flows to the Yenisei.

Ural 1,575 mi. (2,536 km). Rises in Russia and flows through Kazakhstan to Caspian Sea.

Vistula 675 mi. (1086 km). Polish river that flows via Warsaw and Gdansk to Baltic Sea.

Volga 2,290 mi. (3,687 km). Russian river that flows via Gorki and Volgograd (Stalingrad) to Caspian Sea. Longest river in Europe.

Volga-Baltic Canal 685 mi. (1,110 km). Network of canals and improved waterways connecting the Volga with Baltic Sea near St. Petersburg.

Volga-Don Canal (Lenin Canal) 62 mi. (100 km). Last link in Russian waterway system that connects the Baltic, Black, White, and Caspian Seas, and the Sea of Azov; opened in 1952.

Welland Canal 27 mi. (43 km). Canal (first built 1824–29) to overcome 327 ft. (100 m) drop from Lake Ontario to Erie; current canal built 1913–32. Part of St. Lawrence Seaway.

Willamette 294 mi. (473 km). Oregon river that flows to the Columbia at Portland.

Yangtze (Chang Jiang) 3,720 mi. (5,989 km). Chinese river that flows via Wuhan, Nanjing, and Shanghai to East China Sea.

Yazoo 169 mi. (272 km). River in Mississippi that flows to the Mississippi.

Yellow (Huang He) 2,903 mi. (4,674 km). Chinese river that flows to Bo Hai (Yellow Sea).

Yenisei 2,566 mi. (4,131 km) Russian river that flows to Kara Sea. Combined length with Angara (Upper Tunguska) River is 3,650 mi. (5,877 km).

Yukon 1,979 mi. (3,186 km). Rises in Yukon Territory and flows through Alaska to Bering Sea.

Zambezi 1,700 mi. (2,737 km). Rises in Zambia and flows through Angola, Namibia, Zambia, Zimbabwe, and Mozambique to Mozambique Channel.

Islands and Archipelagos of the World

Åland Is. (Ahvenanmaa) 60°N, 20°E. Finnish archipelago of more than 6,000 islands between Finland and Sweden.

Aleutian Is. 51°-55°N, 163°W-166°E. Chain between Pacific Ocean and Bering Sea stretching 2,700 km: Unimak, Fox Is., Andreanof Is., Rat Is. and Near Is. (Alaska) and Komandorskiye Ostrova (Russia).

Andaman and Nicobar Is. 12°N, 93°E. Union Territory of India comprising some 300 islands in two major archipelagos stretching 725 km north-south in the Bay of Bengal off the coast of Myanmar.

Anticosti 50°N, 63°W. Canadian island in Gulf of St. Lawrence.

Antigua and Barbuda 17°N, 62°W. Two-island Caribbean country.

Antilles' name for the Caribbean islands from Cuba to Trinidad and Tobago, but not including the Bahamas. Greater Antilles: Cuba, Jamaica, Hispaniola, and Puerto Rico. Lesser Antilles: Leeward Is. Virgin Is., Antigua and Barbuda, and Dominica) and Windward Is. (Martinique, St. Lucia, St. Vincent, Grenada, Barbados, Trinidad and Tobago, and Aruba).

Aran Is. 53°N, 10°W. Three islands—Inishmore, Inishmaan, and Inisheer—off western Ireland.

Aruba 12°N, 70°W. Dutch Caribbean island 30 km north of Venezuela.

Major Rivers of the World, by Length

River	Length Miles	Length km	Source	Outflow
Nile	4,145	6,673	Tributaries of Lake Victoria, E. Africa	Mediterranean Sea
Amazon	4,000	6,440	Andes Mts., Peru	Atlantic Ocean
Mississippi-Missouri	3,740[1]	6,021[1]	Confluence of Jefferson, Madison, and Galatin R., Montana	Gulf of Mexico
Changjiang (Yangtze)	3,720	5,989	Kunlun Mts., China	China Sea
Yenisei-Angara	3,650[2]	5,877[2]	Lake Baikal, Russia	Kara Sea (Arctic Ocean)
Amur-Argun	3,590[2]	5,780[2]	Khingan Mts., China	Tatar Strait
Ob-Irtysh	3,360[2]	5,410[2]	Altai Mts., China	Gulf of Ob (Arctic Ocean)
Plata-Parana	3,030[2]	4,878[2]	Confluence of the Paranaiba and Grande rivers, Brazil	Atlantic Ocean
Huang He (Yellow)	2,903	4,674	Kunlun Mts., China	Gulf of Chihli (Yellow Sea)
Congo (Zaire)	2,900	4,669	Confluence of the Luapula and Lualaba rivers, Zaire	Atlantic Ocean
Lena	2,730	4,395	Baikal Mts., Russia	Laptev Sea (Arctic Ocean)
MacKenzie	2,635[2]	4,242[2]	Headwaters of Finlay Rivers, British Columbia, Canada	Beaufort Sea (Arctic Ocean)
Mekong	2,600	4,186	T'ang-ku-la Mts., Tibet	South China Sea
Niger	2,600	4,186	Guinea	Gulf of Guinea
Missouri	2,315	3,725	Confluence of Jefferson, Madison, and Montana Galatin rivers, Montana	Mississippi River
Mississippi	2,348[3]	3,780[3]	Lake Itasca, northwestern Minnesota	Gulf of Mexico
Murray-Darling	2,330	3,751	Great Dividing Range, Australia	Indian Ocean
Volga	2,290	3,687	Valdai Hills, Russia	Caspian Sea
Madeira	2,013	3,241	Confluence of the Mamore and Beni rivers, Bolivia/Brazil	Amazon River
São Francisco	1,988	3,201	Minas Gerais State, Brazil	Atlantic Ocean
Yukon	1,979	3,186	Confluence of Lewes and Pelly rivers, Yukon Territory, Canada	Bering Sea
Rio Grande	1,885	3,035	San Juan Mts., southwestern Colorado	Gulf of Mexico
Purus	1,860	2,995	Andes Mts., Peru	Amazon River
Tunguska, Lower	1,860	2,995	North of Lake Baikal, Russia	Yenesei River
Indus	1,800	2,898	Himalayas, Tibet	Arabian Sea
Danube	1,776	2,859	Confluence of Breg and Brigach rivers, Germany	Black Sea
Brahmaputra	1,770	2,850	Himalayas, Tibet	Ganges River
Salween	1,750	2,818	Tibetan Plateau, Tibet	Bay of Bengal
Para-Tocantins	1,710[2]	2,753[2]	Goias State, Brazil	Atlantic Ocean
Zambezi	1,700	2,737	Northwestern Zambia	Mozambique Channel
Paraguay	1,610	2,592	Mato Grosso State, Brazil	Parana River
Kolyma	1,320	2,130	Kolyma Mts., Russia	Arctic Ocean
Nelson-Saskatchewan	1,600	2,576	Rocky Mts., Canada	Hudson Bay
Orinoco	1,600	2,576	Sierra Parima Mts., Venezuela	Atlantic Ocean
Amu Darya	1,578	2,541	Pamir Mts., Uzbekistan/Turkmenistan	Aral Sea
Ural	1,575	2,536	Ural Mountains, Russia	Caspian Sea

River	Length Miles	km	Source	Outflow
Ganges	1,560	2,512	Himalayas, India	Bay of Bengal
Euphrates	1,510	2,431	Confluence of the Murat Nehri and Kara Su rivers, Turkey	Shatt-al-Arab
Arkansas	1,450	2,335	Central Colorado	Mississippi River
Colorado	1,450	2,335	Northern Colorado	Gulf of California
Dneiper	1,420	2,286	Valdai Hills, Russia	Black Sea
Atchafalaya-Red	1,400	2,254	Eastern New Mexico	Gulf of Mexico
Syr Darya	1,370	2,206	Tien Shan, China/Kyrghyzstan	Aral Sea
Kasai	1,338	2,154	Central Angola	Congo (Zaire) River
Irrawaddy	1,300	2,093	Confluence of Mali and Nmai rivers, Myanmar	Bay of Bengal
Ohio-Allegheny	1,300	2,093	Pennsylvania	Mississippi River
Orange	1,300	2,093	Lesotho	Atlantic Ocean
Columbia	1,243	2,001	Columbia Lake, British Columbia, Canada	Pacific Ocean
Tigris	1,180	1,900	Eastern Turkey	Shatt-al-Arab
Rhine	820	1,320	Confluence of Hinterrhein and Vorderrhein rivers, Switzerland	North Sea
St. Lawrence	800	1,288	Lake Ontario	Gulf of St. Lawrence

1. From the mouth of the Mississippi, up the Missouri to the Red Rock River in Montana. 2. Includes the length of tributaries that are part of the main trunk stream. 3. From the mouth of the Mississippi, up to its source in Minnesota.
Source: U.S. Dept. of Commerce, National Oceanic and Atmospheric Administration.

Ascension 7°S, 14°W. Island of the British Crown Colony of St. Helena about 1,100 km northwest of St. Helena, 2,250 kilometers east of Brazil and 2,500 km west of Africa.

Auckland Is. 51°S, 166°E. Group about 300 km south of New Zealand.

Azores/Açores 37°-40°N, 25°-31°W. Portuguese Atlantic group 1,400 km west of Portugal; first settled in 1430's.

Baffin 68°N, 70°W. Largest Canadian Arctic island, on Davis Strait opposite Greenland.

Bahamas 21°-27°N, 71°-79°W. Chain of 2,700 islands and cays stretching 800 km southeast of Florida; shared by Bahamas and Turks and Caicos (British); Columbus's first American landfall in 1492.

Balearic Is. 39°N, 3°E. Sixteen Spanish Mediterranean 16 islands: Majorca, Minorca and Ibiza.

Bali 9°S, 115°E. Predominantly Hindu Indonesian island east of Java.

Banks 73°N, 121°W. Westernmost large Canadian Arctic island, on Beaufort Sea.

Barbados 13°N, 60°W. Island nation about 150 km east of southern Antilles.

Bermuda 32°N, 65°W. British dependency of 138 coral islands, 20 inhabited, 900 km east of North Carolina.

Bismarck Archipelago 5°S, 150°E. Papua New Guinea archipelago: Admiralty Is., New Britain, and New Ireland; formerly a German colony.

Block 41°N, 72°W. Island between Long Island Sound and Atlantic Ocean, 15 km off Rhode Island.

Borneo 0°N/S, 114°E. Large equatorial Southeast Asian island shared by Indonesia, Malaya and Brunei.

Canary Is. 28°N, 16°W. Spanish archipelago of seven islands 100 km west of Morocco. Inhabited since antiquity (Latin: Fortunatae Insulae); colonized by the Spanish in 1400's.

Cape Verde Is. 15°-17°N, 23°-25°W. 10-island nation 500 km west of Senegal. Settled by Portuguese in mid-1400's.

Capri 41°N, 14°E. Italian island in Bay of Naples.

Caroline Is. 5°-10°N, 130°-166°E. Micronesian group of more than 600 islands: Belau (Palau), Kusaie, Ponape, Satawal, Truk, and Yap.

Cayman Is. 20°N, 81°W. British dependency of three main islands 240 km south of Cuba.

Chagos Archipelago 6°S, 72°E. Part of the British Indian Ocean Territory 600 km south of the Maldives. Diego Garcia has been a UK/U.S. military base since the 1970's when its 1,500 inhabitants—the descendents of slaves—were deported.

Channel/Santa Barbara Is. 34°N, 120°W. Eight-island group off Los Angeles.

Channel Is. 49°N, 2°W. Group in English Channel near France: Jersey, Guernsey, Alderney, and Sark. They are dependent territories of the English Crown, as successor to William the Conqueror, duke of Normandy, but not part of the UK.

Chatham Is. 44°S, 176°W. Polynesian group 860 km east of New Zealand from where they were settled around 1500.

Chincha Is. 14°S, 76°W. Group of three Peruvian islands; important source of guano before synthetic fertilizers.

Christmas 10°S, 106°E. Australian dependency 360 km south of Java.

Cocos/Keeling Is. 12°S, 97°E. Australian archipelago of 27 coral atolls 2,800 km northwest of Perth, settled in 19th century.

Comoros 12°S, 44°E. Indian Ocean nation of three islands about 325 km east of Mozambique.

Cook Is. 8°-23°S, 156°–167°W. Group of 15 islands 3,200 km northeast of New Zealand: Rarotonga.

Corsica 42°N, 9°E. French Mediterranean island.

Cuba 21°N, 80°W. Northernmost Caribbean island, 1,250 km east-west; largest of 1,200 islands in Cuban archipelago.

Cyclades/Kikláhdes 37°N, 25°E. Greek Aegean archipelago of about 220 islands; so-called because they encircle sacred island of Delos.

Devil's 5°N, 52°W. Island off French Guiana; used as penal colony until 1938.

Dodecanese/Sporádhes 36°N, 27°E. Greek Aegean archipelago of 12 islands, including Samos, Kos, and Ródhos.

Dominica 16°N, 61°W. Caribbean island nation.

Easter Island/Isla de Pascua/Rapa Nui 27°07'S, 109°22'W. The most remote island on Earth, Rapa Nui is the eastern tip of Polynesia, about 3,700 km west of Chile, which administers it, and 1,600 km east of Pitcairn Island. Settled by Marquesans around the fourth century, it is famous for its thousand carved statues, some 10 meters tall.

Elba 43°N, 10°E. Italian island where Napoleon was briefly exiled.

Ellesmere Island, Nunavut Territory 79°N, 82°W. Cape Columbia (83°08'N) is the northernmost point in Canada.

Faeroe Is. 62°N, 7°W. Group of 18 islands about 118 km north-south, 320 km north of the Shetlands and halfway between Norway and Iceland; settled in seventh century they are an autonomous part of Denmark.

Falkland Is./Islas Malvinas 51°-53°S, 57°- 62°W. British Crown Colony of 340 islands about 600 km east of Argentina. Claimed by French sailors from St. Mâlo (hence Malvinas), contested by Spanish, settled by English. An Argentine invasion in 1982 failed.

Faylakah 29°N, 48°E. Persian Gulf island off Kuwait.

Fernando de Noronha 4°S, 32°W. Atlantic island about 500 km east of Brazil.

Fernando Po 3°S, 9°E. Former name for Bioko, Equatorial Guinea.

Fiji Is. 16°-19°S, 178°W-177°E. Pacific country of about 330 islands, a third inhabited, about 1,770 km north of New Zealand.

Florida Keys 24°-25°N, 80°-82°W. Chain of coral islands running 240 km west from tip of Florida: Key Largo, Islamorada, Key West, and Dry Tortugas.

Frisian Is. 53°-55°N, 5°-8°E. Chain of North Sea islands, 18 inhabited, off the Netherlands, Germany, and Denmark: Rømø, Sylt, Terschelling, Vlieland and Texel.

Galápagos 1°S, 91°W. Archipelago of 60 volcanic islands about 430 km across and 1,000 km west of Ecuador; known for its diverse flora and fauna and Charles Darwin's research there in 1835.

Gotland 57°N, 18°E. Swedish Baltic island, thought to be the homeland of the Goths.

Hainan 19°N, 109°E. Chinese island between South China Sea and Gulf of Tonkin.

Hawaiian Is. 19°-28°N, 155°-178°W. Polynesian chain comprising eight large and 124 smaller islands stretching 2,400 km from Hawaii to Midway and Kure. Settled in eighth century from the Marquesas. U.S. state: Hawaii, Maui, Lauai, Molokai, Oahu, Kaui, and Nihau.

Hebrides/Western Isles 57°N, 7°W. Islands off the west coast of Scotland. Inner Hebrides: Skye, Mull, and

Islay; 210-km-long Outer Hebrides: Lewis, North Uist, and South Uist.

Hispaniola 19°N, 71°W. Caribbean island divided between Haiti and Dominican Republic.

Hokkaido 43°N, 143°E. Northernmost of main Japanese islands.

Hong Kong 22°N, 114°E. Chinese island at mouth of Pearl River, 145 km southeast of Guangzhou (Canton).

Honshu 36°N, 136°E. Largest of main Japanese islands; cities include Tokyo.

Indonesia From the Greek meaning "Indian islands," the name applies to the archipelagic nation of 18,108 islands: Sumatra, Java, Sulawesi, Bali, Malaku Is., and parts of Borneo, Timor, and New Guinea.

Ionian Is. 39°N, 21°E. Greek Adriatic archipelago of seven islands: Kerkira (Corfu), Kefallinia, Zákinthos, and Odysseus's Itháki.

Jamaica 18°N, 75°W. Caribbean island nation about 175 km south of Cuba.

Jan Mayen 71°N, 8°W. Norwegian island 400 km east of Greenland.

Java 7°S, 110°E. Indonesian island east of Sumatra.

Juan Fernandez Is. 33°S, 80°W. Three-island group 650 km west of Chile. Alexander Selkirk, model for Daniel Defoe's Robinson Crusoe, was marooned on Más a Tierra 1705–09.

Kerguelen/Desolation Is. 49°-50°S, 69°-71°E. French Indian Ocean territory of 300 islands and islets, including Crozet Is., about 4,500 km southeast of South Africa.

Komandorskiye Ostrova 55°N, 167°E. Russian group at western tip of Aleutians.

Krakatoa 6°S, 105°E. Volcanic Indonesian island west of Java.

Kuril Is. 44°-51°N, 146°-155°E. Chain of some 56 islands stretching about 1,200 km between Japan and Russia.

Kyushu 33°N, 131°E. Southernmost of main Japanese islands.

Lakshadweep/Laccadive Is. 8°-12°N, 71°-74°E. Indian archipelago of 12 atolls about 250 km west of India.

Leeward Is. see *Antilles*.

Line Is. 6°N-11°S, 162°-152°W. Group of islands straddling the Equator (Line) south of Hawaii and belonging variously to the U.S., Great Britain and Kiribati.

Lofoten Is. 69°N, 15°E. Northern Norwegian archipelago.

Long Island 41°N, 73°W. New York island, 190 km long, between Atlantic Ocean and Long Island Sound.

Madeira 33°N, 17°W. Portuguese Atlantic archipelago of four main islands about 500 km west of Morocco: discovered in 1400's.

Madeleine, Iles de la 47°N, 61°W. Canadian group in Gulf of St. Lawrence.

Maldive Is. 7°N-1°S, 73°E. Country of 26 archipelagos stretching 823 km north-south about 670 km southwest of Sri Lanka.

Malta 36°N, 14°E. Strategic island nation in central Mediterranean south of Sicily.

Maluku (Moluccas)/Spice Is. 2°N-8°S, 124°-131°E: Indonesian archipelago; in the 16th century, sole source of cloves, nutmeg, and mace, and a major goal of European merchants.

Man, Isle of 54°N, 4°W. Irish Sea crown dependency of Great Britain.

Manhattan 41°N, 74°W. New York island at confluence of Hudson River/Long Island Sound.

Manitoulin 46°N, 83°W. Canadian island in Lake Huron.

Mariana Is. 13°-20°N, 146°E. Micronesian archipelago 2,400 km east of the Philippines comprising Commonwealth of the Northern Mariana Is. (Saipan, 15°N, 146°E), and Guam (13°N, 144°E).

Marquesas Is. 7°-10°S, 138°-141°W. French Polynesian archipelago of 12 islands about 1,200 km northeast of Tahiti.

Marshall Is. 5°-15°N, 161°-172°E. Micronesian group of 34 atolls and islands including Ratak and Ralik chains. Bikini was a nuclear test site in the 1940–50's.

Martha's Vineyard 41°N, 71°W. Massachusetts island south of Cape Cod.

Martinique 15°N, 61°W. French Caribbean island.

Matsu (26°N, 120°E) and **Quemoy** (24°N, 118°E) Chinese coastal islands about 250 km apart; administered and garrisoned by Taiwan since 1950.

Mauritius 20°S, 58°E. Indian Ocean island 800 km east of Madagascar. Part of Mascarene Archipelago, with Réunion.

Melanesia from the Greek meaning "black islands;" Pacific islands south of Micronesia and west of Polynesia—

including New Guinea, the Solomons, New Hebrides, and Fiji.

Micronesia from the Greek meaning "small islands;" Pacific islands north of the equator between Hawaii and the Philippines.

Nantucket 41°N, 70°W. Massachusetts island south of Cape Cod. Major 19th-century whaling port.

Nauru 1°S, 167°E. Island nation 2,300 km northeast of Sydney, Australia.

New Caledonia 18°-22°S, 163-168°E. Pacific island that forms, with Loyalty Is., French overseas territory.

Newfoundland 48°N, 56°W. Large Canadian Atlantic island south of Labrador.

Novaya Zemlya 74°N, 57°E. New Land; Russian archipelago comprising two main islands, 960 km long, between Barents and Kara Seas.

Novosibirskiye Ostrova 75°N, 142°E. New Siberian Is.; Russian group between Laptev and East Siberian Seas.

Orkney Is. 59°N, 3°W. Group of more than 20 islands, 85 km north-south, 10 km north of Scotland.

Outer Banks, North Carolina 35°N, 76°W. Barrier islands—Roanoke, Pea, Bodie, Hatteras, Ocracoke, and Portsmouth—stretching 145 km north-south off North Carolina between the Atlantic Ocean and Albemarle and Pamlico Sounds.

Ouessant, Ile d' (Ushant) 48°N, 5°W. Atlantic island off northwest France at entrance to English Channel.

Paracel Is. 17°N, 112°E. South China Sea group about 400 km east of Vietnam; also claimed by China and Taiwan.

Philippines Southeast Asian nation of more than 7,000 islands: Luzon, Samar, Palawan, Mindanao, Sulu Archipelago, Zamboanga.

Pitcairn 25°S, 130°W. British colony (with Ducie, Henderson and Oeno Is.) halfway between Tahiti and Easter Island. HMS Bounty mutineers arrived in 1790.

Polynesia from the Greek meaning "many islands;" Pacific islands within a triangle drawn between Hawaii, New Zealand and Easter Island.

Pribilof Is. 57°N, 170°W. Alaskan Bering Sea group.

Prince Edward 46°N, 63°W. Canadian island province in Gulf of St. Lawrence and connected to Nova Scotia by bridge.

Puerto Rico 18°N, 66°W. Easternmost and fourth largest of Greater Antilles.

Qeshm 26°N, 56°E. Iranian island in Strait of Hormuz at the mouth of the Persian Gulf.

Queen Charlotte Is. 51°N, 129°W. Canadian group off British Columbia.

Queen Elizabeth Is. 74°-82°N, 60°-125°W. Northernmost Canadian Arctic archipelago: Ellesmere Is., Parry Group and Sverdrup Group.

Réunion 21°S, 56°E. French Indian Ocean island 690 km east of Madagsacar; part of Mascarene Archipelago, with Mauritius.

Ryukyu Is. 24°-31°N, 123°-131°E. Japanese chain stretching 1,000 km between Taiwan and Kyushu. Okinawa was a major World War II battleground.

St. Helena 15°S, 6°W. British Atlantic island where Napoleon was exiled and died.

St. Lawrence Is. 64°N, 171°W. Alaskan Bering Sea island south of Bering Strait.

St. Lucia 14°N, 61°W: Second largest of Windward Is.

St. Pierre & Miquelon 47°N, 56°W. French Atlantic islands southwest of Newfoundland, Canada.

Sakhalin 51°N, 143°E. Russian island, 950 km long, between Sea of Japan and Sea of Okhostk.

Samoa Is. 13°-14°S, 168°-173°W. Pacific group divided between Western Samoa and American Samoa.

Sardinia 40°N, 9°E. Italian island in western Mediterranean.

Severnaya Zemlya 80°N, 98°E. Russian group (four main islands) discovered in 1913, between Kara and Laptev Seas.

Seychelles 4°-5°S, 56°E. Indian Ocean republic of 115 islands extending 1,200 km northeast-southwest about 1,600 km east of Kenya.

Shetland Is. 61°N, 1°W. British group of about 100 islands 80 km northeast of the Orkneys.

Shikoku 33°N, 133°E. Smallest of four main Japanese islands.

Sicily 37°N, 14°E. Italian island in central Mediterranean.

Singapore 1°N, 104°E. Island nation off tip of Malay Peninsula at east end of Strait of Malacca.

Society Is. 16°-18°S, 148°-154°W. French Polynesian archipelago, 750-km long, including Tahiti; settled around 500 B.C.

Socotra 13°N, 54°E. Yemeni Indian Ocean island about 250 km northeast of Somalia.

Solomon Is. 156°-171°E, 5°-13°S. Melanesian archipelago of about 1,000 islands stretching 1,400 km southeast from New Guinea. Guadalcanal was major World War II battleground.

South Georgia Is. 54°S, 37°W; and South Sandwich Is.: 56°S, 26°W. British dependent territory 1,500 km east of the Falklands.

South Orkney Is. 61°S, 44°-46°W. British group about 1,440 km southeast of South America.

South Shetland Is. 61°-64°S, 54°-63°W. Four-group chain, 540-km long, about 120 km north of the Antarctic Peninsula.

Spitsbergen 79°N, 20°E: Norwegian Atlantic island; forms, with Bear Island (74°N, 19°E), dependency of Svalbard.

Spratly Is. 9°N, 112°E. South China Sea archipelago about 500 km southeast of Vietnam; also claimed by China, Taiwan, Malaysia, and the Philippines.

Sulawesi (Celebes) 2°S, 121°E. Indonesian island between Borneo and Maluku Is.

Sulu Archipelago 5°-7°N, 120°-122°E. Philippine archipelago of about 900 islands between Celebes and Sulu Seas.

Sumatra 0°, 100°E. Largest and westernmost island in Indonesia.

Tierra del Fuego 54°S, 69°W. Island shared by Chile and Argentina between the Atlantic and Pacific Oceans; separated from South America by Strait of Magellan, and north of Cape Horn (55°59'S, 67°16'W).

Tongan (Friendly) Is. 15°-23°S, 173°-177°W. Polynesian country of 171 islands (36 inhabited) stretching 1,000 km north-south about 2,000 km northeast of New Zealand.

Trinidad, Isla 39°S, 62°W. Brazilian island 1,200 east of Brazil.

Trinidad and Tobago 10°N, 61°W. Caribbean nation group off Venezuela.

Tristan da Cunha 37°S, 12°W. British Atlantic group about 2,800 km east southeast of South Africa.

Tsushima 34°N, 129°E. Japanese island in Korean (or Tsushima) Strait.

Tuamotu Archipelago 14°-23°S, 134°-149°W. French Polynesian chain of 80 islands, 1,700 km long, east of Tahiti.

Vancouver 50°N, 126°W. Largest island on west coast of Canada; part of British Columbia.

Vanuatu (New Hebrides) 13°-20°S, 166°-170°E. Melanesian island nation, 900 km long.

Victoria 71°N, 114°W. Canadian Arctic island.

Volcano Is. (Kazan-Retto) 25°N, 141°E. Japanese group of three islands 1,100 km southwest of Tokyo. Iwo Jima was a major World War II battleground.

Wake Is. 19°N, 177°E. U.S. Pacific atoll, 1,900 km west of Midway: Wilkes, Wake and Peale Islands.

Wight, Isle of 51°N, 1°W. British English Channel island off Portsmouth and Southampton.

Windward Is. see *Antilles*.

Wrangel Island (Ostrov Vrangelia) 71°N, 180°E/W. Russian island in East Siberian Sea.

Mountain Ranges

Adirondacks New York. Mt. Marcy, 1,629m (5,344′).

Altai Shan China, Kazakhstan, Mongolia, and Russia. Gora Belukha (Russia, Kazakhstan) 4,506m (14,784′).

Ahaggar (Hoggar) Mts. SE Algeria. Tahat, 2,918m (9,573′).

Alaska Range S Alaska. Denali (Mt. McKinley) 6,194m (20,320′); highest point in North America.

Aleutian Range SW Alaska. Mt. Katmai, 2,047m (6,715′).

Alps European range that runs in a 660-mi. arc from France through Italy, Switzerland, Germany, Liechtenstein, Austria, Slovenia, Croatia, and Bosnia and Herzegovina. Ranges include Maritime, Ligurian, Cottian, Graian, Dauphiné, Savoy, Pennine, Lepontine, Rhaetian, Bernese, Noric, Hohe Tauern, Carnic, Dolomites, Julian, Karawanken, and Dinaric Alps. Mont Blanc (France), 4,807m (15,711′).

Andes South American range (cordillera) divided into 12 smaller ranges that run 7,240 km (4,500 mi.) through Argentina, Chile, Bolivia, Peru, Ecuador, Colombia, and Venezuela. Ranges include Cordillera Apalobamba, Cordillera Real, Cordillera Blanca, Cordillera Huayhuash,

Cordillera Central, Cordillera Occidental, Cordillera Oriental, Sierra Nevada del Cocuy, Sierra Nevada de Santa Marta, Sierra Nevada de Merida, and Central Highlands of Venezuela. Aconcagua (Argentina), 6,962m (22,385′); highest point in South America.

Apennines Italy. Corno Grande, 2,912m (9,554′).

Appalachians North American chain divided into Blue Ridge, Allegheny, Berkshire Hills, Taconic, Green, White, Longfellow, Notre Dame Mts. Mt. Mitchell (N.C.), 2,037m (6,684′).

Ararat (Agri Dagi) mountain in E Turkey upon which Noah's Ark is said to have landed. 5,165m (16,945′).

Athos, Mt. Greece. 2,033m (6,667′).

Atlas Mts. 1,900-km.-long (1,200-mi.) North African range in Morocco, Algeria, and Tunisia. Toubkal (Morocco), 4,165m (13,665′).

Balkan Mountains Bulgaria. Botev Peak, 2,375m (7,793′).

Barisan Mts. Indonesia (Sumatra). Kerintji, 3,807m (12,483′).

Black Hills South Dakota, Wyoming. Harney Peak (S.Dak.), 2,207m (7,242′)

Brooks Range N. Alaska. Mount Isto, 2,762m (9,060′).

Cantabrian Mts. Spain. Torre de Cerredo, 2,648m (8,688′).

Carpathian Mts. range, including Transylvanian Alps, in Poland, Slovakia, Ukraine, and Romania. Gerlachovka (Slovakia), 2,655m (8,711′).

Cascade Range Range between Sierra Nevada and Coast Mountains in California, Oregon, and Washington. Mt. Rainier, 4,392m (14,410′).

Caucasus Mts. Range between Black and Caspian Seas in Azerbaijan, Armenia, Georgia, and Russia. Mt. Elbrus (Russia, Georgia), 5,633m (18,481′).

Cerro Chirripo Costa Rica; highest mountain in Central America, 3,820m (12,533′).

Cévennes France. Mt. Mezenc, 1,754m (5,755′).

Coast Mts. British Columbia. Extension of U.S. Cascade Range. Mt. Waddington, 4,016m (13,177′).

Coast Ranges mountains in California, Oregon, Washington, British Columbia, Yukon Terr., and Alaska. Includes San Jacinto Mts., Olympic Range, Vancouver Is., Queen Charlotte Is., Alexander Archipelago, and St. Elias and Chugach Mts. Mt. Logan (Yukon Terr.), 5,959m (19,550′); highest point in Canada.

Daxue Shan Central China. Minya Konka (Gonggashan), 7,590m (24,900′).

Drakensberg Range South Africa, Lesotho. Thabana Ntlenyana (Lesotho), 3,482m (11,425′).

Elburz (Alborz) Mts. N Iran. Damavand, 5,670m (18,602′).

Ellsworth Mts. Antarctic range, including Heritage and Sentinel Ranges. Vinson Massif, 4,897m (16,066′); highest point in Antarctica.

Fujiyama (Mt. Fuji) tallest mountain in Japan; 3,776m (12,389′).

Ghats, Western range in SW India. Anai Mudi, 2,695m (8,841′). Separated from Eastern Ghats, Mahendra Giri, 1,501m (4,924′) by the Deccan.

Great Dividing Range E Australia. Mt. Kosciuszko, 2,228m (7,310′), highest point in Australia.

Guiana Highlands Venezuela, Guyana and Brazil. Mt. Roraima (Venezuela), 2,772m (9,094′). Site of world's highest waterfalls; Angel Falls, 980m (3,212′).

Harz Mts. Germany. Brocken, 1,143m (3,747′).

Himalayas Asian range that runs in a 2,414-km (1,500-mi.) arc in Pakistan, India, Tibet, Nepal, Sikkim, and Bhutan. Mt. Everest, 8,850m (29,035′); highest point on Earth.

Hindu Kush Afghanistan, Pakistan. Tirich Mir (Pakistan), 7,695m (25,230′).

Jotunheimen Norway. Galdhopiggen, 2,469m (8,098′).

Jura Mts. France, Switzerland. Mt. Neige (France), 1,723m (5,652′).

Karakoram India, Pakistan. K2 (Mt. Godwin-Austin; Chogori), 8,611m (28,250′). K2 is so called after a 19th-century surveyor's identification; it was the second mountain listed in the Karakoram (K). Balti porters in the region now call it Ketu.

Kenya (Kirinyaga) mountain in central Kenya. 5,199m (17,058′).

Kilimanjaro mountain rising on the border between Tanzania (where the peak is) and Kenya. 5,895m (19,340′); highest point in Africa.

Kunlun Shan China. Includes Altun Shan and Qiliang Shan (Nan Shan) ranges. Kongur (Kung-ko-erh), 7,719m (25,326′).

Laurentian Mts. Quebec. Mt. Tremblant, 1,190m (3,905′).

Mackenzie Mts. Yukon Territory and Northwest Territories. Mt. Sir James McBrien, 2,758m (9,049′).

Mauna Kea highest mountain in Hawaii. 4,205m (13,796′). If measured from its base on the on the floor of the Pacific, it is 9,698m (31,796′)—taller than Mt. Everest.

Mauna Loa Hawaii. 4,169 m (13,677′).

Olympus, Mt. highest mountain in Greece and home of the gods of Greek myth; 2,917m (9,570′).

Ouachita Mts. Arkansas and Oklahoma. Magazine Mt., 840m (2,753′).

Ozarks Arkansas, Missouri, and Oklahoma. Hare Mt., 726m (2,380′).

Pamirs (Pamir Knot) Afghanistan, China, Tajikistan. Pik Samani (Communism Peak), Tajikistan, 7,495m (24,590′). Surrounded by Tian Shan, Kunlun Shan, Himalayas, Karakoram, and Hindu Kush.

Parnassus, Mt. Greece, at south end of Pindus Mts.; sacred to the god Apollo and the Muses. 2,457m (8,062′).

Pegunungan Maoke New Guinea. Puncak Jaya (Irian Jaya, Indonesia), 5,030m (16,502′).

Pennines England. Cross Fell, 893m (2,930′).

Pikes Peak Colorado. "America's Mountain," in Rockies. 4,300m (14,109′).

Pindus Mts. Albania and Greece. Smólikas Oros (Greece), 2,637m (8,652′).

Pisgah (Nebo), Mt. Jordan. 806m (2,644′).

Pontic Mts. N Turkey. Kaçkar, 3,942m (12,933′).

Pyrenees range between Atlantic and Mediterranean on border between France, Spain, and Andorra. Pico de Aneto, 3,404m (11,168′).

Queen Maud Mts. Ross Dependency, Antarctica. Mt. Kirkpatrick, 4,529m (14,860′).

Rhodope Mts. Bulgaria and Greece. Musala (Bulgaria), 2,925m (9,596′).

Rocky Mts. 6,500-km-long (4,000-mi.) North American chain running from Alaska through Yukon Territory, British Columbia, Alberta, Idaho, Montana, Wyoming, Utah, Colorado, New Mexico, and Arizona. Divided into Arctic Rockies (Brooks Range and Mackenzie Mts.), Northern Rockies (Purcell, Selkirk, and Cariboo Mts.), Middle Rockies (Bighorn and Uinta Mts., Wind River, Absaroka, Wasatch, and Teton Ranges), and Southern Rockies (Front Range, Sangre de Cristo, San Juan, and Sawatch Mts.). Mt. Elbert (Colorado, Sawatch Range, 4,399m (14,433′).

Ruwenzori (Mountains of the Moon) Uganda, Zaire. Mt. Stanley (Zaire), 5,109m (16,763′).

San Bernardino Mts. S California. San Gorgonio Mt., 3,508m (11,502′).

San Gabriel Mts. S California. San Antonio Peak, 3,074m (10,080′).

Sayan Mts. Russia. Munku-Sardyk, 3,490m (11,451′).

Sierra Madre Occidental 1,125-km (700 mi.) range in Mexico. Nevada de Colima, 4,340m (14,239′). Sierra Madre Oriental runs along the east coast of Mexico.

Sierra Madre del Sur Mexico, Guatemala. Volcan Tacan, 4,092m (13,425′).

Sierra Maestra Cuba. Pico Turquino,1,993m (6,540′).

Sierra Nevada 645-km (400-mi.) range in eastern California. Mt. Whitney, 4,418m (14,494′).

Sierra Nevada Spain. Mulhacen, 3,477m (11,408′).

Sinai (Horeb), Mt. mountain in the Gebel Musa of Egypt's Sinai Peninsula, where Moses is said to have received the Ten Commandments. 2,287m (7,497′).

Soback-san South Korea. Ch'eonwhang-bong, 1,915m (6,283′).

Southern Alps New Zealand. Mt. Cook, 3,754m (12,316′).

Sulaiman Range Pakistan. Takht-i-Sulaiman ("Throne of Solomon"), 3,443m (11,295′).

Taeback-san South Korea. Sorak-san, 1,708m (5,604′).

Taurus Mts. Turkey. Erciyas Dag, 3,916m (12848′).

Tian Shan China, Kyrgyzstan. Includes Dzungarian, Kungei, Täläss, Terskei, and Trans-Ili ranges (ala-tau). Pobeda Peak, 7,439m (24,407′).

Tibesti Mts. Chad. Emi Koussi, 3,415m (11,204′).

Transantarctic Mts. Antarctica. Mt. Markham, 4,354m (14,275′).

Ural Mts. 2,640-km-long (1,640-mi.) chain in Russia and Kazakhstan that forms boundary between Europe and Asia. Narodnaya (Russia), 1,895m (6,215′).

Virunga Mts. volcanic chain in Rwanda, Uganda, and Zaire. Karisimbi (Rwanda, Zaire), 4,507m (14,787′).

Vosges Mts. France. Mt. Guebwiller, 1,424m (4,672′).

Washington, Mt. in New Hampshire's White Mts.; peak is the windiest place on Earth. 1,917m (6,288′).

Wind River Range Wyoming. Gannett Peak, 4,207m (13,804′).

Wrangell Mts. S Alaska. Mt. Bona, 5,005m (16,421′).

Zagros Mts. Iran. Zardeh Kuh, 4,550m (14,021′).

Glossary of Geographical Terms

abyssal plain a relatively flat area in the deepest part of the ocean with an average depth of 3.1 miles.

Antarctic Circle a parallel of latitude at 66°32'S, south of which the sun does not rise on the southern winter solstice (about June 22), and does not set on the southern summer solstice (about December 22). The phenomenon is due to the angle of the Earth's inclination toward the sun.

archipelago a group of islands.

Arctic Circle a parallel of latitude at 66°32'N, a point on the Earth's surface north of which the sun does not set on the northern summer solstice (about June 22), and does not rise on the northern winter solstice (about December 22). The phenomenon is due to the angle of the Earth's inclination toward the sun.

atoll a coral island in the shape of a ring around a central lagoon.

basin a natural depression in the land.

bay a curved indentation of a sea or lake into the land. In practice, bays are considered to be bigger than coves and smaller than gulfs.

bight a bay formed by a bend in the coastline.

canyon a deep valley in the Earth's surface formed by a stream or river.

coastal plain a gently sloping lowland bordering the sea.

continent the largest continuous landmasses on the Earth's surface. In common usage, the seven continents are Africa, Antarctica, Asia, Australia, Europe, North America, and South America.

continental divide The ridgeline on a continent (as in the Americas) on one side of which all water flows into the Pacific, and all water on the other side flows into the Atlantic.

continental shelf a gently sloping (ca. 1°) underwater plain extending out from the land to the edge of a continental slope; often a continuation of a coastal plain.

continental slope a more sharply inclined (2°–5°) area of the seafloor that plunges toward the abyssal plain.

delta a triangular-shaped piece of land formed by sediment at the mouth of a river.

desert a location where the rate of evaporation exceeds the rate or precipitation.

dune a hill or ridge of sand deposited by wind.

equator a parallel on the Earth's surface midway between the North and South Poles. Parallels of latitude are measured in degrees north or south of the equatorial parallel, 0°.

erosion the wearing away of the Earth's surface by natural processes such as wind, running water, waves, or ice.

estuary an area in which freshwater from a river meets salt water from the sea.

fjord a long, narrow inlet of the ocean with steeply sloping sides.

floodplain flat, low-lying land along either side of a river that is subject to flooding.

glacier a large mass of ice moving, often imperceptibly, down a valley or slope.

gorge an especially narrow and steep-walled canyon.

gulf a curved indentation of a sea or lake into the land. In general, gulfs are bigger than bays and cut more deeply into the land.

hemisphere one half of the Earth's surface, however it is divided. For example, the Northern Hemisphere lies north of the equator; the Southern Hemisphere, south of the equator.

inlet an indentation in the shore of a sea or an ocean or in the bank of a river. Also, a narrow waterway that connects a lagoon to a larger body of water or which passes between two peninsulas.

hill a natural rise in the land, usually with a more gentle rise and lower maximum elevation than a mountain.

international date line an artificial line along roughly 180° meridian, with some deviations. Crossing the date line from east to west, a day is lost; crossing from west to east, a day is gained.

island a piece of land surrounded entirely by water.

isthmus a narrow strip of land that joins two larger land masses and is surrounded by water on two sides.

lagoon a shallow pool or pond completely or almost completely separated from the sea.

lake an enclosed body of water. Most lakes contain freshwater although there are notable exceptions, including the Great Salt Lake, the Caspian Sea, Aral Sea, and Dead Sea.

latitude the angular distance between a point on the surface of the Earth and the equatorial plane running through the middle of the Earth. Latitude is measured in degrees, minutes, and tenths of minutes or (more rarely) seconds (up to 90°) north or south of the equator. A circle connecting all the points of the same latitude is known as a parallel of latitude.

leeward the direction or side sheltered from the wind. (See *windward.*)

longitude the angular distance between a point on the surface of the Earth and a plane running vertically through the Earth and intersecting the north and south poles. By convention, the prime meridian (0°) runs through Greenwich, England. Longitude is measured in degrees, minutes and tenths of minutes or (more rarely) seconds (up to 180°) east or west of the prime meridian. A line connecting all the points of the same longitude from pole to pole is called a meridian.

magnetic pole poles toward (North) and away from (South) which a magnetized compass needle points; not the same as true north, the location of the North Pole.

mountain a natural rise in the land characterized by a sharp vertical rise from the surrounding land and a summit much smaller in area than the base.

ocean the largest continuous bodies of salt water on the Earth's surface, which collectively cover 70 percent of the Earth's surface. By convention, the world ocean is divided into five smaller oceans: Atlantic, Arctic, Indian, Pacific,and Southern.

peninsula a piece of land connected to a larger landmass and surrounded on three sides by water.

plain an area of the Earth's surface characterized by uninterrupted flat or gently rolling terrain.

plateau an area of flat or nearly flat terrain generally separated from the surrounding land by a steep slope.

prairie level or rolling land generally covered with grasses, with few trees.

rain forest a forest that receives more than 1.8 meters (70 inches) of rain per year.

range a single line of connected mountains. A chain is usually regarded as a series of parallel ranges.

reef a line of rock, coral, or sand in the sea usually exposed at low tide and covered at high tide.

ridge a relatively long stretch of elevated land, or the line that connects the summits of a mountain range.

rise a raised area of the abyssal plain.

river a continuous stream of water that flows into a lake, sea, enclosed depression, or another river.

savanna a portion of land in the Tropics or subtropics with only scattered trees but whose grasses can survive with scant rainfall.

sea a large body of salt water, smaller than an ocean but larger than a gulf.

sound a body of water that separates an island from the mainland or that connects two oceans, seas, or other bodies of water. Sounds are generally long and narrow.

steppe a portion of land with little rainfall, extreme temperature variations, and drought-resistant vegetation.

strait a narrow body of water that connects two large bodies of water.

tide the rise and fall of the surface of the ocean and of bays, gulfs, and other bodies of water connected to the ocean. Tides are caused by the gravitational pull of the moon, which passes over the same meridian of the Earth about once every 24 hours and 50 minutes. The length of time between successive high (or low) tides is about 12 hours and 25 minutes.

trench a depression in the abyssal plain formed at the junction of two tectonic plates, the bases of which are often very deep below the surface of the water.

Tropic of Cancer a parallel of latitude at 23°30'N, a point on the Earth's surface where the sun's rays strike the Earth perpendicularly on the northern summer solstice (about June 22). This marks the northern limit of the Tropics.

Tropic of Capricorn a parallel of latitude at 23°30'S, a point on the Earth's surface where the sun's rays strike the Earth perpendicularly on the southern summer solstice (about December 22). This marks the southern limit of the Tropics.

tsunami a wave generated by an undersea earthquake. Generally unnoticed at sea, these waves can reach great heights and wreak enormous destruction as they near shallow water and the land.

tundra an area of treeless plain near or above the Arctic Circle. Tundra subsoil is permanently frozen, but the soil thaws enough to support the growth of mosses, lichens, and some small flowering shrubs.

valley a long depression in the land, usually open at one end.

wetland a location in which the soil is saturated with water for much or all of the year. Different types of wetlands include bogs, marshes, potholes, swamps, and tidal flats.

windward the direction or side facing the wind.

HISTORY

World History

The Peopling of the World (ca. 150000–15000 B.C.) 210
The Last Ice Age and the Neolithic Revolution (ca. 15000–3000 B.C.) 211
The Dawn of Civilization (ca. 3000–1500 B.C.) 212
From the Bronze Age to the Iron Age (ca. 1500–500 B.C.) 213
The First Imperial Era 216
A Second Age of Empires 220
The World on the Eve of European Expansion 224
European Expansion 229
Expansion of the European Hegemony 234
Triumph and Tragedy of Western Hegemony 239
The Modern World 246

Major Wars in History

Greco-Persian Wars 253
The Peloponnesian Wars 253
The Punic Wars 253
The Crusades 254
The Hundred Years War 255
Wars of the Roses 256
The Thirty Years War 256
English Civil Wars 257
War of the Spanish Succession 257
War of the Austrian Succession 257
The Seven Years War 258
The American Revolution 258
The Wars of the French Revolution 260
The Napoleonic Wars 261
The Crimean War 261
The American Civil War 261
The Franco-Prussian War 265
World War I 265
World War II 268

Times Focus:
Is War Our Biological Destiny?
By Natalie Angier 271

History of the United States

The Age of Exploration 272
The First European Colonies 272
The Colonies in the 18th Century 273
The Federalist Era 276
The Early National Period 277
Slavery and the Road to Civil War 279
Reconstructing the Union 281
The Age of Industry 283
The Turbulent 1890's 284
The Progressive Era (1900–17) 285
The Roaring Twenties and the New Deal 287
Post-War America 288
The Rise of the Conservative Movement 291

HISTORY

World History

The Peopling of the World (ca. 150000–15000 B.C.)

Africa is the cradle of humanity. An early human species, Homo erectus ("Java Man," "Peking Man," and others) evolved in Africa and migrated to Eurasia perhaps a million years ago. These very early humans used fire, created stone weapons and tools, and were successful in occupying a wide range of habitats. Nevertheless, all non-African populations of Homo erectus eventually died out without leaving descendents. Human beings of fully modern type—members of our own species, Homo sapiens—evolved from Homo erectus through various transitional stages in the savannah lands of eastern Africa about 150 millennia ago. Homo sapiens was a highly social and adaptable species, fully capable of using complex language. Modern humans moved out from the original species homeland on the eastern plains of Africa to occupy much of eastern, northern, and southern parts of the continent; the special challenges of the rain forest environment slowed the movement of humans into the western regions of Africa.

Around 105,000 years ago, taking advantage of one of the periodic eras of warm, wet climate that can turn the deserts of northern Africa into a relatively green and pleasant landscape, modern humans migrated northward through Egypt and out of Africa via the Sinai Peninsula to the Middle East. There they apparently met and coexisted with humans of a different and older species—Neanderthals (Homo neandertalensis)—that had a simpler and less flexible culture and tool technology.

Following the coast of southern Asia, modern humans were in India and Southeast Asia by 90,000 years ago. (Ocean levels were generally much lower at the time, because a vast amount of water was locked up in the glaciers of the Ice Age; much of Southeast Asia was dry land, part of an exposed continental shelf. Any traces that these early people might have left of their coastal migrations would now be submerged off the present-day coastlines of Asia.) Sometime between 65,000 and 40,000 years ago, humans crossed miles of open ocean (probably on rafts) to reach New Guinea and Australia. No later than 50,000 years ago, other populations migrated from the Middle East across the plains of Central Asia to China and northeastern Asia, eventually making it to the islands of Japan. As Homo sapiens spread to East and Southeast Asia, remnant populations of Homo erectus, such as "Peking Man" and "Java Man," were displaced and became extinct.

Humans made their way into Europe beginning around 40,000 years ago, challenging the existing populations of Neanderthals there. Whether from superior social organization and technology, from outright human extermination of the Neanderthal competitors, or from some other cause (or combination of causes), the last Neanderthals became extinct around 30,000 years ago, and humans of our own species were in undisputed possession of the Eurasian continent. The early human occupants of Europe and northern Asia of the Paleolithic ("Old Stone Age") period, roughly 40,000 to 12,000 years ago, devised highly sophisticated means of dealing with the cold glacial environment, including the efficient hunting of large animals; the processing of hides and the creation of cut and sewn hide and fur garments; the use of fire for heating, cooking, and light; and the creation of warm shelters from the elements. The "tool kit" of these Paleolithic Homo sapiens was far more elaborate than that of earlier human species, and included not only a wide range of edged tools and projectile points, but also such important devices as spear-throwers, awls, needles, and hammers, made of carefully chosen materials (such as antler and bone) and skillfully crafted.

Using this technology, some humans moved as far as northeasternmost Eurasia, and from there across a broad plain of open land connecting Eurasia with North America (a "land bridge" where the Bering Strait now separates the two continents), introducing humans to the Americas around 15,000 years ago. The timing of human settlement of the Americas is much debated. Some scholars adhere to a conservative view that dates the event to around 13,500 years ago, with the appearance in the archaeological record of the Clovis Culture complex (originally identified in New Mexico but found widely in North America), characterized by distinctive and finely made projectile points. Others rely on apparently securely dated sites that predate the Clovis Culture by at least several thousand years, including some in South America, to argue for a considerably earlier migration.) With this migration, or series of migrations, all of the main land masses of Earth except for icebound Antarctica had become human habitats. Settlement of the Indo-Pacific archipelagos soon followed, with the ancestors of the Austronesian-speaking peoples setting out from the Fujian coast of China around 7000 B.C. to settle Taiwan, the Philippines, Indonesia, and onward to Melanesia, Micronesia, and Polynesia.

In the course of these migrations, humans became adapted to specific habitats (hot, cold, sunny, light-deprived, and so on), while widely separated populations developed in genetic isolation from one another. These two factors combined allowed the evolution of superficial traits of skin color, hair color and texture, eyelid shape, and others that are the external defining characteristics of human "races." All humans during the millennia of the great migrations also demonstrated the shared human capacity for the creation of culture and art of great diversity and refinement, from the cave paintings and ivory sculptures of prehistoric Europe to the equally ancient rock art of Australia.

All humans at that time shared the basic lifestyle of hunting and gathering. Animals, birds and fish were hunted and trapped for food, shellfish were gathered in oceans and rivers, and great numbers of plants were identified and harvested for use as food, fiber, medicine, dyes, and for other purposes. It was a potentially rich and abundant way of living, but one that depended on low population density and little population growth. The latter probably resulted from prolonged nursing of children (which suppresses maternal fertility), as well as from high infant and child mortality. Even very slow growth in population density was probably a significant spur to the great migrations that peopled the earth, as bands of out-migrants left populated areas in search of new hunting and gathering grounds.

The end of the last ice age 12,000–11,000 years ago led in some places to unprecedented population growth, which had momentous consequences for human history.

The Last Ice Age and the Neolithic Revolution (ca. B.C.)

Beginning about 10,000 B.C., a strong global warming period in the earth's climate began to melt the huge glaciers that had covered much of northern Eurasia and North America for thousands of years. Some results of this warming trend, which lasted for several millennia and resulted in the rapid retreat of glaciers and permafrost to far northern latitudes, included the creation of vast steppes or prairies south of the retreating glaciers that were the ideal habitat for huge herds of horses, bison, and other food animals. Further south, warmer, wetter conditions encouraged the growth of food plants and the animals (such as antelope and wild goats) that grazed on them. Humans quickly took advantage of these new food sources, and human numbers and population density began to climb as a result.

At this point, some people in crowded environments began to take a more active role in managing food resources—encouraging certain plant crops, for example, through seeding, weeding, and harvesting plants in certain locations that were well known and over which some form of ownership may have been asserted. This led to the development of a wide range of domesticated plants, including wheat and legumes in Mesopotamia and northwestern India; millet in North China, rice in South China and Southeast Asia; and corn (maize) and beans in Mesoamerica. Neolithic hunters began following, directing, managing and culling herds of horses or wild cattle, protecting them from wild predators to save them for human use. In this way, the first steps toward the domestication of plants and animals were taken. With food management came a tendency to travel less and to settle down more, to guard and enjoy the resources that were under management. Camps became villages, or at least season-long settlements. Animals that acted as scavengers at these settlements (wolves, swine, fowl) were seen to be useful, selected for docility (the fiercer ones were killed, the tamer ones tolerated), and eventually domesticated (as dogs, pigs, and chickens). A more sedentary life reduced the hunter-gatherer nomad's requirement that possessions be light and portable. Pottery was perhaps the most significant consequence of this change; too heavy to carry on nomadic migrations, it greatly improved the possibilities for storing and cooking food in a proto-village environment. Imperceptibly, the people of the post-ice-age world were inventing the Neolithic Revolution.

The full-scale Neolithic ("new stone") culture, evident in the Middle East by 8000 B.C. and found in many parts of the world over the course of time, involves agriculture, particularly the raising of grain crops, and a sharply reduced reliance on wild plants; the domestication of animals for various purposes, and a reduced reliance on wild game; settled life in villages; pottery; water management; the production and use of cloth and of a wide range of well-made stone tools; evidence of belief systems, including ceremonial burial of the dead; and a range of other adaptations to a settled lifestyle. Life for Neolithic villagers may have been harder than it had been for their hunter-gatherer ancestors. Raising, harvesting, storing, and processing grain for food took unremitting toil; so too did the work of animal husbandry. Crowding together in villages, and living in close proximity to domestic animals, exposed farmers to many more diseases than had affected hunter-gatherer bands. But the payoff, for people caught in a cycle of population growth and limited opportunities for migration to unpopulated areas, was that the same land that might support a few hundred hunter-gatherers could support several villages housing thousands of Neolithic farmers.

The Dawn of Civilization (ca. 3000–1500 B.C.)

The transition from prehistoric Neolithic culture to civilization seems to have involved in every case a combination of two things: a culture founded on settled agricultural communities and, on the basis of such settled communities, the development of urban centers with literate religious and social hierarchies whose members asserted control over such matters as irrigation and water control, ritual and religious observances, and the application of military power or legitimized violence, as well as the right to appropriate for their own use a portion of the goods produced by ordinary farmers and workers. The first condition came into being over time in a great many parts of the prehistoric world, including Mesopotamia (the "land between the rivers," i.e. the Tigris and the Euphrates); several of the large river valleys of China; parts of India and Southeast Asia; the Nile Valley and the great bend of the Niger River in Africa; the Danube Valley in Europe; parts of Central America and Mexico, the Mississippi Valley, and the Amazon Basin in the New World; and in the highlands of New Guinea and throughout the islands of the Pacific Ocean. The second condition of civilization, the urban center, eventually appeared in some, but not all, of these Neolithic cultures. It happened first in Mesopotamia in the fourth millennium B.C., but other areas, such as Egypt and the Indus Valley, soon followed. Across Eurasia, the invention and spread of the technologies of metallurgy (by the early third millennium B.C. in Mesopotamia and Egypt, but not until a thousand years later in China) gave the Bronze Age its name.

Mesopotamia The 600–mile-long plain of the Tigris and Euphrates Valleys stretching from Anatolia to the Persian Gulf is the site of the earliest known civilization, which takes its name from the city-state of Sumer. The first of a succession of Mesopotamian civilizations, Sumerian culture first blossomed about 3500 to 3000 B.C. Each of the cities within the Sumerian culture area was a sacred temple city, the realm of a god whose regent on earth was the priest-king. Sumerian culture gave rise to a number of important innovations, including a calendar, the invention of writing (cuneiform, written with a stylus on tablets of soft clay), the plow, the potter's wheel, and wheeled carts. The development of writing, in particular, was an important element in the commercial and administrative success of the Sumerian city-states.

Separate and frequently warring city-states such as Lagash, Nippur, and Ur came under the control of the more northerly Empire of Akkad, whose greatest king was Sargon (ca. 2250 B.C.). The Akkadian Empire in turn fell under the sway of the Babylonian Empire, whose king Hammurabi (ca. 1750 B.C.) conquered all of Mesopotamia and is credited with the first known Code of Laws. Shortly before 1500 B.C. this empire fell under the domination of the Kassites, northern invaders who relied on a new military shock weapon, the horse-drawn chariot.

Egypt The great valley of the Nile, which creates a slender green oasis through the Sahara, had given birth by about 3000 B.C. to a network of farming villages whose population was of urban density, though not yet to cities as such. Tradition, which may incorporate elements of legend, credits the founding of the Egyptian monarchy to Menes (fl. 3100 B.C.), whose conquest of Lower (i.e., northern) Egypt laid the foundation for the Old Kingdom (ca. 3000–2200 B.C.). Political unification, quite different from the autonomous city-states of Sumer, permitted a rapid assimilation of some aspects of Sumerian culture and technology into the indiginous culture of the Nile Valley, while the desert meant relative freedom from invasion. The pharaohs did not rule on behalf of the gods, but were divine beings themselves; the building of their colossal tombs, the pyramids, were great religious works directed by the unitary state. The most famous is the Great Pyramid of Cheops at Gizeh (ca. 2500 B.C.). The development of hieroglyphic writing in Egypt, not much later than the invention of cuneiform writing in Sumer, facilitated both the administrative and the religious roles of the Egyptian monarchy.

The older diversity of the valley reappeared during a century of dissolution and division called the First Intermediate Period, after which the traditions of Menes were revived in the Middle Kingdom (ca. 2100–1800

B.C.). Architecture and sculpture were consciously restorationist, modeled after the Old Kingdom. This period was also the "classical age" of Egyptian literature.

But this age ended with the invasion from Syria-Palestine of a warlike charioteering people known as Hyksos, who ruled during the Second Intermediate Period (ca. 1800– 1600 B.C.). The Eighteenth Dynasty, with its capital at Thebes, at last managed to drive out the Hyksos and reestablish royal authority throughout the valley, initiating the New Kingdom (ca. 1600–1100 B.C.).

The Indus River Basin The Indus Basin, stretching from the Himalayas to the Arabian Sea, had become by about 3000 B.C. another locus of settled agriculture. The emerging Indus culture showed obvious signs of Sumerian influence. The great cities of Harappa and Mohenjo Daro have been excavated, along with many small villages. Small statuary and cylinder seals demonstrate a rich religious, artistic, and commercial life. Some evidence of writing has been discovered, but it remains undeciphered. This Indian civilization flourished from about 2500 to about 1500 B.C. when it was conquered by Central Asian ("Aryan") tribesmen who used chariots and arrows.

The Eastern Mediterranean Around 2000 B.C. three centers of civilization influenced by Mesopotamia and Egypt began to develop: the Canaanites in Syria and Palestine, the Hittites in Asia Minor, and the Minoan civilization on the island of Crete. It is not clear whether Minos was a name or, like "pharaoh" a title; but the palace of Minos, called the Labyrinth, dominated the trading city of Knossos, center of a "sea empire" whose ships were in contact with Italy, Egypt, Asia Minor, and mainland Greece. Yet by about 1500 B.C. the Minoan economy was in decline, possibly because of overexploitation of the Cretan environment as well as the damage wrought by a series of earthquakes, and not long after a Greek prince was ruling at Knossos.

China In China around 1950 B.C., the millet-based agricultural villages of the North China Plain gave rise to the semi-legendary Xia Dynasty, which ushered in the Bronze Age in East Asia. The Xia were overthrown around 1550 B.C. by Tang the Victorious, who established the Shang Dynasty, which endured for 500 years. The Shang Dynasty is noted for its sophisticated bronze vessels, used in worship of the royal ancestors, and for oracle bones inscribed with an early form of Chinese script asking questions of the gods. Shang culture was enriched after around 1350 B.C. by new technologies from western Eurasia, including the chariot, the cultivation of wheat, and sheepraising. Roughly contemporary with the Shang state was the separate Bronze Age culture of the Ba people, characterized by large, highly stylized bronze human statues and masks, with sites in the Sichuan Basin near the present city of Chengdu.

From the Bronze Age to the Iron Age (ca. 1500–500 B.C.)

In the millennium from about 1500 to about 500 B.C., the area of civilized life continued to spread as the civilizations took on their classic form in the "heroic age" of the ancient world. By the mid-first millennium B.C., iron had begun to replace bronze, first for tools and later for weapons, ushering in the Iron Age of classical civilization. The impact of the chariot warriors from the Eurasian steppes, a huge area of grassland stretching from the Black Sea almost to the Pacific Ocean, altered the earliest civilizations in different ways and to different degrees—least in the Near East, most in India.

Egypt Almost immediately after the Hyksos conquerers had been expelled from Egypt proper, the pharaohs of the New Kingdom (1570–1065 B.C.) reconsolidated the monarchy and began an expansion of the empire into Syria. Thutmose I (d. 1495 B.C.) sent an invading army as far as the Euphrates River. His successor Thutmose II (r. ca. 1495–1490 B.C.) did not sustain his father's conquests, and lost power to his half-sister, queen and regent Hatshepsut (d. ca. 1468 B.C.), who maintained her control over the throne during the first twenty years of the reign of Thutmose III (ca. 1500–1436 B.C.). After the death of Hatshepsut in 1468 B.C., Thutmose III again sent armies to the east, winning a great battle at Megiddo in Palestine. The result was an Egyptian empire in Palestine and Syria in which local princes ruled their peoples while Egyptian bureaucrats and garrison commanders oversaw imperial interests, especially the tribute payments. Egyptian control southward along the Nile into the Sudan and Nubia was also reestablished.

The radical religious reforms of Pharaoh Amenhotep IV (r. ca. 1372–1354 B.C.) brought about a period of severe political disruption. The pharaoh changed his name to Akhenaton and led a movement after 1370 B.C. to obliterate the name and memory of all the Egyptian gods save for the sun-god Aton (and his incarnation on Earth, the pharaoh). This almost-monotheistic revolution absorbed the attention of the monarchy to such an extent that it helped the empire to crumble and the dynasty to be overthrown. A rigid traditionalism accompanied the painful recovery of the empire. Akhenaton's son-in-law, Tutankhamen (r. 1361–52 B.C.), sponsored a return to older religious norms, including the return of the god Amon and the eclipse of Aton. Tutankhamen (whose famous tomb was discovered in 1922) was also known as a lawgiver, and as the sponsor of new monumental buildings in the capital at Thebes. But by 1200 B.C. a series of invasions, by Hittites and others, forced the Egyptians to abandon their empire in Palestine and Syria to defend the Nile Valley.

The Third Intermediate Period (1065–525 B.C.) saw Egypt's survival in a cultural and religious sense, with the priesthood exerting control over a series of ineffective monarchs. But the state, weakened by invasions of Libyans from the western desert and Nubians from the Upper Nile, finally fell victim to conquests by the Assyrians (671 B.C.) and the Persians (525 B.C.).

Mesopotamian Empires and the Rise of the Persian Empire The Kassite conquest of the First Babylonian Empire shortly before 1500 B.C. did not lead to substantial changes in the empire, as the northern conquerors adopted the culture and political structure of the conquered. The Assyrians retained their own rulers, under Kassite domination; those rulers eventually took advantage of a series of incursions by other northern horsemen against the Kassites to gain their independence in the First Assyrian Empire (ca. 1150–728 B.C.). The Assyrians were fierce warriors and in the course of establishing the Second Assyrian Empire (728–612 B.C.) they launched attacks on southern Mesopotamia, on Syria and Palestine, and even, briefly, on Egypt. The great Assyrian capital of Nineveh was destroyed, however, in 612 B.C. by the cavalry of an Indo-European people called the Medes. The Medes proceeded to conquer the Assyrian territory east of the Tigris as well as Armenia and eastern Iran, forming a short-lived empire (625–559 B.C.). Assyria's fall permitted the Second Babylonian Empire (625–538 B.C.) to arise in Mesopotamia.

Both Medes and Assyrians fell victim to the Persian Empire (559–331 B.C.). Cyrus the Great (r. 550–533 B.C.) overturned his Median overlord (559 B.C.), conquered King Croesus of Lydia in Asia Minor (546 B.C.) and overthrew King Nebuchadnezzar III of Babylon (538 B.C.). In the next generation a war of succession threatened the empire; unity was restored when Darius I (r. 521–485 B.C.), grandson of Cyrus, came to the throne. Darius brought the empire to its greatest extent, consolidating the conquest of Egypt, and expanding eastward beyond the Indus by 519 B.C. Dividing his empire into 20 "satrapies" (administrative offices), Darius improved communications by building good roads and was farsighted enough to commence the construction of a Mediterranean war fleet.

Under this Persian dynasty's patronage, the religious doctrines of Zoroaster (ca. 628–ca. 551 B.C.) spread through its immense empire. Zoroaster taught a dualist doctrine of a cosmic struggle between the god Ahuramazda, the god of light, truth and peace, and Ahriman, the god of darkness, lies, and discord. Zoroastrian doctrines influenced many later religions.

The People of Israel Tracing their origin to the ancient city of Ur in Mesopotamia and the covenant between their patriarch, Abraham, and their god, Yahweh, the Israelites migrated to Canaan sometime after 1900 B.C. Entering Egypt, probably in the Hyksos period, they dwelt in the Egyptian delta until about 1280 B.C., when, against strong resistance from the pharaoh, Moses led the Hebrews out of Egypt into the desert of Sinai, where, according to the Old Testament, they became God's chosen people in the Sinai covenant. Shortly before 1200 B.C. they occupied parts of Canaan during the decline of Egyptian power there. (This account is based upon biblical narratives; no independent archaeological evidence has yet been discovered for Abraham, Moses, and the other patriarchs.)

The religious league of clans was transformed into the Kingdom of Israel (ca. 1020–922 B.C.) which flourished under the kings Saul (r. ca. 1028–1013 B.C.), David (r. 1013–973 B.C.), and Solomon (r. 973–933 B.C.) largely undisturbed by the neighboring great powers of Egypt and Assyria. But after the death of Solomon, the kingdom divided into Israel in the north and Judah in the south. The northern kingdom fell to the Assyrians under Sargon II (r. 722–705 B.C.) in 721 B.C. Judah held on until the Second Babylonian Empire under Nebuchadnezzar II (r. ca. 605–562 B.C.) destroyed the capital Jerusalem in 587 B.C.

With the establishment of the Persian Empire, the Jews were permitted (538 B.C.) to return to Palestine and to build the second Temple, there to live under the code of law, the Torah.

Greece The Minoan culture of Crete had been in contact with the Greek mainland before 1650 B.C. The people of Greece (called Achaeans) lived in small principalities of which Mycenae, located on the Greek mainland, was preeminent. Adopting the courtly style of the Minoans and the war chariots of the Hyksos, the Achaeans expanded their settlements and with Cretan decline became heirs of Minoan trade with Egypt and Syria.

About 1100 B.C., a second wave of Greek-speaking Dorians invaded from the north and the Achaeans were forced to migrate to the islands and the coast of Asia Minor. In defeat they preserved Mycenaean traditions both socially and in the Homeric epics. Through these great poems the enterprise against Troy became the living symbol of the unity of the Greeks, the mythology of Mycenae provided a common religious background for local cults, and the language of the Achaeans became the norm for the whole Greek world.

By about 750 B.C. the Greek world had recovered from the Dorian invasions. Colonies spread westward to Italy and Sicily and eastward to the northern Aegean and the Black Sea. The lyric poetry of Archilochus (ca. 700 B.C.) and Sappho (ca. 600 B.C.) testifies to a flourishing literary culture. The first philosophers (including Thales, Heraclitus, and Parmenides), later called the pre-Socratics, commenced their speculations on nature and the cosmos; the Pythagoreans taught that mathematics is the foundation of cosmic order. During this period also, the characteristic unit of Greek political life, the city-state or *polis*, developed.

The greatest of these city-states were Athens and Sparta. Sparta emerged in 716 B.C. as conqueror of about 3,200 square miles of territory; by about 610 B.C. Sparta already had the formidable military organization based on strict education for citizenship to inculcate the "savage valor" that Spartans so esteemed. And by 540 B.C. Sparta had formed the Peloponnesian League, uniting all but two of the city-states of the peninsula.

The polis of Athens was, like other Greek cities, dominated by its aristocratic families and characterized by deep inequities. Social grievances led the Athenian leaders to turn over power to Solon, a wealthy merchant and poet, descended from the old kings. Taking office in 594, he cancelled all debts, abolished debt-slavery, encouraged both agriculture and industry, and opened the assembly to all free men. But Athens remained divided among wealthy landowners, a merchant class, and poor peasants, with a large population of slaves.

The Indian Subcontinent The charioteers who invaded the civilization of the Indus Valley called themselves Aryans, a word meaning "noble" in their Sanskrit language. Those they conquered were called sudras, "slaves." The Aryans settled in villages along the Indus, organized in tribal principalities about which almost nothing is known. From about 800 B.C. to about 300 B.C. they moved south along the coast and east across the peninsula to the delta of the Ganges River. There, once the lush jungle vegetation was cleared (using the new tools of the iron age), rice could be cultivated in the rich soil, a food supply sufficient for a very dense and stable population.

The religious classics of Hinduism date to this era. The ancient Vedas, hymns to the gods, date back to about 1000 B.C.—though not written down until much later. The Brahmanas are a body of instructions for rituals, evidence of the rise of an important priestly body, composed over the years 800–600 B.C. Lastly, about 600 B.C. appeared the Upanishads with their stress on asceticism and mysticism. Embodied in this religious literature is the caste system, in which society is divided into four varnas or castes: priests (brahmans), warriors (kshatriyas), artisans (vaisyas), and peasants (originally indistinguishable from slaves: sudras). This system was later to evolve into the fundamental structure of Indian society.

China The late Shang dynasty, known for the extravagance of its royal burials, declined into misrule; the dynasty was overthrown around 1046 B.C. by the ruler of the state of Zhou, centered in the Wei River Valley, northwest of the Shang kingdom (now north-central China). The duke of Zhou served as regent (ca. 1042–1036 B.C.) for the third Zhou ruler, King Cheng (r. 1042–1006 B.C.), and established a system of rule, sometimes loosely described as "feudal," in which the territory of China was parceled out in small states governed by Zhou clansmen and supporters. These states gradually grew larger at the expense of the Zhou royal domain. Zhou authority and territorial control declined drastically after around 770 B.C., and became vestigial during the Warring States Period (ca. 480–221 B.C.), when a handful of large feudal states swallowed up their smaller neighbors.

Despite political turmoil, the Warring States Period was an era of cultural brilliance in philosophy, technology, and the arts. Confucius (ca. 551–479 B.C.), China's first known philosopher, sought a remedy for the political turmoil of his time in an attempted revival of the golden age of the duke of Zhou. Thwarted in his search for a ruler who would put his ideas into practice, Confucius became a teacher whose disciples perpetuated his prescription for good government. Confucius looked to a natural aristocracy of virtue, rather than an hereditary elite, for social leadership; this led centuries later to the Chinese innovation of government by means of a professional civil service recruited through competitive examination. The Taoists, rivals of the Confucian school, rejected government altogether in favor of individual self-cultivation. They claimed as their founder a philosopher named Laozi, who was supposed to have lived in the sixth century B.C.; nothing is known about his life, and he may be wholly legendary.

During this era, the principal states of northern China became known collectively as zhongguo, the "middle kingdoms;" isolated from the high cultures of western Eurasia and India, the Chinese imagined their culture to be at the center of the world, surrounded by zones of ever-increasing barbarism. In this view, the Chinese ruler governed "all under heaven" by authority of the Mandate of Heaven (tian ming). This theory held that a dynastic founder, because of his own virtue, attracted the cosmic force of heaven itself in his support; heaven's mandate was bequeathed to his descendants so long as they cherished the principle of virtuous rule. This political theory, which assumed that exhausted and corrupt dynasties would eventually be overthrown by righteous rebellions, was a force for both dynastic renewal and long-term institutional stability throughout Chinese history.

The Americas The domestication of plants and the creation of Neolithic cultures began in Mexico as early as 7000 B.C., and led to settled village cultures by 2500 B.C. based on the cultivation of squash, beans, chilies, and corn (maize). The earliest civilization in the Americas was that of the Olmec, whose cities lay in the Valley of Mexico, on the coast in the vicinity of Vera Cruz, and in the highlands around Oaxaca. The Olmec cities are marked by large square step-pyramids, and by carvings of enormous stone heads. Olmec culture appears to have begun around 1200 B.C., and to have persisted for some 800 years before being supplanted by the Zapotec.

Meanwhile, to the south, the great civilization of the Maya was beginning to take form in what is known as the late Preclassic Period, beginning around 300 B.C. in the Yucatán Peninsula and adjacent areas of southern Mexico, Belize, Guatemala, and parts of Honduras and El Salvador. Some ancient Maya villages had by this time begun to evolve into cities marked by plazas flanked by pyramids, temples, and palaces.

With the late Olmec, the Zapotec, and the Preclassic Maya, all the hallmarks of Mesoamerican civilization were in place: pyramids and other monumental architecture, a 260-day and 52-year calendar, ritual ballgames, bar-and-dot numbers and hieroglyphic inscriptions, and personal blood sacrifices by members of the ruling elite, together with ritual human sacrifice to nourish the maize goddess and other deities.

The First Imperial Era (ca. 500 B.C.-A.D. 500)

The millennium after 500 B.C. was characterized by the growth of great empires in several parts of the world, including Persia, India, China, and Rome; elsewhere, other polities began to emerge on the stage of world history.

Rival Empires: Persians and Greeks What the Greeks called the Persian Wars (499–479 B.C.) began with a failed revolt of the Greek cities of coastal Asia Minor against the Persian Empire (of which they had become a part in 546 B.C.). To punish the mainland Greek allies of the rebels, the city-states of Athens and Eretria, the Persian Empire made war on Greece, but unsuccessfully. From the Persian point of view the victories of Athens and Sparta in the "Persian Wars" were only a border issue of minor import; but to the Greeks, great battles such as Marathon (490 B.C.) and the fleet engagement at Salamis (480 B.C.) were inspiring symbols of the superiority of their ideals of liberty and free citizenship over the servitude of Eastern despotism.

Under the leadership of Pericles (ca. 495–429 B.C.) Athens transformed itself from the leading power of a naval league into an aggressive conqueror of an Athenian Empire. Athenian aggrandizement allowed Sparta to present itself as the defender of Greek liberties. Athens and Sparta, formerly allies, each at the head of a league of city-states, fought the Peloponnesian War (431–404 B.C.) in which the Spartans won a crushing victory. The history of the war was recorded by the great Greek historian, Thucydides (ca. 460–400 B.C.) Spartan hegemony in Greece lasted only until 387 B.C., when a league of Greek cities with Persian assistance imposed a settlement which made all Greek city-states autonomous (and therefore weak) except for those in Asia under Persian rule. In the midst of this political and military turmoil, Greek culture had flourished: in writing for the theater (Aeschylus, Sophocles, Euripides), philosophy (Socrates, Plato, Aristotle), history (Herodotus, Thucydides), architecture (the Acropolis) and sculpture (Myron, Phidias).

The Empire of Alexander the Great Immediately to the north of the disunited Greek city-states lay the small but militarily powerful kingdom of Macedon, provincial but greatly influenced by Greek civilization. Having conquered the territories of Illyria and Thrace along the northern coast of the Aegean Sea, King Philip (r. 356–330 B.C.) intervened in Greece and forced the formation of a Hellenic League which, under Macedonian influence, began war against Persia (336 B.C.). Philip was assassinated soon after the war began, and his death occasioned the revolt of the Greek cities he dominated. But his son and successor, Alexander the Great (r. 336–323 B.C.) ruthlessly crushed the revolt and then began his conquest of Asia. After winning a great victory in the battle of Issus (in what is now southeastern Turkey, 333 B.C.) over Darius III (r. 336–330 B.C.) of Persia, Alexander declared himself successor to the last Persian emperor under the title King of Asia, continuing rule through the satrapies after the final defeat of the Persians in 330 B.C. In the meantime he added Egypt to his conquests (331 B.C.) and founded the great city of Alexandria. He pushed on into Bactria (modern Uzbekistan) and then to the Indus Valley beyond which his soldiers would not go. When he died of a fever in Babylon in 323 B.C., he had assembled in a dozen years the largest empire the world had known; but his premature death meant the division of the empire among the Diodochi (Alexander's generals who claimed the succession). After half a century of warfare, the successor states became stabilized: the heirs of Antigonus ruled Macedonia, the Ptolemys ruled Egypt, and the descendants of Seleucus inherited Alexander's territories in western Asia.

Rome: From Republic to Empire Shortly before 500 B.C., the small community of Rome broke free from its Etruscan rulers and established a republic. A century of patient expansion against neighboring tribes in central Italy suffered a setback in 390 B.C., when Celts from the Po Valley plundered and burnt the city. But the Roman expansion resumed, and within three generations they had brought under their control all of the Italian peninsula except the Greek cities (Magna Graecia) in the south. These they added by 272 B.C., just as the Diodochi were stabilizing the successor kingdoms to Alexander's empire.

Expansion into southern Italy involved Rome in a struggle with Carthage. Originally a Phoenician colony, the city of Carthage in North Africa had established commercial colonies along the eastern, southern, and northwestern coasts of the Mediterranean and on the Atlantic coasts of Spain and Morocco. In a prodigious series of struggles called the Punic Wars (264–146 B.C.), during which Rome itself narrowly escaped conquest by Hannibal (247–183 B.C.), the Romans utterly vanquished Carthage.

Meanwhile, after the Second Punic War (218–201 B.C.) Rome had become embroiled in the east as Pergamum, Rhodes, and Athens appealed for help against the Diodochi. Rome's eastward expansion began with a war against Macedonia (200–197 B.C.). By 62 B.C. Greece, Macedonia, Asia Minor, Syria, Palestine, Egypt, and the whole North African coast were under Roman rule. The Mediterranean Sea truly became what the Romans called *mare nostrum*: "our sea."

Rather than attempting further conquests in Asia, the Romans looked westward, as Julius Caesar (100–44 B.C.) embarked on the conquest of Gaul (modern France and southern Germany) and of Britain (A.D. 43–84). Eastern defense considerations led to the annexation of Armenia, Mesopotamia, and Assyria (A.D. 114–16). At its greatest extent, the Roman Empire stretched from the North Sea to the Sahara Desert, from the Scottish borderlands to the Persian Gulf.

But in winning their empire, the Romans lost their republic, in which sovereignty had been invested in an elected Senate and the power of government was exercised by magistrates. The tremendous population losses in the Second Punic War, the increase in the slave population with every conquest, the transformation of land tenure from peasant agriculture to huge latifundia (plantations), the rise of a class of financiers, the rivalry of military commanders, the involvement of the military in politics—all overwhelmed the old republican institutions. In the century and a half from 298 B.C. to 133 B.C., the rivalry for power among demagogues and generals meant endless civil war leading to the final victory of the revolutionary adventurer Octavian, who, renamed Augustus (r. 27 B.C-A.D. 14, initiated imperial rule in Rome itself. Augustus initiated the era of the Pax Romana, 200 years of peace under the aegis of the Roman Empire (27 B.C-A.D. 180).

The Roman Empire, East and West, and the Spread of Christianity A lasting legacy of the Roman conquests was the spread of Roman civic tradition into continental Europe and western Asia. The empire became a network of administrative departments centered on cities with central power at Rome; with the external forms of civic life came economic prosperity and the intellectual culture of the Hellenized Roman civilization.

In this milieu, Jesus of Nazareth (ca. 4 B.C.-A.D. 30) was born in the Roman colony of Judea. His followers preached the "good news" (gospel) that God himself had become man and died for man's sins, a message that became the core teaching of the early Christians, as the Romans called them. Christianity soon spread beyond the Jewish world as the preaching of missionaries such as Paul, Barnabas, and Timothy expanded the Christian community through the cities of the Roman world: from Palestine to Syria, Anatolia and Greece, to Africa and Italy; in the second century to Gaul, Germany, Yugoslavia, and Spain. Although the Roman authorities were generally tolerant of all kinds of religious beliefs, the Christians were persecuted because of their secretive practices and their refusal to acknowledge the Roman civic gods; after A.D. 110, adherence to Christianity became a capital offense. Yet the church continued to spread.

When after the death of the Stoic emperor Marcus Aurelius (r. 161–180) the empire fell into civil war, economic decline, and the exhaustion of civic life through excessive taxation and centralized government control, the frontiers became unstable. After A.D. 226 a revived Persian Empire grew aggressive in the east while great confederations of tribes (Goths, Vandals, Allemani, Franks) arose on the Rhine and Danube Rivers. The emperor Diocletian (r. 284–305) attempted to stem the decline with a political and military reorganization, but it was the emperor Constantine (r. 312–37) who saw that much more was needed.

Constantine attempted to provide a new internal principal of spiritual unity to the Roman Empire through Christianity. His "new Rome" of Constantinople was a Christian city from the start; Christianity had progressed from persecution to toleration to favored position to state religion in less than a century. But the state itself was far gone in decline. Visigothic troops sacked Rome in 410 (the first time in 800 years that Rome had been pillaged) then carved out a realm in southern Gaul and Spain by 450. Vandals tore North Africa away from Rome (429–39). Franks reached the Loire by 486, and Saxons, Angles, and Jutes ended Roman rule in Britain.

Meanwhile in the Roman east, imperial control remained intact, but Christianity itself fell into disarray, as peoples in various parts of the eastern empire followed one or another of the heresies that flourished after the formal definition of Christian orthodoxy at the Council of Chalcedon (450).

India and Southeast Asia Alexander's armies had stopped their conquest of Asia at the Indus River. The India that lay beyond was a complex welter of tribal principalities and republics, of which a certain primacy attached to the kingdom of Magadha in the Ganges Valley. In 317 B.C. Chandragupta Maurya (r. 321–297 B.C.), who had met Alexander and was married to a Macedonian princess, attacked and conquered Magadha with the aid of northwestern tribes, founding the Mauryan Empire (317–184 B.C.). Chandragupta subdued the Indus valley as well, and the legitimacy of his rule was recognized by the Diodochus, Seleucus Nicator. By the reign of his grandson Asoka (269–232 B.C.), central and most of southern India had been added to the empire, which extended north to the foothills of the Himalayas and west to the eastern reaches of Afghanistan.

Asoka was known as the Buddhist Emperor, personally devout and publicly the protector and propagator of the religion of the Buddha. Prince Siddhartha Gautama (563–483 B.C.) was a member of the Kshatriya caste; enlightenment came when he left the favored precincts of his father's palace and came face-to-face with the reality of suffering. (The title Buddha, a Sanskrit word meaning "enlightened one," was applied to Gautama after his discovery of religious truth. See World Religions.) The Buddha's disciples lived in communities dedicated to putting into practice his "eightfold path" to holiness, and such monastic communities were fostered and supported by Asoka (ca. 273–233 B.C.).

After the death of Asoka the Mauryan Empire began to crumble into its constituent parts; the last emperor was assassinated by one of his generals in 184 B.C. One of the successor states was the Graeco-Indian kingdom in the north and northwest founded by a general of the Diodoch king of Bactria; another was the Kushan Empire of the first and second centuries A.D., which was the route by which Buddhism expanded into central Asia.

A second Chandragupta (ca. 380–ca. 415) was the founder of the last great Indian imperial regime of the ancient period, the Gupta Empire (320–535 A.D.) which at its greatest extent stretched across the subcontinent from the mouth of the Indus to the mouth of the Ganges. The source of its unity was a revived Hinduism, whose brahmans provided advisers to the emperors and drew up codes of Hindu law that articulated the structures of the caste system. It was the age also of Sanskrit as a literary language, in the drama of Kalidasa (ca. 400–455) and in the final composition (from earlier, partly oral, roots) of the epic poems Mahabharata and Ramayana. The Gupta period was the golden age of Indian science, especially astronomy and mathematics, to which we owe the decimal system and the invention of the number zero. Classic Indian civilization was spread far beyond the political borders of the Gupta realm by Hindu and Buddhist merchants and Buddhist missionaries, to Burma, Thailand, and Indo-China, to the Malay peninsula and beyond into Indonesia. The shores of the Bay of Bengal and of the South China Sea thus became a kind of "greater India."

The First Chinese Empire In 246 B.C., the massed infantry troops, supported by cavalry and chariots, of the northwestern state of Qin, hardened by years of warfare with the nomads of the northern steppes, hurtled eastward to conquer and subjugate, one by one, all of the other feudal principalities, putting an end to the period of the Warring States. These conquests gave rise to the first Chinese Empire under the Qin Dynasty (221–206 B.C.). Qin Shihuangdi ("The First Emperor of Qin," r. 221–210 B.C.) proved more than just a conqueror: he oversaw the completion of the Great Wall along the edge of Inner Mongolia and reorganized the structure of government by dividing the land into regions of civil administration and military garrisons, governed by officials responsible to himself alone. The old nobility was weakened by land confiscations. Scholars and philosophers were persecuted or intimidated; private possession of books was banned. Although the harshness of Qin rule quickly provoked rebellions and the First Emperor's weak successor met his death by assassination (206 B.C.), the structure of imperial rule inaugurated by the Qin would endure for more than two thousand years.

A rebel leader named Liu Bang emerged victorious in the confused and bloody uprisings that brought the Qin Dynasty to an end. Liu (r. 206–195) proclaimed himself emperor of the Han Dynasty, which was to endure (with a brief interregnum, A.D. 7–25, under the usurper Wang Mang) for four centuries, until A.D. 220. The Han founder retained the imperial structure of Qin rule, while moderating its punitive harshness; he opened the way for renewed Confucian participation in government. The greatest Han ruler, Emperor Wu (r. 140–87 B.C.) instituted the practice of choosing officials on the basis of learning and merit. He brought the rich ricelands of the Yangtze River Valley firmly under imperial control, and also greatly extended the boundaries of the empire, conquering south to the South China Sea, southwest to the borders of Burma and Tibet, northeast to northern Korea, and westward to the deserts of Central Asia. He pacified the northern frontier, defeating the Xiongnu tribes, whose descendants, the Huns, would later invade Europe. In an early arms race, the powerful laminated compound bow and cavalry tactics of the northern nomads were countered by Chinese infantry armed with mass-produced crossbows—a refinement of a weapon of Southeast Asian origin. Trade increased along the Silk Route, a network of caravan trails that, through many intermediaries, brought Chinese silk to the Roman Empire and warhorses from Central Asia to China.

The "dynastic cycle" completed its course in the last decades of the Han period, when court corruption, peasant uprisings, and military insurrections led to the overthrow of the last Han emperor in A.D. 220. There followed the Three Kingdoms Period (220–265), when rival states tried without success to reunite the empire, and the period of the Northern and Southern Dynasties (265–589), when northern China was ruled by a succession of short-lived dynasties, often imposed by invaders from the steppes, while southern China was fragmented into short-lived and ineffectual kingdoms. During this period of disunion Buddhism, which had entered China via Central Asia in late Han times, began to establish itself as one of China's major religions. Especially successful were sects of Mahayana ("Greater Vehicle") Buddhism, which promised salvation to the faithful through the mediation of saints called bodhisattvas.

Japan and Korea Around 300 B.C., invaders from southern Manchuria had invaded Japan via the Korean peninsula. These invaders, equipped with horses, bronze weapons, and the wealth produced by rice agriculture, displaced the ancient Jomon culture of the original inhabitants of Japan. This bronze-age Yayoi civilization, which also shows evidence of influence from Austronesian culture via Taiwan and Okinawa, laid the foundations for the subsequent Japanese empire. But for several centuries Japan was divided into small states ruled by military clans, with those associated with the Shinto shrines at Izumo and Ise claiming some degree of primacy.

In Korea the decline of the Chinese colony at Lolang led to the establishment of indigenous kingdoms; three of these—Silla, Paekche, and Koguryo—predominated during the period A.D. 313–668, with Silla ultimately emerging victorious and uniting the whole Korean peninsula under its rule. Chinese cultural influence, via Korea, as well as cultural influence and waves of immigrants from Korea itself, helped to transform the Japanese petty states into a centralized kingdom by the fifth century A.D.

The Americas The Zapotec capital city of Teotihuacán, in the Valley of Mexico, flourished from about A.D. 300 to 900. It was a rich and fertile city of irrigated fields, urban residential districts, and ceremonial pyramids, temples, and administrative buildings, and a population approaching 200,000. Zapotec trade networks extended north to what is now the southwestern United States, and south to the culture area of the Maya.

In the Yucatán and adjacent regions, the era from approximately A.D. 250 to 475 is the Early Classic Period of Mayan civilization. Great cities at Petán, Tikal, and other lowland sites demonstrate that Mayan civilization reached its full flowering near the beginning of the Early Classic period; stelae, altars, lintels, and other stone structures in these cities are replete with inscriptions celebrating the conquests and other deeds of the Mayan kings.

North of the Mexican border, the Hohokam and other cultures of the American Southwest were powerfully influenced by Zapotec civilization. These were provincial areas, with towns and villages linked by ties of trade, administration, and warfare, but they were not independent centers of civilization. In the Mississippi and Ohio Valleys, village-based agrarian centers of the Woodland Culture were sufficiently rich and well organized to construct large earthen mounds for ceremonial purposes.

Africa The Aksum civilization of Ethiopia, the only independent literate culture to arise in the history of Africa beyond the Nile Valley as well as one of the world's earliest Christian cultures, began to flourish during the first century A.D. and reached its zenith in the fourth and fifth centuries A.D. At its height it encompassed an area extending from the fringes of the Sahara in the west, across Ethiopia, and across the Red Sea to the Arabian Desert. The Aksumite economy was based on the cultivation of teff, a grain unique to Ethiopia and still widely cultivated there. The Aksumites built in stone, and inscribed their monuments with a script known as Ge'ez, the precursor of the script still used to write the classical languages of Ethiopia today.

Elsewhere in Africa, most people lived as hunter-gatherers, as pastoral nomads, or in communities of Neolithic farmers. The great migration of Bantu-speaking peoples, which had begun with an expansion from the Congo River Basin in the third millennium B.C., was essentially complete by around A.D. 400. From that time, most of Africa south of the Congo was settled by speakers of Bantu languages, and with earlier populations (such as Khoi-San peoples) displaced to marginal environments.

A Second Age of Empires (A.D. 500–1000)

The appearance in the seventh century of the new religion of Islam, with its militant emphasis on bringing as much of the world as possible into the "realm of submission to God," gave rise to an empire stretching from the Iberian Peninsula to the Indus Valley, but influencing events as well in places as far distant as Ghana and China. It also was a catalyst for the division of Christendom into western and eastern realms.

Under the Tang Dynasty, one of the most brilliant eras of Chinese history, Chinese culture was influenced by that of Central Asia, and spread to Korea and Japan. And in isolation from the Old World, the Mayan civilization of Central America reached its zenith.

The Late Roman Empire and Early Medieval Europe The lapse of direct Roman rule in the West did not imply an immediate "fall" of the Roman Empire so much as a shift of Roman power elsewhere. In the city of Rome, the heir and representative of the Roman Empire was the Catholic Church. The emperor Justinian (r. 527–565) did much to revive the fortunes of the empire, but from a base in Constantinople rather than Rome itself. Maintaining a rough alliance with the Christian Franks in Gaul under their Merovingian dynasty, the emperor Justinian's armies recovered the western provinces: Vandal Africa, Ostrogothic Italy, and the Mediterranean sector of Visigothic Spain. Meanwhile, his jurists codified and preserved the whole body of Roman law that had been built up since the days of the republic. And under imperial patronage there grew up a magnificent cluster of churches whose pinnacle was Hagia Sophia in Constantinople, constructed in 537. The city of Rome itself, however, was well launched on a centuries-long period of decline, with a shrinking population and many buildings disused or in ruins.

The cost of Justinian's efforts was great, and the defense of the West was short-lived. After Justinian's death the empire had neither treasure nor troops enough to save much of Italy from new invaders, the Lombards. The city of Ravenna kept its link with Constantinople, and Rome remained the principality of the popes. Pope Gregory "the Great" (590–604) not only organized the defense of the city but oversaw the work of converting Visigothic Spain and began the restoration of Christianity in faraway Britain through the mission of St. Augustine (354–430) to Kent. In this effort Gregory relied upon the monks who followed the Rule of St. Benedict (ca. 480–547), which provided a uniform way of life for monks living as a community, including vows of poverty, chastity, and obedience, regular and frequent hours of prayer, study of the Bible, and manual work.

The Byzantine Empire In the east lay the empire proper, in the era after Justinian usually called the Byzantine Empire or the Eastern Roman Empire (610–1453). Its wealth and power were based in Asia Minor, its unity dependent upon three factors: Orthodox Christianity (slowly drifting away from Roman Catholicism until the final break with Rome in 1054); Hellenistic culture and the Greek language; and Roman law and administration. Missionary ventures carried Christianity and Byzantine influence to the Serbs and Croats in the Balkans, to the Moravians and Slovaks north of the Danube, and even as far as Kievan Rus, all in the ninth and 10th centuries.

The empire was "byzantine" in the common sense of that word, a world of complex politics involving a wide variety of factors: emperors who were often weak and ineffectual; self-interested palace bureaucrats; powerful generals prone to warlordism; Orthodox prelates engaged in endless struggles with schismatic and heretical clerics; and popular political factions verging on mob rule, often linked to the fortunes of chariot-racing teams in the hippodromes. Yet the empire also prospered through trade, agriculture, and artisanal production of goods. It made brilliant cultural achievements, particularly in the ecclesiastical arts, and managed to survive, in gradually attenuating form, for more than eight centuries.

The empire, which barely held on in the east against Persia, lost large areas to the conquering armies of Islam (see below). Between 636 and 642, Syria, Egypt, and Libya converted to Islam; in a second wave of Islamic expansion (696–711) the rest of North Africa and Spain became part of the world of Islam as well. The Mediterranean seemed on its way to becoming a Muslim lake, threatening both the Byzantine Empire and the emerging successor states to the old Roman Empire in the West.

Charlemagne and His Heirs In the west there arose the Carolingian Empire (751–888). Pepin III (r. 751–768) cooperated with St. Boniface to reform the Frankish Church in close relation with Rome, deposed (with papal approval) the last Merovingian shadow-king, and was himself anointed king. Before his death, Pepin had made Frankish sovereignty felt southward to the Pyrenees and the Mediterranean. His son, Charlemagne (r. 768–814), conquered Lombardy, absorbed Bavaria, expanded into Saxony and beyond the Pyrenees, bringing under his sway an area equal in size to the old Roman Empire in the West. At the same time, to foster missionary endeavors, he ordered the creation of cathedral and monastic schools, drawing heavily for his scholars on Northumbria, the small English kingdom where Celtic and Roman monastic traditions had intermingled. The monasteries, with their libraries and traditions of theological scholarship, kept learning alive during the centuries between the fall of Rome and the rise of medieval monarchies, with their cities and universities.

The pinnacle of Charlemagne's achievements came on Christmas Day in the year 800, when in the city of Rome the pope acclaimed and crowned him as Roman Emperor. But with his death his realm began to disintegrate. By 843 his grandsons divided his realm in three parts with a middle kingdom of the emperor Lothair (r. 855–869) separating the kingdoms of the East and West Franks (lands that much later would become Germany and France). One of the greatest threats to these realms was the Vikings of Scandinavia. Starting in the eighth century, Vikings descended the rivers of eastern Europe to the Caspian, Black and Mediterranean Seas, attacked all along the coast of Western Europe, ravaged the British Isles, established commercial bases between the Baltic and Byzantium, and settled Iceland and Greenland. Eastern Europe was invaded around 900 by the Magyars, who settled in what is now Hungary.

The family of the Carolingians proved unable to lead any effective resistance to the attacks of Vikings, Magyars, and Muslims; military power devolved to local nobles and petty kings. This was the origin of the pattern of decentralized authority and allegiance known as feudalism. Political and military power had become essentially the private possessions of the strong, who became richer as their agricultural land benefited from the use of new technologies (crop rotation, improved horse harness for heavy plows). Under those circumstances, feudalism provided for the grant (from monarch to lords, and from lords to knights) of rights to govern and receive the revenues from certain territories (known as "fiefs"), in return for the remission of some revenues (from knights to lords, and from lords to monarchs), and the provision of military service on demand. This system brought some degree of order to a dangerous and uncertain age. Monarchy was not dead, but the medieval kings' relationship to the nobility had become "firsts amongst equals." King Alfred the Great of Wessex (r. 871–899) defended England against the Danes. Henry the Fowler (r. 919–36) began the Saxon Dynasty of German kings while his son Otto I (r. 936–973) also assumed (962) the title of Emperor; and Hugh Capet (r. 987–996) began the Capetian Dynasty of France, which ruled into the 19th century.

On the fringe of the older Carolingian world, the Scandinavian monarchies were consolidated and converted to Christianity around 1000; an independent and Catholic Kingdom of Poland was established (966); Kievan Rus converted to Christianity (988) under St. Vladimir (r. ca. 956–1015); and in 1001 a Catholic Hungarian kingdom was founded by St. Stephen (r. 997–1038).

The Islamic World To Rome at the height of the empire, the Arabs were not much more than a frontier annoyance; they posed no serious menace. Centuries later, the militant new religion of Islam arose in the Arabian Desert to pose a deadly threat to the heirs of the Roman world. The founder of Islam, Muhammad (or Mohammed) (570–632) was a religious prophet whose revelations came from God; these revelations form the heart of the Muslim sacred book, the Koran. The Koran clearly emerges from the biblical traditions of Abraham, and accepts Jesus as a prophet; but Muhammad is seen as the "Seal of the Prophets," beyond whom no further revelations will be given. (The word Islam means "submission to God"; a Muslim is "one who submits"; for more on Islam, see "Religion.") Muhammad was driven out of Mecca by his enemies in 622; he escaped to Yathrib (now Medina), where he and his followers formed a religious and political community. This event, the hijira, marks the Year 1 of the Muslim calendar. After eight years of desert warfare, Muhammad and his followers returned to capture Mecca (630).

Within two years of Muhammad's death the armies of Islam were marching. Islam divides the world between the Dar al-Islam ("world submissive to God") and the Dar al-Harb ("world at war with God"); conversion of the world is a religious imperative. They detached Syria, Mesopotamia, Egypt, and Libya (636–46) from the Roman Empire, and conquered Persia (637–49). A crisis over the succession to Muhammad was settled in 661, when the old tribal aristocracy triumphed over the family of the prophet and established the Umayyad Dynasty (661–750) of caliphs ("successors") ruling not from Medina but from Damascus and utilizing the old Persian and Roman bureaucracies. This question of succession led to a fundamental split in Islam, between the Shi'a Muslims who remained loyal to the family of the prophet, and who look toward the return of the "hidden Imam" to restore the rightful succession, and the Sunni Muslims who accept the legitimacy of the caliphs. For almost half a century Islam gave its attention to such internal political problems, and to the consolidation of the first wave of conquests; then, with the conversion of the Berbers, Byzantine Africa was brought into the world of Islam (696), as was Visigothic Spain (711). In the same year a Muslim commander established himself in the lower Indus Valley.

A series of revolts protesting the Arabic dominance of the Umayyads led to the establishment of a new dynasty of caliphs, the Abbasid Dynasty (750–1258), descended from a cousin of Muhammad. Arab by descent, the Abbasids nonetheless moved the capital to the new city of Baghdad in Mesopotamia. Persian culture strongly influenced Abbasid politics and literature, while the Islamic scientific and mathematical flowering drew on the scientific and mathematical discoveries of Gupta India (especially the decimal system of numeration and the use of the zero) and ancient Greece as well as on ancient Babylonian astronomy and astrology.

The Umayyads had not been totally overturned; Spain followed their rule when the rest of the empire turned to the Abbasids; after about 800 there were independent Muslim states in Morocco, Tunis, and eastern Persia; and by about 875 in Egypt and Turkistan. Before the year 1000, the caliphs had lost almost all their political power, becoming largely a focus of religious unity, relying even then on members of the ulema, experts in Islamic law and tradition (the hadith). Because Islam in principle does not recognize a distinction between the secular and the sacred, ultimate authority in many Islamic states remains with religious leaders (whose status and opinions are not unlike those of rabbis in Judaism).

India and Africa on the Fringe of Islam After the White Huns (also known as Rajputs) overthrew the Gupta Dynasty in 535, India reverted to its older pattern of a large number of tribal principalities. The Rajputs coexisted with the Hindu princes and established a feudal state across north India east of the Indus Valley, the kingdom of Rajputana. The Sind (or lower Indus Basin) was already in Muslim hands after 711. By the ninth century Buddhism virtually disappeared from India, absorbed into Hinduism; one exception was in the state of the Pala kings, who ruled Bengal and Magadha, in the northeast, into the 12th century. Buddhism remained influential in parts of "greater India:" in the small kingdoms of Burma, in the kingdom of Dvaravati in Siam, in Sri Lanka, and in the Sumatran state of Srivijaya under its Sailendra dynasty. The Sailendra rulers built the Buddhist temple-mandala of Borobudur in central Java ca. 800; the nearby temple of Prambanan was built a century later by the Hindu rulers of the kingdom of Mataram, which succeeded Srivijaya as the dominant trading empire of the East Indies.

At the other extremity of the Muslim world, Muslim traders from Morocco were in contact with the Kingdom of Ghana by about the year 800. Camel caravans crossed the Sahara to the grasslands between the upper Niger and Senegal Rivers, bearing salt and goods from the Mediterranean basin, and returned with gold and ivory from Ghana. Extracting import and export taxes and monopolizing the gold supply, the kings of Ghana exercised an imperial control over the trading cities of the region, growing wealthy and powerful. Yet by 1076 the caliphs in Morocco were able to conquer the region.

At the opposite side of Africa, Muslim Arabs crossed the Red Sea and annexed the Somali coast (ca. 1050) from the ancient Christian kingdom of Ethiopia.

China: Tang and Song Dynasties Three centuries of disunion in China came to an end with the establishment of the Sui Dynasty in 589. The Sui was a short-lived dynasty that paved the way for a long-enduring one. Extravagant expenditures on the Grand Canal linked Hangzhou to the south with the capital at Chang'an to the west, a distance of more than 1,000 miles. This undertaking, combined with a disastrous attempt to conquer Korea and a Turkish invasion of northwestern China, doomed the Sui. It was replaced by the Tang Dynasty (618–907), one of the most glorious eras in all of Chinese history. Buddhism flourished, as did poetry and the fine arts; Tang Chang'an was the largest and most cosmopolitan city in the world by around 700. But in 751 Chinese troops on the westernmost frontier were defeated by an Arab army in the Battle of Talas, and the Tang abandoned much of Central Asia; in 755 China's greatest general at the time, An Lushan (703–757), rebelled against the throne. The rebellion was defeated, but the empire never recovered fully. An imperial persecution of Buddhism in the 840's, during which the wealth of many temples was confiscated, signaled the rise of Neo-Confucianism, reinvigorating China's oldest philosophical tradition. But with the imperial house in disarray, the Tang collapsed in 907.

After five decades of inconclusive attempts to restore central rule, the Song Dynasty was founded in 960, and endured until 1279. But the Song never had firm control of northern China. The northeast was controlled by the Liao Dynasty in the hands of the non-Chinese Khitan people (whose name gives us the word Cathay). They were replaced in the early 12th century by the Jurchen Jin Dynasty, which in 1127 conquered all of northern China, sending the Song emperors south to a new capital at Hangzhou. Although the Song were politically weak, this was nevertheless a time of cultural brilliance, when Chinese landscape painting was perfected, poetry flourished, and urban life (rich from overseas trade from the South China Sea and the Indian Ocean) attained new heights of sophistication. With the old northern aristocratic clans destroyed by the downfall of the Tang and subsequent centuries of barbarian rule, the Song state was run by a modern bureaucratic government recruited from a prosperous and well-educated rural gentry.

Annam, comprising the northern and central parts of what is now Vietnam, capped several centuries of resistance to Chinese domination by driving out the Chinese in 939 and establishing an independent monarchy, though one that in many respects continued to adhere to Chinese Confucian cultural norms.

Japan and Korea In Korea, the state of Silla in 562 put an end to Japanese attempts to carve out colonial enclaves on the peninsula, and then, with Tang support, turned its attention to defeating its rivals Paekche and Koguryo. This process was completed by 670, and Silla grew prosperous with Tang support and cultural influence. But Silla in turn was defeated in 935 by the small western state of Koryo, which established a dynasty ruling all of Korea until 1392. Relatively isolated from Song influence by the intervening states of Liao, and later Jin, the Koryo state became culturally more independent of China.

In Japan, the Yamato clan, which had gradually pressed its claim to recognition as an imperial dynasty on the Chinese model, was firmly established on the throne by the fifth century A.D. Buddhism came to Japan in the following century, along with such continental innovations as the use of Chinese script to write (phonetically) the very different Japanese language (as well as the adoption of Classical Chinese itself as a literary language). In 604 Prince Shotoku (572–622) issued a 17-article "constitution" establishing imperial support for Buddhism and enjoining all aristocrats to respect the imperial throne. The throne thereupon came under the influence of the powerful Soga clan until 645; an early 8th-century restoration movement emphasized emulation of the Chinese model of government. But the principle of appointment to office on the basis of merit never caught on in Japan, which continued to be ruled by a hereditary aristocracy.

Japan's first planned capital city was founded at Nara in 710; by 750 the city was wholly dominated by its rich and powerful Buddhist temples. In response the emperors moved the capital to the new city of Heian-kyo (now Kyoto) in 794; the emperors remained there for over a thousand years. Both Nara and Heian-kyo were built on a grid plan, modeled after the Chinese capital at Chang'an; Heian-kyo especially boasted a glittering cultural life, supported by agrarian wealth from the provinces. The powerful Fujiwara clan gained control of the country's political life through the expedient of making sure that every emperor married a Fujiwara daughter, and abdicated the throne for a life of monastic retirement shortly after producing an heir; the head of the Fujiwara clan thus was always first the regent for and then the father-in-law of one emperor and regent-to-be for the heir-apparent.

The Classic Age of Mayan Culture The period A.D. 475–900 encompasses the Middle Classic and Late Classic periods of Mayan history. Great temple-cities arose throughout the Mayan cultural area, encompassing southern Mexico and the Yucatán, Guatemala, Belize, and parts of Honduras and El Salvador. Cities such as Palenque, Copá, and Tikal, among many others, supported an aristocracy dedicated to warfare and sacrifice to the gods, as well as a priesthood and classes of scribes and artisans. As in the Early Classic Period, the activities of the Mayan rulers were recorded in a hieroglyphic script on stone monuments. Mayan culture was supported by intensive agriculture, especially utilizing the technique of raised crop beds surrounded by irrigation channels. The total population of the Mayan cultural region during the Late Classic era may have been 8 to 10 million people. Remarkably, the Maya reached a high cultural level without the use of metal or wheeled vehicles, and with limited use of domestic animals (mainly dogs and fowl).

Around 900, or slightly before, most of the great Mayan cities suffered precipitous declines, or were abandoned altogether. Many theories have been advanced to explain the sudden decline of Mayan civilization, including prolonged drought, deforestation, excessive devotion of resources to warfare, and the encroachment of the Toltec from the north. In any case, the Post-Classical Mayan world does seem to have come under at least the loose control of the Toltec empire; Toltec and Maya alike would be conquered by the Aztec after about 1300.

Meanwhile, in the Valley of Mexico, the Zapotec civilization, with its cultural center at the great city of Teotihuacán, was supplanted first by the Mixtec and then (around 900) by the Toltec, who built a great capital at Tula, not far from Teotihuacán.

The World on the Eve of European Expansion (A.D. 1000–1500)

The four major centers of Old World civilization that had been established by the year 1000—European Christendom, the Islamic world, India, and China—all underwent tremendous challenges from confederations of warlike Turkish and Mongol tribes in the next 500 years. By the end of the 15th century, Europe had already commenced its expansion to the Americas, to Africa and to southern Asia.

Expansion of the Muslim World: Asia and Africa

The Abbasid dynasty of caliphs of Baghdad had long employed Turkish auxiliaries (rather as the Romans had used German tribes) in their Near Eastern armies; one such army, under their chieftain Mahmud of Ghazni (r. 997–1030), moved out of Afghanistan into the Punjab about the year 1000 and by 1030 established a Muslim dynasty there. Over the next 200 years they spread their conquests over the Rajputs eastward into the plain of the Ganges, establishing their capital at Delhi about the year 1200. Many of the rich Hindu temples were plundered and destroyed by the invaders. Under the sultan of Delhi Ala-ud-din (r. 1296–1316) most of the subcontinent was brought under one rule for the first time since Asoka.

Unable to break the caste tradition, the ruling Turks became a casteless minority of warrior-aristocrats extracting heavy taxes but relying upon the Hindu princes for administration. Though the Hindu temples had been devastated, they were rebuilt, as the Muslim Turks had to permit a practical tolerance for Hinduism. After the death of Ala-ud-din his empire dissolved into a medley of warring kingdoms ruled by Muslim generals or Hindu princes over whom the sultans at Delhi exercised greater or lesser control.

In the "greater India" of Southeast Asia, Islamic influence expanded through trade and Chinese influence through trade and warfare. In Burma, the Buddhist kingdom founded by Anawrahta (r. 1044–77) was destroyed by the Mongol armies of Kublai Khan in 1287, and the land was divided into a number of small principalities. Dvaravati Siam (briefly annexed to Cambodia in the 11th century) was overrun by Thai tribesmen from southwestern China in the 13th century; by 1350 a Thai kingdom of Siam had established its capital at Ayutthaya (north of present-day Bangkok), which was to remain its capital until the end of the 18th century. Over the next century, Siam subdued the independent kingdom of Cambodia to the east and expanded against Burma as well. In the archipelago of Indonesia and curving north into the Philippines, Muslim traders and missionaries spread the Islamic faith. Over 20 Islamic states had been established through religious conversions of rulers by the year 1500, though many of the inhabitants of those states continued to follow indigenous religious beliefs. The Hindu aristoc racy of Java took refuge on the island of Bali, which still preserves elements of pre-Islamic Indonesian culture and where a unique form of Hinduism is still practiced.

Muslim expansion occurred in western Africa as well. The conquest of ancient Ghana by Muslim Berbers in 1076 (who had conquered Morocco 20 years earlier) led to a series of successor states. One of these, Kangaba, had by the 13th century established another trading state of immense size, the Kingdom of Mali, which stretched, in the 14th century, from the Atlantic coast eastward beyond Gao on the Niger. Under Mansa Musa (r. ca. 1312–37) Islam spread through the western savanna, the king himself making a pilgrimage to Mecca in 1324. Farther east, the king of the Songhay people on the great bend of the Niger had already converted to Islam in the 11th century; thus, when the dominance of Mali was replaced in the 15th century by the Kingdom of Songhay, Islam dominated not only the northern coast of Africa but almost the entire belt of savanna south of the Sahara as well.

Also in this period, Bantu-speaking peoples established polities in several parts of central, east, and southern Africa. On the Zimbabwe Plateau, Great Zimbabwe, the largest of some 300 stone complexes in the area, was built between the twelfth and fifteenth centuries. A capital city and trading center of the Kingdom of Makaranga, it may have had nearly 20,000 inhabitants at its height.

Transformation of the Muslim World: The Turks and the Fall of Byzantium Leaders of the Seljuk clan of Turks seized Afghanistan (1037) from the Turkish Muslim rulers of the Punjab, then expanded into Persia and Mesopotamia by 1055. After the battle of Manzikert (1071) the Seljuks took most of Asia Minor from Byzantium, and conquered Syria in 1084, creating an empire that stretched from Egypt to India and endured in some form until 1243. During the 12th century, in the aftermath of the First Crusade (1096–99), the Seljuk Empire dissolved in all but name, becoming a collection of small emirates ruled by princes or generals. The heirs to the Seljuks were another Turkish clan, the Ottomans. In 1326 they drove Byzantine forces entirely out of Asia Minor, thus beginning the Ottoman Empire (1326–1920). By century's end they controlled all of Asia Minor and the Balkans as far north as Bosnia. Half a century later (1453) they took Constantinople, turning Hagia Sophia into a mosque in their renamed capital of Istanbul.

The 11th century had been the apogee of the Eastern Roman Empire (Byzantium) as it conquered the Christian kingdom of Bulgaria (1018) and made Serbia a client state, while to the east Armenia and the Crimea were annexed (1022). But by mid-century the Normans, descendants of Vikings who settled in the French province of Normandy, were establishing themselves in Byzantine Italy (and Muslim Sicily). Furthermore, the battle of Manzikert, which left most of Asia Minor in the hands of the Seljuk Turks, proved a catastrophe from which the empire never recovered, losing both its granary and its military recruiting ground in a single blow. Although the first three crusades (1096–1192) were initially successful in wresting the Holy Land from Islam, the subsequent organization of the territory in the French pattern of small, squabbling and isolated feudal statelets rendered them impotent and hence of only marginal help to Byzantium.

The Fourth Crusade (1202–4) was a disaster, for the crusaders took Constantinople, establishing what is called the Latin Empire (1204–61). In 1261 Michael Palaeologus (1261–82) restored a rump Byzantine state along the shores of the Aegean, and it was against this enfeebled state that the Ottoman Turks expanded. The doom of Constantinople brought Turkish power right to the borders of Hungary, with the Balkans absorbed into the Ottoman Empire for 450 years. In the northeast it was not the Turks but the Mongols whose arrival transformed Christendom. Hungary, Poland, and Kievian Rus were weakened by dynastic struggles from the 11th century on, yet remained independent of the Holy Roman Empire to the west and the Turkish Cumans in the east.

The Mongol Empire (1200–1500) In Mongolia, a young orphan, Temujin (ca. 1162–1227), relied on his personal skills as a warrior, his charisma, his ruthlessness as a conqueror, and his organizational genius to create a great confederation of the Mongol tribes. He took the title Genghis Khan in 1206, and lay claim to leadership of all of the nomadic peoples of Asia—"all who live in felt tents." His confederation grew strong enough to strike at China, the Near East, and Europe at the same time, and his realm extended from Korea to the borders of Persia and Russia. The Mongol conquest of northern China (ruled at that time by Jurchen tribesmen from Manchuria) was completed by Genghis Khan's successors in 1234. The Mongols then turned their attention to Korea, which they conquered in 1231–36, and to the Chinese Song Dynasty in the Yangtze River Valley. The Song defended their territory vigorously, while the Mongols were slowed down as their horsemen learned to cope with wet rice-fields and rivers defended by heavily armed ships; but in 1271 Kublai Khan (1215–94), a grandson of Genghis Khan, proclaimed himself emperor of the Yuan Dynasty of China, and in 1279 the last Song emperor died at sea and the dynasty collapsed. During his reign Kublai Khan tried twice to invade Japan; his armies were defeated by Japan's samurai defenders. An attempt to conquer Java. 2,500 miles to the south, failed when the Mongols were betrayed and forced to withdraw. Nevertheless the expedition resulted in the decline of the Singhasari kingdom in Java and the emergence of the Majapahit Empire which dominated much of what is now Indonesia and the Malay Peninsula, including the growing spice trade, until the arrival of the Portuguese more than 200 years later.

Meanwhile, Mongol armies under another of Genghis Khan's grandsons, Batu (d. 1255), fell upon Europe (1237–40) and advanced beyond Russia into Poland and Hungary and the lands of the German knights on the Baltic. Europe was saved by the death of the Genghis Khan's son and successor, Ögödei Khan (r. 1229–41), which necessitated a khuraltai (conference) in Mongolia of all the Mongol chieftains to choose the next Great Khan. The Mongol armies withdrew from their campaigns in Europe while this conference was in progress. The outcome of the khuraltai was a division of the Mongol Empire into four sub-empires ruled by Genghis Khan's grandsons, which weakened and fragmented the great conqueror's legacy. Still, the "Golden Horde," Batu's Khanate on the lower Volga River, ruled all of south Russia and reduced the north Russian principalities to vassal status. Not until the late 15th century was the prince of Moscow powerful enough to refuse tribute money to the empire of the Golden Horde. Mongol rule in China endured until 1368, and the Ilkhanate of Persia, which converted to Islam, left its mark on Central Asia as well. The Khanate of Chagatai, in Turkestan, lasted until the mid-14th century.

Part of the Mongol Empire was reconstituted in the late 14th century by Timur Leng (ca. 1336–1405, known in Europe as Tamerlane), who claimed descent from Genghis Khan. Assembling a confederation of Turkish and Mongol tribes, Timur conquered much of Turkestan by 1369 and established his capital at Samarkand. Further campaigns brought most of Persia into Timur's empire by 1387, and in 1392 he extended his territory to include Mesopotamia and eastern Anatolia. A campaign in 1398 annexed northwestern India and put an end to the Delhi Sultanate. At his death in 1405 Timur was planning an invasion of China. His empire was divided among his sons, and though Samarkand became one of the greatest cities in the world in the early 15th century, the Timurid empire collapsed after the reign of Timur's grandson, Ulugh Beg (r. 1447–49). The last of the Timurids, Babur (1483–1530) founded the Mogul Dynasty in India.

The Rise of Western Christendom Western Christendom slowly emerged from the ruins of the western Roman Empire and the destruction wrought by barbarian invasions. The Christian conversion of Europe was essentially completed by 1050, as Scandinavia, Poland, and Hungary became Christian kingdoms. (The penetration of Christianity into the lives of the common people did not necessarily follow immediately from the conversion of kings and nobles.) Europe remained divided into feudal kingdoms and domains; its unity, such as it was, was more religious and cultural than political.

Whether the leadership of this society should fall to the popes or the Holy Roman Emperors was settled in the 11th century in the Investiture Struggle in which the papacy emerged victorious. From Pope Gregory VII (r. 1073–85) to Boniface VIII (r. 1294–1303) the papacy gave the lead to western Christendom, often in alliance with reforming monastic leaders. In the 12th and 13th centuries the characteristic Gothic architecture and sculpture of medieval

Europe (which succeeded the earlier Romanesque style) spread across Europe under church patronage while the Leagues of the Peace and the Crusades attempted to limit the warrior ethos of the feudal nobles or channel it to the Christian project of conquering the Holy Land.

In 1066 William of Normandy (ca. 1028–1087), thereafter known as the Conqueror, led an invading army to England, where he defeated the Saxon king Harold Godwinson (r. 1066) at the Battle of Hastings. England was thus transformed into a participant in the world of European monarchical power. The Domesday Book, surveying all of the territory under the control of the new rulers, was a landmark of royal administration. For two centuries the kings of England looked more to the Continent (in their continuing role as dukes of Normandy) than to the British Isles, while the French language made an indelible impact on vernacular English.

In 1215 King John (r. 1188–1216) was forced by his rebellious barons—a powerful and self-confident military aristocracy—to sign a treaty, later known as Magna Carta, that guaranteed aristocratic rights and made the king as much a subject of the law as his people. This event was part of a trend, beginning late in the 12th century in Spain and Italy, and continuing in the 13th century in Germany, England, and France and in the 14th and 15th centuries in Hungary, Poland, and Scandinavia, toward the creation of parliaments, as monarchs (often under political pressure) began to call the elected representatives of the towns to meet in formal sessions along with prelates and nobles to render advice to the throne. (This trend toward parliamentary government had been anticipated two centuries earlier in Iceland, where the althing representative assembly had been established in 930.)

Beginning in 11th-century Italy and 12th-century Netherlands, the commune movement, in which all the inhabitants of a town bound themselves by oath to obey their magistrates, keep the peace, and defend their liberties, revived town life and created the medieval city as a confederation of self-governing guilds. Guilds were associations of craftsmen of one trade or merchants bound together for mutual aid. Fairs held regularly in the towns of Western Europe both reflected and stimulated the reestablishment of trade, while in the Mediterranean, the Italian cities (especially Venice and Genoa) linked the West with Byzantium and the Muslim Near East. The Crusades, ironically, stimulated trade with the Muslim world, while the pax Mongolica reinvigorated trade along the Silk Route between China and Western Asia in the 13th century. (The celebrated journies to China of such missionaries, traders and geographers as William of Rubruck, Marco Polo, Odoric of Pordenone and Ibn Battuta from the mid-13th century on reflected the continued importance of this trade route.) The sea lanes from East Asia, the Spice Islands, and India brought Asian goods to the Persian Gulf and the Red Sea, thence overland to the cities of the Levant and on to Europe.

In the commercial and ecclesiastical towns of Europe, such as Paris, Bologna, Salerno, and Oxford, universities were founded where Greek and Arab learning met with the Christian traditions of the Carolingian schools. The classical philosophy of Aristotle was rethought in Christian terms and gave rise to the legal, philosophic, theological, and scientific work of scholasticism. Prominent 13th-century scholars such as Albertus Magnus, Thomas Aquinas, Bonaventure, Roger Bacon, and Duns Scotus were all members of the newly established religious orders, Franciscans (St. Francis, 1182–1226) and Dominicans (St. Dominic, 1170–1221). Committed to evangelical poverty and combating heresy, they played a role in university life as well.

The development of these social and cultural and religious institutions was accompanied by the first stirrings of European expansion. This was based in part on new economic initiatives, such as the clearing of forests and the cultivation of new farmland able to support an increased population. It also involved bringing peripheral territories firmly into the religious and political orbit of Europe, as with the reconquest of Spain from the Muslims (1085–1492), the conquest of Prussia and Livonia by the Teutonic Knights (1229–1466) and the conversion of Lithuania (1386 and after.

Poland attained its status as the largest state in Christendom with the marriage of its queen Jadwiga (r. 1384–99) to the Grand Duke Jagiello of Lithuania, who ruled as Wladislaw II (1386–1434). In the 15th century the Jagellon Dynasty (1386–1572) controlled the entire region between the Baltic and Black Seas. It was however in a precarious position, exposed to danger from the Teutonic Knights, Tatars, and Hungarians, as well as the Ottomans, Russians, and Swedes. The marriage of Ivan III "the Great" (r. 1462–1505) to the niece of the last Byzantine emperor established the czar's claim to imperial succession as he took the title "czar" (= Caesar or emperor); his conquest of the principality of Novgorod (1478) established a large Russian state northeast of Poland.

All aspects of the political, economic, and social life of

Western Europe were affected by the precipitous decline in population caused by the Black Death, an outbreak of bubonic plague that swept over Europe (1347–51), wiping out perhaps 25 million, a third of the population. The sudden demand for agricultural labor helped to do away with the old feudal structure of land use and gave rise to a tenant peasantry; new economic opportunities arose in cities and towns for those who survived the plague.

The loose unity of western Christendom began to alter in the 14th century in significant ways. First of all, the universality of the papacy was compromised when seven popes in succession (1305–78) preferred to reside at Avignon rather than Rome (the "Babylonian captivity"), in too close an association with the kings of France; then, after the return to Rome there arose a series of disputed elections to the papacy that is called the Great Schism (1378–1417); and finally, with the end of the schism, the popes became more and more involved in the politics of Renaissance Italy.

Meanwhile, while theories of sovereignty derived from the study of Roman law exalted the authorities of kings, royal powers disastrously declined due to chronic feudal violence: the "age of princes" in Germany (1273–1493), the Hundred Years' War in England and France (1337–1453), and the dynastic Wars of the Roses in England (1455–85). Out of the turmoil arose the "new monarchies" of more unified states: the Tudors in England (1485–1603), the Valois in France (1328–1529), and the Spanish branch of the Habsburgs (1504–1700).

In the Italy of the 14th and 15th centuries, increasingly at the mercy of the more powerful monarchical states to the north and west, there began the great cultural transformation known as the Renaissance. Humanists such as Petrarch (1304–74) and Boccaccio (1313–75) sought a revival of the ideals of Greek and Roman antiquity, both pagan (Cicero, Virgil, Tacitus) and Christian (Augustine and the other Church fathers), in an educational movement that sought to unite the values of Hellenism with Christianity. At the same time artists, studying Roman architecture and Hellenistic sculpture on the one hand and the new sciences of anatomy and perspective on the other, created a new visual aesthetic. Florence alone produced the genius of Botticelli and da Vinci in painting, Brunelleschi (1377–1446) in architecture, and Ghiberti (1378–1455) and Donatello (1386–1466) in sculpture; and other city-states had their own artistic geniuses to rival them.

Building on medieval foundations and new navigational discoveries (magnetic compasses, the astrolabe, the quadrant), Prince Henry "the Navigator" of Portugal (1394–1460) and his successors pursued a program of exploration of the coast of Africa, which ultimately led to the discovery of a direct sea route to India, Southeast Asia, and China. The Gulf of Guinea was reached by 1470, the Cape of Good Hope by 1487, and India by 1498. The Spanish monarchs sponsored the voyage of Christopher Columbus (1451–1506) in search of a westward route to the Orient. His three ships reached the Bahamas and inaugurated uninterrupted transatlantic traffic between the "old," known world of Eurasia and Africa and the "new," unknown world of the Americas. By the end of the 15th century Europe was launched on the period of maritime exploration and expansion that would bring much of the world under European rule over the next few centuries, and spread European ideas and technology around the globe.

The Americas At the end of the 15th century, the Americas were home to two great empires, the Aztec in Mexico and the Inca in Peru, as well as smaller states, tribes and communities of hunter-gatherers and village agriculturalists spread from the northern sub-Arctic region to Tierra de Fuego, the southern tip of South America. Contrary to Europeans' initial expectations, the Americas were neither unpopulated nor a trackless wilderness.

In the three centuries after the collapse of the Late Classical Mayan civilization around 900, the Toltec empire had expanded to include most of the old Mayan lands in Mexico and northern Central America. Its capital was in the magnificent temple city of Tula, not far from the old Zapotec city of Teotihuacán. The 12th and 13th centuries saw a series of incursions by diverse tribes known collectively as Chichimecs, whose armed might destroyed the Toltec civilization. One of these tribes, of obscure origins, was known first as the Mexica and later as the Aztec. Eventually rising to a dominant position, the Aztec established a capital at Tenochtitlán (now Mexico City), in the Valley of Mexico, and from about 1360 to about 1470 conquered neighboring peoples and constructed the sanguinary Aztec Empire (ca. 1360–1520). Montezuma I (r. 1440–69) was a ruthless conqueror but a great builder who transformed the capital into a magnificent city of stone. By 1500 the Aztec had expanded south to Guatemala. For their subject peoples the Aztec were a catastrophe, constantly in need of human sacrificial victims to offer to the sun god who required human blood for his nourishment.

Stretching for more than a thousand miles along the towering Andes Mountains that parallel the west coast of

South America lay the empire of the Inca with their capital at Cuzco. It was basically a highland empire, but it controlled contiguous lowland regions as well and traded with the forest peoples of the Amazon Basin to the east. The Inca Empire was a centralized bureaucratic state, assembled through military conquest and sustained by the religious vision of the Inca monarchy; it engaged in extensive road and bridge building and irrigation projects. Begun about 1200, the empire attained its greatest size under Huayna Capac (r. ca. 1493–1527).

China, Japan, and Korea (1300–1500) In China, the Mongols of the Yuan Dynasty (1279–1368) were seen as an alien occupying power; their habit of using foreign, Persian-speaking tax-collectors made them especially hated. The successors to Kublai Khan were mediocre rulers; in 1368 a Chinese nativist rebellion led by a charismatic ex-Buddhist monk named Zhu Yuanzhang succeeded in overthrowing the Mongols and establishing the Ming Dynasty (1368–1644). The early Ming emperors were vigorous and forward-looking; they rebuilt the Great Wall, rerouted the northern section of the Grand Canal to Beijing, built a new southern capital at Nanjing, and sent maritime expeditions on missions of explor-ation and diplomacy throughout the South China Sea and the Indian Ocean as far as Sri Lanka, and beyond, to the Persian Gulf, the Red Sea and the east coast of Africa. These expeditions, under Admiral Zheng He (ca. 1371–ca. 1433), were however abruptly terminated in 1433, criticized by the conservative Confucian bureaucracy as a waste of money and resources. Thus, the Chinese missed by only half a century the chance to confront the Portuguese as rival maritime powers in the Indian Ocean.

In Korea, the Koryo Dynasty did not long survive their Mongol patrons. The last Koryo king in 1388 sent his best general, Yi Songgye (ca. 1335–1408), already famous for his victories over Japanese pirates, to invade China to try to overthrow the Ming Dynasty on behalf of the Mongols. General Yi instead turned back at the border, overthrew the Koryo king, and established his own dynasty, the Kingdom of Choson, which soon proclaimed its support for the Ming emperors. The third Choson (or Yi Dynasty) ruler, King Sejong (r. 1418–50), was Korea's greatest sovereign, a patron of art, science, and technology during whose reign Korean scholars and craftsmen perfected printing with moveable metal type, invented a syllabic script to write vernacular Korean, and equipped Seoul with what was, for a time, the best astronomical observatory in the world. The Choson monarchs tolerated Buddhism, promoted Confucianism, ruled through a very conservative aristocracy, and remained on the throne until 1910.

In Japan, the Fujiwara-dominated aristocrats of Heian-kyo ignored the rise of a provincial warrior aristocracy in the provinces until it was too late. The Fujiwaras were ousted by the western Taira clan in 1160; they in turn were defeated by Minamoto no Yoritomo (1147–99) at the naval battle of Dan-no-Ura in 1185. Yoritomo then took the hereditary title of shogun ("supreme general"), and established a military capital at Kamakura, leaving the emperors to reign but not rule in Heian-kyo. The Minamoto were shunted aside by their own hereditary retainers, the Hojo Clan, in 1229. Amid an imperial succession crisis (1331–33), a general named Ashikaga Takauji (1305–58), overthrew the Hojo, proclaimed himself shogun, and moved the capital to the Muromachi district of Kyoto, putting the emperors firmly in their place once again. The Muromachi shogunate endured until 1568, though with little military power; the shoguns were better known as patrons of Zen Buddhism, Noh theater, and the tea ceremony. With the waning of central authority, Japanese merchants were more free to establish domestic and overseas trade routes which fostered economic prosperity amid political instability. While the Japanese were not major players in foreign trade, by the end of the 1500's there were Japanese merchant communities in ports throughout Asia, including the Philippines, Macao, Malacca, Java, Burma and Thailand.

European Expansion: The First Phase (1500–1650)

During this period, Ottoman Turkey, Safavid Persia, Mogul India, and Ming China remained traditional Asian empires, while a new dynamism infused the emerging nation-states of Europe. Although severe religious and political divisions led to incessant warfare within Europe, the major European powers managed to dominate the sea lanes of the globe and control the coasts and islands of Africa, southern Asia, and the Americas.

The Near East: Ottoman Empire and Safavid Persia Under their sultans Selim I the Grim (r. 1512–20) and Suleiman I the Magnificent (r. 1520–66) the Ottoman Turks added Syria and Egypt to their domains, then from their fortress at Belgrade launched an invasion of Hungary, which climaxed at the battle of Mohacs (1526). This brought three-quarters of the

Hungarian Empire under Turkish rule, either directly or through Ottoman client princes of Transylvania. The Turks moved on to besiege Vienna (1529), halting the campaign because of troubles with Persia in the east. Turkish fleets added the ports of Yemen and Aden on the Persian Gulf and Tripoli, Algeria, and Tunis on the southern shores of the Mediterranean to the Ottoman domain.

Suleiman's successor was Selim II "the Sot" (r. 1566–74), the first in a series of weak sultans who came to the throne between 1566 and 1718 as a result of harem intrigues of wives and eunuchs, and of the specifically Ottoman problem, an inability to prevent the sultans' guard troops, the Janissaries, from acting as a power unto themselves. Ottoman naval power suffered a temporary setback in 1571, when the Holy League (an alliance of the Papacy, Venice, Tuscany, and Spain) triumphed over the Turkish navy in the battle of Lepanto, off the coast of Italy. But the dissolution of the league after the victory meant that Ottoman seapower in the Mediterranean was only temporarily impaired.

In Persia, the native Iranian Safavid Dynasty (1501–1736) came to power. Its founder Shah Ismail seized power from the White Sheep Turks in 1501 and successfully defended Persia from Ottoman expansion into Mesopotamia, a work continued under his son and successor, Shah Tahmasp (r. 1524–76). Shah Abbas I "the Great" (r. 1587–1629) made his capital city of Isfahan into one of the great showplaces of Islamic architecture. The dynasty weakened after his reign, and Ottoman encroachments on Mesopotamia resumed; the Turks succeeded in taking Baghdad (1638).

In the meantime, the Portuguese had established a trading presence in the Persian Gulf at Hormuz in 1507. In 1622 the Portuguese were expelled by Shah Abbas, who invited English merchants to replace them.

Mogul India and the Spice Trade In 1526 Babur (1483–1530), a descendent of Timur Leng, who had already established himself as the ruler of Afghanistan, overthrew the Sultanate of Delhi and extended his dominance east of the Indus. Although Babur, like all the Timurids, was a Turk, because of the long association of his family with the Mongols, his empire came to be called the Mughal Empire (1526–1857; Mughal was a local variant pronunciation of Mongol). Babur then expanded east to the borders of Bengal. Although his son Humayun lost almost all Babur had conquered, his grandson Akbar (r. 1556–1605), contemporary of Philip II of Spain and Elizabeth of England, restored Babur's realm and expanded it further until it included all of India north of the Deccan Plateau highlands of central India. Akbar's empire was both peaceful and prosperous. Most of the Deccan region was added in the reign of his grandson Shah Jahan (r. 1628–58), who also built the Taj Mahal.

In 1497 the Portuguese navigator Vasco da Gama (ca. 1469–1524) began a voyage that took him around Africa's Cape of Good Hope and across the Indian Ocean to Calicut, a major trading entrepôt on the southwestern coast of India. The incentive for the Portuguese (and soon other European) voyages of the Age of Expansion was the trade in spices and other Asian commodities. The European appetite for spices was fueled for the obvious reason that spices make food taste better, as well as for their effectiveness as a preservative (cinnamon was used not only to flavor food, but as an embalming agent for the noble dead), but the idea that they were needed to cover up the taste of rotten food in the era before refrigeration is merely a myth. (No one rich enough to afford spices had to eat spoiled meat.) But spices, carried from the East Indies by Malay, Indian, and Arab ships to Hormuz on the Persian Gulf or Aden at the entrance to the Red Sea, and thence to Europe, became exorbitantly expensive as they passed through the hands of Levantine and Venetian middlemen; this provided ample incentive for western European monarchs to look for direct sea routes to India and the Spice Islands. East Asia became a goal of navigation as well, because the overland Silk Route trade with China had been seriously disrupted by the fall of Constantinople, one of the trade's main transshipment points, in 1453.

After da Gama's second voyage (1502), the Muslim state of Gujarat, allied with Mameluke Egypt, attempted to fend off the newcomers with military force, but at Diu, the Portuguese won a complete victory (1508). The Portuguese viceroy organized the building of a "rosary" of over a dozen forts stretching from Hormuz on the Persian Gulf through Goa to Malacca on the Malay Peninsula. Thus the Portuguese could monopolize the carrying trade in the Indian Ocean as well as divert the spice trade around Africa. From Malacca, captured in 1511, they established trading posts in the Spice Islands (Melaku), China, and Japan. This network provided the route for Christian missionaries as well.

During the 16th century the Portuguese assumed a dominant role in Europe's trade with China and Japan from their trading colony at Macao, on the southeastern coast of China, established in 1557. But Portugal's early near-monopoly on European shipping in Asia was soon challenged. The Spanish conquered the Philippines in a series of campaigns in the mid-16th century, and established a trans-Pacific trade route between Acapulco in New Spain (Mexico) and Manila. The English and the Dutch established their East India Companies in 1600 and 1602, respectively, and in the 17th century the Dutch gradually supplanted the Portuguese in Asia through a combination of war and diplomacy. By 1639 the English were at Madras (now Chennai), the first step in their long involvement with the Indian subcontinent.

East Asia: China, Korea, Japan The late Ming emperors were great patrons of culture, but mediocre rulers. After China's abandonment of long-range ocean voyages in 1433, and the adoption of an inward-looking policy of isolationism, China gradually began a long period of decline as a great power.

Annam, which had briefly (1407–28) been reconquered by China under the vigorous third emperor of the Ming dynasty, in 1558 split into two monarchies, with the Trinh dynasty ruling the kingdom of Tonkin (northern Vietnam) from Hanoi, and the Nguyen dynasty ruling the kingdom of Annam (central Vietnam) from its capital at Hue. The Hindu kingdom of Champa, in southernmost Vietnam, was continually under pressure from the rulers of Annam but retained its independent existence until the mid-17th century, when its last vestiges were absorbed by its northern neighbor.

The danger to China from Mongolia, from where Altan Khan (r. 1543–1583) raided almost annually across the Great Wall, was kept in check by adroit Ming diplomacy, and further allayed by the Mongol acceptance of Tibetan religious authority; with the spread of Lamaism, monasteries absorbed surplus sons who might otherwise have become warriors. But in the northeast, descendants of the 12th-century Jurchen rulers of the Jin Dynasty were forming a new tribal confederation of people who would become known as Manchus. Their chieftain, Nurhachi (r. 1586–1626), took the title of emperor; his son Alatai (d. 1643, also known as Hong Taiji) brought all of Mongolia under his rule, overran Korea in 1627, and took the northeastern Ming outpost of Mukden in 1636.

Within China, a combination of rising imperial expenditures and increasing land tax evasion by the rural gentry eventually destabilized even so rich an empire as the Ming. Factionalism and eunuch intrigues in the capital weakened the dynasty further; popular rebellions broke out and were not thoroughly suppressed. In desperation, the last Ming emperor invited a Manchu army to Beijing to expel a rebel band that had seized the city. Having expelled the rebels, the Manchus refused to leave. The Ming emperor hanged himself, and the Manchus proclaimed the founding of the Qing Dynasty (1644–1911). Ming resistance in southern China was quashed by 1661; all Chinese men were required to braid their hair in a queue as a sign of submission.

During the last decades of the Ming, China began to feel the first effects of European influence. The Jesuit missionary Matteo Ricci (1552–1610) reached Macao in 1582 and Beijing in 1601. Adapting himself to local custom, he became an accomplished Confucian scholar and used that guise as a means of introducing to China such things as the astrolabe, the weight-driven clock, prisms, and the Mercator map of the world. For a brief time Christianity became a vogue among some members of the mandarin class, but imperial disapproval (exacerbated by factional disputes among the Christian missionary orders) discouraged conversions. Under Qing rule the Jesuits were prohibited from preaching, but allowed to remain in China for their technical skills in astronomy, mathematics, painting, and cannon making.

In Korea, the Choson Kingdom was badly shaken by a destructive invasion (1592–98) from Japan. The invasion was finally repelled with Chinese aid, but Korea suffered long-term economic and social damage during the six years of guerrilla warfare and occupation by Japanese and Chinese armies. Conquered by the Manchus in 1627, the Koreans had no difficulty in transferring their loyalty from the Ming to the Qing; Choson remained a loyal vassal of China, and isolated from the rest of the world, until the late 19th century.

Japan borrowed the old Chinese term "Warring States Period" to describe the century from 1467 to 1568, when Muromachi rule dissolved in a welter of mutually hostile feudal domains. Order was gradually restored after 1568 by three remarkable generals: Oda Nobunaga (1534–1582), who was the first Japanese general to use firearms extensively in battle; Toyotomi Hideyoshi (1537–1598), a peasant who rose to rule Japan, only to squander his resources in the fruitless invasion of Korea; and Tokugawa Ieyasu (1543–1616), who defeated a coalition of enemies at the Battle of Sekigahara (near the modern city of Nagoya) in 1600 and established the Tokugawa shogunate, military rulers of Japan until 1868. The Tokugawa period is sometimes known as the Edo Period, after its capital (now Tokyo).

Japan readily absorbed European influence in the sixteenth century. The Portuguese arrived as traders in 1543; another Jesuit, Francis Xavier (1506–52) began his mission to the Japanese in 1549. By the end of the century the number of Catholic converts, including some members of the high military aristocracy, peaked at about 300,000. Thereafter Hideyoshi began to suppress Christianity as a foreign threat, banishing Portuguese missionaries in 1587. The Tokugawa shoguns persecuted Christianity even more fiercely, executing thousands after 1612 and driving the church underground after the Christian Shimabara Uprising of 1637–38 ended in an appalling slaughter. Thereafter no foreigners were allowed in Japan except for a small number of Dutch traders, who were rigorously confined to an island in Nagasaki harbor.

The European Impact on Africa, 1500–1650

The expansion of Portuguese sea power to the African coast profoundly changed Europe's relations with Africa. Earlier Portuguese traders had brought cotton goods and metal manufactures to exchange for ivory and gold as far as the delta of the Niger river. Further south, at the mouth of the Congo, a Bantu-speaking Christian state developed under Portuguese influence after 1483. These early contacts were supplanted by the rapid growth of the slave trade, as the new world of the Americas provided a large market for traffic in human beings. The Portuguese dominated the slave trade to Brazil and New Spain until the Dutch drove them out of the Gold Coast in 1642. African slavery, once an incidental result of tribal warfare, now became a cause of warfare and social dislocation throughout West Africa. First the Portuguese, then the Dutch, English and others encouraged states along the west coast to provide them with captives to be sold as slaves in the Americas.

The trading Kingdom of Songhay, which reached its greatest extent under Askia Mohammed II (r. 1531–37) and Askia Dawud (r. 1549–82), was smashed by a Moroccan invasion in 1591. The fall of Songhay brought decline farther east to the Kingdom of Kanem (Bornu) in the savanna surrounding Lake Chad after 1617. The paradoxical result was the decline of Islamic influence, for with the destruction of the Muslim towns, trade on the old caravan routes across the Sahara dwindled. Farther south, the Portuguese established themselves in southeast Africa in Mozambique (1507), and southwest Africa in Angola (1574). The Dutch established a trading colony at Capetown, at Africa's southern tip, in 1652.

The Americas: Europe's New Provinces

The Treaty of Tordesillas (1494) between Spain and Portugal divided the world by a line 370 leagues west of the Azores (approximately 45°W), establishing monopolies for Spain westward and Portugal eastward of the line. Thus Brazil, first explored separately in 1500 by Vicente Yáñez Pinzón (a veteran of Columbus's 1492 voyage) and Pedro Cabral (ca. 1467–ca. 1520), became Portuguese territory. But it was not immediately clear to Portugal and Spain what to do with their conquests in the Americas. It was increasingly obvious that the New World was not part of Asia, but rather a barrier to reaching Asia by a westbound sea route.

The picture changed entirely in the years 1519–22. In 1520, Ferdinand Magellan (ca. 1480–1521) sailed around the southern tip of South America, bringing the Spanish to the Philippines and the Moluccas across the Pacific. Then in 1521, the conquistador (conqueror) Hernando Cortés (1485–1547) conquered the Aztec Empire. When Francisco Pizarro (1476–1541) toppled the Inca Empire in 1533, Spain acquired a stupendous world empire, the wealth of whose silver mines dwarfed the riches of the Indies.

Organized into two vice-royalties, the Spanish Empire granted *encomiendas* (plantations) to the conquerors; although enslavement of the Indians was forbidden, the Spanish reduced them to serflike status and forced them to work for their new lords. Christian missions were immediately established with such success that more than 20 bishoprics had been created by the mid-16th century. Five universities were flourishing by the middle of the 17th century.

Despite the restrictions of the Treaty of Tordesillas, the new Tudor monarchy of England financed John Cabot's (ca. 1450–ca. 1499) search for a Northwest Passage to the Orient, which took him as far as Newfoundland in 1497; he disappeared on his second voyage. France also sent exploratory ventures to America led by Giovanni da Verrazano (ca. 1485–ca. 1528) in 1524 and Jacques Cartier (1491–1557) in 1534; but it was not until the 17th century that a permanent settlement was established by Samuel de Champlain (1567–1635), who founded New France (1608) with a capital at Quebec on the St. Lawrence River. Missions began in 1615, but the process of christianizing the Indians met with limited success. After 1642, Montreal grew up around the Indian village of Hochelaga, 150 miles farther up the St. Lawrence River from Quebec, and grew into a center of the fur trade on which the economy of New France was based.

Earlier the French had also begun colonizing the

Lesser Antilles, on the fringe of the Spanish Empire, and by 1656 they controlled a dozen of these islands. In a scramble for Caribbean possessions, the Dutch also colonized several of the Antilles Islands, and the English in 1627 settled Barbados, soon establishing a sugar-plantation economy that became a spectacular source of wealth.

England's Queen Elizabeth (1558–1603) did not undertake any large-scale projects of exploration and colonization, but she did encourage courtiers such as Sir Humphrey Gilbert (ca. 1539–83) and Sir Walter Raleigh (1554–1618) in their early, ill-fated attempts at settlement (Roanoke Island, 1585) in North America. She also authorized Sir Francis Drake (1540–96), Sir John Hawkins (1532–95), and other adventurers in their plundering Spanish ships, and she apparently gave Drake her tacit support of his circumnavigation of the globe (1577–80). The rich fisheries off the coast of New England and the Canadian maritime provinces attracted fishermen from many parts of Western Europe long before actual settlements were established. Not until the Stuart Dynasty (1603–49) did English settlement begin in earnest. Henry Hudson, backed by various patrons, made several attempts to find a northern passage from Europe to Asia in 1607–11, during which he explored much of the northern coast of North America. Through grants to commercial companies and individual proprietors, the English established colonies from the Chesapeake to Maine broken only by the Swedes on the lower Delaware River and the Dutch in the Hudson Valley; the Dutch colony of New Amsterdam was established in 1624 and seized by the English in 1664. Chesapeake Bay became the center of a thriving agricultural region based upon tobacco, while New England flourished as a haven for the English Calvinists known as Puritans.

Europe in the Age of the Reformation Throughout the 15th century, leading members of the Catholic Church had called for reform of the clergy, who often led scandalous lives amid great wealth. The sale of God's forgiveness (indulgences) to raise cash for the rebuilding of Rome as a splendid Renaissance city struck some critics as a particular outrage. But not even the powerful voices of the Dutch humanist Desiderius Erasmus (1466–1536) or the English statesman Sir Thomas More (1478–1535) had any impact.

In 1517 the call of the Augustinian monk Martin Luther (1483–1546) for a cleansing of the church swept across northern Germany; the adherence of the Scandinavian monarchies to the new faith made the Baltic almost a Lutheran lake. Luther's assertion that "the just shall live by faith alone" implied that the established priesthood of the Catholic Church and priestly administration of the sacraments by priests were unnecessary for the salvation of believers; Luther's Reformation thus involved fundamental doctrinal issues as well as proposals for secular reform. The English king Henry VIII (1509–47), while anti-Lutheran, severed his realm from the Catholic Church after 1532. Most influential in consolidating the Reformation was John Calvin (1509–64) who, from 1541 until his death, made Geneva a theocratic state, from which Calvinism spread to France, the Low Countries, and the British Isles.

The attempts of the Holy Roman Emperor Charles V (r. 1519–56) to halt the spread of the Reformation were hampered by his need to retain the support of the Lutheran princes in the struggle against the Ottoman Turks and to maintain his dynastic territories against the kings of France, who allied with the Turks against him. Charles V was ruler of the Netherlands and Spain in addition to being the Holy Roman Emperor. At his abdication he divided his inheritance between his brother Ferdinand (r. 1558–64) who received the Holy Roman Empire along with Habsburg holdings in central Europe, and his son Philip II (r. 1556–98), who inherited Spain with its empire both in the New World and Europe, including the Netherlands, Burgundy, Milan, and Naples.

Philip faced rebellion in the Netherlands, and by the end of his reign the northern provinces had all but won their independence. His armada (1588) against England met with disaster, thereby strengthening Queen Elizabeth's rule and the triumph of Protestantism in both England and Scotland. France was badly damaged by the Wars of Religion (1562–98) in which Philip ineffectively intervened on the Catholic side against the Calvinists. The upshot was victory for the Calvinist claimant Henry IV (1589–1610), who embraced Catholicism when he came to the throne but also issued the Edict of Nantes (1598) granting toleration to French Calvinists (Huguenots).

The Counter-Reformation, with the support of Philip II, led a great renewal within the Catholic Church. Spanish religious leadership was exemplified by Ignatius Loyola (1491–1556), who in 1540 founded the Jesuit Order, a fertile source of missionaries, preachers, scholars, and schoolmasters, as well as by the great mystic theologians Theresa of Avila and John of the Cross. Institutionally, the Council of Trent (1545–63) failed to heal the breach with the Protestants but did manage to reform the most glaring abuses in the church and provide an authoritative expression of Catholic belief.

Germany and the Hapsburg Empire were devastated by the Thirty Years' War (1618–48) in which the triumph of the Catholic Habsburgs was prevented by the interventions of Lutheran Sweden, under Gustavus II Adolphus (r. 1611–32) and Catholic France, under the effective leadership of Cardinal Richelieu (Louis XIII chief minister, 1628–42). Britain was shaken by the religious struggle between Anglicans and Puritans, reflected in the political struggle between the Stuart kings and Parliament. This clash resulted in the English Civil Wars (1642–49), in which the victory of the Puritan forces led to the execution of Charles I (r. 1625–49) and the establishment of a military dictatorship under Oliver Cromwell (1649–58).

In Russia during the long reign of Ivan IV the Terrible (r. 1533–84), the entire Volga came under Russian rule and expansion began beyond the Ural Mountains. After Ivan's death the monarchy was weakened by a succession struggle, settled when the national assembly in 1613 elected as czar Michael Romanov (r. 1613–45), founder of the Romanov Dynasty (1613–1917).

In Poland, Sigismund II (r. 1548–72) halted the spread of the Reformation and joined Lithuania and Poland into a single state (1569). But Sigismund was the last of the Jagellonian dynasty and after his death the monarchy became the plaything of other great powers. From 1587 to 1648 two members of the Catholic branch of Sweden's royal family, the Vasas, ruled in Poland.

In 1543 Andreas Vesalius (1514–64) published his great work on anatomy, the first step in the creation of a modern science of medicine. Also in 1543 a Polish priest, Copernicus (1473–1543), published his heliocentric theory of the cosmos, one of the key works of the Scientific Revolution. The process of overturning the old Ptolemaic geocentric cosmology continued with the observational work of the Dane, Tycho Brahe (1546–1601) and the theoretical insights of his scientific heir, the German Johannes Kepler (1571–1630). The movement reached its first climax in the system of the Italian Galileo (1564–1642), the greatest scientist of the age.

The period between 1500 and 1650 was an age of the great flowering of the vernacular literatures of Europe, especially in epic poetry and drama: in England, Edmund Spenser (ca. 1553–99) and William Shakespeare (1564–1616); in Italy, Ludovico Ariosto (1474–1533) and Torquato Tasso (1544–95); in Spain, Miguel de Cervantes (1547–1616), Lope de Vega (1562–1635), and Rodrigo Calderón (ca. 1576–1621); in Portugal, Luíz Vaz de Camoëns (ca. 1524–80). This turbulent age also saw the magnificent flowering of the visual and plastic arts, for example in the work of the painter and sculptor Michelangelo (1475–1564), the sculptor Bernini (1598–1680), and the painters Raphael, Titian (ca. 1490–1576), El Greco (ca. 1541–1614), Velázquez (1599–1660), Rubens (1577–1640), and Rembrandt (1606–69).

Expansion of the European World Hegemony (1650–1815)

In the century and a half after the Thirty Years' War, France dominated Europe both politically and culturally. In the Americas, European colonies matured, with the British dominating North America (though challenged by the French in the St. Lawrence and Mississippi valleys) and the Spanish controlling Mexico and Central America, much of the Caribbean, and South America. In Africa and the Middle East, Western influence grew primarily through trade, an increasing proportion of which was controlled by Britain. In Eurasia, Russia and China acquired huge land empires. In South Asia, British control of India evolved slowly, while the Dutch built a colonial empire in the vast archipelago now known as Indonesia.

Europe in Enlightenment and Revolution Partly in response to the religious controversies of the previous era, there had arisen the philosophical movement known as rationalism, which sought to reconstruct philosophy on the basis of "clear and distinct ideas" (René Descartes, 1596–1650). The Scientific Revolution reached a climax in the achievement of Isaac Newton (1642–1727), whose *Principia Mathematica* (1687) expressed in precise mathematical terms such key ideas as inertia, acceleration, the conservation of energy, and the force of gravity. Newton's commitment to scientific rigor built on the work of such earlier figures as Erasmus and Francis Bacon (1541–1626), and was spurred by competition with contemporaries such as Gottfried Leibniz (1646–1716).

The three streams of political philosophy, rationalism, and scientific reasoning flowed together in the movement known as the Enlightenment, whose adherents sought to understand the world in rational terms without appeal to traditional authority, whether of the divine right of rulers or religious doctrine. The Enlightenment contended that the world could be understood in purely rational terms, and that knowledge of the universe could be put to use for the benefit of humankind; this attitude lay behind the early mechanical and scientific discoveries that led to the Industrial Revolution, first in Britain and later in continental Europe and North America. Nevertheless, the era of the Enlightenment also remained an age of class privilege, economic inequity, and wealth derived from slavery and exploitation.

Louis XIV (r. 1661–1715) was an absolute monarch whose court at Versailles became the model for sovereigns across Europe, establishing a French cultural dominance backed by significant political and military power. In a series of four wars the "Sun King" expanded France's frontiers to the Rhine and his Bourbon dynasty to the throne of Spain. It took alliances of almost all Europe, organized principally by the Dutch stadtholder William III of Orange (r. 1672–1702), to limit his gains. Louis XIV's revocation of the Edict of Nantes (1685) forced the Protestant Huguenots to leave France for Holland, Britain, and Prussia, where they became industrious businessmen and artisans; through their dominance of publishing, especially, they contributed to the spread of the Enlightenment.

In England, the largely Protestant aristocracy, never comfortable with the Catholic faith of the restored Stuarts, drove James II (r. 1685–88) from his throne and invited William III of Orange (related by marriage to English royalty) to reign in his place as William III of England. This event is known as the Glorious Revolution; and it turned England essentially into an aristocratic republic dominated by Parliament, with an unwritten "constitution" that progressively limited the powers of the British monarchy.

In eastern Europe, the age of Louis XIV saw the decline of Polish and Ottoman power and the rise to dominance of Prussia and Russia in the Baltic region and the new Habsburg Empire to the southeast. With the Spanish Habsburgs sliding toward extinction and the Holy Roman Empire virtually obsolete by the Thirty Years' War, the Austrian Habsburgs drove the Ottomans out of Croatia and Hungary (1699) and took Galicia from Poland (1772). Meanwhile, the War of the Spanish Succession (1702–13) which established the Bourbons on the throne of Spain also detached from Spain its holdings in the Spanish Netherlands (roughly modern Belgium) and northern Italy (Milan and Tuscany), awarding both to the Austrian Habsburgs. The heart of Catholic Baroque culture in art and architecture and music, Austria became in the reign of Joseph II (1765–80) the seat of an enlightened despotism as well.

Brandenburg excelled in switching alliances: Frederick William "the Great Elector" (r. 1640–88) gained sovereignty in the Duchy of Prussia from Poland (1660); thus the Hohenzollern dynasty's holdings are usually called Prussia. Under Frederick II "the Great" (r. 1740–86), friend and patron of the French writer Voltaire (1694–1788), Prussia snatched Silesia from the Habsburgs (1748). Participating in the partitions of Poland (1772, 1793, 1795) the Hohenzollerns again doubled the size of their dynastic holdings.

The Seven Years' War (1756–63) was fought on three continents. In the European theater the alliances (Great Britain and Prussia against France, Austria, and Russia) fought to a draw; the war was won by the British overseas. In North America (where it was called the French and Indian War) and India, the British drove out the French and established their hegemony over the areas that had been under French control.

Great Britain and North America Between the crises of the Cromwellian period (1643–60) and the Glorious Revolution (1688) the Stuart kings of England fostered new proprietary grants in the Hudson Valley, in Pennsylvania, and in the Carolinas. Thereafter, the North American colonies became habituated to self-government under their elected assemblies in a period, from the late 1600's to the 1760's, when the home government paid relatively little attention to them. Legally colonies, they became something more like provinces of Great Britain overseas. The Seven Years' War in North America was hard fought, and the death in victory of General Wolfe at the Battle of the Plains of Abraham (near Quebec, 1759) became a rallying point of British colonial sentiment. The war ended with Great Britain realizing nearly all of its objectives, the most important of which was that French Canada came under British rule. When in the aftermath of the war the British government attempted organize its vast new North American holdings (in the "new imperial system"), the old coastal colonies were provoked into rebellion. Their grievances included British efforts to limit settlement beyond the Appalachians, to tax the colonists for the costs of administering the enlarged British holdings, and British appeasement of religious and other grievances of the culturally French portions of Canada. Colonial resistance to these British policies led to rebellion.

The publication of the Declaration of Independence (July 4, 1776) initiated a war that the British found impossible to win in the face of a highly motivated colonial populace supported by French military and financial assistance. The American Revolution was primarily a war for self-government; it did not produce immediate revolutionary social changes in the former colonies, though it did result in the replacement of a monarchy by a republic. The independence of the United States of America was recognized in the Peace of Paris (1783). (For North American developments afterward, see "History of the United States.")

The French Revolution and the Napoleonic Wars

France was the most prosperous state in Europe, but the long series of wars since 1660 combined with the clergy's and the aristocracy's exemption from taxation impoverished the monarchy. As a way out of the impasse, Louis XVI resurrected the old medieval Estates General (1789) in the hope of reaching consensus on reform measures. But the representatives transformed themselves into a constitutional convention called the National Assembly. After abolishing the feudal privileges of the aristocracy, they remodeled the French state into a constitutional monarchy, inspired to some extent by the recent experience of the United States. But they also confiscated church lands, dissolved the monasteries, and attempted to make the church a department of the state, thus alienating many Catholics.

The widespread appeal of the French Revolution to people across Europe frightened the monarchs and encouraged the National Assembly to declare war on them all. The new mass armies of the French, fired by ideology and national pride, easily outmatched the old-fashioned armies of the monarchical states. At home, the war emergency and a revolt in a pro-royalist area (the Vendée) against the newly declared republic were used to justify a Committee of Public Safety led by Georges Danton (1759–94) and Maximilien Robespierre (1758–94). This committee quickly instituted a Reign of Terror (1793–94), marked by guillotine executions of thousands of aristocrats and "enemies of the revolution," beginning with the royal family, including Louis XVI and his wife, Marie Antoinette. The rule of the Directory (1795–99) that followed was overturned by its most daring and charismatic general, the Corsican adventurer and military genius Napoleon Bonaparte (1769–1821), who established a popular and military dictatorship (1799) first in the guise of a republic, then as the French Empire (1804–15).

Several coalitions of nations were formed to stop Napoleon, but he defeated all of them. At its peak, the empire dominated all of Europe from the English Channel to the Ottoman Empire, incorporating some former states into the empire, or turning others into satellites, or enlisting them as allies. But a popular uprising in Spain, supported by Britain, and the catastrophic failure of Napoleon's invasion of Russia (1812) began the crumbling of his empire. By 1814 the anti-French nationalisms that conquest had evoked and the recovery of the monarchs' courage brought Napoleon to defeat, and he was exiled to the Mediterranean island of Elba. When he escaped and returned to France in 1815, initially to a warm welcome from much of the French populace, he resumed his military campaigns but suffered his final defeat at Waterloo (1815) at the hands of the first duke of Wellington (1769–1852). Napoleon was exiled again to the remote island of St. Helena, in the south Atlantic, for the rest of his life.

At the time of the French Revolution, a revolution in European agriculture and industry was also under way, particularly in Great Britain. Landowners were enclosing the commons (the village lands tenant farmers used to graze cattle) and developing new crops, such as the white potato (originally from South America). This produced real gains in agricultural productivity, but also serious agrarian unemployment. Surplus rural workers migrated to the burgeoning cities, where inventors were creating the machinery (the spinning jenny, the waterframe, and the steam engine) that launched the Industrial Revolution. Thus an industrial workforce was born.

Spain, Portugal, and the Americas The Spanish New World colonies, with new viceroyalties of New Granada (1717; roughly modern Venezuela, Colombia, and Ecuador) and La Plata (1776; Bolivia, Paraguay, Uruguay, and Argentina) were governed paternalistically by the king of Spain, in whose name all regulations were sent to the viceroys. After about 1650 the Indian populations of the viceroyalties recovered rapidly from the disasters of the conquest period. While rule remained in the hands of "peninsulares" from the home country and, to a lesser degree, of "creoles" (colonists of Spanish descent), in the towns, the Indians' chief contact with Spanish culture was through church missionaries and bishops who constituted a spiritual elite. Brazil prospered as a Portuguese colony and by 1800 had a population larger than that of Portugal itself.

To the viceroyalty of New Spain (Mexico) was attached the Philippines. No one was sure where in the Pacific lay the treaty line of 1494 so that while the Philippines were in fact on the Portuguese side, it was Spain that claimed them in 1565, founding Manila in 1571, which became the western terminus for the famous "Manila galleon" trade in

Mexican silver and Chinese silk and porcelain. In the course of the 17th and 18th centuries, voyages of English, Dutch, and Spanish mariners discovered the islands of the South Pacific: the Carolines, the Marshalls, Tasmania, New Zealand, and Australia; but before the late 18th century, no settlements of European colonists disturbed their original inhabitants.

Europe and Africa In Africa, the slave trade continued, peaking in the 1780's but with demand dropping decade by decade thereafter. In the early years of the 19th century, Britain, Denmark, and the United States abolished the trade, Britain actively but not always effectively trying to block the trade (still carried on by several other nations) along the African coast. In west Africa, there was an Islamic revival in the savanna as the Fulbe people, over the century after 1670, spread eastward toward Lake Chad in a series of campaigns against Hausa cities.

In the late 1700's, the Zulu nation of southern Africa employed trained infantry units armed with spears to establish a small empire over their neighbors, who still relied on the hurling of javelins. Near the southern tip of the continent, at the Cape of Good Hope, with its Mediterranean climate and its sparse indigenous population of Khoikhoi hunter-gatherers, the Dutch built a Dutch-speaking, Calvinist colony that by 1815 had a population of about 80,000. The pioneering *trekboers* who founded agrarian settlements beyond the Cape found their expansion limited by the resistance of the Xhosa people, and when the colony passed from the Dutch to the British (1814), British governors attempted to halt the expansion in the name of peace. In East Africa, trade reached inland as far as Lake Victoria. This was in the hands of the Nyamwezi people of Tanzania until after 1800 when it was absorbed into the trade network of Oman, an ally of Britain.

The Russian Empire While in one aspect the development of the Russian Empire was an eastward expansion of Europe, in another it was the creation of a huge Eurasian state menacing Europe. Russian pioneers had already reached the Pacific by 1637; expansion into Central Asia brought the Russians up against Chinese expansion westward into the same region. Peace was established in 1689 by the Treaty of Nerchinsk, which set the boundary along the peaks of the Stanovoi Mountains north of the great bend of the Amur River; the Russians evacuated a fort they had constructed on the Amur. This shifted Russian interests farther to the northeast, leading eventually to Russian settlements on the west coast of North America from Alaska to California (1805–1912).

Peter the Great (1689–1725) presided over a revolution from above that autocratically imposed upon his land western modes of manufacturing, political administration, military techniques, court manners, and dress. Russia had already taken eastern Ukraine including Kiev from Poland (1667), and in 1681 they added the portion that their allies the Ottomans had won in the same war. Peter's attempts to gain Azov—the warm-water port on the Black Sea that offered access to the Mediterranean—from the Ottoman Empire proved ineffectual. But in the Great Northern War against Sweden (1700–21), he proved more successful, establishing Russia on the Baltic and founding a new capital at St. Petersburg.

Under Catherine II "the Great" (r. 1762–96), Russia fought a war with the Ottoman Empire and achieved most of the objectives that Peter the Great had attempted a century earlier. The Treaty of Kuchuk Kainarji (1774) established Russia in the Crimea along the north of the Black Sea, granted navigation rights to Russia in Turkish waters, including the Bosporus and Dardanelles Straits into the Mediterranean, and provided a legal basis for Russia to intervene to protect Orthodox Christians in the provinces of Moldavia and Walachia. Catherine also participated in the partitions of Poland (1772, 1793, 1795), which obliterated that ancient state.

In a third stage of expansion during the Napoleonic Wars, Russia took Finland (1809) from Sweden and Bessarabia (1812) from the Ottomans. After repulsing Napoleon's 1812 invasion, Czar Alexander I (r. 1801–25) participated in the great coalition that at last brought Napoleon down, and in 1815 Russian troops participated in the occupation of Paris. Under terms laid down at the Congress of Vienna, central Poland was reconstituted as a nominally independent kingdom, but in a "personal alliance" with the Russian throne and Alexander as its king.

The Ottoman Empire in Decline The Russian ascendancy was paralleled by Ottoman decline. Of the dozen sultans who ruled between 1648 and 1839 only Selim III (r. 1789–1807) was a man of intelligence and vigor. The period began with misleading signs of strength, as the Turks took Podolia from Poland (1672) and advanced against the Habsburgs, a campaign that culminated in the siege of Vienna (1683). The failure of the siege proved the start of a long slow sag in Ottoman fortunes that made it by the 19th century "the sick man of Europe." Facing war after war against Austria and Russia (often in tandem) in the west and Persia in the east, the empire yielded territory, strained its finances, and developed a defensive mentality. Its domestic power waned as well as frontier garrisons meant for defense had to be used to suppress rebellions and endemic banditry.

The year after the siege of Vienna was lifted, the Austrians were victorious in the second Battle of Mohacs (1684), and they were victorious again in the Battle of Zenta (1697); as a result, Hungary and Croatia were detached from Ottoman control. After the Treaty of Kuchuk Kainarji, the Black Sea was no longer a Turkish lake and Russian ships sailed freely through Ottoman waters. Egypt, temporarily independent in 1769, gained its autonomy in 1805, while Serbia became the first Christian Balkan state to gain autonomy. Even Arabia, the original homeland of Islam, slipped from Ottoman rule as the Saud clan provided political and economic support for the puritanical and fundamentalist Wahhabi movement, which sought a return to the theocracy of the original Islamic vision. The Saud clan controlled most of Arabia by the end of the 18th century, but the Egyptians defeated and overthrew them in a series of military campaigns (1811–19) and they remained out of power for most of the 19th century.

The Growth of British Influence in the Middle East and India With the Portuguese control of the Indian Ocean trade routes eclipsed by Dutch and British competitors, and the Dutch concentrating their colonial efforts on the Malay Archipelago and the Spice Islands, British commercial interests grew ascendant in India. Bombay became the headquarters of the East India Company (1661) from which Calcutta was founded (1690). But British gains in India were not uncontested: the French founded their East India Company in 1664 and established a trading post at Pondicherry in 1674. The British gains in India compensated for the declining importance of their trade interests in Safavid Persia.

In the long reign of Aurangzeb (1659–1707), the Mughal empire had reached its greatest territorial extent, principally through conquests in the Deccan plateau in south-central India. But within the empire his rule was weak as local governors grew increasingly independent. The Maratha people of west-central India, under Raja Sivadi, established an independent Hindu state against which the emperor waged inconclusive war until his death. In the Punjab, in northwestern India, the Sikhs—followers of a religion founded by Guru Nanakh (ca. 1469–1539)—became dominant under the militant leadership of Govind Singh.

After Aurangzeb's death Mogul decline became precipitous. The Maratha state became the dominant Indian power, collecting taxes in southern India from 1720 onward. Nadir Shah's invasion (1738) wrested northwestern India from the Moguls, who were unable to reassert control after Nadir Shah's death. In the turmoil the European East India companies began forming private armies of Indian troops ("sepoys") under European officers. After the War of the Austrian Succession (1746–48) French forces ruled virtually the entire south. But in the Indian theater of the Seven Years' War (1756–63), Robert Clive (1725–1774) roundly defeated the French; the Treaty of Paris left but a few holdings to the French. In the aftermath, the English East India Company gained direct control of the rich province of Bengal (1764).

During this struggle the Afghans invaded from the northwest, establishing their rule over the Maratha domains and the Punjab (1761–62). Faced with a choice between the Afghans and the British, most Indian princes gravitated toward the British. The trend toward British domination in India was not halted by Parliament's India Act (1784), which was intended to bring the company under government control and to prohibit it from interfering in Indian affairs or from engaging in war. Between 1786 and 1813, the company's governors-general began a judicial system, gained control over the foreign affairs of most southern principalities in return for British protection, and entered into treaties with Persia and Afghanistan.

The term British Empire probably exaggerates the degree to which Great Britain exercised direct control over India in the 18th and early 19th centuries. In reality, the company ruled directly only certain territories whose princes could not (at least in the judgment of the British) secure peace and order, and established treaty obligations with other princes. There were as yet no Protestant missionaries in India (although Portuguese Catholic missionaries had tended to the needs of Christian communities in Goa and other enclaves for some 300 years), nor the rule of British law. A thin layer of foreign administrators and merchants assumed an odd combination of feelings of British superiority and the trappings of Oriental wealth; Indian culture was largely ignored by the British. To the majority of Indians, meanwhile, the foreigners were outside the caste system and largely irrelevant to the concerns of daily life.

China and Japan, 1650–1800 The Manchu emperors of China, having established the Qing Dynasty, adapted themselves rapidly to the ancient Chinese system of imperial government, maintaining the examination system for the bureaucracy (though sometimes doubling officials, one Manchu, one Chinese). So serene and sensible (and nontheological) did the Manchu state appear to many European Enlightenment political thinkers that it was often held up as a kind of ideal model for the reform of European monarchy.

Taiwan was annexed in 1683 and Tibet was gradually brought under Chinese control (1705–51) with the emperor managing succession of the Dalai Lamas, who functioned as both religious and temporal rulers of Tibet. But the great expansion was into Central Asia, settled diplomatically with the Russians in 1689 to China's advantage. All this was the work of the Kangxi Emperor (1661–1722), a contemporary of Louis XIV. The papacy's finding (1715) that reverence shown toward Confucius or toward one's ancestors was incompatible with Catholic belief led China's rulers to ban proselytizing by Christian missionaries in 1720, though some Jesuits were encouraged to stay on in China as experts in astronomy, painting, architecture, and other technical fields.

Under the Qianlong Emperor (r. 1736–95), China forced Burma (1769) and Nepal (1792) to recognize Chinese overlordship. Burma had only recently been reunited (1753) with British assistance, so the relationship between Burma and China became an avenue of British influence. In Annam (Vietnam), a Confucian ruling elite adopted many features of Chinese culture and recognized China's suzerainty, but the country's rulers permitted Catholic missions, which met with surprising success, especially after Gia Long (r. 1802–20) emerged as emperor of Vietnam.

The whole period was for China one of expansion, economically as well as territorially. In agriculture new crops from the Americas (maize and sweet potatoes, as well as the Mexican chili pepper, which had become an essential element of many Asian cuisines in the 16th century) provided a larger and more diversified food supply, though by the end of the 18th century population was once again pressing up against the limits of food production. Trade with Europe, initially carried in Portuguese ships but later open to ships of all European nations through the Portuguese colony of Macao, was based upon Chinese exports of tea, silk, and porcelain, the latter increasingly produced on a mass basis in imperial and private kilns. There was also some small-scale trade with Japan, carried both by Chinese craft and the Dutch merchants authorized to trade at Nagasaki.

But China showed little interest in the outside world. European trade was restricted after the mid-18th century to the port of Canton, under onerous conditions. No substantial Chinese market for European manufactured goods developed, nor did many Chinese intellectuals show strong interest in European culture. The late 19th-century mission of the British diplomat Lord George MacCartney, which sought diplomatic relations and improved conditions of trade between China and Great Britain, was met with indifference. China, oblivious even to the superiority of European military technology, would soon suffer badly from its imperial self-satisfaction, as Britain began balancing its China trade deficit with a massive trade in opium from Bengal to Canton.

In Japan, the splendid isolation of the Tokugawa period continued. But the internal peace that they enforced left the samurai warriors functionless, increasingly dissolute and in debt to the thriving merchant class. The heyday of the latter in the Genroku Period (1688–1704) led to a flourishing of Japanese literature, including haiku poetry, especially under the master Matsuo Basho (1644–1694), plays by Chikamatsu Monzaemon and others for the Kabuki and Bunraku (puppet theater) stages, and the development of popular art in the form of woodblock prints celebrating the pleasures of urban life. In the last decades of the Tokugawa period there were signs of restiveness against the shogunate, not only from the great clans excluded from power but from the imperial court as well, both merging patriotic feeling and imperial loyalty with a revival of the Shinto religion. Informed of world affairs by the Dutch merchants, who were required to report annually to the shogun, many Japanese increasingly worried about the danger of the Westerners to Japan's isolated development.

Triumph and Tragedy of Western Hegemony (1815–1945)

With the defeat of Napoleon in 1815, Europe entered 100 years of general peace—the so-called Pax Britannica. Europe underwent reforms of land tenure and improvements in agricultural technology, the development of industrial capitalism and the spread of liberal and democratic institutions, and spread its imperial influence worldwide. But the century of peace was followed by 30 years of tumultuous upheaval. Two world wars were waged with new weapons of mass destruction; the interval between them was marked by the subjection of much of Europe to grim totalitarian domination. By 1945, Europe lay devastated, its fate and that of the world in the hands of the two atomic superpowers, liberal-democratic America and communist Russia.

Europe: The Rise of Nationalism After a quarter-century of exhausting warfare against revolutionary France and the imperial ambitions of Napoleon, the conservative monarchs and statesmen of Britain, Austria, Prussia, and Russia made a generous peace with France at the 1815 Congress of Vienna, restoring the Bourbon dynasty but hedging France's borders with an enlarged Netherlands to the north, the Prussians on the Rhine, and the Habsburgs in northern Italy. The achievements of the Congress of Vienna owed much to the Austrian diplomat Prince Metternich (1773–1859), who brokered the establishment of the Concert of Europe, a series of international conferences (to which France was soon admitted) to regulate European affairs, initiating the longest sustained general European peace since Rome's Antonine emperors in the second century A.D. Fearing revolution as the source of war and therefore a threat to themselves, they suppressed liberal and nationalist organizations and sent troops into Italy and Spain to prop up their tottering monarchies. But Britain, supporting America's Monroe Doctrine barring European interference in the affairs of the New World, prevented Spain from intervening effectively against the revolts in Latin America. With the slow collapse of the Ottoman Empire in the Balkans, the powers supported an independent Greece (1829) and autonomy for Serbia, Moldavia, and Walachia.

Liberal revolts in 1830 led to independence for Belgium and a change of dynasty for France; in the same year, however, Russia crushed a Polish revolt and absorbed that state into her empire. Britain, without revolution, carried out a liberal reform of her constitution (1832). Parliament was reformed by abolishing "rotten" or underpopulated boroughs and expanding the electorate by 50 percent (from a tiny base), especially in the new manufacturing centers, by extending the franchise to property-owners and leaseholders of modest means. But Parliament was still dominated by rural constituencies, and it took two more Reform Acts (1867 and 1884) to extend the franchise fairly to urban populations. Equally significant was the repeal (1846) of the Corn Laws, which for centuries had restricted the importation of staple foods into Britain; the repeal was a victory for manufacturers, who supported free trade.

The year 1848 saw liberal and nationalist revolts in many of the capitals of the German and Italian principalities and of the Habsburg realms. Yet none of the 1848 uprisings succeeded in turning monarchies into republics, as the armies remained loyal to their sovereigns. Still the uprisings of 1848 had lasting effects, as feudal restrictions on land tenure, which had locked the peasantry into an unfree status, were abolished throughout central Europe. The 1848 revolt in Paris led to the establishment of a brief Second Republic, then, in a revival of Bonapartism, a Second Empire (1852–70) under Napoleon III (Louis Napoleon Bonaparte, 1808–73).

The years 1848–61 marked the Italian Risorgimento (resurgence). The key figures in the struggle for Italian unification were the radical republican Giuseppe Mazzini (1805–72), Giuseppe Garibaldi (1807–82), who had spent his youth fighting in South America's wars of independence but who turned away from republicanism to embrace a pragmatic constitutional monarchy, and Camillo Benso di Cavour (1810–61), the supporter of the would-be Italian king. After a series of adept military and diplomatic moves, in which Louis Napoleon rendered crucial assistance to Piedmont's conquest of most of Italy, Victor Emmanuel II (1820–78) of Sardinia was crowned king of the Kingdom of Italy in 1861. Transformed from a collection of weak states and dependencies, by 1870 the Kingdom of Italy included Venice and Rome as well, and had become a player in the game of 19th-century European international relations. An incidental effect was to deprive the papacy of its secular territories, except for the tiny enclave of the Vatican in Rome.

The 1870 completion of Italian unification was accomplished with the aid of one of the 19th century's most dominant figures, Prussia's Otto von Bismarck (1815–98), the unifier of Germany. In a series of brief wars, Bismarck incorporated all of non-Habsburg Germany into the German Empire, proclaimed in 1871. In the process Bismarck forced the reform of the Austrian empire, in effect excluding Austria from German affairs and leading to the establishment in 1867 of the "Dual Monarchy" of Austria-Hungary. Another of Bismarck's wars (the

Franco-Prussian War, 1870–71), took Alsace and Lorraine from France, toppled Napoleon III, and led to the formation of France's Third Republic (1871–1940).

In one decade the map of Europe had been transformed, its most powerful state the new Germany which, with rapid industrialization, became stronger still in the years that led up to World War I.

The Troubled Independence of Latin America

The impact of the Napoleonic wars upon Europe's transatlantic provinces (and the newly independent United States as well) was profound. Haiti maintained its independence, gained in 1794 as the result of a slave insurrection-turned-republican movement, against Napoleon's attempt to reconquer it. This in turn led to Napoleon's abandonment of any scheme for a New World empire; Louisiana was therefore sold to the United States. When Joseph Bonaparte (brother of Napoleon) ascended the throne of Spain (1808), Spanish America was thrown into confusion: which king to obey? Juntas loyal to the Bourbon king Ferdinand VII, led by creoles such as Simon Bolivar (1783–1830) and José de San Martín (1778–1850), resisted French rule at first, but then turned against the absolutism of the restored Ferdinand in whose name they had first risen up. In colony after colony the juntas' armies fought for and won their independence: La Plata (Argentina,1810), Chile (1818), New Granada (Ecuador, Colombia, Panama, and Venezuela, 1819), Peru (1821). In separate and more complicated developments, Mexican and Brazilian independence followed in 1822.

The Monroe Doctrine (1823) of the United States, which suited the interests of and was supported by Great Britain, shielded the new states from Spanish repression. But nothing could shield them from the effects of their own inexperience in politics (an effect of Spanish imperial centralization) or from boundary disputes (for New World boundaries too were purely Spanish creations) or from the internal struggles of local leaders (caudillos) seeking autonomy within the new republics. Thus independence was followed by a long period of war, civil war, insurrection, and/or coup.

When the trade links with Spain were cut, the new states found a welcome from Great Britain for their products. British investment fostered mining and industrial development; American investment entered late in the 19th century. The development in the 1880's of adequate methods of refrigeration on steamships meant that beef could join wheat and sugar and coffee as exports. The needs of the Allies in World War I for massive increases in raw materials brought a great increase in trade; large-scale postwar investment from the United States both in industry and in plantation agriculture helped continue economic growth, though this declined sharply after the start of the Great Depression in 1929.

This expansion brought social tension through the growth of both a middle class and agricultural and industrial working classes, adding new elements to the older political instability. In the 1930's governments in Mexico, Argentina, and several other Latin American states followed the "popular front" or "corporate state" models of Europe, and followed Europe's lead also in relying too much on political strongmen. In the Caribbean, the United States played a dominant role, whether as "policeman" or, as after 1934, "good neighbor."

European Empires in Africa For 60 years after the Napoleonic wars, Europeans evinced only small interest in Africa. Liberal economic thought supported free trade rather than empire. Trading forts dotted the west African coasts, while steamboats penetrated only somewhat farther inland and missionaries began evangelization on a small scale. "Cash crop" agriculture depended on European markets for such commodities as nuts and palm products, especially oil for lighting and machine lubrication, but in this early period the plantations tended to be domestic ventures of various African kings and chiefs, who were, with the drying up of the trade in slaves, eager for new sources of revenue. In the south, the expansion of the Zulu nation after 1818 led to disruptions lasting into the 1850's while among the Boers in the Dutch colony at the Cape of Good Hope, the British ban on slavery provoked the Great Trek of some 10,000 settlers into the grassy interior plateau known as the high veld, where they came into conflict with indigenous peoples. This movement of Dutch farmers out of the old Cape Colony paved the way for the arrival of new British settlers and set the stage for later conflicts between the two main groups of Europeans in south Africa. On the east coast the sultan of Oman moved his capital to Zanzibar, the better to control his network of trade in cloves and slaves; the continuation of the slave trade brought increasing British estrangement from their protégé. Along the Mediterranean coast of North Africa, the Ottoman Empire was nominally sovereign though rule in fact was exercised by local beys and sultans whose revenues depended largely on the profits from harassing merchant ships, or accepting payments for safe passage. This provoked armed reactions first by the United States in the Tripolitan War (1801–1805) and again in 1815, by an Anglo-Dutch fleet in the latter year, and finally by the French who in 1830 occupied Algiers and a few other coastal cities.

About 1880 a group of French projects—a railways scheme at Dakar, new trading posts on the Ivory Coast and north of the Congo river—alarmed the other powers into the "scramble for Africa," which brought Britain and Portugal and later Germany into a contest to annex territory, principally to prevent the others from doing the same and gaining some unknown and unpredictable benefit. The Congress of Berlin (1885) sought to put some order into the competition, and by 1900 the entire continent had been divided between European powers, save for the colony of freed American slaves in Liberia and the ancient Christian empire of Ethiopia. Colonial theorists gained the ear of Western governments for grand schemes of great belts of territory, the French to stretch from Dakar to the Red Sea, the British from Capetown to Cairo—even though the construction of the Suez Canal (1859–69) had rendered such schemes economically pointless. One specific and concrete interest was the discovery of gold and diamond deposits in the republic of Transvaal, which led to Britain's conquest of the Boer republics in the Boer War (1889–1901) and her formation (1910) of the Union of South Africa, which through elections Boers soon governed.

The End of Imperial China and the Rise of Japan

If Africa had not yet felt the full impact of European sovereignty, Asia's experience of European rule was no illusion. British rule was established in India, Burma, and Malaya, the Netherlands' in Indonesia, America's in the islands of the Pacific (Hawaii, Samoa, and later the Philippines) and France's in Indochina. Two new provinces of Western civilization grew in Australia and New Zealand. China underwent yet another cycle of imperial decline but with the new element of the presence of the "southern barbarians" (the Europeans) and the aggressive designs of a suddenly modernized Japan.

A succession of wars and rebellions marked the decline of China's power and prestige in the 19th century. Her attempts to maintain Canton as the sole port for Western trade and to end Britain's sale of opium led to the Opium War (1839–42) and a thorough British victory. The Treaty of Nanking opened four more cities to trade and ended the "Canton system." Western nations were now accepted as China's equals rather than treated as tribute-bearing "barbarian" states. A uniform tariff of 5 percent was levied on foreign trade; in addition, Hong Kong was ceded to the United Kingdom. In the aftermath of the war, in 1844 and 1845, the United States gained the right of "extraterritoriality" (exemption from Chinese law) for its citizens, soon extended to all the Western states, and the French gained toleration for Catholic Christianity, soon extended to Protestant Christians as well.

The social and economic dislocations caused by the Opium War in south China culminated in the Taiping Rebellion (1851–64), led by Hong Xiuquan, a failed examination candidate who, having read some Christian missionary pamphlets, imagined himself to be the younger brother of Jesus Christ. A charismatic figure, he raised a huge army and seized much of southern and central China, including the city of Nanjing. To put down the rebellion the Qing emperor resorted to the very dangerous expedient of allowing provincial governors-general to raise their own military units; these were effective but would prove destabilizing in the future. Some Western military assistance helped keep the Taipings away from the trading port of Shanghai.

At the same time China experienced three other major rebellions: Muslim uprisings in the northwest and in Yunnan Province in the southwest, and the millenarian Nian Rebellion in the north-central plains. Total loss of life from all of these rebellions exceeded 20 million; the dynasty itself barely survived. In 1856, in the midst of this turmoil, the Chinese were forced to fight a second war with Europeans, when the British provoked a small affray called the Arrow War. This was settled by the Treaty of Tientsin in 1858, which resulted in the opening of yet another 11 ports, the legalization of the opium trade, and the collection of China's customs by Great Britain. When the Chinese court attempted to delay implementation of the treaty, a British expeditionary force burned the imperial Summer Palace, near Bejing, in 1860 to punish the emperor and force his compliance. With customs revenues under British control, Sir Robert Hart became, in effect, China's finance minister through the years 1863–1908.

Japan's attempt to gain concessions like those of the Western powers and to challenge Chinese control over the Manchu tributary state of Korea led to the third of the China's disastrous foreign wars. Losing the Sino-Japanese War (1894–95), China had to cede Taiwan and certain mainland territories to Japan and recognize the independence of Korea, a prelude to that kingdom's annexation as a Japanese colony in 1910. Meanwhile, in Indochina the

French ignored the protests of China's Qing Dynasty and established protectorates over Annam (1883) and, right on China's border, Tonkin (1893).

After an unsuccessful attempt in 1898 to reform the imperial government, followed by the abortive, anti-Western Boxer Rebellion (1900), discontent with the feebleness of the Manchu government led to the Chinese Revolution (1911), led by Sun Yat-sen (1866–1925). Forced by Western pressure to put aside his leadership of a new China, Sun yielded the presidency of the new Chinese Republic to a Qing Dynasty general, Yuan Shikai (1859–1916). General Yuan promptly made plans to establish yet another new dynasty with himself as founding emperor, but his death permitted the republic to continue, though rent by warlordism and anarchy made more dangerous by modern weapons and mass political organizations.

Japan's rise to great power status was rooted in an extraordinary adaptability. After the American Commodore Matthew Perry forced the opening of Japan to Western trade in 1853–54, antiforeign and pro-imperial sentiment grew until in 1867 young patriots at the court of the teenage emperor Mutsuhito (r. 1867–1912) felt strong enough to end the shogunate and restore imperial control. The emperor's reigning name, Meiji, gave the movement its name: the Meiji Restoration. During his long rule, Japan embarked on a course of furious imitation of Western ways, as earlier they had sometimes imitated the Chinese. The pre-1867 isolationist slogan "revere the emperor, expel the barbarians" gave way to "enrich the state, strengthen the military," a goal realized through the energetic adoption of Western science, technology, industry, and arms. Japan's feudal class structure was abolished; some former samurai declined into poverty, while others became enthusiastic and successful entrepreneurs. The topmost layer of the old samurai class was reconstituted in 1884 as a Japanese peerage so that there might be an upper house on the British model when the Meiji Constitution (1889) established a Diet. But it was the military and industrial spheres that showed most rapid advance, providing the basis for triumphs over China (1895) and much more surprisingly Russia (1905), the takeover of some German holdings in the Pacific and in China's Shandong Province during World War I, and the incursions against China in the 1930's.

India Under the Raj In India, the British kept up the fiction of Mughal rule but proceeded to act more and more like a sovereign power: commencing the repair of the Mogul system of canals (1818) and building roads and irrigation projects; replacing Persian as the language of law courts with English in the higher courts and local tongues in local courts; founding schools whose curriculum was European and whose language of instruction was English; and intervening more and more in matters of local custom and culture.

In the 1840's, warfare in Afghanistan, in the Sind, and against the Sikhs made Britain a true imperial power, the ruling authority in India, protecting Indian princes from subversion and aggression, and annexing territory when princely families died out. After the Great Mutiny (1857–58) of the sepoys (Indian soldiers in the British army), Britain banished the last of the Moguls. Twenty years later came the symbolic climax, the proclamation (1877) of Queen Victoria (r. 1837–1901) as empress of India.

At the same time the British were establishing executive and legislative councils with Indian representation and courts with Indian justices sitting on the bench. And in both world wars, Indian troops fought loyally and with valor on the British side. Nevertheless, the tides of nationalism and anticolonialism that swept through all of Asia in the early 20th century brought a new measure of political awareness to many Indians. The Indian National Congress, first established in 1885, came increasingly under the influence of Mahatma Gandhi (1869–1948). His campaigns of civil disobedience in 1921 and in 1930 presaged the post-war demands that would signal the end of British rule.

Australia and New Zealand More enduring than British India or British rule in Singapore (1819) or Burma (1886) as vehicles of European influence were Australia, a convict colony founded in 1788, that was gradually transformed by generous land grants into the Commonwealth of Australia (1901), and New Zealand, where after 1840 assisted immigration and land grants brought dominion status by 1907. Both fought loyally among Britain's allies in both of the world wars. As in the Americas, in Australia and New Zealand the rights of indigenous inhabitants were ignored in the rush of European settlement; Aborigine rights (in Australia) and Maori rights (in New Zealand) are important political issues in both countries today.

The First World War, 1914–18 World War I had its roots in strains that had been accumulating in Europe since the late 19th century. One of Bismarck's political objectives was to keep France isolated. He encouraged its colonial expansion to compensate for diminished status in Europe and in the hope that imperial rivalry with

Britain would keep those western states apart. He hoped for similar results from Russian and British rivalry in Persia and Afghanistan. To strengthen Germany's position in Europe, he formed the Triple Alliance of Germany, Austria-Hungary, and Italy.

However, France and Russia allied in 1894; a decade later, after settling colonial issues that had nearly brought them to war, France and Britain came to a "friendly understanding." The triangle of alliances that Bismarck had sought to prevent was completed in 1907, when Britain and Russia agreed to establish spheres of influence in Persia. Bismarck's diplomacy was undone by the aggressive foreign policy of Kaiser Wilhelm II (r. 1888–1918) and a naval arms race with Britain.

While colonial disputes generally proved amenable to diplomatic solution, in the Balkans events moved beyond any statesman's ability to control. In the disintegration of Ottoman power there, Serbia, Romania, and Montenegro became independent in 1878 and Bulgaria in 1908. The powers consistently checked Russian advances in the Balkans while the influence of Austria-Hungary grew. Struggling for territory from the Ottomans and from one another, the Balkan states fought a series of three wars in 1912, 1913, and 1914. It was the third, which began with the assassination of Austria's Archduke Franz Ferdinand (1863–1914) in Sarajevo by a Serbian nationalist, that expanded into the catastrophe of World War I.

Outside Europe fighting was slight: German holdings in the Pacific and Africa were taken by British and French imperial forces, and German concessions in China were seized by Japan; Russian and British forces engaged the Ottomans in Mesopotamia and Armenia; and Western-backed Arab revolts further weakened Ottoman strength. But in Belgium and northern France, armies fought through four years of horrifying trench warfare, and on the gigantic eastern front immense armies clashed without resolution until 1917. In February-March of that year a moderate (Menshevik) revolution led by Aleksandr F. Kerensky and others put an end to centuries of czarist autocracy; Nicholas II (r. 1894–1917) abdicated on March 15 and a Provisional Government was established. But the moderates were progressively undermined by the Bolsheviks, led by Vladimir I. Lenin (1870–1924), who seized power in a coup on November 6 (October 24 by the old calendar, hence the term "October Revolution"). Nicholas II and his family were arrested; they were executed, apparently on Lenin's orders, on July 16, 1918. Kerensky fled the country, and many moderate leaders were arrested. The Bolshevik regime took Russia out of the world war, but the country was soon plunged into a civil war between Reds (Bolsheviks and other communists) and Whites (supporters of the old regime). The effect on World War I of Russia's withdrawal from the east was offset in the west by the entry of the United States, provoked by Germany's resumption of unrestricted submarine warfare in a futile attempt to escape the noose of Britain's naval blockade. The fighting ended on November 11, 1918. (see pp. 265–68 for a history of the war.)

The Aftermath of World War I Besides its immense cost in treasure and blood—more than 8 million died in battle and 6 million civilians perished—the war overturned the old European state system as four empires collapsed and were partitioned. Germany, under the Treaty of Versailles (1919) emerged as the Weimar Republic with small territorial losses to France and a resurrected Poland, but burdened with the war guilt clauses and the immense financial reparations they were meant to justify. Russia lost all her western gains since Peter the Great, retreating eastward to build a Leninist communist state on the foundations of the 1917 revolution. Austria-Hungary disappeared utterly, two little republics maintaining only the names of those once great states. By 1923 in Asia Minor a one-party Turkish Republic emerged under Mustafa Kemal Ataturk (1818–1938), replacing the last vestiges of the Ottoman Empire.

The successor states in eastern Europe, whether republican or monarchical in form, readily adopted the parliamentary government of the victorious western Allies, which, in the years after 1848, had steadily democratized the franchise. But most contained substantial ethnic minorities whose rivalries poisoned parliamentary life; tariff barriers that arose everywhere fragmented the old common markets of the empires they replaced, protecting inefficient industries and penalizing those that were efficient; and in agriculture depression was chronic.

To the east the czarist Russian Empire was replaced by the somewhat smaller but still vast Soviet Union. With the death of Lenin in 1924 the dictatorship of the Communist Party turned increasingly into the personal dictatorship of Joseph Stalin (1879–1953), who oversaw the murderous collectivization of agriculture and the forced industrialization of the Five Year Plans, then purged the party, the army and the secret police of all but his own men. Millions died.

Western and central Europe seemed sheltered from these grim developments by the "cordon sanitaire" of the new states of east-central Europe. After a period of postwar adjustment, prosperity returned to the Western democracies, especially in Germany, whose adherence to the Locarno Treaties (1925) presaged an enduring peace. Yet in Italy, whose wartime sacrifices seemed unrewarded by territorial gains and whose economy seemed to dissolve into the chaos of socialist and anarchist and capitalist violence, there arose in 1922 the second (after Lenin) of Europe's interwar dictators, Benito Mussolini (1883–1945). His fascist movement promised a halfway house between liberal individualism and communist class war, stressing a belligerent nationalism with a corporative economy. Mussolini's personal charisma obscured the bombast and incoherence of the Fascist program.

The needs of the Allies in World War I for massive increases in raw materials brought a great increase in trade. Large-scale postwar investment from the United States both in industry and in plantation agriculture helped continue economic growth but with serious decline after 1929 in the rate of growth.

In Latin America, postindependence economic growth and expanding trade with Europe from the late 19th century onward had brought social tension through the growth of both a middle class and agricultural and industrial working classes, adding new elements to the older political instability. In the 1930's governments in Mexico, Argentina, and several other Latin American states followed the "popular front" or "corporate state" models of Europe, and followed Europe's lead also in relying too much on political strongmen. In the Caribbean, the interests of the United States predominated whether as "policeman" or, as after 1934, "good neighbor."

In China, the Nationalist Party of the revolutionary leader Dr. Sun Yat-sen (the Kuomintang, KMT; modern spelling Guomindang), came after his death in 1925 under the control of his Moscow-trained general, Chiang Kai-shek (1887–1975), whose armies gave the KMT military control of south China. Chiang's Northern Expedition (1927–29) reunited most of the country under Nationalist rule, but his decision to try to exterminate his nominal Communist Party allies beginning in Shanghai in 1927 led to a failed series of Communist uprisings and their retreat to the northwest in the Long March (1932–34). In their new stronghold of Yan'an, Mao Zedong (1893–1976) emerged as the party leader and Chiang's chief rival. Their struggle was submerged in the 1930's by the need to oppose the Japanese.

In Japan, the western-style parliamentary government that had been established in the late 19th century broke down in the reign of the Meiji Emperor's grandson Hirohito (always known in Japan by his reign-name, the Showa Emperor, r. 1926–89), as military cliques and gangs came to control government after government and political violence became the order of the day. Japan occupied Manchuria as a protectorate in 1931–32 and invaded China in 1937—the start of World War II in Asia.

The Second World War In much of Europe, the collapse of the world economy after 1929 was exacerbated by the social and ethnic divisions of the successor states, their boundary grievances, and the real or imagined fear of communist revolution. Most of Europe outside the monarchies of the north and west turned to right-wing authoritarian regimes which, though often called "fascist," made little pretense of being ideologically based; they resembled Italy less than they did Latin America. Germany presented a very different and very grievous case; there, the 1933 elevation of Adolf Hitler (1889–1945) to the office of chancellor proved that thuggery, the repellent doctrines of National Socialism (including virulent anti-Semitism), and German nationalistic resentment over the post–World War I settlement were sufficient to establish the Nazi dictatorship in the heart of Europe.

The Western democracies dithered, deluded themselves, and sought peace through appeasement. Having neglected their own military capabilities while Hitler was rebuilding the German war machine, there were few realistic alternatives to appeasement in any case. Domestically, the German persecution of Jews accelerated throughout the 1930's, while Hitler, bent on overturning the Versailles settlement, successfully remilitarized the Rhineland (1936) and absorbed Austria (in a sudden campaign called the Anschluss) and the ethnically German parts of Czechoslovakia (1938), then turned the remainder of Czechoslovakia into a satellite, took the city of Memel from Lithuania, and began demands on Poland (1939). In August 1939 Germany and Russia agreed to partition Poland yet again. With Hitler's invasion of Poland in September, World War II began in Europe. (The Asian phase of World War II had begun two years earlier.)

The European war was, until 1941, an unbroken series of totalitarian triumphs; by June of 1940, when France fell, all of Europe outside Britain was neutral or an ally or satellite of Germany. But in June of 1941 Hitler invaded Russia, and in December Hitler's ally, Japan, attacked the U.S. Navy base at Pearl Harbor, Hawaii. The attack was designed to cripple the American Pacific fleet, thus giving the Japanese a free hand for the invasion of southeast Asia, which brought Japanese forces by mid-1942 to occupy the American Philippines, the Dutch East Indies, British Hong Kong, Malaya, Singapore, and Burma, while French Indochina and independent Thailand collaborated. But the American carrier fleet survived the attack on Pearl Harbor; having failed to defeat the United States in a single blow, the Japanese war effort gradually was ground down by American industrial and military might.

In Europe, German armies penetrated as far east as Leningrad, Moscow and Stalingrad before being fought to a stalemate on the Eastern Front. The grand alliance of Britain and the U.S. with the USSR forced Nazi Germany to fight a two-front war, which ultimately spelled utter defeat in May of 1945—but not before Germany killed 6 million Jews and a like number of Gypsies, homosexuals, handicapped people, Communists and other undesirables during the Holocaust. In Asia, the great powers, especially America, kept up the illusion that China was a great power with Chiang as its ruler, which helped to keep Japanese troops tied down on the Asian mainland. In August 1945, atomic bomb attacks on Hiroshima and Nagasaki, major Japanese cities, hastened Japan's surrender, and World War II came to its end. The United States and the Soviet Union, with Great Britain a very junior partner, bestrode the globe. Japan itself was occupied by American forces. In China, civil war led to the establishment of a Communist state within four years of the end of the war, while Eastern Europe came under the domination of the Soviet Union. A new era in world history had begun. (see pp. 268–70 for a history of the war)

The Modern World (1945–Present)

Planning the Postwar World By the end of 1943, it had become obvious to the leaders of the Allied Powers that, barring some completely unforeseen development, Germany and Japan would be defeated in World War II. The allied leaders – Churchill, Roosevelt, and Stalin – met in a series of conferences not only to plan the later stages of the war, but to establish the outlines of the postwar world. Conferences at Cairo (1943), Casablanca (1944), and Yalta (1945) affirmed the policy of pursuing the war until Germany and Japan had surrendered unconditionally; established a four-power (U.S., U.K., France, and USSR) occupation of Germany; gave the United States responsibility for the occupation of Japan; and permitted the European colonial powers (principally Britain, France, and the Netherlands) to reestablish their empires. The Yalta Conference also had the effect of creating a Soviet sphere of influence in Eastern Europe that would soon be exploited (against the wishes of the Western powers) to install communist governments throughout the region. The Potsdam Conference (1945) recognized the division of Germany into East and West. In effect the cold war had begun before World War II had even ended.

Other wartime conferences had a lasting positive impact on the postwar world. The Dumbarton Oaks Conference (1944) laid down the basic principles of the United Nations; the U.N. Charter was written at the San Francisco Conference in the spring of 1945, signed on June 26, and ratified by the requisite number of countries in October of that year. Meanwhile, the Bretton Woods Conference (1944) established the International Monetary Fund and the International Bank for Reconstruction and Development (the World Bank), both governed by their member countries and associated with the UN as specialized agencies; these immediately began to play a vital role in postwar economic development and financial stabilization.

Realities of the Postwar World The occupation of Germany quickly devolved into a hostile confrontation between the USSR and the Western Allies in a rigidly divided country. Despite earlier agreements, East Germany was cut off from contact with the west, while Berlin, an enclave under four-power occupation surrounded by East Germany, also was divided into eastern and western zones. The American occupation of Japan, designed initially to turn defeated Japan into a democratic, demilitarized, and largely deindustrialized backwater, changed course to promote greater economic reconstruction as Japan came to be seen as a potential ally in the face of communist gains in the Chinese Civil War and the establishment in North Korea of a communist government under Soviet sponsorship.

The reaffirmation of British colonial rule in India, and of French rule in northern and western Africa, and especially the reestablishment of colonial regimes in areas that had been under Japanese control during the war (French Indochina, British Malaya, Dutch Indonesia) was widely resented, and engendered armed independence movements in many of those colonies. America's speedy honoring of its pledge of independence for the Philippines (1946) had the effect of inspiring more urgent calls for decolonization elsewhere.

In Europe, wartime destruction and economic privation began to be alleviated in 1947 with the inauguration of the Marshall Plan, an American foreign-aid program aimed at the rapid rebuilding of the noncommunist countries of Europe. The signatories to the agreement (Austria, Belgium, Denmark, France, West Germany, Great Britain, Greece, Iceland, Italy, Luxembourg, the Netherlands, Norway, Sweden, Switzerland, Turkey, and the United States) formed the Organization for European Economic Cooperation (OEEC), later known as the Organization for Economic Cooperation and Development (OECD). Meanwhile, the American president announced what was to become known as the Truman Doctrine, committing the U.S. to oppose the establishment "by force or outside influence" of dictatorships in Europe. Under this doctrine, American military and political aid helped forestall communist movements in Greece, Turkey, and Italy.

Eastern Europe, the "Iron Curtain," and the Cold War The Soviet Union, devastated by the war, its industrial base and agricultural economy in a shambles, crippled by military and civilian casualties that probably exceeded 20 million deaths, sought to insulate itself behind a zone of friendly and submissive European neighbors so as never again to suffer the kind of invasion that Germany had mounted against the USSR. In Europe, the Soviet Union's interpretation of the wartime Yalta agreements enabled it to move rapidly to depose fledgling democratic governments in the Eastern European countries under Soviet occupation; as early as 1946 Winston Churchill warned that an "Iron Curtain" was being drawn around a Soviet zone in Eastern Europe. Soviet power was made credible with the rapid development of atomic weapons through Russian research, captured foreign scientists, and atomic secrets stolen from the United States during the war. Pro-USSR communist governments were in place in Poland, Czechoslovakia, Hungary, Yugoslavia, Bulgaria, and Romania by 1948. (Communist Yugoslavia, under Josip Broz Tito (1892–1980), pursued a tenuous independence form Soviet control, while Albania under Enver Hoxha (1908–1985) broke with the Soviet Union in 1961 and allied itself with the People's Republic of China thereafter.) Austria and Finland accepted a neutral status highly deferential to the Soviet Union. A popular uprising in Hungary in 1956 was ruthlessly crushed, making clear the USSR's determination to maintain tight control of Eastern Europe.

India and the Partition; Southeast Asia Bowing to intense pressure, in 1946 Britain pledged independence for India. But the issue of how to apportion power between the (Hindu) Congress Party and the Muslim League proved impossible to resolve, and in August 1947 British India was divided into the separate states of India and Pakistan. Communal violence in 1947–48, in which at least 500,000 people died, led to widespread displacement of Hindus from Pakistan to India, and of Muslims from India to Pakistan, the latter comprising the non-contiguous areas of West Pakistan (now Pakistan) and East Pakistan (now Bangladesh); the status of Kashmir remained unresolved. Relations between India and Pakistan have been strained throughout the postindependence period. In 1971 the awkward division of Pakistan into eastern and western halves was resolved through bitter fighting when East Pakistan broke away to become the independent state of Bangladesh.

Burma, administratively separated from India in 1935, became independent in 1947; Sri Lanka gained independence in 1948. Malaya achieved independence in 1957, after the British fought a communist insurgency there from 1948 to the the mid-1950's. In 1963, Malaya joined with Singapore and the former British colonies of Sarawak and British North Borneo (Sabah) to form a new nation, the Federation of Malaysia. Singapore withdrew from the federation in 1965 and became an independent nation thereafter. In Indonesia, a proclamation of independence in 1945 led to four years of fighting as the Dutch attempted to reimpose colonial control; they withdrew in 1949 and the Republic of Indonesia won international recognition. (In 1965 popular backlash against an attempted communist coup in Indonesia led to the slaughter of several hundred thousand people, many of them ethnic Chinese.)

The State of Israel The Zionist movement of the late 19th century had promoted Jewish emigration to the ancient homeland of Israel, more recently known as Palestine. Palestine was part of Great Britain's League of Nations Mandate in the Middle East after World War I. British policy there was governed by the Balfour Declaration of 1917, which pledged support for a Jewish homeland in Palestine provided that the rights of the Palestinian people were protected. After World War II and the Holocaust, support for a Jewish state grew dramatically and became a cornerstone of American policy in the Middle East. The creation of the State of Israel was formally proclaimed on May 14, 1948; but allegations of forced displacement of

Palestinians led to the immediate outbreak of war between Israel and its Arab neighbors. Israel's victory turned out to be only the first round in more than half a century of armed confrontation with the Arab world.

The People's Republic of China In China, the simmering conflict between Communist and Nationalist forces in China broke out into open civil war by 1946, despite American efforts at mediation. With only grudging material support from the USSR, Chinese Communists under the leadership of Mao Zedong defeated the far larger and better equipped Nationalists, whose corruption, ineptitude, and bourgeois orientation proved no match for the simple communist slogan, "Land to the tiller." The Nationalists retreated to Taiwan in 1948–49, and Mao proclaimed the founding of the People's Republic of China in Beijing on October 1, 1949. (A break between the USSR and the People's Republic of China in the late 1950's, over both geopolitical and ideological issues, did not alter American policy assumptions of monolithic international communism. U.S.-Chinese relations were nearly nonexistent before Pres. Richard M. Nixon (1913–1994) initiated a rapprochement in 1973.)

The Cold War Heats Up A Soviet attempt in 1948 to blockade the Western occupied zone of Berlin was met with the Berlin Airlift, which preserved a Western presence in the city. The Berlin Wall was built in 1961 to stem a tide of illegal migration from East to West Germany. (Its fall in 1989 marked the end of the cold war.) The North Atlantic Treaty Organization (NATO, 1949) was founded under American leadership as part of a strategy to contain the Soviet Union; it was countered by the organization of the Eastern-bloc Warsaw Pact (1955). The Soviet Union made a concerted effort to match the United States in production of nuclear weapons and delivery systems; the resulting arms race eventually resulted in the production of enough nuclear weapons by the two powers to obliterate the entire population of the world. The death of Joseph Stalin in 1953 made no appreciable difference in the atmosphere of hostility between the Eastern and Western blocs.

The Korean War In Korea, divided after the war into separate occupation zones roughly north and south of 38° N., the Soviet-backed government led by the veteran Communist Kim Il-sung (1912–1994) rapidly took control in the north, whereas in the south an inept and ill-prepared American occupation squandered the opportunity for democratic development and eventually backed the corrupt right-wing movement of Syngman Rhee (1875–1965). When North Korean troops invaded across the demilitarized zone at the 38th parallel on June 25, 1950, the United States successfully obtained United Nations backing to rescue the south; the Korean War ensued. Hard-pressed at first when China sent troops in support of North Korea, the U.N. forces fought the war to a bloody standoff over the next three years.

Domestically, America's "loss" of China and the stalemate of the Korean War led to purges, orchestrated by Sen. Joseph McCarthy of Wisconsin, of supposed "communist sympathizers" in the State Department. Abroad, in the cold war struggles of the 1950's and 1960's between the U.S. and the USSR for influence in the Third World, America often wound up allied with corrupt, repressive "anticommunist" governments, while the Soviet Union was able to pose as the champion of progressive anticolonial, nationalist, and antiimperial movements. Soviet- and Cuban-backed insurgencies in Latin America countries (including El Salvador, Nicaragua, Peru, Chile, Colombia, and others) drew particular attention from the United States, while repressive rightist regimes in Argentina and Chile engineered the "disappearance" of tens of thousands of political opponents and Brazil fell under military rule.

Decolonization The colonial powers of western Europe were on the whole slow to see the ill effects of trying to maintain the old order. The French effort to retain colonial Indochina led to a debilitating war culminating in a devastating defeat at Dienbienphu in 1954. The terms of the French withdrawal left Vietnam divided between a communist north and a non-communist south. In 1956, the United States blocked a proposal for internationally supervised elections that would likely have resulted in a victory in the south for the northern government of Ho Chi Minh (1890–1969), long-time leader of communist and nationalist anti-French resistance who came to power in the north after the French withdrawal. This set the stage for American involvement in the Vietnam War a few years later. Just as the French withdrew from Indochina, they faced a disaster in Algeria, where an uprising was aimed at driving out the more than 1 million ethnic French settlers there. After eight years of brutal struggle, the French withdrew in 1962.

Meanwhile, in 1956 Great Britain and France went to war with Egypt in an attempt to retain control over the Suez Canal, which had been nationalized by Egypt under its leader Gamel Abdul Nasser (1918–70). The war, opposed by the United States, was a political disaster, and hastened the collapse of British colonial rule everywhere. The outcome bolstered Nasser's socialist regime, already friendly to the USSR for aid in building the Aswan High Dam, while Iraq, Syria, and Libya became anti-Israeli Soviet clients.

The 1950's also saw the beginning of decolonization in Africa, beginning with the independence of Ghana in 1957. Within two decades nearly all of the former European colonies of Africa would be independent; but the anomalies of colonial boundaries transformed into national borders regardless of topography or ethnicity led to severe strains in many of the new states. The civil war that followed Biafra's attempted secession from Nigeria in 1960, and the 40–year civil war in the Sudan between the Arab, Islamic north and the Black, Christian/Animist south, attest to the difficuty of making nations from what had been colonies. Struggles in the Congo, Namibia, Angola, and elsewhere turned into proxy conflicts of the cold war. At the continent's southern tip, the Republic of South Africa, which gained independence from Great Britain in 1961, became an international pariah because of its policy of "apartheid" racial segregation.

The Cuban Revolution The 1959 triumph of Fidel Castro's (b. 1926) communist revolution in Cuba was a bitter blow to the United States, which had supported the old, corrupt regime of Fulgencio Batista. With the support of the CIA, an army of Cuban exiles invaded Cuba at the Bay of Pigs in January 1961, and were immediately killed or taken prisoner by Castro's troops; the hoped-for anti-communist popular uprising failed to occur. The incident was a humiliation for the United States and its new president, John F. Kennedy. Castro thereafter remained one of the most loyal supporters of the Soviet Union and relied on Soviet economic aid to counter the effects of an American-led trade embargo on Cuba.

The Russians took advantage of this alliance in 1962 to place missiles in Cuba that were aimed directly at the United States. An American demand (ultimately successful) that they be removed led, in October 1962, to 10 days of tense confrontation. The Cuban missile crisis, as the incident was called, is generally regarded as having been the most serious single incident of the cold war and, in retrospect, the high water mark of Soviet influence internationally. Thereafter, having looked into the abyss and been daunted by what they saw, both superpowers began efforts to reduce the cold war atmosphere of confrontation. Beginning in the 1960's, a series of agreements between the U.S. and the USSR succeeded in limiting the testing and production of nuclear weapons, and reducing their numbers.

The Vietnam War In South Vietnam, a nationalist, anticolonial, communist-allied movement (Vietminh) became increasingly transformed into a communist-led armed struggle (Vietcong) supported by North Vietnam and dedicated to the overthrow of the American-backed southern government. American military and political advisers sent to South Vietnam by President Kennedy failed to stem the communist insurgency; ground troops followed in 1963–64, in numbers that escalated for the next several years. Relying on poorly informed views of "Asian communism" and fears of a communist revolutionary "domino effect" in Southeast Asia, America found itself embroiled in a war that proved impossible to win in the field and deeply devisive at home. The Vietcong and North Vietnamese Tet offensive of February 1968 was defeated by American and South Vietnamese forces, but the victory was costly both in military terms and in its effect on American public opinion. Later in 1968 President Johnson declined to run for reelection in the face of dwindling public support for the war. American troop reductions began in 1969 as part of a "Vietnamization" program, and in 1972 a cease-fire agreement (never implemented) was signed in Paris between North Vietnam, South Vietnam, the Vietcong, and the United States. Saigon fell to communist forces on April 30, 1975; the last remaining Americans were evacuated, and Vietnam was reunited under communist rule in 1976.

Development in the Third World The post-World War II creation of the new field of development economics was intended to assist the economic growth of the emergent countries of the Third World. The nations of Asia, Africa, and South America have acted in effect as laboratories to test different approaches to development, approaches that have had uneven results. Overemphasis on raising the gross domestic product of target countries has led in many cases to corruption, environmental damage, and extremes of wealth and poverty. This has been exacerbated in cases where exploitation of valuable natural resources, such as petroleum, has led to the squandering or embezzlement of wealth by a small ruling class (Venezuela, Nigeria, Iraq), with little benefit to the country as a whole.

A more comprehensive approach to development that combines investments in infrastructure (water resources, transportation systems, and the like), widely available public education, improved public health, and the empowerment of women, in combination with free trade (facilitated by the World Trade Organization and the General Agreement on Tariffs and Trade or GATT) and the protection of workers (through the International Labor Organization), has been a more effective recipe for rapid and reasonably equitable development. This has been evident especially in Asia, with the postwar recovery of Japan and the development of new "tiger" economies in South Korea, Taiwan, Thailand, Malaysia, and elsewhere. In contrast, client states of the Soviet Union, encouraged to pursue state ownership of industry, subsidized food and housing prices, restraints on foreign trade, and pervasive economic planning, have had far less impressive results. Much of Africa has yet to recover from quasi-socialist experiments in economic planning combined with kleptocratic government, a situation made much more difficult in some parts of the continent by the crippling prevalence of HIV/AIDS.

Social Change in the 1960's The Vietnam War engendered a persistent and powerful antiwar movement, especially among young people, that became part of a more pervasive atmosphere of youth rebellion and social change in the 1960's. Another strong component of that impulse for change was the Civil Rights movement, which embraced both government action (school desegregation, voting rights legislation) and political action with wide public participation ("sit-ins" and "freedom marches," and the formation of groups such as the Rev. Martin Luther King's Southern Christian Leadership Council and the more radical Student National Coordinating Council [SNCC] and the Black Panthers). By the end of the decade the legal structure of segregation had been overturned, and new efforts, such as affirmative action initiatives, were implemented to try to counter the effects of past discrimination.

In the late 1960's and early 1970's, the women's movement sought to emulate the tactics and successes of the Civil Rights movement with an agenda that embraced a spectrum of issues from equal pay for equal work, to coeducation at traditionally male colleges and equal access for women students to school athletic programs, to legalization of abortion.

Abroad, the social ferment of the 1960's also found expression in China. In 1958 Mao Zedong had initiated the Great Leap Forward, an effort at rapid economic development in agriculture and industry that proved to be a costly failure, with between 20 and 30 million people dying in the resulting famine of 1958–61. The country had barely recovered before Mao launched the Great Proletarian Cultural Revolution (1966–68), a bizarre campaign to combat complacency and bureaucratism within the Communist Party and government at all levels by unleashing the revolutionary energies of youthful "Red Guards" and workers' "revolutionary committees." The Cultural Revolution (the chaotic destructiveness of which was not widely understood outside China) in turn helped to inspire student revolts in 1968 in the United States, Western Europe, Japan, and elsewhere.

Demographic and Environmental Issues In 1950 the world's population was about 2.5 billion people; that figure doubled to 5 billion by 1985. This demographic explosion, a result of a complex of factors including improved public health, sanitation, medicine, and nutrition, produced widespread fears that world population growth would soon outstrip food supplies and other global resources. In fact, population growth began to slow in the mid-1980's, as economic growth produced a demographic transition of longer lifespans, reduced infant mortality, and lower fertility rates.

Fears of widespread food shortages were also alleviated beginning in the 1960's by the Green Revolution, involving the development of new varieties of major food plants (especially corn [maize] and rice) that, under the proper conditions, produce far higher yields than older varieties. These high yields come at an environmental price, including increased use of chemical pesticides and fertilizers.

Economic development and population growth have produced a range of environmental effects, from human encroachment on wetlands, forests, and other ecosystems, to production of greenhouse gasses, resource depletion, and production of waste. On the other hand, lack of development also has negative environmental consequences, including deforestation, soil depletion and desertification, and overexploitation of wild species, while development can produce benefits such as substitution of energy-efficient devices for wasteful burning of fuels, and the preservation of selected environments for recreational, aesthetic, and conservation purposes. The postwar period has seen a significant increase worldwide of national parks, UN World Heritage sites, wildlife refuges, and other protected areas. Environmental issues, most especially global warming and associated environmental changes, remain serious challenges for the 21st century, but the rise of environmental science and the beginnings of international cooperation on environmental issues have been major steps forward. Landmarks of this process include the Convention on International Trade in Endangered Species (CITES, 1973); the Treaty on the International Law of the Sea (1983), and an international conference in Rio de Janeiro, Brazil (1992) that produced major agreements on biodiversity and global warming.

The Iranian Revolution and the Rise of Islamism

The CIA-sponsored overthrow of the democratic regime of Mohammad Mossadegh (1880–1967) in 1954 led to the return to power of Mohammad Reza Shah Pahlavi (1919–80), who had been deposed the year before. In 1979 his unpopular and autocratic government fell to a fundamentalist Islamic revolution. The disheartening ordeal of dozens of Americans taken hostage at the U.S. embassy in Teheran played a major role in the defeat of President Jimmy Carter (b. 1924) by Ronald Reagan (1911–2004) in the 1980 presidential election. The subsequent Iran-Iraq war of 1980–88, which cost millions of lives but led to no clear military victory for either side, led the U.S. into the anomalous position of supporting the former Soviet client, Iraq's Saddam Hussein.

The Soviet Union in Afghanistan In 1978 a leftist mililtary coup overthrew the republican government of Afghanistan. A popular anticommunist revolt the next year led to a Soviet invasion to support its client regime; the USSR soon found itself in a Vietnam-style war, fighting amid a hostile population. The U.S.-funded anticommunist forces included religiously-motivated guerrilla fighters from all over the Islamic world, some of whom would later turn against the United States in militant opposition to Western values as they understood them. The Afghan war cost the USSR lives, treasure, and popular support; Soviet forces were withdrawn, under a face-saving agreement, beginning in 1988. After several years of instability, in 1995 the Taliban, a fundamentalist party, came to power and instituted what became the world's strictest and most repressive Islamic government.

Israel and Palestine Israel emerged from wars with Egypt and Syria in 1967 and 1973, and military actions in Lebanon in 1975–76 and 1978, militarily strong and in possession of the West Bank, the Golan Heights, and the Gaza Strip, but no closer to peace with its Arab neighbors. The U.S.-brokered Camp David accords of 1979 led to a peace agreement with Egypt. Palestinian intifada uprisings (including the use of suicide bombers) against Israeli occupation of Gaza and the West Bank, countered by Israeli military action against various Palestinian militarized groups and their backers, have led to a continuing state of unrest in the Palestinian territories. The Oslo Agreement, providing for the withdrawal of Israeli forces from the Palestinian territories, which would have become self-governing under a Palestinian Authority, was signed in 1994 but never completely implemented. The Israeli-Palestinian conflict remains among the world's most intractable political problems.

Post-Mao China and the Limits of Reform The death in September 1976 of Mao Zedong meant the end of the "ten terrible years" of the Cultural Revolution and its aftermath. Mao's widow and several associates (the "Gang of Four") were arrested and tried for their roles in that period of turmoil. China's new leader, Deng Xiaoping (1904–1997), in 1978 ushered in a policy of modernization of industry, education, science, and defense that led to the rapid development of a hybrid socialist-capitalist economy. A student-led democracy movement, demonstrating in Beijing's Tiananmen Square in May-June 1989, was put down with great loss of life, a signal that economic liberalization would not be accompanied by political liberalization. By the early years of the 21st century, China had become a great economic powerhouse, though still under repressive communist rule.

Glasnost, Perestroika, and the Fall of the Soviet Union The resolutely anti-Soviet policies of Pres. Ronald Reagan in the 1980's apparently hastened the cold war's end. With a restless population and a crumbling economy, and still reeling from its disastrous adventure in Afghanistan, Russia found itself unable to sustain the military expenditures needed to keep pace with the U.S. in cold war competition around the world. With Mikahil Gorbachev's (b. 1931) glasnost ("openness") and perestroika ("restructuring") policies in the mid-80's, people in Poland, East Germany, Czechoslovakia, the Baltic states, and elsewhere in Eastern Europe, sensed the end of Russia's will to retain a Soviet empire. In rapid and largely peaceful revolutions, the people of these countries overthrew their governments and demanded the withdrawal of Soviet troops. The fall of the Berlin Wall in November 1989 meant in effect the fall of international communism, and the end of the cold war.

The Computer Revolution and the Information Age The first digital computers, built in the 1940's, were huge, expensive, slow, and extremely limited in their capabilities, but they pointed the way to a transformed future. By the 1950's mainframe computers were processing actuarial data, handling mailing lists, and changing the way the world does business. The invention of the transistor, the integrated circuit, the memory chip, the floppy disk, and other key components made personal computers a reality by the late 1970's. (A crucial event was the introduction of the Apple II, the world's first widely popular personal computer, in 1977.) Since that time speed and memory have steadily increased, and cost has plummetted. The Internet, search engines, and online databases have made vast quantities of information available to virtually anyone, anywhere in the world; e-mail and cell phones have transformed personal communications. Of all changes in the post–World War II period, the computer revolution may prove to have been the most profound.

A remarkable example of the possibilities opened up by new computer technology and applications was the Apollo Program. On July 20, 1969, American astronaut Neil Armstrong (b. 1930) stepped onto the surface of the Moon, an event that marked a technological and propaganda triumph for the United States. Since that time, manned spaceflight has turned out to be expensive, dangerous, and lacking in clear purpose; but unmanned orbital and interplanetary vehicles, notably for broadcasting and telecommunications, military surveillance, remote imaging, and scientific research have become the basis of a multibillion-dollar industry that has contributed substantially to the development of the information age.

Globalization and its Discontents One consequence of the information revolution has been the increasing globalization of the world economy, with manufacturing and service industries easily relocating anywhere in the world where skilled workers can be hired at low cost. This has led to decreased costs for food, clothing, and many other basic goods for much of the world's population. At the same time, it has led to exploitation of ill-paid labor in developing countries; the "flight" of jobs overseas; controlled and subsidized markets for many agricultural goods; and other negative consequences, real and perceived. The question of how nation-states and national markets are to adjust to global manufacturing, transportation, and marketing of goods remains unresolved. Meetings of economic ministers of the world's largest economies (Seattle 1999, Genoa 2001, and others) have been met by massive demonstrations and some rioting aimed especially at what protesters considered the pro-globalization policies of the World Bank and the IMF.

A Single Superpower World With the end of the cold war, the United States had to adjust to being the world's sole superpower, while Europe, China, and Russia had to adapt to finding ways to make their voices heard and their interests taken into account in the face of American military and economic might. America responded to a 1990 Iraqi invasion of Kuwait with the first gulf war (1990–91); an easy American military victory led to Iraq's withdrawal from Kuwait but no lasting change in the Iraqi government. In 1992 a major American intervention under U.N. auspices into an ongoing civil war in Somalia led to limited and short-term gains; American forces were withdrawn in March, 1994 after the downing of an American helicopter led to a deadly ambush of U.S. Marines. In 1994 neither the U.S. nor the U.N. intervened to stop the genocidal killing of ethnic Tutsis by their Hutu neighbors in Rwanda. The limits of America's power as "the world's policeman" were tested by participation in U.N. peacekeeping forces in Bosnia in 1995 and a NATO police action in 1999 designed to halt Serbian "ethnic cleansing" of Albanians in the province of Kosovo.

Undoubtedly the most difficult adjustment for U.S. policy in the new millennium has been the growth of international terrorist organizations, most notably al-Qaeda, that are privately organized and funded with few or no ties to any government or state and that have goals which do not fit into traditional categories of international relations. The destruction of New York's World Trade Center by Al-Qaeda terrorists on September 11, 2001, led to an American response against al-Qaeda bases in Afghanistan, resulting in the overthrow of the Taliban government but neither to the effective social and political rebuilding of Afghanistan nor to the capture or destruction of the Al-Qaeda leadership. The American invasion of Iraq in 2003 led to the downfall of Saddam Hussein's government, but early military success was followed by a long and difficult occupation period that did not necessarily produce any gains in America's war against terrorism.

Major Wars in History

Greco-Persian Wars (500-448 B.C.)

The empire of the Persian king Darius I (r. 521-486 B.C.) stretched from modern Afghanistan to Egypt. Beginning in the early 5th century B.C., Greek cities in Ionia (modern western Turkey and several islands) and Cyprus revolted and the Persians quickly put down the revolt and then moved into Thrace. The mainland Greek cities of Athens and Eretrea had supported the revolt so in 490 B.C. the Persians attacked Greece by sea, but their troops were defeated on the plains of Marathon by the Athenians. After the death of Darius (486 B.C.) his son Xerxes I launched a second invasion (480 B.C.) overland through Thrace and Macedonia. At first successful, the Persians destroyed a brave Spartan force defending the pass at Thermopylae and then marched to Athens. But a Greek fleet defeated the Persian navy at Salamis in 480 B.C., and Greek heavy infantry (*hoplites*) crushed the Persian army at Plataea (479 B.C.), ending the threat to the mainland. Additional fighting followed over many years in Egypt, Asia Minor, and Cyprus. By the end of the war (traditionally 448 B.C.), the Greeks had swept Persia from the Aegean.

The Peloponnesian Wars (431 B.C.–404 B.C.)

The Peloponnesus, the peninsula in southwestern Greece connected to the mainland by the Isthmus of Corinth, was the home of ancient cities including Sparta, Corinth, Pylos and Argos. The Peloponnesian wars were fought on both land and sea between Athens and Sparta, with varying allies on both sides. Athens and Sparta had fought intermittently several decades before (460 B.C.–445 B.C.) but the major conflict broke out with an attack by a Spartan ally, Thebes, on an Athenian ally, Plataea, followed by an invasion of Attica by the Peloponnesians. At first Athens, led by Pericles, avoided direct battle with Sparta and a siege of Athens (431 B.C.) by the Spartans failed as Athens mounted naval raids on the Peloponnesus. In 430-28 B.C. plague killed Pericles and a quarter of Athens's population. Under the leadership of Cleon the Athenians began a more aggressive policy by establishing bases in the Peloponnesus, but they encountered reverses including defeat at Delium (424 B.C.). After the deaths of the Spartan and Athenian leaders Brasidas and Cleon in battle (422 B.C.), peace was won under the Athenian leader Nicias (d. 413 B.C.).

Fighting was soon renewed, however, and an anti-Spartan coalition was defeated at Mantineia (418 B.C.). Alcibiades (d. 413 B.C.) then convinced the Athenians (415 B.C.) to send a large fleet to Sicily but this venture ended in complete disaster (413 B.C.). The heavy loss of ships and personnel changed the war as Sparta began, with Persian support, to compete with the Athenians at sea. Alcibiades, who had defected to Sparta, rejoined Athens and a series of land and sea victories under his command caused the Spartans to sue for peace. Cleophon (d. 404 B.C.), the new Athenian ruler, rejected this request in 410 B.C. and another in 406 B.C. But in 405 B.C., the Spartan commander Lysander (d. 395 B.C.) destroyed the Athenian fleet at the decisive battle of Aegospotami in the Dardanelles. The Spartans sailed to Athens and blockaded the city and port. Athens, dependent on the sea for supplies, capitulated and the ensuing peace made Sparta the greatest power in Greece. Athens, bankrupt and defeated, never thereafter played a major political role in the ancient world.

The Punic Wars (264 B.C.–146 B.C.)

The three Punic Wars were fought between Rome and Carthage, which was located in northern Africa near modern Tunis. (Punic is from the Latin for Carthaginian.) In 264 B.C. Carthage was the great commercial power of the western Mediterranean while Rome was only an Italian power, not even having conquered northern Italy. By 146 B.C., however, Carthage had been destroyed and Rome dominated the Mediterranean world.

The first war (264-241 B.C.) began with the intervention of the two powers in factional conflict on Sicily, then controlled by Carthage. Fought in and around Sicily, this was primarily a naval conflict, with rowed galleys (*triremes* and *quinqueremes*) used to ram or come alongside and board opposing ships. The Romans caught up quickly with Carthaginian sea power and ultimately their fleets were victorious. Their ships had a spiked boarding ramp (the *corvus*, crow) that allowed legionaries to board enemy vessels for close combat. The war concluded with Carthage giving up her possessions in Sicily and her fleet.

The second war (218-201 B.C.) began in Spain with conflict between Roman and Carthaginian allies. Hannibal, the Carthagian commander in Spain, took the city of Sargentum and then began his audacious march from Spain to Italy, crossing the Alps with a force including war elephants. Prevailing in several key battles (notably at Lake Trasimere, 217 B.C., and Cannae, 216

B.C.), he seemed to achieve victory with many Roman colonies and allies coming over to his side. But the Romans followed the cautious policy of Fabius Maximus (d. 203 B.C.), avoiding pitched battles, maintaining key positions, and recapturing places when Hannibal's army left. Over many years in Italy Hannibal was unable to achieve final victory. Beginning in 210, the Roman commander Scipio Africanus (236 B.C.–184/3 B.C.) was triumphant in Spain and carried the war to Africa in 204 B.C. Hannibal was recalled to defend Carthage, but was defeated at Zama (202 B.C.). In the ensuing peace, Carthage gave up its possessions in Spain and its navy, but maintained its commercial activities.

The third war (149-146 B.C.) resulted from Roman concern with Carthage's revived commercial power. Rome supported a rival kingdom in Numidia (modern Algeria); conflict between it and Carthage provided an excuse for Roman intervention, which led to the final destruction of Carthage in 146 B.C. The city was razed, its inhabitants were killed or sold into slavery, and Rome took control of North Africa.

The Crusades (1095–1272)

First Crusade (1095–1099) Jerusalem had been in Islamic hands since the seventh century, but Christian pilgrimages continued, although by the 11th century there was persecution of Christians and the Holy Sepulcher (Tomb of Christ) was despoiled. In 1071 the Seljuk Turks took control of Jerusalem, and in the same year defeated the Byzantine army at Manzikert. The Byzantine Emperor requested help from Latin Christendom but it is uncertain what effect this had. The impetus for the First Crusade was the preaching of Pope Urban II at the Council of Clermont, France in 1095, urging Christians to go to war for the Holy Sepulcher. In addition to religious fervor the possibility of territorial expansion and riches contributed to the enthusiastic response. Norman designs against the Byzantines as well as the Muslims and the interest of Italian cities in increased trade with the east were also factors.

The organized crusade was preceded by a disorganized band (called "The People's Crusade") led by Walter the Penniless and another composed of followers of Peter the Hermit. Their journeys through Byzantium were not entirely peaceful, and their arrival in the Holy Land led to quick defeat. The main force was under the command of noblemen such as Godfrey of Bouillon, Bohemond I, Raymond IV of Toulouse, and Robert II of Flanders. The First Crusade was successful. The Latin Christians took Nicaea in 1097, defeated the Turks at Dorylaeum (1097), took Antioch in 1098, and Jerusalem in 1099. The latter victory was marked by the slaughter of Muslims and Jews. Godfrey of Bouillon was elected defender of the Holy Sepulcher; on his death his brother Baldwin assumed the title King of Jerusalem. Other fiefs were created at Edessa, Tripoli, and Antioch. After the First Crusade, and partly because of enmity with the Byzantines, later (and less successful) crusades were primarily dependent on sea transport rather than the overland route.

Second Crusade (1147–49) After the Turks recaptured Edessa (1144), a new Crusade was preached by St. Bernard of Clairvaux. The Holy Roman Emperor Conrad III and Louis VII of France led the Crusade, both armies pillaging in Byzantine territory en route. Conrad's force arrived first, was forced to retreat by the Turks at Dorylaeum (1147), and joined the French (1148). A joint assault on Damascus miscarried through jealousy among the leaders; Conrad returned home in 1148 and Louis in 1149, the Crusade a failure.

Third Crusade (1189–92) After the recapture of Jerusalem in 1187 by Saladin (1137/38–1193) and the defeat of the Latin princes at Hattin, Pope Gregory VIII asked for a new crusade. It was led by Richard I of England ("The Lion Heart," 1157–99), Philip II of France (1165–1223), and the Holy Roman Emperor Frederick I (1123–90). Frederick left first and encountered difficulties with the Byzantine Emperor, who had made an alliance with Saladin. He forced his way to Asia Minor but died en route and only part of his army continued on. Richard took Cyprus from the Byzantines and joining up with Philip took Acre in 1191. Philip returned home, and Richard moved his base to Jaffa. Jerusalem remained in Muslim hands, but Richard made a truce that permitted access to the city and the Holy Sepulcher.

Fourth Crusade (1202–04) Pope Innocent III (1160/61–1216) preached the Fourth Crusade, which became entirely diverted from its original purpose. The Crusaders arrived at Venice in 1202, and to help pay sea passage to the East agreed to assist the Venetians in capturing the Dalmatian city of Zara (for which they were excommunicated by the Pope). A combination of scheming by aspirants to the Byzantine throne, Venetian pressure, money, and aid for the capture of Egypt led to a plan to overthrow the Byzantine Emperor. The fleet arrived in

1203, and in 1204 the Crusaders stormed and sacked the city, dividing the spoils with the Venetians and setting up a short-lived Latin Empire of Constantinople (1204–61). From the standpoint of the church, this Crusade was a total failure: the Byzantine Empire was undermined and Western resources were diverted from the Holy Land.

After the Fourth Crusade came the sad event of the Children's Crusade in 1212. Mobs of enthusiastic children, led by a charismatic French boy, Stephen of Cloyes, took ship at Marseilles to rescue the cause in which their elders had failed. It is thought that they were sold into slavery by rapacious ship captains.

Fifth Crusade (1217–21) At the Fourth Lateran Council (1215) Pope Innocent III and his successor, Honorius III, called for a new Crusade against the center of Muslim power in Egypt. Under the leadership of John of Brienne, the papal legate Pelagius, Andrew II of Hungary, and Duke Leopold VI of Austria, Crusaders took Damietta in the Nile delta (1219), which was evacuated in 1221 after the defeat of an attempt on Cairo; the Crusaders settled for a truce.

Sixth Crusade (1228-29) The Holy Roman Emperor Frederick II (1194–1250) undertook a largely diplomatic visit to the Holy Land that resulted (1229) in a 10 year treaty that ceded Jerusalem and other holy places; he then crowned himself King of Jerusalem. After the peace expired in 1239 the conflict continued.

Seventh Crusade (1248-54) A treaty with Damascus (1244) restored Palestine to the Christians, but in 1244 the Egyptians and Turks retook Jerusalem and defeated the Christians at Gaza. The fall of Jerusalem prompted Louis IX of France (1214–70), a canonized saint, to launch a new Crusade with the support of Pope Innocent IV, aimed at Egypt. The Crusaders took Damietta in 1249, but an attack on Cairo failed and led to Louis's capture. After his ransom, Louis spent four years shoring up the defenses of the remaining Crusader states.

Eighth Crusade (1270) When Jaffa and Antioch fell to Muslims in 1268, Louis IX of France undertook a new Crusade, cut short when he succumbed to disease in Tunis in 1270.

Ninth Crusade (1271-72) Prince Edward of England, later King Edward I, arrived in North Africa too late to help the French but at Acre he negotiated a truce before returning to England.

Muslims captured Tripoli in 1289 and Acre, the last Christian stronghold, in 1291 effectively ending the Crusaders' presence in the East except for Cypus, which was captured by the Ottoman Turks in the sixteenth century. Thereafter no Crusades were directed toward the Holy Land, although Crusades continued to be preached. Crusade-like campaigns were undertaken in Europe against Muslim incursion in Europe. The most famous of these was the victory of a Christian fleet under the command of John of Austria against the Turks off Lepanto, Greece, 1571. The Crusades to the Holy Land, although ultimately a failure, led to a wide range of influences on the West through contacts with other civilizations, increased commerce, and improved geographical knowledge. They also strengthened monarchs against the Pope, who lost the power to direct these great Christian enterprises.

The Hundred Years War (1337–1453)

The origins of The Hundred Years War can be traced to 1066, when the Duke of Normandy, known as William the Conqueror, invaded and defeated England. The French-speaking Normans now maintained possessions on both sides of the English Channel. In the 14th century, kings of England held the Duchy of Guienne (also called Aquitaine) in southwest France, where they were in conflict with the French kings who were their feudal lords. The immediate causes of the war were the failure of Philip VI to restore part of Aquitaine, English attempts to control Flanders, and Philip's support of Scotland against England.

The war began in 1337, when Edward III of England took the title of King of France, even though it was still held by Philip VI. Invading through the Low Countries, Edward and his son, Edward the Black Prince, won at Crecy with his English archers (1346) and then took Calais (1347). The English captured King John II at Poitiers (1356); by the treaty of Bretigny (1360) they received Calais and Aquitaine and a ransom for the king.

The war began again in 1369 after uprisings against the English in France over taxation. By 1373, most of the lost French territory had been regained. But in 1415 Henry V of England won a great victory at Agincourt as English long bows helped to defeat heavily armored French cavalry. With help from Burgundian allies Henry gained most of France north of the Loire. In 1429, the peasant girl Joan of Arc raised the English siege of Orleans on behalf of the Dauphin, the French king's son, and brought him to Reims to be crowned king. Her execution by the English did not stop French successes, which culminated in the reconquest of Normandy by 1450 and Aquitaine by 1453. The sole English possession remaining in France (until 1558) was Calais. England became engaged in a dynastic war, the Wars of the Roses, and so undertook no further adventures in France. The immense devastation of the war in France helped destroy the power of the feudal nobility and permitted Louis XI to bring the country increasingly under royal authority.

Wars of the Roses (1455–85)

The Wars of the Roses were dynastic conflicts in England between the house of Lancaster, whose symbol was a red rose, and the Yorkists, whose symbol was a white rose. Chronicled by Shakespeare in several history plays, the wars extended intermittently over 30 years, but the amount of fighting was limited. The immediate cause of conflict was the weakness of the Lancastrian King, Henry VI, and the struggle for influence at court between the factions of the Queen, Margaret of Anjou, and Richard, Duke of York. Richard defeated the Lancastrians at St. Albans (1455) and briefly won control of king and government. He rebelled again in 1459; while the Yorkists were initially outmaneuvered, they captured the king in 1460 and Richard was declared Henry's heir. Margaret then raised an army, defeating and killing Richard at Wakefield (1460), and Henry was rescued in 1461. Richard's son Edward took up his claim and won a decisive victory at Mortimer's Cross (1461) and became king as Edward IV (1442–83). The Yorkists had prevailed, but desertions and quarrels among them led to a renewed Lancastrian offensive in 1470. Edward fled England and Henry VI was briefly restored. Edward regained power in 1471 and ruled until 1483. On his death his younger brother, taking the throne as Richard III (1452–85), imprisoned (and may have murdered) Edward's sons. Opposition to Richard provided an opening for Henry Tudor, who had a remote claim to the throne. He defeated Richard at Bosworth Field in 1485, and as Henry VII (1457–1509) founded the Tudor dynasty and brought the Wars of the Roses to an end.

Thirty Years War (1618-48)

Fought with vast destruction and loss of life primarily in Germany, the Thirty Years War, was the complex result of religious conflict, the ambitions of the Hapsburg Holy Roman Empire, and the national interests of European states including France, the Netherlands, Sweden, Denmark, Spain and the German principalities. The Peace of Augsburg (1555) had permitted each ruler to choose the religion of his state and many became Lutheran. In this context the immediate cause of the war was the appointment of the Emperor Matthias' heir apparent, the ardently Catholic Ferdinand, as King of Bohemia (who therefore also became an Elector of the Empire). He was rejected by Protestant Bohemian nobles and the Calvinist Elector of the Palatine was chosen king as Frederick V (1596–1632). The king and his allies were quickly defeated by the imperial forces at White Mountain (1620), and Ferdinand (now Holy Roman Emperor) set about imposing Catholicism in Bohemia and elsewhere. These anti-Protestant developments discomfited both Protestant states and Catholic France, which opposed the extension of Habsburg power. Denmark, with aid from England and the Netherlands, entered the war (1625) for both religious and territorial reasons but was defeated and sued for peace (1629). The Emperor issued the Edict of Restitution (1629), by which all lands secularized since 1552 were restored to the Roman Catholic Church. The evident power of the Counter-Reformation and the Hapsburgs in Germany greatly alarmed Sweden and other Protestant states as well as France. Sweden, under King Gustavus Adolphus, entered the fray (1630) with subsidies from France and the Netherlands. After winning at Breitenfeld (1631) Gustavus was killed at the victory of Luetzen (1632).

After further fighting, the Peace of Prague (1635) seemed to end the conflict, at least for the German states (the Emperor had mostly annulled the Edict of Restitution), but neither the French nor the Spanish were content with this. The French came out openly in support of the Swedes in the last phase of the war, which then became a general European war as Spanish troops entered France from bases in the Spanish Netherlands, France entered Spain, and Portugal declared independence.

Peace negotiations began in 1644, with participation of the contending states and the German principalities, strengthening the rule of nation states in Europe. In the resulting Peace of Westphalia (1648), the independence of the Netherlands and Switzerland was confirmed; France took territories in Alsace and Lorraine; Sweden gained territory in North Germany; and the Holy Roman Empire ceased to have a significant role in international affairs. The Protestant states won a complete victory regarding annexed church lands, the Counter-Reformation was checked, and the Peace of Augsburg was expanded to include Calvinism as well as Catholicism and Lutheranism.

English Civil Wars (1642–51)

The first two Stuart kings of England, James I (1566-1625) and Charles I (1600-49), believed in the divine right of kings to rule without interference. Parliament, however, strove to assert control over taxation and royal expenditures. Charles I, fearing that Parliament would try to limit his power, ruled without it for 11 years. At the same time, Puritans were at odds with the established Anglican church, a situation complicated by the Presbyterianism and shifting alliances of the Scots. War in Scotland (1639) over attempts to institute Anglican practices forced Charles to call two parliaments in 1640 to raise money. The "Short Parliament" was quickly dismissed, and the "Long Parliament" resulted in bitter conflict with the king over constitutional and religious issues, which led to war in 1642. A first encounter between Royalists and Parliamentary forces (Edgehill, 1642), was indecisive, but Oliver Cromwell (1599-1658) and the Scots crushed the Royalists at Marston Moor (1644), and Cromwell was victorious with Parliament's New Model Army at Naseby (1645). The King fled to Scotland and the first war ended in 1646.

Charles began a second war in 1648, this time with Scottish aid; this uprising was quickly defeated, and Parliament and King began negotiations. Army leaders, who were more radical than many members of Parliament, seized power, purging Parliament of their opponents (leaving the "Rump Parliament"); the King was tried and executed (1649) and a Commonwealth instituted. In 1651 Cromwell put down a Royalist rebellion in Ireland, where he slaughtered thousands.

Charles II (1630-85), recognized as King in Scotland, was also proclaimed king of England by the Scots. His large army was defeated by Cromwell in a third war both at Dunbar (1650) and at Worcester (1651). Cromwell became Lord Protector; after his death his son Richard ruled briefly. In 1660 Charles II was restored to the throne.

War of the Spanish Succession (1701–14)

The succession of the childless Charles II of Spain caused widespread concern in Europe. England and Holland were opposed to a Bourbon and the potential union of Spanish and French power; France, England, and Holland were opposed to the Imperial candidate, re-uniting the Austrian and Spanish Habsburgs. Eventually Charles named the grandson of Louis IV as his heir—Philip V of Spain. French commercial and military moves, and the reservation of Philip's right to the French crown (1700) led to war with England, Holland and the Holy Roman Emperor. In Italy, Prince Eugene of Savoy led Imperial forces in outmaneuvering the French. In 1704, with the French menacing Vienna, John Churchill, Duke of Marlborough (1650–1722), marched to Bavaria and with Eugene won the great victory of Blenheim; victories at Ramillies (1706) Oudenard (1708) and finally Malplaquet (1709) followed. After further indecisive moves, England, Holland and France agreed to terms in the Peace of Utrecht (1713). The crowns of France and Spain would remain separate; the Protestant succession in Britain was guaranteed; the Empire received the Spanish Netherlands and Britain retained Gibraltar. France ceded Acadia, Newfoundland, and Hudson Bay—reflecting fighting in the North American part of the conflict, Queen Anne's War—to Britain. The war had significant balance of power results: the containment of France, the eclipse of Spain in Europe, and recognition of British maritime strength.

War of the Austrian Succession (1740–48)

The Holy Roman Emperor Charles VI (1711–40) had other German princes recognize the right of his daughter, Maria Theresa (1717–80), to inherit his Austrian possessions through the Pragmatic Sanction of 1713. When he died, however, several claimants challenged Maria Theresa's rights; in particular, Frederick II, the Great, of Prussia, pressed a claim for Silesia in modern Poland. At first, the Prussians, together with their French, Spanish, Bavarians and Saxons allies, were successful, but Austria managed to detach Prussia and Saxony from the alliance and Austrian armies, aided by the British and Hanoverians forces under the leadership of King George II, ruler of both states, began to enjoy success. The French, after being driven to the west bank of the Rhine began a drive on the Austrian Netherlands, modern Belgium, that was largely successful. Prussia reentered the war against Austria and, despite being politically isolated, the Prussians were able to repel successive Imperial armies. By the Treaty of Aix-la-Chapelle (1748), Prussia was confirmed in control of Silesia, but otherwise, Maria Theresa's rights under the Pragmatic Sanction were recognized, as well as the election of Maria Theresa's husband, Francis I (1708–65), as Holy Roman Emperor.

The war in Europe spread to India and North America. In America, where the war was known as King George's

War, a joint British and colonial force managed to capture the heavily fortified French stronghold of Louisbourg on Cape Breton and the French captured the important British trading post of Madras in southern India. At war's end, both captures were exchanged, leaving Britain and France in a position to pursue their ambitions in both places in the future.

The Seven Years War (1756–63)

This war embodied both the conflict between Prussia and Austria for supremacy in Germany, and the worldwide engagement between Britain and France. In Germany, Frederick the Great preempted an anticipated attack by the Austrians and their allies, France and Russia (and later Sweden), and entered Saxony in 1756 and then Bohemia. At first successful, reverses put the Prussians in difficulties redeemed by victories at Rossbach and Leuthen (1757). Defeat at Rossbach led to a reduction in France's commitment to the European conflict. Britain, under the government of William Pitt the Elder (1758-61) provided heavy subsidies to Prussia, but even with these and his eventual mastery of the Austrians, Frederick was only spared defeat at the hands of the Russians (who briefly occupied Berlin) by the death of his enemy Empress Elizabeth and the accession of the pro-Prussian Peter III. Russia and Sweden made peace with the Prussians in 1762 and the treaty of Hubertusburg (February 1763) between Prussia, Austria and Saxony restored the central European territorial status quo.

In British-French conflict on the continent, the French started with victories but were soon decisively defeated at Krefeld in 1758 and Minden in 1759, ending the French threat to Hanover in Germany. British superiority at sea brought victories off Lagos (Portugal) and Quiberon Bay (Brittany) in 1759. In Portugal, the British helped to repel an invasion from Spain, which had joined France in a Bourbon alliance.

In North America (The French and Indian War), the British seized French Canada with victories at Louisbourg (1758), Quebec (1759) and Montreal (1760). In the Caribbean, the British took Guadaloupe and Martinique from France and Cuba from Spain (and also, in the Pacific, the Philippines). In India, Robert Clive (1725–74) defeated the French at Plessey (1757) and secured Bengal for the East India Company. British victories at Wandiwash (1760) and Pondicherry (1761) weakened the French position in the Carnatic coast (southeast India).

The results of the Seven Years War decisively established Britain as the leading colonial and sea power of the age. According to the Treaty of Paris (1763), the French abandoned their claims to North America and India. Other provisions of the treaty provided for the return of Guadaloupe and Martinique to France, and Cuba and the Philippines to the Spanish; Spain ceded Florida to Britain and received Louisiana from the French.

The American Revolution (1775–83)

1775 Tensions between England and the Colonies had been steadily growing worse since 1773 as colonists—especially in Boston—took drastic actions to protest British taxation problems. On March 20, 1775, a member of the House of Burgesses in Virginia, Patrick Henry (1736–99), delivered a stirring speech. He concluded by saying: "I know not what course others may take, but as for me—give me liberty, or give me death." In Boston, General Thomas Gage decided to move against radical leaders. Troops moved out of the city towards Concord on the night of April 18. Paul Revere and William Dawes, two local patriots, rode out of Boston to warn of the British move. When troops arrived in Lexington in the early morning hours of April 19, a skirmish broke out between the British and armed citizens known as "minutemen." The British then moved on to Concord, where more militia awaited them. After furious fighting, the British retreated back to Boston, where they were surrounded by patriot militia gathered in the hills overlooking the city. The seige of Boston had begun.

On May 10, patriot troops under the joint command of Ethan Allen and Benedict Arnold seized the British strongpoint of Fort Ticonderoga. That same day, the Second Contintental Congress convened in Philadelphia. John Hancock was elected president of the Congress on May 24. The Congress, on June 15, appointed George Washington as commander in chief of a fledgling American army. But on June 17, British forces assaulted patriot positions on Breed's Hill and Bunker Hill and after a furious battle, the patriots retreated. The cost to the British was horrendous, however, as their casualty rate was nearly 50 percent. Washington arrived in Boston on July 2 and took command of a hodge-podge of colonial militia with a troop strength of about 14,000. On August 23 King George III proclaimed America to be in a state of rebellion. As the seige outside Boston continued through summer, an American force led by General Richard Montgomery set out from Fort Ticonderoga on August 28, bound for Canada with the hope of drawing Canada into the war. On September 12, Washington sent Benedict Arnold north to join the invasion. The British countered the American moves by bombarding and burning Falmouth, now called Portland, Maine on October 18. American troops under Generals Montgomery and Arnold begin a seige of Quebec on December 8. On New Year's Eve, 1775, Montgomery launched an attack to break the siege. The assault failed, and Montgomery was killed. The battered Americans were forced to retreat.

1776 On January 1, the enlistments of thousands of militiamen outside Boston expired, and many went home. George Washington had hoped to have 20,000 men in army in a new Continental Army by this date, but only about 10,000 men volunteered. Washington called up other militia units to fill in gaps in the patriot line until new recruits could be found. Washington could not have asked for better recruiting propaganda than a pamphlet published on January 9 in Phildelphia. Entitled *Common Sense*, it was written by a self-educated Englishman newly arrived in America, Thomas Paine. He assailed the monarchy and advocated complete separation between America and Great Britain.

The war moved south on January 20, when the new British commander in Boston, General William Howe, sent infantry units to North Carolina, where they were to operate with militia units loyal to Britain. Washington convened a council of war at his headquarters in Cambridge, Mass., on Feburary 16 and proposed an assault on Boston to break the seige. His fellow generals, however, were opposed, and the plan was dropped. But on March 4, Washington ordered American troops to fortify Dorchester Heights, which overlooks Boston from the south. Artillery brought from Fort Ticonderoga by Henry Knox (1750–1806) was put in place, allowing the Americans to bombard the British garrison. The British briefly considered an assault on the heights, but weather prevented the action. The last British soldiers evacuated the city on March 17. The Americans took possession of the city later that day.

The war then moved to New York. Anticipating a British assault on the city, Washington's army began marching south on April 13 to set up a defense of Long Island. On April 17 the American warship Lexington, under the command of Capt. John Barry, defeated the British warship HMS Edward off the Virginia coast. Barry was later called the founder of the American Navy. An American adventure in Canada, however, was not as successful. A battle at Trois Rivieres on June 8 ended with a devastating American defeat, bringing the Canadian invasion to an end. On July 3, British General Howe and nearly 10,000 British troops sailed into New York harbor to begin preparations for an attack on the city. The following day, in Philadelphia, the Second Continental Congress accepted the final draft of a Declaration of Independence. The vote, by state, was unanimous, although New York abstained.

British forces began their attack on the American army in what is now Brooklyn on the night of August 26. After suffering high casualties, the Americans withdrew across the East River on the night of August 29, and subsequently withdrew from lower Manhattan in early September. On September 29, a mysterious fire consumed huge swaths of the city. On November 16, the last American outpost in Manhattan fell when Fort Washington and its garrison of 3,000 soldiers surrendered. The bedraggled Americans withdrew through New Jersey and into Pennsylvania, with the British hard on their heels. But on the morning after Christmas, December 26, the Americans launched a successful surprise attack on German mercenaries in Trenton.

1777 As the main British force hurried to Trenton, Washington followed up his victory with another surprise attack, this one on January 4 in Princeton. The armies, following the custom of the day, then retired to winter quarters. Washington camped in Morristown, N.J.

In the summer the British launched an offensive from Canada into upper New York. Troops under General Burgoyne captured Fort Ticonderoga without a fight on July 6. On August 16 the Americans responded, when troops under the command of Brigadier General John Stark defeated an enemy detachment in Bennington, Vt. With General Howe now threatening Philadelphia, Washington moved south and paraded his troops through the city on August 24. But on September 11, the British defeated Washington at the Battle of Brandywine, outside Philadelphia, and members of Congress began to flee the city. The British captured the capital on September 23, and on October 4 defeated Washington again at the Battle of Germantown near Philadelphia.

Meanwhile, in northern New York, American troops under Horatio Gates inflicted huge casualties on Burgoyne on September 19 at Bemis Heights. A new

American assault on October 7 led to Burgoyne's surrender in Saratoga on October 17. Gates's victory led to a movement in Congress to appoint him as the army's new commander. And on December 6, the French government revived talks about a prospective alliance with the American rebels. Washington's battered army established winter quarters in Valley Forge, Pa., on December 19.

1778 The French government recognized American independence on January 6 but throughout the harsh winter American soldiers lived in desperate conditions in snowy Valley Forge, where a breakdown in supplies led to terrible suffering among the troops. On April 24 Captain John Paul Jones (1747–92) of the American navy, in command of the warship *Ranger*, defeated the HMS *Drake* in British waters. Both armies prepared for a new campaign, but the British suddenly began withdrawing from Philadelphia on June 16. The Americans reoccupied the city on June 19 and General Benedict Arnold was named military governor. As the British marched from Philadelphia to New York, Washington attacked on June 28 at Monmouth Court House. The battle was a draw, but it proved the Americans were still strong enough to fight. The British withdrawal continued. The Battle of Monmouth was the last major engagement of the war in the north. The French Navy arrived off Newport, R.I., on July 29, but a planned Franco-American offensive fizzled.

1779 An expedition in the west under the command of George Rogers Clark led to an attack on Fort Sackville near Vincennes in the Illinois Territory. The British garrison surrendered a day later. In the south, a new British strategy to move the war to the Carolinas and Georgia showed promise when the American force was defeated on June 20 at Stono Ferry, S.C. John Paul Jones, commanding the warship *Bonhomme Richard*, won a brutal, costly victory over HMS *Serapis* off the coast of England on September 23. On October 9 American and French forces were mauled in an attack on Savannah, Ga.

1780 On May 12 the Americans suffered their worst defeat of the war and Charleston, S.C. surrendered. The British captured nearly 5,000 prisoners, but on June 23 a small British advance in New Jersey was checked, when Americans under the command of Nathanael Greene won the Battle of Springfield. Congress ordered Horatio Gates to rally the Americans in the South, but on August 16 Gates was defeated when he tried to attack Camden, S.C. For the second time in less than four months, an American force was crushed. More terrible news followed when on September 25, Washington discovered that Benedict Arnold had betrayed the cause and tried to hand over the garrison at West Point to the British. Congress approved Washington's selection of Nathanael Greene to reorganize the American army in the South on October 7. That same day, American militia defeated Loyalist American troops at the battle of Kings Mountain, S.C.

1781 Greene, now in the South, divided his army as he prepared to confront British Lord Cornwallis. The detachment under Daniel Morgan stunned the British at the Battle of Cowpens, S.C., on January 17. Greene and Morgan rejoined forces and retreated into Virginia. Greene returned to North Carolina after gathering militia reinforcements, and on March 15, he fought Cornwallis at the Battle of Guilford Courthouse. Though technically a British victory, Cornwallis suffered high casualties. He eventually withdrew, and on April 24, he left Wilmington, N.C. and marched to Virginia. He settled into camp in Yorktown, Va., on August 5. Sensing an opportunity to attack by land and sea, Washington and his French allies marched and sailed from the north. Pinched between the Franco-American armies and the French Navy, the British surrendered on October 19. Though hostilities continued, in essence the war ended with the surrender of Yorktown.

1783 The final peace treaties were signed on September 3 in Paris. The British evacuated New York, their last outpost, on November 25, and Washington bade farewell to his officers in Fraunces Tavern on December 4.

The Wars of the French Revolution (1792-1802)

These wars arose out of the tumultuous changes of the French Revolution (1789) and its impact on the rest of Europe. The Wars of the French Revolution (1792-1802) began as attempts to defend the revolution and then extended into wars of conquest. The peace of 1801-2 is usually taken as the dividing line with the Napoleonic Wars (1803-1815). Napoleon fought as a brilliant commander in the first series of wars and as the absolute ruler of France in the second.

The European powers, fearful of revolutionary ideas, pressed France to restore Louis XVI. But France declared war on Austria in April, 1792; at first falling back before the allied forces, the French won at Valmy (Sept. 1792) and advanced in the Austrian Netherlands and on the Rhine. The execution of Louis XVI (Jan. 1793) and other actions brought the First Coalition (Britain, Holland, Spain, Austria, and Prussia) into being, . The allies pushed into France, but with the aid of a mass military draft, the French expelled them by the end of 1793; Prussia, Holland, and Spain made peace quickly. Fighting continued, with an Austrian offensive (1796), rapid victories of Napoleon in Italy, and the defeat of the French fleet by Admiral Horatio Nelson (1758–1805) at Aboukir (1798) during Napoleon's invasion of Egypt.

The Second Coalition (Russia, Britain, Turkey, Portugal and Naples) was created in 1798 under Russian leadership. The Allies were victorious in north Italy and Switzerland. Returning from Egypt, Napoleon crushed the Austrians at Marengo (1800) and Moreau won at Hohenlinden (1800). Austria was forced out of the war, and Great Britain, victorious still at sea but war-weary, made peace in 1802 (Treaty of Amiens). In France, Napoleon had become First Consul (1799), First Consul for Life (1802), and then Emperor (1804).

The Napoleonic Wars (1806–15)

Napoleon then faced a new so-called Third Coalition (1805) but he crushed the Austrians at Ulm, scored a brilliant victory over the Russians and Austrians at Austerlitz, and defeated Prussia at Jena (1806), entering Berlin in triumph. After defeating Russia at Friedland (1807) he became master of the continent. Napoleon reorganized the map of Europe, with new kings, including his brothers, other family members, allies and some of his officers, placed on new and existing thrones. Britain remained master of the sea, however, with a decisive victory over the French at Trafalgar (1805), again led by Nelson. Napoleon resolved to beat Britain with an economic blockade, the Continental System.

Austria attempted to reopen the war and was beaten at Wagram (1809), but Napoleon faced continuing problems in the Peninsular War in Spain and Portugal, where (1808–14) he was frustrated and his marshals ultimately defeated by the British under Wellington and Spanish and Portuguese regulars and guerrillas. The Russian Czar's rejection of the economically ruinous Continental System was the impetus for the turning point in Napoleon's fortunes. He crossed into Russia with an army of 500,000 in June, 1812 but in September he failed to achieve a decisive victory at Borodino and entered a devastated and burning Moscow, set ablaze by the Russians. Now he had no winter quarters, long supply lines, and few sources of local supply. He began a disastrous retreat and after the crossing of the Berezina River (November) his decimated army was in complete rout. Napoleon abandoned his forces to return to Paris to regroup. A new anti-French coalition was formed, and at Leipzig (Oct. 1813) Napoleon was forced to retreat; he was offered terms (France to return to borders of Rhine and Alps) and refused; the Allies entered Paris in March, 1814. Napoleon abdicated, was exiled to the island of Elba and replaced by Louis XVIII. In March 1815 he escaped and landed at Cannes. Thus began the Hundred Days, when the Allies finally destroyed Napoleon's army at Waterloo, under the Duke of Wellington (1769–1852) and von Blücher (1742–1819). Napoleon died in 1821 in exile on the desolate island of Saint Helena.

Crimean War (1853-56)

Claiming the right to protect Orthodox Christians within the Ottoman Empire, the Russian Czar Nicholas I (1796-1855), sent troops into Moldavia and Wallachia (Romania today), and defeated a Turkish fleet at Sinop on the Black Sea (1853). The British and French, fearing Russian ambitions in the Balkans and the Near East, supported Turkey and declared war on Russia (March, 1854). In September 1854 British, French, Sardinian and Turkish troops landed on the Crimean peninsula (Black Sea) for a bloody year-long siege of the Russian naval base at Sevastopol. The appalling condition of sick and wounded Allied troops was given prominence by Florence Nightingale (1820–1910), leading to important reforms in nursing care. The allies were victorious at Balaklava (immortalized in Tennyson's poem "The Charge of the Light Brigade") and Inkerman. After the capture of strong points overlooking the city, the allies secured Sevastopol in 1855. (The Crimean War also involved fighting in the Caucasus and the Baltic.) Alexander II (1818-1881), Nicholas's son and successor, sued for peace. The Treaty of Paris (1856) provided for the territorial integrity of the Ottoman Empire, the neutralization of the Black Sea, and Russian renunciation of its claim of protection of Orthodox Christians under Turkish rule.

The American Civil War (1861–65)

1861 The Civil War began when the first shots were fired at Fort Sumter on April 12, 1861. Determined to maintain a symbolic presence of federal authority in the heart of the Confederacy, newly installed President Abraham

Lincoln informed the South Carolina government of his intention to send a ship with supplies to Fort Sumter, a garrison in Charleston harbor still in federal hands. Confederates responded by demanding surrender of the fort and when he refused began an artillery assault and the garrison surrendered the next day. On April 15 Lincoln declared the lower South to be in state of "insurrection" and called for 75,000 men to enlist for the purposed of putting down the rebellion. Immediately, four more southern states seceded, and the nation prepared for war.

Despite their lack of training and equipment, the Confederate and Union armies met at the Battle of Bull Run (The First Battle of Manassas) in Virginia on July 21, 1861. After the Union Army under nearly drove the Confederates from the field, the latter rallied and staged a furious counter assault. Exhausted and undisciplined, Union soldiers panicked and began a chaotic retreat to Washington. The loss was deeply embarrassing to the Lincoln administration and greatly boosted morale in the Confederacy.

1862 While the Union Army in Virginia (soon to named the Army of the Potomac), now under the leadership of Gen. George B. McClellan (1826–85), regrouped, the war in the west heated up. Union victory depended on the army controlling the Mississippi River (thereby splitting the Confederacy in two) and seizing the key rail lines vital to the southern economy.

In February 1862 Union troops, led by a virtual unknown named Gen. Ulysses S. Grant (1822–85), seized Forts Henry and Donelson on the Tennessee River. The twin victories gave the Union control of vital communication and transportation routes on the Tennessee and Cumberland Rivers and drove the Confederates out of Kentucky and most of Tennessee.

An extraordinary naval clash occurred on March 8, 1862 when the *Virginia* (Confederate) and *Monitor* (Union) met off Hampton Roads, Virginia. The ensuing battle — the first ever between ironclad vessels – ended in a draw and left both ships badly damaged. The Virginia retreated up the James River where it did no damage, but did prevent McClellan from using the river in his upcoming campaign.

Less than three weeks later, Confederate fortunes in the west suffered another setback. The far west, including California, was secured from Confederate seizure after Union forces triumphed at the Battle of Glorieta Pass (March 26-28, 1862) in New Mexico. Further east, Grant withstood a surprise Confederate attack near Shiloh Church, Tennessee (April 6) and then counter-attacked to drive the Confederates off in retreat. Grant's victory left the Union Army in control of the Mississippi River south to Memphis, Tennessee. Working at the other end of the Mississippi, Union Navy Captain David G. Farragut (1801–1870) captured New Orleans (May 1), dealing a devastating blow to Confederate hopes as it closed the mouth of the Mississippi and put under Union control the South's largest city and most important commercial center.

In the spring of 1862, after lengthy delays (despite Lincoln's constant urging to move on the Confederate capital at Richmond, Va.), McClellan finally commenced his Peninsular Campaign. When the campaign became bogged down with delays, a Confederate force under General Thomas "Stonewall" Jackson (1824–63) went north and threatened an attack on Washington, D.C., prompting Lincoln to withhold 30,000 troops from McClellan to protect the capital.

It was late May before McClellan finally moved on Richmond. The Confederates attacked McClellan's slow moving force of 110,000 in the Battle of Fair Oaks (also called Seven Pines) on May 31-June 1, 1862. Although technically a Union victory the battle proved inconclusive. Yet it was an important turning point in that the Confederate general was severely injured and replaced by Robert E. Lee (1807–70).

Lee recalled Jackson from the Shenandoah Valley and led an offensive against McClellan to separate the Army of the Potomac from its York River base and destroy it. The Seven Days Battle (June 25 - July 1, 1862) was bloody but inconclusive as both armies remained in the field. McClellan's army lay just 25 miles from Richmond, but he refused to move on Lee's weakened army, claiming he had inadequate amounts of intelligence, men and supplies.

Thoroughly frustrated, Lincoln ordered McClellan to abandon the Peninsular Campaign and remove the Army of Potomac to northern Virginia to unite with other forces for a traditional overland assault on Richmond. But Lee moved north and defeated those troops (August 29-30, 1862) in the Second Battle of Bull Run (Second Manassas) before McClellan could join him.

In September McClellan attacked Lee's army which had moved north into Maryland. The Battle of Antietam (Sharpsburg) claimed a total of 6,000 lives and left 17,000 wounded, making it the bloodiest single day of the war. The next day Lee took his tattered army back into Virginia, handing McClellan, who opted not to pursue, a technical victory.

Lincoln issued a preliminary Emancipation Proclamation that declared unless the seceded states returned to the Union by January 1, 1863, their slaves "shall be then, thenceforward, and forever free." Emancipation struck a blow at the foundation of southern society and all but eliminated the possibility that England would intervene in the conflict.

On Nov. 7, after McClellan refused to move against Lee, claiming as always that he lacked sufficient troops and supplies, an exasperated Lincoln relieved him of command and replaced him with General Ambrose E. Burnside (1824–81) who immediately formulated plans for an offensive against Richmond. Yet Burnside's impulsiveness proved almost as ruinous as McClellan's timidity for at the Battle of Fredericksburg (December 13, 1862) he ordered repeated attacks on fortified Confederate positions with disastrous results (nearly 13,000 casualties compared to Lee's 5,300).

Not all the news from the Union battlefields in late 1862 was negative. Union troops turned back an attempt by Confederates, to regain western Tennessee and Kentucky. After months of inconclusive maneuvering, the two forces finally clashed on December 31 in Tennessee in the Battle of Murfreesboro (Stone's River). When the Confederates retreated on January 2, 1863, the west was firmly in the hands of the Union Army for the rest of the war.

1863 The Emancipation Proclamation took effect on January 1, 1863, but it would be no more than a lofty declaration if the Union lost the war. In April 1863, 120,000 soldiers of the Army of the Potomac, now under Gen. Joseph Hooker (1814–79), once again set out to defeat Lee and take Richmond. At Chancellorsville (May 2, 1863) Lee divided his army and led one half in frontal assault against Hooker's center, while "Stonewall" Jackson attacked Hooker's right flank. After three days of bloody fighting the Army of the Potomac was nearly destroyed, and Hooker barely managed to retreat.

But Lee's stunning victory at Chancellorsville came at a very high price as he lost more than 20 percent of his men, including the man he had come to count on most, "Stonewall" Jackson, killed accidentally by his own men.

Despite these losses, Lee took the offensive and plunged into Union territory, crossing through Maryland into Pennsylvania. It was a risky move, but one he hoped would cause such alarm in the North as to force Grant to pull back from the west. Victory on northern soil would demoralize the Lincoln administration and strengthen the hand of "Peace Democrats" who were calling for a negotiated settlement with the Confederacy.

Although slow to react, the Army of the Potomac, now under Gen. George C. Meade, eventually confronted Lee at Gettysburg, a small town at the junction of several major roads. For two days, the two armies clashed in the bloodiest fighting yet. On numerous occasions, each side seemed about to gain the upper hand, only to be turned back. On the third and decisive day, Lee threw caution to the wind and ordered on all-out assault on the heavily fortified Union center. "Pickett's Charge" as it became known, proved gallant, but suicidal as Union forces devastated Gen. George Pickett's 15,000 men as they tried to cross one mile of open field and ascend Cemetery Ridge. The next day, July 4, having lost one-third of his men (28,000 killed, wounded, or missing), Lee removed his tattered army back toward Virginia. Gettysburg was a major Union victory that ensured the Confederate Army would never again threaten the North.

On the day of Lee's retreat, Grant accepted the surrender of Vicksburg where he had been laying siege since mid-May. Vicksburg was the Confederacy's last stronghold on the Mississippi and the victory severed the South in two, leaving the Union in control of the entire Mississippi River.

Ten days later rioting broke out in New York City and lasted for four days before federal troops quelled the violence. Mobs of poor workers, many of them immigrants, took to the streets to protest the imposition of a draft instituted by the Lincoln administration to replenish the dwindling ranks of the Union Army. The riots did millions of dollars in damage and left 119 dead, including more than a dozen blacks blamed by the mob for the war and draft.

Even as rioters in New York blamed African Americans for the bloody war, 54th Massachusetts regiment, a unit made up of free blacks, became one of the first African American units given a chance to fight. Their nighttime assault on Fort Wagner (July 18, 1863), a key Confederate outpost that guarded the harbor in Charleston, S.C., like all others before it, was repulsed with extremely high casualties. But the courage exhibited by the soldiers under fire won them universal praise and did much to undermine the racist belief that blacks would not stand and fight. Eventually, some 180,000 blacks served in the Army (ten percent of the total Union Army), 38,000 of whom died.

In November, Grant and the general he increasingly counted on, William T. Sherman (1820–91), attacked the Confederate army in Tennesee and drove his army back into Georgia. Victory in the Battle of Chattanooga (Nov. 23-25, 1863) boosted northern morale and put most of eastern Tennessee and the vital Tennessee River in Union hands. Already cut in two after the fall of Vicksburg, the Confederacy now faced the prospect of being sliced into thirds.

1864 In the beginning of 1864 Lincoln named Grant commander of all Union armies. He recognized in Grant a commander who understood the key to victory in modern warfare—seek out and destroy the enemy's army rather than seize territory. Grant planned a two-pronged attack to finish off the Confederacy. He sent the 120,000 men of the Army of the Potomac south to destroy Lee's army of 66,000 and to take Richmond. Sherman, a man who shared Grant's understanding of modern warfare, took an army of 90,000 from Tennessee and pushed east to destroy the Confederate force of 60,000 and to seize Atlanta.

In the first clash, known as the Battle of the Wilderness, Grant hurled his army against Lee's for two days (May 5-6). Aided by the rough, wooded terrain and sluggish Union leadership, the Confederates successfully survived Grant's offensive and withdrew. Both sides lost huge numbers of men (18,000 federals to 12,000 Confederates). Unlike his predecessors who customarily opted for rest and recouperation after a major engagement, Grant ordered his army to pursue Lee the very next day. On May 8 the two armies clashed again 10 miles closer to Richmond in the Battle of Spotsylvania Court House, an epic struggle that played out for days and left another 30,000 casualties between the two armies. Lee's army was weakened but remained intact.

Grant continued southward, trying to draw Lee out for a final, decisive battle. Lee worked to keep his army between Grant and Richmond, playing for time and avoiding total defeat. A third major engagement occurred on June 3 at Cold Harbor. Grant again ordered a massive assault against Lee's smaller but heavily entrenched force. The result was the greatest loss of life since Fredericksburg in December 1862. More than 7,000 federals fell compared to fewer than 1,500 Confederates.

After the disaster at Cold Harbor, Grant changed his strategy. He moved his army south past Richmond and seized the vital railroad junction at Petersburg. If he took the town, he would cut Richmond off from the rest of the Confederacy. But Lee kept his exhausted army on the move and managed to dig in around Petersburg before Grant arrived. By now Grant recognized the futility of staging frontal assaults against entrenched troops and settled down for a prolonged siege.

General Sherman faced less resistance. His opponent tried to avoid a direct fight. But Sherman, like Grant, refused to stop in his drive toward Atlanta and took the city on September 2. It was a crushing blow that all but doomed the Confederacy to collapse. Further adding to their woes was the fact that the victory boosted northern morale and helped re-elect Lincoln in November, thereby killing the hope that a war-weary Democrat would win and open peace negations with the Confederacy.

Shortly after seizing Atlanta, Sherman's army embarked on an epic journey across the state of Georgia to deprive the Confederate Army of badly needed supplies and to demoralize the southern people. Six weeks after Lincoln won re-election, as Sherman moved into Georgia, he sent a detachment of troops which all but destroyed the Confederate force at the Battle of Nashville (December 15-16, 1864). Less than a week later, Sherman's army took Savannah. Known as the "March to the Sea," Sherman's 285-mile campaign left a 60-mile wide swath of destruction in its wake. More than $100 million in property was seized or destroyed and the Confederate army had lost a major source of supplies.

1865 With Georgia now in ashes, the stage was set for the final phase of Grant's plan—the crushing of Lee's army between his and Sherman's forces. On February 1, Sherman left Savannah and headed north into South Carolina. He faced almost no opposition and took the city of Columbia, South Carolina on February 17th then continued north into North Carolina where the meager opposition provided by General Joseph E. Johnston's force slowed him only slightly.

By now Grant's nearly nine-month long siege of Lee's army at Petersburg began to take its toll. Cut off from supplies, Lee's men were starving. Thousands had deserted. On April 1, in the Battle of Five Forks, General Philip Sheridan's (1831–88) cavalry and a large force of infantry attacked Lee's right flank and cut off the only remaining railroad line into Petersburg. When Grant attacked all along the Confederate line the next day, he forced Lee to retreat from both Richmond and Petersburg. Lee's one remaining hope was to somehow slip his ragged army west and south to join forces with Johnston in North Carolina. To prevent this, Grant dispatched Sheridan's cavalry which headed them off at a place called Appomattox Courthouse, Virginia. On April 8 Lee made one last attempt to break out, but failed. The next day, April 9, 1865, Lee surrendered. Almost four years to the day that the first shots were fired at Fort Sumter, the Civil War was over.

The Franco-Prussian War (1870-71)

Otto von Bismarck (1815–98), the Prussian Chancellor, believing that a victorious war with France would encourage independent south German states to join with the Prussian-led North German Confederation, goaded the French into declaring war (July 15, 1870) over an attempt to place a German prince on the Spanish throne. A Prussian-led invasion of France under Marshall Helmuth von Moltke (1800–91) resulted in an overwhelming victory at the Battle of Sedan (September 1, 1870) in which 80,000 prisoners were taken, including Napoleon III; the fortress of Metz surrendered October 27, 1870. A provisional French government deposed Napoleon III (1808–73) and declared the Third Republic. Paris was surrounded in September and capitulated on January 28, 1871. The Treaty of Frankfurt (May 10, 1871) resulted in France's loss of most of Alsace and Lorraine and the payment of a heavy indemnity. At Versailles, William I of Prussia (1797–1888) was declared Emperor of Germany. The war transformed Germany, changed the balance of power, and prefigured the First World War.

World War I

On June 28, 1914, a Serb nationalist assassinated the Austrian Archduke Francis Ferdinand, the heir to the Austrian throne, in Sarajevo. This was the flashpoint that led to war, but the causes ran much deeper. The war followed decades of imperialist, economic, and territorial rivalries among the great powers, accompanied by an armaments race empowered by new technology and industrial development. Serbia rejected an ultimatum by Austria-Hungary, which declared war on July 28. Russia mobilized, and was answered by a German declaration of war (August 1). The Germans, believing France was about to attack, declared war on France (August 3) and sent troops through Belgium and Luxembourg. Britain joined the war in response to the German invasion and violation of the treaty of Belgian neutrality. The two sides in the war were the Central Powers (Germany and Austria-Hungary, later joined by Turkey and Bulgaria) and the Allies (France, Great Britain, Russia the Triple Entente countries, Serbia and Belgium, later joined by the U.S. and many other countries). Italy declined to fight with the Central Powers and later joined the Allies.

1914

The Western Front Following mobilization, the Germans and the French acted in accordance with their pre-war battle plans. The German commander Helmuth von Moltke (1848–1916), nephew of the 19th century Prussian commander, carried out the Schlieffen plan, named for its author, a former chief of the German general staff, and launched an invasion of Belgium. During the initial weeks of the war, the Germans were able to keep to their plan's timetable. Despite a setback delivered by the British at Mons, the Germans occupied almost all of Belgium and were soon deep in France. In the course of their occupation, German soldiers were accused of committing atrocities, which were used by the Allies to turn neutral opinion against the Central Powers.

The German plan was formulated on the assumption that the French would stay on the defensive behind a line of fortresses. Since the Germans did not wish to mount a direct assault on the French fortresses, the invasion through Belgium was a way to outflank them. The French, however, in their final pre-war plan, Plan XVII, proposed a massive frontal attack against the German border, leaving the northern border with Belgium largely undefended. The resulting offensive, known as the Battle of the Frontiers, squandered countless French lives against superior German firepower. Meanwhile, the main German force continued to push south towards Paris, although their plan had originally called for a sweep west of Paris. The French and British attacked the German right flank and forced the Germans back at the First Battle of the Marne. The Germans , however, were able to retreat to easily defended positions within France. As the Germans began to fortify their new positions, there began the "Race to the Sea". The initial French retreat had left the northern coast undefended. The French sent troops north to insure that they, and not the Germans, controlled the coast, representing as it did a vital link to

Britain. The Germans too moved to seize the coast, culminating in the First Battle of Ypres in which the Germans suffered heavy casualties. As 1914 ended, the Western Front had assumed the shape, from the sea to the Swiss border, that it would retain until the autumn of 1918. This front was the scene of innumerable casualties on both sides in seemingly unending trench warfare.

The Eastern Front A small German army had been left to guard the Prussian heartland against a larger Russian force. To relieve pressure on the French, the Russians moved swiftly against the Germans. Command in the East was turned over to Paul von Hindenburg (1847–1934) and his chief of staff, Erich Ludendorff (1865–1937). The Russians were forced to split their armies and the numerically inferior Germans were able to defeat them at the Battle of Tannenberg and at the Masurian Lakes. Elsewhere in the east the Central Powers were less successful. A divided Austrian army was unable to defeat Serbia in the south and was itself defeated in Galicia, Austrian Poland.

War Outside Europe The Allies quickly seized Germany's overseas possessions with the exception of German East Africa (modern Tanzania), where resistance continued up to 1918. On the borders of the Ottoman Empire there were three major areas of combat. After years of stalemate, British and Commonwealth troops, aided by Arab rebels, overwhelmed Turkish troops in Palestine and by war's end, the Allies had seized Damascus in Syria. Anglo-Indian troops invaded Mesopotamia (modern Iraq) early in the war to protect British oil interests in the Persian Gulf. After initial successes, an invading army was forced to surrender at Kut al-Amara in 1916 and by war's end the Allies had failed to make a breakthrough on this front. The Turkish war effort was primarily directed against the Russian Trans-Caucasus provinces. The Russians repulsed these attacks and pushed into Turkey. Local support for the invaders triggered massacres of Armenians in the Ottoman Empire. After the outbreak of the Russian Revolution, the Caucasus front collapsed and by war's end German and Turkish troops had invaded the Trans-Caucasus region and Russian Central Asia.

1915

The Western Front As 1915 began, the combatants began to realize that, notwithstanding pre-war predictions, the war would be long. The British in particular realized that they could not rely only on their navy to conduct the war and began to raise and equip a large continental army. The stalemate on the Western Front continued, despite the second battle of Ypres, in which the Germans used poison gas for the first time in the West. Allied offensives—the French in Artois and Champagne, and the British toward Lens and Loos, failed to effect breakthroughs.

The Eastern Front Although denied additional troops from the west, von Hindenburg and Ludendorff finally got permission to mount an offensive against the Russians in conjunction with the Austrians. This offensive proved successful and the Russians were driven from Poland, but the Russian army remained intact. Serbia and Montenegro were overrun by Bulgarian and Austro-Hungarian troops.

Winston Churchill (1871–1974), the British First Lord of the Admiralty, and others had begun to question direct assaults on the Western Front early on. Churchill, a firm believer in sea power, began to lobby for the opening of another front; he proposed a naval attack on the Dardanelles opening the way to Constantinople. Such an attack, it was argued, would drive the Turks out of the war and relieve pressure on the Russians. Although Allied military commanders were reluctant to spare troops from the Western Front a force was collected and dispatched to aid the naval operations. After the navy proved unable to clear the Dardanelles itself, these troops were landed on the European shore of Turkey near the town of Gallipoli. Despite substantial casualties on both sides, the Turks remained in possession of the heights and late in 1915 it was decided to abandon the attack.

The Naval War The British, with substantial naval supremacy, relied on an ever tightening blockade of the Central Powers to drive their enemies to sue for peace. In 1914 a series of engagements designed to eliminate German naval and commercial presence outside Europe had moderate success. Despite a setback at the Battle of Coronel off Chile, this goal was largely accomplished by year's end. Germany feared to risk its battle fleet in a single great battle, and was content to launch a series of raids on British North Sea ports. Finally, in 1916, the Germans steamed out to meet the British high seas fleet at the Battle of Jutland (May 31). The battle was a draw but because the Germans needed to break the blockade, it was essentially a German loss. Mounting German frustration with the British blockade led eventually to unrestricted submarine warfare, which would lead to the United States' entry into the war. Although Allied commerce was disrupted by this warfare, the Germans never possessed sufficient submarines to inflict a serious blow on the Allied cause.

1916

The Western Front In an attempt to weaken the French the German Chief of Staff Erich von Falkenhayn (1861–1922) decided to attack the French fortress town of Verdun, which the French would have to defend, if they chose, at heavy cost. The town was of little strategic importance but the French rose to the bait and resolved to hold the position at all costs. As time passed, however, the Germans lost sight of their original objective and became obsessed with taking the town without regard to their own casualties. In the end, both sides came to invest the battle with an importance far beyond its strategic significance. By the end of 1916 the French had recaptured lost ground and the position was approximately what it was before the attack, at the cost of an estimated 300,000 casualties on both sides. Von Falkenhayn was dismissed.

In order to take pressure off of the French at Verdun the British in June launched a campaign of five months duration known as the Battle of the Somme. The British used tanks for the first time, and after months of deadly attritional warfare the British could claim, in November, small territorial gains and the imposition of heavy casualties on the German field army. But at the end of the year stalemate continued in the West and an estimated 1.2 million men lost their lives, perhaps 650,000 Germans, 400,000 British, and 200,000 French.

The Eastern Front The Russians launched an offensive against the Austrians in southern Poland, but after driving them back a considerable distance, the offensive stalled and there was no general reversal of the Russian losses of 1915. The offensive did, however, prompt Romania, which had been neutral from to declare for the Allies. This proved disastrous. Bulgaria, which had joined the Central Powers, served as a staging ground for a Bulgarian-Turkish invasion of Romania, while German and Austrian troops stopped a Romanian invasion of Hungary and went on the offensive. In a matter of weeks, all of Romania had fallen to the Central Powers, except for a portion close to Russia. Anglo-French troops in Salonika in Greece attempted to put pressure on Bulgaria by marching north, but a small force of Bulgarians and Germans was able to stop them.

The Italian Front Italy joined the Allies in 1916. The Italians launched a series of battles on the Isonzo River. The strategic goal was to breach the Alps and drive on to Vienna. However, those Alps were among the most rugged in Europe and the Austrian position was easily defensible. The Austrians attacked from Trentino, crossing the border and driving on Venice, only to be stopped by resolute defense at Monte Ciova.

1917

The Western Front The French commander since the beginning of the war, Marshall Joseph Joffre (1852–1931), lost the confidence of the government and was replaced in late 1916 by Robert Nivelle (1856–1924), who had convinced his political superiors that he had a formula for breaking the stalemate in the west. His offensive in early 1917 proved a disaster. The offensive in Champagne resulted in little gain, but stretched the morale of the French army to the breaking point, resulting in widespread mutinies. Nivelle was replaced by Philippe Petain (1856–1951), who quickly dealt with soldiers' grievances instituting a policy of rest and retraining that effectively took the French army out of the war for the rest of 1917. The British responded to requests to take pressure off the French by planning a summer offensive in Flanders. This offensive, the Third Battle of Ypres, consisted of a series of engagements, among them the battle for Passchendaele ridge, that resulted in horrific British and Commonwealth losses for little gain. On April 6, the United States declared war on Germany, but needed time to mobilize troops.

The Eastern Front Having crushed Romania, the Central Powers turned on Serbia. Austrian, German, and Bulgarian troops launched an offensive, Amid great hardships, the Serbian army managed to escape and was eventually ferried to Salonika. In March of 1917, revolution broke out in St. Petersburg and within a short period of time, the Tsar abdicated. Power was assumed by Alexander Kerensky (1881–1970), a Socialist committed to continuing the war against the Central Powers. Kerensky's policy was undermined by the Bolsheviks under V.I. Lenin (1870–1924) and Leon Trotsky (1879–1940), who seized power in November. The Bolsheviks offered the Central Powers a truce and in March 1918, the Treaty of Brest-Litovsk was signed, effectively ending the war against the Central Powers in the east, although civil war continued in Russia for years.

The Italian Front The Austrians, re-enforced by Germans, decisively defeated the Italian army at the Battle of Caporetto, driving it back to the River Piave. Timely re-enforcement by British and French troops stabilized the line, but at the cost of weakening the Western Front.

1918 The collapse of Russia in 1917 meant that soldiers were available for a last German offensive in the west. In March of 1918, the Germans attacked the British army near Amiens in an attempt to separate it from the French. After enjoying initial success, the German advance slowed and eventually stalled. Having failed to break the British army, Ludendorff turned against the French army in Champagne, culminating in the Second Battle of the Marne, in which the Germans were stopped short of Paris (July-August). In August, the Allies began a counter offensive that made steady progress at high cost. For the first time in the war American troops distinguished themselves in such battles as St. Mihiel, Chateau Thierry, and the Argonne Forest. The German army was not routed but increasing numbers of German troops surrendered, in part because the Americans represented an accession of power to the Allies that more than offset Russia and in part because of Germany's deteriorating political and military position. Internal opposition to the war grew resulting in strikes and other disturbances in German cities. Finally, the government was forced to ask for an armistice based on principles set forth earlier by U.S. President Woodrow Wilson (1856–1924). Austria, Bulgaria and Turkey sued for peace and the German fleet mutinied at its home port of Kiel. Wilhelm II(1859–1941) left Berlin and went into exile in the Netherlands for the rest of his life. The armistice ending the war was signed by an interim government on November 11, 1918.

Aftermath A peace conference was held in Paris that resulted in 1919 in signing of the Treaty of Versailles ending the war with Germany. (Other treaties were signed with Austria, Hungary, Bulgaria, and Turkey.) The Treaty of Versailles placed the responsibility for the war on Germany and its allies, imposed reparations and military sanctions on Germany, returned Alsace and Lorraine to France, demilitarized the Rhineland, and made other territorial arrangements including several crucial ones in the Middle East that gave Great Britain and France a firm foothold in the oil-rich region. The United States Senate refused to ratify the Treaty of Versailles and with it the League of Nations, simply declaring in 1921 that the war with Germany was over. The treaties that concluded the war in the end satisfied neither victors nor vanquished, and hope for permanent collective security through creation of the League of Nations, which had some successes, ultimately proved ephemeral.

World War II

1939 On September 1, Germany invaded Poland from the west. Britain and France declared war on Germany on September 3. The United States had declared its neutrality on May 1, 1937, when Roosevelt signed the Permanent Neutrality Bill into law, and on September 5 he invoked that law. On September 8, however, President Roosevelt authorized a military buildup. The Soviets invaded Poland from the east on September 17. Warsaw surrendered on September 27, and the Germans and Soviets partitioned Poland on September 29. The Soviets then invaded Finland on November 30. In mid-December, the Royal Navy battled the German warship *Graf Spee* off the South American (Montevideo) coast. The ship's captain scuttled the *Graf Spee* on December 17, giving the British a morale boost.

1940 With little action on the main front, the Germans occupied Denmark and invaded Norway on April 9. The so-called "phony war" in Europe came to an end on May 10 with a massive German invasion of Belgium, the Netherlands, and Luxembourg. British Prime Minister Neville Chamberlain (1869–1940) resigned and was replaced by the First Lord of the Admiralty, Winston Churchill. On May 13, Churchill told Britain and the world that he had "nothing to offer but blood, toil, tears and sweat." German troops crossed into France that same day. On May 26, with the battle in France lost, the British began evacuating their expeditionary force from the port of Dunkirk.

Norway surrendered on June 9; France, on June 22. With Hitler triumphant in Europe, Roosevelt declared a national emergency in the United States on June 27. In preparation for a planned invasion of Britain, the German air force (Luftwaffe) attacked Royal Air Force bases on August 15. The onslaught was massive, but the R.A.F. prevailed. Not long after this pivotal battle, the Germans changed their strategy and began bombing cities. The R.A.F. bombed Berlin on August 25 and 26.

On September 16, President Roosevelt signed the Selective Service Bill, authorizing the draft of Americans between the ages of 21 and 35. With a cross-channel invasion scheduled for September 21, the Germans launched their largest air raid on Britain on September 15, hoping to destroy the R.A.F. The effort failed, and the invasion was postponed. The Luftwaffe continued to bomb England, leading to a massive raid on Coventry on November 14.

1941 British forces in Libya routed the Italians, capturing Tobruk on January 22. The Australians and British followed up with a victory in Benghazi on February 6. On that day, Erwin Rommel (1891–1944) was given command of Germany's Afrika Korps, which was sent to Libya to assist the beleaguered Italians. On March 11, the U.S. Senate passed the Lend-Lease Act, which authorized Roosevelt to send arms and equipment to Britain and other countries opposing the Axis (50 destroyers had already been exchanged in September 1940).

On April 6 German troops invaded Yugoslavia and Greece. Rudolf Hess, the third most-powerful man in Nazi Germany, parachuted into Britain on May 10 on a bizarre, unauthorized mission to broker peace between Germany and the British. The Royal Navy sank the German battleship Bismarck on May 27.

In a move that stunned a world already familiar with the unthinkable, Germany invaded the Soviet Union on June 22. Hitler's huge commitment of men and material to the Eastern Front meant that Britain was safe from invasion. It also changed the war's dynamics. On July 31, the head of the Luftwaffe, Hermann Göring, used the phrase "final solution" in discussing what was to be done with Europe's Jews.

Winston Churchill and President Roosevelt met face to face in Newfoundland on August 9-12 to create an eight-point program of war aims, subsequently named the Atlantic Charter. After Nazi U-boats attacked numerous American ships, Roosevelt issued the order on September 11 to "shoot at sight" any German or Italian ship encountered by American ships or planes.

Germany ordered Jews to wear a Star of David beginning September 13. The following day, more than a half-million Russians surrendered near Kiev. In Asia, Japan's War Minister, Hideki Tojo (1884–1948), was named Prime Minister on October 16, signaling a more aggressive policy toward the United States. On December 6, the new Soviet commander of Moscow, General Georgi Zhukov (1896–1974), launched a massive counter-attack against German forces.

On December 7 Japanese warplanes attacked the U.S. naval base of Pearl Harbor in Hawaii. The United States declared war on Japan the following day. Germany and Italy declared war on the U.S. on December 11.

1942 The German SS, the elite military units of the Nazis, officially adopted a policy of genocide against the Jews on January 20. The Japanese captured the British garrison of Singapore, thought to be impregnable, on February 15. On March 11 U.S. General Douglas MacArthur left the Philippines, soon to fall to the Japanese. He told the Filipinos: "I shall return." The Japanese overran an American garrison on Bataan on April 9. Nearly 75,000 American and Filipino prisoners were captured, and many died during the Bataan Death March. American morale improved on April 18 when General James Doolittle, flying from the carrier USS Hornet, led an air raid on Tokyo. Less than a month later, from May 4–8, U.S. carriers and planes clashed with Japanese forces in the Battle of the Coral Sea. On May 6 American ground forces on Corregidor surrendered.

More than a thousand British aircraft bombed the German city of Cologne during the night of May 30. Thanks to intercepts of Japanese communications, the American fleet won the Battle of Midway on June 4–6. Japan lost four carriers, and America would now go on the offensive in the Pacific. In North Africa, Rommel overran the British garrison of Tobruk in Libya on June 21.

America's 1st Marine Division invaded Guadalcanal on August 7. British forces under the command of General Bernard Montgomery (1887–1976) launched the battle of El Alamein on October 24, beginning the Allied reconquest of North Africa. American and British troops invaded Algeria and Morocco on November 8. Code-named Operation Torch, it was the beginning of major Anglo-American operations against the Germans. In Russia, the Red Army began a major offensive to relieve Stalingrad on November 19.

1943 The Battle of Stalingrad ended with a stunning German surrender on January 31, a turning point of the war in Europe. In the Pacific theater, the Japanese evacuated Guadalcanal on February 9. And in North Africa, the leader of Germany's famed Afrika Korps, Rommel, left the region on March 9 after a string of defeats. Polish Jews in Warsaw launched an uprising on April 19. It would end on May 16, with few survivors.

The Anglo-American conquest of North Africa was completed on May 12 with the surrender of remaining Axis troops. The victorious Allies then invaded Sicily on July 10. Fifteen days later, on July 25, the Italian dictator Benito Mussolini(1883–1945) was overthrown and placed under arrest. Italy ended hostilities with the Allies on September

3, and the American army invaded Salerno on September 9 to fight German forces in Italy. German troops rescued Mussolini from his captors on September 12. The Soviets continued their dramatic westward push, recapturing Kiev on November 6.

U.S. Marines landed on Tarawa in the Gilbert Islands on November 20. Roosevelt, Churchill and Stalin met together for the first time in Tehran, Iran, from November 28 to December 1. The leaders discussed preparations for an invasion of Nazi-held France. Rommel was named to oversee German defenses in France on December 12. Dwight Eisenhower was appointed supreme commander of the Mediterranean unified command on December 24.

1944 Allied troops landed in Anzio on January 22. The Red Army relieved Leningrad on January 27 after a 900-day siege. A million or more civilians most likely died.

American troops entered Rome on June 4 after weeks of bitter fighting. On June 6, American, British and Canadian troops landed in Normandy as part of the long-expected invasion of Hitler's Fortress Europe. Five thousand ships, the largest armada in history, took part in the D-Day invasion, Operation Overlord. Some 150,000 troops were put ashore on five beaches.

U.S. Marines, moving closer to the Japanese home islands, invaded Saipan on June 15. American naval forces sank two Japanese carriers during the Battle of the Philippine Sea on June 19–20. Tojo was ousted as the civilian and military leader of Japan in July.

With the Allies pressing on both the western and eastern fronts, a group of dissident German officers attempted to kill Adolf Hitler on July 20. The plot failed. Among those implicated was Field Marshal Erwin Rommel, who was allowed to commit suicide. American and Free French troops invaded southern France on August 15 in what became known as the "Champagne Campaign." The Russians moved into Poland in late July and into Romania on August 20. The liberation of Paris took place on August 25, with the Free French army leading the way. A new German offensive from the air began on September 8, when a V-2 rocket landed in Britain.

U.S. Marines landed on Peleliu Island in the Pacific on September 15. In a daring but vain move, the Allies tried to get behind German lines by landing paratroops near Arnhem in Holland on September 17 (Operation Market-Garden). Survivors later were evacuated.

On October 2 German troops put down a two-month civilian uprising in Warsaw that was encouraged but not supported by the Soviets. General MacArthur made good on his promise to return to the Philippine Islands as Americans landed there on October 20. A huge naval engagement between American and Japanese warships, the Battle of Leyte Gulf, followed on October 23 to October 26. The Japanese lost 34 ships.

After retreating through France since D-Day, the German army counterattacked through the Ardennes Forest on December 16. The fight which ensued became known as the Battle of the Bulge. On December 22 the commander of the besieged American garrison, General Anthony McAuliffe, gave a one-word answer when Germans demanded his surrender: "Nuts." The siege ended on December 26.

1945 More than a million Soviet troops under Zhukov launched an attack against German troops in Poland on January 12. Stalin, Roosevelt and Churchill met in Yalta from February 4–11 to discuss postwar plans. Royal Air Force and U.S. airplanes firebombed Dresden February 13–15, killing some 50,000 civilians. U.S. Marines landed on Iwo Jima on February 19. On March 7, American troops crossed the Rhine River at Remagen.

The American air force firebombed Tokyo and other Japanese cities on March 9, killing more than 80,000 civilians. On April 1 American forces invaded Okinawa. The Buchenwald concentration camp was liberated on April 11. The following day, President Roosevelt died in Warm Springs, Georgia. Harry Truman succeeded him. Soviet troops reached Berlin on April 23, and on April 25, American and Soviet forces linked up on the Elbe River.

The former dictator of Italy, Benito Mussolini, was captured and killed by Italian irregulars on April 28. Hitler committed suicide on April 30 as Russian troops closed in on his bunker. Germany surrendered on May 7. The allies designated May 8 as V-E Day— Victory in Europe. In his victory speech, Churchill reminded his nation that Japan remained unconquered. Nevertheless, he would be turned out of office on July 26 when British voters chose the Labor Party to lead them.

The atomic bomb was tested successfully in New Mexico on July 16. On August 6, the American warplane *Enola Gay* dropped the bomb on the Japanese city of Hiroshima. Another atomic bomb fell on Nagasaki on August 9. The Japanese surrendered on August 14, and August 15 was designated as V-J Day.

Is War Our Biological Destiny?

By NATALIE ANGIER

In these days of hidebound militarism and round-robin carnage, when even that beloved ambassador of peace, the Dalai Lama, says it may be necessary to counter terrorism with violence, it's fair to ask: Is humanity doomed? Are we born for the battlefield—congenitally, hormonally incapable of putting war behind us? Is there no alternative to the bullet-riddled trapdoor, short of mass sedation or a Marshall Plan for our DNA?

Was Plato right that "Only the dead have seen the end of war"? In the opinion of a number of researchers who study warfare, blood lust and the desire to wage war are by no means innate. To the contrary, recent studies in the field of game theory show just how readily human beings establish cooperative networks with one another, and how quickly a cooperative strategy reaches a point of so-called fixation. Researchers argue that one can plausibly imagine a human future in which war is rare and universally condemned.

The incentive to make war anachronistic is enormous, say the researchers, though they worry that it may take the dropping of another nuclear bomb in the middle of a battlefield before everybody gets the message.

Archaeologists and anthropologists have found evidence of militarism in perhaps 95 percent of the cultures they have examined or unearthed. Time and again groups initially lauded as gentle and peace-loving—the Mayas, the !Kung of the Kalahari, Margaret Mead's Samoans—eventually were outed as being no less bestial than the rest of us.

Warriors have often been the most esteemed of their group, the most coveted mates. Geneticists have found evidence that Genghis Khan, the 13th century Mongol emperor, fathered so many offspring as he slashed through Asia that 16 million men, or half a percent of the world's male population, could be his descendants.

Wars are romanticized, subjects of an endless, cross-temporal, transcultural spool of poems, songs, plays, paintings, novels, films. The battlefield is mythologized as the furnace in which character and nobility are forged. "The rush of battle is a potent and often lethal addiction," writes Chris Hedges, a reporter for *The New York Times*. Even with its destruction and carnage, he adds, war "can give us what we long for in life."

Chimpanzees, which share about 98 percent of their genes with humans, also wage war: gangs of neighboring males meet at the borderline of their territories with the express purpose of exterminating their opponents.

And yet Dr. Frans de Waal, a primatologist and professor of psychology at Emory University, points out that a different species of chimpanzee, the bonobo, chooses love over war, using sex to resolve any social problems that arise. Serious bonobo combat is rare. Bonobos are as closely related to humans as are common chimpanzees, so either might offer insight into the primal "roots" of human behavior.

Even the ubiquitousness of warfare in human history doesn't impress researchers. Indeed, national temperaments seem capable of rapid, radical change. The Vikings slaughtered and plundered; their descendants in Sweden haven't fought a war in nearly 200 years. The tribes of highland New Guinea were famous for small-scale warfare, said Dr. Peter J. Richerson, an expert in cultural evolution at the University of California at Davis. "But when, after World War II, the Australian police patrols went around and told people they couldn't fight anymore, the New Guineans thought that was wonderful," Dr. Richerson said.

Dr. Wilson cites the results of game theory experiments: participants can adopt a cheating strategy to try to earn more for themselves, but at the risk of everybody's losing, or a cooperative strategy with all earning a smaller but more reliable reward. In laboratories around the world, researchers have found that participants implement the mutually beneficial strategy, in which cooperators are rewarded and noncooperators are punished.

As Dr. de Waal and many others see it, the way to foment peace is to encourage interdependency among nations, as in the European Union. "It's not as if Europeans all love each other," Dr. de Waal said. "But you're not promoting love, you're promoting economic calculations."

History of the United States

Prior to the arrival of European colonists, the area now constituting Canada and the United States was inhabited by as many as 1.5 million indigenous peoples, mistakenly called Indians by Europeans who initially believed they had landed in the East Indies. Descendants of migratory peoples who came from Asia (theoretically via a land bridge across the present-day Bering Sea) some 20,000 to 35,000 years earlier, native Americans lived in virtually every region of North America, grouped into countless tribes and bands. Lifestyle and culture varied by region, as did fishing, hunting, gathering, and farming techniques. By the time of Columbus's arrival, many of these peoples had developed sophisticated tools, pottery, and architecture, as well as knowledge of irrigation, agriculture, and medicine.

The Age of Exploration

European explorers probably arrived in North America long before Columbus's famed voyage of 1492. Viking explorer Leif Ericson explored the east coast of North America ca. A.D. 1000, making his way as far south as Newfoundland in present-day Canada, where he established a small settlement. Vikings appear to have traveled as far south as the coast of present-day New England. Centuries later, in 1452 Portuguese explorers Pedro Vásquez and Diogo de Teive were blown off course from the Azores and sent on a voyage that may have taken them to Newfoundland.

These episodic encounters made no discernible impact on North America and its inhabitants. The same cannot be said of the voyages of Christopher Columbus, an Italian in the service of the Spanish crown who came ashore in the Bahamas on October 12, 1492. Columbus's discovery of the New World unleashed a frantic effort by other European powers to establish colonies. The steady influx of migrants bearing European technology, language, religion, culture, and disease brought profound and in some cases catastrophic changes for the indigenous inhabitants of the New World.

Subsequent explorers of note include John Cabot (Giovanni Caboto, 1450–99), who sailed to Newfoundland and Maine in 1497 and claimed the area in the name of King Henry VII of England, and Juan Ponce de León, who in 1513 explored Florida on behalf of the Spanish monarchy. Giovanni de Verrazano (1485–1528), sponsored by Francis I of France, arrived at the Carolinas in 1524 and explored northward to Nova Scotia. Hernando de Soto (1496/97–1542) landed in Florida in 1539 with 600 Spanish soldiers and proceeded to explore as far north as the Carolinas and then west to Oklahoma. The following year fellow Spaniard Francisco Vásquez de Coronado (1510–54) explored New Mexico and Arizona (becoming the first European to see the Grand Canyon), and then northward as far as Kansas. In 1542 Juan Rodríguez Cabrillo (d. 1543) explored the west coast and claimed California for the Spanish crown.

After many failed efforts to establish permanent settlements in these areas, Pedro Ménendez de Avilés of Spain succeeded in establishing St. Augustine in Florida in 1565. Sir Walter Raleigh explored the Carolinas and Virginia in 1584 and returned the following year to establish an English settlement on Roanoke Island. Three years later, in 1587, an expedition bearing additional settlers arrived to find the colony wiped out, presumably by local Indians. These settlers, including Virginia Dare, the first English child born in America, also had vanished by the time a supply ship arrived in 1590.

The First European Colonies

The first successful English settlement was Jamestown, established in Virginia in 1607 by a group of investors called the Virginia Company. The early years were marked by great suffering, sickness, and starvation—many of the original colonists were adventurers intent on making fortunes by finding gold rather than through hard work. A lack of adequate supplies and Indian attacks nearly caused the colony to fail, but effective leadership by Captain John Smith (baptized 1580–1631), land policy reform, and the successful cultivation of tobacco in 1612 led to a gradual improvement in conditions, profits, and the number of English settlers willing to migrate. In 1619 a new charter created the House of Burgesses, the first European-style representative government in North America. That same year, however, slavery was introduced in Virginia with the arrival of 20 Africans.

In 1620 religious dissenters (Separatists), who were suffering persecution under the Church of England, founded a second English colony at Plymouth in Massachusetts. They created a form of self-government called the Mayflower Compact and quickly set about establishing a flourishing colony. In contrast to their fellow colonizers in Jamestown, Plymouth residents benefited from a healthier climate and a sense of religious mission. Settlers also included many families and people dedicated to building a functioning settlement rather than fortune-seeking. The colony was debt-free and self-supporting by 1627.

Farther to the south settlers brought by the Dutch West India Company in 1624 established the colony of New Netherland with a principal town known as New Amsterdam (present-day New York City). It prospered with the development of a booming fur trade with the Iroquois Indians. In 1664 the colony was seized by the English and renamed New York, after the Duke of York, the king's son.

The Massachusetts Bay Colony was established by English Puritans (dissenters who sought to "purify" the Church of England by ridding it of "popish" practices). The first 1,000 emigrants arrived in 1630 and the settlement quickly flourished for the same reasons that marked the rise of nearby Plymouth. Word of its success enticed some 25,000 Puritans to migrate between 1630 and 1640, leading to rapid expansion and the establishment of several new towns outside Boston. When quarrels over religious doctrine led Puritan leaders to expel Roger Williams (1603?–83) and Anne Hutchinson (baptized 1591–1643) for their unorthodox beliefs, the two established new settlements in present-day Rhode Island (1636). Similar circumstances led to new settlements in Connecticut, beginning with Hartford in 1636.

Lord Baltimore (1578/79–1632) founded Maryland in 1632 as a haven for English Catholics, the first of whom arrived in 1634. Like nearby Virginia, the colony quickly established a flourishing economy based on tobacco.

Pennsylvania, too, was founded as a religious haven, in this case for Quakers. William Penn (1644–1718), a wealthy member of the sect, received a massive land grant from the English king, Charles II, in 1661. Penn's colony was unique both for its firmly established principle of religious toleration and relatively benign treatment of Indians. Residents, who numbered 12,000 by 1689, also enjoyed democratic government in the form of an elected legislature.

The last major colony established in the 17th century was Carolina in 1653 (North and South Carolina were not created until 1729). Lacking a major cash crop like tobacco, the colony struggled until the 1690's, when a thriving fur trade and rice cultivation were developed.

Georgia was the last of the 13 original colonies to be settled. Georgia's first settlers, mostly debtors led by James Oglethorpe, arrived in 1733, but the colony struggled and grew slowly as a result of low migration and frequent conflict with Spanish Florida to the south.

Although each colony developed its own distinct character in the 17th century, several common trends emerged. All the colonies experienced conflicts with Indians, who naturally resisted European seizure of their lands. In some cases, attacks by Indians nearly destroyed colonies, as in the case of a war in 1622 that left 357 Virginia colonists dead. But the colonists' technological superiority in military affairs and the devastating effects of European diseases led to the steady decline of the Indian population.

Slavery also took hold in all the colonies, but to a far greater extent in the south, where labor intensive agriculture (tobacco and rice) flourished. By 1700 some 20,500 slaves had been brought to the colonies, a number destined to rise dramatically in the decades to come.

Finally, as the examples of Roger Williams and Anne Hutchinson indicate, the colonies were frequently beset by social conflict. Virginia experienced an uprising of poor farmers in 1676 known as Bacon's Rebellion, while several colonial governments were toppled in the wake of England's "Glorious Revolution" of 1688, when the Stuart dynasty was overthrown. In Salem, Mass., for reasons that still baffle historians, hysteria over witchcraft in 1692 spiraled out of control and led to the executions of 21 accused witches.

The Colonies in the 18th Century

Economy The tumultuous politics of 17th century England (the execution of Charles I, the civil war) left the American colonies substantially unregulated in many matters, especially economic affairs. The stability that followed the accession of William III to the throne in 1689 led to an effort by Crown officials to impose strict regulations on the colonies regarding manufacturing and trade. Guiding these decisions was the theory of mercantilism, which argued that the colonies ought to provide England with raw materials such as timber, tobacco, fur, and fish and a market for sale of finished goods such as clothes, tools, books, and luxury goods. In other words, the colonies were to serve the economic interests of England.

In 1696 the English government established the Board of Trade (1696–1776) to oversee the administration of colonial policy. One of its main purposes was to enforce a series of Navigation Acts regulating colonial trade, the first of which were passed in 1660, 1663, and 1673. They required that all goods sent from the colonies to England be carried on English ships (or ships built in English colonies), that all European goods bound for the colonies must pass through England, and that certain "enumerated articles" produced in the colonies (tobacco, sugar, cotton, indigo, etc.) must be sold only to England.

Despite passage of these laws, England adopted a policy of "salutary neglect" for the decades leading up to the 1760's, allowing the colonies tremendous freedom in economic matters. Colonists developed a thriving "Triangular Trade" in food (fish, grain, meat), slaves, and sugar with north Africa and the West Indies. Shipbuilding also emerged as a major industry in response to the requirement that all goods must travel in British ships.

Population The population of colonial America not only increased dramatically in the 18th century, it also grew increasingly diverse. Some 250,000 Palatine Germans arrived after 1700, settling mainly on the Pennsylvania and Virginia frontiers and in an area outside of Philadelphia that soon became known as Germantown. Immigrants from northern Ireland, the so-called Scotch Irish, totaled more than 200,000 by 1776. Like their German counterparts, they also settled primarily on the frontier. Smaller numbers of settlers from Portugal, Spain, France, Sweden, and many other European nations could be found in the major port cities such as Boston and New York.

During the 18th century there was a sharp increase in the number of slaves imported from Africa and, as was more common, the West Indies. Most of the estimated 500,000 who arrived in this period were sent to the southern colonies.

Religion Beginning in the 1720's, the English colonies experienced an intense revival of religious fervor known as the Great Awakening. It began with revivals in New Jersey and Pennsylvania and eventually spread to New England and the South. Ministers such as Jonathan Edwards (1703–58) preached an evangelical and highly emotional form of Christianity that stressed a person's sinfulness and need for a closer relationship with God. The movement's power diminished by 1745, but not before dramatically increasing church membership and causing lasting splits in several denominations.

England Defeats France The British faced several European rivals in the contest for control of North America. The Spanish controlled Florida and vast areas of the Southwest. The French settlement of New France covered a huge triangle of territory stretching from Nova Scotia to New Orleans to Montana. For much of the 18th century France loomed as the biggest threat to English colonial ambitions, especially in matters related to trade, resulting in three protracted wars between 1689–97, 1701–13, and 1744–48, with much of the action taking place in upper New York, New England, and Canada.

The decisive Anglo-French conflict, called the French and Indian War in America (see "The Seven Years' War" in World History), began in 1754. The fight resulted from a struggle for control of the Ohio River Valley and the rich trade opportunities therein. The French allied themselves with several powerful Indian tribes and enjoyed the upper hand in the early years of warfare. But the British reorganized and proved victorious by 1763. Under the Treaty of Paris (1763) France was forced to cede all of Canada to the English.

The Road to Revolution With peace restored in 1763, English government authorities decided to end the period of "salutary neglect" and reassert control over the American colonies. They were particularly eager to gain control over colonial trade as a means of raising badly needed revenue to pay for the huge cost of the French and Indian War and the anticipated expense of defending the now vastly enlarged colonial frontier. British leaders believed the colonists ought to pay for their own defense, because they stood to gain the most from it. Colonists came to reject this interpretation, arguing that taxation by a government in which they were not represented was unjust. They also resisted taxation because of a severe economic recession that afflicted the colonies through much of the 1760's.

Nevertheless, the English Parliament passed a series of laws that stirred fierce opposition in the colonies. The first was the Proclamation Act of 1763, which prohibited English settlement beyond the Appalachian Mountains. Designed to ensure peace with Indians on the frontier, it angered many colonists eager to acquire western lands. The Sugar Act of 1764 (an extension of the never-enforced Molasses Act of 1733) imposed a duty on foreign molasses, sugar, and other products imported into the colonies. The Currency Act of the same year prohibited the issuance of paper money by colonial governments. Opposition to these measures first emerged in Massachusetts, where leaders denounced "taxation without representation" and organized the first boycott, or nonimportation movement, against English goods. Communication with leaders in other colonies caused the movement to spread.

Colonial opposition to British policy exploded in 1765 with the passage of the Stamp Act, which imposed a tax on a wide range of products, including newspapers, almanacs, legal documents, licenses, and even playing cards. Outraged over this first instance of an "internal" tax on the colonies, colonists formed secret organizations known as the Sons of Liberty, which staged several riots against the agents in charge of collecting the taxes and marking the articles with a special stamp. In October representatives of nine colonies gathered for a Stamp Act Congress in New York, where they drew up resolutions stating their reasons for opposing the act and sent them to England. Hundreds of merchants throughout the colonies joined in a renewed nonimportation effort to put economic pressure on the government. Parliament repealed the Stamp Act in March 1766.

Still determined to rein in the rebellious colonies and generate revenue, Parliament passed the Townshend Acts in 1767, which imposed duties on lead, glass, paint, paper, and tea. It immediately sparked resistance in the form of a renewed nonimportation movement that severely reduced the importation of British goods. Deeply concerned about the loss of trade, Parliament in 1770 limited the duties imposed by the Townshend Acts to tea. Calm returned to the colonies and nonimportation was ended on all goods except tea.

Tensions remained high in places where large contingents of British soldiers were stationed. A serious clash in New York between the Sons of Liberty and soldiers in January 1770 was followed by the "Boston Massacre" on March 5, 1770. Panicky British soldiers opened fire on a jeering crowd, killing five. In spite of the outrage among colonists, tension between England and the colonies diminished substantially over the next few years.

Passage of the Tea Act in 1773 sparked renewed agitation because it granted a monopoly on sales of tea to the British East India Company, a move interpreted as harmful to American merchants and the ongoing effort to boycott tea. In protest, a group of colonial protestors dressed as Indians boarded a merchant ship in Boston Harbor on the night of Dec. 16, 1773, and dumped hundreds of chests of British tea into the harbor, an event known thereafter as the "Boston Tea Party." Parliament reacted by passing the Coercive Acts (called the "Intolerable Acts" in the colonies) in 1774. The legislation closed the port of Boston, drastically altered the colonial charter of Massachusetts, and suppressed town meetings.

In response, 10 of the 11 colonies sent delegates to a Continental Congress, which met in Philadelphia on September 5, 1774. The body issued a "Declaration of Rights and Grievances" that pledged obedience to the king but denied the right of Parliament to tax the colonies. It also renewed the nonimportation effort.

In Massachusetts resistance to the Coercive Acts increased, most notably with the mobilization of the colonial militia in anticipation of a clash with British troops. On April 19, 1775, General Thomas Gage, the colony's military governor, led a force of British troops to Concord, Mass., to seize a large cache of arms and ammunition stored there by the militia. They were attacked by a force of so-called Minute Men and driven back to Boston in two clashes known as the Battles of Lexington and Concord.

The Second Continental Congress convened on May 10, 1775, with many delegates recommending a declaration of independence from Britain. Instead, the body established an army and named George Washington as its commander.

The American Revolution (1775–83)

See "Major Wars in History," pp. 258–60.

The Articles of Confederation

After the war began the Continental Congress urged the former colonies to establish state governments. Eleven of the 13 states drafted constitutions that established representative governments (elected by limited suffrage) with bicameral legislatures and a bill of rights. A national government based on the Articles of Confederation was devised during the war and approved by the Continental Congress on November 15, 1777. Fearing centralized power, the architects of the Articles created a weak national government (in the form of a unicameral Congress) that left most power with the individual states. These included the power to tax and to regulate the economy.

The new Confederation government was ratified by the states in March 1781 but soon proved ineffective. At the end of the Revolution, the new nation was beset by severe economic problems, much of it brought on by the war but also by the chaos of having 13 different trade, tariff, and tax policies established by the individual states. The suffering led to protests like Shay's Rebellion (1786) in Massachusetts by debtors who faced foreclosure on their farms. Moreover, major threats loomed from foreign powers such as Spain, which still controlled Florida and the lower Mississippi. Concerned leaders convened at the Annapolis Conference in 1786, where they approved a resolution calling upon the states to send representatives to a convention to discuss changes to the Confederation government.

The Constitution and New Government The Constitutional Convention gathered in Philadelphia in May 1787 and considered several revisions before agreeing in September to adopt an entirely new form of government. The Constitution of the United States created a strong national government consisting of an executive (president), legislature (Senate and House of Representatives), and judiciary (federal courts, including the Supreme Court). The required nine states ratified the Constitution by June 1788 and the new government took effect in the spring of 1789. Concerns over states' rights and civil liberties led Congress to approve 12 amendments to the Constitution. The states ratified 10 of them, known collectively as the Bill of Rights.

The Federalist Era

George Washington was inaugurated as the nation's first president on April 30, 1789. The most important figure in his administration was Treasury Secretary Alexander Hamilton, whose successful effort to fund the national debt, assume individual state debts, and establish a Bank of the United States did much to restore economic growth, especially in the long term. His decision to impose a tax on whiskey, however, led to a revolt by Pennsylvania farmers known as the Whiskey Rebellion (1794) which ended only after Washington sent federal troops to quell the uprising.

By the mid-1790's opponents of Hamilton's policies united behind Thomas Jefferson, marking the beginning of the first political parties. The Hamilton faction took the name Federalists, while the Jeffersonians tried several names before settling on Republicans (also known as Jeffersonian Republicans, and the forerunner of the modern Democratic party).

Washington's administration faced many challenges, especially in the realm of foreign affairs. Warfare with Indians raged on the frontier, while relations with Spain were strained over boundary disputes in the southeast. Worse was the turmoil caused by the French Revolution and the subsequent war between England and France (1793). Despite a declaration of neutrality, England seized some 150 American ships for trading with the French, an outrage the weak American nation was powerless to stop until ratification of the Jay Treaty in 1795, although England never actually abandoned the practice.

Federalist John Adams was elected president in 1796 after George Washington decided to retire. In 1797 a diplomatic crisis (the XYZ Affair, in which French officials tried to elicit bribes from U.S. diplomats) had many Americans demanding war with France. Adams resisted, but the U.S. was soon embroiled in an undeclared war on the high seas with France (1798–1800). Irritated by criticism from his Jeffersonian adversaries and leery of the influence of radical French émigrés on U. S. politics, Adams signed the Alien and Sedition Acts, a series of constitutionally questionable measures (including making criticism of the government a crime) vigorously challenged by Jefferson and James Madison in their Kentucky and Virginia Resolutions.

Jeffersonian Democracy After a bitter election campaign in 1800, Thomas Jefferson was elected president over John Adams. The peaceful transfer of power from one party (Federalists) to another (Jeffersonian Republicans) marked a major moment in American democracy. Jefferson emphasized a strict interpretation of the Constitution that argued the federal government possessed very limited powers relative to the states. Jefferson ignored this principle, however, when in 1803 cash-strapped France offered to sell the Louisiana Territory to the United States for $15 million. The acquisition of 828,000 square miles (the Louisiana Purchase) doubled the size of the nation and prompted Jefferson to dispatch the Merriwether Lewis and William Clark expedition (1804–06) to explore it. That same year the Supreme Court issued its decision in *Marbury v. Madison*, the first time the Court declared an act of Congress unconstitutional.

With the resumption of the Napoleonic Wars in 1803, U.S. shipping again faced hostility from the French and British, both of whom sought to deny the other access to American trade. The British posed the biggest threat, seizing hundreds of American ships and forcing many crewmen into the British navy. When treaty negotiations failed, Congress, at Jefferson's urging, imposed an embargo (1807) on virtually all foreign commerce. It proved a very controversial measure, as it inflicted heavy damage on the fragile U. S. economy, especially in Federalist-dominated states in the northeast.

The War of 1812 James Madison won the presidency in the election of 1808 and inherited from Jefferson the foreign policy crisis with England. Matters eventually deteriorated to such a point that the U.S. declared war on England on June 18, 1812.

The war represented America's participation in the

global Napoleonic Wars that had arisen from the French Revolution of 1789. Both Britain and France had attacked American commerce, but Britain, the dominant naval power, was responsible for more injuries. In particular, the British did not recognize the right of a person to change nationality and so claimed the right to impress into their navy American sailors whom they claimed were still British subjects.

James Madison had been reelected President in 1812 under the slogan, "Free men, free trade, free ships" and he led a deeply divided country into war. A U.S. attack on Montreal failed, but in the West, U.S. forces were generally successful. Captain Oliver Perry defeated the British fleet on Lake Erie; Detroit, which had fallen to the British, was retaken; and General William Henry Harrison, a future president, defeated the British and an Indian confederacy under Tecumseh at the Battle of the Thames in Canada. Despite these U.S. victories, however, the British were largely successful in blockading American ports.

In 1814, in the wake of Napoleon's defeat in Europe, the British took to the offensive, but were generally unsuccessful. An invasion of New York from Canada was stopped at Plattsburgh; and while an invading army succeeded in taking and burning Washington, D.C., it was repulsed at Baltimore. Finally, a British attack on New Orleans was crushed by another future American president, Andrew Jackson, who became a national hero. The American victory occurred two weeks after a peace treaty had been signed in Ghent, Belgium, in December of 1814. By its terms, Britain finally accepted U.S. independence.

Even as peace negotiations progressed, disgruntled Federalists from New England sent representatives to the Hartford Convention (1814). Embracing a states' rights doctrine, they adopted several resolutions that would have seriously undercut the war effort if Congress had approved them. News of the peace treaty and Jackson's victory deeply embarrassed the convention and brought lasting discredit upon the Federalist Party.

The Early National Period (1815–40)

Peace in 1815 ushered in an era of national pride, westward expansion, and economic growth. To facilitate the latter, Madison won reauthorization of the Bank of the United States in 1816 and signed into a law a high protective tariff. Many states and private companies spurred economic development and westward expansion by building networks of roads and canals, while the development of steamboats after 1811 greatly expanded transportation on rivers. James Monroe, the last of the "Virginia Dynasty" presidents, won the presidency in 1816. Soon after his inauguration in early 1817 he embarked on a national tour that took him through New England and westward to Detroit. The outpouring of enthusiasm and national pride, even in Federalist strongholds in the northeast, led some to dub Monroe's eight years in office as "The Era of Good Feelings." But beneath the surface of this exuberant nationalism lay several divisive issues that call into question the accuracy of the phrase.

Warfare broke out in Spanish Florida in 1818 as a U. S. force invaded, ostensibly in response to threats by Seminole Indians and escaped slaves to the state of Georgia. Led by Andrew Jackson, the force seized most of Florida, forcing the Spanish to cede it to the U.S. in subsequent treaty negotiations. Financial distress set in with the Panic of 1819 and lasted until 1821. Controversy over slavery erupted in 1819 when Missouri applied for statehood, with many northerners opposed to the extension of slavery into the western territories. The resulting Missouri Compromise (or the Compromise of 1820) admitted Missouri as a slave state, but offset it with the admission of Maine as a free state, thus retaining the balance of power between slave and free states in Congress. It also adopted a provision barring slavery from the former Louisiana Territory above the latitude 36′30″, the southern boundary of Missouri.

To ensure American security, Monroe issued the Monroe Doctrine in 1823. It announced that America would not tolerate intervention by European powers into the affairs of recently liberated Latin American nations. In addition, he pledged that America would not intervene in any European wars.

Economic Expansion The 1820's and 1830's witnessed a dramatic transformation of the economy, politics, population, and values of the United States. By the end of the 1820's, the granting of the vote to virtually all white men through the abolition of property requirements made politics far more democratic. Major advances were made in transportation technology with the spread of canals—most notably the Erie Canal in upstate New York (completed 1825)—steamboats, and the first railroads. Similarly, the movement of information was dramatically accelerated with the invention and subsequent spread of the telegraph. Industrial manufacturing achieved prominence with the construction of the first factory town in Lowell, Massachusetts. The onset of mass immigration in the 1830's (especially Irish, Germans, and Scandinavians) added greatly to the nation's demographic diversity and spurred rapid urbanization.

Jacksonian Democracy The election of Andrew Jackson as President in 1828 inaugurated a new era in American democracy. He was the first president elected after expansion of the franchise, and he pledged to represent the interests of the "common man" against the forces of elitism, wealth, and privilege. During his term, the Democratic Party also evolved from the earlier Jeffersonian Republicans and other political factions.

Indian Removal Jackson's two terms as President were marked by several major controversies. The first began in 1830 with Jackson's decision to forcibly remove Indian tribes from the southeast United States to remote settlements in the west. He carried out this program despite a Supreme Court ruling in 1832 that upheld the rights of the tribes. Thousands of Cherokee Indians died during the harsh journey to Oklahoma, an experience that came to be called "The Trail of Tears."

The Nullification Crisis Congress passed a new tariff in 1828 that pleased northern manufacturing interests and angered southern planters. Vice-President and later Senator John C. Calhoun (1782–1850) of South Carolina led the outcry against the tariff and issued a decree that states possessed the right to "nullify" any act of Congress they deemed unjust or unconstitutional. Jackson threatened to use force if South Carolina continued its resistance. Eventually the matter was settled when a new tariff was adopted in 1833.

The Bank War Because he viewed banks as undemocratic institutions that favored the rich over the common man, Jackson decided to destroy the Bank of the United States. The charter for the bank, created in 1792 by Alexander Hamilton, was due to expire in 1836. Congress passed a bill authorizing a new charter in 1832 but Jackson vetoed it. When Congress was unable to override the veto, the Bank ceased operations in 1836.

The Texas Republic Thousands of Americans had moved to northern Mexico in the 1820's at the invitation of the Mexican government. But the abolition of slavery in Mexico in 1829, a ban on further American settlement in 1830, and the assumption of dictatorial powers by Mexican president General Santa Ana in 1835 prompted American settlers to revolt. They set up a provincial government, declared Texas an independent republic, and raised an army. Santa Ana defeated the Americans at the Battle of the Alamo in March 1836 but suffered a crushing defeat at the Battle of San Jacinto a month later. Texans celebrated their independence but hoped for annexation by the United States.

The Abolitionists Expansion of plantations and slave labor into the fertile regions of Georgia, Alabama, Mississippi, Arkansas, Louisiana, and Texas led to a boom in the output of cash crops like tobacco, sugar, rice, and especially cotton. Production of cotton jumped from 1.35 million bales in 1840 to an incredible 4.8 million bales by 1860. Southern cotton by this time accounted for three-fifths of American exports and three-quarters of the world supply of cotton, leading many southerners to boast that "Cotton is King."

The growth of the southern economy, much of it based on the forced labor of slaves, alarmed many northerners who had hoped that slavery in the South would wither away as it had in the North. Beginning in the early 1830's, they formed a movement dedicated to the abolition of slavery. The most notable of them was William Lloyd Garrison (1805–79), who in 1831 founded *The Liberator*, an influential abolitionist newspaper, and in 1833 started the American Anti-Slavery Society. Abolitionists collected thousands of signatures in support of abolition and forwarded them to Congress. Southern congressmen became so exasperated at this mounting attack on slavery that they passed the so-called "Gag Rule" that prohibited the reading of these anti-slavery petitions in Congress. They also denounced abolition as an unconstitutional attack on property rights and an effort to encourage slave uprisings, a sentiment that gained widespread support in 1831 when a slave named Nat Turner (1800-31) led a bloody insurrection in Virginia, killing more than 50 white people.

The Second Great Awakening Abolition was only one of many reform movements that swept antebellum America. Much of this support for reform emanated from the enthusiasm generated by a religious revival known as the Second Great Awakening. Beginning in the 1820's evangelical ministers such as Charles Grandison Finney traveled the country preaching a new doctrine of Christianity that urged individuals to eradicate sinful practices both in their personal lives and in society at large.

Temperance Many people inspired by this upsurge in religious enthusiasm came to see slavery as an evil and joined the abolitionist movement. Many also joined a growing crusade against alcohol. Led by the American

Society for the Promotion of Temperance, founded in 1826, they delivered speeches and published tracts urging their fellow Americans to abstain from drinking. The first law banning alcohol outright was passed in Maine in 1846, followed by 12 more states by 1860.

Women's Rights Some of the most committed reformers in this era were women. Their involvement in abolition and temperance led many to demand greater rights for women. Few states in this era recognized a woman's right to own property, execute contracts, sue for divorce, or vote. In 1848 more than 100 men and women gathered at the first Women's Rights Convention in Seneca Falls, N.Y. and issued a stirring call for an end to laws and customs that kept women subordinate to men.

Manifest Destiny In the mid-1840's many Americans began to see westward expansion and development as the key to the nation's rise to greatness. The construction of canals, railroads, and roads enticed thousands to head west to establish farms or small businesses in trading centers like St. Louis and Cincinnati. Enthusiastic supporters of expansion declared that it was America's "manifest destiny" to become a continental power reaching all the way to the Pacific. That much of this territory was part of Mexico, or controlled by Great Britain, or occupied by Native American tribes did not trouble them. In keeping with this spirit, Congress annexed the Texas republic in 1845 and settled a longstanding border dispute between the U.S. and Great Britain in the Pacific northwest in 1846.

The Mexican War American annexation of the Texas Republic in 1845 triggered war with Mexico. At issue was the border between Mexico and Texas, the Rio Grande or the more northerly Nueces River. Mexican troops attacked American forces under a future American president, Zachary Taylor, in the disputed area, and President James K. Polk asked Congress for a declaration of war. General Taylor's army defeated Santa Ana at Buena Vista. Other American forces seized Santa Fe in present day New Mexico and proceeded to California, where American settlers had already seized power in the name of a separate Great Bear Republic. General Winfield Scott landed at the Mexican port of Santa Cruz and, in a series of battles culminating in the Battle of Chapultepec, commemorated in the Marine Corps Hymn as the "Halls of Montezuma," Scott took Mexico City. Mexico capitulated in the Treaty of Guadelupe Hidalgo (1848), ceding to the United States the territories of Texas, California, and what would become Arizona, Utah, Colorado, and Nevada. The U.S. agreed to pay Mexico about $18 million.

The California gold rush Gold was discovered in January 1848 along the American River in northern California. By August stories of California gold reached the East. Any lingering skepticism was swept aside in December when more than 300 ounces of pure gold arrived in Washington, D.C. Tens of thousands of Americans caught "gold fever" and left farms and workshops for San Francisco. California's population exploded, rising from just 14,000 at the start of 1849 to more than 100,000 by year's end and 220,000 by 1852.

Slavery and the Road to Civil War

In 1849 California's application to be admitted to the Union touched off another political crisis over the issue of slavery. Most northerners were willing to leave slavery alone where it currently existed, but demanded that it be prevented from the new territories. They cited moral opposition to human bondage and the fact that Mexico had abolished slavery in 1829. Most southerners demanded with equal firmness that slaveholders had every right to bring slaves into the west and vehemently opposed any attempt to limit the spread of what was called the "peculiar institution."

The struggle to reach a compromise in the coming months set the stage for the final performances of three legislative giants—westerner Henry Clay of Kentucky, northerner Daniel Webster of Massachusetts, and southerner John Calhoun of South Carolina. As he had done so in the Missouri Compromise in 1820 and the Nullification Crisis of 1832-33, Clay ("the great compromiser") endeavored to broker a deal acceptable to the various factions, sections, and interests by granting each part of what they demanded. Accordingly he drafted an omnibus bill that gave northerners and southerners a portion of their wishes: California admitted as a free state, New Mexico organized into two territories with slavery determined later by popular sovereignty, the Texas border adjusted in exchange for federal assumption of its debt, the slave trade banned in Washington D.C., and a stronger federal fugitive slave law.

The debate over Clay's proposed compromise inspired some of the most renowned speeches in the history of Congress. But the views expressed in them illustrated a hardening of positions on the issue of slavery. On March 4 Calhoun, speaking for southern hardliners, rejected Clay's proposal and demanded that the North accord the South equal rights in the territories, enforce the fugitive slave laws, cease attacking slavery, and accept a constitutional amendment creating two presidents, one northern and one southern, each possessing a veto. Three days later Webster delivered his famous "Seventh of March Address" in which he chastised both southern nationalists and northern abolitionists and spoke passionately on behalf of compromise as a rational course and a patriotic duty. William Seward of New York then delivered an address invoking the authority of "a higher law than the Constitution" (the law of God) to denounce slavery.

The dispute was settled by Illinois Senator Stephen A. Douglas's Compromise of 1850, parts of which appealed to proslavery southerners and others to antislavery northerners. California was admitted as a free state. To offset this concession to slavery's opponents, a second bill organized the southwest as the New Mexico and Utah territories and left the question of slavery to be decided by popular sovereignty when each applied for statehood. Left unexplained was the status of slavery in the years leading to statehood. The most important concession to the South was a new, more stringent Fugitive Slave Act to replace the original one passed in 1793.

Vowing to resist the Fugitive Slave Act, abolitionists formed so-called vigilance committees throughout the North. Some of the earliest and most memorable incidents occurred in Boston, the unofficial headquarters of the abolitionist movement. In early 1851 when word spread that an escaped slave named Shadrach Minkins had been arrested, an incensed black mob broke into the courthouse, overpowered the marshals, and whisked him off to Montreal. When another escaped slave, Thomas Sims, was apprehended in Boston two months later, President Millard Fillmore sent 250 soldiers to guard the courthouse and escort the captive to a ship bound for Georgia. Similar incidents by abolitionist mobs occurred in New York City, Philadelphia, Detroit, Syracuse and many smaller towns.

Sentiment against slavery also was fueled by the publication of the novel *Uncle Tom's Cabin* in 1852. Written by Harriet Beecher Stowe, a member of a prominent abolitionist family, it sold an astonishing 300,000 copies in one year, making it the best-selling book of the era. Its account of slavery's brutality moved the hearts and minds of millions of northerners.

The Kansas-Nebraska Act of 1854 created the Kansas Territory west of Missouri and the Nebraska Territory west of Iowa. The issue of whether slavery would be permitted in these territories would be determined by popular sovereignty. This last provision, intended to placate both North and South by allowing the eventual establishment of Kansas as a slave state (since its soil and climate were similar to neighboring Missouri) and Nebraska as a free state, required the repeal of the Missouri Compromise of 1820 that had barred slavery above 36'30". The bitter fight over this bill intensified sectional animosities.

The political impact of the Kansas-Nebraska controversy became clear in the 1854 midterm elections. Free Soilers, ex-Whigs, and antislavery Democrats in the North formed dozens of local parties under names like the Anti-Nebraska or the People's Party. By far the most popular name, and the one under which they would eventually unite, was Republican Party. Despite their varied names, they shared an overriding commitment to opposing further concessions to southern slave interests.

Antipathy toward slavery in the North competed with rising anti-immigrant sentiment. The latter reached a fever pitch in 1854 with the emergence of a political party whose core constituents were members of secret anti-immigrant societies. Referred to as "Know Nothings," they called for legislation restricting office holding to native-born citizens, barring the use of public funds for parochial schools, and raising the period of naturalization for citizenship from 5 to 21 years. With the Whig party in decline and the Democrats closely associated with the immigrant vote, Know Nothings achieved stunning success in the 1854 elections in Massachusetts, Delaware, and Pennsylvania and polled well in most other northeast and border states.

The controversy over slavery erupted once again in the Kansas Territory in 1855-56. Pro-slavery and anti-slavery settlers flocked to the territory in advance of a vote that would determine the fate of slavery there. Armed conflict between the two sides broke out all across "Bleeding Kansas," resulting in hundreds of deaths. The violence even reached Congress when, in 1857, South Carolina Representative Preston Brooks attacked Senator Charles Sumner of Massachusetts with a cane after the latter delivered a spirited speech denouncing the South for its "crimes against Kansas."

The Dred Scott Decision Passions were further inflamed when the Supreme Court issued its decision in the Dred Scott case. Scott, a slave, had sued for his freedom, arguing that the years he spent with his owner in Illinois and the Wisconsin Territory (where the Missouri Compromise barred slavery) had made him a free man. The southern-dominated Supreme Court, led by Chief Justice Roger B. Taney of Maryland, a slave state, rejected Scott's claim, arguing that slaves were property, not people, and as such, they were not citizens and therefore lacked standing in a court of law. The Court went further and declared that Congress had no authority to regulate slavery in the territories. Many northerners denounced the Court's decision, seeing it as an example of southern dominance of the federal government.

Slavery emerged as a dominant theme in an election for U.S. Senate from Illinois in 1858, when a former congressman named Abraham Lincoln challenged two-term incumbent Stephen Douglas. In accepting the Senate nomination, Lincoln famously warned that "a house divided against itself cannot stand." The two candidates agreed to a series of debates around the state, during which Lincoln, running as the candidate of the new Republican Party, articulated his opposition to the extension of slavery into new territories. Douglas was one of the foremost champions of popular sovereignty. Douglas went on to win the election, but Lincoln emerged as a candidate for national office.

In the fall of 1859 a band of white and black abolitionists led by John Brown (1800–59) staged a raid on a federal arsenal at Harper's Ferry, Va. Their plan had been to move on to the South, arming slaves as they went and touching off a wave of rebellion across the South. But militia and U.S. Marines arrived and stormed their stronghold, killing 10 and taking Brown and the rest as prisoners. All were summarily tried, convicted, and executed. Southerners were enraged by what they perceived as an increasingly aggressive abolitionist movement, while many in the North hailed Brown as a martyr.

The Election of 1860 The breaking point came in the election of 1860. Four candidates vied for the presidency in a contest dominated by the slavery question. Abraham Lincoln, nominee of the Republican Party, won the election. But the details of the results foreshadowed a crisis. Lincoln swept most northern states, but received virtually no support in the South, where the Republican Party was condemned as the party of abolition.

Southerners had threatened secession as far back as the Constitutional Convention, but had always accepted compromise in the end. Not so in 1860, for secessionist-minded southerners now declared that they would not live under a Republican administration. On December 20, 1860, South Carolina declared that the bond between their state and the United States of America "is hereby dissolved." Six more slave states—Florida, Alabama, Georgia, Mississippi, Louisiana, and Texas—quickly followed. Within months Virginia, North Carolina, Tennessee, and Arkansas joined with them to form a new nation, the Confederate States of America. All efforts at compromise failed and war began in April 1861 when the newly elected president, Lincoln, attempted to re-supply Fort Sumter, a federally held garrison in Charleston, South Carolina.

The Civil War (1861-65) See "Major Wars in History," pp. 261–65.

Transformation of the Union While war raged, Republicans took advantage of their dominant position in Congress to enact legislation which had long been opposed by Southerners. Most of these were policies designed to promote westward settlement, industrialization, and a modern financial system. In 1862 Congress passed the Homestead Act, which granted 160 acres of land to any settler who agreed to live on it for five years and improve it. The Morrill Act that same year gave thousands of acres of land to individual states. The money raised from its sale was designated to fund public education, especially to what became known as land grant colleges. To protect Northern manufacturers from foreign competition, Congress raised the tariff on imported goods to its highest level ever. Deeming a transcontinental railroad a national necessity, Congress created two federally chartered railroads, the Union Pacific and the Central Pacific, and provided them with vast tracts of free land and inexpensive loans to finance the project, which was completed in 1869. Finally, the National Bank Acts of 1863 and 1864 established a national banking system whereby member banks could issue treasury notes, or "greenbacks," as currency.

Reconstructing the Union

After critical Northern victories in 1863, Lincoln began to outline a moderate plan for restoring the Southern states to the Union. That December his Proclamation of Amnesty and Reconstruction proposed that all Southerners (except for high-ranking military officers and

Confederate officials) who took an oath pledging loyalty to the Union and support for emancipation would be pardoned. As soon as 10 percent of a state's voters took this oath, they could call a convention, establish a new state government and apply for Congressional recognition.

Under Lincoln's leadership, Congress passed the 13th Amendment abolishing slavery in late January 1865. In March 1865 Congress established the Bureau of Refugees, Freedmen and Abandoned Lands. Known simply as the Freedmen's Bureau, it was to serve as an all-purpose relief agency in the war-ravaged South, providing emergency services, building schools, and managing confiscated lands.

The relief that followed the end of the Civil War quickly changed to despair. On the night of April 14, 1865, just five days after Lee's surrender, Lincoln was shot at close range by Confederate sympathizer John Wilkes Booth. Lincoln died the following day. News of the tragedy elicited an enormous outpouring of grief for the martyred president among citizens of the North and freed slaves in the South.

Lincoln's successor, Andrew Johnson, also promoted a very lenient policy toward the South with an eye toward rapidly restoring the Union. In late May 1865 he issued two proclamations outlining his policy. One offered "amnesty and pardon," including the return of all property, to southerners who took an oath of allegiance to the Constitution and Union. Former Confederate leaders and wealthy planters worth more than $20,000, however, would have to apply to him personally for a pardon. The second set forth extremely lenient terms for ex-Confederate states to gain readmission to the Union. With Congress out of session, Johnson's plan faced little formal opposition. In December 1865, with all 11 former Confederate states having established new governments under his terms, he announced the Union was restored and that reconstruction was "over."

Radical Reconstruction Johnson's actions outraged many northern Republicans who viewed them as far too easy on the South. They noted that in the supposedly "reconstructed" South voters elected to office dozens of ex-Confederate officials and army officers, among them Alexander Stephens, former vice president of the Confederacy. Republicans also observed that new southern state governments, beginning in late 1865 with Mississippi and South Carolina, passed laws or "Black Codes" that limited the civil and economic rights of the former slaves. So-called "Radical Republicans" in Congress repudiated Johnson's Reconstruction plan and refused to recognize the new southern state governments. They then set out to pass a much more aggressive and vindictive plan for reconstructing the South.

The 14th Amendment In June 1866 Radical and moderate Republicans passed the 14th Amendment to the Constitution. A long and complex amendment, it contained five main provisions. First, it defined freedmen (all persons born or naturalized in the United States) as national citizens. Second, all citizens were entitled to "equal protection of the laws" of the states where they lived. Third, all high-ranking former Confederates were prohibited from holding public office, unless pardoned by act of Congress. Fourth, African-American men were granted the right to vote. Fifth, it repudiated the Confederate debt (thus punishing those who lent money to the Confederacy) and denied all claims for compensation by ex-slave owners. The 14th Amendment represented a radical redefining of the role of the federal government as the definer and guarantor of individual civil rights.

The Reconstruction Acts In March 1867 Republicans in Congress passed several Reconstruction Acts and divided the South (except Tennessee) into five military districts, each governed by a military commander empowered with wide authority to keep order and protect individuals, especially freedmen. As soon as order was established, the ex-Confederate states could begin a new, stricter readmission process. Voters, including African-American men but excluding former Confederates, would elect delegates to state conventions. The new state constitutions drawn up by these conventions had to allow universal male suffrage, regardless of race. If a state's voters approved the new constitution, the state could hold elections to fill government office. Finally, if Congress approved the state's constitution and the state legislature ratified the 14th Amendment, the state would be readmitted to the Union.

The Impeachment of Andrew Johnson Radical Republicans came to despise Johnson for his attempts to obstruct their reconstruction plans and began looking for a way to remove him from office. They passed a law (the Tenure of Office Act) requiring the president to seek Congressional approval before removing a cabinet official. When Johnson fired Secretary of War Edwin Stanton, his enemies in Congress voted to impeach him. The trial began in March 1868 and included two months of heated debate and accusation. In the end the Senate failed—by one vote—to convict Johnson and remove him from office.

The 15th Amendment With southern resistance on the rise in 1867–68, many Republicans in Congress argued that an additional amendment was necessary to guarantee unequivocally the right of African-Americans to vote. Consequently they drafted the 15th Amendment. In succinct language it stated "The right of citizens of the United States shall not be denied or abridged by the United States or by any state on account of race, color, or previous condition of servitude." It was passed by Congress in February 1869 and ratified in 1870.

By the early 1870's the northern effort to reshape southern society and protect the rights of the ex-slaves began to lose support. Many northerners had grown tired of the endless debates in Washington over Reconstruction policy. By the end of the decade white Southerners had succeeded in reacquiring political power and using it to deprive the former slaves of their rights.

The Age of Industry

America experienced an industrial boom during the Civil War that continued after the war ended. New technology such as improved steam power generation and sophisticated manufacturing machinery led to an explosion in industrial output. New industries such as steel and oil transformed the economy and added thousands of new jobs.

One of the driving forces behind the industrial revolution was what many termed the "inventive spirit" of the age. Inventiveness was driven by dreams of profit and led to constant improvements in existing products and the creation of whole new industries. Christopher Sholes, for example, was one of dozens of men working on a machine that eventually bore the name "typewriter." Sholes sold his design to the Remington Company and the typewriter soon became a standard piece of equipment found in every office and eventually many homes. Other inventors of note include George Eastman (Kodak camera), William S. Burroughs (adding machine), Isaac Singer (sewing machine), Alexander Graham Bell (telephone), and Thomas Edison (incandescent lightbulb, phonograph, motion picture camera, mimeograph machine, and more). Between 1860 and 1900 American inventors registered nearly 700,000 patents with the U.S. Patent Office, prompting its commissioner to boast in 1892 "America has become known the world around as the home of invention."

Captains of Industry The new industrial economy witnessed the emergence of immensely rich and powerful men such as Andrew Carnegie (steel), John D. Rockefeller (oil), Jay Gould (railroads), J.P. Morgan (finance), and Philip Armour (meatpacking). They were alternately praised for their business genius and success and condemned for their questionable practices and exploitation of workers. Many Americans also grew concerned over the power wielded by these men and the huge corporations and trusts they headed.

Conflict and Crisis Industrialization generated enormous wealth for successful entrepreneurs and investors and raised the standard of living for the average worker. It also brought new freedoms, comforts, styles, and forms of entertainment. But these benefits were accompanied by disturbing trends. Many workers suffered from long hours, dangerous conditions, monotonous work, and low pay.

Farmers likewise complained about the exploitation they suffered at the hands of banks, suppliers, and railroads. The new industrial economy was also marked by instability that produced several recessions and two severe depressions (1873–77 and 1893–97). Political leaders held fast to a laissez-faire policy toward business, with the exception of the Interstate Commerce Act (1887) and Sherman Antitrust Act (1890), both of which proved ineffective.

Labor Movement Wage earners responded to these challenges by engaging in record numbers of boycotts and strikes. The latter frequently turned violent when police or militia confronted strikers. The great railroad strike of 1877 shut down much of the national rail system from Baltimore to Chicago and saw scores of workers killed and millions of dollar of property destroyed. Workers also formed unions to help them achieve shorter hours and better pay. In the 1880's the Knights of Labor, a national industrial organization with hundreds of local union affiliates, emerged as a major force in labor's struggle. Membership soared to 700,000 in 1886 before the organization went into decline and was replaced by the American Federation of Labor.

American farmers likewise turned to organization to address their grievances. Thousands joined the Grange, or Patrons of Husbandry (founded 1867), a fraternal and educational association that became a political force in the Midwest by the mid-1870's. Grange-supported candidates took control of state legislatures and passed several laws regulating railroads. It faded in the 1880's but its spirit was revived in the People's Party in the 1890's.

Westward Expansion The end of the Civil War unleashed a flood of westward migration and settlement. Thousands of Americans and recent immigrants, attracted by cheap land and the perception of widespread opportunity, crossed the Mississippi River to settle on the Great Plains and beyond. Ranching and mining developed, along with farming, as the primary elements of the western economy. Economic development was hastened by the rapid expansion of the railroad system, most notably with the completion of the Transcontinental Railroad in 1869.

Conflict with Native Americans Westward settlement brought increased conflict with Native American tribes who believed they had a right to the lands where they had lived for generations. This was especially true of the eastern tribes that had agreed before 1860 to relocate to so-called "Indian Country," lands west of the Mississippi. Beginning in the 1850's, however, the U.S. government pursued a policy of confining Indian tribes to specific tracts of land known as reservations and in 1867 it established two huge Indian Territories in Oklahoma and the Dakotas. Units of veteran Union Army soldiers were sent west after the Civil War to enforce this policy. Wars broke out repeatedly on the Great Plains and elsewhere as white settlers encroached on Indian land and tribes resisted confinement to reservations. Native Americans lacked the firepower and unity to withstand the army, but nonetheless put up fierce resistance. In the most notable incident, a band of 2,000 Sioux and Cheyenne warriors in June 1876 wiped out a small force under the command of Gen. George A. Custer (1839–76) at the Battle of Little Big Horn in Montana.

Continued conflict led Congress to pass the Dawes Act in 1887. Declaring reservations a failure, it aimed to break up Indian communities and encourage assimilation into white culture by distributing allotments of reservation land to individual Indians who in turn would become farmers. This and subsequent acts led to the reduction of Indian lands from 156 million acres in 1881 to 53 million by 1934 when the policy was ended.

The End of Armed Resistance Large-scale Native American resistance waned in the late 1880's with the surrender of the Apache warrior-chief Geronimo in 1886, and in 1890 the massacre at Wounded Knee, South Dakota. In the latter incident, soldiers opened fire on hundreds of Sioux who had recently fled their reservation, killing nearly 200 men, women, and children. Thereafter, Indians resisted white authority by working to preserve their culture and traditions.

Mass Immigration Immigration soared in the last third of the 19th century to record levels. After 1880 the majority of the newcomers came from southern and eastern Europe, the largest groups being Italian and Jews from the Russian empire. Significant numbers of Chinese immigrants arrived in California. Most newcomers settled in urban areas where they often formed ethnic enclaves known to outsiders as Little Italy or Little Russia. They provided a huge source of cheap labor for the economy and made lasting contributions to American culture.

Just as it did in the antebellum era, mass migration produced hostility among native-born Americans who feared the newcomers as competition for jobs and bearers of strange habits. In 1882 Congressed passed the Chinese Exclusion Act and in 1890, the Federal Immigration Act. The latter established guidelines for admitting immigrants and authorized construction of screening centers, the most famous of which was Ellis Island (1892) in New York Harbor. Still, record numbers of immigrants continued to arrive, hitting a peak of 1,004,756 in 1907.

The Turbulent 1890's

Many of the nation's most pressing social problems came to a head in the 1890's. Two landmark strikes in Homestead, Pa. (1892) and Pullman, Ill. (1894) highlighted the grievances of American workers and the immense power of big business as workers lost both strikes. Frustrated farmers and industrial workers threw their support to a new third party, the Peoples Party (Populist), which garnered 1 million votes in the 1892 presidential election.

Over the next few years national politics was dominated by debate over currency reform and the gold standard. Republicans, conservatives, and industrialists defended the policy of tying American currency to the gold standard. Such a policy benefited businesses and banks by restricting the money supply and keeping inflation low. Democrats, led by a flamboyant congressman from Nebraska, William Jennings Bryan (1860–1925), demanded the unlimited coinage of silver which would benefit farmers and other debtors by increasing the money supply and inflation. Bryan's impassioned "Cross of Gold" speech at the Democratic national convention in 1896 won him the party's presidential nomination. Republican William McKinley won the election handily, but Bryan succeeded in reshaping the ideology of the Democratic party to support activist and interventionist government. Bryan earned his party's nomination again in 1900 and 1908 but lost both elections.

Jim Crow Southerners successfully stripped away most of the civil, political, and economic rights of African Americans. Voting rights were suppressed through tactics such as literacy tests, poll taxes, and the infamous grandfather clause, requiring proof that your grandfather had voted. Segregation received sanction in several decisions by a conservative Supreme Court, most egregiously in *Plessy v. Ferguson* (1896). To discourage resistance, vigilante groups like the Ku Klux Klan waged a campaign of terror that included arson, beatings, and lynchings. Nonetheless African Americans and sympathetic whites founded the National Association for the Advancement of Colored People in 1905 to oppose the oppression.

The Spanish American War America's rise as an industrial power convinced many that it should take a more active role in world affairs—if only to protect national interests overseas. Congress authorized a massive expansion of the navy and promoted a more vigorous foreign policy, especially in matters pertaining to Latin America and the Caribbean.

Encouraged by a jingoistic press, Americans increasingly took an interest in the efforts of Cubans to free themselves from Spanish colonial rule. In addition, many American businesses had substantial investments in Cuba. The American government pressured Spain to end its repression, but resisted calls for military intervention, even after the naval vessel U.S.S. *Maine* exploded and sank in Havana harbor (February 15, 1898), killing 260. But the U.S. press insisted on blaming the Spanish and diplomatic relations rapidly deteriorated. At the request of President McKinley, Congress declared war on April 17, 1898. A weak Spain was no match for the U.S. forces.

The U.S. Pacific fleet under Commodore George Dewey proceeded to the Philippines, where it defeated its larger Spanish counterpart at the Battle of Manila Bay, capturing the island of Guam on the way. American troops later landed, and together with Filipino insurgents, secured control of the Philippines. In the Atlantic, the U.S. fleet blockaded its Spanish opponent at Santiago de Cuba. American troops, led by (among others) future U.S. president Theodore Roosevelt, stormed the heights overlooking Santiago de Cuba at the Battle of San Juan Hill. With the heights in U.S. possession, the Spanish fleet was forced to give battle and was destroyed. By the Treaty of Paris of December, 10, 1898, the Spanish yielded sovereignty to Cuba and gave the U.S. possession of Puerto Rico, Guam, and the Philippines. With some reluctance, and subject to numerous conditions, the United States conceded Cuban independence but decided to retain control of the Philippines and there became embroiled in an insurrection with its former allies, the local insurgents under Emilio Aguinaldo. The insurrection continued at substantial costs to both sides until 1902.

After more than a century of steadfast isolationism, the U.S. was now a global power. The coming years would see repeated military intervention in countries like Haiti (1915–34), the Dominican Republic (1916–24), Nicaragua (1909–10, 1912–25, 1926–33), and Colombia (1904), the latter as a prelude to building the Panama Canal, which opened in 1914.

The Progressive Era (1900–17)

The Progressive Spirit The immense social and economic change brought on by the industrial revolution produced, at the turn of the century, a growing popular demand for reform over a wide range of issues. Americans of all walks of life became concerned over the enormous and unchecked power wielded by large corporations. Equally disturbing was the growing gap between rich and poor, a trend exemplified by the rise of industrial elites such as the Rockefellers, Carnegies, Morgans, and Whitneys and masses of impoverished, slum-dwelling workers. Many Americans likewise decried the corruption and undemocratic aspects of the political system at all levels of government.

Much of this rising concern and demand for reform was generated by the writings of investigative journalists, or "muckrakers," who penned exposes of corporate and political wrongdoing. Ida Tarbell (1857–1944), for example, wrote a scathing exposé of John D. Rockefeller and the corrupt practices of Standard Oil. Upton Sinclair (1878–1968) shocked the nation with his novel, *The Jungle* (1906), which exposed the horrors of Chicago's meatpacking industry. Lincoln Steffens's (1866–1936) book, *Shame of the Cities* (1906), attacked corrupt political machines. Jacob Riis (1849–1914) shed light on the urban poor in *How the Other Half Lives* (1890).

Progressive-era reformers came from widely divergent backgrounds and supported a diverse array of causes, from child labor legislation to prohibition. Some drew their inspiration from religion, others from feminism and socialism. Yet they shared one fundamental belief: that government ought to be used to eradicate social ills and promote equality and the common good.

Political Reform Movements for reform of state government led to the adoption of the initiative and referendum in dozens of states. These forms of direct democracy were intended to allow the people to gain passage of reforms over the opposition of corrupt or out-of-touch legislatures. Similarly, the wide adoption of the recall put pressure on legislators to heed the needs of their constituents, rather than lobbyists and special interests.

Reforms of municipal government saw the adoption of measures designed to undercut the power of corrupt political machines. These included the introduction of nonpartisan elections, direct primaries, the secret ballot, and city manager and city commission forms of government, as well as the expansion of civil service.

On the national level reformers gained adoption of the 17th Amendment to the Constitution (ratified in 1913), which required popular election of U.S. Senators, and the 19th Amendment (ratified in 1920) granting women the right to vote.

Economic Reform Vice President Theodore Roosevelt became president following the assassination of William McKinley in 1901, and he immediately launched an effort to curb the power of large trusts. The Justice Department (under the Sherman Antitrust Act) initiated 44 lawsuits against trusts it charged engaged in unlawful practices. The most famous case resulted in the breakup of the Northern Securities Trust (1904), a massive railroad combination. Roosevelt signed the Elkins Act (1903) and Hepburn Act (1906), which greatly enhanced the power of the Interstate Commerce Commission to regulate the railroad industry. The administration of Roosevelt's successor, William Howard Taft, initiated 90 lawsuits against trusts.

The cause of consumer protection was advanced with the signing of the Pure Food and Drug Act (1906), which prohibited the use of harmful drugs or chemicals in food. The Meat Inspection Act (1906) increased the regulation of the meat industry to prevent the sale of tainted meat.

American workers saw many important gains in this era, mainly in the form of state laws. By 1917 more than two-thirds of the states had adopted laws prohibiting child labor and mandating workmen's compensation. At the federal level, the Roosevelt administration created the Department of Commerce and Labor (1903).

Conservation Concerned over the loss of wilderness lands to the timber, mining, and ranching industries, conservationists called upon the government to take action. An avid outdoorsman, Roosevelt used his presidential authority to set aside 238 million acres of federal lands to protect them from development. He also established wildlife preserves, expanded the national park system, and created the National Conservation Commission (1909). The 1902 Newlands Reclamation Act provided federal funds for dams and large-scale irrigation projects in semi-arid regions of the U.S.

In 1909 President Taft fired Gifford Pinchot, head of the forestry service, when Pinchot accused Secretary of the Interior Richard A. Ballinger of failing to protect forests and other natural resources. The so-called Ballinger-Pinchot controversy caused a major political upheaval and gave many Americans the impression Taft was undermining Roosevelt's conservation achievements.

The Wilson Administration Woodrow Wilson won the 1912 presidential election, a contest that saw Roosevelt mount an insurgent campaign as the candidate of the Progressive Party (Bull Moose Party), while Eugene Debs garnered nearly 1 million votes as candidate for the Socialist Party. Taft finished third (behind Roosevelt) in his bid for re-election.

Wilson added to earlier progressive economic reforms by signing into law several landmark pieces of legislation. The Federal Reserve Act (1913) created a national banking system designed to bring greater stability to banking and the money supply. The Clayton Antitrust Act (1914) supplemented and strengthened the Sherman Act of 1890 by defining a series of specific "unfair methods of competition," making corporate officers liable for illegal actions, and exempting labor unions from antitrust lawsuits. The Federal Trade Commission (FTC) was established to enforce these antitrust measures.

The 16th Amendment to the Constitution (ratified 1913) authorized Congress to impose an income tax, a measure designed to make the wealthy pay a greater share of the nation's tax burden and to eliminate the reliance on tariff revenue to fund government operations.

The War in Europe When World War I broke out in Europe in the summer of 1914, America declared its neutrality, a position Wilson hoped would allow the U.S. to play the role of peacemaker between the Triple Entente (England, France, and Russia) and the Central Powers (Germany and Austria-Hungary). He resisted pressure to declare war on Germany after the sinking of the *Lusitania* (1915) and won re-election in 1916 on the slogan "He Kept

Us Out Of War." But Germany's decision to resume unrestricted submarine warfare (January 31, 1917) against all ships trading with the Allies and the interception of the Zimmerman Telegram, in which Germany encouraged Mexico to wage war against the U.S., prompted Congress to declare war (April 6, 1917).

World War I See "Major Wars in History," pp. 265–68.

Radicalism and Reaction The end of World War I (November 11, 1918) touched off months of domestic unrest, including the biggest strike wave in U.S. history as 4 million workers walked off the job in 1919. Most were angry about attempts by employers to revoke wartime policies that had reduced hours, boosted wages, and recognized unions. The scale of the work stoppages and violence that attended many of them caused widespread alarm and eventually a campaign of repression known as the "Red Scare." Leftist newspapers were closed, union leaders arrested, and hundreds of radicals deported. This conservative mood also led to the ratification (1919) of the 18th Amendment banning the manufacture, sale, or transportation of alcoholic beverages and the rejection of the Versailles Treaty (1920) and U.S. membership in the new League of Nations.

The Roaring Twenties and The New Deal

Republican Warren G. Harding won the election of 1920 on a pledge to restore "normalcy." A poor leader, his administration was rocked by corruption, most notably the Teapot Dome Scandal. Harding died in office (1923) and was succeeded by his vice-president, Calvin Coolidge.

After a sharp recession in 1920-21, the American economy roared until late 1929. Industrial output boomed, and the automobile industry put nearly 27 million cars on the road by 1929. Per capita income rose for nearly everyone except farmers. Rising stock prices on Wall Street enticed millions to invest and to borrow money to do so.

The 1920's also witnessed profound social and cultural changes. The American music form known as jazz became wildly popular, as did the dance called the Charleston, professional boxing, silent movies, and radio. Many women shocked their contemporaries by taking on the so-called "flapper" look, with short hair, short dresses, and subdued bustlines.

Many Americans, especially those not living in urban areas, condemned the ebullient spirit of the era. A revived Ku Klux Klan saw its membership top 5 million by 1926. Congressed passed the National Origins Act in 1924, sharply curtailing immigration for the first time. And in Tennessee, John Scopes was convicted for teaching evolution in science class in the so-called "Monkey Trial" in 1925.

The Crash The stock market crash that began on October 29, 1929 announced the arrival of the Great Depression. After nearly a decade of overheated economic growth, excessive borrowing, and widespread crisis among farmers, the economy slowly but inexorably collapsed. President Herbert Hoover resisted calls for government relief and instead urged Americans to be patient. Hoover eventually signed several relief bills by 1932 but they did little to ease the suffering and boost the economy.

The Great Depression was an economic catastrophe for the United States. Unemployment quickly reached 25 percent—five million people were out of work in 1930, but by 1932, that figure had risen to 13 million. People thrown out of their homes set up makeshift residences called Hoovervilles, a derisive reference to the President who seemed overwhelmed by events. Families waited in long lines for bread. Rural workers left the Dust Bowl of the Plains and headed west in search of work. Mighty companies like General Motors and U.S. Steel saw their stock prices collapse. Banks around the nation failed, causing a run on those institutions by customers who stood to lose their life's savings if their bank closed. In 1929, before the crash, about 600 banks failed. In 1931, nearly 3,000 did. More than 100,000 businesses went under from 1929 to 1932. The despair of the period would sear its way into the souls of all those who lived through it. In 1932, voters turned Hoover out of office, replacing him with a man with a sunny disposition and a determination to change the nation's social contract, Franklin D. Roosevelt of New York.

The New Deal Promising a "new deal" during the campaign, Roosevelt and his advisors entered office committed to a program of bold experimentation to end the Depression. Over the next eight years Roosevelt signed into law some of the most far-reaching legislation in American history. In general, the initiatives fell into three broad categories: relief, recovery and reform.

Relief To relieve suffering, hunger, and homelessness, the New Deal included jobs programs such as the Public Works Administration, which spent $4.3 billion on 34,000 public projects. Related programs included the Civilian Conservation Corps (C.C.C), National Youth Administration (N.Y.A.), and Works Progress Administration (W.P.A.).

Recovery To stimulate economic recovery, the government spent billions on jobs programs and public projects like the Tennessee Valley Authority (1933), a massive water control and hydroelectric project that constructed 16 dams, and Boulder Dam, finished in 1935 and later renamed Hoover Dam, in Nevada. The National Recovery Administration was established to set price, wage, and production codes for business. The Agricultural Adjustment Act aimed to limit farm production and boost farmer income.

Reform The most profound achievements of the New Deal were those that took advantage of the crisis to enact major social and economic legislation. To bring stability to the economy and prevent future crashes, Congress passed the Glass-Steagall Act (which separated banking and investing) and created the Securities and Exchange Commission to regulate dangerous speculative practices on Wall Street. The Wagner Act aimed to improve labor-employer relations by guaranteeing a wide range of rights to workers and unions. Most significant of all was the Social Security Act of 1935 which established pensions for the aged and infirm as well as a system of unemployment insurance.

Though the New Deal did not achieve all of its goals, it changed the nation's political dynamics and built a coalition that would define the nation's politics until the 1970s. Roosevelt and his administration aggressively sought a larger role for government in regulating the nation's economy. Government expanded rapidly under Roosevelt's tenure as new agencies were given unprecedented powers over private industry. In addition, innovations like the Social Security Act led the construction of a social safety net for the unemployed, the young and the disabled. Many of the reforms Roosevelt instituted on a national level had been tried successfully in New York state when Alfred E. Smith was governor in the 1920's.

Franklin D. Roosevelt easily won re-election in 1936. Yet the ultimate goal of the New Deal—ending the Depression—remained elusive as unemployment still hovered at 14 percent as late as 1940. The nation's economy would not recover until America entered World War II.

Neutrality As the threat of war loomed in Europe, Americans supported a policy of strict neutrality. Congress passed three Neutrality Acts in the late 1930's designed to prevent the President from lending money or selling arms to any combatants.

But soon after hostilities broke out in Europe in September 1939, Congress took steps to prepare the U.S. for war, including a massive naval build-up and the institution of a draft in 1940. The Neutrality Act of 1939 allowed the U.S. to sell arms to the Allies. In 1941 Congress passed the Lend-Lease Act to allow Britain to acquire U.S. arms and ships without payment.

The hope that the U.S. could stay out of the war ended with the surprise attack by Japan on the U.S. naval base at Pearl Harbor (December 7, 1941). Congress declared war on December 8. Three days later, Japan's allies Germany and Italy declared war on the U.S.

World War II See "Major Wars in History," pp. 268–70.

Post-War America

Post-War Boom As with the end of the First World War, the end of World War II inaugurated a period of strife. Millions of Americans went on strike in 1946. In response, Republicans, who gained control of Congress in 1946, passed the Taft-Hartley Act (1947) curbing some of organized labor's powers gained under the Wagner Act.

The conversion of the national economy from wartime to peacetime production by 1947 touched off an unprecedented period of prosperity and economic growth. The wartime economy had put billions of dollars into the pockets of American families which they now spent on consumer goods such as cars, radios, and refrigerators, items they could not afford during the Depression and were unavailable during the war. The G.I. Bill and other legislation also stimulated a movement to the suburbs and sent tens of thousands of former soldiers off for a college education.

The election of 1948 featured one of the greatest political upsets in U.S. political history. Virtually every poll showed Republican challenger Thomas E. Dewey defeating President Harry S. Truman. But Truman won and immediately proposed a major domestic legislative agenda called the "Fair Deal," much of which was blocked by Republicans in Congress.

The Cold War Although the Soviet Union and U.S. were allies during World War II, they became bitter adversaries afterward in a geopolitical rivalry that came to be known as the Cold War. Tension first emerged over the Soviet occupation of Eastern Europe, the struggle over the future of Germany, and Soviet backing of communist insurgencies in Greece and Turkey.

The Truman Doctrine To counter the perceived Soviet threat, Truman announced in early 1947 that the

U.S. was committed to the "containment" of communist expansion anywhere in the world. As part of this effort, the administration adopted the Marshall Plan, which provided $12 billion to rebuild nations ravaged by the war. In 1949 the U.S. joined with Great Britain, France, Canada and other European nations to form the North Atlantic Treaty Organization (NATO). Under the terms of the alliance, signatory nations pledged to come to the aid of any member that was attacked.

Fear of the Soviet Union rose sharply with the Soviet blockade of East Berlin (1948-49), the Soviet announcement that they had detonated their first atomic bomb (1949), the arrest of several people accused of spying for the Soviets (1948-50), the overthrow of the pro-U.S. Chinese government by communist revolutionaries (1949), and news that communist North Korea had invaded non-communist South Korea (June 1950). The latter event prompted Truman to intervene militarily.

At the end of World War II, Korea was divided, for administrative purposes, at the 38th parallel between the United States and the Soviet Union, which created separate governments in their zones of occupation. On June, 25, 1950, the northern Communists invaded the south without warning and, within two months, they had driven South Korean and U.S. forces to the southeastern tip of the Korean Peninsula, the Pusan Perimeter. The United Nations supported the south and U.N. forces were placed under the command of U.S. general Douglas MacArthur. MacArthur launched an amphibious assault at Inchon on the western coast of Korea that successfully drove the North Koreans back to the Yalu River, the border between North Korea and China. On November, 26, 1950, however, a large Communist Chinese army counterattacked and drove the U.N. forces back south. By 1951, the front had stabilized along the 38th parallel, the original dividing line between the two Koreas. Negotiations dragged on as fighting continued without material gain to either side. During the negotiations, General MacArthur favored bombing China and was removed for insubordination by Truman in 1951. An armistice was signed on July 27, 1953, but no peace treaty has ever concluded the war.

This atmosphere of fear led to the emergence of Wisconsin Senator Joseph McCarthy (1908–57) in 1950 as the nation's leading anti-communist. His accusations that the U.S. government was riddled with communists earned him wide public support. He held hearings and continued his accusations before being censured by the U.S. Senate in 1954.

Despite the Cold War, the 1950's and early 1960's was a period of unprecedented prosperity. Per capita income rose steadily as did levels of education and homeownership. The latter was most evident in the explosion of suburban housing. Seventy percent of American homes had a television by 1960, with dramatic implications for pop culture, politics, social mores and consumer habits.

Peace and prosperity gave rise to a spirit of optimism and confidence that was reflected in the election of John F. Kennedy as president in 1960. The youngest man ever elected to the office (age 43) and the first Roman Catholic, he brought youth, charisma, and energy to national politics. While much of his administration was dominated by cold war events (a failed invasion in Cuba, the Berlin Wall Crisis, Cuban Missile Crisis, and Vietnam), Kennedy pushed for the space program, civil rights legislation, and efforts to eradicate poverty. His assassination on November 22, 1963 stunned the nation.

The Civil Rights Movement Not all Americans shared in the prosperity and optimism of the post-war period. By the mid-1950's African-Americans in the South began to demand civil rights and an end to state-sponsored discrimination. In 1954 the Supreme Court issued *Brown v. Board of Education*, a landmark decision that declared segregation in schools unconstitutional. One year later the African-American residents of Montgomery, Ala., initiated a boycott of the city's bus lines to protest segregation. In 1957 local resistance to a plan to desegregate the public schools of Little Rock, Ark., led President Dwight Eisenhower to send in federal troops to keep order and protect nine African American students enrolled in the formerly all-white Central High School. As a result of these incidents, Congress passed the Civil Rights Act of 1957, which created a Commission for Civil Rights and strengthened federal protection of voting rights.

The civil rights movement increased its profile and appeal in the early 1960's. Hundreds of African-American college students in places like Greensboro, N.C., staged sit-ins at segregated lunch counters (1960). Civil rights activists also organized Freedom Rides on buses in 1961 to challenge segregated bus stations across the South. In 1962 federal troops were sent to protect James Meredith as he became the first African-American to enroll in the University of Mississippi. The following year Rev. Martin Luther King Jr. of the Southern Christian Leadership Council began leading protest marches in Alabama demanding the right to vote. When a brutal police assault on a march in Birmingham was broadcast on television, it caused a national outcry and eventually led President Kennedy to call for a new Civil Rights Act. In August 1963 King delivered his famous "I Have A Dream" speech during a march on Washington.

Lyndon Johnson became president following Kennedy's assassination. He immediately made passage of a Civil Rights Act a priority and signed it into law on July 2, 1964. The act prohibited segregation of public facilities, created an Equal Employment Opportunity Commission to combat racial discrimination in the workplace, and added protections to voting rights. The following year Johnson signed the Voting Rights Act which led to a dramatic rise in African American voting.

While many rejoiced at these achievements, a more radical faction of the civil rights movement emerged. Preaching a doctrine of separatism and Black Power and rejecting non-violence, they gained significant support among young African-Americans, especially in northern cities. Their frustration led to major riots in Los Angeles, New York, and Detroit. Rioting broke out in more than 100 cities following the assassination of Rev. Martin Luther King, Jr. (April 4, 1968).

The Johnson administration also launched a massive initiative dubbed the War on Poverty. It included expanded welfare and healthcare benefits, education and job training programs, early childhood development initiatives (Head Start), public housing construction, and economic development programs for inner-city communities.

The War in Vietnam American involvement in Vietnam marked the second phase of a war that began in 1946. In the first, the French, who had ruled Indo-China since the 19th century, were defeated by the Vietnamese under Ho Chi Minh. Vietnam was divided at the 17th parallel into the nominally democratic Republic of Vietnam (South Vietnam) and the communist Democratic Republic of Vietnam (North Vietnam). In 1956, an insurgency broke out in the south; the insurgents, the Viet Cong, were supported by the government of North Vietnam. The United States provided aid, including advisors, to the south and, in 1961, the advisors were authorized to fight with South Vietnamese troops. In 1964, in response to purported attacks on U.S. naval vessels, Congress passed, at President Johnson's request, the Gulf of Tonkin Resolution, authorizing the use of force to repel any armed attack on U.S. troops. U.S. troops were dispatched to South Vietnam and bombing missions commenced there, eventually extending to North Vietnam and Cambodia.

At the beginning of 1968, the Viet Cong launched the Tet Offensive (named for the lunar new year during which it occurred). Although U.S. troops crushed the offensive and largely destroyed the Viet Cong, whose place was largely taken by North Vietnamese regulars, sentiment in America turned steadily against the war and, in July of 1968, the United States announced a policy of substituting Vietnamese troops for U.S. soldiers. In 1972, peace talks, which had been going on sporadically since 1968, broke down and President Richard Nixon ordered an intensive bombing campaign against the north. A cease fire agreement was signed in January of 1973, but fighting continued as American troops were withdrawn. A final North Vietnamese offensive in January of 1975 led to a collapse of South Vietnam by April of that year.

Politics and Protest Johnson's accomplishments in the areas of civil rights and poverty eradication were eventually overshadowed by his decision to escalate the war in Vietnam. Isolated protests in 1965 gave way to massive demonstrations in 1967 and 1968 as initial support for the war crumbled in the face of soaring U.S. casualties.

When Johnson nearly lost the New Hampshire primary to anti-war challenger Eugene McCarthy in early 1968, he withdrew his bid for re-election. Senator Robert F. Kennedy, brother of the slain president, then entered the race but was himself assassinated (June 5, 1968) after winning the California primary. Clashes between police and anti-war demonstrators broke out at the Democratic National Convention in Chicago. In November Nixon defeated Democrat Hubert H. Humphrey on a campaign that stressed a return to law and order at home and a dignified solution to the conflict in Vietnam.

The Counterculture Many young Americans grew disillusioned with their society, condemning it as hopelessly materialistic, racist, militaristic, and repressed. They called themselves "hippies" and turned to a counterculture of rock music, radical politics, sexual liberation, and experimentation with drugs.

Years of Crisis (1970–80)

The anti-war movement receded in 1969-70 as Nixon began a sustained removal of American troops from South Vietnam while pressing the North Vietnamese to enter peace talks by launching massive airstrikes against North Vietnamese cities. Protests resumed in May 1970 when

U.S. troops entered Cambodia, suggesting a re-escalation of the conflict. Four students were killed at Kent State University in Ohio when panicky National Guardsmen opened fire on an anti-war rally. The so-called "Pentagon Papers" leaked to the press in June 1971 added to anti-war sentiment by revealing how poorly the war was going and the extent to which the government had covered it up. Nonetheless, on January 27, 1973, North Vietnam and the U.S. announced a truce. In truth, it was merely a temporary stoppage to allow U.S. forces to pull out. North Vietnam soon renewed its offensive and toppled the pro-U.S. government of South Vietnam in April 1975.

The 1970's brought additional foreign policy crises. In the wake of the Arab-Israeli War of 1973, Arab nations cut off oil shipments to the U.S., causing fuel prices to soar and plunging the economy into a period of sustained inflation. In 1979 Islamic nationalists toppled the pro-U.S. government in Iran and seized 58 Americans in the U.S. embassy. That same year Cold War tensions spiked when the Soviet Union invaded neighboring Afghanistan.

Watergate President Nixon had won a landslide reelection victory in 1972, but soon found himself embroiled in a major political scandal. It began when men connected with his re-election campaign were arrested for breaking into Democratic campaign headquarters at the Watergate Hotel in Washington, D.C. During congressional hearings attention eventually shifted to Nixon's role in a cover-up attempt and he resigned from office in August 1974. His vice president, Gerald Ford, became president and subsequently issued a controversial pardon to Nixon.

Economic Crisis The oil embargo and ensuing inflation were not the only troubling economic developments. U.S. manufacturers faced increasing competition from abroad and thousands of factory jobs were lost. The unemployment rate soared while economic growth stagnated. Interest rates rose to a staggering 21 percent, crippling the housing market and discouraging investment. The economic malaise was felt across the country, but most intensely in major cities, leading to an era of budget crises, labor unrest, high crime, and infrastructure deterioration.

Women's Rights The seventies saw record numbers of women enter college and the workplace. Congress passed the Equal Rights Amendment in 1972 and by 1974 it had been ratified by 33 of the needed 38 states. Conservative opposition to the amendment, however, successfully stymied any additional ratifications. Many women also hailed the 1973 Supreme Court decision *Roe v. Wade* that legalized abortion. In 1976 Democrat Jimmy Carter defeated Ford, promising he would never lie to the American people. Carter's presidency was dogged by a poor economy and the Iran hostage crisis. But he also emphasized human rights around the world and tried to broker peace in the Middle East.

The Rise of the Conservative Movement

The Reagan "Revolution" In the election of 1980, former California Governor Ronald W. Reagan defeated Carter, a victory that signaled the emergence of a strong conservative political movement that would exert great influence in the coming decades. The new conservatism combined antagonism toward government regulation and taxes, support for an aggressive foreign policy toward the Soviet Union, and promotion of so-called family values based on Christian morality.

Reagan pursued an economic policy ("Reaganomics") of tax cuts and deregulation. When the disastrous economy of the late 1970's entered a period of record expansion after 1982, Reagan's popularity soared. His tough rhetorical stance against the Soviet Union and massive defense build-up likewise earned him support not only from conservatives, but many disaffected middle-class voters who traditionally had voted Democratic. In 1984 he won re-election in a landslide.

Though many found Reagan charming, his presidency was controversial. Annual budget deficits reached record levels in the 1980's, pushing the national debt to nearly $3 trillion by 1988. Conservative zeal for prosecuting the Cold War also led to the administration's greatest crisis, the Iran-Contra scandal, an illegal scheme that involved arms sales to Iran to secretly fund anti-communist rebels in Nicaragua. A number of Reagan administration officials were convicted for their role in the scheme, but Reagan avoided prosecution. He also later admitted that his administration had traded arms for hostages with Iran.

The election of 1988 brought Reagan's vice president, George H. W. Bush, to the White House. His presidency was largely a continuation of Reagan's conservatism, with some notable exceptions including enactment of the Americans with Disabilities Act and a significant increase in taxes (despite Bush's campaign promise of "no new taxes").

The most significant event during this period was the end of the Cold War, an event occasioned by the tearing down of the Berlin Wall in 1989 and subsequent collapse of the Soviet Union. Bush's popularity soared in 1991 when he successfully organized an international force to fight Iraq after that nation attacked Kuwait. But Bush lost his bid for re-election in 1992 to Democrat William J. Clinton in large measure because voters believed his administration poorly handled a severe economic recession in the early 1990's.

The Clinton Years President Clinton's administration got off to a rocky start when it attempted to craft a plan for universal healthcare coverage. Intense opposition from Republicans and special interests combined to kill the proposal. In 1994, under the leadership of Newt Gingrich, the Republicans took complete control of Congress for the first time in 40 years. The Clinton administration pursued politically moderate policies, many of them supported by Republicans. It ignored concerns of environmentalists and organized labor by signing the North American Free Trade Agreement which lowered tariffs among the United States, Canada, and Mexico. In 1995 Clinton signed the Welfare Reform Act that dramatically reshaped the nation's welfare system, setting time limits for benefits and requiring recipients to work. This popular political strategy, plus a booming economy and rising sense of security engendered by the end of the Cold War, was more than enough to gain Clinton re-election in 1996. His second term was marred by scandal after revelations of an extra-marital affair between Clinton and Monica Lewinsky, a White House intern. The cover-up of the scandal and Clinton's lying to a grand jury led to him becoming only the second President to be impeached and tried by the Senate, a process that ended in acquittal.

George W. Bush The election of 2000 pitted Democrat Albert Gore, the sitting Vice-President, versus Republican George W. Bush, governor of Texas and son of former President Bush. The result was one of the closest and most controversial presidential elections in U.S. history. Gore won the popular vote by 500,000 votes, but the electoral vote tally—the vote that determines the victor—was left unclear because of questions regarding the vote count in Florida. After 36 days of intense debate, vote recounts, and legal maneuvering, the Supreme Court, in the unprecedented *Bush v. Gore* decision, ruled (5–4) against a request for a continuing recount of ballots in Florida, upholding Bush's victory in the state and awarding him the electoral votes that gave him the presidency.

Elected on a conservative platform, Bush pushed for and signed into law a steep cut in taxes, a plan to allow federal funds to be used by religiously-affiliated charities, and a large increase in defense spending. But the event that defined his first term and left a lasting impact on American society and world affairs was the terrorist strike on September 11, 2001. The attack against the Pentagon in Virginia and the World Trade Center in New York City claimed the lives of some 3,000 people and led the U.S. to invade Afghanistan, the nation that harbored the radical Islamic terrorist organization responsible for the plot.

Bush announced that this was but the first phase of a global war on terrorism and soon began making the case for international action against Iraq for violations of the terms of the ceasefire signed at the end of the Gulf War of 1991. The most serious charge was that the government of Saddam Hussein had built an arsenal of weapons of mass destruction and thus posed a threat to regional stability and world peace. Although the United Nations and many European governments questioned these claims and urged restraint, Bush ordered an invasion in March 2003. Joined by forces from Great Britain, the U. S. quickly toppled the government of Saddam Hussein and then commenced a very difficult occupation in an effort to establish a representative Iraqi government. The failure to find evidence of weapons of mass destruction led many to question the wisdom of the decision to invade Iraq.

LAW

A Brief History of Law
Code of Hammurabi 294
Ancient Greece 294
Rome 294
Medieval Law 295
Anglo-American Law 295
The Enlightenment 296

The American Constitutional System 297

Criminal Law and Civil Law
Criminal Law 299
Civil Law 299
The Court System 300
Civil Procedure 300
Criminal Procedure 301

Other Legal Systems 302

Important Supreme Court Decisions 303
Times Focus: *The Supreme Court: Federalism After 9-11*
By Linda Greenhouse 305

Glossary of Legal Terms 308

The Constitution of the United States of America: An Annotated Guide 313
The Bill of Rights 327

LAW

A Brief History of Law

The roots of the American legal system lie in Great Britain and the English common law. However, English law itself borrowed concepts and rules from the legal systems of the ancient world, including early Babylonia, ancient Greece, and Rome. Whether the Roman concept of "criminal intent" that still underlies the entire modern U.S. criminal law, or the more ancient concept of strict liability of an "eye for an eye" found in the Code of Hammurabi and the Old Testament, early law casts an illuminating light on choices we have made in our current system.

Code of Hammurabi

The earliest known figure of great legal importance is Hammurabi (1792–50 B.C.), the king of Bablyonia and creator of one of the most comprehensive early codes of laws. The code, engraved on an eight-foot-tall black stone monument, is well known for its thoroughness and complexity, addressing commercial, family, labor, property, and personal injury law. But it is also known for the harsh dictum, "an eye for an eye," a literal legal punishment. Many other crimes that would seem relatively minor today incurred capital punishment. Rather than attempting any of the more modern aims of the law, such as rehabilitation, Hammurabi's Code mandated simple retribution.

Ancient Greece

Law began to emerge as an instrument of a more humanitarian impulse in Greece during the rule of Solon (ca. 639–ca. 559 B.C.), the Athenian general and statesman who helped lay the groundwork for democracy in Athens. Prior to Solon, the harsh laws of Draco, promulgated in 621 B.C., were in force. Under Draco's laws, most crimes, even idleness, were punishable by death. After his election in 594 B.C., Solon instituted a milder legal regime, in which punishments were calibrated to the seriousness of the crime. Courts also took on a more powerful role under Solon's law. The Roman historian Plutarch suggested that Solon intentionally wrote laws with a measure of ambiguity in order to increase the power of the courts through interpretation—a step that foreshadowed the U.S. lawmakers' proclivity to let the courts decide the application of the general provisions of statutes to specific situations. Finally, Athenian law became more democratic, as Solon reformed the existing social, economic, and political systems in Athens. Solon gave his reforms popular appeal by, among other measures, annulling all mortgages and debts, limiting the amount of land any single citizen could hold, and forbidding all borrowing that could cause a debtor to lose personal liberty.

Rome

Early Roman law, as stated in the Twelve Tables (ca. 450 B.C.), formed the basis for the legal systems that would later influence those of Europe and through Europe the entire world. While some of the rules contained in the Twelve Tables are nearly identical to those of the modern world, such as requiring the accused to appear before a magistrate in the initial stages of a criminal proceeding, others were rooted in their time, such as the prohibition of marriages between plebeians and patricians. Law was made more sophisticated as a method of stabilizing society by Lucius Cornelius Sulla (138–78 B.C.), a Roman general and dictator whose usurpation of power paved the way for the fall of the republic. His *leges corneliae* provided specific punishments for homicide, arson, the intention of killing or stealing, poisoning, and the manufacture and possession of poison. However, his rule was also marked by efforts to check the populist branches of Roman government. For example, Sulla protected the power of the Senate from populist incursions by giving it control of the courts and new measures against the tribunes.

Law continued to be developed during the reign of Augustus (63 B.C.–A.D. 14), who took power in 29 B.C. Augustus established legal principles that would influence Western law, including clear procedures for formalizing contracts, strengthening personal property law, and the presumption that defendants were innocent until proven guilty. Augustus's legal reforms were extensive but were rooted in Roman tradition. Rome technically remained a republic governed by the Senate, but with Augustus as leading man or *princeps*. The term *emperor* derives from the Latin *imperator,* meaning victorious general.

Roman law underwent some of its most important developments under Emperor Justinian I (A.D. 483–565).

Previously disparate Roman legal decisions and laws were now systematized and codified as the *Corpus Juris Civilis* (body of civil law). What was important about Justinian's Code was not necessarily what was new in it, but rather the influence that this systematic restatement of law would have on the development of future legal systems worldwide.

Medieval Law

In the early medieval period, the Germanic tribes' invasion of the Roman Empire resulted in a complex coexistence of Roman and German legal systems. In general, Roman subjects of barbarian kings remained subject to Roman law, while their Germanic neighbors were subject to traditional Germanic laws and customs. A key difference between the two systems was that Roman law retained a notion of the *rei publicae* or common good, whereas Germanic law tended to reduce every good, even justice, to a private right.

During the seventh, eighth, and ninth centuries, the Germanic tribes codified their customary law. The influence of Roman law grew enormously after Charlemagne's establishment of the Holy Roman Empire in A.D. 800 because the Roman Catholic church used Roman law in its tribunals, giving them a uniform system of justice throughout the West. The collapse of the Carolingian empire in the 10th century led to the emergence of feudalism, placing many disputes in the hands of the local lord whose control of the land was seen as giving him the concurrent right to administer justice. Property law, especially in the Anglo-American legal systems, remains influenced by concepts of ownership derived from the Middle Ages. However, modern law has moved away from the medieval treatment of crime, under which harsh punishments were meted out for minor offenses (a thief, for example, might be hanged or have his eyes gouged out).

Legal procedures in the early Middle Ages were heavily influenced by Germanic customs. An accused criminal was often subjected to an "ordeal," such as being bound and thrown into water, to determine guilt or innocence. Over time, largely through the church's influence, judicial procedures on the Continent came to conform to Roman practices, including the use of torture to extract evidence in certain situations. In the 11th century, the founding of the University of Bologna in Italy, which specialized in the teaching of law using Justinian's Code as the basis of instruction, contributed to a revival of Roman law. This revival was aided by the efforts of both stronger monarchies and the church to suppress the jurisdiction of local feudal courts and to replace them with royal and ecclesiastical courts, often administered by clerics and others who had been specifically trained in Roman law.

Anglo-American Law

Anglo-American jurisdictions are said to be "common law" systems rather than "civil law" systems as found on the continent of Europe (see "Civil Law," below). After William the Conqueror invaded England in 1066, he introduced feudal concepts that had taken hold in France, and embarked on what would become a centuries-long struggle to centralize control over justice and taxation. One result was his order to prepare the Domesday Book, an inventory of all the property in his new realm. Subsequent rulers, with greater or lesser success, sought to maintain the supremacy of the royal courts, introducing new ones and modifying old ones as new situations arose. Most significant was the development of "equity jurisdiction" under a series of lord chancellors. Equity filled the gaps in the common-law system and gave faster and more efficient justice than traditional royal courts, which had particularly inflexible procedural rules that often seemed to impede rather than facilitate justice. By the late 15th century, the supremacy of the royal courts was established, but how the different court systems were related to one another was unclear. In the early 17th century, Charles I began to collect taxes without the consent of Parliament, and soon the role of the courts became crucial as the king attempted to use them as the means of collecting taxes. In general, the traditional courts supported Parliament; and with the triumph of Parliament in the English civil wars, the supremacy of the traditional courts with their customary, non-Roman procedures was ensured.

The Common Law Common law stands in contrast to European civil law, which governs society through extensive and specific codes, devised at once by a legislature. Common law evolves as scores of decentralized judges independently make legal decisions on cases. Over time, operative legal principles in cases become clear. Thus legal rules emerge from "case law."

The common law yields a flexible and organic legal system at the cost of precision and clarity. Generations of American and British law students have bemoaned the process of unthreading legal rules from dense cases. The common law does not always hold sway, however. Legislatures are free to overrule judge-made law with statutes, and so there is a balance between statutory and case law on many legal matters. Some scholars have predicted a decline in common-law rules of property, tort, contract, and family law as legislators grow more bold in these areas. Yet basic common-law principles that emerged centuries ago in England are still quite powerful in most U.S. jurisdictions. American common law continues to be made every day by plaintiffs, defendants, lawyers, and judges, and to be amended by statutes passed by citizens and legislators.

The common law borrows its basic foundation from English constitutionalism. While Great Britain has never had a written constitution, it has, for several centuries, relied strongly on laws and judges rather than rules handed down by divine authority. The beginnings of English constitutionalism lie in Magna Carta, the document that English barons and church elders forced King John I to sign in 1215. Magna Carta required King John to refrain from encroaching on feudal rights and to abandon the practice of waging expensive, unsuccessful wars and auctioning off church offices. Between the lines of the charter's 63 brief clauses lay a recognition of individual and communal rights inviolable by any authority. These new rights helped to form the basis of the emerging British constitution.

The common law evolved as a coherent system under a series of jurists. Sir Edward Coke (1552–1634), a chief justice of the King's Bench, helped cement the common law, rather than royal prerogative, as the default law of England. Sir Matthew Hale (1609–76), the lord chief justice under Charles II, helped synthesize the common law into a field of careful study. And Sir William Blackstone (1723–80), a professor of law at Oxford, wrote the four-volume *Commentaries on the Laws of England*, which conclusively demonstrated that English law was comparable to the two other grand legal systems—Roman law and the civil law of Europe.

A century later, the development of common law under the control of British and American judges was chronicled by Oliver Wendell Holmes (1841–1935). In his lectures and book *The Common Law*, Holmes argued provocatively that the common law developed in accordance with social reality and collective desires, rather than clear moral or philosophical precepts. "The life of the law is not logic, but experience," he wrote. Holmes's approach formed the foundation for the early 20th-century legal realist movement, which understood judicial reasoning not as an abstract logical process but instead as a reflection of judges' own personal and political lives and the society of which they are a part.

The Enlightenment

Although the form and process of American law came from the British common law model, dating to the late Middle Ages, many of the ideas underpinning America's legal and political choices came from a more modern period, the Enlightenment. In the 17th and 18th centuries, philosophers began arguing for the power of rational, equality-focused, and humanistic reasoning over the inherited authority of the church and other traditional sources of law. The Enlightenment's impact on the law was therefore deep and lasting. The law now evolved to fit societies that were learning to value rational ideas and the value of individual rights, rather than the divine right of kings or the rigidity of traditional institutions. The law itself became more enlightened, more logical, more systematic, and more humane.

The familiar American rights to "life, liberty, and the pursuit of happiness," included by Thomas Jefferson in the Declaration of Independence, may be traced directly to John Locke (1632–1704), whose *Treatises on Government* helped shape the American notion of a government dedicated to protecting private property and individual liberties. Locke's political and legal theories directly contradicted those of Thomas Hobbes (1588–1679), who believed that life for men in a state of nature was "solitary, poor, nasty, brutish, and short," driving the need for a strong collective state to protect men from themselves. Locke avoided such a dark view, arguing instead that life in the state of nature was fundamentally felicitous, and that the state was necessary only because certain people would never recognize the rights of others to "life, health, liberty, or possessions." The American dedication to natural rights and a government dedicated to protecting them borrows directly from these ideas.

In France, *Spirit of the Laws* (1748), by Charles Louis Montesquieu (1689–1755), contained the basic notion of separation of powers to guarantee the freedom of the individual. The Founding Fathers of the United States emphasized balancing the executive, legislative, and judicial branches, an approach that can be traced directly to Montesquieu, as can their thoughtful approach to avoiding the fate of the Roman republic (the subject of a study by Montesquieu in 1734).

The American legal idea of popular sovereignty can be traced to the work of another French philosopher, Jean-Jacques Rousseau (1712–78). Rousseau's political theory, found in *Of the Social Contract* (1762), was that people were intrinsically good prior to their involvement in a state. They traded their original sovereignty to the state in exchange for protection and social progress, so the state must recognize and obey the collective desires—the people's "general will"—on issues of political and legal significance. Such ideas stood in stark contrast to traditional monarchical or aristocratic theories of the state. They also led the Founding Fathers to base American law on the consent of the people, the limitations of the state, and the embrace of individual rights.

The American Constitutional System

The United States possesses a highly unusual, innovative legal system as complex as it is elegant. The American legal system has several interlocking elements that depend on federalism, which ensures that state legal systems will always have some independent authority to balance against the strength of the federal system. The two interdependent systems share a number of elements. First, each state has explicitly incorporated the British common law as the default set of rules on matters of torts, contracts, and other basic areas of the law. Second, each state as well as the federal government has a constitution, which not only gives citizens individual rights not found in the common law but also governs the operations of the various branches of government. Third, both the states and the federal government have complex and ever-growing bodies of statutory law: rules passed by the legislature which often supplant the common law. The growth of federal statutes (regarding labor, the environment, and consumer protection, among other matters) was one of the principal legal stories of the 20th century. In sum, it is an enormous system with many moving parts, designed for stability rather than agility.

The basic American constitutional system required interpretation and molding before it could take its present form. A strong hand was provided by John Marshall (1755–1835), chief justice of the United States for three decades. Marshall's extraordinary opinion in *Marbury v. Madison* (1803) established the doctrine of "judicial review," which essentially gave the Supreme Court and lower courts final power to consider and reject actions by the legislative and executive branches of government. His decision in *McCulloch v. Maryland* (1819), rejecting the argument that states could trump federal statutes and establishing congressional enactments (in this case, to launch a bank) as the law of the land, had a similar structural impact on the constitutional system.

In contrast with the common law, constitutional law stems exclusively from the U.S. Constitution and the constitutions of the states. In federal constitutional law, two separate documents are at work: the seven articles of the original Constitution, and the amendments subsequently added to the Constitution (including the original ten, the Bill of Rights). The articles deal primarily with the organization and powers of the national government: interstate commerce, claims of the states against the federal government, qualifications for public office, and the checks and balances within the government. The Bill of Rights, on the other hand, focuses on civil liberties, the concepts popularly associated with constitutional law: freedom of speech, religion, and assembly; the right to bear arms; the right against self-incrimination and improper search and seizure; and a variety of other claims individuals may hold against a potentially oppressive government.

The Bill of Rights

The Bill of Rights was not incorporated in the original Constitution, which was a document designed mainly to ensure the stability of the national government. But many of the states had adopted bills of rights, and opponents of ratification of the Constitution insisted on its eventual inclusion.

Freedom of Speech and the Press Today perhaps the paramount constitutional right for Americans, freedom of speech (which includes the broader idea of freedom of expression), has had a fascinating career since the early days of the republic. Despite the explicit guarantee in the First Amendment, it was only nine years before passage of the Alien and Sedition Acts (1798), designed to silence criticism of the Federalist-controlled government by the Jefferson-led Republican Party. The free speech clause was seldom invoked until government repression during World War I led to a flurry of cases. Through the first half of the 20th century, a variety of cases allowed the government to suppress political speech under flexible doctrines such as the "clear and present danger test." In *Dennis v. United States* (1951), for example, defendants were convicted simply of organizing the Communist Party, which was conspiring to overthrow the federal government, without any proof that they had encouraged any direct or immediate acts of violence. This expansive doctrine was abandoned in *Brandenburg v. Ohio* (1969), which allowed the suppression only of speech which incited "imminent lawless action." The only speech that is constitutionally unprotected today is obscenity, criminal speech (such as yelling "Fire!" in a crowded theater when there is no fire), defamatory speech (such as libel), and words that incite violence.

Freedom of Religion Some have speculated that the Founding Fathers intended the "establishment" clause ("Congress shall make no laws respecting the establishment of religion") to protect only active religious dissenters, while still protecting Protestantism as the de facto state religion of the United States. Whatever the original intent, the establishment clause has been interpreted by the Supreme Court as barring almost any state involvement, explicit or implicit, with religion. The three-pronged test announced in *Lemon v. Kurtzman* (1971) required government action to have a secular purpose, to have a neutral effect on religion, and to avoid entanglement between government and religion. The Supreme Court has interpreted the clause, to ban school prayer, government funding of Christmas trees, and aid to religious schools. In recent years, the Rehnquist court has been somewhat less hostile toward government actions that are religion-neutral on the surface, for example by allowing the state prejudicial treatment of Native Americans for smoking peyote at religious ceremonies, and ratifying a state-based school voucher system that would support parochial schools with state money.

Search and Seizure Law Contained in the Fourth Amendment of the Bill of Rights, search and seizure law represents perhaps the most substantial constraint on the everyday exercise of the power of the police. The text of the amendment states, "The right of the people to be secure in their persons, houses, papers and effects, against unreasonable searches and seizures, shall not be violated, and no warrants shall issue, but upon probable cause." The amendment has generated scores of cases on precise questions, such as whether a car's glove compartment or trunk is protected from a search, and exactly what may constitute "probable cause" for a wiretap, a strip search, or a drug test. This area of the law speaks to the Founding Fathers' deep fear of a government and police force that could operate with no controls whatsoever. It embodies a respect for individual rights that would rather allow a person to break the law than be searched without due protections.

The protection against improper searches is strengthened by the *exclusionary rule*, which requires the courts to discard evidence if it has been obtained through constitutionally improper procedures. Examples range from an officer's failure to read a witness a Miranda warning or a detective's failure to obtain a warrant before searching a property. In both cases, unless acceptable extenuating circumstances applied, any evidence found would be inadmissible in court as the "fruit of the poisonous tree." The rule exists primarily to discourage abuses of police power, but it occasionally allows demonstrably guilty defendants to go free. Critics say more efficacious, less costly methods—such as police review boards or a new tort describing police misconduct—could discourage misconduct while saving valuable evidence for trials.

Race and the Civil War Amendments No issue has been more vexatious or more profound in the development of American law than race. The original Constitution considered a slave (no slaves were white), for the purposes of congressional represenation, "three-fifths" of a person. Three constitutional amendments (the 13th, 14th, and 15th) were directly tied to both freeing slaves and ensuring their civil rights. A century of case law then followed, interpreting the rights guaranteed by those amendments. At first, southern Reconstruction denied African Americans the rights supposedly protected by the 14th Amendment's guarantee of equal protection and due process of the law. The Supreme Court's decision in *Plessy v. Ferguson* (1896) that the "separate but equal" doctrine underlying segregation was constitutional effectively rescinded the 14th Amendment for blacks. As the 20th century wore on, a consensus gradually developed that segregation was wrong. The Supreme Court's antisegregation decision in *Brown v. Board of Education* (1954), while a lightning bolt from the court, failed to effect much change over the southern white establishment's policy of "massive resistance." Not until the Civil Rights Act of 1964 did federal action succeed in substantially reversing segregation.

Although blacks were denied the protections of the amendments designed to protect them, two clauses of the 14th amendment became crucial to the development of American law. The "due process" clause gradually was used by the Supreme Court to "incorporate" almost all of the freedoms of the Bill of Rights against the states. The "equal protection" clause has been used to help not only African Americans, but also women, the young, the old, the disabled, and various other demographic, ethnic, and religious groups.

Criminal Law and Civil Law

Citizens may appear in court under two different legal umbrellas: criminal or civil law. In criminal law, the state prosecutes a crime, with the legal result of the dispute, whether imprisonment, a fine, public service, probation, or any other of a variety of punishments, administered directly by the government. In civil law, an individual citizen sues another, often for money damages.

Criminal Law

Criminal law, the field of law that aims to protect society in general, focuses on acts such as murder, rape, theft, and battery, as well as "white-collar" crimes such as fraud and embezzlement. As crimes threaten society rather than just an individual, the prosecution of these crimes is left up to the state and is placed in the hands of prosecutors, who are state employees.

Criminal law leans heavily on the notion of voluntariness. Conviction for many crimes involves a finding of *mens rea*, Latin for "state of mind," as well as *actus reus*, Latin for the "actual act." Hence, for example, the distinction between murder (intentional killing) and manslaughter (killing with lesser degrees of intentionality—by someone who was drunk or someone who meant only to harm, not kill). A prosecution can be derailed by attacks on evidence or on witnesses, or with inventive tools such as the insanity defense, which argues that the defendant lacked the requisite *mens rea*. While widely criticized, such developments are generally consistent with the early framework of criminal law. American criminal law rests considerably on the goal of retribution, answering crimes with simple punishment. From time to time critics have argued for a greater emphasis on improving criminals themselves through rehabilitation, but their success has been modest at best.

Civil Law

Civil law is broader than criminal law, incorporating a variety of different areas of human interaction that may occasion private lawsuits—contracts, injuries, real and personal property, and family relations.

Contract Law Contract law provides for the enforcement and regulation of private agreements, including informal contacts between individuals and complex agreements between large corporations. Because contract law focuses on agreement, contracting parties have substantial latitude to make whatever agreements they want on whatever terms they want, and the law will provide a remedy if the promises made are not kept. Increasingly, contracts are made through the use of standard forms with boilerplate language, such as the terms of agreement one must accept when purchasing a product over the Internet; this practice has produced much controversy about what it means to "agree" to terms which may not be available, read, or understood at the time of contracting.

Tort Law The term *tort* derives from Latin for "twisted" or "turned aside" and applies to any act that "twists away" from reasonable actions, resulting in harm to others. Torts are as diverse as the injuries they cause. A tort can be the placement of a dangerous ladder on a public sidewalk or the sale of a dangerous drug. Tort law includes intentional torts (in which the defendant intended to injure the victim), negligence (in which the defendant has failed to act with reasonable care), and strict liability (in which the defendant is liable for harm caused even in the absence of intent to injure or negligence). Damages in tort cases include both *compensatory damages* such as medical bills and lost wages, and *punitive damages* to deter wrongdoers from potentially dangerous conduct. Tort reformers believe that the field recklessly delivers enormous awards that too lavishly punish corporations, raising insurance rates and prices for everyone. Defenders cite a generation of consumer protections and unprecedented increases in safety, all generated by more vigorous enforcement of tort law.

Property Law Stemming from medieval feudal law, in which landowning lords granted privileges to renting knights and vassals, property law still mediates conflicts between owners, renters, and borrowers. But the subject has branched out to cover, among other mattters, intellectual property (products of the mind, whether novels or computer programs, protected as property); tenants' rights (landlords are now required to provide tenants with not just land, but also certain services, including habitable and safe conditions); and zoning restrictions (local boards are allowed to control property rights for the sake of community standards). Property law becomes especially important in matters of marriage, life, and death, when divorces, wills, trusts, and estates are administered in accordance with centuries of procedures and modern reforms.

Family Law A critical area of the law is the regulation and distribution of legal rights within the private realm of the family. The "hot-button" areas of family law are, sadly, most familiar to those who have experience in troubled homes: divorce, alimony, custody, child support, domestic violence. Other areas help structure some of the more felicitous circumstances of private life, such as marriage and adoption. Like most other areas of the civil and criminal law, family law is almost wholly contained within individual states, and the states' systems of family law vary dramatically. Regarding the division of marital property after a divorce, for instance, the states fall into two categories: "community property" states, in which spouses are entitled to an equal share of much of each other's property; and "equitable distribution" states, where a judge attempts to divide the economic products of the marriage fairly, taking account of the contribution and needs of each spouse. Today the most controversial issue in family law is what constitutes a marriage: whether same-sex marriage or a substitute like civil union should be recognized.

The Court System

Federal Courts Federal courts hear cases involving federal law and significant disputes between citizens of different states. The federal court system has three levels: district courts, circuit courts, and the Supreme Court. Federal district courts have jurisdiction in both civil and criminal matters. Circuit courts of appeals hear cases on appeal from district judges' decisions. The 50 states are organized into 11 circuits, and there are separate appeals courts for the District of Columbia and for such specialties as federal patent issues. A circuit court will hear a case in one of two ways: a panel, usually of three judges, may decide a case; or an *en banc* ruling may be issued by the entire court. A panel decision may be appealed for a full *en banc* hearing. Both district judges and circuit court judges are "Article Three" judges, so called because they are formally chartered by Article Three of the Constitution and are appointed by the president and confirmed by the Senate for life terms. The third and final level is the Supreme Court, which hears most of its cases on a discretionary appeal known as a "writ of certiorari." The Supreme Court receives several thousand writs a year, and accepts only about 150 for review, usually on issues of great legal, social, or political significance.

State Courts Most state court systems roughly parallel the federal system, with three levels: courts of general jurisdiction, which hear all kinds of cases; intermediate appeals courts; and a state supreme court. State court systems also have courts of limited jurisdiction, which hear only certain matters, such as small claims issues. In many states, judges are popularly elected rather than appointed by the legislature or the governor.

Civil Procedure

If a civil lawsuit is initiated, parties will enter the "private law"—the legal processes that occur when one citizen, rather than the government, confronts another. Examples of civil lawsuit include contract disputes, personal injury claims, and divorces.

Getting a Lawyer The first step is to secure legal representation from a lawyer, though it is possible for litigants to file *pro se* lawsuits, in which they represent themselves. In all the American states and the District of Columbia, lawyers are admitted to practice under rules promulgated by the courts, typically requiring graduation from an accredited law school, passing a bar examination, and screening for character and fitness.

Jurisdiction A confusing but important second step is to choose the jurisdiction in which the dispute will be filed and settled. For jurisdiction to be proper, a court must have both subject matter jurisdiction and personal jurisdiction over an issue. Subject matter jurisdiction means the court is chartered to hear the type of issue being raised (federal district courts, for example, can hear only those cases authorized by statute). Personal jurisdiction exists if the event in question occurs in the court's jurisdiction, if one or both of the parties are residents of the jurisdiction, or if a corporation's headquarters are in a jurisdiction. A complaint that would otherwise be in state court may end up in federal court if diversity jurisdiction exists—if the parties are from two different states, for instance.

Filing a Complaint A plaintiff's complaint frames the upcoming litigation. It lays out the parties, describes the facts of the circumstance occasioning the lawsuit, outlines the allegations of the legal issues (the "cause of action"), and makes a demand. A complaint usually is written by a lawyer, and then filed with the court and "served" on the defendant.

The Defendant's Response The defendant does not have to accept the complaint on its face. Often, a defendant (or one's lawyer) files a motion to dismiss, formally requesting that the court dismiss the complaint before litigation even gets under way. There can be several grounds for such a motion, including that the court lacks proper jurisdiction, or that there is no proper legal basis for the claim. Otherwise, the defendant "answers," denying the allegations in the plaintiff's complaint. Defendants can also "counterclaim" against the plaintiff, introducing a new claim of their own related to the original complaint.

Discovery If the court does not dismiss the original complaint, the case goes into the next phase of litigation: the "discovery" of all the evidence relevant to the litigation. This process involves several stages. Potential witnesses are identified and required to provide relevant facts through their written response to interrogatories, or their oral testimony in a deposition. Depositions are made under oath and are usually conducted with lawyers from both parties in the room, with one lawyer questioning the witness in an adversarial fashion. Opposing parties also may subpoena relevant documents. The purpose of discovery is to disclose as much relevant evidence as possible in advance of trial.

During the discovery period, parties have the option to make a motion for summary judgment. Such a motion asks the court to rule that, on the basis of evidence, there is no "genuine issue of material fact," and so no reason to go to court. Summary judgment is intended to allow courts to weed out undeserving cases prior to trial.

Alternative Dispute Resolution In an attempt to avoid unnecessary and expensive litigation, parties may arbitrate or mediate their disputes in advance of trial. Some states require alternative dispute resolution before going to trial, and parties may choose on their own to submit to the process. In mediation, a mediator assists the parties in the effort to find a compromise solution to their dispute. In arbitration, one arbitrator or an arbitration panel decides the case; depending on the path to arbitration and the agreement to arbitrate, the arbitrators' decision may be binding or the dissatisfied party may proceed to trial.

Trial Many people are familiar with the basic elements of trials from countless courtroom dramas on television and in films. However, trials can vary a great deal. Not all have juries, for instance; parties may elect to have a "bench trial" in which only the judge sits. Furthermore, certain trials are very short, such as minor slip-and-fall cases; other trials, such as those between large corporations, can go on for months, with various hearings on certain motions causing the entire trial to take years.

The basic elements of all trials are the same, however. The plaintiff's attorney makes an opening statement, and the defense attorney does the same. The counsel then introduces the first witness and performs a direct examination of him or her. The defense counsel then has an opportunity for a cross-examination, with the plaintiff's counsel having the option of a redirect. This process continues until all the plaintiff's witnesses have been heard. The defense counsel then introduces witnesses, with the same steps being followed in reverse order. After all witnesses have been heard and all the evidence has been introduced, plaintiff and defense make closing arguments, after which the plaintiff has an opportunity for a rebuttal. The jury (or the judge) then removes to consider the case and make a decision. After trial, the losing party may appeal, claiming errors of law in the conduct of the trial or a verdict that is so unreasonable it should not stand.

Criminal Procedure

Criminal procedure shares many elements of civil procedures. However, this critical area of "public law" has some important differences, most stemming from the government's involvement not just as a mediator but as the initiator of the procedures themselves, raising constitutional and ethical issues.

Jurisdiction Most criminal law is state-based, so most criminal trials occur in state courts. However, the growing body of federal criminal law, on issues ranging from racketeering to securities fraud, ensures that federal courts also hear criminal cases.

The Arrest A person is arrested if an officer determines that this person broke the law. Arrest may occur on the spot, if the officer witnesses the instance of lawbreaking, or it may occur after a criminal investigation. In either case, the person becomes an arrestee. After the case of *Miranda v. Arizona* (1966), officers today must always advise arrestees of their constitutional rights, including the right to remain silent and to have an attorney.

The Complaint A high-ranking police officer or a prosecutor, or both, will make a decision to charge the arrestee with a crime. The complaint sets forth the legal grounds for the arrest, as well as any other laws that the arrestee may have broken. The arrestee formally becomes a defendant after the filing of the complaint.

Preliminary Hearings Defendants are first brought before a judge or magistrate, to be informed of the charges against them and advised of their basic rights. Bail is also set, sometimes at a separate bail hearing. This is the amount of money the defendant must pay to be released from jail while the case is tried; the intent of bail is to reduce the chance that a defendant will flee the jurisdiction. If the court determines a high likelihood of flight, bail can be denied altogether. In cases involving crimes of a certain level, a preliminary hearing may also be held, at which the basic elements of the crime are outlined by the prosecutor, and the defendant's lawyer has a chance to cross-examine witnesses. The judge then determines whether or not probable cause exists to charge the defendant. In felony cases, a grand jury of citizens drawn from the jurisdiction decides whether to issue an indictment of the defendant; only the prosecutor appears before the grand jury, whose proceedings are secret. The defendant is then arraigned before the court, where the charges are announced and the trial date is set.

The Trial If the defendant pleads not guilty, the case may go to trial. Frequently, the prosecutor and the defense attorney plea-bargain: the defendant can plead guilty in exchange for a lower charge or lesser punishment. At trial, the defendant can be defended by a public defender or by a private attorney of the defendant's choosing. In criminal trials involving felonies or certain serious misdemeanors, all states provide the constitutionally required trial by a jury of one's peers, which may be waived for a bench trial with only the judge presiding. As in civil proceedings, the prosecutor and defense attorney each make opening statements, present witnesses for direct and cross-examinations, introduce evidence, and make closing statements. If an unfavorable verdict is delivered, a right to appeal exists.

Other Legal Systems

While the common law is naturally most familiar to Americans, several other legal systems exist, which are organized quite differently and which can take different attitudes toward the principles Americans hold most dear, such as individual rights and the authority of judges to make the law.

Civil Law

Best understood in contrast with Anglo-American common law, civil law is the umbrella term for the code-driven legal systems that exist in countries on the European continent or their former colonies. The origin of civil law was Roman law, particularly Justinian's *Corpus Juris Civilis* of the sixth century. Whereas the common law induces legal rules from the decentralized decisions of judges, civil law instead deduces its principles and conclusions from a prefabricated, systematic code. The Napoleonic Code of 1804 is perhaps the most famous modern example. All of the former English colonies, as well as all of the American states (with the exception of formerly French-ruled Louisiana, and with some modifications in states with vestiges of Spanish rule, such as California), follow the common law instead.

Shariah Law

The law of Islam, Shariah law functions in countries that have made Islam the official state religion and works both as a religious and as an ordinary legal code. Shariah legal rules stem from four sources: the Koran's legislative segments; the stories of Muhammad, as related through the *hadith*; the general agreement of Muslims (as reflected in Muhammad's saying, "My nation cannot agree on an error"); and principles arrived at by analogy to other rules. Legal rules themselves are prescriptive and fall into five categories: obligatory, meritorious, permissible, reprehensible, and forbidden. Best understood in contrast with a more passive and decentralized system such as the common law, Shariah law makes an active and ambitious attempt to shape the behavior of Muslim citizens.

Canon Law

Canon law is the body of law that governs in the Roman Catholic Church. Although canon law may generally be traced back to centuries of legal rules in the church courts, its formal embodiment took place in 1917, with the *Codex juris canonici*, which was itself superseded by the Code of Canon Law for the Latin Church, published in 1983. Canon law contains rules for the governance and regulation of both clergy and the church, covering issues such as the qualifications and responsibilities of clergy, rules for marriage, and holy orders. While it does not compare in size with state-based legal systems such as the common or civil law, canon law has had wide influence in countries where the Roman Catholic Church was the state church, and still governs today in the Vatican.

International Law

Several sources are cited for international law in Article 38 of the Statute of the International Court of Justice (1945). First, international conventions such as treaties hold sway over agreements and obligations between different states or political actors. Second, customary law, the general practice of states and intergovernmental organizations, is generally legally binding and recognized by states. Third, general principles of law are seen to be the source of universally applicable rules in any disputes or agreements. Fourth, the judicial decisions and teachings of highly qualified jurists in individual nations are relied upon to inform international law. Taken together, this web of information constitutes international law.

Some scholars have suggested that international law is weaker than might otherwise be supposed. This view stems from the prevailing "realist" school of international relations, which holds that international legal relationships reflect and wholly depend upon underlying power relations. In other words, international law exists at the whim of superpowers; if they choose, international law can be broken, with barely any consequences. Momentum is gaining, however, for the liberal view that international law does exist and does matter. Liberal scholars observe that the United Nations, the International Monetary Fund, the World Bank, the North Atlantic Treaty Organization, and the North American Free Trade Agreement all have rule-making authority. Taken together, these institutions contain many courts where even the powerful United States can be brought up on charges and will, on occasion, comply, lending legitimacy to the independent strength of international law.

Important Supreme Court Decisions

Marbury v. Madison **(1803)** The Court struck down a law "repugnant to the constitution" for the first time and set the precedent for judicial review of acts of Congress. In a politically ingenious ruling on the Judiciary Act of 1789, Chief Justice John Marshall asserted the Supreme Court's power "to say what the law is," while avoiding a confrontation with President Thomas Jefferson. Not until the *Dred Scott* case of 1857 would another federal law be ruled unconstitutional.

Fletcher v. Peck **(1810)** The Court ruled that Georgia could not deprive land speculators of their title, even though the previous owners had obtained the land from the state through fraud and bribery. Arising from the infamous Yazoo land frauds of 1795, this decision followed the Constitution's obligation of contracts clause and was the first time the Court invalidated a state law.

Dartmouth College v. Woodward **(1819)** The Court encouraged business investment with this decision by treating corporate charters as fully protected contracts. Not even the state legislatures that originally granted them could tamper with charters to private corporations, unless the legislature retained the power to do so. Dartmouth College remained a private institution despite New Hampshire's attempt to take it over. This decision, which opened the way for abuse of corporate privileges, would later be modified in the *Charles River Bridge* (1837) and *Munn v. Illinois* (1877) cases.

McCulloch v. Maryland **(1819)** "Broad," as opposed to "strict," construction of the Constitution received high court approval in Chief Justice John Marshall's opinion upholding the constitutionality of the national bank against a challenge by Maryland. This ruling enhanced federal governmental authority by liberally interpreting the power of Congress to make laws "necessary and proper" for its specified powers. At a time when states were trying to tax the Bank of the United States out of existence, this decision also forbade such state interference with the federal government. "The power to tax," Marshall wrote, "involves the power to destroy."

Cohens v. Virginia **(1821)** With this ruling, the Court reiterated its power to hear appeals from state courts, and affirmed the national supremacy of federal judicial power. Virginia's conviction of the Cohens for selling lottery tickets in violation of state law was upheld, but so too was the Cohens' right to appeal to the Court, which Virginia had challenged. Critics of judicial "consolidationalism" were reminded of the Court's comprehensive powers as the ultimate appellate court for all Americans.

Gibbons v. Ogden **(1824)** In a dispute arising from a ferry monopoly in New York, the Court ruled that states could not restrain interstate commerce in any way, and that congressional power to regulate interstate commerce "does not stop at the jurisdictional lines of the several states." The decision helped prevent interstate trade wars, quite common under the Articles of Confederation, from breaking out under the Constitution. Chief Justice Marshall's opinion also confirmed the broad potential power of the Constitution's commerce clause.

Charles River Bridge v. Warren Bridge **(1837)** A key decision for economic development, this case arose when state-chartered proprietors of a toll bridge in Boston objected that a new state-chartered bridge across the Charles River would put them out of business. Chief Justice Roger B. Taney, in his first constitutional ruling, held that state charters implied no vested rights and that ambiguities must be construed in favor of the public, which would benefit from the new toll-free bridge. This decision balanced private property rights against the public welfare.

***Dred Scott v. Sanford* (1857)** Dred Scott, a Missouri slave, sued for his liberty after his owner took him into free territory. The Court ruled that Congress could not bar slavery in the territories. Scott remained a slave because the Missouri Compromise of 1820, prohibiting slavery from part of the Louisiana Purchase, violated the Fifth Amendment by depriving slave owners of their right to enjoy property without due process of law. Scott himself could not even sue, for he was held to be property, not a citizen. This decision sharpened sectional conflict by sweeping away legal barriers to the expansion of slavery.

***Ex Parte Milligan* (1866)** President Abraham Lincoln's suspension of some civil liberties during the Civil War was attacked in this decision, which upheld the right of *habeas corpus*. The Court ruled that the president could not hold military tribunals in areas remote from battle and where civil courts were open and functioning. Milligan's conviction by such a Civil War tribunal in Indianapolis was overturned. The Constitution, admonished the Court, applies "at all times, and under all circumstances."

***Slaughter-House Cases* (1873)** In its first ruling on the Fourteenth Amendment, the Court held that Louisiana's grant of a butcher monopoly did not violate the privileges and immunities of competitors, or deny them equal protection of the laws, or deprive them of property without due process. Only a few rights deriving from "federal citizenship" were subject to federal protection; states still protected most civil and property rights. Federal protection of civil rights, even for former slaves, was very narrowly interpreted in this ruling. But this decision broadly upheld business regulation by states until *Santa Clara Co. v. Southern Pacific Railroad Co.* (1886) applied the Fourteenth Amendment to defense of corporate property rights.

***Munn v. Illinois* (1877)** This decision enabled states to regulate private property in the public interest when the public had an interest in that property. The Court held that laws in Illinois setting maximum rates for grain storage did not violate the Fourteenth Amendment's ban on deprivation of property without due process of law, and did not restrain interstate commerce.

***Civil Rights Cases* (1883)** Racial equality was postponed 80 years by this decision, which struck down the Civil Rights Act of 1875 and allowed for private segregation. The Fourteenth Amendment's guarantee of equal protection, the Court ruled, applied against state action—but not against private individuals, whose discrimination unaided by the states was beyond federal control. Segregation of public facilities was approved soon afterward in *Plessy v. Ferguson* (1896).

***United States v. E. C. Knight Co.* (1895)** The first ruling on the Sherman Antitrust Act of 1890, this decision curtailed federal regulation of monopolies by placing national manufacturers beyond the reach of the Constitution's commerce clause. Only the actual interstate commerce of monopolies, not their production activities, was subject to federal control. The Court's distinction between production and commerce impeded federal regulation of manufacturing until *National Labor Relations Board v. Jones & Laughlin Steel Corp.* (1937).

***Plessy v. Ferguson* (1896)** The "separate but equal" doctrine supporting public segregation by law was affirmed in this ruling, which originated with segregated railroad cars in Louisiana. The Court held that as long as equal accommodations were provided, segregation was not discrimination and did not deprive blacks of equal protection of the laws under the Fourteenth Amendment. This decision was overturned in *Brown v. Board of Education* (1954).

***Lochner v. New York* (1905)** This decision struck down a law in New York placing limits on maximum working hours for bakers. The law violated the Fourteenth Amendment by restricting individual "freedom of contract" to buy and sell labor, and was an excessive use of state police power, the Court held. The ruling was soon modified in *Muller v. Oregon* (1908), which approved state-regulated limits on women's labor after the Court used sociological and economic data to consider the health and morals of women workers.

***Standard Oil Co. of New Jersey v. United States* (1911)** Federal efforts to break up monopolies under the Sherman Antitrust Act had to follow the "rule of reason," according to this ruling. Only those combinations in restraint of trade that were contrary to the public interest, and therefore unreasonable, were illegal. Although the Taft administration's prosecution of Standard Oil was upheld, breaking up one of the nation's leading monopolies, further antitrust suits were impaired by this decision, which facilitated the merger movement of the 1920's.

The Supreme Court: Federalism After 9-11

By LINDA GREENHOUSE

For the last decade, the Supreme Court, under Chief Justice William H. Rehnquist, has engaged in a far-reaching reappraisal of the scope of Congressional authority and the balance of powers between the national government and the states. But recently the Supreme Court's federalism revolution has been overtaken by events.

In case after case, the court has invoked broad theories of the sovereignty of the individual states and a limited view of Congress's authority—creating a new federalism jurisprudence that has become the hallmark of the Rehnquist court. Not since the Supreme Court's resistance to the New Deal crumpled in the late 1930's has the court been so hostile to the exercise of federal power.

It is no coincidence that this federalism revival flourished in a post cold-war atmosphere of tranquillity, when it was easy to regard the federal government as superfluous at best. To many, it seemed a blundering and costly intruder into matters properly rooted at the state and local level. That attitude vanished as suddenly and completely as the twin towers.

A Republican president proposed to give a new Homeland Security Agency authority over state and local as well as federal agencies engaged in domestic defense.

The Supreme Court's attachment to federalism and disaffection from it has often tracked changes in the nation's mood and circumstances. "In a national emergency, you give the national government the power to get done what needs to get done," explained Robert C. Post, a law professor at the University of California at Berkeley who has examined the rise of nationalism during World War I.

Even strong supporters of the court's federalism rulings offer a similar analysis. The events of Sept. 11 "struck at the heart of the federalism revival," said John O. McGinnis, a professor at the Benjamin N. Cardozo School of Law at Yeshiva University. "It brings the country together, he continued, "and federalism, whatever its intellectual claims, doesn't speak to that."

The court responds not only to the domestic mood but to the justices' perception of what message the court needs to send to the wider world, according to Mary L. Dudziak, a legal historian at the University of Southern California. "Federalism jurisprudence might have felt anachronistic and quaint in an era of globalization, but after Sept. 11 it feels dangerous."

The justices are unlikely to repudiate what they have accomplished so far, said Michael S. Greve, director of the federalism project at the American Enterprise Institute, a conservative public policy organization. "It will be more subtle and nuanced, hard to trace," Mr. Greve added. "To sustain ancient constitutional doctrines at a time like this becomes impossible."

The end of the federalism revolution raises another question: will the court overcompensate in favor of the federal government, accepting the government's claims about the need to restrict individual liberties for the sake of national security?

In 1987, one of the court's great civil libertarians, Justice William J. Brennan Jr., offered a sober warning on this point that now sounds particularly timely. Brennan pointed out that America had little practice at sorting out real security risks and needs from exaggerated claims.

"The episodic nature of our security crises" left the country and its judges vulnerable to being "swept away by irrational passion" when the unaccustomed threat arrived, Brennan said.

It is a hard proposition: that only prolonged and intimate exposure to danger can develop the necessary wisdom to deal with it. By Brennan's measure, both the court and country are seriously out of practice. Both are now confronted by the end of a peaceful period that appeared, just days ago, to have no end in sight.

So often in recent years, this court has seemed to have its eye on the past. Now, with the nation, it has been abruptly propelled into an unappealing future where the search for the right balance between order and liberty may well present the Rehnquist court with its greatest test.

***Schenk v. United States* (1919)** The Court unanimously held that limits on freedom of speech during World War I did not violate the First Amendment—if the speech in question represented a "clear and present danger." That famous doctrine of Justice Oliver Wendell Holmes, which approved the arrest of a draft resister for handing out pamphlets to soldiers in wartime, became an important standard for interpreting the First Amendment. But in subsequent cases of this period, the Court added that the mere "bad tendency" of speech to cause danger could be grounds for censorship.

***National Labor Relations Board v. Jones & Laughlin Steel Corp.* (1937)** Under pressure from the public and President Franklin D. Roosevelt, the Court abruptly reversed itself and began approving New Deal legislation. In this case, laws protecting unions and barring "unfair labor practices" were upheld by the "stream of commerce" doctrine that employers who sold their goods and obtained their raw materials through interstate commerce were subject to federal regulation. This ruling overturned *United States v. E. C. Knight Co.* (1895) and became the basis for an expansive understanding of the commerce clause.

***Erie Railroad Co. v. Tompkins* (1938)** The Court held that there could be no federal common law, but rather that federal courts must turn to the law of the state in which they sit when ruling on substantive issues. The case overruled *Swift v. Tyson* (1842), in which Justice Story had argued strongly for a federal common law, in part because of his opinion that federal judges had an almost divine ability to channel the correct rulings, in contrast to more clumsy state courts. *Erie* rejected that view, reestablished state-based federalism at the heart of jurisdiction, attempted to discourage forum-shopping, all while sapping federal judges of their ability to create much law.

***West Virginia Board of Education v. Barnette* (1943)** The Court reversed its earlier ruling in *Minersville School District v. Gobitis* (1940), which had required Jehovah's Witnesses to salute the flag in school. In this case, also brought against a Jehovah's Witness, the Court recognized that refusing to salute the flag did not violate anyone's rights, and that the First Amendment protected the "right of silence" as well as freedom of speech.

***Korematsu v. United States* (1944)** President Franklin D. Roosevelt's executive order No. 9066, which approved the evacuation and internment of 120,000 Japanese-Americans on the West Coast during World War II, was upheld on the grounds of "military necessity" in this ruling. The Court was reluctant to interfere with executive authority in time of national emergency. But in *Ex parte Endo* (1944), the Court held that persons of proven loyalty should not be interned. In August 1988, Congress made a formal apology to former internees and appropriated $1.25 billion in compensation for the 60,000 survivors.

***Dennis v. United States* (1951)** At the height of the postwar "red scare," the Court upheld the conviction of 11 American Communist leaders under the Smith Act of 1940, which made it a crime to belong to organizations teaching or advocating the violent overthrow of the government. The "clear and present danger" doctrine could be disregarded, the Court held, if "the gravity of the 'evil,' discounted by its improbability, justifies such invasion of free speech as is necessary to avoid the evil." More than 100 Communists were indicted as a result, effectively destroying the Communist Party as a political force.

***Youngstown Sheet and Tube Co. v. Sawyer* (1952)** During the Korean War, when President Harry S Truman seized steel plants to keep them operating despite a strike, the Court held that his action was an unconstitutional usurpation of legislative authority. Only an act of Congress, not the president's inherent executive powers or military powers as commander-in-chief, could justify such a sizable confiscation of property, despite the wartime emergency.

***Brown v. Board of Education of Topeka* (1954)** Chief Justice Earl Warren led the Court to decide unanimously that segregated schools violated the equal protection clause of the Fourteenth Amendment. The "separate but equal" doctrine of *Plessy v. Ferguson* (1896) was overruled after a series of cases dating back to *Missouri ex. rel. Gaines v. Canada* (1938) had already limited it. "Separate educational facilities are inherently unequal," held the Court. Efforts to desegregate southern schools after the *Brown* decision met with massive resistance for many years.

***Baker v. Carr* (1962)** Overrepresentation of rural districts in state legislatures, which effectively disfranchised millions of voters, led the Court to abandon its traditional noninterference in drawing legislative boundaries. Citizens in Tennessee deprived of full representation by "arbitrary and capricious" malapportionment were denied equal protection under the Fourteenth Amendment, ruled the Court. All states eventually reapportioned their legislatures in conformance with the "one man, one vote" doctrine of *Reynolds v. Sims* (1964).

***Gideon v. Wainwright* (1963)** Reversing an earlier ruling in *Betts v. Brady* (1942), the Court held that the Sixth

Amendment guaranteed access to qualified counsel, which was "fundamental to a fair trial." Gideon was entitled to a retrial because Florida failed to provide him with an attorney. After this decision, states were required to furnish public defenders for indigent defendants in felony cases. In *Argersinger v. Hamlin* (1972), the ruling was extended to all cases that might result in imprisonment.

***Heart of Atlanta Motel, Inc. v. United States* (1964)** The Court upheld Title II of the Civil Rights Act of 1964, outlawing private discrimination in public accommodations, as a legitimate exertion of federal power over interstate commerce. Congress had "ample power" to forbid racial discrimination in facilities that affected commerce by serving interstate travelers. The Heart of Atlanta Motel was located on two interstate highways, so the Court could sidestep the *Civil Rights Cases* (1883) protection of private discrimination to overrule it.

***New York Times Co. v. Sullivan* (1964)** Rejecting a civil action for libel filed by a city commissioner of Montgomery, Ala., the Court created a wide berth for the press to criticize public figures. In a unanimous opinion written by Justice William J. Brennan, the Court found that even false statements must be protected "if the freedoms of expression are to have the 'breathing space' that they 'need to survive.'" The Court announced a new standard for libel of public figures: actual malice, combined with actual knowledge that such statements are false or reckless disregard of whether they are true or not.

***Griswold v. Connecticut* (1965)** In striking down a Connecticut law of 1879 against the use of contraceptives, the Court established a "right to privacy" that was implied by, though not specifically enumerated in, the First, Third, Fourth, Fifth, Ninth, and Fourteenth Amendments. The case is most notable for laying the groundwork for other legal challenges invoking this newfound right to privacy. Foremost among them is the decision in *Roe v. Wade* (1973) allowing women to choose abortion.

***South Carolina v. Katzenbach* (1966)** South Carolina sued the attorney general, contending that the Voting Rights Act of 1965 encroached on the reserved powers of the states, treated the states unequally, and violated separation of powers. Chief Justice Warren ruled that the Fifteenth Amendment gave Congress broad powers to "use any rational means to effectuate the constitutional prohibition of racial discrimination in voting."

***Miranda v. Arizona* (1966)** Expanding upon *Gideon v. Wainwright* (1963) and *Escobedo v. Illinois* (1964), the Court set forth stringent interrogation procedures for criminal suspects to protect their Fifth Amendment freedom from self-incrimination. Miranda's confession to kidnapping and rape was obtained without counsel and without his having been advised of his right to silence, so it was ruled inadmissible as evidence. This decision obliged police to advise suspects of their rights upon taking them into custody.

***Loving v. Virginia* (1967)** Loving was a white man who had married a black woman and had been convicted under Virginia's law prohibiting interracial marriage. In a unanimous opinion Chief Justice Warren struck down the law as an invidious racial classification prohibited by the Fourteenth Amendment's equal protection clause. The ruling continued the Court's commitment to equality under the law signaled in *Brown v. Board of Education* (1954).

***New York Times Co. v. United States* (1971)** When the *New York Times* and the *Washington Post* published the top-secret Pentagon Papers in 1971, revealing government duplicity in the Vietnam War, the Nixon administration obtained an injunction against the *Times* on grounds of national security. But in a brief *per curiam* opinion, the Court observed that in this case, the government had not met the "heavy burden of showing justification" for "prior restraint" on freedom of the press.

***Roe v. Wade* (1973)** In a controversial ruling, the Court held that state laws restricting abortion were an unconstitutional invasion of a woman's right to privacy. Only in the last trimester of pregnancy, when the fetus achieved viability outside the womb, might states regulate abortion—except when the life or health of the mother was at stake. In *Planned Parenthood of Central Missouri v. Danforth* (1976), the Court added that wives did not need their husbands' consent to obtain abortions.

***United States v. Nixon* (1974)** In a unanimous ruling, the Court held that the secret White House recordings of President Richard M. Nixon's conversations with aides were subject to subpoena in the Watergate cover-up trial. Nixon's claim to "executive privilege" was rejected as invalid because military and national security issues were not at stake, and Chief Justice Warren Burger cited *Marbury v. Madison* (1803) to assert the Court's primacy in constitutional issues. Once the tapes were released, documenting Nixon's obstruction of justice, the president resigned to avoid impeachment.

***University of California Regents v. Bakke* (1978)** Twice refused admission to medical school, Bakke sued the University of California for giving "affirmative action" preference to less-qualified black applicants. In an ambiguous 5-4 ruling, the Court agreed that Bakke's right to equal protection had been denied, that he should be admitted, and that affirmative action quotas should be discarded. But at the same time, the Court recognized race as "a factor" in admissions and hiring decisions. Affirmative action could continue so long as rigid quotas did not constitute, in effect, "reverse discrimination."

Immigration and Naturalization Service v. Chadha **(1983)** The legislative veto, contained in hundreds of federal statutes since 1932, was disallowed in this decision. Congress exceeded its constitutional powers when it blocked the attorney general's suspension of a deportation order for Jagdish Rai Chadha, a Kenyan student who had overstayed his visa. The Court held that the Immigration and Nationality Act's legislative veto provision violated the constitutional separation of powers. Chief Justice Burger recognized that Congress would prefer to delegate authority to the executive branch and reserve the right to veto administrative regulations, but "we have not found a better way to preserve freedom" than the separation of powers.

United States v. Lopez **(1995)** The Court struck down an act of Congress for the first time in 60 years and in so doing sparked the federalism revolution for which the Rehnquist court will be known in the future. Congress had passed the Drug Free School Zones Act under its traditional loose grant of power under the Constitution's "commerce clause," allowing regulation of interstate commerce. In a strongly worded opinion, Chief Justice Rehnquist observed that no obviously commercial activity was involved in the act. Assailed by critics for attempting a return to a retrograde era of state-based federalism, the ruling struck a blow against the "living Constitution" argument, holding instead that anything Congress does must be explicitly authorized by the text.

Bush v. Gore **(2000)** For the first time in the nation's history, the Court found itself in the position of deciding a presidential election. With Florida's decisive 25 electoral votes hanging in the balance, Vice President Al Gore filed suit in state court to begin a recount of ballots in several counties where machines were unable to determine the voters' selection. Governor George W. Bush of Texas appealed the decision to the Supreme Court, which ruled that because there were no uniform standards for how to conduct a recount, doing so would violate the Fourteenth Amendment's guarantee of equal protection. The highly controversial 5-4 decision ended the recount 36 days after Election Day, and with it, Gore's chance of winning the presidency.

Lawrence v. Texas **(2003)** The Court struck down a statute in Texas that made it criminal for two persons of the same sex to engage in sexual acts. In a controversial case, *Bowers v. Hardwick* (1986), the Court had ruled that the constitutional right to privacy does not protect homosexual relations, even between consenting adults in the privacy of their home. In *Lawrence*, the Court overruled *Bowers*, relying on a different view of the history of sodomy statutes and the changes in law and social mores since *Bowers*.

Glossary of Legal Terms

accessory person who helps another person plan, commit, or attempt to escape the consequences of a crime.

acquittal judgment that a person is not guilty of the crime of which he or she has been charged.

actus reus wrongful act, regardless of the intentions behind the act; see *mens rea*.

adjudication final judgment in a legal proceeding; see also *judgment*.

affidavit written statement confirmed by oath or affirmation, for use as evidence in court.

amicus curiae Latin, "friend of the court." a party who joins a case voluntarily in order to present evidence and arguments to the court.

appeal application to a higher court for a decision of a lower court to be reversed, or for a new trial to be granted.

arbitration use of an independent person or body officially appointed to settle a dispute, as an alternative to going to court.

arraignment call to bring someone before a court to answer a criminal charge.

arrest to seize someone by legal authority and take that person into custody.

assault attempted or actual attack on a person that has the potential to result in palpable harm. Aggravated assault involves the use of a weapon; battery results when an attacker makes physical contact with the victim.

attachment court writ authorizing the seizure of property or income in order to obtain payment of damages resulting from a judgment in a legal proceeding.

attorney-client privilege rule that keeps communications between an attorney and his or her client confidential and bars them from being used as evidence in a trial, or even being seen by the opposing party during discovery.

bail amount of money left in the custody of a court by a defendant who has been allowed to remain free while awaiting trial, to ensure that he or she will not flee the jurisdiction.

bar the legal profession; lawyers collectively. Traditionally a partition (actual or symbolic) in a courtroom beyond which most persons may not pass and at which an accused person stands.

bench office of judge or magistrate; a judge's seat in a court of law; judges or magistrates collectively ("the bench").

bench trial in which only a judge, as opposed to a jury of the defendant's peers, presides.

breaking and entering entering a building with criminal intent; the charge does not require actual damage to the building's doors, windows, or locks.

brief formal written document in which a lawyer presents arguments and case law in support of a client in court.

burden of proof obligation to prove a case. A basic principle of U.S. law is that the state (in a criminal action) or the plaintiff (in a civil action) must prove its case; the defendant is considered not guilty (or not liable) until proven guilty (or liable) and does not need to prove his or her innocence.

burglary unlawful presence in a building for the purpose of committing a crime (usuallly theft).

case law law as established by the outcome of former cases. See *common law*.

certiorari writ or order from a higher court consenting to review a decision of a lower court.

civil law system of law concerned with private relations between members of a community rather than criminal, military, or religious affairs; as opposed to criminal law. Also, the reliance on codified statute law typical of European legal systems, contrasted with Anglo-American common law.

circumstantial evidence evidence in a court of law that points indirectly toward someone's guilt but does not conclusively prove it.

class-action suit lawsuit filed or defended by an individual or small group acting on behalf of a larger group of similar individuals—e.g., all persons injured by a particular defective product. All members of the group share in any judgment or settlement.

commerce clause Article 1, section 8 of the U.S. Constitution is commonly referred to as the commerce clause; it gives wide fiscal powers to the federal government.

common law part of law that is derived from long-standing custom and judicial precedent, in contrast to statute law. Common law is the foundation of the Anglo-American legal system.

compensatory damages money awarded in tort law in an attempt to compensate the injured plaintiff for any loss suffered at the hands of the defendant.

complaint initial statement of facts in a civil case, or initial accusation in a criminal case.

consent agreement to do or to refrain from doing some action. Informed consent means that the person understands the consequences of his or her consent.

consent decree court order ratifying an agreement between two or more parties in settlement of a legal case.

conspiracy agreement by two or more persons to break the law.

constitutional law branch of law dealing specifically with questions of whether statutes, regulations, and court rulings conform to the provisions of state constitutions and the federal Constitution.

contract legally binding agreement between two or more parties, enforceable by law.

copyright legal right of the creator of written, visual, or musical material to publish, reproduce, distribute, or perform the material, or authorize others to do so, for a fixed period of time. See also *intellectual property*.

corpus delicti Latin, "body of offense"; the physical evidence that a crime has taken place. Possibly, but not necessarily, a human corpse; a vandalized automobile can be a corpus delicti, for example.

court order directive issued by a court of law, ordering a person to do something or to refrain from doing something; see also *injunction*.

covenant *n.* contract drawn up by deed; a clause in a contract. *v.* to agree, especially by lease, deed, or other legal contract.

criminal intent See *intent; mens rea*.

criminal procedure criminal case in court; also, the rules governing the presentation and evaluation of evidence in a criminal case.

cross-examination questioning of a witness designed to cast doubt upon or discredit testimony the witness has already given in court.

damages sum of money claimed or awarded in compensation for a loss or an injury. See also *compensatory damages; punitive damages*.

defamation act of damaging another person's reputation in writing or in speech. See also *libel; slander*.

defendant person against whom charges or actions are brought in a criminal or civil case.

degree in criminal law, the level of severity of a crime (e.g., murder in the first degree, assault in the third degree), established by statute and specifying particular circumstances for one degree of the crime or another.

deposition pretrial examination of a witness. A witness so examined is said to be "deposed."

discovery pretrial process in which attorneys for both sides in a civil or criminal action assemble their evidence and disclose that evidence to the other party.

double jeopardy prosecution of a person twice for the same offense; prohibited in American law.

due diligence reasonable steps taken by a person to satisfy a legal requirement.

due process fair treatment through the normal judicial system; guaranteed by the Fifth and 14th Amendments to the U.S. Constitution.

eminent domain right of a government or its agent to expropriate private property for public use, with payment of compensation.

equal protection phrase used in section 1 of the 14th Amendment to the U.S. Constitution. Ratified on July 9, 1868, it says in part: "No State shall make or enforce any law which shall abridge the privileges or immunities of citizens of the United States; nor shall any State deprive any person of life, liberty, or property, without due process of law; nor deny to any person within its jurisdiction the equal protection of the laws."

evidence testimony, documents, and objects used to prove questions of fact in a trial.

exclusionary rule rule requiring U.S. courts to discard evidence if it has been obtained through constitutionally improper procedures.

ex parte Latin, "from one party"; refers to a legal action in which only one party to a lawsuit appears to argue a case.

ex rel(atione) Latin, "on the relation of"; refers to a legal action based not on firsthand information but on behalf of another person.

family court court established to deal exclusively with matters of family law, and often operating under strong rules of confidentiality.

felony any serious crime, such as murder, assault, or the theft of property of substantial value, usually punishable by imprisonment. See also *misdemeanor*.

fraud conduct intended to cheat someone by lying, by repeating information known to be wrong, or by concealing relevant information.

grand jury jury, typically of 23 jurors, empaneled by the state to examine whether the evidence supporting a criminal accusation is sufficient for prosecution to proceed.

habeas corpus, writ of Latin, "produce the body"; a writ requiring a person under custody to be brought before a judge or into court.

hearing act of listening to evidence or arguments in a court of law or before an official.

hearsay testimony attributing statements to another person who is not present in court to give testimony or be cross-examined; generally, hearsay is not admissable as evidence.

homicide killing of a person by another person. Not necessarily in itself a crime, but prerequisite to a charge of murder or manslaughter.

indictment formal charge or accusation of a crime, presented by a prosecutor to a grand jury. If the grand jury ratifies the indictment, it becomes a true bill.

intellectual property creative work, invention, or similar intangible good to which rights of ownership can be asserted through copyright or patent.

immunity grant of exemption from prosecution for some crime, thus making irrelevant to that person the constitutional protection against self-incrimination; the person granted immunity can then be compelled to testify against others involved in the case.

injunction court order requiring a person to behave in a specified way. A "cease and desist" order requires the person to stop doing something and refrain from doing it in the future.

intent purpose or intention. A crime committed "with intent" is committed with purpose and forethought.

judgment a court's final ruling in a case; based on, but subsequent to, the verdict of a judge or jury.

judicial review review by a court, especially a state high court or the federal Supreme Court, of the constitutionality of a law, regulation, or legal decision.

jurisdiction legal right of a court to try or adjudicate a case; the jurisdiction of a particular court is usually limited to a specific locality.

jury group of people, representing the public at large, chosen to determine issues of fact at a trial. Also called a petty jury or petit jury. See also *grand jury*.

larceny taking of money or other property by overtly unlawful means. See also *theft*.

liability state of being legally responsible for an act or an omission that causes or leads to loss, damage, injury, or death to another.

libel published false statement that is or may be damaging to a person's reputation. See also *defamation*; *slander*.

lien right to take or keep possession of property belonging to another person until a debt owed by that person is discharged.

litigation process of taking a civil case to court for adjudication. Parties to or subjects of a lawsuit are *litigants*; *to litigate* means to try a civil case at law.

malice aforethought mental state characterized by willingness to do harm to a person through recklessness or violence.

malpractice improper, illegal, or negligent professional treatment or activity, especially by a medical practitioner, lawyer, or public official.

manslaughter killing of a person without prior intent. Manslaughter may be voluntary (such as the consequence of a fight in which someone meant to harm, but not kill, the victim) or involuntary (resulting from negligence, for example by an intoxicated driver).

mens rea Latin, "state of mind"; under common law, a key to whether or not a defendant can be tried for a crime. Insane or severely mentally handicapped people, for example, cannot form criminal intent because they have diminished capacity to understand the consequences of their behavior.

Miranda warning result of the Supreme Court case *Miranda v. Arizona* (1966) stating that the police must inform persons taken into custody of their right to legal counsel and to remain silent under questioning.

misdemeanor lesser crime, usually punishable by a fine, community service, or brief incarceration.

motion request to a trial judge to make a ruling (for example, on the admissability of evidence).

murder intentional killing of a person, with or without premeditation.

negligence failure to use reasonable care, resulting in damage or injury to another.

nolo contendere Latin, "I do not wish to contest"; a plea in which a person does not challenge the charges against him or her but also does not admit guilt or liability.

patent government grant of authority to a person of the sole right, for a limited period of time, to use, manufacture, license, or sell something, usually an invention. See also *intellectual property*.

per curiam Latin, "by the court"; an opinion of a court in which the author of the decision is not identified.

perjury knowingly giving false testimony while under oath.

plaintiff person who files a lawsuit against another person in a civil case.

plea person's answer to a criminal charge: usually "guilty" or "not guilty." See also *nolo contendere*.

plea bargain deal between a prosecutor and a person accused of a crime, whereby the person pleads guilty to a lesser crime, or to the original crime in a lesser degree, to avoid trial and conviction on the original complaint.

power of attorney authority, which may be limited or unlimited, to act for another person in legal or financial matters; a legal document giving such authority to someone.

precedent See *case law*.

preponderance greater or weightier part; civil cases must normally be proved with a preponderance of the evidence, but not necessarily beyond reasonable doubt (as in criminal cases).

probable cause requirement that the police must have a reasonable belief that a person has committed a crime before the person may be arrested, or that a piece of evidence is physically present in a place before the place may be searched and the evidence seized.

probate official proving (verification) of a will. Probate results in the issuing of a verified copy of a will to the executors of an estate. Matters relating to the proving of wills are handled in probate court.

pro bono Latin, "for the [public] good"; services provided without charge (for example, legal services performed without charge on behalf of the indigent).

prosecutor elected or appointed public official responsible for pursuing criminal charges against accused persons in court.

punitive damages damages awarded to a plaintiff with the sole purpose of punishing the defendant for doing wrong.

rape forced sexual intercourse with another person, especially through the use or threat of violence, or intercourse with a person without that person's consent. Statutory rape defines as rape any sexual intercourse with a person below a certain age.

reasonable doubt doubt as to the guilt of a defendant such as might be entertained by a reasonable person in light of all the available evidence. The state is obliged to prove criminal charges beyond a reasonable doubt.

restraining order court order temporarily preventing someone from taking some action, until the validity or permissability of the action can be adjudicated in court.

robbery theft accomplished by means of violence or intimidation. Distinct from burglary. See also *larceny*.

search and seizure law Fourth Amendment to the U.S. Constitution, guaranteeing that "the right of the people to be secure in their persons, houses, papers and effects, against unreasonable searches and seizures, shall not be violated, and no warrants shall issue, but upon probable cause."

self-defense possible defense against charges of violence against another; self-defense is justified if an attack is unprovoked and seems likely to cause actual harm, and safe retreat is impossible.

self-incrimination act of answering questions or offering testimony that might lead to one's own prosecution for a crime. The Fifth Amendment to the U.S. Constitution prohibits the state from forcing a person to testify against himself.

slander spoken false statement that is or may be damaging to a person's reputation. See also *defamation; libel*.

small claims court special court, often with simplified procedures, for civil proceedings involving sums of money below a specified low threshold.

statute of limitations statute prescribing a period of time beyond which certain kinds of legal action (e.g., prosecution for a crime) may no longer be undertaken.

statutory law body of principles and rules written down and pased by a legislative body; statutes often supplant, supplement, or clarify the common law.

subpoena writ ordering a person to attend a court; to summon (someone) with a subpoena or to require (a document or other evidence) to be submitted to a court of law.

summary judgment court ruling that, on the basis of the evidence, there is no "genuine issue of material fact," and thus no reason to proceed with a case.

testimony sworn statements given by a witness in court as evidence in a case.

tort act under civil law whereby one person causes injury to another, or to another's property; tort law deals specifically with torts and damages arising from them.

verdict judge's or jury's finding of the facts of a case.

voir dire French, "to speak the truth"; a preliminary examination of a witness or a potential juror by a judge or a lawyer.

warrant court order directing a public official to do something—for example, to make an arrest, or to search some premises for evidence.

writ legal directive from a court directing some person or some entity to act or refrain from acting in a certain specified way.

The Constitution of the United States of America

An Annotated Guide

On May 25, 1787, 55 delegates from 12 states convened in Philadelphia to attempt the writing of a new constitution to replace the woefully inadequate Articles of Confederation. On September 17th, after 17 weeks of wrangling, compromising, and deal-making, the 42 remaining delegates signed the new document and presented it to the states for ratification. On June 21, 1788, New Hampshire became the ninth state to accept the Constitution and it became the law of the land.

Below is the text of the Constitution and all of the amendments added over two centuries and more. Interspersed between articles and sections are brief explanatory remarks by Stanley I. Kutler, professor emeritus of constitutional history at the University of Wisconsin. The commentary is from *Your Constitution: What It Says, What It Means* (copyright © 1987 by G&H Soho Inc. and reprinted with permission).

Preamble

WE, THE PEOPLE of the United States, in order to form a more perfect union, establish justice, insure domestic tranquillity, provide for the common defense, promote the general welfare, and secure the blessings of liberty to ourselves and our posterity, do ordain and establish this Constitution for the United States of America.

The Preamble embodies long-standing English and colonial beliefs in the social contract or covenant, a notion that society is bound together through the common agreement of the people—the ultimate sovereign. People created governments as part of the social contract to establish political order for the better protection of their liberties. The purposes set forth here reflected the needs of 1787 and also the enduring demands for an ordered, civilized society.

Article I

Section 1 All legislative powers herein granted shall be vested in a Congress of the United States, which shall consist of a Senate and House of Representatives.

At the outset, the Constitution established the concept of separation of powers, providing that the two houses of Congress would exercise "all" legislative powers. English political theory and practice had emphasized that legislative power could not be delegated. In the United States, however, Congress can delegate and has delegated significant power. For example, it has given power to presidents to allow them to respond to national security matters or the need for adjusting tariffs, and to regulatory agencies, such as the Federal Trade Commission or the Federal Communications Commission, that have the expertise to deal with specialized and complex problems.

Section 2 [1] The House of Representatives shall be composed of members chosen every second year by the people of the several States, and the electors in each State shall have the qualifications requisite for electors of the most numerous branch of the State legislature.

The "Great Compromise" resolved the basic division at the Constitutional Convention in 1787. Delegates had split over the apportionment of legislative power for the various states, largely between larger and smaller states. The compromise provided for two separate houses of Congress. The House of Representatives is determined by population and is subject to reelection every two years. The Senate is based on the idea of state equality, with each state having two senators, and its members serve six-year terms (see "section 3(1)"). This section also clearly provided for state control over voting qualifications, but subsequent amendments (15, 19, and 24) and legislation (Voting Rights Act of 1965) have permitted significant federal involvement in this area.

[2] No person shall be a Representative who shall not have attained to the age of twenty-five years, and been seven years a citizen of the United States, and who shall not, when elected, be an inhabitant of that State in which he shall be chosen.

The American Constitution contains state residency requirements for members of Congress, unlike the English system, where members of Parliament typically are not residents of the constituencies they represent.

[3] Representatives and direct taxes shall be apportioned among the several States which may be included within this Union, according to their respective numbers, which shall be determined by adding to the whole number of free persons, including those bound to service for a term of years, and excluding Indians not taxed, three-fifths of all other persons. The actual

enumeration shall be made within three years after the first meeting of the Congress of the United States, and within every subsequent term of ten years, in such manner as they shall by law direct. The number of Representatives shall not exceed one for every thirty thousand, but each State shall have at least one Representative; and until such enumeration shall be made, the State of New Hampshire shall be entitled to choose three; Massachusetts, eight; Rhode Island and Providence Plantations, one; Connecticut, five; New York, six; New Jersey, four; Pennsylvania, eight; Delaware, one; Maryland, six; Virginia, ten; North Carolina, five; South Carolina, five; and Georgia, three.

Sharp sectional differences occurred at the Constitutional Convention, particularly about slavery. Northern delegates agreed to several forms of protection for what the Constitution labels "all other persons." The concessions included arrangements to facilitate the recapture of fugitive slaves, the denial of congressional authority to prohibit the slave trade until 1808, and the above clause, popularly known as the "3/5ths Compromise." It provided that each slave would count as 3/5ths "of all other persons" for purposes of determining the number of representatives for each state and the amount of direct taxation. Following the abolition of slavery, the Fourteenth Amendment, Section 2, superseded this clause.

This section also mandates a federal census every 10 years. Some delegates feared that new sections of the nation would gain influence and power greater than the original states. As such, they favored congressional determination of national apportionment. But the inclusion of the census requirement reflected the framers' faith in republican principles, ensuring support for the idea that representation would be determined by persons, and not property or other interests.

[4] When vacancies happen in the representation from any State, the executive authority thereof shall issue writs of election to fill such vacancies.

The requirement that state governors arrange for the filling of congressional vacancies again indicates the framers' desire to give states control over the election of representatives and senators.

[5] The House of Representatives shall choose their Speaker and other officers, and shall have the sole power of impeachment.

The House impeaches civil officers; the Senate tries them. The analogy is somewhat similar to the idea of a grand jury that indicts, leaving the determination of guilt to another panel. But the analogy is limited. Until the Clinton impeachment in 1998–99 the House only considered impeachment when it believed the evidence would result in conviction.

Section 3 [1] The Senate of the United States shall be composed of two Senators from each State, chosen by the legislature thereof for six years; and each Senator shall have one vote.

The original Constitution provided that state legislatures would choose senators, again recognizing the necessity for some state influence in the affairs of the national government. The method of indirect election presumably would help create a more conservative body, yet this provision is at odds with the framers' supposed fear of state legislatures. The Seventeenth Amendment, which was ratified in 1913, eventually provided for the direct election of senators.

[2] Immediately after they shall be assembled in consequence of the first election, they shall be divided as equally as may be into three classes. The seats of the Senators of the first class shall be vacated at the expiration of the second year, of the second class at the expiration of the fourth year, and of the third class at the expiration of the sixth year, so that one-third may be chosen every second year; and if vacancies happen by resignation or otherwise during the recess of the legislature of any State, the executive thereof may make temporary appointments until the next meeting of the legislature, which shall then fill such vacancies.

[3] No person shall be a Senator who shall not have attained to the age of thirty years, and been nine years a citizen of the United States, and who shall not, when elected, be an inhabitant of that State for which he shall be chosen.

The Senate is a continuing body, unlike the House of Representatives, which assembles a new group every two years. Only one-third of the Senate stands for election every two years. This practice again reflected the framers' belief that the Senate would be the more conservative body, providing stability and continuity in government. The same interpretation can explain the differing age requirement for a senator as opposed to a representative.

[4] The Vice-President of the United States shall be President of the Senate, but shall have no vote, unless they be equally divided.

Every newly elected president seems to promise a greater role and enhanced powers for the vice president. In fact, this clause provides the only constitutional power for that officer: to preside over the Senate and to cast a vote to break a tie vote of the body.

[5] The Senate shall choose their other officers and also a President pro tempore in the absence of the Vice-President, or when he shall exercise the office of President of the United States.

The stipulation that the Senate chooses its own officers gives that body a degree of independence, presumably from the executive. The Twenty-fifth Amendment provided for the selection of a successor in the event the elected vice president succeeded to the presidency. The Senate nevertheless elects a president pro tempore, but largely for honorific reasons.

[6] The Senate shall have the sole power to try all impeachments. When sitting for that purpose, they shall be on oath or affirmation. When the President of the United States is tried, the Chief Justice shall preside; and no person shall be convicted without the concurrence of two-thirds of the members present.

The House of Representatives votes impeachment articles; the Senate tries the issues. House action requires only a majority vote. The requirement of a two-thirds vote for conviction by the Senate offers another example of checks and balances in the Constitution, for a two-thirds vote is not easily gained. The difference in voting requirements indicates that the framers believed that impeachment hearings—inquests into the behavior of public officials—served the public interest. Conviction, however, was not to be achieved as readily. The requirement that the chief justice preside in a presidential impeachment trial provided another check and balance by including the authority of the third branch of government.

[7] Judgment in cases of impeachment shall not extend further than to removal from office, and disqualification to hold and enjoy any office of honor, trust, or profit under the United States; but the party convicted shall, nevertheless, be liable and subject to indictment, trial, judgment, and punishment, according to law.

Impeached officers are subject to subsequent indictment and trial for their alleged crimes. This clause is the basis of the argument that impeachment is not meant to be confined to criminal acts, as ordinary legal procedures could punish such violations adequately.

Section 4 [1] The times, places, and manner of holding elections for Senators and Representatives shall be prescribed in each State by the legislature thereof; but the Congress may at any time by law make or alter such regulations, except as to the places of choosing Senators.

This provision again shows a willingness to give the states a significant measure of control over elections. Congress, as this clause provides, may make exceptions, but the states still largely determine the time, place, and manner of holding elections.

[2] The Congress shall assemble at least once in every year, and such meeting shall be on the first Monday in December, unless they shall by law appoint a different day.

The Twentieth Amendment superseded this section, reflecting modern improvements in transportation and communications.

Section 5 [1] Each House shall be the judge of the elections, returns, and qualification of its own members, and a majority of each shall constitute a quorum to do business; but a smaller number may adjourn from day to day, and may be authorized to compel the attendance of absent members, in such manner, and under such penalties, as each House may provide.

[2] Each House may determine the rules of its proceedings, punish its members for disorderly behavior, and with the concurrence of two-thirds, expel a member.

[3] Each House shall keep a journal of its proceedings, and from time to time publish the same, excepting such parts as may in their judgment require secrecy, and the yeas and nays of the members of either House on any question shall, at the desire of one-fifth of those present, be entered on the journal.

[4] Neither House, during the session of Congress, shall, without the consent of the other, adjourn for more than three days, nor to any other place than that in which the two Houses shall be sitting.

The clauses in this section reinforce the independence of the legislative branch and guarantee each house the right to determine its internal rules. They can be traced back to the English Parliament's long struggle for independence from the Crown; as such, they are basic components of the American doctrine of separation of powers. During the controversy over Reconstruction following the Civil War, Congress's authority to determine its own membership gave that body enormous leverage in determining when the ex-Confederate states could be readmitted to the Union. The courts generally have given Congress almost absolute control over these matters, but in 1968, the Supreme Court held that Congress had no "authority to exclude any person, duly elected by his constituency who meets all the requirements for membership expressly prescribed" in the Constitution. Congress polices the internal behavior of its members and thus may censure, criticize, or change assignments of its members. The Congressional Record offers a public record of the congressional debates and votes.

Section 6 [1] The Senators and Representatives shall receive a compensation for their services, to be ascertained by law and paid out of the Treasury of the United States. They shall, in all cases except treason, felony, and breach of the peace, be privileged from arrest during their attendance at the session of their respective Houses, and in going to and returning from the same; and for any speech or debate in either House they shall not be questioned in any other place.

Under the Articles of Confederation, the states paid the salaries of congressional representatives, thus diminishing legislators' loyalties to the national government. This clause, like similar ones for the executive and judiciary, strengthens the independence of the three branches of government.

The second sentence refers to hard-won privileges and prerogatives secured by Parliament during its lengthy struggles with the English monarchy in the 16th and 17th centuries. Essentially, they provide immunity for what legislators say in Congress and immunity from arrest while they are attending legislative sessions, except if charged with a felony. The "speech and debate" clause has been extended to provide immunity for congressman from libel suits for remarks made in a press release.

[2] No Senator or Representative shall, during the time for which he was elected, be appointed to any civil office under the authority of the United States, which shall have been created, or the emoluments whereof shall have been increased during such time; and no person holding any office under the United States shall be a member of either House during his continuance in office.

The English parliamentary system allows members of the legislature to become ministers of the Crown, or cabinet officers. This clause underlines the principle of separation of powers, for it ensures that no one may simultaneously be a member of Congress and hold a federal civil office.

Section 7 [1] All bills for raising revenue shall originate in the House of Representatives; but the Senate may propose or concur with amendments as on other bills.

The framers of the Constitution to some extent saw the House of Representatives as analogous to the English House of Commons, which traditionally had the exclusive power for originating revenue measures. In practice, the Senate has equal power in revenue matters because of its ability to amend bills.

[2] Every bill which shall have passed the House of Representatives and the Senate shall, before it becomes a law, be presented to the President of the United States; if he approves he shall sign it, but if not he shall return it, with his objections, to that House in which it shall have originated, who shall enter the objections at large on their journal and proceed to reconsider it. If after such reconsideration two-thirds of that House shall agree to pass the bill, it shall be sent, together with the objections, to the other House, by which it shall likewise be reconsidered, and if approved by two-thirds of that House it shall become a law. But in all such cases the vote of both Houses shall be determined by yeas and nays, and the names of the persons voting for and against the bill shall be entered on the journal of each House respectively. If any bill shall not be returned by the President within ten days (Sundays excepted) after it shall have been presented to him, the same shall be a law, in like manner as if he had signed it, unless the Congress by their adjournment prevent its return, in which case it shall not be a law.

This lengthy section involves the president's veto power and his role in legislation. The requirement that two-thirds of each house vote to override presidential objections usually is difficult to secure, thus giving the president a significant role in the lawmaking process. The last part of this section describes what is known as the "pocket veto," which is the president's practice of withholding his signature as Congress adjourns, thereby preventing Congress from overriding his action.

[3] Every order, resolution or vote to which the concurrence of the Senate and House of Representatives may be necessary (except on a question of adjournment) shall be presented to the President of the United States; and before the same shall take effect shall be approved by him, or being disapproved by him, shall be repassed by two-thirds of the Senate and House of Representatives, according to the rules and limitations prescribed in the case of a bill.

In recent times, Congress has used the concurrent resolution to prohibit or recall presidential authority delegated by Congress, which in effect subjects presidential actions to a legislative veto. At times, Congress has provided that the veto of one house is adequate to reject or repudiate an executive action. The Supreme Court ruled in 1983 that such action violated constitutional requirements for bicameralism and for presidential involvement in the legislative process.

Section 8 [1] The Congress shall have power to lay and collect taxes, duties, imposts and excises, to pay the debts and provide for the common defense and general welfare of the United States; but all duties, imposts and excises shall be uniform throughout the United States;

Section 8 enumerates the major powers of Congress. The first grant of power remedied one of the great defects of the government under the Articles of Confederation, namely, the inability of the national government to raise its own sources of revenue. The aims of taxation are broadly stated: to pay the nation's debts, and to provide for the common defense and general welfare. The latter clause in particular has been liberally construed to give Congress great latitude in determining its scope. For example, it has been used to authorize the Social Security system, which is financed by payroll taxes. James Madison believed that the power to tax and spend was limited to the enumerated objects of congressional authority; Alexander Hamilton, however, advanced a broad construction and maintained that the power existed apart from others granted to the national government. History and constitutional law clearly have sustained Hamilton's view.

[2] To borrow money on the credit of the United States;

This clause enables the United States government to utilize deficit financing. Many state constitutions specifically prohibit such practice. This authority, along with the preceding one, and clauses 5 and 6 below, constitute the national government's fiscal powers.

[3] To regulate commerce with foreign nations, and among the several States, and with the Indian tribes;

The "commerce clause" fulfilled one of the basic aims of the Constitutional Convention: to reduce state economic rivalries and establish the national government as arbiter of the national economy and market. Chief Justice John Marshall in *Gibbons v. Ogden* (1824) ruled that "Commerce undoubtedly is traffic, but it is something more—it is intercourse." That statement has been the basis for using the commerce clause as the primary vehicle for expanding the regulatory powers of the national government over the national marketplace. These expanded powers include, for example, rate regulations of various means of transportation, the regulation of stock markets and commodities exchanges, the limitations on monopoly powers, minimum wage and maximum hours laws, the prohibition of child labor products, quality control of food products and medicines, the policing of water and air pollution, and the guarantee of equal access to public accommodations.

[4] To establish an uniform rule of naturalization, and uniform laws on the subject of bankruptcies throughout the United States;

Throughout our history, Congress has regulated aliens and immigrants in a variety of ways, even to the point of exclusion. As early as 1798, responding to charges that aliens represented a subversive threat, Congress imposed severe restrictions on their entry, activities, and ability to acquire citizenship. In the 1880's, Congress responded to west coast political pressures and barred Asians from citizenship. During World War II, Congress amended the law to enable Chinese to acquire citizenship, and then, in 1952, provided that neither race nor sex could be a barrier to naturalization. The Constitution lacked a definition of citizenship until the Fourteenth Amendment stipulated that all persons born or naturalized in the United States were citizens.

The bankruptcy provision again shows the framers' desire that commercial relations be as uniform as possible. But it was not until the post–Civil War period that Congress finally overcame state and sectional concerns and developed effective national bankruptcy legislation.

[5] To coin money, regulate the value thereof, and of

foreign coin, and fix the standard of weights and measures;

[6] To provide for the punishment of counterfeiting the securities and current coin of the United States;

[7] To establish post offices and post roads;

The national government derives its power to handle and protect mail service from clause 7. The provision regarding post roads offered an opening wedge for Congress's role in providing for "internal improvements," such as roads, bridges, and, eventually, railroads. The clause also comprehends a "police power," enabling the federal government to exclude "harmful" items from the mails, such as circulars relating to fraudulent schemes. But the Supreme Court has ruled that Congress may not authorize the Postal Service to prevent or detain the mailing of "political propaganda."

[8] To promote the progress of science and useful arts by securing for limited times to authors and inventors the exclusive right to their respective writings and discoveries;

This clause is the basis for federal patent and copyright laws.

[9] To constitute tribunals inferior to the Supreme Court;

The Constitution does not require any federal courts other than the Supreme Court. The First Congress in 1789 seriously considered using the existing state judiciaries to conduct federal business, with an appeal to the national Supreme Court. Anti-Federalists and those suspicious of expanding the national government vigorously opposed creating a lower federal court system. But the Judiciary Act of 1789 created both federal district courts and intermediate courts of appeal.

[10] To define and punish piracies and felonies committed on the high seas and offenses against the law of nations.

[11] To declare war, grant letters of marque and reprisal, and make rules concerning captures on land and water;

[12] To raise and support armies, but no appropriation of money to that use shall be for a longer term than two years;

[13] To provide and maintain a navy;

[14] To make rules for the government and regulation of the land and naval forces;

[15] To provide for calling forth the militia to execute the laws of the Union, suppress insurrections, and repel invasions;

[16] To provide for organizing, arming and disciplining the militia, and for governing such part of them as may be employed in the service of the United States, reserving to the States respectively the appointment of the officers, and the authority of training the militia according to the discipline prescribed by Congress;

Clauses 10 through 16 form the so-called war powers. These statements underline civilian control over the military, as they empower Congress to provide for the maintenance and governance of military forces. Military appropriations may not be for a period of longer than two years, thus requiring military officials to submit to regular congressional scrutiny.

Chief Justice John Marshall once referred to Congress's power to "declare and conduct a war," thus indicating a notion of resultant and implied powers. The war powers in general have been used to create and sanction extensive authority for the national government in wartime. Much of this authority inevitably has flowed to the president in his capacity as commander in chief under Article II, Section 2. Thus during World War II, President Roosevelt issued an executive order directing the forced evacuation and internment of Japanese-Americans from the West Coast. In more recent times, presidents have on numerous occasions committed American soldiers to combat situations without formal congressional action, claiming that the realities of the moment required prompt action by the nation. The Vietnam War resulted in the War Powers Act of 1973, which requires the president to consult with Congress before committing troops, or to withdraw those troops if directed by congressional resolution.

Clause 15 has significant scope aside from its contribution to the war powers. This clause provided the power necessary to cure what James Madison believed to be a fundamental defect of the Articles of Confederation, that is, the "want of power" to enforce the granted powers of government. In 1795 Congress gave President Washington the authority to decide whether to use military force to quash potential insurrection. That law largely survives today and has been used by various presidents, such as Eisenhower, Kennedy, and Johnson, to maintain order or to ensure the enforcement of federal court orders.

[17] To exercise exclusive legislation in all cases whatsoever over such district (not exceeding ten miles

square) as may, by cession of particular States and the acceptance of Congress, become the seat of the Government of the United States, and to exercise like authority over all places purchased by the consent of the legislature of the State in which the same shall be, for the erection of forts, magazines, arsenals, dock-yards, and other needful buildings;

This section provides for the establishment of a separate district as the site of the national government. The District of Columbia was formed from land cessions by Virginia and Maryland, and Congress has had a primary responsibility for governing the area. In recent years, however, the District has elected its own mayor and city council and has gained more control over its local affairs. The District does not have a voting representative in Congress, but the Twenty-third Amendment enabled residents to vote in presidential elections.

[18] To make all laws which shall be necessary and proper for carrying into execution the foregoing powers, and all other powers vested by this Constitution in the Government of the United States, or in any department or officer thereof.

This is the "necessary and proper" clause, sometimes known as the "elastic clause" in that it provides for an interpretation of congressional powers beyond the simple enumeration of those listed in Section 8. Chief Justice Marshall established the time-honored interpretation of the clause in 1819: "Let the end be legitimate, let it be within the scope of the Constitution, and all means which are appropriate, which are plainly adapted to that end, which are not prohibited, but consistent with the letter and spirit of the Constitution, are constitutional." Marshall's view responded to those who opposed the development of national power beyond those items specifically laid down in the Constitution. Marshall insisted that the Constitution had a vitality that enabled it "to be adapted to the various crises of human affairs." Clearly, Marshall did not intend his words as license for Congress to do whatever it wishes. The formula he enunciated, as well as his published essays at the time, carefully reinforced the notion that the Constitution not only granted power but also prescribed limitations of power, such as those that follow in the next section.

Section 9 [1] The migration or importation of such persons as any of the States now existing shall think proper to admit shall not be prohibited by the Congress prior to the year one thousand eight hundred and eight, but a tax or duty may be imposed on such importation, not exceeding ten dollars for each person.

This clause refers to the importation of slaves, although here, as throughout the document, the framers carefully avoided mentioning slavery. The constitutional stipulation that the slave trade could not be prohibited for 20 years represented another sectional compromise.

[2] The privilege of the writ of habeas corpus shall not be suspended, unless when in cases of rebellion or invasion the public safety may require it.

The writ of habeas corpus is a fundamental guarantee of Anglo-American justice, providing that a person may seek a judicial inquiry into the cause of his detention by authorities. During the Civil War, Lincoln temporarily suspended the writ in Maryland, and Congress eventually approved the action retroactively. The result left unresolved the constitutional issue of which branch had the power to suspend the writ.

[3] No bill of attainder or ex post facto law shall be passed.

A bill of attainder is a legislative judgment that imposes punishment without proper judicial proceedings. The prohibition of attainder reinforces the separation of powers doctrine as it denies Congress any judicial role, except for the Senate's role in impeachment proceedings. Following the Civil War, the Supreme Court ruled that Congress could not impose loyalty oaths as a precondition for the practice in the federal courts. The prohibition against attainders, the Court said, voided any act "which inflicts punishment without a judicial trial." Ex post facto laws retroactively impose penalties; thus all legislation must be prospective in effect.

[4] No capitation or other direct tax shall be laid, unless in proportion to the census or enumeration herein before directed to be taken.

This clause protected the institution of slavery , as it ensured that no form of direct tax would be imposed, except under the three-fifths compromise arrangement.

[5] No tax or duty shall be laid on articles exported from any State.

The inference here is that Congress may never tax exports, a clear reservation to the otherwise broad scope of the federal tax and commerce powers. Southern delegates at the Constitutional Convention feared the possibility of an export tax on cotton. But in general, the provision reflected the framers' desire to encourage economic development and enterprise.

[6] No preference shall be given by any regulation of commerce or revenue to the ports of one State over those of another; nor shall vessels bound to or from one State be obliged to enter, clear or pay duties in another.

Several of these clauses reflect the framers' concern for the development of a national common market that would be unimpeded by artificial state constraints or barriers. This particular section offers a corollary to congressional control over interstate commerce.

[7] No money shall be drawn from the Treasury but in consequence of appropriations made by law; and a regular statement and account of the receipts and expenditures of all public money shall be published from time to time.

Here again, the Constitution reflects the framers' awareness of the long struggle between the Crown and Parliament in England. This provision is designed to prevent unauthorized expenditures by the president, ensuring congressional control of the "purse." There have been exceptions to public accounting of expenditures in recent years. The Central Intelligence Agency's budget and those of other security agencies, for example, are not fully published.

[8] No title of nobility shall be granted by the United States; and no person holding any office of profit or trust under them shall, without the consent of the Congress, accept of any present, emolument, office, or title of any kind whatever from any king, prince, or foreign state.

Since American presidents have become world figures in the 20th century, they have received numerous presents from foreign states. The executive branch and Congress have worked out appropriate rules for the disposition of these gifts.

Section 10 [1] No State shall enter into any treaty, alliance, or confederation; grant letters of marque and reprisal; coin money; emit bills of credit; make anything but gold and silver coin a tender in payment of debts; pass any bill of attainder, ex post facto law or law impairing the obligation of contracts, or grant any title of nobility.

This section clearly repudiates any notion of state sovereignty, for everything denied to the states represents traditional attributes of sovereign power. Historically, the most important clause has been that prohibiting the state from "impairing the obligation of contracts." That language reveals the framers' fears that ever-changing popular majorities would repudiate and overturn contracts and property titles. The original intention seemed to confine the restraint to any interference in private contracts, but John Marshall later extended it to public grants and charters. The contract clause, perhaps as much as any part of the Constitution, fortified the framers' concern for the protection of private property rights.

[2] No State shall, without the consent of the Congress, lay any imposts or duties on imports or exports, except what may be absolutely necessary for executing its inspection laws; and the net produce of all duties and imposts, laid by any State on imports or exports, shall be for the use of the Treasury of the United States; and all such laws shall be subject to the revision and control of the Congress.

[3] No State shall, without the consent of Congress, lay any duty of tonnage, keep troops and ships of war in time of peace, enter into any agreement or compact with another State or with a foreign power, or engage in war, unless actually invaded or in such imminent danger as will not admit of delay.

Clauses 2 and 3 again restrict state power and reject any notions of state sovereignty. States are restrained from interfering with the flow of the national market. Their relations with other states and foreign powers, aside from normal commercial dealings, are subject to congressional control.

Article II

Section 1 [1] The executive power shall be vested in a President of the United States of America. He shall hold his office during the term of four years, and together with the Vice-President, chosen for the same term, be elected, as follows.

Executive power as vested in Article II generally has

been interpreted in a broad, expansive manner. Theodore Roosevelt believed that the president could do "anything that the needs of the Nation demanded unless such action was forbidden by the Constitution and the laws." The 20th-century developments that spurred national consolidation, the growth and complexity of the national market, and the dramatic increase of involvement in world affairs have all resulted in greater activity and responsibility by the chief executive. Basically, the nation has accepted the steadily expanding notion of presidential power and authority; many attempts to limit presidential power in foreign and military affairs have been unsuccessful. Yet political realities and the restraining influences of other branches periodically have served as both informal and formal checks and balances on presidential power. Presidents need congressional appropriations of funds to conduct foreign policy. Also, the Supreme Court in recent times has rejected broad claims of "inherent powers" and "executive privilege" by Presidents Truman, Nixon, and George W. Bush.

The framers specified a four-year presidential term, but they deliberately left open the question of reeligibility. Thomas Jefferson periodically expressed fears that incumbents would serve for life, but until 1940, all presidents followed George Washington's two-term precedent. Franklin D. Roosevelt broke the tradition and was elected for third and fourth terms. In large measure, the Twenty-Second Amendment, limiting presidents to two elected terms, represented a reaction against Roosevelt.

[2] Each State shall appoint, in such manner as the legislature thereof may direct, a number of Electors, equal to the whole number of Senators and Representatives to which the State may be entitled in the Congress; but no Senator or Representative, or person holding an office of trust or profit under the United States shall be appointed an Elector.

[3] The Electors shall meet in their respective States and vote by ballot for two persons, of whom one at least shall not be an inhabitant of the same State with themselves. And they shall make a list of all the persons voted for, and of the number of votes for each; which list they shall sign and certify, and transmit sealed to the seat of government of the United States, directed to the President of the Senate. The President of the Senate shall, in the presence of the Senate and House of Representatives, open all the certificates, and the votes shall then be counted. The person having the greatest number of votes shall be the President, if such number be a majority of the whole number of Electors appointed; and if there be more than one who have such majority, and have an equal number of votes, then the House of Representatives shall immediately choose by ballot one of them for President; and if no person have a majority, then from the five highest on the list the said House shall in like manner choose the President. But in choosing the President the votes shall be taken by States, the representation from each State having one vote; a quorum for this purpose shall consist of a member or members from two-thirds of the States, and a majority of all the States shall be necessary to a choice. In every case, after the choice of the President, the person having the greatest number of votes of the Electors shall be the Vice-President. But if there should remain two or more who have equal votes, the Senate shall choose from them by ballot the Vice-President.

[4] The Congress may determine the time of choosing the Electors and the day on which they shall give their votes, which day shall be the same throughout the United States.

The second, third, and fourth paragraphs in this section established the "Electoral College." The framers' apparent intention was to create an independent body of electors, but in fact, the electors have traditionally followed the election results in their individual states. Each state has electors equal to its delegation of representatives and senators; the "electoral" votes are cast by those representing the victorious candidate. Presidents Abraham Lincoln and Woodrow Wilson received less than a majority of the popular votes because of significant third-party candidacies, but they had decisive margins in the Electoral College. Presidents Rutherford B. Hayes, Benjamin Harrison, and George W. Bush gained electoral college victories, yet they finished second in the popular balloting; none of those elections had a substantial third-party vote. Periodic efforts to abolish the Electoral College have failed, despite serious concerns in recent years of the possibility of a popular choice failing to attain an electoral majority.

The third paragraph resulted in the complex stalemate between Thomas Jefferson and Aaron Burr in 1800–01. Jefferson clearly had been his party's choice for president and Burr for vice president. When party electors met, however, they failed to divert one vote from Burr. The result was a tie, and the House of Representatives finally had to choose between the two. The Twelfth Amendment subsequently was designed to prevent that situation, requiring electors to ballot separately for president and vice president.

[5] No person except a natural-born citizen, or citizen of the United States at the time of the adoption of this Constitution, shall be eligible to the office of President; neither shall any person be eligible to that office who shall not have attained to the age of thirty-five years, and been fourteen years a resident within the United States.

This section has never been litigated. Some candidates for the presidency were born abroad of American parents, but they have generally been regarded as American citizens. Herbert Hoover had not lived in the United States for 14 years prior to his election in 1928, but he had maintained a legal residence.

[6] In case of the removal of the President from office, or of his death, resignation, or inability to discharge the powers and duties of the said office, the same shall devolve on the Vice-President, and the Congress may by law provide for the case of removal, death, resignation, or inability, both of the President and Vice-President, declaring what officer shall then act as President, and such officer shall act accordingly until the disability be removed or a President shall be elected.

Congress has periodically altered the manner of presidential succession beyond the vice president. We have had legislation that variously established the president pro tempore of the Senate, the secretary of state, or the Speaker of the House of Representatives as next in line in the event that the vice president succeeded to the presidency. The problem of determining presidential disability has been difficult. Mindful of intruding on executive independence, Congress historically had been reluctant to find a legislative solution. Finally, Congress devised a formula and proposed it in the form of the Twenty-fifth Amendment, which was ratified in 1967.

[7] The President shall, at stated times, receive for his services a compensation, which shall neither be increased nor diminished during the period for which he shall have been elected, and he shall not receive within that period any other emolument from the United States or any of them.

This clause is essential for the separation of powers and the independence of the executive. Congress may not punish the president by reducing his salary during his elected term; similarly, a Congress composed of the president's friends and allies may not increase his salary in that same period.

[8] Before he enter on the execution of his office he shall take the following oath or affirmation:

"I do solemnly swear (or affirm) that I will faithfully execute the office of President of the United States, and will to the best of my ability preserve, protect, and defend the Constitution of the United States."

This oath binds the president to the Constitution, as it does all civil officers in the United States (see Article VI, Section 3), thus reinforcing the supremacy of the Constitution. When the House of Representatives impeached Andrew Johnson in 1868 and Bill Clinton in 1998, and when the House Judiciary Committee voted impeachment articles against Richard Nixon in 1974, they did so, in part, on the grounds that the presidents had violated their oath.

Section 2 [1] The President shall be Commander in Chief of the Army and Navy of the United States, and of the militia of the several States when called into the actual service of the United States; he may require the opinion, in writing, of the principal officer in each of the executive departments, upon any subject relating to the duties of their respective offices, and he shall have power to grant reprieves and pardons for offenses against the United States, except in cases of impeachment.

The president as commander in chief again asserts the idea of civilian supremacy over the military. Presidents have claimed, and exercised, the prerogative of conducting military policies in their capacity as overall commander. President Abraham Lincoln issued direct orders to his army commanders; President Harry Truman directly ordered the dropping of the atomic bomb; and Presidents Lyndon Johnson and Richard Nixon supervised and directed military attacks on North Vietnam. In 1951 Truman removed General Douglas MacArthur as military commander in Japan and Korea on the grounds that the general had been insubordinate to the president.

Largely for practical reasons, the president has been the beneficiary of a widened scope of national power resulting from the war powers enumerated in Article I, Section 8. Those powers, combined with the president's assumption of wartime leadership sanctioned by this section, have resulted in presidential exercises of power that involve nonmilitary matters. President Truman, for example, justified his seizure of the steel mills as necessary to prevent a strike and maintain essential steel production. The Supreme Court rejected his argument and restored the mills to private owners.

This section also refers to the advisory capacity of the heads of the executive departments—that is, the cabinet. That body, however, has no authority except for what individual presidents may bestow on it.

The president's pardoning power is absolute, and it may be granted even before an individual has been convicted, such as when President Gerald Ford pardoned former President Richard Nixon in 1974.

[2] He shall have power, by and with the advice and consent of the Senate, to make treaties, provided two-thirds of the Senators present concur; and he shall nominate, and, by and with the advice and consent of the Senate, shall appoint ambassadors, other public ministers and consuls, judges of the Supreme Court, and all other officers of the United States whose appointments are not herein otherwise provided for, and which shall be established by law; but the Congress may by law vest the appointment of such inferior officers, as they think proper, in the President alone, in the courts of law, or in the heads of departments.

The president's treaty-making power, together with his ability to send and receive foreign ambassadors, provides the foundation for his authority to conduct the foreign policy of the United States. The stipulation that two-thirds of the Senate must consent to the ratification of a treaty indicates that the Senate, at least, was given some share in the making of such policy. Treaties, according to Article VI, Section 2, are part of the "supreme law of the land"; as such, the framers established a rigorous standard for their incorporation into the fundamental law. The Senate's role in providing "advice" in the formulation of foreign policy is largely dependent upon the president's wishes. President Wilson's failure to consult with the Senate during the formulation of the Treaty of Versailles, establishing the League of Nations, often is cited as a leading cause for the Senate's rejection of the treaty. Since then, presidential consultation with Congress is considered politically imperative.

The Senate also shares power in the appointment of executive and judicial officers, since it must consent to their nomination by the president. As it establishes various offices, Congress may determine what levels of executive officers the Senate must confirm. When the First Congress created the original executive departments, congressmen debated at length whether the president required Senate consent to remove any officers that the Senate had confirmed. By indirection, Congress provided that removal was a matter of presidential discretion.

[3] The President shall have power to fill up all vacancies that may happen during the recess of the Senate, by granting commissions which shall expire at the end of their next session.

This paragraph provides for "recess" appointments; that is, the president may appoint an executive officer, a judge, or an ambassador without consent while the Senate is not in session. Such appointments are rare as they are considered offensive to Congress.

Section 3 He shall from time to time give to the Congress information of the state of the Union, and recommend to their consideration such measures as he shall judge necessary and expedient; he may, on extraordinary occasions, convene both Houses, or either of them, and in case of disagreement between them with respect to the time of adjournment, he may adjourn them to such time as he shall think proper; he shall receive ambassadors and other public ministers; he shall take care that the laws be faithfully executed, and shall commission all the officers of the United States.

Presidents are expected to provide a "State of the Union" message to Congress. The tradition has been that the information is given annually. Washington and John Adams appeared in person, but Jefferson began a practice of submitting written messages, one that continued until Woodrow Wilson's first message in 1913. Today, the president uses the State of the Union report in large measure as a vehicle to communicate with the nation. Earlier, presidents provided a review of the year's important national events and developments; in the 20th century, the message has been a device for articulating the president's agenda.

The requirement that the president "take care that the laws be faithfully executed" basically supplements the oath of office and offers a reference for accountability in the event Congress seeks to impeach and remove the president. This section also has been used by various presidents to justify armed intervention in the case of strikes or defiance of court orders. President William McKinley ordered federal troops to break the Pullman strike in 1894; Dwight D. Eisenhower and John F. Kennedy dispatched soldiers and federal marshals to enforce court-ordered desegregation in the 1950's and 1960's; and Lyndon Johnson did the same to quell urban disorders in 1967.

Section 4 The President, Vice-President and all civil officers of the United States shall be removed from office on impeachment for and conviction of treason, bribery, or other high crimes and misdemeanors.

Andrew Johnson, the 17th president of the United States, was impeached in 1868, but acquitted by one vote in the Senate. In 1974 the House Judiciary Committee voted three articles of impeachment against Richard Nixon, but Nixon resigned before the full House could act. In 1998–99 Bill Clinton was impeached for three alleged offenses but the Senate could not muster even a majority for any of them.

Article III

Section 1 The judicial power of the United States shall be vested in one Supreme Court, and in such inferior courts as the Congress may from time to time ordain and establish. The judges, both of the Supreme and inferior courts, shall hold their offices during good behavior, and shall, at stated times, receive for their services a compensation which shall not be diminished during their continuance in office.

The opening statement of this section is similar to ones in the previous articles for the legislative and executive branches. Judicial power is vested in the courts, meaning that power is separate and distinct and cannot be exercised by other branches. Except for an impeachment trial, Congress has no judicial authority. The Constitution does not mandate the size of the Supreme Court. There is an earlier reference to the Chief Justice of the United States, but that is the only judicial officer specified. Congress has varied the number of justices from five to ten, but since 1869, it has kept the membership at nine. When Franklin D. Roosevelt proposed increasing the Court from nine to 15 members in 1937, public opinion polls reported a widespread belief that his action was "unconstitutional." It was not; no number is mandated in the Constitution.

In 1789 Congress established a lower court system, and it has regularly increased the number of such courts as federal court business has warranted. Federal judges hold their offices for life, dependent on their "good behavior." They may be removed through the impeachment process. The stipulation regarding compensation prevents legislative or executive reprisals against judges who might deliver unpopular opinions.

Section 2 [1] The judicial power shall extend to all cases, in law and equity, arising under this Constitution, the laws of the United States, and treaties made, or which shall be made, under their authority; to all cases affecting ambassadors, other public ministers, and consuls; to all cases of admiralty and maritime jurisdiction; to controversies to which the United States shall be a party; to controversies between two or more States; between a State and citizens of another State; between citizens of different States; between citizens of the same State claiming lands under grants of different States, and between a State, or the citizens thereof, and foreign states, citizens, or subjects.

This section establishes the scope of judicial power, giving to the federal judiciary the right to rule in cases that involve the Constitution, federal laws, or treaties. In addition, the Constitution sets forth a number of other contingencies for federal judicial authority. This section provides an opening for the exercise of judicial review, that is, the power of the judiciary to declare laws unconstitutional. Contemporary comments at the time of the Constitutional Convention generally acknowledged that interpreting laws was the "proper and peculiar province of the courts," including resolving the superiority of the fundamental law over acts of legislative bodies. Chief Justice John Marshall's decision in *Marbury v. Madison* (1803) reinforced this view and since then, judicial review has been an acknowledged fact of American constitutional practice. Marshall rationalized judicial review as resulting from general principles of constitutional government. He declared that the Constitution was the nation's "fundamental" law and that the judiciary had the particular duty "to say what the law is."

[2] In all cases affecting ambassadors, other public ministers and consuls, and those in which a State shall be party, the Supreme Court shall have original jurisdiction. In all the other cases before mentioned the Supreme Court shall have appellate jurisdiction, both as to law and fact, with such exceptions and under such regulations as the Congress shall make.

The Supreme Court has original jurisdiction—that is, it is the court of first instance—in only a few areas. Its jurisdiction is essentially appellate. But Congress determines that jurisdiction, offering one of the few checks on judicial power. Congress may even revoke jurisdiction previously conferred, as it did shortly after the Civil War, although that action had no real consequence at the time.

[3] The trial of all crimes, except in cases of impeachment, shall be by jury; and such trial shall be held in the State where the said crimes shall have been committed; but when not committed within any State, the trial shall be at such place or places as the Congress may by law have directed.

The Sixth Amendment has a similar provision on jury trials. Such trials may be waived by the accused.

Section 3 [1] Treason against the United States shall consist only in levying war against them, or in adhering to their enemies, giving them aid and comfort. No person shall be convicted of treason unless on the testimony of two witnesses to the same overt act, or on confession in open court.

This is the only crime is specifically defined in the Constitution and is borrowed literally from the English Treason Act of 1694. The narrow, strict definition of treason serves to restrain public officials from bringing treason charges against political opponents, such as had been the practice of English monarchs. In that sense, the treason clause serves to legitimate political opposition.

[2] The Congress shall have power to declare the punishment of treason, but no attainder of treason shall work corruption of blood or forfeiture except during the life of the person attained.

Quite simply, a conviction of treason shall not bring punishment on the children or heirs of those convicted.

Article IV

Section 1 Full faith and credit shall be given in each State to the public acts, records, and judicial proceedings of every other State. And the Congress may by general laws prescribe the manner in which such acts, records, and proceedings shall be proved, and the effect thereof.

This section is borrowed from the international law concept of comity. The Constitution requires that states honor one another's laws and judicial decrees. Much of the litigation of the full faith and credit clause has involved the validity of divorce decrees in states other than that in which they have been granted.

Section 2 [1] The citizens of each State shall be entitled to all privileges and immunities of citizens in the several States.

The privileges and immunities provision has been interpreted in a variety of ways, but mostly it has been understood as a restraint on state action. States may not discriminate against citizens of other states in favor of their own. But in certain cases, if the so-called discrimination is uniform, states may have different requirements for outsiders. They may, for example, have a reasonable residency requirement for voting or practicing law, and they may require lower fees for college tuition or less expensive licenses for hunting and fishing.

[2] A person charged in any State with treason, felony, or other crime, who shall flee from justice, and be found in another State, shall, on demand of the executive authority of the State from which he fled, be delivered up, to be removed to the State having jurisdiction of the crime.

The requirement of extradition of criminally accused or convicted persons marked another attempt to cement the union of states. But extradition is not mandatory, as governors have some discretionary power to deny another state's request.

[3] No person held to service or labor in one State, under the laws thereof, escaping into another, shall, in consequence of any law or regulation therein, be discharged from such service or labor, but shall be delivered up on claim to the party to whom such service or labor may be due.

This section applied to escaped slaves or indentured servants. Together with the "three-fifths" arrangement in Article I, it represented a crucial element in the sectional compromise that produced the Constitution. Congress enacted a fugitive slave law in 1793, and reinforced it with subsequent laws through the 1850's. Many northern states and officials supported abolitionist efforts to aid fugitive slaves and refused to comply with the various laws providing for recapture, thus sharpening the sectional controversy.

Section 3 [1] New States may be admitted by the Congress into this Union; but no new State shall be formed or erected within the jurisdiction of any other

State; nor any State be formed by the junction of two or more States or parts of States, without the consent of the legislatures of the States concerned as well as of the Congress.

This section has been interpreted by the Supreme Court as guaranteeing the admission of new states as equal members of the Union.

[2] The Congress shall have power to dispose of and make all needful rules and regulations respecting the territory or other property belonging to the United States; and nothing in this Constitution shall be so construed as to prejudice any claims of the United States or of any particular State.

The section originally applied to governing territories of the United States. But it also has been used to sustain the inherent power of the nation to acquire new territory, such as was done with the Louisiana Purchase in 1803. As the United States expanded across the continent in the 19th century, Congress regularly provided territorial laws and constitutions prior to the granting of statehood. During the long controversy over slavery, much attention focused on whether Congress could prohibit slavery in the territories. Antislavery forces relied on this paragraph, but supporters of slavery contended that such prohibition interfered with one's property rights, in violation of the Fifth Amendment.

Section 4 The United States shall guarantee to every State in this Union a republican form of government, and shall protect each of them against invasion, and on application of the legislature, or of the executive (when the legislature cannot be convened), against domestic violence.

Protecting the states from domestic violence or the threat of foreign invasion certainly was one of the great objects of the Constitution. The fear of domestic insurrection and the possibility of anarchy generated the drive for a constitutional convention in 1786–87. This section supplements other sections of the Constitution that give the national government authority to defend public order. The phrase, "republican form of government," has had no satisfactory, conclusive definition other than that it repudiates any monarchial or totalitarian form of government.

Article V

The Congress, whenever two-thirds of both Houses shall deem it necessary, shall propose amendments to this Constitution, or, on the application of the legislatures of two-thirds of the several States, shall call a convention for proposing amendments, which in either case shall be valid to all intents and purposes as part of this Constitution, when ratified by the legislatures of three-fourths of the several States, or by conventions in three-fourths thereof, as the one or the other mode of ratification may be proposed by the Congress; provided that no amendment which may be made prior to the year one thousand eight hundred and eight shall in any manner affect the first and fourth clauses in the Ninth Section of the First Article; and that no State, without its consent, shall be deprived of its equal suffrage in the Senate.

The Articles of Confederation required unanimous consent of the states for any amendment. The process is made easier in the Constitution; still, the requirement for a two-thirds vote of both houses, or the application of two-thirds of the states, plus the ratification of three-fourths of the states, usually ensures great difficulty for the passage of an amendment. No constitutional amendment has ever been successfully proposed by the states. The amending process is, like the Electoral College, an important vestige of state power. The three-fourths requirement for ratification does not necessarily reflect majoritarianism, for that number of states may represent less than half the population. Similarly, one-fourth plus one of the states that might block an amendment can represent a population number far less than one-fourth.

Article VI

[1] All debts contracted and engagements entered into, before the adoption of this Constitution, shall be as valid against the United States under this Constitution as under the Confederation.

This section was designed to maintain the continuity of the United States and announced that the government under the new Constitution would honor whatever public debts had been incurred since 1776. In this manner, the framers of the new government hoped to establish public credit, both at home and abroad.

[2] This Constitution, and the laws of the United States which shall be made in pursuance thereof, and all treaties made, or which shall be made, under the authority of the United States, shall be the supreme

law of the land; and the judges in every State shall be bound thereby, anything in the Constitution or laws of any State to the contrary notwithstanding.

The "supremacy clause" emphasizes the paramount authority of the Constitution, national laws, and treaties over state laws, and it has been called "the linchpin" of the constitutional system. The clause has been the basis for national preemption of authority over the states in a variety of matters. The provision for judicial enforcement, in part, supported arguments on behalf of the judiciary's special role in interpreting the Constitution.

[3] **The Senators and Representatives before mentioned and the members of the several State legislatures, and all executive and judicial officers both of the United States and of the several States, shall be bound by oath or affirmation to support this Constitution; but no religious test shall ever be required as a qualification to any office or public trust under the United States.**

Again, the framers sought to bind the nation to the Constitution as fundamental law. Alexander Hamilton wrote in *The Federalist Papers* that all governmental officers were "incorporated into the operations of the national government as far as its just and constitutional authority extends, and will be rendered auxiliary to the enforcement of its laws." Thus state officials are as responsible for maintaining the integrity of national laws as national officials. The proviso that no religious tests could be imposed as a qualification to office-holding underlined the framers' strong sentiments against any kind of religious establishment. In 1962 the Supreme Court struck down a longstanding Maryland law requiring notary publics to declare their belief in God in order to secure a state license.

Article VII

The ratification of the conventions of nine States shall be sufficient for the establishment of this Constitution between the States so ratifying the same.

The stipulation that only nine states needed to ratify the Constitution in order to make it effective again marked a reaction against the requirement for unanimity to amend the Articles of Confederation. Practically speaking, however, the original union needed the participation of key states such as New York and Virginia, which were among the last to ratify. After those states ratified, the Constitution went into effect in 1788, although North Carolina and Rhode Island stayed out of the Union for several more years. The requirement of conventions stemmed from a belief that the Constitution needed the consent of the "sovereign people," thus rationalizing a bypass of the state legislatures.

The Bill of Rights

During the process of ratification from 1787 to 1789, proponents of the new Constitution found it necessary to promise that they would support a Bill of Rights as the first order of business for the new government. Nearly everyone agreed that the national government was restricted to the powers delegated by the Constitution; as such, many supporters of the Constitution believed that a Bill of Rights was superfluous and unnecessary. Still, James Madison, the leading architect of the Constitution, considered it politically expedient to provide such amendments to counter fears of the new government and to discredit a budding movement for a new convention that might impose added restrictions on national powers. Congress submitted 12 amendments to the states in September 1789, and two years later, the requisite number of states ratified 10.

Unquestionably, the Bill of Rights originally applied only against action by the federal government. Madison and others failed in their attempt to ensure similar guarantees against state action. Chief Justice John Marshall confirmed that the amendments referred only to the national government. But since 1925 the Supreme Court has steadily expanded the doctrine that the Fourteenth Amendment "incorporated" the Bill of Rights and has applied the restrictions of the Bill of Rights against the states. In that year, the Court declared: "[W]e may and do assume that freedom of speech and of the press—which are protected by the First Amendment from abridgment by Congress—are among the fundamental personal rights and 'liberties' protected by the due process clause of the Fourteenth Amendment from impairment by the states." That incorporation subsequently extended to the religion guarantees and various rights of the criminally accused.

Amendments to the Constitution

The first 10 amendments, known collectively as the Bill of Rights, were adopted in 1791.

Amendment I

Congress shall make no law respecting an establish-

ment of religion, or prohibiting the free exercise thereof; or abridging the freedom of speech or of the press; or the right of the people peaceably to assemble, and to petition the government for a redress of grievances.

The religion clauses of the First Amendment reflected widespread antagonism toward official support for religion. As colonists, Americans had resented compulsory taxes levied on behalf of the Church of England, despite the fact that the settlers belonged to a variety of sects. Following the Revolution, many states repealed the taxes and incorporated provisions against the establishment of religion in their new state constitutions. In many states, and certainly in the minds of James Madison and other framers of the Constitution, the nonestablishment of religion meant opposition to any nonpreferential aid to religion as well. Constitutional interpretation of the establishment clause has varied. Traditionally, we have accepted tax exemption for religious groups, as well as the maintenance of chaplains for the military and various legislatures. Yet direct aids such as tuition grants for parochial schools or government support for religious activity, including public school prayers, have been held to violate the establishment clause. Since 1971 the Court has tried to invoke a three-pronged test for determining when governmental action does not violate the establishment clause. Such a statute, the Court said, "must have a secular legislative purpose; second, its principal or primary effect must be one that neither advances nor inhibits religion; finally, the statute must not foster 'an excessive government entanglement with religion.' "

The free exercise clause offers a historical lesson on the need for tolerance in a diverse, pluralistic society. Religious expression is protected by the Constitution; as such, a state cannot compel children to attend high school and thereby defy their parents' religious beliefs. But the courts have held that the free exercise clause cannot justify actions that violate "social duties or [are] subversive of good order." Accordingly, the Supreme Court upheld a congressional act prohibiting polygamy in the territories of the United States.

Few constitutional clauses have been subjected to as many doctrinal theories and abstract formulas as the free speech clause of the First Amendment. The best evidence indicates that the framers intended to prohibit any "prior restraints" on political speech. As understood at the time, the common law of "seditious libel" allowed government officials to prosecute political dissenters, yet the government could not formally restrict such activity in advance. After a number of prosecutions under the Sedition Act of 1798, however, prosecutions for seditious libel became discredited, and generally, there was an understanding that political dissent had a legitimate place in the American political order.

The diverse political world of the 20th century, aided by improved communications, often made the First Amendment a key battleground for the assertion of constitutional rights and privileges. The courts have responded with varied doctrines on the permissibility of speech, including "tests" to determine whether particular speeches or writings offer a "clear and present danger," whether they represent a "bad tendency" or a "clear and probable danger," whether there is an absolute prohibition against any governmental restraint upon expression of opinion, or whether the competing demands of individual rights and the security needs of the state must be "balanced" on a case-by-case basis. The net result has been inconsistency, and decisions have been reached depending on the facts of individual cases, the climate of opinion at a given moment, and the different values of the judges.

Speech is understood to be more than verbal and more than political. Courts have protected "symbolic speech," such as the wearing of protest badges or carrying picketing signs. For some judges, however, such activity is "conduct," and not speech, and thus not protected by the First Amendment. In recent years, "commercial speech" has found protection in the First Amendment as courts have ruled that states may not prohibit advertising of prescription drugs or legal services.

The right of assembly and petition clause of this amendment largely has been understood as "cognate to those of free speech and free press and is equally fundamental." Still, there are restrictions. An assemblage can be subject to requirements of a peaceful social order, such as the unimpeded flow of traffic. "The constitutional guarantee of liberty," the Supreme Court held in 1965, "implies the existence of an organized society maintaining public order, without which liberty itself would be lost in the excesses of anarchy."

Amendment II

A well-regulated militia being necessary to the security of a free State, the right of the people to keep and bear arms shall not be infringed.

The historical record is somewhat ambiguous as to whether the framers intended that the "right to bear arms" be considered separate from the concerns for the maintenance of a militia. Many of the political figures of the period regarded a "people's militia" as an alternative to a standing army. In any event, courts have sustained a variety of regulations regarding the registration and concealment of firearms and the prohibition of some weapons.

Amendment III

No soldier shall, in time of peace, be quartered in any house without the consent of the owner, nor in time of war, but in a manner to be prescribed by law.

This amendment reflected colonial and revolutionary era problems, when the British Crown required Americans to quarter troops and pay for the soldiers' maintenance. In some cases, the British insisted on quartering soldiers in private dwellings, thus violating the ancient maxim that a "man's house is his castle." The amendment also demonstrated again the framers' concern for civilian control of the military.

Amendment IV

The right of the people to be secure in their persons, houses, papers, and effects, against unreasonable searches and seizures, shall not be violated, and no warrants shall issue but upon probable cause, supported by oath or affirmation, and particularly describing the place to be searched, and the persons or things to be seized.

This amendment also had its roots in British imperial practices. The Crown often would issue general warrants, or writs of assistance, allowing for indiscriminate searches and seizures as officials sought to suppress smuggling or illegal trade. In the past century, the courts have applied this amendment with the self-incrimination clause of the Fifth Amendment to exclude the unreasonable seizure of evidence from being introduced as evidence against a defendant. But court decisions have varied on the meaning of "unreasonable," and, in fact, courts have ruled that there can be permissible arrest and searches and seizure of evidence without a warrant. Common sense, for example, dictates that airline passengers submit themselves and their baggage to some examination before boarding. Wiretapping and other forms of electronic surveillance have presented modern challenges for the Constitution. President Richard Nixon's attorney general contended that the government had "inherent power" to maintain electronic surveillance of alleged political subversives and need not apply to the courts for a proper warrant. The Supreme Court responded by asserting that neither the Constitution nor any statute justified such an extravagant doctrine. The requirement of a warrant, the Court concluded, "is justified in a free society to protect constitutional values" and would reassure the public "that indiscriminate wiretapping and bugging of law-abiding citizens cannot occur."

All of this changed in 2001 with passage of the Patriot Act only 45 days after the 9-11 attacks. Congress authorized government agencies to search any individual's financial and medical records, Internet searches, and travel patterns without a warrant, nor do they have to show cause.

Amendment V

No person shall be held to answer for a capital, or otherwise infamous crime, unless on a presentment or indictment of a grand jury, except in cases arising in the land or naval forces, or in the militia, when in actual service in time of war or public danger; nor shall any person be subject for the same offense to be twice put in jeopardy of life or limb; nor shall be compelled in any criminal case to be a witness against himself, nor be deprived of life, liberty or property, without due process of law; nor shall private property be taken for public use without just compensation.

The Fifth Amendment is at the heart of procedural guarantees for accused persons. It is a summary of English and colonial legal developments, most notably with the due process of law clause that stems directly from Magna Carta of 1215. The double jeopardy prohibition provides a barrier to the massed resources of the state, which may not, the Supreme Court has ruled, subject a person to "repeated attempts to convict [him], . . . thereby subjecting him to embarrassment, expense and ordeal and compelling him to live in a continuing state of anxiety and insecurity, as well as enhancing the possibility that even though innocent he may be found guilty."

The provision against self-incrimination developed as part of the accusatorial rather than inquisitional system of criminal justice. It reflects a reaction against torture or other inhumane means of gaining information from the accused. In recent years, the Supreme Court has asserted that the provision dictates "a fair state-individual balance by requiring the government to leave the individual alone until good cause is shown for disturbing him and by requiring the government in its contest with the individual to shoulder the entire load." Individuals, however, can be compelled to testify in exchange for immunity from prosecution.

Due process of law originally applied in a general way to procedures, including proper notice and hearing in civil cases, and as a supplement to the specific provisions of the Fourth and Sixth Amendments for criminal cases. But the due process clause also developed a substantive content to serve, the Supreme Court has said, as a "bulwark also against arbitrary legislation." Courts have invoked the due process clause against legislation, which "given even the fairest possible procedure in application to individuals, [might] nevertheless destroy the enjoyment of" life, liberty, or property.

The Fifth Amendment specifically protects an individual's right to hold and enjoy lawful property. The last clause explicitly guarantees that private property cannot be appropriated for public use without fair compensation.

Amendment VI

In all criminal prosecutions, the accused shall enjoy the right to a speedy and public trial, by an impartial jury of the State and district wherein the crime shall have been committed, which district shall have been previously ascertained by law, and to be informed of the nature and cause of the accusation; to be confronted with the witnesses against him; to have compulsory process for obtaining witnesses in his favor, and to have the assistance of counsel for his defense.

The provision for a speedy and public trial represented a reaction to the arbitrary forms of justice practiced in royal prerogative courts in England. A speedy public trial affects both the defendant and the society, giving the former a hearing in reasonable time and also providing the society with a trial before evidence grows cold and witnesses die or disappear. The defendant's right to know the charges, to be confronted with witnesses, and to challenge witnesses and evidence with his own, again formed a reaction against arbitrary justice in England and extended the concepts of due process of law. Prosecutors, for example, cannot offer anonymous reports of undercover agents as evidence of criminal behavior; the witness must be produced for cross-examination. In 2004 the Supreme Court ruled (*Hamdi v. Rumsfeld*) that U.S. citizens detained as "enemy combatants" in the Bush administration's war on terror have the right to a lawyer; to learn of the evidence against them; and to confront their accusers in a court of law.

Amendment VII

In suits at common law, where the value in controversy shall exceed twenty dollars, the right of trial by jury shall be preserved, and no fact tried by a jury shall be otherwise reexamined in any court of the United States, than according to the rules of the common law.

Critics of the Constitution during the ratification process pointed to the omission of a guarantee of a jury trial in civil matters. The amendment also provides some limits to judicial power, for it stipulates that the courts cannot reconsider the facts of a case on appeal.

Amendment VIII

Excessive bail shall not be required, nor excessive fines imposed, nor cruel and unusual punishments inflicted.

The provision against excessive bail again involves the procedural rights of the criminally accused. It has been interpreted as part of the presumption of innocence and as sometimes necessary to enable an accused to prepare an adequate defense. The cruel and unusual punishments clause has served (with other constitutional provisions) to challenge the death penalty. Judicial rulings in this area often have been contradictory, but by the mid-1970's, the Supreme Court had held that the death sentence "for the crime of murder" was not unconstitutional under the Eighth Amendment.

Amendment IX

The enumeration in the Constitution of certain rights shall not be construed to deny or disparage others retained by the people.

This amendment was designed to allay fears that the partial listing of individual rights might be inadequate to protect all the rights of the people. In recent years, some Supreme Court justices have used the amendment to advance a right of individual privacy.

Amendment X

The powers not delegated to the United States by the Constitution, nor prohibited by it to the States, are reserved to the States respectively, or to the people.

The Tenth Amendment was intended to summarize the Bill of Rights as a series of statements restricting Congress to the powers granted to it by the Constitution. But as Chief Justice Marshall noted in 1819, the amendment does not confine Congress to powers "expressly delegated," as it did in the Articles of Confederation. In fact, opponents of the new Constitution lobbied hard to confine the national government to "expressly" enumerated powers. But James Madison insisted that some powers had to be "admitted by implication." That omission served Marshall's doctrine of "broad construction" of the Constitution when he interpreted the meaning of the "necessary and proper" clause (Article I, Section 8, Clause 18).

Many decisions over the last 20 years, however, offer ample testimony to the persistent vitality of federalism and the recognition of state authority, without unduly hindering the need for national action and uniformity.

Later Amendments

Amendment XI [Adopted Jan. 8, 1798]

The judicial power of the United States shall not be construed to extend to any suit in law or equity, commenced or prosecuted against one of the United States by citizens of another State, or by citizens or subjects of any foreign state.

The Supreme Court ruled in 1793 that it had jurisdiction to hear a suit against Georgia by a citizen of another state. That decision provoked violent reaction protests and actions in various states and Congress promptly responded with this amendment. The amendment established sovereign immunity for the states; nevertheless, other rulings have permitted a variety of suits, particularly against state officials. Since 1824, the Supreme Court has held that governmental officers can claim no immunity when acting in alleged violation of a constitutional right.

Amendment XII [Adopted Sept. 25, 1804]

[1] The Electors shall meet in their respective States and vote by ballot for President and Vice-President, one of whom, at least, shall not be an inhabitant of the same State with themselves; they shall name in their ballots the person voted for as President, and in distinct ballots the person voted for as Vice-President, and they shall make distinct lists of all persons voted for as President and of all persons voted for as Vice-President, and of the number of votes for each; which lists they shall sign and certify, and transmit sealed to the seat of the government of the United States, directed to the President of the Senate. The President of the Senate shall, in the presence of the Senate and House of Representatives, open all the certificates and the votes shall then be counted. The person having the greatest number of votes for President shall be the President, if such number be a majority of the whole number of Electors appointed; and if no person have such majority, then from the persons having the highest numbers not exceeding three on the list of those voted for as President, the House of Representatives shall choose immediately, by ballot, the President. But in choosing the President the votes shall be taken by States, the representation from each State having one vote; a quorum for this purpose shall consist of a member or members from two-thirds of the States, and a majority of all the States shall be necessary to a choice. And if the House of Representatives shall not choose a President whenever the right of choice shall devolve upon them, before the fourth day of March next following, then the Vice-President shall act as President, as in the case of the death or other constitutional disability of the President.

[2] The person having the greatest number of votes as Vice-President shall be the Vice-President, if such number be a majority of the whole number of Electors appointed; and if no person have a majority, then from the two highest numbers on the list the Senate shall choose the Vice-President; a quorum for the purpose shall consist of two-thirds of the whole number of Senators, and a majority of the whole number shall be necessary to a choice. But no person constitutionally ineligible to the office of President shall be eligible to that of Vice-President of the United States.

This amendment resulted from the electoral tie between Thomas Jefferson and Aaron Burr in the election of 1800. The electors clearly intended Jefferson to be President, but they inadvertently all cast their ballots for the "ticket," thus creating a tie. The Twelfth Amendment superseded Article II, Section 1, and provides that electors vote separately for president and vice president. If no candidate receives a majority of the electoral vote, the House of Representatives chooses between the three leading candidates (as opposed to five in Article II), but the balloting is by states, with each having only one vote.

Amendment XIII [Adopted Dec. 18, 1865]

Section 1 Neither slavery nor involuntary servitude, except as a punishment for crime whereof the party shall have been duly convicted, shall exist within the United States, or any place subject to their jurisdiction.

Section 2 Congress shall have power to enforce this article by appropriate legislation.

Congress proposed a Thirteenth Amendment to the states early in 1861, providing that no future amendment would authorize the abolition of slavery. Only three states ratified this amendment before the Civil War erupted in April 1861. The amendment eventually adopted in 1865 was a radical act, for it abolished all slavery—which was, of course, private property—without compensation. In subsequent years, the amendment was interpreted to prohibit peonage, which is compulsory service for payment of debts. The second section provided Congress with substantive enforcement powers. Consequently, Congress enacted the Civil Rights Act of 1866 to ensure equality of treatment for newly freed slaves.

Amendment XIV [Adopted July 28, 1868]

Section 1 All persons born or naturalized in the United States, and subject to the jurisdiction thereof, are citizens of the United States and of the State wherein they reside. No State shall make or enforce any law which shall abridge the privileges or immunities of citizens of the United States; nor shall any State deprive any person of life, liberty or property, without due process of law; nor deny to any person within its jurisdiction the equal protection of the laws.

Section 2 Representatives shall be apportioned among the several States according to their respective numbers, counting the whole number of persons in each State, excluding Indians not taxed. But when the right to vote at any election for the choice of Electors for President and Vice-President of the United States, Representatives in Congress, the executive and judicial officers of a State, or the members of the legislature thereof, is denied to any of the male inhabitants of such State, being twenty-one years of age, and citizens of the United States, or in any way abridged except for participation in rebellion or other crime, the basis of representation therein shall be reduced in the proportion which the number of such male citizens shall bear to the whole number of male citizens twenty-one years of age in such State.

Section 3 No person shall be a Senator or Representative in Congress, or elector of President and Vice-President, or hold any office, civil or military, under the United States or under any State, who, having previously taken an oath as a member of Congress, or as an officer of the United States, or as a member of any State legislature, or as an executive or judicial officer of any State, to support the Constitution of the United States, shall have engaged in insurrection or rebellion against the same, or given aid or comfort to the enemies thereof. But Congress may, by a vote of two-thirds of each House, remove such disability.

Section 4 The validity of the public debt of the United States, authorized by law, including debts incurred for payment of pensions and bounties for services in suppressing insurrection or rebellion, shall not be questioned. But neither the United States nor any State shall assume or pay any debt or obligation incurred in aid of insurrection or rebellion against the United States, or any claim for the loss or emancipation of any slave; but all such debts, obligations, and claims shall be held illegal and void.

Section 5 The Congress shall have power to enforce, by appropriate legislation, the provisions of this article.

The Fourteenth Amendment represents the most substantial and fundamental change in the Constitution since the ratification of the first 10 amendments. A great majority of the nation's constitutional history of the past century can be viewed from the perspective and interpretation of this amendment.

When written, the Fourteenth Amendment was understood to be the centerpiece of efforts to reconstruct the nation following the Civil War. At that time, attention focused on Sections 2, 3, and 4, dealing with postwar loyalty and claims matters. Section 2 repealed the infamous "three-fifths compromise" (Article I, Section 2), but it also provided for the reduction of congressional representation for those states that racially discriminated against the voting rights of its citizens. This clearly was designed to guarantee suffrage for the freedmen; but Congress never has reduced any state's representation in accordance with this provision.

Section 1 has had enduring relevance and meaning for American constitutional development. The first sentence defined citizenship—one of the notable omissions of the original Constitution—and was designed specifically to settle the status of the newly freed slaves. National citizenship is given primacy, and state citizenship derives from it. The scope is generous. Children born of foreign nationals, even those only temporarily living in the United States, are citizens of the nation. So although the United States denied citizenship to Japanese immigrants in the late 19th and early 20th centuries, their children born here automatically become citizens.

The privileges and immunities and due process clauses are designed to prevent violations of those guarantees, in the same manner as citizens are protected against federal intrusions in these areas. Since 1925, the Supreme Court consistently has ruled that the Fourteenth Amendment incorporates most of the Bill of Rights—for example, free speech, free press, no establishment of religion, and right to counsel—and secures those rights against state action.

The "equal protection of the laws" clause might well be the most vital part of the amendment during the last century. It has been used to strike down discriminatory racial, gender, and age practices and laws, residency requirements, discrepancies in criminal proceedings and sentences, and the apportionment of voting districts.

Amendment XV [Adopted Mar. 30, 1870]

Section 1 The right of citizens of the United States to vote shall not be denied or abridged by the United States or by any State on account of race, color, or previous condition of servitude.

Section 2 The Congress shall have power to enforce this article by appropriate legislation.

The last of the trio of post Civil War amendments supplemented Section 2 of the Fourteenth Amendment in its attempt to extend suffrage to the freedmen. But in 1876, the Supreme Court ruled that the Fifteenth Amendment did "not confer the right [to vote] . . . upon anyone." Instead, the justices held that the amendment merely prohibited discrimination on the grounds of race. As a result, for nearly 80 years, southern states devised a series of literacy and educational requirements that were stringently applied against blacks as a means of denying them suffrage. Through much of that period, the Court ignored the reality of such practices or only partially prohibited them. Post–World War II demands for the political rights of blacks resulted in several congressional acts to ensure the franchise. The climax came in the Voting Rights Act of 1965, when Congress, under authority of Section 2, granted federal authorities the right to suspend state discriminatory practices and provided federal registrars and poll-watchers to secure suffrage rights. The legislation and the use of the Fifteenth Amendment represented a significant reversal of the traditional constitutional recognition of state supervision of voting rights.

Amendment XVI [Adopted Feb. 25, 1913]

The Congress shall have power to lay and collect taxes on incomes, from whatever source derived, without apportionment among the several States, and without regard to any census or enumeration.

This amendment resulted from the Supreme Court's conflicting views on the constitutionality of an income tax. In 1895, the Court held income taxes unconstitutional as they were direct taxes, and thus violated provisions in Article I stipulating that direct taxes be apportioned among the states according to population. However, the national government's expanded role and responsibilities in the early 20th century required expanded sources of income. The progressive income tax promised to be the most lucrative and equitable and there was widespread support for an amendment.

Amendment XVII [Adopted May 31, 1913]

Section 1 The Senate of the United States shall be composed of two Senators from each State, elected by the people thereof, for six years; and each Senator shall have one vote. The electors in each State shall have the qualifications requisite for electors of the most numerous branch of the State legislatures.

Section 2 When vacancies happen in the representation of any State in the Senate, the executive authority of such State shall issue writs of election to fill such vacancies: Provided that the legislature of any State may empower the executive thereof to make temporary appointments until the people fill the vacancies by election as the legislature may direct.

Section 3 This amendment shall not be so construed as to affect the election or term of any Senator chosen before it becomes valid as part of the Constitution.

This amendment provided for the direct election of senators and superseded the provisions in Article I, Section 3, directing that state legislatures choose senators. The amendment reflected one of the reform drives of the Progressive Movement in the early 20th century.

Amendment XVIII [Adopted Jan. 29, 1919]

Section 1 After one year from the ratification of this article the manufacture, sale, or transportation of intoxicating liquors within, the importation thereof into, or the exportation thereof from the United States and all territory subject to the jurisdiction thereof, for beverage purposes, is hereby prohibited.

Section 2 The Congress and the several States shall

have concurrent power to enforce this article by appropriate legislation.

Section 3 This article shall be inoperative unless it shall have been ratified as an amendment to the Constitution by the legislatures of the several States, as provided in the Constitution, within seven years from the date of the submission hereof to the States by the Congress.

The prohibition amendment resulted in a first-time challenge to the constitutionality of a constitutional amendment. One of the nonratifying states contended that the amendment invaded state sovereignty and that it was really a legislative act, not a constitutional amendment relating to the nature of governmental power. The Supreme Court rejected the argument, and in subsequent cases upheld the amendment against challenges that its enforcement violated aspects of other constitutional guarantees, such as those in the Fourth and Fifth Amendments.

The Eighteenth Amendment marked the first time that Congress stipulated that the proposed amendment must be ratified within seven years. Such a provision is discretionary for Congress.

Amendment XIX [Adopted Aug. 26, 1920]

Section 1 The right of citizens of the United States to vote shall not be denied or abridged by the United States or by any State on account of sex.

Section 2 Congress shall have power to enforce this article by appropriate legislation.

The woman's suffrage amendment can be grouped with the three preceding ones as reflecting some of the key reform drives of the Progressive Era. By that time, a number of states, particularly western ones, had granted women the right to vote. The amendment became effective in time for the 1920 presidential election.

Amendment XX [Adopted Feb. 6, 1933]

Section 1 The terms of the President and Vice-President shall end at noon on the 20th day of January, and the terms of Senators and Representatives at noon on the 3d day of January, of the years in which such terms would have ended if this article had not been ratified; and the terms of their successors shall then begin.

Section 2 The Congress shall assemble at least once in every year, and such meeting shall begin at noon on the 3d day of January, unless they shall by law appoint a different day.

Section 3 If, at the time fixed for the beginning of the term of the President, the President-elect shall have died, the Vice-President-elect shall become President. If a President shall not have been chosen before the time fixed for the beginning of his term or if the President-elect shall have failed to qualify, then the Vice-President-elect shall act as President until a President shall have qualified; and the Congress may by law provide for the case wherein neither a President-elect nor a Vice-President-elect shall have qualified, declaring who shall then act as President, or the manner in which one who is to act shall be selected, and such person shall act accordingly until a President or Vice-President shall have qualified.

Section 4 The Congress may by law provide for the case of the death of any of the persons from whom the House of Representatives may choose a President whenever the right of choice shall have devolved upon them, and for the case of death of any of the persons from whom the Senate may choose a Vice-President whenever the right of choice shall have devolved upon them.

Section 5 Sections 1 and 2 shall take effect on the 15th day of October following the ratification of this article.

Section 6 This article shall be inoperative unless it shall have been ratified as an amendment to the Constitution by the legislatures of three-fourths of the several States within seven years from the date of its submission.

This amendment, reflecting improved transportation and communications facilities, reduced the gap between the November elections and the inauguration of the president and the beginning of a new Congress. It thereby eliminated the "lame-duck" session of Congress that regularly occurred between the November elections and the expiration of the old Congress the following March.

Section 3 reinforced Congress's right to determine the presidential succession in the absence of both a president and avice president. For much of the 19th century, the president pro tempore of the Senate stood next in succession. In the 1880's, Congress determined that the secretary of state would be the successor. But in 1947, Congress again changed the law, providing for the speaker of the House to assume office in such a contingency. The theory was that it would be best to have an elected official, rather than an appointed one, succeed to the presidency.

Amendment XXI [Adopted Dec. 5, 1933]

Section 1 The eighteenth article of amendment to the

Constitution of the United States is hereby repealed.

Section 2 The transportation or importation into any State, territory, or possession of the United States for delivery or use therein of intoxicating liquors, in violation of the laws thereof, is hereby prohibited.

Section 3 This article shall be inoperative unless it shall have been ratified as an amendment to the Constitution by conventions in the several States, as provided in the Constitution, within seven years from the date of the submission hereof to the States by the Congress.

The Twenty-First Amendment not only marked the first repeal of a constitutional amendment, but for the first time, Congress required ratification by conventions rather than by state legislatures. The courts have sustained Section 2 by requiring passenger trains to honor state prohibition laws.

Amendment XXII [Adopted Feb. 26, 1951]

Section 1 No person shall be elected to the office of President more than twice, and no person who has held the office of President, or acted as President, for more than two years of a term to which some other person was elected President shall be elected to the office of President more than once. But this Article shall not apply to any person holding the office of President when this Article was proposed by the Congress, and shall not prevent any person who may be holding the office of President, or acting as President, during the term within which this Article becomes operative from holding the office of President or acting as President during the remainder of such term.

Section 2 This article shall be inoperative unless it shall have been ratified as an amendment to the Constitution by the legislatures of three-fourths of the several States within seven years from the date of its submission to the States by the Congress.

This amendment resulted from a combination of resentment and concern after Franklin D. Roosevelt shattered the two-term tradition and was reelected to third and fourth terms. It did not become effective until Dwight D. Eisenhower's term. There was periodic talk of its repeal then, and again in the 1980's, but such efforts have made little headway. Nevertheless, many commentators view the amendment as in effect creating a "lame duck" and greatly weakened presidency during the second term.

Amendment XXIII [Adopted Apr. 3, 1961]

Section 1 The District constituting the seat of Government of the United States shall appoint in such manner as the Congress may direct:

A number of electors of President and Vice President equal to the whole number of Senators and Representatives in Congress to which the District would be entitled if it were a State, but in no event more than the least populous State; they shall be in addition to those appointed by the States, but they shall be considered, for the purposes of the election of President and Vice-President, to be electors appointed by a State; and they shall meet in the District and perform such duties as provided by the twelfth article of amendment.

Section 2 The Congress shall have power to enforce this article by appropriate legislation.

The amendment grants residents of the District of Columbia the right to vote in presidential elections. Together with the Twenty-Fourth Amendment, it fulfilled the demands of the 1950's and 1960's for making suffrage as democratic and broad as possible.

Amendment XXIV [Adopted Jan. 23, 1964]

Section 1 The right of citizens of the United States to vote in any primary or other election for President or Vice-President, for electors for President or Vice-President, or for Senator or Representative in Congress, shall not be denied or abridged by the United States or any State by reason of failure to pay any poll tax or other tax.

Section 2 The Congress shall have power to enforce this article by appropriate legislation.

Congress in this amendment sought to eliminate another barrier to black voters in southern states. States-rights' arguments had defeated previous legislative attempts to abolish the poll tax dating back to 1939. Two years after the adoption of this amendment, the Supreme Court invoked the equal protection clause of the Fourteenth Amendment to invalidate the requirement of a poll tax in state elections.

Amendment XXV [Adopted Feb. 10, 1967]

Section 1 In case of the removal of the President from office or of his death or resignation, the Vice-President shall become President.

Section 2 Whenever there is a vacancy in the office of

the Vice-President, the President shall nominate a Vice-President who shall take office upon confirmation by a majority vote of both Houses of Congress.

Section 3 Whenever the President transmits to the President pro tempore of the Senate and the Speaker of the House of Representatives his written declaration that he is unable to discharge the powers and duties of his office, and until he transmits to them a written declaration to the contrary, such powers and duties shall be discharged by the Vice-President as Acting President.

Section 4 Whenever the Vice-President and a majority of either the principal officers of the executive departments or of such other body as Congress may by law provide, transmit to the President pro tempore of the Senate and the Speaker of the House of Representatives their written declaration that the President is unable to discharge the powers and duties of his office, the Vice-President shall immediately assume the powers and duties of the office as Acting President.

Thereafter, when the President transmits to the President pro tempore of the Senate and the Speaker of the House of Representatives his written declaration that no inability exists, he shall resume the powers and duties of his office unless the Vice-President and a majority of either the principal officers of the executive department or of such other body as Congress may by law provide, transmit within four days to the President pro tempore of the Senate and the Speaker of the House of Representatives their written declaration that the President is unable to discharge the powers and duties of his office. Thereupon Congress shall decide the issue, assembling within forty-eight hours for that purpose if not in session. If the Congress, within twenty-one days after receipt of the latter written declaration, or, if Congress is not in session, within twenty-one days after Congress is required to assemble, determines by two-thirds vote of both Houses that the President is unable to discharge the powers and duties of his office, the Vice-President shall continue to discharge the same as Acting President; otherwise the President shall resume the powers and duties of his office.

This amendment was designed to deal with the problem of presidential disability and succession. In 1973 criminal charges forced Vice President Spiro Agnew to resign. President Richard Nixon invoked this amendment to nominate Gerald Ford as Agnew's successor, and Congress confirmed his selection. Less than a year later, following Nixon's resignation, Ford followed the amendment to nominate Nelson Rockefeller as vice president.

Before this amendment established a procedure for determining disability, Presidents Eisenhower, Kennedy, and Johnson had informal arrangements with their vice presidents in the event they were incapacitated. When President Ronald Reagan was hospitalized for a few days in 1985, he publicly transferred power to his vice president. The subject of presidential disability, obviously, is a very sensitive one, opening the possibility that a politically protagonistic Congress might deal unfairly with a president only marginally disabled. Presumably, the requirement for a two-thirds vote is designed to safeguard against that contingency. In 1918 President Woodrow Wilson suffered a stroke, and serious questions were raised about his ability to conduct the nation's affairs. This amendment would have provided a procedure for inquiring into the president's effectiveness in such a case.

Amendment XXVI [Adopted June 30, 1971]

Section 1 The right of citizens of the United States, who are eighteen years of age or older, to vote shall not be denied or abridged by the United States or by any State on account of age.

Section 2 The Congress shall have power to enforce this article by appropriate legislation.

In 1970 Congress passed a voting rights act lowering the voting age to 18 in both federal and state elections. But the Supreme Court quickly ruled that Congress lacked legislative authority to determine requirements for state elections. Congress responded with this amendment to eliminate confusion. The unusually quick ratification by the states resulted from pressures generated by the Vietnam War, especially the growing belief that if young people could serve in the military they should be entitled to all the rights and privileges of adults.

Amendment XXVII [Adopted May 18, 1992]

No law, varying the compensation for the services of the Senators and Representatives, shall take effect until an election of Representatives shall have intervened.

First proposed as an amendment in 1789 along with the first ten amendments but ratified by only six states. In 1982 Gregory Watson, a University of Texas student, began a campaign to have it submitted to the states again and it was finally approved in 1992.

LITERATURE & DRAMA

World Literature 338

Literature of the Ancient World...........338

Medieval Europe................................339

Renaissance Europe 339

17th Century Europe..........................340

18th Century Europe..........................340

19th Century Europe..........................341

Late-19th Century and 20thCentury Europe 341

Russian Literature............................342

Latin-American Literature.................343

Chinese Literature 344

Japanese Literature 345

Indian Literature...............................346

African Literature..............................347

English Poetry...........................348

The English Novel.....................354

American Literature 358

Colonial Period through the 18th Century 358

18th Century Enlightenment and Revolution 359

The 19th Century 359

Transcendentalism, Romanticism, and the American Renaissance.........360

Late 19th- through Early 20th Century Literature 362

Mid-to Late 20th Century and Beyond ..365

Times Focus: *New Wave of Writers Reinvents Literature By Michiko Kakutani 366*

Popular Literature....................368

Mystery Fiction 369

Romance Novels 372

Science Fiction and Fantasy 373

History of Western Drama 374

Greek Drama 374

Roman Drama 375

Medieval Drama (ca. 500–1500) 375

Theater of the Italian Renaissance (ca. 1300–1600) 376

Elizabethan and Jacobean Drama (1558–1642) 376

William Shakespeare 377

French Neoclassical Theater and Molière 379

Restoration Drama (1660–1700)..........380

18th Century Drama..........................380

19th Century American Drama............381

Modern Drama in Europe 381

Modern American Drama 382

British and American Theater since 1960 383

World Theater 384

Glossary of Literary Terms........384

LITERATURE

World Literature

Literature of the Ancient Western World

Western literature begins with the Babylonian poem *Gilgamesh*, composed probably ca. 2000 B.C. but known most completely from Akkadian-language clay tablets in the library of King Assurbanipal at Nineveh (r. 668–626 B.C.). It presents a mythical account of the exploits of an ancient king of southern Mesopotamia; some of its episodes parallel other accounts in ancient Middle Eastern literature such as the biblical narrative of Noah and the Flood. *Gilgamesh* tells of a king who, through the actions of the gods and his friendship with the "wild man" Enkidu, learns to forsake the tyranny with which he had ruled his subjects. Contemporary with the Gilgamesh epic is a cycle of hymns to the Sumerian goddess Inanna (2000 B.C.), known to the Babylonians as Ishtar and a precursor of the Greek goddess Aphrodite.

The most important work of early Egyptian literature is the *Book of Going Forth by Day* (earliest portions ca. 2300–2100 B.C.; also known as the "Egyptian Book of the Dead"), a collection of incantations and spells (in many different versions) placed in tombs as guides for the dead in their journey to the afterlife. Ancient Egyptian literature is also rich in poetry, including love poems, hymns to the gods, and evocations of daily life, written over a period of many centuries from the late third millennium to the early first millennium B.C. The story of "The Sailor and the Wonder Island," from the Middle Kingdom (2022–1850 B.C.) has some parallels with the later Greek myth of Atlantis. (For the Hebrew Bible, a work of great literary as well as religious and historical importance, see "The Bible.")

Greek literature begins with Homer (ca. 800 B.C.), by tradition a blind poet who composed and sang the two great epic poems, *The Iliad* and *The Odyssey*, that are considered the cornerstones of western literature. The background of both is the Trojan War, believed to have been fought around 1100 B.C. and, according to Homer, caused by the abduction of Helen, wife of the Greek king, Menelaus, by Paris, a Trojan prince. *The Iliad* tells the story of the 10-year siege of Troy by the Greeks with all of the action centered on the final year, and the fierce warrior and demigod Achilles as the central character. *The Odyssey* relates the story of Odysseus, a wily Greek leader who after the success of his scheme to penetrate the walls of Troy with a wooden horse, is forced by the god Poseidon to wander for 10 years before he can return home to Ithaca, his beloved wife, Penelope, and his faithful son, Telemachus. Both epics are filled with gripping scenes of war, love, loyalty, and betrayal—all the elements we have come to associate with brilliant stories that help to illuminate the human experience. Although Homer is always credited as the author, some scholars believe they are the work of more than one person.

Another important poet of this period was Hesiod (ca. 700 B.C.), whose poem *Theogony* is a leading source of information about the deities of ancient Greek religion, and whose *Works and Days* celebrates the pleasures of agrarian and pastoral life. Other important early Greek poets were Archilocus (ca. 650 B.C.); Alacaeus (ca. 620–580 B.C.); Sappho (fl. ca. 612 B.C.), the first woman poet known by name; and Anacreon (sixth century B.C.).

Greek literary work of the high classical period was dominated by writing for the theater: the tragedies of Aeschylus, Sophocles, and Euripides, and the comedies of Aristophanes and Menander (see *Drama*). Their contemporary Pindar (518–446 B.C.) was considered the greatest poet of his age, famed for celebratory choral verse (lyric odes), while Demosthenes (384–322 B.C.) was regarded as the greatest orator. Expository prose writing also flourished in classical Greece, reaching hitherto unknown levels of logical and rhetorical power in the histories of Herodotus (ca. 484–425 B.C.) and Thucydides (ca. 470–425 B.C.) and in the philosophical and scientific works of Plato, Aristotle, and Euclid, among many others.

Poetry blossomed in the Hellenic Period that followed the end of the Classical Greek era (conventionally dated to the death of Aristotle). Theocritus (fl. 270 B.C.) was the inventor of the pastoral ode, while Appollonius Rhodius (fl. third century B.C.) wrote epic poetry in Homeric style, including the *Argonautica*. Hundreds of Hellenic poems are preserved in the Greek *Anthology*, which has as its core the first-century B.C. collection *The Garland* edited by the poet Meleager (ca. 140–70 B.C.), and was augmented by a series of editors over the next millennium. Among the many poets represented in the earlier (and generally finer) layers of the anthology, particularly with short, epigrammatic verses, are Callimachus (ca. 300–240 B.C.), Antipater of Sidon (ca. 130 B.C.), Philodemus (110–40 B.C.), and Lucilius (99–55 B.C.).

Latin writing prior to the first century was largely derivative of, or reactive against, Greek literature, and did not cohere into a Latin literature as such. The situation changed drastically in the last century of the Roman Republic, with the lyric love poetry of Catullus (84–54 B.C.) constrasting with the *De Rerum Natura* ("The Nature of Things") and other long expository poems by Lucretius (95–54 B.C.). Latin prose came of age in the works of Cicero (106–43 B.C.) and Julius Caesar (ca. 100–44 B.C.). Virgil (70–19 B.C.), the greatest of the Latin epic poets, is known for his long pastoral poems, the *Eclogues* and the *Georgics*, but especially for his epic masterpiece, the *Aeneid*, which tells the story of the founding of Rome by Aeneas, a prince of Troy driven away by the Greek conquest in the Trojan War.

Horace (65–8 B.C.) was the greatest master of Latin lyric poetry; his *Odes and Epistles* take brilliant advantage of the grammatical complexities and expressive possibilities of Latin. The republican era of Latin literature effectively comes to an end with Ovid (43 B.C.–A.D. 19), who forsook an official career for his poetry, and spent the last decade of his life in exile on the Black Sea. His amatory and erotic verse, *Amores* ("The Loves") and *Ars Amatoria* ("The Art of Love"), won him fame and notoriety; his *Metamorphoses* ("Transformations") are meditations on the ceaseless changes that affect gods, humans, and the natural world.

Medieval Europe

The earliest medieval European literature was written in Latin, and, whether prose, poetry, or drama, predominantly expressed Christian themes. Vernacular literature first appeared ca. 800 with the now fragmentary epic in High German, the *Lay of Hildebrand*. Much of Europe's literature before the 12th century, including epics and ballads, was communicated orally, and Old Norse (Norwegian) oral poetry migrated to Iceland, where heroic narratives called "eddas" were written down from ca. 1100 to ca. 1350. France's national epic, the *Chanson de Roland*, appeared ca. 1100, followed during the ensuing century by Spain's *Cantar del Mio Cid* and at the turn of the 13th century by Germany's *Nibelungenlied*.

The Christian romance form, based largely on British-Celtic Arthurian legend, also appeared in 12th-century France, where its leading practitioner was Chrétien de Troyes. In Germany, Wolfram von Eschenbach composed his long great romance *Parzival* about 1220. During this same period lyric poetry was developed by the troubadours in southern France and spread to northern France and to Germany, where its exponents were known as "minnesingers." In the 13th century, allegorical fable and romance arose in France, best represented by the long symbolic poem of courtly love, *Roman de la Rose*.

The French lyric tradition was also picked up in Sicily, where the first sonnets are believed to have been composed in the 13th century, leading to the northward spread of a "sweet new style" and the birth of a great Italian vernacular (Tuscan) literature. Its supreme poetic voice was the Florentine politician Dante Alighieri (1265–1321), creator, in the early 14th century, of one of the transcendent works of world literature, *The Divine Comedy*, an allegorical tour of heaven, hell, and purgatory that embodies all medieval Christianity within the limits of the poet's own time and country.

Dante entitled his poem of three books, 100 cantos, and more than 14,000 intricately rhymed lines simply *La Commodia*, indicating that it was a positive or happy pilgrimage by the poet (representing Dante himself) from darkness, or ignorance, to a glimpse of the ultimate light and truth emanating from the heavenly God. He is guided by the Roman poet Virgil through the nine circles of hell and seven stages of purgatory, all astonishingly imagined and vividly populated by historical persons and the poet's own acquaintances. And when the pagan Virgil can take him no farther, Beatrice, Dante's ideal human, now become celestial, leads him triumphantly, though less dramatically, through the radiant spheres of Paradise.

Later in that century, another Tuscan, Petrarch, wrote a series of sonnets that became for centuries the foundation for that international verse form. His contemporary, Giovanni Boccaccio, produced the volume of tales, *The Decameron*, that is the foundation for all prose storytelling.

After the troubadours, lyric poetry became a profession, consummately practiced in 15th-century France by Francois Villon. In 1499 the first European novel, *La Celestina*, probably by Fernando de Rojas, appeared in Spain.

Renaissance Europe

Literature in the Tuscan dialect flourished during the reign of Lorenzo de'Medici, prince of Florence in the late 15th century; in the 16th century two of the greatest humanistic works appeared: Ludovico Ariosto's epic

Orlando Furioso (1516), and Baldassare Castiglione's *The Courtier* (1528), a series of dialogues on courtly requirements and behavior. Niccolò Machiavelli's *The Prince* (1513), expressing a ruthlessly pragmatic view of statecraft and centralized power, is one of history's most enduring political treatises. Among the best Italian lyric poets of the 16th century were Torquato Tasso, who also wrote an epic of the First Crusade; and Michelangelo Buonarotti (the great painter and sculptor).

The Italian Renaissance moved to France, where it so influenced lyric poetry that a group of poets known as the Pléiade, led by Pierre de Ronsard (1524–85), reacted by dedicating themselves to writing verse that was more distinctly French. Other important 16th-century French literary figures wrote prose. François Rabelais (1490–1553) composed four extended comic, socially incisive tales about the father-and-son giants Gargantua and Pantagruel between 1532 and 1552. Michel de Montaigne (1533–92) was the first great modern essayist, who commented, from a classical, humanist, skeptical perspective, on a great range of subjects.

In Spain the late 16th century and the 17th century are known as a Golden Age of literature, and its poets, including Garcilaso de la Vega (1503?–36), were also inspired by the Italian tradition. A new genre, the chivalric novel, had arisen early in the 16th century, and led ironically to the great masterpiece of all Spanish literature, Miguel de Cervantes's (1547–1616) *Don Quixote de la Mancha* (1605–15), a mock-chivalric, all-encompassing novel of an idealistic but all-too-flawed "knight's" adventures.

The hero of the novel (in two books—Parts I and II, published a decade apart), is an old gentleman who has been so addled by his reading of romances that he fancies himself a knight and undertakes, in the company of his peasant "squire," Sancho Panza, to spread his noble influence across Spain—a panorama richly and hilariously imagined. This allows the narrator to observe all Spanish society, and ultimately, all humanity, under the dual lenses of illusion and reality, in a work identified as the first modern novel by many and as the greatest novel by some.

Before the Protestant Reformation in the 16th century, Catholic humanist writing, embracing a modern, skeptical view of church organization and materialism, took hold in northern Europe, including Martin Luther's Germany. The greatest humanists were Thomas More in England and, in Holland, Desiderius Erasmus (1466?–1536), who promoted church reform and further challenged the institution in his satirical book *The Praise of Folly* (1509).

17th-Century Europe

In France the 17th century was a period of growing political and cultural influence during which, under rigid state control, literary language and sensibility were refined and confined to an almost doctrinal Classicism. The greatest Classical writers were playwrights of the middle and late century: the tragedians Pierre Corneille and Jean Racine and the comedian Molière (see *Drama*). The leading nondramatic poets were the satirist (and critic) Nicolas Boileau-Despreaux (1636–1711) and the great fable-writer Jean de La Fontaine (1621–95). Distinguished prose was exhibited in the *Maximes* of François, duc de La Rochefoucauld (1613–80), and the *Pensées* of Blaise Pascal (1623–62). In 1678 Madame de La Fayette (1634–92) produced the first significant French novel, *La Princesse de Clèves*. Nine years earlier, *Simplicissimus*, considered the first German novel, had been published by Hans Jakob von Grimmelshausen (1625–76).

18th-Century Europe

In early 18th-century Germany, French-influenced Classicism brought linguistic and stylistic restrictions such as had been introduced in France. Throughout Europe this would be the Age of the Enlightenment, a time of secular, rationalist vision, when science and humankind were being emphasized more than religion and God.

The Enlightenment was most fully realized in France, where Voltaire (1694–1778) was its dominant voice; his most famous literary work is the satirical tale *Candide* (1759). Another essential figure in this movement was Denis Diderot (1713–84), essayist on the arts and science, novelist and editor of the 28-volume *Encyclopédie*, the very emblem of the age.

A contemporary writer whose original views departed from those of the Enlightenment was Jean-Jacques Rousseau (1712–78), who exhorted humanity to renounce society and rediscover its natural goodness and equality. His *Social Contract* (1762) incorporates these ideas into a political treatise. In addition, he was the author of an important and influential novel, *La Nouvelle Héloise* (1761)

The Enlightenment influenced German rationalist and classicist literature, but more important in the country's literary history is the *Sturm und Drang* ("storm and stress") movement that followed as a reaction. Influenced by Rousseau, *Sturm und Drang* emphasized emotion over reason and self-expression over social norms, and it celebrated nature. Its greatest exponent—one of the great figures in all literature—was Johann Wolfgang von Goethe (1749–1832), whose early play, *Götz von Berlichingen* (1773), and novel, *The Sorrows of Young Werther* (1774), were central to the movement. Its other major voice was Friedrich von Schiller (1759–1805), first heard in the 1781 drama *Die Räuber*. Goethe and Schiller both represented a new and more genuine period of German Classicism. Schiller's most famous work is the play *Wilhelm Tell*; Goethe's is the great dramatic investigation of God and man, *Faust* (1808, 1832), a long poem presented in two parts and in a remarkable variety of styles and poetic meters. Goethe's broad and deep sensibility embraced science, music, philosophy, politics, and theology. He changed the Faust legend from that of a man who loses his soul after bargaining with the devil to grow in power and knowledge, to that of one who defeats Satan's claim on him when he reaches beyond wordliness to divine redemption. Goethe's Faust, then, is more than a Romantic rebel; he is a type of the European, or Western, man, whose mind and soul are caught between the self, the created world, and its Creator.

19th-Century Europe

Although the French Revolution of 1789 is the great political event at the source of European Romanticism, the movement in fact arrived sooner in Germany than in France. Early German Romantics were the lyric poet (and novelist) Novalis, (1772–1801), and Heinrich von Kleist (1777–1811), a poetic dramatist and the most accomplished author of a newly popular form, the novella (*The Marquise of O and Other Stories* (1810–11). E.T.A. Hoffmann (1776–1822) applied grotesque and supernatural subject matter to this form.

In Germany the philosopher Friedrich von Schlegel (1772–1829) and in France the novelist and literary hostess (Madame) Germaine de Stahl (1766–1817) advocated a new, and international, literature of feeling. Their wish was fulfilled in France by the poetry of Alphonse de Lamartine (1790–1869) and consummately by the writing of Victor Hugo (1802–85), who gained fame as a poet, a dramatist, and especially a novelist (*Notre Dame de Paris* (1832), *Les Misérables* (1862)). Hugo's contribution to a distinguished period of French drama was accompanied by the achievements of Alfred de Vigny and Alfred de Musset. As a popular historical novelist he was rivaled by Alexandre Dumas *père* (1802–70) who wrote *The Three Musketeers* (1844) and *The Count of Monte Cristo* (1845).

From Britain to Russia, the novel came of age in the 1800's. While George Sand (Amandine Dupin, 1804–76) steadily produced romantic works, French fiction was becoming dominated by a series of extraordinary realistic novelists. The earliest of these, Stendhal (1785–1842), author of *The Red and the Black* (1831), was both romantic and realist, for he wrote vividly but unflinchingly about passion and society. French society, in all its colors and textures, its flaws and wonders, was the special study of Honoré de Balzac (1799–1850), whose prolific output of novels and stories is known as *La Comédie Humaine*. He was followed by the quintessential French realist, Gustave Flaubert (1821–80), whose *Madame Bovary* (1857) depicts a heroine whose illusory romanticism is doomed in a dull provincial world.

French poetry, too, departed from strictly Romantic pathos as the mid-century approached. Perhaps the most original French poetic voice of the century was that of Charles Baudelaire (1821–67), who was also an aesthete, a Symbolist, and in some degree a romantic in his sensitivity to emotional pain and the corruption that infected beauty. His *Fleurs du Mal* (1857) is a landmark of European poetry.

The "Young Germany" movement was an organized reaction against Romantic poetry, and its most significant figure was Heinrich Heine (1797–1856). Although political in outlook—immersed in the French Revolution and critical of German nationalism—he was a splendid love poet and the finest German lyric poet of the century. In France the second half of the century was the period of Symbolist and Decadent poetry, both influenced by Baudelaire. Paul Verlaine (1844–96) belonged to the first movement in his early career and the second in later life. His protégé as a Symbolist (and also his lover) was Arthur Rimbaud (1854–91). The latter's dreamlike verse differed from the elliptically phrased, pessimistic symbolism of Stephan Mallarmé (1842–98).

In fiction, the literary movement that succeeded realism was naturalism, which depicted humanity, often in disturbing detail, as determined by nature and environment. Its well-known practitioners were Émile Zola (1840–92) and Guy de Maupassant (1850–93). Zola's Rougon-Macquart sequence of novels, including *Nana* (1880), examined the life of the lower classes. De Maupassant's masterly, brief, often bitter short stories have always been widely read. An important later naturalist was the German playwright, novelist, and poet Gerhart Hauptmann (1862–1946)

Late-19th and 20th-Century Europe

In southern Europe the careers of two major writers straddled the border of the 20th century. Italy's Gabriele D'Annunzio (1863–1938) first made his mark as a sensuous poet in the 1880's, and soon turned to writing novels, then plays. A nationalist and Word War I airforce hero. D'Annunzio's reputation is besmirched by his embrace of fascism. A contemporary literary star in Spain was Miguel de Unamuno (1864–1936), a philosopher turned novelist and poet who searched for political and religious certainty.

The leading French poets of the early 20th century were Paul Claudel (1868–1955), a mystical Catholic who was also a major playwright; Paul Valéry (1871–1945), who picked up the Symbolist tradition; and Guillaume Appollinaire (1880–1918), a modernist influenced by Cubist painting. The great novelists were Marcel Proust (1871–1922), whose seven-novel sequence, *Remembrance of Things Past*, published from 1913 until after his death, is one of the greatest achievements in psychological literature; and André Gide (1869–1951), a writer who examined individual freedom (*The Immoralist*, 1902) and increasingly explored technical innovation.

The men widely regarded as the Germany's greatest 20th-century poet and novelist, Rainer Maria Rilke and Thomas Mann, were both born in 1875. Like Appollinaire, Rilke (d. 1926) was inspired by modern art and was a strongly visual poet who explored both spirituality and erotic love. Mann (d. 1955), who moved to America during the Nazi regime, was a profound, wide-ranging writer who explored eroticism and the meaning of art in novels such as *The Magic Mountain* (1924).

Mann's contemporary, Hermann Hesse (1875–1962), was a psychological, symbolic novelist whose spiritual interest was directed to the East (*Siddhartha*, 1922). One of the most distinct voices in 20th-century fiction is that of a Czech Jew who wrote in German, Franz Kafka (1883–1924). The nightmarish anxiety that entraps his characters in works such as *The Metamorphosis* (1917) seemed to represent the political and psychological conditions of the age.

In the years before the 1930's civil war, poetry flourished in Spain, including that of two Andalusian poets, Juan Ramon Jiménez (1881–1958; 1956 Nobel Prize), and Federico García Lorca (1898–1936), a compassionate and popular surrealist poet and dramatist who was killed by Revolutionary forces.

The French novel continued to develop in many directions. In the 1920's and 30's two profound Catholic writers, François Mauriac (1885–1970) and Georges Bernanos (1888–1948), emerged, followed by the politically tumultuous works of André Malraux (1901–76), best known for *La Condition Humaine* (1933); and the innovative, sometimes obscene and bigoted, novels of Céline (1894–1961). Soon there appeared the great French existentialist philosopher novelists, for whom modern life was godless and without intrinsic meaning: Jean-Paul Sartre (1905–80), whose first, and most famous, novel was *Nausea* (1938); and Albert Camus (1913–60), whose first, and most famous, novel was *The Stranger* (1942). In 1937 another major writer grouped with the existentialists, the Irishman Samuel Beckett (1906–89), moved to Paris and soon began writing novels and plays in French.

Italy, too, produced important novelists toward the mid-century, including Alberto Moravia (1907–90), a close observer of uprooted modern humanity; and Italo Calvino (1923–85), who wrote in both realistic and fantastic modes. The Spanish novelist Camilo José Cela (b. 1916) won a Nobel Prize in 1989, as did the Italian poet Eugenio Montale (1896–1981) in 1975.

After the Second World War a main current in French fiction was experimental, often depriving the reader of familiar patterns of time, plot, even character—the *nouveau roman*, represented by authors such as Romain Gary (1914–80), Marguerite Duras (1914–96), and Alain Robbe-Grillet (b. 1922). Understandably, German writers examined a society devastated by the experience of Nazism and war. Heinrich Böll (1917–85) and Günter Grass (b. 1927) were internationally popular novelists in the late 20th century. Grass's novel *The Tin Drum* (1961) helped to earn him the Nobel Prize.

Russian Literature

Except for some oral secular poems, the earliest Russian literature, after the introduction of Christianity in 988, was almost entirely religious, until the nation's first great work, the heroic *Song of Igor's Campaign*, was completed 1187. The first significant work with a known author was a late 14th-century epic imitative of the Igor tale, *Beyond the River Don*, by Sophonia of Ryazin, which celebrated a victory over the Tatars. The following centuries produced some interesting travel writing, more dogmatic religious writing and some political polemics, but Russian literature did not begin to hit stride until Czar Peter the Great welcomed Westernization in the second half of the 17th century. The first theater opened in 1662, and a new poetic style and prose fiction were introduced.

In the 18th century, a specific Russian literary language was developed, codified by Mikhail Lomonosov (1711–65), who was distinguished amid a thriving crop of poets. The first native dramatist was Aleksandr Sumarokov (1718–77). Empress Catherine the Great, whose reign began in

1762, felt the breath of the European Enlightenment and herself wrote plays, though she also punished writers who displeased her.

Romantic poetry was introduced to Russia through the translations and original poems of Vasily Zhukovsky (1783–1852), clearing a path for Russia's greatest poet, Aleksandr Pushkin (1799–1837), who was a superb lyric and narrative poet and a complexly ironic composer of parodies. His most famous works are the great verse-novel *Eugene Onegin*, (1823–31), a tragic tale of love and egotism; and the historical drama *Boris Godunov* (1831).

The first important 19th-century Russian fiction writer, Nikolai Gogol (1809–52), known for his stories and the novel *Dead Souls* (1842), has been hailed as both the first Russian realist and as a comic fantasist. A parade of great prose artists followed. A chief "Westernizer" was Ivan Turgenev (1818–83), a controversial critic of Russian society, best known for *Fathers and Sons* (1862). His contemporary was the brilliant novelist Fyodor Dostoyevsky (1821–81), author of *Crime and Punishment* (1866) and *The Brothers Karamazov* (1880). A more realistic, yet no less profound and emotionally vivid writer was Leo Tolstoy, (1828–1910), whose historical *War and Peace* (1865–69) and passionate *Anna Karenina* (1874–77) are among the world's greatest novels. And the compassionate, moral tales of Anton Chekhov are among the world's best short stories, while his sad, realistic, internationally produced plays are the finest written by any Russian.

Writers such as the novelist and poet Andrei Bely (1880–1934) formed a significant Symbolist movement around the turn of the 20th century. A reactive movement, that of the "acmeists," emphasized precision in poetry. Its principal voice was Osip Mandelstam (1892–1938). He and Maxim Gorky (1868–1936) were the last important writers to express themselves before the Communist revolution of 1917—although Gorky's "social realism" (as revealed in the play *The Lower Depths*, 1902) was in fact a forerunner of Soviet literature.

Bolshevism stifled artistic expression, yet some writing of distinction was produced in the following decades, including the epic novels of Mikhail Sholokhov (1905–84), the stories of Isaac Babel (1894–1940), and the satirical works of Mikhail Bulgakov (1891–1940) and Aleksey Tolstoy (1883–1945). After the death of Josef Stalin a more tolerant period of expression was marked by the 1954 publication of Ilya Ehrenburg's (1891–1967) novel *The Thaw*. Boris Pasternak's (1890–1960) famous *Dr. Zhivago* followed in 1957. And the poems of Yevgeny Yevtushenko (b. 1933) became well known outside his homeland. The powerfully anti-Soviet work of Aleksandr Solzhenitsyn (b. 1918), however, beginning with the novel *A Day in the Life of Ivan Denisovich* (1962), led to his exile in 1974. He later returned to a Russia in which he was free to express his religious beliefs, along with another member of the Tolstoy family, Tatyana Tolstaya (b. 1951), whose spiritually informed short stories continued to move that distinguished Russian form forward.

Latin-American Literature

The effective beginning of literature in Latin America is the appearance in Chile in 1569 of the epic poem *La Araucana* by a native Spaniard, Alonso de Ercilla y Zúñiga (1533–94); it is a tribute to the Indian tribe with whom the Spanish had warred. This pattern was reversed in the 17th century, when a Mexican-born poet, Juan Ruiz de Alarcón (1581?–1639), moved to Spain and became one of that country's greatest dramatists. A much later Mexican, writing near the end of colonial times, José Joaquín Fernández de Lizardi (1776–1827), published the first Latin-American novel, *The Itching Parrot*, in 1816–30.

In the first half of the 19th century the Ecuadorian José Joaquin Olmedo (1780–1847) celebrated the continent's independence movement and its great hero in the poem *La Victoria Junín: Canto a Bolívar* (1825). The Venezualan-born Andres Bello (1781–1865) wrote poetry about agrarian life. The next generation of poets were primarily Romantics, who expressed the ideal of freedom in an age of political independence. Chief among them were the Argentinians Esetban Echevarría (1805–51) and Domingo Faustino Sarmiento (1811–88), both of whom protested against a tyrannical ruler. And out of their romantic enthusiasm for their land emerged the South American tradition of gaucho (or cowboy) literature, in particular *Martin Fierro* (1872), Argentina's national epic, by José Hernández (1834–86). Meanwhile, in Peru, Ricardo Palma (1833–1919) introduced another traditional Latin-American genre, the historical anecdote.

The novel flourished in the latter part of the century, the most popular being the tragic *Maria* (1867) by Colombia's Jorge Isaacs (1837–95). Brazil produced several important novelists, including the realists Aluisio Azevedo (1857–1913) and Joaquim Maria Machado de Assis (1839–1908).

As the century drew to a close, writers embraced an experimental style known as *modernismo*. The Mexican poet and story-writer Manuel Guittierez Najera (1859–95) and the Cuban poet (and, in spite of the movement's contrary trend, revolutionary warrior) José Martí (1853–95) were principal initiators. The most important *modernista* was Nicaragua's Rubén Darío (1867–1916), a poet whose influence was felt strongly even in Spain.

Modernismo influenced a group of women lyrical poets in the early decades of the 20th century, including Chile's Gabriela Mistral (1889–1957), who in 1945 became the first Latin American to win the Nobel Prize in Literature. Another Chilean poet, Pablo Neruda (1904–73), would receive that honor in 1971.

Both nonfiction and fiction prose writers in the 20th century were affected by the Mexican Revolution of 1910 and inclined to address economic and social conditions. The outstanding novel of that uprising was Matriana Azuela's (1873–1952) *The Underdogs* (1915). A less prominent uprising was depicted by the Brazilian novelist Euclides da Cunha (1866–1909) in *Rebellion in the Backlands* (1902), which also described the harsh penurious living conditions of provincial people. Such problems were also addressed in a series of "Indian" novels, including *Birds Without a Nest* (1889) by Clorinda Matto de Turner (1852–1909) and *Peru and The Indian* (1935) by Gregorio Lopez de Fuentes (1897–1966) in Mexico.

Many novelists in the first half of the century wrote about the challenges of life in specific environments. Among them, Ricardo Guiraldes (1886–1927) wrote about the gauchos of the Argentine pampas, Jóse Eustasio Rivera (1889–1928) about the Colombian jungle, Manuel Gálvez (1882–1962) about urban social problems in Argentina, and Jorge Amado (b. 1912) about the hardships of cacao-harvesting in Brazil.

Since the 1960's Latin-American literature—fiction, especially—has burst forth with such creativity that the period has been called "El Boom." One of century's greatest Spanish-American writers, Argentina's Jorge Luis Borges (1899–1986), wrote only short tales, poems, and essays. His tales, though—fantastic, symbolic, elusive, and allusive—are something like a new literary form.

The new direction in Latin-American literature can be seen in the surrealism of Guatemalan novelist Miguel Ángel Asturias (1899–1974), a 1967 Nobel laureate. He is linked with the great trend of the time, "Magical Realism," a term introduced by Cuban novelist Alfonso Carpentier (1904–80) and signifying a blend of fantasy and reality. The most thoroughgoing, most widely read magical realist is Gabriel García Márquez (b. 1928), Colombian author of *One Hundred Years of Solitude* (1967) and a 1982 Nobel winner. Other exponents are the Mexican Carlos Fuentes (b. 1928) and, at least partially, the Chilean Isabel Allende (b. 1942). The most admired Brazilian novel of the last half century is *The Devil to Pay in the Backlands* (1956) by João Guimarães Rosa (1908–67). Peru's leading contemporary novelist is Mario Vargas Llosa (b. 1936) After Neruda, Latin America's premier poet has been Mexico's Octavio Paz (1914–98), who became his country's first Nobel laureate in 1990.

Chinese Literature

The earliest surviving Chinese writings, dating from the 13th century B.C., are divination records inscribed on animal bones and turtle shells ("oracle bones"); despite their considerable historical value, they do not amount to literature in the usual sense of the term. Literary values can be seen in some inscriptions on bronze ritual vessels dating to the Western Zhou period (ca. 1046–771 B.C.), commemorating feasts, wars, royal gifts to aristocrats, and similar events.

Three books represent the foundation of the Chinese literary tradition. The *Shujing* ("Book of Documents"), a collection of historical accounts, contains some material that may date to the early Western Zhou period as well as later materials. The *Chunqiu* ("Chronicle of Springs and Autumns") is a chronicle of the aristocratic state of Lu for the years 722–481 B.C. The *Shijing* ("Book of Poetry") preserves over 300 poems from the Zhou period, comprising liturgical hymns, folk songs, elite poetry, and other types.

These three works were regarded as classics of great literary and moral value by Confucius (Kongzi, 551–479 B.C.), whose own teachings were recorded in the *Lunyü* ("Analects of Confucius") by his followers over a long period of time, ca. 450–250 B.C. The period after about 400 B.C. saw a dramatic increase in the production and circulation of written documents of all kinds, and marks the first great age of Chinese philosophical literature. Important philosophical works include eponymous books by the Confucian followers Mengzi ("Mencius," ca. 387–303 B.C.) and Xunzi (ca. 307–235 B.C.); the *Mozi*, ascribed to a rival of Confucius and compiled in stages ca. 400–200 B.C.; the Daoist classics *Laozi* or *Daodejing* ("The Way and Its Power"), ascribed to the legendary "Lao Dan," sixth century B.C., but actually dating from ca. 320–220 B.C.; and *Zhuangzi*, third century B.C.; and the works of "Legalist" thinkers Shang Yang ("Lord Shang"), fourth century B.C., and Han Feizi (d. 233 B.C.). Narrative nonfiction and protofiction flourished in such collections as the *Guoyü* ("Narratives of the States"), *Zhanguoce* ("Intrigues of the Warring States"), and the

Guanzi ("Book of Master Guan"). A southern tradition of poetry is preserved in the *Chuci* ("Elegies of Chu"), the earliest portions of which are ascribed to the statesman-poet Qu Yuan (fourth century B.C.).

In the Han Dynasty (206 B.C.–A.D. 220), most of the works mentioned above were edited into the form in which they are presently known. A tradition of historical writing was established by Sima Qian (ca. 145–90 B.C.) in the *Shiji* ("Records of the Historian") and Ban Biao (A.D. 3–54) and his son Ban Gu (32–92) in the *Han shu* ("History of the [Former] Han Dynasty"); their works served as the model for subsequent official dynastic histories compiled throughout the imperial era. Poetry flourished as folk lyrics were collected and edited by the official Music Bureau, and named poets worked in several genres, including the characteristically *Han fu* ("rhapsody") style of long, rococo narrative verse.

The great age of Chinese poetry was the Tang Dynasty (618–907), during which the principal genre was highly formal *shi* ("regulated verse"). In a time of poetic genius, the greatest figures included Wang Wei (699–761), Li Bo (or Li Bai, 701–762), Du Fu (712-770), the courtesan-poet Xue Tao (768–831), and Bo Juyi (or Bai Juyi, 772–846). The poet and essayist Han Yü (768–824) led a movement in favor of classical simplicity in prose writing. The art of Chinese fiction advanced in the Tang, with the rise of short stories, often ghost stories or "tales of the strange" with Buddhist or Daoist themes.

Poets of the Song Dynasty (960–1279) favored the *ce* ("song lyric") form; the greatest master of the age was Su Shi (or Su Dongpo, 1036–1101). Classical poetry continued to be written into the 20th century, but with few exceptions it failed to match the brilliance of Tang and Song verse. Under the Mongol Yuan Dynasty (1270–1368) writers turned their attention to the theater, and *qu* ("Chinese opera") scripts became a major genre of literary creation.

Fiction, though despised as "vulgar" by the elite, flourished under the Ming (1368–1644) and Qing (1644–1911) dynasties, when China's major novels were written: *Sanguozhi yanyi* ("Romance of the Three Kingdoms") by Luo Guanzhong (ca. 1330–1400); *Shuihu zhuan* ("Water Margin," also called "Outlaws of the Marsh") by Luo Guanzhong and Shi Nai'an (ca. 1296–1370); *Xiyouji* ("Journey to the West") by Wu Cheng'en (1500–1582), incorporating earlier narratives; the anonymous satirical and erotic classic *Jinpingmei* ("Plum Blossoms in a Golden Vase"), ca. 1618; and the greatest of all, *Hong lou meng* ("Dream of the Red Chamber") by Cao Xueqin (1715–1763).

Following the Republican revolution of 1911, a vernacular literature movement led by Chen Duxiu, Hu Shi , and others led to an outpouring of essays, criticism, translations, and fiction in the new style. The leading master of the new prose was Lu Xun (pen name of Zhou Shuren, 1881–1936), whose short stories helped define an age. Prominent novelists including Ba Jin (pen name of Li Feigan, b. 1904), Guo Moruo (1892–1978), Mao Dun (pen name of Shen Yanbing, 1896–1981), Lao She (pen name of Shu Shuyu, 1899–1966), and Ding Ling (pen name of Jiang Bingzhi, 1904–86) combined social consciousness with a tendency toward romanticism derived from 19th-century Western fiction. The best-known works of these writers include Ba Jin's *Jia* ("Family," 1931) and Lao She's *Luotuo xiangzi* ("Rickshaw," 1936).

Mao Zedong's "Yan'an Talks on Art and Literature" (1943) served notice to artists and writers that their work was expected to serve the interests of the Communist Party; the result was a decades-long literary drought. After Mao's death in 1976, older writers such as Liu Binyan (b. 1925) and Wang Meng (b. 1934) began to write more freely, joined by younger writers such as the novelist Mo Yan (b. 1956; *Red Sorghum* and other novels) and the "misty" poets including Bei Dao (b. 1949) and Mang Ke (b. 1950). A Chinese diaspora literature also began to flourish in the last decades of the 20th century; leading figures include Gao Xingjian (b. 1940, resident of France), author of *Soul Mountain* and other novels; Jung Chang (b. 1952, resident of England), author of *Wild Swans*; and Anchee Min (b. 1957, resident of the U.S.), author of *Red Azalea*.

Japanese Literature

The foundational works of Japanese literature date from the eighth century A.D. Two works of history, the *Kojiki* ("Record of Ancient Matters," 712, written in Classical Chinese) and the *Nihon shoki* or *Nihongi* ("Chronicle of Japan," 720, written in Japanese) recount the history of Japan from its mythical beginnings and underpin the imperial clan's claim to rule. The *Man'yōshuō* ("Book of Ten Thousand Leaves," ca. 759) is Japan's first anthology of poetry. Its more than 4,500 poems include works in both "long poem" (*chōka*) and "short poem" (*tanka*) form, on a wide range of subjects including bereavement, erotic longing, and other emotion-laden themes.

By the early 10th century, with the publication of the anthology *Kokinshō* ("Ancient and Modern Writings," edited by Ki no Turayuki (ca.868–945) and others, the world of Japanese poetry was and would remain dominated by the *tanka*, verse of 31 syllables arranged in five lines of 5, 7, 5, 7, and 7 syllables. The development of a syllabic script (*kana*) for writing Japanese opened the literary world to women writers (men were expected to write prose in formal Classical Chinese, whereas women could write informally in Japanese). The most celebrated writers of the Heian Period (794–1185) were women, including Murasaki Shikibu (ca. 973–?), author of the *Tale of Genji*; and Sei Shōnagon (ca. 966–?), whose *Pillow Book* gives us an intimate picture of Heian court society. The poetic travel diary (e.g., Ki no Turayuki's *Tosa Nikki*) was a favorite genre of Heian authors.

The establishment of samurai military rule in 1185 led to the popularity of novels with military themes, most famously the *Tale of Heike* (anon., ca. 1240). Zen Buddhism influenced many literary works of the Kamakura Period (1185–1333), including belles-lettres essays by Kamo Chōmei (1155–1216, *Hojoki*, "The Ten-Foot-Square Hut") and Yoshida Kenkō (1283–1352, *Tsurezuregusa*, "Essays in Idleness"). The slow, formal, Zen-influenced musical drama known as *Nō* flourished in the ensuing Muromachi Period (1336–1573), with scripts by Zeami (1363–1443) and Sōami (d. 1545). The popularity of *renga* linked-verse (Sogi, 1422–1502, was its greatest practitioner) led to the development of *haiku*, a 17–syllable, 3–line form (5–7–5, essentially the first three lines of a *tanka*). The *haiku* form developed further during the Tokugawa Period (1601–1868); its finest practitioner was Matsuo Bashō (1644–1694), whose poetic travel diary *Oku no hosomichi* ("Narrow Road to the Interior") is one of the great masterpieces of Japanese literature.

Urban culture flourished during the Tokugawa Period, leading to new markets for popular literature and theater. Ihara Saikaku (1642–1693) was known for "Life of an Amorous Woman" and other racy, satirical stories; Chikamatsu Monzaemon (1653–1725), Japan's greatest playwright, wrote scripts used in both *bunraku* puppet theater and *kabuki* live drama.

With the Meiji Restoration (1868) and the creation of modern Japan, literature changed markedly. Western literary forms influenced the essayist Fukuzawa Yōkichi (1835–1901), the novelist and critic Mori ōgai (1862–1922), and others. Yosano Akiko (1878–1942) brought a modernist sensibility to *tanka* poetry in *Midaregami* ("Tangled Hair") and other collections. Other important 20th-century poets include Takamura Kotarō (1883–1956), Nishiwaki Junzaburō (1894–1982), and Ibaragi Noriko (b. 1926).

Twentieth-century Japan also produced many important novelists and short-story writers, including Natsume Sōseki (1867–1916; *Botchan*); Akutagawa Ryōnosuke (1892–1927), whose short story "Rashōmon" was the basis for Kurosawa Akira's famous film; Tanizaki Junichirō (1886–1965; *The Makioka Sisters*); Dazai Osamu (pen name of Tsushima Shuji, 1909–48), who wrote *Ningen Shikkaku* ("Disqualified as a Human"); Kawabata Yasunari (1899–1972, *Snow Country*; *House of the Sleeping Beauties*), who won the 1968 Nobel Prize in Literature; and Mishima Yukio (1925–1970, *Temple of the Golden Pavilioni*), who combined literary genius with theatrical right-wing politics.

The postwar generation of Japanese writers includes Abe Kobo (1924–1993, *Woman in the Dunes*); Oe Kenzaburo (b. 1935, *The Silent Cry*), who won the 1994 Nobel Prize in Literature; Murakami Haruki (b. 1949, *A Wild Sheep Chase*); and Banana Yoshimoto (b. 1964, *Kitchen*). Japan today is home to a very diverse and vibrant literary scene.

Indian Literature

The earliest surviving works of literature from the Indian subcontinent are the Vedas. These were written in Sanskrit, and are dated from 1500 to 1200 B.C. Written in verse, the Vedas contain the essential beliefs and laws of Hinduism. The Upanishads, composed between the eighth and sixth centuries B.C. were written as commentaries on the Vedas.

Two epics, the *Ramayana* and the *Mahabharata*, both written in Sanskrit, are the foundations of Indian mythology. The *Ramayana* (Romance of Rama), made up of seven books and probably written around 300 B.C. by Valmiki, tells the story of the life of Rama, from his birth, to his marriage to Sita, through his quest to rescue Sita from captivity by the demon Ravana, and to their reunion. The *Ramayana* is the source of much Indian literature and dance.

The *Mahabharata* (Great Epic of the Bharata Dynasty), composed between 300 B.C. and A.D. 300 and consisting of close to 100,000 verses, tells the story of the great war between the Pandavas and the Kauravas. The *Bhagavadgita*, contained within the *Mahabharata* and probably one of the later additions to the text (thought to have been written in the first or second century A.D.), is written as a dialogue between Prince Arjuna, one of the Pandavas, and Krishna, who acts as his charioteer in battle.

Bankim Chandra Chatterjee (1838–94) is credited with having first introduced European models of narrative structure to Indian literature. Chatterjee's novels, the most memorable of which are written in Bengali, include *Durgesnandini* and *Rajsimha* (1881). The first Indian writer of modern times to achieve international recognition was Rabindranath Tagore (1861–1941). Born in Calcutta, Tagore, who wrote in Bengali, achieved success first as a poet and later as a novelist and painter. His collection *Gitanjali* was published in English translation in 1910. Tagore won the Nobel Prize in 1913.

R.K. Narayan (1906–2001) was one of the first major Indian literary figures to write in English. Much of his work takes place in Malgudi, a fictitious town in South India. Among his novels are *Swami and Friends* (1935), *The English Teacher* (1945), and *A Tiger for Malgudi* (1983).

Salman Rushdie, born in Bombay in 1947, first rose to international prominence with the publication of his second novel, *Midnight's Children* (1981), which uses magical realism to chronicle the history of India after the end of British rule. Rushdie's other works include *The Satanic Verses* (1988), *The Moor's Last Sigh* (1995), and *The Ground Beneath Her Feet* (1999).

The literature of the Indian subcontinent appears today in many languages, including Bengali, Hindi, Tamil, and others. It is, however, those writing in English, many of whom live abroad, who have achieved the greatest international acclaim. Among this group are Amitav Ghosh, born in Calcutta in 1956, whose book *Shadowlines* chronicles the effects of partition; and Arundhati Roy (b. 1961), whose first novel, *The God of Small Things* (1998), won the Booker Prize.

African Literature

A rich and diverse oral literary tradition in Africa extends from the distant past to the present time. Marked by wordplay and musical accompaniment, this tradition comprised myths, folktales, dramas, poems, songs, parables, riddles, and other forms. Since ancient African languages were exclusively oral, written literature on the continent did not begin until Arab conquests in North Africa brought Arabic language and culture to the continent. A poet of African birth, Antar, wrote in Arabic in the sixth and seventh centuries.

The first evidence of indigenous written African literature is in the East African Swahili language in the mid-17th century, and from 1728 there is a manuscript of a Swahili epic, *Ubendi wa Tambuka*. This work, as well as 19th-century poems in the Hausa languge of Nigeria, was set down in Arabic script. After the arrival of Europeans, the Latin alphabet was used, and many Africans, including several writers who escaped slavery, wrote in European languages. The most important and thorough early account of the life of a freed slave was published in 1789 by a Nigerian who had been shackled and sent to the American South, and later lived free in England: *The Interesting Narrative of the Life and Adventures of Olaudah Equiano or Gustavus Vassa, the African*. In the late 19th century, the Angolan poet Caetano da Costa Alegre of São Tomé became the first African to write literature in Portuguese.

In the 20th century African writing blossomed in both native and colonial tongues, in fiction, poetry, and drama. The first African writer to be read internationally was Thomas Mofolo of Lesotho (South Africa), who wrote novels in the Sotho language, including *Chaka* (1925), about a Zulu warrior. In 1934 James Mbotela published the first Swahili work of fiction; and beginning in 1939, Olorunfemi Fagunwa of Nigeria wrote a series of groundbreaking novels in Yoruba. Among native-language poets, Tanzania's Shaaban Robert Swahili and South Africa's S. E. K Mqhayi in Xhosa stand out. Perhaps the finest African poet of the first half century was Jean-Joseph Rabéarivelo of Madagascar, who wrote dreamy, imagistic poems in French.

Ironically, the French language gave a voice to a group of writers who expressed alienation from their African roots. These were the poets of the *négritude* movement, which arose in the 1930's, and whose most famous exponent was Léopold Senghor, who would become the first president of Senegal.

A boom in African writing coincided with the independence movement after World War II, and much of the literature is charged with reaction against colonial influence. The principal novelists have written in French and English. In the 1950's, two Cameroonians, Ferdinand Oyono (*Houseboy*, 1956) and Mongo Beti (*The Poor Christ of Bomba*, 1956), wrote novels critical of French cultural impositions; and two Nigerians published important books of fiction in English: Amos Tutuola's folklore-rooted tales have been popular well beyond Africa, and Chinua Achebe's *Things Fall Apart* (1958) became a famous novel about the clash of European and native sensibilities. Among novels in English, the Mau Mau rebellion in Kenya is the background for *Weep Not Child* (1964), by Ngugi Wa Thiong'o; and exile is a theme of South African Es'kia Mphahlele's *The Wanderers* (1971). More recently, the Nigerian Ben Okri has applied the magic-realism motif in his novels, including *The Famished Road* (1991).

The *négritude* movement in poetry endured into the 1950's and 1960's in the writings of Tchicaya U Tam'si of the Congo and David Diop of Senegal. Agostinho Neto, the first Angolan president, was a leading Portuguese-language poet. Significant English-language poets since the

1960's have included Christopher Okigbo of Nigeria, Okot p'Bitek of Uganda, Kofi Awoonor of Ghana, and Dennis Brutus of South Africa.

Another important Nigerian poet is Wole Soyinka, better known as a playwright and the first African to win a Nobel Prize in Literature (1986). His works, ranging from the comic (*The Lion and the Jewel*, 1963) to the intellectually complex (*Death and the King's Horsemen*, 1975), are inflected by Yoruba culture yet satirically focused on contemporary politics.

Two separate traditions of African writing are the Afrikaans and English literature produced by white South Africans. In the 20th century, Afrikaans literature was distinguished by a strong poetic tradition, particularly the "Poets of the 30's." Another group, the "writers of the 60's," included poets and novelists such as André P. Brink Better known in the West are the English-language novelists Alan Paton (*Cry, the Beloved Country*, 1948) and two Nobel laureates, Nadine Gordimer (1991) and J. M. Coetzee (2003).

English Poetry

Old English Poetry (ca. 428–1100)

The earliest English, or Anglo-Saxon, poetry celebrated the heroic deeds, physical accomplishments, courage, and success in battle of kings and warriors in the period between the arrival of the Angles and Saxons in the fifth century and their conversion to Christianity in the seventh century. But this poetry does not survive in original form. The earliest recorded poems, written, like all Old English poetry, in alliterative verse-form, in which sounds at the beginnings of words are repeated in each line, are from the second half of the seventh century: the secular paean to kings, "Widstith"; and the nine-line "Caedmon's Hymn," the first in a centuries-long tradition of English Christian devotional poems. Caedmon, a Northumbrian monk, is the first known English poet. "The Dream of the Rood," in which the rood, or Christ's cross, describes its experience to the dreamer, was written in the early eighth century, and is considered the best example of the Anglo-Saxon devotional poem. While it is often ascribed to the second known English poet, Cynewulf, there is doubt as to whether he is actually its author.

The Heroic Epic The finest example of the Old English heroic epic, a narrative verse form depicting the deeds of a valorous hero, and the longest existing poem of its day, is *Beowulf*, written in the eighth century. *Beowulf* records an older pagan tale of slaying a monster. Set in Scandinavia, it is overlaid with Christian elements, including a judging God and a biblical lineage for the monster Grendel, but remains a celebration of courage and honor, the virtues of a harsh, pre-Christian heroic age. Later examples of heroic poems include the *Battle of Maldon* (undated) and the *Battle of Brunanburgh* (undated).

Middle English Poetry (1100–1500)

Middle English poetry first flourished in the 14th century, although some short lyrical poems, poems of an emotionally expressive nature, appeared as early as the 12th and 13th centuries; and long verse romances, narratives about kings and knights and sexual love, were also written in the 13th century. The elegy and the allegory were also popular during this period.

The Middle English Lyric Examples of anonymous lyrics abound into the 15th century. Among these lyrics, which have themes of nature (especially of springtime), love, and Christian piety, are "The Cuckoo Song" and "Westron Wind." Numerous short ballads, narrative verse meant to be sung or spoken aloud, such as "Barbara Allen," "Lord Randall," and "Sir Patrick Spens," appear from about 1200 to 1700.

Romance, Elegy, and Allegory These three forms rose to prominence in the Middle English period. The romance, a narrative in which knights and other characters of chivalry are the main actors, is exemplified by *Sir Gawain and the Green Knight* (ca. 1380–1400), the story of a brave knight who must defend the honor of King Arthur and his court after its invasion by the mysterious Green Knight. Sir Gawain's testing reveals the limitation of manly virtue and leads him to a religious epiphany. The elegy, a poem of mourning written to commemorate the death of a person and often used as a meditation on death or life, is exemplified by *The Pearl* (ca. 1360), believed to have been occasioned by the death of the poet's daughter. *Sir Gawain* and *The Pearl* are believed to have been written by the same person, but, as is the case with so many works of this period, their author remains anonymous. The allegory, in which virtues or states of being are represented as persons or other objective forms, is exemplified by *Piers Plowman* (ca. 1362), which may have been written, or partly written, by William Langland, of whom little is known. The poem is an account of the Plowman's dream vision of the history of Christianity and its current, somewhat corrupted, state.

Geoffrey Chaucer Considered the first great English poet, Geoffrey Chaucer (ca. 1343–1400) was a Londoner who wrote in a Middle English dialect. His *Canterbury Tales*, a narrative cycle told by 22 richly varied travelers brought together on a religious pilgrimage, is one of the greatest works of English literature—ribaldly comic in parts, yet profound and vivid in its portrayal of medieval life and character. Although Chaucer never completed this work, which he began in 1386, it develops unity and artistic resonance from the interplay, even quarreling, between the characters, and through their tendency to respond to the stories of others in their own stories. Chaucer's other poems include the love story *Troilus and Criseide* (ca. 1385), and *The Parliament of Fowls*.

The Tudor Period (1485–1603)

The era of Tudor England, which began in 1485 with the accession of King Henry VII and lasted through the death of Elizabeth I in 1603, saw a modernizing of the English language, allowing it to reflect the humanist ideas and images of the European Renaissance. Fittingly, the sonnet, the 14-line form first developed in Italy, began to carve its deep impression into English poetry in the 16th century.

The English Sonnet and Blank Verse During the Tudor period, nearly all sonnets were love poems, often expressing disappointment or despair. The earliest English practitioners were Thomas Wyatt (1503–42), a distinguished lyric poet, and Henry Howard, Earl of Surrey (1517–47), who wrote the first sonnets with an "English" rhyme-scheme, which arranged the poem in three four-line sections and one two-line section rather than the Italian pattern of eight and six lines. Howard also composed the first English *blank verse,* unrhymed 10–syllable lines with a regular meter, usually iambic pentameter (a set of an unstressed syllable followed by a stressed syllable, repeated five times). Philip Sidney (1554–86) followed Howard with a similarly patterned sequence of love sonnets, *Astrophel and Stella*.

Elizabethan Poetry The greatest nondramatic Elizabethan poet was Edmund Spenser (1552–99), whose romantic and allegorical *The Faerie Queene* (1590–96) is one of the great English epics and stands apart from all other 16th-century narrative poetry. Its six books are each dedicated to a courtly virtue, and its strong ecclesiastical views mark it as the first masterly English Protestant poem. Among Spenser's innovations was the nine-line stanza that is named for him. He, too, wrote a sonnet sequence, *Amoretti*.

The leading Elizabethan dramatists, Christopher Marlowe (1564–93) and, greatest of all English writers, William Shakespeare (1564–1616), were also significant lyric and narrative poets. Marlowe's *Hero and Leander* retold a classical Greek love story. Shakespeare used the Roman poet Ovid as the source of two narrative poems of his early career, the mythological *Venus and Adonis* (1593) and *The Rape of Lucrece* (1594). His 154-sonnet sequence, written in the 1590s and addressed to both a young man and a woman, is the crown of that Elizabethan tradition.

The Seventeenth Century

The turn of the 17th century brought with it the reign of James I (1603–25) and introduced two new traditions in English poetry that would endure until the century's end: the Metaphysical style originated by John Donne and the Cavalier style embraced by the followers of Ben Jonson.

Donne and the Metaphysical Poets John Donne (1572–1631) created a poetry of intellectual and spiritual reaching, which in a later period was labeled "metaphysical." Donne's poetry was witty, and sometimes abrupt in manner, allowing content to take precedence over form. Within his poetry he made unusual imagistic and intellectual connections. Donne, a clergyman, wrote beautiful religious poetry, including the *Holy Sonnets*. But his equally trenchant poems of physical love would inspire others who wrote in this tradition.

Other poets of the Metaphysical school included George Herbert (1593–1633), who approached God with more certainty than Donne, but with similar leaps of imagery. In poems such as "Easter Wings" and "The Altar," he used lines shaped to depict his subject. Richard Crashaw (1613–49), a convert to Catholicism, was influenced by Italian poetry and wrote idiosyncratic, baroque, passionately devotional verse that incorporated notably Italian Catholic flesh-and-blood images. Other members of the Metaphysical school were Henry Vaughan (1621–95), Thomas Traherne (ca. 1636–74), and Abraham Cowley (1618–67).

Jonson and the Cavalier Poets Ben Jonson (1572–1637), born the same year as Donne, wrote spare, smooth lines modeled on classical poetry that were in striking contrast to those of the Metaphysical poets. Jonson's poems included satires, a celebrated tribute to a great house ("To Penshurst"), and a powerful memorial to Shakespeare. But it was his lyrics addressed to women ("To Celia") that influenced the casual yet polished style of the Cavalier poets. In addition to being a poet, Jonson was also a leading Jacobean playwright.

Jonson was not himself a Cavalier poet in the sense in which Donne was a Metaphysical poet. The term *Cavalier* refers to supporters of Charles I, the king beheaded in 1649 during Oliver Cromwell's Puritan Revolution, eight years after Jonson's death. But the Cavalier poets modeled their work on the classical beauty of Jonson's verse. The first and finest of the Cavalier poets, Robert Herrick (1591–1673), was one of a group of Jonson's companions and admirers who called themselves "Sons of Ben." He and the later Cavaliers were informed by the ideal of courtly love and by upper-class sophistication. Their mostly lyrical poems were witty, and well-crafted. Herrick's lyrics, mainly short and sometimes epigrammatic, were often concerned with the natural things and the females that delighted him. These two subjects were often addressed in the same poem: "To the Virgins, to Make Much of Time" ("Gather ye rosebuds while ye may"); or "Corinna's Going-A-Maying." These direct addresses to women and urges to "seize the day" ("*carpe diem*") were repeated by later Cavalier poets such as Edmund Waller (1606–87; "Go, lovely rose"), John Suckling (1609–42; "Why so pale and wan, fond lover?"), and Richard Lovelace (1618–57; "To Althea, from Prison"). The greatest *carpe diem* poem, "To His Coy Mistress," was composed by Andrew Marvell (1621–78), who wrote in both the Cavalier and Metaphysical traditions. A creator of lyrics, odes, and dialogues that married playful wit with deep significance, he has been called England's most important minor poet.

The Restoration and 18th Century

With the restoration of the monarchy in the person of Charles II in 1660, freedom of expression, in such forms as satire and staged drama, was again possible. The later decades of the 17th century introduced an age of mordant satire and wit that endured into the second half of the 18th century, in which poetry focused on human behavior and political developments. Although the poets of these times were generally unrestrained in their personal attacks, their style was moderated, simplified, and cool, reflecting the peaceful era that followed the heat and turbulence of civil war. Because this period was compared to the post–civil war reign of Augustus Caesar, and because its poetic style was in good part derived from the great Roman poets of that time, it is known as the neoclassical or Augustan period of English poetry. This movement, in the age of rationalism, emphasized order and restraint in imagination, along with an emphasis on human society more than communion with the divine, a belief, in Alexander Pope's words, that "the proper study of mankind is man."

John Milton and the Neoclassical Period John Milton (1608–74) is considered the most important poet of the neoclassical period. Milton restored a rich and resonant style to English poetry, and, as is true of Spenser in the previous century, his epic poetry sets him apart from the traditions of his time. He produced *Paradise Lost*, considered the greatest English epic, in 1667. In soaring blank verse, *Paradise Lost* presents the fall of Satan and of Adam and Eve, and thus the origin of evil. Although a theological argument with the pronounced intention to "justify the ways of God to men," *Paradise Lost* is a powerfully dramatic and descriptive poem, especially vivid in its portrayal of Satan. A second epic, *Paradise Regained* (1671), describes the redemptive triumph of Christ. In addition to these long poems and the poetic drama *Samson Agonistes* (1671), Milton wrote some of the best English sonnets.

Satire in the Neoclassical Period Satire rose in full force when Samuel Butler (1612–80) published Part I of *Hudibras*, his three-part ridicule of religious and political nonconformists (i.e., Cromwell and the Puritans) two years after the monarchy returned. This scalding poem is also a burlesque of the romantic idealism expressed in such poems as Spenser's *Faerie Queene*.

The original neoclassicist and finest satiric poet of the period, as well as a leading dramatist, was John Dryden (1631–1700). In earlier decades an "occasional" poet, a celebrator of public events, his career as a satirist began with a mock-heroic poem, "Mac Flecknoe," which lampooned a rival playwright, and continued with his masterpiece, *Absalom and Achitophel* (1681), an account of the "popish plot" against King Charles II. Dryden's stylish wit and his mastery of the heroic couplet—pairs of rhymed, 10-syllable lines—greatly influenced later poets. He was also an influential and masterly composer of odes, such as "To Mrs. Anne Killegrew" and "Alexander's Feast."

Best known as a prose satirist, Jonathan Swift (1667–1745), author of the timeless *Gulliver's Travels,* was also a distinguished poet, whether he was mocking his fellow humans or praising his beloved "Stella." However, the title of greatest English satirical poet belongs to Swift's friend Alexander Pope (1688–1744). A neoclassicist and literary descendant of Dryden, whose heroic couplets he picked up and mastered, Pope updated the satirical and didactic forms and styles of the Roman poet Horace. He ridiculed the upper class in the mock-epic *The Rape of the Lock* (1712–14) and contemporary poets in *The Dunciad* (1728); defined the literary principles of the age in *An Essay on Criticism*; and argued for classical order in all things in *An Essay on Man* (1733).

The Late Eighteenth Century and Nature Poetry

Samuel Johnson (1709–84), who, like Swift, is known primarily for his prose (and for his conversation), also made his mark as a poet, particularly with *The Vanity of Human Wishes* (1749). Oliver Goldsmith's *The Deserted Village* (1770), was a reaction against the destruction of small farms and village life as a result of the Enclosure Acts. Its rural theme is indicative of a tendency for poets in the mid and late 18th century to express feelings, often melancholy, about nature or in natural settings. Thomas Gray's "Elegy Written in a Country Churchyard" (1751), a meditation on the anonymity of the rural dead, is a famous example of this trend, and the poem is considered a harbinger of the Romantic movement. William Collins's "Ode to Evening" (1746) is another example of this trend toward nature as a subject. This wave of nature poetry, in fact, began earlier in the century with James Thomson's *The Seasons* (1726–27), and was picked up toward the century's end by William Cowper, particularly in his long poem about country life, *The Task* (1785), and by George Crabbe, whose realistic depiction of poverty and inhumanity in the countryside in *The Village* (1783) is a stark alternative to Goldsmith's idealized view.

The Romantic Period

In the Romantic period, the focus of poetry moved even further away from society, toward nature and the individual expressing inner feelings. Arising in the wake of the French Revolution, Romanticism tilted to the political left, embraced nationalistic yearnings, and expressed rebellious impulses. Its poets reached beyond 18th-century restraints to commune with realities and absolute principles, such as love, beauty, and truth, that existed outside the boundaries of everyday life.

Although the Romantic period in English poetry is traditionally assigned a starting date, 1798, when William Wordsworth and Samuel Taylor Coleridge published *Lyrical Ballads*, groundbreaking Romantic poems had already been written by then by William Blake in England and Robert Burns in Scotland.

The "Pre-Romantics" William Blake (1757–1827), whose first poems were published in 1783, was a visionary poet-artist who, both in lyrics (*Songs of Innocence*, 1789; and *Songs of Experience*, 1794) and in long prophetic and narrative poems, was characteristically Romantic in his deep concern for economic oppression, his simple diction, and his use of symbolism. Robert Burns, who died in 1796, took plainness of language even further than Blake by producing in Scots dialect the lyrics, especially love poems, for which he is well known.

The First Generation of Romantic Poets These predecessors notwithstanding, the year 1798 remains a boundary line for the Romantic movement. In a manifesto-like preface to the second edition (1800) of *Lyrical Ballads*, William Wordsworth (1770–1850) explicitly separated poetry's future from its neoclassical past, prescribing that poems should deal with "common life" in "language really used by men," and pronouncing poetry to be "the spontaneous overflow of powerful feelings." These remained qualities of the English Romantic poetry that thrived for the next three decades and lingered until Wordsworth's death.

Wordsworth's output comprised short lyric poems, meditative odes, such as "Tintern Abbey" and "Intimations of Immortality," and long poems, including the masterly, autobiographical *The Prelude*, completed in 1805 but published posthumously. Samuel Taylor Coleridge (1772–1834) also wrote meditative verse but is best known for narrative poems tinged by supernatural effects, particularly "The Rime of the Ancient Mariner," which was published in *Lyrical Ballads*.

The Second Generation of Romantic Poets The relative brevity of the Romantic era was caused in part by the early deaths of three of its greatest poets of the second generation, Lord Byron, Percy Bysshe Shelley, and John Keats. The eldest of these, Byron (George Gordon, 1788–1824), was a notorious lover and enormously popular writer in his own time, regarded best for his long narrative and satirical poems (*Childe Harold's Pilgrimage*, 1812–18; *Don Juan*, 1819–24) and known for his creation of the rebellious, immoral "Byronic hero." Shelley (1792–1822) was a more philosophical poet who believed in the transforming power of love. He was a composer of lyrics and politically inflected poems such as "Ode to the West Wind," and his advocacy of the romantic impulse to overcome human limitations is well expressed in the title of his great verse-drama *Prometheus Unbound* (1820), which offers the possibility of humanity's moral triumph over evil.

Keats (1795–1821) was a poet of sensuous and emotional experience to whom life was "a vale of soul-making." He pronounced, in "Ode on a Grecian Urn," the quintessentially Romantic sentence: "Beauty is truth, truth beauty." Yet his beautiful works also expressed the sadness that accompanies human yearning.

Walter Scott (1771–1832), a Scotsman who achieved distinction as a novelist and as a narrative lyric poet, is also considered a Romantic poet. Like other Romantics, including Keats, Scott sometimes reached into the medieval past for themes. Other notable lyric poets of the period were Robert Southey (1774–1843), Walter Savage Landor (1775–1864), Leigh Hunt (1784–1859), and the Irishman Thomas Moore (1779–1852).

The Victorian Age (1837–1901)

During the long reign of Queen Victoria, from 1837 to 1901, England was transformed into the most vigorous industrial, capitalist society ever known, and its empire gained its farthest reach. It was an age in which the population shifted from the land to the cities and the advance of science encroached on the ground of religious certainty. These matters roiled the poetic imagination and diversified poetic points of view.

Faith and Doubt in Victorian Poetry During the Victorian age, religion was subject to experimentation, renunciation, and doubt. The dominant, longest-lived poet of the period, Alfred, Lord Tennyson (1809–92), absorbed, early in his career, the age's uncertainty about material and scientific progress. Tennyson, racked by the death of his best friend, expressed his melancholy and longing for faith in his first successful volume of poems; then, in an extended elegy for that friend, *In Memoriam A. H. H.* (1850), Tennyson embraced faith. Tennyson found further assurance in his country's distant past, most thoroughly explored in his epic *Idylls of the King* (1859–62).

Faith and doubt were also pervasive issues for the other great Victorian poets, Robert Browning (1812–89) and Matthew Arnold (1822–88). As a young man, Browning made the transition from atheism to belief, and he has often been misconstrued as having harbored a Pollyannaish certainty that, as he once wrote, "God's in his heaven—/ All's right with the world." In fact, he was a writer of psychological depth, keenly aware of human corruption and fully conscious of the implications of Darwin's science, whose belief in a transcendent God was buffeted from many sides. Arnold is considered the emblematic Victorian poet of doubt and alienation, particularly for his most famous poem, "Dover Beach," in which he spoke hauntingly of an "eternal note of sadness."

Pre-Raphaelites and Others Between Tennyson and Browning, particularly, there is an obvious dissociation of poetic style. While Tennyson wrote within the great tradition of fluid and sonorous English verse, Browning's diction was more colloquial, his rhythms less regular, and his poetic modes more experimental, all of these traits apparent in his brilliant dramatic monologues, such as "My Last Duchess." Both styles had followers. Dante Gabriel Rossetti (1828–82), for example, leader of the "Pre-Raphaelite" artistic-poetic movement (which advocated an earlier, simpler style of painting than was prevalent at the time) was a poet of rich color and smooth meter. His sister, Christina Rossetti (1830–94), was a lyrical poet of strong religious sensibility. Browning's wife, Elizabeth Barrett Browning (1806–61), was best known for an extended series of love sonnets, as was the later Victorian George Meredith (1828–1909). Edward FitzGerald (1809–83) translated and revised the 12th-century *Rubaiyat of Omar Khayam* (1857–59); his version, recognized for its polished beauty, quickly gained great popularity. Algernon Charles Swinburne (1837–1909), a Pre-Raphaelite in his early career, later became entranced by the sound of words and metrical experiment. Like his contemporary and friend, Matthew Arnold, Arthur Hugh Clough (1819–61), experienced his own bouts of religious skepticism, which he addressed, somewhat ironically, in his verse.

Late Victorian and Early 20th-Century Poetry

In late Victorian times a number of strains ran independently through English poetry. In the 1890's, one of the great novelists of the second half of the 19th century, Thomas Hardy (1840–1928), brought his dark but compassionate vision to the writing of lyric poetry, and over the next 30 years developed into a major poet. In the same decade, A. E. Housman (1859–1936) published a wistful and classically spare volume of lyrics, *A Shropshire Lad* (1896); and the end-of-the-century "decadents," chief among them Oscar

Wilde (1854–1900) and Ernest Dowson (1867–1900), rose to prominence. Meanwhile, a poet of an altogether different sensibility and style, Rudyard Kipling (1865–1936), writing rhythmically about the imperial British soldier, emerged and began to win great popularity.

Oscar Wilde, Ernest Dowson, and the Decadents

The term *decadent* refers to a school of writing, most popular in France but present in England as well, in which art took precedence over nature. The Decadents produced poems that rejected Victorian convention and reflected the somewhat antisocial ideal of "art for art's sake." The two most important poets of the British Decadent movement were Oscar Wilde and Ernest Dowson. Dowson, the iconic English Decadent, was a sonorous, incantatory poet who characteristically expressed the loss of love, youth, and beauty, and a weariness with life that may have contributed to his dissipation and early death. Oscar Wilde, whose novel *The Picture of Dorian Gray* exemplifies the Decadent school's preoccupation with art and decay, looked back to the work of Pre-Raphaelites as a model for his verse.

Gerard Manley Hopkins and Sprung Rhythm

The most influential poet of the Victorian age, the Jesuit priest Gerard Manley Hopkins (1844–99), is often not considered a Victorian at all. Because of his extraordinary break with the poetic traditions of his era, and because he was not published until 1918, long after his death, he is instead often grouped among poets of the 20th century. His originality included the development of an irregular "sprung" meter in which poetic feet of varying syllables are used in an attempt to mirror the rhythms of prose, that changed poetic rhythm; a precise diction that was partly invented; and the extensive, forceful use of alliteration. Hopkins's verse is at times bright and at times somber. He is considered one of the language's most powerful religious poets. Like many of his predecessors, he was a great composer of sonnets.

World War I and the End of the Victorian Age

World War I had a profound impact on the direction of English poetry. Kipling's patriotic poems, featuring stoically virtuous troops in India and other far-flung places, yield in modern memory to the palpable expressions of combat experience by England's World War I poets. One of these, Rupert Brooke (1887–1915), still sang patriotically, "there's a corner in of some foreign field / That is forever England"; but others, Wilfred Owen (1893–1918; "Anthem for Doomed Youth"), Siegfried Sassoon (1886–1967), and Isaac Rosenberg (1890–1918), wrote with darker realism and increasing bitterness. Their vivid lines, like the Great War itself, delivered a decisive finish to Victorian times.

The Twentieth Century after World War I.

British poetry after the First World War has been more diverse in style and intention than that of any previous century. The Modernist movement arrived in the 1910's and 1920's. With it came the use of new, irregular meters and forms and an unprecedented range of diction and subjects. These were used to effectively mirror the breaking with the past, the concern with alienation and a fractured world, and the breaking down of England's imperial power that rose after the World War I.

Neither of the two most influential figures of "English" poetry in the 20th century were English. William Butler Yeats (1865–1939), an Irishman, is often considered the century's greatest English-language poet (see "Irish Literature"). However it was the work of the American-born and -educated T.S. Eliot (1888–1965), who settled in England in his 20's, that most profoundly shaped the poetry of the English Modernist movement. His technique presented a clear break with the poetic past. Eliot's breakthrough has long been identified with two early poems, "The Love Song of J. Alfred Prufrock" (1915) and *The Waste Land* (1922). In these, Eliot presented fresh, sometimes jarring, images, diverse literary allusions, snatches of conversation, and a variety of scenes in disconnected and ironic juxtaposition. In Eliot's poetry, the spiritual and emotional dislocation of the modern world was represented in form as well as content.

Although Eliot exerted a profound influence on poets of the following generations, not all important 20th-century British poetry was affected by Eliot's revolutionary innovations. His contemporaries Edwin Muir (1887–1959), Robert Graves (1895–1985), and D. H. Lawrence (1885–1930) all found ways to address the changing world without using Eliot as their model. Muir, a Scotsman, and Graves each wrote traditional lines with traditional diction but a distinctive voice, and each sought to understand the present in relation to the classical past. Graves, especially, was influenced by Thomas Hardy. The novelist Lawrence also produced several books of increasingly significant poetry, expressing the same intimacy with the force and beauty of nature that is reflected in his poetic prose. For a model he looked well past Eliot to the free verse of an earlier, American "modernism."

It was the next generation of Modernist poets, those born in the first decade of the 20th century, that owed so much to Eliot. Coming of age in the 1930's, these poets saw a different kind of wasteland from that which Eliot had written of—economic depression—and wrote poetry that leaned sharply to the political left. The finest of these was W. H. Auden (1907–73), who moved to New York early on and grew to be a poet with a wide range of concerns who combined technical dexterity with straightforward but eloquent diction. His contemporaries included Stephen Spender (1909–95), who later wrote of his disillusion with communism; and two Irish natives educated in England: C. Day Lewis (1904–72), who would one day be poet laureate, and Louis MacNeice (1907–63), a poet known for his sad and sometimes ironic depictions of modern life.

Dylan Thomas (1914–53), born in Wales, is often included in discussions of the Modernist period. Thomas's language was not colloquial or restrained, but energetic, resonant, sensuous, and full of life. In his use of alliteration and original phrasing, Thomas looked back to Hopkins; and in his fashion, Thomas, too, celebrated nature with religious fervor. To Thomas, who incorporated Freudian thought into his poetry, all nature, all sexuality, and all love are linked to death.

New Apocalypse Poetry and "The Movement" By the mid- to late 20th century, British poetry had begun to coalesce into a series of movements. The exuberance and surrealism of Thomas, George Barker (1913–91), and others were placed under the heading of "New Apocalypse" poetry, which was followed in the 1950's by a reaction labeled simply "The Movement" and included Philip Larkin (1922–85), Donald Davie (b. 1922), and Thom Gunn (b. 1929). Their poems were subdued, ironic and "antiromantic." Larkin, like Robert Graves before him, was much influenced by Thomas Hardy, and is regarded as the chief successor to Hardy in the expression of a pessimistic sensibility. Some of Larkin's concerns were shared by John Betjeman (1906–84), poet laureate from 1972 to 1984; and the distinctly "English," nonmodernist tradition that they wrote in has been impressively taken up by the working-class poet Tony Harrison (b. 1937).

Hughes and MacDiarmid Ted Hughes (1930–98), whose work does not fall neatly into any one school, was Betjeman's successor as poet laureate. Hughes was perhaps the most distinguished English poetic voice of the second half of the 20th century. Greatly influenced by Lawrence, Hughes was a poet of nature, but the nature he wrote of was an often ferocious one, a nature that reveals a deep and troubling undercurrent beneath all creation, including humanity. The chief Scottish poet after Muir was Hugh MacDiarmid (1892–1978), a nationalist, communist, and leader of the "Scottish Renaissance."

Contemporary Irish Poets In recent times, extraordinary contributions to poetry in English have come from Ireland, particularly Northern Ireland, which has produced Seamus Heaney (b. 1939), winner of the 1995 Nobel Prize and widely considered the finest living English-language poet, and his onetime pupil, Paul Muldoon (b. 1951), who settled in America and received a 2003 Pulitzer Prize.

The English Novel

The English novel emerged in the 18th century. Its forerunners included long prose stories dating back to Roman times and such later classics as Cervantes's *Don Quixote* and Swift's *Gulliver's Travels*. The term *novel*, implying the newness of the form, is derived from the Italian *novella*, which identified realistic medieval prose tales such as those contained in Boccaccio's *Decameron*.

At its most basic level, the novel is defined as an extended prose narrative. Elements of the novel include characterization, plot, and theme. Characterization involved the creation and depiction of lifelike characters to act within the narrative. *Plot* involved a series of causally linked events, usually broken into the three-part structure of beginning, middle, and end. Theme was the unifying idea behind the novel. Early on, realism was an essential ingredient of the novel, as was the depiction of interior consciousness. In languages other than English, the novel is most often called a *roman*, implying a link to the romances of the Medieval period (see "English Poetry"). Traditionally, *romans* looked back to a romanticized or magical past for their subjects, whereas novels looked to the realistic present, though these distinctions faded as the forms progressed.

The 18th-Century English Novel

The French novel appeared earlier than the English novel. Madame de La Fayette's *La Princesse de Clèves* (1678), a psychologically detailed love story, is generally thought to have been the first novel in France, and writers in England were able to draw on it as a model for the new form. *Moll Flanders* (1722) by Daniel Defoe (1660–1731), the story of a thieving prostitute, is sometimes considered the first English novel; because *Moll Flanders* lacks a depiction of interior consciousness, the claim belongs more accurately to *Pamela* (1740), by Samuel Richardson (1689–1761), an epistolary novel, or novel written in the form of letters. With the publication of Richardson's highly regarded *Clarissa Harlowe* (1747–48), also an epistolary novel, the English novel had become firmly established as a literary form. Among the innovations that Richardson introduced were a focus on character and moral choice.

Even as Richardson established moral choice as one of the criteria for the novel, his contemporary, Henry Fielding (1707–54), recognizing the form's power for innovation, used it to satirize Richardson's work. Fielding's novel *Shamela* (1741) is a send-up of *Pamela*. Fielding, who is considered the first great English novelist, continued to develop the form throughout his career with picaresque novels—novels that depict the adventures of a rascal through a series of loosely connected episodes—such as *Joseph Andrews* (1742) and *Tom Jones* (1749), both of which depict ordinary English life, and both of which were conceived of as "comic epics in prose."

The tradition of great comic fiction established by Fielding was picked up by the Irish-born Laurence Sterne (1713–68), whose *Tristram Shandy*, published between 1760 and 1767, is perversely whimsical in its variety of styles, moods, and devices, and marks the first instance in which development of character and exploration of the inner self take primacy over plot. The Scottish-born Tobias Smollett (1721–71) returned to the episodic tradition in his novels of international land-and-sea escapades and his mature *Humphrey Clinker* (1771), a realistic adventure story set in England and Scotland.

The 19th-Century English Novel

In the 19th century, the novel flourished in Britain, as well as in France, Russia, and the United States. The first important British novelists of the century, the Scotsman Walter Scott (1771–1832) and the Englishwoman Jane Austen (1775–1817), were close contemporaries but radically different in style. Scott was a lyric and narrative poet whose transition to novel writing produced well-plotted romances of Scottish life and introduced the historical novel in Britain. Scott's works include his "Waverley novels" (among them *Rob Roy* and *The Heart of Midlothian*, both 1818; *Ivanhoe*, 1820, which takes place during the Crusades), the first and most famous of his historical novels. Scott's work was aligned with the Romantic movement then thriving in English poetry. Austen, whose first novel, *Sense and Sensibility*, was published in 1811, wrote completely outside the Romantic movement, producing novels of manners that were largely concerned with the social customs and conventions of provincial society. These circumscribed stories, which include *Pride and Prejudice* (1813), *Mansfield Park* (1814), *Emma* (1816), and, published after she died in 1817, *Northanger Abbey* and *Persuasion*, are masterly in form, witty, satirical, and sharply observant of character and manners.

The Romantic Novel The Romantic novel reached its pinnacle at the beginning of the Victorian age when, in 1847, the Brontë sisters each published one of the most enduringly popular novels in English literature: Charlotte Brontë's (1816–55) *Jane Eyre* and Emily Brontë's (1818–48) *Wuthering Heights*. Both novels were tales of passionate love. *Wuthering Heights*, Emily Brontë's only novel, is an intense and eerie account of the relationship between a gentlewoman and a Gypsy foundling. It is considered to be one of England's finest examples of the novel for its clarity of structure and streamlined plot.

The Satirical Novel The satirical novel *Vanity Fair* by William Makepiece Thackeray (1811–61) was published in 1848. Although Thackeray called *Vanity Fair* "a novel without a hero," it has a heroine, of sorts, in Becky Sharp, a winning, though not admirable, character who serves as a vehicle for lampooning the English upper class. Because of its concern with the interior life of its characters, *Vanity Fair* is considered an early forerunner of the psychological novel, a form that would grow in popularity as the 19th century progressed.

Charles Dickens (1812–70), perhaps the most widely read English novelist of all time, had an unmatched genius for creating richly mannered and comic characters, most of whom populate his vividly portrayed, socially diverse London. Raising his voice against poverty and industrial depersonalization, Dickens was, like Thackeray, a great satirist. He was also a brilliant master of plot, though many of his books, written hurriedly in magazine installments, are overly sentimental and structurally flawed. His best-known novel is *David Copperfield* (1850), but his most critically acclaimed works are *Bleak House* (1853), *Hard Times*, (1854) and *Great Expectations* (1861).

The Psychological Novel George Eliot (1819–80), the pen name of Mary Ann Evans, set her novels in small towns far from Dickens's London. Her psychologically probing novels reflect the Victorian uncertainty about religious faith. In them, she presented highly intelligent, fully realized characters with the moral challenge to live meaningful lives. Her novel *Middlemarch* (1872) is sometimes called the greatest English novel because of its scope, its richly drawn characters, and its psychological insight. Other works include *Silas Marner* (1861) and *The Mill on the Floss* (1860). Eliot's work represents the full flowering of the psychological novel.

The Late Victorian Novel The Victorian age brought with it the expansion of the British Empire, the Industrial Revolution, and breakthroughs in science that created a new understanding of the world. Many novels of this period reflect a resulting loss of certainty and religious consolation. The work of two novelists of the late Victorian age, Thomas Hardy and Henry James, reflect the questions of this changing era.

Thomas Hardy (1840–1928) began his career as a novelist and later turned to poetry. Hardy's novels, which include *The Return of the Native* (1878), *Tess of the D'Urbervilles* (1891), and *Jude the Obscure* (1896), are set in "Wessex," his name for Dorsetshire. In Hardy's worldview, nature is beautiful but harsh, and aligned with cosmic fate to mock human aspiration.

Henry James (1843–1916) was born and educated in America but resettled in England at the age of 33. He was fascinated with the schism between the old, genteel, sophisticated world of Europe and the relative innocence of America. In early novels such as *The Portrait of a Lady* (1881) and later ones such as *The Ambassadors* (1903) and *The Golden Bowl* (1904), he explored the psychological complexity of characters on the boundary between the old and new worlds. In his "middle period" he focused on political themes in books such as *The Bostonians* (1886), then wrote a series of short "dramatic" novels such as *What Maisie Knew* (1897). Among James's innovations was the technique of writing from a character's point of view. He was the originator of the technique of "stream of consciousness" which would so profoundly effect the novel in the 20th century.

The Novel in the 20th Century

The historical events of the 20th century brought with them enormous changes to the development of the novel. The Victorian issues of imperialism, a new social order engendered by the Industrial Revolution, and loss of religious consolation continued to return as literary themes. World War I brought with it a fractured worldview. Experiments in form and subject matter reflected this changing world.

Novels of the Edwardian Age (1901–1914) During the period between the death of Queen Victoria and the advent of World War I—in England, the Edwardian age—two novelists made concerns about Victorian imperialism the subject matter of their most famous novels. Despite the fact that English was his third language, Joseph Conrad (1857–1924), a Pole, is considered the first great 20th-century English novelist and a masterly prose stylist. His earliest important novels, *The Nigger of the Narcissus* (1897) and *Lord Jim* (1900), and several brilliant novellas, including *Youth* (1902), *Heart of Darkness* (1902), *Typhoon* (1903), and *The Secret Sharer* (1909), are set on the sea. *Heart of Darkness*, his most important work, is especially concerned with the fruits of imperialism. Some of Conrad's finest works, such as *Nostromo* (1904), *The Secret Agent* (1907), and *Under Western Eyes* (1911), are overtly political novels. A master of narrative technique, using, for example, multiple points of view, and of keen psychological insight, Conrad examined the isolation and moral conduct of men confronting the human condition.

E. M. Forster (1879–1970) made his mark between the turn of the century and the end of World War I. Indeed, Forster, who died at 91 in 1970, published fiction only between 1905 and 1924, when his last and best novel, *A Passage to India*, which examines the British Raj, appeared. In this and other social novels, including *A Room with a View* (1908) and *Howards End* (1910), he exposes the barren emotional life of the English middle class and explores the difficulties of personal relationships. Forster was one of several experimental writers and artists collectively known as the Bloomsbury Group, the most famous of which was Virginia Woolf.

The Early Modern Novel While many novelists rose to prominence during and just after World War I, two, D. H. Lawrence (1885–1930) and Virginia Woolf (1882–1941), exemplify the novel's shifting subject matter and form.

Lawrence's first major novel was the autobiographical

Sons and Lovers (1913), followed by *The Rainbow* (1915) and *Women in Love* (1921). He was a groundbreaker (and enormously controversial) in his celebration of sensuality. Lawrence was an original, impassioned stylist, and a latter-day romantic who scorned social convention and reacted against industrialism and intellectualism that divorced humanity from nature.

Virginia Woolf, E. M. Forster's close associate in the Bloomsbury Group, departed from Forster's traditional storytelling techniques and developed stream-of-consciousness narrative well beyond the innovations of Henry James. Stream of consciousness, in which the reader has access to all aspects of a character's mental processes, allows the reader to experience a character with enormous immediacy and closeness. In the novels *Mrs. Dalloway* (1925), *To the Lighthouse* (1927), and *The Waves* (1931), this style became increasingly poetic and free-ranging, and was a perfect vehicle with which Woolf could examine time, change, and the interior lives of characters seeking both to know themselves and to form valuable relationships with others. Stream of consciousness was also used by James Joyce (1882–1941) in his masterpiece *Ulysses* (1922).

The Recent English Novel No writer or group of writers has claimed a preeminent place in English fiction in the period since the 1930's, a time during which novelists writing in English have approached the complex and bewildering modern world from varied political, religious, and geographical directions.

An indication of this variety might begin with two prominent novelists born in the first decade of the 20th century, Evelyn Waugh (1903–66) and Graham Greene (1904–91), both of them Catholic in faith and theme but with altogether disparate political views and literary styles. For Waugh, the leading satirist of his time and a thoroughgoing conservative, the church represented a depth of values rooted in the distant past. After directing his devastating wit at British society in books like *Vile Bodies* (1930) and the British military in *Put Out More Flags* (1942), Waugh wrote his most famous novel, *Brideshead Revisited* (1945), about an aristocratic Catholic family, and a highly regarded trilogy of World War II entitled *Sword of Honour* (1952–61). Greene's road to Catholicism emerged out of the leftist atmosphere of the 1930's. He was a master composer of thrillers and spy stories that he labeled "entertainments," and his more important works are soul-searching novels such as *The Power and the Glory* (1940) and *The Heart of the Matter* (1948).

The century's first years also produced two persistent chroniclers of English society as it changed during their lives: C. P. Snow (1905–80), who between 1940 and 1970 produced a sequence of 11 novels, *Strangers and Brothers*; and Anthony Powell (1905–2000), who from 1951 to 1975 published 12 under the collective title *A Dance to the Music of Time*. Again, these men observed very different worlds. Snow wrote of one man rising from the lower class to political power. Powell, with homage to Marcel Proust, chronicled, with depth and humor, the shifting realities of upper-class life.

George Orwell (1903–50), who eloquently represented the left wing, is more highly regarded as an essayist than as a novelist, but in 1949, the year before his death, he completed the most widely read English novel of the century's second half, *Nineteen Eighty-Four*, his chilling warning against totalitarianism. Five years later, William Golding (1911–93) produced another much-read novel, as chilling in its way—*Lord of the Flies*, a symbolic tale of accumulating cruelty and barbarism among boys stranded on a Pacific island. It was Golding's first novel and it is by far his most famous, although he published many more significant novels and won the Nobel Prize in 1983.

During the 1950's, a highly talented, diverse, and bountiful crop of new English novelists appeared. Among them were Muriel Spark (b. 1918), Iris Murdoch (1919–99) and Doris Lessing (b. 1919), none of whom were born in England. The Scottish Spark, like Greene a Catholic convert, shares with him a keen awareness of evil, and focuses on fallen humanity's disturbing misbehavior. Her best-known novel, replicated on stage and in film, is the brief *The Prime of Miss Jean Brodie* (1961). Murdoch, a philosopher turned fiction writer, also examined evil but, much influenced by Plato, might be called a novelist of "the good," a principle that she keeps permanently in view even while depicting the limitations of human nature. Murdoch wove entertaining plots as webs in which characters struggle with the duality of spiritual and sexual yearning. She won early acclaim for *The Bell* (1958) and *A Severed Head* (1961) and wrote novels prolifically thereafter, including *Henry and Cato* (1976) and *The Sea, The Sea* (1978). Lessing came to London from Rhodesia in 1949 and soon wrote the first of five novels in the *Children of Violence* sequence (1952–69), an extended, autobiographically based psychological and social portrait of the character Martha Quest. These and other novels, particularly *The Golden Notebook* (1962) established her as a major feminist writer, as well as a chronicler of the changing sensibilities of her time. She later shifted modes from realism to fantasy in *A Briefing for a Descent into Hell* (1971) and *The Memoirs of a Survivor* (1974) and to science fiction in a series of five novels under the general title *Canopus in Argos* (1979–83).

A group of male novelists who began publishing in the 1950's became known, along with certain playwrights and poets, as the "angry young men," for their protest against the meanness of postwar society and against the old order clinging to its authority. These included Alan Sillitoe (b. 1928), John Wain (1925–94), John Braine (1922–87), and Kingsley Amis (1922–95), who is best known for his sharply amusing first novel, *Lucky Jim* (1954).

In the second half of the 20th century, numerous British novelists arrived in England from points all around the imperial compass. Among them, from Dominica in the Caribbean came Jean Rhys (1890–1979), author of *Wide Sargasso Sea* (1966); from South Africa came Angus Wilson (1913–91), author of *No Laughing Matter* (1967); from Ireland, William Trevor (b. 1928), an accomplished short story writer; from Trinidad, the ethnic Indian V. S. Naipaul (b. 1932), author of *A Bend in the River* (1979); and from India, Salman Rushdie (b. 1947) author of *Satanic Verses* (1988). Notable English novelists currently writing include Margaret Drabble (b. 1939), A.S. Byatt (b. 1936), Ian McEwan (b. 1948), and Martin Amis (b. 1949), son of Kingsley.

American Literature

Colonial Period through the 18th Century

Origins Locating a starting point for the diverse collection of genres and voices known as American literature has provoked lively debate for centuries. The Viking Leif Ericson's voyage to Newfoundland in 1001 became fodder for two Norse fables that might be considered the first texts of North American origin. But many critics now mark America's literary origins with the performance of oral literature by Native Americans such as the Zuni and Navajo, both tribes of the southwest U.S. European exploration narratives by such figures as Christopher Columbus (1451–1506) and Alvar Núñez Cabeza de Vaca (1490–1556) gave Europeans a first glimpse of indigenous cultures, but the 18 million indigenous peoples speaking roughly 200 distinct languages in North America at the time had been sharing stories perhaps for millennia.

Not transcribed until the 19th century, these included creation myths and trickster tales (the latter most notably featuring the figure of the coyote), and were woven with natural imagery. The Zuni "Talk Concerning the First Beginning" speaks of a mammalian birth of the world through a "fourth womb," for example.

Literature in the Colonies

Mainstream American literature dates from the early 17th century with the arrival of European settlers in North America, beginning with the small, precariously situated colonial presence in Jamestown, Virginia, founded in 1607. In 1619 passengers on the *Mayflower* arrived in Plymouth, Massachusetts. Like those in Jamestown, these settlers learned survival and agricultural tactics from Native Americans. Diarists recorded the hardships they suffered as well as their encounters with indigenous tribes. Mary White Rowlandson (1637–1711) wrote a captivity narrative about her three-month detention with Native Americans during King Philip's War (1675–78); became one of the first best sellers from the New World and helped prepare the soil that would later give life to the genre of the western.

The Pilgrims in Plymouth were motivated to leave England in part for Separatist religious causes. As a result, much of the early literature to emerge from the colonies was religious in tone and content. One of the most influential early American men of letters was William Bradford (1590–1657), who served as governor of the Plymouth Colony for a total of 33 years and bestowed upon the settlers the name "Pilgrims." His *Of Plymouth Plantation* reads more like a theological treatise on Christianity than the history it purports to be. The Pilgrims were soon followed by the Puritans, who attempted to create a religious utopia in the Massachusetts Bay Colony. As John Winthrop (1588–1649), the colony's governor for a dozen years, put it (in a nod to the New Testament), they strove to craft "a city upon a hill." Anne Bradstreet (1612–72), who came to the colonies with Winthrop, earned the distinction of being the first colonial subject, male or female, to publish a book of poetry. Indeed, she was one of the first women writing in English to achieve success in the literary market, and her critical reception has endured. Her poetry eschews religious zealotry in favor of a more nuanced treatment of her own spirituality and also treats themes of family life.

John Cotton (1585–1652) established the justification for the Puritan way of life by publishing an influential sermon and contributing a preface to the *Bay Psalm Book* of 1640. Cotton gained recognition for pursuing the case of heresy against Anne Hutchinson (1591–1643) for her doctrinal differences with him and other leaders. Later in the century, a prolific clergyman and poet named Edward Taylor (1642–1729) crafted such works as "The Psalm Paraphrases" and "God's Determinations." In the same era, Cotton Mather (1663–1728) fulfilled his destiny as the grandson of two Puritan leaders and the son of Increase Mather (1639–1723), pastor of the Old North Church and president of Harvard, by writing many influential documents, including a definitive ecclesiastical history of New England, *Magnalia Christi Americana* (1702). Less admirable but equally momentous was his approval of the Salem witch trials in 1692. The sermon form that gained popularity in New England traces its roots to Cicero's oratory and shares much with other performance arts. Jonathan Edwards (1703–58) stepped forward as the last great religious orator of colonial New England. His "Sinners in the Hands of an Angry God" caused many of those who heard it to swoon with fear, and marked the last time that religious writing would constitute the center of American literature.

18th-Century Enlightenment and Revolution

The most distinctive and enduring voice in colonial America belonged to Benjamin Franklin (1706–90), who subscribed to the Enlightenment faith in the rational, scientific mind. He set in motion the restless American narrative of upward mobility with his autobiography. J. Hector St. John de Crèvecoeur (1735–1813) fueled this narrative by attempting to describe the American character for Europeans in his *Letters from an American Farmer* (1782). Franklin and Crèvecoeur helped colonial Americans articulate a coherent national identity full of patriotism that would ignite with the War of Independence.

Revolution inspired the political writings of the editor and writer Thomas Paine (1735–1826), who became a leading voice in the revolutionary movement with his pamphlet "Common Sense," published in 1776. In the same year, Thomas Jefferson (1743–1826), who would become the third president of the new United States and was the leading writer of the Revolution, wrote the first draft of the Declaration of Independence, outlining a rational, legal argument for a break with the English throne. It is widely held to be the most vital document of American political letters. Next most important is *The Federalist* (1787–88) of Alexander Hamilton, James Madison, and John Jay, a series of essays urging adoption of the Constitution.

In this climate of revolutionary freedom, Olaudah Equiano (1745–97), who had served masters in America, the West Indies, and England, published the first American slave narrative. The title, *The Interesting Narrative of the Life of Olaudah Equiano, or Gustavus Vassa the African, Written by Himself* (1789), displays pride in the remarkable achievement of reading and writing, which were outlawed for slaves. Equally powerful was the work of another former slave, the poet Phillis Wheatley (1753–84), who earned the distinction of becoming the first published black American.

Early American Novels The most democratic of genres, the novel, flourished on American soil, rapidly catching on with the masses. To their dismay, the elite could not wield control over its widely and quickly disseminated messages. The three most popular novelists of the 18th century were Hannah Webster Foster (1758–1840), Susanna Haswell Rowson (1762–1824), and Charles Brockden Brown (1771–1810), all of whom specialized in the seduction narrative, a particularly troubling form for the arbiters of culture and morals. Many such volumes claimed that the moral contained within their pages would outweigh the perils of the subject matter for their young readers.

The 19th Century

American literature exploded onto the world stage from the turn of the 19th century through the Civil War, as American writers rushed to distinguish themselves from their European forebears and define a distinct American character for themselves. By 1800 Americans found the country charming and baffling by turns. The resulting prose, poetry, and essays expose a complex ambivalence about the same contradictions Charles Dickens, the Frenchman Alexis de Tocqueville, and other distinguished visitors witnessed, along with a profound thirst for a coherent national identity.

The Role of the Frontier Frontier mythology emerged to fill what seemed a worrisome void to the country's first citizens—the lack of an artistic and historical identity like the identities cultivated in Europe over millennia. Frontier fiction drew upon forms and characters from travel narratives and captivity diaries, wherein the land and its indigenous occupants could be portrayed as alternately magnificent and brutal and the American could declare his independence over and over again, reinventing himself and his context. The land supported the lofty democratic ideals of a population that soared from 5.3 million in 1800 to 31.4 million ca. 1860.

In the first three decades of the 19th century, novelists such as Washington Irving (1783–1859) and James Fenimore Cooper (1789–1851) furnished portraits of American lands and struggles. Both were masters of the picaresque, a form known for panoramic landscapes, characters from the lower rungs of society, and freedom from convention. *Rip Van Winkle* (1819), Irving's most famous contribution to the American literary canon, is a shrewd metaphor for life in America in the early years following the American Revolution: if a citizen slept too long, he would run the risk of waking to an unrecognizable country.

Cooper's *Leatherstocking Tales*, a series of novels featuring the hero Natty Bumppo (called Hawkeye), were very popular adventure stories about the epic hazards and glories of westward expansion. The sentimental and nostalgic images of the frontier in such novels as *The Last of the Mohicans* (1826) would ignite a collective vision of the contours of a wild and self-reliant American spirit. America gained recognition as a literary entity in its own right when it inspired Noah Webster (1758–1843) to compile the new *American Dictionary of the English Language* (1828), but critics abroad scoffed.

Transcendentalism, Romanticism, and the American Renaissance

Romanticism originated in Germany as a late 18th-century reaction against the cold, clinical mind-set of Enlightenment reason. In the world constructed by the American Romantic writer, the individual reigns supreme, but not at the expense of civility—a departure from European Romantics such as Byron. The Americans imagined a community in which individuality leads to unity, not chaos. The Romantic literary movement in America was informed by Transcendentalism, which blossomed in New England as a reform movement in Unitarianism under the prominent abolitionist minister William Ellery Channing (1780–1842). He argued for the presence of the divine within each human being, who must be trained to listen to intuitive thoughts. The Transcendentalists believed in the unity of God and a divine presence in the world linking nature and people. This marked a departure from New England Calvinism, which cast sin as the defining characteristic of humanity; and from 18th-century Enlightenment rationalism, which renounced spirituality. Transcendentalism built upon the emerging ideals of optimism, opportunity, and self-reliance in the American democracy at a time when the United States was deeply divided on the morality of its laws, particularly those concerning slavery. Romanticism and Transcendentalism characterized an intense flowering of all the literary arts that has inspired critics to refer to the period from about 1830 to 1865 as an "American Renaissance."

The Essay Transcendentalism found its most direct expression in the essays and other nonfiction works of thinkers and artists centered in Concord, Mass. Ralph Waldo Emerson (1803–82) began his writing career in good-natured defiance of old traditions. In a talk that would ultimately appear in print as "The Divinity School Address" (1838), Emerson declared a break from Harvard's traditional theologians, and he would find himself effectively prevented from sharing his controversial views at the university until after the Civil War. His Transcendental view proposed that God was dead in church but very much alive in nature and the individual.

Emerson's most famous works include *Nature*, published in 1836; and "Self-Reliance," in 1841. As part of the Transcendental Club, he cofounded a periodical called *The Dial*, published from 1840 to 1844, with the freethinking author of *Women in the Nineteenth Century (1845)*, Margaret Fuller, as a vehicle for the expression of Transcendentalist views.

No single writer evokes the sights and sounds of Concord, or better uses the natural landscape to promote his philosophy, than Henry David Thoreau (1817–62), Emerson's close friend. Thoreau began his two-year experiment in living at Walden Pond in 1845; writing about it in *Walden* (1854), he advocates a spiritually exuberant but materially spartan life. In 1849 he delineated the platform for peaceful resistance that would inspire future generations, in an essay later titled "Civil Disobedience."

Poetry The early 19th century saw meaningful innovation in poetry, as well as an exploration and celebration of democratic ideals. The poet William Cullen Bryant

(1794–1878), a prominent leader of Unitarianism, is best known for "Thanatopsis," which praised divine nature and inspired Emerson and Thoreau, although he is more often classified with the Knickerbocker School of New York writers than with Transcendentalism's Concord cabal. Bryant helped fashion a distinctly American voice in literature, as did Henry Wadsworth Longfellow (1807–82), who was best known for *Evangeline* (1847), *Hiawatha*, (1855), and "Paul Revere's Ride" (1861).

Walt Whitman (1819–92) offers a poetic voice that may be said to encapsulate and call into being the American character more effectively than that of any other poets of the century, or perhaps of any century. His *vers libre* or "free verse" poems broke away from conventional meters and rhyme. Whitman got his start in journalism with the *Brooklyn Daily Eagle* in 1841, and his poems share with works of journalism a gift for keen observation. In 1855 he first published his magnum opus, *Leaves of Grass*, which he would add to and revise for decades. In this equal-opportunity collection, a prostitute occupies the same poetic space as the president of the United States. Emerson shared Whitman's enthusiasm for a home-grown American poetic voice, but is better known for his essays than his poetry.

Emily Dickinson (1830–86) seldom left her home in Amherst, Massachusetts, after age 30, but her spiritual searching and devoted observation of nature made her poems very much of their time and place. Her witty, epigrammatic style is also reminiscent of the 17th-century English Metaphysical poets, whom Dickinson admired. At the same time her unlikely images that multiply meanings in tightly worked lyrics anticipate 20th-century poetic trends. With very few exceptions, Dickinson's 1,000-plus extant poems, many written in a burst of creativity around 1860, were not published until after her death, close to the turn of the century.

Edgar Allan Poe (1809–49) left his mark on both poetry and the short story. His was the world of the Romantic individual locked in personal consciousness. In one of the most famous American poems, "The Raven" (1845), Poe's narrator construes the bird's parroted responses as a message of doom, suggesting that humans require no outside source of fear—they most often frighten themselves.

Poe's fascination with the supernatural, alternative realities, and the power of the human mind to perceive and deceive makes his tales early examples of the modern-day horror, science fiction, and detective-story genres. A number of his most famous stories, including "The Fall of the House of Usher," appeared in *Burton's Gentleman's Magazine* while he was its coeditor from 1839 to 1840.

The novelist and short-story writer Nathaniel Hawthorne (1803–82) commanded the world's respect for the subtlety of his often melancholic, anxiety-riddled narratives. Hawthorne imagined the recent past of his Puritan and colonial forebears and gave voice to the dark underside of life in the new republic, which was often fraught with alienation and despair. In 1850 he published *The Scarlet Letter*, which, like much of his work, employs rich symbolism and allegory to highlight the profound moral dilemma of evil and guilt: the scarlet *A* for adultery metamorphoses as sympathies shift. The Romantic fiction writers offered nuanced character studies, moving well beyond setting and plot to psychological interiority.

Louisa May Alcott (1832–88) grew up in a world steeped in Transcendentalism. Her father, Bronson Alcott (1799–1888), was a school reformer in Concord and elsewhere and a frequent contributor to *The Dial*. His daughter shared his passion for philosophy and education. She was memorialized as "the children's friend" at her funeral, primarily for *Little Women* (1868), one of the most popular works of children's literature ever published. She has never fallen into obscurity, unlike so many other 19th-century women who wrote about the domestic sphere.

The fiction of Herman Melville (1819–91) combines the adventure of the frontier narrative with the symbolism and psychological interiority of Hawthorne's character studies. In Melville's novels—such as *Typee* (1846) and *Moby-Dick; or, the Whale* (1851), and short stories and novellas, such as *Billy Budd, Sailor*, which drew on his own maritime adventures—authority is no guarantee of morality. Both Hawthorne and Melville struggled to make a financial success of writing. At the time of Melville's death in 1891, he had a stronger following in England than in his own country, but since the early 20th century scholars have considered his contribution to American letters to be virtually unparalleled.

Women's Domestic Fiction Hawthorne railed against what he called "those damned scribbling women," who wrote domestic or sentimental fiction. While *The Scarlet Letter* was a best seller in 1850, it sold only in the thousands of copies; that same year the novelist Susan Warner (1819–85) published *The Wide, Wide World*, whose 14 editions in two years exceeded any previous book's sales in the United States, and it became an exceptional publishing sensation in England as well. Domestic or sentimental fiction enjoyed its greatest popularity in America from 1820 through 1870, beginning with Catharine Sedgwick's *New-England Tale* (1822). Stemming from the 18th-century novel of sensibility, the genre promoted reliance on the goodness of human nature and the power of feelings as a guide to proper behavior. It took its place alongside conduct manuals for young girls and women. The stories generally focused on the plight of a heroine in an economically precarious situation whose redemption often comes with self-mastery. In sentimental fiction, sacrifice through marriage, family, and service to God takes precedence over personal happiness, or stands as the fastest routes to that happiness.

The novelist Harriet Beecher Stowe (1811–96) resists classification in this genre because her themes transcend the hearth, although her work would be readily accessible to a reading public hungry for sentimental fiction. The sentimental aspects of her writing helped her advocate for causes, primarily for the abolition of slavery. In 1851 *Uncle Tom's Cabin* sold 1 million copies within the year, another unprecedented literary success in the United States.

The Slave Narrative One slave who found freedom and wrote about his experiences was Frederick Douglass (1818–95), who published *Narrative of the Life of Frederick Douglass, an American Slave: Written by Himself* in 1845. Reading and writing proved the former slave's salvation: Douglass was forced to learn in secrecy and by his wits. He eloquently depicts the dehumanizing effects of bondage, writing what is often considered one of the finest examples of the slave narrative genre. In describing the efforts of an overseer to break his spirit, Douglass turns the tables to show that it was the slaveholders, not the slaves, who were the brutes to be feared. Douglass toured much of the United States and Europe speaking about his experiences and working for the emancipation of slaves.

Another slave who wrote a powerful account of the hazards of life for a black person in antebellum America was Harriet Ann Jacobs (1813–97), also known as Linda Brent, the author of *Incidents in the Life of a Slave Girl* (1861). Jacobs survived her enslavement by hiding in the crawlspace of an attic on her owner's property for several years. She used sentimental conventions to describe the plight of a black woman intent on keeping her virtue in an immensely cruel and dehumanizing system. A spin-off of the slave narrative is the narrative from a "free" black woman. Harriet Wilson (1827–63) published *Our Nig: Or, Sketches from the Life of a Free Black, in a Two-Story White House, North, Showing that Slavery's Shadows Fall Even There*, the first novel by an African-American woman, in 1859. It features the horrible mistreatment of a slave/servant in the North and appealed, to the humane sensibilities of white northern women.

Late 19th- through Early 20th-Century Literature

In 1867 the cattle route known as the Chisholm Trail would fuel the genre of the western; and the completion of the Union Pacific–Central Pacific Railroad in 1869 and the Klondike Gold Rush of 1896 would expand the frontiers of America's literary imagination. Alexander Graham Bell's invention of the telephone in 1876 would propel Americans into the future; the advent of motion pictures at the turn of the 20th century would forever alter the production of art and literature both at home and abroad. Add a "Rough Rider" for a president in Theodore Roosevelt, who ascended to power in 1901; the advent of Orville Wright's flying machine in 1903; Henry Ford's Model T in 1908; Albert Einstein's theory of relativity in 1905, and a world war lurking on the horizon, and you have a country and a world hurtling into a new era at the turn of the 20th century, a time of excitement and anticipation as well as conflict, secularism, industrialization, and alienation.

Naturalism Naturalism depicted the chaos of modern human life with rational, scientific objectivity in an exploration of Darwinian theories of biological and environmental determinism. Like Romanticism, the movement began in Europe and focused on the disadvantaged in society, as in Émile Zola's 1885 novel about French mine workers, *Germinal*. As America became more mechanized, the social radicalism of the trend flourished. Many of its practitioners came of age in the heyday of muckraking journalism, which exposed the horrors of working life at the time. Upton Sinclair (1878–1968) honed his skills in this training ground, telling about factory atrocities of the meatpacking industry in *The Jungle* (1906). Stephen Crane, native of New Jersey, changed the genre of war writing with *The Red Badge of Courage* (1895). His *Maggie: A Girl of the Streets* (1893) depicted the immigrant experience.

The masters of naturalism include Frank Norris (1870–1902), who was born in Chicago but spent most of his life in San Francisco. Theodore Dreiser (1871–1945), a protégé of Norris, was born in Indiana, the ninth child of German immigrants. His concern with the plight of the working class led him to spend most of his life as a socialist; shortly before he died, he joined the American Communist Party. Dreiser's *Sister Carrie* (1900) and *An American Tragedy* (1925) reveal the profound dissatisfactions of the materialist life in an America with a torn social fabric utterly beyond individual control.

The Californian novelist Jack London (1876–1916) explored the potential for adaptation to one's environment in such novels as *The Call of the Wild* (1903) and *White Fang* (1906). He gained equal fame for his real-life adventures and for his literary achievements, becoming the most commercially successful writer of the period.

Realism The line separating naturalism and realism often seems blurred, but they have quite distinct aims. Realism attempts to capture reality as faithfully as possible, almost photographically. Instead of focusing on the dark and seemingly inevitable chaos in the offing, the realist project concerns itself with the immediate present, the verifiable fact, and the search for truth. With roots in journalism and a lifelong series of editorial positions at literary magazines, Ohio-born William Dean Howells (1837–1920) was best known for *The Rise of Silas Lapham* (1885). Henry James (1843–1916), the scion of an old and powerful New York family, refined psychological interiority into high art, particularly in such works as *The Portrait of a Lady* (1881). His characters occupied high social strata, yet they could cut absurd (though ethically superior) figures next to their European counterparts, especially in *The American* (1877). James reigned over a set of American writers, philosophers, architects, artists, and philanthropists known as the "cosmopolitans," training his eye on the bustling transatlantic traffic of the day. He examined the American character laid bare before the scrutiny and ridicule of ancestral Europe, routinely lampooning its democratic cousin abroad. James's protégée, the Pulitzer Prize–winning novelist Edith Wharton (1862–1937), examined American personalities, mores, and ethics, sharing his fascination with the social elite. She crafted chilling and illuminating portraits of the social order in the United States, most notably in *The Age of Innocence* (1919), *Ethan Frome* (1911), and *The House of Mirth* (1905).

Regionalism The use of vernacular and dialect aids realist characterization, which trumped plot in the regionalist movement and figured in regional or local-color fiction. The master of vernacular was Missouri-born Mark Twain (Samuel Clemens, 1835–1910), who served as a Confederate soldier. His humor, which he used to depict life on the Mississippi River, demonstrates realism's distinction from the dour naturalist model. His unflinching honesty debunked outmoded ways of thinking about the country. Twain was a great and influential innovator with his frequent use of authentic vernacular language. His work also exemplified popular frontier humor, and *Adventures of Huckleberry Finn* (1884) is often considered to be the best novel produced by an American.

A literary renaissance centered in Chicago flourished at the end of the 19th century and start of the 20th and also challenged the East's literary monopoly. Hamlin Garland (1860–1940) documented the unromanticized truth of pioneer subsistence. Sherwood Anderson (1876–1941) spun character studies set in the quiet desolation of small-town midwestern American life, most famously in *Winesburg, Ohio* (1919). Carl Sandburg (1878–1967), whose *Chicago Poems* emerged in print in 1916, won two Pulitzers. Vachel Lindsay (1879–1931), of Springfield, Illinois, traveled the country on foot performing his poetry for the masses. *Spoon River Anthology* (1915) by Edgar Lee Masters (1869–1950), conjures up voices of tiny Spoon River in dramatic monologues. The Chicago poets used experimental techniques to animate overlooked members of society.

Late 19th- and early 20th-century regional voices often belonged to women. Willa Cather's *O, Pioneers!* (1913), *My Antonía* (1918), and *Death Comes for the Archbishop* (1927) made high art out of life on the prairie and in the American Southwest. Like Wharton, Cather gave texture and nuance to the life experienced by women as the nation struggled with women's suffrage. In the same vein, Kate Chopin (1851–1904) and Charlotte Perkins Gilman (1860–1935) wrote narratives that illuminated the great dissatisfaction that even affluent women could feel with their lives—dissatisfaction that could lead to mental illness and suicide. Both Chopin's *The Awakening* and Gilman's *The Yellow Wallpaper* appeared in 1899.

In the heyday of regionalism, a group in Nashville, Tennessee, group taking its name from a Vanderbilt University literary magazine, *The Fugitive*, launched a challenge to northern values of urban industrial life and cast off the charges of southern racism and provincialism. The "Fugitives" were led by the poet and critic John Crowe Ransom (1888–1974), the poet Allen Tate (1899–1979), and novelist Robert Penn Warren (1905–89). They were affiliated with New Criticism and attentive to formal patterns.

The South also blossomed with tart, insightful, humorous, and haunting fiction by Katherine Anne Porter (1890–1980), Eudora Welty (1909–2001), and Flannery O'Connor (1925–64). More recently, Wallace Stegner (1909–93) has crafted several brilliant and effective character studies set in the West in *Angle of Repose* (1971) and *Crossing to Safety* (1987).

Modernism and Its Discontents Modernism reached its height in the 1920's, though it began before World War I and dominated the arts at least through the 1940's. Along with scientists such as Werner Heisenberg and philosophers such as Edmund Husserl, modernists believed that what we call objective reality is shaped by perception. The new human sciences of psychology, anthropology, and linguistics exposed the mental and social dimensions of reality. Artists tried to capture the ways in which dreams, culture, and language color perception. Cubism in painting, with its rejection of three-dimensional perspective; and jazz in music, with its improvisation and syncopation, began to dismantle familiar structures of visual and aural experience. Modernist writers brought analogous stylistic innovations to the page.

The era's epistemological uncertainty, along with the upheavals of war and technological change, bred anxious despair about the disintegration of Western civilization as well as breathless expectation of a radically different future. Influenced by the technological enthusiasm of the Italian Futurists, Ezra Pound (1885–1972) enjoined aspiring poets to "make it new." Pound presided over the Imagist movement of the 1910's, which ushered in a spare poetic style that broke with traditional prosody and discursive rhetoric. Like the "objective correlative" described by T. S. Eliot (1888–1965), the Imagist poem elicits a reader's emotions through associations in the material world. In addition to writing his own extensive opus, most notably the unfinished long poem of 30 years' labor, *The Cantos*, Pound mentored many important Modernist poets, including Eliot, whose poem *The Waste Land* (1922) famously captures the tenor of Modernism. It is a collage of fragments—myths, legends, symbols, overheard voices—from many different cultures, some in other languages, that its neurotic speaker "shores up against the ruins" of modern urban life.

Many American intellectuals, including Pound and Eliot, sought refuge in Europe from what they saw as the culturally impoverished, socially repressive United States. Gertrude Stein (1874–1946) hosted a number of them, bringing together the artists in her life as much as in her work. An avant-garde poet, fiction writer, and dramatist herself, Stein was also a discerning, forward-looking collector of paintings by the likes of Pablo Picasso and Henri Matisse, and her adopted home in Paris served as a salon for these and other artists, including expatriate Americans such as Ernest Hemingway (1899–1961)and F. Scott Fitzgerald (1896–1940). Stein's phrase for the decimated youth of World War I, the "lost generation," would eventually be applied to such American exiles, whose European adventures Hemingway's *The Sun Also Rises (1926)* and Fitzgerald's *Tender Is the Night* (1934) are fictionalized in Hemingway's journalistic style of direct statement and concrete detail might be compared to Imagist poetry. Writing in a more conventional style, Fitzgerald chronicled the libertine lifestyle of the "roaring" 1920's, with its speakeasies and flappers, in *The Great Gatsby* (1925) and other works.

In fiction and drama, William Faulkner (1897–1962) and Eugene O'Neill (1888–1953) (see Drama) may be considered America's modernist masters. Faulkner's *The Sound and the Fury* (1929) exhibits two key innovations of the period: stream-of-consciousness narration and multiple points of view. Depicting the same circumstances from four points of view, the text reads as if it were the transcription of characters' interior monologues, including apparently random thoughts usually omitted from rational discourse. Other renowned works by Faulkner include *Light in August* (1932) and *Absalom, Absalom!* (1936).

The Great Depression of the 1930's made the "high" Modernism of the previous decade seem especially removed from the real hardships of everyday life. Pound's fascist sympathies and anti-Semitism, especially in the years leading up to World War II, confirmed suspicions of modernists' conservative politics at a time when many artists were leaning left. William Carlos Williams (1883–1963), once published as an Imagist poet, began to object to his colleagues' elitism. Instead of the models many in the "lost generation" adopted abroad, he sought a uniquely American voice in his poetry and largely stuck to native shores. Even as he documented the humble and home-grown, however, Williams let the unadorned image speak, in true Modernist style. John Dos Passos (1896–1970) also put Modernist technique in the service of progressive politics. His *U.S.A.* trilogy, which explored the degradations of the economic and social divide under capitalism in the United States between 1900 and 1930, juxtaposed newspaper headlines and popular songs with the stories of his fictional characters in a manner reminiscent of Cubists' collages and the montage style of film, a modern form by definition. Experiences as a manual laborer enabled John Steinbeck (1902–68) to write proletarian novels from the heart. Especially moving and enduring is *The Grapes of Wrath* (1939), the story of a dispossessed farm family fleeing the Dust Bowl for California.

The Beats of the 1950's rejected the establishment in all its guises, including the Modernist literature that had gone mainstream by that time. Although Beat literature employed open forms akin to the Modernists' free verse, the Beats prized uncensored, spontaneous self-expression whereas the Modernists favored an impersonal, crafted lyricism. *Howl* (1956) by Allen Ginsberg (1926–97), for example, seemingly blurts out all aspects of the author's private life—sexual encounters, drug experiments, episodes of mental illness—in incantatory Whitmanesque catalogs. Jack Kerouac (1922–69) so urgently wanted to capture raw moments of inspiration that he typed on continuous rolls of paper parts of *On the Road* (1957), a *roman à clef* depicting the cross-country joyrides of Beats such as Kerouac, Ginsberg, and the novelist William S. Burroughs (1914–97). Kerouac defined this distinctly American group of artists as "beaten" down by the conformist postwar suburban lifestyle and capable of a certain "beatitude" through altered states induced by drugs, sex, music, and Eastern mysticism.

The Harlem Renaissance African-American writers left the constraints of the slave narrative as they migrated from the rural South searching for opportunity in the cities of the North. In 1892 Frances Harper's sentimental novel *Iola Leroy* was the best-selling of all African-American women's writings of the 19th century. In 1899 Charles Chesnutt (1858–1932) published *The Conjure Woman* and *The Wife of His Youth and Other Stories of the Color Line*, which neatly bridged antebellum and postbellum American life. In 1903 W. E. B. DuBois (1868–1963) contributed a controversial, landmark book called *The Souls of Black Folk* about life and opportunity for African Americans in the United States. By the 1920's, a community in northern New York City known as Harlem had become a mecca for men and women of color, including musicians and artists, spawning what became known as the Harlem Renaissance of culture and artistic expression.

In the vitality of this environment, a number of talented writers flourished, including Langston Hughes (1902–67), the brave poet of such works as *The Weary Blues* (1926); Nella Larsen (1891–1964), best known for her sobering account of the perils of assimilation in America in the 1929 novel *Passing*, and Zora Neale Hurston (1891–1960). Hurston was raised in all-black Eatonville, Florida, to which she returned to do research, having studied with the anthropologist Franz Boaz and become a folklorist and novelist. She is best known for *Their Eyes Were Watching God* (1937). Additional stars of the Harlem Renaissance include Claude McKay (1889–1948), the poet Countee Cullen (1903–46), and Jean Toomer (1894–1967).

They all paved the way for such masterly novelists and essayists as Richard Wright (1908–60) and James Baldwin (1924–87), who depicted racial struggles throughout the civil rights era. Like many modern writers, James Baldwin spent time in self-imposed exile, particularly in Paris, and his experiences abroad translated into remarkable perspective in his writings. *The Fire Next Time* (1963) takes stock of American race relations on the 100th anniversary of the Emancipation Proclamation. The collection of essays contains a jeremiad to a nation that might self-destruct if it cannot heal its own racial wounds. Martin Luther King Jr., Malcolm X, Maya Angelou (b. 1928), Alice Walker (b. 1944), and Toni Morrison (b. 1931) flesh out Baldwin's portrait of a nation still very much in need of change.

Mid- to Late 20th Century and Beyond

The responsibilities of technology and the challenges of modernity in a diverse democracy have provided most of the fodder for the postmodern American novel. The coming-of-age narrative or bildungsroman began in Germany but caught fire in the United States, perhaps because the nation had to come of age rather violently and quickly in the late 19th and 20th centuries. *The Catcher in the Rye* (1951) by J. D. (Jerome David) Salinger (b. 1919) stands as the quintessential 20th-century American bildungsroman; but Philip Roth (b. 1933), John Winslow Irving (b. 1942), Bernard Malamud (1914–86), Jamaica Kincaid (b. 1949), Amy Tan (b. 1952), Maxine Hong Kingston (b. 1940), and many others have added to the canon. For scope, range, and sheer talent, it is hard to surpass Vladimir Nabokov (1899–1977), who was foreign-born but captured America's love affair with youth, Hollywood, sex, and materialism in the scandalous *Lolita* (1955). Kurt Vonnegut

New Wave of Writers Reinvents Literature

By MICHIKO KAKUTANI

Sixty-one years ago, in a famous essay, Philip Rahv divided American writers into two groups: "palefaces," like Henry James and T. S. Eliot, with high brows, oversize superegos and self-conscious, philosophical sensibilities; and "redskins," like Whitman and Dreiser, with earthier styles and noisier, more populist outlooks. The first group specialized in heady, cultivated works, rich in symbolism and allegory; the second favored a blunter, more emotional naturalism.

At their worst, Rahv argued, "palefaces" were snobbish, pedantic and effete, while "redskins" tended to fall prey to conformity, sentimentality and a crude anti-intellectualism. It was the view of Rahv—the editor of *Partisan Review* and one of his generation's most influential critics—that "the national literature" had been crippled by "the ills of a split personality." The question, he went on, was whether "history will make whole again what it has rent asunder."

The answer, it turns out, is an exuberant yes. It's clear now that the most exciting writers at work today—both in the United States and abroad—have transcended Rahv's great artistic schism and done so with remarkable energy and elan.

Such masters of the contemporary novel as Don DeLillo, Toni Morrison, Thomas Pynchon, and Salman Rushdie—along with a new generation of writers like Dave Eggers, David Foster Wallace, and Zadie Smith—have discovered a myriad of ways to fuse the cerebral and the visceral, the high and the low, the world of ideas and the world of raw experience. Like Rahv's "redskins," these writers are hot-wired to the gritty world around them, rendering it with uncommon spontaneity and vigor. At the same time, their books boast a "paleface" fascination with complexity and philosophical nuance; they are highly self-referential works of art, replete with arcane references and complex literary games.

At their best, writers like Mr. Eggers and Ms. Smith combine a mandarin love of ornate, even byzantine prose with the vernacular energy of the streets, tossing together the literary and the colloquial with hyperventilated glee. They tend to be magpies, lifting bits and pieces from virtually every recent literary school—from the French nouveau roman, from the magical realists, from Kafka and Borges, from Barthes and Barthelme and Barth—while putting the chilly innovations of the avant-garde at the service of a more capacious social vision.

Mr. Eggers's *Heartbreaking Work of Staggering Genius* uses all the latest postmodern hardware: his account of his parents's deaths and his rearing of his eight-year old brother is prefaced with a coy discussion of the major themes of the book, "Rules and Suggestions for Enjoyment of this Book" and an emotional flow chart; it demonstrates, however, that such devices can enhance, rather than undermine, the emotional power of his story.

Mr. Wallace's 1,079-page novel *Infinite Jest* employs jokes, soliloquies, run-on footnotes and a proliferating series of subplots to give the reader a carnivalesque portrait of a toxic postmillennial America. And Mark Z. Danielewski's new novel *House of Leaves* uses poems, screenplay excerpts, playful typography, assorted appendices, and a succession of stories within stories to create a novelistic mosaic that simultaneously reads like a thriller and like a strange, dreamlike excursion into the subconscious.

Mr. Rushdie's *Midnight's Children* and *The Moor's Last Sigh* address no less a subject than the history of the Indian subcontinent over the last 50 years. Mr. DeLillo's *Underworld* does the same for America in the second half of the 20th century. Slavery and its dark legacy stand at the center of Ms. Morrison's masterpiece *Beloved*. And the consequences of imperialism form the pivot of Zadie Smith's *White Teeth*, a remarkable first novel that explores the impact of public events on private lives with Dickensian energy and skill.

Even such seemingly self-contained forms as the memoir and the bildungsroman are being reinvented by these writers. Mr. Eggers's *Heartbreaking Work* bears about as much resemblance to most autobiographies as Laurence Sterne's *Tristram Shandy* does to the traditional novel, and Moses Isegawa's new novel *Abyssinian Chronicles* opens out from a fairly conventional coming of age story into an alarming, multifaceted tableau of life in Idi Amin's Uganda.

With his Pulitzer Prize-winning 1997 novel *American Pastoral*, Mr. Roth grappled shrewdly with the big subjects he had once spurned as unmanageable: the book renounced the solipsistic mirror games that had distinguished so much of his earlier fiction to create a resonant parable of American innocence and disillusion: through the prism of one man's life, it told the story of what happened to the nation in the tumultuous decades between World War II and Vietnam, and the aftermath of the 60's.

It was also in 1997, which can now be seen as a kind of watershed year in American fiction, that two of our postmodern masters brought out their finest novels to date, novels that evinced a new emotionality and ardor. Mr. Pynchon's *Mason & Dixon* was a sprawling, darkly comic epic that showed the novelist moving beyond his love of allegory and cartoonish farce to create two wonderfully human heroes (based on the surveyors who mapped the Mason-Dixon line, dividing the North and South) and a richly detailed portrait of early America in all its promise and menace. Mr. DeLillo's dazzling, virtuosic *Underworld* similarly revealed a new sympathy and attention to character on the author's part: in tracing the crisscrossing, tangential lives of dozens of people who witnessed the famous Giants-Dodgers game that decided the 1951 pennant race, the novel conjured up a jazzy, synesthetic vision of this country in the waning decades of the last millennium.

Younger writers who grew up reading Mr. DeLillo, Mr. Pynchon and Mr. Roth (along with novelists like Faulkner, Nabokov, and Joyce) were at the same time assimilating that earlier generation's innovations, and developing distinctive voices of their own. Children of the 60's and 70's, such writers as Mr. Wallace, Mr. Eggers, Mr. Danielewski, Dale Peck, Richard Powers, and Alex Garland had grown up with discontinuity and flux. Chaos was not intimidating to them; it was simply how things were.

As a result, they've tackled the crazy, multifarious reality they see around them head-on, trying to cram all its information-age effluvia willy-nilly into the pages their books. This is why their books often flaunt a smorgasbord of techniques, transforming the comic and the tragic, the hallucinatory and the naturalistic from mutually exclusive genres into stylistic modes that can be shrugged on and off at will. This is why their books often have an encyclopedic air to them: *House of Leaves* bristles with lists of photographers and girls, interpolated passages of gibberish, and collage-like asides about architecture and construction.

Music-inspired strategies surface in many pale-red works, offering, perhaps, a structural form that's fluid enough to accommodate these authors' nonlinear proclivities. In "Martin and John," Dale Peck uses the technique of theme and variation to create a portrait of his hero: we hear John—a hustler turned author—tell us his story directly, and then we hear his story again, as refracted through the fictions he's written. In *A Heartbreaking Work*, Mr. Eggers reprises events in different keys to try to convey to the reader the emotional fallout of his parents' deaths. And in *Infinite Jest*, Mr. Wallace juxtaposes three storylines (concerning a tennis instructor's family, a former Demerol addict and a group of radicals who want to get their hands on a movie reputed to be so entertaining that it causes audiences to die of pleasure) to build a musical echo chamber of shared motifs.

In merging Rahv's paleface and redskin traditions, such writers are creating a literature that's both brainy and potent, a literature fecund with ideas and in sync with the invisible thrum of the zeitgeist. The finest pale-red books not only capture our cultural vertigo, they also attest to the vitality of literature today. They prove that rumors of the novel's demise—repeatedly promulgated by scholars like Harold Bloom and Alvin Kernan—are vastly exaggerated, that literature has managed to survive deconstruction and decanonized curriculums, the dot-com revolution and the siren call of Hollywood, that young authors continue to revere the art of writing even as they reinvent its form.

(b. 1922), Norman Mailer (b. 1923), John Updike (b. 1932), John Cheever (1912–82), Raymond Carver (1938–88), Joyce Carol Oates (b. 1938), Tim O'Brien (b. 1946), T. C. Boyle (b. 1948), Barbara Kingsolver (b. 1955), and Don DeLillo (b. 1936) have all shown tremendous talent and courage describing war, prejudice, gender relations, and other topics of great importance in a wild and varied nation.

Postmodernism A common characteristic of postmodern fiction and poetry is an awareness of the unreliability of representation. Gone is the realist faith in the capacity of writing to capture external reality, but gone too are the Modernists' earnest efforts to document perception. Though postmodern authors may write in a realist mode or use modernist techniques, they often do so self-consciously. This self-consciousness produces a pastiche of styles; a mixing of genres and registers, including allusions to mass culture; adaptations of earlier modes, as in magic realism's interpolation of fantasy interludes amid everyday life; a fascination with chance and randomness; and self-reflexivity, or art about art, called metafiction in the novel. An example of self-reflexivity in poetry is *Self-Portrait in a Convex Mirror* (1975) by John Ashbery (b. 1927), with its central image of a painter painting a distorted reflection of himself while the poet comments on the composition of the poem. The incommensurability of words with what they represent in a poststructuralist universe evinces world-weary resignation, ironic detachment or even giddiness in postmodern literature. Still, the critique of power structures that followed from poststructuralism has helped open the postmodern canon to women and multiethnic authors.

Multimedia approaches and the continued challenges of war and technology, as well as unprecedented and expanding access to art and literary production with the Internet and online publishing, should ensure that the literary landscape will continue to shift radically in the 21st century.

Popular Literature

Popular literature is simply writing read by a wide audience. More pejoratively, literary critics have sometimes used *popular* to distinguish supposedly formulaic and disposable writing from unique and valuable art. Always appealing to readers and lucrative for the publishing industry, popular literature now commands academic regard among scholars of cultural studies.

The history of popular literature is the story of how large numbers of readers have obtained and consumed texts. Books remained largely out of the reach of most people's skills and means until the 18th century, when in England small paper-covered "chapbooks" usually containing 24 pages of oral-traditional folklore were sold by itinerant peddlers or "chapmen." Also called "penny histories," these little books offered much cheaper diversions than the hardback, multivolume, professionally written novels enjoyed by the middle and upper classes at the time. In the 19th century charity schools and compulsory public education created a mass readership in Europe and the United States. This reading public began to look beyond the family Bible for entertainment, and the market responded with gripping tales produced inexpensively for the cash-strapped lower classes. From around 1830 in the United States, family-friendly "story papers" such as *Tip Top Weekly* and the *Fireside Companion* provided romances for women, adventure tales for men, and stories for children, primarily boys, in an affordable newspaper format enabled by the new steam-powered rotary press.

The dime novel of the late 19th century and the pulp magazine of the early 20th combined the hallmarks of popular literature—expendability, irresistibility, and affordability. Dime novels were billed as "Books for the millions!" by their original publisher, Beadle and Adams, and were imitated by many other publishing houses such as the long-lived Street and Smith. Priced between five and 25 cents, these small, approximately 100-page, paper-covered volumes appeared at regular intervals in numbered sequence. This presentation qualified them for periodical-rate postage, which, together with the new transcontinental railway, kept national distribution costs down and the ever-expanding readership among the poor affordably supplied. Publishers also economized by employing a stable of unrecognized, meagerly compensated authors writing anonymously under house pseudonyms. The American frontier was a favorite setting, and recurring heroes such as Deadwood Dick won readers loyalty. Around the turn of the 20th century, European publishers jumped on the American dime-novel bandwagon, but the parade slowed during World War I and halted entirely by 1933. While the Great Depression contributed to the dime novel's demise, competition from the new mass media of film and radio played a part, too. Readers of little means turned to pulp magazines, which offered more and bigger pages covered with glossy color illustrations, at the same price as dime novels. Subsidized by many advertisers and printed on cheap untrimmed wood-pulp paper, the "pulps" saw their heyday in the 1920's and 30's following publisher Frank A. Munsey's early success with the fiction magazine *Argosy* in the 1890's.

Since 1950 or so, popular literature has often been equated with the common paperback genres of western, horror, romance, mystery, fantasy, and science fiction. This division of the field solidified in the days of pulp magazines, when publishers marketed separate periodicals under clearly defined niche titles such as *Western Story*, *Love Story*, *Detective Story*, and *Astounding Science Fiction*. Paperbacks as we know them today first appeared in the 1930's from Penguin Books in England and Pocket Books in the United States. In the tradition of popular literature, these books were designed for low price rather than long life. Portability also made them popular with soldiers in World War II. Reprints of major works by recognized authors appeared in paperback after more expensive hardback editions; however, the often anonymous writers of so-called paperback originals wrote to order for a familiar hero or series. To draw a mass audience, these strictly softcover novels had dramatic cover illustrations and were sold at drugstores and newsstands rather than in bookstores. Mystery, romance, and science fiction remain most steeped in these traditional practices of popular literature. Sometimes dismissed as formula fiction, novels in these genres indeed tend to follow well-established conventions. Fans and scholars alike find varied and complicated functions beneath this apparent simplicity, however. Some note that the very predictability of these books can offer a reassuring anchor amid personal turmoil or cultural upheaval. Such novels can even help to make social change more acceptable, for example, by adapting familiar plots and settings to new roles for women and ethnic minorities. For readers well versed in a favorite genre, aesthetic pleasure lies in observing writers' innovation within conventional constraints.

Mystery Fiction

Urbanization began in Europe and North America about the same time that a mass readership for popular literature emerged. City living kindled the interest of 18th- and 19th-century readers in the new urban crime-fighting organizations. These included the Bow Street Runners in London, the Sûreté Nationale in Paris, and the Pinkerton private investigation agency, which orginated in Chicago. Bookworms seeking a thrill eagerly consumed police accounts such as *Richmond: Or, Scenes in the Life of a Bow Street Runner* (1827); the *Mémoires* (1828–29) of François Eugène Vidocq (1775–1857), first chief of the Sûreté; and the monthly *Police Gazette* of Allan Pinkerton (1819–94). Early mysteries often drew upon characters and cases from real-life police work. English novelist Wilkie Collins (1824–89) modeled Sergeant Cuff in *The Moonstone* (1868) after Scotland Yard detective Jonathan Whicher, who had solved a similar case. Old Sleuth, hero of a fiction series starting in 1872 in the *Fireside Companion* and continuing in the dime novel *Old Sleuth Weekly*, which lasted until 1918, is thought to have been based on Allan Pinkerton.

The greater anonymity afforded by urban life meant that bringing a criminal to justice sometimes necessitated feats of detection that could make for a good story. More than a strong arm, mental muscle began to characterize the quintessential crime fighter. The famous ratiocination of C. Auguste Dupin—a dectective created by Edgar Allan Poe (1809–49)—surpasses that of real police officers like Vidocq, whose inferior powers Dupin belittles in "Murders in the Rue Morgue" (1841). In this story, along with two others featuring Dupin, Poe inaugurated a common pattern in mystery fiction: a slower-witted sidekick narrates for mystified readers how a cerebral amateur detective solves an apparently impossible crime mishandled by the police.

Sherlock Holmes The well-known stories of the eccentric savant Sherlock Holmes and the simpler everyman Dr. Watson, written by Sir Arthur Conan Doyle (1859–1930), certainly fit this pattern. A physician himself, Conan Doyle represented crime detection as a diagnostic science, modeling Holmes after one of his own medical school teachers, Dr. Joseph Bell. The first Holmes story, *A Study in Scarlet*, appeared serially in 1887, and Conan Doyle continued to recount the great detective's cases primarily in magazines. Having written these stories out of financial need, the author grew weary of his creations long before the public's appetite for Holmes and

Watson was satisfied. "The Final Problem" (1893) attempted to dispense with Holmes, but he soon came back by popular demand for an eventual total of 60 narratives by Conan Doyle himself, not to mention many by imitators and parodists. Conan Doyle's first short-story collection, *The Adventures of Sherlock Holmes*, appeared in 1892; his most acclaimed Holmes novel is *The Hound of the Baskervilles* (1902). Other novels featuring Holmes include *The Sign of Four* (1892) and *The Valley of Fear* (1915). To this day, Sherlock Holmes and Dr. Watson live on in the imagination of fans who write letters addressed to the fictional detective's address, 221B Baker Street.

Nick Carter One of America's earliest and most enduring detectives, Nick Carter was a figure of great learning and brilliance—like Sherlock Holmes—as well as a man of action, adventure, and strength in the tradition of popular narrative. He debuted in 1886 in story papers, appeared from 1889 to 1915 in his own dime-novel series, *Nick Carter Detective*, which totaled 800 issues, and survived in pulp magazines, paperback originals, radio shows, and movies as late as the 1970's.

Classic Detective Fiction The classic "whodunit" flowered in the 1920's and 30's—sometimes called the "Golden Age" of mystery novels. In the tradition of Poe and Conan Doyle, Golden Age mysteries narrate the intellectual exercise of determining who committed an improbable murder. During the social and economic upheaval of the decades between the wars, the solution of such puzzles offered rationality and order in fiction. Readers also took comfort in the Golden Age's typically upper-class settings, vicariously partaking of financial ease and social privilege. Clichés like "the butler did it in the library" date from this period, when murder infiltrated the English manor house. The era's fictional sleuths operated as leisured amateurs or even hailed from the aristocracy themselves. The grande dame of classic detective fiction, Agatha Christie (1890–1976), introduced the retired inspector Hercule Poirot in *The Mysterious Affair at Styles* (1920). Another writer in Christie's cohort, Dorothy L. Sayers (1893–1957), brought forth a titled detective, Lord Peter Wimsey, in *Whose Body?* (1923). One legacy of the period is today's "cozy" mystery. Often set in a reassuringly predictable English village, a "cozy" treats murder as an unpleasant aberration that an affable amateur can explain. Christie's sleuth Miss Jane Marple, an elderly spinster-knitter of St. Mary Meade, anticipated this trend. The present-day American anglophile Martha Grimes, who titles her stories after English country pubs, preserves the "cozy" conventions most faithfully.

Some of Christie's and Sayers's contemporaries across the Atlantic cultivated Golden Age sensibilities as well. Writing as a team under the pen name Ellery Queen, the cousins Frederic Dannay (1905–82) and Manfred B. Lee (1905–71) created a literary empire with their codetectives Ellery Queen and his father, Richard Queen. The erudite Ellery is a writer by trade but spends his time helping Richard, a New York City police inspector, solve crimes. The two men lead a refined home life on Manhattan's upper East Side. Beginning with *The Roman Hat Mystery* (1929), Ellery Queen solved crimes in 40 novels and short-story collections, 10 films, a weekly radio show of nine years' duration, and television series and specials. Dannay also lent the famous name to his influential *Ellery Queen's Mystery Magazine*, which fostered the careers of many now legendary mystery writers during his 40-year editorship. Another American author, Rex Stout (1886–1975), found great success with the reclusive genius Nero Wolfe, whose taste for rare orchids and gourmet food places him in the tradition of great Golden Age detectives with their upper-crust trappings.

Hard-Boiled Detective Fiction America's indigenous mystery genre is "hard-boiled" detective fiction. The adjective *hard-boiled* described World War I drill sergeants before being applied to the similarly tough, unsentimental but righteous postwar detectives (or "dicks") of stateside popular literature. Whereas Golden Age novels offered a fantasy of wealth and charm, hard-boiled fiction painted a picture of gritty mean streets, with a lone-wolf private investigator in the environment of organized crime and police corruption during Prohibition. Cynical about the law, such crime fighters operated by their own codes of honor. Like latter-day knights-errant, they enshrined the little guy against fallible institutions and the Depression-era establishment that kept many people down while insulating those at the top from hardship. The hard-boiled style began in the pulp magazine *Black Mask* with the macho man of action Race Williams, created by Carroll John Daly (1885–1958). Originally publishing adventure stories of all kinds, *Black Mask* eventually specialized in detective fiction and became nearly synonymous with the hard-boiled school, especially under editor Joseph T. "Cap" Shaw (1874–1952) from 1926 to 1936. The fast-paced, violent tales of hard-boiled suspense, as opposed to the genteel, intellectual narratives of Golden-Age puzzle solving, arose from America's pulp-magazine roots. *Black Mask* also published stories by Dashiell Hammett (1894–1961) and Raymond Chandler (1888–1959). Along with Hammett's Sam Spade and Contin-ental Op, Chandler's Philip Marlowe epitomized the hard-boiled hero's tough softness. "Down these mean streets," Chandler's credo went, "a man must go who is not himself mean, who is neither tarnished nor afraid." Perry Mason, the famous lawyer invented by Erle Stanley Gardner (1889–1970), another *Black Mask* regular, plays by his own rules and defends against injustice like any hard-boiled detective. All three writers set many of their cases in the rough-and-tumble world of Los Angeles and San Francisco.

Variations on the hard-boiled style continued during and after World War II. Mike Hammer, the dectective created by Mickey Spillane (b. 1918) is most directly descended from Daly's Race Williams. Hammer's disdain for women harks back to Williams's machismo, and, as his name would suggest, Hammer retaliates against crime with sometimes extreme violence, eschewing the moral high ground of Chandler's hard-boiled ideal. Often called "noir" fiction, many detective stories of the 1940's and 1950's adopted a darker outlook. The protagonists no longer uphold justice and order but find themselves subject to the crime and chaos that surround them. The present-day writer James Ellroy (b. 1948) keeps the noir mood alive by setting novels of cruelty and corruption in Los Angeles during the 1950's.

Police Procedurals and Crime Novels There are two mystery subgenres that do not focus on a great detective, action hero, or spy. "Police procedurals" document a whole squad's daily grind in solving a case. The 87th Precinct in Ed McBain's procedurals, for example, has five detectives, plus a lieutenant, desk sergeant, and clerk. Writing under the pen name McBain, the New Yorker Evan Hunter (Salvatore A. Lombino, b. 1926) conducted his research in squad cars and crime labs in order to portray police work as realistically as possible. Another subgenre, the crime novel or "whydunit," explores the psychology of a criminal rather than the solution of a crime. Whereas the detective in a whodunit champions justice in a world of distinct right and wrong, the killer in a whydunit may lead an apparently innocuous life in a murkier world of moral ambiguity. Prominent practitioners of the crime novel include expatriate American Mary Patricia Plangman (1921–95), writing as Patricia Highsmith, and the Belgian-born Georges Simenon (1903–89). One of the most prolific and best-selling novelists of all time, Simenon also wrote classic detective fiction about Inspector Jules Maigret of the Paris Sûreté.

Other examples of mystery fiction put a twist on the classic form by varying the age, gender, race, ethnicity, sexual orientation, occupation, or historical context of the crime solver. The adventures of the famous juvenile detectives Frank and Joe Hardy (the Hardy Boys) and Nancy Drew started in 1927 and 1930 under the pen names Franklin W. Dixon and Carolyn Keene, respectively. The Americans Edward L. Stratemeyer (1862–1930) and his daughter Harriet Stratemeyer Adams (1892–1982), as well as many ghost writers employed by the Stratemeyer Literary Syndicate, composed volumes in these ongoing, perennially popular series. The women's movement of the 1970's opened the door for widely known female sleuths of American authors: Sue Grafton (b. 1940) created Kinsey Millhone; Sara Paretsky (b. 1947) created V[ictoria] I[phigenia] Warshawski; and Patricia Cornwell (b. 1956) created Kay Scarpetta. Even before Conan Doyle created Sherlock Holmes, the American Anna Katherine Green (1846–1935), famous for *The Leavenworth Case* (1878) and other Ebenezer Gryce mysteries, brought us two women crime solvers Amelia Butterworth (Gryce's assistant) and Violet Strange. The path-breaking African-American author Chester Himes (1909–84) began writing about two black detectives, "Coffin" Ed Johnson and "Grave Digger" Jones, in the language of his adopted country, France, in 1957. These two Harlem crime fighters appeared in seven additional novels in English. Walter Mosley (b. 1952) found considerable success in the 1990's with his series about an African-American investigator, Ezekiel "Easy" Rawlins set in Mosley's hometown, Los Angeles. The Native American Tony Hillerman (b. 1925) conveys Navajo culture through mysteries involving a tribal police captain, Joe Leaphorn; and his sergeant, Jim Chee. The openly gay Dave Brandstetter, an insurance investigator, is the creation of American Joseph Hansen (b. 1923). A boom in mysteries solved by sleuths with alternative sexualities—such as lesbians Cassandra Reilly and Pam Nielsen, created by American Barbara Wilson (b. 1950)—has followed Hansen's early success. British author Edith Mary Pargeter (1913–95), writing as Ellis Peters, set the sleuthing a holy man, Brother Cadfael, in the medieval period. Peters's monastic crime solver follows the venerable British tradition of G[ilbert] K[eith] Chesterton (1874–1936), who created Father Brown.

Annual awards honoring achievement in all varieties of mystery fiction began in the 1950's. The Mystery Writers of America appoints a committee of its members to choose the year's best novel, which wins an Edgar Allan Poe ("Edgar") award. The Crime Writers' Association of Great Britain has a panel of external critics determine the winner of its yearly Gold Dagger award. Mystery Writers of America has also recognized lifetime accomplishment in mystery writing by Agatha Christie, Rex Stout, Ellery Queen, Erle Stanley Gardner, Georges Simenon, John le Carré, Ed McBain, Tony Hillerman, and Mickey Spillane with its Grand Master award. The Crime Writers' Association bestows a similar honor, the Diamond Dagger.

Romance Novels

Romance once referred to all genres of popular literature in Europe. In medieval times tales intended for a wide audience were called romances because they were written not in Latin, the lingua franca of the elite, but in regional tongues of the common folk such as French, Spanish, and Italian—the romance languages derived from the Roman tongue. Recounting a knight's feats of valor and devotion to his lady, these stories combined action, adventure, and love. Modern romance novels focus more exclusively on a love relationship and often have a female protagonist. This new perspective evolved during the 17th and 18th centuries as women readers became more common and women writers more popular. Early chroniclers of love such as the Frenchwoman Madeleine de Scudéry (1607–1701) and the Englishwoman Aphra Behn (1640–89), who fictionalized the sex scandals of their rich and famous contemporaries, were among the first female professional writers. England's Mary de la Rivière Manley (1663–1724) and Eliza Haywood (1693–1756) wrote cautionary tales for the feminine reading public about virgins seduced and abandoned by wealthy and powerful men. Susanna Rowson Haswell (1762–1824) wrote *Charlotte Temple* (1791), a sentimental tale of seduction and betrayal that was an early publishing sensation. It saw nearly 200 editions in America after the author emigrated from England.

Narratives of the 19th and 20th centuries, written by or for women, elaborated the romantic theme and female focus. A typical plot emerged when the Englishman Samuel Richardson (1689–1761) wrote *Pamela: Or, Virtue Rewarded* (1740), in which a vulnerable but spunky heroine reforms a worldly man and they marry. Set in the authors' native England, these novels also provide templates for the gothic and regency settings of today's historical romance fiction. Eleanor Hibbert (1906–93), writing as Victoria Holt, summoned up the gothic's eerie castles and supernatural events from *Jane Eyre* and its popular precursor *The Mysteries of Udolpho* (1794), written by another Englishwoman, Ann Radcliffe (1764–1823). The novels of the `British writer Georgette Heyer (1902–74) recall Austen's genteel English countryside in the 1810's, during the regency of the Prince of Wales, later George IV.

A heroine's romantic adventures ending in marriage became the stock-in-trade for much popular literature of the 19th and 20th centuries. Some of this literature was devoted exclusively to affairs of the heart, such as the longest-running Bertha Clay Library and New Bertha M. Clay Library (1900–32), whose titles referred to a pen name under which different authors wrote. Pulp magazine romances began with Street and Smith's *Love Story* in 1921. Harlequin became synonymous with the mass market romance paperback sold in groceries and drugstores. This Canadian house specialized exclusively in romance titles in 1964, and acquired its competitor across the Atlantic in 1971. With the purchase of Simon & Schuster's romance line, Silhouette, in 1985, Harlequin became the only major publisher of traditional series romances. Other numbered series, such as Bantam's Loveswept line, market the works of individual authors.

Though the basic formula remains the same, the romance genre has diversified with changing times. The American Kathleen Woodiwiss's *Flame and the Flower* (1972) introduced explicit sex between the virginal heroine and the older love interest. The force of sexual encounters in "bodice-rippers" attracted criticism for normalizing violence against women and implying that women find rape arousing. By the 1980's, cover art reflected the industry's response. Bare-chested muscle-bound men replaced fainting heroines' ripped bodices, and sex scenes became somewhat more consensual. The age gap between partners also closed. Contemporary romances such as those by the American author Nora Roberts, who has placed 69 titles on the *New York Times* best-seller list, often feature older, sexually experienced career women.

Romance fiction dominates popular literature in English today. Defining its genre as novels with a central love story and an emotionally satisfying, optimistic ending, Romance Writers of America counts more than 50 million regular readers in North America alone. In 2002 romance generated sales of more than 1.5 billion copies, which constituted more than half the popular paperback fiction market.

Science Fiction and Fantasy

Fantasy became a distinct genre in the 18th century. Rather than depicting people and events as they appear, fantasy invents enchanted locales inhabited by witches, wizards, ghosts, werewolves, vampires, and demons. It can include everything from the work of J. R. R. Tolkien (1892–1973), who created a mythology for his ancestral England, to the horrifying or "dark" fantasy of the American Stephen King (b. 1947).

Science fiction emerged after the scientific revolution. It leads into possible futures or along alternate time streams and features spaceships, ray guns, teleportation, robots, androids, cyborgs, and aliens. Though science fiction's wonders generally do not exist, its writers extrapolate empirical understandings of the physical, biological, or social environment. For example, many scholars credit the Englishwoman Mary Shelley (1797–1851) with writing the first science fiction novel in 1818, when she set Dr. Victor Frankenstein's creation of a monster in a laboratory. Victor's experiments extend 18th-century theories of electricity as the life force, so reanimating a corpse through "galvanism" would have seemed plausible to Shelley's readers. The inventions of fantasy, by contrast, are logically impossible.

As the Industrial Revolution brought technology into the daily lives of millions, science fiction came to dominate speculative literature. Steam-powered factories and railroads transformed the agrarian societies of Europe and the United States so quickly that the present seemed strange and the future likely to become more so . As novelists tried to imagine what lay ahead, some believed technology would be a positive force while others had doubts. France's Jules Verne (1828–1905) started by equipping benign heroes with exciting futuristic machines, beginning with *Five Weeks in a Balloon* (1863), the first of what he called his "scientific-didactic" novels. The misanthropic Captain Nemo in *Twenty Thousand Leagues under the Sea* (1870), however, qualifies Verne's earlier vision of benevolent science. By contrast, his optimistic countryman Edward Bellamy (1850–98) imagined a utopia free from class privilege or sexism in his best seller of 1888, *Looking Backward, 2000–1887*. Bellamy anticipated telephones, television, automobiles, and automated industry transforming society for the better. England's H. G. Wells (1866–1946) responded to him with characteristic gloom in *When the Sleeper Wakes* (1899). Wells projected a future of ever more destructive weapons, a theme also evident in *War of the Worlds* (1898), *The War in the Air* (1908), and most horrifyingly in *The World Set Free* (1914), which envisions the weaponization of nuclear energy. Even the first of Wells's "scientific romances," as he called them, *The Time Machine* (1895), warned of our planet's ultimate demise.

Both science fiction and fantasy blossomed into popular genres through magazines. In his periodical *Science and Invention,* Hugo Gernsback (1884–1967) included stories involving made-up inventions that he called "scientific-tion." Gernsback went on to publish a pulp magazine, *Amazing Stories*, devoted entirely to "science fiction." Gernsback's foundational role is recognized each year with the Hugo Award for best science fiction, still the most prestigious prize, along with the Nebula award, given by the Science Fiction and Fantasy Writers of America. Even before Gernsback's *Amazing Stories* began in 1926, the American author Edgar Rice Burroughs (1875–1950) had been writing about life on Mars, on Venus, and at the center of the Earth for *All-Story*, *Argosy*, and other general-interest pulps.

"Space opera," a successful formula, pitted good against evil in epic struggles at the intergalactic frontiers of human expansion. The American E. E. "Doc" Smith (1890–1965) cultivated a devoted readership for these thrilling action adventures. One of Smith's fans, American John W. Campbell Jr. (1910–71), went on to foster "golden age" of science fiction through *Astounding Stories*, which came under his editorship in 1938. The American authors Robert Heinlein (1907–88); Theodore Sturgeon (1918–85); Isaac Asimov (1920–93), who was born in Russia; A. E. van Vogt (1912–2000), who migrated from Canada; and many others rallied to Campbell's editorial vision. Campbell's "hard" approach to science fiction insisted on scientific plausibility, and he encouraged philosophical speculation about the human interface with technology. Destined for fame as the author of *2001: A Space Odyssey* (1968), the English-born Arthur C. Clarke (b. 1917) got his start in *Astouding Stories* under Campbell as well. Campbell also raised the profile of fantasy through another pulp, *Unknown*. Only *Weird Tales*, the primary outlet for the legendary fantasist H. P. Lovecraft (1890–1937), exceeds *Unknown* in significance. A number of fantasy writers elaborated on Lovecraft's Cthulhu mythos, a system of gods and demons based in his native New England.

The mushroom clouds that ended World War II fundamentally changed science fiction and fantasy. Writers began to look to the technological future more soberly, and readers wanted to escape into fantastic alternative worlds. Splitting the atom for a superweapon had been a common fictional topic until life and art converged with horrifying results in Hiroshima and Nagasaki. Naive faith in technological progress, or in humankind for that matter, no longer seemed tenable. Pessimism peaked in the 1960's in the British science fiction magazine *New Worlds* under the editorship of Michael Moorcock (b. 1939). His New Wave science fiction abandoned the traditional adventure format to experiment with literary style. Instead of sending a hero into outer space to fight evil and expand civilization, New Wave stories explore the inner space of individuals caught in oppressive societies. Two important New Wave authors are the Englishmen Brian Aldiss (b. 1926) and J. G. Ballard (b. 1930).

The postwar period brought other reactions against the pulp fiction typified by *Amazing* and *Astounding* magazines, the latter of which became *Analog* in 1960. *Galaxy* rose to prominence in the 1950's with a "soft," often satiric turn away from the pulps' swashbuckling technophilia. *The Magazine of Fantasy and Science Fiction* emphasized literary quality, and Isaac Asimov's *Science Fiction Magazine* prized innovation. By appearing in the new digest format and including both science fiction and fantasy, these two publications survived the capture of the popular literature market by paperbacks, which brought the two genres to a new generation. The paperback juggernaut also kept up-and-coming authors such as the Californian Philip K. Dick (1928–82) writing furiously. Often set in a dystopian future California, Dick's novels inspired the "cyberpunk" writers of the 1980's, who combined computers, information theory, and biotechnology with a countercultural edge. The American William Gibson (1948–) has provided the prime example with his first novel of cyberspace, *Neuromancer* (1984).

Now that space exploration and the Internet have become realities, science fiction is crossing over into the mainstream and converging with fantasy. Today's realism can look a lot like yesterday's science fiction, and hard scientific speculation no longer defines the genre as it blurs into fantasy. The American Ray Bradbury (b. 1920) has ceased to be regarded as a niche author, for example, even though his most famous novel, *Fahrenheit 451* (1953), first appeared in the science fiction magazine *Galaxy* and he wrote extensively for the fantasy pulp *Weird Tales*. The American Ursula K. LeGuin (b. 1929) has a similar reputation as a literary artist who happens to write science fiction and fantasy. The third in her young-adult *Earthsea* trilogy even won the National Book Award. Crossing over into the mainstream is a sign of the increasing respectability and widening appeal of these two popular genres.

History of Western Drama

Greek Drama (ca. Fifth Century B.C.)

Western drama originated in ancient Greece when, legend has it, one member of the chorus, Thespis, stepped aside and conversed with the rest—hence the term *thespian*. More than entertainment, drama for the Greeks was a vital part of the community's cultural life. It was derived from the dithyramb, a choral hymn and dance performed in honor of Dionysus, god of fertility and wine. Tragic and, later, comic playwriting competitions dating from 534 B.C. were held in Athens (and later in other cities) during the City Dionysia, an annual festival in honor of Dionysus.

Greek Festivals and Theaters The City Dionysia was a five-day festival that began with two days of pageantry in the name of Dionysus and ended with three days of drama. Three competing playwrights were each given a day on which to present their tetralogies, sets of four plays consisting of three tragedies and a brief satiric play called a satyr play. The tragedies almost always drew on familiar stories of the gods and heroes of Greek culture, often from stories found in the *Iliad* and the *Odyssey*. The productions consisted of two actors (later three actors) and a chorus. The satyr plays were bawdy, comic looks at mythology featuring choruses costumed to resemble satyrs, the half-man, half-goat minions of Dionysus.

Beyond writing the plays, the competing playwrights were responsible for creating the music, scenery, and costumes. They were also responsible for the directing and choreography, and in most cases acted in the productions as well. Each play interspersed narrative or dialogue elements, or both, with dance-songs performed by a chorus.

All of the participants in the plays wore elaborate masks and costumes, allowing actors to assume the roles of the different characters.

Greek theaters were semicircular stone structures built into slopes of hills. Each theater had a central area called an *orchestra*, or dance space, where the chorus performed. At the back of the orchestra was the *skene*, a structure believed to have been used first as a storage area, later as a scenic background for plays, and finally as a raised stage. The area where the audience sat was called the *theatron*, or "seeing place." The theaters typically held between 14,000 and 19,000 audience members, though some held even more (indeed, the theater at Epidaurus held 25,000 audience members).

Tragic Playwrights Although there were many tragic playwrights, the work of only three survives from the fifth century B.C.: that of Aeschylus (ca. 523–456 B.C.), Sophocles (ca. 496–406 B.C.) and Euripides (ca. 480–406 B.C.). Each is credited with an innovation that changed the form of theater. Aeschylus is said to have introduced a second actor to the stage, and was instrumental in the transition from the early dithyramb form to the tragic form. He is thought to have written some 90 plays, of which 70 fragments still exist. His *Oresteia* follows Orestes as he avenges his father's murder by his mother, and exemplifies Aeschylus's concerns with issues of vengeance and justice. The *Oresteia* is the only trilogy that survives intact. Sophocles introduced a third actor and increased the size of the chorus from 12 to 15 members. He is thought to have written some 123 plays, of which only seven have survived. Euripides is credited with having introduced realistic characterization and dialogue. He has 19 surviving plays.

Comic Playwrights The comic playwrights Aristophanes (ca. 450–388 B.C.) and Menander (ca. 342–292 B.C.) show a division in comic styles. Their work is categorized as Old Comedy (Aristophanes) and New Comedy (Menander). Old Comedy, typified in Aristophanes's masterpiece, *The Frogs*—which satirizes Aeschylus and Euripides and puts them onstage as characters—showed the world in chaos. New Comedy introduced stock characters, and in this way provided a direct link to the comedies of Rome and later the stock characters of the Italian commedia dell'arte.

Drama and Aristotle's Poetics After the fifth century B.C., with the defeat of Athens in the Peloponnesian War, the golden age of the Greek tragedy faded. In writing on fifth-century drama in his *Poetics*, considered the most important tract on Western drama ever written, Aristotle (384–322 B.C.) defined the elements of drama. He introduced the term *catharsis*—the purging of spectators' emotions through pity and fear—and the concept of the unities of time, place, and action—that the action of a play should take place within no more than 24 hours, have but one location, and have only one main plot. His work would inform Western drama for centuries to come.

Roman Drama

The theater of the Roman Empire was, to a large degree, a transfer of Greek theater into a Roman vernacular. Plays, though performed at Roman festivals, were set in Greece; actors wore costumes similar to those worn in Greek theater; and most of the surviving Roman plays are adaptations of Greek plays. However, whereas drama in ancient Greece was intrinsically tied to religious experience, drama in the Roman Empire increasingly found value as entertainment. Farce, typified in the works of Plautus (ca. 254–184 B.C.) and Terence (ca. 195–159 B.C.), was a popular form, and the chorus of Greek theater diminished in importance.

Spectacle in Roman Drama Whereas in Greek theater action took place offstage, in Roman theater, which relied heavily on spectacle, action took place directly onstage. In Seneca's (ca. 4 B.C.–A.D. 65) *Medea*, for example, Medea kills her children onstage. Euripides' Medea, by contrast, kills her children offstage. The audience hears the events taking place offstage but does not see them.

With the fall of Rome in the fifth century, theater fell into a void for nearly 800 years. The rise of Christianity saw the festivals of Rome become incorporated in the Christian liturgical calendar, giving birth to what would be the liturgical drama of the late Middle Ages.

Medieval Drama (ca. 500–1500)

As the Christian church rose to power during the Middle Ages, a new style of drama that celebrated the life of Christ and Christian principles emerged. By the late Middle Ages (ca. 1300–1500), with the rise in the importance of craft and trade guilds and of universities, these plays began to be performed outside of churches, often outdoors at festivals where they were produced and performed by the guilds in the towns in which they were presented.

Mystery Plays Mystery plays, also called liturgical plays or cycle plays, had their roots in Christian liturgy and in the church calendar. They enacted moments from the life of Christ, and were performed in cycles. The most popular mystery plays were connected to Easter and depicted events involved in Christ's resurrection. Also popular were plays performed during the Christmas season, depicting scenes about the birth of Christ. Special stages were erected for the plays, and the festivals at which they were performed began with processions through the town.

Morality Plays Morality plays dramatized Christian morals by portraying scenes in which actors personified allegorical characters. One actor might take the role of Goods or Fellowship, while another might enact the role of Sloth. The best known of these plays, *Everyman* (ca. 1500), shows the character of Everyman summoned by Death and accompanied on his journey by actors personifying the material elements of his earthly life, such as Kindred and Fellowship. By the time Everyman reaches Death, only Good Deeds remains as his companion. Morality plays, though first performed by guild members, eventually were performed by professional actors who traveled from town to town.

Theater of the Italian Renaissance (ca. 1300–1600)

During the Italian Renaissance theater developed along two lines: the courtly theater in which the scenic arts flourished and for which new theaters were built; and the improvisational theater of commedia dell'arte. Within the courtly theater there were few playwrights of significance. Among them were Ludovico Ariosto (1474–1533) and Niccolò Machiavelli (1469–1527), both of whom modeled their work after that of the Romans. Plays were often performed at court with amateur performers who were usually courtiers. Although there are few memorable plays from this period, a number of innovations were made in terms of scenic design that influenced theater throughout Europe for centuries to come, including scenes painted on backdrops and the proscenium arch, a frame at the very front of the stage that hid the mechanisms for moving scenery. The proscenium has remained in place in theaters through modern times.

Commedia dell'Arte Commedia dell'arte was exuberant, largely improvisational theater, dependent on actors rather than on playwrights. It was performed by touring acting troupes throughout Italy, and later throughout Europe. The productions were generally farces, and, while dialogue was improvised, the plots were standardized. Many of the standard plots were laid out in Flaminio Scala's *Teatro delle favole rappresentative (The theater of stage plots)*. Each plot had a main story, usually involving a pair of youthful lovers, and a comic subplot that was moved along by the characters of comic servants, or *zanni*. Performances relied on visual humor and set comic bits called *lazzi*. With the exception of the young lovers, all actors wore masks. Actors had some scripted speeches that they could draw upon and insert where appropriate, but because of the improvisational dialogue, every performance was different. Music, dance, and acrobatics were often incorporated into the action.

Commedia dell'arte troupes were made up of between eight and 12 members and included women as well as men. Each performer took on the role of a commedia character, often playing the same role throughout his or her career. The roles were the same throughout all troupes—among them were the middle-aged Pantalone; the maid, Colombina; and the servant, Arlecchino (Harlequin).

By the late 16th century, commedia dell'arte troupes had begun to tour throughout Europe. Commedia reached the peak of its popularity by the mid-17th century, though it continued to be performed until the mid-18th century. Commedia's influence was far-reaching and can be seen in the work of, among others, Molière and Shakespeare.

Elizabethan and Jacobean Drama (1558–1642)

In the early part of the 16th century English drama was still beholden to the conventions and practices of the medieval stage. Performances were given by companies that were under the patronage of wealthy gentlemen and were presented both to the court and to the general public. The performances combined elements of popular entertainment with a wide range of source material including biblical stories, romantic tales, classical myths, and English folklore. They often took place on temporary stages consisting of a simple platform, or on pageant wagons that could travel from town to town. In 1559, however, Queen Elizabeth I prohibited plays that dealt with political or religious subjects, forbade the presentation of the medieval cycle plays, and made local authorities responsible for the performances that took place in their area. In addition, she passed a number of laws that were designed to keep the growing number of theatrical companies under close supervision. It was with these developments that the first professional companies appeared, and with them, the need for playwrights and permanent theaters.

Elizabethan Playwrights In the 1580's the University Wits, a group of highly educated playwrights influenced by an interest in the classical ideal of ancient Greece and Rome that was common throughout Renaissance Europe, appeared in London. They elevated the English language and introduced Senecan devices such as the use of soliloquies, ghosts, and confidantes. The best-known of these playwrights were Christopher Marlowe (ca. 1564–1593), a great innovator in the use of iambic pentameter; and Ben Jonson (1572–1637) who, like Shakespeare, did not have a university education, but was perhaps the most ardent of the period's playwrights in following the classical ideal.

Elizabethan Theaters The late 16th- and early 17th-century theaters were generally divided into two categories: public (open-aired; outdoor) and private (closed roof; indoor). By the middle of the 1600's, professional companies performed in both. James Burbage built the first permanent public theater (the Theatre) in 1576, and by the start of the English Civil War in 1642 there were as many as nine others competing for business. These theaters included, among others, the Globe, the Swan, the Rose, and the Fortune. The layout of the public theaters is still a matter of speculation, but it is generally thought that they consisted of a raised platform stage that could be surrounded on three sides by standing spectators. Surrounding the standing audience were two galleries of seated spectators. To the rear of the stage was a wall with doors leading to a backstage area. Above the doors was a gallery used for musicians, and above that a tower contain stage machinery. Covering the stage was a painted canopy that was supported by columns and referred to as the "heavens." The private, or indoor, theaters were the venue of choice for the more classically-minded playwrights such as Ben Jonson. The best-known of these theaters was the Blackfriars Playhouse.

Theater Companies Although Elizabethan and Jacobean theater companies operated under the patronage of noble or wealthy gentlemen, most still relied on the public for support. These companies, like the Italian commedia dell'arte troupes, generally operated according to a profit-sharing system. Most company members had multiple responsibilities within the company, such as playwriting, business management, costuming, or acting. Some companies owned their own theaters. Women were not allowed to perform; female roles were played by male actors. A high level of competition existed among the various companies, making it necessary for companies to perform often and maintain a large repertory of plays. Commissioned plays became the property of the company once the playwright's fee was paid. Plays were tightly guarded and rarely published. Rather, the actors would be given the lines for their individual parts alone, and the play would come together as a whole only during its presentation.

William Shakespeare Although much speculation and debate surround the identity of William Shakespeare, official documents and literary references lend valid evidence of his existence.

In 1564 William Shakespeare was born to John and Mary Arden Shakespeare on April 23, as scholars infer from his christening date, April 26. As Shakespeare grew up and attended school in Stratford, his father worked at a number of local government jobs to support the family and became one of the town's most noted citizens. At age 18, William married Anne Hathaway, another citizen of Stratford, and in 1585 they had a twin son and daughter, Hamnet and Judith. One year after the birth of his first two children, Shakespeare left his family in Stratford and traveled to London to pursue his career as an actor and playwright.

In London, between 1589 and 1591, Shakespeare wrote his first plays, a trilogy chronicling the reign of King Henry VI. But in 1592 the plague that swept through the city, killing thousands and forcing all theaters closed by official decree until 1594, compelled Shakespeare to retreat to the outer areas of London.

As his career advanced, a friendly competition arose between Shakespeare and his contemporary Christopher Marlowe, author of *The Jew of Malta* (published posthumously in 1633), *The Tragical History of Dr. Faustus* (1588), and other plays, as both playwrights attempted to win the favor of English audiences. Despite the rarity of theatrical performances during the time of the plague, Shakespeare continued to write plays and, ultimately, 154 sonnets.

In 1593, one year before London's theaters reopened, Christopher Marlowe was killed in a bar fight, leaving Shakespeare as the preeminent playwright of the era. When the theaters did reopen, acting troupes returned to business,

Timeline for Shakespeare's Writings

Year Written	Play and Publication Date
1590–1591	*2 Henry VI* (pub. 1594), *3 Henry VI* (Pub. 1594)
1591–1592	*1 Henry VI* (pub. 1623)
1592–1593	*Richard III* (pub. 1597), *Venus and Adonis* (pub. 1593)
1592–1593	*The Comedy of Errors* (pub. 1623), *The Rape of Lucrece* (pub. 1594), *Titus Andronicus* (pub. 1594), *The Taming of the Shrew* (pub. 1623)
1594	*Two Gentlemen of Verona* (pub. 1623)
1594–1595	*Love's Labour's Lost* (pub. 1598), *Romeo and Juliet*
1595-1596	*Richard II* (pub. 1597)
1595–1596	*A Midsummer Night's Dream* (pub. 1600)
1596–1597	*King John* (pub. 1623)
1596–1597	*The Merchant of Venice* (pub. 1600)
1597–1598	*1 Henry IV* (pub. 1598)
1598	*2 Henry IV* (pub. 1600)
1598–1599	*Much Ado about Nothing* (pub. 1600)
1598–1599	*Henry V* (pub. 1600),
1596–1600	*Julius Caesar* (pub. 1623), *As You Like It* (pub. 1623)
1599–1600	*Twelfth Night* (pub. 1623)
1600–1601	*The Merry Wives of Windsor* (pub. 1602)
1600–1601	*Hamlet* (pub. 1603)
1601–1602	*Troilus and Cressida* (pub. 1609)
1602–1603	*All's Well That Ends Well* (pub. 1623)
1604–1605	*Measure for Measure* (pub. 1623), *Othello* (pub. 1622)
1605–1606	*King Lear* (pub. 1608), *Macbeth* (pub. 1623)
1606–1607	*Antony and Cleopatra* (pub. 1623)
1607–1608	*Coriolanus* (pub. 1623), *Timon of Athens* (pub. 1623),
1608-1609	*Pericles* (pub. 1609)
1609–1610	*Cymbeline* (pub. 1623)
1610–1611	*The Winter's Tale* (pub. 1623)
1611–1612	*The Tempest* (pub. 1623)
1612–1613	*Henry VIII* (pub. 1623)
1613	*The Two Noble Kinsmen* (pub. 1634)

and the troupe with which Shakespeare worked as an actor and writer of plays for the rest of his career, the Lord Chamberlain's Men, came together. In 1599 the Globe Theatre—the theater most regularly used for Shakespeare's performances—opened for exclusive use by the Lord Chamberlain's Men. In 1601, the year of John Shakespeare's death, and the year William Shakespeare wrote *Hamlet*, his history *Richard II* played at the Globe Theatre. At about the same time, the earl of Essex attempted a rebellion against Queen Elizabeth. Because of the content of *Richard II*, many felt that Essex's party had instigated this performance as an incentive to rebellion, thus implicating Shakespeare as a sympathizer to the earl of Essex and his cause. After the failed rebellion an investigation into Shakespeare's actions disclosed no irregularities, and ultimately the authorities brought no charges against him.

Queen Elizabeth died in 1603, leading to accession of James I (James VI of Scotland) and ushering in the Jacobean period in England. King James was a great supporter of the theater, and after he saw a performance of Shakespeare's comedy *As You Like It*, he issued a royal order to change the name of the Lord Chamberlain's Men to the King's Men.

Shakespeare's artistic production was astounding, not only in number but in quality: the 38 plays and the poems and sonnets are a trove of both astounding insights into human character and arguably the most magnificent poetry ever written in the English language.

Shakespeare died on April 23, 1616. It seems an unlikely coincidence that his death took place on his 52nd birthday. Yet, since we can infer the date from the date of his burial (April 25) and from an inscription on a statue carved in his honor a few years after he died, scholars have more or less agreed on April 23 as the correct date of his death.

The Shakespeare Controversy Some people believe that Shakespeare was not a real person, but the pseudonym of another author of the Elizabethan era. Others believe that because the works are so brilliant they cannot possibly be the work of one man, and therefore bear the mark of many writers. The controversy endures today as the Calvin Hoffman Prize, worth almost 1 million British pounds, is still offered as an incentive for researchers to investigate and uncover a concrete answer to the question of Shakespeare's identity.

Some people have suggested that Francis Bacon wrote much of what we attribute to Shakespeare, since Bacon possessed the range of cultural knowledge exhibited in Shakespeare's works and was often seen in the royal court.

Another popular choice for the real identity of Shakespeare is the 17th earl of Oxford, Edward de Vere, whose life seems to be reflected in a number of Shakespeare's works. Edward de Vere, like Francis Bacon, was a member of the English secret service under Queen Elizabeth. It is worth noting that Queen Elizabeth paid de Vere a large sum annually to head the theater wing of the royal secret service.

Many people prefer a more obvious choice for Shakespeare's identity, the playwright, poet, and translator Christopher Marlowe, Shakespeare's rival. Marlowe and Shakespeare always competed with each other to turn out popular plays, all of which followed a similar poetic style—a blank verse version of iambic pentameter. Marlowe, like Bacon and de Vere, was a member of the English secret service and participated in a number of government operations. When he was accused of heresy after writing against certain corrupt English officials, Marlowe was imprisoned and subsequently bailed out by the English secret service. Only a few days later, Marlowe was suspiciously murdered in a bar fight. Just two weeks after this suspicious death, a London publisher received the poem *Venus and Adonis* with the title page acknowledging the author as W. Shakespeare. *Venus and Adonis* is the first publication of any work with Shakespeare's name on it, and this same work had been submitted to the same publisher months before, anonymously—thus, the controversy. Those who accept the theory of Christopher Marlowe as Shakespeare believe that Marlowe's death was more a cover than an actual event and that he continued writing for the rest of his days under the pseudonym "William Shakespeare."

The abundant theories notwithstanding, several local government and church documents from Stratford-upon-Avon in the 16th century mention John Shakespeare and his various business and government dealings in addition to the births of his children. Nevertheless, the search continues for the identity of the author of William Shakespeare's works. Today the most commonly accepted theory is that Shakespeare—who is also called simply the Bard or the Poet (to attest to his supreme standing in the world of poetry)—did exist and wrote his own dramatic and poetic works.

Jacobean Theater Shortly after the ascension of James I (1566–1625) to the throne in 1603, a new kind of dramatist emerged in England. The work of these technically skilled playwrights was highly polished but lacked the profundity of the work of their Elizabethan predecessors. The Jacobean playwrights were more interested in sensation and thrills than in illuminating universal truths. The work of this period is often described as decadent. John Ford (ca. 1586–1639), in *Tis Pity She's a Whore* (1629) treats themes of incestuous love sympathetically. Other writers of note were John Fletcher (ca. 1579–1625), Francis Beaumont (ca. 1585–1616), and John Webster (ca. 1580–ca. 1632), whose plays *The White Devil* (1609) and *The Duchess of Malfi* (1613) are still often produced.

In general, the theater in England began to decline after Shakespeare's death in 1616, and when civil war broke out in 1642 the theaters were effectively closed. By the time theatrical activity reemerged in 1660, the great theater culture that had marked the Elizabethan and Jacobean stages and the genius of Shakespeare had vanished, and English theater was forced to begin anew.

French Neoclassical Theater and Molière (1500–1700)

The neoclassical movement encouraged imitation of classical works and adherence to classical literary rules, and eventually led to French plays written in the classical manner. By 1550, plays by Sophocles, Euripides, Aristophanes, Terence, and Seneca, as well as critical works by Horace and Aristotle, including Aristotle's *Poetics*, had been translated into French. During this time the Pleiade, a group of French intellectuals, formalized rules of French grammar and poetry with the goal of developing the French language into a vehicle for classical works and defining the neoclassical ideal.

The Neoclassical Ideal Realized By the 17th century, a group of highly learned and technically proficient playwrights led the neoclassical movement. Chief among them was Pierre Corneille (1606–1684). In *Le Cid* (1636), Corneille adapted a sprawling Spanish play, compressing the original into the neoclassical five-act structure. In addition, he attempted to adhere to the unities by reducing the original play's many locations to four settings in a single town, and the original play's many years into the course of a single day. Despite Corneille's efforts, *Le Cid* was still criticized for not adhering closely enough to the three unities and for lacking verisimilitude. Jean Racine (1639–99) was later credited with perfecting the neoclassical tragedy with *Phedra* (1677).

Molière Jean-Baptiste Poquelin (1622–73), who took the name Molière, was an actor, manager, and dramatist who combined the exuberance of the touring acting companies with the ideas of the neoclassicists. He was considered the greatest comic playwright of France and perhaps all of Europe, and his work (together with the tragedies of Racine) marks the high point in French neoclassical theater. Molière was highly educated, but he abandoned a promising career at court in 1643 to join the acting company Théâtre Illustre. He eventually became the head of the company and soon began to write its plays. Among Molière's numerous plays are the comedies *Tartuffe* (1664), *The Misanthrope* (1666), *The Miser* (1668), *The Learned Ladies* (1672), and *The Imaginary Invalid* (1673). His work was often controversial, both reflecting and commenting on the social and religious hypocrisies of his day. His full-length plays, often written in verse, adhered to the five-act structure and the three unities espoused by the neoclassicists. Molière worked in the theater until his death, directing and often performing the leading role in his plays himself.

Restoration Drama (1660–1700)

In 1660 the restoration of Charles II to the English throne after his exile in continental Europe paved the way for the reopening of theaters and the reestablishment of English drama. For the first time, women were allowed to perform on the British stages. New theaters were built using innovations, such as the proscenium arch, from the Italian theaters. The new theaters were opened only with a mandate from the king. Audiences, mostly from the upper class, were more sophisticated than in earlier times. Plays often made allusions to gossip of the day, so that to a large degree Restoration theater was an insider's theater.

Restoration Comedy Plays of the Elizabethan and Jacobean periods were performed in the Restoration period but were often rewritten versions. Even many of Shakespeare's tragedies were reworked with happy endings. Restoration comedies reflected the worldly-wise sensibility of the period. These comedies of manners were set in London, not in the country or in the courts where dramas of earlier periods had been set. They often involved sexual intrigue among characters who were members of the upper class. For the first time, characters spoke in a conversational style, displaying sparkling wit and jaded sensibilities. Two playwrights of note during the Restoration period were the poet John Dryden (1631–1700) and William Congreve (1670–1729), whose *Love for Love* (1695) and *The Way of the World* (1695) are considered masterpieces of the form.

18th-Century Drama

In the 18th century the identity of each of London's theaters was strongly shaped by actor-managers. In 1747 the actor David Garrick (1717–79) became manager, with John Lacy, of the Drury Lane Theatre. Garrick, considered the greatest actor of his day, was instrumental in bringing spectacle to the stage. His style of acting, much admired throughout Europe, included the use of pauses in action to heighten dramatic tension, and elaborate costumes (such as, famously, a trick wig with hair that stood on end at the moment when Hamlet sees his father's ghost). In 1728 *The Beggars Opera* by John Gay (1685–1732) opened at the Lincoln's Inn Fields Theatre, launching a new dramatic form, the ballad opera, which combined social and political satire with popular song. Comedies that rejected sentimentality and drew on the Restoration form were also popular. *The School for Scandal* by Richard Brinsley Sheridan (1751–1816) was first performed in 1771. *She Stoops to Conquer* by Oliver Goldsmith (1730–1774) was first performed in 1773.

Melodrama The 19th century saw the height of the melodramatic form, as well as various technological innovations in theatrical effects (particularly in lighting), and the rise of the English music hall. In melodrama every aspect of a production—including costuming, sets, lighting, and acting—served the purpose of expressing dramatic content. Now the stage setting of a dark night or a lonely forest became symbolic of a character's emotional state. Plot took precedence over characterization, with virtuous heroes or heroines beset by disasters and under attack by sinister villains. Limelight, originally used to create atmosphere and later as a focused spotlight, was first used in the mid-19th century.

English Music Hall Music halls at first were eating or drinking establishments that catered to a lower- or middle-class clientele and that also provided entertainment. But as they attracted larger audiences, halls were built specifically for the purpose of entertainment. The performances at music halls consisted of separate acts such as jugglers, dancers, magicians, and singers. Music hall, more affordable than the theater and aimed at a less sophisticated audience, soon rivaled theater in popularity. In America vaudeville was the equivalent of English music hall entertainment.

19th-Century American Drama

Vaudeville, the Minstrel Show, and the Musical Revue During the 19th century, drama in the United States evolved in a manner similar to that in England. Stylish comedies imported from England were produced in theaters in urban centers throughout the country, as were ballad operas and melodramas. By the mid-19th century vaudeville, the American counterpart to music hall entertainment, had developed into a genre of its own. It reached its height in the late 19th century, then declined in popularity in the 1920's with the advent of talking films.

Vaudeville bills, like those in music halls, comprised separate acts that usually included singers, dancers, and comedians, as well as jugglers, musicians, or magicians. Like music hall entertainment, vaudeville grew out of a need for a popular form of entertainment for working-class audiences—often audiences made up of frontier workers in the American West. The minstrel show, at first a part of vaudeville and later an event unto itself, consisted of songs, comic bits, skits, and stories depicting caricatures of slaves. Minstrel shows were first staged by white performers wearing blackface; later there were some African-American minstrel troupes as well. The first minstrel show was performed by T. D. Rice (1806–60), who first sang and danced his "Jim Crow" act in 1828. Burlesque—shows that featured satirical or slapstick humor and striptease acts—was also popular during the 19th century. Musical revues such as the Ziegfeld Follies, which included music, dancing, and spectacle, became popular in the early 20th century.

Modern Drama in Europe

European Modern Drama (1880–1920) This period was marked by revolutionary, idea-driven styles sparked first by playwrights and then by the directors and institutions that interpreted and presented the writers' works. During the modern period, European theatrical movements were no longer localized within any given country; they were broadened to include or correspond with movements throughout Europe. Among the movements were realism, naturalism, symbolism, and expressionism.

Henrik Ibsen and Psychological Realism Henrik Ibsen (1828–1906) is considered the first modern playwright. His later plays, most notably *A Doll's House* (1879), were revolutionary: realistic, written in colloquial prose, set in the domestic world, and displaying an until then unseen concern with psychology. Because of the realistic nature of the dialogue, the emotionally intimate content, and the domestic settings, actors could no longer rely on the presentational styles popular in the mainstream 18th- and 19th-century theater. Sets no longer were designed for a painterly effect, but rather reproduced in a detailed way the interiors where scenes took place. The idea of the fourth wall—audiences viewed action onstage as though a fourth wall had become invisible, thereby giving them a window onto private action—was adopted.

Theaters of the Modern Era Venues for the new realistic theater sprang up throughout Europe. In Paris the Théâtre Libre opened under the direction of André Antoine. In Berlin the Freie Bühne opened under the direction of Otto Brahm (1856–1912). In Russia the Moscow Art Theater, under the direction of Konstantin Stanislavski (1856–1938), presented the new acting style necessitated by the work of Anton Chekhov (1860–1904). In London the Independent Theater presented work by, among others, George Bernard Shaw (1856–1950). In Copenhagen the Scandinavian Experimental Theater opened under the direction of the Swedish playwright August Strindberg (1849–1912).

August Strindberg's best-known early play, *Miss Julie*, was a work in the naturalistic style. In it a wealthy girl seduces her father's servant. Strindberg used the play to examine the schism between the old and the new eras, and its form mirrored the radicalism of its content—the play is written without acts and calls for a sparsely furnished stage. *Miss Julie* was considered so controversial that its opening in Stockholm was canceled and it was instead first produced in 1893 at the Théâtre Libre in Paris. Strindberg's later plays *The Ghost Sonata* and *The Dream Play* rejected realism, relying heavily instead on symbols in an attempt to portray internal reality on the stage.

Anton Chekhov, like Ibsen, used the stage to explore the psychology of his characters. His dialogue was subtle and often understated. When first presented in the traditional 19th-century acting style in St. Petersburg, his play *The Seagull* had met with failure. It was only when *The Seagull* was produced at the Moscow Art Theater in 1898 under the direction of Stanislavski, whose method called upon actors to identify with the characters they played in a search for emotional truth, that it met with success.

Symbolism, Expressionism, and the Birth of the Avant-Garde The playwright Maurice Maeterlinck (1862–1949) came to epitomize the Symbolist movement, whereby experience and ideas were evoked through the use of images, with his play *Pelléas* and *Mélisande*. Franz Wedekind (1864–1918) sparked the expressionist movement, which distorted action and images in order to stress the subjectivity of experience, with his play *Spring Awakening*. Alfred Jarry (1873–1907), whose play *Ubu roi* was first produced in 1896, is considered the forefather of such avant-garde theatrical movements as surrealism and theater of the absurd, although it was not until more than a generation after *Ubu roi* was first produced that these movements would find their names.

European Modern Drama (1920–1960) During the period between World War I and World War II, theater increasingly became a venue for social and political protest. In Russia agitprop drama (propaganda-driven theater) developed. First in Switzerland and later in Germany the Dada movement found its way to theater. It aimed to promote social change through acts of simultaneity and spontaneity, in which public displays, such as the disruption of a parliamentary debate, became theater. Such displays necessitated audience participation, breaking down further what theater could be or mean. At the same time theater itself became a subject for drama. Luigi Pirandello (1867–1936) wrote *Six Characters in Search of an Author* (1921), in which six characters interrupt the rehearsal of a play; it became an instant classic. As the 20th century progressed, theater became increasingly influenced by theory.

Bertolt Brecht and Epic Theater Bertolt Brecht (1898–1956), influenced by agitprop, saw theater as a force for social change. He created epic theater, which consciously rejected Aristotle's classical vision of catharsis. For Brecht, theater, the importance of which lay in its social relevance, was a forum for making the spectator not only feel but think as well. To this end he employed the alienation effect, devised to remind audiences that they were watching a theatrical production. His productions called attention to the mechanics of theater: signs gave scene information, scene changes were fully visible to the audience, and his company (the Berliner Ensemble) practiced a nonnaturalistic style of acting. Among Brecht's plays were *The Caucasian Chalk Circle*, *Mother Courage and Her Children*, and *The Good Person of Setzuan*. Brecht, in collaboration with the composer Kurt Weill (1900–50), updated John Gay's 18th-century ballad opera *The Beggar's Opera*, for their *Threepenny Opera*.

Antonin Artaud and the Avant-Garde In France Dada evolved into surrealism in the work of, among others, Jean Cocteau (1889–1963). Theater of cruelty was a term first employed by Antonin Artaud (1896–1949) in his collection of essays *The Theater and Its Double* (1938), considered the most important work of theater criticism since Aristotle's *Poetics*. In *The Theater and Its Double* Artaud called for theater that would completely involve the audience. To witness theater meant to participate in it, and by participating, the audience was forced to confront itself. Artaud sought to move not through logic but through invoking "communicative delirium," a collective, almost religious, fervor in the audience. *The Theater and Its Double* became the manifesto of the next generation of avant-garde playwrights, including the absurdists Eugène Ionesco (1909–94) and Jean Genet (1910–86).

Samuel Beckett After World War II drama began to reflect an even more fractured view of the world. *Waiting for Godot*, by the Irish playwright Samuel Beckett (1906–89), was first produced in 1953. In the play two tramps, Vladimir and Estragon, are trapped on a road, waiting for the arrival of Godot. In this vacant world they are forced to repeat the same patterns over and over. Though the play did not meet with immediate success, it went on to become the seminal work of the second half of the 20th century.

The Angry Young Men In England the drama of the mid-20th century evolved with less obvious experimentation than it did in the rest of Europe. Its experimentation at first lay in content rather than in style. *Look Back in Anger* by John Osborne (1929–1994), was first produced in 1956. This stylistically realistic play, which followed the struggles of its main character, Jimmy Porter, raised highly charged questions about class and social roles. It gave rise to the generation of so-called angry young men—playwrights such as John Arden (b. 1930) and Arnold Wesker (b. 1932), whose work called into question the accepted political and social norms of the times.

Modern American Drama

Modern drama in America was formed by many of the same forces that influenced modern European drama. However, because American theater developed in a country where the two world wars had not been fought, it allowed for a coherence in theatrical traditions uninterrupted by war. American modern theater was as subversive as its European counterpart, but not so extreme in its expression.

Eugene O'Neill, Thornton Wilder, and Tennessee Williams Eugene O'Neill was the most important playwright in bringing new European ideas of theater to America. Although his primary influence was expressionism, O'Neill's work is marked by an interest in psychology and virtuosity in a variety of styles. *The Emperor Jones* (1920) employs Symbolist techniques; *The Hairy Ape* (1922) employs expressionist techniques; *Long Day's Journey into Night* (1943), which was not produced until 1956, three years after O'Neill's death, uses realism paired with psychological symbols to paint a brutally honest portrait of a family.

Thornton Wilder's best-known plays are *Our Town* (1938) and the highly theatrical *The Skin of Our Teeth* (1942). Tennessee Williams, also influenced by expressionism, paired realism with psychological symbols to comment on American culture, the nature of memory, and the vulnerability of the artist in the modern world. All these playwrights had successful Broadway productions of their work, but the first production of Tennessee Williams's *Summer and Smoke* in 1952 at the Circle in the Square Theater is said to mark the beginning of the off-Broadway movement.

The Group Theatre and Method Acting In the 1920's experimental theater in New York was localized in Greenwich Village. Eugene O'Neill's company, the Provincetown Players, was originally part of the Washington Square Players (later known as the Theatre Guild). The Neighborhood Playhouse became a venue not only for plays but also for dance and avant-garde performances. The Group Theatre, founded in 1931, had a social and political agenda, reacting to the enormous unemployment and extreme working conditions of the times. The work of Clifford Odets (1906–63) reflects this agenda. Odets's most famous play, *Waiting for Lefty* (1935), draws on agitprop techniques to dramatize the concerns of union workers.

The Group Theatre employed an Americanized version of Stanislavski's approach to acting which became known simply as the Method. Method acting used emotional recall—in which actors drew on their own experiences to imbue a character with life—to create genuine emotion and highly realistic performances. The Group Theatre disbanded in 1941, but its influence continues to this day.

British and American Theater since 1960

British Theater In the 1960's the social concerns and experimentation of the earlier generation gave rise to an explosion of new playwrights. In England Harold Pinter (b. 1930), whose plays combine the fractured worldview of Samuel Beckett with a kind of realism akin to that of the "angry young men," rose to prominence with such plays as *The Caretaker* (1960) and *The Homecoming* (1965). Pinter's plays, imbued with a sense of menace, often take place in a vague world where naturalistic dialogue is paired with an unexplained or mysterious situation. The comic playwright Joe Orton (1933–67) used sex farce as a tool to satirize the social norms of the times in such plays as *Entertaining Mr. Sloane* (1964) and *What the Butler Saw* (1969). Tom Stoppard (b. Zlin, Czechoslovakia, 1937) combines high theatricality with dazzling linguistic invention to explore philosophical matters such as the nature of reality in *Rosencrantz and Guildenstern are Dead* (1967), *The Real Thing* (1982), and *Arcadia* (1993).

American Theater Arthur Miller (b. 1915), whose plays comment on societal injustices, rose to prominence when his play *All My Sons* was produced in 1947. Other plays include *The Crucible* (1953), which used the Salem witch hunts to comment on McCarthyism; and *Death of a Salesman* (1949), which introduced the tragic everyman, Willy Loman.

A profusion of new types of theater arose during the 1960's. Happenings, whose roots can be traced to the Dadaist spontaneous theater of Europe in the 1930's, gave birth to performance art, in which experimental theater companies such as the Living Theater, the Open Theatre, Mabou Mines, the Wooster Group, and Richard Foreman's Ontological-Hysteric Theatre expanded the boundaries of what were considered theatrical events. The playwrights best able to navigate a path between the experimental and popular theater of the 1960's and 1970's are Sam Shepard (b. 1943), who in plays such as *Buried Child* (1978) and *True West* (1980) combines a surreal, poetic style with a realistic setting to explore concern for American identity and mythology; Edward Albee (b. 1928), who rose to prominence in the 1960's and for over four decades has produced such masterpieces as *The Zoo Story* (1959), *Who's Afraid of Virginia Woolf?* (1962), *A Delicate Balance* (1966), and *Three Tall Women* (1991); and David Mamet (b. 1947), who in signature work such as *American Buffalo* (1976) and *Glengarry Glen Ross* (1983) uses vernacular patterns and rhythms to create recognizable characters and an emblematic American speech. Contemporary American theater exhibits a globalization of styles, drawing upon theater forms from the world over.

World Theater

Although countless forms of theater are found throughout the world, the traditions that have most influenced Western drama are found in India, China, and Japan.

Two of South India's classical dance forms, *bharata natyam* (performed by women) and *khatakali* (performed by men) combine systems of movements and gestures to create characters and tell stories.

In China, Peking opera, in existence since the late 18th century, uses male and female actors, elaborate costumes and makeup, mime, stylized gestures, and acrobatics to tell stories set in China's past.

Three traditional Japanese theater forms, *noh*, *bunraku*, and *kabuki*, are very different in style and origins. *Noh*, dating from the 14th century and originally performed only for the samurai class, exhibits the austerity and restraint of Zen Buddhism. Its goal is to inspire an emotional state through meditating on a related event from the past. Movement and song within *noh* plays are more important than spoken text, and every movement has a codified meaning. Actors wear masks and brightly colored, stylized costumes. The less esoteric *bunraku* and *kabuki* both date from the 17th century. *Banruku*, a form of puppet theater, operates according to strict conventions. Puppets are manipulated by black-clothed puppeteers. The story is told by a narrator and is accompanied by music. Puppets vary in size and complexity according to their importance in the story. *Kabuki* was originally performed for the lower classes, although it became popular among the samurai class as well. The characters in *kabuki* are made up of types—villains, courageous heroes, etc. The stories often involve erotic subjects or heroic exploits, and many are drawn from *bunraku* plays. Actors wear elaborate makeup, and each character has a traditional costume. Acrobatics and stylized gestures are employed.

Glossary of Literary Terms

Note: *When discussions of poetic meter arise, universal symbols are used: "–" for a stressed syllable, "⌣" for an unstressed syllable.*

acrostic poem in which the initial letters of each line form a word when read downward. When composed in prose, the first letters of each paragraph spell a word.

Shining down on our faces
Under the bright blue sky we sit
Nightfall ends its warm embrace

allegory story in which persons or places represent abstract, often moral, concepts. John Bunyan's *The Pilgrim's Progress*, in which Christian, on his journey to the Celestial City, must pass through such locations as the Slough of Despond and meet such characters as the Giant Despair, is a famous English Christian allegory. One may enjoy an allegorical work of verse or prose for its literal story or for the lesson it implies.

alliteration repetition of one consonant sound at the beginning of words or of stressed syllables.

Sally sells seashells at the seashore.

allusion appeal to the knowledge shared by the author and reader, usually an implicit reference to a preexisting work of literature or, a art, a person, or a historical event.

anamnesis "recalling to mind" (Greek); in a work of literature, a look back to events or people from a previous existence. See also *flashback*.

anapest in poetry, a metrical foot consisting of two unstressed syllables followed by one stressed syllable, giving a sense of galloping or steady motion.

⌣ ⌣ – ⌣ ⌣ – ⌣ ⌣ – ⌣ ⌣ –
With a leap and a bound the swift Anapests throng.
—Samuel Taylor Coleridge, "Metrical Feet"

antagonist in drama or fiction, the character who opposes the main character (protagonist).

antihero character who does not possess the typical traits of a literary hero. An antihero tends to be stupid, clumsy, or unlucky—one for whom heroic deeds seem impossible.

apostrophe technique in which a speaker addresses a dead, absent, or inanimate subject as if it were present or able to understand.

Death, be not proud, though some have call'd thee
Mighty and dreadful, for thou art not so;
—John Donne

assonance repetition of the same or similar vowel sounds.

She eats each peach with speed.

bildungsroman "formation novel" (German); a novel that chronicles the development of a hero or heroine from youth to maturity.

blank verse poetic form consisting of unrhymed iambic pentameter lines.

bowdlerize to delete words or passages of a work considered obscene, improper, or unfit for children; named for Thomas Bowdler, who performed this operation on an 1818 edition of Shakespeare.

burlesque most general term for a literary work that uses comic imitation to ridicule persons or events or another literary work A burlesque of a literary work can be a parody, which applies a serious literary style to a trivial subject; or a travesty, which treats a serious subject in low terms. A burlesque of a person can be a caricature or, if extended, a lampoon.

caesura pause or break within a line of poetry indicated by either punctuation or a natural pause in the syntax. In an analysis of poetic lines, it is indicated by two slashes (//).

Of foot and heart,// and did invite
Me to its game.// 'Its seemed to bless
Itself in me;
—Marvell, "The Nymph Complaining for the Dearh of her Fawn"

catharsis according to Aristotle in his *Poetics*, the effect that a Greek tragedy has on its audience of purging or relieving the emotions of fear and pity that the play arouses. The term has also been applied to the experience of the tragic hero. At the end of Sophocles' *Oedipus Rex*, for example, Oedipus gouges out his own eyes to purge himself of his sins.

comedy primarily associated with drama, this form originated in Greek antiquity as a means of celebrating fertility and the god Dionysus. Aristotle wrote in his *Poetics* that comedy was the opposite of tragedy in that it deals with everyday life in a humorous way. Frequently comedies start with misfortune and end with pleasure, whereas classical tragedies open with kings or heroes living in a lofty state and end with their misfortune. Forms of comedy include comedy of errors, comedy of manners, romantic comedy, and black comedy.

connotation implied or suggested meaning of a word as opposed to its literal meaning (denotation).

consonance close repetition of consonant sounds.

Deep with the first dead lies London's daughter
—Dylan Thomas

couplet in poetry, two successive rhyming lines.

But if thou live rememb'red not to be,
Die single, and thine image dies with thee.
—Shakespeare, sonnet no. 3

dactyl in poetry, a metrical foot consisting of one stressed syllable followed by two unstressed syllables.

– ˘ ˘ – ˘ ˘ – ˘ ˘ – ˘ ˘
Ever to come up with Dactyl's trisyllable.
—Samuel Taylor Coleridge, "Metrical Feet"

denotation most literal meaning of a word.

dénouement unraveling of a plot's complications after the climax of a story.

deus ex machina "god out of a machine" (Latin); originally, the resolution of a plot in Greek tragedy by the intervention a god lowered to the stage on a machine; by extension, the resolution of a conflict or difficult situation, in literature or elsewhere, by any unexpected or contrived device or event (for example, a violent storm). The term is often used pejoratively.

dramatic irony theatrical technique whereby the audience knows something that one or more characters in a play are unaware of, causing anticipation for the moment of revelation. For example, in Shakespeare's comedy *Twelfth Night*, Olivia, a rich countess, falls in love with Cesario, who is actually a woman named Viola disguised as a man.

dramatic unities in classical theory, the requirements for a properly constructed play, particularly a tragedy. Aristotle, in the *Poetics*, insisted upon "unity of action": a plot that is well ordered, excludes extraneous events, and is focused on the protagonist. Seventeenth-century French neoclassicists, feeling that a play should not strain the limitations of the stage, added that it should possess unity of place (unfolding in one location) and unity of time (taking place within one day).

elegy poem that laments the death of an individual or other sad event.

enjambment one line of poetry running into another, unseparated by end punctuation.

Let my left remember, and your right close
And your mouth open near the gate.
—Amichai, "If I Forget Thee, Jerusalem"

epic long narrative poem telling the story of heroic characters and often representing critical events in the history of a race or nation. Homer's *Iliad* and *Odyssey* and John Milton's *Paradise Lost* are among the greatest epics.

epigram any terse statement or, in poetry, a brief, usually rhymed, often two-lined, witty observation.

Know then thyself, presume not God to scan;
The proper study of mankind is Man.
—Pope, *An Essay on Man*

epigraph quotation preceding a literary work or part of a work, indicating a theme for what is to follow and sometimes providing a title.

epiphany term, notably applied in literature to the stories in James Joyce's *Dubliners*, that indicates a sudden realization or revelation taking place in a character, usually at a story's end.

fable story, often satirical or pointed toward a moral, in which animals have human characteristics. Examples are tales by Aesop and La Fontaine and George Orwell's *Animal Farm*.

farce comic drama that relies heavily on "low" comedy. A farce can contain slapstick (physical) comedy, buffoonery, absurd events and situations, and exaggerated characters and personalities. Whereas a classic comedy aims toward a happy ending, a farce primarily seeks to make its audience laugh.

figurative language nonliteral language, also called "figures of speech," used to express meaning or insight. In figurative language, something or someone is often presented as or compared to something that in literal terms is quite different. For specific kinds of figures of speech, see *metaphor*, *metonymy*, *simile*, and *synechdoche*.

figure of speech See *figurative language*.

flashback literary device common in modern fiction and drama that uses events from an earlier time to provide additional information about current characters or events.

foot in poetry, a group of syllables forming a metrical unit. Poems traditionally have been written in lines with a specific number of feet in a specific meter. Thus a poem written in iambic pentameter would consist of lines of five feet in iambic meter, that is, five feet containing two syllables, the first stressed and the second unstressed. A four-foot line would be tetrameter; a six-foot line would be hexameter, and so on. When illustrated for the reader, metrical feet are divided by a slash (/).

foreshadowing presentation of clues in a narrative to indicate later events.

free verse in poetry, a form with no regular line length or meter, intended to imitate the rhythms of natural speech.

hamartia ancient Greek term for the tragic flaw in the protagonist of a tragedy, as described by Aristotle. Hamartia is the cause of the hero's downfall. In Greek tragedy, this flaw was often hubris, or pride that leads a character to disregard the superiority or moral authority of a god or gods.

hubris in Greek tragedy, the characteristic of the hero which causes him to ignore warnings by the gods or oppose their commands.

hyperbole extreme exaggeration for rhetorical effect.

> *I told you a million times that I would not be*
> *home on Saturday.*

iamb in poetry, a metrical foot containing an unstressed syllable followed by a stressed syllable. One of the most commonly used metrical patterns, iambs most closely imitate the normal speech pattern of English.

> ˘ ¯ ˘ ¯ ˘ ¯ ˘ ¯
> *Iambics march from short to long.*
> —Coleridge, "Metrical Feet"

imagery appeal to any of the five senses to create a mental impression for the reader.

irony literary mode, tone, or attitude of which there are many variations, but which fundamentally involves parallel or opposite ways of seeing or knowing that in some way oppose each other. Irony may involve events of which the result is the opposite of what is anticipated, a character's saying one thing but meaning another, or a character's unawareness of a certain situation or fact critical to his or her well-being. Irony may be comic or cosmic, as when the gods control events with intentions that are contrary to those of hopelessly striving humans.

melodrama play in which absolutely good and evil characters are opposed, and in which the evil characters usually threaten the well-being of the good, but, in the end, good survives or triumphs and evil is defeated or punished.

metaphor comparison of two unlike objects or ideas in which the writer states that one is the other.

> *My eyes are flowers for your tomb*
> —Thomas Merton

meter in poetry, the pattern of unstressed and stressed syllables. See *iamb*, *trochee*, *dactyl*, *anapest*, and *spondee*. Lines in a given poem often have a regular number of metrical units, or feet. See *foot*.

metonymy figure of speech in which something represents an entity or person with which it is typically associated.

> *The White House says it will not tolerate such behavior.*

monologue single person speaking alone, especially on stage or in a poem. In a dramatic monologue, such as one written by the Victorian poet Robert Browning, an implied listener is present but silent. See also *soliloquy*.

novel extended (generally, more than 100 pages) work of prose fiction, usually, in distinction from the older romance form, realistic in setting. A novel may have one or more plots, may narrate current or historical events, and almost always contains dialogue between characters. Cervantes's *Don Quixote*, published in early 17th-century Spain, is often considered the first novel. In English, the earliest novels were written in the 18th century.

novella work of prose fiction, longer than a short story but shorter than a novel, and thus often between 50 and 100 pages long. Examples are several works by Joseph Conrad, including *The Heart of Darkness* and *The Secret Sharer*. These are also called short novels or novelettes.

ode long lyric poem, grand in tone and typically marking a ceremonious occasion.

onomatopoeia word used to represent a sound.

boom; buzz; plop; woof

oxymoron combination, for effect, of two inherently contradictory words.

Darkness visible —Milton, *Paradise Lost*
It was the best of times, it was the worst of times.
—Dickens, *A Tale of Two Cities*

parody imitation of a specific work, style, or idea, in which certain characteristics are exaggerated to call attention to the ridiculous nature of what is imitated. See *burlesque*.

pastoral poem literally about shepherds or, more generally, about rural life. It may be lyrical, elegiac, narrative, satirical, or dramatic. Spenser's *Shepherd's Calendar* and Milton's *Lycidas* are examples.

pentameter line of poetry containing five metrical units, or feet. See *foot* and *meter*.

personification literary device in which human qualities are attributed to an inanimate object.

In the faint moonlight, the grass is singing
—Eliot, *The Waste Land*

picaresque term describing a usually satirical story or novel focusing on a rogue (*picaro*) who may serve many masters and often experiences many adventures.

plot sequence of events in a work of fiction, a drama, or a narrative poem.

prose written or spoken language with no restrictions imposed (as in poetry) by rhyme, meter, or length and structure of lines.

roman à clef "key novel" (French), a novel in which the characters portray real people. In some cases, a key to the characters has been published with the book to provide the reader with the true identities of the characters.

romance literary form containing characters who seem removed from the real world by fantasy or improbability. The romance was originally a medieval European literary form narrating, in verse or prose, the adventures of knights and kings, often involving a religious quest and including a love theme. The term is also applied to historical novels such as those of Walter Scott or other unrealistic novels of adventure or love.

saga heroic prose or verse narrative, originally appearing in Norse and Icelandic medieval literature, telling of historical or legendary events, the reigns of kings, or the life of a family.

satire work of literature that pokes fun at an institution or idea. A satire is intended to be critical and humorous, and may also seek to reform what it attacks by forcing those associated with it to see its ridiculous qualities. For example, Horace Miner's satirical article "Body Ritual among the Nacirema" illustrates how the "Nacirema" ("American" spelled backward) pay particular attention to how they look and insist upon ridiculous rituals to make their bodies look better.

setting where and when a story takes place.

simile figure of speech comparing two unlike objects or ideas, generally employing the words *like* or *as*.

Helen, thy beauty is to me
Like those Nicae barks of yore
—Edgar Allan Poe, "To Helen"

soliloquy in theater, a speech delivered by a character, alone on stage, often expressing his or her deepest thoughts and feelings. The most famous soliloquy is Hamlet's "To be or not to be . . ."— a speech in which he reveals his internal struggle as he contemplates suicide.

sonnet 14–line lyric, rhymed poem, usually in iambic pentameter. The form originated in 13th-century Sicily and was made famous and internationally influential by the Tuscan Petrarch in the 14th century. Although sonnets continue to be written in various rhyme schemes, these poems have traditionally had rhyme patterns called Petrarchan or Italian (divided into an octave rhymed *abbaabba* and a sestet rhymed *cdecde*) and Shakespearean or English (comprising three quatrains and a couplet: *abab cdcd efef gg*). The English sonnet was actually introduced in the 16th century by Henry Howard, earl of Surrey, who, like Petrarch in Italy and several other 16th-century English poets—Wyatt, Sidney, Spenser, and Shakespeare—wrote a sequence of love sonnets.

spondee in poetry, a metrical foot consisting of two consecutive stressed syllables.

From long to long in solemn sort
Slow Spondee stalks, strong foot!
—Coleridge, "Metrical Feet"

Spondaic feet are used less frequently than the others in poetry and, when used, bring a certain emphasis. These two lines from Coleridge's poem are written in iambs until the last metrical foot.

symbolism literary technique in which an object is used to represent one or more ideas or concepts.

synecdoche representation of the whole of an object using only a part of the object.

All hands on deck!

Here the hands, being the most important parts of bodies being summoned to labor, represent the men.

tone the attitude—comic, somber, ironic—that an author or character expresses.

tragedy first defined by Aristotle in his *Poetics* as a drama that imitates serious and great events, in which a tragic flaw (hamartia) leads to a hero's downfall, and in which the events arouse fear and pity in the audience, followed by a purgation (catharsis) of these emotions. These characteristics remained applicable, but only partly so, as tragedy developed in later cultures, such as Elizabethan and Jacobean England—the time of Shakespeare. The tragedies of that period might include comic elements, and in them the causes of catastrophe are not as sharply defined. Still later, in the 19th century, tragedies would focus on middle-class rather than aristocratic characters, and would not necessarily end with the death of a hero. Tragedy can now be defined as a drama that starts with fortune and happiness and ends with misfortune and displeasure.

tragic flaw See *hamartia*.

tragicomedy play in which gravely serious and lighter elements or scenes are combined, particularly one in which, as in Shakespeare's *Merchant of Venice*, the plot poses danger to the main character but turns toward a happy ending.

trochee (pronounced tro-kee) in poetry, a metrical foot consisting of a stressed syllable followed by an unstressed syllable.

– ᴗ – ᴗ – ᴗ –
Trochee trips from long to short
—Coleridge, "Metrical Feet"

vernacular native language. In literature, vernacular refers to works, particularly in medieval times, that were written in the local language or dialect rather than in Greek or Latin.

verse term used to describe the forms and patterns of poetic language, involving any number of specifications of meter, rhyme, and length, and arrangement of lines.

zeugma "yoking" (Greek); literary device in which one word (such as an adjective or a verb) is applied grammatically to two others (such as two nouns).

Dost sometimes counsel take—and sometimes tea.
—Pope, *The Rape of the Lock*

Zeugma tends to show comic or ironic variation. In the example above, the character is equally businesslike when he takes counsel and relaxed when he takes tea.

MATHEMATICS

History of Mathematics 390

Branches of Mathematics 392

Mathematical Formulas 393

Numbers and Number Systems 396

Probability 398

Glossary of Mathematical Terms 398

MATHEMATICS

History of Mathematics

The roots of mathematics date from ancient Egypt and Babylonia, although the discipline owes most to the ancient Greeks. Greek mathematical works were translated into Arabic and Latin, and were later adopted and expanded upon by Western Europeans.

Early Arithmetic As early as 30,000 years ago, people scratched tally marks representing numbers on bone or rock. A different system of recording numbers was also used in the Middle East from at least 8,000 years ago; quantities of trade goods were counted with small pieces of hardened clay, now called tokens.

Arithmetic was performed by manipulating small objects, such as tokens, to determine sums or differences. This method was enhanced by having objects represent tens—that is, one object stands for 10 objects—and others ones. Counting boards, simple devices that preceded abaci, improved on this idea by marking one part of a tablet for the ones, another for tens, and a third for hundreds. In an abacus (3000 B.C.), a similar idea is used, but the counters are strung on wires, making them easy to move and hard to lose.

By 2000 B.C. the simple mathematics of counting and whole-number arithmetic led to what conceptually was algebra—although not easily recognized as such because symbols were not employed. In Mesopotamia of that era, simple quadratic equations (such as $x^2 + 2 = 3x$) could be solved.

Measurement and Geometry Standards for length and weight are known to have existed 5,000 years ago. In Egypt, methods were developed to measure property and to restore boundaries after the annual Nile flood. Construction of pyramids and temples required knowledge of how to measure angles.

Measurement soon led to a practical sort of geometry. Formulas were developed for area and volume in Egypt, Mesopotamia, and China. The Pythagorean theorem and its relation to right angles were also recognized to varying extents in these early civilizations, starting ca. 1850 B.C. By 1750 B.C. Egyptian mathematicians could calculate volumes of many figures, including a pyramid with its top removed (a truncated pyramid). In a few instances, the early mathematicians recognized that one idea followed from another—the beginnings of proof.

Proof became central to geometry in the Greek civilization starting soon after 600 B.C. By A.D. 300 it was possible for Euclid of Alexandria (ca. 325–ca. 265 B.C.) to gather all known results of geometry and arithmetic and arrange them into a logical system. Some results were proved directly from a few simple rules (called axioms and postulates) and from the definitions of geometric shapes. The mathematics of Euclid remains the basis of geometry today, although some of the reasoning behind the results has been improved by modern mathematicians.

Mathematics in the East Some ideas of Greek mathematics followed conquest and trade into India, but for the most part mathematics developed independently in Asia. The Chinese improved notation with decimal fractions (ca. A.D. 5), and also introduced a form of negative numbers (ca. A.D. 200). Several Chinese mathematicians calculated the ratio of the distance around a circle to the distance across, which we now call π (pi), to many decimal places, beginning as early as A.D. 263.

Indian mathematicians introduced a numerical relative of geometry, called trigonometry ("triangle measuring"). By about A.D. 800 the Indians' recognition that zero is a number, seemingly a small advance, allowed the development of the flexible system of place-value, decimal numeration used around the world today.

Beginnings of Algebra Another Greek innovation was the use of symbols to represent very general problems. The originator of this approach, Diophantus (ca. 210–ca. 290) is often called the "father of algebra," although his book of problems is named *Arithmetica*.

In 835, the Arab mathematician Muhammad Al-Khwarizmi (ca. 780–ca. 850) wrote the work *Al-jabr wa'l muqábalah* ("restoring and simplifying"), known in the West as *Algebra*. This work introduced methods for finding the solutions to equations of the first and second degree (linear equations and quadratics, respectively).

Mathematic Renaissance European mathematics had a rebirth in the 15th century, aided by the institution of symbols for operations and relationships (such as +, −, and =). Geometry was enriched by the studies of perspective made by Renaissance painters, starting with Leon Battista Alberti (1404–72) in 1436. The need for better computation, especially for navigation, led to the invention of logarithms by John Napier (1550–1617) in 1614.

By the 17th century, algebra had reached the level taught in high school today, and mathematics was moving into new fields, such as analytic geometry. This field, which combines geometry and algebra into a single entity, was invented independently by Pierre de Fermat (1601–65) in 1636 and René Descartes (1596–1650) in 1637, and became the basis of nearly all subsequent mathematics. In 1639 the idea of perspective led to a new kind of geometry, called projective geometry, which showed that geometry did not have to depend on measurement. Another new field of mathematics, which started during the Renaissance and was revived in the 17th century, was probability, developed largely in correspondence between Fermat and Blaise Pascal (1623–62) ca. 1660.

Rise of Calculus As early as Greek mathematics, some problems had been solved by breaking a geometric figure into an arbitrarily large number of tiny pieces and then mathematically re-combining the pieces. Variations on this idea were used to find the distance around a circle or to determine the area or volume of an irregular figure. This general idea became the basis of a new method for solving problems based upon the infinitely small, which we now call calculus.

In 1665 and 1666, Sir Isaac Newton (1643–1727) expanded on methods of approximation developed by earlier mathematicians, creating the first version of calculus. About 10 years later, Gottfried Wilhelm von Leibniz (1646–1716) developed the same mathematical tools, using different symbols and words with somewhat different meanings. Leibniz published his first account in 1684 and Newton his first public account in 1687, although Newton had circulated manuscripts much earlier. Most of the symbolism and language used today derive from Leibniz.

19th-Century Reform Although many physical and mathematical problems were solved with calculus, some applications appeared to produce nonsensical or contradictory results. Furthermore, it was obvious that the inner logic of the infinitely small was unclear. Throughout the 19th century, even as the applications of calculus continued to be largely successful, some mathematicians sought to put calculus on a logical basis. Eventually this was accomplished by a program that eliminated the infinitely small and replaced it with rules derived from arithmetic.

Geometry also experienced a revolution in the 19th century. Mathematicians found that there exist geometries as logical as the geometry of the ancient Greeks but which follow different rules. This new non-Euclidean geometry greatly expanded mathematics, which no longer seemed to need an obvious connection to reality. Einstein's general relativity theory of 1916 showed that the true geometry of space may be non-Euclidean.

Nineteenth-century mathematicians also looked for the simplest concepts that underlie arithmetic, algebra, geometry, and logic. Abstract mathematics and symbolic logic are concerned with the implications of these underlying rules, not with entities of the real world or even idealized entities.

Crisis in Foundations Late in the 19th century, the search for a logical basis for mathematics led to inclusion of the infinitely large. Because this work generally dealt with infinite sets of points, the beginning part of this change in mathematics was called set theory.

Set theory led to contradictory results that were harder to eliminate than the contradictions that had surfaced in the early work with calculus. Several different groups of mathematicians tried to resolve the contradictions. These efforts came to a halt as logicians first proved that not all problems could be solved within mathematics; then that reducing problems to arithmetic did not eliminate contradictions, since any complete system of arithmetic will contain contradictions itself; and finally that the basis of modern mathematics is consistent with diametrically opposed statements.

Mathematics Today These results have not deterred mathematicians from solving old and new problems using all the tools developed in the long history of the subject. In the 20th century, applied methods of statistical inference ("confidence intervals" and other techniques) have been highly developed and widely applied, through computer programs, in the sciences, engineering, and social sciences. There have also been dramatic advances in the ancient science of geometry, such as the development of fractal geometry, in which patterns of smaller parts (such as a coastline seen very close up) relate in complex ways to the whole seen at a distance. These and other modern developments in mathematics and statistics mean that, while students today study some math that is thousands of years old, their lives are affected by up-to-date mathematical techniques embodied in powerful computational packages.

Branches of Mathematics

The growth of mathematics from counting, measuring, and reasoning led to the development of a discipline with many parts. As late as the 19th century, a mathematician might be familiar with and work in all of these, but the different branches have since grown so complex and diverse that modern mathematicians have to specialize.

Algebra

The first encounters with algebra in school concern writing and solving equations—mathematical statements that use a letter or another symbol to represent an unknown quantity. For example, the equation $2x + 3 = 11$ is the statement that twice the unknown amount plus three equals eleven. Solving the equation is based on applying procedures (called algorithms) to reduce the equation to a statement of the form x equals an amount—in this case $x = 4$. The determined amount is called a solution.

As algebra becomes more sophisticated, equations with several solutions occur and the answers form a solution set. New algorithms are needed to find solutions; complex equations, such as those involving powers higher than the fifth, cannot be solved with any general algorithms, although such equations do have solution sets.

Modern or abstract algebra is not concerned with solving specific equations or inequalities, however. Instead, it deals with systems where equations obey general rules, such as $a + b = b + a$ or $a(b + c) = ab + ac$. The letters no longer represent unknown numbers but are variables that may stand for anything from a given class—numbers, points, operations, and so forth. Each small set of rules for operating with the variables describes a particular kind of structure, called by such names as *groups*, *rings*, and *fields*.

Analytic Geometry

Analytic geometry is one name for a subject that in high school might be called "graphing" or "coordinate geometry." Today it is largely a stepping-stone from algebra to calculus, although in its earliest form it was used to model problems from geometry in terms of numbers and equations.

The basic idea of analytic geometry is that points in a space can be located by numbers. The space may be a simple straight line, with one point for 0 and another for 1. In that case, the location of a point is just its distance from 0 with the distance from 0 to 1 used as the unit of measure. Typically distance to the right is represented as a positive number, while distance to the left is negative.

Two lines meeting at 0 can be used to locate points in a two-dimensional space; three such lines locate points in three dimensions. It is conventional to have the lines all meet at right angles. Points in two dimensions require two numbers for location (x,y); three dimensions require three numbers (x,y,z). The mathematician also extends this method of location to spaces of more than three dimensions; even though it is impossible to imagine some large number of lines all intersecting at right angles, it is easy to write the location of a point as a string of numbers.

Calculus

Calculus is a method for handling quantities that change value, such as velocity and acceleration; or that are defined by very general curves, such as the area of a figure bounded by curves. As arithmetic deals with numbers and algebra with variables, calculus handles functions. A function is a rule for obtaining one number from others.

For example, to calculate the number of gallons used in driving a specific number of miles in a car that gets 30 miles per gallon, one can state the rule $g = 30m$, where g is the number of gallons and m the number of miles. The function is the actual rule, and g and m are variables used in stating the rule.

Calculus in its simplest form solves two kinds of problems concerning rules for deriving one number from another. What is the formula for the rate of change of the derived number? The answer to this question is called the derivative, and this part of calculus is the derivative calculus. The other problem is based on the graph of the original rule. What is the formula for the area of the region between the graph and the horizontal axis? The answer to this question is called the integral, hence the integral calculus.

Geometry

Geometry means "earth measuring," although it was Felix Klein (1849–1925) in 1872 who gave the definition that is the basis of present-day understanding: geometry is the study of those properties of figures that remain invariant under a particular group of transformations.

Egyptian and Mesopotamian mathematicians found many practical rules for lengths, areas, and volumes. The Greeks established geometry as reasoning about the properties of figures. Euclid arranged the various proofs concerning figures formed from curves with no width and surfaces with no depth into a powerful axiomatic system that was the basis of geometry for the next 2,000 years. Euclid's geometry was based on five postulates, of which the fifth concerned parallel lines.

In the 1800's, mathematicians discovered a self-consistent system of geometry different from that logically established by Euclid. The basis of this non-Euclidean geometry differs from plane Euclidean geometry in that many lines through a point can be parallel to a line not through the point; or, equivalently, in that the sum of angles in a triangle is less than two right angles (180°).

Measurement

Any method of assigning a number, called the measure, to an entity on the basis of multiples of a unit amount can be called measurement. Most measures are rational or real numbers because measurement normally is applied to continuous amounts; measurement of a discrete set is called counting. To measure a line segment, for example, a unit length is placed on the segment a number of times until the unit extends beyond the segment. The unit that extends beyond is subdivided to determine the fraction that is beyond the end. The concept is generalized for measurement of any quantity that can vary in amount, such as electric current.

Network or Graph Theory

Figures called networks can be formed by connecting distinct points by line segments or arcs. Shapes and sizes do not count. The points are called the vertices of the network, and the connections are sometimes called edges, terminology inspired by networks that define polyhedrons in three-dimensional space. In a network all vertices are connected—you can travel via the edges to any vertex from any other—and edges do not intersect except at vertices. The theory can also deal with edges that are directed—a message can travel in a specific way on a specific edge. This theory has become increasingly important for dealing with problems of communication, including the Internet, but it also has many applications in understanding trade or other systems of two-way interactions.

Number Theory

Number theory (sometimes called arithmetic or higher arithmetic) is the study of properties of the natural numbers, especially those connected with solution of diophantine equations, divisibility (division with 0 remainder), and prime numbers. Studied for its own sake since the time of the Hellenic author Diophantus (ca. 200–ca. 299), number theory in recent years has had important applications in codes used for protecting information transmitted by computer.

Probability and Statistics

Probability is concerned with numbers that reflect the concept of chance. The theory is built on the idea that an event that occurs a certain number of times (called successes) in so many tries has a probability that is the ratio of the successes to the number of tries. Thus an event with no chance of happening has a probability of 0, and one that always happens has a probability of 1. In a coin toss where heads and tails have equal probability, the probability of heads is 1/2. The probability that any of a die's six faces will face up is 1/6.

Set Theory

Set theory studies the properties of sets, fundamental objects used to define all other concepts in mathematics. A set is determined by its elements; two sets are deemed equal if they have exactly the same elements. The language of set theory is based on the relation called membership. We say that A is a member of B, or that set B contains A as its element. In practice, one considers sets of numbers, points, functions, and so on.

Mathematical Formulas

Most formulas needed in solving everyday problems are collected below, with special emphasis on formulas relating to measurements, as these are used in everything from sewing to building a house. However, some important formulas from algebra, graphing, and trigonometry are at the end. Additional formulas can also be found in "Basic Laws of Physics."

General

The **distance** d, given the rate r and the time t:

$$d = rt$$

Length

The **perimeter (distance around)** p **of any polygon** (closed plane figure with straight sides that do not cross), given the lengths of the sides a, b, c, and so forth:

$$p = a + b + c + \ldots$$

Perimeter p **of a rectangle,** given the length l and the width w:

$$p = 2l + 2w$$

Perimeter p **of a square,** given the length of a side s:

$$p = 4s$$

Circumference (distance around) C **of a circle,** given the diameter d (distance across) or the radius r (distance from the center to the circle):

$$C = \pi d$$
$$\text{or } C = 2\pi r$$

The number π is an infinite decimal that begins 3.14159 . . . and is often approximated as either 3.14 or as 22/7.

Area

In each of the following, the area (amount of surface) is A. For three-dimensional figures, A is the total surface area.

Rectangle, given the length l and the width w:

$$A = lw$$

Square, given the length of a side s:

$$A = s^2$$

Circle, given the radius r:

$$A = \pi r^2$$

Triangle, given the base b and the height h:

$$A = \tfrac{1}{2}\, bh$$

Right triangle, given the lengths a and b of the two sides (legs) that form the right angle:

$$A = \tfrac{1}{2}\, ab$$

Parallelogram, given the base b and the height h:

$$A = bh$$

Trapezoid, given the two bases B and b and the height h:

$$A = \tfrac{1}{2}\, h\,(B + b)$$

Kite, given the lengths of the two diagonals D and d:

$$A = \tfrac{1}{2}\, Dd$$

Regular polygon (polygon with all sides of equal length and all angles of equal measure), given the perimeter p and the apothem a (the distance from the center of the regular polygon to one of its sides):

$$A = \tfrac{1}{2}\, ap$$

Equilateral triangle (all sides the same length), given the length of a side s:

$$A = \frac{s^2\sqrt{3}}{4}$$

Heron's formula Any triangle, given half the length of the perimeter (the semiperimeter) s and the lengths of the sides a, b, and c:

$$A = \sqrt{s(s-a)(s-b)(s-c)}$$

Right circular cylinder (a cylinder with a circular region as its base whose sides make a right angle with the base), given the radius r of the base and the height h of the cylinder:

$$A = 2\pi r(h + r)$$

Right circular cone (a cone with a circular region as its base, whose altitude makes a right angle with the base), given the radius r of the base and the slant height l of the cone (the shortest distance from the tip of the cone to the circle of the base):

$$A = \pi r(l + r)$$

Sphere, given the radius r:

$$A = 4\pi r^2$$

Volume

In each of the following, the volume (space enclosed) is V.

Cube, given the length of an edge e:

$$V = e^3$$

Right rectangular prism (box), given the length l, the width w, and the height h:

$$V = lwh$$

Prism, given the area of the base B and the height h:

$$V = Bh$$

Right circular cylinder, given the radius r of the base and the height h:

$$V = \pi r^2 h$$

Right circular cone, given the radius r of the base and the height h:

$$V = \tfrac{1}{3}\, \pi r^2 h$$

Pyramid, given the area of the base B and the height h:

$$V = \tfrac{1}{3}\, Bh$$

Sphere, given the radius r:

$$V = \tfrac{4}{3}\, \pi r^3$$

Algebra

If a, b, and x are any numbers or variables ("unknowns"):

$$(a+b)^2 = a^2 + 2ab + b^2$$
$$(a-b)^2 = a^2 - 2ab + b^2$$
$$x^2 - a^2 = (x+a)(x-a)$$
$$x^3 - a^3 = (x-a)(x^2 + ax + a^2)$$
$$x^3 + a^3 = (x+a)(x^2 - ax + a^2)$$

If a, b, c, and d are any numbers or variables except that neither b nor d can be zero:

$$a/b + c/d = (ad + bc)/bd$$
$$a/b - c/d = (ad - bc)/bd$$
$$a/b \times c/d = ac/bd$$
$$a/b \div c/d = ad/bc \ (c \neq 0)$$

Quadratic formula for the solutions of a second degree polynomial equation in one variable of the form $ax^2 + bx + c = 0$:

$$x = \frac{-b \pm \sqrt{b^2 - 4ac}}{2a}$$

Laws of exponents, given that a, b, x, and y are numbers or variables:

$$a^x a^y = a^{x+y} \qquad (a^x)^y = a^{xy}$$
$$(ab)^x = a^x b^x \qquad (a/b)^x = a^x/b^x$$
$$a^x/a^y = a^{x-y} \qquad a^{-x} = \frac{1}{a^x}$$
$$a^0 = 1 \qquad a^1 = a.$$

Laws of logarithms, given that a, b, x, and y are positive numbers; c is any real number; and $a \neq 1$, $b \neq 1$.

$$\log_a (xy) = \log_a x + \log_a y \qquad \log_a 1/x = -\log_a x$$
$$\log_a (x/y) = \log_a x - \log_a y \qquad \log_a (x^c) = c \log_a x$$
$$\log_b x = (\log_a x)/(\log_a b) \qquad \log_a 1 = 0$$
$$\log_a a = 1 \qquad a^{\log_a x} = x$$
$$\log_a (a^c) = c$$

Graphs

In a rectangular (Cartesian) coordinate plane, where the horizontal axis is x and the vertical axis is y:

Slope of a line, m, given two particular points (x_1, y_1) and (x_2, y_2) where $x_1 \neq x_2$:

$$m = (y_2 - y_1)/(x_2 - x_1)$$

Point-slope equation of a line, given the slope m and a point on the nonvertical line (x_1, y_1):

$$y - y_1 = m(x - x_1)$$

Slope-intercept equation of a line, given the slope m and the y-intercept b (the number on the y axis where the line crosses the y axis):

$$y = mx + b$$

Distance d between any two points, (x_1, y_1) and (x_2, y_2):

$$d = \sqrt{(x_2 - x_1)^2 + (y_2 - y_1)^2}.$$

Trigonometry

In a right triangle whose two shorter sides (or legs) are a and b, opposite angles A and B respectively, and whose longest side (or hypotenuse, always the side opposite the right angle, C) is c:

Pythagorean theorem:

$$c^2 = a^2 + b^2$$

Trigonometric functions:

sine: $\sin A = a/c$	cosine: $\cos A = b/c$
tangent: $\tan A = a/b$	cotangent: $\cot A = b/a$
secant: $\sec A = c/b$	cosecant: $\csc A = c/a$

In any triangle labeled such that side a is opposite angle A, side b is opposite angle B, and side c is opposite angle C:

Angle sum:

$$A + B + C = 180°$$

Law of sines:

$$(\sin A)/a = (\sin B)/b = (\sin C)/c$$

Law of cosines:

$$c^2 = a^2 + b^2 - 2ab \cos C$$

If x is any real number or a measure of an angle in degrees, the following statements are true.

Defining trigonometric identities:

$$\tan x = \sin x/\cos x \qquad \csc x = 1/\sin x$$
$$\cot x = \cos x/\sin x \qquad \cot x = 1/\tan x$$
$$\sec x = 1/\cos x$$

Trigonometric identities of symmetry:

$$\sin(-x) = -\sin x \qquad \cos(-x) = \cos x$$
$$\tan(-x) = -\tan x \qquad \cot(-x) = -\cot x$$
$$\sec(-x) = \sec x \qquad \csc(-x) = -\csc x.$$

Pythagorean identities:

$$\sin^2 x + \cos^2 x = 1$$
$$\tan^2 x + 1 = \sec^2 x$$
$$\cot^2 x + 1 = \csc^2 x$$

Sum and difference formulas: If x and y are any two real numbers or measures of angles:

$$\sin(x+y) = \sin x \cos y + \cos x \sin y$$
$$\cos(x+y) = \cos x \cos y - \sin x \sin y$$
$$\tan(x+y) = (\tan x + \tan y)/(1 - \tan x \tan y)$$
$$\sin(x-y) = \sin x \cos y - \cos x \sin y$$
$$\cos(x-y) = \cos x \cos y + \sin x \sin y$$
$$\tan(x-y) = (\tan x - \tan y)/(1 + \tan x \tan y)$$

Numbers and Number Systems

Counting, or Natural, Numbers

The counting numbers (1, 2, 3, 4, and so forth) are the numbers used in counting. The whole numbers are the counting numbers with 0 added to the set, or 0, 1, 2, 3, 4, ... These distinctions are somewhat elastic; mathematicians use the term *natural numbers*, but sometimes they include 0 and sometimes not. There are two ways to define these kinds of numbers—by matching sets with the same number of members (which permits 0), and by starting with 1 and defining the numbers as 1, 1 + 1 = 2, 2 + 1 = 3, and so forth.

These numbers can be shown in order as equally spaced points on a line that extends indefinitely, which is called a number line.

0 1 2 3 4 5 6 7 8 ...

Integers

Integers are a set of numbers consisting of the whole numbers (or natural numbers including 0) and their opposites, Two numbers at equal distances from 0 on the number line are called opposites.

Integers are also known as the positive and negative whole numbers. When the real numbers are arranged in order on a line from least to greatest, all the numbers greater than 0 (on the same side of 0 as 1) are positive numbers. All the numbers less than 0 (on the opposite side of 0 from 1) are negative numbers. The integers extend infinitely in both directions, so they can be shown as ... –3, –2, –1, 0, +1, +2, +3, ...

...-4 -3 -2 -1 0 +1 +2 +3 +4...

Real Numbers

A rational number is any number that can be represented as the ratio of an integer to a nonzero integer. The positive and negative fractions (with integral parts), such as 1/2 or 2/3 or 22/7, are rational numbers, but so are all the integers. If you divide the numerator of the fraction by the denominator, the answer will be the rational number expressed as a decimal fraction. As decimals, rational numbers either terminate (that is, become a string of 0s after some decimal place, such as 0.25 = 0.2500000...) or repeat a finite pattern over and over (such as 0.33 ... = 1/3 or 0.142857142857142857... = 1/7).

Greek mathematicians from ca. 400 B.C. discovered that that some numbers, such as the diagonal of a square whose sides are rational numbers, are not rational. Any real number that cannot be represented as the ratio of two integers is an irrational number. When real numbers are expressed as infinite decimals, any decimal that fails to repeat the same finite pattern of digits over and over represents an irrational number.

The totality of rational numbers and irrational numbers constitutes the real numbers. The real numbers are most easily pictured as all the numbers that can be represented as points on the number line, filling in all of the points between the integers. Another way to define the real numbers is as all numbers that can be represented by decimal fractions. Note that two different decimals can equal the same real number, as, for example, 2.0000 ... and 1.99999...

Complex Numbers

Multiplying a number by itself produces a square of that number. For real numbers the square is always positive; for example, not only does $3^2 = 9$, but also $(-3)^2 = 9$. For a given positive number p, the square root is a number that, when multiplied by itself, has the product p. For example, the two square roots of 9 are +3 and –3.

The square roots of the negative numbers are called imaginary numbers. To avoid inconsistencies, imaginary numbers are expressed in terms of the square root of –1, known as i. Examples include $2i$, $-i$, $i/3$, and $4i\sqrt{2}$. The existence and utility of such numbers is beyond question, but the name (to contrast with real numbers) was coined when mathematicians doubted that such numbers made sense.

A complex number is the sum of a real number and an imaginary number, expressed usually as $x + iy$ where i is the square root of negative 1. All numbers are included among the complex numbers. For real numbers, y is 0; for integers, x is an integer and y is 0; and so forth.

While real numbers are shown on a number line, complex numbers require a plane. The usual y axis is replaced by an iy axis. On the plane of complex numbers, the imaginaries occupy the vertical or y axis, while the real numbers are on the horizontal or x axis. The other complex numbers form the other parts of the plane.

Fractions, Decimals, and Percents

To find the equivalent of a fraction in decimal form, divide the numerator (top number) by the denominator (bottom number). To change from a decimal to a percent, multiply by 100. To change from a percent to a decimal, divide by 100.

Fraction	Decimal	Percent (%)
1/16	0.0625	6.25
1/8 (= 2/16)	0.125	12.5
3/16	0.1875	18.75
1/4 (= 2/8 = 4/16)	0.25	25.0
5/16	0.3125	31.25
1/3	0.3 . . .	33 1/3
3/8 (= 6/16)	0.375	37.5
7/16	0.4375	43.75
1/2 (= 2/4 = 4/8 = 8/16)	0.5	50.0
9/16	0.5625	56.25
5/8 (= 10/16)	0.625	62.5
2/3	0.6 . . .	66 2/3
11/16	0.6875	68.75
3/4 (= 6/8 = 12/16)	0.75	75.0
13/16	0.8125	81.25
7/8 (= 14/16)	0.875	87.5
15/16	0.9375	93.75
1 (= 2/2 = 4/4 = 8/8 = 16/16)	1.0	100.0

Large Numbers

There are two primary naming systems for large numbers. The United States and France (among others) use one system, while Germany and Great Britain use the other. (Googol and googolplex, invented by the nephew of the mathematician and author Edward Kasner, are rarely used outside the United States.)

Number of zeroes after 1	American name	British name
6	million	million
9	billion	milliard
12	trillion	billion
15	quadrillion	1,000 billion
18	quintillion	trillion
21	sextillion	1,000 trillion
24	septillion	quadrillion
27	octillion	1,000 quadrillion
30	nonillion	quintillion
33	decillion	1,000 quintillion
100	googol	googol
googol	googolplex	googolplex

Prefixes Used in the International System of Units

Prefix	Abbrev.	Factor by which unit is multipled	Scientific notation
yotta-	Y	1,000,000,000,000,000,000,000,000	10^{24}
zetta-	Z	1,000,000,000,000,000,000,000	10^{21}
exa-	E	1,000,000,000,000,000,000	10^{18}
peta-	P	1,000,000,000,000,000	10^{15}
tera-	T	1,000,000,000,000	10^{12}
giga-	G	1,000,000,000	10^{9}
mega-	M	1,000,000	10^{6}
kilo-	k	1,000	10^{3}
hecto-	h	100	10^{2}
deka-	da	10	10^{1}
deci-	d	0.1	10^{-1}
centi-	c	0.01	10^{-2}
milli-	m	0.001	10^{-3}
micro-	ct	0.000 001	10^{-6}
nano-	n	0.000 000 001	10^{-9}
pico-	p	0.000 000 000 001	10^{-12}
femto-	f	0.000 000 000 000 001	10^{-15}
atto-	a	0.000 000 000 000 000 001	10^{-18}
zepto-	z	0.000 000 000 000 000 000 001	10^{-21}
yocto-	y	0.000 000 000 000 000 000 000 001	10^{-24}

Probability

Probability is the measure of how likely it is that some event will occur. The simplest form of probability is based on the ratio of a selected outcome (called a success) to the total number of possibilities. For example, if you toss one die one time, only one face (from the six possible faces) can land facing up; the probability is 1/6 for a selected face to be a success. If an outcome never occurs, then its probability is 0, but if it always occurs, the ratio becomes 1.

Any result of an experiment or observation that can lead to success or failure is called an event. Events that cannot be simplified further are called simple; those that can be decomposed into simple events are compound.

For many events in ordinary life, such as weather, probability is based on analysis of past events. For example, a meteorologist might determine that a certain weather pattern has previously led to rain about 2 times in 10; this probability is expressed as a 20 percent chance of rain. For the toss of a die, chances that any one face will land up are thought to be equal for any toss, so the past history is not considered.

Probability theory is the mathematical formulation of these ideas, and requires outcomes that can be enumerated. For example, tossing a coin twice has four possible outcomes. Representing heads with H and tails with T, the only possible outcomes to that experiment (discounting the coins landing on edge) are HH, HT, TH, and TT. These four outcomes form what is called the sample space for that experiment. Each of the simple events, such as HH, is a sample point. A compound event, such as getting one head and one tail, is represented by several sample points (in this case two, HT and TH). Thus, while the simple event of getting two heads has a probability of 1/4, the probability of the compound event of getting one head and one tail has a probability of 2/4, or 1/2.

It is possible to compute the probability of some compound events from known probabilities of other events. If two events cannot occur at the same time, they are mutually exclusive and the probability of one or the other of the events is just the sum of the probabilities of the two events. For example, when one die is tossed, the probability of getting a face up with fewer than three dots is 1/3 (since there are two successful outcomes out of six), while the probability of getting exactly five dots is 1/6. Since these two events are mutually exclusive, the probability of getting fewer than three dots or five dots is 1/3 + 1/6 = 1/2.

Often a person wants to know the probability that two events will both occur. For example, one might want to know if on a particular day it will rain and also if a friend will telephone. These events appear to be unconnected in any way, and are called independent. For these independent events, the probability that one and the other will happen is the product of the probabilities. For example, if the probability of rain is 40 percent (or 2/5—40 percent expressed as a fraction); and if your friend calls every other day on the average, for a probability of 50 percent (or 1/2); and if these are independent events, the probability that it will rain and your friend will call is 2/5 times 1/2, which is 2/10, or 1/5. (For percents, one calculates 0.4 times 0.5 = 0.20, which is the same result, since 20 percent expressed as a fraction is 1/5).

Finally, we must consider the probability of dependent events — for example, determining if on a given day it will rain and if you will wash your car. Since these events can be connected in one way or another, they are not independent. In the instance of dependent events like these, you cannot multiply the probabilities to determine if both will happen on the same day.

Glossary of Mathematical Terms

absolute value distance of a number from 0. Indicated by vertical lines, as in |−6|. Distance is always a positive number or 0, so absolute value is always nonnegative: |−6| = 6, |3/4| = 3/4, and |0| = 0.

algebra branch of mathematics that substitutes letters for numbers.

algebraic expression expression that contains at least one variable.

algorithm step-by-step procedure for solving a mathematical problem.

analytic geometry idea that graphs and equations are two different ways of expressing the same concepts.

angle union of two rays with a common end point.

arc portion of the circumference of a circle

area number of square units covering a shape or figure.

arithmetic branch of mathematics usually concerned with the four numerical operations (adding, subtracting, multiplication, and division).

average single number that represents in some way a typical member of a collection. The arithmetic mean, usually called the mean, is commonly used as the average. The mean of *n* numbers is the sum of the numbers divided by *n*. Another number commonly used is the median. A median is the middle number for a set with an odd number of members, but if there are an even number of members there is no middle number, and the median is half the sum of the two numbers nearest the middle. Sometimes another measure of central tendency, called the mode, is used; this is the number in the set that occurs most frequently.

axiom self-evident and necessary truth.

axes vertical and horizontal lines that make up the quadrants of a coordinate plane. The vertical axis is typically referred to as the *y* axis, and the horizontal axis is usually referred to as the *x* axis.

biconditional statement "if-then" statement that is true in both directions.

binomial polynomial equation with two terms usually joined by a plus or minus sign.

bisect divide into two equal parts.

calculus branch of mathematics involving derivatives and integrals.

cardinality number of elements in a set.

circumference distance around a circle.

coefficient factor of a term.

collinear word describing points that lie in a straight line.

commutative property the order of elements in a calculation makes no difference in the outcome, i.e. $ab = ba$.

complement set of elements in the universal set that are not in the current set.

complementary angles two angles that combine for a total of 90 degrees.

conditional statement "if-then" statement. The "if" section has a condition that must be met; the "then" section results if the condition is true.

constant value that does not change.

coordinates ordered grouping of numbers that corresponds to a point on a line, a line on a plane, or a plane in space.

cosine in a right triangle, the ratio of the length of the side adjacent to an acute angle to the length of the hypotenuse.

cube and cube root multiplying a number by itself twice produces the cube of that number, which can be indicated with the exponent ^{3}; for example, $4^3 = 4 \times 4 \times 4 = 64$. For a given number, the cube root is the number that, when multiplied by itself twice, has the product that is the number. For example, the cube root of 64 is +4 and of −64 is −4.

decimal our common way of writing numbers is based on 10, and is called decimal, from the Latin word for ten. For whole numbers the digit farthest right shows ones, the next left shows tens, and so on, with each place indicating the next higher power of 10. A decimal point at the right of a whole number marks the beginning of a decimal fraction with places continuing as tenths, hundredths, thousandths, and so on. To convert a common fraction such as 3/4 to its decimal equivalent, divide the numerator ("top number") by the denominator ("bottom number"); for example, for 3/4 the decimal equivalent is 0.75.

decimal fraction fraction expressed in decimal notation. For example, 1/4 is expressed as the decimal fraction 0.25.

degree unit of measurement for an angle.

denominator bottom number of a fraction.

derivative slope of the tangent line to a curve at any instant *a*.

diameter length of the line that passes through the center of a circle, cutting it in half.

discontinuous function that cannot be drawn without a gap.

disjoint sets two or more sets with no elements in common.

dividend number that is being divided.

divisor number that is doing the dividing.

elements individual items or objects in a set.

empty set set with no contents, also known as a null set.

equation statement composed of two equal mathematical expressions, joined by an equals (=) sign.

equilateral having all sides equal.

exponent number that gives reference to the repeated multiplication required. For example, the exponent of 2^3 is $2 \times 2 \times 2$, or 8.

expression mathematical statement using numbers, variables, and operations.

factor as a noun, a factor is one of the numbers used to form a particular product. As a verb, to factor is to locate all factors of the number. For example, the factors of 12 are 1, 2, 3, 4, 6, and 12. In most cases only prime number factors are found and they are often shown as forming the product, which for 12 is $2 \times 2 \times 3$.

factorial number multiplied by every integer less than the number, down to 1. Represented by the symbol !. For example, 3! equals $3 \times 2 \times 1$, or 6.

finite not infinite.

finite set set whose cardinality is a finite number; a set whose number of elements is countable.

formula mathematical sentence that expresses the relationship between two or more variables.

fraction a *common fraction* is a type of numeral that represents division of two numbers, with the one being divided into (the numerator) above a short line and the one being divided by (the denominator) below the line. For example, the fraction 3/4 means that 3 (the numerator) is to be divided by 4 (the denominator). If the numerator is larger than the denominator, as in 5/2, the fraction is called *improper*. The same numbers can be represented as *decimal fractions* by carrying out the division: 3/4 is the same as 0.75, and 5/2 is the same as 2.5. Different fractions can show the same number; for example 2/3 and 8/12 are two different common fractions for the same number. Fractions can be added or subtracted if they have the same denominator, by adding or subtracting the numerators. Fractions can be multiplied by multiplying their numerators and their denominators separately. For division, the fraction that is being divided into another number is replaced by its reciprocal, and then the two numbers are multiplied.

geometry branch of mathematics that studies lines, angles, shapes, and their properties.

hypotenuse longest side of a right-angled triangle.

imaginary numbers square roots of negative numbers.

infinite having no limit or end.

integer whole number, positive or negative, including zero.

intersection what is common between two sets.

interval set containing all the points between two end points.

irrational number number that cannot be expressed as the ratio of two integers.

least common denominator addition or subtraction of fractions requires that fractions have the same denominator. Calculations are simplest if that denominator is the smallest natural number that will suffice, a number called the least common denominator. For example, the least common denominator of 2/3 and 1/4 is 12, since 12 is the smallest number that can be divided evenly by both 3 and 4.

line straight infinite path joining an infinite number of points.

line segment straight path that has a beginning and an end (end points).

linear equation equation whose graph is a line.

logarithm power to which a base must be raised to produce a given number.

matrix array of numbers in columns and rows.

mean See *average*.

median See *average*.

mode See *average*.

monomial algebraic expression consisting of a single term.

natural numbers regular counting numbers.

negative number number that is less than zero.

noncollinear word describing points that do not all lie in a straight line.

null set See *empty set*.

numeral written symbol corresponding to a number.

numerator top number in a fraction.

obtuse angle angle measuring between 90 and 180 degrees.

octagon polygon with eight sides.

odd number whole number that is not divisible by 2.

operation addition, subtraction, multiplication, or division.

ordered pair set of two numbers, with the x-coordinate listed first and the y-coordinate listed second.

parallel word describing two or more lines that never intersect.

parallelogram quadrilateral that has both sets of opposite sides that are parallel.

percent numeral showing a ratio of a number to 100. For example, 35 percent denotes a ratio of 35 to 100. This can be expressed as a common fraction, 35/100, or more commonly as a decimal fraction, 0.35. The rule for rewriting a percent as a decimal is to drop the percent sign and move the decimal point two places to the left; for example, 5.6 percent becomes 0.056 as a decimal. To add, subtract, multiply, or divide ratios indicated by percents, first change all the percents to decimals. The symbol for percent is %.

perpendicular word describing two intersecting lines that form a right angle (90 degrees).

pi (π) an infinite decimal that begins 3.14159265358…, often approximated by 3.14 or by 22/7. π is the ratio of the circumference of any circle to its diameter.

plane set of points joined to form a flat surface.

polygon line segments joined to form a closed figure.

polynomial algebraic expression with more than one term.

power the power of a number is the value of a numeral indicated by an exponent, shown as a superscript numeral. For example, 8 is the third power of 2, shown as 2^3.

prime number natural number greater than 1 that has no divisors other than itself and 1. Non-prime natural numbers are called composite numbers. Thus, 2, 3, 5, 7, 11, 13, 17, 19 are the prime numbers less than 20; and 4, 6, 8, 9, 10, 12, 14, 15, 16, and 18 are composite numbers. (The number 1 is neither prime nor composite.)

probability likelihood of an event.

product sum obtained when two or more numbers are multiplied together.

proof demonstration that, given certain axioms, a certain statement is true.

proportion correct statement that two ratios are equal. A proportion can be written in fraction form, such as 3/4 = 9/12.

Pythagorean theorem theorem that relates the three sides of a right triangle, as $a^2 + b^2 = c^2$.

quadratic equation second-degree polynomial equation in one variable of the form $ax^2 + bx + c = 0$

quotient solution to a division problem.

radical number shown with the sign $\sqrt{\ }$. For example $\sqrt{2}$, the positive square root of 2, can also be called radical 2. In this notation, the number 2 is said to be inside or under the radical, and such a number is called a radicand. For roots other than square roots, the same sign is used with a small numeral greater than 2 written in the V of the radical sign. The small numeral, called an index, shows which root is indicated: 3 for the cube root, 4 for the fourth root, etc. When a radical has an even index, it always means the positive root.

radius line segment from the center of a circle to any point on the circle.

range difference between the largest and smallest numbers in a set.

ratio amount of one entity with respect to another, usually expressed as a fraction. Ratios are essentially the same as rates, such as miles per gallon.

rational number number that can be expressed as the ratio of two integers.

ray straight line with one end point.

real numbers combined set of rational and irrational numbers.

reciprocal number obtained when a given number is divided into 1. For example, the reciprocal of 5 is 1 divided by 5, or 1/5. For common fractions, the reciprocal can be obtained by interchanging numerator and denominator, so the reciprocal of 3/7 is 7/3.

rectangle parallelogram with four right angles.

rhombus parallelogram with four equal sides.

right angle 90-degree angle.

scientific notation system of writing numbers as the product of a number between 1 and 10 and a power of 10. A number such as 2.398×10^9 takes less space and, if you know the system, is easier to read than 239,800,000. Negative exponents provide scientific notation for small numbers: 0.00000087 in scientific notation is 8.7×10^{-7}.

set defined collection of items or objects.

slope steepness of a line, determined from two points on the line.

solution substitution for the variable that will make the equation true.

square and square root multiplying a number by itself produces a square of that number, which can be indicated with the exponent 2. For real numbers the square is always positive; not only does $3^2 = 9$ but also $(-3)^2 = 9$. For a given positive number, the square root is a number that when multiplied by itself has the product that is the original number. Positive numbers have two square roots, one positive and one negative. For example, the two square roots of 9 are +3 and −3. Square roots of negative numbers are called imaginary.

subset set, all of whose elements are also elements of another set.

supplementary angles two angles whose sum equals 180 degrees.

tangent in a right angle, the ratio of lengths of the side opposite angle *x* to the side adjacent to angle *x*.

term See *monomial.*

trapezoid quadrilateral with exactly two parallel sides.

triangle three-sided polygon.

trigonometric function function that includes algebraic operations and any of the six trigonometric definitions (sine, cosine, tangent, cosecant, secant, cotangent).

trigonometry branch of mathematics that deals with the relationships between the sides and angles of triangles, and the calculations based on them

trinomial algebraic equation with three terms.

union joining of two or more sets into a master set, without creating multiples of any single item.

variable symbol that represents an unknown quantity.

whole number number that does not contain a fraction.

MEDIA

Electronic Media

Radio 404

The Evolution of Broadcasting 404

The Business of Broadcasting (1919–26) 404

The Era of Network Radio (1927–47) 406

Network Radio Programming 408

Television 411

Inventing Television (1927–47) 411

The Rise of Commercial Television (1948–59) 412

The Era of Network Television (1955–83) 415

Television Programming in the Network Era (1960–83) 417

The Cable Era (1984–2004) 420

The Three Major Networks Today . . . 424

Television in the Digital Era 426

The Digital Future 429

Print Media

Newspapers 430

Newspapers in Colonial America 430

The Penny Press 431

The Rise of the Modern Newspaper . 431

Consolidation 432

Magazines 433

The 19th Century 433

The 20th Century 434

Magazines Today 434

ELECTRONIC MEDIA

Radio

The Evolution of Broadcasting

Early Uses of Radio The earliest practical applications of wireless technology involved communication between ships and land-based stations to coordinate information about cargo pickup schedules, shipping routes, and weather conditions. Wireless technology made its most dramatic impact by saving lives in several well-publicized maritime disasters. The most famous of these occurred in April 1912 when the ocean liner *Titanic* struck an iceberg while on its maiden voyage across the Atlantic. Most of the passengers and crew perished, but a ship that had picked up the *Titanic*'s distress signal from 50 miles away rescued nearly 700 survivors.

In the years leading up to World War I, such events led hobbyists to purchase radio equipment and build their own transmitters and receivers. Thousands of these amateurs, eager to communicate with fellow radio enthusiasts, began experimental broadcasts, first using Morse code, then soon venturing into the transmission of voice and music. Radio corporations that had been formed to promote and capitalize on point-to-point communication began to glimpse the commercial potential of broadcasting to American homes. David Sarnoff (1891–1971), the future chairman of RCA, began his career as commercial manager of American Marconi, where he was credited with writing a 1916 memo that first recommended "a plan of development which would make radio a 'household utility' in the same sense as the piano or phonograph." As he observed the rapidly expanding market for household goods, Sarnoff proposed manufacturing a receiver that could take its place in the home as a "Radio Music Box," transforming radio from an instrument of two-way communication into a source of domestic amusement for the American family.

With the explosion of interest in radio the U.S., Congress passed the Radio Act of 1912, which established public policy and standards of operation in an attempt to impose order on the airwaves. This legislation gave the government priority and control over radio communication, including the licensing of transmitters. The government exercised its control upon the country's entry into World War I. There were more than 8,500 licensed amateurs in 1917 when the government ordered all amateur transmissions to cease and the navy assumed operational control of all radio stations for the duration of the war. To promote research and innovation, the government also untangled the welter of competing patents by suspending proprietary license agreements and creating a patents pool that gathered together the many patents held by individuals and corporations that were necessary for the operation of radio.

The Business of Broadcasting, 1919–1926

The Creation of RCA At the end of World War I the question of whether or not radio in the U.S. should be defined as a matter of public service or of private enterprise caused a serious debate in business and government circles. In the war's aftermath, with radio essentially operating under government control, some thought American radio might follow the model of the postal service and continue as a business operated solely by the federal government. European countries had begun to adopt this model by establishing radio as a state monopoly. On the other hand, the prospect of a government monopoly in the U.S. provoked strenuous opposition from amateur radio operators, manufacturers, and those companies that had stations seized by the government during the war.

But if radio was not to be operated as a government monopoly, how would the U.S. foster the growth of companies able to compete against British Marconi, the world's leading radio corporation? British Marconi held key patents and dominated manufacturing and sales in the United States through its subsidiary, American Marconi. Public opinion strongly opposed foreign ownership of American radio, so placing radio in the hands of American owners became a national priority. Without a government monopoly to coordinate the development of radio, however, the marketplace had produced a tangled mess of competing patents and proprietary license agreements that stalled technological advances.

General Electric, a titan of the electric industry, solved the problem by engineering an American radio monopoly upon the foundation of a new company that would soon become the industry leader. With the federal government still in control of American Marconi stations seized during the war and spurred by a growing sentiment against foreign ownership, British Marconi sold its holdings in American Marconi to GE in 1919. In October 1919 GE established the Radio Corporation of America as a subsidiary and transferred all tangible assets of American Marconi to the new company. Through this arrangement, GE planned to manufacture equipment, while RCA would sell receivers and operate the company's radio stations.

The chief obstacle to manufacturing quality radio receivers was that AT&T controlled key patents to De Forest's Audion tube. This problem was solved in 1920 when GE, RCA, and AT&T signed a patents pooling agreement that provided for the cross licensing of each company's patents. United Fruit, which controlled several radio patents because of its shipping interests, joined the pool in 1921. Westinghouse, GE's chief competitor and the last major company that might have competed with this growing alliance, joined the pool and acquired a stake in RCA in 1921.

By 1922 all the pieces of an American radio monopoly had been assembled. The companies in the patents pool became the majority shareholders in RCA. GE was the largest shareholder with 25.8 percent of the company's stock, followed by Westinghouse with 20.6 percent, and AT&T and United Fruit, both of which owned roughly four percent. With control of nearly 2,000 patents necessary for the manufacture of radio transmitters and receivers, the companies in the patents pool carved up the radio industry for themselves. GE and Westinghouse manufactured radio receivers, which were sold exclusively by RCA. AT&T, through its Western Electric subsidiary, manufactured and sold transmitters. From this intricate set of alliances a viable radio industry was born.

Broadcasting Booms Quickly Once the patents pool had established a viable industry structure for radio manufacturing, factory-assembled receivers began to arrive in the marketplace. Designed to compete with phonographs as a domestic amusement and to complement household furnishings, the new receivers brought radio out of father's workshop and into the family parlor, where it began the transition from an astonishing gadget into a medium for the masses.

Westinghouse became the first manufacturer to move into broadcasting when it established regularly scheduled evening broadcasts from 100-watt station KDKA in Pittsburgh. The first broadcast reported the returns on election night, November 2, 1920. By offering a regular program service, Westinghouse hoped to sell receivers and to promote the company's brand name. Soon the radio craze was sweeping the nation. In 1921 there were only 30 stations conducting regular broadcasts; by the end of 1922 there were 600. Radio manufacturers and dealers offered programs in order to tempt people into buying radio sets. Universities, churches, and newspapers began broadcasting in order to extend their service to their communities. In 1921 one in every 500 American households had a radio set; by 1926 there was one radio for every six households.

Advertising Comes to Radio As stations expanded their programming they faced the inescapable question of how a program service should be financed. In European countries the answer was to subsidize program service through taxes or license fees paid by owners of receivers. In the U.S. the answer had to be found in the marketplace. By applying insights from the telephone industry, AT&T introduced two concepts—commercial sponsorship and networks—that transformed the radio business. In 1922 AT&T opened radio station WEAF in New York City, where it introduced the concept of *toll broadcasting*. In the telephone business, AT&T charged customers a toll for the length of time they used its long-distance telephone wires. AT&T proposed the same model for radio, offering to sell time by the minute to anyone who wanted to use its station. The first commercial—a 10-minute sales pitch for an apartment complex in Queens—appeared on WEAF during the evening of August 28, 1922. By 1923 Gimbels department store and other New York businesses were taking a less direct route to consumers, forgoing the extended sales pitch and instead sponsoring entertainment programs.

The next step for AT&T was to use its telephone wires in order to interconnect individual stations. This network (or "chain," as it was then called) gave sponsors access to a larger audience—and allowed AT&T to charge higher rates for advertising. By 1924, WEAF had become the flagship of a 20-station network operating as far west as Chicago.

AT&T's innovations were not without controversy. Many Americans were alarmed by the rise of radio advertising and distrusted the expansion of networks. Much early advertising was *institutional*; companies hoped that a listener's gratitude for a particular program would translate into goodwill for the company and its products. Critics and politicians argued that it would be inappropriate for radio to bring *direct* advertising, in which a sponsor blatantly promoted its products, into American homes, but direct advertising soon appeared. Others argued that broadcasting was an inherently local phenomenon and that networks would inevitably undermine radio's local character. AT&T grew tired of the controversy and of the competition in the radio industry. In 1926 the telephone company sold station WEAF to RCA and withdrew from the patents pool. In the years to follow, AT&T's innovative use of advertising and networking would serve as the essential financial structure of broadcasting.

The Need for Regulation Radio grew so quickly that by 1925 listeners in many cities complained that signal interference had begun to dim the appeal of listening. Some of this was caused by the equipment of the day—transmitters drifted from their intended frequency, receivers were hard to tune—but the most pressing problem was that too many stations shared a narrow band of the spectrum. Most transmitters of the era were not terribly powerful; at 100–500 watts, they could send a reliable signal 20–50 miles. As more ambitious stations began to transmit with ratings as high as 5,000 watts, however, they overpowered weaker signals even at a distance.

Washington recognized the need for new legislation, but broadcasting presented both technical and social challenges that changed with each new innovation. Secretary of Commerce Herbert Hoover held four annual conferences between 1922 and 1925, but no clear consensus emerged. Congress wasn't able to pass a comprehensive new radio bill until February 1927.

The Radio Act of 1927 left many questions unanswered, but it created the Federal Radio Commission (F.R.C.), a temporary agency charged with bringing order to the airwaves. In order to operate, radio stations needed a license from the F.R.C., which was responsible for assigning transmission frequencies, determining the location and power of a station's transmitter, and setting up signal coverage areas. The Radio Act also stipulated that licensees bear a responsibility to society, but refrained from specifying those obligations. Because there were vastly more applicants than available channel frequencies, those fortunate enough to be selected for a broadcast license would be expected to operate in the "public interest, convenience, and/or necessity." These vague and virtually unenforceable expectations became the cornerstone of broadcasting policy in America. By imposing order on the airwaves while limiting the public obligations of broadcasters, the legislation cleared the ground for the expansion of commercial radio and the rise of networks.

The Era of Network Radio, 1927–47

The Rise of National Networks Broadcasting began as a local event. Each station operated independently and devised its own solution to the challenges of addressing an audience, providing a program service, and financing its operations. Radio listeners heard voices from their own communities, voices that sounded like their own, and music they recognized from church or the local dance hall. This changed with the emergence of NBC and CBS as national networks in the late 1920's. By making news and entertainment available simultaneously to listeners across the nation, networks transformed radio into the central cultural medium of American society.

NBC The era of network radio began in September 1926 when RCA, led by chairman David Sarnoff, formed the National Broadcasting Company (NBC), with ownership held by RCA (50 percent), GE (30 percent), and Westinghouse (20 percent). The first network broadcast took place on November 15, 1926, originating from RCA's New York station, WEAF. The four-hour program, featuring singers, orchestras, and comedians, was broadcast live from the Grand Ballroom of the Waldorf-Astoria Hotel in New York over a network of 21 affiliate stations stretching as far west as Kansas City. In January 1927, NBC added a second network originating from its other New York station, WJZ, and the two networks were designated as NBC-Red and NBC-Blue. By the end of 1928, as NBC added affiliates and programs, both networks offered full-time coast-to-coast programming.

Backed by the financial resources of its wealthy corporate patrons, NBC entered the radio business with overwhelming advantages. NBC directly owned and operated 10 stations that formed the core of its networks. The majority of these were powerful stations, broadcasting on exclusive, clear-channel frequencies at 50,000 watts with signals that could be heard for hundreds of miles. Independently owned stations joined the network as affiliates. NBC supplied these stations with live programs that no independent station could afford to produce on its own. By coordinating stations around the country, NBC was able to accumulate listeners and then sell access to this newly created mass audience to advertisers. For the evening hours, when more people listened to radio, NBC supplied programs sponsored by national advertisers. The network paid affiliates a fee to broadcast the programs and charged the advertisers a much larger fee for access to a national audience. Because these stations needed to fill many hours each day, NBC also produced "sustaining" programs that affiliates could purchase in order to sell time to local advertisers. By 1933, the two NBC networks had 52 full-time and 36 part-time affiliates, or 15 percent of all the stations in the country.

CBS Unlike NBC, which was the favored child of America's largest companies, the Columbia Broadcasting System (CBS) was an orphan when William S. Paley (1901–90) purchased a controlling interest in September 1928. Paley courted new affiliates by offering more generous contracts than those being dangled by NBC. Instead of requiring affiliates to purchase sustaining programs, CBS gave away this basic program service free of charge. In exchange, CBS asked for "option time," a guaranteed number of hours in the affiliate's evening schedule. An NBC affiliate might choose not to air some of the network's programs, but CBS could guarantee sponsors that their advertisements would reach a national audience. During Paley's first year CBS had only 17 affiliates, but by 1933 it had surpassed NBC with 91 affiliates, or 16 percent of all stations.

NBC and CBS defined the successful radio network: a central corporate structure based in New York, live production from New York studios, a stable of powerful stations owned and operated by the network, affiliate contracts with the strongest stations in the largest remaining markets, and exclusive original programming that appealed to listeners. By the early 1930's, any station that wanted to compete in its local market felt it necessary to affiliate with either NBC or CBS.

The Federal Communications Commission

When Franklin D. Roosevelt became president in 1933, he appointed a commission that proposed streamlining the federal regulation of radio by creating a permanent Federal Communications Commission (F.C.C.) with responsibility for the regulation of radio and television, along with interstate telephone and telegraph use. As a result, Congress passed the Communications Act of 1934, which would govern American communications policy for the next six decades. This milestone legislation called for the F.C.C. to administer a national communications policy capable of inspiring confidence among industry leaders and the general public by establishing technical standards and operational protocols.

Virtually all of the F.C.C.'s power over the radio and television industries resided in its authority for granting broadcast licenses to local stations. Rather than support a highly centralized form of broadcasting like the national public service networks being established in European countries, American communications policy celebrated the fundamental principle of "localism," convinced that American democracy would be served best by independent local stations operating without excessive government supervision. The agency's power of enforcement came from its ability to revoke, or refuse to renew, the license of a local station—something that has happened rarely.

The Communications Act of 1934 recognized that broadcasting takes place over frequencies of the electromagnetic spectrum that constitute a rare public resource. In exchange for granting a license to use these scarce frequencies, the F.C.C. has a right to make certain demands of broadcasters. Moreover, since radio and television signals bring the public world directly into the home, broadcasters should bear a social responsibility that isn't demanded of publishers or theater owners. This responsibility was articulated as a demand that stations operate in the "public interest, convenience and necessity." In practice, this meant that stations added a few noncommercial, public service programs—religious or community information programs—usually tucked away in early morning or late evening hours that were undesirable to advertisers. With the public interest fulfilled by a few token programs, stations were free to pursue commercial interests.

By the late 1930's, members of Congress had begun to pressure the F.C.C. to investigate the monopolistic practices of the networks. Local stations complained about the increasingly restrictive terms of network affiliation contracts, which had tilted heavily in favor of the networks as network programming gained popularity and NBC and CBS acquired leverage as a result. Spurred by Congress, the F.C.C. conducted hearings on the structure and practices of network radio, which were known at the time as "chain broadcasting." The three-year investigation resulted in the 1941 publication of the F.C.C.'s *Report on Chain Broadcasting*. A report that might have questioned the very legitimacy of commercial networks essentially left the network system intact, choosing instead to concentrate criticism on RCA's undue influence in operating two networks. The report called for the divorcement of the two NBC networks, a decision that RCA vigorously appealed. In October 1943, NBC reluctantly sold its Blue network for $8 million to Life Savers candy tycoon Edward J. Noble (1884–1961). In 1944 Noble christened this new network the American Broadcasting Company (ABC), and it would eventually become a viable third network.

Network Radio Programming

National radio networks didn't conquer American radio overnight. Many local stations created popular programs starring local celebrities, and some of these lasted for decades. Independent stations with powerful signals introduced programs that appealed to regional tastes. Radio made a particularly strong impression on once-isolated rural listeners. In the 1920's these listeners embraced country-and-Western music when Chicago station WLS began broadcasting the "National Barn Dance" and Nashville station WSM debuted the "Grand Ole Opry." The signals from these 50,000-watt clear-channel stations could be heard throughout the Midwest and South.

Most local stations were on the air for 12–18 hours each day and couldn't afford to create original programs day-in and day-out. They filled many of those hours with recordings—musical phonograph records or wax-disc "transcriptions" of speeches and talk—but embraced the networks because only the networks had the financial resources to supply new, live programs on a daily basis. As these local stations relayed the network signal, network radio helped listeners negotiate local, regional, and national identities by addressing them as members of a mass audience—a national audience for news, entertainment, and, of course, brand-name goods.

Broadcast News Beginning in 1933, President Roosevelt used radio to speak directly to Americans in a series of "Fireside Chats." Roosevelt's informal speaking style and naturalistic approach to radio introduced a more intimate style of political communication that departed significantly from the grand traditions of political oratory. Radio also brought a new intimacy to the coverage of news events, as demonstrated by the emotions stirred up by radio coverage of the 1935 trial of Bruno Hauptmann, the man convicted of kidnapping the baby of aviation hero Charles Lindbergh.

Radio not only presented the news, but also brought immediacy to the coverage of world events by enabling reporters to report directly from the scene. As reporters bore witness to current events, they brought a distant world closer to radio listeners. Nowhere was this more evident than in the period 1939–41, when reporters for CBS and NBC covered the war in Europe, using short wave radio to send live reports across the Atlantic ocean. Standing on a rooftop during the withering nightly bombardments of the London blitz, CBS's Edward R. Murrow (1908–65) brought the war to American radio listeners, sharing not only his personal impressions and encounters with Londoners, but also the sounds of air-raid sirens, police whistles, and explosions—a city under siege in the very moment of its distress.

Entertainment and Advertising In learning to entertain a national audience, the radio networks introduced virtually every genre that has subsequently appeared on television. The networks deserve little credit for actually inventing these genres, because advertising agencies handled the production of nearly all entertainment programs during the era of network radio, when each program had only a single sponsor. Agencies wanted programs to be compatible with their clients' marketing goals, while networks wanted to minimize operating expenses and so saw themselves primarily as conduits for advertisers to reach consumers. The agencies hired performers and staff, supervised writing and rehearsals, contracted for studio facilities, and presented the finished product with the sponsor's commercials integrated into the flow of the program. The line separating entertainment and advertising was seldom apparent to radio listeners who grew accustomed to a fictional character's casual mention of a product, or a star's complete identification with a sponsor. Many programs bore the name of the sponsor, and many stars represented a single brand for years at a time. One of radio's most popular performers gleefully introduced himself each week as Bob "Pepsodent" Hope. His movie partner, Bing Crosby, hosted *Kraft Music Hall* for a decade (1936–46).

Daytime Programs In order to advertise products to women, agencies invented programs for the daytime schedule, when the listening audience was composed largely of housewives. These programs were designed to encourage audience loyalty, while accommodating a preoccupied listener who might be doing housework or taking care of children. The origins of the morning talk show can be found in programs that intended to be the radio equivalent of *Good Housekeeping* magazine. Hosted by cheerful men and women who spoke directly to homemakers, these programs offered genial conversation, recipes, health information, and household advice. Hosts like Mary Margaret McBride (1899–1976) became celebrities and established long careers with these broadcasts.

The *soap opera*, as its name suggests, was invented to serve the needs of companies like Procter and Gamble that intended to sell household cleaning supplies to women consumers. Inspired by the structure of serialized fiction in newspapers and magazines, soap operas wove characters into dense emotional entanglements that continued from one daily 15-minute installment to the next. Irna Phillips (1901–73) is credited with creating the first daytime soap opera, *Painted Dreams*, which debuted in 1930. In a long career, Phillips produced many of the most enduring soap operas on radio and television—including *Guiding Light*, which aired for five decades—and trained more than one generation of soap opera writers and producers. The husband-and-wife team of Frank and Anne Hummert were the most prolific producers of radio soap operas. In order to meet the overwhelming demand for daily dramas during the era of network radio, they employed a staff of more than 30 writers.

Prime Time Radio The networks and advertisers referred to the evening hours as *prime time* because the largest audiences tuned in during the evening, so networks could charge the highest rates for advertising during this period. In developing prime time, the networks essentially created a new cultural experience for Americans, who learned to gather around the radio in the evening hours in order to share a central cultural experience with their own families and a nation of fellow listeners. The most popular prime time programs became cultural institutions and their stars the icons of American entertainment.

The *musical-variety* genre was transplanted almost directly from vaudeville and often featured vaudeville performers or popular singers as hosts. Rudy Vallee, Ed Wynn, Eddie Cantor, and Fred Allen were among the most successful early stars; Jack Benny, George Burns and Gracie Allen, Bob Hope, and Bing Crosby had the greatest success. Many of the era's big band orchestras—led by Benny Goodman, Glenn Miller, the Dorsey Brothers, Duke Ellington, and others—appeared in their own programs or were featured on others.

Alongside professional entertainers and musicians, listeners also enjoyed hearing people like themselves—average Americans—appear on network radio. Listeners flocked to "amateur hour" programs that gave aspiring performers a shot at fame and fortune. The most celebrated of these was *Major Bowes and His Original Amateur Hour,* which premiered in 1934 and introduced, among others, a young singer from New Jersey named Frank Sinatra. The quiz or game show was another innovative genre that allowed nonprofessionals to appear on radio. It is not surprising that many of these programs—*Stop the Music!*, *Quiz Kids*, and *Truth or Consequences*—were transplanted directly to television. In a celebrity-obsessed culture, talent competitions and quiz shows have allowed anonymous Americans to grasp fame, if only temporarily.

Broadcasting's most enduring entertainment genre—the *situation comedy*—also has roots in the comic routines of vaudeville, but came to stand by itself as writers and performers crossed vaudeville's comic sketches with the ongoing storylines of serialized fiction. The most popular and influential of all the programs in the first decade of network radio—and the progenitor of the situation comedy—was *Amos 'n' Andy*. Created and performed by Freeman Gosden (1899–1982) and Charles Correll (1890–1972), *Amos 'n' Andy* centered on the lives of two African-American friends who have migrated from the South to an all-black neighborhood in a northern city (originally the south side of Chicago, later changed to Harlem), where they operate the Fresh Air Taxi Company. It was no secret to radio listeners that Gosden and Correll were white men speaking in comic black dialect.

By the end of 1929, *Amos 'n' Andy* (broadcast in 15-minute installments six evenings a week) had become the most important program in radio, the inspiration for many people to purchase their first radio set. Because of its success in building a loyal following of 40 million listeners, many elements of *Amos 'n' Andy* came to define the situation comedy: a familiar setting; central characters surrounded by a recurring cast of comic characters; and an episodic structure that introduces and resolves a new comic incident each time. This format gave rise to a few sitcoms set in a workplace or a public setting, such as *Duffy's Tavern,* and inspired an endless series of situation comedies revolving around the experiences of a family. This pattern began with *The Rise of the Goldbergs* (later known as *The Goldbergs*), the *Fibber McGee and Molly Show*, *Easy Aces*, *The Aldrich Family*, and *The Adventures of Ozzie and Harriet*, and to this day shows no sign of ending. Many of the most popular comedies of the era—*The Jack Benny Program*, *The George Burns and Gracie Allen Show*, *The Edgar Bergen and Charlie McCarthy Show*—featured celebrity performers playing themselves in comic episodes.

Prime time network radio relied on two dramatic formats: dramatic series and anthology dramas. A dramatic series presented the adventures of a hero or a tale of mystery in 30-minute episodes; these series were most directly influenced by pulp fiction and comic strips—westerns (*The Lone Ranger*, *The Cisco Kid*, *Gunsmoke*), detective shows (*The Shadow*), police series (*Dragnet*), and tales of suspense and the supernatural (*Light's Out*, *Inner Sanctum*, *Suspense*). Many of these series either moved directly to television or served as the unacknowledged influence of subsequent television programs.

Anthology dramas were more prestigious. They often had a famous host who introduced each week's performance and a 60-minute slot in the network schedule. The stories generally consisted of adaptations of famous novels, Broadway plays, or Hollywood movies; performers often were stars of Hollywood or the New York theater. *Lux Radio Theatre*, hosted by Cecil B. DeMille, featured movie adaptations performed by movie stars, who spoke to DeMille about their latest theatrical releases. The best of these drama series was the *Mercury Theater of the Air*, a program created by Orson Welles and John Houseman using members of their New York theater troupe. The *Mercury Theater* featured many skillful adaptations of novels and plays, designed to take advantage of the storytelling opportunities offered by radio, but is best remembered for a notorious dramatization of H. G. Wells's *War of the Worlds* on October 30, 1938. By expertly mimicking a typical network broadcast interrupted repeatedly by news accounts of a Martian invasion, the broadcast panicked certain credulous listeners and made a national celebrity out of Welles.

With such an array of programs, radio listeners began to organize their daily routines around the broadcast schedule. Soon ratings services, such as Hooperatings and A.C. Nielsen, came forward to provide networks and advertisers with information about the nature and size of audiences, using modern social scientific research techniques to shed light on the habits of listeners.

The creation of national networks was an unprecedented achievement in American history. For the first time, Americans scattered throughout the country, who until recently had been isolated by geography and regional differences, experienced the same events at exactly the same moment, and this clearly changed the way people felt about what it meant to be an American. As radio entwined individual listeners into a national civic culture, it also introduced them to other forms of national culture—a culture of popular entertainment created by Hollywood movies and radio programs and a culture of consumption created by advertising and mass-produced goods. In the United States, where the federal government had allowed private companies to control broadcasting, radio helped to create a national culture that is an unruly mixture of politics, advertising, and popular culture.

Radio After Television The cultural role of radio changed dramatically with the full-scale launch of network television in 1948. Following a period of transition, mass-market advertisers began to shift their national advertising budgets to television, and the networks followed by eliminating popular radio programs during the early 1950's. Radio stations adapted to the loss by introducing the disk jockey—record-spinners whose personalities gave a station its identity. In place of individual programs, radio stations began to offer "formats" aimed at fans of particular musical genres. The format with the broadest appeal came to be known as Top 40. By concentrating on the best-selling records of the day, the Top 40 format established a powerful link between the radio and recording industries and helped fuel the explosive growth of rock 'n' roll, as affluent teenagers became radio's most lucrative audience in the 1950's.

The invention of the transistor in 1947 played a significant role in the transformation of radio by allowing manufacturers to make smaller, more portable radio receivers and to improve the reception and tuning of radios in automobiles. After decades as a piece of furniture, the radio receiver cast off its mooring and floated into the public world. Inexpensive, lightweight, battery-operated transistor radios, made affordable by competition from Japanese manufacturers beginning in the early 1960's, brought radios directly into the hands of millions of listeners, including children and teenagers who made their own program choices. The automobile radio, which had been seen as a luxury before World War II, gradually became a necessity in the postwar years.

By the early 1960's, Americans used radio differently than ever before. The possibilities for "out-of-home" listening gave radio a new cultural role as the mobile accompaniment for everyday life. Radio advertisers began to target listeners during "drive time," the hours spent commuting to and from work with only the automobile radio for company. As radio receivers became more mobile, the medium of radio reclaimed its local roots. Local news, weather, and traffic reports—continuously updated throughout the day—made the radio station a secure anchor for listeners in motion, the only source for authoritative, real-time reports on local conditions (symbolized by the traffic helicopter's "eye-in-the-sky" surveillance). The immediacy of local radio has made it an indispensable source of information during emergencies and natural disasters.

The 1970's gave birth to the "FM revolution" in which new stations transmitting hi-fidelity stereo signals on the

FM band of the spectrum presented a fresh alternative to AM stations that had drifted into repetitive commercial formulas. In the early 1960's, there were fewer than 1,000 FM stations on the air; by 1976 there were nearly 4,000. Listeners familiar with the rich sound of hi-fi stereos and drawn to the more ambitious rock albums of the late 1960's and 1970's welcomed stations that dispensed with the hit-driven Top 40 format and played obscure tracks from albums or entire albums by artistically ambitious musicians.

As FM stations became the preferred choice for listening to music, many AM stations struggling to find a new identity reinvented themselves in the late 1980's by shifting to all-news and talk formats. In the early 1980's there were fewer than 200 AM stations devoted entirely to news and talk; by the late 1990's there were nearly 1,000. While much of the programming at these stations features local hosts speaking to local audiences, the rise of talk radio has created national celebrities like Howard Stern, Don Imus, Dr. Laura Schlesinger, and Rush Limbaugh, whose programs are syndicated to hundreds of stations.

In the 21st century, the prospects for noncommercial radio are stronger than ever, even as commercial radio becomes increasingly homogenized. National Public Radio, with its extensive network of affiliated stations, has grown over the past quarter-century to play a vital role in the national media. Local community access stations, using low-power transmitters and operated by dedicated volunteers, have introduced a distinctively local voice to the airwaves in many communities and keep alive the free-form programming abandoned by commercial FM stations. Meanwhile, as a result of government deregulation over the past two decades, local commercial stations have been absorbed into massive chains. A company like Clear Channel Communications, which now owns more than 1,000 local stations in all 50 states, eliminates decision making at the local level, enforcing limited music playlists designed according to market research.

New digital services bypass local stations altogether by broadcasting directly from satellites to individual receivers. Although the services require consumers to purchase a special receiver and pay a monthly subscription fee, they have grown in popularity by providing a wide range of commercial-free programming that contrasts sharply with the homogenized content and aggressive commercialism of local radio. Only time will tell how satellite radio will affect the radio industry and the role of radio in American culture.

Television

Inventing Television, 1927–1947

On the foggy morning of September 7, 1927, in a small house at 202 Green Street in San Francisco, an obscure young inventor named Philo T. Farnsworth (1906–71) transmitted the image of a triangle across a crowded laboratory, where it appeared on a receiver placed behind a partition on the far side of the room. Farnsworth's invention, registered with the U.S. Patents Office in January 1927 as an "Image Dissector" tube, scanned the image electronically, using a focused electron beam, and sent the signal through the air to the awaiting receiver. Farnsworth had invented electronic television.

Beginning with his distinctive name, Philo T. Farnsworth seems to have been conjured from fiction for his role as the quintessential American inventor. He grew up on a remote farm in Utah, and it was there as a teenage radio enthusiast tilling his family's fields that he first conceived of a method for scanning an image electronically in order to send pictures along radio waves. In the great tradition of American inventors, he began as an amateur, with no formal scientific training. He wasn't a scientist; he was a brilliant and eccentric tinkerer consumed by a singular ambition. With a small financial stake from a few California businessmen and the aid of a tiny staff—his young wife, Pem, her brother Cliff, and two engineers—he achieved at the age of 21 what had so far eluded scientists at America's greatest corporations. When it came time to demonstrate his electronic television to his investors, Farnsworth answered their eternal question—"When are we going to see some dollars in this gadget?"—by making the image of a dollar sign appear before their eyes on a small television screen.

RCA and Television From a wood-paneled office in a New York skyscraper 3,000 miles away, RCA commercial manager David Sarnoff also saw dollar signs, in his mind's eye, when he thought about television. He brought Russian-born scientist Vladimir Zworykin (1889–1982) from Westinghouse in 1929 to supervise television research at RCA. Starting with an annual budget of more than $100,000, Zworykin and his staff worked feverishly to develop a proprietary television system for which RCA would control all underlying patents. Zworykin soon introduced an electronic television receiver, which he called a Kinescope. Even with this breakthrough, RCA trailed Farnsworth, because Zworykin had not succeeded in creating an electronic television camera. Like all previous television systems, the RCA camera relied upon a mechanical device for scanning images. In the end RCA resorted to infringing on Farnsworth's patents and was forced to pay a licensing fee after a protracted lawsuit. But RCA would win in the end.

The key to establishing RCA's dominance depended on providing a program service through the NBC network. NBC had conducted experimental broadcasts from the Empire State Building as early as 1932. On April 30, 1939 NBC became the first network to launch regular television service with its inaugural telecast of the opening day ceremonies at the New York World's Fair. The following day RCA television sets went on sale in New York department stores; a set with a seven-by-ten-inch screen sold for $1,000. NBC followed its debut with daily broadcasts and highly promoted live events beamed to a few thousand receivers in the New York area. A Columbia-Princeton baseball game in May and a Giants-Dodgers game from Ebbets Field in June are considered to be the first sports telecasts in America.

Televised events had few viewers but captured public attention through accounts in newspapers and magazines or displays of television sets at trade shows and department stores. The goal was to sell TV sets by stimulating curiosity about the new medium. These broadcasts—and similar ones by CBS and independent stations—were still experimental. There were no industry-wide technical standards for television broadcasting. A TV set purchased one day could be obsolete the next. This problem was solved by the F.C.C. in April 1941, but the onset of the war ended production of new electronic equipment.

Postwar Developments The F.C.C. was anxious to pave the way for a quick launch of television once the war ended. During 1944–45 the commission conducted hearings to establish a policy for the allocation of television channels. Many historians believe that these hearings were the single most important event in determining the eventual structure of the television industry. The critical issue at stake was whether television broadcasting should remain in the VHF (Very High Frequency) band of the spectrum, where there were only 13 available channels, or should move to the UHF (Ultra High Frequency) band, which had a much greater channel capacity. These hearings offered the last opportunity to shift U.S. television to the UHF band without disrupting manufacturers, station owners, and consumers.

In May 1945 the F.C.C. approved a system of 13-channel VHF broadcasting and reserved UHF for experimental broadcasts. By selecting a system that restricted the number of available channels, the F.C.C. created an artificial scarcity that guaranteed fierce competition for channel slots. High demand for a limited number of channels essentially eliminated the possibility of exploring alternative forms of television such as theater television, subscription-based television, or noncommercial broadcasting. The channel allocation decision ensured that television would adopt the model of network radio—commercially supported programs broadcast to home receivers by stations linked to a few national networks.

Despite the intense expectations for television in the 1940's, commercial television was slow to develop after the war. The F.C.C. had received 116 station applications from 50 cities by the end of 1945, but two years later there were still only 16 stations on the air and fewer than 200,000 TV sets in the country. The electronics industry needed time to retool for consumer markets, and lingering uncertainty over technical standards made manufacturers and consumers wary about moving forward.

The Rise of Commercial Television, 1948–1959

It is difficult to comprehend the speed with which television swept across the American landscape during the 1950's. The television networks had introduced regular prime time schedules in the fall of 1948, and by the end of 1949 1 million American households, or just 2 percent of the population, had a television set. By 1954, however, more than half of all Americans had TV sets in their homes, as the number of households with television jumped to 26 million. By 1959 the television set was as common as a refrigerator in American homes; 44 million households, or 86 percent of the population, had TV sets and the average household had one switched on for nearly six hours a day.

As a technology and a cultural medium, television was almost ideally suited to capitalize on the social changes taking place in the United States after World War II. The postwar baby boom led to an explosion in the number of young families with children. Many of these families took advantage of low-cost government loans to purchase homes in the fast-growing suburbs. Rising wages enabled these families to participate in an expanding economy that gave Americans access to consumer goods that had seemed like unattainable luxuries before the war—a brave new world of automobiles and appliances. Innovations in marketing and more efficient transportation meant that Americans participated in a national culture of consumption, with nationally advertised brand-name goods replacing local products, and retail chains popping up alongside local businesses.

Early TV Programming In the beginning much of network television was broadcast live. Videotape wasn't invented until 1956 and didn't come into widespread use by broadcasters until the 1960's. Some programs were produced on film, but CBS and NBC initially discouraged the practice in order to promote the value of the network program service. Any station with an antenna could buy a B western and slap it on the air, but only the networks could afford to deliver live programs on a regular basis.

Over the course of the 1950's the networks gradually shifted from programs produced live in New York to those shot on film in Hollywood, but a unique appeal of television during the 1950's was the experience of immediacy offered by live broadcasts. Many of the live program formats of the early 1950's were imported directly from radio, including soap operas, quiz programs, talent contests, and talk shows. The reputation of the early 1950's as the "Golden Age" of American television rests upon fading memories of programs produced live in the era before videotape, shows that disappeared into the ether, never to be seen again.

The *comedy-variety* format represented by television's first breakout hit, *The Texaco Star Theater* (1948), starring Milton Berle (1908–2002), kept the traditions of vaudeville alive into the television era. The raucous comic sketches and musical numbers, the performances of acrobats, magicians, pantomimes, and plate-spinners on *Texaco Star Theater*, *The Colgate Comedy Hour* (1950), *The Red Skelton Show* (1951), and the critically acclaimed, *Your Show of Shows* (1950), starring Sid Caesar (b. 1922) and Imogene Coca (1908–2001), made few concessions to the new medium of television. Comedian Jackie Gleason (1916–87) is best remembered as Ralph Kramden from the situation comedy *The Honeymooners* (1955), but he became a star playing a range of hilarious characters on his comedy-variety series, *The Jackie Gleason Show* (1952). The most durable of these series began in 1948 as *Toast of the Town* and, after taking on the name of its host in 1955, continued until 1971 as *The Ed Sullivan Show*.

Early television's most prestigious entertainment programs were the *live dramas* broadcast on CBS and NBC. Programs such as *Kraft Television Theatre* (1947), *Studio One* (1948), *Philco TV Playhouse* (1948), and *Playhouse 90* (1956) presented plays written for television and performed live. A playwright fortunate enough to see his work produced on a live network drama literally could become an overnight sensation. Writers like Paddy Chayefsky (author of *Marty*), Reginald Rose (author of *Twelve Angry Men*), Rod Serling (author of *Requiem for a Heavyweight*), and Horton Foote (author of *A Trip to Bountiful*) launched their careers in these early TV dramas.

The most influential television series of the early 1950's was *I Love Lucy*, which debuted on CBS in October 1951 and spent four of its six seasons as the highest-rated series on television. The remarkable popularity of *I Love Lucy*—in its initial network broadcasts and countless reruns—established the *family sitcom* as television's essential genre for decades to come. Veterans of movies, radio, and nightclubs, the married team of Lucille Ball (1911–89) and Desi Arnaz (1917–86) came to television as Lucy and Ricky Ricardo, a young married couple living in a converted brownstone in Manhattan. In each episode Ricky pursued his career as an entertainer, while Lucy wreaked havoc simply by resisting her confinement in the straightjacket of wifely duties. *I Love Lucy* placed an indelible stamp on the situation comedy. In a medium experienced primarily by families in their homes, marriage and family life became the wellspring of television comedy. A definitive moment in the early history of network television came in January 1953 when 44 million viewers tuned in to witness the birth of the Ricardo's baby, Little Ricky. That was 15 million more viewers than had watched President Eisenhower's inauguration the day before.

A Three-Network Universe The chief beneficiaries of television's explosive growth during the 1950's were the networks, which expanded by turning virtually every new television station into a network outlet. As with radio, local stations joined the national TV networks to get access to network programs and to share in the income from national advertising.

Four networks introduced regular prime time schedules in 1948, but an F.C.C. decision ensured that NBC and CBS would hold an insurmountable lead over the smaller networks, ABC and Du Mont. In spite of the many deliberations that preceded the resumption of commercial television after World War II, a significant question still hadn't been answered. How many miles apart should stations be located when assigned to the same or adjacent channels? Stations in the more crowded urban areas along the East Coast discovered that their signals frequently interfered with one another.

Faced with this grave problem, the F.C.C. froze the licensing of new stations beginning in September 1948 and lasting for four years, until the commission delivered its historic *Sixth Report and Order* in May 1952. Although there were no new licenses distributed during the years of the freeze, American television was hardly frozen. Stations licensed prior to the freeze went on the air, and advertisers and the public were drawn to the new medium. The number of stations rose from 50 in 1948 to 108 in 1952, and the number of TV sets in the U.S. increased from 1.2 million to 15 million.

During the period of the freeze, NBC and CBS effectively seized control of the television industry by establishing owned-and-operated stations in major cities (the F.C.C. allowed each network to own five) and by signing affiliate contracts with the vast majority of these early TV stations. By solidifying their positions in local markets during a period of limited competition, the former radio networks built an insurmountable advantage over their weaker rivals. In attempting to limit station interference, the F.C.C. created another form of artificial scarcity by determining that most American cities could support no more than three stations. In effect, this ruling meant that there would be only three viable television networks in the United States. As a result of its inability to sign affiliates, the fourth network, Du Mont, left the air in 1955.

NBC Leads the Way NBC's prime time schedule was heavily oriented toward live programs, including the drama and comedy-variety series described above. In spite of its reliance on these familiar formats, NBC also introduced several key programming innovations.

Sylvester "Pat" Weaver (1908–2002) served as NBC's chief programmer from 1949 to 1953 and as president from 1953 to 1955. His programming strategies expanded the network schedule outside of prime time, into the "fringe" time periods of early morning and late night, by introducing *Today* and *Tonight* (later *The Tonight Show*). These innovative and influential programs played upon the medium's intimacy by blending information, news, advice, and conversation in an informal setting. At the same time, they allowed NBC to claim even more time in the daily schedules of its affiliate stations.

Weaver is also credited with promoting the "magazine concept" of television advertising, in which advertisers paid to have individual commercials placed within a program—as ads appear in a magazine—instead of serving as a program's sole sponsor. Following the pattern established in radio, advertisers had dominated early television production by purchasing broadcast time from the networks and hiring advertising agencies to produce the programs that filled these slots. Since TV networks served mainly as conduits for programs produced by advertisers, the networks exercised surprisingly little control over the structure and content of most television programming. By limiting advertisers to individual commercials in programs produced by the network, Weaver began to shift the balance of power toward the networks.

Weaver departed from another tradition imported from radio when he argued that regularly scheduled series succeeded in creating a viewing habit, but also threatened "to reduce the importance of network service in the lives of the people." He championed special event programs which he called "spectaculars"—prestigious live programs modeled after Broadway dramas, musicals, and variety revues. By raising the cost of production beyond the reach of most individual sponsors, these productions also supported Weaver's goal of reducing sponsor influence. NBC's most celebrated "spectacular" was the 1955 broadcast of *Peter Pan*, starring Mary Martin. Aired just days after the play had completed its Broadway run, the program drew a record audience of 65 million viewers.

ABC Finds Hollywood ABC entered television as a distant third-place network, lagging far behind NBC and CBS in affiliates and earnings. In 1951 United Paramount Theaters—the theater chain once owned by Paramount Pictures—offered to purchase the network; the F.C.C. approved the merger in 1953. At the time, ABC had only 40 affiliates among the 354 stations in the country. Led by chairman Leonard Goldenson (1905–99), who had come of age in the movie business, ABC turned to Hollywood in order to compete with the more established networks, which had a firm grip on TV's big stars and corporate sponsors.

Goldenson and the other United Paramount executives had long-established relationships with executives at the Hollywood studios, so it made sense for ABC to cultivate the movie industry as a neglected source of television programming. ABC gambled first on independent producer Walt Disney, whose *Disneyland* television series premiered in October 1954. *Disneyland* was an immediate hit, launching a top-10 song and a craze for coonskin caps with its chronicle of the legendary Davy Crockett, and creating fanatical interest in the Disneyland theme park, which was shown under construction in several episodes. In 1956 ABC established its most profitable Hollywood alliance with Warner Brothers. The venerable Hollywood studio delivered ABC's first hit drama, the western, *Cheyenne*, and followed with a string of hits: westerns, such as *Maverick*, *Bronco*, *Sugarfoot*, and detective series such as *77 Sunset Strip*.

ABC now stocked its schedule with filmed, hour-long action-adventure series produced in Hollywood, and by the late 1950's its profits were growing by more than 20 percent per year. ABC's clear success with filmed series convinced the other networks to follow suit. In 1953, 80 percent of prime time programs were produced and broadcast live, most originating in New York. By 1958, 80 percent of prime time belonged to filmed programs made in Hollywood. In pursuit of higher ratings, the three networks began to copy each other's hits and take fewer risks. A popular genre, such as the western in the wake of *Gunsmoke* (1955), would be replicated until viewers became exhausted and moved on to something else. In 1958 more than 25 westerns filled prime time each week. The networks had settled on the staples of the network schedule: family sitcoms and dramas with cowboys and cops (later to include doctors and lawyers).

The Era of Network Television, 1955–1983

The Network Monopoly By 1960, American television had become synonymous with network television. Of the 515 television stations licensed by the F.C.C. to serve the "public interest" of its community, 96 percent were affiliated with a national network. Federal communications policy espoused a principle of "localism," but local stations were unable to resist the financial incentives to join a network. With the exception of a few independent stations in the largest cities, television viewers had no alternative to the networks. Over the next two decades, on any given evening, nearly 95 percent of those watching television were tuned into one of the three networks.

By monopolizing television in America, the networks set the terms that governed virtually every aspect of the television industry. In order to join the networks, stations signed increasingly restrictive affiliate contracts requiring them to hand over the most valuable portions of their schedules to the networks. In creating a national audience for commercial broadcasting, the networks controlled the largest advertising market in history. This allowed them to charge higher and higher rates to national brand-name advertisers for access to that market. For studios and independent producers, the networks were the only game in town. In exchange for scheduling a television series in prime time, networks began demanding an ownership stake, a percentage of any money earned by program-related merchandise or subsequent sales of the series for "off-network" reruns in domestic and foreign markets.

Many Americans watched the growing network monopoly with alarm. The airwaves were supposed to be a public domain, licensed by the F.C.C. on behalf of the American people, but they had become nothing more than an advertising medium. Politicians and intellectuals raised a litany of complaints about network programs and practices: broadcasters had failed to live up to their public service obligations; in pursuing the highest possible ratings, the networks settled for the lowest common denominator in entertainment; the range of programs had narrowed alarmingly; there was too much violence on television; the networks lacked socially responsible programs—news and current affairs, or educational programs for children. CBS journalist Edward R. Murrow summed up the protests when he complained that this powerful medium was being used simply "to distract, delude, amuse, and insulate us."

Scandals Such criticism never caused the public to question the fundamental legitimacy of a profit-driven television system sponsored entirely by advertising. The greatest threat came as a result of the "quiz show scandals" of the late 1950's. Beginning in 1955, several high-stakes quiz shows—including *The $64,000 Question*, *The $64,000 Challenge*, and *Twenty-One*—became popular hits in prime time. In the third season, disgruntled contestants began to claim that producers often rigged the programs to favor contestants who seemed to appeal to viewers. The scandals eventually led to a grand jury investigation and a full-blown congressional hearing. But the howls of outrage gradually subsided and nothing much happened. Since the quiz shows were among the last network programs still produced by advertising agencies, the scandal actually served to strengthen the networks, by giving them the leverage needed to remove sponsors once and for all from the production process.

The F.C.C. Challenge The F.C.C. had sanctioned the system of commercial broadcasting and allowed the networks to monopolize television. Under the Kennedy administration, the F.C.C. began to look seriously at the criticisms of the television networks.

F.C.C. Chairman Newton Minow (b. 1926) addressed the National Association of Broadcasters convention in May 1961, just months after taking office. Minow condemned the entire output of the American television industry, referring to American television, in his famous phrase, as a "vast wasteland." Minow admonished station owners and network executives to recall what had been lost in the rush to win the highest ratings: "Your obligations are not satisfied if you look only to popularity as the test of what to broadcast. You are not only in show business.... It is not enough to cater to the nation's whims—you must also serve the nation's needs."

Network News In commercial terms, the network news divisions were a "loss leader"—not a source of income, but one of prestige and network identity, an effort to serve the public service mandate. Edward R. Murrow at CBS was the most celebrated figure in television news, host of the groundbreaking documentary series, *See It Now*, and the interview show, *Person to Person*. Murrow's thorough critique of Senator Joseph McCarthy on *See It Now* in March 1954 is credited with turning the tide of public opinion against the senator's destructive anticommunist investigations. The debates between Richard Nixon and John F. Kennedy during the 1960 presidential campaign were a milestone, giving television a central role in the electoral process that would continue to develop in convention coverage and political advertising.

The regular evening news programs didn't play a truly prominent role at the networks until they were expanded from 15 to 30 minutes in 1963. *The CBS Evening News* with Walter Cronkite and NBC's *The Huntley-Brinkley Report* with Chet Huntley and David Brinkley became flagship programs for their networks. Network news coverage of desegregation efforts in the South and the war in Vietnam provided unexpected momentum to the civil rights and antiwar movements during the 1960's by bringing shocking or emotionally charged pictures of these events into American homes.

The networks and their news divisions achieved new public stature in the aftermath of the Kennedy assassination on November 22, 1963. For the next three days, the networks suspended their regular programming and devoted themselves to coverage of the breaking news, followed by the memorial service and funeral. Americans huddled around their television sets in search of information and comfort. The promise of television as a national medium was fulfilled, at least for a moment, as it united a nation in a form of public ceremony that would have been unimaginable a generation earlier. Television has returned to this ceremonial function occasionally over the years—in moments of national celebration, like the moon landing in 1969, or mourning, like the space shuttle Challenger explosion in 1986—allowing an entire nation to experience a single event.

Public Broadcasting The few gems of news and current affairs programs nearly always faded, however, beneath the shadow of entertainment programs designed to generate advertising revenue. Activists and politicians argued that the United States must have an alternative to commercial television. A 1967 report funded by the Carnegie Commission recommended establishing a fourth network, a noncommercial public network built upon the educational stations already in operation around the country. With President Johnson's support, Congress passed the Public Broadcasting Act in 1967, creating a Corporation for Public Broadcasting to coordinate the country's loosely organized public radio and television stations. But Congress did not work out an adequate system of funding for public broadcasting, which has survived by cobbling together government allocations, corporate underwriting, grants, and direct contributions from viewers. As a result, public broadcasting in the U.S. has been directed toward a middle-class audience likely to make contributions, and has had difficulty serving a more diverse public.

New Regulations By the end of the 1960's, a political consensus had emerged—the networks had to be reined in. Along with the steady drumbeat of criticism from advocacy groups, Congress heard the complaints of station owners, advertisers, and producers who protested the network's stranglehold over American television. As a result, the F.C.C. and Congress took a number of steps in the early 1970's that restricted network practices for the first time in history. The Prime-Time Access Rule set limits on the number of hours in which a network could require its affiliates to air network programs. As a result, stations gained control over 10 additional hours of their weekly schedules, which meant advertising revenue lost to the networks would be regained by the stations. The Financial Interest and Syndication Rules prohibited networks from demanding ownership in the programs they broadcast. At the same time, the F.C.C. ruled that a network could produce no more than two hours of its weekly prime time schedule. Networks would have to seek programs from outside producers, and producers no longer would feel pressure to share their profits with a network. Finally, Congress passed a law banning cigarette advertising on television, which went into effect January 2, 1971 (giving the networks one final windfall from cigarette ads during the New Year's Day football games). This was a significant blow to the bottom line at the networks, which received 20 percent of their advertising revenue from cigarette manufacturers.

Television Programming in the Network Era (1960–83)

In an age before VCRs and remote controls, the experience of television was beyond the control of individual viewers, who had no choice but to build their lives around the network schedule. If you wanted to watch a program, you had to make plans to be in front of a TV when it aired. As a result, one of the defining achievements of this period was the ability to create a mass audience on a scale that had never been achieved before.

When the Beatles first appeared on *The Ed Sullivan Show* in February 1964, the event drew 73 million viewers, more than 40 percent of the total population. It's an astonishing figure—and a good measure of the band's popularity—but it's less astonishing when weighed against the fact that a routine episode of *The Beverly Hillbillies* aired two weeks earlier drew 70 million viewers. With a national audience divided among just three networks, the typical audience for a long-running hit series always numbered tens of millions of people. Still, television during this period achieved several milestones of "event" television, producing audiences that are likely never to be equaled. Some of these events were ceremonial—the Kennedy assassination coverage or the moon landing—and attracted a nearly universal audience because the networks temporarily suspended regular programming. Some, such as the Super Bowl starting in the 1970's, were transformed into national events by television.

Some entertainment programs in which there was intense viewer involvement in the story and characters could have a single episode of a series turn into a national event. The first of these involved the final episode of *The Fugitive*, which aired in August 1967 and was viewed by 51 million people, or 27 percent of the population. A decade later, 69 million people (32 percent of the population), tuned in for the final episode of the miniseries *Roots* (1977), and in 1980, 83 million people (38 percent of the population) watched the episode of *Dallas* that answered the previous season's cliffhanger question, "Who Shot J.R.?"

Although the networks competed with one another for ratings, they otherwise faced virtually no competition and perceived little incentive for innovation. In a world of limited choice, they reasoned, viewers don't watch particular programs; they simply watch television. Ratings revealed that every day at the same time the number of television sets turned on is remarkably constant—regardless of what is on the air. So the networks operated according to a theory of "Least Objectionable Programming." Under these conditions, network programmers worried less about creating exceptional programs to attract viewers than about supplying the least objectionable program on the air at any given moment.

With the F.C.C. scrutinizing network television in the 1960's for its failure to achieve its utopian promise, much of the blame fell on ABC, which came under attack as the network most responsible for the shift to filmed comedies and formulaic action series. In spite of its influence, however, ABC fell into a distant third place during the 1960's, losing money every year between 1963 and 1971. Television settled back into a two-network race between NBC and CBS.

NBC and Movies Robert Kintner (1909–80) took over programming at NBC in 1956 and served as network president from 1958 to 1965. Kintner supervised the expansion of NBC news and the shift to color broadcasting (completed in 1965). Programming under Kintner followed the network's traditional reliance on dramas and comedy-variety. NBC formed a strong alliance with the production company MCA-Universal, whose drama series came to dominate the network's schedule well into the 1970's. NBC also took the lead in bringing feature films to prime time. In 1960 the Screen Actors Guild agreed to a collective bargaining agreement that allowed movies made after 1948 to be shown on television for the first time. NBC introduced recent Hollywood movies to prime time in September 1961 with the premiere of *NBC Saturday Night at the Movies*. Hollywood movies became an increasingly important component of prime time schedules; each network scheduled movies at least two nights a week in the 1960's.

When the Hollywood studios began to license their recent feature films for television in the early 1960's, they set off a bidding war that raised the cost of all programming. In 1965 the average price for network rights to a feature film reached $400,000; in three years that figure had doubled. As an alternative to movies, NBC joined with MCA-Universal to develop several long-form program formats, including the 90-minute episodic series (*The Virginian*), the made-for-TV movie, and the movie series (*The NBC Mystery Movie* in 1971, which initially featured a rotation of *Columbo*, *McCloud*, and *McMillan and Wife*).

CBS Holds the Lead The ratings leader throughout the 1960's, however, was CBS, which owed its success largely to the programming philosophy of James T. Aubrey (1918–94), who served as president from 1959–65. The Aubrey philosophy was simple: count on situation comedies first, last, and always. The most popular CBS situation comedies offered a reassuring depiction of the contemporary family (*The Dick Van Dyke Show*, *The Andy Griffith Show*, *Family Affair*, *My Three Sons*) or a revival of rural vernacular humor (*The Beverly Hillbillies*, *Green Acres*, *Petticoat Junction*, *Mr. Ed*, *Gomer Pyle U.S.M.C.*). To maintain audience loyalty, Aubrey also showed great faith in long-term hits, many of which dated back, in one incarnation or another, to television's earliest days: *Gunsmoke*, *The Red Skelton Hour*, *The Ed Sullivan Show*, *The Lucy Show*.

Viewed in retrospect, what is striking about this list is how little it says about the many social upheavals of the decade—movements for civil rights and women's rights, for consumer rights and environmental protection, youth culture and antiwar protest. Faced with these changes in society, television entertainment offered escapist fantasy. The family sitcoms of the 1950's were replaced by the fantasy sitcoms of the 1960's: *Bewitched*, *I Dream of Jeannie*, *The Addams Family*, *The Munsters*, *Mr. Ed*. As the nation found itself tangled in the Vietnam war, television offered military service comedies that wouldn't have looked out of place in World War II: *McHale's Navy*, *Gomer Pyle*, and *Hogan's Heroes*. CBS made a modest effort to catch up to the revolution taking place in youth culture by signing the comic duo of Tom and Dick Smothers in 1967 for *The Smothers Brothers Comedy Hour*, but the decision eventually backfired on the network. When the stars became more vocal in their opposition to the Vietnam war and the Nixon administration, CBS abruptly cancelled the series in 1970.

Nielsen and the Changing Audience For nearly two decades Nielsen based its ratings on the number of households viewing a given program. This emphasis on bulk ratings—the sheer number of viewers watching a program—helped to reinforce a lowest common denominator approach to programming, because it ignored distinctions in the viewing audience. In the late 1960's, however, Nielsen began to register demographic differences among viewers, particularly differences in age and income. Some network executives reasoned that they could charge higher advertising rates for programs that attract viewers who were more likely to be active consumers. Instead of relying on habitual viewing patterns to attract the largest quantity of viewers, networks for the first time recognized the value of creating distinctive programs in order to attract young, urban viewers, who tended to have more disposable income.

CBS President Robert Wood (1925–86) and vice president for programming Fred Silverman (b. 1937) decided to reposition CBS as a network for the young, urban viewer. In a period of two years, 1969–71, they swept aside nearly a dozen successful programs that appealed largely to the network's older viewers—*The Jackie Gleason Show*, *The Red Skelton Hour*, *Petticoat Junction*, and others. In the 1970–71 season, CBS introduced *The Mary Tyler Moore Show* and *All In The Family*, iconoclastic series that took the sitcom genre in new directions.

As the character Mary Richards, a single woman working as a producer in a Minneapolis television station, Mary Tyler Moore infused the spirit of the women's movement into a comedy of the workplace. In structure and style, *All in the Family* was more familiar—a family sitcom with jokes and punch lines, built around an outrageous lead character, Archie Bunker, played emphatically by Carroll O'Connor. But producer Norman Lear introduced a raw, confrontational edge to the family comedy. In confrontations between the working-class bigot, Archie, and his liberal daughter and son-in-law, Lear addressed the most controversial political and social issues of the day.

Striking a chord with television viewers, *All in the Family* became television's top-rated program between 1971 and 1975. In 1972 CBS added the antiwar comedy, *M*A*S*H*, to its roster. Within a few years, CBS had exchanged its rural sitcoms for a schedule that appealed to younger viewers: *Maude*, *Good Times*, *The Jeffersons*, *Rhoda*, and *The Bob Newhart Show*. Led by these comedies, CBS dominated the ratings until the last-place network, ABC, engineered an improbable revival in the late 1970's.

ABC Revived When Fred Pierce (b. 1933) was named ABC president in 1974, he presided over a perennial third-place network that had grown accustomed to haphazard imitation of its network rivals. Under his leadership, however, ABC rode an unprecedented wave of popular success that carried the network to first place in just three years.

In 1975 Pierce convinced Fred Silverman to leave CBS and take over programming at ABC. Soon ABC's programming was aimed squarely at younger viewers and families: warm family comedy (*Eight is Enough*, *Happy Days*), wacky farce (*Laverne and Shirley*, *Three's Company*, *Soap*), high-concept action (*Charlie's Angels*, *The Six Million Dollar Man*), and escapist fantasy (*The Love Boat*, *Fantasy Island*). Through some ineffable blend of intuition, audience research, and accident, ABC's program choices seemed almost perfectly attuned to popular taste for several years in the late 1970's—the final years before cable and home video began to disperse the vast network audience. As they had in the 1950's, critics labeled ABC programs crass and formulaic, but those easy criticisms still don't explain ABC's complete dominance of the ratings; in 1979, 14 of the top 20 programs on television belonged to ABC.

Sports and news played a central role in ABC's reemergence during the 1970's—particularly by attracting new affiliates and contributing to the network's profile as a national institution—and Roone Arledge (1931–2002) is the central figure in the history of both. As president of ABC Sports beginning in 1968, he was the person most responsible for creating *Monday Night Football* in 1970 and for shaping ABC's stellar Olympics coverage over the years. Arledge revolutionized television sports coverage, moving sports to the center of American culture by making sports competition meaningful for the non-sports-fan. He gave each game a storyline and developed ABC's trademark "up close and personal" style to bring out the character and personality of athletes. He was also a showman, unafraid to burnish the spectacle of sports television with multiple camera angles and flashy graphics or to use outlandish personalities like Howard Cosell, who often overshadowed the sports they covered. He brought these traits to ABC News when he was appointed president in 1977. He presided over the creation of *World News Tonight* in 1978 and *Nightline* in 1979 and eventually transformed ABC News into the most respected network news organization.

The Miniseries ABC's most innovative and influential programming achievement in the 1970's was the development of the miniseries. The first miniseries, *Rich Man, Poor Man* (1976), became a sensation. The 12-episode adaptation of Irwin Shaw's 1970 best seller told a sweeping story unlike anything seen before on American television. Its dark romance ranged over decades, with a story measured out in weekly cliffhangers that kept viewers dangling in suspense, waiting anxiously for the story to resume. The milestone in the miniseries format was ABC's broadcast of *Roots*, the powerful adaptation of Alex Haley's multigenerational saga of an African-American family's historical journey from slavery to freedom. Because miniseries have a clear beginning and end, they lend themselves to innovative forms of scheduling. This was the case with *Roots*, a 12-hour series that Fred Silverman chose to show on eight consecutive frigid nights in January 1977.

Prime Time Soaps While each of the networks added miniseries to their schedules, they also recognized that the format's central appeal rested in addictive, ongoing storylines—which the networks had perfected in their daytime soap operas. The answer was to bring the qualities of the daytime soaps into prime time. CBS led the way with *Dallas*, *Knot's Landing*, and *Falcon Crest*. ABC countered with *Dynasty*. These prime-time soap operas, which introduced the strategy of the season-ending cliffhanger that leaves viewers in eager anticipation, became the most popular television dramas of the late 1970's and early 1980's.

End of an Era In retrospect, the predominance of continuous, open-ended storylines in television series of the late 1970's and 1980's looks like a characteristic of a lost age. Open-ended storylines require a high degree of viewer involvement, so networks today fear that a viewer who misses one or two episodes may never return. The strategy of scheduling prime-time soap operas and miniseries developed when the networks could take their audiences for granted. Both formats survived into the 1980's, but they have largely disappeared from television because networks consider them to be too risky in an age when viewers have choices beyond the three networks.

On February 28, 1983, a record 106 million people—47 percent of all Americans—watched the final episode of *M*A*S*H*, which concluded its 10-year run on CBS. At the time, the average American home received 14 television channels; the same home today has more than 50. The *M*A*S*H* finale represents the end of the era of network monopoly, because for the last time almost half of all Americans gathered to watch a single television program

The Cable Era (1984–2004)

The first three decades of network television in America represent a period of remarkable stability for the television industry. Once the basic structure of the television industry had been established, the television seasons rolled past with comforting familiarity. The networks constructed their schedules around regular weekly series that seemed best suited for the purposes of delivering a predictable number of viewers to the advertisers. New series debuted each fall. Some found an audience and survived; most were cancelled. And the cycle started all over again. The three networks battled one another for ratings supremacy, because each ratings point translated into millions of dollars in advertising revenue, but little happened to challenge the fundamental logic of the television business. Under these conditions, the networks were among the country's most stable corporations. In the six decades since NBC and CBS were founded, they had never changed owners; ABC hadn't changed since 1953. And then suddenly, in the period of six months in 1985, all three networks changed ownership. By the end of the 1990's, ABC and CBS had changed owners yet again. Behind these drastic changes were several technological advances now familiar to everyone.

Cable Television Cable television began in the 1940's and 1950's as community antenna television (CATV), a solution to reception problems in geographically isolated towns where people had trouble receiving television signals with a home antenna. The answer was to erect a large antenna tower in a high location and distribute the signal to subscribers using coaxial cable. Before cable, the networks had benefited from the fact that the stronger VHF signals tended to belong to network affiliates, while newer independent channels got stuck with the weaker UHF channels. (UHF channels were even segregated onto a separate tuner knob on TV sets of the era). Because a large community antenna could receive distant signals and amplify the weaker UHF channels, it created a situation in which cable viewers received more channels than those typically available over the air, and each channel arrived with a strong, clear signal. By adding a satellite dish to the master antenna, cable system operators had the potential to liberate television viewers from all geographical constraints inherent in over-the-air broadcasting.

HBO, Turner, et al. The turning point for cable television came during the 1970's when several corporations began to distribute program services by satellite, making it possible to reach audiences on a national—and eventually international—scale without the need for local affiliate stations. Time, Inc. was the first to launch a satellite-based service when it premiered Home Box Office (HBO) in 1975. The service began on a small scale, with only a few hundred viewers for its initial broadcast, but demonstrated that subscription service of movies and special events could be a viable economic alternative to commercial broadcasting. By the end of the decade, other subscription-based movie channels, including Showtime, The Movie Channel, and HBO's own spin-off network, Cinemax, had followed suit.

In 1976 Ted Turner (b. 1938) transformed a modest Atlanta independent station, WTCG, into the first cable-era "superstation," WTBS, by distributing its signal across the country via satellite. Turner's station later was joined by other satellite-distributed independent stations, including WGN from Chicago and WWOR from New York.

The next five years saw the birth of many networks created expressly for cable that were not burdened by the requirement to broadcast from a specific location or to fulfill a public service expectation. If the major networks were department stores, stocking a wide assortment of programs for a variety of customers, the new cable networks were boutiques, created to provide a distinct product to a discerning customer. Following decades of *broadcasting*, the cable networks introduced *narrowcasting* to the television industry.

Narrowcasting Networks Between 1976 and 1981 several cable networks emerged to offer an alternative to the major networks. Some networks provided a program service or addressed an audience that had been neglected by the broadcast networks. C-Span (introduced 1979) provided commercial-free coverage of the U.S. Congress. The Christian Broadcasting Network (CBN) was the most successful of many networks devoted to religious programming. Black Entertainment Television (BET) aimed at young, African-American viewers who had rarely been served well by the broadcast networks. Other cable networks selected a particular element of Big Three programming as the basis for an entire network; the goal was to capture the segment of the mass audience drawn to a particular element of the network schedule. ESPN attracted an audience of adult males by delivering a steady stream of sporting events and sports news. Nickelodeon offered programs for children. The Weather Channel actually introduced a new way to watch television. Instead of tuning in for a program, viewers paused in the midst of other television viewing to monitor weather conditions.

CNN Launched in 1980 by Ted Turner, who was emerging as the iconoclastic leader of the cable network revolution, Cable News Network (CNN) directly challenged the broadcast networks by delivering national and international news on a round-the-clock basis. As the commercial value of network time had soared over the years, the networks had come to devote less time to news programs and had grown reluctant to preempt regular programs for ongoing coverage of news events. In place of the networks' condensed and packaged newscasts, CNN used lightweight video equipment and satellite hook-ups to present live coverage of events in real time. As a result, CNN became the viewer's choice for breaking news and ongoing coverage of criminal trials and government hearings. CNN's coverage of the 1991 Gulf War, when CNN reporters speaking by telephone from a Baghdad hotel delivered live reports during the first night's bombardment, proved to be a milestone for the network. The influence of CNN can be observed directly in the rise of competing news networks like Fox News and MSNBC and indirectly in the intense media coverage of emotionally charged events like the trial of O.J. Simpson and the Clinton-Lewinsky scandal.

MTV The premiere of MTV in 1981 was a godsend for the music, advertising, and cable television industries. Created by Warner Communications, the first of the movie and television companies to operate cable delivery systems, MTV introduced a new approach to television by adopting the programming model that radio had developed following the decline of the radio networks. After the shift to all-music formats, radio listeners no longer tuned in to a station to hear a particular program, but to locate a type of music that suited their tastes. MTV adapted this approach to television—with affable young hosts who served as "veejays" and music videos featuring popular musicians. The early influence of MTV on music and style is nearly impossible to exaggerate. The network sparked a recovery in the slumping music industry, while creating countless new stars. MTV also represented a boon to the advertising industry, because television never before had been an effective medium for advertising to teenagers. MTV essentially created a new audience where the Big Three had failed. With its distinctive logo and promotions, its programming and personalities, MTV was more than a television network; it was a brand, an identity for its young viewers and, therefore, an ideal vehicle for advertising.

In essence, everything on MTV during its early days was an advertisement. Music videos were supplied to the network by the music industry, which saw an unprecedented opportunity to promote record sales. Music videos blurred the distinction between advertising and programming—and no one seemed to mind.

HSN The introduction of Home Shopping Network in 1985 and its competitor, QVC, in 1986, showed that cable networks could eliminate programs and commercials entirely by selling directly to customers. Home shopping networks have been among the most profitable networks in the television industry. Along with the other cable networks of this period, they introduced a new operational model to the television business.

The Power of the MSOs The cable systems that brought these networks into American homes became a new force in the television industry. Companies that operated cable systems in several cities around the county, such as Telecommunications, Inc., Cablevision, Comcast, and Warner-Amex, became known as *multiple system operators* (MSOs). These companies started by controlling the hardware of cable distribution—the network of cables that connected the master antenna or satellite receiver to individual households. The costs of wiring cities for cable were enormous, and many of these companies took on huge debts to finance the installation process. While raking in the steady income from cable subscribers, MSOs used their growing control over distribution to exercise new leverage in the television industry. By deciding which networks to carry on their systems, MSOs transformed themselves into the gatekeepers of cable television. An entrepreneur might launch a network, but it was doomed to failure unless the MSOs elected to carry it. Many of these MSOs used this leverage to invest directly in cable networks.

The Impact of Cable Before the 1980's, regulatory concerns hampered the widespread adoption of cable TV in America. But in 1984 Congress passed the Cable Communications Policy Act, which lifted most federal regulatory restraints from the cable industry, with the exception of "must-carry" provisions that required cable operators to have local stations on their systems. Cable service soon expanded rapidly. In 1978 only 17 percent of American households had cable; by 1989 cable penetration had reached 57 percent.

Television viewers subscribed to cable in part because cable offered a solution to the problem of program scarcity associated with the era of network monopoly. Given the choice of dozens of new networks, viewers began drifting away from the broadcast networks. In 1984 the Big Three still claimed 80 percent of the nation's TV audience, but that was already a sharp drop from the days when they could count on more than 90 percent of the audience. As competition has increased, the broadcast networks' share of the total audience has spiraled downward each year. In 2004 there are six broadcast networks, and together they account for just 54 percent of the total audience.

New Technologies During the era of network monopoly, viewers not only had a limited choice of programs, they also had no control over the flow of television programming or the schedule imposed by the networks. New technologies—inexpensive television sets, videocassette recorders (VCRs), and remote control devices—gave viewers a measure of autonomy from television programmers, and control over the way television could be experienced.

Multiple TV Sets In 1981, for the first time a majority of American households contained more than one television set. The availability of multiple sets in the home changes the dynamic of television viewing by freeing family members to make choices based on their individual tastes, rather than the need to conform to a common taste or, more likely, to the taste of the person who controls the TV. This created an incentive for networks to provide programs for children and teenagers, who were able to make their own choices about what to watch.

VCRs Videocassette recorders became a common feature in American homes during the 1980's. Home video recorders awaited the development of the videocassette by Sony in the 1970's. The consumer market for home VCRs developed slowly at first because Sony and its rival Matsushita developed incompatible systems (Betamax and VHS, respectively). The market also stalled because of a lawsuit filed in 1976 by Disney and Universal against Sony, charging that home videotaping represented a violation of copyright. The issue was settled in Sony's favor by a 1984 Supreme Court decision, and the consumer market for VCRs exploded (although Sony's Betamax system eventually lost out and faded from the consumer market). In 1982, 4 percent of households owned a VCR; in 1984, the number had risen to 19 percent; by 1988 60 percent of American households owned a VCR. (As of 2002, that figure had risen to 94 percent.)

VCRs allowed users to tape TV programs and watch them at their convenience, a practice that came to be known as "time-shifting." The use of the VCR for time-shifting, like the evident popularity of cable, grew from viewer frustration with network television and the rigidity of the TV schedule.

The Remote The remote control device became popular during the 1980's, and it has had a significant impact on the manner in which people experience television. Industry researchers quickly began to observe new viewing patterns that they described as "grazing." Many viewers used the remote control to avoid watching commercials, while others learned to scan restlessly through the channels, not watching entire programs, but looking for an arresting image or sound that entices them to stop on a particular channel. As one result, many cable networks crafted a signature visual style, using distinctive logos, graphic designs, and other techniques, that made the network immediately identifiable to the restless, remote-control-enhanced television viewer.

Home Video Other video technologies introduced during the 1980's also helped to alter the relationship of people to television, creating a growing awareness of a distinction between television and video. Camcorders have made people aware that video can be a technology for recording one's own experiences, creating an archive of personal memories. Video games, introduced during the 1980's but not to achieve their full impact until the 1990's, have initiated people into a new relationship with the video screen, a participatory mode of engagement. This interactive relationship with the screen was reinforced by the spread of the home computer during the 1980's. Each of these technologies would have a much greater impact in the years to come, but from the beginning they changed the way that people used their television sets. They broke the link that had made television seem like the natural use for video technology, revealing that television is just an effective way for certain industries to capitalize on the technology.

Deregulation During the 1980's, the most dramatic changes in the television industry were the result of a new approach and philosophy in the federal government's approach to the regulation of communication industries.

Under the Reagan administration the F.C.C. pursued a policy to reduce the federal oversight of broadcasting and allow market forces to govern the conduct of media corporations. From a regulatory perspective, Reagan-era F.C.C. chairman Mark Fowler (b. 1941) famously asserted, television is no different from a toaster or any other household appliance. Under his administration the F.C.C. relaxed or removed many of the long-standing rules that governed the broadcasting industries, including the public service obligations.

The old rules that had created stability in the broadcast industries by preventing stations from being easily bought and sold were relaxed. License terms were extended in 1981 from three to five years. The license renewal process was simplified and scrutiny of licensees (which had never been particularly stringent) became virtually nonexistent; a station could renew its license by sending in a postcard. For years station owners were restricted by the "5-5-5 rule" that limited any single entity to owning no more than five AM radio stations, five FM stations, and five TV stations. After first increasing the limit to seven, in 1985 the F.C.C. raised the limit to 12 television stations. The cap for radio stations was eventually raised to 40. The changes in license procedures and ownership limits created a seller's market for station licenses—a speculative market in licenses that led to a rapid turnover in stations—and encouraged consolidation in the broadcasting industries as large media corporations accumulated more and more stations.

These changes also produced a sharp increase in the number of television stations, as corporations invested in station chains. At the time of the F.C.C.'s actions to limit the power of networks in 1970, there were 862 stations in the country, only 82 of which operated independently of the three networks. By 1995, there were 1,532 stations, and 450 of these were independent of the three networks. One result of this growth in stations was the development of a first-run syndication market—a market for programs sold directly to stations, bypassing the networks. The first-run syndication market led to the proliferation of game shows (*Wheel of Fortune*, *Jeopardy!*) and talk shows (among which the most celebrated is *The Oprah Winfrey Show*, which entered national syndication in 1986).

As regulatory changes heated up the broadcasting business, a general trend of mergers and acquisitions swept through the industry, aided by the use of leveraged buyouts and relaxed enforcement of antitrust laws by the Reagan-era Justice Department. This climate gave rise to the series of mergers and acquisitions that saw the three major networks change hands in 1985–86 and also saw the introduction of a fourth broadcast network, Fox. In 1985 the media conglomerate, News Corporation, owned by Rupert Murdoch (b. 1931), purchased Twentieth Century-Fox studios. In 1986 Murdoch then purchased six television stations, which served as the foundation for launching the Fox network in 1987. Because Fox began by programming just a few nights each week, it technically did not meet the F.C.C. definition of a full-fledged network, and therefore was not constrained by the rules that prohibited a network from producing its own programs. Although Fox began with many fewer affiliates than the major networks, it quickly began to attract viewers by concentrating on programs with youth appeal: *The Simpsons*, *Beverly Hills 90210*, *Melrose Place*, *Married With Children*, and *The X-Files*.

The networks lobbied for an end to the financial-interest-and-syndication rules that had kept them out of the studio business and the lucrative syndication market since the early 1970's. They pointed to the loophole that Fox had squeezed through in order to produce its own programs and argued that increased competition in the television industry—particularly from foreign-owned companies that were not governed by such restrictions—placed them at a competitive disadvantage.

The financial-interest-and-syndication rules were gradually repealed between 1991 and 1995. The policy change not only gave networks the opportunity to produce many of their own programs, but also provided an incentive for further integration of the media industries by encouraging studio-network mergers. Two new broadcast networks debuted in 1995: Time-Warner's WB network and Viacom's United Paramount Network (UPN). As with Fox, these networks began with stations owned by the studios and then recruited affiliates from among the many stations not affiliated with the three major networks. Like Fox, these networks created programs to siphon off viewers from the dominant networks, with schedules aimed heavily at younger viewers and African Americans.

The Telecommunications Act of 1996 eliminated most of the remaining barriers to consolidation in the media and communication industries. It also eliminated all ownership limits on radio stations, which has paved the way for a radical consolidation of the radio industry. Another significant policy change that encourages concentration is the F.C.C.'s 1999 decision to approve "duopolies," or the owning of more than one television station in a single market. The F.C.C. still limits an individual company to owning stations that cover no more than 35 percent of the nation's households—but some companies have exceeded the cap without penalty. Under the Bush administration the F.C.C. has proposed removing the cap altogether—along with virtually all remaining ownership limits in radio and television.

The Three Major Networks Today

NBC NBC entered the 1980's mired in third place, at the depths of its fortunes as a television network. In 1981 Grant Tinker (b. 1926) became NBC chairman and together with programming chief Brandon Tartikoff (1949–97) led NBC on a three-year journey back to respectability by continuing the commitment to quality programming, including such acclaimed series as *Hill Street Blues*, *Cheers*, *St. Elsewhere*, *Family Ties*, and *Miami Vice*. The turning point for NBC came in 1984, when Tartikoff convinced comedian Bill Cosby (b. 1937) to return to series television with *The Cosby Show*. Network profits climbed from $48 million in 1981 to $333 million in 1985.

General Electric purchased RCA—and with it NBC—in 1985 for $6.3 billion. GE chairman Jack Welch (b. 1935) named Robert Wright (b. 1943) to replace Tinker as network chairman. Many observers of the media industries were dubious about GE's ability to operate a television network. General Electric was a vast conglomerate based in Fairfield, Conn., a manufacturer of medical equipment, power turbines, airplane engines, and appliances that had diversified into such businesses as the financing of commercial and consumer loans. Little in GE's recent history foretold success in programming a television network. Nearly two decades later much has changed in the television business, but Robert Wright is still chairman, and NBC has been the dominant network in the United States for much of the past two decades, a model of stability in an otherwise turbulent business.

NBC has consistently led all networks in attracting the 18- to 49-year-old adults most coveted by advertisers—winning this demographic in seven of the eight years from 1995 to 2003—and has helped to reorient the entire broadcasting industry toward the pursuit of this segment of the audience. Led by a Thursday night lineup that has launched such hits as *The Cosby Show*, *Cheers*, and *L.A. Law* in the 1980's, and *Seinfeld*, *Friends*, and *E.R.* in the 1990's, NBC has the highest advertising rates of any broadcast network and has long been the most profitable, generating profits of $700–800 million from its prime-time schedule in the 2002–03 season. NBC's dominance extends to virtually every part of the schedule, where its self-produced entertainment and news programs have led the ratings during much of the past decade: *The Today Show* and *Meet The Press* in the mornings, *NBC Nightly News* among evening newscasts, *The Tonight Show with Jay Leno*, *Late Night with Conan O'Brien*, and *Saturday Night Live* in late night. Over the same period, NBC has been responsible for many of television's most acclaimed series, easily overshadowing the other broadcast networks with a mounting pile of Emmy nominations for *E.R.*, *The West Wing*, *Law and Order*, *Homicide: Life on the Streets*, *Frasier*, *Seinfeld*, and *Will and Grace*.

Due to the strength of its network programming, NBC's 14 owned-and-operated television stations contribute another $1 billion in annual advertising revenue. Still, the audience for over-the-air broadcasting continues to shrink in the United States as audiences are dispersed among cable channels and competing forms of home entertainment. Like other media companies, NBC has diversified well beyond its original base in broadcasting in order to reach these elusive viewers. NBC now controls several cable channels, including CNBC, a business news network available in 175 million households worldwide; MSNBC, a 24-hour news network owned jointly with Microsoft; and Bravo, a network targeted at upscale viewers. In order to reach the growing Latino audience in the U.S., NBC purchased Telemundo, the second-largest U.S. Spanish-language broadcast network, in April 2002. With international markets as important as the domestic market to GE's bottom line, NBC programming now reaches viewers in one hundred countries on six continents. All told, NBC Television and Cable operations generate annual revenues of $7.1 billion (still only 5 percent of GE's annual sales) and operating profits of $1.7 billion.

In May 2004 GE officially merged with Vivendi Universal Entertainment in a deal valued at $14 billion. The new company, NBC Universal, gives GE control of the Universal movie studio, the USA Network and other cable channels, a television production unit responsible for the network's lucrative *Law and Order* franchise, and Vivendi's interest in the Universal Studios theme parks. By integrating additional cable networks and a major studio with its broadcast network, NBC Universal will compete as a fully integrated media conglomerate.

ABC The new era of corporate mergers and acquisitions dawned at ABC when Capital Cities Communications acquired the network in 1985 for $3.5 billion. This was a big leap for Capital Cities, a media corporation with interests in local television stations and magazine and newspaper publishing, and annual revenues of slightly more than $1 billion. Following the merger, severe cost-cutting measures were instituted throughout the network, but most of the network management remained in place. Capital Cities also made far-sighted investments in the cable networks A&E, The History Channel, Lifetime, and ESPN (which ABC had purchased in 1984).

The Capital Cities team placed Robert Iger (b. 1951) in charge of network programming in 1989. Iger's four years at the head of ABC Entertainment kicked off the network's last great period of ratings dominance. Iger inherited *thirtysomething* and *Roseanne* and added several other series that became hits: *Doogie Howser*, *NYPD Blue*, *Family Matters*, *Full House*, *America's Funniest Home Videos*, and *Home Improvement*. In the target market of 18- to 49-year-old adults, ABC won the prime-time ratings race three times during Iger's tenure. ABC moved into first place in the network ratings for the 1994–95 season.

ABC came under the control of the Walt Disney Co. in August 1995, when Disney acquired the network's parent company, Capital Cities/ABC, for $19 billion. Disney's merger of a major studio with a broadcast network figured to be the model for the television industry of the future, as companies jockeyed for position following the end of the F.C.C.'s financial-interest-and-syndication rules. The enticement of media synergy drove Disney to acquire ABC, and the Disney-ABC alliance has served as a model for the subsequent consolidation of networks and studios throughout the television industry.

As a result of its absorption into the Disney empire, ABC is now a highly diversified corporation with extensive U.S. and international interests in broadcasting and cable. The ABC Broadcasting group consists of 10 television and 55 radio stations that are owned and operated by ABC, a television network with 225 affiliate stations, a basic radio network that provides programming for 4,600 affiliate stations, and two specialized radio program services—ESPN Radio and Radio Disney. The ABC Cable Networks group oversees a number of cable networks that are either wholly or partially owned by Disney: ABC Family, A&E Television Networks (which include A&E, Biography, and the History Channel), E! Entertainment Television, ESPN Networks (including ESPN International, which reaches 119 million households outside the U.S.), Lifetime and Lifetime Movies, the Soap Network, Toon Disney, and the Disney Channel and its international versions (seen in 56 countries). In addition to its own sports and news production, ABC now oversees all network and syndicated television production at Disney.

The goal of the Disney-ABC alliance was to create the conditions for mutually beneficial cooperation among the company's separate divisions. Disney now has the ability to distribute its movies and television programs through a range of television networks that provide opportunities for the "repurposing" of content (as the industry refers to the practice of recycling content from one network or medium to another) and targeted access to different types of viewers—the Disney Channel for children, Lifetime for women, ESPN for men. When synergy works, as it does for ABC's sports and children's programming, it allows for convenient cross-promotion of Disney products and more efficient use of resources. ABC has stocked its Saturday morning schedule with children's programs originally produced for Disney's premium cable channel. These programs are then distributed to the international Disney channels and sold on home video. ESPN and ABC Sports have combined to purchase broadcast rights to NBA basketball and NFL football and now share production facilities and personnel. ESPN has become the world's most valuable cable network, generating more than $500 million per year and establishing a brand name that Disney has successfully exploited by creating additional ESPN cable channels, an ESPN magazine, and ESPN Zone restaurants.

The Achilles' heel of synergy in the television business is that success still depends on having a strong broadcast network at the core. ABC has had no such luck. ABC was the first-place network at the time of the merger, but its ratings soon began a downward slide. In just two seasons, ABC fell from first to third in the ratings. Operating income dropped from $400 million to $100 million in the first two years of Disney ownership, and the network has posted significant losses in subsequent years. Except for the improbable success of 1999–2000, when *Who Wants To Be a Millionaire?* (aired as many as four times a week) carried the network into first place, ABC's prime-time ratings have never recovered—in part because the network has failed to use opportunities like the fluke success of

Millionaire to develop new hits. Over the past two seasons, ABC has dropped into fourth place in the ratings.

CBS During the 1980's, CBS was still controlled by the aging patriarch William S. Paley, who had founded the network six decades earlier. In the competitive business environment of the 1980's, CBS found itself under continuous threat of a corporate takeover, including one launched by cable mogul Ted Turner. To defend itself, the CBS board recruited Lawrence Tisch (1923–2003), the president of CBS's largest shareholder, Loew's Inc., to become president and CEO in 1986. Tisch immediately set about doing exactly what a corporate raider would have done: he slashed budgets—including that of the network's venerable news division—reduced personnel, and sold off assets like CBS Records.

CBS, which had been near the top of the network ratings for the entire history of television, found itself drifting into unfamiliar last-place territory during the late 1980's. The network's identity with older viewers began with its most prominent program, the news magazine *60 Minutes*, which has been on the air since 1968. A top-10 hit for much of its network run, *60 Minutes* rose to number one during the years 1991–94, and helped to carry the network back to the top, accompanied by such older-skewing dramas as *Murder, She Wrote*; *Dr. Quinn, Medicine Woman*; *Walker, Texas Ranger*, and the situation comedies *Murphy Brown* and *Designing Women*.

For a decade after the Tisch takeover, CBS continued to operate as an independent corporation, the last network to resist becoming a subsidiary of a larger conglomerate. That ended in November 1995, when Westinghouse purchased the network for $5.4 billion. Like General Electric, its former partner in the alliance that had created the radio industry so many years before, Westinghouse was a highly diversified company with a long history in broadcasting as the owner of a large group of radio and TV stations. CBS was a Westinghouse subsidiary for four mostly undistinguished years before the media conglomerate Viacom acquired Westinghouse's media properties (the network and stations) in a September 1999 deal valued at $50 billion.

By adding the CBS network to Paramount Communications, which it had acquired in 1994, Viacom created a fully integrated media conglomerate in order to keep pace with its chief competitors at Disney, Fox, and Time Warner. Viacom led one of the major developments in television during the cable era—the transformation of cable networks into consumer brands. By creating a clearly identifiable identity and a loyal fan base for such channels as Nickelodeon and MTV, Viacom has succeeded in manufacturing new brand names that can be used to market movies, music, books, magazines, and merchandise. Viacom is dedicated to achieving the same results with the other cable networks that it has acquired or developed over the years: VH1, Comedy Central, Country Music Television (CMT), TV Land, Spike, and Black Entertainment Television (BET).

Viacom is the only media conglomerate with two broadcast networks—CBS and the United Paramount Network (UPN). In addition, Viacom owns the subscription cable channels Showtime, The Movie Channel, Flix, and the Sundance Channel. Through its acquisitions Viacom now owns and operates 39 television stations in 15 of the top 20 television markets, and Infinity Broadcasting, which controls more than 180 radio stations concentrated in the 50 largest radio markets in the United States. Alongside these television properties, Viacom's many other divisions include Paramount Pictures and Paramount Television, producing movies and television programs; King World, the leading producer and distributor of first-run syndication programs; Viacom Outdoor, the largest billboard company in America; Blockbuster, the leading home video retail chain; the publisher Simon & Schuster; and Paramount Parks, a chain of theme parks.

Network C.E.O. and president Les Moonves (b. 1953) arrived at CBS in 1995 from Warner Bros. Television, where he had been the head of the studio that produced such hits as *Friends* and *E.R.* In 2000 he introduced the first reality-genre sensation, *Survivor*, and *C.S.I.: Crime Scene Investigation*, which displaced *E.R.* as the highest rated drama on television. *C.S.I.* has spawned highly rated spin-offs *C.S.I.: Miami* and *C.S.I.: New York*.

Television in the Digital Era

Just as the introduction of cable and home video compelled the television industry to change over the past two decades, the proliferation of digital technologies promises to transform American television in the years to come. Although it is tempting to make predictions about the future of television, the ground is littered with failed predictions from the past. For nearly 20 years before most Americans ever saw a television broadcast, they heard that television was just around the corner. For more than a decade now, we've heard about a fabled 500-channel television universe, a Shangri-la yet to be discovered. Modesty is essential when forecasting the future of technology. If history is any guide, one can safely predict only that new technologies will disrupt the status quo—particularly as people, through their collective actions, choose how to incorporate new technologies into their lives—and that media corporations will figure out how to profit from any change that takes place.

Broadcasting vs. Narrowcasting The broadcast networks still attract the largest audiences of any mass medium in America. The leading networks—currently CBS and NBC—average 12 to 14 million viewers in prime time, and a top 10 series can draw 20 to 25 million viewers each week. A splashy, well-publicized event still can assemble an audience of unparalleled size; the final episode of *Seinfeld* attracted 76 million viewers in May 1998. By contrast, Lifetime, the cable network with the highest ratings during prime time, averages only 2 million viewers. Most other cable networks have cause for celebration when they break the million-viewer barrier. Even the news networks that appear to play a prominent role in national political discourse—CNN and Fox—average between 700,000 and 1 million viewers.

No single competitor threatens the viability of the broadcast networks, but their audiences are gradually slipping away with each passing year, and television as a cultural medium is being changed in the process. In place of broadcasting, the television and advertising industries have supported a shift to narrowcasting—the segmentation of the mass audience into smaller demographic categories. For many advertisers selling goods and services to a mass market, it is still efficient to reach the large concentrations of viewers made available by a top-rated prime-time series. But even mass-market companies like McDonald's and Coca-Cola often find it more effective to target specific consumers with advertising messages designed for them. In other words, it's more efficient for advertisers to speak to consumers who are interested in what they have to say.

As a result, it is virtually impossible to make any generalized assumptions about the television audience. The Nielsen ratings reveal that African-American and white households typically prefer different programs. At times there is virtually no overlap between the 10 highest-rated programs for the two races. The growth of leading Spanish-language network Univision and rival Telemundo during the 1990's provides another glimpse of the segmentation of the mass audience. In cities with large Latino populations, Univision programs—most produced in Mexico City or another Latin American media capital—can equal the ratings for programs on the broadcast networks.

Unlike the broadcast networks, the cable networks cannot afford a full schedule of original programs. Cable networks rely on network reruns, but also have begun to concentrate their efforts on developing one or two signature programs that create an identity for the entire network—such as *Biography* on A&E, or the police drama *The Shield* on FX. Another strategy is for a cable network to concentrate marketing and promotion budgets to raise the profile of a single series in order to create a phenomenon that attracts media attention and draws viewers, prompted by media coverage, to the network. Such programs include Bravo's *Queer Eye for the Straight Guy*, and MTV's *The Osbournes*.

During the 1990's, the broadcast networks have seen their status as the source of quality programs eroded by HBO, which has developed a reputation for creating the most innovative television series: *The Larry Sanders Show*, *Sex and the City*, *The Sopranos*, *Curb Your Enthusiasm*, *The Wire*, *Deadwood*, and *Six Feet Under*. As a subscription service, HBO doesn't have to provide a full program service or attract an audience for advertisers; it simply has to give people a reason to pay the cost of subscribing. This leads HBO to focus on creating a few series that attract inordinate attention from critics and the media. It frees HBO from the scheduling constraints of the broadcast networks. HBO doesn't have to premiere all of its series at one time in the fall or commission 22 episodes per season. HBO allows its producers to concentrate on making 12 high-quality episodes, instead of struggling to provide 22. Most worrisome for the broadcast networks, HBO's acclaimed series siphon off the viewers most prized by the advertisers—upscale 18- to 49-year-olds. HBO doesn't sell these audiences to advertisers, but if they're watching HBO, they aren't available for the broadcast networks.

The Fate of the Broadcast Networks While ABC's prime-time ratings have collapsed and the network has floundered, the larger ABC organization has achieved some notable success over the past few years. The owned-and-operated TV and radio stations are profitable for ABC, as they are for all broadcast networks. Corporate synergy has worked in sports and children's programming. The most obvious successes are in Disney's cable television group. While broadcast networks have only a single source of revenue—advertising sales—cable networks earn money from advertising and from charging transmission fees to cable and satellite delivery systems, which are passed along to viewers as higher service rates. For the most successful networks, such as Disney's ESPN, these transmission fees can be raised by as much as 20 percent annually.

Even as ABC struggles, several of Disney's cable networks, including ESPN, the Disney Channel, A&E, and Lifetime have seen steady growth in revenues and profits. The many networks owned by Viacom provide advertisers with the ability to target television viewers from cradle to grave: Nick Jr. for preschoolers; Nickelodeon for preteens; MTV for teens; Comedy Central, VH1, Spike, and UPN for young adults; Nick-at-Nite, CMT, and CBS for adults.

A diversified portfolio of broadcast and cable networks allows the parent companies of ABC, NBC, and CBS to reconstitute much of the audience lost to the traditional broadcast networks over the past two decades. Although the audience for the broadcast networks continues to shrink, the five companies that control the broadcast networks still reach more than 80 percent of viewers in prime time when counting the ratings for their combined broadcast and cable networks. This explains why half of the top 50 cable networks have changed hands since 1990 and why most are now controlled by the five companies that already own broadcast networks.

Cable networks also allow companies to spread operating costs and extend their global reach. NBC has achieved greater efficiency and reach for CNBC by expanding CNBC Europe and CNBC Asia Pacific (both of which are jointly owned with Dow Jones, the publisher of the *Wall Street Journal*) through a range of localized services using the resources of partners in Japan, Australia, Singapore, Hong Kong, Sweden, and several other countries. The 24-hour news network MSNBC uses the resources of NBC News to provide programming for both cable and the Internet. Viacom's MTV, with several unique regional services, reaches nearly 400 million subscribers in more than 160 countries and territories. Cable networks also lend themselves to the establishment of brand identities and to cross-promotional opportunities, as networks like ESPN, MTV, and Nickelodeon have proven for NBC's competitors.

The competition in prime time has increased over the past several years as the audience has continued to shrink, the advertising market has flattened, programming costs have risen, new program formats have been introduced, and new networks compete for viewers. There are now six broadcast networks and dozens of cable channels competing for the attention of viewers. Because viewers are more dispersed, the networks have relied on programs that are easily promoted, such as the reality formats that offer a low-cost, highly marketable alternative to episodic series. The success of nonscripted series like ABC's *Who Wants to Be a Millionaire?* and *The Bachelor*, CBS's *Survivor*, and Fox's *American Idol* and *Joe Millionaire* have shown the value of less expensive alternatives to scripted series. The focus has shifted from building long-term audience commitment to series, as they once did, to going after big ratings—even if they are temporary and can't be repeated with regularity.

Because viewers are widely dispersed over 50 or more channels, it has become difficult to introduce a new conventional scripted series. NBC has not had a breakout hit since *Will and Grace* debuted in 1998. The only scripted series to become immediate hits over the past several years have been *C.S.I.* and its spin-off, *C.S.I. Miami*, on CBS. As a result of the difficulty in launching new series, the cost of holding together a prime-time schedule has increased dramatically over the past several years. NBC has been forced to spend lavishly in order to keep in place its most successful series. As it becomes more difficult than ever to turn a scripted series into a hit, producers of existing series find themselves with considerable bargaining leverage. When *E.R.* came up for renewal in 2000, NBC paid Warner Bros. Television a record $13 million per episode. In order to lure *Friends* back for a final season in 2003–04, NBC paid Warner Bros. $10 million per episode and reduced its order to only 18 episodes.

Over the past few years there has been a return to weekly dramas in which each episode is neatly concluded, such as the *Law and Order* and *C.S.I.* franchises. Over the past few years NBC has used repeats of the *Law and Order* franchise to plug holes in its schedule, even filling entire nights with back-to-back episodes. In the summer of 2003, for instance, 20 percent of NBC's entire prime-time schedule consisted of *Law and Order*. One industry analyst estimated that the *Law and Order* franchise accounted for $180 million of the network's prime-time profits in 2001–02, or 25 percent of its total profits for prime time. *Law and Order* has been extremely profitable in syndication for its studio, Universal, but NBC has not shared in these profits or those of many other prime-time series, because it has been the only network without a large in-house production unit. The solution was to acquire Universal's parent company and create NBC Universal.

The Digital Future

HDTV Any number of new digital technologies could alter the way that television programs are produced, distributed, and viewed. The most obvious transition will be the shift from the conventional, analog television of the past half-century to digital, high-definition television (HDTV), which achieves photo-quality images due to a scan rate of up to 1,080 lines (the NTSC standard for conventional TV has been 525 lines). Since the F.C.C. approved a digital television standard for the United States in 1996, the transition to digital television has occurred more slowly than some had predicted, but it has gained momentum recently. As consumers adopt the technology, networks and local stations have picked up the pace in switching from analog to digital broadcasting. Aside from providing higher quality image and sound, digital transmission opens up possibilities for providing many more television channels—or for the transmission of additional information—using techniques of digital compression.

File Sharing The spread of networked home computers elicits wild mood swings in the television industry, as it does in all media industries. On the one hand, the industry has worked to develop various forms of interactive television (dating back to Warner-Amex trials in Ohio during the 1970's), and the growth of the Internet makes some form of interactivity seem inevitable—especially as bandwidth increases and the Internet becomes a plausible delivery system for television. But the industry also worries about the potential loss of revenue from consumers who make digital files of television programs and distribute them over the Internet. With the ease of file sharing on peer-to-peer networks, the music industry has seen CD sales drop by nearly 40 percent since 2000. It only makes sense that TV programs will become ripe for file-sharing once more consumers have the necessary bandwidth needed to transmit larger files.

DVRs A greater concern for the television industry lies in the public's adoption of digital video recorders (DVR). Introduced by companies like TiVo and Replay, digital video recorders are essentially networked computers capable of selecting television programs and recording them as digital files. Unlike conventional VCRs, a viewer doesn't need to program a digital recorder to record a certain program at a certain time. A viewer simply selects a title and the digital video recorder finds the program and records it from any channel at any time—whether it's prime time or the middle of the night. This feature ends the tyranny of the program schedule once and for all, allowing the DVR user to make all the programming decisions about what to watch and when to watch it. From the perspective of the television industry, the most threatening feature of the digital video recorder is its ability to skip commercials by leaping ahead in 30-second increments—not scan through a commercial as VCR users have learned to do, but to avoid commercials entirely.

As Americans integrate digital technologies into their lives, television will not be able to exist as it has for the past 50 years. Will television be able to continue as an advertiser-supported medium? What will happen to television programming? Will we see more limited-run series? Will networks continue to provide programs transmitted on a regular schedule or will they shift to a model of "video-on-demand" that would look more like the publishing or recording industry, in which an array of products are made available for the selection of consumers? Is it possible to imagine television audiences dispersing so much that the cultural experience of television looks more like the experience of books and music—in which people pursue their own narrowly defined tastes and seldom come together to form a mass audience? In its history, television has never been anything but a mass medium. Perhaps that will change in the years to come.

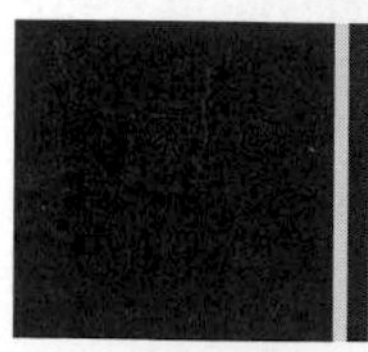

PRINT MEDIA

Newspapers

The origins of news writing date back to China and the Roman Empire before the birth of Christ. In China's Han dynasty (206 B.C. to A.D. 220), sheets called *tipao* were passed among government officials, while in the Forum of Rome, daily reports called *acta diurna* were posted, relating noteworthy events both local and throughout the Empire.

The chief limitation to a regular news service was, of course, the difficulty in production. Every sheet had to be hand-written, a laborious, time-consuming process that greatly restricted the dissemination of news. That problem, and many others, was solved by the invention of the printing press in 1436 by a German named Johannes Gutenberg (d. 1468). The printing press, arguably the most influential invention in human history, enabled production of news sheets much more easily, and at much lower cost.

However, news was not disseminated on a regular basis. Instead it was reserved for occasional postings about single, noteworthy events. Many of these one-time reports, often in pamphlet form, were printed throughout the 16th and 17th centuries. The first regular news sheet appeared in Venice, a major sea power at the time, with a trade network that required frequently updated reports. These sheets, called *gazette* or *avisi*—*gazette* comes from *gazetta,* a Venetian coin—were disseminated weekly as early as 1566, and were borne on merchant vessels to many ports in the Mediterranean and beyond.

The oldest surviving printed weekly newspaper appeared in Strasbourg, Germany, in 1609. Printed weeklies caught on quickly, popping up in Frankfurt and Vienna in 1615, Hamburg in 1616, Berlin in 1617, and Amsterdam in 1618. The first English newspaper was published in 1621, followed over the next two decades by papers in France, Italy, and Spain. The first daily newspaper, *Einkommende Zeirungen* ("Incoming News"), appeared in Leipzig in 1650; the first English daily, *The Daily Courant*, was published in London from 1702–35.

These early papers were mostly assembled from letters sent from other cities, so the news was not particularly timely. Most were printed with government permission, so their news reports focused on events outside their nation or community rather than risk offending the powers that be.

The first society to practice what might be termed freedom of the press was in the England of the 1640's, in the years leading to that nation's Civil War. The conflict between Parliament and King Charles I, which seemed to weaken the king's stature, encouraged several publications to turn their focus from foreign shores to the conflict at home. Following the execution of the king, however, the Protectorate of Cromwell greatly limited the press once again.

Newspapers in Colonial America

The sense that the press could criticize government was borne across the Atlantic to the American colonies, but the theory often withered before reality. In fact, the first issue of America's first newspaper was also the last. *Public Occurrences, Both FORREIGN and DOMESTICK*, printed in Boston on Sept. 25, 1690, made several impolitic statements and was suppressed.

Fourteen years later came America's second printed paper, the *Boston News-Letter*, which survived from its first printing in 1704 until 1776. It was followed in 1719 by the *Boston Gazette* and the *American Weekly Mercury*, printed in Philadelphia. Benjamin Franklin printed the *Pennsylvania Gazette* (also in Philadelphia) starting in 1729. Other papers appeared in Maryland and Virginia in the following decade, and by 1765 all 13 colonies except for Delaware and New Jersey had weekly papers. Boston had four of its own, and New York, three.

News in these pages was scant, with most weeklies four pages long and featuring reprocessed news from Europe. Criticism of colonial administration was rare. Yet one printer dared to criticize, and John Peter Zenger's *New York Weekly Journal*, first printed in 1733, was to have a significant effect on the history of the United States.

After arguing against some of the governor's policies, Zenger was arrested in November 1734 under the charge of seditious libel. During the trial the following August, the judge instructed the jury that, according to the definition of seditious libel, truth afforded no protection against libel of the government. Zenger's attorney, however, made a stirring argument, defending "the liberty both of exposing and opposing arbitrary power... by speaking and writing truth." The jury decided that Zenger was innocent.

Zenger's acquittal was a major victory for freedom of the press in the colonies; without it, many other papers that were critical of the colonial administration over the next four decades might have been silenced. Newspapers played a major part in fueling the fires of revolution. For example, the home of Benjamin Edes, editor of the *Boston Gazette,* served as the center of organization for the Boston Tea Party in 1773.

Following the Revolution, freedom of the press, along with other freedoms, was guaranteed in the First Amendment of the Constitution, ratified in 1787. Still, partisan conflict between the major political parties of the period led to the passage of the Sedition Act in 1798, the most dire threat to freedom of the press in American history. Passed under the presidency of Federalist John Adams, it threatened to punish "any false, scandalous and malicious writing" against the government, including the Congress and the president. During the act's short life, 25 people were arrested and 10 convicted. When Thomas Jefferson ascended to the presidency following the 1800 election, the Sedition Act was allowed to lapse.

The Penny Press

Technological advances in the early Industrial Revolution affected the business of newspapers along with the rest of society. In September 1833 a small paper in New York called the *Sun* went on sale for a penny. The cheap price enabled the lower classes to buy and read the news. By 1835 the *Sun*, printed on a new steam press, was selling 15,000 copies a day, substantially higher than the circulation of other papers in New York.

Within a few years, several cities—including Boston, Philadelphia, and Baltimore—added penny papers. No longer was the common man priced out of ready daily information. Instead, thanks to the low price of printing allowed by better technology, papers could be made more cheaply and quickly. Publishers could reach more customers and sell more advertising. Newspapers became successful businesses.

Content changed as well—sensationalism crept into newspapers. Accounts from police court were common, especially among the penny press, and eventually some publishers improved their content by hiring employees to report and write news stories. This practice had been seen in England before, but it was in the mid-19th century that the practice became common in America. The *New York Herald*, for example, employed dozens of reporters to cover the Civil War.

Another technological innovation that aided reporting and news-gathering was the invention of the telegraph by Samuel Morse in 1844, which enabled news to travel long distances almost instantly, permitting next-day coverage of faraway events. With the completion of the trans-Atlantic cable in 1866, newspapers had similar access to news from Europe.

The Rise of the Modern Newspaper

During the second half of the 19th century new technology and a better-educated public led to tremendous growth in the number of newspapers. Approximately 3,000 papers existed in the U.S. in 1860; 20 years later, the total had reached about 7,000. During this time the modern "pyramid" style of news writing was also devised. This style discarded the earlier form—a narrative and frequently unfocused account—and instead placed the most important facts near the story's beginning. Thus, the first sentence of a news story, called the "lead," contains the essential facts for the reader. Additional facts and details follow, with the least important information placed at the end.

The late 19th century was the most colorful period of American journalism. In many cities, newspapers competed using tough tactics. Nowhere was this more evident than in New York, where two newspaper barons, Joseph Pulitzer (1847–1911) and William Randolph Hearst (1863–1951), vied for the lucrative market.

Pulitzer, a native of the Austro-Hungarian Empire, emigrated to America during the Civil War and eventually started work as a reporter at a German-language paper in St. Louis. In 1878 he bought a small paper at a fire sale price, which he combined with another paper to form the *St. Louis Post-Dispatch*. The new paper prospered, but Pulitzer wanted other challenges, so he purchased the *New York World* in 1883. The *World* quickly differentiated itself from its competitors with stories that focused on lively human interest, gossip and scandal, with a healthy dose of stunts. In 1889 a *World* reporter named Nellie Bly—whose real name was Elizabeth Cochran—set out to circumnavigate the world in less than 80 days, the time required by Phileas Fogg, the protagonist of Jules Verne's novel *Around the World in Eighty Days*. Bly succeeded, returning to New

York 72 days after her departure to considerable *World*-sponsored fanfare.

This new style of journalism was much admired by William Randolph Hearst. The California native began his newspaper empire with the *San Francisco Examiner*, which was owned by his father. Hearst acquired the *New York Journal* in 1895, by which time Pulitzer had headed the *New York World* for 12 years. Almost immediately after Hearst's entry into the market, the two papers engaged in a circulation war in which each owner sought to out-sensationalize the other. Hearst hired away several of the *World's* star reporters, and both papers cut prices to a penny. Their stories and stunts were a significant cause of the furor that led the U.S. into the Spanish-American War in 1898.

This style of rabid sensationalism was dubbed "yellow journalism," a term derived from a comic strip called "The Yellow Kid" that, naturally, both papers believed was their sole right to publish. Still, such journalism sold, and both newspapers regularly sold more than 1 million copies per day. (Only four contemporary newspapers—*USA Today*, *The Wall Street Journal*, *The New York Times*, and the *Los Angeles Times*—exceed or approach that mark.) Some newspapers, such as *The New York Times*, disdained "yellow" tactics, and eventually Pulitzer tired of them as well.

Consolidation

The first half of the 20th century saw a steep decline in the number of American newspapers, a trend caused by attrition and by the development of corporations that owned papers in many cities. Scripps-Howard, another media behemoth, boasted 25 newspapers by 1929. Hearst eventually accrued 20 daily newspapers in the U.S., plus some Sunday editions, as well as magazines, a newsreel operation, and other interests.

Newspaper Advertising Expenditures
(including national, retail and classifieds)

Year	Amount
1950	$2.0 billion
1960	$3.6 billion
1970	$5.7 billion
1980	$14.8 billion
1990	$32.3 billion
2000	$48.7 billion
2003	$44.9 billion (projected)

Source: Newspaper Association of America

Consolidation may have been good for the owners of the media outlets, but not necessarily for the readers. This limitation of viewpoints prompted New Yorker columnist A.J. Liebling to famously quip, in 1961, "Freedom of the press is guaranteed only to those who own one."

In the second half of the 20th century, newspapers's adversarial role with the government became more controversial. *The New York Times* won a Supreme Court battle to publish the Pentagon Papers, top secret government documents, in 1971. The next year, *Washington Post* reporters Robert Woodward and Carl Bernstein wrote a series on the Watergate scandal that is credited with leading to the resignation of President Richard Nixon. About the same time, in an effort to attract more readers, many newspapers expanded beyond hard news, adding sections to covering fashion, food, science, home design, real estate, and other lifestyle topics.

In recent years, the growth of television and the rise of the Internet have reduced both the number of papers and their circulation. In 1960 there were 1,763 daily newspapers in the U.S., with a circulation of 58.9 million. By 2002, those numbers had dwindled to 1,457 daily papers with a circulation of 55.2 million. Newspapers still attract

Top 10 Newspapers by Reported Circulation
(as of March 31, 2004)

Paper	Owner	Circulation
1. *USA Today*	Gannett	2,635,412
2. *The Wall Street Journal*	Dow Jones	2,101,017
3. *New York Times*	New York Times Co.	1,677,003
4. *Los Angeles Times*	Tribune Publishing Co.	1,392,672
5. *The Washington Post*	Washington Post Co.	1,025,579
6. *Chicago Tribune*	Tribune Publishing Co.	1,002,398
7. *New York Daily News*	New York Daily News	802,103
8. *Denver Post/ Rocky Mountain News*	E.W. Scripps	783,274
9. *Philadelphia Inquirer*	Knight Ridder	769,257
10. *Dallas Morning News*	Belo Corporation	755,912

Source: Audit Bureau of Circulations

a well-educated, affluent customer—about 60 percent of daily readers are college educated and earn more than $75,000. But they are having a hard time reaching new, younger readers who get their news for free on the Internet, if they read news at all. In an effort to attract the 18–34 year old crowd, some newspapers have started publishing special editions aimed at the MTV generation. In Chicago, Dallas, Boston and New York, free daily newspapers with snazzy graphics, pretty pictures and nuggets of news are distributed on the street. Several other papers have hired young, hip reporters to cover culture and entertainment with a nod toward Gen X and Y. Sections with weather reports, movie listings, sports scores, and consumer advice have all been beefed up.

As circulation declined newspapers became more and more dependent on advertising for their revenues (see table), particularly from local sources.

Today, both national and regional daily newspapers are owned by large media conglomerates. Such entities as Gannett, Knight Ridder, Tribune Co. and The New York Times Company own a number of the top newspapers in the U.S. The Tribune Co., for example, owns the *Los Angeles Times*, the *Chicago Tribune* and *Newsday*, a New York daily, plus other papers. News Corporation, the parent of Fox Entertainment Group, publishes numerous English-language newspapers, including the *New York Post.*

With the advent of the Internet, modern technology has provided yet another means for newspapers, media companies, and advertisers to reach their customers. Instead of being obliterated by the digital age, however, newspapers have adapted to it, and most major papers provide much of their content online.

Magazines

The first magazines, single sheets covered front and back with opinion, gossip, and shipping news, circulated in the coffeehouses of early 18th century London. Such literary giants as Daniel Defoe (*The Review*, 1704–13) and Samuel Johnson (*The Rambler*, 1750–52) wrote and edited some of these publications. The most successful practitioners of the trade were Joseph Addison (1672–1719) and Sir Richard Steele (1672–1729), who collaborated on *The Tatler* (1709–11) and *The Spectator* (1711–14). Most of the copy for these early periodicals was written by the editors themselves.

Inspired by their linguistic cousins across the Atlantic, colonial Americans started their own magazines. Benjamin Franklin's *General Magazine* published poetry and political articles, among other things, but ended its run in 1741 after only six issues.

The 19th Century

Only in the mid-19th century did magazines take on their modern form. These magazines presented more opinion and culturally focused content than newspapers, and they also targeted the wealthy, literate class. Among the more noteworthy magazines were *The Knickerbocker*, which ran from 1833 to 1865, and *Harper's Magazine*, which debuted in 1850. Harper's serialized stories and novels from prominent authors including Charles Dickens and William Makepeace Thackeray. *The Atlantic Monthly*, launched in 1857, was notable for commissioning short stories by Mark Twain and Bret Harte. Both the *Atlantic Monthly* and *Harper's* are still published today.

The advances in technology brought about by the Industrial Revolution greatly affected the magazine trade. Improved machinery and more efficient production allowed publishers to print their magazines at a lower cost. This meant magazines could be sold for lower prices and attract more readers. With more readers came more advertising, and magazines turned from organs of commentary for the upper class to periodicals of interest for the masses.

Other famous magazines of the late 19th century included *McClure's* and *Munsey's Magazine*, which were among the first to target the general public in earnest. Soon after its launch in 1893, *McClure's* published works by authors such as Sir Arthur Conan Doyle and Rudyard Kipling. The magazine later distinguished itself through its muckraking articles. Muckraking was the turn-of-the-century term for a journalistic crusade, particularly against large corporations. Ida Tarbell wrote several stories in *McClure's* in the early 1900's that painstakingly exposed the questionable practices of John D. Rockefeller's monopolistic Standard Oil Company, becoming one of the creators of modern investigative journalism. *McClure's* folded in 1929.

Stylistically, magazines of this time were rather gray, with few pictures and lots of text. As artistic techniques improved, illustrations began to break the visual monotony. Cartoons provided one of the chief methods of magazine illustration. Thomas Nast, the founding father of political cartoons, doodled for *Harper's* in the late 19th century. Nast was also responsible for connecting American political parties with animals, and for the image of Uncle Sam, the gray-bearded figure who is symbolic of America. The rise of photography near the end of the century provided a startling innovation that made magazines more eye-catching—an improvement not lost on advertisers.

The 20th Century

One group of prominent contemporary magazines trace their history to the early 20th century. Henry Luce and Briton Hadden founded a weekly magazine called *Time* in 1923; they followed this successful venture with a business-focused magazine named *Fortune* in 1930. Six years later came an illustrated magazine called *Life*, and these three publications formed the cornerstone of what is now Time Warner, one of the world's most powerful media organizations. The company added *Sports Illustrated*, one of today's top circulation magazines, in 1954.

The New Yorker is another contemporary magazine that dates from the 1920's (the first issue was published on February 21, 1925). Upon foundation the magazine's object was to concentrate coverage on New York City, but the *New Yorker* soon broadened its scope to include short stories, poetry, cartoons, and news in its content.

In the 1960's magazines also served as a laboratory for experimental styles of journalism. Several writers, including Norman Mailer, Tom Wolfe, Gay Talese, and Hunter S. Thompson, practiced an innovative form of writing and reportage that came to be called "New Journalism." It broke away from the patterns of conventional journalism because it applied the narrative techniques of novels to nonfiction articles. These techniques included a focus on capturing dialogue and the author becoming a participant, rather than an observer, in the story.

Magazines Today

High-quality color and photography may be the most obvious differences between today's magazines and their predecessors of a century ago, but the layouts of magazines have adapted to the behavior of modern readers in other ways as well; stories jump across pages, eye-catching sidebars break out related content, and numerous quickly-read items are packed together at the front. Advertising takes up substantial portions of magazines, not least because advertising accounts for a substantial portion of magazine revenues. In 2003 advertisers spent approximately $11.8 billion on magazine advertising in the U.S., according to media agency Universal McCann.

The contemporary magazine industry is remarkable for the number of niche publications that seek a very specific audience. In 2000 the U.S. was served by more than 12,000 magazine titles, according to *Advertising Age*, a trade publication. While a magazines such as *Time* or *Newsweek* targets a large general audience, thousands of smaller publications aim for a niche audience with titles ranging from *Luxury Pools*, to *Redneck World*, to *Budget Travel*. With the exception of the occasional mass market magazine such as *In Style* for women and *Maxim* for men, the almost 1,000 new magazines launched annually are usually small-scale ventures. There are also hundreds of trade magazines for every industry from media to machinery that concern themselves with a particular business.

Top 10 Magazines in Paid Circulation, 2003

Magazine	Average Circulation
AARP The Magazine	22.0 million
Reader's Digest	11.0 million
TV Guide	9.0 million
Better Homes and Gardens	7.6 million
National Geographic	6.6 million
Good Housekeeping	4.8 million
Family Circle	4.6 million
Woman's Day	4.3 million
Time	4.1 million
Ladies' Home Journal	4.1 million

Source: Audit Bureau of Circulations

MEDICINE

A Brief History of Medicine . . . 436

Medicine in Antiquity 436

Medicine During the Dark Ages 437

The Renaissance Through the 18th Century 437

19th-Century Contributions 438

20th Century Contributions 440

Disease. 442

Common Diseases 443

Times Focus: *Success Stories Abound in Efforts to Prevent and Control Cancer By Jane E. Brody* 448

Estimated New Cancer Cases and Deaths. 450

Times Focus: *The Hard Facts of Hypertension By Jane E. Brody*. 452

Well-Known Genetic Diseases 457

Selected Vitamin-Deficiency Diseases 461

Diagnostic Tests 462

Common Blood Tests 465

Medications. 466

Side Effects. 466

Commonly Prescribed Medications . . 467

Immunization 468

MEDICINE

A Brief History of Medicine

The practice of medicine began long before the advent of written records. Prehistoric people in every culture had ideas on the causes of illness, often placing responsibility on gods, evil spirits, or angry ancestors. To cope with pain and disability, they tried various remedies, ranging from magical incantations to rational strategies.

More than 10,000 years ago people practiced trepanation: a hole was made in the skull bone, possibly in hopes of alleviating the effects of head injuries or symptoms of mental illness. The Iceman, who lived some 5,300 years ago and whose mummified body was discovered in the Italian Alps in 1991, appears to have been familiar with a natural antibiotic. He was carrying the fruit of the fungus *Piptoporus betulinus*, which contains oils toxic to the parasitic whipworm *Trichuris trichiura*. An autopsy of the Iceman's body revealed that his intestine was infested with *Trichuris* eggs.

Medicine in Antiquity

Beginning around the time of the Iceman, civilizations formed in the Middle East and people started to use numbers, pictures, and words to record information. The scientific study of medicine began as slowly information was disseminated from one healer to another and from one civilization to another.

Mesopotamia Clay tables from early civilizations in Mesopotamia contain diagnostic treatises with subsections covering gynecology, pediatrics, and convulsive disorders. Skin lesions, venereal disease, and fevers were described, and some of the described treatments were similar to modern treatments for the same conditions. Surgeries were performed and the earliest known legal code, the Code of Hammurabi, composed by the ruler of Babylon around 1700 B.C., included laws pertaining to the liability of physicians who "used the knife."

Egypt Papyruses from ancient Egypt, dating from 3000 B.C. to 1200 B.C., include methods for diagnosing pregnancy and the sex of a fetus, accurate descriptions of diseases, and rational treatment of various diseases. Particularly well known are the Ebers Papyrus (ca. 1550 B.C. but possibly based on papyri dating back to 3000 B.C.), which describes a wide range of diseases plus more than 700 remedies, and the Edwin Smith Papyrus (also ca. 1550 B.C.), which details 48 surgical cases of wounds of the head and upper body, showing particularly astute knowledge of fractures.

Greece In Greece, nonmagic medicine based on empirical knowledge emerged around 500 B.C. Hippocrates (ca. 460–ca. 377 B.C.), today often referred to as the Father of Medicine, is credited with establishing medicine as a scientific undertaking. He wrote the first clinical description of diphtheria, recognized that tuberculosis occurs most commonly between the ages of 18 and 35, and stated "those naturally very fat are more liable to sudden death than the thin." The Hippocratic Oath, dating from around the time of Hippocrates, pledges physicians to do their best for patients, to avoid doing harm, and to keep secret information about their patients; it continues to serve as a code of conduct for today's physicians.

Around 300 B.C., the Greek physician Herophilus (ca. 335–280 B.C.), who practiced in Alexandria, Egypt, where dissections of human corpses were permitted, founded the first school of anatomy. He differentiated between sensory and motor nerves and established that the brain is the center of the nervous system. He made important observations about organs such as the liver and ovaries, and he invented a water clock to measure the pulse of arterial blood.

Rome By the beginning of the Christian era, the Romans had created a widespread empire that included lands from Gaul (France) through Greece and as far east as Syria. But the center of their empire, Rome, was crowded, dirty, and the frequent victim of epidemics of smallpox, bubonic plague, and other diseases. The Romans adopted important public health measures, building aqueducts to bring freshwater into the city and sewers to carry away wastes. Public baths were established to encourage personal hygiene and special buildings were set aside for care of the sick. War injuries advanced surgery: Roman surgeons could surgically reduce limb fractures, tie ligatures around blood vessels, and cauterize wounds to stop bleeding.

The most influential physician of ancient Rome was Galen (ca. 130–ca. 200). He used pulse readings in diagnosing problems, showed that different parts of the spinal cord control different muscles, and demonstrated that arteries contain blood, not air as had been believed. But his misconceptions were many. For instance, he stated that pores connect the two sides of the heart and the liver is the main organ of the blood system. In numerous writings on physiology, anatomy, disease, and drugs, Galen brought together his ideas and those of predecessors and contemporaries. For more than 1,400 years, these writings were considered infallible and were the basis of medical education in Europe.

Medicine During the Dark Ages

Following the collapse of the Roman Empire in the fifth century, medical knowledge withered in Europe. Religious teachings about the causes of disease—and about other knowledge—were paramount; questioning these teachings risked charges of heresy and blasphemy. Dissections of human corpses were forbidden and experimental investigations suppressed. The great pestilences of the period were considered the will of God. Infirmaries were founded, but they were crowded, unsanitary places where care consisted of little more than kindness to the dying.

Arabic Contributions Meanwhile, Arab physicians preserved, adopted, and expanded on the rational ideas of the ancient Greeks and Romans. Razi (Rhazes: ca. 860–ca. 925) was the first to write a scientific paper about infectious diseases and the first to describe smallpox; he used opium as an anesthetic, plaster of Paris for casts, and animal guts for sutures. His multivolume *al-Hawi* (Comprehensive Book) included all the medical knowledge of the time, including work handed down from earlier times. Another vast encyclopedia of medical information, the *Qanum* (Canon of Medicine) was written by Ibn Sina (Avicenna, 980–1037), who recognized that tuberculosis is a contagious disease and that some diseases are spread through water or soil. In the Islamic empire, medicinal plants were avidly collected; the number of drugs used to treat illness increased greatly and pharmacy became a separate vocation. Beginning in the late eighth century, hospitals providing both medical care and medical apprenticeships were opened in major cities of the empire.

The Renaissance Through the 18th Century

A revival of learning took place in Europe beginning in the early 13th century. Classical medical texts as well as works by Razi, Ibn Sina, and other Islamic scholars were translated from Arabic or Greek into Latin, and physicians such as Taddeo Alderotti (1223–95) urged their colleagues to read these texts. Major centers for the study of medicine opened in Paris and Montpellier in France and Bologna in Italy.

By the end of the 1400's the Renaissance was well under way. The invention of printing in Europe led to books on surgery and medicinal plants. Experimentation became more common, as did dissection of human corpses. Seafaring explorations also influenced medical history—for instance, a monk who accompanied Christopher Columbus described for Europeans how Native Americans smoked tobacco for medicinal purposes; sailors introduced smallpox to the Americas and brought syphilis into Europe.

Anatomy Medical knowledge increased dramatically as the modern study of anatomy began in the 16th century. Andreas Vesalius (1514–64) dissected human and animal cadavers, demonstrating that Galen's descriptions of human anatomy were based on the dissection of animals whose structure differs markedly from that of humans. In 1543 Vesalius published *De Humani corporis fabrica* ("On the Structure of the Human Body"), the first work to accurately illustrate human anatomy.

Gabriele Falloppio (1523–62), a student of Vesalius, described the tubes between the ovary and the uterus, now called Fallopian tubes, as well as previously unknown structures in the skull and inner ear. Bartolomeo Eustachio (1513–74) described tooth structure at different ages and the tube that connects the middle ear to the back of the throat, today known as the Eustachian tube. Hieronymus Fabricius (ca. 1533–1619) helped found embryology. He compared the anatomy of embryos of dogs, cats, horses, and humans, and was the first to describe the placenta. He also provided detailed descriptions of the semilunar valves in blood veins. This led to the discovery of blood circulation by his student William Harvey (1578–1657). Harvey's *Anatomical Study on the Movement of the Heart and Blood in Animals*, published in 1628, accurately explained that the heart pumps blood into arteries, the arteries carry the blood throughout the body, and the veins return the blood to the heart.

One of the most important medical tools, helping physicians understand anatomy and identify signs of disease, has been the compound microscope, invented in 1590. News of this invention traveled quickly, and curious people began studying ever-tinier structures. Marcello Malpighi (1628–94) discovered blood capillaries and nephrons (structures in the kidney where urine is formed). In 1655 Robert Hooke (1635–1703) discovered cells. In the 1670's, using single-lens microscopes he made himself, Antoni van Leeuwenhoek (1632–1723) became the first person to see blood cells, sperm cells, and one-celled organisms.

Understanding normal anatomy led to the scientific study of diseased organs. This field of pathological anatomy was founded by Giovanni Morgagni (1682–1771), who carefully related his postmortem findings to detailed clinical records of patients' symptoms. Symptoms came to be viewed as "the cry of the suffering organs" and people with a technical bent looked for ways to detect organ abnormalities in living patients. In a 1761 paper, Leopold Auenbrugger (1722–1809), who recognized that the sounds of lungs full of air differ from those of lungs containing fluid, introduced percussion—tapping on a patient's chest and listening to the resulting sounds. In the early 1800's René Laënnec (1781–1826) invented the stethoscope to detect abnormal heartbeats and other chest sounds.

Study of Disease Interest in epidemiology—the causes of disease—developed, nurtured by the epidemics of plague and other diseases that killed huge numbers of Europeans during this period. Paracelsus (Theophrastus Bombastus von Hohenheim, 1493–1541) attacked the widely held belief, handed down from ancient Greece, that disease results from internal disturbances of four bodily "humors" (blood, phlegm, yellow bile, and black bile). He stated that external agents cause disease; for example, in his *On Diseases of Miners*—the earliest book on occupational diseases—he wrote that inhaling metallic dust causes silicosis ("miner's disease"). Paracelsus also pioneered the use of chemicals to fight diseases, advocating the use of specific medicines for specific diseases.

The 1546 work *De contagione et contagiosis morbis* ("On Contagion and Contagious Diseases") by Girolamo Fracastoro (1483–1553) proposed that epidemic diseases are spread by tiny particles, with contagion occurring by either direct contact, indirect contact via infected items, or without contact from a distance. Fracastoro also identified typhus and gave syphilis its name.

Physiology Modern physiology began with Harvey's discovery of blood circulation. Also in the 17th century, men such as Thomas Wharton (1614–73) and Regnier de Graaf (1641–73) initiated the study of glands and their secretions. Around 1670 Thomas Willis (1621–75) was the first to recognize diabetes mellitus when he noted that patients whose urine has a sweet taste suffer from fatigue and other symptoms. Later, Luigi Galvani (1737–98) showed that nerves conduct electricity and that electric stimuli cause muscle contractions. Antoine Lavoisier (1743–94) studied breathing, proving that muscles need less oxygen at rest than when working.

Improved treatment The 18th century saw the rise of modern hospitals, establishment of the first medical school in what would become the United States, and introduction of new medical practices and technologies. John Floyer (1649–1734) introduced the concept of measuring the pulse and created a special watch for this purpose. Dominique Amel (1679–1730) invented the fine-point syringe. James Lind (1716–94) found that ingesting lemon juice could prevent and cure scurvy. William Withering (1741–99) discovered the value of digitalis in treating edema and suggested its efficacy in treating heart disease. One of the most far-reaching advancements in the fight against disease occurred in 1796, when Edward Jenner (1749–1823) used fluid from a cowpox infection to give a young boy immunity against smallpox—a technique that Jenner called vaccination.

19th-Century Contributions

Medical advances occurred on many fronts during the 19th century. Of fundamental importance was the growing effect on medicine of the scientific method: observing a phenomenon, forming a hypothesis or possible explanation of the phenomenon, designing experiments to test the hypothesis, carefully observing and studying the experimental results to determine if they support the hypothesis—and if not, why not. As a result, many long-used remedies were found worthless or too harmful and were discarded; the use of addictive opium to soothe pain and the use of poisonous mercury to cure syphilis are examples.

The connection between filth and disease was firmly established, leading to improved sanitation and other public health measures. John Snow (1813–58) traced a number of cholera cases to a specific water pump in London—the first time that water pollution was proven to cause illness. More and more communities began treating water supplies with chlorine, first used to purify water in 1800.

The germ theory of disease, which holds that bacteria and other microbes ("germs") cause infectious diseases, was established independently by Louis Pasteur (1822–95) and Robert Koch (1843–1910) in the 1870's. This soon led to isolation of the causative agents of diphtheria, gonorrhea, tuberculosis, cholera, and other scourges—and sounded the death knell for theories that ascribed disease to such factors as spontaneous generation and alien spirits.

In 1892 came the first indication that some agents of disease are smaller than bacteria—indeed, so small that they cannot be seen with light microscopes. The discovery was confirmed in 1898 by Martinus Beijerinck (1851–1931), who named the agents "filterable viruses."

Diagnostic advances Diagnoses became more accurate as physicians applied new knowledge of human anatomy and physiology. In the 19th century scientists recognized that all organisms are composed of cells. Charles Bell (1774–1842) discovered the functions of nerves and showed that a nerve is not a single unit but a collection of filaments within a common sheath. William Beaumont (1785–1853) experimentally studied digestion in the exposed stomach of a wounded man, greatly advancing understanding of the process. Thomas Addison (1793–1860) helped found endocrinology when he reported that a form of anemia (now called pernicious anemia) was related to a fatal disease of the adrenal glands—the first time that anyone demonstrated that the adrenals are necessary for life. Jean Pierre Flourens (1794–1867) discovered the functions of the cerebellum and Paul Broca (1824–80) discovered the part of the brain that controls speech.

Claude Bernard (1813–78), often considered the founder of experimental medicine, investigated carbohydrate metabolism, discovering the ability of the liver to change glycogen to sugar and showing that blockage of the pancreatic duct prevents digestion of fats. Bernard also found that oxygen is not carried in solution in the blood but is bound to the red blood cells. He also proposed that in order to survive, a body maintains a stable internal environment even though external conditions change, a concept later termed *homeostasis*.

Numerous diseases, both acute and chronic, were carefully described for the first time: "shaking palsy" by James Parkinson (1755–1824), for whom the disease is now named; the facial paralysis now known as Bell's palsy, by Charles Bell; hemophilia, by Johann Schonlein (1793–1864); Hodgkin's disease, a cancer of the lymph nodes, by Thomas Hodgkin (1798–1866); and so on.

New tools New tools included the stethoscope, invented by René Laënnec (1781–1826) in 1816 and used to investigate the lungs and heart; the ophthalmoscope, invented independently by Charles Babbage (1792–1871) and Herman Helmholtz (1821–94) in mid-century and used to view the interior of the eye; and the sphygmograph, the predecessor of the modern sphygmometer, used to measure blood pressure, invented by Etienne-Jules Marey (1830–1904) in 1863. Endoscopy, or passing an instrument into a hollow organ in order to view its interior, had its beginnings in 1877 with the invention of a cystoscope to view the urinary bladder; candlelight was its source of illumination.

Until the 1860's, doctors used very long thermometers to take a patient's temperature, a process that took about 20 minutes. In 1866 Thomas Allbutt (1836–1925) introduced the short, efficient clinical thermometer. Its use was advanced by Carl Wunderlich (1815–77), who showed that fever is a symptom, not a disease.

In 1895, as the century neared its end, Wilhelm Röntgen discovered x-rays and how the radiation could be used to create a "shadow picture" revealing bone structure. Medicine diagnosis was revolutionized, for doctors could now examine a patient's insides without cutting into the body.

A critical advance in medical treatment occurred in the 1840's, when doctors and dentists discovered anesthetics that deadened pain without causing harmful side effects. In 1842 Crawford Long (1815–78) painlessly removed a tumor from a patient's neck after the patient sniffed ether. In 1844 Horace Wells (1815–48) used nitrous oxide as an anesthetic in dentistry. In 1847 James Young Simpson (1811–70) discovered the anesthetic properties of chloroform and began using the substance to relieve the pain women experience during childbirth.

Illness and death in hospitals decreased markedly with the introduction of antiseptic practices. In 1847 Ignaz Semmelweiss (1818–65) ordered doctors to wash their hands in a chlorine solution before each examination of a patient. In the late 1860's Joseph Lister (1827–1912) introduced the use of carbolic acid on surgical instruments, wounds, and bandages, decreasing the death rate in his surgery from 49 percent to about 15 percent. Around 1890 William Halsted (1852–1922) introduced the practice of wearing sterilized rubber gloves during surgery.

Elucidation of the germ theory of disease led to the development of vaccines for diseases other than smallpox. In 1879 Louis Pasteur accidentally discovered that bacteria could be weakened, which prevents them from causing disease but still enables them to trigger immunity in infected individuals. Using weakened anthrax bacteria taken from the blood of diseased animals, Pasteur developed the first artificially produced vaccine in 1881. Vaccines for rabies (1885), cholera (1893), plague (1897), and typhoid (1897) soon followed.

Chewing willow bark had been a successful method of combating fever for more than 2,000 years. Starting in 1838, chemists tried to produce a safe derivative of the active ingredient. Success came in 1893, when Felix Hoffmann (1868–1946) found acetylsalicylate. His employer, the Bayer pharmaceutical company, named the new drug "aspirin" and began selling it in 1899. Other drugs in the physician's medicine cabinet included digitalis for heart ailments, amyl nitrate for angina, quinine for malaria, and sedatives such as chloral hydrate and paraldehyde.

20th-Century Advances

When the 20th century began, life expectancy in the United States was 47 years. By 2000 average length of life had increased to almost 77 years. This steady improvement was due largely to a decline in deaths during childhood, the development of drugs to combat infectious diseases, improved nutrition, and better environmental sanitation. Public health measures, including pasteurization, inspection of food supplies, and fluoridation of water supplies, also were of great value.

Basic discoveries Enormous strides in basic biological sciences—microbiology, biochemistry, genetics, and so on—coupled with technological advances led to explosive growth of pharmaceuticals and the development of new surgical techniques. For instance, the first indication that viruses can cause disease in humans came in 1901, when Walter Reed (1851–1902) and an associate proved that a virus causes yellow fever. Development of electron microscopes in the 1930's gave scientists their first glimpse of viruses, and tissue culture techniques enabled researchers to grow viruses in the laboratory, for drug testing, preparation of vaccines, and other purposes.

Another type of disease-causing agent was first isolated in 1982 by Stanley Prusiner (b. 1942). Called *prions*, these particles consist solely of a protein. For reasons not yet understood, they can be transformed into abnormal shapes capable of destroying cells. Prions cause spongiform encephalopathies, fatal diseases characterized by the breakdown of brain tissue. These diseases include bovine spongiform encephalopathy, popularly called "mad cow disease," and Creutzfeldt-Jakob disease in humans.

In 1901 Jokichi Takamine (1854–1922) became the first scientist to isolate a hormone, adrenalin. Isolation and, subsequently, synthesis made it easier to identify the roles played by hormones in diseases and led to improved treatments. The therapeutic use of hormones began in 1921, when Frederick Banting (1891–1941) and colleagues injected insulin, a hormone produced by certain pancreatic cells, into a person with diabetes.

In the first decade of the 20th century, scientists realized that certain "accessory food factors" are essential for good health. In 1911 Casimir Funk (1884–1967) found the first of these factors, B, and in a 1912 paper proposed the factors be called *vitamins*. The discovery of vitamins A (1913), D (1922), E (1922), C (1928), and K (1934) followed; it was shown that vitamin B actually is a complex of several vitamins, and synthesis led to widespread availability of the substances.

Rise of genetics Nineteenth-century developments in genetics went largely unnoticed until 1900, when three botanists independently rediscovered basic laws of heredity published by Gregor Mendel (1822–84) in 1866. In 1902 Walter Sutton (1877–1916) correctly suggested that chromosomes—discovered and named in the late 1800's—carry Mendel's "hereditary units," later named genes.

By 1911 Thomas Hunt Morgan (1866–1945) had discovered that mutations could occur in the hereditary material; by the 1940's scientists had established that all organisms as well as viruses can mutate. Meanwhile, other research demonstrated that exposure to x-rays, radioactive materials, and various chemicals increases the mutation rate. Scientists began identifying the connections between genes and disease. Today it is known that some harmful mutations cause disease while others increase susceptibility to disease or influence progression of a disease. Specific genes have been linked to illnesses from Alzheimer's disease to osteoporosis to Tay-Sachs disease; more than a dozen genes have been identified as being related to muscular dystrophy, and more than 600 cancer-related genes have been identified.

Genetic engineering, the deliberate alteration of an organism's genetic material, began in 1973. By inserting specific human genes into bacteria or yeast, it became possible to manufacture large quantities of important human compounds: insulin, for people who have diabetes; erythropoietin, for treating anemia; tissue plasminogen activator

(TPA), for dissolving blood clots; and so on. Researchers also took the first steps in *gene therapy*, transferring normal genes into the cells of people who suffer from diseases caused by defective genes. In 1990 a 4-year-old girl became the first person to undergo gene therapy, receiving a blood transfusion containing billions of cells with copies of the gene that would enable her body to made adenosine deaminase, an enzyme essential for a healthy immune system.

New medications At the beginning of the 20th century, pneumonia and tuberculosis were the leading causes of death in the United States. By the century's end, thanks to modern drug development, these and most other common bacterial infections had been brought under control, at least in the United States and other developed nations. Paul Ehrlich (1854–1915) helped found modern chemotherapy (the use of chemicals to fight disease) when he synthesized Salvarsan and in 1910 successfully used it to cure syphilis. In 1932 Gerhard Domagk (1895–1964) discovered that the red textile dye Prontosil protected against deadly *Staphylococcus* and *Streptococcus bacteria*. Prontosil was the first drug that could be used against a variety of bacteria; later, more powerful drugs, called sulfonamides or sulfa drugs, were derived from Prontosil. They would eventually be largely replaced by safer and more effective antibiotics.

The first antibiotic, penicillin,was developed by Alexander Fleming (1881-1955) in 1928. Its disease-fighting potential was recognized in the early years of World War II, and it saved the lives of many wounded soldiers. Today a number of penicillins are available, including ampicillin, amoxicillin, and oxacillin, and they are among the most widely used antibiotics. Other antibiotics include cephalosporins (for example, cephalothin), tetracyclines (tetracycline), macrolides (erythromycin), aminoglycosides (streptomycin), quinolones (ciprofloxacin), and glycopeptides (vancomycin). Unfortunately, bacteria evolve rapidly, developing strains resistant to one or more antibiotics and requiring researchers to search for new drugs to combat the "superbugs."

Other drugs added to the pharmaceutical arsenal included corticosteroids, to treat rheumatoid arthritis; antabuse, to prevent alcoholics from drinking; cyclosporine, to prevent rejection of transplanted organs; antidepressants and antipsychotics, for mental problems; and thrombolytic drugs to dissolve blood clots. Some new offerings actually were ancient drugs in new form. In 1950, for instance, reserpine was introduced for treatment of high blood pressure; the drug had long been used in India in the form of snakeroot.

New technologies Twentieth-century technologies such as computers, electronics, fiber optics, lasers, and ultrasound were all incorporated into medicine, making diagnoses much more accurate and treatments safer and more effective. Mammography for diagnosing breast cancer was introduced in 1913, the electroencephalogram (EEG) for recording brain waves in 1929, the heart-lung machine for performing open-heart surgery in 1953, the implantable pacemaker for regulating heartbeat in 1958, the CT scan for producing three-dimensional images of internal organs in 1972, balloon angioplasty for unclogging diseased arteries in 1977, and the lithotripter for breaking up kidney stones in 1980.

Successful transplantation of organs from one person to another began in 1954, when a team of physicians at Peter Bent Brigham Hospital in Boston transplanted a kidney from a young man into his identical twin. Two years later, the first successful bone marrow transplant took place, also between identical twins. Successful transplants of various organs between nonrelated individuals followed, including the pancreas (1966), liver (1967), heart (1967), lung (1983), and small intestine (1990).

Great advances also occurred in the construction of artificial body parts. Aluminum, titanium, plastic resins, and three-dimensional computer modeling were used to build sophisticated limbs and joints. An artificial kidney was first used in 1943, the first artificial heart was implanted in 1969, and artificial skin was introduced in 1981. As the century neared its end, artificial blood vessels were being successfully tested in dogs.

Alternative therapies Modern Western medicine has not been without its critics. Patients complain about assembly-line atmospheres in doctors' offices, improper or ineffective treatments, too many operations inexcusably botched, the debilitating side effects of many drugs, and health care costs that spiral higher and higher. In recent decades factors such as these helped fuel interest in alternative forms of medicine.

Herbalism, the use of potions derived exclusively from plants, has been practiced in China, India, and other places for thousands of years.*Acupuncture*, the insertion of needles into specific points on the body to stimulate and balance the flow of energy through the body, has been used in China for more than 2,000 years.*Ayurvedic medicine*, which focuses on natural diet, herbs, exercise, and such therapies as massage, has been practiced in India for at least 4,000 years. *Homeopathy*, treating a disease with minuscule doses of the natural substances that in larger amounts would bring on the disorder, was developed in the early 1800's. *Chiropractic*, manipulation of the spine to treat spinal and nervous disorders, began in 1895. *Biofeedback*, learning to detect and consciously control physiological functions, developed in the mid-1900's.

New scientific evidence supported the effectiveness of some alternative therapies. For example, acupuncture was found to ease chronic back pain and arthritic pain in some patients; migraine sufferers who learned relaxation techniques had fewer migraines and needed less medication to cope with their headaches. Physicians began integrating certain alternative therapies with conventional medicine—recommending biofeedback and stress-management techniques to heart patients, offering hypnosis programs to people who wanted to quit smoking, and referring patients to chiropractors and acupuncturists.

Current and Future Developments Humans continue to face major health challenges. Many infectious diseases have been brought under control in developed countries but remain huge epidemics elsewhere. Some of these diseases, such as malaria, tuberculosis, and dengue fever, actually are increasing and spreading to new regions. AIDS, Lyme disease, and other emerging diseases discovered only in recent decades have created new medical battlefields. So, too, has the growing resistance of ever-mutating germs to antibiotics; physicians have few weapons to combat once-treatable organisms such as *Streptococcus pneumoniae*, a major cause of bacterial pneumonia.

People are living longer, resulting in a growing incidence of arthritis, Alzheimer's disease, congestive heart failure, and other diseases of the elderly. High-risk behaviors such as illicit drug use and limited access to health care are additional issues. Preventable illnesses kill many millions of people annually. Tobacco use is the leading cause of preventable death in the United States, causing approximately 440,000 premature deaths annually. Globally, more than 6 million children under age five die every year from diarrhea, pneumonia, and other preventable diseases; they could be saved if malnutrition and poor sanitary conditions were eradicated and basic medical treatments were provided.

On the positive side, there is hope that some of the world's worst diseases may soon be brought under control. Under the auspices of the World Health Organization (WHO), elimination and eradication programs are in place for polio, leprosy, guinea-worm disease (dracunculiasis), river blindness (onchocerciasis) and Chagas' disease. Results have been encouraging. After the Global Polio Eradication Initiative was launched in 1988, the number of polio cases fell by over 99 percent—from an estimated 350,000 cases in 1988 to 1,919 in 2002; the number of polio-infected countries decreased from more than 125 to seven.

Greater emphasis on prevention has helped reduce the incidence of polio and other dreaded diseases, and should have an increasing impact on lifestyle diseases—lung cancer due to smoking, diabetes due to overeating, and so on. Better understanding of human biology, genetics, and psychology should lead to improved preventive measures, diagnostic tools, and therapies. Genetic engineering, computerization, miniaturization, and other technological advances also will continue to improve diagnosis and treatment.

Through past millennia, human life span has increased as people have learned how to prevent and treat illness. By the beginning of the 21st century, average life span had exceeded 80 years in some countries. There is much reason to believe that future medical advances will increase not only life span but also quality of life.

Disease

Disease can be defined as a disturbance or abnormality in which part of the body is not functioning properly, thereby making a person physically or mentally ill and possibly leading to death. The most common types of diseases include:

Infectious diseases, which are caused by viruses, bacteria, fungi, and other organisms, and transmitted from person to person—or from animal to person. Examples: common cold, influenza, chickenpox, measles, tuberculosis, AIDS.

Hereditary diseases, which are transferred from parent to child via the genes. Examples: Down syndrome, hemophilia, sickle cell anemia.

Degenerative diseases, which result from a general breakdown of body structures and natural aging processes. Examples: certain types of arthritis and cardiovascular disease.

Hormonal disorders, resulting from an insufficiency or excess of hormones—chemicals that act as messengers in the body. Examples: diabetes, hypoglycemia, hypothyroidism, Graves' disease.

Environmental diseases, caused by chemical and physical agents such as radiation, smoke, drugs, and poisons. Examples: allergies, asbestosis, bysinosis, lead poisoning.

Deficiency diseases, caused by the lack of vitamins or other essential nutrients. Examples: beriberi, scurvy, pellagra, rickets.

Mental and emotional illnesses, caused by chemical, genetic, and environmental factors. Examples: anxiety, bipolar disorder, dementia, schizophrenia.

Frequently, two or more factors are responsible for a disease or its progression. For instance, when a person who smokes and is a heavy drinker develops throat cancer, it is probable that the cancer was caused by both tobacco and alcohol. A study in India reported in 2003 found that smokers are four times as likely as nonsmokers to die of tuberculosis.

The most common disease is cardiovascular disease. The World Health Organization (WHO) estimated that of the 56.6 million deaths that occurred worldwide in 2001, 29.3 percent were caused by heart attacks or strokes. In the United States, cardiovascular diseases account for about 40 percent of all deaths.

Some diseases have plagued humans since prehistoric times. Others are new. For example, in March 2003 WHO issued warnings of a previously unknown but deadly form of viral pneumonia; named SARS (severe acute respiratory syndrome), it appeared to have originated in southern China in late 2002; by mid-June 2003, thanks to modern airplane travel, the virus had spread to 30 countries, infecting 8,439 people and killing 812. Global transport of people and goods also accelerates the spread of diseases long confined to certain areas. By 2002 West Nile virus, a disease unknown in the United States prior to 1999, had spread to at least 39 states. Thirty mosquito species were known to carry the virus.

In *World Health Report* 2002, WHO identified the top 10 health risks in terms of the burden of disease they cause. These risks are responsible for more than one-third of all deaths worldwide. They are: underweight, unsafe sex, high blood pressure, tobacco consumption, alcohol consumption, unsafe water, sanitation and hygiene, iron deficiency, indoor smoke from solid fuels, high cholesterol, and obesity.

Common Diseases

AIDS Acquired immune deficiency disease (AIDS) is caused by human immunodeficiency virus (HIV). The disease was discovered in 1981 and the causative agent was identified in 1983. By 2003 an estimated 42 million people were infected worldwide and more than 20 million people had died of the disease. A United Nations report

Leading Causes of Death, Worldwide, 2001*

	Number	Percent
Total Population	6,122,210,000	
Deaths, all causes	**56,554,000**	**100.0**
Cardiovascular diseases	16,585,000	29.3
Infectious and parasitic diseases	10,937,000	19.3
Cancer	7,115,000	12.6
Respiratory infections	3,947,000	7.0
Perinatal conditions	2,504,000	4.4
Neuropsychiatric disorders	1,023,000	1.8
Diabetes mellitus	895,000	1.6
Maternal conditions	509,000	0.9
Nutritional deficiencies	477,000	0.8

* Estimates.

Source: World Health Organization, *World Health Report* 2002.

Leading Causes of Death, United States, 2001*

	Number	Death Rates per 100,000 Population
Deaths, all causes	**2,417,798**	**849.0**
Cardiovascular diseases	699,697	245.7
Cancer	553,251	194.3
Cerebrovascular diseases	163,601	57.4
Chronic lower respiratory infections	123,974	43.5
Accidents	97,707	34.3
Diabetes mellitus	71,252	25.0
Influenza and pneumonia	62,123	21.8
Alzheimer's disease	53,679	18.8
Kidney diseases	39,661	13.9
Septicemia	32,275	11.3

* Preliminary data based on estimation procedures.

Source: U.S. Dept. of Health and Human Services, National Center for Health Statistics, *National Vital Statistics Reports*, March 14, 2003.

presented in 2002 predicted that unless prevention programs were greatly expanded, AIDS would claim an additional 68 million lives by 2020. Sub-Saharan Africa has been the region hardest hit by the HIV/AIDS pandemic; more than two-thirds of all people with HIV/AIDS are in this region. In the United States, an estimated 900,000 people were living with HIV/AIDS in 2002.

HIV is spread through contact with infected body fluids such as blood and semen. Infected people may harbor the virus within their bodies for several years or even longer before developing symptoms of AIDS. Though symptomless, they can still infect others. Worldwide, most HIV transmission occurs during sexual relations between heterosexual partners. In the United States, the majority of transmission has been between homosexual partners. Transmission among drug addicts who share infected needles is another significant route of transmission in many countries.

In the body, HIV invades immune system cells called T-helper lymphocytes. The viruses reproduce in the cells and send out new viruses to attack additional T-helper lymphocytes. Eventually, the lymphocytes are destroyed, leaving the patient vulnerable to *Pneumocystis carinii* and other "opportunistic" pathogens.

No cure for AIDS is known. Researchers are working on preventative AIDS vaccines, but none are expected to be ready for market in the near future. Meanwhile, drug therapies introduced in the mid-1990's have been extremely effective in controlling AIDS progression for some patients. However, the medications are expensive, putting them beyond the reach of the vast majority of the world's HIV-positive people.

Allergies Allergies are overreactions of the immune system to foreign substances. Any substance that triggers an allergic reaction is called an allergen. Pollen, mold spores, dust mites, foods, medications, chemicals, and animal dander are common allergens. Allergens cause the body to produce and release histamine and other "mediator" compounds. These compounds affect local tissues and organs, causing symptoms of the reaction.

Symptoms may include itchy or blistering skin, stuffy or runny nose, sneezing, shortness of breath, red or swollen eyes, headache, swelling of the lips or tongue, nausea, vomiting, or diarrhea. If the release of mediator compounds is sudden or extensive, the allergic reaction may be severe, resulting in anaphylactic shock. Each year in the United States, more than 400 people die from

Discovery Dates and Effects of Human Pathogens

Year	Pathogen	Disease
1975	Human parvovirus B19	*Erythema infectiosum* (fifth disease), chronic hemolytic anemias
1976	Cryptosporidium parvum	Acute and chronic diarrhea
1977	Ebola virus	Ebola hemorrhagic fever
1977	Legionella pneumophilia	Legionnaire's disease
1977	Hantaan virus	Hemorrhagic fever with renal syndrome
1977	Campylobacter jejuni	Enteric diseases
1980	Human T-lymphotropic virus 1 (HTLV-1)	T-cell lymphoma-leukemia
1981	Toxin-producing strains of *Staphylococcus aureus*	Toxic shock syndrome
1982	Escherichia coli O157:H7	Hemorrhagic colitis; hemolytic uremic syndrome
1982	HTLV-II	Hairy cell leukemia
1982	Borrelia burgdorferi	Lyme disease
1983	Human immunodeficiency virus (HIV)	AIDS (acquired immune deficiency syndrome)
1983	Helicobacter pylori	Peptic ulcer disease
1988	Hepatitis E	Enterically transmitted non-A, non-B hepatitis
1992	Vibrio cholerae O139	Epidemic cholera
1992	Bartonella henselae	Cat-scratch disease (bacillary angiomatosis)
1995	Hepatitis G virus	Parenterally transmitted non-A, non-B hepatitis
1997	Avian influenza, type A (H5N1)	Influenza
2003	SARS virus	SARS (severe acute respiratory syndrome)

allergic reactions to penicillin, and more than 50 die from allergic reactions to bee and fire ant stings.

Measures such as staying away from poison ivy and eliminating certain foods from the diet can prevent many problems. Medications such as antihistamines and corticosteroids are helpful in treating allergic reactions. Prompt injection of the hormone epinephrine (adrenaline) can stop anaphylactic shock, saving the person's life.

Alzheimer's disease This progressive degenerative condition is characterized by forgetfulness in early stages and, as the disease progresses, increasingly severe debilitating symptoms that create demanding care-giving needs. In the United States, an estimated 4 million people, most of them elderly, have Alzheimer's disease, and the disease causes about 50,000 deaths annually.

The cause of Alzheimer's disease is unknown, but genetic abnormalities appear to play a role. There is a gradual degeneration of brain tissue. Areas involved with memory are damaged first, then structures involved with emotion and control of behavior. No cure yet exists. Treatment consists of alleviating symptoms and providing long-term care. Death usually occurs 10 to 15 years following onset of the disease.

Amyotrophic lateral sclerosis (ALS) ALS is a fatal disorder of the nervous system. Its cause is not known. It involves the progressive deterioration and death of the nerve cells that control the muscles. In its early stages, weakness in the limbs is the primary symptom. Gradually, cramping and twitching develop and the person has difficulty walking and carrying out everyday tasks. Weakening of muscles in the throat make speaking and swallowing difficult. When the diaphragm and chest muscles involved in breathing become affected, the person may require a ventilator. There is no cure for ALS; treatment consists of relieving symptoms and using physical therapy to slow muscle atrophy.

An estimated 30,000 Americans have ALS; about 50 percent die within three years of the first symptoms. ALS is also known as Lou Gehrig's disease because the New York Yankee star was one of its most famous victims.

Anthrax This infectious disease is caused by the bacterium *Bacillus anthracis*. People contract it by inhaling bacterial spores, touching infected animals or animal parts (infected cattle hide, for example), or eating infected meat; the disease does not spread from one person to another.

Early symptoms vary depending on the source of infection. Anthrax bacteria that colonize the skin form a dark sore. Intestinal anthrax induces vomiting and abdominal pain. Inhaled spores are the most dangerous; they cause breathing difficulties, change into actively dividing cells, and pass quickly from the lungs into the lymph and blood. Swift diagnosis and treatment with antibiotics are critical in preventing death.

Arthritis Arthritis is a generic term that encompasses more than 100 different diseases, all of which cause pain, stiffness, and usually swelling in the joints. According to the National Arthritis Foundation, arthritis affects nearly 43 million Americans and is the leading cause of physical disability. Although it affects people of all ages, it most commonly develops as people get older.

The causes of most types of arthritis are unknown, although certain factors—particularly excess weight and joint injuries caused by accidents or overuse—increase risk. Genetic factors can increase risk for some types of arthritis. The most common types of arthritis include osteoarthritis, rheumatoid arthritis, and gout.

Osteoarthritis is a degenerative disease that involves the breakdown of cartilage and bone, particularly in the fingers and weight-bearing joints such as the spine, hips, and knees. Treatments include regular exercise, medication, and if a joint is seriously deformed, surgery.

Rheumatoid arthritis, the most severe form of arthritis, is an *autoimmune disorder* in which the immune system attacks joint tissues, causing inflammation that can eventually lead to serious damage, including bone erosion and dislocated joints. In some cases, the heart, lungs, and eyes also are affected. Effects of the disease can be limited by regular exercise during periods of remission and by rest and anti-inflammatory medications during attacks. Juvenile rheumatoid arthritis is the most common type of arthritis in children. It often is mild, disappearing after several years, but serious cases can last a lifetime.

Gout results from an accumulation of uric acid in the blood, which leads to deposits of uric acid crystals in a joint. Typically, the first joint to be affected is the one in the big toe; other joints of the extremities—fingers, wrist, knee, and ankle—often become affected as well. Attacks, which last for days, can be extremely painful. Fortunately, gout generally can be successfully controlled. Uric acid is a waste product of the digestion of compounds called purines; avoiding foods rich in purines prevents or reduces the severity of attacks. During attacks, anti-inflammatory and corticosteroid drugs counteract joint inflammation and pain.

Asthma More than 20 million Americans are estimated to have asthma, an immune disorder that affects the muscles around the bronchial tubes leading to the lungs. In a reaction to certain stimuli, the muscles tighten, narrowing the airways and causing them to become inflamed and clogged. The person finds breathing difficult, and wheezes and coughs. In severe episodes, the person finds it almost impossible to breathe and requires immediate medical attention.

Most asthma attacks are caused by allergies to inhaled substances such as pollen, dust, and animal dander. Food allergies, infections, and emotional stress also can cause attacks. There is no cure for asthma, and proper management is essential. People with the disease can avoid substances and situations that act as triggers. They also can learn to recognize early warning signs and take medications to reduce underlying inflammation and prevent or relieve narrowing of the airways.

Autoimmune diseases More than two dozen known diseases result from immune system malfunctions that cause disease-fighting cells to attack the body's own tissues. What initiates such autoimmune diseases is usually not known. However, their incidence appears to be increasing, particularly in industrialized nations. In the United States, 14 million to 22 million people are believed to be affected. About twice as many women as men developed autoimmune diseases.

Symptoms of an autoimmune disease can vary widely, as can the disease's course. Some patients develop mild cases, while in others the disease causes severe damage and can be fatal. Mild symptoms may be treated with nonsteroidal anti-inflammatory drugs (NSAIDs). Stronger anti-inflammatory compounds, including corticosteroids, are prescribed for severe symptoms. Common autoimmune diseases include:

Addison's disease Affects adrenal glands; causes a deficiency of adrenal hormones, which can be life threatening if not treated.

Crohn's disease Affects intestinal wall; causes chronic diarrhea, abdominal pain, rectal bleeding; increases risk of colon cancer.

Graves' disease Affects thyroid; most common cause of hyperthyroidism, or overactive thyroid.

Multiple sclerosis Affects brain, spinal cord; causes partial or complete paralysis and muscle tremors.

Myasthenia gravis Affects synapses between nerves and muscles, causing muscle weakness.

Psoriasis Affects skin, forming red patches covered with white scales.

Rheumatoid arthritis Affects connective tissue, joints; characterized by pain, stiffness, inflammation, swelling.

Systemic lupus erythematosus (lupus) Affects connective tissue, joints, kidneys, blood vessel walls, mucous membranes (such as those surrounding the lungs); causes joint pain, skin rashes, chest pain, enlarged lymph nodes.

Cancer This group of diseases is characterized by the unrestrained growth of cells. Physicians describe the extent or spread of a cancer using a process called staging. This aids in determining the most appropriate treatment and in assessing the prognosis. One system widely used for many types of cancer classifies cancers into four stages. In this system, stage I is early stage cancer with no involvement of lymph nodes and no spread of the cancer from its original site (metastases); stage IV is advanced cancer, with both lymph node involvement and distant metastases.

Cancer afflicts people of all ages and races, although about 77 percent of all cases are diagnosed at ages 55 and above. Cancers vary greatly in cause, symptoms, response to treatment, and possibility of cure.

The International Agency for Research on Cancer estimated that there were 5.3 million new cases of cancer and 3.5 million cancer deaths worldwide in 2000. In the United States, more than 1.2 million new cases were diagnosed in 2002 and more than 550,000 people died of the disease. A U.S. male has a 1 in 2 probability of developing invasive cancer at some time during his life; a female 1 in 3.

Bladder cancer Smoking is the main risk factor for cancer of the urinary bladder; exposure to certain hazardous chemicals in the workplace also places people at risk. Warning signs include blood in the urine, pain during urination, and frequent urination. Early stage cancer can often be removed surgically. Additional treatment may include chemotherapy and radiation.

Breast cancer The most common, though not the deadliest, cancer among women is breast cancer. Risk factors include advancing age, obesity, physical inactivity, alcohol use, hormone replacement therapy, a family history of breast cancer, and inherited susceptibility genes, particularly mutated *BRCA1* or *BRCA2* genes. Early detection of the tumor—typically by breast self-examination or, more effectively, by mammography—is critical in improving a person's survival rate. Treatment options include removal of the tumor (lumpectomy) or the entire breast (mastectomy), radiation, chemotherapy, and hormone therapy.

Cervical cancer Sexually transmitted diseases (STDs), particularly genital warts, appear to be the major cause of cancer of the cervix (the lower opening of the uterus). Tobacco use and obesity also increase risk. The first noticeable symptom generally is abnormal bleeding or discharge from the vagina. Treatment may include surgical removal of the tumor, cyrotherapy (freezing the cancerous cells), radiation, and chemotherapy.

Colorectal cancer Major factors that increase the risk of cancer of the rectum and colon include increasing age, inflammatory bowel disease, and familial history of colorectal cancer. Obesity, smoking, physical inactivity, alcohol consumption, and high-fat or low-fiber diets also increase risk. Symptoms include rectal bleeding, blood in the stool, and lower abdominal cramps. Because symptoms generally are not noticeable until the disease is advanced, people age 50 or more are advised to have periodic fecal occult blood tests and sigmoidoscopies or colonoscopies. Surgery is the most common treatment; chemotherapy and radiation may also be used.

Leukemia Leukemia affects bone marrow, the lymph system, and other tissues involved in forming white blood cells, resulting in excessive production of abnormal white blood cells. The cause is unknown, though exposure to viruses, radiation, and certain hazardous chemicals (benzene, for example) increase risk. Common symptoms include fatigue, fever, weight loss, swollen lymph nodes, a tendency to bleed, and pain in the bones and joint. Treatment options include chemotherapy, radiation, and bone marrow transplants.

Lung cancer The leading cause of cancer deaths in the United States and worldwide is lung cancer. The great majority of these deaths could be prevented if people did not use tobacco. Initial symptoms often are not noticeable until the lung cancer has grown for five to 10 years; they include chronic coughing, shortness of breath, wheezing, and chest or shoulder pain. Treatment may include surgical excision of part or all of the affected lung, radiation, and chemotherapy.

Lymphoma Cancers that develop in lymph tissue fall into two main categories: Hodgkin's disease and non-Hodgkin's lymphoma. Risk factors are unclear, though viruses or other infectious agents are believed to play a role in at least some cases. The first noticeable symptom of lymphoma usually is a swelling of lymph glands; fever, night sweats, itching, fatigue, and weight loss also are common symptoms. Treatment may involve chemotherapy, radiation, and, in advanced stages, bone marrow transplants.

Melanoma This is the deadliest type of skin cancer, and it may also occur in the eyes and in other areas where melanocytes (pigment-producing cells) are found. The major risk factors include certain inherited characteristics (light-colored skin, blond or red hair, blue eyes) and exposure to natural and artificial sunlight. Most often, the first noticeable sign of melanoma is a mole that has one or more ABCD characteristics: Asymmetry, Border irregularity, Color variation, and Diameter greater than that of a pencil. If caught early, before it has penetrated deeper levels of the skin or spread to other parts of the body, melanoma is very treatable. Treatment options include surgical excision of the melanoma and, if the cancer has spread, chemotherapy, radiation, and immunotherapy.

Ovarian cancer Major risk factors for cancer of the ovaries include advancing age, familial history of breast or ovarian cancer, and the use of fertility drugs and hormone replacement therapy. The most common symptom is an enlarged abdomen due to accumulation of fluid. Treatment options include surgical removal of the ovaries and other female sex organs, radiation, and chemotherapy.

Pancreatic cancer Risk factors for cancer of the pancreas include tobacco use, advancing age, and obesity; pancreatitis, diabetes, and cirrhosis may also be factors. Symptoms usually are not noticeable until the disease has metastasized. Surgery, chemotherapy, and radiation may help ease pain and prolong survival.

Prostate cancer Increasing age is a leading risk factor for cancer of the prostate gland. Other risk factors are a family history of the disease and ethnicity—African-American men have the world's highest incidence rates of prostate cancer. Noticeable symptoms generally develop after the disease has advanced, and include difficulty urinating, pain during urination, and pain in the lower back, pelvis, or upper thighs. Treatment may include surgery, hormone therapy, chemotherapy, and radiation.

Uterine cancer Cancer of the uterus (other than cervical cancer) typically begins in the lining, or endometrium. The major risk factor is exposure to the hormone estrogen; obesity, diabetes, and hypertension also increase risk. The first noticeable symptom generally is abnormal bleeding or discharge from the vagina. Treatment involves removal of the uterus and perhaps

Success Stories Abound in Efforts to Prevent and Control Cancer

By *JANE E. BRODY*

Anyone who has recently lost a loved one to cancer may be inclined to think that little progress has been made in conquering this complex disease. That would be very wrong.

The advances in the last 50 years in understanding the causes of cancer and in detecting and treating it have turned many once fatal cancers into curable and, sometimes, preventable diseases.

In 1953, the American Cancer Society published what was to become an annual analysis of "Cancer Facts and Figures." It stated that the "only means of curing cancer are by X-rays, radium and surgery," that the cancer society was "studying the smoking habits of 200,000 men to determine if there is any connection between lung cancer and smoking," that "the number of cancer patients who were cured last year could have been doubled by early diagnosis and prompt treatment" and that "last year cancer took the lives of some 3,200 children."

Progress on Many Fronts Today, we know that cancer is not one disease, but at least 100 different diseases, perhaps even thousands of diseases, each unique to an individual. Accordingly, there are scores of treatment combinations, each created to cure or arrest a particular type of cancer. Treatments include hundreds of drugs, immunotherapy and advanced forms of radiation that are often combined with surgery to cure once-fatal cancers, including childhood leukemia, Hodgkin's disease, non-Hodgkin's lymphoma, melanoma and many formerly fatal cancers of the breast, colon and prostate.

Today we know that smoking causes more cancers than any other single factor and, nearly 40 years after this fact became clear, smoking still causes an overwhelming majority of cases of lung cancer, the leading cause of cancer deaths in men and women. Up to 90 percent of the 157,200 lung cancer deaths that will occur this year could have been prevented if people did not smoke.

Avoiding the primary cause of lung cancer remains critically important, because there is not yet any effective way to screen for early signs of the disease, which is usually not detected until it is advanced.

The cancer society's old recommendation for regular chest X-rays has long been abandoned as useless in screening for early cancer. Even with the most advanced treatments today, just 15 percent of lung cancer patients survive five years.

In contrast, amazing progress has been made in treating childhood cancers, although their causes remain a mystery. Even though far more children are alive in the United States now than in 1952, fewer than half the number who died of cancer that year will be killed by cancer in 2003, about 1,500 children from birth to 14 years old. Just since the mid-1970's, survival rates for children with acute lymphocytic leukemia, the most common childhood cancer and one that in the 1950's was always fatal, have increased to 85 percent from 53 percent. Cure rates for some less common childhood cancers approach 100 percent.

In another striking example of progress, as recently as a decade ago, the survival rate for women who developed inflammatory breast cancer, a particularly aggressive form, was only 15 percent. Today, with modern combinations of chemotherapy, followed by surgery, more chemotherapy and radiation, about 70 percent of women who develop this cancer can expect to beat it.

And for the more common forms of breast cancer, researchers have proved that the once-universal treatment, radical mastectomy, is in most cases no more effective (and sometimes less effective) than a lumpectomy, an operation that is much less involved, followed by radiation therapy and often chemotherapy.

Early Detection After cancer has escaped from its site of origin, the ability to cure it plummets sharply. Although some cancers are so aggressive that early detection may not be helpful, in most cases it is lifesaving. For example, when colorectal cancer is detected while still apparently localized, 90 percent of patients are alive five years later, and most are cured.

But after this cancer has spread to adjacent organs or lymph nodes, the five-year survival rate drops, to 65 percent, and when the cancer has spread to other distant organs, the rate drops, to 9 percent.

The statistics are equally striking for breast cancer. For women with cancer that is diagnosed as localized, the five-year survival rate today is 97 percent, up from 72 percent half a century ago. For regional spread at diagnosis, the rate is 78 percent, and for distant spread, 23 percent.

Half a century ago, the American Cancer Society, among others, said it believed, "Early curable cancer often betrays itself by one of seven danger signals." The society listed those as "a sore that does not heal, a lump or thickening, unusual bleeding or discharge, a change in a wart or mole, persistent indigestion or difficulty in swallowing, persistent hoarseness or cough, a change in normal bowel habits."

Now we know that these symptoms often signal, not early, but advanced disease. We know that in their early stages, most cancers cause no symptoms. Because of that, "early, curable cancer" requires submitting to regular examinations that can disclose footprints of possible cancers or even cellular changes that have not yet become full-scale cancers.

Perhaps the most striking example of this is the Pap smear for early detection of cervical cancer, once a leading cause of cancer deaths in women. The Pap smear can disclose changes in cervical cells that preclude invasive cancer, permitting treatment that prevents cancer.

Because of the Pap smear, the incidence of cervical cancer has declined steadily. Death rates have declined nearly 80 percent since the 1930's. Now precancer of the cervix is detected far more often than actual cancer. An estimated 4,100 Americans will die of the cancer this year.

With any luck, the P.S.A. (for prostate specific antigen) blood test will have similar effects. As a cause of an estimated 28,900 deaths this year, prostate cancer remains the second leading cause of cancer deaths, after lung cancer, in American men. Black men and those with close relatives who had the disease are especially at risk.

As with most other cancers, early localized prostate cancer usually produces no symptoms. More and more, it is being found when the blood test suggests trouble, prompting biopsies. Since the advent of the test, death rates from prostate cancer have declined. Today, 85 percent of prostate cancers are detected at localized and regional stages, and virtually all of those men survive their cancers at least five years.

Other common cancers that lend themselves to early detection include breast cancer (mainly through routine mammograms), colorectal cancer (especially through colonoscopy, which can detect and remove precancerous lesions, as well as early cancers), and skin cancers (through visual vigilance).

One of the cancer society's seven danger signs remains important to early detection, a change in a wart or mole, possibly signaling the start of a melanoma, the most deadly form of skin cancer.

Recognition of these changes and, sometimes, removal of moles even before changes occur, have resulted in the diagnosis of 82 percent of melanomas while they are still localized and have a five-year survival rate of 96 percent.

Another change is worth noting. Fifty years ago, one American in seven died of cancer. Today, it is one in four. The difference reflects two facts. The leading cause of death, heart disease, has drastically declined as a cause of death since 1970, especially in men, and the life expectancy of Americans continues to climb. With longer lives and more escapes from deaths from heart disease, more people will develop cancer, which is primarily a disease of older people, and die from it.

The job of conquering cancer is far from over, but to accomplish it will require the joint efforts of researchers, clinicians and especially every one of you.

other female sex organs. If metastasis has occurred, radiation and chemotherapy may also be used.

Cardiovascular disease Diseases of the heart and blood vessels kill more than 16 million people worldwide and account for 30 percent of the total number of deaths each year. Additional millions are disabled, frequently in their prime years. In the U.S., an estimated 61.8 million people live with cardiovascular disease. Heart disease and stroke, the main components of cardiovascular disease, account for nearly 40 percent of all deaths in the nation.

Decades of research show that lifestyle, beginning in childhood, is the main cause of cardiovascular disease. The major risk factors are high blood pressure, tobacco use, poor dietary habits, especially the intake of saturated fat, elevated blood cholesterol, lack of physical activity, obesity, and diabetes.

Lifestyle changes are the first line of prevention and treatment of cardiovascular disease. Medical interventions range from drugs to surgery. For example, a bypass operation may be performed to reduce a person's risk of a heart attack. In this operation, a blood vessel from elsewhere in the body is used to reroute blood around a blocked coronary artery (one of two arteries that arise from the aorta and supply the tissues of the heart with blood).

Atherosclerosis This condition is characterized by

Estimated New Cancer Cases and Deaths by Site and Sex, United States, 2003

Site	New cases			Deaths		
	Total	Male	Female	Total	Male	Female
All Sites	**1,334,100**	**675,300**	**658,800**	**556,500**	**285,900**	**270,600**
Skin[1]	58,800	32,300	26,500	9,800	6,200	3,600
Oral	27,700	18,200	9,500	7,200	4,800	2,400
Lung, bronchus, and other respiratory	185,800	102,200	83,600	163,700	93,400	70,300
Breast	212,600	1,300	211,300	40,200	400	39,800
Esophagus	13,900	10,600	3,300	13,000	9,900	3,100
Stomach	22,400	13,400	9,000	12,100	7,000	5,100
Small intestine	5,300	2,700	2,600	1,100	600	500
Colon, rectum, and anus	151,500	74,500	77,000	57,600	28,500	29,100
Liver and bile passages	24,100	14,800	9,300	17,900	10,500	7,400
Pancreas	30,700	14,900	15,800	30,000	14,700	15,300
Other digestive organs	4,500	1,400	3,100	1,900	700	1,200
Urinary (bladder, kidney, etc.)	91,700	63,300	28,400	25,100	16,400	8,700
Leukemia	30,600	17,900	12,700	21,900	12,100	9,800
Lymphoma	61,000	32,300	28,700	24,700	12,900	11,800
Multiple myeloma	14,600	7,800	6,800	10,900	5,400	5,500
Bone and joints	2,400	1,300	1,100	1,300	700	600
Endocrine system	23,800	6,600	17,200	2,300	1,100	1,200
Eye	2,200	1,100	1,100	200	100	100
Brain, other nervous system	18,300	10,200	8,100	13,100	7,300	5,800
Ovary	25,400	—	25,400	14,300	—	14,300
Uterus	52,300	—	52,300	10,900	—	10,900
Other genital, female	6,000	—	6,000	1,600	—	1,600
Prostate	220,900	220,900	—	28,900	28,900	—
Testis	7,600	7,600	—	400	400	—
Other genital, male	1,400	1,400	—	200	200	—
All other plus unspecified sites[2]	30,300	14,100	16,200	42,300	21,700	20,600

Note: Except for bladder, figures for invasive cancer only. Carcinoma in situ of the breast accounts for about 55,700 new cases annually and melanoma carcinoma in situ accounts for about 37,700 cases annually. 1. Melanoma and other nonepithelial skin cancers only; highly curable basal cell and squamous cell skin cancers account for more than 1 million new cases annually. 2. More deaths than cases suggests lack of specificity in recording underlying causes of death on death certificate. **Source**: American Cancer Society, *Cancer Facts & Figures*, 2003.

the deposition of fatty material called plaque on the inner walls of the arteries. As plaque builds up, the arterial channel narrows and blood flow is reduced. Usually there are no noticeable symptoms until plaque buildup is significant. Indeed, the first symptoms may be those of a heart attack or stroke. Treatment options include lifestyle changes, drugs to lower blood pressure or cholesterol, and surgery.

Heart attack A heart attack, or coronary event, occurs when the blood supply to the heart muscles is blocked. An uncomfortable pressure, fullness, squeezing, or pain in the center of the chest that lasts for two minutes or more may be a sign of a heart attack. Sweating, dizziness, nausea, fainting, or shortness of breath may also occur.

Many people who have heart attacks go into sudden cardiac arrest, in which the heart stops beating and begins to fibrillate (quiver). Unless its rhythm is rapidly restored by a defibrillator, the patient's oxygen-starved brain will begin to die.

Heart failure In this disease, the heart's pumping power is weaker than normal. Blood moves through the heart and body sluggishly, and pressure in the heart increases. The muscles surrounding the chambers of the heart respond by stretching, which keeps the blood moving but gradually weakens the muscles. The kidneys may then cause the body to retain water and sodium, resulting in fluid buildup in arms, legs, feet, or other organs—a condition known as congestive heart failure. Important warning signs of heart failure include swollen feet and ankles, fatigue, dizziness, rapid or irregular heartbeats, and shortness of breath. Heart failure often is a progressive condition, worsening over time and ultimately fatal. Treatment options include lifestyle changes, medication, and surgery.

Hypertension The pressure of blood against the walls of arteries is recorded as two numbers—the systolic pressure (as the heart beats) over the diastolic pressure (as the heart relaxes between beats). Normal blood pressure is less than 120 milliliters of mercury systolic and less than 80 milliliters mercury diastolic.

Nearly 50 million Americans have high blood pressure. If left untreated, high blood pressure can lead to strokes, heart attacks, and kidney failure. Conversely, controlling elevated blood pressure can cut strokes 35 to 40 percent and heart attacks 20 to 25 percent. Often, dietary and other lifestyle changes are sufficient to keep blood pressure controlled. If not, if may be necessary to add blood pressure medications such as diuretics, ACE inhibitors, beta blockers, or calcium channel blockers.

Stroke A stroke occurs when the blood supply to the brain is blocked, usually by a clot. The primary signal of a stroke is a sudden, temporary weakness or numbness of the face, arm, or leg on one side of the body. Other signals include temporary loss of speech, difficulty in speaking or understanding speech, temporary vision problems (particularly in one eye), unsteadiness, or unexplained dizziness.

Prompt medical attention may increase a person's chances of survival and limit the amount of disability. Treatment, involving drugs or surgery, is aimed at stopping the stroke and preventing another stroke.

Cerebral palsy This disorder is characterized by damage to the areas of the brain that regulate movement. It results from damage to the brain before, during, or soon after birth. Poor oxygen supply to the brain, trauma, severe dehydration, and maternal infections such as rubella are among the factors that may result in cerebral palsy, but often the precise cause of the damage cannot be identified.

The most common form of the disorder is spastic cerebral palsy, in which the arm and leg muscles become stiff and weak. In the ataxic form, the sense of balance and depth perception are affected, resulting in coordination difficulties and unsteady movements. The choreoathetoid form is characterized by abrupt, jerky, spontaneous movements. Some individuals have symptoms of more than one of these forms, indicating damage to more than one area of the brain; this is called mixed cerebral palsy. The severity of cerebral palsy varies greatly. There is no cure. Drugs, surgery, and therapy are used to minimize its effects.

Cholera The bacterium *Vibrio cholerae* causes this infectious disease, which is typically spread via contaminated food and drinking water. Cholera is rare in the United States but common in Asia, Africa, and Latin America. For example, an epidemic in Latin America during the 1990's infected 1.3 million people, killing 12,000.

Blood Pressure Guidelines for Adults*

Category	Systolic Pressure**		Diastolic Pressure**
Normal	Less than 120	and	Less than 80
Prehypertension	120 to 139	or	80 to 89
Stage 1 hypertension	140 to 159	or	90 to 99
Stage 2 hypertension	160 or greater	or	100 or greater

* Age 18 and older. **Millimeters of mercury. **Source:** National Heart, Lung and Blood Institute, 2003.

The Hard Facts of Hypertension

By JANE E. BRODY

Over the course of their remaining lives, Americans now 55 or over face a 90 percent chance of developing high blood pressure, or hypertension, a major risk factor for heart attacks, strokes, congestive heart failure, circulatory failure, kidney disease, and loss of vision. This finding emerged from a 22-year follow-up study of 1,298 residents of Framingham, Mass., who were from 55 to 65 in 1976.

If applied to the whole population, the risk of developing hypertension represents a huge public health burden, in addition to the costs to the health of those affected. Hypertension is a primary or contributing cause of more than 10 percent of American deaths each year. Complicating the picture is more bad news: of the 50 million Americans with hypertension, only 27 percent are receiving treatment that restores blood pressure to normal.

What Is Normal? Despite three decades of efforts to educate physicians and the public, there is still profound ignorance about what is normal blood pressure. And many physicians seem reluctant to provide adequate treatment and guidance. Your blood pressure should be measured at every visit to a health professional, regardless of the reason for the visit.

In most cases, hypertension is a silent disease, producing either no symptoms or symptoms readily attributed to other causes—headaches, ringing in the ears, lightheadedness, fatigue. The only way to be sure your pressure is normal is to have it taken.

The test is fast, cheap, noninvasive and painless. A cuff is wrapped around your upper arm, inflated to temporarily stop blood flow and then slowly deflated as the examiner listens through a stethoscope to your blood flowing through an artery just above the elbow, recording the number when a pulse noise is first heard and the number when the noise stops.

The two numbers, expressed in millimeters of mercury, represent the force of blood pushing against the walls of your arteries when your heart pumps, the systolic pressure, and when your heart rests between beats, the diastolic pressure. The final reading is the systolic pressure (the higher number) over the diastolic. Hypertension is defined as a systolic blood pressure of 140 or more, a diastolic pressure of 90 or more, or both. Both numbers are important; when either is elevated, so is the risk of developing heart and blood vessel disorders. Contrary to the practice of some physicians, bringing only the diastolic pressure down to normal is not enough to protect against complications.

Further, when a person already has a disease affected by hypertension, like heart or kidney disease, current medical guidelines call for lowering blood pressure even more, well below the 140-over-90 cutoff.

Finally, Some Good News How people live can make a big difference in their risk of becoming hypertensive. Several factors have already proved effective in controlling blood pressure. Other minor influences that can help keep blood pressure under control are continually being discovered.

First, the main actors: diet, weight control and exercise. In a major collaborative study sponsored by the National Heart, Lung and Blood Institute, the so-called DASH diet rich in fruits, vegetables and low-fat dairy products and moderate in fat, saturated fat, red meat, sweets and sugar-containing drinks not only lowered blood pressure, it lowered blood levels of L.D.L. cholesterol and homocysteine, each increasing the risk of heart disease. In a second study, a reduction in dietary sodium combined with the DASH diet was even more effective in lowering blood pressure than DASH alone. The DASH diet can also help prevent another major contributor to hypertension: being overweight. The third main factor in preventing hypertension, regular physical activity, can also help control the second, being overweight. Even among those who already have hypertension, aerobic activities like brisk walking, jogging, lap-swimming and cycling at least five days a week can reduce blood pressure. If nondrug measures are not enough to bring high blood pressure under control, there are now numerous effective and safe drugs that can drastically reduce the risks associated with this condition.

For more information, see the booklet "High Blood Pressure: What You Should Know About It and What You Can Do to Help Your Doctor Treat It," available on the Web at www.hypertensionfoundation .org.

Symptoms include severe diarrhea and vomiting. Without treatment, the person becomes dehydrated, which can lead to kidney failure, shock, and death. Treatment consists of antibiotics and rapid replacement of fluids. Cholera vaccines are available, but they provide only limited protection; they are not available in the United States.

Common cold More than 200 different viruses, about one-third of them rhinoviruses, cause contagious respiratory illnesses known as the common cold. Generally, an infection is short-lived, lasting about a week. Symptoms include a runny nose, sore throat, sneezing, and occasional coughing. There are no proven preventative measures and no known cure; over-the-counter cold remedies may relieve symptoms.

Cold viruses often spread as infected individuals cough or sneeze, releasing virus-laden droplets in the air. People become infected by breathing in the viruses or touching contaminated items (furniture, clothing, and so on) and rubbing their contaminated hands against their mouth, nose, or eyes. Frequent hand washing and keeping one's hands away from the mouth, nose, and eyes—where the viruses thrive—help reduce one's risk of catching a cold.

Congenital problems Congenital disorders are defects or malformations that are present at birth. In many cases, the cause is unknown. However, some factors are associated with an increased chance of developing certain congenital disorders. For example, alcohol or drug abuse during pregnancy or maternal viral infection can increase the risk of congenital heart disease. Down syndrome may cause congenital malformations of the heart or gastrointestinal system.

Treatment is based on the severity of the problem. Mild problems may not require any treatment; others may be treated with medication or surgery.

Dengue fever This infectious disease is caused by four different dengue viruses and transmitted by the *Aedes aegypti* mosquito. Symptoms include fever, headache, vomiting, and severe joint and muscle pain. Symptoms typically disappear within a week, and the disease is rarely fatal. No cure has been developed; treatment is mostly palliative—making patients as comfortable as possible and encouraging them to drink large amounts of fluids.

Worldwide, more than 100 million cases of dengue fever occur annually. Most cases are in tropical and subtropical regions, particularly Southeast Asia. U.S. cases are usually brought in from other countries.

As a result of an infection, a person develops immunity to the implicated virus. If the person later contracts a different dengue virus, he or she is at risk of dengue hemorrhagic fever, a much more dangerous disease that is often fatal, especially among young children.

Diabetes Diabetes mellitus is a group of diseases characterized by high blood sugar levels that result from the body's inability to make or use insulin, a hormone produced by the pancreas that plays a vital role in metabolism. Symptoms include increased thirst and urination, hunger, weight loss, fatigue, and blurred vision. Diabetes can lead to debilitating and life-threatening complications including blindness, memory problems, kidney disease, heart disease, nerve damage, and amputations.

The most common type is type 2 diabetes, previously called adult-onset diabetes. It usually develops because the body fails to use insulin properly. It occurs in people, including children, who are overweight; other risk factors include high cholesterol, high blood pressure, ethnicity, and a family history of diabetes. Treatment includes a healthy diet, weight loss, and regular exercise. Many patients require daily insulin injections.

Type 1 diabetes, formerly called juvenile diabetes, usually develops in childhood. It is caused by the inability of the pancreas to produce insulin. Genetic predisposition combined with exposure to viruses are the main risk factors. Treatment consists of carefully monitored insulin replacement, typically via needles or a special pump.

A small percentage of pregnant women develop gestational diabetes, sometimes labeled type 3, as a result of changing hormonal levels. Blood sugars often return to normal after delivery, but almost half of the women who experience gestational diabetes develop type 2 diabetes later in life.

Diphtheria The bacterium *Corynebacterium diphtheriae* causes this highly contagious infectious disease, which is spread mainly by coughing. Once a leading childhood disease, diphtheria is now rare in developed countries due to widespread vaccination.

Symptoms include sore throat, fever, coughing, and headache. As the disease progresses, tissues in respiratory passages may swell, making breathing difficult. The toxin produced by the bacteria may damage nerves and the heart muscle, leading to heart failure and death. Treatment consists of antibiotics to kill the bacteria and antibodies to neutralize the toxin.

Eating disorders Several mental health disorders are characterized by insufficient or excessive consumption of foods. These disorders are much more prevalent among females, particularly teenage girls and young women, than among males.

People who starve themselves because of a pathological fear of weight gain suffer from anorexia nervosa. Excessive weight loss and malnutrition result, and anorectics have many symptoms associated with chronic starvation, including low blood pressure, slow heartbeat, constipation, osteoporosis, weakened immunity, and failure to menstruate. Treatment is often difficult, and death occurs in about 6 percent of cases.

Bulimia nervosa is an abnormal, rapid consumption of large amounts of food (bingeing) followed by self-induced vomiting or the use of laxatives to get rid of the food (purging). The person may experience rapid fluctuations in weight, but the weight generally remains close to normal. Other symptoms may include swollen salivary glands, erosion of tooth enamel, dehydration, and electrolyte imbalances. Treatment generally includes psychiatric counseling to break the binge-purge cycle.

Binge eating disorder is characterized by eating abnormally large amounts of food, which leads to significant weight gain. People with this problem tend to be older than anorectics and bulimics, and their numbers are more evenly divided among men and women. Treatment consists of behavior therapy.

Emphysema This debilitating, often fatal disease is characterized by the enlargement and destruction of alveoli—the tiny air sacs that make up the lungs. This obstructs the exchange of oxygen and carbon dioxide with the blood, leading to coughing, breathing difficulties, rapid heartbeat, and—in advanced cases—mental problems. Smoking is the most important cause of emphysema. Air pollution also increases the risk.

Damage caused by emphysema cannot be reversed. However, regular exercise, medication, and giving up smoking can slow progression of the disease. A lung or heart/lung transplant may be used in certain severe cases.

Encephalitis Encephalitis is a viral inflammation of the brain. While some infections are mild, with few if any specific symptoms, others can be deadly. Early symptoms often include headaches, fever, and nausea. If the disease progresses, the person may suffer seizures, paralysis, mental confusion, and coma. Often the disease is accompanied by viral meningitis.

Mosquitoes carry some of the most dangerous types of encephalitis, including equine encephalitis, West Nile encephalitis, and St. Louis encephalitis. In other cases, encephalitis develops as a secondary complication of other viral diseases, including chickenpox, herpes, mumps, polio, and rubella. Treatment depends on the type and severity of the disease. It may include antiviral drugs and steroids to combat brain swelling.

Food-borne illnesses An estimated 76 million illnesses caused by food poisoning occur in the United States each year. Generally, the result is diarrhea and other temporary disorders of the digestive tract. But the illnesses can lead to more serious consequences, including about 325,000 hospitalizations and 5,000 deaths in the United States each year. People most at risk are pregnant women, children, those with compromised or suppressed immune systems, and the elderly.

Most food-related illnesses can be avoided—by washing fresh fruits and vegetables, cooking meat thoroughly, drinking only pasteurized milk, and common-sense hygiene.

Microbial contamination is the most common cause of food-borne illnesses. Pesticides, heavy metals, and other chemical agents that enter the food supply can also cause gastrointestinal, as well as neurologic and respiratory, symptoms.

See also *Prion diseases* and *Worms and disease*.

Genetic diseases Hundreds of diseases are due wholly or in part to genetic errors—mutations in genes that result in physical, chemical, or mental abnormalities. Genes work in pairs; in many cases, one form of the gene is stronger, or dominant, while another form is weaker, or recessive. If an individual inherits a mutated dominant gene or two copies of a mutated recessive gene, the result may be an inherited disease or increased susceptibility to disease. For example, Tay-Sachs disease is caused by a single recessive gene; the recessive gene must be inherited from both parents for the disease to develop. Although genetic diseases usually are inherited from parents, they also can appear as a result of a new mutation in either the mother's egg or father's sperm.

Abnormal genes on the X chromosome cause x-linked diseases. A female inherits two X chromosomes, one from each parent. A male inherits an X chromosome from his mother and a Y chromosome from his father. If the male inherits an abnormal gene on the X chromosome, the gene will express itself. Hemophilia is a well-known example. The genes responsible are located on the X chromosome.

A female must inherit two copies of a recessive form to develop hemophilia, but a male need inherit only one.

In some cases, genetic disease occurs because an individual receives an abnormal number of chromosomes (the structures on which genes are located). For example, in Klinefelter syndrome, a male is born with an extra X chromosome.

Often, multiple genes may be involved in any one disease. For example, more than a dozen genes related to muscular dystrophy and more than 600 cancer-related genes have been identified. Many disorders—autism, for example—are believed to have a genetic component even though this has not yet been proven.

Hemorrhagic fevers These dangerous viral infections are characterized by bleeding (hemorrhaging). Each is commonly linked to a specific geographic region. For instance, outbreaks of Lassa fever have been limited to West Africa, while hantavirus pulmonary syndrome occurs mostly in the western United States. As a group, they are most common in tropical regions. The diseases spread to humans in various ways. Lassa fever and hantavirus are carried by rodents and spread in their droppings and saliva. Ebola, an exceptionally virulent African disease, is usually spread via the blood or secretions of an infected person.

The first symptoms of hemorrhagic fevers are flulike, including fever, headache, nausea, and fatigue. The symptoms may be mild and taper off after several days or become increasingly severe. Not all cases progress to hemorrhaging. Fatality rates vary with the disease. Treatment is mostly palliative; maintaining appropriate fluid balance, blood pressure, and oxygen status is often critical.

Hepatitis Inflammation of the liver, called hepatitis, can be caused by excessive alcohol use or the use of certain medications. However, hepatitis usually results from one of several viruses, particularly hepatitis viruses A, B, and C. The disease can be acute (short-term) or chronic (long-term).

Hepatitis A is spread primarily by fecal contamination of food and water and through person-to-person contact. Inflammation lasts only a few weeks and may be asymptomatic, which makes its frequency difficult to estimate. People who have had the disease do not get it again. Vaccines are available to prevent the disease.

Hepatitis B is generally transmitted via contact with the blood of an infected person during sex, during birth, or through contaminated needles and syringes. It can cause a chronic infection leading to cirrhosis of the liver, liver cancer, liver failure, and death. A vaccine is available, and medical groups recommend that all newborns be vaccinated.

Some Food-borne Bacteria That Can Cause Serious Illnesses

Bacteria	Serious illnesses that can result	Foods in which the bacteria may be found
Campylobacter	Arthritis; blood poisoning; Guillain-Barre syndrome (paralysis); chronic diarrhea; meningitis; inflammation of the heart, gallbladder, pancreas, and colon	Poultry, raw milk, meat
E. coli O157:H7	Kidney failure, neurologic disorders	Meat, especially ground beef; raw milk; produce
Listeria	Meningitis, blood poisoning, stillbirths	Soft cheese and other dairy products; meat, including poultry; seafood; fruits and vegetables
Salmonella	Arthritis, blood poisoning; inflammation of joints, heart, thyroid, pancreas, spleen, gallbladder, and colon	Meat, including poultry; eggs; dairy products; seafood; fruits and vegetables
Shigella	Kidney failure, neurologic disorders, pneumonia, blood poisoning, inflammation of the joints and spleen	Salads, milk and other dairy products, fruits and vegetables
Vibrio vulnificus	Blood poisoning	Seafood
Yersinia enterocolitica	Pneumonia; inflammation of the joints, vertebrae, lymphatic glands, liver, and spleen	Pork, dairy products

WHO estimates that some 350 million people worldwide are chronically infected with hepatitis B.

Hepatitis C is spread through exposure to infected body fluids. Major risks include unprotected sex and sharing contaminated needles. No vaccine is available. WHO estimates that 170 million people are chronic carriers. In the United States, hepatitis C is the leading cause of chronic liver disease and the main reason for liver transplants.

Influenza Several types of viruses cause this highly contagious disease, commonly called the flu. The viruses are spread from one person to another via airborne droplets released during coughing and sneezing. They lodge in the lungs and breathing passages, causing fever, chills, sore throat, coughing, headache, fatigue, and weakness. Most symptoms subside in several days, but complications, particularly pneumonia, can occur. Treatment consists of bed rest and plenty of fluids; antiviral drugs may be prescribed.

Vaccination to avoid infection is strongly recommended for people age 50 and older; people with heart disease, diabetes, or immune system problems; residents of nursing homes; family members and caregivers of such individuals; and health care workers. Unfortunately, the flu vaccine only protects against certain viral strains; evolution of a new strain can result in a worldwide epidemic. One of the worst such epidemics, the 1917–18 "Spanish flu," killed some 20 million people.

Leprosy (Hansen's disease) Known since ancient times, leprosy is a chronic disease caused by the bacterium *Mycobacterium leprae*. Once widespread, the number of infected people has declined rapidly since the early 1990's. According to WHO, at the beginning of 2003 there were about 534,000 leprosy patients worldwide, primarily in the tropics; between 1 million and 2 million people were disabled due to past and present leprosy. Of the approximately 300 new cases of leprosy identified in the United States each year, the vast majority develop among immigrants who acquired the disease in their home countries.

Although infectious, leprosy is not very contagious. In most people, the immune system easily fights off the bacteria. Leprosy primarily damages the skin, peripheral nerves, eyes, and mucous membrane of the upper respiratory system, resulting in numbness, muscle weakness, blindness, and internal damage to the nose. Left untreated it can cause permanent disfigurement, especially of the face, hands, and feet, which historically cause people to fear the afflicted and expel them from society. Today, the disease is easy to treat with a combination of antibiotics.

Lyme disease Named after Lyme, Connecticut, where it was first reported, Lyme disease is caused by the spirochete bacterium *Borrelia burgdorferi*. It is transmitted to humans through the bite of ticks, including the deer tick *Ixodes dammini*. Its symptoms often mimic those of other diseases, and may include pain, diarrhea, nausea, swollen glands, difficulty swallowing, and coughing. A rash may appear several days after infection; the hallmark of Lyme disease is a bull's-eye rash—a round ring with a central clearing. As the disease advances, it may produce a painful joint condition known as Lyme arthritis.

Prevention includes performing tick checks after walking in woods and other areas infested with ticks. Vaccines are available, but they are not completely effective. Antibiotics usually cure the illness.

Malaria This infectious disease is caused by single-celled *Plasmodium* protists, including *P. falciparum*, *P. vivax*, *P. malariae*, and *P. ovale*. The parasites are usually transmitted from infected to noninfected people via the bite of female *Anopheles* mosquitoes; about 60 species of *Anopheles* can serve as vectors. The parasites take up residence in the victim's red blood cells.

The disease is characterized by episodes of chills and fever followed by profuse sweating; shaking and fatigue are other common symptoms. Repeated bouts can result in severe anemia, dehydration, and death. Infants, children, and pregnant women are at greatest risk of severe illness and death.

Treatment with chloroquine or other drugs that kill the *Plasmodium* has become more difficult in recent years. The parasites have become resistant to the drugs, and the *Anopheles* mosquitoes have become resistant to insecticides. Efforts to produce a malaria vaccine have been extensive but unsuccessful.

Malaria is most common in tropical and subtropical lands, particularly sub-Saharan Africa and Southeast Asia. It is both a cause of poverty and a result of poverty. Each year, between 300 million and 500 million acute cases are diagnosed and 1.5 million to 2.7 million people die of the disease. Almost all of the approximately 1,000 Americans who contract malaria each year get the disease while traveling abroad.

Measles (rubeola) An itchy rash consisting of small, reddish raised spots characterizes this highly contagious viral disease. Measles epidemics were once common, afflicting thousands of people, particularly young children, annually. Since the 1960's vaccination has greatly reduced its incidence, to about 100 cases a year in the United States. People who contract measles develop a natural immunity to the disease.

Initial symptoms include fever, coughing, a runny nose, and red eyes. Several days later the rash begins, usually on the face and neck and then spreading to the trunk and limbs. The rash typically fades in about a week. Treatment is palliative, keeping the patient comfortable while his or her immune system combats the virus.

In some cases, secondary bacterial infections or viral encephalitis develop. As a result, measles is sometimes, though rarely, fatal.

Meningitis This is an inflammation of the membranes (called meninges) that envelop the brain and spinal cord. It can result from a broad variety of bacterial, viral, fungal, and protozoan infections, including AIDS, brucellosis, cat-scratch disease, chickenpox, herpes, Lyme disease, malaria, mumps, rubella, syphilis, toxoplasmosis, trichinosis, and tuberculosis. The viruses that cause encephalitis can also infect the meninges.

Early symptoms include headache if the meninges around the brain are infected, and back pain if the spinal cord is infected. If the disease progresses, the patient may experience fever, vomiting, confusion, paralysis, and coma. Treatment depends on the causative agent and disease severity; it may include antibiotics (bacterial meningitis) or other medications.

Meningitis can also have noninfectious causes: brain disorders (cancer, multiple sclerosis, stroke), medications (including nonsteroidal anti-inflammatory drugs such as ibuprofen and naproxen), lead poisoning, and adverse reac-

Well-known Genetic Diseases

Disease	Cause	Symptoms
Cystic fibrosis	Mutated recessive gene	Glands produce abnormal secretions, resulting in lung inflammation, infection, and damage.
Down syndrome	Extra copy of chromosome 21	Physical abnormalities, mental retardation.
Fragile-X syndrome	Mutated recessive gene on X chromosome	Mental retardation.
Hemophilia	Mutated recessive gene on X chromosome	Blood does not clot properly; excessive bleeding from small wounds and increased susceptibility to bruising.
Huntington's disease	Mutated dominate gene	Deterioration of nerve cells in the brain, interfering with mental abilities and control of muscles.
Klinefelter syndrome	Extra copy of X chromosome in male	Problems with speaking and language skills.
Muscular dystrophy	Depends on the form; the two most common, Duchenne muscular dystrophy and Becker muscular dystrophy, are caused by a mutated recessive gene on the X chromosome.	Progressive weakening and deterioration of muscles.
Sickle cell anemia	Mutated recessive gene	Misshapen ("sickled") red blood cells, causing insufficient oxygen delivery to cells.
Tay-Sachs disease	Mutated recessive gene	Inability to produce a vital enzyme, resulting in progressive damage to the nervous system.
Von Willebrand's disease	Mutated dominant gene	Abnormal blood clotting, with excessive bleeding from small wounds and increased susceptibility to bruising.
Wilson's disease	Mutated recessive gene	Inability to process copper, resulting in progressive damage to the liver and other organs

tions to antibiotics, chemotherapy, and certain vaccines. These cases usually are mild and do not require treatment.

Mental illness

Among the commonest illnesses are those characterized by impaired psychological functioning and a significantly decreased ability to cope with emotions, thinking, and other basics of everyday life. According to the National Institute of Mental Health, four of the 10 leading causes of disability in the United States and other developed countries are mental disorders: major depression, bipolar disorder, schizophrenia, and obsessive-compulsive disorder. The institute has indicated that an estimated 22 percent of Americans age 18 and older—more than 44 million people—suffer from a diagnosable mental disorder in a given year. (see also *Psychology*.)

The causes of mental illness are gradually being identified. Some illnesses involve abnormal brain chemistry, such as an excess or deficiency of the neurotransmitter dopamine. Others develop after great trauma, such as that caused by child abuse, rape, or war. Genetics appears to play an important role and viruses are suspected of triggering or causing at least some problems.

Treatment generally involves medications, psychotherapy, or some combination of the two.

Anxiety disorders Excessive, chronic apprehension, tension, or uncertainty resulting from imagined or unreal threats are the hallmarks of anxiety disorders. The illnesses include general anxiety disorder, obsessive-compulsive disorder, panic disorder, phobias, and post-traumatic stress disorder.

Attention deficit/hyperactivity disorder (ADHD) ADHD is the most treated childhood-onset mental disorder in the United States, affecting an estimated 2 million children. Boys are two to three times more likely than girls to have ADHD. About half the children with ADHD retain symptoms throughout their adulthood.

Autism Evidence of this developmental disorder appears by the age of three. Autistic individuals have difficulty relating emotionally to other people, difficulty in communicating with others, and poor cognitive and language skills. They exhibit compulsive, ritualistic behavior and are easily upset by even slight changes in their surroundings or daily schedule.

Depression Depression is marked by feelings of extreme sadness, hopelessness, and inadequacy. Individuals often experience disturbed sleep and weight change. Most people who commit suicide suffer from depression.

Bipolar disorder, formerly known as manic depression, is characterized by alternating periods of abnormally intense elation and depression, with episodes lasting a week or longer.

Dissociative disorders Individuals separate, or dissociate themselves from, their identity and other aspects of their personality. They may have multiple personalities, each with its own set of temperaments, responses, and even memories. Dissociation is believed to be a mechanism for coping with physical abuse or other severe trauma.

Schizophrenia A loss of contact with reality, irrational fears, delusions, hallucinations, bizarre behavior, and a restricted range of emotions characterize schizophrenia. Both genetic and environmental factors appear to be involved in causing the disorder, with severity varying significantly among individuals.

Oral diseases

A normal person's mouth harbors some 400 species of bacteria, which combine with saliva to form a sticky, colorless film called plaque. The plaque accumulates on teeth and gums, as does its hardened product, tartar. This leads to tooth decay and periodontal (gum) disease. Many of these problems can be prevented by good oral hygiene, including daily brushing and flossing as well as regular checkups in which the dentist or dental hygienist removes plaque. Proper diet and avoidance of tobacco also help keep teeth and gums healthy.

Periodontal disease is the most frequent cause of tooth loss in adults. It is progressive; the earlier it is treated, the less the damage. In its early form, called *gingivitis*, plaque builds up along the gum line; toxins released by the bacteria cause the gums to become red, swollen, and prone to bleeding. In the advanced stages of the disease, called *periodontitis*, the bacterial toxins deepen the openings between the gums and the roots of the teeth, and corrode the bone and ligament that anchor the teeth in the jaw.

In addition, periodontal disease can easily release bacteria into the bloodstream. This can exacerbate problems in other parts of the body. For instance, people with periodontal disease are more likely to suffer a stroke or fatal heart attack than those without periodontal disease.

Other common oral diseases include small sores called cankers and cold sores. Cankers, of unknown cause, form singly or in clusters and generally heal by themselves. Cold sores, caused by the *Herpes simplex* virus, are highly contagious; acyclovir ointment fights the virus and aspirin or ointment containing benzocaine may help relieve pain. Trench mouth is a painful inflammation of the gums caused by bacteria whose rapid growth is triggered by stress, poor diet, smoking, or other factors. Treatment options include careful cleaning of teeth, painkillers, and antibiotics.

Osteoporosis This condition is characterized by a progressive decrease in bone density. The person may experience back pain, stooped posture, increased curvature of the spine, and an ever-greater likelihood of fractures. Osteoporosis is particularly common in post-menopausal women. An estimated 10 million women in the United States have osteoporosis; millions more have low bone mass and thus are at risk of developing the disease. Aging, physical inactivity, poor nutrition, smoking, and genetics are major risk factors.

Prevention should begin in childhood, with a diet containing sufficient calcium and vitamin D, both critical for building strong bones. Weight-bearing and strength-building exercises are important throughout life. Calcium supplements and certain medications help build and maintain bone mass. The drug calcitonin is used to treat osteoporosis.

Parkinson's disease This degenerative disease, which usually begins between ages 45 and 65, is characterized by the gradual deterioration of brain cells that control muscles. The cells stop producing the chemical dopamine, which serves as a messenger to transmit impulses from one nerve cell to the next. As dopamine production is reduced, the person experiences tremors in a hand. Tremors may gradually appear in the other hand as well as the arms and legs. As the disease progresses, muscle stiffness, difficulty walking, stooped posture, reduced sense of smell, and decreased facial expression become noticeable. About 50 percent of the people develop dementia.

The cause of Parkinson's disease is unknown. Nor is there a known cure. Treatment is designed to slow progression and reduce the severity of tremors.

Parkinsonism is a disorder with similar characteristics except that its causes are known. These include viral encephalitis, head injury, brain tumors, use of the illicit drug MPTP, and certain medications that interfere with the action of dopamine. Treating the underlying problem may result in a cure.

Pneumonia Various bacteria, viruses, and fungi cause this inflammatory lung disease. Common symptoms include coughing that produces sputum, which may contain blood; fever; chills; and chest pain. Severity ranges from mild to life threatening. For example, so-called walking pneumonia is a mild form of bronchial pneumonia that infects a relatively small area of the bronchi. In contrast, double pneumonia involves inflammation of both lungs. An estimated 2 million Americans develop pneumonia each year, and about 50,000 of them die from the disease.

Vaccines are available to prevent certain types of pneumonia and are recommended for people who are particularly susceptible to the disease, including individuals age 65 and older. Antibiotics are used to treat bacterial pneumonia but are not effective against viral pneumonia. Antifungal drugs are used to fight pneumonia caused by fungi.

In addition to microscopic organisms, pneumonia can be caused by inhaling food, liquids, or toxic chemicals. A common form of such aspiration pneumonia develops after a person inhales stomach acid during vomiting.

Poliomyelitis "Polio" is an infectious disease caused by three types of polioviruses that attack the central nervous system. The great majority of people who are infected are asymptomatic or experience only mild flulike symptoms that disappear in a few days and require no medical intervention. They are, however, a potential threat for others because polioviruses are excreted in their feces.

A small percentage of people develop major polio, with weakness or paralysis developing in certain muscles. Permanent disability can result, though often may be prevented or limited through an intensive program of physical therapy, to rebuild and maintain strength and muscle tone.

Polio is highly contagious and was once widespread in the United States. Vaccines introduced beginning in 1955 eradicated polio in the United States and the rest of the Western Hemisphere and are now part of routine childhood immunizations. Since 1988 the World Health Organization has led a worldwide vaccination effort to eliminate polio completely. In 2001 only 537 cases of polio were reported.

Prion diseases Misfolded proteins called prions appear to be the cause of a group of degenerative diseases of the central nervous system known as transmissible spongiform encephalopathies (TSEs). Prions are not organisms; they have no cell structure and no genetic material (DNA or RNA). They are infectious, however; prions can pass to humans and certain animals that eat the remains of infected organisms. The prions may incubate for years before beginning to destroy brain tissue, leaving parts of the brain porous and spongy and leading to dementia and loss of muscle control.

The best-known TSE is bovine spongiform encephalopathy (BSE)—so-called mad cow disease. In 1996 it was discovered that BSE can pass from infected meat to humans. The humans develop a disease similar to the TSE Creutzfeldt-Jakob disease (CJD), called variant CJD (vCJD). Other human TSEs are kuru, Gerstmann-Straussler syndrome, and fatal familiar insomnia. All are rare but fatal.

Rocky Mountain spotted fever Caused by the bacterium *Rickettsia rickettsii* and spread by ticks, Rocky Mountain spotted fever causes high fever, headache, fatigue, and a rash that spreads across most of the body. Approximately 1,000 cases are reported in the United States each year. If treated early with antibiotics, a patient usually recovers without serious problems. But if treatment is delayed, complications may include damage to the heart, lungs, liver, and kidneys.

Rubella Also known as German measles, rubella is a contagious viral disease that prior to the introduction of a vaccine in 1969 was very common among children. Its symptoms are mild and include low fever, swollen lymph nodes, and a rash. Treatment includes rest, fluids, and painkillers. Rubella infection poses serious problems for women in the early stages of pregnancy. The virus can pass through the placenta to the fetus, causing miscarriage, stillbirth, or permanent mental and physical disabilities in the infant.

Sexually transmitted diseases (STDs) More than 65 million Americans have an incurable STD. An additional 15 million become infected with one or more STDs each year, roughly half of whom contract lifelong infections. STDs are difficult to track, in part because many infected people do not have symptoms and remain undiagnosed, though able to infect others.

The most prevalent STDs are the human papilloma viruses, which causes warts and genital cancers; trichomoniasis, caused by a protozoan; chlamydia, caused by a bacterium; genital herpes, caused by a virus; and gonorrhea, caused by a bacterium. Syphilis is another STD caused by a bacterium, but the number of cases has declined significantly, and the U.S. Centers for Disease Control and Prevention hope to soon reduce cases to 1,000 or fewer per year.

People who have STDs have a significantly increased risk of becoming infected with HIV, the virus that causes AIDS, in part because they may have open sores that provide the virus with an easy route of entry to the body.

Prevention—practicing safe sex—is of critical importance in controlling the spread of STDs. Most STD cases caused by bacteria can be treated with antibiotics. There is no known cure for viral STDs.

In addition to STDs, some other diseases can be sexually transmitted. These include amebiasis, giardiasis, hepatitis, salmonellosis, scabies, and shigellosis.

Smallpox This is a highly contagious, deadly disease caused by *Variola* viruses. Its symptoms include high fever, headache, muscle pain, and a rash that develops into oozing pustules that contain viruses able to infect others. People who recover have permanent scars from the pustules.

Smallpox once caused deadly epidemics. In the 20th century alone, experts estimate, it took up to a half billion lives. But by 1979, due to worldwide vaccination programs, smallpox had been eradicated in nature. By 2002 the only known stocks of *Variola* were kept in research laboratories in the United States and Russia, although there are fears that samples may have slipped into the hands of other countries or terrorists.

Tuberculosis (TB) TB, which usually infects the lungs, is caused by the bacterium *Mycobacterium tuberculosis*. Except for young children, few people become ill soon after *M. tuberculosis* enters their body. Their immune system kills most of the bacteria. The rest of the bacteria are confined by white blood cells, not causing problems but remaining alive in a state of dormancy. In most cases, these bacteria do not cause any problems. But if a person's immune system is compromised by poor nutrition, unhealthy living conditions, aging, cancer, or certain infections, the bacteria may start to multiply; the person becomes sick and can spread the germs when he or she coughs or sneezes.

Left untreated, TB gradually destroys the lungs. Treatment consists of at least six months of daily antibiotic therapy; generally, this results in a complete cure. However, many patients stop taking the drugs after several weeks because their symptoms disappear. Not only do they risk developing active TB in the future, but they increase the likelihood that the TB they develop, and pass on to others, will be drug-resistant and difficult to treat. Since the mid-1990's, WHO has recommended "directly observed treatment strategy" (DOTS), in which health care workers watch patients take their medications to ensure the antibiotics are taken as instructed.

About 95 percent of the world's TB cases occur in developing countries, with China and India heading the list. Each year, some 8 million infected people become sick and nearly 3 million die.

Typhoid Also known as enteric fever, typhoid is caused by the bacterium *Salmonella typhi*. It is spread via food or liquids contaminated with the feces and urine of infected people. The disease causes flulike symptoms, including headache, joint pain, and prolonged fever. If untreated, complications such as pneumonia and internal bleeding may occur. Treatment consists of antibiotics. Although rare in developed nations, it is estimated that each year there are 17 million typhoid cases worldwide, with 600,000 deaths. Multidrug resistant strains of *S. typhi* have been reported in parts of Asia, Latin America, and the Middle East, where the disease is common.

Vitamin-related diseases Consuming too little or too much of a vitamin can interfere with cell building and other basic physiological processes, resulting in potentially fatal disease. For instance, a lack of biotin (a B vitamin) causes skin problems, nausea, and depression. Too much vitamin A can cause liver and nerve damage, dry skin, hair loss, blurred vision, and birth defects.

Vitamin deficiency diseases are most common in poor lands where proper nutrition is difficult to achieve. However, these diseases are not unknown in the United States and other developed countries. For instance, alcoholics are at high risk of vitamin B1 and folic acid deficiencies. Also, certain diseases such as cystic fibrosis and Crohn's disease interfere with absorption of some vitamins; this problem, like other vitamin deficiencies, can be resolved with vitamin supplements.

Selected Vitamin-Deficiency Diseases

Disease	Cause	Major Symptoms
Beriberi	Vitamin B1 (thiamine) deficiency	Muscle cramps, nerve or heart abnormalities; in advanced cases, coma and death.
Night blindness	Vitamin A deficiency	Difficulty seeing in dim light; can cause blindness.
Pellagra	Niacin (a B vitamin) deficiency together with a deficiency of the amino acid tryptophan	Rash and other skin abnormalities, diarrhea, nausea; in advanced cases, mental problems and death.
Rickets	Vitamin D deficiency	Abnormal bone growth, weakened bones.
Scurvy	Vitamin C deficiency	Swollen gums, loose teeth, infection, irritability, bleeding, anemia.

Worms and disease A variety of parasitic worms can take up residence in the human body. They commonly enter through the skin or via contaminated food and water. Depending on the parasite and the number of worms present, an infected person may be asymptomatic, have mild symptoms, or experience life-threatening difficulties.

Guinea worms The worm *Dracunculus medinensis* causes guinea worm disease, or dracunculiasis. People become infected by drinking water contaminated with *Dracunculus* larvae. In the body, the worms grow to adults up to 3 feet (90 centimeters) long. The worms migrate to the surface of the body and a blister and ulceration develop on the skin where each worm emerges. The person typically experiences painful swelling, fever, nausea, and vomiting. Ulcers often become infected with bacteria, which causes disabling complications. A worm can be removed surgically or by slowly pulling it out—a process that can take months. No medication is available to prevent or treat infection.

People in poor communities in remote parts of Africa are most commonly affected by Guinea worm disease. An international effort to eradicate the disease was begun in 1986. By 2002, as a result of educating and encouraging people to make the behavioral changes necessary to stop disease transmission, the number of infected individuals was reduced by 98 percent, from 3.5 million to 55,000 reported cases.

Hookworms An estimated 1 billion people who live in moist tropical and subtropical areas where sanitation is poor are infected with small roundworms of the genus *Necator*. Worm larvae present in the soil can penetrate the skin and travel to the intestines, where they mature; the adult worms produce huge numbers of eggs that are excreted in feces. Abdominal pain and diarrhea are common symptoms; however, many infected people are symptomless. Oral medications are available to treat the infection.

Pinworms Pinworm infection, or enterobiasis, is

caused by certain roundworms that live in the intestine. Infections are common among children, who typically ingest the worms when sucking their thumbs or eating food contaminated with fecal matter. Itching in the anal or vaginal area is the most common symptom. Infections can be cured with medication, but children are often reinfected.

Schistosomiasis Also known as bilharziasis, *schistosomiasis* is caused by several species of the flatworm Schistosoma. People become infected by swimming or bathing in contaminated freshwater. Once established in a person's body, the worms produce great numbers of eggs, which elicit an immune system response. This eventually results in internal bleeding and irreversible tissue damage. Globally, an estimated 200 million people are infected, mainly in the tropics and subtropics. About 120 million show symptoms of schistosomiasis, with 20 million suffering severe consequences of the infection. Treatment consists of daily doses of the medication praziquantel.

Tapeworms Several species of parasitic flatworms known as tapeworms can infect humans. The most common are the beef tapeworm, *Taenia saginata*; pork tapeworm, *Taenia solium*; and fish tapeworm, *Diphyllobothrium latum*. Infection—rare in North America but common in Asia, eastern Europe, and Latin America—can be prevented by prolonged freezing or thorough cooking of meat and fish. In the human body, the tapeworms attach themselves to the intestinal wall, where some species may attain lengths of 25 feet (7.6 meters) or more. Common symptoms include abdominal pain and diarrhea, but many infected people are symptomless. Treatment consists of praziquantel.

Trichinosis Larvae of the tiny roundworm *Trichinella spirali* live in the muscle tissue of many mammals. A person becomes infected by eating undercooked or poorly smoked meat, especially pork, from infected animals. The larvae mature into adult worms in the person's intestines. When the adult worms reproduce, new larvae move into the blood and to the muscles, where they form cysts. Swollen upper eyelids, muscle pains, fever, fatigue, and weakness are common symptoms. Treatment consists of antiparasitic medicines. The disease is rare in the United States.

Whipworms Whipworm infection, also known as trichuriasis, is caused by the small roundworm *Trichuris trichiura*. It is most common in subtropical and tropical regions where sanitation is poor; an estimated 800 million people are infected worldwide. Whipworm eggs are ingested orally, via contaminated food or unclean hands. The eggs develop into worms in the intestines. Most people have no noticeable symptoms but if a large number of worms are present, abdominal pain and diarrhea may occur. Treatment consists of antiparasitic medicines.

Yellow fever A virus transmitted by mosquito bites causes this infectious disease. Initial symptoms are flulike and disappear after a few days. In some cases, the fever returns, accompanied by nausea, vomiting, bleeding, jaundice, and delirium. There is no cure; treatment is palliative. However, a highly effective vaccine is available; people visiting tropical areas of Africa and Latin America where the disease is a problem should be vaccinated prior to travel.

Diagnostic Tests

Health care professionals rely on a broad variety of diagnostic tests to look for the presence of disease or injury, to pinpoint its cause, and to monitor its course. Diagnostic tests also help determine the appropriate treatment and, subsequently, the effectiveness of therapy. Some tests are invasive, requiring at least minor surgery, while others are noninvasive. Common diagnostic tests include:

Amniocentesis This common prenatal test involves insertion of a needle through the mother's abdomen and into the amniotic sac that surrounds the fetus. A sample of fluid, which contains fetal cells, is removed from the sac. The fetal cells are then tested for genetic defects such as Down syndrome. The procedure also can be used to identify the sex of the fetus. Chorionic villus sampling (CVS) provides similar information but can be performed earlier in the pregnancy.

Angiography In this procedure, a thin tube, or catheter, is passed through the skin into a blood vessel and a contrast dye is introduced into the bloodstream, allowing visualization of blood vessels. Angiography is commonly used to examine the coronary arteries of the heart and arteries that carry blood to the brain. It also is used to view blood vessels in the lungs, liver, kidney, spleen, and legs.

Biopsy In a biopsy, a tissue sample is extracted and examined microscopically. Depending on the site, the sample may be removed surgically or through a needle. Biopsies are performed to look for abnormal cells damaged by injury or disease. Biopsy is a standard procedure for confirming a diagnosis of cancer.

Blood tests Numerous laboratory tests can be performed on blood. Which tests are performed depends on what the physician wishes to check. For example, enzyme-linked immunosorbent assay (ELISA) looks for the presence of antibodies to HIV in the blood; positive results indicate that the person is infected with HIV, the virus that causes AIDS. For the most common blood tests, such as those for cholesterol levels and red blood cell count, laboratories establish a so-called normal result range. Typically, 95 percent of healthy patients fall within a laboratory's normal range. This means that 5 percent of healthy patients fall outside the normal range. Results may also be outside the normal range for non-illness-related factors such as age, dietary habits, physical activity, pregnancy, use of prescription and nonprescription drugs, and alcohol intake. It is therefore critical that the physician carefully evaluate results.

Bone density tests These imaging techniques are used to measure bone density—an important aid in detecting osteoporosis, a disease characterized by brittle, easily fractured bones. The best-known test is dual-energy x-ray absorptiometry (DEXA), which uses photons given off by x-rays to measure photon absorption by the bone. The more radiation absorbed, the denser the bone.

Bone scan In this imaging technique, a radioisotope (radioactive material) that concentrates in bones is injected into the patient's bloodstream. After an hour or more, during which the bones pick up the radioisotope, special equipment is used to detect radiation emissions and translate them into images. These bone scans can be used to detect abnormalities such as stress fractures, arthritis, and tumors.

Colonoscopy and sigmoidoscopy These endoscopic procedures allow the examination of the inside of the large intestine. They are commonly used to screen for colon cancer and to detect polyps, infectious bowel disease, and other abnormalities. In sigmoidoscopy, a thin, flexible tube called a sigmoidoscope is passed through the anus and into the large intestine to inspect its lower 10 to 12 inches (25–30 centimeters). Colonscopy allows examination of the entire large intestine and sometimes the lower part of the small intestine. Both procedures can also be done to obtain tissue samples for biopsies or stool samples for microscopic examination.

CT Computer tomography is an imaging technique that uses X rays to take pictures—tomograms or, more commonly, CAT scans—of the body. The pictures are reconfigured by a computer to produce 3-D images. CT is particularly helpful in locating tumors, organ injuries, abscesses, and fluid accumulation.

Culture To identify bacteria or other disease-causing agents, samples of blood or other fluids or tissues are placed in laboratory dishes containing special culture media that encourage the growth of microorganisms. For example, if cholera is suspected, a stool sample or a swab from the patient's rectum is cultured. The diagnosis is confirmed by isolation of the organism *Vibrio cholerae* from the culture.

Electrocardiogram For an ECG, small metal sensors are placed on the skin to record the electrical activity of the heart. The information is transmitted to a machine that creates a graph of the data. ECGs are used to diagnose heart attacks and other heart problems, to detect noncardiac problems such as potassium deficit, to monitor patients recovering from heart problems, to determine the effectiveness of pacemakers and certain heart medications, and in exercise stress tests to determine a person's fitness for strenuous exercise. An echocardiogram is another test used for many of the same purposes. In this test, sound waves emitted from a device placed on the chest bounce off the heart; the echoes are then converted into images.

Electromyogram In electromyography, small needle sensors, or electrodes, are inserted into a selected muscle; they record the electrical activity of the muscle at rest and when contracting. The data are displayed on a screen or printed as a graphic record (electromyogram, or EMG) for study. Test results aid in diagnosing muscular, nerve, and neuromuscular diseases, including muscular dystrophy, amyotrophic lateral sclerosis, and myasthenia gravis.

Endoscopy This technique uses a thin, flexible tube with a mounted camera to show internal anatomy through a television monitor, providing "virtual tours" of the inside of joints and other body parts. Instruments may be passed through the tube to obtain fluid or tissues samples for laboratory examination. In some tests, the tube is inserted through a natural opening in the body. For instance, in a cystoscopy an endoscope called a cystoscope is passed through the urethra and into the urinary bladder. In other cases, endoscopy requires minor surgery. In arthroscopy, for example, an arthroscope is inserted through a small incision into a knee or other joint. See also *Colonoscopy* and *sigmoidoscopy*.

Fecal occult blood test In this test, samples of a person's stool (feces) are examined microscopically and chemically to detect occult blood ("hidden" blood not visible to the naked eye). The test detects bleeding in the digestive tract, which may be caused by a variety of disorders such as hemorrhoids, ulcerative colitis, inflammatory bowel disease, and cancer. It is recommended that all individuals age 50 or older have the test annually, to screen the colon and rectum for premalignant growths and cancer.

Imaging Production of an image using X rays, sound waves or other signals. These techniques enable physicians to obtain highly detailed views of internal organs without surgery. See *Bone density tests, Bone scan, CT, MRI, Ultrasound*, and *X rays*.

Mammogram Images of the internal tissues of the breasts (mammary glands) are produced by passing low-dose X rays through the breasts. Abnormalities show up as masses, shadows, and other distortions. The test is used to detect benign and malignant tumors and to monitor breast cancer patients during and following treatment. Women age 50 and older are urged to have a mammogram every year. A newer test is digital mammography, which records the X rays on digital film that can then be manipulated for more precise study of the images.

MRI Magnetic resonance imaging uses a combination of a strong magnetic field and radio waves to measure the distribution and chemical bonds of the protons in the body's hydrogen atoms. A computer translates measurements into 3-D images. MRI is frequently used to view the brain and other soft tissues.

Myelogram The spinal column can by studied by injecting a dye into the cerebrospinal fluid that surrounds the spinal cord. X rays are used to track the flow of the dye and to identify abnormalities, including tumors, arthritic bone spurs, and herniated disks.

Pap smear For a Papanicolaou (Pap) test, a small sample of cells is scraped from the female patient's cervix. The cells are examined microscopically for signs of cancer or inflammation. Women age 21 and older are urged to have regular Pap smears.

PSA test The prostate-specific antigen (PSA) test is a screening test for prostate cancer. It measures the blood level of the protein PSA, which is made by the prostate. PSA level fluctuates naturally over time, and cancer is not the sole factor that can raise the level. It is recommended that males over age 50 have the PSA test annually.

Pulmonary function tests These measure the lungs' capacity to hold air and to inhale and exhale air. The patient is asked to do certain breathing exercises while breathing through a mouthpiece. The tests help diagnose and assess the severity of breathing ailments. They also are used to determine whether a patient has restrictive lung disease, which primarily interferes with breathing in, or obstructive lung disease, which primarily inhibits breathing out.

Scratch tests These tests are used to identify allergies—sensitivities to substances in the environment, called allergens. Scratches are made on the surface of the person's skin, and a small amount of a suspected allergen is applied. If the person is allergic to the substance, the skin usually reddens and swells within about 15 minutes. Alternate techniques include pricking the skin or injecting the allergen between layers of the skin.

Spinal tap Also called a lumbar puncture, this procedure involves inserting a thin needle into the spinal canal and removing a sample of cerebrospinal fluid for analysis. The test helps diagnose disorders of the brain and spinal cord, including infections, tumors, bleeding, and multiple sclerosis. Spinal taps are also used therapeutically, to introduce medication into the cerebrospinal fluid.

Ultrasound Ultrasound imaging, or sonography, beams high-frequency sound waves at the body's organs. The echoes that bounce back are translated into computer images. Because it doesn't use X rays, sonography is recommended for use on pregnant women. It is well suited for examining soft tissue, such as the gall bladder, liver, heart, and thyroid gland. Doppler ultrasound images blood flow in blood vessels, enabling the detection of blockages and aneurysms.

Upper GI series Sometimes referred to as the barium swallow, the upper gastrointestinal series is used to examine the esophagus, stomach, and upper part of the small intestine. It detects structural abnormalities, inflammation, tumors, hiatal hernia, and other problems. The patient swallows a liquid containing barium sulfate, a dye

Common Blood Tests

Substance	Test Description	Result Indications
Blood Urea Nitrogen (BUN)	Measures the concentration of nitrogen in the form of urea in the blood; used to evaluate the rate at which blood is filtered across blood vessels in the kidney.	Elevated levels may indicate kidney dysfunction.
Cholesterol: high density lipoprotein (HDL)	Measures "good" cholesterol: HDL helps prevent cholesterol buildup in arteries.	Elevated levels may counteract the negative effects of high LDL levels.
Cholesterol: low density lipoprotein (LDL)	Measures "bad" cholesterol: LDL is the primary source of cholesterol buildup and blockage in arteries.	Elevated levels are a major risk factor for cardiovascular disease.
Cholesterol, total	Measures blood levels of cholesterol, a fatlike substance found in all cells. Total blood cholesterol is the sum of HDL and LDL.	Elevated levels suggest an increased risk of cardiovascular disease.
C-reactive protein	Measures the amount of a protein linked to artery disease.	The lower the level the better; elevated levels are associated with increased risk of heart attack or stroke.
Creatinine	Measures the amount of creatinine, a waste product of muscle breakdown that is excreted by the kidneys.	Elevated levels, especially accompanied by high BUN levels, may indicate renal failure or other kidney problems, dehydration, or hyperthyroidism.
Glucose	Measures the level of sugar in the blood.	Elevated levels are associated with diabetes, medications such as steroids, and eating before the test.
Hemoglobin (Hgb)	Measures the amount of oxygen- carrying hemoglobin contained within the red blood cells (RBCs).	Low levels suggest anemia, which can be due to a variety of causes. High Hgb may indicate lung disease or excessive production of RBCs; living at high altitudes elevates Hgb.
Iron	Measure blood levels of iron. Iron is essential for the formation of red blood cells.	Abnormal results may indicate bleeding, anemia, malabsorption, malnutrition, liver disease, cancer, infection, or other problems.
Platelets (PLT)	Estimates the number of platelets (cell fragments critical in initiating blood clotting).	Elevated levels may indicate bleeding or excessive production by the bone marrow. Low levels may result from acute blood loss, infections, bone marrow failure, or usage of certain drugs.
Potassium	Measures blood levels of potassium. Potassium regulates muscle activity, including contraction of heart muscles.	Abnormal levels may indicate kidney disease.
Prothrombin time (PT), Activated partial thromboplastin time (APTT)	Measure the time needed for a clot to form after certain reagents are added to the blood sample.	Abnormalities may indicate problems with anticoagulant drug therapy.

Substance	Test Description	Result Indications
Sodium	Measures the amount of sodium in the blood.	Elevated levels may result from dehydration, diabetes, or excessive salt intake. Low levels may result from heart or kidney dysfunction, use of diuretic or diabetes drugs, vomiting, or diarrhea.
Thyroid hormones	Measure the blood levels of thyroxine (T4) and triiodothyronine (T3), hormones that regulate body metabolism.	Elevated levels suggest an underactive thyroid; low levels suggest an overactive thyroid.
Triglycerides	Measures trigylcerides, a form of fat carried in the blood on very-low density lipoprotein (VLDL).	Elevated triglycerides, usually accompanied by low HDL cholesterol levels, may be associated with heart disease and pancreatitis.
Uric acid	Measures the blood levels of uric acid, a breakdown product of building blocks of DNA and RNA.	Elevated levels are associated with gout, kidney problems, and the use of certain diuretics.
White blood cells (WBC)	Measures the number of white blood cells in a unit of blood. A WBC differential count measures the different types of white blood cells (lymphocytes, monocytes, and so on).	A high WBC may be a sign of infection. A low WBC may indicate bone marrow disease or an enlarged spleen.

that coats the interior of the gastrointestinal tract. X rays are used to view the flow of the barium sulfate.

Urinalysis The chemical, physical, and microscopic analysis of urine often is a first step in diagnosing kidney disorders, urinary bladder infections, and certain metabolic diseases. For example, the presence of bacteria such as *Escherichia coli* or *Proteus vulgaris* signals a bladder infection (cystitis). Excessive glucose is a symptom of diabetes mellitus. Bilirubin—an orange-yellow pigment formed when red blood cells are broken down, and normally excreted in bile—suggests possible liver disease.

X-rays X-ray pictures, or radiographs, are two-dimensional images commonly used to detect bone fractures and displacements, dental problems, and tumors in certain organs. They are the most widely used diagnostic imaging technique.

Medications

Prescription drugs ease pain, combat infections, control blood pressure, relieve allergy symptoms, and play numerous other important roles in health care. They make up the fastest-growing health-care expenditure in the United States. In 1980 the nation spent $12 billion on drugs. By 2000 the nation's pharmaceutical tab had risen to $121.8 billion, as retail pharmacies filled 2.9 billion prescriptions. An aging population and the introduction of new therapies for chronic conditions helped fuel the increasing demand for drugs. Additionally, newer drugs tended to be much costlier than older medications.

Side effects

Every medication has possible side effects. These can range from slight nausea or temporary drowsiness to kidney failure and other deadly conditions. The side effects can vary depending on the size of the dose and on the patient's genetic makeup, body size, age, and overall health. People with one medical problem may not be able to take medication designed to treat another medical problem. For example, the cholesterol reducer simvastatin (Zocor) can lead to kidney failure in people with severe infections.

Side effects are among the most common causes of hospitalization in the United States. To avoid or limit such problems, it is important that patients know the common side effects of any medication, including over-the-counter medications, that they are taking. Medications should be taken as directed, problems should be reported promptly to the physician, and expired drugs should be discarded.

Some drugs interact with foods, causing side effects or inhibiting the effectiveness of the drugs. For example, antidepressants known as MAO inhibitors can cause severe headaches and potentially fatal increases in blood pressure in people who consume foods high in tyramine (many cheeses, yogurt, cured meats, red wine, and so on).

Additionally, drugs taken during the same time period can interact with one another, sometimes in deadly fashion. For instance, certain blood pressure medications can dangerously increase levels of lithium in people taking lithium drugs to combat manic depression. Pain relievers such as ibuprofen can reduce the effectiveness of diuretics. Alcohol consumption increases the risk of seizures among people taking the antidepressant bupropion hyudrochloride (Wellbutrin). Thus it is also important that patients inform all their doctors about all prescription and over-the-counter medications they are taking, including herbal remedies and weight loss pills.

Commonly Prescribed Medications

A medication has a chemical name that describes its molecular structure, a generic (nonproprietary) name, and a brand (proprietary) name. In the following list, which is by no means inclusive, the generic name is followed by a brand name in parentheses.

Acne therapy Substances used to treat a common skin condition characterized by pimples and pus-filled pockets on the face and upper torso. Isotretinoin (Accutane), antibiotics such as tetracycline and doxycycline.

Analgesics Substances that relieve pain. Prescription analgesics include both narcotics, such as Oxycodone (OxyContin) and hydrocodone/APAP, and non-narcotics, such as Sumatriptan succinate (Imitrex Oral) and Tramadol (Ultram). The most widely used over-the-counter analgesics are nonsteroidal anti-inflammatory drugs (NSAIDs), such as aspirin and ibuprofen.

Antianxiety medications Substances used to treat panic, phobias, and other anxiety disorders. Alprazolam (Xanax), clonazepam (Klonopin), diazepam (Valium).

Antiarthritics Substances used to reduce symptoms of osteoarthritis. Celecoxib (Celebrex), rofecoxib (Vioxx).

Antibiotics Substances that destroy or inhibit the growth of bacteria. Amoxicillin/clavulanae (Augmentin), Azithromycin (Zithromax), Ciprofloxacin (Cipro), Levofloxacin (Levaquin).

Antidepressants Substances used to treat depression. There are three types:

Selective serotonin reuptake inhibitors (SSRIs) Fluoxetine (Prozac), paroxetine (Paxil), sertraline (Zoloft), Citalopram (Celexa).

Tricyclic antidepressants Clomipramine (Norpramin, Pertofrane), imipramine (Tofranil).

Monoamine oxidase inhibitors (MAOIs) Bupropion HCL (Wellbutrin SR), Venlafaxine (Effexor XR), Isocarboxazid (Marplan), phenelzine sulfate (Nardil).

Antihistamines Substances that interfere with the action of histamines, which play a critical role in allergic reactions. Loratadine (Claritin), fexofenadine (Allegra), cetirizine (Zyrtec).

Antihypertensives Substances used to combat high blood pressure. There are four types:

Angiotensin-converting enzyme (ACE) inhibitors Benazepril (Lotensin), captopril (Capoten), enalapril maleate (Vasotec), lisinopril (Zestril).

Beta blockers Acebutolol (Sectral), metoprolol (Lopressor), penbutolol (Levatol).

Calcium channel blockers Amlodipine (Norvasc), diltiazem (Dilacor), verapamil (Verelan).

Diuretics Thiazides such as chlorothiazide (Diuril) and chlorthalidone (Thalitone), potassium-sparing diuretics such as amiloride (Midamor) and spironolactone (Aldactone).

Antimanic medications Substances that treat bipolar disorder. Gabapentin (Neurontin), divalproex sodium (Depakote), lithium citrate (Cibalith-S).

Antiplatelet medications Substances that destroy or interfere with blood platelets, to prevent excessive blood clotting and help prevent strokes caused by blood clots. Clopidogrel (Plavix), ticlopidine (Ticlid), aspirin.

Antipsychotic Substances that alleviate the symptoms of schizophrenia and other psychotic states. Olanzapine (Zyprexa), Risperidone (Risperdal), chlorpromazine (Thorazine).

Antiulcerants Substances that prevent or treat ulcers. Omepravole (Prilosec), Lansoprazole (Prevacid), Rabeprazole (Aciphex), Ranitidine (Zantac).

Asthma therapy Substances that prevent or treat asthma. Leukotriene modifiers such as montelukast sodium (Singulair), inhaled corticosteroids such as beclomethasone (Beclovent), beta-adrenergic agonists such as albuterol (Proventil), mast cell stabilizers such as cromolyn (Gastrocrom).

Bone density therapy Substances used to treat osteoporosis. Bisphosphonates such as alendronate (Fosamax), calcium and vitamin D supplements.

Bronchodilator Substances that relax and widen respiratory passages leading to the lungs, relieving wheezing and bronchial spasms. Albuterol (Proventil), salmeterol xinafoate (Serevent).

Cholesterol reducers Substances that lower cholesterol and trigylceride levels. Statins, including lovastatin, simvastatin (Zocor), pravastatin (Pravachol), and atorvastatin (Lipitor); fibric acid derivatives such as fenofibrate (TriCor); bile acid binders such as cholestyramine (Prevalite).

Contraceptives Hormone medications that prevent fertilization of an egg by a sperm. Ethinyl estradiol (Ortho Tri-Cyclen).

Diabetes therapy Substances that lower blood sugar levels in people with type II diabetes. Metformin (Glucophage), pioglitazone (Actos), rosiglitazone maleate (Avandia).

Estrogen replacement Substances that treat symptoms of menopause. Conjugated estrogens (Premarin, Prempro).

Hormone therapy Substances used to treat endocrine gland disorders. For example, levothyroxine (Synthroid) is used to replace thyroid hormones in people with an underactive thyroid gland.

Sedatives Substances that calm or tranquilize, reducing anxiety and inducing sleep. Zolpidem (Ambien), temazepam (Restoril).

Sexual function therapy Substances used to treat impotence in men. Sildenafil citrate (Viagra).

Steroids Substances that treat inflammation by suppressing the immune system. For example, respiratory steroids such as fluticasone propionate (Flovent, Flonase) provide relief from allergy symptoms. Topical steroids are applied to the skin to treat inflammatory skin diseases.

Immunization

When bacteria or viruses invade the body, they trigger a counterattack, or immune response. This response includes synthesizing antibody proteins that combine with antigen molecules on the surface of the invader, destroying the invader. Secondarily, the body forms long-lived "memory cells." If again exposed to the same antigen at a later time, the memory cells immediately go into action, releasing antibodies. This is the basis for immunity to certain infectious disease and the basis for immunization programs that vaccinate against diseases.

Vaccines consist of dead or weakened bacteria or viruses. When a person is inoculated with a vaccine for a specific disease, the vaccine stimulates the production of antibodies without producing the disease. Some vaccines provide lifelong immunity. In other cases, immunity can begin to fade over time, requiring booster shots. The three most widely recommended vaccines for adults are:

Tetanus, diphtheria (Td) vaccine To combat tetanus and diphtheria. One dose booster every 10 years.

Influenza vaccine To combat the flu. One dose annually for individuals age 50 and older. For younger adults, one dose annually for those with medical or exposure indications. Medical indicators include chronic cardiovascular and pulmonary conditions, certain chronic metabolic conditions, and women who will be in the second or third trimester of pregnancy during influenza season.

Pneumococcal vaccine To combat pneumonia and other pneumococcal bacteria. One dose for individuals age 65 and older. For younger adults, one dose for those with medical or exposure indications. Medical indicators include chronic pulmonary disorders (excluding asthma), cardiovascular disease, chronic liver or kidney disease, and immunosuppressive conditions.

Childhood and Adolescent Vaccines: Recommended Immunization Schedule, 2003

Age	Vaccines
Birth	Hepatitis B
1 to 4 months	Hepatitis B
2 months	Diphtheria, tetanus, pertussis (DTaP); haemophilus B (Hib); polio; pneumonia and other pneumococcal bacteria (PCV)
4 months	DTaP, Hib, polio, PCV
6 months	DTaP, Hib, PCV
6 to 18 months	Hepatitis B, polio
6 months to 18 years	Influenza (yearly)
12 to 15 months	Hib; measles, mumps, rubella (MMR), PCV
12 to 18 months	Chickenpox (varicella)
15 to 18 months	DTaP
2 to 18 years	Hepatitis A series
4 to 6 years	DTaP, polio, MMR
11 to18 years	Tetanus, diphtheria (Td)

Note: It generally takes several doses of each vaccine for full protection. In some cases, there is a range of acceptable ages for vaccination. For example, the third dose of hepatitis B vaccine may be given between 6 and 18 months of age. Children who have not been vaccinated against hepatitis B in infancy may begin the series during any childhood visit. **Source:** American Academy of Pediatrics.

MYTHOLOGY

Classical Mythology 470

Olympian Gods of Classical Mythology *470*

Other Figures in Classical Myth and Legend *471*

Mesopotamian Mythology 479

Egyptian Mythology 480

Norse Mythology 481

MYTHOLOGY

"Mythology" refers to stories that convey the beliefs of a particular culture at a particular time. Myths, which usually refer to the actions of divinities, can be distinguished from legends (which tell of heroic deeds and historical events, real or imagined) and folktales (stories, often humorous or exaggerated, involving ordinary people). Mythologies usually originated in preliterate oral traditions, at a remote but indeterminate time period. At some point they are written down and become systematized, though because of their oral roots variant and sometimes contradictory versions persist.

This section presents an overview of four traditions of mythology: those of the Classical world (Greece and Rome); Mesopotamia (the ancient Middle East); Egypt; and the Norse world of northernmost Europe. All four have had an influence on subsequent European religion, literature, art, and cultural life.

Classical Mythology

The prehistoric Indo-European settlers of the Greek peninsula and the Aegean islands brought some myths with them from their original homeland in western Central Asia, and borrowed others from their Mediterranean neighbors. With the development of literacy in Greece in the Archaic Period (ca. 800–480 B.C.), the myths began to be written down. Early sources for Greek mythology include the *Iliad* and the *Odyssey*, attributed to Homer (8th century B.C.); Hesiod's *Theogony* (ca. 700 B.C.); the so-called *Homeric Hymns* (7th–6th century B.C.); and the surviving great works of ancient Greek theater, which often involve the interactions of humans and gods.

Greek trade and the establishment of Greek colonies in Sicily and elsewhere spread Greek myths throughout the Mediterranean world; the conquests of Alexander the Great (d. 323 B.C.) carried Greek culture far into Asia. When the Romans conquered Greece and the Hellenic world during the second and first centuries B.C., they absorbed much of Greek culture; they equated many of the Greek deities, and stories of their deeds, to figures in their own pantheon. The two most important Roman sources for classical mythology and legends are Virgil's *Aeneid* (unfinished; from ca. 30 B.C.) and Ovid's *Metamorphoses* (completed A.D. 8).

In what follows, deities and legendary figures are listed by their Greek (or, in a few cases, customary English) names, followed by their Roman names in parentheses. Entries for figures that appear only in Roman myth are italicized in boldface.

Olympian Gods of Classical Mythology

Aphrodite (Venus) Goddess of love, beauty, and sensuality; patron of courtesans. Aphrodite is the daughter of Zeus and Dione in one account; in another she is born out of the foam created when Cronus castrates Uranus and throws his genitals into the sea. Aphrodite is the wife of Hephaestus but has numerous lovers, including Adonis, Anchises, with whom she has a son, Aeneas, and Ares, with whom she has Eros (Cupid) and three other children (see *Ares*).

Apollo (Apollo) God of healing, oracles, the sun, poetry, and music; son of Zeus and Leto; twin brother of Artemis. Apollo is one of the most prominent gods in Greek myth with many roles and attributes and a multitude of children and lovers, most notably Asclepius by Coronis. Apollo symbolizes order and the rational as opposed to the irrational world of Dionysus.

Ares (Mars) God of war; son of Zeus and Hera. Unmarried Ares' most famous of many lovers is Aphrodite, with whom he sires Phobus (Panic), Deimos (Fear), Harmonia (Harmony), and Eros (Cupid). Ares is often accompanied by Enyo (Horror) and Eris (Strife).

Artemis (Diana) Virgin goddess of the hunt, wild animals, and animal and human young; daughter of Zeus and Leto; twin sister of Apollo. Artemis is usually accompanied by a group of nymphs and often appears with a bow and arrow.

Athena (Minerva) Virgin goddess of wisdom, war, crafts, and city life; protector of Athens. The daughter of Zeus and Metis (see *Metis* for birth), Athena springs from the head of Zeus in full armor with a helmet and spear. Athena gives the olive tree as a gift to Athens. She also gives mankind the loom, the plough, and the flute. (See also *Nike*.)

Demeter (Ceres) Goddess of the harvest, grain, earth, and fertility; daughter of Cronus and Rhea; mother of

Persephone. During the third of the year when Persephone is held by Hades in the underworld (see *Persephone*), Demeter will not allow anything to grow.

✳**Dionysus** (Bacchus, Liber) God of the vine, wine, and fertility; closely associated with theater, particularly tragedy; son of Zeus and Semele; husband of Ariadne. Dionysus's followers are maenads (also Bacchae),a drunk, frenzied, ecstatic mob of women, and satyrs, mythical creatures that are half man and half goat.

Hephaestus (Vulcan) God of fire, smiths, and crafts; son of Zeus and Hera or of Hera alone in some accounts; cuckolded husband of Aphrodite. Born lame, Hephaestus is ejected from Olympus, once by Hera and again by Zeus. Hephaestus is responsible for fashioning some of the most important objects in myth, including the chains that held Prometheus and armor for Achilles, Heracles, and Aeneas. He also crafts the first woman, Pandora.

Hera (Juno) Goddess of marriage and family; daughter of Cronus and Rhea; mother of Ares (by Zeus) and Hephaestus (by Zeus in some accounts and alone in others). Hera is often seen in myth as the vengeful wife of the adulterous Zeus, causing havoc for his lovers and illegitimate children, most famously Heracles (Hercules).

Hermes (Mercury) Trickster god; messenger god; god of commerce; patron of travelers and thieves; son of Zeus and Maia. Hermes is often seen in myth wearing a winged helmet and winged sandals, and carrying a caduceus, a herald's staff entwined with snakes.

✳**Hestia** (Vesta) Virgin goddess of fire and the hearth; daughter of Cronus and Rhea. Hestia is the protector of the home, the household and the hearth.

Poseidon (Neptune) God of the sea and earthquakes; son of Cronus and Rhea; husband of the nymph Amphitrite. Poseidon is closely associated with horses and classically seen carrying a trident. He is one of the less benevolent gods, responsible for unpredictable and destructive forces.

Zeus (Jupiter, Jove) Chief Olympian god; son of Cronus and Rhea. Zeus ousts Cronus and the other Titans from Olympus and takes control as the supreme sky god while his brothers Poseidon and Hades take over the sea and underworld, respectively. Zeus often appears in myth having affairs (see *Danae, Europa, Io, Leda, Semele*), much to the dismay of his typically jealous wife, Hera.

✳**Note:** In some accounts, Dionysus replaces Hestia as the 12th Olympian god. Hades' realm is the underworld, so he is not considered one of the 12 Olympians.

Other Figures in Classical Myth and Legend

Achilles Hero of the Trojan War in Homer's *Iliad*; son of Thetis (sea nymph) and Peleus (mortal). Thetis dips Achilles in the river Styx at birth making him invulnerable except for the heel by which he is held. Fighting for the Greeks at Troy, Achilles kills Hector and is killed by Paris, who shoots an arrow into his heel.

Adonis Lover of Aphrodite. Adonis is a young man so beautiful that both Aphrodite and Persephone want to have him. When he is killed by a boar, a compromise allows him to live in the celestial world with Aphrodite for half the year and in the underworld with Persephone the other half.

Aegisthus See *Clytemnestra* and *Orestes*.

Aeneas Legendary Trojan warrior; son of Aphrodite and Anchises; lover of Dido. Aeneas is the hero of Virgil's *Aeneid*, in which he is depicted as the father of the Roman people.

Aeolus God of the winds. In Homer's *Odyssey*, Aeolus gives Odysseus a bag of wind and warns him not to open it. Odysseus's men untie the bag, releasing dangerous winds that cause a great setback in the journey home.

Agamemnon King of Mycenae and leader of the Greeks in the Trojan War; son of Atreus; husband of Clytemnestra; father of Orestes, Electra, and Iphigeneia; brother of Menelaus. (See also *Clytemnestra, Iphigeneia,* and *Orestes*.)

Agave Daughter of Cadmus and Harmonia. In Euripides' *Bacchantes*, Agave's son Pentheus disrespects Dionysus. The god drives Agave insane, compelling her and her sisters to tear Pentheus to pieces.

Ajax Hero of the Trojan War in Homer's *Iliad*; son of Telemon. Ajax kills himself when the prize of Achilles' armor goes to Odysseus instead of him.

Amphitrite Goddess of the sea; a Nereid (sea nymph); wife of Poseidon.

Anchises Trojan prince. Anchises is a lover of Aphrodite, with whom he has a son, Aeneas. Hearing of the affair, Zeus cripples Anchises with a thunderbolt.

Andromeda Daughter of Cepheus and Cassiopeia; wife of Perseus. When Cassiopeia boasts that her daughter is more beautiful than the Nereids, an oracle demands that Andromeda be sacrificed to defuse the wrath of Poseidon. She is about to be killed by a sea monster, when Perseus, flying past on his winged sandals, rescues her and gains her hand in marriage.

Antigone Daughter of Oedipus and Jocasta; sister of Eteocles, Ismene, and Polynices. In a fight for power, Eteocles and Polynices kill each other. In Sophocles' *Antigone*, Antigone performs funeral rites for Polynices against the orders of her uncle Creon, the new king. He sentences her to be buried alive in a cave, where she hangs herself. When Haemon, Creon's son and Antigone's fiancé, finds out, he kills himself, causing Creon's wife to kill herself.

Antiope (Hippolyta) Queen of the Amazons; mother of Hippolytus by Theseus. Theseus abducts Antiope and takes her to Athens, causing the Amazons to invade in retaliation.

Arachne A young woman who challenges Athena to a weaving contest. When Athena finds no flaw in Arachne's work, she tears it up and beats her. Arachne kills herself; Athena then turns her into a spider.

Argus 1) Hundred-eyed monster that Hera sends to guard Io to whom Zeus has taken a liking. 2) Odysseus's faithful dog, which drops dead upon seeing him after his 20-year absence.

Ariadne Daughter of King Minos of Crete. After she shows Theseus how to overcome the Minotaur, the two run away together. In one version of the story, Theseus then abandons her; in another she dies, and in another she becomes the mistress of Dionysus.

Asclepius (Aesculapius) God of medicine; deified son of Apollo and Coronis (mortal). The centaur Chiron was his mentor, and he is usually seen carrying a staff entwined by a snake.

Atalanta Beautiful girl who could outrun men. Atalanta says that she will only marry the suitor who can beat her in a foot race; losers will be killed. Hippomenes, distracting her by dropping golden apples from Aphrodite, wins her hand.

Atlas A Titan in some accounts and a giant in others; brother of Prometheus. Atlas sides with the Titans in their battle with Zeus. When Zeus emerges the victor, he condemns Atlas to bear the weight of the world on his shoulders.

Bellerophon Slayer of the Chimera (see *Chimera*). With a golden bridle from Athena, Bellerophon mounts Pegasus and slays the monster. Bellerophon remains the master of Pegasus until he tries to ride the winged horse up Mount Olympus and is punished by Zeus.

Bellona Roman goddess of war. Bellona is the wife of Mars in some accounts, his sister in others.

Cadmus Legendary founder of Thebes; father of Agave, Autonoe, Ino, Polydorus, and Semele. With his wife, Harmonia, Cadmus begins an ill-fated bloodline whose woes are popular subjects of myth.

Calydonian boar Legendary boar hunted by heroes, including Theseus, Jason, Castor, and Pollux (the Dioscuri) and Nestor.

Calypso Sea nymph. A marooned Odysseus spends seven years living on an island with her. She offers him immortality to stay, but he chooses to return home.

Cassandra Daughter of Priam and Hecuba, king and queen of Troy. Cassandra promises to marry Apollo if he gives her the gift of prophesy. When she backs out of the deal, Apollo gives her the ability but makes it so that no one will believe her. She is taken by Agamemnon at the end of the Trojan War. (See also *Clytemnestra*.)

Cassiopeia See *Andromeda*.

Castor Son of Leda and Tyndareus; mortal brother of the immortal Pollux (together known as the Dioscuri), Helen, and Clytemnestra (see *Leda*). Popular subjects of myth, the brothers figure in the story of Jason and the Argonauts and Theseus's abduction of their sister Helen. When Castor dies, Pollux splits his immortality with him so that they can remain together alternating days in the world and the underworld.

Centaur Mythical creature with the head and torso of a man and the body of a horse. Centaurs are mountain and forest dwellers often seen harassing nymphs and maidens passing through the woods.

Cephalus Husband of Procris. Eos (Dawn) falls in love with him and tries in vain to lure him away. Another story tells how jealous Procris, having heard that Cephalus was unfaithful, went to spy on him hunting in the woods. Cephalus hears a noise and hurls his javelin, accidentally killing his wife.

Cerberus Three-headed dog guarding the gates of Hades; offspring of Typhon and Echidna. Heracles captures the beast in the last of his labors.

Chaos The void from which Gaea (Earth) and all things in the universe came. This creation story is most famously told in Hesiod's *Theogony*.

Charon Ferryman of the dead. For the price of an obol, Charon steers the boat that carries the dead across the rivers Acheron or Styx in the underworld.

Charybdis Dangerous whirlpool mentioned in the *Odyssey* positioned near Scylla in the Strait of Messina.

Chimera Mythical creature with the head of a lion, the

body of a goat and a snake for a tail; offspring of Typhon and Echidna. The hero Bellerophon, riding his steed Pegasus, slays the Chimera, who is ravaging the city of Lycia.

Chiron Centaur son of Cronus. Chiron was Asclepius's mentor in the art of healing and reared Achilles and Theseus. When Heracles accidentally shoots him with an arrow, Chiron decides to relinquish his immortality to Prometheus.

Chloris (Flora) Goddess of flowers and fertility; personification of spring and the wife of Zephyrus, the west wind.

Circe Daughter of Helios (Sun). Circe turns Odysseus's men into swine when they land on her island. Swearing to do Odysseus no harm, she sleeps with him and releases his men from the spell. They remain on her island for a year.

Clytemnestra Daughter of Leda and Tyndareus; wife of Agamemnon; sister of Castor and half sister of Helen and Pollux (see *Leda*). In the first play of Aeschylus's *Oresteia*, she and her lover, Aegisthus, murder Agamemnon and his mistress, Cassandra, upon their return from Troy. She and Aegisthus are killed by her son Orestes, who plots with her daughter Electra in the second play of the trilogy.

Creon See *Antigone*.

Cronus (Saturn) Son of Uranus and Gaea; leader of the Titans; husband of Rhea; father of Zeus, Hera, Demeter, Poseidon, Hestia, and Hades. After Cronus ousts his father from the heavens, he swallows all his children to prevent them from ousting him. Rhea saves Zeus, who grows up to battle his father, release his siblings and hurl Cronus and his Titan allies into the underworld.

Cumaean Sibyl seer loved by Apollo. She agrees to sleep with Apollo in exchange for long life. When she refuses to follow through, Apollo grants her long life but not extended youth. She shrivels to the size of an insect.

Cyclopes One-eyed giants; children of Uranus and Gaea. Imprisoned by Uranus and then freed by Zeus, the Cyclopes become the blacksmiths of the gods, assisting Hephaestus. (See also *Polyphemus*.)

Daedalus Legendary inventor and architect who builds the Labyrinth to hold the Minotaur on Crete. When the hero Theseus slays the Minotaur and runs off with King Minos's daughter, the king imprisons Daedalus and his son, Icarus, in the Labyrinth. Daedalus builds wings so they can escape. Icarus flies too close to sun and his wings, held together by wax, melt, sending him plummeting to his death in the sea below. (See also *Pasiphae*.)

Danae Mother of Perseus; lover of Zeus. Zeus comes to Danae as a shower of gold and impregnates her. A prophesy warned her father, Acrisius, of Danae's offspring. When he discovers the baby Perseus, he locks them both in a chest and sets it adrift at sea. They are retrieved by a fisherman's net near the island of Seriphus.

Daphne A nymph loved by Apollo. When Daphne refuses Apollo's advances, he tries to rape her. She begs her father, the river god Peneus, to save her. He turns her into a laurel tree. The laurel becomes a symbol of Apollo.

Deianeira Wife of Heracles. Heracles battles the river god Achelous for Deianeira's hand in marriage. The Centaur Nessus tricks her into poisoning her husband. Heracles dies and she hangs herself.

Dido Queen of Carthage. In Virgil's *Aeneid*, Dido falls in love with Aeneas. When he sails away without her, she throws herself on a funeral pyre.

Echidna Monster with the head of a nymph and the body of a serpent; mate of Typhon. Mother of many creatures involved in the labors of legendary heroes, including Cerberus, Chimera, Hydra, the Nemean Lion, and the Sphinx.

Echo Mountain nymph. When Echo tries to run interference for the unfaithful Zeus, Hera condemns her to say nothing more than a repetition of the last words she hears. She falls in love with Narcissus. When he rejects her, she shrivels up until only her voice remains.

Electra See *Clytemnestra*.

Enyo Goddess of war and violence. Enyo, meaning "horror," is often a companion of Ares, having varying familial relationships to him in different accounts.

Eos (Aurora) Goddess of the dawn; daughter of Titans Theia and Hyperion; sister of Helios (Sun) and Selene (Moon); mother of the winds Boreas, Eurus, Zephyrus, and Notus. Pictured as "rosy-fingered" and beautiful, Eos has many lovers including Ares and Orion. (See also *Cephalus*.)

Erinyes, Eumenides (Furiae) The Furies, tormentors of the guilty. The Furies are a trio of female spirits born out of the spilled blood of Uranus when he is castrated by Cronus.

Eris (Discordia) Goddess of strife; sister and companion of Ares. The causes of the Trojan War can be traced back to Eris's handiwork at the wedding of Peleus and Thetis when she throws the golden apple of discord into the mix.

Eros (Cupid, Amor) God of sexual love. Eros is the son of Ares and Aphrodite in some accounts; in others, the god was among the first to come out of Chaos along with Gaea. A mischievous winged boy in many stories, Eros usually carries a bow and arrow with which he inspires love or indifference in his victims.

Europa Daughter of King Agenor of Phoenicia; mother of Minos, Rhadamanthus, and Sarpedon by Zeus. Zeus comes to Europa in the form of a white bull and carries her off to Crete, where he keeps her as his mistress. She later marries King Asterius of Crete.

Eurydice See *Orpheus*.

Fates (Greek, Moirae: Clotho, Atropos, Lachesis; Roman, Parcae: Decuma, Nona, Morta) Daughters of Zeus and Themis (Law). Often depicted spinning thread, the three goddesses are responsible for the destinies of all.

Gaea Earth goddess; among the principal deities to come out of Chaos. Gaea is the mother of Uranus (Sky) and Pontus (Sea) and, from her coupling with Uranus, the Titans.

Graces (Greek, Charites; Roman, Gratiae) Daughters of Zeus and Eurynome (an Oceanid). Aglaia, Euphrosyne, and Thalia, usually seen together, represent splendor, joy, and blossoming, respectively.

Hades, Pluto (Orcus, Pluto) God of the dead; son of Cronus and Rhea; husband of Persephone. When Zeus overthrows Cronus, he divides control of the universe with his two brothers leaving Poseidon to lord over the sea and Hades the underworld.

Harmonia Daughter of Ares and Aphrodite. (See *Cadmus*.)

Harpies Malevolent female spirits depicted as birds with human heads. Meaning "snatchers," the Harpies are associated with Hades's taking of bodies. (See also *Phineus*).

Hebe (Juventas) Goddess of youth and cupbearer of the gods; daughter of Zeus and Hera. Hebe marries the deified hero Heracles.

Hecate Goddess of night, darkness, and crossroads. Hecate is often associated with witchcraft and malevolence, but she can also be a benevolent force, as in the case of Persephone, whom she saves from Hades. She is closely associated with both Artemis and Selene.

Hector Legendary Trojan prince; son of Priam and Hecuba; husband of Andromache; father of Astyanax; brother of Paris. When Hector kills Patroclus in Homer's *Iliad*, Achilles kills Hector and drags his body from the back of a chariot until Priam convinces Achilles to let him give Hector a proper burial.

Hecuba Wife of King Priam of Troy; mother of Hector and Paris.

Helen Daughter of Zeus and Leda; sister of Pollux and half sister of Castor and Clytemnestra (see *Leda*). Helen, known for her amazing beauty, was first abducted by Theseus and rescued by her brothers, Castor and Pollux. She marries Menelaus, king of Sparta, and has a daughter, Hermione. Paris, prince of Troy, abducts her (or she willingly goes with him), and so begins the Trojan War.

Helios (Sol) Sun god; son of Titans Hyperion and Theia; brother of Selene (Moon) and Eos (Dawn); father of Circe and Pasiphae, among others. Helios drives the chariot of the sun across the sky. In a story told by Ovid, he lets his son Phaethon drive the chariot. Phaethon loses control, nearly crashes and scorches vast areas of the earth.

Heracles (Hercules) Deified hero; son of Zeus and Alcmene. Constantly persecuted by jealous Hera, Heracles is driven mad and kills his wife, Megara, and their children. An oracle orders him to perform 12 labors to redeem himself: in order, the Nemean lion, Lernaean hydra, Ceryneian hind, Erymanthian boar, Augean stables, Stymphalian birds, Cretan bull, horses of Diomedes, girdle of Hippolyta, cattle of Geryon, apples of the Hesperides and Cerberus. He succeeds and marries Deianeira ,who, fooled by Nessus, accidentally poisons and kills him. After death Heracles is made immortal and marries the goddess Hebe. (See also *Cerberus, Chiron, Hydra, Jason,* and *Prometheus*.)

Hermaphroditus Beautiful son of Hermes and Aphrodite. In Ovid a nymph, Salmacis, falls in love with Hermaphroditus and, clinging to him, prays that they never be separated. Her wish is granted, and they become one being, half male and half female.

Hippolytus Son of Theseus and Antiope (Hippolyta), queen of the Amazons. Theseus leaves Antiope for Phaedra. In Euripides' *Hippolytus*, Phaedra falls in love with Hippolytus. When he rejects Phaedra's advances, she tells Theseus that he raped her and then kills herself. Theseus orders the death of his son only to find out too late that he was innocent.

Horae (Eunomia, Dike, Irene; in another version, Thallo, Auxo and Carpo) The seasons; daughters of Zeus and Themis. The Horae are goddesses of agriculture and universal order.

Hydra Nine-headed monster; offspring of Typhon and Echidna. Eight of its heads are mortal but will grow back as two when cut off; the ninth is immortal. In Heracles' second labor, he kills the Hydra by burning the stumps of the eight mortal heads so they cannot grow back and burying the immortal one.

Hypnos (Somnus) God of sleep; son of Nyx (Night) and Erebus (Darkness); brother of Thanatos (Death).

Icarus See *Daedalus*.

Ino Daughter of Cadmus and Harmonia; wife of King Athamas of Orchomenus. Ino raises the god Dionysus, offspring of her sister Semele and Zeus. Jealous Hera drives Ino and her husband insane, and they kill their children. She jumps into the sea to commit suicide and is turned into Leucothea, a sea goddess.

Io Lover of Zeus. Zeus turns Io into a heifer to spare her from Hera's wrath. Suspicious Hera places the heifer under the guard of the hundred-eyed Argus. Io is freed by Hermes, but Hera sends a gadfly to torment her. After a long journey, she regains her normal form and has a son by Zeus, Epaphus, an ancestor of Heracles.

Iphigeneia Daughter of Agamemnon and Clytemnestra. Agamemnon is ordered to sacrifice his daughter so the Greek ships can make it safely to Troy. Hearing that her husband has sacrificed Iphigeneia, Clytemnestra murders Agamemnon upon his return from Troy.

Iris Messenger goddess, particularly for Zeus and Hera; goddess of the rainbow.

Janus Roman god of the gate. Janus is depicted with two faces looking in opposite directions from gateways and doorways. Representing beginnings and endings, Janus presides over agricultural cycles, the onset and conclusion of battle, births and marriages.

Jason Son of Aeson; raised by Chiron. King Pelias of Iolcus sends Jason on a seemingly impossible quest for the Golden Fleece because it is prophesized that Jason will kill him. Along with heroes such as Heracles, Orpheus, Castor, and Pollux, Jason sets out on the ship *Argo*. With the help of the sorceress Medea, Jason takes the fleece and returns with Medea to Iolcus, where Jason kills King Pelias. They are banished from the city and move to Corinth, where after a few years Jason tries to leave Medea and marry another. In Euripides' *Medea* , Medea kills their children and flees to Athens. (See also *Calydonian boar*.)

Jocasta See *Oedipus*.

Laertes Father of Odysseus.

Laius See *Oedipus*.

Lares Roman household gods protecting the home, family and the hearth; patron spirits of travelers and crossroads. The Lares are usually seen in the plural, often as a pair of spirits. (See also *Penates*.)

Leda Lover of Zeus; wife of Tyndareus. Zeus comes to Leda in the form of a swan and impregnates her right around a time when she has also been with her mortal husband. She gives birth to four children, Pollux and Helen by Zeus (from an egg, in some accounts) and Castor and Clytemnestra by Tyndareus. (See also *Helen, Castor*, and *Clytemnestra*.)

Leto Daughter of Titans Coeus and Phoebe; mother of Artemis and Apollo. When Zeus falls in love with Leto and she becomes pregnant, Hera chases her away until she finally lands on Delos, where she gives birth to the divine twins, Artemis and Apollo.

Medea Daughter of King Aeetes of Colchis. A sorceress and lover of Jason, Medea uses her power to aid Jason in his quest for the Golden Fleece. (See also *Jason*.)

Medusa The only mortal of the three Gorgons, winged creatures with snakes for hair that turn anyone who looks at them into stone. When legendary hero Perseus beheads Medusa, the winged horse, Pegasus, and the giant Chrysaor spring from her neck.

Menelaus Legendary king of Sparta; son of Atreus; husband of Helen; brother of Agamemnon. When the Trojan prince Paris abducts his wife, Helen, Menelaus enlists Agamemnon to lead the Greek forces in a war against Troy.

Metis Goddess of wisdom; mother of Athena. When Metis becomes pregnant by Zeus, he swallows Metis to protect his offspring and Athena is born from his head.

Midas King of Phrygia. Granted one wish by Dionysus, Midas asks that everything he touches turn to gold. Unable to eat or drink, he realizes his folly and has the wish reversed.

Minos King of Crete; son of Zeus and Europa; husband of Pasiphae; father of Ariadne, Phaedra, and others. Minos is a main player in many of the legends of Crete (see *Ariadne, Daedalus, Minotaur, Pasiphae*). The great king and lawmaker becomes a judge of the dead after his death.

Minotaur Mythical creature with the body of a man and the head of a bull kept by King Minos of Crete in the

Labyrinth; offspring of Pasiphae and a bull (see *Pasiphae* for birth). The Minotaur is killed by the Athenian hero Theseus.

Muses Nine daughters of Zeus and Mnemosyne (Memory) that serve as inspiration for the arts and sciences. Each muse is assigned a particular art: Calliope, epic poetry; Clio, history; Erato, love poetry; Euterpe, lyric poetry; Melpomene, tragedy; Polyhymnia, music and song; Terpsichore, dance; Thalia, comedy; and Urania, astronomy.

Narcissus Beautiful son of Liriope (nymph) and Cephisus (river god). When Narcissus rejects the advances of a nymph, the goddess of love, Aphrodite, damns him to fall in love with his own reflection. (See also *Echo*.)

Nemesis Goddess of vengeance, justice, and retribution; daughter of Nyx (Night).

Nereids Sea nymphs; daughters of Nereus and Doris (an Oceanid). Often numbered at 50, many Nereids have roles in Classical mythology, most notably Thetis, mother of Achilles, and Amphitrite, wife of Poseidon.

Nereus Sea god; son of Pontus and Gaea; husband of Doris (an Oceanid), father of the Nereids.

Nestor King of Pylos and hero of the Trojan War. In Homer's *Iliad* Nestor is portrayed as the voice of wisdom for the Greeks.

Nike (Victoria) Goddess of victory. She is usually winged and often seen as an aspect of Athena.

Niobe Wife of Amphion. Niobe boasts that she is better than Leto because she has seven sons and seven daughters while Leto only has two. Unfortunately, Leto's two children are Artemis and Apollo who avenge Niobe's hubris by killing all of her children.

Nyx (Nox) Personification of night; mother of Hypnos (Sleep), Thanatos (Death), and Nemesis (Vengeance), among others. Nyx is one of the principal entities to arise out of Chaos.

Oceanids Sea nymphs; daughters of the Titans Oceanos and Tethys. The most famous Oceanids in myth include Metis, mother of Athena, and Doris, mother of the Nereids.

Oceanos Sea god; Titan son of Uranus and Gaea; husband of Tethys; father of the Oceanids.

Odysseus King of Ithaca and hero of the Trojan War; son of Laertes; husband of Penelope; father of Telemachus. In Homer's *Iliad* Odysseus is the most clever of the Greeks. His lengthy return home from the war is the subject of Homer's *Odyssey*. (See *Aeolus, Argus, Calypso, Charybdis, Circe, Penelope, Polyphemus, Scylla, Sirens,* and *Telemachus*.)

Oedipus Legendary king of Thebes; son of Laius and Jocasta, king and queen of Thebes; father of Antigone, Eteocles, Ismene, and Polynices. In Sophocles' *Oedipus the King*, Oedipus was abandoned as a child and raised in Corinth. As an adult he returns to Thebes and unwittingly kills his father and marries his own mother after solving the riddle of the Sphinx. When the truth is revealed, he blinds himself and goes into exile.

Orestes Son of Agamemnon and Clytemnestra. In Aeschylus's trilogy, the *Oresteia*, Orestes avenges his father's death by killing Clytemnestra and her lover, Aegisthus, who plotted Agamemnon's murder. Orestes is tormented by the Furies for the murders but is eventually released from their persecution by a jury in a court presided over by Athena.

Orion Son of Poseidon. Orion is a giant and a great hunter with whom Eos falls in love. In one version, Artemis disapproves of the union and kills Orion. He is made into a constellation.

Orpheus Great musician and poet; son of the muse Calliope and Apollo (in some versions); husband of Eurydice. Having been bitten by a snake, Eurydice dies on their wedding day. Orpheus convinces Hades with his beautiful music to let him escort her out of Hades on the condition that he does not look back at her until they have left the underworld. He turns around accidentally and Eurydice is sent back to Hades permanently. Orpheus is later ripped to pieces by a group of maenads, followers of Dionysus.

Pan (Faunus, Inuus) God of flocks, the forest, and fertility. He is depicted in myth as a satyr (see *Satyr*) and sexual aggressor, often seen chasing nymphs in the woods.

Pandora The first woman. Zeus enlists Hephaestus to create Pandora. When Prometheus steals fire from Olympus and gives it to man, Zeus sends Pandora to Prometheus's brother Epimetheus along with a jar that she is ordered not to open. Curiosity gets the better of her, and she opens the jar, releasing evil and misery into the world. The only thing remaining in the jar when she closes the lid is hope.

Paris Prince of Troy; son of Priam and Hecuba; brother of Hector. Paris's kidnapping of Helen causes the Trojan War. In Homer's *Iliad* he kills Achilles by shooting an arrow into the Greek warrior's weak heel.

Pasiphae Wife of King Minos of Crete; mother of Ariadne, Phaedra, and others. When Minos insults Poseidon, the god inspires Pasiphae to yearn for a bull. She enlists Daedalus to construct a wooden cow that she hides in to mate with the animal. The offspring of this union is the Minotaur. (See also *Daedalus*, *Minos*, and the *Minotaur*.)

Patroclus Greek hero of the Trojan War. Patroclus is the constant companion of Achilles. When Hector kills Patroclus, Achilles reenters the fighting, killing Hector and many others in a spree of vengeance.

Pegasus Winged horse; offspring of the gorgon Medusa and Poseidon. Along with the giant Chrysaor, Pegasus springs from Medusa's neck when Perseus decapitates her. (See also *Bellerophon*.)

Peleus Father of Achilles; husband of Thetis. Attended by the gods, the wedding of Peleus and Thetis is a popular theme in myth.

Penates Roman household gods; protectors of home, family, and hearth. Always seen in the plural, the Penates are often worshipped along with the Lares (see *Lares*).

Penelope Wife of Odysseus. Besieged by suitors throughout Odysseus's 10-year absence after the Trojan War, she remains faithful. She tells the suitors that she cannot remarry until she has finished weaving a shroud, but every night she unravels the work she has done, thus never finishing.

Persephone (Proserpina) See *Demeter*.

Perseus Son of Zeus and Danae (see *Danae* for birth). Challenged by King Polydectes, who is trying to get rid of him, Perseus sets out with various magical items from the gods (winged sandals, a special sword, and others) to slay the gorgon Medusa. When he returns with the gorgon's head to find Polydectes pursuing his mother, Perseus holds up the head and turns the king and his men into stone. (See also *Andromeda* and *Medusa*.)

Phaedra Daughter of Minos and Pasiphae. See *Hippolytus*.

Phaethon See *Helios*.

Phineus Legendary king of Salmydessus. Apollo gives Phineus the gift of prophesy but forbids him to reveal what he sees. When Phineus discloses details about the future, Zeus blinds him and sends the Harpies to snatch away anything he tries to eat. Jason and the Argonauts thwart the Harpies in exchange for information about the future of their journey.

Pollux (Greek, Polydeuces) See *Castor*.

Polynices See *Antigone*.

Polyphemus Cyclops encountered by Odysseus in the *Odyssey*. Odysseus and his men escape the cave of Polyphemus by blinding the one-eyed giant and hiding under his sheep as they go out to pasture.

Priam King of Troy; husband of Hecuba; father of Hector and Paris.

Priapus God of gardens, vines, flocks, and fertility. Statues of Priapus with an exaggerated phallus were often placed in Greek and Roman gardens.

Procris See *Cephalus*.

Prometheus Creator of man; son of the Titan Iapetus. Having fashioned man out of earth and water, Prometheus steals fire from Olympus and gives it to mortals. As punishment Zeus chains Prometheus to a rock with a bird incessantly pecking at his immortal liver. He is eventually freed by Heracles. Prometheus is also responsible for providing man with crafts, medicine, writing, and many other gifts.

Psyche Personification of the soul. Eros falls in love with Psyche, a beautiful nymph. Aphrodite forbids the affair, so Eros will only come to her in the dark when she cannot see who he is. Curious Psyche tries to get a look at him, but a drop of oil from her lamp falls and wakes him. He leaves her, but they are eventually reunited.

Pygmalion Sculptor in myth. Pygmalion creates a statue of a beautiful woman, which he calls Galatea. He falls in love with it and prays to Aphrodite that he find a wife like the statue. Aphrodite, impressed with his work, makes Galatea real.

Pyramus The Romeo and Juliet of Ovid's *Metamorphoses*, Pyramus and Thisbe grow up next door to each other and fall in love. Their parents forbid them to marry, so they elope. Thisbe encounters a lioness, bloody from the hunt, at the meeting spot and runs away, leaving behind her veil. When Pyramus sees the veil and the lioness, he assumes Thisbe has been killed and stabs himself. When Thisbe sees Pyramus dying, she stabs herself and they die in each other's arms.

Remus See *Romulus*.

Rhea See *Cronus*.

Romulus Legendary founder of Rome; son of Mars and Rhea Silvia (priestess); twin brother of Remus. Abandoned as infants, the twins Romulus and Remus are nursed by a she-wolf and eventually found and raised by a shepherd. They grow up to co-found a city, but a power struggle leads to Romulus killing Remus. The new city is thus called Rome after its sole leader. Romulus is deified as Quirinus after his death. (See also *Sabines*.)

Sabines When Romulus founds Rome, bandits and other riffraff populate the city, but they have no women to marry. At a festival Romulus abducts all the young Sabine women from a nearby community to couple with the Roman men.

Satyr Creature with the head and torso of a man and the horns, tail, legs, and hooves of a goat. Satyrs are the lascivious and gluttonous followers of Dionysus, often seen in the woods pursuing nymphs.

Scylla Sea monster situated across from Charybdis in the Strait of Messina. In the *Odyssey* six of Scylla's 12 dog heads snatch and devour six of Odysseus's men as they sail by.

Selene (Luna) Moon goddess; daughter of Titans Hyperion and Theia; sister of Helios and Eos. Selene is often associated with magic.

Semele Daughter of Cadmus and Harmonia; mother of Dionysus by Zeus. When Zeus displays his divine form to Semele, she is scorched by the splendor and dies. Zeus saves the unborn Dionysus and sews him into his thigh.

Sirens Nymphs with the heads and torsos of women and the wings and lower bodies of birds whose song lures passing sailors to their destruction on nearby rocks. Odysseus escapes unharmed by plugging his crew's ears with wax. He decides to be tied to the mast so he can hear the beautiful music but pass safely.

Sisyphus Underworld figure. As punishment for wronging the gods, Sisyphus is damned to eternally push a boulder up a hill only to have it roll back down once it reaches the top.

Tantalus Underworld figure; father of Niobe; ancestor of the doomed house of Atreus (see *Agamemnon*, *Clytemnestra*, and *Orestes*). As punishment for trying to trick the gods into eating his son Pelops, Tantalus is damned to spend eternity surrounded by plentiful food and water that he can see but cannot reach.

Tartarus The lowest level of the underworld. Tartarus is one of the principal entities to arise from Chaos. Wrongdoers, most notably the Titans after being defeated by Zeus, are banished to Tartarus.

Telemachus Son of Odysseus and Penelope. Telemachus helps Odysseus slay his mother's suitors in the *Odyssey*.

Terminus Roman god of boundaries and borders.

Tethys Titan; daughter of Uranus and Gaea; wife of Oceanos; mother of the Oceanids.

Thanatos Personification of death; son of Nyx (Night); brother of Hypnos (Sleep).

Themis Titan goddess of justice; daughter of Uranus and Gaea; mother of the Horae (Seasons) and the Moirae (Fates) by Zeus.

Theseus Legendary Athenian hero; son of Aegus (a mortal) and Poseidon with Aethra, who was impregnated by both on the same night. The stories of Theseus are similar to other heroes such as his cousin Heracles. Theseus is sent away as an infant, returns to find glory and performs a collection of labors. His most notable feat is the slaying of the Minotaur. (See also *Antiope*, *Ariadne*, *Calydonian boar*, *Castor*, *Chiron*, *Daedalus*, *Helen*, *Hippolytus*, and the *Minotaur*.)

Thetis See *Achilles*.

Thisbe See *Pyramus*.

Tiresias Prophet of myth. Blinded by the gods (either Athena or Hera in different versions) but given the gift of prophesy, Tiresias plays a role in many myths, particularly in the story of Oedipus.

Titans 12 children of Uranus and Gaea who make up the second generation of gods. The daughters are Eurybia, Phoebe, Rhea, Tethys, Theia, and Themis. The sons are Coeus, Crius, Cronus, Hyperion, Iapetus, and Oceanus. They form several pairings, the most notable being Cronus and Rhea, who beget Zeus and other Olympians. The Titans are defeated by Zeus and his allies and banished to Tartarus.

Triton Sea god; son of Poseidon and Amphitrite. In the plural Tritons are the half-man half-fish companions of the sea nymphs, the Nereids.

Tyche (Fortuna) Goddess of fortune, fate, and chance; daughter of Zeus in one version and Tethys and Oceanus in another. She is depicted with a wheel of fortune.

Uranus God of the sky; son and husband of Gaea (Earth); father of the Titans with Gaea. When the Titan Cronus castrates Uranus, Aphrodite is born from his blood.

Mesopotamian Mythology

Mesopotamia, the land "between the rivers" in the Tigris and Euphrates valleys (now Iraq and adjacent areas), was home to the world's earliest civilizations. The Sumerians, whose cities date back to around 4000 B.C., had a well-developed agricultural and mercantile economy and a rich religious life. A succession of other peoples, both Indo-European and Semitic, including the Hittites, Akkadians, Babylonians, and Assyrians, absorbed and added to the basic elements of Sumerian culture. There are many points of similarity between Mesopotamian mythology and events recorded in the Hebrew Bible, notably an account of a great world-engulfing flood.

The Sumerians and later Mesopotamian peoples recorded their myths (and much other information besides) in cuneiform writing inscribed on clay tablets. The main surviving sources of this mythology are the creation myth and cosmogony (account of the origin of the universe) in the Babylonian *Enuma Elish* (ca. 1000 B.C.), and the epic of *Gilgamesh*, a legendary king, known in its most complete form from tablets dating to the seventh century B.C. The myths in these sources have deep oral roots, and exist in several different and often inconsistent versions.

In the material below, deities are listed by their Sumerian names, with Akkadian, Babylonian, or Assyrian counterparts in parentheses.

Major Figures in Mesopotamian Myth and Legend

An (Anu) Personification of sky; husband of Ki (Earth); father of Enlil. An is a pivotal figure in creation myths but plays a much smaller role in later myths.

Apsu Personification of sweet water. In the Sumerian cosmogony, Apsu (masculine) and Tiamat (feminine) are the first entities to arise from the primordial oceans. From their union comes An and Enki. Apsu is killed by Enki.

Dumuzi (Tammuz) Shepherd god; god of vegetation; husband of Inanna. Inanna banishes him to the underworld, but he is given new life one day a year. This story is similar to those of the Egyptian Osiris and several Greek figures such as Persephone and Adonis.

Enki (Ea) God of the earth, groundwater, fecundity, and magic. Enki is crafty and the trickster among the gods but well disposed toward humans, to whom he gives the arts.

Enkidu Companion of Gilgamesh. Enkidu is a wild man molded from clay and sent by the gods to temper Gilgamesh, who had become a tyrannical king. They become best friends and share many adventures. Enkidu falls ill and dies after angering the gods.

Enlil Supreme sky god controlling storms and the destinies of men; son of An. Enlil is the equivalent of the Greek Zeus, king of the gods, who can be both a friendly and destructive force in human affairs.

Ereshkigal Goddess of death; sister of Inanna. Ereshkigal rules Kur, the underworld.

Gilgamesh King of Uruk; most popular legendary hero of Mesopotamian myth. Gilgamesh has many adventures, including slaying Humbaba, guardian of the forest; slaying the bull of heaven sent by Anu (An) at the request of Ishtar (Inanna), angry because Gilgamesh rejects her advances; and in a quest for eternal life, visiting the immortal Utnapishtim (Ziusudra).

Humbaba In the story of Gilgamesh, guardian of the forest in the domain of Shamash (Utu). Gilgamesh kills Humbaba, angering Enlil.

Inanna (Ishtar) Sumerian goddess of love and war; daughter of An; sister of Ereshkigal. Known for having a multitude of lovers, most notably Dumuzi (Tammuz), and for attempting to take control of the underworld from Ereshkigal.

Ki (Ninhursag) Supreme earth goddess; personification of Mother Earth; wife of An (Sky).

Kingu Second husband of Tiamat after Apsu. Tiamat intends to make Kingu the supreme deity, giving him the tablets of destiny, but they are both defeated by Marduk.

Marduk Son of Ea (Enki); protector of Babylon. A powerful figure in later Mesopotamian myth, Marduk defeats Tiamat and Kingu, becoming the supreme deity responsible for the arrangement of the universe in its current form.

Siduri Goddess of the vine. Gilgamesh comes to her in his quest for eternal life, and she tells him to eat, drink, enjoy life, and accept his mortality.

Tiamat Personification of salt water. See *Apsu*.

Urshanabi Ferryman of Utnapishtim (Ziusudra). Urshanabi helps Gilgamesh across perilous waters to the land where Utnapishtim lives in immortal bliss.

Utu (Shamash) Sun god responsible for justice among gods and men.

Ziusudra (Utnapishtim, Atrahasis) The Mesopotamian Noah, the only mortal spared from the universal flood. In his quest for eternal life, Gilgamesh goes to Utnapishtim (Ziusudra), who was made immortal, to find out how to overcome death; he tells Gilgamesh that he cannot.

Egyptian Mythology

Egyptian civilization grew from local cultures stretched along hundreds of miles of the Nile Valley, nourished by the annual flooding of the river. When these areas were unified in the Old Kingdom around 3000 B.C., a great deal of cultural diversity remained, and this is reflected in the complex and often contradictory myths that survive in Egyptian written sources. Despite internal differences, much of Egyptian religion was concerned with life, death, renewal, and the afterlife. The sun plays a large role in Egyptian mythology, with four major deities representing different aspects of the sun: Atum, Amon, Aten, and Ra.

The two most important Egyptian cosmogonies are identified with two principal pharonic cities, Heliopolis and Hermopolis. In the Heliopolitan cosmogony, the primoridal waters give birth to Atum (the Sun). From his mucus (or semen) comes Shu (Air) and Tefnut (Moisture). Shu and Tefnut beget Geb (Earth) and Nut (Sky), who beget two gods, Osiris and Seth, and two goddesses, Isis and Nephthys. These nine deities are the core pantheon, joined by other gods such as Horus, son of Isis and Osiris. The Hermopolitan cosmogony features four god-goddess pairs: Kuk and Kauket (darkness), Huh and Hauhet (limitlessness), Amon and Amaunet (invisibility), and Nun and Naunet (primordial waters).

When the pharaoh Menes (also called Narmer) united Upper and Lower Egypt to found the Old Kingdom (ca. 2575–2130 B.C.), he joined together the two pantheons; in his system, Ptah spoke the eight Hermopolitan gods into existence, and then engendered the nine Heliopolitan deities. These and other deities, with just some of their attributes and myths, are listed below.

Major Figures in Egyptian Mythology

Amon Sun and wind god. With his female counterpart, Amaunet, Amon represented the principle of invisibility in the Hermopolitan cosmogony. As Amon-Ra he became a very powerful deity in later dynasties.

Anubis Jackal-headed god of mummification.

Apis A great bull that was identified with Ptah.

Aten Personification of the sun disk. The pharaoh Amenhotep IV, who renamed himself Akhenaten, declared Aten the sole higher power. After Akhenaten's death (1350 B.C.), the cult of Aten declined.

Atum Sun god, particularly of the setting sun; chief deity and creator god. In the Heliopolitan cosmogony, Atum comes from Nun, the primordial waters, and creates Shu (Air) and Tefnut (Moisture).

Bastet Cat goddess; goddess of vengeance; daughter of Ra; consort of Ptah. The cult of Bastet did not arise until around 1000 B.C.

Geb (Seb) See *Nut*.

Hapi Personification of the annual flooding of the Nile.

Hathor Goddess of love and fertility; daughter of Ra. Hathor is depicted as a cow and thought to be present at births. Many pharaohs deemed themselves the son of Hathor. In some accounts of the story of the eye of Ra, she becomes Sekhmet (see *Sekhmet*).

Horus Sky god; god of horizons; son of Isis and Osiris. Horus, often depicted as a falcon, was the most popular and powerful deity at times, with many pharaohs claiming to be an incarnation of the god.

Isis Goddess of love; wife and sister of Osiris; mother of Horus. Isis is often associated with the Mesopotamian Inanna/Astarte/Ishtar and the Greek Aphrodite. See also *Osiris*.

Khnum Ram-headed god of the Nile's rising water. In older accounts Khnum creates the gods and mankind on his potter's wheel.

Ma'at Goddess of truth and justice. Her symbol is a feather that is weighed against the heart of the dead to decide the fate of the soul.

Mut Vulture goddess; consort of Amon. Mummies wore a Mut amulet.

Nephthys Daughter of Geb and Nut; sister of Isis, Osiris, and Seth. Nephthys is depicted as the companion of the dead as they make their journey to be judged in the afterlife.

Nut Personification of sky; daughter of Shu and Tefnut; wife of Geb (Earth); mother of Isis, Osiris, Seth, and Nephthys. In the Heliopolitan cosmogony, Nut is separated from Geb (Sky from Earth) by Shu (Air).

Osiris God of the underworld and judge of the dead; son of Geb and Nut. Osiris's brother Seth cuts him into pieces, and he is reconstituted and resurrected by his sister Isis, with whom he fathers the god Horus. Osiris is also a fertility god associated with the flooding of the Nile.

Ptah Earth god. Ptah is the primordial hill that appears out of water and speaks the rest of the gods into existence in the Memphite theology. In another account he creates the gods and universe from mud.

Ra Sun god, particularly the midday sun. In the Heliopolitan cosmogony, Ra (along with his other two aspects, Atum and Khepri) emerges out of Nun, the primordial waters, and creates Shu (Air) and Tefnut (Moisture). In later dynasties Ra takes on the form Amon-Ra and becomes a very powerful deity. (See also *Sekhmet.*)

Sekhmet Personification of feminine power; goddess of war and vengeance. Sekhmet, depicted as a lioness, is created from the eye of Ra to destroy mankind. Ra changes his mind and stops her before she has completely ravaged the earth. In some versions Ra turns Hathor into Sekhmet for the task.

Seth Malevolent god of storms, foreign lands, and destructive forces; son of Geb and Nut. Seth was the patron of the desert land of Upper Egypt and was at times the chief god, while Horus ruled at other times. Seth is often seen engaged in a power struggle with Horus in myth. (See also *Osiris.*)

Shu Personification of air; husband of Tefnut (Moisture); father of Geb (Earth) and Nut (Sky). In the Heliopolitan cosmogony he is one of the deities created by Atum. (See also *Nut.*)

Tefnut See *Shu.*

Thoth God of wisdom, writing, and the moon. Worshipped in Hermopolis, he was depicted as a baboon. Some accounts make Thoth the son of Ra.

Norse Mythology

Norse mythology is the pre-Christian religion of the Scandinavian people of Norway, Sweden, Denmark, and Iceland in the first millennium A.D. The main sources for Norse myth are the Icelandic Eddas (sagas), which were written down in the mid-13th century A.D. but based on stories that had been developing for nearly a thousand years earlier. Norse myth resembles other European and Middle Eastern mythologies in many ways.

The creation myth involves a primordial gap out of which the basic elements arise, just as in Greco-Roman and Mesopotamian mythology. There are also several generations of gods. In Norse myth the two most important races of gods are the Vanir and the Aesir. The Aesir are the ruling body living in Asgard, the realm of the gods. There are other clearly delineated realms in the Norse cosmogony, most importantly Midgard, the realm of man; Hel, the underworld; and Valhalla, the land where slain warriors go to live for eternity among the gods. Elves, dwarves, the Vanir gods, and giants all have their own realms.

One of the most important assumptions in Norse myth is that there will be a final conflict between gods and giants called Ragnarok. In this battle many gods will be killed and some will survive to create and rule over a new universe. Many entries below refer to stories in Norse myth that have already "happened," as well as stories of that figure's fate at Ragnarok.

Major Figures in Norse Mythology

Aegir God of the sea; husband of Ran, with whom he has nine daughters, the Waves; entertainer and brewer of the gods, often seen hosting feasts in his underwater hall.

Balder God of light; son of Odin and Frigg; husband of Nanna; father of Forseti. Balder is a benevolent deity, loved by all except jealous Loki. Loki tricks Balder's blind brother Hodur into killing him with mistletoe, Balder's only mortal weakness. Nanna then kills herself. It is said that Balder will be resurrected after Ragnarok. (See also *Valio*)

Bragi God of poetry; son of Odin and Frigg; husband of Idun. Wise Bragi is the patron of skalds (poets); he is depicted with runes carved on his tongue.

Fenrir Wolf Offspring of Loki and Angrboda (giantess). It is prophesized that the giant wolf will cause the destruction of the world, so the gods trick the beast into magical fetters. At Ragnarok Fenrir will break free and devour Odin.

Forseti God of justice; son of Balder and Nanna. Forseti lives in Glitnir, a palace that serves as a divine courtroom.

Freyja Goddess of love, fertility, and childbirth; daughter of Njord; sister (and possible consort) of Freyr; wife of Od (maybe another form of Odin). Freyja travels on a chariot drawn by two cats or the boar Hildeswin. Freyja and Freyr along with their father, Njord, are sent by the Vanir to live among the Aesir in a hostage exchange. (See also *Frigg.*)

Freyr God of peace, prosperity, and fertility; lord of the elves (alfs); son of Njord; husband of Gerd (beautiful giantess); brother (and possible consort) of Freyja. Freyr travels around in a magical ship, the Skidbladner, or a chariot pulled by the boar Gullinborsti. His loyal servant is Skirnir. Freyr is to be killed by the giant Surt at Ragnarok. (See also *Freyja.*)

Frigg (Frigga, Fricka) Goddess of fertility, motherhood and sensuality; wife of Odin; mother of Balder, Bragi, Hodur, and Hermod. Frigg's home in Asgard is called Fensalir. Frigg and Freyja may be different forms of the same goddess.

Gerd See *Freyr*.

Heimdall Watchman of the Aesir gods. Heimdall stands guard at the Bifrost, the bridge to Asgard, where he waits for the coming of Ragnarok, which he will announce with his horn, the Gjallar. At Ragnarok Heimdall and Loki will kill each other. As Rig, he creates the three races of man—the slaves, the peasants, and the nobles/warriors.

Hel (Hella, Holle) Goddess of the underworld; daughter of Loki and Angrboda (giantess); sister of Fenrir and Jormurgandr. She is depicted as half living woman and half rotting corpse.

Hodur God of darkness and winter; son of Odin and Frigg. (See also *Balder* and *Vali*.)

Idun Goddess of eternal youth; wife of Bragi. Idun is the keeper of the golden apples of youth that the gods must eat when they feel they are aging. In one story she is abducted by a giant. Without Idun's fruit the gods begin aging and send Loki to retrieve her.

Jormurgandr Midgard serpent; offspring of Loki and Angrboda (giantess); sibling of Fenrir and Hel. The serpent is cast out of heaven by Odin and left to grow as the destructive force of the oceans. At Ragnarok Jormurgandr and Thor will kill each other.

Loki Shape-changing god of mischief and often destruction; husband of Sigyn; with Angrboda (giantess) father of Fenrir, Hel, and Jormurgandr. Loki is a giant who is made one of the Aesir by Odin. After causing the death of Balder, the gods chain Loki to three rocks where he remains until Ragnarok. In the conflict he will lead the opposition against the gods. (See also *Balder, Heimdall,* and *Idun*.)

Nanna See *Balder*.

Njord God of wind, sea, and fire. (See also *Freyja* and *Freyr*.)

Norns Fates. The Norns are three sisters (Urd, Verdandi, and Skuld) responsible for the destinies of gods and men.

Odin (Woden, Wotan) Chief god of the Aesir; god of wisdom, poetry, and war; husband of Frigg; father of Balder, Brag, Hodur, and Hermod (with Frigg), Thor (with the goddess Jord), Vali (with Rind), and Vidar (with Grid). Odin is often depicted as an aged warrior with one eye, having sacrificed the other for knowledge. He is accompanied by two ravens, Hugin (Thought) and Munin (Memory), who tell him what is going on in the world, and served by the Valkyries and the horse Sleipnir. At Ragnarok Odin will be devoured by Fenrir. (See also *Tyr*.)

Ran Sea goddess of the drowned; wife of Aegir; mother of the Waves. Ran catches drowned sailors in her net and tends to them.

Sif Wife of Thor; mother of Ullr. She is depicted with golden hair and was probably originally a fertility or harvest goddess.

Sigurd Greatest hero of Germanic legend. The story of Sigurd's heroic feats and his freeing of the Valkyrie Brunhilde from a magical sleep imposed by Odin is told in the Saga of the Volsungs.

Skadi Goddess of skis and snowshoes; daughter of the giant Thiassi. Skadi goes to take revenge on the Aesir gods who killed her father. To appease her she is allowed to marry one of them but must choose only seeing their feet. She picks the aged Njord thinking he is the handsome Balder. Skadi and Njord separate, and she goes on to marry Odin and then Ullr.

Thor (Donnar) God of thunder and fertility; son of Odin and Jord (earth goddess); husband of Sif; stepfather of Ullr. Thor's attributes are a mighty hammer (Mjollnir) that causes lightning, a belt that doubles his already massive strength and a chariot pulled by two goats. Thor was the most popular god among common people. At Ragnarok Thor will slay the Midgard serpent but then die from its venom.

Tyr (Tiw, Ziw) God of war and justice. Tyr is the original leader of the gods before Odin ousts him. Tyr is one-handed because the other is bitten off by the wolf Fenrir while the gods are binding the beast. At Ragnarok he and the hound Garm will kill each other.

Ullr God of justice, archery, dueling, skis, and snowshoes; son of Sif (also called the stepson of Thor). When Skadi leaves Njord, she marries Ullr.

Vali Son of Odin and Rind. At one-day old Vali kills Hodur to avenge the death of Balder. He will survive Ragnarok and rule with Vidar when the new world is created.

Valkyries Maidens serving Odin. The Valkyries were responsible for dooming warriors to die and transporting them to Valhalla.

Vidar God of vengeance; son of Odin and Grid (giantess). At Ragnarok Vidar will slay the wolf Fenrir to avenge the death of his father. He is one of the gods that will survive to rule when the conflict is over and the new world is created.

PHILOSOPHY

Branches of Philosophy 484

History of Western Philosophy 484

Pre-Socratic Philosophers of Ancient Greece 484

Hellenistic and Roman Philosophy . . 488

Medieval Philosophy 488

Early Modern Philosophy 490

The Enlightenment 491

19th Century Philosophy 492

20th Century Philosophy 493

PHILOSOPHY

Philosophy (Greek, "love of wisdom") attempts to understand basic questions of the human condition rationally, without resorting to superstition or myth. Some of those questions are: What is the world? Does God exist? What is truth? What is knowledge? What is the best form of government? What gives life meaning?

These questions have never been settled to widespread satisfaction. As a result, many people have the impression that philosophical inquiry is futile.

Yet the study of philosophy has deeply affected most people, even those who are not themselves philosophers. Most branches of knowledge (such as physics, biology, and the social sciences) are highly specialized studies of questions that were originally discussed by philosophers. Today, philosophers continue to debate the basic assumptions that make these specialized studies possible. Philosophy also considers how different branches of knowledge ought to relate to a question, when they seem to overlap and conflict with one another. For example, *bioethics* (a branch of philosophy) asks whether a problem, such as euthanasia, should be a matter of medical science, of individual rights, or of government.

Branches of Philosophy

Philosophical inquiry may be directed at practically any field of study. There is, for example, *political philosophy* (the philosophy of politics) and *natural philosophy* (the philosophy of nature, or science). As a more general field of study, philosophy is traditionally broken down into four major branches:

Metaphysics (Greek, "after physics") seeks to describe the ultimate nature of reality. It asks questions that go beyond physics; it considers the ultimate nature of spiritual or nonphysical entities, such as ideas and emotions. It also debates fundamental questions about existence that are often accepted as self-evident by the hard sciences.

Epistemology, or theory of knowledge, is closely associated with metaphysics, and considers how people come to know what they know. It is the study of the nature, source, and limits of understanding.

Logic is the branch of philosophy devoted to understanding and expressing the rules of reasoning and inference. Logic originated with Aristotle, who introduced the use of variables as a tool for describing logical argument in general terms.

Ethics is the study of principles for proper human behavior. It is primarily concerned with establishing moral guidelines and debating their usefulness.

Aesthetics is sometimes counted as a fifth branch of philosophy. It is concerned with the nature and benefits of art, beauty, and other sensual experiences.

History of Western Philosophy

Pre-Socratic Philosophers of Ancient Greece

Although their surviving written work is fragmentary, ancient Greek thinkers of the seventh to fifth centuries B.C. are usually credited with founding Western philosophy. Most of their work is known to us only through references made by other writers, especially Aristotle.

The pre-Socratics sought explanations over and above those offered by mythology. Most of these philosophers believed they could find rational explanations for the behavior of natural phenomena. The most common object of their inquiries was the nature of matter. These musings were thus the beginning of both *ontology* (the search for a rational explanation of the nature of existence) and science. Some pre-Socratics also made major advances in the early development of mathematics and ethics.

Although the word *pre-Socratic* appears to slight the achievements of Greek philosophers preceding Socrates, it also implies that Socrates' achievements did not arise out of a vacuum. His thinking was heavily influenced by those who came before him.

The Milesian School: The First Greek Philosophers The work of Thales of Miletus (ca. 625–ca. 545 B.C.), renowned as an astronomer and statesman as well as a metaphysician, is traditionally regarded as the starting point of Western philosophy. He and his disciples Anaximander (ca. 610–ca. 540 B.C.) and Anaximenes (fl. ca. 545) suggested that everything in the world derives from a single "original principle." Thales argued that the source of all things is water, presumably because it was believed that Earth floated on water. Also, water is known to assume various forms as solid, liquid, and gas.

Although no philosopher after Thales agreed that all things come from water, Thales successfully proposed a problem that intrigued all who came later. Perhaps the world works according to definite rational principles, and perhaps the nature of those principles could be discovered through observation of the natural world.

Anaximander argued that the source of all things could not itself be a material. Instead he proposed that it is something called "the boundless." Anaximenes, by contrast, argued that the source of all things is air, of which all other substances (such as fog, water, earth, metal) are condensed forms.

Pythagoreanism In Croton (now Crotona), on the Italian peninsula, Pythagoras (ca. 570–ca. 495 B.C.) founded a school of philosophy, which survived through the fourth century B.C. It is now impossible to distinguish the achievements of Pythagoras himself from those of the school named after him. The Pythagoreans are credited with discovering the famous geometrical theorem defining the relative lengths of the sides of a right triangle. They also discovered the mathematical basis of musical pitch, which is the foundation of our understanding of harmony. Socrates and Plato were influenced by the Pythagorean belief that mathematics should be a model for true human understanding.

Heraclitus (late fifth century B.C.) lived in Ephesus, not far from Miletus; he appeared to be interested in taking up the problems proposed by the Milesians. He proposed that the source of all things is fire. This belief was probably metaphorical, because Heraclitus loved paradox; fire needs to consume in order to exist. Heraclitus appeared to believe that existence is by nature paradoxical; the definition of anything seems to depend on its opposite: hot depends on cold, up depends on down, and so on. He is credited with the often-quoted line, "You can never step in the same river twice, for fresh waters are ever flowing in."

The Eleatic School and the Nature of Being Philosophers of the Eleatic school were the first Westerners to articulate a problem that has occupied philosophers ever since: the notion that there is a marked difference between the "real" world, accessible only through reason, and the mundane world that humans normally perceive and experience, accessible through the senses.

Parmenides (b. ca. 515 B.C.) argued that the concepts of "being" and "not-being" are so exclusive that nothing can be understood about not-being. In other words: nothing can come out of nothing. It then follows that any change is impossible, because change implies that something previously nonexistent has come into being. Motion is also logically impossible, because motion can happen only if change is possible. The real world must be thus one in which change and motion exist only as illusions.

Zeno of Elea (ca. 490–ca. 430 B.C.), Parmenides's most famous pupil, came up with a series of paradoxes that illustrate the theory of an unchanging universe. These paradoxes seek to prove that motion is impossible because time and space can be divided into an infinite series of parts. For example, in order for an arrow to reach its target, it must first cover half the distance to the target, then half of the remaining distance, then half of that remainder, and so on. Since time is infinitely divisible, the arrow will always have a little more distance to travel before it reaches its target. Hence, the arrow will never reach its target.

Advances in Natural Philosophy Despite the largely impractical theories of the Eleatic school, natural philosophers continued to pursue the investigation of matter, basing their theories (at least in part) on observation and experience. Some of the theories developed were remarkably sophisticated and useful.

Empedocles (ca. 495–ca. 435 B.C.) proposed four natural sources of existence (earth, fire, water, and air) which reside in different proportions in all things and are transformed by the forces of harmony and discord. In response to Parmenides's theories, Empedocles also proposed that the four elements exist in constant and unchanging quantities in the universe—an early statement of the conservation of matter, a principle of Newtonian physics.

Anaxagoras (ca. 500–ca. 428 B.C.) further expanded the list of elements, proposing that they are infinite in number. The universe was originally a homogeneous mixture of all the elements, until they were set into motion and order by "mind." This mind is characterized as being capable not only of acting on matter; it could also mix itself into matter, being the distinguishing feature of animate matter, or living organisms.

Leucippus (late fifth century B.C.) posited that the world consists of nothing but empty space containing indivisible atoms. His pupil Democritus (ca. 460–ca. 370 B.C.) developed a more complete system to explain the entire physical universe through atomic structure. Atoms, in his view, have various shapes and sizes accounting for the visual characteristics of, and interactions between, objects, as well as the emotions and ethical character of men.

The Sophists In the fifth century B.C., Greek learning expanded in almost every direction. It became more and more difficult for learned men to keep up with new developments and to educate the next generation. Also, the ability to influence others through the use of rational argument was increasingly prized, mostly for arguing legal cases, but also for advancing one's political agenda in the more democratic city-states. In this environment, teachers called Sophists began to travel from town to town in the Greek-speaking world. Usually they made their living by charging fees for giving instructional speeches on rhetoric, logic, and ethics.

The teachings of the Sophists varied widely; there was no "school" of sophistry. But in general, Sophists tended to use skilled argument and logic to expound on the political and ethical issues of the day. The Sophists were less concerned with natural philosophy. Some found the more paradoxical teachings of Heraclitus and the Eleatics very useful for confusing opponents in a debate.

Of the Sophists, Protagoras (ca. 490–ca. 420 B.C.) was the most well known. His famous dictum that "Man is the measure of all things" emphasized the relativity of truth. Since each person is a judge of truth, the relative "correctness" of any argument depends entirely on the speaker's ability to persuade. Protagoras professed to be able to teach people, through rhetorical skill, how to transform the weaker argument into the stronger, whether or not the weaker argument is true.

Socrates

It would be difficult to overestimate the influence of Socrates of Athens (469–399 B.C.) on the development of Western philosophy—particularly in the fields of ethics and epistemology. Nearly every major philosopher interested in these fields has addressed basic questions as formulated by Socrates.

Most Athenians of his time regarded Socrates as one of the Sophists, but Socrates was not a traveling lecturer and accepted no fees for instruction. He was preoccupied by philosophical questions that he debated freely and frequently in public gathering places. He also attracted a following of bright young men, which his enemies found threatening. At the age of 70, Socrates was convicted by the Athenian assembly on charges that he was impious, introduced false gods, and corrupted the youth. These crimes brought the penalty of death. Rather than escape and live in exile, as his friends had arranged and urged, Socrates chose to accept the sentence of the assembly and drink poison hemlock about one month after his conviction.

Socrates' philosophical beliefs are known primarily through the dialogues written by his disciple Plato. Although Socrates is featured as a character in most of Plato's dialogues, there is general agreement among philosophers (beginning with Aristotle) that not all of Plato's dialogues reflect the beliefs of Socrates alone. The dialogues, especially those written later in Plato's life, more closely reflect Plato's own philosophy. Perhaps only the early dialogues reflect the thinking of Socrates without much Platonic embellishment.

In the early Platonic dialogues Socrates is usually looking for the definition of a virtue such as "piety" (in the *Euthypro*) or "courage" (in the *Laches*). Professing ignorance of the matter, Socrates asks his querent to supply a definition. Then through a round of questioning Socrates tests the definition, and all participants find it wanting. The querent is then urged to alter the definition, and the new definition is tested. This usually goes on for a couple of rounds until the querent professes to be in a state of *aporia*, or helplessness. None of his definitions avoids self-contradiction. The dialogue ends with no definition holding up under this *Socratic method* of questioning. But the actual exercise of creating and dismissing the definitions may have been in some way enlightening for all participants.

Although the exact nature of Socrates' underlying assumptions is a matter of debate, it is possible to make some general observations about Socratic principles that are not controversial. Socrates loathed the title Sophist, mostly because some of the Sophists, such as Protagoras, were relativists. They felt that truth could be claimed by the argument that swayed the most people. Socrates did not accept the notion that truth can be relative or changeable. Since a mathematician knows with certainty that a good geometric proof admits no contradiction, Socrates believed that important ethical ideas should aspire to a similar standard of certainty.

Additionally, Socrates frequently characterized virtue as a form of knowledge that should be learned. He believed that anyone who goes through a process of self-scrutiny and ultimately discovers the true nature of virtue, *must act virtuously*. In a sense, he believed that bad behavior is a form of ignorance.

Finally, the Socratic method itself appears to arise from an assumption that an individual cannot understand virtue without going through this process of rigorous self-examination. Socrates himself stated before the Athenian assembly, in his self-defense, that life without self-examination "is not worth living." (*Apology* 38a)

Plato

Plato's (427–347 B.C.) primary contribution to philosophy is a series of about 24 pieces of writing that have come to be known as Platonic dialogues. These dialogues are neither plays nor philosophical treatises. Instead, they are a peculiar literary form designed to reflect the importance of the Socratic method of teaching: discussing and answering probing questions. As such, these dialogues contain no explicit message; readers are left to form their own opinion based on the arguments presented. Because of this method of presentation, Plato's actual philosophy and its differences from Socratic thought are both subjects of debate among scholars.

The most well-known passage in Plato's written work, and also the most debated, is the "Allegory of the Cave" section of the *Republic*. In the allegory, normal human perception is depicted as analogous to the perception of slaves chained since birth in a position where they are facing the wall of a cave. On the wall shadow play is enacted by puppets paraded in front of a fire, but the slaves' chains don't permit them to look backward and see the source of the shadow play or the firelight. Supposing one of the slaves were freed from his chains and looked backward, he would come to understand that the shadows have no existence of their own that does not derive from the firelight and the puppets. This freed slave might later even travel out of the cave to witness daylight and look upon the world illuminated by the sun. Yet if he went back into the cave and tried to convince his fellow slaves that they perceived only illusions, they would be angry with him and perhaps kill him for disrupting their illusion. (This is a clear allusion to the life and death of Socrates.)

The point of the allegory is to describe how reality might be quite different from normal perception. Theories of existence (*ontology*) that argue that reality is different from normal perception are known as *realism*. To this day, the Allegory of the Cave remains the best known justification of a realist ontology.

Several of Plato's dialogues present a theory of *forms* that is also characteristic of Plato's thought. According to this theory, there may be a class of existence for ideal and unchanging versions of the things we know, and Plato calls these unchanging ideals "forms (*ideai*)." Presumably, there is a form for table that is an ideal table and never changes. More important, there are forms for virtues, such as piety, justice, and courage, all of which add up to the highest form (the sun in the allegory) of "the good." According to Plato, these forms should be the object of a philosopher's study.

Aristotle

Plato's other lasting contribution to the development of philosophy, besides the dialogues, was the founding of the Academy (387 B.C.), a school dedicated to philosophical and political learning. The school lasted nine centuries, until Emperor Justinian closed it and every other remnant of the Greek philosophical schools in A.D. 529. The most famous and influential product of the Academy, Aristotle (384–322 B.C.), set up a rival school, the Lyceum, in 335 B.C.

Aristotle produced a massive body of work on widely divergent topics. His writings shaped philosophical and scientific inquiry for centuries. Unlike Socrates and Plato, who were both focused on finding unifying principles through abstract reason, Aristotle was much more open to contemplating and understanding the complexities of nature as perceived by the senses. Aristotle traveled widely, collecting biological data wherever he went, and he took an interest in the pre-Socratics' work on the nature of matter.

He opposed Plato's theory of forms, suggesting that they are not fixed and absolute. The highest form, or "the good," means different things for different creatures. Virtue and happiness both derive from realizing one's individual nature, and thus for humans, who are highly social and adaptable, this can mean many different things. Some of the most realized humans are those who develop humanity's peculiar gift for thought and contemplation, but it would be ridiculous to expect the same virtue from a turtle. Consequently, Aristotle's ethics stresses discovering *how* to achieve personal happiness, rather than defining *what* correct behavior is for everyone.

Another of Aristotle's contributions to the development of philosophy was his structured analysis of logic. He defined a *syllogism* as a logical argument consisting of a major premise, a minor premise, and a conclusion: all men are mortal; Socrates is a man; therefore, Socrates is mortal.

Perhaps Aristotle's most widely-read work is his esoteric treatise on aesthetics, the *Poetics*. According to his analysis of tragic poetry (a section on comedy was either lost or never completed), the theatrical audience experiences *katharsis* (purgation) of the heightened emotions of pity and fear as the tragic hero, a basically good but flawed aristocrat, is brought down by his own "error of judgment" (*hamartia*).

Hellenistic and Roman Philosophy

After Aristotle, philosophy spread out from the domain of cultured aristocrats in Athens and entered the imagination of a wider audience, one that seemed eager for a supplement to pagan religious beliefs in more troubled times. The popular philosophies of the Hellenistic and Roman periods were often less intellectually rigorous than Athenian philosophy, but far more influential on the culture and history of the period. Still, the figure of Socrates remained highly influential, not so much because of his reasoning, as because of his exemplary life.

Skepticism All Hellenistic philosophies took an interest in epistemology and tended to question the basis of knowledge. The Skeptics were most extreme in this regard, denying even the possibility of knowledge.

Pyrrho of Elis (ca. 360–ca. 275 B.C.) was the most influential of the Skeptics. According to one source he traveled to India with Alexander's army, and there he encountered philosophies that denied the existence of the physical world. Pyrrho believed that existence is impossible to prove, and happiness is possible only through emotional indifference to events in the apparent world. After Pyrrho, Skepticism was widely adopted by the scholars in the Academy of Athens founded earlier by Plato.

Epicureanism Named for Epicurus of Samos (341–270 B.C.), Epicureanism was essentially agnostic, professing no knowledge of any world outside of the physical one. Given the lack of a divine directive for human behavior, the Epicureans turned to personal pleasure as a source of happiness.

Many have since misinterpreted the Epicurean attitude toward pleasure as a ruling principle. The original Epicureans were not hedonistic. They believed that pleasure consisted in removing pain from life, resulting in tranquility. This would be best achieved by satisfying only a limited number of desires, the ones that would cause pain if not satisfied.

Stoicism Although Stoicism is often described as inferior to the great philosophies of the Athenian period, Stoic thinkers are the source of many lasting and influential ideas, such as beliefs in the fundamental equality of all persons (universal brotherhood) and the concept of natural rights. The Stoics also admired Socrates because he remained focused on universal, timeless principles despite personal hardship and eventual martyrdom. Similar ideas were later widely accepted by, and considered characteristic of, Christianity.

Zeno of Citium (334–262 B.C.) founded Stoicism, teaching in the porticos (or *stoa*) of Athens. He was influenced by the teachings of Pyrrho, but stopped short of Pyrrho's radically negative theory of knowledge. Zeno's ideas were furthered by many who came later, including Chrysippus (ca. 280–207 B.C.), and the Romans Seneca (3 B.C.–A.D.65), Epictetus (ca. 55–ca. 135 A.D.), and Emperor Marcus Aurelius (A.D. 121–180).

The Stoics believed that people are alone among all beings in that they possess the ability to understand and react to the reason (*logos*) that orders the universe. People cannot control the world, but they can seek to understand and live by the principles that govern the world. Like the Skeptics, the Stoics sought to develop an emotional indifference to their environment, because it signaled an acceptance of the order of things.

Medieval Philosophy

Medieval philosophy covers a vast time period: from the fall of the Roman Empire in the fourth and fifth centuries to the dawn of the Renaissance in the 15th century. During most of that time the climate in Europe was not hospitable to philosophical ideas, mostly due to Christian hostility to pagan beliefs. Major Christian thinkers were often inspired by Greek philosophy, but they were checked by a faith that subordinated reason to divine revelation as a source of knowledge. As time went on, most manuscripts of Greek philosophy were either destroyed or allowed to disintegrate. It was not until the 12th century that scholars regained access to copies of Greek manuscripts preserved in the Islamic world.

The predominant philosophical debate throughout this period was, in fact, related to the predominant debate of the Hellenistic and Roman periods: to what extent should one trust philosophical reason as a source of knowledge? Before the rise of Christianity, this debate was purely epistemological: is knowledge possible? But Christianity supplied a challenge to reason that was quite different from that of Skepticism. Christians professed profound certainty of some forms of knowledge, knowledge based on divine revelation through faith, not based on reason. But from time to time Christian thinkers emerged making various claims about the usefulness of reason along with faith.

Early Medieval Philosophical Theology Saint Augustine of Hippo (354–430) was perhaps the first significant Christian philosopher. His interest in non-Christian philosophy emboldened other educated Christians to read philosophy as well. His thinking drew heavily from Plotinus (205–71), whose mixture of Platonic, Aristotelian, and Stoic beliefs came to be known as *Neoplatonism*. Plotinus believed that the order (*logos*) of the universe emanated from a single spiritual entity, and Augustine, in his major work, *The City of God*, identified these features with the Christian godhead.

Saint Anselm of Canterbury (1033–1109) promoted reason as an important and valuable counterpart to revelation, a position that helped to pave the way for later Scholasticism. Anselm used Aristotelian logic to produce three proofs of the existence of God. One of those proofs, known as the "ontological argument for the existence of God," was remarkably original. It deduced God's existence from humanity's ability to understand God as a being so great that it is impossible to conceive of one greater. According to the argument, people would not have the capacity to understand this concept if God did not exist.

Scholasticism In the 12th century, an increase in urban development led to major changes in the centers of learning, which were evolving from religious institutions into universities. The universities of Paris and Oxford were founded in 1150 and 1168 respectively, and their curricula began to place greater emphasis on disciplines that had come down from the Greek philosophers, such as logic, dialectic, and the natural sciences.

Aristotle was the most influential ancient philosopher during the high Middle Ages, thanks to the appearance of new translations of and commentaries on his work from the Arab Islamic world. Chief among the Arab sources were Ibn Sina, known as Avicenna (980–1037), and later, Ibn Rushd, known as Averroës (1126–98).

Saint Thomas Aquinas (1225–74) was a Dominican monk whose interest in Aristotle caused him to write a complete systematic Christian theology, the *Summa Theologiae*, based on Aristotelian principles. He constructed five arguments proving the existence of God, all based on reason. He also argued that, ultimately, both reason and revelation were viable and parallel pathways to knowledge of God. The former is accessible only to a few, but the latter is available to all.

The Divergence of Philosophy and Theology Late in the medieval period more philosophers at the leading universities began to suggest that reason might be more important than revelation, and that scholarship should pursue reason even if it diverged from accepted theology. A group at the University of Paris known as the Latin Averroists (for their adherence to principles articulated in Averroës's commentaries on Aristotle), led by Siger de Brabant (ca. 1240–84), were among the most vocal proponents of this position. Augustinians and other churchmen cited this development as proof that pagan and Islamic influences were leading to the disintegration of the Christian faith.

William of Ockham (ca. 1285–1347), was a Franciscan monk whose interpretations of Aristotle introduced the possibility of greater conflict between scholars and the church. His logical principle, known as *Ockham's razor*, maintains that when choosing between possible explanations of a phenomenon, the simplest explanation is best. Following his principle (and Aristotle), Ockham dismissed the notion that categories of thought, universals, or ideals were real things. He asserted that they were instead only intellectual constructs. (By contrast, Augustine and Aquinas had seen universals as an important bridge between spiritual reality and reason.) Ockham's position became known as *nominalism*, because he believed these categories of thought were only names (*nomoi*) and had no existence, spiritual or otherwise.

Early Modern Philosophy

Whereas medieval philosophy was overwhelmingly associated with and influenced by the Christian church, philosophical inquiry in the 15th and 16th centuries took quite a different direction, due to social and technological changes. As secular state power displaced the power of the church in Europe, many philosophers focused anew on political and social theory. Rapid advances in technology and geographical exploration went hand in hand with new leaps in natural philosophy; and the invention of the printing press allowed more people to read and participate in the major philosophical debates of the time.

Renaissance Political Theorists As the power of the Christian church waned, many philosophers turned from theology to the study of social morality and political power. Among the most prominent of political thinkers was Niccolò Machiavelli (1469–1527), whose examinations of political power echoed those of the Sophists. Machiavelli suggested that the power and authority of the state was often more important than individual morality or liberty, and that life could be improved only through the effective application of power. Others, like Thomas Hobbes (1588–1679) saw government and the rule of law as an antidote to the natural state of man, a war of all against all in which life was "nasty, brutish, and short."

Renaissance Humanism One of the defining movements of the Renaissance, Humanism was not strictly a philosophical school. Rather, it represented a broad worldview that placed humanity and reason at the center of the universe. It gave humans pride of place in the natural world by virtue of their superior faculties of reason. New translations of the complete works of Plato played a role in the new focus on Humanism, as did renewed appreciation for the works of the Stoics and Skeptics. Humanism prompted a resurgence of the dialogue form of philosophical writing, which was a style more in keeping with the broadly artistic and literary nature of the movement.

Early Empiricism Until at least the early 18th century, philosophy still encompassed the fields of inquiry that would later splinter off into mathematics, physics, and other sciences. The medieval image of a God-driven universe was challenged by new scientific discoveries and philosophical descriptions of a world that obeyed only mechanical and mathematical rules.

This changing view of the world was also reflected in epistemology. Sir Francis Bacon (1561–1626), was one of the first proponents of Empiricism, a philosophic school that stressed sensory experience and rigorous observation as the true path to knowledge. He was extremely skeptical of any claim to knowledge based on any other authority. In his view, only "bodies" (material objects) exist and these must conform only to natural laws, or "forms."

Like Bacon, René Descartes (1596–1650) sought to establish a system of knowledge that rejected the authority of the church and all previous philosophy. But Descartes did not place his greatest trust in information obtained through the senses. In his *Meditations on First Philosophy* (1641) his skepticism extended to refute naive empiricism. He maintained that the senses must be doubted, because when we dream we think we are taking in sensory information, when, in fact, we are not. Also, Descartes invented an additional reason to be skeptical of almost all knowledge. Suppose there is an omnipotent evil demon with the power to deceive people at every turn! How could one know that any information is not being skewed by such a demon?

Descartes's response gave rise to one of the most famous phrases found in the history of philosophy. He reasoned that even in the case of an evil demon's deception, the demon could not have the power to make Descartes doubt his own existence, as long as he remains a thinking being. The thinker knows his thoughts are the thoughts of a being with existence: "I think; therefore I am." (Latin: *cogito ergo sum*) On this foundation Descartes proceeded to build a rational philosophy, i.e. a philosophy based on reason, rather than experience.

Despite the apparent primacy of reason in Descartes's thinking, most would agree that the philosophical system he subsequently built contained vestiges of medieval Christian thinking. Most heavily criticized is Descartes's view of humans as exceptional beings, the only ones possessing minds composed of a wholly different substance from matter. This view is commonly characterized as mind-body dualism, and it appears to reflect Christian beliefs more than either reason or science. It fails to explain the mutual dependence of mind and body and their coincidence in space and time.

Baruch Spinoza's (1632–77) earliest writings were expositions of Descartes. Like his mentor's philosophy, Spinoza's thinking was firmly entrenched in the rationalist school. But unlike Descartes, Spinoza was Jewish (and at odds with orthodox Jewish beliefs). Consequently, he was far less influenced by medieval Christian patterns of thinking about God and the world. As a result, Spinoza's highly original philosophy was much more true to the spirit of a hyperrational age.

Spinoza resolved a host of philosophical difficulties by defining God as one and the same as nature and all existing matter. This view is often characterized as *pantheism*, a belief that all things are divine. Accordingly, the question of God's existence is settled, since everything that exists is itself God by definition. Matter may appear in different forms, but the differences are not substantial. Instead, they are characterized as local and finite extensions of God that differ in various "attributes," and God's attributes are infinite. Many of Spinoza's contemporaries were uncomfortable with his theology, and they interpreted his views as atheism in disguise.

Spinoza's philosophy resolves the issue of mind-body dualism by characterizing mind as only the "idea" form of the body. Body and mind are simply parallel extensions of two attributes of God. In essence they are one and the same thing, looked at from two different perspectives.

The Enlightenment

Isaac Newton's (1642–1727) mathematical analysis of the natural world seemed to validate human reason as the key to understanding all existence. Having confirmed the power of empirical research for understanding the world, intellectuals renewed their interest in using empirical methods to understand reason itself—to describe the origin of the force that had laid bare the secrets of nature. The interest in empiricism was strong in Britain, despite the scientific credentials of many rationalist philosophers such as Descartes and Gottfried Wilhelm Leibniz (1646–1716). In philosophies of Locke, Berkeley, and Hume, British Empiricism would stand as the quintessential philosophical movement of the Enlightenment, were it not for the monumental achievement of Immanuel Kant, who later resolved many of the debates between rationalists and empiricists.

The Enlightenment also brought a shift in the major themes of political philosophy, responding to the dawn of new democratic governments. Philosophers moved away from the analysis and defense of state power and focused instead on individual morality and the role of ordinary citizens.

British Empiricism The school of British Empiricism inquired into the process by which humans came to possess knowledge about the world. John Locke (1632–1704), an acquaintance of both Newton and Robert Boyle, presented his theory of knowledge in *Essay Concerning Human Understanding* (1689). He asserted that there are no innate ideas or knowledge independent of interaction with the world. Knowledge begins when human sense organs are influenced by entities in the world mechanically, producing mental impressions of reality upon which humans reflect. The mind, on which the impressions are imprinted, was characterized by Locke as a blank slate (Latin: *tabula rasa*) at birth.

Locke's *Second Treatise of Government* was a highly influential account of liberal political theory. It detailed both the rights and responsibilities of citizens to their government on the basis of a "social contract," motivated by the desire for civilization rather than the "state of nature." Government by mutual consent is necessary to protect life, liberty, and property, and as long as the government fulfills its side of the agreement, citizens owe their allegiance and obedience in return. Locke's version of the social contract was later contested by Jean-Jacques Rousseau (1712–78), who stated that the common man was attracted to such an agreement only to find himself later in chains. According to Rousseau, the "state of nature" was superior to subjection to modern governments.

Irish philosopher and Anglican bishop George Berkeley (1685–1753) took Locke's theory of knowledge to an interesting metaphysical conclusion. If one accepts the assertion that there are no innate ideas independent of interaction with the senses, then it is also impossible to assert that matter exists. If knowledge of existence depends on perception, and that perception is an idea in the mind, then the only thing that must exist is the idea. Without perception matter does not exist, because we cannot know that it exists.

The third major British Empiricist, David Hume (1711–76), pushed the theories of Locke and Berkeley to their extreme limits, provoking the interest of Kant. Hume was ultimately skeptical that any knowledge is possible. Since everything we know depends on the experience of perceptions, we can make only educated deductions about how the world behaves. But these deductions are not knowledge. They do not carry the certainty of an irrefutable proof. For example, we can believe wholeheartedly that the sun will rise tomorrow, but there is no way we can know that it will, just because it has always done so before. Certainty is beyond our grasp.

For many, the work of German thinker Immanuel Kant (1724–1804) is synonymous with Enlightenment philosophy. After reading David Hume, Kant began to work on *Critique of Pure Reason* (1781, revised 1787), the foundation of Kant's theory of knowledge. Kant was troubled by empiricism and extreme skepticism primarily because they fail to explain how the achievements of mathematics are possible. Also, empiricism does not explain why almost all people share the experiences of space and time without significant differences in their understanding of them.

Kant observed that there is a difference between the temporal priority of experience and the logical priority of experience. In other words, Kant agrees that knowledge depends on experience, but he does not believe that this dependence prevents us from understanding certain features of thought that must have preceded experience in order for learning to take place. These features of mind can be deduced *after* knowledge is gained, even though they are not detected by the senses beforehand. They cannot be observed independently of experience, but their existence cannot be denied. Such features are the common human experience of space and time, and the logical truths of mathematics. They are an integral part of the way people think. Their logical necessity is due not to coincidence, but to the way human thought works. Hence they will always behave the same way for everybody. Kant's resolution of the main difficulties between the rationalists and the empiricists is often characterized as *idealism*, because it retains the notion that ideal metaphysical realities, such as time and space, can be known, even in a world where knowledge depends on experience.

Similarly, Kant's moral philosophy sought to resolve the contradiction between free will and determinism. Kant reasoned that the individual will is necessarily determined; that is, it must be subject to some force that gives it direction. People may think that they are free to make individual choices, but that is an illusion, usually at the service of some passion of the senses. It is only when one conditions the will to follow some "ideal," or rationally determined duty, that one can know freedom. The best solution is to search for the best ideal and dedicate yourself to the service of that ideal. Kant's formulation of this ideal, known as the "categorical imperative," states that one's actions should be governed by "maxims," and those maxims should be such that everyone follows them. In other words, rules that would serve everyone are the best rules to govern individual behavior, and training yourself to live by such rules is the key to freedom.

19th Century Philosophy

The greatest commonality among the various philosophical movements of the 19th century was their operation under the broad shadow of Kant. The first wave of Kantians, known as Idealists, sought to broaden metaphysics beyond Kant's very modest list of structures (such as space, time, and mathematical deductions) that guide human understanding. Growing disillusion with the hopes of the Enlightenment, coupled with the growing extravagance of the claims of the Idealists, prompted a reaction against Idealism, and against philosophy itself, in intellectual circles. By the end of the century, especially in continental Europe, philosophy became a weapon for attacking the notion that people are rational beings. Instead, according to such thinkers as Nietzsche and Freud, people merely use the guise of rationality to achieve irrationally motivated ends.

German Idealism By opening up a new space for philosophy to discuss the metaphysics of mind, Kantianism gave rise to a series of more mystical speculations about the ultimate nature of humankind and anything else that might be universal about the human experience. Georg Wilhelm Hegel (1770–1831) extended this discussion to the point that mind is characterized as a universal and *evolving* entity. Just as Kant deduced the structure of the human mind after the fact of knowledge, Hegel sought to determine the course of universal mind by analyzing the course of history. He concluded that universal mind is on an inexorable course toward self-awareness, although the path from ignorance to pure self-awareness is not marked by a straight line. Instead, the course of history has been a series of social upheavals marked by philosophical confusions that must be resolved before the next historical epoch can begin.

Hegel often coined new phrases in service to his philosophy, prompting a great deal of debate—about both his intended meaning and its value. To this day there is very little agreement among philosophers about either, yet there is no doubt that Hegelian speculation had a strong impact on some of the great minds of the 19th century, including Schopenhauer, Marx, Kierkegaard, Darwin, Nietzsche, and Freud.

Reaction to Idealism: Søren Kierkegaard and Karl Marx Both the Danish philosopher Søren Kierkegaard (1813–55) and Karl Marx (1818–83) attended Friedrich Schelling's (1775–1854) lectures in Berlin propounding his distinctive version of German Idealism. Both reacted against Idealism in highly individual yet influential directions.

Although he was not a pastor, Kierkegaard was a Lutheran theologian. As such, he was mostly interested in the individual's relationship to God, which he viewed as parallel to the Idealists' characterization of the relationship between the individual and the universal. Kierkegaard saw the various claims of the Idealists as extravagant, and he gravitated to a more skeptical view in which universals are beyond the reach of human knowledge. Likewise, he saw God as an entity that humans cannot really know. Rather than languish in despair, however, Kierkegaard saw this gap in human understanding as an opportunity for faith. Kierkegaard maintained that faith is an extremely important concept undervalued in philosophical circles. In fact, it is only through faith that people can meet the various challenges they face in an irrational life filled with uncertainties.

Karl Marx accepted much of Hegel's characterization of history, but Marx sought to change the story from its "fairy tale" version into a real account of actual historical forces struggling to liberate people from the chains of oppression. Marx called his version of Idealism "historical materialism" to highlight the differences. For Marx the key to materialism was understanding the economic forces that determine human interest. The ultimate hope for human liberation depends on the common working people understanding their economic interests and taking control of their destiny through collective action.

Friedrich Nietzsche (1844–1900) As Kierkegaard had done earlier, intellectuals in continental Europe at the end of the century (such as Sigmund Freud) were taking a greater interest in the exploration of the irrational mind. Building on the thought of Arthur Schopenhauer (1788-1866), Friedrich Nietzsche characterized philosophy as part of a grand deception designed to prevent people from recognizing the truth about human nature.

According to Nietzsche, Western Judeo-Christian values were invented to subvert a prior and more important moral order. In the world of nature, strength wins out and weakness is eliminated. Yet Judaism and Christianity conspire to assure people that weakness has its own strengths and morality is rewarded in a future life that is, in fact, nonexistent. Almost all of philosophy (with the exception of Schopenhauer) has conspired with this inverted value system to justify Judeo-Christian morality. Metaphysics is merely the creation of a false world that proceeds according to rules people prefer, rather than according to the rule of nature. In response, intellectual thought should be primarily negative and antimetaphysical. Philosophical critique should strip away false metaphysics and expose the real, physical world in all of its naked brutality.

20th Century Philosophy

Independent Visions of Philosophy Philosophy in the 20th century was dominated by what is commonly called analytic philosophy (Anglo-American) and continental philosophy (European), but a number of individual voices, not associated strongly with any particular school, also made significant contributions. At the turn of the century, Henri Bergson (1859–1941) developed a philosophy that distinguished between the intellect, which uses reason and analysis to know the world, and intuition, which enables man to identify with entities in the world and which provides a basis for metaphysical knowledge. Bergson shared this metaphysical inclination with Alfred North Whitehead (1861–1947), who promoted a "speculative philosophy" whose primary goal was the definition of universal ideas that would explain the general nature of reality.

John Dewey (1859–1952), the dominant American philosopher of the early 20th century, came from the school of Pragmatism, a descendant of Positivism and other anti-Idealistic schools of thought. Dewey and his followers adopted the position that reality and human responses to it were constantly evolving; in light of that state of change, philosophy's primary task should be to find practical solutions to human problems. Dewey's pursuit of this goal made him an influential figure in the philosophy of education in the 20th century.

Analytic Philosophy The first major branch of analytic philosophy was *Logical Positivism,* which emerged at the University of Vienna in 1923. This branch was influenced heavily by the work of David Hume and the new logical system of Bertrand Russell (1872–1970) and A. N. Whitehead. The Logical Positivists argued for a strictly scientific approach to philosophy, which was newly redefined by Ludwig Wittgenstein (1889–1951) as "the logical clarification of thoughts," and focused in particular on the structure and use of human language. The Positivists claimed that unverifiable statements were meaningless, and thus practically all metaphysical inquiry had no value due to its purely speculative nature.

Later, however, Logical Positivists such as Wittgenstein and G. E. Moore (1873–1958) contributed to the development of *Linguistic Analysis*, which focused on the language people used in daily existence instead of the rarefied and artificial language of Logical Positivism. Wittgenstein asserted that the ambiguous and highly contextual nature of language is what produces most philosophical problems—thus, the ultimate question of philosophy is to ask why a person uses a particular word or expression in a given situation.

Continental Philosophy While the analytic philosophers turned their attention to language as a tool and construct of human reason, philosophers of the continental school retained a more metaphysical orientation. Elucidating on Kant's proposition that only phenomena, not things-in-themselves, are perceivable, Edmund Husserl (1859–1939) developed the phenomenological method. His method, and the whole school of *Phenomenology*, attempted to describe phenomena through intuition in the immediate moment of experience, divorced from metaphysical and scientific presumptions. Martin Heidegger (1889–1976), who worked with Husserl at Freiburg University, discussed phenomenology as a method of access to being. His early works did much to influence philosophers in not only phenomenology, but many other fields, including existentialism (e.g. Sartre), and postmodernism (e.g. Foucault).

Existentialism, the last major development in 20th-century philosophy, owed a direct debt to Kierkegaard's studies of human anxiety and despair. Karl Jaspers (1883–1969) rejected the existentialist label but nonetheless worked within its boundaries, inquiring into the question of individual Being. In his view, one's Being was revealed most clearly in extreme situations or states of mind, such as despair and suffering—occasions when the individual was confronted with the temporal nature of his or her own existence. Jean-Paul Sartre (1905–80), on the other hand, embraced the existentialist label, and his literary and philosophical works are perhaps more closely associated with Existentialism than any other individual. Sartre denied the existence of God, and thus the existence of any essential or preexisting human nature; people, therefore, exist in a state of total freedom and are responsible only to themselves. In most people, said Sartre, recognition of this fact leads not to a feeling of liberation, but rather to a state of overwhelming indecision and anxiety, and subsequently to a perverse immersion in behaviors and institutions that negate that freedom and responsibility.

RELIGION

Judaism 496

Christianity 498

Islam 506

Hinduism 508

Buddhism 511

Other World Religions...............513

Glossary of Religious Terms......518

The Bible 519

RELIGION

Judaism

Judaism is the oldest of the world's three major monotheistic religions and a forerunner of Christianity and Islam. Modern Judaism evolved from the ancient religion of the Hebrews, whose law, culture, and religious practices were influenced in turn by Mesopotamian and Babylonian culture.

Scripture

The Bible The Hebrew Bible consists of 24 books. These include the five books of the Torah, or Law (also known by the Greek *Pentateuch*, five books); the eight books of the Former and Latter Prophets (*Nevi'im*); and the eleven books of Writings (*Ketuvim*) (see Books of the Bible). Composed between the 10th and second centuries B.C. and based in part on oral traditions, the various books of the Hebrew Bible include the creation story, the laws and the history of the Jewish people, prophecies about the fate of God's chosen people depending on their acceptance of God and his law, and stories, poems, and proverbs.

The Talmud The Talmud, a collection of rabbinical commentary dating from A.D. 200 onward, is divided into two major parts, the *Mishna* ("repeated study" or oral law), and the *Gemara* ("completion"), a supplemental commentary on the Mishna. The Talmudic tradition has continued through the centuries and constitutes not only commentary on the law (*Halakah*), but also stories from the Bible, parables, and legends (*Haggadah*) illustrating religious principles, as well as information on a wide range of secular subjects such as astronomy and geography.

Kabbalah Also of note is a body of Jewish mystical literature known as the *Kabbalah* ("tradition"). The Kabbalah movement arose in 11th-century France; it is, among other things, an esoteric system for understanding the Scriptures, based on the conviction that words, letters, and numbers in the Scriptures contain mysteries interpretable by the adept.

Belief and Practice

God Jews believe in a single, all-powerful God; in the Hebrew Bible he is referred to by the four-letter name YHWH (reconstructed as the modern name *Yahweh*). Because pronouncing this name aloud was considered taboo, in Scripture God is more frequently addressed as *Adonai* ("my great lord") or referred to by generic names for God such as *Elohim*. Central to Jewish belief is the idea that the Hebrew people have a unique and privileged relationship with God, as demonstrated by God's covenant with them, his law, and his direct intervention on numerous occasions in the history of the Jewish people.

Law Judaism is distinctive for its body of law, which offers an extensive system of guidance and regulation of religious practice as well as daily social conduct. Jews believe that although God guides human destiny, the humanity of mankind is defined by the ability of individuals to make ethical choices in keeping with God's law. The failure to act according to God's law is sin, and a basic tenet of Jewish faith is that sin is a willful act; so, too, is turning, or returning, to God. At the core of Jewish law are the Ten Commandments, given directly to Moses by God, and the large body of law contained in the Torah itself; these are supplemented by the teachings of the prophets as well as the centuries of oral law and biblical commentary codified in the Talmud.

Dietary Restrictions Devout Jews observe a detailed set of dietary rules and restrictions. The rules for *kosher* ("ritually correct") food preparation and consumption include prohibitions against eating specific animals (including pork and shellfish); guidelines for the slaughter, butchering, and inspection of meat; and a prohibition against mixing meat and dairy products. Some scholars speculate that thousands of years ago many of these rules may have served a practical hygienic purpose, but their true significance may lie in the obligation of God's chosen people to obey him in all things, however seemingly unimportant. Today the dietary laws are often understood to represent only ritual purity, and therefore many Jews do not adhere to all of these rules.

Prayer and Worship Devout Jews generally pray at dawn, noon, and dusk; some also pray at bedtime. Among the more traditional sects of Judaism, individuals (mostly males) also make use of special objects and clothing in prayer. These include *tefillin*, small boxes containing handwritten passages of Scripture, which are strapped to the forehead and the upper left arm; *talit*, or prayer shawls, which cover the head and upper body during prayer to show humility before God; and *kippah* (more commonly known by the Yiddish term *yarmulke*), or skullcaps. The Jewish Sabbath (day of rest) is observed from sunset Friday to sunset Saturday; many religious Jews worship in synagogues, where a *rabbi* (teacher or master) leads them in readings from Scripture, prayer, and singing.

Rites of Passage Jewish males are traditionally circumcised eight days after birth; the ceremony also marks the occasion at which they receive their name. At age 13, their official coming-of-age is marked with a ceremony known as a *bar mitzvah* ("son of the commandment"). Some branches of Judaism hold a similar ceremony for women, called a *bat mitzvah*, celebrated between age 12 and 18.

Schools and sects

Orthodox Judaism is the most rigorous, and smallest, branch of Judaism, with an estimated 400,000 adherents. Orthodox Jews may keep entirely separate kitchens for milk and meat, refuse to operate electric and mechanical devices on the Sabbath, and often attend temple services or hold prayer sessions every day. Orthodox services are generally conducted entirely in Hebrew; men and women are required to pray separately, even when not in temple. Many orthodox (or so-called ultra-orthodox) communities, especially self-contained communities such as those of the Hasidic Jews (located in large numbers in New York and in Israel), impose strict dress codes. Hasidism emerged in late 18th-century Poland and Lithuania. The Hasidim ("the pious") are strict observers of Jewish religious laws. Today there are several sects, all of which stress prayer and direct mystical experience of God.

Reform Judaism traces its origins to the 18th century; it was strongly influenced by the writings of Moses Mendelssohn (1729–86), who advocated a movement to integrate Judaism with mainstream European culture. Reform Judaism has a liberal interpretation of Jewish doctrine and ritual, and is especially prevalent in the United States. Men and women may worship together, and many worship services are conducted in local vernacular languages. Dietary and other laws (such as wearing tefillin or talit during prayer) are often not observed. Women can become rabbis in Reform Judaism.

Conservative Judaism combines elements of doctrinal reform with more traditional observance. Conservative Judaism rose in Europe and the United States in the late 19th century in response to the Reform movement, and sought to preserve more of the ancient observances of the old orthodoxy, but without losing touch with modern culture and behavior. Conservative Jews have been slower to question tradition than Reform Jews, but over time have come to accept many of the same changes, including the ordination of female rabbis. About one-third of affiliated Jews in the USA belong to Conservative institutions.

History

The Bible recounts the story of the Jewish people from the creation. (There is, however, relatively little archaeological and independent textual evidence corroborating the earliest history of the Jewish people, so that the historical reliability of the biblical account is uncertain.) In the historical narrative, the foundation of Jewish faith began with the exodus from Egypt and the transmission of the Ten Commandments (the Decalogue) from God to his people through Moses, probably sometime between 1450 and 1290 B.C. The people of Israel conquered and settled in Canaan—the promised land—and were ruled by a succession of judges. The monarchical period under Samuel and David dates to the 11th and 10th centuries B.C. Israel (the Northern Kingdom) and Judah (the Southern Kingdom) continued under separate rulers until the fall of Israel in 722 B.C. Judah was conquered by Babylonians, and the First Temple of David in Jerusalem destroyed in 586 B.C. The Babylonian captivity marks the start of the Jewish Diaspora, or dispersal. Exile lasted until 538 B.C., and the Second Temple was dedicated in 516 B.C. Under Seleucid rule, the Maccabees successfully resisted efforts to suppress Judaism (168–142 B.C.). Under Roman rule (63 B.C.–A.D. 135), there were several revolts, the first of which resulted in the destruction of the Second Temple (A.D. 70). With the loss of the land and especially the temple, which had formerly been the center of Judaism, the Jewish religion was reconstructed and continued by the rabbinate.

The early Middle Ages saw the flourishing of the Talmudic tradition. Following the rise of Islam, Judaism evolved into two distinct strains, the Sephardim, centered in Spain, and the Ashkenazim, a term that applied to Jews from Northern France through Germany, Poland, and Russia. The long history of persecution of Jews in Europe, includes expulsion from France (1306) and Spain (1492), and the pogroms of the 19th century in eastern Europe, culminating in the Nazi regime's attempt to eradicate all Jews during the Holocaust.

Zionism was a European Jewish political movement of the late 19th century, expounded in works such as Theodor Herzl's *The Jewish State*. A response to the Diaspora, the rise of European nationalism, and the growing problem of anti-Semitism, the Zionist search for a Jewish homeland led eventually to the birth of the state of Israel in 1948. Though Israel is a secular republic, religious parties play an active role in politics, and the Orthodox rabbinate has a role in defining civil status, such as marriage.

Holidays

The Jewish calendar is lunar, so the dates of Jewish holidays vary in relation to the standard solar calendar each year. Rosh Hashanah, the Jewish New Year, occurs in the seventh lunar month. Ten days later is Yom Kippur, the Day of Atonement, which is celebrated with fasting and prayers seeking God's forgiveness. These two holidays are together referred to as the High Holy Days.

The festival of Sukkot, a celebration of the harvest, is celebrated from the 15th through the 22nd days of the seventh lunar month. Hanukkah is celebrated over an eight-day period in the ninth lunar month; it commemorates the rededication of the Second Temple in 165 B.C. Purim, celebrated in the 12th lunar month, just before the beginning of spring, recalls events from the book of Esther (a Persian queen of Jewish origin who saved the Hebrews). Passover (*Pesach*) is celebrated for an entire week in the first lunar month; it commemorates the flight of the Hebrews from Egypt. Central to the Passover celebration is a meal called the *Seder* ("order"), which consists of a number of symbolic foods, and to which many Jews often invite non-Jews.

Geography and numbers

There are an estimated 14 million Jews in 134 countries, the overwhelming majority of whom live in the United States (5.8 million) and Israel (4.3 million). There are an estimated 2.4 million Jews in Europe.

Christianity

Christianity was founded by followers of Jesus of Nazareth, who was born a Jew in Bethlehem ca. 4 B.C. Details of his life before about A.D. 26–28 are obscure. According to the four Gospels of the New Testament, Jesus was baptized by John the Baptist, who recognized Jesus as the Messiah (Hebrew *Mashiah*, "anointed one"). Jesus' ministry of teaching, healing and miracles, which lasted only a few years, was conducted primarily in Galilee in northwest Palestine. After a fateful journey to Jerusalem, he was tried and executed by the Roman authorities, who together with members of Jewish priestly circles were concerned with the civil and religious consequences of Jesus' preaching of the Kingdom of God. According to Christian belief, Jesus rose from the dead on the third day, appeared to the disciples at various places, and then ascended to heaven. Christians believe that Jesus, the Son of God, died on the cross as an offering and sacrifice for the salvation of humankind; those who believe in him will be saved.

Scripture

Christian Bibles consist of two parts: the Old Testament and the New Testament. The Protestant Old Testament includes the text of the Hebrew Bible, with some books renamed and in a different order (see Books of the Bible); Roman Catholic and other Christian religions add some additional books from the *Septuagint*, the Greek translation of the Hebrew Bible (third century B.C.). The New Testament of 27 books is accepted by both the Roman Catholic and Protestant churches.

Belief and Practice

Although Christian churches and sects vary greatly in structure, practice, and certain points of faith, a few core beliefs and rituals are common to most.

The Trinity This fundamental Christian doctrine states that God has three natures, or exists equally in three persons: God the Father, God the Son (Jesus), and God the Holy Spirit. God the Father is the all-powerful creator of the world, who continues to govern his creation and judge mankind. Jesus, also called Christ (Greek for "anointed one") is God in the flesh; Christians believe his crucifixion removed the stain of Adam's original sin from mankind. The Holy Spirit is generally viewed as a distinct part or aspect of God that provides strength and guidance to followers of Christianity.

Each of these is properly viewed as only one aspect of a singular God. However, this concept is difficult to grasp even for many Christians, among whom it may be accepted as a mystery beyond human understanding; and some adherents of other religions view the doctrine of the Holy

Trinity as evidence of polytheism in Christianity. The doctrine of the Trinity poses special difficulties for the rigorously monotheistic adherents of the other two religions of the tradition of Abraham—Judaism and Islam.

The Sacraments Central to the practice of most Christians are seven sacraments: baptism, the anointing or immersion of persons in water (often soon after birth) to symbolically cleanse them of sin and welcome them to the Christian church; confirmation, the sacrament by which an adult Christian confirms the sacrament of baptism and enters into full church membership; marriage; ordination, or entry into the clergy; the sacrament of the sick, the anointing and absolution of the sick and dying; the confession of sins; and communion, or the ceremonial sharing of bread and wine in memory of Jesus' Last Supper with his disciples.

The Afterlife Christians believe that each human possesses an eternal soul, which after the death of the body is judged by God and then rewarded (in heaven) or punished (in hell) according to that individual's actions in life. Many Christians (particularly Roman Catholics and some Eastern Orthodox believers, but not most Protestants) also believe in purgatory, an intermediate state in which some less-pure souls are prepared for entry into heaven.

Schools and sects

Roman Catholic Church The Roman Catholic Church is the largest Christian denomination in the world, claiming more than 17 percent of the total world population. Worldwide, there are more than 1 billion Roman Catholics; in the U.S. there are 63.7 million, or 22 percent of the U.S. population

Early Christians based the organization of their church on the political structure of the Roman Empire and accepted the bishop of Rome (later known as the pope, from the Latin *papa*, "father") as the leader of the worldwide Christian community. Christianity was granted legal toleration within the Roman Empire under the emperor Constantine (ruled 312–27), and was proclaimed the official religion of the empire in 380. The church flourished in the fourth and fifth centuries amid the political decline of Rome, and also found fertile ground in the empire's new eastern capital, Constantinople. After the fall of the Roman Empire the church continued to embody its language, architecture and other cultural features.

The pope continues to lead the Catholic Church from Vatican City in Rome. Bishops (and, at a higher level of organization, archbishops) administer church affairs in a given region; certain bishops are elevated to the College of Cardinals, which advises the pope and comes together after his death to choose a successor. Priests are male and (except in a few splinter organizations within the Catholic Church that have rejected the authority of Rome) must be and remain unmarried. Orders of nuns and monks, most of whom take lifelong vows of charity, chastity, poverty, and obedience, provide educational and charitable services. Local churches operate parochial elementary schools, and regional bodies and religious orders operate high schools and administer seminaries and church-related colleges.

Eastern Catholicism The various churches of Eastern Catholicism hold doctrinal beliefs and liturgical practices that are generally similar to those of the Roman Catholic Church, but they regard themselves as co-equal with what they call the "Roman Rite" church, and do not recognize the primacy of the Roman church and its pope. In general, Eastern Catholic Churches exist in areas where Eastern Orthodox Churches are dominant; the Eastern Catholic churches in those countries and regions have chosen Roman forms of belief and practice without uniting with the Roman Church.

There are 22 Eastern Catholic Churches, divided into several broad categories, as follows: Byzantine Rite Churches: Albanian, Bulgarian, Belarussian, Croatian, Georgian, Greek, Hungarian, Italo-Albanian, Melkite, Romanian, Russian, Ruthenian, Slovak, and Ukrainian; Armenian Rite Church; Alexandrian Rite Churches: Coptic and Ethiopic; Antiochene Rite Churches: Maronite, Syrian, Syro-Malankar; Chaldean Rite Churches: Chaldean, Syro-Malabar. The Maronite Church (which recognizes the primacy of the Roman pope) is centered in Lebanon, and has played an important political and social role in that country in the 20th century. The Chaldean Rite churches have historical roots in common with the Nestorian Church (see below); there is a large community of Chaldean Catholics (mostly of Iraqi origin) in the United States, particularly in the Detroit area.

With the resurgence of the Orthodox Church in Russia, Ukraine, and other areas following the fall of the Soviet Union, leaders of the Eastern Catholic Churches have complained of interference and repression at the hands of Orthodox authorities.

Roman Rite Churches The term *Roman Rite Church* is used by Eastern Catholic Churches to refer to Rome as one of (in their view) many co-equal Catholic Churches, each with its own rites and traditions. In modern parlance, however, the term is also used to denote former Roman Catholic Churches that have broken with the Vatican but still adhere to Roman Catholic rites and practices. Some of these split with Rome over doctrinal and political issues in the 19th century (for example, the Polish Roman Rite Church, established in Scranton, Pennsylvania, in the 1890's by church leaders of Polish descent). Other Roman Rite churches broke with Rome over objections to the reforms and modernizations decreed by the Vatican II Council (1962–65); these churches tend to adhere to the Latin Mass rather than using vernacular language at worship.

Eastern Orthodox Church In 1054, the bishops of Rome (representing the Western church) and Constantinople (representing the Eastern church) excommunicated each other, creating a major schism that remains to this day. The word *orthodox* means "correct belief" and is applied to the Eastern church because it has attempted to keep its beliefs and practices unchanged. Monasticism is of great importance in the Orthodox tradition; monasteries serve as focal points of Orthodox spirituality and as centers for the study and preservation of ancient beliefs, rituals, and practices.

Orthodox Churches are organized hierarchically, in a manner similar to the Roman Catholic churches, although the Orthodox community rejects the supreme authority of the Catholic pope and subscribes to a decentralized model of decision making in important church matters; archbishops and bishops possess special spiritual authority and administer church affairs. There are 15 independent churches within the Orthodox community. Four of them —those of Constantinople, Alexandria, Antioch, and Jerusalem—occupy a position of primacy because of their antiquity. They are ruled by patriarchs, of whom the patriarch of Constantinople (known as the Ecumenical Patriarch) is recognized as senior, though without any powers comparable to those of the pope in the Roman Catholic Church. The churches of Bulgaria, Georgia, Romania, Russia, and Serbia are also headed by patriarchs; the heads of the churches in Albania, Cyprus, Greece, Poland, Slovakia, and the U.S. are known as metropolitans.

Orthodox religious observances tend to be solemn and elaborate, and ancient liturgies have been carefully preserved in their original languages such as Greek, Slavonic, Armenian, and Georgian. The display and veneration of religious images known as icons is a distinctive feature of Orthodox Churches. Orthodox clergy are male, and in most churches they are allowed to marry. Because of differences in calculating feast days, Easter and other movable feasts may occur on different dates in the Orthodox Church than in Western churches.

In the U.S., many Orthodox Churches have served as cultural centers for immigrants seeking to preserve their own ethnic heritage. At the same time, however, many denominations are active members of ecumenical groups such as the National Council of Churches. The two largest Orthodox Churches in the U.S. today are Greek and Russian, respectively. The next largest represent Armenians and Syrians.

The Coptic Church The Coptic Church is the indigenous and independent Christian church of Egypt. It broke from the Orthodox Church in A.D. 450 after theological disputes over how to define the human and divine natures in Christ; the Coptic Monophysite position rejects the idea of the duality of Christ's nature. The Coptic Church thereafter was headed by its own leader, known as the pope of Alexandria and patriarch of the See of St. Mark, rivaled by the Orthodox patriarch of Alexandria (who continued to lead those Egyptian Christians who remained within the Orthodox community).

The Coptic Church uses the Coptic language (descended from the ancient language of Pharonic Egypt) in its liturgies, but has tended increasingly to employ vernacular Arabic in other church activities. As in Orthodox Christianity, monasticism plays an important role in church life; monks must be celibate, but married men may be ordained to the clergy (though single clergymen may not marry). Coptic Christians make up 9.4 percent of the population of Egypt, and have suffered persecution in the late 20th century at the hands of Islamic militants. There is also a Coptic community among Egyptian immigrants in the United States.

The Ethiopian Orthodox Church Despite its name, the Ethiopian Orthodox Church is affiliated, not with the Orthodox community, but with the Coptic Church of Egypt. The ancient Ethiopian kingdom of Aksum converted to Christianity in the fourth century and sided with the Coptic Church at Alexandria in the disputes over Monophysitism in the mid-fifth century. The Ethiopian Church is independent, but is similar in beliefs and practices to the Coptic Church. Its liturgical language is Amharic. About half the population of Ethiopia is Christian, the overwhelming majority of them adherents of the Ethiopian Orthodox Church; church members are also a presence in Ethiopian overseas communities in Europe and the United States.

The Nestorian Church Nestorianism takes its name from Nestorius (d. A.D. 451), an influential monk and bishop of Constantinople who denied that Mary could be the "mother of God" (as she had become popularly known) because the complete Trinity had always existed. He was condemned as a heretic in 431; some communities of Syrian Christians rejected his condemnation and followed his teachings. The Nestorian Church, which used Syriac as its liturgical language, was the most prominent form of Christianity in Central Asia between the sixth and 14th centuries, with communities as far east as Mongolia and China. However, it lost ground to Islam thereafter and declined to relative insignificance, with remnant communities surviving into modern times in India, Iraq, and the United States. Since the 16th century some Nestorian Churches, such as the one in Malabar in southwest India, have reunited with the Roman Catholic Church.

Protestant Churches Protestant denominations number in the hundreds. There is no single governing authority for all of them, and they vary widely in organization and in forms of worship. Most, however, teach that Christian belief and worship should follow the simple model outlined in the New Testament, without the pageantry and ritual added by later generations. The term *protestant* is now commonly understood as referring to the churches that developed from the objections of Martin Luther and other reformers to Catholic practices; the specific early use of the term (1529) referred to protests against an edict of the Holy Roman Empire prohibiting cities and principalities from choosing their own religion. The belief in Scripture as the sole definitive source of Christian wisdom and guidance (rather than the creeds and doctrines of the Catholic Church) is often referred to as the Protestant Principle. Martin Luther's expansion of the New Testament injunction that "the just shall live by faith" (to which Luther added, "alone") implies the rejection of a separate priesthood in favor of "the priesthood of all believers." Most Protestant denominations also stress the singular importance of Jesus as a connection between man and God, and reject or downplay the veneration of Mary and the saints. Some Protestant denominations are described as evangelical, meaning that they emphasize Scriptural authority, the responsibility of believers for the personal acknowledgment of sin and the experience of salvation, and the obligation of believers to spread the message of Christian salvation to others.

Adventist Churches sprang up in the U.S. in the 1840's, a time of fervent religious revival and widespread prophecies of the end of the world. Adventists anticipate and prepare for the world's end and the second coming of Jesus Christ. The largest Adventist group, the Seventh-day Adventists, is one of the most dynamic religious groups in the world today, claiming a worldwide membership of 12 million. As their name suggests, they worship on Saturday rather than Sunday. They operate parochial schools, colleges, medical schools, and hospitals.

Anabaptist Churches Anabaptist, which means "re-baptizers," refers to a group of radical churches and sects that arose during the Reformation and embraced the doctrine of adult baptism for believers. The first group was the Swiss Brethren (1525); other well-known groups include the Mennonites (followers of Menno Simons, 1496–1561, the Netherlands); the Hutterites (followers of Jacob Hutter, d. 1536, Moravia); and Melchiorites (followers of Melchior Hoffman ca. 1500–ca. 1543, Germany); the Amish originated (late 17th century) as a sect of the Swiss Brethren. Beliefs include the need to separate from civil authority, and pacifism; hence members would not swear oaths and would not bear arms in the service of temporal leaders. These groups were persecuted in Europe by both Protestants and Catholics, and many believers emigrated to North America, especially to Pennsylvania and the Great Plains of the U.S. and Canada; there are also groups in other countries. The groups differ in some matters of doctrine and the extent to which they interact with the larger community. In the United States the Old Order Amish in Pennsylvania, for example, maintain deeply committed to traditional ways, including the use of horses and buggies and distinctive plain dress.

Baptist Churches are collectively the largest Protestant denomination in the United States. Baptists trace their theological roots back to radical reformers in Europe in the 1500's, but the number of Baptists in the world was tiny until the 1800's, when Baptist faith and practice became predominant in the American South (both for whites and for African Americans). Baptists are still most heavily represented in the southern and border states.

Local Baptist congregations have great independence, determining many of their own policies. At the same time, these churches share many practices. They agree that the rite of baptism should be administered only to those who have reached an age of independent judgment. Consequently, Baptist children are not included in membership totals until after baptism (which usually occurs no earlier than age six or seven).

Most Baptists take a strong stand on the authority of the Bible, and many (though not all) believe that it should be interpreted literally. Baptists have traditionally been strong supporters of separation of church and state; and Baptist denominations have mounted energetic international missionary campaigns.

The Southern Baptist Convention, a predominantly white church, is the largest Protestant denomination in the United States. The two National Baptist Conventions and the Progressive National Baptist Convention are predominantly African-American churches. Together they account for the religious affiliation of more African Americans than any other family of churches.

Christian Churches and Churches of Christ trace their origins to a great religious awakening in 1800 on the Pennsylvania and Kentucky frontiers. Discouraged by sectarian competition among Methodists, Presbyterians, and others, leaders of the revival did not seek to form a denomination but to reestablish a single nondenominational Christian Church. In time they became a denomination themselves. In the 1870's the Churches of Christ and the Christian Church (Disciples) split over questions of using musical instruments in worship and over the issue of centralizing some church functions. The Churches of Christ opposed both instrumental music and national organization. The Disciples allowed instrumental music and established a central missionary board to coordinate mission work; they also have a long history of cooperation and discussion with other denominations. A third group, the Christian Churches and Churches of Christ, split from the Disciples in the 1920's–30's. They allow instrumental music but are theologically more conservative than the Disciples.

Church of Christ, Scientist Christian Scientists, as adherents are often known, follow the teaching of Mary Baker Eddy (1821–1910), who founded the church in 1879 in Boston and wrote *Science and Health with a Key to the Scriptures*, which remains a major source of the church's basic doctrines. Christian Science asserts that sickness and other adversities exist only in the mind and that disciplined spiritual thinking can correct them. Thus, Christian Scientists refuse most or all medical treatment. Christian Science practitioners help adherents deal with illness but do not serve as clergy. The church publishes the influential newspaper *The Christian Science Monitor*, and operates many reading rooms open to the public. Christian Science has had declining membership since the 1970's.

Episcopal Churches are descendants of the Church of England, which was established as a separate church by King Henry VIII in 1534. Churches descending from the English church make up the worldwide Anglican Communion. The American church takes its name from the Latin *episcopus*, bishop; this suggests its hierarchical organization. In colonial times the Church of England was established in the southern colonies and had some influence in the middle colonies, but was less welcome in New England, where Reformed churches were predominant. During the American Revolution, many Church of England members and clergy remained loyal to England, and thousands migrated to Canada. Those who remained were under suspicion, and some were persecuted. After the Revolution, a small group of Anglicans loyal to the United States gradually revived the church, and it gained considerable influence—in eastern cities, many families of wealth and power were Episcopalian. The Episcopal Church accommodates a wide spectrum of belief and practice. It shares much with other Protestant denominations, yet its worship services retain strong elements of pre-Reformation Catholic tradition, especially in the "high church" wing of the denomination.

The Religious Society of Friends was established by the English mystic George Fox (1624–91) in the mid-1600's. Known popularly as **Quakers**, Friends were persecuted in England for refusing to take oaths or to serve as combatants in war, but under the protection of William Penn (1644–1718), many settled in Pennsylvania. According to Fox, they were called Quakers because they were admonished to "tremble at the word of the Lord." In Pennsylvania the Quakers set themselves apart, dressing plainly and avoiding worldly amusements. In Philadelphia many became influential businesspeople, known for "doing well by doing good."

The most distinctive doctrine of the Friends is that of the Inner Light, the spark of God in each individual. Traditionally the Friends have had no church buildings (services are held in Meeting Houses) and no clergy; leadership is granted to certain individuals by common consent. Worship meetings are characterized by silent meditation, which might be interrupted from time to time by spontaneous statements by any member of the group who feels "moved by the Spirit" to speak. Some Quaker groups in America have moved away from this original austerity, and have adopted clergy, sermons, and singing at worship services. Friends have organized remarkable world relief and peace organizations, by which they are perhaps best known to outsiders.

Holiness Churches grew from a religious revival in the late 1800's, primarily in Methodist congregations. The originators of the movement objected to the excessive bureaucracy of established denominations and sought to refocus attention on the need for deep personal change. They placed great emphasis on the teachings of Methodism's founder, John Wesley, that those who are saved may aspire to the gift of complete sanctification, or holiness. Around 1900, groups of especially intense Holiness worshipers began experiencing further "gifts of the Spirit." From these experiences grew the first Pentecostal Churches with their emphasis on speaking in tongues. Many who began as adherents of Holiness Churches became Pentacostalists, but the Holiness Churches rejected Pentecostal worship as extremist.

Jehovah's Witnesses are an active sect whose members are under a strong obligation to undertake personal missionary activities. Jehovah's Witnesses displaying the magazine *The Watchtower* on street corners, or speading their message through door-to-door encounters, have made the sect a familiar part of American life. They have no clergy (all members are considered ministers and missionaries), and meet not in churches but in plain buildings that always are called Kingdom Hall. They were founded by Charles Taze Russell (1852–1916) in western Pennsylvania in the 1870's. The Witnesses preach a slightly unorthodox form of the Christian message, holding that events of Armageddon and the Second Coming of Christ have already begun, and that the end of the world (which they regard as imminent) will bring one final opportunity for believers to be saved. They refuse blood transfusions and some other forms of medicine on biblical grounds, and, considering human government to be illegitimate, refuse to perform military service, pledge alliegance to the flag, or take oaths; these positions have often resulted in the sect's persecution. They claim more than 6 million members worldwide, of whom about a quarter live in the U.S.

Lutheran Churches trace their churches back to the German reformer Martin Luther (1483–1546), who sought to reform the doctrine and practice of the Roman Christian Church in Europe. In a set of 95 theses that he nailed to the door of the church at Wittenberg in 1517, he detailed his complaints against the Roman Church and his proposals for addressing them. He stressed a Scripture-based faith and a redemptive Christ; he complained about corruption among the clergy and advocated worship in the language of the people rather than in Latin. He also came to favor a married, rather than a celibate, clergy. The Church of Rome considered Luther disloyal and eventually drove him out; he then helped establish independent churches in northern Germany.

Immigrants from Germany and Scandinavia brought the Lutheran faith to North America, concentrating first in Pennsylvania. Later immigrants settled in the upper Midwest. Most Lutheran churches retain the altar and vestments of the Roman Church, and emphasize preaching and congregational participation in worship services.

Methodist Churches trace their origins to John Wesley (1703–91), a minister in the Church of England who sought to bring a new sense of warmth and commitment to individuals' religious life. He urged his followers to set aside regular times to study the Bible and pray together, earning his followers the then-pejorative title "Methodists" because of their discipline and seriousness. Wesley himself remained in the Church of England his whole life, but his followers began to develop independent organizations both in England and the United States. On the American frontier, Methodist "circuit riders" traveled from settlement to settlement, ministering to pioneer families. By 1820 Methodism was the largest religious denomination in the United States, and it remained the largest Protestant church until the 1920's.

The United Methodist Church accounts for nearly two-thirds of the Methodists in America. This denomination is made up of not only traditional Methodists but also several churches of German origin whose beliefs and spirit accorded well with Methodism. The two "African" churches (the African Methodist Episcopal Church and the African Methodist Episcopal Zion Church) and the Christian Methodist Church are predominantly African-American churches, and they account for nearly all of the remaining third of the Methodist group.

Pentecostal Churches share a belief that God grants believers special spiritual gifts—especially the experience called "speaking in tongues," a common feature of Pentecostal services. ("Speaking in tongues" refers to speaking words, not necessarily of any known language, under direct divine inspiration.) Pentecostal Churches trace their origin to the day of Pentecost (from the Greek meaning "50th day," i.e. the seventh Sunday after Easter), described in the New Testament book, Acts of the

Apostles, when early Christians received ecstatic or mystical powers. Modern Pentecostalism began in the early 1900's, when members of some Holiness churches received the gift of tongues (see "Holiness Churches").

Pentecostal congregations tend to be small, yet the Pentecostal faith experienced rapid growth in the later decades of the 20th century, and Pentecostal beliefs had an impact on Roman Catholic, Lutheran, Episcopal, and other denominations, who reported a growth among adherents of "charismatic renewal," a movement based on spiritual gifts. The two Churches of God in Christ and the United Pentecostal Church are predominantly African-American denominations. The Assemblies of God is the largest predominantly white denomination. Many Pentecostal organizations are regional or purely local. Because of this loose organization, there are likely to be many thousands of Pentecostal believers not included in national membership counts because their local congregations are not affiliated with a regional or national group.

Reformed Churches trace their descent to the French-born reformer John Calvin (1509–64). These churches were especially significant in the early settlement of the present-day United States. The Pilgrims and Puritans who settled in New England established the Congregational Church, which is a main component of today's United Church of Christ. New York was settled by the Dutch, who established the present-day Reformed Church in America. Later, immigrants of Scottish and Scotch-Irish descent established a strong Presbyterian Church. Presbyterians differ from Congregationalists in matters of church governance but share many points of theology and practice. Reformed Church buildings are generally simple and sparsely adorned. Similarly, worship in these churches is austere and simple. Reformed Churches generally value a well-educated clergy and have played a role in the founding of many universities, including Harvard, Yale, and Princeton.

The Presbyterian Church (USA) is the result of several mergers between smaller churches that had been separated by regional and doctrinal differences. The United Church of Christ includes, in addition to Congregational Churches, descendants of German Reformed Churches and of the Evangelical and Reformed Church (also of German descent). The Reformed Church in America and the Christian Reformed Church are both of Dutch descent.

The Salvation Army, a religious and charitable organization founded in England in 1865 by William and Catherine Booth (and took the name Salvation Army in 1878), shares the core beliefs of other evangelical churches. It is most familiar to outsiders through its work among the homeless and the poor and its fundraising on the streets, especially before Christmas. As its name suggests, the Salvation Army is organized on military lines (symbolizing the organization's "warfare against evil"). Full-time uniformed personnel, organized in military ranks, are expected to devote their lives to its service and to accept a regime of poverty, austerity, and chastity (or marital fidelity; the organization encourages marriage within its ranks). The religious services do not follow a set form, although music and singing are often emphasized.

Unitarian Universalist Association Unitarianism was an outgrowth of New England Congregationalism in the late 1700's and early 1800's. Unitarians assert God's unity and repudiate the doctrine of the Trinity. They also interpret other Christian beliefs in a liberal, figurative manner. Universalism was a separate movement emphasizing the availability of God's care to all people, not only to a small chosen group. In 1961 Unitarian and Universalist organizations merged. Many traditional Christians do not acknowledge Unitarian Universalists as Christians, and many adherents would agree with that judgment.

Other Christian Churches

Among other denominations there is a wide variety of religious belief and practice. Some are large, such as the Mormons (below), and others are very small, perhaps a single local congregation that reports as a separate and independent church body. Many groups do not recognize any organizational or doctrinal authority beyond the individual congregation, thereby making it difficult to generalize about them. Some groups are heterodox offshoots from the Pentecostal family. (See also "Folk Religions" and "New Religions," below.)

The Church of Jesus Christ of Latter-day Saints, known popularly as the Mormon Church, was "established anew," according to Mormon doctrine, on April 6, 1830, by a 19th-century American prophet named Joseph Smith (1805–44). Smith, who grew up in western New York State, reported direct revelations from God. The Book of Mormon, which Smith said was given to him as a set of golden tablets by the Angel Moroni, and which he translated, tells of a visit by the resurrected Jesus Christ to pre-Columbian America. Smith assembled a community of believers that settled first in western New York and later in Ohio, Missouri, and Illinois. Wherever they went, the Mormons aroused the antagonism of neighboring non-

Mormons, in part because Mormons allowed men to take more than one wife. Persecution peaked with the murder of Smith himself in 1844.

The next great leader of the church was Brigham Young (1801–77), who led the majority of Mormons westward to settle in the then-uninhabited basin by the Great Salt Lake. There the church grew and prospered. To this day, the majority of religiously affiliated people in Utah are Mormons. There are also many adherents in surrounding states, especially Colorado and Idaho.

About half of the church's 11.4 million members live in the United States, but the Mormons' missionary work goes on around the globe. Since about 1900, the church has encouraged converts to stay in their own countries and organize congregations there. The Community of Christ, formerly the Reorganized Church of Jesus Christ of Latter-day Saints, is the largest of the groups that did not make the trek to the Great Salt Lake. Its headquarters are in Independence, Missouri, which Smith had designated as the site of a great future temple. Members of the Community of Christ (Reorganized Church) recognize their organizational and spiritual descent from the Church of Jesus Christ of Latter-day Saints but do not consider themselves Mormons.

History

At the time of his death, Jesus had a small handful of followers among Jews, but his teachings were not widely accepted among the larger Jewish community. Christianity began to outgrow its origins as a Jewish sect when the disciples of Jesus, particularly under the leadership of the Apostle Paul, preached to non-Jewish gentiles throughout the Roman Empire. Jesus' teachings were remembered in oral tradition and recorded and amplified in many writings. The 27 books recognized as the canonical New Testament were written in Greek from about A.D. 50 to the early second century A.D. (see "Books of the Bible.") The New Testament includes the four gospels, the Acts of the Apostles, the letters of Paul and others, and Revelations.

Christians were widely persecuted by Roman authorities, because they refused to accept either the secular authority or the civic religion of the empire, until the emperor Constantine legalized the religion in 313; in 380 Christianity became the official religion of the Roman Empire by proclamation of the Emperor Theodosius. Christianity also spread beyond the Roman Empire to parts of Central Asia, India, and northern Ethiopia.

Disputes over theological issues such as the nature of the Trinity and the person of Christ were resolved at a series of Ecumenical ("universal") Councils, convened by the pope and attended by bishops of most or all of the leading Christian communities. The first four of these councils—at Nicaea (325), Constantinople (381), Ephesus (431), and Chalcedon (451) were of particular importance in establishing certain Christian beliefs as orthodox and casting out others as heretical. The consolidation of Christian doctrine is reflected in the Anthanasian Creed, an extended statement of faith formerly widely used in western churches (fourth or fifth century A.D., after the time of St. Athanasius himself); and in the Nicene Creed, widely used today in liturgies (it was known in the fifth century, i.e. later than the Council of Nicaea).

In 1054 the Eastern and Western churches split over differences of theology, politics, geography, and language. The issues ranged from debates over the nature and form of the sacrament of the Eucharist (the Christian sacrificial ceremony of bread and wine) and debates about clerical celibacy to the pope's objections to the patriarch of Constantinople taking the title Ecumenical Patriarch and the patriarch's objections to the crowning of emperors of the Holy Roman Empire by the pope, in contradistinction to the Roman emperor at Constantinople. The division between Catholic and Orthodox grew steadily in complexity, bitterness, and intransigence, and only recently have leaders on both sides shown a sustained willingness to enter into dialogue to heal the breach.

Meanwhile, the papacy in Rome acquired the nature of a civil authority; and within the Western church ascetic and spiritual traditions competed with secular ones. In the 16th century, papal authority was challenged by such reform-minded priests as Martin Luther and John Calvin, abetted by England's King Henry VIII, who transferred authority over the church in England from the pope to himself. Sectarian wars engulfed Europe for more than a century as Catholics and Protestants vied for temporal and spiritual power.

European explorers and colonists spread Christianity to the Americas, as well as to Asia and Africa. (In some places in both Asia and Africa, the Europeans encountered well-established indigenous Christian communities adhering to older rites such as Nestorianism or Syrian Orthodoxy.) The Spanish and Portuguese brought Catholicism to Latin America, while North America became a haven for Protestant denominations from northern Europe. Since the mid-1800's, Protestant and

Catholic evangelists have carried out energetic missionary programs to Africa and East Asia.

Geography and numbers

Christianity is the most populous and most widespread religion in the world, with almost 2 billion adherents in 260 countries. Europe is home to more than 555 million Christians (76 percent of the region's population), but Latin America has proportionally the highest number of Christian adherents—93 percent of the population. There are more Christians in Africa (360 million) and Asia (303 million) than in North America (255 million).

Islam

The precepts of Islam were revealed through the prophet Muhammad, who was born ca. 570 at Mecca in western Saudi Arabia and died in 632 in the city of Medina. Muslims trace their descent from Abraham; but unlike Jews, who trace their descent through Isaac, the son of Abraham's wife, Sarah, Muslims trace their decent through Ishmael, Abraham's son by his servant Hagar. The word *Islam* , Arabic "surrender" or "submission," suggests an adherent's (known as a Muslim) total obedience to the will of God.

Scripture

The Koran ("recitation") consists of 114 chapters, known as suras. Muslims view the text as the infallible word of God as revealed to Muhammad and transcribed by his followers over the course of the last 23 years of his life. Chapters are arranged by length, from shortest to longest, and cover a wide range of topics. The Koran includes versions of historical episodes from the Jewish and Christian Bibles, including the stories of Adam and Eve, Abraham, Moses, and David; but the Koran focuses on the significance of these events, rather than the historical details, which are expected to be familiar to the reader. The Koran recounts the virgin birth of Jesus, but does not portray him as the son of God. The Scripture also recounts events in the life of Muhammad and offers practical guidance in daily matters and religious law. According to Muslim tradition, Muhammad's first *caliph* ("successor"), his son-in-law Ali, began the process of standardizing the text shortly after Muhammad's death. In orthodox belief, the Koran was dictated to Muhammad by God in Arabic, and may be read and recited only in that language; translations of the Koran are considered to have no status as scripture.

Belief and Practice

Allah The very definition of a Muslim is one who submits to God. God is referred to as Allah, although this word—a contraction of *al* (the) and *ilah* (God)—merely means "the God." It is not the name of God, who is often said to have "99 names," such as The Merciful, The Just, and The Compassionate. Muhammad viewed himself and was seen by his followers not as a divine figure, but as the last in a line of prophets, following Abraham, Moses, and Jesus.

Five Pillars of Islam A Muslim's relations with God are regulated by the Five Pillars of Islam:

Profession of Faith (*Shahadah*) This is a single sentence that essentially makes a person a Muslim: "There is no God but Allah, and Muhammad is his messenger." These are the first words spoken to a newborn Muslim, and they are recited daily throughout a person's life.

Prayer (*Salat*) Most Muslims pray five times daily: before dawn, midday, midafternoon, sunset, and nighttime; some Shiite Muslims combine these into three prayers. Prayers are announced by a *muezzin* who calls from the top of a minaret. The call begins with "Allahu akbar" ("God is supreme") and continues, "I witness that there is no God but God; I witness that Muhammad is the messenger of God; hasten to prayer." Muslims are expected to perform ritual purification before prayer, washing their hands, arms, face, neck, and feet. Prayer is performed facing *qiblah*, the direction of Mecca; inside a mosque this is indicated by an arched niche known as a *mihrab*. Prayer typically consists of passages from the Koran recited in Arabic from memory, in standing, bowing, prostrate, and sitting postures. Friday is a day of public prayer, but not necessarily a day of rest, and services in a mosque will usually include a sermon by religious leader.

Charity (*Zakat*) Devout Muslims are obligated to give a portion of their wealth to the poor. The actual percentage varies, but is usually about 2.5 percent yearly—and this is based on all of a Muslim's possessions, not only their annual income. They are also expected to provide other forms of charity whenever the opportunity arises.

Fasting during Ramadan (*Sawm*) Muslims are required to abstain from food, liquid, tobacco, and sex between dawn and dusk during the ninth month of the

Muslim calendar, Ramadan, in remembrance of the time of Muhammad's first revelations. Due to the lunar Muslim calendar, the month begins 11 days earlier each year.

Pilgrimage to Mecca (*Hajj*) Every Muslim is expected to visit Mecca once in his or her lifetime, unless prevented by poverty or illness, and only Muslims may enter the city. About 2 million people make the journey each year: either the "lesser pilgrimage," which is simply a visit to Mecca to worship in the great mosque and visit nearby holy sites, or a "greater pilgrimage" which involves several ritual visits to the Kabah (below) over a period of several days, interspersed with reenactments of events from the lives of Abraham, Hagar, and Muhammad. Completing the pilgrimage gives a Muslim the status of *hajji* or *hajjiyah* (male or female pilgrim).

Schools and sects

Sunni Islam The overwhelming majority of Muslims (83 percent, or 934 million people) are Sunnites. The name derives from *sunna*, meaning "tradition" or "example," and refers to the teachings of Muhammad in the Koran and authoritative *hadiths* ("recollections" by Muhammad's followers). Saudi Arabia and Egypt are the main centers of power in the Sunni world.

Shiite Islam Shiites, or "partisans," represent another 16 percent (180 million) of the worldwide Muslim community. The original division between Sunni and Shiite Islam revolved around the question of Muhammad's caliph (successor); Shiites believed that succession should be strictly hereditary, descending directly from Muhammad. Since then the two divisions have developed further differences about deeper issues of faith and the practice of Islam. Iran is the center of Shiite Islamic power, although there are also significant Shiite communities in parts of Iraq, Syria, Yemen, and non-Arab countries such as Pakistan and India.

Sufism Sufism is essentially Islamic mysticism, a branch of the religion that promotes a simple existence and seeks a direct experience of God. It emerged in response to a perceived "worldliness" overtaking Islam in its early years of development. A traditional Sufi disciple (*fakir* in Arabic, *darwish* in Persian) pursues spiritual studies with a Sufi leader, or *shaykh*. Throughout their history, Sufi orders (*tariqah*) have incorporated a variety of techniques to produce a mystical state of *sana* ("extinction" or loss of self), including breathing techniques, counting on rosaries, playing music, and spinning or dancing (the English phrase *whirling dervish* comes from the circular dance of the Mawlawiya order). Because many orthodox Muslims view Sufism as a folk religion, on a lower order than "true" Islam, it is not practiced openly in many parts of the world.

History

Muhammad, the founder and first prophet of Islam, was born ca. A.D. 570 in Mecca. The city was already a holy place for a variety of local religious practices, and the home of the Kabah ("cube"), which housed hundreds of images of tribal gods, as well as a black meteorite believed to have been sent by heaven (and still the central focus of a Muslim's pilgrimage to the city). Muhammad was raised by his uncle and became a trader, traveling throughout the Arabian Peninsula and gaining exposure to a variety of religions, including Judaism, Christianity, and Zoroastrianism. At the age of 25 he married his employer, the widow Khadija.

At age 40, in a cave at Mount Hira, Muhammad claimed he received his first visitation from the angel Gabriel, who ordered him to recite the word of God to others. The first people Muhammad shared these messages with were his wife, his cousin Ali, and his friend Abu Bakr, known now as the first Muslims. Most of Muhammad's "recitations" promoted compassion, kindness, honesty, and charity. Others, however, promoting monotheism, prohibiting statues and images, and railing against unfair contracts and usury, provoked resistance from powerful businesspeople in Mecca. In 615 some of Muhammad's followers fled to Ethiopia; in 619 Khadija died, and a year later Muhammad experienced the Night Journey (or Night of Ascent), a vision of being guided by Gabriel through Heaven into the presence of God.

In 622 Muhammad and his followers were invited by the city of Yathrib (now Medina; in Arabic, *madinat an-nabi*, "city of the prophet") to leave Mecca. Their journey is called the *Hegira* ("flight" or "migration") and marks year 1 in the Muslim calendar. In Yathrib, Muhammad fought against and ultimately banished or executed his Jewish opponents and their political allies, took control of Yathrib, and built the first Islamic mosque (*masjid*). In 624 citizens of Yathrib defeated opponents from Mecca at Badr, and Muhammad returned to Mecca to rule. His followers destroyed the images of tribal gods in the Kabah and marketplace, and began the institutionalization of

Islam. Muhammad continued to extend Islamic control in Arabia until his death in Yathrib in 632.

Under a succession of secular and theocratic caliphates, Islam swept east and west from Arabia. Muslims reached the Indus River in 713, and most of North Africa was Muslim by the end of the seventh century. Islam's advance in France was stopped in 733 at the Battle of Tours; Muslims remained in Spain until 1492. Islamic armies captured the Byzantine capital of Constantinople in 1453, and controlled much of southeastern Europe until the 19th century. In the east, Muslims swept through India at the end of the 10th century and reached the East Indies in the 15th century.

The arts, architecture, and technology flourished in the golden age of Islam and Islamic learning and culture was responsible for the transmission of much of classical philosophy and science to the West. From the 18th to 20th centuries, many traditionally Islamic countries came under Western cultural and political influence. In the 20th century, some traditionally Islamic countries such as Turkey opted for a secular state; others such as Saudi Arabia and Iran came under strict fundamentalist rule.

Holidays

Id al-Adha (Day of Sacrifice) recalls Abraham's sacrifice of a ram in place of his son; celebrated during 12th lunar month, the month of the Hajj. Id al-Fitr (Day of Breaking the Fast) is observed after the end of Ramadan. Muharram (first month of Muslim year) commemorates Muhammad's migration to Yathrib (Medina); in Shiite branch, it also commemorates of death of Husayn, son of Muhammad's son-in-law Ali. Muhammad's birthday is celebrated on the 12th day of the third month of the year.

Geography and numbers

With 1.1 billion adherents in 184 countries, Islam is the second-largest religion in the world. It is the dominant religion throughout the Middle East, North Africa, Central Asia, Afghanistan, Pakistan, and Indonesia, the country with the largest number of adherents (172 million people). There are 104 million Muslims in India—11 percent of that country's population.

Hinduism

Modern Hinduism evolved from ancient Vedism, a religion of Indo-European origin dating from the second millennium B.C. The term *Hinduism*, however, was not introduced until the early 19th century (by British writers), and it properly refers to the past 2,000 years of this complex polytheistic religion and philosophy.

Scripture

The earliest sacred books of Hinduism are the Vedas, which preserve in written form the chants of the priestly class of the *Aryan* ("noble") people, who brought Vedism to the Indian subcontinent. The Vedas, which date to about 1500 B.C., are revered by Hindus as the authoritative source of religious truth, even though they are not widely read by practitioners and are not a common source of guidance in daily life or in religious practice. The four central texts are: the *Rig Veda* ("hymn knowledge"), the oldest and most important of the Vedas, consisting of chants to the Aryan gods; the *Yajur Veda* ("ceremonial knowledge"), chants to be performed in conjunction with religious ceremonies and sacrifices; the *Sama Veda* ("chant knowledge"), musical elaborations of chants; and the *Atharva Veda* ("knowledge from Atharva," a Vedic teacher), practical and protective charms and chants.

In addition to the four core texts, the collective term *Vedas* also commonly encompasses: the *Brahmanas* and *Aranyakas*, ceremonial rules appended in later centuries to each of the earlier collections; and the *Upanishads*, a collection of approximately 100 works in prose and poetry written over hundreds of years. Most of the Upanishads are in dialogue form and constitute an exploration of basic Hindu philosophical and spiritual concepts, such as *karma* and *samsara* (see below). In contrast to the oldest Vedic texts, which were traditionally restricted to the priestly class, the Upanishads insist that spiritual mastery is not dependent on heredity, but is available to all who practice sufficient discipline and meditation.

Other key Hindu texts include epic mythological poems such as the *Ramayana* and the *Mahabharata*. The *Bhagavad Gita* is part of the *Mahabharata*, but is of such great importance it is often printed and studied on its own: written in dialogue form like the Upanishads, the *Bhagavad Gita* teaches that action and duty (*dharma*)—in accordance with one's station in life—are paths to spiritual perfection just as surely as are prayer and sacrifice.

Belief and Practice

Hindu worship is largely an individual or family matter. There are striking regional differences in the relative importance of Hindu gods, the ways in which they are worshipped, and in various other Hindu practices. Still, some basic concepts are common to most Hindu schools and sects, many of which are articulated in the Upanishads:

Atman and Brahman often defined as "soul" and "divine spirit," but in the Upanishads they carry deeper meanings. Brahman is both the source and substance of all existence; as the "self" of living beings, it is referred to as Atman. The ultimate spiritual goal of Hinduism is understanding and experiencing that there is no difference between Atman and Brahman, between one's self and the rest of the universe.

Maya is frequently used to describe the world in the Upanishads; commonly translated as "illusion" but derived from a root with the dual connotation of "magic" and "matter." Maya implies that the world is real and substantial, but at the same time is not separated into individual things; rather, it is of a singular spiritual nature that shifts and changes.

Karma refers to the moral consequences of every act in life; Karma is not inherently good or bad, except in relation to the person who experiences it.

Samsara is the Hindu cycle of birth and rebirth in life; a person's path through and rebirth into this cycle is determined by their karma.

Moksha means "freedom" or "liberation"; breaking free of the endless cycle of Samsara. One achieves Moksha by freeing oneself from such selfish traits as egotism and anger, and even losing all sense of one's individuality. Moksha is the ultimate goal of Hindu practice, achieving the recognition that one's self is inseparable and indistinguishable from Brahman.

In addition to the spiritual goal of Moksha, Hindus also believe in the pursuit of worldly goals, including Dharma, or social and religious duty; Artha, or economic security and power; and Kama, or pleasure.

The Upanishads describe these concepts, but the texts are not strictly a guide to achieving Moksha. The daily practice of Hinduism is more directly influenced by the *Bhagavad Gita*, which portrays a dialogue between Prince Arjuna and his adviser, Krishna. Arjuna struggles with the dilemma of whether or not he should fight against his cousins, who are threatening his rule. Krishna reveals himself as an incarnation of the god Vishnu and advises Arjuna to act in accordance with his princely role and fight; the dialogue teaches that acting in accordance with one's station in society is a form of worship, and a path to oneness with the universe.

Caste The traditional Hindu caste system provides a framework for this process. This system divides society into four primary (and hundreds of subsidiary) castes defined by occupation and social standing: *brahmins* are the highest, priestly class; *kshatriyas* are the aristocracy and protectors of society; *vaishyas* are merchants, landowners, moneylenders, and sometimes artisans; and *shudras* are laborers. Beyond the caste system are the *dalit*, untouchables or outcasts. India's modern constitution outlawed the caste system, and urbanization has accelerated the intermingling and intermarriage of castes, but the system is still of great importance in Indian society (for example, many arranged marriages are based in part on considerations of caste) and is particularly important in rural areas and the conservative southern parts of India.

Yoga A yoga is an active path to spiritual perfection, each one viewed as appropriate to a different caste and personality type. A yoga may also be referred to as a *marga* ("way"). Three are spoken of in the Upanishads: Jnana Yoga ("knowledge yoga"), meditation and systematic study of Hindu texts and the teaching of gurus; Karma Yoga ("Action Yoga"), the unselfish performance of social duties; and Bhakti Yoga ("devotion yoga"), devotion to an external entity, which may be a god, a guru, or even (more rarely) a spouse or parent. A vast number of other yogic traditions have been developed over the centuries, among them Hatha Yoga ("force yoga") and its many schools, which utilize stretching, breathing, and balancing exercises to achieve spiritual perfection.

Hindu Deities Hinduism has three primary theistic traditions revolving around the cults of anthropomorphic gods. Vishnu is the force of preservation; Shiva is a god of destruction; and Brahma represents the creative force. These three are often linked together in the *Trimurti*, or "triple form." Hindus also pay tribute to different incarnations of the gods, such as Rama or Krishna, both incarnations of Vishnu. Many (mostly male) Hindu gods also have animal companions and female consorts who represent different forces and may be worshipped in their own right.

Hindus have a deep respect for all living things and honor many animals as manifestations of particular deities. The most revered animal is the cow; that Muslims butcher cows is often cited as one of the reasons for conflict between Hindus and Muslims, although many Hindus today do eat beef.

Schools and Sects

Hinduism comprises myriad religious cults and various schools of philosophy, with no central authoritative body or hierarchy. The principle of religious toleration is reflected in the Hindu belief that Christianity, Islam, and other religions offer, at best, alternative paths to the same goal (or at worst, paths that are simply inadequate, rather than wrong or evil). Schools are differentiated by their adherence to different practices (such as types of yoga), or in the case of devotional Hinduism, the way of the majority of Hindus, by the god or gods to which they pay primary respect.

History

The oldest Hindu writings are Vedic texts associated with a group of invaders (probably from southeastern Europe or somewhere in the region between the Black and Caspian Seas) known as the Aryans, who conquered much of India in the second millennium B.C. The invaders also brought with them a strict caste system, the Sanskrit language, and a family of gods with obvious ties to other European deities (the Aryan father of the gods, Dyaus Pitr, was clearly the same figure as the Roman Jupiter or the Greek Zeus). Over many centuries, the Vedic religion assimilated local customs and folk religions, including the ideas of Karma and reincarnation.

The end of the first millennium B.C. marked a major transformation in Vedism, as ascetics challenged the religion and the power of the priests. Prominent among these reformers were Vardhamana, the founder of Jainism, and Siddhartha Gautama, later known as the Buddha. During this volatile period some Brahman priests propounded the doctrine that there is a Dharma (duty) for each stage of a person's life. This was an argument, in effect, for social responsibility; among other things it inveighed against the increasingly widespread phenomenon of men abandoning society for a life of religious rigor and austerity. Eremitism, in this view, was contrary to Dharma unless the person had reached an "appropriate" stage of life.

Between the second century B.C. and the fourth century A.D., the epics *Ramayana* and *Mahabharata* were developed (probably initially for oral performance, and later stabilized and standardized in written form), cults of Vishnu and Shiva grew in power, and Hinduism spread to southeast Asia. From the fourth to 11th century, devotional (*bhakti*) Hinduism exploded in popularity as religious leaders adapted their practices to vernacular languages, such as Tamil, rather than the traditional Sanskrit. Muslim power in northern India also began to increase, and many Hindus in areas that are now Pakistan, Bangladesh, and Kashmir were forced to convert to Islam. Christian ideas also made inroads in the subcontinent in the 19th century, especially under the influence of the British East India Company.

The 19th and 20th centuries also brought the struggle for Indian independence, often linked to a Hindu revival by major leaders and reformers. The best known of these leaders was Mohandas Gandhi, who brought the Hindu ascetic tradition and the principle of passive resistance (*satyagraha*) to bear on the social and political reform movement in India.

After the separation of Pakistan from India in 1947, the gulf between Hindus and Muslims in the region widened. Violent clashes continued into the 21st century, especially in the disputed territory of Kashmir. In India, secularization and urbanization have led to the decline (though by no means the disappearance) of many traditional Hindu practices, including discrimination against untouchables and caste separation. There has also been a decline in the importance of the traditionally privileged priestly class.

Holidays

Because of the vast number of Hindu gods and the variety of schools and practices, there are few holidays common to all Hindus. Some of the more important festival days include Dipavali, "festival of lights," sacred to Lakshmi, goddess of prosperity; Holi, a spring festival; and Dashara, a harvest festival.

Geography and Numbers

Hinduism has an estimated 820 million adherents worldwide. With deep roots in India, and lacking a missionary tradition and any widely recognized means of converting from another religion to Hinduism, it is found almost nowhere outside of India and neighboring countries except in expatriate Indian communities.

Buddhism

The central tenets of Buddhism were developed by Siddhartha Gautama, who was born into a royal Hindu family in present-day Nepal around 563 B.C. After observing the suffering of ordinary people in the world, he left home and embarked on a long period of travel, study, and meditation; he eventually experienced enlightenment, earning the name *Buddha*, or "awakened one." He founded an order of monks and taught a philosophy of escape from life's endless cycle of suffering through nonviolence, compassion, and moderate living, until his death in 483 B.C.

Scripture

Of primary importance to all Buddhists is the *Tipitaka*, the "three baskets" or collections of Buddhist thought. These are often treated as the exact words of the Buddha, although most of the texts were not written down by his companions until years after his death. The first "basket" is the *sutras*, teachings of the Buddha in the form of sermons or dialogues; the second is the *vinaya*, or rules of monastic life; and the third is the *abhidharma*, a more systematic presentation of the lessons of the randomly organized sutras. Some schools of Buddhism make use of additional texts: the Mahayana school utilizes new sutras written centuries after the Buddha's death (though maintaining at least the pretense that these sutras represent "recovered" teachings of the Buddha), and Vajrayana Buddhism makes use of Tantric texts as well as the *Tenjur*, a collection of commentaries on a wide range of subjects such as medicine and grammar.

Belief and Practice

Because Buddhism emerged in the midst of Hindu culture, the two religions share many beliefs and concepts, such as ahimsa, or nonviolence, and samsara, the endless cycle of birth and rebirth. The Buddhist nirvana is roughly equivalent to the Hindu *moksha*, a break or escape from samsara (contrary to popular Western usage, it does not represent a spiritual or otherworldly paradise). A key difference between the religions is the Buddhist insistence that nothing is permanent, not even the universal spirit (*Brahman*) and self (*Atman*) of Hindu belief. The key Buddhist concept meaning "no permanent identity" is expressed in Sanskrit as *anatman*, or "no-Atman." The Buddha taught that the universe is constantly changing, and all things will eventually decay and disappear; therefore desire is infinite and insatiable, because nothing can be held on to forever; as a result, peace and enlightenment are only possible through renouncing desire and accepting the impermanence of existence.

In further contrast to the overwhelming complexity and multiplicity of Hindu gods and beliefs, the central truths and teachings of Buddhism—those held in common by practically all schools and sects—are summarized quite simply in the Three Jewels, the Four Noble Truths, and the Noble Eightfold Path:

The Three Jewels Three things constitute the essential heart of Buddhism: the Buddha, the ideal model to which humans should aspire; the Dharma, or the overall Buddhist worldview and way of life; and the Sangha, or the Buddhist community of monks and nuns.

The Four Noble Truths The Buddhist worldview is summarized in four simple statements: (1) All life entails suffering; (2) Suffering is caused by desire; (3) Desire can be overcome; and (4) The means for overcoming desire is the Noble Eightfold Path.

The Noble Eightfold Path These eight steps are meant to be practiced simultaneously rather than consecutively, and together they constitute a systematic method for understanding the universe, living compassionately, and achieving peace and enlightenment. They are: right views, right intentions, right speech, right conduct, right work, right effort, right meditation, and right contemplation. The term *right* may also be interpreted as "true" or "correct" and implies a distinction between the teachings of the Buddha and those of other religions and philosophies.

A hallmark of Buddhist practice has always been the monastic order, although the importance of monastic life—and even the proper interaction of monks with society at large—differs substantially between schools and sects. Buddhist temples are primarily for individual meditation and other forms of individual prayer and worship. Collective rituals play a smaller part in the lives of most Buddhists than they do in the lives of Jews, Christians, Muslims, or Hindus, though the importance of collective rituals in Buddhism varies in different sects.

Schools and Sects

Theravada Buddhism This form of Buddhism (the name means "Doctrine of the Elders") predominates today in Sri Lanka, Myanmar, Thailand, Laos, and Cambodia and claims to adhere most closely to the tenets of the early Buddhist sects. Special importance is attached to monastic life, and followers maintain a conservative view of the Buddha's teachings. The Theravada ideal is the arhat, a person who has achieved perfect enlightenment and cessation of desire, and so will enter nirvana upon his death. Theravada Buddhism thus places great emphasis on individual religious cultivation within the supportive environment of the monastic community. Theravada monks retain characteristics of Hindu sannyasins, or wandering ascetics, including their characteristic orange or burgundy robes. Because the monks must beg for food, their monasteries are often located in the center of towns instead of remote locations. Theraveda Buddhism is also called Hinayana, "Lesser Vehicle."

Mahayana Buddhism A defining characteristic of the Mahayana ("Greater Vehicle") school is its focus on compassion for others rather than personal progress toward enlightenment. This is expressed most clearly by the Mahayana ideal of the bodhisattva, or "enlightenment being," a person who, though having attained perfection of enlightenment and cessation of desire, consciously postpones entry into nirvana in order to help others. Mahayana Buddhism is also more liberal than Theravada in its approach to religious practice, which (much as in Hinduism) may include meditation, ritual, sacred objects, or even devotion to a deity, according to one's personality and station in life. This school's many sects account for the majority of Buddhists worldwide. It has been highly influential in China, Korea, and Japan. Many Mahayana schools were first developed in China, and some of those became dominant in the spectrum of Japanese Buddhism.

Among the more significant Mahayana schools to achieve particular prominence in Japan are Shingon (Chinese *zhen'yan*, "true word"), which emphasizes chanted mantras; Jodo (Chinese *qingtu*, "pure land"), a devotional Buddhism for laypeople that offers rebirth into the Western Paradise of Amitabha Buddha, a Bodhisattva of pure compassion; and the Nichiren School, named for its 13th-century founder, which focuses on the creation of a peaceful society on earth and which takes as its fundamental scripture the Lotus Sutra, a Mahayana scripture that predicts the eventual salvation of all sentient beings. Nichiren Buddhism is the basis for the New Religion (see below) known as Soka Gakkai which has succeeded in winning many converts in the West. Zen Buddhism is one of the most widely recognized Mahayana schools; it takes its name from the Japanese pronunciation of the Chinese word *chan* ("meditation," itself a transcription of the Sanskrit word *dhyana*), denoting the seventh step of the Noble Eightfold Path. Zen emphasizes meditation techniques as the most important path to satori, or enlightened experience.

Vajrayana Buddhism This school, also referred to as Tantric Buddhism, is regularly treated as the third major school of Buddhism, though it shares many features of Mahayana Buddhism and may also be considered a form of Mahayana. Vajrayana Buddhism places great emphasis on ritual, including the use of prayer wheels, mantras (chants), mudras (hand gestures), and mandalas (visible icons of the universe). Music and dance are also often included in Vajrayana ceremonies. Tibetan or Lamaistic Buddhism is a major, and probably the best-known, school of Vajrayana Buddhism; its most important sect is led by the Dalai Lama, who is believed to be the spiritual emanation of Avalokteshvara, the bodhisattva of compassion.

History

In its first few centuries of development, Buddhism benefited greatly from the support of rulers in northeast India, particularly King Asoka the Great of the Maurya dynasty (ruled 269–232 B.C.), who saw the new religion as a way to weaken the powerful Hindu priestly caste. From the second century B.C. to the seventh century A.D., however, Buddhism steadily declined in India as bhakti (devotional) Hinduism grew in popularity; in some cases Hinduism even assimilated Buddhism by portraying the Buddha as an incarnation of the Hindu god Vishnu. Meanwhile Buddhism, particularly in its Theravada form, had spread to Burma and Sri Lanka, and remains the dominant religion in those countries, as well as in Thailand, Laos, and Cambodia.

Buddhism entered China in the first century A.D. and spread to Korea no later than the fourth century, achieving great prominence under the Unified Kingdom of Silla (668–935) and reaching its peak in the Koryo Dynasty (A.D. 918–1392). From Korea Buddhism spread to Japan in the mid-sixth century. Buddhist temples dominated the Japanese capital during the Nara Period (710–785), and Buddhism (augmented from time to time by new sects borrowed from China) became thoroughly assimilated to Japanese life in the ensuing Heian Period (795–1185); it remains an influentual part of Japanese culture. In India, Mahayana Buddhism experienced a tremendous revival under the Pala Kings (eighth to 12th century A.D.) but subsequently collapsed along with that dynasty; meanwhile it had spread under Pala influence to Sumatra and Java. Since 1900, however, there has been a resurgence of Buddhism in India, thanks to its adoption by many Indian intellectuals, an influx of displaced Tibetan Buddhists and the mass conversion of hundreds of thousands of Hindu untouchables.

Geography and Numbers

There are an estimated 362 million people in more than 120 countries who adhere to Buddhist beliefs and practices. Mahayana Buddhists account for about 53 percent of all Buddhists, mostly in Japan, Korea, and China; Theravada Buddhists account for 35 percent, in Southeast Asia and Sri Lanka. Lamaist Buddhists account for the remainder in Tibet and Mongolia.

Other World Religions

Baha'i

Baha'i was founded in Iran in the mid-19th century by Husayn Ali (1817–92), known by followers as *Baha'u'llah* ("Glory of God"), a divine messenger prophesied by the earlier religion of Babism.

Husayn Ali was a devoted follower of Babism, an Iranian religion led by Siyyid Ali Muhammad (1819–50), also known as Bab (meaning "gate" or "door"). Bab claimed to be the last Imam, or hereditary successor of the prophet Muhammad's son Ali; Muslim leaders considered this to be heresy and ultimately executed Bab and persecuted his followers. Husayn Ali was imprisoned and later exiled from Iran, but declared himself in 1863 to be a divine messenger whose coming was foretold by Bab. Baha'i was spread to Europe and North America by Baha'u'llah's son, and expanded rapidly worldwide beginning in the 1960's. Baha'i is still treated as a heretical sect by many Muslims, and persecution of its followers continues in Iran and elsewhere.

A central doctrine of Baha'i is that all of the religions of the world are in agreement and that their respective prophet-founders revealed the will of God in forms appropriate to their particular time and place in history. Baha'i believers advocate a single world government and are staunch supporters of organizations such as the United Nations. There is no priesthood in Baha'i, and worship is often performed at followers' homes; however, there are organized Baha'i assemblies as well as large houses of prayer in several countries. The headquarters is in Haifa, Israel, Baha'u'llah's home in the final years of his life.

Unique Baha'i scriptures include many collections of writings by Baha'u'llah, including the *Kitab-i-Iqan* ("Book of Certainty"), *Kitab-I-Aqdas* ("Book of Holiness"), and *The Hidden Worlds*, a collection of ethical teachings. In addition, Baha'i followers also read from the scriptures of other religions in their worship services.

The Baha'i calendar is unique, comprising 19 months of 19 days each (plus four extra days). The last month of the year is a period of fasting similar to Islam's Ramadan (although it occurs at a fixed time each year, from March 2 through March 20).

There are approximately 6 million members of the Baha'i faith in more than 200 countries.

Confucianism

Confucianism takes its name from the sixth-century B.C. scholar and civil servant Kong Qiu or Kongzi ("Master Kong"; sometimes written as Kung Fu-Tzu and Latinized as "Confucius" by 17th-century Jesuit missionaries in China), but he is not the "founder" of Confucianism in the same sense that the Buddha was the founder of Buddhism. Rather, Confucius was responsible for systematizing and teaching a scholarly tradition and code of ethical conduct that had roots hundreds of years in the past, particularly in China's ancient cult of ancestor worship. The teachings of Confucius, as recorded in the *Analects* (the collected teachings of Confucius, written down by disciples over a long period after the Master's death) advocate a humanitarian ethical system focused on five values: *Ren* (reciprocal human-feeling); *Yi* (righteousness); *Li* (propriety, including ritually correct behavior); *Zhi* (knowledge); and *Xin* (trustworthiness). Collectively these values contribute to the paramount Confucian virtues of *Xiao* (filial piety); and *Wen* (culture or civilization; also civil as opposed to military power).

Confucianism remained primarily a philosophical school of thought for many centuries, but began to develop into more of a religious system (complete with ceremonies, festivals, and temples) in the first century A.D., partially in response to the growing influence of Buddhism in China. Today it is widely viewed in China as an equal part of a religious triad with Buddhism and Taoism (below); Confucius is often portrayed in religious images next to Laozi and the Buddha. There are about 6.3 million self-identified Confucianists in various countries around the world, but in a sense anyone who is culturally Chinese is to some degree a Confucianist.

Druze Community

The Druze community (also called Muwahhiddun, "unitarians") originated in Egypt in 1017, when Hamza ibn Ali, leader of a heretical sect of Ismaili Shiite Muslims, declared that the present Caliph, al-Hakim, was the sole, ubiquitous and timeless incarnation of God. After al-Hakim's death Hamza developed the main doctrinal lines of the Druze faith in a series of letters to the community. Hamza also moved the main center of the community to Greater Syria and entrusted it to a series of five leaders ("missionaries") who were considered embodiments of cosmic principles. The Druze believe in human reincarnation and in the return of al-Hakim in human form some time in the future, an event that will bring to a close the present age and inaugurate a new messianic era.

The Druze community remains a vital presence in Lebanon, Syria, Jordan, and Israel, but in modern times its adherents have been subject to occasional persecution by both Muslims and Maronite Christians.

Jainism

Jainism is a polytheistic religion established in India by Nataputta Vardhamana (known as Mahavira, or "great man") in the sixth century B.C. Jainism shares many features of Buddhism, including the principle of ahimsa (nonviolence), although its practitioners are generally committed to a more austere way of living than Buddhists. Important practices include devotional acts toward Jainist saints (*tirthankaras*), fasting, and pilgrimages to various temples. There are four major Jainist branches, each of which adheres to a different set of scriptures. Almost all of the world's 4.3 million Jainists live in India.

Native American Religions

The Native American religions of North America have deep historical roots, with a wide range of beliefs about the natural and spirit worlds and highly developed ceremonial practices. Native American tribal religions practiced today include those of the Navajo, with chant complexes; the Lakota, with seven sacred ceremonies; the Iroquis Longhouse religion; and many others. Some beliefs and practices, such as the Sun Dances of the Great Plains, are shared by more than one tribe. The largest organized inter-tribal religion is the Native American Church ("peyote church"), dating to the 19th century. In Saturday all-night rituals incorporating prayer, singing and contemplation around an earth altar and fire, the psychoactive peyote cactus is used sacramentally; this religion includes both tribal and Christian elements. While many ancient Native American religious practices continue today, the lack of careful recording in the early days of European exploration means that the pre-contact forms of most Native American religions are difficult to retrieve completely.

Parsiism

Parsiism has its roots in Zoroastrianism, an ancient Iranian religion whose central focus is on the struggle between good and evil. Its monotheistic tendencies are thought to have influenced Judaism and Christianity. Parsis ("Persians") migrated to India between the 10th and 15th centuries A.D., and live mainly around Bombay and in Gujurat, where they have prospered as merchants. There are today several hundred thousand Parsis in India and elsewhere, including North America.

Shintoism

Shinto (literally "way of the gods") evolved from ancient Japanese religious traditions that focused on the worship of kami, spirits who created the world and continue to inhabit the islands of Japan. Many kami are identified with forces of nature, such as wind or fire, or with specific individual trees, mountains, lakes, and other natural features. Deceased people also become minor kami, and are venerated by their descendants. Although some Shinto texts date from the eighth century, none is considered authoritative; Shinto is largely a religion of practice rather than doctrine or scripture, and places particular emphasis on worshipping the gods in a state of physical and ritual purity. Shinto underlies many Japanese folk festivals, and is the spiritual basis of the national sport of sumo wrestling. Shintoism became a state religion during the reign of the Meiji emperor in the 19th century, and the emphasis of state Shinto on the divinity of the Japanese emperor contibuted to the country's destructive imperialist nationalism before and during World War II. State Shinto was repudiated (along with the emperor's claim to divine status) in the postwar period, but remains controversial in such manifestations as official visits to Tokyo's Yasukuni Shrine, where the spirits of Japan's war dead are venerated. Today Shrine Shinto is the dominant strain of Shinto practice in Japan, while Folk Shinto remains locally important in rural areas. There are also many sects and offshoots of Shinto, some of which are considered to fall within the family of New Religions (see below). Because Shinto is intimately associated with the Japanese nation itself, and contains no provisions for missionary activity or conversion, virtually all Shinto believers are Japanese, and almost all of them live in Japan.

Sikhism

The Sikh ("learner") religion was founded by Guru Nanak in the early 16th century. A monotheistic religion that draws on both Hindu and Islamic beliefs, it advocates a search for eternal truth and, while believing in reincarnation, rejects the notion of divine incarnation. It was led by a succession of 10 gurus, the last of whom declared himself the last human guru. Sikhs now follow the sacred text known as *Guru Granth Singh*, or Collection of Sacred Wisdom. There are nearly 24 million Sikhs in the world; most of them live in the Punjab region of India, but there are significant Sikh immigrant communities in the United States, Canada, and Great Britain.

Taoism

The legendary founder of Taoism (also spelled Daoism) is Laozi (old spelling Lao Tzu; probably a wholly mythical figure but traditionally dated ca. 600 B.C.), whose name means "old master." According to tradition, he is the sole author of the core Taoist text, the *Daodejing* (old spelling *Tao Te Ching* "The Way and its Power"). Modern scholarship has established, however, that the book is a work of anonymous, and probably multiple, authorship from the late fourth century B.C. The *Daodejing*, also known as the *Book of Laozi*, is a collection of 81 brief, poetic chapters that discuss, often through challenging paradoxes, the nature of the Dao (Tao), the source and essence of all being. An eponymous collection of writings by Zhuangzi (old spelling Chuang Tzu; ca. 300 B.C.) is another important Taoist text. From the beginning, Taoism included elements of both religion and philosophy. It advocated a political ideal of simplicity and austerity, with the state being ruled by a sage-king empowered by his complete oneness with the Dao itself to act with wu-wei, or nonintentionality: effortlessly effecting his actions while seeming to do nothing. Self-cultivation was central to early Daoist practice, with sagehood and immortality its religious goals.

Beginning in the third century A.D., undoubtedly under the influence of Buddhism, Taoism took on more of the overt trappings of organized religion and gave rise to various sects through divine revelations granted to their founders. The two most important sects, the Heavenly Masters Sect and the Highest Clarity Sect, organized networks of temples, ordained clergy and were governed by hereditary leaders. These sects remain a vital part of religious life in Taiwan, and in many overseas Chinese communities are experiencing a dramatic revival in post-Mao China, and have thousands of active priests serving hundreds of temples. Taoist beliefs and practices have also been incorporated into some East Asian sects of Buddhism and many different forms of Chinese Folk Religion and New Religions.

Folk Religions

Worldwide, hundreds of millions of people believe in and participate in the rituals of what are known as "folk religions." While the term is a loose and elastic one, it generally implies a faith that draws selectively on disparate traditions, has little or no formal organization beyond the level of individual communities or congregations, and lacks (at least by comparison with mainstream religions) a highly developed written canon or formal theology. Some splinter groups of mainstream religions (such as Pentecostal snake-handling congregations) can be considered to fall into the category of folk religions. Of the many types of folk religions in the world today, the best known and most widespread are Chinese folk religions and New World sects that meld African religious traditions and Catholicism.

Chinese folk religions consist of a blend of ancient ancestor worship with elements of Buddhism, Confucianism, and Taoism and the worship of particular deities. One of the most important of these folk religions, widespread in the coastal provinces of southeastern China as well as on Taiwan and in overseas Chinese communities in Southeast Asia, involves the worship of the Queen of Heaven (Tian Hou, also known as Mazu, "Mother Ancestor"), venerated as the protector goddess of mariners.

There are many other Chinese folk religions, often devoted to a single deity or a particular type of religious practice; these sects range in size from single temples with a few hundred believers to large denominations with hundreds of temples and tens of thousands of believers. The vast majority of believers in Chinese folk religions live in China, the rest in scattered Chinese communities around the world.

New World folk religions African religious beliefs, especially those of the Yoruba people who now live in West Africa in Nigeria and Benin, were brought to the New World with the slave trade. These traditions mixed with Catholicism in various Caribbean and South American countries to produce new syncretic religions. Among these are Voodoo, developed in Haiti, which blends beliefs from Dahomey, the Yoruba people, and the Bakongo with French Catholicism; Santeria, developed in Cuba, synthesizing Yoruba traditions and Spanish Catholicism, and Candomblé, found in Brazil, melding Yoruba beliefs, Portuguese Catholicism, and native Brazilian religious elements.

New Religions

The term *new religion* applies to a variety of more or less organized religious systems that grew up in the 19th and 20th centuries. New religions are distinguished from folk religions in that they usually have a known founder and a written body of scripture. These religions are also often characterized by a synthesis of various Asian traditions (Hinduism, Buddhism, Confucianism, and Taoism) with modern Western religion, philosophy, mysticism, and spirituality. The number of adherents of new religions worldwide is unknown, but probably rises into the hundreds of millions. Some of the most widely known of these religions include:

Cao Dai Founded by Ngo Van Chieu (1878–1926) in Vietnam, Cao Dai followers believe that all religions teach essentially the same path to spiritual perfection, but that Cao Dai offers the clearest revelation of God's truth. Cao Dai borrows many features from Buddhism (vegetarianism, avoidance of alcohol and drugs) and Confucianism (self-cultivation and learning), but also has a rigid power structure based on Catholicism, complete with a pope, cardinals, and a headquarters called the Holy See, located near Ho Chi Minh City. It is also unusual in that it includes Winston Churchill, Victor Hugo, and the Chinese leader Sun Yat-sen among its pantheon of saints.

Ethical Culture Society Founded in New York in 1876 by Felix Adler, the Ethical Culture Society seeks to retain and build upon the ethical and moral teachings of Judaism and Christianity while purging those faiths of all supernatural, theological, and metaphysical elements. The society continues to exist, with a small number of branches; it is probably best known today for its commitment to liberal education.

Falun Gong Founded by Li Hongzhi (b. China 1951), and based on Qigong, exercises derived from Chinese martial arts, and meditation, it is part of a continuum of generally similar religious movements stretching back to the Yellow Turban and Five Pecks of Rice movements in the Latter Han Dynasty (second century A.D.) and the White Lotus sect that surfaced repeatedly as an ideology of peasant rebellion from the 14th to the 19th centuries. The name means "law-wheel energy" and refers to the *falun*, a spiritual wheel in the abdomen that, when spinning in one direction, absorbs energy from the universe; when spinning in other direction, it releases energy to the practitioner and others. Li Hongzhi moved to the U.S. in 1996; Falun Gong is now practiced worldwide but is banned in China.

International Society for Krishna Consciousness Society ("Hari Krishnas") A neo-Hindu religion founded in the United States in 1965 by the Indian Hindu missionary (itself an anomalous concept within Hinduism) Abhay Charan De (1896–1977). It has succeeded in winning many converts among young people in America and Europe; Hari Krishnas in their pink robes have become a familiar sight in public places throughout the Western world, drumming, dancing, and chanting in praise of Lord Krishna. The movement has made energetic, but only partially successful, efforts to win acceptance within the wider Hindu community.

Neo-Paganism Refers to a variety of practices based on nature-based religions of early European cultures. One of the best-known is Wicca. Both male and female practitioners may refer to themselves as witches, but contrary to popular misconceptions, Wicca is not Satan worship. Other Neo-Pagan groups include the Druids, whose beliefs and practices represent a supposed revival of Celtic religion practiced in the British Isles and France two thousand years ago, and Goddess Worship, which attempts to revive the religion of the Mother Goddess of prehistoric times (exemplified by paleolithic so-called Venus statues). The cult of the Goddess aims at recovering an era of matriarchy prior to the development of aggressive, patriarchal societies. Goddess Worship has been associated with some elements of the feminist movement in North America and Western Europe.

Rastafarianism Refers to a group of related movements taking their name from Ethiopian nobleman Ras Tafari (1891–1975), later known as that country's Emperor Haile Selassie and worshipped as a divine being. Rastafarians believe the Bible carries special messages for people of African descent, and encourages them to free themselves from any form of oppression. Because of its focus on the Bible, Rastafarian belief and practice shares many features of Christianity and Judaism: the Rastafarian God is known as Jah (related to Yahweh and Jehovah); the practice of allowing one's hair to grow in deadlocks is related to the biblical prohibition, followed by Orthodox Jews, against the cutting of hair on the side of a male's head; and many Rastafarians follow dietary restrictions based on Hebrew law, including the avoidance of pork and shellfish. A unique component of Rastafarianism is the use of *ganja* (marijuana) as a sacramental herb.

Soka Gakkai "Value Creation Society" founded by Makiguchi Tsunesaburo as an organization to enhance the role of Buddhist values in Japanese society and associated from the beginning with the Nichiren School of Japanese Buddhism, it became an independent religious group in 1937. In Japan it became highly influential in the post–World War II period through its political arm, the Komeito ("Clean Government Party"). Under the leadership of Ikeda Daisaku (b. 1928), Soka Gakkai became an international movement, gaining converts in the United States, Europe, and elsewhere. Its principal devotional practice is chanting the mantra *namu myoho renge kyo* ("praise to the wonderful law of the lotus").

Tenrikyo ("Religion of Heavenly Truth") founded in the mid-19th century by Nakayama Miki after she received what she identified as divine revelations. A blend of Buddhist and Shinto beliefs, Tenrikyo emphasizes positive thinking and social service for its adherents. Many of its believers live in the dedicated community of Tenri City, near Osaka. The sect has amassed substantial wealth over the years and is now known for its patronage of culture and the arts.

Theosophy This ancient Greek Christian term ("divine wisdom") was revived in the 19th century by Mme. Helena Blavatsky (1831–91) and others for a new religion (the Theosophical Society, 1875) based on mysticism, spiritualism, and an eclectic mix of philosophies. Theosophy teaches that established religions exemplify the enduring truths of Theosophy, but in attenuated form; that there is an enduring spiritual realm beyond the manifest world , which can with appropriate practices be called upon directly; and that it is possible for practitioners to attain extraordinary spiritual gifts. Theosophy in the 20th century became increasingly associated with Indian philosophy, religious beliefs, and practices such as yoga. It also gave rise to offshoots such as the Church Universal and Triumphant (founded by Mark and Elizabeth Clare Prophet) and the I AM Religious Movement, both of which blend Theosophical beliefs (such as messages from the "Ascended Masters") with American patriotism.

Transcendental Meditation a set of meditation techniques, based on Indian practices modified for Western audiences and promulgated in the 1950's and 60's by Maharishi Mahesh Yogi, Transcendental meditation became well known for a time because the Maharishi's followers included such figures as the Beatles and Mia Farrow, but it now is largely passé.

Unification Church (Korean *Tongilgyo*) is a new religion founded in Korea by the Reverend Sun-myung Moon (b. 1920). Unification Church is largely based on Christianity, but modified by new interpretations of the Bible divinely revealed to Rev. Moon. Members of the Unification Church are expected to live highly disciplined lives within the organization and to be obedient in all things to the founder and members of the church hierarchy; mass weddings of couples selected for each other by the church are perhaps the most conspicuous practice of the sect in the eyes of the outside world. The Unification Church's cultlike aspects have given rise to the derisive nickname "Moonies" for its adherents.

Glossary of Religious Terms

adhan call to prayer (Isl.)

anosticism belief that the existence of God can be neither proved nor disproved

ahimsa nonviolence to living things (Hind.)

animism belief that animals and other common objects possess souls, or are inhabited by other supernatural entities

Annatta/Anatman "no-Atman" (see Hinduism); the nonexistence of an individual soul (Bud.)

arhat "perfect being," or one who has attained nirvana (Bud.)

ashram religious retreat (Hind.)

atheism absence of belief in God

Atman divine spirit common to all living things (Hind.)

avatar earthly manifestation of Hindu deity (Hind.)

Ayatollah leader of Shiite sect; teacher and judge (Isl.)

baptism immersion in water to symbolize cleansing of sins, admission into church (Chr.)

bhakti acts of devotion (esp. to deity) (Hind.)

bodhi enlightenment (Bud.)

Brahman source and substance of universe (Hind.)

bushido spiritual code of samurai class

caliph literally, "successor"; a religious and political leader claiming succession from Muhammad (Isl.)

canon religious doctrine; authoritative religious texts

caste social and religious division of hindu society (Hind.)

dharma spiritual and social obligations (Hind., Bud.)

dhyana meditation (Hind., Bud.)

ecumenical pertaining to Christian church as a whole

Eucharist Holy Communion

fatwa an authoritative judgement in Islamic law (Isl.)

hadith an authoritative "recollection" of Muhammad's teachings (Isl.)

hajj pilgrimage to Mecca (Isl.)

Imam leader of the Muslim community; may also be used as honorary title for prayer leader in mosque (Isl.)

jihad "struggle"; crusade to spread Islamic faith (Isl.)

karma law of moral cause-and-effect, determining one's path through cycle of rebirth (Hind., Bud.)

koan mysterious or paradoxical story or question intended to spark enlightened thought by disrupting flow of everyday, logical thought (Bud.)

kosher "ritually correct," pertaining to dietary laws of Judaism (Jud.)

Lama monk or priest (Bud.)

mandala complex, ritually powerful design used in temples and other Buddhist art (Bud.)

mantra word or sound used to facilitate meditation (Hind., Bud.)

midrash nonliteral explanation of Jewish scripture

moksha "liberation" or release from cycle of rebirth and everyday suffering (Hind.)

muezzin person who calls Muslims to prayer (Isl.)

Mullah title for teacher of religious law (Isl.)

nirvana escape from cycle of rebirth (Bud.)

pantheism worship of all gods; belief that God exists in all things in the universe

polytheism worship of more than one god

sacrament religious rite that confers divine grace on the practitioner

samadhi transcendental union of individual with the object of their meditation (Bud.)

samsara cycle of birth and rebirth (Hind., Bud.)

sangha worldwide community of Buddhists; also monastic order founded by the Buddha (Bud.)

satori enlightenment (Bud.)

shari'ah Koranic law and regulations (Isl.)

Shiite smaller of two branches of Islam; defining belief is that succession of Islamic leaders should descend from Ali, son-in-law of the prophet Muhammad (Isl.)

Sunni larger of two branches of Islam; believes that succession from Muhammad is not necessarily based on heredity (Isl.)

sura a chapter of the Koran (Isl.)

Tao the "Way" of spiritual awareness and enlightenment

Yin and Yang two opposite but complementary forms of cosmic energy, present in different proportions in all things

yoga spiritual practice or discipline, involving any number of different techniques (physical, philosophical, or devotional) to achieve higher awareness (Hind.)

The Bible

The Bible (Greek *biblia*, books) contains the fundamental texts of the Jewish and Christian religions. The product of a long history of oral and written tradition reaching back to the second millennium B.C., the Bible has been one of the most influential books in history, shaping the religion, literature, and politics of much of the world for two millennia. It has been translated into numerous languages and has been a source of history, religion, and guidance for hundreds of millions of people.

Since the rise of Christianity in the early first millennium A.D., the Bible has been divided into two parts to reflect the Christian belief that humankind's relationship to God was changed by Jesus Christ. The Old Testament, which contains the Jewish scriptures, tells the story of the creation of the world and how the first man and woman disobeyed God and were cast out of the Garden of Eden; it describes the history of the Hebrew people and their relation to God over more than a thousand years. The New Testament includes narratives of the life, ministry, death, and resurrection of Jesus, stories about his followers, and letters to young churches. It emphasizes Jesus' message of justice and love, and asserts his divinity as the Son of God.

Types of Bibles

The Hebrew Bible The Hebrew Bible dates, in its earliest parts, to before 1000 B.C. and includes material composed as late as the second century B.C. It contains the holy writings of the Jewish people, who developed a monotheistic religion in which they are the chosen people of God who has made a covenant with them. The Hebrew Bible consists of 24 books divided into three sections: the Law (Torah), the first 5 books; the Prophets (Nevi'im); and Writings (Ketuvim). (See *World Religions*.) In their present form the scriptures are believed to have passed through a long history of oral tradition before being written down in Hebrew with a few passages in Aramaic. The standard Hebrew Bible is called the Masoretic or "transmitted," text (MT).

The Septuagint Beginning in the third century B.C., the Hebrew Bible was translated into Greek to serve the extensive communities of Greek-speaking Jews in the Eastern Mediterranean. Known as the Septuagint, Greek for "seventy", a reference to the number of writers said to have been engaged in its translation, it is referred to by the Latin number seventy, LXX. Differing from the standard Hebrew bible, it includes additional books and sections of books and is partly based on alternative textual sources.

The Old Testament The Septuagint was not only the bible of Greek-speaking Jews, it was also the bible used in the early Christian church. After the Hebrew Bible became standardized about 100 A.D., Jews turned away from the Septuagint; its preservation in various versions resulted largely from its use by the Christian church. The Septuagint was translated into Latin and other languages and it is often the text to which the New Testament writers refer in connecting the story of Jesus' life to earlier events. The Old Testament of the Roman Catholic Church is based on its books and their order. The Septuagint was first referred to as the Old Testament (by contrast with the New Testament) by Tertullian (ca. 160–230 A.D.) and Origen (ca. 185–254 A.D.) The books in the Septuagint not included in the standard Hebrew Bible are referred to as the Apocrypha (Greek hidden) or as the deuterocanonical books, i.e. those added secondarily, or later, to the canon.

At the time of the Reformation, Martin Luther, John Calvin, and others decided that the proper Old Testament was not the entire book derived from the Septuagint, but rather the shorter and older Hebrew Bible. The Protestant Old Testament now contains, in translation, the text of the Hebrew Bible, but the order of the books is that of the Septuagint. The deuterocanonical books and parts of books in the Roman Catholic Old Testament were dropped from the Protestant Old Testament; these are reprinted in many (but not all) Protestant Bibles as the Apocrypha. The Apocrypha are deemed by many Protestants to be worthy of consideration, but of less authority than the books in the Hebrew Bible.

The New Testament The New Testament consists of 27 books, all written in Greek in the first and second centuries (even though Jesus and his early followers spoke Aramaic); the books were first listed as the New Testament by Bishop Athanasius of Alexandria in A.D. 367. Both Protestant and Roman Catholic churches accept the same books of the New Testament, although Martin Luther and others held some of the New Testament books to be less authoritative. The four Gospels (meaning "good news"), each attributed to one of Christ's earliest followers, tell stories of Jesus' birth, baptism, teaching, death, and resurrection. The story of the spread of Christianity in the first century is told in the Acts of the Apostles and the epistles (letters) of St. Paul and other followers of Jesus. These writings also present early statements of Christian belief.

English Translations of the Bible The Bible has been the subject of numerous translations into English and many other languages. In the late fourth century A.D. St. Jerome, translating the Old Testament from the Hebrew, provided a standard Latin text of the Bible called the Vulgate or "common text." The earliest complete English Bible was that of John Wycliffe (1324–1384) in 1382. In 1526 the New Testament of William Tyndale (1484–1536) was published. (Both Wycliffe and Tyndale were executed for their efforts to make the Bible available to the common people.) The most famous of English Bibles is the King James Version. In 1604 James I of England approved a new translation of the Bible to replace two others in use, the Geneva Bible and the Bishops' Bible. Fifty-four translators were organized into six groups: three for the Old Testament, two for the New Testament, and one for the Apocrypha. Rules were drawn up to guide the work, and the entire new translation was ready in 1611; for the New Testament especially it draws heavily on Tyndale's translation. The King James Version, noted for its powerful language, has remained in use, although replaced in many churches by newer versions, since its publication.

In modern times, many new translations have appeared. A revision of the King James Version was published in England in 1885, with an American version in 1901. The Revised Standard Version was published 1946–1957. The New English Bible, a new translation rather than a revision of previous translations, was published 1970. The first Roman Catholic Bible in English completely translated from original Hebrew and Greek sources, the New American Bible, was published in 1970. The Good News Bible (American Bible Society) appeared in 1970, the New Revised Standard Version in 1990, and the evangelical New Living Translation in 1996. It can be expected that new translations will continue to appear because of the availability of new early manuscripts, because of the changing English language, and for doctrinal reasons.

The Bibles used today have elements to ease their use that are not in older Bibles and original manuscripts. The present chapter divisions are attributed to Cardinal Hugo de San Caro, 1248; verse divisions in the New Testament are attributed to Robert Estienne (Stephanus), 1551. Most of the punctuation and some paragraphing is modern.

The Bible as it is known today represents only a small proportion of the religious literature produced during Old and New Testament times. There is a vast sea of extra-canonical writings and different versions of canonical books, some known for centuries, some discovered more recently, such as the Dead Sea Scrolls (discovered 1947–1956 and shedding light on Judaism, the languages of Palestine and the transmission of Old Testament texts), and no doubt others yet to be discovered. For the New Testament there are noncanonical writings of many types, such as gospels (The Gospel of Paul, the Gospel of Mary, and many others), acts (The Acts of Andrew and others), letters, and apocalypses. Among the manuscripts studied extensively that provide information on the piety and practices of early Christians is the Gospel of Thomas, found at Nag Hammadi, Egypt, in 1945; this is a collection of 114 sayings attributed to Jesus.

The Books of the Bible

The books of the Old and New Testaments and the Apocrypha are described here in the order in which they are found in the Protestant Bible.

Old Testament

The Old Testament includes narrative histories, law, prayers, proverbs, poems, and wisdom literature. Some of this probably dates to before 1000 B.C. in written form; the latest material, part of Daniel, dates from the second century B.C. Much of the Old Testament is based on oral traditions, which takes the timeline even further back. Most of the books are of uncertain authorship, although they are by tradition attributed to Moses, the prophets, kings and other authors. The books went through a long series of redactions and often date in their canonical forms from long after the times of their presumed authors. Moreover, there is relatively little archaeological and independent textual evidence corroborating the historical narratives in the Old Testament for the earliest times, so that the historical reliability of these is uncertain. Nonetheless, the Old Testament has for Jewish, Christian, and many other readers, even those who do not accept it as the literal word of God, an essential religious unity

Genesis The Bible's first book describes God's creation of the world and its creatures in six days; on the seventh day God rests. He sees the disobedience of Adam and Eve in the Garden of Eden and the downward spiral of human events, and provides a new beginning with a destructive flood and the salvation of Noah. The second part of the book tells the stories of Abraham and Sarah, blessed by God and sent to find a new land, and the generations that follow: Isaac, Jacob, and Joseph in Egypt.

Exodus Tells the story of the Israelites' escape from slavery in Egypt. Moses is saved from Pharaoh's edict to kill Jewish male infants; his mother sets him afloat in the Nile and he is discovered and adopted by a princess. God commands Moses to ask Pharaoh for the Jews' freedom, but Pharaoh refuses; God sends plagues upon Egypt, ending with the slaughter of the first-born. (Passover was instituted to celebrate God's passing over the houses of the Israelites during this event.) The Israelites leave Egypt and are saved from pursuing Egyptians by the miraculous parting of the Red Sea. At Mt. Sinai Moses receives God's ten commandments, laws for society and civil life, and ceremonial laws. There God and Israel enter into a covenant: God promises to protect Israel and the Israelites promise to obey God's laws. At God's command a tabernacle is built to accompany the Israelites.

Leviticus Sets out detailed rules to govern Israelite life: the forms of sacrifices; the laws of purity (such as which animals may be eaten); the Day of Atonement; and the code of holiness, including teachings on sexual relations, festivals, ritual objects, and social matters. All of these laws were given to Moses by God. Leviticus explains the woes that have befallen Israel as a result of the people's sins, and stresses atonement.

Numbers Describes Moses' census of the Israelites; laws and cultic matters, including the priestly and temple duties of the Aaronites and Levites; travel from Sinai to Kadesh (south of Canaan); an abortive rebellion against Moses' leadership; travel from Kadesh to the plains of Moab east of the Jordan; and the preparations for conquest of Canaan, including a second census, the appointment of Joshua as leader, and detailed laws for the promised land.

Deuteronomy Composed of discourses or sermons of Moses. The first is a summary of events at Sinai and the camp at Moab, with a call for faithfulness: the people should live their lives in relation to the one true God revealed to them. The second tells of the Ten Commandments and gives an explanation of the first commandment; urges Israel to remain faithful, and presents detailed instructions for communal life. A third section recapitulates the first two, calls for faithfulness (equated to goodness and life) and warns of disobedience (equated to wickedness and death). Deuteronomy concludes with the final words and instructions of Moses linking the people to God, their past, and their future in the new land.

Joshua The Lord appointed Joshua to lead the Israelites across the Jordan; Joshua relays God's commands to the people. In a long series of battles the Israelites conquer Jericho, other cities, and much but not all of the land of Canaan that had been promised to them. The land is divided among the tribes, including tribes east of the Jordan, and cities of refuge and cities for the Levites are designated. Joshua's farewell address, prior to his death in old age, implores the Israelites to follow God.

Judges Describes the history of the Jewish people from the conquests of Joshua to the time of Samuel and the beginning of the monarchy (late 11th century B.C.) The most important judges were military rulers as well as administrators. The Israelites lived among pagan peoples in the parts of Canaan that they had conquered. In a repetitive historical pattern, the Israelites were idolatrous and worshiped the gods of their neighbors; God oppressed them with defeats and slavery but then sent a judge to save the penitent and bring peace. The thankless Israelites would then fall back into their faithless ways. Ultimately the land became completely lawless; the disasters concluded with a civil war against the Benjaminites.

Ruth Naomi and her husband leave Bethlehem during a famine for the Moabite country, where their two sons marry. After the deaths of her husband and sons, Naomi vows to return to her own land. Ruth, one of her Moabite daughters-in-law, demonstrates her loyalty and love by returning with Naomi to Judah. There, she marries her kinsman Boaz, to whom she bears a son, Obed, the grandfather of David.

1 Samuel and 2 Samuel Samuel, dedicated from birth to God's service, was the last person to rule in Israel before the monarchy. At the request of the people for a king, Samuel first anointed Saul. He, however, was disobedient to God, and so Samuel secretly anointed David, a young shepherd; the life and kingship of David, the ideal ruler, are the focus of the books. The events recounted include the combat with Goliath; David's rise to power in conflict with Saul and his family (in which his innocence of wrongdoing is stressed); various battles and revolts; David's conquest of Jerusalem, the city in which God has chosen to be worshiped by his people; the prophecy of perpetual rule for David's line; and his infidelity with Bathsheba.

1 Kings and 2 Kings These two books relate the history of the 400 years of the Jewish monarchy, beginning with the death of David and the start of the reign of Solomon (about 965 B.C.). The narrative also describes the period of the dual monarchy (Israel and Judah) and ends with the destruction of Jerusalem and the Babylonian captivity in 586 B.C. The faithfulness of each of the kings to the law of God as given to Moses is judged. Most of the kings (and all of those of Israel, which broke away from the House of David) fall short, and their repeated failures to keep the covenant of God are used to explain such disasters as the fall of Jerusalem.

1 Chronicles and 2 Chronicles 1 and 2 Chronicles cover genealogies from Adam to Saul; the reign of David, including his preparations for building the temple; the reign of Solomon (the beginning of 2 Chronicles), including the building and dedication of the temple; and the Davidic kings ending with the Babylonian conquest and exile. The main focus is on David as the founder of worship at the temple, and Solomon as its builder; the later kings of the southern kingdom are evaluated primarily on their loyalty to the temple and temple worship.

Ezra The first part of Ezra deals with the rebuilding of Jerusalem and the temple according to the decree of the Persian ruler Cyrus (late 6th century B.C.), by which Jews were permitted to return from exile. There is local opposition to reconstruction, but after confirmation from the later Persian ruler Darius the rebuilding is completed with the encouragement of Haggai and Zechariah. The second part of the book concerns Ezra's mission from Babylon to Jerusalem in the mid fifth (or early fourth) century B.C. He goes to renew and reform the temple and its rites. The Jews had been guilty of idolatry and had mixed with the local population and taken foreign wives, a practice forbidden by Ezra. The books of Ezra and Nehemiah were originally one in the Hebrew bible.

Nehemiah Nehemiah, a cupbearer to Persian King Artaxerxes, asks permission to return to Jerusalem to rebuild the walls (ca. 455 B.C.). He is allowed to go with other Jews; arriving in Jerusalem, he surveys the walls and plans their reconstruction, succeeding brilliantly in the face of opposition from neighboring communities and even from within Jerusalem. The covenant is renewed; Nehemiah institutes legal and religious reforms and remains as governor for many years, later returning for a second term.

Esther Tells the story of Esther, the foster-child of Mordecai, who becomes Queen to Ahasuerus, King of Persia. Through her beauty and courage, she foils a plot of the courtier Haman to kill all the Jews, her people, in the Kingdom. Instead, Haman is executed, the Jews are saved and avenge themselves on their enemies, and Mordecai becomes great at court. The days of salvation are to be celebrated always as the feast of Purim.

Job Examines the questions of God's nature and his relationship to humans. In particular, Job raises the question of why the righteous should suffer; he has been visited by dreadful calamities which imply that he is wicked. Yet according to the covenant calculation of righteousness equals salvation, this should not be, since he is a righteous man. So perhaps God is not a benevolent creator after all, although Job continues to engage with him. The book contains Job's laments, dialogues with friends, God's direct speeches to Job from the tempest (whirlwind) and Job's response, in which he says that he is comforted and has reached a new understanding.

Psalms The Psalms are a varied collection of songs and prayers that have long played an important liturgical role in synagogues and churches. The Psalter, as the book is called, was well known in medieval times. The psalms are of various types: some are spoken or sung by individuals, and some by groups; some celebrate and praise God, and others are petitions for divine help. The psalter includes some discernible subcollections, as indicated by the repetition of some psalms (e.g. 14 and 53) and the titles of certain psalms. Until the 19th century the psalms were taken to be personal lyrics of King David, but it is now known that they were composed over a long period.

Proverbs Traditionally called the Proverbs of Solomon although their collection dates to no earlier than the sixth century B.C. It is a compilation of collections of poems and sayings such as "Sayings of the Wise" and "The Words of King Lemuel" offering advice on an enormous range of matters, usually with a moral point, relevant to the ancient world. There is also a poem about the capable (or virtuous) wife. A key theme of Proverbs is the virtue of wisdom, personified by a woman (equated with righteousness), as opposed to folly (equated to evil).

Ecclesiastes The "Speaker," who describes himself as king (perhaps administrator) over Jerusalem, seeks to grasp the elusive meaning of human existence, and expresses his lifelong search of wisdom in a series of insightful maxims.

Song of Solomon The "Song of Songs," attributed to Solomon, but probably compiled after mid-sixth century B.C., is a book of love poems between a man and a woman, with a chorus of daughters of Jerusalem; the poems are filled with powerful erotic imagery. The book is traditionally interpreted as an allegory of the relation of God to his people.

Isaiah This book is usually regarded as three distinct but related works: First Isaiah deals with the period of Isaiah's prophecies in Judah in the second half of the eighth century B.C. (chs. 1-39); Second Isaiah (chs. 40-55), deals with the sixth to fifth centuries B.C.; and Third Isaiah (chs. 56-66) with the period after the exile. First Isaiah is concerned with the political and military developments in the world of Judah. Isaiah interprets events concerning Jerusalem and the continuity of the House of David in terms of sin, and military defeat as the form of God's punishments. But punishments are not final: justice can be restored and the people purified. Second Isaiah's author is concerned with the Babylonian captivity and exiles' feeling that God is neglectful or absent; Isaiah gives hope for the future. The victories of Cyrus the Persian, who permitted the exiles to return to Jerusalem and rebuild the temple, are seen as ordained by God. Third Isaiah, reflecting conditions in the Holy Land after the return from exile, deals with ritual matters, repentance, and promises of final salvation.

Jeremiah Born about 645–640 B.C., Jeremiah is one of the greatest prophets. His book contains long personal confessions and laments, prophecies against the nations, and restoration prophecies; the core message includes a sternly moral call to true repentance: outward ceremonies and confessions are inadequate in God's sight. After the rise of Babylon Jeremiah prophesied accommodation rather than revolt but his message went unheeded and Jerusalem was destroyed; the prophet at first remained in Jerusalem but was later taken to Egypt. Jeremiah made enemies throughout his career with his harsh prophecies; he was imprisoned and efforts were made to kill him.

Lamentations Attributed to the prophet Jeremiah but of uncertain authorship, Lamentations contains five elegies for Jerusalem and the temple, destroyed by the Babylonians 586 B.C. The fall of the city and the extreme suffering of the people are attributed to the Israelites' failure to be true to God, but the book expresses the ultimate hope of regaining God's favor. In poetic form, four of the book's chapters have 22 verses (three are acrostics with lines beginning with each of the letters of the Hebrew alphabet).

Ezekiel Ezekiel (sixth century B.C.) was taken to Babylon after the capture of Jerusalem (597 B.C.) by Nebuchadnezzar; in exile he felt the call to prophesy. His book has three parts. The first includes oracles of judgment against Jerusalem and Judah before the final destruction of Jerusalem in 586 B.C. In the second part, there are oracles against foreign nations, including Judah's neighbors, Egypt and Tyre. But the God who acts in history gives salvation as well as judgment; his desire is to bring the nations to righteousness. In the third part, after the destruction of Jerusalem and the fulfillment of his oracles, Ezekiel's prophecies, such as the story of the valley of dry bones coming to life, focus on restoration and redemption: the return of Israel to the promised land. Ezekiel also has visions of the restoration of the temple, its regulations, the priestly order, and the distribution of land.

Daniel The first section includes narratives set in the Babylonian and Persian courts, the best known of which is Daniel in the lions' den, thrown in by the ahistorical Darius the Mede for his piety but saved by an angel of the lord. The second part is an apocalypse, in which God's visions to Daniel, interpreted by an angel, provide a prophecy of history and offer comfort: the pious martyrs will shine in the resurrection. The "son of man" who appears in one vision is used in the New Testament as a title for Jesus.

The Minor Prophets ("The Twelve")

Hosea Active from middle eighth century B.C. to the fall of the Northern Kingdom (721 B.C.), Hosea describes symbolically and historically the relationship of God to his faithless people, who are idolatrous sinners. The awful punishment of God is prophesied, but God will forgive the repentant.

Joel Describes the devastation of a locust plague, characterizing the locusts as an army; there is also drought. But for a repentant Israel the Lord will reverse this agricultural devastation and in the ideal future time will redeem Israel and defeat all its enemies.

Amos A herdsman of Tekoa in Judah, Amos was the earliest of the prophets (fl. ca. 750 B.C.) whose words were collected and later written down. Proclaiming God's judgment on Israel and its neighbors for grievous religious and social sins, he foresees God's punishment of Israel with drought, plagues, military defeat and exile.

Obadiah Obadiah prophesies the total and final destruction of Edom for its participation in the Babylonian destruction of Jerusalem: the Edomites, held to be the descendants of Jacob's brother Esau, are kin who betrayed Judah. The book, the shortest in the Old Testament (21 verses), is in poetry except for the final three verses.

Jonah God tells Jonah to go to the Assyrian capital, Nineveh, and denounce its wickedness. Instead Jonah sails to Tarshish; en route the ship is threatened by a God-sent storm. As propitiation, Jonah is thrown into the water and swallowed by a great fish. Freed by God, he goes to

Nineveh, where he preaches with success but protests God's forgiveness of the repentant Ninevites; God instructs him on the need for mercy.

Micah Punishments for evil-doing in the cities of Samaria and Jerusalem (capitals of Israel and Judah) are prophesied and a future reign of God's peace centered on Mt. Zion in Jerusalem is foreseen. The rupture between God and his people because of their wickedness is described; it will be followed by ultimate reconciliation.

Nahum Describes the wrath and power of God and vividly prophesies the destruction of Nineveh. Its aim may have been to encourage the Judean king to join in revolt against Assyria through faith in God's purpose to destroy it.

Habakkuk Laments the success of the wicked and God's use of the Babylonians to wreak punishments; but God assures him that the righteous will triumph. The book concludes with a prayer, perhaps used liturgically in the temple, depicting God as a powerful warrior.

Zephaniah Zephaniah (seventh century B.C.) prophesies against idolatry and other sins of Judah and Jerusalem; the Israelites and foreign peoples will all be laid waste by God on the awful Day of the Lord. Only repentance can save; God will leave a small remnant of the humble and righteous in Jerusalem and he will establish his kingdom over the earth.

Haggai The Lord, through his prophet Haggai, tells the leaders of Judah of his wrath because the temple has not been rebuilt. In his anger God damages Israel's harvests, but once the people begin rebuilding the temple, they have God's blessing and his temple will again be glorious.

Zechariah Zechariah reports the word of the Lord in seven visions, said to have occured in 519 B.C., that represent the Jewish community and a rebuilt temple. God is angry with his people for their failures, but is ready to forgive the repentant builders. The two last sections of Zechariah, oracles of Judah's triumph and the Day of the Lord, are later additions.

Malachi Attacks inferior and inadequate sacrifices, faithlessness, and marrying foreign wives. A "messenger of the covenant" (also identified as Elijah) will come to clear a path for the Lord who will cast down evildoers while the righteous will rejoice; this prophecy in the last book of the Old Testament greatly influenced later Jewish and Christian messianic thought.

New Testament

The New Testament includes 27 books: four gospels, the Acts of the Apostles, 21 letters (epistles), and Revelation; these are accepted as canonical by the Roman Catholic and Protestant churches, although some scholars and a few churches argue for a smaller canon. The New Testament books were written in Greek during the years from about A.D. 50 to the first half of the second century A.D. The arrangement of the books, adopted in the fourth century A.D., is roughly in chronological order of subject, rather than date of writing: the story of Jesus (gospels), the beginning of the church (Acts), advice to churches and the beginnings of Christian theology (letters), and the future vision of hope (Revelation). Aside from the genuine letters of Paul, little is known about the actual authors of the New Testament books; the traditional attributions result from the custom of writers assigning works to revered predecessors or from later decisions by church fathers.

The Gospels The earliest gospel ("good news") is that of Mark, about A.D. 70 (the time of the destruction of the Second Temple in Jerusalem by the Romans); Luke wrote about A.D. 80-85, Matthew, about A.D. 90 , and John during the late first century A.D. Mark gathered sayings of Jesus and stories of his life and ministry from the oral traditions of the early church. Later, Matthew and Luke wrote their gospels using Mark as a source and a collection of Jesus' sayings. The first three gospels, similar in contents and in order, are called the synoptic ("seen together") gospels. John, by contrast, may not have known of the synoptics when he wrote; in any event his gospel is different in tone and focus from the other three. The four canonical gospels were collected about the mid-second century A.D.; at that time, the Acts of the Apostles, originally part of Luke, was treated as a distinct work.

Matthew Begins by saying that Jesus, descended from Abraham, is the Messiah. The story of his birth in Bethlehem is described: the adoration of the Magi, the wrath of Herod, and the flight of Mary, Joseph, and Jesus to Egypt. Jesus' baptism by John is followed by his ministry: the Sermon on the Mount, miracles, and the recognition of Jesus as the Messiah by his disciples. His journey to Jerusalem and conflict with the priestly elite is followed by his death, resurrection, and appearance to the disciples. Matthew contrasts the Old Testament time of prophecy with the era of God's fulfillment in Jesus; the believer needs to receive Jesus to be part of God's eternal kingdom.

Mark Starts with John's baptism of Jesus, then tells of Jesus' ministry: his preaching, teaching, and healing, and the activities of his disciples. The miracles of calming the waters, of feeding the multitudes with loaves and fishes, and others are described. Mark then focuses on Jesus' journey to Jerusalem, death, and resurrection. In Mark's rendering, those who hear Jesus, even his disciples, do not fully understand who he is; it is only with the crucifixion that Jesus and his mission are fully understood and he is recognized as the son of God.

Luke Luke begins with the birth of John the Baptist and continues with the story of Jesus' birth, including the annunciation, the manger, and the shepherds. Jesus' ministry begins after his baptism by John. Luke describes the conflicts with the Pharisees (an observant Jewish group), the journey to Jerusalem, Jesus' death, resurrection and appearances to the disciples, and his ascension. Luke emphasizes Jesus' concern with the poor and the duties of the rich to the poor. Several gospel incidents and parables are found only in Luke, such as the boy Jesus in the temple, the appearance to two disciples on the road to Emmaus, and the stories of the Good Samaritan and the prodigal son.

John John starts with the assertion that Jesus is the Word, the God from eternity embodied in humankind. The focus is not on the everyday moral and religious implications of Jesus' teaching, but rather on his claims to be the Messiah, the Light of the World, the Son of God. While including miracles and healing, John omits parables, the Sermon on the Mount, the instruction to pray the Lord's Prayer, and the institution of the Last Supper. The gospel emphasizes the conflict of Jesus with the Pharisees, and more broadly Jesus versus the Jews, a focus that may reflect the writer's era, when clearer distinctions between Jews and Christians had developed. The gospel ends with Jesus' death, resurrection, and appearances to the disciples, including his appearance by the Sea of Galilee to Peter and others.

Acts of the Apostles Written about A.D. 80–85, Acts is by the same author as Luke. It begins where Luke ends, with the Ascension of Jesus, and recalls his words that the disciples will bear witness in Jerusalem, to Judah and Samaria, and thence to the "ends of the earth." The book describes the earliest years of the church: its rapid growth among the Jews, the conversion of Paul, outreach to the Gentiles, and doctrinal controversies. Paul's missions in Asia Minor and Greece, and his trials in Jerusalem and Caesarea are detailed; the book ends with his final preaching and imprisonment in Rome.

Letters

Letters are the dominant form of literature in the New Testament: they provide early statements of Christian theology as well as advice and counsel to churches and individuals. Collections of Pauline letters were circulated among congregations by about A.D. 100. Of the 21 letters, 13 attributed to Paul are listed first: nine to churches (ordered by descending length), and four to individuals. Then come Hebrews and the seven "general" or "catholic" letters, either written to general audiences or to unidentified individuals. Today only nine letters are widely regarded as genuinely Paul's: Romans, 1 & 2 Corinthians, Galatians, Philippians, 1 Thessalonians, and Philemon. The "pastorals" (1 & 2 Timothy and Titus) are usually regarded as non-Pauline; opinions vary on 2 Thessalonians, Ephesians, and Colossians.

Romans Written to the church in Rome probably between A.D. 55 and 58. Paul defends his gospel to the Gentiles, answering questions and challenges raised by Jewish Christians in Rome. He writes that Jesus' obedience benefits all groups, not just Jews: through the first Adam all became sinners, through the last Adam (Jesus) all were granted grace. The law that God gave to the Israelites was not wrong; rather the lack was in sinful humans, whose sin is forgiven by God's grace that now supersedes the law. Gentiles can become righteous, and in the end Jews and Gentiles will be one. Those with gifts should use them to the benefit of the church, and all should respect the state for preserving order and providing a frame for witness. In closing, Paul tells the Roman congregation that he will visit them on his way to a projected (unrealized) mission to Spain.

1 Corinthians Paul founded the congregation at Corinth, on the isthmus between mainland Greece and the Peloponnesus, about A.D. 50/51; he wrote them at least five letters. This second letter (the first is lost) was written about A.D. 54 from Ephesus. Paul gives advice on problems that were endangering the congregation's communal life. Some people claimed special status because of supposed religious wisdom; a man had an incestuous relationship; there were disorders at the Lord's Supper; and Paul has received an inquiry from the congregation about his ideas on sexuality and marriage. Paul responds that God's revealed wisdom sets aside individual claims to status. Worldly matters are transient, but not unimportant, and Christians must behave in a worthy manner; he says that whatever is done should be done in love, with an awareness of the grace bestowed on Christians by their faith both in the present and for eternity.

2 Corinthians This letter is thought to be a composite of at least two letters by Paul to the church in Corinth, one (chs. 1–9) written in A.D. 55 , and a second (chs. 10-13) about a year later. Paul first refers to a "tearful letter," now lost, assailing the congregation for not disciplining a member with whom Paul had been in conflict. But Paul assures the Corinthians of his care and devotion, and writes of the Christian message and the Christian ministry, including his own struggles, and the need for generosity in supporting other congregations. He attacks rival missionaries and their false claims, asserts the truth of the faith he preached, and promises the Corinthians another visit.

Galatians Written by Paul between A.D. 50 and 55 to the churches in Galatia (central or southern Anatolia). Paul admonishes these Christians not to stray from the gospel of faith in favor of a return to circumcision and the Mosaic law advocated by competing Jewish-Christian missionaries. Paul says that the new faith in Jesus Christ completely supersedes the old covenant: it is by faith that Christians are saved, not by the law. In this argument Paul provides the earliest statement of gentile Christian theology as distinct from Judaism.

Ephesians Probably written by a disciple of Paul intent on continuing his teaching, in A.D. 80-90, the destination is traditionally regarded as Ephesus, a port city in western Asia Minor where Paul had lived and preached. The author writes that God's plan from eternity will be accomplished through Christ, who is Lord not only of humanity but the whole universe. Within the church members must behave in godly fashion, speak the truth, love one another, and stand firm against the superhuman powers of evil. Some elements of this book may have been used in early liturgies.

Philippians Written by Paul from prison (probably in Ephesus, about A.D. 55). Paul rejoices in the faith of the congregation at Philippi (a city in northeastern Greece), urges on them conduct worthy of the gospel, and thanks them for their generosity. The letter as it now exists may be a composite (probably edited before A.D. 90) of several of Paul's letters to the Christians at Philippi.

Colossians Probably written by a follower of Paul to the church at Colossae (in Asia Minor), this letter gives thanks for the faith of the Colossians, reminds them that Christ embodies all wisdom, urges them therefore to reject concerns with planets, stars, and dietary laws, and commands them to embody Christian virtues.

1 Thessalonians This letter of Paul to the church in Thessalonica (present-day Thessaloniki in northeastern Greece) was composed about A.D. 50; it is the earliest book in the New Testament. Writing probably from Corinth, Paul and his colleagues Timothy and Sylvanus assure the church in Thessalonica, where Paul had earlier preached, of their affection and urge the members to be steadfast in faith, love, and hope. Paul emphasizes final (eschatological) things, and affirms that Christians who die prior to the Second Coming of Christ, as well as those who are then alive, will share in the new life in Christ.

2 Thessalonians Christians at Thessalonica are told that those who cause them to suffer will be punished at the last day and the faithful will rest; that the coming of Christ is not necessarily imminent—the wicked one whom Jesus will destroy must come first; and that Christians must not be idle, but should work in order to eat.

1 Timothy, 2 Timothy, and Titus These three letters deal with similar congregational matters and are often grouped as the "pastoral letters." Sharply admonitory in tone, they urge godly church officers and leaders to demonstrate exemplary moral and religious purity, as compared to the unacceptable social, religious, and sexual behavior of heretics; they instruct congregants, men and women, old and young, on their duties. The unknown author, writing perhaps early second century A.D., attempts to convey the continuity of Paul's teachings and message, thereby stabilizing and strengthening the church in the generations following the fervor of the apostolic age.

Philemon Paul's letter to Philemon (probably in Colossae) is the shortest (25 verses) of his letters. Paul writes on behalf of Philemon's slave Onesimus (= Gk. useful), who fled to Paul after wronging his master in some way. Paul, in his imprisonment in Ephesus about A.D. 55, converts Onesimus and appeals to Philemon to receive him not as a slave but as a member of the new fellowship of Jesus.

Hebrews This anonymous work, in the form of a sermon rather than a letter, was apparently aimed at encouraging Christians after the first generation. It presents a carefully developed series of comparisons between the Old Testament and Christianity to show the nature and purpose of the new faith. The author says that before, God spoke through the prophets, but now he has spoken through his son; the old faith had an earthly temple and sacrifices; the new is transcendent and eternal, with a single sacrifice for the world. Christians must be firm in their hope, and confident of their salvation.

James Traditionally ascribed to James the brother of Jesus, this general ("catholic") letter is intended for the guidance of the whole church. James emphasizes keeping the commandment to love one's neighbor, which entails especially caring for the poor and the oppressed; warns the rich; and emphasizes the importance of works as well as faith.

1 Peter Attributed to Peter but probably written late first century A.D. by another author, this letter affirms the truth of the faith and proclaims a new birth into a living hope through the resurrection. Christians may suffer from the loss of old attachments, but all, including the marginalized, are full members of the new community of believers and should aspire to live worthily in the faith.

2 Peter Ascribed to Peter but probably written by another author early second century A.D. Christians are exhorted to behave rightly, avoiding the sins of scoffers, evildoers and false prophets, in order to prepare for the Day of the Lord. Then judgment will be rendered and a new heaven and earth will be instituted. The Day has not yet come because God in his patience wishes all to repent.

John, the Letters of These three letters may have been written toward the end of the first century A.D. The first and longest asserts Jesus' role as the son of God who became man, the source and beginning of Christianity, and the bringer of eternal life; those who believe in him are the children of God and should not behave as sinners do. 2 John is a very brief letter addressed to "the Lady chosen by God and her children" (possibly a symbolic reference to churches) that emphasizes the importance of obeying the command to love one another, and to acknowledge that Jesus has come in human form. 3 John, also brief, is addressed to a Gaius: it commends him for his kindness and hospitality to fellow Christians, and criticizes a church leader who has not received others appropriately.

Jude Traditionally ascribed to Jude, a brother of Jesus; exhorts the faithful to be steadfast against heretics and false prophets in their midst. With their manifold personal and religious sins they are condemned, as were the false prophets of the Old Testament. The date of this short letter is unknown; it refers to remembering the words of the apostles, suggesting post-apostolic times.

Revelation Written about A.D. 95, John's revelations of visions from Christ were accepted as prophetic by the early church; this John is not the same as the author of the Gospel or the letters. The book describes allegorically the struggle between good and evil, reflecting the actual conflict between Christians and the Roman Empire. The vivid images include angels, the scroll with seven seals, savage beasts and plagues, the battle of Armageddon, and John's final vision of a new heaven and earth: a New Jerusalem, the rule of God, and the salvation of his faithful people.

Apocrypha

The Apocrypha, originally scriptures of the Septuagint, were part of the early Christian Bible. They remain part of the Roman Catholic Old Testament and, with some additional books, of Orthodox Old Testaments, but are noncanonical (although of historical interest) in Protestant churches. Of Jewish origin, they were written in Hebrew, Aramaic, and Greek during the period 300 B.C. to A.D. 100, and mostly from about 200 B.C. to A.D. 70 (the date of the destruction of the Second Temple by the Romans). They do not form part of the standard Hebrew Bible, which under rabbinic influence after A.D. 70 was standardized on the principle that revelation, beginning with Moses, ended with Ezra. The Apocrypha are listed here with the names and in the order used when they are printed in a separate section in Protestant Bibles.

The First Book of Esdras Focuses on the temple and temple worship, including a Passover celebration after Josiah's religious reforms (ca. 620 B.C.); the restoration of the temple (520–516 B.C.); and, years later, Ezra's preaching against mingling with the heathen local population and taking non-Jewish wives. An alternative version of part of 2 Chronicles, all of Ezra, and part of Nehemiah, probably dating to the late second century B.C.

The Second Book of Esdras A Jewish apocalypse written under the name of Ezra after the Roman destruction of Jerusalem (A.D. 70). Its seven visions (the beginning and ending parts of the book are Christian additions) deal in allegorical form with the suffering of God's chosen people, his slowness in bringing justice, Ezra's dictation of the Hebrew holy books destroyed in Jerusalem, and the last times: the messianic age, resurrection, and final judgment.

Tobit Concerns the sufferings of Jews in the diaspora. God hears the prayers of the pious blind Tobit and his relative Sarah, beset with a demon. The angel Raphael, in disguise, helps Tobit's son Tobias, who marries Sarah, to defeat the demon and restore Tobit's sight. Thus God helps the righteous, and Jews will one day reunite in Jerusalem. Probably in written in Aramaic before the second century B.C.; the setting in eighth century B.C. Nineveh is anachronistic.

Judith A message of faith in God's deliverance of oppressed Jews. A beautiful and pious widow, Judith goes to the camp of Holofernes, the Assyrian general besieging Bethulia, arranges to be alone with him and decapitates him. The Assyrians retreat, Judith is honored, and celebrations and offerings are made at the temple. Possibly written in the Maccabean era (second to first century B.C.).

The Rest of the Chapters of the Book of Esther These additions provide religious content to Esther's story, which in the original Hebrew does not mention God. The additions include a dream of Mordecai and prayers of Mordecai and Esther. God responds to Esther's piety and saves his people from the destruction planned by Haman.

The Wisdom of Solomon Praises wisdom and righteousness and warns against the evils of repression and idolatry. The wicked may prosper in this life, but they face condemnation at the heavenly judgment, of which they are unaware, and at which they will witness the final salvation of the righteous and oppressed. Other themes are the role of wisdom in governance and in history, and the origins of idolatry. Written in Greek, possibly first century A.D., probably to support Jews in a time of persecution.

Ecclesiasticus, or the Wisdom of Jesus Son of Sirach. A lengthy treatise on morals and behavior written by a tutor to the wealthy in Jerusalem about 180 B.C., it provides a picture of Palestinian Jewish society prior to the Maccabean revolt. Its primary purpose is to give advice on a huge range of matters great and small, from the fear of the Lord to good table manners. Jewish heroes are described in a section beginning "Let us now praise famous men."

Baruch From Babylonia Baruch sends the temple vessels back to the high priest in Jerusalem, along with the people's funds for sacrifices. There is a prayer of confession and repentance for the people's falling away from God; a hymn to wisdom, personified as a woman and identified with the Torah; and a psalm of comfort for those in exile. Possibly second century B.C. and anachronistically ascribed to Baruch, the scribe of Jeremiah.

Jeremiah, A Letter of A diatribe against idols: they are constructed by Gentiles of metal, wood and stone and thus, human-created, could not be gods; Jews must avoid them and believe instead in the true God of Israel. Probably fourth century B.C., possibly in Babylonia but attributed to the prophet Jeremiah, late seventh to early sixth century B.C.

The Song of the Three Includes a prayer for forgiveness and salvation, brief narrative material, and a hymn sung by three youths as they survive the fiery furnace. Probably added to the earlier versions of Daniel between the Maccabean revolt (167–164 B.C.) and the publication of the LXX translation of Daniel (100 B.C.).

Daniel and Susanna The beautiful Susanna is falsely accused of adultery by two lecherous elders who covet her. Condemned to death, Susanna calls on God in her innocence; Daniel intervenes to save her by confronting the elders and exposing their lies. An addition to Daniel, probably second century B.C.

Daniel, Bel, and the Snake Daniel, a valued counselor, proves to the Babylonian king that the idol Bel is not a god; sacrifices are actually secretly eaten by the priests. He also shows that a living snake is not a god by killing it with cakes of pitch. But for worshiping Israel's God he is thrown into the lion's den; he survives with God's protection. Probably added to the earlier versions of Daniel between the Maccabean revolt (167–164 B.C.) and the publication of the LXX translation of Daniel (100 B.C.).

Manasseh, the Prayer of This short prayer of repentance asserts God's majesty and compassion and asks forgiveness for the supplicant's transgressions.

The First Book of the Maccabees Details the history of the Jewish revolt against Antiochus IV Epiphanes, Seleucid King of Syria, whose reign began in 175 B.C. and who repressed Judaism and instituted Hellenistic cults. The family of the Maccabees took the lead in winning Judean freedom, and this book, with many references to Jewish history, attributes the revolt's success to their leadership and faith in God. Written between 104 B.C. and the beginning of Roman rule in 63 B.C.

The Second Book of the Maccabees 2 Maccabees focuses on the defilement of the temple, for which Jewish Hellenizers are held responsible. God sends punishments upon his people for these sins; but repentance brings redemption in the revolt led by Judas Maccabeus. This book promises the resurrection of the righteous dead, a theological idea of late Judaism.

SCIENCE & TECHNOLOGY

Astronomy

History of Astronomy 530
Techniques of Astronomy 532
Contents of the Universe 534
Glossary of Astronomical Terms . . . 545
Times Focus: *"Dark Energy" May Be Splitting the Universe* *by Dennis Overbye* 547

Biology

History of Biology 548
Times Focus: *How Did Life Begin?* *By Nicholas Wade* 550
Taxonomy 551
Basic Life Processes 551
Cell Biology 552
The Human Body 556
Times Focus: *How Does the Brain Work? By Sandra Blakeslee* 562
Evolution 565
Genetics 567
Times Focus: *The End of Evolution* *By Nicholas Wade* 568
Ecology 570
Times Focus: *Managing Planet Earth: Environmental Challenges Lie Ahead* *By Andrew Revkin* 572
Biochemistry 576

Chemistry

History of Chemistry 577
The Elements 579
Glossary of Chemistry Terms 591

Geology

History of Geology 593
Historical Geology 594
Physical Geology 597
Structural Geology 598
The Earth in Upheaval 600
Paleontology 602
Times Focus: *Seven Million Year Old Fossil Pushes Back Human Origins* *By John Noble Wilford* 604

Physics

History of Physics 605
Times Focus: *What Happened Before the Big Bang? By Dennis Overbye* . . 607
Times Focus: *Demolition Derby of Physics Jars Loose Clues on Subatomic Glue By James Glanz* . . 612
Basic Laws of Physics 613
Subatomic Particles 617
Glossary of Physics Terms 619
Times Focus: *Zillions of Universes? Or Did Ours Get Lucky?* *By Dennis Overbye* 623

Psychology

Areas of Psychological Research 625
A Brief History of Psychology 625
Disorders 628
Common Treatments 631

Technology

History of Significant Technologies . 633
Times Focus: *Human or Computer? Take This Test By Sara Robinson* . . 645
History of Computing 646
Times Focus: *Teaching Computers To Work in Unison* *By Steve Lohr* 657
Glossary of Computer and Internet Terms 659
History of Home Video Games 666
Times Focus: *Does Science Matter?* *By William J. Broad and James Glanz* . 668

ASTRONOMY

History of Astronomy

Ancient Astronomy

The roots of astronomy extend to before written records, but it is clear that humans have always observed the sky. The earliest known records of astronomical observations come from the Sumerian and Babylonian cultures (in what is modern-day Iraq) and date from as far back as 3000 B.C. Careful observations by court-sponsored astronomers led to the first known star maps, the zodiac, and many of the other constellations still referred to today, as well as the sexigesimal (base-60) counting system on which our angular measures are based. Babylonian astronomers knew the length of the year to high precision. These measurements were probably used for political and agricultural purposes. During the same epoch, a number of astronomical monuments, including the well-known Stonehenge, were being constructed around what is now Great Britain as calendar devices. Egyptian astronomers undertook similar cataloging and mapping work, using stars as references in alignment of construction projects like the Great Pyramids. Greek philosophers were the first to speculate on the structure of the universe, but were constrained by philosophical traditions relying on pure geometrical forms. Aristotle (ca. 350 B.C.), established a model of the universe constructed of nested spheres in which the Earth lay at the center, while the Sun, Moon, planets and stars moved around the Earth in constant motion each with its own rate. Although this corresponded crudely to the observations, especially of planetary motions, the philosophical tradition relied more heavily on spheres as building blocks than on the matching the observations. Some Greek "natural philosophers," though, did make more detailed measurements and surmises about the structure of space. For instance, Pythagoras (ca. 500 B.C.) and Plato (ca. 400 B.C.) made strong arguments, based on the shape of the Earth's shadow during lunar eclipses and the changing view of the sky as one traveled north or south, that the Earth was a sphere. Eratosthenes (ca. 200 B.C.) estimated the diameter of the Earth to high precision based on the angle of sunlight observed at different locations. Aristarchus (ca. 280 B.C.) is the first person known to have proposed that the Earth orbits the Sun. One of the outstanding problems noted by Greek astronomers was the motions of the planets ("wanderers"), objects which moved with respect to the background stars. The culmination of ancient astronomical endeavors was the work of Ptolemy (ca. A.D. 140), whose great work *Syntaxis* was an attempt to match the complicated motions of the planets about the Earth. In his model, Ptolemy proposed that the Sun, Moon, planets, and stars moved around the stationary Earth on circular orbits onto which were placed smaller circles that carried the planets eastward, then briefly westward ("retrograde"), then eastward again relative to the fixed stars. In melding the tradition of Aristotle with an attempt to match what was actually observed, Ptolemy ensured his place in astronomical history.

The Middle Ages

The decline of Greek and Roman influence throughout the ancient Middle East spelled the end of real astronomical progress for the following 13 centuries. Several cultures in the Americas constructed astronomical monuments similar to those found in Europe. Most notable was the role played by Islamic astronomers during this period when much of Europe was stagnating. In the Mediterranean basin, the rising Islamic societies fostered scientific collaboration at the same time that the religious customs of Islam relied on precise astronomical calculations. As a result, Islamic astronomers made precise catalogs of stellar brightness and developed trigonometric tools. Much of the work revolved around refining Ptolemy's system of planetary motion. Many of the names given to stars descend either directly from or as modified versions of the names given them by Islamic scholars during this time.

At the same time, other cultures were making measurements of astronomical phenomena. In particular, Chinese courts noted the appearance of comets and "guest stars" (supernovas).

Renaissance Astronomy: The Copernican Revolution

A complete revision of thinking about the universe began with the speculative work of the Polish cleric Nicolaus Copernicus in the early 16th century. Copernicus was the first modern astronomer to propose that the Sun was the center of the universe, and that the Earth orbited the Sun like the other planets. He correctly attributed the daily motions of the Sun and stars to the rotation of the Earth, annual changes in the appearance of the sky to the orbital motion of the Earth about the Sun, and retrograde motion to the relative speeds of planets as they orbited the Sun. But his model still relied on the perfect circular orbits preferred by Aristotle, and as a result his predictions, published in 1543 in *De Revolutionibus* as he lay dying, were no more accurate at predicting planetary positions than the 1,300-year-old geocentric model of Ptolemy. Nonetheless, he laid the groundwork for the revolutionary changes that were to occur in the understanding of the cosmos over the following 200 years.

The great Danish astronomer Tycho Brahe was concerned that both the Ptolemaic and Copernican models failed to accurately reproduce careful observations. During the last 30 years of the 16th century, Tycho undertook the most accurate observations of planetary and stellar positions that had ever been made, in an attempt to prove his own model of the universe in which the Earth lay stationary at the center while the other planets orbited the Sun. When Tycho died suddenly in 1601, the data came into the possession of the talented German mathematician Johannes Kepler. Based on his analysis of Tycho's data, Kepler was able to show that planets orbit Sun on elliptical paths (rather than circular paths as had been assumed for nearly two millennia), that planets moved faster along their orbits when closer to the Sun, and that there was a precise mathematical relation between a planet's distance from the Sun and the time to complete at orbit. These results, published in 1609 and 1619, are known as Kepler's laws of planetary motion. So precisely could Kepler's results predict the locations of planets that they lent great support to Copernicus's Sun-centered universe.

In 1608, as Kepler labored to interpret Tycho's data, a usable telescope design was invented by the Dutch lens maker Hans Lippershey. The following year, the Italian empirical scientist Galileo built his own version of the device and made the first careful observations of astronomical objects with a telescope. With the telescope, he observed the Moon's physical geologic features, sunspots, the changing illumination of Venus as it orbited the Sun, and moons of Jupiter in orbit around that planet. These provided strong evidence in support of a Sun-centered universe and against several tenets of Aristotelian thought that held that all objects beyond the Earth were perfect and unchanging and that all objects orbited the Earth. In 1633 Galileo was famously tried and exiled for flouting Catholic doctrine; which relied heavily on the Earth-centered universe, but his work stands today as a crucial moment in scientific history, when observation became paramount to belief.

Post-Renaissance Astronomy: The 17th and 18th Centuries

In the aftermath of the Copernican revolution, when precise observations showed convincingly that the Earth orbited the Sun, astronomy flourished. The most important developments came from the work of Isaac Newton, the brilliant, eccentric, and moody English physicist and mathematician. Newton established his laws of motion, which were equally applicable to the motions of objects on Earth as to the motions of planets about the Sun, thereby unifying what to ancient philosophies were considered separate physical realms. He constructed the law of universal gravitation, which described in a precise mathematical form the forces that held the planets in orbit about the Sun. While developing these laws, he also invented calculus, which would turn out to be an invaluable tool for making predictions of the motions of astronomical bodies. His work was published in 1687 as the *Principia*. Newton also applied his talents to optics and invented the reflecting telescope, a design used in modified form on all large modern telescopes.

Newton's law of gravity was put to use by his friend Edmund Halley even before the *Principia* was published. Halley had collected observations of comets made in previous centuries. Using Newton's methods, he argued that a number of comet observations were actually of the same comet, and in 1705 he predicted the comet's return would occur in 1758. For the success of this prediction, the comet is now known as Halley's Comet.

Despite the successes of Kepler's and Newton's laws, both were able to predict only the relative distances from each planet to the Sun, not the absolute distances. The distance from the Earth to the Sun was referred to as an astronomical unit, and both sets of laws could show for instance that Mars orbited the Sun at an average distance of one-and-a-half astronomical units, but the absolute number of miles or meters in an astronomical unit remained unknown. In 1672 the Italian astronomer Giovanni Cassini made the first accurate attempt at determining this scale when he and an assistant measured the projected position of Mars against distant background stars from two different locations on Earth. Their result of about 87 million miles for the astronomical unit agrees with the modern number to better than 10 percent accuracy. (Using this number and comparing observed and predicted appearances of Jupiter's moons, the Danish astronomer Roemer made the first accurate estimate of the speed of light in 1676.) In 1716 Halley showed that a more accurate measure of the astronomical unit could be made if observers in different locations on Earth recorded the passage of the planet Venus across the face of the Sun, an event that would occur twice in the 18th century, first in 1761 and again in 1769. Halley did not live to see these events, but several hundred astronomers positioned around the Earth did, finding a result of about 95 million miles, in very close agreement with the modern accepted value of about 93 million miles.

In 1781 the German-English astronomer William Herschel discovered the planet Uranus, the first planet found since antiquity. In several following years, Herschel applied himself to measuring the dimensions of the Milky Way, the large grouping of stars to which the Sun belongs. Herschel incorrectly found that the Sun lay at the center of the Milky Way, but he demonstrated that the Sun lay in the plane of a flattened disklike structure that was substantially thinner than it was wide.

19th- and Early 20th-Century Astronomy: The Birth of Astrophysics

The 19th century continued much of the empirical study of the 18th century. In 1801 the Italian astronomer Giuseppe Piazzi discovered the first asteroid, a rocky object smaller than a planet orbiting the Sun in the gap between Mars and Jupiter. In 1838 the German mathematician and astronomer Freidrich Bessel made the first successful observation of the distance to another star by measuring the tiny apparent shift in the star's position when observed from different sides of the Earth's orbit. And in a great triumph for Newton's law of gravity, the planet Neptune was discovered independently by German and French astronomers in 1846 based on small perturbations in the orbit of Uranus.

The most important developments in astronomy during this time were those that occurred outside of traditional astronomical observations. In 1800 Herschel discovered that the Sun produced light outside the range of colors detectable with the human eye. In 1814 the German Joseph Fraunhofer split sunlight into its constituent colors with a prism and identified the element sodium in the Sun, the first time that the chemical composition of an astronomical object was made. In 1842 the Austrian Christian Doppler showed that the motion of an object could be inferred from a shift in the wavelengths of light received from that object. In 1865 the Scottish physicist James Clark Maxwell showed formally that visible light was a subset of the wavelike phenomenon by which charged particles interact, known as electromagnetic radiation. In the 1880's the Austrian physicists Josef Stefan and Ludwig Boltzmann showed that the energy output of an object was directly related to that object's temperature. In 1893 the German physicist Wilhelm Wien showed that the temperature of an object could be determined by determining the color that an object emitted most intensely. And many developments in quantum mechanics, beginning with the work of Danish physicist Neils Bohr in 1913, showed that details of an object's spectrum could be used to deduce it's chemical composition. Although seemingly peripheral to astronomy, these developments allowed astronomers for the first time to interpret the light they collected from astronomical objects and marked the birth of modern astrophysics.

The Last 100 Years

The past century has seen remarkable progress in the understanding of the structure of stars, the galaxy, and the universe. Technological advances and the beginning of the space age have led to a detailed reconnaissance of the solar system. Similar advances in telescope and detector technology have meant great leaps in the quality and quantity of astronomical data. The results of this work are highlighted below.

Techniques of Astronomy

As in other sciences, progress in astronomy comes from the comparison between the predictions of physical theories and the results of observations. Astronomy is nearly unique, however, in that most of the objects under study are not directly accessible, mainly because of the huge distances separating the Earth and even nearby astronomical objects.

Direct Sampling and Spacecraft Reconnaissance

Direct sampling has occurred only within the solar system, and thus far has been limited to: surface measurements (pre-Apollo) and sample returns from the Moon (approximately 1,000 pounds of rock returned by the

U.S. Apollo missions); planetary surface and atmospheric measurements by U.S. and Soviet spacecraft that have landed on Mars and Venus; atmospheric sampling by a single probe descending into Jupiter's upper atmosphere; and several spacecraft encounters with smaller objects in the solar system such as Halley's Comet and the asteroid Eros. Missions to sample Titan (the largest of Saturn's moons) and to return comet material from Comet Wild-2 are currently under way.

Some samples of the solar system enter the Earth's atmosphere as meteors; intact meteorites have been recovered, mostly samples of asteroids but including several samples of the Moon and Mars. High-altitude aircraft and Earth-orbiting spacecraft have collected smaller samples of solar system dust.

Even for objects in the solar system, the vast majority of study has been done from Earth-based observatories or by spacecraft using remote sensing techniques. The same techniques used for reconnaissance of the Earth, including imaging of geological features, tracking of weather patterns, radar study of surface features, and spectroscopic measurements of temperature and atmospheric composition, have been used to study planets, moons, comets, and asteroids.

Indirect Sampling

With the exception of bodies in the solar system, all the objects studied by astronomers are too far away for direct sampling or spacecraft reconnaissance. The spacecraft that has traveled the farthest from Earth, *Voyager 1*, has covered only one four-thousandth of the distance to the nearest star during its quarter-century-long flight. For all practical purposes, astronomical objects beyond the solar system are out of reach and must be studied from afar. All information is gleaned from the collection, analysis, and interpretation of electromagnetic radiation, energy given off by all objects in the universe. The visible light to which human eyes are sensitive represents a small portion of the electromagnetic spectrum. The electromagnetic spectrum is broken up into six bands (for largely historical reasons): radio, infrared, visible, ultraviolet, X-ray, and gamma-ray. Successive bands probe progressively hotter or more energetic phenomena (with a few exceptions).

Radio—Infrared—Visible—Ultraviolet—X-ray—Gamma-ray
Low Energy ◄────► High Energy
Long Wavelength ◄────► Short Wavelength

Some details of the various bands are given here:

Radio radiation is the lowest-energy electromagnetic radiation. It is emitted by cold gas and the early universe. Radio radiation passes freely through the Earth's atmosphere and is detectable from ground-based observatories.

Infrared radiation is emitted by planets, cool stars, stars that are forming, dust and gas in star-forming regions, and the cores of active galaxies. It is blocked by water and carbon dioxide in the Earth's atmosphere, so infrared observatories must be placed on high mountains, in aircraft, or in space.

Visible radiation ("light") is emitted by stars and reflected by planets. It passes freely through the Earth's atmosphere and is detectable from ground-based observatories.

Ultraviolet radiation is emitted by hot stars and gas. Ozone in the upper atmosphere prevents it from penetrating to ground level. Ultraviolet observatories must be placed in space.

X radiation is emitted by the remnants of hot stars, the Sun's corona, and galaxy clusters. Atoms in the upper atmosphere block these emissions, so X-ray observatories must be placed in space.

Gamma radiation is emitted when stellar collisions occur, from the regions around black holes, and in supernova explosions. It is blocked by the upper atmosphere, so gamma-ray observatories must be placed in space.

Astronomers must collect and detect electromagnetic radiation in order to analyze and interpret the physical conditions in distant astronomical sources.

Collection of radiation is done through the use of a telescope. A telescope consists of one or more optical elements serving to collect as much electromagnetic radiation as possible. Performance of a telescope is determined by the size of the main radiation-collecting element (usually a mirror or lens). The larger the size, the more radiation is collected. Larger telescopes can be used to detect fainter objects than smaller telescopes. In addition to this collecting ability, the size of the telescope also determines the level of detail that can be discerned in an observation: the larger the main optical element, the finer the detail. The Earth's atmosphere tends to smear out this detail through the bending of light ("twinkling"), though advanced engineering techniques have been developed to counter atmospheric effects. Telescopes in space are not affected by the Earth's atmosphere; thus the Hubble space telescope is able to produce images with stunning detail despite being much smaller than many modern ground-based telescopes.

The radiation collected with a telescope is then fed through telescope optics to a detector. The ability to detect an astronomical source depends on the efficiency of the detector at collecting radiation as well as the inherent random signal in a detector ("noise"). The human eye was used as the first astronomical detector. The eye is about 1 percent efficient at detecting visible light (99 percent is not detected); it has no sensitivity outside the visible part of the electromagnetic spectrum; and it has no ability to accumulate light over time. Astronomers used photographic film as a detector throughout much of the 20th century; film can be made to detect about 10 percent of the visible or infrared radiation striking it, and long exposures could be made in order to collect as much light as possible from a faint source. For the past 25 years, astronomers have used Charge-Coupled Devices (CCDs) as detectors of infrared, visible, and X-ray radiation. These solid-state devices have efficiencies of nearly 100 percent and produce a digital record of the detection that is especially convenient for analysis using computers. Detection of X rays and gamma rays requires specialized hardware, and detection of radio radiation requires specialized receivers. These typically have lower efficiencies than CCDs.

The collected and detected electromagnetic radiation is then used in a variety of ways. Astronomers undertake three basic types of collection and detection. Imaging involves focusing the electromagnetic radiation on the detector in order to have a representation of the source's physical appearance and distribution in space. Spectroscopy involves passing the collected radiation through an optical element that spreads the light out into its constituent wavelengths, after which it is sent to the detector. From spectroscopic studies, it is possible to determine the temperature, chemical composition, and motion of an astronomical source. Photometry is the very careful measurement of the quantity of electromagnetic radiation emitted by a source.

Examples of important telescopes studying each wavelength band are given below.

Gamma ray: Compton Gamma Ray Observatory
Four specialized instruments for detecting gamma radiation, operation in Earth orbit (1991–2000)

X-ray: Chandra X-Ray Observatory 1.3 meters, operation in Earth orbit (1999–)

Ultraviolet: Lyman FUSE 0.4 meter, operation in Earth orbit (1999–)

Visible: Single—Keck I 10 meters, Mauna Kea, Hawaii, 1993–; Multiple—Very Large Telescope (VLT) 16.4 meters (4–8.2-meter mirrors), Cerro Paranal, Chile (1997–)

Infrared: SIRTF (Space Infrared Telescope Facility) 0.85 meter, Earth-trailing orbit (2003–); SOFIA (Stratospheric Observatory for Infrared Astronomy) 2.5 meters, housed in Mountain View, Calif., but operation from airplane (2005–)

Radio: Single—Arecibo 305 meters, Arecibo, Puerto Rico (1963–); Multiple—Very Long Baseline Array, 10 locations across North America/Pacific, 5,800 miles

---

Contents of the Universe

The contents of the universe range in size from individual gas atoms and dust grains up to enormous clusters and superclusters of galaxies. As in other sciences, astronomers develop classifications for objects, organizational boundaries that suggest common origins or physical processes. These classifications change as additional data are collected. For instance, until 1995 only the planets around the Sun were known, and the classification "planet" was suitable for objects orbiting the Sun. Over the past 9 years, more than 100 planets have been discovered orbiting stars outside the solar system, as well as some planet-mass objects that are not in orbit around stars.

Solar System Summary

The solar system comprises a single star, the Sun, and all of the objects that orbit the Sun. The largest objects that orbit the Sun are referred to as planets. These planets are grouped broadly into two categories: the terrestrial planets and the Jovian planets. The terrestrial planets are the four closest to the Sun: Mercury, Venus, Earth, and Mars. These are composed primarily of silicon-based rock and metals. The Earth is the largest of the terrestrial planets, slightly more massive than Venus, 10 times as massive as Mars, and nearly 20 times the mass of Mercury. Earth has a substantial atmosphere dominated by nitrogen and oxygen; Venus and Mars have atmospheres dominated by carbon dioxide; Mercury has no appreciable atmosphere.

The Jovian planets include Jupiter, Saturn, Uranus, and Neptune. Jupiter, at more than 300 times the Earth's mass, is the largest object in the solar system besides the Sun. Jupiter and Saturn are composed mostly of hydrogen gas. Uranus and Neptune, each approximately 15 times the mass of Earth, are composed of icy cores surrounded by substantial hydrogen atmospheres.

Pluto, the farthest planet from the Sun, does not fit into either the terrestrial or the Jovian category. It is composed primarily of ice, and with a mass only 0.2 percent of the Earth it is much smaller than the Moon. Pluto is now thought to belong to a much larger class of objects found beyond the orbit of Neptune (see the Kuiper Belt, below). For the time being, it continues to be classified as the ninth planet.

All of the planets except Mercury and Venus have moons, or natural satellites, in orbit around them. Only three moons are known to orbit the terrestrial planets: the Moon, in orbit around the Earth; and two much smaller objects in orbit about Mars. The Jovian planets, however, are accompanied by large numbers of moons. As of this writing, Jupiter holds the record with 61 moons, ranging in size from larger than Mercury to as small as a kilometer in diameter. Saturn, Uranus, and Neptune have 31, 27, and 13 known moons, respectively. Pluto is orbited by a single moon, Charon, which, with a diameter half that of Pluto, is the largest moon relative to the planet it orbits.

Planet Details

Mercury (Average distance from Sun: 0.38 AU. Mass: 0.055 Earth masses. Diameter: 0.38 Earth diameters. Orbit time: 88 days. Rotation time: 59 days.)

Mercury is the planet closest to the Sun and, as such, orbits the Sun in the shortest time. Usually obscured from view from Earth by the Sun's glare, it is sometimes visible on Earth's horizon just after sunset, when it is called the Evening Star, or just before dawn, when it is called the Morning Star. About 14 times per century, Mercury can also be seen crossing directly in front of the Sun's disk.

The U.S. *Mariner 10* space probe provided the first detailed pictures of Mercury's surface during flybys in 1974 and 1975. *Mariner 10* mapped about 35 percent of the planet's heavily cratered, moonlike surface. No space probe has visited the planet since, though NASA will send the *Messenger* orbiter there in 2004, and the European Space Agency plans to send the Bepi-Columbo orbiter-lander mission to Mercury in 2009.

Mercury is a waterless, airless world that alternately bakes and freezes as it orbits the Sun. The high temperatures on the sunlit side mean that the planet cannot retain a substantial atmosphere. The small numbers of atmospheric particles that have been detected are thought to consist of atoms streaming out from the Sun as well as atoms knocked off surface rock by the fast-moving solar atoms; the total mass of these particles is thought to be less than 1,000 kilograms. Without a substantial atmosphere, temperatures are poorly regulated. On Mercury's sunlit side temperatures reach 850°F (450°C) and plummet to –300°F (–180°C) on the dark side. The extremes of temperature are largely due to Mercury's slow rate of rotation: one single rotation is two-thirds of a Mercury year, or 59 days for a rotation compared with 88 days for a revolution. Mercury's axis is almost perpendicular to its plane of rotation, so any single place on the planet sees dawn only once every 176 days—the planet must rotate three times and go through two of its "years" before a new day dawns.

Mercury's surface is scarred with hundreds of thousands of craters. Many such craters were probably formed during the early history of the solar system, when large numbers of asteroids and comets were slamming into planetary surfaces. Many areas have had the craters smoothed over by ancient lava flows, however. This indicates extensive volcanic activity on Mercury during and after the time when the craters formed. The surface is also crisscrossed by huge cliffs, or scarps. These probably formed as Mercury's surface cooled and shrank. Some of the scarps are up to 1.2 miles (1.9 kilometers) high and 932 miles (1,500 kilometers) long.

Mercury is so dense that astronomers think that its rocky outer crust is very thin and that the planet is mostly iron. It probably was once larger. During the early bombardment, it is conjectured that a large planetesimal or protoplanet (about a sixth of the size of the early planet) hit Mercury so hard that it ripped most of the rocky crust away.

Venus (Average distance from Sun: 0.72 AU. Mass: 0.82 Earth masses. Diameter: 0.95 Earth diameters. Orbit time: 224 days. Rotation time: 243 days.)

As seen in the night sky from Earth, Venus is second only to the Moon in brightness. Venus, named for the Roman goddess of love, is the planet that passes closest to Earth (24,000,000 miles, or 39,000,000 kilometers). Since it is between Earth and the Sun, Venus, like Mercury, is seen either just before sunrise or just after sunset.

Because of its proximity to Earth and its position between Earth and the Sun, Venus became (in 1962) the first planet beyond Earth to be studied in situ by a space probe (*Mariner 2*). The pull of the Sun's gravity makes Venus and Mercury "downhill" from the Earth; one must travel against the Sun's gravity to reach other planets. Since 1962 numerous U.S. and Soviet spacecraft have visited Venus. Soviet space probes *Venera 13* and *Venera 14* were the first to make a soft landing and send back pictures from the Venusian surface.

The Venusian atmosphere is 96.4 percent carbon dioxide and 3.4 percent nitrogen. Thick clouds shroud the planet's surface from direct view. The Venusian clouds range from about 28 to 37 miles (45 to 60 km) above the planet's surface and are differentiated into three layers. Droplets of sulfuric acid and water have been identified in the clouds.

The clouds and high level of carbon dioxide in the atmosphere have combined to trap heat in the lower atmosphere of Venus. This is an extreme form of the greenhouse effect and is responsible for high temperatures in the lower atmosphere, 870°F (460°C)—hot enough to melt lead. The atmospheric pressure at the surface is 92 times that of Earth. The atmospheric CO_2 is so efficient at trapping heat that there is little variation of temperature between night and day.

One feature of the Venusian upper atmosphere is markedly different from that of Earth. The atmosphere superrotates on Venus—that is, the atmosphere above the clouds moves 60 times faster than the planet rotates—whereas the Earth and its atmosphere rotate at the same speed. So, high winds and steady upper-atmosphere winds—100 mph (160 km/hr) or faster—are a dominant factor in Venusian weather. But at ground level, winds are calmer, with an average closer to 2 mph (3.6 km/hr).

Soviet space probes that soft-landed on Venus have provided photographs of the planet's surface. Radar maps of 99 percent of the Venusian surface, completed by the U.S. Pioneer spacecraft (from 1978 to 1993), and Magellan (from 1989 to 1994), now give a detailed picture of features as small as 350 ft. (100 m) in diameter. More than a thousand Venusian mountains, volcanoes, rifts, basins, impact craters, and other features have been identified.

About 10 percent of the surface is highland terrain, 70 percent rolling uplands, and 20 percent lowland plains. There are two major highland areas: one about half the size of Africa and located in the equatorial region and the other, about the size of Australia, located to the north. The highest mountain on Venus—Maxwell Montes—is in the northern highlands and is higher than Earth's Mt. Everest. Volcanic activity has dominated Venusian geology, as the planet is covered with volcanic domes and lava channels. It is not clear whether such volcanic activity continues at the present time.

Like Earth, Venus is thought to have an internal structure. The crust, however, is much thicker than that of Earth, perhaps twice as deep on the average, making the crust of Venus about 60 mi. (100 km) thick. Below the crust is a large layer called the mantle; below the mantle is a core thought to be molten nickel-iron, similar to Earth's outer core.

Earth (Average distance from Sun: 1 AU = 93 million miles = 150 million km. Mass: 13 trillion trillion pounds = 5.9 trillion trillion kilograms. Diameter: 7,900 miles = 12800 km. Orbit time: 365.25 days. Rotation time: 24 hours.)

Earth is the third planet from the Sun and the only one in the solar system known to harbor life. From space, our planet appears as a bright blue-and-white sphere—blue because some 70 percent of the surface is covered by water, and white because clouds cover about half the planet's surface.

The Moon is Earth's only natural satellite. It is over one-quarter the size of Earth in diameter (2,160 mi. or 3,476 km). At an average distance of 238,000 mi. (380,000 km), it is the brightest object in Earth's nighttime sky. The Moon regularly changes in appearance as seen from Earth.

The Moon is slightly egg-shaped, and the same side of the satellite always faces Earth—this side being the elongated small end. As a result, the Moon's rotation and revolution are synchronized. The side we do not see is called the far side (not the dark side—all parts of the moon undergo 14 Earth days of light, followed by 14 days of darkness).

Over a decade of exploration of the Moon by space probes was capped by the landing of two U.S. astronauts on the Moon on July 20, 1969. A total of six two-man crews of American astronauts eventually landed on the Moon between 1969 and 1972, and they brought back some 842 pounds (382 kg) of samples of Moon rocks. Study of these rocks has led to a far greater understanding of the Moon's history and of the formation of the solar system. Analysis of the Moon's composition has led to the hypothesis that the Moon formed when the collision of a large protoplanet stripped material from the Earth's crust.

The world the astronauts found was airless and devoid of life. Temperatures on the Moon range from up to 273°F (134°C) on the bright side to –274°F (–170°C) on the unlighted side. A mixture of fine powder and broken rock blankets the Moon's surface. The near side also has large regions (called maria, or seas) of solidified lava. The lunar surface is pockmarked with craters and larger impact basins, the largest about 1,300 miles (2,100 km) across, and is broken by huge mountain ranges. Some craters at the poles may contain frozen water in their depths.

Mars (Average distance from Sun: 1.52 AU. Mass: 0.11 Earth masses. Diameter: 0.53 Earth diameters. Orbit time: 1.88 years. Rotation time: 1.03 days.)

Mars is the outermost of the four terrestrial planets and has a distinctive reddish coloring, coming from iron oxide in the Martian soil. The Romans named the planet after their god of war, and the two irregularly shaped satellites of Mars have been named after the horses—Deimos (terror) and Phobos (fear)—that pulled the war god's chariot. Earth lies directly between Mars and the Sun once every 780 days, though because of the eccentric shape of Mar's orbit, its closest approach to Earth (33,800,000 mi., or 54,500,000 km) comes at 15- or 17-year intervals.

The so-called canals on Mars—later found to be optical illusions—were first observed by 19th-century astronomers and led to the widespread belief that there was life on Mars. (In 1900 the French Academy offered a prize to the first person to find life on any planet except Mars, presumably because everyone knew that there was life on that planet.) The planet thus became the target of numerous space probes, both U.S. and Soviet, from the early years of interplanetary exploration.

The first successful flyby of Mars was achieved by the U.S. spacecraft *Mariner 4* in 1965. The Soviets became the first to land a probe successfully on the surface of Mars, in 1971, but the probe malfunctioned and stopped transmitting after only 20 seconds. It was not until 1976, when the U.S. *Viking 1* and *Viking 2* landers touched down on Mars, that extensive study of the planet from its surface became possible. The *Viking 1* lander continued to function until 1983. *Pathfinder* landed on Mars on July 4, 1997. Using a remote-controlled robot called Sojourner, whose travels to Martian rocks were televised, the *Pathfinder* mission reported the details of the weather and geology of Mars. In January 2004, the U.S. landed twin rover spacecraft (*Spirit* and *Opportunity*) to study Martian geology and to test for the past presence of water on the Martian surface.

The big question of whether there is (or was) life on Mars has yet to be answered with certainty. The Viking landers conducted three experiments on Martian soil to check for biological processes. Some of the tests yielded positive results, but these could also be explained by the soil chemistry. The lack of other evidence of organic molecules adds to the case against life on Mars. A British spacecraft, *Beagle II*, was set to conduct further biological experiments in 2004, but the craft failed to land safely on the Martian surface.

Orbiting satellites have mapped the entire planet down to a resolution of 500–1,000 ft. (150–300 m), and in smaller regions have imaged surface features 1.5 ft. (0.5 m) across. The planet's surface is heavily cratered, and there is extensive evidence of once-active volcanoes. There are also such spectacular features as Olympus Mons (an extinct volcano three times as high as Earth's Mt. Everest); mammoth canyons, one of which is four times deeper than the Grand Canyon and as wide as the U.S.; and a gigantic basin (larger than Alaska) in the southern hemisphere that was probably created by a single, huge asteroid. The planet has ice caps at both poles (water ice with some frozen carbon dioxide), and the ice caps advance and recede with changes in the seasons.

But the most intriguing aspect of the Martian surface is that water once flowed there in great quantities. Parts of the terrain apparently have sedimentary origins, and there are many long channels, complete with smaller tributary channels and islands, that extend for hundreds of kilometers. Scientists speculate that Mars once had a much thicker atmosphere, made up of gases vented during volcanic eruptions, which would have made it possible for water in its liquid state to exist on the surface. Martian atmospheric pressure is now so low, however, that surface water would immediately vaporize. It is conjectured that in the past, water flowed through the channels to lowland areas and then sank into the Martian regolith, or upper soil layer, since there is no geologic evidence that standing bodies of water ever existed. In 2002 the orbiting *Mars Odyssey* detected signs of a large amount of water ice just below soil level in the south polar region. In early 2004 the European spacecraft *Mars Express* began an orbital survey of the water content as far as 2.5 miles (4 km) below the Martian surface.

Mars is too small to sustain continual volcanic activity. Its atmosphere apparently thinned out after volcanic activity ceased. Atmospheric pressure is now just seven one-thousandths of that on Earth at sea level, and the predominant gas is carbon dioxide, which is relatively heavy. A small amount of water vapor in the atmosphere is enough to form some clouds, small patches of fog in some valleys, and occasionally even patches of frost. Surface temperatures vary from a high of about 70°F (20°C) during summer at the equator to a low of about –220°F (–140°C) during winter at the poles. By far the most pronounced feature of Martian weather is dust storms, which regularly engulf the entire planet for a period of several months.

Jupiter (Average distance from Sun: 5.20 AU. Mass: 318 Earth masses. Diameter: 11.2 Earth diameters. Orbit time: 11.9 years. Rotation time: 9 hours 56 minutes.)

Jupiter is the largest planet in the solar system. It has 2.5 times more mass than all the other planets of the solar system together and is 11 times as large as Earth in diameter. Jupiter is so large that scientists believe it almost became a star: as the gases and dust contracted to form the planet, gravitational forces created tremendous pressure and temperature inside the core—as high as tens of thousands of degrees. But there was not enough mass available to create the temperatures needed to start a fusion reaction such as that of the Sun (above 27,000,000°F, or 15,000,000°C, at the Sun's core); thus Jupiter has been slowly cooling down ever since. Even so, Jupiter radiates about as much power times as much heat as it receives from the Sun.

The first object to reach Jupiter from Earth was *Pioneer 10*. It returned the first close-up pictures of the giant planet in 1973. Subsequently, the more sophisticated space probes *Voyager 1* and *Voyager 2* passed by Jupiter in 1979 and sent back images and more data on the planet. One of the most exciting discoveries by *Voyager 1* was that Jupiter has a faint but extensive ring system that extends almost 186,000 miles (300,000 km) out from the planet's surface. The Galileo spacecraft found another faint ring at 1 million miles (1.6 million km) in 1998. A probe released from the Galileo spacecraft arrived at Jupiter on December 7, 1995, finding winds of 435 mph (700 km/hr) and much less water vapor than expected. Scientists later determined that the probe had arrived in what amounts to a Jovian desert. In September 2003, Galileo's mission ended with a final plunge into Jupiter's atmosphere.

The most prominent features of Jupiter are its colorful cloud layers. Because the planet spins so fast (one rotation in just under 10 hours), its clouds tend to form bands that give the planet a striped appearance. Darker bands are called belts; light ones are zones. Clouds at higher altitudes are carried eastward by jet streams; those at lower levels are blown westward.

There are numerous eddies and swirls in Jupiter's atmosphere, but none can compare with the Great Red Spot, apparently a massive hurricane (rotating counterclockwise) located in the southern hemisphere near the equator. The Great Red Spot was first observed some 300 years ago, and this storm continues unabated today. Since 1938 three smaller white ovals have been observed to the south of the Great Red Spot.

Jupiter's cloud tops are extremely cold (about –202°F, or –130°C), but temperatures increase deeper inside the atmosphere. The interior of Jupiter is largely a mystery, since no information has been gleaned from direct observations. Jupiter's density is only about one-fourth that of the terrestrial planets, indicating that it is composed of light atoms, more than 90 percent hydrogen. Although hydrogen normally is a gas on Earth, it takes on somewhat more exotic forms at the high pressures inside Jupiter. Below a gaseous cloud layer, the hydrogen is compressed into a liquid and then a liquid metal. At the very center of the planet there may be a small core of rocklike and icelike material, no more than a few times the mass of the Earth. There is nothing like a solid surface anywhere near the cloud tops. Most of Jupiter is just an unusual gaseous-liquid atmosphere. Jupiter's extremely rapid rotation, combined with its large metallic hydrogen interior, gives rise to the strongest magnetic field in the solar system.

Jupiter is now known to have 61 moons, many of them quite small (less than 6 miles in diameter). The four largest are the Galilean moons, so called because the Italian scientist Galileo first observed them. The Galilean moons are Ganymede, Callisto, Europa, and Io—after the Roman god Jupiter's cupbearer (Ganymede) and three of Jupiter's inamorata. Ganymede is the largest moon in the solar system and is larger even than the planets Pluto and Mercury. It is a huge, cratered ball of ice and may have a core of solid silicate rock with liquid water between the thick ice covering and the core. Callisto, with an orbit outside that of Ganymede, is also covered with ice and is riddled with thousands of craters. Europa, which orbits inside Ganymede, is about the size of our Moon and has a smooth surface marked by networks of cracks. The most interesting of Jupiter's moons are Io, which orbits closest to Jupiter, and Europa.

Io undergoes the most intense volcanic activity known, heated it is thought by tidal energy generated by gravitational tugs from Jupiter, Europa, and Ganymede. One giant volcano may have been erupting for the past 19 years. Orange-red patches on Io's mottled surface are apparently molten sulfur beds, but most other parts of Io's surface are cold (about −229°F, or −145°C).

Europa, on the other hand, is covered in ice, but some have speculated that a liquid ocean beneath the ice could contain life. The liquid, which probably contains salts like oceans on Earth, could be heated by the same tidal forces that propel Io's volcanoes.

Saturn (Average distance from Sun: 9.54 AU. Mass: 95 Earth masses. Diameter: 9.5 Earth diameters. Orbit time: 29.4 years. Rotation time: 10 hours 40 minutes.)

Saturn is the sixth planet of the solar system and the second largest, after Jupiter. The outermost of the planets that can be identified easily in Earth's nighttime sky with the unaided eye, Saturn has a pale yellowish color and is not nearly so bright as Mars. Saturn's spectacular ring system, which makes it one of the most interesting of the planets, is visible through even a small telescope. Its rings are more extensive than those of any other planet.

Like Jupiter, Saturn is composed of densely compacted hydrogen, helium, and other gases. Liquid or metallic hydrogen probably exists underneath the planet's thick atmosphere, and scientists believe there is a solid core of rock about two times the size of Earth at its center. Saturn's high rotational speed makes it the most oblate (flattened) of all the planets; it is almost 6,800 miles (11,000 km) wider at the equator than on a line through the poles.

Exploration of Saturn began in 1979 with the first flyby (*Pioneer 11*), but the *Voyager 1* (1980) and *Voyager 2* (1981) missions provided the first detailed look at the planet. Scientists have spent years sifting through the data gathered. Though there were important new findings, many questions about Saturn remain unanswered. The Cassini-Huygens probe, due to begin orbiting Saturn in mid-2004, should provide many answers.

The Voyagers found a huge storm thousands of miles across on Saturn, along with a wide band of extremely high winds—up to 1,000 miles (1,600 km) per hour—at the equator. Winds in this band all travel in the direction of the planet's rotation (unlike bands of wind on Jupiter). The Voyagers also discovered a vast hydrogen cloud circling the planet above the equator.

The Voyagers' most exciting discoveries concern the planetary rings. Previously, about six different rings had been identified within the ring system, but *Voyager 1* pictures show as many as 1,000 separate rings. Narrow rings can even be seen within the Cassini Division, once thought to be an empty gap between the two major parts of the ring system. Some rings are not circular, and at least two rings are intertwined, or "braided." A strange new phenomenon was also discovered in the rings. *Voyager 1* pictures clearly show dark, radial fingers—"spokes"—moving inside the rings in the direction of rotation. Scientists speculate that they are made of ice crystals.

Voyager 2 pictures show that Saturn has far more than 1,000 rings—perhaps as many as 100,000 or more. One of the brightest rings is under 152 meters (500 ft.) thick. *Voyager 2* also found seasonal differences between the planet's two hemispheres and photographed a storm 4,000 miles (6,500 km) wide.

Twelve of Saturn's moons were known before the arrival of the Voyagers, and instruments aboard the space probe helped locate five new ones in the 1980's. In 1990 an 18th moon, later named Pan, was located in images made by *Voyager 2*. The discovery of 12 small moons of Saturn, found with ground-based telescopes, was reported in 2001, and another new moon was spotted in 2003, bringing the total number of moons to 31. Most of Saturn's moons are relatively small and composed of rock and ice. All but one of the small moons are pockmarked by meteor craters, and in some cases the moons appear to have been cracked by collisions with especially large meteors. But Voyager pictures show that one moon, Enceladus, is smooth in large regions apparently unmarked by collisions with meteors. Scientists believe that Enceladus is being pulled and stretched by the combined gravities of a nearby moon and Saturn itself. Tidal forces have apparently heated the core of Enceladus and made its surface soft enough to smooth over any craters formed by meteor impacts.

Titan, Saturn's largest moon (3,000 mi., or 4,800 km, in diameter), is one of the few moons in the solar system known to have an atmosphere of any substance. Scientists suspect that at least some precursors of life may have formed there. For this reason *Voyager 1* was guided to within about 2,500 miles (4,000 km) of Titan during the Saturn flyby. Though Titan's surface was obscured by dense clouds, the Voyagers' sensors nevertheless returned a considerable amount of information about the moon and its atmosphere. Titan's atmosphere is composed mostly of nitrogen, like that of Earth, with only a small percentage of methane and carbon monoxide. Atmospheric pressure is at least 1.5 times that on Earth, and temperatures range around −294°F (−181°C). Titan in fact appears to be a frozen version of Earth before life evolved. The Huygens probe will descend to Titan's surface in early 2005.

The possibility of oceans of liquid methane (or of nitrogen or methane rain) on Titan was a matter of considerable controversy for some time after *Voyager 1* investigated the moon. But Titan is "dry," at least in the regions investigated. Pools of liquid methane might still exist in other low-lying regions, but it is unlikely that either methane or nitrogen condenses to liquid form on Titan.

Uranus (Average distance from Sun: 19.2 AU. Mass: 14.5 Earth masses. Diameter: 4.0 Earth diameters. Orbit time: 84 years. Rotation time: 17 hours 14 minutes.)

Uranus is the seventh planet in the solar system and the third of the gas giants. The planet is barely visible in Earth's nighttime sky (it looks like a faint star), and for that reason it went undiscovered until 1781.

Nearly the same size as Neptune and only about 5 percent of Jupiter's mass, Uranus is a faintly greenish color, perhaps because its atmosphere contains methane. The planet's axis of rotation is tipped over on its side. Astronomers discovered a system of nine faint rings in 1977, and *Voyager 2* found two more rings in 1986. There are thought to be 21 moons of Uranus. Among these, Caliban and Sycorax were found in 1997; a still unnamed moon was noticed in 1999 by a researcher studying a photograph taken in 1986 by *Voyager 2*. Three more discovered later in 1999 have been named Prospero, Setebos, and Stephano.

Uranus's atmosphere is very cold (–355°F, or –215°C). No clouds have been observed. Scientists speculate that, as on Jupiter and Saturn, temperatures and pressures increase dramatically down through the outer layer of atmosphere. At some point the hydrogen and helium would be sufficiently compressed to form a liquid or slushy surface "crust." Underneath this crust, they believe, is a mantle of solidified methane, ammonia, and water; and inside this mantle, a rocky core of silicon and iron about 10 times as massive as Earth. The core is thought to be hot, probably about 12,000°F (7,000°C).

Neptune (Average distance from Sun: 30.1 AU. Mass: 17.1 Earth masses. Diameter: 3.8 Earth diameters. Orbit time: 165 years. Rotation time: 16 hours 6 minutes.)

The last of the gas giants, Neptune is the eighth planet in the solar system. It was discovered in 1846 after mathematical calculations based on irregularities in the orbit of Uranus provided astronomers with the correct location of the planet. Neptune, like Uranus, has been surrounded by considerable uncertainty because of its enormous distance from Earth. The visit by *Voyager 2* in 1989 contributed greatly to improved understanding of the planet.

Neptune is a pale bluish color, but it has a clear atmosphere and is very cold at the cloud tops (about –365°F or –220°C). Scientists believe Neptune has a three-layered structure similar to that of Uranus: a crust of solidified or liquid hydrogen and helium that gradually thins outward into an atmosphere; a mantle of solidified gases and water; and a hot, rocky core (about 12,000°F or 7,000°C) some 15 times as massive as Earth. But one aspect of Neptune remains a mystery. Despite similarities with Uranus, Neptune has been found to radiate 2.7 times as much heat as it receives from the Sun (at a rate of 0.03 microwatts per ton of mass). Uranus, on the other hand, does not emit as much excess heat. As a result, Neptune is about the same temperature as Uranus, despite being 50 percent farther from the Sun.

Neptune has 11 known moons: Triton and Nereid, discovered from Earth; six others discovered by *Voyager 2*; and three more newly spotted in 2002. Triton is the largest moon and has an atmosphere. Triton is unusual in that it travels in a direction opposite that of Neptune's rotation, suggesting that it had a different origin from the planet. Triton also has volcanic activity: geysers of nitrogen rising as high as 5 miles (8 km).

Pluto (Average distance from Sun: 39.5 AU. Mass: 0.002 Earth masses. Diameter: 0.18 Earth diameters. Orbit time: 248 years. Rotation time: 6.4 days.)

Main components of atmosphere: methane and nitrogen (quantities unknown). The ninth and outermost (most of the time) known planet of the solar system is a ball of frozen gases probably only about the size of Earth's Moon. Pluto was discovered in 1930 as a result of an extensive search by Clyde Tombaugh. Because of its relatively small size and chaotic orbit (which at times crosses inside Neptune's orbit), some scientists think that Pluto is not really a planet at all. Instead, they theorize that Pluto is one of the large comets in the Kuiper Belt, discovered outside the orbit of Neptune over several years beginning in 1992.

Today Pluto is about as close to the Sun as it ever gets and possesses a thin atmosphere, but it is expected to freeze solid as the planet moves away from the Sun. Pluto has one known moon, Charon, discovered in 1978. Charon is about half the size of Pluto. Pluto and Charon rotate and revolve synchronously like a double planet system.

Smaller Objects in the Solar System

In addition to the nine planets, a large number of smaller objects orbit the Sun.

Asteroids, small objects with compositions similar to the terrestrial planets, are found primarily in the asteroid belt, a band lying between the orbits of Mars and Jupiter. Smaller numbers are found in orbits that cross those of the terrestrial planets, including Earth's orbit, and leading or trailing several planets. The largest of the asteroids, Ceres, is nearly half the diameter of Pluto, though most are much smaller, with diameters of several kilometers. More than 200,000 asteroids are now known.

Comets are icy bodies, composed mostly of water ice and carbon dioxide ice. When far from the Sun, comets are essentially in deep freeze, but if a comet's orbit carries it closer to the Sun than Jupiter, significant amounts of the ice evaporate and trail away from the main body of the comet, forming the comet's distinctive tail. As the ice evaporates, small solid grainlike particles mixed in with the ice are also released. The main body of a comet may be only a few kilometers in diameter, but upon close approach to the Sun, the tail may extend for millions of kilometers. Upon leaving the inner solar system, a comet returns to deep freeze. Two different locations are recognized as sources of comets. Long-period comets, ones that take more than several hundred years to complete an orbit of the Sun, are thought to come from the Oort Cloud, a large group of as many as a million comets located 50,000 times farther from the Sun than Earth, halfway to the next nearest star. Small gravitational perturbations occasionally sling one or more of these in toward the Sun. Some end up on long, repeating elliptical orbits; others make a single pass by the Sun and are flung out of the solar system, while some crash into the Sun. Short-period comets move on elliptical orbits that take them out no farther than the orbit of Pluto. The source of short-period comets is now thought to be a recently discovered group of icy objects just outside of Neptune's orbit called the Kuiper Belt. The first Kuiper Belt object was discovered in 1992, and hundreds have now been discovered, including four with at least one-third the diameter of Pluto. Many astronomers now believe that Pluto is merely the largest member of the Kuiper Belt, though a consensus on whether Pluto should continue to be classified as a planet has not been reached.

Extrasolar Planets

Astronomers have long suspected that planets were not unique to our solar system, and numerous searches for planets around other stars have been undertaken. In 1995 the first detection of an extrasolar planet around a Sun-like star was announced. The discovery was made by looking for very small shifts in the spectrum of the star 51 Pegasi as the star wobbled back and forth under the gravitational influence of a much smaller object in orbit around it. From the time it took for the star to complete one wobble, it was determined that the planet orbited much closer to 51 Pegasi than Mercury's distance from the Sun, completing an orbit in only four days. From the strength of the gravitational pull, the planet was found to have a mass about one-half that of Jupiter. Since this discovery, more than 100 more extrasolar planets have been found around ordinary stars. Many of the planets orbit their star at very small distances, but the search has now turned up systems similar to the solar system, with Jovian-sized planets at large distances from their stars. The techniques presently being used are not capable of finding Earth-size planets, so it is not yet possible to know whether terrestrial planets exist around other stars.

Stars

The Life Cycles of Stars Stars are spheres of gas that generate energy by nuclear fusion. Their life cycles are responsible for the rich chemical complexity of the universe and are intimately connected to the existence of life. Since soon after the beginning of the universe, stars have been forming and then producing heavy elements as a byproduct of energy generation at their cores. When their nuclear fuel is exhausted, some of these fusion products are released back into space, in the process enriching the interstellar medium, the raw materials for formation of subsequent generations of stars.

The Interstellar Medium and Star Formation The space between stars is vast (typically tens of trillions of miles between pairs of stars), and that space is not empty. Astronomers refer to this space as interstellar space; the material distributed throughout interstellar space is referred to as the interstellar medium (ISM). The ISM is composed of thinly spread gas atoms, mostly hydrogen with a smaller amount of helium, and traces of other elements, as well as a small amount of dusty solid material. Conditions in the ISM are extreme: atoms are so thinly spread that a cube-shape region 500 miles on a side contains only about a gram of matter. Forming a star from such diffuse material requires compacting interstellar gas by a trillion trillion times. Most star formation occurs in denser accumulations of interstellar gas called Giant Molecular Clouds (GMCs), so called because they contain enough raw material, mostly in the form of hydrogen molecules, to make hundreds of thousands of stars. In these clouds, the gas can be thousands of times denser than average but even colder, reaching temperatures of 10 Kelvins (less than –400° F). GMCs are found in the spiral arms of our galaxy (see the Milky Way). The formation of individual stars occurs in denser clumps within GMCs, where gravity pulls together the million trillion trillion kilograms of interstellar matter necessary to make a star. This accumulated matter is known as a protostar, enough raw material to make a star but not yet producing energy through nuclear fusion. Although there are tantalizing clues, astronomers have yet to definitively observe the initial gravitational infall needed to form a protostar, though later stages have been seen. Observations also show that collapse is accompanied by the formation of a disk of interstellar material around the protostar's equator; this protoplanetary disk is presumably the material from which planets form.

As more material accumulates, the central temperature of the protostar reaches the millions of degrees necessary for hydrogen atoms to combine to form helium. The mass of helium produced in these reactions is smaller than the initial hydrogen; the difference is converted to energy (see Physics: $E = mc^2$). The onset of fusion marks the true birth of the star. After a period during which the star settles into its final configuration and surrounding cloud material is cleared away, the star becomes a stable main-sequence star, steadily converting hydrogen to helium in its hottest central regions. Within GMCs, stars form in groups of hundreds or thousands of stars, and a GMC may experience multiple episodes of star formation. The smallest stars have masses of about 1/12 the Sun's mass. Below this mass, the center of a hydrogen gas sphere does not reach high enough temperatures to fuse hydrogen into helium; an object below this mass is known as a brown dwarf. Stars form with masses up to about 100 times the Sun's mass. The smaller the mass, the more stars of that mass there are; stars smaller than the Sun are the most common; high-mass stars are rare.

The Main Sequence Once the structure of a star stabilizes, it steadily converts hydrogen to helium in its core. This phase in a star's life, known as the main sequence, lasts far longer than a star's formation or death. The stable structure arises from the balance between gravity, trying to compress the star; and internal pressure, generated by energy released in the nuclear reactions, pushing outward. Since the fuel for nuclear fusion is hydrogen, and since stars are made of enormous quantities of this fuel, the main-sequence stage can continue for millions or billions of years. Although high-mass stars contain more hydrogen fuel than low-mass stars, they have higher power outputs and run through the available hydrogen faster. The highest-mass stars use up their nuclear fuel in a few million years; the Sun has enough fuel to last 10 billion years; the smallest stars will take hundreds of billions of years to run through their fuel.

Post-Main-Sequence Evolution and Star Death

As hydrogen is replaced by helium in a stellar core, a star enters the post-main-sequence stage. The core shrinks and becomes hotter, allowing helium fusion to begin, increasing the nuclear reaction rate and power output of the star. The star's outer layers expand to 100–1,000 times the main-sequence diameter and become cooler. This is known as the red giant phase.

In lower-mass stars like the Sun, atoms as massive as carbon and oxygen are formed at the core. The expanded outer layers begin to flow away from the core, dispersing back into interstellar space during the planetary nebula phase. The remaining stellar core, composed of carbon, oxygen, and electrons, has about the mass of the Sun but with a diameter about the same as Earth. This remnant of a low-mass star's life is a white dwarf. The large gravitational force trying to collapse the core is offset by a quantum effect, electron degeneracy pressure, which prevents electrons from occupying the same space and as a result provides an outward force to hold up the core.

In higher-mass stars, central pressures are high enough to allow additional fusion reactions, producing heavier elements like silicon, sulfur, and iron. The resulting internal structure is onionlike, with layers of earlier fusion products lying atop the stellar core. When iron is formed in the core, no other fusion reactions can occur without removing pressure from the system, and the core rapidly collapses. If the core mass is less than three times the mass of the Sun, collapse is halted by neutron degeneracy pressure when the core is about 10 kilometers across. The resulting high-density object is a neutron star. As neutron pressure halts collapse of the core, the resulting rebound ejects the star's outer layers back into interstellar space in a supernova explosion. The interstellar medium is thereby enriched with heavy elements, including elements such as carbon, oxygen, iron, sulfur, and phosphorous, which are crucial to life on Earth. The Sun and Earth presumably formed from supernova-enriched interstellar gas.

In stars where the core mass exceeds three times the Sun's mass, even neutron pressure cannot halt the collapse once all core fuel sources have been exhausted. The core collapses to an infinitely dense mass called a black hole. The gravitational force within a few tens of kilometers of such a stellar black hole is so strong that even light cannot escape from it. The precise fate of the star's outer layers is not clear. Since high-mass stars are rare, few possible stellar black holes have been identified, and none has been observed during the collapse phase.

The Milky Way Galaxy

The Sun is one of several hundred billion stars that belong to the Milky Way galaxy (in astronomical usage known as "the Galaxy"), a vast accumulation of gravitationally associated stars, star-forming material, and other matter. The common name Milky Way dates from antiquity and refers to the white "spilled milk" appearance of the Galaxy, easily seen from dark viewing sites cutting across the nighttime sky. In the 17th century, Galileo used a telescope to show that this light band was actually made up of a large number of individual stars. Studies were made throughout the 18th and 19th centuries in attempts to measure the scale of the Galaxy, but incorrect interpretations of the data led to underestimates of the Galaxy's extent and mistakenly placed the Sun at the Galaxy center. In the early 20th century, work by American astronomers Henrietta Leavitt and Harlow Shapley showed that the Sun was located about halfway out from the center of the Galaxy's flattened disk of stars, about 24,000 light-years (144 quadrillion miles) from the Galactic Center and a similar distance from the disk's outer edge. This disk is just one of several components of the Galaxy.

The Galactic Disk The Milky Way is a spiral galaxy, distinguishable by its prominent, bright, flattened disk of stars, all orbiting about the Galactic Center in the same direction (clockwise as viewed from the North Galactic Pole). This disk contains most of the stars in the Galaxy and nearly all of the interstellar gas and dust. The thickness of the disk ranges from a few hundred light-years for the youngest stars and star-forming clouds to a few thousand light-years for the oldest disk stars. The diameter of the disk is some 100,000 light-years. The disk is thus extremely thin, with a width-to-height ratio of more than 1,000 (comparable to a sheet of letter-size paper). The disk is the site of most star formation in the Galaxy.

To an observer outside the Galaxy, the disk would stand out because of the young, blue, massive stars that have recently formed there. These stars tend to be found along one of at least four arclike spiral arms extending outward from the center of the Galactic Disk. In these arms, star-forming material is accumulated and compressed into the Giant Molecular Clouds (GMCs) where new stars are formed. From studies of chemical composition (see Stellar Evolution), astronomers have identified stars with ages up to 10 billion years in the disk. Older disk stars have lower abundances of metals than the stars just emerging from molecular clouds. The Sun, with an age of approximately 5 billion years, lies in the middle of the continuum of disk star ages; presumably the Sun formed out of a molecular cloud in a galactic spiral arm some 5 billion years ago.

Despite the apparent crowding of stars along the Milky Way disk, the typical separation between stars is quite large. In the Sun's vicinity, the separation between stars is several light-years (1 light-year = 6 trillion miles), and the chance for stellar close encounters is extremely small during the lifetime of the Galaxy.

The Sun travels in a roughly circular orbit about the Galaxy at a speed of 220 km/s (about 140 miles/second). A single orbit about the Galaxy at this speed, 24,000 light-years from the center, takes approximately 240 million years. Applying Newton's law of gravity, astronomers can use the speed of the Sun at this distance to determine the Galaxy's matter content interior to the Sun's orbit. Similar observations of the motions of stars located elsewhere yield information about the matter distribution in other parts of the Galaxy. These observations indicate the presence of a thinly populated, though massive, halo of material extending well beyond the Galactic Disk (see below).

The Galactic Halo Surrounding the Galactic Disk is a diffuse Galactic Halo. The halo is roughly spherical and contains widely spaced old stars and almost no star-forming gas. Many of the halo stars are found in dense concentrations of stars called Globular Clusters. These are the oldest structures in the Galaxy, with stellar ages of approximately 15 billion years, and are thought to have formed before the Galactic Disk. By counting stars, astronomers estimate that the stellar mass of the halo is only a few percent that of the disk. However, motions of stars in the outer Galactic Disk imply the presence of large amounts of matter that does not give off light; mass estimates range up to as much as 10 times the mass of the Galactic Disk, bringing the Galaxy's mass to more than a trillion times that of the Sun. The presence of this Dark Matter Halo has prompted searches for exotic subatomic particles or a large population of compact but non-light-emitting dead stars. These searches have, thus far, been inconclusive at best.

The Galactic Bulge Within approximately 2,000 light-years of the Galactic Center, the shape of the Galaxy changes. A separate component, the Galactic Bulge, is the prominent feature. The bulge is about 1,000 light-years thick, nearly as thick as it is wide, shaped somewhat like a football. The bulge contains both old and young stars and also has significant amounts of star-forming gas. Stars are up to a thousand times closer together in the bulge than they are in the disk. The stellar density and presence of gas and dust in the bulge makes observations confusing, and little is known about the Galaxy on the far side of the bulge. Because dense clouds of gas and dust block visible-wavelength starlight, astronomers typically use long-wavelength infrared or radio-wavelength light to probe the bulge structure. The bulge is dynamically distinct from the disk; bulge stars move on elongated orbits about the Galactic Center, with no tendency toward the ordered motion seen in the disk.

By studying the motion of stars very near to Galactic Center, astronomers have discovered that a very large mass, several million times more massive than the Sun, lies within the inner few tenths of a light-year of the Galaxy. This information, combined with observations of powerful X-rays and gamma rays emerging from the Galactic Center, implies the presence there of a massive black hole. Studies of other galaxies seem to show that black holes are a common galaxy feature, so it is not surprising that the Milky Way should house one as well.

Other Galaxies

Considerable debate raged among astronomers during the 18th and 19th centuries about whether all of the contents of the universe lay within the Milky Way or whether the Milky Way was but one of numerous stellar swarms. In 1923 Edwin Hubble measured the distance to what is now known as the Andromeda Galaxy, showing that it lay well outside the confines of the Milky Way and establishing that the Milky Way was but one of an enormous number of galaxies. The visible universe is thought to contain perhaps hundreds of billions of galaxies.

Galaxies are classified into several morphological types. A spiral galaxy has a structure similar to that of the Milky Way: a bright, flattened disk of stars, gas, and dust showing evidence of spiral arms, along with a bulge and diffuse halo. The Milky Way is at the large extreme of spiral galaxy sizes and masses—most spiral galaxies have smaller disks and fewer stars. Elliptical galaxies do not have disks. Instead, they are roughly the shape of a football or basketball, with stars orbiting the galaxy center in random directions. Elliptical galaxies contain mostly old stars, have little gas or dust, and show no evidence of ongoing star formation. The largest elliptical galaxies have masses 100 times that of the Milky Way; the smallest, dwarf spheroidals, may only have one millionth the mass of the Milky Way. Galaxies that do not fit the spiral or elliptical descriptions are classified as irregular galaxies. These tend to be smaller than spiral galaxies and have asymmetric shapes.

Some galaxies exhibit energetic activity originating near their cores, including strong outputs of high-energy X rays and enormous jets of radio radiation. These phenomena are caused by material plunging into a galaxy's central black hole. These active galaxies provide a link to an earlier phase in the evolution of galaxies. In addition to finding the distances to galaxies, Hubble found that galaxies tended to be moving away from the Milky Way and that the farther away they were the faster they were moving. This relation, now known as Hubble's law, serves as the most valuable indicator of large distances in the universe. Light from galaxies located far from the Milky Way may have left those galaxies billions of years ago, so we are seeing these galaxies as they were long ago. Some very distant galaxies can be detected only because of the energetic activity at their centers. These distant, active galaxies, known as quasars, represent an earlier time in the evolution of galaxies when more gas was available to fuel the activity associated with galactic black holes.

Typical separations between large galaxies are millions of light-years, but many galaxies are found in galaxy clusters, concentrations of tens to thousands of galaxies extending over 10 million to 20 million light-years in diameter. On scales of 100 hundred million light-years, galaxies are found in superclusters. On even larger scales, superclusters are arranged in gigantic sheets, separated by even larger voids with very small numbers of galaxies.

The Universe

Astronomy at its core tries to determine the origins of the universe, and observations have helped to constrain the conditions in the early universe. Three key observations underpin the understanding of the early universe. First, Hubble's law (see Galaxies) shows that all galaxies are moving away from one another. This results from the expansion of the universe, and implies that the universe evolved from an earlier dense, compact point. Second, the universe is observed to be composed of roughly 75 percent hydrogen (by number) and 25 percent helium. Third, a faint glow of radio-wavelength radiation is observed coming from every direction in the universe.

Taken together, these observations make up strong evidence for the standard picture of the early universe, the Big Bang. All of the data support the idea that the universe began in a hotter, denser state than we currently find it. Cosmic expansion is the most direct by-product, as space continues to stretch outward, carrying galaxies along with it and away from one another. The abundance of hydrogen and helium is naturally explained as having formed during the first extremely hot moments after the Big Bang, when the universe was hot enough to produce matter from energy and fuse hydrogen into helium. The radio glow seen in all directions, known as cosmic background radiation, is the remnant of heat from the Big Bang, weakened by the stretching of space since the Big Bang.

The speeds of galaxies combined with their distances from one another gives an estimate of the time they have been receding from one another and therefore of the time since the Big Bang. Careful measurements of the recession rate and the cosmic background radiation combine to give an age of the universe of 13.7 billion years. For comparison, the Sun and solar system formed in the Milky Way 4.5 billion years ago.

The standard picture of the Big Bang does not explain several observations. For instance, the cosmic background radiation is incredibly smooth in all directions. This is a problem since there are regions of the universe that cannot have had contact with one another at the time the background radiation was produced. To explain this, a period of rapid expansion, known as inflation, has been proposed. Inflation puts all points in the universe much closer together during the earliest instants after the Big Bang, and causes them to expand more rapidly during those first fractions of a second.

Recent observations may force a revision of astronomers' understanding of the universe. The gravitational pull of galaxies on one another should have caused the cosmic expansion to slow over the past 13.7 billion years. New observations of distant galaxies seem to show that, on the largest scales, the rate with which galaxies are moving away from one another is increasing rather than decreasing. This cosmic acceleration is as yet unexplained.

Glossary of Astronomical Terms

asteroid one of many small rocky or metallic objects remaining from the formation of the solar system, most of which are found in the asteroid belt, the region between Mars and Jupiter.

Big Bang beginning of the expansion of the universe from a high-density, high-temperature state.

black hole infinitely dense remnant of a massive star that results from the inability of the star to support itself against gravity; also, similar but more massive objects often found in the centers of galaxies.

brown dwarf sphere of hydrogen gas too small to begin nuclear fusion.

charge-coupled device (CCD) sensitive solid-state detector capable of recording visible light and other types of electromagnetic radiation.

comet icy remnant of the formation of the solar system, composed primarily of water ice as well as a smaller portion of rocky material; sublimation of the ices when a comet approaches the Sun produces the distinctive cometary tail.

cosmic background radiation electromagnetic radiation resulting from the time after the Big Bang when radiation could flow freely throughout the universe.

dark matter any of a number of possible constituents of the universe evidenced by a gravitional effect on other matter but not producing any discernable radiation.

detector part of a telescope system in which light from an astronomical source is actually collected.

electromagnetic radiation energy emitted by all objects with a temperature above absolute zero.

electromagnetic spectrum all of the possible forms of electromagnetic radiation, including gamma rays, X rays, ultraviolet radiation, visible light, infrared, and radio waves.

galaxy large collection of stars and gasses, bound together by gravitational force, containing as many as hundreds of billions of stars.

gamma rays the most energetic form of electromagnetic radiation.

globular cluster group of up to millions of stars that orbit the cores of spiral galaxies out of the galactic plane.

inflation period just after the Big Bang during which the universe was thought to expand exponentially.

infrared radiation electromagnetic waves emitted by relatively cool astronomical objects, such as forming stars and planets.

interstellar medium gas and dust found in the regions between stars in a galaxy; this is the raw material from which stars form.

Jovian planet large planet composed primarily of light atoms such as hydrogen. The Jovian planets in the solar system are Jupiter, Saturn, Uranus, and Neptune; most extrasolar planet candidates are thought to be similar.

Kuiper Belt collection of small icy bodies found beyond the orbit of Neptune and thought to be the source of short-period comets.

metals in the astronomical sense, any atom heavier than helium and therefore necessarily a product of stellar fusion.

meteor object that glows brightly from frictional heating as it plunges through Earth's atmosphere; a "shooting star."

meteorite any portion of a meteor that survives intact all the way to the Earth's surface.

main sequence portion of a star's life during which hydrogen fusion is the main source of energy production; this is generally the longest stage in a star's life.

Milky Way galaxy in which the Sun and solar system reside; "the Galaxy."

molecular cloud large, dense collection of interstellar gas and dust in which stars form.

Moon Earth's only natural satellite.

moon natural satellite of a planet.

neutron star compact remnant of a star massive enough to become a supernova but not so massive that a black hole forms.

nuclear fusion production of heavy atomic nuclei from lighter atomic nuclei; the process by which hydrogen is converted to helium in the core of the Sun.

Oort Cloud large spherical swarm of comets orbiting the Sun at a distance of about 10,000 astronomical units, thought to be the source of long-period comets.

planet relatively large object that orbits a star but is incapable of producing energy by nuclear fusion.

planetary nebula escaping outer layers of a dying low-mass star.

planetesimal one of a large number of small objects present in the early solar system that collided to form the cores of planets.

protostar collection of accumulating interstellar material that will become a star but has not yet begun producing energy by nuclear fusion.

quasar high-luminosity core of an active galaxy.

radio waves the lowest-energy band of the electromagnetic spectrum.

red giant cool, high-luminosity, large-radius star resulting from the onset of helium fusion in the core of a low-mass star.

spiral arm one of a number of extended structures in the plane of a spiral galaxy in which interstellar material is denser than average and in which young stars are found.

solar system planets and other objects that orbit the Sun.

star sphere of gas, mostly hydrogen, that produces energy by nuclear fusion.

supernova explosion resulting from the collapse and rebound of a high-mass star after nuclear fusion has completed in the stellar core.

telescope device for collecting electromagnetic radiation.

terrestrial planet small, rock- and metal-based planet, including Mercury, Venus, Earth, Mars.

ultraviolet radiation band of the electromagnetic spectrum slightly more energetic than visible light.

visible light form of electromagnetic radiation to which the human eye is sensitive.

white dwarf compact core left over after a low-mass star has shed its outer envelope as a planetary nebula.

X rays band of the electromagnetic spectrum just less energetic than gamma rays.

"Dark Energy" May Be Splitting the Universe

By DENNIS OVERBYE

By comparing maps of heat emanating from the fading remnants of the Big Bang to maps of the modern universe, astronomers in 2004 believe they have uncovered evidence that some "dark energy" is wrenching the universe apart.

The new research provides independent confirmation of one of the strangest astronomical findings in years, that based on studies of distant exploding stars the expansion of the universe is speeding up.

The simplest explanation, astrophysicists say, is that space is imbued with a repulsive, or antigravitational, force first hypothesized in 1917 by Einstein and known as the cosmological constant. But nobody understands this so-called dark energy, although speculations have blossomed in the physics literature in the last few years.

Using the maps, a multinational team of 33 astrophysicists, led by Dr. Ryan Scranton of the University of Pittsburgh, found what the members called "the shadow of dark energy" in the form of a slight boost in the energy of the radiation from the Big Bang as it passed through huge clouds of galaxies.

The astronomers said their results represented an important validation of dark energy and the emerging consensus of a universe dominated by mysterious dark matter and even more mysterious dark energy, which is geometrically "flat." That means that parallel lines drawn across the cosmos will not meet.

The results were obtained by combining information from the Sloan Digital Sky Survey, which is mapping the distances and positions of more than a million galaxies, with the Wilkinson Microwave Anisotropy Probe of NASA. The probe, a satellite, is busy mapping the intensity of a faint cosmic microwave radiation that fills the sky and is presumed to represent heat emanating from the remains of the Big Bang when the universe was only 380,000 years old.

The cosmic radiation is rippled with hot and cool spots. Some are a result of lumps in the primordial cosmic gravy and are the seeds of galaxies and other conglomerations of matter. But other hot spots, theorists point out, may be generated by the passage of microwaves through the modern universe.

As a microwave passes through a large cloud of galaxies, its energy will first increase, as a rolling marble speeds up when it hits a dip in the road. Later, as the microwave leaves the cloud, gravity will take away some energy, as the marble climbs out of the dip.

In a universe that is geometrically "flat" and with no dark energy, those effects will cancel out. No net change in the energy of the microwaves will occur.

But in an accelerating universe, the effects will not always cancel out. In the largest agglomerations of matter, so-called superclusters that are forming, the microwaves will gain energy and thus appear hotter.

In such systems, tens of millions of light-years across, the force of dark energy that is trying to push apart the cloud is winning the battle over the gravity trying to pull together the galaxies. As a result, the cloud becomes less dense rather than more dense as the microwaves pass through it, explained Dr. Andrew J. Connolly, a team member from the University of Pittsburgh.

It takes less energy for them to climb back out than they acquired falling in. So the microwaves should be slightly hotter, by a minuscule fraction of a degree.

The effect is known as the Integrated Sachs-Wolfe effect, after Dr. Arthur M. Wolfe, who is now at the University of California in San Diego, and Dr. Rainer K. Sachs, who is now at the University of California at Berkeley, who first investigated the effects of lumps in the universe on the cosmic microwaves in 1967.

In recent months, several groups, including those led by Dr. Stephen Boughn of Haverford College in Pennsylvania, Dr. Michael R. Nolta of Princeton and Dr. Pablo Fosalba of the Institute of Astrophysics in Paris, have reported promising correlations between cosmic hot spots and sky catalogs of radio sources and X rays, as well as galaxy maps.

The Sloan survey aims to map more than a million galaxies, out to a distance of 1.5 billion light-years, over a quarter of the sky.

BIOLOGY

Biology is the study of living creatures—also called organisms. Organisms are distinguished from nonliving matter by their structure and their ability to carry out certain processes. They are composed of one or more cells that are highly organized and able to maintain a relatively constant internal environment. They can assimilate and use energy, in complex series of chemical reactions that make up metabolism. They can grow and reproduce, using information encoded in their genetic material. They can respond to their environment and adapt to changes in that environment.

These characteristics are shared by all of the more than 1.8 million known kinds of organisms present on Earth. The organisms are tremendously diverse, ranging from microscopic bacteria to giant whales and sequoia trees, from green plants to black bears, from mushrooms to manatees.

A Word about Viruses Because they are unable to accomplish life's processes by themselves, viruses are not considered living organisms. They are able to metabolize and reproduce only when they are within living cells. Thus, all viruses are parasites, and many of them cause disease.

Much smaller than the smallest bacteria, most viruses consist only of a strand or two of a nucleic acid—DNA or RNA—wrapped in a protein coat. Some also have a lipid envelope outside the coat. A virus reproduces and spreads because once its nucleic acid is inside a cell, the virus uses the cell's own DNA to produce additional copies of itself.

Numerous Disciplines Originally the study of living creatures was informal, revolving around knowledge useful for hunting, farming, and early medicine. Following the scientific revolution of the 17th century, biology was formalized and came to consist of three broad categories: zoology (study of animals), botany (study of plants), and taxonomy (classification of organisms). Later, additional disciplines had their beginnings, including microbiology (study of organisms visible only with a microscope), genetics (study of how traits are inherited), molecular biology (study of chemistry used by organisms), ecology (study of interactions between organisms and their environment), and ethology (study of animal behavior). Numerous subdisciplines also developed. Some scientists focus on specific organisms; for instance, herpetologists study reptiles and pomologists study fruits. Other scientists are concerned with structure and functions; for instance, cytologists study cells and plant pathologists study plant diseases.

In recent years the lines between disciplines have blurred, owing mainly to advances in molecular biology and the development of new technologies, such as the ability to sequence genomes (the complete complement of species' DNA). Information science has been applied to biology to create the field of bioinformatics, which is concerned with the development and maintenance of databases of biological information. Such databases help scientists compare disparate genomes, examine evolutionary relationships, predict the structure and function of newly discovered proteins, and better understand the complexity of life.

History of Biology

Although at its inception biology was not yet what we think of as a science, it can be said to have begun when our ancestors observed other animals and plants, learning which to avoid and which to eat. Early hunter-gatherers had to know this kind of biology to stay alive. When farming began about 11,000 years ago, humans needed to know even more about the growth and development of the organisms they domesticated, as well as about the insects, fungi, and other pests that attacked crops.

A more systematic approach to biology started with the Greek philosophers about 2,500 years ago. Aristotle (384–322 B.C.) is considered the "father of biology" for his classification of animals and for performing the first known biology experiments, dissecting plants and animals and studying the development of the chick in its egg. His student Theophrastus (ca. 372–286 B.C.) laid the foundation of botany, describing and classifying more than 500 plants and also describing the ways plants can germinate and grow. In Roman times, Lucretius (99–55 B.C.) proposed one of the earliest theories of evolution. But biology, other than medical knowledge, made little progress until after the Middle Ages.

In the 15th and 16th centuries Europeans explored the Americas and some of the Pacific islands, and regular contact between Europe and southern Africa and eastern Asia was instituted. As a result European scholars were exposed to a great variety of plants and animals that were new to them. They responded with books describing and classifying both newfound and familiar plants and animals, starting as early as 1530. A few years later the first botanical gardens began to be established. When the scientific revolution of the 17th century began, scientists undertook more detailed experiments in biology. For example, Jan van Helmont (1579–1694) carefully measured the weight of soil in a tub as a willow grew there, establishing that the increase in mass of the willow was much greater than any diminution of mass of the soil.

Also in the 17th century, biologists began to use an important new tool, the microscope (probably invented in 1595). A previously unseen world opened, beginning with capillaries (1660), cells (1665), the tiny organs of insects (1669) and plants (1675), sperm (1667), protists (1673), and bacteria (1683). Microscopic studies contributed to increasingly sophisticated methods of classification of organisms; in 1735 these methods took the basic shape that taxonomy has retained until today, although with many refinements and improvements.

In the 19th century, biology advanced with two overarching theories that have been central to the science ever since. A number of scientists from as early as 1668 had performed experiments to show that life arises only from life and is not spontaneously generated from nonliving matter. In 1838 and 1839, Matthias Schleiden (1804–81) and Theodor Schwann (1810–82) concluded that living things are composed of cells and that reproduction always begins with cells. Since then the cell theory has been confirmed over and over, whether for single-celled bacteria or protists or for the largest organisms, giant trees and whales. About the same time, Charles Darwin (1809–82) began to formulate his theory of evolution by natural selection, published as *The Origin of Species* in 1859. Darwin's theory provides a framework in time and space that can be used to analyze almost all biological topics ranging from animal behavior to changes in the chemicals that cells employ in respiration.

A third unifying idea also began in the mid-19th century, but few knew of it at the time. Gregor Mendel (1822–84) had by 1865 discovered from experiment the basic laws of heredity, but his work was described to a local scientific society and published in its journal. In 1900, Mendel's work was rediscovered and the science of genetics began. Chromosomes were recognized as the carriers of genes (the units of heredity) as early as 1902. In 1907, Thomas Hunt Morgan (1866–1945) began a long series of experiments with fruit flies that detailed the relationship between heredity and development of traits in organisms.

Biologists also pursued the details of basic life processes (respiration, nutrition, synthesis, excretion, transport, regulation, growth, reproduction). As early as 1779, Jan Ingenhousz (1730–99) recognized the essentials of photosynthesis, which is the basis of both respiration and nutrition for nearly all forms of life; however, the chemical pathways involved were not firmly identified until 1957. The role of vitamins in nutrition began to be understood in 1901, chemical control of life processes through hormones began to be unraveled in 1902, and the chemical transmission of nerve impulses was first identified in 1920. Similarly, the chemical bases of metabolism and respiration were uncovered during the first half of the 20th century, and the details of growth and development became one of the main advances off the second half of that century.

Other 20th-century advances involved the recognition of the study of complex interactions of organisms in particular environments, which became the science of ecology; and of animal behavior, or the science of ethology.

Biology obtained a new basis in the advances of genetics, which began with the study of heredity at the beginning of the 20th century and reached a high point when the human genome (totality of genes) was almost completely deciphered, as announced in 2003. Along the way, advances in genetics had included the recognition that genes are found in the DNA of chromosomes (1944), the discovery of the structure of DNA (1953), working out the genetic code (1961–68), the invention of genetic engineering by inserting genes from one species into another (1972–73), deciphering the genomes of viruses (1977), using DNA to unravel evolutionary relationships (1981), sequencing the genome of a bacterium (1995), and cloning the first mammal with a set of genes taken from an adult body cell (1997).

How Did Life Begin?

By NICHOLAS WADE

The origin of life is biology's most daunting problem. Scientists are good at understanding processes that they can study. But life emerged 3.5 billion to 4 billion years ago. Even the rocks of that era have mostly vanished.

Some progress is being made at reconstructing the process that led to the first living cells. But it consists of conjectures of varying plausibility, not proof.

Modern cells are so complex that it is hard to conceive how they could have assembled spontaneously from the chemicals available on the primitive earth. A recent approach to the problem, developed by Günter Wächtershaüser, a Munich chemist and patent lawyer, goes as follows. Forget the sophisticated molecules that run today's cells—the DNA that stores information, the RNA that runs operations, the proteins that serve as structural material and controllers of chemical metabolism; and forget about the cell membrane. All these must have come later.

Life must have started in the simplest possible way, as a cycle, a natural chemical reaction that repeated itself, spinning off by-products, some of which stayed around to maintain and develop the cycle.

Where did this cycle start? Dr. Wächtershaüser favors some mineral surface like iron pyrites, also known as fool's gold. A natural catalyst, the iron pyrites could have assembled chemicals like carbon monoxide into biological building blocks.

At some stage, the little cycle acquired a cover of protective chemicals, to separate its own reactions from the general milieu. When the cover eventually enveloped the cycle and broke free of the mineral surface, the first cell was born.

Dr. Wächtershaüser and others have shown that important components of today's biochemistry can be formed on iron pyrite surfaces, notably pyruvate, the fuel for a basic energy-producing reaction known as the citric acid cycle.

Another approach to the origin of life concerns RNA, the close chemical cousin of DNA. RNA performs all of the trickiest operations in the cell, whether retrieving information from the DNA or turning this information into proteins.

Biologists have long supposed that RNA was the pivotal actor in the earliest cells and later delegated most of its information-storage duties to DNA, a less versatile but stabler chemical. The concept gained credence when Dr. Thomas R. Cech and Dr. Sidney Altman discovered independently that RNA could act as an enzyme, a catalyst of chemical activities, as well as store genetic information.

This dual property of RNA seems in principle to resolve a thorny paradox of life, that DNA requires a protein catalyst for its replication, and the protein requires DNA to make it, implying that neither could exist without the other's being there first. RNA could have performed both functions.

Chemists have not yet devised an RNA molecule that can replicate itself. But they have shown that RNA molecules can copy short pieces of RNA. That bolsters the idea that before DNA there was an RNA world in which RNA, or some similar precursor, ran the show.

The subunits of RNA molecules are themselves complex chemicals. It is not easy to see how the first RNA molecules could have come into existence. But a clay called montmorillonite, formed from weathered volcanic ash and familiar in many households as cat litter, has the interesting property of catalyzing the formation of RNA from its subunits.

Researchers from the Massachusetts General Hospital reported that montmorillonite clay has another property possibly relevant to the origin of life. It makes droplets of fat molecules rearrange themselves into small bubbles, similar to the membranes that make up the walls of living cells.

Often the clay particles are incorporated into the bubbles, the research team found, with any attached RNA molecules. "Mineral particles may have greatly facilitated the emergence of the first cells," they said.

In a second experiment, the researchers found that they could make their protocells divide by forcing them through fine holes in a filter. A natural counterpart to this process would be water currents' forcing bubbles through rock pores.

Researchers are a long way from reconstructing any plausible path for the origin of life. But they have not given up. And they always conclude, no matter how fragmentary their evidence, that life is possible.

Taxonomy

Classification of organisms is called taxonomy. It is part of the field of systematics, which studies the diversity of organisms and relationships among groups of organisms, both living and extinct. Systematics is closely related to the study of evolution, which is the causal agent for both diversity and relationships among organisms.

Organisms are classified by using the binomial system of nomenclature, which became standard after Carolus Linnaeus (1707–78) used it to identify plants in *Species Plantarum*, first published in 1753. In this system, each kind, or species, of organism is given a two-word (binomial) name consisting of the organism's genus and species.

Classification is hierarchical, with small, related groups clustered together in a larger group. The main groups are species, genus, family, order, phylum, and kingdom. The species is generally the smallest unit in the system (subspecies are recognized in some instances). Members of a species are closely related genetically and almost identical in structure and behavior. Similar species are grouped into a genus. For instance, genus *Otus* includes not only a number of species of screech owls but also species such as the Puerto Rican owl, *O. nudipes*; and the Palau owl, *O. podarginus*.

Similarly, all genera of owls are grouped in the family Strigidae and order Strigiformes. Owls are grouped with all other birds in the class Aves. Together with other vertebrates, they are part of the phylum Chordata. And together with all other animals, they make up the kingdom Animalia.

Any particular group of organisms is referred to as a taxon. For example, owls form a taxon at the levels of family and order; and insects, which are all classified in class Insecta, form a taxon at the level of class.

As biological knowledge increases, taxonomic disagreements are resolved and revisions often are made in how organisms are classified.

Viruses, though generally not considered living organisms, are classified in a similar hierarchical scheme, with groups identified by the type of nucleic acid that forms their core: double-stranded DNA, single-stranded DNA, double-stranded RNA, ordinary single-stranded RNA, and negative-sense single-stranded RNA. In addition, there are two groups known as reverse-transcribing viruses because they alter the DNA of the host cell to match the viral nucleic acid, which may be either RNA or DNA. Within each group are families of viruses, a classification usually based on the type of host that the virus infects.

As biologists learned more about organisms, they recognized that many organisms are neither plant nor animal, so the number of kingdoms was gradually expanded and then separated into three domains. The domains, described in the table below, are Archaea, Prokarya, and Eukarya. It is now believed that the original life-forms were Archaea and that early in life's history the Prokarya separated from them. At a later date, the Eukarya also separated from the Archaea.

Examples of Classification

Kingdom	Animalia	Animalia	Plantae
Phylum or division	Chordata	Arthropoda	Anthophyta
Subphylum	Vertebrata	Crustacea	Angiospermae
Class	Mammalia	Malacostraca	Dicotyledoneae
Order	Primates	Decapoda	Rosales
Family	Hominidae	Nephropidae	Leguminosae
Genus	*Homo*	*Homarus*	*Lathyrus*
Species	*sapiens*	*americanus*	*odoratus*
Common name	human	Atlantic lobster	sweet pea

Basic Life Processes

All living organisms must perform certain life processes in order to survive. Some processes are common to all organisms; others are unique to certain groups.

Making or Obtaining Food Green plants and algae are autotrophs. In the presence of light, they produce their own food, in a complex series of reactions that make up the process of photosynthesis. The process takes place in special cell structures, typically chloroplasts, that contain the light-absorbing pigment chlorophyll. Briefly, photosynthesis converts carbon dioxide, water, and light energy into glucose sugar and oxygen; the light energy is changed into chemical energy that holds the glucose molecule together.

Without photosynthesis, life as we know it would not exist. Animals and other heterotrophs depend, directly or indirectly, on autotrophs for their food. Herbivores, such as cows and sea urchins, are heterotrophs that feed directly on green plants and algae. Carnivores, such as lions and spiders, feed mainly on the flesh of other animals. Omnivores, including humans and bluebirds, eat both plants and animals.

Chemical Synthesis In numerous chemical reactions, an organism makes, or synthesizes, molecules needed to maintain structure, grow, and carry out chemical processes. For instance, plant cells convert some of the glucose created during photosynthesis into cellulose, a complex carbohydrate that is the main constituent of plant cell walls. The human body takes phosphorus obtained from meat and other foodstuffs and incorporates it in nucleic acid molecules.

Cellular Respiration Every living cell needs a continuous supply of energy to perform life processes. During a series of many reactions that make up respiration, food molecules are broken down, releasing energy in the form of adenosine triphosphate (ATP).

Excretion Metabolism produces various waste products that must be removed, or excreted, from an organism. The oxygen produced during photosynthesis is a waste product; although the organism uses some of the oxygen for respiration, most is released into the atmosphere (by land plants) or water (by algae). In birds, the metabolism of proteins produces uric acid, an insoluble waste excreted as a thick paste.

Coordination and Regulation An organism's functions must be coordinated to maintain a stable internal environment. This requires coordination of internal processes as well as regulation of responses to changes in the external environment. In plants, for example, chemicals called auxins and gibberellins work together to elongate stems. If one side of a dahlia stem is in the shade, auxins concentrate there; the cells on the shaded side grow faster and longer, causing the stem to gradually bend toward the light. In animals, nerve cells and chemicals called hormones regulate many aspects of physiology and behavior.

Growth and Reproduction All organisms grow in size. Plants grow only at the tips of their shoots and leaves, whereas humans grow throughout their entire length. In most plants, growth goes on indefinitely, whereas humans grow only to a certain point in their development.

Reproduction is not necessary for an individual organism but is essential if a species, or type of organism, is to continue to exist. Asexual reproduction involves only one parent and results in offspring that are genetically identical to the parent. For instance, a strawberry plant can reproduce asexually by sending out a special stem that runs along the ground; a daughter plant develops at the end of the stem, developing roots and leaves and eventually producing runner stems of its own. Strawberry plants, like all plants and animals, also reproduce sexually. Sexual reproduction typically involves two parents and results in offspring that are not genetically identical to either parent. This promotes variability, which is the basis of evolution.

Cell Biology

A basic concept of biology is that all organisms are composed of one or more cells, and that cells arise only from other cells. A bacterium consists of a single cell, whereas an elephant is made up of trillions of cells. Almost all cells are microscopic; the largest of the few visible to the naked eye is only 0.03 inch (0.76 millimeter) in diameter.

Although each type of cell is unique, all cells share four characteristics. First, every cell is enclosed in a thin cell membrane, which provides shape and acts as a barrier between the cell and its environment. The membrane is semipermeable, composed largely of lipids (fats, oils, and fatty substances such as cholesterol), with embedded proteins that regulate the transport of molecules into and out of the cell.

Second, all cells are filled with cytoplasm. The fluid portion of cytoplasm, called cytosol, contains nutrients, enzymes, and other dissolved materials vital for cell metabolism. Also in the cytoplasm are specialized structures called organelles, held in place by a network of protein filaments.

Third, within the cytoplasm of all cells are organelles called ribosomes, which manufacture proteins for the cell. Some of the proteins are structural components; others are enzymes that control chemical reactions in the cell.

Fourth, all cells contain chromosomes composed of DNA, which encodes instructions for making the hundreds or even thousands of different proteins found in a cell.

Major Taxons, with Representative Species

Domain Archaea

Discovered in the 20th century, archaea are one-celled organisms that look like bacteria but are genetically different. As with bacteria, the genetic material is not contained within a nucleus and there are no other membrane-bound organelles. Unlike bacteria, archaea lack the sugar-polypeptide compound peptidoglycan in the cell wall. Also, the composition and assembly of flagella (filaments that extend from the organism and that are used in propulsion) differ in the two groups. Archaea were once believed to live almost exclusively in extreme environments such as hot springs and deep-sea hydrothermal vents, but they are now recognized as being widespread.

Kingdom Euryarcheota Extreme halophiles (salt-lovers), extreme thermophiles (heat-lovers), methanogens (which metabolize methane instead of oxygen)
Kingdom Crenarcheota Extreme thermophiles, nonthermophiles
Kingdom Korarcheota Extreme thermophiles

Domain Prokarya

Discovered the 17th century, following the invention of the microscope, prokaryotes are better known by their common name, bacteria. Unlike archaea, they have peptidoglycan in the cell wall. And unlike eukaryotes, they lack a distinct nucleus and any other membrane-bound organelles. Bacteria are much more common than archaea and live in almost every type of environment (there are more bacteria in your mouth than there are people on Earth). The group, which in some classification schemes is called Monera, includes both autotrophs (which produce their own food) and heterotrophs (which depend directly or indirectly on autotrophs). The classification and naming of large taxons are in flux.

Kingdom Proteobacteria Purple bacteria, nitrifying bacteria (Nitrosomonas, Nitrobacter), nitrogen-fixing bacteria (Azotobacter), pseudomonads, enteric bacteria (Escherichia, Enterobacter), myxobacteria, rickettsia
Kingdom Gram-positive bacteria Cocci (spherical): Staphylococcus; bacilli (rod-shaped): Bacillus; Mycoplasma
Kingdom Spirochetes Long, slender, tightly coiled bacteria: Spirillum, Treponema
Kingdom Chlamydiae Parasitic: Chlamydia
Kingdom Cyanobacteria Blue-green algae-like autotrophs: Anabaena, Nostoc
Kingdom Green sulfur bacteria Photosynthetic: Chlorobium
Kingdom Green nonsulfur bacteria Thermophiles: Chloroflexus
Kingdom Flavobacteria and relatives Flavobacteria, bacteriodes
Kingdom Hyperthermophiles Extreme heat-lovers: Aquifex, Thermotoga

Domain Eukarya

First classified by the ancient Greeks, eukaryotes include unicellular, filamentous, colonial, and multicellular species—everything from amoebas to humans. The genetic material is contained within a nucleus delineated by a nuclear membrane, and cells also contain a variety of additional membrane-bound organelles.

Kingdom Protista The simplest eukaryotes. Most are one-celled, but some species are colonial or multicellular. The algae are autotrophs; other protists are heterotrophs. Protists live mainly in aquatic habitats.
Phylum Mastigophora flagellates: Trypanosoma
Phylum Ciliophora ciliates: Paramecium, Vorticella
Phylum Sporozoa amoeboid parasites: Balantidium, Plasmodium
Phylum Sarcodina amoeboids: Amoeba, foraminifera, radiolarians
Phylum Euglenophyta flagellate algae: Euglena, Volvox
Phylum Chrysophyta golden algae, diatoms
Phylum Pyrrhophyta fire algae; dinoflagellates: Gonyaulax, Ceratium
Phylum Chlorophyta green algae: sea lettuce, Spirogyra
Phylum Phaeophyta brown algae: kelps
Phylum Rhodophyta red algae: Porphyra
Phylum Myxomycota acellular slime molds: Physarum

Kingdom Fungi One-celled and multicellular heterotrophs with cell walls made of chitin. They reproduce asexually by spores and sexually by conjugation.
Division Zygomycota bread molds: Rhizopus
Division Ascomycota sac fungi: morels, truffles, yeasts
Division Basidiomycota club fungi: bracket fungi, mushrooms, puffballs, rusts
Division Mycomycota fungi that appear in lichens, in symbiotic relationships with algae

Kingdom Plantae Multicellular autotrophs that carry out photosynthesis. Cells contain a large central vacuole and have walls made of cellulose. Most species live in terrestrial habitats.
Division Bryophyta hornworts, liverworts, mosses
Division Lycopodiophyta club mosses, quillworts, spike mosses
Division Sphenophyta horsetails: Equisetum
Division Filicophyta ferns
Division Cycadophyta cycads
Division Ginkgophyta ginkgo
Division Coniferophyta conifers: cypresses, pines, redwoods, yews
Division Anthophyta angiosperms: flowering plants
- **Class Monocotyledoneae** monocots (have a single cotyledon, or seed leaf): grasses, irises, lilies, onions, orchids, palms
- **Class Dicotyledoneae** dicots (two cotyledons): apples, cacti, carrots, geraniums, legumes, maples, mints, oaks, poppies, roses, sunflowers

Kingdom Animalia Multicellular heterotrophs. The cells do not have cell walls.
Phylum Porifera sponges
Phylum Cnidaria coelenterates
- **Class Hydrozoa** hydroids: Hydra
- **Class Scyphozoa** jellyfish: Aurelia, Cassiopaea
- **Class Anthozoa** corals, sea anemones

Phylum Ctenophora comb jellies, sea gooseberries
Phylum Platyhelminthes flatworms
- **Class Turbellaria** turbellarians: planarians (Dugesia)
- **Class Trematoda** flukes: Clonorchis, Fasciola, Schistosoma
- **Class Cestoda** tapeworms: Diphyllobothrium, Taenia

Phylum Nematoda roundworms: Ascaris, Trichinella
Phylum Rotifera rotifers: Philodina
Phylum Bryozoa moss animals
Phylum Brachiopoda lamp shells: Hemithyris, Lingula
Phylum Nemertea ribbon worms: Baseodiscus, Lineus
Phylum Phoronida horseshoe worms: Phoronis

Major Taxons, with Representative Species (continued)

Phylum Annelida segmented worms
Class Polychaeta bristleworms: Eunice, Nereis
Class Oligochaeta earthworms: Lumbricus
Class Hirudinea leeches: Hirudo
Phylum Onychophora velvetworms: Peripatopsis, Peripatus
Phylum Mollusca mollusks; the soft body usually is enclosed in a hard shell secreted by a tissue called the mantle.
Class Polyplacophora chitons: Callistoplax, Chiton
Class Bivalvia bivalves: clams, mussels, oysters, scallops
Class Scaphopoda tusk shells: Cadalus, Dentalium
Class Gastropoda nudibranchs, slugs, snails
Class Cephalopoda nautiluses, octopuses, squids
Phylum Arthropoda arthropods
Class Merostomata horseshoe crabs: Limulus
Class Crustacea barnacles, crabs, lobsters, shrimps
Class Arachnida harvestmen, mites, scorpions, spiders, ticks
Class Chilopoda centipedes: Geophilus, Lithobius
Class Diplopoda millipedes: Glomeridesmus, Hirudisoma
Class Insecta insects: ants, bees, beetles, bristletails, butterflies, dragonflies, flies, grasshoppers, mayflies, silverfish, springtails, termites
Phylum Tardigrada water bears: Echiniscus
Phylum Chaetognatha arrowworms: Ferosagitta, Mesosagattia
Phylum Echinodermata echinoderms
Class Crinoidea feather stars, sea lilies
Class Asteroidea sea stars (starfish)
Class Ophiuroidea basket stars, brittle stars
Class Echinoidea heart urchins, sand dollars, sea urchins
Class Holothuroidea sea cucumbers
Phylum Hemichordata acorn worms
Phylum Chordata
Subphylum Urochordata tunicates: sea squirts
Subphylum Cephalochordata lancelets
Subphylum Vertebrata vertebrates
Class Agnatha jawless fish: hagfish, lampreys
Class Chondrichthyes cartilaginous fish: rays, sharks, skates
Class Osteichthyes bony fish: bass, eels, salmon, seahorses, trout, tuna
Class Amphibia amphibians
Order Gymnophiona caecilians
Order Caudata newts, salamanders
Order Anura frogs, toads
Class Reptilia reptiles
Order Chelonia tortoises, turtles
Order Crocodylia alligators, caimans, crocodiles, gavial
Order Rhynchocephalia tuataras
Order Squamata lizards, snakes
Class Aves birds
Order Struthioniformes ostriches
Order Rheiformes rheas
Order Casuariiformes cassowaries, emus
Order Apterygiformes kiwis
Order Tinamiformes tinamous
Order Sphenisciformes penguins
Order Gaviiformes divers, loons
Order Podicipediformes grebes
Order Procellariiformes albatrosses, fulmars, petrels, shearwaters
Order Pelecaniformes anhingas, boobies, cormorants, frigatebirds, pelicans
Order Ciconiiformes bitterns, herons, ibises, spoonbills, storks
Order Phoenicopteriformes flamingos
Order Anseriformes ducks, geese, screamers, swans
Order Falconiformes birds of prey: condors, falcons, hawks, osprey, vultures
Order Galliformes fowl: curassows, grouse, hoatzins, pheasants, quail, turkeys
Order Gruiformes bustards, coots, cranes, hemipodes, rails
Order Charadriiformes auks, gulls, jacanas, murres, plovers, puffins, stilts, terns
Order Columbiformes doves, pigeons, sandgrouse
Order Psittaciformes cockatoos, lories, parakeets, parrots
Order Cuculiformes cuckoos, roadrunners, turacos
Order Strigiformes owls
Order Caprimulgiformes goatsuckers, nighthawks, nightjars, poorwills, potoos
Order Apodiformes hummingbirds, swifts
Order Coliiformes colies, mousebirds
Order Trogoniformes quetzals, trogons
Order Coraciiformes bee-eaters, hoopoes, hornbills, kingfishers, motmots, rollers
Order Piciformes barbets, honeyguides, jacamars, puffbirds, toucans, woodpeckers
Order Passeriformes perching birds: blackbirds, chickadees, finches, jays, larks, mockingbirds, nuthatches, sparrows, swallows, thrushes, tits, warblers, wrens
Class Mammalia mammals
Order Monotremata echidnas, platypuses
Order Marsupialia marsupials: bandicoots, kangaroos, koalas, numbats, opossums, wallabies, wombats
Order Insectivora insectivores: moles, shrews, solenodons, tenrecs
Order Dermoptera flying lemurs
Order Chiroptera bats
Order Primates primates: chimpanzees, gorillas, humans, lemurs, monkeys, tarsiers
Order Endentata edentates: anteaters, armadillos, sloths
Order Pholidota pangolins
Order Lagomorpha hares, pikas, rabbits
Order Rodentia rodents: beavers, capybara, chinchillas, hamsters, mice, muskrats, porcupines, rats, prairie dogs, squirrels
Order Cetacea dolphins, porpoises, whales
Order Carnivora carnivores: bears, cats, dogs, foxes, hyenas, mongooses, otters, raccoons, skunks, weasels
Order Pinnipedia seals, sea lions, walruses
Order Tubulidentata aardvarks
Order Proboscidea elephants
Order Hyracoidea hyraxes
Order Sirenia dugongs, manatee
Order Perissodactyla odd-toed hoofed mammals: horses, rhinoceroses, zebras
Order Artiodactyla even-toed hoofed mammals: antelopes, buffaloes, camels, cattle, deer, giraffes, goats, hippopotamuses, pigs, sheep

Homeostasis and Enzymes

If the internal environment of a cell (or an organism as a whole) changes significantly, the cell dies. Thus, it is important that a cell maintains homeostasis: a relatively stable internal environment regardless of changes in the external environment.

Cells perform many metabolic reactions to maintain homeostasis. Proteins called enzymes act as catalysts of these reactions. Enzymes are very specific; many catalyze only a single reaction whereas others are able to catalyze a few closely related reactions. Some enzymes break compounds into smaller molecules. Others act to combine small molecules into a larger molecule. In either process, the enzymes are neither changed nor destroyed; they can be reused again and again.

If temperature, acidity, or other environmental conditions vary outside a narrow range, the rate of a catalytic reaction is affected. For instance, in humans, the optimal temperature for catalytic reactions is normal body temperature, approximately 98.6° F. If body temperature gets too cold, enzymes are unable to bind to molecules quickly enough and the rate of the reaction will decrease, possibly to levels that cannot sustain life. If body temperature rises too high, the heat causes enzymes to denature and lose their catalytic ability.

Cell Transport

Cells obtain nutrients and other needed materials from their environment, and excrete wastes and other substances into the environment. These materials must move through the cell membrane, which is selectively permeable; that is, it controls the passage of materials between the cell and its environment, allowing some substances in while keeping others out. Two basic methods transport materials through the membrane.

Passive transport, including diffusion and osmosis, requires no energy. Small molecules such as oxygen, carbon dioxide, and water plus ions such as those of sodium and calcium pass freely across the membrane, from an area of

Additional Specialized Cell Structures

Organelle	Description	Function
Cell wall	Rigid structure exterior to the cell membrane; found in most organisms other than animals	Protection, support
Chloroplast	Contains chlorophyll, a pigment needed for photosynthesis; present in plants and protists called algae	Site of photosynthesis
Cilium	Hairlike projection; common in archaea, bacteria, protists, and animals	Locomotion (single-celled organisms), movement of cells or materials (multicellular organisms)
Endoplasmic reticulum (ER)	Extensive network of convoluted membranes; found in protists, fungi, plants, and animals	Rough ER helps synthesize proteins and lipids; smooth ER metabolizes carbohydrates and lipids, stores calcium, and breaks down poisons
Flagellum	Whiplike projections; found in archaea, bacteria, protists, and animals	Locomotion (single-celled organisms), movement of materials (multicellular organisms)
Golgi body	Stack of flattened, membrane-bound sacs; found in most protists, fungi, plants, and animals	Modifies food molecules manufactured in the ER
Mitochondrion	Oblong, with highly folded interior; present in protists, fungi, plants, and animals	Site of cell respiration
Nucleus	Central structure surrounded by a membrane; largest organelle in a cell; present in protists, fungi, plants, and animals	Contains the genetic material DNA, which directs operations of the cell, including cell division
Vacuole	Found in some animals; common in protists, fungi, and plants.	Storage of food or water

higher concentration to an area of lower concentration.

Active transport moves substances from an area of low concentration to an area of high concentration. The cell must expend energy for active transport. For example, in a process called endocytosis, human white blood cells engulf harmful invaders, which it then destroys. In a reverse process, exocytosis, a cell can expel large waste molecules. Another type of active transport relies on membrane proteins called pumps. They capture molecules from one side of the membrane and release them on the other side.

Cell Division

Cells create new cells in a process known as cell division. The two basic types of cell division, which differ in their end results, are mitosis and meiosis.

Mitosis Mitosis results in two new daughter cells that are structurally and functionally like the parent cell, with exactly the same chromosome material. In amoebas and other one-celled protists, mitosis is a form of asexual reproduction, producing new organisms and thereby increasing the population. In animals and other many-celled organisms, mitosis results in growth and in the replacement of dead and injured cells.

The cells in these organisms are diploid: that is they contain a double set of chromosomes (2n). For example, muscle, skin, and other body cells of a human contain 46 chromosomes each arranged in 23 pairs. During a series of mitotic phases, these chromosomes are duplicated (4n). The two double sets of chromosomes move to opposite sides of the parent cell and the parent cell cleaves along its center, forming two diploid (2n) cells.

Meiosis In a series of phases somewhat different from those of mitosis, meiosis produces reproductive cells, or gametes, that are not exact copies of the parent cell. Most importantly, they are haploid (n), containing only one chromosome of each pair found in the parent cell. For example, human eggs and sperm each contain 23 chromosomes. When a sperm (n) unites with an egg (n), the result is a fertilized egg that is diploid (2n).

Types of Cells and Tissues All cells carry on fundamental activities such as cellular respiration. However, the cells that make up a multicellular organism are specialized to perform specific functions for the whole organism. For example, in humans nerve cells are specialized for coordinating body activities whereas red blood cells are designed to carry oxygen.

Specialized cells are organized in groups called tissues, which perform a common task. Muscle cells form muscle tissue, which causes movement; nerve cells form nerve tissue, and so on.

In turn, various kinds of tissues are bound together to form a unit known as an organ, which accomplishes more complex tasks. Your stomach, for example, contains muscle tissue that helps churn food and other tissues that manufacture acids and enzymes necessary to digest the food. Organs are further organized into organ systems, such as the digestive system of an animal or the root system of a tree. Some organs function in more than one system; for example, some cells in the liver manufacture a chemical used in digestion and other cells have an excretory function. Most important, all the systems work together to maintain the organism's homeostasis.

The Human Body

Like other animals, a human begins from a single cell, the fertilized egg. By the time the human reaches adulthood, the body consists of some 100 trillion cells. Each is part of an organ system designed to perform essential life functions.

The Circulatory System

This system transports useful materials to every cell in the body and carries wastes away from the cells. It has three parts: blood, a heart, and blood vessels.

Blood An average adult contains 5 to 6 quarts of blood, a fluid tissue that carries materials throughout the body. The blood consists of plasma, a yellowish liquid containing dissolved substances such as salts and proteins, and three types of cells or cell fragments: red blood cells, white blood cells, and platelets.

Red blood cells (RBCs), or erythrocytes, are the most numerous type of blood cell; a normal adult has about 25 billion RBCs. Produced in the bone marrow, they differ from other cells in that they do not have nuclei as adults. RBCs contain hemoglobin, a reddish protein-iron compound that binds to oxygen during circulation through the lungs, then releases the oxygen to cells elsewhere in the body.

White blood cells (WBCs), or leukocytes, also manufactured in the bone marrow, are larger than RBCs and have nuclei. They help protect the body from bacteria and other disease-causing organisms. They are an important part of the immune system, described below.

Platelets are colorless cell fragments produced in the bone marrow and involved in clotting. When a blood vessel is cut or broken, the damaged tissue sends out a chemical signal that causes platelets to aggregate at that location. The platelets secrete an enzyme that starts the clotting process. The end result is a clot that prevents blood from leaking out of the vessel. Over time, the tissue repairs itself and the clot dissolves.

The Heart The human heart is a large muscular organ with four chambers. Two small, thin-walled chambers called atria at the top of the heart receive blood from the veins, then move the blood to the lower chambers of the heart. These are large, thick-walled chambers called ventricles, which pump blood to the body cells through arteries. Between the atria and ventricles lie valves, flaps of tissue that maintain blood flow in one direction.

Circulation The left and right sides of the heart act independently, as two separate pumps. Blood from body cells flows through the vena cava to the right atrium. This blood is rich in carbon dioxide and deficient in oxygen. It flows into the left ventricle, which pumps it through the pulmonary artery to the lungs. Here, carbon dioxide is excreted and oxygen is absorbed into the blood.

The oxygen-rich blood flows through the pulmonary vein to the left atrium and then into the left ventricle. When the ventricle contracts, the blood is pumped through the body's largest artery, the aorta, to the rest of the body cells—including, via coronary arteries, cells that make up the heart's own muscles.

To keep blood flowing properly, the atria and ventricles must alternately contract and relax at precisely the correct time. A signal to contract originates from a group of cells in the right atrium called the sinoatrial node. The signal first reaches the atria and they contract, moving blood into the ventricles. The signal then reaches another group of cells in the right atrium called the atrioventricular node, which relays the signal to the ventricles and causes them to contract, forcing the blood out of the heart. After this wave of contractions, the heart muscles relax and blood again fills the atria.

The period when heart muscles contract is called systole; the period of relaxation is diastole. When doctors measure blood pressure, they report both values, with the pressure during systole higher than that during diastole. Normal blood pressure is 120/80.

Blood vessels The human circulatory system is a closed system, meaning that blood never leaves the network of blood vessels, which consists of arteries, veins, and capillaries.

Arteries carry blood away from the heart. Because they receive a large volume of blood from the heart under very high pressure, the arteries have thick, muscular walls that allow them to expand during systole and contract during diastole. This rhythmic expansion and contraction of arteries is a person's pulse, and can be used to measure the number of times the heart contracts each minute.

Veins carry blood toward the heart. The blood has traveled a significant distance since being pumped from the heart; therefore, pressure in the veins is much lower than in arteries. For this reason, veins have much thinner walls than arteries. However, because the pressure is low, there is a risk that blood might flow backward when the heart relaxes. To prevent such backflow, veins contain valves, similar in purpose to the valves in the heart. In addition, veins are sometimes embedded in skeletal muscle, such as the thigh, so that as the muscle contracts, it squeezes the veins and assists in moving the blood back to the heart.

As blood travels from the heart, the arteries that carry it branch from one another and get progressively smaller as they spread to all parts of the body. Eventually the smallest arteries attach to microscopic capillaries. Every cell is located in close proximity to a capillary.

Capillary walls are only one cell thick, allowing materials to diffuse into and out of the blood. Materials move from the blood into intercellular space, the space between cells, which contains intercellular fluid—the cells' aqueous environment. From this fluid, cells absorb vital gases and nutrients and deposit metabolic wastes, which are picked up by the blood. At their distal end, capillaries connect to tiny veins, which join to form progressively larger veins that return the blood to the heart.

The Immune System

This system protects the body from invaders, such as viruses and bacteria. The system includes the lymphatic system and various white blood cells (WBCs).

Lymphatic system The lymphatic system has a network of vessels that drain intracellular fluid from the intracellular space and return it to the blood. The lymph vessels are not connected to the heart and do not benefit from its contraction. They, like many veins, are embedded in skeletal muscle and rely on muscle contractions to move the lymphatic fluid (intracellular fluid inside lymph vessels). Also like veins, lymph vessels contain valves that prevent backflow. The lymph vessels deliver the fluid into large veins in the chest, where the fluid again becomes part of the blood.

Connected to lymph vessels are small masses of spongy tissue called lymph nodes, which remove contaminants such as bacteria and dead cells from lymphatic fluid. In addition, the nodes are homes for certain types of WBCs.

White blood cells A healthy human typically has 5,000 to 9,000 WBCs per milliliter of blood. When bacteria or other foreign particles are present, however, WBCs rapidly proliferate. Unlike RBCs, WBCs can move on their own; they frequently pass through the walls of blood vessels and go into intercellular space and the lymphatic system in search of invaders.

Most WBCs are granulocytes. These are phagocytes ("eating cells"), moving like amoebas to surround and engulf foreign particles. Monocytes, the smallest group of WBCs, move out of blood and into intercellular space whenever an infection develops. There they turn into phagocytic macrophages and destroy invaders. Monocytes also destroy worn-out RBCs.

Lymphocytes are WBCs more common in the lymph system than in the blood. There are two classes: T cells and B cells. Helper T cells and suppressor T cells regulate the immune response, including the activities of B cells. Killer T cells kill cells they attack, such as body cells infected with viruses. B cells produce antibodies, highly specific proteins secreted in response to foreign chemicals called antigens, such as protein molecules on the surface of bacteria. The antibodies bind to and inactivate the antigens. Some B cells, called memory cells, have learned to recognize a specific invader and patrol the body to defend against it. If the invader reappears, the memory cells trigger a massive defense. This reaction protects a person from getting certain diseases more than once, and is the basis of vaccination against disease.

The Respiratory System

This system obtains oxygen from the environment and gets rid of carbon dioxide and water vapor. Its function can be divided into two parts: breathing, which carries air into and out of the lungs; and gas exchange, during which the blood trades carbon dioxide and water vapor for oxygen.

Drawing air into the lungs from the environment—a process called inhalation—begins with a signal that travels from the respiratory center of the brain to the diaphragm, a dome-shaped muscle that lies beneath the lungs, separating the thoracic (chest) and abdominal cavities. The diaphragm contracts, pushing downward and decreasing the pressure on the lungs, allowing them to inflate. This in turn decreases pressure in the respiratory passages. Air is forced through the nasal passages and mouth and passes through the throat and trachea (windpipe) into the two bronchial tubes that lead to the lungs.

In each lung, the bronchial tube branches into smaller and smaller tubes, ending in millions of tiny air sacs surrounded by capillaries. The air sacs, or alveoli, are the site of gas exchange. Because there is a higher concentration of oxygen in the inhaled air than in the blood in the capillaries, oxygen diffuses from the alveoli into the blood, where RBCs immediately bind it to their hemoglobin molecules. Conversely, concentrations of carbon dioxide and water are higher in the blood than in the air, so these substances diffuse into the alveoli.

As gas exchange is completed, the diaphragm relaxes and moves upward. Pressure on the lungs increases, causing them to deflate and resulting in exhalation—expulsion of air out of the lungs. The air follows the same path it took during inhalation.

The Digestive System

The human digestive system is designed to take in and break down large food molecules into small molecules that can be absorbed into the blood and distributed to the cells of the body.

Organs of the digestive system Two groups of organs are involved in digestion. One group, the gastrointestinal tract, also known as the alimentary canal, begins with the mouth and includes the esophagus, stomach, small intestine, and large intestine. Food enters through the mouth; is digested in the mouth, stomach, and small intestine and is absorbed into the blood from the intestines. Undigested material forms feces, which are expelled through the anus, the distal opening of the tract. Food is pushed down through the tract by muscles in the organ walls. By contracting and relaxing in sequence, the muscles create a wavelike movement called peristalsis. In addition to moving matter through the tract, peristalsis helps mix food with digestive juices.

The second group of digestive organs makes enzymes and other substances needed for digestion, and secretes these substances into the gastrointestinal tract. These accessory organs include the salivary glands, gastric glands, intestinal glands, liver, gallbladder, and pancreas.

The Digestive process Food undergoes both chemical and mechanical digestion. Chemical digestion uses enzymes to change the chemical properties of food so it can be absorbed into the blood. Mechanical digestion breaks food into small pieces, increasing the surface area that enzymes can work on, and thereby speeding the rate of chemical digestion.

Digestion begins in the mouth. Teeth bite, tear, crush, and grind food. Salivary glands secrete saliva into the mouth, which wets the food, making it easier to mechanically digest and swallow. Saliva also contains amylase, an enzyme that chemically breaks down complex starches into sugar molecules.

When a person swallows, food passes into the esophagus and is moved by peristalsis into the stomach. As muscles in the stomach's wall contract and relax, food is churned and broken into even smaller particles. Gastric glands embedded in the stomach walls secrete hydrochloric acid, which kills bacteria in the food; and pepsin, an enzyme that chemically breaks proteins into smaller amino acid chains.

When the proteins have been sufficiently digested, a round muscle at the base of the stomach opens, allowing the food to be pushed into the small intestine. In the duodenum, the upper portion of the small intestine, an alkaline solution secreted by the pancreas neutralizes the stomach acids, preventing damage to intestinal tissues. The pancreas also secretes the enzyme trypsin, which continues to break down protein molecules, plus enzymes that digest lipids and complex carbohydrates. Finally, glands embedded in the intestinal walls secrete enzymes that finish the digestion of proteins and carbohydrates.

In the jejunum and ileum, the middle and lower portions of the small intestine, the walls have millions of tiny fingerlike projects called villi. Fully digested sugars, lipids, and proteins are absorbed into the blood through the walls of the villi.

The large intestine, shorter in length but larger in diameter than the small intestine, serves three important functions. Beneficial bacteria that make the large intestine their home manufacture and secrete vitamins necessary for human metabolism. Vitamins, minerals, and much of the water that was mixed into the food during digestion are absorbed into the blood through the organ's walls. And undigested materials and dead bacteria are stored in the large intestine until it is ready to be excreted.

The Excretory System

As by-products of metabolism, cells create wastes. These wastes must be disposed of before they accumulate to toxic levels. Organs involved in excretion include the lungs, which, as mentioned above, excrete carbon dioxide and water vapor; and the skin, liver, and urinary system.

The skin One waste product of metabolism is heat energy. To dissipate excess heat, the body takes advantage of the large surface area of the skin—the body's largest organ, accounting for about 12 percent of a person's weight. As blood flows through vast numbers of capillaries just under the skin's surface, heat is transferred from the blood to the skin and eventually to the environment. During periods of exertion, when more heat than normal is generated, glands in the skin produce sweat, a solution of salts and water, to expedite heat transfer. The sweat absorbs large amounts of heat energy and evaporates, releasing that heat into the environment.

The liver The liver is the largest internal organ in the human body, weighing an average of 55 ounces (1,560 grams). In addition to other vital functions, it performs two excretory functions. It produces enzymes that detoxify the blood, breaking down alcohol and other harmful substances into inactive or less toxic compounds. The liver also breaks down excess amino acids, forming urea. These breakdown materials are carried by the blood to the kidneys for excretion.

The Urinary System

This system removes wastes from the blood and excretes them into the environment. The system's pivotal organs are the two kidneys, bean-shaped structures at the back of the upper abdomen. Each kidney has about a million nephrons, microscopic structures where water, urea, salts, and other substances diffuse out of the blood. Substances needed by the body are reabsorbed by the blood. The remaining materials form urine. The urine produced in each kidney empties into a ureter, a tube that carries the fluid to the urinary bladder. This muscular sac stores the urine until it is excreted through a tube called the urethra.

The Musculoskeletal System

Skeletal muscles and bones work together to perform functions such as support, protection, and locomotion.

Bones The body contains 206 bones. The longest is the thighbone, or femur, which grows to an average length of 19.88 inches (50.5 centimeters). The smallest is the stapes, the innermost of three tiny bones in the middle ear, only 0.07 inch (1.8 millimeter) long. Bones give the body its shape and support and protect various organs. For example, the skull protects the brain, and the rib cage prevents lung and heart damage.

Bones are made from cells that secrete long, strong fibers of a protein called collagen. These fibers are reinforced by calcium and phosphorous deposits, which make bone hard and able to support large amounts of weight. The long bones, such as those in the arms and legs, have hollow spaces that are filled with bone marrow. Part of this bone marrow manufactures blood cells.

Muscles Muscles generate movement. Skeletal muscles, numbering about 700, are considered to be voluntary muscles. Their movement requires signals from the nervous system, but the person can usually control the signals and hence the movement, whether it involves bending a leg, raising the eyebrows, or moving the fingers over the keys of a piano.

In addition to the voluntary muscles that are part of the musculoskeletal system, the body contains cardiac and visceral muscles. Cardiac muscle, found exclusively in the heart, is unique in that it does not require signals from the brain to contract and relax; it generates its own signals from cells within the heart. Visceral, or smooth, muscles are found in the stomach, diaphragm, intestines, arterial walls, and other internal organs. Like cardiac muscle, they are involuntary; however, their function is regulated by a part of the brain called the medulla oblongata.

Movement Movement of the skeleton occurs at a joint, where two bones meet. Tough elastic connective tissue called a ligament connects the two bones. The ends of the bones are covered with pads of flexible tissue called cartilage, which acts as a cushion, preventing damage to the bones as they rub against each other during movement. A slippery fluid also is present to lubricate the joint.

Skeletal muscle is anchored to a bone by tough connective tissue called a tendon. Because skeletal muscles cause movement only when they contract, they are present in pairs that allow opposite movement. For example, the biceps muscle on the upper side of the arm pulls the forearm toward the upper arm when it contracts, making the arm bend. To straighten the arm, the triceps on the underside of the upper arm contracts.

The Nervous System

This system controls body functions, telling structures what to do and when to do it. The nervous system monitors the internal and external environment and coordinates responses to changes. Its overriding objective is to maintain the stable state called homeostasis.

Neurons The nervous system is made up of neurons, cells that transmit electrochemical signals throughout the body. Sensory neurons receive information—changes in light, pressure on the skin, arterial blood volume, and so on—and carry the information to the brain or spinal cord. Interneurons, located in the brain and spinal cord, act as bridges, transmitting impulses from sensory neurons to motor neurons. Motor neurons carry instructions to tissues and effect change, such as causing a hand to jerk away from a hot stove or causing an eye to blink.

Although they differ greatly in shape and size, neurons typically have three main parts. The cell body contains the nucleus and carries out most metabolic processes. Branched projections called dendrites receive impulses from other cells and carry them toward the cell body. The axon conducts impulses away from the cell body.

Neurons that function in a particular area are often bundled together. These bundles are called nerves. The longest human nerve is the sciatic nerve, which extends along the back of the leg from the buttocks to the ankle; some of its branches measure more than 3.3 feet (1 meter) in length.

Signal transmission The terminal branches of an axon do not actually touch the dendrites of another neuron. Rather, the two cells are separated by a tiny space called the synapse.

Within a neuron, a signal is transmitted electrically, through the movement of positively charged ions. At a synapse, neurons must rely on chemical rather than electrical signals. Chemicals called neurotransmitters are synthesized by a neuron and released to transmit a signal to specific receptors on the receiving cell. Several dozen substances that can act as neurotransmitters have been identified, each with different functions. For example, acetylcholine is released from the tips of motor neurons and is responsible for moving skeletal muscles. Serotonin, produced in the brain and spinal cord, is believed to play an inhibitory role in sleep.

Parts of the nervous system The nervous system has two main parts. The central nervous system consists of the brain and spinal cord. The latter is a hollow cylinder of nerve tissue within the backbone. It is connected to muscles, glands, and other body parts by 31 pairs of spinal nerves.

The peripheral nervous system includes all neurons outside of the brain and spinal cord. It can be subdivided into the somatic nervous system, over which we have voluntary control; and the autonomic nervous system, which serves muscles—such as those of the diaphragm and bladder—that generally are not under our voluntary control. The autonomic nervous system also controls glands and their release of chemicals.

The brain The brain weighs about 3 pounds (1.4 kilograms) and consists of two types of cells: about 100 billion neurons and ten to fifty times that many glial cells, which surround the neurons and provide support and electrical insulation. The brain has seven major regions, of which the largest are the cerebrum, cerebellum, and medulla oblongata.

The largest portion of the human brain is the cerebrum, which is separated by a long fissure into right and left hemispheres. The cerebrum interprets sensory impulses it receives from the eyes and other sense organs. It is responsible for consciousness, language, memory, thinking, and personality. It also controls the movement of voluntary muscles.

The cerebellum, located below the posterior part of the cerebrum, regulates body movements, muscle coordination, and balance. It helps us repeat learned movements such as playing a trumpet or swinging a baseball bat.

The medulla oblongata, the lowermost portion of the brain, is connected to the spinal cord. It controls involuntary activities such as breathing, heartbeat, and swallowing.

The sense organs These structures gather information about the external environment and send the information to the central nervous system, which processes the information and determines a response. The organs include the ears, which detect sounds; the eyes, which detect light radiation; receptors in the nasal cavities of the nose, which detect smell; receptors in the skin that detect pressure; and taste buds, which detect chemicals in food. Other sense organs detect body position and temperature.

The Endocrine System

Working closely with the nervous system is the endocrine system, which is composed of glands that produce and secrete hormones, compounds that help coordinate and regulate body activities. Hormones are secreted directly into the blood. Although the blood carries them to every cell in the body, only certain cells have the appropriate receptor proteins on their outer membrane to allow the hormones to activate a change.

Some glands, such as the pituitary, serve only an endocrine function. Others, such as the pancreas, have additional functions. Also, organs such as the heart, liver, and kidneys contain tissues that secrete hormones.

Controlling secretion Hormone secretion is primarily controlled by a feedback mechanism in which the secretion is controlled by another factor. An example is the maintenance of sugar levels in the blood. As we consume food, our blood sugar level rises. In response, the pancreas secretes insulin, which lowers the blood sugar level. As a result of the decrease, the pancreas stops secreting insulin.

A more complex feedback mechanism is involved in control of cellular metabolism. The pituitary releases thyroid-stimulating hormone (TSH) in response to decreased metabolic levels. TSH stimulates the thyroid to increase secretion of thyroxine. Thyroxine stimulates metabolism but also inhibits the pituitary from releasing TSH. As TSH levels drop, the thyroid decreases its secretion of thyroxine and the metabolic rate in cells is again altered.

Reproductive Systems

The male and female reproductive systems produce gametes, or sex cells—eggs in females, sperm in males. The male system is designed to deliver sperm into the female's system, where under proper conditions an egg and sperm unite, forming a zygote, or fertilized egg, that contains all the genetic material needed to develop into a new human being. The female's reproductive system also provides the environment in which the fertilized egg develops over a period of about nine months into an infant ready to be born.

Male reproductive system The main organs are two testes that lie in the scrotum, a sac of skin outside the lower abdomen. Beginning during puberty, the testes produce the hormone testosterone. This initiates sperm production within the testes, in a vast network of seminiferous tubules. Testosterone also is responsible for the develop-

How Does the Brain Work?

By SANDRA BLAKESLEE

In the continuing effort to understand the human brain, the mysteries keep piling up. Consider what scientists are up against. Stretched flat, the human neocortex—the center of our higher mental functions—is about the size and thickness of a formal dinner napkin. With 100 billion cells, each with 1,000 to 10,000 synapses, the neocortex makes roughly 100 trillion connections and contains 300 million feet of wiring packed with other tissue into a one-and-a-half-quart volume in the brain.

These cells are arranged in six very similar layers, inviting confusion. Within these layers, different regions carry out vision, hearing, touch, the sense of balance, movement, emotional responses and every other feat of cognition. More mysterious yet, there are 10 times as many feedback connections—from the neocortex to lower levels of the brain—as there are feedforward or bottom-up connections.

Added to these mysteries is the lack of a good framework for understanding the brain's connectivity and electrochemistry. Researchers do not know how the six-layered cortical sheet gives rise to the sense of self. They have not been able to disentangle the role of genes and experience in shaping brains. They do not know how the firing of billions of loosely coupled neurons gives rise to coordinated, goal-directed behavior. They can see trees but no forest.

They do think they have solved one long-standing mystery, though. Most neuroscientists are convinced the mind is in no way separate from the brain. In the brain they have found a physical basis for all our thoughts, aspirations, language, sense of consciousness, moral beliefs and everything else that makes us human. All of this arises from interactions among billions of ordinary cells. Neuroscience finds no duality, no finger of God animating the human mind.

So what have neuroscientists been doing? Like a child who takes apart his father's watch, they have dissected the brain and now have almost all the pieces laid out before them. There are thousands of clues about what makes the brain tick.

But how to put it back together? How to understand something so complex by examining it piecemeal? Even harder, how to integrate the different levels of analysis? Some brain events occur in fractions of milliseconds while others, like long-term memory formation, can take days or weeks. One can study molecules, ion channels, single neurons, functional areas, circuits, oscillations and chemistry. There are neural stem cells and mechanisms of plasticity, which involve how the brain changes with experience or recovers from injury.

New research tools continue to drive progress. In the late 1970's, researchers mostly placed sharp-tipped electrodes into single cells and measured firing patterns. By the 1990's, they had machines that could take images of brain activity while people spoke, read, gambled, solved moral dilemmas or, as in a recent study, had orgasms.

Unfortunately, studies like these, while fascinating, tend to feed the fires of a huge disagreement within the brain sciences; is the brain made up of discrete modules that pass information among themselves? Or is it more loosely organized so that varied pockets of distant neurons fire together when called upon to perform a particular task? In mapping the brain, some researchers say that areas dedicated to aspects of language, arm movements or face recognition are hard-wired modules.

Other researchers say that such areas are surprisingly flexible. For example, the human face recognition area is where expert bird watchers distinguish features of closely related species or car experts decide if a 1958 or 1959 Plymouth had bigger fins.

While the two sides in this debate agree that the brain is prewired to some degree at birth, the nature of that prewiring is uncertain. What do genes expressed in the brain do? How do genes influence behavior? What is innate and what is flexible? What is the role of culture in shaping a brain?

One of the most exciting developments is the recent exploration of the frontal lobes. Located behind the forehead, the frontal lobes help create the social brain, melding emotions, cognition, error detection, the body, volition and an autobiographical sense of self. Special circuits containing spindle cells appear to broadcast messages—this feels right, this does not feel right—to the rest of the brain. Researchers are finding that emotions arise from body states as well as brain states, confirming that the supposed distinction between mind and body is illusory.

Others are delving into individual differences. What makes one person empathic, another mean or shy or articulate or musical? How do genes relate to temperament and how is a baby's brain constructed from early experience? Specialized cells called mirror neurons seem to help babies imitate the world to learn gestures, facial expressions, language and feelings.

Brain chemistry is no longer the study of neuromodulators as "juices" that make us feel good or awake. Substances like serotonin, dopamine and norepinephrine play crucial roles in learning, updating memories and neuropsychiatric disease.

The question of free will is on the table. Some of our behavior is conscious, but most of it is notoriously unconscious. So although we make choices, is free will mostly an illusion? And what is consciousness? In seeking an explanation, a new mystery has emerged. Many scientists now believe that the brain basically works by simulating reality. The sights, sounds and touches that flow into the brain are put in the framework of what the brain expects on the basis of previous experience and memory.

In the words of many neuroscientists, all these mysteries are terrific job security.

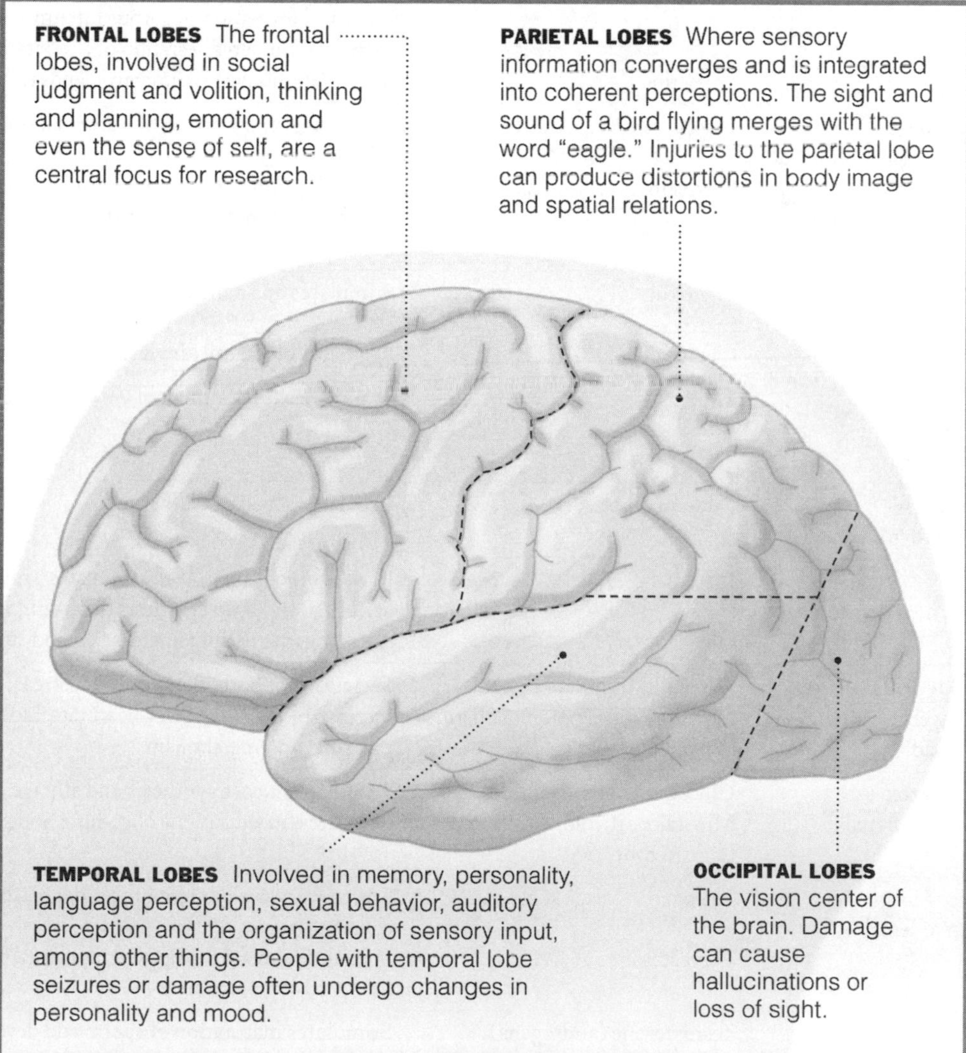

FRONTAL LOBES The frontal lobes, involved in social judgment and volition, thinking and planning, emotion and even the sense of self, are a central focus for research.
PARIETAL LOBES Where sensory information converges and is integrated into coherent perceptions. The sight and sound of a bird flying merges with the word "eagle." Injuries to the parietal lobe can produce distortions in body image and spatial relations.
TEMPORAL LOBES Involved in memory, personality, language perception, sexual behavior, auditory perception and the organization of sensory input, among other things. People with temporal lobe seizures or damage often undergo changes in personality and mood.
OCCIPITAL LOBES The vision center of the brain. Damage can cause hallucinations or loss of sight.

The New York Times

Endocrine Glands and Their Secretions

Gland and Its Location	Hormones	Major Effects
Pituitary: anterior lobe at the base of the brain	Growth hormone	Stimulates cell growth and division by prompting protein synthesis.
	Thyroid-stimulating hormone (TSH)	Stimulates thyroid to produce thyroxine.
	Adrenocorticotropic hormone (ACTH)	Stimulates adrenal cortex to secrete hormones.
	Follicle-stimulating hormone (FSH)	In female: stimulates follicle development in ovaries and secretion of estrogen. In male: stimulates sperm production.
	Luteinizing hormone (LH)	In female: stimulates discharge of mature egg from ovary and formation of corpus luteum. In male: stimulates secretion of testosterone.
	Prolactin	In female: stimulates mammary glands to secrete milk.
Hypothalamus Part of the brain (its hormones are stored in the pituitary until secreted into the bloodstream)	Vasopressin	Stimulates reabsorption of water in kidneys.
	Oxytocin	In female: stimulates uterine contractions during childbirth; stimulates mammary glands to produce milk.
Thyroid In neck, wrapped around the trachea	Thyroxin	Stimulates and controls metabolic rate.
	Calcitonin	Regulates blood calcium levels.
Thymus Under the breastbone just above the heart	Thymosin	Stimulates development of white blood cells.
Parathyroids Embedded in thyroid gland	Parathormone	Regulates blood calcium level.
Pancreas In abdomen, near the stomach	Insulin	Lowers blood sugar level; stimulates protein, glycogen, and lipid synthesis in certain cells.
	Glucagon	Antagonist to insulin: increases blood sugar level.
Adrenals: Medulla Innermost layers of adrenal, located atop kidneys	Adrenaline (epinephrine) and Noradrenaline (norepinepherine)	Secretions of both increase under stress; they increase blood sugar level, heart rate, blood pressure, and metabolism.
Adrenals: Cortex Outer layers of adrenals	Glucocorticoids	Stimulate glucose synthesis and storage.
	Mineralocorticoids (aldosterone)	Regulate concentrations of sodium and potassium.
Ovaries In abdomen of females	Estrogen	Stimulates development of secondary sex characteristics.
	Progesterone	Stimulates breast development; maintains uterine lining during pregnancy.
Testes In scrotum of males	Testosterone (androgens)	Stimulates maturation of sperm and development of secondary sex characteristics.

ment of facial hair, increased muscle mass, and other secondary sex characteristics of men. Atop each testis is the epididymis, where sperm mature and are stored.

The penis is designed for delivering sperm inside the female reproductive system. It contains spongy tissue that can fill with blood, causing the penis to become erect. It also contains the urethra, a tube that carries semen—a mixture of sperm and fluids—out of the body during waves of muscle contraction called ejaculation.

During ejaculation, millions of sperm leave the epididymis through the vas deferens, tubes that carry them to the urethra. Almost simultaneously, accessory organs release fluids into the urethra. These fluids provide a medium in which the sperm can swim through the female reproductive system, plus sugar, which nourishes the sperm.

Female reproductive system Eggs are produced in the two ovaries. Beginning at puberty the ovaries also produce the hormone estrogen, which stimulates development of breasts, growth of genital hair, and other secondary sex characteristics of women.

Each immature egg, or ovum, is contained in a separate follicle in the ovary. During the menstrual cycle, one egg matures and its follicle ruptures, releasing the egg into the fallopian, or uterine, tube. The egg travels through the tube to the uterus (sometimes called the womb), a muscular organ capable of changing shape and dilating. It is here that an embryo develops into a fetus. When fully developed, the fetus is pushed from the uterus through a muscular tube, the vagina, to the outside.

Menstrual cycle The female reproductive system prepares itself for pregnancy on a regular cycle called the menstrual cycle. The cycle begins at puberty and continues until about age 50, when the cycle ceases, a stage called menopause.

The menstrual cycle lasts about 28 days, its stages regulated by a variety of hormones. In the first stage, the walls of the uterus thicken with blood vessels, preparing it to nourish an embryo. About a week later, a follicle in one of the ovaries bursts, releasing an egg into the fallopian tube. The egg travels toward the uterus, where the lining continues to thicken.

If the egg isn't fertilized, the uterine lining begins to break down and slough off the blood vessels constructed during earlier stages of the cycle. This tissue passes out of the body through the vagina, constituting the characteristic menstrual flow.

Fertilization and embryo development As an egg travels through the fallopian tube, it may meet and be fertilized by a sperm. The menstrual cycle then ceases. About seven days after fertilization, the fertilized egg has divided numerous times and developed into a young embryo. The embryo implants itself in the uterine wall, where it will reside and grow until birth.

One section of the young embryo forms a network of blood vessels similar to those in the thickened uterine wall. The two sets of blood vessels—one from the embryo, the other from the mother—form the placenta, a temporary organ that allows materials such as nutrients and wastes to move from one set of vessels to the other. Basically, the placenta acts as the embryo's organs of respiration, digestion, and excretion.

After approximately two months, most major organ systems have begun to form in the embryo and it takes on a human appearance. Now called a fetus, it is about 1 inch (2.5 centimeters) long and weighs about 0.035 ounce (1 gram). Between now and birth it will grow to 14 to 21 inches (35 to 50 centimeters) in length and increase in weight to 106 to 140 ounces (3,000 to 4,000 grams).

Evolution

Evolution is the change in organisms from generation to generation. Modern evolutionary theory states that the millions of different kinds of organisms on Earth today did not come into existence in their present form but descended from earlier forms as a result of genetic change. This theory began in the mid-19th century with the work of Charles Darwin and Alfred Russel Wallace (1823–1913). Darwin's observations of fossils and living organisms during a five-year voyage around the world aboard H.M.S. *Beagle* led him to conclude that new species arose as existing species gradually changed in response to environmental conditions. Wallace, working in the Malay Archipelago, reached a similar conclusion and communicated his findings to Darwin. Darwin presented his and Wallace's theory before the Linnaean Society in London in 1858 and published the theory in 1859 as *The Origin of Species*.

Their theory states that natural selection is the main force in evolution. Organisms with the most favorable inherited traits have an advantage, making them more likely to survive, reproduce, and pass on their traits to the next generation. In species that reproduce sexually, individuals vary in size, coloration, physiology, and other characteristics. Some of these variations are acquired characteristics resulting from differences in environmental factors—as in a human who develops bulging muscles from weight lifting, for example. Such characteristics are not inherited by offspring. Other variations, however, are genetic and can be passed from one generation to the next during reproduction—differences in the proteins that regulate metabolism in muscle cells, for instance.

Evidence of Evolution

A vast body of evidence supports the theory of evolution by natural selection.

The Fossil Record Fossils, the remains of organisms from past geologic ages, can be dated, either roughly by observing their position in layers of rock (older fossils are found below newer fossils) or more exactly by radioactive dating and other techniques. By arranging fossils along a time line, scientists can sometimes see gradual changes from simple to more complex life-forms. In some cases, scientists can see the evolution through various intermediate forms over millions of years and compare those transitional forms with the present organism. A well-documented example is the horse. The earliest known species lived some 60 million years ago; it was a small creature less than 20 inches (50 centimeters) high at the shoulders. Successive rock layers have yielded fossils of ever-larger horse species, culminating in the horses of today. As size changed, so did other aspects of the horses' anatomy; teeth became adapted to eating grass, the bones of the lower leg fused, and multiple toes evolved into a single toe surrounded by a hoof.

Comparative anatomy Organisms that are closely related, such as mammals, share similar anatomical structures. For instance, although they are used very differently, a bat's wing, a dog's foreleg, a seal's flipper, and a human's arm are composed of the same bones arranged in similar ways. They all have a humerus bone in the upper arm, radius and ulna in the lower arm, wrist carpals, hand metacarpals, and finger phalanges. Such homologous structures, scientists believe, are explained by common ancestry.

In contrast, some organisms have analogous structures, which look similar externally but have different internal structures. The wings of a bat, a buzzard, and a butterfly all serve the same purpose, but they are completely different in origin.

Evolutionary theory predicts that certain anatomical mutations may occur but others will not. For instance, because birds evolved from reptiles some 150 million years after mammals evolved from an earlier group of reptiles, a mutant mammal with feathers is an impossibility. However, since whales evolved from legged mammals, it is possible for a whale to be born with limbs, as does indeed occur on rare occasions.

Comparative embryology Similarities in the early stages of development also are evidence of common ancestry. For example, early in their embryonic development, fish, chickens, and humans all have a tail (as well as gill slits and similar shapes). In the human embryo, most of the tail vertebrae normally disappear by the eighth week in a process called programmed cell death. But four of the tail vertebrae remain; normally they fuse to form the irregular tapering bone called the coccyx at the distal end of the spine.

The human coccyx is an example of a vestigial organ—one that appears to serve no useful function but suggests a common ancestry with organisms in which the homologous structure is functional. The coccyx is homologous to the functional tail of other primates. Similarly, the eyes of blind cave-dwelling salamanders are homologous to those of related species that live in a world of light.

Comparative biochemistry The biochemical similarity of basic processes in all living organisms is additional evidence of common descent. All organisms use DNA and RNA as the hereditary material that directs the operation of cells. In every species, the DNA molecule has the same components and even uses the same code to carry information.

In all known species, proteins are built from the same 20 amino acids, even though there are about 250 naturally occurring amino acids. All organisms possess similar respiratory proteins. All aerobic organisms—from bacteria to humans—use cytochrome c, evidence that all these organisms descended from a common ancestor that used this compound for respiration. Furthermore, the cytochrome of humans and cows is more alike than that of humans and fish, suggesting that humans and cows are more closely related than are humans and fish. In a similar manner, hemoglobins and other blood proteins can be used to infer evolutionary relationships among species.

Biogeography During Earth's history, the continents have slowly changed their relative positions as a result of plate tectonics (movement of pieces, or plates, of Earth's crust). For millions of years before 200 million years ago, all the continents were joined together in a single supercontinent, now called Pangaea. Evidence includes a fossil fern from that time found in Africa, South America, Australia, and India; there is no way the fern could have spread unless the continents were somehow joined.

Populations of a species that are separated for a long period of time gradually evolve along different paths. Darwin recognized this when he observed 13 species of finches on the Galápagos Islands. Each species was slightly different. For example, some species had small, thin beaks and fed on small seeds; others had larger, thicker beaks that allowed them to eat large seeds.

A dramatic example of such divergent evolution is seen in Australia, which has had the longest separation from other continents. It has the most distinctive of all plants and animals. Most familiar is the great divergence of marsupials that evolved there, in an environment free of competition from the placental mammals that came to be the dominant mammals on other continents.

Genetics

Genetic information is carried in cell structures called chromosomes. A chromosome is composed of DNA and associated proteins. (An exception is certain viruses, in which RNA is the hereditary material.)

The basic unit of inheritance is the gene. It consists of a specific segment of a DNA (or RNA) molecule. All the genes of an organism can be thought of as constituting the blueprint for the organism, determining all its anatomical and physiological characteristics.

Structure of DNA and RNA

A molecule of DNA, or deoxyribonucleic acid, consists of repeating subunits called nucleotides. Each nucleotide has three parts: a phosphate unit (phosphorus bonded to oxygen), a sugar unit, and a nitrogen base. The sugar is deoxyribose. There are four types of nitrogen bases: adenine (A), thymine (T), guanine (G), and cytosine (C). Because of their chemical properties, adenine and thymine always bond together and guanine and cytosine always bond together.

In 1953, James Watson (b. 1928) and Francis Crick (1916–2004) determined that the DNA molecule resembles a long, twisted ladder—a shape called a double helix. The sides of the ladder are composed of alternating sugar and phosphate units. Each "rung" consists of a pair of nitrogen bases: A-T, T-A, G-C, or C-G. The two bases are held together by weak hydrogen bonds that can be readily broken by enzymes in the cell, so that the DNA molecule can unwind and duplicate itself during cell reproduction.

A molecule of RNA, or ribonucleic acid, also is a chain of nucleotides. However, it commonly is single-stranded; its sugar is ribose; and instead of thymine it contains the base uracil (U), which pairs with adenine. Also unlike DNA, RNA exists in several forms, the best known of which are three forms involved in protein synthesis: messenger RNA (mRNA), ribosomal RNA (rRNA), and transfer RNA (tRNA).

Nonchromosomal DNA In addition to making up chromosomes, DNA can be found in other cell structures: plant chloroplasts and plant and animal mitochondria. Mitochondrial DNA is inherited from the female parent; it is passed to offspring solely via the egg cell.

The Genetic Code and Protein Synthesis

The sequence of nucleotides in a gene or in mRNA is the genetic code needed by cells for protein synthesis. It spells out the sequence of amino acids in a protein. The basic unit of the genetic code is the codon, a sequence of three nucleotides on a DNA or mRNA molecule that codes for a specific amino acid. For example, TTT is a DNA codon for phenyalanine and AGG is a codon for arginine. If a DNA molecule includes the sequence TTTAGGTTT, it is translated into a protein with a phenyalanine-arginine-phenyalanine sequence.

The gene can be thought of as the template, or pattern, for the manufacture of mRNA. This process takes place in the nucleus. The mRNA leaves the nucleus and in the cytoplasm attaches to ribosomes (made partly of rRNA). Amino acids are brought to the ribosomes by tRNA. In a process called translation, the amino acids are linked together in the order coded by mRNA to form the protein.

Mutations An alteration, or mutation, in the genetic code may change the order of amino acids in a protein and

The End of Evolution?

By NICHOLAS WADE

The most improbable item in science fiction movies is not the hardware but the people. Strangely, they always look and behave just like us. Yet the one safe prediction about the far future is that human evolution will be a lot further along.

Recently population geneticists, rummaging in DNA's ever-fascinating attic, set dates on two important changes in humans.

Dr. Alan R. Rogers of the University of Utah estimated that the ancestral human population had acquired black skin, as a protection against the sun, at least 1.2 million years ago, and therefore that it must have shed its fur some time before that.

Clothing came long after we were naked. Dr. Mark Stoneking, of the Institute for Evolutionary Anthropology in Leipzig, addressed this question by calculating when the human body louse, which lives only in clothing, not in hair, evolved from the human head louse: between 72,000 and 42,000 years ago.

So have we attained perfection and ceased to evolve?

Many geneticists think that is unlikely, though it's hard to say where we are headed or how fast. Until the agricultural revolution 10,000 years ago, people lived in small populations with little gene flow between them. That is the best situation for rapid evolution, said Sewall Wright, a founder of population genetics. But Sir Ronald A. Fisher, another founder of the discipline, argued that large populations with random mating—what globalization and air travel are helping to bring about—were best for rapid evolution.

Considering that the common ancestor of humans and chimpanzees lived only 5 to 6 million years ago, human evolution seems to have been quite rapid. And our evolution put on an extra spurt just 50,000 years ago, when we may have perfected language, made our first objets d'art and dispersed from our ancestral homeland in northeast Africa.

Despite the medical advances and creature comforts that shelter people in rich countries, natural selection remains at work. Microbes and parasites still nip at our heels, forcing the human genome to stay in constant motion. It is clearly in the throes of adapting to malaria, a disease that seems to have struck only in the last 8,000 years; the protective gene that has sickle-cell anemia as a side effect is a sign of a hasty patch.

It seems reasonable to predict that the human physical form will stay in equilibrium with its surroundings. If the ozone layer thins, pale skin will be out and dark skin de rigeur. If climate heats up, the adaptations for living in hot places will spread, though it could take tens or hundreds of generations for a new gene to become widespread.

Sexual selection, too, is at work. This powerful process, first recognized by Darwin, works on traits that are attractive to the other sex and help the owner's genes spread into the next generation. The peacock's tail has been created by the sexual preference of generations of peahens.

Though features like the peacock's tail are chosen for aesthetic, or arbitrary, reasons, they often seem to be correlated with health, and indeed their owners are chosen as mates because these features advertise good immune systems or freedom from parasites. So if sexual selection in people becomes more intense as people have a wider choice of mates, that suggests a terribly Panglossian forecast: we will become more healthy and ever more beautiful.

Most animals struggle to survive in harsh environments beset by accidents and predators. Humans got that problem largely under control long ago but live in a fiercer jungle—that of human society. Indeed, social intelligence—the ability to keep track of a society's hierarchy and what obligations an individual owed to others or had due—may have been a factor in the increase of human brain size.

Society, and the knowledge needed to survive in it, seems to get ever more complex, suggesting that human social behavior will continue to evolve. Unfortunately, evolution has no concept of progress, so behavioral change is not always for the better.

Given all the possibilities for human evolutionary change, it is hard to know which path our distant descendants will be constrained to tread.

hence the biochemical properties of the protein. This can have serious consequences. If a mutation occurs in a body cell, such as a liver cell, all cells produced from that cell will contain the mutation. If a mutation occurs in a precursor to an egg or sperm cell, it can be passed on to offspring.

Hundreds of human diseases are caused wholly or in part by such genetic errors. For instance, more than 600 cancer-related genes have been identified. The normal genes are involved in numerous different activities, but when mutated they may help promote development of a malignant growth.

Genomes

The full complement of genetic material in a virus or organism is called a genome. The first genome to be sequenced was that of a bacterial virus, consisting of 5,375 bases; this sequencing was accomplished in 1977. The first genome of an organism to be sequenced, the bacterium *Haemophilus influenzae*, consists of 1.8 million bases and includes 1,743 genes. In 2001, two groups working independently published rough drafts of the human genome, which consists of about 3 billion bases and appears to have 30,000 to 40,000 genes.

Genetic Engineering

The deliberate alternation, or engineering, of an organism's genetic material may involve changing the sequence of bases in a species' DNA. Or it may involve moving DNA from one species to another. For example, when the human gene that directs production of the hormone insulin is inserted into the DNA of bacteria, the bacteria—and all their descendants—produce human insulin. This process has made it possible to manufacture large quantities of insulin and other hormones, tissue plasminogen activator (for dissolving blood clots), several types of interferon (for treating hepatitis B and other diseases), and other substances.

Patterns of Inheritance

The scientific study of inheritance can be said to have begun in the mid-19th century with the work of Gregor Mendel. He crossbred garden pea plants and kept meticulous records of certain traits of parent plants (P generation) and of first and second offspring (filial) generations (F1 and F2 generations).

Mendel developed several theories that have since been proved and today are known as basic principles of heredity. It is important to note that Mendel's work was accomplished before scientists knew about chromosomes, genes, and DNA.

Principle of Segregation When Mendel crossbred two parent plants from strains that always bred true to type—for example, a tall plant and a short plant—he found that the F1 generation all resembled one parent; in this case, they all were tall. However, when he allowed a plant from the F1 generation to self-pollinate, its offspring (F2 generation) had a ratio of approximately three tall plants for every one short plant.

Mendel concluded that each plant possessed two inheritance factors for height. In parent plants, the two factors were alike, but the F1 plants were hybrid. That is, the two factors for the trait were different. The factors separated (segregated) when the plant produced sex cells, and one factor from each parent was passed to the offspring.

Principle of dominance Today we know that a gene can exist in more than one form. A particular form is called an allele. In pea plants, there are two alleles that control height.

Mendel noted that one factor (allele) for a trait may appear to be "stronger" than another factor. He called this the dominant form, and the "weaker" factor the recessive form. In pea plants, the allele for tallness is dominant and the allele for shortness is recessive; therefore, hybrid plants will be tall.

The crosses can be described in shorthand using T for tall and t for short, with TT and tt indicating purebred plants and Tt representing hybrid plants:

TT × tt → 100% Tt
Tt × Tt → 25% TT + 50% Tt + 25% tt

Principle of independent assortment When Mendel tracked more than one trait, he found that each trait acted in accordance with the principle of segregation; one trait did not appear to have any influence on the other trait. He concluded that each trait segregates independently of the other traits.

Non-Mendelian inheritance patterns Organisms contain many traits that do not exhibit the predictable patterns discovered by Mendel.

In some cases, there is incomplete dominance; neither gene is dominant over the other. A well-known example is four-o'clock flowers. When a four o'clock plant with red flowers (RR) is crossed with a plant that has white flowers (WW), the hybrid offspring have pink flowers (RW). A cross of two hybrids produces an F2 generation with the same ratios as above:

RW × RW ➜ 25% RR + 50% RW + 25% WW

Other hybrids may display codominance, as seen in shorthorn cattle. If a pure red cow is bred with a pure white bull, the offspring has a roan coat with both red and white hairs.

Some traits have multiple alleles. An example is the major human blood alleles, of which there are three: A, B, and O. Neither A nor B is dominant over the other but both are dominant over O. Thus, a person with type A blood may have two A alleles or an A and an O allele. A person with type B blood has two B's or BO. A person with AB blood has an A and a B. And a person with type O blood has two O alleles.

Although Mendel's principle of independent assortment says that traits are inherited independently from one another, genes on the same chromosome usually are inherited together.

Certain genes are carried on the sex chromosomes. In females, who have two X chromosomes, the laws of dominance apply. Males have an X chromosome inherited from the mother and a Y chromosome received from the father. The two chromosomes are not alike; there are numerous genes on the X chromosome and comparatively few on the Y chromosome. One important gene on the X chromosome codes for factor VIII, a protein needed to make blood clot. Lack of factor VIII results in the life-threatening condition known as hemophilia. A female may have a normal gene and an abnormal one, but the normal gene is dominant, so she is healthy. A male, who has only one X chromosome, will have hemophilia if that chromosome carries the abnormal gene.

Ecology

Ecology is the study of how organisms interact with their environment—both with other living things and with the air, water, and other physical aspects of their surroundings. Although it is a relatively young science, ecology is based on work done over more than 2,000 years, starting with efforts of Theophrastus (ca. 372–286 B.C.), who described relationships within communities of organisms. The term *ecology* was coined by Ernst Haeckel (German, 1834–1919), who gave its first definition in 1866. In the early part of the 20th century, plant and animal populations were studied separately until scientists realized that interrelationships among all types of living organisms are a fundamental aspect of ecology. Today, ecological studies are based on the concepts of ecosystems, a term coined in 1935 by Arthur Tansley (1871–1955).

Ecosystems, Biomes, and Habitats

An ecosystem consists of a community of organisms and the physical environment in which they live. Ecosystems vary greatly in size, ranging from small ponds to coral reefs to the vast expanse of coniferous forests. All the members of a species that live within an ecosystem constitute a population.

A group of ecosystems occupying a large area of land and having characteristic climate, soil, and mixture of plants and animals is called a biome. Major biomes include desert, chapparal, savanna, tropical rain forest, temperate grassland, temperate deciduous forest, taiga, and tundra. Biomes merge gradually with their neighbors in transition zones called ecotones. Some evidence suggests that the greatest diversity of species, long believed to exist in rain forests, may actually be present in the ecotones between rain forests and savannas.

The particular kind of surroundings in which individuals of a species normally live is their habitat. The habitat consists of both living and nonliving components, including competitors, predators, soil, water, and so on. Some organisms, such as blue whales, have habitats as large as an ocean. Others, such as butterflies and sea anemones, have habitats the size of a meadow or tide pool. Very small habitats, such as the ground beneath a rock, are called microhabitats.

Within its habitat, an organism occupies a unique position, or niche. For instance, five species of North American warblers all live in spruce forests and eat insects. But they feed in different parts of the trees—for example, Cape May warblers look for food in the uppermost parts of a tree whereas bay-breasted warblers feed mainly on somewhat lower branches. Because they occupy slightly different niches, they can coexist.

Interactions Within a Community

Interactions in a community occur between members of the same species (intraspecific) and between members of different species (interspecific). Most interactions fall into three categories: competition, predation, and symbiosis.

Competition Competition may involve any resource needed to live, grow, or reproduce. It generally is greatest among members of the same species because all their needs are identical. An acorn eaten by one gray squirrel means one fewer acorn for other gray squirrels in the community. But it also means one fewer acorn for white-breasted nuthatches that live in the same community.

If competition for a resource is significant and one species is better adapted for acquiring the resource, it may eventually crowd out the other species. The introduction of nonindigenous species into a community is a serious issue because it often leads to loss of native species and significant change in the habitat. For example, purple loosestrife, a native of Eurasia, has crowded out native plants in many North American wetlands in part because of its reproductive edge: a single plant may produce as many as 250,000 seeds. Kudzu, a native of Asia nicknamed "the plant that ate the South," has strong, tough vines that can grow up to 60 feet (18 meters) in just one season, smothering any vegetation in its path.

Predation Lions, snakes, and eagles are examples of predators—organisms that hunt and eat other organisms. Those that have the best techniques for obtaining food are the ones most likely to grow and reproduce. Predation affects the size of prey populations and the diversity of species within a community. One reason nonindigenous species often are a serious problem is a lack of natural predators in their new homes. Purple loosestrife is such a species, whereas in its native habitats its populations are kept in check by a leaf-eating beetle and root-eating weevil. Parasitism is a variety of predation; a parasite feeds on prey but often weakens rather than kills its host. Some parasites, such as wheat rust, have very specific host requirements. Others, such as mistletoe, parasitize a variety of species.

Symbiosis Two organisms of different species may live together in a long-term association in which neither organism is harmed and one or both may benefit.

Commensalism is a symbiotic relationship in which one species benefits while the other is neither helped nor harmed. Suckerfish (Remora) use a flat suction disk behind the head to attach to the underside of sharks and other fish. This arrangement does not affect the larger fish, but the suckerfish obtains food, feeding on material that drops from the host's mouth.

Mutualism is a relationship that benefits both species. A sea anemone attached to the back of a shell housing a hermit crab camouflages and protects the crab. In turn, as the crab moves about the sea anemone gains a larger feeding range.

Adaptations

Every organism has certain characteristics that adapt it for life in a certain environment. These include structural adaptations, based on how the organism is built; physiological adaptations, based on how the parts of the organism operate; and behavioral adaptations, based on the things an organism does. A bald eagle's structural adaptations that aid in predation include sharp eyesight to locate prey, strong feet with sharp claws to grasp prey, and a hooked bill for tearing flesh. Physiological adaptations include production of enzymes needed to digest flesh. A behavioral adaptation is the eagle's tendency to sit on a high branch overlooking a river where salmon and other prey swim. From this perch, the eagle can see fish underwater and small movements up to a mile away.

Some organisms are highly adapted to a particular niche. This adaptation makes it difficult for them to cope if their environment is altered. Many endangered species facing extinction fall into this category. Other organisms are able to thrive in a variety of niches. Norway rats are an example, living in habitats as diverse as wharves, salt marshes, garbage dumps, sewers, and many types of human dwellings.

Biodiversity

All the living organisms on Earth make up the biosphere. The variety of these organisms is called Earth's biodiversity. Biodiversity can be measured in three different but equally important ways: the variety of genes within a species, the variety of genes among all the species on Earth, and the variety of ecosystems that provide homes for these species.

Biodiversity provides the oxygen needed by most lifeforms for metabolism, rich soils in which plants can grow, systems for breaking down wastes, clean water, chemicals that humans can use as pharmaceuticals, and raw materials for clothing, homes, and other human needs.

The greater the degree of biodiversity, the more stable and resilient Earth's ecology. However, with humanity's spread, increasing population, and overconsumption, biodiversity has come under attack. Introduced species, habitat degradation, overhunting, deforestation, and pollution imperil species, speed the rate of extinction, and decrease biodiversity.

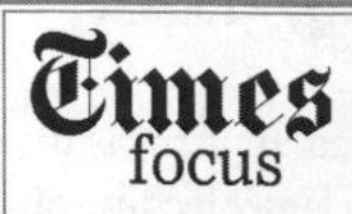

Managing Planet Earth: Environmental Challenges Lie Ahead

by Andrew Revkin

Nearly 70 years ago, a Soviet geochemist, reflecting on his world, made a startling observation: through technology and sheer numbers, he wrote, people were becoming a geological force, shaping the planet's future just as rivers and earthquakes had shaped its past. Eventually, wrote the scientist, Vladimir I. Vernadsky, global society, guided by science, would soften the human environmental impact, and earth would become a "noosphere," a planet of the mind, "life's domain ruled by reason."

Today, a broad range of scientists say, part of Vernadsky's thinking has already been proved right: people have significantly altered the atmosphere and are the dominant influence on ecosystems and natural selection. The question now, scientists say, is whether the rest of his vision will come to pass. Choices made in the next few years will determine the answer.

Aided by satellites and supercomputers, and mobilized by the evident environmental damage of the last century, humans have a real chance to begin balancing economic development with sustaining earth's ecological webs. Communities and countries face concrete choices in the next decade that are likely to determine the quality of human life and the environment well into the 22nd century. Human activity is such a pervasive influence on the planet's ecological framework that it is no longer possible to separate people and nature. Emissions of heat-trapping carbon dioxide, whether from an Ohio power plant or a Bangkok taxicab, contribute to global warming. Seafood lovers dining in Manhattan bistros prompt fishing vessels to sweep Antarctic waters for slow-growing Chilean sea bass. Shoppers in Tokyo seeking inexpensive picture frames send loggers deep into Indonesian forests.

In the book *Great Transition: The Promise and Lure of the Times Ahead*, published by the Stockholm Environment Institute, a group of top geographers, economists, engineers and other experts concludes that the same inventiveness that accelerated the human ascent can be harnessed to soften human impact. The need for a new approach is urgent, the researchers say, because a surge of growth in quickly industrializing regions of Asia and the Americas could have environmental effects that exceed those of the industrialization of the West. More pressure for change comes from southern Africa and other pockets of extreme poverty where the brutal calculus of Malthus still holds sway.

Even in the industrialized north, after generations of prosperity, people are hemmed in by concrete, seeing commuting times grow and starting to question their definition of progress. As a result, countless communities, from the charred fringes of the Amazon to the spreading suburbs of Seattle, are balancing growing needs and limited resources. If development does not change course, the new book concludes, "the nightmare of an impoverished, mean, destructive future looms."

Human Imprints from Pole to Pole Evidence abounds now that the world is a human-dominated place. By flooding the atmosphere with synthetic chemicals and heat-trapping carbon dioxide and other greenhouse gases, for example, people damaged the protective ozone layer and contributed to a warming climate, scientists have said. The ozone depletion became vividly and unexpectedly evident in the 1980's, when a gaping hole was detected over Antarctica. The hole will shrink in the next 50 years because of a ban on ozone-eating chlorofluorocarbons. Other damage will not be so easy to repair.

Long before they are cataloged, thousands of plant and animal species are likely to be driven to extinction as forests, wetlands, mountain slopes and other habitats are exploited or harmed by climate change. Satellites that map vegetation and the nighttime signature of human activity—fire and light—show that people have altered more than one-third of the terrestrial landscape. Once it is changed, it is usually changed forever.

Where progress is seen, too often it is only in a slowing rate of destruction, ecologists say. For example, new satellite surveys show that forest loss in the tropics through the 1990's occurred at a rate 23 percent less than previous estimates. But losses still add up to some

14 million acres a year, with 5 million more acres visibly damaged.

The human imprint is evident almost everywhere. In the South Atlantic, fleets illuminate so much of the ocean to attract squid that the illuminated area dwarfs the megalopolis of São Paulo. The squid harvest has in part grown because commercial fish stocks have been overfished. Altogether, scientists have found that two-thirds of commercial marine fish species are fully exploited or diminishing, prompting companies to move down the food chain.

Aquaculture is a fast-growing alternative, but often causes damage like the destruction of coastal mangroves in southern Asia to make way for shrimp farms. Also, in many cases, farmed species are fed fish meal made of other fish. So the cultivation still indirectly depletes the oceans.

Hydrologists estimate that people appropriate half the world's flowing fresh water. Across the American West in the last 20 years, circular patches made by great rotating irrigation rigs have peppered the land like an expanding checkerboard, marking the draining of aquifers under the plains.

Scientists have concluded that humans not only now dominate the planet, but have also become the dominant driver of natural selection, the machinery of evolution. The main influence, experts say, is the continuing chemical arms race against germs and pests, which kills most, but leaves a resistant minority behind. Also, by wittingly and unwittingly moving myriad species around the globe, humans have become a biological blender, carrying West Nile virus to America and overrunning the Bordeaux countryside in France with American bullfrogs that residents say do not even taste good.

Troubling Trends Projections for the next two generations do not bode well for easing environmental problems. Even with the population bomb predicted in the 1960's substantially defused, the human population is likely headed for at least nine billion before leveling off. Most of the growth will be in poor countries, and as people there pursue prosperity, consumption of natural resources will rapidly increase.

Car companies are racing to build factories to assemble sport utility vehicles in India, even as its once-legendary rail system, plagued by mismanagement, is deteriorating and losing freight and passengers, said Dr. Rajendra K. Pachauri, director general of the Tata Energy Research Institute of India. The private organization assesses energy and environmental problems in India.

"In the last 10 years, every major manufacturer has set up facilities in India," Dr. Pachauri said. "They see it as a major market. They have the buzz of the people. This is something that should cause real concern."

Depending on how power is generated, bringing electricity to the two billion people in the world who still lack it could greatly increase emissions of greenhouse gases. But, experts note, the options available to those who remain off the grid also cause harm. The two billion people who cook on wood or dung fires live in acrid clouds of toxic smoke and deplete forests. In India, Dr. Pachauri said, millions of people light their homes with kerosene, using government-subsidized fuel. Together, cooking fires and sputtering lanterns create indoor pollution that causes asthma and other ailments and that, in India alone, is estimated to kill 600,000 women a year.

Dr. Pachauri's group has experimented with distributing solar-powered lanterns to rural communities. Other projects push cleaner ovens that use less-polluting fuels. But the question of how to take good ideas from pilot projects to the new norm remains largely unsolved.

Then there are the costs. For example, about a billion people have no clean water. More than twice that number live where raw sewage flows unchecked. When even countries like the United States lag tens of billions of dollars in improving their sewage systems, experts say the prospects of big investments elsewhere are dim.

Learning to Harvest More from Less If farming does not change drastically in the next few decades, enormous ecological damage will result, many scientists say. Farming has already produced the biggest global imprint of humanity, affecting half the earth's habitable land. The challenge now will be to double agricultural

productivity without using substantially more land. There are signs this can be achieved. In an extraordinary experiment several years ago, in Yunnan Province, China, rice farmers were recruited to intersperse two varieties on 8,000 acres instead of planting one. The total yield rose 17 percent, and the occurrence of rice blast, the most harmful disease in the world's biggest crop, fell 94 percent.

Recognizing a good thing, China has expanded the work to 250,000 acres, said Dr. Christopher C. Mundt, a plant pathologist at Oregon State University who helped conduct the research.

"Perhaps more important," he added, "the Chinese are taking the general concept of diversification into related approaches" to other crops.

The key to the next green revolution, Dr. Mundt said, will be abandoning most of the industrial model of agriculture of the 20th century and shifting to a "biological model based on management of ecological processes" like applying fertilizer and water only as needed. Such efforts are being made in agriculture, forestry, fisheries and other fields around the world. But, once again, experts say the challenge lies in moving to the scales needed to avert widespread harm.

The Megalopolis As Eco-Strategy Another focal point for experts who envision a managed earth is cities. In many ways, they are where the battle will be won or lost. Cities are where almost all remaining population growth will occur, demographers say. The roster of megacities, those with populations exceeding 10 million, is widely expected to climb, from 20 today to 36 by 2015.

These vast metropolises have been widely characterized as a nightmarish element of the new century, sprawling and chaotic and spawning waste and illness. But increasingly, demographers and other experts say that cities may actually be a critical means of limiting environmental damage. Most significantly, they say, family size drops sharply in urban areas. For the poor, access to health care, schools and other basic services is generally greater in the city than in the countryside. Energy is used more efficiently, and drinking and wastewater systems, although lacking now, can be built relatively easily.

And for every person who moves to a city, that is one person fewer chopping firewood or poaching game.

Still, many cities face decisions now that may permanently alter the quality of human lives and the environment. The pivotal nature of these times is perfectly illustrated by Mexico City, which is just behind Tokyo atop the list of megacities. The sprawling megalopolis, where traffic is paralyzed, is about to choose in a referendum between double-decking its downtown highways or expanding its subway system. One course could encourage sprawl and pollution; the other would conserve energy, experts say.

Chances of Change: "Pernicious Fad" or Real Prospect? Some environmentalists say the whole notion of sustainable development is an oxymoron, that the Western industrial model of endless growth, however packaged, cannot possibly persist without grievous environmental damage. At the same time, some business leaders still scoff at the effort. In a new PricewaterhouseCoopers survey of Fortune 1000 executives' attitudes toward sustainable development, one corporate vice president for environmental affairs called the concept "a pernicious fad."

Some skeptics note that even if cleaner, less destructive industries take hold everywhere, the sheer volume of economic growth could still cause big problems. But a durable line of pragmatic optimists from science, business and environmental groups, for now, holds center stage. They say that cleaning the environment and reducing poverty are not only required from an ethical standpoint, but also because they are in humanity's self-interest. Hundreds of businesses, though still a minority, have added sustainability managers to their executive roster.

Prof. Jeffrey D. Sachs, director of the Columbia University Earth Institute, said the world was quickly shifting from a model in which wealth was derived mainly through exploiting resources.

"Most growth now comes from increased knowledge, not from the mining of nature," Professor Sachs said. "And knowledge isn't limited in the way that, say, soil fertility is."

Environmental Trends

Megacities By 2015, demographers predict, the number of cities with more than 10 million people—so-called megacities—will rise to 36, from about 20 today. Megacities are notorious for pollution and sprawling slums. But people who live in them tend to have smaller families and greater opportunities for jobs and educations. And environmental improvements can come quickly to cities. For example, in Mexico City, left, the percentage of days violating pollution standards has fallen to less than 20 percent, from 50 percent. Now the city is considering a mass transit program that would bring further improvements.

Food Supplies Demographers are lowering their estimates for how much the population of the world will increase before it stabilizes, but even so they predict 50 percent growth by the end of the century. Demand for food will grow even faster, as people in developing countries start consuming more meat and fish. Aquaculture, once thought of as a solution, has produced problems of its own. In Thailand and elsewhere, shrimp farms have replaced valuable mangrove ecosystems. In China, however, a recent experiment in mixing rice varieties in a single field greatly increased yields, without added chemicals.

Falling Forests In the tropics, forests continue to fall before farmers, loggers and timber processors like the sawmill on a branch of the Amazon River in Brazil. But new surveys show that in the 1990's the rate of cutting was 23 percent less than earlier estimates. Some timber companies have gained certification from environmental groups as managing forests with care. Companies that buy their wood, like the Gibson guitar company, promote their products as environmentally friendly. Environmental groups are working with growers of cocoa, bananas, coffee and other commodities to adopt similar programs. And some conservationists now say that judicious logging can actually benefit the plants and animals that live in the forest.

Exploiting and Protecting Land Humans have altered great swaths of the planet for agriculture and settlements, putting extreme pressure on many ecosystems. Close to a third of the world's land surface has been converted for human use. The United Nations estimates that an additional one-third of lands could be converted in the next 100 years. Far less land is protected from development.

	% of land converted	% of land protected[1]
North America	27%	11.1%
Europe and Russia	35	4.7
Asia (excl. Middle East)	44	6.0
Middle East/North Africa	12	2.1
Central America and Carribean	28	6.1
Sub-Saharan Africa	25	6.0
Oceania	9	7.1
South America	33	7.4

Note: 1. Parks, reserves, wildlife refuges.
Source: World Resources Institute

U.S. Waste and Recycling Almost a third (30 percent) of waste in the U.S. is recycled, 55 percent goes to landfills, and 15 percent is burned.

Consumer electronics Televisions, stereos, computers, phones and other electronic products are a small but rapidly growing portion of the waste stream: over 2 million tons in 2000. 21 percent of computers and related equipment are recycled; virtually all TV's, video and audio units are discarded. Lead accounts for 4 percent of material in electronic products.

Paper Almost half is recycled.

Plastic Waste volume is growing fast. Very little of it is recycled.

Metals About one-third of them are recycled.

Glass Its use has declined because of plastics.

Wood Only about 4 percent of it is recycled.

Biochemistry

Biochemistry is the study of chemical compounds and processes that occur in living organisms. Like nonliving components of our world, organisms are composed of atoms and molecules that interact in a vast variety of chemical reactions. The sum of all the chemical reactions that occur in the cells of an organism is called metabolism. It includes both anabolic reactions, in which energy is used to build matter used for growth and repair; and catabolic reactions, in which compounds are broken down to release energy. Reactions generally occur in a sequence of steps that make up a metabolic pathway. For example, the sugar glucose is broken down in a 10-step reaction called glycolysis.

Compounds of Living Organisms

Four major groups of chemicals are found in living organisms: carbohydrates, lipids, proteins, and nucleic acids. These are called organic compounds; the term means that each molecule contains one or more carbon atoms.

Carbohydrates Carbohydrate molecules consist of carbon (C), hydrogen (H), and oxygen (O), typically with a two-to-one proportion of hydrogen atoms to oxygen atoms. For example, the simple sugar glucose has the formula $C_6H_{12}O_6$. Linking together hundreds or thousands of simple sugar molecules forms more complex carbohydrates, called polysaccharides. The main sources of energy for most organisms are the carbohydrates sugar, starch, and glycogen. The carbohydrate cellulose is the main structural component of plants. It is the most common organic compound on Earth.

Lipids Lipid molecules contain carbon, hydrogen, and oxygen, in a ratio different from that found in carbohydrates. Some lipids also contain elements such as nitrogen (N) and phosphorus (P). Fats, oils, and waxes are lipids. They are important energy-storage molecules and structural components of cells.

Proteins Proteins are large, complex molecules composed of amino acid molecules. An amino acid molecule has at least one amino group (NH2) and one carboxyl group (COOH). The molecules are linked together to form peptides; a polypeptide is a long chain of amino acids; proteins consist of one or more polypeptide chains. Soluble proteins function mainly as enzymes, which promote biological reactions, or as carriers—for instance, hemoglobin carries oxygen. Other proteins are fibrous and insoluble; they are mainly structural materials, forming cell membranes, muscles, cartilage, hair, and so on.

Nucleic acids The molecules of nucleic acids are composed of repeated units called nucleotides. Each nucleotide consists of a phosphate group, a 5-carbon sugar, and a nitrogen base. The nucleic acids, deoxyribonucleic acid (DNA) and ribonucleic acid (RNA), carry the genetic material of an organism.

Other compounds Combinations of the above are common. For instance, lipoproteins are proteins that contain lipid groups in their molecules, and glycoproteins are proteins that have sugar as part of their molecules.

Hormones are chemicals produced in minute amounts by endocrine glands. They turn on, turn off, speed up, or slow down activities. Some hormones are steroids, fatty compounds synthesized from cholesterol. Other hormones are nitrogen-containing compounds such as proteins, peptides, and amino acid derivatives.

Neurotransmitters are chemicals that transmit signals across spaces that separate one nerve cell from another. They are derived from precursor proteins.

History of Biochemistry

Biochemistry has its beginnings in the 18th century when scientists discovered that plants give off oxygen and, in the presence of light, absorb carbon dioxide. During the same period, Antoine-Laurent Lavoisier (1743–94) demonstrated that animals need oxygen and that respiration involves the oxidation of compounds. In 1828, Friedrich Wöhler (1800–82) synthesized the organic compound urea from an inorganic compound, establishing that the chemistry of living organisms was essentially the same as that of nonliving materials such as minerals.

The first amino acid, asparagine, was isolated in 1806; the first hormone, adrenaline (epinephrine), in 1897; and the first neurotransmitter, acetylcholine, in 1920. The discovery and synthesis of hundreds of biological compounds over the past two centuries have been accompanied by elucidation of the major pathways of metabolism, such as those involved in photosynthesis and respiration. It is now known that seemingly minor changes in a complex molecule may have dramatic consequences. For instance, many if not all cancers result from changes in the structure of nucleic acid molecules.

In recent years, biochemical research has increasingly been part of interdisciplinary efforts involving cell biology, molecular biology, genetics, and immunology. The synthesis of biochemical compounds such as insulin and other hormones has dramatic medical consequences. Other advances in biochemistry are critical to genetic engineering and agriculture.

CHEMISTRY

Chemistry is the study of the nature of matter, the way substances can change and interact with one another, and the energy flows that result when these changes take place. Following a long period of impressive development in the 18th and 19th centuries, chemistry has become one of the great scientific disciplines, an expansive enterprise of exploration, analysis, and application. Chemical methods are essential to the working of modern economies, and chemical knowledge and processes relate the discipline to many other pure and applied sciences, including agronomy, biology, ecology, metallurgy and solid-state physics. The main branches of chemistry include *organic chemistry*, the study of carbon compounds including those essential to living beings; *inorganic chemistry*, the study of compounds other than those containing carbon; *physical chemistry*, in which the laws of physics are used to study chemical substances and processes; and *analytic chemistry*, the study of the constituents of a substance and their relative amounts. There are also many more specialized fields, such as electrochemistry, photochemistry, quantum chemistry, and others. Biochemistry, the study of the chemistry of biological processes, has developed into a separate discipline.

History of Chemistry

The early development of applied chemical processes can be dated to the Neolithic Revolution (about 6000 B.C.), which brought the spread of sedentary agriculture and a rise in population. The first metal to be extracted from ore by heating was probably copper. Both copper and lead were in use by 4000 B.C., and bronze, a combination of tin and copper produced by 3000 B.C., gave its name to the Bronze Age. Silver was produced as a by-product of smelting lead, and iron was made by about 1000 B.C. (the Iron Age). Pottery making was another early chemical process: by 3000 B.C. kilns were in use that had temperatures high enough to cause chemical changes in clays to produce durable pottery. Dyes were also made by chemical means.

Greek Science In Greece in the first millennium B.C., an atomic theory of matter was developed, but the theory that dominated chemistry for centuries was Aristotle's view that there are four elements: earth, air, fire, and water. They could be transformed one into the other, and in turn all were composed of the fundamental primary matter. In reality Aristotle's theories explained relatively little, but they held sway in the West as late as the 16th century.

Alchemy In Alexandria, Egypt, chemical practices in the early centuries A.D. were linked to alchemy (the attempt to turn base metals into gold). It was believed that the end product of the maturation of metals in the earth was gold, and that this process might be accelerated in the laboratory. The center of alchemical work later shifted to the Islamic world, and finally to Europe, where alchemical ideas held sway into the 17th century. China also had a long alchemical tradition, which contributed to the development of early forms of gunpowder. Throughout its history alchemy was bound up with a series of philosophical and mystical beliefs. Although the alchemists did not succeed in their goal, many laboratory techniques were developed in their efforts that were later used for more productive purposes.

The Scientific Revolution The beginnings of the scientific revolution in the West and the ultimate rise of scientific chemistry can be traced generally to the 16th and 17th centuries, when Nicolaus Copernicus and Galileo Galilei challenged the idea of the Earth as the center of the universe. Experimental science too hold in the 17th century and Robert Boyle (1627–91) took the lead in the study of how chemical reactions occur. Evangelista Torricelli (1608–47) demonstrated the possibility of a vacuum, formerly thought impossible. Boyle's protégé Robert Hooke (1635–1703), who improved the microscope, prepared regular experiments for the meetings of the Royal Society in London. Sir Isaac Newton (1642–1727) proposed his theory of gravity. These developments had a profound influence on the development of modern chemistry.

The Chemical Revolution Between 1770 and 1790, the so-called chemical revolution gave birth to modern chemistry. Early in the century, the process of combustion, perhaps the most obvious of chemical reactions, was explained by the theory of phlogiston, which was believed to be a common constituent of matter but one so hard to detect that it could be noticed only when phlogiston left a burning substance and ashes remained. This view seemed to explain many chemical phenomena, but became increasingly hard to accept as new discoveries proliferated. Joseph Black (1728-99) discovered carbon dioxide in 1755; Joseph Priestley (1733–1804) discovered oxygen in 1774; and Henry Cavendish (1731–1810) discovered that water was hydrogen and oxygen in 1784 (all of these gases were known by different names at the time). However, the chemical revolution is most closely associated with the name of the great French chemist Antoine-Laurent Lavoisier (1743–94). He demonstrated the true nature of combustion and definitively overthrew the phlogiston theory, worked with others to reform chemical nomenclature from its older alchemical roots, and introduced the modern idea of an element as a substance that could not be decomposed. His famous textbook, called in English *Elements of Chemistry*, was published in 1789. The work of Lavoisier and his colleagues is the foundation of chemistry as a science.

Chemistry and Industrialization During the 19th century there were many developments that still mark chemistry as a science. By the end of the 19th century more than 80 elements were known, as compared with some 32 at the end of the 18th. Early in the century, the chemical atomic theory held that each element had a different atom and that therefore elements could not be transmuted, as had been the goal of alchemy. Robert Bunsen (1811–99) developed his gas burner, and Bunsen and Gustav Robert Kirchhoff (1824–87) developed the atomic spectrograph, with which elements could be identified by their characteristic wavelengths. Dmitry Mendeleyev (1834–1907) developed the first satisfactory periodic table of the elements, later much revised and extended. In the latter half of the 19th century studies of molecular structure and the optical activity of molecules flourished. The nature of carbon bonds was discovered, and the organic chemical industry grew rapidly. Perhaps the most important aspect of 19th-century chemistry from the standpoint of the average person was the rise of the chemical industries and the crucial role they played in industrialization and economic modernization. The 19th century also saw the professionalization of chemistry as a discipline and career.

Modern Chemistry The 20th century provided the chemical developments that in large part define the modern world. Building on the discovery of radioactive substances in the late 19th century, scientists studied the nature of radioactivity. The concept of the electron was elucidated by Joseph Thomson (1856–1940), and the structure of the atom, using quantum-theoretic ideas, was developed by Neils Bohr (1885–1962). The nature of the chemical bond through valence electrons was understood. This activity in chemistry (and physics) created the nuclear age. Industrial and practical chemistry continued to develop throughout the century, beginning notably with the Haber-Bosch process used to produce ammonia for fertilizers and other uses prior to World War I. Among new drugs were the sulfanilamide drugs and penicillin (first produced in quantity during World War II), which revolutionized medicine in war and peace. The chemistry of materials continued to flourish. In the postwar period there was also increased concern about the negative environmental effects of chemistry, and there is now a focus on "green chemistry" to alleviate these.

Applications of Chemistry

Enormous chemical industries underpin modern industry, commerce, and agriculture. The table on page 579 shows the top 20 industrial chemicals produced in the United States. Two of these of particular importance are described here.

Sulfuric Acid Most people know sulfuric acid (H_2SO_4) only from the high school chemistry laboratory, where it provides a lesson in the careful handling of dangerous chemicals, and from the one common consumer product that contains it, lead-acid automobile batteries. But in fact sulfuric acid is the most important industrial chemical in the world, and the most commonly used strong acid; nearly all manufactured products depend on sulfuric acid in some way. About 40 million metric tons are produced in the United States each year, far exceeding the amount of other important industrial chemicals. Sulfuric acid is used in the production of agricultural fertilizers (the largest volume use), and in metal processing and refining, electroplating, water treatment, petroleum refining, and the removal of oxides from iron and steel prior to galvanizing and electroplating.

Ammonia and Feeding the World Ammonia (NH_3) is a pungent, colorless gas that is soluble in water; it is a familiar household cleanser. But its main use is much more important: manufactured ammonia is used primarily to produce nitrogen fertilizers, which are of immense importance in feeding the world's population: it is estimated that some 40 percent of the world's protein needs are produced with nitrogen fertilizers. Fritz Haber (1868–1934), after years of experimentation, developed the first successful process (1908) to produce ammonia from the elements, a feat for which he won the Nobel Prize for Chemistry (1918). Carl Bosch (1874–1940) provided the engineering to bring the first commercial plant on line in 1913. The Haber process uses nitrogen, separated from liquid air; and hydrogen, produced usually from a hydrocarbon. An iron catalyst is used to speed up the reaction, which is undertaken at about 4,500 degrees Celsius and an air pressure equivalent to several hundred times normal atmospheric pressure. (Nitrogen-fixing bacteria perform a similar function under normal pressure and temperature conditions.) The production of ammonia is one of the most widespread applied chemical processes. There are hundreds of plants that produce ammonia in 80 countries, with an estimated production (in 2000) of 130 million metric tons. More than half of ammonia production is in developing countries, and about 85 percent of worldwide production is used to make nitrogen fertilizers; India and China together account for more than one-third of nitrogen fertilizer production. Ammonia is used for other products as well, including dyes, resins, and explosives.

Top 20 Industrial Chemicals Produced in U.S.

Rank	Chemical	Production (in 10^9 kg)
1.	Sulfuric acid	39.62
2.	Ethylene	25.15
3.	Lime	20.12
4.	Phosphoric acid	16.16
5.	Ammonia	15.03
6.	Propylene	14.45
7.	Chlorine	12.01
8.	Sodium hydroxide	10.99
9.	Sodium carbonate	10.21
10.	Ethylene chloride	9.92
11.	Nitric acid	7.99
12.	Ammonium nitrate	7.49
13.	Urea	6.96
14.	Ethylbenzene	5.97
15.	Styrene	5.41
16.	Hydrogen chloride	4.34
17.	Ethylene oxide	3.87
18.	Cumene	3.74
19.	Ammonium sulfate	2.60
20.	1,3-Butadiene	2.01

Source: *Chemical Engineering News*

The Elements

The elements are the basic building blocks of the chemical world. Elements are known by abbreviations of one to three letters, most often from their modern names but sometimes from earlier (especially Latin) names. For example, aluminum has the abbreviation Al, from its name in English, whereas gold has the abbreviation Au, from the Latin word for gold, *aurum*. An element is defined by the number of protons (positively charged particles) in its atomic nucleus. This number is the atomic number of the element. There are at present more than 100 known elements. Elements 1 through 94 are observed in nature; the elements beyond 94, not all of which have been observed, are produced in nuclear facilities and research laboratories. Elements above 83 (bismuth) decay radioactively. The highest atomic number of an element that has been observed to date is 116; elements 113 and 115 have not yet been produced.

Atomic Structure

An atoms's nucleus contains *neutrons*, which have no electric charge, as well as *protons*. Each neutron weighs approximately as much as a proton. An element's atoms all have the same number of protons, but some atoms of an element can have different numbers of neutrons. Different combinations of neutrons with the fixed number of protons that defines the element are called *isotopes* of the element. The total of protons and neutrons of an element or one of its isotopes is the *mass number* of the element. In addition to the particles in the nucleus of an atom, there are negatively charged *electrons*, which have very little mass, in orbit around the nucleus. The *atomic weight* of an element is its weight as compared with one-twelfth of the weight of the principal isotope of carbon, carbon 12, which is used as the standard atomic mass unit, or amu. The atomic weight in tables is the average atomic weight of an element's known isotopes, adjusted for the frequency with which they occur. Thus, the atomic weight of carbon, which would be 12.00 if all carbon were isotope 12, is given as 12.017 because there are small amounts of carbon 13 and carbon 14 in every sample of carbon. The chemical activity of an element is produced by the electrons in outer orbits, called valence electrons; in chemical reactions, the nucleus is not changed. Elements are thus the building blocks of chemical reactions.

The Periodic Table

The periodic table arranges the elements in an orderly fashion that reflects their underlying atomic characteristics. The term "period" refers to the rows of the table, which group elements in such a way that elements in the columns, progressively heavier, have similar chemical characteristics. The periodic table shown here is the so-called "long form" in current use. Each entry shows the chemical symbol for the element, its name, its atomic number (which is equal to the number of protons in the nucleus), and its atomic weight. For elements that do not occur in nature, the most common known isotope is listed.

The current periodic table stems from the first successful early periodic table, compiled in 1869 by Dmitry Mendeleyev. Mendeleyev built on the considerable knowledge developed by chemists in the 18th and 19th centuries about the elements (more than 50 were known at the time) and their characteristics, including atomic weights and spectrographs.

The Modern Form of the Periodic Table The long form of the table reflects our current knowledge of atomic structure and the many new elements found in the 20th century, including those synthesized in nuclear facilities. The table consists of seven rows of 2, 8, 8, 18, 18, 32, and 32 elements, respectively. The elements are arranged by atomic number, rather than by atomic weight. Most elements are classed as metals, i.e., substances with good electrical and heat conductivity. These are divided into groups: alkali metals, alkaline earth metals, transitional metals, and other metals. The table also includes nonmetals, toward the right-hand side, and the noble gases in the last column on the right. Two elements are classed as liquids: mercury and bromine. Elements with atomic numbers higher than uranium have been produced in nuclear facilities and laboratories; two elements with atomic numbers smaller than that of uranium that occur naturally in very small traces (technetium and promethium) are also shown here as human-created, which is how

THE PERIODIC TABLE OF THE ELEMENTS

6 — atomic number
C — chemical number
12.01 — atomic mass
Carbon — name of element

(transition metals: III B – II B; nonmetals: III A – VII A)

	alkali metals I A	alkaline earth metals II A	III B	IV B	V B	VI B	VII B	VIII	VIII	VIII	I B	II B	III A	IV A	V A	VI A	VII A	noble gases O
Period 1	1 H 1.01 Hydrogen																	2 He 4.00 Helium
Period 2	3 Li 6.94 Lithium	4 Be 9.01 Beryllium											5 B 10.81 Boron	6 C 12.01 Carbon	7 N 14.01 Nitrogen	8 O 16.00 Oxygen	9 F 19.00 Fluorine	10 Ne 20.18 Neon
Period 3	11 Na 22.99 Sodium	12 Mg 24.31 Magnesium											13 Al 26.98 Aluminum	14 Si 28.09 Silicon	15 P 30.97 Phosphorus	16 S 32.07 Sulfur	17 Cl 35.45 Chlorine	18 Ar 39.95 Argon
Period 4	19 K 39.10 Potassium	20 Ca 40.08 Calcium	21 Sc 44.96 Scandium	22 Ti 47.88 Titanium	23 V 50.94 Vanadium	24 Cr 52.00 Chromium	25 Mn 54.95 Manganese	26 Fe 55.85 Iron	27 Co 58.93 Cobalt	28 Ni 58.70 Nickel	29 Cu 63.55 Copper	30 Zn 65.39 Zinc	31 Ga 69.72 Gallium	32 Ge 72.61 Germanium	33 As 74.92 Arsenic	34 Se 78.96 Selenium	35 Br 79.90 Bromine	36 Kr 83.80 Krypton
Period 5	37 Rb 85.47 Rubidium	38 Sr 87.62 Strontium	39 Y 88.91 Yttrium	40 Zr 91.22 Zirconium	41 Nb 92.91 Niobium	42 Mo 95.94 Molybdenum	43 Tc (98) Technetium	44 Ru 101.07 Ruthenium	45 Rh 102.91 Rhodium	46 Pd 106.4 Palladium	47 Ag 107.87 Silver	48 Cd 112.41 Cadmium	49 In 114.82 Indium	50 Sn 118.71 Tin	51 Sb 121.74 Antimony	52 Te 127.60 Tellurium	53 I 126.90 Iodine	54 Xe 131.29 Xenon
Period 6	55 Cs 132.91 Cesium	56 Ba 137.33 Barium	Lanthanide series (see below)	72 Hf 178.49 Hafnium	73 Ta 180.94 Tantalum	74 W 183.85 Tungsten	75 Re 186.21 Rhenium	76 Os 190.23 Osmium	77 Ir 192.22 Iridium	78 Pt 195.08 Platinum	79 Au 196.97 Gold	80 Hg 200.59 Mercury	81 Tl 204.38 Thallium	82 Pb 207.2 Lead	83 Bi 208.98 Bismuth	84 Po (209) Polonium	85 At (210) Astatine	86 Rn (222) Radon
Period 7	87 Fr (223) Francium	88 Ra 226.03 Radium	Actinide series (see below)	104 Rf (261) Rutherfordium	105 Db (262) Dubnium	106 Sg (263) Seaborgium	107 Bh (262) Bohrium	108 Hs (265) Hassium	109 Mt (266) Meitnerium	110 (269)	111 (272)	112 (277)		114 (281)		116 (292)		

rare earth elements—Lanthanide series	57 La 138.91 Lanthanum	58 Ce 140.12 Cerium	59 Pr 140.91 Praseodymium	60 Nd 144.24 Neodymium	61 Pm (145) Promethium	62 Sm 150.4 Samarium	63 Eu 151.96 Europium	64 Gd 157.25 Gadolinium	65 Tb 158.93 Terbium	66 Dy 162.50 Dysprosium	67 Ho 164.93 Holmium	68 Er 167.26 Erbium	69 Tm 168.93 Thulium	70 Yb 173.04 Ytterbium	71 Lu 174.97 Lutetium
Actinide series	89 Ac 227.03 Actinium	90 Th 232.04 Thorium	91 Pa 231.04 Protactinium	92 U 238.03 Uranium	93 Np 237.05 Neptunium	94 Pu (244) Plutonium	95 Am (243) Americium	96 Cm (247) Curium	97 Bk (247) Berkelium	98 Cf (251) Californium	99 Es (252) Einsteinium	100 Fm (257) Fermium	101 Md (258) Mendelevium	102 No (259) Nobelium	103 Lr (260) Lawrencium

they were first identified. The lanthanide and the actinide series do not fit neatly into the column structure of the table, and are usually shown separately from the rows of which they are a part. Hydrogen and helium are placed as shown because of their special characteristics, hydrogen as a gas and helium as a noble gas.

Finding New Elements In the first third of the 20th century, 88 elements were known, up through uranium (92), with four elements missing. The first of these, technetium (43), was produced in 1937; francium (87) was produced in 1939; astatine (85) in 1940; and promethium (61) in 1945. The extent to which new elements (the transuranic elements) can be produced beyond the elements up to 92 is limited by the basic properties of nature. These fundamental forces suggest an upper bound to the periodic table of about 125 elements. The reactions involved in nuclear synthesis are complex, and success in finding a new element requires a balancing of the production of a new element with its ability to survive long enough to be identified. In general, the heavier the new element, the more likely it is to decay by fission, and therefore the less likely are the prospects for its survival. The first transuranic element to be produced and identified was neptunium (93), by Edwin M. McMillan (1907–91) and Phillip H. Abelson (b. 1913) at Berkeley, Calif., in 1940. Neptunium was produced by bombarding uranium with neutrons in the Berkeley cyclotron (neptunium also occurs naturally in minute quantities in uranium ores). The element with the highest atomic weight thought to have been observed as of 2003 is 116.

The Elements

The known elements are described here in alphabetical order. Following the name of the element, the symbol is given in parentheses. The atomic number and weight of each element can be found in the periodic table. The generally accepted discoverers of the elements found in modern times are given together with the date of the discovery and the country in which it took place.

Actinium (Ac) Actinium is the first of the radioactive rare-earths, the metals 89–102, which are called collectively the *actinides* and are grouped in a separate row in the periodic table. Discovered by André Debierne (1899, France), who extracted it from uranium ore, it is a soft, silvery-white metal used in research. Actinium glows in the dark and is named from the Greek *aktinos*, or "ray."

Aluminum (Al) Aluminum, a soft workable metal, is the most abundant metal in the Earth's crust. Its name is from the Latin *alumen*, "bitter salt." It was known in ancient times in the form of alum (potassium aluminum sulfate), and has been used in medicine to stop bleeding, in papermaking, and to fix dyes in cloth making. The first metal was obtained in 1825 (Hans Christian Oersted, Denmark), but the aluminum metal industry was begun only late in the 19th century when a process was developed to extract the metal from its salts by electric current. Today, aluminum and its alloys have many uses, including metal parts for houses, cars, aircraft, and drink cans. Compounds are used in paper treatment and water purification. Aluminum is still produced with heavy input of electricity, which makes recycling this metal especially advantageous.

Americium (Am) A radioactive rare-earth element, discovered by Glenn T. Seaborg and others (1944, U.S.) and named for America. Am-241, produced by nuclear reactors, is the source of ionizing radiation in smoke detectors.

Antimony (Sb) A *metalloid*, antimony has characteristics of both metals and nonmetals. It was known in ancient times and used for vases, as a cosmetic, as a glaze, and for medicinal purposes (although it is now known to be toxic to humans). Its name is from the Greek, *antimonos* ("not alone"), and its symbol is from the Latin *stibium* for antimony sulfide; the only significant modern use of antimony is in flame retardants.

Argon (Ar) Discovered in 1894 by William Ramsay and John Strutt (England), argon is a noble gas whose name derives from the Greek *argos*, "idle." Obtained from liquid air, argon is completely unreactive in ordinary conditions, but is important commercially as an inert atmosphere in lightbulbs and for metallurgical processes.

Arsenic (As) Arsenic (thought to be from the Greek *arsenikon*, for a yellow mineral) compounds were known in ancient times, and were used for purposes including gilding; the element itself was discovered by Albertus Magnus in the 13th century. Arsenic, which is essential in trace amounts for some animals, has a long history as a poison. Its modern uses include gallium arsenide semiconductors and specialized glasses.

Astatine (At) A member of the halogen group, astatine (after the Greek for "unstable") was discovered (1940, U.S.) by Dale R. Corson and others. Little is known about this dangerously radioactive element, whose longest-lived isotope has a half-life of eight hours.

Barium (Ba) An abundant alkaline earth element, barium was first isolated by Humphry Davy (1808, England) and named for the Greek *barys*, "heavy." Many of its compounds are toxic to humans, but barium sulfate can be ingested for X-ray medical diagnosis. Other uses are in lubricants and alloys.

Berkelium (Bk) Berkelium was first produced in 1947 by Glenn T. Seaborg and others (U.S.) at the University of California at Berkeley and named after the university. It is a radioactive, silver-colored metallic transuranic element; the 243 isotope has a half-life of five hours. There is no known use for berkelium, and it is not found in nature.

Beryllium (Be) Beryllium, discovered (1798, France) by Nicholas Louis Vauquelin, is named after one of its minerals, beryl. The element beryllium is toxic when breathed or swallowed; it is used primarily as an alloy with copper and nickel. When beryl is of high quality it is a well-known gemstone, emerald.

Bismuth (Bi) Bismuth (after the German *weisse masse*, "white mass," referring to an ore) was discovered in the Middle Ages and used to craft caskets and other objects, sometimes alloyed with lead, with which it was confused until the 18th century. Its principal current use is as a catalyst for the production of synthetic fibers ; it also yields a pearl color in cosmetics.

Bohrium (Bh) Bohrium is a radioactive transfermium metal named after Neils Bohr, the Nobel Prize–winning Danish physicist. Credit for its discovery is shared by the Laboratory for Heavy Ion Research (1981, Germany) and Yuri Oganessian and others (1976, Russia). Uses: research.

Boron (B) Boron, from the Arabic *buraq*, "borax" (sodium borate), is essential to plants. The element was discovered independently (1808) by Louis-Joseph Gay-Lussac and Louis-Jacques Thenard (France) and Humphry Davy (England), but borax was known at least since the early Middle Ages, when it was used in metalwork and in medicine; more recently it was used as a bleaching agent in household detergents. Boron is now used in making heat-resistant glass and ceramic glazes, and as an additive to fertilizers.

Bromine (Br) Bromine, a member of the halogen group, was isolated by Antoine-Jerome Ballard (France, 1826); it is named from the Greek word for "stench," *bromos*. Bromine is highly toxic; bromides, used in 19th-century medicine, are only mildly so. Bromine is used in industry to make compounds for pharmaceuticals, pesticides such as methyl bromide, and fire extinguishers. Bromine is implicated in ozone destruction and many of its uses are being phased out; the production of methyl bromide, for example, will eventually cease by international treaty.

Cadmium (Cd) Discovered by Friedrich Strohmeyer (1817, Germany), and named after the Latin for the mineral calamine (*cadmia*), cadmium is highly toxic to humans and poses dangers from accumulation in the environment. It is used in nickel-cadmium batteries and to electroplate steel for protection from seawater; many other uses have been discontinued.

Calcium (Ca) Calcium is essential to most living things, and is the most abundant metal in the human body, primarily in bone. Elemental calcium was discovered by Humphry Davy (1808, England), and named after the Latin for "lime," *calx*. In metallic form it is soft and silvery, a member of the alkaline earth metal group. Since ancient times, calcium, as calcium oxide (lime), has been mixed with sand and water to produce mortar. Calcium is now used as lime in metallurgy, chemicals, water treatment, and the production of cement. Calcium metal is also used in metallurgy and alloys. Gypsum, a hydrated calcium sulfate, is used as plaster.

Californium (Cf) Highly radioactive rare-earth (actinide) element produced in 1950 in Berkeley, California by Stanley G. Thompson and others, and named after the university and state. It is produced in nuclear reactors and has limited uses as a neutron emitter in mineral prospecting and cancer therapy.

Carbon (C) Carbon has been known since ancient times in various forms such as coal, charcoal, peat, the soft crystal graphite, and the hard crystalline form diamond; its name is from the Latin for "charcoal," *carbo*. Carbon forms very strong bonds to itself which are resistant to chemical attack, and the resulting chains of carbon atoms form compounds that are found in all living cells. Carbon represents 23 percent of human body mass, and most of our food is made up of carbon compounds. An entire field, organic chemistry, is devoted primarily to the study of carbon compounds (of which some 20 million are known). Carbon has several isotopes, the most common of which is carbon 12, which makes up 99 percent of carbon; carbon 13 amounts to about 1 percent. (Small amounts of carbon 14 exist; this is radioactive with a half-life of 5,730 years and is used to date archeological material.) Carbon is used industrially in ironmaking, printing, as activated charcoal in water treatment, and as fibers to strengthen laminates in aerospace and in sports equipment. The most substantial industrial use of carbon is as fuel: enormous amounts of carbon are extracted from the earth in the form of fossil fuels, and the resulting increase in carbon in the atmosphere has led to global warming. In 1985 *fullerenes*, a new form of carbon, were produced. These are polyhedral (approximately spherical) structures composed of carbon 60; *nanotubes* are cylindrical forms of fullerenes.

Cerium (Ce) A soft gray reactive rare-earth metal, cerium was discovered 1803 or 1804 by Jöns Jacob Berzelius and Wilhelm Hisinger in Sweden and independently by Martin Klaproth in Germany. Widely available in mineral form, it is used in carbon-arc electrodes for floodlights, in catalytic converters, in glass as a filter for ultraviolet rays, and in self-cleaning ovens. It is named after the asteroid Ceres, which in turn was named after the Roman goddess of agriculture.

Cesium (Cs) Discovered (1860, Germany) by Robert Bunsen and Gustav Kirchhoff, and named after the Latin for "sky blue," *caesius*, for the blue rays of its atomic spectrum. Cesium from minerals has specialized industrial uses in enhancing catalytic reactions, as a glass coating, and in medical diagnosis. Cesium-137, a radioactive isotope produced in nuclear reactors, is environmentally dangerous (it was emitted at Chernobyl).

Chlorine (Cl) Chlorine is a greenish-yellow gas (C_2) that is highly reactive and dangerous; it is a member of the halogen group. As chloride (a chlorine atom with a negative electron) it is essential to many living things, including humans. It was identified as an element (1810, England) by Humphry Davy, and named after the Greek for "greenish-yellow," *chloros*. The first significant use of chlorine was as a bleach in the late 18th century (hydrochloric acid had been used earlier by alchemists). Chlorine today is used in the chemical industry, in manufacturing polyvinylchlorides (PVCs), in water purification (one of the most effective of public health measures), bleaching and other uses. The production of chlorofluorocarbons, harmful to the ozone layer, is being phased out.

Chromium (Cr) Chromium is an essential trace metal in humans and other species. Discovered (1798, France) by Nicholas Louis Vauquelin, it is named after the Greek for "color," *chroma*, for its bright compounds. Used in stainless steel and other alloys, it can also be used to coat steel for car parts ("chrome").

Cobalt (Co) Cobalt, a constituent of vitamin B12, is essential to humans, and cobalt minerals have been used since ancient times to produce a deep rich blue in glass and other materials. The element itself was isolated in 1739 (Sweden) by Georges Brandt; it is thought to be named after the German for goblin, *Kobald*, so called by miners who were fooled into thinking one of its ores was silver. Cobalt is widely used in alloys for such varied products as razor blades, jet engines, and magnets (cobalt maintains its magnetism at high temperatures). It is a blue pigment in glass, ceramics, and jewelry; a radioactive isotope, Co 60, is used in medicine and to irradiate food.

Copper (Cu) Copper is essential to living things, in which it forms part of important enzymes; in large amounts it can be toxic. It was known and worked in ancient times; its name and symbol derive from the Latin name for Cyprus, *Cuprum*, where copper was mined. It has been used for 10,000 years, worked from natural nuggets, and has been mined and smelted for 7,000 years and used as copper or in an alloy with tin to produce bronze. Copper is an excellent conductor of heat and electricity, and most copper is now destined for electrical equipment. Other uses are in construction and industrial machinery.

Curium (Cm) Highly radioactive rare-earth element produced in 1944 by Glenn T. Seaborg and others (U.S.). Curium 242, produced from plutonium in reactors, is used as an energy source in pacemakers, navigational buoys, and space missions. It is named after Pierre and Marie Curie.

Dubnium (Db) A radioactive transfermium element reported in 1967 by Georgy Flerov and others (Russia) and named after the city in which they worked, Dubna. Uses: research.

Dysprosium (Dy) A soft, bright silvery rare-earth metal, it has limited uses in halide lamps and as a neutron absorber in nuclear reactors. Its name (from the Greek, *dysprositos*) means "hard to get"; its discoverer, Paul-Émile Lecoq de Boisbaudran (1886, France), found it difficult to isolate.

Einsteinium (Es) Discovered from analysis of the debris of the first thermonuclear explosion at Eniwetok, 1952, by Albert Ghiorso and others (U.S.), this actinide element does not occur naturally; it is named after Albert Einstein. Uses: research.

Erbium (Er) A bright, silvery rare-earth metal. It is used in optical fibers, protective goggles, as an alloy in magnetic resonance imaging (MRI) machines, and to tint glass pink. Discovered 1843 by Carl Gustav Mosander (Sweden) and named after Ytterby, Sweden.

Europium (Eu) A soft, silvery rare-earth metal that is

highly reactive with oxygen and water. It produces red emissions in TV tubes and in low-energy light bulbs provides both red and blue emissions. Isolated from a form of samarium in 1901 by Eugène-Anatole Demarçay (France).

Fermium (Fm) Discovered from analysis of the debris of the first thermonuclear explosion at Eniwetok, 1952, by Albert Ghiorso and others (U.S.), this highly radioactive actinide element does not occur naturally; it is named after the Nobel Prize–winning physicist Enrico Fermi. Uses: research.

Fluorine (F) Fluorine is a pale yellow gas (F_2) that is highly reactive and dangerous. The form found in nature, fluoride (F-), is stable and is essential for humans in small amounts. Elemental fluorine was isolated (1886, France) by Henri Moissan; it is named after the Latin *fluere* ("to flow") because its mineral fluorspar (calcium fluoride) melts when heated. Fluorspar was used in preindustrial times in metallurgy and in glass etching. Today, fluoride is best known as an additive to water and toothpaste to prevent tooth decay. It is also an element in non-stick pan coatings, and has uses in the nuclear, electrical, and chemical industries. Its use in chlorofluorocarbons, harmful to the ozone layer, is being phased out.

Francium (Fr) Discovered (1939, France) by Marguerite Perey and named after France. It is an unstable, highly radioactive element; the longest-lived isotope (223) has a half-life of only 22 minutes. Uses: research.

Gadolinium (Gd) Gadolinium is a soft, silvery rare-earth metal used in alloys in magnets and electronic components, and as a neutron regulator in nuclear reactors. Discovered in 1880 by Jean-Charles Gallissard de Marignac (Switzerland); named after an early investigator of rare-earth minerals, Johan Gadolin (Sweden).

Gallium (Ga) A soft, silver-white metal, Gallium was discovered (1875, France) by Paul-Émile Lecoq de Boisbaudran and named after the Latin for "France," *Gallia*. Especially as gallium arsenide, it has semiconductor properties and is used in light-emitting diodes (LEDs), supercomputers, and cell phones.

Germanium (Ge) A silver-white semi-metal, germanium has few uses except in specialized lenses and infrared detectors, although it was the first element to be used in transistors. Discovered (1886, Germany) by Clemens A. Winkler and named after the Latin for the country, *Germania*.

Gold (Au) Gold occurs naturally in surface waters and on land. It also occurs underground, often in quartz veins or pyrites. The most malleable of all elements, its ready availability and easy workability made it one of the first metals used in prehistoric times. The word "gold" is originally Anglo-Saxon and its symbol is from the Latin for gold, *aurum*. Gold's sparkling beauty and sunlike color have led people to attribute magical and religious properties to it, and it has from ancient times been the basis of monetary systems. In addition to its uses in jewelry and the decorative arts, gold has electronics and aerospace applications; it is relatively unreactive and a good conductor of electricity. Gold is usually mixed with other elements to harden it—pure gold is called 24 karat gold; an alloy of 75 percent gold is called 18 karat gold. Most gold produced is mined, principally in the U.S., Canada, Russia, and South Africa.

Hafnium (Hf) Discovered by George Charles de Hevesy and Dirk Koster (1923, Denmark) and named after the Latin name for Copenhagen, *Hafnia*, hafnium is a silvery metal used for control rods in nuclear plants as a neutron absorber; it is also used for alloys and ceramics. Because of the difficulty of separating it from zirconium, to which it is chemically similar, it was one of the last non-radioactive elements to be discovered.

Hassium (Hs) A radioactive transfermium element synthesized in 1984 by Peter Armbruster and others (Germany) and named after the state of Hesse.

Helium (He) Helium, a colorless, odorless and unreactive noble gas, is the second-most abundant element in the universe, after hydrogen. It was discovered (1868, England) by Norman Lockyer and (1868, observing an eclipse in India) by Pierre J. C. Janssen, through analysis of the sun's spectrum, and is named after the Greek *helios*, "sun." It was then discovered that the element also existed on earth, in uranium minerals. The principal uses of helium are cooling low-temperature instruments, such as the magnets in magnetic resonance imaging and providing inert atmospheres for industrial processes; it is also provides the lift in lighter-than-air craft.

Holmium (Ho) A soft, bright silvery rare-earth metal. From the Latin name for Stockholm, *Holmia*. Independently discovered in 1878 by Marc Delafontaine and Louis Soret (Switzerland) and by Per Teodor Cleve (Sweden), it has limited uses in nuclear reactors as a control and in lasers.

Hydrogen (H) The first element in the periodic table and the most abundant element in the universe (80 percent), hydrogen fuels the stars, including our Sun. The lightest of gases, odorless and highly flammable, it was discovered in 1766 by Henry Cavendish (England), but its properties were recognized earlier. Hydrogen's name comes from Greek words meaning "forming water," (H_2O), *hydro* and *genes*. Hydrogen is essential to life, is found in most molecules in living cells, and is a part of DNA, the bases of which are joined by hydrogen bonds. About 10 percent of human body mass is hydrogen. Hydrogen is also a component of common acids, such as sulfuric, nitric, and hydrochloric acids. Its main industrial use is in the production of ammonia for fertilizers. Hydrogen is a constituent of atmospheric water vapor, the most potent greenhouse gas, which keeps earth more than 300 degrees C (800 degrees F) warmer than it would be otherwise. Its form in the atmosphere is generally H_2.

Indium (In) Indium is a soft, silvery metal discovered (1863, Germany) by Ferdinand Reich and Hieronymous Richter, and named for the Latin for "indigo," *indicum*, for its bright color in the atomic spectrum. Its main use is in low-melting alloys for fire-sprinkling systems.

Iodine (I) Named after the Greek for "violet" (the color of its fumes), *iodes*, the element was first identified by Bernard Courtois (1811, France). It is essential to many animal species, and iodide is added to table salt to prevent iodine deficiency in humans, especially goiter (enlarged thyroid gland). Iodine is used in pharmaceuticals (especially as a disinfectant), and in animal feed, photographic chemicals, dyes, and catalysts.

Iridium (Ir) A hard, silvery metal of the platinum group, Iridium was discovered by Smithson Tennant (1803, England) and named, for its colorful salts, after the Greek goddess of the rainbow, Iris. Modern uses include spark plug tips, electrode coatings, and aircraft engine parts.

Iron (Fe) Iron is a soft, workable metal that is the most abundant element on Earth (it makes up most of Earth's molten core). Named for the Anglo-Saxon for "iron," *iren*, its symbol is from the Latin *ferrum*. It is essential to most living things, and an iron deficiency in humans leads to anemia. Iron was known in ancient times, when it was worked from nuggets, probably from meteorites, found on the surface. About 3,500 years ago the technique of smelting from ores was discovered in the Middle East and the use of iron transformed human societies. Iron still accounts for perhaps 90 percent of refined metals, and has more uses as iron, steel (which includes carbon), stainless steel (with chromium and nickel), and other alloys than any other metal.

Krypton (Kr) Krypton, a noble (chemically inert) gas, was discovered in 1898 by William Ramsay and Morris Travers (England); its name is from the Greek for "hidden," *kryptos*. Except under very cold conditions, it reacts only with fluorine gas. Extracted from liquid air, it is used in specialized lighting such as flash lamps.

Lanthanides The lanthanides are the metallic elements with atomic numbers 57–70. They are named after lanthanum, element 57, and in the long form of the periodic table are shown grouped in a separate row. Lutetium, element 71, is traditionally included with the lathanides, but it is actually a member of the next grouping in the periodic table. The lanthanides are commonly called the rare-earth elements, but many of them are not in fact rare. They generally occur together in rare-earth minerals, and 19th century chemists had great difficulties in isolating the separate elements. (Indeed, the name of one, dysprosium, is from the Greek meaning "hard to get.") Among the many minerals in which rare-earth elements are found, the two most important sources are monazite, which is a phosphate ore, and bastnasite, a flouride carbonate ore. The principal sources of rare-earth elements are the U.S. and China, but they are produced in many other countries as well. Among the specialized uses of lanthanides are in fluorescent lighting, high–intensity lighting, and specialized magnets. The lanthanides, many of which are soft, silvery metals, are similar chemically because as the atomic number increases and the number of electrons increases, the extra electrons are added, not, as expected, to the outer ring but to inner orbits. Swedish chemists were active in analyzing the rare-earths, and three of them (terbium, erbium, and ytterbium) are named after Ytterby, a village near Vauxholm where, in 1787, a rock was found that led later to some of the rare-earths. (Yttrium, which is not a rare-earth, is also named after the village.)

Lanthanum (La) Named after the Greek *lanthanein*, "to be hidden." Discovered (1839, Sweden) by Carl Gustav Mosander. Lanthanum is a reactive, silver-white metal, the first of the lathanide group of the periodic table, it is found in ores with other rare-earth metals. As a metal it has no commercial uses, but its alloys are used in carbon-arc electrodes and to increase the refractive index in glass.

Lawrencium (Lr) A transfermium element produced by Albert Ghiorso and others (1961, U.S.) and named after Ernest O. Lawrence, the inventor of the cyclotron. Uses: research.

Lead (Pb) Lead is a soft, ductile gray metal that has been known and used since ancient times. The name *lead* is Anglo-Saxon in origin, and its symbol is from the Latin, *plumbum*. Lead is harmful and even fatal to humans and other animals when it accumulates in the body, and for this reason many of its uses (in paints and as an additive in gasoline, for example) have been phased out. The Romans used lead extensively in water pipes and other products; and in the Middle Ages lead was added as a sweetener to wine. Current uses of lead are primarily for electrodes in vehicle storage batteries, in TV and computer screens as a shield against radiation, and in medicine as protection against X rays.

Lithium (Li) Lithium, the first of the alkali group of metals, was discovered (1817, Sweden) by Johan August Arfvedson and named for the Greek *lithos*, "stone." A soft, silvery metal, it has many uses, including the production of glass, lithium batteries, and a strong, light alloy with aluminum for airplanes. Lithium carbonate is used in the treatment of mental illness, and an unknown amount is used as lithium hydride in the production of nuclear weapons.

Lutetium (Lu) Densest of the elements grouped as rare-earths and discovered in 1907 by Georges Urbain (France), it is a transition element in the periodic table. Mostly used for research purposes, small amounts are used in magnetic bubble memories and in oil refining. From *Lutetia*, the Roman name for Paris.

Magnesium (Mg) Magnesium is an essential element for both animals and plants, in which it is part of the chlorophyll molecule. Recognized as an element by Joseph Black (1755, Scotland) and named after a district in Greece, Magnesia, its main commercial uses are as an alloy with aluminum for car and plane bodies and to remove sulfur in steel production.

Manganese (Mn) Essential to all species, including humans, manganese was identified as an element by John Gottlieb Gahn (1774, Sweden). Its name may be from the Latin for "magnet," *magnes*, as one of its minerals is slightly magnetic. It is used in steel alloys, in which it is essential for strength and wear resistance. The U.S. is 100 percent import dependent for manganese. Produced mainly in South Africa, Gabon, Russia, and Australia, manganese is also widely found in nodules on the ocean floor.

Meitnerium (Mt) Produced in 1982 by Peter Armbruster and others (Germany) and named after the Austrian physicist Lise Meitner. Uses: research.

Mendelevium (Md) A transferium element produced in 1955 by Albert Ghiorso and others (U.S.), it is named after Mendeleyev, who developed the early periodic table. Uses: research.

Mercury (Hg) A liquid, silvery metal with a melting point of –390 degrees C (–380 degrees F), Mercury was known and used in ancient times (indeed, as mercury sulfide (HgS) it was used to produce red color in cave paintings more than 30,000 years ago). It has long fascinated humans because of its silvery, liquid quality and its ability to dissolve gold to form an amalgam. Found throughout the atmosphere and ecosystem, it is ubiquitous in living things. Tolerated in small amounts, in larger amounts it is highly poisonous and has caused sickness and death through its use in medicine, commerce, and industry. These harmful uses have included its application in gilding, in making felt hats, and in making mirrors. Many uses of mercury (including thermometers) have been phased out, and it is currently used in limited quantities in electrical equipment, specialized batteries for small electronic devices, and fluorescent lights.

Molybdenum (Mo) An essential trace element for plants and animals, molybdenum was identified by Peter Jacob Hjelm (1781, Sweden). Earlier, an ore was mistaken for lead ore, and so the element inappropriately bears the Greek name for "lead," *molybdos*. It has many industrial uses, especially for alloys, such as "moly steel," which has high strength and resists wear and corrosion.

Neodymium (Nd) Isolated in 1885 by Karl Auer in Vienna, neodymium is a silver-white rare-earth metal. It is alloyed with iron and boron to make magnets used in cars and trucks, and to produce a purple tint in glass. Its name, from the Greek *neos didymos*, means "new twin," referring to its discovery with praeseodymium.

Neon (Ne) Neon was discovered in 1898 by William Ramsay and Morris Travers (England); its name is from the Greek for new, *neos*. Relatively rare, it is found in the atmosphere, sea, and land. Neon is completely unreactive with known chemicals because of its complete outer electron shell; it is one of the noble or inert gases. Uses: neon lights, low-temperature refrigerants.

Neptunium (Np) Edward McMillan and Philip Abelson (U.S.) announced the discovery of the first transuranic element in 1940. It is named after the planet Neptune, which follows Uranus in the solar system. Minute quantities are found in nature. Uses: nuclear facilities and research.

Nickel (Ni) Nickel was discovered as an element by Alex Fredrik Cronstedt (Stockholm, 1751), but nickel-tin alloys were known in ancient times. It takes its name, "Devil's copper," for a seemingly useless nickel-containing ore known to German copper miners, kupfernickel. Much of the nickel mined from the surface of the earth may have arrived in meteorites; there is also nickel in the Earth's core. Its first modern use was as a base for silver plating (19th century). Its main current use is as a component of stainless steel alloys; it is also used in a variety of other alloys with chromium, copper, and molybdenum, and it is still used in coinage in many countries.

Niobium (Nb) A steel-gray, corrosion-resistant metal, it is named after Niobe, daughter of Tantalus in Greek mythology, because of niobium's chemical similarity to tantalum. Discovered by Charles Hatchett (1801, England), most niobium now comes from Brazil; it has specialized uses as an alloy in stainless steel and other metals, and in the production of anodes. Its alloys with tin and titanium are superconducting.

Nitrogen (N) Nitrogen exists in compounds and in the form of N_2, an odorless, colorless, unreactive gas that composes 78 percent of the air we breathe. Nitrogen was identified as the main constituent of air by Daniel Rutherford (1772, Scotland); it is named after the Greek *nitron* and *genes*, for "niter" (saltpeter), which is potassium nitrate, and "forming." Nitrogen is essential for life; it is part of DNA, amino acids, and the body messenger nitric oxide. Plants require nitrogen, which must be "fixed" (combined with oxygen or hydrogen) for them by bacteria as part of the nitrogen cycle. Commercially nitrogen is produced by liquefication of air and is used to make ammonium nitrates for fertilizer and for many other chemical compounds. Nitrogen is also used as a supercoolant and an inert atmosphere.

Nobelium (No) A transfermium element named after the founder of the Nobel prizes, Alfred Nobel, it was produced by Albert Ghiorso and others, (1958, U.S.).

Osmium (Os) Osmium (from the Greek *osme*, "smell") was discovered in 1803 by Smithson Tennant (England) during investigations into platinum. A sparkling, silvery metal, osmium is the densest metal known but is hard to work. Its few uses include microscope slide stains, catalysis, and alloys. Osmium tetroxide gives off a pungent odor.

Oxygen (O) Oxygen is a colorless and odorless reactive gas that exists naturally as O_2. Oxygen was discovered as an element by Joseph Priestley (1774, England) and named for the Greek for "acid-forming,"*oxy* and *genes*. Oxygen makes up one-fifth of the air; it is essential for sustaining animal life through the respiratory process, which brings oxygen to the blood, and as a constituent of many important compounds in our bodies including DNA. On Earth oxygen is formed by the photosynthesis of carbon dioxide and water by plants (it is also formed as part of the fuel cycle of stars). Oxygen used commercially is produced from liquefied air and is used primarily in steelmaking and chemical production; other uses include water purification and medicine. Ozone consists of three oxygen atoms, O_3.

Palladium (Pd) A silvery, malleable metal that is one of the platinum group, palladium was discovered by William Wollaston (1802, England) and named after the asteroid Pallas. Produced primarily as a by-product of mining other metals, it is used in jewelry, cars, electronics, dental fillings, and catalytic convertors.

Phosphorus (P) Phosphorus (Greek for "bringer of light") was isolated by Hennig Brandt (1669, Germany). In the form of phosphates, phosphorus is essential to all living cells. Most is calcium phosphate in bones, and there are also the organophosphates in key molecules such as ATP (adenosine triphosphate), which is a source of chemical energy in the body. Phosphorus itself is highly toxic. Commercial and industrial uses of phosphate include fertilizers, detergents, flameproofing, rat poison, and tracer bullets. Excess phosphates in water produce eutrophication (the growth of algae), and the use of phosphates is now regulated in many countries.

Platinum (Pt) From the Spanish for "little silver," *platina*, platinum was known and worked in some ancient New World societies but was used rarely in Old World civilization. It became widely known in Europe during the 18th century. Nuggets occur naturally, and it is also mined, obtained as a by-product from copper and nickel refining, and recycled. A bright, silvery, dense metal, it is used primarily for jewelry, with other principal uses in catalytic convertors and in the chemical and electronics industries.

Plutonium (Pu) Discovered by Glenn T. Seaborg and others (1940, U.S.) and named for the planet Pluto. Plutonium was the fissile material in the first atomic weapon tested (July, 1945) and the second used in war. Plutonium is a byproduct of nuclear reactors, and its handling and storage are a considerable environmental challenge. It is used for weapons, in research, and as a power source for pacemakers and space equipment.

Polonium (Po) Discovered in 1898 (France) by Marie Curie and named after her native country, Poland, polonium is a dangerously radioactive element. Produced in research facilities, small amounts are used as a heat source for satellites.

Potassium (K) Potassium, named after *kalium*, the Middle Latin for potash (potassium carbonate), was identified as an element by Humphry Davy (1807, England). It is a soft metal in the alkali metal group. Potassium is essential for most living things; in the human body its many functions include transmitting nerve impulses. Before the industrial era potassium salts were used for flavoring and preserving food and improving soil. Most potassium produced today goes into fertilizers, because of plants' need for the element. Other uses are in glass manufacturing, detergents, and pharmaceuticals.

Praeseodymium (Pr) Isolated in 1885 by Karl Auer in Vienna, praeseodymium is a soft silver-yellow rare-earth metal used to color glass used in protective goggles and in electrodes for carbon arc lighting. The name (from the Greek, *prasios didymos*) means "green twin" and refers both to the color of its oxide and its discovery with neodymium.

Promethium (Pm) Identified in 1945 by J. Marinsky and others (U.S.), promethium is a radioactive rare-earth metal produced in nuclear reactors; traces are also found naturally. Named for Prometheus, the mythical Greek who stole fire from the gods, it is used in luminous paint but has few other applications.

Protactinium (Pr) Discovered in 1900 by William Crookes (England), it decays to actinium. Its name, "precursor to actinium," is from the Greek *protos*, "first." Intensely radioactive, it occurs naturally in uranium ores including pitchblende. Uses: nuclear facilities and research.

Radium (Ra) Discovered by Pierre and Marie Curie (1898, France), radium is a highly radioactive alkaline earth; it causes some of the natural background radiation of Earth. In metallic form soft and silvery and named for the Latin *radius*, "ray," it was very widely used for luminous dials and medicinal purposes before its dangers to humans were understood. Uses: research.

Radon (Rn) Radon, a noble (chemically inert) gas that is highly radioactive, was discovered in 1900 by Friedrich Ernst Dorn (Germany). A decay product of uranium and other elements, it is part of natural background radiation. Accumulations in mines and basements can be a health hazard. The name is from radium with the suffix *-on* for the noble gases. Uses: research.

Rare-earths, See *Lanthanides*.

Rhenium (Re) Discovered in 1925 by Walter Noddack and Ida Tacke (Germany) and named after the Latin name for the Rhine River, *Rhenus*. It is a silvery metal that is the last stable, non-radioactive, naturally-occurring element to be discovered. It is used in alloys for lamp filaments and as a catalyst in chemical processes.

Rhodium (Rh) A member of the platinum group of metals, rhodium was discovered by William Wollaston (1803, England) and named, after the Greek *rhodon*, for the rose color of rhodium chloride. A hard, silvery metal obtained as a byproduct of copper and nickel refining, almost all rhodium is used in catalytic converters for cars.

Rubidium (Rb) Discovered by Robert Bunsen and Gustav Kirchhoff (1861, Germany), it is an alkali metal, named after the Latin *rubidius* for the deep red lines in its atomic spectrum. Uses: research.

Ruthenium (Ru) A silvery metal, discovered (1840, Russia) by Karl Klaus and named after the Latin for Russia. Obtained as a byproduct of nickel refining, it has specialized uses in electronics, chemicals, and as an alloy in platinum for jewelry.

Rutherfordium (Rf) Transfermium element produced by Albert Ghiorso and others (1969, U.S.) with an earlier claim by researchers in Dubna, Russia (1964). It is named after the New Zealand chemist Ernest Rutherford. Uses: research.

Samarium (Sm) A silver-white rare-earth metal discovered in 1879 by Paul-Émile Lecoq de Boisbaudran (France). Found in minerals, it is alloyed with cobalt to produce magnets and is also used in ceramics, glass, and lasers. It is named for the Russian engineer V. E. Samarsky.

Scandium (Sc) A soft, silver-white metal, scandium was discovered (1879, Sweden) by Lars Frederik Nilson and named after the Latin for Scandinavia, *Scandia*. It has specialized uses as a neutron filter in nuclear reactors, in mercury vapor lamps, and in oil refining.

Seaborgium (Sg). Produced in 1974 by teams in Dubna, Russia (Georgy Flerov and others) and Berkeley, California (Ghiorsi and others). Named after Glenn T. Seaborg (U.S.), a leading investigator of transuranium elements. Uses: research.

Selenium (Se) Selenium is an essential element for humans, although in excessive doses it is toxic. Discovered (1817, Sweden) by Jöns Jacob Berzelius, it is named after the Greek for "moon," *selene*. It exists in two forms, a silver metal and a red powder, and is used in electronics, in the glass industry, in animal feeds, and as a red pigment.

Silicon (Si) Elemental silicon was first obtained by Jöns Jacob Berzelius (1824, Sweden); its name is derived from the Latin for "flint," *silex* or *silicus*. Early humans made flint from silicon dioxide (silica), and many ancient civilizations made glass from sand. Silicon is used in many ways: as sand in construction, as pure silicon in computer chips, as quartz (silicon dioxide) with its many uses, and as a raw material for the steel and chemical industries. Opal, agate, and rhinestone are gemstones that are forms of silica.

Silver (Ag) Silver is from the Anglo-Saxon *siolfur*, and takes its symbol from the Latin *argentum*. Silver has been known and worked since ancient times in the Old and New Worlds. It is rarely found as the metal; it must be mined from ore and refined, so that although silver is more abundant than gold, it came into use later. A principal use for silver, in which it is alloyed with copper, is in jewelry and tableware. Silver salts are used in still and movie films and prints. Silver, which conducts heat and electricity very well, is widely used in the electrical industry; it also has uses as a disinfectant in medicine. It is found in the food chain in generally harmless amounts, which accumulate in humans.

Sodium (Na) Sodium is a soft, silvery metal named after the English word "soda"; its symbol is from the Latin *natrium* (soda). Sodium is essential to animals; among other functions it moves electric impulses along nerve fibers. Although discovered as an element in the 19th century (Humphry Davy, 1807, England) it has been known in its compounds sodium carbonate ("soda") and sodium chloride (table salt) since biblical times. Table salt is now iodized to prevent thyroid disease, and packets of glucose and salt are used in developing countries to prevent dehydration in young victims of diarrhea and other diseases. Sodium is also an important industrial element. Sodium compounds are widely used in glassmaking, the chemical industry, and metallurgy, and in the manufacture of fire extinguishers; sodium metal is employed in chemical manufacturing, metallurgy, and street lamps.

Strontium (Sr) An alkaline earth element, strontium was first isolated by Humphry Davy (1808, England) and named for the Scottish village of Strontian. It is a constituent of some shelled sea animals and stony corals. The isotope Strontium-90, produced by above-ground nuclear tests, is highly dangerous. Strontium has limited specialized uses in flares, glass for TV screens, and as a power source for remote navigation as well as space and weather stations.

Sulfur (S) Sulfur is essential to all living things, and in humans it is part of the essential amino acid methionine and of vitamin B1. In ancient times it was used for matches, in making wine, and in bleaching cloth; it was also a component of the "Greek fire" of Byzantium and gunpowder. Its name is derived from the Sanskrit and Latin terms *sulvere* and *sulfurium*, for sulfur. Today it is a leading industrial chemical; most of it goes into sulfuric acid, which has an enormous range of uses in phosphate fertilizers, removing rust, and producing paints, detergents, fuels, and many other commodities.

Tantalum (Ta) Discovered by Anders Ekeburgy (1802, Sweden), and named after the mythical King Tantalus; obtained by mining and as a by-product of tin production. Tantalum is easy to work and resists corrosion; it is used to coat other metals, in specialized alloys, and for surgical implants.

Technetium (Tc) Discovered by Emilio Segrè and Carlo Perrier (1937, Italy), although possibly found earlier in Germany (1925), it is a radioactive metal occurring naturally in only minute amounts. Its name is from the Greek *tekhnetos*, "artificial." It is primarily a by-product of nuclear reactors. Uses: medical diagnosis; research.

Tellurium (Te) Discovered (1783, Romania) by Franz Joseph Müller and named for the Latin for "earth," *tellus*, tellurium is a silver-white semi-metal. Uses: specialized alloys with copper, stainless steel, and lead.

Terbium (Tb) A soft, silvery rare-earth element; more costly and less common than most rare-earth elements, Terbium has limited commercial use in magnets, lasers, and lighting. Isolated in 1843 by Carl Gustav Mosander (Sweden) and named after Ytterby, Sweden.

Thallium (Tl,) Discovered (1861, England) by William Crookes, and named (from the Greek *thallos*, "green shoot") after the green line in its atomic spectrum, thallium is a soft, silver-white metal. It has a few specialized uses in lenses and photoelectric cells. Toxic to humans, its use as a pesticide is banned in many countries

Thorium (Th) Discovered by Jöns Jakob Berzelius (Sweden) in 1829, and named after Thor, the Germanic god of war. It occurs naturally in several minerals; its radioactivity was discovered in 1898. Thorium has uses in metallurgy, oil refining, and photoelectric cells.

Thulium (Tm) Isolated by Per Teodor Cleve (1874, Sweden) and named after Thule, the ancient name for Scandinavia. A soft, bright, silvery metal, it is more expensive than other chemically similar rare-earth metals and so has few practical applications.

Tin (Sn) Tin has been known since ancient times; it symbol is from the Latin, *stannum*. Its main use for millennia was to produce bronze, its alloy with copper; it was also anciently used for tinplating; modern "tin cans" are coated with a thin layer of tin. Tin is also used in a wide range of metal alloys to produce engine parts, bearings, and superconducting magnets, and in glassmaking.

Titanium (Ti) Discovered by Martin Klaproth (1795, Germany), titanium was produced as a metal only in 1910 (U.S.). Named for the Titans of Greek mythology, titanium is an unusually strong, easily worked metal that is essential to aircraft engines and frames. It has other commercial uses, such as power plant condensers and architectural sheeting, and is used for replacement parts and pins in the human body, in which it bonds with bone. Titanium dioxide is used in paints.

Transfermium Elements The transfermium elements are the elements beyond fermium (100), from 101 on up to the most recently discovered. These elements have all been produced in the course of research; they are created by bombarding isotopes of elements with subatomic particles. Many have very short half-lives of less than a second. Relatively little is known about them beyond the fact that they have been observed in experimental conditions, the atomic number, isotopes, and in a few cases something about compounds. The elements from 101 through 111 are relatively unstable; then there is a predicted "island of stability" from 112 to 118. As of 2002, the highest-numbered element to be produced is 116; all the elements up to that except 113 and 115 have also been produced. A claim was made in 1999 by scientists at the Lawrence Berkeley National Laboratory for the discovery of element 118, but this claim was apparently based on incorrect and possibly manipulated data and has been withdrawn. During the cold war, priority of discovery and naming were hotly contested for several transfermium elements between teams at Dubna, Russia, and Berkeley, California. Elements without presently agreed-on names use words representing the digits of the atomic number: ununnilium for element 110 (i.e., one, one, zero + ium, the suffix for "metal").

Tungsten (W) A silver-gray metal discovered in 1783 by the de Elhuyar brothers (Spain). It is very hard and resistant to corrosion, with the highest melting point of any metal, 61,700 degrees F (34,100 degrees C). Tungsten is used to make heavy steel alloys for armaments and has been regarded as a strategic mineral since World War I. The United States is dependent on imports for tungsten, primarily from China and Russia. Other uses of tungsten include drilling and abrasives. It is named after the Swedish *tung sten*, "heavy stone," and its abbreviation is from its alternative name, wolfram.

Ununbiium (Uub) A transfermium element produced in 1996 by Peter Armbruster and others (Germany), it is below mercury in the periodic table. No formal name yet assigned. Uses: research.

Ununhexium (Uuh) A transfermium element produced in 2000 at Dubna, Russia. No formal name yet assigned. Uses: research.

Ununnilium (Uun) A transfermium element produced in 1994 by Peter Armbruster and others (Germany), with earlier Russian and American claims. No formal name yet assigned. Uses: research.

Ununquadium (Uuq) A transfermium element discovered by Huri Oganessian and others (1998, Russia). No formal name yet assigned. Uses: research.

Unununium (Uuu) A transfermium element produced in 1994 by Peter Armbruster and others (Germany), it is below gold in the periodic table. No formal name yet assigned. Uses: research.

Uranium (U) Uranium is a naturally radioactive rare-earth metal that was identified by Eugène Pelicot (France) in 1841 and named after the planet Uranus, which is named for the Greek god of the sky. Its radioactive nature was not understood until 1896 (Henri Becquerel, France). Uranium is abundant in mineral ores; it is widely mined, and the most important use is fuel for nuclear reactors. Nuclear fission occurs when the proportion of the U-235 isotope, naturally only about 1 percent, is increased. The fission of nuclear weapons (the first atomic bomb dropped in wartime was a uranium bomb) is controlled in nuclear power plants by neutron absorbers such as heavy water.

Vanadium (V) Vanadium is essential as a trace element for humans and some other animals. Discovered by Andrés del Rio (1801, Mexico), it is named after the Scandinavian goddess of beauty, Vanadis. A silvery metal, vanadium is mainly used in steel alloys to provide strength and rustproofing.

Xenon (Xe) Xenon, a noble (chemically inert) gas, was discovered in 1898 by William Ramsay and Morris Travers (England); its name is from the Greek for "stranger," *xenos*. Produced from liquid air, it is used in biocidal lamps, flash lamps, and other lighting.

Ytterbium (Yb) Named after Ytterby, Sweden, the soft, silvery-white rare-earth metal was isolated by Jean Charles Gallissard de Marignac (Switzerland) in 1878. Chemically similar to other rare-earths, it has few commercial applications.

Yttrium (Y) Isolated by Johan Gadolin (1794, Finland) and named after the village of Ytterby, Sweden, yttrium is a soft, silvery metal obtainable from ores. It is used in many metal alloys and provides the red color in TV monitors. The radioactive isotope yttrium-90 is used in cancer therapy.

Zinc (Zn) Zinc is essential for animals and plants; it is in hundreds of enzymes and in the transcription factors through which RNA is synthesized, and zinc deficiency is a risk in developing countries. As a metal, zinc has been known since ancient times; alloyed with copper, it produces brass. The modern use of zinc is mainly in galvanizing steel; other uses are in castings, in making brass, and in batteries. Zinc oxide is used in pigments, as a catalyst in rubber production, and in sunscreen.

Zirconium (Zr) Discovered by Martin Klaproth (1789, Germany), it is named after the Arabic word for "gold colored," *zargun*. It is widely found in ores, and is used for ceramics and heat resistant furnace linings; as a metal, it does not absorb neutrons and is used for tubing in nuclear reactors. Zircons are gems, known in ancient times, containing zirconium.

Glossary of Chemistry Terms

acid compound that contains hydrogen and dissociates in water, producing hydrogen ions. Among the most common *acids* is sulfuric acid (H^2SO4). Alternative definitions: a substance that tends to release a proton (Lowry-Brønsted); a substance that accepts two electrons from a base (Lewis).

analytic chemistry the branch of chemistry in which the constituents of substances, and their relative amounts, are analyzed.

anion a negatively charged ion. In electrolysis, anions move to the anode.

atom the smallest part of an element that exists chemically. Atoms have a nucleus of protons and neutrons that is surrounded by electrons that move in orbits, or, more precisely, regions of space, around the nucleus.

atomic number the number of protons (positively charged particles) in the nucleus of an atom. Elements are defined by their atomic numbers; all atoms of an element have the same number of protons.

atomic weight weight of an element as compared with 1/12 of the weight of the principal isotope of carbon, carbon 12. Also called relative atomic mass.

atomic mass unit 1/12 of the weight of the principal isotope of carbon, carbon 12; this is the standard atomic mass unit, or amu. Symbol = u.

base compound that reacts with an acid to produce water and a salt. Alternative definitions: a substance that tends to accept a proton (Lowry-Brønsted); a substance that yields two electrons to an acid (Lewis).

boiling point the phase transition between liquid and gas.

catalyst a substance that increases the rate of a chemical reaction without undergoing any permanent chemical change.

cation a positively charged ion. In electrolysis, cations move to the cathode.

electrochemistry the study of chemical reactions and properties relating to ions in solution, including electric cells and electrolysis.

electrolysis the production of a chemical reaction by passing an electric current through an electrolyte. In electrolysis, positive ions (cations) move to the cathode, and negative ions (anions) move to the anode.

electrolyte a liquid that conducts electricity through the presence of positive or negative ions

electron negatively charged particles in orbit around the nucleus of an atom. Electrons have very little mass compared with protons and neutrons.

element a substance that cannot be decomposed into simpler substances; it is defined by the number of protons (the atomic number) in its atoms.

free radical an atom or group of atoms with an unpaired valence electron; most free radicals are highly reactive.

freezing point phase transition between liquid and solid.

gas a state of matter in which the molecules are not held together, but move freely; a gas takes the shape of its container regardless of the quantity of molecules.

inorganic chemistry study of chemical properties and reactions in compounds not containing carbon.

ion an atom or group of atoms that has gained or lost an electron. If an electron is lost, the ion is positively charged (cation), and if an electron is gained, the ion is negatively charged (anion).

isotope an element's atoms all have the same number of protons, but some atoms of an element can have different numbers of neutrons. Different combinations of neutrons with the fixed number of protons that defines the element are called isotopes of the element

liquid state of matter between solid and gas, in which the three-dimensional regularity of the solid is lost but the complete disorganization of the gaseous state is not reached. The phase transition between solid and gas is the melting point, and between liquid and gas the boiling point.

mass number the total of protons and neutrons in an atom of an element or one of its isotopes is the mass number of the element or the isotope.

melting point the phase transition between liquid and solid.

mole unit of the amount of a substance in the SI notation system. It is defined as the amount of a substance that contains as many elementary entities as there are atoms in 0.012 kilograms of carbon 12. The entities can be atoms, molecules, ions, electrons, etc.; and they must be specified. Abbreviation: mol.

molecule particle composed of atoms of elements that are combined in a whole-number ratio. Molecules can be composed of atoms of the same element (e.g., ozone, O_3), or, more commonly, of different elements (e.g., table salt, NaCl).

neutron an element's nucleus contains neutrons, which have no electric charge, as well as protons. Each neutron weighs approximately as much as a proton.

organic chemistry the branch of chemistry in which carbon compounds and their reactions are studied.

periodic table the periodic table arranges the elements in groups according to their atomic weights; the "periods" are the rows of elements, which group elements in such a way that elements in the columns, progressively heavier, have similar chemical properties.

pH a logarithmic scale for expressing the acidity or alkalinity of a solution, introduced in 1909 by Søren Sørensen (1868–1939). The term stands for "potential of hydrogen." A pH of 7 is neutral; acids are less than 7, and bases are greater than 7.

phase change the movement of a substance from one phase to another, e.g. from solid to liquid or liquid to gas.

photochemistry the study of chemical reactions that are caused by light.

polymer a substance that has large molecules composed of repeating structural units. There are natural polymers, such as rubber, and many synthesized polymers, such as those that make most plastics.

proton positively charged particle in the nucleus of an atom. The number of protons in an element's atoms is the atomic number of the element.

reagent a substance reacting with another substance. In the laboratory reagents are used in analysis or experiments.

salt a compound produced by the reaction of an acid and a base, in which hydrogen in the acid is replaced by metal or other positive ions.

SI system the International System of Units used in chemistry and other sciences. The initials are from the French, Système International d'Unités.

solid state of matter in which there is three-dimensional regularity of the components (which may be atoms, molecules, or ions), due to the nearness of the components and the strength of the forces between them. At the melting point, a solid turns into a liquid.

valence electron an electron in one of the outer ("valence") shells of an atom that takes part in forming chemical bonds.

GEOLOGY

Geology is the study of Earth, its substances, makeup, forms, processes, and history. Geology is a great unifying discipline, built on the sciences of physics, chemistry, and biology, and using everything from astronomy and climatology to mathematics. Through geology, we come to understand the life cycle of our planet and thus explore the processes that bring about other bodies in our solar system and universe.

The field breaks down into two significant areas: historical geology, which delves into the formation and physical evolution of Earth; and physical geology, which describes the state of the planet and its physical structures and systems.

Historical geology begins before Earth itself was whole, when the processes that formed the materials of today's Earth had just begun. It introduces us to the geologic time scale, the system by which scientists measure and classify the "ages of Earth." Through this study, we can begin to glimpse the enormousness of the time scale that underlies the science of geology. We see how what we call "prehistory" in fact dwarfs the almost infinitesimally short span of human existence on Earth, only a part of which we call "history."

Physical geology studies the formation of the largest structures on earth—from the highest mountain ranges to the deepest trenches on the ocean bottom—as well as smaller-scale objects such as rocks, minerals, and crystals.

History of Geology

Speculation about the origin and composition of Earth is as old as humanity. Most religions contain some form of creation myth, and many hold that the natural forces governing the planet are embodied by gods and spirits. In antiquity, various philosophers propounded theories of the natural world. Anaximander (610–ca. 546 B.C.) recognized that Earth is curved, but thought it cylindrical. Pythagoras (ca. 569–ca. 480 B.C.) correctly noted that Earth is a sphere. Xenophanes (ca. 570–480 B.C.), noting seashells on mountaintops, was among the first to recognize that Earth's surface rises and falls over time. Aristotle (384–322 B.C.) offered plausible, but incorrect, theories for volcanoes, earthquakes, fossils, and other natural phenomena. Theophrastus (372–287 B.C.) classified a number of rocks and minerals, and Pytheas (fl. 300 B.C.) described the tides and noted that they are controlled by the moon. Eratosthenes (ca. 276–ca. 194 B.C.) calculated the size of Earth with reasonable precision. In China, Zhang Heng (A.D. 78–139) developed a primitive seismograph.

Before the 18th-century Enlightenment most European scientists were heavily influenced by religious belief, including the Judeo-Christian story of creation. Scholars attempted to fix the age of Earth through a careful and literal reading of the Bible, concluding that creation took place about 6,000 years ago (far short of the present-day estimate of 4.6 billion years). Another biblical story with geologic import concerned Noah's great flood, which was used by many scientists at that time to explain a number of observable geologic phenomena, such as the existence of marine fossils on mountaintops. Believing that great singular events such as the flood—either natural or divine in origin—were responsible for the formation of Earth, this school of thought came to be known later as catastrophism.

In the 17th century a few scientists developed ideas that we still believe to be correct today. The French philosopher René Descartes (1596–1650) was among the first to suggest that Earth is much older than biblical chronologies indicate. The Danish scientist Nicolas Steno (1638–86) correctly explained fossils as the remains of long-dead organisms and introduced the idea that layers of rock, called strata by geologists, were deposited at different times, with older layers lying below more recent ones (1669).

In the 18th century, the French polymath Georges-Louis Leclerc, comte de Buffon (1707–88), proposed (1778) that instead of the Judeo-Christian period of six days, creation took six epochs; and Earth might be about 75,000 years old instead of 6,000 years old—privately he thought it was even older. In Scotland in 1785, an amateur geologist, James Hutton (1726–97), suggested that Earth's strata must have formed gradually. He claimed that cataclysmic events had not contributed in any significant way to the overall structure of the planet—a principle that we now call uniformitarianism. Simply stated, Earth's history is a long, gradual development that can be explained in terms of natural forces that are still observable today. This idea became a cornerstone of modern geology.

Hutton had little influence initially, but another Scot, Sir Charles Lyell (1797–1875), expanded on and popularized Hutton's ideas and work. He argued strongly that one could explain geologic history perfectly well by pointing to the geological processes—the action of wind and water, earthquakes, and volcanoes—presently at work and observable on Earth. Lyell rejected the short time line derived from the Bible and proposed a much greater period for the development and evolution of Earth. Lyell's notion of a vastly great "geologic time" had a profound effect on science well beyond the study of geology and on our very understanding of its place in the world. The length of geologic time made possible the evolutionary theory of Lyell's good friend Charles Darwin. It provided the time scale necessary for natural selection to take place.

Historical Geology

Formation of Earth

Although Hutton described Earth as having "no vestige of a beginning," that purely uniformitarian view was not accepted by most geologists. As with many ideas in earth science, one of the first to propose a scientific explanation of Earth's beginnings was Comte Buffon, who suggested in 1745 that Earth was created from material splashed from the sun when a comet struck it. Buffon's theory, however, assumed an impossibly large comet. In 1755 the German philosopher Immanuel Kant (1724–1804) proposed an idea that, with many adjustments by astronomers, became the basis of the modern theory of Earth's formation. He said that Earth and the other planets coalesced from a dust cloud around the sun.

The modern version of Kant's theory is as follows: A mass of gas and dust slowly condensed under the force of gravity into a spinning disk. This solar nebula continued to coalesce, with the sun forming at the center of the disk, and planets coming together out of the material in the outer regions. Earth and the other planets assembled as a result of countless collisions of smaller bodies, some mere microscopic specks and others as large as minor planets. The growing planet swept up and incorporated most of the debris in its path as it orbited the sun, and generated an extremely high temperature from the energy of all those impacts and explosions.

This violent infancy of bombardment and collision brought most of Earth's minerals (some continue to arrive as dust or impacts from space), while the high temperature melted the entire planet. During this period, gravity drew heavier elements into the interior of the new planet, whereas lighter ones remained near the surface. As the planet cooled, Earth took on a three-part form: a thin crust, the surface of Earth; a solid mantle that makes up the main part of the planet; and a liquid core of molten metal (high pressure also created a solid inner core within the molten outer core).

Composition of the Earth

In their study of the Earth, scientists distinguish a number of distinct layers from the inner core—the center of which is about 6,400 km (roughly 4,000 miles) below the surface—to the farthest limit of the atmosphere, about 1,000 km (600 miles) above the surface. This section describes these layers, from the innermost to the outermost.

Core The core consists of two parts—one solid, the other liquid—both thought to be a mixture of iron and a lighter element, probably sulfur or oxygen. The solid inner core begins about 4,650 km (2,890 miles) from the surface, and the liquid outer core at about 2,900 km (1,800 miles) from the surface.

Mantle The bulk of the Earth—roughly two-thirds of its mass—is composed of the mantle, which extends from the outer core to within about 90 km (55 miles) of the Earth's surface below the higher mountains, and to within only 5 to 8 km (3 to 5 miles) of the Earth's surface below some areas of the oceans. Silicon dioxide constitutes almost half of the mantle, and there is an abundance of magnesium oxide, some iron oxide, and smaller amounts of oxides of other metals. (Although silicon dioxide is known as quartz when found in the Earth's crust, under the heat and pressure of the mantle it may have very different properties from the form we know.) Part of the upper mantle is somewhat fluid and is known as the asthenosphere.

Lithosphere Formerly called the crust, the lithosphere is the outermost solid layer of the Earth. Under the continents, the crust varies from 30 to 90 km (19 to 55 miles) in thickness, while under the oceans it is generally only 5 to 8 km (3 to 5 miles) thick. Continental and oceanic crust differ from each other in thickness and composition. Continental crust consists of granite and other relatively light rocks; oceanic crust is made up chiefly of basalt. The crust is separated from the mantle by the Mohorovičić discontinuity, or Moho.

Hydrosphere Water exists on Earth in all three states—solid, liquid, and vapor—and is found on the surface, within the crust, and in the atmosphere. The overwhelming majority of Earth's water, over 97 percent, is contained in the oceans. Another 2 percent is the vast fields of polar ice and the glaciers and ice caps that exist in mountains and other high-altitude regions. The remaining portion is found in surface water—rivers, lakes, streams, etc.—and groundwater and soil water. The abundant presence of water is, of course, what distinguishes Earth from the other planets in the solar system. The unique conditions that allow so much water to exist in liquid form on Earth are the same conditions that make life possible.

Water—virtually all of it seawater—covers about 71 percent of the Earth's surface and thereby constitutes a distinct layer of the Earth. Seawater varies in composition from place to place, but on average it is about 3.5 percent salts—that is, evaporating 100 pounds of seawater would yield 3.5 pounds of salt. Sodium chloride (ordinary table salt) constitutes 2.7 percent of seawater, or 77.8 percent of total solids in seawater.

Atmosphere The atmosphere is the gaseous layer that envelopes the Earth. The lower atmosphere consists of the troposphere and the stratosphere. The *troposphere* has an average thickness of about 11 km (7 miles), although it is only 8 km (5 miles) at the poles and as much as 16 km (10 miles) around the equator. Most clouds and weather phenomena occur in this region. The composition of dry air at sea level is: nitrogen, 78.08 percent; oxygen, 20.05 percent; argon, 0.93 percent; and carbon dioxide, 0.03 percent. There are also lesser amounts of neon, helium, krypton, and xenon. These proportions change with altitude, lighter gases being more common at higher altitudes, but they are approximately the same everywhere on Earth at the same altitude. There are also variable quantities of water vapor, dust particles, and other compounds whose proportions change from place to place at the same altitude—fewer dust particles being found over oceans, and less water vapor over deserts. Temperature decreases with altitude in the troposphere.

The *stratosphere* is found between 11 km and 50 km (7–30 miles) out from the Earth's surface. Temperatures in this region rise slightly as altitude increases, to a maximum of about 0°C (32°F). Virtually coextensive with the stratosphere is the *ozonosphere*, or ozone layer, the region in which most of the atmosphere's ozone is found. Because ozone absorbs most of the sun's ultraviolet radiation, it is vital to the continued existence of life on the planet.

Beyond the stratosphere is the upper atmosphere, or *ionosphere*, so called because it is the layer in which atmospheric gases have been ionized by solar radiation. The ionosphere reflects certain wavelengths back to the surface, making it possible to transmit radio waves around the curve of the Earth. The ionosphere is further divided into the *mesosphere*, between 50 km and 80 km (30–50 miles), in which the temperature decreases with altitude to –90°C (–130°F); and the *thermosphere*, from about 80 km to 450 km (50–280 miles), in which the molecular temperature increases to as much as 1,475°C (2,690°F). To spacecraft traveling in the atmosphere, as the space shuttle does, however, the temperature seems cold because the molecules are so widely spaced. Beyond the thermosphere is the *exosphere*, extending to about 1,000 km (600 miles). In this layer, temperature no longer has the customary meaning.

Geologic Time

The life of our planet is measured in immense blocks of time called eras, period, epochs, and ages. These mark the development of Earth and form the geologic time scale. The planet's origin is generally put at about 4.6 billion years ago, the age of the oldest meteorites found. To appreciate the true length of geologic time, we can think of those 4.6 billion years as represented by a single year. The oldest fossil records go back only about 40 days, and humans' presence on the planet only about two hours. Modern humans would exist for only about five minutes of that year. As Lyell and Darwin demonstrated, the vastness of geologic time makes the notion of evolution possible and comprehensible.

One of the major divisions in the history of life occurs at the beginning of the Cambrian period, when most of the main groups of animals appear for the first time in the geologic record. As a result, geologists often speak of the period before this as Precambrian time (4.6 billion years ago to 542 million years ago, also known sometimes as the Precambrian epoch). More than 88 percent of Earth's history is Precambrian. Of the remaining time, when Earth has been home to animal life as we know it, the part that includes humans and their ancestors is less than 1 percent.

Geologic Time Scale

Eon, Period, or Epoch	Organisms	Beginning of interval (millions of years ago)
HADEAN EON	No evidence of life	4,600.0
ARCHEAN EON	Monerans (bacteria and blue-green algae); Archaea	3,800.0
PROTEROZOIC EON	Protists; algae; and soft-bodied creatures similar to jellyfish or worms	2,500.0
PHANEROZOIC EON		
Cambrian period	Tiny fossils with skeletons followed by animals with shells, notably trilobites	542.0
Ordovician period	Brachiopods (shellfish similar to clams), corals, starfish, and some organisms called sea scorpions and conodonts that have no modern counterparts	488.3
Silurian period	Snails, clams and mussels, ammonoids (similar to the nautilus), jawless fish, sea scorpions, land plants and animals (club mosses, land scorpions); modern groups of algae and fungi	443.7
Devonian period	Spiders, amphibians, jawed fish, lobe-finned fish, sharks, lungfish, and ferns	416.0
Carboniferous period	Insects, land snails, amphibians, early reptiles, sea lilies, giant club mosses, and seed ferns	359.2
Permian period	Mammal-like reptiles and fin-backed reptiles, cycads, ginkgoes, and conifers	289.0
MEZOZOIC ERA		
Triassic period	Marine reptiles (plesiosaurs and ichthyosaurs), crocodiles, frogs, turtles, early mammals, and early dinosaurs	251.0
Jurassic period	Dinosaurs (such as stegosaurs), pterosaurs (such as pterodactyl), early birds, dinoflagellates, diatoms, early flowering plants	199.6
Cretaceous period	Dinosaurs (such as tyrannosaurs, triceratops, and apatosaurs), salamanders, modern bony fishes, mosasaurs (marine reptiles), flowering plants, placental and marsupial mammals	145.5
CENOZOIC ERA		
Palaeogene period		
Paleocene epoch	Early primates, early horses, rodents, sycamore	65.8
Eocene epoch	Whales, penguins, roses, bats, camels, early elephants, dogs, cats, weasels	57.8
Oligocene epoch	Deer, pigs, saber-toothed cats, monkeys	36.6
Neogene period		
Miocene epoch	Seals, dolphins, grasses, daisies, asters, sunflowers, lettuce, giraffes, bears, hyenas, early apes	23.03
Pliocene epoch	Apes, *Ardipithecus* and *australopithecines* (early hominids), *Homo habilis* and *rudolfensis* (first human species), mammoths, giant sloths and armadillos	5.2
Pleistocene epoch	*Homo erectus* and other early human species, modern humans; large mammals such as giant bison and beavers; many kinds of hoofed animals	1.6
Holocene epoch	Modern humans and flora and fauna of today	0.01 (11,000 years)

Plate Tectonics

This scientific theory describes the drifting and shifting of large parts of Earth's crust and upper mantle, called plates. These complex motions cause the formation of mountains and abysses, of volcanoes and earthquakes, and of the very location of Earth's landmasses today. The plates move at an extremely slow pace—perhaps only a few centimeters each year, and the great distances now between them further deepen our appreciation of the length of geologic time.

In 1912 the German meteorologist Alfred Wegener (1880–1930) became the first to make a convincing case for these motions, although a few earlier scientists had recognized some parts of the concept. Wegener began with two simple observations: first, that the coastlines of some continents, such as Africa and South America, appear to fit together like the pieces of a jigsaw puzzle; and second, that many land species (contemporary ones and also those found in the fossil record) of widely disparate continents bear striking resemblances to one another. Wegener postulated that the continents must have at one time been joined together. Most earlier geologists and paleontologists had explained the similarities of coastline shapes as coincidence and the similar species as the result of "land bridges" which had once existed across oceans, but which had subsequently sunk into the sea floor.

Continental Drift Wegener gradually refined his theories and described a single, great protocontinent, which he dubbed Pangaea after the Greek for "whole Earth." This massive body was surrounded by a single vast ocean, Panthalassa, or "universal sea." For reasons that he was not at that time able to determine, Pangaea broke apart and pieces drifted slowly into place around the globe. This theory is known as *continental drift*. As refined by Wegener and later geologists, the theory states that toward the end of the Carboniferous period, Pangaea broke into two main bodies. The northernmost one, encompassing modern Europe, North America, and Asia, is called Laurasia. The southern one, Gondwanaland, contained Africa, South America, the Indian subcontinent, Australia, and Antarctica.

At the time of Wegener's death, however, many remained unconvinced. After World War II the idea of continental drift gained wide acceptance, first in a modified form called seafloor spreading and later as a part of plate tectonics.

Seafloor Spreading One of the unexplained parts of continental drift concerned the great mountain chains and deep trenches found at the bottom of the oceans. The first to be recognized was the mid-atlantic ridge, which matches in general shape both the coastlines on each side of the Atlantic Ocean. A trench runs through the crest of this ridge. Other oceans have similar features, which are connected to form a worldwide mid-Oceanic ridge and also deep, curved trenches near chains of islands, such as the Marianas trench and the Philippine trench in the Pacific. In 1962 the American oceanographer Harry Hammond Hess (1906–69) proposed that the ocean floor is created at the mid-Oceanic ridge and then spreads, widening the oceans. Sometimes the spreading pushes continents farther apart, but in places the ocean floor away from the ridges plunges into deep trenches. In the early 1960's the record of changes over long periods of time in Earth's magnetic field, found preserved in the rock of the ocean floor and in rocks on continents, confirmed both seafloor spreading and relative changes in the positions of the continents. The best explanation was that Earth's crust is broken into giant plates that move with respect to one another, sometimes carrying continents along.

Convergence and Divergence The action and interaction of the plates, both gradually and in occasional sudden outbursts, have created most of the familiar features of the landscape. When the leading edge of one plate meets another plate, we call it convergence, and this is largely responsible for the creation of most mountain ranges. When plates pull apart, a process called divergence, hot molten rock wells up into the void between them. This happens generally under the oceans and is how new material is commonly brought from Earth's interior to the crust or surface. Sometimes, the plates neither come together nor pull apart, but simply move past each other, rubbing together along the edges. These transforms, as they are called, constitute the great geologic faults that we tend to fear, like the San Andreas Fault. The sudden spasms of activity lead to earthquakes, volcanic eruptions, and other natural cataclysms.

Physical Geology

The lithosphere is composed overwhelmingly of rock, or fragments of rock. (The specific scientific study of rocks is called petrology.) Most rock occurs in deposits called beds, which can form in a vertical plane as well as the more common horizontal plane. Rocks, in turn, are made up of minerals, although for the most part, minerals are not rocks. A mineral is a naturally occurring element or compound that has a precise chemical formula. Geologists classify rocks in three main groups, sorted by the process of formation: igneous, sedimentary, and metamorphic.

Igneous rocks are rocks that have formed by solidifying or crystallizing from a molten state, either lava (molten rock on Earth's surface) or magma (molten rock below the surface). Igneous rocks that form from lava are generally called volcanic rocks. Igneous rocks are often subcategorized according to texture, and in addition to the fine-grained rocks such as basalt, lava can also form glassy rocks, typified by obsidian. The speed of cooling normally determines the texture of the rocks, with glasses formed by very quick cooling. Since magma cools more slowly at depth than it does on the surface, rocks that crystallize far deeper within Earth, called plutonic rocks, typically form larger mineral crystals than the fine-grained surface-cooled rocks.

Sedimentary rocks are created by accumulation of deposited materials, including particles and fragments of rocks (sand or gravel), shells of sea animals, and chemical precipitates such as salt from evaporating water. The deposits slowly cement together over long periods of time. Examples of sedimentary rocks include sandstone, shale, and limestone. Sedimentary rocks often capture and contain fossils, footprints, and other clues to evolution.

Metamorphic rocks form as the result of heat, pressure, and chemical activity on igneous or sedimentary rock. These processes are slow and complex, highlighted by the recrystallization of the minerals of the rock. Without melting, the chemical elements and compounds reorganize under the influence of intense heat and pressure. Sometimes, even new minerals can be formed. As a result, metamorphic rocks are largely characterized by a regular crystalline structure, as opposed to the more random internal structure of igneous or sedimentary rocks. The regular patterned structure is typical of rocks like mica or gneiss, which tend to shear off cleanly (a property called cleavage) when broken. These rocks typically form under the more extreme conditions of metamorphism, and their minerals are arranged in roughly parallel lines (foliation), giving the rocks something of a banded appearance.

Minerals

Minerals are naturally occurring substances with characteristic and uniform chemical compositions and physical properties. A few minerals are elements (e.g., gold, iron, and silver), but most are chemical compounds. Minerals are generally obtained by mining on land, although there is some ocean mining. Approximately 3,700 minerals have been discovered.

Minerals can be conveniently divided into two types: fuel and nonfuel minerals. Fuel minerals are coal, oil, and natural gas. Some common and widely used nonfuel minerals are so heavy and bulky that production tends to be relatively local; these minerals include crushed stone and sand and gravel for construction.

Other minerals are traded internationally; the United States is wholly dependent on imports from other countries for at least 14 nonfuel minerals. Strategic minerals are those deemed essential to the functioning of an economy, particularly with respect to wartime conditions. A strategic mineral is one which has key applications in defense or the civilian economy, which cannot be easily replaced by other substances, and for which there are few or no available domestic supplies. Only some nonfuel minerals are strategic; others are widely found and produced.

Structural Geology

Photographs of Earth from airplanes and satellites, as well as those taken from the surface of the moon or from cameras in space, display the great landmasses and the connected world ocean. There are mountains and canyons, fertile plains and swamplands, vast barren deserts and wide inland lakes. Although hidden from sight, similar variety exists at the bottom of the ocean. The processes that gave rise to each of these features are common, yet each locality, each type, has its own unique geologic history.

Folds, Faults, and Joints

Earth's surface is often deformed by tremendous pressures and forces. The resulting structures make up a major area of study for structural geologists. Faults and folds, which exist at the meeting point between various geologic planes and beds, hold special interest, as they are often the site of ongoing seismic activity.

Folds are deformed arrangements of stratified rock. Specialized terms for measuring and describing them include *strike*, the compass direction of the line made by the leading edge of an inclined bed; and *dip*, the angle of inclination of the bed from an imaginary horizontal plane. Where the *limbs*, or two sides of a fold, angle down, away from each other and from the central axis, the fold is called an *anticline*. Where they fold up, toward each other, it is called a *syncline*. The Appalachian Mountains in the eastern United States are characterized by complex fold structures.

Joints are long cracks or fractures common to most rock beds on the surface of Earth. Some joints result from folding or other deforming processes. Others are caused by contraction during the cooling of igneous rock, or when moist earth dries. Some are vertical, while others are parallel to the topographic surface of the area. The origin of these horizontal joints is uncertain, although possibly they are produced when rocks that have formed under great pressure at depth find their way to the surface through natural uplift, where they release some of that pressure.

Faults, like joints, are also breaks in Earth's crust. The critical difference is that a joint is a stable separation, but in a fault there either is or has been movement of rock on one side of the break in relation to the other. Faults are classified according to the type of movement they exhibit—vertical, horizontal, or sideways.

The San Andreas Fault is a well-known example of a fault. This fault, which is actually a system of smaller faults, extends from the Gulf of Mexico to northern California, a distance of roughly 600 miles, and continues into the Pacific. The *fault line* represents the meeting point of two large-scale sections of the lithosphere, the Pacific and the North American plates. Most earthquakes tend to happen along fault lines, and the San Andreas Fault is very active and has been the site of some significant events, such as the great earthquakes of 1906 and 1989 in San Francisco.

Other common geologic structures are formed by the fluctuation of forces beneath the surface of Earth, acting on a crust where the material varies in density and flexibility. We see a variety of upwellings and depressions—called, variously, domes, plateaus, basins, and esplanades—that formed through these geologic processes combined with erosion by wind and water.

Mountains

Mountains occur largely in long chains called ranges and in closely located groups called clusters. Occasionally one mountain appears to be isolated from all the others. The principles of plate tectonics provided geologists with the first reasonable explanations for the sources of mountains. Mountains are formed by a variety of complex processes, and each mountain range or cluster has a unique origin.

Volcanic Mountains Some of the least complex mountains are volcanic; these form out of accumulation of material—magma, lava, ash, and other debris—that is released from the interior of Earth during a cataclysmic fissure or other event. Some of the iconic mountains of the world—Fuji, Kilimanjaro, Etna, Rainier—are volcanic mountains. Although volcanic mountains can appear in clusters, as they do in the Pacific Northwest of America, they do not arise in great chains and ridges like other forms of mountains. Where mountains appear in clusters or along ranges, they are formed from magma created by one plate sliding under another (along the west coasts of the Americas) or by a plate moving over a rising plume of magma (a "hot spot") from deep in Earth's interior.

Folded Mountains The collisions of Earth's plates of crust that give rise to some volcanoes are related to the activity that causes folded mountains. These occur when plates push against each other also. Most of the great ranges of our world, such as the Alps and Himalayas, are folded mountains. In each case, a long period in which sedimentary material is built up is followed by the vertical uplifting of the mountains that results from compression, thrusting, and faulting of lithospheric plates. Much of this accumulation occurs in subsidence areas (where the crust has lowered), such as geosynclines, which are long, troughlike depressions, sometimes underlying large bodies of water.

Block Mountains The origin of block mountains (sometimes called fault-block mountains) is also caused by collision of plates. Plates or sections of the crust collide and exert pressure against each other or pull apart, causing tension. When rock sections break, the results include large differences in elevation between the sections. Such processes are responsible for many of the rift valleys in Africa and for the Basin and Range region of the American West. The midocean ridges are also caused by plates moving apart from each other.

Last, mountains and ranges can be the result of a combination of processes that may include faulting, folding, and some igneous or volcanic element. Scientists describe these as complex mountains.

Glaciers

Glaciers are vast sheets of ice and rock that advance and recede across Earth's surface. They are found throughout the world at very high elevations, as well as in the high-latitude regions approaching the poles. Although they are an uncommon feature of the current landscape, glaciers played a major role in the geology of the relatively recent past and are responsible for many of the landforms and formations we take for granted today.

In order to form, glaciers require not only consistently cold temperatures, but also a significant amount of snowfall. The snow provides the raw material that accumulates to maintain the mass of the glacier. In some regions, such as parts of Antarctica, there is no permanent snow or ice cover on the land, because even though the temperature is sufficiently low, the region is too dry.

Once snow settles on the ground, it tends to undergo a structural transformation and is recrystallized into granules of ice. It is this new ice that becomes part of a glacier. Glaciers are said to "flow" or to behave like "rivers of ice," but this flow usually occurs very slowly. Glacial advance is tremendously slow, ranging from a few inches to several miles annually, although it is punctuated by periods of greater velocity, called surges, which are possibly attributable to the breaking up of damlike accumulations of ice and rock at the leading edge of the ice sheet. The movement of ice sheets is partly due to the instability of the ice, which creates a certain plasticity. Some motion also results from the slippage of the entire ice sheet over the surface of the bed underneath it. As with rivers or streams, the central portion of a glacier tends to advance faster than the edges.

An ice age is a period of large-scale glaciation. Ice ages have occurred regularly throughout the history of the planet. The last one, which occupied the Pleistocene epoch and is believed to have ended as recently as 11,000 years ago, saw an enormous sheet of ice advance downward from the North Pole and spread across a major percentage of the Northern Hemisphere. In North America, the ice traveled down as far as New York in the East, Wisconsin in the Midwest, and Montana and Washington in the West. In Europe, it covered Scandinavia, northern Germany, Russia, and the British Isles. The Andes of South America, as well as major Asian mountain ranges, were also overtaken.

Many geologic features of today—including the sharply cut fjords of Scandinavia, the long lateral ridges of the northeastern United States, and large inland bodies of water such as the Great Lakes—are relics of the last ice age. The Pleistocene epoch probably had numerous periods of glaciation, with periods in between when the ice sheets shrank or receded. Scientists believe that we may be in just such an interglacial period and that in the not too distant future, another ice age is likely to be upon us.

The Earth in Upheaval

The apparent solidity and constancy of the land mask continued activity and upheaval. Just as the atmosphere can produce catastrophic phenomena such as hurricanes and gales, the lithosphere is also the site of cataclysmic events, from terrible earthquakes and volcanic eruptions to more commonplace landslides and sinkholes.

Earthquakes

Tension and compression build up in the Earth's crust, particularly along faults, where large masses of rock or tectonic plates push against each other. When the pressure is released, it usually happens quite suddenly, and the resulting vibrations, or seismic waves, are observed as an earthquake (the word *seismic* means "shaking" and simply refers to earthquakes). Several kinds of seismic waves are produced. Surface waves—also called L waves—travel along Earth's surface. Body waves, which travel through the interior, can be either compressional waves (P waves) or shear waves (S waves), which displace material in different directions and at different speeds as they travel. P waves are back-and-forth waves, essentially the same as sound waves; but for S waves the movement of rock is perpendicular to the movement of the wave, similar to ocean waves.

There are thousands of tiny earthquakes annually. Most are gentle tremors detectable only by sensitive seismographs, but each year a few are of moderate or greater intensity. Major earthquakes are dangerous and destructive, causing buildings or rock formations to fall, often resulting in great loss of life. The point of origin of an earthquake's energy is called its focus, and the depth of the focus below the surface of Earth is the focal depth. The point on the surface directly above a quake's focus is the epicenter, and the location of an earthquake is defined by both the epicenter and the focal depth.

Major earthquakes have occurred frequently around the Pacific Rim and running through the Indian subcontinent to the Mediterranean region. Some places hit by disastrous earthquakes have been California, Alaska, Peru, El Salvador, Iran, Turkey, the islands of the southern Pacific, China, and especially Japan.

Measuring Earthquakes The size of an earthquake is generally reported in the United States using the Richter scale, a system developed by the seismologist Charles Richter (1900–85) in 1935. The Richter scale measures the magnitude of an earthquake, that is, the size of ground waves generated by an earthquake as shown on a measuring device called a seismograph. Each whole number on the scale represents a tenfold increase (or decrease) in magnitude: a magnitude 6 earthquake produces a ground wave 10 times greater than a magnitude 5.

This does not mean, however, that a magnitude 6 earthquake has 10 times the energy as one of magnitude 5. Measuring the actual energy requires instruments placed at the site of the earthquake. Various methods have been developed for inferring energy from magnitude, and these suggest that one change in magnitude corresponds to a thirty- to sixtyfold change in energy. According to these proportions, the energy of a magnitude 8 earthquake, a very serious event, can be 1 million to 10 million times as much as that of a magnitude 4 earthquake, one that can be felt but causes almost no damage.

Richter Scale and Effects Near the Epicenter

Note: The epicenter is the point on Earth's surface above the center of the quake

Below 2.5 Not felt except by a very few.

2.5 to 3.5 Felt only by a few persons at rest, especially on upper floors of buildings.

3.5 to 4.5 At lower levels or farther from the quake, it is felt by many people, sometimes quite noticeably indoors, especially on upper floors of buildings. At somewhat higher levels or nearer to the epicenter, during the day the quake is felt indoors by many but outdoors by few. Sensation is like heavy truck striking building. At the highest level, the earth movement is felt by nearly everyone, with many awakened if the quake occurs during the night. Disturbances of trees, telephone poles, and other tall objects can sometimes be noticed.

4.5 to 6.0 Felt by all. Some heavy furniture moved; there will be a few instances of fallen plaster or damaged chimneys. Other slight local damage may occur. At higher level, however, everybody runs outdoors. At the upper level, while damage is still negligible in buildings of good design and construction, there can be moderate damage even to well-built ordinary structures; there will be considerable damage to poorly built or badly designed structures.

6.0 to 7.0 Destructive earthquake. Damage may be slight in specially designed structures, but will be considerable in ordinary buildings, often with partial collapse. Damage will be great in poorly built structures, including collapse of chimneys, factory stacks, columns, monuments, and walls. At the upper level, damage is likely to be considerable even in specially designed structures. Most ordinary buildings will be shifted off foundations. Even the ground will be cracked conspicuously.

7.0 to 8.0 Major earthquake. Worldwide, about 10 of these occur each year. Some well-built wooden structures will be destroyed. Most masonry and frame structures will be destroyed along with their foundations. Ground becomes badly cracked.

8.0 and above Great earthquakes. These occur once every five to 10 years. Few if any masonry structures remain standing. Bridges are destroyed. Broad fissures appear in ground. At the highest levels and near the epicenter, damage total. Waves seen on solid ground. Heavy objects thrown upward into air.

Volcanoes

A volcano is an opening, called a vent or fissure, in Earth's crust through which solid rock fragments propelled by gases and lava (molten rock) escape from Earth's interior. The term *volcano* is used to describe both the vent itself and the mountain of accumulated discharged materials that builds up around it. The solid material is usually called ash or cinders when the pieces are small, but larger rocks are called bombs. When large amounts of ash, bombs, lava, or gases escape destructively, the process is called an eruption of the volcano. Volcanic eruptions can be both beautiful and horrific. History has seen untold thousands of lives lost and entire pockets of civilization wiped out by volcanic eruptions. Names like Vesuvius, Tambora, Krakatoa, Pinatubo, and Mount St. Helens echo as reminders of Earth's inherent instability and destructive power.

An active volcano either is currently erupting or has erupted in the very recent past (that is, in recorded history) and is considered likely to do so again, as Hawaii's Kilauea is. A volcano is dormant (sleeping) if it is not currently erupting but is believed likely to erupt at some point in the future. Many of the volcanic mountains in the American Northwest are considered dormant. We say a volcano is extinct if it has not erupted in historical time, and if geologists believe it unlikely to erupt in the future, because of a lack of seismic activity or other indicators of subsurface volatility. Africa's Mount Kilimanjaro is considered extinct.

Molten rock below Earth's surface, or magma, tends to rise because liquid rock is less dense than the surrounding solid rock and because magma contains gas under pressure. It collects in pockets or reservoirs under the surface, where its heat causes more of the surrounding rock to melt. Pressure builds in these reservoirs, and the magma and gases eventually force their way up through the surface, either through existing vents or fissures or through structurally weak sections of the crust. Some eruptions seem slow, with lava seeping and flowing gently through cracks in the surface; others are more like massive detonations, spewing great plumes of ash, rock, and steam over large areas of land and into the atmosphere. Either way, volcanic eruptions invariably alter the landscape, sometimes by blasting away large peaks and structures and always by depositing quantities of new material in the form of lava and debris, which build up new land formations. The vent becomes enlarged into a hole in the Earth called a crater. Sometimes an exploded volcano forms a caldera, a large-scale crater created by the collapse of underground magma reservoirs below the volcano.

Eruptions are categorized using the names of historically notable volcanoes or volcanic regions. The quietest eruptions are called Hawaiian and involve gentle emanations of lava and the ejection of debris with some small explosions. Somewhat more dramatic are Strombolian eruptions (after Stromboli in the Mediterranean), with constant recurring explosions and a relatively mild discharge of heavy, viscous lava. Plinian eruptions (after the Roman naturalist Pliny the Elder, killed in an eruption of Vesuvius in A.D. 79 that was described in detail by his nephew, Pliny the Younger) are still more explosive. Immediately prior to these eruptions, the magmatic pressure builds up behind a plug that has naturally formed in the vent that would have been the natural channel to the surface. Eventually, the dam bursts, ejecting material and vapor with great velocity. The most violent eruptions are the Peleean (named for a destructive eruption of Mount Pelée on Martinique in 1902), in which enormous clouds of fine ash and cinder, small bits of molten lava, and superheated steam are propelled sidewise from the eruption, destroying all in the path of the blast.

As catastrophic as volcanoes can be, they are also a mechanism by which valuable elements and minerals, including iron, magnesium, and potassium, are brought from Earth's interior to the surface. Volcanic soils are tremendously rich in these materials and are therefore very fertile. In addition, the study of volcanoes, much like the study of earthquakes, has engendered a much deeper understanding of the mechanisms and processes at work in Earth's interior.

Paleontology

Paleontology is the science of prehistoric life, generally defined as organisms that lived more than 10,000 years ago, prior to the end of the most recent ice age. The science is based on the nature and distribution of fossils, the remains or traces of organisms. In addition to satisfying our curiosity about organisms that lived long ago, paleontology provides evidence to support the concepts of evolution and continental drift (the idea that the positions of the continents have changed over time as a result of plate tectonics). It also helps to support the theory that impacts of asteroids and comets have been instrumental in wiping out significant portions of Earth's life at intervals in our planet's history—so-called mass extinctions. Economically, the study of fossils is valuable in searching for deposits of oil, coal, and other minerals, and in locating limestone and other materials used for construction and building.

The science has subdisciplines, such as paleobotany, the study of ancient plants; paleozoology, the study of ancient animals; and taphonomy, the study of the biological, chemical, and physical processes that lead to an organism's fossilization or its disintegration. Paleontology also relates to other disciplines that study the Earth's past, such as paleogeography, which focuses on Earth's geography as it existed during past eras; paleoecology, which considers the relationships between fossil organisms and the environment in which they lived; and paleoclimatology, the study of ancient climates.

The History of Paleontology

Ancient peoples knew of fossils, and presented various explanations to account for them. Some cultures turned fossils into mythological creatures and described giants that once terrorized Earth. In Greece, Herodotus (ca. 484–ca. 425 B.C.) and others realized that fossil seashells found in mountains were the remains of once-living creatures; but Aristotle (ca. 384–ca. 322 B.C.) suggested that fossils were natural accidents, produced much as crystals are produced, a theory that held sway for many centuries.

The scientific study of fossils began in the 17th century. In 1667 Nicolaus Steno (1638–86) showed that fossils previously believed to be serpent tongues were shark teeth. He proposed that sediments are deposited in horizontal layers, or strata; that strata represent different ages; and that fossils are remains of living creatures from those ages. William Smith (1769–1839) showed that each rock layer has its own distinctive mix of fossils. In 1815, Smith published the first geologic map of England, proving the value of using fossils to define the order of rock layers.

Georges Cuvier (1769–1832), often called the founder of paleontology, discovered that species become extinct, identified pterosaurs as flying reptiles, and was the first scientist to systematically compare the anatomy of fossils and living organisms.

In South America during the 1830's, Charles Darwin (1809–82) examined the fossil remains of giant sloths and other extinct animals, and found fossils of ocean life high in the Andes. His publication in 1859 of *On the Origin of Species*, which proposed that a process he called natural selection is the main force in evolution, profoundly influenced paleontologists. They began looking for ancestors of modern organisms as well as "missing links"—intermediate, transitional forms between known species. The first such link, discovered in Germany in 1861, was *Archaeopteryx*, a primitive bird with characteristics of both its flightless reptile ancestors and modern birds.

Radioactive dating, computer imaging, molecular genetics, and other technologies introduced in the 20th century greatly expanded the study of fossils. Today, new fossil finds are filling blanks in the biological record and pushing back the dawn of life.

Fossils

More than 1 million species of fossil organisms have been identified. These range from microscopic bacteria to giant dinosaurs and tree ferns. Evidence of truly ancient fossils, much of it controversial, suggests that Earth may have had simple bacteria-like life as long as 3.5 billion years ago.

Fossil Types There are two basic types of fossils. Body fossils are either actual remains of organisms or remains in which original chemicals have been replaced by other chemicals, typically silicon dioxide and other minerals from water seeping through the buried remains. Shells, bones, teeth, and petrified wood are common body fossils. Softer tissues, such as those that compose worms, are less likely to be preserved; they often are eaten by animals or broken down by bacteria and other decomposers. Thus the abundance of a species in the fossil record does not necessarily indicate its relative abundance during the age in which it lived.

Trace fossils are marks made by the activities of ancient organisms, such as footprints, burrows, leaf imprints, chemical traces, and tooth marks on bones. They reveal much about anatomy as well as the habits and habitats of their creators. For example, footprint size and the distance between prints in a track provide clues to the size, weight, and speed of the animal that made the track. Pollen from plants preserved in bog sediments in northern Europe demonstrates that cold-adapted species once lived much closer to the equator than they do today.

Dating Fossils The age of a fossil may be determined using relative and absolute dating methods. Relative dating methods compare the ages of various fossils, indicating their relative ages but not their actual ages. For example, stratigraphy is based on the fact that in an undisturbed sequence of rock layers, fossils in lower layers are older than those in upper layers. Amino acid racemization uses the fact that amino acids—the building blocks of proteins—exist in two mirror-image forms, L and D. Amino acids in living things are of the L-form. At death, the L-form racemizes, or changes, into the D-form at a more or less steady rate, though this rate varies from site to site depending on environmental conditions. Thus the greater the extent of racemization, the older the fossil.

The discovery of radiation and radioactive decay led in the 20th century to the development of absolute dating methods that provide specific ages for fossils. These methods are based on the fact that radioactive isotopes decay at a specific rate, called a half-life. For instance, potassium 40 (half-life approximately 1.25 billion years) decays into argon 40 and calcium 40. Potassium-argon dating is usually used to date fossils found in volcanic rock or ash deposits, which are rich in potassium. Another technique, electron spin resonance dating, uses the changes that background radiation indirectly makes, at a predictable rate, in the magnetic field of crystalline minerals. It is used to date calcium carbonate in shells, teeth, and coral.

Dinosaurs The fossil organisms of greatest appeal to laypeople are dinosaurs, land-dwelling reptiles that evolved from reptiles called thecodonts about 225 million years ago. Scientists have named approximately 700 species of dinosaurs. The smallest was *Compsognathus longipes*, a chicken-sized dinosaur that lived about 145 million years ago. The heaviest included *Brachiosaurus*, which lived about 150 million years ago and weighed as much as 70 to 90 tons. The longest may have been *Seismosaurus*, a long-necked plant eater that lived about 150 million years ago and reached lengths of more than 130 feet (39 meters).

Dinosaurs are classified in two groups. Ornithischia, or bird-hipped dinosaurs, had pelvic bones arranged like those of a bird hip, with the pubic bone bent backward. They were plant eaters with hooflike claws. This group included the duck-billed hadrosaurs, plated stegosaurids, beaked ceratopsians, and long-snouted iguanodontids.

The second group is the Saurischia, or lizard-hipped dinosaurs. Their pelvic bones were arranged like those of a lizard hip, with the pubic bone pointing forward. There were two main subgroups. The Theropoda were fast, agile hunters; they included *Tyrannosaurus rex*, *Velociraptor*, *Allosaurus*, and the ancestors of modern birds. The Sauropodomorpha were plant eaters with massive bodies, long tails, and front legs smaller than the back legs. *Brachiosaurus* was a well-known example.

Seven Million Year Old Fossil Pushes Back Human Origins

By JOHN NOBLE WILFORD

In 2004 French scientists digging in Chad, in Central Africa, uncovered a skull, virtually complete and almost seven million years old, that belonged to an individual about the size of a chimpanzee. It is, they say, the earliest known member of the human family, by perhaps as much as a million years. The discovery may be the most important fossil discovery in decades, and a critical turning point in the study of human origins.

The scientists said it was too early to know whether the skull represented a species on a direct ancestral line to humans. The braincase is apelike, but the face and teeth are more like those of a human. The cranial capacity is similar to that of living chimps. Some of its characteristics suggest that the skull is closely related to the last common ancestor of humans and chimps and may yield an understanding of what those apelike creatures were like.

The specimen is sufficiently distinct from apes and other human precursors, or hominids, to be given a new genus and species name, *Sahelanthropus tchadensis*, by the discovery team, headed by Dr. Michel Brunet of the University of Poitiers in France. Informally, the hominid is being called Toumai, a name often given to children born close to the dry season.

The discovery site, in the Djurab Desert in Chad, is more than 1,500 miles west of the more familiar fossil beds of East Africa, in Ethiopia, Kenya and Tanzania. The absence of volcanic ash layers at the fossil site prevented the discoverers from dating the specimens in absolute terms and with the usual scientific methods. But a comparison of other fossils found at the site with similar ones from well-dated sites in East Africa yielded an estimate of six million to seven million years for the Chad fossils.

Molecular biological studies have indicated that the divergence between chimps and humans occurred five million to seven or eight million years ago. *Orrorin tugenensis*, a specimen reported in Kenya two years ago, had until now claimed the title of earliest hominid, at about six million years. An *Ardipithecus ramidus*, which lived about 5.8 million years ago in Ethiopia, was a close competitor. *Sahelanthropus tchadensis*, said Dr. Brunet, "is seven million years old, so the divergence between human and chimp must be even older than we thought before"

The Chad discovery opens a window on a fateful period in evolutionary history about which the fossil record has been sparse. None of the other early specimens include almost complete skulls, which are considered more revealing of a fossil species' place in the hominid family. Toumai is about three million years older than the next-oldest hominid skull.

Dr. Daniel E. Lieberman, a Harvard paleontologist, noted that most research on early hominids has been based on data from East Africa and South Africa. Thus the Chad skull is exciting and challenging because of its age and location as well as for its mosaic of primitive and advanced characteristics.

The specimen's face is essentially that of a *Homo habilis*, Dr. Lieberman pointed out, all the more puzzling because *Australopithecus afarensis*, the Lucy species that lived 3.2 million years ago, has a decidedly chimp-like face. Several scientists said the discovery thus seemed to undermine the simplest linear models of hominid evolution.

Dr. Bernard Wood, a paleoanthropologist at George Washington University, said that he favored a "bushy" model of hominid evolution over a simple linear model. The many branches reflect evolutionary diversity in response to new or changed circumstances.

So Dr. Wood said the bushy, or untidy, model "would predict that at six to seven million years ago we are likely to find evidence of creatures with hitherto unknown combinations of hominid, chimp and even more novel features." He further predicted that Toumai was "just the tip of an iceberg of taxonomic diversity during hominid evolution five to seven million years ago."

Dinosaurs became extinct around 65 million years ago during a mass extinction known as the Cretaceous-Tertiary or K/T event. It is believed that the event resulted from the collision of an asteroid with Earth, at a point on the northwest coastline of the Yucatán Peninsula in Mexico. A crater 106 miles (170 kilometers) across formed, shooting billions of tons of matter into the atmosphere, which blotted out the sun and caused global temperatures to plummet.

PHYSICS

According to the *Oxford Dictionary of Physics*, physics is "the study of the laws that determine the structure of the universe with reference to the matter and energy of which it consists. It is concerned with the forces that exist between objects, and the interrelationship between matter and energy. Until the early 20th century, physics was divided into six diverse areas of study: heat, light, magnetism, sound, and electricity. Since then quantum mechanics and Einstein's theory of relativity have become separate fields of inquiry." Modern physics also includes other subdivisions that are useful. Matter and energy are manifest in the interactions of subatomic particles and the nuclei of atoms as well as in the materials (condensed matter) that make up solids, liquids, and other forms of matter, leading to the branches of study known respectively as particle physics, nuclear physics, and condensed-matter physics. Relativity theory also predicted the expansion of the universe, linking physics for the first time to cosmology, the study of the universe as a whole. Recently the links between physics, astronomy, and cosmology have become tighter; nuclear and particle physics are needed to explain the stars and galaxies. At the same time, physicists who study advanced concepts such as string theory, which replaces particles with strings, now look to astronomy to validate their work.

History of Physics

Physics in Antiquity and the Middle Ages

The ancient Greeks tried, sometimes successfully, to explain materials and motion on the basis of observation and reasoning. One successful explanation, advocated by Democritus of Abdera (ca. 470–380 B.C.) and others, is that all matter is composed of small particles called atoms. Their theories proposed that different atoms have different shapes and that all materials can be based on atoms of fire, air, water, and earth. Today scientists recognize that most matter is made from combinations of nearly 100 different atoms, usually joined to form larger particles called molecules. (Traditionally there are 92 elements, although only 88 or so are normally found on Earth; there is hardly any astatine, francium, or protactinium, and no promethium or technitium. Some transuranic elements are manufactured in relatively large amounts, notably plutonium, americium, and californium. Neptunium, although considered artificial, may exist in greater supply on Earth than astatine, owing to some natural creation. Other synthetic elements are not stable enough to be counted.)

Aristotle The most complete Greek theory of physics, incorporating the ideas of earlier writers as well as his own, is that of Aristotle (384–322 B.C.). Most of what Aristotle thought about physics is now recognized as incorrect. Aristotle rejected atoms because any space between atoms must be empty, but he had based his theories on the idea that a vacuum cannot exist. He thought that an object in motion requires a continuing force to keep it in motion. If an object is moving fast enough, he conjectured, air rushing to prevent a vacuum behind the object could provide the necessary force for a time, but that force would gradually diminish. So a thrown object could travel through the air, but eventually would drop to the ground. The object slows and falls, in Aristotle's view, because the natural place for material objects containing earth or water is toward the center of Earth.

Aristotle remained the main influence on physics for the next 2,000 years. Although some Chinese philosophers developed ideas of motion similar to those we use today, they were unknown in the Arab world or in Europe. Arabic scholars followed the ideas of Aristotle and other Greek philosophers, but they also advanced beyond Greek concepts in some areas of physics, notably optics (the science of light). Aristotle had believed that light travels from an object to the eye, but other influential writers of antiquity, such as Euclid (fl. ca. 300 B.C.) and Ptolemy (ca. 100–170), thought that light proceeds from the observer to the object. The decisive arguments in favor of Aristotle's view were made by Alhazen (Al-Haytham, 965–ca. 1040) around 1020. Alhazen extended the laws of reflection from those applying to flat mirrors, which had been known to Ptolemy, to cover curved mirrors and lenses.

In the Middle Ages, physics began to free itself from some of Aristotle's inaccurate ideas about motion. The French philosopher Jean Buridan (ca. 1295–ca. 1358) was the first to propose that a body in motion contained a mysterious inner force, called impetus, that maintains motion for a time. As a body moves, the impetus dissipates, especially if some force opposes the motion, speeding dissipation.

The Scientific Revolution

Near the end of the 16th century, Galileo Galilei (1564–1642) accepted Aristotelian ideas and such modifications as impetus at first, but he soon brought a radical concept to studies of motion. Instead of trying to explain why objects move as they do, he experimented and then described exactly how they move. He also used experiment to determine how forces affect objects that do not move. Although he made some errors, his basic conclusion in 1590—that an object in motion continues to move in a straight line until stopped by a force—is still accepted. His other famous conclusion—that light bodies and heavy bodies fall through the same distance in the same amount of time—is also true. He had established it by experiment, and announced the correct mathematical law governing falling (distance increases with the square of time) in 1638.

Other scientists continued in the same vein as Galileo during the 17th century. The German astronomer Johannes Kepler (1571–1630) advanced optics and showed in 1604 that the intensity of light diminishes as the square of the distance from its source. In 1643 the Italian physicist Evangelista Torricelli (1608–47), with the invention of the barometer, showed that Aristotle had been wrong about the vacuum, since a vacuum forms above the mercury column in the original barometer. Blaise Pascal experimented with the vacuum and with fluids, establishing that in a fluid, force is transmitted in all directions and always acts perpendicular to the surface of the container (1654, published 1662). Isaac Newton experimented with breaking light into its components (1665) and reported that white light is the combination of the colored lights of the rainbow (1675).

This period when experiments began to dominate physics is known as the scientific revolution. It culminated in 1687 when Newton's *Principia* emerged. Newton improved on Galileo's laws of motion and combined them with a mathematical law of gravity. The combination was sufficient to explain not only the motions of objects on Earth, but also the motions of the heavenly bodies (see Law of Gravity and Newton's Laws of Motion). Newton (and independently Leibniz) had also invented a new mathematical tool, the calculus. Throughout the 18th century, Newtonian physics and calculus were combined to develop systematically a wide range of topics in physics, ranging from acoustics to detailed orbits of the planets. Some scientists believed that if the exact position and momentum of every point in space were known, the future of the universe could be predicted exactly as well.

Electromagnetism Although Newton's work explained how gravity functioned, it did not explain why material objects attract each other with this force. There were also other forces that were unexplained, and less was known of their rules. As early as 1600 William Gilbert applied the experimental method to two of these forces, identifying and differentiating between magnetism and static electricity. A hundred years later, scientists began to attempt to tease from nature the secrets of these forces. Weak electric charges were made by rubbing glass tubes with silk or by similar means at first. In 1729 another English experimenter, Stephen Gray (1666–1736), was the first to recognize that these weak charges could travel from one material to another through substances that were later called conductors. He soon showed that when conductors do not carry away the charge, almost anything—even a human being—could be charged with electricity. A French experimenter, Charles Du Fay (1698–1739), was the first to recognize that there are two kinds of charge and that like charges repel, whereas different charges attract, each other (1733).

The English and French experimenters and their assistants also began to build up charges strong enough to produce the first recognized shocks. In 1746 the invention of the way to store static electricity (called a Leiden jar after the site of its discovery) permitted experiments with much more powerful charges. In 1751 Benjamin Franklin connected the small shocks from Leiden jars with the powerful shock of lightning, proving his theory by flying a kite in a thunderstorm and conducting the charge down the wet string. In 1769 a Scottish scientist, John Robison (1739–1805), showed that the repulsive force caused by charge obeys an inverse-square law like the law for loss of intensity of light over distance.

What Happened Before the Big Bang?

By DENNIS OVERBYE

Like baseball, the universe makes its own time. There is no outside timekeeper. Space and time are part of the universe, not the other way around, thinkers since Augustine have said, and that is one of the central lessons of Einstein's general theory of relativity.

In explaining gravity as the "bending" of space-time geometry, Einstein's theory predicted the expansion of the universe, the primal fact of 20th-century astronomy. By imagining the expansion going backward, like a film in reverse, cosmologists have traced the history of the universe back to a millionth of a second after the Big Bang that began it all.

But to ask what happened before the Big Bang is like asking who was on base before the first pitch was thrown out in a game between the Yankees and the Red Sox. There was no "then" then.

Still, this has not stopped theorists from trying to imagine how the universe made its "quantum leap from eternity into time," as the physicist Dr. Sidney Coleman of Harvard once put it.

Some physicists speculate that on the other side of Time Zero is another universe going backward in time. Others suggest that creation as we know it is punctuated by an eternal dance of clashing island universes.

In their so-called quantum cosmology, Dr. Stephen Hawking, the Cambridge University physicist and author, and his collaborators envision the universe as a kind of self-contained entity, a crystalline melt of all possibilities existing in "imaginary time."

All these will remain just fancy ideas until physicists have married Einstein's gravity to the paradoxical quantum laws that describe the behavior of subatomic particles. Such a theory of quantum gravity, scientists agree, is needed to describe the universe when it was so small and dense that even space and time become fuzzy and discontinuous.

At this moment there are two pretenders to the throne of that ultimate theory putative "theory of everything," which posits that the ultimate constituents of nature are tiny vibrating strings rather than points. String theorists have scored some striking successes in the study of black holes, in which matter has been compressed to catastrophic densities similar to the Big Bang, but they have made little progress with the Big Bang itself.

String's lesser-known rival, called loop quantum gravity, is the result of applying quantum strictures directly to Einstein's equations. This theory makes no pretensions to explaining anything but gravity and space-time. But recently Dr. Martin Bojowald of the Max Planck Institute for Gravitational Physics in Golm, Germany, found that using the theory he could follow the evolution of the universe back past the alleged beginning point: instead of having a "zero moment" of infinite density, the universe behaved as if it were contracting from an earlier phase.

Theorists of both stripes hope that they will discover that they have been exploring two faces of a single idea, yet unknown, which might explain how time, space and everything else can be built out of nothing.

The physicist Dr. John Archibald Wheeler of Princeton, the preeminent poet-adventurer in physics, has put forth his own proposal. According to quantum theory's famous uncertainty principle, the properties of a subatomic particle like its momentum or position remain in abeyance, in a sort of fog of possibility until something measures it or hits it.

Likewise he has wondered out loud if the universe bootstraps itself into being by the accumulation of billions upon billions of quantum interactions—the universe stepping on its own feet, microscopically, and bumbling itself awake. It's a notion he calls "it from bit" to emphasize a proposed connection between quantum mechanics and information theory.

One implication of Wheeler's quantum genesis, if it is correct, is that the notion of the creation of the universe as something far away and long ago must go. "The past is theory," Dr. Wheeler once wrote. "It has no existence except in the records of the present."

If the creation of the universe happens outside time, then it must happen all the time. The Big Bang is here and now, the foundation of every moment.

And you are there.

A new source of electric charge began to be developed in Italy during the 1770s and 1780s when Luigi Galvani (1737–1798) investigated charge produced in the muscles of animals, which Alessando Volta (1745–1827) recognized as the result of chemical interactions. Volta in 1800 built a chemical device (similar to a modern automobile battery) that produced the first current electricity.

Meanwhile a parallel set of experiments with magnets began in 1749 when the English experimenters John Canton (1718–72) and John Michell (1724–93) developed stronger magnets than occur in nature. Michell immediately used his magnets to derive the mathematical laws of attraction and repulsion. In 1751 Benjamin Franklin showed that electric charge can produce magnetism. In 1785 the French physicist Charles Coulomb (1736–1806) carefully measured both electric and magnetic forces and also found that both obey exactly the same inverse-square laws. As early as 1807 the Danish physicist Hans Christian Oersted (1777–1851) began to search for a deeper connection between electricity and magnetism, which he found in 1820 when he observed that an electric current affects a magnetized needle. The recognition that electricity and magnetism are closely connected quickly led to the discovery of the laws governing electromagnetism (see Laws of Current Electricity) as well as to devices that combined the two forces to produce motion (electric motors), powerful electric currents (generators, or dynamos), and powerful electromagnets.

Light At the same time as charge and magnetism were being analyzed, there were apparently unrelated studies concerning light. As early as 1678, the Dutch physicist Christiaan Huygens (1625–95) had proposed a theory of light based on waves. But in 1704 Newton published *Opticks*, which summarized his view that light consists of small particles. About a hundred years later the study of light experienced several rapid advances. In 1800 and 1801 two forms of invisible light were discovered: infrared by William Herschel and ultraviolet by Johann Ritter (1776–1810). Also in 1801, the English scientist Thomas Young (1773–1829) conducted experiments that convinced scientists everywhere that light must be a wave phenomenon, a view reinforced in 1808 when the French physicist Etienne Malus (1775–1812) discovered polarized light, a form of light in which waves are confined to a plane.

It was already known that electric charge could in some circumstances produce light (in lightning, for example). In 1839 the French physicist Edmond Becquerel (1820–91) determined that the opposite also occurs in some circumstances; light produces electric current, known as the photovoltaic effect. A few years later Michael Faraday showed that a magnetic field changes the polarization of light (1845). With these discoveries in mind James Clerk Maxwell concluded that light consists of waves incorporating both electricity and magnetism—that is, electromagnetic waves. He predicted that electromagnetic waves exist in the electromagnetic spectrum below infrared and above ultraviolet radiation. In 1873 Maxwell published a complete mathematical theory of electromagnetism.

There were still mysteries. While setting up the equipment to produce and detect radio waves (the long electromagnetic waves predicted by Maxwell) in 1887, the German physicist Heinrich Hertz (1857–94) observed that light shining on the apparatus affects the size of an electric spark. Further investigation with more energetic electromagnetic radiation revealed that the amount of charge released by the metal depends on the frequency rather than the intensity of the radiation, a finding which made no sense at first. The problem was resolved in 1905 when Albert Einstein proved that light, as Newton had proposed, behaves in this case as a particle instead of as a wave.

Heat As early as 1724 scientists tried to explain heat and cold with the idea that heat is an unusual component of matter, similar to a liquid, which they called caloric. Caloric persisted throughout the 18th century until a decisive experiment by Benjamin Thompson (Count Rumford, 1753–1814) showed that heat is closely connected to motion. Scientists since have believed heat to be an effect of the motion of molecules in any substance (cold is simply the absence of heat, or slower molecular motions), but it was not until 1860 that James Clerk Maxwell and, independently, the Austrian physicist Ludwig Boltzmann (1844–1906) worked out the mathematical theory of such particles.

Meanwhile, physicists were discovering the general laws of heat. The French physicist Sadi Carnot (1796–1832), after studying the still new steam engines, established mathematically in 1824 that work is done as heat passed from a high temperature to a lower one and that the maximum amount of work possible depends only on the temperature. Heat was recognized as a form of energy, along with motion, electricity, light, and stored, or potential, energy. Several English and German physicists measured exactly the amount of heat produced by motion, work that led to the laws of thermodynamics ("movement of heat"). With the new understanding of heat the British physicist William Thomson (Baron Kelvin, 1824–1907) recognized in 1851 that the total absence of heat would produce a specific coldest temperature, absolute zero.

Experimentalists used various methods to lower temperatures nearly to absolute zero, liquefying air in 1878, hydrogen in 1895, and helium, the element that has the coldest known transition from a gas to a liquid, in 1908.

With liquid helium near absolute zero, strange new forms of matter could be created. One of the most important is matter that superconducts—an electric current started in a ring of a superconducting material will continue around the ring as long as the temperature is maintained at a few degrees above absolute zero. Since the Dutch physicist Heike Kamerlingh-Onnes (1853–1926) discovered the first form of superconductivity in 1911, other materials, called high-temperature superconductors, have been found (starting in 1986), although none are superconducting at temperatures above –200°F (–130°C). Liquid helium itself was found to have unusual properties similar to those of superconductors, such as superfluidity. Like some very cold gases, first produced in 1995, liquid helium is a Bose-Einstein condensate (BEC), matter in which the atoms merge into a single superatom, first predicted by Albert Einstein in 1924.

Relativity Maxwell's theory of electromagnetism (proposed in 1873) assumed that electromagnetic waves must be motions in some all-pervasive but undetectable substance, which was called ether. Various attempts were made to define the properties of ether and, in a famous failed experiment of 1888, to determine Earth's motion through the ether. The Polish-American physicist Albert Michelson (1852–1931) and the American physicist Edward Morley (1838–1923) used a sensitive device invented by Michelson to measure the speed of light in the direction of Earth's motion through space and perpendicular to that motion, but failed to find any difference, suggesting that ether was a flawed concept. When Einstein developed the special theory of relativity (1905), however, he concluded that electromagnetic waves do not need ether to explain their properties. He took as a postulate that light travels through a vacuum at the same speed under all conditions; thus you cannot determine how Earth is moving by looking for variations in the speed of light that such motion would cause. He also observed that physical laws as measured should be the same for two entities moving with respect to each other with no change in velocity. From these ideas he concluded that the universe can be described in terms of four-dimensional space-time and that matter and energy are related by the famous equation $E = mc^2$, where E is energy, m is mass, and c is the speed of light in a vacuum. Relativity theory also showed that time can be viewed as a dimension related to the dimensions of space. A definition of modern physics, then, might be that it is the study of matter-energy in space-time.

Next Einstein considered what happens if one entity is accelerated with relation to the other. He based this theory, the general theory of relativity, on the idea that no test can determine a difference between gravitational force and the force produced by acceleration, called inertia.

The general theory of relativity, which resulted from this postulate in 1915, is a description of gravity in terms of the curvature of space-time. Einstein's theory explained previously observed, but unexplained, changes in the orbit of Mercury and in 1919 described how light from a star was bent by the sun's gravitational field. Almost as soon as the general theory was published, it became clear that the theory as originally formulated predicted an expanding universe and also predicted the existence of what we now call black holes (1917), stars that have collapsed into points with such a strong gravitational force that light cannot escape. In 1979 another effect predicted by the theory, the lensing effect caused by the gravitational force of an entire galaxy, was observed for the first time; since then, gravitational lenses have become one of the principal tools astronomers use to observe the early universe.

Einstein thought in 1917 that the universe should be static, but assumed that gravity would cause the universe to be contracting. He interpreted his original equations as showing a universe that is slowly collapsing. To resolve this, he added a "cosmological constant" to the equations for general relativity to provide a small force opposing gravity. Einstein was clearly wrong about the possibility of gravitational collapse, for the Dutch physicist Willem de Sitter (1872–1934) showed in 1919 that Einstein's equations without the cosmological constant actually predicted an expanding universe. When expansion of the universe was observed by astronomers in the 1920's, Einstein abandoned the cosmological constant. In recent years, however, astronomers have detected an acceleration of the expansion of the universe. The mysterious force that causes this expansion is called "dark energy." Some physicists think that dark energy is evidence suggesting that the Einstein's cosmological constant was correct and should be reinstated.

Particles and Quantum Theory Several Greek and Roman writers had a theory that matter is made from small, indivisible particles; this theory was revived in 1803 as atomic theory by the British chemist John Dalton (1766–1844). During the 19th century, the idea of indivisible atoms came to be accepted, but near the end of the century evidence emerged that atoms themselves are made from even smaller particles. The electron was discovered by the English physicist J. J. Thomson (1856–1940) in 1897 and measured to be smaller by far than the smallest atom. Two years later, Thomson showed that the electron is a part of the atom.

Because electrons have a negative charge, but atoms are electrically neutral, it was apparent that there must be some particle (or other entity) in the atom with a positive charge to neutralize the charge of the electron. By 1911 the New Zealand-born British physicist Ernest Rutherford (1871–1937) had established that the positive charge is carried by a particle much heavier than the electron; he named this new particle the proton. The Danish physicist Niels Bohr (1885–1962) developed the mathematical theory of hydrogen, which has the simplest atom, in 1913. He found that the theory was correct in terms of experiment only if he used the idea that electrons can travel in only a few orbits and that they must be able to change from one orbit to another instantly (giving off or absorbing light in the process).

The idea that light energy has only separate (discrete) levels had first been used in 1900 to explain the spectrum of light emitted as a body is heated. The discrete levels were called quanta by the German physicist Max Planck (1858–1947), who had developed this theory. In 1905 Einstein used the same idea to explain the phenomenon discovered by Hertz in 1887, showing that light behaves like particles (quanta of light). Bohr showed that electron orbits are also quanta. Thus the theory of particle behavior is called the quantum theory.

Quantum theory advanced rapidly in the 1920s, beginning with the idea of the French physicist Louis de Broglie (1892–1987) that particles such as the electron have a wave aspect. The following year the Pauli exclusion principle (see Two Basic Laws of Quantum Physics) and the matrix theory of the electron were established, along with the concept of particle spin. In 1926 the German physicist Erwin Schrödinger developed the equation of the electron wave. In 1927 the Heisenberg uncertainty principle was introduced. During this period, the only known particles were the photon, electron, and proton, but in 1930 Wolfgang Pauli (1900–58) proposed the neutrino, which was followed by dozens of other particles (see Subatomic Particles). Quantum theory was cast into the more precise form called quantum electrodynamics in 1947, when several physicists developed mathematical techniques to resolve problems with the original quantum theory.

Nuclear Physics Radioactivity, which was discovered in 1896 by the French physicist Henri Becquerel (1852–1908), was the key to discovery of the proton and the concept that each atom has a positive nucleus surrounded by negative electrons. The study of the nucleus could not advance much until the discovery, in 1932, of the neutral particle the neutron, which is part of the nucleus in all atoms but the simplest hydrogen atom. Different forms of the same element, called isotopes, have the same number of protons in the nucleus, but different numbers of neutrons.

The French wife-and-husband team Irène Joliot-Curie (1897–1956) and Frédéric Joliot-Curie (1900–58) showed in 1934 that an element can be changed to a radioactive isotope by bombarding the atoms with neutrons. In 1937 the Italian-American physicist Emilio Segrè used the same idea to produce a previously unknown artificial element, technetium. In 1940 the first artificial element with an atomic number higher than that of uranium was created and named neptunium, element 93. The following year element 94, plutonium, joined the list. Today there are artificial elements through element 116.

In 1938 the German physicist Otto Hahn (1879–1968) and the Austrian physicist Lise Meitner (1878–1968) discovered that the large uranium atom could break into pieces (fission) when stuck with a neutron, releasing additional neutrons and other forms of energy in the process. This discovery led to the atomic, or nuclear fission, bomb and nuclear power (see Technology). Also in 1938 two physicists, Hans Bethe and Carl von Weizsäcker, proposed that in the intense heat and pressure of the interior of a star, hydrogen nuclei combine with each other to form helium (fusion), releasing energy in the process. This process also led to the development of a fusion bomb (the hydrogen bomb, 1952).

In the last decades of the 20th century physicists developed the standard model of elementary particles. This model incorporates three of the four fundamental forces in nature: the strong and weak nuclear forces and electromagnetic force (the other force is gravity). In the model, bosons mediate the forces: gluons, for the strong nuclear force; the photon for electromagnetism; and W and Z particles for the weak nuclear force. Within this model, the weak and electromagnetic forces have been combined into electroweak theory. The standard model has thus far met all experimental challenges, but it has some gaps in addition to the omission of gravity: in particular, the strong and electroweak forces are called grand unified theories (GUTs). Beyond grand unified theories, a great challenge for physicists is a "theory of everything" (TOE) that would account for all of the fundamental forces in nature.

Condensed Matter Nuclear and particle physics apply to what occurs within atoms and in isolated subatomic particles but do not explain the behavior of surface interactions, of clusters of small numbers of atoms or molecules, of complex molecular structures such as colloidal solutions or foams, or of electromagnetic phenomena in solids or liquids. Physicists have come to refer to the branch of the science that is concerned with the collective behavior of many particles as "condensed matter" physics. Today condensed matter physics is one of the most active areas of the science.

Although scientific studies of magnetism and static electricity began in 1600, the first accurate theory of the cause of magnetism was that of the French physicist André-Marie Ampère (1775–1836) in 1825. Michael Faraday (1791–1867) recognized in 1845 that there are several magnetic effects, including diamagnetism (opposition to a magnetic field), paramagnetism (which disappears when a magnetic field is removed), and ferromagnetism (the familiar "permanent" magnetism that can be induced in iron and some other metals). Another major advance occurred in 1907 when the French physicist Pierre-Ernest Weiss (1865–1940) explained ferromagnetism as the effect produced when many small regions, called domains, become aligned by a magnetic field.

Early experimenters with static electricity observed that some substances—notably metals—conduct electricity and others are insulators. But not until 1900 did the German physicist Paul Drude (1863–1906) establish that in conductors some electrons are free to move away from their atoms, carrying negative charge with them. When quantum theory was developed, the Russian-German physicist Arnold Sommerfeld (1868–1951) developed in detail the theory of how electrons behave in a conductor. But there were still mysteries unsolved, for superconductivity was not explained until 1957, and high-temperature superconductivity still lacks a satisfactory explanation.

Understanding how conductors and insulators work led to a better understanding of semiconductors. This provided the background for the development in 1947 of the transistor and for subsequent applications of semiconductors, including some types of lasers and light-emitting diodes. Today condensed-matter physicists are applying the concept of spin to produce the effective disk drives in modern computers and look forward to using the electronics of spin, called spintronics, to develop improved devices that accomplish the tasks of transistors and their variants better and faster.

Physics and Other Disciplines Physics is a fundamental underpinning of most science other than the studies of human beings and some theories concerning living organisms, and sometimes physics becomes completely combined with parts of other sciences. Three notable examples are combinations of physics with astronomy, earth science, and biology.

Astrophysics is the study of stars, gas clouds, and other astronomical bodies, based on the application of the laws of physics, including energy production, composition, and evolution. While a broad view of astrophysics would include virtually all of astronomy, the disciple was originally concerned primarily with energy production and the development of stars from gas clouds through several stages such as red giants or white dwarfs to concluding explosions as supernovas or collapse into burned-out cinders or black holes. In recent years, the evolution of the universe as a whole (cosmology) has become a central focus of many astrophysicists; cosmology includes the development of subatomic particles in the early universe and the possible roles of subatomic particles and physical forces in such concepts as dark matter or the unknown energy that is accelerating the expansion of the universe.

Geophysics is the study of the structure of Earth based on the application of physical laws to Earth's shape, seismology, electromagnetic properties, oceans, and atmosphere. The methods of geophysics have revealed Earth's layered structure, consisting of inner and outer cores, mantle, and crust, and have provided the theoretical basis of plate tectonics. In recent years, the definition of geophysics has been stretched to include the physical

Demolition Derby of Physics Jars Loose Clues on Subatomic Glue

By JAMES GLANZ

Particle physicists are known as the demolition crews of the very small, smashing tiny bits of matter together to find the even tinier bits that they are made of. So it may come as a surprise that the field has recently found a powerful new engine of discovery: gluing it all back together again, sometimes in weird ways that seldom occur in nature, if ever.

The glue linking these discoveries is the "strong force," which is normally relegated to holding together quarks, the building blocks of particles like protons and neutrons. But theorists have long suspected that the strong force has a wild side and that it should be able to take the subatomic equivalent of a Tudor chimney here, an Art Deco facade there, and stick them together into new particle types.

Hints of those strange creations began turning up recently. Although quarks normally congregate in twos and threes, several laboratories said in 2003 that they were seeing what appeared to be ungainly clumps of five quarks.

In one paper, the High Energy Accelerator Research Organization in Tsukuba, Japan (KEK, for its Japanese acronym) describes what the researchers believe were two pairs of quarks dancing close enough to form a single new particle.

The finding at KEK, which followed a related discovery at the Stanford Linear Accelerator Center, could also turn out to be a rare combination of just two quarks called charmonium, some theorists believe. Either way, the results are expected to lend fresh insights on the strong force, widely considered among the most opaque and intractable parts of the Standard Model, the theory physicists use to explain matter's basic structure.

A full understanding of the strong force has eluded theorists. Although physicists know that protons and neutrons are made of groups of three quarks, the demolition experts of science have not been able to knock a quark free. That is because the strong force does not become weaker—in contrast to gravity or electrical forces—the farther the particles are apart. They can never escape the sticky embrace of another quark.

The particles that transmit the strong force from quark to quark are called gluons. They spend part of the time in the guise of other quarks. That means that heavy particles like protons and neutrons are also filled with these more evanescent quarks winking in and out of existence.

There are eight different kinds of gluons, each with a different type of "charge." And there are six varieties of quarks: up, down, top, bottom, charm and strange.

When physicists have no hope of passing the high-energy frontier in collisions, efforts such as the BaBar experiment at Stanford use a different strategy: creating vast numbers of particles that are closely monitored when they decay into other products, with an eye to measuring their properties precisely and finding exotica.

Scientists like to call this the luminosity frontier. BaBar, for example, has created some 150 million B-meson pairs, particles made of a bottom quark and an up or down one.

When Dr. Antimo Palano was checking a decay process, he saw a small bump in the data sample. He added more data, and the signal kept getting bigger. What was the particle? Dr. Palano and some colleagues believe that it was a long-sought type of D-meson that contains a charm quark and a strange quark.

If that interpretation turns out to be right, it will shed light on the workings of the strong force. Calculations suggest the mesons are tethered as if by a rubber band, with one of the quarks behaving as if it were nearly massless.

But Dr. Frank Close of Oxford, suggested that the particle's surprising mass could be explained more easily if it were a kind of molecule of two other mesons, whirling about each other and exchanging still other particles that help them stick together.

Add it all up, and it has been a hot time for those who study the strong force, said Dr. Close, who added that scientists had moved nearer to understanding the mysterious glue of the atomic nucleus.

properties of planets other than Earth as well as of the satellites of planets.

Biophysics is the study of such physical processes as transport of materials in living organisms, growth of such organisms, and their structural stability in terms of the laws of physics. Of particular concern are transport of ions across cell membranes and the mechanisms of protein folding along with the physics of such imaging techniques as CT, MRI, and PET scans.

String Theory and Supersymmetry Although quantum theories of particle physics explain many phenomena and allow interactions to be calculated to a high degree of accuracy, some of the mathematics involved has been viewed as questionable. Positive and negative infinities are added in such a way that their difference nearly cancels, but leaves a tiny amount that is exactly the amount measured by experiment. Also, physicists since Einstein have hoped to develop a unified theory that would include relativity and quantum mechanics as the logical outgrowth. Several developments since 1970 have attempted to resolve the mathematics and unify the various theories. The first was string theory, which replaced the concept of particles with one-dimensional strings whose properties are mathematically tractable, but only in spaces with more than four dimensions. In 1974 this was joined with a theory that every particle has a partner—if one particle represents matter, then the other represents force, and vice versa. This symmetry, called supersymmetry, called for a wide range of new particles that had not been previously observed, implying that the unobserved particles may be too massive to be created easily. Two years later the recognition that certain strings behave like the graviton, a particle predicted by general relativity theory, led to combining relativity with string theory in a theory called supergravity. By 1984 string theory and supersymmetry had also been combined to create superstring theory—strings instead of particles, very massive and unknown partners for every known string, and all in ten- or eleven-dimensional space. The dimensions above the three known dimensions of space and the dimension of time are also unobserved and thought to be curled so tightly that they are too small to observe. In 1995 the American physicist Edward Witten (b. 1951) extended the symmetric theory of supergravity to a theory in which the fundamental entities are membranes in eleven-dimensional space. Variations on this concept, known as M theory or brane theory, remain the most popular concept of the underlying reality of the universe, called the "theory of everything," for today's theoretical physicists, although these theories are hampered by the inability of experimenters to prove or disprove them.

Basic Laws of Physics

Key Terms

Mass is a measure of the amount of matter; it is proportional to weight. Near the surface of Earth it is roughly equivalent to weight.

Velocity measures how an object changes position with time.

Acceleration is how an object changes velocity with time.

Momentum is the product of mass and velocity.

Energy is the ability to do work.

Law of Gravity

The gravitational force between any two objects is proportional to the product of their masses and inversely proportional to the square of the distance between them. If F is the force, G is the number that represents the ratio (the gravitational constant), m and M are the two masses, and r is the distance between the objects:

$$F = \frac{GmM}{r^2}$$

In metric measure, the gravitational constant is 0.0000000000667390 (6.67390×10^{-11}) newton m^2/kg^2, so another way of writing the basic law of gravity is

$$F = \frac{0.0000000000667390mM}{r^2}$$

This law implies that objects falling near the surface of Earth will fall with the same rate of acceleration (ignoring drag caused by air). This rate is 32.174 feet per second per second (ft/sec^2), or 9.8 m/sec^2, and is conventionally labeled g. Applying this rate to falling objects gives the velocity, v, and distance, d, after any amount of time, t, in seconds. If the object starts at rest and 32 ft/sec^2 is used as an approximation for g,

$$v = 32t$$
$$d = 16t^2$$

For example, after 3 seconds, a dropped object that is still falling will have a velocity of 32 × 3 = 96 feet per second and will have fallen a distance of 16 × 32 = 144 feet.

If the object has an initial velocity v_0 and an initial height above the ground of a, the equations describing the velocity and the distance, d, above the ground (a positive velocity is up and a negative velocity is down) become

$$v = v_0 - 32t$$

and

$$d = -16t^2 + v_0 t + a$$

After 3 seconds, an object tossed in the air from a height of 6 feet with a velocity of 88 feet per second will reach a speed of 88 – 96 = –8 feet per second, meaning that it has begun to descend, and will have a height of (–16 × 9) + (88 × 3) + 6 = –144 + 264 + 6 = 126 feet above the ground.

The maximum height, H, reached by the object with an initial velocity v_0 and initial height a is

$$H = a + \frac{v_0^2}{64}$$

For the object tossed upward at 88 feet per second from a height of 6 feet, the maximum height reached would be 6 + $88^2/64$ = 6 + 121 = 127 feet. Therefore, after 3 seconds, the object has just reached its peak and has fallen back only 1 foot.

Albert Einstein's general theory of relativity introduced laws of gravity more accurate than those just given, which were discovered by Sir Isaac Newton. Newton's gravitational theory is extremely accurate for most practical situations, however. For example, Newton's theory is used to determine how to launch satellites into proper orbits.

Newton's Laws of Motion

Newton's laws of motion apply to objects in a vacuum and are not easily observed in the real world, where forces such as friction tend to overwhelm the natural motion of objects. To obtain realistic solutions to problems, however, physicists and engineers begin with Newton's laws and then add in the various forces that also affect motion.

1. *Any object at rest tends to stay at rest.* A body in motion moves at the same velocity in a straight line unless acted upon by a force. This is also known as the law of inertia. Note that this law implies that an object will travel in a curved path only so long as a force is acting on it. When the force is released, the object will travel in a straight line. A weight on a string swung in a circle will travel in a straight line when the string is released, for the string was supplying the force that caused circular motion.

2. *The acceleration of an object is directly proportional to the force acting on it and inversely proportional to the mass of the object.* This law, for an acceleration a, a force F, and a mass m, is more commonly expressed in terms of finding the force when you know the mass and the acceleration. In this form it is written as

$$F = ma$$

The implication of this law is that a constant force will produce acceleration, which is an increase in velocity. Thus a rocket, which is propelled by a constant force as long as its fuel is burning, constantly increases in velocity. Even with an infinite supply of fuel, the rocket would eventually cease to increase in velocity, however, because Einstein's other relativity theory, the special theory of relativity, states that no object can exceed the speed of light in a vacuum (see Conservation of Mass-Energy, below). Nevertheless, even a small force, constantly applied, can cause a large mass to reach velocities near the speed of light if enough time is allowed.

3. *For every action there is an equal and opposite reaction.*

Conservation Laws

Many results in physics come from various conservation laws. A conservation law is a rule that a certain entity must not change in amount during a certain class of operations. All such conservation laws treat closed systems. Anything added from outside the system could affect the amount of the entity being conserved.

Conservation of Momentum In a closed system, momentum stays the same. This law is equivalent to Newton's third law. Since momentum is the product of mass and velocity, if the mass of a system changes, then the velocity must change. For example, consider a person holding a heavy anchor in a stationary rowboat in the water. The momentum of the system is 0, since the masses have no velocity. Now the person in the rowboat tosses the anchor toward the shore. The momentum of the anchor is now a positive number if velocity toward the shore is measured as positive. To conserve momentum, the rowboat is accelerated in the opposite direction, away from the shore. The positive momentum of the anchor is balanced by the negative momentum of the rowboat and its cargo. In terms of two masses, m and M, and matching velocities v and V,

$$mv = MV$$

Conservation of Angular Momentum An object moving in a circle has a special kind of momentum, called angular momentum. As noted above, motion in a circle requires some force. Angular momentum combines mass, velocity, and acceleration (produced by the force). For a body moving in a circle, the acceleration depends on both the speed of the body in its path and the square of the radius of the circle. The product of this speed, the mass, and the square of the radius is the angular momentum of the mass.

In a closed system, angular momentum is conserved. This effect is used by skaters to change their velocity of spinning. Angular momentum is partly determined by the masses of a skater's arms combined with the rate of rotation and the square of the radius to the center of mass of each arm (the point that can represent the total mass of the arm). When skaters bring their arms close to their body, this would tend to reduce the angular momentum, because the center of mass is closer to the body. But, since angular momentum is conserved, the rate of rotation has to increase to compensate for the decreased radius. Because the rate depends on the square of the radius, the rate increases dramatically.

Conservation of Mass In a closed system, the total amount of mass appears to be conserved in all but nuclear reactions and other extreme conditions.

Conservation of Energy In a closed system, energy appears to be conserved in all but nuclear reactions and other extreme conditions. Energy comes in very many forms: mechanical, chemical, electrical, heat, and so forth. As one form is changed into another (excepting nuclear reactions and extreme conditions), this law guarantees that the total amount remains the same. Thus, when you change the chemical energy of a dry cell into electrical energy and use that to turn a motor, the total amount of energy does not change (although some becomes heat energy—see Laws of Thermodynamics, below).

Conservation of Mass-Energy Einstein discovered that his special theory of relativity implies that energy and mass are related. Consequently, mass and energy by themselves are not conserved, since one can be converted into the other. Mass and energy appear to be conserved in ordinary situations because the effect of Einstein's discovery is very small most of the time. The more general law, then, is the law of conservation of mass-energy: The total amount of mass and energy must be conserved. Einstein found the following equation that links mass and energy:

$$E = mc^2$$

In this equation, E is the amount of energy, m is the mass, and c is the speed of light in a vacuum.

One instance of energy changing to mass occurs in Einstein's equation for how the mass increases with velocity. If m_0 is the mass of the object when it is not moving, v is the velocity of the object in relation to an observer who is considered to be at rest, and c is the speed of light in a vacuum, then the mass, m, is given by the equation

$$m = \frac{m_0}{\sqrt{1 - \frac{v^2}{c^2}}}$$

This accounts for the rule that no object can exceed the speed of light in a vacuum. As the object approaches this speed, so much of the energy is converted to mass that it cannot continue to accelerate.

In both nuclear fission (splitting of the atomic nucleus) and nuclear fusion (the joining of atomic nuclei, producing the energy of a hydrogen bomb), mass is converted into energy.

Conservation for Particles Many properties associated with atoms and subatomic particles are also conserved. Among them are charge, spin, isospin, and a combination known as CPT: charge conjugation, parity, and time.

First and Second Laws of Thermodynamics

First Law This is the same as the law of conservation of energy. It is a law of thermodynamics, or the movement of heat, because heat must be treated as a form of energy to keep the total amount of energy constant. All bodies contain heat as energy no matter how cold they are, although there is not much heat at temperatures close to absolute zero.

Second Law Heat in a closed system can never travel from a low-temperature region to one of higher temperature in a self-sustaining process. *Self-sustaining* in this case describes a process that does not need energy from outside the system to keep it going. In a refrigerator, heat from the cold inside of the refrigerator is transferred to a warmer room, but energy from outside is required to make the transfer happen, so the process is not self-sustaining.

The second law has many implications. One of them is that no perpetual motion machine can be constructed. Another is that all energy in a closed system eventually becomes heat that is diffused equally throughout the system, so that one can no longer obtain work from the system.

The equations that describe the behavior of heat also can be applied to order and therefore to information. The word *entropy* refers to diffuse heat, disorder, or lack of information. Another form of the second law of thermodynamics is that in a closed system, entropy always increases.

Laws of Current Electricity

Key Terms When electrons flow in a conductor, the result is electric current. The amount of current is based on an amount of electric charge called the coulomb, which is the charge of about 6.25 quintillion (6.25×10^{18}) electrons. When 1 coulomb of charge moves past a point in 1 second, it creates a current of 1 ampere. Just as a stream can carry the same amount of water swiftly through a narrow channel or slowly through a broad channel, the energy of an electric current varies depending on the difference in charge between places along the conductor. This is called potential difference and is measured in volts. The voltage is affected by the nature of the conductors. Some substances conduct an electric current much more easily than others. This resistance to the current is measured in ohms. Electric power is the rate at which electricity is used.

Ohm's Law Electric current is directly proportional to the potential difference and inversely proportional to resistance. If you measure current, I, in amperes, potential difference, V, in volts, and resistance, R, in ohms, then the current is equal to the potential difference divided by the resistance.

$$I = \frac{V}{R}$$

Law of Electric Power If electric power, P, is measured in watts, then the power is equal to the product of the current measured in amperes and the potential difference measured in volts.

$$P = IV$$

Laws of Light and Electromagnetic Radiation

Key Terms Light is a part of a general form of radiation known as electromagnetic waves, or, when thought of as particles, photons. Here, electromagnetic radiation is considered as a wave phenomenon for the most part. The velocity of a wave is how fast the wave travels as a whole. The wavelength is the distance between one crest of the wave and the next crest. The frequency is how many crests pass a particular location in a unit of time. One crest passing each second is called a hertz.

Law of Electromagnetic Energy The energy of an electromagnetic wave depends on a small number known as Planck's constant. Measured in joules per hertz (energy per frequency), Planck's constant is 6.67259×10^{-34}. The energy is equal to the product of Planck's constant and the frequency. Using E for energy, h for Planck's constant, and f for frequency,

$$E = hf$$

When thought of in terms of the particles called photons, the energy of a photon obeys the same law. The law of wave motion and the law of electromagnetic energy can be combined with the speed of light in a vacuum (c) to give

$$\mathrm{E} = \frac{hc}{l}$$

The energy of a photon is the product of Planck's constant and the speed of light, divided by the wavelength (l) of the photon.

Inverse-Square Law All radiation obeys an inverse-square law, which is similar to the law of gravity. The intensity of the radiation decreases as the inverse of the square of the distance from a point source of radiation.

Two Basic Laws of Quantum Physics

When one considers effects on very small masses and at very small distances, it is necessary to recognize that objects behave differently from their action at sizes and distances one can observe directly. Since these effects occur in discrete steps based upon Planck's constant times the frequency, called the quantum—which is the size by which energy changes in steps (instead of continuously)—the science of such effects is called quantum physics. Small masses act sometimes like particles and sometimes like waves. Two laws in particular that describe the behavior of small masses are basic and easily stated.

Heisenberg's Uncertainty Principle It is impossible to specify completely the position and momentum of a particle, such as an electron, at the same time.

Pauli's Exclusion Principle Two particles of matter cannot be in the same exact state. Particles of matter include the electron, neutron, and proton. Bosons, particles of force, do not obey Pauli's exclusion principle. (see Subatomic Particles.)

Subatomic Particles

The idea of an atom goes back to the ancient Greek philosophers, who thought that matter was composed of tiny indivisible particles. The concept was put on a scientific basis by John Dalton (1766–1844) in 1803 and became the foundation of chemistry. Nearly a hundred years later, experiments by J. J. Thomson (1856–1940) in 1899 were the first to show that atoms are not indivisible after all. In the past hundred years, physics at almost all levels has been completely revolutionized by the study of the particles that make up atoms or that are smaller than atoms. In the last decades of the 20th century physicists developed the standard model of elementary particles. This model incorporates three of the four fundamental forces in nature: the strong and weak nuclear forces and electromagnetic force (the other force is gravity). In the model, bosons mediate the forces: gluons for the strong nuclear force, the photon for electromagnetism, and W and Z particles for the weak nuclear force. Within this model, the weak and electromagnetic forces have been combined into electroweak theory. The standard model has thus far met all experimental challenges, but it has some gaps in addition to the omission of gravity: in particular, the strong and electroweak forces are not completely unified. Theories that attempt to unify the strong and electroweak forces are called grand unified theories (GUTs). Beyond grand unified theories, a great challenge for physicists is a "theory of everything" (TOE) that would account for all of the fundamental forces in nature. Below is a list of all the most important subatomic particles, in the chronological order of their discovery.

1897 Electron The first subatomic particle to be identified, also by J. J. Thomson, was the electron, a low-mass particle that can be found in the outer reaches of the atom. One property of the electron is charge, the response to electric or magnetic fields. The charge of a single electron is always the same, and is identified as −1 (negative one). Each atom consists of a cloud of electrons around a center of positive charge, which is called the nucleus.

1905 Photon The photon is the particle that carries the electromagnetic force. This concept began with Albert Einstein (1879–1955) in 1905, when he established that light acts sometimes as a particle instead of as waves. Although we usually think of the photon as the particle of light, it is also the particle form of radio waves, X rays, or gamma rays. The mass of the photon is 0.

1911 Proton At least one proton is always found in the nucleus of every atom. The proton has a charge that is the same in size as that of the electron, but responds in the opposite direction to an electric or magnetic field. This charge is +1 (positive one). Each proton is almost 2,000 times as heavy as an electron, or about the same as the mass of a single hydrogen atom.

1924 Bosons While matter is made from subatomic particles, the forces that act on matter are also produced by subatomic particles. The particles that create these forces are collectively called bosons because the mathematics of the behavior of this type of particle was worked out originally by Satyendranath Bose (1894–1974) in 1924, although it was put into final form by Einstein. The observed bosons are the photon, pions, gluons, W particles, and Z particles. Bosons that are predicted, but that have not been observed, include the Higgs particle and the graviton.

1925–26 Quantum Mechanics The basic theory of subatomic particles, called quantum mechanics, was developed in two different forms, in 1925 by Werner Heisenberg (1901–76) and in 1926 by Erwin Schrödinger (1887–1961). Although the two forms appear very different, they produce the same results.

1926 Fermions All the particles that make up matter are called fermions, as opposed to the bosons that create forces. The fermions include all the leptons and quarks as well as the particles made from quarks (see below). Fermions are named for Enrico Fermi (Italian-American, 1901–54), who first worked out the mathematics of their interactions in 1926. Fermions all obey the Pauli exclusion principle (see Basic Laws of Physics, earlier in this chapter); that is, they occupy a definite space. Two fermions cannot be in the same place at the same time.

1930 Antiparticles When Paul A. M. Dirac (1902–84) completed his mathematical version of the theory of the electron in 1930, he observed that one solution to his equations predicted a particle that would be a mirror image of the electron, exactly the same as the electron but with a positive instead of a negative charge. The particle, discovered two years later in 1932, was named the positron. The same equations predicted mirror images for all subatomic particles. These particles are called antiparticles, so another name for positron is antielectron.

1932 Neutron The neutron is very much like a neutral proton, with just slightly more mass. Neutrons are stable when they are found in atoms, but decay into other particles when left to themselves.

1935 Muon The muon is now recognized as a high-energy analogue to the electron with a mass about 200 times that of the electron.

1947 Pion (Predicted in 1935.) A pion carries the strong force that holds the nucleus of atoms together, but since each pion appears and disappears almost instantly, the pions are not usually counted as part of the nucleus. In the same year that the pion was found, theoreticians were able to work out a comprehensive theory of the electron, called quantum electrodynamics (QED).

1950 Strange Particles Starting in 1950 experimenters observed a number of previously undetected particles that did not behave as particles were expected to. Because these particles have masses greater than that of the proton and neutron, they were called hyperons. Other unexpected particles, about the size of the pion, were classed as mesons. A classification scheme for the hyperons, developed in 1961, helped physicists understand them better, but their essential difference was already labeled "strangeness."

1955 Neutrinos Neutrinos are thought to be among the most common particles in the universe, but they interact with ordinary matter so weakly that they are very difficult to observe. Predicted in 1930, neutrinos were thought to have no rest mass, but Canadian experiments in 2001 indicate that they have a very small mass equal to less than about 10^{-7} of the mass of an electron. Different neutrinos are associated with electrons, muons, and tauons.

1964–95 Quarks Murray Gell-Mann (b. 1928) and several other physicists determined that a way to explain the properties of protons, neutrons, mesons, and hyperons is to think of the heavy particles as made from combinations of light ones, just as the atom is made from combinations of electrons, protons, and neutrons. The smaller particles are quarks; there are six of them in all. Two quarks, known as up and down, form protons and neutrons. The top quark is the most massive—about as heavy as an atom of gold—and was the last to be detected. (First version of theory in 1964, evidence for top quark in 1995.)

1965–73 Gluons The eight different bosons that produce a force between quarks known as the color force are called gluons. The color force is also the basis of the strong force that holds the nucleus together. Because of the color force, the study of quarks and gluons is today called quantum chromodynamics (QCD).

1974 J/psi Particle Like the strange hyperons, the J/psi particle is a heavy particle that appears at high energies. It also is produced by a different kind of quark, the charm quark. The odd name J/psi comes from the particle's having been discovered independently by two investigators, of whom one called it J and the other named it psi.

1983 W and Z Particles The particles that produce the weak force are called W and Z. At high energies, however, the weak force merges with the electromagnetic force, so that W and Z are to some extent analogues to the photon, although they could not be more different, since the photon has a 0 rest mass and both W particles and the single Z particle are very massive.

1995 Antiatoms Since antiparticles have all the properties of ordinary particles except for being mirror images, it is possible to create an antiatom by combining subatomic antiparticles. This was accomplished in 1995 with the production of a few antiatoms of antihydrogen made by causing an antielectron (positron) to orbit an antiproton.

(Not Yet Observed) Graviton and Higgs Particle A particle that produces gravitational force by its exchange between all kinds of particles is known as the graviton, but so far it is known only in theory. The Laser Interferometer Gravitational Wave Observatory (LIGO) that began operations in 2000 seeks to observe gravity waves, the wave version of the graviton. The Higgs particle is the main undetected particle of the standard model of subatomic particles. Physicists believe that the Higgs, named after Peter Higgs (b. 1919), who predicted it in 1964, confers mass on all other particles.

Glossary of Physics Terms

alternating current electric current in which an electric field flows first in one direction and then the opposite way at a constant frequency (in the United States, 60 cycles per second). It is produced by switching current back and forth at the source. Current supplied over power lines is alternating current because AC voltages can be stepped up for transmission and down for distribution to users, allowing current to travel farther with less loss.

anode positive electrode. In an electron tube the anode attracts electrons from the cathode.

atom electrically neutral particle that is the smallest part of a chemical element. Atoms are formed by a nucleus of at least one proton and, except for the hydrogen atom, one or more neutrons, surrounded by a cloud of exactly as many electrons as protons.

boiling point temperature at which the vapor pressure of a liquid equals that of the surrounding gas or vapor. At this temperature, a phase change begins, as the liquid boils and changes to a vapor (gas) state at a given pressure.

Bose-Einstein condensate phase of matter occurring at extremely low temperatures in systems consisting of large numbers of atoms in the same quantum state, so that they act like a single entity or superatom. The atoms must be bosons (particles with integral spin, which can apply to either atomic nuclei or atoms). The first Bose-Einstein condensate was created in 1995 by physicists at the Joint Institute of Laboratory Astrophysics, in Boulder, Colo.

capillary action process by which liquid in a very narrow tube rises against the pull of gravity. When the surface of a liquid is in contact with a solid, the liquid is elevated or depressed depending upon the relative attraction of the molecules of the liquid for each other or for those of the solid.

cathode negative electrode. In a vacuum tube, electrons flow from the cathode to the anode.

centripetal and centrifugal force centripetal force acts on a body to cause it to move in a circular path. A satellite circling the earth is held by the centripetal force of the Earth's gravity. Inertia tends to keep the body moving straight, and this is referred to as centrifugal force.

Cerenkov radiation any charged particle traveling faster than light moves in a liquid or solid medium produces a wake of electromagnetic radiation called Cerenkov radiation or Cerenkov light. The phenomenon was discovered in 1934 by Pavel A. Cerenkov (Russian, 1904–90).

charge property of matter that gives rise to electrical phenomena. The unit of charge is that of the proton or the electron; the proton is designated as positive (+1) and the electron as negative (–1). All other charged elementary particles have charges equal to +1 or –1, except quarks, whose charge can be 1/3 or 2/3. Every charged particle is surrounded by an electric force field so that it attracts any charge of opposite sign brought near it and repels any charge of the same sign. This force is responsible for holding protons and electrons together in atoms and for chemical bonding.

colloid combination of two materials in which one is in a gas, liquid, or solid phase (called the medium) and the other is dispersed through the first in tiny clusters of atoms or molecules or in very large molecules. A colloid in which liquid or solid particles are dispersed in a gas is also called an aerosol; one with gas in a liquid or solid is a foam; one with liquid particles in another liquid is an emulsion; and solid particles in a liquid form a sol. Gels are colloids in which both elements have a three-dimensional structure throughout the material. Examples of colloids include the aerosols fog (water in air) and smoke (soot in air); the foams whipped cream (air in milk) and Styrofoam (air in styrene); the emulsion mayonnaise (oil in egg); the gel gelatin (protein in water); and the sol ruby glass (metal in glass).

convection process in which heat is transported by the movement of a fluid. Responding to gravitational force, parts of a fluid such as air that are denser than surrounding parts sink. The sinking fluids displace hotter, less dense material and cause it to rise, transporting heat. From the point of view of someone surrounded by the fluid, as we are by air, it is more obvious that the less dense fluid is rising than that the denser fluid is sinking. Thus people say "hot air rises," although that occurs only because cold air sinks. When a fluid is heated from the bottom, the unheated fluid sinks and the heated fluid is pushed away—but then the previously unheated fluid becomes heated.

crystal solid with a regular geometric shape, with a defined internal structure, and enclosed by symmetrically arranged plane surfaces that intersect at definite and characteristic angles. The particles (atoms, ions, or molecules) in a crystal have a regular three-dimensional repeating arrangement in space, called the crystal structure.

decay spontaneous disintegration of the nucleus of an atom, such as an isotope of uranium, by the emission of particles, usually with the emission of electromagnetic radiation. The half-life of a radioactive substance is the time that is required for half of the quantity of the substance to decay.

density mass of a substance per unit of volume, which can be measured in units such as pounds per cubic inch or kg/m^3. It is commonly confused with weight; lead is denser than water, not heavier. Density is often compared with that of water. Such a comparison, made with the densest water—at 39.2°F (4°C)—is called relative density (formerly specific gravity). Relative density of lead is about 11 (it is 11 times as dense as water); the lightest metal, lithium, has a relative density of about 0.5, so it floats on water.

diffraction bending or spreading of waves (such as light) when a wave encounters either an object or an opening; some of the wave near the edges of the object or opening is bent. The diffracted waves interfere with each other, producing reinforcement or weakening.

direct current electric current in which the net flow of charge is in one direction.

Doppler effect apparent change in the frequency of a wave with the relative motion between source and observer (after Christian Doppler, 1803–53). For example, sound from an approaching vehicle, such as a siren, is perceived as having a higher pitch because more sound waves per second are perceived by the human ear; the apparent pitch falls as the vehicle passes and moves away from the observer. Light from distant galaxies is affected by a related phenomenon. As the universe expands, electromagnetic waves emitted in the distant past become longer in wavelength, shifting frequencies lower, which for visible light is toward the red.

efficiency measure that applies to any transformation of energy by an engine, machine, etc., from one form to another. It is the ratio of the amount of work done to the amount of energy used to produce the work. Since work and energy are measured in the same unit (in scientific notation, the joule), this ratio is a pure number, most commonly expressed as a percent. No transformations in the real world have 100 percent efficiency.

energy measure of a system's ability to do work (measured in joules).

entropy measure of the unavailability of a system's energy to do work. In a closed system entropy tends to increase (the second law of thermodynamics), resulting in less energy available to do work. In a more general sense, all ordered systems tend to become less ordered—that is, to increase in entropy: solids crumble; liquids and gases diffuse.

evaporation change of a liquid to a gas below the boiling point. Evaporation occurs from the surface of a liquid, where the force attracting molecules of the liquid to each other holds most molecules in the liquid, but a few move fast enough to escape into the gas phase. Evaporation increases with temperature because the average speed of molecules is greater at higher temperatures.

field in physics a field assigns to every point in space an amount—often the size of a force—and a direction, for example the direction in which a force acts. Typical fields include gravitational, electric, and magnetic fields.

fluorescence light produced by a material that was induced by incident radiation. A fluorescent light is one in which a gas in a glass tube coated with a fluorescent substance is excited by electrons, resulting in the emission of photons of ultraviolet radiation converted to visible light by the coating in the tube.

force any push or pull; that is, a quantity that changes the motion of a body if it is free to move. Force has both magnitude and direction; the magnitude is measured in pounds or newtons. A force acting on a mass produces acceleration proportional to the force unless balanced by a force in the opposite direction. Physicists generally recognize four fundamental forces: gravity, electromagnetism, and two atomic-level forces: the strong force, which holds the atomic nucleus together; and the weak force, which is associated with beta particle emission and particle decay.

frequency number of waves per second; it is measured as hertz (Hz): 10 Hz is 10 cycles per second. Frequency is determined by wavelength and the speed at which a wave travels.

friction resistance to the movement of one object past another with which it is in contact. Friction is dependent on the size of the force holding the objects together. For an object sliding on top of another, this is the weight (or force of gravity). An increase in the weight causes an increase in resistance. Friction is also dependent to some degree on the smoothness of the surfaces; generally, rougher surfaces have more friction, i.e., require a greater force to move one object past another.

half-life time in which one-half of the original quantity of a radioactive element will decay. Radioactive elements decay atom by atom in random events. Which individual atom decays is inherently unpredictable, but statistically the change follows a specific decay function for each isotope of an element.

incandescence light emitted by heating a material to a high temperature. In the common lightbulb a tungsten filament, usually in an inert gas, is heated to a high temperature to produce light.

inertia property that causes objects to resist any change in their motion. Objects at rest tend to stay at rest unless acted upon by an external force, and objects in motion continue in motion unless acted upon by an external force. This is a statement of Newton's first law of motion.

ion atom or group of atoms that either gains one or more electrons, and thus becomes negatively charged (anion), or loses one or more electrons, becoming positively charged (cation).

isotope substance formed from atoms that each have the same number of protons and neutrons per atom. Elements usually exist in several different isotopes. The number of protons in each atom determines which element it is and most of the properties; the number of neutrons determines the specific isotope. The number that is the sum of the protons and neutrons per atom is combined with the element name to identify a specific isotope. For example, two isotopes of carbon are carbon 12, with six protons and six neutrons; and carbon 14, with six protons and eight neutrons.

kinetic energy energy of motion.

mass measure of an object's inertia, that is, its resistance to acceleration. Inertial mass is exactly equivalent to gravitational mass, measurable by the force between two bodies separated by a given distance. The international standard of mass is a 1-kg platinum-iridium cylinder.

melting point temperature, usually measured at a pressure of 1 bar, at which a solid becomes liquid. The melting point is the same temperature as the freezing point, at which liquids become solid.

noise random changes in a signal being received at a detector. A mixture of sound or electromagnetic waves of random amplitude and frequency is called white noise.

osmosis process of diffusion of a solvent such as water through a semipermeable membrane that will transmit the solvent but impede most dissolved substances. Normally the flow of solvent is from the more dilute solution to the more concentrated solution; flow will stop when the solutions are of equal concentration. Movement of water in plants and animals is determined to a large extent by osmosis.

period time that it takes for an oscillation or wave motion to repeat. Period (p) is the reciprocal of the frequency (f): $p = 1/f$. Any repeated motion, as for a pendulum or vibrating atom, similarly has a period—the amount of time for one repetition.

phase of matter traditionally matter exists in three states or phases—solid, liquid, and gas—but the modern view is that there are five phases of matter: the three traditional states plus plasma and Bose-Einstein condensates. For most elements and compounds, phases of matter change in response to heating.

phosphorescence light produced by causes other than increasing the heat of a substance that persists after the source of excitation has been removed.

photoelectric effects various electrical effects caused by light. The photoelectric (or photoemissive) effect occurs when electromagnetic waves strike a substance and liberate electrons from its surface In the photovoltaic effect a current flows across the junction of two dissimilar materials when light falls upon it. In the photoconductive effect, an increase in the electrical conductivity of a semi-conductor is caused by radiation.

piezoelectricity electric current caused by a mechanical force. When a mechanical force is applied to both sides of any of various nonconducting crystals such as quartz or Rochelle salt, positive charge builds on one face and negative charge on the opposite face, inducing a small electric current, in a circuit. The effect also works in reverse. Applying a current changes the shape of the crystal or other material as the faces repel or attract each other. These properties give rise to a variety of applications in acoustic and other devices such as microphones and quartz clocks.

pitch highness or lowness of a sound to an observer; higher pitches correspond to higher frequencies; pitch can also be affected by the loudness of a sound.

plasma one of the five phases of matter, consisting of a low-density, fully ionized gas with approximately equal numbers of positive and negative ions. Plasmas are electrically conductive and affected by magnetic fields. Interstellar gases, as well as the matter inside stars, is believed to be in the form of plasma. The study of plasma is important in the attempt to produce a controlled thermonuclear reaction as an energy source.

polarized light electromagnetic field confined to two dimensions, also called plane-polarized light. The electromagnetic field of unpolarized light vibrates in all directions perpendicular to the line of travel. One use of polarizing materials is in certain kinds of sunglasses, which absorb horizontally polarized light reflected off surfaces such as water.

potential energy energy stored in a system or body as a result of its position or shape; examples are gravitational, electrical, chemical, and nuclear energy. A rock on the edge of a cliff has potential energy because of its position in the Earth's gravitational field.

power rate at which work is done or energy transferred. It is measured scientifically in watts (joules/second). In common usage, it is sometimes measured in horsepower (1 horsepower = 745.7 watts)

radiation emission and transmission of energy through space or a material medium; also the radiated energy. Generally the term is applied to the electromagnetic spectrum, which (from longest to shortest waves) includes radio, microwave, infrared, visible light, ultraviolet, X rays, and gamma rays; or to radioactivity, which includes streams of electrons or alpha particles as well as gamma rays.

radioactivity radiation produced by decay from one element to another or by nuclear fusion or fission. The disintegration of certain atomic nuclei is accompanied by the emission of alpha particles (helium nuclei), beta particles (electrons or positrons), or gamma radiation (short-wavelength electromagnetic radiation). Natural radioactivity is the disintegration of naturally occurring radioisotopes. Radioactivity can also be induced by bombarding the nuclei of normally stable elements in a particle accelerator to produce radioactive isotopes.

refraction deflection of a ray of light as it passes obliquely from one medium to another in which its speed is different. The incoming ray is the incident ray, and the deflected ray is the refracted ray. Other electromagnetic waves and sound waves can also be refracted.

spectrum rainbow or any of various related electromagnetic displays. A rainbow is just the spectrum of visible light. The complete electromagnetic spectrum includes (from longest to shortest waves) radio, microwave, infrared, visible light, ultraviolet, X-ray, and gamma-ray emissions. The emission (or "bright line") spectrum of a body is the characteristic radiation pattern produced when the body is heated, bombarded by electrons or ions, or absorbing photons; the lines in the spectrum can be used to identify elements with the spectroscope. The absorption (dark line) spectrum is the reverse of the emissions spectrum; it is produced by white light passing through a gas not hot enough to be incandescent.

specific heat amount of heat needed to raise the temperature of 1 gram of a substance, at a given pressure, by 1°C. For water at sea level, this is 4.187 joules (1 Calorie). Different substances have different specific heats.

spin quantum characteristic of particles best described as intrinsic angular momentum that is not associated with rotation. The quantum values of spin are restricted to integer or half-integer multiples of $h/2$, where h is Planck's constant. Because of spin, particles also have their own intrinsic magnetic moments.

sublimation change of a substance directly from a solid to a gas without first becoming a liquid. This process is most familiar from frozen carbon dioxide, known as dry ice. Water ice also sublimes slowly at temperatures below 32°F (0°C).

surface tension property of liquids in which the liquid appears to be bounded by a thin elastic skin. Molecules in a liquid attract each other from all directions, but at the surface of a liquid there are attractive forces only from below. The unbalanced attraction creates the illusion of a skin at the surface.

suspension mixture in which finely divided particles of solid or liquid are suspended in a liquid or gas.

temperature measure of the average energy of motion in the atoms or molecules of a substance. As more heat is added to a system, its temperature rises. Temperature determines the direction of heat flow: heat transfers from a higher-temperature system to a lower one until the two systems are at the same temperature and thus in thermal equilibrium.

tunneling quantum-mechanical effect by which a particle can penetrate a barrier into a region of space that would be forbidden according to ordinary classic mechanics. Tunneling occurs because of the wavelike properties of particles; the wave associated with a particle can leak or decay through the barrier, and there is a finite probability of finding the particle on the other side. The theory of tunneling is the basis of the tunnel diode, used in electronic applications.

Zillions Of Universes? Or Did Ours Get Lucky?

By DENNIS OVERBYE

Cosmology used to be a heartless science, all about dark matter lost in mind-bending abysses and exploding stars. But whenever physicists and astronomers gather, the subject that roils discussions tends to be not dark matter or the fate of the universe. Rather it is about the role and meaning of life in the cosmos.

Cosmologists held a debate on the question during a 2003 conference at Case Western Reserve University.

According to a notion known as the anthropic principle, certain otherwise baffling features of the universe can only be understood by including ourselves in the equation. The universe must be suitable for life, otherwise we would not be here to wonder about it.

The features in question are mysterious numbers in the equations of physics and cosmology, denoting, say, the amount of matter in the universe or the number of dimensions, which don't seem predictable by any known theory. They are like the knobs on God's control console, and they seem almost miraculously tuned to allow life.

A slight change from the present settings could cause all stars to collapse into black holes or atoms to evaporate, negating the possibility of biology.

If there were only one universe, theorists would have their hands full trying to explain why it is as it is.

But the anthropic principle suggests that there could be zillions of possible universes. This view has been bolstered in recent years by a theory of the Big Bang, known as inflation, which implies that our universe is only one bubble in an endless chain of them, and by string theory—the so-called theory of everything—whose equations seem to have an almost uncountable number of solutions, each representing a different possible universe.

Only a few will be conducive to life, the anthropic argument goes, but it is no surprise to find ourselves in one of them. We live where we can live.

Some scientists regard the anthropic principle as more philosophy than science. Others regard it as a betrayal of the Einsteinian dream of predicting everything about the universe.

Dr. Steven Weinberg, a Nobel laureate from the University of Texas, is among the most prominent of theorists who have reluctantly accepted, at least provisionally, the anthropic principle as a kind of tragic necessity in order to explain the gnarliest knob of all.

Called the cosmological constant, it is a number that measures the amount of cosmic repulsion caused by the energy in empty space. That empty space should be boiling with such energy is predicted by quantum theory, and astronomers in the last few years have discovered that some cosmic repulsion seems to be accelerating the expansion of the universe.

In 1989 Dr. Weinberg used the anthropic principle to set limits on the value of the constant. Suppose instead of being fixed by theory, it was random from universe to universe. In that case the value of the cosmological constant in our universe may just be an "environmental effect," he explained, and we shouldn't expect to be able to predict it exactly.

Dr. Alex Vilenkin, a Tufts University physicist, suggested at the conference that the anthropic reasoning was a logical attempt to apply probabilities to cosmology, using all the data, including the fact of our own existence. Dr. John Peacock, a University of Edinburgh cosmologist, argued that the anthropic principle was not a retreat from physics, but an advance. The existence of an ensemble of universes with different properties, he explained, implies a mechanism to produce variation, a kind of cosmic genetic code.

But Dr. David Gross, director of the Kavli Institute for Theoretical Physics in Santa Barbara, Calif., questioned whether the rules of the anthropic game were precise enough. What were the parameters that could vary from universe to universe? How many could vary at once? What was the probability distribution of their values, and what was necessary for "life"?

Nobody who adheres to the anthropic principle, Dr. Gross said, would hold on if there were "an honest old-fashioned calculation" that explained the cosmological constant.

Dr. Weinberg agreed that it was too soon to give up hope for such a breakthrough.

ultrasound sound beyond the range of human hearing, at frequencies greater than 20,000 cycles/second. Unlike audible sound, in which high intensity produces discomfort, ultrasound can increase in pressure (intensity) with little impact on human hearing. Ultrasound is widely used for medical and industrial imaging and testing: objects are scanned with ultrasound and the echoes recorded and analyzed.

vacuum region of space with very few atoms or other particles. A true or perfect vacuum would be a region of space that contains no matter, but in practice this is unattainable. The uncertainty principle permits subatomic particles to appear out of nothing and disappear before violating any physical laws. Thus any vacuum contains virtual particles.

viscosity property of a fluid's resistance to flow; a higher viscosity means a slower flow. The cause of viscosity is internal molecular friction.

wave disturbance in space or a medium with a periodic form, such as electromagnetic waves and sound waves. The main characteristics of waves are speed of propagation, frequency, amplitude, and wavelength.

work a force that causes an object to move produces work, which is the product of the force and the distance moved. Work is measured in joules, the same unit used to measure energy.

PSYCHOLOGY

Areas of Psychological Research

Psychology (literally, "study of the mind") is the scientific study of mental processes and behavior in humans and other animals. Psychiatry, on the other hand, is the branch of medicine that specializes in mental illness. Psychology is intimately related to the biological and social sciences. There are five main branches of psychological study:

Biopsychology examines the biological foundations of behavior and mental processes, or the interconnect between the body and the mind. Important subfields in biopsychology include behavioral genetics (the study of how various characteristics and mental illnesses are inherited), behavioral neuroscience (the study of the links between behavior and the brain and nervous system), cognitive neuroscience (the study of how activities in the brain correspond to operations of the mind), comparative psychology (the study of behavior among different animal species, including humans), ethology (the study of animal behavior in natural habitats), evolutionary psychology (the study of the origins of various human behaviors), and psychopharmacology (the study of how drugs affect mental functions and behavior).

Clinical psychology is concerned with the study, diagnosis, and treatment of mental illnesses and other behavioral and emotional disorders. This is the largest field of psychological study; the goal is to design non-drug-related treatments for all types of psychological disturbances. Clinical psychologists have developed many successful forms of therapy, including psychoanalysis and behavioral therapy.

Cognitive psychology is the scientific study of how people acquire, process, and use information. Cognitive psychologists examine how people learn, how they solve problems, and how their brains store important information.

Developmental psychology examines mental and behavioral changes as people age. Researchers compare people of different ages and track individuals over time to learn how both nature (inherited qualities) and nurture affect human development.

Social psychology is the study of how people think, feel, and behave in social situations. Social psychologists observe individuals in both laboratory and real-world social settings to determine how people interact with one another.

A Brief History of Psychology

Psychology emerged as a formal discipline in the late 19th century, but its intellectual origins date back to early Greek philosophers such as Socrates, Plato, and Aristotle, who debated human perception (epistemology), motivation (ethics), and the organization of the mind (associationism). In the 17th century, the philosopher René Descartes (1596–1650) theorized that the body and mind are two separate entities (dualism); Thomas Hobbes (1588–1679) and John Locke (1632–1704) disagreed, arguing that all thoughts and sensations are physical processes occurring within the brain (monism).

Psychology also has roots in the pseudoscience of the 18th century and the early 19th century. Franz Joseph Gall (1758–1828) introduced the study of phrenology, which explored the alleged relationship between psychological traits and the bumps on a person's head. More important, Franz Anton Mesmer (1734–1815) developed the theory of mesmerism, which used magnetic fields to put patients into a trance, and was the precursor to the more legitimate science of hypnotism.

The physiological roots of modern psychology date to the late 19th century, when naturalist Charles Darwin (1809–82) and his theories of natural selection invited comparisons between humans and animals in later psychological research. Concurrently, surgeon Paul Broca (1824–80) and neurologist Carl Wernicke (1848–1904) discovered the relationship between physical damage to the brain and specific changes in behavior, while neurologist Jean-Martin Charcot (1825–93) discovered that patients with certain nervous disorders could be cured through hypnosis.

The Birth of Modern Psychology

The birth of modern psychology is often said to have occurred in 1879 at the University of Leipzig, where physiologist Wilhelm Wundt (1832–1920) established the first laboratory dedicated to the scientific study of the mind. Wundt taught thousands of students, established the first scholarly psychological journal, and introduced the scientific method to psychological studies.

Wundt's progress was mirrored in the United States by William James (1842–1910), a professor at Harvard University who in 1875 offered the first academic course in psychology. In 1890 James published *Principles of Psychology*, a groundbreaking two-volume work that solidified his position as the founder of American psychology. Like Wundt, James taught many students who made their own contributions to the burgeoning field of psychology.

James also developed one of the first schools of psychological thought, known as functionalism, which proposed that the goal of psychology is to investigate the function of consciousness—the purpose of human thought. This goal was contradicted by the proponents of structuralism, led by one of Wundt's former students, Edward Bradford Titchener (1867–1927). Structuralists believed that the goal of psychology is to identify the basic elements of consciousness, and thus define consciousness itself.

Other scholars followed Wundt and James in developing the new field of psychological study. In 1885 Hermann Ebbinghaus (1850–1909) pioneered the study of memory, using nonsense syllables to examine how humans retain information. In 1896 Lightner Witmer (1867–1956) opened the first psychological clinic; he later founded the field of clinical psychology. In 1905 Alfred Binet (1851–1911) devised the first intelligence test; this test was later revised by Stanford University psychologist Lewis Madison Terman (1877–1956), and is now known as the Stanford-Binet intelligence test. In 1912 Max Wertheimer (1880–1943) inspired the gestalt psychology movement, which theorized that people tend to perceive organized patterns that are different from the sum of isolated sensations.

Psychoanalysis

The most influential early figure was Sigmund Freud (1856–1939). A neurologist by training, Freud formulated the form of psychotherapy known as psychoanalysis, which became one of the most influential schools of thought in the 20th century.

Freud developed his theories when treating patients who appeared to suffer from certain ailments but had nothing physically wrong with them. He discovered that these patients' symptoms would often disappear through the use of hypnosis, or even just through talking. In his book *The Interpretation of Dreams* (1889), Freud proposed that people are primarily motivated by unconscious forces; by finding a suitable outlet for these unconscious motivations, a person can develop a more healthy personality.

To probe the unconscious mind, Freud developed the technique of free association. In this form of psychotherapy, patients recline on a couch and talk about their dreams or anything else that comes to mind; the analyst then interprets these thoughts to determine their psychological significance and reveal their underlying latent content.

Freud's Theory of Sexuality In 1905 Freud published the landmark work *Drei Abhandlungen zur Sexualtheorie* (*Three Essays on the Theory of Sexuality*), which extended the conventional concept of sexuality to include a variety of erotic impulses, starting in earliest childhood. Freud contended that a fixation on sexual aims or objects, when expressed openly, can result in a perversion; the same fixation, when repressed, can produce a neurosis. In this way, Freud concluded, sexuality is the prime mover in a great deal of human behavior.

Neo-Freudian Thought Freud's theories dominated psychological thought in the early 20th century, although many of his followers (dubbed neo-Freudians) did not share Freud's emphasis on sex as the primary motivating factor for human behavior.

The most notable was Carl Jung (1875–1961), who had been one of Freud's most devoted adherents. They severed all relations when Jung published his *Psychology of the Unconscious* (1912), in which he theorized that all humans experience a collective unconscious that contains universal memories (called archetypes) from their shared past. Jung developed the concept of attitude types, in which he differentiated two classes of people: extroverted (outward-looking) and introverted (inward-looking). He also explored how any one of four functions of the mind—thinking, feeling, sensation, and intuition—can predominate in any given person. Jung made the ideas of extroversion and introversion part of all psychological discourse.

Karen Horney (1885–1992) disagreed with Freud's view of female psychology as an offshoot of male psychology, in particular the notion of penis envy; instead, she argued that male-dominated culture was the source of much female psychiatric disturbance. Alfred Adler (1870–1937) believed that people are motivated by feelings of inferiority (the inferiority complex) and are influenced by birth order in the family, sometimes leading to sibling rivalry. And other researchers, led by Hermann Rorschach (1884–1922), developed projective tests designed to uncover various aspects of the unconscious psyche.

Behaviorism

Not all psychologists accepted Freud's theories of unconscious motivation; many rejected the method of introspection and turned their attention to the direct observation of human behavior. This approach, first developed in the early 20th century, was known as behaviorism.

The Law of Effect and Classical Conditioning In 1898 Edward Lee Thorndike (1874–1949) conducted a series of experiments on how animals learned various behaviors. This led him to propose the law of effect, which states that behaviors that lead to a positive outcome are repeated, whereas those followed by a negative outcome are abandoned.

In 1906 Ivan Pavlov (1849–1936) expanded on Thorndike's theory when he discovered that dogs would salivate in anticipation of food, based on the ringing of a bell before being fed. He named this form of learning *classical conditioning*, in which a person or animal comes to associate one stimulus with another. Later research found that this basic process explains how people form certain fears and prejudices.

These early studies were codified in 1913, when an animal psychologist, John Watson (1878–1958), published a paper entitled "Psychology as the Behaviorist Views It," followed the next year by the book *Behaviorism: An Introduction to Comparative Psychology*. Watson redefined psychology as an objective branch of natural science with its goal the predication and control of behavior; he stressed observational technique and the use of animals in psychological research.

After Watson, the primary proponent of behaviorism was B. F. Skinner (1904–90), who coined the term *reinforcement* to describe how animal and human behavior is motivated, in a process he called *operant conditioning*. Skinner and his followers applied these theories to attempt to modify behavior in the workplace, the classroom, and other social settings; this technique became known as behavior modification.

Post-Behaviorist Psychology

By the middle of the 20th century, many psychologists found it difficult to resolve the diametrically opposed theories of psychoanalysis and behaviorism. This led to the new fields of exploration known as humanistic psychology and cognitive psychology.

Humanistic Psychology In an attempt to bridge the gap between the dark forces of the unconscious mind and the effects of reinforcement on behavior, psychologists in the 1950's and 1960's developed the "third force" known as humanistic psychology. This new movement was aimed at a better understanding of the conscious mind, free will, and the human capacity for self-reflection and growth.

The humanistic movement was led by Carl Rogers (1902–87), who believed that all humans are born with a drive to achieve their full capacity. He developed a nondirective technique known as person-centered therapy, which helped patients clarify their sense of self to facilitate their individual healing process.

Concurrently, Abraham Maslow (1908–70) proposed a hierarchy of needs that humans are motivated to fulfill, in ascending order. At the bottom of the hierarchy are basic physiological needs, such as hunger, thirst, and sleep; ascending the hierarchy, humans attempt to fulfill the needs for safety and security, the needs for belonging and love, and the needs for status and achievement. Once these needs are met, people strive for self-actualization, the ultimate state of personal fulfillment.

Cognitive Psychology Other psychologists moved beyond behaviorism to study cognition, the mental processes involved in acquiring, storing, and using forms of knowledge. This new field of cognitive psychology was based partially on the work of psychologist Jean Piaget (1896–1980) in the 1920's. Piaget explored how children think and reason, and theorized about a predictable series of cognitive stages. Piaget's work was supplemented in the late 1950's by the observations of the linguist Noam Chomsky (b. 1928), who theorized that the human brain is "hardwired" for language as a product of evolution.

Later researchers, influenced by the pioneering work of the computer scientist Alan Turing (1912–54), compared human thought to the information-processing abilities of computers. In 1943 Donald O. Hebb (1904–85) published *The Organization of Behavior: A Neuropsychological Theory*, which defined a consolidation theory that explained thought processes in terms of interconnected neurons and synapses. George A. Miller (b. 1920) explored the concept of short-term memory, which can hold only seven "chunks" of information at a time.

Disorders

Mental Disorders

Researchers estimate that just over 22 percent of U.S. citizens aged 18 or older, or about 44 million adults, suffer from a diagnosable mental disorder in any given year. The acknowledged authoritative guide to the various types of mental illnesses is the *Diagnostic and Statistical Manual of Mental Disorders*, 4th edition (DSM-IV), published by the American Psychiatric Association, which describes more than 300 different mental and addictive disorders.

Anxiety involves the inability to cope with excessive apprehension, worry, and fear. Symptoms are long-lasting and often socially disruptive; treatment involves systematic desensitization and training in social skills.

Acute stress is typically caused by exposure to a traumatic event that threatened death or serious injury, and typically occurs within four weeks after the event. Symptoms include a sense of numbing or detachment, a reduction in awareness of one's surroundings, depersonalization, or dissociative amnesia; the event is often reexperienced in dreams, illusions, or flashbacks.

Generalized anxiety (GAD) involves constant anxiety about routine events in one's life; this is an excessive and long-lasting anxiety that is not related to any one specific event or object. Approximately 4 million Americans aged 18 to 54, or about 2.8 percent of all adults, suffer from GAD.

Obsessive-compulsive disorder (OCD) involves having upsetting and unwanted thoughts (obsessions) or feeling compelled to perform certain repetitive behaviors (compulsions). The first symptoms of OCD often begin during childhood or adolescence.

Panic disorder and resultant panic attacks are marked by a sudden, intense terror, often manifested in such physical symptoms as rapid heartbeat, shortness of breath, chest pain, dizziness, and sweating. About one in three people with panic disorder will also develop agoraphobia. (See below, Phobias.)

Post-traumatic stress disorder (PTSD) involves anxiety and stress about traumatic events in one's past. This disorder frequently occurs after violent personal assaults, such as rape, mugging, domestic violence, terrorism, natural disasters, or accidents. About a third of Vietnam veterans experienced PTSD at some point after the war.

Phobias are persistent, intense, and irrational fears and the subsequent avoidance of a specific object, activity, or situation. Common phobias include fear of closed spaces (claustrophobia), fear of heights (acrophobia), fear of snakes (orphiophobia), fear of spiders (arachnophobia), and so on. Also common are social phobia, the fear of embarrassment; and agoraphobia, the fear of being in any place or situation where escape might be difficult or help unavailable in the event of a panic attack.

Childhood Disorders

Many psychological disorders found in children involve physiological or genetic components, although many of these disorders have no physical causes.

Asperger's disorder is a milder variant of autistic disorder, characterized by social isolation and eccentric behavior, as well as impaired social interaction and verbal communication. Treatment is typically psychotherapy and various drug therapies.

Attention deficit hyperactivity disorder (ADHD) is one of the most common mental disorders in children and adolescents, affecting an estimated 4.1 percent of youngsters aged nine to 17. Symptoms include difficulty in paying attention, not seeming to listen when spoken to directly, inability to follow through on tasks or finish schoolwork, persistent fidgeting, and excessive talking. Treatment is typically medication (stimulants) and behavior therapy.

Autistic disorder, also known as autism, affects a child's ability to communicate, form relationships with others, and respond appropriately to the environment. It often manifests itself in restricted and repetitive patterns of behavior, interests, and activities. Autism is about four times more common in boys than in girls, although girls tend to have more severe symptoms and greater cognitive impairment; treatment is typically drug therapy (antipsychotics and antiepileptics) and certain dietary restrictions.

Conduct disorder is a repetitive and persistent pattern of behavior in which age-appropriate societal norms are violated. Children with conduct disorder frequently engage in bullying and are often cruel to other children and animals.

Oppositional defiant disorder is a pattern of hostile and defiant behavior, lasting at least six months. Children with this disorder often lose their temper, argue with adults, and refuse to comply with adults' requests or rules.

Separation anxiety is characterized by inappropriate and excessive anxiety concerning separation from home, family members, or close friends. Children with separation anxiety disorder worry about losing, or about possible harm befalling, those close to them.

Tourette syndrome (or Tourette's disorder) is a neurological disorder characterized by tics—involuntary, rapid, and sudden movements or vocalizations that occur repeatedly. It is currently believed to be caused by an abnormal metabolism of the neurotransmitters dopamine and serotonin; Tourette's is genetically transmitted, with affected parents having a 50 percent chance of passing the gene on to their children. The most common treatment is drug therapy, typically with haloperidol, pimozide, and other neuroleptics.

Cognitive Disorders

Cognitive disorders involve a significant loss of mental functioning, typically a result of a medical condition, substance abuse, or adverse reactions to medication. The goal of treatment is to control or reverse the cause of the symptoms, which varies with the specific condition.

Delirium is excessively confused or disorganized thinking. This is often manifested in a reduced ability to maintain attention to external stimuli, and sometimes in a reduced level of consciousness.

Dementia is characterized by impaired memory and difficulties in such functions as speaking, abstract thinking, and the ability to identify familiar objects. The most common cause of dementia among people aged 65 and older is Alzheimer's disease, affecting an estimated 4 million Americans; the duration of illness, from onset of symptoms to death, averages 8-10 years.

Multi-infarct dementia (MID) occurs when blood clots block small blood vessels in the brain and destroy brain tissue. MID is a common cause of dementia in the elderly; high blood pressure and advanced age are likely risk factors. The disease can also cause migraine-like headaches, stroke, and psychiatric disturbances.

Dissociative disorders involve a sudden, often temporary disturbance in one's consciousness, memory, and identity. Treatment is a combination of drug therapy and psychotherapy.

Depersonalization disorder is the third most common psychological symptom and frequently occurs when one is in life-threatening danger; it can also occur as a symptom in other psychiatric disorders. One has a chronic feeling of being detached from one's body or mental processes; common objects and familiar situations seem strange or foreign. Treatment is warranted only if the disorder is persistent, recurring, or especially distressing.

Dissociative amnesia is an inability to recall important personal information, a memory loss that is too extensive to be explained by normal forgetfulness. With treatment, most patients recover the missing memories and resolve their amnesia; however, some never break through the barriers to reconstruct their missing past.

Dissociative fugue is one or more episodes of amnesia in which the loss of one's identity or the formation of a new identity coincides with sudden departure from home or work. A fugue might last from hours to weeks to months; most episodes are brief and self-limited.

Dissociative identity disorder (DID), also known as multiple personality disorder (MPD), is characterized by a person's having two or more distinct personalities that alternate in their control of his or her behavior. Drug therapy may help to manage specific symptoms; psychotherapy is a more effective treatment.

Eating Disorders

An eating disorder is a severe disturbance in eating behavior. These disorders occur mostly among young women in Western societies and certain parts of Asia. Treatment typically involves a short-term intervention to restore body weight and long-term therapy (often accompanied by antidepressants) to prevent relapse.

Anorexia nervosa is characterized by a disturbed sense of body image and a morbid fear of obesity. People with anorexia nervosa often refuse to eat adequately or even to maintain a normal body weight.

Bulimia nervosa is characterized by binge eating followed by self-induced vomiting or the use of laxatives, diuretics, or other medications to prevent weight gain. Patients are overly concerned about their body shape and weight.

Binge eating is characterized by eating excessive amounts of food without subsequent purging. It occurs most commonly in obese persons. Affected persons also tend to be older; nearly half are male.

Factitious Disorders

People with factitious disorders intentionally fake physical or psychological symptoms in order to receive medical attention and care. Factitious disorders are not to be confused with somatoform disorders, in which one actually believes that he or she has a (nonexistent) physical illness. The most extreme and chronic factitious disorder is Munchausen syndrome, which involves the repeated and often convincing fabrication of a physical illness by a person who wanders from hospital to hospital for treatment. Patients with this type of disorder are rarely treated successfully.

Mood Disorders

Mood disorders, also called affective disorders, are conditions in which a person regularly experiences moods that are inconsistent with events, or shifts in mood from one extreme to another. In any given year, nearly 18.8 million American adults—9.5 percent of the population aged 18 and older—have a mood disorder; nearly twice as many women as men are affected by this type of disorder. Treatment with antidepressant drugs is often effective.

Bipolar disorder, also known as manic-depressive illness, is characterized by a person's mood alternating between the extremes of mania (an overexcited, hyperactive state) and depression. There are two primary types of bipolar disorder. *Bipolar I* disorder is characterized by alternating manic and depressive episodes. *Bipolar II* disorder is characterized by depressive episodes alternating with hypomanic periods, when the patient's mood is generally brighter and the patient has less need for sleep.

Cyclothymic disorder is a less extreme type of bipolar disorder, in which mild hypomanic and mini-depressive episodes follow an irregular course. This disorder is commonly a precursor of bipolar II disorder, but it can also occur as extreme moodiness in the affected person.

Dysthymic disorder is characterized by a chronic mild depression that persists for several years. This disorder often begins in childhood or adolescence; affected persons are typically perceived as gloomy, pessimistic, humorless, and introverted.

Depression is by far the most common psychological disorder today, and the leading cause of emotional disability in the U.S. Symptoms of depression may include feelings of sadness, hopelessness, and worthlessness, as well as changes in appetite, sleep patterns, and energy level, all lasting for two or more weeks. Persons with major depressive disorder typically lose interest in people and activities, experience little pleasure or enjoyment from normal activities, and find that even simple tasks become difficult.

Personality Disorders

Personality disorders are enduring and inflexible behavior patterns that impair normal social functioning. People with personality disorders have a poor perception of themselves or others, which commonly manifests itself in weak impulse control, troubled social relationships, and inappropriate emotional responses. These disorders are classified by three primary clusters of personality types: odd/eccentric, dramatic/erratic, and anxious/inhibited.

Odd/Eccentric Personalities in this cluster include paranoid (cold, distant, and suspicious), schizoid (introverted, withdrawn, and prone to daydreaming), schizotypal (emotionally detached, often expressing oddities of thinking, such as clairvoyance).

Dramatic/Erratic Personalities in this cluster include antisocial (often called psychopathic or sociopathic: callously disregardful of the rights and feelings of others); borderline (unstable in self-image, relationships, and behavior); histrionic (often called hysterical: dramatically and conspicuously seeking attention); and narcissistic (possessing an exaggerated sense of superiority).

Anxious/Inhibited Personalities in this cluster include avoidant (hypersensitive to rejection, fearful of starting new relationships), dependent (surrendering responsibility for major areas of their lives to others), obsessive-compulsive (overly orderly, inflexible, and unable to adapt to change).

Other Personality Types Personality types not falling within the three major clusters include cyclothymic (alternating high spirits with gloom and pessimism), depressive (morose, worried, and self-conscious), and passive-aggressive (employing inept or passive behaviors in an attempt to avoid responsibility or to control or punish others).

Psychotic Disorders

People with psychotic disorders lose touch with reality; symptoms may include delusions and hallucinations, disorganized thinking and speech, bizarre behavior, a diminished range of emotional responses, and social withdrawal. People who suffer from psychotic disorders often experience an inability to function in one or more important areas of life.

Schizophrenia is actually a group of disorders marked by severely disturbed thinking, perception, and behavior. It significantly impairs one's ability to communicate and relate to others, and disturbs most aspects of daily functioning. Typical symptoms include disorganized thought and language, hallucinations, and muted emotional expression (called flat affect); these symptoms usually last more than six months. The major types of schizophrenic disorder include catatonic, disorganized, paranoid, residual, and undifferentiated. Treatment with neuroleptic drugs is common.

Shared psychotic disorder is typified by delusions that occur in the context of a relationship with another person who already has his or her own delusions.

Somatoform Disorders

Somatoform disorders are characterized by the presence of physical symptoms that cannot be explained by a medical condition or have no identifiable physical cause. Such symptoms typically result from psychological conflicts or distress—psychological conditions taking a physical form.

Conversion disorder, also known as hysteria, is characterized by the loss of physical functioning without any physiological reason, typically the result of emotional conflict. Symptoms appear suddenly and at times of extreme psychological stress; patients often have a lack of concern over these symptoms (known as *la belle indifférence*).

Hypochondriasis (hypochondria) involves fear that one will develop a serious disease, typically misinterpreting minor physical symptoms as evidence of a major illness. Hypochondria typically lasts at least six months and causes significant distress.

Somatization disorder is a condition in which the patient has numerous physical complaints, persisting for several years, that have no physical cause. Common complaints include chronic pain and problems with the digestive, nervous, or reproductive systems; a lifetime history of sickliness is often found, although no specific disease is ever linked to the symptoms. This disorder typically begins before the age of 30, and occurs more often in females.

Substance-Related Disorders

Substance-related disorders, often called addictions, typically result from the abuse of drugs, medications, or other toxic substances. The most common substance-related disorders include alcohol dependence, amphetamine dependence, cannibis dependence, cocaine dependence, hallucinogen dependence, inhalant dependence, nicotine dependence, opoid dependence, phencyclidine dependence, and sedative dependence.

Common Treatments

Before the dawn of modern psychology, mental illness was thought to be the result of possession by demons, and treatment ranged from trephaning (the drilling of a hole in the head) to exorcism, torture, and hanging—all designed to release evil spirits from the body. Today there are three primary forms of treatment for patients with mental disorders: organic treatments, psychotherapy, and drug therapy.

Organic Treatments

Older forms of organic treatments involve some sort of physical approach to mental illness, but have gradually fallen out of favor.

Electroconvulsive therapy (ECT) uses electrical current, passed through the patient's brain for several seconds, to deliberately induce a controlled seizure; treatments are typically repeated over a period of several weeks. This treatment is most commonly used to treat severe depressions that has not responded to other forms of treatment; it is also sometimes used to treat schizophrenia. This is a controversial treatment, with major side effects such as confusion and memory loss.

Psychosurgery is the surgical removal or destruction of sections of the brain, in order to reduce severe and chronic psychiatric symptoms. The best-known psychosurgical procedure is the lobotomy, which was widely performed in the 1940's and early 1950's. As no research has proved this technique effective, and because it can produce drastic changes in personality and behavior, psychosurgery is now rarely performed.

Psychotherapy

Psychotherapy is a nonorganic treatment that is psychodynamic in nature, focusing on the resolution of internal psychic conflict. Unlike organic treatments, psychotherapy produces no physical side effects, although it can cause psychological damage when improperly administered; it also typically takes longer to produce noticeable results.

Behavioral therapy does not focus on past experiences, but instead helps the patient change abnormal behavior by applying established principles of conditioning and learning. This type of therapy has proved effective in treating phobias, obsessive-compulsive disorder, and other behavioral disorders.

Cognitive therapy attempts to identify patterns of irrational thinking that cause a person to behave abnormally. The patient learns to perceive people, situations, and self in a more realistic way, and thus develops improved problem-solving and coping skills. Cognitive therapy is commonly used to treat depression, panic disorder, and some personality disorders.

Group therapy brings a number of people together, under the guidance of a therapist, to discuss their individual problems; by sharing their feelings and experiences with others, group members learn that their problems are not unique and receive group support. Psychodrama is a type of group therapy in which participants act out emotional conflicts.

Humanistic and existential therapy These therapies treat mental illnesses by helping the patient achieve personal growth and meaning in life. The best-known humanistic therapy is client-centered therapy, in which the therapist provides no advice, instead restating the observations of the patient in nonjudgmental terms. Existential therapy encourages the patient to confront basic questions about the meaning of his or her life, in a journey toward discovery of personal uniqueness.

Psychodynamic therapy is used to untangle the sources of unconscious conflict and subsequently restructure the patient's personality. The first psychodynamic therapy was psychoanalysis, which typically involves the patient lying on a couch and saying whatever comes to mind (free association); some therapists may use hypnosis to uncover repressed memories. This type of treatment is lengthy and expensive, with multiple sessions often taking place over a period of several years. For this reason, classical psychoanalysis is not so widely practiced today as in previous years.

Drug Therapy

Drug therapy is a newer form of organic treatment, first introduced in the mid-1950's. Psychotherapeutic drugs help relieve the symptoms of many common mental disorders, although relapse may occur when their use is discontinued.

Antipsychotic drugs, also called neuroleptics, are powerful tranquilizers primarily used to treat schizophrenia; they work by diminishing symptoms such as delusions, hallucinations, and thought disorder. The most commonly prescribed antipsychotic drugs are the phenothiazines; other popular antipsychotics include thioxanthenes, butyrophenomes, and indoles. Side effects may include dry mouth, blurred vision, and tardive dyskinesia, typified by involuntary movements of the lips, mouth, and tongue.

Antianxiety drugs, typically benzodiazepines such as Valium or other minor tranquilizers, are used to treat anxiety, insomnia, and other stress-related disorders. These newer drugs replace barbiturates, the previous antianxiety drugs of choice, which produced more severe side effects and were more likely to be abused. Benzodiazepines can also be addictive, however, and can also cause drowsiness and impaired coordination.

Antidepressant drugs help relieve symptoms of depression. There are three major classes of antidepressant drugs: tricyclics and tetracyclics, monoamine oxidase (MAO) inhibitors, and selective serotonin-selective reuptake inhibitors (SSRIs), such as Prozac. Side effects may include dizziness, blurred vision, dry mouth, difficult urination, drowsiness, and sexual dysfunction.

Antimanic drugs help control the mania related to bipolar disorder. The most common antimanic drug is lithium carbonate, also known as lithium. Side effects may include nausea, vertigo, and increased thirst and urination; long-term use may result in kidney damage.

TECHNOLOGY

Technology is the application of different crafts, skills and aspects of applied science for the creation of objects and tools people need for the maintenance and improvement of subsistence, work, and pleasure. The earliest technologies were practiced or developed through trial and error, and their practitioners did not necessarily understand why particular methods or materials worked better than others. For example, early potters did not know the chemistry behind ceramics and had no way of measuring the heat used in firing; but they produced excellent pots based on craft knowledge. In the past several hundred years, especially, technology has become increasingly allied with science.

But even when a new technology appears to come directly from a scientific theory—the laser, for example—it is built on many of the technologies that preceded it, traceable back to the earliest stone tools and fire if one looks hard enough.

History of Significant Technologies

Stone Tools Ancestors of humans began to improve rocks to make better tools about 2.5 million years ago. These first tools, called Oldowan pebble tools, were medium-size rocks broken to have a sharp edge. About a million years later, other ancestors began to create specialized tool shapes. The hand ax, or biface, had sharpened edges on both sides and a characteristic teardrop form. Starting about 200,000 years ago, Neandertals and early humans developed points for spears, and stone knives and awls. Small points for arrowheads date from about 25,000 B.C. Other small stone tools, called microliths, were introduced about 18,000 B.C. Some microliths were mounted in wood.

Fire The earliest evidence that humans used fire is more than 1.5 million years old, but it is impossible to tell when people began to make fire with sparks or friction. Hearths in Africa and Israel, well-defined places used over and over again for small fires, are at least 750,000 years old and possibly older. By 40,000 B.C. fireplaces with walls were built and stone lamps made. Although wood was the main fuel, people also burned bone where wood was scarce, and early stone lamps burned animal fat. By about A.D. 300 people in China began to burn coal and later natural gas and petroleum. As forests were replaced by fields, coal became the fuel of choice in both Asia and Europe. Air pollution from coal burning has been the main impetus for replacing coal with natural gas and oil as a source of heat since the mid-twentieth century.

Baskets and Cloth It is thought that woven baskets preceded cloth and pottery and led to both (a basket lined with clay to hold a liquid may have been the earliest pot, although this theory is mostly speculation). The earliest woven cloth was made either from the flax plant (linen) or from wool. Cotton and silk fibers were introduced about 3000 B.C. In each case, short fibers needed to be spun together to make yarn. For centuries spinning was accomplished with a simple weight turned by hand as the spinner added bits of fiber to the yarn. A better method, using the spinning wheel, originated in China around A.D. 1000, reaching Europe by at least 1280. In the 18th century, the spinning jenny, a device that could spin several strands of yarn at once and that was powered by water or steam, heralded the Industrial Revolution. This was followed by power looms that wove the yarn into cloth.

In the 19th and 20th centuries, scientists developed plastics that resembled the silk spun by caterpillars and spiders—rayon, nylon, Dacron, and polyester.

Ceramics and Glass Clays heated to high temperatures permanently harden into ceramics. The earliest, dating from about 28,000 B.C., were made in Moravia (Czech Republic) and are small statues of animals. Bricks made from clay were first dried in the sun, but by 23,000 B.C. were also fired to harden them. Coatings used on ceramics, called glazes, made them shiny. About 2000 B.C. in Egypt one glaze material was melted separately and cooled to form glass. Another type of ceramic, formed when water bonds particles of powdered rock, is the basis of plaster (7000 B.C.) and concrete, the latter first made by the Romans.

Bow and Arrow The early history of bows used to propel small spears called arrows is unclear. Some evidence points to use in Spain and North Africa about 25,000 B.C., but the earliest direct evidence (preserved arrow shafts) dates from 8500 B.C. The arrow was only one of several weapons that strike at a distance—boomerangs, slings, and blowpipes are all ancient—but became the weapon of choice in most societies until the advent of firearms. Bows were improved in several steps. The Persians sometime before 500 B.C. replaced wooden bows with bows made from horn and animal tendons. Bows so powerful that unaided human strength could not draw them were developed—crossbows that were drawn with levers, pulleys, or cranks. Large versions of crossbows were an early form a catapult, the first weapon of mass destruction. A very effective crossbow, the arbalest, was developed as a weapon of war in the 14th century, but quickly lost out to firearms, which were introduced to Europe about that time.

Metals Most metals combine easily with nonmetals, so elemental metals are rare in nature. Early humans discovered the few metals that are relatively common "native" minerals—gold, copper, and silver. These are all shiny and flexible and can be used for decoration.

Copper is hard enough to form tools. The earliest evidence for copper use dates from 8000 B.C., but copper was not melted and cast until about 1,500 years later. Common copper ores break down easily with heat, releasing metallic copper. Smelting—making metal from an ore—of copper-had begun by about 4500 B.C. in the Near East. A period of using copper extensively for weapons and tools lasted about 500 years from about 3500 B.C.

This brief Copper Age ended when a better metal, the alloy bronze, was introduced about 3000 B.C., starting the more familiar Bronze Age, which lasted more than 1,500 years. Bronze, usually copper alloyed with tin, is stronger and harder than copper.

The Bronze Age ended after people in Anatolia discovered how to smelt and work iron, which is even harder and stronger than bronze. Early iron had too high a melting point to be cast, so it was hammered into shape ("wrought"). The Chinese, about 300 B.C., discovered that mixing charcoal with iron reduces the melting point enough so that it can be cast. About 400 years later cast iron was rediscovered in Greece, but cast iron did not begin to replace wrought iron in the West until the 12th century.

Steel, the very strong, hard alloy of iron and carbon, was made in small amounts for most of iron's history. Inexpensive processes for making large quantities of steel were discovered only in the 19th century, the best known being the Bessemer process of 1856. Steel gradually replaced iron as the main metal for structural uses.

Aluminum, known since 1825, gradually became the second most common metal in use after an electrochemical extraction discovered in 1888 dramatically lowered production costs.

Boats and Ships Using rafts of logs or reeds tied together or simple dugouts, canoes made by hollowing large tree trunks, humans crossed deep water to Japan as early as 100,000 years ago. There is evidence for regular trade between the mainland and various islands by 11,500 B.C., the end of the last Ice Age. Since wood is seldom preserved, the earliest physical evidence for canoes is from 7500 B.C.; the oldest complete canoe preserved, in Paris, is from 4300 B.C.

Canoes are usually propelled by paddles, but can also use sails. The earliest use of sails has been dated to the second half of the fourth millennium B.C. in Egypt. Sails were gradually improved, from flat sails to "bags of wind," to complex arrangements of several types of sails on different masts on the same ship. Triangular sails could easily be moved to catch the wind from different directions. The wind was too fickle for warships, however, so in antiquity warships in battle used banks of oars (an oar is a paddle that pivots on a fixed point, providing the mechanical advantage of a lever).

By 3000 B.C. the technique of joining planks to form a hull was in use. This was replaced by the modern technique of building an internal framework and then planking it, a process whose evolution began about the seventh century A.D. Early sailing ships were steered with a large paddle, but the Chinese introduced a stern-mounted rudder around the start of the common era. The kind of vessel we would recognize as a "modern" sailing ship with a combination of square sails (set perpendicular to the centerline of the hull) and fore-and-aft (set parallel to the centerline) did not come into being until about 1400. The wooden sailing ship reached its peak for speed and size with the ships-of-the-line of the late seventeenth century and the merchantman in the nineteenth century.

Ships propelled by steam (as early as 1783 in France) and with steel hulls (1843 in England) gradually replaced wooden-hulled sailing ships. In their first decades, these were propelled by paddle wheels, generally mounted on either side of the hull amidships or at the stern. Although people had experimented with screw propulsion for centuries, it was not until the 1830s and 1840s that practical screw propellers were developed. In 1836, working independently, Francis Petit Smith, a British farmer; and Swedish-American inventor John Ericsson (1803–89), secured patents for ships' propellers, and the first ship built with a screw, aptly named *Archimedes*, was launched in 1838. The next major advance in marine propulsion was the development of the steam turbine engine by English designer Charles Parsons (1854–1931) in 1897. But two decades later the diesel engine began to replace steam turbines as well. Large oceangoing ships continued to use steam turbines until after World War II, but in the 1950's nearly all ships shifted to diesel power. Diesel ships are more fuel-efficient, although they emit more particulate pollution.

Canals and Locks Canals for irrigation were built about 6000 B.C. in the Middle East soon after the "agricultural revolution." The need to transport stone from quarries to sites of temples and pyramids produced the first transportation canals in Egypt. Egyptians also built the first canal intended to connect major waterways, a canal from the Nile to the Red Sea, as early as 2000 B.C.

Canals helped unify China. The Magic Canal of 219 B.C., by linking two key rivers in the interior, made much of interior China accessible to the sea. China's Grand Canal, which links Beijing and Hangzhou, is a series of canals the genesis of which can be traced to the fifth century B.C. and which was gradually extended to reach its full length of 1,100 miles in 1293.

Although early transportation canals connected bodies of water at the same level, it soon became apparent that some canals could not be level. At places where canal levels changed, water flowed rapidly downhill. Going uphill, boats had to unload all their goods and passengers for towing through such sections, called spillways or stanches. Boats were often lost in the process and goods stolen by people waiting on the shore for any disaster. In 983, in response to the losses at spillways, a Chinese official invented the first canal lock. Gates across the canal are closed and opened to raise or lower water levels in a small section of the canal, allowing a boat to move from one canal level to another. Similar canal locks were introduced in Europe during the 14th century.

The great age of canal building in Europe began in France in the 17th century and continued in England (18th century) and the United States (19th century). Inexpensive shipping of goods by canal was one crucial element of the Industrial Revolution, although most canals became unnecessary after the introduction of railroads and the internal combustion engine. The notable exceptions connect large bodies of water—the Panama Canal (completed 1914) between two oceans, the Suez Canal (completed 1869) between two seas, and the St. Lawrence Seaway (completed 1959) connecting the Great Lakes to the Atlantic Ocean.

Wheels Rotary motion dates from early drills used in making beads. The first wheels were potter's wheels, used to rotate the clay as it was made into a symmetrical vessel. Soon after the introduction of the potter's wheel (about 4000 B.C.), wheels replaced runners on sledges in Mesopotamia, creating the first carts. Early cart and chariot wheels were made by joining three or four wooden boards and carving the edge into a circle. A strip of wood or metal might be placed around the rim to reduce wear. By 1800 B.C. the weight of the wheel was reduced by connecting spokes to the rim, leaving open space within the wheel. The first wheels were attached to axles that rotated with the wheel. Later wheels rotated about fixed axles, with friction reduced by small rolling devices called bearings, in occasional use since the Roman Empire.

Wheels were also used for grinding grain into flour; the grain was placed under the flat face of a heavy wheel as it rotated against a fixed surface. Another application of the wheel is for transmitting rotary motion from one place to another, especially when two or more wheels are connected at their rims by projections called teeth, an arrangement called a gear. Gears of two different sizes are used to change speed of rotation and rotational force.

Papyrus, Parchment, and Paper Writing began somewhat before 3000 B.C. While people in Mesopotamia pressed cuneiform symbols into clay tables, Egyptians painted hieroglyphs on material made by pounding stems of a reed, called papyrus. Parchment, a treated animal skin invented in Turkey about 250 B.C., gradually replaced papyrus in the Roman Empire. Meanwhile in China, paper, a material similar to papyrus, was prepared from pounded cloth fibers. At first paper was used for cleaning or as a packing material, but by A.D. 100 paper was used for writing Chinese. The secret of making paper from rags slowly spread from China, reaching the Arab world in 751 and Europe in 1150. After printing was introduced in the 15th century, the need for paper rose dramatically. An industry was built around collecting used cloth to feed paper mills. Paper was made one sheet at a time until 1798, when French inventor Nicolas-Louis Robert (1761–1828) developed the first continuous process for making paper, commercialized in 1807 by the Fourdrinier brothers. In 1850 the first attempts to produce paper from ground wood began in Germany and England; although the earliest versions were unsuccessful, improved versions of ground-wood paper are still used for newsprint and most books.

Water Mills and Windmills In 25 B.C. the Roman architect Vitruvius (ca. 90 B.C.–ca. 20 B.C.) described the use of a wheel with paddles pushed by running water as a source of power for grinding grain. A similar wheel for operating a bellows was described in China as invented in A.D. 31. The Vitruvian water wheel had a horizontal axis and used gears to reduce speed and increase power enough to turn a millstone. The use of such mills, sometimes placed on boats—it was easier to anchor a floating mill over a fast-moving stream than to build a stationary one that projected over the water—increased throughout the Roman Empire and the Middle Ages. Toward the end of the Roman Empire, however, a more efficient water mill was invented; the water was retained in a small pond and allowed to flow over the paddles, adding the force of the water's weight to that of its movement. Thousands of such mills were built all over the world. The mills were also adapted to many purposes, including making thread and cloth, sawing wood, and forging iron. They remained the basic source of power for factories until the development of the steam engine in the 19th century.

Windmills were inspired more by sailing ships than by water mills. The first windmills, about A.D. 600 in what is now Iran, had a vertical axis from which several sails extended. By protecting the sails on one side of the axis from the wind, the wind turned the axis. European windmills, which date from the 12th century, were based on angled sails on a horizontal axis. The sails had to face the wind, but all the sails received the wind's force at once. These became the familiar Dutch windmills, used to pump water and increase the amount of dry land for farming. The fantail, which aims the windmill into the wind automatically, was added in 1745.

As electricity became common, water mills and windmills were nearly abandoned. Hydroelectric power is produced in a way similar to water mills, except that the mill pond is replaced with a giant reservoir and water wheels are replaced with turbines. In recent years, there has been a rising movement to generate electricity with windmills. The earliest, built in 1929 in France, used a rotor 66 feet in diameter and generated about 10 kW. Today windmills with aerodynamic designs are grouped together in wind farms. More than 30,000 windmills in farms located in mountain passes, at sea, or wherever winds are common generate about a million kW each year.

Clocks In ancient Egypt and Mesopotamia sundials were used to measure the time of day by the position of a shadow, while water clocks measured the passage of time by the level of water flowing from a vessel. About A.D. 725 Chinese inventors improved the accuracy of the water clock with a device called an escapement, a gear mechanism that permits a small amount of water to flow and then briefly stops the flow (the sound of the escapement stopping and starting is the familiar tick of a clock). Shortly before 1280 an unknown European inventor recognized that an escapement could be used to slow a falling weight and make it fall at a uniform average speed. Clocks using this method are still in use. The first large town clocks, built in the 14th century, were all powered by falling weights. Hours were sounded by striking bells. Such clocks kept only approximate time, however. Dials with hour hands were added to town clocks, but the first clocks accurate enough to use a minute hand were not built until the 17th century.

Several mechanisms were added to escapements to improve accuracy, but not until the pendulum was introduced were good timekeepers developed. Leonardo da Vinci, Galileo, and others recognized that the regular swing of a pendulum could be used to regulate a clock, but the first to make accurate clocks—to within ten to fifteen seconds per day—according to this idea were Dutch scientist Christiaan Huygens (1629–95) and the Dutch clockmaker Salomon Coster, starting in 1656. An alternative to the falling weight, the watch spring, was devised by English scientist Robert Hooke (1635–1703) in 1658. This type of clock achieved great accuracy with the marine chronometer of English clockmaker John Harrison (1693–1776) in 1759.

In 1927 the quartz crystal was introduced as an electronic form of pendulum. Clocks driven by electric motors instead of falling weights or springs and modulated by quartz crystals are by far the most common today. While these are sufficiently accurate for most purposes, the atomic clock (1949), which uses the natural vibration period of an atom to regulate time (1949), is the basis of modern timekeeping. By 1993 the best atomic clocks were accurate to within one second in three million years.

Gunpowder and Guns The first mention of gunpowder—an explosive mixture of saltpeter, charcoal, and sulfur—is in a Chinese book published about A.D. 850. For about 300 years, the primary use of gunpowder involved devices such as firecrackers used to create loud noises, but by 1150 gunpowder explosions were also used to power the first rockets. In 1221 gunpowder bombs laced with destructive shrapnel were used in war. After this application, the use of bombs and rockets spread throughout Asia and Europe, where the first forms of cannon were built early in the 14th century.

Small arms are first mentioned in 1381. The charge of gunpowder in early small arms (muskets) and cannon was ignited with a match, but about 1500 muskets incorporating a wheel-lock that strikes a spark from flint were invented. Improvements gradually led to the flintlock shortly before 1700. In 1807 Scottish clergyman Alexander Forsyth (1769-1843) developed percussion gunpowder, which explodes when struck. A small amount of this material contained in a thin metal cup is called a percussion cap. Since about 1840 nearly all firearms use percussion caps. Today the cap is part of a cartridge that also contains the gunpowder and the bullet.

Printing About A.D. 600 the Chinese began using ink to transfer images carved in a wood block to paper or other materials. At first text was handled by carving the entire page in a mirror image onto a block. Whole books were printed by this method in the ninth century. By 1050, however, Chinese printers had begun to compose pages from individual carved characters for words, the first form of movable type. Movable type became even more useful when applied to European languages, since only the limited forms of the alphabet—twenty-six letters in the case of modern English—needed to be cast. About 1440 Johannes Gutenberg (1397–1468) created the first European books printed with cast metal movable type. Gutenberg's method, with improvements, was the main form of printing until the nineteenth century. The development of the rotary press in 1812 quadrupled the speed of printing, a rate that was quickly improved upon. In 1884, German printer Ottmar Mergenthaler (1854–99) invented the Linotype, which cast a single line of type (hence the name) at a time. Twenty years later another printing innovation made a fundamental change; in offset printing, the image is first transferred to a rubber roller and then to the page. The original type is usually pressed into a plate that might have 16 to 48 pages on it. Other 20th-century techniques changed the way type is cast and introduced photographic methods for setting type and for making the plates.

The advent of the computer made new forms of printing possible and also produced a need for versatile printers that could be used to print pages from a computer display. In 1971 printers were introduced for which a computer controlled separate elements in an array, called a dot matrix. The computer and printer select a particular set of the elements from the matrix, forming each individual letter. Four years later IBM introduced the first printer to use a laser to create images by a process similar to xerographic copying. The following year IBM developed a different computer-controlled printer, the ink jet, which uses either heat-produced bubbles or a crystal to fling tiny drops of ink onto the page in precise patterns.

Rockets and Jet Engines The Chinese observed that explosions of gunpowder in a container could propel the container some distance. By A.D. 1150 they had controlled the explosion enough to propel a container with a sustained burning. These first rockets were used for fireworks but soon also employed in warfare. By 1380 the use of military rockets had reached Italy, but rocket technology fell behind the development of cannon. Rockets maintained a modest role in warfare until the end of World War II, when large, liquid-fueled V-2 rockets were used by Germany against England.

By then, the basic science behind rocket propulsion was understood. Newton's third law of motion established that expelling material in one direction exerts an equal force in the opposite direction. This self-contained process does not require air or water to act against, as a propeller does; rockets work even in the vacuum of space.

World War II also brought new propulsion systems to aircraft. In Germany and England aircraft designers replaced the propeller with jet engines that expelled jets of hot gases to obtain thrust. The difference between a jet engine and a rocket is that the jet heats atmospheric air to create the fast-moving gases that propel it, while a rocket carries all its own fuel and does not need air to operate. Jet engines enabled greater speeds than could be obtained from propellers. Rocket planes were attempted by the Germans toward the end of the war, but were unsuccessful. Since then, however, experimental rocket-propelled aircraft have set all atmospheric records for speed and height. Starting in 1957, rockets were successfully used to propel artificial satellites and space probes, including spacecraft carrying people.

Calculators The first calculators were based on moving counters (the counting board) or moving beads on a string (the abacus) to add or subtract. Counting boards were used in Europe throughout antiquity and the abacus in Asia from at least A.D. 300. Although it is possible to multiply or divide with these tools, it is not very efficient. In the 17th century, English mathematicians developed the first effective mechanical methods for multiplying and dividing. John Napier (1550–1617) was the force behind a simple device called Napier's bones, which was based on a medieval algorithm for multiplication of whole numbers. Napier also invented logarithms, which became the basis of the slide rule (1621). A slide rule uses two logarithmic scales which can be aligned to give approximate results of any multiplication, division, or power. At essentially the same time as the slide rule, the German inventor Wilhelm Schickard (1592–1635) built what is generally recognized as the first calculating machine, a device based on Napier's bones—but only one of the Shickard machines was ever built.

Blaise Pascal (1623–62) invented the adding machine. Pascal's device used gears to accomplish mechanically the kinds of calculation done by hand with an abacus. He made and sold about 50 of the machines, starting in 1642. In 1694 Gottfried Leibniz (1646–1716) developed a calculator that could perform all four arithmetic operations and even extract square roots. Like Pascal's adding machine, it was based on gears, but it contained an additional gear for multiplication and division. Leibniz made only two working models, but his device became the basis for one of the first commercially successful desk calculators in 1820. The next improvement in design replaced the additional multiplication gear with built-in times tables (1889), followed by calculators using electric motors to turn the gears (1902, introduced commercially in the United States in 1922).

After the transistor was invented (1947), it became possible to dispense with gears completely. Logic gates in transistors translate decimal numerals into binary and back, and electric charges moving through the transistors replace the moving gears. The modern handheld calculator (1971 to the present) combines transistorized calculations with electronic displays.

Steam Engines The power of steam to move objects was recognized in antiquity. Heron of Alexandria (ca. A.D. 10—ca. 75) built a toy that rotated as steam issued from nozzles, the prototype of the steam turbine. The first serious efforts to take advantage of the great expansion in volume as water is vaporized took place at the end of the 17th century. French-English engineer Denis Papin (1647–1712) and English inventor Thomas Savery (1650–1715) each invented pumps powered by the expansion of steam. In 1710 English entrepreneur Thomas Newcomen (1663–1729) combined Papin's concept of steam lifting a piston with Savery's pump to create the first practical steam engine, which he sold for pumping water out of mines.

Scottish engineer James Watt (1736–1819) became interested in the Newcomen engine and produced a much improved version (1776). The original Watt engine, like the Newcomen engine, moved a cylinder back and forth—reciprocating motion—but Watt developed ways to convert the output to rotary motion as well as methods for improving power and control. Watt's steam engines not only replaced water for powering mills, but also were used to power boats and vehicles, and by 1882 were being used to generate electric power.

In addition to the reciprocating steam engine, the steam turbine, a sophisticated version of Heron's toy, began to be used for powering boats and generating electricity (1884). Steam turbines replaced most reciprocating steam engines in the first half of the 20th century, but later in the century the steam turbine was often replaced by diesel engines.

Flight Although Leonardo da Vinci and others designed various forms of flying machines with wings that flapped or rotating propellers, the first actual flight by humans came in balloons. Both hot air and hydrogen balloons were introduced in 1783, the former by the Montgolfier brothers (Joseph-Michel, 1740–1810; and Jacques-Étienne, 1745–99) and the latter by French scientist Jacques Charles (1746–1823). Even after balloons that can be steered, called dirigibles, were developed in 1852, balloons failed to become a major form of transportation, although they have contributed to scientific advances and have also had occasional use in warfare.

A more promising start for human flight occurred in 1853 when a glider built by the English inventor Sir George Cayley (1773–1857) carried a full-grown human 900 feet. By the end of the 19th century, a number of inventors had recognized that a combination of a glider, a lightweight engine, and a propeller similar to that found on ships could be used for sustained flight. But the first inventions along this line failed because of poor control mechanisms.

The Wright brothers (Wilbur, 1867–1912; and Orville, 1871–1948) became the first to solve the control problem. After successful experiments with gliders, they achieved powered flight in 1903. Although their original method of control by warping the wings of the aircraft was soon replaced by a system of small flaps, their success marks the beginning of heavier-than-air flight. Before World War I started in 1914, the first shipment of air cargo and the first passenger airline had started. World War I produced many pilots as reconnaissance and fighter planes entered battles. After the war, these pilots and others carried mail, demonstrated aircraft, and set new records for long-distance flight. Airplanes became larger and more reliable. As World War II started (1939), the Pan American Clipper provided regular passenger service from California to Hawaii. Air power was much more important during World War II and again the end of the war left many pilots available for commercial flight.

Another approach to flight had roots extending back to Leonardo's designs and some of Sir George Cayley's experiments—the helicopter. In the 1930's Spanish inventor Juan de La Cierva (1895–1936) established with his autogiro that a large propeller, called a rotor, can provide enough lift for a heavier-than-air craft. In 1936 German engineer Heinrich Focke developed the first successful craft to use a rotor both for lift and propulsion. His helicopter could rise nearly vertically and fly either forward or backward. But the helicopter did not become practical until the designs of Russian-American Igor Sikorsky (1889–1972) at the close of World War II.

Electric Power Electricity was known in antiquity and became an important subject for scientific investigation as early as 1600 with English scientist William Gilbert's (1544–1603) studies of magnetism and electrical attraction. The electric charge then known resulted from rubbing one substance (such as amber—in Greek, "electron") with another (such as wool). Despite extensive experiments with electricity in the 18th century, no successful applications were developed. At the end of the century, however, Italian scientists Luigi Galvani (1738–98) and Alessandro Volta (1745–1827) discovered that certain chemical reactions produce an electric charge. Volta recognized that this effect can be employed to make a continuous transfer of charge, the first known electric current. Shortly after Volta announced his first chemical battery in 1800, English chemist Humphry Davy (1778–1829) used electric current to heat metal so that it glowed and to produce visible arcs between two conductors. By 1807 Davy had shown that electric current is powerful enough to separate compounds into their components, finding half a dozen new elements by electrolysis.

A connection between electricity and magnetism had long been suspected, but was not established until 1820 when Danish scientist Hans Christian Oersted (1777–1851) reported that a magnetic compass needle responds to an electric current. Other scientists immediately began to extend Oersted's discovery, notably French physicist André-Marie Ampère (1775–1836) and English chemist Michael Faraday (1791–1867). Faraday and American physicist Joseph Henry (1797–1878) independently discovered that a moving magnetic field generates an electric current (first published by Faraday in 1831). Unlike the electric battery, which ceases operation after several hours, the generator can produce a continuous current so long as the magnet keeps moving.

The first practical application of electric current was telegraphy in 1837. By 1873 the first electric motor was demonstrated—a generator reversed so that current produced motion instead of motion producing current. In 1879 both Thomas Edison (1847–1931) and English inventor Joseph Swan (1828–1914) developed practical lights powered by electric current. Edison quickly began to build electric generating stations and power grids to capitalize on his invention. Soon electric power was available to thousands of homes.

Edison's power plants developed a form of electric current called direct current (DC) in which electrons flow through a conductor in a single direction. Another form of electric current, alternating current (AC), is produced as electrons swish back and forth in the conductor. Beginning in 1884, Croatian-American engineer Nikola Tesla (1856–1943) developed motors and other devices using AC that are now the basis of the modern electrical grid.

Photography See "Photography" in *Arts*.

Telegraph and Telephone The possibility of transmitting messages with electric current was recognized soon after William Sturgeon (1783–1850) invented the electromagnet in 1825. Three methods using this process, which came to be called telegraphy, were introduced in 1837—in the United States, Germany, and England. After a dramatic demonstration of the American system in 1844 by inventor Samuel F. B. Morse (1791–1872), the Morse version came to dominate rapid communication in the remainder of the 19th century. Morse's method relied on a simple binary code using short pulses (dots) and longer ones (dashes) known as Morse code.

Alexander Graham Bell (1847–1922) and other inventors attempted to use a varying electric current instead of simple pulses to transmit voice. Bell's telephone, patented in 1876, used a metal membrane that vibrated in response to changes in electromagnetic force. Within two years a commercial telephone system was in operation in New Haven, Connecticut, the beginning of a worldwide network. The microphone, invented by Emile Berliner (1851–1929), proved a more effective way to translate sound waves into electric currents, and was the first in many improvements to the telephone.

Radio In 1888 Heinrich Hertz (1857–94) showed that invisible electromagnetic waves could be produced and detected at a distance. By 1894 several researchers had demonstrated that Hertz's wave could be detected over distances ranging from 30 to 180 feet. One of these researchers, Italian inventor Guglielmo Marconi (1874–1937) extended the distance and used the waves, which he named radio waves, to transmit Morse code. He demonstrated wireless telegraphy across the Atlantic in 1901. Wireless soon became an important way to transmit messages to and between ships. Inventors also recognized that the same principles behind voice transmission through the telephone could be used with radio waves. The Canadian-American physicist Reginald Fessenden (1866–1932) was the first to succeed in transmitting voice (1903), although signals were quite weak. A key improvement was the invention of the triode vacuum tube (or valve; 1907) by American inventor Lee De Forest (1873–1961) which could amplify weak signals. By 1920, the first radio station in the United States was broadcasting both voice and music. The initial development of radio was based on Fessenden's method of amplitude modulation (AM), which used changes in the intensity of waves to transmit signals. The American physicist Edwin Howard Armstrong (1890–1954), who had contributed many of the technical improvements to AM radio, developed a method that eliminated interference by transmitting signals by varying frequency (frequency modulation, or FM; patented 1933). FM radio was limited in distance by the curvature of Earth, while AM signals reflect from the ionosphere to travel much farther.

Motion Pictures See "Film" in *Arts.*

Television Transmission of images over wires preceded broadcast television. As early as 1884 the German inventor Paul Nipkow (1860–1940) created a method based on a rotating disk that broke images into varying electrical pulses that could be reconstructed using a second disk. Several inventors used versions of the Nipkow disk for early television. The British engineer John Logie Baird (1888–1946) was most successful, transmitting still images in 1925, moving images in 1926, and images across the Atlantic in 1928. The British Broadcasting System (BBC) used Baird's method for the first wireless television. But the future of television was not with the electromechanical Nipkow disk. In 1927 American inventor Philo T. Farnsworth (1906–71) created the first all-electronic television. By 1936 the BBC was broadcasting an all-electronic version. Today television uses electronic cameras of various types to create images, which are broadcast along with sound by FM signals (or transmitted over coaxial cables or fiber cables). The images are reconstructed by various electronic means, ranging from a cathode-ray tube that produces images by directing electrons toward a phosphorescent screen to displays of all modern types.

Railroads The idea of rolling carts along fixed grooves or rails for more efficient ground transportation is of great antiquity. By the 16th century, wooden wagonways were used in mines to carry out ore or coal; donkeys or oxen could pull several linked carts because of the smooth ride on the rails. By the start of the 19th century, animal-drawn trains rode iron-covered rails to bring heavy goods to canals, where they could be loaded onto boats.

Early steam engines were too heavy to use for travel on poor 19th-century roads, but rail lines could handle the heavy locomotives, the first vehicles to power travel by rotating the wheels. Several inventors in England designed and built early locomotives, starting with Richard Trevithick (1771–1833) in 1804. By 1825 the first railroad with a regular schedule for passengers and freight was in service in England. The first transcontinental line in the United States was completed in 1869.

Although a few steam-powered locomotives are still in operation, most are now powered by electric (1879) or diesel (1912) engines. Starting in the 1970's, engineers in Japan and Germany began experimenting with trains using magnetic levitation (maglev) technology. Maglev trains, which float on a magnetic field above a guideway in which magnets are turned off and on to pull it forward, are capable of reaching speeds of 500 km/hr (300 mph).

Rubber Native Americans discovered that the sap of a tropical tree (latex) hardens into a substance that bounces, which they used to make balls for games. Hardened latex became known to Europeans after the second voyage of Columbus, but Europeans did not pay much attention to it. After French explorer Charles de la Condamine (1701–74) rediscovered it in 1730, however, it came to be used in making flexible hoses. The substance acquired the name rubber after British chemist Joseph Priestley (1733–1804) noticed in 1770 that it could be used as an eraser to rub out pencil marks. Other uses of rubber were slow to develop because natural rubber is unstable in both heat and cold. In 1823 the Scottish inventor Charles Macintosh (1766–1843) found a way to use rubber to waterproof cloth, resulting in the raingear called a mackintosh.

In 1839 the American inventor Charles Goodyear (1800–60) discovered a way to make a tough form of rubber that resisted environmental changes. He named the process vulcanization. Rubber bands of vulcanized rubber were introduced as early as 1845. Air-filled tires using vulcanized rubber were developed by Scottish veterinarian John Dunlop in 1887 for use on his son's tricycle, but soon Dunlop was manufacturing the tires for bicycles and carriages. The very first automobiles used rubber tires.

In 1931 the Du Pont laboratories began marketing a synthetic rubber called neoprene. As World War II restricted access to tropical sources of natural rubber, other artificial forms of rubber were created. Since 1960 more synthetic than natural rubber has been used in the world market.

Skyscrapers The first buildings had only one floor, but by Roman times apartment houses five stories tall were being built (ca. 100 B.C.). The first office building recognized as a skyscraper was William Le Baron Jenney's (1832–1907) Leiter Building (Chicago, eight stories) of 1879. The Leiter Building's iron frame, not its height, gives it this distinction. Tall buildings without an iron or steel skeleton had to have progressively thicker walls and fewer and smaller windows for lower floors. Another Chicago building built a decade later was twice as tall as the Leiter Building: lacking an internal frame, it had walls six feet thick and narrow slits for windows on the first floor.

By the end of the 19th century, the tallest office building had reached 30 stories, or 435 feet. Taller buildings awaited improvement in elevators. Early elevators were effective to about 20 floors, but the modern cable elevator, introduced in 1900, had no obvious limits. Famous skyscrapers of New York, such as the Chrysler Building and the Empire State Building, were built in the early 1930's. Even taller buildings such as the twin towers of the World Trade Center (New York, 1,368 feet) and the Sears Tower (Chicago, 1,450 feet) were built in 1972 and 1973. As of 2004 the tallest skyscraper, at 1,667 feet, is the Taipei Financial Center in Taiwan (built 2003).

Sound Recording In 1877 Thomas Alva Edison recorded and played back his voice with a device that used a needle attached to a diaphragm to make a groove in waxed paper. Later that year he was able to record several minutes of speech by using a cylinder on which a much longer continuous groove could be made by the same method. In recording, the depth of the groove reflected the movements of the diaphragm that were caused by spoken words. During playback, the same needle transmitted the pattern of groove depths back to the diaphragm, which reproduced the original words. Edison called his device a phonograph and intended it to record dictation, but soon recorded music became its principal application.

Various alternatives to Edison's phonograph were invented in the 1880s, including the Dictaphone (1885, words recorded in a belt), Alexander Graham Bell's gramophone (1886, shellac cylinders with grooves that veered back and forth), and Emile Berliner's gramophone (1888, shellac discs using Bell's groove system). Berliner's discs, which could be reproduced by stamping, soon dominated the new industry. Sound quality was greatly improved after 1924 when electric microphones and amplification were introduced.

An alternative technology, recording sound as changes in magnetism, was patented in 1898 by Danish inventor Valdemar Poulsen (1869–1942). Poulsen's device used a steel wire, but in the early 1930's German engineers improved sound quality by using a coated tape instead of a wire.

Recording sound as changes in grooves or magnetism is an analog process, but the first digital system, the compact disc (CD), was introduced in 1982. A laser is used to detect tiny pits in a rapidly rotating disk, which are then transformed into analog sound for loudspeakers by an electronic system. Although CDs continue to be the main commercial medium for sound recording, much home recording today is done by copying digital files from a computer onto a magnetic disk, for example with MP3 (short for Motion Picture Experts Group, Layer 3, or MPEG-3), which was introduced in 2000.

Internal Combustion Engine In a steam engine, water is boiled outside the engine itself and the steam is introduced into the engine's cylinders to propel a piston up and down. The engine used on most automobiles, small nonelectric machinery, and propeller-driven airplanes is called an internal combustion engine because an explosion of fuel inside the cylinder moves the piston. The first such engine, invented by Belgian engineer Jean-Joseph Lenoir (1822–1900), used an electric spark to explode coal gas. Because the piston movement consists of a compression stroke (which also draws fuel and air from the tank) followed by a combustion stroke (ignition from the spark plug), the Lenoir engine is the first example of a two-stroke engine.

The German inventor Nikolaus Otto (1832–91) first improved the Lenoir engine and then in 1876 developed the more complex four-stroke engine, which adds a separate intake and exhaust step to the two strokes of the Lenoir engine. Because the four-stroke engine is more fuel-efficient and easier to lubricate, improved versions of the Otto engine are used in most automobiles and larger machinery. Early Otto engines ran on coal gas, but in 1893 German inventor Wilhelm Maybach (1846–1929) developed a carburetor that mixed gasoline with air, leading to internal combustion engines that burn gasoline. Many modern engines use fuel injection just outside the cylinder instead of a carburetor.

Not all internal combustion engines run on gasoline. In 1892 the French-German engineer Rudolf Diesel (1858–1913) patented an engine in which the compression of air creates a temperature high enough to ignite less volatile oils than gasoline; some diesel engines, for example, run on cooking oil. No spark plug is needed, but air must be much more compressed than in a gasoline engine. Diesel engines can be either four-stroke (used in some automobiles and trucks) or two-stroke (used in trains and large ships). Diesel engines get more energy from their lower-cost fuel, and produce less carbon dioxide than gasoline engines, but their particulate emissions are greater than those from gasoline engines.

Refrigeration and Air Conditioning The first machine to cool air was the refrigerator, invented by French engineer Ferdinand Carré (1824–1900). It was based on two physical principles: as a gases expands, its temperature falls; and heat travels from warmer to cooler material. Carré used the expansion of ammonia gas to lower the temperature inside an insulated box. He pumped the cool ammonia back to a higher pressure outside the box, raising its temperature. The effect was to pump heat from inside the box to outside.

Reducing air temperature lowers the amount of water vapor that air can hold. In 1902 American engineer Willis H. Carrier (1876–1950) used this effect to reduce humidity in a printing plant so that ink would dry faster. Instead of cooling the interior of an insulated box, he forced air through the refrigerated chamber, lowering both humidity and temperature. Soon he was hired by other manufacturers to condition the air in their plants. In 1921 Carrier invented an air conditioner that used a better pump to circulate the gas through the pipes; on the basis of this invention, he formed a company to manufacturer air conditioners. In 1924 a department store in Detroit, Michigan, became the first air-conditioned public building. Motion picture theaters soon became the biggest users of air conditioning equipment. The first home units were built as early as 1928, but home air conditioning did not become common until after World War II.

Plastics Synthetic materials that resemble such natural materials as amber, ivory, and rubber are called plastics, from the Greek word meaning "to mould." These materials are composed of small molecular units, called monomers, linked together to form polymers. Plastics are polymers that under heat or pressure can be molded or otherwise shaped easily, producing fibers or thin films as well as solid objects. The first plastics were Celluloid (1871) and rayon (1924). Celluloid is easily shaped, but flimsy, easily melted, and flammable. It was invented by American chemist John Hyatt (1837-1920) in 1869 as a replacement for ivory in billiard balls, but soon thin films of Celluloid became the basis for photographic film.

In 1906 the Belgian-American chemist Leo Baekeland (1863–1944) discovered a synthetic material that he first used as a hard varnish. When molded and heated, however, it turned into a plastic that did not melt. He named the new material Bakelite, and by 1917 it began to replace natural materials in many applications. The plastics polystyrene and polyvinyl chloride were invented in 1930, polyethylene in 1933, nylon in 1935, and polyurethane in 1944. Some new plastics, such as Kevlar, invented by American chemist Stephanie Kwolek (b. 1923) in 1964, are tougher than any natural materials previously used in such applications as bulletproof vests or lightweight canoes.

Solar Power Nearly all energy used on Earth comes ultimately from the sun. Photosynthesis in plants provides all food and fossil fuels, winds blow from unequal solar heating, and water flows in part because solar evaporation lifts water molecules into the air. "Solar power" refers to ways to tap sunlight directly.

In 1883 a French experiment demonstrated that sunlight captured with a parabolic mirror could heat water enough to power a small steam engine. Solar water heaters were first used in the United States in the 1890s. In 1948 a house in Dover, Mass., was heated by collecting solar heat in flat plates containing water, which was then pumped into the house to warm it, but the house was not sufficiently warmed on cloudy days and the method was judged a failure. The method, however, has since been refined and used on many houses, most effectively in mild climates.

Direct conversion of sunlight into electricity started in 1954. The devices that accomplish this feat are called photovoltaic (or solar) cells and the first ones used silicon technology, similar to transistors. Other materials have since been used, improving efficiency in some instances to 37 percent (with gallium compounds) in 1989. Most uses of this form of solar power were isolated installations such as lighthouses or artificial satellites, or small appliances such as watches and calculators, although several experimental automobiles have been powered this way. More recently homes have used solar panels for power. These are usually connected to the local power grid; they sell any excess power to the grid and buy power when the sun is not shining. Larger installations based on this concept have also been connected to the power grid, starting in 1994 in Spain.

Radar As early as 1900, Nikola Tesla (1856–1943) suggested using radio waves to detect objects, which is the basic principle of radar. At the time, however, there was no way to produce electromagnetic waves between the short length of infrared waves and very long radio waves. Radio waves were used to detect objects as early as 1904, but the waves were too long to locate objects precisely. By 1935, however, British physicist Robert Watson-Watt (1892–1973) and coworkers were observing airplanes from as far as 15 miles away using short-wave radio.

In 1920, American physicist Albert W. Hull (1880–1966) had developed the first vacuum tube to produce more energetic than short waves. Watson-Watt and others secretly developed improved versions of microwaves during the late 1930's and early 1940's, which were used to great effect during World War II. Radar detects aircraft, ships, and other objects by bouncing microwaves from the surface, collecting the echoes, and using the time between the initial signal and the echo to determine distance.

After World War II radar was used to measure the motion of planets. Weather prediction relies on radar to observe storms. Radar from satellites and space probes has also been used to map features on earth and other planets.

Nuclear Power In 1938 the German physicist Otto Hahn (1879–1968) and Austrian physicist Lise Meitner (1878–1968) discovered that the large uranium atom could break into pieces (fission) when struck with a neutron, releasing additional neutrons and other forms of energy in the process. In a sufficiently large mass of uranium, the secondary neutrons will also strike atoms to start a chain reaction. Within the next two years, physicists around the world determined which isotope of uranium works best for fission and how to use more stable elements, such as beryllium and carbon, to control the chain reaction. World War II had started and with it a largely American effort—although enlisting scientists from all over the world—to find a way to use the energy from nuclear fission in war. The first controlled chain reaction, in a device called a nuclear reactor, was built by Enrico Fermi (1901–54) in 1942.

The wartime emphasis was on developing the fast release of a vast amount of energy—the first atomic (nuclear fission) bombs in 1945. After the war, however, physicists looked to controlled nuclear fission in a reactor as a source of power—energy from the chain reaction in the form of heat could be used to power steam turbines that would generate electricity. In the early 1950's, Great Britain, the United States, and the Soviet Union began work on such power plants, with the first small plant becoming operational in the Soviet Union in 1954. The United States had two small plants delivering electricity in 1955. England opened the first full-scale nuclear power plant, called Calder Hall, in 1956. Many predicted that nuclear power would be cheap and plentiful, although early production was more expensive than other forms of electric power. Although nuclear power did not become less expensive than other forms of power, partly because of the difficulty and enormous costs of disposing of radioactive waste from reactors, it soon became one of the most common types of new electric power plants.

Microwave Ovens During World War II the special vacuum tubes used to produce microwaves were greatly improved for radar. The American engineer Percy L. Spencer (1894–1970) observed that an operating microwave tube melted the candy bar in his pocket. After experimenting by using microwaves to pop corn, he patented the idea of cooking with microwaves in 1945. Two years later a microwave oven the size of a home refrigerator went on sale, intended for restaurants to cook or reheat food. The first microwave oven designed for home use was marketed in 1955, but it was not until 1967 that an inexpensive home unit was available. After that, the microwave oven became a fixture in most kitchens.

Microwaves used in ovens are radio waves in the 2.5 gigahertz range, which are absorbed by molecules of water, fat, or sugar, but not by molecules of glass, plastic, or ceramics. The energy from the microwaves causes molecules that absorb it to vibrate faster, raising the temperature of the food. For most foods, the microwaves will penetrate the entire food item, so the temperature rise is nearly uniform throughout.

Robotics The concept of a mechanical person or animal goes back to antiquity. Greek and Chinese inventors made clever moving statues that could duplicate the actions of a person or animal, such as playing a musical instrument or flapping wings and crowing. Such devices are called automatons. Most worked by some form of clockwork, wound with a spring or powered by flowing water.

Automatons appear lifelike, but whenever they are activated, they repeat the same motions as the time before; they do not react to their environment. A device that accomplishes tasks similar to those a human can perform and that reacts to at least some changes in the environment is called a robot. Robots may or may not be made to resemble humans, although many have parts that are similar to human arms, hands, or eyes. The first robot to be manufactured and sold (in 1962, but based on a 1954 design) was an arm that performed repetitive tasks in automobile factories. The earliest models could be programmed to perform different tasks, but lacked sensors to recognize sizes or shapes of objects. Although called robots, their capabilities were about the same as a player piano, which plays different songs when different music rolls are inserted. Soon, however, robot arms that could distinguish the objects by weight or temperature or shape became available.

Another group of useful robots began with the space program. The best examples are the various Mars rovers, such as Sojourner, Spirit, and Opportunity, which move through the landscape, detecting obstacles and compensating for them, and also sample and analyze rocks and soil. Because of the time lag for signals to reach Mars from Earth and return, the rovers had to be given robot skills.

In some companies today, robots deliver mail, following a programmed path, but also sensing obstacles and avoiding them. There are also robot vacuum cleaners, pool cleaners, and lawn mowers available. None of the working robots so far resemble humans or animals very much, but toys are another matter. Toy manufacturers have developed humanoid robots that can sense some of their environment and react, as well as robotic pets whose behavior seems similar to that of real animals.

Lasers A laser is a device that produces an intense and focused beam of light waves that are all aligned with each other. Although Albert Einstein (1879–1955) described the science behind the laser as early as 1917, it was not until 1960 that American physicist Theodore Maiman (b. 1927) built the first working laser. In some ways the action of a laser is similar to the chain reaction that powers a nuclear reactor—one photon of light absorbed in an energized molecule releases two or more that are exactly the same as the first. By reflecting such photons back and forth, but allowing some to escape in one direction, the energy of the laser emerges as a beam of identical photons.

Maiman's laser used the molecules of a ruby to create its beam. Improvements in design started quickly and by 1965 a laser was built that could be adjusted to different wavelengths of light. In 1970 the first carbon-dioxide lasers could cut through metals or be used for welding. Applications proliferated. As early as 1962 a laser was used in eye surgery, where lasers have become a common tool. Perhaps the most common uses of lasers today are in barcode scanners, CD and DVD players, and fiber-optic communications. Special tools for farmers and carpenters use lasers as aids in leveling fields or measuring distances.

Displays When used in the context of electronic devices, a display is the visual medium for communicating changing information to the device's user. The earliest displays were purely mechanical, such as the small cards with numerals showing the indicated operations of old-fashioned cash registers. Similarly, early calculators often had numbers on the rims of wheels; the wheels turned independently to indicate a numeral with several digits.

Today nearly all displays are completely electronic. In some early meters, a pattern of individual lights was used to display different numbers, but such numbers are hard to read and their display used a lot of power. The earliest computers used patterns of electric lights turned off or on as displays. The cathode-ray tube (CRT), which works by having a beam of electrons paint a picture with fluorescing dyes on a glass screen, was introduced as a display as early as 1911. By the time early computers were being built, the

Human or Computer? Take This Test

By SARA ROBINSON

As chief scientist of the Internet portal Yahoo, Dr. Udi Manber had a profound problem: how to differentiate human intelligence from that of a machine.

His concern was more than academic. Rogue computer programs masquerading as teenagers were infiltrating Yahoo chat rooms, collecting personal information or posting links to Web sites promoting company products. Spam companies were creating havoc by writing programs that swiftly registered for hundreds of free Yahoo e-mail accounts then used them for bulk mailings. "What we needed," said Dr. Manber, "was a simple way of telling a human user from a computer program."

The roots of Dr. Manber's philosophical conundrum lay in a paper written 50 years earlier by the mathematician Dr. Alan Turing, who imagined a game in which a human interrogator was connected electronically to a human and a computer in the next room. The interrogator's task was to pose a series of questions that determined which of the other participants was the human.

Dr. Turing suggested that a machine could be said to think if the human interrogator could not distinguish it from the other human.

The Turing test, as it is now called, spawned a vibrant field of research known as artificial intelligence. But while today's computers are capable of feats Dr. Turing never imagined, yet in many simple tasks, a typical 5-year-old can outperform the most powerful computers.

Indeed, the abilities that require much of what is usually described as intelligence, like medical diagnosis or playing chess, have proved far easier for computers than seemingly simpler abilities: those requiring vision, hearing, language or motor control.

In a September 2000 Dr. Manber discussed his problem with a group of computer science researchers at Carnegie Mellon University. The result was a long-term project that is now beginning to bear fruit. Dr. Manuel Blum, a professor of computer science at Carnegie Mellon who took part in the Yahoo discussions, realized that the failures of artificial intelligence might provide exactly the solution Yahoo needed. Why not devise a new sort of Turing test, he suggested, that would be simple for humans but would baffle sophisticated computer programs.

Dr. Manber liked the idea, so Dr. Blum, with his Ph.D. student Luis von Ahn and others devised a collection of cognitive puzzles based on the challenging problems of artificial intelligence. The puzzles have the property that computers can generate and grade the tests even though they cannot pass them. The researchers decided to call their puzzles Captchas, an acronym for Completely Automated Public Turing Test to Tell Computers and Humans Apart (on the Web at www.captcha.net).

One puzzle, called Gimpy, consists of a display of seven distorted, overlapping words chosen at random from a dictionary of simple words. Solving the puzzle requires identifying three of the seven words and typing them into the box provided. The Carnegie Mellon group also created a simplified version of Gimpy—a single distorted word displayed against a complicated background, which has been used as part of Yahoo's registration process.

As a cryptographer, Dr. Blum was familiar with the constant efforts of cryptographic researchers to advance the field by cracking codes to discover their weaknesses.

He hoped to start a similar dynamic for Captchas, spurring researchers to try to create better Captchas while building computer programs that crack existing ones.

"Captchas are useful for companies like Yahoo, but if they're broken it's even more useful for researchers," Dr. Blum said, and later he got his wish. Dr. Jitendra Malik of Berkeley and Greg Mori, a student, devised a computer program that could crack Gimpy—both the simple version used by Yahoo and the harder one on Captcha's Web site.

Since its inception several years ago, the Captcha effort has been building. Other research teams have joined the Captcha effort, trying to make and break better Captchas and using the ideas behind Captchas for new lines of research. While this Captcha conflict continues, the researchers hope that their techniques for recognizing objects against cluttered backgrounds will have other practical applications like automated recognition of military targets or detection of trademark infringements on the Internet.

CRT was already used in television. The first commercial computers to use CRTs were introduced in 1960, although they displayed only numbers and characters. By 1973 a small computer was available commercially that also displayed pictures on a CRT. Early personal computers could display only two colors—often green and black—with what were termed monochrome CRTs, but the Apple II of 1977 used a color television set to display images.

Meanwhile, all-electronic displays other than the CRT had been invented and were gaining in popularity. The American engineer Nick Holonyak, Jr. (b. 1928) developed a form of transistor that produces light, the light-emitting diode (LED). Unlike the bulky, heavy, fragile, and energy-greedy CRT, the LED is small enough to be used to display results on handheld calculators or in meters of various types—although these must be monochrome (usually reddish orange in early applications). The first handheld calculator to use an LED display was marketed in 1971.

A different electronic technology, based on liquid crystals, which had been known to chemists since 1888, came to the fore. A practical liquid-crystal display (LCD) was patented in 1971 and used as a display on a digital watch. The following year an LCD display was used for one of the first video games. By 1983 the LCD, which is lightweight and of low power consumption, made possible the first laptop computer. Early LCDs were monochrome—usually shades of gray—but by 1979 a method had been developed to make a color LCD, leading to a television set with a tiny color LCD display in 1985. As LCDs improved, they began to be used for computer monitors instead of CRTs and for flat-screen television.

A different concept, the plasma display, was conceived in 1964 at the University of Illinois, but took many years to bring to fruition. It remains a costly alternative, but with what many find the sharpest and brightest effects. The basic concept of a plasma display is the same as for a fluorescent light—a highly ionized gas emits ultraviolet light that then stimulates dyes called phosphors to light up. In the display, hundreds of thousands of tiny fluorescent cells can each be lit in three separate colors—red, green, or blue.

Nanotechnology In 1959 the American physicist Richard Feynman (1918–88) proposed that useful electronic devices could be built one atom at a time and that the smallest devices might consist of as few as seven atoms. Although Feynman did not specify exact methods for making small tools, his speech is considered the founding document of nanotechnology, the art of creating useful objects whose size is less than 100 nanometers—a single atom may be about half a nanometer in size or somewhat less, down to about 0.1 nanometer. The word *nanotechnology* was coined in 1974, but no working devices less than 100 nanometers in size were created until the 1980's.

Chemists have also contributed to nanotechnology. In the 1990's they devised chemicals that when combined would self-assemble their molecules into particular configurations. Silicon has been fabricated into dust particles that can detect chemicals or that emit tiny jolts of electricity when exposed to light, providing a power source for nanomotors. One of the most dramatic ideas in nanotechnology is based on using the DNA molecule as a computer. Experimental DNA computers can in a test tube detect enzymes produced by cancer cells and on their own release a form of chemotherapy only when the proper combination of enzymes is present.

History of Computing

The history of computing contains four distinct generations, along with a rich prehistory of mechanical computing devices. Each generation is characterized by dramatic improvements in the technology used to build computer hardware, the internal organization of computer systems, and the computers' programming languages.

The Mechanical Era: 1623–1940

Computers as we know them had their beginnings in the so-called computing machines of the early 17th century. These machines were like crude calculators, designed to automate complex mathematical calculations, but had no memory or data storage. In fact, these machines did not even have a way to output the results of their calculations, other than dials or indicators.

Babbage's Difference and Analytical Engines Charles Babbage (1792–1871) is often referred to as the "father of computing," due to his development of two separate computing machines—the Difference Engine and the Analytical Engine. The initial prototype of the Difference Engine was produced in 1822, and Babbage started work on the full machine in 1823. The Difference Engine was conceived as a steam-powered, fully automatic machine, capable of printing the results of its computations on paper.

The Difference Engine was never completed; Babbage ceased work on it in 1834 because he had an idea for a better calculating machine. This new machine, to be called the Analytical Engine, was a parallel decimal computer that could operate on words of 50 decimals and was capable of storing 1,000 such numbers. The Analytical Engine included a number of built-in operations, including conditional control that enabled the machine to execute instructions in a specific order. The instructions themselves were entered into the machine on punch cards, thus introducing the input method used in computers through the 1970's.

The Birth of International Business Machines Herman Hollerith (1860–1929) first came to prominence in 1886, when he constructed the first electromechanical adding and sorting machine. This machine, which he dubbed a "tabulator," was put to its first commercial use in 1890 for the U.S. Census Bureau. Hollerith's tabulator could read census data that had been punched into rectangular cardboard cards, later known as punch cards. The use of these punch cards significantly reduced the incidence of data entry errors and increased the speed of data entry; in addition, a stack of punch cards served as a crude form of data storage.

Based on this success, Hollerith formed the Tabulating Machine Company in 1896. In 1911 the Tabulating Machine Company merged with the International Time Recording Company and the Computing Scale Company to form the Computing-Tabulating-Recording Company (C-T-R); in 1924, the name of the company was changed to International Business Machines (I.B.M.). By the end of the 20th century I.B.M. had more than 300,000 employees and revenues exceeding $88 billion.

Early 20th-Century Computers: The Dawn of the Digital Age

In spite of U.S. Patent Director Charles Duell's in famous claim in 1899 that "everything that can be invented has already been invented," new calculating and computing machines continued to be invented after the turn of the century. These new machines were the forerunners of the modern computer, electrifying formerly mechanical devices, adding storage capability (and the ability to manipulate the stored results), and developing the capability of printing the results on paper.

Zuse's Binary Computing Machines In 1936 scientist Konrad Zuse (1910–95), with assistance from Helmut Schreyer (1912–84), began construction of the Z1, the world's first programmable binary computer. The Z1, built in Zuse's bedroom (and overflowing into his parents' living room), was controlled by perforated strips of discarded movie film. This machine (originally dubbed the V1, but retroactively renamed Z1 after World War II) was completed in 1938, and is the ancestor of all modern computers.

Perhaps the most important development of the Z1 is the adoption of the binary system—also called digital computing. Zuse went on to develop the Z2, Z3, and Z4, which further refined the processes originally incorporated into the Z1.

Stibitz's Complex Number Calculator In 1937 George Stibitz (1914–95,) of Bell Labs constructed one of the first binary computers, a 1-bit binary adder built for demonstration purposes only. Stibitz spent the next few years improving the device, which when completed in 1939 was dubbed the Complex Number Calculator (and was later called the Bell Labs Model 1). The Complex Number Calculator used electromagnetic relays, and was the first computing machine to be used over normal telephone lines, setting the stage for the future linking of computers and communications systems.

Desch and Mumma's Electronic Accumulator The next major leap in computing technology involved the use of vacuum tubes as on/off valves. This enabled calculations to be made electronically rather than mechanically, which resulted in a significant increase in calculating speed.

The first use of the vacuum tube in a computing device was in 1938, when Joseph Desch (1907–87) and Robert Mumma (b. 1905) built a machine they called the Electronic Accumulator. This machine primed the world for true first-generation computers, and would be the dominant switching technology for the next 20 years.

First-Generation Computers: 1940–56

The first generation of true computers used vacuum tubes and electronic circuits to replace the mechanical switches and moving parts of mechanical calculators. While these first computers were physically massive and operationally complicated, they delivered on the promise of handling increasingly large and complex calculations and were essential to deciphering secret codes in World War II and developing America's atomic energy program in the years after.

The Turing Machine The first true computer was strictly theoretical. In 1937 the Cambridge mathematician

Alan Turing (1912–54, England), in a paper on the mathematical theory of computation, conceived of the idea for a "universal machine" capable of executing any describable algorithm. This theoretical machine, dubbed the Turing Machine, formed the basis for the concept of "computability," separate from the process of calculation.

Colossus The first fully electronic computer to actually be built was named Colossus. Commissioned to crack the secret code used by German Enigma cipher machines, Colossus was completed in December of 1943 by Thomas Flowers (1905–98) at London's Post Office Research Laboratories. Ten Colossus machines were built over the course of the war, but all were destroyed immediately after completing their work, to keep the design from falling into enemy hands.

Harvard Mark I The Harvard Mark I, more formally known as the Automatic Sequence Controlled Calculator (ASCC), was the world's first fully programmable computer. It was an electromechanical machine that executed commands in a step-by-step fashion; instructions were fed into the machine by means of paper tape, punch cards, or switches.

The Mark I, partially financed by IBM, was developed by Howard Aiken (1900–73) and James W. Bryce (1880–1949) at Harvard University, where it occupied an entire building. The Mark I was completed in 1944, and was kept in operation for more than 15 years. During World War II it was employed by the U.S. Navy to run repetitive calculations for various mathematical tables.

ENIAC The most famous first-generation computer was arguably the Electronic Numerical Integrator and Computer, or ENIAC. ENIAC was developed as a result of a wartime commission by the U.S. Army Ordinance Corps to design an electronic machine that could quickly compute firing and bombing tables. John W. Mauchly (1907–1980) and J. Presper Eckert, Jr. (1919–1995) of Pennsylvania's Moore School of Engineering began work on ENIAC in 1943, and the machine was completed in 1946.

Compared with today's computers, ENIAC was a monster. It was composed of 30 separate units (plus power supply and forced-air cooling); weighed over 30 tons; and contained more than 18,000 vacuum tubes, 1,500 relays, and hundreds of thousands of resistors, capacitors, and inductors.

On completion, ENIAC was put into service for calculations involved in the design of the hydrogen bomb. It served as the nation's main computational workhorse through 1952, and was finally dismantled in 1955.

UNIVAC After the success of ENIAC, Mauchly and Eckert decided to go into business for themselves. In 1948 they began development on the Universal Automatic Computer, or UNIVAC—one of the first large computers developed for business use, not war use. In 1950 Mauchly and Eckert sold their company to Remington Rand Inc.; in 1951 the U.S. Census Bureau accepted delivery of the first UNIVAC computer.

Second-Generation Computers: 1956–63

The second generation of computers was characterized by the shrinking size and increased computing power made possible by the replacement of vacuum tubes and large electronic circuits with smaller transistors and integrated circuits. These second-generation computers were the first that were powerful enough to handle interpreted programming languages, such as FORTRAN and COBOL, and dominated information processing in the late 1950's and early 1960's.

Introducing the Transistor The transistor—short for transfer resistor—was developed at AT&T Bell Laboratories in 1947 by Walter H. Brattain (1902–87), William Shockley (1910–89), and John Bardeen (1908–91), who would be awarded the 1956 Nobel Prize in physics for their work. The transistor's small size, high yield, low heat production, and low price helped to make the next generation of computers run 1,000 times faster than the previous generation.

Transistorized Computers Building on Brattain and others' groundbreaking research, the first completely transistorized computer, TRADIC, was developed by Bell Laboratories in 1953. Another early transistorized computer was the Transistorized Experimental Computer (TX-0), developed at MIT's Lincoln Laboratories in 1956.

Third-Generation Computers: 1964–71

The third generation of computing is based on the development of the integrated circuit. It was this generation of computer that gained widespread acceptance in corporate America, and led to the growth of data processing.

Introducing the Integrated Circuit (IC) Chip The integrated circuit (IC) is a single electronic circuit on a single slice of silicon. The first IC was developed by two teams of scientists, working independently of each other, at Fairchild Semiconductor and Texas Instruments. The Texas Instruments team, led by Jack St. Clair Kilby (b. 1923), developed their IC in December of 1958. The following year the Fairchild team—consisting of Jean Hoerni (1924–97), Kurt Lehovec (b. 1918), and Robert N. Noyce (1927–90)—successfully completed their IC project. The first commercial implementation of this technology hit the market in 1961.

Moore's Law In 1965 Gordon Moore (b. 1929), then a scientist at Fairchild., in an article for the 35th anniversary issue of *Electronics* magazine, wrote what would later be dubbed "Moore's Law," which predicted that integrated circuits would double in complexity every year, while prices would stay the same. Moore's Law proved remarkably accurate in the years to come. (By the end of the 20th century, however, the rate of change had slowed down, and Moore's Law was revised to state that integrated circuits would double in complexity every 18 months while remaining at the same price.)

Computers in the Corporate World Third-generation computers were both powerful and affordable enough to be adopted by large corporations around the world. From the mid-1960's on, formerly manual tasks were automated by large mainframe computers, creating a new profession that became known as data processing. The most popular uses of these third-generation computers included inventory management, payroll management, file management, and report generation.

During this period the computer landscape was dominated by one company: IBM. IBM's dominance of the business market was even more profound outside the U.S.; at one point in the 1960's, 90 percent of the installed computers in the European market were IBM models.

Fourth-Generation Computers: 1972–Present

Fourth-generation computing is characterized by the use of the microprocessor, which is a computer processing unit (CPU) contained in an integrated circuit on a tiny piece of silicon. This generation of computers remains the longest to date, 30 years and counting at the start of the new millennium. During the fourth generation, improvements in computing have come from increases in speed and power, not from entirely new technology.

Introducing the Microprocessor The development of the microprocessor fueled a revolution in computing, and enabled the creation and popularization of the so-called personal computer. Now that the brains of the computer could be contained in a thumbnail-sized chip, computers could be made smaller and lighter than ever before and thus be used for a greater variety of practical applications.

Exactly who invented the microprocessor is open to debate. Independent engineer Gilbert Hyatt (b. 1938) filed for a patent for microprocessor technology in 1970, as did three engineers from Intel, led by Marcian E. Hoff (b. 1937). A year earlier Ray Holt (b. 1945) developed the onboard flight computer for the U.S. Navy's F-14A "Tomcat" fighter jet—a "computer on a chip" that was more powerful than Intel's first microprocessor. This controversy was similar to the one surrounding the invention of the integrated circuit; Hyatt was eventually awarded the patent in 1990.

Intel's Microprocessors Intel Corporation was founded in 1968 by three former employees of Fairchild Semiconductor: Gordon Moore, Robert Noyce, and William Shockley. Intel would soon become one of the world's largest technology companies, and one of the three founding fathers of personal computing technology.

4-Bit Microprocessors Intel released its first microprocessor, the 4001, in October 1970. It was followed a month later by the 4002, and then the 4003, all 4-bit processors. The 4004 chip, released in November 1971, contained the equivalent of 2,300 transistors.

8-Bit Microprocessors Development of new microprocessor technology was fast and furious. Just five months after the release of the 4004 chip, in April 1972, Intel released its first 8-bit processor, the 8008, which contained the equivalent of 3,500 transistors.

Intel's next chip, the 8080, was released in January 1974. The 8080 was an 8-bit processor that was 10 times faster than the 8008, and contained the equivalent of 6,000 transistors. It was this chip that led to the development of the world's first personal computers.

IBM System/370 IBM quickly capitalized on the miniaturization enabled by the development of the microprocessor. In 1971 IBM released the System/370 family of computers, the first mainframe machines to be powered by microprocessor chips.

Personal Computing: The Early Years

Microprocessor technology enabled the construction of

more powerful mainframe computers, and of smaller, lower-priced machines that came to be known as personal computers. The first personal computers were sold in kit form for the hobbyist market, but these smaller, easier-to-use computers soon gained a foothold with both business users and general consumers.

Hobby Computers The earliest personal computers were based on Intel's 8-bit microprocessors, and were designed strictly for hobbyists. The first of these, the Mark 8, was actually a how-to project introduced in the July 1974 issue of *Radio Electronics* magazine, based on a design by Jonathan Titus.

Altair 8800: The World's First Personal Computer In 1975 a New Mexico-based company called MITS (Micro Instrumentation and Telemetry) released what is generally regarded as the world's first true personal computer, the Altair 8800. The Altair was based on Intel's 8080 microprocessor, contained 256 bytes of memory, and sold for $395 in kit form, or $498 assembled. Two thousand Altair 8800s were sold in the first year of release.

CP/M: The First Personal Computer Operating System All personal computers used a special type of program—called an operating system—that controlled the machine's most basic operations. The primary operating system for these first personal computers was called CP/M (Control Program for Microcomputers). It was developed in 1974 by Gary Kildall (1942–94) and John Torode of Digital Research specifically for the 8080 microprocessor.

Tandy Enters the Fray As it became apparent that personal computers had mainstream appeal, many manufacturers and retailers sought to offer their own computer models for the hobbyist and home markets. One of the most successful of these early entrants was Tandy Corporation, which began selling computers through its Radio Shack retail stores in 1977.

Tandy TRS-80 Tandy's first personal computer was dubbed the TRS-80. It included a built-in keyboard, cassette storage, and 4Kb RAM. The TRS-80 was based on the Zilog Z80 chip, and sold for $599 (without a monitor); it could be hooked up to any black-and-white television set.

Tandy Color Computer In 1980 Tandy released its first color computer, named simply the Color Computer, or "coco" for short.

Commodore Sets Sail Commodore Business Machines was a major player in the calculator and office machines market. When the personal computer market took off, it sought to complement its business machine offerings with a line of business- and home-oriented personal computers.

Commodore PET The Commodore PET was released in 1977. It was based on a 1-MHz MOS 6502 processor, had 8 Kb of RAM, and displayed monochrome text on a 9-inch monitor. Programs were loaded into the system on audiocassettes. The PET sold for $795, and was an overnight success.

Commodore VIC-20 The first of Commodore's true home computers was the VIC-20, released in 1981. It combined the computer and the keyboard in a single unit that could be connected to any color television set, contained 5Kb of RAM, and was targeted at a mass market with a price of $300. It was the industry's first million-unit seller, with production peaking at 9,000 units per day.

Commodore 64 The Commodore 64 was released in January 1982. The C-64 was built on the MOS 6502 microprocessor, contained 64Kb RAM, and sold for $595. It sold more than 17 million units over the course of its lifetime.

Other Early Players The promise of the home market inspired many manufacturers to offer their own proprietary low-priced personal computers. The late 1970's and early 1980's saw a plethora of such machines released, although few would be considered long-term financial successes.

Apple Apple Computing was a major player from the very beginning of the personal computer era, with its Apple I (1976) and Apple II (1977) machines targeted at the business, home, and education markets.

Atari Over the course of the 1970's Atari became known for its coin-operated and home videogames. When the personal computer burst onto the scene, Atari decided to build on its success with games and migrate development to the personal computer platform. Atari ended up releasing two personal computer models in 1978. The Atari 400 and the Atari 800 were both powered by the MOS 6502 microprocessor and had more of a video game than a business feel; neither machine was fully accepted by the marketplace.

Osborne Adam Osborne (1939–2003) introduced the world's first portable computer, the Osborne I, in 1981. The Osborne I wasn't all that portable, however; it weighed more than 23 pounds and had a built-in 5-inch monochrome display, 64Kb RAM, and two floppy disk drives. It ran the CP/M operating system and sold for $1,795, and met with moderate success, ultimately losing the marketplace to IBM and IBM-compatible computers.

KayPro Like Osborne's, KayPro's main offering (the KayPro II) was a heavy portable computer. The KayPro II, released in 1982, came with a larger 9-inch monochrome display and ran the CP/M operating system. Also like the Osborne, the KayPro computer ultimately lost the format war to IBM.

Texas Instruments The TI 99/4 was Texas Instruments' initial entry into the burgeoning personal computer market. Released in 1979, it used TI's 16-bit 9940 microprocessor, but at $1,150 was significantly overpriced for the market. In 1980, TI replaced this initial unit by the more affordable TI 99/4A, which featured color graphics and a $525 price tag.

Sinclair In 1979 Sinclair Research introduced the ZX80 personal computer, based on Zilog's Z80 microprocessor. It featured 1Kb of RAM, had a membrane keyboard, and sold for $199. The low price of this model made it quite popular among the hobbyist crowd.

The IBM PC

The most important development in the history of personal computers was the entry of IBM into the marketplace. The initial IBM PC was an unparalleled success, driven by a combination of three factors—Intel's fast and affordable microprocessor chip, IBM's open architecture and marketing power, and Microsoft's operating system.

The Microprocessor: Intel

The heart of the IBM PC was an Intel microprocessor chip. Over the course of the years Intel has provided many different microprocessors, supplying more power and faster speeds for new generations of personal computers.

Intel 8086/8088 Intel's 8086, released in 1978, was the first commercially successful 16-bit processor. When it was found to be too expensive to include in early personal computers, Intel developed (in 1979) an 8-bit version of the chip, dubbed the 8088. It was this chip, the 8088, that was chosen by IBM for use in the first IBM PC.

Intel 80286/80386/80486 The so-called x86 family of microprocessors, based on Intel's earlier 8086 chip, was designed to replace the 8088 in newer IBM-compatible PCs and introduced 16-bit processors to the world of personal computing. The first chip in this family was the 80186, released in 1982, although it saw little use in personal computers; it was better suited for self-contained controller devices. It was Intel's next chip, the 80286, that met with widespread acceptance among PC manufacturers. Also released in 1982, the 80286 contained the equivalent of 134,000 transistors. The 80286 was succeeded by the 80386 in 1985, and the 80486 in 1989.

The Hardware: IBM

IBM, with its history of mainframe computing, legitimized the personal computing industry. IBM wasn't a fly-by-night company, and it didn't sell kits for hobbyists; it sold a ready-to-use, relatively easy-to-use, fully functioning computer through traditional retail stores—and was a name that consumers could trust.

The Original IBM PC IBM released its first personal computer—called, simply enough, the IBM PC—in August 1981. The standard model had 64Kb RAM and a single 160Kb single-sided floppy disk drive, and sold for $1,565 (without the green-on-black monochrome display). It was sold through IBM's established network of retail stores.

IBM initially hoped to sell 240,000 units in a five-year period. It received that many orders in the machine's first month of release. In fact, the IBM PC was so successful that its hardware technology and operating system became the standards for the industry; other operating systems, such as CP/M, soon disappeared from the personal computer landscape.

Compaq and Other Clones Competing computers that were functionally compatible with the IBM PC were called clones. The first of these clone computers was released by Compaq in 1982. The Compaq Portable—actually more of a "luggable"—was the size of a small suitcase and several times the weight. It included a built-in 9-inch monochrome monitor, 128Kb RAM, and a detachable keyboard. It sold for $3,590.

The Operating System: Microsoft

Microsoft Corporation was founded in 1975 by Bill Gates (b. 1955) and Paul Allen (b. 1953). Their first product was a version of the BASIC programming language that they sold to MITS for use in its Altair computers, but the key to their long-lasting success was their contract with IBM to supply an operating system for the original IBM PC.

PC-DOS and MS-DOS The operating system that Microsoft supplied to IBM was called PC-DOS. (A variant of this operating system was sold to clone manufacturers as MS-DOS; PC-DOS and MS-DOS were operationally identical.) Microsoft began work on MS-DOS/PC-DOS in 1980. More accurately, that was when Microsoft acquired an operating system called QDOS (for Quick and Dirty Operating System) from a small company called Seattle Computer Products. QDOS was essentially a 16-bit version of the older CP/M operating system developed for Intel's 8086 microprocessor; Microsoft reworked the code to IBM's specs, and PC-DOS was born.

Versions of PC/MS-DOS powered IBM-compatible personal computers through the early 1990s, when it was replaced by another Microsoft operating system—Windows.

Microsoft Windows Whereas DOS was a text-based operating system, Windows was graphical—and supported the click-and-drag operation of a mouse. The first version of Windows, launched in November 1985, required more power than machines of that era could deliver, and had little impact on the market. A more fully functional version, Windows 2.0, was released in 1987. But it was version 3.0, released in 1990, that introduced true multitasking to the personal computing environment, and eventually led to the demise of PC/MS-DOS.

OS/2 OS/2 (Operating System 2) was designed as a 32-bit graphical replacement for PC-DOS, to be used on IBM's PS/2 computers. Although IBM and Microsoft jointly developed the operating system, a falling-out between the two giants resulted in IBM marketing OS/2 for its higher-end PCs, and Microsoft further developing the code into its Windows NT operating system.

Apple Computing

While the story of the personal computer is primarily a story about IBM and compatible computers, there is a secondary story—that of Apple Computing, and the company's proprietary computers.

Apple Computer, Inc., was founded in 1976 by Steven Jobs (b. 1955) and Steven Wozniak (b. 1950), two former game programmers at Atari. They built their first computer (the prototype for the Apple I) in Jobs's garage; by the mid-1980's, Apple had become the fastest-growing company in history, generating, at its peak (in 2000), almost $8 billion in revenues.

Apple I, II, and III The first computer from Apple, dubbed the Apple I, was released in 1976. It was based on the MOS 6502 microprocessor, and sold for $666.66.

Apple's second computer, the Apple II, was introduced in April 1977. Like the Apple I, the Apple II used the MOS 6502 chip, but it included an integrated keyboard and color graphics. The selling price was $1,295.

The next iteration, the Apple III, was released in 1980, but was less successful than its predecessors. This was partly due to the unit's higher price and business focus; depending on configuration, the Apple III sold for between $4,340 and $7,800

LISA Breaking off from the Apple I/II/III line of computers, in 1983 Apple introduced the LISA computer. LISA (Largely Integrated Systems Architecture) was the first personal computer to use a graphical user interface (GUI), complete with icons and pull-down menus, and also the first to have a mouse for users' input.

Macintosh Apple released the first Macintosh computer in January 1984, supported by an attention-getting advertisement during that year's Super Bowl broadcast. Based on Motorola's 68000 microprocessor, it incorporated many features of the failed LISA project, including an icon-driven GUI and mouse input. Priced at $2,495, it was an immediate success, and in various incarnations remains the core of Apple's line of computers

Personal Computing in the 1990's

As the personal computer industry moved into the 1990's, machines became both more affordable and more powerful, and software programs became much easier to use. The decade continued to be dominated by Intel microprocessors, IBM-compatible hardware, and Microsoft software and operating systems.

Microprocessor Power Microprocessor development in the 1990's was ruled by Moore's Law; every year saw the introduction of a new chip that was faster and lower-priced than its predecessor—and most of these chips were from Intel.

Intel Pentium Family Instead of following the 80486 chip with an 80586 model, Intel took the opportunity to introduce an entirely new family of microprocessor chips, called the Pentium, that contained the equivalent of 1.5 million transistors. The first Pentium chip was released in 1993, in both 60-Mhz and 66-MHz versions; increasingly faster versions of this chip were released throughout the 1990's.

In 1995 Intel released the next chip in the Pentium family, the Pentium Pro, which contained the equivalent of 5.5 million transistors and operated at up to 200 MHz. This was followed, in 1997, by the Pentium II, which contained the equivalent of 7.5 million transistors and operated at was capable of 300-MHz speeds.

Intel's Pentium III chip was released in 1999. The initial version of this microprocessor operated at 500 MHz, and contained the equivalent of 9.5 million transistors. Intel released the Pentium 4 in 2000; it contained the equivalent of 42 million transistors, and operated at speeds up to 1.5 Ghz.

AMD and Other Competitors While Intel dominated the market for microprocessor chips, it wasn't the only manufacturer out there. Intel's chief competitor, Advanced Micro Devices (AMD), was founded in 1969, and for the next 20 years produced microprocessors for proprietary devices. In 1991 AMD decided to challenge Intel in the personal computer marketplace with its AM386 microprocessor, which competed head-to-head with Intel's 80386 chip.

Another competitor in the microprocessor market was Cyrix, a division of National Semiconductor, which released chips to compete with Intel's 80486 and Pentium series. Cyrix was less successful than AMD in carving out a market niche, and in 1999 the company was acquired by Taiwanese chipset manufacturer VIA.

PC Hardware: Growth, Consolidation, Contraction The market for personal computer hardware experienced significant expansion in the 1990's—and significant contraction.

PC Industry Consolidates As the 1990's started, there were dozens of PC manufacturers, including Acer, IBM, Compaq, CompuAdd, Dell, Gateway, Hewlett Packard, Northgate, and Zeos. With the market growing at annual rates in excess of 10 percent, there seemed to be room for everyone. But as the decade progressed, competition became fierce, and the industry saw a consolidation. Minor players dropped by the wayside, and even major players found reason to consolidate—one example was the acquisition of Compaq by Hewlett Packard.

Postmillennium Technology Slump The technology market was on a definite roll, and PC hardware manufacturers were benefiting from the seemingly endless growth. In 2000, however, the bubble burst, and the technology market crashed to reality. PC sales actually declined for the first time in memory, as corporations and individuals alike put the brakes to their tech spending. The slump continued into 2003, and it remains to be seen when—or if—the computer hardware market will return to its former glory.

Windows Even during the darkest period of the technology slump, one company continued to log record profits. Microsoft, thanks primarily to the income from its Windows operating system, weathered the slump well, and continued to dominate the PC operating systems market—as it had all decade long.

Microsoft released a series of new Windows versions over the course of the decade, starting with Windows 3.0 in 1990 and continuing with Windows 95, Windows 98, Windows Me, and Windows XP. The company also released two versions of Windows designed for the corporate market, Windows NT and Windows 2000.

Open Source Competition As dominant as Microsoft was in the operating systems arena, it has never been fully without competition. In the early days of the PC era, that competition came from DOS clones such as Digital Research's DR DOS; in the late 1990's, competition came from an offshoot of the UNIX operating system called Linux.

Linux Linux, first introduced in 1991, is an open source variant of the established UNIX operating system, which was developed by Ken Thompson (b. 1943) and Dennis Ritchie in 1975. The Linux operating system was developed by (and named for) Linus Torvalds (b. 1970), a second-year student of computer science at the University of Helsinki. Torvalds permitted his operating system to be distributed free; it subsequently gained ground as alternative to Windows on enterprise and Web servers.

The Open Source Software Movement Concurrent with the rise of Linux, other application developers were touting the acceptance of open source software—applications whose underlying code lies in the public domain, and could be distributed free of charge. The open source movement believes that when programmers can modify and redistribute program code at no cost, the software evolves faster than it would if distributed through traditional commercial means. This movement, whose members are quite vocal in the software community, has yet to make major inroads against commercial software; the lack of central control inherent in the concept actually discourages large corporations from adopting free software of this type.

Enter the Internet

During the 1990's, the biggest impact on personal computing came not from hardware or software, but from a virtual network called the Internet. The Internet changed the way computer users communicated and accessed information, and led to a new "Internet economy" composed of companies seeking to exploit the commercial applications of the Internet space.

Before the Internet: ARPANET The Internet was born of a previous network called ARPANET. The U.S. Department of Defense created ARPANET in 1969 to research the concept of networking multiple computers together. Since it connected computers from various research universities, it soon evolved into a giant electronic post office, with researchers using the network to collaborate on projects and discuss topics of general interest.

The Birth of the Internet By 1981 more than 200 host computers were connected to ARPANET, with new hosts being added every 20 days. The term *Internet* was first used in 1982 to describe this evolving network, and by the mid-1980's the use of Internet-based e-mail and newsgroups was common at most major universities.

The Commercial Internet Is Born ARPANET was decommissioned in 1990, leaving only the vast network-of-networks that we now known as the Internet. At that time the Internet was still primarily a university-level phenomenon, however, as commercial traffic was banned from the National Science Foundation's NFSNET, which served as the Internet's backbone. The NSF lifted this ban on commercial traffic in 1991, clearing the way for the commercial Internet of the 1990's and beyond.

Once the Internet was opened to commercial use, the Internet service provider (ISP) was born. ISPs served as a "middleman," connecting home users to the Internet backbone. The typical home user accessed their ISP by using a personal computer to dial into the provider, over normal phone lines.

Now that both home and business PC users could connect to the Internet, the number of Internet users began a decade of dramatic growth. By 1995 there were 25 million users connected to the Internet, worldwide; the number of users exploded to 527 million by the end of 2001.

Commercial Services Connect to the Net America Online (AOL) and the other commercial online services initially positioned themselves as proprietary services separate from the Internet, but user demand eventually forced these private services to allow their users access to the public Internet. The first online service to connect to the Internet was Prodigy, in 1995; CompuServe and AOL soon followed suit. Today, America Online can be viewed as the largest ISP, respective of the proprietary content it offers its users.

E-mail If the Internet itself was a "killer app" for home computer users, the killer app of the Internet was e-mail. Users indulged their desire to communicate with one another by sending and receiving, by the dawn of the new millennium, more than 500 million e-mail messages a day. The most popular e-mail programs were Microsoft Outlook, Outlook Express, and Eudora.

World Wide Web The World Wide Web was invented in 1989 at Switzerland's CERN Particle Physics Library, by Tim Berners-Lee (b. 1955). Originally developed to enable scientists to collaborate on research projects, the Web applied the concept of hypertext linking to the Internet and added colorful graphics and multimedia applications to the end-user experience. The Web soon became the dominant part of the Internet, used for everything from research to shopping to personal expression.

Internet Applications By the mid-1990's Microsoft had a monopoly on desktop applications. Since most computer users already had these applications installed in their machines, they no longer functioned as killer apps. Now it was the Internet that was driving computer adoption, especially that graphical collection of servers that made up the World Wide Web.

The first software developed to surf the Web was Mosaic, a Web browser developed at the University of Illinois by undergraduate student Marc Andreessen (b. 1971). Mosaic was available free of charge over the Internet, but was soon supplanted by the more fully featured Netscape browser, also developed by Andreessen at his new company, Netscape Communications. Over the next few years users would be subjected to the so-called browser wars, with Netscape fending off a similar Web browser from Microsoft. Microsoft's Internet Explorer would ultimately win the browser wars, in part because Microsoft integrated the browser into its Windows operating system.

The other Internet killer app of 1990's was the e-mail client, typified by Microsoft's Outlook Express. Outlook Express, like other e-mail programs, could also post and read messages to and from Usenet newsgroups.

At the dawn of the new millennium, it appeared that the next killer app was the instant messaging program. Instant messengers—such as AOL Instant Messenger, ICQ, and Microsoft Messenger—let users exchange private messages in real time over the Internet, and quickly supplanted the earlier Internet public chat programs.

Searching the Web Perhaps the most common user activity on the Web was searching—for information, names and addresses, or whatever else the user needed to find.

Accordingly, one of the most-visited Web sites was a searchable directory of other Web sites called Yahoo! The Yahoo! site was created in 1994 by two Stanford University students, Jerry Yang (b. 1968) and David Filo (b. 1966), and eventually grew into a full-fledged information and services portal.

Other popular search sites of the 1990's included Alta Vista, Excite, Hotbot, and Lycos. Moving into the 21st century, the most popular search site was Google, which provided a fast and accurate search without the portal trappings found at Yahoo! and other similar sites.

e-Shopping Also important to the popularization of the Internet was the development of online retailers, commonly called e-tailers. One of the first of these e-tailers—and ultimately the most successful—was Amazon.com, founded in 1995 by Jeff Bezos (b. 1964). Although Amazon.com was founded as an online book retailer (with the slogan "the world's largest bookstore"), the company later expanded its merchandise mix to offer music, movies, clothing, and electronics.

Another powerful force in e-tailing is eBay. Founded in 1995 by Pierre Omidyar (b. 1967), eBay enables users to buy and sell items through automated online auctions. It was one of the few Internet businesses to show revenues and profit from day one; in 2002 eBay was host to more than $14 billion in auction transactions.

The Dot-com Explosion—and Implosion During the late 1990's the promise of Internet riches inspired an investment boom heretofore unknown in U.S. and global markets. Each week saw IPOs from dozens of so-called dot-com companies, offering all manner of goods and services online.

Unfortunately, the vast majority of these dot-com companies had weak business models, and never turned a profit — surviving, instead, on venture capital money and the paper profits realized from skyrocketing stock prices. In 2000, when the bottom dropped out of the stock market, the dot-com bubble burst, and thousands of dot-com companies were forced to close their doors.

Peer-to-Peer on the Internet One factor that contributed to the growth of the Internet is the concept of peer-to-peer (P2P) computing. When a computer is connected (over the Internet) to a P2P network of computers, the users of that computer can directly access the files stored on all the network's PCs, and then transfer selected files to their PC—all without accessing a central server. This technology is used in a number of popular file-sharing networks, for the sharing of MP3 audio files.

Instant Messaging Another service driven by P2P technology is instant messaging. Instant message services enable you to send short electronic messages back and forth to other online users, in real time, without the need to enter a public chat room.

P2P Groupware and Other Future Applications P2P technology has also driven a new type of software program, dubbed groupware. Groupware enables multiple users to work together on group projects, over the Internet or a corporate network. Traditional groupware programs, such as Lotus Notes, require the group to be connected by a central server. P2P groupware, such as Groove, enables users' PCs to connect directly to the other PCs in their group, independent of any central server or corporate network. This type of arrangement provides increased user freedom, while at the same time reducing the company's server workload.

The Dark Side of Personal Computing

The Internet proved invaluable in connecting millions of users together in a global community. Unfortunately, the benefits of this increased communication and community were partly offset by the increased dangers of the connected computer.

Computer Viruses Some of the most damaging incidents in the computing world have been caused by computer viruses—software programs designed for destruction. ICSA Labs found that in 2001, there were 113 infections per 1,000 computers in North America. That year 2.3 million computers were infected by the SirCam virus alone, and another million computers were hit by CodeRed. To date, more than 53,000 different viruses have been identified and cataloged—with another half-dozen or so appearing every day.

Computer Attacks Any computers connected to the Internet—especially those with a persistent broadband connection—are also at risk of attack from other users. Unless proper firewall software is in place, a computer can be victim to data theft, data destruction, data diddling, computer hijacking, and denial-of-service attacks that overload a computer or network by bombing it with thousands of simultaneous requests for data.

Most computer attacks are aimed at large Web sites or corporate computer networks. Some attacks are executed using other computers that have been hijacked by the use of virus-like backdoor software. These "zombie" computers are then remotely controlled to participate in the attack, providing a degree of anonymity to the cracker behind the entire scheme.

E-Mail Spam A more common annoyance to all Internet users is the increase in unsolicited commercial e-mail messages, or spam. The average Internet user today receives twice as many e-mails as he or she sends. In 2001 at least 20 percent of these messages were junk e-mail, nearly double the number from the previous year. By 2006, the amount of junk e-mail received by the average Internet user will increase to 1,400 pieces each year—up from 700 pieces, on average, in 2001—totaling 206 billion individual messages.

Green Card Lottery The first large-scale commercial spam came on April 12, 1994, when Laurence Canter (b. 1953) and Martha Siegel (1948–2000), two technology-savvy immigration lawyers from Scottsdale, Arizona, flooded all 6,000 Usenet newsgroups with a spam known as the "Green Card Lottery." This spam message advertised the services of their law firm for obtaining green cards for immigrants; Canter and Siegel purportedly generated close to $200,000 from the mailing.

Spam Today It took less than a year for spam to migrate from the Usenet to the realm of Internet e-mail. Today, unfortunately, spam is a fact of everyday Internet life. Spammers now send out millions of e-mails at a time, thanks to specialized spam software and the availability of millions of e-mail addresses on CD-ROM. The problem is so severe that some states have enacted antispam legislation, and the federal government is considering ways to block the onslaught of junk messages.

Computing Gets Small

As computing moved into the mid-1990's, users wanted to take their information with them wherever they went—they didn't want to be tied to an immovable desktop computer. The result was a profusion of portable computing devices, from notebook PCs to handheld devices.

The Evolution of Portable Computing The history of portable computing is one of increasingly smaller devices, enabled by the shrinking size of microprocessor chips and peripheral devices.

Early Portable PCs Early portable PCs—such as the Osborne 1, the KayPro II, and the Compaq Portable—were portable only in the sense that they could be picked up and carried. They weren't small and they weren't light, and consequently didn't see much portable use.

The Shrinking Laptop Over the years portable computers became truly portable—and gained the new designation of laptop or (for even smaller models) notebook computers. The typical laptop computer of the late 1990's featured a 14-inch LCD screen that folded over a standard-size keyboard into a 4-inch-thick package that weighed just a few pounds. This new portable PC operated on either AC or battery power, with the built-in batteries lasting for three hours or more—enough power to last through a typical plane flight.

Handheld Computing Handheld computers, also called palmtops or personal digital assistants (PDAs), incorporate many of the essential functions of a laptop computer, but with a much smaller screen and without a keyboard. Instructions are entered by tapping the touch-sensitive screen with a pen-like stylus; most people use their PDAs to store contact and schedule information, and to send and receive e-mail.

The First Handheld Computer The very first handheld computer, Hewlett-Packard's HP95LX, was introduced with limited success in 1991. It weighed 11 oz., and used the DOS operating system. Subsequent models, all DOS-based, were released through 1994.

Apple Newton In 1993 Apple entered the PDA market with the Newton MessagePad. The Newton's notoriously poor handwriting recognition, however, resulted in poor marketplace acceptance; the product was finally pulled from the market in 1998.

PalmPilot The first truly successful PDA was the PalmPilot 1000, released in 1996 from Palm Inc. (later acquired by 3Com Corp.). The first-generation PalmPilot offered simple schedule and contact management capabilities, accessed with a stylus and touchpad. Subsequent models added more advanced features, including a color display and built-in wireless modem.

Handspring and Compatibles/Competitors It wasn't long before the PalmPilot had marketplace competition. The most direct competition came from Handspring, a company founded by former Palm developers. The Handspring Visor, first released in 1999, used the Palm operating system, but offered more advanced features and met with widespread market acceptance.

Microsoft Windows CE In 1996 Microsoft introduced a version of its Windows operating system for handheld devices. Windows CE was designed for devices that included (small) built-in keyboards, and featured scaled-scaled down versions of Microsoft's key desktop applica-

Teaching Computers To Work In Unison

By STEVE LOHR

Computers do wondrous things, but computer science itself is largely a discipline of step-by-step progress as a steady stream of innovations in hardware, software and networking pile up. It is an engineering science whose frontiers are pushed ahead by people building new tools rendered in silicon and programming code rather than the breathtaking epiphanies and grand unifying theories of mathematics or physics.

Yet computer science does have its revelatory moments, typically when several advances come together to create a new computing experience. One of those memorable episodes took place in December 1995 at a supercomputing conference in San Diego. For three days, a prototype called I-Way linked more than a dozen big computer centers in the United States to work as a single machine on computationally daunting simulations, like the collision of neutron stars and the movement of cloud patterns around the globe.

The participants recall those few days as the first glimpse of what many computer scientists now regard as the next big evolutionary step in the development of the Internet, known as grid computing.

The idea of lashing computers together to tackle computing chores for users who tap in as needed has been around since the 1960's. But to move the concept of distributed computing utilities, or grids, toward practical reality has taken years of continuous improvement in computer processing speeds, data storage and network capacity. Perhaps the biggest challenge, however, has been to design software able to juggle and link all the computing resources across far-flung sites, and deliver them on demand.

The creation of this basic software—the DNA of grid computing—has been led by Dr. Ian Foster, a senior scientist at the Argonne National Laboratory and a professor of computer science at the University of Chicago, and Dr. Carl Kesselman, director of the center for grid technologies at the University of Southern California's Information Sciences Institute. They have worked together for more than a decade and, a year after the San Diego supercomputing conference, they founded the Globus Project to develop grid software.

In 2003, grid computing moved further toward the commercial mainstream when the Globus Project released new software tools that blend the grid standards with a programming technology called Web services, developed mainly in corporate labs, for automated computer-to-computer communications.

The heart of the grid problem is managing and linking computing resources. The long-term vision is that anyone with a desktop machine or handheld computer can have the power of a supercomputer at his or her fingertips. And small groups with shared interests could find answers to computationally complex problems as never before.

That grand vision, however, is perhaps a decade or more away. Dr. Larry Smarr, the former director of the National Center for Supercomputing Applications at the University of Illinois, compares the state of grid computing now to the Web in 1994.

The grid is widely regarded as the next stage for the Internet after the World Wide Web. The promise of the grid is to add a problem-solving system to the Web's multimedia retrieval system.

Computer scientists say the contribution of Dr. Foster and Dr. Kesselman to grid computing is roughly similar to that made by Tim Berners-Lee to the development of the Web. Mr. Berners-Lee came up with the software standards for addressing, linking and sharing documents over the Web.

The wisdom of their work, according to computer scientists, lies in its farsighted simplicity, designing a set of minimalist standards in an open-source model that others can build upon. It is the same design philosophy, they note, found in the original Internet and the Web.

Today, most grid projects remain the province of supercomputing centers and university labs. The research centers are linked by network connections about 20 times as fast as the standard high-speed connections and are equipped with storage systems able to handle vast data files and high-performance computers.

"Like nearly everything in computer science, the work we've done on the Globus software is incremental," says Dr. Foster. "But it is having an impact. There are thousands of people doing collaborative, computing-intensive work in a variety of fields that they could not do before."

tions, including Word and Excel. Windows CE proved more than the consumer wanted, however, as the Windows CE devices were larger and harder to use than the competing Palm PC; they had only limited market success.

Microsoft Pocket PC Four years later, in 2000, Microsoft released a new handheld operating system, dubbed Pocket PC. The new Pocket PC devices were almost identical to Palm devices in size and functionality; they had the added benefit of being application- and document-compatible with Microsoft's desktop applications.

Computing Goes Wireless As computing moved into the new millennium, users of portable computing devices had conflicting desires. They wanted a constant connection to the Internet (or to their corporate network); they also wanted to remain untethered by cables and connections. The solution was the development of wireless networking technology, which enabled users to connect without cables.

Wi-Fi The most popular wireless connection technology proved to be that based on the IEEE 802.11 standard, otherwise known as Wi-Fi. Wi-Fi operates in the unlicensed 2.4-GHz RF spectrum, and allows devices to connect at 11 Mbps—a little over a tenth the speed of a wired Ethernet network, but more than adequate for surfing the Internet and sending files back and forth. Thanks to steadily decreasing prices of Wi-Fi equipment, one can now find wireless nodes on corporate networks, wireless home networks, and public wireless access points in various hotels, airports, and coffeeshop locations. Many new notebook and handheld PCs come with Wi-Fi technology built in, so users can easily connect their portable devices to any nearby Wi-Fi network.

Bluetooth Bluetooth is a wireless technology that both competes with and complements Wi-Fi. Designed by the portable phone manufacturer Ericsson as a cable replacement technology, Bluetooth lets devices connect over short distances at 1 Mbps, using the same 2.4-GHz RF band used by Wi-Fi. While Bluetooth's transmission speed is much less than that of Wi-Fi, Bluetooth-enabled devices also consume much less power—making the technology ideal for small, portable devices. Today, Bluetooth wireless technology is used to connect wireless headsets to cellular and traditional phones, and printers, scanners, keyboards, and mice to personal computers.

Supercomputing

Although the personal computer was the technology story of the 1980's and 1990's, larger computers continued to evolve—into faster, more powerful machines called supercomputers. Supercomputers are used by universities, governments, and corporations to solve complex mathematics and physics problems, forecast the weather, and create sophisticated computer animation.

Cray Computers Seymour Cray (1925–96, USA) was the inventor behind the first commercial supercomputer. Finished in 1976, his Cray-1 contained 200,000 ICs and could perform at 160 million flops (floating point operations per second; a million flops is called a megaflop). Its price was approximately $8.8 million.

Throughout the 1980's and 1990's Cray delivered faster and more powerful supercomputers, including the Cray X-MP (1982, 500 megaflops), the Cray-2 (1985, 1.9 gigaflops), and the Cray C90 (1991, 16 gigaflops). Cray Research merged with Silicon Graphics, Inc., in 1996.

IBM Supercomputers IBM Corporation has long been at the forefront of computer development. IBM's supercomputers include Deep Blue (1996; 1 teraflop), ASCI White (2000; 12.3 teraflops), and the planned ASCI Purple (2005; 100 teraflops) and Blue Gene/L (2005; 200 teraflops).

NEC ESS Supercomputer In December 2002 NEC shocked the world when it announced the launch of its Earth Simulator System (ESS) supercomputer. It promised operation at 35.6 teraflops, and will be used for climatological research; it can, with remarkable precision, predict the path of a typhoon or the likelihood of a volcanic eruption.

The Fifth Generation

Today's computers are all of the fourth generation. Upcoming fifth-generation computers will be even more powerful, and will incorporate some rudimentary form of artificial intelligence. This new generation will also be characterized by distributed computing—where multiple computers connect together to deliver the power of a supercomputer.

Distributed Computing Distributed computing is already in place today. Several distributed computing projects connect hundreds or thousands of personal computers together, harnessing the combined power of their microprocessors while the PCs would otherwise be off-duty. Among the most publicized distributed computing projects are SETI@home, which uses home PCs to analyze radiotelegraph data for signs of extraterrestrial intelligence; the Cancer Research Project, which is charged with finding drug compounds that can disable the proteins that promote cancer; and evolution@home, which seeks to uncover the genetic causes for the distinction of species.

Pervasive Computing While supercomputers will continue to get bigger, other types of computers will get smaller. Thanks to the shrinking size (and price) of microprocessor chips, we will soon see miniature computers incorporated into a variety of household, automotive, and portable devices.

The result of all this computing power being embedded into all types of items will be what some are calling pervasive computing. With pervasive computing, virtually every device you own will be "smart." Your refrigerator will contain a microprocessor to tell you when you're running out of your favorite beverage; your watch will contain a microprocessor (and Bluetooth radio transmitter) to compute your heart rate and inform your doctor if you have a heart attack. Cheap microprocessors will be embedded in product bar codes to create radio frequency identification (RFID) tags that alert store managers when stocks run low. All your credit cards and even your driver's license will employ microprocessors to enable better tracking and smart transactions.

It remains to be seen whether the average citizen is ready for—or needs—this type of pervasive computing. The only sure thing is that computers will continue to get smaller, faster, and more powerful—and become more and more integrated into the fabric of everyday lives.

Glossary of Computer and Internet Terms

802.11 more accurately described as IEEE 802.11, the radio frequency (RF)-based technology used for home and small business wireless networks, and for most public wireless Internet connections. There are various subsets of the 802.11 standard; the most popular is 802.11b, which uses the 2.4-GHz RF band and is more commonly known as Wi-Fi.

address the location of an Internet host. An e-mail address might take the form johndoe@xyz.com; a Web address might look like www.xyztech.com. See also URL.

adware stealth software that tracks your online activity and sends that data to a marketing or advertising company.

anonymizer a Web site or service that enables anonymous Web browsing or e-mail communications.

anti-aliasing a technique used to smooth the ragged edges from electronic type or graphic images.

applet a small program, typically embedded in a Web page that a user can quickly download and launch, thus enhancing the Web page's content.

application a computer program designed for a specific task or use, such as word processing, accounting, or missile guidance.

artificial intelligence (AI) the capability of machines to be programmed to perform human functions. The primary AI functions are expert systems, programs that contain a body of knowledge (contributed by experts) that the machine can draw on to solve specific types of problems; natural language interfaces that make it possible for users to access a computer's database with commands entered in ordinary written or spoken language (for example, "Give me a list of countries bordering the Atlantic Ocean"); and speech recognition, speech synthesis, and optical recognition systems that enable computers to understand spoken commands, make speech, and interpret visible images (such as bar codes on retail goods).

ASCII (American Standard Code for Information Interchange) the numerical code used by personal computers.

assembly language the computer programming language that translates between higher-level programming languages and machine language. Assembly language has the same commands as machine language, but is more accessible because it enables programmers to use names instead of numbers.

attachment a file, such as a Word document or graphic image, attached to an e-mail message.

backbone a high-speed connection that forms a major pathway within a network, or over the Internet.

backup the process of creating a compressed copy of computer data that can be restored to its original location if the original data have somehow been erased or corrupted.

bandwidth the amount of data, graphics, sound, and other information that can be transmitted through cyberspace at a certain time. Bandwidth is measured in kilobits per second (kbps). Most telephone modems have a bandwidth of 56 kbps (or simply 56k); cable modems and DSL can offer bandwidths of more than 1 megabit per second (Mbps).

BASIC (Beginner's All-purpose Symbolic Instruction Code) an early programming language that is still among the simplest and most popular of programming languages today.

baud rate a transmission rate used in sending data from one computer to another, with a baud approximately equal to one bit per second.

beta a prerelease version of a software program, typically in the process of being tested for bugs. The process of testing software before its public release is called beta testing.

binary information consisting entirely of zeros and ones. In the computer world, also refers to files (such as image files) that are not simply ASCII text files.

BIOS the basic input/output system that interacts with computer hardware. The BIOS sits between computer hardware and the PC operating system.

bit in the binary system, a bit (binary digit) either of the digits 0 or 1. It is the basic unit for storing data, with "off" representing 0 and "on" representing 1.

blog short for "Weblog," a diarylike Web site, usually containing the personal thoughts of the site's owner as well as links to other sites of interest.

Bluetooth the specification for a wireless connection technology operating in the unlicensed 2.4-GHz radio frequency band. Originally intended to be a "wire replacement" technology for both computers and cellular phones, the Bluetooth specification has since been expanded to compete somewhat with the more powerful Wi-Fi wireless networking standard.

boot the process of turning on a computer system.

broadband a high-speed Internet connection (faster than a typical dial-up connection), accomplished via ISDN, cable, DSL, satellite, T1, or T3 lines.

browser a program that translates the hypertext markup language of the World Wide Web into viewable Web pages. The two most common browsers today are Microsoft's Internet Explorer and Netscape Navigator.

buffer any memory location where data can be stored temporarily while the computer is doing something else.

bug an error in a software program or the hardware.

bulletin board system (BBS) an electronic online meeting and messaging system, accessible by dial-in modem connections, popular in the 1980's and pre-Internet 1990's. Freestanding BBSs have been mostly superseded by Internet-based message boards and communities.

burner a device that writes CD-ROMs or DVD-ROMS.

byte a group of eight bits that together represent one character, whether alphabetic, numeric, or other. A byte is the smallest accessible unit in a computer's memory.

C a high-level programming language, particularly popular among personal computer programmers.

C++ an object-oriented version of the C programming language.

cable modem a high-speed, broadband Internet connection via digital cable TV lines.

cache pronounced "cash," the place on a hard drive or in memory where a software program temporarily stores data. If a user needs to access that data again, it can be read from the cache rather than from its original location.

cathode-ray tube (CRT) the display device, or monitor, similar to a television screen, used with most desktop computers.

CD-R (Compact Disc Recordable) a type of CD drive that lets you record once onto a disc, which can then be read by any CD-ROM drive or audio CD player.

CD-ROM (Compact Disc Read-Only Memory) a CD that can be used to store computer data. A CD-ROM, similar to an audio CD, stores data in a form readable by a laser, resulting in a storage device of great capacity and quick accessibility.

CD-RW (Compact Disc Rewritable) a type of CD that can be recorded, erased, and rewritten to by the user, multiple times.

central processing unit (CPU) the group of circuits that directs the entire computer system by (1) interpreting and executing program instruction and (2) coordinating the interaction of input, output, and storage devices.

chat text-based real-time Internet communication, typically consisting of short one-line messages back and forth between two or more users. Users gather in chat rooms or channels.

client in a client/server relationship between two devices, the device that pushes or pulls data from the other device (the server).

client/server computing a relationship between two or more computers where one computer (the server) serves as the host for all data and applications, and all other machines (the clients) access the server for all key operations.

clustering connecting two or more computers to behave as a single computer. Thanks to clustering, two or more computers can jointly execute a function, activity can be distributed evenly across a computer network, and systems can respond gracefully to unexpected failures.

complimentary metal oxide semiconductor (CMOS) pronounced "see-moss," this is a small, 64-byte memory chip on the computer motherboard that stores information a PC needs in order to boot up.

computer a programmable device that can store, retrieve, and process data. The computer's brain is the microprocessor, which is capable of doing math, moving data around, and altering data after storing it in binary code.

computer virus a computer program or piece of program code that attaches itself to other files and then replicates itself, or causes the computer to perform some damaging or malicious act.

computer-aided design (CAD) a type of software that automates complex drafting tasks.

computer-aided engineering (CAE) a type of software that automates complex engineering tasks.

computer-aided manufacturing (CAM) a type of software that automates complex manufacturing tasks.

cookie a small file created on a hard disk by a Web site visited. Cookie files contain small pieces of information that can be read and altered by that site or other Web sites, thereby making it possible to identify users who have been to the site before.

cracker an individual who maliciously breaks into another computer system. (Not to be confused with a hacker, who typically does not have malicious intent.)

cursor the highlighted area or pointer that tracks with the movement of a mouse or arrow keys onscreen.

cyberspace an all-encompassing term for online world of the Internet and other computer networks.

data information that is convenient to move or process.

database either a program for arranging facts in the computer and retrieving them (the computer equivalent of a filing system) or a file set up by such a system.

desktop publishing a type of software application that enables the creation of visually appealing printed newsletters, reports, and other similar documents.

digital a means of transmitting or storing data using "on" and "off" bits, expressed as "1" or "0."

digital subscriber line (DSL) a high-speed Internet connection that uses the ultrahigh-frequency portion of ordinary telephone lines, allowing users to send and receive voice and data on the same line at the same time.

directory an area or data structure in which information is stored regarding the location and contents of files or file structures. On the Web, a directory is a hand-assembled collection of Web pages, sorted by category; Yahoo! is currently the biggest directory on the Internet.

disk a device that stores data in magnetic or optical format.

disk drive a mechanism for retrieving information stored on a magnetic disk. The drive rotates the disk at high speed and reads the data with a magnetic head similar to those used in tape recorders.

disk operating system (DOS) The standard operating system for older IBM-compatible PCs, available in two near-identical formats: MS-DOS and PC-DOS.

diskette a portable or removable disk.

distributed computing a form of peer-to-peer computing where multiple computers are connected together to harness their total processing power; typically used for large projects that would otherwise require use of a supercomputer.

domain the identifying portion of an Internet address. In e-mail addresses, the domain name follows the @ sign; in Web site addresses, the domain name follows the www. Domain names are followed by a period and a zone that indicates the type of organization. Commercial entities end with .com; educational institutions end with .edu; government bodies end with .gov; and other organizations end with .org.

domain name system (DNS) the system used to translate Internet domain and host names to IP addresses.

driver a support file that tells a program how to interact with a specific hardware device, such as a hard disk controller or video display card.

DSL See *digital subscriber line*.

DVD an optical disc, similar to a CD, that can hold a minimum of 4.7GB, enough for a full-length movie.

e-commerce electronic commerce, or business conducted over the Internet.

e-mail electronic mail, a means of corresponding to other computer users over the Internet through digital messages. Also spelled *email*.

e-tailer a retailer engaging in e-commerce; an online merchant.

emoticon a cluster of punctuation marks commonly used in online chat, postings, and e-mail to signify a facial expression or emotional response. For example, :-) represents a smile, and :-(a frown.

encryption a method of encoding files so only the recipient can read the information. Encryption is necessary for transmitting secure data like credit card numbers over computer networks.

Ethernet the most common computer networking protocol; Ethernet is used to network, or hook computers together so they can share information.

extensible markup language (XML) a universal format for structured documents and data transmitted on the Web.

file any group of data treated as a single entity by the computer, such as a word processor document, a program, or a database.

file allocation table (FAT) a special section of a hard disk that stores tracking data to help an operating system locate files.

file transfer protocol (FTP) an older protocol for downloading files from the Internet, pre-Web.

firewall computer hardware or software with special security features to safeguard a network server (or individual computer connected to a network, or to the Internet) from damage by authorized or unauthorized users.

FireWire a high-speed bus used to connect digital devices, such as digital cameras and video cameras, to a computer system. Also known as iLink and IE-1394.

folder a way to group files on a disk; each folder can contain multiple files or other folders (called subfolders). In the DOS and Windows operating systems, folders were originally called directories.

frequently asked questions (FAQ) a file that contains answers to the most common questions for a particular forum or service.

GIF pronounced "jif," a common file format for image files on the Internet.

gigabyte (GB) one billion bytes.

Gopher a pre-Web method of organizing material on Internet servers.

graphical user interface (GUI) a system that uses graphical symbols called icons to represent available functions. These icons are generally manipulated by a mouse and/or a keyboard.

groupware software that enables groups of users to work together by providing communication, workflow, and task-sharing functions.

hacker an individual who enjoys exploring the details of computer systems and programming code, typically by "hacking" into those systems and programs—but without causing any intentional damage. (Not to be confused with a cracker, who engages in intentionally malicious behavior.)

hard disk a sealed cartridge containing magnetic storage disk(s) that holds much more memory—up to more than 100 gigabytes—than floppy disks. Usually a hard disk is built into the computer, but it can be a peripheral.

hardware the physical equipment, as opposed to the programs and procedures, used in computing.

hit a single request from a Web browser to view an item (typically a Web page) stored on a Web server.

home page the first or main page of a Web site.

host the computer used to run programs and store files for remote users or over a network.

hover the act of selecting an item by placing a cursor over an icon without clicking.

hub hardware used to network computers together, usually over an Ethernet connection.

hyperlink a connection between two tagged elements in a Web page, or separate sites, that makes it possible to click from one to the other.

hypertext a system of organizing information based on its relationship to other information, rather than linear or alphabetical orders. Hypertext allows users to link related Web pages and to store information in more than one place.

hypertext markup language (HTML) the scripting language used to create documents on the World Wide Web (WWW).

hypertext transfer protocol (HTTP) the protocol used to transfer World Wide Web pages from one computer to another.

icon a graphic symbol on the display screen that represents a file, peripheral, or some other object or function.

instant messaging text-based real-time one-on-one communication over the Internet. Not to be confused with chat, which can accommodate multiple users, instant messaging (IM) typically is limited to just two users.

integrated circuit an entire electronic circuit contained on one piece of silicon. The first integrated circuit began with a single board (originally plastic), onto which strips of conducting material were sprayed; electronic components could then be inserted directly onto the board.

Internet the global "network of networks" that connects millions of computers and other devices around the world.

Internet protocol (IP) the protocol that defines how data are sent through routers to different networks, by assigning unique IP addresses to different devices.

Internet Relay Chat (IRC) an Internet-based network of chat servers and channels that facilitates real-time public chat and file exchanges.

Internet service provider (ISP) a company that provides end-user access to the Internet via its central computers and local access lines.

intranet a private network of computers, using Internet protocols, accessible only by members of the network.

Java a computer language developed by Sun Microsystems that produces programs that run on almost any computer or operating system. Its compatibility and ease of use make it popular for Web applets.

JavaScript a scripting language used to create advanced Web page functionality, such as rollovers, pull-down menus, and other special effects.

JPG/JPEG a common file format for photographic images on the Internet.

kilobyte (K) a unit of measure for data storage or transmission equivalent to 1,024 bytes; often rounded to 1,000.

ligh-emitting diode (LED) an electronic device that lights up when electricity is passed through it.

link a hypertext connection that allows a user to jump from one Internet site to another by pointing and clicking. On the World Wide Web, links are often underlined or highlighted.

Linux a Unix-like operating system that runs on many different types of computers. There are many different flavors of Linux, many of which are freely distributed under open source guidelines.

liquid crystal display (LCD) a flat-screen display where images are created by light transmitted through a layer of liquid crystals.

local area network (LAN) a system that enables users to connect PCs to one another or to minicomputers or mainframes.

macro a series of instructions in a simple coding language, used to automate procedures in a computer application, document, or template.

mainframe computer generally the largest, fastest, and most expensive kind of computer, usually costing millions of dollars and requiring special cooling. Mainframe computers can accommodate hundreds of simultaneous users and normally are run around the clock; typically they are owned by large companies.

malware "malicious software," shorthand for any virus, Trojan, or worm.

megabyte (MB) one million bytes.

megahertz (MHz) a measure of microprocessing speed; 1 MHz equals 1 million electrical cycles per second.

memory temporary electronic storage for data and instructions, using electronic impulses on a chip.

microcomputer a computer based on a microprocessor chip. Also known as a personal computer.

microprocessor a complete central processing unit assembled on a single silicon chip.

MIDI (musical instrument digital interface) a file format for sound and music on the Internet.

minicomputer a midsize computer, sized between a workstation (or microcomputer) and a mainframe.

MIPS (million instructions per second) a measure of computer processing speed.

MPEG Motion Picture Experts Group, a file format for high-quality video in small file sizes.

modem (modulator-demodulator) a device capable of converting a digital signal to an analog signal, which can be transmitted via a telephone line, reconverted, and then "read" by another computer.

monitor the display device on a computer, similar to a television screen.

Mosaic the very first Web browser, developed in 1993 by the National Center for Supercomputing Applications (NCSA) at the University of Illinois.

motherboard the largest printed circuit board in a computer, housing the CPU chip and controlling circuitry.

mouse a small handheld input device connected to a computer and featuring one or more button-style switches. When moved around a desk, the mouse causes a symbol on the computer screen to make corresponding movements.

multimedia the combination, usually on a computer, of interactive text, graphics, audio, and video.

netiquette the etiquette of the Internet.

network an interconnected group of computers.

newbie inexperienced user.

newsgroup a discussion forum on the Usenet segment of the Internet. Newsgroups are typically arranged by category of interest; to read, respond to, or post information on a newsgroup, a user must have a program known as a newsreader.

node any single computer connected to a network.

Open Source software for which the underlying programming code is available (free) for users to make changes to it and build new versions incorporating those changes.

operating system a sequence of programming codes that instructs a computer about its various parts and peripherals and how to operate them. Operating systems, such as Windows or Linux, deal only with the workings of the hardware and are separate from software programs.

parallel a type of external port used to connect printers and other similar devices.

path the collection of folders and subfolders (listed in order of hierarchy) that hold a particular file.

peer-to-peer (P2P) a communications network where two or more computers work together as equals, without the benefit of a central server.

peripheral a device connected to the computer that provides communication or auxiliary functions.

personal computer a computer used by an individual at home, in the office, or on the road.

personal digital assistant (PDA) a handheld device that organizes personal information, combining computing and networking features. A typical PDA includes an address book and a to-do list.

pixel the individual picture elements that combine to create a video image.

pixelization the stair-stepped appearance of a curved or angled line in a digital image

Plug and Play (PnP) hardware that includes its manufacturer and model information in its ROM, enabling Windows to recognize it immediately upon startup and install the necessary drivers if they are not already set up.

Pocket PC Microsoft's handheld computer operating system and hardware platform, similar to the competing Palm OS.

port an interface on a computer to which one can connect a device. Personal computers have various types of ports. Internally, there are several ports for connecting disk drives, display screens, and keyboards. Externally, there are ports for connecting modems, printers, mice, and other peripheral devices.

Post Office Protocol (POP) a protocol used to retrieve e-mail from a mail server.

Pretty Good Privacy (PGP) one of the most popular tools for public-key encryption.

printer the piece of computer hardware that creates hard-copy printouts of documents.

program as a noun, a prepared set of instructions for the computer, often with provisions for the operator to choose among various options. As a verb, to create such a set of instructions.

protocol an agreed-upon format for transmitting data between two devices.

public key cryptography (PKC) a means of encrypting data and messages using a combination of public and private keys.

random-access memory (RAM) a temporary storage space in which data may be held on a chip rather than stored on disk or tape. The contents of RAM may be accessed or altered at any time during a session, but will be lost when the computer is turned off.

read-only memory (ROM) a type of chip memory, the contents of which have been permanently recorded in a computer by the manufacturer and cannot be altered by the user.

reduced instruction set computing (RISC) a type of microprocessor that gains speed by using fewer instructions than the Complex Instruction Set (CISC) chip.

resolution the degree of clarity an image displays. The term is most often used to describe the sharpness of bit-mapped images on monitors, but also applies to images on printed pages, as expressed by the number of dots per inch (dpi).

root the main directory or folder on a disk.

router a piece of hardware or software that handles the connection between two or more networks.

scanner a device that converts paper documents or photos into a format that can be viewed on a computer and manipulated by the user.

script language an easy-to-use pseudo-programming language that enables the creation of executable scripts composed of individual commands.

search engine a Web server that indexes Web pages, then makes the index available for user searching. Search engines differ from directories in that the indexes are generated using programs called spiders, while directories are assembled manually. Search engine indexes typically include many more Web pages than are found in directories.

serial a type of external port used to connect communication devices, such as modems, PalmPilots, etc.

server the central computer in a network, providing a service or data access to client computers on the network.

shareware a software program distributed on the honor system; providers make their programs freely accessible over the Internet, with the understanding that those who use them will send payment to the provider after using them. See also *freeware*.

Small Computer System Interface (SCSI) pronounced "skuzzy," the standard port for Macintosh computers, also common in PCs and Unix boxes.

software the programs and procedures, as opposed to the physical equipment, used in computing.

spam junk e-mail. As a verb, it means to send thousands of copies of a junk e-mail message.

spider a software program that follows hypertext links across multiple Web pages, but is not directly under human control. Spiders scan the Web, looking for URLs, automatically following all the hyperlinks on pages accessed. The results from a spider's search are used to create the indexes used by search engines.

spreadsheet a program that performs mathematical operations on numbers arranged in large arrays; used mainly for accounting and other record keeping.

spyware software used to surreptitiously monitor computer use (i.e., spy on other users).

static RAM (SRAM) random-access memory that retains data bits in its memory as long as power is being supplied.

streaming refers to the continuous transmission of data, typically audio or video, so it can be processed as a steady stream. With streaming, the client browser or plug-in can start displaying the data as sound and pictures before the entire file has been transmitted.

Structured Query Language (SQL) a computer language used to send queries to databases.

supercomputer the fastest (and biggest and most expensive) of the mainframe class of computers, usually used for complex scientific calculations.

Telnet an older protocol used to log in to and access data stored on an Internet server.

terabyte (TB) one trillion bytes.

terminal a device with a screen and keyboard that relies on a mainframe or another computer for intelligence.

transistor a small piece of semiconducting material (material that conducts electricity better than, say, wood but not as well as metal). Flows of electrons within the transistor can be controlled, enabling it to act as an electronic "switching" device, recoding information in the form of an "on" or an "off" signal.

Transmission Control Protocol/Internet Protocol (TCP/IP) the protocol used for communications on the Internet; coordinates the addressing and packaging of the data packets that make up any communication.

Trojan horse a malicious program that pretends to be another, harmless program or file.

universal serial bus (USB) an external bus standard that supports data transfer rates of 12 Mbps and can connect up to 127 peripheral devices, such as keyboards, modems, and mice. USB also supports hot plugging and plug-and-play installation.

UNIX A multi-user, multitasking operating system designed to run on a wide variety of computers, from microcomputers to mainframes.

unsolicited commercial e-mail (UCE) spam.

upgrade to add a new or improved peripheral or part to a system's hardware. Also, to install a newer version of an existing piece of software.

URL (Uniform Resource Locator) the address that identifies a Web page to a browser. Also known as a Web address.

Usenet a subset of the Internet that contains thousands of topic-specific newsgroups.

vaporware new computer software that has been announced but never seems to be released.

Veronica stands for Very Easy Rodent Oriented Net-wide Index to Computerized Archives; an early method of indexing and searching Gopher servers.

virus a computer program segment or string of code that can attach itself to another program or file, reproduce itself, and spread from one computer to another. Viruses can destroy or change data and in other ways sabotage computer systems.

warez pronounced "wheres," this is illegally distributed software, from which normal copy protection has been cracked or removed.

Web page an HTML file, containing text, graphics, or mini-applications, viewed with a Web browser.

Web site an organized, linked collection of Web pages stored on an Internet server and read using a Web browser. The opening page of a site is called a home page.

Wide Area Information Servers (WAIS) a software program that enables the indexing of huge quantities of information across the Internet and other networks.

wide area network (WAN) a connection between two or more local area networks (LANs). Wide area networks can be made up of interconnected smaller networks spread throughout a building, a state, or the globe.

Wi-Fi the 802.11b wireless networking standard; short for "wireless fidelity."

Windows the generic name for all versions of Microsoft's graphical operating system.

Wireless Equivalent Privacy (WEP) the encryption and security protocol for Wi-Fi networks.

wireless LAN (WLAN) a local area network composed of wireless connections between devices.

workstation a high-performance computer with advanced graphics capabilities designed for use by scientists and engineers.

World Wide Web (WWW) a vast network of information, mainly from business, commercial, and government resources, that uses a hypertext system for quickly transmitting graphics, sound, and video over the Internet.

worm a parasitic computer program that replicates but does not infect other files.

The History of Home Video Games

First Generation: 1972–77

In 1966 Ralph Baer (b. 1922), an employee of the defense contractor Sanders Associates, first came up with the concept of a "television gaming apparatus." Originally designed to develop the reflexes of military personal, this device included both a chase game and a video tennis game, and could be attached to a normal television set.

Magnavox licensed Baer's game and on January 27, 1972, launched the Odyssey videogame console—the world's first home video game system. Priced at $100, the Odyssey featured simple black-and-white graphics, enhanced by plastic overlays for the television screen. This pioneering game system was not a lasting success, however; it sold only 200,000 units over its three-year life.

That same year, inspired by Baer's original video tennis game, Atari released an electronic arcade game called PONG, which became a huge success. Unfazed by Odyssey's short shelf life, in 1975 Atari released a home version of PONG, under the Sears Tele-Games label. The $100 game system was Sears's best-selling item during the 1975 Christmas season, with sales of more than $40 million. Atari released its own branded PONG unit in 1976.

In August 1976 Fairchild Camera and Instrument leveraged its position as the creator of the microchip to release the first programmable home video game system, based on the 8-bit F8 processor. The Channel F Video Entertainment System sold for $169 and accepted $20 "Videocart" game cartridges; it displayed its games in 16 colors.

RCA's Studio II followed Fairchild to market in January 1977 at a price of $149. Even though the Studio II used the same 8-bit COSMAC 1802 microprocessor that was used in NASA's *Voyager* and *Galileo* spacecraft, its chunky black-and-white graphics were notably inferior to those of the Channel F, and the unit was discontinued in 1979.

Second Generation (Golden Age): 1977–82

The "golden age" of home video games was launched in October 1977, when Atari released its own programmable video game system. Priced at $199, Atari's Video Computer

System (VCS), later known as the Atari 2600, was based on an 8-bit Motorola 6507 microprocessor, with 256 bytes of RAM. On the market through 1990, the Atari VCS went on to sell more than 25 million units over its product life. Over the course of its production run, 40 different manufacturers created more than 200 different games for the system, selling more than 120 million cartridges of popular games such as Space Invaders, Asteroids, and Pac-Man.

One of Atari's first competitors in the programmable video game market was Bally, which launched the Bally Professional Arcade in 1977. Even though the Bally unit had better graphics than the Atari VCS, it sold at a higher price ($350) and failed to catch on.

Magnavox jumped into the programmable video game market with Odyssey². Launched in 1978, Odyssey² featured an integrated membrane keyboard. The Odyssey² was more popular in Europe than in the U.S., where the parent company Philips Electronics marketed it as the Videopac.

Atari faced a more serious competitor in 1980, when Mattel launched its Intellivision video game system. Intellivision featured better graphics than the VCS, and was the first video game system to use a 16-bit microprocessor—the General Instruments 1600. Intellivision became known for its proprietary sports titles, such as Major League Baseball, NFL Football, NHL Hockey, and NBA Basketball, even though the lack of third-party games contributed to its second-place showing against the Atari 2600.

Third Generation: 1982–84

The third generation of video games became known as the "dark ages," not because of any new technology, but rather because of the precipitous drop in sales that started in 1982. The crash was caused by too many derivative or poor-quality game cartridges from too many manufacturers. Many third-party game developers went out of business during this period, and even established companies lost money on unsold inventory.

The most prominent third-generation game system was Coleco's Colecovision. Launched in 1982 at a price of $199, Colecovision featured high-quality graphics and used an 8-bit Z-80A microprocessor with 8K RAM. Colecovision's main claim to fame is that it offered high-quality versions of arcade favorites: *Donkey Kong*, *Defender*, *Frogger*, *Joust*, *Spy Hunter*, and *Zaxxon*.

Atari responded to Coleco by releasing the $299 Atari 5200 SuperSystem, which was based on the graphics and audio chips found in the Atari 400 personal computer. Games for the 5200 were essentially improved releases of older 2600 (VCS) games; this lack of new games failed to excite consumers, and the 5200 was lost amid the overall market crash of 1982.

Fourth Generation: 1985–89

Following the crash of 1982–84, the home video game industry experienced a rebirth with the introduction of a new generation of game units driven by two technological innovations—less expensive memory chips and higher-power 8-bit microprocessors. These developments enabled game designers to produce home video game consoles that could successfully compete at a quality level equal to that of arcade machines.

In 1983 Nintendo had released the Famicon ("family computer") video game system to the Japanese market. The console was a hit, selling 2.5 million units in its first year, and Nintendo began negotiations with Atari to distribute the system in the United States. These talks fell through, and Nintendo decided to distribute the system itself in the U.S., under the name Nintendo Entertainment System (NES).

The $199 NES was based on an 8-bit Motorola 6502 microprocessor and shipped with a version of the hit arcade game *Super Mario Bros*. Quantities of the NES were shipped into the New York market in time for Christmas 1985, and national distribution followed early in 1986. Nintendo sold more than 3 million NES units in its first two years of release; it is estimated that, over its entire product life, more than 65 million NES consoles were sold worldwide, along with 500 million cartridges.

In 1989, Sega released its first game system in the United States, the Sega Master System (SMS). The SMS had two cartridge ports; one in a standard cartridge configuration, and a second port that accepted small credit card–shaped cartridges. The system was capable of using both ports at any given time, and Sega used this feature to produce plug-in 3-D glasses for use with certain games.

Also released in 1989 was the first programmable handheld game system, Nintendo's GameBoy. Priced at $100, GameBoy featured a black-and-white LCD screen, and came prepackaged with a Tetris cartridge. With more than 100 million units shipped in various configurations, GameBoy holds the honor of being the world's all-time best-selling video game system.

Does Science Matter?

By WILLIAM J. BROAD and JAMES GLANZ

Through its rituals of discovery, science has extended life, conquered disease and offered new sexual and commercial freedoms. It has pushed aside demigods and demons and revealed a cosmos more intricate and awesome than anything produced by pure imagination.

But there are new troubles in the peculiar form of paradise that science has created, as well as new questions about whether it has popular support to meet the future challenges of disease, pollution, security, energy, education, food, water and urban sprawl.

The public seems increasingly intolerant of grand, technical fixes, even while it hungers for new gadgets and drugs. It has also come to fear the potential consequences of unfettered science and technology in areas like genetic engineering, germ warfare, global warming, nuclear power and the proliferation of nuclear arms.

Tension between science and the public has thrown up barriers to research involving deadly pathogens, stem cells and human cloning. Some of the doubts about science began with the environmental movement of the 1960's.

Science has also provoked deeper unease by disturbing traditional beliefs. Some scientists, stunned by the increasing vigor of fundamentalist religion worldwide, wonder if old certainties have rushed into a sort of vacuum left by the inconclusiveness of science on the big issues of everyday life.

The disaffection can be gauged in opinion surveys. In 2003, a Harris poll found that the percentage of Americans rating scientists as having "very great prestige" had declined nine percentage points in the last quarter-century, from 66 to 57 percent. Another Harris poll found that most Americans believe in miracles, while half believe in ghosts and a third in astrology—hardly an endorsement of scientific rationality. In this atmosphere of ambivalence, research priorities have become increasingly politicized, some scientists say.

As the world marches into a century born amid fundamentalist strife in oil-producing nations, a divisive political climate in the United States and abroad and ever more sophisticated challenges to scientific credos like Darwin's theory of evolution, it seems warranted to ask a question that runs counter to centuries of Western thought: Does science matter? Do people care about it anymore?

The Context: Breakthroughs And Disenchantment Clearly, science has mattered a lot, for a long time. Advances in food, public health and medicine helped raise life expectancy in the United States in the past century from roughly 50 to 80 years. So too, world population between 1950 and 1990 more than doubled, now exceeding six billion. Biology discovered the structure of DNA, made test-tube babies and cured diseases. And the decoding of the human genome is leading scientists toward a detailed understanding of how the body works, possibly offering new treatments for cancer and other diseases.

In physics, breakthroughs produced digital electronics and subatomic discoveries. American rocket science put men on the moon, probed distant planets and lofted hundreds of satellites, including the Hubble Space Telescope.

But major problems also arose: acid rain, environmental toxins, the Bhopal chemical disaster, nuclear waste, global warming, the ozone hole, fears over genetically modified food and the fiery destruction of two space shuttles. Such troubles have helped feed social disenchantment with science.

When the cold war ended, the physical sciences began to lose luster and funding. After spending $2 billion, Congress killed physicists' preeminent endeavor, the enormous Superconducting Super Collider particle accelerator.

At the same time, industry spending on research soared to twice that of the federal government, about $180 billion in 2003, according to the National Science Foundation. One result is that Americans see more drugs, cell phones, advanced toys, innovative cars and engineered foods and less news about the fundamental building blocks and great shadowy vistas of the universe.

The main exceptions to the downward trend in the federal science budget are for health and weapons. In 2003, spending on military research hit $58 billion, higher in fixed dollars than during the cold war.

Meanwhile, other countries are spending more on research, taking some of the glory that America once monopolized.

The Contradictions: New Challenges, but Also Threats Despite the explosion in the life sci-

ences, cancer still darkens many lives, and the flowering of biotechnology has fed worries about genetically modified foods and organisms as well as the pending reinvention of what it means to be human. Many people worry that the growing power of genetics will sully the sanctity of human life.

Experts also worry about terrorists using advances in biology for intentional harm, perhaps on vast new scales.

The physical sciences, without the space race and the cold war, and perhaps facing intrinsic limits as well as declining budgets, are slightly adrift. Some observers worry that physics has entered a phase of diminishing returns. Other experts disagree, noting that scientific fields rise and fall in cycles and that physics may be poised for new strides.

Despite the decline in prestige recorded in the recent Harris poll, scientists still top the list of 22 professions in terms of high status, ahead of doctors, teachers, lawyers and athletes.

The Competition: The Battles Increase Over Darwin's Theory A simple number jars many scientists: about two-thirds of the public believe that alternatives to Darwin's theory of evolution should be taught in public schools alongside this bedrock concept of biology itself.

The organized opposition to the mainstream theory of evolution has become vastly more sophisticated and influential than it was, say, 25 years ago. The leading foes of Darwin espouse a theory called "intelligent design," which holds that purely random natural processes could never have produced humans. These foes are led by a relatively small group of people with various academic and professional credentials, including some with advanced degrees in science and even university professorships.

Backers of intelligent design say they are simply pointing up shortcomings in Darwin's theory. Scientists have publicly rallied in response, recently staving off an effort at the Texas State Board of Education to have intelligent design taught alongside evolution.

Science has, in fact, sold itself from the start as something more than a utilitarian exercise in developing technologies and medicines. Einstein—who often used religious and philosophical language to explain his discoveries—seemed to tell humanity something fundamental about the fabric of existence. More recently, the cosmologist Stephen Hawking said that discovering a better theory of gravitation would be like seeing into "the mind of God."

Such rhetorical flourishes are as much derided as admired by the bulk of working scientists, who as a culture have drifted closer to the thinking of Steven Weinberg, another Nobel Prize winner in particle physics, who famously wrote that "the more the universe seems comprehensible, the more it also seems pointless."

That view helps some observers explain how science has come into bitter conflict with particular religious groups, especially biblical literalists.

The Future: Urgent Goals for Governments
Industry looks to short-term goals and has proven highly adept at using science to take care of itself and consumers. A far more uncertain issue is whether the federal government can successfully address issues of human welfare that lie well beyond the industrial horizon—years, decades and even centuries ahead.

An urgent goal, experts say, is to develop new sources of energy, which will become vitally important as oil becomes increasingly scarce. Another is to better understand the nuances of climate change. Another is to develop ways of countering the spread of nuclear arms and germ weapons.

The world will also need a new science of cities, to help coordinate planning in areas like waste, water use, congestion, highways, hazard mitigation and pollution control.

Whether the complex challenges of today generate a new era of scientific greatness, several scientists said, may depend on how a deeply conflicted public answers the question of whether science still matters.

In many ways, it all boils down to "a schism between people who have accepted the modern scientific view of the world and the people who are fighting that," said Dr. David Baltimore, the Nobel Prize-winning biologist.

Some experts warn that if support for science falters and if the American public loses interest in it, such apathy may foster an age in which scientific elites ignore the public weal and global imperatives for their own narrow interests, producing something like a dictatorship of the lab coats.

"For any man to abdicate an interest in science," Jacob Bronowski, the science historian, wrote, "is to walk with open eyes towards slavery."

Fifth Generation: 1989–95

The fifth generation of home video game systems was ushered in by the 1989 American release of NEC's TurboGrafx-16. (The system was launched in Japan in 1988 as the PC Engine.) Although the TurboGrafx-16 was advertised as a 16-bit system, it actually used an 8-bit microprocessor, assisted by a 16-bit graphics chip and 64K RAM; it was notable as the first game console to have a CD player attachment.

More formidable was the Sega Genesis game system (sold as the Mega Drive in Japan). Released to the U.S. market in 1989, Genesis was the first true 16-bit game system, using a Motorola 68000 microprocessor. Genesis was priced at $199, and ran excellent translations of Sega arcade hits; sales received a significant boost with the 1991 release of the *Sonic the Hedgehog* game.

To compete with the Sega Genesis, Nintendo launched its own 16-bit system in 1991. The Super NES, known as the Super Famicon in Japan, sold for $199 and included the Super Mario World cartridge. The initial U.S. production run of 300,000 units sold out overnight; over the course of its product life, more than 46 million Super NES units were sold worldwide.

Sixth Generation: 1995–98

The sixth generation of home video games featured high-powered microprocessors and dedicated graphics processors that enabled extremely realistic graphics and game play. These game consoles outperformed the much higher-priced personal computer systems of the day.

The Sega Saturn, released in May of 1995, achieved its high graphics quality by using twin 32-bit microprocessors and CD-ROM-based games. The Saturn's high $399 price and lack of third-party games led to its being overshadowed by Sony's upcoming game console.

In September 1995 Sony released its first video game system, the Playstation, to the U.S. market. The Playstation was priced at $299, $100 less than the competing Sega Saturn, and incorporated a 32-bit microprocessor designed to produce polygon graphics. Backed with a massive advertising campaign, the Playstation unseated both Nintendo and Sega to become the leading home video game system; to date, it has sold more than 50 million units worldwide.

In 1996, five years after the release of the Super NES, Nintendo released its own sixth-generation game system, the Nintendo 64. The Nintendo 64 used a 64-bit microprocessor (hence the name), and was priced at just $150, significantly lower than its competition. The launch was hugely successful, with 1.7 million units sold in the first three months of release.

Next Generation: 1998–Present

Sega upped the video game ante in 1999 with the release of its Dreamcast system. Incorporating a 128-bit microprocessor and 26MB memory, the Dreamcast ran on Microsoft's Windows CE platform. Dreamcast had strong sales until Sony's release of its Playstation 2; continuing financial problems led Sega to discontinue production in March 2001.

Building on the success of the first-generation Playstation, Sony released the Playstation 2 (PS2), powered by a 128-bit "Emotion Engine" microprocessor and 32MB memory. In the first two days of its March 2000,Japanese launch, Sony sold more than 1 million units. Released in the United States in October 2000, the $200 console sold out its initial run of 500,000 units within a matter of hours. Three years after the PS2's launch, worldwide console sales had reached 60 million units, making it the dominant video game system in the current market.

Microsoft entered the video game market in November 2001 with its widely anticipated Xbox system. The Xbox incorporated a 733MHz Pentium III microprocessor, 64MB RAM, a 10GB hard drive, and built-in Ethernet support. Microsoft initially shipped 1.1 million units to retailers; in its first two years of release, almost 10 million units were sold worldwide.

Also released in November 2001 was Nintendo's latest game system, the GameCube. Priced at $199, $100 less than Xbox, the GameCube was Nintendo's first noncartridge system, instead running small-diameter CD-ROM discs. Nintendo sold more than 500,000 GameCubes in the first week of release; after two years on the market, total worldwide sales reached 13 million units.

SPORTS

Baseball **672**
History *672*
Rules of the Game................ *675*
Baseball Hall of Fame............. *676*
Glossary of Baseball Terms *684*
Basketball **686**
Rules and Conduct of Play *686*
History of Basketball *687*
Glossary of Basketball Terms........ *691*
Basketball Hall of Fame *693*
Football **697**
Rules and Conduct of Play *697*
College Football.................. *698*
Professional Football.............. *701*
Professional Football Hall of Fame.... *704*
Super Bowl Results *707*
Glossary of Football Terms.......... *708*
Ice Hockey **710**
History *710*
Equipment, Rules, & Field of Play.... *711*
Glossary of Ice Hockey Terms *712*
The Stanley Cup *714*
Hart Trophy Winners.............. *715*
Vezina Trophy Winners *716*
Golf **717**
History *717*
Rules of the Game................ *718*
Glossary of Golf Terms *719*
The Masters *721*
The U.S. Open Championship *722*
P.G.A. Championship.............. *722*
The British Open *723*
U.S. Women's Grand Slam Champions *724*
U.S. Women's Open Champions *724*
Tennis **725**
History of Tennis *725*
Rules of the Game................ *727*
Glossary of Tennis Terms........... *728*
Men's Grand Slam Champions....... *730*
Women's Grand Slam Champions *732*
Soccer **734**
History *734*
Rules of the Game................ *734*
Glossary of Soccer Terms *735*
World Cup Results *737*
Horse Racing **739**
Origins *739*
The Basics...................... *739*
History *740*
Glossary of Horse Racing Terms *742*
Kentucky Derby Winners *744*
Olympic Games **745**
History *745*
Summer Games, 1896–2008 .... *746*
Winter Games, 1924–2006 .... *749*
Times Focus: *When the Games Began: Olympic Archeology By John Noble Wilford* *752*
Track & Field **753**
Boxing **756**
History *756*
Notable Heavyweight Champions..... *757*
Olympic Boxing *758*
Swimming **760**
History *760*
The Sport of Swimming............ *760*
The Olympics *761*
Auto Racing **763**
Formula One.................... *763*
NASCAR........................ *763*
Indy Car *764*
Le Mans *765*
Indianapolis 500 Winners........... *766*

BASEBALL

History

Origins

Although no scholar has pinpointed the exact origins of baseball in America, most agree that it began to evolve in the early 17th century out of a family of English folk games including rounders, stoolball, and cricket. American historian David Hackett Fischer believes that bittle-battle, a game popular in southeastern England, is perhaps the most direct ancestor of the sport that claims to be America's pastime. Played with four bases, a pitcher, and a batter in the Massachusetts Bay Colony in the early 1600's, within a century bittle-battle became known as the Massachusetts Game. As early as 1791, as evidenced by the recently unearthed "Pittsfield Prohibition," the game was common enough to be a nuisance to town elders, who were forced to issue a bylaw for "the Preservation of the Windows in the New Meeting House in said Town." Because the sport was unorganized and only played informally, several versions of the game existed.

In the 19th century a somewhat different game was being played in New York City: batters hit from a corner of the diamond, for example, rather than midway between bases, and runners could not be put out by being plunked (or "soaked") with the ball. In 1845 the New York game was codified by a young bank clerk named Alexander Cartwright, who proposed 20 rules of play that covered everything from punctuality to distance between bases ("42 paces") to a balk rule and the institution of foul lines. His own club, the Knickerbocker Base Ball club, adopted these rules, which proved very popular. The club issued a challenge to any other club willing to abide by their rules. The New York Nine accepted the challenge, and on June 19, 1846, the first base ball contest was played at Elysian Field in Hoboken, N.J. With Cartwright, his team's best player, serving as umpire, the Knickerbockers succumbed by a score of 23-1. Umpire Cartwright's most memorable decision was fining a player six cents for swearing.

Professionalization: 1850–1900

Base-ball, as it was known in the 19th century, spread from the Northeast, where it had achieved craze status among English, Irish, and German immigrants, to the South and West, thanks to the enthusiasm of Union soldiers in the Civil War period and the burgeoning era of railroad expansion.

In 1869 the first professional club was formed in Cincinnati. In 1876 an eight-team league—the National League of Professional Baseball Clubs—was founded at a meeting held at the Grand Central Hotel in New York City. A 70-game schedule was announced; the first game took place in Philadelphia; the gloveless defenders committed 19 errors, but baseball was on its way. Players like first basemen Cap Anson and Dan Brouthers, the indefatigable pitcher Hoss Radbourn, and the matinee idol outfielder Mike "King" Kelly became the game's early superstars, while the game continued to tinker with its rules—initially eight balls constituted a walk, then seven, then six, then four. The league settled on three strikes as an out and permitted pitchers to deliver the ball overhand.

The game's popularity made it an attractive business venture. The National League owners fought off several competing leagues and maintained strict control over the players. But in 1901 one competing circuit, the American League, offered players greater freedom of movement among the other clubs, and grew into a rival that the National League could not vanquish. So a settlement was worked out whereby owners in both leagues agreed not to raid each other's talent and to honor the reserve clause, which bound players to teams in perpetuity. By 1903 the first World Series between the two leagues was played.

In 1908 a commission was formed to determine the true origins of baseball and a myth was born: that Abner Doubleday of Cooperstown, N.Y., drew up the rules and dimensions of play on a sandlot in that town. The apocryphal story made baseball a totally American game, quite in contrast to its international roots.

Dead Ball and Scandal: 1901–1920

With the two eight-team leagues in agreement, baseball flourished. New stars emerged—Ty Cobb as a base-thief and expert hitter, Cy Young and Christy Mathewson as scintillating pitchers, Nap Lajoie and Eddie Collins as hard-hitting second basemen. The use of gloves brought defensive stars to the fore, like Boston's third baseman

Jimmy Collins. Colorful owners and managers, from the White Sox's penny-pinching Charles Comiskey to Philadelphia's austere Connie Mack to the swaggering New York Giant John McGraw, gave the game great character and provided theater and vituperation for hungry sportswriters. The appearance of box scores in daily newspapers helped spread the excitement across the land, as fans could track more easily how their teams were doing.

The game, however, seemed to belong to the pitchers, as fewer and fewer runs were scored. The owners began to fear that the public would lose interest; the ball was livened in 1912; the spitball, a pitch that used the deceptive properties of saliva, was outlawed in 1920, after Cleveland shortstop Ray Chapman was hit in the temple and killed by a pitch from New York Yankee Carl Mays.

But what nearly derailed baseball was not low run production or a fatal injury but a betting scandal that rocked the country. In 1919 eight members of the Chicago White Sox (forever known as "The Black Sox") were involved in a scheme concocted by a New York gambler named Arnold Rothstein to throw the World Series to the underdog Cincinnati Reds. In the end, the baseball owners, worried about the integrity of the game, hired a commissioner, Judge Kenesaw Mountain Landis. His first action was to banish from the game, for life, all eight of the Chicago players, one of whom, Shoeless Joe Jackson, was one of the greatest players of all time.

Baseball was back on safe moral ground, and a young slugger named George Herman "Babe" Ruth revitalized and revolutionized the sport with his prodigious home runs and huge personality. After leading his Boston Red Sox to a World Series victory in 1918 on the strength of both his pitching and hitting, Ruth was sold to the rival Yankees for cash and a line of credit by Red Sox owner Harry Frazee. In his first year as a Yankee, Ruth reached theretofore unimaginable heights, knocking 54 home runs, more than any other team in the league that year and 35 more than runner-up George Sisler. Ruth gave up pitching, and the Yankees built a house for him—Yankee Stadium. Radio broadcasts—the first of which was heard on Pittsburgh's KDKA radio in 1922—helped baseball capitalize on the game's newfound integrity and its larger-than-life superhero. In 1927 Ruth hit 60 home runs, a record that would stand for 34 years.

War, Growth, and Stability: 1920–1960

Baseball remained constant for decades, with the same 16 teams divided into two leagues.

American League: Boston Red Sox, Chicago White Sox, Cleveland Indians, Detroit Tigers, New York Yankees, Philadelphia Athletics, St. Louis Browns, Washington Senators.

National League: Boston Braves, Brooklyn Dodgers, Chicago Cubs, Cincinnati Reds, New York Giants, Philadelphia Phillies, Pittsburgh Pirates, St. Louis Cardinals.

The New York Yankees dominated baseball through this era, producing a seemingly endless succession of great players—Ruth, Lou Gehrig, Joe DiMaggio, Mickey Mantle. The game weathered the Depression in the 1930's and in 1939 the National Baseball Hall of Fame was founded in the game's mythical birthplace, Cooperstown, N.Y. Inducted in the first class were Ty Cobb, Honus Wagner, Walter Johnson, Babe Ruth, and Christy Mathewson. In 1941 DiMaggio mesmerized the country with a 56-game hitting streak; by season's end, the era's other great hitter, Boston's Ted Williams, finished the year with a .406 batting average, connecting for four hits on the last day of the season. Williams remains the last player to hit over .400 over a full season.

Many players left the sport to serve in the military during World War II. In 1942 President Roosevelt specifically approved baseball's continuance during the war in a "green light" letter to Commissioner Landis. So weakened was the league, however, that the lowly St. Louis Browns made their only World Series appearance (a loss) in 1944. When the war was over, the economy began to boom, the stars came back, and baseball returned to its pinnacle.

With President Truman having desegregated the armed forces toward the end of the war, it was only a matter of time before baseball also ended its exclusionary racial policy. In 1947 Jackie Robinson, a college-educated four-star athlete from California, broke the color barrier by taking the field for the Brooklyn Dodgers. Robinson was followed by other black stars, including Larry Doby, Don Newcombe, Roy Campanella, and one of the greatest players of all time, Willie Mays. Soon after, the game opened to Latin American players as well, further broadening the appeal of baseball.

One victim of the racial integration of baseball, however, was what were known then as the "Negro Leagues," which operated in more than two dozen cities from around 1920 to about 1950. The Kansas City Monarchs, the Chicago American Giants, and the Detroit Stars were among the most successful teams, and the exploits of many players—Josh Gibson, Buck Leonard, Oscar

Charleston, Cool Papa Bell, and Ray Dandridge—earned them induction into the Hall of Fame. But attendance slumped badly when young Negro League stars, such as the Birmingham Black Barons's Willie Mays, began signing major league contracts. Baseball was becoming America's game.

Television began to appear in many American homes in the 1950's, and baseball looked for ways to either protect itself from the new technology or profit by it. Television as well as air travel made the country smaller, and baseball, which since its inception had never been played professionally west of St. Louis, expanded in 1958, when the Dodgers and the New York Giants moved to California. The Yankees continued their dominance on the field, racking up 25 American League pennants and 18 World Series titles between 1921 and 1960.

Expansion and Labor Unrest: 1961–1980

The 16-team major leagues expanded to 18 for the 1961 season with the addition of the Los Angeles Angels and the new Washington Senators (who replaced the old Senators, who had moved to Minnesota to become the Twins). As a result, the regular season was extended from 154 to 162 games. Roger Maris of the Yankees hit his 61st home run on the last day of the 1961 season to break Ruth's record, a feat that earned Maris a place in the record book with an asterisk (since removed) explaining the longer season. Two more teams—the New York Mets and the Houston Colt .45s—joined the majors in 1962. That year the Mets, under legendary manager Casey Stengel, who earlier steered the Yankees to 10 pennants in 12 years, set a new record for futility by going 40-120 in their debut season. Seven years later, with the crosstown Yankees falling on hard times, the "Miracle" Mets won the World Series in an upset of the powerful Baltimore Orioles.

In the 1970's two mini-dynasties emerged, one in each league. The brash, young Oakland A's, with slugger Reggie Jackson, pitchers Catfish Hunter, Blue Moon Odom, and Vida Blue, won three consecutive World Series early in the decade, and were followed by Cincinnati's Big Red Machine, led by catcher Johnny Bench and second baseman Joe Morgan. In 1973 the American League, in an effort to boost attendance, instituted the designated hitter rule, which allowed another person to hit in the pitcher's place.

End of the Reserve Clause It was also a period of player unrest. Because of the reserve clause, players had no freedom to seek a more profitable position with another team. An outfielder named Curt Flood, frustrated by an unwanted trade from St. Louis to Philadelphia, filed suit against baseball in 1970, alleging that baseball violated antitrust laws. The courts sided with management, but the victory was short-lived. A's pitcher Jim "Catfish" Hunter, after a falling-out with owner Charlie Finley, became baseball's first free agent, so declared by an independent arbitrator. The nascent player's union watched intently as a player at the peak of his abilities offered his services to the highest bidder, something that had been prohibited previously by the reserve clause. Hunter signed with the Yankees (headed by new owner George Steinbrenner) for five years and $3.75 million. The next year, 1976, the same arbitrator ruled in favor of two more players, Dave McNally and Andy Messersmith. These steps opened the way for free agency to be negotiated as a part of the collective bargaining agreement. Salaries for players began to skyrocket.

Free Agency, Records, and Internationalization: 1980–2004

With free agency came increases in salaries and hard-fought labor battles between owners and players, with strikes or lockouts marking the end of almost every collective bargaining agreement. The movement of free agents to the highest bidder raised the issue of competitive imbalance. The "large market" teams that could afford more, better players were in danger of overwhelming the "small market" teams.

Because of labor strife, the last seven weeks of the 1994 season and post-season was cancelled. It was the first year without a World Series since 1904. As the influx of money from television and licensing rights continued, baseball expanded. Following the addition of teams in 1994 and 1998, there are currently 30 major league teams. As the talent spread more thinly, records began to fall, and in 1998 Mark McGwire of the St. Louis Cardinals broke Roger Maris's record by slugging 70 home runs. San Francisco Giants outfielder Barry Bonds hit 73 home runs three years later.

The Yankees returned to dominance in the late 1990's under the managerial hand of Joe Torre and a stable of quality pitchers. In the National League, the Atlanta Braves won 12 straight division titles but only one World Series. In the late 1990's the game's popularity abroad began to register in the States—accomplished Japanese players Hideo Nomo, Ichiro Suzuki, and Hideki Matsui signed lucrative contracts to play for American teams. Regular season games were played in Mexico, Japan, and Puerto Rico as ownership began to market the sport more aggressively. In 2002 a long-dreaded contract negotiation was worked out between the owners and the player's union with no stoppage of play. In the 2003 season, Barry Bonds won an unprecedented sixth Most Valuable Player award.

With the issues of competitive imbalance still being debated, baseball entered the 2004 season with several franchises in deep financial trouble—Milwaukee and Montreal among them. Concerns were also growing that performance-enhancing drugs and nutritional supplements were harming the game's integrity and possibly the health of its participants.

Rules of the Game

Although bookshelves groan with the weight of volumes analyzing baseball strategy, *The Official Baseball Rules*, in paragraphs 1.01-1.03, define the game and its objectives plainly:

1.01. Baseball is a game between two teams of nine players each, under the direction of a manager, played on an enclosed field under jurisdiction of one or more umpires.

1.02. The objective of each team is to win by scoring more runs than the opponent.

1.03. The winner of the game shall be that team which shall have scored the greater number of runs at the conclusion of a regulation game.

The Playing Field The infield is a 90-foot square and the outfield is the area formed by extending two foul lines radiating left and right from one corner of the square, which is home base. The other bases, first, second, and third, occupy the three other corners of the square (called a "diamond") and the are ordered counterclockwise. Batters at home plate attempt to hit the offering of the opposition pitcher, who stands 60 feet six inches away and throws the ball in an attempt to make the batter swing and miss or hit the ball to one of the pitcher's eight supporting defenders, including his catcher, who is positioned behind home plate to receive the pitches. Home plate is a five-sided white rubber surface set flush to the ground 17 inches wide and 17 inches long, with the two back corners removed so that the plate comes to a point. The defensive positions, in addition to the pitcher and catcher, are four infielders (at first, second, and third bases, and one between second and third base, called a shortstop) and three outfielders, usually spaced equally apart in what are called left, center, and right fields.

Balls, Strikes, Outs Pitches that the umpire deems have passed over home plate and at a height between the batter's knees and upper chest are considered hittable and will be called a strike if the batter does not swing. Three strikes, whether called so by the umpire or swung at and missed or fouled off by the batter, constitute an out. Four pitches out of the strike zone and not swung at are called balls, and earn the batter a free pass to first base. Balls hit into the air and caught before hitting the ground are outs, as are balls hit on the ground that are relayed to a base before the batter/runner arrives. Three outs per team per try (or half inning), and the teams switch sides for the completion of the inning

Running the Bases Runs are scored when a player progresses safely from home to first, second, and third and back to home. Runners trying to get to first base can be called out if the ball reaches a defensive player who is touching the base before they arrive. At second, third, and at home plate, runners have to be tagged out by the defender with the ball or a glove with the ball in it, unless there are runners on all the bases behind the lead runner, in which case a forceout is applicable—merely touching the base before the runner's arrival will suffice. A regulation game is nine innings; if the score is tied, extra innings will be played until one team has the advantage in runs. In the event of inclement weather, a minimum of five innings can constitute a complete game.

On the Field Today In today's game, there are usually four umpires, and team rosters consist of 25 players, including, on average, 10 pitchers. The nine players who start a game assume one of the aforementioned nine defensive positions and, on offense, bat in a specified order. In the American League, since 1973, the pitcher does not bat, but is replaced in the lineup by a designated hitter, who does not play the field.

Baseball Hall of Fame

Player/Position/Year Inducted	Games	At Bats	HRs	Avg.	Hits	RBIs
Aaron, Henry (Hank) OF 1982 *All-time leader in home runs and RBI*	3,298	12,364	755	.305	3,771	2,297
Anson, Adrian (Cap) 1B 1939 *Managed 20 years, 1879-98, winning five pennants*	2,523	10,278	97	.333	3,418	2,076
Aparicio, Luis SS 1984 *Led AL in stolen bases nine years in a row (1955-64)*	2,599	10,230	83	.262	2,677	791
Appling, Luke SS 1964 *Batted .388 in 1936*	2,422	8,857	45	.310	2,749	1,116
Ashburn, Richie OF 1995 *Hit .300 or more nine times*	2,189	8,365	29	.308	2,574	586
Averill, Earl OF 1975 *232 hits in 1936*	1,669	6,358	238	.318	2,020	1,165
Baker, Frank (Home Run) 3B 1955 *Batted .363 in six World Series*	1,575	5,985	96	.307	1,838	1,013
Bancroft, Dave SS 1971 *Handled 984 chances in 1922*	1,913	7,182	32	.279	2,004	591
Banks, Ernie SS, 1B 1977 *Consecutive M.V.P. awards, 1958-59*	2,528	9,421	512	.274	2,583	1,636
Beckley, Jake 1B 1971 *244 career triples, mostly in 19th century*	2,386	9,527	88	.308	2,931	1,575
Bench, Johnny C 1989 *Hit .529 in 1976 World Series; NL M.V.P. 1970, 1972*	2,158	7,658	389	.267	2,048	1,376
Berra, Lawrence (Yogi) C, OF 1972 *Three M.V.P. awards, 1951, 1954, 1955*	2,120	7,555	358	.285	2,150	1,430
Bottomley, Jim 1B 1974 *12 RBI in one game, 1924*	1,991	7,471	219	.310	2,313	1,422
Boudreau, Lou SS 1970 *M.V.P. in 1948; managed 16 years*	1,646	6,030	68	.295	1,779	789
Bresnahan, Roger C, OF 1945 *212 stolen bases; first catcher elected to Hall of Fame*	1,430	4,478	26	.279	1,251	530
Brett, George 3B, 1B 1999 *Hit .300 11 times; 13-time all-star; hit .390 in 1980*	2,707	10,349	317	.305	3,154	1,595
Brock, Lou OF 1985 *938 stolen bases; batted .391 in three World Series*	2,616	10,332	149	.293	3,023	900
Brouthers, Dan 1B 1945 *Seven slugging and five batting titles during 19th century*	1,673	6,711	106	.342	2,296	1,296
Burkett, Jesse OF 1946 *Led NL in batting three times and in hits four times*	2,072	8,430	75	.341	2,873	952
Campanella, Roy C 1969 *Three M.V.P. awards, 1951, 1953, 1955*	1,215	4,205	242	.276	1,161	856
Carey, Max OF 1961 *738 stolen bases*	2,476	9,363	70	.285	2,665	800
Carter, Gary C 2003 *11-time All-Star (1975, 1979-88); won three gold gloves*	2,296	7,971	324	.262	2,092	1,225
Cepeda, Orlando 1B 1999 *Seven-time All-star; NL M.V.P. 1967; .499 career slugging percentage*	2,124	7,927	379	.297	2,351	1,365

Player/Position/Year Inducted	Games	At Bats	HRs	Avg.	Hits	RBIs
Chance, Frank 1B 1946 *Managed Chicago (NL) to four pennants in five years, 1906–10*	1,286	4,295	20	.297	1,274	596
Clarke, Fred OF 1945 *223 career triples, hit .300 or better 11 times*	2,245	8,588	67	.315	2,708	1,015
Clemente, Roberto OF 1973 *Career average of over 18 outfield assists per season*	2,433	9,454	240	.317	3,000	1,305
Cobb, Ty OF 1936 *Batted .320 or better in 23 straight years*	3,035	11,429	117	.367	4,191	1,938
Cochrane, Mickey C 1947 *Two M.V.P. awards, 1928 and 1934*	1,482	5,169	119	.320	1,652	832
Collins, Eddie 2B 1939 *Hit .340 or better 10 times; led AL in fielding nine times*	2,826	9,949	47	.333	3,315	1,300
Collins, Jimmy 3B 1945 *Led NL in home runs, 1898*	1,728	6,796	64	.294	1,997	982
Combs, Earle OF 1970 *Averaged 127 runs scored per season*	1,454	5,748	58	.325	1,866	629
Connor, Roger 1B 1976 *Held all-time HR record before Babe Ruth*	1,998	7,798	136	.318	2,480	1,078
Crawford, Sam OF 1957 *312 triples, best ever*	2,517	9,580	97	.309	2,964	1,525
Cronin, Joe SS 1956 *M.V.P. in 1930; managed 1933–47*	2,124	7,579	170	.301	2,285	1,424
Cuyler, Hazen (Kiki) OF 1968 *Led NL in runs scored twice, stolen bases four times*	1,879	7,161	127	.321	2,299	1,065
Davis, George SS 1998 *Hit over .300 nine years in a row (1893–1901)*	2,376	9,035	73	.295	2,665	1,435
Delahanty, Ed IF, OF 1945 *Batted .410 in 1899*	1,835	7,505	101	.346	2,596	1,464
Dickey, Bill C 1954 *Catcher on eight AL-pennant-winning teams*	1,789	6,300	202	.313	1,969	1,209
DiMaggio, Joe OF 1955 *56 game hitting streak in 1941*	1,736	6,821	361	.325	2,214	1,537
Doby, Larry, OF 1998 *Led AL in HR twice; seven-time all-star (1949–55); first black man to play in AL*	1,533	5,348	253	.283	1,515	969
Doerr, Bobby 2B 1986 *Led AL in slugging 1944*	1,865	7,093	223	.288	2,042	1,247
Duffy, Hugh OF 1945 *Batted .438 in 1894*	1,736	7,062	103	.328	2,314	1,299
Evers, Johnny 2B 1946 *NL M.V.P. in 1914*	1,783	6,134	12	.270	1,658	538
Ewing, Buck C, IF, OF 1939 *Regarded as the greatest player of the 19th century*	1,315	5,363	70	.303	1,625	733
Ferrell, Rick C 1984 *Led AL catchers at times in putouts, assists, fielding average, and double plays*	1,884	6,028	28	.281	1,692	734
Fisk, Carlton C 2000 *Hit 20 or more home runs 8 times*	2,499	8,756	376	.269	2,356	1,330
Flick, Elmer OF 1963 *Led AL in triples 1905-07*	1,484	5,603	47	.315	1,767	756

Player/Position/Year Inducted	Games	At Bats	HRs	Avg.	Hits	RBIs
Fox, Nellie 2B 1997 *Led AL in putouts, 1951-60*	2,367	9,232	35	.288	2,663	790
Foxx, Jimmie 1B, 3B 1951 *Slugged over .700 three seasons*	2,317	8,134	534	.325	2,646	1,921
Frisch, Frank 2B, 3B 1947 *Hit .300 or better 11 years in a row (1921–31)*	2,311	9,112	105	.316	2,880	1,244
Gehrig, Lou 1B 1939 *Played in 2,130 consecutive games; first player to hit 4 HRs in one game*	2,164	8,001	493	.340	2,721	1,990
Gehringer, Charlie 2B 1949 *60 doubles in 1936*	2,323	8,860	184	.320	2,839	1,427
Goslin, Leon (Goose) OF 1968 *100+ RBI 11 years*	2,287	8,655	248	.316	2,735	1,609
Greenberg, Hank 1B 1956 *58 home runs in 1938; 63 doubles in 1934*	1,394	5,193	331	.313	1,628	1,276
Hafey, Charles (Chick) OF 1971 *NL batting title (.349) in 1931*	1,283	4,625	164	.317	1,466	833
Hamilton, Billy OF 1961 *Scored 196 runs in 1894, with a .509 on-base average and 99 stolen bases*	1,591	6,269	40	.344	2,159	739
Hartnett, Charles (Gabby) C 1955 *Played on four NL pennant winners, managed one*	1,990	6,432	236	.297	1,912	1,179
Heilmann, Harry OF, 1B 1952 *Batted .403 in 1923*	2,147	7,787	183	.342	2,660	1,539
Herman, Billy 2B 1975 *57 doubles in 1935*	1,922	7,707	47	.304	2,345	839
Hooper, Harry OF 1971 *375 career stolen bases*	2,308	8,785	75	.281	2,466	817
Hornsby, Rogers 2B, IF 1942 *Batted .424 in 1924; nine slugging titles*	2,259	8,173	301	.358	2,930	1,584
Jackson, Reggie 1993 *Played in 5 World Series and 11 divisional playoffs in 21 years; World Series M.V.P. 1977*	2,820	9,864	563	.262	2,584	1,702
Jackson, Travis SS 1982 *Batted over .300 six times in 1920's and 1930's*	1,656	6,086	135	.291	1,768	929
Jennings, Hugh SS 1945 *Batted .398 in 1896*	1,285	4,905	18	.312	1,531	840
Kaline, Al OF 1980 *3,007 career hits*	2,834	10,116	399	.297	3,007	1,583
Keeler, Willie OF 1939 *Batted .424 in 1897; 495 career stolen bases*	2,123	8,591	33	.341	2,932	810
Kell, George 3B 1983 *AL batting champ (.343) in 1949*	1,795	6,702	78	.306	2,054	870
Kelley, Joe OF 1971 *Averaged 151 runs scored, 1894–96*	1,845	7,018	65	.319	2,242	1,193
Kelly, George 1B 1973 *Led NL in RBI, 1920 and 1925*	1,622	5,993	148	.297	1,778	1,020
Kelly, Mike (King) OF, C 1945 *Two batting titles, 1884 and 1886; 315 career stolen bases*	1,463	5,923	69	.307	1,820	794
Killebrew, Harmon 1B, 3B, OF 1984 *40+ home runs eight years*	2,435	8,147	573	.256	2,086	1,584

Player/Position/Year Inducted	Games	At Bats	HRs	Avg.	Hits	RBIs
Kiner, Ralph OF 1975 *Second highest home run per at bat ratio of all-time*	1,472	5,205	369	.279	1,451	1,015
Klein, Chuck OF 1980 *44 outfield assists in 1930*	1,753	6,486	300	.320	2,076	1,201
Lajoie, Napoleon 2B 1937 *Batted .422 in 1901*	2,480	9,589	82	.338	3,242	1,599
Lazerri, Tony IF 1991 *Batted .300 or better five times; clutch hitter in World Series*	1,740	6,297	178	.292	1,840	1,191
Lindstrom, Fred 3B, OF 1976 *231 hits in 1928*	1,438	5,611	103	.311	1,747	779
Lombardi, Ernie C 1986 *Two NL batting titles, 1938 and 1942*	1,853	5,855	190	.306	1,792	990
Mantle, Mickey OF 1974 *52 home runs in 1956, 54 in 1961*	2,401	8,102	536	.298	2,415	1,509
Manush, Heinie OF 1964 *Hit .378 in 1926*	2,009	7,653	110	.330	2,524	1,173
Maranville, Rabbit SS, 2B 1954 *23-year career; hit .308 in two World Series*	2,670	10,078	28	.258	2,605	884
Mathews, Eddie 3B 1978 *1,444 career walks*	2,388	8,537	512	.271	2,315	1,453
Mays, Willie OF 1979 *Slugged over .600 six seasons*	2,992	10,881	660	.302	3,283	1,903
Mazeroski, Bill 2B 2001 *Eight-time gold glove winner. Turned a record 1,706 double plays.*	2,163	7,755	138	.260	2,016	853
McCarthy, Tommy OF 1946 *Averaged 122 runs scored, 1888-94*	1,275	5,128	44	.292	1,496	666
McCovey, Willie 1B, OF 1986 *Hit 18 career grand slams*	2,588	8,197	521	.270	2,211	1,555
McPhee, Bid 2B 2000 *Considered greatest second baseman of the 19th century, though he played without a glove*	2,135	8,291	53	.279	2,250	727
Medwick, Joe OF 1968 *Won NL triple crown in 1937*	1,984	7,635	205	.324	2,471	1,383
Mize, Johnny 1B 1981 *Four-time NL home run champ*	1,884	6,443	359	.312	2,011	1,337
Molitor, Paul DH 2004 *Seven-time All-Star; 1993 World Series M.V.P.*	2,683	10,835	234	.306	3,319	1,307
Morgan, Joe 2B 1990 *Won back-to-back M.V.P. Awards (1975–76)*	2,649	9,277	268	.271	2,517	1,133
Murray, Eddie 1B 2003 *Third player ever with 3,000 hits and 500 HRs*	3,026	11,336	504	.287	3,255	1,917
Musial, Stan OF, 1B 1969 *725 doubles and 177 triples*	3,026	10,972	475	.331	3,630	1,951
O'Rourke, Jim OF 1945 *Batted .300+ eleven times in the 19th century*	1,774	7,435	51	.310	2,304	830
Ott, Mel OF 1951 *Averaged 121 RBI 1929-38*	2,732	9,456	511	.304	2,876	1,860
Perez, Tony 1B 2000 *His 1,652 RBIs are the most ever by a Latin player.*	2,777	9,778	379	.279	2,732	1,652

Player/Position/Year Inducted	Games	At Bats	HRs	Avg.	Hits	RBIs
Puckett, Kirby OF 2001	1,783	7,244	207	.318	2,304	1,085
Led Minnesota Twins to World Series wins in 1987 and 1991.						
Reese, Harold (Pee Wee) SS 1984	2,166	8,058	126	.269	2,170	885
Finished in the top ten of M.V.P. balloting nine times						
Rice, Sam OF 1963	2,404	9,269	34	.322	2,987	1,078
Only 18 strikeouts per 154 games						
Rizzuto, Phil SS 1994	1,661	5,816	38	.273	1,588	563
AL M.V.P. in 1950; Played in 9 World Series						
Robinson, Brooks 3B 1983	2,896	10,654	268	.267	2,848	1357
16 consecutive Gold Gloves, 1960-75						
Robinson, Frank OF 1982	2,808	10,006	586	.294	2,943	1812
M.V.P. in both leagues; AL triple crown in 1966						
Robinson, Jackie 2B 1962	1,382	4,877	137	.311	1,518	734
First black player in MLB; Rookie of the Year 1947; M.V.P. and batting champ, 1949						
Roush, Edd OF 1962	1,967	7,363	68	.323	2,376	981
Two NL batting titles, 1917 and 1919						
Ruth, George (Babe) OF, P 1936	2,503	8,399	714	.342	2,873	2211
Slugged .847 1920-21						
Schalk, Ray C 1955	1,760	5,306	12	.253	1,345	594
176 stolen bases						
Schmidt, Mike 3B 1995	2,404	8,352	548	.267	2,234	1,595
Led NL in homers 8 times; won 10 Gold Gloves						
Schoendienst, Albert (Red) 1989	2,216	8,479	84	.289	2,449	773
Managed Cardinals to two pennants and 1967 World Series crown						
Sewell, Joe SS, 3B 1977	1,902	7,132	49	.312	2,226	1,051
Only 22 strikeouts in his last 2,500 at bats, 1929–33						
Simmons, Al OF 1953	2,215	8,761	307	.334	2,927	1,827
Drove in over 100 runs in each of his first 11 years, 1924–34						
Sisler, George 1B 1939	2,055	8,267	100	.340	2,812	1,175
Batted .400 1920-22						
Slaughter, Enos OF 1985	2,380	7,946	169	.300	2,383	1,304
52 doubles in 1939						
Smith, Ozzie SS 2002	2,573	9,396	28	.262	2,460	793
Won 13 Gold Gloves; 15-time All-Star						
Snider, Edwin (Duke) OF 1980	2,143	7,161	407	.295	2,116	1,333
Averaged 41 home runs, 1953-57						
Speaker, Tris OF 1937	2,789	10,195	117	.345	3,514	1,529
Led AL in doubles eight times						
Stargell, Willie OF, 1B 1988	2,360	7,927	475	.282	2,232	1,540
National League M.V.P. in 1979						
Terry, Bill 1B 1954	1,721	6,428	154	.341	2,193	1,078
Hit .401 in 1930						
Thompson, Sam OF 1974	1,410	6,005	128	.331	1,986	1,299
166 RBI in 1887, 165 in 1895						
Tinker, Joe SS 1946	1,805	6,441	31	.263	1,695	782
Played in four World Series with Chicago Cubs						
Traynor, Pie 3B 1948	1,941	7,559	58	.320	2,416	1,273
100+ RBI seven years						

Player/Position/Year Inducted	Games	At Bats	HRs	Avg.	Hits	RBIs
Vaughan, Joseph (Arky) SS 1985 *Hit .385 in 1935*	1,817	6,622	96	.318	2,103	926
Wagner, Honus SS 1936 *Eight batting titles, four in a row 1906–09*	2786	10,427	101	.329	3,430	1,732
Wallace, Bobby SS 1953 *Handled 6.1 chances per game at shortstop*	2,386	8,652	35	.267	2,314	1,121
Waner, Lloyd OF 1967 *234 hits in 1929*	1,992	7,772	28	.316	2,459	598
Waner, Paul OF 1952 *62 doubles in 1932*	2,549	9,459	112	.333	3,152	1,309
Wheat, Zack OF 1959 *Batted .375 at age 36 in 1924*	2,410	9,106	132	.317	2,884	1,261
Williams, Billy OF 1987 *30+ home runs in five seasons*	2,488	9,350	426	.290	2,711	1,475
Williams, Ted OF 1966 *Last .400 hitter in majors, .406 in 1941*	2,292	7,706	521	.344	2,654	1,839
Wilson, Lewis (Hack) OF 1979 *56 home runs and 190 RBI in 1930*	1,348	[illegible]	244	.307	1,461	1,062
Winfield, Dave OF 2001 *Member of both the 3,000-hit and 400-home run club.*	2,973	11,003	465	.283	3,110	1,833
Yastrzemski, Carl (Yaz) OF, 1B 1989 *Won Triple Crown in 1967; won batting titles in 1963, 1967, and 1968*	3,308	11,988	452	.285	3,419	1,844
Youngs, Ross OF 1972 *Killed at age 30; .398 on-base average in four World Series, 1921–24*	1,211	4,627	42	.322	1,491	592
Yount, Robin SS, OF 1999 *The only player ever to win AL M.V.P. awards at shortstop (1982) and center field (1989).*	2,856	11,008	251	.285	3,142	1,406

Hall of Fame Pitchers

Player/Year Inducted	W	L	ERA	Games	Innings	Strikeouts
Alexander, Grover Cleveland 1938 *Won 30 games three years; led NL in ERA five times*	373	208	2.56	696	5,190	2,198
Bender, Charles (Chief) 1953 *Led AL in winning percentage three seasons*	210	127	2.46	459	3,017	1,711
Brown, Mordecai (Three-Finger) 1949 *1.04 ERA in 1906*	239	130	2.06	481	3,172	1,375
Bunning, Jim 1996 *Struck out 1,000 batters in each league*	224	184	3.27	591	3,760	2,855
Carlton, Steve (Lefty) 1994 *Four-time Cy Young Award winner (1972, 1977, 1980, 1982)*	329	244	3.22	741	5,217	4,136
Chesbro, Jack 1946 *41 wins in 1904*	198	132	2.68	392	2,897	1,265
Clarkson, John 1963 *53 wins in 1885, with 623 innings pitched*	326	177	2.81	531	4,536	2,015
Coveleski, Stan 1969 *Led AL in ERA in 1925, 2.84*	215	142	2.88	450	3,093	981
Cummings, Williams (Candy) 1939 *Inventor of the curveball*	21	22	2.78	43	372	37

Player/Year Inducted	W	L	ERA	Games	Innings	Strikeouts
Dean, Jay (Dizzy) 1953 *30 wins in 1934*	150	83	3.03	317	1,966	1,155
Drysdale, Don 1984 *56 2/3 consecutive scoreless innings, 1968*	209	166	2.95	518	3,432	2,486
Eckersley, Dennis 2004 *Only pitcher with 100 complete games and 100 saves*	197	171	3.50	1,071	3,286	2,401
Faber, Urban (Red) 1964 *Led AL in ERA in 1921 and 1922*	254	212	3.15	669	4,088	1,471
Feller, Bob 1962 *Led AL in wins six times, in shutouts seven*	266	162	3.25	570	3,827	2,581
Fingers, Rollie 1992 *341 saves over 17 years; AL M.V.P. in 1981*	114	118	2.90	944	1,701	1,299
Ford, Edward (Whitey) 1974 *25–4 in 1961, 24–7 in 1963*	236	106	2.75	498	3,170	1,956
Galvin, James (Pud) 1965 *46 wins in 1883 and 1884*	365	310	2.85	705	6,003	1,807
Gibson, Bob 1981 *1.12 ERA in 1968, seven straight wins in World Series play*	251	174	2.91	528	3,885	3,117
Gomez, Vernon (Lefty) 1972 *Led AL in shutouts three years*	189	102	3.34	368	2,503	1,468
Grimes, Burleigh 1964 *Last legal spitball pitcher, he won 20+ five times*	270	212	3.53	617	4,180	1,512
Grove, Robert (Lefty) 1947 *Led AL in ERA nine times, in strikeouts seven*	300	141	3.06	616	3,941	2,266
Haines, Jesse 1970 *Twice led NL in shutouts, 1921 and 1927*	210	158	3.64	555	3,209	981
Hoyt, Waite 1969 *1.83 in 84 World Series innings*	237	182	3.59	674	3,763	1,206
Hubbell, Carl 1947 *26–6 in 1936; 1.66 ERA in 1933*	253	154	2.97	535	3,589	1,678
Hunter, Jim (Catfish) 1987 *21 or more wins, 1971–75*	224	166	3.26	500	3,448	2,012
Jenkins, Ferguson 1991 *Cy Young Award winner in 1971; three-time all-star*	284	226	3.34	664	4,499	3,192
Johnson, Walter 1936 *36-7, 1.14 ERA in 1913*	417	279	2.17	802	5,914	3,508
Joss, Addie 1978 *Averaged 21–11, 1.66 ERA in years 1904–08*	160	97	1.89	286	2,327	920
Keefe, Tim 1964 *Averaged 37 wins 1883–85*	342	225	2.62	600	5,049	2,564
Koufax, Sandy 1972 *95–27, 1.85 ERA for seasons 1963-66*	165	87	2.76	397	2,324	2,396
Lemon, Bob 1976 *Won 20 or more seven times*	207	128	3.23	460	2,850	1,277
Lyons, Ted 1955 *Pitched 27 shutouts, but never won 20 games*	260	230	3.67	594	4,161	1,073
Marichal, Juan 1983 *Only 1.8 walks per nine innings over career*	243	142	2.89	471	3,509	2,303
Marquard, Richard (Rube) 1971 *73–23 in years 1911–13*	201	177	3.08	536	3,307	1,593
Mathewson, Christy 1936 *79 career shutouts*	373	188	2.13	635	4,780	2,502

Player/Year Inducted	W	L	ERA	Games	Innings	Strikeouts
McGinnity, Joe 1946	247	144	2.64	466	3,459	1,068
35–8 in 1904, with an ERA of 1.61						
Newhouser, Hal 1992	207	150	3.06	488	2,993	1,796
Led AL in victories three years in a row (1944–46)						
Nichols, Charles (Kid) 1949	361	208	2.95	620	5,056	1,873
Won 30 or more games seven times, 1891-94, 1896-98						
Niekro, Phil 1997	318	274	3.35	864	5,404	3,342
Knuckleballer pitched until age 48; five-time all-star						
Palmer, Jim 1990	268	152	2.86	558	3,948	2,212
Won Cy Young Award 1973, 1975, 1976						
Pennock, Herb 1948	240	162	3.61	617	3,558	1,227
162–90 as a New York Yankee, 1923–33						
Perry, Gaylord 1991	314	265	3.10	777	5,352	3,534
Won Cy Young Award in both leagues						
Plank, Eddie 1946	326	194	2.35	623	4,496	2,246
1.32 ERA in seven World Series games						
Radbourn, Charles (Old Hoss) 1939	309	195	2.67	528	4,535	1,830
60–12 in 1884, with 679 innings pitched						
Rixey, Eppa 1963	266	251	3.15	692	4,495	1,350
Won 25 games in 1922						
Roberts, Robin 1976	286	245	3.41	676	4,689	2,357
28–7 in 1952; five-time NL leader in complete games						
Ruffing, Charles (Red) 1967	273	225	3.80	624	4,344	1,987
.645 winning percentage as a New York Yankee						
Rusie, Amos 1977	243	160	3.07	462	3,770	1,957
Won 30+ games three years						
Ryan, Nolan 1999	324	292	3.19	807	5,386	5,714
Threw seven no-hitters; struck out 300 or more six times; struck out 200 or more 15 times						
Seaver, Tom 1992	311	205	2.86	656	4,782	3,640
Won 20 or more games five times; won Cy Young Award 1969, 1973, 1975						
Spahn, Warren 1973	363	245	3.09	750	5,244	2,583
Won 20 or more games 13 times, including 23 at age 42						
Sutton, Don 1998	324	256	3.26	774	5,280	3,574
Won 15 or more games eight years in a row (1969–76)						
Vance, Clarence (Dazzy) 1955	197	140	3.24	442	2,697	2,045
60–15 over two years—1924, 1925						
Waddell, George (Rube) 1946	193	143	2.16	407	2,961	2,316
349 strikeouts in 1904						
Walsh, Ed 1946	195	126	1.82	430	2,964	1,736
40–15 in 1908 with 11 shutouts; all-time ERA leader						
Ward, Monte 1964	161	101	2.10	291	2,462	920
47 wins in 1879; 40 wins in 1880; played 1,825 games as a hitter						
Welch, Mickey 1973	307	210	2.71	565	4,802	1,850
44–11 in 1885						
Wilhelm, Hoyt 1985	143	122	2.52	1070	2,254	1,610
227 career saves; first relief pitcher elected to Hall of Fame						
Willis, Vic 1995	249	205	2.63	513	3,996	1,651
Won 20 games eight times; 45 complete games in 1902						
Wynn, Early 1972	300	244	3.54	691	4,564	2,334
Led AL in shutouts at age 40 in 1960						
Young, Cy 1937	511	313	2.63	906	7,359	2,799
All-time leader in wins, losses, complete games, and innings pitched.						

Glossary of Baseball Terms

all-star a player chosen, either by fan vote or by a manager, to play on a roster representing his league against the opposing league in an exhibition game played at the mid-season break in July.

backstop a screen behind home plate that protects spectators from being hit by errant pitches or foul balls; also a synonym for the catcher.

balk a motion by the pitcher deemed by an umpire to be an illegal attempt to deceive a baserunner; when a balk is called, the ball is dead and all base runners advance to the next base.

box the rectangle in which the batter stands—batter's box; or the area fielded by the pitcher, as when a pitch is hit "back to the box," a term that dates to the 19th century, when the pitcher threw from a boxed area rather than from a mound.

breaking ball an all-inconclusive term used to describe any of a family of pitches intended to swerve in some fashion—a curve ball, slider, screwball, sinker, forkball.

bunt a batted ball that is intentionally hit softly and to a short distance so as either to allow the batter to reach first base safely or to advance another runner while the bunter is retired at first base.

change-up a pitch thrown intentionally at a slower speed than preceding pitches so as to disrupt the batter's timing.

cleanup the fourth hitter in the lineup who, if all three runners reach base before him, is then set to "clean up" all the bases by virtue of a homerun; this position is usually reserved for the team's most powerful hitter.

closer the pitcher who comes in to pitch toward the end of the game to preserve a lead.

curve a pitch thrown with a downward snap of the wrist, intended to impart a spin to the ball that will force it to curve as it approaches the plate.

cycle a batter's feat that requires the hitting of a single, double, triple, and home run in the same game—"hitting for the cycle."

designated hitter (or DH) a position created in 1973 in the American League (and still in practice only there), whereby one player is designated to play offense only, batting for the pitcher, who plays defense only.

double a hit that results in the batter reaching second base safely without fielder error.

doubleheader when two teams play twice in succession on the same day.

double play when one pitched ball results in the making of two outs, either by virtue of a strikeout and a base runner being thrown out, or when a batter hits the ball and two runners are called out on the bases.

error a defensive mistake, deemed avoidable by an official scorer, that results in either a batter reaching base safely or having his at bat extended.

fastball a pitch thrown for maximum speed.

foul ball the result of a pitched ball hitting a bat but going into foul territory; it is a strike until there are two strikes, in which case it does not count as a strike.

grand slam a home run with runners on all three bases, resulting in four runs.

ground-rule double a hit that, because of a mutually agreed-upon rule particular to the ball park the game is being played in, results in the batter being awarded second base; e.g., when a ball hit fairly bounces into the stands and out of play.

grounder a batted ball that bounces one or more times in the infield.

hit-and-run a play usually ordered by the manager whereby a base runner runs for the next base when the pitch is made and the hitter tries to hit the ball into play in an attempt to advance the runner two bases or avoid a double play by virtue of the base runner's head start toward the next base.

home run when a batter either hits the ball out of the field of play in fair territory or when the batter is able to advance all around the bases to score before the defense can retrieve the batted ball and get him out on the base paths.

hot corner third base, so-called because of the hard hits often directed to that part of the field.

infield fly rule a ball hit high in the air above the infield with runners on first or first and second with less than two out, at which time an umpire calls the batter automatically out so that fielders cannot intentionally let the ball drop safely and then try to turn a double play; runners advance at their own risk once an the infield fly rule is invoked by the umpire.

inning one of nine units that constitute a regular-length game, consisting of one turn on offense by each team for a duration necessary for them to make three outs. If the game is tied after the ninth inning, the game continues in extra innings until a winner is decided.

K the official scorer's shorthand for a strikeout; a backwards K denotes that the batter struck out without swinging at the third strike.

knuckleball a pitch gripped by only the finger tips or in some cases the knuckles, meant to put as little spin on the ball as possible, resulting, ideally, in the ball fluttering slowly and unpredictably toward the plate.

line drive a ball hit sharply with very little elevation (sometimes called "a rope").

mound a packed dome of dirt, 60 feet six inches from the back of home plate, from which a pitcher throws the ball; in the center of the mound is a rectangular slab of rubber that the pitcher uses to push himself toward the plate (using the power of his leg) when throwing the ball.

no-hitter a game in which a pitcher or pitchers for one team do not allow a base hit by the opposition.

out play in which a batter or a runner is retired.

perfect game a nine-inning (or greater) complete game victory by one pitcher who does not allow a single runner to reach first base safely by any means.

pick-off when a pitcher or catcher throws behind a runner on base, resulting in that runner being tagged out before returning to his base.

pinch-hit to take a turn at bat in place of another player, who is then removed from the game.

relief pitcher any pitcher who enters the game after the starting pitcher has been removed, usually because of ineffectiveness, injury, or fatigue, but sometimes for strategic purposes.

sacrifice when a batter intentionally makes an out in order to advance a base runner or when an out leads to the advantageous advance of a runner; a sacrifice does not count as an official at bat.

slider a pitch that is nearly as fast as a fastball and which breaks nearly as much as a curve, ideally confusing the batter as to whether it is a fastball or a curve that is being thrown, confounding his timing.

stolen base when a base runner advances from one base to the next by running at the moment of the pitch and, if the pitch is not hit, makes it to the next base before the catcher can make a throw to a fielder covering that base.

strikeout when a batter gets his third strike, either swinging and missing or judged by the umpire to be hittable and in the strike zone.

Texas Leaguer a batted ball that loops over the infielders and drops safely in front of the outfielders, so named because of one (perhaps apocryphal) player's knack for making such hits while playing in a league in Texas.

triple when a batter hits the ball safely in such a way as to enable him to make it to third base.

triple play when a ball in play leads to three base runners being called out.

umpires the official arbiters of a game, usually four in number, positioned behind home plate, and at first, second, and third base.

walk when a batter receives, in one at bat, four pitches that are deemed out of the strike zone by the umpire, and at which the batter does not swing, in which instance he is awarded first base with no official at bat charged.

warning track usually a cinder path in front of the outfield wall, that when stepped on will alert an outfielder that he is approaching the boundary of the playing field.

BASKETBALL

Unlike most modern sports, which evolved from other games (as football did from rugby), basketball can be attributed to a single inventor. Dr. James Naismith, a physical education instructor at the Young Men's Christian Association (YMCA) Training School—now Springfield College—in Springfield, Mass., devised the game in December 1891 as an indoor athletic alternative for the winter months. Naismith's invention was a noncontact sport in which two teams of players attempted to toss a soccer ball into peach baskets hung from the railings at opposite ends of the gymnasium. Because the railings were 10 feet high—not 12 or 14 feet—the basket has been forever set at that height.

Basketball was an immediate success, catching on at other YMCAs and schools in the East. Today it is one of the most popular team sports in the United States and throughout the world. Young men and women compete at every level from the playground to youth, scholastic, collegiate, and professional leagues. Spectators throng to arenas to enjoy the game's fast-paced action and competitive drama.

Rules and Conduct of Play

The rules created by Dr. Naismith are basic to basketball today, though there have been major refinements and notable improvements in the equipment. His original 13 rules included a prohibition against running with the ball. Most formal competition is still held indoors on a wooden floor. Outdoors, the surface is typically made of asphalt or concrete. The court, which varies in size depending on the level of competition, measures up to 94 feet (28.7 meters) long and 50 feet (15.2 meters) wide. It is divided into offensive and defensive halves by a midcourt line. The baskets are metal hoops, or rims, measuring 18 inches (45.7 centimeters) in diameter and set 10 feet (3.05 meters) above the floor. The rims are attached to wood or fiberglass backboards, supported by a post or stanchion, at opposites ends of the court. An open cord net hangs from each rim. An official basketball is 30 inches (76 centimeters) in circumference—slightly smaller for women—inflated with air, and made of leather or rubber.

A basketball team consists of five players plus substitutes and coaches. Each team defends one goal, or basket, at its back. Players advance the ball toward the opposite goal by passing it to a teammate or dribbling it while in motion. Members of the opposing team try to prevent them from scoring a basket. A successful shot at the basket, called a field goal, is generally counted as two points. If attempted from behind a line marked on the floor (the distance varying by level of competition), a successful shot is worth three points. If a shot is missed, usually caroming off the rim or backboard, a defensive player may catch the rebound and, with teammates, advance the ball toward the opposite basket. An offensive player who captures a rebound may simply shoot again, pass to a teammate, or dribble away. After each basket, possession of the ball goes to the opposing team.

Pushing, holding, and other forms of physical contact are limited. Excessive contact may be called a foul by the referees. If the fouled player was touched while attempting a shot, he is awarded uncontested attempts at the basket, called foul shots or free throws, from a distance of 15 feet (4.6 meters). Each successful foul shot is worth one point. If a team collectively commits a certain number of fouls in a period of time (five fouls in a professional quarter, seven fouls in a collegiate half), then the other team takes foul shots for every additional foul, even if not committed in the act of shooting.

A pro basketball game has four 12-minute quarters. There are limits on the amount of time a team may take to advance the ball past the midcourt line (8 seconds) and to make an attempt at the basket (24 seconds).

History of Basketball

The introduction of metal rims, backboards, nets, and a larger ball—all in the mid-1890's—fueled enthusiasm for Dr. Naismith's invention. The new game of basketball was especially popular with young women, and in 1896 the first women's intercollegiate game was held between Stanford and California. The first men's college game was contested in 1897, the same year in which five-player teams became standard. A rule change allowing players to dribble was adopted in 1900 (before which players could advance the ball only by passing), adding speed, excitement, and more scoring to the game.

Men's College Basketball

The sport quickly spread in popularity and early college games had various numbers of players on each side. By 1900 five-a-side was standard. At the 1904 Olympic Games in St. Louis, a number of schools played the first "College Basket Ball Championship"—won by Hiram College of Ohio—and soon this became an annual event sponsored by various groups, eventually evolving in the 1930's into the annual N.C.A.A. (National Collegiate Athletic Association) men's basketball tournament, and the N.I.T. (National Invitational Tournament), initially a more prestigious event than the N.C.A.A. title.

The growth of college basketball paralleled that of college football: the sport began as a student-centered and -operated activity, and became at many schools a semi-professional enterprise with paid coaches running the squads. During the first three decades of the 20th century, the most successful coaches were Joseph Raycroft of the University of Chicago, Walter "Doc" Meanwell of the University of Wisconsin, George Keogan of the University of Notre Dame, and Ward "Piggy" Lambert of Purdue University. Among the outstanding players were John Schommer (Chicago), Charles "Stretch" Murphy and John Wooden (Purdue), and Hank Luisetti (Stanford). In addition, Dr. James Naismith continued to coach for many years at the University of Kansas, and a number of his players became famous coaches: Forrest "Phog" Allen at Kansas and Adolph Rupp at the University of Kentucky.

During its first two decades, college basketball remained a campus sport played mainly in school facilities. In the 1930's, however, with the popularity of double-header games at city arenas, college basketball gained many new fans as well as media attention. Schools in urban areas began to produce some of the best teams: City College of New York (C.C.N.Y.), New York University (N.Y.U.), Long Island University (L.I.U.), and DePaul University in Chicago. The urban influence on college basketball was both positive and negative: the city schools often had African-American youngsters on their teams and helped integrate the sport. (Jackie Robinson, in fact, played basketball at U.C.L.A. from 1939 to 1941.) But city arenas also attracted large numbers of gamblers and fans betting on games.

The 1940's should have been college basketball's best era to date—the sport had become more exciting because of talented big men like George Mikan of DePaul, as well as the increased use of the jump shot and the fast break—but gambling scandals overwhelmed it. Law enforcement agencies discovered that many players on the late-1940's and early-1950's championship teams of C.C.N.Y. and Kentucky, and on many other nationally ranked squads, took bribes from gamblers to fix the outcomes of games. Moreover, the players had engaged in fixing games for a number of years, and their coaches, among the most famous in the sport—Clair Bee (L.I.U.), Nat Holman (C.C.N.Y.), and Adolph Rupp (Kentucky)—probably knew about their players' malfeasance and chose not to report it to the authorities.

Despite the scandals and their repercussions—some players went to prison and some schools deemphasized the sport—college basketball remained popular in the 1950's, particularly on college campuses in the Midwest and on the West Coast. Outstanding players such as Wilt Chamberlain (Kansas), Oscar Robertson (Cincinnati), and Jerry West (West Virginia) emerged, and such superb teams as the University of San Francisco Dons, led by Bill Russell and K.C. Jones, won N.C.A.A. championships. Toward the end of the 1950's, John Wooden, the coach at U.C.L.A., began to build excellent squads. Because his school had a history of integration and because he was the first college coach to recruit outstanding players from all regions of the country, his teams came to dominate their conference and then the N.C.A.A. tournament, winning nine out of 10 national titles from 1964 to 1973. Led by such players as Lew Alcindor (later known as Kareem Abdul-Jabbar), Bill Walton, Walt Hazzard, and Lucius Allen, U.C.L.A. dominated college basketball longer than any school has ever done.

U.C.L.A.'s reign was interrupted in 1966 by Texas Western (now the University of Texas at El Paso). In the N.C.A.A. final game, Texas Western's all-black starting five easily beat the all-white Kentucky lineup and, symbolically, ended segregation in college basketball. In 1969 an event with far-reaching consequences occurred when University of Detroit basketball star Spencer Haywood challenged the rule forbidding players from leaving school to play in the N.B.A. before their class graduated. Haywood won his case and changed the future of college basketball: from the 1970's to the present, increasing numbers of players, including a majority of stars, depart school early for the pros. By the late 1990's, players were jumping directly from high school to the professional game, bypassing college completely.

The most memorable on-court event of the 1970's took place in the N.C.A.A. final game of 1979. The Michigan State Spartans, led by Earvin "Magic" Johnson, played the Indiana State Sycamores, starring Larry Bird. The contest, won by Michigan State, drew the highest TV ratings of any game in college basketball history. It also helped elevate the N.C.A.A. men's basketball tournament to national event status, now nicknamed "March Madness."

In the early 1980's, ESPN began televising a multitude of college basketball games, and this greatly increased the popularity of the sport. The network also prompted the creation of new conferences of universities seeking air time for their teams. The alliance between ESPN and the Big East was particularly fruitful and in the 1980's helped promote the basketball programs of schools such as Georgetown and Villanova, which won N.C.A.A. titles in 1984 and 1985, respectively. By the end of the decade, the N.C.A.A. signed its first $1 billion-plus contract with a TV network (CBS) to televise the men's and women's basketball tournaments. The current contract, a multiyear deal, is worth more than $6 billion.

By 1990 college basketball was awash in money but also in corruption. A shadowy world of "street agents" and under-the-table payments came to exist and continues to the present. Some of the best teams and players participated in the corruption. The University of Michigan's "Fab Five," led by Chris Webber, were involved in six-figure under-the-table payments; other schools and players had other problems. Some scandals, such as at the University of Minnesota, involved academic fraud.

Yet, through all the scandals, the fans, especially the students at prominent basketball schools, loved the sport and their teams, and followed them avidly. As a result, many universities built new and grandiose arenas and spent millions on their basketball programs. All of this was far from the game's modest origins in Springfield, Mass. From that casual beginning to college basketball's highly organized and commercialized present is the trajectory of the sport.

On the court, college basketball is similar to the professional game but with several major differences. First and foremost is the element of time: a college game stretches over two 20-minute halves, rather than the four 12-minute quarters in its professional version. Furthermore, the shot clock lasts 35 seconds in college rules, compared to 24 seconds in the pros. The longer shot clock and the shorter game mean that college basketball features less scoring than its professional cousin, but in the eyes of many observers, the emphasis on rapid passing and player movement in the collegiate game make for better viewing.

Women's college basketball

Women's college basketball is almost as old as the men's game; in fact, its earliest proponent, Maude Sherman, married Dr. James Naismith, the sport's inventor. Unfortunately, because of the Victorian conventions against females playing contact sports, the rules of women's basketball were different from the evolving men's game. Until the 1970's, most women played what was termed "girl ball": six players per team, three confined to each half the court, with restrictions on dribbling and ball-handling. Nevertheless, the game thrived in various regions of the country, particularly in high schools and colleges in Iowa and some adjacent states.

In the early 1970's, the associations in charge of women's sports sanctioned the use of the five-a-side, full-court game, along with a 30-second shot clock. Then, in 1973, the passage of Title IX, which mandated equal opportunities in college sports for all students, began the transformation of women's basketball into a major intercollegiate sport. The Association of Intercollegiate Athletics for Women (A.I.A.W.) organized regional tournaments and a national championship; outstanding teams from Delta State University (Mississippi) and Immaculata College (Pennsylvania) emerged, along with stars such as Ann Meyers (U.C.L.A.), Nancy Lieberman (Old Dominion University), and Lynette Woodward (Kansas).

In the early 1980's the N.C.A.A. pushed the A.I.A.W. aside and took over the sport, promoting the championship tournament on television, and paralleling the women's teams to the men's squads of their universities (but permitting underfunding of the women's teams). From the late 1980's to the present, those schools willing to fund their women's teams at a high level have amassed the best records and the most N.C.A.A. titles: the University of Tennessee, the University of Connecticut, and Stanford have all won multiple crowns.

Professional Basketball

Professional basketball was born in 1898, as several teams began barnstorming the eastern states to compete for pay against local squads. The first collegiate association, the Eastern Intercollegiate League, was formed in 1902. Basketball was introduced as an Olympic demonstration sport in the Summer Games of 1904, spreading interest to Europe and Asia.

Other notable innovations in the early years included a limit of five personal fouls per player per game (1908–09) and a change in the penalty for walking or double-dribbling from foul shots to loss of ball possession (1923). The results were a reduction in rough play and shorter breaks in the action. More changes in the early 1930's, including the 10-second rule (for advancing the ball past midcourt) and a 3-second rule (prohibiting a player from remaining inside the foul lane), further contributed to the evolution of the game.

1920's and 1930's By the 1920's, basketball tournaments were being held in high schools and colleges across the country. Company teams and touring professionals built grassroots followings. Among the top pro teams of the era were the Original Celtics, featuring such stars as Nat Holman and Joe Lapchick (both of whom would become prominent coaches), and the Harlem Globetrotters, a talented and flamboyant all-black team founded in 1927 by promoter Abe Saperstein. Before the integration of the National Basketball Association later in the century, the Globetrotters frequently beat top teams in invitational events. Later, after the growth and integration of the N.B.A. took away their best players and talent base, the Globetrotters turned into a traveling basketball carnival, and they have entertained audiences in more than 100 countries with their on-court stunts and clowning routines.

It was not until the mid-1930's, however, with developments at the college level, that basketball began to emerge as a major spectator sport. In 1934 a sportswriter named Ned Irish promoted a college doubleheader at New York's Madison Square Garden that drew a large crowd. College basketball became a regular event at the Garden and elsewhere, prompting many universities to build arenas or launch programs.

Another turning point came in 1936, when the team from Stanford University traveled east to compete at Madison Square Garden and stunned the basketball establishment with its fast-paced, freewheeling style of play. Stanford featured the dynamic Hank Luisetti, whose running one-handed shot revolutionized offensive play (replacing the standard two-hand set shot) and delighted spectators. With the 1937–38 season came elimination of the jump ball after each field goal, further accelerating the pace of the game.

In 1938 Madison Square Garden held the first major postseason intercollegiate playoff, the National Invitation Tournament (NIT), and the National Collegiate Athletic Association (N.C.A.A.) organized its own championship the following year. The NIT is still held at the end of every season, but the winner of the N.C.A.A. tournament is recognized as the official collegiate champion.

The 1930's also witnessed the birth of organized competition at the international level. An official governing body, the International Amateur Basketball Federation (FIBA), was established in 1932 in Geneva, Switzerland (later moved to Munich, Germany). In 1936 basketball became a full medal sport for men at the Olympic Games in Berlin, with teams from 22 nations taking part.

1940's and 1950's The National Basketball League (NBL), founded in 1937 and based in the Midwest, was the most successful of several early professional leagues. Interest in the pro game lagged until 1946, however, when the new Basketball Association of America (BAA) was launched. With franchises in 11 major cites, including Toronto, the BAA attracted fans eager to see former college players compete. Four NBL franchises jumped to the BAA in 1948, and the expansion was completed in 1949—thereby creating the National Basketball Association. The N.B.A. dates its foundation to the creation of the BAA, in 1946. The original N.B.A. included 17 franchises in three divisions. George Mikan of the Minneapolis Lakers, at 6'10" the game's first great "big man," was a major gate attraction who helped ensure the success of the league. Mikan dominated the pro game until his retirement in 1956, leading his team to five N.B.A. championships.

Several developments in the early 1950's—combined with the ever-improving skills of the players—contributed to the growth of the N.B.A.. The first black players were drafted into the N.B.A. in 1950, bringing a new segment of talent that would grow only more vital. Before the 1954–55 season, the N.B.A. introduced the 24-second rule to eliminate stalling; with more shots came more excitement. The arrival of professional basketball was perhaps most clearly symbolized by the election of the first members of the Basketball Hall of Fame in 1959, a list appropriately headed by Naismith. (The original Hall of Fame building, located on the campus of Springfield College, did not open until 1968.)

Aside from Mikan's Minneapolis Lakers (later to become the Los Angeles Lakers), top N.B.A. teams of the 1950's included the Boston Celtics (champions in 1957 and 1959), Syracuse Nationals (1955), Philadelphia Warriors (1956), St. Louis Hawks (1958), and perennial powers New York Knickerbockers and Fort Wayne Pistons.

The mantle of the game's top center passed from Mikan to Bill Russell in the latter part of the decade. After leading the University of San Francisco to N.C.A.A. titles in 1955 and 1956, Russell teamed with passing wizard Bob Cousy and other members of the Boston Celtics in winning the first two of many N.B.A. championships. Other outstanding players of the decade included Bob Pettit, Cliff Hagan, Dolph Schayes, Clyde Lovellette, and "Easy" Ed Macauley.

1960's By the early 1960's, the N.B.A. had 10 franchises across the United States, with annual attendance reaching several million. The print and broadcast media expanded coverage, and the game's top players became highly paid celebrities. As players also increased in height and athletic ability, the style and tempo of play also evolved. The dunk shot, or simply dunk, in which a player leaps high off the floor, extends the ball over the basket, and jams it through the hoop, became a common and crowd-thrilling part of the game. The fast break, featuring skilled dribbling and deft passing at top speed, became another trademark of modern pro basketball.

A new league, the American Basketball Association (ABA), was founded in 1967 with 11 teams. The ABA gained a following by luring graduating college stars or established pros and by introducing such innovations as the three-point shot and a red-white-and-blue ball. The league continued operations until after the 1975–76 season, when its strongest franchises were absorbed into the N.B.A..

The Boston Celtics dominated the N.B.A. in the 1960's, establishing one of the great dynasties in professional sports by capturing nine titles in 10 years. Coached by Red Auerbach and led by Russell, Cousy, John Havlicek, and a host of other future Hall of Famers, the Celtics demonstrated that smart, unselfish team play wins championships.

Russell's supremacy at the center position was challenged by a bigger, stronger new talent, the 7'1" Wilt Chamberlain. Once scoring an astonishing 100 points in a game, Chamberlain was an almost unstoppable scoring threat for the Philadelphia 76ers and later the Los Angeles Lakers. Among the other N.B.A. greats of the 1960's were Jerry West, Elgin Baylor, and Oscar Robertson.

1970's The decade of the 1970's marked a period of expansion, realignment, and competitive parity for the N.B.A.. In 1970 the league expanded from 14 teams in two divisions to 17 teams in four divisions (two divisions each in Eastern and Western conferences). Then in 1976, with the merger of former ABA franchises, the total increased to 22. With growth came a new balance of power. The Celtic dynasty, with championships in 1974 and 1976, could hardly be declared dead, but no team won consecutive N.B.A. crowns through the course of the decade. The New York Knicks were the only other team to capture two titles (1970 and 1973).

Center Kareem Abdul-Jabbar was the preeminent player of the decade, earning league M.V.P. honors six times; he would go on to become the leading scorer in N.B.A. history, retiring with 38,387 points in 1989. Other Hall of Famers from the 1970's included Bill Walton, Julius "Dr. J" Erving, Willis Reed, Walt Frazier, Rick Barry, Nate "Tiny" Archibald, Dave Cowens, Pete Maravich, Calvin Murphy, and Bob McAdoo.

1980's Although the N.B.A. continued its expansion in the 1980's, reaching 27 teams by the 1989–90 season, the league faced declining game attendance and television ratings as the decade commenced. At least two factors contributed to a rebound in fan interest by mid-decade. One was the adoption of the three-point field goal before the 1979-80 season, which added an exciting dimension to the game. More important, perhaps, was the compelling rivalry that developed between the Los Angeles Lakers, led by Magic Johnson and Abdul-Jabbar, and the Boston Celtics, with Larry Bird. The Lakers won five championships during the 1980's, the Celtics three. Johnson and Bird each captured three M.V.P. awards. Marquee players of the decade also included Erving and Moses Malone of the Philadelphia 76ers (champions in 1983), Isiah Thomas of the Detroit Pistons (champions in 1989 and 1990), Dominique Wilkins of the Atlanta Hawks, and a young Michael Jordan.

1990's–Present By 1991, a century after its birth, basketball had attained a following that James Naismith could hardly have imagined. The professional game was an entertainment and merchandising industry. Standout players hailed from far-flung parts of the globe.

No individual better symbolized the success of professional basketball than Michael Jordan, an international media celebrity, endorser of consumer products, millionaire many times over, and perhaps the sport's greatest-ever player. The 6'6" Jordan, a shooting guard, carried the Chicago Bulls to six N.B.A. championships during the 1990's, won the league scoring title 10 times, and was named M.V.P. five times. As Jordan's career waned, younger stars—Shaquille O'Neal and Kobe Bryant—restored the Lakers to preeminence with three consecutive league crowns (2000–02). Charles Barkley, Karl Malone, Hakeem Olajuwon, David Robinson, John Stockton, and Tim Duncan were other top stars.

The 21st century promised increasing globalization at virtual every level of play. Already N.B.A. rosters were filled with talented foreign players. Olympic and international amateur tournaments were closely contested. And Naismith's game was being played in schools and playgrounds around the world.

The N.B.A. today comprises 29 teams in the United States and Canada, organized in two conferences (Eastern and Western) with two divisions each. In the 2004–5 season, a new team will join the league in Charlotte, N.C., bringing the N.B.A. to a total of 30 teams. The N.B.A. season lasts from October to June, with each team playing 82 regular-season games. The top teams compete in multiple rounds of post-season playoffs, culminating in a best-of-seven championship series.

Women's Professional Basketball The development of women's basketball at the college level and in the summer Olympics prompted the creation of two women's leagues in the late 1990's. The American Basketball League (ABL) began operations in 1996 and was followed a year later by the WN.B.A., a women's league operated under the auspices of the N.B.A.. The WN.B.A.'s marketing clout proved to be a decisive edge, and the ABL folded in 1999. The WN.B.A. plays a summer schedule that fits in the N.B.A. off-season. In the 2003 season, the WN.B.A. had 14 teams divided into two conferences.

Glossary of Basketball Terms

assist a pass that directly leads to a field goal by a teammate. Assists are an individual statistic.

blocked shot when a defensive player interferes with an opponent's shot attempt by swatting or tipping the ball out of its desired trajectory.

double-dribble a violation in which a player dribbles the ball with two hands or stops dribbling and then resumes; the ball is awarded to the opposing team.

dribbling repetitive bouncing of the ball with one hand, while the player is in motion or standing still.

field goal a successful shot at the basket during the normal course of play; generally worth two points, or three points if shot from beyond a designated distance (the three-point line).

foul an infraction for improper physical play that is determined by the game officials. There are several types of fouls, including reaching in, blocking, charging, and over the back, among others. If a player commits six fouls in the course of the game, he is said to have fouled out, and must leave the court for the remainder of the contest. If a foul is committed on an offensive player in the act of shooting, the shooter is normally entitled to two foul shots, the exceptions being a single foul shot if the player's original attempt was successful, or three foul shots if the shooter was fouled beyond the three-point line.

foul lane the painted area under the basket, bordered by the end line and the foul line; players must stand outside the area during foul shots and may not spend more than three consecutive seconds inside it during active play.

foul shot an uncontested attempt at the basket, taken from the foul line at a distance of 15 feet; one or two shots may be awarded for a personal foul (three if a player is fouled while attempting a three-point shot).

free throw another name for a foul shot.

goaltending when a defensive player touches a shot attempt off of its trajectory after the ball has reached the height of its arc. As a result of a goaltending infraction, the shooting team is awarded the value of the shot attempt. Goaltending is also given when a player slaps the backboard or if the ball is touched directly above the goal, even by an offensive player.

jump ball method of putting the ball into play in which a referee tosses the ball in the air and two opposing players attempt to tap it to a teammate and gain possession.

man-to-man defense a strategy in which each defensive player is responsible for guarding a single offensive opponent.

officials in the N.B.A. there are three officials who enforce the rules of the game.

position the role performed by a player. Each team has five players on the court at any time, and any combination may be employed based on the game situation. Standard starting lineups include two guards, two forwards, and a center. Each of these is occasionally referred to by a number one through five that indicates the player's role.

point guard (1) the primary ballhandler on offense. The point guard brings the ball up the court and seeks to pass the ball to other players for scoring opportunities. Their most important statistic is assists, though good shooting is also helpful. Quickness, vision, and passing ability, not height, are premium requisites.

shooting guard (2) along with the small forward, one of the primary scoring positions. The shooting guard's job is to score points, either by jump shots or by driving to the basket. Usually taller than point guards, but still quick and good shooters.

small forward (3) another of the main scoring positions, slightly taller than the shooting guard, but equally capable of scoring from inside or outside. A player who combines speed and agility with some size.

power forward (4) a player who is a main scoring threat close to the basket, and concentrates on rebounding on the defensive and offensive ends of the floor. These players are tall and strong.

center (5) the tallest players on the court. Primary duty is on defense and rebounding, and most scoring is accomplished near the basket. A dominant center displays an uncommon mix of size, agility, and skill.

rebound recovering the ball after a missed shot. Also an individual (and very underrated) statistic.

roster a list of all of the players on a team. N.B.A. teams have 12 players.

shot clock the device that tracks the time the offensive team has to attempt a shot. This 24-second period commences with the offense's gaining possession of the ball. The clock is reset by such things as offensive rebounds, among others. If the offense does not shoot the ball before the 24 seconds elapses, the team suffers a shot clock violation, and the defending team takes possession.

steal when a defender intercepts or grabs the ball from the opposing team; a defensive statistic.

technical foul a violation called for a procedural violation or, at the discretion of the referee, misconduct; penalized by one foul shot and possession of the ball for the nonoffending team.

three-point play a two-point field goal followed by a successful foul shot; made possible by the commission of a defensive foul as the offensive player is making a successful field goal attempt.

three-point shot a field goal worth three points because the shooter released the ball from behind the three-point line.

traveling a violation in which a player advances the ball by taking three steps without dribbling; possession is awarded to the opposing team; also known as walking.

turnover when the offensive team loses possession of the ball through a variety of methods, including passing the ball out of bounds, traveling, or double dribbling; a negative statistic, as a team that commits many turnovers will attempt fewer shots.

zone defense a strategy in which each defensive player is assigned a specific area of the court and must guard any opponent who enters that area; the zone configuration may take any of several forms, such as a 2-1-2, 1-3-1, or 2-3. In the N.B.A., zone defenses were only recently permitted by the rules.

Naismith Memorial Basketball Hall of Fame

The Basketball Hall of Fame elected its first members (including Dr. James Naismith, the game's originator) in 1959, but it did not have a physical home until February 17, 1968. In 1985 the Hall of Fame moved to larger quarters in Springfield, Mass. The Basketball Hall of Fame includes players from all basketball levels, including college, women's, and foreign leagues. Career statistics are given only for players who played some portion of their career in the N.B.A..

Player (Year Elected)	Games	Points	FG%	FT%	Rebs.	Assts.
Archibald, Nate (Tiny) (1991)	876	16,481	.467	.810	2,046	6,476
Averaged 18.8 ppg over 13 seasons; six-time All-Star						
Arizin, Paul J. (1977)	713	16,266	.421	.810	6,129	1,665
N.B.A. scoring leader in 1952 (25.4 ppg) and 1957 (25.6 ppg)						
Barry, Rick (1987)	794	18,395	.449	.900	5,168	4,017
(A.B.A. Statistics)	226	6,884	.477	.880	1,695	935
N.B.A. all-time free-throw percentage leader						
Baylor, Elgin (1976)	846	23,149	.431	.780	11,463	3,650
Named to N.B.A. All-Star First Team 10 times						
Bellamy, Walt (1993)	1,043	20,941	.516	.632	14,241	2,544
N.B.A. Rookie of the Year in 1962						
Bing, Dave (1990)	901	18,327	.441	.775	3,420	5,397
N.B.A. Rookie of the Year 1967, M.V.P. 1976						
Bird, Larry (1998)	897	21,791	.496	.886	8,974	5,695
N.B.A. Rookie of the Year 1980. N.B.A. M.V.P. 1984, 1985, and 1986. 12-time All-star						
Bradley, Bill (1982)	742	9,217	.448	.840	2,533	2,363
Averaged 30.2 ppg in 83 games at Princeton University						
Chamberlain, Wilt (1978)	1045	31,419	.540	.511	23,924	4,643
Holds N.B.A. single-game records for points (100) and rebounds (55); led league in scoring 1959-66						
Cousy, Bob (1970)	924	16,960	.375	.803	4,786	6,955
Led N.B.A. in assists eight consecutive seasons (1953-60)						
Cowens, Dave (1991)	766	13,516	.460	.783	10,444	2,950
Seven-time All-star; three-time All-defensive team						
Cunningham, Billy (1986)	654	13,626	.446	.720	6,638	2,625
(A.B.A. Statistics)	116	2,684	.483	.791	1,343	680
Coached Philadelphia 76ers to 454-196 record in eight years						
Davies, Bob (1969)	462	6,594	.378	.759	9801	2,050
N.B.L. M.V.P., 1947						
DeBusschere, Dave (1982)	875	14,053	.432	.699	9,618	2,497
N.B.A. All-Defensive team six consecutive seasons (1969-74)						
Drexler, Clyde (2004)	1,086	22,195	.472	.788	6,677	6,125
Nine-time All-star; led Houston Cougars to Final Four in 1982 and 1983						
English, Alex (1997)	1,193	25,613	.507	.832	6,538	4,351
Eight-time all-star; Averaged 21.5 points per game over 15 seasons						
Erving, Julius (Dr. J) (1993)	836	18,364	.507	.777	5,601	3,224
(A.B.A. Statistics)	407	11,662	.504	.778	4,924	1,952
A.B.A. M.V.P. 1974-76; N.B.A. M.V.P., 1981						
Frazier, Walt (Clyde) (1987)	825	15,581	.490	.786	4,830	5,040
N.B.A. All-Defensive team seven consecutive seasons (1969-75)						
Fulks, Joe (1977)	489	8,003	.302	.766	1,3821	587
B.A.A. scoring leader in 1947 (23.2 ppg)						

Player (Year Elected)	Games	Points	FG%	FT%	Rebs.	Assts.
Gallatin, Harry (1991)	682	8,843	.398	.773	6,684	1,208
Seven-time All-Star						
Gervin, George (Iceman) (1996)	791	20,708	.511	.844	3,607	2,214
(A.B.A. Statistics)	269	5,887	.480	.831	1,995	584
All-N.B.A. team five years in a row (1978-82)						
Gola, Tom (1975)	698	7,871	.431	.760	5,605	2,953
One of only two major-college players with over 2,000 points and 2,000 rebounds in career						
Goodrich, Gail (1996)	1,031	19,181	.456	.807	3,279	4,805
Scored 42 points in 1965 N.C.A.A. Final; averaged 18.6 points per game over 14 years in N.B.A.						
Greer, Harold (Hal) (1981)	1,122	21,586	.452	.801	5,665	4,540
Scored 19 points in one quarter of 1968 All-Star game						
Hagan, Cliff (1977)	746	13,447	.450	.798	5,019	2,236
(A.B.A. Statistics)	94	1,423	.496	.807	436	398
Helped St. Louis to 1958 championship with 27.7 ppg in playoffs						
Havlicek, John J. (Hondo) (1983)	1,270	26,395	.439	.815	8,007	6,114
Averaged 20.8 ppg; member of 8 N.B.A. championship teams						
Hawkins, Connie (1992)	499	8,233	.467	.785	3,971	2,052
(A.B.A. Statistics)	117	3,295	.515	.765	1,479	504
Four-time All-Star; ABA M.V.P. 1969						
Hayes, Elvin (1990)	1,303	27,313	.452	.670	16,279	2,398
Led league in scoring (1969) and rebounds per game (1970, 1974)						
Heinsohn, Tom (1986)	654	12,194	.405	.790	5,749	1,318
Played for eight N.B.A. championship teams and coached two others						
Houbregs, Robert J. (1987)	281	2,611	.404	.721	1,552	500
N.C.A.A. Player of the Year, 1953						
Issel, Dan (1993)	718	14,659	.506	.797	5,707	1,804
(A.B.A. Statistics)	500	12,823	.488	.786	5,426	1,103
Averaged 33.7 points per game in senior year at Kentucky, 1969-70						
Jabbar, Kareem Abdul (1995)	1,560	38,387	.559	.721	17,440	5,660
Six-time N.B.A. M.V.P.. All-time N.B.A. leader in scoring, games, minutes, field goals						
Jeannette, Buddy (1994) (B.A.A.-N.B.A.)	139	997	.341	.781	N.A.	287
Won N.B.L. M.V.P. three times						
Johnson, Earvin (Magic) (2002)	906	17,707	.520	.848	6,559	10,141
Led Lakers to five N.B.A. championships; 3-time N.B.A. M.V.P. (1987, 1989, 1990); 12-time All-Star						
Johnston, Neil (1990)	516	10,023	.444	.768	5,856	1,269
Named to four straight all-N.B.A. First Teams (1953-56)						
Jones, K.C. (1989)	676	5,011	.387	.647	2,399	2,908
High scorer in 1955 N.C.A.A. finals (24 pts); held Tom Gola scoreless for 21 mins.						
Jones, Sam (1983)	871	15,411	.456	.803	4,305	2,209
Member of 10 N.B.A. championship teams						
Lanier, Bob (1992)	959	19,248	.514	.767	9,698	3,007
Eight-time All-Star; N.B.A. M.V.P., 1974						
Lloyd, Earl (2003)	560	4,682	.356	.750	3,609	810
First African-American to play in a N.B.A. game, 1950						
Lovellette, Clyde (1988)	704	11,947	.443	.756	6,663	1,165
Three-time All-American at University of Kansas (1950-52)						
Lucas, Jerry Ray (Luke) (1979)	829	14,053	.499	.783	12,942	2,730
N.B.A. Rookie of the Year and field-goal percentage leader (.527) in 1964						

Player (Year Elected)	Games	Points	FG%	FT%	Rebs.	Assts.
Macauley, Edward (Easy Ed) (1960)	641	11,234	.436	.761	2,079	1,667
N.B.A. All-Star Game M.V.P., 1951						
Malone, Moses (2001)	1,329	27,409	.491	.769	16,212	1,796
Three-time M.V.P., 12-time All-Star. Averaged 20 points per game 11 straight seasons.						
Maravich, Pete (Pistol) (1987)	658	15,948	.441	.820	2,747	3,563
N.C.A.A. career record holder for points scored (3667) and scoring avg. (44.2 ppg)						
Martin, Slater (1981)	745	7,337	.364	.762	2,3021	3,160
Played in seven straight All-Star Games, 1953-59						
McAdoo, Bob (2000)	852	18,787	.503	.754	8,048	1,951
N.B.A. Rookie of the Year (1973); led league in scoring 1974, 1975, and 1976.						
McGuire, Dick (1993)	738	5,921	.389	.644	2,784	4,205
Averaged 8.0 ppg.						
McHale, Kevin (1999)	971	17,335	.554	.798	7,122	1,670
Seven-time All-Star; won Sixth Man Award twice; won 3 N.B.A. Championships: 1981, 1984, 1986						
Mikan, George L. (1959)	439	10,156	.404	.782	4,1671	1,245
Three-time N.B.A. scoring leader (1949, 1950, 1952)						
Mikkelson, Vern (1995)	699	10,063	.403	.766	5,9401	1,515
Six time N.B.A. All Star; won 4 N.B.A. Championships: 1950, 1952, 1953, & 1954						
Monroe, Earl (The Pearl) (1990)	926	17,454	.464	.807	2,796	3,594
N.B.A. Rookie of the Year, 1968						
Murphy, Calvin (1993)	1,002	17,949	.482	.892	2,103	4,402
Set single-season free throw percentage record with .958 in 1980-81						
Parish, Robert (2003)	1,611	23,334	.537	.721	14,715	2,180
Nine-time N.B.A. All-Star (1981-87, 1990-91). Won 3 N.B.A. Championships (1981, 1984, & 1986)						
Petrovic, Drazen (2002)	290	4,461	.506	.841	669	701
Averaged 15.4 ppg and 43.7% from 3-pt range over 4 years before being killed in auto accident						
Pettit, Bob (1970)	792	20,880	.436	.761	12,849	2,369
Led N.B.A. in scoring (25.7 ppg) and rebounds (1164) in 1956						
Phillip, Andy (1961)	701	6,384	.368	.695	2,3951	3,759
Led N.B.A. in assists, 1951 and 1952						
Pollard, Jim (1977)	438	5,762	.360	.750	2,4871	1,417
Started four N.B.A. All-Star Games						
Ramsey, Frank (1981)	623	8,378	.402	.804	3,410	1,136
Member of seven N.B.A. championship teams						
Reed, Willis (1981)	650	12,183	.476	.747	8,414	1,186
1970 N.B.A. Most Valuable Player, All-Star Game M.V.P. and Playoff M.V.P.						
Risen, Arnie (1998)	637	7,633	.381	.699	5,011	1,058
Three-time N.B.A. All-star (1953, 1954, and 1955)						
Robertson, Oscar (1979)	1,040	26,710	.485	.838	7,804	9,887
N.B.A. M.V.P. 1964; Member of All-N.B.A. First team, 1961-69						
Russell, Bill (1974)	963	14,522	.440	.561	21,620	4,100
Five-time N.B.A. Most Valuable Player; 32 rebounds in one half vs. Philadelphia, 1957						
Schayes, Adolph (Dolph) (1972)	996	18,438	.380	.849	11,2561	3,072
N.B.A. Coach of the Year (1966)						
Sharman, Bill (1974)	711	12,665	.426	.883	2,779	2,101
Led N.B.A. in free-throw percentage seven seasons						
Stokes, Maurice (2004)	202	3,315	.351	.698	3,492	1,062
Rookie of the Year (1955–56); hurt badly in freak accident after three N.B.A. seasons						

Player (Year Elected)	Games	Points	FG%	FT%	Rebs.	Assts.
Thomas, Isiah, (2000)	979	18,822	.452	.759	3,478	9,061
N.B.A. Rookie of the Year (1982); 12-time All-Star; M.V.P. of the 1990 Finals						
Thompson, David (1996)	509	11,264	.504	.778	1,921	1,631
(ABA Statistics)	83	2,158	.515	.794	525	308
N.C.A.A. player of the year 1974 and 1975; ABA Rookie of the Year, 1976						
Thurmond, Nate (1984)	964	14,437	.421	.667	14,464	2,575
1,000+ rebounds 1964-69, 1970-73						
Twyman, Jack (1982)	823	15,840	.450	.778	5,421	1,969
Led N.B.A. in field-goal percentage, 1958 (.452)						
Unseld, Wes (1988)	984	10,624	.509	.633	13,769	3,822
Named N.B.A. Most Valuable Player and Rookie of the Year in same year (1969)						
Walton, Bill (1993)	468	6,215	.521	.660	4,923	1,590
N.B.A. M.V.P. in 1976						
Wanzer, Robert (1987)	502	5,891	.388	.800	1,6521	1,575
Free-throw percentage leader, 1952 (.904)						
West, Jerry Alan (1979)	932	25,192	.474	.814	5,376	6,238
N.B.A. M.V.P. in 1970; .805 free throw percentage in 13 years in the playoffs						
Worthy, James (2003)	926	16,320	.521	.769	4,707	2,791
M.V.P. of 1988 N.B.A. Finals.						
Wilkens, Lenny (1989)	1,077	17,772	.432	.774	5,030	7,211
600+ assists 6 consecutive seasons						
Yardley, George (1996)	472	9,063	.422	.780	4,220	815
First player in N.B.A. history to score 2,000 points in a season						

Note: All statistics for N.B.A. career unless otherwise noted. NBL = National Basketball League. ABA = American Basketball Association. N.C.A.A. (National Collegiate Athletic Association) 1. Does not include seasons played prior to 1950-51 when the N.B.A. first began keeping statistics for rebounds. 2. The National Basketball League did not keep statistics for field-goal percentage, rebounds, or assists.

Hall of Fame Coaches

Anderson, W. Harold, 1984
Auerbach, Arnold J. "Red," 1968
Barry, Justin "Sam," 1978
Blood, Ernest A., 1960
Brown, Larry, 2002
Cann, Howard G., 1967
Carlson, Dr. H. Clifford, 1959
Carnesecca, Lou, 1992
Carnevale, Ben, 1969
Carril, Pete, 1997
Case, Everett, 1981
Chaney, John, 2001
Conradt, Jody, 1998
Crum, Denny, 1994
Daly, Chuck, 1994
Dean, Everett S., 1966
Diddle, Edgar A., 1971
Drake, Bruce, 1972
Gaines, Clarence, 1981
Gardner, James H. "Jack," 1983
Gill, Amory T. "Slats," 1967
Hannum, Alex, 1998
Harshman, Marv, 1984
Haskins, Don, 1997
Hickey, Edgar S., 1978
Hobson, Howard A., 1965
Holzman, William "Red," 1985-86
Iba, Henry P. "Hank," 1968
Julian, Alvin "Doggie," 1967
Keaney, Frank W., 1960
Keogan, George E., 1961
Knight, Bob, 1991
Krzyzewski, Mike, 2001
Kundla, John, 1995
Lambert, Ward L., 1960
Litwack, Harry, 1975
Loeffler, Kenneth D., 1964
Lonborg, Arthur C., 1972
McCutchan, Arad A., 1980
McGuire, Al, 1992
McGuire, Frank J., 1976
Meanwell, Dr. Walter E., 1959
Meyer, Raymond J., 1978
Miller, Ralph, 1987
Moore, Billie, 1999
Nikolic, Aleksandar, 1998
Olson, Lute, 2002
Ramsay, Jack, 1992
Rupp, Adolph F., 1968
Sachs, Leonard D., 1961
Shelton, Everett F., 1979
Smith, Dean, 1982
Summitt, Pat, 2000
Taylor, Fred R., 1985-86
Teague, Bertha, 1984
Thompson, John, 1999
Wade, L. Margaret, 1984
Watts, Stanley H., 1985-86
Wilkens, Lenny, 1998
Wooden, John R., 1972
Woolpert, Phil, 1992
Wootten, Morgan, 2000

FOOTBALL

Football, or American football, as it is known in the rest of the world, evolved from soccer and rugby in the late 19th century. On November 6, 1869, Rutgers and Princeton played a soccer-like game that would eventually evolve into modern football. During the next seven years, rugby gained in popularity at eastern colleges, while soccer fell from favor. In 1876 the rules of American football became different enough from rugby that they were codified. At that time, a field goal and a touchdown were each worth four points.

Since then, American football has continued to diverge from its international cousins. Today there are hundreds of rules that differentiate American football from the version played around the world, the most ironic being that very little of the American game uses the feet.

With periodic breaks in the action, football is uniquely suited for television. Football's symbiotic relationship with television has fueled its rise to the most popular sport in the United States and one of the most popular forms of entertainment in the world.

Rules and Conduct of Play

Although football's myriad rules have evolved substantially in the sport's first century, the differences among the high school, college, and professional games are few. A football field, itself now commonly regarded in the United States as a unit of measurement, is 100 yards long, demarcated every five yards by white stripes that run the width of the field (160 feet). At either end of the 100 yards are 10-yardlong end zones. At the center of the rear boundary of each end zone is a U-shaped goalpost with a crossbar 10 feet high and two uprights 18 1/2 feet apart. The surface is grass or a synthetic facsimile. The middle of the field is the 50-yard line; numbers decrease on either side of the center stripe until they reach the 0-yard line, or the goal line.

The object of the game is to move the football into the end zone (a touchdown), or to get close enough so as to kick the ball between the uprights (a field goal). A touchdown is worth six points and carries with it the right to attempt an extra point (kicking the ball between the uprights from the 2 1/2 yard line) or a two-point conversion (moving the ball across the goal line again from the 2 1/2 yard line). A field goal is always worth three points. The defense can score by pushing an offensive player backward into his own end zone. This uncommon method of scoring is called a safety, and is worth two points.

Each team has 11 players on the field at once. The offensive team tries to advance the ball, and the defensive team seeks to stop them by tackling the player with the ball before he can advance down the field. The offensive team has four chances (or downs) to advance the ball 10 yards (a first down). If they achieve this goal, they are rewarded with four more downs to advance another 10 yards. If they fail, they must give the ball to the other team. At any time, the offensive team has the option of punting (i.e. kicking) the ball to the defensive team. Most teams do this on fourth down when it seems unlikely that they will get a first down.

The defense may also take possession by catching a pass intended for an offensive player (an interception), or by picking up the ball after it has been dropped by an offensive player (a fumble). Any player on either team may pick up a fumbled football.

The game is played in four 15-minute quarters, with a break for halftime. The teams switch ends of the field between the first and second quarters and the third and fourth quarters. The game commences with one team kicking the ball to the other team (the kickoff). After every touchdown and field goal, the team that scores kicks off again. At the game's conclusion, the team with the most points wins.

Positions

The *quarterback* is the player who runs the offense on the field. He signals the start of play and either hands the ball to a running back or he retreats several steps into a pocket formed by the offensive line and attempts to throw the ball to an eligible receiver. Alternatively, he can run with the ball himself. Quarterbacks are usually tall with a strong arm.

The *running backs* carry the ball most frequently on running plays. Often divided into two roles: the fullback, a player who specializes in blocking, and the tailback or halfback, who will run the ball most often. These players normally align behind the quarterback and offensive line.

The primary duty of the *wide receivers* is to catch passes. They align outside—often 10 to 12 yards—the offensive line, and are almost always the swiftest players on the offense. They try to run well-designed pass routes or patterns to separate themselves from defenders.

The *offensive line* is a set of five players whose responsibility is to protect the quarterback and block defenders to clear lanes for the running backs. The *center* initiates each play by snapping the ball to the quarterback. The center is flanked by two players called *guards*, and outside the guards are two *tackles*.

The defensive team is divided into three different units. The defensive players on the line of scrimmage are known as the defensive line. They are often separated into nose tackles (who align directly over or near the offensive center), tackles, and ends.

Linebackers are a group of defenders who usually begin each play immediately behind the defensive linemen or outside the linemen on the line of scrimmage. They are responsible for stopping running plays, covering short pass routes, and rushing the quarterback.

The *defensive backs*, known collectively as the secondary, have the primary responsibility of preventing the offense from progressing by the pass. In standard situations, the secondary numbers four players: two *cornerbacks*, a *strong safety*, and a *free safety*. In likely passing plays, defenses may choose a package of players called the "nickel" (an extra defensive back) or even the "dime" (two extras) at the expense of linebackers or linemen.

College Football

Origins

American football originated in the second half of the 19th century, evolving out of the British games of soccer and rugby. During the 1870's, teams played various versions of the game, the home squad often dictating the rules. Early contests included Princeton against Rutgers in 1871 and Princeton versus Yale in 1873. The student captain was in charge of the team on and off the field. At Yale, Walter Camp proved to be a brilliant captain and, after his graduation in 1881, he stayed in New Haven and continued to run the squad as the "graduate manager."

Camp, often called the "Father of Football," worked to codify the on-field rules and to institute daily practice routines and game strategies. Because, above all, he wanted his teams to win, sometimes he enlisted athletes who were paid for playing football at Yale. Yale's rivals, as well as other schools taking up the game, also wanted to win, and soon many rosters featured "ringers" (non-students) and "tramp athletes" (ringers who sold their services to more than one school during a season and/or over a number of seasons).

By the 1890's, football moved off-campus and grew in popularity with the sporting press and the general public. The annual Thanksgiving Day contests in New York City, usually featuring Yale and Princeton, attracted significant media attention and large crowds. From this popularity came the first football stadium at Harvard in 1903. Unfortunately the on-field game, featuring the "flying wedge" formation where the offensive team linked arms and tried to trample their opponents, resulted in many injuries and some deaths. In 1906, President Theodore Roosevelt invited the college presidents of the major Ivy League schools to the White House and insisted that they change the rules to eliminate violent play. Later that year, representatives of 28 schools with football teams met in New York City and formed the group that evolved into the National Collegiate Athletic Association (N.C.A.A.). After 1906 the rules became more uniform and outlawed fighting and open brutality; the new rules also allowed a limited version of the forward pass but kept the rugby-sized ball. Fullback plunges into the line became the main offensive weapon.

Early Success

During the first two decades of the 20th century, college football increased in popularity, not only in the Northeast but even more so in the Midwest. The largest schools in the Midwest—Michigan, Minnesota, Wisconsin, Illinois, Purdue, Chicago, and Northwestern—formed a conference (the forerunner of the Big Ten) in 1895, and these universities began to produce some of the best football teams in the country. Directing the on-field game were the graduate managers, who at many schools, had become full-time, well-paid coaches and athletic directors. The media promoted the teams and focused public attention on the most successful and famous coaches and the best players. From 1899 to 1924, Amos Alonzo Stagg won seven Big Ten championships for the University of Chicago with his "Monsters of the Midway"; Glenn "Pop" Warner invented the single wing and, from 1907 to 1914, won at Carlisle Institute (where few of his players were college students); and Fielding Yost had great success at the University of Michigan during the first decades of the century. The greatest player of the era was the Native American athlete Jim Thorpe, who played at Carlisle from 1908 to 1911. College football—unlike other organized sports, notably major and minor league baseball—was open to all minority groups, including African Americans. In the mid-1910's Paul Robeson at Rutgers and Fritz Pollard at Brown were football stars, their schools amenable to their playing and attending as long as they helped their teams win.

The Roaring Twenties and Great Depression

In the 1920's, a decade of economic prosperity, college football expanded dramatically. Many schools, particularly in urban areas and in the South and Southwest, started or enlarged their teams, while many of the established football powers built huge stadiums and began organizing student and alumni activities around the games, particularly the new phenomenon of Homecoming.

The sporting press loved the hoopla of college football, and national sportswriters such as Grantland Rice turned the era's stars into national heroes. Before ever seeing him play, Rice called Harold "Red" Grange, an outstanding running back at the University of Illinois, "The Galloping Ghost of the Illini." But Rice's greatest creation was "The Four Horsemen of Notre Dame," a swift but small backfield for the decade's most popular team, the Fighting Irish of the University of Notre Dame. Their innovative and entrepreneurial coach, Knute Rockne, aided by the media, turned the teams of a small Catholic school in northern Indiana into a national phenomenon. The more games and championships that Rockne's teams won, the greater their popularity among regular fans. The Fighting Irish also created college football fans of millions of people, particularly working-class Catholics who previously had no interest in football or college. A decade later, Warner Brothers made a saccharine movie about this team and its coach, *Knute Rockne—All-American*, with future president Ronald Reagan portraying Rockne's greatest player, George Gipp.

The Great Depression of the 1930's erased some small college football programs, but the big ones persevered and, thanks to the new medium of radio, became even more popular. Notre Dame, West Point, and the Naval Academy allowed free broadcasts of their games and developed huge national followings, but even the schools that charged the broadcasters reached large local and regional audiences. In the mid-1930's tourism promoters in a number of warm weather cities started the Sugar, Cotton, and Orange Bowls (the Rose Bowl, the "Grand-Daddy of the Bowls," had begun in 1903). The bowl promoters invited the most successful teams to participate in this extra game that took place after the regular season. This system remains in place in the modern college game. Another continuing tradition is the Heisman Trophy. In 1934 the Downtown Athletic Club of New York City created the annual trophy to honor the year's best college player. During these years, the Southeastern and Southwestern conferences, in an attempt to lure athletes from the football-rich high schools of the north, offered the first athletic scholarships.

In 1934 the rules committee of the coaches association shrank the size of the football, and the forward pass started to become a major offensive weapon, particularly in the Southwest Conference, featuring passers such as "Slinging" Sammy Baugh and Davey O'Brien of Texas Christian University. Yet, in the North, running backs and fierce linemen still dominated the game, producing national champions at the University of Minnesota under coach Bernie Bierman, a.k.a. "Hammer of the North," and outstanding teams at Fordham University, led by their "Seven Blocks of Granite" line.

World War II and Its Aftermath

During World War II, many schools curtailed their football programs but various armed forces training camps fielded teams to play the college squads still operating. In addition, through the cooperation of draft boards around the country, West Point and the Naval Academy produced the best teams of the war era. Coach Earl "Red" Blaik's Black Knights of the Hudson, with Heisman Trophy winners Felix "Doc" Blanchard and Glenn Davis leading the running attack, captured national championships in 1944 and 1945.

After the war, college football exploded in popularity.

Hundreds of schools entered or reentered the sport, and more than 50 new bowl games began. Atop this chaotic situation stood the traditional powers, particularly teams from Big Ten and Pacific Coast Conference universities. Cheating was rampant, with coaches often employing professional athletes and not pretending that their players were students. Ruthless buccaneers like Paul "Bear" Bryant emerged, winning at every stop—in Bryant's case at Maryland, Kentucky, Texas A & M, and eventually his alma mater, Alabama. Among the great players of the era—Heisman winners and runners-up—were Notre Dame quarterback Johnny Lujack and end Leon Hart; Southern Methodist running backs Doak Walker and Kyle Rote; Georgia's Charley Trippi; and North Carolina's Charlie "Choo-Choo" Justice.

In the 1950's, for the first time, the N.C.A.A. permitted all of its members to award athletic scholarships, bringing them in line with the conferences already allowing them. However, the Ivy League schools, terming athletic scholarships as pay-for-play, refused to grant them and dropped out of big-time football. In 1952 tailback Dick Kazmaier of Princeton was the last Heisman Trophy winner from the league that had invented American college football.

In this decade, the N.C.A.A. also gained control of all televising of college football games and parceled them out to schools across the country—but did not allow the most popular teams, like Notre Dame, to appear more than a few times a season. Coach Bud Wilkinson's Oklahoma Sooners dominated their conference, but Big Ten teams, notably coach Woody Hayes's Ohio State Buckeyes and Clarence "Biggie" Munn's Michigan State Spartans challenged Oklahoma for the top spot in the national ranking. Ohio State players Vic Janowicz and Howard "Hopalong" Cassidy won Heismans, as did Billy Vessels of Oklahoma. In addition, many black players entered big-time college football at this time; because southern and southwestern schools still excluded them, Big Ten universities were able to bring many excellent African-American players north to suit up for their teams.

The Full Integration of College Football

In 1961 Ernie Davis of Syracuse was the first black athlete to win the Heisman. A few years before, the great Jim Brown of Syracuse had finished far from the top spot because of the prejudiced voting of southern sportswriters. In the 1960s, as civil rights issues became more important politically, so did black athletes at major schools: the University of Southern California won championships with Mike Garrett and O.J. Simpson (both Heisman winners). At the end of the decade, schools below the Mason-Dixon Line began to recruit black players—Jerry Levias at Southern Methodist was the first African American to play in the Southwest Conference. Black athletes speeded the integration of many colleges in the South and Southwest and, equally important, helped the fans of those teams accept integration. For most football fans, winning trumped racism, and if black players could bring championships, the fans wanted them on their teams. "Bear" Bryant of Alabama, after losing a game to a U.S.C. squad led by black running back Sam Cunningham, integrated the Crimson Tide in the early 1970's, and Alabama fans cheered as the team added more national championships to its list.

In this era, TV coverage of intercollegiate football changed. Roone Arledge began producing telecasts for ABC-TV, and he portrayed college football as a spectacle, not just a contest on a field. He employed many more cameras than had been used before, and his crews frequently focused on coaches and cheerleadeers on the sidelines, fans in the crowd, as well the on-field action. Arledge wanted the TV audience to stay tuned to the game—and the ads—whether the score was lopsided or not; he wanted the spectacle to transcend the sport. His approach came to dominate television coverage of college sports as did the increasing intrusion of commercial sponsors.

The Final Decades of the Century

In 1973 the N.C.A.A. changed athletic scholarships from a guaranteed four-year grant to a one-year contract renewed at the behest of the athlete's coach, in effect, making a football player an employee of his athletic department and under the strict control of his coach. The new system rewarded martinets like Ohio State's Woody Hayes, who put his players through long, grueling practices and demanded absolute obedience. In the 1970's his Buckeyes won Big Ten titles and played in Rose Bowls, and his running back Archie Griffin garnered two Heisman Trophies (and remains the only multiple Heisman winner). But Hayes's career ended in 1978 when he ran onto the field during a bowl game between Ohio State and Clemson and punched a player on the opposing squad. Other outstanding Heisman winners of the 1970's and their national championship teams were Tony Dorsett at Pitt, Johnny Rodgers at Nebraska, and Charles White at USC.

In 1976 61 of the major football schools formed the College Football Association. Dissatisfied with the

N.C.A.A.'s control of the sport, they sought more autonomy over and revenue from their football programs. Two CFA schools, the universities of Georgia and Oklahoma, challenged the N.C.A.A.'s monopoly on telecasts of college football games in court. In a series of verdicts, ending with an almost unanimous 1984 Supreme Court decision, the CFA schools prevailed, and the N.C.A.A. lost control of televising college football. As a result, many national and local networks began broadcasting the games, and many schools, seeking better payouts, moved the scheduling of contests from the traditional Saturday afternoon spot to night games, then games on other days and nights of the week.

In the 1980's the University of Miami Hurricanes, with such excellent quarterbacks as Bernie Kosar and Vinny Testaverde, rose to the top of the polls, and won national titles in 1983, 1987, and 1989. Other excellent teams of the decade were coach Barry Switzer's Oklahoma Sooners and coach Joe Paterno's Penn State Nittany Lions. The articulate Paterno, a graduate of Brown University, was often pointed to as an exemplary coach; he accepted the acclaim and also criticized the increasing corruption in his sport. Many critics and two major reform groups, the Knight Commission and the N.C.A.A. Presidents' Commission, suggested reforms; however, they could never convince powerful coaches and athletic directors to agree to any meaningful changes in the college sports system.

The Contemporary Era

In the 1990's the on-field game came to resemble a version of professional football, and an increasing number of coaches shuttled back and forth between college and N.F.L. teams. Many players considered themselves in minor league training for the N.F.L. and, as a result, the graduation rates of the best teams were often very low. Coach Bobby Bowden's Florida State Seminoles won conference titles, bowl games, and two national championships in the 1990's, and also featured many players who did not graduate and some who acquired criminal records while in college.

At the end of the century, the division between the have and have-not teams in college football increased, and the rich schools and conferences took the lion's share of revenue from television and the bowl games. The haves codified their status when they endorsed the Bowl Championship Series (BCS) in 1992 and convinced the N.C.A.A. to give them semi-autonomous status a few years later. This situation contributed to the demise of the Southwest Conference in 1996 and major shifts in other leagues. In 2003 the Big East football conference, only formed in 1990, lost two important members, Miami and Virginia Tech, to the Atlantic Coast Conference, and this started a domino effect with stronger conferences considering raids on weaker ones to replace departed schools. Because power and greed seem to motivate the men and women running the major conferences and schools, many more changes in college football likely will occur in the first decades of the 21st century. And the game will become increasingly commercial and professional, with more coaches earning more than $1 million a year, and their players detached from regular student life. Yet fans will continue to love college football, attend games and watch them on TV, and the sport will remain an important part of their lives. No other higher education system in the world has produced such an unusual institution as American intercollegiate football.

Professional Football

From its roots in rugby and soccer, American football began its own history in 1876, with the first set of rules. By 1902 the sport had already seen its first professional player (William "Pudge" Heffelfinger, in 1892), its first all professional team (the Allegheny Athletic Association, in 1896), and its first night game (1902, Elmira, N.Y.). But interest in the pro game was largely limited to the Great Lakes states.

Backward passes, or laterals, were always a part of the game, remnants of the sport's rugby ancestry. It wasn't until 1906 that the forward pass was legalized. However, until 1933, the forward pass had to be thrown from five yards behind the line of scrimmage. Other notable rule changes over time included reducing the value of a field goal from four points to three. As for the value of a touchdown, it was raised from four points to five in 1898 and raised again to six points in 1909. Though there have been literally hundreds of changes to the rules and equipment since then, today's game has much in common with its ancestor.

1920's and 1930's

The American Professional Football League was formed in 1920, and adopted a constitution a year later for its 22 franchises. In 1922 the association changed its name to the National Football League. Two extant N.F.L. franchises predate the league's existence: the Arizona (formerly St. Louis, formerly Chicago) Cardinals (1899), and the Green Bay Packers (1919). The number of franchises fluctuated as high as 23 clubs in 1925 and as low as eight teams in 1932, as the Depression took its toll on the league.

The sport first attracted national attention in 1925, when All-America quarterback Red Grange, from the University of Illinois, signed a contract with the Chicago Bears. A then-record crowd of 36,000 people watched the "Galloping Ghost" play his first pro game at Wrigley Field. The Bears then went on a barnstorming tour across the country that brought crowds of 73,000 to the Polo Grounds for a game against the New York Giants and 75,000 to the Los Angeles Coliseum for an exhibition against the L.A. Tigers.

The N.F.L. changed the forward pass rule in 1933, so that the ball could be thrown from anywhere behind the line of scrimmage. The rule change increased the importance of the quarterback position, giving rise to passers like "Slingin'" Sammy Baugh. In 1935 the N.F.L. adopted a draft, with teams choosing players from college's game in inverse order of finish; a year later, the Philadelphia Eagles chose Heisman Trophy winner Jay Berwanger, a University of Chicago running back, with the first pick.

N.F.L. attendance topped 1 million for the first time in 1939. Also that year, the league's first game was televised, a game between the Eagles and the Brooklyn Dodgers. Fewer than one thousand people owned television sets at the time, but this paved the way for football to become a fixture in American living rooms.

1940's and 1950's

World War II decimated several franchises, forcing some teams to merge with each other for a season or longer. In 1943, the era of specialization began when the league adopted free substitution. Amended in 1946, it was restored in 1950, allowing players to play only offense or defense, and to go out of the game for a play or longer and then return. The league also approved a 10-game schedule and made helmets mandatory. Five years later, the Los Angeles Rams painted horns on their helmets, becoming the first team to add emblems to their headgear.

The rival All-America Football Conference started play in 1946 with eight teams, three of which (Cleveland Browns, Baltimore Colts, and San Francisco 49ers) were welcomed into the N.F.L. in 1949. This began the N.F.L.'s hegemony over competitive leagues by appropriating their strongest assets. The A.A.F.C. folded in 1950, and its players were allocated to N.F.L. franchises through a special draft.

That same year, the Los Angeles Rams, and later the Washington Redskins, negotiated deals to have all their games televised. In 1951 the Rams televised only road games in an attempt to increase attendance. Later that year, the DuMont Network paid $75,000 to televise the N.F.L. Championship game coast to coast. NBC paid $100,000 for the 1955 title game, and in 1956 CBS began broadcasting regular season games on Sunday afternoons.

On December 28, 1958, the Baltimore Colts and New York Giants played for the N.F.L. title in what many still deem the greatest football game ever played. The game went into overtime (a first for the title game) before Colts fullback Alan Ameche scored the winning touchdown.

1960's and 1970's

The N.F.L. was at a crossroads in 1960. After longtime Commissioner Bert Bell died of a heart attack, league owners could not agree on a successor. Finally, on the 23rd ballot, they settled on Rams general manager Pete Rozelle. Over the next three decades, Rozelle would guide the league through unprecedented growth, surpassing even baseball, the national pastime, as America's favorite sport.

The N.F.L. faced competition from another upstart league, the American Football League, which was scheduled to launch in the fall of 1960. But the N.F.L. eviscerated its would-be rival, awarding N.F.L. franchises to Minnesota (which then withdrew from the A.F.L.) and to Dallas (home of A.F.L. president Lamar Hunt's Dallas Texans).

Even though the A.F.L.'s two-year-long antitrust suit against the N.F.L. failed in 1962, the new league's high-scoring offenses attracted fans and television money. ABC signed a five-year deal in 1960, and NBC took over A.F.L. broadcasts in 1965 for $36 million over the next five years. In 1965 the A.F.L.'s New York Jets signed Alabama quarterback Joe Namath to a three-year, $427,000 deal, a record salary for any football player. The deal sparked a bidding war between the two leagues as they spent a combined $7 million on their 1966 draft choices.

The champions of each league squared off in the first A.F.L.-N.F.L. World Championship game in 1967. The contest wouldn't be dubbed "Super Bowl" for another year, and the game wasn't a sellout. In the first title game, the Green Bay Packers defeated the Kansas City Chiefs 35-

10. Bart Starr led the Packers to a second championship a year later over the Oakland Raiders. In 1969 Namath roiled the football world again by predicting the Jets would defeat the heavily favored Baltimore Colts in Super Bowl III. His prediction was correct, and the shocking upset brought credibility to the younger league.

Unable to vanquish its newest competitor, the N.F.L. consumed it in a merger of the two leagues. In 1970 Baltimore, Cleveland, and Pittsburgh joined the 10 A.F.L. teams to form the American Football Conference. The remaining 13 teams made up the National Football Conference. From 1972 to 1980, the former A.F.L. teams dominated. The Miami Dolphins completed football's only undefeated season in 1972 and repeated as champions in 1973. They were succeeded by the Pittsburgh Steelers, whose "Steel Curtain" defense won four championships (1974, 1975, 1978, and 1979), and the Oakland Raiders (1976 and 1980).

The N.F.L.'s relationship with television changed forever because of what came to be known as the "Heidi" game. On November 17, 1968, NBC cut away in the last minute of the Jets-Raiders game so the beloved children's movie could start on time. The Raiders scored two touchdowns in the last 42 seconds for a come-from-behind 43-32 win. Since then, any time a football game has run past its scheduled ending time, the networks have delayed the programming that follows it until the contest's completion.

Football also conquered prime-time television with the advent of Monday Night Football in 1970. It would become the longest-running prime-time series in the network's history. Meanwhile, the Super Bowl began its rise from curiosity to the most-watched event in world history. By 1971 the TV audience of 24 million homes was the largest ever for a one-day sports event. Two years later, a record 75 million people tuned in. In 1978 the Super Bowl audience topped 102 million.

Another rival league, the World Football League, started operation in 1974, with franchises concentrated in the Sun Belt and Canada. The W.F.L. scored a coup by signing three Miami Dolphins stars to lucrative contracts, but the league folded after only two seasons.

The N.F.L. extended its season from 14 to 16 games in 1978 and added a second wildcard team in each conference to the playoff structure. The two wildcard teams played each other, with the winner advancing to the eight-team playoffs. Additional rule changes outlawed the head slap and allowed defenders to make contact with receivers only once; wide receivers were prohibited from blocking a defender in the back.

1980's to the present

In 1982 an astounding 73 percent of American homes tuned in to the Super Bowl, making it the highest-rated sports event in history. The 1986 Super Bowl drew a record 127 million viewers, a greater overall number of people, but a slightly lower percentage of the total. Although competition from more networks and channels has fractured the TV audience since then, the Super Bowl is routinely the most-watched television program of the year.

Other off-the-field developments played pivotal roles in the N.F.L.'s recent history. Players' strikes in 1982 and 1987 shortened those seasons to nine and 15 games respectively; in 1987 the owners hired replacement players for three games before the regulars returned. Those strikes resulted in increased free agency for players, but allowed clubs some leeway to retain "franchise players."

The new labor agreements maintained the N.F.L.'s system of revenue-sharing, ballyhooed as the saving grace for small market teams like Green Bay and Cincinnati. But they did nothing to stop the trend of owners hijacking franchises and moving them to the city with the most favorable deal. The Raiders moved from Oakland to Los Angeles in 1982, and returned to Oakland in 1995. Los Angeles, the nation's second-largest media market, was left without a team, as that same year, the Rams departed for St. Louis, which had been ditched in 1987 by the Cardinals, who had fled to Phoenix.

Baltimore Colts owner Robert Irsay surreptitiously packed his team into moving vans in the middle of the night of January 14, 1984, and opened shop the next day in Indianapolis. Recognizing Baltimore's hunger for Sunday afternoon entertainment, Cleveland Browns owner Art Modell moved his team there in 1996 and renamed it the Ravens. The N.F.L. responded by awarding an expansion franchise, also called the Browns, to Cleveland to begin play in 1999. The Houston Oilers relocated to Nashville in 1998, and changed their name to the Titans the year after. In 2002 jilted Houston received an expansion franchise, bringing the total number of N.F.L. teams to 32.

To accommodate all the moving and expanding, the league realigned each conference from three divisions to four in 2002, preserving traditional rivalries while imposing some geographic order. Because the number of division champions increased from six to eight, the number of playoff wildcard teams, which had been increased to six in 1990, was reduced to four, keeping the total number of playoff teams at 12.

Two other rival leagues came and went quickly: the U.S.F.L., which won an antitrust suit against the N.F.L. in 1986, but was awarded damages of only $1, and soon went out of business; and the X.F.L., a joint venture of NBC and pro wrestling impresario Vince McMahon. The first week of the 2001 X.F.L. season drew large crowds and ratings, but the poor quality of play could not sustain that level of interest, and the league folded after its first year.

Meanwhile, the N.F.L. spread its influence across the globe. After exhibition games in London (1986), Tokyo (1989), Berlin (1990), and Montreal (1990) drew sizable crowds, the league launched the World League of American Football in 1990, scuttled it in 1993, reintroduced it in 1995 with six European franchises, and renamed it N.F.L. Europe in 1998.

All the while, the television money kept rolling in, with networks paying record sums for broadcast rights. The latest multibillion-dollar contracts with CBS, Fox, ABC, and ESPN last through the 2005 season.

There were also developments on the field. Miami's Dan Marino rewrote the record book for quarterbacks, though he ended his career without ever winning a Super Bowl. San Francisco's Jerry Rice became the all-time leader in receptions and receiving yards in 1995, then continued to play past his 40th birthday for the Raiders. Chicago Bear running back Walter Payton broke Jim Brown's record for career rushing yards in 1987, and Emmitt Smith of the Cowboys surpassed Payton's record in 2002.

The NFC returned to dominance, winning 13 straight Super Bowls from the 1984 to the 1996 seasons, most of them in blowouts. Quarterback Joe Montana orchestrated Bill Walsh's pass-first West Coast offense to perfection to lead the San Francisco 49ers to four Super Bowls.

The N.F.L.'s desire for parity has kept more teams in the playoff hunt late into the season, but critics say it has led to an overall mediocrity. A total of seven different teams appeared in the 2000–2003 Super Bowls, with four different winners.

Professional Football Hall of Fame

Alphabetical listing includes enshrinee's name, year of enshrinement, position, and the teams he played or coached for.

Herb Adderley (1980) CB, Packers, Cowboys.
George Allen (2002) Coach, Rams, Redskins.
Lance Alworth (1978) WR, Chargers, Cowboys.
Doug Atkins (1982) DE, Browns, Bears, Saints.
Morris (Red) Badgro (1981) E, Yankees, Giants, Dodgers.
Lem Barney (1992) CB, Lions.
Cliff Battles (1968) RB, QB, Braves, Redskins.
Sammy Baugh (1963) QB, Redskins.
Chuck Bednarik (1967) C, LB, Eagles.
Bert Bell (1963 Charter) Commissioner, N.F.L. Founder/coach, Eagles, Steelers.
Bobby Bell (1983) LB, DE, Chiefs.
Raymond Berry (1973) E, Colts.
Charles W. Bidwill, Sr. (1967) Owner/president, Cardinals.
Fred Biletnikoff (1988) WR, Raiders.
George Blanda (1981) QB, PK, Bears, Colts, Oilers, Raiders.
Mel Blount (1989) CB, Steelers.
Terry Bradshaw (1989) QB, Steelers.
Bob Brown (2004) T, Eagles, Rams, Raiders.
Jim Brown (1971) FB, Browns.
Paul E. Brown (1967) Coach and GM, Browns, Bengals.
Roosevelt Brown (1975) OT, Giants.
Willie Brown (1984) CB, Broncos, Raiders.
Buck Buchanan (1990) DT, Chiefs.
Nick Buoniconti (2001) LB, Patriots, Dolphins.
Dick Butkus (1979) LB, Bears.
Earl Campbell (1991) RB, Oilers, Saints.
Tony Canadeo (1974) RB, Packers.
Joe Carr (1963) N.F.L. President.
Dave Casper (2002) TE, Raiders, Oilers, Vikings.
Guy Chamberlin (1965) E, Bulldogs, Staleys, Yellowjackets, Cardinals. Coach, Bulldogs, Yellowjackets, Cardinals.
Jack Christiansen (1970) DB, Spartans, Lions.
Earl (Dutch) Clark (1970) DB, Spartans, Lions, Rams.
George Connor (1975) OT, DT, LB, Bears.
Jimmy Conzelman (1964) QB, Staleys, Independents, Badgers, Panthers. Owner, Steamrollers, Cardinals.
Lou Creekmur, (1996) OL, Lions.
Larry Csonka (1987) RB, Dolphins, Giants.
Al Davis (1992) President, Owner, General Manager, Coach, Raiders. Commissioner, A.F.L.

Willie Davis (1981) DE, Browns, Packers.
Len Dawson (1987) QB, Steelers, Browns, Texans, Chiefs.
Eric Dickerson (1999) RB, Rams, Colts, Raiders, Falcons.
Dan Dierdorf (1996) OT, Cardinals.
Mike Ditka (1988) TE, Bears, Eagles, Cowboys.
Art Donovan (1968) DT, Colts, Yankees, Texans.
Tony Dorsett (1994) RB, Cowboys, Broncos.
John (Paddy) Driscoll (1965) QB, Pros, Staleys, Cardinals, Bears.
Bill Dudley (1966) RB, Steelers, Lions, Redskins.
Albert Glen (Turk) Edwards (1969) OT, Braves, Redskins.
Carl Eller (2004) DE, Vikings, Seahawks.
John Elway (2004) QB, Broncos.
Weeb Ewbank (1978) Coach, Colts, Jets.
Tom Fears (1970) E, Rams.
Jim Finks (1995) President, Vikings, Bears, Saints.
Ray Flaherty (1976) Coach, Redskins, Yankees.
Len Ford (1976) DE, E, Dons, Browns, Packers.
Dan Fortmann (1965) G, Bears.
Dan Fouts (1993) QB, Chargers.
Frank Gatski (1985) C, Browns, Lions.
Bill George (1974) LB, Bears, Rams.
Joe Gibbs (1996) Coach, Chargers, Redskins.
Frank Gifford (1977) RB, Giants.
Sid Gillman (1983) Coach, Rams, Chargers, Oilers.
Otto Graham (1965) QB, Browns.
Harold (Red) Grange (1963 Charter) RB, Bears, Yankees.
Bud Grant (1994) Coach, Vikings.
(Mean) Joe Greene (1987) DT, Steelers.
Forrest Gregg (1977) OL, Packers, Cowboys.
Bob Griese (1990) QB, Dolphins.
Lou Groza (1974) OT, PK, Browns.
Joe Guyon (1966) RB, Bulldogs, Indians, Independents, Cowboys, Giants.
George Halas (1963) Founder, Coach, player, Staleys. President, Coach, player, Bears.
Jack Ham (1988) LB, Steelers.
Dan Hampton (2002) DE/DT, Bears.
John Hannah (1991) G, Patriots.
Franco Harris (1990) RB, Steelers, Seahawks.
Mike Haynes (1997) CB, Patriots, Raiders.
Ed Healey (1964) OT, Independents, Bears.
Mel Hein (1963) C, Giants.
Ted Hendricks (1990) LB, Colts, Packers, Raiders.
Wilbur (Pete) Henry (1963) OT, Bulldogs, Giants, Maroons.
Arnie Herber (1966) QB, Packers, Giants.
Bill Hewitt (1971) E, Bears, Eagles.
Clarke Hinkle (1964) RB, Packers.
Elroy (Crazylegs) Hirsch (1968) HB, E, Rockets, Rams.
Paul Hornung (1986) HB, Packers.
Ken Houston (1986) S, Oilers, Redskins.
Cal Hubbard (1963) OT, Giants, Packers, Pirates.
Sam Huff (1982) LB, Giants, Redskins.
Lamar Hunt (1972) Founder, AFL; Owner Texans, Chiefs.
Don Hutson (1963) E, Packers.
Jimmy Johnson (1994) CB, 49ers.
John Henry Johnson (1987) RB, 49ers, Lions, Steelers, Oilers.
Charlie Joiner (1996), WR, Oilers, Bengals, Chargers.
Deacon Jones (1980) DE, Rams, Chargers, Redskins.
Stan Jones (1991) G, DT, Bears, Redskins.
Henry Jordan (1995) DT, Packers.
Sonny Jurgensen (1983) QB, Eagles, Redskins.
Jim Kelly (2002) QB, Bills.
Leroy Kelly (1994) RB, Browns.
Walt Kiesling (1966) G, Eskimos, Maroons, Cardinals, Bears, Packers, Pirates. Coach, Pirates, Steelers.
Frank (Bruiser) Kinard (1971) OT, Dodgers, Yankees.
Paul Krause (1998) S, Vikings, Redskins.
Early (Curly) Lambeau (1963) Founder, Packers. Coach, Packers, Cardinals, Redskins.
Jack Lambert (1990) LB, Steelers.
Tom Landry (1990) Coach, Cowboys.
Dick (Night Train) Lane (1974) DB, Rams, Cardinals, Lions.
Jim Langer (1987) C, Dolphins, Vikings.
Willie Lanier (1986) LB, Chiefs.
Steve Largent (1995) WR, Seahawks.
Yale Lary (1979) DB, Lions.
Dante Lavelli (1975) E, Browns.
Bobby Layne (1967) QB, Bears, Bulldogs, Lions, Steelers.
Alphonse (Tuffy) Leemans (1978) RB, Giants.
Marv Levy (2001) Coach, Chiefs, Bills.
Bob Lilly (1980) DT, Cowboys.
Larry Little (1993) G, Chargers, Dolphins.
Vince Lombardi (1971) Coach, GM, Packers, Redskins.
Howie Long (2000) DL, Raiders.
Ronnie Lott (2000) DB, 49ers, Raiders, Jets.
Sid Luckman (1965) QB, Bears.
William Roy (Link) Lyman (1964) T, Bulldogs, Yellowjackets, Bears.
Tom Mack (1999) OG, Rams.
John Mackey (1992) TE, Colts, Chargers.
Tim Mara (1963) Founder, President, Giants.
Wellington Mara (1997) Owner, Giants.

Gino Marchetti (1972) DE, Texans, Colts.
George Preston Marshall (1963) Founder, President, Braves (Redskins).
Ollie Matson (1972) RB, Cardinals, Rams, Lions, Eagles.
Don Maynard (1987) WR, Giants, Titans, Jets, Cardinals.
George McAfee (1966) RB, Bears.
Mike McCormack (1984) OT, Yankees, Browns.
Tommy McDonald (1998) WR, Eagles, Cowboys, Rams, Falcons, Browns.
Hugh McElhenny (1970) RB, 49ers Vikings, Giants, Lions.
John (Blood) McNally (1963) RB, Badgers, Eskimos, Maroons, Packers, Pirates, Packers.
Mike Michalske (1964) G, Yankees, Packers.
Wayne Millner (1968) E, Redskins. Coach, Eagles.
Bobby Mitchell (1983) WR, RB Browns, Redskins.
Ron Mix (1979) OT, Chargers, Raiders.
Joe Montana (2000) QB, 49ers, Chiefs.
Lenny Moore (1975) WR, RB, Colts.
Marion Motley (1968) RB, Browns, Steelers.
Mike Munchak (2001) G, Oilers.
Anthony Muñoz (1998) T, Bengals.
George Musso (1982) OT, G, Bears.
Bronko Nagurski (1963) RB, Bears.
Joe Namath (1985) QB, Jets, Rams.
Earle (Greasy) Neale (1969) Coach, Eagles.
Ozzie Newsome (1999) TE, Browns.
Ernie Nevers (1963) RB, Eskimos, Cardinals.
Ray Nitschke (1978) LB, Packers.
Chuck Noll (1993) Coach, Steelers.
Leo Nomellini (1969) DT, 49ers.
Merlin Olsen (1982) DT, Rams.
Jim Otto (1980) C, Raiders.
Steve Owen (1966) T, Cowboys, Giants. Coach, Giants.
Alan Page (1988) DT, Vikings, Bears.
Clarence (Ace) Parker (1972) QB, Dodgers, Yankees.
Jim Parker (1973) OL, Colts.
Walter Payton (1993) RB, Bears.
Joe Perry (1969) RB, 49ers, Colts.
Pete Pihos (1970) E, Eagles.
Hugh (Shorty) Ray (1966) Supervisor of Officials.
Dan Reeves (1967) Owner, Rams.
Mel Renfro (1996), CB, Cowboys.
John Riggins (1992) RB, Jets, Redskins.
Jim Ringo (1981) C, Packers, Eagles.
Andy Robustelli (1971) DE, Rams, Giants.
Art Rooney (1964) Founder, President, Pirates, Steelers.
Dan Rooney (2000) President, Steelers.
Pete Rozelle (1985) Commissioner, N.F.L..
Bob St. Clair (1990) OT, 49ers.
Barry Sanders (2004) RB, Lions.
Gale Sayers (1977) RB, Bears.
Joe Schmidt (1973) LB, Lions. Coach, Lions.
Tex Schramm (1991) GM, Cowboys.
Lee Roy Selmon (1995) DE, Buccaneers.
Billy Shaw (1999) OG, Bills.
Art Shell (1989) OT, Raiders.
Don Shula (1997) Coach, Colts, Dolphins.
O.J. Simpson (1985) RB, Bills, 49ers.
Mike Singletary (1998) LB, Bears.
Jackie Slater (2001) OT, Rams.
Jackie Smith (1994) TE, Cardinals, Cowboys.
John Stallworth (2002) WR, Steelers.
Bart Starr (1977) QB, Packers.
Roger Staubach, (1985) QB, Cowboys.
Ernie Stautner (1969) DT, Steelers.
Jan Stenerud (1991) PK, Chiefs, Packers, Vikings.
Dwight Stephenson (1998) C, Dolphins.
Ken Strong (1967) RB, Stapletons, Giants, Yankees.
Joe Stydahar (1967) OT, Bears.
Lynn Swann (2001) WR, Steelers.
Fran Tarkenton (1986) QB, Giants, Vikings.
Charley Taylor (1984) WR, RB, Redskins.
Jim Taylor (1976) RB, Packers, Saints.
Lawrence Taylor (1999) LB, Giants.
Jim Thorpe (1963) RB, Bulldogs, Indians, Maroons, Independents, Giants, Bulldogs, Cardinals.
Y.A. Tittle (1971) QB, Colts, 49ers, Giants.
George Trafton (1964) C, Staleys, Bears.
Charley Trippi (1968) RB, QB, Cardinals.
Emlen Tunnell (1967) DB, Giants, Packers.
Clyde (Bulldog) Turner (1966) C, LB, Bears.
Johnny Unitas (1979) QB, Colts, Chargers.
Gene Upshaw (1987) G, Raiders.
Norm Van Brocklin (1971) QB, Rams, Eagles.
Steve Van Buren (1965) RB, Eagles.
Doak Walker (1986) RB, Lions.
Bill Walsh (1993) Coach, 49ers.
Paul Warfield (1983) WR, Browns, Dolphins.
Bob Waterfield (1965) QB, Coach, Rams.
Mike Webster (1997) C, Steelers.
Arnie Weinmeister, (1984) DT, Yankees, Giants.
Randy White (1994) DT, Cowboys.
Dave Wilcox (2000) LB, 49ers.
Bill Willis (1977) G, MG, Browns.
Larry Wilson (1978) DB, Cardinals.
Kellen Winslow (1995) TE, Chargers.
Alex Wojciechowicz (1968) C, LB, Lions, Eagles.
Willie Wood (1989) S, Packers.
Ron Yary (2001) OT, Vikings.
Jack Youngblood (2001) DE, Rams.

Super Bowl Results, 1967–2004

Super Bowl	Location	Winning Team	Losing Team
I	Jan. 15, 1967 Memorial Coliseum, Los Angeles, California	Green Bay Packers 35	Kansas City Chiefs 10
II	Jan. 14, 1968, Orange Bowl, Miami, Florida	Green Bay Packers 33	Oakland Raiders 14
III	Jan. 12, 1969, Orange Bowl, Miami, Florida	New York Jets 16	Baltimore Colts 7
IV	Jan. 11, 1970, Tulane Stadium, New Orleans, Louisiana	Kansas City Chiefs 23	Minnesota Vikings 7
V	Jan. 17, 1971, Orange Bowl, Miami, Florida	Baltimore Colts 16	Dallas Cowboys 13
VI	Jan. 16, 1972, Tulane Stadium, New Orleans, Louisiana	Dallas Cowboys 24	Miami Dolphins 3
VII	Jan. 14, 1973, Memorial Coliseum, Los Angeles, California	Miami Dolphins 14	Washington Redskins 7
VIII	Jan. 13, 1974, Rice Stadium, Houston, Texas	Miami Dolphins 24	Minnesota Vikings 7
IX	Jan, 12, 1975, Tulane Stadium, New Orleans, Louisiana	Pittsburgh Steelers 16	Minnesota 6
X	Jan. 18, 1976, Orange Bowl, Miami Florida	Pittsburgh Steelers 21	Dallas Cowboys 17
XI	Jan. 9, 1977, Rose Bowl, Pasadena, California	Oakland Raiders 32	Minnesota Vikings 14
XII	Jan. 15, 1978, Louisiana Superdome, New Orleans	Dallas Cowboys 27	Denver Broncos 10
XIII	Jan, 21, 1979, Orange Bowl, Miami, Florida	Pittsburgh Steelers 35	Dallas Cowboys 31
XIV	Jan. 20, 1980, Rose Bowl, Pasadena, California	Pittsburgh Steelers 31	Los Angeles Rams 19
XV	Jan. 25, 1981, Louisiana Superdome, New Orleans	Oakland Raiders 27	Philadelphia Eagles 10
XVI	Jan. 24, 1982, Pontiac Silverdome, Pontiac, Michigan	San Francisco 49ers 26	Cincinnati Bengals 21
XVII	Jan. 30, 1983, Rose Bowl, Pasadena, California	Washington Redskins 27	Miami Dolphins 17
XVIII	Jan, 22, 1984, Tampa Stadium, Tampa, Florida	Los Angeles Raiders 38	Washington Redskins 9
XIX	Jan. 20, 1985, Stanford Stadium, Stanford, California	San Francisco 49ers 38	Miami Dolphins 16
XX	Jan 26, 1986 Louisiana Superdome, New Orleans	Chicago Bears 46	New England Patriots 10
XXI	Jan. 25, 1987, Rose Bowl, Pasadena, California	New York Giants 39	Denver Broncos 20
XXII	Jan 31, 1988, Jack Murphy Stadium, San Diego, California	Washington Redskins 42	Denver Broncos 10
XXIII	Jan. 22, 1989, Joe Robbie Stadium, Miami Florida	San Francisco 49ers 20	Cincinnati Bengals 16
XXIV	Jan. 28, 1990, Louisiana Superdome, New Orleans, Louisiana	San Francisco 49ers 55	Denver Broncos 10
XXV	Jan. 27, 1991, Tampa Stadium, Tampa, Florida	New York Giants 20	Buffalo Bills 19
XXVI	Jan. 26, 1992, Hubert H. Humphrey Metrodome, Minneapolis, Minnesota	Washington Redskins 37	Buffalo Bills 24
XXVII	Jan. 31, 1993, Rose Bowl, Pasadena, California	Dallas Cowboys 52	Buffalo Bills 17
XXVIII	Jan. 30, 1994, Georgia Dome, Atlanta, Georgia	Dallas Cowboys 30	Buffalo Bills 13
XXIX	Jan. 29, 1995, Joe Robbie Stadium, Miami, Florida	San Francisco 49ers 49	San Diego Chargers 26
XXX	Jan. 28, 1996, Sun Devil Stadium, Tempe, Arizona	Dallas Cowboys 27	Pittsburgh Steelers 17
XXXI	Jan. 26, 1997, Louisiana Superdome, New Orleans	Green Bay Packers 35	New England Patriots 21
XXXII	Jan. 25, 1998, Qualcomm Stadium, San Diego	Denver Broncos 31	Green Bay Packers 24
XXXIII	Jan. 31, 1999, Pro Player Stadium, Miami, Florida	Denver Broncos 34	Atlanta Falcons 19
XXXIV	Jan. 30, 2000, Georgia Dome, Atlanta, Georgia	St. Louis Rams 23	Tennessee Titans 16
XXXV	Jan. 28, 2001, Raymond James Stadium, Tampa, Florida	Baltimore Ravens 34	New York Giants 7
XXXVI	Feb. 3, 2002, Louisiana Superdome, New Orleans	New England Patriots 20	St. Louis Rams 17
XXXVII	Jan. 26, 2003, Qualcomm Stadium, San Diego	Tampa Bay Buccaneers 48	Oakland Raiders 21
XXXVIII	Feb. 1, 2004, Reliant Stadium, Houston	New England Patriots 32	Carolina Panthers 29

Glossary of Football Terms

blitz a defensive strategy in which one or more linebackers or defensive backs, in addition to the defensive line, attempt to overwhelm the quarterback's protection by attacking from unexpected locations or situations.

block clearing a path for a teammate by obstructing or hitting an opponent.

clock the device that measures the time of a game. The game is divided into four 15-minute quarters with a 12-minute halftime. The clock continues to run after any play in which the ball carrier is tackled on the field, but will stop on any incomplete pass. When the ball carrier goes out of bounds during the last two minutes of the first half and the last five minutes of the second half, the clock will also halt.

cornerbacks the defenders primarily responsible for preventing the offense's wide receivers from catching passes, accomplished by remaining as close to the opponent as possible during pass routes. Cornerbacks are usually the fastest players on the defense.

defense the unit that must stop the opposing offense from moving the ball down the field and scoring. Unlike the offense, which is limited by rules in its deployment, the defense may align in any formation and may move without restriction before the snap. There are several kinds of standard defenses, including the 4-3 (four linemen and three linebackers), the 3-4 (three linemen and four linebackers), goal line, nickel, and dime, among others.

defensive backs a label applied to cornerbacks and safeties, or the secondary in general.

end zone an area 10 yards deep at either end of the field bordered by the goal line and the boundaries.

field goal an attempt to kick the ball through the uprights, worth three points. It is taken by a specialist called the place kicker. Distances are measured from the spot of the kick plus 10 yards for the depth of the end zone.

formation the alignment selected by the offense for the chosen play. In obvious passing situations, the offense may spread five wide receivers across the field; or on short yardage plays, the offense may opt for three tight ends and two running backs packed close to the offensive line.

first down the first play in a set of four downs, or when the offense succeeds in covering 10 yards in the four downs.

fumble when a player loses possession of the ball before being tackled, normally by contact with an opponent. Either team may recover the ball. The ground cannot cause a fumble.

goal line the line that divides the end zones from the rest of the field. A touchdown is awarded if the ball breaks the vertical plane of the goal line while in possession or if a receiver catches the ball in the end zone.

huddle a gathering of the offense or defense to communicate the upcoming play decided by the coach.

interception a pass caught by a defensive player instead of an offensive receiver. The ball may be returned in the other direction.

lateral a pass or toss behind the originating player to a teammate as measured by the lines across the field. Although the offense may only make one forward pass per play, there is no limit to the number of laterals at any time.

line of scrimmage an imaginary line, determined by the ball's location before each play, that extends across the field from sideline to sideline. Seven offensive players must be on the line of scrimmage, though the defense can set up in any formation. Forward passes cannot be thrown from beyond the line of scrimmage.

man/zone coverage the system that defenses employ to prevent the offense from passing the ball. In man coverage, the defender focuses on a single offensive player. In zone coverage, defenders are spread around the field, each with a section of responsibility. Frequently, coverages employ both strategies simultaneously some players in man coverage, others in zone.

officials in the N.F.L., seven officials, distinguished by black-and-white striped shirts, that rule on the game. The referee is the head official. Others are the umpire, head linesman, line judge, side judge, field judge, and back judge.

pass when the ball is thrown to a receiver who is farther down the field. A team is limited to one such forward pass per play. Normally this is the duty of the quarterback, although technically any eligible receiver can pass the ball.

pass routes/patterns the path that an offensive player runs to clear opposing defenders and receive a pass. These can be complex. Some more common routes include the slant, post, curl, in, out, and streak.

penalty a rules violation that is spotted and enforced by the officials. Penalty costs vary.

play action a type of offensive play in which the quarterback pretends to hand the ball to a running back before passing the ball. The goal is to fool the secondary into weakening their pass coverage.

play clock visible behind the end zone at either end of the stadium. Once a play is concluded, the offense has 40 seconds to snap the ball for the next play. The duration is reduced to 25 seconds for game-related stoppages such as penalties. Time is kept on the play clock. If the offense does not snap the ball before the play clock elapses, they incur a 5-yard penalty for delay of game.

possession when a player is judged to have control of the football. On pass receptions, the receiver must place two feet inside the boundaries to establish possession.

punt a kick, taken by a special teams player called the punter, that surrenders possession to the opposing team. This is normally done on fourth down when the offense deems gaining a first down unlikely.

receiver an offensive player who may legally catch a pass, almost always wide receivers, tight ends, and running backs. Only the two outermost players on either end of the line of scrimmage—even wide receivers who line up distantly from the offensive line—or the four players behind the line of scrimmage (such as running backs, another wide receiver, and the quarterback) are eligible receivers. If an offensive lineman, normally an ineligible receiver, is placed on the outside of the line of scrimmage because of an unusual formation, he is considered eligible but must indicate his eligibility to game officials before the play.

run a type of offensive play in which the quarterback, after accepting the ball from center, either keeps it and heads upfield or gives the ball to another player, who then attempts to move ahead with the help of blocking teammates.

sack a play in which the defense tackles the quarterback behind the line of scrimmage on a pass play.

safety 1) the most uncommon scoring play in football. When an offensive player is tackled in his own end zone, the defensive team is awarded two points and receives the ball via a kick. 2) a defensive secondary position divided into two roles, free safety and strong safety.

snap the action that begins each play. The center must snap the ball between his legs, usually to the quarterback, who accepts the ball while immediately behind the center or several yards farther back in a formation called the shotgun.

special teams the personnel that take the field for the punts, kickoffs, and field goals, or a generic term for that part of the game.

strong/weak an offensive formation is said to be strong or weak based on which side—counting out from the center—has the most players. The strong side, most frequently decided by the location of the tight end, has more players. The opposing defense also has players devoted to roles based on the offensive formation (such as strong safety and weakside linebacker), and will adjust its alignment accordingly before the play begins.

tackle 1) a term for both an offensive and defensive player. The offensive tackles line up on the outside of the line, but inside the tight end, while the defensive tackles protect the interior of their line. 2) the act of forcing a ball carrier to touch the ground with any body part other than the hand or feet. This concludes a play.

tight end an offensive player who normally lines up on the outside of either offensive tackle. Multiple tight ends are frequently employed on running plays where the offense requires only a modest gain. Roles vary between blocking or running pass routes.

timeout a timeout stops the clock and confers a break of varying duration. Either team may call a timeout between plays. Each team has three timeouts per half, which cannot be carried over to the second half.

touchdown scored when the ball breaks the vertical plane of the goal line. Worth six points and the scoring team can add a single additional point by kick or two points by converting from the 2-yard line with an offensive play.

ICE HOCKEY

History

Ice hockey evolved from the summertime sports of field hockey and Irish hurling, but the name "hockey" comes from the French word *hoquet*, which means "bent stick," or "shepherd's crook." The original game was brought by British soldiers to North America, where it was revised in the 1870's to use a flat puck instead of a ball. As the century progressed, the sport moved from the summertime fields to wintertime ice.

By the late 19th century, hockey was very popular in Canada. In 1892 the governor general of Canada, Lord Stanley, for a price of less than $50, purchased a silver cup lined with gold and declared that it should be awarded each year to the best amateur hockey team. This cup soon came to be called the Stanley Cup, and the trophy continues to be given to the champion of the National Hockey League (N.H.L.), the world's preeminent hockey league.

In the late 19th and early 20th centuries teams from all over Canada fought (often literally) for the Stanley Cup. As there was no overall league, any team could compete for the Cup. In its infancy, teams from 17 different leagues challenged for the Cup before the National Hockey Association (predecessor of the N.H.L.) took possession of the trophy in 1910. Since 1926, only N.H.L. teams have competed for the Stanley Cup.

The early days of hockey are filled with colorful stories. One club, the Dawson City Klondikers from the Yukon, traveled on dogsleds, bicycles, stagecoaches, and a boat just to reach a train to take them on a 23-day journey to vie for the Stanley Cup. Their travels came to an end against the legendary Ottawa Silver Seven, led by Frank McGee. In the second game of the series, McGee scored 14 goals—a record that still stands. Ottawa, as might be expected, won the series.

Hockey had a number of stars in the years prior to the N.H.L.. Fred "Cyclone" Taylor, one of the first players to realize the financial potential of his talent, barnstormed through packed exhibitions in the United States. Taylor was a member of the famous Renfrew Millionaires, the best team money could buy in 1910. (Money couldn't buy victory, however, for despite their name, the Millionaires never won the Stanley Cup.)

By the time the N.H.L. was born in 1917, hockey games were wild events in Canada, replete with rowdiness, fights, and airborne fruit in barnlike arenas. At first, the N.H.L. was just another league trying to attract players and spectators to make money on the growing popularity of the fast and brutal game. But by 1926 the N.H.L. took full control of the Stanley Cup and expanded to a collection of 10 teams, including the New York Rangers, the Chicago Black Hawks, and the Detroit Cougars.

Through the years, teams dropped out of the league until, by 1938, there were six teams remaining. The same six teams made up the N.H.L. for nearly three decades, until 1967, when the league expanded to 12 clubs. The six long-time members from 1938 to 1967 are known the Original Six: the Boston Bruins, Chicago Black Hawks, Detroit Red Wings, New York Rangers, Montreal Canadiens, and Toronto Maple Leafs.

Of the Original Six, the Montreal Canadiens were the most dominant club, chiefly drawing their talent from the French Canadian players of the province of Quebec. Maurice "Rocket" Richard, the first player to score 50 goals in a season, won eight Stanley Cups with the Canadiens. The Canadiens are hockey's most honored club, having captured the Stanley Cup 23 times since the foundation of the N.H.L..

As hockey matured into the middle of the century, the N.H.L. became a glamour sport in cities where players were heroes on ice. Gordie Howe of the Detroit Red Wings was a tough, dominating competitor who played until he was 52 years old. When he retired, he held the records for career goals, assists, and points.

On November 1, 1959, goalie Jacques Plante of the Canadiens, after being hit in the face by the puck in an earlier game, donned a fiberglass mask for protection. This innovation, scoffed at by his contemporaries, soon became standard equipment for goalies. In the modern N.H.L., goalies wear helmets remarkable both for their protective and decorative qualities.

Other stars of this era are the "Golden Jet" Bobby Hull, a fast skater and powerful shooter who played for Chicago, and Boston's Bobby Orr, a superbly fluid defenseman whose attacking prowess revolutionized the sport.

In 1967 the N.H.L. doubled in size, adding franchises in Los Angeles, Oakland, Minnesota, Philadelphia, Pittsburgh, and St. Louis. In 1970 the league again expanded, to Buffalo and Vancouver, and then in 1972 two more teams were introduced in Atlanta and Long Island, New York.

In 1972 a new league was founded to compete with the N.H.L.—the World Hockey Association (the WHA). By offering huge salaries to superstars such as Bobby Hull and Bruins goaltender Gerry Cheevers, the league gained instant credibility. Still, the WHA only lasted until 1980, at which time four teams—Edmonton, Hartford, Quebec, and Winnipeg—joined the N.H.L.. One of those teams, the Edmonton Oilers, featured a young player named Wayne Gretzky, who, on the way to shattering nearly every scoring record, deservedly acquired the moniker the "Great One." In the 1981–82 season, Gretzky scored 92 goals (still a record) and had 120 assists for a total of 212 points. In the 1985–86 season, Gretzky notched 52 goals and 163 assists for a combined 215 points, a record that may never be broken. During the 1980's, the Oilers won five Stanley Cups, four under Gretzky's leadership.

Yet the most memorable hockey achievement of the 1980's, at least to American eyes, was the gold medal team at the 1980 Winter Olympics in Lake Placid. The unheralded American squad, formed almost entirely of collegians, shocked the formidable and experienced Soviet Union in the semifinals and beat Finland to win the gold medal.

As the N.H.L. developed its own brand of hockey on smaller rinks, foreign players learned a different style of play on the larger rinks common in Europe. By the 1990's, many European players entered the N.H.L. from nations such as Russia, Finland, Sweden, and the Czech Republic, and the influx of talent transformed the league. But the biggest star was Canada's Mario Lemieux, who became the league's premier player as Gretzky entered the latter stages of his career. Lemieux's Pittsburgh Penguins won consecutive Stanley Cups in the early 1990's.

In recent years, the league expanded into Sunbelt markets such as Miami, Tampa, Nashville, and Dallas. At the end of the 2002–03 season, the N.H.L. boasted 30 teams.

Equipment, Rules, and Field of Play

In hockey, two teams use hooked sticks to propel a vulcanized rubber puck in opposite directions. The idea is for each team to shoot the puck into a net, called a goal. The net for each team is at opposite ends of the ice playing surface, also called a rink.

The puck is one inch thick and three inches in diameter, and it weighs between 5 1/2 to 6 ounces. For all N.H.L. games, the pucks, supplied by the home team, must be frozen.

In the N.H.L., sticks cannot measure longer than 63 inches from heel to end of the shaft. The blade length cannot measure more than 12 1/2 inches. The blade must be between two and three inches wide, and the curve of the blade cannot be more than a half inch.

Each team of five players plus a goaltender tries to send the puck into a net (called a goal) defended by the other team. Every time the puck goes into the net, the attacking team scores a goal. The game is 60 minutes long, divided into three 20-minute periods. (In lower levels, games can be shorter—divided into 15-, 12-, 10-minute or shorter periods.) At the end of the game, whichever team has the most goals wins.

The goal is a rectangle framed by red metal posts and backed by a white net. It measures six feet wide by four feet high and defended by the goaltender, a player with a stick and a glove who wears thick padding all over his body. If the puck passes completely over the goal line (usually, but not always, hitting the net) a goal is scored. It cannot be deliberately batted in with any part of the body or skate. It can get deflected in.

Hockey was first played on frozen ponds and lakes, but now the sport is contested in cozy arenas with smooth ice surfaces that are not at the mercy of the elements. During the intermissions between periods, the ice is resurfaced by a tractorlike machine called a Zamboni, which scrapes away the old chipped ice and lays down a light layer of water that immediately freezes smooth.

Through the years and across the world, ice surfaces have come in many different sizes. The official rink now in the N.H.L. is 200 feet long by 85 feet wide, with rounded corners. In the old days of the N.H.L., some surfaces were smaller; the rink at the venerable Boston Garden was 191 feet by 83 feet. European rinks (and those used in the Olympics) are larger—200 feet by 100 feet—making skating skills even more important.

The rules of hockey encourage skill; the rules do not

permit the puck to fly back and forth across the ice without anyone touching it. The concept of hockey is to create an exciting game that thrives on quick, slick passing, hard hitting, and precise movement. Through the use of lines painted onto the ice, the playing surface requires that the puck move from player to player without long passes. These painted lines are covered with thin layers of ice.

The Red Line is a one-foot-wide line that dissects the surface from side to side, dividing the rink into two equal halves.

There are two one-foot-wide Blue Lines—60 feet from each goal, running the width of the ice, from board to board.

There is another two-inch-wide red line that serves as the goal line, running the width of the ice, from board to board.

The Red Line and the two Blue Lines are on the ice to prevent a team, or players, from moving forward or ahead of the play too fast (too far in front of the puck carrier).

An infraction is called in two cases:

If an offensive player crosses the attacking Blue Line before the puck, it is offsides. Both of the player's skates have to be completely over the line for offsides to be called by a linesman, an official situated on the Blue Line who closely watches for such infractions.

If there is a two-line pass. For instance, if the puck is behind the defensive Blue Line and it is passed over the Blue Line and the Red Line, it is a two-line pass. This also applies if the puck is behind Red Line and it is passed over the Red Line and the Attacking Blue Line.

When offsides occurs, play is suspended by the game officials and there is a face-off, in which a puck is dropped between two opposing players.

Icing is called when a player is behind the Red Line and he sends the puck all the way into the offensive zone, beyond the goal line, and the first person to touch it is a player other than the goalie on the other team. As soon as the puck is touched by such a player, play is stopped. If the goalie touches the puck or the puck passes through the crease in front of the goal, the icing is waved off, or not called. The linesman is the one who will wave off an icing. When icing is called, the puck is returned for a face-off to the defensive zone of the team that iced it.

The area inside the Blue Line back to the rounded end of the rink is considered one team's defensive zone. Alternatively, it is called the others team's attacking zone. The area between the blue lines is called the neutral zone.

There is a semicircular crease in front of each goal, which most goalies consider their sacred territory. An offensive player may skate through the crease if he causes no contact with anyone.

There are five red circles on the ice where most of the face-offs will occur. A face-off restarts play following a penalty, an infraction such as offsides, or a puck that flies over the Plexiglas that surrounds the rink. The chosen method is dropping the puck between two opposing players; frequently, the face-off is won by the player who reacts quickest. When the infraction occurs (or a puck is lost) near a face-off circle, the puck is dropped in that circle. At the game's start, the beginning of each period, or after a goal, the play commences with a face-off in the center circle, in the middle of the rink.

Hockey is unique among the major sports in that teams frequently play without the same number of players. (In soccer, expulsions occur but are relatively rare.) Penalties are given for various physical infractions that go beyond the sport's permissive rules of contact. Penalties include high-sticking, roughing, and cross-checking, among others. Such penalties result in a stint in an isolated area called the penalty box, during which time the offender's team must operate a player short. The ensuing period, when teams have different numbers of players, is called a power play, and provides an excellent scoring opportunity to the larger team. Combinations of penalties may cause strange game situations such as four-on-four and even three-on-three (not counting the goalie). During a power play, the short-handed team may ice the puck without penalty (i.e. play the puck in such a way that would normally cause icing in an even-strength situation).

Glossary of Ice Hockey Terms

assist a pass that leads to a goal by a teammate. Although usually assists are passes, they are also given for unintentional deflections. Up to two assists can be awarded: one for the final pass and another for the preceding pass.

Blue Lines the blue lines located 60 feet from each goal, running the width of the ice, from board to board.

center one of three players on a forward line, the center is flanked by two wingers. The center is frequently the most skilled offensive player.

check to collide with an opponent in an attempt to knock him off balance or into the boards.

defensemen the two players whose main responsibility is to prevent scoring opportunities for the other team. Defensemen usually take their shifts in set pairs.

face-off how play begins each period or in a restart after an infraction or penalty. The puck is dropped between two opposing players who battle for control of it with their sticks.

five-hole the space between a goaltender's legs. So named because the other primary scoring areas are in the upper left, upper right, lower left, and lower right corners of the goal. Many goals are scored because a goalie does not close this gap quickly enough.

forwards the primary offensive players, divided into centers and wingers. Some forwards are known for their defensive abilities and are employed against the opposing team's most skilled attackers. Normally a unit of three players who take their shifts together.

goal 1) the only scoring play in hockey, given when the puck completely crosses an imaginary plane formed by the goal line, the posts, and the crossbar. In situations when the play happens too quickly, a goal judge (who sits behind each goal) and instant replay may be consulted to determine whether a goal was scored. 2) a statistic that tracks the number of a player's goals in the course of a season.

goal line the narrow red line that stretches from side to side across the ice near the end of the rink. This line is used to determine icing and goals.

icing sending the puck the length of the ice without it being touched. Icing is called when a player behind the Red Line hits the puck through the offensive zone and past the goal line and the first person to touch the puck is a defender other than the goaltender. When icing is whistled, the puck is returned for a face-off to the defensive zone of the team that iced it.

line change to switch the team's on-ice personnel during a stoppage in play or during the game. Because of the speed of hockey, players tire quickly, and line changes must be made frequently so that a team is not caught with exhausted, ineffective players.

linesmen the two game officials whose primary job is to determine offsides and icing calls. Normally found hovering about the Blue Lines.

offsides a violation called if an offensive player crosses the attacking Blue Line before the puck. When this occurs, the play is stopped and there is a face-off outside the zone.

one-timer to immediately redirect the puck with the stick without first controlling it. Although applied to passes, the term is most often used in relation to such shots. The chief benefit of a one-time shot is that the quick release allows the goalie little preparation.

overtime the period of play following a game that ends in a tie after three periods. In the regular season, the teams play one five-minute overtime. If still scoreless after five minutes, the game is tied. In the playoffs, the game continues in 20-minute periods until a goal is scored.

penalties a group of infractions that normally incur a two-minute stay in the penalty box for the offender. For severe penalties, called majors, the sentence may last four minutes. Penalties include boarding, charging, holding, cross-checking, and roughing, among others.

penalty shot a one-on-one attempt against the goalkeeper, given after the referee decides an attacker with an otherwise clear breakaway is victimized by a defender's penalty. In such cases, the referee awards a penalty shot instead of a penalty (and possible power play).

point 1) for an individual player, points are assists plus goals. 2) during the regular season, team standings are maintained by awarding points, with two points for a win, one for a tie or overtime loss, and nothing for a loss in regulation.

power play the period of time when one team has more players than the other, due to one or more penalties. Most frequently power plays are on 5-on-4, not counting the goalies, but other situations also occur. Power plays end if a goal is scored by the advantaged team, unless the penalty that caused the power play was determined to be a major rather than minor.

plus/minus a statistic unique to hockey, the plus/minus rating is an indication of a individual player's offensive and defensive value. A point is added for every goal scored for his team when the player is on the ice (power play goals excepted) and, similarly, a point is subtracted for every goal scored against.

puck a flat, frozen disk of vulcanized rubber.

Red Line a one-foot-wide line, running the width of the ice from board to board, that divides the ice surface into halves. This is also called "center ice."

referee the game officials with the power to judge penalties and otherwise guide the action. Recently the N.H.L. switched to employing two referees per game instead of one.

save when a goaltender prevents the puck from entering his goal, either by catching the puck in a glove or stopping or deflecting it with part of his body or his stick.

shift the length of a player's turn on the ice before a line change; usually no more than 90 seconds.

shorthanded when a team has fewer players on the ice than the opposing team because of one or more penalties. When a team with fewer players manages to score a goal, it is called a shorthanded goal.

slap shot the hardest kind of shot in hockey, when a player draws back his stick well off the ice to fiercely strike the puck. The fastest shots are often more than 90 miles per hour.

tie the result if the score is equal after regulation and five minutes of overtime. Both teams receive one point.

wingers two of the three forwards on a line (along with the center). The two types are right and left wing.

wrist shot a type of shot so named because the impetus is provided by the player's hands alone. In other words, the player does not lift his stick to strike the puck. An accurate, quickly released shot is very useful near the goal.

Zamboni a large tractorlike machine that treats the ice surface between periods. It scrapes off chipped ice and lays down a thin layer of water that immediately freezes smooth.

The Stanley Cup

Season	Champion
1917–18	Toronto Arenas
1918–19	No decision
1919–20	Ottawa Senators
1920–21	Ottawa Senators
1921–22	Toronto St. Pats
1922–23	Ottawa Senators
1923–24	Montreal Canadiens
1924–25	Victoria Cougars
1925–26	Montreal Maroons
1926–27	Ottawa Senators
1927–28	New York Rangers
1928–29	Boston Bruins
1929–30	Montreal Canadiens
1930–31	Montreal Canadiens
1931–32	Toronto Maple Leafs
1932–33	New York Rangers
1933–34	Chicago Blackhawks
1934–35	Montreal Maroons
1935–36	Detroit Red Wings
1936–37	Detroit Red Wings
1937–38	Chicago Blackhawks
1938–39	Boston Bruins
1939–40	New York Rangers
1940–41	Boston Bruins
1941–42	Toronto Maple Leafs
1942–43	Detroit Red Wings
1943–44	Montreal Canadiens
1944–45	Toronto Maple Leafs
1945–46	Montreal Canadiens

Season	Champion
1946–47	Toronto Maple Leafs
1947–48	Toronto Maple Leafs
1948–49	Toronto Maple Leafs
1949–50	Detroit Red Wings
1950–51	Toronto Maple Leafs
1951–52	Detroit Red Wings
1952–53	Montreal Canadiens
1953–54	Detroit Red Wings
1954–55	Detroit Red Wings
1955–56	Montreal Canadiens
1956–57	Montreal Canadiens
1957–58	Montreal Canadiens
1958–59	Montreal Canadiens
1959–60	Montreal Canadiens
1960–61	Chicago Blackhawks
1961–62	Toronto Maple Leafs
1962–63	Toronto Maple Leafs
1963–64	Toronto Maple Leafs
1964–65	Montreal Canadiens
1965–66	Montreal Canadiens
1966–67	Toronto Maple Leafs
1967–68	Montreal Canadiens
1968–69	Montreal Canadiens
1969–70	Boston Bruins
1970–71	Montreal Canadiens
1971–72	Boston Bruins
1972–73	Montreal Canadiens
1973–74	Philadelphia Flyers
1974–75	Philadelphia Flyers

Season	Champion
1975–76	Montreal Canadiens
1976–77	Montreal Canadiens
1977–78	Montreal Canadiens
1978–79	Montreal Canadiens
1979–80	New York Islanders
1980–81	New York Islanders
1981–82	New York Islanders
1982–83	New York Islanders
1983–84	Edmonton Oilers
1984–85	Edmonton Oilers
1985–86	Montreal Canadiens
1986–87	Edmonton Oilers
1987–88	Edmonton Oilers
1988–89	Calgary Flames
1989–90	Edmonton Oilers
1990–91	Pittsburgh Penguins
1991–92	Pittsburgh Penguins
1992–93	Montreal Canadiens
1993–94	New York Rangers
1994–95	New Jersey Devils
1995–96	Colorado Avalanche
1996–97	Detroit Red Wings
1997–98	Detroit Red Wings
1998–99	Dallas Stars
1999–00	New Jersey Devils
2000–01	Colorado Avalanche
2001–02	Detroit Red Wings
2002–03	New Jersey Devils
2003–04	Tampa Bay Lightning

Hart Trophy Winners, 1924–2004

The league's most valuable player is chosen by a poll of the Professional Hockey Writers' Association.

Season	Player	Team
1924	Frank Nighbor	Ottawa Senators
1925	Billy Burch	N.Y. Americans
1926	Nels Stewart	Montreal Maroons
1927	Herb Gardiner	Montreal
1928	Howie Morenz	Montreal
1929	Roy Worters	N.Y. Americans
1930	Nels Stewart	Montreal Maroons
1931	Howie Morenz	Montreal
1932	Howie Morenz	Montreal
1933	Eddie Shore	Boston
1934	Aurel Joliat	Montreal
1935	Eddie Shore	Boston
1936	Eddie Shore	Boston
1937	Babe Siebert	Montreal
1938	Eddie Shore	Boston
1939	Toe Blake	Montreal
1940	Ebbie Goodfellow	Detroit
1941	Bill Cowley	Boston
1942	Tom Anderson	N.Y. Americans
1943	Bill Cowley	Boston
1944	Babe Pratt	Toronto
1945	Elmer Lach	Montreal
1946	Max Bentley	Toronto
1947	Maurice Richard	Montreal
1948	Buddy O'Connor	N.Y. Rangers
1949	Sid Abel	Detroit
1950	Charlie Rayner	N.Y. Rangers
1951	Milt Schmidt	Boston
1952	Gordie Howe	Detroit
1953	Gordie Howe	Detroit
1954	Al Rollins	Toronto
1955	Ted Kennedy	Toronto
1956	Jean Béliveau	Montreal
1957	Gordie Howe	Detroit
1958	Gordie Howe	Detroit
1959	Andy Bathgate	N.Y. Rangers
1960	Gordie Howe	Detroit
1961	Bernie Geoffrion	Montreal
1962	Jacques Plante	Montreal
1963	Gordie Howe	Detroit
1964	Jean Béliveau	Montreal

Season	Player	Team
1965	Bobby Hull	Chicago
1966	Bobby Hull	Chicago
1967	Stan Mikita	Chicago
1968	Stan Mikita	Chicago
1969	Phil Esposito	Boston
1970	Bobby Orr	Boston
1971	Bobby Orr	Boston
1972	Bobby Orr	Boston
1973	Bobby Clarke	Philadelphia
1974	Phil Esposito	Boston
1975	Bobby Clarke	Philadelphia
1976	Bobby Clarke	Philadelphia
1977	Guy Lafleur	Montreal
1978	Guy Lafleur	Montreal
1979	Bryan Trottier	N.Y. Islanders
1980	Wayne Gretzky	Edmonton
1981	Wayne Gretzky	Edmonton
1982	Wayne Gretzky	Edmonton
1983	Wayne Gretzky	Edmonton
1984	Wayne Gretzky	Edmonton
1985	Wayne Gretzky	Edmonton
1986	Wayne Gretzky	Edmonton
1987	Wayne Gretzky	Edmonton
1988	Mario Lemieux	Pittsburgh
1989	Wayne Gretzky	Los Angeles
1990	Mark Messier	Edmonton
1991	Bret Hull	St. Louis
1992	Mark Messier	N.Y. Rangers
1993	Mario Lemieux	Pittsburgh
1994	Sergei Fedorov	Detroit
1995	Eric Lindros	Philadelphia
1996	Mario Lemieux	Pittsburgh
1997	Dominik Hasek	Buffalo
1998	Dominik Hasek	Buffalo
1999	Jaromir Jagr	Pittsburgh
2000	Chris Pronger	St. Louis
2001	Joe Sakic	Colorado
2002	Jose Theodore	Montreal
2003	Peter Forsberg	Colorado
2004	Martin St. Louis	Tampa Bay

Vezina Trophy Winners, 1927–2004

The Vezina Trophy is awarded to the league's best goalkeeper and is selected by a poll of the league's general managers. The winner receives $10,000.

Season	Player	Team
1927	George Hainsworth	Montreal
1928	George Hainsworth	Montreal
1929	George Hainsworth	Montreal
1930	Tiny Thompson	Boston
1931	Roy Worters	N.Y. Americans
1932	Charlie Gardiner	Chicago
1933	Tiny Thompson	Boston
1934	Charlie Gardiner	Chicago
1935	Lorne Chabot	Chicago
1936	Tiny Thompson	Boston
1937	Normie Smith	Detroit
1938	Tiny Thompson	Boston
1939	Frank Brimsek	Boston
1940	Dave Kerr	N.Y. Rangers
1941	Turk Broda	Toronto
1942	Frank Brimsek	Boston
1943	Johnny Mowers	Detroit
1944	Bill Durnan	Montreal
1945	Bill Durnan	Montreal
1946	Bill Durnan	Montreal
1947	Bill Durnan	Montreal
1948	Turk Broda	Toronto
1949	Bill Durnan	Montreal
1950	Bill Durnan	Montreal
1951	Al Rollins	Toronto
1952	Terry Sawchuk	Detroit
1953	Terry Sawchuk	Detroit
1954	Harry Lumley	Toronto
1955	Terry Sawchuk	Detroit
1956	Jacques Plante	Montreal
1957	Jacques Plante	Montreal
1958	Jacques Plante	Montreal
1959	Jacques Plante	Montreal
1960	Jacques Plante	Montreal
1961	Johnny Bower	Toronto
1962	Jacques Plante	Montreal
1963	Glenn Hall	Chicago
1964	Charlie Hodge	Montreal
1965	Terry Sawchuk/Johnny Bower	Toronto
1966	Lorne Worsley/Charlie Hodge	Montreal
1967	Glenn Hall/ Denis Dejordy	Chicago
1968	Lorne Worsley/Rogie Vachon	Montreal
1969	Jacques Plante/Glenn Hall	St. Louis
1970	Tony Esposito	Chicago
1971	Ed Giacomin/Gilles Villemure	N.Y. Rangers
1972	Tony Esposito/Gary Smith	Chicago
1973	Ken Dryden	Montreal
1974	Bernie Parent	Philadelphia
	Tony Esposito	Chicago
1975	Bernie Parent	Philadelphia
1976	Ken Dryden	Montreal
1977	Ken Dryden/Michel Larocque	Montreal
1978	Ken Dryden/Michel Larocque	Montreal
1979	Ken Dryden/Michel Larocque	Montreal
1980	Bob Sauvé/Don Edwards	Buffalo
1981	Richard Sevigny/Denis Herron/ Michel Larocque	Montreal
1982	Bill Smith	N.Y. Islanders
1983	Pete Peeters	Boston
1984	Tom Barrasso	Buffalo
1985	Pele Lindbergh	Philadelphia
1986	John Vanbiesbrouck	N.Y. Rangers
1987	Ron Hextall	Philadelphia
1988	Grant Fuhr	Edmonton
1989	Patrick Roy	Montreal
1990	Patrick Roy	Montreal
1991	Ed Belfour	Chicago
1992	Patrick Roy	Montreal
1993	Ed Belfour	Chicago
1994	Dominik Hasek	Buffalo
1995	Dominik Hasek	Buffalo
1996	Jim Carey	Washington
1997	Dominik Hasek	Buffalo
1998	Dominik Hasek	Buffalo
1999	Dominik Hasek	Buffalo
2000	Olaf Kolzig	Washington
2001	Dominik Hasek	Buffalo
2002	Jose Theodore	Montreal
2003	Martin Brodeur	New Jersey
2004	Martin Brodeur	New Jersey

GOLF

History

Golf's physical requirements are modest. Players come in all shapes, sizes, and ages, and golf's mix of challenge, and the consequent rewards and punishments, has made it one of the most ubiquitous individual sports. Golf has gained such popularity, in fact, that its most famous shots weren't even hit on this planet.

It is also a sport of wealth. A golf outing costs substantially more than most other sports, and private clubs demand steep membership fees for the right to enjoy their courses. This is particularly true in the United States, but in places such as Scotland, the home of golf, the sport is more egalitarian. At the professional level, elite players compete for considerable prize money on a number of circuits, or tours, under the watchful eye of an international television audience.

However, despite the million-dollar purses at the professional level and a worldwide explosion in popularity, the sport's beginnings were anything but glamorous.

Golf originated in Scotland, the northern part of the island of Great Britain, during the 15th century. In its primitive incarnation, golfers struck a rock around a primitive course with an equally primitive stick or club.

Facing invasion from his English neighbors to the south, in 1457 Scotland's King James II prohibited his subjects from playing golf so they could concentrate on more martial pursuits such as archery. Setting a trend that would continue until the present, the golfers played on, and the ban was finally lifted in 1502 with the ascension of King James VI (known to history as James I) to the throne of both England and Scotland. With royal patronage, the sport prospered.

The first golf club was formed near Edinburgh in 1744, and the members named themselves The Gentlemen Golfers of Leith. Setting another trend, the club codified a list of 13 rules, including stipulations about how golfers should deal with water hazards and lost balls. Revisions were made and two more rules added in 1775.

St. Andrews, a picturesque town on the North Sea, has the cachet of being the most important center of golf. The St. Andrews Society of Golfers, founded in 1754, was and still is among the most prestigious clubs in the sport. The course at St. Andrews, with its 18 holes, inspired the modern standard, and the club received the designation of "Royal & Ancient" in 1834 from King William IV. In 1897 the Royal & Ancient Golf Club of St. Andrews, or the R&A, created a Rules of Golf Committee to write the official Rules of Golf.

Early courses were almost always by the sea, with windswept dunes and junglelike rough that devoured wayward shots. The term still applied to such seaside courses is links, or linksland, yet the word *links* is often used now (incorrectly) to describe any golf course. Equipment of golf's early era seems ancient compared to the technological marvels of modernity. Balls were constructed from a horsehide sphere filled with compacted feathers, and clubs were usually manufactured from a variety of materials, including persimmon, hickory, beech, and iron. Later advances of the Industrial Revolution made metal club heads more common, and balls were fabricated from gutta percha, a rubberlike material produced by an Asian tree.

Not until 1766 was a golf club formed outside Scotland, and the first outside of Britain, borne by the tide of imperialism, was created in Bangalore, India, in 1820. During the 19th century, clubs sprang up in Australia, Canada, South Africa, Hong Kong, India, France, Ireland, and the United States.

The first significant tournament was the British Open, first contested in 1860. Old Tom Morris won the Open in 1862, 1864, and 1867, but his feats were were surpassed by his son—Young Tom, of course— who captured four straight tournaments starting in 1869. With the sparse number of paying tournaments, professional players frequently bet with their opponents or worked at golf-related jobs such as making clubs.

During the first years of the 20th century there was a marked improvement in equipment, including one-piece rubber balls, dimpled balls, steel-shafted clubs, and groove-faced irons. By then, golf had been firmly established in the United States. In 1894 the United States Golf Association (USGA) was created. American courses, normally distant from the coastlines distinctive to British golf, were instead carved from the countryside. The differences between British and American golf were not limited to the style: a 30-year dispute between the R&A and the USGA—about a number of rules and the standard golf ball—lasted until 1951. Modern golf is jointly supervised by the two organizations.

With the increasing number of tournaments, the Professional Golfers Association (P.G.A.) of America was organized in 1916. Initially, the association played a series of contests only in the winter months, but by 1944 the tour had expanded to include 22 events. The growth of the professional tour fueled the rise of several notable golfers, first and foremost American Bobby Jones, who won the Grand Slam in 1931. (At that time, the Grand Slam—winning all four major tournaments in a calendar year—consisted of the U.S. and British Amateurs and the U.S. and British Opens.) Other great players include Walter Hagen and Sir Henry Cotton.

Eventually, four tournaments acquired more importance than the others, and these became known as the majors. They are the U.S. and British Opens, the P.G.A. Championship, and the Masters. The Masters is unique among the majors in that it is the only tournament played at the same club—Augusta National in Augusta, Ga.—every year.

Although the P.G.A. tour attracted most early interest in golf, women also became well-known players. The first U.S. women's amateur championship was held in 1895. In the first half of the 20th century, England's Joyce Wethered, and Americans Glenna Collett Vare and Babe Didrikson Zaharias were the most successful players. (In the 1932 Summer Olympics, Zaharias, the premier female athlete of the age, won gold medals in the javelin and hurdles and a silver medal in the high jump.) The Ladies Professional Golf Association (L.P.G.A.) was formed in 1950.

Three dominant players emerged in the 1960's back on the P.G.A. tour: Americans Arnold Palmer and Jack Nicklaus, and South Africa's Gary Player. The three men won a combined 34 professional majors in their careers. Palmer won seven, and Player captured nine, but Nicklaus's 18 majors remains the standard for all future golfers. Their reign lasted from Palmer's Masters breakthrough in 1958 until Nicklaus's stunning Masters victory in 1986, when he was 46 years old.

For all of these three men's success on the lush courses of earth, the most famous golf shots in history were taken on the moon. During the Apollo 14 mission in 1971, astronaut Alan Shepherd took two swings with an improvised 6-iron formed with a club head he smuggled onto the spacecraft.

Although many good golfers had moments to shine after Nicklaus's run concluded, there were no truly exceptional players until the arrival of Eldrick "Tiger" Woods in the late 1990's. Woods, three-time U.S. amateur champion, won the Masters in 1997 at the age of 21 and has since added seven more majors to his resumé. His total of eight already surpasses that of the legendary Palmer. Combining superior athleticism and a keen competitive mind, Woods is a threat to surpass Nicklaus's record 18 majors.

Rules of the Game

Golf is contested on a course, usually consisting of 18 holes, though some smaller courses have only nine holes. To finish the hole, the golfer, with the aid of an implement called a club, must guide a small, spherical ball into a round opening (the hole) several hundred yards away. The goal of golf is to complete each hole in as few strokes as possible, and a stroke is counted whenever the golfer contacts with the ball with a club. (There are several types of clubs, each with a particular form and function.) Scores are tracked by the hole, and the player's overall score is an addition of all the strokes for all the holes. A player who needs 73 strokes to complete an 18-hole course has done better than someone who required 76 strokes.

For each hole, there is a number called par against which players must test themselves. Par measures the standard number of strokes necessary to finish the hole. The longest holes are par 5, the shortest holes are par 3, and the most common holes are par 4. To determine the total par for the course, the figures are added for each hole. A course with a par of 72, for example, sets a standard of 72 shots to complete all 18 holes. Par varies with the length of the course, but usually ranges from 70 to 72. A par 72 course could, for example, have 14 par 4 holes, two par 5 holes, and two par 3 holes.

Play on each hole begins from what is called a tee box, where a golfer sets the ball on a small, raised peg called a tee. On most par 4 and par 5 holes, the first shot is called a drive, and players seek to hit the ball into the center of a clear lane of grass called the fairway. With the second shot, players want to hit the ball onto a close-cut, amorphous area called the green, which is where the hole is located. On tee shots on par 3's, players aim for the green from the start. Once on the green, players use a club called a putter to direct the ball into the hole. When the ball drops into the hole, the hole is complete. Typically, par 3 holes are 250 yards or less in distance from the tee box to the green, while par 4 holes range up to around 475 yards, with longer holes being par 5.

Certain terms are assigned to a particular score on each hole. On a par 4 hole, for example, if the hole is finished in only three strokes, the player has made a "birdie," that is, scored a stroke below par.

Golf is not as simple as it sounds. The act of consistently swinging a club to strike a stationary round ball so that it flies where you want befuddles even the best golfers. Furthermore, courses are designed to offer tricky obstacles: there are bunkers, low pits filled with sand that can trap poor shots, and there is rough—thick grass—to punish any misses of the fairway and green. Other hazards, such as creeks and lakes, also abound.

Glossary of Golf Terms

ace a hole in one; when a player's tee shot drops into the hole, a rare event.

away a term that describes the golfer who will play first following the tee shot. The player whose ball is farthest from the hole plays first.

ball the small spherical object that players must guide around the golf course with the aid of their clubs. Balls can weigh no less than 1.62 ounces and must be at least 1.68 inches in diameter.

birdie to complete a hole in one stroke less than the par, e.g. needing three strokes to finish a par 4. A good thing.

bogey to complete a hole in one stroke more than the par, e.g. needing five strokes to finish a par 4. A bad thing. Each additional stroke above par merits an appellation, such as "double bogey" or even "quadruple bogey."

bunker the low areas filled with sand that line the fairways and surround the greens. Bunkers, also called sand traps, present various difficulties to the player because of their depth, positioning, or sand quality.

caddy the assistant who carries the player's clubs and is allowed to dispense advice.

club one of the implements with which a player strikes the ball. Clubs consist of the grip, the shaft, and the club face, the part of the club that contacts with the ball. Players may carry only 14 clubs in their bag during a round.

clubhouse the building that serves the main nonplaying functions, such as changing rooms and dining, of a golf club and course. The clubhouse is where a round begins (at the nearby 1st tee) and ends (after the 18th hole). On many courses, the hole layout returns to the clubhouse area between the 9th and the 10th holes.

course the layout of holes, usually 18, that players must progress through to complete a round.

cut the separation of the contending golfers from the rest after the second round of a tournament. Normally, slightly less than half of the players after two rounds of play are allowed to compete in the final two rounds of a four-round tournament, and the rest are cut and eliminated from the tournament.

draw a shot made with sidespin that causes the ball to drift from right to left when hit by a right-handed golfer. Often an intentional shot used to circumvent obstacles. Its opposite is a fade.

driver the longest hitting club, normally used for the tee shot or drive.

eagle completing a hole in two strokes less than par, such as finishing a par 5 in three strokes. A double eagle, also known as an "albatross," is three strokes below par.

fade to strike a ball with spin so that, when hit by a right-handed golfer, the ball drifts from left to right. Normally an intentional shot. Its opposite is the draw.

fairway the long, sometimes narrow lane of short grass that is the target of most tee shots and drives. Although mounds and slopes may affect the player's lie, usually the fairway is a better place from which to take the second shot than the rough.

flag the brightly colored banner atop the flagstick that marks the hole, removed or tended once players have steered their balls onto the green.

front and back nine a phrase that divides the course into its first nine holes (the front) and its last nine holes (the back).

Grand Slam to win all four of golf's major tournaments in the same calendar year. No golfer has ever won the modern Grand Slam, which consists of the Masters, the U.S.

Open, the British Open, and the P.G.A. Championship.

green the close-cut area of grass, often with small mounds and subtle curves, where the hole is placed. Once the players have reached the green, they try to putt the ball into the hole.

handicap a measure of a player's skill level as compared to par. A player who averages 78 strokes on a par 72 course is said to have a 6 handicap, while a player who averages par is said to be a "scratch" golfer. Handicaps are also adjusted by course difficulty.

hole a single portion of a golf course. Typically there are 18 holes on a course, although smaller courses may have only nine. Also, the hole is the round space on the green, 4 1/4 inches in diameter and at least 4 inches deep, into which the ball must drop to complete one hole. A flag marks the hole so that it can be seen from a distance.

hook an errant shot that, when made by a right-handed golfer, will force the ball to drastically fly from right to left, not straight, because of poor club contact. Its opposite is a slice.

iron a series of clubs with metal faces of varying angles. Irons range from the 1-iron to the 9-iron, with the higher numbers indicating a higher loft to the club. A 9-iron will send the ball higher and a much shorter distance than a 1-iron. Irons are used on some tee shots (such as on a par 3) and until the players reach the green.

lie the positioning of a ball on the ground with respect to the ease with which a player will take the next shot. With a good lie, for example, the ball may rest on flat area, while with a bad lie, the ball may be buried in thick rough.

links a generic word often used incorrectly to describe any golf course. Specifically, the word applies to a seaside course, particularly in Britain, with sandy soil.

match play a type of contest, different from the stroke play seen in most professional tournaments, in which players compete by the hole, not by the shot. If one player scores better on a hole than his opponent, that player wins the hole. Whoever wins the most holes wins the match.

out and back a phrase used to describe courses that reach their farthest point from the start at the end of the 9th hole and do not return to the clubhouse until the 18th hole.

par the standard number of strokes to complete the hole or the course. Par also means to finish a hole in the standard number of strokes.

penalty a punishment, usually a number of strokes added to the players score, assessed if the player loses a ball or hits the ball into a water hazard, among other infractions.

putter the flat-faced club golfers use to strike, or putt, the ball into the hole once on the green.

rough the thick, grassy areas that border the fairway and the greens, and ordinarily a bad place to discover your ball.

round the completion of the course, whether it be nine or 18 holes. A player who needs 79 strokes to finish an 18 hole course is said to have played a round of 79.

rules the laws that legislate how golf must be played.

score the number of strokes necessary to complete a hole or a round. To total a score for a round, add up the number of strokes for each hole.

scorecard the record sheet on which a player tracks his or her score.

short game a term that describes the skills of golf near and on the greens, mainly chipping, escaping bunkers, and putting.

slice a bad shot that, because of the club's facing when meeting the ball, makes a right-handed golfer's shot curve drastically from left to right instead of going straight.

stroke a single contact of the ball with any club.

stroke play a type of competition in which the number of strokes, not the number of holes (as in match play), determines the winner. The player with the lowest number of strokes wins. This is the most common method of scoring in tournament play.

swing the physical process of striking the ball, and one of the most analyzed movements in human history. Despite years of practice, even top professionals have troublesome moments with their swings.

tee shot the shot that begins the hole, taken from an area called the tee box. On a tee shot, the ball is placed upon a small raised peg, made of wood or plastic, called a tee. The player who scored better on the previous hole plays first.

tour a series of tournaments in which players compete, usually based on their relative skills or regions. The most prestigious tours are the P.G.A. Tour, in the United States, and the European P.G.A. Tour.

tournament a competition of golfers. On the P.G.A. tour, a tournament consists of four rounds, with one round a day from Thursday to Sunday. After the first two rounds, many players are eliminated at the cut. To determine the champion, the scores for all four rounds are added together and the player with the fewest strokes wins. The scoring system is similar for tournaments on other tours, though such tours as the Seniors and the L.P.G.A. may not play four rounds.

water hazards areas on the golf course covered by water. When a shot falls into the water, the player can play it as it lies if found, but if the ball is lost, the player incurs a one-stroke penalty and must shoot again.

wedge the most lofted clubs, used to produce high short shots. The pitching wedge has the least loft, followed by the sand wedge, and then comes the lob wedge. The sand wedge has a flange that makes it useful for blasting the ball out of a bunker.

woods a set of clubs used on the tee or for long shots from the fairway to the green. The driver is considered the 1-wood, and other common woods include the 3-wood and the 5-wood. In the past, these were made from wood, but now are formed from metal.

yardage a measurement of distance from the tee, or one's current position on a hole, to the flag. The yardage of each hole varies by the position of the tee box: men's tees are farther back than the women's tees. To determine the complete course yardage, the yardage for each hole is added, with a total usually around 6,500 to 7,000 yards (give or take a few hundred).

The Masters

Year	Winner
1934	Horton Smith
1935	Gene Sarazen
1936	Horton Smith
1937	Byron Nelson
1938	Henry Picard
1939	Ralph Guldahl
1940	Jimmy Demaret
1941	Craig Wood
1942	Byron Nelson
1943	Not held
1944	Not held
1945	Not held
1946	Herman Keiser
1947	Jimmy Demaret
1948	Claude Harman
1949	Sam Snead
1950	Jimmy Demaret
1951	Ben Hogan
1952	Sam Snead
1953	Ben Hogan
1954	Sam Snead
1955	Cary Middlecoff
1956	Jack Burke Jr.
1957	Doug Ford
1958	Arnold Palmer
1959	Art Wall Jr.
1960	Arnold Palmer
1961	Gary Player
1962	Arnold Palmer
1963	Jack Nicklaus
1964	Arnold Palmer
1965	Jack Nicklaus
1966	Jack Nicklaus
1967	Gay Brewer Jr.
1968	Bob Goalby
1969	George Archer
1970	Billy Casper
1971	Charles Coody
1972	Jack Nicklaus
1973	Tommy Aaron
1974	Gary Player
1975	Jack Nicklaus
1976	Ray Floyd
1977	Tom Watson
1978	Gary Player
1979	Fuzzy Zoeller
1980	Seve Ballesteros
1981	Tom Watson
1982	Craig Stadler
1983	Seve Ballesteros
1984	Ben Crenshaw
1985	Bernhard Langer
1986	Jack Nicklaus
1987	Larry Mize
1988	Sandy Lyle
1989	Nick Faldo
1990	Nick Faldo
1991	Ian Woosnam
1992	Fred Couples
1993	Bernhard Langer
1994	José María Olazábal
1995	Ben Crenshaw
1996	Nick Faldo
1997	Tiger Woods
1998	Mark O'Meara
1999	José María Olazábal
2000	Vijay Singh
2001	Tiger Woods
2002	Tiger Woods
2003	Mike Weir
2004	Phil Mickelson

The U.S. Open Championship

Year	Winner
1895	Horace Rawlins
1896	James Foulis
1897	Joe Lloyd
1898	Fred Herd
1899	Willie Smith
1900	Harry Vardon
1901	Willie Anderson
1902	Laurie Auchterlonie
1903	Willie Anderson
1904	Willie Anderson
1905	Willie Anderson
1906	Alex Smith
1907	Alex Ross
1908	Fred McLeod
1909	George Sargent
1910	Alex Smith
1911	John McDermott
1912	John McDermott
1913	Francis Ouimet
1914	Walter Hagen
1915	Jerome Travers
1916	Charles Evans Jr.
1917	Not held
1918	Not held
1919	Walter Hagen
1920	Edward Ray
1921	James M. Barnes
1922	Gene Sarazen
1923	Robert T. Jones Jr.
1924	Cyril Walker
1925	W. MacFarlane
1926	Robert T. Jones Jr.
1927	Tommy Armour
1928	Johnny Farrell
1929	Robert T. Jones Jr.
1930	Robert T. Jones Jr.
1931	Billy Burke
1932	Gene Sarazen
1933	Johnny Goodman
1934	Olin Dutra
1935	Sam Parks, Jr.
1936	Tony Manero
1937	Ralph Guldahl
1938	Ralph Guldahl
1939	Byron Nelson
1940	Lawson Little
1941	Craig Wood
1942	Not held
1943	Not held
1944	Not held
1945	Not held
1946	Lloyd Mangrum
1947	Lew Worsham
1948	Ben Hogan
1949	Cary Middlecoff
1950	Ben Hogan
1951	Ben Hogan
1952	Julius Boros
1953	Ben Hogan
1954	Ed Furgol
1955	Jack Fleck
1956	Cary Middlecoff
1957	Dick Mayer
1958	Tommy Bolt
1959	Billy Casper
1960	Arnold Palmer
1961	Gene Littler
1962	Jack Nicklaus
1963	Julius Boros
1964	Ken Venturi
1965	Gary Player
1966	Billy Casper
1967	Jack Nicklaus
1968	Lee Trevino
1969	Orville Moody
1970	Tony Jacklin
1971	Lee Trevino
1972	Jack Nicklaus
1973	Johnny Miller
1974	Hale Irwin
1975	Lou Graham
1976	Jerry Pate
1977	Hubert Green
1978	Andy North
1979	Hale Irwin
1980	Jack Nicklaus
1981	David Graham
1982	Tom Watson
1983	Larry Nelson
1984	Fuzzy Zoeller
1985	Andy North
1986	Ray Floyd
1987	Scott Simpson
1988	Curtis Strange
1989	Curtis Strange
1990	Hale Irwin
1991	Payne Stewart
1992	Tom Kite
1993	Lee Janzen
1994	Ernie Els
1995	Corey Pavin
1996	Steve Jones
1997	Ernie Els
1998	Lee Janzen
1999	Payne Stewart
2000	Tiger Woods
2001	Retief Goosen
2002	Tiger Woods
2003	Jim Furyk
2004	Retief Goosen

P.G.A. Championship

Year	Winner
1916	James M. Barnes
1917	Not held
1918	Not held
1919	James M. Barnes
1920	Jock Hutchison
1921	Walter Hagen
1922	Gene Sarazen
1923	Gene Sarazen
1924	Walter Hagen
1925	Walter Hagen
1926	Walter Hagen
1927	Walter Hagen
1928	Leo Diegel
1929	Leo Diegel
1930	Tommy Armour
1931	Tom Creavy
1932	Olin Dutra
1933	Gene Sarazen
1934	Paul Runyan
1935	Johnny Revolta
1936	Denny Shute
1937	Denny Shute
1938	Paul Runyan
1939	Henry Picard
1940	Byron Nelson
1941	Vic Ghezzi
1942	Sam Snead
1943	Not held
1944	Bob Hamilton
1945	Byron Nelson
1946	Ben Hogan
1947	Jim Ferrier
1948	Ben Hogan
1949	Sam Snead
1950	Chandler Harper
1951	Sam Snead
1952	Jim Turnesa
1953	Walter Burkemo
1954	Chick Harbert
1955	Doug Ford
1956	Jack Burke
1957	Lionel Hebert
1958	Dow Finsterwald
1959	Bob Rosburg
1960	Jay Hebert
1961	Jerry Barber
1962	Gary Player
1963	Jack Nicklaus
1964	Bobby Nichols
1965	Dave Marr
1966	Al Geiberger
1967	Don January
1968	Julius Boros
1969	Ray Floyd
1970	Dave Stockton
1971	Jack Nicklaus
1972	Gary Player
1973	Jack Nicklaus
1974	Lee Trevino
1975	Jack Nicklaus
1976	Dave Stockton
1977	Lanny Wadkins
1978	John Mahaffey
1979	David Graham
1980	Jack Nicklaus
1981	Larry Nelson
1982	Raymond Floyd
1983	Hal Sutton
1984	Lee Trevino
1985	Hubert Green
1986	Bob Tway
1987	Larry Nelson
1988	Jeff Sluman
1989	Payne Stewart
1990	Wayne Grady
1991	John Daly
1992	Nick Price
1993	Paul Azinger
1994	Nick Price
1995	Steve Elkington
1996	Mark Brooks
1997	Davis Love III
1998	Vijay Singh
1999	Tiger Woods
2000	Tiger Woods
2001	David Toms
2002	Rich Beem
2003	Shaun Micheel
2004	Vijay Singh

The British Open

Year	Winner
1860	Willie Park
1861	Tom Morris Sr.
1862	Tom Morris Sr.
1863	Willie Park
1864	Tom Morris Sr.
1865	Andrew Strath
1866	Willie Park
1867	Tom Morris Sr.
1868	Tom Morris Jr.
1869	Tom Morris Jr.
1870	Tom Morris Jr.
1871	Not held
1872	Tom Morris Jr.
1873	Tom Kidd
1874	Mungo Park
1875	Willie Park
1876	Bob Martin
1877	Jamie Anderson
1878	Jamie Anderson
1879	Jamie Anderson
1880	Robert Ferguson
1881	Robert Ferguson
1882	Robert Ferguson
1883	Willie Fernie
1884	Jack Simpson
1885	Bob Martin
1886	David Brown
1887	Willie Park Jr.
1888	Jack Burns
1889	Willie Park Jr.
1890	John Ball
1891	Hugh Kirkaldy
1892	Harold H. Hiltoni
1893	William Auchterlonie
1894	John H. Taylor
1895	John H. Taylor
1896	Harry Vardon
1897	Harold H. Hilton
1898	Harry Vardon
1899	Harry Vardon
1900	John H. Taylor
1901	James Braid
1902	Alexander Herd
1903	Harry Vardon
1904	Jack White
1905	James Braid
1906	James Braid
1907	Arnaud Massy
1908	James Braid
1909	John H. Taylor
1910	James Braid
1911	Harry Vardon
1912	Edward (Ted) Ray
1913	John H. Taylor
1914	Harry Vardon
1915	Not held
1916	Not held
1917	Not held
1918	Not held
1919	Not held
1920	George Duncan
1921	Jock Hutchison
1922	Walter Hagen
1923	Arthur G. Havers
1924	Walter Hagen
1925	James M. Barnes
1926	Robert T. Jones Jr.
1927	Robert T. Jones Jr.
1928	Walter Hagen
1929	Walter Hagen
1930	Robert T. Jones Jr.
1931	Tommy D. Armour
1932	Gene Sarazen
1933	Denny Shute
1934	Henry Cotton
1935	Alfred Perry
1936	Alfred Padgham
1937	Henry Cotton
1938	R.A. Whitcombe
1939	Richard Burton
1940	Not held
1941	Not held
1942	Not held
1943	Not held
1944	Not held
1945	Not held
1946	Sam Snead
1947	Fred Daly
1948	Henry Cotton
1949	Bobby Locke
1950	Bobby Locke
1951	Max Faulkner
1952	Bobby Locke
1953	Ben Hogan
1954	Peter Thomson
1955	Peter Thomson
1956	Peter Thomson
1957	Bobby Locke
1958	Peter Thomson
1959	Gary Player
1960	Kel Nagle
1961	Arnold Palmer
1962	Arnold Palmer
1963	Bob Charles
1964	Tony Lema
1965	Peter Thomson
1966	Jack Nicklaus
1967	Roberto DeVicenzo
1968	Gary Player
1969	Tony Jacklin
1970	Jack Nicklaus
1971	Lee Trevino
1972	Lee Trevino
1973	Tom Weiskopf
1974	Gary Player
1975	Tom Watson
1976	Johnny Miller
1977	Tom Watson
1978	Jack Nicklaus
1979	Seve Ballesteros
1980	Tom Watson
1981	Bill Rogers
1982	Tom Watson
1983	Tom Watson
1984	Seve Ballesteros
1985	Sandy Lyle
1986	Greg Norman
1987	Nick Faldo
1988	Seve Ballesteros
1989	Mark Calcavecchia
1990	Nick Faldo
1991	Ian Baker-Finch
1992	Nick Faldo
1993	Greg Norman
1994	Nick Price
1995	John Daly
1996	Tom Lehman
1997	Justin Leonard
1998	Mark O'Meara
1999	Paul Lawrie
2000	Tiger Woods
2001	David Duval
2002	Ernie Els
2003	Ben Curtis
2004	Todd Hamilton

U.S. Women's Grand Slam Champions, 1972–2004

Until 1979, women's golf had two major championships: The LPGA and the U.S. Women's Open. The duMaurier Classic became the third major in 1979, and the Nabisco Championship was added in 1983. In 2001, the Women's British Open replaced the duMaurier. In the table below, the tournaments are listed in the order in which they occur during the year.

Year	Nabisco Championship	L.P.G.A. Championship	U.S. Women's Open	du Maurier Classic[1]
1972		Kathy Ahern	Susie Berning	
1973		Mary Mills	Susie Berning	
1974		Sandra Haynie	Sandra Haynie	
1975		Kathy Whitworth	Sandra Palmer	
1976		Betty Burfeindt	JoAnne Carner	
1977		Chako Higuchi	Hollis Stacy	
1978		Nancy Lopez	Hollis Stacy	
1979		Donna Caponi	Jerilyn Britz	Amy Alcott
1980		Sally Little	Amy Alcott	Pat Bradley
1981		Donna Caponi	Pat Bradley	Jan Stephenson
1982		Jan Stephenson	Janet Anderson	Sandra Haynie
1983	Amy Alcott	Patty Sheehan	Jan Stephenson	Hollis Stacy
1984	Juli Inkster	Patty Sheehan	Hollis Stacy	Juli Inkster
1985	Alice Miller	Nancy Lopez	Kathy Baker	Pat Bradley
1986	Pat Bradley	Pat Bradley	Jane Geddes	Pat Bradley
1987	Betsy King	Jane Geddes	Laura Davies	Jody Rosenthal
1988	Amy Alcott	Sherri Turner	Liselotte Neumann	Sally Little
1989	Juli Inkster	Nancy Lopez	Betsy King	Tammie Green
1990	Betsy King	Beth Daniel	Betsy King	Cathy Johnston
1991	Amy Alcott	Meg Mallon	Meg Mallon	Nancy Scranton
1992	Dottie Pepper	Betsy King	Patty Sheehan	Sherri Steinhauer
1993	Helen Alfredsson	Patty Sheehan	Lauri Merten	Brandie Burton
1994	Donna Andrews	Laura Davies	Patty Sheehan	Martha Nause
1995	Nanci Bowen	Kelly Robbins	Annika Sorenstam	Jenny Lidback
1996	Patty Sheehan	Laura Davies	Annika Sorenstam	Laura Davies
1997	Betsy King	Chris Johnson	Alison Nicholas	Colleen Walker
1998	Pat Hurst	Se Ri Pak	Se Ri Pak	Brandie Burton
1999	Dottie Pepper	Juli Inkster	Juli Inkster	Karrie Webb
2000	Karrie Webb	Juli Inkster	Karrie Webb	Meg Mallon
				Women's British Open[1]
2001	Annika Sorenstam	Karrie Webb	Karrie Webb	Se Ri Pak
2002	Annika Sorenstam	Se Ri Pak	Juli Inkster	Karrie Webb
2003	Patricia Meunier-Lebouc	Annika Sorenstam	Hilary Lunke	Annika Sorenstam
2004	Grace Park	Annika Sorenstam	Meg Mallon	Karen Stupples

Note: 1. The Women's British Open replaced the duMaurier Classic as the fourth major in 2001. **Source:** LPGA

U.S. Women's Open Champions, 1946-71

Year	Champion	Year	Champion	Year	Champion	Year	Champion
1946	Patty Berg	1953	Betsy Rawls	1958	Mickey Wright	1964	Mickey Wright
1947	Betty Jameson	1954	Babe Zaharias	1961	Mickey Wright	1965	Carol Mann
1948	Babe Zaharias	1955	Fay Crocker	1962	Murle Breer	1969	Donna Caponi
1949	Louise Suggs	1956	Kathy Cornelius	1963	Mary Mills	1970	Donna Caponi
1950	Babe Zaharias	1957	Betsy Rawls	1966	Sandra Spuzich	1971	JoAnne Carner
1951	Betsy Rawls	1959	Mickey Wright	1967	Catherine LaCoste		
1952	Louise Suggs	1960	Betsy Rawls	1968	Susie Berning		

TENNIS

"I had one thought," said the famed tennis player, "and that was to put the ball across the net."

The statement is attibuted not to a young man of the modern day, but to Helen Wills Moody, an American woman who won 19 Grand Slam singles titles between 1923 and 1938 while bearing an impassive expression that earned her the nickname "Little Miss Poker Face." The quote reveals the essence of tennis: At root, the sport, often derided as a pursuit for the country club set, demands of its practicioners incredible determination and focus. For in its most glamorous incarnation, singles play, tennis pits two opponents against each other, with no teammates, no clock, and (usually) no excuses. It is no wonder that the sport's champions, whether long ago or recent, have demonstrated a prodigious will along with their more obvious ability to hit like hammers and run like rabbits.

History of Tennis

The history of tennis is shrouded, like many sports, in an uncertain past. Some speculate that predecessors of tennis were played in ancient Egypt, Greece, and Rome. Yet the first concrete evidence of the sport's origins dates to medieval times, when the sport was played in walled courtyards by French monks. Those monastic players apparently divided their quadrangles with a rope, the forerunner of the modern net. This early form of the game was often called "jeu de paume," paume meaning the hand, which indicates the hands were used to strike the ball. Later, however, players employed gloves and short bats or paddles. Despite initial royal and even ecclesiastical obstacles to the sport, it is said that in the 13th century more than 1,800 courts existed in France. Tennis jumped across the Channel to England, where it was popular among the royalty.

The assemblage of terms that are particular to tennis may have their roots in this time. The truth is, no one knows for sure how words like *love* or *deuce*, not to mention the curious scoring system, came about. It is believed that the word *tennis* itself stems from the French *tenez*, or "take this," which was apparently shouted before the serve. The word *love* may be derived from *l'oeuf*, the French for egg, or from the Dutch/Flemish *lof*, or honor. The term *deuce* likely stems from the French a *deux du jeu*, or two points away from game. It is also not clear where the 15, 30, and 40 stem from, but theories assert score was kept on a clock face (with "45" being gradually shortened to "40") or a way to keep track of money while gambling on the match.

By 1500 the paddle used to hit the ball now included a head strung with animal intestines, and the game reached an early peak not long after. Despite innovations, the game then became less popular, so that by 1800 the game barely existed in France.

Yet tennis made a resurgence in the 19th century. In 1874 Major Walter Wingfield of the British army developed a new version of tennis with modified rules. He chose to patent the game under the unfortunate name of "sphairisitke," from the Greek for "ball game." Wingfield's version was not only played outdoors, without walls, but on a court shaped like an hourglass, narrow in the middle and wider on either end.

Neither Wingfield's obscure name for the sport nor his hourglass court left much of an imprint on history. In 1877 the All-England Croquet Club at Wimbledon contested its first lawn tennis championships, played according to a newly codified standard of rules that abandoned the hourglass court. The chosen dimensions, 78 feet long and 27 feet wide, and the created rules have stood almost untouched since that time. This initial competition was the predecessor to the modern Grand Slam tournament of Wimbledon held every summer.

Like other sports invented in Europe, tennis quickly spread to other nations. The U.S. Lawn Tennis Assocation, predecessor to the modern U.S. Tennis Association, was formed in 1881, while the British Lawn Tennis Association was created in 1888. An international body, the International Tennis Federation, was founded in 1913.

The newfangled sport of lawn tennis quickly surpassed its old ancestor, although its form indoor tennis, variously called Real Tennis or Court Tennis, is still played in places.

Yet it pales in comparison to its offspring. In the early 20th century, regular international competitions had begun, and the sport was even included in the program of the 1896 Olympic Games.

Modern Tennis

At the beginning of the 20th century, tennis was a preserve for the wealthy. The few tournaments that existed were contested by rich amateurs. The divide between amateur and professional would last, in fact, for nearly seven more decades. Only in 1968 were the top tournaments—the Australian, the French, Wimbledon, and the U.S. championships—made open to professionals. This period following 1968 is called the Open Era. Before that time, professional players could not compete in the most prestigious competitions of their sport, although many won the events while still amateurs.

Early stars of the pre-Open Era include Bill Tilden and Don Budge, who, in 1938, was the first person to win all four majors in the same year (the Grand Slam). Among women, Suzanne Lenglen and Helen Wills Moody rose to prominence. Yet star players could not earn a living playing amateur-only tournaments. So the professionals gave up such events and earned their wages with more unusual methods. As an example, Tilden won seven U.S. singles championships and three Wimbledons before turning pro in 1931. He conducted barnstorming tours, racing from match to match, often overnight, and played until he neared 50 years of age.

In mid-century, top players included Bobby Riggs, Jack Kramer, and Pancho Gonzales, plus several Australians, among them Roy Emerson and the great Rod Laver. Laver won the Grand Slam—all four major tournaments in a calendar year—in 1962.

Then came 1968, and the beginning of the Open Era. There is no better indication of the massive changes wrought by the coming of the Open Era than the U.S. Open champion in 1968: Arthur Ashe, an African American in a sport that had been historically almost exclusive to whites. After the Open Era, the game of tennis became more popular, freed from its image of being only for those rich, white, and amateur. It became a sport of the middle class.

With the added popularity of professional tennis came more tournaments and prize money. Four tournaments have historically held, in one form or another, more importance than the rest, and these are called the Grand Slams, or Slams, though winning the Grand Slam means winning all four of these in a single calendar year. There are differences in surfaces among the Slams, differences that affect how the tennis is played. In the calendar year, the first is the Australian Open, played on hardcourts in Melbourne during January, the Australian summer. Next is the French Open, played on clay, the slowest surface, in Paris in early June, and it is followed a few weeks later by Wimbledon, contested at the club's London location on the fastest surface, grass. Finally, around Labor Day comes the U.S. Open, played on the hardcourts at the U.S. Tennis Center in New York City.

In international competition, there is the Davis Cup, first contested in 1900, in which countries compete against one another's teams in both singles and doubles. Tennis is also featured in the Olympic Games.

Following the advent of the Open Era, a stable of superb players sprang to worldwide attention. First among the great men's stars was an old one, Laver, who won a second Grand Slam in 1969 (still the last man to win the Grand Slam). Laver has a claim to being the best male player in history. Other male stars included Jimmy Connors (eight Slams, including five U.S. Opens), Bjorn Borg (11 Slams, including five straight Wimbledon titles and six French Opens), and John McEnroe (seven Slams).

Two early female stars, Billie Jean King (12 Slams) and Australia's Margaret Court (a record 24 Slams, including the Grand Slam in 1970) dominated the early post–Open Era years. King was a driving force behind the formation of the Women's Tennis Association (WTA) in 1970. They were soon followed by two more superlative players, Chris Evert (18 Slams) and Martina Navratilova (also 18 Slams), a Czech who became a naturalized American.

Although the Open Era brought many changes to the game, the rules have been essentially unchanged for more than a century. The court is the same size as that prescribed by the All-England Croquet Club in 1877. Also remaining is the quirky scoring system. The only substantial rule change was the introduction of the tiebreaker in the 1970's.

Although the rules are almost the same, modern competitors are essentially playing a different sport than that seen immediately after the coming of the Open Era. Technology has revolutionized tennis in the last 25 years, not always for the better in the eyes of some critics. As recently as 1980, Sweden's Bjorn Borg won his last Wimbledon title with a wooden racket. Not long after, new materials were used to manufacture the rackets. High-tech composites permitted larger faces and lighter weights. The result has been a dramatic surge in the speed of the sport, as more athletic players zip shots back and forth over the net. In modern tennis, the rewarding virtues are shot power and quickness, which is necessary to pursue the blistering shots. Men regularly serve at around 130 miles per hour, while women customarily climb above 100 mph.

The last years of the 20th century saw dominant players arise in both the men's and women's game. Germany's Steffi Graf won 22 Slams in her career, second only to Court, and she enjoyed the most decorated year in tennis history in 1988, when she not only won the Grand Slam, but added a gold medal at the Summer Olympics in Seoul. Her nickname,"Fraulein Forehand," bestowed due to her punishing forehand stroke, symbolized the power and speed of the new game. Among men, American Pete Sampras won a record 14 Slams, including seven Wimbledons, his last Slam being a surprising U.S. Open title in 2002 (however, he never won the French Open.)

Although Margaret Court won more Slams than Graf, Graf faced stiffer competition throughout her career. Sampras's total haul of 14 Slams surpasses that of Emerson (who won 12) and Laver's 11, but Sampras did not miss six years of Grand Slam competition because he was a professional, as did Laver. Other great players of the late 80's and 90's include Boris Becker, Ivan Lendl, Andre Agassi, Monica Seles, and Martina Hingis.

Contemporary men's tennis is governed by two associations, the ITF and the ATP, while the women's game is run by the WTA. These tours host regular events around the world, each with its own schedule, and come together at the majors. As the 21st century begins, a new crop of players, particularly on the women's side, has emerged. For example, American sisters Venus and Serena Williams have combined for 10 Slams in their young careers.

Rules of the Game

A tennis match is contested either by single opponents (singles) or by two players per side (doubles). A coin toss determines who will begin the match with the serve.

Singles tennis is played on a court measuring 78 feet long and 27 feet wide, with a number of lines that have attached rules. A three-foot-high net stretches across the center of the court, dividing the surface into two equal halves. The only items of equipment necessary to play are a round ball, usually yellow, and a hand-held device called a racket, which has a web of taut strings. A tennis ball is a hollow rubber sphere covered with a synthetic felt fabric. It usually weighs about 2 ounces and has a diameter of just over 2 1/2 inches. Tennis rackets generally measure from 27 to 32 inches in length and weigh between 10 and 11 ounces. The frames, once made of wood, are now typically made of graphite and fiberglass with nylon strings.

The basic action of tennis is relatively simple. With the racket, players hit the ball over the net and the ball is similarly returned by the opponent. The ball can bounce only once and always on the receiving side of the court, and it must land within the boundaries. However, players can hit the ball while they, or the ball, is above a portion of the playing surface that is not legal. Players want to avoid hitting the ball outside of the legal surface or into the net.

The essential unit of scoring is the point. If a player makes a shot that the opponent cannot return (either by not reaching the ball at all or allowing it to bounce twice), the player wins the point. If the player makes a mistake, such as hitting the ball outside of the legal area ("out") or into, and not over, the net, the player loses the point. A ball that hits the net and still drops over into the opponent's half of the court is a legal shot. This legal area is either half of the court, including the lines. If the ball bounces on one of the lines, it is considered "in" and the opponent must return the ball or lose the point.

One addition to this is the serve, the action that commences each point. On the serve, one player strikes the ball, usually overhead, with the racket. On the serve alone the ball must land in a smaller box—the service box—outlined by small lines on the opponent's side of the court. If a player misses this box or hits the ball into the net, it is said to be a "fault." The player may serve again, but if the second serve is also in error, the player incurs a "double fault" and loses the point.

Following the serve, play continues in the specified manner until a player makes a mistake or hits a shot the opponent cannot return, and the point is awarded.

Scoring is one of the more confusing elements of tennis. To win a game, players must capture a certain number of points. If no points have been taken, the player has "0," or "love," a term specific to tennis. The first point is considered to be "15," the second "30," and the third "40."

(The source of these terms is a matter of some debate, but they harken back to medieval times.) As an example, a player who has won two points in a particular game will have "30." The fourth point, although unnamed, will win the game but for one notable exception.

At any time, the score of the game is usually read as a combination of numbers, such as 30-40, with the first number indicating the score of the person with the serve, and the second the person receiving the serve. In the case of 30-40, the player with the serve has won two points, and the player receiving has won three.

To win a game, a player has to win by at least two points. This is a problem if the players are tied at 40, in which case a mechanism called "deuce" begins. Following deuce, the game continues until one player has captured two more points than the other. If, at deuce, a player wins the next point, he/she is said to have the advantage. If, at advantage, that player wins another point, he/she wins the game. If the opponent wins the point, the game returns to deuce, and the process begins again.

For the next game, the serve goes to the other player. After every two games, players switch sides on the court.

The outcome of a match, however, is not determined by who wins the most games, but by who wins the majority of sets. In men's singles, the player who wins three out of a maximum five sets wins the match, while in women's singles, the victor takes two out of a maximum three sets.

Players win sets by winning games. To take a set, the player must capture six games while winning the set by at least two games. If the players are tied at six games in any set except the last set of the match (fifth set if men's, third if women's), then they proceed to a tiebreaker, which, of course, must be won by two points. In the final set of a match, there is no tiebreaker, and players continue to compete in games until one has captured two more games than the other. (This can take a long time.) When a player has won a majority of the possible sets, he/she wins the match.

Doubles tennis is played in almost precisely the same manner, but with two players a side. The major change is the inclusion of alleys on either flank of the court, which add nine feet to the legal width, making the court 78 feet by 36 feet.

Glossary of Tennis Terms

ace a legal serve that is not touched by the opponent. The server wins the point.

backhand one of the two common strokes in tennis, along with the forehand. In a backhand, the player faces the net with the shoulder of the racket-holding arm and swings the racket across the body to strike the ball.

baseline the lines on opposite ends of the court that serve as the far boundaries; usually four inches thick.

break when the player with the serve loses the game.

chair umpire a courtside official who sits in a high chair overlooking the net and presides over the match.

court the playing surface, of a uniform 78 feet in length but with a width that varies according to the number of players. For singles, the court is 27 feet wide, while for doubles the alleys on either side increase the dimension to 36 feet. A three-foot net divides the court across the middle, and the court can be made of concrete, grass, clay, or other materials.

deuce when a game is tied at 40. The player who wins the next point is said to have the advantage, and wins the game if he or she also scores the next point. The player without the advantage can return the game to deuce by scoring the following, point, however. The system arises because, by the rules of tennis, a player can only win a game by at least two points.

double fault if both the first and second serves result in faults, giving the opponent the point.

doubles when teams of two players compete against each other. In doubles, the alleys on either side of the court come into play, widening the legal surface by nine feet, to 36 feet.

drop shot a light shot hit with significant spin that, because of its positioning, forces the opponent to come toward the net.

fault an errant serve, called if the ball hits the net or misses the service box. A serve that strikes the top of the net and lands in the service box results in a let.

foot fault when the foot of the server enters the court before the serve is finished.

forehand one of the two main shots in tennis, executed with the shoulder of the arm without the racket facing the net, and swinging the racket forward to strike the ball. Normally a player's strongest, most powerful stroke.

gallery the name for the area where the crowd sits; also used to describe the crowd itself.

game the incremental unit of scoring to determine the progress of a set. To win a game, a player must win at least two more points than the opponent. Scores begin at 0, or love, and progress to 15, 30, and then 40. A point won at 40 will win the game, unless the game is at deuce.

in when a struck ball lands inside the legal boundaries of the court. If the ball hits the lines, it is considered "in."

let when the served ball hits the net and lands in the service box. The server is allowed to serve again without a fault.

line the white stripes that delineate the legal portions of the court. The outer lines are thicker to ease identification of whether the ball is in or out.

line judge the officials who determine whether balls land inside or outside the court. The baseline judges, service line judges, and sideline judges are all line judges.

lob a high return hit above and beyond an opponent who is close to the net. The shot forces the opponent to move backward to play the ball.

love a term unique to tennis that means zero points in the context of a game or in a set. Perhaps based on the French term for egg, *l'oeuf*, but no one really knows.

match a singles or doubles contest with an outcome determined by the number of sets won. In women's tennis, the winner is the player who wins two out of a maximum three sets, while in men's competition, the victor will win at least three of five sets.

match point the point where if a player wins, he or she wins the whole match. The terms game point and set point are also used to describe points where a player can win a game or set respectively.

net the obstacle that divides the court in two across the center. The net is three feet high in the middle and slightly higher at the court's edges. A ball must pass over the net into the opponent's court to be a legal shot. The term net is also relevant to a style of play in which players come close to the net to reduce the angle of their opponent's possible returns.

out when a ball lands outside the legal boundaries of the court.

passing shot when a player returns the ball past an opponent who is rushing to the net.

point the smallest unit of scoring in tennis, the accumulation of which determine the result of games. Players win points thusly: hitting the ball into the opposing player's court without it being returned by the opponent; if the opponent hits a ball out of the court or into the net; if the opponent double faults.

serve the action that begins every point. A player tosses the ball in the air and strikes the ball at high velocity into the diagonally opposite service box, a space. If the first serve results in a fault, the second serve is normally slower, as the server will want to avoid a double fault.

set the units that determine the outcome of a match. To take the set, a player must win two more games than opponent and at least six games in total. If tied at six games, there is a tiebreaker to determine the set winner, with the exception if it is the last and decisive set of the match, in which case the players must continue to play until one has won two more games than the other.

singles when one player plays against another player. In these games, the court is 27 feet wide.

smash a powerful overhead shot used to return a poor, high soft shot by the opponent.

tiebreaker the mechanism to determine the winner of a set tied at six games apiece. The first player to win seven points in the tiebreaker wins the game and the set, but the tiebreaker must be won by two points, and therefore may be extended until a winner is determined.

topspin when a ball is struck with spin so that it dips toward the court after being hit. This permits the ball to be hit with more power, as the ball is more likely to dive down and remain in play.

umpire the official seated in a chair on one side of the court, facing along the length of the net, who rules on the play of the game. The umpire is assisted by judges, posted with close views of the lines, to determine the legality of shots and serves.

underspin when the ball is hit with spin back toward the striking player; also called a slice. The underspin causes the ball to lose speed and bounce softly.

unforced error a shot that does not enter the opponent's court, either hitting the net or landing outside the boundaries.

volley a shot made before the ball bounces in a player's court, usually hit when close to the net. A half-volley is a shot made immediately after the ball bounces.

winner a point won when a shot lands in the opposing court and is not returned by the opponent.

Men's Grand Slam Champions

Year	Australian Champion	French Champion	Wimbledon Champion	U.S. Champion
1920	Pat O'Hara Wood	—	Bill Tilden	Bill Tilden
1921	Rhys H. Gemmell	—	Bill Tilden	Bill Tilden
1922	Pat O'Hara Wood	—	Gerald L. Patterson	Bill Tilden
1923	Pat O'Hara Wood	—	William M. Johnston	Bill Tilden
1924	James Anderson	—	Jean Borotra	Bill Tilden
1925	James Anderson	René Lacoste	René Lacoste	Bill Tilden
1926	John Hawkes	Henri Cochet	Jean Borotra	René Lacoste
1927	Gerald Patterson	René Lacoste	Henri Cochet	RenéLacoste
1928	Jean Borotra	Henri Cochet	René Lacoste	Henri Cochet
1929	John C. Gregory	René Lacoste	Henri Cochet	Bill Tilden
1930	Gar Moon	Henri Cochet	Bill Tilden	John H. Doeg
1931	Jack Crawford	Jean Borotra	Sidney B.Wood Jr.	H. Ellsworth Vines
1932	Jack Crawford	Henri Cochet	Ellsworth Vines	H. Ellsworth Vines
1933	Jack Crawford	John H. Crawford	Jack Crawford	Fred Perry
1934	Fred J. Perry	Gottfried von Cramm	Fred Perry	Fred Perry
1935	Jack Crawford	Fred J. Perry	Fred Perry	Wilmer L. Allison
1936	Adrian Quist	Gottfried von Cramm	Fred Perry	Fred Perry
1937	Vivian B. McGrath	Henner Henkel	Don Budge	Don Budge
1938[1]	Don Budge	Don Budge	Don Budge	Don Budge
1939	John Bromwich	W. Donald McNeill	Bobby Riggs	Bobby Riggs
1940	Adrian Quist	No competition	Not Held	Donald McNeill
1941	Foreigners excluded	Bernard Destremau	Not Held	Bobby Riggs
1942	Foreigners excluded	Bernard Destremau	Not Held	Frederick Schroeder
1943	Foreigners excluded	Yvon Petra	Not Held	Joseph R. Hunt
1944	Foreigners excluded	Yvon Petra	Not Held	Frank Parker
1945	Foreigners excluded	Yvon Petra	Not Held	Frank Parker
1946	John Bromwich	Marcel Bernard	Yvon Petra	Jack Kramer
1947	Dinny Pails	Joseph Asboth	Jack Kramer	Jack Kramer
1948	Adrian Quist	Frank Parker	Bob Falkenburg	Pancho Gonzales
1949	Frank Sedgman	Frank Parker	Ted Schroeder	Pancho Gonzales
1950	Frank Sedgman	Budge Patty	Budge Patty	Arthur Larsen
1951	Richard Savitt	Jaroslav Drobny	Dick Savitt	Frank Sedgman
1952	Ken McGregor	Jaroslav Drobny	Frank Sedgman	Frank Sedgman
1953	Ken Rosewall	Ken Rosewall	Vic Seixas	Tony Trabert
1954	Mervyn Rose	Tony Trabert	Jaroslav Drobny	E. Victor Seixas Jr.
1955	Ken Rosewall	Tony Trabert	Tony Trabert	Tony Trabert
1956	Lew Hoad	Lew Hoad	Lew Hoad	Ken Rosewall
1957	Ashley Cooper	Sven Davidson	Lew Hoad	Malcolm Anderson
1958	Ashley Cooper	Mervyn Rose	Ashley Cooper	Ashley J. Cooper
1959	Alex Olmedo	Nicola Pietrangeli	Alex Olmedo	Neale Fraser
1960	Rod Laver	Nicola Pietrangeli	Neale Fraser	Neale Fraser
1961	Roy Emerson	Manuel Santana	Rod Laver	Roy Emerson
1962[1]	Rod Laver	Rod Laver	Rod Laver	Rod Laver
1963	Roy Emerson	Roy Emerson	Chuck McKinley	Rafael Osuna
1964	Roy Emerson	Manuel Santana	Roy Emerson	Roy Emerson
1965	Roy Emerson	Fred Stolle	Roy Emerson	Manuel Santana

Men's Grand Slam Champions (cont'd)

Year	Australian Champion	French Champion	Wimbledon Champion	U.S. Champion
1966	Roy Emerson	Tony Roche	Manuel Santana	Fred Stolle
1967	Roy Emerson	Roy Emerson	John Newcombe	John Newcombe
1968	Bill Bowrey	Ken Rosewall	Rod Laver	Arthur Ashe
1969[1]	Rod Laver	Rod Laver	Rod Laver	Rod Laver
1970	Arthur Ashe	Jan Kodes	John Newcombe	Ken Rosewall
1971	Ken Rosewall	Jan Kodes	John Newcombe	Stan Smith
1972	Ken Rosewall	Andres Gimeno	Stan Smith	Ilie Nastase
1973	John Newcombe	Ilie Nastase	Jan Kodes	John Newcombe
1974	Jimmy Connors	Bjorn Borg	Jimmy Connors	Jimmy Connors
1975	John Newcombe	Bjorn Borg	Arthur Ashe	Manuel Orantes
1976	Mark Edmondson	Adriano Panatta	Bjorn Borg	Jimmy Connors
1977	Roscoe Tanner[2] Vitas Gerulaitis[2]	Guillermo Vilas	Bjorn Borg	Guillermo Vilas
1978	Guillermo Vilas	Bjorn Borg	Bjorn Borg	Jimmy Connors
1979	Guillermo Vilas	Bjorn Borg	Bjorn Borg	John McEnroe
1980	Brian Teacher	Bjorn Borg	Bjorn Borg	John McEnroe
1981	Johan Kriek	Bjorn Borg	John McEnroe	John McEnroe
1982	Johan Kriek	Mats Wilander	Jimmy Connors	Jimmy Connors
1983	Mats Wilander	Yannick Noah	John McEnroe	Jimmy Connors
1984	Mats Wilander	Ivan Lendl	John McEnroe	John McEnroe
1985	Stefan Edberg	Mats Wilander	Boris Becker	Ivan Lendl
1986	Moved to Jan. 1987	Ivan Lendl	Boris Becker	Ivan Lendl
1987	Stefan Edberg	Ivan Lendl	Pat Cash	Ivan Lendl
1988	Mats Wilander	Mats Wilander	Stefan Edberg	Mats Wilander
1989	Ivan Lendl	Michael Chang	Boris Becker	Boris Becker
1990	Ivan Lendl	Andrés Gomez	Stefan Edberg	Pete Sampras
1991	Boris Becker	Jim Courier	Michael Stich	Stefan Edberg
1992	Jim Courier	Jim Courier	Andre Agassi	Stefan Edberg
1993	Jim Courier	Sergi Bruguera	Pete Sampras	Pete Sampras
1994	Pete Sampras	Sergi Bruguera	Pete Sampras	Andre Agassi
1995	Andre Agassi	Thomas Muster	Pete Sampras	Pete Sampras
1996	Boris Becker	Yevgeny Kafelnikov	Richard Krajicek	Pete Sampras
1997	Pete Sampras	Gustavo Kuerten	Pete Sampras	Patrick Rafter
1998	Petr Korda	Carlos Moya	Pete Sampras	Patrick Rafter
1999	Yevgeny Kafelnikov	Andre Agassi	Pete Sampras	Andre Agassi
2000	Andre Agassi	Gustavo Kuerten	Pete Sampras	Marat Safin
2001	Andre Agassi	Gustavo Kuerten	Goran Ivanisevic	Lleyton Hewitt
2002	Thomas Johansson	Albert Costa	Lleyton Hewitt	Pete Sampras
2003	Andre Agassi	Juan Carlos Ferrero	Roger Federer	Andy Roddick
2004	Roger Federer	Gaston Gaudio	Roger Federer	—

1. Grand Slam winner. 2. Two tournaments were held in 1977, the first in January, the second in December.

Women's Grand Slam Champions

Year	Australian Champion	French Champion	Wimbledon Champion	U.S. Champion
1920	Not held	Suzanne Lenglen	Suzanne Lenglen	Molla Bjurstedt Mallory
1921	Not held	Suzanne Lenglen	Suzanne Lenglen	Molla Bjurstedt Mallory
1922	Margaret Molesworth	Suzanne Lenglen	Suzanne Lenglen	Molla Bjurstedt Mallory
1923	Margaret Molesworth	Suzanne Lenglen	Suzanne Lenglen	Helen Wills
1924	Sylvia Lance	Diddie Vlasto	Kathleen McKane	Helen Wills
1925	Daphne Akhurst	Suzanne Lenglen	Suzanne Lenglen	Helen Wills
1926	Daphne Akhurst	Suzanne Lenglen	Kathleen McKane Godfree	Molla Bjurstedt Mallory
1927	Edna Boyd	Kea Bouman	Helen Wills	Helen Wills
1928	Daphne Akhurst	Helen Wills	Helen Wills	Helen Wills
1929	Daphne Akhurst	Helen Wills	Helen Wills	Helen Wills
1930	Daphne Akhurst	Helen Wills Moody	Helen Wills Moody	Betty Nuthall
1931	Coral Buttsworth	Cilly Aussem	Cilly Aussem	Helen Wills Moody
1932	Coral Buttsworth	Helen Wills Moody	Helen Wills Moody	Helen Jacobs
1933	Joan Hartigan	Margaret Scriven	Helen Wills Moody	Helen Jacobs
1934	Joan Hartigan	Margaret Scriven	Dorothy Round	Helen Jacobs
1935	Dorothy Round	Hilde Sperling	Helen Wills Moody	Helen Jacobs
1936	Joan Hartigan	Hilde Sperling	Helen Jacobs	Alice Marble
1937	Nancye Wynne Bolton	Hilde Sperling	Dorothy Round	Anita Lizane
1938	Dorothy Bundy	Simone Mathieu	Helen Wills Moody	Alice Marble
1939	Emily Westacott	Simone Mathieu	Alice Marble	Alice Marble
1940	Nancye Wynne Bolton	Not Held	Not Held	Alice Marble
1941	Not Held	Not Held	Not Held	Sarah Palfrey Cooke
1942	Not Held	Not Held	Not Held	Pauline Betz
1943	Not Held	Not Held	Not Held	Pauline Betz
1944	Not Held	Not Held	Not Held	Pauline Betz Cooke
1945	Not Held	Not Held	Not Held	Sarah Palfrey Cooke
1946	Nancye Wynne Bolton	Margaret Osborne	Pauline Betz	Pauline Betz
1947	Nancye Wynne Bolton	Patricia Todd	Margaret Osborne	Louise Brough
1948	Nancye Wynne Bolton	Nelly Landry	Louise Brough	Margaret Osborne duPont
1949	Doris Hart	Margaret Osborne duPont	Louise Brough	Margaret Osborne duPont
1950	Louise Brough	Doris Hart	Louise Brough	Margaret Osborne duPont
1951	Nancye Wynne Bolton	Shirley Fry	Doris Hart	Maureen Connolly
1952	Thelma Long	Doris Hart	Maureen Connolly	Maureen Connolly
1953[1]	Maureen Connolly	Maureen Connolly	Maureen Connolly	Maureen Connolly
1954	Thelma Long	Maureen Connolly	Maureen Connolly	Doris Hart
1955	Beryl Penrose	Angela Mortimer	Louise Brough	Doris Hart
1956	Mary Carter	Althea Gibson	Shirley Fry	Shirley Fry
1957	Shirley Fry	Shirley Bloomer	Althea Gibson	Althea Gibson
1958	Angela Mortimer	Zsuzsi Kormoczy	Althea Gibson	Althea Gibson
1959	Mary Carter Reitano	Christine Truman	Maria Bueno	Maria Bueno
1960	Margaret Smith	Darlene Hard	Maria Bueno	Darlene Hard
1961	Margaret Smith	Ann Haydon	Angela Mortimer	Darlene Hard
1962	Margaret Smith	Margaret Smith	Karen Hantze Susman	Margaret Smith
1963	Margaret Smith	Lesley Turner	Margaret Smith	Maria Bueno
1964	Margaret Smith	Margaret Smith	Maria Bueno	Maria Bueno
1965	Margaret Smith	Lesley Turner	Margaret Smith	Margaret Smith

Women's Grand Slam Champions (cont'd)

Year	Australian Champion	French Champion	Wimbledon Champion	U.S. Champion
1966	Margaret Smith	Ann Jones	Billie Jean King	Maria Bueno
1967	Nancy Richey	Francoise Durr	Billie Jean King	Billie Jean King
1968	Billie Jean King	Nancy Richey	Billie Jean King	Virginia Wade
1969	Margaret Smith Court	Margaret Smith Court	Ann Jones	Margaret Smith Court
1970[1]	Margaret Smith Court	Margaret Smith Court	Margaret Smith Court	Margaret Smith Court
1971	Margaret Smith Court	Evonne Goolagong	Evonne Goolagong	Billie Jean King
1972	Virginia Wade	Billie Jean King	Billie Jean King	Billie Jean King
1973	Margaret Smith Court	Margaret Smith Court	Billie Jean King	Margaret Smith Court
1974	Evonne Goolagong	Chris Evert	Chris Evert	Billie Jean King
1975	Evonne Goolagong	Chris Evert	Billie Jean King	Chris Evert
1976	Evonne Goolagong Cawley	Sue Barker	Chris Evert	Chris Evert
1977	Kerry Melville Reid[2] Evonne Goolagong Cawley[2]	Mima Jasuovec	Virginia Wade	Chris Evert
1978	Chris O'Neil	Virginia Ruzici	Martina Navratilova	Chris Evert
1979	Barbara Jordan	Chris Evert Lloyd	Martina Navratilova	Tracy Austin
1980	Hana Mandlikova	Chris Evert Lloyd	Evonne Goolagong Cawley	Chris Evert Lloyd
1981	Martina Navratilova	Hana Mandlikova	Chris Evert Lloyd	Tracy Austin
1982	Chris Evert Lloyd	Martina Navratilova	Martina Navratilova	Chris Evert Lloyd
1983	Martina Navratilova	Chris Evert Lloyd	Martina Navratilova	Martina Navratilova
1984	Chris Evert Lloyd	Martina Navratilova	Martina Navratilova	Martina Navratilova
1985	Martina Navratilova	Chris Evert Lloyd	Martina Navratilova	Hana Mandlikova
1986	Moved to Jan. 1987	Chris Evert Lloyd	Martina Navratilova	Martina Navratilova
1987	Hana Mandlikova	Steffi Graf	Martina Navratilova	Martina Navratilova
1988[1]	Steffi Graf	Steffi Graf	Steffi Graf	Steffi Graf
1989	Steffi Graf	Arantxa Sanchez	Steffi Graf	Steffi Graf
1990	Steffi Graf	Monica Seles	Martina Navratilova	Gabriela Sabatini
1991	Monica Seles	Monica Seles	Steffi Graf	Monica Seles
1992	Monica Seles	Monica Seles	Steffi Graf	Monica Seles
1993	Monica Seles	Steffi Graf	Steffi Graf	Steffi Graf
1994	Steffi Graf	Arantxa Sánchez Vicario	Conchita Martinez	Arantxa Sánchez Vicario
1995	Mary Pierce	Steffi Graf	Steffi Graf	Steffi Graf
1996	Monica Seles	Steffi Graf	Steffi Graf	Steffi Graf
1997	Martina Hingis	Iva Majoli	Martina Hingis	Martina Hingis
1998	Martina Hingis	Arantxa Sánchez Vicario	Jana Novotna	Lindsay Davenport
1999	Martina Hingis	Steffi Graf	Lindsay Davenport	Serena Williams
2000	Lindsay Davenport	Mary Pierce	Venus Williams	Venus Williams
2001	Jennifer Capriati	Jennifer Capriati	Venus Williams	Venus Williams
2002	Jennifer Capriati	Serena Williams	Serena Williams	Serena Williams
2003	Serena Williams	Justine Henin-Hardenne	Serena Williams	Justine Henin-Hardenne
2004	Justine Henin-Hardenne	Anastasia Myskina	Maria Sharapova	—

1. Grand Slam winner. 2. Two tournaments were held in 1977, the first in January, the second in December.

SOCCER

History

Commonly known as "football" outside North America, soccer is the world's most popular sport. The word *soccer* is derived from "association football," the traditional name for the game in the British Commonwealth countries. Although ball-kicking games can be traced at least as far back as ancient Greece and China, modern soccer originated in 19th-century England. The Football Association laid down the first set of rules in 1863, and the first organized league was established in 1888. Carried outside Britain by sailors and expatriates, the game quickly caught on in the rest of Europe, South America, and Asia. The Fédération Internationale de Football Association (FIFA), the world's official governing body for the sport, was founded in 1904, with headquarters in Paris (later moved to Zurich). Soccer became a medal sport in the Olympic Games of 1908. In 1930 FIFA organized the World Cup, a tournament contested every four years to determine international soccer supremacy.

The World Cup is the most coveted prize in soccer. The month-long quadrennial tournament culminates more than two years of qualifying play in six world regions. A total of 198 national teams entered competition for the 2002 World Cup, of which 32 qualified for the final tournament. More than 2 billion television viewers were estimated to have watched the 2002 final, in which Brazil defeated Germany to capture its record fifth title.

World Cup competition for women began in 1991, with tournaments also held every four years. The United States has won twice.

Rules of the Game

Soccer is played according to the same basic rules almost everywhere. The field, or "pitch," is rectangular in shape, measuring 100–130 yards (91-119 meters) long and at least 50 yard (46 meters) wide. Each team consists of 11 players, including a goalkeeper. The goalkeeper is the only player who may touch the ball with the hands or arms, and only within a designated area. The other players attempt to advance the ball by kicking, or sometimes heading, it to a teammate. The object is to force the ball into the opponent's goal—24 feet (7.3 meters) wide and 8 feet (2.4 meters) high—at the far end of the field. In high-level competition, a match lasts 90 minutes and is played in 45-minute halves.

Combining speed, skill, and chesslike strategy, soccer attracts numerous players and spectators throughout the world. Professional clubs play in domestic leagues before passionate crowds. Concurrent with league play, top clubs may compete in annual continent-wide tournaments, such as the European Cup and South America's Copa Libertadores (Liberator's Cup).

In the United States, the growth of soccer has taken place largely at the amateur level—community youth leagues, high schools, and colleges—since the 1960's. U.S. professional leagues (mostly notably the North American Soccer League, 1966–84 and the present Major League Soccer) have had passing success.

Club Soccer

Although the World Cup is considered the premier event in soccer, it is a competition that is held only once every four years. Most daily interest in the game is devoted to club soccer. Every year, clubs all over the world compete in domestic leagues, domestic cups, and in regional cup competitions. At the elite levels, these leagues and clubs command hundreds of millions of dollars in television fees, attendance revenues, and salaries.

Domestic leagues are typically organized in a fashion similar to American baseball: a top division, in which the best clubs and players are concentrated, with lower tiers underneath. However, clubs in the lower leagues are not affiliated with the top-level teams, as in the minor leagues of American baseball. Furthermore, teams move up and down in these divisions through a system of promotion and relegation. For example, Italy's highest division is called Serie A, and underneath are Serie B and Serie C. At the end of every season, the worst four teams in Serie A are relegated to Serie B for the following year, while the top four teams in Serie B are promoted to Serie A.

Another differentiating feature between American sports and international club soccer is the form of player movement. Players customarily change teams through payment of a transfer fee between clubs, although switching via a trade or free agency is also possible. For the best players, transfer fees can be exorbitant: in the summer of 2002, Spain's Real Madrid purchased Brazilian forward Ronaldo, fresh off a dominating (and victorious) performance in the 2002 World Cup, from Italy's Inter Milan in a package that totaled more than $40 million.

Perhaps the most significant aspect of club soccer is that, unlike American sports leagues, where the goal is a single championship, international soccer clubs pursue several trophies, of varying worth, in a single year.

Domestic leagues typically involve a home-and-away round robin, which in a league of 20 teams, such as Spain's La Liga, consists of 38 games. Three points are awarded for a win and one for a draw, and the club with the most points at the end of the season is the champion.

In most countries there is also a knockout cup competition similar to the collegiate basketball tournaments in the United States, but without a seeding system. In some nations, these have a long and significant history: England's Football Association Cup, for example, has been played since 1872, and participants include top-notch clubs such as London's Tottenham Hotspur, teams from several lower professional divisions, and amateur squads. While such cup titles add to the trophy case, they are not as coveted as the league titles.

The elite clubs also compete across international borders in regional competitions. The European Champions Cup is contested by the best teams from all members of UEFA, the European soccer federation. In South America top clubs fight for the Copa Libertadores. These are the most prestigious trophies a club can win in their respective regions.

In the United States, Major League Soccer entered its eighth year of competition in 2003. Although the league continues to struggle, MLS has achieved stability through close scrutiny of expenses and player salaries. The league has bred a number of key contributors to the U.S. national team and has sold several players to foreign clubs. Also, the WUSA, a women's league, began play in 2001, but folded after the 2003 season.

Glossary of Soccer Terms

arc the D-shaped line at the top of the penalty area. The line demarcates a circular distance of 10 yards from the penalty spot.

cap an appearance for a country's national team, so named because, in the past, players were awarded with celebratory headwear.

card a disciplinary system available to the referee. The yellow card is given for overly tough fouls or for persistent fouling by a single player. On violent fouls, such as a lunging tackle from behind, the referee may choose to show a red card, thereby expelling the offending player from the game. Two yellow cards incurred by the same player during the course of a match equals a red card.

corner kick a free kick taken from either corner of the field by the attacking team, awarded when the ball crosses the end line after being last touched by a defender. As with any free kick, the defending team must be at least 10 yards from the spot of the kick.

cross an attacking pass from either side of the field into the penalty area. Frequently aimed at the heads of forwards.

defenders the group of players whose primary duty is to prevent the opposition's attackers from scoring goals. Customarily defenders come in several flavors, including center backs, right or left backs, and sweepers.

draw when the match is tied at game's end. In league play both teams will receive one point in the standings.

extra time an added 30-minute period of play, used only in some tournaments (such as the knockout stage of the World Cup) if the contest is tied after regulation. If there is no score after 30 minutes, the game is usually decided by a penalty shootout.

formation a team's alignment of players on the field. This is described with a set of three numbers, representative of the defenders, midfielders, and forwards, that add up to 10. (The goalkeeper is not considered.) In a 4-4-2 formation, for example, there will be four defenders, four midfielders and two forwards. There is no restriction on a team's formation, and these change based on the game situation.

forwards the players who operate closest to the opposing goal, forwards are the most frequent goalscorers and playmakers; sometimes called strikers.

foul an infraction decided by the referee; usually given for body contact that does not touch the ball first. The fouled team is awarded a free kick. (see *card*)

free kick the action that returns the ball to play after a foul. The victimized team is allowed a 10-yard circle free of enemy defenders. Near the opposing goal, free kicks offer good shooting opportunities. A penalty kick is a free kick taken from the penalty spot.

friendly an exhibition match.

goal the only kind of scoring play in soccer, worth one unit each. The entire ball must cross the goal line—the line underneath the crossbar that links the goalposts—to be counted as a goal. The goal itself is a rectangle 24 feet wide and eight feet high.

goal area a box set within the larger penalty area, from which goal kicks are taken by the defending team. The goal area extends six yards into the field of play.

goalkeeper the player responsible for stopping or blocking shots at his team's goal. The goalkeeper is also the only player allowed to use the hands, but this ability is limited to the penalty area. A keeper who touches the ball with the hands while outside the area risks a yellow or even a red card.

goal kick the kick that restarts play after the attacking team knocks the ball over the end line. This kick is usually taken by the goalkeeper.

goal line the line that marks either end of the field. If the ball exits the field over the goal line, the result is either a corner kick (if last touched by the defending team) or a goal kick. If the entire ball crosses the goal line in the area surrounded by the goal structure, a goal is awarded. Outside of the goal, the goal line is often called simply the end line.

halfway line the line that divides the field in half across the center.

handball intentionally touching the ball with one's hand; strictly forbidden in soccer, the exception being the goalkeeper while in the penalty area. If the balls hits the hand, and the referee determines the player did not touch the ball intentionally, then the referee often lets play continue. Otherwise, if the referee judges a handball, the result is a free kick for the other team.

midfielders the set of players who are equally responsible for defense and attack. Primary duties include winning the ball from the opposing team and creating scoring chances for their own team. The generic term covers a set of varying roles, including wingers, attacking midfielders, and defensive midfielders, among others.

offside an infraction at the moment the ball is passed by a teammate, and the offensive player does not have two opposing defenders (usually counting the goalkeeper as one) between him or her and the goal line. The attacker is considered offside, and this infraction awards a free kick to the defending team. This is the much misunderstood offside rule. Defenses often try to catch attackers in offside situations via a maneuver called the offside trap, in which several defending players simultaneously move away from their own goal. Of course, there are instances when an attacker, timing movement carefully, is said to beat the offside trap, usually obtaining a one-on-one chance against the goalkeeper.

own goal when a defending player, normally by deflection, knocks the ball into his team's goal.

penalty a serious infraction, decided by the referee, who determines that a defender handled the ball or fouled an attacking player in the penalty area. The victimized team is given a free kick from the penalty spot with only the goalkeeper to beat.

penalty area a box that begins 18 yards outside either goalpost, at right angles to the goal line, and extends 18 yards into the field of play. The penalty area has two rules attached. A goalkeeper may touch the ball only with the hands while inside the box, and a foul on the attacking team inside the penalty area results in a penalty.

penalty spot a small circle 12 yards from the goal line, at the center of the box or penalty area, from which penalties are taken.

referee the official who judges and enforces the rules of the game. He or she is aided by two assistants whose primary responsibility is to determine offside infractions. A fourth official, on the sideline, supervises substitutions.

shootout the act of taking alternating penalty kicks to decide a game. Each team receives five attempts (or more if the tie persists) from the penalty spot.

stoppage time the period of time at the end of either half to account for substitutions, injuries, and time-wasting.

substitutions in most league play, three substitutions per game. The player removed cannot return to the match.

In friendly matches, usually only five substitutions are permitted, though this limit may be raised with the agreement of both teams.

tackle a defender's attempt to take the ball from an offensive player.

through ball a pass that splits the opposing defense to an onrushing attacker; often used to describe passes that beat the offside trap.

throw in the action that restarts play after the ball goes over the touchline. The player grasps the ball with two hands and throws it back onto the field.

time game time of two 45-minute halves, usually counting up from zero, with stoppage time added at the end of each half. Goals are tracked only by the minute of their scoring, i.e. the 65th minute, not 64:22.

touchline the boundary that borders either side of the field. If the entire ball goes over the touchline, the team that did not touch the ball last is awarded a throw in.

World Cup (women)

Year	Host Country	Championship Game
1991	China	United States 2, Norway 1
1995	Sweden	Norway 2, Germany 0
1999	U.S.	United States 0 (5), China 0 (4) (ET)
2003	U.S.	Germany 2, Sweden 1 (ET)

World Cup (men)

Year	Host Country	Final Score, Championship Game	Leading Scorer, Country (goals)
1930	**Uruguay**	**Uruguay 4, Argentina 2**	**Guillermo Stábile, Arg. (8)**
Thirteen nations (only 4 from Europe) participate in the first World Cup. The host country, celebrating the centennial of national independence, wins the final before 95,000 spectators.			
1934	**Italy**	**Italy 2, Czechoslovakia 1 (ET)**	**Three Players with 4 Goals**[1]
The World Cup comes to Europe; defending champion Uruguay does not attend. A qualifying round reduces the field from 31 teams to 16. Giuseppe Meazza leads Italy to the title.			
1938	**France**	**Italy 4, Hungary 2**	**Leonidas, Brazil (7)**
Italy, behind the great Meazza, successfully defends its crown. Leonidas, a preeminent center-forward of the prewar era, carries Brazil to a third-place finish.			
1950	**Brazil**	**Uruguay 2, Brazil 1**[2]	**Ademir, Brazil (9)**
After cancellations in 1942 and 1946 due to World War II, 33 nations participate in qualifying play—15 in the tournament. Uruguay, led by Juan Schiaffino and Obdulio Varela, stuns the home crowd in the final match in Rio de Janeiro's Maracana stadium.			
1954	**Switzerland**	**West Germany 3, Hungary 2**	**Sandor Kocsis, Hun. (11)**
Hungary, featuring Kocsis and Ferenc Puskas, dominates the tournament, but West Germany scores the winning goal with six minutes to play in one of the most dramatic finals ever.			
1958	**Sweden**	**Brazil 5, Sweden 2**	**Just Fontaine, France (13)**
The first internationally televised Cup sees the emergence of Brazil's Pelé, only 17, as a major star. He scores three goals in the semifinal and two more in the final against the host country.			
1962	**Chile**	**Brazil 3, Czechoslovakia 1**	**Six Players with 4 Goals**[3]
Brazil successfully defends its title behind goal scorers Garrincha and Vava (four each for the tournament). Pelé is injured in an early match and sees little action.			
1966	**England**	**England 4, West Germany 2 (ET)**	**Eusébio, Port. (9)**
The host team—with Bobby Charlton, captain Bobby Moore, Geoff Hurst, and goalkeeper Gordon Banks—thrills its fans with an extra time victory in the final; Hurst scores a hat trick.			

Year	Host Country	Final Score, Championship Game	Leading Scorer, Country (goals)
1970	**Mexico**	**Brazil 4, Italy 1**	**Gerd Müller, W. Ger. (10)**

This tournament features a welcome return to attacking football. Standouts include Pelé and Jairzinho of Brazil, Cubillas of Peru, and German Gerd Müller, the tourney's leading scorer. Brazil keeps the Jules Rimet Trophy (named for the World Cup's founder) after winning for the third time.

Year	Host Country	Final Score, Championship Game	Leading Scorer, Country (goals)
1974	**West Germany**	**West Germany 2, Netherlands 1**	**Grzegorz Lato, Pol. (7)**

The host country, led by sweeper Franz Beckenbauer and goal-scorer Paul Breitner, defeats Holland, featuring Johan Cruyff and an innovative team style known as "Total Football."

Year	Host Country	Final Score, Championship Game	Leading Scorer, Country (goals)
1978	**Argentina**	**Argentina 3, Netherlands 1 (ET)**	**Mario Kempes, Arg. (6)**

More than 100 nations participate in qualifying play, but the host wins again. Kempes (two goals in final), and Daniel Passarella power the blue-and-white.

Year	Host Country	Final Score, Championship Game	Leading Scorer, Country (goals)
1982	**Spain**	**Italy 3, West Germany 1**	**Paolo Rossi, Italy (6)**

The number of final-round qualifiers is increased from 16 to 24, divided into six groups. Behind Rossi and goalkeeper/captain Dino Zoff, Italy wins its third World Cup.

Year	Host Country	Final Score, Championship Game	Leading Scorer, Country (goals)
1986	**Mexico**	**Argentina 3, West Germany 2**	**Gary Lineker, Eng. (6)**

Argentina's Diego Maradona (5 goals, 5 assists) emerges as the king of world soccer, dominating the tournament. The final between Argentina and West Germany, with three goals in the last 20 minutes, is one of the most exciting ever.

Year	Host Country	Final Score, Championship Game	Leading Scorer, Country (goals)
1990	**Italy**	**West Germany 1, Argentina 0**	**Salvatore Schillaci, Italy (6)**

Midfielder Lothar Matthäus and striker Jürgen Klinsmann lead a powerful German squad, which wins the Cup on a penalty with only five minutes to play against the defending champions.

Year	Host Country	Final Score, Championship Game	Leading Scorer, Country (goals)
1994	**United States**	**Brazil 0 (3), Italy 0 (2) (ET)**	**Hristo Stoitchkov, Bulgaria, Oleg Salenko, Russia (6)**

In the first World Cup hosted by the United States, Romario propels Brazil to its fourth Cup. The title match against Italy, led by Roberto Baggio, is decided by penalty kicks after a scoreless tie in regulation and 30 minutes of extra time.

Year	Host Country	Final Score, Championship Game	Leading Scorer, Country (goals)
1998	**France**	**France 3, Brazil 0**	**Davor Suker, Croatia (6)**

The field expands to 32 teams in eight groups. The host country, surprisingly, wins for the sixth time. Midfielder Zinedine Zidane, who scores twice in the final, is France's inspirational player.

Year	Host Country	Final Score, Championship Game	Leading Scorer, Country (goals)
2002	**South Korea/Japan**	**Brazil 2, Germany 0**	**Ronaldo, Brazil (8)**

The men's tournament is held in Asia for the first time. Ronaldo scores twice in the second half of the final—the first-ever World Cup meeting between the soccer powers—as Brazil beats Germany for its fifth title.

(ET) = Extra Time, a 30-minute period played if the game is tied after regulation.

Notes: 1. Conen (Germany), Schiavio (Italy), and Nejedly (Czechoslovakia) 2. Uruguay's upset of Brazil in the 1950 World Cup was the decisive final match of a four-team round robin group, not a single championship game. 3. Albert (Hungary), Garrincha (Brazil), V. Ivanov (Soviet Union), Jerkovic (Yugoslavia), L. Sánchez (Chile), Vavá (Brazil).

HORSE RACING

Origins

The sport of thoroughbred horse racing has a worldwide appeal that is second only to soccer. Racing can be found across five continents, with particular interest in England and France and their former colonies, especially Australia, South Africa, and Hong Kong. Japan, too, has developed a flourishing horse racing industry. In the United States there are more than 100 tracks and in 2002 $15.1 billion was wagered in America alone.

It is an ancient sport as well, tracing back to the time of the domestication of the horse. Humans may have raced horses as early as 4500 B.C. The Olympic Games first featured racing (with both chariots and riders) in the seventh century B.C. One of the key moments in "modern" racing occurred in the 12th century, when English knights returned from the crusades with Arabian horses. These faster horses became popular, and over time many more were imported from their native lands and bred to stouter English mares.

During the 16th and 17th centuries, the royalty of Europe improved the speed and stamina of their horses by importing stallions from more distant regions. England's Charles II formalized the rules of racing in the mid-17th century. In the last decade of the 17th century and the early part of the 18th century, three stallions of Arabian blood achieved prominence: the Byerly Turk, the Darley Arabian, and the Godolphin Arabian (aka the Godolphin Barb).

The Basics

An average thoroughbred weighs about 1,000 pounds and is a little more than five feet tall. Many races are restricted by age. Horses' ages are determined by the year in which they were born, i.e. every horse in the Northern Hemisphere officially has January 1 as his/her birthday. Males are called colts until they turn five, after which they are called horses. Similarly, females are known as fillies until they turn five, then later as mares. A castrated male horse is called a gelding. Horses generally begin racing at two or three years of age.

Types of Races

Races can be run on either dirt courses or grass courses, called turf. They are run at short distances (called sprints) or longer distances (known as routes). Any race of at least a mile is considered a route. Steeplechase is a closely related sport that features thoroughbreds running longer distances over hurdles. They are sometimes run at the same tracks but more often are run at "hunt meets" around the country.

Races fall into four categories:

Maiden races are races for horses who have yet to win a race. A horse who wins his first race "breaks his maiden."

Claiming races are races in which each horse is for sale for a certain predetermined price before the race takes place. This brings together horses of similar ability.

In allowance races, the horses are not for sale but they do have to meet certain conditions to enter. (For example, they have not won two races in their career.) These are the races in which very good horses usually compete once they have broken their maidens but are not ready (or good enough) to compete in stakes.

Stakes races are the cream of the crop. They offer the highest purses (prize money paid by the track), and they feature the best horses. The Kentucky Derby and the Breeders' Cup races are the most prestigious stakes races in America.

Breeding

The industry of breeding racehorses is a huge business worldwide. More than 35,000 foals were registered in the United States in 2003. Successful sires can command tens of thousands of dollars in stud fees for getting mares in foal. Currently, the stud fee for the great sire, Storm Cat, is $500,000 for a live foal. The offspring can be sold for up to millions, particularly at the famous horse sales at Keeneland in Lexington, Ky., and Saratoga Springs, N.Y. The most expensive yearling ever sold at auction was Seattle Dancer in 1985 for $13.1 million. Breeding today is conducted with serious scientific knowledge with every aspect of a horse's lineage being evaluated.

Betting

There is betting on nearly all the thoroughbred racing in America. Bets include win (horse must finish first), place (horse must finish first or second), or show (horse must run first, second, or third). Also very popular are wagers like the double (pick the winners of two consecutive races) and the exacta (pick the first and second place horses in a given race). There are many other exotic wagers to choose from. A certain percentage of each dollar bet (called the takeout) goes to the racetrack. The rest of the pool of money on each wager is divided up among the winners. This is called parimutuel wagering.

History

1890's–1930

These years were a transitional time for racing as the sport moved from stamina intensive heats covering long distances for older horses to one focused on younger horses running much shorter distances for faster times.

A dominant sprinter called Domino became one of the first great modern champions when he broke the all-time earnings record as a two-year-old in 1893. His best son was Colin, who was undefeated in 15 starts; for 80 years he was the only major thoroughbred to retire undefeated.

Regret was the first filly to win the Kentucky Derby in 1915, going wire-to-wire as the favorite.

In 1919 a maiden named Sir Barton became the first horse to win the Kentucky Derby, the Preakness, and the Belmont Stakes. There was no "Triple Crown" at the time, however, as that distinction didn't exist until later. The honor was awarded to Sir Barton retroactively.

That same year also saw a big red colt named Man O'War race for the first time. Before he was done, he would win 19 of his 20 races and own track records at five different distances. By the middle of his career, few horses would even show up to face him. Man O'War's lone loss, at Saratoga, was so shocking that it forever changed the parlance of sports: his victor was a horse named Upset. The last race of Man O'War's career was a match race thrashing of Sir Barton. Many consider Man O'War the best horse to ever don two pairs of shoes.

1930's

The Depression was a boom time for racing, as many states opened racetracks to help attract money to empty coffers. Famous tracks such as Santa Anita, Del Mar, Keeneland, Hialeah, and Gulfstream Park opened during the decade.

In 1930 Gallant Fox, trained by Sunny Jim Fitzsimmons, won the Derby, Preakness, and Belmont (the Preakness came first at that point) and the achievement was dubbed as the Triple Crown. Gallant Fox continued the tradition of great horses, losing at Saratoga when he lost to a 100-1 shot named Jim Dandy in that year's Travers Stakes.

Five years later, Gallant Fox's son Omaha, also trained by Fitzsimmons, became the third horse to win the Triple Crown. Gallant Fox remains the only Triple Crown winner to sire a Triple Crown winner.

The best rivalry of the decade pitted War Admiral against Seabiscuit. War Admiral was a regally bred son of Man O'War who won the Triple Crown in 1937. Many thought War Admiral to be the best horse since his sire. Seabiscuit was a grandson of Man O'War, and his career had modest beginnings, as he was beaten in claiming races as a two-year-old and did nothing to distinguish himself in the first half of his third year. However, he blossomed under the care of Silent Tom Smith and set nine track records. He beat Man O'War in their famous match race in the fall of 1938 and closed out his career by returning from injury to win the Santa Anita Handicap, a prize that had eluded him until then.

1940's

The 1940's saw the emergence of four more Triple Crown winners, two of whom carried the devil's red and blue silks of Kentucky's Calumet Farm. Whirlaway, trained by Ben Jones, was first in 1941, and he went on to pass Seabiscuit's all-time earnings mark in 1942, when he captured Horse of the Year for the second time.

The tempermental Count Fleet, the 1943 Triple Crown winner, never finished off the board in 21 career starts.

Assault suffered from a series of physical ailments, but none prevented him from earning the decade's third Triple Crown in 1946. His rivalry with the extremely popular former claimer Stymie was among the best of the decade, with Assault winning five of their eight meetings, though it was Stymie who ended the decade as the all-time money earner.

Stymie's record didn't last long. Calumet Farm's Citation, trained by Jimmy Jones and usually piloted by Eddie Arcaro, won the Triple Crown in 1948 as part of his famous 16-race winning streak. He set the earnings record and became the first horse to earn more than $1 million with victory in the Hollywood Gold Cup in 1951.

1950's

Alfred Vanderbilt's Native Dancer, known as the Gray Ghost, would have retired a perfect 22 for 22 had he not encountered bad luck in the 1953 Kentucky Derby, which he lost by a head to Dark Star. He was named Horse of the Year as both a two-year-old and a four-year-old.

Tom Fool won the honor in the year between, 1953. He was a perfect 10 for 10 as a four- and five-year-old.

Nashua and Swaps fought one of the great rivalries in racing's storied history. Nashua was the two-year-old champion of 1954 but Swaps upset him in the 1955 Derby. They hooked up for a match race in 1956, and Nashua achieved his revenge, winning by more than six lengths.

Many consider the 1957 Kentucky Derby the greatest ever. Gallant Man appeared the winner, but jockey Bill Shoemaker misjudged the finish line, allowing Iron Liege to pass him. Bold Ruler and Round Table were also in the field. Bold Ruler went on to win the Preakness and was named top horse in 1957. Round Table won 43 of 66 races on both turf and dirt during his career and was Horse of the Year in 1958.

1960's

The late-blooming gelding Kelso, trained by Carl Hanford and owned by Mrs. Richard C. duPont, dominated racing in the early part of the decade, winning Horse of the Year five years in a row from 1960 through 1964. He retired as the all-time money earner with nearly $2 million in combined purses.

The Canadian-bred Northern Dancer won the Kentucky Derby in a record time of two minutes flat but was denied the Triple Crown when he lost the 1964 Belmont to Quadrangle. Overall, he would win 14 of 18 races and later become one of the most influential stallions of the century. Ogden Phipps's Buckpasser was another horse that earned more than $1 million. He missed the Triple Crown in 1966 but was Horse of the Year anyway and won 25 of 31 races overall.

One of the greatest races of the decade saw Buckpasser take on Dr. Fager and Damascus in the 1967 Woodward Stakes. Damascus won that day and would win Horse of the Year. In 1968 it was Dr. Fager's turn to win the honor as he proved himself one of the most versatile and talented horses of the decade.

1970's

The advent of Off-Track Betting facilities as well as the growing popularity of state lotteries and other forms of legalized gambling started to erode the numbers of people who would go see live racing. However, wager amounts only kept increasing.

In 1970 Bill Shoemaker broke Johnny Longden's record for most wins by a jockey (6,032). Shoe's record of 8,833 stood until 1999, when Laffit Pincay Jr. surpassed him.

Secretariat, believed by many to be the greatest horse in history, won the Triple Crown in 1973. A big red colt by Bold Ruler, Secretariat had been a champion two-year-old and was wildly popular during his Triple Crown run. He set a track record that still stands in winning the Kentucky Derby in 1:59 2/5, and in the Belmont he beat the second place horse by 31 lengths. When ESPN named its 50 greatest athletes of the century nearly three decades later, Secretariat was the only nonhuman on the list.

Ruffian was a beautiful black filly who was undefeated in 10 career starts and had never seen the tail of another horse during a race. She took on Derby winner Foolish Pleasure in a match race in 1975. In one of the sport's darkest moments, she broke down during the running, and she is buried near the finish line at Belmont Park.

Seattle Slew was another undefeated two-year-old, who went on to win the Triple Crown in 1977.

The great rivalry of the 70's pitted Harbor View Farm's Affirmed against Calumet Farm's Alydar. As two-year-olds, Affirmed beat Alydar in four of six races. At three years, Affirmed also got the best of his rival, winning each of the Triple Crown races with Alydar in second each time. Alydar did achieve a measure of revenge over Affirmed in a controversial win by disqualification in the Travers.

In the 1979 Jockey Club Gold Cup, Affirmed took on Spectacular Bid, who had won both the Derby and Preakness. Affirmed won by three-quarters of a length in the last race of his career. He would retire as the all-time money earner with $2.3 million, a record soon to be broken by Spectacular Bid, who never lost another race after that and won 26 of 30 races with nearly $2.8 million in earnings.

1980's

No filly had won the Kentucky Derby since Regret, but two horses accomplished the feat in the 80's: Genuine Risk in 1980 and D. Wayne Lukas's Winning Colors in 1988.

A six-year-old gelding named John Henry made quite a

splash in 1981, winning stakes races on both coasts on both turf and dirt. The temperamental and beloved star raced through age nine, banking nearly $6.6 million in the process.

The biggest story of the decade though, was the advent of the Breeders' Cup, a series of high-purse championship races to be held in one day toward the end of the year at a rotating site. The inaugural event took place in 1984 and was an instant success.

John Henry's earnings record was surpassed a few years later by Alysheba. The latter's bid for the Triple Crown was denied by his rival Bet Twice, but he raced again as a four-year-old and was Horse of the Year. In his final start, Alysheba won the Breeders' Cup Classic, a race he was denied by a nose as a three-year-old. He finished with almost $6.7 million in earnings.

One of the most exciting races in the history of the Breeders' Cup occurred earlier that day. Ogden Phipps's bay filly Personal Ensign, trained by Shug McGaughey, became the first horse since Colin to retire undefeated, a perfect 10 for 10, including a victory over the boys in the Whitney. She barely beat Winning Colors in the Distaff.

The decade went out with a bang with a great rivalry between California-bred Sunday Silence and New York-bred Easy Goer. Easy Goer was a champion as a two-year-old and he denied Sunday Silence the Triple Crown but in the end, it was Sunday Silence who owned a 3-1 record over his adversary, with wins in the Derby, Preakness, and the Breeders' Cup.

1990's through present

Allen Paulson's Cigar, trained by Bill Mott and ridden by Jerry Bailey, was the horse of the 90's. He was Horse of the Year twice, equaled the great Citation's win streak of 16 races in a row and won just a hair under $10 million.

Skip Away fell just short of Cigar's earnings record but was a star from ages three through six, winning Horse of the Year in 1998.

Serena's Song set a record for money won by a filly or mare by earning just under $3.3 million and beating males twice in the process.

In recent years, several horses have gone into the Belmont with a chance to become the first Triple Crown winner since Affirmed. All have seen their bids fall short. They include Silver Charm in '97, Real Quiet in '98, Charismatic '99, War Emblem in '02, Funny Cide in '03, and Smarty Jones in '04.

The Triple Crown

Much of the interest in American racing is centered on the Triple Crown, a series of three races in the spring for three-year-olds. It consists of the Kentucky Derby, run at 1 1/4 miles at Churchill Downs on the first Saturday in May; the Preakness, contested two weeks after at 1 3/16 miles at Pimlico in Baltimore; and the Belmont Stakes, held three weeks after that at 1 1/2 miles at New York's Belmont Park. Only 11 horses have won all three Triple Crown races:

1919—Sir Barton
1930—Gallant Fox
1935—Omaha
1937—War Admiral
1941—Whirlaway
1943—Count Fleet
1946—Assault
1948—Citation
1973—Secretariat
1977—Seattle Slew
1978—Affirmed

Glossary of Horse Racing Terms

across the board a bet to win, place and show on the same horse. A $2 bet across the board costs $6. If your horse wins you cash all three tickets. If he finishes second, you cash your place and show tickets. If he finishes third, you just cash your show bet.

apprentice a jockey in training who does not have to carry as much weight as an experienced rider until he/she wins a certain number of races and has raced for a certain amount of time.

backstretch the straight stretch of track on the far side of the oval away from the grandstand. Also sometimes refers to the people who take care of the horses who generally live and/or work over there where the barns are.

box a bet in which all possible combinations are played. A two horse exacta box covers both horses in first and second.

broodmare a female horse used for breeding.

card the slate of a given day's races is sometimes known as the card, or race card.

chalk informal term for the race favorite

check when a horse gets into trouble during a race, i.e. the hole he was going for disappears, he has to "check," pull back losing his momentum.

closer a horse whose running style is to make a run in the latter stage of a race.

dam the mother of a horse.

dead heat a tie between two horses.

derby a stakes race for three-year old horses.

even money a horse whose odds are 1 to 1, i.e said to be at even money; you bet $2 to make $4.

fast a term that means the track is dry.

favorite the horse that is most popular in the betting.

firm the grass equivalent of a fast track.

furlong an eighth of a mile.

good a dirt or turf course rated just below fast or firm, with a little bit of moisture in it.

hand four inches. Horses heights are given in hands.

handicap 1) to evaluate each horses' chances of winning a race based on the past performances. 2) a type of stakes race in which each horse is assigned a weight to carry based on how good he or she is, theoretically evening out the chances of each one winning.

home stretch the straight ground that leads from the final turn to the finish line.

in the money a horse who runs first, second, or third finishes in the money.

jumper a steeplechase horse, also called a jumper.

juvenile two year-old fillies and colts are called juveniles.

length about eight feet. Lengths are used in race charts and by race callers to explain how far ahead or behind a horse is during the running of a race.

long shot a horse with a small chance of winning and high odds.

meet or meeting a collection of races or days of races organized by the same organization at the same location.

morning line an estimate a track employee makes as to how the public will bet in a given race. These estimates will run in the track program.

mudder a horse who likes to run on off-tracks, i.e., in the mud.

muddy a track that is thoroughly wet but has no standing water.

oaks A stakes race for three-year-old fillies, the female equivalent of a derby (though fillies may contest derbies also).

pace race tempo. A horse who runs quickly early sets a fast pace.

paddock the area where the horses are saddled before the race.

past performances a detailed account of a horse's previous races.

photo finish when two horses finish so close that a photograph is required to determine which one has crossed the wire first.

post the position of the horse in the starting gate. The first spot is also known as the one post, etc.

quarter pole a pole placed one quarter of a mile from the finish line.

silks the costume (cap and jacket) worn by the jockey in the designated colors of the owner he or she is riding for.

sloppy a track condition that indicates soaked through dirt with some water on top.

sire the father of a horse.

stallion a male horse used for breeding

starting gate the mechanical contraption with slots for each horse where the horses start each race.

stewards racetrack officials whose job it is to enforce the rules.

tack a rider's racing gear.

tote board electronic board that indicates the betting odds of each horse.

trip a horse's journey during a race. If a horse is blocked in or stumbles or is carried wide around a turn he or she is said to have had a bad trip.

valet a person who assists the riders with their clothes and equipment.

walkover when only one horse is entered in a race (or the field scratches down to one) and one horse must race around by himself as a formality.

yearling a horse in his/her first year, i.e. before New Year's Day of the following year.

yielding a grass course soaked through with moisture.

Kentucky Derby Winners

2004	Smarty Jones	1971	Canonero II	1938	Lawrin	1905	Agile
2003	Funny Cide	1970	Dust Commander	1937	War Admiral	1904	Elwood
2002	War Emblem	1969	Majestic Prince	1936	Bold Venture	1903	Judge Himes
2001	Monarchos	1968	Forward Pass	1935	Omaha	1902	Alan-a-Dale
2000	Fusaichi Pegasus	1967	Proud Clarion	1934	Cavalcade	1901	His Eminence
1999	Charismatic	1966	Kauai King	1933	Brokers Tip	1900	Lieut. Gibson
1998	Real Quiet	1965	Lucky Debonair	1932	Burgoo King	1899	Manuel
1997	Silver Charm	1964	Northern Dancer	1931	Twenty Grand	1898	Plaudit
1996	Grindstone	1963	Chateaugay	1930	Gallant Fox	1897	Typhoon II
1995	Thunder Gulch	1962	Decidedly	1929	Clyde Van Dusen	1896	Ben Brush
1994	Go For Gin	1961	Carry Back	1928	Reigh Count	1895	Halma
1993	Sea Hero	1960	Venetian Way	1927	Whiskery	1894	Chant
1992	Lil E. Tee	1959	Tomy Lee	1926	Bubbling Over	1893	Lookout
1991	Strike the Gold	1958	Tim Tam	1925	Flying Ebony	1892	Azra
1990	Unbridled	1957	Iron Liege	1924	Black Gold	1891	Kingman
1989	Sunday Silence	1956	Needles	1923	Zev	1890	Riley
1988	Winning Colors	1955	Swaps	1922	Morvich	1889	Spokane
1987	Alysheba	1954	Determine	1921	Behave Yourself	1888	MacBeth II
1986	Ferdinand	1953	Dark Star	1920	Paul Jones	1887	Montrose
1985	Spend A Buck	1952	Hill Gail	1919	Sir Barton	1886	Ben Ali
1984	Swale	1951	Count Turf	1918	Exterminator	1885	Joe Cotton
1983	Sunny's Halo	1950	Middleground	1917	Omar Khayyam	1884	Buchanan
1982	Gato del Sol	1949	Ponder	1916	George Smith	1883	Leonatus
1981	Pleasant Colony	1948	Citation	1915	Regret	1882	Apollo
1980	Genuine Risk	1947	Jet Pilot	1914	Old Rosebud	1881	Hindoo
1979	Spectacular Bid	1946	Assault	1913	Donerail	1880	Fonso
1978	Affirmed	1945	Hoop, Jr.	1912	Worth	1879	Lord Murphy
1977	Seattle Slew	1944	Pensive	1911	Meridan	1878	Day Star
1976	Bold Forbes	1943	Count Fleet	1910	Donau	1877	Baden Baden
1975	Foolish Pleasure	1942	Shut Out	1909	Wintergreen	1876	Vagrant
1974	Cannonade	1941	Whirlaway	1908	Stone Street	1875	Aristides
1973	Secretariat	1940	Gallahadion	1907	Pink Star		
1972	Riva Ridge	1939	Johnstown	1906	Sir Huon		

OLYMPIC GAMES

The Olympic Games are held every four years—in summer and winter—at a different site. Athletes from nearly every country compete for personal and national honor in a variety of sports. Television broadcasts show the Games in every corner of the globe, with recent audiences estimated to exceed 3 billion people.

The Olympics originated in ancient Greece, beginning in 776 B.C., as a festival to honor Zeus. They are named for the town of Olympia, a sacred site in the western Peloponnesus where athletes converged from far-flung city-states for a month-long festival of religious rites and athletic competition. The Olympics were revived in 1896, when athletes from 14 nations gathered in Athens, Greece, for the first modern Games. With exceptions for World War I (1916) and World War II (1940 and 1944), the modern Summer Games have been held every four years since 1896. The Olympic Winter Games, featuring competition in skiing, skating, ice hockey, and other cold-weather sports, commenced in 1924. The Winter and Summer Games followed the same quadrennial cycle through 1992, after which a staggered two-year interval was instituted.

Like their ancient predecessors, the modern Olympics were conceived as a celebration of peace, international cooperation, and pure love of sport. These ideals have often proved elusive, however, as political rancor—to the point of boycott and terrorist violence—has marred several Games. The original restriction that only amateur athletes could compete, rigorously enforced by the modern founders, has also been relaxed. Although Olympic athletes today receive no direct remuneration for taking part, highly paid professionals now are allowed to compete in most sports. Whereas ancient Olympic champions were crowned with olive wreaths, hailed as heroes, and enshrined in a sacred grove, modern Olympic champions are awarded gold medals—silver for runners-up and bronze for third-place finishers—and some earn lucrative commercial endorsements after the Games. Still, the athletes compete for national pride as much as for individual honor, and the ranking of nations by number of medals won (while not an official statistic) is closely watched. The rivalry among countries is often intense, yet most participants enjoy the spirit of celebration, friendly competition, and shared love of sport that prevails at most Games.

The International Olympic Committee (I.O.C.), based in Lausanne, Switzerland, is the governing authority of the Summer and Winter Games. In addition to establishing and administering the Olympic rules, the I.O.C. selects the host cities every four years, accepts or rejects new sports and events on the Olympic program, and oversees the efforts of various other bodies. These include the National Olympic Committee (N.O.C.) for each participating country, the Olympic Organizing Committee (O.O.C.) for each host city, and the International Federation (IF) governing competition in each sport. Each N.O.C., such as the United States Olympic Committee, is responsible for the representation of its respective country, including all necessary arrangements when it hosts the Games. The O.O.C., in conjunction with the N.O.C., raises funds, constructs venues, and oversees the myriad logistical details involved with the two-and-a- half weeks of competition, such as living quarters, dining, transportation, and communication. Federations for the individual sports establish the rules of play, monitor venue construction, supervise competition, and are responsible for officiating or judging. They also lobby the I.O.C. for the addition of new events to the Olympic program.

History

Ancient Games

The Olympics were sacred to the ancient Greeks, and nothing was allowed to interfere with them—not even war. A truce was called and trade ceased during the month-long festival; no one bearing arms could enter Olympia. According to historians, competition in the first 13 Olympics consisted of only one footrace—called the stade—of about 200 yards (183 meters), or the length of the stadium. The first known Olympic champion was a cook named Coroebus from the nearby city of Elis.

The Games were held at four-year intervals, called "Olympiads," which later Greeks began numbering from the first Panhellenic festival in 776 B.C. Over the centuries, other events were added to the program, including the double-stade and longer footraces; wrestling; the five-event pentathlon (jumping, javelin, sprinting, discus, and wrestling); boxing; chariot and horse races; and the pancration (a brutal combination of wrestling and boxing). Only men were allowed to compete, and in the nude. The Games attracted as many as 40,000 spectators, but women were not allowed to attend. In addition to athletic events, the Olympic festivals included contests in music, poetry, and oratory. (Exhibitions and performances in the arts remain an official, if often overlooked, part of the modern Olympic program.)

By the fifth century B.C., Olympia was the holiest site in Greece, and the ceremonial Games reached their peak. In 146 B.C., after Greece became part of the Roman empire, the Olympics were moved to Rome, and the original purpose was largely forgotten. The Games finally were banned in A.D. 393 by the Roman emperor Theodosius I, a convert to Christianity, who deemed them pagan.

Modern Games

A modern version of the Olympics was the idea of a French aristocrat named Pierre de Coubertin in the 1880's. Coubertin had advanced educational programs in France according to the Greek ideal of physical and mental training. Excavations at ancient Olympia fired Courbertin's imagination, and he began pursuing the idea of an Olympic revival. By 1894 he had won the support of an international athletic congress and succeeded in creating the I.O.C., of which he became the first secretary-general. The first modern Olympic Games were held in 1896 in Athens, and moved to other cities every four years.

Summer Games, 1896–2008

Year	Olympiad	Host City, Country	Nations Represented	Athletes Men	Athletes Women	Events
1896	**I**	**Athens, Greece**	**14**	**245**	**—**	**43**

King George I of Greece opens the first modern Games on April 6, before a crowd of 80,000. James Connolly of the U.S. becomes the first Olympic champion in more than 1,500 years with his victory in the triple jump. Spyridon Louis, a Greek shepherd, is hailed as a national hero for winning the marathon. The United States takes 11 of 43 events; the host country wins 10.

Year	Olympiad	Host City, Country	Nations Represented	Athletes Men	Athletes Women	Events
1900	**II**	**Paris, France**	**24**	**1,206**	**19**	**87**

Coinciding with the Paris World's Fair, the competition is spread out over five months. The Paris Games gain wider international acceptance than the Athens revival—a thousand more athletes participated—but the public takes scant notice. Women make their first appearance: the first female champion is Britain's Charlotte Cooper in tennis. Alvin Kraenzlein of the United States. wins four track-and-field competitions. France leads all countries with 25 victories in 87 events.

Year	Olympiad	Host City, Country	Nations Represented	Athletes Men	Athletes Women	Events
1904	**III**	**St. Louis, U.S.A.**	**13**	**681**	**8**	**89**

The first Olympics held in the United States, the St. Louis Games are overshadowed by another World's Fair. Again the events are spread out over months, and again the public lacks interest. The cost and time of travel also limit participation. Americans dominate competition, earning 70 gold medals (awarded for the first time); Archie Hahn wins three sprint races, Ray Ewry repeats as champion in three jumping events, and Thomas Hicks captures the marathon.

Year	Olympiad	Host City, Country	Nations Represented	Athletes Men	Athletes Women	Events
1908	**IV**	**London, England**	**22**	**1,999**	**36**	**109**

After an interim Games (later declared unofficial) at Athens in 1906, the Olympics open a new chapter in London. Without the distraction of a world exhibition, the 1908 Games entertain an avid public at specially constructed venues. Held from April to October, they include the first official Opening Ceremony. The host country again wins the most events, 56. In a dramatic marathon, Italy's Dorando Pietri collapses near the finish line, is helped across it by officials, and then disqualified; John Joseph Hayes of the United States is declared the winner.

Year	Olympiad	Host City, Country	Nations Represented	Athletes Men	Athletes Women	Events
1912	**V**	**Stockholm, Sweden**	**29**	**2,490**	**57**	**102**

A model of efficiency and organization, these Games feature the best facilities yet and attract large crowds. For the first time, athletes from every continent participate. The standout is Native American Jim Thorpe, winner of both the pentathlon and decathlon. The I.O.C. strips Thorpe of his medals a year later for alleged violation of the rules of amateurism—only to restore them posthumously in 1982. Sweden and the United States lead all nations with 24 gold medals each.

Year	Olympiad	Host City, Country	Nations Represented	Athletes Men	Athletes Women	Events
1916	**VI**	**Berlin, Germany**	——————**Canceled due to war**——————			

Germany, unanimously selected to host the VI Olympics, believes that any war will be short and proceeds with preparations. But the prolonged Great War forces cancellation.

1920	**VII**	**Antwerp, Belgium**	29	2,591	78	154

War-weary Belgium revives the Olympic spirit. The Central Powers (Germany, Austria, Turkey, Bulgaria, and Hungary) are excluded, and an atmosphere of peace prevails. The Olympic flag and Athletes' Oath are introduced. The Finnish distance runner Paavo Nurmi takes three gold medals and one bronze; Italy's Nedo Nadi wins five golds in fencing; and France's tennis star Suzanne Lenglen takes two golds and a bronze. U.S. athletes claim 41 first-place finishes.

1924	**VIII**	**Paris, France**	44	2,956	136	126

Growing acceptance of the Games is reflected by increases in the number of nations, athletes, spectators, and journalists who attend. "Firsts" in Paris include an Olympic Village to house the athletes, live radio broadcasts, and introduction of the Olympic motto. Nurmi, "the Flying Finn," is the star with five gold medals; American swimmer Johnny Weissmuller claims three. The United States again leads all nations by winning 45 events.

1928	**IX**	**Amsterdam, Holland**	46	2,724	290	109

The Olympic flame is lit during the Opening Ceremony for the first time. Track-and-field and gymnastics events for women are added to the program. Athletes from a record 28 countries, including the first from Asia, win gold medals. The United States tops the list with 22; Germany, reinstated after 16 years, finishes second with 10. Nurmi and Weissmuller add to their medal totals and legends.

1932	**X**	**Los Angeles, U.S.A.**	37	1,281	127	116

Worldwide depression and the cost of travel keep many countries away, but the facilities—including the 100,000-seat Los Angeles Coliseum—are top-notch. Innovations include the three-level podium for medal ceremonies and automatic timing for track events. Mildred "Babe" Didrikson, perhaps the greatest female athlete of the century, wins two gold medals and one silver in track and field. Americans continue their domination, winning 44 events.

1936	**XI**	**Berlin, Germany**	49	3,738	328	129

The first torch relay belies the spirit of the so-called Nazi Olympics. Hitler stages a lavish Games as a giant propaganda event, seeking to prove Aryan supremacy. The undisputed star, however, is Jesse Owens, an African American whose record four gold medals in track and field embarrass the German leader. The host country nevertheless wins the most events, 33.

1940	**XII**	**Tokyo, Japan**	——————**Canceled due to war**——————			

The IOC feels that holding the Games in Asia will enhance the Olympic movement, but Japan resigns as host after the outbreak of war with the U.S.S.R. in 1937. Helsinki is chosen as the new site, but World War II forces cancellation.

1944	**XIII**	**London, England**	——————**Canceled due to war**——————			

London is designated as the site of the 1944 Games, but continued fighting in Europe and Asia make the event impossible.

1948	**XIV**	**London, England**	59	3,714	385	136

Facilities are modest as London recovers from war, but attendance and enthusiasm run high. Japan and Germany are barred, and the U.S.S.R. refuses to take part. The 1948 Games are the first to be broadcast on home television. Fanny Blankers-Koen of the Netherlands wins four gold medals in sprints and hurdles. American Bob Mathias, 17, becomes the youngest male to win an athletic event, taking the first of his two decathlon titles. The United States wins 38 gold medals.

1952	**XV**	**Helsinki, Finland**	69	4,407	518	149

The atmosphere in Helsinki makes the 1952 Games one of the most memorable, even though the Soviet bloc nations insist on separate quarters. The most impressive achievement belongs to Czech distance runner Emil Zátopek, who wins the 5,000 meters, 10,000 meters, and the marathon. U.S. sprinter and hurdler Harrison Dillard repeats his double-gold performance of 1948; Soviet gymnast Viktor Chukarin wins four gold medals and two silvers. U.S. athletes earn 40 golds.

1956	**XVI**	**Melbourne, Australia**	67	2,813	371	145

The first Olympics in the Southern Hemisphere, the 1956 Games are held in November-December (Australian summer) and present training problems for some athletes. Several countries withdraw over the Soviet invasion of Hungary, the Suez

<table>
<tr><th>Year</th><th>Olympiad</th><th>Host City, Country</th><th>Nations Represented</th><th>Athletes Men</th><th>Athletes Women</th><th>Events</th></tr>
<tr><td colspan="7">crisis, and other world events. Soviet gymnast Larissa Latynina wins four of her country's 37 gold medals, plus a silver and bronze. American discus thrower Al Oerter wins the first of his four straight Olympic golds.</td></tr>
<tr><td>1960</td><td>XVII</td><td>Rome, Italy</td><td>83</td><td>4,738</td><td>610</td><td>150</td></tr>
<tr><td colspan="7">The Olympics return to the city where the ancient Games ended; satellite TV broadcasts begin. More countries win medals (44) than at any previous Games; the U.S.S.R. tops the list with 43 golds and 103 medals in all. Standouts include the barefoot Ethiopian marathoner Abebe Bikila; Soviet gymnasts Latynina and Boris Shakhlin; and sprinter Wilma Rudolph, decathlete Rafer Johnson, and light-heavyweight boxer Cassius Clay (later Muhammad Ali), all of the United States.</td></tr>
<tr><td>1964</td><td>XVIII</td><td>Tokyo, Japan</td><td>93</td><td>4,457</td><td>683</td><td>163</td></tr>
<tr><td colspan="7">The Olympics come to Asia, and a resurgent Japan spends heavily on new sports facilities and city infrastructure. World and Olympic records are broken almost daily. Don Schollander of the United States becomes the first swimmer to earn four gold medals in one Games. Abebe Bikila, this time running in shoes, becomes the first to repeat as marathon champion. Latynina boosts her career medal count to a record 18, including 9 gold. U.S. athletes win 90 medals, 36 gold.</td></tr>
<tr><td>1968</td><td>XIX</td><td>Mexico City, Mexico</td><td>112</td><td>4,750</td><td>780</td><td>172</td></tr>
<tr><td colspan="7">Political and social unrest—in the host country, the United States, and elsewhere—intrude as never before. Two African-American track stars give the black power salute at the medal ceremony. Mexico City's high altitude is the bane of distance runners but contributes to a total of 34 world and 38 Olympic records. Most astounding is Bob Beamon's mark (29'-2?") in the long jump. Debbie Meyer, also of the United States, becomes the first swimmer to win three individual events. Czech gymnast Vera Cáslavská earns six medals, four of them gold.</td></tr>
<tr><td>1972</td><td>XX</td><td>Munich, West Germany</td><td>122</td><td>6,659</td><td>1,171</td><td>195</td></tr>
<tr><td colspan="7">The Olympic spirit is shattered in an assault by Palestinian terrorists that leaves 11 Israeli athletes, one policeman, and the five terrorists dead. Under a pall, the Games continue two days later. Two swimmers stand out: Mark Spitz of the United States wins a record seven gold medals, and Australian Shane Gould takes three golds (and five medals in all). Soviet gymnast Olga Korbut is the darling of the Games, and the U.S.S.R. stuns the U.S. in men's basketball. Soviet athletes take home 50 gold medals.</td></tr>
<tr><td>1976</td><td>XXI</td><td>Montreal, Canada</td><td>92</td><td>4,781</td><td>1,247</td><td>198</td></tr>
<tr><td colspan="7">Twenty-four African nations boycott because of the participation of New Zealand, whose rugby team had played a match in racially segregated South Africa. Security is heavy and some facilities unfinished, but the XXI Olympics go smoothly. Romanian gymnast Nadia Comaneci, only 14, dazzles judges and charms audiences. Soviet athletes garner 125 medals, 49 gold. For the first time, a host country fails to win a gold medal.</td></tr>
<tr><td>1980</td><td>XXII</td><td>Moscow, U.S.S.R.</td><td>80</td><td>4,093</td><td>1,124</td><td>203</td></tr>
<tr><td colspan="7">Political controversy again mars the Games, the first held in a communist country. The United States leads a large-scale boycott over Soviet military action in Afghanistan, reducing the number of participating nations to the lowest total since 1956. Aleksandr Dityanin continues the Soviet tradition of excellence in gymnastics with a record eight medals. Heavyweight boxer Teófilo Stevenson of Cuba wins his third straight gold. The U.S.S.R. hauls 197 medals, the most ever.</td></tr>
<tr><td>1984</td><td>XXIII</td><td>Los Angeles, U.S.A.</td><td>140</td><td>5,230</td><td>1,567</td><td>221</td></tr>
<tr><td colspan="7">Supported by some 30 commercial sponsors, the L.A. Games are the first privately funded Olympics in history. The Soviet Union leads a retaliatory boycott, but participation is wider than ever. American Carl Lewis equals Jesse Owens's feat of four gold medals in track and field. Britain's Daley Thompson repeats as decathlon champion. Joan Benoit of the U.S. wins the inaugural women's marathon. The U.S. leads all nations with 174 medals.</td></tr>
<tr><td>1988</td><td>XXIV</td><td>Seoul, South Korea</td><td>159</td><td>6,279</td><td>2,186</td><td>237</td></tr>
<tr><td colspan="7">Returning to Asia, the Games are restored to near-full participation by I.O.C. member nations; only Cuba and Ethiopia stay away. Ben Johnson of Canada is stripped of his gold medal for the 100 meters after testing positive for banned substances. America's Florence Griffith-Joyner dominates the women's sprints, swimmer Matt Biondi wins five golds, and Greg Louganis repeats as champion in both diving events. U.S. athletes earn 132 medals in all.</td></tr>
</table>

Year	Olympiad	Host City, Country	Nations Represented	Athletes Men	Athletes Women	Events
1992	XXV	**Barcelona, Spain**	169	6,659	2708	257

For the first time in 20 years, every country with an N.O.C. is represented. Among them are a united Germany, four Balkan states, and a "Unified Team" (EUN) representing former Soviet republics. EUN athletes take 112 medals, 45 gold. Gymnast Vitaly Scherbo accounts for six of the golds. Men's basketball is open to professionals, and the American "Dream Team" dominates. Splendid facilities and cultural events contribute to one of the best Games ever.

Year	Olympiad	Host City, Country	Nations Represented	Athletes Men	Athletes Women	Events
1996	XXVI	**Atlanta, U.S.A.**	197	6,797	3,523	271

The centennial modern Games are disrupted by a bomb explosion in the Olympic complex that kills one person and injures 110 others. In competition, a record 79 countries earn medals and 53 win gold; the United States tops the list with 101 in all, 44 gold. Runners Michael Johnson of the U.S. and Marie-José Pérec of France both achieve a difficult double, winning the 200 meters and the 400 meters. U.S. women gymnasts are surprise winners in the team event.

Year	Olympiad	Host City, Country	Nations Represented	Athletes Men	Athletes Women	Events
2000	XXVII	**Sydney, Australia**	199	6,582	4,069	300

Upbeat, positive, and bigger than ever, the Sydney Games go off without a hitch. North and South Korea march together in the Opening Ceremony. The percentage of women competitors (38 percent) is the highest ever. Cathy Freeman, an Australian Aborigine, lights the Olympic torch and becomes a national hero with a victory in the 400 meters. Russian gymnast Aleksei Nemov wins six medals. Sprinter Marion Jones takes three gold and two bronze, contributing to the U.S. total of 97.

Year	Olympiad	Host City, Country	Nations Represented	Athletes Men	Athletes Women	Events
2004	XXVIII	**Athens, Greece**				
2008	XXIX	**Beijing, China**				

Winter Games, 1924–2006

Year	Olympiad	Host City, Country	Nations Represented	Athletes Men	Athletes Women	Events
1924	I	**Chamonix, France**	16	245	13	16

Originally called International Winter Sports Week, the festival is officially sanctioned as the first Olympic Winter Games by the I.O.C. in 1925. U.S. speed skater Charles Jewtraw wins the first gold; Finland's Clas Thunberg medals in all five speed skating events. Norway and Finland combine for 28 of the 48 medals.

Year	Olympiad	Host City, Country	Nations Represented	Athletes Men	Athletes Women	Events
1928	II	**St. Moritz, Switzerland**	25	438	26	14

The original idea that one nation should host the Summer and Winter Games in the same year is abandoned. Inclement weather disrupts a number of events. Norway's Sonja Henie, 15, wins the first of three straight singles figure skating competitions; Thunberg adds two more gold medals. Norway claims 15 medals in all, six gold.

Year	Olympiad	Host City, Country	Nations Represented	Athletes Men	Athletes Women	Events
1932	III	**Lake Placid, U.S.A.**	17	231	21	14

The Games go on despite worldwide depression, but participation is down and more than half of all competitors are American or Canadian. Americans John Shea and Irving Jaffee sweep the speed skating events with two golds each, and the host country wins six of the 14 events.

Year	Olympiad	Host City, Country	Nations Represented	Athletes Men	Athletes Women	Events
1936	IV	**Garmisch-Partenkirchen, Germany**	28	588	80	17

Adolf Hitler declares open the first of two Olympic festivals on German soil in 1936. Alpine skiing events are added to the program. Norway's Ivar Ballangrud wins three gold medals and one silver in the four speed skating events, and Henie skates to her third title. The Norwegians garner 15 medals in all.

Year	
1940	**Canceled due to war**
1944	**Canceled due to war**

Year	Olympiad	Host City, Country	Nations Represented	Athletes Men	Athletes Women	Events
1948	V	**St. Moritz, Switzerland**	28	592	77	22

Neutral Switzerland is awarded the Games; St. Moritz, with facilities intact, is again the host. Germany and Japan are barred. Slalom and downhill events for men and women are added. France's Henri Oreiller wins two golds and a bronze in Alpine skiing. Norway and Sweden tie with four gold medals and 10 in all.

Year	Olympiad	Host City, Country	Nations Represented	Athletes Men	Athletes Women	Events
1952	VI	**Oslo, Norway**	30	585	109	22

The first held in a Scandinavian country, the 1952 Games attract large, enthusiastic crowds. Speed skater Hjallis Andersen of the home team captures three gold medals. Andrea Mead of the U.S. wins the slalom and giant slalom. American Dick Button repeats as men's figure skating champion. Norway tops all nations with 16 medals, seven gold.

Year	Olympiad	Host City, Country	Nations Represented	Athletes Men	Athletes Women	Events
1956	VII	**Cortina D'Ampezzo, Italy**	32	688	132	24

The first Winter Games to be telecast live, the Cortina Olympics also feature the debut of the U.S.S.R.—which immediately wins more medals (seven gold, 16 in all) than any other country. The individual star is Austria's Toni Sailer, who wins all three men's Alpine skiing events.

Year	Olympiad	Host City, Country	Nations Represented	Athletes Men	Athletes Women	Events
1960	VIII	**Squaw Valley, U.S.A.**	30	522	143	27

The Winter Games come to California, and Walt Disney produces the opening and closing ceremonies. Biathlon and women's speed skating are added to the program. The U.S. hockey team upsets the U.S.S.R. to win gold, but the Soviets lead all nations with 21 medals.

Year	Olympiad	Host City, Country	Nations Represented	Athletes Men	Athletes Women	Events
1964	IX	**Innsbruck, Austria**	36	891	200	34

Mild weather threatens competition, and Austrian troops haul in snow from higher elevations. East and West Germany compete as a combined team. The U.S.S.R. again heads the medals list, with 25 (11 gold); Lydia Skoblikova wins all four women's speed skating events.

Year	Olympiad	Host City, Country	Nations Represented	Athletes Men	Athletes Women	Events
1968	X	**Grenoble, France**	37	947	211	35

An unlikely host, the industrial city of Grenoble stages events in widespread locations. Jean-Claude Killy of the host country sweeps men's Alpine skiing. The Soviet pairs figure skating team of Beloussova and Protopopov repeats as champions. Women's figure skater Peggy Fleming wins the only U.S. gold. Norway earns 14 medals.

Year	Olympiad	Host City, Country	Nations Represented	Athletes Men	Athletes Women	Events
1972	XI	**Sapporo, Japan**	35	800	206	35

The first held outside Europe or the United States, the Sapporo Games are the most extravagant to date. Austrian skiing star Karl Schranz is barred for violating the I.O.C.'s rules of amateurism. Dutch speed skater Ard Schenk is the outstanding male athlete with three golds. The U.S.S.R. wins the medals race with 16 in all, eight gold.

Year	Olympiad	Host City, Country	Nations Represented	Athletes Men	Athletes Women	Events
1976	XII	**Innsbruck, Austria**	37	892	231	37

The Games return to Innsbruck after voters in Denver, the IOC's initial choice, reject plans. West Germany's Rosi Mittermaier takes two golds and a silver in women's Alpine skiing; Austrian daredevil Franz Klammer thrills spectators in the men's downhill. Dorothy Hamill of the United States earns gold in figure skating. Soviet athletes win 27 medals, 13 gold.

Year	Olympiad	Host City, Country	Nations Represented	Athletes Men	Athletes Women	Events
1980	XIII	**Lake Placid, U.S.A.**	37	839	233	38

Outstanding performances overshadow transportation problems. America's Eric Heiden wins all five men's speed skating events. Ingemar Stenmark of Sweden and Hanni Wenzel of tiny Liechtenstein win the slalom and giant slalom for men and women. The U.S. hockey team stuns the U.S.S.R. and later wins gold against Finland. Soviet athletes capture 22 medals in all.

Year	Olympiad	Host City, Country	Nations Represented	Athletes Men	Athletes Women	Events
1984	XIV	**Sarajevo, Yugoslavia**	49	1,000	274	39

The city will be decimated by civil war in following years, but the 1984 Games are remembered for a spirit of friendliness and goodwill. Standouts include Finland's Marja-Liisa Hämäläinen in Nordic skiing, East Germany's Katarina Witt and America's Scott Hamilton in figure skating, and the British ice dancing team of Torvill and Dean. East Germany leads all with nine gold medals.

Year	Olympiad	Host City, Country	Nations Represented	Athletes Men	Athletes Women	Events
1988	XV	**Calgary, Canada**	57	1,110	313	46
The Games are expanded from 12 to 16 days, new skiing events are added, and demonstration sports are included for the first time. Finnish ski jumper Matti Nykänen soars to three golds, Italy's charismatic Alberto Tomba takes two Alpine events, and Katarina Witt repeats in figure skating. The U.S.S.R. tallies 29 medals, 11 gold.						
1992	XVI	**Albertville, France**	64	1,313	488	57
Most former Soviet republics participate as the "Unified Team" (EUN), but several compete under their own flags. The two Germanys are reunited and top all nations with 26 medals. Norwegians win every men's cross-country skiing race. Bonnie Blair of the United States and Gunda Niemann of Germany win two golds each in women's speed skating.						
1994	XVII	**Lillehammer, Norway**	67	1,217	522	61
The two-year interval between Winter and Summer Games is instituted, and the atmosphere is festive. Newly independent Soviet republics compete as separate teams. Still, Russia tops the medals list with 23, 11 of them gold; Lyubov Yegorova wins three golds in women's cross-country skiing. Norway's Johann Koss triples in speed skating.						
1998	XVIII	**Nagano, Japan**	72	1,488	814	68
Snowboarding, curling, and women's hockey are added to the program. Norway's Bjorn Dählie wins three gold medals in Nordic skiing, bringing his career total to a record eight, plus four silver. At 15, American figure skater Tara Lipinski becomes the youngest to win an individual event. German athletes take home 29 medals, 12 gold.						
2002	XIX	**Salt Lake City, U.S.A.**	77	1,513	886	78
With nearly 2,400 athletes, the 2002 Winter Games are the largest yet. A record 18 countries win gold medals; Germany heads the list with 12 (35 medals overall). A judging scandal mars the pairs figure skating competition, and two sets of gold medals are awarded. Croatia's Janica Kostelic wins three gold medals and one silver in women's Alpine skiing.						
2006	XX	**Turin, Italy**				

The Summer Program

(Sydney, 2000)
Archery: 4 events (2 men, 2 women)
Badminton: 5 events (2 men, 2 women, 1 mixed)
Baseball: 1 tournament (men)
Basketball: 2 tournaments (1 men, 1 women)
Boxing: 12 weight classes (men)
Canoe/Kayak: 16 events (12 men, 4 women kayak)
Cycling: 18 events (11 men, 7 women)
Diving: 8 events (4 men, 4 women)
Equestrian: 6 events (mixed)
Fencing: 10 events (6 men, 4 women)
Field Hockey: 2 tournaments (1 men, 1 women)
Gymnastics: 18 events (9 men, 9 women)
Handball: 2 tournaments (1 men, 1 women)
Judo: 14 weight classes (7 men, 7 women)
Modern Pentathlon: 2 events (1 men, 1 women)
Rowing: 14 events (8 men, 6 women)
Sailing: 11 classes (3 men, 3 women, 5 mixed)
Shooting: 17 events (10 men, 7 women)
Soccer: 2 tournaments (1 men, 1 women)
Softball: 1 tournament (women)
Swimming: 32 events (16 men, 16 women)
Synchronized Swimming: 2 events (women)
Table Tennis: 4 events (2 men, 2 women)
Taekwondo: 8 weight classes (4 men, 4 women)
Tennis: 4 events (2 men, 2 women)
Track and Field: 46 events (24 men, 22 women)
Triathlon: 2 events (1 men, 1 women)
Volleyball: 4 tournaments (1 men, 1 women)
Water Polo: 2 tournaments (1 men, 1 women)
Weightlifting: 15 weight classes (8 men, 7 women)
Wrestling, Freestyle: 8 weight classes (men)
Wrestling, Greco-Roman: 8 weight classes (men)

The Winter Program

(Salt Lake City, 2002)
Alpine Skiing: 10 events (5 men, 5 women)
Biathlon: 8 events (4 men, 4 women)
Bobsledding: 3 events (2 men, 1 women)
Cross-Country Skiing: 12 events (6 men, 6 women)
Curling: 2 tournaments (1 men, 1 women)
Figure Skating: 4 events (1 men, 1 women, 2 mixed pairs)
Freestyle Skiing: 4 events (2 men, 2 women)
Ice Hockey: 2 tournaments (1 men, 1 women)
Luge: 3 events (1 men, 1 women, 1 doubles mixed)
Nordic Combined: 3 events (men)
Short Track Speed Skating: 8 events (4 men, 4 women)
Skeleton: 2 events (1 men, 1 women)
Ski Jumping: 3 events (men)
Snowboarding: 4 events (2 men, 2 women)
Speed Skating: 10 events (5 men, 5 women)

When the Games Began: Olympic Archaeology

By JOHN NOBLE WILFORD

Opening day of the ancient Greek games was a spectacle to behold, a celebration of the vigor and supercharged competitiveness that infused the creative spirit of one of antiquity's most transforming civilizations.

People by the thousands from every corner of the land swarmed the sacred grounds, where altars and columned temples stood in homage to their gods. They came from cities that were often bitter rivals but shared a religion, a language and an enthusiasm for organized athletics.

A closer study of ancient texts, art and artifacts, and deeper archaeological excavations are giving scholars new insights into the early games and just how integral athletics was to ancient Greek life.

Organized athletics were so popular that nothing was allowed to stand in the way. When it was time for the games, armies of rival cities usually laid down their weapons in a "sacred truce."

In athletics, scholars are finding, the ancient Greeks expressed one of their defining attributes: the pursuit of excellence through public competition. "Of all the cultural legacies left by the ancient Greeks," Dr. Edith Hall of the University of Durham in England has written, "the three which have had the most obvious impact on modern Western life are athletics, democracy and drama."

Dr. Donald G. Kyle, a professor of ancient history at the University of Texas in Arlington, said that long before the Greeks, others engaged in competitive sports like running and boxing. Contemporaries of the Greeks in Egypt and Mesopotamia put on lavish entertainments at court, with acrobats and athletes performing, and also promoted some sports as part of military training.

But the Greeks took athletics out to the wider public and to regularly scheduled competitions. They spread their games as they colonized Sicily and southern Italy and Alexander the Great conquered Eastern lands. "The Greeks linked their games to recurring religious festivals," Dr. Kyle said, "and this regularized and institutionalized athletics."

Dr. Stephen G. Miller of Berkeley has sifted through literature, art; and recent archaeology to compile a comprehensive history of sports in ancient Greece and their relationship with social and political life. Dr. Miller dates the origin of Greek organized athletics to the beginning of the eighth century B.C.

Much of the new research draws heavily on texts of ancient writers, inscriptions on stadium walls and statue bases, and artifacts excavated from ruins at the sites of the contests, including the stones of starting lines and turning points for races. Vase paintings often depict the pentathlon, five competitions that a single winner had to excel in. Archaeologists have also recovered the jumping weights and discuses of athletes and jars that held the olive oil they rubbed on their bodies.

Fans of the modern Olympics would find striking differences at the original games. There were no team sports and no second-place prizes. Fouls were punished by flogging. The athletes were allowed to accept cash and valuable gifts before and after competing.

Women were prohibited from watching or taking part in the games, except as owners in the horse races. In later years, though, some separate contests were staged for women in honor of Hera, the wife of Zeus. Unmarried girls ran a footrace wearing the Greek equivalent of a gym tunic that left the right breast bare.

The most obvious difference in the early games was the nudity of the young men. Some scholars have suggested that ancient Greece was a highly body-conscious society, in which the robust nudity of young men was itself an aspect of competitiveness.

By the fourth century A.D., with the spread of Christianity and the waning of belief in the ancient Greek gods, Dr. Miller wrote, the games "ceased completely to play any meaningful role in society."

It was not until 1896 that they were revived in their modern, international form, a tribute to the competitive spirit of ancient Greece. The 2004 Olympic games in Athens are a reminder of exuberance and pageantry of the original Greek games and the land where it all began.

TRACK AND FIELD

Track and Field consists of running, jumping, and throwing events. Often there is an outdoor 400-meter track made of synthetic materials that encloses an area called the field where many of the jumping and throwing events take place. There are also smaller indoor tracks where events take place. More than 200 nations have track and field teams, making it one of the most popular sports in the world. Track and Field meets are also very popular at the high school, college, and amateur levels. The first university meet took place in 1864 between Oxford and Cambridge. The New York Athletic Club hosted the first amateur meet in the U.S. in 1868.

Track Events Races at various distances between 50 and 10,000 meters are run. Cross-country races and road races are held outside the main track. Additionally, there are hurdle events, where runners leap over fences and steeplechase races, which are run over longer distances and contain water jumps in addition to hurdles. There are also walking races, where competitors must use a strict walking technique, and relay races. In the latter, four runners each run a section of a race, passing a baton to a teammate as they finish their portion.

Marathons, while not a standard part of track meets, are also very popular. The concept of the marathon was born in 490 B.C., when a Greek messenger named Phillippides ran from Marathon to Athens to deliver good news about a battle against the Persians. After the hilly run (about 40 km, or 25 miles), Phillippides shouted "Nike" (victory) then collapsed and died. When the Olympics were born again in 1896 in Athens, a race from Marathon to Athens was included to commemorate Phillippides' run. In 1924 the distance of the race was standardized at 26 miles, 385 yards.

Jumping Events There are four main jumping events. In the long jump, competitors have a running start to make a leap into a sand-filled area. The triple jump consists of three continuous jumps, the first two of which occur on the runway and the third of which lands in the sand. In these events, the athlete who travels farthest wins.

In the high jump and pole vault, the idea is to jump as high as possible, over a crossbar. High jumpers jump with one foot on the ground, pole vaulters use a fiberglass pole to help propel themselves over the bar.

Throwing Events There are four events where an athlete attempts to throw an object as far as possible. The *discus* is a frisbee-shaped object that weighs at least 4.4 lbs. for men and 2.2 lbs. for women. The *hammer* is a steel wire that connects a metal ball and a handle. It weighs 16 lbs. In the *shot-put*, a metal ball (called the shot) that weighs 16 lbs. for men and 8 lbs., 13 ounces for women is thrown. In these three events, competitors start from an area called the cage and throw as far as they can into a certain area. The *javelin* is the only throwing event that uses a runway. The javelin can be made out of metal or wood and is at least 8 1/2 feet for men and 7 feet, 3 inches for women.

Combined Events In addition to the individual events, there are also combined competitions, where an individual competes in different events over a day or two and gets points based on each. In the ancient Olympic games, the *pentathlon* was a main event. It included the long jump, discus and javelin throwing, running and wrestling. Today, the two most important combined events are the *decathlon* for men, consisting of 10 events, and the *heptathlon* for women, a seven-event competition.

On the first day of the decathlon, athletes do a 100-meter run, long jump, shot-put, high jump, and 400-meter run. Day two consists of the high hurdles, discus, pole vault, javelin and an 800-meter run.

The heptathlon's first day events are the high hurdles, high jump, shot put, and 200 meter run. Day two includes the long jump, the javelin throw and an 800-meter run.

The Olympics

In many ways, the history of track and field is the history of the Olympics.

1896 Athens Americans won gold medals in nine of the 12 track and field events. Americans Thomas Burke, Ellery Clark, and Robert Garrett each won two gold medals. American Robert Garrett won the shot with a throw of 36'9-3/4". Burke won the 100-meter race with a time of 12.0.

1900 Paris American Alvin Kraenzlein won four gold medals, in the 60-meter dash, the 100-meter, and 200-meter hurdles, and the long jump. American Ray Ewry won three gold medals for the high jump, standing long jump, and standing triple jump. Through subsequent Olympics Ewry finished his career with a total of eight gold medals. American Francis Jarvis won the 100-meter race with a time of 11.0.

1904 St. Louis American Archie Hahn won the 60-meter, 100-meter, and 200-meter dash. American Ray Ewry also won three gold medals, as did American Harry Hillman. Hahn won the 100-meter dash with a time of 11.0.

1908 London American Melvin Sheppard won three gold medals for the 800-meter race, the 1500-meter, and for a relay. American Ray Ewry won gold medals in the standing high jump and the long jump. American Ralph Rose won the shot put, as he had in 1904 in St. Louis. In the marathon Italian Dorando Pietri fell four times on his final lap inside the stadium. Officials helped him across the finish line to the cheers of the crowd but he was disqualified because of the help. Reginald Walker of South Africa won the 100-meter dash with a time of 10.8.

1912 Stockholm American Jim Thorpe won the pentathlon and decathlon but was stripped of his gold medals a year later when it was revealed he had earlier been paid for playing baseball. Hannes Kolehmainen of Finland won three gold medals. American Ralph Cook Craig won the 100-meter race with a time of 10.8.

1920 Antwerp Tug-of-war made its final appearance as an Olympic event, and was won by the British. Athletes from Finland won three of the four throwing events, only American Patrick Ryan, by winning the hammer throw, was able to upset the Finns. American Charles Paddock won the 100-meter race with a time of 10.8.

1924 Paris Finnish runner Paavo Nurmi won five gold medals, including the 5,000-meter race only an hour after winning the 1,500. American Matthew McGrath was 45 years old when he won the silver in the hammer throw. Harold Abrahams of Great Britain won the 100-meter race with a time of 10.6.

1928 Amsterdam Women participated in track and field events for the first time. American Elizabeth Robinson won the 100-meter race with a time of 12.2. American John Kuck won the shot put. Canadian Percy Williams won gold medals in the 200-meter and the 100-meter race. He won the 100-meter race with a time of 10.8.

1932 Los Angeles Mildred "Babe" Didrikson, who later became a legendary professional golfer, won two gold medals, in the 80-meter hurdles and the javelin, and a silver medal for the javelin. Stanislawa Walasiewicz won the women's 100-meter race with a time of 11.9. In the men's competition, athletes ran an extra lap in the 3,000-meter steeplechase because of a mistake by the lap counter. This caused American Joseph Mcluskey to fall from second to third. Eddie Tolan, 5'5", won the 100-meter and the 200-meter race. Tolan's win in the 100-meter race was decided by a photograph, as both Tolan and silver medal winner Ralph Metcalfe had a time of 10.38.

1936 Berlin Jesse Owens won four gold medals, including a friendly rivalry in the long jump with German Luz Long. The Germans dominated the throwing events except for the discus, which was won by American Kenneth Carpenter. Hans Woellke of Germany won the shot with a throw of 53'1-3/4". American Helen Stephens won the women's 100-meter race with a time of 11.5. Owens won the men's 100-meter race with a time of 10.3.

1948 London Fanny Blankers-Koen of the Netherlands won four gold medals. The mother of two, Blankers-Koen was known as the "flying housewife." Micheline Ostermeyer won two gold medals, in the women's shot and discus events. Blankers-Koen won the women's 100-meter race with a time of 11.9. American Harrison Dillard won the men's 100-meter race with a time of 10.3.

1952 Helsinki Emil Zatopek of Czechoslovakia won gold medals in the 5,000-meters, the 10-meters and the marathon. Past Olympic star Fanny Blankers-Koen fell over a hurdle in the 80-meters hurdles and left the track in tears. She never competed again. Australian Marjorie Jackson won two gold medals, in the 200-meter and 100-meter race. In the 100-meter race, Jackson had a world record time of 11.5. American Lindy Remigino won the men's 100-meter race with a time of 10.4.

1956 Melbourne Australian Betty Cuthbert won two individual gold medals and a third as a member of a relay team. Cuthbert won the women's 100-meter race with a time of 11.5. Soviet Vladimer Kuts won the men's 5,000-meter and 10,000-meter events. American Robert Morrow won two gold medals including the men's 100-meter race with a time of 10.5.

1960 Rome American Wilma Rudolph, who suffered from polio as a child, won two individual gold medals in sprints and a third as a member of a relay. Rudolph won the women's 100-meter race with a time of 11.0. Ethiopian runner Abebe Bikila won the marathon barefoot. Don Thompson of Great Britain set an Olympic record winning the 50-kilometer walk in 4:25.30. American Rafer Johnson won the decathlon. Armin Hary of Germany won the men's 100-meter race with a time of 10.2.

1964 Tokyo Tamara Press of the Soviet Union won two gold medals, in the women's shot-put and the discus. Australia's Betty Cuthbert, who won three gold medals in 1956, won the first ever women's 400-meter race. Peter Snell of New Zealand won two gold medals, in the men's 800-meter and 1,500-meter race. American Wyomia Tyus won the women's 100-meter race with a time of 11.4. Bob Hayes, who later went on to star for the Dallas Cowboys in the N.F.L., won the men's 100-meter race with a time of 10.0.

1968 Mexico City American Dick Fosbury unveiled a new approach to high jumping by going over shoulders first. This new technique, dubbed the Fosbury Flop, helped him win the gold medal. American Al Oerter became the first athlete to win the same event four Olympics in a row when he won the discus. One of the most memorable moments came in the medal ceremony for the 200-meter race, won by American Tommie Smith, when Smith and bronze medalist John Carlos raised black gloved fists as a demonstration for black rights. American Wyomia Tyus won the women's 100-meter race with a time of 11.0. American Jim Hines won the men's 100-meter race with a time of 9.9.

1972 Munich Lasse Viren of Finland won the 5,000-meter and 10,000-meter race. American Frank Shorter won the marathon by more than two minutes. Renate Stecher of East Germany won the women's 200-meter and 100-meter races. She won the 100-meter race with a time of 11.07. Valeriy Borsov won the men's 200-meter and 100-meter races. He won the 100-meter race with a time of 10.14.

1976 Montreal American Bruce Jenner set a world record while winning the decathlon. Cuban Alberto Juantorena won the 400-meter and 800-meter race. Tatyana Kazankina of the Soviet Union won the women's 800-meter and 1,500-meter race. Annegret Richter of West Germany won the women's 100-meter race with a time of 11.08. Hasely Crawford of Trinidad and Tobago won the men's 100-meter race with a time of 10.06.

1980 Moscow Wladyslaw Kosakiewicz won the pole vault with a world record jump of 18'11-1/2". Ludmilla Kondratyeva of the Soviet Union won the women's 100-meter race with a time of 11.06. Miruts Yifter of Ethiopia won two gold medals, in the 5,000-meter and 10,000-meter race. Allan Wells of Great Britain won the men's 100-meter run with a time of 10.25.

1984 Los Angeles American Carl Lewis won four gold medals, three individual medals and one as a member of a relay. Sebastian Coe of Great Britain won the men's 1,500-meter race for the second straight Olympics, having won in Moscow. American Edwin Moses, who won the 400-meter hurdles in 1976 but was absent in the boycott of 1980, won the even again in LA. American Valerie Brisco-Hooks won two gold medals, in the 200-meter and 400-meter race. American Evelyn Ashford won the women's 100-meter race with a time of 10.97. Lewis won the men's race with a time of 9.99.

1988 Seoul American Florence Griffith-Joyner won three gold medals and a silver. American Jackie Joyner-Kersee won two gold medals, in the long jump and the heptathlon. Griffith-Joyner won the women's 100-meter race with a time of 10.54. In the men's race Canadian Ben Johnson, the apparent winner, was disqualified for taking performance-enhancing drugs. American Carl Lewis won the men's 100-meter race with a time of 9.92.

1992 Barcelona The 10,000-meter men's final featured a controversial finish in which one Moroccan runner who had been lapped obstructed Kenyan Richard Chelimo, who was then passed by Khalid Skah, also of Morocco. Skah was first disqualified but then given the gold medal. Michael Stulce won the men's shot-put with a throw of 71'2". American Gail Devers won the women's 100-meter race with a time of 10.82. Linford Christie of Great Britain won the men's 100-meter race with a time of 9.96.

1996 Atlanta The track program was altered to allow American Michael Johnson to run the 200-meter and 400-meter race. He won both events, setting a world record for the 200-meter race. American Carl Lewis won the ninth gold medal of his Olympic career by wining the long jump. Jose-Marie Perek won the women's 200-meter and 400-meter race. American Gail Devers won the women's 100-meter race with a time of 10.94. Canadian Donovan Bailey won the men's 100-meter race with a time of 9.84.

2000 Sydney American Marion Jones won three gold medals and two bronze, and performed spectacularly in the third leg of the 4x400 relay, giving the American team an insurmountable lead. Romanian Mihaela Melinte, the women's hammer throw world record holder, was escorted away from the competition after testing positive for steroids. Jones won the women's 100-meter race with a time of 10.75. Maurice Green won the men's 100-meter race with a time of 9.87.

BOXING

Boxing is a sport in which two people in a ring, using padded gloves, fight with their fists. When done professionally, for a purse, it is also called prizefighting. It is also sometimes called pugilism, after the Latin term for a boxer. The ring is a 16 to 20 foot square, with three ropes across each of its four sides. Fighters are broken into many different weight classes, which differ between the amateur and professional ranks.

The idea in professional boxing is to knock the opponent out. This is accomplished either by a knockout, beating the opponent so that he can not stand up within a count of 10, or a technical knockout, beating the opponent to a point where the referee or the ringside doctor decides it would be unsafe for him to continue. If no knockout occurs, judges determine the winner. Fights are scored based on the boxers' performance in each round. A win obtained this way is called a decision. Officials may also score a fight as a draw.

Hitting below the belt, behind the head, or while the opponent is down are prohibited. Intentionally using one's head, legs, or elbows as a weapon are also illegal and will result in a loss of points or a disqualification.

Professional Boxing Professional matches are set up by promoters—an individual or group of individuals who make all the arrangements for a fight. State and local commissions regulate the sport at the professional level. Each of these commissions belongs to one or more of the following organizations: the World Boxing Council (WBC), the World Boxing Association (WBA), or the International Boxing Federation (IBF). Each of these organizations has its own list of champions and contenders that are sometimes the same and sometimes different.

Amateur Boxing The rules of amateur boxing are less brutal than the pros, with more of an emphasis placed on landing blows as opposed to hurting the opponent. Amateurs also wear protective headgear and there are fewer, shorter rounds. In the United States amateur boxing is governed by the U.S.A. Amateur Boxing Federation (U.S.A./A.B.F.). They hold their own tournaments, select the Olympic team, and provide the rules for the very popular Golden Gloves tournament, which is held annually across the country.

History of Boxing

In one form or another, boxing has existed for more than 6,000 years. It gained popularity in the Middle East and Africa and spread throughout the world. In ancient Greece fighters, tethered together and sitting on opposing stones, hit each other bare-fisted until one was knocked out. A less brutal version of boxing was included in the ancient Olympics in 688 B.C.

The Romans maximized the concept of bloody entertainment by allowing weapons, including one called a myrmex which meant, "limb piercer." The Romans, who invented the ring by marking a circle on the ground, eventually abolished boxing in 30 B.C. for being too violent.

Boxing reappeared in 17th century England and the game took a big leap forward in 1719, when James Figg, an expert fencer, opened a boxing academy. Before Figg, the sport was a combination of wrestling and boxing. He invented modern boxing by using his fencer's skill to parry and counterpunch. One of his students, Jack Broughton, was English champion from 1729 to 1750. Broughton drew up the first set of formal rules, including stopping a fight for 30 seconds after a knockdown.

In the mid-1860's the Marquess of Queensberry, an English nobleman, sponsored a new set of rules for boxing that are still the basis for boxing rules today. They include the use of gloves instead of bare fists, and mandate three-minute rounds with a one- minute rest period in between.

In the United States in the mid-19th century, boxers still fought with bare fists. One of most famous fights pitted John L. Sullivan against Jake Kilrain in 1889. Sullivan, despite throwing up in the 44th round, won in the 75th round. It was the last of the great bare-knuckles fights. In 1892 Sullivan fought and defeated Gentleman Jim Corbett under the Queensberry rules.

Although boxing is divided into many weight categories, and women's boxing has gained popularity in recent years, the heavyweights have garnered the most attention.

Notable Heavyweight Champions

1890's Gentleman Jim Corbett reigned for most of the decade, but on March 17, 1897, in Carson City, Nevada, Corbett lost to Englishman Bob Fitzsimmons in the 14th round, when Fitzsimmons hit Corbett in his stomach with a knockout called the "solar plexus" blow. Jim Jeffries beat Fitzsimmons in 1899, and then in a classic fight Jeffries beat challenger Tom Sharkey on November 3, 1899, at Coney Island.

1900's Jeffries retired in 1904, and then Jack Johnson, a charismatic black fighter, reigned for most of the decade. The boxing establishment tried to find a "white hope" to win back the title, but Johnson was too good.

1910's Jeffries came out of retirement to fight Johnson on July 4, 1910, in Reno, Nevada. Johnson won in the 15th round. Promoters continued searching for a "white hope" to beat Johnson and finally in 1915, in the last scheduled 45-round bout in history, Jess Willard, 6'6" tall from Kansas was able to beat Johnson, who was 37 years old and out of shape. Willard won in the 26th round. In 1919 Willard was battered by Jack Dempsey of Manassa, Colorado, losing in three rounds.

1920's This decade was the golden age of boxing. Jack Dempsey ranked with New York Yankees' slugger Babe Ruth in terms of adulation. Known as the Manassa Mauler, Dempsey beat French fighter Georges Carpentier on July 2, 1921, in a fight that produced the first million-dollar gate. In 1923 Dempsey knocked out Luis Angel Firpo of Argentina in two brutal rounds. Dempsey lost two fights, in 1926 at the Sesquicentennial Stadium of Philadelphia and in 1927 at Soldiers Field in Chicago, both to Gene Tunney.

1930's After Tunney retired, Max Schmeling won a tournament for the title when Jack Sharkey was disqualified in the finals for hitting Schmeling below the belt. Schmeling lost the rematch to Sharkey two years later. On June 19, 1936, Schmeling knocked out the young rising heavyweight Joe Louis in Yankee Stadium. Louis came back to win the world championship from Jim Braddock in Chicago on June 22, 1937. On June 22, 1938, Louis avenged his loss to Schmeling by knocking out Schmeling in the first round, in a fight that has massive political implications as Adolf Hitler had held up Schmeling as an example of Aryan racial superiority.

1940's Joe Louis began fighting so much that writers referred to his opponents as "the bum of the month." On June 18, 1941, Louis took on light-heavyweight champion Billy Conn at the Polo Grounds in New York. Conn was winning the fight with speed and boxing skills until he decided to slug it out with Louis in the 13th round. Louis knocked him out. Louis served in the army during World War II. Then he went on to win other fights, including a memorable victory against future champion Jersey Joe Walcott. Louis retired in 1949.

1950's After Louis retired, the title changed hands a couple of times before Jersey Joe Walcott was knocked out by Rocky Marciano on September 23, 1952. Marciano, a brutal puncher, never lost a fight in his career. He retired in 1955. Former Olympic middleweight Floyd Patterson beat Archie Moore to win a heavyweight elimination tournament and the championship on November 30, 1956. On June 26, 1959, at Yankee Stadium, Swedish fighter Ingemar Johansson knocked Patterson down seven times in the third round to win the title.

1960's Patterson regained his title by beating Johannson in two rematches and then on September 5, 1962, he lost a first-round knockout to Sonny Liston, an ex-con with ties to underworld figures. On February 25, 1964, in Miami, Florida, Liston lost to Cassius Clay, a charismatic fighter from Louisville, who later became a Muslim and changed his name to Muhammad Ali. Ali beat Liston in a rematch, and then, as a conscientious objector, refused to be drafted into the military. He spent a year fighting in Europe. In 1967 Ali was stripped of his titles and banned from fighting because he was convicted of avoiding the draft.

1970's Joe Frazier beat Jimmy Ellis in New York on Febuary 16, 1970, to cap a three-year tournament to find a new champion. As court victories went his way, Ali began a comeback in Georgia against Jerry Quarry on October 26, 1970, and after that win he was on a collision course with Joe Frazier. Frazier won the first fight, on March 8, 1971, at Madison Square Garden. Then George Foreman beat Joe Frazier in two rounds to win the heavyweight title on January 22, 1973, in Kingston, Jamaica. On October 29, 1974, Ali, who won the rematch against Frazier in the meantime, upset the heavily favored Foreman in a fight in Zaire that Ali dubbed "the rumble in the jungle." Using a style he called rope-a-dope, Ali stood on the ropes and let Foreman punch himself out for seven rounds. In the eighth, Ali knocked out Foreman. Ali then won another fight against Frazier that was dubbed the Thrilla in Manila.

In the late 1970's Ali lost to, then beat Leon Spinks to regain his title.

1980's On October 2, 1980, Larry Holmes, an old sparring partner of Ali, beat him to win the title. Holmes held the title until September 22, 1985, when he lost to lightheavyweight champion Michael Spinks in Las Vegas. A dispute over the title created more than one champion, and Trevor Berbick was one of the champions, until he lost to 20-year-old Mike Tyson on November 22, 1986. Tyson was an epic powerhouse early in his career, often winning by spectacular knockouts in the first few minutes of fights. On June 27, 1988, Tyson beat Michael Spinks in 91 seconds.

1990's to the present On February 11, 1990, James "Buster" Douglas scored one of the biggest upsets in history when he knocked Tyson out in the 10th round in Tokyo, Japan. In 1992 Tyson was convicted of rape in Indiana. He served three years in jail. Douglas lost to Evander Holyfield, who lost to Riddick Bowe, who refused to fight Lennox Lewis, who was then crowned champion. The title was disputed among many governing bodies, and at one point 45-year-old George Foreman won the title from one of the governing bodies. After getting out of jail, Tyson twice lost to Holyfield. Once he bit Holyfield's ear in frustration at taking a beating.

Olympic Boxing

Olympic boxing is a single elimination tournament. There is no seeding. Five judges, using a computerized system, judge each fight. Fights consist of four two-minute rounds. Prior to the 2000 Olympics, rounds were three-minutes each. The weight divisions have changed several times. As of the 2000 Olympics, they are:

Light Flyweight	106 pounds/48 kg
Flyweight	112.5 pounds/51 kg
Bantamweight	119.5 pounds/54 kg
Featherweight	126 pounds/57 kg
Lightweight	132 pounds/60 kg
Light Welterweight	140 pounds/63.5 kg
Welterweight	148 pounds/67 kg
Light Middleweight	156 pounds/71 kg
Middleweight	165.5 pounds/ 75 kg
Light Heavyweight	179 pounds/81 kg
Heavyweight	200.5 pounds/91 kg
Super Heavyweight	more than 200.5 pounds/91 kg

Notable Olympic Matches

1904 St. Louis Boxing was actually an event in the 1904 Olympics, although by the time the tournament was held, the athletes from Europe had all gone home. Only American boxers competed. In the bantamweight division, there were only two competitors.

1908 London Johnny Douglas of Great Britain won the middleweight title. The referee for the final was Douglas's father. Douglas is remembered as a great athlete who also was captain of Britain's cricket team.

1912 Stockholm There was no boxing in the 1912 Olympics because boxing was illegal in Sweden.

1920 Antwerp Eight weight divisions, from flyweight to heavyweight, were contested. Three Americans won gold medals and two boxers from Great Britain, including middleweight Harry Mallin, won gold medals.

1924 Paris In the middleweight quarterfinals, reigning champion Harry Mallin of Great Britain initially lost to Roger Brouse of France, but upon revealing bite marks on his chest, Mallin was awarded a controversial victory. Mallin went on to win his second gold medal.

1928 Amsterdam Controversial decisions in the featherweight, flyweight, and middleweight divisions marred the games. After American Hyman Miller lost a controversial flyweight decision to Marcel Santos of Belgium, the American team threatened to withdraw from the competition.

1932 Los Angeles Two Americans, two boxers from Argentina, and two from South Africa won gold medals. Santiago Lovell of Argentina won the heavyweight gold medal.

1936 Berlin German Willy Kaiser won the flyweight division and German Herbert Runge won the heavyweight division. Two fighters from France also won gold medals.

1948 London Lazlo Papp of Hungary won his first of three gold medals by winning the middleweight division. In the finals, he fought hometown favorite John Wright of Great Britain. Papp called it the hardest fight of his career. Rafael Iglesias of Argentina won the heavyweight division, which went up from 175 pounds to 176-1/4 pounds.

1952 Helsinki Lazlo Papp of Hungary moved down a division and won the gold medal in the light middleweight division. American Floyd Patterson, who would later go on to win the world heavyweight championship in professional boxing, won the middleweight gold medal. The silver medalist in the heavyweight division, Ingemar Johansson of Sweden, beat Patterson in 1959 to win Patterson's professional championship.

1956 Melbourne Lazlo Papp of Hungary became the first Olympic boxer to win three medals in a career when he won the middleweight division. Three fighters from the Soviet Union won gold medals, as well as two German fighters and two Americans. American Peter Rademacher won the heavyweight division, which increased to 178-1/2 pounds.

1960 Rome American Cassius Clay, who later changed his name to Muhammad Ali, won the gold medal in the light heavyweight division. Clay beat Polish fighter Zbigniew Pietrzykowski to win the gold medal. Later, Ali went on to become one of the most famous heavyweight professional fighters in history. Three Italians also won gold medals, including Franco De Piccoli, who won the heavyweight division.

1964 Tokyo Joe Frazier, who went on to become Muhammad Ali's epic professional opponent, won the gold medal in the heavyweight division. Three fighters from Poland won gold medals and three fighters from the Soviet Union won gold medals.

1968 Mexico City When American George Foreman won the gold medal in the heavyweight division, he paraded around the ring waving a miniature American flag. This patriotic gesture was long remembered from these turbulent times. Foreman went on to become a great professional champion who beat Joe Frazier and lost to Muhammad Ali. Two Mexican fighters won gold medals.

1972 Munich Cuban heavyweight Teofilo Stevenson began a historic three-Olympic reign of the heavyweight division. The statuesque Stevenson was most impressive in his first Olympics, beating top competition including American Duane Bobick. In later Olympics, boycotts affected his level of competition.

1976 Montreal Five Americans won gold medals including Michael Spinks in the middleweight division and his brother, Leon Spinks, in the light heavyweight division. Both Spinks brothers went on to win the professional heavyweight championship. Sugar Ray Leonard, who went on to have a storied professional career, won the gold medal in the light-welterweight division. Teofilo Stevenson of Cuba won the gold medal in the heavyweight division.

1980 Moscow The United States boycotted. Six Cuban fighters won gold medals. Teofilo Stevenson of Cuba won his third gold medal in the heavyweight division.

1984 Los Angeles The Soviet Union boycotted. An extra weight division, superheavyweight (more than 200 pounds) was added. This redefined the heavyweight competition as being for fighters between 178-1/2 pounds and 200 pounds. Americans won nine gold medals. American Tyrell Biggs won the super-heavyweight division, American Henry Tillman won the heavyweight division, and American Pernell Whitaker won the lightweight division.

1988 Seoul American Roy Jones Jr. clearly out-boxed his Korean opponent, Park Si Hun, but he lost a decision in the light-middleweight division. Three Americans won gold medals, including Ray Mercer, who won the heavyweight division. Canadian Lennox Lewis, won the gold medal in the superheavyweight division.

1992 Barcelona Cuban fighters won seven of 12 gold medals. Felix Savon of Cuba won the heavyweight, division and Cuban Roberto Balado Mendez won the superheavyweight division. American Oscar de la Hoya won the light middleweight division.

1996 Atlanta Cuban fighters won four gold medals. Felix Savon of Cuba won the heavyweight division and Vladimir Klichko of Ukraine won the super-heavyweight division. American David Reid won the light-middleweight division.

2000 Sydney Felix Savon of Cuba won his third gold medal by taking the heavyweight division. For the first time since 1948, the American team did not win a gold medal.

SWIMMING

History

In relics from the ancient world, there are a number of references to swimming. An Egyptian hieroglyphic depicting a swimmer dates to 2500 B.C. and mosaics in early Middle Eastern civilizations and in Pompeii depict men doing the dog paddle stroke, which they presumably learned from watching animals move about in the water.

In the first century A.D. swimming gained popularity in Britain and competitive races were introduced in Japan. But swimming fell out of favor, particularly in Europe, with the rise of the plagues of the Middle Ages.

In time, swimming regained its popularity. In 1837 swim competitions were held in London. The English swam with their heads over the water and their arms under the water, coordinating both hands to pull the water at the same time while using a frog kick. This evolved into the modern breaststroke.

In 1844 in a 130-foot pool in London, two American Indians, Flying Gull and Tobacco, demonstrated an overhand stroke that enabled them to cover the distance in an amazing 30 seconds. The swimming style was described at the time as "totally un-European."

This overhand stroke was more common elsewhere in the world. Between 1870 and 1890—depending on the historian—an Englishman, J. Walter Trudgen, on a trip to South America, noticed that South American Indians had an overhand stroke that was faster than the traditional British stroke. When he returned to England, he began teaching this overhand arm stroke, but he continued to teach the frog kick.

Frederick Cavill, a well-known swimmer in England, moved to Australia in 1878 and a few years later took a trip to the South Seas. On an island in the South Seas, Cavill noticed swimmers using an overhand stroke with an up-and-down kicking motion. Back in Australia, Cavill taught his sons the new stroke, and they soon were setting swimming records. One of the Cavill boys described the style as "like crawling through the water." This stroke became known as the Australian crawl.

Competitive swimming became important after it was included as part of the first modern Olympics in 1896. In the early 1900's, American Johnny Weissmuller invented a slightly modified version of the Australian crawl. This is the front crawl that is accepted as the fastest stroke in the world. Today, swimmers compete at many levels, from local swim clubs to high school meets to major college competitions.

The Sport of Swimming

Swimming competitions are held at swim meets, where different teams come together and compete in different events. International swim meets are held in pools that are 164 feet (50 meters) long and are divided into between six and 10 lanes. In the United States, pools half as long are also common for some meets.

There are five kinds of races: backstroke, breaststroke, butterfly, freestyle, and individual medley. In freestyle, a swimmer can choose any stroke though the front crawl is almost always selected because it is the fastest. The medley consists of equal distances of the butterfly, backstroke, breaststroke, and the front crawl.

Freestyle races are held at various distances between 100 meters and 1,500 meters. Individual medley races are either 200 or 400 meters. For the other three strokes, races are either 100 or 200 meters. Some races are also contested in open water. In the United States, open water races are held at five, 10, and 15 kilometers. International open water races are held over 25 kilometers.

Team relays are also a popular event at swim meets. Four team members each swim a different stroke the same distances (100 or 200 meters). The strokes are backstroke, breaststroke, butterfly, and front crawl.

Basic Strokes

The most popular stroke in swimming is the *front crawl*. The swimmer reaches the arms, one at a time in a sweeping, overhead motion while doing a flutter kick—moving the legs up and down with slightly bent knees.

The *backstroke* is similar to the crawl but is performed upside down, on the back.

The *breaststroke* is performed facedown and uses both arms simultaneously sweeping forward in the water. The breaststroke also has a special kick that involves drawing the feet toward the backside and pressing the feet back.

In the *butterfly*, the arms simultaneously swing above the head. This is accompanied by a dolphin kick—similar to the flutter kick but with more of a knee bend and where the legs move up and down at the same time.

The *sidestroke* is done on the side, moving the arms up and back with a scissor kick. In a scissors kick, the swimmer opens and closes the extended legs like scissors.

The Olympics

1896 Athens Four freestyle events are held with competitors either swimming breast stroke or Trudgen stroke. Alfred Hajos of Hungary wins the 100-meter freestyle with a time of 1:22.2.

1900 Paris Swimming competition is held in the Seine River. Two events were held—underwater swimming and the 200-meter obstacle race—that are no longer held. Backstroke was added as an event. In 1900 there was no 100-meter freestyle race. Frederick Lane of Australia wins the 200-meter freestyle with a time of 2:25.2.

1904 St. Louis American Charles Daniels wins three gold medals, two individual medals, and one as a member of a relay team. Most swimmers are swimming the crawl in freestyle events, so breaststroke is added as an event. Zoltan Halmay of Hungary wins the 100-yard freestyle with a time of 1:02.8. This is the only year that the Olympics swim races are measured in yards.

1908 London British swimmer Henry Taylor wins three gold medals, two individual medals, and one as a member of a relay team. American Charles Daniels wins the 100-meter freestyle with a time of 1:05.6.

1912 Stockholm Women compete in Olympic swimming for the first time. Australian Fanny Durack wins the women's 100-meter freestyle with a time of 1:22.2. American Duke Kahanamoku, a self-taught Hawaiian who brought the classic six-beat swimming style into prominence, wins the men's 100-meter freestyle. The six-beat style includes six flutter kicks during each cycle of the arms. Kahanamoku wins the 100-meter freestyle with a time of 1:03.4

1920 Antwerp American Ethelda Bleibtrey wins the women's 100-meter freestyle with a time of 1:13.6. American Duke Kahanamoku wins the men's 100-meter freestyle with a time of 1:01.4

1924 Paris American Johnny Weissmuller wins three gold medals. Weissmuller goes on to a legendary career setting world records in 67 different events. Later Weissmuller starred as Tarzan in many movies. American Ethel Lackie won the women's 100-meter freestyle with a time of 1:12.4. Weissmuller won the 100-meter freestyle with a time of 59.0.

1928 Amsterdam Hilde Schrader of Germany wins the women's 200-meter breaststroke, setting a world record. American Albina Osipowich wins the women's 100-meter freestyle with a time of 1:11.0. American Johnny Weissmuller won the men's 100-meter freestyle with a time of 58.6.

1932 Los Angeles American Helene Madison wins the two gold medals including the women's 100-meter freestyle with a time of 1:06.8. In the 100-meter race, she has a time of 1:06.8. Clarence "Buster" Crabbe wins the 400-meter freestyle and used his fame to land in the movies. Japan's Yasuji Miyazaki won the men's 100-meter freestyle with a time of 58.2.

1936 Berlin Japan and the United States dominates the men's swimming events, winning all but three of the medals in the men's individual events. Hendrika Mastenbroek of Holland wins the women's 100-meter freestyle with a time of 1:05.9.

1948 London Denmark's Greta Andersen wins the women's 100-meter freestyle with a time of 1:06.3. In the 400-meter freestyle race, however, Andersen faints and has to be rescued. Walter Ris of the United States wins the 100-meter freestyle with a time of 57.3.

1952 Helsinki Hungary's Katalin Szoke wins the women's 100-meter freestyle with a time of 1:06.8. American Clark Scholes wins the men's 100-meter freestyle with a time of 57.4.

1956 Melbourne This Olympics marks the introduction of the butterfly stroke as a separate event. Developed in the 1930's, the butterfly double-overhand arm stroke was combined with a frog kick and used to compete in and dominate breaststroke races. A dolphin kick—keeping the legs together and using a hip through toes double kick—was added to the stroke to make it more efficient. In 1953 breaststroke and butterfly were made into separate competitions. Dawn Fraser of Australia wins the women's 100-meter freestyle with a time of 1:02.0. Murray Rose of Australia becomes the first man to win two individual gold medals in swimming since Johnny Weissmuller in 1924. Australia's John Henricks wins the men's 100-meter freestyle with a time of 55.4.

1960 Rome Medley relay events are added for this Olympics. A medley is a race in which all four strokes—butterfly, backstroke, breaststroke, and freestyle—are each swum. In a relay race, each swimmer swims a different stroke. Australian Dawn Fraser wins the women's 100-meter freestyle with a time of 1:01.2. Australia's John Devitt wins the men's 100-meter freestyle with a time of 55.2.

1964 Tokyo Individual medley races are added. An individual medley is a race in which one swimmer swims each of the four strokes. American Don Schollander wins four gold medals two in individual events and two in relays. Australian Dawn Fraser wins the women's 100-meter freestyle with a time of 59.5. Schollander wins the men's 100-meter freestyle with a time of 53.4.

1968 Mexico City American Debbie Meyer wins three individual gold medals for the 200-meter freestyle, 400-meter freestyle, and 800-meter freestyle. American Jan Henne wins the women's 100-meter freestyle with a time of 1:00.0. Australian Michael Wenden wins the men's 100-meter freestyle with a time of 52.2.

1972 Munich American Mark Spitz puts in the most dominant performance in Olympic history, winning gold medals in four individual events while setting world records. He wins three more gold medals as a member of three relay teams. Australian Shane Gould wins three gold medals, a silver medal, and a bronze in the women's events. American Sandra Neilson wins the women's 100-meter freestyle with a time of 58.59. Spitz wins the men's 100-meter freestyle with a time of 51.22.

1976 Montreal The United States and East Germany dominate the swimming events. Only the 200-meter breaststroke in both the men's and women's events are won by a competitor who wasn't German or American. American John Naber wins two individual gold medals and two as a member of a relay team. He also wins a silver medal. Naber breaks the two-minute barrier for 200 backstroke by swimming it in 1:59.19. Kornelia Ender of East Germany wins four gold medals and a silver medal. Ender wins the women's 100-meter freestyle with a time of 55.65. American Jim Montgomery wins the men's 100-meter freestyle with a time of 49.99.

1980 Moscow East German Rica Reinisch won three gold medals in women's events. Barbara Krause of East Germany wins the 100-meter freestyle with a time of 54.79. Jorg Woithe of East Germany wins the men's 100-meter freestyle with a time of 50.40.

1984 Los Angeles American Mary T. Meagher wins two individual gold medals and a third as a member of a relay team. West German Michael Gross wins the 100-meter butterfly and the 200-meter butterfly, setting world records in both. Canadian Alex Baumann sets world records in two events, winning the 200-meter medley and the 400-meter medley. American Carrie Steinseifer wins the women's 100-meter freestyle with a time of 55.92. American Ambrose Gaines wins the men's 100-meter freestyle with a time of 49.80.

1988 Seoul A short sprint—the 50-meter freestyle—is added. Kristin Otto of East Germany wins six gold medals; four individual gold medals and two as a member of a relay team. American Matt Biondi wins five gold medals, silver, and a bronze. Otto won the wins 100-meter freestyle with a time of 54.93. Biondi wins the men's 100-meter freestyle with a time of 48.63.

1992 Barcelona Yevgeniy Sadovyi of the Unified Team wins three gold medals in the men's competition and Hungarian Kriszitina Egerzegy wins three gold medals in the women's competition. Yong Zhuang of China wins the women's 100-meter freestyle with a time of 54.64. Alexander Popov of the Unified Team wins the men's 100-meter freestyle with a time of 49.02.

1996 Atlanta American women are dominant, winning seven of 16 gold medals, and five silver medals. American Amy van Dyken wins four gold medals, two in individual events and two as a member of a relay team. Michelle Smith of Ireland wins three gold medals and a bronze. American Gary Hall Jr. wins two gold medals on relay teams and two individual silver medals. Le Jingyi of China wins the women's 100-meter freestyle with a time of 54.50. Alexander Popov wins the men's 100-meter freestyle with a time of 48.74.

2000 Sydney High-tech body suits were worn by many swimmers and 15 world records are broken or tied. The Americans are dominant winning 14 gold medals. American Lenny Krayzelburg wins three gold medals in backstroke events. Inge de Bruijn won the women's 100-meter freestyle with a time of 54.33. Pieter van den Hoogenband of the Netherlands wins the men's 100-meter freestyle with a time of 48.30.

AUTO RACING

The sport of automobile racing is almost as old as automobiles themselves, dating back to the 1890's. There are many types of racing, differentiated by the characteristics of the vehicles involved. The stock cars seen in NASCAR, for example, outwardly resemble something that might be found in any garage in America. Formula One and Indy car circuits are designed for low-slung cars seen nowhere else but a race track. There are vehicles built for extreme speed called dragsters that can reach speeds of more than 300 miles per hour for a few seconds. One of the world's most famous races, the 24 Hours of Le Mans held annually in Le Mans, France, is an endurance race. But the three styles of racing that attract the most attention are Formula One, NASCAR, and Indy cars.

Because of the tremendous cost involved in building and maintaining a team of cars, almost all professional racing teams have corporate sponsors who support them in exchange for displaying logos on the cars. All three of these racing circuits award a championship, for both teams and individuals, based on points accumulated through high-place finishes. Some drivers have had success in more than one of the three types of racing.

Formula One

The world's most popular form of auto racing is Formula One (F1). Formula One cars are designed according to specifications of the sport's governing body, the Federation Internationale de l'Automobile (FIA). The FIA was established in 1904 and supervised its first major event (called a Grand Prix) in 1906 near Le Mans, France. The first Grand Prix series was held in 1920. The circuit now covers 18 events in locations as diverse as Malaysia, Monaco, Germany, and the United States, with races usually ranging from 150 to 200 miles. Although Formula One cars can reach high speeds on straightaways, courses have frequent turns that require vehicles to be nimble as well as fast.

Drivers belong to teams that provide and outfit the cars. Only nine teams—each with multiple cars and drivers—participated in the 2004 Formula One season, including Italy's Ferrari (the dominant team of the previous half decade), and two British teams, Williams and McLaren, plus others.

Some of the sport's biggest stars include the Argentinian Juan Manuel Fangio, who raced in the 1950's, Scotland's Jackie Stewart, a star of the 1960's and 1970's, Brazil's Ayrton Senna, a brilliant driver who died in a crash during the 1994 San Marino Grand Prix, and Germany's Michael Schumacher, who established himself in the 1990's and 2000's as one of the great Formula One drivers of all time.

NASCAR

While the National Association for Stock Car Automobile Racing ranks among the fastest-growing of all sports in terms of popularity with the public, the sport originated with a very specific activity. Stock car racing grew out of the bootlegging communities of the South, where the quest to transport illegal moonshine past the authorities led naturally to the development of fast cars. Competing bootleggers who bragged about having fast cars would race against one another. One account says the first race was contested in the mid-1930's in a town near Atlanta, Georgia.

By the 1940's, thousands of spectators attended these races. In 1947 Bill France, who promoted a race in Daytona Beach, Fla., gathered racing promoters throughout the region to organize a racing circuit that became NASCAR. In 1949 the first race in the Strictly Stock Division series was held at the 116-mile Beach & Road Course at Daytona Beach. Red Byron won in an Oldsmobile.

In the first two years of NASCAR, modified older cars were used, but in 1949 the organization began racing the same kinds of vehicles sold in automobile showrooms. Nine models of cars—Buick, Cadillac, Chrysler, Ford, Hudson, Kaiser, Lincoln, Mercury, and Oldsmobile—competed in the first Strictly Stock Division race. As manufacturers realized that victories helped sell cars, they began upgrading their stock cars for the public. Hudson drivers won 22 of 37 races in 1953 after Hudson introduced its "Twin H" carburetor setup. Then in 1955 Chevrolet introduced the legendary 355 "small block" V8 engine still employed by General Motors racing teams. Over time, NASCAR loosened rules so that stock cars became something different from the cars sold on showroom floors.

In 1958 the final beach road race was held in Daytona Beach. The Daytona International Speedway opened in 1959, and three other major racetracks—in Hanford, Calif.; Concord, N.H., and Hampton, Ga.—opened within the next year. Racing in the early 1960's was marked by the "engine wars," as Ford, Chevrolet, and others spent millions of dollars on research and development. In 1964 Richard Petty used a Plymouth hemispherical combustion engine, or a "hemi," to win the Daytona 500.

In 1951 the name of the circuit changed to the NASCAR Grand National Series and that title remained until RJ Reynolds began sponsoring the series in 1972. For more than three decades, the NASCAR circuit was also known as the Winston Cup Series, after an RJ Reynolds cigarette brand. In a change symbolic of NASCAR's broadening appeal, cellular phone company Nextel took over the titular sponsorship of the circuit in 2004. For 10-year naming rights to the NASCAR Nextel Cup series, the company paid $700 million.

The first race of the NASCAR season is also the biggest, the Daytona 500, which is held in mid-February. The series ends with the Ford 400 in Homestead, Fla. in mid-November, with almost weekly races throughout the season.

Contemporary NASCAR engines are restricted to 358 cubic inches and require a restrictor plate that limits the flow of air to the engine. This decrease in air flow restricts the car to 450 horsepower. Cars weigh a minimum of 3,400 pounds and employ a steering system on oval left-turn tracks that forces them to turn right in order to go straight. This modification makes turning left easier.

Notable NASCAR drivers

Dale Earnhardt won seven series championships and is considered by many as the most talented driver in NASCAR history. Earnhardt's aggressive style earned him the nickname, "The Intimidator." He died in a crash in the last lap of the 2001 Daytona 500.

Jeff Gordon won three cup series (in 1995, 1997, 1998) and the Daytona 500 twice.

Junior Johnson was one of the most famous of the bootleg racers. He was arrested at his father's still in 1956 and spent two years in jail. Johnson won 50 races between 1953 and 1966, and later became a prominent car owner.

Lee Petty won 54 races. His son Richard, who went on to become the greatest NASCAR driver, was in Lee Petty's pit crew.

Richard Petty, known to racing fans as "The King," won 200 NASCAR races, seven cup series championships, and seven victories in the Daytona 500. In 1967 Petty won 27 of 48 races, including 10 in a row.

Edward Glenn "Fireball" Roberts, considered the greatest driver never to win the cup series, won the Daytona 500 in 1962. He died in a racing accident in 1964.

Darrell Waltrip won three cup championships, in 1977, 1981, 1982. He is the only five-time winner of the Coca Cola 600 at the Charlotte (N.C.) Motor Speedway.

Joe Weatherly won two cup championships, in 1962 and 1963. He was also an accomplished motorcycle racer. He died in a crash in 1964.

Cale Yarborough won three consecutive championships (1976–78), and won the Daytona 500 four times.

Indy Car

Indy car racing is the fastest multimile automobile racing in the world. Like Formula One cars, Indy cars have an open cockpit, one seat, and an engine in the rear. Each year racers compete in more than two dozen races, from oval tracks to closed-off city streets. The Indianapolis 500 is the premier event, held each Memorial Day weekend in Indiana.

In 1906 Carl Fisher, frustrated at the unreliability of automobiles, decided to build a racetrack in Indianapolis to entice car manufacturers to make better vehicles. His creation, built on a 300-acre plot of land, was the Indianapolis Motor Speedway. The original 2.5-mile track was surfaced with bricks. Of this original surface, only a yard-wide strip remains to serve as the finish line. Because of this unusual feature, the track is also known as the Brickyard.

The first race at Indianapolis was held in August 1909. In 1911 the Indianapolis Motor Speedway hosted a 500-mile race, the first Indianapolis 500. Ray Haroun, with an average speed of 74.59 miles per hour, won the race. The contest proved popular with the public, and new grandstands were added as the event grew in prestige.

In 1916, during World War I, only 21 cars competed in a race that was reduced to only 300 miles. After America entered the war, during the next two years the track was closed and served as an aviation repair depot and landing field for planes flying coast to coast through the Midwest.

Following the conflict, racing returned in earnest. The 1919 race was won by Howdy Wilcox, who was the first to drive more than 100 miles per hour. He won $50,000 in that race, in which three drivers died. The 1920 race was won by Gaston Chevrolet, driving a Monroe. In 1925 Pete DePaolo won by averaging more than 100 mph for the first time. In 1927 Fisher sold the speedway to World War I flying ace Eddie Rickenbacker for $750,000.

Racing, like everything else, suffered during the Great Depression, and the speedway was again closed during the World War II. In 1946, as the grandstands stood in disrepair and the track was overgrown with weeds, Rickenbacker sold it to Tony Hulman, who supervised the Indianapolis 500 for 30 years. Hulman spent millions of dollars to renovate the track, and the race took on renewed significance.

In 1955 Bill Vukovich, the winner of the two previous races, died while leading the race in the 57th lap. In 1956 an eight-story control tower was added, as were new seats, tunnels, and safer pit areas. And in 1957 a 15 car accident killed driver Pat O'Connor. After that, rollbars were required in all cars, and drivers were mandated to wear fireproof uniforms. In the 1960's the circuit mandated that methanol be used instead of gasoline because it is much less flammable.

Early Indy cars were made of heavy sheet metal. Modern cars are fabricated from aluminum and carbon fiber. Since drivers had trouble keeping these lighter cars on the track, wings were added to both the front and rear of the vehicle. These have the opposite effect of airplane wings—rather than giving lift, they produce downward force that keeps the car on the ground.

The two major models of race cars are Penskes and Lolas. The British-built Cosworth-Ford engine was the standard Indy car engine but the Ilmor-Ford engine has also become popular in recent years.

A. J. Foyt was among the biggest names in the sport in the 1960's and 1970's, winning four Indianapolis 500's – in 1961, 1964, 1967, 1977. A few racing families have achieved a high profile in the sport, including the Unsers. Al and Bobby Unser won the race seven times between them, and Al Unser Jr. won the race in 1992 and 1994.

A feud between two competing groups in the 1990's diminished the importance of the Indianapolis 500 for several years. The Championship Auto Racing Team (CART) was formed in 1978 after a dispute with the United States Auto Racing Club, which was operating Indy car racing. Court cases and rejected entries marked the feud, which took new meaning in 1994, when the Indy Racing League (IRL) was formed by Tony George, president of the Indianopolis Motor Speedway. By 1996 the feud deepened and CART planned the U.S. 500 for the Michigan Motor Speedway on the same day as the Indianapolis 500.

For four years, the U.S. 500 was held the same day, but in 2000 CART cleared its schedule for two weeks, and CART drivers are again participating in the Indianapolis 500. Helio Castroneves of CART won in 2001 and 2002, and his CART colleague Gil de Ferran won the 2003 race, beating Castroneves by 0.299 seconds.

Le Mans

Auto racing originated as a way of testing the new vehicles for speed and endurance. In 1923 the Automobile Club of the Sarthe, which had established the first French Grand Prix, decided to organize a race that would test not only around-the-clock endurance but also auto headlights, which were still in their infancy. The result was the first 24 Hours of Le Mans race, originally called the Grand Prix of Endurance. The first race began at 4 p.m. May 26, 1923, during a tempestuous rain storm accompanied by bursts of hail.

Thirty-five cars from 18 different manufacturers entered that race. When it ended at 4 p.m. the following day, the winner was a Chenard and Walcker "Sport" driven by Andre Lagache and Rene Leonard. The car covered 2,209.536 kilometers at an average speed of 92.064 kilometers per hour, about 57.2 miles an hour.

The 24 Hours of Le Mans is still a major test of the endurance of an auto, driven continuously at high speeds. Teams originally included only two drivers. Since 1977, a team has been allowed, but not required, to have three drivers. Prequalifying sessions take place in early May, with qualifying rounds a month later and the race itself on a weekend in mid-June.

Indianapolis 500 Winners, 1911–2004

Year	Winner	Time	MPH
Under AAA Sanction			
1911	Ray Harroun	6:42.08	74.602
1912	Joe Dawson	6:21.06	78.719
1913	Juses Goux	6:35:05	75.933
1914	Rene Thomas	6:03:45	82.474
1915	Ralph DePalma	5:33:55	89.840
1916	Dario Resta	3:34:17[1]	84.001
1919	Howard Wilcox	5:40:42	88.050
1920	Gaston Chevrolet	5:38:32	88.618
1921	Tommy Milton	5:34:34	89.621
1922	Jimmy Murphy	5:17:30	94.484
1923	Tommy Milton	5:29:50	90.954
1924	L.L. Corum, Joe Boyer	5:05:23	98.234
1925	Peter DePaolo	4:56:39	101.127
1926	Peter Lockhart	4:10:14[2]	95.904
1927	George Souders	5:07:33	97.545
1928	Louis Meyer	5:01:33	99.482
1929	Ray Keech	5:07:25	97.585
1930	Billy Arnold	4:58:39	100.448
1931	Louis Schneider	5:10:27	96.629
1932	Fred Frame	4:48:03	104.144
1933	Louis Meyer	4:48:00	104.162
1934	William Cummings	4:46:05	104.863
1935	Kelly Petillo	4:42:22	106.240
1936	Louis Meyer	4:35:03	109.069
1937	Wilbur Shaw	4:24:07	113.580
1938	Floyd Roberts	4:15:58	117.200
1939	Wilbur Shaw	4:20:47	115.035
1940	Wilbur Shaw	4:22:31	114.277
1941	Floyd Davis, Mauri Rose	4:20:36	115.117
1946	George Robson	4:21:16	114.820
1947	Mauri Rose	4:17:52	116.338
1948	Mauri Rose	4:10:23	119.814
1949	Bill Holland	4:07:15	121.327
1950	Johnnie Parsons	2:46:55[3]	124.002
1951	Lee Wallard	3:57:38	126.244
1952	Troy Tuttman	3:52:41	128.922
1953	Bill Vukovich	3:53:01	128.740
1954	Bill Vukovich	3:49:17	130.840
1955	Bob Sweikert	3:53:59	128.209
Under USAC Sanction			
1956	Pat Flaherty	3:53.28	128.490
1957	Sam Hanks	3:41.14	135.601
1958	Jim Bryan	3:44:13	133.791
1959	Rodger Ward	3:40:49	135.857
1960	Jim Rathmann	3:36:11	138.767
1961	A.J. Foyt, Jr.	3:35:37	139.131
1962	Roger Ward	3:33:50	140.293
1963	Parnelli Jones	3:29:35	143.137
1964	A.J. Foyt, Jr.	3:23:35	147.350
1965	Jim Clark	3:19:05	150.686
1966	Graham Hill	3:27:52	144.317
1967	A.J. Foyt, Jr.	3:18:14	151.207
1968	Bobby Unser	3:16:13	152.882
1969	Mario Andretti	3:11:14	156.867
1970	Al Unser	3:12:37	155.749
1971	Al Unser	3:10:11	157.735
1972	Mark Donohue	3:04:05	162.962
1973	Gordon Johncock	2:05:26[4]	159.036
1974	Johnny Rutherford	3:09:10	158.589
1975	Bobby Unser	2:54:55[5]	149.213
1976	Johnny Rutherford	1:42:52[6]	148.725
1977	A.J. Foyt, Jr.	3:05:57	161.331
1978	Al Unser	3:05:54	161.363
1979	Rick Mears	3:08:47	158.899
1980	Johnny Rutherford	3:29:59	142.862
1981	Bobby Unser	3:35:41	139.084
1982	Gordon Johncock	3:05:09	162.029
1983	Tom Sneva	3:05:03	162.117
1984	Rick Mears	3:30:21	163.612
1985	Danny Sullivan	3:16:06	152.982
1986	Bobby Rahal	2:55:43	170.722
1987	Al Unser	3:04:59	162.175
1988	Rick Mears	3:27:10	144.809
1989	Emerson Fittipaldi	2:59:01	167.581
1990	Arie Luyendyk	2:41:18	185.984[7]
1991	Rick Mears	2:50:01	176.457
1992	Al Unser, Jr.	3:43:05	134.477
1993	Emerson Fittipaldi	3:10:50	157.207
1994	Al Unser, Jr.	3:06:29	160.872
1995	Jacques Villeneuve	3:15:18	153.616
1996	Buddy Lazier	3:22:46	147.956
1997	Arie Luyendyk	3:25:43	145.827
1998	Eddie Cheever	3:26:40	145.155
1999	Kenny Brack	3:15:51	153.176
2000	Juan Montoya	2:58.59	167.607
2001	Helio Castroneves	3:31.54	141.574
2002	Helio Castroneves	3:00:11	166.499
2003	Gil de Ferran	3:11:57	156.291
2004	Buddy Rice	3:14:55[8]	138.518

1. 300 miles (scheduled). 2. 400 miles (rain). 3. 345 miles (rain). 4. 332.5 miles (rain). 5. 435 miles (rain). 6. 255 miles (rain). 7. Track record. 8. 450 miles (rain). **Source**: Indianapolis Motor Speedway Hall of Fame and Museum.

REFERENCE LIBRARY

A Writer's Guide 768

Eight Parts of Speech 768
Basic Sentence Grammar 772
Punctuation 784
Mechanics 793
Spelling 795
Using Capitals 799

Languages 801

Language Families 801

Crossword Puzzles 805

How to Solve the New York Times *Crossword Puzzle* by Will Shortz . . 805
Concise Crossword Dictionary By Will Shortz 806

Nations of the World 813

Nations of the World, A–Z 813
The United Nations 859

U.S. States and Cities 861

U.S. States 861
The 50 Largest U.S. Cities, 2000 876

Awards and Prizes 883

Academy Awards 883
Emmy Awards 890
Tony Awards 893
Grammy Awards 898
Pulitzer Prizes 901
Nobel Prizes 911

Weights and Measurements . . . 921

Systems of Measurement 921

Dictionary of Food 925

Cereals and Grains 925
Fruit 926
Vegetables 929
Herbs 933
Spices 933
Salt 933
Fungi 933
Fish 934
Animal Foods 936
Dairy Foods 937
Chocolate, Coffee, and Tea 938
Nuts 939

Wine: A Primer 940

A Brief History of Wine 940
Regions 940
Wine and Food 944
Wine Glossary 945

Guide to Nutrition 948

Food and Nutrition 948
Diet and Dieting 949
The Value of Vitamins and Minerals 950
Burning off Calories 952
Body Mass Index 954

Biographical Dictionary 955

A WRITER'S GUIDE

The Eight Parts of Speech

Sentence elements consist primarily of a subject and predicate. Grammarians classify the words in each element as parts of speech. The eight parts of speech are *nouns, verbs, pronouns, adjectives, adverbs, conjunctions, prepositions,* and *interjections*. We classify words as one or another part of speech according to the role they play in a sentence.

Nouns

Nouns are the names for people, places, animals, things, ideas, actions, states of existence, colors and so forth. In sentences, nouns serve as *subjects, objects* and *complements.*

Nouns may also be *appositives*; that is, they can identify another noun or pronoun, usually by naming it again in different words. In the following sentence bold indicates the appositive (or noun in apposition):

My mother, a ***police lieutenant****, works late every night.*

Common nouns name ordinary things: *ability, democracy, justice, rope, baseball, desks, library, beauty*.

Proper nouns are the names of persons, places, and things. Always capitalize proper nouns: *Amtrak, Germany, Donald A. Stone, Greek Orthodox, State Department, General Dynamics, the Rolling Stones, New York.*

Compound nouns consist of two or more words that function as a unit. They include such common nouns as *heartache, mother-in-law, father-in-law, great-grandmother,* and *worldview*. Compound nouns also may be proper nouns—*International Business Machines, Federal Bureau of Investigation, Suez Canal and Sacramento, California*.

Verbs

Verbs report action, condition, or state of being. Verbs are the controlling words in predicates, but verbs themselves are controlled by subjects.

Number and person The *number* of the subject determines the form of its verb. If a subject is only one thing, it is *singular*. If it is more than one, it is *plural*: *dog* is singular; the plural form is *dogs*. Verbs reflect these differences in subjects by taking a singular or a plural form.

In the *first-person singular*, I speak or write of myself. In the *first-person plural*, we speak or write of ourselves. In the *second-person singular and plural* (the forms are the same), you are addressed. In the *third-person singular*, someone speaks or writes about somebody or something who is not being addressed. In the *third-person plural*, someone speaks or writes about more than one person or object.

	Singular	Plural
First person	I	we
Second person	you	you
Third person	she	they

In the present tense the only change that takes place is in the third person singular; a final *–s* is added to the common form of the verb. Most but not all verbs will add this *–s* in the third person singular.

	Singular	Plural
First person	I build.	We build.
Second person	You build.	You build
Third person	He builds.	They build.

Helping verbs or auxiliary verbs enable a single verb to express a meaning that it could not express by itself. A verb phrase is the helping verb plus the main verb. The final word in a verb phrase, the main verb, carries the primary meaning of the verb phrase. Sometimes more than one helping verb accompanies the main verb. In the following sentences, the verb phrases are bold; HV appears over each helping verb, and MV appears over each main verb.

HV MV
He ***is biking*** *to Vermont from Boston.*

HV MV
They ***will arrive*** *in time for the game.*

HV HV MV
Cy Young ***has*** *always* ***been considered*** *one of the best pitchers in baseball history.*

Notice that sometimes words not part of the verb phrase come between the helping verb and the main verb.

Typical helping verbs include: *be, being, been, is, am, are, was, were, do, did, does, has, have, had, must, may, can, shall, will, might, could, would, should*.

Particles are short words that never change their form no matter how the main verb changes. They sometimes look like other parts of speech, but they always go with the verb to add a meaning that the verb does not have by itself.

Harry made ***up*** *with Gloria.*

She filled ***out*** *her application.*

Tenses Verbs show whether the action of the sentence is taking place now, took place in the past, or will take place in the future. English has three simple tenses—present, past, and future.

Present: *She* ***works*** *every day.*

Past: *She* ***worked*** *yesterday.*

Future: *She* ***will work*** *tomorrow.*

Irregular verbs form the simple past tense by changing a part of the verb other than the ending.

Present: *We* ***grow*** *tomatoes every year on our kitchen window shelf.*

I ***run*** *four miles every day.*

I ***go*** *to the grocery store every Saturday morning.*

Past: *We* ***grew*** *corn back in Iowa.*

In 1981 Coe ***ran*** *the mile in three minutes and forty-six seconds.*

I ***went*** *to the grocery store last Saturday.*

Form the future tense of verbs by adding *will* or *shall* to the common form of the present.

Present: *I often* ***read*** *in bed.*

Future: *I* ***shall read*** *you a story before bedtime.*

She ***will read*** *you the ending tomorrow morning.*

Pronouns

A pronoun takes the place of a noun and can serve as subject, object, and complement in sentences. Sentences must always make clear what nouns the pronouns stand for. A pronoun that lacks a clear antecedent (the word for which the pronoun substitutes) causes confusion.

Personal pronouns refer to one or more persons: *I, you, he, she, it, we, they*.

Indefinite pronouns indicate a member of a group without naming which one we mean: *all, any, anyone, each, everybody, everyone, few, nobody, someone.*

Reflexive pronouns refer to the noun or pronoun that is the subject of the sentence; they always end in *–self* or *–selves*: *myself, himself, herself, yourself, ourselves*.

She allowed ***herself*** *no rest.*

He loved ***himself*** *more than he loved anyone else.*

Intensive pronouns have the same form as reflexive pronouns; they add special emphasis to nouns and other pronouns.

I ***myself*** *have often made that mistake.*

President Harding ***himself*** *played poker and drank whiskey in the White House during Prohibition.*

Demonstrative pronouns point out nouns or other pronouns that come after them: *this, that, these, those*.

That *is the book I want.*

Are ***those*** *the books you bought?*

Relative pronouns join word groups containing a subject and verb to nouns or pronouns that the word groups describe: *who, whom, that, which*.

Ian McEwan is the writer ***who*** *won the award for his novel* Atonement.

The tools ***that*** *I lost in the lake cost me a fortune to replace.*

The doctor ***whom*** *you recommended has left town.*

Possessive pronouns show possession or special relations: *my, his, her, your, our, their, its*. Unlike possessive nouns, possessive pronouns have no apostrophes.

Their *cat sets off* ***my*** *allergies.*

The fault was ***ours****, and the worst mistake was* ***mine****.*

Interrogative pronouns introduce questions: *who, which, what*.

What *courses are you taking?*

Who *kept score?*

Which *of the glasses is mine?*

Like nouns, pronouns can be singular or plural, depending on the noun form they replace.

Adjectives

Adjectives modify nouns and pronouns. That is, they help describe nouns and pronouns in a sentence by answering questions such as *which one, what kind, how many, what size, what color, what condition, whose*. Adjectives appear in boldface in the sentences below.

The ***bright yellow*** *sun shone through the* ***gloomy*** *clouds.*

Six *camels trudged across a* ***vast white*** *desert* ***one scorching*** *afternoon.*

Adjectives usually come immediately before, but sometimes immediately after, the words they modify.

The ***tired, thirsty, impatient*** *horse threw its rider.*

The horse, ***tired, thirsty,*** *and* ***impatient,*** *threw its rider.*

Subject complements An adjective modifying the subject of a sentence sometimes appears on the opposite side of a linking verb from the subject.

The horse looked ***tired, thirsty,*** *and* ***impatient.***

My friend was ***ill,*** *and I was* ***worried.***

In these examples, the adjectives are subject complements.

Articles The articles *a, an,* and *the* function as adjectives.

He sent me ***the*** *card in* ***an*** *old envelope.*

A and *an* are indefinite and singular. The article *a* appears before words that begin with a consonant sound; *an* appears before words that begin with a vowel sound.

a dish, a year, an apple, an entreaty, a European, a historian, an enemy, a friend, an umbrella, a union, an understanding, an hour

Degree In comparisons, adjectives show degree or intensity by the addition of an *–er* or *–est* ending or by the use of *more* or *most* or *less* or *least*.

Present and past participles of verbs often serve as adjectives:

The trip was both ***exhausting*** *and* ***rewarding.***

The ***gathering*** *night was filled with stars.*

Tired *and* ***discouraged,*** *she dropped out of the marathon.*

A noun can serve as an adjective.

Cigarette *smoking harms our lungs.*

People who drive gas guzzlers worsen the ***energy*** *crisis.*

Adjectives can also serve as nouns. All the words in boldface in the sentence below are normally adjectives, but here they clearly modify an implicit noun, *people* or *persons*. The words therefore assume the function of the implicit noun and become nouns themselves.

The ***unemployed*** *are not always the* ***lazy*** *and* ***inept.***

Avoid Adjectives When the Sentence Requires Adverbs Common speech sometimes accepts adjectival forms in an adverbial way; avoid this colloquial usage in writing.

Nonstandard: *He hit that one* ***real good.***

Revised: *He hit that one really well.*

Nonstandard: *She* ***sure*** *made me work hard for my grade.*

Revised: *She certainly made me work hard for my grade.*

Adverbs

Adverbs usually modify verbs, adjectives, and other adverbs, but they sometimes modify prepositions, phrases, clauses, and even whole sentences.

Adverbs answer questions such as *how, how often, to what degree (how much), where,* and *when.*

Wearily *he drifted* ***away.***

She did ***not*** *speak* ***much today.***

Adverbs may modify by affirmation or negation. *Not* is always an adverb.

He will ***surely*** *call home before he leaves.*

They shall ***not*** *pass.*

We will ***never*** *see anyone like her again.*

Many adverbs end in *–ly*, and you can make adverbs of most adjectives simply by adding *–ly* to the adjective form.

Adjective	Adverb
large	largely
crude	crudely
beautiful	beautifully

However, a great many adverbs do not end in *–ly*:

often, sometimes, then, when, anywhere, anyplace, somewhere, somehow, somewhat, yesterday, Sunday, before, behind, ahead, seldom

Note also that many adjectives already end in *–ly*.

costly, stately, lowly, homely, measly, manly, womanly, terribly, honestly

Conjunctive adverbs such as *accordingly, consequently, hence, however, indeed, meanwhile, moreover, nevertheless, on the other hand,* and *therefore* connect ideas logically between clauses.

Descartes said, "I think, ***therefore*** *I am."*

He opposed her before she won the primary election; ***however,*** *he supported her afterward in her campaign.*

Swimming exercises the heart and muscles; ***on the other hand,*** *swimming does not control weight as well as jogging and biking do.*

Degree Adverbs, like adjectives, show degrees by the addition of an *–er* or *–est* ending or by the use of *more* or *most* or *less* or *least*. Whether modifying an adjective or another adverb, the words *more, most, less,* and *least* are themselves adverbs.

Conjunctions

Conjunctions join words or groups of words like clauses or phrases.

Coordinating conjunctions (coordinators) join elements of equal weight or function. The common coordinating conjunctions are *and, but, or, for,* and *nor*. Some writers now include *yet* and *so*.

She was tired ***and*** *happy.*

The town was small ***but*** *pretty.*

They must be tired, ***for*** *they have climbed all day long.*

You may take the green ***or*** *the red.*

He would not leave the table, ***nor*** *would he stop insulting his host.*

Correlative conjunctions are conjunctions used in pairs. They also connect sentence elements of equal value. The familiar correlatives are *both... and, either... or, neither... nor,* and *not only... but also*.

Neither *the doctor* ***nor*** *the police believed his story.*

Henry Yip ***not only*** *baked the brownies* ***but also*** *ate every last one of them.*

Subordinating conjunctions (subordinators) join dependent or subordinate sections of a sentence to independent sections or to other dependent sections. The common subordinating conjunctions are *after, although, as, because, if, rather than, since, that, unless, until, when, whenever, where, wherever* and *while*.

Although *the desert may look barren and dead, vigorous life goes on there.*

He always wore a hat ***when*** *he went out in the sun.*

Prepositions

Prepositions are words that, with nouns or pronouns, form prepositional phrases and work as modifiers, often specifying place or time. The noun or pronoun is the *object* of the preposition. In the following sentence the prepositions are underlined and their objects are bold.

Suburban yards ***throughout*** *America now provide homes* ***for*** *wildlife that once lived only* ***in*** *the country.*

The preposition, its noun, and any modifiers attached to the noun make up a *prepositional phrase*, which acts as adjective or adverb. Prepositions allow the nouns or pronouns that follow them to modify other words in the sentence. Common prepositions include:

about, below, including, under, above, beneath, inside, underneath, across, beside, into, until, after, beyond, like, up, against, by, near, upon, along, despite, of, via, amid, during, on, with, among, except, over, within, as, excluding, since, without, at, following, throughout, before, from, to, behind, in, toward

Some prepositions consist of more than one word.

according to, except for, instead of, along with, in addition to, on account of, apart from, in case of, up to, as to, in front of, with respect to, because of, in place of, with reference to, by means of, in regard to, by way of, in spite of

Prepositions usually come before their objects. But sometimes, especially in questions, they do not. Grammarians debate whether prepositions should end a sentence. Most writers favoring an informal style will now and then use a preposition to end a sentence.

Formal: ***In*** *what state do you live?*

Informal: *What state do you live* ***in****?*

Interjections

Interjections are forceful expressions, usually written with an exclamation point, though mild ones may be set off with commas. They are not used often in formal writing except in dialogue.

Hooray! Ouch! Oh, no! Wow!

"Wow!" Davis said. "Are you telling me that there's a former presidential adviser who hasn't written a book?"

How Words Act as Different Parts of Speech

A word that acts as one part of speech in one sentence may act as other parts of speech in other sentences or in other parts of the same sentence. The way the word is used will determine what part of speech it is.

The ***light*** *glowed at the end of the pier.* (noun)

As you ***light*** *the candle, say a prayer.* (verb)

The ***light*** *drizzle foretold heavy rain.* (adjective)

Basic Sentence Grammar

Sentence Structure

The *subject* is the part of the sentence that names what the sentence is about. The *predicate* is the part of the sentence that makes a statement or asks a question about the subject. Every sentence contains at least one subject and one predicate that fit together to make a statement, ask a question, or give a command.

Subject The subject and the words that describe it are often called the *complete subject*. Within the complete subject, the word (or words) that serve as the focus of the sentence may be called the *simple subject*.

In the following examples, the complete subjects are underscored and the simple subjects are in boldface.

*The quick brown **fox** jumps over the lazy dog.*

*The huge black **clouds** in the west predicted a violent storm.*

A *compound subject* has two or more subjects joined by a connecting word such as *and* or *but*.

*Thoughtful **acts** and kind **words** have distinguished his administrative career.*

Predicate The predicate asserts something about the subject. The predicate, together with all the words that help make a statement about the subject, is often called the *complete predicate*. Within the complete predicate, the word (or words) that reports or states conditions, with all describing words removed, is called the *simple predicate* or the *verb*. A verb expresses action or a state of being.

In the following sentences, complete predicates are underlined and simple predicates (the *verbs*) are in boldface.

*The quick brown fox **jumps** over the lazy dog.*

*The huge black clouds in the west **predicted** a violent storm.*

*Thoughtful acts and kind words **have** distinguished his administrative career.*

In a *compound predicate*, a connecting word joins two or more verbs.

*The huge black clouds in the west **predicted** a violent storm and **ended** our picnic.*

Other Predicate Parts In addition to verbs, complete predicates may also include sentence elements that modify, or help describe, other elements.

Direct objects The *direct object* tells who or what receives the action done by the subject and expressed by the verb. Not every sentence has a direct object, but transitive verbs (from the Latin *trans*, meaning "across") require one to complete their meaning. A transitive verb carries action from the subject across to the direct object. In the examples below, direct objects are in boldface; transitive verbs are underlined.

*Catholic missionaries established the **school**.*

*I have read that **story**.*

*We heard the distant **voice**.*

A verb that does not carry action to a direct object is an intransitive verb. An *intransitive verb* reports action done by a subject, but it is not action done to anything. The following verbs are intransitive.

*The ship **sank** within three hours after the collision.*

*She **jogs** to keep fit.*

Indirect objects Sometimes, in addition to a direct object, a predicate also includes a noun or pronoun specifying to whom or for whom the action is done. This is the *indirect object*. It appears after the verb and before the direct object. Indirect objects are usually used with verbs such as *give, ask, tell, sing,* and *write*.

*The tenants gave the **manager** their complaints.*

*Tell the **teacher** your idea.*

*Jack asked **George** an embarrassing question.*

Phrases A *phrase* is a group of related words without a subject and a predicate.

*They **were watching** the game.*

*The child ran **into the lake**.*

Grinning happily, *she made a three-point shot.*

To succeed in writing, *you must be willing to revise again and again.*

English sentences contain three basic types of phrases: prepositional phrases, verb phrases, and absolute phrases.

Prepositional phrases always begin with a preposition and always end with a noun or pronoun that serves as the object of the proposition. The noun or pronoun in the phrase can then help to describe something else in the sentence. A prepositional phrase generally serves as an adjective or an adverb in the sentence in which it occurs.

Adjective prepositional phrase: *The tree **in the yard** is an oak.*

Adverb prepositional phrase: *He arrived **before breakfast**.*

Verb phrases are combinations of verbs including a main verb and one or more auxiliary verbs. Verb phrases also can serve as *verbals*. Verbals include words formed from verbs that do not function as verbs in sentences. There are three kinds of verbals: infinitives, participials, and gerunds.

Infinitives and infinitive phrases The infinitive of any verb except the verb *to be* is formed when the infinitive marker to is placed before the common form of the verb in the first-person present tense.

Verb	Infinitive
go	to go
make	to make

Infinitives and infinitive phrases function as nouns, adjectives, and adverbs. In the sentences below, examine the various ways the infinitive phrase *to finish his novel* can function.

***To finish his novel** was his greatest ambition.* (noun, the subject of the sentence)

*He made many efforts **to finish his novel**.* (adjective modifying the noun *efforts*)

*He rushed **to finish his novel**.* (adverb modifying the verb *rushed*)

Participles and participial phrases *Present participles* suggest some continuing action. *Past participles* suggest completed action. To form the present participle of verbs add *–ing* to the common present form of the verb. (The present participle *being* is formed from the infinitive *to be*.) To form the past participle add *–ed* to the common present form of the verb. Past participles are frequently irregular. That is, some past participles are formed not by an added *–ed*, but by an added *–en* or by a change in the root of the verb.

Verb	Past Participle
bike	biked
drive	driven
fight	fought

Because they do represent action, participles serve in a wide variety of ways. They can be part of a verb phrase. Participles can act as adjectives. In the sentence below, the participial phrase modifies the subject.

***Insulted by the joke**, the team stormed out of the banquet.*

Gerunds and gerund phrases A *gerund* is the present participle used as a noun. A *gerund phrase* includes any words and phrases attached to the gerund so that the whole is a noun serving as a subject or an object.

***Walking** is one of life's great pleasures.* (subject)

*He worked hard at **typing the paper**.* (object)

Absolute phrases consist of a noun or pronoun attached to a participle without a helping verb. It modifies the whole sentence in which it appears. (Including a helping verb would make the participle part of a verb phrase.)

***Her body falling nearly a hundred miles an hour**, she pulled the ripcord and the parachute opened with a heavy jerk.*

***Falling nearly a hundred miles an hour**, she pulled the ripcord, and the parachute opened with a heavy jerk.*

*The storm came suddenly, **the clouds boiling across the sky**.*

Clauses A *clause* is a group of grammatically related words containing both a subject and a predicate. An *independent clause* can usually stand by itself as a complete sentence. A *dependent*, or *subordinate*, clause often cannot stand by itself because it is introduced by a subordinating conjunction or a relative pronoun and therefore the clause alone does not make sense. In the sentences below, the independent clauses are in boldface, the dependent clauses in italics.

***She ran in the marathon** because she wanted to test herself.*

*When we had done everything possible, **we left the wounded to the enemy**.*

Noun clauses A *noun clause* is a clause that acts as a subject, object, or complement.

Subject: ***That English is a flexible language** is both its glory and its pain.*

Object: *He told me **that English is a flexible language**.*

Complement: *His response was **that English is a flexible language**.*

Adjective clauses An *adjective* (or *adjectival*) *clause* modifies a noun or pronoun. A relative pronoun connects the adjective clause to the word it modifies.

*The contestant **whom he most wanted to beat** was his father.*

Here, the adjective clause modifies the noun *contestant*; the relative pronoun *whom*, which stands for its antecedent *contestant*, serves as the direct object of the infinitive to *beat*.

*The computer **that I wanted** cost too much money.*

Here the adjective clause modifies the noun *computer*; the relative pronoun *that* serves as the direct object of the verb *wanted*.

> *The journey of Odysseus,* ***which is traceable even today on a map of Greece and the Aegean Sea,*** *made an age of giants and miracles seem close to the ancient Greeks.*

The adjective clause modifies *journey*; the relative pronoun *which* serves as the subject of the verb phrase *is visible*.

Adverb clauses An *adverb* (or *adverbial*) *clause* serves as an adverb, frequently (but not always) modifying the verb in another clause. The subordinators *after, when, before, because, although, if, though, whenever, where,* and *wherever*, as well as many others, can introduce adverb clauses.

> ***After we had talked for an hour,*** *he began to look at his watch.* (The adverb clause modifies the verb *began*.)
>
> *He ran as swiftly* ***as he could.*** (The adverb clause modifies the adverb *swiftly*.)
>
> *The desert was more yellow* ***than he remembered.*** (The adverb clause modifies the adjective *yellow*.)

Sentence Types

Grammarians classify sentences by numbers of clauses and how the clauses are joined. The basic sentence types in English are simple, compound, complex, and compound-complex. Another classification of sentences is by purpose: declarative, interrogative, imperative, and exclamatory.

Simple sentences A simple sentence contains only one clause, and that clause is independent, able to stand alone grammatically. A simple sentence may have several phrases, a compound subject, and a compound verb. The following are simple sentences, each with one independent clause.

> *The bloodhound is the oldest known breed of dog.*
>
> *He staked out a plot of high ground in the mountains, cut down the trees, and built his own house with a fine view of the valley below.*
>
> *Historians, novelists, short-story writers, and playwrights write about characters, design plots, and usually seek the dramatic resolution of a problem.*

Compound sentences A compound sentence contains two or more independent clauses, usually joined by a comma and a coordinating conjunction such as *and, but, nor, or, for, yet,* or *so*. A compound sentence does not contain a dependent clause. Sometimes a semicolon, a dash, or a colon joins the independent clauses.

> *The sun blasted the earth, and the plants withered and died.*
>
> *He asked directions at the end of every street; his wife sighed in frustration.*

A compound sentence also may consist of a series of independent clauses joined by commas or semicolons, usually but not always with a conjunction before the last clause.

> *They searched the want ads, she visited real estate agents, he drove through neighborhoods seeking for-sale signs, and they finally located a house big enough for them and their pet rattlesnakes.*
>
> *The trees on the ridge behind our house change in September: the oaks redden; the maples pass from green to orange; the pines grow darker.*

Complex sentences A complex sentence contains one independent clause and one or more dependent clauses. In the following sentences, the dependent clause is in boldface type.

Sentence Classification by Purpose

We also classify sentences by the kind of information they convey—by whether they are statements, questions, commands or exclamations. End punctuation helps identify the purpose of the sentence.

Sentence type	Meaning	Example	End Punctuation
Declarative	Makes a statement	*He stopped watching "Law and Order" reruns.*	Period
Interrogative	Asks a question	*Did he stop watching "Law and Order" reruns?*	Question mark
Imperative	Gives a command/ Makes a request	*Please stop watching "Law and Order" reruns.*	Period
Exclamatory	Expresses strong emotion	*I'll smash the TV if you don't stop watching "Law and Order" reruns!*	Exclamation point

He consulted the dictionary ***because he did not know how to pronounce the word.***

She asked people ***if they approved of what the speaker said.***

Compound-complex sentences A compound-complex sentence contains two or more independent clauses and at least one dependent clause. In the following sentences, boldface type indicates dependent clauses.

She discovered a new world in international finance, but she worked so hard investing other people's money ***that she had no time to invest any of her own.***

After Abraham Lincoln was killed, *the government could not determine* ***how many conspirators there were;*** *and* ***since John Wilkes Booth, the assassin, was himself soon killed,*** *he could not clarify the mystery,* ***which remains to this day.***

Correct Verb Usage

Verbs can take a variety of forms, depending on how we use them.

Basic Tense There are three basic tenses in English—present, past, and future.

Simple present The simple present of most verbs is the dictionary form, which is also called the present stem. Usually, to form the third-person singular from the simple present, add *–s* or *–es* to the present stem.

I run	we run	I go	we go
you run	you run	you go	you go
he runs	they run	she goes	they go

The simple present has several uses. It makes an unemphatic statement about something happening or a condition existing right now.

The earth ***revolves*** *around the sun.*

The car ***passes*** *in the street.*

It expresses habitual or continuous or characteristic action.

Porters ***carry*** *things.*

Dentists ***fill*** *teeth and sometimes* ***pull*** *them.*

It expresses a command indirectly, as a statement of fact.

Periodicals ***are*** *not to be taken out of the room.*

It reports the content of literature, documents, movies, musical compositions, works of art, or anything else that supposedly comes alive in the present each time it is experienced by an audience.

Macbeth ***is driven*** *by ambition, and he* ***is haunted*** *by ghosts.*

The Parthenon in Athens ***embodies*** *grace, beauty, and calm.*

Simple past To form the simple past of regular verbs, add *–d* or *–ed* to the present stem. The simple past does not change form.

I escaped	we escaped
you escaped	you escaped
he escaped	they escaped

Sometimes the simple past is irregular. Irregular verbs form the simple past tense not with *–d* or *–ed* but by some other change, often a change in an internal vowel.

Infinitive: *to run*

I ran	we ran	I brought	we brought
you ran	you ran	you brought	you brought
she ran	they ran	he brought	they brought

Simple future Use the helping verbs *shall* and *will* to make the simple future.

I shall go	we shall go
you will go	you will go
she will go	they will go

Traditional grammar holds that *shall* should be used for the first person, *will* for the second and third persons. In practice, this distinction is often ignored; most people write: "I will be 25 years old on my next birthday."

The Three Perfect Tenses In addition to the simple present, past, and future, English verbs have three perfect tenses—the *present perfect*, the *past perfect*, and the *future perfect*. The *perfect* tense expresses an act that will be completed before an act reported by another verb takes place. For that reason, a verb in the *perfect tense* should always be thought of as paired with another verb, either expressed or understood.

Present perfect In the *present perfect* tense, the action of the verb started in the past. The present perfect is formed by the helping verb *has* or *have* plus the past participle.

She ***has loved*** *architecture for many years, and now she takes architecture courses in night school.*

I ***have worked*** *hard for this diploma.*

Past perfect The *past perfect* tense reports an action completed before another action took place. The past perfect is also formed with the past participle, but it uses the helping verb *had*.

I ***had worked*** *twenty years before I saved any money.*

The past perfect, like the present perfect, implies another act that is not always stated in the sentence.

*He **had told** me that he would quit if I yelled at him. I yelled at him, and he quit.*

Future perfect The *future perfect* tense reports an act that will be completed by some specific time in the future. It is formed by the helping verb *shall* or *will* added to *have* or *has* and the past participle.

*I **shall have worked** 50 years when I retire.*

*He **will have lived** with me 10 years next March.*

The Progressive Form The *progressive* form shows that an action continues during the time that the sentence reports, whether that time is past, present, or future. It is made with the present participle and a helping verb that is a form of *to be*.

Present progressive: *I am working.*
Past progressive: *I was working.*
Future progressive: *They will be working.*
Present perfect progressive: *She has been working.*
Past perfect progressive: *We had been working.*
Future perfect progressive: *They will have been working.*

Here are some more examples of progressive forms:

*I **am writing** a new book.*

*I **was making** soup in the kitchen when the house caught fire.*

*They **will be painting** the garage tomorrow afternoon.*

Principal Parts of the Most Common Irregular Verbs Many verbs are *irregular*: their past tense and their past participle are not formed simply by an added –*ed*. If the verb is regular, a dictionary will list only the present form. Form both the past and the past participle by adding –*d* or –*ed* to this form. If the verb is irregular, a dictionary will give the forms of the principal parts.

The most important irregular verb is *to be*, often used as a helping verb. It is the only English verb that does not use the infinitive as the basic form for the present tense.

Common Irregular Verbs

Present	Past	Past participle
awake	awoke	awoke/awakened
become	became	become
begin	began	begun
blow	blew	blown
break	broke	broken
bring	brought	brought
burst	burst	burst
choose	chose	chosen
cling	clung	clung
come	came	come
dive	dived	dived
do	did	done
draw	drew	drawn
drink	drank	drunk
drive	drove	driven
eat	ate	eaten
fall	fell	fallen
fly	flew	flown
forget	forgot	forgotten/forgot
forgive	forgave	forgiven
freeze	froze	frozen
get	got	gotten/got
give	gave	given
go	went	gone
grow	grew	grown
hang (things)	hung	hung
hang (people)	hanged	hanged
know	knew	known
lay (to put)	laid	laid
lie (to recline)	lay	lain

Present	Past	Past participle
lose	lost	lost
pay	paid	paid
ride	rode	ridden
ring	rang	rung
rise	rose	risen
say	said	said
see	saw	seen
set	set	set
shake	shook	shaken
shine	shone/shined	shone/shined
show	showed	shone
sing	sang	sung
sink	sank	sunk
sit	sat	sat
speak	spoke	spoken
spin	spun	spun
spit	spat/spit	spat/spit
steal	stole	stolen
strive	strove/strived	striven/strived
swear	swore	sworn
swim	swam	swum
swing	swung	swung
take	took	taken
tear	tore	torn
tread	trod	trod/trodden
wake	woke	waked/woke/wakened
wear	wore	worn
weave	wove	woven
wring	wrung	wrung
write	wrote	written

	Singular	Plural
Present:	I am	we are
	you are	you are
	she is	they are
Past:	I was	we were
	you were	you were
	it was	they were
Past perfect:	I had been	we had been
	you had been	you had been
	he had been	they had been

Mood The mood of a verb expresses the attitude of the writer. Verbs have several moods—indicative, subjunctive, imperative and conditional.

Indicative mood The indicative is used for simple statements of fact or for asking questions about fact. It is by far the most common mood of verbs in English.

*The tide **came** in at six o'clock and **swept** almost to the foundation of our house.*

***Can** he **be** serious?*

Subjunctive mood The subjunctive conveys a wish, a desire, or a demand in the first or third person, or it makes a statement contrary to fact.

*I wish I **were** a bird.*

*Helen wishes she **were** home.*

*He asked that she never **forget** him.*

*If only I **were** in Paris tonight!*

The subjunctive form for most verbs differs from the indicative only in the first and third person singular. The present subjunctive of the verb *to be* is *were* for the first, second, and third persons, singular and plural.

***Were** she my daughter, I would not permit her to date a member of a motorcycle gang.*

*If we **were** born with wings, we could learn to fly.*

When the subjunctive is used with the verb *to be* to express commands or wishes in the third person singular or the future tense in the first or third person, the verb form is *be*.

*If I **be** proved wrong, I shall eat my hat.*

*If this **be** treason, make the most of it!*

Use the subjunctive in clauses beginning with *that* after verbs that give orders or advice or express wishes or requests.

*He wishes that she **were** happier.*

*She asked that he **draw** up a marriage contract before the wedding.*

In the examples above, a request appears in a *that* clause. Since no one can tell whether a request will be honored or not, the verb clause is in the subjunctive. *Should* and *had* may also express the subjunctive.

***Should** he step on a rattlesnake, his boots will protect him.*

***Had** he taken my advice, he would not have eaten raw cranberries.*

Do not confuse the conditional with the past subjunctive:

Incorrect: *I wish we **would have** won the tournament.*

Correct: *I wish we **had** won the tournament.*

Imperative mood The imperative expresses a command or entreaty in the second person singular or plural, and the form of the verb is the same as the indicative.

In the imperative sentence, the *subject* of the verb is always *you*, but *you* is usually understood, not written out.

***Pass** the bread.*

***Watch** your step!*

Sometimes *you* is included for emphasis.

*You **give** me my letter this instant!*

Conditional mood The conditional makes statements that depend on one another; one is true on condition of the other's being true. A conditional sentence contains a clause that states the condition and another that states the consequence of the condition. Most conditional statements are introduced with *if*.

***If** communist governments had been able to produce enough food for their people, they would not have collapsed in 1989.*

***If** you will be home tonight, I'll come to visit.*

*Even **if** the strike is settled, the workers will still be angry.*

Like the indicative, the conditional requires no changes in ordinary verb forms. Distinguish the conditional from the subjunctive. Use the subjunctive only for conditions clearly contrary to fact.

If the circumstances are in the past, use the subjunctive for conditions that were clearly not factual and the indicative for conditions that may have been true. Use *would* or *could* as a helping verb for statements that give the supposed consequences of conditions that were not factual.

*If he **were** there that night, he **would have had** no excuse.*

He was not there; the *if* clause uses the subjunctive, and the clause stating the consequences uses *would*.

*If he **was** there, he **had** no excuse.*

He may have been there; we do not know. If he was indeed there, he had no excuse. The indicative mood is used in both clauses as a simple statement of fact.

Use the past perfect in past conditional statements when the condition states something that was not true.

If Hitler ***had stopped*** *in 1938, World War II* ***would not have come*** *as it did.*

Avoid using the conditional in both clauses.

Incorrect: *If she* ***would have gone*** *to Paris, she* ***would have had*** *a good time.*

Correct: *If she* ***had gone*** *to Paris, she* ***would have had*** *a good time.*

Do not confuse the conditional with the past subjunctive.

Incorrect: *I wish we* ***would have won*** *the tournament.*

Correct: *I wish we* ***had won*** *the tournament.*

Active and Passive Voice Use verbs in the active voice in most sentences; use verbs in the passive voice sparingly and only for good reason.

The voice of a transitive verb tells whether the subject is the actor in the sentence or is acted upon. (A transitive verb carries action from an agent to an object. A transitive verb can take a direct object; an intransitive verb does not take a direct object.) Intransitive verbs cannot be passive.

When transitive verbs are in the *active voice*, the subject does the acting. When transitive verbs are in the *passive voice*, an agent—either implied or expressed in a prepositional phrase—acts upon the subject.

Active: *He burned the* arroz con pollo.

Passive: *The* arroz con pollo ***was burned*** *by him.*

The arroz con pollo *was burned.*

Readers usually want to know the agent of an action; that is, they want to know *who* or *what* does the acting. Since the passive often fails to identify the agent of an action, it suggests evasion of responsibility.

Active: *The senator* ***misplaced*** *the memo.*

Passive: *The memo* ***was misplaced.***

Use the passive when the recipient of the action in the sentence is much more important to the statement than the doer of the action.

My car ***was stolen*** *last night.*

Who stole your car is not known. The important thing is that the car was stolen.

Scientific researchers generally use the passive voice throughout reports on experiments to keep the focus on the experiment rather than on the experimenters.

When the bacteria ***were isolated,*** *they* ***were treated*** *carefully with nicotine and* ***were observed*** *to stop reproducing.*

Infinitives The infinitive is the present tense of a verb with the marker *to*. Grammatically, the infinitive can complete the sense of other verbs, serve as a noun, and form the basis of some phrases.

The *present infinitive*, which uses the infinitive marker *to* along with the verb, describes action that takes place at the same time as the action in the verb the infinitive completes.

He wants ***to go.***
He wanted ***to go.***
He will want ***to go.***

The *present perfect infinitive*, which uses the infinitive marker *to*, the verb *have* and a past participle, describes action prior to the action of the verb whose sense is completed by the infinitive. The present perfect infinitive often follows verb phrases that include *should* or *would*.

I would like ***to have seen*** *her face when she found the duck in her bathtub.*

An *infinitive phrase* includes the infinitive and the words that complete its meaning.

He studied ***to improve his voice.***

Sometimes the infinitive marker is omitted before the verb, especially after such verbs as *hear, help, let, see* and *watch*.

They watched the ship ***sail*** *out to sea.*

In general, avoid split infinitives. A *split infinitive* has one or more words awkwardly placed between the infinitive marker *to* and the verb form. The rule against split infinitives is not absolute: some writers split infinitives and others do not. But the words used to split infinitives can usually go outside the infinitive, or they can be omitted altogether.

Split infinitive: *He told me* ***to*** *really* ***try*** *to do better.*

Enrique wanted ***to*** *completely* ***forget*** *his painful romance.*

Revised: *He told me* ***to try*** *to do better.*

Enrique wanted ***to forget*** *his painful romance completely.*

Correct Pronoun Usage

Pronouns take the places of nouns in sentences. Most pronouns require an antecedent to give them content and meaning. The *antecedent* is the word for which the pronoun substitutes. The antecedent usually appears earlier in the same sentence or in the same passage. In the following example, the antecedent for the pronoun *it* is *snow*.

The snow fell all day long, and by nightfall it was three feet deep.

Pronoun Reference Rewrite sentences with pronouns that do not refer clearly to their antecedents or that are widely separated from them.

Confusing:

*Albert was with Emanuel when **he** got the news that **his** rare books had arrived.*

Who got the news? Did the rare books belong to Emanuel, or did they belong to Albert?

Improved:

*When Albert got the news that **his** rare books had arrived, **he** was with Emanuel.*

Generally, personal pronouns refer to the nearest previous noun, but don't risk a potentially unclear antecedent. Revise the sentence.

Pronoun Agreement Pronouns must agree with their antecedents in number and gender. Singular antecedents require singular pronouns. Plural antecedents require plural pronouns.

*The house was dark and gloomy, and **it** sat in a grove of tall cedars that made **it** seem darker still.*

*The cars swept by on the highway, all of **them** doing more than 55 miles per hour.*

Use a singular pronoun when all the parts of a compound antecedent are singular and the parts are joined by *or* or *nor*. Notice, too, how the pronouns in the following examples also agree with their antecedents in *gender*, or sexual reference in grammar.

*Either Ted or John will take **his** car.*

*Neither Judy nor Linda will lend you **her** scalpel.*

Antecedents of unknown gender Do not use the masculine singular pronoun to refer to a noun or pronoun of unknown gender.

Awkward:

*Any teacher must sometimes despair at the indifference of **his** students.*

Common Errors in Verbs

	Faulty	Correct
Irregular verbs		
Avoid confusing simple past with past participle.	*I **seen** her last night.* *He **done** it himself.*	*I **saw** her last night.* *He **did** it himself.* *He **had done** it himself.*
Don't try to make irregular verbs regular.	*She **drawed** my picture.* *We **payed** for everything.*	*She **drew** my picture.* *We **paid** for everything.*
Transitive and intransitive verbs		
Don't confuse *lay* (transitive) with *lie* (intransitive).	*I **lay** awake every night.* *I **lay** my books on the desk when I came in.* *I **laid** down for an hour.*	*I **lie** awake every night.* *I **laid** my books on the desk when I came in.* *I **lay** down for an hour.*
Don't confuse *set* (transitive) with *sit* (intransitive).	*He pointed to a chair, so I **set** down.* *She **sat** the vase on the table.*	*He pointed to a chair, so I **sat** down.* *She **set** the vase on the table.*
Tense		
Don't shift tenses illogically.	*The car **bounced** over the curb and **comes** crashing through the window.*	*The car **bounced** over the curb and **came** crashing through the window.*
Mood		
Don't confuse conditional with past subjunctive.	*I wish he **would have** arrived sooner.* *I would have been here if you **would have told** me you were performing.*	*I wish he **had** arrived sooner.* *I would have been here if you **had told** me you were performing.*

Everybody can have what ***he*** *wants to eat.*

Such language, though grammatically correct, is now viewed as sexist. Avoid sexist language by changing nouns and pronouns to plural forms, or revise the sentence in some other way.

Improved:

Any teacher must sometimes despair at the indifference of students.

Teachers must sometimes despair at the indifference of their students.

When referring to the whole, collective nouns—*team, family, audience, majority, minority, committee, group, government, flock, herd* and many others—use singular pronouns.

The team won ***its*** *victory gratefully.*

The committee disbanded when ***it*** *finished its business.*

However, if the members of the group indicated by a collective noun are considered as individuals, use a plural pronoun.

The hard-rock band broke up and began fighting among ***themselves*** *when* ***their*** *leader quit.*

Pronouns without references

Pronouns such as *this, that, they, it, which* and *such* sometimes refer not to a specific antecedent, but to the general idea expressed by a whole clause or sentence. Using pronouns in this way is imprecise and often misleading.

Andy Warhol once made a movie of a man sleeping for a whole night, which was a tiresome experience.

Was the movie tiresome to watch? Or was making the movie the tiresome experience?

"It" as Pronoun and Expletive

The pronoun *it* always has an antecedent; the expletive *it* serves as a grammatical subject when the real subject comes after the verb or is understood.

Pronoun:

In rural America when a barn burns, ***it*** *often takes with* ***it*** *a year's hard work for a farm family.*

Expletive:

In rural America, when a barn burns, ***it*** *is difficult for a farm family to recover from the loss.*

The expletive *it* serves as the grammatical subject of the independent clause that it begins. Avoid using the expletive it and the pronoun it one after the other.

Weak:

What will happen to the kite? If ***it*** *is windy,* ***it*** *will fly.*

Improved:

What will happen to the kite? ***It*** *will fly if the wind blows.*

The expletive *it* does not require an antecedent. But other pronouns used without antecedents are both awkward and unclear.

Some Rules for Using Pronouns

* The subject of a dependent clause is always in the subjective case, even when the dependent clause serves as the object for another clause.

Dr. Hiromichi promised the prize to ***whoever*** *made the best grades.*

Leave the message with ***whoever*** *comes into the house first.*

* Objects of prepositions, direct objects, and indirect objects always take the objective case.

She called ***him*** *and* ***me*** *fools.*

It was a secret between ***you*** *and* ***me****.*

* When a noun follows a pronoun in an appositive construction, use the case for the pronoun that you would use if the noun were not present. The presence of the noun does not change the case of the pronoun.

He gave the test to ***us*** *students.*

We *students said that the test was too hard.*

* *Than* and *as often* serve as conjunctions introducing implied clauses. In these constructions the idea that follows a pronoun at the end of a sentence is understood, not stated. The case of the pronoun depends on how the pronoun is used in the clause if it were written. (Implied clauses are sometimes called elliptical clauses.)

Throughout elementary school, Elizabeth was taller than ***he****.*

The Sanchezes are much richer than ***they****.*

* Pronouns that are the subjects or the objects of infinitives take the objective case.

I believe ***them*** *to be tedious and ordinary.*

* Use the possessive case before a gerund (an *–ing* verb form used as a noun). Use the subjective or objective case with present participles used as adjectives.

Gerund:

His *returning the punt 96 yards for a touchdown spoiled the bets made by the gamblers.*

Present participle:

They remembered ***him*** *laughing as he said goodbye.*

* Pronouns agree in case with the nouns or pronouns with which they are paired.

Compound:
***She** and Carla ran a design studio.*

Appositive: *The captain chose two crew members, **her** and **me**, to attempt the rescue.*

*The last two crew members on board, Carla and **I**, drew the first watch.*

Using Adjectives and Adverbs Correctly

Adverbs and Adjectives with Verbs of Sense

Verbs of sense (*smell, taste, feel* and so on) can be linking or nonlinking. Decide whether the modifier after a verb of sense serves the verb (adverb) or the subject (adjective).

Adverb: *I felt **badly**.* (referring to the sense of touch)

Adjective: *I felt **bad** because she heard me say that her baby looked like a baboon.* (referring to emotions)

Distinguishing Adjectives and Adverbs Spelled Alike Not every adverb is an adjective with *–ly* tacked to the end of it. In standard English, many adverbs do not require the *–ly*, and some words have the same form whether they are used as adjectives or as adverbs.

Words that are both adjectives and adverbs: *fast, hard, only, right, straight*.

Using Adjectives and Adverbs for Comparison

Writers often use adjectives and adverbs to compare. Usually an *–er* or an *–est* ending on the word or the use of *more* or *most* along with the word indicates the degree, amount, or quality.

The simplest form of the adjective or the adverb is the positive degree, the form used when no comparison is involved. This is the form found in a dictionary.

To compare two things, use the *comparative* degree. Form the comparative degree of many adjectives by adding the suffix *–er*, or by using the adverb *more* or *less* with the positive form. Use the adverb *more* or *less* to form the comparative of most adverbs.

Use the *superlative* degree of both adjectives and adverbs to compare more than two things. Form the superlative of an adjective by adding the suffix *–est* to the positive form, or by using the adverb *most* or *least* with the positive form. The adverb *most* or *least* is used to form the superlative degree of an adverb.

Formal grammatical rules reserve the *–er* and *–est* endings for comparative and superlative degrees of adjectives and adverbs of no more than two syllables. Yet common usage for these modifiers of degree draws on suffix endings interchangeably with the forms *more* and *most*, *less* and *least*.

Irregular adjectives and adverbs Some adjectives and adverbs are irregular; they change form to show degree.

Positive	Comparative	Superlative
bad	worse	worst
good	better	best
little	less	least
many/much	more	most
far	farther	farthest

Using degrees correctly

* Do not use the superlative for only two things or units.

Not: *Of the two brothers, John was the quickest.*

But: *Of the two brothers, John was the quicker.*

* Do not use the comparative and superlative degrees with absolute adjectives. *Absolutes* are words that in themselves mean something complete or ideal, such as *unique, half, infinite, impossible, perfect, round, square, destroyed,* and *demolished*. If something is unique, it is the only one of its kind. We cannot say, "Her dresses were more unique than his neckties." Either something is unique or it is not. No degrees of uniqueness are possible. "The answer to your question is *more impossible* than you think," is also wrong. Something is either possible or impossible; it cannot be *more* or *less* impossible.

* Avoid using the superlative when no comparison is stated.

Dracula *is the **scariest** movie!*

The scariest movie ever filmed? The scariest movie ever viewed? The scariest movie ever shown in town? In common speech expressions such as *scariest movie* or *silliest thing* often do not in fact compare the movie or the thing with anything else. In writing, such expressions take up space without conveying any precise meaning.

* Avoid adding an unnecessary adverb to the superlative degree of adjectives.

Not: *She was the very brightest person in the room.*

But: *She was the brightest person in the room.*

Not: *The interstate was the most shortest way to Nashville.*

But: *The interstate was the shortest way to Nashville.*

* Avoid making illogical comparisons with adjectives and adverbs. Illogical comparisons occur when writers leave out some necessary words.

Illogical: *The story of the* Titanic *is more interesting than the story of any disaster at sea.*

This comparison makes it seem that the story of the *Titanic* is one thing and that the story of any disaster at sea is something different. In fact, the story of the *Titanic* is about a disaster at sea. Is the story of the *Titanic* more interesting than itself?

Corrected: *The story of the* Titanic *is more interesting than the story of any other disaster at sea.*

Overuse of Adjectives and Adverbs Too many adjectives or adverbs can weaken the force of a statement. Strong writers put an adjective before a noun or pronoun only when the adjective is truly needed. They rarely put more than one adjective before a noun unless they need to create some special effect or unless one of the adjectives is a number or part of a compound noun, such as *high school* or *living room*.

The ***clean*** *and* ***brightly lit*** *dining car left a* ***cold*** *and* ***snowy*** *Moscow well stocked with* ***large*** *and* ***sweet fresh red*** *apples,* ***many*** *oranges,* ***long green*** *cucumbers,* ***delicious chocolate*** *candy, and countless other* ***well-loved*** *delicacies.*

Improved: *The dining car left Moscow well stocked with* ***fresh*** *apples, oranges, cucumbers;* ***chocolate*** *candy; and* ***other little*** *delicacies.* — Hedrick Smith

Use adverbs in the same careful way. Instead of piling them up, use strong verbs that carry the meaning.

Weak: *The train* ***went very swiftly*** *along the tracks.*

Improved: *The train* ***sped*** *along the tracks.*

Misplaced Modifiers Most adjectives and adjectival clauses and phrases should stand as close as possible to the words that they modify. Misplacing the modifier can lead to unintended, and usually confusing and humorous, results.

In general it is easier to separate adverbs and adverbial phrases from the words that they modify than adjectives from the words that they modify.

Dangling Participles Introductory participles and participial phrases must modify the grammatical subject of the sentence. Participles that do not modify the grammatical subject are called dangling or misplaced participles. A dangling participle lacks a noun to modify.

Incorrect:

Driving along Route 10, the sun shone in Carmela's face.

(The sun is driving along Route 10?)

Using elaborate charts and graphs, the audience understood the plan.

(The audience used the charts?)

Running down the street, the fallen lamppost stopped her suddenly.

(The lamppost ran down the street?)

Revised:

Driving along Route 10, Carmela found the sun shining in her face.

or

As Carmela drove along Route 10, the sun shone in her face.

Using elaborate charts and graphs, the mayor explained the plan to the audience.

or

Because the mayor used elaborate charts and graphs, the audience understood the plan.

Running down the street, she saw the fallen lamppost, which stopped her suddenly.

or

As she ran down the street, the fallen lamppost stopped her suddenly.

Informal usage frequently accepts use of an introductory participle as a modifier of the expletive *it*, especially when the participle expresses habitual or general action.

Walking in the country at dawn, it is easy to see many species of birds.

The statement expresses something that might be done by anyone. Many writers and editors would prefer this revision: "Walking in the country at dawn is an easy way to see many species of birds."

Prepositional Phrases Prepositional phrases used as adjectives seldom give trouble. Prepositional phrases used as adverbs, however, are harder to place in sentences, and misplaced adverbial phrases can lead readers astray.

Confusing:

He saw the first dive bombers approaching ***from the bridge of the battleship.***

The multipurpose knife was introduced to Americans ***on television.***

He ran the 10-kilometer race from the shopping mall through the center of town to the finish line by the monument ***in his bare feet.***

Revised:

From the bridge of the battleship, *he saw the first dive bombers approaching.*

The multipurpose knife was introduced ***on television*** *to Americans.*

In his bare feet *he ran the 10-kilometer race from the shopping mall through the center of town to the finish line by the monument.*

or

From the shopping mall through the center of town to the finish line by the monument he ran the 10-kilometer race ***in his bare feet.***

Clauses A misplaced clause is one that modifies the wrong element of the sentence.

Confusing: *Professor Peebles taught the course on the English novel that most students dropped after three weeks.*

Revised: *Professor Peebles taught the course on the English novel, a course that most students dropped after three weeks.*

Placing Adverbs Correctly Adverbs can modify what precedes or what follows them. Avoid the confusing adverb or adverbial phrase that seems to modify both the element that comes immediately before it and the element that comes immediately after it.

Confusing:

To read a good book ***completely*** *satisfies her.*

To speak in public ***often*** *makes her uncomfortable.*

Revised:

She is ***completely*** *satisfied when she reads a good book.*

or

She is satisfied when she reads a good book ***completely.***

or

When she speaks in public ***often,*** *she feels uncomfortable.*

or

Often *she feels uncomfortable when she speaks in public.*

Be cautious when you use adverbs to modify whole sentences. Some adverbs are much more ambiguous when they modify full sentences.

Confusing: ***Hopefully*** *he will change his job before this one gives him an ulcer.*

Who is doing the hoping?

Revised: *We hope he will change his job before this one gives him an ulcer.*

Confusing: ***Briefly,*** *Tom was the source of the trouble.*

Does the writer wish to say, briefly, that Tom was the

Forming Degrees of Adjective and Adverb Modifiers

Modifier	Positive Degree (One object is)	Comparative Degree (Of two objects, one is)	Superlative Degree (Of three or more objects, one is)
fast (adjective)	*Pia's dog was fast.*	*Pia's dog was faster than Juan's cat.*	*Rebecca's snake was the fastest animal in the neighborhood.*
sophisticated (adjective)	*Joan's analysis of* Moby-Dick *was sophisticated.*	*Joan's analysis of* Moby-Dick *was more sophisticated than Emily's.*	*Joan's analysis of* Moby-Dick *was the most sophisticated in her class*
quickly (adverb)	*Eben ran quickly.*	*Rita ran more quickly than Eben.*	*Of the students in the class, Wilson ran most quickly.*
eloquently (adverb)	*The mayor spoke eloquently in support of the arts.*	*The governor spoke even more eloquently than the mayor.*	*The children's performance spoke most eloquently to support the City Art Center.*

source of the trouble? Or was Tom the source of the trouble, but only briefly?

Revised: *To put it briefly, Tom was the source of the trouble.*

Put Limiting Modifiers in Logical Places In speaking, modifiers can work in illogical places because the sense is clear from tone of voice, gesture or general context. In writing, the lack of logic that results from misplacement of modifiers can cause confusion. Limiting modifiers, words such as *merely, completely, fully, perfectly, hardly, nearly, almost, even, just simply, scarcely* and *only,* must stand directly before the words or phrases they modify.

Confusing: *He **only** had one bad habit, but it **just** was enough to keep him in trouble.*

Revised: *He had **only** one bad habit, but it was **just** enough to keep him in trouble.*

PUNCTUATION

End Marks

Period

Use a period after a sentence that makes a statement, gives a mild command or makes a mild request, or asks a question indirectly. Simple statements end with a period.

Statement: *The building burned down last night*

Mild command: *Lend me a car, and I'll do the shopping.*

Indirect question:
She asked me where I had gone to college and who my adviser was.

Question Mark

Use a question mark after a direct question, but not after an indirect question.

Who wrote Wuthering Heights*?*

She wanted to know who wrote Wuthering Heights.

If a question ends with a quoted question, one question mark serves for both the question in the main clause and the question that is quoted.

What did Juliet mean when she cried, "O Romeo, Romeo! Wherefore art thou Romeo?"

For a quoted question before the end of a sentence that makes a statement, place a question mark before the last quotation mark and put a period at the end of the sentence.

"What did the president know and when did he know it?" became the great question of the Watergate hearings.

Occasionally a question mark changes a statement into a question.

You expect me to believe a story like that?

He drove my car into your kitchen?

Exclamation Point

Use exclamation points sparingly to convey surprise, shock, or some other strong emotion.

The land of the free! This is the land of the free! Why, if I say anything that displeases them, the free mob will lynch me, and that's my freedom. — D. H. Lawrence

Moon, rise! Wind, hit the trees, blow up the leaves! Up, now, run! Tricks! Treats! Gangway! — Ray Bradbury

Commands showing strong emotion also use exclamation points.

Stay away from the stove!

Help!

Avoid using too many exclamation marks.

Commas

With Independent Clauses Use commas to set off independent clauses joined by the common coordinating conjunctions *and, but, or, nor, for, yet,* and *so*.

Her computer broke down, and she had to write with a pencil.

He won the Heisman Trophy, but no professional team drafted him.

The art majors could paint portraits, or they could paint houses.

Some writers do not separate short independent clauses with a comma.

He stayed at home and she went to work.

With Long Introductory Phrases and Clauses Use commas after long introductory phrases and clauses.

After he had sat in the hot tub for three hours, the fire department had to revive him.

If you plan to lose 50 or more pounds, you should take the advice of a doctor.

A short opening phrase does not require a comma after the phrase.

After the game I drifted along with the happy crowd.

In their coffeehouses 18th-century Englishmen conducted many of their business affairs.

Always put a comma after an introductory subordinate clause.

When we came out, we were not on the busiest Chinatown street but on a side street across from the park. —Maxine Hong Kingston

Commas also set off introductory interjections, transitional expressions, and names in direct address.

Yes, a fight broke out after the game.

Nevertheless, we should look on the bright side.

Pablo, why are you doing this?

With Clauses and Phrases That Modify

Setting off absolutes An absolute is set off from the rest of the sentence by a comma. An absolute is a phrase that combines a noun with a present or past participle and that serves to modify the entire sentence.

The bridge now built, *the British set out to destroy it.*

The snake slithered through the tall grass, ***the sunlight shining now and then on its green skin.***

Setting off participial modifiers Use commas to set off participial modifiers at the beginning or end of a sentence.

Having learned that she failed the test, *Marie had a sleepless night.*

We climbed the mountain, ***feeling the spring sunshine and intoxicated by the view.***

With Nonrestrictive Clauses and Phrases Use commas to set off nonrestrictive clauses and phrases. *Nonrestrictive clauses and phrases* can be lifted out of sentences without any resultant change in the primary meaning of the sentences. The paired commas that set off a nonrestrictive clause or phrase announce that these words provide additional information.

My dog Lady, ***who treed a cat last week,*** *treed the mailman this morning.*

In the midst of the forest, ***hidden from the rest of the world,*** *stood a small cabin.*

Setting off a phrase or a clause with commas can often change the meaning of a sentence. In this sentence the commas make the clauses nonrestrictive.

The commencement speaker, who was a sleep therapist, spoke for three hours.

There was only one commencement speaker, and that speaker happened to be a sleep therapist.

The commencement speaker who was a sleep therapist spoke for three hours.

In this sentence, the absence of commas means that there must have been more than one speaker. The clause is restrictive: it defines the noun and is essential to its meaning. The writer must single out the one who spoke for three hours.

With Items in a Series ("Serial Comma") Use commas to separate items in a series. A *series* is a set of nouns, pronouns, adjectives, adverbs, phrases, or clauses joined by commas and a final coordinating conjunction. The serial comma, before the coordinating conjunction at the end of a series, is often necessary to avoid confusion so most style guides recommend using it. Newspaper style, including that of *The New York Times*, often omits the serial comma.

With: *Winston Churchill told the English people that he had nothing to offer them but blood, toil, sweat, and tears.*

Without: *Lincoln's great address commended government of the people, by the people and for the people.*

With Two or More Adjectives Use commas to separate two or more adjectives before a noun or a pronoun if you can use the conjunction *and* in place of the commas.

Lyndon Johnson flew a short, dangerous combat mission in the Pacific during World War II.

(Lyndon Johnson flew a short ***and*** *dangerous combat mission in the Pacific during World War II)*

With Direct Quotations Use a comma with quotation marks to set off a direct quotation from the clause that names the source of the quotation. When the source comes first, the comma goes before the quotation marks. When the quotation comes first, the comma goes before the last quotation mark.

She said, "I'm sorry, but all sections are full."

"But I have to take the course to graduate," he said.

Do not use a comma if the quotation ends in a question mark or an exclamation point.

"Do you believe in fate?" he asked.

"Believe in it!" she cried. "It has ruled my life."

In some cases, a colon can precede a quotation. (See *colons*.)

Parenthetical Elements are words, phrases or clauses that add further description to the main statement the sentence makes. Always set such elements off by paired commas: i.e., a comma at the beginning of the element and another at the end.

Brian Wilson, however, was unable to cope with the pressures of touring with the Beach Boys.

Senator Cadwallader, responding to his campaign contributions from the coal industry, introduced a bill to begin strip-mining operations in Yellowstone National Park.

With Numbers, Names, and Dates Use a pair of commas to separate parts of place names and addresses.

At Cleveland, Ohio, the river sometimes catches fire.

Commas are used to separate the day from the year.

On October 17, 1989, the largest earthquake in America since 1906 shook San Francisco.

No comma is necessary when the day of the month is omitted.

Germany invaded Poland in September 1939.

Some writers use a form of the complete date that requires no comma at all.

She graduated from college on 5 June 1980.

Commas separate digits by hundreds except for years and references to page numbers.

Jackson received 647,276 votes in the 1828 presidential election.

The entry for Tennessee is on page 2304.

Checklist: Avoiding Unnecessary Commas

* A comma should not separate a subject from its verb or a verb from its object or complement unless a nonrestrictive clause or phrase intervenes.

Incorrect:

The tulips that I planted last year, suddenly died.

Revised:

The tulips that I planted last year, which grew rapidly, suddenly died.

* Do not separate prepositional phrases from what they modify. A prepositional phrase that serves as an adjective is not set off by commas from the noun or pronoun that it modifies.

Incorrect: *The book, about terrorists, was simplistic.*

* A prepositional phrase that serves as an adverb is not set off from the rest of the sentence by commas.

Incorrect: *He swam, with the current, rather than against it.*

* Do not divide a compound verb with a comma.

Incorrect: *He ran, and walked 20 miles.*

* But if the parts of a compound verb form a series, set off the parts of the verb with commas.

He ran, walked, and crawled 20 miles.

* Do not use a comma after the last item in a series unless the series concludes a clause or phrase set off by commas.

He loved books, flowers, and people and spent much of his time with all of them.

Three "scourges of modern life," as Roberts calls the automobile, the telephone, and the polyester shirt, are now ubiquitous.

* Avoid commas that create false parenthesis.

Incorrect: *A song called, "Faded Love," made Bob Wills famous.*

Semicolons

Semicolons are punctuation marks stronger than a comma, but weaker than a period. Use semicolons sparingly.

* Use a semicolon to join independent clauses that are closely related in meaning. A coordinating conjunction or a conjunctive adverb may precede the semicolon.

Silence is deep as eternity; speech is shallow as time.

— Thomas Carlyle

In the first draft I had Bigger going smack to the electric chair; but I felt that two murders were enough for one novel.

— Richard Wright

In the first sentence above, the semicolon helps stress the relation between the two clauses. In the second sentence the semicolon emphasizes the connection between the two independent clauses.

* Use a semicolon to join independent clauses separated by a conjunctive adverb, such as *however*, *nevertheless*, *moreover*, *then* and *consequently*. Conjunctive adverbs connect ideas between clauses, but these adverbs cannot work without appropriate punctuation. In these cases place a semicolon before the conjunctive adverb, and a comma after it.

He had biked a hundred miles in ten hours; nevertheless, he now had to do a marathon.

Sheila had to wait at home until the plumber arrived to fix the water heater; consequently, she was late for the exam.

* Use semicolons to separate various elements in a series when some of those elements contain commas.

They are aware of sunrise, noon and sunset; of the full moon and the new; of equinox and solstice; of spring and summer, autumn and winter. — Aldous Huxley

* Use semicolons to separate elements that contain other marks of punctuation as well.

The assignment will be to read Leviticus 21:1-20; Joshua 5:3-6; and Isaiah 55:1-10.

Apostrophes

Apostrophes form the possessive case of all nouns and of many pronouns. Apostrophes indicate omitted letters in words written as contractions. In only rare cases do apostrophes form plurals, so a good rule is not to use an apostrophe to make a word plural.

Forming a Possessive To form a possessive, add an apostrophe plus *s* to a noun or pronoun, whether it is singular or plural, unless the plural already ends in *s*; then add an apostrophe only.

Singular: *a baby's smile, the woman's hat*

Plural: *the men's club, the children's books, everyone's park, the robbers' plans*

Many writers add both an apostrophe and a final s to one-syllable singular nouns already ending in –s and to nouns of any number of syllables if the final s is a hard sound (as in *kiss*). *The New York Times Manual of Style and Usage* recommends this style as well.

*Keats***'s** *poetry, Ross***'s** *flag, Elvis***'s** *songs, the kiss***'s** *power*

However, other style manuals consider *Keats' poetry, Ross' play, Elvis' song, kiss' power* correct.

The *Times* suggests dropping the *s* after the apostrophe if a word ends in two sibilant sounds (*ch, sh, j, s,* or *z*) separated only by a vowel sound: *Kansas' climate, the sizes' range*).

Sometimes the thing possessed precedes the possessor. Sometimes the sentence may not name the thing possessed, but the reader easily understands its identity. Sometimes both the *of* form and an apostrophe plus *s* or a personal possessive pronoun can indicate possession.

*The motorcycle is the student***'s***.*

*Is the tractor Jan Stewart***'s***?*

*I saw your cousin at Nicki***'s***.*

Other Common Uses of Apostrophes Proper names of some geographical locations and organizations do not take apostrophes, even though possession is implied.

Kings Point, St. Marks Place, Harpers Ferry, Department of Veterans Affairs

For hyphenated words and compound words and word groups, add an apostrophe plus *s* to the last word only.

my father-in-law's job, the editor-in-chief's responsibilities

Use apostrophes with concepts of duration and monetary value.

An hour's wait, two minutes' work

To express joint ownership by two or more people, use the possessive form for the last name only; to express individual ownership, use the possessive form for each name.

McGraw-Hill's catalog

Felicia and Elias's house

Felicia's and Elias's houses

The city's and the state's finances

Showing omission In a contraction—a shortened word or group of words formed when some letters or sounds are omitted—the apostrophe serves as a substitute for omitted letters.

it's	(for *it is* or *it has*)
weren't	(for *were not*)
here's	(for *here is*)
comin'	(for *coming*)
you're	(for *you are*)

Apostrophes can also substitute for omitted numbers: *The '50s were a decade of relative calm; the '60s were much more turbulent.* *The New York Times* uses the apostrophe in these dates (1960's, 1970's).

Special uses of apostrophes for plurals *The New York Times Manual of Style and Usage* suggests the use of an apostrophe to show the plural form of an abbreviation, a number or a letter:

two TV's, the new Delta 747's, mind your p's and q's

Many writers, however, omit the apostrophe in these cases.

Quotation Marks

Direct quotations Use quotation marks, and other required punctuation, to indicate a direct quotation. A direct quotation repeats the exact words of a speaker or of a text. Direct quotations from written material may include whole sentences or only a few words or phrases.

James Baldwin wrote of his experiences during his childhood, "The only white people who came to our house were welfare workers and bill collectors."

In writing dialogue, use quotation marks to enclose everything a speaker says. When one person continues speaking, use quotation marks again if the quoted sentence is interrupted.

"I don't know what you're talking about," he said. "I did listen to everything you told me."

No comma precedes the quotation when it completes the meaning of the sentence and the existing initial capital letter in the quotation is made into a lowercase letter:

James Baldwin wrote of his childhood experiences that "the only white people who came to our house were welfare workers and bill collectors."

Indirect quotations An indirect quotation is a paraphrase, that is, an expression in one's own words of the meaning of someone else's words. Do not use quotation marks with an indirect quotation.

Casey said that he enjoyed blowing the whistle more than anything else he did as a locomotive engineer.

Odette asked if she could borrow my car.

Single quotation marks set off quotations within quotations.

What happened when the faculty demanded an investigation of dishonest recruiting practices in the athletic department? The coach at the university said, "I know you're saying to me, 'We want an honest football team.' But I'm telling you this: 'I want a winning football team.' "

Placing punctuation with quotation marks

Convention calls for the placement of some marks of punctuation inside closing quotation marks. Other cases do require punctuation outside quotation marks.

* Periods always belong inside quotation marks.
* Commas always belong inside quotation marks.
* Semicolons always belong outside quotation marks.
* Exclamation points belong inside quotation marks if they are part of the statement or title quoted but outside quotation marks if they are end marks for the entire sentence.
* Question marks belong inside quotation marks if they are part of the question or title quoted but outside quotation marks if they are end marks for the entire sentence.

Enclosing Titles *The New York Times Manual of Style and Usage* recommends quotation marks around all titles and does not recommend italics for any titles. Most writers and publications use quotation marks only for certain titles, such as essays, book chapters or sections, short poems, short stories, songs, articles in periodicals, radio or television program episodes, and all unpublished works. They use italics for all other titles, including books, films, and artworks.

The chapter was called "Another Question of Location."

Robert Herrick wrote the poem "Upon Julia's Clothes."

Special Use of Quotation Marks Use quotation marks to show that someone else has used a word or phrase in a special way that others may not use or agree with completely.

George had the "privilege" of working his way through school by cleaning bathrooms.

For them, getting "saved" is clearly only the first step.
— Frances Fitzgerald

Avoid quotation marks to apologize for the informality of certain expressions.

Apologetic:

Many people in California are "laid back."

You can accomplish great things only if you "keep your nose to the grindstone."

I thought he was "cute."

It is better simply to avoid using slang, clichés, and expressions that call for an apology, and take time to think of a better way of expressing the thought.

Revised:

Many people in California pride themselves on living for pleasure without taking anything too seriously.

You can accomplish great things only if you pay attention to what you are doing.

I thought he was attractive.

But if you have a good reason for using a cliché or a slang expression and are sure you can justify its use, use it—without quotation marks.

Italics

Italic, a typeface in which the characters slant to the right, is used to set off certain words and phrases.

Works of art and literature Many publications use italics for titles of books, magazines, journals, newspapers, plays, films, artworks, long poems, pamphlets, and other short works published separately, and for musical works. (Note that if surrounding text is italic, as here, the titles are set in roman, or plain text.)

Joan Didion, a former editor of Vogue *and the* National Review, *received glowing reviews in* The New York Times *for her novel* A Book of Common Prayer.

Since newspapers use italics sparingly, *The New York Times Manual of Style and Usage* recommends quotation marks, not italics, for titles of works of art. According to the *Times*, names of newspapers and magazines take neither italics nor quotation marks.

Foreign terms Italicize most foreign words and phrases that are either absent from an English dictionary or included but labeled foreign.

> *They are wise to remember, however, one thing. He is Sinatra. The boss.* Il Padrone. — Gay Talese

> *Memphis, in fact, was definitely the mecca, yardstick and* summum bonum. — Terry Southern

Many common foreign words require no italics: rigor mortis (Latin), pasta (Italian), sombrero (Spanish), foie gras (French).

Some foreign words are still borderline, and some writers underline them while others do not. Examples are *ex nihilo* (Latin for "from nothing"), *imprimatur* (Latin for "Let it be printed"), and *Weltanschauung* (German for "worldview").

Dictionaries offer some help. By labeling as *French* a phrase like *mise-en-scène*, for example, a dictionary guides your decision to underline. Some dictionaries have special sections headed "Foreign Words." Others italicize foreign words when they appear. Use judgment about the borderline words. Consider the audience and the expectations that readers may bring to the writing. Be consistent in italicizing foreign words and phrases that appear more than once.

Words used as words Italicize words or phrases used as words rather than for the meaning they convey.

> *And if the word* integration *means anything, this is what it means: that we, with love, shall force our brothers to see themselves as they are to cease fleeing from reality and begin changing it.* — James Baldwin

Letters used alone also require underlining to show italics.

> *The word bookkeeper has three sets of double letters: double* o, *double* k, *and double* e.

Some writers use quotation marks to show that words are being used as words.

> *When I was in graduate school in the late fifties, "criticism" was still a fighting word.* — Gerald Graff

Italics for emphasis Use italics sparingly to show the kind of emphasis desired if the words were spoken. An occasional word in italics helps emphasize a point.

> *That advertisers exploit women's subordination rather than cause it can be clearly seen now that* male *fashions and toiletries have become big business.* — Ellen Wills

In written dialogue, writers may use italics to emphasize words to show rhythms of speech used by characters.

> *The lady, however, regarded it very placidly. "I shouldn't have gone if she* had *asked me."* — Henry James

Other uses of italics By convention, the names of ships often appear in italics, as do the names of air and space vehicles. The names of trains do not. (*The New York Times Manual of Style and Usage* does not follow this convention.)

> *I packed my valise, and took passage on an ancient tub called the* Paul Jones *for New Orleans.* — Mark Twain

Many style manuals also recommend the use of italics for court cases. (*The New York Times Manual of Style and Usage* requires neither italics nor quotation marks for court cases.)

> *In* Brown v. Board of Education of Topeka *(1954), the U.S. Supreme Court ruled that segregation in public schools was unconstitutional.*

Dashes

The dash (–) sets off words, phrases, and sometimes whole sentences so that they receive special emphasis. Think of the dash as a very strong pause intended to give special emphasis to what follows—and sometimes to what comes immediately before.

> *I think this is the most extraordinary collection of human talent, of human knowledge, that has ever been gathered at the White House—with the possible exception of when Thomas Jefferson dined alone.* — John F. Kennedy

> *Coca-Cola, potato chips, and brevity—these are the marks of a good study session in the dorm.*

Sometimes dashes are paired—as in this sentence—and sometimes, as in the sentence above about study in the dorm, they are not.

When used in pairs, dashes serve to separate parenthetical statements more closely related to the sentence than parentheses would allow but less closely related than a pair of commas would imply.

> *What she gets—and enjoys—from me is a youthful perspective.* — Judith Viorst

> *A Wisconsin man traveling on horseback had the lower parts of his boots—brand new ones, be it noted—eaten by wolves, but managed to save his toes.* — Richard Erdoes

Colons

Colons can link independent clauses when the second clause restates or elaborates on the first. In this usage the colon emphasizes the second clause.

Until recently, women in Switzerland had an overwhelming political disadvantage: they could not vote.

Of this I am sure: Martin will arrive late, talk loudly, and eat too much.

Colons provide a formal way of introducing direct quotations. In this usage the colon provides additional separation between the statement before the quotation and the quotation itself.

"Don't speak of it," she said in a reciting voice and choosing her words sadly and carefully: "It was a stroke."
— V. S. Pritchett

Colons usually introduce block quotations, which are set off from regular text by spaces and indents, especially if the introduction previews the quotation.

Dickens had contempt for lazy people. Here is the way he introduces Mrs. Witterly in Nicholas Nickleby*:*

> *The lady had an air of sweet insipidity, and a face of engaging paleness; there was a faded look about her, and about the furniture, and about the house altogether.*

Colons also introduce itemized lists.

During its first four years the Virginia venture had failed to meet three basic needs: political stability, economic prosperity and peaceful Indian relations. — Alden T. Vaughan

By convention, colons separate a main title from the subtitle. Capitalize the first word of the subtitle.

Doing Without: Meeting the Energy Crisis in the 1980's

Colons intervene between Bible chapters and verses.

Young writers should take Proverbs 12:1 as a motto.

Indicate the time of day using a colon between the hour and the minutes.

He woke up at 6:30 in the morning.

Colons follow salutations in business letters.

Dear Mr. Clinton:

Parentheses

Parentheses always work in pairs to set off information that breaks the flow of thought within a sentence or a paragraph. Parentheses enclose material that is not as important as material set off by commas or dashes.

The first money you get for a book will probably be your advance; as a rule, half of that is paid when you sign your contract (or as soon thereafter as the legal department and the accounting department fill out the appropriate forms), and the other half comes due when you deliver a satisfactory manuscript.

When parentheses enclose a whole sentence, a period comes after the sentence but before the final parenthesis.

At another barrier a seaman held back Kathy Gilnagh, Kate Mullins and Kate Murphy. (On the Titanic *everyone seemed to be named Katherine.)* — Walter Lord

A sentence that appears inside parentheses within a sentence is neither capitalized nor ended with a period.

He was trying to memorize Kandahar (that's how he spent the long hours on the flight over), and one thing he knew for sure was that the city had lots of intersections.
— Mark Bowden

But a question mark or an exclamation point may follow a parenthetical sentence within a sentence.

John Henry (did he really swing a 40-pound hammer?) was a hero to miners fearing the loss of their jobs to machines.

Parentheses can enclose many kinds of numbers within a text. In some forms of annotation, parentheses enclose page numbers of a book referred to throughout a paper. Parentheses also can be used for numbered lists.

Stevens writes that the demands of their offices turn the best university presidents into machines (43).

Fernandez insists that (1) *university presidents don't work as well as machines,* (2) *university presidents don't do any real work at all, and* (3) *universities would be better off if faculty committees ran them.*

Use parenthetical numbers sparingly because the numbers interrupt the flow of thought.

Brackets

Use brackets to set off material within quoted matter that is not part of the quotation.

Samuel Eliot Morison has written, "This passage has attracted a good deal of scorn to the Florentine mariner [*Verrazano*]*, but without justice."*

In this sentence, a writer is quoting Morison, whose sentence does not include the name of the "Florentine mariner." The writer adds the name—Verrazano—but places it in brackets.

Sometimes material in brackets explains or corrects a quotation.

Vasco da Gama's man wrote in 1487, "The body of the church [*it was not really a church but a Hindu shrine*] *is as large as a monastery."*

Brackets also surround words inserted within a quotation to make it fit the style or grammar of a sentence.

According to Ann Banks, he said, "I went back to the country and farmed a crop of tobacco with my dad that next year [but] I didn't make half as much as I'd been making at the factory."

The bracketed word *but* makes the sentence read smoothly. It eliminates the need for an ellipsis. (See *ellipses*.)

Brackets may enclose the word *sic* (Latin for "thus") after quoted matter that looks like a mistake. *Sic* lets the reader know that the quotation is presented exactly as it appears in its source and that the writer is aware of the error it contains.

The dean said, "Those kids is [sic] going to get kicked out of school for saying, 'I don't know no [sic] grammar.'"

Brackets are sometimes used to enclose editorial notes, page numbers, or other documentation inserted in a text.

Slashes

As a rule, use the slash only to show divisions between lines of poetry when you quote more than one line of a poem as part of a sentence. Poetry shown as a block quotation replicates the original lines and does not require slashes.

Sophocles wrote of the uncertainty of human knowledge: "No man can judge that rough unknown or trust in second sight/For wisdom changes hands among the wise."

Occasionally the slash shows that something happened over a couple of calendar years.

The book sold well in 1988/89.

But it is usually better to use this wording.

The book sold well in 1976 and 1977.

The book sold well in 1988–89.

Some writers use the slash to substitute for the conjunction *or* or as a marker between the words *and* and *or* when the words suggest options.

The winner will be chosen by lot, and he/she will drive a new car home.

You can buy the toaster oven and/or the microwave.

Most writers however, consider such usage awkward. It is usually better to paraphrase the sentence.

The winner, to be chosen by lot, will drive a new car home.

You can buy the toaster oven or the microwave, or both.

Do not use a slash to show alternative pronouns; it produces a clumsy sentence.

Ellipses

Use three spaced periods, called an ellipsis, to indicate words omitted from a quoted passage.

Full quotation:

In America, which is a successful society, we can all be celebrities in some little sphere, and we are very impressed with ourselves. — David Brooks

Edited quotation:

In his article on what he calls our superiority complex, Brooks argues that in America, "which is a successful society . . . we are very impressed with ourselves."

In general, do not use ellipses to replace words left out at the beginning or the end of a quotation.

Use an ellipsis at the end of a sentence to suggest that the ending of the thought is either unclear or extremely obvious. Add a fourth spaced period for an ellipsis at the end of a sentence.

Oh God, I'm scared. I wish I could die right now with the feeling I have because I know Momma's going to make me mad and I'm going to make her mad, and me and Presley's gonna fight . . . "Richard, you get in here and put your coat on. Get in here or I'll whip you." — Dick Gregory

Hyphens

* Use the hyphen in constructions like *three-mile hike* and *30-car train* and to avoid confusion in words like *re-form* (meaning form again).
* Do not use hyphens in compound modifiers when the meaning is clear without them: *sales tax bill; foreign aid plan; C minor concerto*. But: *pay-as-you-go plan* and *earned-income tax credit*. Hyphens inserted hastily or automatically can be misleading, since the first word may relate at least as much to the third word as to the second. For example: *airport departure lounge; fast breeder reactor; national health insurance*. Also, use no hyphen in these forms: *navy blue skirt; dark green paint*.
* In some compounds, the hyphen should be used to avoid ambiguity or absurdity: *unfair-practices charge*, not *unfair practices charge*. Note the separation of an otherwise solid compound in *small-business man* (not *small businessman*) and *parochial-school teacher* (not *parochial schoolteacher*).
* Never use a hyphen after an adverb ending in *ly*: *a newly married couple; an elegantly furnished house; a perfectly explicit instruction*. But an adjective ending in *ly* may take the hyphen if it is useful: *gravelly-voiced; grizzly-maned*.
* Use a hyphen with the modifiers *ill*(-) and *well*(-) when they precede a noun. An example: *He wore a well-tailored*

gray suit. But omit the hyphen when the words follow the noun they modify: *The suit was well tailored*.

* Some other compound modifiers, typically those beginning with nouns, keep their hyphens regardless of position in a sentence: *They are health-conscious; The purchase was tax-free; The party describes itself as family-oriented; Stylebook editors are awe-inspiring*.

* Use no hyphens in a title consisting of a principal noun with modifiers: *commander in chief; lieutenant general; attorney general; director general; editor in chief; delegate at large; secretary general*. But use the hyphen in a title that joins two equal nouns: *secretary-treasurer*.

* When a modifier consisting of two or more words is bound together by quotation marks, the hyphen is redundant; thus *poison-pill defense* and *"poison pill" defense* are both acceptable, but *"poison-pill" defense* is not. A long phrase serving as a contrived modifier is best set off by quotation marks rather than hyphens: *her "fed up with business as usual" theme*.

* Use the *suspensive* hyphen, rather than repeat the second part of a modifier, in cases like this: *On successive days there were three-, five-, and nine-inch snowfalls*.

* Some house numbers in Queens take the hyphen: *107-71 111th Street*.

* Use the hyphen in a compound denoting national origin: *Italian-American; Japanese-American*. But *French Canadian* and *Jewish American*, for example, take no hyphen because both phrases denote current group membership rather than origin.

Joining Hyphens can join two nouns to make one compound word: *clerk-typist, scholar-poet, composer-conductor, writer-editor.*

Use a hyphen to link a noun with an adjective, an adverb, or another part of speech to form a compound noun: *accident-prone, cat-hater, break-in, first-rate.*

Hyphens also join nouns designating family relations and compounds of more than two words: *brother-in-law, stay-at-home, sister-in-law, stick-in-the-mud.*

Hyphen: Dos and Don'ts

Hyphenate	Do Not Hyphenate
compound adjectives preceding noun: *well-tailored suit; high-quality fabric*	modifiers following noun: *suit was well tailored; fabric is high quality*
after adjective ending in *ly*: *gravelly-voiced; grizzly-maned*	after adverb ending in *ly*: *highly paid job; newly married couple*
to avoid ambiguity: *unfair-practices charge; parochial-school teacher*	when meaning is clear: *sales tax bill; C minor concerto; foreign aid bill*
ages: *a three-year-old; two-year-old baby; eight-to-ten-year-olds*	ages: *She is three years old; they are eight and ten years old.*
colors: *bluish-green; black-and-white movie*	colors: *emerald green; dark red; navy blue; movie was in black and white*
noun+modifier: *tax-free; health- conscious*	noun+modifier: *commander in chief; secretary general*
numbers: *three-inch-high statue; ten-foot pole; 16th-century cathedral; second-best finish*	numbers: *it is three inches high; cathedral from 16th century; 20 percent; 20 percent increase*
three-, five-, and nine-inch snowfalls	*snowfalls of three, five, and nine inches*
nationality: *African-American man; Italian-American*	nationality: *He is African American; French Canadian; Jewish American*
noun+gerund: *A decision-making boss can be difficult.*	noun+gerund: *Decision making is difficult; decision maker*
relations: *great-grandfather; sister-in-law*	relations: *half brother; foster child; granddaughter; stepmother*
vice-chancellor	*vice president*
co-opt, co-worker, intra-arterial, multi-institutional, mid-July, pro-life, re-create, un-English	Close most words with prefixes such as: *ante, anti, co, intra, micro, mid, multi, non, post, pre, re, semi, sub, un*

In general, a compound that would be hard to decipher at a glance should be hyphenated. To avoid incongruity, a compound noun that is ordinarily solid should be separated when the first part is modified by an adjective: *businessman*, for example, becomes *small-business man; sailmaker* becomes *racing-sail maker; schoolteacher* becomes *public-school teacher*.

Modifiers Use hyphens to avoid confusion in meaning with modifiers.

She was a parochial school principal. (meaning that her ideas were narrow)

She was a parochial-school principal. (meaning that she was in charge of a parochial school)

When a compound modifier is formed by an adjective before a noun, it is usually hyphenated: *They wore well-tailored gray suits*. But the hyphen is sometimes omitted when the phrase follows what it modifies: *The suits were well tailored*.

Prefixes A hyphen joins a prefix and a capitalized word.

un-American, pre-Columbian

Some prefixes are attached with hyphens even though the main word is not capitalized.

all-conference, self-interest

Most prefixes, however, are not attached by hyphens. Simply join the prefix to the stem with no punctuation.

antisocial, nonjudgmental, superpower, atypical, postwar, undersea, extracurricular, preliterate

In some cases retain the hyphen to distinguish meanings or aid pronunciation.

anti-inflammatory, re-create

Some proper nouns that are joined to make an adjective are hyphenated.

a Mexican-American heritage, the Sino-Japanese agreement

Some numbers are hyphenated.

30-odd, twenty-five

Mechanics

Numbers

Style manuals have varying rules for when to spell out numbers and when to use figures. Many (including *The New York Times Manual of Style and Usage*) recommend spelling out the first nine *cardinal* and *ordinal* numbers. Some guides call for spelling out numbers up to one hundred and round numbers over one hundred but using figures for 100 and over.

Always try not to start a sentence with a number, but if you must, spell the number out.

Using Figures Use figures for statistical comparisons, quantitative information, dates, times of day, and addresses.

In writing about some subjects where numbers are frequent, write them as figures.

The original plan for the house called for a dining room that would be 18 by 25 feet and a living room that would be 30 by 34 feet with plate-glass windows at each end.

In nontechnical writing, use figures to express percentages, but spell out *percent*.

Nearly 60 percent of those who went to the polls voted to reject the referendum.

Dates that include the year usually appear as figures, but some writers prefer to spell them out.

October 9, 1893	*the ninth of October 1893*
The 1960's or *the 1960s*	*the nineteen-sixties*

Always express the time of day in figures followed by the abbreviation A.M. or P.M. With the less technical forms *in the morning* or *in the evening*, spell out the numbers.

6:00 A.M., 8:15 P.M.

a quarter past eight in the evening

Street and highway numbers almost always appear as figures.

1 Park Avenue

Interstate 80

Abbreviations

As a general rule, spell out most words rather than abbreviate them.

Spell out the names of countries, cities, boroughs, and states and the words *Avenue, Boulevard, Highway, Street, River* and *Mountains* and words like them used as parts of proper names in formal writing.

The Catskill Mountains of New York flank the Hudson River.

Not: *The Catskill Mts. of N.Y. flank the Hudson Riv.*

Veterans Highway crosses Deer Park Avenue.

In addressing envelopes use street and state abbreviations as recommended in postal codes.

Spell out the names of months and days of the week, and spell out people's names.

> **Not:** *In Sept. and Oct. Chas. visits the botanical gardens every Sun.*

> **But:** *In September and October, Charles visits the botanical gardens every Sunday.*

Use an ampersand only if it is part of an official name.

> *The pistol was a Smith & Wesson.*

Spell out the words *pages, chapter, volume,* and *edition* and the names of courses of study.

> *Chapter 16 in the 11th edition of the textbook presents new developments in open-heart surgery.*

> *Freshman Composition 102 is a prerequisite for Communications 201.*

Use abbreviations for *page, chapter,* and *edition* in footnotes, endnotes and bibliographical references in certain documentation systems such as the one set forth by the American Psychological Association. The APA requires the abbreviation *p* (for page) or *pp.* (for pages) in quoting a passage from a source and in citing an article in a monthly or bimonthly magazine on the references page.

Unfamiliar abbreviations Abbreviations may impair readability, since a general audience may be unfamiliar with them. But in some technical writing such as memos or reports intended for a limited audience, you may use abbreviations that are standard to that audience.

> **Not:** *Dr. Ruth and SOL Dean Th. Luciano discussed the std. Rules about hab. Corp. proceedings in the pol. Cts. as they might apply to studs. arrested on DWI charges in the commercial dist. Alg. Mass. Ave.*

> **But:** *Dr. Ruth Smith and Thomas Luciano, dean of the School of Law, discussed the standard rules about habeas corpus proceedings in the police courts as they might apply to students arrested on charges of driving while intoxicated in the commercial district along Massachusetts Avenue.*

Use the abbreviation *Inc., Corp., Co.,* or *Bros.* only when it is part of the official title of a company.

> *Tiffany & Co. sells extravagantly expensive jewelry.*

Familiar titles The general guideline about avoiding abbreviations does not apply to commonly abbreviated titles that always precede the person's name. These include *Mr., Mrs, Ms., Dr., St., the Rev., the Hon., Sen., Rep.,* and *Fr.*

> *Dr. Epstein and Dr. Kwang consulted on the operation.*

> *The Rev. Dr. Karl Barth performed the marriage.*

Many women prefer the title *Ms.* instead of *Miss* or *Mrs.* Strictly speaking, *Ms.* is not an abbreviation, since it does not stand for a word. But it is used in the same way *Mr.* and *Mrs.* are used—before a name. The title *Miss* is not an abbreviation, so it is not followed by a period. It always precedes the name.

Some abbreviations follow a proper name only. Usually they indicate academic or professional degrees or honors. Use a comma between the name and the abbreviation. A space follows the comma.

> *Robert Robinson, Jr.*
> *Kai-y Hsu, Ph.D.*
> *Maria Tiante, M.D.*
> *Elaine Leff, C.P.A., L.L.D.*
> *Michael Bartlett, Esq.*

But spell out titles used without proper names.

> *Mr. Carew asked if she had seen the doctor.* (*not* dr.)

Notice that when an abbreviation ends a sentence, the period at the end of the abbreviation itself will serve as the period of the sentence. If a question mark or an exclamation point ends the sentence, use such a punctuation mark *after* the period in the abbreviation.

> *Is it true that he now wants to be called Stanley Martin, Esq.?*

Acronyms Abbreviate the name of an agency or organization named frequently, to make the repetition less tedious. Abbreviations of agency names that can be pronounced as words are called *acronyms*.

Many government agencies are regularly referred to by acronyms or abbreviations, especially in publications that mention them frequently. Often these abbreviations are so well known that they do not require any explanation.

> *The F.B.I. entered the case immediately at the request of the C.I.A.*

The New York Times Manual for Style and Usage recommends the use of periods in abbreviations when the letters stand for separate words:

> *F.B.I., I.B.M., N.L.R.B.*

However, in acronyms the *Times Manual* omits periods:

> *NASA, NATO*

Broadcasting services, radio stations, and networks omit periods in all their abbreviations and call letters:

> *ABC, WOR, CNN, WNBC*

Other Common Abbreviations Abbreviate words typically used with times, dates and figures.

6:00 P.M. *A.D. 1066* *9:45 A.M.*
6000 r.p.m. *498 B.C.*

Note that instead of B.C., many writers now use B.C.E., "Before the Common Era." If a year stands alone, without B.C. or B.C.E., it is assumed to be A.D., although some writers still use C.E. when clarity requires it.

Latin Abbreviations In text, use English translations rather than Latin abbreviations.

compare	not	cf.
for example	not	e.g.
and others	not	et al.
and so on, and so forth and the rest	not	etc.
in the same place	not	ibid.
that is	not	i.e.

Although current documentation systems for research use a minimum of abbreviations, the short Latin forms may appear in older sources. Check a dictionary for unfamiliar Latin abbreviations.

Spelling

Important Spelling Rules

"ei" versus "ie"

The familiar rule is *i* before *e* except after *c* or when sounded like *a* as in *neighbor* or *weigh*.

In deciding between the combinations *ei* and *ie*, then, consider the previous letter and the sound of the word. When these letters sound like the *ee* in *see*, usually place the *i* before *e*.

believe, relieve, grief, chief, yield, wield

When the letters are preceded by *c*, the spelling is nearly always *ei*.

receive, deceive, ceiling, conceit

When the sound is like *ay* in *bay* or *May*, the spelling is nearly always *ei*.

neigh, feign, neighbor, weigh

Exceptions: *seize, caffeine, codeine, stein, weird, foreign, height, forfeit, pietism, sierra, pierce, pier, pie, pied, fiery, sieve*

Suffixes

Words ending in a silent –e Before adding the suffix *–ing*, drop a final silent *–e* from the root word.

force/forcing, surprise/surprising, manage/managing, hope/hoping, scare/scaring, come/coming, pave/paving, become/becoming, fume/fuming

Exceptions:

dye/dyeing (to avoid confusion with dying)
hoe/hoeing (to avoid mispronunciation)
shoe/shoeing (to avoid mispronunciation and confusion with showing)

Always drop a final silent *–e* on a root word before the suffix *–ible*.

force/forcible

Some roots drop the *e* before the suffix *-able*; others retain the e.

observe/observable, advise/advisable, move/movable (sometimes *moveable*), *argue/arguable, debate/debatable*

knowledge/knowledgeable, manage/manageable, peace/peaceable, notice/noticeable, change/changeable, embrace/embraceable

In the second set of examples, the *e* is retained to keep the soft sound of the *c* and *g*.

Before adding a suffix, always drop a final silent *–e* preceded by another vowel.

argue/argument, true/truly

Words ending in –y When adding the suffix *–ing* to a word ending in *–y*, retain the *–y*.

study/studying, rally/rallying, enjoy/enjoying, cry/crying, ready/readying, steady/steadying, lay/laying

When a final *–y* follows a consonant in the root word, change the *y* to *i* before adding an ending other than *–ing*.

merry/merriment, merriest, merrier
happy/happier, happiness, happiest
rally/rallies, rallied, rallier

To form the past tense of verbs ending in a final *–y* preceded by a vowel, generally keep the final *y* and add the suffix *–ed*.

play/played, dismay/dismayed, enjoy/enjoyed

Exceptions: *pay/paid, say/said, lay/laid*

Words ending in a consonant With most words of one syllable ending in a consonant immediately preceded by a vowel, double the final consonant.

grip/gripping, quip/quipped, stun/stunning, quit/quitting, plan/planned, sad/saddest, scar/scarring

The Hundred Words Most Frequently Misspelled

1. accommodate	51. performance
2. achievement	52. personal
3. acquire	53. personnel
4. all right	54. possession
5. among	55. possible
6. apparent	56. practical
7. argument	57. precede
8. arguing	58. prejudice
9. belief	59. prepare
10. believe	60. prevalent
11. beneficial	61. principal
12. benefited	62. principle
13. category	63. privilege
14. coming	64. probably
15. comparative	65. proceed
16. conscious	66. procedure
17. controversy	67. professor
18. controversial	68. profession
19. definitely	69. prominent
20. definition	70. pursue
21. define	71. quiet
22. describe	72. receive
23. description	73. receiving
24. disastrous	74. recommend
25. effect	75. referring
26. embarrass	76. repetition
27. environment	77. rhythm
28. exaggerate	78. sense
29. existence	79. separate
30. existent	80. separation
31. experience	81. shining
32. explanation	82. similar
33. fascinate	83. studying
34. height	84. succeed
35. interest	85. succession
36. its, it's	86. surprise
37. led	87. technique
38. lose	88. than
39. losing	89. then
40. marriage	90. their
41. mere	91. there
42. necessary	92. they're
43. occasion	93. thorough
44. occurred	94. to, too, two
45. occurring	95. transferred
46. occurrence	96. unnecessary
47. opinion	97. villain
48. opportunity	98. women
49. paid	99. write
50. particular	100. writing

If the root word ends with two consecutive consonants or with a consonant preceded by two consecutive vowels, do not double the final consonant before suffixes that begin with vowels.

tight/tighter, stoop/stooping, straight/straightest, sing/singer, deep/deepened, creep/creeping, crawl/crawler

If the root word has more than one syllable, and if the accent of the root falls on the last syllable, usually double the final consonant.

occur/occurrence, refer/referred, rebut/rebutting, concur/concurring

But if the final consonant of the root is preceded by a consonant or by two consecutive vowels, or if the accent shifts from the final syllable of the root when the suffix is added, don't double the final consonant.

depart/departing, ferment/fermenting, repair/repairing, refer/reference

Spelling varies if the final consonant is *–l*. The increasing preference for the words listed below and others is not to double the final *–l*.

cancel/canceling, pencil/penciling, travel/traveled, unravel/unraveled

Prefixes are letters attached to the beginnings of words that change their meanings. Prefixes do not require changing the spelling or the root word.

appear/disappear   *create/procreate*
eminent/preeminen   *satisfy/dissatisfy*
operate/cooperate   *spell/misspell*
usual/unusual

Before root words beginning with vowels, prefixes ending in vowels sometimes require a hyphen.

un-American   *co-op*

Forming Plurals To show plurality, simply add a final *–s*.

grove/groves, boat/boats, cobra/cobras, bank/banks, scientist/scientists, gasp/gasps

Exceptions based on endings When the singular of a noun ends in *–s*, *-x*, *-ch*, or *–sh*, add *–es* to form the plural.

kiss/kisses, Marx/the Marxes, Mr. Jones/the Joneses, church/churches, dish/dishes

If a noun ends in *–y* preceded by a consonant, change the *y* to *i* and add *–es* to form the plural; if the final *y* is preceded by a vowel, keep the *y* and add *–s* to make the plural.

beauty/beauties, sally/sallies, city/cities, ray/rays, boy/boys, joy/joys, valley/valleys

When a noun ends in –*o* in the singular, form the plural by adding –*s* or –*es*. The best practice here is to look these plurals up in the dictionary.

hero/heroes, solo/solos, tomato/tomatoes, folio/folios, flamingo/flamingos or flamingoes, piano/pianos

To form the plurals of some nouns ending in –*f*, change the final *f* to *v* and add –*es*. If a silent *e* follows the *f*, also change the *f* to *v*.

leaf/leaves, hoof/hooves, knife/knives

Many nouns ending in *f* form the plural by the standard addition of –s

chief/chiefs, roof/roofs

Irregular plurals Some nouns have irregular plurals formed by changes in internal vowels or the addition of endings that don't include –*s*.

child/children, goose/geese, man/men, woman/women, ox/oxen, tooth/teeth, mouse/mice

Some nouns are the same in the singular and plural.

deer/deer, fish/fish or fishes, fowl/fowl or fowls, moose/moose

Compound nouns generally form plurals by the addition of –*s* or –*es*.

babysitter/babysitters, millrace/millraces

But when the first element of the compound is the most important word, –*s* or –*es* is added to it.

attorney general/attorneys general, mother-in-law/mothers-in-law, father-in-law/fathers-in-law, court-martial/courts-martial, passerby/passersby

To form the plurals of many Latin and Greek words with the singular ending –*um* or –*on*, drop these endings and add –*a*.

addendum/addenda, criterion/criteria, datum/data, medium/media, phenomenon/phenomena

The plurals of a few nouns ending in –*is* are formed by changing this ending to –*es*.

analysis/analyses, basis/bases, crisis/crises, thesis/theses

Some words with Latin roots ending in a vowel and an *x* may change to –*ices* when the plural is formed.

appendix/appendices, index/indices (math), vortex/vortices

But –*es* is the preferred ending for the plurals of these words.

appendixes, indexes (book), vortexes

A few English words with Latin roots ending in –*us* form their plurals by changing the –*us* to –*i*.

alumnus/alumni, tumulus/tumuli, cumulus/cumuli, hippopotamus/hippopotami or hippopotamuses, calculus/calculi, cactus/cacti

Even fewer words with Latin roots ending in –*a* form their plurals by changing the –*a* to –*ae*.

alumna/alumnae

Homophones

The source of many spelling problems are homophones, words that sound alike or nearly alike but have different meanings and different spellings.

affect, effect	foreword, forward
all, awl	hear, here
complement, compliment	its, it's
council, counsel	lead, led
discreet, discrete	lightening, lightning
made, maid	sea, see
pail, pale	stationary, stationery
pair, pare	straight, strait
plain, plane	vain, vane, vein
principal, principle	way, weigh
rain, reign, rein	who's, shoes

Commonly Confused Words

✦ It's — Its ✦

it's: it is — *It's too quiet.*
it has — *Tell us if **it's** true*
It's been a week since I saw her.

Hint: *It's* always stands for *it is* or *it has*, and nothing else.

its: possession or ownership by some nonhuman thing

*The Raggedy-Ann doll lost **its** stuffing.*

*As winter approached, the tree lost **its** leaves.*

Hint: Replace *its* with *his* or *her* to see if the possessive pronoun is correct in the sentence.

*The tree lost **his** leaves.*

(His gives the sense of ownership; since trees have no male or female qualities, *its* is correct in the sentence.)

its': This form does not exist.

✦ Two — Too — To ✦

two: the number 2

too: 1. One meaning is "very," "more than enough," "excessively" or "in a great degree.

*The color is **too** dull.*

*My cousin is **too** tall.*

2. Too means "also" as well.

*Let me go, **too**.*

*Will the mayor, **too**, speak at the luncheon?*

Hint: When *too* (meaning "also") is an interrupting word or appears at the end of a sentence, use a comma before it.

*I shook President Carter's hand, **too**.*

to: 1. *To* shows direction. It means "toward," "for," or "at."

*Carry the milk **to** the refrigerator.*

***To** me he is always fair.*

2. *To* is the first word in an infinitive. (An infinitive is the starting point of any verb used in a sentence.)

To run (infinitive) *in track meets, you must begin* *to train* (infinitive) *your legs.*

✦ There — Their — They're ✦

there: a place — Was it there?

Hint: There often starts a sentence. It is sometimes followed by *are, were, is,* or some other verb.

***There** was a good movie at the Rialto.*

***There** are too many books, and there is too little time to read them.*

their: ownership (possession) by a group

*It's **their** car.*

*Was it **their** house that burned?*

they're: they are

Hint: They're always means *they are*. Substitute the two words for the contraction to see if the sentence is correct.

***They're** late again! (They + are late again.)*

✦ Your — You're ✦

your: ownership. It means "belonging to you."

*Is that **your** car?*

*Give **your** husband the car keys.*

you're: you are

*When **you're** out of town, call.*

Hint: You're always means *you are*. Substitute the two words for the contraction to see if the sentence is correct.

✦ Who's — Whose ✦

who's: the contraction for *who is* or *who has*

***Who's** at the door?*

*Tell him **who's** on the phone.*

Hint: Who's always means *who is*. Substitute the two words for the contraction to see if the sentence is correct.

Whose: possession. It asks a question (belonging to whom?) or it refers to some person or thing named earlier in the sentence.

***Whose** dime is that?*

*The man **whose** briefcase was lost offered a reward.*

✦ Principal — Principle ✦

principal: 1. a head person at a school

*The **principal** speaks to the students each day.*

2. a major sum of money

*The **principal** he invested earned $1,250 interest.*

3. a descriptive word that means "most important"

*Rice is still the **principal** food for many people.*

principle: a rule, a major belief, a basic idea or truth

*One **principle** for success is hard work.*

*As a woman of **principle**, she refused a bribe.*

Hint: Principle and *rule* both end in *–le*: if you use *principle*, make sure it means *rule*.

✦ Loose — Lose ✦

loose: rhymes with *moose*. It means "not tight, freer"; sometimes it means "set free."

*A **loose** shoelace is dangerous.*

*You should **loose** the hand brake before driving your car.*

lose: rhymes with *whose*. It means "to misplace" or "not to win or keep."

*If you **lose** the registration form, you will have to pay another fee.*

✦ No — Know ✦

no: negative; not any

*I have **no** information about it.*

know: to understand, to be acquainted with

*I **know** the principles of chemistry.*

✦ Then — Than ✦

then: at a certain time

*The folksinger performed, and **then** we left the party.*

than: a comparing word

*She is taller **than** her brother.*

✦ Lead — Led ✦

lead: 1. rhymes with *weed*. It means to show the way.

*A good instructor will **lead** you to discover important values.*

2. rhymes with *fed*. It is a grayish metal.

*A **lead** pencil contains graphite and no lead at all.*

led: rhymes with *fed*, too. This *led* is the past tense of *lead*. It means showed the way.

*He **led** us through the back alleys of Los Angeles.*

Using Capitals

The First Word of a Sentence The capital letter at the beginning of a sentence signals the reader that a new unit of thought is about to begin. Together with the punctuation mark at the end of the previous sentence, it makes reading easier.

Chile and Peru are squabbling over strong liquor called pisco. Each country claims to be the parent country of the grape-based drink.

In sentence fragments used for special effects, capitalize the first word.

But aside from good hair grooming, they are oblivious to everything but each other. Everybody gives them a once-over. Disgusting! Amusing! How touching! — Tom Wolff

After a Colon Many writers do not capitalize the first word of an independent clause that follows a colon.

It should be clearly understood: facts can change, and new interpretations can, at any moment, alter our interpretations of them.

But some writers do capitalize the first word after a colon.

The answer is another question: How many days must go by before millions of people notice they are not eating?

The New York Times usually does not capitalize after a colon.

The first word in an independent clause following a semicolon is never capitalized unless it is a proper noun.

All in all, however, outside support counted for little; the men of the village did the work themselves.

Proper Nouns and Their Abbreviations Proper nouns are the names of specific people, places, or things — names that set off the individual from the species. Proper nouns include names like *Melissa* (instead of the common noun *person*), *Spain* (instead of the common noun *country*) and *Empire State Building* (instead of the common noun *building*).

Names and nicknames of people Wolfgang Amadeus Mozart, Ella Fitzgerald, John F. Kennedy, Phish, Bugsy

Names of places Italy, the United States of America, the Panama Canal, Back Bay, the North Shore, the Irunia Restaurant, the Sierra Nevada, the Great Lakes

Official names of organizations, organized events, courses The Authors' Guild of America, the University of Notre Dame, Cumberland College, Fort Motor Company, the Roman Catholic Church, the American Red Cross, the NCAA, the N.A.A.C.P., History 351: Old South and Civil War

Days of the week, months, special days Monday, July, Christmas, Labor Day, Yom Kippur, Pearl Harbor Day

Ethnic groups, nationalities, and their languages Greeks, Chinese, Americans, Turks, Chinese, English, Arabic. The words *blacks* and *whites* generally are not capitalized when they are used to refer to ethnic groups, but many writers follow individual choice in this matter.

Members of religious bodies and their sacred books and names Jews, Christians, Baptists, Holy Bible, God, Allah, Hindus, Jesus Christ, Holy Spirit, the Koran, the Torah.

Religious terms Many religious terms such as *sacrament, altar, priests, rabbi, preacher* and *holy water* are not capitalized. The word *Bible* is capitalized (though *biblical* is not), but it is never capitalized when it is used as a metaphor for an essential book.

The Daily Racing Form *was for many years called the* ***bible*** *of horse racing enthusiasts.*

Pronoun references to a deity worshiped by people in the present are sometimes capitalized, although some writers use capitals only to prevent confusion.

God helped Abraham carry out ***His*** *law.*

Do not capitalize pronoun references to deities no longer worshiped.

The Roman god Jupiter led a tempestuous love life that often got ***him*** *into deep trouble with* ***his*** *wife, Juno.*

Historical events, names of movements, and titles of works World War II, the Louisiana Purchase, Impressionism, the Bill of Rights, *Moby-Dick*

Other proper nouns Sometimes words not ordinarily capitalized take capitals when they are used as parts of proper names.

My ***aunt*** *is arriving this afternoon.*
My ***Aunt Lou*** *tells fantastic stories that I think she makes up.*

I graduated from ***high school*** *in 1989.*
I went to ***Lenoir City High School.***

* *Mother, Father, Cousin, Brother,* and *Sister* may replace proper names in speech and writing.

I still miss ***Mother****, although she has been dead for years.*

I asked my ***mother*** *to wake me at 5:00 A.M.*

* Some titles that may be capitalized before a proper name are often not capitalized when they are used after the name.

Everyone knew that ***Governor*** *Cleveland was the most likely candidate for the Democratic nomination.*

The most likely candidate for the Democratic nomination was Grover Cleveland, ***governor*** *of New York.*

Writers and editors do not agree on the capitalization of titles. *President of the United States*, or the *President* (meaning the chief executive of the United States), is frequently but not always capitalized. Practice varies with other titles also: *speak to the Governor, speak to the governor, the President of the university, the president of the university.*

In general, editors and writers are tending to capitalize less, but it is all-important to be consistent.

* Words derived from proper nouns generally keep the capitals of the original words.

Reaganomics, Siamese cat

* When proper names describe or identify common nouns, the nouns that follow are generally not capitalized.

Russian history, French fries, Philadelphia cheese steak

* Brand names and trademarks are capitalized

Apple computer, Band-Aid, Big Mac

* Abbreviations used as parts of proper names usually take capitals.

T. S. Eliot; Sammy Davis, Jr.; Maria Lopez, M.D.

Names of regions Capitalize names of regions if they are well established, like the Midwest and Central Europe, but do not capitalize directions, as in *turn south.*

Months and days of the week Capitalize names of months and days of the week; do not capitalize seasons, such as summer.

Capitalization in Dialogue and Quotations

Capitalize the first word in quoted spoken dialogue.

"Calm down," he shouted. "I spent just 30 minutes learning to drive this motorcycle, and we're already doing a hundred miles an hour."

Indirect quotations and questions require no capitals for words attributed to a speaker or writer.

She said that jazz was one of the many contributions of blacks to world culture.

Capitalize the first word of quotations from printed sources if the quotation is introduced as dialogue.

Jim, the narrator of My Antonia*, concludes: "Whatever we had missed, we possessed together the precious, the incommunicable past."*

When a quotation from a printed source is only an element in a sentence, not a sentence on its own, do not capitalize the first word.

Jim took comfort in sharing with Antonia "the precious, the incommunicable past."

LANGUAGES

Human beings are unique in their use of language. Many other animals communicate by vocal and visual signals; in some (apes, whales, parrots) communication is highly developed. But only humans have the innate, hard-wired ability to employ a large vocabulary of words with a complex grammar to create language itself. Fully developed language is thought to have been an evolutionary innovation of Homo sapiens, separating us from all ancestral human and hominid species and facilitating the spread of our species around the globe.

Languages themselves are highly changeable, in vocabulary, pronunciation, and (more slowly) grammar. Words fall into disuse; others are coined or borrowed; pronunciations change both over time and geographically, as populations disperse. If a population of speakers of a given language becomes divided geographically and the two new populations have little or no contact with each other, in just a few tens of generations their speech will have diverged so widely that it will no longer be mutually intelligible: one language will have become two. The relatedness of the two languages will still be apparent, however.

Language Families

Languages that are related by descent from a common ancestor are said to belong to the same language family. The study of language families began in the late 18th century, when an official of the British East India Company, Sir William Jones (1746–94), noticed that Sanskrit, Greek, and Latin have many similarities in vocabulary and grammar. Jones proposed that all three (and thus all other languages descended from them as well) were derived from an extinct ancestral language, now known as proto-Indo-European. All languages descended from proto-Indo-European are members of the Indo-European language family. As the study of the historical development of languages progressed, many other language families were discovered. Scholars recognized that language families come into existence as populations migrate and become geographically separated, so that their original language splits into new but related languages, which themselves evolve separately and can split and resplit again.

Traces of linguistic relatedness disappear over long periods of time. Few or perhaps none of the language families known at present can be dated back further than the end of the last ice age, some 12,000 years ago. Attempts by some linguists to discover much older "superfamilies" of languages remain highly controversial. Even well-established language families can arouse controversy. Some linguists tend to lump languages together, in part on the basis of common grammar; others, insisting on commonly evolved vocabulary as the criterion for relatedness, tend to split languages into smaller families.

The physical distribution of languages within language families (supplemented now by genetic DNA studies, which generally confirm the linguistic evidence) can be used to trace the movement of populations over the past several thousand years. Examples include the spread of Indo Europeans from somewhere near the Black Sea to India, Europe, and beyond; the spread of Austronesians from southeastern China to Indonesia, and from there eastward to the islands of the Pacific and westward to Madagascar; and the spread of Turks from eastern Central Asia westward to Anatolia and beyond.

Most languages can be can be classified as members of a language family or subfamily. A few (Basque is the most famous example) are linguistic isolates; there are also a number of hybrid forms (pidgins and creoles) that cross linguistic boundaries.

Eurasia

Indo-European embraces about 150 languages spoken by some 3 billion people worldwide; it is the most widely distributed language family, evidence of a persistent Indo-European drive for territorial expansion throughout history. It comprises several subfamilies, including *Indo-Iranian* (Sanskrit, Hindi, Bengali, Sinhalese, Pashto, Farsi, and others); *Italic* or *Romance* (Latin, Italian, French, Spanish, Portuguese, Catalan, Romanian, and others); *Germanic* (Gothic, German, Dutch, English, Swedish, Icelandic, and others); *Celtic* (Gaelic, Welsh, Breton, and others); *Baltic* (Latvian, Lituanian, and others); *Slavic*

(Slavonic, Russian, Polish, Czech, Serbo-Croation, and others); and Albanian, Greek, and Armenian.

Other language families of Eurasia include *Caucasian* (Georgian, Circassian, Chechen, the several languages of the *Kartavelian* subfamily, and many others) and *Uralic* (Finnish, Estonian, Hungarian, and Saami). *Turkic* (Turkish, Uzbek, Uighur, and others), *Mongolic* (such as Mongolian, Buryat, and Kalmyk), and *Tungusic* (Manchu and others) are grouped together by some linguists as the *Altaic* language family, and the Uralic and Altaic families are sometimes combined as the *Uralic-Altaic* language family; but those amalgamations are not accepted by all authorities. Korean and Japanese are sometimes also described as Altaic languages; this identification is highly controversial. Despite obvious similarities and many years of research, no organic link between Korean and Japanese has been proven; some authorities conclude that Korean is linguistically isolated, and Japanese is part of the small *Koguryoic* language family (along with Okinawan and several extinct languages of Korea and northeastern China). The smallest of the world's language families is *Chukchi-Kamchatkan* (also known as *Paleo-Siberian*), comprising five languages spoken by fewer than 25,000 people in northeastern Siberia.

Elamo-Dravidian includes Tamil, Malayalam, Kannada, and other languages of South India. *Sinitic* includes all dialects of Chinese (Mandarin, Guangdong (Cantonese), Min, Wu, Hakka, and others). These are more like independent languages than dialects of a single language, except that they can all be written mutually intelligibly with Chinese characters, which are not closely tied to particular pronunciations. Some authorities combine the Sinitic languages with the *Tibeto-Burman* language family to form *Sino-Tibetan*.

Austroasiatic contains some 250 languages spoken in mainland Southeast Asia, including Vietnamese, Khmer (Cambodian), Mon, and Tai. (Some linguists, however, propose that Tai and closely related languages, such as Lao, belong instead in the Sino-Tibetan family.)

Southeast Asia and the Pacific Islands

Austronesian (also called *Malayo-Polynesian*) family includes several hundred languages spoken in Southeast Asia and the islands of the Indian and Pacific Oceans, ranging from Malagasy (spoken in Madagascar, off the coast of Africa) to Hawai'ian and Maori in the Pacific, and reflecting a strong seafaring heritage. The family is divided into two groups, *Western Austronesian* and *Eastern Austronesian*. Western Austronesian (including Malay, Indonesian, Javanese, Tagalog, and many others) languages are spoken by more than 300 million people. The Eastern Austronesian subfamily is further divided into *Micronesian* and *Polynesian* languages.

Papuan language family of New Guinea (and also nearby island groups of the Moluccas and Melanesia) includes several hundred languages divided into at least six subfamilies. The *Australian* languages of the aboriginal peoples of Australia, isolated from external contact for perhaps 40,000 years, are divided into several families and subfamilies.

Africa

The languages of Africa (and the adjacent Middle East) are divided into four families. *Afro-Asiatic* includes Berber, Coptic, Hausa, and the languages of the *Semitic* subfamily (Hebrew, Arabic, Aramaic, and Amharic). The *Nilo-Saharan* family, found in northeastern, eastern, and central Africa, includes (among many others) Turkana, Masai, Dinka, Mangbetu, Efe, and the numerous languages of the *Eastern Sudanic* (including Nubian) and *Central Sudanic* subfamilies. The *Niger-Kordofanic* family is found widely in west, central, and southern Africa. It has two main branches, *Kordofanic* and *Niger-Congo*; the latter includes the subfamilies *West Atlantic* (Wolof, Fulani), *Gur* (or *Voltaic*), *Mande*, *Kwa* (Ewe, Yoruba, Igbo, Ashanti), *Benue-Congo*, and *Adamawa*. The Benue-Congo group includes hundreds of languages of the *Bantu* subfamily (Swahili, Zulu, Xhosa, Sotho, Setsuana), reflecting a historic expansion of the Bantu peoples southward and eastward from an original homeland in the Congo basin. Finally, Africa is home to the *Khoisan* family, ancient languages (San and others) spoken by peoples largely displaced by the Bantu expansion; these languages are known for their distinctive "click" sounds.

The Americas

The language families of the Americas include *Eskimo-Aleut* (including Inuktatut, the language of the Inuit, as well as Aleut); *Na-Dene* (Athabascan and Navajo); and, according to the controversial theory of the late Joseph Greenberg, *Amerind*, which includes all other Native American languages. Other authorities divide these languages into numerous families (which Greenberg regarded as subfamilies), including, in North America and Mexico, *Algonquian-Wakashian* (eastern and northern woodlands and Pacific Northwest, including Algonquin, Delaware, Cheyanne, Cree, Salish, Nootka, and Kwakiutl); *Penutian* (central and coastal California into Mexico and Central America; includes the widespread Mayan languages); *Hokan-Siouan* (widely distributed, including Choktaw, Seminole, the Iroquois languages, Cherokee, Lakota, and many others); and *Aztec-Tanoan* (southwestern North America and Mexico, including Paiute, Shoshone, Comanche, Hopi, Nahuatl, and many others). The languages of Central America, the Caribbean, and South America are, according to many bewildering and contradictory schemes, divided into dozens of proposed families and subfamilies, the most prominent of which include *Mixtecan* and *Toltecan* (Mexico and Central America); *Cariban* and *Arawakan* (Caribbean); and *Chibchan*, *Ge*, *Quechua*, *Aymara*,*Araukanian*, and *Tupi-Guarani* (South America).

Isolates, Pidgins, and Creoles

A few languages are classified as *isolates*, unrelated to others; examples include Basque or Euskara (a survival from the time before the Indo-Europeans expanded into Europe); the extinct Etruscan language of Italy; Korean; Burushaski, spoken in Kashmir; Gilyak, spoken on the island of Sakhalin off the eastern coast of Siberia, and a dozen or so others.

Pidgins are simplified languages often used for trading purposes between peoples with no common language (the word *pidgin* itself derives from the English word *business*); South China Coast Pidgin is a well-known example. Pidgins can evolve into creoles, independent languages that combine features of two or more parent languages; examples include Jamaican (with English and West African roots), Haitian (French and West African), and Hawai'ian Creole (combining Hawai'ian and English with Japanese, Tagalog, and other Asian languages).

Major Languages of the World Today

Chinese is the native language of more than 1.2 billion people, principally in China, but also in ethnic Chinese communities worldwide. All dialects of Chinese are written in essentially the same way, using Chinese characters (hanzi), which are not closely tied to particular pronunciations. Major dialects include Mandarin, also known as *guoyu* ("national language") or *putonghua* ("ordinary speech"); Guangdong (Cantonese, widely spoken in southern and southeastern China, and in many Chinese communities overseas); Min (Fujian Province, Taiwan, and in Southeast Asia overseas Chinese communities); Wu (Shanghai and nearby regions); and Hakka (southeastern China and Southeast Asian overseas Chinese communities). Chinese is also an official language of the United Nations.

Hindi, an official language of India, has some 450 million native speakers; this number rises by at least another 50 million if lumped together with the similar Urdu (an official language of Pakistan); collectively these and other closely related lanugages are known as Hindustani. Hindustani is also spoken in Malaysia, Singapore, Trinidad, Guayana, South Africa, Mauritius, and other countries with large expatriate Indo-Pakistani communities.

English is the native language of some 450 million people or more in the British Isles, the United States, Canada, Australia, South Africa, Philippines, India, Nigeria, Oceania, many Caribbean countries, and others. English is used as a second language to some degree by another 1.5 billion people; it is an official language of 58 countries and the United Nations.

Spanish is the official language of 21 countries, including Spain, Mexico, Colombia, Argentina, and many other nations of Central and South America and the Caribbean; native speakers total about 350 million, including about 20 million in the United States. Spanish is also an official language of the United Nations.

Malay and Indonesian Malay is spoken as a first language by some 33 million people in Malaysia and on the Indonesian island of Sumatra. Indonesian, closely similar to Malay, is the official language of Indonesia but the second language of most people who speak it—who might be native speakers of Javanese, Sundanese, Balinese, or any of 700+ other languages spoken in Indonesia. About 230 million people regularly use Malay or Indonesian as a first or second language.

Bengali is the official language of Bangladesh, and also widely spoken in the Indian state of West Bengal. There are significant Bengali-speaking communities in Great Britain and the United States. Native speakers total about 200 million.

Arabic is the native language of some 200 million people in North Africa and the Middle East, and, as the language of the Koran is studied throughout the Islamic world. It is an official language of the United Nations and of 25 countries worldwide.

Portuguese is spoken by only 10 million people in Portugal, but by about 160 million more in eight additional countries and territories where it is an official language: Brazil; Angola and four other countries in Africa; East Timor, an island Southeast Asia; and the special administrative region of Macau, on the southeastern coast of China.

Russian is the native language of about 160 million people. It is the official language of Russia and Belarus (together 130 million native speakers), and widely used also in Ukraine (17 million) and Kazakhstan (8 million), as well as Uzbekistan, Kyrgyzstan, and Moldova; it is an official language of the United Nations.

Japanese is the official language of Japan, where it is spoken by more than 125 million people. Significant Japanese-speaking populations are also found in Brazil and the United States.

German is an official language of six European countries (Germany, Austria, Switzerland, Luxembourg, Liechtenstein, and Belgium); there are sizable German-speaking populations in Poland, Russia, Brazil, and the United States. Native speakers total nearly 120 million.

Turkish Standard (Anatolian) Turkish, plus closely related dialects and languages including Azeri, Kyrgyz, Kazakh, Türkmen, Tartar, Uighur, and Uzbek, have approximately 120 million native speakers. Turkish languages are spoken across a huge span of central Eurasia, including Turkey, Azerbaijan, Kazakhstan, Kyrgyzstan, Turkmenistan, Uzbekistan, and the province of Xinjiang in northwestern China. There are significant Turkish-speaking populations in Iran, Russia, Germany, and the United States.

French has some 90 million native speakers in France, Switzerland, Belgium, Canada, Ivory Coast, Congo, Cameroon, Madagascar, and in French overseas territories and possessions from Martinique to New Caledonia. It is widely used as a second language, especially in West Africa. French is an official language of the United Nations, and of 32 countries.

Vietnamese is spoken primarily in Vietnam, with sizable Vietnamese-speaking populations in the neighboring countries of Cambodia and Laos, as well as in the United States. Native speakaers total about 80 million people.

Korean is spoken primarily in North and South Korea, with significant Korean-speaking populations in Japan, Russia, China, and the United States. Native speakers total about 72 million people.

Tamil is the principal language of the province of Tamil Nadu, in southeastern India; it is also spoken by a large minority population of Sri Lanka, concentrated in the northern and eastern parts of that country. There are about 66 million native speakers of Tamil.

Persian includes Farsi, the official language of Iran, plus the closely related languages of Tajik (Tajikistan and parts of Afghanistan) and Dari (spoken by nearly half the population of Afghanistan). There are about 55 million native speakers of various dialects of Persian.

CROSSWORD PUZZLES

How to Solve *The New York Times* Crossword Puzzle

By Will Shortz

A crossword puzzle is a battle between the puzzle maker and editor on one side and the solver on the other. But in this battle, unlike most battles, both sides have the same goal—for the solver to win. A perfect puzzle may put up lots of resistance. It may, in fact, seem impossible at first. Ideally, though, in the end the solver should triumph and think, Oh, how clever I am!

The perfect level of difficulty, of course, differs from person to person. This is why, as editor, I vary the difficulty of the weekday *Times* crossword from easy-medium on Monday up to what the actor and puzzle aficionado Paul Sorvino calls "the bitch mother of all crosswords" on Saturday. (He said this as a compliment.) The goal is to have something for everyone. I advise new solvers to begin on Monday and see how far through the week they can go. The *Sunday Times* puzzle, while larger than its weekday counterpart, averages only Thursday-plus in difficulty.

Step 1 in solving any crossword is to begin with the answers you're surest of and build from there. The fill-in-the-blank clues are easy to spot and often the easiest to solve. Focus in the early stages on the three-, four-, and five-letter words, because the English language has relatively few of these, and the same ones tend to repeat a lot in puzzles. This is especially so for vowel-heavy words like ALEE, IOTA, EEL, AGO, OREO, etc. Watch for the celebrity names (UMA, ARTE, ENO, AGEE) and geographical names (ADA, AMES, ELON, ORONO) that crop up with unusual frequency. Once you have a few crossing letters in the longer answers, you'll be more likely to get them from their clues.

Don't be afraid to guess. At the same time, don't be afraid to erase an answer that isn't working out. For the clue "Butcher's offering," I once watched a solver successively guess T-BONE, CHUCK, and STEAK before finally hitting upon the correct answer, SHANK. Don't assume that because you have a few crossing letters your answer is necessarily correct. And if nothing seems to cross the answer you have filled in, be very wary.

Mental flexibility is a great asset in solving crosswords. Let your mind wander. The clue "Present time" might suggest NOWADAYS, but in a different sense it might lead to the answer YULETIDE. Similarly, "Life sentences" could be OBIT; "Inside shot" is X-RAY; and my all-time favorite clue, "It turns into a different story" (15 letters), results in the phrase SPIRAL STAIRCASE.

The *New York Times* crossword has not printed hints like "2 wds." and "3 wds." since the early 1950's, so be on your toes for multiword answers. One answer that always seems to trip solvers up is R-A-N-D-R, which was clued as "Leave time?" when it first appeared in a *Times* puzzle several years ago. Afterward lots of solvers called and wrote me saying that they couldn't find the word RANDR in their dictionaries, and where did I get it? I had to inform them gently that the answer was three words, R AND R, as in the time when one goes on leave.

A question mark at the end of a clue can mean several things. In the above clue for R AND R, it means "This clue is tricky! Be careful!" It can also indicate that the answer only loosely fits the clue. For example, "Cause for a head-slap?" (BONER). Making a boner may or may not be cause for slapping one's forehead. When question marks appear at the ends of the clues for all the long answers in a puzzle, usually the marks are signals for related puns.

No matter how tricky or misleading the clues, they will always follow a fairly strict set of rules. Most important, a clue and its answer will always be expressed in the same part of speech and as a rule must be interchangeable in a sentence, with the same meaning each way.

If a crossword answer is not a Standard English word, the clue will usually signal this fact. Thus, a slangy answer will have a slangy clue. The clue for an abbreviated answer will contain the tag "Abbr." or else a word that is not usually abbreviated ("Entrepreneur's deg." = M.B.A.). Similarly, words that are strictly foreign will be signaled either directly ("Boy: Sp." = NINO) or indirectly ("Son, in Sonora"). By convention, diacritical marks are ignored in American crosswords, so don't worry about that tilde in "niño."

True crossword cognoscenti observe the bylines on the crosswords and prepare themselves accordingly. Cathy Millhauser, a frequent *Times* constructor, is famous for puns. In a puzzle called "M-M-M" she changed N sounds to M's at the end of familiar phrases, like SAVINGS AND LOAM, AMERICA ON-LIME and AS CRAZY AS A LOOM. Knowing her tendencies helps you nail one or two of the long puns, and you have a big advantage in getting the others.

The constructor's age is sometimes reflected in a puzzle. The late Frances Hansen, one of *The Times*'s longest-running crossword contributors, produced elegant grids full of classical knowledge, while Brendan Emmett Quigley, 26, a guitarist for a rock band in Boston, conveys a younger, more pop-cultured sensibility.

If you get stuck on a puzzle, a time-honored technique is to put it aside and return later. Perhaps the brain works subconsciously on problems in the interim. Whatever the case, a fresh look at a tough puzzle almost always brings new answers.

A question I am asked often is this: "Is it cheating to use references?" In reply I always quote Will Weng, one of my predecessors as *Times* crossword editor: "It's your puzzle. Solve it any way you want." And is it cheating to call *The Times*'s 900 number to get answers? Well, of course! But what nobody knows won't hurt you.

Concise Crossword Dictionary

by Will Shortz

By their nature crossword puzzles tend to have shorter, more vowel-heavy words than the English language does as a whole. Short words are necessary to make the vocabulary in the grid interlock. And though most modern crosswords eschew obscurity, even well-made puzzles, by necessity, may have a few answers that ordinary people have never heard of. Below is a list of almost 600 short, difficult words that often appear in crosswords (words like these are sometimes called "crosswordese"), along with common clues that are used for them. The great majority of words in crosswords are ones you already know. Memorizing this modest list of rare but frequently encountered puzzle words will instantly make you a substantially better solver.

AAR — Swiss river (also AARE)
ABBE — French cleric
ABELE — White poplar
ABIES — "____ Irish Rose"
ABRI — Hillside shelter
ACER — Maple genus
ACIS — Galatea's beloved
ACTA — Recorded proceedings
ADA — City in Oklahoma
ADAK — Alaskan island
ADANO — Hersey's "A Bell for ____"
ADAR — Jewish month
ADE — Fruit drink; humorist George
ADIT — Mine entrance
ADZ — Shaping tool (also ADZE)
AEDES — Mosquito genus
AERIE — Eagle's nest (also AERY)
AESIR — Pantheon in Norse mythology
AGA — Turkish leader (also AGHA)
AGANA — Guam's capital, old-style
AGAR — Culture medium; journalist-writer Herbert
AGEE — Writer James
AGIO — Currency exchange premium
AGON — Literary conflict; Stravinsky ballet
AGORA — Ancient Greek marketplace
AGRA — Taj Mahal city
AGUE — Chills and fever
AINU — Japanese aborigine
AIRE — River in Yorkshire
AISNE — French river
AIT — River island
ALAE — Winglike part
ALAI — Kyrgyzstan's ____ Mountains; jai ____
ALAR — Winged; banned apple spray
ALB — Church vestment
ALEE — Toward shelter
ALETA — Prince Valiant's wife
ALGA — Tiny pond plant
ALOP — Askew
ALOU — Baseball family name
ALTAI — Asia's ____ Mountains
ALUM — Astringent; graduate, for short

ALVA Thomas Edison's middle name
AMAH Oriental nurse
AMATI Italian violinmaker
AMES Iowa university town; singer Ed
A MOI Belonging to me, in France
AMUR River in northeastern Asia
ANA Literary collection; Santa ____
ANAIS Diarist Nin
ANI Black cuckoo
ANIL Indigo-yielding plant
ANILE Old-womanish
ANION Negatively charged particle
ANO Year in Spain
ANOA Celebes ox
ANSA Looped handle
ANTA Theater group
ANYA Author Seton
APIA Samoa's capital
APIS Sacred bull of ancient Egypt
APOD Footless animal
APSE Church recess
ARA Southern constellation; coach Parseghian
ARAL Asia's ____ Sea
ARAM Composer Khachaturian
ARAN Ireland's ____ Islands
ARECA Betel palm
ARETE Mountain rdge
ARI Shipping magnate Onassis; former White House spokesman Fleischer
ARIL Seed covering
ARON Elvis Presley's middle name
ARRAS Tapestry
ARTEL Old Soviet peasants' cooperative
ARUM Calla lily family
ASANA Yoga position
ASE Peer Gynt's mother; enzyme suffix
ASOR Ancient Hebrew musical instrument
ASSAI Very, in music
ASSAM State in northeastern India
ASTA Nick and Nora Charles's dog in *The Thin Man*
ASTI Italian wine region
ATLE Tamarisk salt tree
ATLI Norse king
ATON Egyptian solar diety (also ATEN)
ATRI Italian bell town
ATTU Westernmost of the Aleutian Islands
AUDE French river
AUGER Hole-boring tool
AVAL Grandparental
AWN Grain bristle
AXEL Skater's jump
AXIL Leaf angle
AXON Nerve-cell process
AYIN Hebrew letter
AYN Author Rand
BAHT Thai money
BEDE "Venerable" monk
BELEM Brazilian city
BEY Governor in the Ottoman Empire
BOLA Gaucho's weapon
BOLO Philippine knife; ____ tie
BRAE Scottish hillside
BREN Clip-fed machine gun
CAEN Normandy city
CANA Where Jesus performed his first miracle
CANEA Former capital of Crete
CARIB West Indies native
CHA Oriental tea
CEBU Philippine island
CERE Cover with wax: Obs.
CERES Goddess of agriculture; largest asteroid
CLIO Muse of history
COHO Great Lakes salmon
COIR Coconut fiber
CONTE French story
COR Heart
COS Type of lettuce; business grps.
CREE Algonquian Indian
CREEL Fisher's basket
DACE Carplike fish
DADA Art movement
DADO Part of a pedestal
DAG Former U.N. Secretary General ____ Hammarskjöld
DAIL Irish parliament
DEE Scottish river; actress Ruby or Sandra
DELE Remove, to a typesetter
DENE Sand hill
DEVA Hindu deity
DEY Former Algerian ruler; actress Susan
DIDO Queen of Carthage; prank
DOGE Old Venetian magistrate
DREI German four
DUMA Russian legislature
DYAD Pair
DYNE Unit of force

EBON Black, in poetry
EBRO Spanish river
ECCE Behold, in old Rome
ECLAT Brilliant display
ECOLE French place of learning
ECRU Beige
ECTO Outer: Prefix
ECU Old French coin
EDA Author LeShan
EDDA Icelandic literary work
EDE Dutch city
EDEMA Swelling
EDER German river
EDH Old English letter (also ETH)
EDIE Singer Adams
EDILE Old Roman magistrate
EDO Former name of Tokyo
EDOM Biblical country
EER Always, in poetry
EERO Architect Saarinen
EFT Young newt
EGER German river
EGIS Protection (also AEGIS)
EIN German article (also EINE)
EIS Frozen water: Ger.
E LA Guido's note
ELAM Biblical kingdom
ELATER Click beetle
ELATH Israeli port on the Gulf of Aqaba (also ELAT, EILAT)
ELBA Island of Napoleon's exile
ELBE German river
ELD Antiquity
ELEA Zeno of ____
ELEMI Fragrant resin
ELEVE French student
ELI Biblical high priest
ELIA Charles Lamb's pen name
ELIS Home of the ancient Olympics; Yale students
ELL Building wing; pipe joint
ELOI *The Time Machine* people
ELON North Carolina university
ELS Overhead trains; golfer Ernie
ELSA *Born Free* lioness; Lohengrin's love
ELUL Jewish month
ELVER Young eel
ELY English cathedral town; Tarzan player Ron
EME Scottish uncle
EMIR Mideast leader (also EMEER, AMIR, AMEER)
EMO Comic Philips
EMS German spa; type widths
ENA Bambi's aunt; Alfonso's queen
ENERO January: Sp.
ENG Chang's conjoined twin; H.S. class
ENID City in Oklahoma; Arthurian lady; author Bagnold
ENNA Sicilian city
ENNS Austrian river
ENO Rock musician Brian
ENOL Organic compounds
ENOS Son of Seth
ENS Type widths; nav. officer
ENTO Inner: Prefix
ENYO Ares' mother
EOS Greek goddess of the dawn
EOSIN Rose-colored dye
EPEE Fencing sword
EPHAH Hebrew measure
EPI Finial ornament; prefix with center
EPODE Lyric poem
EPOS Grand poetry
ERATO Muse of lyric poetry
ERDA Norse earth goddess
ERE Before
ERG Energy unit
ERGOT Plant fungus
ERI Silkworm (also ERIA); "____ Tu" (aria)
ERIS Goddess of discord
ERN Sea eagle (also ERNE)
EROS Greek god of love
ERS Bitter vetch; hesitation sounds
ERSE Scottish Gaelic
ESAU Twin brother of Jacob
ESKER Glacial ridge
ESNE Anglo-Saxon slave
ESS Double curve; feminine suffix
ESSE Existence
ESSENE Dead Sea scrolls writer
ESTE Italian commune; Renaissance family name
ESTER Organic compounds
ESTES ____ Park, Colo.; Sen. Kefauver
ESTOP Prevent by law
ETAH Greenland settlement
ET AL And others: Lat.
ETAPE Public warehouse

ETE French summer
ETNA Sicilian volcano
ETO W.W. II zone: Abbr.
ETON English college; type of jacket or collar
ETTA Singer James or Jones
ET TU "____, Brute!"
ETUDE Practice piece in music
ETUI Needle case
EVOE Bacchanalian cry
EWER Pitcher
EXE River in Devon
FALA F.D.R.'s dog
FARO Card game
FRA Monk
GAEA Mother of the Titans
GAM Attractive leg, slangily; school of whales
GAR Needlefish
GARE Railway station: Fr.
GASPE Canadian peninsula
GAT Gangster's gun
GHEE Liquid butter, in India
GNAR Snarl, growl
GNU African antelope
GOA Former Portuguese colony in India
HARI W.W. I spy Mata ____
HEBE Greek goddess of youth
HEL Loki's daughter
HEMO Blood: Prefix (also HEMA)
HEART Afghanistan city
HESSE German state; *Steppenwolf* author
HOREB Biblical mountain
IAGO *Othello* villain
IAMB Verse foot
IBEX Wild goat
IBO Nigerian tribesman
ICI Here: Fr.
IDA Mountain on Crete
IDEO Thought: Prefix
IGLU Eskimo home: Var.
ILA Dockworkers' org.
ILE ____ de France
ILIA Hip bones
ILO Worldwide workers' grp.
INEE Arrow poison
INGE Dramatist William
INO Daughter of Cadmus, in Greek mythology
IN RE Concerning
IOLA Kansas town
IOLE Hercules' captive
IONA Scottish isle; New Rochelle college
IONIA Asia Minor district
IPSE ____ dixit
IRADE Muslim decree
ISAK Author Dinesen
ISER Czech river
ISERE French river
ISSEI Japanese-American
ISTLE Rope fiber
ITEA Virginia willow
ITER Roman road
ITO Japanese statesman; Simpson judge Lance
IYAR Hebrew month
JETE Ballet jump
KEIL German canal
KEPI Military cap
KOLA Nut with caffeine
KRAAL Enclosure for cattle in South Africa
KRONA Icelandic money
KUDU African antelope
LAC Resin in sealing wax; Fond du ____, Wis.
LAE New Guinea port
LAIC Secular
LAR Roman household god
LEA Meadow
LEDA Mother of Castor and Pollux
LEHR Glassmaker's oven
LEK Albanian money
LEN Author Deighton
LENA Russian river; singer Horne
LENE Smooth sound
LER Celtic god of the sea
LETO Apollo's mother
LETT Native of Latvia
LEU Romanian money
LEV Bulgarian coin
LEVI Jacob's son
LEYTE Philippine island
LIANA Tropical climbing plant (also LIANE)
LIRA Turkish money; former Italian currency
LIS French flower
LOBO Timber wolf
LODI Town in New Jersey or California
LOKI Mischief-making Norse god
LST W.W. II craft: Abbr.
LYS French/Belgian river
MAKO Variety of shark

MARL	Crumbly soil
MARU	Japanese ship name
MEDE	Ancient Persian
MENE	Part of writing on a wall, in Daniel
MERL	Blackbird
MHO	Unit of electrical conductance
MIL	Wire measure
MISE	____ en scene (the staging of a play)
MITER	Bishop's headdress
MOA	Extinct flightless bird
MORO	Philippine tribesman; 1960's-70's Italian P.M. Aldo ____
NACRE	Mother-of-pearl
NAE	Scottish refusal
NAHA	Okinawa port
NAIAD	Water nymph
NANA	Zola novel; child's caretaker
NARD	Aromatic plant that yields an ointment
NEB	Bird's beak
NEBO	Biblical mount
NEE	Born: Fr.
NEF	Ship clock
NENE	Hawaiian goose
NESS	Headland; Eliot in *The Untouchables*
NEVA	Leningrad's river
NEVE	Glacial snowfield; actress Campbell
NEY	Napoleon's marshal at Waterloo
NEZ	____ Percé Indians; pince-____
NIB	Pen point
NIDE	Brood of pheasants
NIDI	Nests of eggs
NIPA	East Indian palm
NISAN	Hebrew month
NISI	Not yet final, at law
NOH	Japanese drama
NONES	Canonical hour
NORIA	Waterwheel
NORN	One of the three Norse Fates
OAST	Kiln
OBE	British award: Abbr.
OBEAH	Witchcraft
OBI	Japanese sash
OBOL	Ancient Greek coin
OCA	Edible root in South America
ODA	Harem room
ODEA	Concert halls
ODER	German-Polish border river
ODETS	Playwright Clifford
ODIN	Supreme Norse deity
OGEE	Double curve, in molding
OHM	Unit of resistance
OISE	River of France
OKA	Russian river
OKAPI	Relative of the giraffe
OKIE	Migratory Dust Bowl worker
OLAND	Warner ____, Charlie Chan portrayer
OLID	Foul-smelling
OLIO	Medley
OLLA	Earthenware jar
OLOR	Swan genus
OMAR	Persian poet and mathematician
OMER	Ancient Hebrew measure
OMOO	Melville novel
OMRI	Ahab's father; actor Katz
ONDE	French wave
ONER	Unique person or thing
OONA	Mrs. Charlie Chaplin
OPA	W.W. II ration board agcy.; ____-Locka, Fla.
OPAH	Colorful moonfish
OPE	Unlock: Poetic
OPS	Roman goddess of plenty; photo ____
ORA	Mouths
ORAN	Algerian port
ORCA	Killer whale
ORD	California's Fort ____
ORDO	Church calendar
OREL	Russian city; pitcher Hershiser
ORIEL	Bay window
ORLE	Heraldic bearing
ORNE	French department
ORO	Spanish gold
ORONO	Maine university town
ORT	Table scrap
OSAR	Glacial ridge
OSIER	Willow
OSS	C.I.A. predecessor
OSSA	Greek mountain
OSTIA	Port of ancient Rome
OTHO	Holy Roman emperor
OTIC	Ear-related
OTO	Oklahoma tribe (also OTOE)
OUSE	English river
OVA	Eggs
PACA	Spotted brown rodent
PAS	Dance step; fathers
PEKOE	Black tea

PELEE Martinique volcano
PERI Persian sprite
PES Footlike part
PHON Loudness measure
PHOT Light unit
PIA ____ mater (brain cover); actress Zadora
PICA Type measure
PIMA Arizona Indian; strong-fibered cotton
PLIE Ballet bend
POI Hawaiian dish
POILU French soldier in W.W. I
PROA Malay outrigger
PTAH Egyptian deity
PULE Whimper
PULI Hungarian dog
PYE English poet laureate
QADI Muslim magistrate (also CADI)
RAE Arctic explorer John; actress Charlotte
RAGA Indian music
RALE Harsh breathing
RAMA Incarnation of Vishnu
RAMIE Sturdy cloth fiber
RANA Indian prince
RANI Hindu queen (also RANEE)
RAO Indian novelist
RAREE ____ show (amusing spectacle)
RATEL Nocturnal animal of Africa and India
RAVI Sitarist Shankar
REBEC Medieval musical instrument
REN Stimpy's partner in cartoons
RENI Italian painter Guido
REO Antique auto
RES Thing at law; musical notes
RET Soak flax
RETE Network
RHEA Ostrichlike bird
RHEE First president of Korea
RIA Narrow inlet
RIAL Mideast money (also RIYAL)
RIATA Gaucho's lariat (also REATA)
RIEN Nothing: Fr.
RIGA Latvia's capital
RIVA Kentucky Derby winner ____ Ridge
ROC Fabled bird of *The Arabian Nights*
ROE Caviar; ____ v. Wade
ROO Aussie hopper; *Winnie-the-Pooh* baby
ROTA Roster
ROTI Roasted: Fr.
ROTO Old newspaper section
RUR Karel Capek drama
RYA Scandinavian rug
SABRA Native Israeli
SAC Algonquian Indian; pouch
SAGO Starchy foodstuff
SAKI H. H. Munro's pen name
SANA Capital of Yemen (also SANAA)
SARD Semiprecious stone
SARI Hindu dress
SEC Dry, as wine; part of a min.
SEGO Utah's state flower
SEL Salt: Fr.
SERA Antitoxins; evening in Italy
SERAC Glacial ridge
SERAI Mideast inn
SERE Dry and withered
SERT Spanish muralist José María ____
SES French possessive
SETA Bristle
SETI One of two Egyptian pharaohs
SHEM Son of Noah
SIENA City of Tuscany
SIMI California's ____ Valley
SIVA Hindu god (also SHIVA)
SLOE Blackthorn fruit; ____ gin fizz
SMA Wee, in Scotland
SMEE Captain Hook's assistant
SMEW Eurasian diving duck
SNA Scottish snow
SNEE Old-fashioned dagger
SOMA *Brave New World* drug
SORA Marsh bird
SPEE Graf ____ (historic German battleship)
SRA Mrs.: Spanish
SRI Hindu honorific
SRO Theater box-office sign
SRTA Spanish miss: Abbr.
STELE Inscribed pillar (also STELA)
STEN British submachine gun
STERE Cubic dry measure
STET "Let it stand," to a typesetter
STILE Set of steps over a fence or wall
ST. LO Normandy town
STOA Greek portico
STOAT Brown ermine
STOL Aircraft acronym
STRAD Classic violin

SURA Chapter in the Koran
SUSA Capital of ancient Elam
SUVA Fiji's capital
TABU Forbidden: Var.
TAEL Oriental weight
TARA *Gone With the Wind* plantation
TARE Weight allowance
TARN Mountain lake
TARO Tropical tuber
TASS Soviet news agency
TASSE French cup
TAT Make lace
TAV Hebrew letter
TEC Gumshoe
TERA Trillion: Prefix
TIA Aunt: Sp.
TIC Spasm; ____-tac-toe
TIKI Polynesian carving; "Kon-____"
TIO Spanish uncle
TITI Small South American monkey
TIU Teutonic deity
TOLE Lacquered metalware
TOPEE Pith helmet (also TOPI)
TOR Craggy hill
TORI Geometric doughnuts; actress Spelling
TORTE Rich cake
TRE Italian three
TRET Waste allowance
TYPEE Melville novel
UBER Over: Ger.
UDO Japanese vegetable
UELE River to the Ubangi
UKASE Edict
ULAN ____ Bator, Mongolia
ULEE Peter Fonda title role
ULU Eskimo knife
UMBO Projecting stud at the center of a shield
UNA Heroine of Spenser's *The Faerie Queene*; Spanish article
UNAU Two-toed sloth
UNCAS *The Last of the Mohicans* character
U NU Burma's first prime minister
UPAS Javanese poison tree
URAL Russian river or mountain
URE River in Yorkshire
UREY Chemistry Nobelist Harold
URI Swiss canton; mentalist Geller
URIAH Dickens's "____ Heep"
UTE Colorado Indian; sport ____ (vehicle)
UVEA Iris layer
VOLE Short-tailed rodent
WADI Dry river bed
WEIR Small dam
WEN Cyst
YALU Korean river
YSER Belgian river
ZARF Coffee cup holder
ZED Last letter, in England and Canada

NATIONS OF THE WORLD

The following section presents major facts about all the nations of the world, including statistics on each nation's geography, people, government, and economy.

Sources include the annual *World Factbook* published by the Central Intelligence Agency, the United Nations, the U.S. Census Bureau, and the U.S. Department of State.

Afghanistan

Geography Location: Southern Asia, north and west of Pakistan, east of Iran. **Area**: 250,000 sq. mi. (647,500 sq km). **Border countries**: China, Iran, Pakistan, Tajikistan, Turkmenistan, Uzbekistan. **Natural resources**: natural gas, petroleum, coal, copper, chromite, talc, barites, sulfur, lead, zinc, iron ore, salt, precious and semiprecious stones. **People Population**: 28,717,213 (July 2003 est.). **Nationality**: noun: Afghan(s); adjective: Afghan. **Ethnic groups**: Pashtun 44%, Tajik 25%, Hazara 10%, minor ethnic groups (Aimaks, Turkmen, Baloch, and others) 13%, Uzbek 8%. **Religions**: Sunni Muslim 84%, Shi'a Muslim 15%, other 1%. **Languages**: Pashtu 35%, Afghan Persian (Dari) 50%, Turkic languages (primarily Uzbek and Turkmen) 11%, 30 minor languages (primarily Balochi and Pashai) 4%, much bilingualism. **Government Government type**: transitional. **Independence**: 19 August 1919 (from UK control over Afghan foreign affairs). **National holiday**: Independence Day, 19 August (1919). **Economy G.D.P.**: $19 billion (2002 est.). G.D.P.—per capita: $700 (2002 est.). **Currency**: afghani (AFA).

Albania

Republic of Albania

Geography Location: Southeastern Europe, bordering the Adriatic Sea and Ionian Sea, between Greece and Serbia and Montenegro. **Area:** 11, 100 sq. mi. (28,748 sq km.). **Border countries:** Greece, The Former Yugoslav Republic of Macedonia, Serbia and Montenegro. **Natural resources:** petroleum, natural gas, coal, chromium, copper, timber, nickel, hydropower. **People Population:** 3,582,205 (July 2003 est.). **Nationality:** noun: Albanian(s); adjective: Albanian. **Ethnic groups:** Albanian 95%, Greek 3%, other 2% (Vlach, Gypsy, Serb, and Bulgarian) (1989 est.). **Religions:** Muslim 70%, Albanian Orthodox 20%, Roman Catholic 10%. **Languages:** Albanian (Tosk is the official dialect), Greek. **Government Government type:** emerging democracy. **Capital:** Tirana. **Independence:** 28 November 1912 (from Ottoman Empire). **National holiday:** Independence Day, 28 November (1912). **Economy G.D.P.:** purchasing power parity—$14 billion (2002 est.). **G.D.P.—per capita:** purchasing power parity—$4,500 (2002 est.). **Currency:** lek (ALL)

Algeria

People's Democratic Republic of Algeria

Geography Location: Northern Africa, bordering the Mediterranean Sea, between Morocco and Tunisia. **Area**: 919,591 sq. mi. (2,381,740 sq km). **Border countries**: Libya, Mali, Mauritania, Morocco, Niger, Tunisia, Western Sahara. **Natural resources**: petroleum, natural gas, iron ore, phosphates, uranium, lead, zinc. **People Population**: 32,818,500 (July 2003 est.). **Nationality**: noun: Algerian(s); adjective: Algerian. **Ethnic groups:** Arab-Berber 99%, European less than 1%. **Religions:** Sunni Muslim (state religion) 99%, Christian and Jewish 1%. **Languages:** Arabic (official), French, Berber dialects. **Government Government type:** republic. **Capital:** Algiers. **Independence:** 5 July 1962 (from France). **National holiday:** Revolution Day, 1 November (1954). **Economy G.D.P.:** purchasing power parity—$167 billion (2002 est.). **G.D.P.—per capita:** purchasing power parity—$5,300 (2002 est.). **Currency:** Algerian dinar (DZD).

Andorra

Principality of Andorra

Geography Location: Southwestern Europe, between France and Spain. **Area:** 174 sq. mi. (450 sq km). **Border countries:** France, Spain **Natural resources:** hydropower, mineral water, timber, iron ore, lead. **People Population:** 69,150 (July 2003 est.). **Nationality:** noun: Andorran(s); adjective: Andorran. **Ethnic groups:** Spanish 43%, Andorran 33%, Portuguese 11%, French 7%, other 6% (1998).

Religions: Roman Catholic (predominant). **Languages:** Catalan (official), French, Castilian, Portuguese. **Government Government type:** parliamentary democracy. **Capital:** Andorra la Vella. **Independence:** 1278 (was formed under the joint suzerainty of the French count of Foix and the Spanish bishop of Urgel). **National holiday:** Our Lady of Meritxell Day, 8 September (1278). **Economy G.D.P.:** purchasing power parity—$1.3 billion (2000 est.). **G.D.P.—per capita:** purchasing power parity—$19,000 (2000 est.). **Currency:** euro (EUR)

Angola

Republic of Angola

Geography Location: Southern Africa, bordering the South Atlantic Ocean, between Namibia and Democratic Republic of the Congo. **Area:** 481,352 sq. mi. (1,246,700 sq km). **Border countries:** Democratic Republic of the Congo (of which 225 km is the boundary of discontiguous Cabinda Province), Republic of the Congo, Namibia, Zambia. **Natural resources:** petroleum, diamonds, iron ore, phosphates, copper, feldspar, gold, bauxite, uranium. **People Population:** 10,766,471 (July 2003 est.). **Nationality:** noun: Angolan(s); adjective: Angolan. **Ethnic groups:** Ovimbundu 37%, Kimbundu 25%, Bakongo 13%, mestico (mixed European and Native African) 2%, European 1%, other 22%. **Religions:** indigenous beliefs 47%, Roman Catholic 38%, Protestant 15% (1998 est.). **Languages:** Portuguese (official), Bantu and other African languages. **Government Government type:** republic, nominally a multiparty democracy with a strong presidential system. **Capital:** Luanda. **Independence:** 11 November 1975 (from Portugal). **National holiday:** Independence Day, 11 November (1975). **Economy G.D.P.:** purchasing power parity—$16.9 billion (2002 est.). **G.D.P.—per capita:** purchasing power parity—$1,600 (2002 est.). **Currency:** kwanza (AOA).

Antigua and Barbuda

Geography Location: Caribbean, islands between the Caribbean Sea and the North Atlantic Ocean, east-southeast of Puerto Rico. **Area: 170** sq. mi. (443 sq km (Antigua 280 sq km; Barbuda 161 sq km). **Natural resources:** NEGL; pleasant climate fosters tourism **People Population:** 67,897 (July 2003 est.). **Nationality:** noun: Antiguan(s), Barbudan(s); **adjective:** Antiguan, Barbudan. **Ethnic groups:** black, British, Portuguese, Lebanese, Syrian. **Religions:** Christian, (predominantly Anglican with other Protestant, and some Roman Catholic). **Languages:** English (official), local dialects. **Government Government type:** constitutional monarchy with UK-style parliament. **Capital:** Saint John's. **Independence:** 1 November 1981 (from UK). **National holiday:** Independence Day (National Day), 1 November (1981). **Economy G.D.P.:** purchasing power parity—$750 million (2002 est.). **G.D.P.—per capita:** purchasing power parity—$11,000 (2002 est.). **Currency:** East Caribbean dollar (XCD)

Argentina

Argentine Republic

Geography Location: Southern South America, bordering the South Atlantic Ocean, between Chile and Uruguay. **Area:** 1,068,298 sq. mi. (2,766,890 sq km). **Border countries:** Bolivia, Brazil, Chile, Paraguay, Uruguay. **Natural resources:** fertile plains of the Pampas, lead, zinc, tin, copper, iron ore, manganese, petroleum, uranium. **People Population:** 38,740,807 (July 2003 est.). **Nationality:** noun: Argentine(s); adjective: Argentine. **Ethnic groups:** white (mostly Spanish and Italian) 97%, mestizo, Amerindian, or other nonwhite groups 3%. **Religions:** nominally Roman Catholic 92% (less than 20% practicing), Protestant 2%, Jewish 2%, other 4%. **Languages:** Spanish (official), English, Italian, German, French. **Government Government type:** republic. **Capital:** Buenos Aires. **Independence:** 9 July 1816 (from Spain). **National holiday:** Revolution Day, 25 May (1810). **Economy G.D.P.:** purchasing power parity—$391 billion (2002 est.). **G.D.P.—per capita:** purchasing power parity—$10,200 (2002 est.). **Currency:** Argentine peso (ARS).

Armenia

Republic of Armenia

Geography Location: Southwestern Asia, east of Turkey. **Area:** 11,506 sq. mi. (29,800 sq km). **Border countries:** Azerbaijan-proper, Azerbaijan-Naxcivan, Georgia, Iran, Turkey. **Natural resources:** small deposits of gold, copper, molybdenum, zinc, alumina. **People Population:** 3,326,448; *note:* Armenia's first census since independence was conducted in October 2001; official results are not expected until late 2003 (July 2003 est.). **Nationality:** *noun:* Armenian(s); *adj.:* Armenian. **Ethnic groups:** Armenian 93%, Azeri 1%, Russian 2%, other (mostly Yezidi Kurds) 4% (2002); *note:* as of the end of 1993, virtually all Azeris had emigrated from Armenia. **Religions:** Armenian Apostolic 94%, other Christian 4%, Yezidi (Zoroastrian/animist) 2%. **Languages:** Armenian 96%, Russian 2%, other 2%. **Government Government type:** republic. Capital: Yerevan. **Independence:** 21 September 1991 (from Soviet Union). **National holiday:** Independence Day, 21 September (1991). **Economy G.D.P.:** purchasing power parity—$12.6 billion (2002 est.). **G.D.P.—per capita:** purchasing power parity—$3,800 (2002 est.). **Currency:** dram (AMD)

Australia

Commonwealth of Australia

Geography Location: Oceania, continent between the Indian Ocean and the South Pacific Ocean. Area: 2,967,897 sq. mi. (7,686,850 sq km). Natural resources: bauxite, coal, iron ore, copper, tin, gold, silver, uranium, nickel, tungsten, mineral sands, lead, zinc, diamonds, natural gas, petroleum. **People Population:** 19,731,984 (July 2003 est.). **Nationality:** *noun:* Australian(s); *adj.:* Australian. **Ethnic groups:** Caucasian 92%, Asian 7%, aboriginal and other 1%. **Religions:** Anglican 26.1%, Roman Catholic 26%, other Christian 24.3%, non-Christian 11%, other 12.6%. **Languages:** English, native languages. **Government Government type:** democratic, federal-state system recognizing the British monarch as sovereign. Capital: Canberra. **Independence:** 1 January 1901 (federation of UK colonies). **National holiday:** Australia Day, 26 January (1788). **Economy G.D.P.:** purchasing power parity—$528 billion (2002 est.). **G.D.P.—per capita:** purchasing power parity $27,000 (2002 est.). **Currency:** Australian dollar (AUD)

Austria

Republic of Austria

Geography Location: Central Europe, north of Italy and Slovenia. **Area:** 32,377 sq. mi. (83,858 sq km). **Border countries**: Czech Republic, Germany, Hungary, Italy, Liechtenstein, Slovakia, Slovenia, Switzerland. **Natural resources:** iron ore, oil, timber, magnesite, lead, coal, lignite, copper, hydropower. **People Population:** 8,188,207 (July 2003 est.). **Nationality:** *noun:* Austrian(s); *adj.:* Austrian. **Ethnic groups:** German 88%, non-nationals 9.3% (includes Croatians, Slovenes, Hungarians, Czechs, Slovaks, Roma), naturalized 2% (includes those who have lived in Austria at least three generations). **Religions:** Roman Catholic 78%, Protestant 5%, Muslim and other 17%. **Languages:** German. **Government Government type:** federal republic. Capital: Vienna. **Independence:** 1156 (from Bavaria). **National holiday:** National Day, 26 October (1955). **Economy G.D.P.:** purchasing power parity—$226 billion (2002 est.). **G.D.P.—per capita:** purchasing power parity—$27,700 (2002 est.). **Currency:** euro (EUR).

Azerbaijan

Geography Location: Southwestern Asia, bordering the Caspian Sea, between Iran and Russia, with a small European portion north of the Caucasus range. **Area:** 33,436 sq. mi. (86,600 sq km). **Border countries**: Armenia (with Azerbaijan-proper), Armenia (with Azerbaijan-Naxcivan exclave), Georgia, Iran (with Azerbaijan-proper), Iran (with Azerbaijan-Naxcivan exclave), Russia, Turkey. **Natural resources:** petroleum, natural gas, iron ore, nonferrous metals, alumina. **People Population:** 7,830,764 (July 2003 est.). **Nationality:** *noun:* Azerbaijani(s); *adj.:* Azerbaijani. **Ethnic groups:** Azeri 90%, Dagestani 3.2%, Russian 2.5%, Armenian 2%, other 2.3% (1998 est.). **Religions:** Muslim 93.4%, Russian Orthodox 2.5%, Armenian Orthodox 2.3%, other 1.8% (1995 est.). *note:* religious affiliation is still nominal in Azerbaijan; percentages for actual practicing adherents are much lower. **Languages:** Azerbaijani (Azeri) 89%, Russian 3%, Armenian 2%, other 6% (1995 est.). **Government Government type:** republic. Capital: Baku (Baki). **Independence:** 30 August 1991 (from Soviet Union). **National holiday:** Founding of the Democratic Republic of Azerbaidzhan, 28 May (1918). **Economy G.D.P.:** purchasing power parity—$27 billion (2002 est.). **G.D.P.—per capita:** purchasing power parity—$3,500 (2002 est.). **Currency:** Azerbaijani manat (AZM).

Bahamas, The

Commonwealth of The Bahamas

Geography Location: Caribbean, chain of islands in the North Atlantic Ocean, southeast of Florida, northeast of Cuba. **Area:** 5,382 sq. mi. (13,940 sq km). **Natural resources:** salt, aragonite, timber, arable land **People Population:** 297,477 *note:* estimates for this country explicitly take into account the effects of excess mortality due to AIDS; this can result in lower life expectancy, higher infant mortality and death rates, lower population and growth rates, and changes in the distribution of population by age and sex than would otherwise be expected (July 2003 est.). **Nationality:** *noun:* Bahamian(s); *adj.:* Bahamian. **Ethnic groups:** black 85%, white 12%, Asian and Hispanic 3%. **Religions:** Baptist 32%, Anglican 20%, Roman Catholic 19%, Methodist 6%, Church of God 6%, other Protestant 12%, none or unknown 3%, other 2%. **Languages:** English, Creole (among Haitian immigrants). **Government Government type:** constitutional parliamentary democracy. Capital: Nassau. **Independence:** 10 July 1973 (from UK). **National holiday:** Independence Day, 10 July (1973). **Economy G.D.P.:** purchasing power parity—$5.2 billion (2002 est.). **G.D.P.—per capita:** purchasing power parity—$17,000 (2002 est.). **Currency:** Bahamian dollar (BSD).

Bahrain

Kingdom of Bahrain

Geography Location: Middle East, archipelago in the Persian Gulf, east of Saudi Arabia. **Area:** 239 sq. mi. (620 sq km). **Border countries**: Saudi Arabia, Qatar. **Natural**

resources: oil, associated and nonassociated natural gas, fish, pearls. **People Population:** 667,238 *note:* includes 235,108 non-nationals (July 2003 est.). **Nationality:** *noun:* Bahraini(s); *adj.:* Bahraini. **Ethnic groups:** Bahraini 63%, Asian 19%, other Arab 10%, Iranian 8%. **Religions:** Shi'a Muslim 70%, Sunni Muslim 30%. **Languages:** Arabic, English, Farsi, Urdu. **Government Government type:** constitutional hereditary monarchy. Capital: Manama. **Independence:** 15 August 1971 (from UK). **National holiday:** National Day, 16 December (1971). **Economy G.D.P.:** purchasing power parity—$9.8 billion (2002 est.). **G.D.P.—per capita:** purchasing power parity—$14,000 (2002 est.). **Currency:** Bahraini dinar (BHD).

Bangladesh

People's Republic of Bangladesh

Geography Location: Southern Asia, bordering the Bay of Bengal, between Burma and India. **Area:** 55,598 sq. mi. (144,000 sq km). **Border countries**: Burma, India. **Natural resources:** natural gas, arable land, timber, coal. **People Population:** 138,448,210 (July 2003 est.). **Nationality:** *noun:* Bangladeshi(s); *adj.:* Bangladeshi. **Ethnic groups:** Bengali 98%, tribal groups, non-Bengali Muslims (1998). **Religions:** Muslim 83%, Hindu 16%, other 1% (1998). **Languages:** Bangla (official, also known as Bengali), English. **Government Government type:** parliamentary democracy. Capital: Dhaka. **Independence:** 16 December 1971 (from West Pakistan). **National holiday:** Independence Day, 26 March (1971). **Economy G.D.P.:** purchasing power parity—$239 billion (2002 est.). **G.D.P.—per capita:** purchasing power parity—$1,700 (2002 est.). **Currency:** taka (BDT).

Barbados

Geography Location: Caribbean, island in the North Atlantic Ocean, northeast of Venezuela. **Area:** 166 sq. mi. (431 sq km). **Natural resources:** petroleum, fish, natural gas. **People Population:** 277,264 (July 2003 est.). **Nationality:** *noun:* Barbadian(s) or Bajan (colloquial); *adj.:* Barbadian or Bajan (colloquial). **Ethnic groups:** black 90%, white 4%, Asian and mixed 6%. **Religions:** Protestant 67% (Anglican 40%, Pentecostal 8%, Methodist 7%, other 12%), Roman Catholic 4%, none 17%, other 12%. **Languages:** English. **Government Government type:** parliamentary democracy; independent sovereign state within the Commonwealth. Capital: Bridgetown. **Independence:** 30 November 1966 (from UK). **National holiday:** Independence Day, 30 November (1966). **Economy G.D.P.:** purchasing power parity—$4 billion (2002 est.). **G.D.P.—per capita:** purchasing power parity—$14,500 (2002 est.). **Currency:** Barbadian dollar (BBD).

Belarus

Republic of Belarus

Geography Location: Eastern Europe, east of Poland. **Area:** 80, 154 sq. mi. (207,600 sq km). **Border countries**: Latvia, Lithuania, Poland, Russia, Ukraine. **Natural resources:** forests, peat deposits, small quantities of oil and natural gas, granite, dolomitic limestone, marl, chalk, sand, gravel, clay. **People Population:** 10,322,151 (July 2003 est.). **Nationality:** *noun:* Belarusian(s); *adj.:* Belarusian. **Ethnic groups:** Belarusian 81.2%, Russian 11.4%, Polish, Ukrainian, and other 7.4%. **Religions:** Eastern Orthodox 80%, other (including Roman Catholic, Protestant, Jewish, and Muslim) 20% (1997 est.). **Languages:** Belarusian, Russian, other. **Government Government type:** republic. Capital: Minsk. **Independence:** 25 August 1991 (from Soviet Union) **National holiday:** Independence Day, 3 July (1944). **Economy G.D.P.:** purchasing power parity—$85 billion (2002 est.). **G.D.P.—per capita:** purchasing power parity—$8,200 (2002 est.). **Currency:** Belarusian ruble (BYB/BYR).

Belgium

Kingdom of Belgium

Geography Location: Western Europe, bordering the North Sea, between France and the Netherlands. **Area:** 11,780 sq. mi. (30,510 sq km). **Border countries**: France, Germany, Luxembourg, Netherlands. **Natural resources:** coal, natural gas. **People Population:** 10,289,088 (July 2003 est.). **Nationality:** *noun:* Belgian(s); *adj.:* Belgian. **Ethnic groups:** Fleming 58%, Walloon 31%, mixed or other 11%. **Religions:** Roman Catholic 75%, Protestant or other 25%. **Languages:** Dutch (official) 60%, French (official) 40%, German (official) less than 1%, legally bilingual (Dutch and French). **Government Government type:** federal parliamentary democracy under a constitutional monarch. Capital: Brussels. **Independence:** 4 October 1830 a provisional government declared independence from the Netherlands; 21 July 1831 the ascension of King Leopold I to the throne. **National holiday:** Independence Day, 21 July (1831). **Economy G.D.P.:** purchasing power parity—$297.6 billion (2002 est.). **G.D.P.—per capita:** purchasing power parity—$29,000 (2002 est.). **Currency:** euro (EUR).

Benin

Republic of Benin

Geography Location: Western Africa, bordering the Bight of Benin, between Nigeria and Togo. **Area:** 43,483 sq. mi. (112,620 sq km). **Border countries**: Burkina Faso, Niger, Nigeria, Togo. **Natural resources:** small offshore oil deposits, limestone, marble, timber. **People Population:**

7,041,490. **Nationality:** *noun:* Beninese (singular and plural); *adj.:* Beninese. **Ethnic groups:** African 99% (42 ethnic groups, most important being Fon, Adja, Yoruba, Bariba), Europeans 5,500. **Religions:** indigenous beliefs 50%, Christian 30%, Muslim 20%. **Languages:** French (official), Fon and Yoruba (most common vernaculars in south), tribal languages (at least six major ones in north). **Government Government type:** republic under multiparty democratic rule. Capital: Porto-Novo is the official capital; Cotonou is the seat of government. **Independence:** 1 August 1960 (from France). **National holiday:** National Day, 1 August (1960). **Economy G.D.P.:** purchasing power parity—$7.3 billion (2002 est.). **G.D.P.—per capita:** purchasing power parity—$1,070 (2002 est.). **Currency:** Communaute Financiere Africaine franc (XOF).

Bhutan

Kingdom of Bhutan

Geography Location: Southern Asia, between China and India. **Area:** 18,147 sq. mi. (47,000 sq km). **Border countries**: China, India. **Natural resources:** timber, hydropower, gypsum, calcium carbide **People Population:** 2,139,549 *note:* other estimates range as low as 810,000 (July 2003 est.) **Nationality:** *noun:* Bhutanese (singular and plural); *adj.:* Bhutanese. **Ethnic groups:** Bhote 50%, ethnic Nepalese 35% (includes Lhotsampas—one of several Nepalese ethnic groups), indigenous or migrant tribes 15%. **Religions:** Lamaistic Buddhist 75%, Indian- and Nepalese-influenced Hinduism 25%. **Languages:** Dzongkha (official), Bhotes speak various Tibetan dialects, Nepalese speak various Nepalese dialects. **Government Government type:** monarchy; special treaty relationship with India. Capital: Thimphu. **Independence:** 8 August 1949 (from India). **National holiday:** National Day (Ugyen WANGCHUCK became first hereditary king), 17 December (1907). **Economy G.D.P.:** purchasing power parity—$2.7 billion (2002 est.). **G.D.P.—per capita:** purchasing power parity—$1,300 (2002 est.). **Currency:** ngultrum (BTN); Indian rupee (INR).

Bolivia

Republic of Bolivia

Geography Location: Central South America, southwest of Brazil. **Area:** 424,162 sq. mi. (1,098,580 sq km). **Border countries**: Argentina, Brazil, Chile, Paraguay, Peru. **Natural resources:** tin, natural gas, petroleum, zinc, tungsten, antimony, silver, iron, lead, gold, timber, hydropower. **People Population:** 8,586,443 (July 2003 est.). **Nationality:** *noun:* Bolivian(s); *adj.:* Bolivian. **Ethnic groups:** Quechua 30%, mestizo (mixed white and Amerindian ancestry) 30%, Aymara 25%, white 15%. **Religions:** Roman Catholic 95%, Protestant (Evangelical Methodist). **Languages:** Spanish (official), Quechua (official), Aymara (official). **Government Government type:** republic. Capital: La Paz (seat of government); Sucre (legal capital and seat of judiciary). **Independence:** 6 August 1825 (from Spain). **National holiday:** Independence Day, 6 August (1825). **Economy G.D.P.:** purchasing power parity—$21 billion (2002 est.). **G.D.P.—per capita:** purchasing power parity—$2,500 (2002 est.). **Currency:** boliviano (BOB).

Bosnia and Herzegovina

Geography Location: Southeastern Europe, bordering the Adriatic Sea and Croatia. **Area:** 19,776 sq. mi. (51,129 sq km). **Border countries**: Croatia, Serbia and Montenegro. **Natural resources:** coal, iron, bauxite, manganese, forests, copper, chromium, lead, zinc, hydropower. **People Population:** 3,989,018 (July 2003 est.). **Nationality:** *noun:* Bosnian(s); *adj.:* Bosnian. **Ethnic groups:** Serb 37.1%, Bosniak 48%, Croat 14.3%, other 0.6% (2000) *note:* Bosniak has replaced Muslim as an ethnic term in part to avoid confusion with the religious term Muslim—an adherent of Islam. **Religions:** Muslim 40%, Orthodox 31%, Roman Catholic 15%, Protestant 4%, other 10%. **Languages:** Croatian, Serbian, Bosnian. **Government Government type:** emerging federal democratic republic. Capital: Sarajevo. **Independence:** 1 March 1992. **National holiday:** National Day, 25 November (1943). **Economy G.D.P.:** purchasing power parity—$7.3 billion (2002 est.). **G.D.P.—per capita:** purchasing power parity—$1,900 (2002 est.). **Currency:** marka (BAM).

Botswana

Republic of Botswana

Geography Location: Southern Africa, north of South Africa. **Area:** 231,803 sq. mi. (600,370 sq km). **Border countries**: Namibia, South Africa, Zimbabwe. **Natural resources:** diamonds, copper, nickel, salt, coal, iron ore, silver. **People Population:** 1,573,267. **Nationality:** *noun:* Motswana (singular), Batswana (plural) *adj.:* Motswana (singular), Batswana (plural). **Ethnic groups:** Tswana (or Setswana) 79%, Kalanga 11%, Basarwa 3%, other 7%. **Religions:** indigenous beliefs 85%, Christian 15%. **Languages:** English (official), Setswana. **Government Government type:** parliamentary republic. Capital: Gaborone. **Independence:** 30 September 1966 (from UK). **National holiday:** Independence Day (Botswana Day), 30 September (1966). **Economy G.D.P.:** purchasing power parity—$15.1 billion (2002 est.). **G.D.P.—per capita:** purchasing power parity—$9,500 (2002 est.). **Currency:** pula (BWP).

Brazil

Federative Republic of Brazil

Geography Location: Eastern South America, bordering the Atlantic Ocean. **Area:** 3,286,475 sq. mi. (8,511,965 sq km). **Border countries**: Argentina, Bolivia, Colombia, French Guiana, Guyana, Paraguay, Peru, Suriname, Uruguay, Venezuela. **Natural resources:** bauxite, gold, iron ore, manganese, nickel, phosphates, platinum, tin, uranium, petroleum, hydropower, timber. **People Population:** 182,032,604. **Nationality:** *noun:* Brazilian(s); *adj.:* Brazilian; **Ethnic groups:** white (includes Portuguese, German, Italian, Spanish, Polish) 55%, mixed white and black 38%, black 6%, other (includes Japanese, Arab, Amerindian) 1%. **Religions:** Roman Catholic (nominal) 80%. **Languages:** Portuguese (official), Spanish, English, French. **Government Government type:** federative republic. Capital: Brasilia. **National holiday:** Independence Day, 7 September (1822). **Economy G.D.P.:** purchasing power parity—$1.34 trillion (2002 est.). **G.D.P.—per capita:** purchasing power parity—$7,600 (2002 est.). **Currency:** real (BRL).

Brunei

Negara Brunei Darussalam

Geography Location: Southeastern Asia, bordering the South China Sea and Malaysia. **Area:** 2,228 sq. mi. (5,770 sq km). **Border countries**: Malaysia. **Natural resources:** petroleum, natural gas, timber. **People Population:** 358,098 (July 2003 est.). **Nationality:** *noun:* Bruneian(s); *adj.:* Bruneian. **Ethnic groups:** Malay 67%, Chinese 15%, indigenous 6%, other 12%. **Religions:** Muslim (official) 67%, Buddhist 13%, Christian 10%, indigenous beliefs and other 10%. **Government Government type:** constitutional sultanate. Capital: Bandar Seri Begawan. **Independence:** 1 January 1984 (from UK). **National holiday:** National Day, 23 February (1984). **Economy G.D.P.:** purchasing power parity—$6.5 billion (2002 est.). **G.D.P.—per capita:** purchasing power parity—$18,600 (2002 est.). **Currency:** Bruneian dollar (BND).

Bulgaria

Republic of Bulgaria

Geography Location: Southeastern Europe, bordering the Black Sea, between Romania and Turkey. **Area:** 42,822 sq. mi. (110,910 sq km). **Border countries**: Greece, The Former Yugoslav Republic of Macedonia, Romania, Serbia and Montenegro, Turkey. **Natural resources:** bauxite, copper, lead, zinc, coal, timber, arable land. **People Population:** 7,537,929 (July 2003 est.). **Nationality:** *noun:* Bulgarian(s); *adj.:* Bulgarian. **Ethnic groups:** Bulgarian 83.6%, Turk 9.5%, Roma 4.6%, other 2.3% (including Macedonian, Armenian, Tatar, Circassian) (1998). **Religions:** Bulgarian Orthodox 83.8%, Muslim 12.1%, Roman Catholic 1.7%, Jewish 0.1%, Protestant, Gregorian-Armenian, and other 2.3% (1998). **Languages:** Bulgarian, secondary languages closely correspond to ethnic breakdown. **Government Government type:** parliamentary democracy. **Capital:** Sofia. **Independence:** 3 March 1878 (from Ottoman Empire). **National holiday:** Liberation Day, 3 March (1878). **Economy G.D.P.:** purchasing power parity—$50.6 billion (2002 est.). **G.D.P.—per capita:** purchasing power parity—$6,600 (2002 est.). **Currency:** lev (BGL).

Burkina Faso

Geography Location: Western Africa, north of Ghana. **Area:** 105,869 sq. mi. (274,200 sq km). **Border countries**: Benin, Cote d'Ivoire, Ghana, Mali, Niger, Togo. **Natural resources:** manganese, limestone, marble; small deposits of gold, antimony, copper, nickel, bauxite, lead, phosphates, zinc, silver. **People Population:** 13,228,460. **Nationality:** noun: Burkinabe (singular and plural); adj.: Burkinabe. **Ethnic groups:** Mossi over 40%, Gurunsi, Senufo, Lobi, Bobo, Mande, Fulani. **Religions:** indigenous beliefs 40%, Muslim 50%, Christian (mainly Roman Catholic) 10%. **Languages:** French (official), native African languages belonging to Sudanic family spoken by 90% of the population. **Government Government type:** parliamentary republic. Capital: Ouagadougou. **Independence:** 5 August 1960 (from France). **National holiday:** Republic Day, 11 December (1958). **Economy G.D.P.:** purchasing power parity—$13.6 billion (2002 est.). **G.D.P.—per capita:** purchasing power parity—$1,080 (2002 est.). **Currency:** Communaute Financiere Africaine franc (XOF); note—responsible authority is the Central Bank of the West African States.

Burundi

Republic of Burundi

Geography Location: Central Africa, east of Democratic Republic of the Congo. **Area:** 10,745 sq. mi. (27,830 sq km). **Border countries**: Democratic Republic of the Congo, Rwanda, Tanzania. **Natural resources:** nickel, uranium, rare earth oxides, peat, cobalt, copper, platinum (not yet exploited), vanadium, arable land, hydropower. **People Population:** 6,096,156. **Nationality:** *noun:* Burundian(s); *adj.:* Burundian. **Ethnic groups:** Hutu (Bantu) 85%, Tutsi (Hamitic) 14%, Twa (Pygmy) 1%, Europeans 3,000, South Asians 2,000. **Religions:** Christian 67% (Roman Catholic

62%, Protestant 5%), indigenous beliefs 23%, Muslim 10%. **Languages:** Kirundi (official), French (official), Swahili (along Lake Tanganyika and in the Bujumbura area). **Government Government type:** republic. Capital: Bujumbura. **Independence:** 1 July 1962 (from UN trusteeship under Belgian administration). **National holiday:** Independence Day, 1 July (1962). **Economy G.D.P.:** purchasing power parity—$3.8 billion (2002 est.). **G.D.P.—per capita:** purchasing power parity—$600 (2002 est.). **Currency:** Burundi franc (BIF).

Cambodia

Kingdom of Cambodia

Geography Location: Southeastern Asia, bordering the Gulf of Thailand, between Thailand, Vietnam, and Laos. **Area:** 69,900 sq. mi. (181,040 sq km). **Border countries**: Laos, Thailand, Vietnam. **Natural resources:** timber, gemstones, some iron ore, manganese, phosphates, hydropower potential. **People Population:** 13,124,764. **Nationality:** *noun:* Cambodian(s); *adj.:* Cambodian. **Ethnic groups:** Khmer 90%, Vietnamese 5%, Chinese 1%, other 4%. **Religions:** Theravada Buddhist 95%, other 5%. **Languages:** Khmer (official) 95%, French, English. **Government Government type:** multiparty democracy under a constitutional monarchy established in September 1993. Capital: Phnom Penh. **Independence:** 9 November 1953 (from France). **National holiday:** Independence Day, 9 November (1953). **Economy G.D.P.:** purchasing power parity—$19.7 billion (2002 est.). **G.D.P.—per capita:** purchasing power parity—$1,500 (2002 est.). **Currency:** riel (KHR).

Cameroon

Republic of Cameroon

Geography Location: Western Africa, bordering the Bight of Biafra, between Equatorial Guinea and Nigeria. **Area:** 183,568 sq. mi. (475,440 sq km). **Border countries**: Central African Republic, Chad, Republic of the Congo, Equatorial Guinea, Gabon, Nigeria. **Natural resources:** petroleum, bauxite, iron ore, timber, hydropower. **People Population:** 15,746,179. **Nationality:** *noun:* Cameroonian(s); *adj.:* Cameroonian. **Ethnic groups:** Cameroon Highlanders 31%, Equatorial Bantu 19%, Kirdi 11%, Fulani 10%, Northwestern Bantu 8%, Eastern Nigritic 7%, other African 13%, non-African less than 1%. **Religions:** indigenous beliefs 40%, Christian 40%, Muslim 20%. **Languages:** 24 major African language groups, English (official), French (official). **Government Government type:** unitary republic; multiparty presidential regime (opposition parties legalized in 1990) *note:* preponderance of power remains with the president. Capital: Yaounde. **Independence:** 1 January 1960 (from French-administered UN trusteeship). **National holiday:** Republic Day (National Day), 20 May (1972). **Economy G.D.P.:** purchasing power parity—$27 billion (2002 est.). **G.D.P.—per capita:** purchasing power parity—$1,700 (2002 est.). **Currency:** Communaute Financiere Africaine franc (XAF).

Canada

Geography Location: Northern North America, bordering the North Atlantic Ocean on the east, North Pacific Ocean on the west, and the Arctic Ocean on the north, north of the conterminous US. **Area:** 3,851,794 sq. mi. (9,976,140 sq km). **Border countries**: US. **Natural resources:** iron ore, nickel, zinc, copper, gold, lead, molybdenum, potash, diamonds, silver, fish, timber, wildlife, coal, petroleum, natural gas, hydropower. **People Population:** 32,207,113 (July 2003 est.). **Nationality:** *noun:* Canadian(s); *adj.:* Canadian. **Ethnic groups:** British Isles origin 28%, French origin 23%, other European 15%, Amerindian 2%, other, mostly Asian, African, Arab 6%, mixed background 26%. **Religions:** Roman Catholic 46%, Protestant 36%, other 18% *note:* based on the 1991 census. **Languages:** English 59.3% (official), French 23.2% (official), other 17.5% **Government Government type:** confederation with parliamentary democracy. Capital: Ottawa. **Independence:** 1 July 1867 (from UK). **National holiday:** Canada Day, 1 July (1867). **Economy G.D.P.:** purchasing power parity—$923 billion (2002 est.). **G.D.P.—per capita:** purchasing power parity—$29,400 (2002 est.). **Currency:** Canadian dollar (CAD).

Cape Verde

Republic of Cape Verde

Geography Location: Western Africa, group of islands in the North Atlantic Ocean, west of Senegal. **Area:** 1,556 sq. mi. (4,033 sq km). **Natural resources:** salt, basalt rock, limestone, kaolin, fish. **People Population:** 412,137 (July 2003 est.). **Nationality:** *noun:* Cape Verdean(s); *adj.:* Cape Verdean. **Ethnic groups:** Creole (mulatto) 71%, African 28%, European 1%. **Religions:** Roman Catholic (infused with indigenous beliefs); Protestant (mostly Church of the Nazarene). **Languages:** Portuguese, Crioulo (a blend of Portuguese and West African words). **Government Government type:** republic. Capital: Praia. **Independence:** 5 July 1975 (from Portugal). **National holiday:** Independence Day, 5 July (1975). **Economy G.D.P.:** purchasing power parity—$600 million (2002 est.). **G.D.P.—per capita:** purchasing power parity—$1,400 (2002 est.). **Currency:** Cape Verdean escudo (CVE).

Central African Republic

Central African Republic

Geography Location: Central Africa, north of Democratic Republic of the Congo. **Area:** 240,533 sq. mi. (622,984 sq km). **Border countries**: Cameroon, Chad, Democratic Republic of the Congo, Republic of the Congo, Sudan. **Natural resources:** diamonds, uranium, timber, gold, oil, hydropower. **People Population:** 3,683,538. **Nationality:** *noun:* Central African(s); *adj.:* Central African. **Ethnic groups:** Baya 33%, Banda 27%, Mandjia 13%, Sara 10%, Mboum 7%, M'Baka 4%, Yakoma 4%, other 2%. **Religions:** indigenous beliefs 35%, Protestant 25%, Roman Catholic 25%, Muslim 15% *note:* animistic beliefs and practices strongly influence the Christian majority. **Languages:** French (official), Sangho (lingua franca and national language), tribal languages. **Government Government type:** republic. Capital: Bangui. **Independence:** 13 August 1960 (from France). **National holiday:** Republic Day, 1 December (1958). **Economy G.D.P.:** purchasing power parity—$4.7 billion (2002 est.). **G.D.P.—per capita:** purchasing power parity—$1,300 (2002 est.). **Currency:** Communaute Financiere Africaine franc (XAF); note—responsible authority is the Bank of the Central African States.

Chad

Republic of Chad

Geography Location: Central Africa, south of Libya. **Area:** 495,753 sq. mi. (1.284 million sq km). **Border countries**: Cameroon, Central African Republic, Libya, Niger, Nigeria, Sudan. **Natural resources:** petroleum (unexploited but exploration under way), uranium, natron, kaolin, fish (Lake Chad). **People Population:** 9,253,493 (July 2003 est.). **Nationality:** *noun:* Chadian(s); *adj.:* Chadian. **Ethnic groups:** 200 distinct groups; in the north and center: Arabs, Gorane (Toubou, Daza, Kreda), Zaghawa, Kanembou, Ouaddai, Baguirmi, Hadjerai, Fulbe, Kotoko, Hausa, Boulala, and Maba, most of whom are Muslim; in the south: Sara (Ngambaye, Mbaye, Goulaye), Moundang, Moussei, Massa, most of whom are Christian or animist; about 1,000 French citizens. **Religions:** Muslim 51%, Christian 35%, animist 7%, other 7%. **Languages:** French (official), Arabic (official), Sara (in south), more than 120 different languages and dialects. **Government Government type:** republic. Capital: N'Djamena. **Independence:** 11 August 1960 (from France). **National holiday:** Independence Day, 11 August (1960). **Economy G.D.P.:** purchasing power parity—$10 billion (2002 est.). **G.D.P.—per capita:** purchasing power parity—$1,100 (2002 est.). **Currency:** Communaute Financiere Africaine franc (XAF); note—responsible authority is the Bank of the Central African States.

Chile

Republic of Chile

Geography Location: Southern South America, bordering the South Pacific Ocean, between Argentina and Peru. **Area:** 292,259 sq. mi. (756,950 sq km). **Border countries**: Argentina, Bolivia, Peru. **Natural resources:** copper, timber, iron ore, nitrates, precious metals, molybdenum, hydropower. **People Population:** 15,665,216 (July 2003 est.). **Nationality:** *noun:* Chilean(s); *adj.:* Chilean. **Ethnic groups:** white and white-Amerindian 95%, Amerindian 3%, other 2%. **Religions:** Roman Catholic 89%, Protestant 11%, Jewish NEGL%. **Languages:** Spanish. **Government Government type:** republic. Capital: Santiago. **Independence:** 18 September 1810 (from Spain). **National holiday:** Independence Day, 18 September (1810). **Economy G.D.P.:** purchasing power parity—$151 billion (2002 est.). **G.D.P.—per capita:** purchasing power parity—$10,000 (2002 est.). **Currency:** Chilean peso (CLP).

China

People's Republic of China

Geography Location: Eastern Asia, bordering the East China Sea, Korea Bay, Yellow Sea, and South China Sea, between North Korea and Vietnam. **Area:** 3,705,392 sq. mi. (9,596,960 sq km). **Border countries**: Afghanistan, Bhutan, Burma, Hong Kong, India, Kazakhstan, North Korea, Kyrgyzstan, Laos, Macau, Mongolia, Nepal, Pakistan, Russia (northeast), Russia (northwest), Tajikistan, Vietnam. **Natural resources:** coal, iron ore, petroleum, natural gas, mercury, tin, tungsten, antimony, manganese, molybdenum, vanadium, magnetite, aluminum, lead, zinc, uranium, hydropower potential (world's largest). **People Population:** 1,286,975,468 (July 2003 est.). **Nationality:** *noun:* Chinese (singular and plural). *adj.:* Chinese. **Ethnic groups:** Han Chinese 91.9%, Zhuang, Uygur, Hui, Yi, Tibetan, Miao, Manchu, Mongol, Buyi, Korean, and other nationalities 8.1%. **Religions:** Daoist (Taoist), Buddhist, Muslim 1%-2%, Christian 3%-4%; *note:* officially atheist (2002 est.) **Languages:** Standard Chinese or Mandarin (Putonghua, based on the Beijing dialect), Yue (Cantonese), Wu (Shanghaiese), Minbei (Fuzhou), Minnan (Hokkien-Taiwanese), Xiang, Gan, Hakka dialects, minority languages (see Ethnic groups entry). **Government Government type:** Communist state. Capital: Beijing. **Independence:** 221 BC (unification under the Qin or Ch'in Dynasty 221 BC; Qing or Ch'ing Dynasty replaced by the Republic on 12 February 1912; People's Republic established 1 October 1949). **National holiday:** Anniversary of the Founding of the People's Republic of China, 1 October (1949). **Economy**

G.D.P.: purchasing power parity—$5.7 trillion (2002 est.). **G.D.P.—per capita:** purchasing power parity—$4,400 (2002 est.). **Currency:** yuan (CNY).

Colombia

Republic of Colombia

Geography Location: Northern South America, bordering the Caribbean Sea, between Panama and Venezuela, and bordering the North Pacific Ocean, between Ecuador and Panama. **Area:** 439,734 sq. mi. (1,138,910 sq km). **Border countries**: Brazil, Ecuador, Panama, Peru, Venezuela. **Natural resources:** petroleum, natural gas, coal, iron ore, nickel, gold, copper, emeralds, hydropower. **People Population:** 41,662,073 (July 2003 est.). **Nationality:** *noun:* Colombian(s); *adj.:* Colombian. **Ethnic groups:** mestizo 58%, white 20%, mulatto 14%, black 4%, mixed black-Amerindian 3%, Amerindian 1%. **Religions:** Roman Catholic 90%. **Languages:** Spanish. **Government Government type:** republic; executive branch dominates government structure. Capital: Bogota. **Independence:** 20 July 1810 (from Spain). **National holiday:** Independence Day, 20 July (1810). **Economy G.D.P.:** purchasing power parity—$268 billion (2002 est.). **G.D.P.—per capita:** purchasing power parity—$6,500 (2002 est.). **Currency:** Colombian peso (COP).

Comoros

Union of the Comoros

Geography Location: Southern Africa, group of islands at the northern mouth of the Mozambique Channel, about two-thirds of the way between northern Madagascar and northern Mozambique. **Area:** 838 sq. mi. (2,170 sq km). **Natural resources:** NEGL. **People Population:** 632,948 (July 2003 est.). **Nationality:** *noun:* Comoran(s); *adj.:* Comoran. **Ethnic groups:** Antalote, Cafre, Makoa, Oimatsaha, Sakalava. **Religions:** Sunni Muslim 98%, Roman Catholic 2%. **Languages:** Arabic (official), French (official), Shikomoro (a blend of Swahili and Arabic). **Government Government type:** independent republic. Capital: Moroni. **Independence:** 6 July 1975 (from France). **National holiday:** Independence Day, 6 July (1975). **Economy G.D.P.:** purchasing power parity—$441 million (2002 est.). **G.D.P.—per capita:** purchasing power parity—$720 (2002 est.). **Currency:** Comoran franc (KMF).

Congo, Democratic Republic of the

Democratic Republic of the Congo

Geography Location: Central Africa, northeast of Angola. **Area:** 905,564 sq. mi. (2,345,410 sq km). **Border countries**: Angola(of which 225 km is the boundary of Angola's discontiguous Cabinda Province), Burundi, Central African Republic, Republic of the Congo, Rwanda, Sudan, Tanzania, Uganda, Zambia. **Natural resources:** cobalt, copper, cadmium, petroleum, industrial and gem diamonds, gold, silver, zinc, manganese, tin, germanium, uranium, radium, bauxite, iron ore, coal, hydropower, timber. **People Population:** 56,625,039. **Nationality:** *noun:* Congolese (singular and plural); *adj.:* Congolese or Congo. **Ethnic groups:** over 200 African ethnic groups of which the majority are Bantu; the four largest tribes—Mongo, Luba, Kongo (all Bantu), and the Mangbetu-Azande (Hamitic) make up about 45% of the population. **Religions:** Roman Catholic 50%, Protestant 20%, Kimbanguist 10%, Muslim 10%, other syncretic sects and indigenous beliefs 10%. **Languages:** French (official), Lingala (a lingua franca trade language), Kingwana (a dialect of Kiswahili or Swahili), Kikongo, Tshiluba. **Government Government type:** dictatorship; presumably undergoing a transition to representative government. Capital: Kinshasa. **Independence:** 30 June 1960 (from Belgium). **National holiday:** Independence Day, 30 June (1960). **Economy G.D.P.:** purchasing power parity—$34 billion (2002 est.). **G.D.P.—per capita:** purchasing power parity—$610 (2002 est.). **Currency:** Congolese franc (CDF).

Congo, Republic of the

Republic of the Congo

Geography Location: Western Africa, bordering the South Atlantic Ocean, between Angola and Gabon. **Area:** 132,046 sq. mi. (342,000 sq km). **Border countries**: Angola, Cameroon, Central African Republic, Democratic Republic of the Congo, Gabon. **Natural resources:** petroleum, timber, potash, lead, zinc, uranium, copper, phosphates, natural gas, hydropower. **People Population:** 2,954,258. **Nationality:** *noun:* Congolese (singular and plural); *adj.:* Congolese or Congo. **Ethnic groups:** Kongo 48%, Sangha 20%, M'Bochi 12%, Teke 17%, Europeans and other 3%. *note:* Europeans estimated at 8,500, mostly French, before the 1997 civil war; may be half that in 1998, following the widespread destruction of foreign businesses in 1997. **Religions:** Christian 50%, animist 48%, Muslim 2%. **Languages:** French (official), Lingala and Monokutuba (lingua franca trade languages), many local languages and dialects (of which Kikongo has the most users). **Government Government type:**republic. Capital: Brazzaville. **Independence:** 15 August 1960 (from France). **National holiday:** Independence Day, 15 August (1960). **Economy G.D.P.:** purchasing power parity—$2.5 billion (2002 est.). **G.D.P.—per capita:** purchasing power parity—$900 (2002 est.). **Currency:** Communaute Financiere Africaine franc (XAF); note—responsible authority is the Bank of the Central African States.

Costa Rica

Republic of Costa Rica

Geography Location: Middle America, bordering both the Caribbean Sea and the North Pacific Ocean, between Nicaragua and Panama. **Area:** 19,730 sq. mi. (51,100 sq km). **Border countries**: Nicaragua, Panama. **Natural resources:** hydropower. **People Population:** 3,896,092 (July 2003 est.). **Nationality:** *noun:* Costa Rican(s); *adj.:* Costa Rican. **Ethnic groups:** white (including mestizo) 94%, black 3%, Amerindian 1%, Chinese 1%, other 1%. **Religions:** Roman Catholic 76.3%, Evangelical 13.7%, Jehovah's Witnesses 1.3%, other Protestant 0.7%, other 4.8%, none 3.2%. **Languages:** Spanish (official), English spoken around Puerto Limon. **Government Government type:** democratic republic. Capital: San Jose. **Independence:** 15 September 1821 (from Spain). **National holiday:** Independence Day, 15 September (1821). **Economy G.D.P.:** purchasing power parity—$32.3 billion (2002 est.). **G.D.P.—per capita:** purchasing power parity—$8,500 (2002 est.). **Currency:** Costa Rican colon (CRC).

Cote d'Ivoire

Republic of Cote d'Ivoire

Geography Location: Western Africa, bordering the North Atlantic Ocean, between Ghana and Liberia. **Area:** 124,502 sq. mi. (322,460 sq km). **Border countries**: Burkina Faso, Ghana, Guinea, Liberia, Mali. **Natural resources:** petroleum, natural gas, diamonds, manganese, iron ore, cobalt, bauxite, copper, hydropower. **People Population:** 16,962,491. **Nationality:** *noun:* Ivorian(s); *adj.:* Ivorian. **Ethnic groups:** Akan 42.1%, Voltaiques or Gur 17.6%, Northern Mandes 16.5%, Krous 11%, Southern Mandes 10%, other 2.8% (includes 130,000 Lebanese and 20,000 French) (1998). **Religions:** Christian 20-30%, Muslim 35-40%, indigenous 25-40% (2001). *note:* the majority of foreigners (migratory workers) are Muslim (70%) and Christian (20%). **Languages:** French (official), 60 native dialects with Dioula the most widely spoken. **Government Government type:** republic; multiparty presidential regime established 1960. Capital: Yamoussoukro; note—although Yamoussoukro has been the official capital since 1983, Abidjan remains the commercial and administrative center; the US, like other countries, maintains its Embassy in Abidjan. **Independence:** 7 August (1960) (from France). **National holiday:** Independence Day, 7 August (1960). **Economy G.D.P.:** purchasing power parity—$24.5 billion (2002 est.). **G.D.P.—per capita:** purchasing power parity—$1,500 (2002 est.). **Currency:** Communaute Financiere Africaine franc (XOF); note—responsible authority is the Central Bank of the West African States.

Croatia

Republic of Croatia

Geography Location: Southeastern Europe, bordering the Adriatic Sea, between Bosnia and Herzegovina and Slovenia. **Area:** 21,824 sq. mi. (56,542 sq km). **Border countries:** Bosnia and Herzegovina, Hungary, Serbia and Montenegro, Slovenia. **Natural resources:** oil, some coal, bauxite, low-grade iron ore, calcium, natural asphalt, silica, mica, clays, salt, hydropower. **People Population:** 4,422,248 (July 2003 est.). **Nationality:** *noun:* Croat(s), Croatian(s); *adj.:* Croatian. **Ethnic groups:** Croat 89.6%, Serb 4.5%, Bosniak 0.5%, Hungarian 0.4%, Slovene 0.3%, Czech 0.2%, Roma 0.2%, Albanian 0.1%, Montenegrin 0.1%, others 4.1% (2001). **Religions:** Roman Catholic 87.8%, Orthodox 4.4%, Muslim 1.3%, Protestant 0.3%, others and unknown 6.2% (2001). **Languages:** Croatian 96%, other 4% (including Italian, Hungarian, Czech, Slovak, and German). **Government Government type:** presidential/parliamentary democracy. Capital: Zagreb. **Independence:** 25 June 1991 (from Yugoslavia). **National holiday:** Statehood Day, 25 June (1991). **Economy G.D.P.:** purchasing power parity—$38.9 billion (2002 est.). **G.D.P.—per capita:** purchasing power parity—$8,800 (2002 est.). **Currency:** kuna (HRK).

Cuba

Republic of Cuba

Geography Location: Caribbean, island between the Caribbean Sea and the North Atlantic Ocean, 150 km south of Key West, Florida. **Area:** 42,803 sq. mi. (110,860 sq km). **Border countries**: US Naval Base at Guantanamo Bay *note:* Guantanamo Naval Base is leased by the US and thus remains part of Cuba. **Natural resources:** cobalt, nickel, iron ore, copper, manganese, salt, timber, silica, petroleum, arable land. **People Population:** 11,263,429 (July 2003 est.). **Nationality:** *noun:* Cuban(s); *adj.:* Cuban. **Ethnic groups:** mulatto 51%, white 37%, black 11%, Chinese 1%. **Religions:** nominally 85% Roman Catholic prior to CASTRO assuming power; Protestants, Jehovah's Witnesses, Jews, and Santeria are also represented. **Languages:** Spanish. **Government Government type:**Communist state. Capital: Havana. **Independence:** 20 May 1902 (from Spain 10 December 1898; administered by the US from 1898 to 1902). **National holiday:** Independence Day, 10 December (1898); note—10 December 1898 is the date of independence from Spain, 20 May 1902 is the date of independence from US administration; Rebellion Day, 26 July (1953). **Economy G.D.P.:** purchasing power parity—$25.9 billion (2002 est.). **G.D.P.—per capita:** purchasing power parity—$2,300 (2002 est.); **Currency:** Cuban peso (CUP).

Cyprus

Republic of Cyprus

Geography Location: Middle East, island in the Mediterranean Sea, south of Turkey. **Area:** 3,571 sq. mi. (9,250 sq km) (of which 3,355 sq km are in the Turkish Cypriot area). **Natural resources:** copper, pyrites, asbestos, gypsum, timber, salt, marble, clay earth pigment. **People Population:** 771,657 (July 2003 est.). **Nationality:** *noun:* Cypriot(s); *adj.:* Cypriot. **Ethnic groups:** Greek 85.2%, Turkish 11.6%, other 3.2% (2000). **Religions:** Greek Orthodox 78%, Muslim 18%, Maronite, Armenian Apostolic, and other 4%. **Languages:** Greek, Turkish, English. **Government Government type:** republic. Capital: Nicosia. **Independence:** 16 August 1960 (from UK); note—Turkish Cypriot area proclaimed self-rule on 13 February 1975. **National holiday:** Independence Day, 1 October (1960); note—Turkish Cypriot area celebrates 15 November (1983) as Independence Day. **Economy G.D.P.:** Greek Cypriot **area:** purchasing power parity—$9.4 billion (2001 est.); Turkish Cypriot **area:** purchasing power parity—$787 million (2002 est.). **G.D.P.—per capita:** Greek Cypriot **area:** purchasing power parity—$15,000 (2001 est.); Turkish Cypriot **area:** purchasing power parity—$6,000 (2002 est.). **Currency:** Greek Cypriot **area:** Cypriot pound (CYP); Turkish Cypriot **area:** Turkish lira (TRL).

Czech Republic

Geography Location: Central Europe, southeast of Germany. **Area:** 30,387 sq. mi. (78,866 sq km). **Border countries**: Austria, Germany, Poland, Slovakia. **Natural resources:** hard coal, soft coal, kaolin, clay, graphite, timber. **People Population:** 10,249,216 (July 2003 est.). **Nationality:** *noun:* Czech(s); *adj.:* Czech. **Ethnic groups:** Czech 81.2%, Moravian 13.2%, Slovak 3.1%, Polish 0.6%, German 0.5%, Silesian 0.4%, Roma 0.3%, Hungarian 0.2%, other 0.5% (1991). **Religions:** Roman Catholic 39.2%, Protestant 4.6%, Orthodox 3%, other 13.4%, atheist 39.8%. **Languages:** Czech. **Government Government type:** parliamentary democracy. Capital: Prague. **Independence:** 1 January 1993 (Czechoslovakia split into the Czech Republic and Slovakia). **National holiday:** Czech Founding Day, 28 October (1918). **Economy G.D.P.:** purchasing power parity—$155.9 billion (2002 est.). **G.D.P.—per capita:** purchasing power parity—$15,300 (2002 est.). **Currency:** Czech koruna (CZK).

Denmark

Kingdom of Denmark

Geography Location: Northern Europe, bordering the Baltic Sea and the North Sea, on a peninsula north of Germany (Jutland); also includes two major islands (Sjaelland and Fyn). **Area:** 16,629 sq. mi. (43,094 sq km). **Border countries**: Germany. **Natural resources:** petroleum, natural gas, fish, salt, limestone, stone, gravel and sand. **People Population:** 5,384,384 (July 2003 est.). **Nationality:** *noun:* Dane(s); *adj.:* Danish. **Ethnic groups:** Scandinavian, Inuit, Faroese, German, Turkish, Iranian, Somali. **Religions:** Evangelical Lutheran 95%, other Protestant and Roman Catholic 3%, Muslim 2%. **Languages:** Danish, Faroese, Greenlandic (an Inuit dialect), German (small minority). *note:* English is the predominant second language. **Government Government type**: constitutional monarchy. Capital: Copenhagen. **National holiday**: none designated; Constitution Day, 5 June is generally viewed as the National Day. **Economy G.D.P.:** purchasing power parity—$155.5 billion (2002 est.). **G.D.P.—per capita:** purchasing power parity—$29,000 (2002 est.). **Currency:** Danish krone (DKK).

Djibouti

Republic of Djibouti

Geography Location: Eastern Africa, bordering the Gulf of Aden and the Red Sea, between Eritrea and Somalia. **Area:** 8,494 sq. mi. (23,000 sq km). **Border countries**: Eritrea, Ethiopia, Somalia. **Natural resources:** geothermal areas. **People Population:** 457,130 (July 2003 est.). **Nationality:** *noun:* Djiboutian(s); *adj.:* Djiboutian. **Government Government type:** republic. Capital: Djibouti. **Independence:** 27 June 1977 (from France). **National holiday:** Independence Day, 27 June (1977). **Economy G.D.P.:** purchasing power parity—$619 million (2002 est.). **G.D.P.—per capita:** purchasing power parity—$1,300 (2002 est.). **Currency:** Djiboutian franc (DJF).

Dominica

Commonwealth of Dominica

Geography Location: Caribbean, island between the Caribbean Sea and the North Atlantic Ocean, about one-half of the way from Puerto Rico to Trinidad and Tobago. **Area:** 290 sq. mi. (754 sq km). **Natural resources:** timber, hydropower, arable land. **People Population:** 69,655 (July 2003 est.). **Nationality:** *noun:* Dominican(s); *adj.:* Dominican. **Ethnic groups:** black, mixed black and European, European, Syrian, Carib Amerindian. **Religions:** Roman Catholic 77%, Protestant 15% (Methodist 5%, Pentecostal 3%, Seventh-Day Adventist 3%, Baptist 2%, other 2%), none 2%, other 6%. **Languages:** English (official), French patois. **Government Government type**: parliamentary democracy; republic within the Commonwealth. Capital: Roseau. **Independence**: 3 November 1978 (from UK). **National holiday**: Independence Day, 3 November

(1978). **Economy G.D.P.:** purchasing power parity—$380 million (2002 est.). **G.D.P.—per capita:** purchasing power parity—$5,400 (2002 est.). **Currency:** East Caribbean dollar (XCD).

Dominican Republic

Geography Location: Caribbean, eastern two-thirds of the island of Hispaniola, between the Caribbean Sea and the North Atlantic Ocean, east of Haiti. **Area:** 18,815 sq. mi. (48,730 sq km). **Border countries**: Haiti. **Natural resources:** nickel, bauxite, gold, silver. **People Population:** 8,715,602 (July 2003 est.). **Nationality:** *noun:* Dominican(s); *adj.:* Dominican. **Ethnic groups:** white 16%, black 11%, mixed 73%. **Religions:** Roman Catholic 95%. **Languages:** Spanish. **Government Government type:** representative democracy. Capital: Santo Domingo. **Independence:** 27 February 1844 (from Haiti). **National holiday:** Independence Day, 27 February (1844). **Economy G.D.P.**: purchasing power parity—$53 billion (2002 est.). **G.D.P.—per capita**: purchasing power parity—$6,100 (2002 est.). **Currency**: Dominican peso (DOP).

East Timor

Democratic Republic of Timor-Leste

Geography: **Location:** Southeastern Asia, northwest of Australia in the Lesser Sunda Islands at the eastern end of the Indonesian archipelago; note—East Timor includes the eastern half of the island of Timor, the Oecussi (Ambeno) region on the northwest portion of the island of Timor, and the islands of Pulau Atauro and Pulau Jaco. **Area:** 7,336 sq. mi. (15,007 sq km). **Border countries**: Indonesia. **Natural resources:** gold, petroleum, natural gas, manganese, marble. **People** Population:997,853. **Nationality:** *noun:* Timorese; *adj.:* Timorese. **Ethnic groups:** Austronesian (Malayo-Polynesian), Papuan, small Chinese minority. **Religions:** Roman Catholic 90%, Muslim 4%, Protestant 3%, Hindu 0.5%, Buddhist, Animist (1992 est.). **Languages:** Tetum (official), Portuguese (official), Indonesian, English. *note:* there are about 16 indigenous languages; Tetum, Galole, Mambae, and Kemak are spoken by significant numbers of people **Government Government type:** republic. Capital: Dili. **Independence:** 28 November 1975 (date of proclamation of independence from Portugal); note—20 May 2002 is the official date of international recognition of East Timor's independence from Indonesia. **National holiday:** Independence Day, 28 November (1975). **Economy G.D.P.:** purchasing power parity—$440 million (2001 est.). **G.D.P.—per capita:** purchasing power parity—$500 (2001 est.). **Currency:** Indonesian Rupiah (IDR).

Ecuador

Republic of Ecuador

Geography Location: Western South America, bordering the Pacific Ocean at the Equator, between Colombia and Peru. **Area:** 109,483 sq. mi. (283,560 sq km). **Border countries:** Colombia, Peru. **Natural resources:** petroleum, fish, timber, hydropower. **People Population:** 13,710,234 (July 2003 est.). **Nationality:** *noun:* Ecuadorian(s); *adj.:* Ecuadorian. **Ethnic groups:** mestizo (mixed Amerindian and white) 65%, Amerindian 25%, Spanish and others 7%, black 3%. **Religions:** Roman Catholic 95%. **Languages:** Spanish (official), Amerindian languages (especially Quechua). **Government Government type:** republic. Capital: Quito. **Independence:** 24 May 1822 (from Spain). **National holiday:** Independence Day (independence of Quito), 10 August (1809). **Economy G.D.P.:** purchasing power parity—$41.7 billion (2002 est.). **G.D.P.—per capita:** purchasing power parity—$3,100 (2002 est.). **Currency:** US dollar (USD).

Egypt

Arab Republic of Egypt

Geography Location: Northern Africa, bordering the Mediterranean Sea, between Libya and the Gaza Strip, and the Red Sea north of Sudan, and includes the Asian Sinai Peninsula. **Area:** 386,660 sq. mi. (1,001,450 sq km). **Border countries**: Gaza Strip, Israel, Libya, Sudan. **Natural resources:** petroleum, natural gas, iron ore, phosphates, manganese, limestone, gypsum, talc, asbestos, lead, zinc. **People Population:** 74,718,797 (July 2003 est.). **Nationality:** *noun:* Egyptian(s); *adj.:* Egyptian. **Ethnic groups:** Eastern Hamitic stock (Egyptians, Bedouins, and Berbers) 99%, Greek, Nubian, Armenian, other European (primarily Italian and French) 1%. **Religions:** Muslim (mostly Sunni) 94%, Coptic Christian and other 6%. **Languages:** Arabic (official), English and French widely understood by educated classes. **Government Government type:** republic. Capital: Cairo. **Independence:** 28 February 1922 (from UK). **National holiday:** Revolution Day, 23 July (1952). **Constitution:** 11 September 1971. **Legal system:** based on English common law, Islamic law, and Napoleonic codes; judicial review by Supreme Court and Council of State (oversees validity of administrative decisions); accepts compulsory ICJ jurisdiction, with reservations. **Executive branch:** president nominated by the People's Assembly for a six-year term, the nomination must then be validated by a national, popular referendum; prime minister appointed by the president. **Legislative branch:** bicameral system consists of the People's Assembly and the Advisory Council. **Judicial branch:** Supreme Constitutional Court. **Economy G.D.P.:**

purchasing power parity—$268 billion (2002 est.). **Industries:** textiles, food processing, tourism, chemicals, hydrocarbons, construction, cement, metals. **Agriculture—products:** cotton, rice, corn, wheat, beans, fruits, vegetables; cattle, water buffalo, sheep, goats. **Currency:** Egyptian pound (EGP).

El Salvador

Republic of El Salvador

Geography **Location:** Middle America, bordering the North Pacific Ocean, between Guatemala and Honduras. **Area:** 8,124 sq. mi. (21,040 sq km). **Border countries**: Guatemala, Honduras. **Natural resources:** hydropower, geothermal power, petroleum, arable land. **People** **Population:** 6,470,379 (July 2003 est.). **Nationality:** *noun:* Salvadoran(s); *adj.:* Salvadoran. **Ethnic groups:** mestizo 90%, Amerindian 1%, white 9%. **Religions:** Roman Catholic 83%. *note:* there is extensive activity by Protestant groups throughout the country; by the end of 1992, there were an estimated 1 million Protestant evangelicals in El Salvador. **Languages:** Spanish, Nahua (among some Amerindians). **Government** **Government type:** republic. Capital: San Salvador. **Independence:** 15 September 1821 (from Spain). **National holiday:** Independence Day, 15 September (1821). **Economy** **G.D.P.:** purchasing power parity—$30 billion (2002 est.). **G.D.P.—per capita:** purchasing power parity—$4,700 (2002 est.). **Currency:** US dollar (USD).

Equatorial Guinea

Republic of Equatorial Guinea

Geography **Location:** Western Africa, bordering the Bight of Biafra, between Cameroon and Gabon. **Area:** 10,830 sq. mi. (28,051 sq km). **Border countries**: Cameroon, Gabon. **Natural resources:** oil, petroleum, timber, small unexploited deposits of gold, manganese, uranium, titanium, iron ore. **People** **Population:** 510,473 (July 2003 est.). **Nationality:** *noun:* Equatorial Guinean(s) or Equatoguinean(s); *adj.:* Equatorial Guinean or Equatoguinean. **Ethnic groups:** Bioko (primarily Bubi, some Fernandinos), Rio Muni (primarily Fang), Europeans less than 1,000, mostly Spanish. **Religions:** nominally Christian and predominantly Roman Catholic, pagan practices. **Languages:** Spanish (official), French (official), pidgin English, Fang, Bubi, Ibo. **Government** **Government type:** republic. Capital: Malabo. **Independence:** 12 October 1968 (from Spain). **National holiday:** Independence Day, 12 October (1968). **Economy** **G.D.P.:** purchasing power parity—$1.27 billion (2002 est.). **G.D.P.—per capita:** purchasing power parity—$2,700 (2002 est.). **Currency:** Communaute Financiere Africaine franc (XAF); note—responsible authority is the Bank of the Central African States.

Eritrea

State of Eritrea

Geography **Location:** Eastern Africa, bordering the Red Sea, between Djibouti and Sudan. **Area:** 46,842 sq. mi. (121,320 sq km). **Border countries**: Djibouti, Ethiopia, Sudan. **Natural resources:** gold, potash, zinc, copper, salt, possibly oil and natural gas, fish. **People** **Population:** 4,362,254 (July 2003 est.). **Nationality:** *noun:* Eritrean(s); *adj.:* Eritrean. **Ethnic groups:** ethnic Tigrinya 50%, Tigre and Kunama 40%, Afar 4%, Saho (Red Sea coast dwellers) 3%, other 3%. **Religions:** Muslim, Coptic Christian, Roman Catholic, Protestant. **Languages:** Afar, Amharic, Arabic, Tigre and Kunama, Tigrinya, other Cushitic languages. **Government** **Government type:** transitional government. *note:* following a successful referendum on independence for the Autonomous Region of Eritrea on 23-25 April 1993, a National Assembly, composed entirely of the People's Front for Democracy and Justice or PFDJ, was established as a transitional legislature; a Constitutional Commission was also established to draft a constitution; ISAIAS Afworki was elected president by the transitional legislature; the constitution, ratified in May 1997, did not enter into effect, pending parliamentary and presidential elections; parliamentary elections had been scheduled to take place in December 2001, but were postponed indefinitely; currently the sole legal party is the People's Front for Democracy and Justice (PFDJ). Capital: Asmara (formerly Asmera). **Independence:** 24 May 1993 (from Ethiopia). **National holiday:** Independence Day, 24 May (1993). **Economy** **G.D.P.:** purchasing power parity—$3.3 billion (2002 est.). **G.D.P.—per capita:** purchasing power parity—$740 (2002 est.). **Currency:** nakfa (ERN).

Estonia

Republic of Estonia

Geography **Location:** Eastern Europe, bordering the Baltic Sea and Gulf of Finland, between Latvia and Russia. **Area:** 17,413 sq. mi. (45,226 sq km). **Border countries**: Latvia, Russia. **Natural resources:** oil shale, peat, phosphorite, clay, limestone, sand, dolomite, arable land, sea mud. **People** Population:1,408,556 (July 2003 est.). **Nationality:***noun:* Estonian(s); *adj.:* Estonian. **Ethnic groups:** Estonian 65.3%, Russian 28.1%, Ukrainian 2.5%, Belarusian 1.5%, Finn 1%, other 1.6% (1998). **Religions:** Evangelical Lutheran, Russian Orthodox, Estonian Orthodox, Baptist, Methodist, Seventh-Day Adventist, Roman Catholic, Pentecostal, Word of Life, Jewish.

Languages: Estonian (official), Russian, Ukrainian, Finnish, other. **Government Government type**: parliamentary republic. Capital: Tallinn. **Independence**: regained on 20 August 1991 (from Soviet Union). **National holiday**: Independence Day, 24 February (1918); note—24 February 1918 was the date of independence from Soviet Russia, 20 August 1991 was the date of reindependence from the Soviet Union. **Economy G.D.P.:** purchasing power parity—$15.2 billion (2002 est.). **G.D.P.—per capita:** purchasing power parity—$10,900 (2002 est.). **Industries:** engineering, electronics, wood and wood products, textile; information technology, telecommunications. **Agriculture—products:** potatoes, vegetables; livestock and dairy products; fish. **Currency:** Estonian kroon (EEK).

Ethiopia

Federal Democratic Republic of Ethiopia

Geography Location: Eastern Africa, west of Somalia. **Area:** 435,184 sq. mi. (1,127,127 sq km). **Border countries**: Djibouti, Eritrea, Kenya, Somalia, Sudan. **Natural resources:** small reserves of gold, platinum, copper, potash, natural gas, hydropower. **People Population:** 66,557,553. **Nationality:** *noun:* Ethiopian(s); *adj.:* Ethiopian. **Ethnic groups:** Oromo 40%, Amhara and Tigre 32%, Sidamo 9%, Shankella 6%, Somali 6%, Afar 4%, Gurage 2%, other 1%. **Religions:** Muslim 45%-50%, Ethiopian Orthodox 35%-40%, animist 12%, other 3%-8%. **Languages:** Amharic, Tigrinya, Oromigna, Guaragigna, Somali, Arabic, other local languages, English (major foreign language taught in schools). **Government Government type:** federal republic. Capital: Addis Ababa. **Independence:** oldest independent country in Africa and one of the oldest in the world—at least 2,000 years. **National holiday:** National Day (defeat of MENGISTU regime), 28 May (1991). **Economy G.D.P.:** purchasing power parity—$50.6 billion (2002 est.). **G.D.P.—per capita:** purchasing power parity—$750 (2002 est.). **Currency:** birr (ETB).

Fiji

Republic of the Fiji Islands

Geography Location: Oceania, island group in the South Pacific Ocean, about two-thirds of the way from Hawaii to New Zealand. **Area:** 7,054 sq. mi. (18,270 sq km). **Natural resources:** timber, fish, gold, copper, offshore oil potential, hydropower. **People Population:** 868,531 (July 2003 est.). **Nationality:** *noun:* Fijian(s); *adj.:* Fijian. **Ethnic groups:** Fijian 51% (predominantly Melanesian with a Polynesian admixture), Indian 44%, European, other Pacific Islanders, overseas Chinese, and other 5% (1998 est.). **Religions:** Christian 52% (Methodist 37%, Roman Catholic 9%), Hindu 38%, Muslim 8%, other 2%. *note:* Fijians are mainly Christian, Indians are Hindu, and there is a Muslim minority (1986). **Languages:** English (official), Fijian, Hindustani. **Government Government type:** republic. *note:* military coup leader Maj. Gen. Sitiveni RABUKA formally declared Fiji a republic on 6 October 1987. Capital: Suva. **Independence:** 10 October 1970 (from UK). **National holiday:** Independence Day, second Monday of October (1970). **Economy G.D.P.:** purchasing power parity—$4.7 billion (2002 est.). **G.D.P.—per capita:** purchasing power parity—$5,500 (2002 est.). **Currency:** Fijian dollar (FJD).

Finland

Republic of Finland

Geography Location: Northern Europe, bordering the Baltic Sea, Gulf of Bothnia, and Gulf of Finland, between Sweden and Russia. **Area:** 130,127 sq. mi. (337,030 sq km). **Border countries**: Norway, Sweden, Russia. **Natural resources:** timber, copper, zinc, iron ore, silver. **People Population:** 5,190,785 (July 2003 est.). **Nationality:** *noun:* Finn(s); *adj.:* Finnish. **Ethnic groups:** Finn 93%, Swede 6%, Sami 0.11%, Roma 0.12%, Tatar 0.02%. **Religions:** Evangelical Lutheran 89%, Russian Orthodox 1%, none 9%, other 1%. **Languages:** Finnish 93.4% (official), Swedish 5.9% (official), small Sami- and Russian-speaking minorities. **Government Government type:** republic. Capital: Helsinki. **Independence:** 6 December 1917 (from Russia). **National holiday:** Independence Day, 6 December (1917). **Economy G.D.P.:** purchasing power parity—$136.2 billion (2002 est.). **G.D.P.—per capita:** purchasing power parity—$26,200 (2002 est.). **Currency:** euro (EUR).

France

French Republic

Geography Location: Western Europe, bordering the Bay of Biscay and English Channel, between Belgium and Spain, southeast of the UK; bordering the Mediterranean Sea, between Italy and Spain. **Area:** 176,460 sq. mi. (547,030 sq km). **Border countries**: Andorra, Belgium, Germany, Italy, Luxembourg, Monaco, Spain, Switzerland. **Natural resources:** coal, iron ore, bauxite, zinc, potash, timber, fish. **People Population:** 60,180,529 (July 2003 est.). **Nationality:** *noun:* Frenchman(men), Frenchwoman (women); *adj.:* French. **Ethnic groups:** Celtic and Latin with Teutonic, Slavic, North African, Indochinese, Basque minorities. **Religions:** Roman Catholic 83%-88%, Protestant 2%, Jewish 1%, Muslim 5%-10%, unaffiliated 4%. **Languages:** French 100%, rapidly declining regional dialects and languages (Provencal, Breton, Alsatian, Corsican, Catalan, Basque, Flemish). **Government Government type:** republic. Capital: Paris. **Independence:** 486 (unified by Clovis). **National holiday:** Bastille Day, 14 July (1789). **Economy G.D.P.:** purchasing power parity—$1.54 trillion (2002 est.). **G.D.P.—per capita:** purchasing power parity—$25,700 (2002 est.). **Currency:** euro (EUR).

Gabon

Gabonese Republic

Geography Location: Western Africa, bordering the Atlantic Ocean at the Equator, between Republic of the Congo and Equatorial Guinea. **Area:** 103,348 sq. mi. (267,667 sq km). **Border countries**: Cameroon, Republic of the Congo, Equatorial Guinea. **Natural resources:** petroleum, manganese, uranium, gold, timber, iron ore, hydropower. **People** Population:1,321,560. **Nationality:** *noun:* Gabonese (singular and plural); *adj.:* Gabonese. **Ethnic groups:** Bantu tribes including four major tribal groupings (Fang, Bapounou, Nzebi, Obamba), other Africans and Europeans 154,000, including 10,700 French and 11,000 persons of dual nationality. **Religions:** Christian 55%-75%, animist, Muslim less than 1%. **Languages:** French (official), Fang, Myene, Nzebi, Bapounou/Eschira, Bandjabi. **Government Government type:** republic; multiparty presidential regime (opposition parties legalized in 1990). Capital: Libreville. **Independence:** 17 August 1960 (from France). **National holiday:** Founding of the Gabonese Democratic Party (PDG), 12 March (1968). **Economy G.D.P.:** purchasing power parity—$7 billion (2002 est.). **G.D.P.—per capita:** purchasing power parity—$5,700 (2002 est.). **Currency:** Communaute Financiere Africaine franc (XAF); note—responsible authority is the Bank of the Central African States.

Gambia, The

Republic of The Gambia

Geography Location: Western Africa, bordering the North Atlantic Ocean and Senegal. **Area:** 4,363 sq. mi. (11,300 sq km). **Border countries**: Senegal. **Natural resources:** fish. **People Population:** 1,501,050 (July 2003 est.). **Nationality:** *noun:* Gambian(s); *adj.:* Gambian. **Ethnic groups:** African 99% (Mandinka 42%, Fula 18%, Wolof 16%, Jola 10%, Serahuli 9%, other 4%), non-African 1%. **Religions:** Muslim 90%, Christian 9%, indigenous beliefs 1%. **Languages:** English (official), Mandinka, Wolof, Fula, other indigenous vernaculars. **Government Government type**: republic under multiparty democratic rule. Capital: Banjul. **Independence**: 18 February 1965 (from UK). **National holiday**: Independence Day, 18 February (1965). April 1970. **Economy G.D.P.:** purchasing power parity—$2.6 billion (2002 est.). **G.D.P.—per capita:** purchasing power parity—$1,800 (2002 est.). **Currency:** dalasi (GMD).

Georgia

Geography Location: Southwestern Asia, bordering the Black Sea, between Turkey and Russia. **Area:** 26,911 sq. mi. (69,700 sq km). **Border countries**: Armenia, Azerbaijan, Russia, Turkey. **Natural resources:** forests, hydropower, manganese deposits, iron ore, copper, minor coal and oil deposits; coastal climate and soils allow for important tea and citrus growth. **People Population:** 4,934,413 (July 2003 est.). **Nationality:** *noun:* Georgian(s); *adj.:* Georgian. **Ethnic groups:** Georgian 70.1%, Armenian 8.1%, Russian 6.3%, Azeri 5.7%, Ossetian 3%, Abkhaz 1.8%, other 5%. **Religions:** Georgian Orthodox 65%, Muslim 11%, Russian Orthodox 10%, Armenian Apostolic 8%, unknown 6%. **Languages:** Georgian 71% (official), Russian 9%, Armenian 7%, Azeri 6%, other 7%. *note:* Abkhaz is the official language in Abkhazia. **Government Government type:** republic. Capital: T'bilisi. **Independence:** 9 April 1991 (from Soviet Union). **National holiday:** Independence Day, 26 May (1918); note—26 May 1918 is the date of independence from Soviet Russia, 9 April 1991 is the date of independence from the Soviet Union. **Economy G.D.P.:** purchasing power parity—$15 billion (2002 est.). **G.D.P.—per capita:** purchasing power parity—$3,100 (2001 est.). **Currency:** lari (GEL).

Germany

Federal Republic of Germany

Geography Location: Central Europe, bordering the Baltic Sea and the North Sea, between the Netherlands and Poland, south of Denmark. **Area:** 137,803 sq. mi. (357,021 sq km). **Border countries**: Austria, Belgium, Czech Republic, Denmark, France, Luxembourg, Netherlands, Poland, Switzerland. **Natural resources:** iron ore, coal, potash, timber, lignite, uranium, copper, natural gas, salt, nickel, arable land. **People Population:** 82,398,326 (July 2003 est.). **Nationality:** *noun:* German(s); *adj.:* German. **Ethnic groups:** German 91.5%, Turkish 2.4%, other 6.1% (made up largely of Serbo-Croatian, Italian, Russian, Greek, Polish, Spanish). **Religions:** Protestant 34%, Roman Catholic 34%, Muslim 3.7%, unaffiliated or other 28.3%. **Languages:** German. **Government Government type:** federal republic. Capital: Berlin. **Independence:** 18 January 1871 (German Empire unification); divided into four zones of occupation (UK, US, USSR, and later, France) in 1945 following World War II; Federal Republic of Germany (FRG or West

Germany) proclaimed 23 May 1949 and included the former UK, US, and French zones; German Democratic Republic (GDR or East Germany) proclaimed 7 October 1949 and included the former USSR zone; unification of West Germany and East Germany took place 3 October 1990; all four powers formally relinquished rights 15 March 1991. **National holiday:** Unity Day, 3 October (1990). **Economy G.D.P.:** purchasing power parity—$2.184 trillion (2002 est.). **G.D.P.—per capita:** purchasing power parity—$26,600 (2002 est.). **Currency:** euro (EUR).

Ghana

Republic of Ghana

Geography Location: Western Africa, bordering the Gulf of Guinea, between Cote d'Ivoire and Togo. **Area:** 92,100 sq. mi. (239,460 sq km). **Border countries:** Burkina Faso, Cote d'Ivoire, Togo. **Natural resources:** gold, timber, industrial diamonds, bauxite, manganese, fish, rubber, hydropower. **People Population:** 20,467,747. **Nationality:** *noun:* Ghanaian(s); *adj.:* Ghanaian. **Ethnic groups:** black African 98.5% (major tribes—Akan 44%, Moshi-Dagomba 16%, Ewe 13%, Ga 8%, Gurma 3%, Yoruba 1%), European and other 1.5% (1998). **Religions:** indigenous beliefs 21%, Muslim 16%, Christian 63%. **Languages:** English (official), African languages (including Akan, Moshi-Dagomba, Ewe, and Ga). *note:* there are 9,500 Liberians, 2,000 Sierra Leoneans, and 1,000 Togolese refugees residing in Ghana (2002) **Government Government type:** constitutional democracy. Capital: Accra. **Independence:** 6 March 1957 (from UK). **National holiday:** Independence Day, 6 March (1957) **Economy G.D.P.:** purchasing power parity—$42.5 billion (2002 est.). **G.D.P.—per capita:** purchasing power parity—$2,100 (2002 est.). **Currency:** cedi (GHC).

Greece

Hellenic Republic

Geography Location: Southern Europe, bordering the Aegean Sea, Ionian Sea, and the Mediterranean Sea, between Albania and Turkey. **Area:** 50,942 sq. mi. (131,940 sq km). **Border countries:** Albania, Bulgaria, Turkey, The Former Yugoslav Republic of Macedonia. **Natural resources:** bauxite, lignite, magnesite, petroleum, marble, hydropower potential. **People Population:** 10,665,989 (July 2003 est.). **Nationality:** *noun:* Greek(s); *adj.:* Greek. **Ethnic groups:** Greek 98%, other 2%. *note:* the Greek Government states there are no ethnic divisions in Greece. **Religions:** Greek Orthodox 98%, Muslim 1.3%, other 0.7%. **Languages:** Greek 99% (official), English, French. **Government** type: parliamentary republic; monarchy rejected by referendum 8 December 1974. Capital: Athens. **Independence:** 1829 (from the Ottoman Empire). **National holiday:** Independence Day, 25 March (1821). **Economy G.D.P.:** purchasing power parity—$201.1 billion (2002 est.). **G.D.P.—per capita:** purchasing power parity—$19,000 (2002 est.). **Currency:** euro (EUR).

Grenada

Geography Location: Caribbean, island between the Caribbean Sea and Atlantic Ocean, north of Trinidad and Tobago. **Area:** 131 sq. mi. (344 sq km). **Natural resources:** timber, tropical fruit, deepwater harbors. **People Population:** 89,258 (July 2003 est.). **Nationality:** *noun:* Grenadian(s); *adj.:* Grenadian. **Ethnic groups:** black 82%, mixed black and European 13%, European and East Indian 5% , and trace of Arawak/Carib Amerindian. **Religions:** Roman Catholic 53%, Anglican 13.8%, other Protestant 33.2%. **Languages:** English (official), French patois. **Government Government type:** constitutional monarchy with Westminster-style parliament. Capital: Saint George's. **Independence:** 7 February 1974 (from UK). **National holiday:** Independence Day, 7 February (1974). **Economy G.D.P.:** purchasing power parity—$440 million (2002 est.). **G.D.P.—per capita:** purchasing power parity—$5,000 (2002 est.). **Currency:** East Caribbean dollar (XCD).

Guatemala

Republic of Guatemala

Geography Location: Middle America, bordering the North Pacific Ocean, between El Salvador and Mexico, and bordering the Gulf of Honduras (Caribbean Sea) between Honduras and Belize. **Area:** 42,042 sq. mi. (108,890 sq km). **Border countries:** Belize, El Salvador, Honduras, Mexico. **Natural resources:** petroleum, nickel, rare woods, fish, chicle, hydropower. **People Population:** 13,909,384 (July 2003 est.). **Nationality:** *noun:* Guatemalan(s); *adj.:* Guatemalan. **Ethnic groups:** Mestizo (mixed Amerindian-Spanish or assimilated Amerindian—in local Spanish called Ladino), approximately 55%, Amerindian or predominantly Amerindian, approximately 43%, whites and others 2%. **Religions:** Roman Catholic, Protestant, indigenous Mayan beliefs. **Languages:** Spanish 60%, Amerindian languages 40% (23 officially recognized Amerindian languages, including Quiche, Cakchiquel, Kekchi, Mam, Garifuna, and Xinca). **Government Government type:** constitutional democratic republic. Capital: Guatemala. **Independence:** 15 September 1821 (from Spain). **National holiday:** Independence Day, 15 September (1821). **Economy G.D.P.:**

purchasing power parity—$48 billion (2002 est.). **G.D.P.—per capita:** purchasing power parity—$3,700 (2002 est.). , **Currency:** quetzal GTQ), US dollar (USD), others allowed.

Guinea

Republic of Guinea

Geography Location: Western Africa, bordering the North Atlantic Ocean, between Guinea-Bissau and Sierra Leone. **Area:** 94,927 sq. mi. (245,857 sq km). **Border countries**: Cote d'Ivoire, Guinea-Bissau, Liberia, Mali, Senegal, Sierra Leone. **Natural resources:** bauxite, iron ore, diamonds, gold, uranium, hydropower, fish. **People Population:** 9,030,220 (July 2003 est.). **Nationality:** *noun:* Guinean(s); *adj.:* Guinean. **Ethnic groups:** Peuhl 40%, Malinke 30%, Soussou 20%, smaller ethnic groups 10%. **Religions:** Muslim 85%, Christian 8%, indigenous beliefs 7%. **Languages:** French (official), each ethnic group has its own language. **Government Government type:** republic. Capital: Conakry. **Independence:** 2 October 1958 (from France). **National holiday:** Independence Day, 2 October (1958). **Economy G.D.P.:** purchasing power parity—$15.9 billion (2002 est.). **G.D.P.—per capita:** purchasing power parity—$2,000 (2002 est.). **Currency:** Guinean franc (GNF).

Guinea-Bissau

Republic of Guinea-Bissau

Geography Location: Western Africa, bordering the North Atlantic Ocean, between Guinea and Senegal. **Area:** 13,946 sq. mi. (36,120 sq km). **Border countries**: Guinea, Senegal. **Natural resources:** fish, timber, phosphates, bauxite, unexploited deposits of petroleum. **People** Population:1,360,827 (July 2003 est.). **Nationality:** *noun:* Guinean(s); *adj.:* Guinean. **Ethnic groups:** African 99% (Balanta 30%, Fula 20%, Manjaca 14%, Mandinga 13%, Papel 7%), European and mulatto less than 1%. **Religions:** indigenous beliefs 50%, Muslim 45%, Christian 5%. **Languages:** Portuguese (official), Crioulo, African languages. **Government Government type:** republic, multiparty since mid-1991. Capital: Bissau. **Independence:** 24 September 1973 (unilaterally declared by Guinea-Bissau); 10 September 1974 (recognized by Portugal). **National holiday:** Independence Day, 24 September (1973). **Economy G.D.P.:** purchasing power parity—$1.1 billion (2002 est.). **G.D.P.—per capita:** purchasing power parity—$800 (2002 est.). **Currency:** Communaute Financiere Africaine franc (XOF); note—responsible authority is the Central Bank of the West African States; previously the Guinea-Bissau peso (GWP) was used.

Guyana

Co-operative Republic of Guyana

Geography Location: Northern South America, bordering the North Atlantic Ocean, between Suriname and Venezuela. **Area:** 83,000 sq. mi. (214,970 sq km). **Border countries**: Brazil, Suriname, Venezuela. **Natural resources:**bauxite, gold, diamonds, hardwood timber, shrimp, fish. **People Population:** 702,100. **Nationality:** *noun:* Guyanese (singular and plural); *adj.:* Guyanese. **Ethnic groups:** East Indian 50%, black 36%, Amerindian 7%, white, Chinese, and mixed 7%. **Religions:** Christian 50%, Hindu 35%, Muslim 10%, other 5%. **Languages:** English, Amerindian dialects, Creole, Hindi, Urdu. **Government Government type:** republic within the Commonwealth. Capital: Georgetown. **Independence:** 26 May 1966 (from UK). **National holiday:** Republic Day, 23 February (1970). **Economy G.D.P.:** purchasing power parity—$2.7 billion (2002 est.). **Currency:** Guyanese dollar (GYD).

Haiti

Republic of Haiti

Geography Location: Caribbean, western one-third of the island of Hispaniola, between the Caribbean Sea and the North Atlantic Ocean, west of the Dominican Republic. **Area:** 10,714 sq. mi. (27,750 sq km). **Border countries**: Dominican Republic. **Natural resources:** bauxite, copper, calcium carbonate, gold, marble, hydropower.

People Population: 7,527,817. **Nationality:** *noun:* Haitian(s); *adj.:* Haitian; **Ethnic groups:** black 95%, mulatto and white 5%. **Religions:** Roman Catholic 80%, Protestant 16% (Baptist 10%, Pentecostal 4%, Adventist 1%, other 1%), none 1%, other 3% (1982) *note:* roughly half of the population also practices Voodoo. **Languages:** French (official), Creole (official). **Government Government type:** elected government. Capital: Port-au-Prince. **Independence:**1 January 1804 (from France). **National holiday:** Independence Day, 1 January (1804). president elected by popular vote for a five-year term; prime minister appointed by the president, ratified by the National Assembly. **Legislative branch:** bicameral National Assembly. **Judicial branch:** Supreme Court. **Economy G.D.P.:** purchasing power parity—$12 billion (2002 est.). **G.D.P.—per capita:** purchasing power parity—$1,700 (2002 est.). **Currency:** gourde (HTG).

Holy See (Vatican City)

The Holy See (State of the Vatican City)

Geography Location: Southern Europe, an enclave of Rome (Italy). **Area:** 0.17 sq. mi. (0.44 sq km). **Border coun-**

tries: Italy. **Natural resources:** none. **People Population:** 911 (July 2003 est.). **Nationality:** *noun:* none; *adj.:* none. **Ethnic groups:** Italians, Swiss, other. **Religions:** Roman Catholic. **Languages:** Italian, Latin, French, various other languages. **Government Government type:** ecclesiastical . Capital: Vatican City. **Independence:** 11 February 1929 (from Italy). *note:* on 11 February 1929, three treaties were signed with Italy which, among other things, recognized the full sovereignty of the Vatican and established its territorial extent; however, the origin of the Papal States, which over the years have varied considerably in extent, may be traced back to the 8th century. **National holiday:** Coronation Day of Pope JOHN PAUL II, 22 October (1978). **Economy** Overview: This unique, noncommercial economy is supported financially by an annual tax on Roman Catholic dioceses throughout the world, as well as by special collections (known as Peter's Pence); the sale of postage stamps, coins, medals, and tourist mementos; fees for admission to museums; and the sale of publications. Investments and real estate income also account for a sizable portion of revenue. The incomes and living standards of lay workers are comparable to those of counterparts who work in the city of Rome. **Currency:**euro (EUR).

Honduras

Republic of Honduras

Geography Location: Middle America, bordering the Caribbean Sea, between Guatemala and Nicaragua and bordering the Gulf of Fonseca (North Pacific Ocean), between El Salvador and Nicaragua. **Area:** 43,278 sq. mi. (112,090 sq km). **Border countries**: Guatemala, El Salvador, Nicaragua. **Natural resources:** timber, gold, silver, copper, lead, zinc, iron ore, antimony, coal, fish, hydropower. **People Population:** 6,669,789. **Nationality:** *noun:* Honduran(s); *adj.:* Honduran. **Ethnic groups:** mestizo (mixed Amerindian and European) 90%, Amerindian 7%, black 2%, white 1%. **Religions:** Roman Catholic 97%, Protestant minority. **Languages:** Spanish, Amerindian dialects. **Government Government type:** democratic constitutional republic. Capital: Tegucigalpa. **Independence:** 15 September 1821 (from Spain). **National holiday:** Independence Day, 15 September (1821). **Economy G.D.P.:** purchasing power parity—$17.6 billion (2002 est.). **G.D.P.—per capita:** purchasing power parity—$2,600 (2002 est.). **Currency:** lempira (HNL).

Hungary

Republic of Hungary

Geography Location: Central Europe, northwest of Romania. **Area:** 35,919 sq. mi. (93,030 sq km). **Border countries**: Austria, Croatia, Romania, Serbia and Montenegro, Slovakia, Slovenia, Ukraine. **Natural resources:** bauxite, coal, natural gas, fertile soils, arable land. **People Population:** 10,045,407 (July 2003 est.). **Nationality:** *noun:* Hungarian(s); *adj.:* Hungarian. **Ethnic groups:** Hungarian 89.9%, Roma 4%, German 2.6%, Serb 2%, Slovak 0.8%, Romanian 0.7%. **Religions:** Roman Catholic 67.5%, Calvinist 20%, Lutheran 5%, atheist and other 7.5%. **Languages:** Hungarian 98.2%, other 1.8%. **Government Government type:** parliamentary democracy. Capital: Budapest. **Independence:** 1001 (unification by King Stephen I). **National holiday:** Saint Stephen's Day, 20 August. **Economy G.D.P.:** purchasing power parity—$134.7 billion (2002 est.). **G.D.P.—per capita:** purchasing power parity—$13,300 (2002 est.). **Currency:** forint (HUF).

Iceland

Republic of Iceland

Geography Location: Northern Europe, island between the Greenland Sea and the North Atlantic Ocean, northwest of the UK. **Area:** 39,768 sq. mi. (103,000 sq km). **Natural resources:** fish, hydropower, geothermal power, diatomite. **People Population:** 280,798 (July 2003 est.). **Nationality:** *noun:* Icelander(s); *adj.:* Icelandic. **Ethnic groups:** homogeneous mixture of descendants of Norse and Celts 94%, population of foreign origin 6%. **Religions:** Evangelical Lutheran 87.1%, other Protestant 4.1%, Roman Catholic 1.7%, other 7.1% (2002). **Languages:** Icelandic, English, Nordic languages, German widely spoken. **Government Government type**: constitutional republic. Capital: Reykjavik. **Independence**: 1 December 1918 (became a sovereign state under the Danish Crown); 17 June 1944 (from Denmark). **National holiday**: Independence Day, 17 June (1944). **Economy G.D.P.:** purchasing power parity—$7 billion (2002 est.). **G.D.P.—per capita:** purchasing power parity—$25,000 (2002 est.). **Currency:** Icelandic krona (ISK).

India

Republic of India

Geography Location: Southern Asia, bordering the Arabian Sea and the Bay of Bengal, between Burma and Pakistan. **Area:** 1,269,340 sq. mi. (3,287,590 sq km). **Border countries**: Bangladesh, Bhutan, Burma, China, Nepal, Pakistan. **Natural resources:** coal (fourth-largest reserves in the world), iron ore, manganese, mica, bauxite, titanium ore, chromite, natural gas, diamonds, petroleum, limestone, arable land. **People Population:** 1,049,700,118 (July 2003 est.). **Nationality:** *noun:* Indian(s); *adj.:* Indian. **Ethnic groups:** Indo-Aryan 72%, Dravidian 25%, Mongoloid and other 3% (2000). **Religions:** Hindu 81.3%, Muslim 12%, Christian

2.3%, Sikh 1.9%, other groups including Buddhist, Jain, Parsi 2.5% (2000). **Languages:** English enjoys associate status but is the most important language for national, political, and commercial communication; Hindi is the national language and primary tongue of 30% of the people; there are 14 other official **languages:** Bengali, Telugu, Marathi, Tamil, Urdu, Gujarati, Malayalam, Kannada, Oriya, Punjabi, Assamese, Kashmiri, Sindhi, and Sanskrit; Hindustani is a popular variant of Hindi/Urdu spoken widely throughout northern India but is not an official language. **Government Government type:** federal republic. Capital: New Delhi. **Independence:** 15 August 1947 (from UK). **National holiday:** Republic Day, 26 January (1950). **Economy G.D.P.:** purchasing power parity—$2.66 trillion (2002 est.). **G.D.P.—per capita:** purchasing power parity—$2,540 (2002 est.). **Currency:** Indian rupee (INR).

Indonesia

Republic of Indonesia

Geography Location: Southeastern Asia, archipelago between the Indian Ocean and the Pacific Ocean. **Area:** 741,097 sq. mi. (1,919,440 sq km). **Border countries**: East Timor, Malaysia, Papua New Guinea. **Natural resources:** petroleum, tin, natural gas, nickel, timber, bauxite, copper, fertile soils, coal, gold, silver. **People Population:** 234,893,453 (July 2003 est.). **Nationality:** *noun:* Indonesian(s); *adj.:* Indonesian. **Ethnic groups:** Javanese 45%, Sundanese 14%, Madurese 7.5%, coastal Malays 7.5%, other 26%. **Religions:** Muslim 88%, Protestant 5%, Roman Catholic 3%, Hindu 2%, Buddhist 1%, other 1% (1998). **Languages:** Bahasa Indonesia (official, modified form of Malay), English, Dutch, local dialects, the most widely spoken of which is Javanese. **Government Government type:** republic. Capital: Jakarta. **Independence:** 17 August 1945 (proclaimed independence; on 27 December 1949, Indonesia became legally independent from the Netherlands). **National holiday:** Independence Day, 17 August (1945). **Economy G.D.P.:** purchasing power parity—$663 billion (2002 est.). **G.D.P.—per capita:** purchasing power parity—$3,100 (2002 est.). **Currency:** Indonesian rupiah (IDR).

Iran

Islamic Republic of Iran

Geography Location: Middle East, bordering the Gulf of Oman, the Persian Gulf, and the Caspian Sea, between Iraq and Pakistan. **Area:** 636,294 sq. mi. (1.648 million sq km). **Border countries**: Afghanistan, Armenia, Azerbaijan-proper, Azerbaijan-Naxcivan exclave, Iraq, Pakistan, Turkey, Turkmenistan. **Natural resources:** petroleum, natural gas, coal, chromium, copper, iron ore, lead, manganese, zinc, sulfur. **People Population:** 68,278,826 (July 2003 est.). **Nationality:** *noun:* Iranian(s); *adj.:* Iranian. **Ethnic groups:** Persian 51%, Azeri 24%, Gilaki and Mazandarani 8%, Kurd 7%, Arab 3%, Lur 2%, Baloch 2%, Turkmen 2%, other 1%. **Religions:** Shi'a Muslim 89%, Sunni Muslim 10%, Zoroastrian, Jewish, Christian, and Baha'i 1%. **Languages:** Persian and Persian dialects 58%, Turkic and Turkic dialects 26%, Kurdish 9%, Luri 2%, Balochi 1%, Arabic 1%, Turkish 1%, other 2% **Government Government type:** theocratic republic. Capital: Tehran. **Independence:** 1 April 1979 (Islamic Republic of Iran proclaimed). **National holiday:** Republic Day, 1 April (1979) *note:* additional holidays celebrated widely in Iran include Revolution Day, 11 February (1979); Noruz (New Year's Day), 21 March; Constitutional Monarchy Day, 5 August (1925). **Economy G.D.P.**: purchasing power parity—$456 billion (2002 est.). **G.D.P.—per capita**: purchasing power parity—$7,000 (2002 est.). **Currency**: Iranian rial (IRR).

Iraq

Republic of Iraq

Geography Location: Middle East, bordering the Persian Gulf, between Iran and Kuwait. **Area:** 168,754 sq. mi. (437,072 sq km). **Border countries**: Iran, Jordan, Kuwait , Saudi Arabia, Syria, Turkey. **Natural resources:** petroleum, natural gas, phosphates, sulfur. **People Population:** 24,683,313 (July 2003 est.). **Nationality:** *noun:* Iraqi(s); *adj.:* Iraqi. **Ethnic groups:** Arab 75%-80%, Kurdish 15%-20%, Turkoman, Assyrian or other 5%. **Religions:** Muslim 97% (Shi'a 60%-65%, Sunni 32%-37%), Christian or other 3%. **Languages:** Arabic, Kurdish (official in Kurdish regions), Assyrian, Armenian. **Government Government type**: in transition following April 2003 defeat of SADDAM Husayn regime by US-led coalition. Capital: Baghdad. **Independence**: 3 October 1932 (from League of Nations mandate under British administration). **National holiday**: Revolution Day, 17 July (1968). **Economy G.D.P.:** purchasing power parity—$58 billion (2002 est.). **G.D.P.—per capita:** purchasing power parity—$2,400 (2002 est.). **Currency:** Iraqi dinar (IQD).

Ireland

Geography Location: Western Europe, occupying five-sixths of the island of Ireland in the North Atlantic Ocean, west of Great Britain. **Area:** 27,135 sq. mi. (70,280 sq km). **Border countries**: UK. **Natural resources:**zinc, lead, natural gas, barite, copper, gypsum, limestone, dolomite, peat, silver. **People Population:** 3,924,140 (July 2003 est.). **Nationality:** *noun:* Irishman(men), Irishwoman(women), Irish (collective plural); *adj.:* Irish. **Ethnic groups:** Celtic,

English. **Religions:** Roman Catholic 91.6%, Church of Ireland 2.5%, other 5.9% (1998) **Languages:** English is the language generally used, Irish (Gaelic) spoken mainly in areas located along the western seaboard. **Government Government type:** republic. Capital: Dublin. **Independence:** 6 December 1921 (from UK by treaty). **National holiday:** Saint Patrick's Day, 17 March. **Economy G.D.P.:** purchasing power parity—$118.5 billion (2002 est.). **G.D.P.—per capita:** purchasing power parity—$30,500 (2002 est.). **Currency:** euro (EUR).

Israel

State of Israel

Geography Location: Middle East, bordering the Mediterranean Sea, between Egypt and Lebanon. **Area:** 8,019 sq. mi. (20,770 sq km). **Border countries**: Egypt, Gaza Strip, Jordan, Lebanon, Syria, West Bank. **Natural resources:** timber, potash, copper ore, natural gas, phosphate rock, magnesium bromide, clays, sand. **People Population:** 6,116,533 (July 2002 est.). *note:* includes about 187,000 Israeli settlers in the West Bank, about 20,000 in the Israeli-occupied Golan Heights, more than 5,000 in the Gaza Strip, and fewer than 177,000 in East Jerusalem (February 2003 est.) (July 2003 est.). **Nationality:** *noun:* Israeli(s). *adj.:* Israeli. **Ethnic groups:** Jewish 80.1% (Europe/America-born 32.1%, Israel-born 20.8%, Africa-born 14.6%, Asia-born 12.6%), non-Jewish 19.9% (mostly Arab) (1996 est.). **Religions:** Jewish 80.1%, Muslim 14.6% (mostly Sunni Muslim), Christian 2.1%, other 3.2% (1996 est.). **Languages:** Hebrew (official), Arabic used officially for Arab minority, English most commonly used foreign language. **Government Government type:** parliamentary democracy. Capital: Jerusalem; note—Israel proclaimed Jerusalem as its capital in 1950, but the US, like nearly all other countries, maintains its Embassy in Tel Aviv. **Independence:** 14 May 1948 (from League of Nations mandate under British administration). **National holiday:** Independence Day, 14 May (1948); note—Israel declared independence on 14 May 1948, but the Jewish calendar is lunar and the holiday may occur in April or May. **Economy G.D.P.:** purchasing power parity—$122 billion (2002 est.). **G.D.P.—per capita:** purchasing power parity—$19,000 (2002 est.). **Currency:** new Israeli shekel (ILS).

Italy

Italian Republic

Geography Location: Southern Europe, a peninsula extending into the central Mediterranean Sea, northeast of Tunisia. **Area:** 116,305 sq. mi. (301,230 sq km). **Border countries**: Austria, France, Holy See (Vatican City), San Marino, Slovenia, Switzerland. **Natural resources:** mercury, potash, marble, sulfur, natural gas and crude oil reserves, fish, coal, arable land. **People Population:** 57,998,353 (July 2003 est.). **Nationality:** *noun:* Italian(s); *adj.:* Italian. **Ethnic groups:** Italian (includes small clusters of German-, French-, and Slovene-Italians in the north and Albanian-Italians and Greek-Italians in the south). **Religions:** predominately Roman Catholic with mature Protestant and Jewish communities and a growing Muslim immigrant community. **Languages:** Italian (official), German (parts of Trentino-Alto Adige region are predominantly German speaking), French (small French-speaking minority in Valle d'Aosta region), Slovene (Slovene-speaking minority in the Trieste-Gorizia area). **Government Government type:** republic. Capital: Rome. **Independence:** 17 March 1861 (Kingdom of Italy proclaimed; Italy was not finally unified until 1870). **National holiday:** Republic Day, 2 June (1946). **Economy G.D.P.:** purchasing power parity—$1.438 trillion (2002 est.). **G.D.P.—per capita:** purchasing power parity—$25,000 (2002 est.). **Currency:** euro (EUR).

Jamaica

Geography Location: Caribbean, island in the Caribbean Sea, south of Cuba. **Area:** 4,243 sq. mi. (10,991 sq km). **Natural resources:** bauxite, gypsum, limestone. **People Population:** (2,695,867 (July 2003 est.). **Nationality:** *noun:* Jamaican(s); *adj.:* Jamaican. **Ethnic groups:** black 90.9%, East Indian 1.3%, white 0.2%, Chinese 0.2%, mixed 7.3%, other 0.1%. **Religions:** Protestant 61.3% (Church of God 21.2%, Baptist 8.8%, Anglican 5.5%, Seventh-Day Adventist 9%, Pentecostal 7.6%, Methodist 2.7%, United Church 2.7%, Brethren 1.1%, Jehovah's Witness 1.6%, Moravian 1.1%), Roman Catholic 4%, other, including some spiritual cults 34.7%. **Languages:** English, patois English. **Government Government type:** constitutional parliamentary democracy. Capital: Kingston. **Independence:** 6 August 1962 (from UK). **National holiday:** Independence Day, first Monday in August (1962). **Economy G.D.P.:** purchasing power parity—$10 billion (2002 est.). **G.D.P.—per capita:** purchasing power parity—$3,900 (2002 est.). **Currency:** Jamaican dollar (JMD).

Japan

Geography Location: Eastern Asia, island chain between the North Pacific Ocean and the Sea of Japan, east of the Korean Peninsula. **Area:** 145,882 sq. mi. (377,835 sq km). **Natural resources:** negligible mineral resources, fish. **People Population:** 127,214,499 (July 2003 est.). **Nationality:** *noun:* Japanese (singular and plural); *adj.:* Japanese. **Ethnic groups:** Japanese 99%, others 1% (Korean

511,262, Chinese 244,241, Brazilian 182,232, Filipino 89,851, other 237,914) (2000). **Religions:** observe both Shinto and Buddhist 84%, other 16% (including Christian 0.7%). **Languages:** Japanese. **Government** **Government type:** constitutional monarchy with a parliamentary government. Capital: Tokyo. **Independence:** 660 BC (traditional founding by Emperor Jimmu). **National holiday:** Birthday of Emperor AKIHITO, 23 December (1933). **Economy** **G.D.P.:** purchasing power parity—$3.55 trillion (2002 est.). **G.D.P.—per capita:** purchasing power parity—$28,000 (2002 est.). **Currency:** yen (JPY).

Jordan

Hashemite Kingdom of Jordan

Geography **Location:** Middle East, northwest of Saudi Arabia. **Area:** 34,445 sq. mi. (92,300 sq km). **Border countries**: Iraq, Israel, Saudi Arabia, Syria, West Bank. **Natural resources:** phosphates, potash, shale oil. **People** **Population:** 5,460,265 (July 2003 est.). **Nationality:** *noun:* Jordanian(s); *adj.:* Jordanian. **Ethnic groups:** Arab 98%, Circassian 1%, Armenian 1%. **Religions:** Sunni Muslim 92%, Christian 6% (majority Greek Orthodox, but some Greek and Roman Catholics, Syrian Orthodox, Coptic Orthodox, Armenian Orthodox, and Protestant denominations), other 2% (several small Shi'a Muslim and Druze populations) (2001 est.). **Languages:** Arabic (official), English widely understood among upper and middle classes. **Government** **Government type:** constitutional monarchy. Capital: 'Amman. **Independence:** 25 May 1946 (from League of Nations mandate under British administration). **National holiday:** Independence Day, 25 May (1946). **Economy** **G.D.P.:** purchasing power parity—$22.8 billion (2002 est.). **G.D.P.—per capita:** purchasing power parity—$4,300 (2002 est.). **Currency:** Jordanian dinar (JOD).

Kazakhstan

Geography **Location:** Central Asia, northwest of China; a small portion west of the Ural River in eastern-most Europe. **Area:** 1,049,151 sq. mi. (2,717,300 sq km). **Border countries**: China, Kyrgyzstan, Russia, Turkmenistan, Uzbekistan. **Natural resources:** major deposits of petroleum, natural gas, coal, iron ore, manganese, chrome ore, nickel, cobalt, copper, molybdenum, lead, zinc, bauxite, gold, uranium. **People** **Population:** 16,763,795 (July 2003 est.). **Nationality:** *noun:* Kazakhstani(s); *adj.:* Kazakhstani. **Ethnic groups:** Kazakh (Qazaq) 53.4%, Russian 30%, Ukrainian 3.7%, Uzbek 2.5%, German 2.4%, Uighur 1.4%, other 6.6% (1999 census). **Religions:** Muslim 47%, Russian Orthodox 44%, Protestant 2%, other 7%. **Languages:** Kazakh (Qazaq, state language) 64.4%, Russian (official, used in everyday business, designated the "language of interethnic communication") 95% (2001 est.). **Government** **Government type:** republic. Capital: Astana; note—the government moved from Almaty to Astana in December 1998. **Independence:** 16 December 1991 (from the Soviet Union). **National holiday:** Republic Day, 25 October (1990). **Economy** **G.D.P.:** purchasing power parity—$105 billion (2002 est.). **G.D.P.—per capita:** purchasing power parity—$6,300 (2002 est.). **Currency:** tenge (KZT).

Kenya

Republic of Kenya

Geography **Location:** Eastern Africa, bordering the Indian Ocean, between Somalia and Tanzania. **Area:** 224,962 sq. mi. (582,650 sq km). **Border countries**: Ethiopia, Somalia, Sudan, Tanzania, Uganda. **Natural resources:** gold, limestone, soda ash, salt, rubies, fluorspar, garnets, wildlife, hydropower. **People** **Population:** 31,639,091. **Nationality:** *noun:* Kenyan(s); *adj.:* Kenyan. **Ethnic groups:** Kikuyu 22%, Luhya 14%, Luo 13%, Kalenjin 12%, Kamba 11%, Kisii 6%, Meru 6%, other African 15%, non-African (Asian, European, and Arab) 1%. **Religions:** Protestant 45%, Roman Catholic 33%, indigenous beliefs 10%, Muslim 10%, other 2% *note:* a large majority of Kenyans are Christian, but estimates for the percentage of the population that adheres to Islam or indigenous beliefs vary widely. **Languages:** English (official), Kiswahili (official), numerous indigenous languages. **Government** **Government type:** republic. Capital: Nairobi. **Independence:** 12 December 1963 (from UK). **National holiday:** Independence Day, 12 December (1963). **Economy** **G.D.P.:** purchasing power parity—$32 billion (2002 est.). **G.D.P.—per capita:** purchasing power parity—$1,020 (2002 est.). **Industries:** small-scale consumer goods (plastic, furniture, batteries, textiles, soap, cigarettes, flour), agricultural products processing; oil refining, cement; tourism. **Agriculture—products:** tea, coffee, corn, wheat, sugarcane, fruit, vegetables; dairy products, beef, pork, poultry, eggs. **Currency:** Kenyan shilling (KES).

Kiribati

Republic of Kiribati

Geography **Location:** Oceania, group of 33 coral atolls in the Pacific Ocean, straddling the equator; the capital Tarawa is about one-half of the way from Hawaii to Australia; note—on 1 January 1995, Kiribati proclaimed that all of its territory lies in the same time zone as its Gilbert Islands group (GMT +12) even though the Phoenix Islands and the Line Islands under its jurisdiction lie on the other side of the International Date Line. **Area:** 277 sq. mi. (811 sq km). **Natural resources:** phosphate (production discontinued in 1979). **People**

Population: 98,549 (July 2003 est.). **Nationality:** *noun:* I-Kiribati (singular and plural); *adj.:* I-Kiribati. **Ethnic groups:** predominantly Micronesian with some Polynesian. **Religions:** Roman Catholic 52%, Protestant (Congregational) 40%, some Seventh-Day Adventist, Muslim, Baha'i, Latter-day Saints, and Church of God (1999). **Languages:** I-Kiribati, English (official). **Government Government type:** republic. Capital: Tarawa. **Independence:** 12 July 1979 (from UK). **National holiday:** Independence Day, 12 July (1979). **Economy G.D.P.:** purchasing power parity—$79 million—supplemented by a nearly equal amount from external sources (2001 est.). **G.D.P.—per capita:** purchasing power parity—$840 (2001 est.). **Currency:** Australian dollar (AUD).

Korea, North

Democratic People's Republic of Korea

Geography Location: Eastern Asia, northern half of the Korean Peninsula bordering the Korea Bay and the Sea of Japan, between China and South Korea. **Area:** 46,541 sq. mi. (120,540 sq km). **Border countries**: China, South Korea, Russia. **Natural resources:** coal, lead, tungsten, zinc, graphite, magnesite, iron ore, copper, gold, pyrites, salt, fluorspar, hydropower. **People Population:** 22,466,481 (July 2003 est.). **Nationality:** *noun:* Korean(s); *adj.:* Korean. **Ethnic groups:** racially homogeneous; there is a small Chinese community and a few ethnic Japanese. **Religions:** traditionally Buddhist and Confucianist, some Christian and syncretic Chondogyo (Religion of the Heavenly Way). *note:* autonomous religious activities now almost nonexistent; government-sponsored religious groups exist to provide illusion of religious freedom. **Languages:** Korean. **Government Government type:** authoritarian socialist; one-man dictatorship. Capital: Pyongyang. **Independence:** 15 August 1945 (from Japan). **National holiday:** Founding of the Democratic People's Republic of Korea (DPRK), 9 September (1948). **Economy G.D.P.:** purchasing power parity—$22 billion (2002 est.). **G.D.P.—per capita:** purchasing power parity—$1,000 (2002 est.). **Currency:** North Korean won (KPW).

Korea, South

Republic of Korea

Geography Location: Eastern Asia, southern half of the Korean Peninsula bordering the Sea of Japan and the Yellow Sea. **Area:** 38,023 sq. mi. (98,480 sq km). **Border countries**: North Korea. **Natural resources:** coal, tungsten, graphite, molybdenum, lead, hydropower potential. **People Population:** 48,289,037 (July 2003 est.). **Nationality:** *noun:* Korean(s); *adj.:* Korean. **Ethnic groups:** homogeneous (except for about 20,000 Chinese). **Religions:** Christian 49%, Buddhist 47%, Confucianist 3%, Shamanist, Chondogyo (Religion of the Heavenly Way), and other 1%. **Languages:** Korean, English widely taught in junior high and high school. **Government Government type:** republic. Capital: Seoul. **Independence:** 15 August 1945 (from Japan). **National holiday:** Liberation Day, 15 August (1945). **Economy G.D.P.:** purchasing power parity—$931 billion (2002 est.). **G.D.P.—per capita:** purchasing power parity—$19,400 (2002 est.). **Currency:** South Korean won (KRW).

Kuwait

State of Kuwait

Geography Location: Middle East, bordering the Persian Gulf, between Iraq and Saudi Arabia. **Area:** 6,880 sq. mi. (17,820 sq km). **Border countries**: Iraq, Saudi Arabia. **Natural resources:** petroleum, fish, shrimp, natural gas. **People Population:** 2,183,161. *note:* includes 1,291,354 non-nationals (July 2003 est.). **Nationality:** *noun:* Kuwaiti(s); *adj.:* Kuwaiti. **Ethnic groups:** Kuwaiti 45%, other Arab 35%, South Asian 9%, Iranian 4%, other 7%. **Religions:** Muslim 85% (Sunni 70%, Shi'a 30%), Christian, Hindu, Parsi, and other 15%. **Languages:** Arabic (official), English widely spoken. **Government Government type:** nominal constitutional monarchy. Capital: Kuwait. **Independence:** 19 June 1961 (from UK). **National holiday:** National Day, 25 February (1950). **Economy G.D.P.:** purchasing power parity—$34.2 billion (2002 est.). **G.D.P.—per capita:** purchasing power parity—$15,000 (2002 est.). **Currency:** Kuwaiti dinar (KD).

Kyrgyzstan

Kyrgyz Republic

Geography Location: Central Asia, west of China. **Area:** 76,641 sq. mi. (198,500 sq km). **Border countries**: China, Kazakhstan, Tajikistan, Uzbekistan. **Natural resources:** abundant hydropower; significant deposits of gold and rare earth metals; locally exploitable coal, oil, and natural gas; other deposits of nepheline, mercury, bismuth, lead, and zinc. **People Population:** 4,892,808 (July 2003 est.) **Nationality:** *noun:* Kyrgyzstani(s); *adj.:* Kyrgyzstani. **Ethnic groups:** Kyrgyz 52.4%, Russian 18%, Uzbek 12.9%, Ukrainian 2.5%, German 2.4%, other 11.8%. **Religions:** Muslim 75%, Russian Orthodox 20%, other 5%. **Languages:** Kyrgyz—official language, Russian—official language, *note:* in December 2001, the Kyrgyzstani legislature made Russian an official language, equal in status to Kyrgyz. **Government Government type:** republic. Capital: Bishkek.

Independence: 31 August 1991 (from Soviet Union). **National holiday:** Independence Day, 31 August (1991). **Economy** **G.D.P.:** purchasing power parity—$13.5 billion (2002 est.). **G.D.P.—per capita:** purchasing power parity—$2,800 (2002 est.). **Currency:** Kyrgyzstani som (KGS).

Laos

Lao People's Democratic Republic

Geography **Location:** Southeastern Asia, northeast of Thailand, west of Vietnam. **Area:** 91,429 sq. mi. (236,800 sq km). **Border countries**: Burma, Cambodia, China, Thailand, Vietnam. **Natural resources:** timber, hydropower, gypsum, tin, gold, gemstones. **People** **Population:** 5,921,545 (July 2003 est.). **Nationality:** *noun:* Lao(s) or Laotian(s); *adj.:* Lao or Laotian. **Ethnic groups:** Lao Loum (lowland) 68%, Lao Theung (upland) 22%, Lao Soung (highland) including the Hmong ("Meo") and the Yao (Mien) 9%, ethnic Vietnamese/Chinese 1%. **Religions:** Buddhist 60%, animist and other 40% (including various Christian denominations 1.5%). **Languages:** Lao (official), French, English, and various ethnic languages. **Government** **Government type:** Communist state. Capital: Vientiane. **Independence:** 19 July 1949 (from France). **National holiday:** Republic Day, 2 December (1975). **Economy** **G.D.P.:** purchasing power parity—$9.9 billion (2002 est.). **G.D.P.—per capita:** purchasing power parity—$1,700 (2002 est.). **Currency:** kip (LAK).

Latvia

Republic of Latvia

Geography **Location:** Eastern Europe, bordering the Baltic Sea, between Estonia and Lithuania. **Area:** 24,749 sq. mi. (64,589 sq km). **Border countries**: Belarus, Estonia, Lithuania, Russia. **Natural resources:** peat, limestone, dolomite, amber, hydropower, wood, arable land. **People** **Population:** 2,348,784 (July 2003 est.). **Nationality:** *noun:* Latvian(s); *adj.:* Latvian. **Ethnic groups:** Latvian 57.7%, Russian 29.6%, Belarusian 4.1%, Ukrainian 2.7%, Polish 2.5%, Lithuanian 1.4%, other 2%. **Religions:** Lutheran, Roman Catholic, Russian Orthodox. **Languages:** Latvian (official), Lithuanian, Russian, other. **Government** **Government type:** parliamentary democracy. Capital: Riga. **Independence:** 21 August 1991 (from Soviet Union). **National holiday:** Independence Day, 18 November (1918); note—18 November 1918 is the date of independence from Soviet Russia, 21 August 1991 is the date of independence from the Soviet Union. **Economy** **G.D.P.:** purchasing power parity—$20 billion (2002 est.). **G.D.P.—per capita:** purchasing power parity—$8,300 (2002 est.). **Currency:** Latvian lat (LVL).

Lebanon

Lebanese Republic

Geography **Location:** Middle East, bordering the Mediterranean Sea, between Israel and Syria. **Area:** 4,015 sq. mi. (10,400 sq km). **Border countries**: Israel, Syria. **Natural resources:** limestone, iron ore, salt, water-surplus state in a water-deficit region, arable land. **People** **Population:** 3,727,703 (July 2003 est.). **Nationality:** *noun:* Lebanese (singular and plural); *adj.:* Lebanese . **Ethnic groups:** Arab 95%, Armenian 4%, other 1%. **Religions:** Muslim 70% (including Shi'a, Sunni, Druze, Isma'ilite, Alawite or Nusayri), Christian 30% (including Orthodox Christian, Catholic, Protestant), Jewish NEGL%. **Languages:** Arabic (official), French, English, Armenian. **Government** **Government type:** republic. Capital: Beirut. **Independence:** 22 November 1943 (from League of Nations mandate under French administration). **National holiday:** Independence Day, 22 November (1943). **Economy** **G.D.P.:** purchasing power parity—$19.3 billion (2002 est.). **G.D.P.—per capita:** purchasing power parity—$5,400 (2002 est.). **Currency:** Lebanese pound (LBP).

Lesotho

Kingdom of Lesotho

Geography **Location:** Southern Africa, an enclave of South Africa. **Area:** 11,718 sq. mi. (30,355 sq km). **Border countries**: South Africa. **Natural resources:** water, agricultural and grazing land, some diamonds and other minerals. **People** **Population:** 1,861,959. *note:* estimates for this country explicitly take into account the effects of excess mortality due to AIDS; this can result in lower life expectancy, higher infant mortality and death rates, lower population and growth rates, and changes in the distribution of population by age and sex than would otherwise be expected (July 2003 est.). **Nationality:** *noun:* Mosotho (singular), Basotho (plural); *adj.:* Basotho. **Ethnic groups:** Sotho 99.7%, Europeans, Asians, and other 0.3%. **Religions:** Christian 80%, indigenous beliefs 20%. **Languages:** Sesotho (southern Sotho), English (official), Zulu, Xhosa. **Government** **Government type:** parliamentary constitutional monarchy. Capital: Maseru. **Independence:** 4 October 1966 (from UK). **National holiday:** Independence Day, 4 October (1966). **Economy** **G.D.P.:** purchasing power parity—$5.6 billion (2002 est.). **G.D.P.—per capita:** purchasing power parity—$2,700 (2002 est.). **Currency:** loti (LSL); South African rand (ZAR).

Liberia

Republic of Liberia

Geography **Location:** Western Africa, bordering the North Atlantic Ocean, between Cote d'Ivoire and Sierra Leone.

Area: 43,000 sq. mi. (111,370 sq km). **Border countries**: Guinea, Cote d'Ivoire, Sierra Leone. **Natural resources:** iron ore, timber, diamonds, gold, hydropower. **People Population:** 3,317,176 (July 2003 est.). **Nationality:** *noun:* Liberian(s); *adj.:* Liberian. **Ethnic groups:** indigenous African tribes 95% (including Kpelle, Bassa, Gio, Kru, Grebo, Mano, Krahn, Gola, Gbandi, Loma, Kissi, Vai, Dei, Bella, Mandingo, and Mende), Americo-Liberians 2.5% (descendants of immigrants from the US who had been slaves), Congo People 2.5% (descendants of immigrants from the Caribbean who had been slaves). **Religions:** indigenous beliefs 40%, Christian 40%, Muslim 20%. **Languages:** English 20% (official), some 20 ethnic group languages, of which a few can be written and are used in correspondence. **Government Government type:** republic. Capital: Monrovia. **Independence:** 26 July 1847. **National holiday:** Independence Day, 26 July (1847). **Economy G.D.P.:** purchasing power parity—$3.5 billion (2002 est.). **G.D.P.—per capita:** purchasing power parity—$1,100 (2002 est.).;

Libya

Great Socialist People's Libyan Arab Jamahiriya

Geography Location: Northern Africa, bordering the Mediterranean Sea, between Egypt and Tunisia. **Area:** 679,359 sq. mi. (1,759,540 sq km). **Border countries**: Algeria, Chad, Egypt, Niger, Sudan, Tunisia. **Natural resources:** petroleum, natural gas, gypsum. **People Population:** 5,499,074. *note:* includes 166,510 non-nationals (July 2003 est.). **Nationality:** *noun:* Libyan(s); *adj.:* Libyan. **Ethnic groups:** Berber and Arab 97%, Greeks, Maltese, Italians, Egyptians, Pakistanis, Turks, Indians, Tunisians. **Religions:** Sunni Muslim 97%. **Languages:** Arabic, Italian, English, all are widely understood in the major cities. **Government Government type:** Jamahiriya (a state of the masses) in theory, governed by the populace through local councils; in fact, a military dictatorship. Capital: Tripoli. **Independence:** 24 December 1951 (from Italy). **National holiday:** Revolution Day, 1 September (1969). **Economy G.D.P.:** purchasing power parity—$41 billion (2002 est.). **G.D.P.—per capita:** purchasing power parity—$7,600 (2002 est.). **Currency:** Libyan dinar (LYD).

Liechtenstein

Principality of Liechtenstein

Geography Location: Central Europe, between Austria and Switzerland. **Area:** 62 sq. mi. (160 sq km). **Border countries**: Austria, Switzerland. **Natural resources:** hydroelectric potential, arable land. **People Population:** 33,145 (July 2003 est.). **Nationality:** *noun:* Liechtensteiner(s); *adj.:* Liechtenstein. **Ethnic groups:** Alemannic 86%, Italian, Turkish, and other 14%. **Religions:** Roman Catholic 76.2%, Protestant 7%, unknown 10.6%, other 6.2% (June 2002). **Languages:** German (official), Alemannic dialect. **Government Government type:** hereditary constitutional monarchy on a democratic and parliamentary basis. Capital: Vaduz. **Independence:** 23 January 1719 Imperial Principality of Liechtenstein established; 12 July 1806 established independence from the Holy Roman Empire. **National holiday:** Assumption Day, 15 August. **Economy G.D.P.:** purchasing power parity—$825 million (1999 est.). **G.D.P.—per capita:** purchasing power parity—$25,000 (1999 est.). **Currency:** Swiss franc (CHF).

Lithuania

Republic of Lithuania

Geography Location: Eastern Europe, bordering the Baltic Sea, between Latvia and Russia. **Area:** 25,174 sq. mi. (65,200 sq km). **Border countries**: Belarus, Latvia, Poland, Russia (Kaliningrad). **Natural resources:** peat, arable land. **People Population:** 3,592,561 (July 2003 est.). **Nationality:** *noun:* Lithuanian(s). *adj.:* Lithuanian. **Ethnic groups:** Lithuanian 80.6%, Russian 8.7%, Polish 7%, Belarusian 1.6%, other 2.1%. **Religions:** Roman Catholic (primarily), Lutheran, Russian Orthodox, Protestant, Evangelical Christian Baptist, Muslim, Jewish. **Languages:** Lithuanian (official), Polish, Russian. **Government Government type**: parliamentary democracy. Capital: Vilnius. **Independence**: 11 March 1990 (independence declared from Soviet Union); 6 September 1991 (Soviet Union recognizes Lithuania's independence). **National holiday**: Independence Day, 16 February (1918); note—16 February 1918 is the date of independence from German, Austrian, Prussian, and Russian occupation, 11 March 1990 is the date of independence from the Soviet Union. **Economy G.D.P.:** purchasing power parity—$29.2 billion (2002 est.). **G.D.P.—per capita:** purchasing power parity—$8,400 (2002 est.). **Currency:** litas (LTL).

Luxembourg

Grand Duchy of Luxembourg

Geography Location: Western Europe, between France and Germany. **Area:** 998 sq. mi. (2,586 sq km). **Border countries**: Belgium, France, Germany. **Natural resources:** iron ore (no longer exploited), arable land. **People Population:** 454,157 (July 2003 est.). **Nationality:** *noun:* Luxembourger(s); *adj.:* Luxembourg. **Ethnic groups:** Celtic base (with French and German blend), Portuguese, Italian, Slavs (from Montenegro, Albania, and Kososvo) and European (guest and resident workers). **Religions:** 87% Roman Catholic, 13% Protestants, Jews, and Muslims

(2000). **Languages:** Luxembourgish (national language), German (administrative language), French (administrative language). **Government Government type:** constitutional monarchy. Capital: Luxembourg. **Independence:** 1839 (from the Netherlands). **National holiday:** National Day (Birthday of Grand Duchess Charlotte) 23 June. **Economy G.D.P.:** purchasing power parity—$20 billion (2002 est.). **G.D.P.—per capita:** purchasing power parity—$44,000 (2002 est.). **Currency:** euro (EUR).

Macedonia, The Former Yugoslav Republic of

The Former Yugoslav Republic of Macedonia

Geography Location: Southeastern Europe, north of Greece. **Area:** 9,781 sq. mi. (25,333 sq km). **Border countries**: Albania, Bulgaria, Greece, Serbia and Montenegro. **Natural resources:** chromium, lead, zinc, manganese, tungsten, nickel, low-grade iron ore, asbestos, sulfur, timber, arable land. **People Population:** 2,063,122, *note:* a census was taken 1-15 November 2002, but results are not yet available (July 2003 est.). **Nationality:** *noun:* Macedonian(s); *adj.:* Macedonian. **Ethnic groups:** Macedonian 66.6%, Albanian 22.7%, Turkish 4%, Roma 2.2%, Serb 2.1%, other 2.4% (1994). **Religions:** Macedonian Orthodox 67%, Muslim 30%, other 3%. **Languages:** Macedonian 70%, Albanian 21%, Turkish 3%, Serbo Croatian 3%, other 3%. **Government Government type:** parliamentary democracy. Capital: Skopje. **Independence:** 8 September 1991 referendum by registered voters endorsing independence (from Yugoslavia). **National holiday:** Uprising Day, 2 August (1903); note—also known as Saint Elijah's Day and Ilinden. **Economy G.D.P.:** purchasing power parity—$10 billion (2002 est.). **G.D.P.—per capita:** purchasing power parity—$5,000 (2002 est.). **Currency:** Macedonian denar (MKD).

Madagascar

Republic of Madagascar

Geography Location: Southern Africa, island in the Indian Ocean, east of Mozambique. **Area:** 226,656 sq. mi. (587,040 sq km). **Natural resources:** graphite, chromite, coal, bauxite, salt, quartz, tar sands, semiprecious stones, mica, fish, hydropower. **People Population:** 16,979,744 (July 2003 est.). **Nationality:** *noun:* Malagasy (singular and plural); *adj.:* Malagasy. **Ethnic groups:** Malayo-Indonesian (Merina and related Betsileo), Cotiers (mixed African, Malayo-Indonesian, and Arab ancestry—Betsimisaraka, Tsimihety, Antaisaka, Sakalava), French, Indian, Creole, Comoran. **Religions:** indigenous beliefs 52%, Christian 41%, Muslim 7%. **Languages:** French (official), Malagasy (official). **Government Government type:** republic. Capital: Antananarivo. **Independence**: 26 June 1960 (from France). **National holiday**: Independence Day, 26 June (1960). **Economy G.D.P.:** purchasing power parity—$12.6 billion (2002). **G.D.P.—per capita:** purchasing power parity—$760 (2002 est.). **Currency:** Malagasy franc (MGF).

Malawi

Republic of Malawi

Geography Location: Southern Africa, east of Zambia. **Area:** 45,745 sq. mi. (118,480 sq km). **Border countries**: Mozambique, Tanzania, Zambia. **Natural resources:** limestone, arable land, hydropower, unexploited deposits of uranium, coal, and bauxite. **People Population:** 11,651,239, *note:* estimates for this country explicitly take into account the effects of excess mortality due to AIDS; this can result in lower life expectancy, higher infant mortality and death rates, lower population and growth rates, and changes in the distribution of population by age and sex than would otherwise be expected (July 2003 est.). **Nationality:** *noun:* Malawian(s); *adj.:* Malawian. **Ethnic groups:** Chewa, Nyanja, Tumbuka, Yao, Lomwe, Sena, Tonga, Ngoni, Ngonde, Asian, European. **Religions:** Protestant 55%, Roman Catholic 20%, Muslim 20%, indigenous beliefs 3%, other 2%. **Languages:** English (official), Chichewa (official), other languages important regionally. **Government Government type:** multiparty democracy. **Capital:** Lilongwe. **Independence:** 6 July 1964 (from UK). **National holiday:** Independence Day (Republic Day), 6 July (1964). **Economy G.D.P.:** purchasing power parity—$7.2 billion (2002 est.). **G.D.P.—per capita:** purchasing power parity—$670 (2002 est.). **Currency:** Malawian kwacha (MWK).

Malaysia

Geography Location: Southeastern Asia, peninsula and northern one-third of the island of Borneo, bordering Indonesia and the South China Sea, south of Vietnam. **Area:** 127,317 sq. mi. (329,750 sq km). **Border countries**: Brunei, Indonesia, Thailand. **Natural resources:** tin, petroleum, timber, copper, iron ore, natural gas, bauxite. **People Population:** 23,092,940 (July 2003 est.). **Nationality:** *noun:* Malaysian(s); *adj.:* Malaysian. **Ethnic groups:** Malay and other indigenous 58%, Chinese 24%, Indian 8%, others 10% (2000). **Religions:** Muslim, Buddhist, Daoist, Hindu, Christian, Sikh; note—in addition, Shamanism is practiced in East Malaysia. **Languages:** Bahasa Melayu (official), English, Chinese dialects (Cantonese, Mandarin, Hokkien, Hakka, Hainan, Foochow), Tamil, Telugu, Malayalam, Panjabi, Thai; note—in addition, in East Malaysia several indigenous languages are spoken, the largest are Iban and Kadazan. **Government Government type:** constitutional monarchy, *note:* Malaya (what is now Peninsular Malaysia) formed 31

August 1957; Federation of Malaysia (Malaya, Sabah, Sarawak, and Singapore) formed 9 July 1963 (Singapore left the federation on 9 August 1965); nominally headed by the paramount ruler and a bicameral Parliament consisting of a nonelected upper house and an elected lower house; Peninsular Malaysian states—hereditary rulers in all but Melaka, George Town (Penang), Sabah, and Sarawak, where governors are appointed by the Malaysian Government; powers of state governments are limited by the federal constitution; under terms of the federation, Sabah and Sarawak retain certain constitutional prerogatives (e.g., the right to maintain their own immigration controls); Sabah—holds 20 seats in House of Representatives, with foreign affairs, defense, internal security, and other powers delegated to federal government; Sarawak—holds 28 seats in House of Representatives, with foreign affairs, defense, internal security, and other powers delegated to federal government. Capital: Kuala Lumpur. **Independence:** 31 August 1957 (from UK). **National holiday:** Independence Day/Malaysia Day, 31 August (1957). **Economy G.D.P.:** purchasing power parity—$210 billion (2002 est.). **G.D.P.—per capita:** purchasing power parity—$9,300 (2002 est.). **Currency:** ringgit (MYR).

Maldives

Republic of Maldives

Geography Location: Southern Asia, group of atolls in the Indian Ocean, south-southwest of India. **Area:** 116 sq. mi. (300 sq km). **Natural resources:** fish. **People Population:** 329,684 (July 2003 est.). **Nationality:** *noun:* Maldivian(s); *adj.:* Maldivian. **Ethnic groups:** South Indians, Sinhalese, Arabs. **Religions:** Sunni Muslim. **Languages:** Maldivian Dhivehi (dialect of Sinhala, script derived from Arabic), English spoken by most government officials. **Government Government type:** republic. Capital: Male. **Independence:** 26 July 1965 (from UK). **National holiday:** Independence Day, 26 July (1965). **Economy G.D.P.:** purchasing power parity—$1.25 billion (2002 est.). **G.D.P.—per capita:** purchasing power parity—$3,900 (2002 est.). **Currency:** rufiyaa (MVR).

Mali

Republic of Mali

Geography Location: Western Africa, southwest of Algeria. **Area:** 478,765 sq. mi. (1.24 million sq km). **Border countries**: Algeria, Burkina Faso, Guinea, Cote d'Ivoire, Mauritania, Niger, Senegal. **Natural resources:** gold, phosphates, kaolin, salt, limestone, uranium, hydropower, *note:* bauxite, iron ore, manganese, tin, and copper deposits are known but not exploited. **People Population:** 11,626,219 (July 2003 est.). **Nationality:** *noun:* Malian(s); *adj.:* Malian. **Ethnic groups:** Mande 50% (Bambara, Malinke, Soninke), Peul 17%, Voltaic 12%, Songhai 6%, Tuareg and Moor 10%, other 5%. **Religions:** Muslim 90%, indigenous beliefs 9%, Christian 1%. **Languages:** French (official), Bambara 80%, numerous African languages. **Government Government type:** republic. Capital: Bamako. **Independence:** 22 September 1960 (from France). **National holiday:** Independence Day, 22 September (1960). **Economy G.D.P.:** purchasing power parity—$9.8 billion (2002 est.). **G.D.P.—per capita:** purchasing power parity—$860 (2002 est.). **Currency:** Communaute Financiere Africaine franc (XOF); note—responsible authority is the Central Bank of the West African States.

Malta

Republic of Malta

Geography Location: Southern Europe, islands in the Mediterranean Sea, south of Sicily (Italy). **Area:** 124 sq. mi. (316 sq km). **Natural resources:** limestone, salt, arable land. **People Population:** 400,420 (July 2003 est.). **Nationality:** *noun:* Maltese (singular and plural); *adj.:* Maltese. **Ethnic groups:** Maltese (descendants of ancient Carthaginians and Phoenicians, with strong elements of Italian and other Mediterranean stock). **Religions:** Roman Catholic 98%. **Languages:** Maltese (official), English (official). **Government Government type:** republic. Capital: Valletta. **Independence:** 21 September 1964 (from UK). **National holiday:** Independence Day, 21 September (1964). **Economy G.D.P.:** purchasing power parity—$7 billion (2002 est.). **G.D.P.—per capita:** purchasing power parity—$17,000 (2002 est.). **Currency:** Maltese lira (MTL).

Marshall Islands

Republic of the Marshall Islands

Geography Location: Oceania, group of atolls and reefs in the North Pacific Ocean, about one-half of the way from Hawaii to Australia. **Area:** 70 sq. mi. (181.3 sq km). **Natural resources:** coconut products, marine products, deep seabed minerals. **People** population: 56,429 (July 2003 est.). **Nationality:** *noun:* Marshallese (singular and plural); *adj.:* Marshallese. **Ethnic groups:** Micronesian. **Religions:** Christian (mostly Protestant). **Languages:** English (widely spoken as a second language, both English and Marshallese are official languages), two major Marshallese dialects from the Malayo-Polynesian family, Japanese. **Government Government type:** constitutional government in free association with the US; the Compact of Free Association entered into force 21 October 1986. Capital: Majuro. **Independence:** 21 October 1986 (from the US-administered UN trusteeship). **National holiday:** Constitution Day, 1 May (1979).

Economy G.D.P.: purchasing power parity—$115 million (2001 est.). **G.D.P.—per capita:** purchasing power parity—$1,600 (2001 est.). **Currency:** US dollar (USD).

Mauritania

Islamic Republic of Mauritania

Geography Location: Northern Africa, bordering the North Atlantic Ocean, between Senegal and Western Sahara. **Area:** 397,954 sq. mi. (1,030,700 sq km). **Border countries**: Algeria, Mali, Senegal, Western Sahara. **Natural resources:** iron ore, gypsum, copper, phosphate, diamonds, gold, oil, fish. **People Population:** 2,912,584 (July 2003 est.). **Nationality:** *noun:* Mauritanian(s); *adj.:* Mauritanian. **Ethnic groups:** mixed Maur/black 40%, Maur 30%, black 30%. **Religions:** Muslim 100%. **Languages:** Hassaniya Arabic (official), Pulaar, Soninke, Wolof (official), French. **Government Government type:** republic. Capital: Nouakchott. **Independence:** 28 November 1960 (from France). **National holiday:** Independence Day, 28 November (1960). **Economy G.D.P.:** purchasing power parity—$5.3 billion (2002 est.). **G.D.P.—per capita:** purchasing power parity—$1,900 (2002 est.). **Currency:** ouguiya (MRO).

Mauritius

Republic of Mauritius

Geography Location: Southern Africa, island in the Indian Ocean, east of Madagascar. **Area:** 718 sq. mi. (2,040 sq km). **Natural resources:** arable land, fish. **People Population:** 1,210,447 (July 2003 est.). **Nationality:** *noun:* Mauritian(s); *adj.:* Mauritian. **Ethnic groups:** Indo-Mauritian 68%, Creole 27%, Sino-Mauritian 3%, Franco-Mauritian 2%. **Religions:** Hindu 52%, Christian 28.3% (Roman Catholic 26%, Protestant 2.3%), Muslim 16.6%, other 3.1%. **Languages:** English (official), Creole, French (official), Hindi, Urdu, Hakka, Bhojpuri. **Government Government type:** parliamentary democracy. Capital: Port Louis. **Independence:** 12 March 1968 (from UK). **National holiday:** Independence Day, 12 March (1968). **Economy G.D.P.:** purchasing power parity—$13.2 billion (2002 est.). **G.D.P.—per capita:** purchasing power parity—$11,000 (2002 est.). **Currency:** Mauritian rupee (MUR).

Mexico

United Mexican States

Geography Location: Middle America, bordering the Caribbean Sea and the Gulf of Mexico, between Belize and the US and bordering the North Pacific Ocean, between Guatemala and the US. **Area:** 761,603 sq. mi. (1,972,550 sq km). **Border countries**: Belize, Guatemala, US. **Natural resources:** petroleum, silver, copper, gold, lead, zinc, natural gas, timber. **People Population:** 104,907,991 (July 2003 est.). **Nationality:** *noun:* Mexican(s); *adj.:* Mexican. **Ethnic groups:** mestizo (Amerindian-Spanish) 60%, Amerindian or predominantly Amerindian 30%, white 9%, other 1%. **Religions:** nominally Roman Catholic 89%, Protestant 6%, other 5%. **Languages:** Spanish, various Mayan, Nahuatl, and other regional indigenous languages. **Government Government type:** federal republic. Capital: Mexico (Distrito Federal). **Independence:** 16 September 1810 (from Spain). **National holiday:** Independence Day, 16 September (1810). **Economy G.D.P.:** purchasing power parity—$900 billion (2002 est.). **G.D.P.—per capita:** purchasing power parity—$9,000 (2002 est.). **Currency:** Mexican peso (MXN).

Micronesia, Federated States of

Federated States of Micronesia

Geography Location: Oceania, island group in the North Pacific Ocean, about three-quarters of the way from Hawaii to Indonesia. **Area:** 271 sq. mi. (702 sq km). **Natural resources:** forests, marine products, deep-seabed minerals. **People Population:** 108,143 (July 2003 est.). **Nationality:** *noun:* Micronesian(s); *adj.:* Micronesian; Chuukese, Kosraen(s), Pohnpeian(s), Yapese. **Ethnic groups:** nine ethnic Micronesian and Polynesian groups. **Religions:** Roman Catholic 50%, Protestant 47%. **Languages:** English (official and common language), Trukese, Pohnpeian, Yapese, Kosrean, Ulithian, Woleaian, Nukuoro, Kapingamarangi. **Government Government type:** constitutional government in free association with the US; the Compact of Free Association entered into force 3 November 1986; economic provisions of the Compact are being renegotiated. Capital: Palikir. **Independence:** 3 November 1986 (from the US-administered UN Trusteeship). **National holiday:** Constitution Day, 10 May (1979). **Economy G.D.P.:** purchasing power parity—$277 million, *note:* G.D.P. is supplemented by grant aid, averaging perhaps $100 million annually (2002 est.). **G.D.P.—per capita:** purchasing power parity—$2,000 (2002 est.). **Currency:** US dollar (USD).

Moldova

Republic of Moldova

Geography Location: Eastern Europe, northeast of Romania. **Area:** 13,012 sq. mi. (33,843 sq km). **Border countries**: Romania, Ukraine. **Natural resources:** lignite, phosphorites, gypsum, arable land, limestone. **People Population:** 4,439,502 (July 2003 est.). **Nationality:** *noun:* Moldovan(s); *adj.:* Moldovan. **Ethnic groups:** Moldovan/Romanian 64.5%, Ukrainian 13.8%, Russian 13%, Jewish 1.5%, Bulgarian 2%, Gagauz and other 5.2% (1989 est.), *note:* internal disputes with ethnic Slavs in the Transnistrian region. **Religions:** Eastern Orthodox 98%, Jewish 1.5%, Baptist and other 0.5% (2000). **Languages:** Moldovan (official, virtually the same as the Romanian language), Russian (official), Gagauz (a Turkish dialect). **Government Government type:** republic. Capital: Chisinau. **Independence:** 27 August 1991 (from Soviet Union). **National holiday:** Independence Day, 27 August (1991). **Economy G.D.P.:** purchasing power parity—$11 billion (2002 est.). **G.D.P.—per capita:** purchasing power parity—$2,500 (2002 est.). **Currency:** Moldovan leu (MDL).

Monaco

Principality of Monaco

Geography Location: Western Europe, bordering the Mediterranean Sea on the southern coast of France, near the border with Italy. **Area:** 1.21 sq. mi. (1.95 sq km). **Border countries**: France. **Natural resources:** none **People Population:** 32,130 (July 2003 est.). **Nationality:** *noun:* Monegasque(s) or Monacan(s); *adj.:* Monegasque or Monacan. **Ethnic groups:** French 47%, Monegasque 16%, Italian 16%, other 21%. **Religions:** Roman Catholic 90%. **Languages:** French (official), English, Italian, Monegasque. **Government Government type:** constitutional monarchy. Capital: Monaco. **Independence:** 1419 (beginning of the rule by the House of Grimaldi). **National holiday:** National Day (Prince of Monaco Holiday), 19 November. **Economy G.D.P.:** purchasing power parity—$870 million (1999 est.). **G.D.P.—per capita:** purchasing power parity—$27,000 (1999 est.). **Currency:** euro (EUR).

Mongolia

Geography Location: Northern Asia, between China and Russia. **Area:** 604,247 sq. mi. (1.565 million sq km). **Border countries**: China, Russia. **Natural resources:** oil, coal, copper, molybdenum, tungsten, phosphates, tin, nickel, zinc, wolfram, fluorspar, gold, silver, iron, phosphate. **People Population:** 2,712,315 (July 2003 est.). **Nationality:** *noun:* Mongolian(s); *adj.:* Mongolian. **Ethnic groups:** Mongol (predominantly Khalkha) 85%, Turkic (of which Kazakh is the largest group) 7%, Tungusic 4.6%, other (including Chinese and Russian) 3.4% (1998). **Religions:** Tibetan Buddhist Lamaism 96%, Muslim (primarily in the southwest), Shamanism, and Christian 4% (1998). **Languages:** Khalkha Mongol 90%, Turkic, Russian (1999). **Government Government type:** parliamentary. Capital: Ulaanbaatar. **Independence:** 11 July 1921 (from China). **National holiday:**Independence Day/Revolution Day, 11 July (1921). **Economy G.D.P.:** purchasing power parity—$5 billion (2002 est.). **G.D.P.—per capita:** purchasing power parity—$1,840 (2002 est.). **Currency:** togrog/tugrik (MNT).

Morocco

Kingdom of Morocco

Geography Location: Northern Africa, bordering the North Atlantic Ocean and the Mediterranean Sea, between Algeria and Western Sahara. **Area:** 172,413 sq. mi. (446,550 sq km). **Border countries**: Algeria, Western Sahara, Spain (Ceuta), Spain (Melilla). **Natural resources:** phosphates, iron ore, manganese, lead, zinc, fish, salt. **People Population:** 31,689,265 (July 2003 est.). **Nationality:** *noun:* Moroccan(s); *adj.:* Moroccan. **Ethnic groups:** Arab-Berber 99.1%, other 0.7%, Jewish 0.2%. **Religions:** Muslim 98.7%, Christian 1.1%, Jewish 0.2%. **Languages:** Arabic (official), Berber dialects, French often the language of business, government, and diplomacy. **Government Government type:** constitutional monarchy. Capital: Rabat. **Independence:** 2 March 1956 (from France). **National holiday:** Throne Day (accession of King MOHAMED VI to the throne), 30 July (1999). **Economy G.D.P.:** purchasing power parity—$115 billion (2002 est.). **G.D.P.—per capita:** purchasing power parity—$3,900 (2002 est.). **Currency:** Moroccan dirham (MAD).

Mozambique

Republic of Mozambique

Geography Location: South-eastern Africa, bordering the Mozambique Channel, between South Africa and Tanzania. **Area:** 309,494 sq. mi. (801,590 sq km). **Border countries**: Malawi, South Africa, Swaziland, Tanzania, Zambia, Zimbabwe. **Natural resources:** coal, titanium, natural gas, hydropower, tantalum, graphite. **People Population:** 17,479,266, *note:* estimates for this country explicitly take into account the effects of excess mortality due to AIDS; this can result in lower life expectancy, higher infant mortality and death rates, lower population and growth rates, and changes in the distribution of population by age and sex than would otherwise be expected; the 1997 Mozambican census reported a population of 16,099,246 (July 2003 est.), **Nationality:** *noun:* Mozambican(s); *adj.:* Mozambican. **Ethnic groups:** indigenous tribal groups 99.66% (Shangaan, Chokwe, Manyika, Sena, Makua, and others), Europeans 0.06%, Euro-Africans 0.2%, Indians 0.08%. **Religions:** indigenous beliefs 50%, Christian 30%, Muslim 20%. **Languages:** Portuguese (official), indigenous dialects. **Government Government type:** republic. Capital: Maputo. **Independence:** 25 June 1975 (from Portugal). **National holiday:** Independence Day, 25 June (1975). **Economy**

G.D.P.: purchasing power parity—$19.2 billion (2002 est.). **G.D.P.—per capita:** purchasing power parity—$1,000 (2002 est.). **Currency:** metical (MZM).

Myanmar

Union of Burma

Geography **Location:** Southeastern Asia, bordering the Andaman Sea and the Bay of Bengal, between Bangladesh and Thailand. **Area:** 261,969 sq. mi. (678,500 sq km). **Border countries**: Bangladesh, China, India, Laos, Thailand. **Natural resources:** petroleum, timber, tin, antimony, zinc, copper, tungsten, lead, coal, some marble, limestone, precious stones, natural gas, hydropower. **People** **Population:** 42,510,537, *note:* estimates for this country take into account the effects of excess mortality due to AIDS; this can result in lower life expectancy, higher infant mortality and death rates, lower population and growth rates, and changes in the distribution of population by age and sex than would otherwise be expected (July 2003 est.). **Nationality:** *noun:* Burmese (singular and plural); *adj.:* Burmese. **Ethnic groups:** Burman 68%, Shan 9%, Karen 7%, Rakhine 4%, Chinese 3%, Indian 2%, Mon 2%, other 5%. **Religions:** Buddhist 89%, Christian 4% (Baptist 3%, Roman Catholic 1%), Muslim 4%, animist 1%, other 2%. **Languages:** Burmese, minority ethnic groups have their own languages. **Government** **Government type:** military regime. Capital: Rangoon (regime refers to the capital as Yangon). **Independence:** 4 January 1948 (from UK). **National holiday:** Independence Day, 4 January (1948). **Economy** **G.D.P.:** purchasing power parity—$70 billion (2002 est.). **G.D.P.—per capita:** purchasing power parity—$1,660 (2002 est.). **Currency:** kyat (MMK).

Namibia

Republic of Namibia

Geography **Location:** Southern Africa, bordering the South Atlantic Ocean, between Angola and South Africa. **Area:** 318,259 sq. mi. (825,418 sq km). **Border countries**: Angola, Botswana, South Africa, Zambia. **Natural resources:** diamonds, copper, uranium, gold, lead, tin, lithium, cadmium, zinc, salt, vanadium, natural gas, hydropower, fish; *note:* suspected deposits of oil, coal, and iron ore. **People** **Population:** 1,927,447, *note:* estimates for this country explicitly take into account the effects of excess mortality due to AIDS; this can result in lower life expectancy, higher infant mortality and death rates, lower population and growth rates, and changes in the distribution of population by age and sex than would otherwise be expected (July 2003 est.). **Nationality:** *noun:* Namibian(s); *adj.:* Namibian. **Ethnic groups:** black 87.5%, white 6%, mixed 6.5%. *note:* about 50% of the population belong to the Ovambo tribe and 9% to the Kavangos tribe; other ethnic groups are: Herero 7%, Damara 7%, Nama 5%, Caprivian 4%, Bushmen 3%, Baster 2%, Tswana 0.5%. **Religions:** Christian 80% to 90% (Lutheran 50% at least), indigenous beliefs 10% to 20%. **Languages:** English 7% (official), Afrikaans common language of most of the population and about 60% of the white population, German 32%, indigenous **languages:** Oshivambo, Herero, Nama. **Government** **Government type:** republic. Capital: Windhoek. Administrative divisions: 13 regions; Caprivi, Erongo, Hardap, Karas, Khomas, Kunene, Ohangwena, Okavango, Omaheke, Omusati, Oshana, Oshikoto, Otjozondjupa. **Independence:** 21 March 1990 (from South African mandate). **National holiday:** Independence Day, 21 March (1990). **Economy** **G.D.P.:** purchasing power parity—$12.6 billion (2002 est.). **G.D.P.—per capita:** purchasing power parity—$6,900 (2002 est.). **Currency:** Namibian dollar (NAD); South African rand (ZAR).

Nauru

Republic of Nauru

Geography **Location:** Oceania, island in the South Pacific Ocean, south of the Marshall Islands. **Area:** 8 sq. mi. (21 sq km). **Natural resources:** phosphates, fish. **People** **Population:** 12,570 (July 2003 est.). **Nationality:** *noun:* Nauruan(s); *adj.:* Nauruan. **Ethnic groups:** Nauruan 58%, other Pacific Islander 26%, Chinese 8%, European 8%. **Religions:** Christian (two-thirds Protestant, one-third Roman Catholic). **Languages:** Nauruan (official, a distinct Pacific Island language), English widely understood, spoken, and used for most government and commercial purposes. **Government** **Government type:** republic. Capital: no official capital; government offices in Yaren District. **Independence:** 31 January 1968 (from the Australia-, NZ-, and UK-administered UN trusteeship). **National holiday:** Independence Day, 31 January (1968). **Economy** **G.D.P.:** purchasing power parity—$60 million (2001 est.). **G.D.P.—per capita:** purchasing power parity—$5,000 (2001 est.). **Currency:** Australian dollar (AUD).

Nepal

Kingdom of Nepal

Geography **Location:** Southern Asia, between China and India. **Area:** 54,363 sq. mi. (140,800 sq km). **Border countries**: China, India. **Natural resources:** quartz, water, timber, hydropower, scenic beauty, small deposits of lignite, copper, cobalt, iron ore. **People** **Population:** 26,469,569 (July 2003 est.). **Nationality:** *noun:* Nepalese (singular and plural); *adj.:* Nepalese. **Ethnic groups:** Brahman, Chetri, Newar, Gurung, Magar, Tamang, Rai, Limbu, Sherpa, Tharu, and others (1995). **Religions:** Hinduism 86.2%, Buddhism 7.8%, Islam 3.8%, other 2.2%, *note:* only official Hindu state in the world (1995). **Languages:** Nepali (official; spoken by 90% of the population), about a dozen other languages and about 30 major dialects; note—many in government and business also speak English (1995). **Government Government type:** parliamentary democracy and constitutional monarchy. Capital: Kathmandu. **Independence:** 1768 (unified by Prithvi Narayan Shah). **National holiday:** Birthday of King GYANENDRA, 7 July (1946). **Economy G.D.P.:** purchasing power parity—$36 billion (2002 est.). **G.D.P.—per capita:** purchasing power parity—$1,400 (2002 est.). **Industries:** tourism, carpet, textile; small rice, jute, sugar, and oilseed mills; cigarette; cement and brick production. **Agriculture—products:** rice, corn, wheat, sugarcane, root crops; milk, water buffalo meat. **Currency:** Nepalese rupee (NPR).

Netherlands

Kingdom of the Netherlands

Geography Location: Western Europe, bordering the North Sea, between Belgium and Germany. **Area:** 14,413 sq. mi. (41,526 sq km). **Border countries**: Belgium, Germany. **Natural resources:** natural gas, petroleum, arable land. **People Population:** 16,150,511 (July 2003 est.). **Nationality:** *noun:* Dutchman(men), Dutchwoman(women); *adj.:* Dutch. **Ethnic groups:** Dutch 83%, other 17% (of which 9% are non-western origin mainly Turks, Moroccans, Antilleans, Surinamese and Indonesians) (1999 est.). **Religions:** Roman Catholic 31%, Protestant 21%, Muslim 4.4%, other 3.6%, unaffiliated 40% (1998). **Languages:** Dutch (official language), Frisian (official language). **Government Government type:** constitutional monarchy. Capital: Amsterdam; The Hague is the seat of government. **Independence:** 1579 (from Spain); note—the northern provinces of the Low Country concluded the Union of Utrecht, but it was 1648 before Spain finally recognized their independence. **National holiday:** Queen's Day (Birthday of Queen-Mother JULIANA in 1909 and accession to the throne of her oldest daughter BEATRIX in 1980), 30 April. **Economy G.D.P.:** purchasing power parity—$434 billion (2002 est.). **G.D.P.—per capita:** purchasing power parity—$26,900 (2002 est.). **Currency:** euro (EUR).

New Zealand

Geography Location: Oceania, islands in the South Pacific Ocean, southeast of Australia. **Area:** 103,738 sq. mi. (268,680 sq km). **Natural resources:** natural gas, iron ore, sand, coal, timber, hydropower, gold, limestone. **People Population:** 3,951,307 (July 2003 est.). **Nationality:** *noun:* New Zealander(s); *adj.:* New Zealand. **Ethnic groups:** New Zealand European 74.5%, Maori 9.7%, other European 4.6%, Pacific Islander 3.8%, Asian and others 7.4%. **Religions:** Anglican 24%, Presbyterian 18%, Roman Catholic 15%, Methodist 5%, Baptist 2%, other Protestant 3%, unspecified or none 33% (1986). **Languages:** English (official), Maori (official). **Government Government type:** parliamentary democracy. Capital: Wellington. **Independence:** 26 September 1907 (from UK). **National holiday:** Waitangi Day (Treaty of Waitangi established British sovereignty over New Zealand), 6 February (1840). **Economy G.D.P.:** purchasing power parity—$78.8 billion (2002 est.). **G.D.P.—per capita:** purchasing power parity—$20,200 (2002 est.). **Currency:** New Zealand dollar (NZD).

Nicaragua

Republic of Nicaragua

Geography Location: Middle America, bordering both the Caribbean Sea and the North Pacific Ocean, between Costa Rica and Honduras. **Area:** 49,998 sq. mi. (129,494 sq km). **Border countries**: Costa Rica, Honduras. **Natural resources:** gold, silver, copper, tungsten, lead, zinc, timber, fish. **People Population:** 5,128,517 (July 2003 est.). **Nationality:** *noun:* Nicaraguan(s); *adj.:* Nicaraguan. **Ethnic groups:** mestizo (mixed Amerindian and white) 69%, white 17%, black 9%, Amerindian 5%. **Religions:** Roman Catholic 85%, Protestant. **Languages:** Spanish (official), *note:* English and indigenous languages on Atlantic coast. **Government Government type:** republic. Capital: Managua. **Independence:** 15 September 1821 (from Spain). **National holiday:** Independence Day, 15 September (1821). **Economy G.D.P.:** purchasing power parity—$12.8 billion (2002 est.). **G.D.P.—per capita:** purchasing power parity—$2,500 (2002 est.). **Currency:** gold cordoba (NIO).

Niger

Republic of Niger

Geography Location: Western Africa, southeast of Algeria. **Area:** 489,189 sq. mi. (1.267 million sq km). **Border countries**: Algeria, Benin, Burkina Faso, Chad, Libya, Mali, Nigeria. **Natural resources:** uranium, coal, iron ore, tin, phosphates, gold, petroleum. **People Population:** 11,058,590 (July 2003 est.). **Nationality:** *noun:* Nigerien(s); *adj.:* Nigerien. **Ethnic groups:** Hausa 56%, Djerma 22%, Fula 8.5%, Tuareg 8%, Beri Beri (Kanouri) 4.3%, Arab, Toubou, and Gourmantche 1.2%, about 1,200 French expatriates. **Religions:** Muslim 80%, remainder indigenous beliefs and Christian. **Languages:** French (official), Hausa, Djerma. **Government Government type:** republic. Capital:

Niamey. **Independence:** 3 August 1960 (from France). **National holiday:** Republic Day, 18 December (1958). **Economy G.D.P.:** purchasing power parity—$8.8 billion (2002 est.). **G.D.P.—per capita:** purchasing power parity—$830 (2002 est.). **Currency:** Communaute Financiere Africaine franc (XOF); note—responsible authority is the Central Bank of the West African States.

Nigeria

Federal Republic of Nigeria

Geography Location: Western Africa, bordering the Gulf of Guinea, between Benin and Cameroon. **Area:** 356,668 sq. mi. (923,768 sq km). **Border countries**: Benin, Cameroon, Chad, Niger. **Natural resources:** natural gas, petroleum, tin, columbite, iron ore, coal, limestone, lead, zinc, arable land. **People Population:** 133,881,703, *note:* estimates for this country explicitly take into account the effects of excess mortality due to AIDS; this can result in lower life expectancy, higher infant mortality and death rates, lower population and growth rates, and changes in the distribution of population by age and sex than would otherwise be expected (July 2003 est.). **Nationality:** *noun:* Nigerian(s); *adj.:* Nigerian. **Ethnic groups:** Nigeria, which is Africa's most populous country, is composed of more than 250 ethnic groups; the following are the most populous and politically influential: Hausa and Fulani 29%, Yoruba 21%, Igbo (Ibo) 18%, Ijaw 10%, Kanuri 4%, Ibibio 3.5%, Tiv 2.5%. **Religions:** Muslim 50%, Christian 40%, indigenous beliefs 10%. **Languages:** English (official), Hausa, Yoruba, Igbo (Ibo), Fulani. **Government Government type:** republic transitioning from military to civilian rule. Capital: Abuja; note—on 12 December 1991 the capital was officially transferred from Lagos to Abuja; most federal government offices have now made the move to Abuja. **Independence:** 1 October 1960 (from UK). **National holiday:** Independence Day (National Day), 1 October (1960). **Economy G.D.P.:** purchasing power parity—$113.5 billion (2002 est.). **G.D.P.—per capita:** purchasing power parity—$875 (2002 est.). **Currency:** naira (NGN).

Norway

Kingdom of Norway

Geography Location: Northern Europe, bordering the North Sea and the North Atlantic Ocean, west of Sweden. **Area:** 125,182 sq. mi. (324,220 sq km). **Border countries**: Finland, Sweden, Russia. **Natural resources:** petroleum, copper, natural gas, pyrites, nickel, iron ore, zinc, lead, fish, timber, hydropower. **People Population:** 4,546,123 (July 2003 est.). **Nationality:** *noun:* Norwegian(s); *adj.:* Norwegian. **Ethnic groups:** Norwegian, Sami 20,000. **Religions:** Evangelical Lutheran 86% (state church), other Protestant and Roman Catholic 3%, other 1%, none and unknown 10% (1997). **Languages:** Norwegian (official), *note:* small Sami- and Finnish-speaking minorities. **Government Government type:** constitutional monarchy. Capital: Oslo. **Independence:** 7 June 1905 Norway declared the union with Sweden dissolved; 26 October 1905 Sweden agreed to the repeal of the union. **National holiday:** Constitution Day, 17 May (1814); note—on 14 January 1814 Denmark ceded Norway to Sweden; resisting Swedish domination, Norwegians adopted a new constitution four months later; on 14 August 1814 Norway was proclaimed independent but in union with Sweden; on 7 June 1905 Norway declared the union with Sweden dissolved. **Economy G.D.P.:** purchasing power parity—$143 billion (2002 est.). **G.D.P.—per capita:** purchasing power parity—$31,800 (2002 est.). **Currency:** Norwegian krone (NOK).

Oman

Sultanate of Oman

Geography Location: Middle East, bordering the Arabian Sea, Gulf of Oman, and Persian Gulf, between Yemen and UAE. **Area:** 82,031 sq. mi. (212,460 sq km). **Border countries**: Saudi Arabia, United Arab Emirates, Yemen. **Natural resources:** petroleum, copper, asbestos, some marble, limestone, chromium, gypsum, natural gas. **People Population:** 2,807,125, *note:* includes 577,293 non-nationals (July 2003 est.). **Nationality:** *noun:* Omani(s); *adj.:* Omani. **Ethnic groups:** Arab, Baluchi, South Asian (Indian, Pakistani, Sri Lankan, Bangladeshi), African. **Religions:** Ibadhi Muslim 75%, Sunni Muslim, Shi'a Muslim, Hindu. **Languages:** Arabic (official), English, Baluchi, Urdu, Indian dialects. **Government Government type:** monarchy. Capital: Muscat. **Independence:** 1650 (expulsion of the Portuguese). **National holiday:** Birthday of Sultan QABOOS, 18 November (1940). **Economy G.D.P.:** purchasing power parity—$22.4 billion (2002 est.). **G.D.P.—per capita:** purchasing power parity—$8,300 (2002 est.). **Currency:** Omani rial (OMR).

Pakistan

Islamic Republic of Pakistan

Geography Location: Southern Asia, bordering the Arabian Sea, between India on the east and Iran and Afghanistan on the west and China in the north. **Area:** 310,402 sq. mi. (803,940 sq km). **Border countries**: Afghanistan, China, India, Iran. **Natural resources:** land, extensive natural gas reserves, limited petroleum, poor quality coal, iron ore, copper, salt, limestone. **People Population:**

150,694,740 (July 2003 est.). **Nationality:** *noun:* Pakistani(s); *adj.:* Pakistani. **Ethnic groups:** Punjabi, Sindhi, Pashtun (Pathan), Baloch, Muhajir (immigrants from India at the time of partition and their descendants). **Religions:** Muslim 97% (Sunni 77%, Shi'a 20%), Christian, Hindu, and other 3%. **Languages:** Punjabi 48%, Sindhi 12%, Siraiki (a Punjabi variant) 10%, Pashtu 8%, Urdu (official) 8%, Balochi 3%, Hindko 2%, Brahui 1%, English (official and lingua franca of Pakistani elite and most government ministries), Burushaski, and other 8%. **Government Government type:** federal republic. Capital: Islamabad. **Independence:** 14 August 1947 (from UK). **National holiday:** Republic Day, 23 March (1956). **Economy G.D.P.:** purchasing power parity—$311 billion (2002 est.). **G.D.P.—per capita:** purchasing power parity—$2,100 (FY01 est.). **Currency:** Pakistani rupee (PKR).

Palau

Republic of Palau

Geography Location: Oceania, group of islands in the North Pacific Ocean, southeast of the Philippines. **Area:** 177 sq. mi. (458 sq km). **Natural resources:** forests, minerals (especially gold), marine products, deep-seabed minerals. **People Population:** 19,717 (July 2003 est.). **Nationality:** *noun:* Palauan(s); *adj.:* Palauan. **Ethnic groups:** Palauan (Micronesian with Malayan and Melanesian admixtures) 70%, Asian (mainly Filipinos, followed by Chinese, Taiwanese, and Vietnamese) 28%, white 2% (2000 est.). **Religions:** Christian (Roman Catholics 49%, Seventh-Day Adventists, Jehovah's Witnesses, the Assembly of God, the Liebenzell Mission, and Latter-Day Saints), Modekngei religion (one-third of the population observes this religion, which is indigenous to Palau). **Languages:** English and Palauan official in all states except Sonsoral (Sonsoralese and English are official), Tobi (Tobi and English are official), and Angaur (Angaur, Japanese, and English are official). **Government Government type:** constitutional government in free association with the US; the Compact of Free Association entered into force 1 October 1994. Capital: Koror; note—a new capital is being built about 20 km northeast of Koror. Administrative divisions: 16 states; Aimeliik, Airai, Angaur, Hatobohei, Kayangel, Koror, Melekeok, Ngaraard, Ngarchelong, Ngardmau, Ngatpang, Ngchesar, Ngeremlengui, Ngiwal, Peleliu, Sonsoral. **Independence:** 1 October 1994 (from the US-administered UN Trusteeship). **National holiday:** Constitution Day, 9 July (1979). **Economy G.D.P.:** purchasing power parity—$174 million, *note:* G.D.P. estimate includes US subsidy (2001 est.). **G.D.P.—per capita:** purchasing power parity—$9,000 (2001 est.). **Currency:** US dollar (USD).

Panama

Republic of Panama

Geography Location: Middle America, bordering both the Caribbean Sea and the North Pacific Ocean, between Colombia and Costa Rica. **Area:** 30,193 sq. mi. (78,200 sq km). **Border countries**: Colombia 225 Costa Rica 330 km. **Natural resources:** copper, mahogany forests, shrimp, hydropower. **People Population:** 2,960,784 (July 2003 est.). **Nationality:** *noun:* Panamanian(s); *adj.:* Panamanian. **Ethnic groups:** mestizo (mixed Amerindian and white) 70%, Amerindian and mixed (West Indian) 14%, white 10%, Amerindian 6%. **Religions:** Roman Catholic 85%, Protestant 15%. **Languages:** Spanish (official), English 14%, *note:* many Panamanians bilingual. **Government Government type:** constitutional democracy. Capital: Panama. **Independence:** 3 November 1903 (from Colombia; became independent from Spain 28 November 1821). **National holiday:** Independence Day, 3 November (1903). **Economy G.D.P.:** purchasing power parity—$17.3 billion (2002 est.). **G.D.P.—per capita:** purchasing power parity—$6,000 (2002 est.). **Currency:** balboa (PAB); US dollar (USD).

Papua New Guinea

Independent State of Papua New Guinea

Geography Location: Oceania, group of islands including the eastern half of the island of New Guinea between the Coral Sea and the South Pacific Ocean, east of Indonesia. **Area:** 178,259 sq. mi. (462,840 sq km). **Border countries**: Indonesia. **Natural resources:** gold, copper, silver, natural gas, timber, oil, fisheries. **People Population:** 5,295,816 (July 2003 est.). **Nationality:** *noun:* Papua New Guinean(s); *adj.:* Papua New Guinean. **Ethnic groups:** Melanesian, Papuan, Negrito, Micronesian, Polynesian. **Religions:** Roman Catholic 22%, Lutheran 16%, Presbyterian/Methodist/London Missionary Society 8%, Anglican 5%, Evangelical Alliance 4%, Seventh-Day Adventist 1%, other Protestant 10%, indigenous beliefs 34%. **Languages:** English spoken by 1%-2%, pidgin English widespread, Motu spoken in Papua region, *note:* 715 indigenous languages. **Government Government type:** constitutional monarchy with parliamentary democracy. Capital: Port Moresby. **Independence:** 16 September 1975 (from the Australian-administered UN trusteeship). **Economy G.D.P.:** purchasing power parity—$1.2 billion (2002 est.). **G.D.P.—per capita:** purchasing power parity—$2,300 (2002 est.). **Currency:** kina (PGK).

Paraguay

Republic of Paraguay

Geography Location: Central South America, northeast of Argentina. **Area:** 157,046 sq. mi. (406,750 sq km). **Border countries**: Argentina 1,880, Bolivia 750, Brazil 1,290 km. **Natural resources:** hydropower, timber, iron ore, manganese, limestone. **People Population:** 6,036,900 (July 2003 est.). **Nationality:** *noun:* Paraguayan(s); *adj.:* Paraguayan. **Ethnic groups:** mestizo (mixed Spanish and Amerindian) 95%. **Religions:** Roman Catholic 90%, Mennonite, and other Protestant. **Languages:** Spanish (official), Guarani (official). **Government Government type:** constitutional republic. Capital: Asuncion. **Independence:** 14 May 1811 (from Spain). **National holiday:** Independence Day, 14 May (1811). **Economy G.D.P.:** purchasing power parity—$25 billion (2002 est.). **G.D.P.—per capita:** purchasing power parity—$4,200 (2002 est.). **Currency:** guarani (PYG).

Peru

Republic of Peru

Geography Location: Western South America, bordering the South Pacific Ocean, between Chile and Ecuador. **Area:** 496,224 sq. mi. (1,285,220 sq km). **Border countries**: Bolivia, Brazil, Chile, Colombia, Ecuador. **Natural resources:** copper, silver, gold, petroleum, timber, fish, iron ore, coal, phosphate, potash, hydropower, natural gas. **People Population:** 28,409,897 (July 2003 est.). **Nationality:** *noun:* Peruvian(s); *adj.:* Peruvian. **Ethnic groups:** Amerindian 45%, mestizo (mixed Amerindian and white) 37%, white 15%, black, Japanese, Chinese, and other 3%. **Religions:** Roman Catholic 90%. **Languages:** Spanish (official), Quechua (official), Aymara. **Government Government type:** constitutional republic. Capital: Lima. **Independence:** 28 July 1821 (from Spain). **National holiday:** Independence Day, 28 July (1821). **Economy G.D.P.:** purchasing power parity—$132 billion (2002 est.). **G.D.P.—per capita:** purchasing power parity—$4,800 (2002 est.). **Currency:** nuevo sol (PEN).

Philippines

Republic of the Philippines

Geography Location: Southeastern Asia, archipelago between the Philippine Sea and the South China Sea, east of Vietnam. **Area:** 115,830 sq. mi. (300,000 sq km). **Natural resources:** timber, petroleum, nickel, cobalt, silver, gold, salt, copper. **People Population:** 84,619,974 (July 2003 est.). **Nationality:** *noun:* Filipino(s); *adj.:* Philippine. **Ethnic groups:** Christian Malay 91.5%, Muslim Malay 4%, Chinese 1.5%, other 3%. **Religions:** Roman Catholic 83%, Protestant 9%, Muslim 5%, Buddhist and other 3%. **Languages:** two official languages—Filipino (based on Tagalog) and English; eight major dialects—Tagalog, Cebuano, Ilocan, Hiligaynon or Ilonggo, Bicol, Waray, Pampango, and Pangasinense. **Government Government type:** republic. Capital: Manila. **Independence:** 4 July 1946 (from US). **National holiday:** Independence Day (from Spain), 12 June (1898); note—12 June 1898 is the date of independence from Spain, 4 July 1946 is the date of independence from the US. **Economy G.D.P.:** purchasing power parity—$356 billion (2002 est.). **G.D.P.—per capita:** purchasing power parity—$4,200 (2002 est.). **Currency:** Philippine peso (PHP).

Poland

Republic of Poland

Geography Location: Central Europe, east of Germany. **Area:** 120,726 sq. mi. (312,685 sq km). **Border countries**: Belarus, Czech Republic, Germany, Lithuania, Russia (Kaliningrad Oblast), Slovakia, Ukraine. **Natural resources:** coal, sulfur, copper, natural gas, silver, lead, salt, amber, arable land. **People Population:** 38,622,660 (July 2003 est.). **Nationality:** *noun:* Pole(s); *adj.:* Polish. **Ethnic groups:** Polish 97.6%, German 1.3%, Ukrainian 0.6%, Belarusian 0.5% (1990 est.). **Religions:** Roman Catholic 95% (about 75% practicing), Eastern Orthodox, Protestant, and other 5%. **Languages:** Polish. **Government Government type:** republic. Capital: Warsaw. **Independence**: 11 November 1918 (independent republic proclaimed). **National holiday**: Constitution Day, 3 May (1791). **Economy G.D.P.**: purchasing power parity—$368.1 billion (2002 est.). **G.D.P.—per capita:** purchasing power parity—$9,500 (2002 est.). Currency: zloty (PLN).

Portugal

Portuguese Republic

Geography Location: Southwestern Europe, bordering the North Atlantic Ocean, west of Spain. **Area:** 35,552 sq. mi. (92,391 sq km). **Border countries**: Spain. **Natural resources:** fish, forests (cork), tungsten, iron ore, uranium ore, marble, arable land, hydropower. **People Population:** 10,102,022 (July 2003 est.). **Nationality:** *noun:* Portuguese (singular and plural); *adj.:* Portuguese. **Ethnic groups:** homogeneous Mediterranean stock; citizens of black African descent who immigrated to mainland during decolonization number less than 100,000; since 1990 East Europeans have entered Portugal. **Religions:** Roman Catholic 94%, Protestant (1995). **Languages:** Portuguese. **Government Government type:** parliamentary democracy. Capital: Lisbon. **Independence:**

1143 (independent republic proclaimed 5 October 1910). **National holiday:** Portugal Day, 10 June (1580). **Economy G.D.P.:** purchasing power parity—$182 billion (2002 est.). **G.D.P.—per capita:** purchasing power parity—$18,000 (2002 est.). **Currency:** euro (EUR).

Qatar

State of Qatar

Geography Location: Middle East, peninsula bordering the Persian Gulf and Saudi Arabia. **Area:** 4,247 sq. mi. (11,437 sq km). **Border countries**: Saudi Arabia 60 km. **Natural resources:** petroleum, natural gas, fish. **People Population:** 817,052 (July 2003 est.). **Nationality:** *noun:* Qatari(s); *adj.:* Qatari. **Ethnic groups:** Arab 40%, Pakistani 18%, Indian 18%, Iranian 10%, other 14%. **Religions:** Muslim 95%. **Languages:** Arabic (official), English commonly used as a second language. **Government Government type:** traditional monarchy. Capital: Doha. **Independence:** 3 September 1971 (from UK). **National holiday:** Independence Day, 3 September (1971). **Economy G.D.P.:** purchasing power parity—$17.2 billion (2002 est.). **G.D.P.—per capita:** purchasing power parity—$21,500 (2002 est.). **Currency:** Qatari rial (QAR).

Romania

Geography Location: Southeastern Europe, bordering the Black Sea, between Bulgaria and Ukraine. **Area:** 91,699 sq. mi. (237,500 sq km). **Border countries**: Bulgaria, Hungary, Moldova, Serbia and Montenegro, Ukraine (north), Ukraine (east). **Natural resources:** petroleum (reserves declining), timber, natural gas, coal, iron ore, salt, arable land, hydropower. **People Population:** 22,271,839 (July 2003 est.). **Nationality:** *noun:* Romanian(s); *adj.:* Romanian. **Ethnic groups:** Romanian 89.5%, Hungarian 6.6%, Roma 2.5%, Ukrainian 0.3%, German 0.3%, Russian 0.2%, Turkish 0.2%, other 0.4% (2002). **Religions:** Eastern Orthodox (including all sub-denominations) 87%, Protestant 6.8%, Catholic 5.6%, other (mostly Muslim) 0.4%, unaffiliated 0.2% (2002). **Languages:** Romanian (official), Hungarian, German. **Government Government type:** republic. Capital: Bucharest. **Independence:** 9 May 1877 (independence proclaimed from Turkey; independence recognized 13 July 1878 by the Treaty of Berlin; kingdom proclaimed 26 March 1881; republic proclaimed 30 December 1947). **National holiday:** Unification Day (of Romania and Transylvania), 1 December (1918). **Economy G.D.P.:** purchasing power parity—$166 billion (2002 est.). **G.D.P.—per capita:** purchasing power parity—$7,400 (2002 est.). **Currency:** leu (ROL).

Russia

Russian Federation

Geography Location: Northern Asia (that part west of the Urals is included with Europe), bordering the Arctic Ocean, between Europe and the North Pacific Ocean. **Area:** 6,592,745 sq. mi. (17,075,200 sq km). **Border countries**: Azerbaijan, Belarus, China (southeast), China (south), Estonia, Finland, Georgia, Kazakhstan, North Korea, Latvia, Lithuania (Kaliningrad Oblast), Mongolia, Norway, Poland (Kaliningrad Oblast), Ukraine. **Natural resources:** wide natural resource base including major deposits of oil, natural gas, coal, and many strategic minerals, timber. *note:* formidable obstacles of climate, terrain, and distance hinder exploitation of natural resources. **People Population:** 144,526,278 (July 2003 est.). **Nationality:** *noun:* Russian(s); *adj.:* Russian. **Ethnic groups:** Russian 81.5%, Tatar 3.8%, Ukrainian 3%, Chuvash 1.2%, Bashkir 0.9%, Belarusian 0.8%, Moldavian 0.7%, other 8.1% (1989). **Religions:** Russian Orthodox, Muslim, other. **Languages:** Russian, other. **Government Government type:** federation. Capital: Moscow. **Independence:** 24 August 1991 (from Soviet Union). **National holiday:** Russia Day, 12 June (1990). **Economy G.D.P.:** purchasing power parity—$1.35 trillion (2002 est.). **G.D.P.—per capita:** purchasing power parity—$9,300 (2002 est.). **Currency:** Russian ruble (RUR).

Rwanda

Rwandese Republic

Geography Location: Central Africa, east of Democratic Republic of the Congo. **Area:** 10,170 sq. mi. (26,338 sq km). **Border countries**: Burundi, Democratic Republic of the Congo, Tanzania, Uganda. **Natural resources:** gold, cassiterite (tin ore), wolframite (tungsten ore), methane, hydropower, arable land. **People Population:** 7,810,056, *note:* estimates for this country explicitly take into account the effects of excess mortality due to AIDS; this can result in lower life expectancy, higher infant mortality and death rates, lower population and growth rates, and changes in the distribution of population by age and sex than would otherwise be expected (July 2003 est.). **Nationality:** *noun:* Rwandan(s); *adj.:* Rwandan. **Ethnic groups:** Hutu 84%, Tutsi 15%, Twa (Pygmoid) 1%. **Religions:** Roman Catholic 56.5%, Protestant 26%, Adventist 11.1%, Muslim 4.6%, indigenous beliefs 0.1%, none 1.7% (2001). **Languages:** Kinyarwanda (official) universal Bantu vernacular, French (official), English (official), Kiswahili (Swahili) used in commercial centers. **Government Government type:** republic; presidential, multiparty system. Capital: Kigali. **Independence:** 1 July 1962 (from Belgium-administered UN trusteeship). **National holiday:**

Independence Day, 1 July (1962). **Economy G.D.P.:** purchasing power parity—$9 billion (2002 est.). **G.D.P.—per capita:** purchasing power parity—$1,200 (2002 est.). **Currency:** Rwandan franc (RWF).

Saint Kitts and Nevis

Federation of Saint Kitts and Nevis

Geography Location: Caribbean, islands in the Caribbean Sea, about one-third of the way from Puerto Rico to Trinidad and Tobago. **Area:** 104 sq. mi. (261 sq km). **Natural resources:** arable land. **People Population:** 38,763 (July 2003 est.). **Nationality:** *noun:* Kittitian(s), Nevisian(s); *adj.:* Kittitian, Nevisian. **Ethnic groups:** predominantly black; some British, Portuguese, and Lebanese. **Religions:** Anglican, other Protestant, Roman Catholic. **Languages:** English. **Government Government type:** constitutional monarchy with Westminster-style parliament. Capital: Basseterre. **Independence:** 19 September 1983 (from UK). **National holiday:** Independence Day, 19 September (1983). **Economy G.D.P.:** purchasing power parity—$339 million (2002 est.). **G.D.P.—per capita:** purchasing power parity—$8,800 (2002 est.). **Currency:** East Caribbean dollar (XCD).

Saint Lucia

Geography Location: Caribbean, island between the Caribbean Sea and North Atlantic Ocean, north of Trinidad and Tobago. **Area:** 239 sq. mi. (616 sq km). **Natural resources:** forests, sandy beaches, minerals (pumice), mineral springs, geothermal potential. **People Population:** 162,157 (July 2003 est.). **Nationality:** *noun:* Saint Lucian(s); *adj.:* Saint Lucian. **Government Government type:** Westminster-style parliamentary democracy. Capital: Castries. Administrative divisions: 11 quarters; Anse-la-Raye, Castries, Choiseul, Dauphin, Dennery, Gros-Islet, Laborie, Micoud, Praslin, Soufriere, Vieux-Fort. **Independence:** 22 February 1979 (from UK). **National holiday:** Independence Day, 22 February (1979). **Economy G.D.P.:** purchasing power parity—$866 million (2002 est.). **G.D.P.—per capita:** purchasing power parity—$5,400 (2002 est.). **Currency:** East Caribbean dollar (XCD).

Saint Vincent and the Grenadines

Geography Location: Caribbean, islands between the Caribbean Sea and North Atlantic Ocean, north of Trinidad and Tobago. **Area:** 131 sq. mi. (389 sq km). **Natural resources:** hydropower, cropland. **People Population:** 116,812 (July 2003 est.). **Nationality:** noun: Saint Vincentian(s) or Vincentian(s); adj.: Saint Vincentian or Vincentian. **Ethnic groups:** black 66%, mixed 19%, East Indian 6%, Carib Amerindian 2%, other 7%. **Religions:** Anglican 47%, Methodist 28%, Roman Catholic 13%, Hindu Seventh-Day Adventist, other Protestant. **Languages:** English, French patois. **Government Government type:** parliamentary democracy; independent sovereign state within the Commonwealth. Capital: Kingstown. **Independence:** 27 October 1979 (from UK). **National holiday:** Independence Day, 27 October (1979). **Economy G.D.P.:** purchasing power parity—$339 million (2002 est.). **G.D.P.—per capita:** purchasing power parity—$2,900 (2002 est.). **Currency:** East Caribbean dollar (XCD).

Samoa

Independent State of Samoa

Geography Location: Oceania, group of islands in the South Pacific Ocean, about one-half of the way from Hawaii to New Zealand. **Area:** 1,104 sq. mi. (2,944 sq km). **Natural resources:** hardwood forests, fish, hydropower. **People Population:** 178,173 (July 2003 est.). **Nationality:** *noun:* Samoan(s); *adj.:* Samoan. **Ethnic groups:** Samoan 92.6%, Euronesians 7% (persons of European and Polynesian blood), Europeans 0.4%. **Religions:** Christian 99.7% (about one-half of population associated with the London Missionary Society; includes Congregational, Roman Catholic, Methodist, Latter-Day Saints, Seventh-Day Adventist). **Languages:** Samoan (Polynesian), English. **Government Government type:** constitutional monarchy under native chief. Capital: Apia. **Independence:** 1 January 1962 (from New Zealand-administered UN trusteeship). **National holiday:** Independence Day Celebration, 1 June (1962); note—1 January 1962 is the date of independence from the New Zealand-administered UN trusteeship, 1 June 1962 is the date that independence is celebrated. **Economy G.D.P.:** purchasing power parity—$1 billion (2002 est.). **G.D.P.—per capita:** purchasing power parity—$5,600 (2002 est.). **Currency:** tala (WST).

San Marino

Republic of San Marino

Geography Location: Southern Europe, an enclave in central Italy. **Area:** 23 sq. mi. (61.2 sq km). **Border countries:** Italy. **Natural resources:** building stone. **People Population:** 28,119 (July 2003 est.). **Nationality:** *noun:* Sammarinese (singular and plural); *adj.:* Sammarinese. **Ethnic groups:** Sammarinese, Italian. **Religions:** Roman Catholic. **Languages:** Italian. **Government Government type:** independent republic. Capital: San Marino. **Independence:** 3 September 301. **National holiday:** Founding of the Republic, 3 September (301). **Economy**

G.D.P.: purchasing power parity—$940 million (2001 est.). **G.D.P.—per capita:** purchasing power parity—$34,600 (2001 est.). **Currency:** euro (EUR).

Sao Tome and Principe

Democratic Republic of Sao Tome and Principe

Geography **Location:** Western Africa, islands in the Gulf of Guinea, straddling the Equator, west of Gabon. **Area:** 371 sq. mi. (1,001 sq km). **Natural resources:** fish, hydropower. **People** **Population:** 175,883 (July 2003 est.). **Nationality:** *noun:* Sao Tomean(s); *adj.:* Sao Tomean. **Ethnic groups:** mestico, angolares (descendants of Angolan slaves), forros (descendants of freed slaves), servicais (contract laborers from Angola, Mozambique, and Cape Verde), tongas (children of servicais born on the islands), Europeans (primarily Portuguese). **Religions:** Christian 80% (Roman Catholic, Evangelical Protestant, Seventh-Day Adventist). **Languages:** Portuguese (official). **Government** **Government type:** republic. Capital: Sao Tome. **Independence:** 12 July 1975 (from Portugal). **National holiday:** Independence Day, 12 July (1975). **Economy** **G.D.P.:** purchasing power parity—$200 million (2002 est.). **G.D.P.—per capita:** purchasing power parity—$1,200 (2002 est.). **Currency:** dobra (STD).

Saudi Arabia

Kingdom of Saudi Arabia

Geography **Location:** Middle East, bordering the Persian Gulf and the Red Sea, north of Yemen. **Area:** 756,982 sq. mi. (1,960,582 sq km). **Border countries**: Iraq, Jordan, Kuwait, Oman, Qatar, UAE, Yemen. **Natural resources:** petroleum, natural gas, iron ore, gold, copper. **People** **Population:** 24,293,844, *note:* includes 5,576,076 non-nationals (July 2003 est.). **Nationality:** *noun:* Saudi(s); *adj.:* Saudi or Saudi Arabian. **Ethnic groups:** Arab 90%, Afro-Asian 10%. **Religions:** Muslim 100%. **Languages:** Arabic. **Government** **Government type:** monarchy. Capital: Riyadh. **Independence:** 23 September 1932 (Unification of the Kingdom). **National holiday:** Unification of the Kingdom, 23 September (1932). **Economy** **G.D.P.:** purchasing power parity—$242 billion (2002 est.). **G.D.P.—per capita:** purchasing power parity—$10,500 (2002 est.). **Currency:** Saudi riyal (SAR).

Senegal

Republic of Senegal

Geography **Location:** Western Africa, bordering the North Atlantic Ocean, between Guinea-Bissau and Mauritania. **Area:** 75,749 sq. mi. (196,190 sq km). **Border countries**: The Gambia, Guinea, Guinea-Bissau, Mali, Mauritania. **Natural resources:** fish, phosphates, iron ore. **People** **Population:** 10,580,307 (July 2003 est.). **Nationality:** *noun:* Senegalese (singular and plural); *adj.:* Senegalese . **Ethnic groups:** Wolof 43.3%, Pular 23.8%, Serer 14.7%, Jola 3.7%, Mandinka 3%, Soninke 1.1%, European and Lebanese 1%, other 9.4%. **Religions:** Muslim 94%, indigenous beliefs 1%, Christian 5% (mostly Roman Catholic). **Languages:** French (official), Wolof, Pulaar, Jola, Mandinka. **Government** **Government type:** republic under multiparty democratic rule. Capital: Dakar. **Independence:** 4 April 1960 (from France); complete independence was achieved upon dissolution of federation with Mali on 20 August 1960. **National holiday:** Independence Day, 4 April (1960). **Economy** **G.D.P.:** purchasing power parity—$16.2 billion (2002 est.). **G.D.P.—per capita:** purchasing power parity—$1,500 (2002 est.). **Currency:** Communaute Financiere Africaine franc (XOF); note—responsible authority is the Central Bank of the West African States.

Serbia and Montenegro

Serbia and Montenegro

Geography **Location:** Southeastern Europe, bordering the Adriatic Sea, between Albania and Bosnia and Herzegovina. **Area:** 39,517 sq. mi. (102,350 sq km). **Border countries**: Albania, Bosnia and Herzegovina, Bulgaria, Croatia (north), Croatia (south), Hungary, The Former Yugoslav Republic of Macedonia, Romania. **Natural resources:** oil, gas, coal, antimony, copper, lead, zinc, nickel, gold, pyrite, chrome, hydropower, arable land. **People** **Population:** 10,655,774, *note:* a census was taken in Serbia 1-15 April 2002 (July 2003 est.). **Nationality:** *noun:* Serb(s); Montenegrin(s); *adj.:* Serbian; Montenegrin. **Ethnic groups:** Serb 62.6%, Albanian 16.5%, Montenegrin 5%, Hungarian 3.3%, other 12.6% (1991). **Religions:** Orthodox 65%, Muslim 19%, Roman Catholic 4%, Protestant 1%, other 11%. **Languages:** Serbian 95%, Albanian 5%. **Government** **Government type:** republic. Capital: Belgrade. **Independence:** 27 April 1992 (Federal Republic of Yugoslavia or FRY formed as self-proclaimed successor to the Socialist Federal Republic of Yugoslavia or SFRY). **National holiday:** Republic Day, 29 November. **Economy** **G.D.P.:** purchasing power parity—$25.3 billion (2002 est.). **G.D.P.—per capita:** purchasing power parity—$2,370 (2002 est.). **Currency:** new Yugoslav dinar (YUM); note—in Montenegro the euro is legal tender; in Kosovo both the euro and the Yugoslav dinar are legal (2002).

Seychelles

Republic of Seychelles

Geography **Location:** Eastern Africa, group of islands in the Indian Ocean, northeast of Madagascar. **Area:** 176 sq. mi.

(455 sq km). **Natural resources:** fish, copra, cinnamon trees. **People Population:** 80,469 (July 2003 est.). **Nationality:** *noun:* Seychellois (singular and plural); *adj.:* Seychellois. **Ethnic groups:** mixed French, African, Indian, Chinese, and Arab. **Religions:** Roman Catholic 86.6%, Anglican 6.8%, other Christian 2.5%, other 4.1%. **Languages:** English (official), French (official), Creole. **Government Government type:** republic. Capital: Victoria. **Independence:** 29 June 1976 (from UK). **National holiday:** Constitution Day (National Day), 18 June (1993). **Economy G.D.P.:** purchasing power parity—$626 million (2002 est.). **G.D.P.—per capita:** purchasing power parity—$7,800 (2002 est.). **Currency:** Seychelles rupee (SCR).

Sierra Leone

Republic of Sierra Leone

Geography Location: Western Africa, bordering the North Atlantic Ocean, between Guinea and Liberia. **Area:** 27,699 sq. mi. (71,740 sq km). **Border countries:** Guinea, Liberia. **Natural resources:** diamonds, titanium ore, bauxite, iron ore, gold, chromite. **People Population:** 5,732,681 (July 2003 est.). **Nationality:** *noun:* Sierra Leonean(s); *adj.:* Sierra Leonean. **Ethnic groups:** 20 native African tribes 90% (Temne 30%, Mende 30%, other 30%), Creole (Krio) 10% (descendants of freed Jamaican slaves who were settled in the Freetown area in the late-18th century), refugees from Liberia's recent civil war, small numbers of Europeans, Lebanese, Pakistanis, and Indians. **Religions:** Muslim 60%, indigenous beliefs 30%, Christian 10%. **Languages:** English (official, regular use limited to literate minority), Mende (principal vernacular in the south), Temne (principal vernacular in the north), Krio (English-based Creole, spoken by the descendants of freed Jamaican slaves who were settled in the Freetown area, a lingua franca and a first language for 10% of the population but understood by 95%). *note:* Rwanda is the most densely populated country in Africa. **Government Government type:** constitutional democracy. Capital: Freetown. **Independence:** 27 April 1961 (from UK). **National holiday:** Independence Day, 27 April (1961). **Economy G.D.P.:** purchasing power parity—$2.8 billion (2002 est.). **G.D.P.—per capita:** purchasing power parity—$580 (2002 est.). **Currency:** leone (SLL).

Singapore

Republic of Singapore

Geography Location: Southeastern Asia, islands between Malaysia and Indonesia. **Area:** 244 sq. mi. (692.7 sq km). **Natural resources:** fish, deepwater ports. **People Population:** 4,608,595 (July 2003 est.). **Nationality:** *noun:* Singaporean(s); *adj.:* Singapore. **Ethnic groups:** Chinese 76.7%, Malay 14%, Indian 7.9%, other 1.4%. **Religions:** Buddhist (Chinese), Muslim (Malays), Christian, Hindu, Sikh, Taoist, Confucianist. **Languages:** Chinese (official), Malay (official and national), Tamil (official), English (official). **Government Government type:** parliamentary republic. Capital: Singapore. **Independence:** 9 August 1965 (from Malaysian Federation). **National holiday:** Independence Day, 9 August (1965). **Economy G.D.P.:** purchasing power parity—$105 billion (2002 est.). **G.D.P.—per capita:** purchasing power parity—$24,000 (2002 est.). **Currency:** Singapore dollar (SGD).

Slovakia

Slovak Republic

Geography Location: Central Europe, south of Poland. **Area:** 18,859 sq. mi. (48,845 sq km). **Border countries:** Austria, Czech Republic, Hungary, Poland, Ukraine. **Natural resources:** brown coal and lignite; small amounts of iron ore, copper and manganese ore; salt; arable land. **People Population:** 5,430,033 (July 2003 est.). **Nationality:** *noun:* Slovak(s); *adj.:* Slovak. **Ethnic groups:** Slovak 85.7%, Hungarian 10.6%, Roma 1.6% (the 1992 census figures underreport the Gypsy/Romany community, which is about 500,000), Czech, Moravian, Silesian 1.1%, Ruthenian and Ukrainian 0.6%, German 0.1%, Polish 0.1%, other 0.2% (1996). **Religions:** Roman Catholic 60.3%, atheist 9.7%, Protestant 8.4%, Orthodox 4.1%, other 17.5%. **Languages:** Slovak (official), Hungarian. **Government Government type:** parliamentary democracy. Capital: Bratislava. **Independence:** 1 January 1993 (Czechoslovakia split into the Czech Republic and Slovakia). **National holiday:** Constitution Day, 1 September (1992). **Economy G.D.P.:** purchasing power parity—$66 billion (2002 est.). **G.D.P.—per capita:** purchasing power parity—$12,200 (2002 est.). **Currency:** Slovak koruna (SKK).

Solomon Islands

Geography Location: Oceania, group of islands in the South Pacific Ocean, east of Papua New Guinea. **Area:** 10,985 sq. mi. (28,450 sq km). **Natural resources:** fish, forests, gold, bauxite, phosphates, lead, zinc, nickel. **People Population:** 509,190 (July 2003 est.). **Nationality:** *noun:* Solomon Islander(s); *adj.:* Solomon Islander. **Ethnic groups:** Melanesian 93%, Polynesian 4%, Micronesian 1.5%, European 0.8%, Chinese 0.3%, other 0.4%. **Religions:** Anglican 45%, Roman Catholic 18%, United (Methodist/Presbyterian) 12%, Baptist 9%, Seventh-Day Adventist 7%, other Protestant 5%, indigenous beliefs 4%. **Languages:** Melanesian pidgin in much of the country is lingua franca; English is official but spoken by only 1%-2% of the population. *note:* 120 indigenous languages. **Government Government type:** parliamentary democracy tending toward anarchy. Capital: Honiara. **Independence:** 7 July 1978 (from UK). **National holiday:** Independence Day, 7 July (1978). **Economy G.D.P.:** purchasing power parity—$800 million (2001 est.). **G.D.P.—per capita:** purchasing power parity—$1,700 (2001 est.). **Currency:** Solomon Islands dollar (SBD).

Somalia

Geography Location: Eastern Africa, bordering the Gulf of Aden and the Indian Ocean, east of Ethiopia. **Area:** 246,201 sq. mi. (637,657 sq km). **Border countries**: Djibouti, Ethiopia, Kenya. **Natural resources:** uranium and largely unexploited reserves of iron ore, tin, gypsum, bauxite, copper, salt, natural gas, likely oil reserves. **People Population:** 8,025,190, *note:* this estimate was derived from an official census taken in 1975 by the Somali Government; population counting in Somalia is complicated by the large number of nomads and by refugee movements in response to famine and clan warfare (July 2003 est.). **Nationality:** *noun:* Somali(s); *adj.:* Somali. **Ethnic groups:** Somali 85%, Bantu and other non-Somali 15% (including Arabs 30,000). **Religions:** Sunni Muslim. **Languages:** Somali (official), Arabic, Italian, English. **Government Government type:** no permanent national government; transitional, parliamentary national government. Capital: Mogadishu. **Independence:** 1 July 1960 (from a merger of British Somaliland, which became independent from the UK on 26 June 1960, and Italian Somaliland, which became independent from the Italian-administered UN trusteeship on 1 July 1960, to form the Somali Republic). **National holiday:** Foundation of the Somali Republic, 1 July (1960); note—26 June (1960) in Somaliland. **Economy G.D.P.:** purchasing power parity—$4.1 billion (2001 est.). **G.D.P.—per capita:** purchasing power parity—$550 (2001 est.). **Industries:** a few light industries, including sugar refining, textiles, petroleum refining (mostly shut down), wireless communication. **Agriculture—products:** cattle, sheep, goats; bananas, sorghum, corn, coconuts, rice, sugarcane, mangoes, sesame seeds, beans; fish. **Currency:** Somali shilling (SOS).

South Africa

Republic of South Africa

Geography Location: Southern Africa, at the southern tip of the continent of Africa. **Area:** 471,444 sq. mi. (1,219,912 sq km). **Border countries**: Botswana, Lesotho, Mozambique, Namibia, Swaziland, Zimbabwe. **Natural resources:** gold, chromium, antimony, coal, iron ore, manganese, nickel, phosphates, tin, uranium, gem diamonds, platinum, copper, vanadium, salt, natural gas. **People** Population 42,768,678. *note:* South Africa took a census October 1996 that showed a population of 40,583,611 (after an official adjustment for a 6.8% underenumeration based on a postenumeration survey); estimates for this country explicitly take into account the effects of excess mortality due to AIDS; this can result in lower life expectancy, higher infant mortality and death rates, lower population and growth rates, and changes in the distribution of population by age and sex than would otherwise be expected (July 2003 est.). **Nationality:** *noun:* South African(s); *adj.:* South African. **Ethnic groups:** black 75.2%, white 13.6%, Colored 8.6%, Indian 2.6%. **Religions:** Christian 68% (includes most whites and Coloreds, about 60% of blacks and about 40% of Indians), Muslim 2%, Hindu 1.5% (60% of Indians), indigenous beliefs and animist 28.5%. **Languages:** 11 official languages, including Afrikaans, English, Ndebele, Pedi, Sotho, Swazi, Tsonga, Tswana, Venda, Xhosa, Zulu. **Government Government type:** Republic. Capital: Pretoria; note—Cape Town is the legislative center and Bloemfontein the judicial center. **Independence:** 31 May 1910 (from UK). **National holiday:** Freedom Day, 27 April (1994). **Economy G.D.P.:** purchasing power parity—$432 billion (2002 est.). **G.D.P.—per capita:** purchasing power parity—$10,000 (2002 est.). **Currency:** rand (ZAR).

Spain

Kingdom of Spain

Geography Location: Southwestern Europe, bordering the Bay of Biscay, Mediterranean Sea, North Atlantic Ocean, and Pyrenees Mountains, southwest of France. **Area:** 194,884 sq. mi. (504,782 sq km). **Border countries**: Andorra, France, Gibraltar, Portugal, Morocco (Ceuta), Morocco (Melilla). **Natural resources:** coal, lignite, iron ore, uranium, mercury, pyrites, fluorspar, gypsum, zinc, lead, tungsten, copper, kaolin, potash, hydropower, arable land. **People Population:** 40,217,413 (July 2003 est.). **Nationality:** *noun:* Spaniard(s); *adj.:* Spanish. **Ethnic groups:** composite of Mediterranean and Nordic types. **Religions:** Roman Catholic 94%, other 6%. **Languages:** Castilian Spanish (official) 74%, Catalan 17%, Galician 7%, Basque 2%. **Government Government type:** parliamentary monarchy. Capital: Madrid. **Independence:** the Iberian peninsula was characterized by a variety of independent kingdoms prior to the Moslem occupation that began in the early 8th Century A. D. and lasted nearly seven centuries; the small Christian redoubts of the north began the reconquest almost immediately, culminating in the seizure of Granada in 1492; this event completed the unification of several kingdoms and is traditionally considered the forging of present-day Spain. **National holiday:** Hispanic Day, 12 October. **Economy G.D.P.:** purchasing power parity—$828 billion (2002 est.). **G.D.P.—per capita:** purchasing power parity—$20,700 (2002 est.). **Currency:** euro (EUR).

Sri Lanka

Democratic Socialist Republic of Sri Lanka

Geography Location: Southern Asia, island in the Indian Ocean, south of India. **Area:** 25,332 sq. mi. (65,610 sq km). **Natural resources:** limestone, graphite, mineral sands, gems, phosphates, clay, hydropower. **People Population:** 19,742,439 (2003 est.), *note:* since the outbreak of hostilities between the government and armed Tamil separatists in the mid-1980s, several hundred thousand Tamil civilians have fled the island; as of yearend 2000, approximately 65,000 were housed in 131 refugee camps in south India, another 40,000 lived outside the Indian camps, and more than 200,000 Tamils have sought refuge in the West (July 2003 est.). **Nationality:** *noun:* Sri Lankan(s); *adj.:* Sri Lankan. **Ethnic groups:** Sinhalese 74%, Tamil 18%, Moor 7%, Burgher, Malay, and Vedda 1%. **Religions:** Buddhist 70%, Hindu 15%, Christian 8%, Muslim 7% (1999). **Languages:** Sinhala (official and national language) 74%, Tamil (national language) 18%, other 8%. *note:* English is commonly used in government and is spoken competently by about 10% of the population **Government Government type:** republic. Capital: Colombo; note—Sri Jayewardenepura Kotte is the legislative capital. **Independence:** 4 February 1948 (from UK). **National holiday:** Independence Day, 4 February (1948). **Economy G.D.P.:** purchasing power parity—$73.7 billion (2002 est.). **G.D.P.—per capita:** purchasing power parity—$3,700 (2002 est.). **Currency:** Sri Lankan rupee (LKR).

Sudan

Republic of the Sudan

Geography Location: Northern Africa, bordering the Red Sea, between Egypt and Eritrea. **Area:** 967,495 sq. mi. (2,505,810 sq km). **Border countries**: Central African Republic, Chad, Democratic Republic of the Congo, Egypt , Eritrea, Ethiopia, Kenya, Libya, Uganda. **Natural resources:** petroleum; small reserves of iron ore, copper, chromium ore, zinc, tungsten, mica, silver, gold, hydropower. **People Population:** 38,114,160 (July 2003 est.). **Nationality:** *noun:* Sudanese (singular and plural); *adj.:* Sudanese. **Ethnic groups:** black 52%, Arab 39%, Beja 6%, foreigners 2%, other 1%. **Religions:** Sunni Muslim 70% (in north), indigenous beliefs 25%, Christian 5% (mostly in south and Khartoum). **Languages:** Arabic (official), Nubian, Ta Bedawie, diverse dialects of Nilotic, Nilo Hamitic, Sudanic languages, English *note:* program of "Arabization" in process. **Government Government type:** authoritarian regime—ruling military junta took power in 1989; government is run by an alliance of the military and the National Congress Party (NCP), formerly the National Islamic Front (NIF), which espouses an Islamist platform. Capital: Khartoum. **Independence:** 1 January 1956 (from Egypt and UK). **National holiday:** Independence Day, 1 January (1956). **Economy G.D.P.:** purchasing power parity—$52.9 billion (2002 est.). **G.D.P.—per capita:** purchasing power parity—$1,420 (2002 est.). **Currency:** Sudanese dinar (SDD).

Suriname

Republic of Suriname

Geography Location: Northern South America, bordering the North Atlantic Ocean, between French Guiana and Guyana. Area 63,039 sq. mi. (163,270 sq km). **Border countries:** Brazil, French Guiana, Guyana. **Natural resources:** timber, hydropower, fish, kaolin, shrimp, bauxite, gold, and small amounts of nickel, copper, platinum, iron ore. **People Population:** 435,449 (July 2003 est.). **Nationality:** *noun:* Surinamer(s); *adj.:* Surinamese. **Ethnic groups:** Hindustani (also known locally as "East Indians"; their ancestors emigrated from northern India in the latter part of the 19th century) 37%, Creole (mixed white and black) 31%, Javanese 15%, "Maroons" (their African ancestors were brought to the country in the 17th and 18th centuries as slaves and escaped to the interior) 10%, Amerindian 2%, Chinese 2%, white 1%, other 2%. **Religions:** Hindu 27.4%, Muslim 19.6%, Roman Catholic 22.8%, Protestant 25.2% (predominantly Moravian), indigenous beliefs 5%. **Languages:** Dutch (official), English (widely spoken), Sranang Tongo (Surinamese, sometimes called Taki-Taki, is native language of Creoles and much of the younger population and is lingua franca among others), Hindustani (a dialect of Hindi), Javanese. **Government Government type:**constitutional democracy. Capital: Paramaribo. **Independence:** 25 November 1975 (from Netherlands). **National holiday:** Independence Day, 25 November (1975). **Economy G.D.P.:** purchasing power parity—$1.5 billion (2002 est.). **G.D.P.—per capita:** purchasing power parity—$3,500 (2002 est.). **Currency:** Surinamese guilder (SRG).

Swaziland

Kingdom of Swaziland

Geography Location: Southern Africa, between Mozambique and South Africa. **Area:** 6,703 sq. mi. (17,363 sq km). **Border countries**: Mozambique, South Africa. **Natural resources:** asbestos, coal, clay, cassiterite, hydropower, forests, small gold and diamond deposits, quarry stone, and talc. **People Population:** 1,161,219. *note:* estimates for this country explicitly take into account the effects of excess mortality due to AIDS; this can result in lower life expectancy, higher infant mortality and death rates, lower population and growth rates, and changes in the distribution of population by age and sex than would otherwise be expected (July 2003 est.). **Nationality:** *noun:* Swazi(s); *adj.:* Swazi. **Ethnic groups:** African 97%, European 3%. **Religions:** Zionist (a blend of Christianity and indigenous ancestral worship) 40%, Roman Catholic 20%, Muslim 10%, Anglican, Bahai, Methodist, Mormon, Jewish and other 30%. **Languages:** English (official, government business conducted in English), siSwati (official). **Government** **Government type:** monarchy; independent member of Commonwealth. Capital: Mbabane; note—Lobamba is the royal and legislative capital. **Independence:** 6 September 1968 (from UK). **National holiday:** Independence Day, 6 September (1968). **Economy** **G.D.P.:** purchasing power parity—$4.8 billion (2002 est.). **G.D.P.—per capita:** purchasing power parity—$4,400 (2002 est.). **Currency:** lilangeni (SZL).

Sweden

Kingdom of Sweden

Geography **Location:** Northern Europe, bordering the Baltic Sea, Gulf of Bothnia, Kattegat, and Skagerrak, between Finland and Norway. **Area:** 173,731 sq. mi. (449,964 sq km). **Border countries**: Finland, Norway. **Natural resources:** zinc, iron ore, lead, copper, silver, timber, uranium, hydropower. **People** **Population:** 8,878,085 (July 2003 est.). **Nationality:** *noun:* Swede(s); *adj.:* Swedish. **Ethnic groups:** indigenous **population:** Swedes and Finnish and Sami minorities; foreign-born or first-generation immigrants: Finns, Yugoslavs, Danes, Norwegians, Greeks, Turks. **Religions:** Lutheran 87%, Roman Catholic, Orthodox, Baptist, Muslim, Jewish, Buddhist. **Languages:** Swedish. *note:* small Sami- and Finnish-speaking minorities. **Government** **Government type:** constitutional monarchy. Capital: Stockholm. **Independence:** 6 June 1523 (Gustav VASA elected king). **National holiday:** Flag Day, 6 June. **Economy** **G.D.P.:** purchasing power parity—$227.4 billion (2002 est.). **G.D.P.—per capita:** purchasing power parity—$25,400 (2002 est.). **Currency:** Swedish krona (SEK).

Switzerland

Swiss Confederation

Geography **Location:** Central Europe, east of France, north of Italy. **Area:** 15,942 sq. mi. (41,290 sq km). **Border countries**: Austria, France, Italy, Liechtenstein, Germany. **Natural resources:** hydropower potential, timber, salt. **People** **Population:** 7,318,638 (July 2003 est.). **Nationality:** *noun:* Swiss (singular and plural); *adj.:* Swiss. **Ethnic groups:** German 65%, French 18%, Italian 10%, Romansch 1%, other 6%. **Religions:** Roman Catholic 46.1%, Protestant 40%, other 5%, none 8.9% (1990). **Languages:** German (official) 63.7%, French (official) 19.2%, Italian (official) 7.6%, Romansch (official) 0.6%, other 8.9%. **Government** **Government type:** federal republic. Capital: Bern. **Independence:** 1 August 1291 (Founding of the Swiss Confederation). **National holiday:** Founding of the Swiss Confederation, 1 August (1291). **Economy** **G.D.P.:** purchasing power parity—$231 billion (2002 est.). **G.D.P.—per capita:** purchasing power parity—$31,700 (2002 est.). **Currency:** Swiss franc (CHF).

Syria

Syrian Arab Republic

Geography **Location:** Middle East, bordering the Mediterranean Sea, between Lebanon and Turkey. **Area:** 71,498 sq. mi. (185,180 sq km). **Border countries**: Iraq, Israel, Jordan, Lebanon, Turkey. **Natural resources:** petroleum, phosphates, chrome and manganese ores, asphalt, iron ore, rock salt, marble, gypsum, hydropower. **People** **Population:** 17,585,540 (July 2002 est.). *note:* in addition, about 40,000 people live in the Israeli-occupied Golan Heights—20,000 Arabs (18,000 Druze and 2,000 Alawites) and about 20,000 Israeli settlers (February 2003 est.) (July 2003 est.). **Nationality:** *noun:* Syrian(s); *adj.:* Syrian. **Ethnic groups:** Arab 90.3%, Kurds, Armenians, and other 9.7%. **Religions:** Sunni Muslim 74%, Alawite, Druze, and other Muslim sects 16%, Christian (various sects) 10%, Jewish (tiny communities in Damascus, Al Qamishli, and Aleppo). **Languages:** Arabic (official); Kurdish, Armenian, Aramaic, Circassian widely understood; French, English somewhat understood. **Government** **Government type:** republic under military regime since March 1963. Capital: Damascus. **Independence:** 17 April 1946 (from League of Nations mandate under French administration). **National holiday:** Independence Day, 17 April (1946). **Economy** **G.D.P.:** purchasing power parity—$59.4 billion (2002 est.). **G.D.P.—per capita:** purchasing power parity—$3,500 (2002 est.). **Currency:** Syrian pound (SYP).

Taiwan

Geography **Location:** Eastern Asia, islands bordering the East China Sea, Philippine Sea, South China Sea, and Taiwan Strait, north of the Philippines, off the southeastern coast of China. **Area:** 13,892 sq. mi. (35,980 sq km). **Natural resources:** small deposits of coal, natural gas, limestone, marble, and asbestos. **People** **Population:** 22,603,001 (July 2003 est.). **Nationality:** *noun:* Chinese (singular and plural); *adj.:* Chinese. **Ethnic groups:** Taiwanese (including Hakka) 84%, mainland Chinese 14%, aborigine 2%. **Religions:** mixture of Buddhist, Confucian, and Taoist 93%, Christian 4.5%, other 2.5%. **Languages:** Mandarin Chinese (official), Taiwanese (Min), Hakka dialects. **Government Government type:** multiparty democratic regime headed by popularly-elected president and unicameral legislature. Capital: Taipei. **National holiday:** Republic Day (Anniversary of the Chinese Revolution), 10 October (1911). **Economy G.D.P.:** purchasing power parity—$406 billion (2002 est.). **G.D.P.—per capita:** purchasing power parity—$18,000 (2002 est.). **Currency:** new Taiwan dollar (TWD).

Tajikistan

Republic of Tajikistan

Geography Location: Central Asia, west of China. **Area:** 55,251 sq. mi. (143,100 sq km). **Border countries**: Afghanistan, China, Kyrgyzstan, Uzbekistan. **Natural resources:** hydropower, some petroleum, uranium, mercury, brown coal, lead, zinc, antimony, tungsten, silver, gold. **People Population:** 6,863,752 (July 2003 est.). **Nationality:** *noun:* Tajikistani(s); *adj.:* Tajikistani. **Ethnic groups:** Tajik 64.9%, Uzbek 25%, Russian 3.5% (declining because of emigration), other 6.6%. **Religions:** Sunni Muslim 85%, Shi'a Muslim 5%. **Languages:** Tajik (official), Russian widely used in government and business. **Government Government type:** republic. Capital: Dushanbe. **Independence:** 9 September 1991 (from Soviet Union). **National holiday:** Independence Day (or National Day), 9 September (1991). **Economy G.D.P.:** purchasing power parity—$8 billion (2002 est.). **G.D.P.—per capita:** purchasing power parity—$1,250 (2002 est.). **Currency:** somoni.

Tanzania

United Republic of Tanzania

Geography Location: Eastern Africa, bordering the Indian Ocean, between Kenya and Mozambique. **Area:** 364,900 sq. mi. (945,087 sq km). **Border countries**: Burundi, Democratic Republic of the Congo, Kenya, Malawi, Mozambique, Rwanda, Uganda, Zambia. **Natural resources:** hydropower, tin, phosphates, iron ore, coal, diamonds, gemstones, gold, natural gas, nickel. **People Population:** 35,922,454 *note:* estimates for this country explicitly take into account the effects of excess mortality due to AIDS; this can result in lower life expectancy, higher infant mortality and death rates, lower population and growth rates, and changes in the distribution of population by age and sex than would otherwise be expected (July 2003 est.). **Nationality:** *noun:* Tanzanian(s); *adj.:* Tanzanian. **Ethnic groups:** mainland—native African 99% (of which 95% are Bantu consisting of more than 130 tribes), other 1% (consisting of Asian, European, and Arab); Zanzibar—Arab, native African, mixed Arab and native African. **Religions:** mainland—Christian 30%, Muslim 35%, indigenous beliefs 35%; Zanzibar—more than 99% Muslim. **Languages:** Kiswahili or Swahili (official), Kiunguju (name for Swahili in Zanzibar), English (official, primary language of commerce, administration, and higher education), Arabic (widely spoken in Zanzibar), many local languages. *note:* Kiswahili (Swahili) is the mother tongue of the Bantu people living in Zanzibar and nearby coastal Tanzania; although Kiswahili is Bantu in structure and origin, its vocabulary draws on a variety of sources, including Arabic and English, and it has become the lingua franca of central and eastern Africa; the first language of most people is one of the local languages. **Government Government type:** republic. Capital: Dar es Salaam; note—legislative offices have been transferred to Dodoma, which is planned as the new national capital; the National Assembly now meets there on regular basis. **Independence:** 26 April 1964; Tanganyika became independent 9 December 1961 (from UK-administered UN trusteeship); Zanzibar became independent 19 December 1963 (from UK); Tanganyika united with Zanzibar 26 April 1964 to form the United Republic of Tanganyika and Zanzibar; renamed United Republic of Tanzania 29 October 1964. **National holiday:** Union Day (Tanganyika and Zanzibar), 26 April (1964). **Economy G.D.P.:** purchasing power parity—$22.5 billion (2002 est.). **G.D.P.—per capita:** purchasing power parity—$630 (2002 est.). **Currency:** Tanzanian shilling (TZS).

Thailand

Kingdom of Thailand

Geography Location: Southeastern Asia, bordering the Andaman Sea and the Gulf of Thailand, southeast of Burma. **Area:** 198,456 sq. mi. (514,000 sq km). **Border countries**: Burma, Cambodia, Laos, Malaysia. **Natural resources:** tin, rubber, natural gas, tungsten, tantalum, timber, lead, fish, gypsum, lignite, fluorite, arable land. **People Population:** 64,265,276, *note:* estimates for this country explicitly take into account the effects of excess mortality due to AIDS; this can result in lower life expectancy, higher infant mortality and death rates, lower population and growth rates, and changes in the distribution of population by age and sex than would otherwise be expected (July 2003 est.). **Nationality:** *noun:* Thai (singular and plural); *adj.:* Thai. **Ethnic groups:** Thai 75%, Chinese 14%, other 11%. **Religions:** Buddhism 95%, Muslim 3.8%, Christianity 0.5%, Hinduism 0.1%, other 0.6% (1991). **Languages:** Thai, English (secondary language of the elite), ethnic and regional dialects. **Government Government type:** constitutional monarchy. Capital: Bangkok. **Independence:** 1238 (traditional founding date; never colonized). **National holiday:** Birthday of King PHU-

MIPHON, 5 December (1927). **Economy G.D.P.:** purchasing power parity—$429 billion (2002 est.). **G.D.P.—per capita:** purchasing power parity—$6,900 (2002 est.). **Currency:** baht (THB).

Togo

Togolese Republic

Geography Location: Western Africa, bordering the Bight of Benin, between Benin and Ghana. **Area:** 21,927 sq. mi. (56,785 sq km). **Border countries**: Benin, Burkina Faso, Ghana. **Natural resources:** phosphates, limestone, marble, arable land. **People Population:** 5,429,299. *note:* estimates for this country explicitly take into account the effects of excess mortality due to AIDS; this can result in lower life expectancy, higher infant mortality and death rates, lower population and growth rates, and changes in the distribution of population by age and sex than would otherwise be expected (July 2003 est.). **Nationality:** *noun:* Togolese (singular and plural); *adj.:* Togolese. **Ethnic groups:** native African (37 tribes; largest and most important are Ewe, Mina, and Kabre) 99%, European and Syrian-Lebanese less than 1%. **Religions:** indigenous beliefs 51%, Christian 29%, Muslim 20%. **Languages:** French (official and the language of commerce), Ewe and Mina (the two major African languages in the south), Kabye (sometimes spelled Kabiye) and Dagomba (the two major African languages in the north). **Government Government type:** republic under transition to multiparty democratic rule. Capital: Lome. **Independence:** 27 April 1960 (from French-administered UN trusteeship). **National holiday:** Independence Day, 27 April (1960). **Economy G.D.P.:** purchasing power parity—$8 billion (2002 est.). **G.D.P.—per capita:** purchasing power parity—$1,500 (2002 est.). **Currency:** Communaute Financiere Africaine franc (XOF).

Tonga

Kingdom of Tonga

Geography Location: Oceania, archipelago in the South Pacific Ocean, about two-thirds of the way from Hawaii to New Zealand. **Area:** 289 sq. mi. (748 sq km). **Natural resources:** fish, fertile soil. **People Population:** 108,141 (July 2003 est.). **Nationality:** *noun:* Tongan(s); *adj.:* Tongan. **Ethnic groups:** Polynesian, Europeans about 300. **Religions:** Christian (Free Wesleyan Church claims over 30,000 adherents). **Languages:** Tongan, English. **Government Government type:** hereditary constitutional monarchy. Capital: Nuku'alofa. Administrative divisions: 3 island groups; Ha'apai, Tongatapu, Vava'u. **Independence:** 4 June 1970 (from UK protectorate). **National holiday:** Independence Day, 4 June (1970). **Economy G.D.P.:** purchasing power parity—$236 million (2001 est.). **G.D.P.—per capita:** purchasing power parity—$2,200 (2001 est.). **Currency:** pa'anga (TOP).

Trinidad and Tobago

Republic of Trinidad and Tobago

Geography Location: Caribbean, islands between the Caribbean Sea and the North Atlantic Ocean, northeast of Venezuela. **Area:** 1,981 sq. mi. (5,128 sq km). **Natural resources:** petroleum, natural gas, asphalt. **People Population:** 1,104,209 (July 2003 est.). **Nationality:** *noun:* Trinidadian(s), Tobagonian(s); *adj.:* Trinidadian, Tobagonian. **Ethnic groups:** black 39.5%, East Indian (a local term—primarily immigrants from northern India) 40.3%, mixed 18.4%, white 0.6%, Chinese and other 1.2%. **Religions:** Roman Catholic 29.4%, Hindu 23.8%, Anglican 10.9%, Muslim 5.8%, Presbyterian 3.4%, other 26.7%. **Languages:** English (official), Hindi, French, Spanish, Chinese. **Government Government type:** parliamentary democracy. Capital: Port-of-Spain. **Independence:** 31 August 1962 (from UK). **National holiday:** Independence Day, 31 August (1962). **Economy G.D.P.:** purchasing power parity—$11.1 billion (2002 est.). **G.D.P.—per capita:** purchasing power parity—$9,500 (2002 est.). **Currency:** Trinidad and Tobago dollar (TTD).

Tunisia

Tunisian Republic

Geography Location: Northern Africa, bordering the Mediterranean Sea, between Algeria and Libya. **Area:** 63,170 sq. mi. (163,610 sq km). **Border countries**: Algeria, Libya. **Natural resources:** petroleum, phosphates, iron ore, lead, zinc, salt. **People Population:** 9,924,742 (July 2003 est.). **Nationality:** *noun:* Tunisian(s); *adj.:* Tunisian. **Ethnic groups:** Arab 98%, European 1%, Jewish and other 1%. **Religions:** Muslim 98%, Christian 1%, Jewish and other 1%. **Languages:** Arabic (official and one of the languages of commerce), French (commerce). **Government Government type:** republic. Capital: Tunis. **Independence**: 20 March 1956 (from France). **National holiday**: Independence Day, 20 March (1956). **Economy G.D.P.:** purchasing power parity—$63 billion (2002 est.). **G.D.P.—per capita:** purchasing power parity—$6,500 (2002 est.). **Currency:** Tunisian dinar (TND).

Turkey

Republic of Turkey

Geography Location: southeastern Europe and southwestern Asia (that portion of Turkey west of the Bosporus is geographically part of Europe), bordering the Black Sea, between Bulgaria and Georgia, and bordering the Aegean Sea and the Mediterranean Sea, between Greece and Syria. **Area:** 301,382 sq. mi. (780,580 sq km). **Border countries**: Armenia 268 km, Azerbaijan 9 km, Bulgaria 240 km, Georgia 252 km, Greece 206 km, Iran 499 km, Iraq 352 km, Syria 822 km. **Natural resources:** antimony, coal, chromium, mercury, copper, borate, sulfur, iron ore, arable land, hydropower. **People Population:** 68,109,469 (July 2003 est.). **Nationality:** *noun:* Turk(s); *adj.:* Turkish. **Ethnic groups:** Turkish 80%, Kurdish 20% (estimated). **Religions:** Muslim 99.8% (mostly Sunni), other 0.2% (mostly Christians and Jews). **Languages:** Turkish (official), Kurdish, Arabic, Armenian, Greek. **Government Government type:** republican parliamentary democracy. Capital: Ankara. **Independence:** 29 October 1923 (successor state to the Ottoman Empire). **National holiday:** Independence Day, 29 October (1923). **Economy G.D.P.:** purchasing power parity—$468 billion (2002 est.). **G.D.P.—per capita:** purchasing power parity—$7,000 (2002 est.). **Currency:** Turkish lira (TRL).

Turkmenistan

Geography Location: Central Asia, bordering the Caspian Sea, between Iran and Kazakhstan **Area:** 188,456 sq. mi. (488,100 sq km). **Border countries**. Afghanistan 744 km, Iran 992 km, Kazakhstan 379 km, Uzbekistan 1,621 km. **Natural resources:** petroleum, natural gas, coal, sulfur, salt **People Population:** 4,775,544 (July 2003 est.). **Nationality:** *noun:* Turkmen(s) *adj.:* Turkmen. **Ethnic groups:** Turkmen 77%, Uzbek 9.2%, Russian 6.7%, Kazakh 2%, other 5.1% (1995). **Religions:** Muslim 89%, Eastern Orthodox 9%, unknown 2%. **Languages:** Turkmen 72%, Russian 12%, Uzbek 9%, other 7%. **Government Government type:** republic. Capital: Ashgabat. **Independence:** 27 October 1991 (from the Soviet Union). **National holiday:** Independence Day, 27 October (1991). **Economy G.D.P.:** purchasing power parity—$26 billion (2002 est.). **G.D.P.—per capita:** purchasing power parity—$5,500 (2002 est.). **Currency:** Turkmen manat (TMM).

Tuvalu

Geography Location: Oceania, island group consisting of nine coral atolls in the South Pacific Ocean, about one-half of the way from Hawaii to Australia. **Area:** 10 sq. mi. (26 sq km). **Natural resources:** fish. **People Population:** 11,305 (July 2003 est.). **Nationality:** *noun:* Tuvaluan(s); *adj.:* Tuvaluan. **Ethnic groups:** Polynesian 96%, Micronesian 4%. **Religions:** Church of Tuvalu (Congregationalist) 97%, Seventh-Day Adventist 1.4%, Baha'i 1%, other 0.6%. **Languages:** Tuvaluan, English, Samoan, Kiribati (on the island of Nui). **Government Government type:** constitutional monarchy with a parliamentary democracy; began debating republic status in 1992. Capital: Funafuti. **Independence:** 1 October 1978 (from UK). **National holiday:** Independence Day, 1 October (1978). **Economy G.D.P.:** purchasing power parity—$12.2 million (2000 est.). **G.D.P.—per capita:** purchasing power parity—$1,100 (2000 est.). **Currency:** Australian dollar (AUD); note—there is also a Tuvaluan dollar.

Uganda

Republic of Uganda

Geography Location: Eastern Africa, west of Kenya. **Area:** 91,135 sq. mi. (236,040 sq km). **Border countries**: Democratic Republic of the Congo, Kenya, Rwanda, Sudan, Tanzania. **Natural resources:** copper, cobalt, hydropower, limestone, salt, arable land. **People Population:** 25,632,794, *note:* estimates for this country explicitly take into account the effects of excess mortality due to AIDS; this can result in lower life expectancy, higher infant mortality and death rates, lower population and growth rates, and changes in the distribution of population by age and sex than would otherwise be expected (July 2003 est.). **Nationality:** *noun:* Ugandan(s); *adj.:* Ugandan. **Ethnic groups:** Baganda 17%, Ankole 8%, Basoga 8%, Iteso 8%, Bakiga 7%, Langi 6%, Rwanda 6%, Bagisu 5%, Acholi 4%, Lugbara 4%, Batoro 3%, Bunyoro 3%, Alur 2%, Bagwere 2%, Bakonjo 2%, Jopodhola 2%, Karamojong 2%, Rundi 2%, non-African (European, Asian, Arab) 1%, other 8%. **Religions:** Roman Catholic 33%, Protestant 33%, Muslim 16%, indigenous beliefs 18%. **Languages:** English (official national language, taught in grade schools, used in courts of law and by most newspapers and some radio broadcasts), Ganda or Luganda (most widely used of the Niger-Congo languages, preferred for native language publications in the capital and may be taught in school), other Niger-Congo languages, Nilo-Saharan languages, Swahili, Arabic. **Government Government type:** republic. Capital: Kampala. **Independence:** 9 October 1962 (from UK). **National holiday:** Independence Day, 9 October (1962). **Economy G.D.P.:** purchasing power parity—$31 billion (2002 est.). **G.D.P.—per capita:** purchasing power parity—$1,260 (2002 est.). **Currency:** Ugandan shilling (UGX).

Ukraine

Geography Location: Eastern Europe, bordering the Black Sea, between Poland and Russia. **Area:** 233,089 sq. mi. (603,700 sq km). **Border countries**: Belarus, Hungary, Moldova, Poland, Romania (south), Romania (west), Russia 1,576, Slovakia. **Natural resources:** iron ore, coal, manganese, natural gas, oil, salt, sulfur, graphite, titanium, magnesium, kaolin, nickel, mercury, timber, arable land. **People**

Population: 48,055,439 (July 2003 est.). **Nationality:** *noun:* Ukrainian(s); *adj.:* Ukrainian. **Ethnic groups:** Ukrainian 77.8%, Russian 17.3%, Belarusian 0.6%, Moldovan 0.5%, Crimean Tatar 0.5%, Bulgarian 0.4%, Hungarian 0.3%, Romanian 0.3%, Polish 0.3%, Jewish 0.2%, other 1.8% (2001). **Religions:** Ukrainian Orthodox—Moscow Patriarchate, Ukrainian Orthodox—Kiev Patriarchate, Ukrainian Autocephalous Orthodox, Ukrainian Catholic (Uniate), Protestant, Jewish. **Languages:** Ukrainian, Russian, Romanian, Polish, Hungarian. **Government Government type:** republic. Capital: Kiev (Kyyiv). **Independence:** 24 August 1991 (from the Soviet Union). **National holiday:** Independence Day, 24 August (1991); the date of 22 January (1918), the day Ukraine first declared its independence (from Soviet Russia), is now celebrated as Unity Day. **Economy G.D.P.:** purchasing power parity—$218 billion (2002 est.). **G.D.P.—per capita:** purchasing power parity—$4,500 (2002 est.). **Currency:** hryvnia (UAH).

United Arab Emirates

United Arab Emirates

Geography Location: Middle East, bordering the Gulf of Oman and the Persian Gulf, between Oman and Saudi Arabia. **Area:** 31,969 sq. mi. (82,880 sq km). **Border countries**: Oman 410 km, Saudi Arabia 457 km. **Natural resources:** petroleum, natural gas. **People Population:** 2,484,818. *note:* includes an estimated 1,606,079 non-nationals; the 17 December 1995 census presents a total population figure of 2,377,453, and there are estimates of 3.44 million for 2002 (July 2003 est.). **Nationality:** *noun:* Emirati(s); *adj.:* Emirati. **Ethnic groups:** Emirati 19%, other Arab and Iranian 23%, South Asian 50%, other expatriates (includes Westerners and East Asians) 8% (1982) *note:* less than 20% are UAE citizens (1982). **Religions:** Muslim 96% (Shi'a 16%), Christian, Hindu, and other 4%. **Languages:** Arabic (official), Persian, English, Hindi, Urdu. **Government Government type:** federation with specified powers delegated to the UAE federal government and other powers reserved to member emirates. Capital: Abu Dhabi. **Independence:** 2 December 1971 (from UK). **National holiday:** Independence Day, 2 December (1971). **Economy G.D.P.:** purchasing power parity—$53 billion (2002 est.). **G.D.P.—per capita:** purchasing power parity—$22,000 (2002 est.). **Currency:** Emirati dirham (AED).

United Kingdom

United Kingdom of Great Britain and Northern Ireland

Geography Location: Western Europe, islands including the northern one-sixth of the island of Ireland between the North Atlantic Ocean and the North Sea, northwest of France. **Area:** 94,525 sq. mi. (244,820 sq km). **Border countries**: Ireland. **Natural resources:** coal, petroleum, natural gas, tin, limestone, iron ore, salt, clay, chalk, gypsum, lead, silica, arable land. **People Population:** 60,094,648 (July 2003 est.). **Nationality:** *noun:* Briton(s), British (collective plural); *adj.:* British. **Ethnic groups:** English 81.5%, Scottish 9.6%, Irish 2.4%, Welsh 1.9%, Ulster 1.8%, West Indian, Indian, Pakistani, and other 2.8%. **Religions:** Anglican and Roman Catholic 40 million, Muslim 1.5 million, Presbyterian 800,000, Methodist 760,000, Sikh 500,000, Hindu 500,000, Jewish 350,000. **Languages:** English, Welsh (about 26% of the population of Wales), Scottish form of Gaelic (about 60,000 in Scotland). **Government Government type:** constitutional monarchy. Capital: London. **Independence:** England has existed as a unified entity since the 10th century; the union between England and Wales, begun in 1284 with the Statute of Rhuddlan, was not formalized until 1536 with an Act of Union; in another Act of Union in 1707, England and Scotland agreed to permanently join as Great Britain; the legislative union of Great Britain and Ireland was implemented in 1801, with the adoption of the name the United Kingdom of Great Britain and Ireland; the Anglo-Irish treaty of 1921 formalized a partition of Ireland; six northern Irish counties remained part of the United Kingdom as Northern Ireland and the current name of the country, the United Kingdom of Great Britain and Northern Ireland, was adopted in 1927. **National holiday:** Official Birthday of Queen ELIZABETH II, celebrated on the second Saturday in June (1926). **Economy G.D.P.:** purchasing power parity—$1.52 trillion (2002 est.). **G.D.P.—per capita:** purchasing power parity—$25,300 (2002 est.). **Currency:** British pound (GBP).

United States

United States of America

Geography Location: North America, bordering both the North Atlantic Ocean and the North Pacific Ocean, between Canada and Mexico. **Area:** 3,717,797 sq. mi. (9,629,091 sq km). **Border countries**: Canada, Mexico. **Natural resources:** coal, copper, lead, molybdenum, phosphates, uranium, bauxite, gold, iron, mercury, nickel, potash, silver, tungsten, zinc, petroleum, natural gas, timber **People Population:** 290,342,554 (July 2003 est.). **Nationality:** *noun:* American(s); *adj.:* American. **Ethnic groups:** white 77.1%, black 12.9%, Asian 4.2%, Amerindian and Alaska native 1.5%, native Hawaiian and other Pacific islander 0.3%, other 4% (2000) *note:* a separate listing for Hispanic is not included because the US Census Bureau considers Hispanic to mean a person of Latin American descent (including persons of Cuban, Mexican, or Puerto Rican origin) living in the

US who may be of any race or ethnic group (white, black, Asian, etc.). **Religions:** Protestant 56%, Roman Catholic 28%, Jewish 2%, other 4%, none 10% (1989). **Languages:** English, Spanish (spoken by a sizable minority). *note:* data for the US are based on projections that do not take into consideration the results of the 2000 census. **Government Government type:** Constitution-based federal republic; strong democratic tradition. Capital: Washington, DC. **Independence:** 4 July 1776 (from Great Britain). **National holiday:** Independence Day, 4 July (1776). **Economy G.D.P.:** purchasing power parity—$10.4 trillion (2002 est.). **G.D.P.—per capita:** purchasing power parity—$37,600 (2002 est.). **Currency:** US dollar (USD).

Uruguay

Oriental Republic of Uruguay

Geography Location: Southern South America, bordering the South Atlantic Ocean, between Argentina and Brazil. **Area:** 68,039 sq. mi. (176,220 sq km). **Border countries**: Argentina, Brazil. **Natural resources:** arable land, hydropower, minor minerals, fisheries. **People Population:** 3,413,329 (July 2003 est.). **Ethnic groups:** white 88%, mestizo 8%, black 4%, Amerindian, practically nonexistent. **Religions:** Roman Catholic 66% (less than half of the adult population attends church regularly), Protestant 2%, Jewish 1%, nonprofessing or other 31%. **Languages:** Spanish, Portunol, or Brazilero (Portuguese-Spanish mix on the Brazilian frontier). **Government Government type:** constitutional republic. Capital: Montevideo. **Independence:** 25 August 1825 (from Brazil). **National holiday:** Independence Day, 25 August (1825). **Economy G.D.P.:** purchasing power parity—$26.82 billion (2002 est.). **G.D.P.—per capita:** purchasing power parity—$7,900 (2002 est.). **Currency:** Uruguayan peso (UYU).

Uzbekistan

Republic of Uzbekistan

Geography Location: Central Asia, north of Afghanistan. **Area:** 172,741 sq. mi. (447,400 sq km). **Border countries**: Afghanistan, Kazakhstan, Kyrgyzstan, Tajikistan, Turkmenistan. **Natural resources:** natural gas, petroleum, coal, gold, uranium, silver, copper, lead and zinc, tungsten, molybdenum. **People Population:** 25,981,647 (July 2003 est.). **Ethnic groups:** Uzbek 80%, Russian 5.5%, Tajik 5%, Kazakh 3%, Karakalpak 2.5%, Tatar 1.5%, other 2.5% (1996 est.). **Religions:** Muslim 88% (mostly Sunnis), Eastern Orthodox 9%, other 3%. **Languages:** Uzbek 74.3%, Russian 14.2%, Tajik 4.4%, other 7.1%. **Government Government type:** republic; authoritarian presidential rule, with little power outside the executive branch. Capital: Tashkent (Toshkent). **Independence:** 1 September 1991 (from Soviet Union). **National holiday:** Independence Day, 1 September (1991). **Economy G.D.P.:** purchasing power parity—$66.06 billion (2002 est.). **G.D.P.—per capita:** purchasing power parity—$2,600 (2002 est.). **Currency:** Uzbekistani sum (UZS).

Vanuatu

Republic of Vanuatu

Geography Location: Oceania, group of islands in the South Pacific Ocean, about three-quarters of the way from Hawaii to Australia. **Area:** 5,699 sq. mi. (12,200 sq km). **Natural resources:** manganese, hardwood forests, fish. **People Population:** 199,414 (July 2003 est.). **Nationality:** *noun:* Ni-Vanuatu (singular and plural); *adj.:* Ni-Vanuatu. **Ethnic groups:** indigenous Melanesian 98%, French, Vietnamese, Chinese, other Pacific Islanders. **Religions:** Presbyterian 36.7%, Anglican 15%, Roman Catholic 15%, indigenous beliefs 7.6%, Seventh-Day Adventist 6.2%, Church of Christ 3.8%, other 15.7% (including Jon Frum Cargo cult). **Languages:** three official **languages:** English, French, pidgin (known as Bislama or Bichelama), plus more than 100 local languages. **Government Government type:** parliamentary republic. **Capital: Port-Vila. Independence:** 30 July 1980 (from France and UK). **National holiday:** Independence Day, 30 July (1980). **Economy G.D.P.:** purchasing power parity—$563 million (2002 est.). **G.D.P.—per capita:** purchasing power parity—$2,900 (2002 est.). **Currency:** vatu (VUV).

Venezuela

Bolivarian Republic of Venezuela

Geography Location: Northern South America, bordering the Caribbean Sea and the North Atlantic Ocean, between Colombia and Guyana. **Area:** 352,144 sq. mi. (912,050 sq km). **Border countries**: Brazil, Colombia, Guyana. **Natural resources:** petroleum, natural gas, iron ore, gold, bauxite, other minerals, hydropower, diamonds. **People Population:** 24,654,694 (July 2003 est.). **Nationality:** *noun:* Venezuelan(s); *adj.:* Venezuelan. **Ethnic groups:** Spanish, Italian, Portuguese, Arab, German, African, indigenous people. **Religions:** nominally Roman Catholic 96%, Protestant 2%, other 2%. **Languages:** Spanish (official), numerous indigenous dialects. **Government Government type:** federal republic. Capital: Caracas. **Independence:** 5 July 1811 (from Spain). **National holiday:** Independence Day, 5 July (1811). **Economy G.D.P.:** purchasing power parity—$131.7 billion (2002 est.). **G.D.P.—per capita:** purchasing power parity—$5,400 (2002 est.). **Currency:** bolivar (VEB).

Vietnam

Socialist Republic of Vietnam

Geography **Location:** Southeastern Asia, bordering the Gulf of Thailand, Gulf of Tonkin, and South China Sea, alongside China, Laos, and Cambodia. **Area:** 127,243329,560 sq km. **Border countries**: Cambodia, China, Laos. **Natural resources:** phosphates, coal, manganese, bauxite, chromate, offshore oil and gas deposits, forests, hydropower. **People** **Population:** 81,624,716 (July 2003 est.). **Nationality:** *noun:* Vietnamese (singular and plural); *adj.:* Vietnamese. **Ethnic groups:** Vietnamese 85%-90%, Chinese, Hmong, Thai, Khmer, Cham, mountain groups. **Religions:** Buddhist, Hoa Hao, Cao Dai, Christian (predominantly Roman Catholic, some Protestant), indigenous beliefs, Muslim. **Languages:** Vietnamese (official), English (increasingly favored as a second language), some French, Chinese, and Khmer; mountain area languages (Mon-Khmer and Malayo-Polynesian). **Government** **Government type:** Communist state. Capital: Hanoi. **Independence:** 2 September 1945 (from France). **National holiday:** Independence Day, 2 September (1945). **Economy** **G.D.P.**: purchasing power parity—$183.8 billion (2002 est.). **G.D.P.—per capita:** purchasing power parity—$2,300 (2002 est.). **Currency**: dong (VND).

Yemen

Republic of Yemen

Geography **Location:** Middle East, bordering the Arabian Sea, Gulf of Aden, and Red Sea, between Oman and Saudi Arabia. **Area:** 203,850 sq. mi. (527,970 sq km). **Border countries**: Oman, Saudi Arabia. **Natural resources:** petroleum, fish, rock salt, marble, small deposits of coal, gold, lead, nickel, and copper, fertile soil in west. **People** **Population:** 19,349,881 (July 2003 est.). **Nationality:** *noun:* Yemeni(s); *adj.:* Yemeni. **Ethnic groups:** predominantly Arab; but also Afro-Arab, South Asians, Europeans. **Religions:** Muslim including Shaf'i (Sunni) and Zaydi (Shi'a), small numbers of Jewish, Christian, and Hindu. **Languages:** Arabic. **Government** **Government type:** republic. Capital: Sanaa. **Independence:** 22 May 1990, Republic of Yemen established with merger of the Yemen Arab Republic [Yemen (Sanaa) or North Yemen] and the Marxist-dominated People's Democratic Republic of Yemen [Yemen (Aden) or South Yemen]; North Yemen had become independent on NA November 1918 (from the Ottoman Empire) and South Yemen on 30 November 1967 (from the UK). **National holiday:** Unification Day, 22 May (1990). **Economy** **G.D.P.:** purchasing power parity—$15.07 billion (2002 est.). **G.D.P.—per capita:** purchasing power parity—$800 (2002 est.). **Currency:** Yemeni rial (YER).

Zambia

Republic of Zambia

Geography **Location:** Southern Africa, east of Angola. **Area:** 290,583 sq. mi. (752,614 sq km). **Border countries**: Angola, Democratic Republic of the Congo, Malawi, Mozambique, Namibia, Tanzania, Zimbabwe. **Natural resources:** copper, cobalt, zinc, lead, coal, emeralds, gold, silver, uranium, hydropower. **People** **Population:** 10,307,333. *note:* estimates for this country explicitly take into account the effects of excess mortality due to AIDS; this can result in lower life expectancy, higher infant mortality and death rates, lower population and growth rates, and changes in the distribution of population by age and sex than would otherwise be expected (July 2003 est.). **Nationality:** *noun:* Zambian(s); *adj.:* Zambian. **Ethnic groups:** African 98.7%, European 1.1%, other 0.2%. **Religions:** Christian 50%-75%, Muslim and Hindu 24%-49%, indigenous beliefs 1%. **Languages:** English (official), major vernaculars—Bemba, Kaonda, Lozi, Lunda, Luvale, Nyanja, Tonga, and about 70 other indigenous languages. **Government** **Government type:** republic. Capital: Lusaka. **Independence:** 24 October 1964 (from UK). **National holiday:** Independence Day, 24 October (1964). **Economy** **G.D.P.:** purchasing power parity—$8.24 billion (2002 est.). **G.D.P.—per capita:** purchasing power parity—$800 (2002 est.). **Currency:** Zambian kwacha (ZMK).

Zimbabwe

Republic of Zimbabwe

Geography **Location:** Southern Africa, between South Africa and Zambia. **Area:** 150,803 sq. mi. (390,580 sq km). **Border countries**: Botswana, Mozambique, South Africa, Zambia. **Natural resources:** coal, chromium ore, asbestos, gold, nickel, copper, iron ore, vanadium, lithium, tin, platinum group metals. **People** **Population:** 12,576,742. *note:* estimates take into account the effects of excess mortality due to AIDS (July 2003 est.). **Nationality:** *noun:* Zimbabwean(s); *adj.:* Zimbabwean. **Ethnic groups:** African 98% (Shona 82%, Ndebele 14%, other 2%), mixed and Asian 1%, white less than 1%. **Religions:** syncretic (part Christian, part indigenous beliefs) 50%, Christian 25%, indigenous beliefs 24%, Muslim and other 1%. **Languages:** English (official), Shona, Sindebele (the language of the Ndebele, sometimes called Ndebele), numerous but minor tribal dialects. **Government** **Government type:** parliamentary democracy. Capital: Harare. **Independence:** 18 April 1980 (from UK). **National holiday:** Independence Day, 18 April (1980). **Economy** **G.D.P.:** purchasing power parity—$26.07 billion (2002 est.). **G.D.P.—per capita:** purchasing power parity—$2,100 (2002 est.). **Currency:** Zimbabwean dollar (ZWD).

The United Nations

Pres. Franklin D. Roosevelt coined the name "United Nations," which was first used in the "Declaration by United Nations" of Jan. 1, 1942, during World War II, when representatives of 26 countries pledged their governments to continue fighting together against the Axis Powers. From August to October 1944, representatives of China, the Soviet Union, the United Kingdom and the United States met at Dumbarton Oaks, a mansion in Washington, D.C., to discuss creating an international peacekeeping organization. Out of these meetings came a general outline for the United Nations.

At the United Nations Conference on International Organization, which met at San Francisco from Apr. 25 to June 26, 1945, representatives from 50 countries drew up the United Nations Charter and signed it on June 26, 1945.

The United Nations officially came into existence on Oct. 24, 1945, when the charter was ratified by China, France, the Soviet Union, the United Kingdom, and the United States and by a majority of the other signatories.

Purposes The purposes of the United Nations are set forth in Article 1 of the Charter. They are: 1. To maintain international peace and security. 2. To develop friendly relations among nations based on respect for the principle of equal rights and self-determination of peoples. 3. To cooperate in solving international problems of an economic, social, cultural or humanitarian character, and in promoting respect for human rights and fundamental freedoms for all. 4. To be a center for harmonizing the actions of nations in the attainment of these common ends.

Official languages Originally, there were five official languages of the United Nations: Chinese, English, French, Russian and Spanish. Arabic was added to the General Assembly in 1973, to the Security Council in 1982 and to the Economic and Social Council in 1983.

United Nations headquarters United Nations, New York, NY 10017 U.S. U.N. headquarters covers a 16-acre site in New York City along the East River from 42nd to 48th Streets. It consists of the interconnected General Assembly, Secretariat and Dag Hammarskjöld Library buildings.

General Assembly The Assembly consists of all 191 member states, each having one vote. On important issues a two-thirds majority of those present and voting is required; other questions require a simple majority vote. The Assembly also considers and approves U.N. budget and assesses member states according to their ability to pay.

Security Council The Council may investigate any dispute or situation that might lead to international friction, and may recommend terms for their settlement. The Security Council alone has the power to take decisions that member states are obligated under the Charter to carry out.

The Security Council has 15 members: five permanent members, and the General Assembly elects 10 other members for two-year terms. The five permanent members are China, France, Russia, the United Kingdom and the United States. Decisions on matters of procedure require the approval of at least nine of the 15 members. A negative vote by any permanent member on a non-procedural matter is often referred to as the "veto," which results in the rejection of the proposal.

Economic and Social Council (ECOSOC) The Council is the principal organ to co-ordinate the economic and social work of the U.N. and its specialized agencies. It makes recommendations and initiates activities relating to world trade, industrialization, natural resources, human rights, the status of women, population, social welfare, education, health and related matters, science and technology and many other economic and social questions. ECOSOC has 54 members elected for three-year terms by the General Assembly.

International Court of Justice (World Court) The Court is the judicial organ of the U.N. and sits in The Hague, Netherlands. All U.N. member states are automatically members of the Court. It issues judgments on all questions that states refer to it and all matters provided for in the U.N. Charter or in treaties or conventions.

The Court has dealt with a wide variety of subjects, including territorial rights, fishing jurisdiction, territorial sovereignty, and the right of passage through foreign territory. The ICJ has 15 independent judges, of different nationalities, elected by both the General Assembly and the Security Council. Judges hold 9-year terms and may be re-elected.

Secretariat The Secretariat services the other organs of the U.N. and administers the programs and policies they develop. Headed by the Secretary-General, it consists of an international staff of more than 25,000 men and women from over 150 countries.

Secretaries-General: The General Assembly elects the Secretary-General to terms of office of five years (they may be re-elected). The Secretary-General, by tradition, does not come from one of the permanent member states of the Security Council. Those who have served in this post are: Trygve Lie, Norway, Feb. 1, 1946, to Nov. 10, 1952; Dag Hammarskjöld, Sweden, Apr. 11, 1953, to Sept. 17, 1961; U Thant, Burma, Nov. 3, 1961, to Dec. 31, 1971; Kurt Waldheim, Austria, Jan. 1, 1972, to Dec. 31, 1981; Javier Perez de Cuellar, Peru Jan. 1, 1982 to Dec. 31, 1991; Boutros Boutros-Ghali, Egypt, Jan 1, 1992, to Dec. 31, 1996; Kofi Annan, Ghana, Jan. 1, 1997 to present.

United Nations Member States

Country	Joined U.N.
Afghanistan	1946
Albania	1955
Algeria	1962
Andorra	1993
Angola	1976
Antigua and Barbuda	1981
Argentina	1945
Armenia	1992
Australia	1945
Austria	1955
Azerbaijan	1992
Bahamas	1973
Bahrain	1971
Bangladesh	1974
Barbados	1966
Belarus	1945
Belgium	1945
Belize	1981
Benin	1960
Bhutan	1971
Bolivia	1945
Bosnia and Herzegovina	1992
Botswana	1966
Brazil	1945
Brunei Darussalam	1984
Bulgaria	1955
Burkina Faso	1960
Burundi	1962
Cambodia	1955
Cameroon	1960
Canada	1945
Cape Verde	1975
Central African Republic	1960
Chad	1960
Chile	1945
China	1945
Colombia	1945
Comoros	1975
Congo	1960
Congo, Democratic Republic of[1]	1960
Costa Rica	1945
Croatia	1992
Cuba	1945
Cyprus	1960
Czech Republic[2]	1993
Denmark	1945
Djibouti	1977
Dominica	1978
Dominican Republic	1945
East Timor	2002
Ecuador	1945
Egypt	1945
El Salvador	1945
Equatorial Guinea	1968
Eritrea	1993
Estonia	1991
Ethiopia	1945
Fiji	1970
Finland	1955
France	1945
Gabon	1960
Gambia	1965
Georgia	1992
Germany	1973
Ghana	1957
Greece	1945
Grenada	1974
Guatemala	1945
Guinea	1958
Guinea-Bissau	1974
Guyana	1966
Haiti	1945
Honduras	1945
Hungary	1955
Iceland	1946
India	1945
Indonesia	1950
Iran	1945
Iraq	1945
Ireland	1955
Israel	1949
Italy	1955
Ivory Coast	1960
Jamaica	1962
Japan	1956
Jordan	1955
Kazakhstan	1992
Kenya	1963
Kiribati	1999
Kuwait	1963
Kyrgyzstan	1992
Laos	1955
Latvia	1991
Lebanon	1945
Lesotho	1966
Liberia	1945
Libya	1955
Liechtenstein	1990
Lithuania	1991
Luxembourg	1945
Macedonia[3]	1993
Madagascar	1960
Malawi	1964
Malaysia	1957
Maldives	1965
Mali	1960
Malta	1964
Marshall Islands	1991
Mauritania	1961
Mauritius	1968
Mexico	1945
Micronesia	1991
Monaco	1993
Mongolia	1961
Morocco	1956
Mozambique	1975
Myanmar	1948
Namibia	1990
Nauru	1999
Nepal	1955
Netherlands	1945
New Zealand	1945
Nicaragua	1945
Niger	1960
Nigeria	1960
North Korea	1991
Norway	1945
Oman	1971
Pakistan	1947
Palau	1994
Panama	1945
Papua New Guinea	1975
Paraguay	1945
Peru	1945
Philippines	1945
Poland	1945
Portugal	1955
Qatar	1971
Moldova	1992
Romania	1955
Russian Fed.	1945
Rwanda	1962
Saint Kitts and Nevis	1983
Saint Lucia	1979
Saint Vincent and the Grenadines	1980
Samoa	1976
San Marino	1992
São Tome and Principe	1975
Saudi Arabia	1945
Senegal	1960
Seychelles	1976
Sierra Leone	1961
Singapore	1965
Slovakia[2]	1993
Slovenia	1992
Solomon Islands	1978
Somalia	1960
South Africa	1945
South Korea	1991
Spain	1955
Sri Lanka	1955
Sudan	1956
Suriname	1975
Swaziland	1968
Sweden	1946
Switzerland	2002
Syria	1945
Tanzania	1961
Tajikistan	1992
Thailand	1946
Togo	1960
Tonga	1999
Trinidad and Tobago	1962
Tunisia	1956
Turkey	1945
Turkmenistan	1992
Tuvalu	2000
Uganda	1962
Ukraine	1945
United Arab Emirates	1971
United Kingdom	1945
United States	1945
Uruguay	1945
Uzbekistan	1992
Vanuatu	1981
Venezuela	1945
Viet Nam	1977
Yemen[4]	1947
Yugoslavia	1945
Zambia	1964
Zimbabwe	1980

Source: United Nations. 1. Formerly Zaire. 2. Czechoslovakia was an original member of the UN; when the nation split into separate Czech and Slovak Republics, both new republics were admitted as member states on Jan. 19, 1993. 3. Provisionally referred to for all purposes within the UN as "The former Yugoslav Republic of Macedonia" pending settlement of a difference with Greek Macedonia over the name. 4. Includes the former Democratic Yemen (admitted as a separate member in 1967), which merged with Yemen in 1990.

U.S. STATES AND CITIES

U.S. States

This section, a compilation of history and statistics about the 50 United States, the District of Columbia, and U.S. territories and possessions, includes its official motto and other emblems; a summary of geographic, demographic and economic facts; and a list of prominent natives. Statistical sources include the U.S. Census Bureau's 2000 decennial census, intercensal population estimates, and *The Statistical Abstract* (annual). The headings for demographic statistics conform to U.S. Census Bureau usage, except "Black" is used as short for Black or African American, "Indian" is used for American Indian and Alaska Native, and "Pacific Islander" is used for Native Hawaiian and other Pacific Islander. Note that Hispanics may be of any race.

Alabama

www.alabama.gov.

Name Probably after Alabama tribe. **Nickname** Yellowhammer State, Heart of Dixie. **Capital** Montgomery. **Entered union** Dec. 14, 1819 (22nd). **Motto** "We dare defend our rights." **Emblems** *Bird* Yellowhammer. *Song* "Alabama." *Tree* Southern (longleaf) pine. **Land** Total area 52,419 sq. mi (30th), incl. 1,675 sq. mi. inland water. **Borders** Tenn., Ga., Fla., Gulf of Mexico, Miss. **Rivers** Alabama, Chattahoochee, Mobile, Tennessee, Tennessee-Tombigbee Waterway, Tensaw, Tombigbee. **Lakes** Guntersville, Pickwick, Wheeler, Wilson (all formed by Tennessee Valley Authority); Dannelly Res., Martin, Lewis Smith, Weiss. Mountains Cumberland, Lookout, Raccoon, Sand. **People** (July, 2002 est.) 4,486,508 (23rd). Race/Hispanic Origin (2000 Census): White 71.1%. Black 26.0%. Indian 0.5%. Asian 0.7%. Other 0.7%. Two or more races 1.0%. Hispanic 1.7%. **Cities** (2002) Birmingham 239,416. Montgomery 201,425. Mobile 194,862. Huntsville 162,536. Tuscaloosa 79,149. Hoover 64,265. Dothan 58,998. Decatur 53,941. Auburn 45,389. Gadsden 37,966. **Famous natives** Hank Aaron, baseball player. Tallulah Bankhead, actress. William B. Bankhead, politician. Hugo L. Black, jurist. Wernher von Braun (b. Germany), rocket scientist. Nat "King" Cole, singer. W.C. Handy, musician. Frank M. Johnson, Jr., jurist. Helen Keller, author. Coretta Scott (Mrs. Martin Luther) King, reformer. Harper Lee, author. Joe Louis, boxer. Jesse Owens, runner. Leroy Robert "Satchell" Paige, baseball player. Walker Percy, author. George Wallace, politician. Hank Williams, singer. **Tourist information** 1-800-ALABAMA.

Alaska

www.state.ak.us

Name From Aleut alaska and Eskimo alakshak, both meaning "mainland." **Nickname** "The Last Frontier." **Capital** Juneau. **Entered union** Jan. 3, 1959 (49th). **Motto** "North to the future." **Emblems** *Bird* Willow ptarmigan. *Flower* Forget-me-not. *Song* "Alaska's Flag." *Tree* Sitka spruce. **Land** Total area 663,267 sq. mi (1st), incl. 91,316 sq. mi. inland water. **Borders** Arctic Ocean (Chukchi Sea, Beaufort Sea), Yukon, British Columbia, Pacific Ocean, Bering Strait. **Rivers** Colville, Porcupine, Noatak, Yukon, Susitna, Copper, Kobuk, Koyukuk, Kuskokwim, Tanana. **Mountains** Alaska Range (Mt. McKinley 20,320 ft., highest in North America), Aleutian Range, Brooks Range, Kuskokwim, St. Elias. **Other notable features** Aleutian Islands, Alexander Archipelago, Kodiak Island, Nunivak Island, Point Barrow (71°23'N), Pribilof Islands, Seward Peninsula, St. Lawrence Island. **People** (July, 2002 est.) 643,786 (47th). Race/Hispanic Origin (2000 Census): White 69.3%. Black 3.5%. Indian 15.6%. Asian 4.0%. Pacific Islander 0.5%. Other 1.6%. Two or more races 5.4%. Hispanic 4.1%. **Cities** (2002) Anchorage 268,983. Fairbanks 30,780. Juneau 30,751. Sitka 8,835. Ketchikan 7,922. Kenai 6,942. Kodiak 6,334. Bethel 5,471. Wasilla 5,469. Barrow 4,581. **Famous natives** Aleksandr Baranov (b. Russia), first governor of Russian America. Vitus Bering (b. Denmark), explorer. Ernest Gruening (b. N.Y.), governor. Carl Ben Eielson, bush pilot. Walter Hickel (b. Kans.), governor. **Tourist information** (907) 929-2200. www.travelalaska.com.

Arizona

www.az.gov

Name Probably from the Pima or Papago for "place of small springs." **Nickname** Grand Canyon State. **Capital** Phoenix. **Entered union** Feb. 14, 1912 (48th). **Motto** Ditat deus (God enriches). **Emblems** *Bird* Cactus wren. *Flower* Blossom of the saguaro cactus. *Songs* "Arizona March Song," "Arizona." *Tree* Palo verde. **Land** Total area 113,998 sq. mi (6th), incl. 364 sq. mi. inland water. **Borders** Utah, Colo., N.Mex., Sonora, Baja California Norte, Calif., Nev. **Rivers** Colorado, Gila, Little Colorado, Salt, Zuni. **Lakes** Havasu, Mead,

Mohave, Powell, Roosevelt, San Carlos. **Mountains** Black, Gila, Hualpai, Mohawk, San Francisco Peaks (Humphreys Peak 12,633 ft.). **Other notable features** Grand Canyon, Kaibab Plateau, Painted and Sonoran Deserts, Petrified Forest. **People** (July, 2002 est.) 5,456,453 (19th). Race/Hispanic Origin (2000 Census): White 75.5%. Black 3.1%. Indian 5.0%. Asian 1.8%. Pacific Islander 0.1%. Other 11.6%. Two or more races 2.9%. Hispanic 25.3%. **Cities** (2002) Phoenix 1,371,960. Tucson 503,151. Mesa 426,841. Glendale 230,564. Scottsdale 215,779. Chandler 202,016. Tempe 159,508. Gilbert 135,005. Peoria 123,239. Yuma 80,358. **Famous natives** Bruce Babbitt, politician. Cesar Chavez, labor leader. Wyatt Earp (b. Ill.), lawman. Barry Goldwater, politician. Goyathlay (Geronimo), Apache chieftain. Carl T. Hayden, congressman. Eusebio Kino (b. Italy), missionary. Sandra Day O'Connor, jurist. William H. Rehnquist, jurist. **Tourist information** (888) 520-3434. www.arizonaguide.com

Arkansas

www.arkansas.gov

Name From term for Quapaw tribe given by other Indians. **Nickname** Land of Opportunity. **Capital** Little Rock. **Entered union** June 15, 1836 (25th). **Motto** Regnat populus (Let the people rule). **Emblems** *Bird* Mockingbird. *Flower* Apple blossom. *Song* "Arkansas." *Tree* Pine. **Land** Total area 53,179 sq. mi (29th), incl. 1,110 sq. mi. inland water. **Borders** Mo., Tenn., Miss., La., Tex., Okla. **Rivers** Arkansas, Mississippi, Ouachita, Red, St. Francis, White. **Lakes** Beaver, Bull Shoals, Chicot, Dardanelle, Greers Ferry, Greeson, Norfolk, Ouachita. **Other notable features** Ozark Mts. **People** (July, 2002 est.) 2,710,079 (33rd). Race/Hispanic Origin (2000 Census): White 80.0%. Black 15.7%. Indian 0.7%. Asian 0.8%. Pacific Islander 0.1%. Other 1.3%. Two or more races 1.3%. Hispanic 3.2%. **Cities** (2002) Little Rock 184,055. Fort Smith 81,519. Fayetteville 60,732. North Little Rock 60,007. Jonesboro 56,888. Pine Bluff 54,169. Springdale 50,941. Conway 45,915. Rogers 41,545. Hot Springs 36,356. **Famous natives** Maya Angelou, author. Linda Bloodworth-Thomason, television producer/director. Glen Campbell, singer. Hattie W. Caraway, first woman senator. Johnny Cash, singer. Eldridge Cleaver, author. Bill Clinton, U.S. president. William Fulbright (b. Mo.), politician. Douglas MacArthur, general. Dick Powell, actor. Brooks Robinson, baseball player. Winthrop Rockefeller (b. N.Y.), politician/philanthropist. Edward Durrell Stone, architect. C. Vann Woodward, historian. **Tourist information** (800) NATURAL. www.arkansas.com.

California

www.state.ca.us

Name Probably from mythical island in García Ordoñez de Montalvo's 16th-century romance, The Deeds of Esplandián. **Nickname** Golden State. **Capital** Sacramento. **Entered union** Sept. 9, 1850 (31st). **Motto** "Eureka" (I have found it). **Emblems** *Bird* California valley quail. *Flower* Golden poppy. *Song* "I Love You, California." *Tree* California redwood. **Land** Total area 163,696 sq. mi (3rd), incl. 7,736 sq. mi. inland water. **Borders** Oreg., Nev., Ariz., Baja California Norte, Pacific Ocean. **Rivers** American, Colorado, Colorado River Aqueduct, Eel, Friant-Kern Canal, Klamath, Russian, Sacramento, Salinas, San Joaquin. **Lakes** Clear, Goose, Honey, Mono, Owens, Salton Sea, Shasta, Tahoe. Mountains Coast Ranges, Klamath, Lassen Peak, Sierra Nevada (Mt. Whitney 14,494 ft.). Other notable features Catalina Islands, Death Valley (282 ft. below sea level), San Francisco Bay, San Joaquin Valley. **People** (July, 2002 est.) 35,116,033 (1st). Race/Hispanic Origin (2000 Census): White 59.5%. Black 6.7%. Indian 1.0%. Asian 10.9%. Pacific Islander 0.3%. Other 16.8%. Hispanic 32.4%. **Cities** (2002) Los Angeles 3,798,981. San Diego 1,259,532. San Jose 900,443. San Francisco 764,049. Long Beach 472,412. Fresno 445,227. Sacramento 435,245. Oakland 402,777. Santa Ana 343,413. Anaheim 332,642. **Famous natives** Ansel Adams, photographer. Dave Brubeck, musician. Luther Burbank (b. Mass.), horticulturist. John Cage, composer. Joe DiMaggio, baseball player. Robert Frost, poet. Ernest and Julio Gallo (b. Italy), vintners. Pancho Gonzales, tennis player. Samuel Ichiye Hayakawa, politician/educator. William Randolph Hearst, publisher. Steve Jobs, computer entrepreneur. Billie Jean King, tennis player. Allen Lockheed, aviator. Jack London, author. Marilyn Monroe, actress. John Muir (b. Scotland), naturalist. Richard M. Nixon, U.S. president. John Northrop, aviator. Adlai Stevenson, politician. John Steinbeck, author. Levi Strauss (b. Germany), clothier. Edward Teller (b. Hungary), nuclear physicist. Shirley Temple, actress. Earl Warren, politician/jurist. **Tourist information** (800) TO-CALIF. www.gocalif.ca.gov

Colorado

www.colorado.gov

Name For Spanish for the color red. **Nickname** Centennial State. **Capital** Denver. **Entered union** Aug. 1, 1876 (38th). **Motto** Nil sine numine (Nothing without providence). **Emblems** *Bird* Lark bunting. Flower Rocky Mountain Columbine. *Song* "Where the Columbines Grow." *Tree* Colorado blue spruce. **Land** Total area 104,094 sq. mi (8th), incl. 376 sq. mi. inland water. **Borders** Wyo., Nebr., Kans., N.Mex., Ariz., Utah. **Rivers** Arkansas, Colorado, Green, Platte, Rio Grande. **Lakes** Blue Mesa, Dillon, Granby. Mountains Front Range, Laramie, Sangre de Cristo, San Juan, Sawatch Range (Mt. Elbert 14,443 ft.). **People** (July, 2002 est.) 4,506,542 (22nd). Race/Hispanic Origin (2000 Census): White 82.8%. Black 3.8%. Indian 1.0%. Asian 2.2%.

Pacific Islander 0.1%. Other 7.2%. Two or more races 2.8%. Hispanic 17.1%. **Cities** (2002) Denver 560,415. Colorado Springs 371,182. Aurora 286,028. Lakewood 143,754. Fort Collins 124,665. Westminster 103,599. Pueblo 103,411. Arvada 102,190. Centennial 99,447. Boulder 94,167. **Famous natives** Charlie Bent (b. Va.), trapper. "Unsinkable" Molly Brown, Titanic survivor. Scott Carpenter, astronaut. Lon Chaney, actor. Jack Dempsey, boxer. Mamie Eisenhower, first lady. Douglas Fairbanks, actor. Scott Hamilton, ice skater. Anne Parrish, novelist. Lowell Thomas, journalist. Byron R. White, jurist. **Tourist information** (800) COLORADO. www.colorado.com.

Connecticut

www.ct.gov

Name From Mahican word meaning "beside the long tidal river." **Nicknames** Constitution State, Nutmeg State. **Capital** Hartford. **Entered union** Jan. 9, 1788 (5th). **Motto** Qui transtulit sustinet (He who transplanted still sustains). **Emblems** *Bird* American robin. *Flower* Mountain laurel. *Song* "Yankee Doodle." *Tree* White oak. **Land** Total area 5,543 sq. mi (48th), incl. 699 sq. mi. inland water **Borders** Mass., R.I., Long Island Sound, N.Y. **Rivers** Connecticut, Housatonic, Mianus, Naugatuck, Thames. **Lakes** Bantam, Barkhamstead, Candlewood, Waramaug. Other notable features Berkshire Hills, Long Island Sound. **People** (July, 2002 est.) 3,460,503 (29th). Race/Hispanic Origin (2000 Census): White 81.6%. Black 9.1%. Indian 0.3%. Asian 2.4%. Other 4.3%. Two or more races 2.2%. Hispanic 9.4%. **Cities** (2002) Bridgeport 140,104. Hartford 124,558. New Haven 124,176. Stamford 119,850. Waterbury 107,883. Norwalk 84,127. Danbury 76,917. New Britain 71,589. Bristol 60,541. Meriden 58,675. **Famous natives** Benedict Arnold, traitor. P.T. Barnum, showman. Lyman Beecher, theologian. John Brown, abolitionist. Samuel Colt, inventor. Jonathan Edwards, theologian. Charles Goodyear, inventor. Nathan Hale, patriot. Katharine Hepburn, actress. Charles Ives, composer. J.P. Morgan, financier. Ralph Nader, consumer advocate. Frederick Law Olmsted, landscape architect. Harriet Beecher Stowe, author. John Trumbell, artist. Noah Webster, lexicographer. Eli Whitney, inventor. **Tourist information** (800) CT-BOUND. www.tourism.state.ct.us

Delaware

www.delaware.gov

Name For Thomas West, Lord De La Warre, colonial governor of Virginia. **Nicknames** First State, Diamond State. **Capital** Dover. **Entered union** Dec. 7, 1787 (1st). **Motto** "Liberty and Independence." **Emblems** *Bird* Blue hen chicken. *Flower* Peach blossom. *Song* "Our Delaware." *Tree* American holly. **Land** Total area 2,489 sq. mi (49th), incl. 536 sq. mi. inland water. **Borders** Pa., N.J., Atlantic Ocean, Md. **Rivers** Chesapeake & Delaware Canal, Delaware, Nanticoke. **People** (July, 2002 est.) 807,385 (45th). Race/Hispanic Origin (2000 Census): White 74.6%. Black 19.2%. Indian 0.3%. Asian 2.1%. Other 2.0%. Two or more races 1.7%. Hispanic 4.8%. **Cities** (2002) Wilmington 72,503. Dover 32,581. Newark 29,798. **Famous natives** Valerie Bertinelli, actress. John Dickinson (b. Md.), Penman of the Revolution. Eleuthère I. du Pont, manufacturer. Pierre S. ("Pete") du Pont, politician. Morgan Edwards, founder of Brown University (R.I.). Thomas Macdonough, navy officer. Howard Pyle, illustrator. Edward R. Squibb, physician/manufacturer. Christopher Ward, historian. **Tourist information** (800) 441-8846. www.visitdelaware.com.

District of Columbia

www.dc.gov

Name After Christopher Columbus; Columbia was commonly used for the U.S. before 1800. **Became capital** Dec. 1, 1800. **Motto** Justitia omnibus (Justice for all). **Emblems** *Bird* Wood thrush. *Flower* American beauty rose. *Tree* Scarlet oak. **Land** Total area 68 sq. mi., incl. 7 sq. mi. inland water. **Borders** Md., Va. **Rivers** Anacostia, Potomac. **People** (July, 2002 est.) 570,898 (N.A.) Race/Hispanic Origin (2000 Census): White 30.8%. Black 60.0%. Indian 0.3%. Asian 2.7%. Pacific Islander 0.1%. Other 3.8%. Two or more races 2.4%. Hispanic 7.9%. **Famous natives** Edward Albee, playwright. Carl Bernstein, journalist. John Foster Dulles, politician. Duke Ellington, composer. J. Edgar Hoover, FBI director. John Philip Sousa, composer. **Tourist information** (202) 789-7000. www.washington.org.

Florida

www.myflorida.com

Name By Juan Ponce de León for Pascua Florida (Easter festival of the flowers). **Nickname** Sunshine State. **Capital** Tallahassee. **Entered union** Mar. 3, 1845 (27th). **Motto** "In God We Trust." **Emblems** *Bird* Mockingbird. *Flower* Orange blossom. *Song* "Old Folks at Home" ("Swanee River"). *Tree* Sabal palmetto palm. **Land** Total area 65,755 sq. mi (22nd), incl. 11,828 sq. mi. inland water. **Borders** Ga., Atlantic Ocean, Gulf of Mexico, Ala. **Rivers** Apalachicola, Caloosahatchee, Indian, Kissimmee, Perdido, St. Johns, St. Mary's, Suwanee, Withlacoochee. **Lakes** Apopka, George, Okeechobee, Seminole. Other notable features Everglades, Florida Keys, Okefenokee Swamp. **People** (July, 2002 est.) 16,713,149 (4th). Race/Hispanic Origin (2000 Census): White 78.0%. Black 14.6%. Indian 14.6%. Asian 0.3%. Pacific Islander 0.1%. Other 3.0%. Two or more races 2.4%. Hispanic 16.8%. **Cities** (2000) Jacksonville 735,617. Miami 362,470. Tampa 303,447. St. Petersburg 248,232. Hialeah 226,419. Orlando 185,951.

Fort Lauderdale 152,397. Tallahassee 150,624. Hollywood 139,357. Pembroke Pines 137,427. **Famous natives** Mary Bethune, educator/reformer. Faye Dunaway, actress. Chris Evert, tennis player. Zora Neale Hurston, writer. James Weldon Johnson, lawyer/novelist. Osceola, Seminole chief. Sidney Poitier, actor. A. Philip Randolph, labor leader. Edmund Kirby Smith, Confederate general. Joseph Warren "Vinegar Joe" Stillwell, army officer. Ben Vereen, actor/singer. **Tourist information** (888) 735-2872. www.flausa.com.

Georgia

www.georgia.gov

Name For King George II of England 1732. **Nicknames** Empire State of the South, Peach State. **Capital** Atlanta. **Entered union** Jan. 2, 1788 (4th). **Motto** "Wisdom, justice, moderation." **Emblems** *Bird* Brown thrasher. *Flower* Cherokee rose. *Songs* "Georgia," "Georgia on My Mind." *Tree* Live oak. **Land** Total area 59,425 sq. mi (24th), incl. 1,519 sq. mi. inland water. **Borders** Tenn., N.C., S.C., Atlantic Ocean, Fla., Ala. **Rivers** Altamaha, Apalachicola, Chattahoochee, Flint, Ocmulgee, Oconee, Savannah, Suwanee. **Lakes** Clark Hill, Harding, Hartwell, Seminole, Sidney Lanier, Sinclair, Walter F. George, West Point Lake. Other notable features Blue Ridge Mountains (Mount Enotah 4,784 ft.), Okefenokee Swamp. **People** (July, 2002 est.) 8,560,310 (10th). Race/Hispanic Origin (2000 Census): White 65.1%. Black 28.7%. Indian 0.3%. Asian 2.1%. Pacific Islander 0.1%. Two or more races 1.4%. Hispanic 5.3%. **Cities** (2002) Atlanta 424,868. Augusta 193,101. Columbus 185,948. Savannah 127,691. Athens 102,663. Macon 95,862. Roswell 79,031. Albany 76,325. Marietta 62,020. Warner Robins 52,565. **Famous natives** James Brown, singer. Erskine Caldwell, author. James Earl ("Jimmy") Carter, U.S. president. Ray Charles, musician. Ty Cobb, baseball player. James Dickey, poet. Martin Luther King, Jr., minister/reformer. Sidney Lanier, author. Little Richard, musician. Carson McCullers, author. Alexander McGillivray, Creek chief. Margaret Mitchell, author. Elijah Muhammad, religious leader. Flannery O'Connor, author. Burt Reynolds, actor. Jackie Robinson, baseball player. Tomochichi, Yamacraw chief. Ted Turner (b. Ohio), businessman. Joanne Woodward, actress. **Tourist information** (800) VISIT-GA. www.georgia.org

Hawaii

www.hawaii.gov

Name Of unknown origin, perhaps from Hawaii Loa, traditional discoverer of islands, or from Hawaiki, the traditional Polynesian homeland. **Nicknames** Aloha State, Paradise of the Pacific. **Capital** Honolulu. **Entered union** Aug. 21, 1959 (50th). **Motto** Ua mau ke ea o ka aina i ke pono (The life of the land is perpetuated in righteousness). **Emblems** *Bird* Nene (Hawaiian goose). *Flower* Pua aloalo (hibiscus). *Song* "Hawaii Ponoi." *Tree* Kukui (candlenut). **Land** Total area 10,931 sq. mi (43rd), incl. 4,508 sq. mi. inland water. Surrounded by Pacific Ocean. **Rivers** Kaukonahua Stream, Wailuku Stream. **Lakes** Halulu, Kolekole, Salt Lake, Waiia Res. Other notable features Pearl Harbor. Hualalai, Kilauea, Mauna Kea (13,796 ft.), and Mauna Loa volcanoes. Main islands Hawaii, Kauai, Lanai, Maui, Molokai, Oahu. **People** (July, 2002 est.) 1,244,898 (42nd). Race/Hispanic Origin (2000 Census): White 24.3%. Black 1.8%. Indian 0.3%. Asian 41.6%. Pacific Islander 9.4%. Other 1.3%. Two or more races 21.4%. Hispanic 7.2%. **Cities** (2002) Honolulu 378,155. Hilo 40,759. Kailua 36,513. Kaneohe 34,970. Waipahu 33,108. Pearl City 30,976. Waimalu 29,371. Mililani Town 28,608. Kahului 20,146. Kihei 16,749. (Note: The Census Bureau does not keep statistics on cities other than Honolulu between decennial censuses because most Hawaiian cities are not incorporated). **Famous natives** Bernice P. Bishop, philanthropist. Sanford B. Dole, statehood advocate. Charlotte (b. Ohio) and Luther Halsey Gulick, Camp Fire Girls founders. Don Ho, singer. Daniel J. Inouye, politician. Duke Kahanamoku, swimmer. Victoria Kaiulani, last heiress presumptive to Hawaiian throne. Kamehameha I, king. Kamehameha III, king. Liliuokalani, queen. Bette Midler, singer. **Tourist information** (800) GOHAWAII. www.gohawaii.com.

Idaho

www.idaho.gov

Name Means "gem of the mountains." **Nickname** Gem State. **Capital** Boise. **Entered union** July 3, 1890 (43rd). **Motto** Esto perpetua (May it last forever). **Emblems** *Bird* Mountain bluebird. *Flower* Syringa. *Song* "Here We Have Idaho." *Tree* Western white pine. **Land** Total area 83,570 sq. mi (14th), incl. 823 sq. mi. inland water. **Borders** British Columbia, Mont., Wyo., Utah, Nev., Oreg., Wash. **Rivers** Bear, Clearwater, Payette, Salmon, Snake. **Lakes** American Falls Res., Coeur d'Alene, Pend Oreille. Mountains Bitterroot Range, Centennial, Clearwater, Salmon River, Sawtooth Range (Castle Peak 11,820 ft.), Wasatch Range. Other notable features Grand Canyon of the Snake River. **People** (July, 2002 est.) 1,341,131 (39th). Race/Hispanic Origin (2000 Census): White 91.0%. Black 0.4%. Indian 1.4%. Asian 0.9%. Pacific Islander 0.1%. Other 4.2%. Two or more races 2.0%. Hispanic 7.9%. **Cities** (2002) Boise City 189,847. Nampa 60,259. Pocatello 51,242. Idaho Falls 51,096. Meridian 39,067. Coeur d'Alene 36,259. Twin Falls 35,633. Lewiston 30,487. Caldwell 29,466. Moscow 21,674. **Famous natives** Joseph, Nez Percé chief. Ezra Taft Benson, politician.

Gutzon Borglum, sculptor. Frank Church, politician. Ezra Pound, poet. Harmon Killebrew, baseball player. Jerry Kramer, football player. Sacagawea (Bird Woman), Shoshone interpreter. Lana Turner, actress. **Tourist information** (800) 635-7820. www.visitid.org.

Illinois

www.illinois.gov

Name Corruption of iliniwek ("tribe of the superior men"), natives of region at time of earliest French explorations. **Nickname** Prairie State. **Capital** Springfield. **Entered union** Dec. 3, 1818 (21st). **Motto** "State sovereignty—national unity." Slogan "**Land** of Lincoln." **Emblems** *Bird* Cardinal. *Flower* Violet. *Song* "Illinois." *Tree* White oak. **Land** Total area 57,914 sq. mi (25th), incl. 2,331 sq. mi. inland water. **Borders** Wis., Lake Michigan, Ind., Ky., Mo., Iowa. **Rivers** Fox, Illinois, Illinois Waterway, Kankakee, Kaskaskia, Mississippi, Ohio, Rock, Vermillion, Wabash. **Lakes** Carlyle, Crab Orchard. Other notable features Charles Mound (1,235 ft.), Little Egypt. **People** (July, 2002 est.) 12,600,620 (5th). Race/Hispanic Origin (2000 Census): White 73.5%. Black 15.1%. Indian 0.2%. Asian 3.4%. Other 5.8%. Two or more races 1.9%. Hispanic 12.3%. **Cities** (2002) Chicago 2,886,251. Aurora 156,974. Rockford 151,068. Naperville 135,389. Joliet 118,423. Peoria 112,670. Springfield 111,834. Elgin 96,539. Waukegan 91,323. Cicero 84,254. **Famous natives** Jane Addams, reformer (Nobel Peace Prize, 1930). Ernie Banks, baseball player. Saul Bellow, author (Nobel Prize, 1976). Harry A. Blackmun, jurist. Ray Bradbury, author. Gwendolyn Brooks, poet. William Jennings Bryan, politician. Edgar Rice Burroughs, novelist. St. Frances Xavier Cabrini (b. Italy). Clarence Darrow, lawyer. Miles Davis, musician. John Dos Passos, novelist. Enrico Fermi (b. Italy), nuclear physicist (Nobel Prize, 1938). Robert Louis ("Bob") Fosse, choreographer. Milton Friedman, economist (Nobel Prize, 1976). Benny Goodman, musician. Ernest Hemingway, novelist. Charlton Heston, actor. William Holden, actor. Abraham Lincoln, U.S. President (b. Kentucky). Vachel Lindsay, poet. Archibald MacLeish, poet. Ludwig Mies van der Rohe (b. Germany), architect. Charles W. Post, cereal manufacturer. Ronald Reagan, U.S. president. Carl Sandburg, poet. Albert G. Spalding, merchant. John Paul Stevens, jurist. Gloria Swanson, actress. **Tourist information** (800) 2-CONNECT. www.enjoyillinois.com.

Indiana

www.state.in.us/tourism

Name For the land of Indians by early settlers, who found many distinct tribes living in region. **Nickname** Hoosier State. **Capital** Indianapolis. **Entered union** Dec. 11, 1816 (19th). **Motto** "The Crossroads of America." **Emblems** *Bird* Cardinal. *Flower* Peony. *Song* "On the Banks of the Wabash, Far Away." *Tree* Tulip tree. **Land** Total area 36,418 sq. mi (38th), incl. 551 sq. mi. inland water. **Borders** Lake Michigan, Mich., Ohio, Ky., Ill. **Rivers** Kankakee, Ohio, Tippecanoe, Wabash, White, Whitewater. **Lakes** Freeman, Shafer. **People** (July, 2002 est.) 6,159,068 (14th). Race/Hispanic Origin (2000 Census): White 87.5%. Black 8.4%. Indian 0.3%. Asian 1.0%. Other 1.6%. Two or more races 1.2%. Hispanic 3.5%. **Cities** (2002) Indianapolis 783,612. Fort Wayne 210,070. Evansville 119,081. South Bend 106,558. Gary 100,945. Hammond 81,413. Bloomington 69,987. Muncie 67,195. Lafayette 60,594. Anderson 58,853. **Famous natives** Larry Bird, basketball player. Hoagy Carmichael, composer. Eugene V. Debs, politician/organizer. Theodore Dreiser, author. Benjamin Harrison, U.S. president. Jimmy Hoffa, union leader. Michael Jackson, singer. David Letterman, comedian. Carole Lombard, actress. Cole Porter, composer. Ernie Pyle, journalist. Knute Rockne (b. Norway), football coach. Paul Samuelson, economist (Nobel Prize, 1960). Booth Tarkington, author. Kurt Vonnegut, author. Wendell L. Willkie, politician. **Tourist information** (888) ENJOYIN. www.state.in.us/tourism

Iowa

www.iowa.gov

Name For Iowa tribe. **Nickname** Hawkeye State. **Capital** Des Moines. **Entered union** Dec. 28, 1846 (29th). **Motto** "Our liberties we prize and our rights we will maintain." **Emblems** *Bird* Eastern goldfinch. *Flower* Wild rose. *Song* "The Song of Iowa." *Tree* Oak. **Land** Total area 56,272 sq. mi (26th), incl. 402 sq. mi. inland water. **Borders** Minn., Wis., Ill., Mo., Nebr., S.Dak. **Rivers** Big Sioux, Des Moines, Mississippi, Missouri. **Lakes** Okoboji, Rathburn Res., Red Rock, Saylorville Res., Spirit, Storm. Other notable features Ocheyedan Mound (1,675 ft.). **People** (July, 2002 est.) 2,936,760 (30th). Race/Hispanic Origin (2000 Census): White 93.9%. Black 2.1%. Indian 0.3%. Asian 1.3%. Other 1.3%. Two or more races 1.1%. Hispanic 2.8%. **Cities** (2002) Des Moines 198,076. Cedar Rapids 122,514. Davenport 97,777. Sioux City 84,131. Waterloo 67,742. Iowa City 63,816. Council Bluffs 58,640. Dubuque 57,031. Ames 50,913. West Des Moines 49,961. **Famous natives** Norman E. Borlaug, agronomist (Nobel Peace Prize, 1970). William F. ("Buffalo Bill") Cody, scout/showman. George Gallup, pollster. Josiah B. Grinnell (b. Vt.), abolitionist. Herbert Hoover, U.S. president. Harry L. Hopkins, politician. John L. Lewis, labor leader. John R. Mott, religious leader. Billy Sunday, baseball player/evangelist. John Wayne, actor. Meredith Wilson, composer. Grant Wood, painter. **Tourist information** (800) 345-IOWA. www.traveliowa.com.

Kansas

www.accesskansas.org

Name For Kansa or Kaw, "people of the south wind." **Nickname** Sunflower State. **Capital** Topeka. **Entered union** Jan. 29, 1861 (34th). **Motto** Ad astra per aspera (To the stars through adversity). **Emblems** *Bird* Western meadowlark. *Flower* Wild native sunflower. *Song* "Home on the Range." *Tree* Cottonwood. **Land** Total area 82,277 sq. mi (15th), incl. 462 sq. mi. inland water. **Borders** Nebr., Mo., Okla., Colo. **Rivers** Arkansas, Kansas, Missouri, Republican, Saline, Smoky Hill, Solomon. **Lakes** Kanapolis, Malvern, Perry, Pomona, Tuttle Creek, Waconda. Other notable features Flint Hills. **People** (July, 2002 est.) 2,715,884 (32nd). Race/Hispanic Origin (2000 Census): White 86.1%. Black 5.7%. Indian 0.9%. Asian 1.7%. Other 3.4%. Two or more races 2.1%. Hispanic 7.0%. **Cities** (2002) Wichita 355,126. Overland Park 158,430. Kansas City 146,978. Topeka 122,103. Olathe 101,413. Lawrence 81,604. Shawnee 52,715. Salina 45,969. Manhattan 43,794. Lenexa 41,249. **Famous natives** "Buffalo Bill" Cody. Walter Chrysler, carmaker. Robert Dole, politician. Amelia Earhart, aviator. Dwight David Eisenhower (b. Tex.), general/U.S. president. Dennis Hopper, actor. William Inge, playwright. Nancy Landon Kassebaum, politician. Alf Landon, politician. Edgar Lee Masters, poet. James Naismith, inventor of basketball. Carry Nation (b. Ky.), prohibitionist. Charlie ("Bird") Parker, musician. Damon Runyon, writer. Gale Sayers, football player. William Allen White, the Sage of Emporia, editor. **Tourist information** (800) 252-6727. www.travelks.com.

Kentucky, Commonwealth of

www.kentucky.gov

Name Corruption of the Iroquois kenta-ke (meadow land) or Wyandot kah-ten-tah-teh (land of tomorrow). **Nickname** Bluegrass State. **Capital** Frankfort. **Entered union** June 1, 1792 (15th). **Motto** "United we stand, divided we fall." **Emblems** *Bird* Cardinal. *Flower* Goldenrod. *Song* "My Old Kentucky Home." *Tree* Tulip poplar. **Land** Total area 40,409 sq. mi (37th), incl. 681 sq. mi. inland water. **Borders** Ind., Ohio, W.Va., Va., Tenn., Mo., Ill. **Rivers** Cumberland, Kentucky, Licking, Ohio, Tennessee. **Lakes** Barkley, Barren River Res., Dewey, Grayson Res., Laurel Res., Nolin Res., Rough Res. Mountains Appalachian (Black Mt. 4,145 ft.), Cumberland. Other notable features Tennessee Valley. **People** (July, 2002 est.) 4,092,891 (26th). Race/Hispanic Origin (2000 Census): White 90.1%. Black 7.3%. Indian 0.2%. Asian 0.7%. Other 0.6%. Two or more races 1.1%. Hispanic 1.5%. **Cities** (2002) Lexington-Fayette 260,512. Louisville 251,399. Owensboro 54,176. Bowling Green 50,226. Covington 42,983. Hopkinsville 29,279. Richmond 28,093. Frankfort 27,660. Henderson 27,426. Jeffersontown 26,156. **Famous natives** Muhammad Ali, boxer. Alben W. Barkley, politician. Daniel Boone (b. Pa.), frontiersman. Louis D. Brandeis, jurist. Kit Carson, frontiersman. Henry Clay, politician. Jefferson Davis, president of Confederate States of America. D.W. Griffith, director. John Marshall Harlan, jurist. Abraham Lincoln, U.S. president. Col. Harland Sanders, entrepreneur. Frederick M. Vinson, jurist. Robert Penn Warren, author. **Tourist information** (800) 225-TRIP or (800) 255-PARK. www.kytourism.com.

Louisiana

www.louisiana.gov

Name For King Louis XIV. **Nickname** Pelican State. **Capital** Baton Rouge. **Entered union** Apr. 30, 1812 (18th). **Motto** "Union, justice, confidence." **Emblems** *Bird* Eastern brown pelican. *Flower* Magnolia. *Songs* "Give Me Louisiana," "You Are My Sunshine." *Tree* Bald cypress. **Land** Total area 51,840 sq. mi (31st), incl. 8,278 sq. mi. inland water. **Borders** Ark., Miss., Gulf of Mexico, Tex. **Rivers** Atchafalaya, Mississippi, Ouachita, Pearl, Red, Sabine. **Lakes** Bistineau, Borgne, Caddo, Catahoula, Grand, Maurepas, Pontchartrain, Salvador, White. Other notable features Bayou Barataria, Bayou Bodcau, Bayou D'Arbonne, Driskill Mt. (535 ft.). **People** (July, 2002 est.) 4,482,646 (24th). Race/Hispanic Origin (2000 Census): White 63.9%. Black 32.5%. Indian 0.6%. Asian 1.2%. Other 0.7%. Two or more races 1.1%. Hispanic 2.4%. **Cities** (2002) New Orleans 484,674. Baton Rouge 225,702. Shreveport 199,033. Lafayette 111,272. Lake Charles 70,726. Kenner 70,502. Bossier City 57,156. Monroe 52,360. Alexandria 45,856. New Iberia 35,506. **Famous natives** Louis "Satchmo" Armstrong, jazz musician. Pierre Beauregard, Confederate general. Terry Bradshaw, football player. Braxton Bragg, Confederate general. Truman Capote, author. Clyde Cessna, aviator. Michael DeBakey, surgeon. Fats Domino, singer. Lillian Hellman, author. Mahalia Jackson, singer. Jean Baptiste Le Moyne, sieur de Bienville (b. Canada), founded New Orleans. Jerry Lee Lewis, singer. Huey P. Long, senator. Ferdinand Joseph La Menthe "Jelly Roll" Morton, musician. Leonidas K. Polk, clergyman/Confederate general. Henry Miller Shreve (b. NJ), riverboat captain. Edward D. White, Jr., jurist. **Tourist information** (800) 33-GUMBO. www.louisianatravel.com.

Maine

www.maine.gov

Name Either for Maine in France or to distinguish mainland from islands in the Gulf of Maine. **Nickname** Pine Tree State. **Capital** Augusta. **Entered union** Mar. 15, 1820 (23rd). **Motto** Dirigo (I direct). **Emblems** *Bird* Chickadee. *Flower*

White pinecone and tassel. *Song* "State of Maine Song." *Tree* Eastern white pine. **Land** Total area 35,385 sq. mi (39th), incl. 4,523 sq. mi. inland water. **Borders** Quebec, New Brunswick, Atlantic Ocean, N.H. **Rivers** Alagash, Androscoggin, Aroostock, Kennebec, Machias, Penobscot, Piscataqua, Salmon Falls, St. John. **Lakes** Chamberlain, Chesuncook, Grand, Moosehead, Rangeley, Sebago. Other notable features Longfellow Mts. (Mt. Katahadin 5,268 ft.), Mt. Desert Island, Penobscot Bay. **People** (July, 2002 est.) 1,294,464 (40th). Race/Hispanic Origin (2000 Census): White 96.9%. Black 0.5%. Indian 0.6%. Asian 0.7%. Other 0.2%. Two or more races 1.0%. Hispanic 0.7%. **Cities** (2002) Portland 64,249. Lewiston 34,690. Bangor 31,473. South Portland 23,324. Auburn 23,203. Biddeford 20,942. Augusta 18,560. Saco 17,634. Westbrook 16,103. Waterville 15,629. **Famous natives** Cyrus H.K. Curtis, publisher. Hannibal Hamlin, politician. Sarah Orne Jewett, novelist. Henry Wadsworth Longfellow, poet. Sir Hiram and Hudson Maxim, inventors. Edna St. Vincent Millay, poet. Edmund S. Muskie, politician. John Knowles Paine, composer. Kenneth Roberts, novelist. Edward Arlington Robinson, poet. Nelson Rockefeller, politician. Marguerite Yourcenar (b. France), author. **Tourist information** (800) 533-9595. www.visit-maine.com.

Maryland

www.maryland.gov

Name For Henrietta Maria, queen consort of Charles I. **Nickname**s Old Line State, Free State. **Capital** Annapolis. **Entered union** Apr. 28, 1788 (7th). **Motto** Fatti maschii, parole femine (Manly deeds, womanly words). **Emblems** *Bird* Baltimore oriole. *Flower* Black-eyed Susan. *Song* "Maryland, My Maryland." *Tree* White oak. **Land** Total area 12,407 sq. mi (42nd), incl. 2,633 sq. mi. inland water. **Borders** Pa., Del., Atlantic Ocean, Va., D.C., W.Va. **Rivers** Chester, Choptank, Nanticoke, Patapsco, Patuxent, Pocomoke, Potomac, Susquehanna. Other notable features Allegheny Mts., Blue Ridge Mts., Chesapeake Bay. **People** (July, 2002 est.) 5,458,137 (18th). Race/Hispanic Origin (2000 Census): White 64.0%. Black 27.9%. Indian 0.3%. Asian 4.0%. Other 1.8%. Two or more races 2.0%. Hispanic 4.3%. **Cities** (2002). Baltimore 651,154. Gaithersburg 56,300. Frederick 56,063. Rockville 52,573. Bowie 52,123. Hagerstown 36,659. Annapolis 36,196. College Park 25,320. Salisbury 24,645. Greenbelt 22,006. **Famous natives** Russell Baker, journalist. Benjamin Banneker, surveyor. Eubie Blake, pianist. Rachel Carson, biologist/author. Stephen Decatur, navy officer. Frederick Douglass, abolitionist. Billie Holiday, singer. Johns Hopkins, financier/philanthropist. Francis Scott Key, lawyer/poet. Thurgood Marshall, jurist. H.L. Mencken, writer. Charles Willson Peale, artist. William Pinckney, statesman. James Rouse, urban planner. Babe Ruth, baseball player. Upton Sinclair, author. Roger B. Taney, jurist. Harriet Tubman, abolitionist. John Waters, filmmaker. **Tourist Information** (800) MD-IS-FUN. www.mdisfun.org.

Massachusetts, Commonwealth of

www.mass.gov

Name For Massachuset tribe, whose **name** means "at or about the great hill." **Nickname** Bay State. **Capital** Boston. **Entered union** Feb. 6, 1788 (6th). **Motto** Ense petit placidam sub libertate quietem (By the sword we seek peace, but peace only under liberty). **Emblems** *Bird* Chickadee. *Flower* Mayflower. *Song* "All Hail to Massachusetts." *Tree* American elm. **Land** Total area 10,555 sq. mi (44th), incl. 2,715 sq. mi. inland water. **Borders** Vt., N.H., Atlantic Ocean, R.I., Conn., N.Y. **Rivers** Cape Cod Canal, Connecticut, Merrimack, Taunton. Other notable features Buzzard's Bay, Cape Ann, Cape Cod, Cape Cod Bay, Connecticut Valley, Elizabeth Islands, Martha's Vineyard, Monomoy Island, Nantucket Island. **People** (July, 2002 est.) 6,427,801 (13th). Race/Hispanic Origin (2000 Census): White 84.5%. Black 5.4%. Indian 0.2%. Asian 3.8%. Other 3.7%. Two or more races 2.3%. Hispanic 2.3%. **Cities** (2002) Boston 589,281 Worcester 174,962. Springfield 151,915. Lowell 104,901. Cambridge 101,807. Brockton 95,437. New Bedford 94,088. Fall River 92,660. Lynn 89,590. Quincy 89,187. **Famous natives** John Adams, U.S. president. John Quincy Adams, U.S. president. Samuel Adams, patriot. Horatio Alger, clergyman/author. Susan B. Anthony, suffragette. Clara Barton, nurse. Leonard Bernstein, composer. George Herbert Walker Bush, U.S. president. John ("Johnny Appleseed") Chapman, pioneer. Richard Cardinal Cushing, prelate. Bette Davis, actress. Emily Dickinson, poet. Ralph Waldo Emerson, author. Marshall Field, merchant. R. Buckminster Fuller, inventor/engineer. John Hancock, patriot. Oliver Wendell Holmes, jurist. Winslow Homer, painter. John F. Kennedy, U.S. president. Jack Kerouac, author. Cotton Mather, theologian. Samuel Eliot Morison, historian. Samuel Morse, inventor. Thomas P. "Tip" O'Neill, congressman. Edgar Allan Poe, poet/author. Paul Revere patriot/silversmith. Louis Sullivan, architect. Henry David Thoreau, author. **Tourist information** (800) 227-MASS. www.mass-vacation.com

Michigan

www.michigan.gov

Name From the Fox mesikami, "large lake." **Nickname**s Wolverine State, Lake State. **Capital** Lansing. **Entered union** Jan. 26, 1837 (26th). **Motto** Si quaeris peninsulam amoenam circumspice (If you are looking for a beautiful peninsula, look around you). **Emblems** *Bird* Robin. *Flower* Apple blossom. *Song* "Michigan, My Michigan." *Tree* White pine. **Land** Total area 96,716 sq. mi (11th), incl. 39,912 sq. mi. inland water. **Borders** Lake Superior, Ontario, Lake Huron, Lake Erie, Ohio, Ind., Lake Michigan, Wisc. **Rivers** Brule, Detroit, Kalamazoo, Menominee, Montreal, Muskegon, St. Joseph, St. Mary's. **Lakes** Burt, Higgins, Houghton, Huron, Manistique, Michigan, Mullett, St. Clair, Superior. Other notable features Isle Royale, Mt. Curwood (1,980 ft.), Saginaw Bay, Traverse Bay, Whitefish Bay. **People** (July, 2002 est.) 10,050,446 (8th). Race/Hispanic Origin (2000 Census): White 80.2%. Black 14.2%. Indian 0.6%. Asian 1.8%. Other 1.3%. Two or more races 1.9%. Hispanic 3.3%. **Cities** (2002) Detroit 925,051. Grand Rapids 196,595. Warren 137,672. Sterling Heights 126,146. Flint 121,763. Lansing 118,588. Ann Arbor 115,213. Livonia 100,341. Dearborn 97,833. Westland 86,282. **Famous natives** Ralph J. Bunche, statesman (Nobel Peace Prize, 1950). Paul de Kruif, bacteriologist. Thomas Dewey, politician. Herbert H. Dow (b. Canada), chemical manufacturer. Edna Ferber, author. Gerald Ford (b. Neb.) U.S. president. Henry Ford, industrialist. Edgar Guest, journalist/poet. Robert Ingersoll, industrialist. Will Kellogg, businessman/philanthopist. Charles A. Lindbergh, aviator. Madonna, singer. Antoine de La Mothe, sieur de Cadillac (b. France), founded Detroit. Pontiac, Ottawa chief. William Upjohn, drug manufacturer. **Tourist information** (888) 784-7328. www.travel.michigan.org

Minnesota

www.state.mn.us

Name From the Sioux minisota, "sky-tinted waters." **Nicknames** North Star State, Gopher State, **Land** of 10,000 **Lakes**. **Capital** St. Paul. **Entered union** May 11, 1858 (32rd). **Motto** L'étoile du nord (Star of the north). **Emblems** *Bird* Common loon. *Flower* Pink and white lady's slipper. *Song* "Hail, Minnesota!." *Tree* Red pine. **Land** Total area 86,939 sq. mi (12th), incl. 7,329 sq. mi. inland water. **Borders** Manitoba, Ontario, Lake Superior, Wisc., Iowa, S.Dak., N.Dak. **Rivers** Minnesota, Mississippi, Red River of the North, St. Croix. **Lakes** Itasca, Lake of the Woods, Leech, Mille Lacs, Red, Winnibigoshish. Other notable features Mesabi Range. **People** (July, 2001 est.) 4,972,294 (21st). Race/Hispanic Origin (2000 Census): White 89.4%. Black 3.5%. Indian 1.1%. Asian 2.9%. Other 1.3%. Two or more races 1.7%. Hispanic 2.9%. **Cities** (2002) Minneapolis 375,635. St. Paul 284,037. Rochester 90,515. Duluth 86,419. Bloomington 84,092. Brooklyn Park 68,128. Plymouth 67,304. Eagan 64,407. Coon Rapids 62,239. Burnsville 60,033. **Famous natives** Warren Burger, jurist. Bob Dylan, musician. F. Scott Fitzgerald, novelist. Judy Garland, actress. J. Paul Getty, businessman. Garrison Keillor, humorist. Sinclair Lewis, author (Nobel Prize, 1930). Paul Manship, sculptor. William and Charles Mayo, surgeons. Eugene McCarthy, politician. Walter F. Mondale, politician. Charles Schulz, cartoonist. Richard W. Sears, merchant. **Tourist information** (800) 657-3700. www.exploreminnesota.com.

Mississippi

www.mississippi.gov

Name From the Ojibwa misi sipi, "great river." **Nickname** Magnolia State. **Capital** Jackson. **Entered union** Dec. 10, 1817 (20th). **Motto** Virtute et armis (By virtue and arms). **Emblems** *Bird* Mockingbird. *Flower* Magnolia. *Song* "Go, Mississippi." *Tree* Magnolia. **Land** Total area 48,430 sq. mi (32nd), incl. 1,523 sq. mi. inland water. **Borders** Tenn., Ala., Gulf of Mexico, La., Ark. **Rivers** Big Black, Mississippi, Pearl, Tennessee, Yazoo. **Lakes** Arkabutla, Grenada, Ross Barnett Res., Sardis. Other notable features Pontotoc Ridge. **People** (July, 2002 est.) 2,871,782 (31st). Race/Hispanic Origin (2000 Census): White 61.4%. Black 36.3%. Indian 0.4%. Asian 0.7%. Other 0.5%. Two or more races 0.7%. Hispanic 1.4%. **Cities** (2002) Jackson 180,881. Gulfport 72,511. Biloxi 49,809. Hattiesburg 45,773. Greenville 40,286. Meridian 39,518. Tupelo 34,975. Southaven 33,161. Vicksburg 26,226. Pascagoula 25,990. **Famous natives** Medgar Evers, civil rights leader. William Faulkner, novelist. Shelby Foote, historian. Jim Henson, puppeteer. B.B. King, musician. Elvis Presley, singer. Leontyne Price, opera singer. Jerry Rice, football player. John C. Stennis, politician. Conway Twitty, singer. Muddy Waters, musician. Eudora Welty, novelist. Ben Ames Williams, novelist. Tennessee Williams, playwright. Richard Wright, author. **Tourist information** (800) WARMEST. www.visitmississippi.org.

Missouri

www.missouri.gov

Name From the Iliniwek missouri, "owner of big canoes." **Nickname** Show Me State. **Capital** Jefferson City. **Entered union** Aug. 10, 1821 (24th). **Motto** Salus populi suprema lex esto (The welfare of the people shall be the supreme law). **Emblems** *Bird* Bluebird. *Flower* Hawthorne. *Song* "Missouri Waltz." *Tree* Dogwood. **Land** Total area 69,704 sq. mi (21st), incl. 818 sq. mi. inland water. **Borders** Iowa, Ill., Ky., Tenn., Ark., Okla., Kans., Nebr. **Rivers** Des Moines, Mississippi, Missouri, Osage, St. Francis. **Lakes** Bull Shoals, Clearwater, Lake of the Ozarks, Lake of the Woods, Table, Wappapella. Other notable features Ozark Mts. (Taum Sauk Mt. 1,772 ft.). **People** (July, 2002 est.) 5,672,579 (17th). Race/Hispanic Origin (2000 Census): White 84.9%. Black 11.2%. Indian 0.4%. Asian 1.1%. Pacific Islander 0.1%. Other 0.8%. Two or more races 1.5%. Hispanic 2.1%. **Cities** (2002) Kansas City 443,471. St. Louis 338,353. Springfield 151,010. Independence 113,027. Columbia 86,981. Lee's Summit 74,948. St. Joseph 73,148. St. Charles 60,755. O'Fallon 59,678. St. Peters 53,596. **Famous natives** Thomas Hart Benton, painter. Yogi Berra, baseball player. George Caleb Bingham (b. Va.), painter. Omar Bradley, general. Adophus Busch (b. Germany), brewer. George Washington Carver, botanist. Walter Cronkite, journalist. Walt Disney, film producer. T.S. Eliot, poet. Walker Evans, photographer. Langston Hughes, poet. Jesse James, outlaw. Marianne Moore, poet. Reinhold Niebuhr, theologian. J.C. Penny, businessman. John J. "Black Jack" Pershing, soldier. Joseph Pulitzer (b. Hungary), publisher. Ginger Rogers, dancer. Casey Stengel, baseball player. Virgil Thompson, composer. Harry S Truman, U.S. president. Mark Twain, writer. Tom Watson, golfer. Shelley Winters, actress. **Tourist information** (800) 877-1234. www.visitmo.com.

Montana

www.discoveringmontana.com

Name From Spanish montaña, "mountainous." **Nicknames** Treasure State, Big Sky Country. **Capital** Helena. **Entered union** Nov. 8, 1889 (41st). **Motto** Oro y plata (Gold and silver). **Emblems** *Bird* Western meadowlark. *Flower* Bitterroot. *Song* "Montana." *Tree* Ponderosa pine. **Land** Total area 147,042 sq. mi (4th), incl. 1,490 sq. mi. inland water. **Borders** British Columbia, Alberta, Saskatchewan, N.Dak., S.Dak., Wyo., Idaho. **Rivers** Kootenai, Milk, Missouri, Musselshell, Powder, Yellowstone. **Lakes** Bighorn, Canyon Ferry, Elwell, Flathead, Ft. Peck. Mountains Absaroka Range, Beartooth Range (Granite Peak 12,799 ft.), Big Belt, Bitterroot Range, Centennial, Crazy, Lewis Range, Little Belt. Other notable features Continental Divide, Missoula Valley. **People** (July, 2002 est.) 909,453 (44th). Race/Hispanic Origin (2000 Census): White 90.6%. Black 0.3%. Indian 6.2%. Asian 0.5%. Pacific Islander 0.1%. Other 0.6%. Two or more races 1.7%. Hispanic 2.0%. **Cities** (2002) Billings 92,008. Missoula 59,518. Great Falls 56,046. Butte-Silver Bow 32,716. Bozeman 29,459. Helena 26,353. Kalispell 15,463. Havre 9,621. Anaconda-Deer Lodge County 9,417. Miles City 8,487. **Famous natives** Gary Cooper, actor. Marcus Daly (b. Ireland), mine owner. Chet Huntley, journalist. Myrna Loy, actress. Mike Mansfield (b. N.Y.), politician/diplomat. Jeanette Rankin, politician/reformer. Charles M. Russell, artist. **Tourist information** (800) VISIT-MT, (800) 548-3390. www.visitmt.com.

Nebraska

www.nebraska.gov

Name From the Oto nebrathka, "flat water." **Nickname** Cornhusker State. **Capital** Lincoln. **Entered union** Mar. 1, 1867 (37th). **Motto** "Equality before the law." **Emblems** *Bird* Western meadowlark. *Flower* Goldenrod. *Song* "Beautiful Nebraska." *Tree* Western cottonwood. **Land** Total area 77,354 sq. mi (16th), incl. 481 sq. mi. inland water. **Borders** S.Dak., Iowa, Mo., Kans., Colo., Wyo. **Rivers** Missouri, North Platte, Republican, South Platte. **Lakes** Harlan Co. Res., Lewis and Clark Lake. Other notable features Pine Ridge, Sand Hills. **People** (July, 2002 est.) 1,729,180 (38th). Race/Hispanic Origin (2000 Census): White 89.6%. Black 4.0%. Indian 0.9%. Asian 1.3%. Other 2.8%. Two or more races 1.4%. Hispanic 5.5%. **Cities** (2002) Omaha 399,357. Lincoln 232,362. Bellevue 46,217. Grand Island 43,010. Kearney 27,910. Fremont 25,188. Norfolk 24,183. Hastings 23,908. North Platte 23,674. Columbus 20,877. **Famous natives** Fred Astaire, dancer. Marlon Brando, actor. William Jennings Bryan, politician. Johnny Carson (b. Iowa), comedian. Willa Cather (b. Va.), author. Loren Eiseley, anthropologist. Henry Fonda, actor. Rollin Kirby, cartoonist. Melvin Laird, politician. Harold Lloyd, actor. Mahpiua Luta (Red Cloud), Oglala Sioux chief. Malcolm X, religious leader. Roscoe Pound, educator. **Tourist information** (877) NEBRASKA. www.visitnebraska.org.

Nevada

www.nv.gov

Name From Spanish, meaning "snow-covered sierra." **Nicknames** Sagebrush State, Silver State. **Capital** Carson City. **Entered union** Oct. 31, 1864 (36th). **Motto** "All for our country." **Emblems** *Bird* Mountain bluebird. *Flower* Sagebrush. *Song* "Home Means Nevada." *Tree* Single-leaf piñon. **Land** Total area 110,561 sq. mi (7th), incl. 735 sq. mi. inland water. **Borders** Oreg., Idaho, Utah, Ariz., Calif. **Rivers** Colorado, Humboldt. **Lakes** Pyramid, Walker, Winnemucca. Other notable features Black Rock Desert, Carson Sink, Humboldt Salt Marsh, Mojave Desert. **People** (July, 2002 est.) 2,173,491 (35th). Race/Hispanic Origin (2000 Census): White 75.2%. Black 6.8%. Indian 1.3%. Asian 4.5%. Pacific Islander 0.4%. Other 8.0%. Two or more races 3.8%. Hispanic 19.7%. **Cities** (2002) Las Vegas 508,604. Henderson 206,153. Reno 190,248. North Las Vegas 135,902. Sparks 73,730. Carson City 54,311. Elko 16,278. Boulder City 15,364. Mesquite 11,264. **Famous natives** Andre Agassi, tennis player. Walter Van Tilburg Clark (b. Me.), author. Sarah Winnemucca Hopkins, interpeter/teacher. John William MacKay, miner. William Morris Stewart (b. N.Y.), lawyer/senator. **Tourist information** (800)NEVADA8. www.travelnevada.com

New Hampshire

www.state.nh.us

Name For English county of Hampshire. **Nickname** Granite State. **Capital** Concord. **Entered union** June 21, 1788 (9th).

Motto "Live free or die." **Emblems** *Amphibian* Spotted newt. *Bird* Purple finch. *Flower* Purple lilac. *Gem* Smoke quartz. *Insect* Ladybug. *Mineral* Beryl. *Song* "Old New Hampshire." *Tree* White birch. **Land** Total area 9,350 sq. mi (46th), incl. 382 sq. mi. inland water. Borders Quebec, Maine, Atlantic Ocean, Mass., Vt. Rivers Connecticut, Merrimack, Piscataqua, Saco, Salmon Falls. Lakes First Connecticut, Francis, Newfound, Ossipee, Sunapee, Winnipesaukee. Other notable features Isles of Shoals, White Mts. (Mt. Washington 6,288 ft., highest peak in Northeast). **People** (July, 2002 est.) 1,275,056 (41st). Race/Hispanic Origin (2000 Census): White 96.0%. Black 0.7%. Indian 0.2%. Asian 1.3%. Other 0.6%. Two or more races 1.1%. Hispanic 1.7%. **Cities** (2002) Manchester 108,398. Nashua 87,705. Concord 41,404. Rochester 29,350. Dover 27,784. Keene 22,714. Portsmouth 21,408. Laconia 16,949. Claremont 13,195. Lebanon 12,788. **Famous natives** Salmon P. Chase, jurist. Ralph Adams Cram, architect. Mary Baker Eddy, founder, Church of Christ, Scientist. Daniel Chester French, sculptor. Horace Greeley, journalist. Sarah Buell Hale, author. Franklin Pierce, U.S. president. Augustus Saint-Gaudens (b. Ireland), sculptor. Alan Shepard, astronaut. Daniel Webster, politician. Eleazar Wheelock (b. Conn.), Dartmouth founder. **Tourist information** (800) FUN-IN-NH. www.visitnh.gov.

New Jersey

www.state.nj.us

Name After English Channel Island of Jersey. **Nickname** Garden State. **Capital** Trenton. **Entered union** Dec. 18, 1787 (3rd). **Motto** "Liberty and prosperity." **Emblems** *Bird* Eastern goldfinch. *Flower* Violet. *Tree* Red oak. **Land** Total area 8,721 sq. mi (47th), incl. 1,304 sq. mi. inland water. **Borders** N.Y., Atlantic Ocean, Del., Pa. **Rivers** Delaware, Hackensack, Hudson, Passaic. **Lakes** Greenwood, Hopatcong, Round Valley Res., Spruce Run. Other notable features Delaware Water Gap, Kittatinny Mts., Palisades, Pine Barrens, Ramapo Mts. **People** (July, 2002 est.) 8,590,300 (9th). Race/Hispanic Origin (2000 Census): White 72.6%. Black 13.6%. Indian 0.2%. Asian 5.7%. Other 5.4%. Two or more races 2.5%. Hispanic 13.3%. **Cities** (2002) Newark 277,000. Jersey City 240,100. Paterson 150,750. Elizabeth 123,279. Trenton 85,650. Camden 79,685. Clifton 79,626. East Orange 69,750. Passaic 68,445. Union City 66,902. **Famous natives** Count Basie, jazz musician. William J. Brennan, jurist. Aaron Burr, politician. Grover Cleveland, U.S. president. James Fenimore Cooper, novelist/historian. Stephen Crane, author. Thomas Edison, inventor. Albert Einstein (b. Germany), nuclear physicist. Waldo Frank, author. Joyce Kilmer, poet. Jerry Lewis, actor. Jack Nicholson, actor. Zebulon Pike, explorer. Molly Pitcher, Revolutionary War heroine. Paul Robeson, actor/singer. Walter Schirra, astronaut. Frank Sinatra, singer. Alfred Stieglitz, photographer. Meryl Streep, actress. Aaron Montgomery Ward, merchant. William Carlos Williams, poet. **Tourist information** (800) VISITNJ. www.state.nj.us/travel/

New Mexico

www.state.nm.us

Name By Spanish explorers after Mexico. **Nickname** **Land** of Enchantment. **Capital** Santa Fe. **Entered union** Jan. 6, 1912 (47th). **Motto** Crescit eundo (It grows as it goes). **Emblems** *Bird* Roadrunner (chaparral bird). *Flower* Yucca. *Songs* "O, Fair New Mexico," "Así es Nuevo Mejico." *Tree* Piñon. **Land** Total area 121,589 sq. mi (5th), incl. 234 sq. mi. inland water. **Borders** Colo., Okla., Tex., Chihuahua, Ariz. **Rivers** Gila, Pecos, Rio Grande, Zuni. **Lakes** Conchas Res., Eagle Nest, Elephant Butte Res., Navajo Res., Ute Res. Mountains Chuska, Guadalupe, Sacramento, San Andres, Sangre de Cristo. Other notable features Carlsbad Caverns, Continental Divide, Staked Plain. **People** (July, 2002 est.) 1,855,059 (36th). Race/Hispanic Origin (2000 Census): White 66.8%. Black 1.9%. Indian 9.5%. Asian 1.1%. Pacific Islander 0.1%. Other 17.0%. Two or more races 3.6%. Hispanic 42.1%. **Cities** (2002) Albuquerque 463,874. Las Cruces 475,015. Santa Fe 65,127. Rio Rancho 56,614. Roswell 44,058. Farmington 40,563. Alamogordo 35,107. Clovis 32,511. Hobbs 28,479. Carlsbad 25,196. **Famous natives** William "Billy the Kid" Bonney (b. N.Y.), outlaw. Peter Hurd, artist. Archbishop Jean Baptiste Lamy (b. France), missionary. Georgia O'Keeffe (b. Wis.), artist. Popé, Tewa Pueblo chief. Harrison Schmitt, astronaut. **Tourist information** (800) 545-2040. www.newmexico.org.

New York

www.state.ny.us

Name For Duke of York, later James II, of England. **Nickname** Empire State. **Capital** Albany. **Entered union** July 26, 1788 (11th). **Motto** Excelsior (Higher). **Emblems** *Bird* Bluebird. *Flower* Rose. *Song* "I Love New York." *Tree* Sugar maple. **Land** Total area 54,556 sq. mi (27th), incl. 7,342 sq. mi. inland water. **Borders** Lake Ontario, Ontario, Quebec, Vt., Mass., Conn., Atlantic Ocean, N.J., Pa., Lake Erie. **Rivers** Allegheny, Delaware, Genesee, Hudson, Mohawk, New York State Barge Canal, Niagara, St. Lawrence, Susquehanna. **Lakes** Cayuga, Champlain, Chautauqua, Erie, George, Oneida, Ontario, Seneca. Mountains Adirondack (Mt. Marcy 5,344 ft.), Allegheny, Berkshire Hills, Catskill, Kittatinny, Ramapo. Other notable features Hudson Valley, Mohawk Valley, Niagara Falls, Palisades, Thousand Islands. **People** (July, 2002 est.) 19,157,532 (3rd). Race/Hispanic Origin

(2000 Census): White 67.9%. Black, 15.9%. Indian 0.4%. Asian 5.5%. Other 7.1%. Two or more races 3.1%. Hispanic 15.1%. **Cities** (2002) New York 8,084,316. Buffalo 287,698. Rochester 217,158. Yonkers 197,234. Syracuse 145,164. Albany 93,779. New Rochelle 72,472. Mount Vernon 68,615. Schenectady 61,420. Utica 59,947. **Famous natives** Woody Allen, director. John Jacob Astor (b. Germany), merchant. Humphrey Bogart, actor. George Burns, actor. Aaron Copland, composer. Agnes de Mille, choreographer. George Eastman, camera inventor. Millard Fillmore, U.S. president. Lou Gehrig, baseball player. George Gershwin, composer. Julia Ward Howe, reformer. Washington Irving, author. Henry James, author. Vince Lombardi, football coach. Groucho Marx, comedian. Herman Melville, author. Ogden Nash, poet/humorist. Eugene O'Neill, playwright. Otetiani "Red Jacket", Seneca chief. Channing E. Phillips, minister/reformer. John D. Rockefeller, industrialist. Norman Rockwell, illustrator. Richard Rodgers, composer. Franklin Delano Roosevelt, U.S. president. Theodore Roosevelt, U.S. president. Jonas Salk, physician. Elizabeth Ann Seton, first American saint. Elizabeth Cady Stanton, suffragette. James Johnson Sweeney, art critic. Martin Van Buren, U.S. president. Mae West, actress. E.B. White, author. Walt Whitman, poet. **Tourist information** (800) CALL-NYS. www.iloveny.com.

North Carolina

www.ncgov.com

Name For King Charles I (Carolus is Latin for Charles). **Nicknames** Tarheel State, Old North State. **Capital** Raleigh. **Entered union** Nov. 21, 1789 (12th). **Motto** Esse quam videri (To be rather than to seem). **Emblems** *Bird* Cardinal. *Flower* Dogwood. *Song* "The Old North State." *Tree* Pine. **Land** Total area 53,819 sq. mi (28th), incl. 5,108 sq. mi. inland water. **Borders** Va., Atlantic Ocean, S.C., Tenn., Georgia. **Rivers** Pee Dee, Roanoke, Yadkin. **Lakes** Buggs Island, High Rock, Mattamuskeet, Norman, Waccamaw. Mountains Black, Blue Ridge, Great Smoky, Unaka. Other notable features Great Dismal Swamp, Mount Mitchell, Outer Banks, Pamlico Sound. **People** (July, 2002 est.) 8,320,146 (11th). Race/Hispanic Origin (2000 Census): White 72.1%. Black 21.6%. Indian 1.2%. Asian 1.4%. Other 2.3%. Two or more races 1.3%. Hispanic 4.7%. **Cities** (2002) Charlotte 580,597. Raleigh 306,944. Greensboro 228,217. Durham 195,914. Winston-Salem 188,934. Fayetteville 124,286. Cary 98,041. Wilmington 90,644. High Point 90,639. Asheville 69,193. **Famous natives** Benjamin Newton Duke and James Buchanan Duke, industrialists/philanthropists. Richard J. Gatling, inventor. Billy Graham, minister. Andy Griffith, actor. O. Henry, writer. Andrew Johnson, U.S. president. William Rufus King, politician. Charles Kuralt, journalist. Meadowlark Lemon, athlete. Dolley Madison, First Lady. Thelonius Monk, musician. Edward R. Murrow, journalist. James Knox Polk, U.S. president. Moses Waddell, Confederate general. Thomas Wolfe, author. **Tourist information** (800) VISIT-NC. www.visitnc.com.

North Dakota

www.discovernd.com

Name For northern section of Dakota territory; dakota is Sioux word for "allies." **Nicknames** Sioux State, Peace Garden State, Flickertail State. **Capital** Bismarck. **Entered union** Nov. 2, 1889 (39th). **Motto** "Liberty and union, now and forever, one and inseparable." **Emblems** *Bird* Western meadowlark. *Flower* Wild prairie rose. *Song* "North Dakota Hymn." *Tree* American elm. **Land** Total area 70,700sq. mi (19th), incl. 1,724 sq. mi. inland water. **Borders** Saskatchewan, Manitoba, Minn., S.Dak., Mont. **Rivers** Missouri, Red River of the North. **Lakes** Ashtabula, Devils, Oahe, Sakakawea. Other notable features Geographical center of North America, Missouri Plateau, Red River Valley, Rolling Drift Prairie. **People** (July, 2002 est.) 634,110 (48th). Race/Hispanic Origin (2000 Census): White 92.4%. Black 0.6%. Indian 4.9%. Asian 0.6%. Other 0.4%. Two or more races 1.2%. Hispanic 1.2%. **Cities** (2002) Fargo 91,240. Bismarck 56,234. Grand Forks 48,546. Minot 35,617. Mandan 16,769. West Fargo 15,801. Dickinson 15,679. Jamestown 15,115. Williston 12,376. Wahpeton 8,586. **Famous natives** Angie Dickinson, actress. John Bernard Flannagan, sculptor. Louis L'Amour, novelist. Peggy Lee, singer. Roger Maris, baseball player. Vihjalmur Stefansson (b. Canada), ethnologist. Lawrence Welk, entertainer. **Tourist information** (800) HELLO-ND. www.ndtourism.com.

Ohio

www.ohio.gov

Name From the Iroquois oheo, "beautiful." **Nickname** Buckeye State. **Capital** Columbus. **Entered union** Mar. 1, 1803 (17th). **Motto** "With God, all things are possible." **Emblems** *Bird* Cardinal. *Flower* Scarlet carnation. *Song* "Beautiful Ohio." *Tree* Buckeye. **Land** Total area 44,825 sq. mi (34th), incl. 3,877 sq. mi. inland water. **Borders** Mich., Lake Erie, Pa., W.Va., Ky., Ind. **Rivers** Cuyahoga, Maumee, Miami, Muskingum, Ohio, Sandusky, Scioto. **Lakes** Berlin Res., Dillon Res., Erie, Mosquito Res., St. Mary's. **People** (July, 2002 est.) 11,421,267 (7th). Race/Hispanic Origin (2000 Census): White 85.0%. Black 11.5%. Indian 0.2%. Asian 1.2%. Other 0.8%. Two or more races 1.4%. Hispanic 1.9%. **Cities** (2002) Columbus 725,228. Cleveland 467,851. Cincinnati 323,885. Toledo 309,106. Akron 214,349. Dayton 162,669. Parma 84,534. Youngstown 80,026. Canton 79,772. Lorain 67,704. **Famous natives** Sherwood

Anderson, writer. Neil Armstrong, astronaut. George Bellows, artist. Ambrose Bierce, author. George Armstrong Custer, army officer. Paul Laurence Dunbar, poet. Thomas A. Edison, inventor. James A. Garfield, U.S. president. John Glenn, astronaut/politician. Ulysses S. Grant, U.S. president/general. Zane Grey, author. Warren G. Harding, U.S. president. Benjamin Harrison, U.S. president. Rutherford B. Hayes, U.S. president. Bob Hope, entertainer. William McKinley, U.S. president. Annie Oakley, markswoman. Ransom Eli Olds, carmaker. Eddie Rickenbacker, pilot. William Sherman, army officer. William Howard Taft, U.S. president/chief justice. Art Tatum, pianist. Tecumseh, Shawnee chief. James Thurber, humorist. Orville Wright, airplane inventor. **Tourist information** (800)BUCKEYE. www.ohiotourism.com

Oklahoma

www.youroklahoma.com

Name From the Choctaw okla humma, "land of the red people." **Nickname** Sooner State. **Capital** Oklahoma City. **Entered union** Nov. 16, 1907 (46th). **Motto** *Labor omnia vincit* (Work overcomes all obstacles). **Emblems** *Bird* Scissor-tailed flycatcher. *Floral emblem* Mistletoe. *Song* "Oklahoma!" *Tree* Redbud. **Land** Total area 69,898 sq. mi (20th), incl. 1,231 sq. mi. inland water. **Borders** Kans., Mo., Ark., Tex., N.Mex., Colo. **Rivers** Arkansas, Canadian, Cimarron, Red. **Lakes** Canton, Lake o' the Cherokees, Oologah, Texoma. Other notable features Ouachita Mts., Ozark Plateau, Staked Plain, Wichita Mts. **People** (July, 2002 est.) 3,493,714 (28th). Race/Hispanic Origin (2000 Census): White 76.2%. Black 7.6%. Indian 7.9%. Asian 1.4%. Pacific Islander 0.1%. Other 2.4%. Two or more races 4.5%. Hispanic 5.2%. **Cities** (2002) Oklahoma City 519,034. Tulsa 391,098. Norman 97,831. Lawton 91,333. Broken Arrow 80,088. Edmond 70,540. Midwest City 54,503. Enid 46,531. Moore 43,739. Stillwater 40,586. **Famous natives** Ralph Ellison, author. Woody Guthrie, reformer/musician. Patrick J. Hurley, diplomat. Karl Jansky, electrical engineer. Mickey Mantle, baseball player. Wiley Post, aviator. Tony Randall, actor. Oral Roberts, evangelist. Will Rogers, humorist. Maria Tallchief, ballerina. Jim Thorpe, athlete. **Tourist information** (800) 652-6552. www.travelok.com

Oregon

www.state.or.us

Name Unknown origin, first applied to Columbia River. **Nickname** Beaver State. **Capital** Salem. **Entered union** Feb. 14, 1859 (33rd). **Motto** "She flies with her own wings." **Emblems** *Animal* Beaver. *Bird* Western meadowlark. *Dance* Square dance. *Fish* Chinook salmon. *Flower* Oregon grape. *Insect* Swallowtail butterfly. *Song* "Oregon, My Oregon." *Stone* Thunderegg. *Tree* Douglas fir. **Land** Total area 98,381 sq. mi (9th), incl. 2,384 sq. mi. inland water. Borders Wash., Idaho, Nev., Calif., Pacific Ocean. Rivers Columbia, Snake, Willamette. Mountains Cascade Range, Coast Range, Klamath. Other notable features Willamette Valley. **People** (July, 2002 est.) 3,521,515 (27th). Race/Hispanic Origin (2000 Census): White 86.6%. Black 1.6%. Indian 1.3%. Asian 3.0%. Pacific Islander 0.2%. Other 4.2%. Two or more races 3.1%. Hispanic 8.0%. **Cities** (2002) Portland 539,438. Salem 140,977. Eugene 140,395. Gresham 94,706. Beaverton 79,768. Hillsboro 75,945. Medford 64,653. Bend 57,010. Springfield 54,035. Corvallis 49,781. **Famous natives** In-mut-too-yah-lat-lat (Joseph), Nez Percé chief. Ursula LeGuin (b. Calif.), author. Edwin Markham, poet. Dr. John McLoughlin, fur trader, "Father of Oregon". Linus Pauling, chemist. John Reed, author. William Simon U'Ren (b. Wis.), lawyer/reformer. **Tourist information** (800) 547-7842. www.traveloregon.com.

Pennsylvania, Commonwealth of

www.state.pa.us

Name For Adm. William Penn, father of William Penn, founder of commonwealth. **Nickname** Keystone State. **Capital** Harrisburg. **Entered union** Dec. 12, 1787 (2nd). **Motto** "Virtue, liberty and independence." **Emblems** *Bird* Ruffed grouse. *Flower* Mountain laurel. *Tree* Hemlock. **Land** Total area 46,055 sq. mi (33rd), incl. 1,239 sq. mi. inland water. **Borders** N.Y., N.J., Del., Md., W.Va., Ohio, Lake Erie. **Rivers** Allegheny, Delaware, Juniata, Monongahela, Ohio, Schuylkill, Susquehanna. **Lakes** Allegheny Res., Erie, Pymatuning Res., Shenango Res. Mountains Allegheny, Kittatinny, Laurel Hills, Pocono. **People** (July, 2002 est.) 12,335,091 (6th). Race/Hispanic Origin (2000 Census): White 85.4%. Black 10.0%. Indian 0.1%. Asian 1.8%. Other 1.5%. Two or more races 1.2%. Hispanic 3.2%. **Cities** (2002) Philadelphia 1,492,231. Pittsburgh 327,898. Allentown 106,105. Erie 102,122. Reading 80,494. Scranton 74,712. Bethlehem 71,749. Lancaster 55,628. Harrisburg 78,540. Altoona 48,490. **Famous natives** Louisa May Alcott, author. Maxwell Anderson, playwright. James Buchanan, U.S. president. Alexander Calder, sculptor. Andrew Carnegie (b. Scotland), industrialist/philanthropist. Mary Cassatt, painter. Wilt Chamberlain, basketball player. Bill Cosby, comedian/philanthropist. Stephen Foster, songwriter. Benjamin Franklin (b. Mass.), inventor/statesman. Robert Fulton, inventor. Milton S. Hershey, chocolatier. George C. Marshall, statesman. Andrew W. Mellon, financier/philanthropist. Robert E. Peary, explorer. Betsy Ross, patriot. Andy Warhol, artist. Johnny Weismuller, swimmer/actor. Benjamin West, painter. **Tourist information** (800) VISIT-PA. www.experiencepa.com.

Rhode Island and Providence Plantations

www.state.ri.us

Name For Rhode Island in Narragansett Bay, **name**d in turn for Mediterranean island of Rhodes. **Nickname**s Ocean State, Little Rhody. **Capital** Providence. **Entered union** May 29, 1790 (13th). **Motto** "Hope." **Emblems** *Bird* Rhode Island red. *Flower* Violet. *Song* "Rhode Island." *Tree* Red maple. **Land** Total area 1,545 sq. mi (50th), incl. 500 sq. mi. inland water. **Borders** Mass., Atlantic Ocean, Conn. **Rivers** Blackstone, Pawcatuck, Providence, Sakonnet. Other notable features Block Island, Narragansett Bay, Aquidneck Island. **People** (July, 2002 est.) 1,069,725 (43rd). Race/Hispanic Origin (2000 Census): White 85.0%. Black 4.5%. Indian 0.5%. Asian 2.3%. Pacific Islander 0.1%. Other 5.0%. Two or more races 2.7%. Hispanic 8.7%. **Cities** (2002) Providence 175,901. Warwick 87,039. Cranston 81,113. Pawtucket 74,033. East Providence 49,658. Woonsocket 43,879. Newport 26,312. Central Falls 19,168. **Famous natives** George M. Cohan, actor/producer. Nathanael Greene, army officer. Galway Kinell, poet. Metacomet (King Philip), Wampanoag chief. Oliver H. Perry and Matthew C. Perry, naval officers. Gilbert Stuart, portraitist. **Tourist information** (800) 556-2484. www.visitrhodeisland.com.

South Carolina

www.myscgov.com

Name For King Charles II (Carolus is Latin for Charles). **Nickname** Palmetto State. **Capital** Columbia. **Entered union** May 23, 1788 (8th). **Motto** *Animis opibusque parati* (Prepared in mind and deed); *Dum spiro spero* (While I breathe I hope). **Emblems** Bird Carolina wren. Flower Yellow jessamine. Song "Carolina." Tree Palmetto. **Land** Total area 32,020 sq. mi (40th), incl. 1,911 sq. mi. inland water. **Borders** N.C., Atlantic Ocean, Ga. **Rivers** Catawba, Congaree, Edisto, Pee Dee, Savannah, Tugalos, Wateree. **Lakes** Greenwood, Hartwell, Keowee, Marion, Murray, Santee Res., Wylie. Other notable features Blue Ridge Mts., Congaree Swamp, Sea Islands. **People** (July, 2002 est.) 4,107,183 (25th). Race/Hispanic Origin (2000 Census): White 67.2%. Black 29.5%. Indian 0.3%. Asian 0.9%. Other 1.0%. Two or more races 1.0%. Hispanic 2.4%. **Cities** (2002) Columbia 117,394. Charleston 98,795. North Charleston 80,691. Greenville 56,181. Rock Hill 54,606. Mount Pleasant 53,096. Sumter 39,382. Spartanburg 39,068. Hilton Head Island 34,601. Goose Creek 30,179. **Famous natives** James F. Byrnes, politician/jurist. John C. Calhoun, politician. Dizzy Gillespie, musician. Althea Gibson, athlete. DuBose Heyward, author. Andrew Jackson, U.S. president. Eartha Kitt, singer. James Longstreet, army officer. Francis Marion, army officer/politician. Charles C. Pinckney and Thomas Pinckney, diplomats. Edward Rutledge and John Rutledge, politicians. Strom Thurmond, politician. **Tourist information** (800) SC-SMILE. www.discoversouthcarolina.com.

South Dakota

www.state.sd.us

Name For southern section of Dakota territory; dakota is Sioux word for "allies." **Nickname** Coyote State, Sunshine State. **Capital** Pierre. **Entered union** Nov. 2, 1889 (40th). **Motto** "Under God the people rule." **Emblems** *Bird* Chinese ring-necked pheasant. *Flower* Pasque . **Land** Total area 77,116 sq. mi (17th), incl. 1,232 sq. mi. inland water. **Borders** N.Dak., Minn., Iowa, Nebr., Wyo., Mont. **Rivers** Cheyenne, James, Missouri, Moreau, White. **Lakes** Belle Fourche Res., Big Stone, Traverse. Other notable features Badlands, Black Hills (Harney Peak 7,242 ft.). **People** (July, 2002 est.) 761,063 (46th). Race/Hispanic Origin (2000 Census): White 88.7%. Black 0.6%. Indian 8.3%. Asian 0.6%. Other 0.5%. Two or more races 1.3%. Hispanic 1.4%. **Cities** (2002) Sioux Falls 130,491. Rapid City 60,262. Aberdeen 24,312. Watertown 20,191. Brookings 18,703. Mitchell 14,626. Pierre 14,012. Yankton 13,440. Huron 11,569.Vermillion 10,065. **Famous natives** Tom Brokaw, journalist. Martha "Calamity" Jane Burk (b. Mo.), frontiers-woman. Alvin Hansen, economist. Hubert H. Humphrey, politician. Ernest O. Lawrence, physicist (Nobel Prize, 1939). George McGovern, politician. Ta-sunko-witko (Crazy Horse), Oglala Sioux chief. Tatanka Iyotake (Sitting Bull), Sioux chief. **Tourist information** (800) SDAKOTA. www.travelsd.com.

Tennessee

www.tennessee.gov

Name For Tenase, principal village of Cherokees. **Nickname** Volunteer State. **Capital** Nashville. **Entered union** June 1, 1796 (16th). **Motto** "Agriculture and commerce." Slogan "Tennessee—America at its best." Poet laureate Richard M. ("Pek") Gunn. **Emblems** *Bird* Mockingbird. *Flower* Iris. *Songs* "When It's Iris Time in Tennessee," "The Tennessee Waltz," My Homeland, Tennessee," "Rocky Top." *Tree* Tulip poplar. **Land** Total area 42,143 sq. mi (36th), incl. 926 sq. mi. inland water. **Borders** Ky., Va., N.C., Ga., Ala., Miss., Ark., Mo. **Rivers** Clinch, Cumberland, Mississippi, Tennessee. **Lakes** Boone, Center Hill, Cherokee, Dale Hollow, Douglass, J. Percy Priest, Watauga. Other notable features Cumberland Mts., Great Smoky Mts., Tennessee Valley, Unaka Mts. **People People** (July, 2002 est.) 5,797,289 (16th). Race/Hispanic Origin (2000 Census): White 80.2%. Black 16.4%. Indian 0.3%. Asian 1.0%. Other 1.0%. two or more races 1.1%. Hispanic 2.2%. **Cities** (2002) Memphis 648,882. Nashville-Davidson 545,915. Knoxville 173,661.

Chattanooga 155,404. Clarksville 105,898. Murfreesboro 74,894. Jackson 60,635. Johnson City 56,767. Franklin 45,175. Kingsport 44,362. **Famous natives** James Agee, author. Davy Crockett, frontiersman. David Farragut, naval officer. Aretha Franklin, singer. Morgan Freeman, actor. Al Gore, (b. Washington, D.C.), politician. Cordell Hull, statesman (Nobel Peace Prize, 1945). Dolly Parton, singer. Sikawyi (Sequoya), Cherokee scholar. Alvin York, soldier. **Tourist information** (800) 836-6200. www.state.tn.us/tourdev

Texas

www.texas.gov

Name From the Caddo tavshas, "friends." **Nickname** Lone Star State. **Capital** Austin. **Entered union** Dec. 29, 1845 (28th). **Motto** "Friendship." **Emblems** *Bird* Mockingbird. *Flower* Bluebonnet. *Songs* "Texas, Our Texas," "The Eyes of Texas." *Tree* Pecan. **Land** Total area 268,581 sq. mi (2nd), incl. 6,784 sq. mi. inland water. **Borders** Okla., Ark., La., Gulf of Mexico, Tamaulipas, Coahuila, Chihuahua, N.Mex. **Rivers** Brazos, Colorado, Natchez, Red, Rio Grande, Sabine, Trinity. **Lakes** Sam Rayburn Res., Texoma, Toledo Bend Res. Other notable features Balcones Escarpment, Diablo Sierra, Edwards Plateau, Guadalupe Mts., Staked Plain, Stockton Plateau. **People** (July, 2002 est.) 21,779,893 (2nd). Race/Hispanic Origin (2000 Census): White 71.0%. Black 11.5%. Indian 0.6%. Asian 2.7%. Pacific Islander 0.1%. Other 11.7%. Two or more races 2.5%. Hispanic 32.0%. **Cities** (2002) Houston 2,009,834. Dallas 1,211,467. San Antonio 1,194,222. Austin 671,873. El Paso 577,415. Fort Worth 567,516. Arlington 349,944. Corpus Christi 278,520. Plano 238,091. Garland 219,646. **Famous natives** Stephen Austin (b. Va.), pioneer. James "Jim" Bowie (b. Ky.), army officer. Carol Burnett, comedian. J. Frank Dobie, folklorist. Dwight D. Eisenhower, U.S. president/general. Samuel Houston (b. Va.), president Republic of Texas/governor State of Texas. Howard Hughes, industrialist/aviator. Lyndon Baines Johnson, U.S. president. Janis Joplin, singer. Barbara Jordan, politician. Audie Murphy, soldier/actor. Chester Nimitz, navy officer. Katherine Anne Porter, author. Samuel T. Rayburn, politician. Mildred "Babe" Didrikson Zaharias, athlete. **Tourist information** (800) 888-8TEX, ext. 728. www.traveltex.com.

Utah

www.utah.gov

Name For Ute Indians. **Nickname**s Beehive State, Mormon State. **Capital** Salt Lake City. **Entered Union** Jan. 4, 1896 (45th). **Motto**: "Industry." **Emblems** *Bird* California Gull. *Flower* Sego lily. *Song* "Utah, We Love Thee." *Tree* Blue spruce. **Land** Total area 84,899 sq. mi (13th), incl. 2,755 sq. mi. inland water. **Borders** Idaho, Wyo., Colo., Ariz., Nev. **Rivers** Bear, Colorado, Green, Sevier. **Lakes** Bear, Great Salt, Utah. Mountains La Sal, Uinta (Kings Peak 13,528 ft.) Wasatch Range. Other notable features Great Salt Lake Desert (Bonneville Salt Flats) Kaibab Plateau. **People** (July, 2002 est.) 2,316,256 (34th). Race/Hispanic Origin (2000 Census): White 89.2%. Black 0.8%. Indian 1.3%. Asian 1.7%. Pacific Islander 0.7%. Other 4.2%. Two or more races 2.1%. Hispanic 9.0%. **Cities** (2002) Salt Lake City 181,266. West Valley City 111,254. Provo 105,170. Sandy 89,244. Orem 83,662. Ogden 78,641. West Jordan 73,355. Layton 60,064. Taylorsville 59,115. St. George 54,049. **Famous natives** Maud Adams, actress. John Moses Browning, inventor. Philo Farnsworth, inventor of TV. Merlin Olsen, football player/actor. Brigham Young (b. Vt.), religious leader. Loretta Young, actress. **Tourist Information** (800) 200-1160. www.utah.gov.

Vermont

www.vermont.gov

Name From French vert mont, "green mountain." **Nickname** Green Mountain State. **Capital** Montpelier. **Entered Union** Mar. 4, 1791 (14th). **Motto** "Freedom and unity." **Emblems** *Bird* Hermit thrush. *Flower* Red Clover. *Song* "Hail, Vermont!" *Tree* Sugar Maple. **Land** Total Area 9,614 sq. mi (45th), incl. 365 sq. mi. inland water. **Borders** Quebec, N.H., Mass., N.Y. **Rivers** Connecticut, Lamoille, Otter Creek, Poultney, White, Winooski. **Lakes** Bomoseen, Champlain, Memphremagog, Willoughby. Other Notable Features Grand Isle, Green Mts. (Mt. Mansfield 4,393 ft.), Taconic Mts. **People** (July, 2002 est.) 616,592 (49th). Race/Hispanic Origin (2000 Census): White 96.8%. Black 0.5%. Indian 0.4%. Asian 0.9%. Other 0.2%. Two or more races 1.2%. Hispanic 0.9%. **Cities** (2002) Burlington 39,466. Rutland 17,098. South Burlington 15,870. **Famous natives** Ethan Allen (b. Conn.), army officer. Chester A. Arthur, U.S. President. Calvin Coolidge, U.S. president. John Deere, industrialist. George Dewey, naval officer. John Dewey, philosopher. Stephen Douglas, politician. James Fisk, financier. Robert Frost (b. Calif.), poet. Rudy Vallee, singer. **Tourist Information** (800) VERMONT. www.travel-vermont.com

Virginia, Commonwealth of

www.virginia.gov

Name For Elizabeth I, called Virgin Queen. **Nickname** Old Dominion, Mother of Presidents, Mother of States. **Capital** Richmond. **Entered union** June 25, 1788 (10th). **Motto** Sic semper tyrannis (Thus always to tyrants). **Emblems** *Bird* Cardinal. *Flower* Dogwood. *Song* "Carry Me Back to Old Virginia." *Tree* Dogwood. **Land** Total area 42,774 sq. mi (35th), incl. 3,180 sq. mi. inland water. **Borders** Md., D.C., Atlantic Ocean, N.C., Tenn., Ky., W.Va. **Rivers** James, Potomac, Rappahannock, Roanoke, Shenandoah, York. **Lakes** Buggs Island, Claytor, Gaston, Leesville. Mountains Allegheny, Blue

Ridge, Cumberland, Unaka. Other notable features Great Dismal Swamp, Shenandoah Valley. **People** (July, 2002 est.) 7,293,542 (12th). Race/Hispanic Origin (2000 Census): White 72.3%. Black 19.6%. Indian 0.3%. Asian 3.7%. Pacific Islander 0.1%. Other 2.0%. Two or more races 2.0%. Hispanic 4.7%. **Cities** (2002) Virginia Beach 433,934. Norfolk 239,036. Chesapeake 206,665. Richmond 197,456. Newport News 180,272. Hampton 145,921. Alexandria 130,084. Portsmouth 99,790. Roanoke 93,873. Suffolk 69,966. Famous natives Richard E. Byrd, explorer/aviator. William Clark, explorer. Jerry Falwell, evangelist. William Henry Harrison, U.S. president. Patrick Henry, Revolutionary patriot. Thomas Jefferson, U.S. president. Joseph E. Johnston, Confederate general. John Paul Jones (b. Scotland), navy officer. Robert E. Lee, Confederate general. Meriwether Lewis, explorer. James Madison, U.S. president. John Marshall, jurist. Cyrus Hall McCormick, inventor. James Monroe, U.S. president. Walter Reed, doctor. Pat Robertson, evangelist/politician. George C. Scott, actor. Thomas Sumter, army officer. Zachary Taylor, U.S. president. John Tyler, U.S. president. Booker T. Washington, educator. George Washington, U.S. president. Woodrow Wilson, U.S. president. **Tourist information** (800) VISIT-VA. www.virginia.org.

Washington

access.wa.gov

Name For George Washington. **Nickname** Evergreen State. **Capital** Olympia. **Entered union** Nov. 11, 1889 (42nd). **Motto** Alki (By and by). **Emblems** *Bird* Willow goldfinch. *Flower* Western rhododendron. *Song* "Washington, My Home." *Tree* Western hemlock. **Land** Total area 71,300 sq. mi (18th), incl. 4,756 sq. mi. inland water. **Borders** British Columbia, Idaho, Oreg., Pacific Ocean. **Rivers** Chehalis, Columbia, Pend Oreille, Snake, Yakima. **Lakes** Baker, Bank, Chelan, Franklin D. Roosevelt, Ross, Rufus Woods. Mountains Cascade Range, Coast Range, Kettle River Range, Olympic. Other notable features Puget Sound, San Juan Islands, Strait of Juan de Fuca. **People** (July, 2002 est.) 6,068,996 (15th). Race/Hispanic Origin (2000 Census): White 81.8%. Black 3.2%. Indian 1.6%. Asian 5.5%. Pacific Islander 0.4%. Other 3.9%. Two or more races 3.6%. Hispanic 7.5%. **Cities** (2002) Seattle 570,426. Tacoma 197,553. Spokane 196,305. Vancouver 149,811. Bellevue 112,894. Everett 97,088. Federal Way 82,174. Kent 81,724. Yakima 73,298. Bellingham 70,480. **Famous natives** Harry L. "Bing" Crosby, singer. Merce Cunningham, choreographer. Bill Gates, businessman. Jimi Hendrix, guitarist. Robert Joffrey, choreographer. Gary Larson, cartoonist. Edward R. Murrow, reporter (b. North Carolina). Theodore Roethke (b. Mich.), poet. Marcus Whitman (b. N.Y.), missionary/pioneer. **Tourist information** (800) 544-1800. access.tourism.wa.gov.

West Virginia

www.wv.gov

Name for western part of Virginia. **Nickname** Mountain State. **Capital** Charleston. **Entered union** June 20, 1863 (35th). **Motto** *Montani semper liberi* (Mountaineers are always free). **Emblems** *Bird* Cardinal. *Flower* Rhododendron maximum (big laurel). *Songs* "The West Virginia Hills," "West Virginia, My Home Sweet Home," "This Is My West Virginia." *Tree* Sugar maple. **Land** Total area 24,230 sq. mi (41st), incl. 152 sq. mi. inland water. **Borders** Ohio, Pa., Md., Va., Ky. **Rivers** Big Sandy, Guayandotte, Kanawha, Little Kanawha, Monongahela, Ohio, Potomac. **Lakes** Summersville Dam. Mountains Allegheny, Blue Ridge, Cumberland. **People** (July, 2002 est.) 1,801,873 (37th). Race/Hispanic Origin (2000 Census): White 95.0%. Black 3.2%. Indian 0.2%. Asian 0.5%. Other 0.2%. Two or more races 0.9%. Hispanic 0.7%. **Cities** (2002) Charleston 51,702. Huntington 49,910. Parkersburg 32,299. Wheeling 30,367. Morgantown 27,342. Weirton 20,027. Fairmont 19,026. Beckley 17,006. Clarksburg 16,498. Martinsburg 15,119. **Famous natives** Newton D. Baker, politician. Pearl Buck, novelist (Nobel Prize, 1938). John W. Davis, politician. Dwight Whitney Morrow, lawyer/"diplomat. Michael Owens, manufacturer. Walter Reuther, labor leader. Cyrus Vance, statesman. Jerry West, basketball player. Charles "Chuck" Yeager, pilot. **Tourist information** (800) CALL-WVA. www.callwva.com.

Wisconsin

www.wisconsin.gov

Name From the Ojibwa wishkonsing, "place of the bearer." **Nickname** Badger State. **Capital** Madison. **Entered union** May 29, 1848 (30th). **Motto** "Forward." **Emblems** *Bird* Robin. *Flower* Wood violet. *Song* "On, Wisconsin!" *Tree* Sugar maple. **Land** Total area 65,498 sq. mi (23rd), incl. 11,188 sq. mi. inland water. **Borders** Minn., Lake Superior, Mich., Lake Michigan, Ill., Iowa. **Rivers** Black, Chippewa, Menominee, Mississippi, St. Croix, Wisconsin. **Lakes** Chippewa, Du Bay, Mendota, Michigan, Superior, Winnebago. Other notable features Apostle Islands, Door Peninsula, Green Bay. **People** (July, 2002 est.) 5,441,196 (20th). Race/Hispanic Origin (2000 Census): White 88.9%. Black 5.7%. Indian 0.9%. Asian 1.7%. Other 1.6%. Two or more races 1.2%. Hispanic 3.6%. **Cities** (2002) Milwaukee 590,895. Madison 215,211. Green Bay 101,515. Kenosha 92,513. Racine 80,712. Appleton 70,633. Waukesha 66,186. Oshkosh 63,464. Eau Claire 62,361. Janesville 60,921. **Famous natives** King Camp Gillette, inventor/businessman. Eric Heiden, speed skater. Harry Houdini (b. Hungary), magician. Robert La Follette, politician. Liberace (Wladziu Valentino), pianist. Alfred Lunt, actor. Joseph R. McCarthy, politician. Spencer Tracy, actor. Thorstein Veblen, economist. Orson Welles, director. Laura Ingalls Wilder, novelist. Thornton Wilder, author. Frank Lloyd Wright, architect. **Tourist information** (800) 432-TRIP or (800) 372-2737. www.travelwisconsin.com.

Wyoming

www.wyoming.gov

Name From the Delaware maugh-wau-wa-ma, "large plains" or "mountains and valleys alternating." **Nickname** Equality State. **Capital** Cheyenne. **Entered union** July 10, 1890 (44th). **Motto** "Equal rights." **Emblems** *Bird* Meadowlark. *Flower* Indian paintbrush. *Song* "Wyoming." *Tree* Cottonwood. **Land** Total area 97,814 sq. mi (10th), incl. 713 sq. mi. inland water. **Borders** Mont., S.Dak., Nebr., Colo., Utah, Idaho. **Rivers** Bighorn, Green, North Platte, Powder, Snake, Yellowstone. **Lakes** Bighorn, Yellowstone. Mountains Absaroka, Bighorn, Black Hills, Laramie, Owl Creek, Teton Range, Wind River Range, Wyoming Range. **People** (July, 2002 est.) 498,703 (50th). Race/Hispanic Origin (2000 Census): White 92.1%. Black 0.8%. Indian 2.3%. Asian 0.6%. Pacific Islander 0.1%. Other 2.5%. Two or more races 1.8%. Hispanic 6.4%. **Cities** (2002) Cheyenne 53,658. Casper 50,024. Laramie 26,885. Gillette 21,130. Rock Springs 18,464. Sheridan 15,946. Green River 11,628. Evanston 11,448. **Famous natives** James Bridger (b. Va.), pioneer. J.C. Penney, businessman. Jackson Pollock, painter. Nellie Tayloe Ross (b. Mo.), politician. **Tourist information** (800) CALL-WYO. www.wyomingtourism.org.

50 Largest U.S. Cities, 2000

Between 1990 and 2000, the westward movement of the U.S. population again revealed its strength as four cities in the so-called Rust Belt (Buffalo, Cincinnati, Pittsburgh and Toledo) fell from the list of the 50 largest cities in the U.S. They were replaced by Colorado Springs, Las Vegas, Mesa, Ariz. and Wichita, Kansas.

Following are brief descriptions of the 50 largest cities in the U.S. according to numbers from the 2000 Census. They are set forth in alphabetical order.

Albuquerque, New Mexico

Population 448,607 (2000). **Rank**: 35th. **Race/ Hispanic Origin** (2000): White 71.6%. Black 3.1%. Indian 3.9%. Asian 2.2%. Pacific Islander 0.1%. Other 14.8%. Two or more races 4.3%. Hispanic 39.9%. **Location**: 35°05'N, 106°47'W. **County**: Bernalillo. **Terrain and climate** *Elev*.: 5,300 ft. *Area*: 127.2 sq. mi. (329.4 sq km). *Avg. daily min. temp*.: Jan.: 22.3°F/-5.3°C; *avg. daily max*. July: 92.8°F/33.7°C. *Avg. annual*: rainfall, 8.12"; snowfall, 11". **Visitor info**: (505) 842-9918 or (800) 284-2282. www.cabq.gov.

Atlanta, Georgia

Population 416,474 (2000). **Rank**: 39th. **Race/ Hispanic Origin** (2000): White 33.2%. Black 61.4%. Indian 0.2%. Asian 1.9%. Other 2.0%. Two or more races 1.2%. Hispanic 4.5%. **Location**: 33°50'N, 84°24'W. **County**: Fulton. **Terrain and climate** *Elev*.: 1,034 ft. *Area*: 131.2 sq. mi. (339.80 sq km). *Avg. daily min. temp*.: Jan.: 32.6°F/0.3°C; *avg. daily max*. July: 87.9°F/31°C. *Avg. annual*: rainfall, 48.61"; snowfall, 2"; clear days, 108; precipitation days, 116. **Visitor info**: (800) ATLANTA. www.atlanta.net.

Austin, Texas

Population 656,562 (2000). **Rank**: 16th. **Race/ Hispanic Origin** (2000): White 65.4%. Black 10.0%. Indian 0.6%. Asian 4.7%. Pacific Islander 0.1%. Other 16.2%. Two or more races 3.0%. Hispanic 30.5%. **Location**: 30°20'N, 97°45W. Counties: Travis, Williamson **Terrain and climate** *Elev*.: 570 ft. *Area*: 232 sq. mi. (600.9 sq km). *Avg. daily min*. temp.: Jan.: 38.8°F/3.8°C; *avg. daily max*. July: 95.4°F/35.2°C. *Avg. annual*: rainfall, 31.50"; snowfall, 1"; clear days, 115; precipitation days, 82. **Visitor info**: (866) GO-AUSTIN or (512) 583-7234. www.austintexas.org.

Baltimore, Maryland

Population 651,154 (2000). **Rank**: 17th. **Race/Hispanic Origin** (2000): White 31.6%. Black 64.3%. Indian 0.3%. Asian 1.5%. Other 0.7%. Two or more races 1.5%. Hispanic 1.7%. **Location**: 39°18'N, 76°37'W. County: independent city within Baltimore County. **Terrain and climate** *Elev*.: 155 ft. *Area*: 80.3 sq. mi. (208 sq km). *Avg. daily min*. temp.: Jan.: 24.3°F/-4.2°C; *avg. daily max*. July: 87.1°F/30.6°C. *Avg. annual*: rainfall, 43.39"; snowfall, 22"; clear days, 106; precipitation days, 112. **Visitor info**: (877) BALTIMORE. www.baltimore.org.

Boston, Massachusetts

Population 589,141 (2000). **Rank**: 20th. **Race/ Hispanic Origin** (2000): White 54.5%. Black 25.3%. Indian 0.4%. Asian 7.5%. Pacific Islander 0.1%. Other

7.8%. Two or more races 4.4%. Hispanic 14.4%. **Location**: 42°20'N, 71°05'W. County: Suffolk.**Terrain and climate** *Elev*.: 10 ft.*Area*: 47.2 sq. mi. (122.2 sq km). *Avg. daily min. temp*.: Jan.: 22.8°F/-5.1°C; *avg. daily max*. July: 81.8°F/27.6°C. *Avg. annual*: rainfall, 43.81"; snowfall, 42"; clear days, 99; precipitation days, 128. **Visitor info**: (888) 733-2678 or (617) 536-4100. www.bostonusa.com

Charlotte, North Carolina

Population 540,828 (2000). **Rank**: 26th. **Race/Hispanic Origin** (2000): White 58.3%. Black 32.7%. Indian 0.3%. Asian 3.4%. Pacific Islander 0.1%. Other 3.6%. Two or more races 1.7%. Hispanic 7.4%. **Location**: 35°16'N, 80°46'W. County: Mecklenburg. **Terrain and climate** *Elev*.: 665 ft.*Area*: 152.1 sq. mi. (393.9 sq km).*Avg. daily min. temp*.: Jan.: 30.7°F/-0.7°C; *avg. daily max*. July: 88.3°F/31.2°C.*Avg. annual*: rainfall, 43.16"; snowfall, 6"; clear days, 111; precipitation days, 111. **Visitor Info**: (800) 231-4636 or (704) 331-2700. www.visitcharlotte.org.

Chicago, Illinois

Population 2,896,016 (2000). **Rank**: 3rd. **Race/Hispanic Origin** (2000): White 42.0%. Black 36.8%. Indian 0.4%. Asian 4.3%. Pacific Islander 0.1%. Other 13.6%. Two or more races 2.9%. Hispanic 26.0%. **Location**: 41°53'N, 87°40'W. County: Cook.**Terrain and climate** *Elev*.: 623 ft.*Area*: 228.1 sq. mi. (590.8 sq km). *Avg. daily min. temp*.: Jan.: 13.6°F/-10.2°C; *avg. daily max*. July: 83.3°F/28.5°C. *Avg. annual*: rainfall, 33.34"; snowfall, 40"; clear days, 94; precipitation days, 123. **Visitor info**: (877) CHICAGO. or (312) 744-2400. www.877chicago.com.

Cleveland, Ohio

Population 478,403 (2000). **Rank**: 33rd. **Race/Hispanic Origin** (2000): White 41.5%. Black 51.0%. Indian 0.3%. Asian 1.3%. Other 3.6%. Two or more races 2.2%. Hispanic 7.3%. **Location**: 41°28'N, 81°43'W. County: Cuyahoga.**Terrain and climate** Elev.: 805 ft. *Area*: 79 sq. mi. (204.6 sq km). *Avg. daily min. temp*.: Jan.: 18.5°F/-7.5°C; *avg. daily max*. July: 81.7°F/27.6°C. *Avg. annual*: rainfall, 35.40"; snowfall, 52"; clear days, 70; precipitation days, 156. **Visitor Info**: (800) 321-1001 or (216) 621-4110.www.travelcleveland.com

Colorado Springs, Colorado

Population 360,890 (2000). **Rank**: 48th. **Race/Hispanic Origin** (2000): White 80.7%. Black 6.6%. Indian 0.9%. Asian 2.8%. Pacific Islander 0.2%. Other 5.0%. Two or more races 3.9%. Hispanic 12.0%. **Location**: 38°48'N, 104°42'W. County: El Paso.**Terrain and climate** *Elev*. 6,145 ft. *Area* 183.2 sq. mi. (474.5 sq km).*Avg. daily min. temp*.: Jan.: 16.1°F/−8.8°C; *avg. daily max*. July: 86.5°F/30.3°C.*Avg. annual:* rainfall, 16.24"; snowfall, 51"; clear days, 129; precipitation days, 98. **Visitor info**: (800) 888-4748. www.coloradosprings-travel.com.

Columbus, Ohio

Population 711,470 (2000). **Rank**: 15th. **Race/Hispanic Origin** (2000): White 67.9%. Black 24.5%. Indian 0.3%. Asian 3.4%. Pacific Islander 0.1%. Other 1.2%. Two or more races 2.6%. Hispanic 2.5%. **Location**: 39°57'N, 83°01'W. Counties: Fairfield, Franklin. **Terrain and climate** *Elev*.: 833 ft.*Area*: 186.8 sq. mi. (483.8 sq km).*Avg. daily min. temp*.: Jan.: 19.4°F/-7°C; *avg. daily max*. July: 84.4°F/29.1°C. *Avg. annual*: rainfall, 36.97"; snowfall, 28"; clear days, 75; precipitation days, 136. **Visitor info**: (800) 345-4FUN. www.experiencecolumbus.com.

Dallas, Texas

Population 1,188,580 (2000). **Rank**: 8th. **Race/Hispanic Origin** (2000): White 50.8%. Black 25.9%. Indian 0.5%. Asian 2.7%. Other 17.2%. Two or more races 2.7%. Hispanic 35.6%. Location: 32°50'N, 96°50'W. Counties: Collin, Dallas, Denton, Kaufman, Rockwall. **Terrain and climate** *Elev*.: 596 ft.*Area*: 331.4 sq. mi. (858.3 sq km).*Avg. daily min*. temp.: Jan.: 33.9°F/1°C; *avg. daily max*. July: 97.8°F/36.5°C.*Avg. annual*: rainfall, 34.16"; snowfall, 3"; clear days, 138; precipitation days, 79. **Visitor info**: (800) CDALLAS or (214) 571-1000 www.visitdallas.com

Denver, Colorado

Population 554,636 (2000). **Rank**: 25th. **Race/Hispanic Origin** (2000): White 65.3%. Black 11.1%. Indian 1.3%. Asian 2.8%. Pacific Islander 0.1%. Other 15.6%. Two or more races 3.7%. Hispanic 31.7%. **Location**: 39°45'N, 105°00'W. County: Denver. **Terrain and climate** *Elev*.: 5,280 ft.*Area*: 106.8 sq. mi. (276.6 sq km).*Avg. daily min*. temp.: Jan.: 15.9°F/-8.9°C; *avg. daily max*. July: 88°F/31°C. Avg. annual: rainfall, 15.31"; snowfall, 60"; clear days, 115; precipitation days, 88. **Visitor info**: (800) 233-6837 or (303)-892-1505 www.denver.org

Detroit, Michigan

Population 951,270 (2000). **Rank**: 10th. **Race/Hispanic Origin** (2000): White 12.3%. Black 81.6%. Indian 0.3%. Asian 1.0%. Other 2.5%. Two or more races

2.3%. Hispanic 5.0%. **Location**: 42°23'N, 83°05'W. County: Wayne. **Terrain and climate** *Elev.*: 581 ft. *Area*: 135.6 sq. mi. (351.2 sq km). *Avg. daily min.* temp.: Jan.: 16.1°F/-8.8°C; *avg. daily max.* July: 83.1°F/28.3°C. *Avg. annual*: rainfall, 30.97"; snowfall, 39"; clear days, 75; precipitation days, 133. **Visitor info**: (800) DETROIT or (313) 202-1800.www.visitdetroit.com

El Paso, Texas

Population 563,662 (2000). **Rank**: 23rd. **Race/ Hispanic Origin** (2000): White 73.3%. Black 3.1%. Indian 0.8%. Asian 1.1%. Pacific Islander 0.1%. Other 18.2%. Two or more races 3.4%. Hispanic 76.6%. **Location**: 31°50'N, 106°30'W. County: El Paso. **Terrain and climate** *Elev.*: 3,700 ft. *Area*: 239.7 sq. mi. (620.8 sq km). *Avg. daily min. temp.*: Jan.: 30.4°F/-0.8°C; *avg. daily max.* July: 95.3°F/"35.1°C. *Avg. annual*: rainfall, 7.82"; snowfall, 5"; clear days, 194; precipitation days, 45. **Visitor info**: (800) 351-6024 or (915) 534-0600.www.visitelpaso.com/

Fort Worth, Texas

Population 534,694 (2000). **Rank**: 27th. **Race/ Hispanic Origin** (2000): White 59.7%. Black 20.3%. Indian 0.6%. Asian 2.6%. Pacific Islander 0.1%. Other 14.0%. Two or more races 2.7%. Hispanic 29.8%. **Location** 32°45'N, 97°25'W. County: Tarrant. **Terrain and climate** *Elev.*: 670 ft. *Area*: 258.5 sq. mi. (670.3 sq km). *Avg. daily min. temp.*: Jan.: 33.9°F/1°C; *avg. daily max.* July: 97.8°F/36.5°C. *Avg. annual*: rainfall, 29.45"; snowfall, 1.4"; clear days, 137; precipitation days, 78. **Visitor info**: (800) 433-5747 or (817) 336-8791. www.fortworth.com.

Fresno, California

Population 427,652 (2000). **Rank**: 37th. **Race/ Hispanic Origin** (2000): White 50.2%. Black 8.4%. Indian 1.6%. Asian 11.2%. Pacific Islander 0.1%. Other 23.4%. Two or more races 5.2%. Hispanic 39.9%. **Location** 36°47'N, 119°50'W. County: Fresno. **Terrain and climate** *Elev.* 328 ft.; *Area*: 99.4 sq. mi. (257 sq. km). *Avg. daily min. temp.* Jan.: 37.4°/3°C; *avg. daily max.* July: 98°.7F/37°C. *Avg. annual* rainfall: 10"; snowfall 0"; clear days: 200; precipitation days: 44 . **Visitor info**: (800) 788-0836 or (559) 233-0836.www.fresnocvb.org.

Honolulu, Hawaii

Population 371,657 (2000). **Rank**: 46th. **Race/ Hispanic Origin** (2000): White 19.7%. Black 1.6%. Indian 0.2%. Asian 55.9%. Pacific Islander 6.8%. Other 0.9%. Two or more races 14.9%. Hispanic 4.4%. **Location**: 21°19'N, 157°52'W. County: Honolulu. **Terrain and climate** *Elev.*: 15 ft. *Area*: 25.3 sq. mi. (65.52 sq km). *Avg. daily min. temp.*: Jan.: 65.3°F/18.5°C; *avg. daily max.* July: 87.1°F/30.6°C. *Avg. annual rainfall*: 23.47"; snowfall: 0"; clear days: 90; precipitation days: 102. **Visitor info**: (877) 525-OAHU.www.gohawaii.com

Houston, Texas

Population 1,953,631 (2000). **Rank**: 4th. **Race/ Hispanic Origin** (2000): White 49.3%. Black 25.3%. Indian 0.4%. Asian 5.3%. Pacific Islander 0.1%. Other 16.5%. Two or more races 3.1%. Hispanic 37.4%. **Location**: 29°50'N, 95°20'W. Counties: Fort Bend, Harris, Montgomery. **Terrain and climate** *Elev.*: 49 ft. *Area*: 572.7 sq. mi. (1,483.3 sq km). *Avg. daily min. temp.*: Jan.: 40.8°F/4.8°C; *avg. daily max.* July: 93.6°F/34.2°C. *Avg. annual* rainfall: 44.77"; snowfall: 0"; clear days: 94; precipitation days: 107. **Visitor info**: (800) 4HOUSTON. www.houston-spacecityusa.com

Indianapolis, Indiana

Population 791,926 (2000). **Rank**: 12th. **Race/ Hispanic Origin** (2000): White 69.3%. Black 25.3%. Indian 0.3%. Asian 1.4%. Pacific Islander 0.0%. Other 2.0%. Two or more races 1.6%. Hispanic 3.9%. **Location** 39°42'N, 86°10'W. County: Marion. **Terrain and climate** *Elev.*: 808 ft. *Area*: 352 sq. mi. (911.7 sq km). *Avg. daily min. temp.*: Jan.: 17.8°F/-7.8°C; *avg. daily max.* July: 85.2°F/29.5°C. *Avg. annual* rainfall: 39.12"; snowfall: 21"; clear days: 90; precipitation days: 122. **Visitor info**: __1-800-323-4639 or (317) 639-4282. www.visitindy.info.

Jacksonville, Florida

Population 735,617 (2000). **Rank**: 14th. **Race/ Hispanic Origin** (2000): White 64.5%. Black 29.0%. Indian 0.3%. Asian 2.8%. Pacific Islander 0.1%. Other 1.3%. Two or more races 2.0%. Hispanic 4.2%. **Location**: 30°15'N, 81°38'W. County: Duval. **Terrain and climate** *Elev.*: 31 ft. *Area*: 840 sq. mi. (1,967.6 sq km). *Avg. daily min. temp.*: Jan.: 41.7°F/ °C; *avg. daily max.* July: 90.7°F/29.5°C. *Avg. annual* rainfall: 52.77"; snowfall: 0"; clear days: 98; precipitation days: 116. **Visitor info**: 1-800-733-2668 or (904) 353-9736. www.visitjacksonville.com

Kansas City, Missouri

Population 441,545 (2000). **Rank**: 36th. **Race/Hispanic Origin** (2000): White 60.7%. Black 31.2%. Indian 0.5%.

Asian 1.9%. Pacific Islander 0.1%. Other 3.2%. Two or more races 2.4%. Hispanic 6.9%. **Location**: 39°07'N, 94°38'W. Counties: Cass, Clay, Jackson, and Platte. **Terrain and climate** *Elev.*: 744 ft. *Area*: 316.4 sq. mi. (819.5 sq km). *Avg. daily min. temp.*: Jan.: 17.2°F/-8.2°C; *avg. daily max.* July: 88.5°F/31.3°C. Avg. annual rainfall: 29.27"; snowfall: 5.9"; clear days: 132; precipitation days: 97. **Visitor info**: (800) 767-7700. www.visitkc.com

Las Vegas, Nevada

Population 478,434 (2000). **Rank**: 32nd. **Race/Hispanic Origin** (2000): White 69.9%. Black 10.4%. Indian 0.7%. Asian 4.8%. Pacific Islander 0.4%. Other 9.7%. Two or more races 4.1%. Hispanic 23.6%. Location: 36° 05'N, 115°10'W. County: Clark. **Terrain and climate** *Elev.*: 2,162 ft. *Area*: 83.3 sq. mi. (215.7 sq km). *Avg. daily min. temp.*: Jan.: 33.6°F/0.9°C; *avg. daily max.* July: 105.9°F/41.1°C. *Avg. annual* rainfall: 4"; snowfall: 1"; clear days: 211; precipitation days: 26. **Visitor info**: (877) VISIT-LV or (702) 892–7575. www.vegasfreedom.com.

Long Beach, California

Population: 461,522 (2000). **Rank**: 34th. **Race/Hispanic Origin** (2000): White 45.2%. Black 14.9%. Indian 0.8%. Asian 12.0%. Pacific Islander 1.2%. Other 20.6%. Two or more races 5.3%. Hispanic 35.8%. **Location**: 33°46'N, 118°10'W. County: Los Angeles. **Terrain and climate** *Elev.*: 35 ft. *Area*: 49.8 sq. mi. (129 sq km). *Avg. daily min. temp.*: Jan.: 44.3°F/6.8°C; *avg. daily max.* July: 83°F/28.3°C. *Avg. annual* rainfall: 12"; snowfall: 0"; clear days: 143; precipitation days: 35. **Visitor info**: (800) 4LB-STAY or (562) 436-3645. www.visitlongbeach.com

Los Angeles, California

Population 3,694,820 (2000). **Rank**: 2nd. **Race/Hispanic Origin** (2000): White 46.9%. Black 11.2%. Indian 0.8%. Asian 10.0%. Pacific Islander 0.2%. Other 25.7%. Two or more races 5.2%. Hispanic 46.5%. **Location**: 34°00'N, 118°10'W. County: Los Angeles. **Terrain and climate** *Elev.*: 104 ft. *Area*: 465.9 sq. mi. (1206.7 sq km). *Avg. daily min. temp.*: Jan.: 47.3°F/8.5°C; *avg. daily max.* July: 75.3°F/24°C. *Avg. annual* rainfall: 14.85"; snowfall: 0"; clear days: 143; precipitation days: 35. **Visitor info**: (800) 228-2450. www.visitlanow.com

Memphis, Tennessee

Population 650,100 (2000). **Rank**: 18th. **Race/Hispanic Origin** (2000): White 34.4%. Black 61.4%. Indian 0.2%. Asian 1.5%. Pacific Islander 0.0%. Other 1.5%. Two or more races 1.0%. Hispanic 3.0%. **Location**: 35'07'N, 90°00'W. County: Shelby. **Terrain and climate** *Elev.*: 307 ft. *Area*: 264.1 sq. mi. (684 sq km). *Avg. daily min. temp.*: Jan.: 30.9°F/-0.6°C; *avg. daily max.* July: 91.5°F/33°C. *Avg. annual rainfall*: 51.57"; snowfall: 6"; clear days: 118; precipitation days: 106. **Visitor info**: (800) 873-6282 or (901) 543-5300.www.memphistravel.com.

Mesa, Arizona

Population 396,375 (2000). **Rank**: 42nd. **Race/Hispanic Origin** (2000): White 81.7%. Black 2.5%. Indian 1.7%. Asian 1.5%. Pacific Islander 0.2%. Other 9.7%. Two or more races 2.8%. Hispanic 19.7%. **Location**: 33°N, 112°W. County: Maricopa. **Terrain and climate** *Elev.*: 1,241 ft. *Area*: 124.62 sq. mi. *Avg. daily min temp.*: Jan.: 35.6°F/2°C; *avg. daily max.* July: 104.3°F/40.16°C. *Avg. annual*: rainfall, 7.52"; snowfall, 0"; clear days, 320; precipitation days, 45. **Visitor info**: (480) 827-4700 or (800) 283-6372. www.visitmesa.com

Miami, Florida

Population 362,470 (2000). *Rank*: 47th. Race/Hispanic Origin (2000): White 66.6%. Black 22.3%. Indian 0.2%. Asian 0.7%. Other 5.4%. Two or more races 4.7%. Hispanic 65.8%. **Location**: 25°45'N, 80°15'W. County: Dade. **Terrain and climate** *Elev.*: 12 ft. *Area*: 34.3 sq. mi. (88.8 sq km). *Avg. daily min. temp.*: Jan.: 59.2°F/15.1°C; *avg. daily max.* July: 88.7°F/31.5°C. *Avg. annual* rainfall: 57.55"; snowfall: 0"; clear days: 76; precipitation days: 129. **Visitor info**: (800) 933-8448 or (305) 539-3000.www.miamiandbeaches.com.

Milwaukee, Wisconsin

Population 596,974 (2000). **Rank**: 19th. **Race/Hispanic Origin** (2000): White 50.0%. Black 37.3%. Indian 0.9%. Asian 2.9%. Pacific Islander 0.1%. Other 6.1%. Two or more races 2.7%. Hispanic 12.0%. **Location**: 43°09'N, 87°58'W. County: Milwaukee. **Terrain and climate** *Elev.*: 581 ft. *Area*: 95.8 sq. mi. (248.1 sq km). *Avg. daily min. temp.*: Jan.: 11.3°F/-11.5°C; *avg. daily max.* July: 79.8°F/26.5°C. Avg. annual rainfall: 30.94"; snowfall: 45"; clear days: 96; precipitation days: 122. **Visitor info**: (800) 554-1448 or (414) 273-7222. www.milwaukee.org

Minneapolis, Minnesota

Population 382,618 (2000). **Rank**: 45th. **Race/Hispanic Origin** (2000): White 65.1%. Black 18.0%.

Indian 2.2%. Asian 6.1%. Pacific Islander 0.1%. Other 4.1%. Two or more races 4.4%. Hispanic 7.6%. **Location**: 44°58'N, 93°20'W. County: Hennepin. **Terrain and climate** *Elev.*: 828 ft. *Area:* 55.1 sq. mi. (142.7 sq km). *Avg. daily min. temp.*: Jan.: 2.4°F/-16.4°C; *avg. daily max.* July: 83.4°F/28.5°C. *Avg. annual* rainfall: 26.36"; snowfall: 46"; clear days: 100; precipitation days: 113. **Visitor info**: (888)_676-6757 www.minneapolis.org.

Nashville, Tennessee

Population 569,891 (2000). **Rank**: 22nd. **Race/ Hispanic Origin** (2000): White 67.0%. Black 25.9%. Indian 0.3%. Asian 2.3%. Pacific Islander 0.1%. Other 2.4%. Two or more races 2.0%. Hispanic 4.6%. **Location**: 36°12'N, 86°46'W. County: Davidson. **Terrain and climate** *Elev.*: 605 ft. *Area*: 479.5 sq. mi. (1241.9 sq km). *Avg. daily min. temp.*: Jan.: 27.8°F/-2.3°C; *avg. daily max.* July: 89.8°F/32.1°C. *Avg. annual* rainfall: 48.49"; snowfall: 10.7"; clear days: 103; precipitation days: 119. **Visitor info**: (800) 657-6910 or (615) 743-3000. www.nashvillecvb.com.

New Orleans, Louisiana

Population 484,674 (2000). **Rank**: 31st. **Race/ Hispanic Origin** (2000): White 28.1%. Black 67.3%. Indian 0.2%. Asian 2.3%. Pacific Islander 0.0%. Other 0.9%. Two or more races 1.3%. Hispanic 3.1%. **Location**: 30°00'W., 90°05'W. Parish: Orleans. **Terrain and climate** *Elev.*: 30 ft. *Area*: 199.4 sq. mi. (516.4 sq km). *Avg. daily min. temp.*: Jan.: 43°F/6.1°C; *avg. daily max.*: July: 90.7°F/32.6°C. *Avg. annual* rainfall: 59.74"; snowfall: 0.2"; clear days: 109; precipitation days: 113. **Visitor info**: (800) 672-6124. www.www.visitneworleans.info.

New York City, New York

Population 8,008,278 (2000). **Rank**: 1st. **Race/ Hispanic Origin** (2000): White 44.7%. Black 26.6%. Indian 0.5%. Asian 9.8%. Pacific Islander 0.1%. Other 13.4%. Two or more races 4.9%. Hispanic 27.0%. **Location**: 40°45'N, 74°00'W. Counties: Bronx, Kings, New York, Queens, and Richmond. **Terrain and climate** *Elev.*: 87 ft. *Area*: 301.5 sq. mi. (780.9 sq km). *Avg. daily min. temp.*: Jan.: 25.6°F/-3.5°C; *avg. daily max.* July: 85.3°F/29.6°C. *Avg. annual* rainfall: 44.12"; snowfall: 29"; clear days: 107; precipitation days: 121. **Visitor info**: (212) 484-1200. www.nycvisit.com.

Oakland, California

Population 399,484 (2000). *Rank*: 41st. **Race/Hispanic Origin** (2000): White 31.3%. Black 35.7%. Indian 0.7%. Asian 15.2%. Pacific Islander 0.5%. Other 11.7%. Two or more races 5.0%. Hispanic 21.9%. **Location**: 37°50'N, 122°18'W. County: Alameda. **Terrain and climate** *Elev.*: 42 ft. *Area*: 53.9 sq. mi. (139.6 sq km). *Avg. daily min. temp.*: Jan.: 43.4°F/6.3°C; *avg. daily max.* July: 70.6°F/29.6°C. *Avg. annual* rainfall: 18.03"; snowfall: N.A.; clear days: N.A; precipitation days: N.A. **Visitor info**: (800) 262-5526 or (510) 839-9000.www.oaklandcvb.com.

Oklahoma City, Oklahoma

Population 506,132 (2000). **Rank**: 29th. **Race/ Hispanic Origin** (2000): White 68.4%. Black 15.4%. Indian 3.5%. Asian 3.5%. Pacific Islander 0.1%. Other 5.3%. Two or more races 3.9%. Hispanic 10.1%. **Location**: 35°25'N, 97°30'W. Counties: Canadian, Cleveland, McClain, Oklahoma. **Terrain and climate** *Elev.*: 1,304 ft. *Area*: 604 sq. mi. (1,564.4 sq km). *Avg. daily min.* temp.: Jan.: 25.2°F/-3.7°C; *avg. daily max.* July: 93.5°F/34.1°C. *Avg. annual*: rainfall, 30.89"; snowfall, 9"; clear days, 141; precipitation days, 81. **Visitor info**: (800) 225-5652 or (405) 297-8912. www.okccvb.org.

Omaha, Nebraska

Population 390,007 (2000). **Rank**: 44th. **Race/ Hispanic Origin** (2000): White 78.4%. Black 13.3%. Indian 0.7%. Asian 1.7%. Pacific Islander 0.1%. Other 3.9%. Two or more races 1.9%. Hispanic 7.5%. **Location**: 41°15'N, 95°55'W. County: Douglas. **Terrain and climate** *Elev.*: 982 ft. *Area*: 99.3 sq. mi. (257.2 sq km). *Avg. daily min. temp.*: Jan.: 10.2°F/-12.1°C; *avg. daily max.* July: 88.5°F/31.3°C. *Avg. annual* rainfall: 30.34"; snowfall: 32"; clear days: 113; precipitation days: 99. **Visitor info**: (866) YES-OMAHA. www.visit omaha.com.

Philadelphia, Pennsylvania

Population 1,517,550 (2000). **Rank**: 5th. **Race/ Hispanic Origin** (2000): White 45.0%. Black 43.2%. Indian 0.3%. Asian 4.5%. Other 4.8%. Two or more races 2.2%. Hispanic 8.5%. Location: 40°00'N, 75°10'W. County: Philadelphia. **Terrain and climate** *Elev.*: 28 ft. *Area*: 136 sq. mi. (352.2 sq km). *Avg. daily min. temp.*: Jan.: 23.8°F/-4.5°C; *avg. daily max.* July: 86.1°F/30°C. Avg. annual rainfall: 41.42"; snowfall: 20"; clear days: 92; precipitation days: 116. **Visitor info**: (800) CALL-PHL or (215) 636-3300. www.gophila.com.

Phoenix, Arizona

Population 1,321,045 (2000). **Rank:** 6th. **Race/Hispanic Origin** (2000): White 71.1%. Black 5.1%. Indian 2.0%. Asian 2.0%. Pacific Islander 0.1%. Other 16.4%. Two or more races 3.3%. Hispanic 34.1%. **Location:** 33°30'N, 112°04'W. County: Maricopa. **Terrain and climate** *Elev.*: 1,117 ft. *Area*: 375 sq. mi. (971.3 sq km). *Avg. daily min. temp.*: Jan.: 44.4°F/6.8°C; *avg. daily max.* July: 107.5°F/41°C. *Avg. annual* rainfall: 7.11"; snowfall: 0"; clear days: 214; precipitation days: 34. **Visitor info:** (877) CALL-PHX or (602) 254-6500. www.visitphoenix.com.

Portland, Oregon

Population 529,121 (2000). **Rank:** 28th. **Race/Hispanic Origin** (2000): White 77.9%. Black 6.6%. Indian 1.1%. Asian 6.3%. Pacific Islander 0.4%. Other 3.5%. Two or more races 4.1%. Hispanic 6.8%. **Location:** 45°35'N, 122°40'W. Counties: Clackamas, Multnomah, Washington. **Terrain and climate** *Elev.*: 39 ft. *Area*: 113.9 sq. mi. (295 sq km). *Avg. daily min. temp.*: Jan.: 33.5°F/0.8°C; *avg. daily max.* July: 79.5°F/26.3°C. *Avg. annual* rainfall: 37.39"; snowfall: 7"; clear days: 69; precipitation days: 152. **Visitor info:** (877) PORTLAND. www.travel-portland.com.

Sacramento, California

Population 407,018 (2000). **Rank:** 40th. **Race/Hispanic Origin** (2000): White 48.3%. Black 15.5%. Indian 1.3%. Asian 16.6%. Pacific Islander 0.9%. Other 11.0%. Two or more races 6.4%. Hispanic 21.6%. **Location:** 38°33'N, 121°30'W. County: Sacramento. **Terrain and climate** *Elev.*: 25 ft. *Area*: 97.3 sq. mi. (252 sq km). *Avg. daily min. temp.*: Jan.: 37.9°F/3.2°C; *avg. daily max.* July: 93.3°F/34°C. *Avg. annual* rainfall: 17.87"; snowfall: 0.1"; clear days: 193; precipitation days: 57. **Visitor info:** (800) 292-2334 or (916) 264-7777. www.sacramentocvb.org.

San Antonio, Texas

Population 1,144,646 (2000). **Rank:** 9th. **Race/Hispanic Origin** (2000): White 67.7%. Black 6.8%. Indian 0.8%. Asian 1.6%. Pacific Islander 0.1%. Other 19.3%. Two or more races 3.7%. Hispanic 58.7%. **Location:** 29°30'N, 98°30'W. County: Bexar. **Terrain and climate** *Elev.*: 701 ft. *Area*: 304.5 sq. mi. (788.7 sq km). *Avg. daily min. temp.*: Jan.: 39°F/3.8°C; *avg. daily max.* July: 96.3°F/35.7°C. *Avg. annual* rainfall: 29.13"; snowfall: 0.5"; clear days: 110; precipitation days: 81. **Visitor info:** (800) 447-3372 or (210) 270-8700. www.sanantoniovisit.com.

San Diego, California

Population 1,223,400 (2000). **Rank:** 7th. **Race/Hispanic Origin** (2000): White 60.2%. Black 7.9%. Indian 0.6%. Asian 13.6%. Pacific Islander 0.5%. Other 12.4%. Two or more races 4.8%. Hispanic 25.4%. **Location:** 32°43'N, 117°10'W. County: San Diego. **Terrain and climate** *Elev.*: 13 ft. *Area*: 329 sq. mi. (852.1 sq km). *Avg. daily min. temp.*: Jan.: 48.4°F/9.1°C; *avg. daily max.* July: 75.6°F/24.2°C. Avg. annual rainfall: 9.32"; snowfall: 0"; clear days: 150; precipitation days: 41. **Visitor info:** (619) 236-1212. www.sandiego.org.

San Francisco, California

Population 776,733 (2000). **Rank:** 13th. **Race/Hispanic Origin** (2000): White 49.7%. Black 7.8%. Indian 0.4%. Asian 30.8%. Pacific Islander 0.5%. Other 6.5%. Two or more races 4.3%. Hispanic 14.1%. **Location:** 37°47'N, 122°30'W. County: San Francisco. **Terrain and climate** *Elev.*: 155 ft. *Area*: 46.4 sq. mi. (120.2 sq km). *Avg. daily min. temp.*: Jan.: 41.5°F/5.2°C; *avg. daily max.* July: 71°F/21°C. *Avg. annual* rainfall: 19.71"; snowfall: 0"; clear days: 162; precipitation days: 67. **Visitor info:** (415) 391-2000. www.sfvisitor.org.

San Jose, California

Population 894,943 (2000). **Rank:** 11th. **Race/Hispanic Origin** (2000): White 47.5%. Black 3.5%. Indian 0.8%. Asian 26.9%. Pacific Islander 0.4%. Other 15.9%. Two or more races 5.0%. Hispanic 30.2%. **Location:** 37°20'N, 121°53'W. County: Santa Clara. **Terrain and climate** *Elev.*: 65 ft. *Area*: 169.2 sq. mi. (438.2 sq km). *Avg. daily min. temp.*: Jan.: 41.1°F/5°C; *avg. daily max.*: July: 81.5°F/27.5°C. Avg. annual rainfall: 13.86"; snowfall: 0"; clear days: N.A.; precipitation days: N.A. **Visitor info:** (888) SAN JOSE. www.sanjose.org.

Seattle, Washington

Population 563,374 (2000). **Rank:** 24th. **Race/Hispanic Origin** (2000): White 70.1%. Black 8.4%. Indian 1.0%. Asian 13.1%. Pacific Islander 0.5%. Other 2.4%. Two or more races 4.5%. Hispanic 5.3%. **Location:** 47°41'N, 122°15'W. County: King. **Terrain and climate** *Elev.*: 450 ft. *Area*: 83.6 sq. mi. (216.5 sq km). *Avg. daily min. temp.*: Jan.: 34.3°F/1.2°C; avg. *daily max.*: July: 75.2°F/24°C. *Avg. annual* rainfall: 38.85"; snowfall: 15"; clear days: 57; precipitation days: 160. **Visitor info:** (206) 461-5840. www.seeseattle.org.

St. Louis, Missouri

Population 348,189 (2000). **Rank**: 49th. **Race/ Hispanic Origin** (2000): White 43.8%. Black 51.2%. Indian 0.3%. Asian 2.0%. Other 0.8%. Two or more races 1.9%. Hispanic 2.0%. **Location**: 38°40'N, 90°12'W. County: independent city. **Terrain and climate** *Elev.*: 564 ft. *Area*: 61.4 sq. mi. (159 sq km). *Avg. daily min. temp.*: Jan.: 19.9°F/-6.7°C; *avg. daily max.* July: 89°F/31°C. *Avg. annual* rainfall: 33.91"; snowfall: 18"; clear days: 105; precipitation days: 108. **Visitor info**: (800) 325-7692 or (314) 421-1023. www.explorestlouis.com.

Tucson, Arizona

Population 486,699 (2000). **Rank**: 30th. **Race/ Hispanic Origin** (2000): White 70.2%. Black 4.3%. Indian 2.3%. Asian 2.5%. Pacific Islander 0.2%. Other 16.8%. Two or more races 3.8%. Hispanic 35.7%. **Location**: 32°14'N, 110°59'W. County: Pima. **Terrain and climate** *Elev.*: 2,584 ft. *Area*: 125 sq. mi. (324.8 sq km). .: Jan.: 38.1°F/3.3°C; *avg. daily max.* July: 98.5°F/3.3°C. *Avg. annual* rainfall: 11.14"; snowfall: 2"; clear days: 198; precipitation days: 50. **Visitor info**: (800) 638-8350 or (520) 624-1817. www.visittucson.org.

Tulsa, Oklahoma

Population 393,049 (2000). **Rank**: 43rd. **Race/Hispanic Origin** (2000): White 70.1%. Black 15.5%. Indian 4.7%. Asian 1.8%. Pacific Islander 0.1%. Other 3.5%. Two or more races 4.4%. Hispanic 7.2%. **Location**: 36°10'N, 96°00'W. Counties: Osage, Tulsa. **Terrain and climate** *Elev.*: 676 ft. *Area*: 186.1 sq. mi. (482 sq km). *Avg. daily min.* temp.: Jan.: 24.8°F/-4°C; *avg. daily max.* July: 93.9°F/34.3°C. Avg. annual rainfall: 38.77"; snowfall: 9"; clear days: 127; precipitation days: 90. **Visitor info**: (800) 558-3311 or (918) 585-1201. www.visittulsa.com.

Virginia Beach, Virginia

Population 425,257 (2000). **Rank**: 38th. **Race/ Hispanic Origin** (2000): White 71.4%. Black 19.0%. Indian 0.4%. Asian 4.9%. Pacific Islander 0.1%. Other 1.5%. Two or more races 2.7%. Hispanic 4.2%. Location: 36°54'N, 75°58'W. County: independent city. **Terrain and climate** *Elev.*: 12 ft. *Area*: 225.9 sq. mi. (585.1 sq km). *Avg. daily min. temp.*: Jan.: 31.7°F/-0.1°C; *avg. daily max.* July: 86.9°F/30.5°C. *Avg. annual* rainfall: 45.22"; snowfall: 7"; clear days: 110; precipitation days: 115. **Visitor info**: (800) VA-BEACH. www.vbfun.com.

Washington, D.C.

Population 572,059 (2000). **Rank**: 21st. **Race/ Hispanic Origin** (2000): White 30.8%. Black 60.0%. Indian 0.3%. Asian 2.7%. Pacific Islander 0.1%. Other 3.8%. Two or more races 2.4%. Hispanic 7.9%. **Location**: 38°52'N, 77°00'W. County: independent city. **Terrain and climate** *Elev.*: 30 ft. *Area*: 62.7 sq. mi. (162.4 sq km). *Avg. daily min. temp.*: Jan.: 27.5°F/-2.5°C; *avg. daily max.* July: 87.9°F/31°C. *Avg. annual* rainfall: 39"; snowfall: 16"; clear days: 101; precipitation days: 111. **Visitor info**: (202) 789-7000. www.washington.org.

Wichita, Kansas

Population 344,284 (2000). **Rank**: 50th. **Race/ Hispanic Origin** (2000): White 75.2%. Black 11.4%. Indian 1.2%. Asian 4.0%. Pacific Islander 0.1%. Other 5.1%. Two or more races 3.1%. Hispanic 9.6%. **Location**: 37°42'N, 97°20'W. County: Sedgwick. **Terrain and climate** *Elev.*: 387.1 ft. *Area*: 140.2 sq. mi. (363.1sq km). *Avg. daily min. temp.*: Jan.: 19.2°F/-7.1°C; *avg. daily max.* July: 92.8°F/33.8°C. *Avg. annual* rainfall: 29"; snowfall: 16"; clear days: 279; precipitation days: 86. **Visitor info**: (800) 288-9424 or (316) 265-2800.www.visitwichita.com.

AWARDS AND PRIZES

Academy Awards 1928–2003

The "Oscars" are officially known as the Academy of Motion Picture Arts and Sciences Awards. They were inaugurated in 1928 as part of Hollywood's drive to improve its less-than-respectable image. Academy librarian and eventual executive director Margaret Herrick remarked that the statuette looked like her uncle Oscar, and the nickname has stuck ever since. Membership in the Academy (currently over 3,000) is by invitation only, with members divided into 13 branches. Each branch selects up to five nominees for awards in its area of expertise; the entire membership makes "Best Film" nominations and then votes on all the categories. Major awards are shown in the chart. Awards for Best Cinematography and for Best Foreign Language Film are shown in a separate table. Awards for actors and directors are named for films winning Best Picture except where otherwise indicated.

Year	Best picture	Best director	Best actor	Best actress	Best supporting actor	Best supporting actress
1928	*Wings*	Frank Borzage, *Seventh Heaven* Lewis Milestone, *Two Arabian Knights*	Emil Jannings, *The Way of All Flesh, The Last Command*	Janet Gaynor, *Seventh Heaven, Sunrise, Street Angel*	No Awards Given	No Awards Given
1929	*The Broadway Melody*	Frank Lloyd, *The Divine Lady*	Warner Baxter, *In Old Arizona*	Mary Pickford, *Coquette*	No Awards Given	No Awards Given
1930	*All Quiet on the Western Front*	Lewis Milestone	George Arliss, *Disraeli*	Norma Shearer, *The Divorcee*	No Awards Given	No Awards Given
1931	*Cimarron*	Norman Taurog, *Skippy*	Lionel Barrymore, *A Free Soul*	Marie Dressler, *Min and Bill*	No Awards Given	No Awards Given
1932	*Grand Hotel*	Frank Borzage, *Bad Girl*	Wallace Beery, *The Champ* Fredric March, *Dr. Jekyll and Mr. Hyde*	Helen Hayes, *The Sin of Madelon Claudet*	No Awards Given	No Awards Given
1933	*Cavalcade*	Frank Lloyd	Charles Laughton *The Private Life of Henry VIII*	Katharine Hepburn, *Morning Glory*	No Awards Given	No Awards Given
1934	*It Happened One Night*	Frank Capra	Clark Gable	Claudette Colbert	No Awards Given	No Awards Given
1935	*Mutiny on the Bounty*	John Ford, *The Informer*	Victor McLaglen, *The Informer*	Bette Davis, *Dangerous*	No Awards Given	No Awards Given
1936	*The Great Ziegfeld*	Frank Capra, *Mr. Deeds Goes to Town*	Paul Muni, *The Story of Louis Pasteur*	Luise Rainer	Walter Brennan, *Come and Get It*	Gale Sondergaard, *Anthony Adverse*
1937	*The Life of Emile Zola*	Leo McCarey, *The Awful Truth*	Spencer Tracy, *Captains Courageous*	Luise Rainer, *The Good Earth*	Joseph Schildkraut,	Alice Brady, *In Old Chicago*
1938	*You Can't Take It With You*	Frank Capra	Spencer Tracy, *Boys Town*	Bette Davis, *Jezebel*	Walter Brennan, *Kentucky*	Fay Bainter, *Jezebel*

Year	Best picture	Best director	Best actor	Best actress	Best supporting actor	Best supporting actress
1939	*Gone With the Wind*	Victor Fleming	Robert Donat, *Goodbye, Mr. Chips*	Vivien Leigh,	Thomas Mitchell, *Stagecoach*	Hattie McDaniel
1940	*Rebecca*	John Ford, *The Grapes of Wrath*	James Stewart, *The Philadelphia Story*	Ginger Rogers, *Kitty Foyle*	Walter Brennan, *The Westerner*	Jane Darwell, *The Grapes of Wrath*
1941	*How Green Was My Valley*	John Ford	Gary Cooper, *Sergeant York*	Joan Fontaine, *Suspicion*	Donald Crisp	Mary Astor, *The Great Lie*
1942	*Mrs. Miniver*	William Wyler	James Cagney, *Yankee Doodle Dandy*	Greer Garson	Van Heflin, *Johnny Eager*	Teresa Wright
1943	*Casablanca*	Michael Curtiz	Paul Lukas, *Watch On The Rhine*	Jennifer Jones, *The Song of Bernadette*	Charles Coburn, *The More the Merrier*	Katina Paxinou, *For Whom the Bell Tolls*
1944	*Going My Way*	Leo McCarey	Bing Crosby	Ingrid Bergman, *Gaslight*	Barry Fitzgerald	Ethel Barrymore, *None But the Lonely Heart*
1945	*The Lost Weekend*	Billy Wilder	Ray Milland	Joan Crawford, *Mildred Pierce*	James Dunn, *A Tree Grows in Brooklyn*	Anne Revere, *National Velvet*
1946	*The Best Years of Our Lives*	William Wyler	Fredric March	Olivia De Havilland, *To Each His Own*	Harold Russell	Anne Baxter, *The Razor's Edge*
1947	*Gentleman's Agreement*	Elia Kazan	Ronald Colman, *A Double Life*	Loretta Young, *The Farmer's Daughter*	Edmund Gwenn, *Miracle on 34th Street*	Celeste Holm
1948	*Hamlet*	John Huston, *The Treasure of the Sierra Madre*	Laurence Olivier	Jane Wyman, *Johnny Belinda*	Walter Huston, *The Treasure of the Sierra Madre*	Claire Trevor, *Key Largo*
1949	*All the King's Men*	Joseph L. Mankiewicz, *A Letter to Three Wives*	Broderick Crawford	Olivia De Havilland, *The Heiress*	Dean Jagger, *Twelve O'Clock High*	Mercedes McCambridge,
1950	*All About Eve*	Joseph L. Mankiewicz	José Ferrer, *Cyrano de Bergerac*	Judy Holliday, *Born Yesterday*	George Sanders	Josephine Hull, *Harvey*
1951	*An American in Paris*	George Stevens, *A Place in the Sun*	Humphrey Bogart, *The African Queen*	Vivien Leigh, *A Streetcar Named Desire*	Karl Malden, *A Streetcar Named Desire*	Kim Hunter, *A Streetcar Named Desire*
1952	*The Greatest Show on Earth*	John Ford, *The Quiet Man*	Gary Cooper, *High Noon*	Shirley Booth, *Come Back, Little Sheba*	Anthony Quinn, *Viva Zapata!*	Gloria Grahame, *The Bad and the Beautiful*
1953	*From Here to Eternity*	Fred Zinnemann	William Holden, *Stalag 17*	Audrey Hepburn, *Roman Holiday*	Frank Sinatra	Donna Reed,
1954	*On the Waterfront*	Elia Kazan	Marlon Brando	Grace Kelly, *The Country Girl*	Edmond O'Brien, *The Barefoot Contessa*	Eva Marie Saint,

Year	Best picture	Best director	Best actor	Best actress	Best supporting actor	Best supporting actress
1955	*Marty*	Delbert Mann	Ernest Borgnine	Anna Magnani, *The Rose Tattoo*	Jack Lemmon, *Mister Roberts*	Jo Van Fleet, *East of Eden*
1956	*Around the World in 80 Days*	George Stevens, *Giant*	Yul Brynner, *The King And I*	Ingrid Bergman, *Anastasia*	Anthony Quinn, *Lust for Life*	Dorothy Malone, *Written on the Wind*
1957	*The Bridge on the River Kwai*	David Lean	Alec Guinness	Joanne Woodward, *The Three Faces of Eve*	Red Buttons, *Sayonara*	Miyoshi Umeki, *Sayonara*
1958	*Gigi*	Vincente Minnelli	David Niven, *Separate Tables*	Susan Hayward, *I Want to Live!*	Burl Ives, *The Big Country*	Wendy Hiller, *Separate Tables*
1959	*Ben-Hur*	William Wyler	Charlton Heston	Simone Signoret, *Room at the Top*	Hugh Griffith,	Shelley Winters, *The Diary of Anne Frank*
1960	*The Apartment*	Billy Wilder	Burt Lancaster, *Elmer Gantry*	Elizabeth Taylor, *Butterfield 8*	Peter Ustinov, *Spartacus*	Shirley Jones, *Elmer Gantry*
1961	*West Side Story*	Jerome Robbins, Robert Wise	Maximilian Schell, *Judgment At Nuremberg*	Sophia Loren, *Two Women*	George Chakiris	Rita Moreno
1962	*Lawrence of Arabia*	David Lean	Gregory Peck, *To Kill a Mockingbird*	Anne Bancroft, *The Miracle Worker*	Ed Begley, *Sweet Bird of Youth*	Patty Duke, *The Miracle Worker*
1963	*Tom Jones*	Tony Richardson	Sidney Poitier *Lilies of the Field*	Patricia Neal, *Hud*	Melvyn Douglas, *Hud*	Margaret Rutherford, *The V.I.P.s*
1964	*My Fair Lady*	George Cukor	Rex Harrison	Julie Andrews, *Mary Poppins*	Peter Ustinov, *Topkapi*	Lila Kedrova, *Zorba the Greek*
1965	*The Sound of Music*	Robert Wise	Lee Marvin *Cat Ballou*	Julie Christie, *Darling*	Martin Balsam, *A Thousand Clowns*	Shelley Winters, *A Patch of Blue*
1966	*A Man for All Seasons*	Fred Zinnemann	Paul Scofield	Elizabeth Taylor, *Who's Afraid of Virginia Woolf?*	Walter Matthau, *The Fortune Cookie*	Sandy Dennis, *Who's Afraid of Virginia Woolf?*
1967	*In the Heat of the Night*	Mike Nichols, *The Graduate*	Rod Steiger	Katharine Hepburn, *Guess Who's Coming to Dinner*	George Kennedy, *Cool Hand Luke*	Estelle Parsons, *Bonnie and Clyde*
1968	*Oliver!*	Carol Reed	Cliff Robertson, *Charly*	Katharine Hepburn *The Lion in Winter* Barbra Streisand, *Funny Girl*	Jack Albertson, *The Subject Was Roses*	Ruth Gordon, *Rosemary's Baby*
1969	*Midnight Cowboy*	John Schlesinger	John Wayne, *True Grit*	Maggie Smith, *The Prime of Miss Jean Brodie*	Gig Young, *They Shoot Horses, Don't They?*	Goldie Hawn, *Cactus Flower*
1970	*Patton*	Franklin J. Schaffner	George C. Scott	Glenda Jackson, *Women in Love*	John Mills, *Ryan's Daughter*	Helen Hayes, *Airport*
1971	*The French Connection*	William Friedkin	Gene Hackman	Jane Fonda, *Klute*	Ben Johnson, *The Last Picture Show*	Cloris Leachman, *The Last Picture Show*

Year	Best picture	Best director	Best actor	Best actress	Best supporting actor	Best supporting actress
1972	*The Godfather*	Bob Fosse, *Cabaret*	Marlon Brando	Liza Minnelli, *Cabaret*	Joel Grey, *Cabaret*	Eileen Heckart, *Butterflies are Free*
1973	*The Sting*	George Roy Hill	Jack Lemmon *Save the Tiger*	Glenda Jackson, *A Touch of Class*	John Houseman, *The Paper Chase*	Tatum O'Neal, *Paper Moon*
1974	*The Godfather, Part II*	Francis Ford Coppola	Art Carney, *Harry And Tonto*	Ellen Burstyn, *Alice Doesn't Live Here Anymore*	Robert De Niro	Ingrid Bergman, *Murder on the Orient Express*
1975	*One Flew Over the Cuckoo's Nest*	Milos Forman	Jack Nicholson	Louise Fletcher	George Burns, *The Sunshine Boys*	Lee Grant, *Shampoo*
1976	*Rocky*	John G. Avildsen	Peter Finch, *Network*	Faye Dunaway, *Network*	Jason Robards, *All the President's Men*	Beatrice Straight, *Network*
1977	*Annie Hall*	Woody Allen	Richard Dreyfuss, *The Goodbye Girl*	Diane Keaton	Jason Robards, *Julia*	Vanessa Redgrave, *Julia*
1978	*The Deer Hunter*	Michael Cimino	Jon Voight, *Coming Home*	Jane Fonda, *Coming Home*	Christopher Walken	Maggie Smith, *California Suite*
1979	*Kramer vs. Kramer*	Robert Benton	Dustin Hoffman,	Sally Field, *Norma Rae*	Melvyn Douglas, *Being There*	Meryl Streep, *Kramer vs. Kramer*
1980	*Ordinary People*	Robert Redford	Robert De Niro, *Raging Bull*	Sissy Spacek, *Coal Miner's Daughter*	Timothy Hutton	Mary Steenburgen, *Melvin and Howard*
1981	*Chariots of Fire*	Warren Beatty, *Reds*	Henry Fonda, *On Golden Pond*	Katharine Hepburn, *On Golden Pond*	John Gielgud, *Arthur*	Maureen Stapleton, *Reds*
1982	*Gandhi*	Richard Attenborough	Ben Kingsley	Meryl Streep, *Sophie's Choice*	Louis Gossett Jr., *An Officer and a Gentleman*	Jessica Lange, *Tootsie*
1983	*Terms of Endearment*	James L. Brooks	Robert Duvall, *Tender Mercies*	Shirley MacLaine	Jack Nicholson	Linda Hunt, *The Year of Living Dangerously*
1984	*Amadeus*	Milos Forman	F. Murray Abraham	Sally Field, *Places in the Heart*	Haing S. Ngor, *The Killing Fields*	Peggy Ashcroft, *A Passage to India*
1985	*Out of Africa*	Sydney Pollack	William Hurt, *Kiss of the Spider Woman*	Geraldine Page, *The Trip to Bountiful*	Don Ameche, *Cocoon*	Anjelica Huston, *Prizzi's Honor*
1986	*Platoon*	Oliver Stone	Paul Newman, *The Color of Money*	Marlee Matlin, *Children of a Lesser God*	Michael Caine, *Hannah and Her Sisters*	Dianne Wiest, *Hannah and Her Sisters*
1987	*The Last Emperor*	Bernardo Bertolucci	Michael Douglas, *Wall Street*	Cher, *Moonstruck*	Sean Connery, *The Untouchables*	Olympia Dukakis, *Moonstruck*
1988	*Rain Man*	Barry Levinson	Dustin Hoffman	Jodie Foster, *The Accused*	Kevin Kline, *A Fish Called Wanda*	Geena Davis, *The Accidental Tourist*
1989	*Driving Miss Daisy*	Oliver Stone, *Born on the Fourth of July*	Daniel Day-Lewis, *My Left Foot*	Jessica Tandy	Denzel Washington, *Glory*	Brenda Fricker, *My Left Foot*

Year	Best picture	Best director	Best actor	Best actress	Best supporting actor	Best supporting actress
1990	*Dances with Wolves*	Kevin Costner	Jeremy Irons, *Reversal of Fortune*	Kathy Bates, *Misery*	Joe Pesci, *Goodfellas*	Whoopi Goldberg, *Ghost*
1991	*The Silence of the Lambs*	Jonathan Demme	Anthony Hopkins	Jodie Foster	Jack Palance, *City Slickers*	Mercedes Ruehl, *The Fisher King*
1992	*Unforgiven*	Clint Eastwood	Al Pacino, *Scent of a Woman*	Emma Thompson, *Howards End*	Gene Hackman	Marisa Tomei, *My Cousin Vinny*
1993	*Schindler's List*	Steven Spielberg	Tom Hanks, *Philadelphia*	Holly Hunter, *The Piano*	Tommy Lee Jones *The Fugitive*	Anna Paquin, *The Piano*
1994	*Forrest Gump*	Robert Zemeckis	Tom Hanks	Jessica Lange, *Blue Sky*	Martin Landau, *Ed Wood*	Dianne Wiest, *Bullets Over Broadway*
1995	*Braveheart*	Mel Gibson	Nicolas Cage *Leaving Las Vegas*	Susan Sarandon, *Dead Man Walking*	Kevin Spacey, *The Usual Suspects*	Mira Sorvino, *Mighty Aphrodite*
1996	*The English Patient*	Anthony Minghella	Geoffrey Rush, *Shine*	Frances McDormand, *Fargo*	Cuba Gooding Jr., *Jerry Maguire*	Juliette Binoche
1997	*Titanic*	James Cameron	Jack Nicholson, *As Good as it Gets*	Helen Hunt, *As Good as it Gets*	Robin Williams *Good Will Hunting*	Kim Basinger, *L.A. Confidential*
1998	*Shakespeare in Love*	Steven Spielberg, *Saving Private Ryan*	Roberto Benigni *Life is Beautiful*	Gwyneth Paltrow	James Coburn, *Affliction*	Judi Dench
1999	*American Beauty*	Sam Mendes	Kevin Spacey	Hilary Swank *Boys Don't Cry*	Michael Caine, *The Cider House Rules*	Angelina Jolie, *Girl, Interrupted*
2000	*Gladiator*	Steven Soderbergh, *Traffic*	Russell Crowe	Julia Roberts, *Erin Brockovich*	Benicio Del Toro, *Traffic*	Marcia Gay Harden, *Pollock*
2001	*A Beautiful Mind*	Ron Howard	Denzel Washington, *Training Day*	Halle Berry, *Monsters Ball*	Jim Broadbent, *Iris*	Jennifer Connelly
2002	*Chicago*	Roman Polanski	Adrien Brody	Nicole Kidman, *The Hours*	Chris Cooper, *Adaptation*	Catherine Zeta-Jones, *Chicago*
2003	*The Lord of the Rings: Return of the King*	Peter Jackson	Sean Penn, *Mystic River*	Charlize Theron, *Monster*	Tim Robbins, *Mystic River*	Renee Zellweger, *Cold Mountain*

Source: Academy of Motion Picture Arts & Sciences. www. oscar.org

Academy Awards for Best Foreign Language Film, 1956–2003

Year	Film, Country	Director
1956	*La Strada*, Italy	Federico Fellini
1957	*The Nights of Cabiria*, Italy	Federico Fellini
1958	*Mon Oncle*, France	Jacques Tati
1959	*Black Orpheus*, France/Italy/ Brazil	Marcel Camus
1960	*The Virgin Spring*, Sweden	Ingmar Bergman
1961	*Through A Glass Darkly*, Sweden	Ingmar Bergman
1962	*Sundays and Cybele*, France	Serge Bourgignon
1963	*8 1/2*, Italy	Federico Fellini
1964	*Yesterday, Today, and Tomorrow*, Italy/France	Vittorio de Sica
1965	*The Shop on Main Street*, Czechoslovakia	Jan Kadar
1966	*A Man and a Woman*, France	Claude Lelouch
1967	*Closely Watched Trains*, Czechoslovakia	Jiri Menzel
1968	*War and Peace*, USSR	Sergei Bondarchuk
1969	*Z*, France/Algeria	Constantin Costa-Gavras
1970	*Investigation of a Citizen Above Suspicion*, Italy	Elio Petri
1971	*The Garden of the Finzi-Continis*, Italy	Vittorio de Sica
1972	*The Discreet Charm of the Bourgeoisie*, France	Luis Buñuel
1973	*Day For Night*, France/Italy	François Truffaut
1974	*Amarcord*, Italy/France	Federico Fellini
1975	*Dersu Uzala*, USSR/Japan	Akira Kurosawa
1976	*Black and White in Color*, France/Switzerland/Ivory Coast	Jean-Jacques Annaud
1977	*Madame Rosa*, France	Moshe Mizrahi
1978	*Get Out Your Handkerchiefs*, France	Bertrand Blier
1979	*The Tin Drum*, Germany	Volker Scholondorff
1980	*Moscow Does Not Believe in Tears*, USSR	Vladimir Menshov
1981	*Mephisto*, Austria/ Germany/ Hungary	Istvan Szabo
1982	*To Begin Again*, Spain	Jose Luis Garcia
1983	*Fanny and Alexander*, Sweden	Ingmar Bergman
1984	*Dangerous Moves*, France	Richard Dembo
1985	*The Official Story*, Argentina	Luis Puenzo
1986	*The Assault*, Netherlands	Fons Rademakers
1987	*Babette's Feast*, Denmark	Gabriel Axel
1988	*Pelle the Conqueror*, Denmark	Bille August
1989	*Cinema Paradiso*, Italy	Giuseppe Tornatore
1990	*Journey of Hope*, Switzerland	Xavier Koller
1991	*Mediterraneo*, Italy	Gabriel Salvatores
1992	*Indochine*, France	Regis Wargnier
1993	*Belle Époque*, Spain	Fernando Trueba
1994	*Burnt by the Sun*, Russia	Nikita Mikhalkov
1995	*Antonia's Line*, Netherlands	Marlene Gorris
1996	*Kolya*, Czech Republic	Jan Sverak
1997	*Character*, Netherlands	Mike van Diem
1998	*Life is Beautiful*, Italy	Roberto Benigni
1999	*All About My Mother*, Spain	Pedro Almodóvar
2000	*Crouching Tiger, Hidden Dragon*, China	Ang Lee
2001	*No Man's Land*, Bosnia & Herzegovina	Danis Tanovic
2002	*Nowhere in Africa*, Germany	Caroline Link
2003	*The Barbarian Invasions*, Canada	Denys Arcand

Academy Awards for Cinematography, 1928–2003

Year	Cinematographer, Film
1928	Charles Rosher, Karl Struss, *Sunrise*
1929	Clyde DeVinna, White Shadows, *In the South Seas*
1930	Joseph T. Rucker, Willard Van Der Veer, *With Byrd at the South Pole*
1931	Floyd Crosby, *Tabu*
1932	Lee Garmes, *Shanghai Express*
1933	Charles Bryant Lang Jr., *A Farewell to Arms*
1934	Victor Milner, *Cleopatra*
1935	Hal Mohr, *A Midsummer Night's Dream*
1936	Gaetano Gaudio, *Anthony Adverse*
1937	Karl Freund, *The Good Earth*
1938	Joseph Ruttenberg, *The Great Waltz*
1939	Gregg Toland, *Wuthering Heights*
	Ernest Haller, Ray Rennahan, *Gone With the Wind*

Year	Cinematographer, Film
1940	George Barnes, *Rebecca*
	George Perinal, *Thief of Baghdad*
1941	Arthur Miller, *How Green Was My Valley*
	Ernest Palmer, Ray Rennahan, *Blood & Sand*
1942	Joseph Ruttenberg, *Mrs. Miniver*
	Leon Shamroy, *The Black Swan*
1943	Arthur Miller, *The Song of Bernadette*
	Hal Mohr, W. Howard Greene, *The Phantom of the Opera*
1944	Joseph LaShelle, *Laura*
	Leon Shamroy, *Wilson*
1945	Harry Stradling, *The Picture of Dorian Gray*
	Leon Shamroy, *Leave Her to Heaven*
1946	Arthur Miller, *Anna and the King of Siam*
	Charles Rosher, Leonard Smith, Arthur Arling, *The Yearling*
1947	Guy Green, *Great Expectations*
1948	William Daniels, *The Naked City*
	Joseph Valentine, William V. Skall, Winton Hoch, *Joan of Arc*
1949	Paul C. Vogel, *Battleground*
	Winton Hoch, *She Wore a Yellow Ribbon*
1950	Robert Krasker, *The Third Man*
	Robert Surtees, *King Solomon's Mines*
1951	William C. Mellor, *A Place in the Sun*
	Alfred Gilks, John Alton (ballet), *An American in Paris*
1952	Robert Surtees, *The Bad and the Beautiful*
	Winton Hoch, Archie Stout, *The Quiet Man*
1953	Burnett Guffey, *From Here to Eternity*
	Loyal Griggs, *Shane*
1954	Boris Kaufman, *On the Waterfront*
	Milton Krasner, *Three Coins in the Fountain*
1955	James Wong Howe, *The Rose Tattoo*
	Robert Burks, *To Catch a Thief*
1956	Joseph Ruttenberg, *Sombody Up There Likes Me*
	Lionel Lindon, *Around the World in 80 Days*
1957	Jack Hildyard, *The Bridge on the River Kwai*
1958	Sam Leavitt, *The Defiant Ones*
	Joseph Ruttenberg, *Gigi*
1959	William C. Mellor, *The Diary of Anne Frank*
	Robert L. Surtees, *Ben-Hur*
1960	Freddie Francis, *Sons and Lovers*
	Russell Metty, *Spartacus*
1961	Eugene Shuftan, *The Hustler*
	Daniel L. Fapp, *West Side Story*
1962	Jean Bourgoin, Walter Wottitz, *The Longest Day*
	Freddie Young, *Lawrence of Arabia*

Year	Cinematographer, Film
1963	James Wong Howe, *Hud*
	Leon Shamroy, *Cleopatra*
1964	Walter Lassally, *Zorba the Greek*
	Harry Stradling, *My Fair Lady*
1965	Ernest Laszlo, *Ship of Fools*
	Freddie Young, *Dr. Zhivago*
1966	Haskell Wexler, *Who's Afraid of Virginia Woolf?*
	Ted Moore, *A Man for All Seasons*
1967	Burnett Guffey, *Bonnie and Clyde*
1968	Pasqualino De Santis, *Romeo and Juliet*
1969	Conrad Hall, *Butch Cassidy and the Sundance Kid*
1970	Freddie Young, *Ryan's Daughter*
1971	Oswald Morris, *Fiddler on the Roof*
1972	Geoffrey Unsworth, *Cabaret*
1973	Sven Nykvist, *Cries and Whispers*
1974	Fred Koenekamp, Joseph Biroc, *The Towering Inferno*
1975	John Alcott, *Barry Lyndon*
1976	Haskell Wexler, *Bound for Glory*
1977	Vilmos Zsigmond, *Close Encounters of the Third Kind*
1978	Nestor Almendros, *Days of Heaven*
1979	Vittorio Storaro, *Apocalypse Now*
1980	Geoffrey Unsworth, Ghislain Cloquet, *Tess*
1981	Vittorio Storaro, *Reds*
1982	Billy Williams, Ronnie Taylor, *Gandhi*
1983	Sven Nykvist, *Fanny & Alexander*
1984	Chris Menges, *The Killing Fields*
1985	David Watkin, *Out of Africa*
1986	Chris Menges, *The Mission*
1987	Vittorio Storaro, *The Last Emperor*
1988	Peter Biziou, *Mississippi Burning*
1989	Freddie Francis, *Glory*
1990	Dean Semler, *Dances With Wolves*
1991	Robert Richardson, *JFK*
1992	Philippe Rousselot, *A River Runs Through It*
1993	Janusz Kaminski, *Schindler's List*
1994	John Toll, *Legends of the Fall*
1995	John Toll, *Braveheart*
1996	John Seale, *The English Patient*
1997	Russell Carpenter, *Titanic*
1998	Janusz Kaminski, *Saving Private Ryan*
1999	Conrad L. Hall, *American Beauty*
2000	Peter Pau, *Crouching Tiger, Hidden Dragon*
2001	Andrew Lesnie, *The Lord of the Rings: The Fellowship of the Ring*
2002	Conrad L. Hall, *Road to Perdition* (posthumous)
2003	Gus Van Sant, *Elephant*

The Emmy Awards, 1951–2003

The Academy of Television Arts and Sciences, formed in 1946, presented the first Emmy Awards in 1949. The number and names of awards have changed over the years, but since 1965, the Academy has recognized an outstanding comedy and drama, as well as an actor and an actress in a comedy and in a drama.

Year	Comedy	Drama	Comedy Actor	Comedy Actress	Drama Actor	Drama Actress
1951	*The Red Skelton Show*	*Studio One*	Sid Caesar	Imogene Coca	(1)	(1)
1952	*I Love Lucy*	*Robert Montgomery Presents*	Thomas Mitchell	Helen Hayes	(1)	(1)
1953	*I Love Lucy*	*The U.S. Steel Hour*	Donald O'Connor, *Colgate Comedy Hour*	Eve Arden, *Our Miss Brooks*	(1)	(1)
1954	*Make Room for Daddy*	*The U.S. Steel Hour*	Danny Thomas, *Make Room for Daddy*	Loretta Young, *The Loretta Young Show*	(1)	(1)
1955	*The Phil Silvers Show*	*Producers' Showcase*	Phil Silvers, *The Phil Silvers Show*	Lucille Ball, *I Love Lucy*	(1)	(1)
1956	*The Phil Silvers Show*	*Requiem for a Heavyweight*	Sid Caesar, *Caesar's Hour*	Nanette Fabray, *Caesar'sHour*	Robert Young, *Father Knows Best*	Loretta Young, *The Loretta Young Show*
1957	*The Phil Silvers Show*	*Gunsmoke*	Robert Young, *Father Knows Best*	Jane Wyatt, *Father Knows Best*	(1)	(1)
1958 –59	*The Jack Benny Show*	(2)	Jack Benny, *The Jack Benny Show*	Jane Wyatt, *Father Knows Best*	Raymond Burr, *Perry Mason*	Loretta Young, *The Loretta Young Show*
1959 –60	*"Art Carney Special"*	*Playhouse 90*	*Robert Stack, The Untouchables*	*Jane Wyatt, Father Knows Best*	(1)	(1)
1960 –61	*The Jack BennyShow*	"Macbeth," *Hallmark Hall of Fame*	Raymond Burr, *Perry Mason*	Barbara Stanwyck, *The Barbara Stanwyck Show*	(1)	(1)
1961 –62	*The Bob Newhart Show*	*The Defenders*	E.G, Marshall, *The Defenders*	Shirley Booth, *Hazel*	(1)	(1)
1962 –63	*The Dick Van Dyke Show*	*The Defenders*	E.G. Marshall, *The Defenders*	Shirley Booth, *Hazel*	(1)	(1)
1963 –64	*The Dick Van Dyke Show*	*The Defenders*	Dick Van Dyke, *The Dick Van Dyke Show*	Mary Tyler Moore, *The Dick Van Dyke Show*	(1)	(1)
1964 –65	(3)	(3)	(3)	(3)	(3)	(3)
1965 –66	*The Dick Van Dyke Show*	*The Fugitive*	Dick Van Dyke, *The Dick Van Dyke Show*	Mary Tyler Moore, *The Dick Van Dyke Show*	Bill Cosby, *I Spy*	Barbara Stanwyck, *The Big Valley*
1966 –67	*The Monkees*	*Mission: Impossible*	Don Adams, *Get Smart*	Lucille Ball, *The Lucy Show*	Bill Cosby, *I Spy*	Barbara Bain, *Mission: Impossible*
1967 –68	*Get Smart*	*Mission: Impossible*	Don Adams, *Get Smart*	Lucille Ball, *The Lucy Show*	Bill Cosby, *I Spy*	Barbara Bain, *Mission: Impossible*

Year	Comedy	Drama	Comedy Actor	Comedy Actress	Drama Actor	Drama Actress
1968–69	*Get Smart*	*NET Playhouse* (NET)	Don Adams, *Get Smart*	Hope Lange, *The Ghost and Mrs. Muir*	Carl Betz, *Judd for the Defense*	Barbara Bain, *Mission: Impossible*
1969–70	*My World & Welcome to It*	*Marcus Welby, M.D.*	William Windom *My World & Welcome to It*	Hope Lange, *The Ghost and Mrs. Muir*	Robert Young, *Marcus Welby, M.D.*	Susan Hampshire *The Forsyte Saga*
1970–71	*All in the Family*	*The Senator* (segment), *The Bold Ones*	Jack Klugman, *The Odd Couple*	Jean Stapleton, *All in the Family*	Hal Holbrook, *The Senator* (segment), *The Bold Ones*	Susan Hampshire, *The First Churchills*
1971–72	*All in the Family*	"Elizabeth R" *Masterpiece Theatre*	Carroll O'Connor, *All in the Family*	Jean Stapleton, *All in the Family*	Peter Falk, *Columbo*	Glenda Jackson, "Elizabeth R" *Masterpiece Theatre*
1972–73	*All in the Family*	*The Waltons*	Jack Klugman, *The Odd Couple*	Mary Tyler Moore, *The Mary Tyler Moore Show*	Richard Thomas, *The Waltons*	Michael Learned, *The Waltons*
1973–74	*M*A*S*H*	"Upstairs, Downstairs," *Masterpiece Theatre*	Alan Alda, *M*A*S*H*	Mary Tyler Moore *The Mary Tyler Moore Show*	Telly Savalas, *Kojak*	Michael Learned, *The Waltons*
1974–75	*The Mary Tyler Moore Show*	"Upstairs, Downstairs," *Masterpiece Theatre*	Tony Randall, *The Odd Couple*	Valerie Harper, *Rhoda*	Robert Blake, *Baretta*	Jean Marsh, "Upstairs, Downstairs," *Masterpiece Theater*
1975–76	*The Mary Tyler Moore Show*	*Police Story*	Jack Albertson, *Chico & the Man*	Mary Tyler Moore, *The Mary Tyler Moore Show*	Peter Falk, *Columbo*	Michael Learned, *The Waltons*
1977–78	*All in the Family*	*The Rockford Files*	Carroll O'Connor, *All in the Family*	Jean Stapleton, *All in the Family*	Edward Asner, *Lou Grant*	Sada Thompson, *Family*
1978–79	*Taxi*	*Lou Grant*	Carroll O' Connor, *All in the Family*	Ruth Gordon, *Taxi*	Ron Leibman, *Kaz*	Mariette Hartley, *The Incredible Hulk*
1979–80	*Taxi*	*Lou Grant*	Richard Mulligan, *Soap*	Cathryn Damon, *Soap*	Ed Asner, *Lou Grant*	Barbara Bel Geddes, *Dallas*
1980–81	*Taxi*	*Hill Street Blues*	Judd Hirsch, *Taxi*	Isabel Sanford, *The Jeffersons*	Daniel Travanti, *Hill Street Blues*	Barbara Babcock *Hill Street Blues*
1981–82	*Barney Miller*	*Hill Street Blues*	Alan Alda, *M*A*S*H*	Carol Kane, *Taxi*	Daniel Travanti, *Hill Street Blues*	Michael Learned, *Nurse*
1982–83	*Cheers*	*Hill Street Blues*	Judd Hirsch, *Taxi*	Shelley Long, *Cheers*	Ed Flanders, *St. Elsewhere*	Tyne Daly, *Cagney & Lacey*
1983–84	*Cheers*	*Hill Street Blues*	John Ritter, *Three's Company*	Jane Curtin, *Kate & Allie*	Tom Selleck, *Magnum P.I.*	Tyne Daly, *Cagney & Lacey*
1984–85	*The Cosby Show*	*Cagney & Lacey*	Robert Guillaume, *Benson*	Jane Curtin, *Kate & Allie*	William Daniels, *St. Elsewhere*	Tyne Daly, *Cagney & Lacey*
1985–86	*The Golden Girls*	*Cagney & Lacey*	Michael J. Fox, *Family Ties*	Betty White, *The Golden Girls*	William Daniels, *St. Elsewhere*	Sharon Gless, *Cagney & Lacey*

Year	Comedy	Drama	Comedy Actor	Comedy Actress	Drama Actor	Drama Actress
1986 –87	*The Golden Girls*	*L.A. Law*	Michael J. Fox, *Family Ties*	Rue McClanahan, *The Golden Girls*	Bruce Willis, *Moonlighting*	Sharon Gless, *Cagney &Lacey*
1987 –88	*The Wonder Years*	*thirtysomething*	Michael J. Fox, *Family Ties*	Beatrice Arthur, *The Golden Girls*	Richard Kiley, *A Year in the Life*	Tyne Daly, *Cagney &Lacey*
1988 –89	*Cheers*	*L.A. Law*	Richard Mulligan, *Empty Nest*	Candice Bergen, *Murphy Brown*	Carroll O'Connor, *In the Heat of the Night*	Dana Delany, *China Beach*,
1989 –90	*Murphy Brown*	*L.A. Law*	Ted Danson, *Cheers*	Candice Bergen, *Murphy Brown*	Peter Falk, Columbo	Patricia Wettig, *thirtysomething*
1990 –91	*Cheers*	*L.A. Law*	Burt Reynolds, *Evening Shade*	Kirstie Alley, *Cheers*	James Earl Jones, *Gabriel's Fire*	Patricia Wettig, *thirtysomething*
1991 –92	*Murphy Brown*	*Northern Exposure*	Craig T. Nelson, *Coach*	Candice Bergen, *MurphyBrown*	Christopher Lloyd,*Avonlea*	Dana Delany, *China Beach*,
1992 –93	*Seinfeld*	*Picket Fences*	Ted Danson, *Cheers*	Roseanne Arnold, *Roseanne*	Tom Skerritt, *Picket Fences*	Kathy Baker, *Picket Fences*
1993 –94	*Frasier*	*Picket Fences*	Kelsey Grammer, *Frasier*	Candice Bergen, *Murphy Brown*	Dennis Franz, *NYPD Blue*	Sela Ward, *Sisters*
1994 –95	*Frasier*	*NYPD Blue*	Kelsey Grammer, *Frasier*	Candice Bergen, *Murphy Brown*	Mandy Patinkin, *Chicago Hope*	Kathy Baker, *Picket Fences*
1995 –96	*Frasier*	*E.R.*	John Lithgow, *Third Rock From the Sun*	Helen Hunt, *Mad About You*	Dennis Franz, *NYPD Blue*	Kathy Baker, *Picket Fences*
1996 –97	*Frasier*	*Law & Order*	John Lithgow, *Third Rock From the Sun*	Helen Hunt, *Mad About You*	Dennis Franz, *NYPD Blue*	Gillian Anderson, *The X-Files* (Fox)
1997 –98	*Frasier*	*The Practice*	Kelsey Grammer, *Frasier*	Helen Hunt, *Mad About You*	Andre Braugher, *Homicide*	Christine Lahti, *Chicago Hope*
1998 –99	*Ally McBeal*	*The Practice*	John Lithgow, *Third Rock From the Sun*	Helen Hunt, *Mad About You*	Dennis Franz, *NYPD Blue*	Edie Falco, *The Sopranos*
1999 –2000	*Will and Grace*	*The West Wing*	Michael J. Fox, *Spin City*	Patricia Heaton, *Everybody Loves Raymond*	James Gandolfini, *The Sopranos*	Sela Ward, *Once and Again*
2000 –01	*Sex and the City*	*The West Wing*	Eric McCormack, *Will and Grace*	Patricia Heaton, *Everybody Loves Raymond*	James Gandolfini, *The Sopranos*	Edie Falco, *The Sopranos*
2001 –02	*Friends*	*The West Wing*	Ray Romano, *Everybody Loves Raymond*,	Jennifer Aniston, *Friends*	Michael Chiklis, *The Shield* (FX)	Allison Janney, *The West Wing*
2002 –03	*Everybody Loves Raymond*	*The West Wing*	Tony Shalhoub, *Monk*	Edie Falco, *The Sopranos*	James Gandolfini, *The Sopranos*	Debra Messing, *Will & Grace*

Notes: 1. Before 1965, the Academy did always not give separate acting awards for comedy and drama. 2. Playhouse 90 was best drama of one hour or longer; Alcoa-Goodyear Theatre was best drama of less than one hour. 3. In 1964, the Academy gave acting awards to Dick Van Dyke *forThe Dick Van Dyke Show*, Lynn Fontaine and Alfred Lunt for "The Magnificent Yankee" *Hallmark Hall of Fame*, and Barbra Streisand for *My Name is Barbra*. It also gave Achievements in Entertainment awards to these programs.
www.emmys.tv

The Tony Awards, 1947–2004

The Tony Awards are presented each year by the American Theatre Wing for distinguished achievement in the Broadway theater. Named for Antoinette Perry, an actress, producer, director, and chairman of the American Theatre Wing who died in 1946, the Tonys were first presented in 1947. Listed here is a selection of major awards for each year: best play (author), performance by an actor in a play, performance by an actress in a play, best musical (composer and lyricist), performance by an actor in a musical, performance by an actress in a musical.

PLAYS

Year	Best Play	Best Actor	Best Actress
1947	no award	José Ferrer, *Cyrano de Bergerac* Fredric March, *Years Ago*	Ingrid Bergman, *Joan of Lorraine* Helen Hayes, *Happy Birthday*
1948	*Mister Roberts*, Thomas Heggen and Joshua Logan	Henry Fonda, *Mister Roberts* Paul Kelly, *Command Decision* Basil Rathbone, *The Heiress*	Judith Anderson, *Medea*; Katharine Cornell, *Antony and Cleopatra*; Jessica Tandy, *A Streetcar Named Desire*
1949	*Death of a Salesman*, Arthur Miller	Rex Harrison, *Anne of the Thousand Days*	Martita Hunt, *The Madwoman of Chaillot*
1950	*The Cocktail Party*, T. S. Eliot	Sidney Blackmer, *Come Back, Little Sheba*	Shirley Booth, *Come Back, Little Sheba*
1951	*The Rose Tattoo*, Tennessee Williams	Claude Rains, *Darkness at Noon*	Uta Hagen, *The Country Girl*
1952	*The Fourposter*, Jan de Hartog	José Ferrer, *The Shrike*	Julie Harris, *I Am a Camera*
1953	*The Crucible*, Arthur Miller	Tom Ewell, *The Seven Year Itch*	Shirley Booth, *Time of the Cuckoo*
1954	*The Teahouse of the August Moon*, John Patrick	David Wayne, *The Teahouse of the August Moon*	Audrey Hepburn, *Ondine*
1955	*The Desperate Hours*, Joseph Hayes	Alfred Lunt, *Quadrille*	Nancy Kelly, *The Bad Seed*
1956	*The Diary of Anne Frank*, Frances Goodrich and Albert Hackett	Paul Muni, *Inherit the Wind*	Julie Harris, *The Lark*
1957	*Long Day's Journey Into Night*, Eugene O'Neill	Fredric March, *Long Day's Journey Into Night*	Margaret Leighton, *Separate Tables*
1958	*Sunrise at Campobello*, Dore Schary	Ralph Bellamy, *Sunrise at Campobello*	Helen Hayes, *Time Remembered*
1959	*J.B.*, Archibald Macleish	Jason Robards, *The Disenchanted*	Gertrude Berg, *A Majority of One*
1960	*The Miracle Worker*, William Gibson	Melvyn Douglas, *The Best Man*	Anne Bancroft, *The Miracle Worker*
1961	*Becket*, Jean Anouilh	Zero Mostel, *Rhinoceros*	Joan Plowright, *A Taste of Honey*
1962	*A Man for All Seasons*, Robert Bolt	Paul Scofield, *A Man for All Seasons*	Margaret Leighton, *Night of the Iguana*
1963	*Who's Afraid of Virginia Woolf*, Edward Albee	Arthur Hill, *Who's Afraid of Virginia Woolf*	Uta Hagen, *Who's Afraid of Virginia Woolf*
1964	*Luther*, John Osborne	Alec Guiness, *Dylan*	Sandy Dennis, *Any Wednesday*
1965	*The Subject Was Roses*, Frank Gilroy	Walter Matthau, *The Odd Couple*	Irene Worth, *Tiny Alice*
1966	*Marat*/Sade, Peter Weiss	Hal Holbrook, *Mark Twain Tonight!*	Rosemary Harris, *The Lion in Winter*

Year	Best Play	Best Actor	Best Actress
1967	*The Homecoming*, Harold Pinter	Paul Rogers, *The Homecoming*	Beryl Reid, *The Killing of Sister George*
1968	*Rosencrantz and Guildenstern are Dead*, Tom Stoppard	Martin Balsam, *You Know I Can't Hear You When the Water's Running*	Zoe Caldwell, *The Prime of Miss Jean Brodie*
1969	*The Great White Hope*, Howard Sackler	James Earl Jones, *The Great White Hope*	Julie Harris, *Forty Carats*
1970	*Borstal Boy*, Frank McMahon	Fritz Weaver, *Child's Play*	Tammy Grimes, *Private Lives* (R)
1971	*Sleuth*, Anthony Shaffer	Brian Bedford, *The School for Wives* (R)	Maureen Stapleton, *Gingerbread Lady*
1972	*Sticks and Bones*, David Rabe	Cliff Gorman, *Lenny*	Sada Thompson, *Twigs*
1973	*That Championship Season*, Jason Miller	Alan Bates, *Butley*	Julie Harris, *The Last of Mrs. Lincoln*
1974	*The River Niger* Joseph A. Walker	Michael Moriarty, *Find Your Way Home*	Colleen Dewhurst, *A Moon for the Misbegotten* (R)
1975	*Equus*, Peter Shaffer	John Kani, *Sizwe Banzi Is Dead* Winston Ntshona, *The Island*	Ellen Burstyn, *Same Time, Next Year*
1976	*Travesties*, Tom Stoppard	John Wood, *Travesties*	Irene Worth, *Sweet Bird of Youth* (R)
1977	*The Shadow Box*, Michael Cristofer	Al Pacino, *The Basic Training of Pavlo Hummel*	Julie Harris, *The Belle of Amherst*
1978	*Da*, Hugh Leonard	Barnard Hughes, *Da*	Jessica Tandy, *The Gin Game*
1979	*The Elephant Man*, Bernard Pomerance	Tom Conti, *Whose Life Is It Anyway?*	Constance Cummings, *Wings* Carole Shelley, *The Elephant Man*
1980	*Children of a Lesser God*, Mark Medoff	John Rubinstein, *Children of a Lesser God*	Phyllis Frelich, *Children of a Lesser God*
1981	*Amadeus*, Peter Shaffer	Ian McKellen, *Amadeus*	Jane Lapotaire, *Piaf*
1982	*The Life and Adventures of Nicholas Nickleby*, David Edgar	Roger Rees, *The Life and Adventures of Nicholas Nickleby*	Zoe Caldwell, *Medea* (R)
1983	*Torch Song Trilogy*, Harvey Fierstein	Harvey Fierstein, *Torch Song Trilogy*	Jessica Tandy, *Foxfire*
1984	*The Real Thing*, Tom Stoppard	Jeremy Irons, *The Real Thing*	Glenn Close, *The Real Thing*
1985	*Biloxi Blues*, Neil Simon	Derek Jacobi, *Much Ado About Nothing* (R)	Stockard Channing, *Joe Egg* (R)
1986	*I'm Not Rappaport*, Herb Gardner	Judd Hirsch, *I'm Not Rappaport*	Lily Tomlin, *The Search for Signs of Intelligent Life in the Universe*
1987	*Fences*, August Wilson	James Earl Jones, *Fences*	Linda Lavin, *Broadway Bound*
1988	*M. Butterfly*, David Henry Hwang	Ron Silver, *Speed-The-Plow*	Joan Allen, *Burn This*
1989	*The Heidi Chronicles*, Wendy Wasserstein	Philip Bosco, *Lend Me a Tenor*	Pauline Collins, *Shirley Valentine*
1990	*The Grapes of Wrath*, Frank Galati	Robert Morse, *Tru*	Maggie Smith, *Lettice and Lovage*
1991	*Lost in Yonkers*, Neil Simon	Nigel Hawthorne, *Shadowlands*	Mercedes Ruhl, *Lost in Yonkers*
1992	*Dancing at Lughnasa*, Brian Friel	Judd Hirsch, *Conversations with My Father*	Glenn Close, *Death and the Maiden*
1993	*Angels in America: Millennium Approaches*, Tony Kushner	Ron Leibman, *Angels in America: Millennium Approaches*	Madeline Kahn, *The Sisters Rosensweig*

Year	Best Play	Best Actor	Best Actress
1994	*Angels in America: Perestroika*, Tony Kushner	Stephen Spinella, *Angels in America: Perestroika*	Diana Rigg, *Medea* (R)
1995	*Love! Valour! Compassion!*, Terrence McNally	Ralph Fiennes, *Hamlet* (R)	Cherry Jones, *The Heiress* (R)
1996	*Master Class*, Terrence McNally	George Grizzard, *A Delicate Balance* (R)	Zoe Caldwell, *Master Class*
1997	*Last Night of Ballyhoo*, Alfred Uhry	Christopher Plummer, *Barrymore*	Janet McTeer, *A Doll's House* (R)
1998	*Art*, Yasmina Reza	Anthony La Paglia, *A View From the Bridge* (R)	Marie Mullen, *The Beauty Queen of Leenane*
1999	*Side Man*, Warren Leight	Brian Dennehy, *Death of a Salesman* (R)	Judi Dench, *Amy's View*
2000	*Copenhagen*, Michael Frayn	Stephen Dillane, *The Real Thing*	Jennifer Ehle, *The Real Thing*
2001	*Proof*, David Auburn	Richard Easton, *The Invention of Love*	Mary-Louise Parker, *Proof*
2002	*The Goat or Who Is Sylvia?*, Edward Albee	Alan Bates, *Fortune's Fool*	Lindsay Duncan, *Private Lives*
2003	*Take Me Out*, Richard Greenberg	Brian Dennehy, *Long Day's Journey Into Night* (R)	Vanessa Redgrave, *Long Day's Journey Into Night* (R)
2004	*I Am My Own Wife*, Doug Wright	Jefferson Mays, *I Am My Own Wife*	Phylicia Rashad, *A Raisin in the Sun*

MUSICALS

Year	Best Musical	Best Actor	Best Actress
1947	no award	no award	no award
1948	no award	Paul Hartman, *Angel in the Wings*	Grace Hartman, *Angel in the Wings*
1949	*Kiss Me Kate*, Cole Porter (M&L)	Ray Bolger, *Where's Charley?*	Nanette Fabray, *Love Life*
1950	*South Pacific*, Richard Rodgers(M), Oscar Hammerstein (L)	Ezio Pinza, *South Pacific*	Mary Martin, *South Pacific*
1951	*Guys and Dolls*, Frank Loesser (M&L)	Robert Alda, *Guys and Dolls*	Ethel Merman, *Call Me Madam*
1952	*The King and I*, Richard Rodgers (M), Oscar Hammerstein (L)	Phil Silvers, *Top Banana*	Gertrude Lawrence, *The King and I*
1953	*Wonderful Town*, Leonard Bernstein (M), Betty Comden, and Adolph Green (L)	Thomas Mitchell, *Hazel Flagg*	Rosalind Russell, *Wonderful Town*
1954	*Kismet*, Alexander Borodin (M), adapted by Robert Wright and George Forrest (L)	Alfred Drake, *Kismet*	Dolores Gray, *Carnival in Flanders*
1955	*The Pajama Game*, Richard Adler and Jerry Ross (M&L)	Walter Slezak, *Fanny*	Mary Martin, *Peter Pan*
1956	*Damn Yankees*, Richard Adler and Jerry Ross (M&L)	Ray Walston, *Damn Yankees*	Gwen Verdon, *Damn Yankees*
1957	*My Fair Lady*, Frederick Loewe (M), Alan Jay Lerner (L)	Rex Harrison, *My Fair Lady*	Judy Holliday, *Bells Are Ringing*
1958	*The Music Man*, Meredith Willson (M&L)	Robert Preston, *The Music Man*	(tie) Thelma Ritter, Gwen Verdon, *New Girl in Town*
1959	*Redhead*, Albert Hague (M), Dorothy Fields (L)	Richard Kiley, *Redhead*	Gwen Verdon, *Redhead*

Year	Best Musical	Best Actor	Best Actress
1960	(tie) *Fiorello*, Jerry Bock (M), Sheldon Harnick (L); *The Sound of Music*, Richard Rodgers (M), Oscar Hammerstein (L)	Jackie Gleason, *Take Me Along*	Mary Martin, *The Sound of Music*
1961	*Bye, Bye, Birdie*, Charles Strouse (M), Lee Adams (L)	Richard Burton, *Camelot*	Elizabeth Seal, *Irma la Douce*
1962	*How to Succeed in Business Without Really Trying*, Frank Loesser (M&L)	Robert Morse, *How to Succeed in Business Without Really Trying*	(tie) Anna Maria Alberghetti, *Carnival*; Diahann Carroll, *No Strings*
1963	*A Funny Thing Happened on the Way to the Forum*, Stephen Sondheim (M&L)	Zero Mostel, *A Funny Thing Happened on the Way to the Forum*	Vivien Leigh, *Tovarich*
1964	*Hello, Dolly!* Jerry Herman (M&L)	Bert Lahr, *Foxy*	Carol Channing, *Hello, Dolly!*
1965	*Fiddler on the Roof*, Jerry Bock (M), Sheldon Harnick (L)	Zero Mostel, *Fiddler on the Roof*	Liza Minnelli, *Flora, the Red Menace*
1966	*Man of La Mancha*, Mitch Leigh (M), Joe Darion (L)	Richard Kiley, *Man of La Mancha*	Angela Lansbury, *Mame*
1967	*Cabaret*, John Kander (M), Fred Ebb (L)	Robert Preston, *I Do! I Do!*	Barbara Harris, *The Apple Tree*
1968	*Hallelujah, Baby!* Jule Styne (M), Betty Comden & Adolph Green (L)	Robert Goulet, *The Happy Time*	Patricia Routledge, *Darling of the Day* Leslie Uggams, *Hallelujah, Baby!*
1969	*1776*, Sherman Edwards (M&L)	Jerry Orbach, *Promises, Promises*	Angela Lansbury, *Dear World*
1970	*Applause*, Charles Strouse (M), Lee Adams (L)	Cleavon Little, *Purlie*	Lauren Bacall, *Applause*
1971	*Company*, Stephen Sondheim (M&L)	Hal Linden, *The Rothschilds*	Helen Gallagher, *No, No Nannette* (R)
1972	*Two Gentlemen of Verona* [best score: *Follies*, Stephen Sondheim (M&L)]	Phil Silvers, *A Funny Thing Happened on the Way to the Forum* (R)	Alexis Smith, *Follies*
1973	*A Little Night Music*, Stephen Sondheim (M&L)	Ben Vereen, *Pippin*	Glynis Johns, *A Little Night Music*
1974	*Raisin*, [best score: *Gigi*, Frederick Loewe (M), Alan Jay Lerner (L)]	Christopher Plummer, *Cyrano*	Virginia Capers, *Raisin*
1975	*The Wiz*, Charlie Smalls (M&L)	John Cullum, *Shenandoah*	Angela Lansbury, *Gypsy* (R)
1976	*A Chorus Line*, Marvin Hamlisch (M), Edward Kleban (L)	George Rose, *My Fair Lady* (R)	Donna McKechnie, *A Chorus Line*
1977	*Annie*, Charles Strouse (M), Martin Charnin (L)	Barry Bostwick, *The Robber Bridegroom*	Dorothy Loudon, *Annie*
1978	*Ain't Misbehavin'* [best score: *On the Twentieth Century*, Cy Coleman (M) Betty Comden and Adolph Green (L)]	John Cullum, *On the Twentieth Century*	Liza Minnelli, *The Act*
1979	*Sweeney Todd*, Stephen Sondheim	Len Cariou, *Sweeney Todd*	Angela Lansbury, *Sweeney Todd*
1980	*Evita*, Andrew Lloyd Webber (M), Tim Rice (L)	Jim Dale, *Barnum*	Patti LuPone, *Evita*
1981	*42nd Street*, [best score: *Woman of the Year*, John Kander (M), Fred Ebb (L)]	Kevin Kline, *The Pirates of Penzance*	Lauren Bacall, *Woman of the Year*
1982	*Nine*, Maury Yeston (M&L)	Ben Harney, *Dreamgirls*	Jennifer Holliday, *Dreamgirls*
1983	*Cats*, Andrew Lloyd Webber (M), T.S. Eliot (L)	Tommy Tune, *My One and Only*	Natalia Makarova, *On Your Toes*
1984	*La Cage Aux Folles*, Jerry Herman (M&L)	George Hearn, *La Cage Aux Folles*	Chita Rivera, *The Rink*
1985	*Big River*, Roger Miller (M&L)	No award	No award

Year	Best Musical	Best Actor	Best Actress
1986	*The Mystery of Edwin Drood*, Rupert Holmes (M&L)	George Rose, *The Mystery of Edwin Drood*	Bernadette Peters, *Song and Dance*
1987	*Les Misérables*, Claude-Michel Schönberg (M); Herbert Kretzmer & Alain Boublil (L)	Robert Lindsay, *Me and My Girl*	Maryann Plunkett, *Me and My Girl*
1988	*The Phantom of the Opera* [best score: *Into the Woods*, Stephen Sondheim (M&L)]	Michael Crawford, *The Phantom of the Opera*	Joanna Gleason, *Into the Woods*
1989	Jerome Robbins' *Broadway* [best score: no award]	Jason Alexander, Jerome Robbins' *Broadway*	Ruth Brown, *Black and Blue*
1990	*City of Angels*, Cy Coleman (M) David Zippel (L)	James Naughton, *City of Angels*	Tyne Daly, *Gypsy* (R)
1991	*The Will Rogers Follies*, Cy Coleman (M); Betty Comden and Adolph Green (L)	Jonathan Pryce, Miss Saigon	Lea Salonga, *Miss Saigon*
1992	*Crazy for You*, [best score: *Falsettos*, William Finn (M&L)]	Gregory Hines, *Jelly's Last Jam*	Faith Prince, *Guys and Dolls* (R)
1993	*Kiss of the Spider Woman* [best score: (tie) *Kiss of the Spider Woman*, John Kander (M) and Fred Ebb (L); *Tommy*, Pete Townshend (M&L)]	Brent Carver, *Kiss of the Spider Woman*	Chita Rivera, *Kiss of the Spider Woman*
1994	*Passion*, Stephen Sondheim (M&L)	Boyd Gaines, *She Loves Me* (R)	Donna Murphy, *Passion*
1995	*Sunset Boulevard*, Andrew Lloyd Webber (M&L)	Matthew Broderick, *How to Succeed in Business Without Really Trying* (R)	Glenn Close, *Sunset Boulevard*
1996	*Rent*, Jonathan Larson (M&L)	Nathan Lane, *A Funny Thing Happened on the Way to the Forum* (R)	Donna Murphy, *The King and I* (R)
1997	*Titanic*, Maury Yeston (M&L)	James McNaughton, *Chicago* (R)	Bebe Neuwirth, *Chicago* (R)
1998	*The Lion King*, [best score: *Ragtime*, Stephen Flaherty & Lynn Ahrens (M&L)]	Alan Cumming, *Cabaret* (R)	Natasha Richardson, *Cabaret* (R)
1999	*Fosse*, [best score: *Parade*, Jason Robert Brown (M&L)]	Martin Short, *Little Me* (R)	Bernadette Peters, *Annie Get Your Gun* (R)
2000	*Contact* [best score: *Aida*, Elton John (M) and Tim Rice (L)]	Brian Stokes Mitchell, *Kiss Me Kate* (R)	Heather Headley, *Aida*
2001	*The Producers*, Mel Brooks (M&L)	Nathan Lane, *The Producers*	Christine Ebersole, *42nd Street* (R)
2002	*Thoroughly Modern Millie*, [best score: *Urinetown: The Musical*, Mark Hollmann (M); Mark Hollman and Greg Kotis (L)]	John Lithgow, *Sweet Smell of Success*	Sutton Foster, *Thoroughly Modern Millie*
2003	*Hairspray*, Scott Whittman, Marc Shaiman (M&L)	Harvey Fierstein, *Hairspray*	Marissa Jaret Winokur, *Hairspray*
2004	*Avenue Q*, Robert Lopez and Jeff Marx (M&L)	Hugh Jackman, *The Boy From Oz*	Idinia Menzel, *Wicked*

M = music; L = lyrics, R = revival. **Note:** Since 1971 "Musical" and "Score" have been separate categories. However, the winner of the Tony for Best Musical usually wins the award for Best Score, except where otherwise indicated.
Source: Isabelle Stevenson, The Tony Award 1989; American Theatre Wing.

The Grammys, 1958–2002

The "Grammys" are officially known as the National Academy of Recording Arts and Sciences Awards. Winners (in almost 70 categories) are selected yearly by the 6,000 or so voting members of the academy. The five award categories listed below have remained fairly constant over the years, although the overall "Best Vocal Performance" awards were phased out in 1968. From that year on, we list "Best Pop Vocal Performance" (male and female), except where indicated.

Year	Record of the year	Album of the year	Song of the year	Best male vocal performance	Best female vocal performance
1958	Domenico Modugno, "Nel Blu Dipinto di Blu (Volare)"	Henry Mancini, *The Music from Peter Gunn*	Domenico Modugno, "Nel Blu Dipinto di Blu (Volare)"	Perry Como, "Catch a Falling Star"	Ella Fitzgerald, *Ella Fitzgerald Sings the Irving Berlin Songbook*[2]
1959	Bobby Darin, "Mack the Knife"	Frank Sinatra, *Come Dance with Me*	Jimmy Driftwood, "The Battle of New Orleans"	Frank Sinatra, "Come Dance with Me"	Ella Fitzgerald, "But Not for Me"
1960	Percy Faith, "Theme from a Summer Place"	Bob Newhart, *Button-Down Mind*	Ernest Gold, "Theme from Exodus"	Ray Charles, "Georgia on My Mind"	Ella Fitzgerald, "Mack the Knife"
1961	Henry Mancini, "Moon River"	Judy Garland, *Judy at Carnegie Hall*	Henry Mancini, Johnny Mercer, "Moon River"	Jack Jones, "Lollipops and Roses"	Judy Garland, *Judy at Carnegie Hall*
1962	Tony Bennett, "I Left My Heart in San Francisco"	Vaughn Meader, *The First Family*	Leslie Bricusse, Anthony Newley, "What Kind of Fool Am I?"	Tony Bennett, "I Left My Heart in San Francisco"	Ella Fitzgerald, *Ella Swings Brightly with Nelson Riddle*
1963	Henry Mancini, "The Days of Wine and Roses"	Barbra Streisand, *The Barbra Streisand Album*	Henry Mancini, Johnny Mercer, "The Days of Wine and Roses"	Jack Jones, "Wives and Lovers"	Barbra Streisand, *The Barbra Streisand Album*
1964	Stan Getz, Astrud Gilberto, "The Girl from Ipanema"	Stan Getz, Astrud Gilberto, *Getz/Gilberto*	Jerry Herman, "Hello, Dolly!"	Louis Armstrong, "Hello, Dolly!"	Barbra Streisand, "People"
1965	Herb Alpert & the Tijuana Brass, "A Taste of Honey"	Frank Sinatra, *September of My Years*	Paul Francis Webster, Johnny Mandel, "The Shadow of Your Smile"	Frank Sinatra, "It Was a Very Good Year"	Barbra Streisand, *My Name is Barbra*
1966	Frank Sinatra, Strangers in the Night	Frank Sinatra, *A Man and His Music*	John Lennon, Paul McCartney, "Michelle"	Frank Sinatra, "Strangers in the Night"	Eydie Gorme, "If He Walked into My Life"
1967	5th Dimension, "Up, Up and Away"	The Beatles, *Sgt. Pepper's Lonely Hearts Club Band*	Jim Webb, "Up, Up, and Away"	Glen Campbell, "By the Time I Get to Phoenix"	Bobbie Gentry, "Ode to Billie Joe"
1968	Simon & Garfunkel, "Mrs. Robinson"	Glen Campbell, *By the Time I Get to Phoenix*	Bobby Russell, "Little Green Apples"	Jose Feliciano3, "Light My Fire"	Dionne Warwick, "Do You Know the Way to San Jose?"
1969	5th Dimension, "Aquarius/Let the Sunshine In"	Blood, Sweat & Tears, *Blood, Sweat & Tears*	Joe South, "Games People Play"	Harry Nilsson[4], "Everybody's Talkin'"	Peggy Lee, "Is That All There Is?"
1970	Simon & Garfunkel, "Mrs. Robinson"	Simon & Garfunkel, *Bridge over Troubled Water*	Paul Simon, "Bridge over Troubled Water"	Ray Stevens[4], "Everything is Beautiful"	Dionne Warwick, "I'll Never Fall in Love Again"

Year	Record of the year	Album of the year	Song of the year	Best male vocal performance	Best female vocal performance
1971	Carole King, "It's Too Late"	Carole King, *Tapestry*	Carole King, "You've Got a Friend"	James Taylor[5], "You've Got a Friend"	Carole King, "Tapestry"
1972	Roberta Flack, "The First Time Ever I Saw Your Face"	George Harrison, Ravi Shankar, Bob Dylan et al, *Concert for Bangladesh*	Ewan McColl, "The First Time Ever I Saw Your Face"	Harry Nilsson, "Without You"	Helen Reddy, "I Am Woman"
1973	Roberta Flack, "Killing Me Softly with His Song"	Stevie Wonder, *Innervisions*	Norman Gimbel, Charles Fox, "Killing Me Softly with His Song"	Stevie Wonder, "You Are the Sunshine of My Life"	Roberta Flack, "Killing Me Softly with His Song"
1974	Olivia "Newton-John, I Honestly Love You"	Stevie Wonder, *Fulfillingness' First Finale*	Marilyn & Alan Bergman, Marvin Hamlisch, "The Way We Were"	Stevie Wonder, "Fulfillingness' First Finale"	Olivia Newton-John, "I Honestly Love You"
1975	Captain & Tennille, "Love Will Keep Us Together"	Paul Simon, *Still Crazy After All These Years*	Stephen Sondheim, "Send in the Clowns"	Paul Simon, "Still Crazy after All These Years"	Janis Ian, "At Seventeen"
1976	George Benson, "This Masquerade"	Stevie Wonder, *Songs in the Key of Life*	Bruce Johnston, "I Write the Songs"	Stevie Wonder, "Songs in the Key of Life"	Linda Ronstadt, "Hasten Down the Wind"
1977	The Eagles, "Hotel California	Fleetwood Mac, *Rumours*	Barbra Streisand, Paul Williams, "Evergreen"	James Taylor, "Handy Man"	Barbra Streisand, "Evergreen"
1978	Billy Joel, "Just theWay You Are"	Various artists, *Saturday Night Fever*	Billy Joel, "Just the Way You Are"	Barry Manilow, "Copacabana (At the Copa)"	Anne Murray, "You Needed Me"
1979	The Doobie Brothers, "What a Fool Believes"	Billy Joel, *52nd Street*	Kenny Loggins, Michael McDonald, "What a Fool Believes"	Billy Joel, "52nd Street"	Dionne Warwick, "I'll Never Love This Way Again"
1980	Christopher Cross, "Sailing"	Christopher Cross, *Christopher Cross*	Christopher Cross, "Sailing"	Kenny Loggins, "This Is It'	Bette Midler, "The Rose"
1981	Kim Carnes, "Bette Davis Eyes"	John Lennon/Yoko Ono, *Double Fantasy*	Donna Weiss, Jackie DeShannon, "Bette Davis Eyes"	Al Jarreau, "Breakin' Away"	Lena Horne, *The Lady and Her Music Live on Broadway*
1982	Toto, "Rosanna"	Toto, *Toto IV*	Johnny Christopher, Mark James, Wayne Carson, "Always on My Mind"	Lionel Richie, "Truly"	Melissa Manchester, "You Should Hear How She Talks About You"
1983	Michael Jackson, "Beat It"	Michael Jackson, *Thriller*	Sting, "Every Breath You Take"	Michael Jackson, "Thriller"	Irene Cara, *Flashdance... What a Feeling*
1984	Tina Turner, "What's Love Got to Do with It?"	Lionel Richie, *Can't Slow Down*	Graham Lyle, Terry Britten, "What's Love Got to Do with It?"	Phil Collins, "Against All Odds (Take a Look at Me Now)"	Tina Turner, "What's Love Got to Do with It?"
1985	USA for Africa, "We Are the World"	Phil Collins, *No Jacket Required*	Michael Jackson, Lionel Richie, "We Are the World"	Phil Collins, "No Jacket Required"	Whitney Houston, "Saving All My Love for You"
1986	Steve Winwood, "Higher Love"	Paul Simon, *Graceland*	Various, "That's What Friends Are For"	Steve Winwood, "Higher Love"	Barbra Streisand, *The Broadway Album*

Year	Record of the year	Album of the year	Song of the year	Best male vocal performance	Best female vocal performance
1987	Paul Simon, "Graceland"	U2, *The Joshua Tree*	Linda Ronstadt, James Ingram, "Somewhere Out There"	Sting, "Bring on the Night"	Whitney Houston, "I Wanna Dance with Somebody (Who Loves Me)"
1988	Bobby McFerrin, "Don't Worry, Be Happy"	George Michael, *Faith*	Bobby McFerrin, "Don't Worry, Be Happy"	Bobby McFerrin, "Don't Worry, Be Happy"	Tracy Chapman, "Fast Car"
1989	Bette Midler, "Wind Beneath My Wings"	Bonnie Rait, *Nick of Time*	Bette Midler, "Wind Beneath My Wings"	Michael Bolton, "How Am I Supposed to Live Without You"	Bonnie Raitt, "Nick of Time"
1990	Phil Collins, "Another Day in Paradise"	Quincy Jones, *Back on the Block*	Julie Gold, "From a Distance"	Roy Orbison, "Oh, Pretty Woman"	Mariah Carey, *Vision of Love*
1991	Natalie Cole, "Unforgettable"	Natalie Cole , *Unforgettable*	Irving Gordon, "Unforgettable"	Michael Bolton, "When a Man Loves a Woman"	Bonnie Raitt, *Something to Talk About*
1992	Eric Clapton, "Tears in Heaven"	Eric Clapton, *Unplugged*	Eric Clapton, "Tears in Heaven"	Eric Clapton, "Tears in Heaven'	k.d. Lang, "Constant Craving"
1993	Whitney Houston, "I Will Always Love You"	Whitney Houston, *The Bodyguard*	Alan Menken and Tim Rice, " A Whole New World"	Sting, "If I Ever Lose My Faith in You"	Whitney Houston, "I Will Always Love You"
1994	Sheryl Crow, "All I Wanna Do"	Tony Bennett, *MTV Unplugged*	Bruce Springsteen, "Streets of Philadelphia"	Elton John, "Can You Feel the Love Tonight"	Sheryl Crow, "All I Wanna Do"
1995	Seal, "Kiss From a Rose"	Alanis Morissette, *Jagged Little Pill*	Seal, "Kiss From a Rose"	Seal, "Kiss From a Rose"	Annie Lennox, *"No More "I Love Yous"*
1996	Eric Clapton, "Change the World"	Celine Dion, *Falling Into You*	Wayne Kirkpatrick and Tommy Sims, "Change the World"	Eric Clapton, "Change the World"	Toni Braxton, "Unbreak My Heart"
1997	Shawn Colvin, "Sunny Came Home"	Bob Dylan, *Time Out of Mind*	Shawn Colvin and John Leventhal, "Sunny Came Home"	Elton John, "Candle in the Wind" 1997	Sarah McLachlan, "Building a Mystery"
1998	Celine Dion, "My Heart Will Go On"	Lauryn Hill, *The Miseducation of Lauryn Hill*	James Horner and Will Jennings, "My Heart Will Go On"	Eric Clapton, "My Father's Eyes"	Celine Dion, "My Heart Will Go On"
1999	Santana, "Smooth"	Santana, *Supernatural*	Itaal Shur and Rob Thomas, "Smooth"	Sting, "Brand New Day"	Sara McLachlan, "I Will Remember You"
2000	U2, "Beautiful Day"	Steely Dan, *Two Against Nature*	U2 "Beautiful Day"	Sting, "She Walks This Earth"	Macy Gray, "I Try"
2001	U2, "Walk On"	Various artists, *O Brother, Where Art Thou?*	Alicia Keys, "Fallin'"	James Taylor, "Don't Let Me Be Lonely Tonight"	Nelly Furtado, "I'm Like a Bird"
2002	Norah Jones, "Don't Know Why"	Norah Jones, *Come Away With Me*	Norah Jones, "Don't Know Why"	John Mayer, "Your Body is a Wonderland"	Norah Jones, "Don't Know Why"
2003	Coldplay, "Clocks"	Outkast, *Speakerboxxx/ The Love Below*	Luther Vandross & Richard Marx, "Dance with My Father"	Justin Timberlake, "Cry Me a River"	Christina Aguilera "Beautiful"

1. Awarded to the composer, rather than the performer, of the song. 2. Awarded for an album, rather than an individual song. 3. Award given for "Best Contemporary Pop Vocal Performance." 4. Award given for "Best Vocal Performance Contemporary." 5. From 1971 on, all awards are for "Best Pop Vocal Performance." **Source**: National Academy of Recording Arts and Sciences; www.grammy.com.

Pulitzer Prizes

Named for the man who created the endowment, Joseph Pulitzer (1847–1911), a Hungarian-born American newspaper publisher. He ran the *St. Louis Post-Dispatch* and the *New York World* at the end of the 19th century and helped to create many bedrock technologies of modern journalism—some good, some a bit sleazy. He also endowed the famous school of journalism at Columbia University. The Pulitzer Prize for Reporting is the oldest prize given in journalism and was first awarded in 1917 together with the Pulitzer Prizes for History and Biography.

Pulitzer Prize for Public Service in Newspaper Journalism, 1918–2004

Year	Paper
1918	*New York Times*
1919	*Milwaukee Journal*
1920	No award
1921	*Boston Post*
1922	*New York World*
1923	*Memphis Commercial Appeal*
1924	*New York World*
1925	No award
1926	*Columbus* (Ga.) *Enquirer Sun*
1927	*Canton* (Ohio) *Daily News*
1928	*Indianapolis Times*
1929	*New York Evening World*
1930	No award
1931	*Atlanta Constitution*
1932	*Indianapolis News*
1933	*New York World-Telegram*
1934	*Medford* (Oreg.) *Mail Tribune*
1935	*Sacramento Bee*
1936	*Cedar Rapids Gazette*
1937	*St. Louis Post-Dispatch*
1938	*Bismarck* (N.D.) *Tribune*
1939	*Miami Daily News*
1940	*Waterbury* (Conn.) *Republican & American*
1941	*St. Louis Post-Dispatch*
1942	*Los Angeles Times*
1943	*Omaha* (Nebr.) *World-Herald*
1944	*The New York Times*
1945	*Detroit Free Press*
1946	*Scranton* (Pa.) *Times*
1947	*Baltimore Sun*
1948	*St. Louis Post-Dispatch*
1949	*Nebraska State Journal*
1950	*Chicago Daily News* and *St. Louis Post-Dispatch*
1951	*Miami Herald* and *Brooklyn Eagle*
1952	*St. Louis Post-Dispatch*
1953	*Whiteville* (N.C.) *News Reporter* and *Tabor City* (N.C.) *Tribune*
1954	*Newsday* (Garden City, N.Y.)
1955	*Columbus* (Ga.) *Ledger* and *Sunday Ledger-Enquirer*
1956	*Watsonville* (Calif.) *Register-Pajaronion*
1957	*Chicago Daily News*
1958	*Arkansas Gazette*
1959	*Utica Observer-Dispatch* and *Utica Daily Press* (N.Y.)
1960	*Los Angeles Times*
1961	*Amarillo* (Tex.) *Globe-Times*
1962	*Panama City* (Fla.) *News-Herald*
1963	*Chicago Daily News*
1964	*St. Petersburg Times*
1965	*Hutchinson* (Kans.) *News*
1966	*Boston Globe*
1967	*Louisville Courier Journal* and *Milwaukee Journal*
1968	*Riverside* (Calif.) *Press-Enterprise*
1969	*Los Angeles Times*
1970	*Newsday* (Garden City, N.Y.)
1971	*Winston-Salem Journal and Sentinel*
1972	*New York Times*
1973	*Washington Post*
1974	*Newsday* (Garden City, N.Y.)
1975	*Boston Globe*
1976	*Anchorage Daily News*
1977	*Lufkin* (Tex.) *News*
1978	*Philadelphia Inquirer*
1979	*Point Reyes* (Calif.) *Light*
1980	*Gannett News Service*
1981	*Charlotte Observer*
1982	*Detroit News*
1983	*Jackson* (Miss.) *Clarion-Ledger*
1984	*Los Angeles Times*
1985	*Fort Worth Star-Telegram*
1986	*Denver Post*
1987	*Pittsburgh Press*
1988	*Charlotte Observer*
1989	*Anchorage Daily News*
1990	*Philadelphia Inquirer* and *Washington* (N.C.) *Daily News*
1991	*Des Moines Register*
1992	*Sacramento Bee*
1993	*Miami Herald*
1994	*Akron Beacon Journal*

1995	*Virgin Islands Daily News*
1996	*Raleigh News and Observer*
1997	*New Orleans Times-Picayune*
1998	*Grand Forks* (N.D.) *Herald*
1999	*Washington Post*
2000	*Washington Post*
2001	*The Oregonian* (Portland, Ore.)
2002	*New York Times*
2003	*The Boston Globe*
2004	*New York Times*

Pulitzer Prize for National Reporting, 1942–2004

Year	Winner, Newspaper
1942	Louis Stark, *New York Times*
1943	No award
1944	Dewey L. Fleming, *Baltimore Sun*
1945	James B. Reston, *New York Times*
1946	Edward A. Harris, *St. Louis Post-Dispatch*
1947	Edward T. Folliard, *Washington Post*
1948	Bert Andrews, *New York Herald Tribune*
	Nat S. Finney, *Minneapolis Tribune*
1949	C.P. Trussell, *New York Times*
1950	Edwin O. Guthman, *Seattle Times*
1951	No award[1]
1952	Anthony Leviero, *New York Times*
1953	Don Whitehead, *Associated Press*
1954	Richard Wilson, *Des Moines Register and Tribune*
1955	Anthony Lewis, *Washington Daily News*
1956	Charles L. Bartlett, *Chattanooga Times*
1957	James B. Reston, *New York Times*
1958	Relman Morin, *Associated Press*
	Clark Mollenhoff, *Des Moines Register and Tribune*
1959	Howard Van Smith, *Miami News*
1960	Vance Trimble, *Scripps-Howard Newspaper Alliance*
1961	Edward R. Cony, *Wall Street Journal*
1962	Nathan G. Caldwell and Gene S. Graham, *Nashville Tennessean*
1963	Anthony Lewis, *New York Times*
1964	Merriman Smith, *United Press International*
1965	Louis M. Kohlmeier, *Wall Street Journal*
1966	Haynes Johnson, *Washington Evening Star*
1967	Stanley Penn & Monroe Karmin, *Wall Street Journal*
1968	Howard James, *Christian Science Monitor*
	Nathan K. (Nick) Kotz, *Des Moines Register* and *Minneapolis Tribune*
1969	Robert Cahn, *Christian Science Monitor*
1970	William J. Eaton, *Chicago Daily News*
1971	Lucinda Franks and Thomas Powers, *United Press International*
1972	Jack Anderson, (Syndicated columnist)
1973	Robert Boyd and Clark Hoyt, *Knight Newspapers*
1974	James R. Polk, *Washington Star-News*
	Jack White, *Providence Journal and EveningBulletin*
1975	Donald L. Bartlett and James B. Steele, *Philadelphia Inquirer*
1976	James Risser, *Des Moines Register*
1977	Walter Mears, *Associated Press*
1978	Gaylord D. Shaw, *Los Angeles Times*
1979	James Risser, *Des Moines Register*
1980	Bette Swenson Orsini and Charles Stafford, *St. Petersburg Times*
1981	John M Crewdson, *New York Times*
1982	Rick Atkinson, *Kansas City Times*
1983	Staff, *Boston Globe*
1984	John Noble Wilford, *New York Times*
1985	Thomas J. Knudson, *Des Moines Register*
1986	Arthur Howe, *Philadelphia Inquirer*; Craig Flournoy and George Rodrigues, *Dallas Morning News*
1987	Staff, *Miami Herald*; Staff, *New York Times*
1988	Tim Weiner, *Philadelphia Inquirer*
1989	Donald L. Bartlett and James B. Steele, *Philadelphia Inquirer*
1990	Ross Anderson, Bill Dietrich, Mary Ann Gwinn, and Eric Nalder, *Seattle Times*
1991	Marji Lundstrom and Rochelle Sharpe, *Gannet News Service*
1992	Jeff Taylor and Mike McGraw, *Kansas City Star*
1993	David Maraniss, *Washington Post*
1994	Eileen Welsome, *Albuquerque Tribune*
1995	Tony Horwitz, *Wall Street Journal*
1996	Alix M. Freedman, *Wall Street Journal*
1997	Staff, *Wall Street Journal*
1998	Russell Carollo and Jeff Nesmith, *Dayton* (Ohio) *Daily News*
1999	Staff, *New York Times*
2000	Staff, *Wall Street Journal*
2001	Staff, *New York Times*
2002	Staff, *Washington Post*
2003	Alan Miller and Kevin Sack, *Los Angeles Times*
2004	Staff, *Los Angeles Times*

1. The board decided that Arthur Krock of *The New York Times* deserved the prize but he could not accept because he was a board member.

Pulitzer Prize for International Reporting, 1942–2004

Year	Winner, Newspaper
1942	Lawrence Edmund Allen, *Associated Press*
1943	Ira Wolfert, *North American Newspaper Alliance, Inc.*
1944	Daniel DeLuce, *Associated Press*
1945	Mark S. Watson, *Baltimore Sun*
1946	Homer William Bigart, *New York Herald Tribune*
1947	Eddy Gilmore, *Associated Press*
1948	Paul W. Ward, *Baltimore Sun*
1949	Price Day, *Baltimore Sun*
1950	Edmund Stevens, *Christian Science Monitor*
1951	Keyes Beech, *Chicago Daily News*
	Homer William Bigart, *New York Herald Tribune*
	Marguerite Higgins, *New York Herald Tribune*
	Relman Morin, *Associated Press*
	Fred Sparks, *Chicago Daily News*
	Don Whitehead, *Associated Press*
1952	John M. Hightower, *Associated Press*
1953	Austin Wehrwien, *Milwaukee Journal*
1954	Jim G. Lucas, *Scripps-Howard Newspaper Alliance*
1955	Harrison E. Salisbury, *New York Times*
1956	William Randolph Hearst Jr., Kingsbury Smith, and Frank Conniff, *International News Service*
1957	Russell Jones, *United Press*
1958	Staff, *New York Times*
1959	Joseph Martin and Philip Santora, *New York Daily News*
1960	A.M. Rosenthal, *New York Times*
1961	Lynn Heinzerling, *Associated Press*
1962	Walter Lippmann, *New York Herald Tribune Syndicate*
1963	Hal Hendrix, *Miami News*
1964	Malcolm W. Browne, *Associated Press*
	David Halberstam, *New York Times*
1965	J. A. Livingston, *Philadelphia Bulletin*
1966	Peter Arnett, *Associated Press*
1967	R. John Hughes, *Christian Science Monitor*
1968	Alfred Friendly, *Washington Post*
1969	William Tuohy, *Los Angeles Times*
1970	Seymour M. Hersh, *Dispatch News Service*
1971	Jimmie Lee Hoagland, *Washington Post*
1972	Peter R. Kann, *Wall Street Journal*
1973	Max Frankel, *New York Times*
1974	Hedrick Smith, *New York Times*
1975	William Mullen (reporter), Ovie Carter (photographer), *Chicago Tribune*
1976	Sydney H. Schanberg, *New York Times*
1977	No award
1978	Henry Kamm, *New York Times*
1979	Richard Ben Cramer, *Philadelphia Inquirer*
1980	Joel Brinkley (reporter), Jay Mather (photographer), *Louisville Courier-Journal*
1981	Shirley Christian, *Miami Herald*
1982	John Darnton, *New York Times*
1983	Thomas L. Friedman, *New York Times*
	Loren Jenkins, *Washington Post*
1984	Karen Elliott House, *Wall Street Journal*
1985	Josh Friedman and Dennis Bell (reporters) and Ozier Muhammad (photographer), *Newsday* (Garden City, N.Y.)
1986	Lewis M. Simons, Pete Carey, and Katherine Ellison, *San Jose Mercury News*
1987	Michael Parks, *Los Angeles Times*
1988	Thomas L. Friedman, *New York Times*
1989	Glenn Frankel, *Washington Post*
	Bill Keller, *New York Times*
1990	Nicholas D. Kristof and Sheryl WuDunn, *New York Times*
1991	Caryle Murphy, *Washington Post*
	Serge Schmemann, *New York Times*
1992	Patrick J. Sloyan, *Newsday* (Garden City, N.Y.)
1993	John F. Burns, *New York Times*
	Roy Gutman, *Newsday* (Garden City, N.Y.)
1994	Team of reporters, *Dallas Morning News*
1995	Mark Fritz, *Associated Press*
1996	David Rohde, *Christian Science Monitor*
1997	John F. Burns, *New York Times*
1998	Staff, *New York Times*
1999	Staff, *Wall Street Journal*
2000	Mark Schoofs, *Village Voice* (N.Y. City)
2001	Ian Johnson, *Wall Street Journal*
	Paul Salopek, *Chicago Tribune*
2002	Barry Bearak, *New York Times*
2003	Kevin Sullivan and Mary Jordan, *Washington Post*
2004	Anthony Shadid, *Washington Post*

The Pulitzer Prize for Fiction, 1918–2004

Year	Author, Title
1918	Ernest Poole, *His Family*
1919	Booth Tarkington, *The Magnificent Ambersons*
1920	No award
1921	Edith Wharton, *The Age of Innocence*
1922	Booth Tarkington, *Alice Adams*
1923	Willa Cather, *One of Ours*
1924	Margaret Wilson, *The Able McLaughlins*
1925	Edna Ferber, *So Big*
1926	Sinclair Lewis, *Arrowsmith*
1927	Louis Bromfield, *Early Autumn*
1928	Thornton Wilder, *The Bridge of San Luis Rey*
1929	Julia Peterkin, *Scarlet Sister Mary*
1930	Oliver LaFarge, *Laughing Boy*
1931	Margaret Ayer Barnes, *Years of Grace*
1932	Pearl S. Buck, *The Good Earth*
1933	T.S. Stribling, *The Store*
1934	Caroline Miller, *Lamb in His Bosom*
1935	Josephine Winslow Johnson, *Now in November*
1936	Harold L. Davis, *Honey in the Horn*
1937	Margaret Mitchell, *Gone With the Wind*
1938	John Phillips Marquand, *The Late George Apley*
1939	Marjorie Kinnan Rawlings, *The Yearling*
1940	John Steinbeck, *The Grapes of Wrath*
1941	No award
1942	Ellen Glasgow, *In This Our Life*
1943	Upton Sinclair, *Dragon's Teeth*
1944	Martin Flavin, *Journey in the Dark*
1945	John Hersey, *A Bell for Adano*
1946	No award
1947	Robert Penn Warren, *All the King's Men*
1948[1]	James A. Michener, *Tales of the South Pacific*
1949	James Gould Cozzens, *Guard of Honor*
1950	A.B. Guthrie Jr., *The Way West*
1951	Conrad Richter, *The Town*
1952	Herman Wouk, *The Caine Mutiny*
1953	Ernest Hemingway, *The Old Man and the Sea*
1954	No award
1955	William Faulkner, *A Fable*
1956	MacKinlay Kantor, *Andersonville*
1957	No award
1958	James Agee, *A Death in the Family*
1959	Robert Lewis Taylor, *The Travels of Jaimie McPheeters*
1960	Allen Drury, *Advise and Consent*
1961	Harper Lee, *To Kill a Mockingbird*
1962	Edwin O'Connor, *The Edge of Sadness*
1963	William Faulkner, *The Reivers*
1964	No award
1965	Shirley Ann Grau, *The Keepers of the House*
1966	Katherine Anne Porter, *Collected Stories*
1967	Bernard Malamud, *The Fixer*
1968	William Styron, *The Confessions of Nat Turner*
1969	N. Scott Momaday, *House Made of Dawn*
1970	Jean Stafford, *Collected Stories*
1971	No award
1972	Wallace Stegner, *Angle of Repose*
1973	Eudora Welty, *The Optimist's Daughter*
1974	No award
1975	Michael Shaara, *The Killer Angels*
1976	Saul Bellow, *Humboldt's Gift*
1977	No award
1978	James Alan McPherson, *Elbow Room*
1979	John Cheever, *The Stories of John Cheever*
1980	Norman Mailer, *The Executioner's Song*
1981	John Kennedy Toole, *A Confederacy of Dunces*
1982	John Updike, *Rabbit Is Rich*
1983	Alice Walker, *The Color Purple*
1984	William Kennedy, *Ironweed*
1985	Alison Lurie, *Foreign Affairs*
1986	Larry McMurtry, *Lonesome Dove*
1987	Peter Taylor, *A Summons to Memphis*
1988	Toni Morrison, *Beloved*
1989	Anne Tyler, *Breathing Lessons*
1990	Oscar Hijuelos, *The Mambo Kings Play Songs of Love*
1991	John Updike, *Rabbit at Rest*
1992	Jane Smiley, *A Thousand Acres*
1993	Robert Olen Butler, *A Good Scent From a Strange Mountain*
1994	E. Annie Proulx, *The Shipping News*
1995	Carol Shields, *The Stone Diaries*
1996	Richard Ford, *Independence Day*
1997	Steven Millhauser, *Martin Dressler: The Tale of an American Dreamer*
1998	Philip Roth, *American Pastoral*
1999	Michael Cunningham, *The Hours*
2000	Jhumpa Lahiri, *Interpreter of Maladies*
2001	Michael Chabon, *The Amazing Adventures of Kavalier & Clay*
2002	Richard Russo, *Empire Falls*
2003	Jeffrey Eugenides, *Middlesex*
2004	Edward P. Jones, *The Known World*

In 1948, the name of the category was changed from "The Novel" to "Fiction." 2. Awarded posthumously.

The Pulitzer Prize for Drama, 1918–2004

Year	Author, Title
1918	Jesse Lynch Williams, *Why Marry*
1919	No award
1920	Eugene O'Neill, *Beyond the Horizon*
1921	Zona Gale, *Miss Lulu Bett*
1922	Eugene O'Neill, *Anna Christie*
1923	Owen Davis, *Icebound*
1924	Hatcher Hughes, *Hell-Bent Fer Heaven*
1925	Sidney Howard, *They Knew What They Wanted*
1926	George Kelly, *Craig's Wife*
1927	Paul Green, *In Abraham's Bosom*
1928	Eugene O'Neill, *Strange Interlude*
1929	Elmer L. Rice, *Street Scene*
1930	Marc Connelly, *The Green Pastures*
1931	Susan Glaspell, *Alison's House*
1932	George S. Kaufman, Morrie Ryskind, and Ira Gershwin, *Of Thee I Sing*
1933	Maxwell Anderson, *Both Your Houses*
1934	Sidney Kingsley, *Men in White*
1935	Zoe Akins, *The Old Maid*
1936	Robert E. Sherwood, *Idiot's Delight*
1937	Moss Hart and George S. Kaufman, *You Can't Take It With You*
1938	Thornton Wilder, *Our Town*
1939	Robert E. Sherwood, *Abe Lincoln in Illinois*
1940	William Saroyan, *The Time of Your Life*
1941	Robert E. Sherwood, *There Shall Be no Night*
1942	No award
1943	Thornton Wilder, *The Skin of Our Teeth*
1944	No award
1945	Mary Chase, *Harvey*
1946	Russel Crouse and Howard Lindsay, *State of the Union*
1947	No award
1948	Tennessee Williams, *A Streetcar Named Desire*
1949	Arthur Miller, *Death of a Salesman*
1950	Richard Rodgers, Oscar Hammerstein II, and Joshua Logan, *South Pacific*
1951	No award
1952	Joseph Kramm, *The Shrike*
1953	William Inge, *Picnic*
1954	John Patrick, *The Teahouse of the August Moon*
1955	Tennessee Williams, *Cat on a Hot Tin Roof*
1956	Albert Hackett, Frances Goodrich, *The Diary of Anne Frank*
1957	Eugene O'Neill, *Long Day's Journey Into Night*
1958	Ketti Frings, *Look Homeward, Angel*
1959	Archibald MacLeish, *J.B.*
1960	Jerome Weidman and George Abbott (book); Jerry Bock (music); and Sheldon Harnick (lyrics), *Fiorello!*
1961	Tad Mosel, *All the Way Home*
1962	Frank Loesser and Abe Burrows, *How to Succeed in Business Without Really Trying*
1963	No award
1964	No award
1965	Frank D. Gilroy, *The Subject Was Roses*
1966	No award
1967	Edward Albee, *A Delicate Balance*
1968	No award
1969	Howard Sackler, *The Great White Hope*
1970	Charles Gordone, *No Place to Be Somebody*
1971	Paul Zindel, *The Effect of Gamma Rays on Man-in-the-Moon Marigolds*
1972	No award
1973	Jason Miller, *That Championship Season*
1974	No award
1975	Edward Albee, *Seascape*
1976	Michael Bennett; Nicholas Dante & James Kirkwood (book); Marvin Hamlisch (music); and Edward Kleban (lyrics), *A Chorus Line*
1977	Michael Cristofer, *The Shadow Box*
1978	Donald L. Coburn, *The Gin Game*
1979	Sam Shepard, *Buried Child*
1980	Lanford Wilson, *Talley's Folly*
1981	Beth Henley, *Crimes of the Heart*
1982	Charles Fuller, *A Soldier's Play*
1983	Marsha Norman, *'night Mother*
1984	David Mamet, *Glengarry Glen Ross*
1985	Stephen Sondheim (music and lyrics); James Lapine (book), *Sunday in the Park With George*
1986	No award
1987	August Wilson, *Fences*
1988	Alfred Uhry, *Driving Miss Daisy*
1989	Wendy Wasserstein, *The Heidi Chronicles*
1990	August Wilson, *The Piano Lesson*
1991	Neil Simon, *Lost in Yonkers*
1992	Robert Schenkkan, *The Kentucky Cycle*
1993	Tony Kushner, *Angels in America: Millennium Approaches*
1994	Edward Albee, *Three Tall Women*
1995	Horton Foote, *The Young Man From Atlanta*
1996	Jonathan Larson, *Rent*
1997	No award
1998	Paula Vogel, *How I Learned to Drive*
1999	Margaret Edson, *Wit*
2000	Donald Margulies, *Dinner With Friends*
2001	David Auburn, *Proof*
2002	Suzan-Lori Parks, *Topdog/Underdog*
2003	Nilo Cruz, *Anna In the Tropics*
2004	Doug Wright, *I Am My Own Wife*

The Pulitzer Prize for History, 1917–2004

Year	Author, Title
1917	J.J. Jusserand, *With Americans of Past and Present Days*
1918	James Ford Rhodes, *A History of the Civil War*
1920	Justin H. Smith, *The War with Mexico*
1921	William Sowden Sims, with Burton J. Hendrick, *The Victory at Sea*
1922	James Truslow Adams, *The Founding of New England*
1923	Charles Warren, *The Supreme Court in United States History*
1924	Charles Howard McIlwain, *The American Revolution*
1925	Frederic L. Paxson, *A History of the American Frontier*
1926	Edward Channing, *The History of the United States*
1927	Samuel Flagg Bemis, *Pinckney's Treaty*
1928	Vernon Louis Parrington, *Main Currents in American Thought*
1929	Fred Albert Shannon, *The Organization and Administration of the Union Army, 1861–1865*
1930	Claude H. Van Tyne, *The War of Independence*
1931	Bernadotte E. Schmitt, *The Coming of the War: 1914*
1932	John J. Pershing, *My Experiences in the World War*
1933	Frederick J. Turner, *The Significance of Sections in American History*
1934	Herbert Agar, *The People's Choice*
1935	Charles McLean Andrews, *The Colonial Period of American History*
1936	Andrew C. McLaughlin, *The Constitutional History of the United States*
1937	Van Wyck Brooks, *The Flowering of New England*
1938	Paul Herman Buck, *The Road to Reunion 1856–1900*
1939	Frank Luther Mott, *A History of American Magazines*
1940	Carl Sandburg, *Abraham Lincoln: The War Years*
1941	Marcus Lee Hansen, *The Atlantic Migration, 1607–1860*
1942	Margaret Leech, *Reveille in Washington*
1943	Esther Forbes, *Paul Revere and the World He Lived In*
1944	Merle Curti, *The Growth of American Thought*
1945	Stephen Bonsal, *Unfinished Business*
1946	Arthur Meier Schlesinger Jr., *The Age of Jackson*
1947	James Phinney Baxter III, *Scientists Against Time*
1948	Bernard DeVoto, *Across the Wide Missouri*
1949	Roy Franklin Nichols, *The Disruption of American Democracy*
1950	Oliver W. Larkin, *Art and Life in America*
1951	R. Carlyle Buley, *The Old Northwest*
1952	Oscar Handlin, *The Uprooted*
1953	George Dangerfield, *The Era of Good Feelings*
1954	Bruce Catton, *A Stillness at Appomattox*
1955	Paul Horgan, *Great River: The Rio Grande in North American History*
1956	Richard Hofstadter, *The Age of Reform*
1957	George F. Kennan, *Russia Leaves the War: Soviet American Relations, 1917–1920*
1958	Bray Hammond, *Banks and Politics in America*
1959	Leonard D. White, with Miss Jean Schneider, *The Republican Era: 1869–1901*
1960	Margaret Leech, *In the Days of McKinley*
1961	Herbert Feis, *Between War and Peace: The Potsdam Conference*
1962	Lawrence H. Gipson, *The Triumphant Empire: Thunder Clouds in the West*
1963	Constance McLaughlin Green, Washington, *Village and Capital, 1800–1878*
1964	Sumner Chilton Powell, *Puritan Village*
1965	Irwin Unger, *The Greenback Era*
1966	Perry Milleri, *Life of the Mind in America*
1967	William H. Goetzmann, *Exploration and Empire*
1968	Bernard Bailyn, *The Ideological Origins of the American Revolution*
1969	Leonard W. Levy, *Origins of the Fifth Amendment*
1970	Dean Acheson, *Present at the Creation*
1971	James MacGregor Burns, *Roosevelt, The Soldier of Freedom*
1972	Carl N. Degler, *Neither Black Nor White*
1973	Michael Kammen, *People of Paradox*
1974	Daniel J. Boorstin, *The Americans: The Democratic Experience*
1975	Dumas Malone, *Jefferson and His Time*
1976	Paul Horgan, *Lamy of Santa Fe*
1977	David M. Potter[1], *The Impending Crisis*
1978	Alfred D. Chandler Jr., *The Visible Hand: The Managerial Revolution in American Business*
1979	Don E. Fehrenbacher, *The Dred Scott Case*
1980	Leon F. Litwack, *Been in the Storm So Long*
1981	Lawrence A. Cremin, *American Education*
1982	C. Vann Woodward (ed.), *Mary Chesnut's Civil War*
1983	Rhys L. Isaac, *The Transformation of Virginia, 1740–1790*
1985	Thomas K. McCraw, *Prophets of Regulation*
1986	Walter A. McDougall, *The Heavens and the Earth: A Political History of the Space Age*
1987	Bernard Bailyn, *Voyagers to the West*

Year	Author, Title
1988	Robert V. Bruce, *The Launching of Modern American Science 1846–1876*
1989	Taylor Branch, *Parting the Waters*
	James M. McPherson, *Battle Cry of Freedom: The Civil War Era*
1990	Stanley Karnow, *In Our Image*
1991	Laurel Thatcher Ulrich, *A Midwife's Tale*
1992	Mark E. Neely Jr., *The Fate of Liberty*
1993	Gordon S. Wood, *The Radicalism of the American Revolution*
1995	Doris Kearns Goodwin, *No Ordinary Time: Franklin and Eleanor Roosevelt*
1996	Alan Taylor, *William Cooper's Town*
1997	Jack N. Rakove, *Original Meanings: Politics and Ideas in the Making of the Constitution*
1998	Edward J. Larson, *Summer for the Gods: The Scopes Trial and America's Continuing Debate Over Science and Religion*
1999	Edwin G. Burrows and Mike Wallace, *Gotham: A History of New York City to 1898*
2000	David M. Kennedy, *Freedom From Fear: The American People in Depression*
2001	Joseph P. Ellis, *Founding Brothers: The Revolutionary Generation*
2002	Louis Menand, *The Metaphysical Club: A Story of Ideas in America*
2003	Rick Atkinson, *An Army at Dawn: The War in North Africa, 1942–1943*
2004	Steven Hahn, *A Nation Under Our Feet: Black Political Sturggles in the Rural South from Slavery to the Great Migration*

Notes: No award given in 1919, 1984, or 1994. 1. Awarded posthumously.

The Pulitzer Prize for Biography/ Autobiography, 1917–2004

Year	Author, Title
1917	Laura E. Richards and Maude Howe Elliott, with Florence Howe Hall, *Julia Ward Howe*
1918	William Cabell Bruce, *Benjamin Franklin, Self-Revealed*
1919	Henry Adams, *The Education of Henry Adams*
1920	Albert J. Beveridge, *The Life of John Marshall*
1921	Edward Bok, *The Americanization of Edward Bok*
1922	Hamlin Garland, *A Daughter of the Middle Border*
1923	Burton J. Hendrick, *The Life and Letters of Walter H. Page*
1924	Michael Idvorsky Pupin, *From Immigrant to Inventor*
1925	M.A. DeWolfe Howe, *Barrett Wendell and His Letter*
1926	Harvey Cushing, *The Life of Sir William Osler*
1927	Emory Holloway, *Whitman*
1928	Charles Edward Russell, *The American Orchestra and Theodore Thomas*
1929	Burton J. Hendrick, *The Training of an American. The Earlier Life and Letters of Walter H. Page*
1930	Marquis James, *The Raven*
1931	Henry James, *Charles W. Eliot*
1932	Henry F. Pringle, *Theodore Roosevelt*
1933	Allan Nevins, *Grover Cleveland*
1934	Tyler Dennett, *John Hay*
1935	Douglas S. Freeman, *R.E. Lee*
1936	Ralph Barton Perry, *The Thought and Character of William James*
1937	Allan Nevins, *Hamilton Fish*
1938	Odell Shepard, *Pedlar's Progress*
	Marquis James, *Andrew Jackson*
1939	Carl Van Doren, *Benjamin Franklin*
1940	Ray Stannard Baker, *Woodrow Wilson, Life and Letters, vols. 7 & 8*
1941	Ola Elizabeth Winslow, *Jonathan Edwards*
1942	Forrest Wilson, *Crusader in Crinoline*
1943	Samuel Eliot Morison, *Admiral of the Ocean Sea*
1944	Carleton Mabee, *The American Leonardo: The Life of Samuel F.B. Morse*
1945	Russell Blaine Nye, *George Bancroft*
1946	Linnie Marsh Wolfe, *Son of the Wilderness*
1947	William Allen White, *The Autobiography of William Allen White*
1948	Margaret Clapp, *Forgotten First Citizen: John Bigelow*
1949	Robert E. Sherwood, *Roosevelt and Hopkins*
1950	Samuel Flagg Bemis, *John Quincy Adams and the Foundations of American Foreign Policy*
1951	Margaret Louise Coit, *John C. Calhoun*
1952	Merlo J. Pusey, *Charles Evan Hughes*
1953	David J. Mays, *Edmund Pendleton 1721-1803*
1954	Charles A. Lindbergh, *The Spirit of St. Louis*
1955	William S. White, *The Taft Story*
1956	Talbot Faulkner Hamlin, *Benjamin Henry Latrobe*

Year	Author, Title
1957	John F. Kennedy, *Profiles in Courage*
1958	Douglas Southall Freeman, John Alexander Carroll, Mary Wells Ashworth, *George Washington, vols. 1–4*; and *vol. 7, written after Dr. Freeman's death in 1953.*
1959	Arthur Walworth, *Woodrow Wilson, American Prophet*
1960	Samuel Eliot Morison, *John Paul Jones*
1961	David Donald, *Charles Sumner and the Coming of the Civil War*
1962	No award
1963	Leon Edel, *Henry James*
1964	Walter Jackson Bate, *John Keats*
1965	Ernest Samuels, *Henry Adams*
1966	Arthur M. Schlesinger Jr., *A Thousand Days*
1967	Justin Kaplan, *Mr. Clemens and Mark Twain*
1968	George F. Kennan, *Memoirs*
1969	Benjamin Lawrence Reid, *The Man From New York: John Quinn and His Friends*
1970	T. Harry Williams, *Huey Long*
1971	Lawrance Thompson, *Robert Frost*
1972	Joseph P. Lash, *Eleanor and Franklin*
1973	W.A. Swanberg, *Luce and His Empire*
1974	Louis Sheaffer, *O'Neill, Son and Artist*
1975	Robert A. Caro, *The Power Broker*
1976	R.W.B. Lewis, *Edith Wharton: A Biography*
1977	John E. Mack, *A Prince of Our Disorder: The Life of T.E. Lawrence*
1978	Walter Jackson Bate, *Samuel Johnson*
1979	Leonard Baker, *Days of Sorrow and Pain*
1980	Edmund Morris, *The Rise of Theodore Roosevelt*
1981	Robert K. Massie, *Peter the Great*
1982	William S. McFeely, *Grant: A Biography*
1983	Russell Baker, *Growing Up*
1984	Louis R. Harlan, *Booker T. Washington*
1985	Kenneth Silverman, *The Life and Times of Cotton Mather*
1986	Elizabeth Frank, *Louise Bogan: A Portrait*
1987	David J. Garrow, *Bearing the Cross: Martin Luther King, Jr. and the Southern Christian Leadership Conference*
1988	David Herbert Donald, *Look Homeward: A Life of Thomas Wolfe*
1989	Richard Ellmann[1], *Oscar Wilde*
1990	Sebastian de Grazia, *Machiavelli in Hell*
1991	Steven Naifeh, Gregory White Smith, *Jackson Pollock*
1992	Lewis B. Puller Jr., *Fortunate Son*
1993	David McCullough, *Truman*
1994	David Levering Lewis, *W.E.B. DuBois*
1995	Joan D. Hedrick, *Harriet Beecher Stowe*
1996	Jack Miles, *God: A Biography*
1997	Frank McCourt, *Angela's Ashes*
1998	Katharine Graham, *Personal History*
1999	A. Scott Berg, *Lindbergh*
2000	Stacy Schiff, *Véra (Mrs. Vladimir Nabokov)*
2001	David Levering Lewis, *W.E.B. DuBois (vol. 2)*
2002	David McCullough, *John Adams*
2003	Robert A. Caro, *Master of the Senate*
2004	William Taubman, *Khruschev: The Man and His Era*

1. Awarded posthumously.

The Pulitzer Prize for Poetry, 1922–2004

Pulitzer Prizes in poetry were first awarded in 1922. The Poetry Society awarded prizes in 1918 to Sara Teasdale for *Love Songs*, and in 1919 to Margaret Widdemer for *Old Road to Paradise* and to Carl Sandburg for *Corn Huskers.*

Year	Author, Title
1922	Edward Arlington Robinson, *Collected Poems*
1923	Edna St. Vincent Millay, *The Ballad of the Harp-Weaver; A Few Figs from Thistles; Eight Sonnets in American Poetry, 1922, A Miscellany*
1924	Robert Frost, *New Hampshire: A Poem with Notes and Grace Notes*
1925	Edward Arlington Robinson, *The Man Who Died Twice*
1926	Amy Lowell[1], *What's O'Clock*
1927	Leonora Speyer, *Fiddler's Farewell*
1928	Edward Arlington Robinson, *Tristram*
1929	Stephen Vincent Benét, *John Brown's Body*
1930	Conrad Aiken, *Selected Poems*
1931	Robert Frost, *Collected Poems*
1932	George Dillon, *The Flowering Stone*
1933	Archibald MacLeish, *Conquistador*
1934	Robert Hillyer, *Collected Verse*
1935	Audrey Wurdemann, *Bright Ambush*
1936	Robert P. Tristram Coffin, *Strange Holiness*
1937	Robert Frost, *A Further Range*

Year	Author, Title
1938	Marya Zaturenska, *Cold Morning Sky*
1939	John Gould Fletcher, *Selected Poems*
1940	Mark Van Doren, *Collected Poems*
1941	Leonard Bacon, *Sunderland Capture*
1942	William Rose Benét, *The Dust Which Is God*
1943	Robert Frost, *A Witness Tree*
1944	Stephen Vincent Benét[1], *Western Star*
1945	Karl Shapiro, *V-Letter and Other Poems*
1947	Robert Lowell, *Lord Weary's Castle*
1948	W.H. Auden, *The Age of Anxiety*
1949	Peter Viereck, *Terror and Decorum*
1950	Gwendolyn Brooks, *Annie Allen*
1951	Carl Sandburg, *Complete Poems*
1952	Marianne Moore, *Collected Poems*
1953	Archibald MacLeish, *Collected Poems 1917–1952*
1954	Theodore Roethke, *The Waking*
1955	Wallace Stevens, *Collected Poems*
1956	Elizabeth Bishop, *Poems—North & South*
1957	Richard Wilbur, *Things of This World*
1958	Robert Penn Warren, *Promises: Poems 1954-1956*
1959	Stanley Kunitz, *Selected Poems 1928–1958*
1960	W.D. Snodgrass, *Heart's Needle*
1961	Phyllis McGinley, *Times Three: Selected Verse From Three Decades*
1962	Alan Dugan, *Poems*
1963	William Carlos Williams, *Pictures from Breughel*
1964	Louis Simpson, *At the End of the Open Road*
1965	John Berryman, *77 Dream Songs*
1966	Richard Eberhart, *Selected Poems*
1967	Anne Sexton, *Live or Die*
1968	Anthony Hecht, *The Hard Hours*
1969	George Oppen, *Of Being Numerous*
1970	Richard Howard, *Untitled Subjects*
1971	William S. Merwin, *The Carrier of Ladders*
1972	James Wright, *Collected Poems*
1973	Maxine Kumin, *Up Country*
1974	Robert Lowell, *The Dolphins*
1975	Gary Snyder, *Turtle Island*
1976	John Ashberry, *Self-Portrait in a Convex Mirror*
1977	James Merrill, *Divine Comedies*
1978	Howard Nemerov, *Collected Poems*
1979	Robert Penn Warren, *Now and Then*
1980	Donald Justice, *Selected Poems*
1981	James Schuyler, *The Morning of the Poem*
1982	Sylvia Plath, *The Collected Poems*
1983	Galway Kinnell, *Selected Poems*
1984	Mary Oliver, *American Primitive*
1985	Carolyn Kizer, *Yin*
1986	Henry Taylor, *The Flying Change*
1987	Rita Dove, *Thomas and Beulah*
1988	William Meredith, *Partial Accounts: New and Selected Poems*
1989	Richard Wilbur, *New and Collected Poems*
1990	Charles Simic, *The World Doesn't End*
1991	Mona Van Duyn, *Near Changes*
1992	James Tate, *Selected Poems*
1993	Louise Glück, *The Wild Iris*
1994	Yusef Komunyakaa, *Neon Vernacular*
1995	Philip Levine, *Simple Truth*
1996	Jorie Graham, *The Dream of the Unified Field*
1997	Lisel Mueller, *Alive Together: New and Selected Poems*
1998	Charles Wright, *Black Zodiac*
1999	Mark Strand, *Blizzard of One*
2000	C.K. Williams, *Repair*
2001	Stephen Dunn, *Different Hours*
2002	Carl Dennis, *Practical Gods*
2003	Paul Muldoon, *Moy Sand and Gravel*
2004	Franz Wright, *Walking to Martha's Vineyard*

Note: No award given in 1946. 1. Awarded posthumously.

The Pulitzer Prize for General Nonfiction, 1962–2004

Year	Author, Title
1962	Theodore H. White, *The Making of the President, 1960*
1963	Barbara W. Tuchman, *The Guns of August*
1964	Richard Hofstadter, *Anti-Intellectualism in American Life*
1965	Howard Mumford Jones, *O Strange New World*
1966	Edwin Way Teal, *Wandering Through Winter*
1967	David Brion Davis, *The Problem of Slavery in Western Culture*
1968	Will and Ariel Durant, *Rousseau and Revolution*
1969	René Jules Dubos, *So Human An Animal*
	Norman Mailer, *The Armies of the Night*

Year	Author, Title
1970	Erik H. Erikson, *Gandhi's Truth*
1971	John Toland, *The Rising Sun*
1972	Barbara W. Tuchman, *Stilwell and the American Experience in China, 1911–45*
1973	Robert Coles, *Children of Crisis, vols. 2 & 3* Frances Fitzgerald, *Fire in the Lake*
1974	Ernest Becker[1], *The Denial of Death*
1975	Annie Dillard, *Pilgrim at Tinker Creek*
1976	Robert N. Butler, *Why Survive? Being Old in America*
1977	William N. Warner, *Beautiful Swimmers*
1978	Carl Sagan, *The Dragons of Eden*
1979	Edward O. Wilson, *On Human Nature*
1980	Douglas R. Hofstadter, *Gödel, Escher, Bach: an Eternal Golden Braid*
1981	Carl E. Schorske, *Fin-de Siècle Vienna: Politics and Culture*
1982	Tracy Kidder, *The Soul of A New Machine*
1983	Susan Sheehan, *Is There No Place on Earth for Me?*
1984	Paul Starr, *The Social Transformation of American Medicine*
1985	Studs Terkel, *The Good War*
1986	Joseph Lelyveld, *Move Your Shadow* J. Anthony Lukas, *Common Ground*
1987	David K. Shipler, *Arab and Jew*
1988	Richard Rhodes, *The Making of the Atomic Bomb*
1989	Neil Sheehan, *A Bright and Shining Lie*
1990	Dale Maharidge, Michael Williamson, *And Their Children After Them*
1991	Bert Holldobler, Edward O. Wilson, *The Ants*
1992	Daniel Yergin, *The Prize: The Epic Quest for Oil, Money and Power.*
1993	Garry Wills, *Lincoln at Gettysburg*
1994	David Remnick, *Lenin's Tomb: The Last Days of the Soviet Empire*
1995	Jonathan Weiner, *The Beak of the Finch*
1996	Tina Rosenberg, *The Haunted Land*
1997	Richard Kluger, *Ashes to Ashes*
1998	Jared Diamond, *Guns, Germs, and Steel: The Fates of Human Societies*
1999	John McPhee, *Annals of the Former World*
2000	John W. Dower, *Embracing Defeat: Japan in the Wake of World War II*
2001	Herbert P. Bix, *Hirohito and the Making of Modern Japan*
2002	Diane McWhorter, *Carry Me Home: Birmingham, Alabama, the Climactic Battle of the Civil Rights Revolution*
2003	Samantha Power, *"A Problem From Hell": America and the Age of Genocide*
2004	Anne Applebaum, *Gulag: A History*

1. Awarded posthumously.

The Pulitzer Prize for Music, 1943–2004

Year	Author, Title
1943	William Schuman, *Secular Cantata No. 2, A Free Song*
1944	Howard Hanson, *Symphony No. 4, Opus 34*
1945	Aaron Copland, *Appalachian Spring*
1946	Leo Sowerby, *The Canticle of the Sun*
1947	Charles Ives, *Symphony No. 3*
1948	Walter Piston, *Symphony No. 3*
1949	Virgil Thomson, Music for the film, *Louisiana Story*
1950	Gian-Carlo Menotti, Music for the opera *The Consul*
1951	Douglas S. Moore, Music for the opera, *Giants in the Earth*
1952	Gail Kubik, *Symphony Concertante*
1953	No award
1954	Quincy Porter, *Concerto for Two Pianos and Orchestra*
1955	Gian-Carlo Menotti, *The Saint of Bleecker Street* (opera)
1956	Ernest Toch, *Symphony No. 3*
1957	Norman Dello Joio, *Meditations on Ecclesiastes*
1958	Samuel Barber, *Vanessa (opera)*
1959	John LaMontaine, *Concerto for Piano and Orchestra*
1960	Elliott Carter, *Second String Quartet*
1961	Walter Piston, *Symphony No. 7*
1962	Robert Ward, *The Crucible* (opera)
1963	Samuel Barber, *Piano Concerto No. 1*
1964	No award
1965	No award
1966	Leslie Bassett, *Variations for Orchestra*
1967	Leon Kirchner, *Quartet No. 3*
1968	George Crumb, *Echoes of Time and the River* orchestral suite
1969	Karel Husa, *String Quartet No. 3*

Year	Author, Title
1970	Charles Wuorinen, *Time's Encomium*
1971	Mario Davidovsky, *Synchronisms No. 6 for Piano and Electronic Sound*
1972	Jacob Druckman, *Windows*
1973	Elliott Carter, *String Quartet No. 3*
1974	Donald Martino, *Notturno (chamber music)*
1975	Dominick Argento, *From the Diary of Virginia Woolf*
1976	Ned Rorem, *Air Music: Ten Etudes for Orchestra*
1977	Richard Wernick, *Visions of Terror and Wonder*
1978	Michael Colgrass, *Deja Vu for Percussion Quartet and Orchestra*
1979	Joseph Schwantner, *Aftertones of Infinity*
1980	David Del Tredici, *In Memory of a Summer Day*
1981	No award
1982	Roger Sessions, *Concerto for Orchestra*
1983	Ellen Taaffe Zwilich, *Symphony No. 1*
1984	Bernard Rands, *"Canti del Sole" for Tenor and Orchestra*
1985	Stephen Albert, *Symphony RiverRun*
1986	George Perle, *Wind Quintet IV*
1987	John Harbison, *The Flight Into Egypt*
1988	William Bolcom, *12 New Etudes for Piano*
1989	Roger Reynolds, *Whispers Out of Time*
1990	Mel Powell, *Duplicates: A Concerto for Two Pianos and Orchestra*
1991	Shulammit Ran, *Symphony*
1992	Wayne Peterson, *The Face of the Night, The Heart of the Dark*
1993	Christopher Rouse, *Trombone Concerto*
1994	Gunther Schuller, *Of Reminiscences and Reflections*
1995	Morton Gould, *Stringmusic*
1996	George Walker, *Lilacs*
1997	Wynton Marsalis, *Blood on the Fields*
1998	Aaron Jay Kernis, *String Quartet No. 2*
1999	Melinda Wagner, *Concerto for Flute, Strings, and Percussion*
2000	Lewis Spratalan, *Life is a Dream, Opera in Three Acts: Act II, Convert Version*
2001	John Corigliano, *Symphony No. 2 for String Orchestra*
2002	Henry Brant, *Ice Field*
2003	John Adams, *On the Transmigration of Souls*
2004	Paul Moravec, *Tempest Fantasy*

The Nobel Prizes

First awarded in 1901, the Nobel Prizes were established through a bequest of $9.2 million from Alfred Bernhard Nobel (1833–96), a Swedish chemical engineer and the inventor of dynamite and other explosives, and by a gift from the Bank of Sweden. Nobel's will directed that the interest from the fund be divided annually among people who have made significant discoveries or inventions in the fields of chemistry, physics, and physiology or medicine, as well as to that author who has "produced in the field of literature the most outstanding work of an idealistic tendency," and to that individual or group that has "done the most or the best work for fraternity between nations, for the abolition or reduction of standing armies and for the holding and promotion of peace congresses." In 1968, the 300th anniversary of the Bank of Sweden, an additional prize for outstanding work in the economic sciences was established; it was first granted the following year.

Nobel Peace Prize Recipients

1901 Jean-Henri Dunant (Switzerland)
1902 Elie Ducommun (Switzerland)
1903 Sir William R. Cremer (U.K.)
1904 Institute of International Law
1905 Baroness Bertha S.F. von Suttner (Austria)
1906 Theodore Roosevelt (U.S.)
1907 Ernesto T. Moneta (Italy); Louis Renault (France)
1908 Klas P. Arnoldson (Sweden); Fredrik Bajer (Denmark)
1909 Auguste M.F. Beernaert (Belgium); Paul H.B.B. D'Estournelles de Constant (Baron Constant de Rebecque) (France)
1910 Permanent International Peace Bureau
1911 Tobias M.C. Asser (Netherlands); Alfred H. Fried (Austria)
1912 Elihu Root (U.S.)
1913 Henri Lafontaine (Belgium)
1914–1916 No awards given.
1917 International Committee of the Red Cross
1918 No award.
1919 Woodrow Wilson (U.S.)
1920 Léon Victor A. Bourgeois (France)
1921 Karl H. Branting (Sweden); Christian L. Lange (Norway)
1922 Fridtjof Nansen (Norway)
1923–24 No award.

1925 Sir Austen Chamberlain (U.K.); Charles G. Dawes (U.S.)
1926 Aristide Briand (France) and Gustav Stresemann (Germany)
1927 Ferdinand Buisson (France); Ludwig Quidde (Germany)
1928 No award.
1929 Frank B. Kellogg (U.S.)
1930 L.O. Nathan Söderblom (Sweden)
1931 Jane Addams (U.S.); Nicholas M. Butler (U.S.)
1932 No award.
1933 Sir Norman Angell (Ralph Lane) (U.K.)
1934 Arthur Henderson (U.K.)
1935 Carol von Ossietzky (Germany)
1936 Carlos Saavedra Lamas (Argentina)
1937 Lord Edgar Algernon R.G. Cecil (U.K.)
1938 Nansen International Office for Refugees
1939–1943 No awards given.
1944 International Committee of the Red Cross
1945 Cordell Hull (U.S.)
1946 Emily G. Balch (U.S.); John R. Mott (U.S.)
1947 The Friends Service Council (U.K.) and The American Friends Service Committee (U.S.)
1948 No award.
1949 Lord John Boyd Orr (U.K.)
1950 Ralph Bunche (U.S.)
1951 Léon Jouhaux (France)
1952 Albert Schweitzer (France)
1953 George C. Marshall (U.S.)
1954 Office of the U.N. High Commissioner for Refugees
1955–1956 No awards given.
1957 Lester B. Pearson (Canada)
1958 Georges Pire (Belgium)
1959 Philip J. Noel-Baker (U.K.)
1960 Albert J. Lutuli (South Africa)
1961 Dag Hammarskjöld (Sweden)
1962 Linus C. Pauling (U.S.)
1963 International Committee of the Red Cross and League of Red Cross Societies
1964 Martin Luther King, Jr. (U.S.)
1965 United Nations Children's Fund (UNICEF).
1966–1967 No awards given.
1968 René Cassin (France)
1969 International Labour Organization
1970 Norman Borlaug (U.S.)
1971 Willy Brandt (Federal Republic of Germany)
1972 No award
1973 Henry A. Kissinger (U.S.) and Le Duc Tho (Democratic Republic of Viet Nam)
1974 Seán MacBride (Ireland); Eisaku Sato (Japan)
1975 Andrei Sakharov (USSR)
1976 Betty Williams, Mairead Corrigan (Northern Ireland)
1977 Amnesty International
1978 Anwar el-Sadat (Egypt) and Menachem Begin (Israel)
1979 Mother Teresa (India)
1980 Adolfo Pérez Esquivel (Argentina)
1981 Office of the United Nations High Commissioner for Refugees
1982 Alva Myrdal (Sweden) and Alfonso Garcia Robles (Mexico)
1983 Lech Walesa (Poland)
1984 Desmond M. Tutu (South Africa)
1985 Int'l Physicians for the Prevention of Nuclear War
1986 Elie Wiesel (U.S.)
1987 Oscar Arias Sánchez (Costa Rica)
1988 United Nations Peacekeeping Forces
1989 Dalai Lama (Tibet)
1990 Mikhail Gorbachev (USSR)
1991 Aung San Suu Kyi (Myanmar)
1992 Rigoberta Menchú (Guatemala)
1993 Pres. F. W. de Klerk and Nelson Mandela (South Africa)
1994 Yitzhak Rabin (Israel), Shimon Peres (Israel), Yasir Arafat
1995 Joseph Rotblat (U.K. b. Poland)
1996 Bishop Carlos Ximenes Belo (Australia, b. East Timor) and Jose Ramos-Horta (East Timor)
1997 The International Campaign to Ban Landmines and Jody Williams (U.S.)
1998 John Hume (Ireland) and David Trimble (Ireland)
1999 Doctors Without Borders (Médecins Sans Frontières)
2000 Kim Dae Jung (South Korea)
2001 United Nations and Kofi Annan (Ghana)
2002 Jimmy Carter (U.S.)
2003 Shirin Ebadi (Iran)

Nobel Prizes in Physiology or Medicine

1901 Emil A. von Behring (Germany) Marburg Univ.
1902 Sir Ronald Ross (U.K.) University College
1903 Niels R. Finsen (Denmark) Finsen Medical Light Institute
1904 Ivan P. Pavlov (Russia) Military Medical Academy
1905 Robert Koch (Germany) Institute for Infectious Diseases
1906 Camillio Golgi (Italy) Pavia Univ., and Santiago Ramon Y Cajal (Spain) Madrid Univ.
1907 Charles L.A. Laveran (France) Institute Pasteur
1908 Il'ja I. Mecnikov (Russia) Institut Pasteur (Paris), and Paul Ehrlich (Germany) Goettingen Univ. and Royal Institute for Experimental Therapy
1909 Emil R. Kocher (Switzerland) Berne Univ.

1910 Albrecht Kossel (Germany) Heidelberg Univ.
1911 Allvar Gullstrand (Sweden) Uppsala Univ.
1912 Alexis Carrel (France) Rockefeller Institute for Medical Research (New York)
1913 Charles R. Richet (France)
1914 Robert Bárány (Austria) Vienna Univ.
1915–1918 No awards
1919 Jules Bordet (Belgium) Brussels Univ.
1920 Schack A.S. Krogh (Denmark) Copenhagen Univ.
1921 No award
1922 Sir Archibald V. Hill (U.K.) London Univ.; Otto F. Meyerhof (Germany) Kiel Univ.
1923 Sir Frederick G. Banting (Canada) Toronto Univ. and John J.R. Macleod (Canada) Toronto Univ.
1924 Willem Einthoven (Netherlands) Leyden Univ.
1925 No award
1926 Johannes A.G. Fibiger (Denmark) Copenhagen Univ.
1927 Julius Wagner-Jauegg (Austria) Vienna Univ.
1928 Charles J.H. Nicolle (France) Institut Pasteur
1929 Christiaan Eijkman (Netherlands) Utrecht Univ.; Sir Frederick G. Hopkins (U.K.) Cambridge Univ.
1930 Karl Landsteiner (Austria) Rockefeller Institute of Medical Research (New York)
1931 Otto H. Warburg (Germany) Kaiser-Wilhelm Institut
1932 Sir Charles S. Sherrington (U.K.) Oxford Univ. and Lord Edgar D. Adrian (U.K.) Cambridge Univ.
1933 Thomas H. Morgan (U.S.) California Institute of Technology
1934 George H. Whipple (U.S.) Rochester Univ., George R. Minot (U.S.) Harvard Univ., and William P. Murphy (U.S.) Harvard Univ.
1935 Hans Spemann (Germany) Univ. of Freiburg
1936 Sir Henry H. Dale (U.K.) National Institute for Medical Research, and Otto Loewi (Austria) Graz Univ.
1937 Albert von Szent-Györgyi Nagyrapolt (Hungary) Szeged Univ.
1938 Corneille J.F. Heymans (Belgium) Ghent Univ.
1939 Gerhard Domagk (Germany) Munster Univ.
1940–1942 No awards given.
1943 Henrik C.P. Dam (Denmark) Polytechnic Institut; Edward A. Doisy (U.S.) St. Louis Univ.
1944 Joseph Erlanger (U.S.) Washington Univ. and Herbert S. Gasser (U.S.) Rockefeller Institute for Medical Research
1945 Sir Alexander Fleming (U.K.) London Univ., Sir B. Chain (U.K.) Oxford Univ., and Lord Howard W. Florey (U.K.) Oxford Univ.
1946 Hermann J. Muller (U.S.) Indiana Univ.
1947 Carl F. Cori (U.S.) Washington Univ. and his wife Gerty T. Cori (U.S.) Washington Univ.; Bernardo A. Houssay (Argentina) Institute of Biology and Experimental Medicine
1948 Paul H. Müller (Switzerland) Laboratory of the J.R. Geigy Dye-Factory Co.
1949 Walter R. Hess (Switzerland) Zurich Univ.; Antonio Caetano de Abreu F.E. Moniz (Portugal) Univ. of Lisbon
1950 Edward C. Kendall (U.S.) Mayo Clinic, Tadeus Reichstein (Switzerland) Basel Univ., and Philip S. Hench (U.S.) Mayo Clinic
1951 Max Theiler (Union of South Africa) Laboratories Division of Medicine and Public Health, Rockefeller Foundation (New York)
1952 Selman A. Waksman (U.S.) Rutgers Univ.
1953 Sir Hans A. Krebs (U.K., b. Germany) Sheffield Univ.; Fritz A. Lipmann (U.S., b. Germany) Harvard Medical School and Massachusetts General Hospital
1954 John F. Enders (U.S.) Harvard Medical School and Research Division of Infectious Diseases, Children's Medical Center; Thomas H. Weller (U.S.) Research Division of Infectious Diseases, Children's Medical Center; and Frederick C. Robbins (U.S.) Western Reserve Univ.
1955 Axel H.T. Theorell (Sweden) Nobel Medical Institute
1956 Andre F. Cournand (U.S., b. France) Cardio-Pulmonary Laboratory, Columbia Univ. Division. Bellevue Hospital; Werner Forssman (Germany) Mainz Univ. and Bad Kreuznach; and Dickinson W. Richards (U.S.) Columbia Univ.
1957 Daniel Bovet (Italy, b. Switzerland) Chief Institute of Public Health
1958 George W. Beadle (U.S.) California Institute of Technology, and Edward L. Tatum (U.S.) Rockefeller Institute for Medical Research; Joshua Lederberg (U.S.) Wisconsin Univ.
1959 Severo Ochoa (U.S.) New York Univ. College of Medicine, and Arthur Kornberg (U.S.) Stanford Univ.
1960 Sir Frank M. Burnet (Australia) Walter and Eliza Hall Institute for Medical Research, and Sir Peter B. Medawar (U.K.) Univ. College
1961 Georg von Békésy (U.S., b. Hungary) Harvard Univ.
1962 Francis H.C. Crick (U.K.) Institute of Molecular Biology, James D. Watson (U.S.) Harvard Univ., and Maurice H.F. Wilkins (U.K.) University of London
1963 Sir John E. Eccles (Australia) Australian National Univ. Sir Alan L. Hodgkin (U.K.) Cambridge Univ., and Sir Andrew F. Huxley (U.K.) University of London
1964 Konrad Block (U.S., b. Germany) Harvard Univ. and Feodor Lymen (Germany) Max-Planck-Institut fur Zellchemie

1965 Francois Jacob (France), André Lwoff (France), and Jacques Monod (France), Institut Pasteur

1966 Peyton Rous (U.S.) Rockefeller Univ.; Charles B. Huggins (U.S.) Ben May Laboratory for Cancer Research, Univ. of Chicago

1967 Ragnar Granit (Sweden, b. Finland) Karolinska Institutet, Haldan K. Hartline (U.S.) Rockefeller Univ., and George Wald (U.S.) Harvard Univ.

1968 Robert W. Holley (U.S.) Cornell Univ., Har G. Khorana (U.S., b. India) Univ. of Wisconsin, and Marshall W. Nirenberg (U.S.) National Institutes of Health

1969 Max Delbrück (U.S., b. Germany) California Institute of Technology, Alfred D. Hershey (U.S.) Carnegie Institution of Washington, and Salvador Luria (U.S., b. Italy) M.I.T.

1970 Sir Bernard Katz (U.K.) University College, Ulf von Euler (Sweden) Karolinska Institutet, and Julius Axelrod (U.S.) National Institutes of Health

1971 Earl W. Sutherland, Jr. (U.S.) Vanderbilt Univ.

1972 Gerald M. Edelman (U.S.) Rockefeller Univ. and Rodney R. Porter (U.K.) Oxford Univ.

1973 Karl von Frisch (W. Germany) Zoologisches Institut der Universitat Munchen; Konrad Lorenz (Austria) Osterreichische Akademie der Wissenschaften, Institut fur vergleichende Verhaltensforschung, and Nikolaas Tinbergen (U.K.) University Museum

1974 Albert Claude (Belgium) Université Catholique de Louvain, Christian de Duve (Belgium) Rockefeller Univ. (New York), and George E. Palade (U.S., b. Romania) Yale Univ.

1975 David Baltimore (U.S.) M.I.T., Renato Dulbecco (U.S., b. Italy) Imperial Cancer Research Fund Laboratory (London), and Howard M. Temin (U.S.) Univ. of Wisconsin

1976 Baruch S. Blumberg (U.S.) Institute for Cancer Research, and D. Carleton Gajdusek (U.S.) National Institutes of Health

1977 Roger Guillemin (U.S., b. France) Salk Institute, and Andrew V. Schally (U.S., b. Poland) Veterans Administration Hospital, New Orleans; Rosalyn Yalow (U.S.) Veterans Administration Hospital, Bronx

1978 Werner Arber (Switzerland) Biozentrum der Universitat, Daniel Nathans (U.S.) John Hopkins Univ., and Hamilton O. Smith (U.S.) John Hopkins Univ.

1979 Alan M. Cormack (U.S., b. South Africa) Tufts Univ., and Sir Godfrey N. Hounsfield (U.K.) Central Research Laboratories, EMI

1980 Baruj Benacerraf (U.S., b. Venezuela) Harvard Medical School; Jean Dausset (France) Université de Paris, Laboratoire Immuno-Hemetologie; and George D. Snell (U.S.) Jackson Laboratory

1981 Roger W. Sperry (U.S.) California Institute of Technology; David H. Hubel (U.S., b. Canada) Harvard Medical School, and Torsten T. Wiesel (Sweden) Harvard Medical School

1982 Sune K. Bergström (Sweden) Karolinska Institute, Bengt I. Samuelsson (Sweden) Karolinska Institute, and Sir John R. Vane (U.K.) Wellcome Research Laboratories

1983 Barbara McClintock (U.S.) Cold Spring Harbor Laboratory

1984 Niels K. Jerne (Denmark) and Georges J.F. Köhler (W. Germany) of the Basel Institute for Immunology; and César Milstein (U.K. and Argentina) Medical Research Council Laboratory of Molecular Biology (Cambridge)

1985 Michael S. Brown (U.S.), and Joseph L. Goldstein (U.S.), Univ. of Texas Health Science Center at Dallas

1986 Stanley Cohen (U.S.) Vanderbilt Univ., and Rita Levi-Montalcini (Italy and U.S.) Institute of Cell Biology of the C.N.R. (Rome)

1987 Susumu Tonegawa (U.S.) MIT

1988 Sir James W. Black (U.K.) King's College Hospital Medical School, Gertrude B. Elion (U.S.) Welcome Research Laboratories, and George H. Hitchings (U.S.) Wellcome Research Laboratories

1989 J. Michael Bishop and Harold E. Varmus (U.S.) Univ. of California, San Francisco

1990 Joseph E. Murray (U.S.) Brigham and Women's Hospital (Boston), and E. Donnall Thomas (U.S.), Fred Hutchinson Cancer Research Center (Seattle)

1991 Erwin Neher (Germany) Max-Planck Institute for Biophysical Chemistry, Göttingen, and Bert Sakmann (Germany) Max-Planck Institute for Medical Research, Heidelberg,

1992 Edmond H. Fischer (U.S.) and Edwin G. Krebs (U.S.), both of the Univ. of Washington

1993 Richard J. Roberts (U.K.), New England Bio Labs, and Phillip A. Sharp (U.S.), MIT

1994 Alfred G. Gilman (U.S.) Univ. of Texas Southwestern Medical Center, and Martin Rodbell (U.S.) National Institute of Environmental Health Sciences

1995 Edward B. Lewis (U.S.) California Institute of Technology, Eric F. Wieschaus (U.S.) Princeton Univ., and Christiane Nüsslein-Volhard (Germany) Max-Planck Institute in Tübingen

1996 Peter C. Doherty (Australia) St. Jude's Medical Center in Memphis, and Rolf Zinkernagel (Switzerland) University of Zurich

1997 Stanley B. Prusiner (U.S.), Univ. of California

1998 Robert F. Furchgott (U.S.), SUNY Health Science Center; Louis J. Ignarro (U.S.), UCLA School of Medicine; and Ferid Murad (U.S.), Univ. of Texas

1999 Günter Blobel (U.S., b. Germany), Rockefeller Univ.
2000 Arvid Carlsson (Sweden), Univ. of Gothenburg; Paul Greengard (U.S.), Rockefeller Univ., N.Y.; and Eric Kandel (U.S.), Columbia Univ.
2001 Leland H. Hartwell (U.S.), Fred Hutchinson Cancer Research Center, Seattle, and R. Timothy Hunt (U.K.) and Sir Paul M. Nurse (U.K.)
2002 Sydney Brenner, (U.K.), Molecular Sciences Institute, H. Robert Horvitz, (U.S.), M.I.T., and John E. Sulston, (U.K.), Wellcome Trust Sanger Institute
2003 Paul C. Lauterbur (U.S.) and Peter Mansfield (U.K.)

Nobel Prizes in Economic Sciences

1969 Ragnar Frisch (Norway) Oslo Univ. and Jan Tinbergen (Netherlands) Netherlands School of Economics
1970 Paul A. Samuelson (U.S.) M.I.T.
1971 Simon Kuznets (U.S.) Harvard Univ.
1972 Sir John R. Hicks (U.K.) All Souls College, and Kenneth J. Arrow (U.S.) Harvard Univ.
1973 Wassily Leontief (U.S.) Harvard Univ.
1974 Gunnar Myrdal (Sweden), Friedrich A. von Hayek (U.K.)
1975 Leonid Kantorovich (USSR) Academy of Sciences, and Tjalling C. Koopmans (U.S.) Yale Univ.
1976 Milton Friedman (U.S.) Univ. of Chicago for
1977 Bertil Ohlin (Sweden) Stockholm School of Economics, and James E. Meade (U.K.) Cambridge Univ.
1978 Herbert A. Simon (U.S.) Carnegie-Mellon Univ.
1979 Theodore W. Schultz (U.S.) Univ. of Chicago, and Sir Arthur Lewis (U.K.) Princeton Univ.
1980 Lawrence R. Klein (U.S.) Univ. of Pennsylvania
1981 James Tobin (U.S.) Yale Univ.
1982 George J. Stigler (U.S.) Univ. of Chicago
1983 Gerard Debreu (U.S.) Univ. of California
1984 Sir Richard Stone (U.K.) Cambridge Univ.
1985 Franco Modigliani (U.S.) M.I.T.
1986 James M Buchanan Jr. (U.S.) Center for Study of Public Choice
1987 Robert M. Solow (U.S.) M.I.T.
1988 Maurice Allais (France) Centre d'analyse économique
1989 Trygve Haavelmo (Norway) Univ. of Oslo
1990 Harry Markowitz (U.S.) Baruch College (of the City Univ. of New York; William F. Sharpe (U.S.) Stanford Univ.; and Merton Miller (U.S.) Univ. of Chicago
1991 Ronald H. Coase (U.K.) Univ. of Chicago Law School
1992 Gary S. Becker (U.S.), Univ. of Chicago
1993 Robert W. Fogel (U.S.), Univ. of Chicago, and Douglass C. North (U.S.), Washington Univ.
1994 John F. Nash (U.S.) Princeton Univ., John C., Harsanyi (U.S., b. Hungary) Univ. of California, and Reinhard Selten (Germany) Univ. of Bonn
1995 Robert E. Lucas, Jr., (U.S.) Univ. of Chicago
1996 James A. Mirrlees (U.K.) Cambridge, Univ. and William Vickrey (U.S., b. Canada), Columbia Univ.
1997 Robert Merton (U.S.), Harvard University, and Myron Scholes (U.S.), Stanford University
1998 Amartya Sen (India), Cambridge Univ. and Harvard Univ.
1999 Robert A. Mundell (U.S.,b. Canada), Columbia University
2000 James J. Heckman (U.S.), Univ. of Chicago and Daniel L. McFadden (U.S.), Univ. of California
2001 George A. Akerlof (U.S.) Univ. of California, A. Michael Spence (U.S.), Stanford Univ., and Joseph E. Stiglitz (U.S.), Columbia Univ
2002 Daniel Kahneman, (U.S. and Israel), Princeton University and Vernon L. Smith, (U.S.), George Mason University
2003 Robert F. Engle (U.S.), New York University, and Clive W. Granger (U.K.)

Nobel Prizes in Chemistry

1901 Jacobus H. Van't Holt (Netherlands) Berlin Univ.
1902 Hermann E. Fischer (Germany)
1903 Svante A. Arrhenius (Sweden) Stockholm Univ.
1904 Sir William Ramsay (U.K.) London Univ.
1905 Johann F.W.A. von Baeyer (Germany) Munich Univ.
1906 Henri Moissan (France) Sorbonne Univ.
1907 Eduard Buchner (Germany) Agricultural College
1908 Lord Ernest Rutherfold (U.K.) Victoria Univ.
1909 Wilhelm Ostwald (Germany) Leipzig Univ.
1910 Otto Wallach (Germany) Goettingen Univ.
1911 Marie Curie (France) Sorbonne Univ.
1912 Victor Grignard (France) Nancy Univ.; Paul Sabatier (France) Toulouse Univ.
1913 Alfred Werner (Switzerland) Zurich Univ.
1914 Theodore W. Richards (U.S.) Harvard Univ.
1915 Richard M. Willstätter (Germany) Munich Univ.
1916–1917 No awards given.
1918 Fritz Haber (Germany) Kaiser-Wilhelm Institut
1919 No award
1920 Walther H. Nernst (Germany) Berlin Univ.
1921 Frederick Soddy (U.K.) Oxford Univ.
1922 Francis W. Aston (U.K.) Cambridge Univ.
1923 Fritz Pregl (Austria) Graz Univ.
1924 No award
1925 Richard A. Zsigmondy (Germany) Goettingen Univ.
1926 The (Theodor) Svedberg (Sweden) Uppsala Univ.
1927 Heinrich O. Wieland (Germany) Munich Univ.
1928 Adolf O.R. Windaus (Germany) Goettingen Univ.
1929 Sir Arthur Harden (U.K.) London Univ., Hans K.A. von Euler-Chelpin (Sweden)

1930 Hans Fischer (Germany) Institute of Technology
1931 Carl Bosch (Germany) Heidelberg Univ. I.G. Farbenindustrie A.G., and Fredrich Bergius (Germany) Heidelberg Univ. and I.G. Farbenindustrie A.G.
1932 Irving Langmuir (U.S.) General Electric Co.
1933 No award
1934 Harold C. Urey (U.S.) Columbia Univ.
1935 Frédéric Joliot and Iréne Joliot-Curie, (France) Institut du Radium
1936 Petrus (Peter) J.W. Debye (Netherlands) Berlin Univ. and Kaiser-Wilhelm-Institut (now Max-Planck-Institut)
1937 Sir Walter N. Haworth (U.K.) Birmingham Univ.; Paul Karrer (Switzerland) Zurich Univ.
1938 Richard Kuhn (Germany) Heidelberg Univ. and Kaiser-Wilhelm-Institut (now Max-Planck-Institut)
1939 Adolf F.J. Butenandt (Germany) Berlin Univ. and Kaiser-Wilhelm-Institut (now Max-Planck-Institut); Leopold Ruzicka (Switzerland) Federal Institute of Technology
1940–1942 No awards
1943 George de Hevesy (Hungary) Stockholm Univ.
1944 Otto Hahn (Germany) Kaiser-Wilhelm-Institut (now Max-Planck-Institut)
1945 Artturi I. Virtanen (Finland) Helsinki Univ.
1946 James B. Sumner (U.S.) Cornell Univ.; John H. Northrop (U.S.) Rockefeller Institute for Medical Research
1947 Sir Robert Robinson (U.K.) Oxford Univ.
1948 Arne W.K. Tiselius (Sweden) Uppsala Univ.
1949 William F. Giauque (U.S.) Univ. of California
1950 Otto P.H. Diels (Germany) Kiel Univ. and Kurt Alder (Germany) Cologne Univ.
1951 Edwin M. McMillan (U.S.) and Glenn T. Seaborg (U.S.) both of Univ. of California
1952 Archer J.P. Martin (U.K.) Nations Institute for Medical Research, and Richard L.M. Synge (U.K.) Rowett Research Institute (Scotland)
1953 Herman Staudinger (Germany) State Research Institute for Macromolecular Chemistry
1954 Linus C. Pauling (U.S.) California Institute of Technology
1955 Vincent du Vigneaud (U.S.) Cornell Univ.
1956 Sir Cyril N. Hinshelwood (U.K.) Oxford Univ. and Nikolaj N. Semenov (USSR) Institute for Chemical Physics of the Academy of Sciences of the USSR
1957 Lord Alexander R. Todd (U.K.) Cambridge Univ.
1958 Frederick Sanger (U.K.) Cambridge Univ.
1959 Jaroslav Heyrovsky (Czechoslovakia) Polaro-Institute of the Czechoslovakia Academy of Science
1960 Willard F. Libby (U.S.) Univ. of California, Los Angeles
1961 Melvin Calvin (U.S.) Univ. of California
1962 Max F. Perutz (U.K.) Laboratory of Molecular Biology, and Sir John C. Kendrew (U.K.) Laboratory of Molecular Biology
1963 Karl Ziegler (Germany) Max-Planck-Institute for Carbon Research, and Giulio Natta (Italy) Institute of Technology
1964 Dorothy C. Hodgkin (U.K.) Royal Society, Oxford Univ.
1965 Robert B. Woodward (U.S.) Harvard Univ.
1966 Robert S. Mulliken (U.S.) Univ. of Chicago
1967 Manfred Eigen (W. Germany) Max-Planck-Institut, Ronald G.W. Norrish (U.K.) Institute of Physical Chemistry, and Sir George Porter (U.K.) The Royal Institution
1968 Lars Onsager (U.S.) Yale Univ.
1969 Sir Derek H.R. Barton (U.K.) Imperial College of Science and Technology, and Odd Hassel (Norway) Kjemisk Institut
1970 Luis F. Leloir (Argentina) Institute for Biochemical Research
1971 Gerhard Herzberg (Canada) National Research Council of Canada
1972 Christian B. Anfinsen (U.S.) National Institutes of Health; Stanford Moore (U.S.) Rockefeller Univ. and William H. Stein (U.S.) Rockefeller Univ.
1973 Ernst O. Fischer (W. Germany) Technical Univ. of Munich, and Sir Geoffrey Wilkinson (U.K.) Imperial College
1974 Paul J. Flory (U.S.) Stanford Univ.
1975 Sir John W. Cornforth (Australia and U.K.) Univ. of Sussex; Vladimir Prelog (Switzerland) Eidgenossische Technische Hochschule
1976 William N. Lipscomb (U.S.) Harvard Univ.
1977 Ilya Prigogine (Belgium) Université Libre de Bruxelles, (Univ. of Texas, U.S.)
1978 Peter D. Mitchell (U.K.) Glynn Research Laboratories
1979 Herbert C. Brown (U.S.) Purdue Univ., and Georg Wittig (Germany) Univ. of Heidelberg
1980 Paul Berg (U.S.) Stanford Univ.; Walter Gilbert (U.S.) Biological Laboratories, and Frederick Sanger (U.K.) MRC Laboratory of Molecular Biology
1981 Kenichi Fukui (Japan) Kyoto Univ. and Roald Hoffman (U.S.) Cornell Univ.
1982 Aaron Klug (U.K.) MRC Laboratory of Molecular Biology
1983 Henry Taube (U.S.) Stanford Univ.
1984 Robert B. Merrifield (U.S.) Rockefeller Univ.

1985 Herbert A. Hauptman (U.S.) Medical Foundation of Buffalo, and Jerome Karle (U.S.) U.S. Naval Research Laboratory

1986 Dudley R. Herschbach (U.S.) Harvard Univ., Yuan T. Lee (U.S.) Univ. of California, and John C. Polanyi (Canada) Univ. of Toronto

1987 Donald J. Cram (U.S.) University of California, Los Angeles, Jean-Marie Lehn (France) Université Louis Pasteur, and Charles J. Pedersen (U.S.) Du Pont Laboratory

1988 Johann Deisenhofer (U.S.) Howard Hughes Medical Institute, Robert Huber (W. Germany) Max-Planck-Institut, and Hartmut Michel (W. Germany) Max-Planck-Institut

1989 Sidney Altman (U.S.) Yale Univ., and Thomas Cech (U.S.) Univ. of Colorado

1990 Elias James Corey (U.S.) Harvard Univ.

1991 Richard R. Ernst (Switzerland) Eidgenössische Technische Hochschule, Zurich

1992 Rudolph A. Marcus (U.S., b. Canada), Cal Tech.

1993 Kary B. Mullis (U.S.); and Michael Smith (Canada), Univ. of British Columbia

1994 George A. Olah (U.S., b. Hungary) Univ. of Southern California

1995 F. Sherwood Roland (U.S.) Univ. of California-Irvine, Mario Molina (U.S.) M.I.T., and Paul Crutzen (Netherlands) Max Planck Institute for Chemistry in Mainz, Germany

1996 Robert F. Curl, Jr., (U.S.) and Richard E. Smalley (U.S.), of Rice University, and Harold W. Kroto (U.K.) of Univ. of Sussex

1997 Paul D. Boyer (U.S.), UCLA and John E. Walker (U.K.), Medical Research Council Laboratory of Molecular Biology; Jens C. Skou (Denmark), Aarhus Univ.

1998 Walter Kohn (U.S., b. Austria), Univ. of California, Santa Barbara; John A. Pople (U.S., b U.K.), Northwestern Univ.

1999 Ahmed H. Zewail (U.S., b. Egypt), CalTech,

2000 Alan J. Heeger (U.S.), Univ. of California at Santa Barbara; Alan G. MacDiarmid (U.S.), Univ. of Pennsylvania; and Hideki Shirakawa (Japan), Univ. of Tsukuba

2001 William S. Knowles (U.S.) and Ryoji Noyori, (Japan), Nagoya Univ.; K. Barry Sharpless (U.S.), Scripps Research Institute, La Jolla, Calif.

2002 John B. Fenn, (U.S.), Virginia Commonwealth University, and Koichi Tanaka, (Japan), Shimadzu Corp.; and Kurt Wüthrich, (Switzerland), Swiss Federal Institute of Technology Zürich, and The Scripps Research Institute, La Jolla, Calif.

2003 Peter Agre (U.S.), Johns Hopkins Univ.; Koichi Tanaka (U.S.), Rockefeller Univ.

Nobel Prizes in Physics

1901 Wilhelm C. Röntgen (Germany) Munich Univ.

1902 Hendrik A. Lorentz (Netherlands) Leyden Univ., and Pieter Zeeman (Netherlands) Amsterdam Univ.

1903 Antoine H. Becquerel (France) Ecole Polytechnique; Pierre Curie (France) Municipal School of Industrial Physics and Chemistry and his wife, Marie Curie, (France, b. Poland)

1904 Lord Rayleigh (John W. Strutt) (U.K.) Royal Institution of U.K.

1905 Philipp E.A. Lenard (Germany) Kiel Univ.

1906 Sir Joseph J. Thomas (U.K.) Cambridge Univ.

1907 Albert A. Michelson (U.S.) Univ. of Chicago

1908 Gabriel Lippman (France) Sorbonne Univ.

1909 Guglielmo Marconi (Italy) Marconi Wireless Telegraph Co., Ltd., and Carl F. Braun (Germany) Strasbourg Univ.

1910 Johannes D. van der Waals (Netherlands) Amsterdam Univ.

1911 Wilhelm Wein (Germany) Würzburg Univ.

1912 Nils G. Dalén (Sweden) Swedish Gas-Accumulator Co.

1913 Heike Kamerlingh-Onnes (Netherlands) Leyden Univ.

1914 Max von Laue (Germany) Frankfurt-am-Main Univ.

1915 Sir William Henry Bragg (U.K.) London Univ. and his son Sir William Lawrence Bragg (U.K.) Victoria Univ.

1916 No award.

1917 Charles G. Barkla (U.K.) Edinburgh Univ.

1918 Max K.E.L. Planck (Germany) Berlin Univ.

1919 Johannes Stark (Germany) Greifswald Univ.

1920 Charles E. Guillaume (Switzerland) International Bureau of Weights and Measurers

1921 Albert Einstein (Germany) Kaiser-Wilhelm-Institut für Physik (now Max-Panck-Institut)

1922 Niels Bohr (Denmark) Copenhagen Univ.

1923 Robert A. Millikan (U.S.) California Institute of Technology)

1924 Karl M.G. Siegbahn (Sweden) Uppsala Univ.

1925 James Franck (Germany) Goettingen Univ., and Gustav Hertz (Germany) Halle Univ.

1926 Jean B. Perrin (France) Sorbonne Univ.

1927 Arthur H. Compton (U.S.) Univ. of Chicago; Charles T.R. Wilson (U.K.) Cambridge Univ.

1928 Sir Own W. Richardson (U.K.) London Univ.

1929 Prince Louis-Victor de Broglie (France) Sorbonne Univ.

1930 Sir Chandrasekhara V. Raman (India) Calcutta Univ.

1931 No award.

1932 Werner Heisenberg (Germany) Leipzig Univ.

1933 Edwin Schrödinger (Austria) Berlin Univ. and Paul A.M. Dirac (U.K.) Cambridge Univ.
1934 No award
1935 Sir James Chadwick (U.K.) Liverpool Univ.
1936 Victor F. Hess (Austria) Innsbruck Univ.; Carl D. Anderson (U.S.) California Institute of Technology
1937 Clinton J. Davisson (U.S.) Bell Telephone Laboratories, and Sir George P. Thomson (U.K.) London Univ.
1938 Enrico Fermi (Italy) Rome Univ.
1939 Ernest O. Lawrence (U.S.) Univ. of California, Berkeley
1940–1942 No awards given.
1943 Otto Stern (U.S.) Carnegie Institute of Technology
1944 Isidor I. Rabi (U.S.) Columbia Univ.
1945 Wolfgang Pauli (Austria) Princeton Univ.
1946 Percy W. Bridgman (U.S.) Harvard Univ.
1947 Sir Edward V. Appleton (U.K.) Dept. of Scientific and Industrial Research
1948 Lord Patrick M.S. Blackett (U.K.) Victoria Univ.
1949 Hideki Yukawa (Japan) Kyoto Imperial Univ.
1950 Cecil F. Powell (U.K.) Bristol Univ.
1951 Sir John D. Cockcroft (U.K.) Atomic Energy Research Establishment, and Ernest T.S. Walton (Ireland) Dublin Univ.
1952 Felix Block (U.S.) Stanford Univ., and Edward M. Purcell (U.S.) Harvard Univ.
1953 Frits (Frederik) Zernike (Netherlands) Groningern Univ.
1954 Max Born (U.K.) Edinburgh Univ.; Walther Bothe (Germany) Heidelbery Univ., Max-Planck-Institut
1955 Willis E. Lamb (U.S.) Stanford Univ.; Polykarp Kusch (U.S.) Columbia Univ.
1956 William Shockley (U.S. Semiconductor Laboratory of Beckman Instruments, Inc., John Bardeen (U.S.) Univ. of Illinois, and Walter H. Brattain (U.S.) Bell Telephone Laboratories
1957 Chen N. Yang (China) Institute for Advanced Study (Princeton, NJ) and Tsung-Dao Lee (China) Columbia Univ.
1958 Pavel A. Cherenkov (USSR) Physics Institute of USSR Academy of Sciences, Il'ja M.Frank (USSR) Academy of Sciences, and Igor J. Tamm (USSR) Univ. of Moscow and Physics Institute of USSR Academy of Sciences
1959 Emillio G. Sergè (U.S.) Univ. of California, Berkeley, and Owen Chamberlain (U.S.) Univ. of California, Berkeley
1960 Donald A. Glaser (U.S.) Univ. of California, Berkeley
1961 Robert Hofstadter (U.S.) Stanford Univ.; Rudolf L. Mössbauer (Germany) Technische Hochschule (Munich), and California Institute of Technology
1962 Lev D. Landau (USSR) Academy of Sciences
1963 Eugene P. Wigner (U.S.) Princeton Univ.; Maria Goeppert-Mayer (U.S.) Univ. of California, La Jolla, and J. Hans D. Jensen (Germany) Univ. of Heidelberg
1964 Charles H. Townes (U.S.) M.I.T., Nikolai G. Basov (USSR) Lebedev Institute for Physics, and Aleksandre M. Prochorov (USSR) Lebedev Institute for Physics
1965 Schin'ichiro Tomonaga (Japan) Toyko Univ., Julian Schwinger (U.S.) Harvard Univ., and Richard P. Feynman (U.S.) California Institute of Technology
1966 Alfred Kastier (France) Ecole Normale Supérieure, Université de Paris
1967 Hans A. Bethe (U.S.) Cornell Univ.
1968 Luis W. Alvarez (U.S.) Univ. of California, Berkeley
1969 Murray Gell-Mann (U.S.) California Institute of Technology
1970 Hannes Alfvén (Sweden) Royal Institute of Technology; Louis Neel (France) Univ. of Grenoble
1971 Dennis Gabor (U.K.) Imperial College of Science and Technology
1972 John Bardeen (U.S.) Univ. of Illinois, Leon N. Cooper (U.S.) Brown Univ., and J. Robert Schrieffer (U.S.) Univ. of Pennsylvania
1973 Leo Esaki (Japan) IBM Thomas J. Watson Research Center (New York), and Ivar Giaever (U.S.) General Electric Co.; Brian D. Josephson (U.K.) Cambridge Univ.
1974 Sir Martin Ryle (U.K.) and Antony Hewish (U.K.), both of Cambridge Univ.
1975 Aage Bohr (Denmark) Niels Bohr Institute, Ben Mottelson (Denmark) Nordita, and James Rainwater (U.S.) Columbia Univ.
1976 Burton Richter (U.S.) Stanford Linear Accelerator Center, and Samuel C.C. Ting (U.S.) M.I.T.
1977 Philip W. Anderson (U.S.) Bell Laboratories, Sir Nevill F. Mott (U.K.) Cambridge Univ. and John H. van Vleck (U.S.) Harvard Univ.
1978 Peter L. Kapitsa (USSR) Academy of Sciences; Arno A. Penzias (U.S.) Bell Laboratories, and Robert W. Wilson (U.S.) Bell Laboratories
1979 Sheldon L. Glashow (U.S.) Lyman Laboratory, Harvard Univ., Abdus Salam (Pakistan) International Centre for Theoretical Physics (Italy) and Imperial College of Science and Technology (London), and Steven Weinberg (U.S.) Harvard Univ.
1980 James W. Cronin (U.S.) Univ. of Chicago, and Val L. Fitch (U.S.) Princeton Univ.
1981 Nicolaas Bloembergen (U.S.) Harvard Univ., and Arthur L. Schawlow (U.S.) Stanford Univ.; Kai M. Siegbahn (Sweden) Uppsala Univ.
1982 Kenneth G. Wilson (U.S.) Cornell Univ.

1983 Subrahmanyan Chandrasekhar (U.S.) Univ. of Chicago; William A. Fowler (U.S.) California Institute of Technology

1984 Carlo Rubbia (Italy) CERN (Switzerland), and Simon van der Meer (Netherlands) CERN (Switzerland)

1985 Klaus von Klitzing (W. Germany) Max-Planck-Institut for Solid State Research

1986 Ernst Ruska (W. Germany) Fritz-Haber-Institut der Max-Planck-Gesellschaft; Gerd Binnig (W. Germany) IBM Zurich Research Laboratory and Heinrich Rohrer (Switzerland) IBM Zurich Research Laboratory

1987 Georg J. Bednorz (Switzerland) IBM Zurich research Laboratory, and Dr. K. Alex Müller (Switzerland) IBM Zurich Research Laboratory

1988 Leon M. Lederman (U.S.) Fermi National Accelerator Laboratory, Melvin Schwartz (U.S.) Digital Pathways, Inc., and Jack Steinberger (Switzerland)

1989 Norman R. Ramsey (U.S.) Harvard Univ.; Hans G. Dehmelt (U.S.) Univ. of Washington, and Wolfgang Paul (W. Germany) Univ. of Bonn

1990 Richard E. Taylor (Can.), Stanford U.; Jerome I. Friedman (U.S.) MIT; and Henry W. Kendall (U.S.) MIT

1991 Pierre-Gilles de Gennes (France), Collège de France, Paris,

1992 George Charpak (France, b. Poland), affiliated with CERN

1993 Joseph H. Taylor (U.S.), Princeton Univ., and Russel A. Hulse (U.S.), Princeton Plasma Physics Laboratory

1994 Clifford G. Shull (U.S.) MIT, and Bertram N. Brockhouse (Canada) McMaster Univ.

1995 Martin L. Perl, (U.S.) Stanford Univ. Linear Accelerator Center, and Frederick Reines (U.S.) Los Alamos National Laboratory

1996 Robert C. Richardson (U.S.) and David M. Lee (U.S.) of Cornell Univ., and Douglas S. Osheroff (U.S.) Stanford Univ.

1997 Steven Chu (U.S.) Stanford Univ., Claude Cohen-Tannoudji (France), Collège de France, and William D. Phillips (U.S.), National Institute of Standards and Technology

1998 Robert B. Laughlin (U.S.), Stanford Univ., Horst L. Störmer (U.S.), Bell Laboratories; Daniel Tsui (U.S.), Princeton Univ.

1999 Gerardus 't Hooft (Netherlands), Univ. of Utrecht, and Martinus J.G. Veltman (Netherlands) Univ. of Michigan

2000 Jack S. Kilby (U.S.), Texas Instruments; Zhores I. Alferov (Russia), A.F. Ioffe Physico-Technical Institute, St. Petersburg, and Herbert Kroemer, (U.S.), Univ. of California at Santa Barbara

2001 Eric A. Cornell (U.S.) and Carl E. Wieman (U.S.) both of the Joint Institute for Laboratory Astrophysics, Boulder, Colo., and Wolfgang Ketterle (Germany), M.I.T.

2002 Raymond Davis Jr., (U.S.), University of Pennsylvania and Masatoshi Koshiba, (Japan), University of Tokyo; and Riccardo Giacconi, (U.S., B. Italy), University of Milan

2003 Alexei Abrikosov (U.S. and Russia), Argonne (Illinois) National Laboratory, Vitaly L. Ginzburg (Russia), P.N. Ledbedev Physical Institute, Moscow, and Anthony J. Leggett (U.S. and U.K.), Univ. of Illinois

Nobel Prizes in Literature

1901 Sully Prudhomme (pen name of René F.A. Prudhomme) (France)

1902 Christian M.T. Mommsen (Germany)

1903 Bjørstjerne M. Bjørnson (Norway)

1904 Frédéric Mistral (France); José Echegaray y Eizaguirre (Spain)

1905 Henryk Sienkiewicz (Poland)

1906 Giosué Carducci (Italy)

1907 Rudyard Kipling (U.K.)

1908 Rudolf C. Eucken (Germany)

1909 Selma O.L. Lagerlöf (Sweden)

1910 Paul J.L. Heyse (Germany)

1911 Count Maurice (Mooris) P.M.B. Maeterlinck (Belgium)

1912 Gerhart J.R. Hauptmann (Germany)

1913 Rabindranath Tagore (India)

1914 No award

1915 Romain Rolland (France)

1916 Carl G.V. von Heidenstam (Sweden)

1917 Karl A. Gjellerup (Denmark); Henrik Pontoppidan (Denmark)

1918 No award

1919 Carl F.G. Spitteler (Switzerland)

1920 Knut P. Hamsun (Norway)

1921 Anatole France (pen name of Jacques A. Thibault) (France)

1922 Jacinto Benavente (Spain)

1923 William Butler Yeats (Ireland)

1924 Wladyslaw S. Reymont (pen name of Reyment) (Poland)

1925 George Bernard Shaw (U.K.)

1926 Grazia Deledda (pen name of Grazia Madesani (Italy)

1927 Henri Bergson (France)

1928 Sigrid Undset (Norway)

1929 Thomas Mann (Germany)

1930 Sinclair Lewis (U.S.)

1931 Erik A. Karlfeldt (Sweden)

1932 John Galsworthy (U.K.)
1933 Ivan A. Bunin (stateless domicile in France)
1934 Luigi Pirandello (Italy)
1935 No award
1936 Eugene G. O'Neill (U.S.)
1937 Roger Martin du Gard (France)
1938 Pearl Buck (pen name of Pearl Walsh) (U.S.)
1939 Frans E. Sillanpää (Finland)
1940–1943 No awards given.
1944 Johannes V. Jensen (Denmark)
1945 Gabriela Mistral (pen name of Lucila Godoy y Alcayaga) (Chile)
1946 Hermann Hesse (Switzerland)
1947 André P.G. Gide (France)
1948 Thomas S. Eliot (U.K.)
1949 William Faulkner (U.S.)
1950 Earl (Bertrand) Russell (U.K.)
1951 Pär Fabian Lägerkvist (Sweden)
1952 François Mauriac (France)
1953 Sir Winston L.S. Churchill (U.K.)
1954 Ernest M. Hemingway (U.S.)
1955 Halldór K. Laxness (Iceland)
1956 Juan R. Jiménez (Puerto Rico, b. Spain)
1957 Albert Camus (France)
1958 Boris L. Pasternak (U.S.S.R.)
1959 Salvatore Quasimodo (Italy)
1960 Saint-John Perse (pen name of Alexis Léger) (France)
1961 Ivo Andric (Yugoslavia)
1962 John Steinbeck (U.S.)
1963 Giorgos Seferis (pen name of Giorgos Seferiadis) (Greece)
1964 Jean-Paul Sartre (France)
1965 Michail A. Sholokhov (U.S.S.R.)
1966 Shmuel U. Agnon (Israel); Nelly Sachs (Germany, domiciled in Sweden)
1967 Miguel A. Asturias (Guatemala)
1968 Yasunari Kawabata (Japan)
1969 Samuel Beckett (Ireland)
1970 Alexander Solzhenitsyn (U.S.S.R.)
1971 Pablo Neruda (pen name of Neftalí Ricardo Reyes Basoalto) (Chile)
1972 Heinrich Böll (West Germany)
1973 Patrick White (Australia, b. U.K.)
1974 Eyvind Johnson (Sweden); Harry Martinson (Sweden)
1975 Eugenio Montale (Italy)
1976 Saul Bellow (U.S.)
1977 Vincente Aleixandre (Spain)
1978 Isaac Bashevis Singer (U.S., b. Poland)
1979 Odysseus Elytis (pen name of Odysseus Alepoudhelis) (Greece)
1980 Czeslaw Milosz (U.S. and Poland)
1981 Elias Canetti (U.K., b. Bulgaria)
1982 Gabriel García Marquez (Colombia)
1983 William Golding (U.K.)
1984 Jaroslav Seifert (Czechoslovakia)
1985 Claude Simon (France)
1986 Wole Soyinka (Nigeria)
1987 Joseph Brodsky (U.S., b. U.S.S.R.)
1988 Naguib Mahfouz (Egypt)
1989 Camilo José Cela (Spain)
1990 Octavio Paz (Mexico)
1991 Nadine Gordimer (South Africa)
1992 Derek Walcott (West Indies, b. St. Lucia)
1993 Toni Morrison (U.S.)
1994 Kenzaburo Oe (Japan)
1995 Seamus Heaney (Ireland)
1996 Wislawa Szymborska (Poland)
1997 Dario Fo, (Italy)
1998 José Saramago (Portugal)
1999 Günter Grass (Germany)
2000 Gao Xingjian (France, b. China)
2001 V.S. Naipaul (U.K., b. Trinidad)
2002 Imre Kertész, (Hungary)
2003 J.M. Coetzee (South Africa)

WEIGHTS AND MEASURES

Systems of Measurement

There are two widely used measurement systems. Most of the world uses a system known as the metric system, or the International System, abbreviated SI, from Système Internationale, its name in French. The United States continues to use a system called U.S. customary measure, which derives from (and differs from) the British imperial series of weights and measures. From time to time, our government has taken steps to change from the customary system to the International System, but these efforts have had limited success. Metric measure is legal in the United States, but nearly everyone continues to use the customary system in everyday life. The International System is generally used in scientific pursuits and increasingly in international trade.

Length or Distance

U.S. customary system

1 foot (ft.)	=	12 inches
1 yard (yd.)	=	3 feet = 36 inches
1 rod (rd.)	=	5.5 yards = 16.5 feet
1 furlong (fur.)	=	40 rods = 220 yards
	=	660 feet
1 mile (mi.)	=	8 furlongs = 1,760 yards
	=	5,280 feet

An international nautical mile is 6,076.1155 feet.

International System The basic unit of length is the meter, which is slightly longer than the yard. Other units of length are decimal subdivisions or multiples of the meter.

1 decimeter (dm)	=	10 centimeters
	=	0.1 meter
1 centimeter (cm)	=	0.01 meter
1 millimeter (mm)	=	0.1 centimeter
	=	0.001 meter
1 micrometer (µm)	=	0.001 millimeter
	=	0.0001 centimeter
	=	0.000001 meter
1 angstrom (Å)	=	0.0001 micrometers
	=	0.0000001 milimeter
1 dekameter (dam)	=	10 meters
1 hectometer (hm)	=	10 dekameters
	=	100 meters
1 kilometer (km)	=	10 hectometers
	=	100 dekameters
	=	1,000 meters

Conversions In 1959 the relationship between between customary and international measures of length was officially defined as follows:

0.0254 meter (exactly)	=	1 inch
0.0245 meter x 12	=	0.3048 meter
	=	1 international foot

This definition, which makes many conversions simple, defines a foot that is shorter (by about 6 parts in 10 million) than the survey foot, which had earlier been defined as exactly 1200/3937, or 0.3048006, meter.

Following the international foot standard, the major equivalents are as listed below:

1 in.	=	2.54 cm = 0.0254 m
1 ft.	=	30.48 cm = .3048 m
1 yd.	=	91.44 cm = 0.9144 m
1 mi.	=	1,609.344 m = 1.609344 km
1 cm	=	0.3937 in.
1 m	=	1.093613 yd. = 3.28084 ft.
1 km	=	0.62137 mi.

Area

U.S. customary system Areas are derived from lengths as follows:

1 square foot	=	144 square inches
1 square yard	=	9 sq. ft.
1 square rod (rd.2)	=	30.25 square yards
	=	272.25 square feet
1 acre	=	160 square rods
	=	4,840 square yards
	=	43,560 sq. ft.
1 square mile	=	640 acres
1 section	=	1 mile square
1 township	=	6 miles square
	=	36 square miles

International System

1 sq. millimeter (mm^2)	=	1,000,000 sq. micrometers
1 sq. centimeter (cm^2)	=	100 mm^2
1 sq. decimeter (dm^2)	=	100 cm^2
1 sq. meter (m^2)	=	10,000 cm^2
1 are (a)	=	100 m^2
1 hectare (ha)	=	100 ares
	=	10,000 m^2

1 sq kilometer (km^2)	=	100 hectares
	=	1,000,000 m^2

Conversions

1 square inch	=	6.4516 cm^2
1 square foot	=	929.0304 cm^2
	=	0.09290304 m^2
1 square yard	=	8,361.2736 cm^2
	=	0.83612736 m^2
1 acre	=	4,046.8564 m^2
	=	0.40468564 hectares
1 square mile	=	2,589,988.11 m^2
	=	258.998811 hectares
	=	2.58998811 km^2
1 cm^2	=	0.1550003 sq. in.
1 m^2	=	1,550.003 sq. in.
	=	10.76391 sq. ft.
	=	1.195990 sq. yds.
1 hectare	=	107,639.1 sq. ft.
	=	11,959.90 sq. yd.
	=	2.4710538 acres
1 km^2	=	247.10538 acres
	=	0.3861006 sq. mi

Cubic Measure

U.S. customary system

1 cu foot (ft.^{3})	=	1,728 cubic inches (in.^{3})
1 cubic yard (yd.^{3})	=	27 cubic feet (ft.^{3})

International System

1 cubic centimeter (cm^3)	=	1,000 cubic millimeters (mm^3)
1 cubic decimeter (dm^3)	=	1,000 cubic centimeters (cm^3)
1 cubic meter (m^3)	=	1,000 cubic decimeters (dm^3)
	=	1,000,000 cubic centimeters (cm^3)

Cubic centimeter is sometimes abbreviated cc and is used in fluid measure interchangeably with milliliter (ml).

Conversions

1 in.^{3}	=	16.387064 cm^3
1 ft.^{3}	=	28.316846592 cm^3
	=	0.028316847 cm^3
1 yd.^{3}	=	764,554.857984 cm^3
	=	0.764554858 m^3
1 cm^3	=	0.06102374 in.^{3}
1 m^3	=	61,023.74 in.^{3}
	=	35.31467 ft.^{3}
	=	1.307951 yd.^{3}

Fluid Volume

U.S. customary system A gallon is equal to 231 cubic inches of liquid or capacity.

1 tablespoon (tbs.)	=	3 teaspoons (tsp.)
	=	0.5 fluid ounce (fl. oz.)
1 cup	=	8 fl. oz.
1 pint (pt.)	=	2 cups = 16 fl. oz.
1 quart (qt.)	=	2 pt. = 4 cups
	=	32 fl. oz.
1 gallon (gal.)	=	4 qt. = 8 pt. = 16 cups
1 bushel (bu.)	=	8 gal. = 32 qt.

International System Fluid-volume measurements are directly tied to cubic measure. One milliliter of fluid occupies a volume of 1 cubic centimeter. A liter of fluid (slightly more than the customary quart) occupies a volume of 1 cubic decimeter, or 1,000 cubic centimeters.

1 centiliter (cL)	=	10 mililiters (mL)
1 deciliter	=	10 cL = 100 mL
1 liter (L)	=	10 dL = 1,000 mL
1 dekaliter (daL)	=	10 L
1 hectoliter (hL)	=	10 daL = 100 L
1 kiloliter (kL)	=	10 hL = 1,000 L

Conversions

1 fluid ounce	=	29.573528 mL = 0.02957 L
1 cup	=	236.588 mL = 0.236588 L
1 pint	=	473.176 mL = 0.473176 L
1 quart	=	946.3529 mL = 0.9463529 L
1 gallon	=	3,785.41 mL = 3.78541 L
1 milliliter	=	0.0338 fluid ounce
1 liter	=	33.814 fluid ounces
	=	4.2268 cups = 2.113 pints
	=	1.0567 quarts = 0.264 gallon

Dry Volume

Conversions

1 pint, dry	=	33.600 cu. in. = 0.551 L
1 quart, dry	=	67.201 cu. in. = 1.101 L

Mass and Weight

Mass is a measure of the quantity of matter in an object and does not vary with changes in altitude or in gravitational force (as on the moon or another planet). Weight, on the other hand, is a measure of the force of gravity on an object and so does change with altitude or gravitational force.

U.S. customary system In customary measure it is more common to measure weight than mass. The most common customary system of weight is avoirdupois:

1 pound (lb.)	=	16 ounces (oz.)
1 (short) hundred-weight (cwt.)	=	100 lb.
1 (short) ton	=	20 hundredweight
	=	2,000 lb.
1 long hundred-weight	=	112 lb.
1 long ton	=	20 long hundredweight
	=	2,240 lb.

A different system called troy weight is used to weigh precious metals. In troy weight the ounce is slightly larger than in avoirdupois, but there are only 12 ounces to the troy pound.

International System Instead of weight, the International System uses measures of mass. The original basic unit was the gram, which was defined as the mass of 1 milliliter (= 1 cm^3) of water at 4 degrees Celsius (about 39°F). Today the official measure of mass is a specific metal object defined as the standard kilogram.

1 centigram (cg)	=	10 milligrams (mg)
1 decigram (dg)	=	10 cg = 100 mg
1 gram (g)	=	10 dg = 100 cg = 1,000 mg
1 kilogram (kg)	=	10 hectograms (hg)
	=	100 dekagrams (dag)
	=	1,000 g
1 metric ton (t)	=	1,000 kg

Conversions Since mass and weight are identical at standard conditions (sea level on Earth), grams and other International System units of mass are often used as measures of weight or converted into customary units of weight. Under standard conditions:

1 ounce	=	28.3495 grams
1 pound	=	453.59 grams
	=	0.45359 kilogram
1 short ton	=	907.18 kilograms
	=	0.907 metric ton
1 milligram	=	0.000035 ounce
1 gram	=	0.03527 ounce
1 kilogram	=	35.27 ounces
	=	2.2046 pounds
1 metric ton	=	2,204.6 pounds
	=	1.1023 short tons

Time

Customary and International System The International System in 1967 adopted a second that is based on the microwaves emitted by the vibrations of hot cesium atoms. A second (abbreviated sec. in customary usage, s in SI usage) is the time it takes the atoms to vibrate exactly 9,192,631,770 times. In the customary measure of time, the day is divided into 24 hours, the hour into 60 minutes, and the minute into 60 seconds. Since the Earth's rotation is gradually slowing, scientists must periodically add a second to a day to keep the year in sequence with their clocks. The change is so small that for almost all practical purposes an International System second and a customary second are the same.

Decimal fractions of time are used to measure smaller time intervals:

millisecond (ms)	=	0.001 second (10^{-3})
microsecond (µs) (10^{-6})	=	0.000001 second
nanosecond (ns)	=	0.000000001 second (10^{-9})
picosecond (ps)	=	0.000000000001 second (10^{-12})

Temperature

U.S. customary system In the U.S, temperature is usually measured in degrees Fahrenheit: water freezes at 32°F and boils at 212°F. The basis of the Fahrenheit scale was 0°F, the coldest temperature that its originator, G. D. Fahrenheit (1686–1736), could obtain under laboratory conditions.

International System The Swedish astronomer Anders Celsius (1701–44) devised the temperature scale that bears his name in 1742. On the Celsius scale, water freezes at 0°C and boils at 100°C. Very low temperatures are measured on the kelvin scale, named for William Thomson, Baron Kelvin (1824–1907). It is also called the absolute scale because absolute zero—0°K (–273.15° C)—is the temperature at which no body can give up heat. The interval of a kelvin equals the interval of a degree Celsius.

Conversions

Fahrenheit to Celsius: Subtract 32 from the temperature and multiply the difference by 5; then divide the product by 9. The formula is: $C = 5/9\,(F - 32)$

Celsius to Fahrenheit: Multiply the temperature by 1.8 (or 9/5), then add 32. The formula is: $F = 9/5\ C + 32$

Celsius to Kelvin: Add 273.15 to the temperature The formula is: $K = C + 273.15$

Force, Work/Energy, Power

U.S. customary system The foot/pound/second system of reckoning includes the following units:

slug = mass to which a force of 1 poundal will give an acceleration of 1 foot per second per second (= approximately 32.17 lb.)

poundal = fundamental unit of force

foot-pound = work done when a force of 1 poundal produces a movement of 1 foot

foot-pound/second = unit of power equal to 1 foot/pound per second

Another common unit of power is horsepower, which is equal to 550 foot-pounds per second.

Thermal work or energy is often measured in British thermal units (Btu). One Btu is defined as the energy required to increase the temperature of 1 pound of water by 1 degree Fahrenheit. The Btu is equal to about 0.778 foot-pound.

International System

In physics, compound measurements of force, work or energy, and power are essential. There are two parallel systems using International System units: the centimeter/gram/second system (cgs) is used for small measurements, and the meter/kilogram/second system (mks) is used for larger measurements. The mks system is the official one for SI. They are described below.

Measurement of force

cgs unit	dyne (dy)	Force required to accelerate a mass of 1 g 1 cm/s^2 (cm/s^2 means "centimeter per second per second")
mks unit	newton (N)	Force required to accelerate a mass of 1 kg l m/s^2

Measurement of work or energy

cgs unit	erg	Dyne-centimeter, i.e., work done when a force of 1 dy produces a movement of 1 cm
mks unit	joule (j)	Newton-meter, i.e., work done when a force of 1 N produces a movement of 1 m (10,000,000 ergs)

Heat energy is also measured using the calorie (cal), which is defined as the energy required to increase the temperature of 1 cubic centimeter (1 ml) of water by 1 degree C. One calorie is equal to about 4.184 joules. The kilocalorie (Kcal or Cal) is equal to 1,000 calories and is the unit in which the energy values of food are measured. This more familiar unit, also commonly referred to as a Calorie, is equal to about 4,184 joules.

Measurement of power

cgs unit	erg/second	Rate of 1 erg per second
mks unit	watt (W)	Joule/second, i.e., a rate of 1 joule per second

Conversions

Measurement of force

1 poundal	=	13,889 dynes
	=	0.13889 newton
1 dyne	=	0.000072 poundal
1 newton	=	7.2 poundals

Measurement of work or energy

1 foot-pound	=	1,356 joules
British thermal unit	=	1,055 joules
	=	252 calories
1 joule	=	0.0007374 ft.-lbs.
1 calorie	=	0.003968 Btu
1 Kilocalorie	=	3.968 Btu

Measurement of power

1 foot-pound/second	=	1.3564 watts
1 horsepower	=	746 watts
	=	0.746 kilowatt
1 watt	=	0.73725 ft.-lb/sec.
	=	0.00134 horsepower
1 kilowatt	=	737.25 ft.-lb./sec.
	=	1.34 horsepower

Electrical Measure

Originally, the basic unit of quantity in electricity was the coulomb. A coulomb is equal to the passage of 6.25 x 1018 electrons past a given point in an electrical system.

The unit of electrical flow is the ampere, which is equal to a coulomb/second, i.e., the flow of 1 coulomb per second. The ampere is analogous in electrical measure to a unit of flow such as gallons-per-minute in physical measure. In SI, the ampere is taken as the basic unit.

The unit for measuring electrical potential energy is the volt, which is defined as 1 joule/ coulomb, i.e., 1 joule of energy per coulomb of electricity. The volt is analogous to a measure of pressure in a water system.

The unit for measuring electrical power is the watt as defined in the previous section. Power in watts (P) is the product of the electrical flow in amperes (I) and the potential electrical energy in volts (E):

$$P = IE$$

Since the watt is such a small unit for practical applications, the kilowatt (= 1,000 watts) is often used. A kilowatt-hour is the power of 1,000 watts over an hour's time.

The unit for measuring electrical resistance is the ohm, which is the resistance offered by a circuit to the flow of 1 ampere being driven by the force of 1 volt. It is derived from Ohm's law, which defines the relationship between flow or current (amperes), potential energy (volts), and resistance (ohms). It states that the current in amperes (I) is proportional to potential energy in volts (E) and inversely proportional to resistance in ohms (R). Thus, when voltage and resistance are known, amperage can be calculated by the simple formula

$$I = \frac{E}{R}$$

DICTIONARY OF FOOD

Cereals and Grains

Humans began to raise cereal crops, plants belonging to the family of grasses, at the dawn of civilization. Indeed, theory has it that grain-growing was at least partly responsible for civilization itself; the labor of growing and tending a crop was too great for a lone individual, but the harvest could support expanding populations. Wild grain fields sprang up around 8000 B.C. in the Middle East, where people aggregated to exploit them. Over the millennia that followed, barley, wheat, and rice came under cultivation in Europe and Asia, maize in the Americas. Cereals are first in importance in the human diet, as an efficient source of carbohydrate energy. In terms of their protein profile, they generally lack only one amino acid, lysine, which can be found in legumes or in meat. So suited to sustaining life are cereals that they can compose from 25 percent to 90 percent of a balanced diet (with the remainder supplying vital trace minerals and vitamins, as well as the missing protein).

The term *cereal* itself deserves a closer look; its supermarket definition as a cold breakfast food (rather than its botanical definition as a grass-family plant) is very recent in origin. Eating "cereal" (typically processed oats, wheat, corn, or rice) for breakfast was an American fashion popularized in the late 19th century. Before that, breakfast—at least for those who could afford it—revolved primarily around eggs and meat. Food reformists such as Sylvester Graham, C. W. Post, and John Henry Kellogg believed that a grain-based diet was physically and even spiritually nourishing. Post's Grape Nuts (1897) and Kellogg's Corn Flakes (1898) were early entrants in what is today a $7 billion-a-year industry.

Barley (*Hordeum vulgare*) is among the most ancient of cereals, possibly preceding even rice. Barley grew wild throughout Mesopotamia; Neolithic peoples discovered that barley malt—dried, roasted grain—could be soaked and fermented to make beer. Though never a primary crop, it was important enough to be featured on coins in Greco-Roman times. Today, it is primarily used for animal feed and beer distillation.

Maize/corn (*Zea mays*) In most countries the crop is called maize; in the United States it is known simply as corn (Other English-speaking countries describe their primary grains—be they wheat, rye, or barley—as corn.) The descendant of a wild grass called teosinte, corn originated in Mexico as early as 5500 B.C. The protective husk that surrounds the kernels prevents it from self-sowing, and thus wherever corn is grown, it is grown by human stewardship. Corn is likely to have arrived in the Old World on Columbus's return voyages, although there are other theories. It was being cultivated widely in Europe and Africa by the late 16th century; indeed, its success in Africa led to a population explosion that sustained the slave trade for years.

Economies that depend on maize as a primary staple crop run the risk of epidemics of pellagra, or niacin deficiency. But the historical Mayan preparation of maize soaked in lime renders niacin available; this process is called nixtamalization,

Today a number of species of corn are cultivated: dent corn for cattle, flint corn, popcorn, and the familiar sweet corn. Cornmeal and cornstarch and any number of other industrial products are derived from the plant.

Oats (*Avena sativa*) came into cultivation relatively recently—about 1000 B.C. in Europe. Like rye, oats thrive in cool climates. Though highly nutritious (with all the protein of, and more fat than, wheat), they are poor in gluten and make poor bread. When not used for animal fodder, oats are commonly ground into oatmeal, which can them be boiled for a porridge or baked into oatcakes; Scotland, Ireland, and Russia all have a long history of cooking with oats in this manner. In the United States, "rolled oats"—processed and flattened to cook more quickly—were developed by the Quaker Company during the late 19th-century cereal craze, and continue to be a popular breakfast option.

Rice (*Oryza*) Rice, which grows in innumerable varieties, has been cultivated in Asia since at least 2500 B.C. It is the "staff of life" of the Eastern hemisphere just as wheat and corn are in the West; after wheat, it is the second most cultivated grain in the world. The labor-intensive rice crop played a major role in the formation of early human settlements and civilization, since constructing its terraces and irrigation channels required extensive cooperation. Rice underpins many subsistence economies, so crop failure can result in disaster. During the green revolution of the 1960's, the International Rice Research Institute concentrated on producing a number of high-yield rice hybrids, called "miracle rices." These had the effect of erasing famine for some years in developing economies; on the other hand the high-input practices associated with the hybrids often damaged the native ecological balance. Like wheat, rice has a number of derivative products that are important throughout the world, such as rice vinegar, rice wine, and rice noodles. Specialty rices important in international cuisine include basmati, jasmine, japonica, and arborio. North American wild rice (*ZizAnia aquatica*), an aquatic grain, is unrelated to Eastern rice.

Rye (*Secale cereale*) Much hardier than its relative, wheat, rye flourished throughout the Middle East and Europe in soils too poor or cold for wheat (it has been called "the wheat of Allah"—a divinely-sent crop for hard conditions). Rye spreads like a weed wherever wheat and barley are grown; mixed crops of wheat and rye (called maslin) were common in the Middle Ages. As a cold-climate crop, rye traditionally has predominated in Russia (in traditional black bread), Germany (in pumpernickel), and Scandinavia. In the United States, the rye bread (commonly flavored with caraway) of Eastern Europe came to be a staple of Jewish delicatessens.

Wheat (*Triticum*) Wheat, a descendant of wild grains, was domesticated as early as 7000 B.C. in the Middle East, and over time became the dominant cereal crop of Western cultures. As with rice, its cultivation played a vital role in persuading humans to forgo a nomadic hunting lifestyle for a settled, agricultural one. Wheat is highly nutritious and a good source of protein (it contains nearly all the essential amino acids), though somewhat laborious to harvest. The wealthy prized its relatively light-colored flour ("wheat" has the same roots as "white"), a prejudice that persists today in the bleaching and refinement of all-purpose flours. Just as fertility and harvest rites from ancient Mesopotamia to medieval Europe centered on the success of the wheat crop, bread too serves as a near-universal symbol of sustenance. In times of hardship only aristocrats could afford wheaten bread (others relied on "lesser" grains like rye and barley).

Triticum aestivum is the most commonly cultivated wheat; cultivars are divided into hard and soft wheats. Hard refers to high-protein wheat, good for forming gluten, the strands of protein that create the texture of well-made bread. (The high protein content of wheat makes it superior among grains for leavened bread.) Soft refers to wheat low in protein, more suitable for cakes and pastries. A particularly hard type of wheat, durum, is essential for milled pastas.

Wheat arrived in the New World with the Spanish explorers and quickly took to the fertile farmlands of North and South America. Today, the United States and Canada are among the world's largest wheat producers. Wheat is the largest grain crop in the world; close to 2 billion metric tons are harvested annually.

Fruit

The term *fruit* can be confusing. Botanically speaking, a "fruit" is the structure that develops from a plant's ovary, providing nutrition and shelter for its seeds. By this definition, eggplants and tomatoes are fruits, just as apples and oranges are. But when speaking of fruit, we tend to mean sweet, succulent, often aromatic fruits suitable for dessert. Fruits have always held a special allure for humans, dating from prehistory when they may have been the only dietary source of sugar available. Nutritionally speaking, fresh fruits and vegetables are abundant in vitamins and minerals and absolutely essential for vitamin C. Two great families of fruit—the *Rutaceae* (including all citrus fruits) and *Rosaceae* (including apples, peaches, plums, etc.)—predominate heavily in a typical modern Western diet.

Apple (*Malus*) Surely the most storied of fruits, from their fabled role in the garden of Eden to the golden apples that started the Trojan war, apples originated in the forests of Alma-Ata ("father of apples") in Kazakhstan. They were known to humans as early as 6000 B.C., were later prized by Egyptians, were cultivated in the Greco-Roman empire (which perfected grafting techniques), and are now grown in temperate zones throughout the world.

Apples must be cross-pollinated by different varieties to bear fruit; as a result the seeds of each apple are genetically different. Should these seeds be planted, no two trees would bear the same fruit. Early orchardists therefore learned to propagate their trees by grafting apple branches onto selected rootstocks, essentially the same practice used today. American apples, however, enjoyed a biodiversity boom, thanks to John Chapman (1774–1845), "Johnny Appleseed," who scattered apple seeds across the Ohio Valley in the 19th century, allowing the wild forms to crossbreed and produce new varieties.

Apple varieties are divided into "dessert apples" and "cider apples." Cider apples may be bitter or sour, but their complexity benefits the resulting alcoholic or nonalcoholic beverage. (What Americans call hard cider is simply called "cider" by everyone else; what Americans call cider, others call juice.) Hundreds of varieties of dessert, or "eating," apples exist, though aggressive marketing has elevated the Red Delicious, Granny Smith, and McIntosh to supremacy in the U.S.

Bananas and plantains (*Musa*) are members of the same species. The term *bananas* refers to the sweet dessert fruit, *plantains* to the starchy, only faintly sweet fruit used extensively in cooking. Bananas—and particularly plantains—are ancient tropical staples, referred to in origin myths across the Pacific. Once they were introduced to the islands of the Caribbean by Spanish explorers, they established themselves so quickly that subsequent generations of newcomers mistook them for native plants. Consumption of bananas in North America began in the mid-19th century, and bananas became extremely popular when the United Fruit Company began to import them from Jamaica in 1885, later spinning off the internationally recognized brand Chiquita.

Blueberries and cranberries are heath shrubs belonging to the *vaccinium* family, native to the Americas. They were gathered wild by Native Americans across the present-day United States. They were not brought into commercial cultivation until around 1910, when a New Jersey botanist developed a variety with plump and almost seedless fruits. Highbush blueberries (*V. corymbosum*) have a somewhat larger fruit; lowbush blueberries (*V. angustifolium*) have more in common with small wild blueberries. Blueberries have received considerable attention in recent years for their antioxidant properties; they are also an excellent source of vitamin C.

Different species of cranberries existed in the New World and the Old, among them the Swedish lingonberry. Native North Americans gathered the American cranberry (*V. macrocarpon*), and used it and other berries in the jerky-like, long-storing food called pemmican. The pilgrims who crossed the North Atlantic in the 17th century found the American cranberry to be much larger than its European counterparts, and benefited from its high vitamin C content. The roast turkey of an American Thanksgiving is invariably served with cranberry sauce or relish, commemorating the discovery of this important native food. Cranberries, which favor highly acidic, boggy conditions, have been grown commercially in the United States, especially in Massachusetts, since the mid-19th century.

Cherry Cultivated cherries are of two types, the sour (*Prunus cerasus*) and the sweet (*Prunus avium*); both originated in western Asia. They made their way across the Mediterranean, arriving in Europe about the first century after Christ. Combined, there are over 1000 varieties. Their uses are distinct: sweet cherries most often are eaten fresh or in desserts; sour cherries become preserves or liqueurs (though there are some uses for the sour cherry as dessert fruits as well). The most popular sweet cherry is the Bing cherry, named by an Oregon orchardist for his Chinese foreman.

Even more so than the plum blossom in China, the cherry blossom is a central symbol in Japan, where it is cultivated ornamentally rather than for fruit.

Dates (*Phoenix dactylifera*) The dates borne by desert date palms are among the earliest domesticated fruits. The wild palms came under human cultivation in the Indus Valley by 4000 B.C. Sugars account for up to 54 percent by weight of a fresh date's nutritional content; consumed with milk for protein, the date constitutes an important staple food. Most dates are imported from the Middle East and North Africa. Though commonly enjoyed fresh where they are grown, most dates are matured and dried for shipping worldwide.

Figs (*Ficus carica*) The cultivation of figs may have begun in Egypt; figs appear in the Sumerian epic *Gilgamesh* (3000 B.C.), and by Greco-Roman times were certainly well established. Each fig is made up of about 1,500 minuscule fruits or "drupelets" that form the fleshy interior of the fig. Pollenization in a majority of varieties depends on a tiny insect, the fig wasp, which lives inside the fruit and travels between trees in the course of its own life cycle. Figs, which grow in warm (but not tropical) regions worldwide, are sold fresh, dried, and canned.

Grapefruit (*Citrus paradisi*) resulted from the refinement of the pomelo (*Citrus grandis*), brought to the Americas in the 1700's by an English sea captain. Grapefruit became a popular breakfast item during the 19th century, eventually making its way to Europe in the 20th century. Ruby red grapefruit developed from a freak mutation in Texas around 1929; tangelos resulted from a cross between grapefruit and orange. A compound present in grapefruits is medically unusual: it affects the uptake of certain drugs by inhibiting a human digestive enzyme, with the result that grapefruit juice is counterindicated in some prescriptions.

Grapes (*Vitis*) Wild grapes abounded in the Black Sea region long before human civilization. By 3000 B.C. they were being cultivated by Sumerians. *Vitis vinifera* was cultivated throughout antiquity for table grapes and especially for wine. In the 16th century wine grapes traveled to the New World, where they joined the native Concord grape, *V. labrusca*, which was mostly eaten fresh or preserved (grape jelly is still made from Concord grapes). American table grapes are dominated by the mild-flavored Thompson seedless variety. Dried grapes are called raisins or, in the case of the Zante variety, currants (confusingly, as fresh currants belong to a completely different family).

Lemon (*Citrus limon*) The lemon was first cultivated in India. Like the orange, it traveled on the heels of Arab exploration, reaching Europe around the ninth century (though some accounts argue it was known to the Roman empire as early as the first century after Christ). Lemons certainly traveled with Columbus and his successors, and were well established in the Americas by 1700. Lemons have an exalted place in the history of scurvy; the age of discovery was nearly over before seamen were finally persuaded that lemons, with their high vitamin C content, were the cure for a disease that plagued every sustained maritime voyage. The British navy required ships to carry lemon juice rations for its sailors around 1800 (the juice was often added to rum rations), and scurvy essentially vanished. The spread of lemons to California was prompted by the Gold Rush of 1849, as miners lured to new territories scarce in food combated scurvy problems of their own.

Although its juice is too acid to appeal as a beverage, the lemon has practically innumerable culinary uses, ranging from marinades and dressings to lemonade, baked desserts, and complementing fish. Meyer lemons (a cross between a lemon and a tangerine) are milder and sweeter, and popular with confectioners.

Lime Limes accompanied lemons and oranges in their spread from Indochina first to Europe and later to the New World. The original lime (*Citrus aurantifolia*) is the small, astringent fruit called key lime in the U.S.; key limes are little cultivated here except in the Florida Keys, for the dessert called key lime pie (made with ordinary limes elsewhere). The lime more commonly seen in the supermarket is the Persian lime (*Citrus latifolia*) a cross between the key lime and the citron, which was developed in Europe about 1920. Limes, which would ripen to yellow, are typically picked green to avoid confusion with lemons.

In the mid-19th century, limes replaced lemons in the conquest of scurvy (although they are less potent a source of vitamin C than lemons), gaining British seamen a new sobriquet: limeys.

Orange (*Citrus sinensis*) Oranges were first grown either in the Indus Valley or in China, and were of two varieties, the sweet and the sour. The sour orange (*Citrus aurantium*) traveled farthest first, accompanying Arab conquests; it was introduced in Sicily around the eighth or ninth century. The sweet (*Citrus sinensis*) did not follow until as late as the 15th century. But within a hundred years, citrus trees were being widely planted in the Spanish New World, and they have flourished in the Americas since. Today, Seville or bitter oranges are grown mainly in Spain for marmalade, which Britain imports in great quantities. The sweet orange, once an expensive rarity found in European Christmas stockings, became a common treat once refrigerated railcars made it more accessible to the public in the 19th century. Today, the orange enjoys global popularity and is the most important fruit worldwide for juice. The method of producing orange juice from frozen concentrate was perfected in the United States in 1945.

A number of United States relatives of the orange are popular as dessert fruits: blood oranges, navel oranges, tangerines, clementines, and mandarin oranges among them.

Papaya (*Carica papaya*) The papaya is native to the Pacific islands, where inhabitants introduced it to European explorers in the 1800's. It now grows in tropical regions worldwide. Aside from the fruit's sweet and faintly scented flesh (often eaten with lime for acidity), papaya plants contain a digestive enzyme, papain, which tenderizes meat and is used in industrial food processing.

Peach (*Prunus persica*) Peaches are an Asiatic fruit, cultivated in China from 2000 B.C. on. They arrived in Europe with the Greeks and Romans, and in America with the 16th-century Spanish explorers. Varieties are divided into freestone (softer flesh, pit removed easily) and clingstone types (pit closely adhering to firmer flesh, especially suited for canning). Nectarines are a smooth-skinned variant of the peach, and apricots (*Prunus armenica*) are a close relative with a very similar history. Apricots, nectarines, and peaches require very particular growing conditions; most U.S. varieties are grown in California. Apricots are particularly versatile, and are widely sold as a dried fruit as well as in preserves and jellies.

Pear (*Pyrus communis*) originated near the Caucasus, like apples, and rapidly spread east and west. At first pears were prized above apples, both in China and in the Greco-Roman empire. Like the apple, pears left to propagate by seed produce wildly different offspring; this is just what happened in colonial America, where pear seeds were planted and developed into a multitude of varieties. Today, commonly marketed pears include the Bosc, Anjou, Seckel, and Bartlett. The round, crisp Asian pear, a close relative, is also becoming popular.

Pineapple (*Ananas comosus*) Despite its striking success as a Hawaiian commodity, the pineapple is not native to the Pacific islands. It originated in Brazil, where Columbian-age explorers were introduced to it and in turn brought it to Europe. Like the papaya, pineapple contains a tenderizing enzyme, bromelin.

Plum (*Prunus domesticus*) Plums are the hardiest and most widespread of the stone-fruit trees, and thrive on every continent except Antarctica. Though the most common plums here are the red to blue-violet Burbank plums, thousands of varieties—especially European, Asian, and native American in origin—exist. Sloes, damsons, and greengages are among them. In China, the plum blossom is one of four sacred flowers (lotus, chrysanthemum, and peony are the others).

Dried plums are called prunes, and are so laxative in effect that prune juice is often prescribed medicinally.

Raspberries (*Rubus idaeus*) and blackberries (*Rubus ulmifolius*) are fruit-bearing brambles native to the cooler regions of Asia, North America, and Europe. They have been cultivated since at least the first century B.C. Raspberries were particularly dear to the Greeks (they were said to take their color from the blood of the nymph Ida, who pricked herself while feeding them to the infant Zeus). Red raspberry leaf tea has been used as a strengthening tonic by pregnant women for centuries. Raspberries occur in colors ranging from yellow to red, purple, and black; the last appear similar to blackberries but are structurally different. American hybrids developed from the raspberry include loganberries (1881) and boysenberries (1920's).

Strawberry (*Fragaria*) Before human cultivation, strawberries grew wild in both Eurasia and the Americas. In early modern Europe, they were considered a symbol of the Virgin Mary. Most of the original Old World strawberries are small, and some are intensely sweet. The modern supermarket strawberry (*F. ananassa*) descended from two American varieties, *F. virginiana* and the Chilean pineapple strawberry (*F. chiloensis*), which occurred on opposite coasts of North America. They were brought together by chance in 18th-century France, and the popular resulting hybrid dominated the market thereafter (though gourmands still hunt out the tiny *fraises de bois*). Strawberry fruits are exceedingly susceptible to disease, which growers try to discourage by placing clean straw beneath the vines (hence the name).

Vegetables

Vegetables have been crucial to the human diet longer than any other food—from before the cultivation of cereal crops, even before the refinement of hunting techniques. Vegetables tend to be the stems, leaves, or roots of plants. Different systems of classification apply; in the supermarket, we tend to speak of "root vegetables" and "leafy greens." Growers classify vegetables by their families: the Brassicas (broccoli, cauliflower), the Solanaceae or nightshades (tomato, potato, eggplant), the Cucurbits (melons and squashes), the Alliums (onion, garlic, shallots). Many consider legumes (such as peas and beans) separate entirely, as they are distinct in their protein-rich nutritional value and broad application both dried and fresh; they are included here for ease of reference.

Avocado (*Persea americana*) Avocados are native to Latin America and the Caribbean. Though known to other cultures since the Spanish conquest, they first gained commercial popularity in the 19th century; now they are cultivated in regions as far flung as Israel and Australia, as well as in the Americas. Unlike any other tree fruit, they ripen only off the branch (the tree itself chemically inhibits ripening). They contain more fat than any other vegetable or fruit and are the principal ingredient in guacamole.

Beans (*Phaseolus*) The term *beans* loosely refers to plants cultivated for their edible seeds or pods, most commonly members of the *Phaseolus* or *Vigna* families. The green or haricot bean and its varietals (*Phaseolus vulgaris*) are the most commonly eaten fresh beans.

The only cultivated bean in Europe prior to the age of discovery was the broad bean, the fava bean (*Vicius faba*), which was widely cultivated throughout the ancient Middle East and the Greco-Roman empire, despite the fact that a small minority of people are lethally allergic to favas.

Perhaps the predominant cultivated bean worldwide is the soybean (*Glycine max*). Widespread throughout Asia, the soybean has been a major staple crop since the third millennium B.C. Nutritionally, soybeans are even more impressive than wheat and rice; they contain 35 percent protein and a complete complement of amino acids. The diversity of derivative soy products—ranging from soy oil, soy sauce, and miso to bean curd, tempeh, and black beans—is probably rivaled only by that of corn.

Beets (*Beta vulgaris*) Beets evolved from a wild root found on Eurasian seashores. The beet was originally grown only for its greens, but beetroot began to find favor in the first century after Christ. (although it wasn't until the 17th century that the familiar red beet was developed). Today the leaves and especially the root are used throughout Europe and North America; beetroot is the principal ingredient in borscht, the beet soup of eastern Europe. Sugar beets, a subspecies of beet, are the second most important source of sugar (after sugarcane) in the world. Swiss chard is a member of the beet family whose leaves strongly resemble beet greens, though they tend to be used more like *Brassica* greens in cooking.

Cabbage (*Brassica oleracea*) Cabbage is the oldest of the cultivated *brassicas*; some accounts place its origins in the Mediterranean, but others report that it was cultivated in China during the Zhou dynasty (500 B.C.). Cabbage thrives in cooler climates; it has been a Russian staple, for example, for at least three centuries. Its cooking odor emanates from an unusually high quantity of sulfurous compounds (as well as the isothiocyanates, or mustard oils, present in varieties like mustard greens). Common varieties include the hardheaded white or green and the red cabbage, as well as the sweet, wrinkle-leaved savoy cabbage. Cabbage's relatives are legion; they include broccoli, cauliflower, and brussels sprouts.

This extended family of *brassicas* are also known as cruciferous vegetables, after the small flower in the shape of a Greek cross that they bear.

Carrots (*Daucus carota*) originated in Afghanistan, but were common in both East and West. They traveled to the Americas with the Spanish conquest. They belong to a family of plants (*Umbelliferae*) better known for its herbs—dill, parsley, cilantro, caraway. The familiar yellow-orange variety developed in 17th-century Holland but did not become popular in the United States until after World War I, when servicemen became familiar with its uses in European cookery. A wild version (*Daucus glochidiatus*) grows in Australia and is used extensively in aboriginal cooking. Carrots are high in beta carotene, the vitamin A precursor.

Chili peppers (*Capsicum*) All the pepper species—sweet or hot—were cultivated in South America from earliest recorded history. The confusion between the hot or sweet pepper fruits (*Capsicum* species) and the peppercorns used for black pepper (*Piper nigrum*) dates from the spice-obsessed Columbus, who hoped his sponsors would consider the new "peppers" as valuable as the old. A global trade in peppers quickly ensued; Spaniards brought them to East Asia via the Philippines, while the Portuguese brought them to India and Southeast Asia. By the end of the 16th century, peppers were being cultivated wherever the climate was warm enough, from equatorial Africa to the South China Sea. Though they quickly became staples of some cuisines, like those of India and China (especially the Szechuan region), Europe was slower to adopt them. Ottoman Turks brought the red pepper to Hungary, where its dried and powdered form became the popular condiment paprika.

The heat of chili peppers derives from the alkaloid known as capsaicin, and is measured in Scoville units. A sweet red pepper registers 0; a jalapeño 2,500–5,000; and a Scotch bonnet or habañero 80,000–300,000 Scoville units.

Eggplant (*Solanum melongena*), known as aubergine in England, is a native of tropical Asia, and gradually traveled the Silk Road to reach western Europe around the 15th century. Some eggplants actually look very like eggs—white and ovoid—though the most familiar supermarket variety, the globe eggplant, has glossy purple-black skin.

The seeds of mature eggplants are somewhat bitter; salting before cooking is thought to draw out the eggplant's native alkaloids and reduce its bitterness. Eggplants, sometimes called "poor man's caviar," have little flavor of their own (or nutritive value), but their creamy flesh readily absorbs oil, which helps saturate the eggplant with the flavor of other ingredients.

Garlic See *Onions.*

Ginger (*Zingiber officinalis*) Gingerroot is a tropical rhizome that has been used for thousands of years and probably originates in Southeast Asia. It can be used fresh, dried, powdered, or candied, and has powerful preservative and antiscorbutic properties. Like black pepper, it was a valuable cash commodity in the medieval spice trade. Portuguese explorers brought ginger to the New World in the 15th century, and it became the first spice to be grown successfully in New World. Jamaican ginger is considered particularly fine in flavor. Though ginger is primarily used fresh in Eastern cuisines, in Europe and the Americas its dried form predominates as a baking ingredient (and as a legacy of medieval spice habits). Ginger beer, ginger ale, and candied ginger are also popular ginger products.

Lettuces (*Lactuca*) Lettuces were known in ancient Egypt and grew wild in the Mediterranean, but were probably first cultivated by the Greeks; the Romans were inveterate salad eaters. They were long considered cooling and medicinal; the milky fluid or latex at their cores had narcotic properties which were later largely bred out. Like so many other crops, lettuce came to the Americas with the Spaniards. Although lettuces are sometimes shredded and cooked in Asian cuisines, they are almost invariably served raw, as salads, in the West. There are hundreds of varieties: Loose leaf, oak leaf, red, and green lettuces; "butterhead" lettuces like Bibb and Boston; "crisphead" lettuce (Iceberg); and "cos" lettuce (Romaine).

Melons (*Cucumis melo*) probably originated in the wild in the Middle East or West Africa, and were not extensively cultivated until late in the first millennium after Christ. The sweet melons familiar today were probably developed in medieval Europe. While cantaloupes or muskmelons, honeydews, and watermelons are popular in the United States (and watermelons are an important source of portable water for African desert farmers), a number of nonsweet melons and gourds are eaten in Asia; e.g., the Chinese bitter melon, winter melon, and fuzzy gourd. Cucumbers are also members of the genus *Cucumis*, and thrive in similar conditions of abundant light and heat.

Olives (*Olea europaea*) are among the most ancient of food crops; wild olive trees were frequented by humans as much as 10,000 years ago. Olive trees traditionally signify peace, and in Greco-Roman times were said to have been a gift of the goddess Athena. The trees, which can live for hundreds of years, thrive in all the temperate regions of the Mediterranean, as well as in California (where they are mainly cultivated for table olives rather than oil). Olives (which are berries rather than fruits) have an unusually high fat content and have been prized for their oil for millennia. Olive oil is sold in a variety of grades: virgin or extra-virgin oil comes from the first pressing of the olives (extra-virgin denotes a lower acid content). "Cold-pressing" means that the oil has been pressed at a temperature lower than 100 degrees F. More heat yields more oil, but of an inferior quality. The lowest grade of oil was once called "pure olive oil," but now simply is referred to as "olive oil."

Table olives. Raw olives contain bitter glucosides, which are removed by curing (for table olives) or pressing (for oil). Table olives can be brine-cured or lye-cured (the most common methods), dry-cured, or sun-cured; they may or may not be fermented afterward.

Onions (*Allium* genus, *Allium cepa*). The term *onion* can be used generally, to refer to the edible Allium genus (garlic, shallots, chives, etc.), or specifically, to refer to the common yellow or white globe onion, *Allium cepa*. Originating in Central Asia, onions were esteemed in ancient Egypt (they were a staple food for pyramid laborers in 3000 B.C.) and widely eaten in Greece and Rome, and later throughout Asia; for some sects in India, they were considered too sacred to eat. Columbus brought them to the Americas in 1493; today they are grown worldwide.

Most *alliums* release volatile disulfides to greater or lesser degrees, when cut. Cut onions release allicin, which causes eyes to tear, although chilling them or rinsing them reduces the effect (and the substance is neutralized entirely in cooking).

The pungency of garlic (*Allium sativum*) comes from another disulfide. Garlic itself is integral to any number of world cuisines, and has important antifungal and antimicrobial properties; but no one can know whether its health-bestowing effects or its powerful odor gave rise to its reputation as a shield against evil spirits.

Other common cultivars are leeks (*Allium porrum*), shallots (*Allium ascalonicum*), and chives (*Allium schoenophasum*). All onions belong to the same family as the ornamental lily.

Peas (*Pisum sativum*) and **lentils** (*Lens culinaris*) are among the oldest of cultivated plants, dating back as far as 8000 B.C. in Mesopotamia. Until the modern era, peas were mainly used in their dry form, as a long-storing, valuable source of protein and carbohydrate. (They are still primarily used this way in India, for example, where few meals are complete without a serving of dahl.) Dried peas were a staple food in medieval Europe (as in "pease porridge hot, pease porridge cold"). Eating fresh green, immature peas came into vogue only in the 18th century, and today even the pods of many popular peas are eaten, e.g., sugar snaps and snow peas.

Potato (*Solanum tuberosum*) Grown in Peru since 3000 B.C., the many species of potato remained in the New World till the arrival of Spanish explorers in the 15th and 16th centuries. Once brought back to Europe, they were stigmatized as a possibly toxic food for the poor. But frequent famines soon made this easily grown staple crop more attractive; heavy promotion by agriculturalists such as Antoine Parmentier (who had witnessed potatoes eaten in Prussia with no ill effects) and the French aristocracy also helped. By the early 19th century Irish farmers had learned that a single acre of potatoes could feed a family of five; with milk, it made for a nutritionally complete meal. A population explosion ensued, which made the potato famines of 1846 and 1848 especially disastrous and prompted mass emigration.

Spinach (*Spinacia oleracea*) originated in Nepal and spread eastward to China and westward to the Middle East before arriving in Europe in the 11th century. The early 20th-century cartoon character Popeye propagated the notion that spinach is a good source of iron. But spinach contains a high quantity of oxalic acid, which inactivates iron; in fact, spinach is not as rich an iron source as comparable greens like kale. Still, its tender texture, brilliant green color, and delicate flavor make it a popular ingredient for salads, sautées, and soufflés.

Squash (*Cucurbita*) Varieties are commonly divided into "summer" squash and "winter" squash. Summer squashes, like crooknecks and zucchini, have thin skins and light-colored flesh. Winter squash, like butternut, acorn, delicata, and all pumpkins, have thick rinds and generally deeper orange flesh. The cucurbits are native to the Americas, where they were grown for human consumption since at least 10,000 B.C. Native Americans learned to grow them in tandem with ecologically complementary beans and corn (the "three sisters"). They arrived in the Old World with the returning Spanish explorers.

Sweet potato (*Ipomoea batatis*) **and Yam** (*Dioscorea*) Frequently confused, the sweet potato and yam are two entirely different species, though both are starchy tubers. The true yam is very ancient; it could have originated in the Jurassic period, before Asia and America split. It can be found throughout both continents. Starchy and bland, the yam is valued more for its hardiness and storage properties than its delectability; West African and Caribbean cuisines make use of it (as well as the sweet potato, confusingly). The South American sweet potato, on the other hand, was embraced by Spanish explorers for its superior flavor, and brought back to Europe for cultivation. They also brought it west to the Philippines, whence it spread to East Asia. Unlike the yam, the sweet potato does not store particularly well.

Most "yams" sold in U.S. supermarkets are actually sweet potatoes. Boiled, mashed, candied, spiced with nutmeg or cinnamon, or even baked in pies, they are among the more popular root vegetables.

Taro (*Colocasia*) Like the sweet potato, taro is a starchy root crop grown in all of the world's tropical regions. Though relatively insignificant in the North American diet, it is a staple in island nations from the West Indies to Japan and Hawaii. Lighter in texture than a potato, the taro root is low in protein and slightly sweet; it is used to make the paste known as *poi* in the South Pacific, as well as being useful for food starch (like arrowroot and cornstarch), mashes, and chips.

Tomato (*Lycopersicon esculentum*) Tomatoes may have been grown in Mexico as early as 1500 B.C., and remained there until the time of Columbus. Upon their arrival in Europe, they were at first treated as a botanical curiosity, unlike any other vegetable or fruit. And as members of the deadly nightshade family (like potatoes), tomatoes had to overcome intense suspicion before they were considered generally edible. But once they were finally adopted into the cuisines of Spain, Portugal, Italy, and, to a lesser extent, France, they became a new staple crop; and they have not been abandoned, since they are a valuable source of vitamins A and C.

Turnips (*Brassica rapa*) **and Rutabagas or Swedes** (*Brassica napobrassica*) were originally Central European root crops; the swedes are milder and larger than the turnips. Since turnips and their kin grow even in poor soil, they often served as a subsistence crop (during the potato famine, many Irish suffered bloating and malnutrition from subsisting on a turnip-only diet). The root and especially the greens are pickled in the Middle East and East Asia.

Herbs

Generally speaking, herbs are the dried leaves of food plants used for flavoring. The two great families of culinary herbs are the loosely termed carrot family (*Umbelliferae*) and the mint family (*Labiatae*).

Carrot-family members, or umbellifers, are easily distinguished by their feathery leaves and umbrella-shaped crowns of seeds. The ones most commonly used are parsley (*Petroselinum crispum*), cilantro (*Coriandrum sativum*), dill (*Anethum graveolens*), fennel (*Foeniculum vulgare*), lovage (*Levisticum officinale*), and chervil (*Anthriscus cerefolium*).

Mint-family members tend to have squarish stems and distinctive two-lipped flowers; many have strongly scented leaves. Among them are the many species of mint (*Mentha* spp.), especially peppermint and spearmint; oregano (*Origanum vulgare*), marjoram (*Origanum marjorana*), rosemary (*Rosmarinum officinale*), basil (*Ocimum basilicum*), savory (*Satureja hortensis*), winter savory (*Statureja montana*), thyme (*Thymus vulgaris*), lavender (*Lavandula vera*), and sage (*Salvia officinalis*).

Two notable herbs not belonging to either family are tarragon (*Artemisia dracunculus*) and sorrel (*Rumex scutatus*).

Herbs have a long history of medicinal use, which could be said to have peaked in medieval Europe. They had any number of uses, ranging from mild sedative effects (e.g., (chamomile and hops) and sore-throat cures (hyssop) to drawing out fevers (feverfew) and strengthening nerves (rosemary). Today, though the scientific establishment tends to decry them, herbs are still used freely (and with varying effectiveness) as medicines—in Latin American botanicas, in Chinese pharmacies, and on the herbal supplement shelf of many ordinary supermarkets, where anyone can find echinacea or St. John's Wort. Others are simply enjoyed as herbal teas, such as lemon balm (*Melissa officinalis*) and lemon verbena (*Aloysia citriodora*)

Spices

Spices are any part of a plant other than the leaves used for flavoring—seeds, berries, hulls, roots—usually dried for storage and sometimes ground to a powder. For centuries, pepper, cinnamon, clove, and nutmeg-mace were grown only on the so-called Spice Islands of Southeast Asia. Via the Silk Road, Arab traders brought them to Europe and the Middle East, where they became valuable commodities (black pepper was even used as currency). A collapse in Silk Road trading led to the great European sea voyages of the 15th–16th centuries, bound for routes to the Spice Isles. Da Gama found his way around Africa, securing a spice monopoly for the Portuguese. The Dutch East India Company assumed control, followed by the British East India Company, whose trade first in spices and later in tea would support an empire.

Black pepper, called the "king of spices," has without question always been the fulcrum of the trade (red peppercorns and white peppercorns are merely the unfermented and hulled forms of the same berry), especially when it centered in the Spice Islands. A number of spices—cumin, caraway, juniper, bay, mustardseed—grew closer to home, from the European perspective. Allspice was discovered in the Americas, as was the tropical orchid vanilla.

Saffron, native to West Asia, is the most expensive of spices, as hours of labor are required to strip millions of saffron crocuses of their three tiny central stigmata that make up the coveted spice.

Salt

Humans cannot live without salt (sodium chloride), a vital nutrient. Fortunately, salt deposits are abundant (sodium is the sixth most common element on Earth). Prehistoric evidence shows that humans first followed animal trails to salt licks, before learning to mine rock salt and evaporate it from brine; even the earliest civilizations knew that salt could be used to preserve food and improve its flavor. In Greco-Roman times, salt's value was so universally recognized that it was commonly used for money (hence *salary*, from Latin *salarium*, salt). Because its purity linked it with the divine, salt took its place in innumerable religious practices—whether it is used to "kosher" a chicken or to bind a newlywed couple together. Today, salt comes in many forms, from common table salt and sea salt to gourmet varieties like fleur de sel, black lava salt, and Maldon crystals.

Fungi

The two most familiar edible classes of fungi are yeasts and mushrooms. Yeasts, microorganisms that inhabit the air everywhere, have been used—knowingly or not—to ferment beverages, leaven breads, and age cheeses since as early as 3500 B.C.

Mushroom reproduction is famously complex. The few species that can be commercially cultivated, are, and in copious numbers—especially button mushrooms and shiitakes. Others (such as the chanterelle, the hen of the woods, the blewit, the puffball, and the black trumpet) are gathered in the wild by amateur mycophiles for whom the uncertainty of the hunt only adds to its allure. The risk of a lethally toxic misidentification is small—but real enough that most mushroom foragers place a high value on experience, information, and reasonable caution.

Mushrooms (and "toadstools," their poisonous equivalents) grow everywhere, though especially in the Northern hemisphere. The first agriculturalists were slow to embrace mushrooms. Lacking chlorophyll, leaves, and roots, parasitic mushrooms feed off dead or living matter. Their mysteriously rapid appearance after rains and their occasionally fatal toxicity were additional deterrents, and they did not become a commonly accepted food until around 900 B.C. in China. Their nutritional value (high in potassium and protein) and exceptional range of flavors ultimately made them an irresistible food source, and today mushrooms form a prized part of cuisines the world over. A few species are especially notable.

Button mushrooms The white common button mushroom (*Agaricus bisporus*) accounts for 87 percent of mushroom sales in the United States (where per capita mushroom consumption in 2001 totaled about four pounds). A brown-skinned variation of *A. bisporus*, the cremini, and its mature version, the portobello, are increasing in popularity. Also widely popular is the closely related but more flavorful *A. campestris*, or field mushroom, also known as champignon de Paris.

Ceps, cèpes, or porcini mushroom (*Boletus edulis*) are among the most sought-after mushrooms of all, the boletes. Dried, fresh, or pickled, boletes are hunted furiously in Europe during their brief summer season.

Morels (*Morchella*) Succulent, veined, and hollow, morels range from yellow to gray to black and are generally the first mushrooms be found in the spring, especially around neglected orchards.

Truffles Prized since Greco-Roman times, truffles are generally the costliest of fungi, commanding prices that average out at about $100 per ounce—a little less for the white truffle (*Tuber magnatum*) than the black truffle (*Tuber melanosporum*). Buried deep beneath the roots of oaks and nut trees, truffles are famously difficult to find and virtually impossible to propagate; truffle hunters use specially trained dogs in place of the pigs who traditionally hunted truffles. The costly whole truffles are typically shaved onto a prepared dish. Truffle shavings and truffle oil (oil in which truffle has been steeped) are more economically accessible ways to enjoy it.

Shiitakes (*Lentinus edodes*) Shiitakes, or black mushrooms, are the fungus most widely used in Asia, as both medicine and food. Shiitakes are thought to confer a number of health benefits, from bolstering the immune system to lowering cholesterol. Sold fresh or dried, they have become one of the most widely available "wild" mushrooms in recent years, as cultivation has grown more reliable.

Fish

Whether eaten raw, cooked, cured, or smoked, pickled, or fermented, the 20,000 species of fish in the world's oceans provide about 15 percent of the protein in the world's diet. Ninety-five million metric tons of fish are captured annually, and about 37 million tons are farmed (China leads in both categories).

Fish have been eaten by humans for at least 100,000 years. Preservation techniques—drying, smoking, salting—have been used since at least the Mesolithic era.

For thousands of years the basic techniques—spear, line and hook, and net—remained the same, changing mainly in scope with the modern era. The most ancient, dedicated fish-eating cultures included Egypt, Japan, and China; in Polynesian and Pacific island culture fish was the principal protein. Around the second millennium B.C., Cretan civilization was based on the sea, but it later abandoned fish consumption; Greeks probably started fishing again around 500 B.C. and became leaders in the craft. Romans, who inherited the tradition, kept live fish in great enclosed *vivaria*; Roman cuisine depended heavily on garum and liquamen, fermented fish-based sauces.

Around the third century after Christ, fish came to be viewed as a symbol of Christ for mainly acronymic reasons: the Greek word for fish, *ichthys*, corresponded to the first letters of the inscription "Jesus Christ, Son of God, Savior" in Greek.

Medieval religious tradition, with its complex system of feast and fast (or meatless) days, promoted more extensive fish consumption in Europe, especially during Lent. (To this day, the custom of fish on Fridays prevails in Christian nations too numerous to mention.) Herring—salted, pickled, or marinated—dominated the fish market.

Fish farming, or aquaculture, has been practiced since at least 1000 B.C., though it has never approached the scale at which it is pursued now. While aquaculture relieves some of the burden of overfishing of wild species, concerns about pollution, the use of antibiotics, and the possible escape of genetically engineered species surround large-scale hatchery operations.

Fish species are often divided between freshwater and saltwater: common freshwater fish found in rivers and streams include bass, trout, and catfish; common American ocean fish are cod, bluefish, swordfish, and grouper. Some species are anadromous (spawning and breeding in freshwater, but growing to maturity in salt). The best known of these is the salmon; others are shad and sturgeon.

Overfishing is a common problem and has endangered a number of species. The most notable recent cases have been swordfish, "Chilean sea bass" (Patagonian toothfish), and sturgeon (the source of caviar). The top 10 species of fish consumed in the United States in 2002 were shrimp, canned tuna, salmon, pollock, catfish, cod, crabs, clams, tilapia, and assorted flatfish.

Cod (*Gadus*) Prolific, easy to catch, and wide-ranging, the cod has played a large role in human history. Dried cod supplied Viking voyages to North America. Basques fished for cod off the legendary Grand Banks of Newfoundland from 1000 to 1500. Later competition between English explorers, the German-based Hanseatic League, and the Basques ended in the Cod Wars of the 1530's.

The English colonies developed a close relationship with the cod, especially in Massachusetts, where it was very abundant, and where colonists grew so rich from it that an honorary cod sculpture was hung by the statehouse. Dried or salted, cod can be stored practically indefinitely, has good flavor, and provides an invaluable source of protein for many poor economies. In the 19th century, cod preserved by refrigeration gave birth to a whole new industry: the fish-and-chips shop. By the mid-20th century Europeans were so voracious for cod that a second set of Cod Wars began; it had to be brokered by NATO to provide a solution to the overfishing. Taken in sum, cod is probably the most important fish food in modern history. Small cod are called scrod. Cod-liver oil is a rich source of vitamin D.

Pollock (*Pollachius virens*). Also called saithe or Boston bluefish, the cheap and abundant pollock is commonly used for frozen or fried fish (though rarely labeled as pollock in those applications). Its bland white flesh is a fair substitute for cod, though grayer and not as fine.

Salmon The Atlantic Salmon (*Salmo salar*) and Pacific salmon(*Oxyrhyncus* spp.) are separate species, though both are anadromous (ocean fish that travel to freshwater to spawn). The wild Atlantic salmon in particular has suffered serious population decline owing to habitat loss, and to the extent that farmed fish account for the majority of Atlantic salmon on the market. Aquaculture has made salmon an affordable luxury for thousands of households, but has been the target of especially intense criticism in recent years because of the use of pesticides, concentrations of waste, and pollution hazards of some salmon farms. A number of fisheries, notably in Alaska, have taken steps to adopt sustainable cultural practices. Fresh and smoked salmon command the largest part of the salmon market, with canned salmon placing a distant third.

Tuna (*Thunnus*) Although tuna is found almost everywhere, it is most popular in North America (in canned form) and Japan (as sashimi). Tuna is a warm-blooded fish that swims constantly to replenish its oxygen stores; it can reach speeds of up to 55 miles per hour, and eats one-tenth its own weight daily. The most important type of tuna is albacore or longfin tuna, which has a lighter-colored meat than other tuna and is the most prized for canning (though yellowfin tuna was successfully popularized when albacore stocks began to diminish in 1926). Bluefin tuna is most popular eaten fresh.

Dolphin-safe is a term commonly heard in the tuna industry. Dolphins run with yellowfin tuna (less so with albacore), and in the mid-1950's tuna boats, alerted to the presence of tuna by the dolphins on the surface, began to catch tuna using encircling nets. Millions of dolphins were killed in the process; in the 1980's consumers protested with a tuna boycott. A U.S. law enacted in 1990 helped to reduce the death rate of dolphins, permitting the term *dolphin-safe* to be used only by companies that eschewed the nets and embraced a set of "dolphin-safe" fishing standards.

Shellfish The term *shellfish* is generally understood to include any aquatic animal with a shell. Crustaceans, which have a hard outer skeleton, include lobster, crab, and shrimp. Hinged and two-shelled bivalves include oysters, scallops, clams, and mussels; they are one class of the soft-bodied mollusks (the cephalopods, squid, and octopus are shell-less mollusks.) Shellfish, a good source of protein and readily available on most seacoasts, have been eaten since prehistoric times. Shrimp ranks high among the top sea foods eaten globally, whether fresh, dried, or as a paste.

Shellfish—especially bivalves—act as natural filters and can be frighteningly efficient disease vectors in contaminated waters, for organisms like the lethal *Vibrio* bacterium or sewage-borne coliform bacteria. Algae bloom—natural, but toxic to humans—occurs each year during the so-called red tides, at which time it is also unsafe to eat shellfish. (The dictum about eating oysters only in months including the letter "R," however, has to do with the oyster's breeding season rather than tide-borne plagues).

Shellfish cultivation has met with increasing success, particularly in the case of freshwater mussels. Oysters have been cultivated since Roman times.

Animal Foods

Hunting for food, one of the first recognizable human skills, predated even the use of tools. By 75,000 B.C., Neanderthals had established successful hunting techniques. For millennia human omnivores foraged for plant foods, and fished and hunted for whatever animal prey was sufficiently slow, small, or easy to outwit. Wild cattle and pigs began to appear around 10,000 B.C., and the first goats were domesticated. Following the dawn of agriculture, the domestication of animals by humans took off rapidly.

Chicken The origins of *Gallus domesticus* are obscure, but chickens were probably domesticated for their meat and eggs in Southeast Asia by 4500 B.C. Easy to raise, mild-flavored, and invaluable for their eggs, chickens have historically been accepted in nearly every meat-eating culture. Most species of chickens were spring-hatching, making "spring chicken" a seasonal luxury. In the mid-19th century, breeds that laid eggs year-round were popularized in the West.

In the 1950's medical advances introduced a drug to defeat coccidiosis, a disease afflicting large flocks of chickens. The battery system of cages was invented, and soon chicken became less expensive than beef. Today, typical commercial chickens reach maturity in 42 days.

Present-day concerns about poultry are those typical of the livestock industry: the use of hormones and antibiotics, confined living conditions, contaminated feed. Hence the abundance of alternatively raised birds and eggs on the market: "organic," "cage-free," "free-range," "raised without antibiotics." However, not all of these terms are legally defined, and none is strictly regulated.

The most common poultry disease is salmonella, which can flourish in imperfect processing environments but is killed at cooking temperatures exceeding 165 degrees F.

The latest news-making poultry threat is avian flu, a highly contagious disease which can be contained only by slaughtering whole flocks and which during 2004 ravaged the poultry industry in Asia.

Historically, ducks (*Anas platyrhynchos*) and geese (*Anser anser*) enjoyed some of the popularity of chickens as small family livestock, though they were never as reliable egg producers, and more difficult to feed. Sales of goose and turkey in particular tend to peak during the holiday season.

Turkey (*Melleagris gallopavo*) Wild turkeys originated in the Americas—they were certainly bred by the Aztec—and they were brought back to Spain in the 15th century with Columbus. They gained instant popularity in Europe, were widely bred, and came back to the Americas with the English colonists who settled Virginia (presumably unaware that turkeys were already there). Although turkey probably was eaten, as the legend has it, in Massachusetts at the first Thanksgiving in 1621, roast turkey didn't become a Thanksgiving tradition until the mid-18th century.

Today's commercial turkey is typically of the breed known as "broad-breasted white"—with white plumage rather than the colored feathers of folk tradition, and a breast so enormous that a mature turkey can scarcely walk; breeders rely on artifical insemination. However, some small producers are responding to consumer's demand for wild or heritage-breed turkeys.

Beef and veal Today's cattle are descended from two strains, *Bos taurus* and *Bos indicus*, of the Middle East's ancient wild auroch. Humans prized the auroch from at least 6500 B.C. for its meat, milk, hide, and draft power. Oxen, castrated cattle, were pulling primitive plows by 4000 B.C. *Bos taurus* and the plow disseminated westward across Europe, developing countless breeds. *Bos indicus*, the humped zebu, radiated across Asia.

The "sacred cow" is no mere idiom; bovines were associated with deities from the earliest times, when their horns were thought to reflect the curve of the crescent moon. The earliest religious prohibitions against eating beef probably arose around 600 B.C.

Each wave of New World colonization starting with Columbus brought European cattle. Semiferal Spanish cattle populated Mexico and traveled north. Docile northern European dairy cattle arrived in the cold Northeast and traveled west. By the early 19th century, huge herds of mixed wild cattle—notably the Texas longhorn—were roaming the plains, and soon dominated the entire frontier economy. In the 1870's, refrigeration turned the beef industry into a nationwide, year-round industry centered in Kansas City and Chicago.

Game generally refers to any fish, bird, or animal that is hunted rather than farmed or cultivated (in a sense, all animals eaten by humans were once "game"). Common game animals eaten today are likely to be deer (venison), rabbit, and pheasant. The wild boar, once popular prey, has largely been supplanted by readily available pork products. Some traditional "game" birds or meats—like duck, or less commonly ostrich or bison—now are bred on farms.

Goat (*Capra hircus*) The goat was almost certainly the first animal to be domesticated by humans, in the Middle East around 9000 B.C. Goats, like the sheep that soon followed them, could forage on poor land unsuitable for cattle. They came to the Americas with Columbus and became popular herding animals throughout Latin America and the Caribbean.

Today, goat meat remains particularly popular in regions where grazing land is scarce, as in parts of Africa and Asia. In North America and Europe, goats are tended mainly for their milk, which is used to make a number of notable yogurts and cheeses.

Lamb and Mutton (*Ovis aries*) Like goats, sheep thrive on nonarable land, and were domesticated early in the Middle East. They were useful for wool, for meat, and for sacrifice (as is evidenced widely throughout the Judeo-Christian tradition). Mutton and lamb are the principal source of protein in the Middle East and North Africa, much as beef is in North America. In Australia and the Americas, wool is more important than meat in the sheep industry. But sheep are valued worldwide for their milk, yogurt, and cheese (notably Roquefort).

Pork (*Sus scrofa*) Wild hogs may first have roamed the Middle East or Southeast Asia; in any case, pigs were being raised for food in China by 4300 B.C. In many ways, the pig is the ideal barnyard animal for meat: it breeds fast (producing litters of 10 after four months of gestation), it grows fast (reaching maturity at six months), it has a sweet and mild-tasting flesh, and it is famously unfussy about what it eats.

This last trait may have to do with some of the strong prejudices against the pig. In a number of societies, garbage-eating pigs were an early sanitation measure; some early civilizations even used them to dispose of human waste. Judaism and Islam both have strong, specific injunctions against the eating of pork that date from the seventh century B.C.

Cultures that embrace the pig as food, on the other hand, embrace it wholly, from snout to hoof. It would be hard to imagine European cuisine without its cured pork products, from Westphalian ham to prosciutto and soppressata. Dependency on the pig has historically been even greater in China, where the word for "meat" and "pork" is the same.

The major health hazard associated with eating swine is trichinosis, caused by the trichinella worm. This is generally avoided by cooking pork to an internal temperature of 140 degrees F, which kills the organism.

Dairy Foods

Sometime between the domestication of sheep and goats (10,000 B.C.) and the domestication of cattle (6500 B.C.), Sumerians discovered the art of dairying. The technique of cheese making was probably honed on goat and sheep milk, and transferred to cows once they had been reliably doemsticated.

Whether a culture was more likely to drink fluid milk or eat solid cheese could well have had something to do with climate. In the warm Mediterranean, perishable milk could not have been stored for long; cheese would have been one feasible means of storage. Greeks and Romans enjoyed a wide variety of cheeses, but considered milk the drink of "barbarians" to the north. By 1000 B.C., dairy products were known throughout Asia.

Climate may have encouraged a sharp division between milk-drinking and non-milk-drinking peoples, but the split was also biologically enforced. Most humans lose the ability to digest milk sugar (lactose) after toddlerhood. Northern Europeans, however, somehow avoided lactose intolerance; they could and did continue to drink milk into adulthood. Where the Europeans went, milk drinking followed; thus it is easy to forget, in a former colony like the United States, that milk-drinking is actually a minority practice around the world. Outside of Europe, yogurt and cheese tended to prevail in dairying regions; lactose breaks down in the fermentation process that produces these foods, making them more stable.

Today, the most popular bovine breed for dairying is the Holstein, followed distantly by Jerseys, Guernseys, Brown Swiss, and a few others. Other dairy animals used worldwide include goat, sheep, and yaks.

Butter Butter could be called a cream product, rather than a milk product. Churning cream drives out water, milk sugar, and some protein (these products are the "buttermilk"); the resulting solid mass, which is at least 80 percent fat, is butter. Some butters are inoculated with specific bacteria to enhance the butter's flavor. These "cultured" butters are popular throughout continental Europe. Most butter sold in American supermarkets is uncultured, or "sweet cream" butter. Both types of butter may be sold salted or unsalted. "Clarified" butter, like the ghee used throughout India, is pure butterfat that has been melted and drawn off from whole butter; clarified butter has a higher smoking point and a much longer shelf life than ordinary butter.

Cheese Cheese is a prehistoric product, thought to have been discovered by humans transporting milk in pouches fashioned from animal stomachs. The enzyme in the stomach linings, rennet, would have curdled the milk, eventually turning it into cheese. Modern cheese manufacturing depends on the same principle: controlled curdling, assisted by the introduction of select bacteria for flavor, followed by forming and aging.

Various livestock other than cows provide milk for cheese, if not for fluid consumption. Goats produce the various types of chèvre (which is merely French for "goat"); sheep produce Pecorino and Roquefort; water buffalo produce mozzarella.

"Raw milk" cheeses are not heated after the curds have formed; soft raw milk cheeses include Camembert, and Brie. Hard raw milk cheeses include Emmental, Parmesan, and Gruyère. U.S.D.A. regulations do not allow the importation of raw-milk cheeses aged less than 60 days, owing to health concerns. Artisanal cheese farms have also sprung up in the United States. to try and circumvent the import ban.

Milk Milk is a whole food, completely capable of sustaining infant life on its own; it is also a perfect haven for bacterial pathogens. Thus, finding a way to preserve fluid milk (other than transforming it into butter, cheese, or yogurt) has been a priority wherever it is drunk. The earliest methods involved drying milk to a powder and rehydrating it. The industrial revolution introduced refrigeration, which helped expand milk into a national industry. Today, most milk found at the supermarket has been subjected to the heat treatment known as pasteurization. A temperature of at least 144 degrees F kills most of the bacteria in milk and extends its shelf life. The "shelf stable" or UHT (ultra high temperature) milks sold in unrefrigerated cartons have been heated even further; they can be stored unopened at room temperature, though their flavor is somewhat affected.

Because it is expensive to produce, bulky to transport, and highly perishable, fluid milk has always been a challenging commodity to produce and regulate in the United States; its price is highly volatile. For this reason, political controversies over milk price-supports versus free trade have characterized the industry for decades. Market intervention has gradually fallen out of favor, and the last 20 years have seen an increasing concentration in the milk industry (as elsewhere in food) in favor of larger producers. Small dairy farmers have struggled to survive by forming cooperatives and producing value-added commodities like cheese, yogurt, and ice cream; others have simply shut down.

The other major controversy in the milk industry is the use of rBST or rBGH (recombinant bovine somatotropin or bovine growth hormone), a hormone that increases milk production up to 15 percent. Many in the industry embrace the increased yields; in fact, as many as 30 percent of U.S. dairy cattle receive the injections. But public advocates contend that rBST is dangerous and cruel for animals, which suffer reduced life expectancy, lameness, mastitis, and other health problems. They also argue that rBST, which profoundly affects the bovine endocrine system, makes milk unsafe for human consumption.

Yogurt After cheese, yogurt is probably the world's most important fermented milk product. *Lactobacillus* bacteria convert milk sugars into lactic acid, which gives yogurt its tangy or sour taste. This makes it more digestible for the lactose-intolerant, and extends its shelf life. For long an exclusively Asian product, yogurt enjoyed a sudden rise to popularity in the West in the 20th century, as the health benefits of its live cultures began to be recognized. Today, U.S. yogurt consumption stands at about 6.5 quarts per capita.

Chocolate, Coffee, and Tea

Chocolate The tropical cacao plant (*Theobroma cacao*) is native to Central America (though it may have grown wild in the Amazon) and may have been cultivated there as early as 1000 B.C. Cacao beans served as currency; the chocolate drink made from cacao was bitter, and important in ceremonial rites. The fall of the Aztec to Cortés introduced Spaniards, and later the rest of Europe, to chocolate, which was consumed copiously as a sweetened beverage. Not until the early 19th century were the complex processes that result in cocoa powder and bar chocolate perfected in Europe. Today, U.S. per capita chocolate consumption averages a bit over four pounds per year.

Coffee (*Coffea arabica*). Coffee is said to have been discovered in the ninth century after Christ by a goatherd from Abyssinia (present-day Ethiopia) who observed his goats dancing after eating the berries. Quickly recognized as a stimulant and an aid to thought and conversation, coffee was popularized and cultivated throughout the Middle East for centuries. In Arabic cultures, it became the social beverage of choice, since alcohol is prohibited to Muslims. In the 17th century, it arrived in Europe and soon enjoyed wide acceptance.

Coffeehouses have always seemed to be hotbeds for intellectual theorizing and political unrest. The 16th-century Turkish government banned the sale of coffee, and 18th-century European monarchs monopolized or taxed it beyond the reach of common people. Enlightenment thinkers would not do without it, and the French and American revolutions are reputed to have had their starts in coffeehouse brainstorming. The most recent surge in coffeeshop activity began in the 1990's, when Starbucks led the nation into a specialty-coffee craze. Although the frenzied pace of expansion appeared to have deflated with the tech bubble economy, the stores and their specialized drinks remain popular.

Despite the rise in coffee drinking, the cost of coffee has been kept so low that independent growers have scarcely been able to survive in recent years. The "fair trade" movement has been especially active in trying to ensure that coffee growing remains an economically viable profession for small farmers. Other terms used in the industry are *shade grown* and *organic*, which indicate that growers have used ecologically sustainable methods in the production of coffee.

Tea Though it had been known for centuries, tea first became popular around A.D. 600 in China and Japan. Tea slowly made its way west with the Turks, but not until the mid-1700's was it introduced into the new coffeehouses of Europe. It rapidly became an obsession in Britain and Russia. The British East India Company amassed a global fortune in the tea trade, and, during its heyday, tea became a symbol of British colonialism. (The Boston Tea Party of 1773 was an open revolt that helped set the stage for the American Revolution.) The company's efforts to force China to trade tea for opium led to the ill-fated Opium Wars of the mid-1800's—and the company's dissolution.

Nuts

We tend to think of nuts as shelled tree seeds, even though the peanut, for example, is a legume and the pine nut a naked seed. All nuts are a valuable source of energy: high in protein and fat, and some carbohydrate. The earliest *Homo sapiens* stored nuts, supplementing hunting and fishing, by 38,000 B.C. Today, nuts are generally viewed as a snack or "dessert" food rather than a primary source of nutrition; nevertheless, their popularity is such that in the United States alone, consumption reached 3.04 pounds per capita in 2002–03 (not including peanuts).

A number of nuts commonly eaten today arose in the New World; the best-known "nut," perhaps, being the peanut of South America. Originating in Brazil, the peanut (*Arachis hypogaea*) has become the most popular nut in the United States, at least partly because of its popularity in the form of peanut butter. (Americans alone eat about eight pounds of peanuts a year). Other South American native nut trees are the cashew (*Anacardium occidentale*) and the brazil nut (*Bertholettia excelsa*); walnuts (*Juglans regia*) and pecans (*Carya pecan*) are North American in origin.

Among the oldest Old World nut trees are almonds (*Prunus dulcis*) and pistachios (*pistacia vera*). With their starchy interiors suitable as a flour substitute, chestnuts (*Castanea sativa*) were once a staple food in the Mediterranean. Other important Mediterranean nuts are hazelnuts or filberts (*Corylus*) and pine nuts or pignoli, which help give pesto its distinctive taste and texture.

The best-known tropical nut is the macadamia (*Macadamia integrifolia*), which originated in Australia. Transplanted to Hawaii in the late 19th century, macadamias throve to the extent that they are now the state's third most important crop. Candlenuts (*Aleurites moluccana*), similar in flavor to macadamias, are widely used in Southeast Asia.

WINE: A PRIMER

A Brief History of Wine

"The peoples of the Mediterranean began to emerge from barbarism when they learned to cultivate the olive and the vine." So wrote the Greek historian Thucydides in the fifth century B.C., and indeed, wine-making is as old as civilization itself. Just as society finds its roots in ancient Mesopotamia, the earliest evidence we have for the cultivation of grapes and the supervised fermentation of their juices dates back to 6000 B.C. in the ancient Middle East. The Egyptians recorded the harvest of grapes on the walls of their tombs; bottles of wine were even buried with pharaohs in order that they might entertain guests in the afterlife. Wine was also considered a drink of the elite in ancient Greece, and it was a centerpiece of the famous symposia, immortalized by Plato and the poets of the period. But it was during the Roman era that wine became popular throughout society. In Roman cities wine bars were set up on almost every street, and the Romans exported wine and wine-making to the rest of Europe. Soon, production and quality of wine in other regions rivaled that of Rome herself: in A.D. 92, Emperor Domitian decreed that all of the vines in the Cahors region (near Bordeaux) be pulled out, ostensibly in favor of the wheat cultivation the empire so desperately needed, but possibly also to quell the competition with Italian wine exports.

After the fall of Rome, wine continued to be produced in the Byzantine Empire in the eastern Mediterranean. It spread eastward to Central Asia along the Silk Route; grape wine was known in China by the eighth century. But the spread of Islam largely extinguished the wine industry in North Africa and the Middle East. Throughout Europe, wine-making was primarily the business of monasteries, because of the need for wine in the Christian sacraments. During this period stronger, more full-bodied wines replaced their sweeter ancient predecessors (which usually were mixed with water before drinking). During the Renaissance, the virtues of various wine regions were appreciated by the increasingly sophisticated wine drinkers, and by the 18th century the wine trade soared, especially in France, where Bordeaux became the preeminent producer of fine wines. The development of distinctive strains of wine grapes led to the production of regional wines with easily recognizable characteristics.

In the New World the first successful wine-making occurred in the 19th century. Somewhat surprisingly, Ohio was the first region in America to successfully cultivate grapes for wine, but it was soon eclipsed by wine production in California. About this time grape cultivation first began in earnest in Australia. In the Old World, Champagne was establishing itself as a favorite luxury beverage; and fortified wines such as ports and sherries were becoming increasingly popular, especially in Britain. But despite the growing success of the industry, there was also a catastrophe: late in the century, the phylloxera epidemic destroyed many old European vines, a disaster that affected wine-making for decades. The plague was overcome by grafting cuttings of European varietal vines onto disease-resistant American rootstock.

Today wine-making is a global industry, with most of the countries of the world producing wine. Machines that can harvest huge areas by day or night have increased production, and modern viticultural science has ensured that the resulting product meets uniform standards, though sometimes at the expense of quality and flavor. Indeed, there has been a recent trend toward more traditional methods of wine-making such as unfiltered wines that preserve more of the grapes' true character.

Regions

While wine-making is indeed a global industry, some regions stand out for the quality and amount of their wine production.

France French wines, despite recent challenges from upstart New World producers, remain the standard by which all others are judged. Indeed, many of the most successful varietals in the world—such as Cabernet Sauvignon and Chardonnay—find their origins in France. Wine-making regions, such as Burgundy, Bordeaux, Chablis, and Champagne, have become synonymous with fine wine, even lending their names to styles of wine produced in other countries. France produces more fine wine than any other nation, and wine-making takes place in a number of clearly defined regions, as the chart below indicates.

While technology has helped bring New World nations renown for the quality of their wines, French winemakers rely as much on traditional methods on science. The great wines of France are most often aged in wooden casks, and this "French oak" is so renowned that one of the first major investments of most up-and-coming wineries in other countries is in barrels made in France.

Wines of France

Region	Location	Principal varietals
Burgundy (Bourgogne)	Central	*Red:* Pinot Noir, Gamay *White:* Chardonnay, Aligote
Chablis	North-central	*White:* Chardonnay
Bordeaux	Southwest	*Red:* Cabernet Sauvignon, Cabernet Franc, Merlot *White:* Semillon
Rhone	South-central	*Red:* Grenache, Mourvedre, Syrah *White:* Roussanne, Marsanne, Viognier
Loire	West	*Red:* Pinot Noir, Cabernet Franc *White:* Sauvignon Blanc, Pinot Gris, Chenin Blanc
Beaujolais	Central	*Red:* Gamay *White:* Chardonnay
Provence	South	*Red:* Cinsault, Grenache, Tibouren, Carignan *White:* Rolle, Ugnin Blanc, Clairette, Bourboulenc
Languedoc	Southwest	*Red:* Carignan, Cinsaut, Grenache, Mourvedre, Syrah *White:* Aramon Roussillon
Champagne	North	Pinot Noir, Pinot Meunier, Chardonnay
Alsace	East	*White:* Riesling, Gerwurztraminer, Pinot Gris, Muscat, Sylvaner, Chasselas, Pinot Blanc
Jura	East-central	*White:* Savagnin, Chardonnay *Red:* Poulsard, Trousseau, Pinot Noir, Gamay
Savoie	East-central	*White:* Altesse, Jacquere, Bergeron (Roussanne), Molette, Chardonnay *Red:* Mondeuse, Gamay, Douce Noir (Dolcetto)
Corsica	South	*Red:* Nielluccio, Sciaccarello, Carignan, Grenache, Cinsault, Alicante *White:* Vermentino, Muscat

The fact that so many wine terms are French in origin, and that so many wines produced abroad carry the names of French varietals, indicates the almost incalculable and enduring importance of France to the global wine-making industry.

Italy Wine-making is as thoroughly entrenched in Italy as it is in France, and the annual volume of wine produced in Italy is second only to that of France. The entire peninsula is planted with vines of wide variety, and Italy exports more wine than any other country.

In addition, French varietals such as cabernet sauvi-

Wines of Italy

Region	Location	Principal varietals
Friuli	Northeast	*White:* Tocai, Pinot Grigio, Pinot Bianco, Ribolla Gialla, Picolit, Verduzzo, Schiopettino, Sauvignon *Red:* Refosco, Pignolo, Tazzelenghe
Veneto	Northeast	*White:* Garganega, Trebbiano, Prosecco, Vespaiola, *Red:* Corvina, Rondinella, Molinara (Valpolicella, Bardolino, Soave, Prosecco)
Piedmont	Northwest	*Red:* Nebbiolo, Barbera, Dolcetto, Brachetto *White:* Arneis, Cortese, Erbaluce, Moscato (Barolo, Barbaresco, Ghemme, Gattinara, Dolcetto d'Alba, Gavi, Moscato d'Asti)
Liguria	Northwest	*White:* Bosco, Vermentino, Pigato, Albarola *Red:* Ormeasco (Dolcetto), Rossese, Sangiovese, Ciliegiolo (Cinqueterre, Ligure di Ponente, Dolceacqua, Golfo di Tigullio, Colli di Luni)
Emilia-Romagna	Central	Lambrusco, Sangiovese di Romagna
Tuscany	Central	*Red:* Sangiovese, Canaiolo *White:* Trebbiano, Vermentino, Vernaccia, Grechetto, Malvasia (Chianti, Brunello di Montalcino, Rosso di Montalcino, Vino Nobile di Montepulciano, Carmignano, Rufina, Vin Santo, Vernaccia di San Gimignano)

gnon, chardonnay, merlot, and sauvignon blanc have been successfully cultivated in Italy, especially in the northern and central regions. The advent of the "Super Tuscans"—Bordeaux-style blends of Cabernet Sauvignon and Merlot—ushered in a revolution in Italian wine-making in the early 1970's.

While France has largely adhered to traditional wine-making technology, Italy's vineyards are among the most modern on the continent. Steel tanks have largely replaced the wooden and cement fermentation vats of the past, and high-tech advancements such as temperature control, filters, and centrifuges are widely accepted. Together with traditional standards for high quality, these modern techniques have helped place Italian wines among the very best in the world.

Wines of Italy (continued)

Region	Location	Principal varietals
Umbria	Central	*Red:* Sangiovese, Sagrantino *White:* Trebbiano, Grechetto, (Orvieto Classico, Sagrantino di Montefalco, Rosso di Montefalco, Rosso Orvietano)
Le Marche (The Marches)	East-central	*Red:* Lacrima, Montepulciano, Sangiovese *White:* Verdicchio, Trebbiano (Rosso Cornero, Verdicchio)
Campania	Southwest	*Red:* Aglianico, Sangiovese, Piedirosso *White:* Falanghina, Fiano, Greco, Coda di Volpe (Greco di Tufo, Taurasi)
Puglia	Southeast	*Red:* Primitivo, Negroamaro, Malvasia Nera, Uva di Troia *White:* Bombino Bianco, Verdeca
Calabria	South	*White:* Greco, Montonico *Red:* Gaglioppo, Magliocco (Ciro Rosso, Crio Bianco) (Locorotondo, Martina Franca, Salice Salentino)
Sicily	South	*White:* Inzolia, Catarratto, Grillo, Grecanico, Malvasia, Zibibbo *Red:* Nero d'Avola, Frappato, Nerello Mascalese
Sardinia	West	*White:* Vermentino, Nuragus, Vernaccia, Mscato, Malvasia *Red:* Monica, Cannonau, Carignano

Spain The wine-making industry in Spain is as ancient and established as that of France. More land is devoted to the cultivations of the grape in Spain than in any other nation, though it is third in the world in total wine production. While Spain, like Italy, has vineyards throughout the country, the annual yields are lower owing to a less favorable climate and persistent droughts.

Spain plants more than 600 grape varieties, though 80 percent of the land is devoted to just 20 varietals. And while Spain has benefited from the relatively recent modernization of its wine-making industry, its wines are still marked by the distinct regional and cultural differences in the country. Spain, it would seem, has a wine for every taste and occasion, from the dry white wines of Galacia to the big reds of Ribera del Duero to the world famous sherries of Jerez.

Wines of Spain

Region	Location	Principal varietals
La Rioja	North	Albarino, Tempranillo, Garnacha, Malvasia, Macabeo
Castile and Leon	North-central	Tinto Fino, Albillo, Mencia
Galicia	North-west	Albarino, Treixadura, Torrontes, Mencia
Levante	East	Bobal, Monastrell
Catalonia Coast	North-east	Tempranillo, Monastrell, Garnacha
Valdepenas	South-central	Airen, Cencibel (Tempranillo)
Andalucia	South	Palomino, Pedro Ximenez

Other European Nations While France, Italy, and Spain, the world's three largest producers of high-quality wine, dominate European wine production, wine is produced throughout Europe. The better German wines tend to be clean and fruity, with more than 80 percent of German vineyards devoted to white grapes. The image of German wines has suffered in part because of the dominance of exports such as the notoriously dull Liebfraumilch, but the Rieslings produced in the vineyards of Mosel-Saar-Ruwer and Rheingau can easily compete with their French counterparts. Austrian wines are becoming more and more popular, and the country's wineries are increasingly important on the international stage. While the wide variety of grapes cultivated might be expected in a country surrounded by notable national traditions of wine-making, the most popular varietal is a grape indigenous to Austria, the Gruner Veltliner, which, at its best, offers a perfume and taste reminiscent of the wines of Alsace, and represents about half of the white wine production in the country. Greece enjoys one of the richest historical traditions of wine-making, and many of the varietals still popular have ancient roots. The industry has modernized to a large extent over the last 40 years, and with some notable results. Portugal is, of course, known for its port wines, for the eponymous wines of the island of Madeira, and as the preeminent producer of corks. Portuguese vintners have resisted the international trend toward importing grapes and standardizing wine-making practices, preferring to cultivate and blend their own indigenous varietals.

United States After France, Italy, and Spain, the U.S. is the world's fourth-largest producer of wine. Although European vines were introduced to Mexico and California under Spanish rule, the English colonies of the Atlantic coast produced little wine, and the quality of domestic wines was poor. There were no indigenous noble vines; the ubiquitous Concord grape is much better suited for grape juice than for wine. Today, however, after more than a century of cultivating grapes imported from Europe, the United States produces some of the world's best wines. All but four of the 50 states boast wineries, and wine-making is an important and successful industry in California, New York, Washington, and Oregon.

California produces 90 percent of American wine. Wine grapes were planted in the 18th century by the Spanish missionary-priest Junipero Serra, and the first commercial winery in the Napa Valley was established in 1861. California's s viticultural areas are found in about two-thirds of the state, from the high-desert region of Temecula near the Mexican border to Lake County along the northern coast. The most important regions are Napa, Sonoma, Santa Barbara, Monterey, San Luis Obispo, Mendocino, and Lake County. Most of the European varietals cultivated here have flourished, with Cabernet Sauvignon, Chardonnay, Pinot Noir, Merlot, Sauvignon Blanc, Syrah, Viognier, Sangiovese, Riesling, and Gerwurztraminer being the most successful and important. Zinfandel, long considered an indigenous grape, is the most commonly planted red wine grape in the state. It has been conclusively shown in recent years (thanks to DNA fingerprinting) to be a direct descendant of the Primitivo grape of southern Italy; however, nowhere else has this grape produced the often interesting and even complex wines that are made in California.

For the last 30 years, California wines have consistently matched or bested their Old World competition in terms of quality, and the best of the state's Cabernet Sauvignons and Chardonnays command prices often in excess of those from estates in Bordeaux and Burgundy. Famously, a Cabernet from the Stag's Leap winery won a 1974 comparative tasting in Paris, an event that marked the arrival of California wines on the international scene. Over the last 15 to 20 years there has been a growing interest in Rhone-style wines, Italian wines based on the Sangiovese grape, and Alsatian whites.

New York is second only to California in U.S. wine production, and there are four major wine-producing regions. Long Island, specifically the North Fork and Hamptons peninsulas, enjoys a maritime climate that its adherents like to compare to that of Bordeaux. This allows the region a longer growing season, and Merlot, Cabernet Franc, and Sauvingnon Blanc do especially well here. The Hudson River, Finger Lakes, and Lake Erie regions are found in upstate New York and, besides the widely planted and indigenous Concord, the most successful varietals have been Riesling, Gerwurztraminer, Chardonnay, and Pinot Noir.

Washington Most of the important Washington wineries are located in the eastern part of the state, where the climate is not as wet, being closer to the Pacific Coast, and the principal growing region here is the Columbia Valley. Most varietals do well here, and white grapes take up the most acreage. Notable successes have been with Riesling, Semillon, Sauvignon Blanc, Cabernet Sauvignon, and Merlot, the latter arguably the most important varietal in the state today. The Austrian Limberger grape has enjoyed a somewhat surprising success here as well.

Oregon The cool climate of Oregon has allowed grapes that suffer from excessive heat to flourish, and the state has become best known for its production of high quality Pinot Noirs. Gamay Noir also does well here, and the region is known too for ice wines made from Riesling and Gerwurztraminer. The principal regions are the Willamette Valley, Umpqua Valley, Rogue River, Illinois Valley, and Applegate Valley.

Australia and New Zealand More than 1,000 wineries dot the Australian continent, spreading through every state and growing every variety of wine, from dry whites to fortified Port-style wines. Australia is now among the top 10 producers of wine in the world and is especially known for its success with Shiraz (Syrah) and Cabernet Sauvignon. The other predominant varietals grown here are Grenache, Mourvedre, Muscat, Semillon, Pinot Noir, Grenache, Riesling, Chardonnay, and Sauvignon Blanc. Australia's sophisticated, pioneering viticulturalists have had a profound influence on wine and wine-making around the world, an influence that grows with each passing year.

New Zealand wines, like their neighbors in Australia, are gaining more and more recognition internationally, and the Sauvignon Blancs produced in this island nation are now among the most acclaimed in the world. Because the wine-producing regions are spread over a distance of about 1,000 miles, grapes are grown in a wide variety of climates and soil types, and distinctive styles have been achieved with Chardonnay, Pinot Noir, Cabernet Sauvignon, Merlot, and Reisling varietals. Thanks to New Zealand's prevailing maritime climate, grapes are afforded a long, slow ripening period that allows the varietals to retain their distinctive flavors.

South Africa Although the first vineyards in South Africa were created by French Huguenots in the late 17th century, it wasn't until the establishment of a major wine cooperative (KWV) near the end of World War I that wine-making in South Africa became a viable industry. Today South Africa has 15 classified wine-growing regions, and the industry benefits from a climate very similar to that of the Mediterranean. Most popular varietals have thrived here—Cabernet Sauvignon, Pinot Noir, Chardonnay, Sauvignon Blanc, and Muscat in particular—but a notable contribution to the international wine market is Pinotage, a clone of Pinot Noir and Cinsault grapes developed in South Africa. Also of note is Hanepoot, a white varietal grown only in South Africa, used to produce fortified wines.

South America After Europe, South America is the world's second most important wine-producing continent. While most South American nations make some wine, Argentina and Chile are the most important producers in the region.

Argentina, which annually produces about four times the quantity of wine that Chile does, has eight distinct wine-growing regions, of which Mendoza is the most important. Thanks to a rich history of Italian immigration, many of the more important reds wines are produced from varietals such as Barbera, Sangiovese, Nebbiolo, Dolcetto, and Lambrusco. Cabernet Sauvignon has also done well here, but the most important grape in Argentina is the French Malbec, which produces wine of world-class status. Because of its international popularity, Chardonnay is also a widely planted varietal.

Chile, with dry summers, enjoys a climate similar to that of the Napa Valley, and produces fruity and exceptionally ripe wines. Chile is especially known on the international stage for well-produced and well-priced—if somewhat uncomplicated—red wines, with those made from Cabernet Sauvignon heading the list. But without a truly unique style of wine-making, Chile's most important contribution to the world of wine is perhaps its wine made from Carmenere (also known as Grand Vidure), a Bordeaux varietal that is especially promising. Other important varietals grown here are Merlot, Syrah, Chardonnay, and Sauvignon Blanc.

Wine and Food

The perceived need to make the perfect match of wine and food is probably the source of more angst to the budding enophile than any other aspect of wine connoisseurship. While there are certain guidelines that will make the enjoyment of both wine and food more satisfying, the main rule of thumb is to drink what you like. Common sense would dictate, however, that you probably would not want to serve a big Châteauneuf du Pape with a dish like Dover sole. The heartiness of the wine would, quite simply, overwhelm the delicate flavor of the fish. Similarly, roast lamb would most likely overpower a light Sancerre, so a better choice would be a rich and more complex Cabernet Sauvignon.

Some General Rules If you are serving more than one wine with dinner, start with the lighter-bodied wine. Red wines high in tannins are mellowed by heavily textured meats such as beef and lamb. Salty foods will also mitigate the bitterness in some wines and make sweet whites taste sweeter, but bitter foods will accentuate astringent tannins. Sweetness in food will make a wine taste less sweet. Also, it is not wise to serve dry wines with sweet foods, as the sweetness emphasizes the wine's acidity. Delicately flavored foods go better with more delicate wines. Earthy wines go well with dishes like sautéed mushrooms. Pairing opposites often works well, too, such as hot Thai or Indian food with a sweet white wine. Fish, especially when cooked and served with citrus fruits, is better suited to a more acidic white wine. And it is always a good bet to pair foods and wines from the same geographic origins.

Below are listed some especially winning combinations of wine and food:

Food	Wine
Lamb	Bordeaux, Zinfandel, Cotes du Rhone
Roast Beef	Burgundy, Barbera, Barolo, Syrah
Pork	Beaujolais, Pinot Noir, Riesling, Gerwurztraminer, Chardonnay
Game birds	Burgundy
Poultry	Most white wines, Beaujolais
Fish	Sauvignon Blanc
Foie Gras	Sauternes
Oysters	Muscadet, Chablis, Champagne, Riesling
Cheese	
Bleu	Sauternes, Port
Mild cheddar	Champagne, Chardonnay
Sharp cheddar	Cabernet Sauvignon, Sauvignon Blanc
Chevre	Gerwurtraminer, Champagne
Gouda	Riesling, Dry Champagne
Gruyere	Chardonnay, Sauvignon Blanc
Monterey Jack	Riesling
Roquefort	Port
Stilton	Port
Swiss	Gerwurtraminer

Wine Glossary

acidity when mentioned on a label, expressed as a measure of the total acid present in the wine. Excessive acidity can cause wines to taste sharp or tart, sometimes to an unpleasant extent. But too little acidity can cause wines to be flat and uninteresting. The typical acidity of a balanced table wine usually falls within the range of 0.6 percent and 0.75 percent of the total volume. Generally speaking, for proper balance the sweeter the wine the higher the total acidity should be.

alcohol by volume law requires that labels clearly show the level of alcohol in the wine. Table wines usually fall within the range of 11.5 percent and 14 percent; dessert wines range from 17 percent to 21 percent.

aperitif most often used to describe any wine that is usually consumed before a meal, but it also signifies a legal classification for wines having a level of 15 percent or more alcohol by volume.

appellation system defines the area where a wine's grapes were grown. Regulations vary from country to country.

astringent descriptive of wines with a harsh, puckery taste that leaves a sensation of dryness in the mouth. Usually caused by excessive tannins in wine.

auslese German dessert wine. *Auslese* is the German word for "selection," here used to describe specially selected, perfectly ripened bunches of grapes that are hand-picked and then pressed separately from other grapes. One of the six categories in the Qualitatswein mit Pradikat (QmP) classification system for fine German wines.

balance subjective term describing wines whose various elements are in harmony, with no single feature dominant. A wine in which the tastes of acid, sugar, tannin, alcohol, and flavor are in accord is said to be "balanced."

blend unless the label identifies a wine as derived completely from a single varietal, wines, generally blended from different lots or barrels. Tradition and regional laws dictate what grape varieties may be blended together to make a certain wine. Varietals, vintages, and barrel varieties can all be blended to create a distinctive wine.

bottled by indicates only that the winery played a very small part in the wine's production, most likely having purchased and bottled wine made somewhere else. However, if the label reads "Estate-Bottled" or "Château-Bottled," the wine was grown in the winery's own vineyards.

bouquet smell or fragrance that has its origins in the wine production or aging methods (as opposed to the fruit itself). *Bouquet* refers to the smell that develops after a wine is bottled; *aroma* is usually the more appropriate term for describing a wine's overall smell.

breathe, breathing process of aeration. When wine is poured into a wineglass, or decanter, the introduction of air releases aromas that become more pronounced as time passes.

brut term exclusively used for champagne describing the driest—or least sweet—wine. Confusion arises over the term *extra dry*, which actually denotes the sweetest of champagnes.

buttery describes the creamy taste of better white wines, particularly Chardonnay. It can also be used to describe the golden color of these wines.

claret old British synonym for Bordeaux wines, increasingly used today as a general reference to light red wines. Even though *claret* sometimes appears on labels, it has no legal definition.

corked term describing wine that has interacted with a defective or moldy cork. Wines spoiled in this manner taste dank or musty, and, unfortunately, since defective corks look the same as good ones at the time of bottling, there is no way to determine if a wine has been affected in this way without actually tasting the wine.

cru, grand cru the French word for growth, *cru* refers to a vineyard of especially high quality, such as a classified growth. *Grand cru* describes an even higher quality of vineyard, and *grand cru classé* is the designation for the most superb wines that originate in the Bordeaux region. *Cru bourgeois* is a category for the châteaux of the Médoc that ranks just below *cru classé*.

cuvée usually refers to a given lot or batch of wine held in a single tank or large cask. Generally the term indicates a specific blend of wines. It is often used on Champagne labels in lieu of a vintage date.

dessert wines wines served after meals, traditionally of two varieties: fortified wine, such as port or sherry, to which alcohol is added in the form of brandy or neutral spirits; and sweet or very sweet wines of any alcohol level, such as muscat or sauternes.

dry term describing the absence of any taste of sugar in wine. *Dry* usually indicates wines with sugars totaling no more than 0.5 percent, though the term is used rather loosely on wine labels.

eau de vie French term meaning "water of life." Describes any colorless, potent brandy or other spirit distilled from fermented fruit juice.

eiswein German word meaning "ice wine." Eiswein is made from late-harvested grapes allowed to freeze on the vine, concentrating the sugars. While it originated in Germany, eiswein is now produced in many countries with cool climates; the English term *ice wine* is often used.

enology (oenology) study of wine and wine-making.

estate-bottled label phrase meaning that the wine was produced and bottled at the winery from grapes owned and farmed by the vineyard owners.

ethyl acetate vinegary smell that indicates the presence of acetic acid in wine. While it can enhance the aroma and taste of some wines—particularly sweet ones—noticeable ethyl acetate is usually considered a flaw.

fermentation chemical process by which yeasts transform the grapes' sugar into alcohol and carbon dioxide. Most of the other elements of the original grape juice are essentially unchanged by the process.

filtering clarifying process in which yeast cells and other impurities are removed after fermentation. Unless indicated as unfiltered on the label, most wines are filtered for clarity and stability.

finish last impressions of flavor left in the mouth after the wine is swallowed.

first growth, second growth, etc. system of classification instituted in 1855 for Bordeaux wines, ranking vineyards according to price from first growths (*premier crus*) through fifth growths (*cinqième crus*). Price was seen as a directly indication of quality, and the system is still respected and in use today, though there are some obvious omissions. For example, the great wines of Pomerol were never classified according to this system.

fruity describes a wine in which fruit flavors dominate the aroma and taste. These wines are usually light in body and easy to drink.

haut French word meaning "high" or "upper." Generally used in a geographical sense, as in Haut-Médoc which is north of the Médoc region in Bordeaux. *Haut* does not mean that the quality of the wine is higher.

hock British term referring to wine from the Rhine regions of Germany.

kabinett first and lowest of the six subcategories of the QmP German wine classification system. These wines are usually the driest and least expensive in this category.

kir aperitif made of white wine that is flavored with a touch of crème de cassis, a black currant-flavored liqueur. When made with Champagne, it is called a kir royale.

late harvest indicates the condition of the fruit rather than a specific calendar date. Grapes harvested late from the vine are higher in sugars. For white wines this usually indicates a sweeter wine; for reds it may indicate a higher alcohol level as well as additional sweetness.

length almost a synonym for "finish," this term indicates how long the flavor lasts in the back of the throat after swallowing.

limited bottling rather nebulous term referring to everything from small lots of special wine to entire vintages of wines from top producers. This is not a legally defined term in the wine industry.

lot number differentiates wines of the same vintage and type bottled at different times, or wines blending vintages or growing regions.

nose character of a wine as determined through the olfactory senses, including the aroma and bouquet.

nouveau French word meaning "new," generally applied to some Beaujolais-type wines. *Nouveau* describes a wine that is young, fresh, fruity, and simple. Nouveau wines are designed not for long aging but for immediate consumption.

old vines term used especially in California to designate wines produced from vines planted in the pre-Prohibition era. Lacking a legal definition, the term implies quality. It is commonly used to describe the higher-quality (and more expensive) zinfandels.

reserve term used liberally by winemakers (and hence of little value), ostensibly to indicate superior wines. When used to describe Champagne it refers to wine reserved for future blending.

sec French term meaning "dry," though on Champagne labels it means that the wine is sweet. *Demi-sec* is a term exclusively for Champagne indicating that the wine is medium-sweet.

spätlese German for "late picking," refers to grapes that are selectively picked at least a week after the main harvest starts for that specific variety. Because these grapes contain more sugar, the resulting wines are rich and sweet. Another QmP category for German wines.

structure interplay of elements creating a tactile impression in the mouth—such as tannin, acid, alcohol, and body.

sur lie French term meaning "on the lees." Lees is the coarse sediment that accumulates during fermentation. *Sur lie* indicates that a white wine has been kept in contact with yeast lees longer than usual in aging and processing. The hoped-for result is a more complex wine with a toasty, roasted-grain flavor.

sweet term describing the sensation of a sugar taste in wine. The intense flavor of fruit or overripe grapes is often described as sweet. The nonsugary sweetness perceived in wine is often the result of varying levels of alcohol, tannin, and acid. Alcohol in a totally dry wine often gives the wine a sweetish taste, as if sugar had been added.

tannin substance in red wines (and some whites) that imparts a bitter or astringent taste. Tannins are derived from grape skins, stems, and seeds, as well as from wood, if the wine is aged in natural casks. Many powerful young red wines have high levels of tannin that take years of aging to soften. Tannins give many big reds their heady character, though if not kept in balance they can leave an unpleasantly bitter aftertaste.

unfiltered indicates that the wine was clarified and stabilized without the filtration process. Unfiltered wines have achieved a trendy status in recent years.

varietal wine named after the single or predominant grape used in its composition. Wines are required by law to include 75–80 percent of the grape in their makeup to be designated a varietal wine. Examples of varietals include Cabernet Sauvignon, Riesling, Pinot Noir, and Sangiovese.

vermouth white wine that has been fortified and flavored with various herbs and spices, most often served as an aperitif and mixed in cocktails.

vin ordinaire literally, "ordinary wine." Also referred to as *vin de table*, or table wine.

vin de pays in French, "country wine." Indicates an ordinary, everyday table wine, often from a locality near where it is served.

viniculture study or science of making wines.

vinifera vine species of European origin, which includes almost all the well-known wine-producing varieties.

vintage the year the grapes used to produce the wine were harvested. In order for a winery to use a vintage date, 95 percent of the grapes used to produce the wine must have been harvested in the stated calendar year.

GUIDE TO NUTRITION

Food and Nutrition

The adage "you are what you eat" neatly summarizes many truths about human health and well-being. Food is the raw material from which the body obtains the substances it needs to grow, reproduce, repair itself, and fight disease. A diet composed of good food choices gives the body the chemical compounds it needs. A diet deficient in essential molecules inhibits or skews basic physiological mechanisms, preventing the body from functioning properly.

Nutrients

Essential nutrients are substances needed by the body to grow and remain healthy. Macronutrients are needed in large amounts; they include proteins, carbohydrates and fats. Micronutrients are needed in very small quantities; they include vitamins and minerals. Two other critical components of a healthy diet are fiber and water.

Proteins The body needs twenty essential amino acids to assemble approximately 10,000 different kinds of proteins. These proteins include enzymes, antibodies, hemoglobin, components of cell membranes and bone, and so on.

Meat, poultry, seafood, legumes, dairy products, nuts, and seeds are rich sources of proteins. Most Americans eat far more protein than necessary, though protein-deficiency diseases are common in some poor countries. Excess dietary protein is broken down and either used as an energy source or converted into fat.

Carbohydrates Carbohydrates—sugar and starches—are the body's primary source of energy. During a complex series of chemical reactions within cells, carbohydrate molecules are broken down to release the energy needed for everything from maintaining body temperature and heartbeat to moving limbs and eyelids. Most excess dietary carbohydrates are converted into fat.

Fats The category of nutrients known as lipids include solid fats, liquid fats (oils), and cholesterol. These substances provide insulation, protect internal organs, maintain healthy skin, and play important roles in vision, hormone production, and the formation of cell membranes. However, excess dietary fat increases the risk of heart disease, diabetes, cancer, and other health problems.

There are two types of dietary fats: saturated and unsaturated. Saturated fats are the so-called "bad" fats. They are found in red meat, lard, dairy products, coconut and palm oil, and egg yolks. Within the body, they raise total blood cholesterol and low-density lipoproteins (LDL), the main source of cholesterol buildup and blockage of arteries. Unsaturated fats, the so-called "good" fats, include polyunsaturated fats and monounsaturated fats. Most come from plant sources. They lower LDL and raise high-density lipoproteins (HDL), which help prevent cholesterol from building up in arteries.

Trans fatty acids (trans fat) are components of unsaturated fats that have been hydrogenated to make them solid at room temperature. They are found in margarines,

Cholesterol and Triglyceride Levels

Blood Level (mg/dL)*	Significance
Total Cholesterol	
Less than 200	Desirable
200-239	Borderline high
240 or higher	High
LDL	
Less than 100	Optimal
100-129	Near optimal
130-159	Borderline high
160-189	High
190 or higher	Very high
HDL	
Less than 40	Low
40-59	Acceptable
60 or higher	Optimal
Triglycerides	
Less than 150	Acceptable
150-199	Borderline high
200 or higher	High

* Milligrams per deciliter of blood.

Source: Lung, and Blood Institute

peanut butter, and commercially baked goods and fried foods. They raise total cholesterol and LDL and may lower HDL.

Cholesterol is an essential component of cell membranes and needed for the production of sex hormones and other important compounds. However, high levels of blood cholesterol increase people's risk for heart disease. Generally, foods high in saturated fats are also high in cholesterol.

Another form of lipids in the blood is triglycerides—fat molecules consisting of three fatty acids joined to a glycerol molecule. They are important in helping to transfer energy from food into body cells, but excessive levels increase heart disease risk.

Vitamins and Minerals These micronutrients are involved in numerous body processes, from building blood cells to transmitting chemical signals and regulating body temperature. A deficiency can result in illness. For example, insufficient intake of the B-vitamin niacin can lead to pellagra, a disease marked by diarrhea, dermatitis, dementia, and if untreated, death; a deficiency of dietary calcium can result in osteoporosis, a disease characterized by brittle, easily broken bones. Excessive doses of vitamins and minerals can also be dangerous. Too much vitamin A can cause nerve damage, hair loss, blurred vision, and birth defects; excessive zinc can cause a copper deficiency by competing with copper at absorption sites in the intestine.

Since the 1940's, the National Academy of Sciences has provided Recommended Daily Allowances (RDAs) for vitamins and minerals. An RDA indicates the amount of a vitamin or mineral that meets the nutrient needs of about 98 percent of all the healthy individuals in a specified gender and age group.

Vitamin and mineral needs change markedly during life. Gender, tobacco use, and whether a woman is pregnant or lactating also affect needs. For instance, a typical teenage female needs about 1200 mg of calcium daily; after age 25, about 800 mg of calcium are considered sufficient. A 7-year-old child needs 13 mg of niacin daily; a 15-year-old boy should have 20 mg daily and a 60-year-old man about 15 mg daily.

Fiber Dietary fiber is a complex mixture of plant materials that are resistant to digestion by the human digestive system. There are two major types: insoluble (cellulose, hemicellulose, lignin) and soluble (gums, mucilages, pectins). Insoluble fiber is found mainly in vegetables, wheat bran, and whole grains. Foods high in soluble fibers include oats, dry beans and peas, and fruits such as apples, oranges, and strawberries.

Fiber provides bulk for the formation of feces, thus hastening the passage of feces through the lower digestive system and helping to prevent constipation and the formation of diverticula (small pouches in the walls of the large intestine). It provides a feeling of fullness, helping to satisfy appetite. Studies also indicate that adequate dietary fiber helps reduce the risk of heart disease and diabetes and may help prevent colon cancer.

Water The human body is one-half to four-fifths water, with water composing about 70 percent of lean muscle, more than 75 percent of the brain, and about 80 percent of the blood. Water carries nutrients and oxygen to cells, cushions joints, helps regulate body temperature, removes wastes, and helps prevent constipation. Some research indicates sufficient water intake reduces the risks of colon cancer, bladder cancer, fatal heart attacks, and kidney stone formation. Insufficient water intake can result in dehydration.

On average, an adult loses about 10 cups of fluid a day—in urine, feces, perspiration, and exhaled breath. Most of this fluid needs to be replaced by drinking water or other non-alcoholic beverages; the rest is obtained from solid foods. Fluid intake should be increased when engaged in intense physical activities or working in warm environments.

Diet and Dieting

Daily nutritional needs vary from one person to the next, and change as a person moves through life's stages. Genetics, chronic diseases, activity levels, and pregnancy can impact nutritional needs; allergies, availability of food, and cultural and religious beliefs can influence which foods are chosen to meet these needs. Nonetheless, certain basic principles should be followed to assure good health, maintain an ideal weight, and reduce the risk of heart disease, cancer, diabetes, and other diseases:

—Eat a variety of foods.

—Do not overeat; keep portions small or moderate-sized.

—Eat plenty of fruits, vegetables, and whole grains.

—Limit intake of sugar, salt, saturated fat, and cholesterol.

—Drink plenty of water.

—Exercise daily.

The Value of Vitamins

Vitamin Adult RDA*	Major Functions	Significant Food Sources
A M: 900mcg (3000 IU) F: 700 mcg (2330 IU)	Helps form skin, bones, and mucous membranes; promotes healthy eyes	Dairy products, fish oil, fruits and vegetables rich in beta-carotene (carrots, mangos, cantaloupe, sweet potatoes, tomatoes, broccoli, spinach)
B1 (thiamine) M: 1.2 mg F: 1.1 mg	Helps cells convert carbohydrates into energy; promotes healthy brain and nerve cells	Whole grains, wheat germ, soybeans, meat, fish, nuts, brewer's yeast
B2 (riboflavin) M: 1.3 mg F: 1.1 mg	Helps cells convert carbohydrates into energy; necessary for growth and production of red blood cells; promotes healthy skin and eyes	Organ meats (liver, tongue, etc.), meats, fish, milk, bread products, fortified cereals, almonds, egg yolks
B3 (niacin) M: 16 mg F: 14 mg	Helps convert food into energy; promotes healthy skin, nerves, and digestive system	Lean meats, poultry, fish, peanuts, wheat germ, dairy products, brewer's yeast
B5 (pantothenic acid) M, F: no RDA; 5 mg is recommended upper limit	Essential for food metabolism and production of hormones	Organ meats, beans, egg yolk, brewer's yeast, whole grains
B6 (pyridoxine) M (19-50): 1.3 mg M (51+): 1.7 mg F (19-50): 1.3 mg F (51+): 1.5 mg	Essential for protein metabolism; involved in synthesis of hemoglobin and neurotransmitters; aids functioning of nervous and immune systems	Fortified cereals, beans, meats, poultry, fish, bananas, green leafy vegetables, nuts
B12 M, F: 2.4 mcg	Essential for red blood cell production, maintains normal functioning of nervous system	Liver, meats, poultry, eggs, dairy products, fortified cereals, fortified soy products
Biotin (a B vitamin) M, F: no RDA; some experts suggest 30 to 100 mcg	Aids in food metabolism and in production of proteins and fatty acids	Liver, cheese, egg yolks, brewer's yeast, peanuts, cauliflower, bananas, tomatoes, whole grains
Choline (a B vitamin) M, F: 425 mg	Promotes fetal brain development, learning, and memory	Liver, egg yolks, wheat germ
Folate (a B vitamin; folic acid is the synthetic form) M, F: 400 mcg	Aids in new cell formation, protein metabolism, and synthesis of DNA and neurotransmitters	Liver, leafy green vegetables (spinach, turnip greens), asparagus, citrus fruits and juices, fortified cereals, beans and peas, peanuts, whole grains
Inositol (a B vitamin) M, F: no RDA available	Aids in transmission of chemical signals, fat and cholesterol use, and cell membrane formation	Whole grains, nuts, liver, vegetables; can be manufactured by the body
C M: 90 mg** F: 75 mg**	Promotes healthy gums and teeth; aids in production of collagen and hormones; helps in healing wounds and absorption of iron; as an antioxidant, combats adverse effects of free radicals	Fresh fruits (especially citrus; also cantaloupe, strawberries, kiwis), green vegetables, tomatoes, potatoes, cauliflower, brussels sprouts

Vitamin Adult RDA*	Major Functions	Significant Food Sources
D*** M, F (19-50): 5 mcg/200 IU M, F (51-69): 10 mcg/400 IU M, F (70+): 15 mcg/600 IU	Maintains normal blood levels of calcium and phosphorus; promotes strong bones and teeth	Cod liver oil, fish (salmon, mackerel, sardines), fortified dairy products; however, most vitamin D used by the body is made therein following exposure to the sun
E M, F: 15 mg	Aids in production of red blood cells; as an antioxidant, combats adverse effects of free radicals	Vegetable oils, whole grains, wheat germ, nuts, leafy green vegetables
K M: 80 mcg F: 65 mcg	Essential for blood clotting; helps build and maintain bones	Dark green vegetables (spinach, broccoli), soybean oil, eggs; intestinal bacteria produce some of the vitamin K needed by the body

Mg = milligrams; mcg = micrograms. * Unless otherwise specified, RDAs provided herein apply to males age 19 and older and females age 19 and older who are neither pregnant nor lactating. ** Smokers need an additional 35 mg. *** Insufficient evidence exists to establish RDAs for vitamin D. Instead, an Adequate Intake (AI) level is provided.
Sources: U.S. Department of Agriculture, National Institutes of Health.

The Value of Minerals

Mineral Adult RDA*	Major Functions	Major Food Sources
calcium M, F: 800 mg	Essential for formation of bones and teeth and for muscle growth and contraction; aids in production of androgen, estrogen, and cortisone; helps in blood blood clotting, heart rhythm, nerve transmission, cell membrane permeability	Leafy green vegetables, watercress, legumes, milk and dairy products, liver, nuts, seafood (salmon, sardines, shellfish)
chromium M, F: 50-200 mcg	Controls blood sugar level	Whole grains, egg yolks
copper M, F: 1.5-3 mg	Facilitates production of enzymes	Oysters, nuts, seeds, whole grains
fluoride M, F: 3.1 mg	Prevents tooth decay	Found naturally in some community water systems; added to water in other areas
iodine M, F: 150 mcg	Aids in production of thyroid hormones	Iodized salt, marine fish, dairy products
iron M: 8 mg F (19-50): 18 mg F (51+): 8 mg	Important in oxygen transport and metabolism	Liver, lean meats, poultry, shellfish (oysters, clams), beans, spinach, fortified cereals and breads
magnesium M (19-30): 400 mg M (31+): 420 mg F (19-30): 310 mg F (31+): 320 mg	Regulates body temperature; helps maintain normal muscle and nerve function; keeps heart rhythm steady; aids in protein synthesis	Leafy green vegetables, avocados, nuts, whole grains, meats, poultry, fish, dried fruit.

Mineral Adult RDA*	Major Functions	Major Food Sources
manganese M, F: 2-5 mg	Aids in bone formation, needed for synthesis of proteins and fatty acids	Legumes, nuts, rice
phosphorus M, F: 800 mg	Aids in bone and soft tissue growth	Dairy products, meats
potassium M, F: 3500 mg	Maintains fluid balance and proper functioning of muscles and nerves; needed for protein and carbohydrate metabolism	Spinach and other cooked greens, potatoes, beans, fruits, milk
selenium M, F: 55 mcg	Protects cells against the effects of free radicals produced during metabolism; essential for normal functioning of the immune system and thyroid gland	Tuna, cod, liver, Brazil nuts, enriched breads and cereals
zinc M: 11 mg F: 8 mg	Helps maintain the immune response, reproductive functions, and enzyme activity	Oysters, fortified cereals, meats, nuts, seeds

Mg = milligrams; mcg = micrograms. * Unless otherwise specified, RDAs provided herein apply to males age 19 and older and females age 19 and older who are neither pregnant nor lactating. Sources: U.S. Department of Agriculture, National Institutes of Health.

How Long Does It Take to Burn Off Calories?

		Minutes of Activity Needed* (based on person weighing 154 pounds)				
Food	Calories Supplied	Reclining (1.3 calories per minute)	Walking (5.2)	Bike riding (8.2)	Swimming (11.2)	Running (19.6)
Breakfast biscuit with egg and sausage	581	447	112	71	52	30
Fast food hamburger, double patty with condiments	576	443	111	70	51	29
Chicken pot pie, frozen entrée, small pie	484	372	93	59	43	25
Pecan pie, commercially prepared, 1 piece	452	348	87	55	40	23
Tuna salad, 1 cup	383	295	74	47	34	20
Pork spareribs, 3 oz.	337	259	65	41	30	17
Turkey, roasted, 1 cup	238	183	46	29	21	12
Beef stew, canned, 1 cup	218	168	42	27	19	11
Rice, white, cooked, 1 cup	205	158	39	25	18	10
Salmon, cooked, 3 oz.	184	142	35	22	16	9
Pizza with cheese, 1 slice	140	108	27	17	12	7
Ice cream, vanilla, 1/2 cup	133	102	26	16	12	7
Cheese, cheddar, 1 oz.	114	88	22	14	10	6
Banana	105	81	20	13	9	5
Apple, raw, with skin	72	55	14	9	6	4

* Approximate. Varies according to rate of activity. For example, the faster a person walks, the greater the number of calories burned per minute.

Food Pyramids Healthy eating plans often are illustrated in the shape of pyramids that outline what to eat each day. Food that should be eaten in the largest quantities comprise the base of a pyramid; those that should be used sparingly make up the small tip of the pyramid.

The most familiar example is the Food Guide Pyramid established by the U.S. Department of Agriculture and Department of Health and Human Services. Others include the Mediterranean, Asian, and Latin American pyramids, the Vegetarian Diet Pyramid, and the Mayo Clinic Healthy Weight Pyramid.

Calories Calories measure the potential energy in the food we eat. Foods vary widely in caloric content, particularly when factors such as processing and condiments are taken into consideration. For instance, one cup of raw strawberries contains 53 calories; one cup of frozen, sweetened, sliced strawberries has 245 calories. Similarly, 1 cup of air-popped popcorn has 31 calories; a similar amount of caramel-coated popcorn has 152 calories.

The number of calories a person burns up during a typical day depends on age, sex, size, and activity level. Teenage boys, many active men, and some very active women consume about 2,800 calories a day. Most children, teenage girls, active women, and many sedentary men burn about 2,200 calories a day. Many sedentary women and some older adults burn about 1,600 calories a day.

If a person takes in more calories than are burned up, the excess is stored as fat. In general, an excess deposit of 3,500 calories equals one pound of fat. To get rid of this pound of fat, the person must burn up the 3,500 calories.

Weight Guidelines One of the most accurate ways to determine the correlation between weight and health risks is body mass index (BMI). A BMI of less than 18.5 is generally considered a signal that an adult is underweight. A health BMI for most adults is between 18.5 and 24.9. A BMI of 25 to 29.9 is considered overweight; one of 30 or more is considered obese. The higher the BMI, the greater the risk of cardiovascular disease, diabetes, cancer, premature death, and other health problems.

Weight-Loss Diets To lose weight, a person must eat fewer calories than he or she burns. How one attempts to do this varies tremendously. Some people use the slow and steady approach of dietary and lifestyle modifications—basically, eating less and exercising more. Others try weight-loss pills, fasting and other rapid-fire approaches, or one of the many weight-loss diets described in books or offered commercially. Some of the most popular weight-loss diets include:

The Atkins diet A high-fat, low-carbohydrate diet with few limits of the amount of food that can be eaten. In the first two weeks, carbohydrates are severely restricted. Without carbohydrates, the body burns stored body fat and goes into a state called ketosis, which tends to decrease appetite. After two weeks, fiber-rich carbohydrates are gradually added to the diet—but no refined sugar, milk, white rice, white potatoes, or products made with white flour.

Weight Watchers A diet in which each food is assigned a point value based on its caloric, fat, and dietary fiber content. For example: one cup of broccoli has 0 points, one slice of bread 2 points, one ounce of chocolate 4 points, and a 6-ounce steak 8 points. No foods are prohibited but the person is expected to eat only a certain number of points each day, based on body weight, with extra points earned by exercising. Weekly meetings in

What Counts as a Serving?

Grains Group
- 1 slice of bread
- 1 cup of ready-to-eat cereal
- 1/2 cup of cooked cereal, rice, or pasta

Vegetable Group
- 1 cup of raw leafy vegetables
- 1/2 cup of other vegetables cooked or raw
- 3/4 cup of vegetable juice

Fruit Group
- 1 medium apple, banana, orange, pear
- 1/2 cup of chopped, cooked, or canned fruit
- 3/4 cup of fruit juice

Milk Group
- 1 cup of milk or yogurt
- 1 1/2 ounces of natural cheese, such as Cheddar
- 2 ounces of processed cheese, such as American

Meat and Beans Group
- 2 to 3 ounces of cooked lean meat, poultry or fish
- 1/2 cup of cooked dry beans or __ cup of tofu counts as 1 ounce of lean meat
- 2 1/2-ounce soyburger or 1 egg counts as 1 ounce of lean meat
- 2 tablespoons of peanut butter or 1/3 cup of nuts counts as 1 ounce of meat

Source: U.S. Department of Agriculture.

which dieters receive support from one another are an important part of the program.

The Ornish Diet A high-fiber, low-fat vegetarian diet that consists mainly of grains, beans, vegetables, and fruits. Nonfat or very low-fat dairy products may be eaten in moderation; eating meat, oils, nuts and seeds, sugar, and most dairy products is discouraged. The quantity of calories is not considered critical but the sources of calories are; less than 10 percent should come from fats.

The Zone diet Somewhat higher in fats and proteins than traditional diets. An individual on the Zone obtains 40 percent of daily calories from carbohydrates such as beans and vegetables, 30 percent from low-fat proteins, and 30 percent from unsaturated fats. Saturated fats and carbohydrates that release glucose quickly (grains, bread, pasta, rice, etc.) are restricted.

All four of these diets have been found to be effective in shedding weight, though with an important caveat: a person needs to stick to the diet. Otherwise, he or she is likely to gain back the lost weight. In addition, the long-term health effects of diets that greatly restrict fat or carbohydrate intake have not yet been determined.

Body Mass Index

BMI	19	20	21	22	23	24	25	26	27	28	29	30	31	32	33	34	35
Height (in.)	Body Weight (pounds)*																
58	91	96	100	105	110	115	119	124	129	134	138	143	148	153	158	162	167
59	94	99	104	109	114	119	124	128	133	138	143	148	153	158	163	168	173
60	97	102	107	112	118	123	128	133	138	143	148	153	158	163	168	174	179
61	100	106	111	116	122	127	132	137	143	148	153	158	164	169	174	180	185
62	104	109	115	120	126	131	136	142	147	153	158	164	169	175	180	186	191
63	107	113	118	124	130	135	141	146	152	158	163	169	175	180	186	191	197
64	110	116	122	128	134	140	145	151	157	163	169	174	180	186	192	197	204
65	114	120	126	132	138	144	150	156	162	168	174	180	186	192	198	204	210
66	118	124	130	136	142	148	155	161	167	173	179	186	192	198	204	210	216
67	121	127	134	140	146	153	159	166	172	178	185	191	198	204	211	217	223
68	125	131	138	144	151	158	164	171	177	184	190	197	203	210	216	223	230
69	128	135	142	149	155	162	169	176	182	189	196	203	209	216	223	230	236
70	132	139	146	153	160	167	174	181	188	195	202	209	216	222	229	236	243
71	136	143	150	157	165	172	179	186	193	200	208	215	222	229	236	243	250
72	140	147	154	162	169	177	184	191	199	206	213	221	228	235	242	250	258
73	144	151	159	166	174	182	189	197	204	212	219	227	235	242	250	257	265
74	148	155	163	171	179	186	194	202	210	218	225	233	241	249	256	264	272
75	152	160	168	176	184	192	200	208	216	224	232	240	248	256	264	272	279
76	156	164	172	180	189	197	205	213	221	230	238	246	254	263	271	279	287

* Pounds are rounded off. Source: National Heart, Lung, and Blood Institute.

BIOGRAPHICAL DICTIONARY

Aaron, Henry (Hank), *b. Mobile, Ala., 1934.* **Baseball player.** Major-league baseball's all-time career home run leader, Aaron smacked 755 round-trippers in a 23-year (1954–76) career with the Milwaukee and Atlanta Braves and the Milwaukee Brewers. "Hammerin' Hank" also ranks first on the all-time lists for runs batted in (2,297) and total bases (6,856). An outstanding all-around player, he repeatedly led the National League in multiple hitting categories and won three Gold Glove awards for his play in the outfield. Aaron appeared in a record-tying 24 All-Star Games and was named the NL's MVP in 1957.

Abdul-Jabbar, Kareem (Lew Alcindor), *b. New York, N.Y., 1947.* **Basketball player.** Kareem Abdul-Jabbar combined height, skill, and athletic ability to become one of the top "big men" in basketball. As a collegian, the 7'2" center led UCLA to three straight NCAA titles, earning All-America honors three times and honored as College Player of the Year twice. As an N.B.A. star with the Milwaukee Bucks and Los Angeles Lakers, he scored the most points in league history (38,387) and was named M.V.P. a record six times. His teams won six N.B.A. championships (1971, 1980, 1982, 1985, 1987, 1988).

Abelard, Pierre, *b. Le Pallet, France, 1079; d. 1142.* **Philosopher and theologian.** Born into a wealthy family, Abelard gave up his aristocratic life to devote himself to the study of philosophy. Early on he distinguished himself with his work on the concept of universals. Later, he fell in love with and secretly married his student, Heloise. After incurring the anger of her uncle, Heloise entered a convent, and Abelard entered the monastic life, where he developed the use of dialectical analysis in philosophical argument.

Acheson, Dean Gooderham, *b. Middletown, Conn., 1893; d. 1971.* **American diplomat and lawyer.** As secretary of state (1949–1953) under President Harry S Truman, Acheson helped shape the postwar policy of containment of Soviet expansionism, including the Marshall Plan for rebuilding Europe and the North Atlantic Treaty Organization to oppose the Soviets militarily. Critics, however, faulted him for failures in Asia, including the Communist victory in China in 1949 and the invasion of South Korea by North Korea in 1950.

Adams, Ansel, *b. San Francisco, Calif., 1902; d. 1984.* **Photographer.** Best known for his technical expertise and innovations, and for documenting and preserving the landscape of the American West, Adams helped found the famous photography group f/64, was granted three Guggenheim Fellowships to photograph America's national parks and monuments, and spent much of his career working with the Sierra Club. Adams developed the zone system of metering and exposure, one of the most important photographic innovations of the 20th century. His best-known works include *Moonrise, Hernandez, New Mexico* (1942); *Mount Williamson* (1945); and countless images of Yosemite.

Adams, Henry, *b. Boston, 1838; d. 1918.* **Historian.** A direct descendant of two U.S. presidents, he eschewed politics in favor of law, then journalism, then history. His nine-volume *History of the United States of America* (1889–91), which covered the Jefferson and Madison administrations, was acclaimed as one of the finest pieces of historical writing. But he is best remembered for his Pulitzer Prize–winning autobiography, *The Education of Henry Adams* (1918).

Adams, John Quincy, *b. Braintree, Mass. 1767; d. 1848.* **Sixth U.S. president, 1825–29.** The first president's son to become president, John Quincy Adams spent his teens in Europe with his father, John Adams, on diplomatic missions for the new nation. As James Monroe's secretary of state, he purchased Florida from Spain, patched relations with Britain, and conceived the Monroe Doctrine. In 1824 Adams was chosen for the presidency by the House of Representatives, after losing both the popular vote and the electoral vote to Andrew Jackson. He was an unpopular president and failed to win a second term. Adams returned to politics in 1830 as congressman from Massachusetts, remaining a powerful antislavery leader until he collapsed and died on the House floor at age 80.

Adams, John, *b. Braintree, Mass., 1735; d. 1826.* **Second U.S. president, 1797–1801.** Adams gained attention by defending British soldiers brought to trial for the Boston Massacre in 1770. During the Revolution, he persuaded the Continental Congress to commission George Washington as commander in chief, declare independence, and put stars and stripes on the flag. Adams wrote the Massachusetts state constitution (1779), negotiated peace with Britain (1782), and served under Washington as the nation's first vice president. Elected president as a Federalist in 1796, Adams built up the navy and kept the peace, while also signing the controversial Alien and Sedition Acts (1798), which permitted the government to deport foreign-born residents and indict anyone who published "false, scandalous, and malicious" writings. Adams lived to see his son John Quincy Adams elected the sixth president in 1824.

Adams, Samuel, *b. Boston, 1722; d. 1803.* **Leader in American Revolution, governor of Massachusetts.** Second cousin to John Adams, he was an early voice in the fight against taxation without representation, helping to encourage the Stamp Act riots. A skillful propagandist, Adams was leader of the Massachusetts radicals and made independence his goal. He helped organize the Boston Tea Party, and he was a member of the provincial congress of Massachusetts and the First Continental Congress, in which capacity he signed the Declaration of Independence. Adams also helped draft the Massachusetts constitution of 1780 and served as both lieutenant governor and governor of the state.

Addams, Jane, *b. Cedarville, Ill., 1860; d. 1935.* **Social reformer.** In 1889, Addams founded Hull House, a pioneering facility that offered education, vocational training, child care, legal aid, and recreational facilities to anyone in need. Her success inspired the settlement house movement, which brought social services to poor urban areas throughout the United States. Addams also spoke out on women's suffrage and labor reform, lobbying for more humane laws governing child labor, juvenile justice, industrial safety, and exploitation of immigrants. A committed peace activist, she campaigned against U.S. entry into World War I and won the Nobel Peace Prize in 1931.

Aeschylus, *b. 524 B.C.; d. 456 B.C.* **Playwright.** The oldest of the three great playwrights of ancient Greece. Aeschylus's *Oresteia* (458 B.C.) trilogy is considered his masterpiece, exemplifying his concerns with justice, cycles of violence, and the importance of civic law. Of his more than 90 plays, only seven survive intact. These include *The Persians* (472 B.C.), *The Suppliants* (c. 463 B.C.), and *Prometheus Bound* (undated). Aeschylus is credited with introducing a second actor to the Greek stage, which in turn allowed dialogue to take place between actors rather than only with the chorus.

Akbar (Abu al-Fath Jalal al-Din Muhammad Akbar), *b. Umarkot, India, 1542; d. 1605.* **Mogul emperor.** Akbar, who assumed power in 1556, was the greatest of the Mogul emperors. The Moguls were descended from the Mongolian tribesmen who had conquered much of Asia in the 13th century. By the 16th century, the Moguls had accepted Islam and were enthusiastic patrons of literature and the arts. At first, Akbar ruled a small area—Punjab and the area around Delhi—but his power quickly spread across the entire Indian subcontinent. He introduced administrative reforms that increased centralization, and he insisted that subject peoples were treated fairly, with religious tolerance for all.

Akhenaton, *r. ca. 1351–34 B.C.* **Egyptian pharaoh.** An 18th-dynasty (New Kingdom) king, Amenhotep IV changed his name to Akhenaton—"He who serves the Aton"—to reflect his worship of a unitary god which, unusually for Egyptian deities, had no human or animal form. Although particulars of the worship are not known, Aton is often regarded as the first manifestation of a monotheistic god. Akhenaton and his wife, Nefertiti, moved from Thebes to Tell el-Amarna, and the empire declined during his rule, because of Akhenaton's preoccupation with his worship of Aton. He was succeeded by his more traditionalist son-in-law, Tutankhamen.

Albee, Edward (Franklin), *b. Virginia, 1928.* **Playwright.** An adopted member of the Albee theater management family, Albee rose to prominence with such plays as the one-act "The Zoo Story" (1959) and "The American Dream" (1961) and the full-length *Who's Afraid of Virginia Woolf* (1962) that plumb the emotional and intellectual depths of individuals trapped together and trapped within American society. The sustained, brilliant but corrosive dialogue of *Virginia Woolf* established him as a major American dramatist. It was followed by *Tiny Alice* (1964). Three later plays, *A Delicate Balance* (1966), *Seascape* (1975) and *Three Tall Women* (1991) won Pulitzer Prizes.

Albertus Magnus, *b. Lauingen an der Donau, Germany, ca. 1200; d. 1280.* **Philosopher, canonized 1931.** The teacher of St. Thomas Aquinas, Albertus, a Dominican bishop, was a philosopher as well as an innovator in the study of the natural world. He brought Aristotelian knowledge to contemporary scientific thought, creating a precedent for the study of science within the Christian church.

Aldrin, Buzz (Edwin Eugene Aldrin, Jr.), *b. Montclair, N.J., 1930.* **Astronaut.** An Air Force pilot who flew dozens of combat missions in Korea, Aldrin earned a Ph.D. from M.I.T. before joining the U.S. space program. As part of the 1966 Gemini 12 flight, Aldrin took a historic 5 1/2-hour walk in space, demonstrating that humans could survive in its vacuum. In 1969, Aldrin, Neil Armstrong, and Michael Collins formed the crew of Apollo 11. In a separate landing vehicle, Armstrong and Aldrin touched down near the Sea of Tranquillity and became the first humans to walk on the moon.

Alexander the Great, *b. Pelle, Macedonia, 356 B,C,: d. 323B.C.* **Macedonian King.** Alexander, who became king of Macedonia in 336 B.C., was one of the greatest military leaders in history. He conquered Greece in 335 B.C., then invaded Persia at the head of a Greek and Macedonian army. He defeated the Persians at the battle of Issus (in modern Turkey) in 333 B.C. The next year Alexander seized Egypt. In 331 B.C., he again defeated the Persians and marched east, arriving in 326 B.C. on the banks of the Indus River. On his death, at age 33, his empire collapsed into several warring states ruled by his generals, who continued Alexander's policy of hellenizing subject populations.

Ali, Muhammad (Cassius Clay), *b. Louisville, Ky., 1942.* **Boxer.** After winning a gold medal at the 1960 Olympics, he won the heavyweight crown with a surprise knockout of Sonny Liston in 1964. A Black Muslim, he changed his name to Muhammad Ali and was stripped of his title for refusing to fight in the Vietnam War (a decision that was eventually reversed in court). Ali won back the belt in 1974 (defeating George Foreman in Zaire in the heavily hyped "Rumble in the Jungle") and again in 1978. Career highlights included three classic bouts with Joe Frazier, including the "Thrilla in Manila" in 1975. Parkinson's disease eventually robbed Ali of the irrepressible wit and graceful motion that were his trademarks.

Allen, Woody (Allen Stewart Konigsberg), *b. Brooklyn, N.Y., 1935.* **American movie director, writer, and actor.** After writing jokes for television and doing standup comedy, he directed film comedies of angst and sex. His multiple Oscar-winner *Annie Hall* (1977) marked a turn toward more sophisticated romantic fare, including *The Purple Rose of Cairo* (1985), *Hannah and Her Sisters* (1986), and *Radio Days* (1987). In a scenario of life imitating art, his messy breakup with Mia Farrow became tabloid fodder.

Ambrose (Saint), *b. Trier, Gaul, 339 or 340; d. 397.* **Bishop,** theologian, Father of the Roman Catholic Church. Raised and educated in Rome, Ambrose became a provincial governor and, though a layman, was persuaded to become bishop of Milan in 374. He then took holy orders and became a great defender of the faith against the Arian heresy, which denied the divinity of Christ. He also established the authority of the church over the emperors in issues of faith and morality. Though Ambrose was not a speculative theologian, his powerful sermons critically influenced Augustine's conversion and were incorporated into books of biblical commentary, including the *Hexaemeron.* His hymns, original in form, helped establish that Christian musical tradition.

Amundsen, Roald, *b. Borge, Norway, 1872; d. 1928.* **Polar explorer.** In 1897–99, Amundsen sailed with Adrien de Gerlachei's *Belgica* expedition—the first to winter in Antarctica—to locate the southern magnetic pole. He was the first person to transit the Northwest Passage (1903–06). In 1910, Amundsen sailed the *Fram* to the coast of Antarctica and with four companions was the first to reach the South Pole, on December 16, 1911. He later transited the Northeast Passage from Norway to Alaska (1918–20), and in 1925 he flew a dirigible over the North Pole. He died when another dirigible crashed in the Arctic.

Andersen, Hans Christian, *b. 1805, Odense, Denmark; d. 1875.* **Fairy-tale writer, novelist, poet.** Andersen grew up poor and intended to be an actor. In 1829 he published a successful travel fantasy, followed, with little success, by plays and, with better success, novels, beginning with *Improvisatoren* (1835). These works are little known outside Denmark, but his fairy tales, which he began publishing in 1835 and produced prolifically throughout his life, are among the most widely read writings in the world. He was an innovatively compelling storyteller, and his tales range from tragically troubling to optimistically triumphant. Among them are "The Ugly Duckling," "The Snow Queen," "The Little Mermaid" and "The Red Shoes."

Anderson, Marian, *b. Philadelphia, Pa., 1897; d. 1993.* **Singer.** Considered the greatest contralto of her era, Anderson was barred from many U.S. venues because she was black. In 1939, after successful European tours, Anderson planned a concert in Washington's Constitution Hall, owned by the Daughters of the American Revolution.

When the D.A.R. refused Anderson, Eleanor Roosevelt resigned from the organization in protest. Denied her stage, Anderson performed at the Lincoln Memorial for 75,000 fans. In 1955, she became the first African American to perform with New York's Metropolitan Opera. Anderson became a goodwill ambassador for the United States and won the Presidential Medal of Freedom (1963).

Anderson, Sherwood, *b. Camden, Ohio, 1876; d. 1941.* **Writer.** Short-story writer whose work influenced writers such as Ernest Hemingway and William Faulkner. His fiction, characterized by patterns of everyday speech and a deep connection to place, is exemplified by his most famous work, *Winesburg, Ohio* (1919), a series of interrelated short stories narrated by a newspaper reporter and all taking place in the fictionalized town of its title.

Ando, Tadeo, *b. Osaka, Japan, 1941.* **Architect.** Ando is self-taught and has no degree in architecture but has read deeply—especially the works of Le Corbusier—and traveled widely, filling sketchbooks with what he has seen. His early buildings were houses, including Azuma House (1977), a small row house in Osaka. Later buildings embody concrete cast in stark geometrical forms and include the Chikatsu-Asuka Historical Museum (1990–94) in Osaka and Church of the Light (1989) in Ibaraki. He won the Pritzker Prize in 1995.

Andrea Palladio, *b. Padua, 1508; d. 1580.* **Italian architect and architectural theorist of the Renaissance.** Of all his contemporaries, he had the longest-lasting influence. In 1536 he was given an opportunity to study the ancient classical buildings in Rome, and his careful measurements, calculations of proportions, and drawings formed the basis of his later seminal buildings and writings. He designed grand houses and churches in Vicenza and Venice, but it is his villas in and around Vicenza that have had the most influence. Among these are the Villa Capra (1560's), known as the Rotonda, and the Villa Barbaro (1550's) in Maser. "Palladian" has entered the lexicon as a term to describe countless buildings ever since. His influence was also spread by his *Four Books on Architecture*, a theoretical work of idealized buildings that ranks among the most important written works in architecture.

Angelico, Fra (Fra Giovanni da Fiesole; Guido di Piero da Mugello), *b. near Vicchio, Italy, c. 1395–1400; d. 1455.* **Painter, illuminator and Dominican friar.** Fra Angelico was one of Florence's most sought-after artists of the early Renaissance. His style, though somewhat conservative, was influenced by Masaccio, and he is admired for strong three-dimensional spatial compositions. He is best known for fresco cycles at the Vatican and St. Peter's in Rome, as well as his fresco of *The Annunciation* (c. 1440–50) at the monastery of S. Marco in Florence.

Angelou, Maya, (Marguerite Johnson), *b. St. Louis, Mo., 1928.* **Poet and memoirist.** Honored throughout her long and prolific career for her poetry, autobiographical work, and contributions to the chronicling of the African-American experience, Angelou, in her early life, also worked as an actor and dancer, traveling throughout Europe and living for a time in Egypt and Ghana, where she worked on the *African Review.* Her memoir, *I Know Why the Caged Bird Sings* (1970), details the racial oppression and violence of her childhood in rural Arkansas. Later memoirs include *The Heart of a Woman* (1981), and *All God's Children Need Traveling Shoes* (1986).

Anthony, Susan B., *b. Adams, Mass., 1820; d. 1906.* **Feminist social reformer.** Working with Elizabeth Cady Stanton, Anthony campaigned successfully to expand New York's Married Women's Property Law (1848), which granted women the right to own property. During the Civil War, they formed the first national women's organization, which also lobbied for a constitutional amendment guaranteeing freedom to African Americans. In 1869, they founded the National Woman Suffrage Association. Anthony cast a ballot in the 1872 presidential election, an act of defiance that landed her in jail. Her crusade for female suffrage succeeded 14 years after her death.

Antony, Mark (Latin: Marcus Antonius), *b. ca. 82 B.C.; d. 30 B.C.* **Roman general and statesman.** Mark Antony was a general under Julius Caesar and a member of the Second Triumvirate along with Octavian (Augustus) and Lepidus after Caesar's assassination. Antony formed an alliance with Cleopatra in Egypt (41 B.C.), but returned to Rome and married Octavian's sister. In 32 B.C. the triumvirate defeated Brutus and Cassius and divided the empire among themselves. When the triumvirate disintegrated, Antony fled to Egypt. He and Cleopatra were defeated by Octavian's forces in the battle of Actium in 31 B.C. and he committed suicide the next year after being falsely told of Cleopatra's death. She too subsequently committed suicide.

Aquinas, Thomas (Saint), *b. Rocca Secca (by Naples), c. 1225; d. 1274.* **Theologian and philosopher.** The greatest figure of scholasticism, a saint of the church, and the founder of what Pope Leo XIII (1879) declared to be the official philosophy of Roman Catholicism. His system, as expressed in the *Summa Theologica* (1267–73) and other writings, is based on the works of Aristotle. The universe is seen as an ordered construct of things, ascending to God, the only necessary and self-sufficient being. The truths of faith and reason are complementary; there are no conflicts between theology and science or philosophy.

Arafat, Yasir (Muhammad 'Abd ar-Ra'uf al-Qudwah al-Husayni), *b. Cairo?, 1929.* **Palestinian political leader.** The founder of Fatah, one of the main military components of the Palestinian Liberation Organization, Arafat became PLO chairman in 1969, and leader of its political arm in 1973. His efforts at diplomacy in the Middle East won him a share of the Nobel Peace Prize (in 1994, with Israel's Yitzhak Rabin and Shimon Peres) and the presidency of the Palestinian Authority (in 1996), but never a lasting peace with Israel nor a full transition to Palestinian self-rule.

Archimedes, *b. ca. 287 B.C., d. ca. 212 B.C.* **Greek mathematician, physicist, and inventor.** Archimedes spent most of his life in Syracuse (on Sicily). He developed the mathematical theory of simple machines, such as the lever and pulley, as well as the basic law of hydrostatics and applied these laws to build practical devices. Archimedes showed how to write numbers as great as one could desire and how to find the areas bounded by parabolic curves. He considered his greatest achievement to be the discovery of how to calculate the volume of a sphere by comparing it with a similar-sized cylinder.

Aristophanes, *b. ca. 448 B.C.; d. ca. 388 B.C.* **Greek playwright.** Considered the greatest comic poet of his time, Aristophanes wrote the only complete existing examples of Greek Old Comedy. Little is known about his life, but Athens became his home and its politics, society, and prominent figures were the subjects of his satire. Aristophanes parodied everything from Socrates and the sophists in *The Clouds* (423 B.C.) to the Peloponnesian War in *Lysistrata* (411 B.C.), in which the women of Athens boycott their husbands until a peace is reached. The other nine of his 11 surviving plays, out of possibly 50 attributed to him, are *The Acharnians* (425 B.C.), *The Knights* (424 B.C.), *The Wasps* (422 B.C.), *The Peace* (421 B.C.), *The Birds* (414 B.C.), *The Thesmophoriazusae* (*The Women at Demeter's Festival*, 411 B.C.), *The Frogs* (405 B.C.), *The Ecclesiazusae* (*The Women in Politics*, 392 B.C.), and *The Plutus* (388 B.C.).

Armstrong, Lance, *b. Dallas, Tx., 1971.* **Cyclist.** Lance Armstrong reached the pinnacle of international road racing only after overcoming a near-fatal case of cancer. After undergoing surgery and intensive chemotherapy treatments for testicular cancer, he returned to training and, in 1999, became only the second American to win the Tour de France. In 2004, he won the Tour de France a sixth straight time, breaking the record for the most Tour victories in history.

Armstrong, Louis Daniel, *b. New Orleans, La., 1901; d. 1971.* **Jazz trumpeter and vocalist.** Also known as "Pops" and "Satchmo." The first important soloist and arguably the most influential musician in the history of jazz. Armstrong's virtuoso trumpet playing, beginning with his Hot Five and Hot Seven ensembles, featured dynamic, brassy, highly imaginative improvisation. He was also the first singer to scat sing on record ("Heebie Jeebies," 1926), when he purportedly dropped his lyric sheet while recording and was forced to improvise nonsense lyrics. Other important recordings include "Muskrat Ramble" (1926), "West End Blues" (1928), "Chinatown, My Chinatown" (1932), and "When the Saints Go Marching In" (1939).

Armstrong, Neil Alden *b. Wapakoneta, Ohio, 1930.* **Astronaut.** A Navy pilot during the Korean War, Armstrong became a test pilot for the National Advisory Committee for Aeronautics, which developed into the National Aeronautics and Space Administration (NASA). Armstrong piloted the first manual docking in space as commander of *Gemini* 8 in 1966. Three years later, on July 20th, Armstrong made world history by becoming the first man to set foot on the surface of the Moon, declaring the accomplishment "...one small step for man, one giant leap for mankind."

Arnold, Benedict, *b. Norwich, Conn., 1741; d. 1801.* **American military leader in the Revolutionary War.** Arnold distinguished himself in engagements against the English but became embittered over slow promotions and fell into debt. He offered his services to the English in 1779 in exchange for a high command and a substantial fee. His treason was discovered, and he went over to the English, commanding engagements in Virginia and Connecticut. After the war he was shunned by London society and his name became synonymous with treason.

Arnold, Matthew, *b. Laleham, England, 1822; d. 1888.* **Poet, critic, essayist.** Arnold composed one of the most beloved English poems, "Dover Beach" (ca. 1851), emblematic of the Victorians' loss of spiritual certainty, as well as "The Forsaken Merman" (1849), "The Scholar Gypsy" (1853), and "Thyrsis" (1866). As a poet he expressed alienation, but as a critic—in *Essays in Criticism* (1865, 1888) and *The Study of Poetry* (1880)— he praised uplifting literature that gives value to human life. He wrote extensively about society and culture (*Culture and Anarchy*, 1869). "Culture" was for him encompassed an openness of mind and appreciation of the arts necessary to combat middle-class "Philistinism."

Arthur, Chester A., *b. Fairfield, Vt., 1829; d. 1886.* **Twenty-first U.S. president, 1881–85.** A true machine politician, Arthur worked for Republican candidates in New York and enjoyed several patronage jobs during the Civil War. President Grant appointed him collector of the port of New York in 1871, and Arthur prospered there until 1879. In 1880 "Half-Breed" Republicans nominated him for vice president; he acceded to the presidency on Sept. 19, 1881, after James A. Garfield was assassinated. Arthur rooted out post office graft and signed the Pendleton Civil Service Act (1883) that established the tradition of permanent federal employment based on merit rather than party affiliation, but Democrats in Congress thwarted the rest of Arthur's initiatives.

Astaire, Fred (Fredrick E. Austerlitz Jr.), *b. Omaha, Neb., 1899; d. 1987.* **Dancer, actor, singer, and film star.** Astaire began his career as a child star working with his sister, Adele. In 1917–31, they were regulars on Broadway, starring in a number of classic shows, including *Oh, Lady Be Good* (1924) and *Funny Face* (1927). Astaire went to Hollywood in 1933, where he was partnered with Ginger Rogers, and the two became icons in a series of dance-musicals, notably *Top Hat* (1935), which established Astaire's debonair image. Astaire's success continued with a number of partners after World War II, on film, record, and television. His seemingly near-effortless style inspired thousands to study in the ballroom studios that bore his name.

Ataturk, Kemal (Mustafa Kemal), *b. 1881 Salonika (now Thessaloníki); d. 1938.* **Turkish leader.** Ataturk, whose last name means "father of Turks," founded the Republic of Turkey and was its first president (1922–38). As a soldier, he patched together the Turkish forces of the vanquished Ottoman Empire at the end of World War I and repelled invasions by Greece, Britain, France, and Italy. As president, he encouraged national and ethnic pride while simultaneously implementing reforms that laid the groundwork for democracy, modernization of the legal and educational systems, and adoption of the Latin alphabet and European-style names.

Attila, *b. 406?; d. 453.* **King of the Huns.** Attila the Hun, also called the Scourge of God, ruled a vast territory extending at one time from Germany well into Asia. Attila ruled from 434 to 445 with his brother, whom he murdered, and then alone until his own death in 453. Attila is best known for his savagery and ongoing conflicts with the Roman Empire, particularly his invasions of Gaul (451) and northern Italy (452). Although he was defeated in Gaul, he moved on to sack many cities in northern Italy; he nearly invaded Rome but for a shortage of provisions and the mediation of Pope Leo I. After Attila's death his empire disintegrated.

Auden, W(ystan) H(ugh), *b. 1907, York, England; d. 1973.* **English-American poet.** In his early career Auden was one of a group of English poets dedicated to new techniques and leftist politics. He attacked his country's social and economic system before settling in New York, where he wrote his famous ruminative poem on the outbreak of World War II, "September 1st, 1939." He was a poet of versatile style, simple yet haunting diction, and a range of themes from love to art to politics; his sensibility combined modern psychological insight and homosexual orientation with Catholic faith. Other noted poems are "Spain 1937," "Lay Your Sleeping Head, My Love," "Musée des Beaux Arts" and "In Memory of W. B. Yeats."

Augustine (of Hippo), *b. 354, Tagaste, Numidia, North Africa; d. 430.* **Roman Catholic theologian, saint, Church father, and doctor.** In his youth, Augustine took a mistress and joined the Manichaean sect—a period lamented in his *Confessions* (401). In Italy after 376, Augustine was influenced by Plato, and, inspired by St. Ambrose, Bishop of Milan, he embraced Christianity in 387. He became a priest and was bishop of Hippo, in Africa, about 395. A strenuous apologist in a sectarian age, he produced profuse writings that are fundamental to Christian teaching, emphasizing the Fall of Man and his dependence on God's saving grace. *City of God* (413–26) is his great apologetic work and treatise on God and history. *On the Trinity* (400–16) is his greatest dogmatic work.

Augustus, (Gaius Octavius, or Octavian) *b. 63 B.C.; d. A.D. 14* , **great-nephew and heir of Julius Caesar, became the first Roman emperor in 27 B.C.** His reign ushered in a period of peace and prosperity for Rome and the golden age of Latin literature. Upon Caesar's murder by the Roman Senate in 44 B.C., Octavian returned to Rome to avenge Caesar's death. He joined Mark Antony and Lepidus to form the Second Triumvirate and defeat their rivals Brutus and Cassius in 42 B.C. When Antony joined forces with Cleopatra in Egypt, Octavian fought and defeated him at the Battle of Actium in 31 B.C., becoming sole ruler, although he kept up the guise of republican rule as princeps civitatis, or "first citizen," until 27 B.C., when he was renamed Augustus. After his death he was deified, leaving behind a system of government that remained in place for centuries.

Austen, Jane, *b. Steventon, Hampshire, England,1775; d. 1817.* **Novelist.** Austen lived and wrote almost anonymously in her family's home. Focusing on young women and their families and the urgency of arranging appropriate marriages, her novels are revered for their precision of language and form; skillful, often satirical, delineation of character and society; and combination of comic intelligence and moral seriousness are fully achieved within a small frame. Her first book, *Sense and Sensibility,* begun in her early twenties, was not published until 1811. It was followed by *Pride and Prejudice* (1813), *Mansfield Park* (1814), *Emma* (1816), *Persuasion,* and *Northanger Abbey* (both 1818).

Austin, Stephen Fuller, *b. Wythe County, Tex., 1793; d. 1836.* **American political leader in early Texas.** Austin founded a settlement in Texas in 1822 and in 1833 went to Mexico City to persuade the Mexican government to grant the settlers self-government. The Mexicans jailed him when he urged the settlers not to wait but to set up their own government. He returned to Texas in 1835 and went to Washington, D.C., where he won military and financial support for the Republic of Texas. He was secretary of state in Sam Houston's cabinet in 1836.

Bach, Johann Sebastian, *b. Eisenach, 1685; d. 1750.* **German composer and organist of the Baroque period.** Bach was the most important member of a large musical family. He was married twice and fathered 20 children, including his sons Carl Philipp Emanuel and Johann Christian, also noted composers. During his life he was best known as an organist and as music director in Leipzig. Later generations discovered that his musical genius perfectly balanced technical mastery, intellectual control, and an almost limitless inventiveness. Notable works include the *Brandenburg Concertos,* Concerto in D Minor for Two Violins, Toccata and Fugue in D Minor, *Die Kunst der Fuge* (*The Art of Fugue*), *Die Wohltemperierte Klavier* (*The Well-Tempered Klavier*), *Goldberg Variations, St. John Passion, St. Matthew Passion,* Cantata No. 140 (*Wachet auf*) (he wrote over 300 cantatas), and Mass in B Minor.

Bacon, Francis, *b. London, 1561; d. 1626.* **Philosopher, writer, statesman.** In public life Bacon became lord chancellor (1618) at the court of James I; dismissed because of bribery charges, he retired to his estate to write. His philosophical work, a foundation of the scientific revolution, is found in the *Novum Organum* (1620) and other books. In opposition to older a priori methods of scholasticism, Bacon championed the inductive method of science, arguing that scientific theories should arise only from careful observation and experiment. His best-known literary works are the *Essays* (1597–1625).

Baker, James Addison, III, *b. Houston, Tex., 1930.* **American statesman.** Baker became under secretary of commerce under President Gerald R. Ford in 1975 and was White House chief of staff (1981–85) under President Ronald Reagan. He was secretary of the treasury (1985–88) in the second Reagan administration and became secretary of state under President George H. W. Bush (1989–92). As secretary of state he served during the Persian Gulf War (1990–91) and organized a Middle East peace conference in 1991.

Balanchine, George (Georgi Melitonovich Balanchivadze), *b. St. Petersburg, Russia, 1904; d. 1983.* **Choreographer and cofounder of the New York City Ballet.** Balanchine studied at Russia's Imperial Theater, first choreographing as a student in 1919. He made his first European tour in 1924 as a dancer/choreographer with Diaghilev's Ballets Russes, remaining with the company for five years. In 1933, he was invited to the U.S. by dance promoter Lincoln Kirstein; a year later, they co-founded the School of American Ballet. The two formed a number of short-lived companies through the 1930's and early 1940's until finally, in 1948, they successfully established the New York City Ballet, for which Balanchine became principal choreographer. Among Balanchine's best known dances are *Serenade* (1934), *Orpheus* (1948), *Agon* (1957), *Jewels* (1967), and *Union Jack* (1976).

Balboa, Vasco Núñez de, *b. Jerez de los Caballeros, Spain, 1475; d. 1519.* **Explorer and conquistador.** Balboa arrived on the Caribbean coast of South America in 1501. In 1510, he founded Darien, Panama, the oldest permanent European settlement on the American mainland. In 1513, he led an expedition across the mountains of Panama and was the first European to see the Pacific; he claimed it and all the lands it touched for Spain. In 1516, he led another expedition that transported two ships from the Caribbean to the Pacific. Accused of treason, he and four allies were beheaded in Panama in 1519.

Baldwin, James, *b. New York City, 1924; d. 1987.* **Novelist, essayist, and playwright.** Baldwin was the child of a poor African-American family in Harlem. He left New York City for Paris in 1948 and first rose to literary prominence in 1953 with the publication of his autobiographical *Go Tell It on the Mountain,* one of the first novels to reveal the pain of racism. Returning off and on to the United States until the time of his death, Baldwin was a participant in the civil rights movement; most of his essays (collected in *Notes of a Native Son*, 1955; *The Fire Next Time*, 1963) and dramatic works (*Blues for Mr. Charlie*, 1964) are powerful commentaries on civil rights and racism.

Ball, Lucille, *b. Jamestown, N. Y., 1911; d. 1989.* **Actress.** One of television's best-loved entertainers, Lucille Ball was also one of most powerful executives in show business. She started out as a Ziegfeld girl, then moved to Hollywood and worked her way up from bit parts to lead roles in B-movies. Stardom seemed to have passed her by, but at the age of 40 she moved from movies to television and starred with her husband, Desi Arnaz, in the pioneering sitcom *I Love Lucy* (1951–57), in which she was finally able to display her genius for slapstick comedy. As owner of Desilu Productions, she was the first woman to head a Hollywood studio.

Baltimore, David, *b. New York City, 1938.* **American scientist and university president.** Baltimore studied the action of viruses in causing cancer, work that has been valuable in treating AIDS. He shared the Nobel Prize in Physiology or Medicine in 1975. He became president of Rockefeller University in 1990 but was forced to resign in 1991 in a controversy over charges that a paper that he had cowritten included fabricated data. In 1996 the fraud charges were rejected by a federal court and in 1997 he became president of the California Institute of Technology.

Balzac, Honoré de, *b. Tours, France, 1799; d. 1850.* **Novelist and short story writer.** A prolific novelist, Balzac wrote for years under various pseudonyms before publishing his first novel under his own name (*Les Chouans*, 1829). He is considered the founder of realism and an innovator in the use of the omniscient point of view, and his work displayed keen observations about French society. His works are collected in the 24 volume *Comédie humaine* (1869–76).

Baraka, Amiri (LeRoi Jones), *b. Newark, N.J., 1934.* **Poet and Playwright.** Baraka first rose to prominence in the 1960's with his collection of poetry, *Preface to a Twenty Volume Suicide Note* (1961), and his play *Dutchman* (1964), His early work focused on African-American rage at racial oppression, and on black nationalism. He went on to found the Black Arts Repertory Theatre in Harlem in 1965. He has published prolifically, counting among his works several volumes of poetry, plays, collections of essays, and short stories.

Bardeen, John, *b. Madison, Wis. 1908; d. 1991.* **American physicist.** In 1947 at Bell Telephone Laboratories, Bardeen, with William Bradford Schockley and Walter H. Brittain, developed the first transistor that eventually replaced larger vacuum tubes, which consumed more power, in electronic applications from consumer products to the emerging computer industry. The three received the Nobel Prize in Physics in 1956. Bardeen's later studies of superconductivity won him a second Nobel Prize in 1972, making him only the scientist to receive two Nobel Prizes in the same field.

Barnard, Christiaan, *b. South Africa, 1922; d. 2001.* **Surgeon** At Groote Schuur Hospital in Cape Town, Barnard caused an international sensation in 1967 when he performed the world's first heart transplant on a human being. His patient, a middle-aged diabetic with incurable heart disease, received the heart of a young accident victim and died 18 days later. But the surgery was a milestone, and its success rate improved markedly by the 1980's, after new drugs were developed to fight the body's rejection of donor organs.

Barnum, P. T. (Phineas Taylor), *b. Bethel, Conn., 1810; d. 1891.* **American showman.** In 1841 Barnum bought Scudder's American Museum in New York City, where he exhibited the midget General Tom Thumb, and the Siamese twins Chang and Eng. In 1871 he created an innovative traveling circus with animals, including Jumbo the elephant, and freaks, and called it "The Greatest Show on Earth." He merged his circus in 1881 with another owned by James Anthony Bailey. The Barnum and Bailey Circus traveled in the United States and abroad and became known internationally.

Barrymore, Ethel (Ethel Blythe), *b. Philadelphia, Pa. 1879; d. 1959.* **Actress.** The "first lady of American theater," Ethel Barrymore had style and wit that made her a star of stage, screen, vaudeville, radio, and television. Her best-known stage roles were in *Alice Sit by the Fire* (1905) and *The Corn Is Green* (1940–42). She won an Academy Award for her supporting role in *None but the Lonely Heart* (1944). In 1928, she appeared in *The Kingdom of God*, the first production staged at New York's Ethel Barrymore Theater.

Barrymore, Lionel (Lionel Blythe), *b. Philadelphia, Pa. 1878; d. 1954.* **Actor.** The oldest son in the first family of American theater, Lionel Barrymore was a star of stage, screen, and radio, as well as a musician and artist. A well-regarded character actor, he is remembered for screen roles in *Captains Courageous* (1937), *Key Largo* (1948), and more than a dozen Dr. Kildare films. He won an Academy Award as Best Actor of 1931 for *A Free Soul*.

Barton, Clara (Clarissa), *b. Oxford, Mass., 1821; d. 1912.* **Founder of the American Red Cross.** During the Civil War, Barton was the "angel of the battlefield," nursing the wounded and navigating enemy lines to deliver supplies. Relief work in Europe during the Franco German War introduced Barton to the International Red Cross. She returned home in 1873, and successfully lobbied for the U.S. to sign the Geneva Convention, allowing medics to treat those wounded in battle and mandating humane treatment for prisoners of war. In 1881, Barton organized the American Association of the Red Cross. She served as its president until 1904, expanding its mission to assist victims of natural disasters.

Baruch, Bernard Mannes, *b. Camden, S.C., 1870; d. 1965.* **American financier.** Speculating on Wall Street (1891–1912), Baruch became immensely wealthy;he then had the leisure to consult on financial and other matters with several generations of American political leaders, beginning with Woodrow Wilson. Before and during World War I he helped find ways of financing war industries, and later, in the administration of Franklin D. Roosevelt, he helped shape economic policies. He continued to offer advice during World War II and in 1946 President Harry S. Truman appointed him ambassador to the United Nations Atomic Energy Commission.

Baryshnikov, Mikhail, *b. Riga, Latvia, 1948.* **Ballet star.** Baryshnikov studied in Riga and then at the Vaganova School in Leningrad, becoming a principal dancer with the Kirov Ballet In 1967–74. He defected while touring Canada in 1974 and was immediately engaged by American Ballet Theatre as a principal dancer; with the exception of one year at New York City Ballet (1978–79), he remained with ABT through 1989, becoming its artistic director in 1980. In 1990, he founded the White Oak Dance Project. He has also appeared in several Hollywood films, and on television as a dramatic actor.

Baudelaire, Charles Pierre, *b. 1821, Paris; d. 1867.* **Poet and critic.** Baudelaire published only one book of poems, *Les Fleurs du Mal* (*Flowers of Evil*), which appeared in 1857 and was expanded in 1861 and 1868. Its bold, sensuous contents introduced French symbolism and defined the beginning of modernism in French poetry. In it he developed a theory of "correspondences" among the senses, and, as its title suggests, explored beauty's evanescence and closeness to decay and evil. Six of its poems were banned as obscene. Baudelaire, whose life was troubled by spiritual, physical and financial turmoil, was also an important critic of literature and art. A volume of his prose poems was published posthumously.

Beard, James, *b. Portland, Ore., 1903; d. 1985.* **Chef.** Beard revolutionized American cooking with his emphasis on fine food prepared with fresh local ingredients. Beard appeared on television's first cooking segment on NBC in 1946; he went on to countless TV and radio appearances, wrote regular food columns for several national magazines, and penned more than a dozen cookbooks. In 1955, he established the James Beard School, one of the world's premier culinary institutes. The foundation bearing Beard's name continues to bestow the most prestigious annual culinary awards in America on the nation's top chefs, restaurants, and cookbooks.

Beardsley, Aubrey (Vincent), *b. Brighton, England, 1872; d. 1898.* **Draftsman and writer.** Beardsley was mentored by the artist Sir Edward Burne-Jones and was a member of the aesthetic movement. His black-and-white ink drawings were influenced by the pre-Raphaelites, art nouveau, and Japanese prints, and often shocked critics with their curious combination of sensual and grotesque elements. Beardsley died of tuberculosis. His work includes *Hamlet patris manem sequiiur* [sic] ("Hamlet following the Ghost of His Father"), (1891), *Salome* (1892), and *A Footnote* (self-portrait) (1896).

Becket,Thomas á, (Thomas of London), *b. London, c. 1118; d. 1170.* Chancellor of England (1155–62) and archbishop of Canterbury (1162–70). As chancellor, he was a favorite of King Henry II. But after his consecration, believing he had to answer to a higher authority, Becket publicly opposed the king's attempt to exert royal authority over the Catholic Church. Becket lived in exile in France (1164–70), but on his return to Canterbury, he was murdered by knights of Henry's court. The matyred Becket was canonized in 1173; his shrine was the object of Catholic pilgrimages for centuries until Henry VIII had it destroyed.

Beckett, Samuel, *b. Dublin, Ireland, 1906; d, 1989.* **Playwright, novelist, short-story writer.** Considered the leading "absurdist writer," Beckett won the Nobel Prize in Literature in 1969, He first achieved worldwide recognition with the production of his play *Waiting for Godot* (1952). Equally facile writing in both English and French, Beckett proved an innovator not only in the sparseness and abstractness of the worlds he created, but also in his sense of wordplay and his ability to create comedy while exploring man's existential isolation and futile quest for meaning. Notable works include the plays *Endgame* (1957) and *Krapp's Last Tape* (1958), the short stories collected in *More Pricks Than Kicks* (1934), and the novels *Murphy* (1938) and the trilogy *Molloy* (1951), *Malone Dies*, and *The Unnameable* (1953).

Bede (Saint) (the Venerable), *b. Jarrow, Northumbria, England 672 or 673; d. 735.* **Monk, historian, theologian; Doctor of the Church.** The Anglo-Saxon Benedictine monastery at Jarrow, where Bede was brought up and which he later joined, was a center of learning, and there he became the greatest historian and leading scholar of the early Middle Ages. His *Ecclesiastical History of the English People,* ending in 731, is celebrated for its thoroughness and accuracy, and in it he introduced into the West the practice dividing dating before and after Christ's birth. He wrote a *History of the Abbots;* an encyclopedia, *De natura reru;,* commentaries on scripture and the Church Fathers; and treatises on astronomy.

Beethoven, Ludwig van, *b. Bonn , 1770; d. 1827.* **German composer and pianist of the late Classical period.** In early 1790's Vienna he drew attention as both a pianist and composer, but his writing was considered odd and difficult. His career began to flourish around 1800, the year of his first symphony. From 1801 to 1811 he grew progressively deaf, but the handicap never inhibited his development as one of the very greatest Western composers. Notable works include Piano Sonatas No. 14, Op. 27, in C♯ Minor (*Moonlight*) (1800–1), Symphony No. 3 in E♭ (*Eroica*), Op. 55 (1803–04), Symphony No. 5 in C Minor, Op. 67 (1804–08), Symphony No. 6 in F (*Pastorale*), Op. 68 (1807–08), Piano Concerto No. 5 in E*b* (*Emperor*), Op. 73 (1809), Symphony No. 9 in D Minor, Op. 125 (1817–23), and Mass in D Major (*Missa Solemnis*), Op. 123, (1819–22). He wrote one opera, *Fidelio* (1805, 1814). Beethoven composed abundantly, with a depth and expansiveness that permanently changed musical form. Considered course in manner, appearance and temperament, he never married.

Begin, Menachem Wolfovitch, *b. Brest-Litovsk, Russia (now Belarus) 1913; d. 1992.* **Zionist leader and prime minister of Israel (1977-83).** During World War II he fled from Europe to Palestine, where he became a military leader and commander of the Irgun, a resistance force that used terrorist tactics against the British. After Israel's independence he became head of the opposition Herut Party (1948-67). He was elected prime minister of Israel In 1977, and though he steadfastly refused to end Israel's occupation of the West Bank and Gaza Strip, he agreed to return the Sinai Peninsula to Egypt. For his role in the historic Camp David Accords, Begin shared the 1978 Nobel Peace Prize with Egyptian President Anwar Sadat.

Bell, Alexander Graham, *b. Edinburgh, Scotland, 1847; d. 1922.* **Scottish born American inventor.** On March 7, 1876, the U.S. Patent office issued a patent on Bell's device that sent intelligible words over a wire by converting sound waves to a varying current of electricity. Some have called it the single most valuable patent in history. Though Bell is generally credited with the invention of the telephone, others made substantial contributions to its invention and subsequent development.

Bellamy, Edward, *b. Chicopee Falls, Mass. 1850; d. 1898.* **American man of letters.** Bellamy had a strong sympathy for working people and felt strongly about the inequality of wealth. His novel, *Looking Backward 2000-1887*, published in 1888, envisioned a country in 2000 that had evolved into a socialistic state that cared for "every citizen from the cradle to the grave." It was a great success and spawned Bellamy clubs, but by the middle 1890's the movement had died.

Bellow, Saul, *b. Lachine, near Montreal, Canada, 1915.* **American author.** The winner of the Nobel Prize for Literature in 1976, Bellow was the dean of a group of

Jewish-American writers whose work had great influence on postwar American literature. His heroes are often eccentric, Jewish intellectual rogues. Three of his books won the National Book Award. *The Adventures of Augie March* (1953), *Herzog* (1964), and *Mr. Sammler's Planet* (1971). *Humboldt's Gift* (1975), won the Pulitzer Prize for fiction (1976).

Benedict (Saint), *b. Nursia (Norcia), Italy, ca. 480; d. ca. 547.* **Founder of the Benedictine monastic order.** Benedict is the most important figure in the history of organized monasticism because he wrote and established the guide—called "The Rule of St. Benedict"—under which monks of his and other orders have been organized ever since. It provided for strong authority under an abbot, combined with prescriptions for all aspects of community life, including daily prayer and manual labor. Benedict emerged from a period as a hermit to organize 12 monasteries with 12 monks each and then, ca. 520, his great monastery at Monte Cassino, between Rome and Naples, where he imposed his rule and lived out his life.

Benny, Jack, (Benjamin Kubelsky) *b. Chicago, Ill., 1894 ; d. 1974.* **Comedian.** Star of stage, radio, television, and film (*The Horn Blows at Midnight*, 1945). Benny got his start in show business while he was still in high school, playing violin for the orchestra of a vaudeville theater. He starred in numerous programs for NBC Radio in the 1930's and 1940's, becoming famous for his miserliness, his screechy violin, and his twenty-year-long mock feud with a fellow comedian, Fred Allen. As host of *The Jack Benny Show* from 1950 to 1965, he was one of a group of ex-vaudevillians and radio stars who came to represent the "golden age" of television.

Bentham, Jeremy, *b. London, 1748; d. 1832.* **Philosopher and political theorist.** The founder of utilitarianism, Bentham held that the fundamental moral principle is the greatest happiness of the greatest number of people, and that actions and policies should be judged in accordance with this principle. In Bentham's view, public welfare was bound up with personal happiness. His major work is *Introduction to the Principles of Morals and Legislation*, (1789). Many 19th-century legislative and legal reforms in criminal law, the justice system, and the extension of the political franchise were influenced by Bentham and his followers.

Benton, Thomas Hart, *b. Neosho, Mo., 1889; d. 1975.* **Painter, illustrator, and lithographer.** An American scene painter, or regionalist, Benton was part of a movement of socially conscious and nationalist artists who rejected academic styles and European modernism. He embraced an illustrational style, seeking to document American life in works such as *City Building*, from the mural series *America Today* (1930); and *The Ballad of the Jealous Lover of Lone Green Valley* (1934).

Benz, Karl, *b. Karlsruhe, Germany, 1844; d. 1929.* **Automotive pioneer.** In 1885, Benz built a three-wheeled vehicle that was the world's first practical automobile powered by an internal combustion engine. Benz & Company started manufacturing four-wheeled cars in 1893, and merged with Daimler-Motoren-Gesellschaft in 1926 to become Daimler-Benz, maker of Mercedes-Benz cars.

Berg, Alban, *b. Vienna, 1885; d. 1935.* **Austrian composer.** While embracing both atonality and the 12-tone method, Berg brought a welcome emotionality to what were often perceived as cold and calculating forms; he became one of the most influential composers of the early 20th century. His early studies with Schoenberg, along with a friendship with another composer, Webern, influenced Berg's entry into the avant-garde. Notable works include *Altenberglieder* (1912); Chamber Concerto for pianoforte, violin, and 14 wind instruments (1923–25); *Lyric Suite* for string quartet (1925–26); *Der Wein* (1929); Violin Concerto (1935); and the operas *Wozzeck* (1914-22) and *Lulu* (1929-35)

Bergman, Ingmar, *b. Uppsala, Sweden, 1918.* **Film and stage director.** A superb visual stylist, Bergman became a master at using film to analyze human psychology as well as to depict such grand themes as alienation, isolation, and the search for God. He first won international acclaim for his explorations of the metaphysical, as in *The Seventh Seal* (1957) and *Virgin Spring* (1960), but then grew fascinated with female psychology, as revealed in *Persona* (1966) and *Cries and Whispers* (1972). In 1982, an older, softer Bergman reaffirmed the positive values of life and love in *Fanny and Alexander*.

Bergman, Ingrid, *b. Stockholm, Sweden, 1915; d. 1982.* **Actress.** In her best-known roles, Ingrid Bergman struck the perfect balance between naturalness and exoticism, self-assurance and vulnerability. She was already a star in Sweden when David O. Selznik brought her to the United States to remake *Intermezzo* in 1939. Bergman gained international stardom as Ilsa Lund, in *Casablanca* (1942), followed by *For Whom the Bell Tolls* (1943), *Notorious* (1946), and *Joan of Arc* (1948). She abandoned Hollywood and her family for the Italian director Roberto Rossellini, with whom she had three children including the actress Isabella Rossellini. Her later films include *Murder on the Orient Express* (1974), for which she won her third Oscar.

Berlin, Irving, (Israel Isidore Baline), *b. Tumen, Russia, 1888; d. 1989.* **Popular composer.** One of the most successful practitioners of American popular song before World War II, with thousands of songs to his credit, Berlin could not read or write music; but employed a secretary to notate the compositions he plunked out on the black keys of his piano. Memorable compositions include "Alexander's Ragtime Band" (1911), "God Bless America" (1918), "Puttin' on the Ritz" (1929), "Cheek to Cheek" (1933), "Isn't This a Lovely Day (To Be Caught in the Rain)" (1935), "Let's Face the Music and Dance" (1936), "White Christmas" (1942), and "There's No Business Like Show Business" (1946).

Berners-Lee, Sir Tim, *b. London, 1955.* **Computer scientist.** Credited with having invented the World Wide Web, Berners-Lee began working in computer science in the 1970's. In the 1980's he developed a program that provided links between files (later known as hypertext). Between 1990 and 1991, he wrote the programs for the first web server and first web browser.

Bernini, Giovanni Lorenzo, *b. Naples, 1598; d. 1680.* **Italian architect, sculptor, painter, and poet of the Baroque.** His enormous baldacchino (begun in 1624), the canopy over the altar in Saint Peter's in Rome , helped to establish his reputation at an early age. *The Ecstacy of St. Teresa* (1646), his statue in the Cornaro Chapel, Santa Maria della Vittoria, Rome, is an example of his mastery of Baroque sculpture. Bernini designed a number of Baroque churches, including San Andrea al Quirinale (1678) in Rome, but he is best known for the magnificent colonnade (1655–67) that forms the piazza in front of the entrance facade of Saint Peter's.

Berra, Lawrence (Yogi), *b. St. Louis, Mo., 1925.* **Baseball player and wordsmith.** The Yankee catcher was one of the best to ever play his position but he is just as famous for his "Yogi-isms," colorful, sometimes convoluted sayings that contain the ring of truth like "it ain't over til it's over," and "the future ain't what it used to be." Berra played from 1947 through 1963, and he holds the record for the most World Series games played (75). He was named Most Valuable Player three times and was elected to the National Baseball Hall of Fame in 1972.

Berry, Chuck (Charles Edward Anderson Berry), *b. St. Louis, Mo, 1926.* **Rock 'n' roll guitarist, vocalist, and songwriter.** Berry defined the instrumental voice of rock 'n' roll, in particular its guitar sound and the straight-ahead 4/4 rock beat. He was also a key shaper of the rock 'n' roll song form, and a surprisingly intelligent lyricist. Key recordings include: "Maybellene" (1955), "Roll Over Beethoven" (1956), "Rock and Roll Music" (1957), "School Day" (1957), "Sweet Little Sixteen" (1958), "Johnny B. Goode" (1958), "Memphis, Tennessee" (1964), and "No Particular Place to Go" (1965).

Bettleheim, Bruno, *b. Vienna, 1903; d. 1990.* **Psychologist.** Imprisoned at Dachau and Buchenwald during the Nazi occupation of Austria, he emigrated to the U.S. in 1939 and published a shocking psychological study of concentration camp prisoners' behavior. A psychology professor at the University of Chicago and director of the Orthogenic School for Children (1944–73), Bettelheim developed a widely accepted theory of autism that blamed parents. After Bettelheim's death by suicide, many of his theories were discredited.

Bevin, Ernest, *b. Winsford, U.K., 1881; d. 1951.* **English labor leader and statesman.** Beginning with a series of manual jobs, Bevin joined the labor movement and in 1911 became a full time official of the Dockers' Union. For the next three decades he was active in labor organizing and in 1940 he joined the cabinet of Winston Churchill as minister of labor and national service. In 1945 he became secretary of state for foreign affairs in the cabinet of the Labour prime minister Clement Atlee, where he helped organize the Berlin airlift and the North Atlantic Treaty Organization.

Billy the Kid (Henry McCarty), *b. New York City(?), 1859; d. 1881.* **American outlaw.** McCarty adopted many names, and only near the end of his life was he known as Billy the Kid. At an early age he took up petty crime in New Mexico. He fought in the Lincoln County War of 1878 and was one of six who ambushed and killed Sheriff William Brady. Captured in 1880, he was convicted of Brady's murder, escaped before being hanged, but was tracked down by Sheriff Pat Garrett and shot in his bedroom at Fort Sumner on July 14, 1881.

Bird, Larry, *b. West Baden, Ind., 1956.* **Basketball player.** Never a great natural athlete, the "hick from French Lick" became one of basketball's all-time greats, with unmatched court sense and passing skills, and a deadly accurate outside shot. After leading Indiana State to the

NCAA finals in 1979 against Magic Johnson and Michigan State, Bird signed with the Boston Celtics and was named Rookie of the Year. In his 12-year career (1980-92), the 6'9" forward led Boston to NBA championships in 1981, 1984, and 1986, and was a three-time league Most Valuable Player (1984, 1985, and 1986).

Birdseye, Clarence, *b. Brooklyn, N.Y., 1886; d. 1956.* **American inventor and entrepreneur.** Birdseye is best known for his method of quick-freezing food to preserve freshness and taste. While in Labrador (1912–17) he observed that fish caught at temperatures of 50 degrees below zero instantly froze and retained their freshness for several months. Though he was not the first to realize the value of quick-freezing he perfected the process for fish and later vegetables and successfully commercialized frozen foods.

Bismarck, Otto von (Otto Eduard Leopold), *b. Schönhausen, Prussia (now Germany), 1815; d. 1898.* **First chancellor of the German Empire (1871–90).** He was known as the Iron Chancellor for his assertion, upon taking office as Prussian prime minister, that German problems would be solved with "blood and iron." As Prussian prime minister, and later as chancellor, Bismarck transformed the weakest of the major European powers into a German empire with Prussia at its head. He presided over 20 years of peace in western Europe, yet managed to redraw the map of the continent with a powerful, unified Germany in its center.

Black, Hugo LaFayette, *b. Harlan, Ala., 1886; d. 1971.* American jurist. As a young lawyer, Black joined the Ku Klux Klan in 1923, but he resigned to run for the U.S. Senate in 1926. He campaigned for Franklin D. Roosevelt in 1932 and backed New Deal legislation in the Senate. Roosevelt appointed him to the Supreme Court in 1937, and after a contentious process he was confirmed. Black believed strongly in the literal meaning of the Constitution and argued for the absolute right of free speech. For three decades on the court he moved far from his early racist roots and was a champion of equal rights for all citizens.

Blackstone, William, *b. London, 1723; d. 1780.* **English jurist and legal scholar.** In 1758 Blackstone was appointed the first professor of English law at Oxford University where his lectures were widely praised. He collected his lectures in four volumes (1765–69) and, though they have been criticized by legal scholars, his *Commentaries* became standard reading for generations of law students. He served in Parliament (1761–70) and was appointed a justice of the Common Pleas in 1770.

Blair, Anthony Charles Lynton, (Tony), *b. Edinburgh, 1953.* **Scottish-born English statesman.** Elected to Parliament in the Labour Party in 1983, Blair rose quickly as he worked to free the party from its close ties to labor unions and give it a broader appeal. He became head of the Labour Party in 1994 and prime minister in the election of 1997 at the age of 44. He oversaw better relations with the European Union, separate parliaments for Scotland and Wales, and peace talks with Northern Ireland. He joined with the United States in the invasion of Iraq in 2003.

Blake, William, *b. London, 1757; d. 1827.* **Poet and artist.** Blake, a romantic who preceded the Romantic era, was trained as an engraver, and all his books after *Poetical Sketches* (1783) were composites of art and poetry. His early lyrics, *Songs of Innocence* (1789) and *Songs of Experience* (1794), are beloved for their simple diction and rhythms and haunting images; but his later long, symbolic, prophetic poems can be difficult reading. Blake was a visionary who developed his own mythical system. He is seen as both a political revolutionary and religious mystic. His prophetic poems include the satirical *Marriage of Heaven and Hell* (ca. 1793), *America* (1793), *The Book of Urizon* (1794), and *Jerusalem* (1804–20).

Boccaccio, Giovanni, *b. Paris, 1313; d. 1375.* **Italian writer.** Born illegitimately, Boccaccio spent his youth in Florence and Naples and became a writer against his merchant father's wishes. His early works were *Il Filocolo* (ca. 1336–38), a prose romance; the narrative poem *Il Filostrato* (ca. 1338–40), based on the Troilus and Cressida legend, and an epic, *Teseida* (1341). His grand achievement was the *Decameron* (1348–53), a volume of prose tales, both tragic and comic, some bawdy, taking place during the Black Death. This panoramic treatment of bourgeois life is one of the first and greatest works of Italian humanism and helped usher in vernacular Italian as a literary language.

Bogart, Humphrey, *b. New York City, 1899; d. 1957.* **American movie actor.** "Bogie" began on the Broadway stage playing society types; went on to Hollywood, where he had a series of routine tough-guy roles; and reached his prime in *High Sierra* (1941), *The Maltese Falcon* (1941), and *Casablanca* (1942), playing introspective outsiders. Movie magic developed when he was paired with Lauren Bacall (later his wife) in *To Have and Have Not* (1944) and *The Big Sleep* (1946). He won an Oscar for *The African Queen* (1951).

Bohr, Niels *b. 1885 d. 1962* **Danish physicist.** Bohr's analysis of the hydrogen atom in 1913 explained the spectrum of glowing hydrogen gas in terms of sudden "quantum leaps" of an electron from one orbit to another. From 1918 to 1943 Bohr led the Copenhagen Institute of Theoretical Physics, which became the principal incubator of quantum theory. Bohr himself developed the philosophical basis of the theory. In 1939 his water-drop model of the nucleus of heavy elements was used to predict the properties of uranium-235, the basis of one type of atomic bomb.

Boleyn (Bullen), Anne, *b. London, England, 1507?; d. 1536.* **Second wife of England's King Henry VIII and mother of Queen Elizabeth I.** The daughter of Sir Thomas Boleyn, who was the Earl of Wiltshire and then Ormonde, Anne Boleyn lived in Henry's court from 1522. Henry's decision to annul his marriage to Catherine of Aragon, his first wife, led to his break with the Catholic Church and the start of the English Reformation. He married Anne in 1533. In 1536, after Anne had suffered a miscarriage and a stillbirth, Henry had her charged with adultery and incest. She was convicted and beheaded.

Bolivar, Simon, *b. Caracas, New Granada (now Venezuela), 1783; d. 1830.* **South American soldier and statesman.** "*El Libertador*" (The Liberator) led independence movements against Spanish rule throughout South America. His daring attack in 1819 liberated Colombia, and led to independence for Venezuela (1821) and Ecuador (1822). Elected president of the Colombian Republic (1821–30), he preferred the soldier's life. He routed the Spanish army in Ayacucho in 1824, adding president of Peru (1824-29) to his resume, and in 1825, he freed Upper Peru, which renamed itself Bolivia in his honor. A better liberator than a president—his authoritarian constitution gave him dictatorial powers—he resigned after several revolts and an assassination attempt.

Bonds, Barry, *b. Riverside, Calif., 1964.* **Star of modern major-league baseball.** Bonds claimed one of the game's most cherished records by smashing 73 home runs in 2001; his slugging percentage that year (.863) also established a new single-season high. In 2002, the San Francisco Giants outfielder won his first batting title with a .370 average, set records for walks (197) and on-base percentage (.582), and was named National League M.V.P. In 2003, he won an unprecedented sixth M.V.P. title.

Bonnard, Pierre, *b. Fontenay-aux-Roses, France, 1867; d. 1947.* **Painter, printmaker, and photographer.** A member of the Nabis and later the Intimists, Bonnard was known for his decorative style and distinctive use of color. In his still lifes, nudes, interior scenes, and images of Montmartre, he documented France's Belle Époque. Later in his career he became interested in landscape scenes and studied French classisist painting. His work includes *The Dining Room* (1913), *The Abduction of Europa* (1919), and *Bowl of Fruit* (c. 1933).

Boone, Daniel *b. Berks County, Pa. 1734; d. 1820.* **American frontiersman.** A hunter and trapper, in 1775 Boone blazed the Wilderness Road through Cumberland Gap in the Appalachians in Kentucky, making possible the first settlements in the so-called West. After Kentucky became a county of Virginia, Boone was made captain of the militia. In 1778 he used his own capture and subsequent adoption by the Shawnee to successfully warn and defend Boonesborough against an attack by the British and Indians. Boone was famous even during his own life, especially owing to a feature in Lord Byron's *Don Juan,* as well as popular legends.

Booth, John Wilkes, *b. Bel Air, Md., 1835; d. 1865.* **American actor and assassin of President Abraham Lincoln.** Booth gained popular success as an actor in the years before and during the Civil War and developed a strong sympathy for the Southern cause. A plot to kidnap President Abraham Lincoln failed, but on the night of April 14, 1865, Booth shot and killed President Lincoln at the Ford Theater in Washington. On April 26 Booth died in a barn in Virginia from a gunshot wound either from soldiers or his own hand.

Borden, Lizzie Andrew, *b. Fall River, Mass., 1860; d. 1927.* **American famously accused of murdering her parents.** Borden's mother died when she was two and she and her sister resented their father's new wife, whom he married several years later. On August 4, 1892, her father and stepmother were murdered with an ax and Borden became the prime suspect. She was tried in 1893 and acquitted. But many doubted her innocence and she was shunned in Fall River after her acquittal. She and her sister left considerable bequests to Fall River in their wills.

Borges, Jorge Luis, *b. Buenos Aires, 1899; d. 1986.* **Short-story writer, poet, essayist.** Educated in Switzerland, Borges later joined the Ultraist "pure poetry" movement in Spain, and, returning to Argentina, published several books of poems. His primary achievement, however, was his short stories, beginning with the sketches in *A Universal History of*

Infamy (1935), followed by *Ficciones* (1944). Many of his tales are fantasies or allegories, including those in *The Book of Imaginary Beings* (1967), *Dr. Brodie's Report* (1970), and *The Book of Sand* (1975).

Bosch, Hieronymous (Hieronimus, Jérôme, Jheronimus), *b. Netherlands ca. 1450; d. 1516.* **Painter and draftsman.** One of the most distinctive artists of his time, Bosch is known for epic and chaotic scenes that illustrate moral lessons. His detailed compositions, filled with fantastic characters in idiosyncratic landscapes, have been difficult to interpret and have produced much speculation. His works include *The Carrying of the Cross* (ca. 1510), *The Garden of Delights* (ca. 1510–15) and *The Temptation of St. Anthony* (middle period).

Boswell, James, *b. Edinburgh, Scotland, 1740; d. 1795.* **Biographer.** Boswell is famous chiefly for his exhaustively detailed biography of the philosopher Samuel Johnson, considered the definitive biography of all time. He also kept detailed journals chronicling his own daily life that are considered examples of excellent writing. It is his use of details within the *Life of Johnson* that allows Johnson to emerge as a fully rounded, complex human being.

Botticelli, Sandro (Filipepi, Alessandro), *b. Florence, Italy, 1444–45; d. 1510.* **Painter and draftsman.** In his lifetime, Botticelli was one of Italy's most admired and innovative painters, but by the time of his death, with the onset of the High Renaissance, his reputation was waning. He did not regain popularity until the 1890's. His most famous painting is *Birth of Venus* (ca. 1484), in which a nude Venus rises from the water on a clamshell. Focusing on mythological and religious scenes, Botticelli combined classical aesthetics with contemporary courtly style. Other well-known images are *Primavera* (1478) and *Mars and Venus* (1485).

Bougainville, Louis-Antoine, Comte de, *b. Paris, 1729; d. 1811.* **French navigator.** Author of a treatise on calculus before joining the army, Bougainville helped negotiate the surrender of Quebec in 1763. He commanded three voyages to the Falkland Islands, where he established a French colony. In 1766, he led the first French circumnavigation of the world. The expedition discovered or rediscovered dozens of Pacific islands and returned with more than 3,000 plant and animal specimens, together with opinions of Tahitian culture that profoundly shaped Enlightenment thinking. Bougainville later served in the French navy during the American and French Revolutions.

Bourke-White, Margaret, *b. Bronx, N.Y., 1904; d. 1971.* **Photographer. One of the most prominent photojournalists in America,** Bourke-White was known for covering difficult, dangerous, and epic events around the world. As a principal photographer for both *Fortune* and *Life* magazines, she developed and mastered the photo-essay form. Her work included coverage of the Dust Bowl and the American South in the 1930's, the birth of India and Pakistan, the bombing of Moscow in 1941, and the end of World War II in Germany. Bourke-White was also the first female war photographer for the U.S. armed forces, and the first woman to fly on a combat mission.

Boyle, Robert, *b. Lismore, Ireland, 1627; d. 1691.* **Irish scientist.** Boyle's experiments with an air pump led to his postulation of the existence of a vacuum and an understanding of the elastic properties of air. Boyle's Law, published in 1662, states that the pressure of a given mass of gas is inversely proportional to its volume when temperature is held constant. He was also a proponent of the theory that matter is composed of corpuscles, or atoms, that are themselves composed of smaller particles.

Bradbury, Ray, *b. Waukegan, Ill 1920.* **Science-fiction writer.** A master of social commentary through science fiction, Bradbury is known both for short-story collections and for novels. Among his short story collections are *The Martian Chronicles* (1950), *The Illustrated Man* (1951), and *The Golden Apples of the Sun* (1953). His novels include *Fahrenheit 451* (1953) and *Something Wicked This Way Comes* (1962). Many of his stories and novels have been adapted for the screen.

Bradstreet, Anne, *b. ca. 1612, Northampton, England; d. 1672.* **Poet.** Bradstreet was born into a Puritan family and moved to the Massachusetts colony when she was eighteen. She wrote poems that focus on domestic and spiritual matters and became one of the first English poets to write in America. Bradstreet's verse was written for her family, and her first volume, *The Tenth Muse Lately Sprung Up in America* (1650) was published in England without her knowledge. Her sequence *Contemplations,* considered today the finest example of her work, was not published until the mid-19th century.

Brahe, Tycho, *b. Knudstrup, Denmark (now Sweden), 1546; d. 1601.* **Astronomer.** Prior to the invention of the telescope he designed and built improved astronomical instruments and made precise measurements of the positions of planets and stars, providing an empirical basis for Kepler's laws of planetary motion. His advanced observatory at Uranienborg was funded by Frederick II of Denmark. Among many other things, he studied a supernova (1572) and the varied inclination of the moon's orbit. Brahe did not fully accept the Copernican heliocentric system, proposing instead that the sun revolved around the Earth and the five known planets revolved around the sun. Out of favor with a later Danish king, he spent his last years in Prague.

Brahms, Johannes, *b. Hamburg, 1833; d. 1897.* **German composer and pianist of the Romantic era.** Brahms's best-received works were his piano pieces, lieder, and other art music; in these genres, he was regarded as the logical successor to Schubert and Schumann (with whose wife, Clara, he fell in love). Notable works include Piano Sonata No. 3 in F Minor, Op. 5 (1853); Symphony No. 1 in C Minor, Op. 68 (1855–76); *Ein Deutsches Requiem* (*German Requiem*), Op. 45 (1857–68); *Liebeslieder Waltzes,* Op. 52 (1868–9); *Hungarian Dances* (1873); Violin Concerto in D Major, Op. 77 (1878); and Piano Concerto No. 2 in B*b* Major, Op. 83 (1878–81).

Brancusi, Constantin, *b. Hobitza, Gorj, Romania, 1876; d. 1957.* **French sculptor, painter and photographer.** An influential modernist sculptor, known for his primitive aesthetic and his sleek abstracted biomorphic forms, he often reworked a single theme, such as an egg, in stone, wood, marble, and bronze, and he was particularly interested in subjects relating to the cycle of birth, life, and death. Among his famous works are *The Kiss* (1909), *Sleeping Muse* (1909–10), *The Newborn* (1915) and *Bird in Space* (1928).

Brandeis, Louis Dembitz, *b. Louisville, Ky., 1856; d. 1941.* **American attorney and jurist.** In his law practice Brandeis represented many who lacked power against corporations or the state and became known as the "people's attorney." He fought for the right to organize unions and for wage and hour laws. In 1916 he was the first Jew nominated to the Supreme Court; soon he was dissenting in cases decided by the conservative court. During the 1930's he supported New Deal legislation when it came before the court. He retired in 1939.

Brando, Marlon, *b. Omaha, Neb., 1924; d. 2004.* **Actor.** Brando grew up in Omaha and Los Angeles. He became a student of Stella Adler at New York's Actor's Studio, and epitomized her "Method" acting style with his performance as Stanley Kowalski in the Broadway production of *A Streetcar Named Desire* in 1947, a role he brought to film in 1951. Movie roles followed: *Viva Zapata!* (1952), Shakespeare's *Julius Ceasar* (1953) and the musical *Guys and Dolls* (1955). He won an Oscar for *On the Waterfront,* and starred in the original biker film, *The Wild One* (both 1954). Brando's reputation declined during the 1960's, but was revived by legendary performances in *The Godfather* (1972) and *Last Tango in Paris* (1973). Long at odds with the film industry, he lived many years in Tahiti, and refused a 1972 Academy Award.

Brecht, Bertolt, *b. Augsburg, Germany, 1898; d. 1956.* **Playwright and director.** Brecht was the founder of the Berliner Ensemble and creator of "epic theater," which saw theater as a forum for social change. Brecht's plays were politically charged and called for a style of heightened theatricality. Brecht collaborated with the composer Kurt Weill on a ballad opera, the *Threepenny Opera* (1928). Other notable works include *The Caucasian Chalk Circle* (1944), *Mother Courage and Her Children* (1941), and *The Good Woman of Setzuan* (1943).

Brennan, William Joseph, Jr., *b. Newark, N.J., 1906; d. 1997.* **American jurist.** A Democrat, Brennan was appointed by the Republican president Dwight D. Eisenhower to the Supreme Court in 1956 after private law practice and service on the New Jersey Supreme Court. His expansive view that the Constitution guaranteed human dignity for all suited the court under Chief Justice Earl Warren and he wrote a number of important decisions. But under Warren's successors he often dissented on the more conservative court. He retired in 1990.

Breton, André, *b. Tinchebray, France, 1896; d. 1966.* **Poet, essayist, critic, and editor.** One of the leaders of the Surrealist movement, and a participant in Dada, its predecessor, Breton, a onetime medical student, was interested in mental illness and was influenced by Freud's ideas about the unconscious. With Louis Aragon and Philippe Soupault he founded the journal *Littérature* which promoted the technique of automatic writing. His best-known works include *Manifeste du surréalisme* (1924), the novel *Nadja* (1928), and *Poèmes* (1948).

Brontë, Charlotte, *b. 1816, Thornton, Yorkshire, England; d. 1855;* and **Emily,** *b. 1818, Thornton; d. 1848.* **Novelists.**

The Brontë family was ravaged by tuberculosis. After Mrs. Bronte's early death, the two eldest sisters died while still children. Their only brother; Emily; and the youngest daughter, Anne, a novelist less talented than her sisters, died between the ages 29 and 31. Charlotte did not reach 40. Charlotte and Emily studied in Brussels and failed at running a school home. They and Anne then published a poetry collection under pseudonyms; and, using these same names, all published novels in 1847. Of these, Charlotte's *Jane Eyre,* about a governess's love for her employer; and Emily's *Wuthering Heights,* describing the tempestuous, tragic relationship between the genteel Catherine Earnshaw and the elemental Heathcliff, are enduring romantic gems. Charlotte's other novels include *Villette* (1853).

Brooks, Gwendolyn, *b. Topeka, Kan., 1917; d. 2000.* **Poet.** The first African-American poet to win the Pulitzer Prize (*Annie Allen*, 1949), Brooks' work, often narrative in nature, addressed the everyday lives of urban blacks. Among her many collections are *The Bean Eaters* (1960), *In the Mecca* (1968), and *Children Coming Home* (1991). In addition to her collections of poetry, Brooks published novels (*Maud Martha*, 1953), memoirs, and children's books. In 1989 Brooks received a lifetime achievement award from the National Endowment for the Arts.

Brooks, Mel, (Melvin Kaminsky), *b. Brooklyn, New York, 1926.* **Writer, director, actor.** Brooks started out doing standup comedy then became a gag writer for the television comedian Sid Caesar in 1950. In the 1960's, he made the award-winning 2000-Year-Old Man comedy records with Carl Reiner, created the television spy spoof *Get Smart* with Buck Henry, and directed his first film, *The Producers* (1968), about the improbable success of a Broadway musical based on the life of Hitler. His most popular films were two genre spoofs made in 1974, *Blazing Saddles* and *Young Frankenstein*. Later parodies of Hitchcock thrillers, *Star Wars*, *Robin Hood*, and *Dracula* were less successful.

Brown, Jim, *b. St. Simon Island, Ga., 1936.* Football player. Brown dominated the National Football League during the 1950's and early 1960's, and is considered the greatest running back in the history of the sport. An All-America player at Syracuse, he was N.F.L. Rookie of the Year in 1957. He led the league in rushing that year as well, as he did in seven of the next eight seasons. By the time he retired in 1965 (to launch a career in Hollywood), Brown had rushed for a record 12,739 yards and 126 touchdowns.

Brown, John, *b. Torrington, Conn., 1800; d. 1859.* **American abolitionist.** Brown was strongly influenced by his father's opposition to slavery and while he sought to make a living from tanning, farming, and wool, he was involved in numerous actions against slavery, notably in Kansas. Deciding that slavery could be destroyed by a military attack, Brown organized a raid that seized the U.S. arsenal in Harper's Ferry, Va., on October 16, 1959. But his small group of 21 was easily defeated by a force led by Robert E. Lee and he was tried and hanged that same year.

Browning, Elizabeth Barrett, *b. Durham, England, 1806; d. 1861.* **Poet.** Chiefly known for her collection *Sonnets from the Portuguese* (1850), which chronicles her love affair with her husband, Robert Browning, Elizabeth Barrett Browning began publishing in 1838 (*Seraphim and Other Poems*). Although ill and a recluse for much of her early life, Browning quickly became well known in literary circles. After their marriage, the Brownings moved to Italy, where Elizabeth spent the rest of her life.

Browning, Robert, *b. Camberwell, England, 1812; d. 1889.* **Poet.** Browning, once a less-known poet than his wife, Elizabeth Barrett, is now recognized as one of the greatest Victorian poets. He failed as a dramatist but mastered the dramatic monologue to express powerful irony and psychological insight in poems such as "My Last Ducchess," "Andrea del Sarto", and "Fra Lippo Lippi." His often colloquial and discordant style affected later poets. Other important poems are *Pippa Passes* (1841), "Love Among the Ruins" (1852), and the long, great narrative, *The Ring and the Book* (1868–69).

Brubeck, Dave, *b. Concord, Calif., 1920.* **Jazz pianist and composer.** He brought a refined intellectualism to the cool jazz idiom, in part from his classical training. Brubeck's style combined complex harmonies with odd time signatures. The Dave Brubeck Quartet had several successful albums, including *Jazz Goes to College* (1954), *Dave Digs Disney* (1957), and *Time Out* (1960). Key recordings include "In Your Own Sweet Way" (1956), "Take Five" (1960), "Blue Rondo a la Turk" (1960), and "Three to Get Ready" (1960).

Bruegel I, Pieter (the Elder), *b. Breda, Netherlands ?, ca. 1525–30; d. 1569.* **Painter and draftsman.** The head of a family of artists who were active for four generations, Bruegel painted highly detailed compositions that include many figures in large spaces. He was one of the first painters of his time to portray common people and nonreligious subjects, as in his famous *Peasant Wedding* (ca. 1568), and he strongly influenced landscape and genre artists of the later 16th century and 17th century. His most important works also include *Battle between Carnival and Lent* (1559) and *Parable of the Blind* (1568).

Brunelleschi, Filippo, *b. Florence, 1377; d. 1446.* **Italian architect, goldsmith, and sculptor of the Renaissance.** Apprenticed as a goldsmith, he also studied geometry and helped to devise the methods for representing perspective on a flat surface. His growing interest in architecture led him to enter the competition to design a dome for the cathedral of Santa Maria del Fiori in Florence in 1418. Brunelleschi's dome was selected to be built and is considered a masterpiece of design and construction, blending a Renaissance dome with a Gothic cathedral. Among his other buildings were the Ospedale degli Innocenti (Foundlings' Hospital, 1419–99), and the churches of San Lorenzo (begun 1418) and Santo Spirito (begun 1436).

Bryan, William Jennings, *b. Salem, Ill., 1860; d. 1925.* **Politician and orator.** Nicknamed the "boy orator of the Platte," Bryan provided a voice for the American heartland throughout his long political career. He sought populist reforms as a congressman from Nebraska but was ousted from office in 1894. Bryan rebounded in 1896, when he railed against the gold standard in his "Cross of Gold" speech, one of the hallmarks of American oratory. The speech swept him to the Democratic presidential nomination. Bryan ran twice more in 1900 and 1908, losing both times. He was secretary of state in the Wilson administration.

Bryant, William Cullen, *b. Cummington, Mass., 1794; d. 1878.* **American poet and journalist.** Bryant wrote the first draft of his best-known poem, "Thanatopsis," when he was 16 and published *Poems*, his widely praised collected work, when he was 27. Moving to New York in 1825 to work in journalism, he became editor in chief and part owner of the *New York Evening Post* in 1829. His paper was an ardent champion of free speech, workers' rights, free trade, and the abolition of slavery, and he helped organize the Republican Party.

Buchanan, James, *b. Mercersburg, Pa., 1791; d. 1868.* **Fifteenth U.S. president, 1857–61.** Considered one of the worst presidents because of his lack of good judgment and moral courage, Buchanan compiled more than 40 years of public service as legislator and diplomat. As president, Buchanan favored "popular sovereignty" over slavery in the territories and was the last of the Doughfaces, or northern politicians submissive to the South. The secession crisis paralyzed Buchanan, who denied both the southern right to secede and the federal government's right to do anything about it; he was relieved to hand Abraham Lincoln the reins in 1860.

Buck, Pearl, *b. Hillsboro, W. Va., 1892; d. 1973.* **Novelist.** Winner of the Nobel Prize for Literature in 1938, She is best known for her novel *The Good Earth* (1931), which was awarded the Pulitzer Prize in 1932. The daughter of missionaries, Buck was raised in China. Buck's novels, among them *Sons* (1932), *A House Divided* (1935), and *The Good Deed* (1969), often address the struggles of Chinese peasants.

Buddha (Gautama, Siddhartha), *b. ca. 563 B.C., Nepal; d. c. 483 B.C.* **"The Enlightened One," the founder of Buddhism.** According to writings from 200 years after he lived, Siddhartha was born in a royal household and grew up in luxury. But seeing death, illness, and old age, at 29 he became an ascetic. Sitting beneath a pipal tree, he passed through the four stages of insight and achieved enlightenment: there is no soul seeking rescue, but only the process of change and death. He spent the rest of his life wandering with a growing band of disciples.

Buffalo Bill (William F. Cody), *b. Scott County, Iowa, 1846; d. 1917.* **Pioneer of the American West.** The legendary Buffalo Bill was a trapper, stagecoach driver, Pony Express rider, and showman. Nicknamed for his skill at hunting buffalo to feed railroad workers, he was also a remarkably adept scout for the Fifth Cavalry as it clamped down on Indian resistance in the West (1868–72). Buffalo Bill's exploits won adulation from journalists and novelists, and persuaded him to cash in on his celebrity. His Wild West Show, featuring a stagecoach robbery, a buffalo hunt, and marksmanship displays, drew audiences worldwide for a decade.

Bunche, Ralph Johnson, *b. Detroit, Mich., 1904; d. 1971.* **American scholar and statesman.** Bunche contributed to the landmark book *An American Dilemma: The Negro Problem and Modern Democracy*, published in 1944 and edited by Gunnar Myrdal. He participated in organizing the United Nations and in 1946 was appointed to the U.N. Secretariat. When the Arab-Israeli War (1948–49) broke out, he negotiated peace agreements which ended the conflict and for which he received the Nobel Peace Prize in 1950. He later directed peacekeeping in the Suez crisis of 1956 and the Congo in 1960.

Bunshaft, Gordon, *b. Buffalo, 1909; d. 1990.* **American architect.** In 1937 Bunshaft joined the firm of Skidmore & Owings—later Skidmore, Owings and Merrill. He rose in the firm to become a full partner in 1949. The firm became known for its command of the modernist idiom with the glass-faced Lever House (1952) on Park Avenue in New York, designed by Bunshaft. His later work included the glass-walled Manufacturers' Trust Company bank (1954), the Chase Manhattan Bank (1961), and the Union Carbide Corporation building (1960), all in New York; and the Beinike Rare Book and Manuscript Library (1963) at Yale University.

Burger, Warren Earl, *b. St. Paul, Minn., 1907; d. 1995.* **American jurist.** Burger practiced and taught law until 1953, when he became an assistant attorney general in the Justice Department. In 1956 he was appointed to the U.S. Court of Appeals in Washington, D.C., and in 1969 he became Chief Justice of the U.S. Supreme Court. His professed goal was to repeal many of the decisions of the Warren Court but in this he largely failed. In fact, in *Roe v. Wade*, legalizing abortion, in which he reluctantly concurred, his court rendered one of its most far-reaching and controversial decisions.

Burgess, Anthony, *b. Manchester, England, 1917; d. 1993.* **Novelist and critic.** Best known for the disturbing, linguistically inventive novel *A Clockwork Orange* (1962), which chronicles the unsuccessful rehabilitation of a violent young man, Burgess was a prolific writer, publishing more than 50 books. In addition to his novels, he produced many works of criticism, biographies, and translations.

Burke, Edmund, *b. Dublin, 1729; d. 1797.* **Statesman and political writer.** He became private secretary to the British prime minister in 1765 and entered parliament the same year. He was among the first to argue for the value of political parties (*Thoughts on the Cause of the Present Discontents*, 1770) and was interested in reform domestically as well as overseas. He called for compromise with the American colonists and spoke in favor of repealing the Stamp Act. His most famous work, *Reflections on the Revolution in France* (1790), opposed the revolution; his work has influenced conservative thought ever since.

Burns, Robert, *b. Alloway, Ayrshire, Scotland, 1759; d. 1796.* **Poet.** Burns, regarded as Scotland's national poet, is the best-known writer of poetic songs in English. A farmer much of his life, he wrote mostly in the Scots-English dialect—a fresh infusion of colloquial verse into a neoclassical age. A scandalous womanizer, he produced illegitimate children and famous love poems, first published in 1786 in *Poems, Chiefly in the Scottish Dialect,* and continuing with such compositions as "Afton Water" (1789) and "A Red, Red Rose" (1796). He is best known for another song, "Auld Lang Syne," but he also wrote excellent satires and the well-regarded narrative "Tam o' Shanter."

Burr, Aaron, *b. Newark, N.J., 1756; d. 1836.* **American politician.** After serving with distinction in the Revolutionary War, Burr practiced law in New York City where he clashed with Alexander Hamilton. He ran as Thomas Jefferson's vice presidential candidate in 1800, but both received the same number of electoral votes and under the Constitution at the time the election was thrown into the House of Representatives which elected Jefferson. Angered by Hamilton's opposition to his later political aspirations, Burr challenged him to a duel on July 11, 1804, in Weehawken, N.J., and killed him. Burr fled a murder charge to the Louisiana Territory, where he hoped to execute a mysterious plan to invade Mexico and establish a separate republic. The plan failed, and he was arrested and tried for treason in 1807, but was acquitted.

Burroughs, Edgar Rice, *b. Chicago, 1875; d. 1950.* **Novelist.** An unsuccessful businessman and advertising copywriter, Burroughs tried his hand at writing fiction and created an enduring folk hero with the appearance of his first Tarzan story in 1912. Twenty-five Tarzan books followed, chronicling the adventures of an English nobleman's son who was abandoned in the African jungle and raised by apes. Tarzan eventually appeared in comic strips, movies, a radio show, and a television series. Burroughs produced some 68 novels in all, and during World War II, working for the *Los Angeles Times*, he became the oldest war correspondent in the South Pacific.

Burton, Richard, (Richard Walter Jenkins) *b. Pantrhdyfen, Wales, 1925; d. 1984.* **Actor.** One of the brightest stars of the British stage during the 1940's and 1950's, and a sensation on Broadway in the role of King Arthur in *Camelot* in 1960, Richard Burton never quite managed to transfer his considerable talent from the stage to the screen. He costarred with Elizabeth Taylor in *Cleopatra* (1963); their subsequent affair and stormy marriage gave him a tabloid immortality. Burton was nominated for seven Oscars and won none.

Bush, George H. W., *b. Milton, Mass., 1924.* **Forty-first U.S. president, 1989–93.** George Herbert Walker Bush served as congressman, senator, and director of the C.I.A. before serving as Ronald Reagan's vice president and then winning the 1988 presidential election. with a pledge of "no new taxes." Despite being criticized for a lack of leadership, he ordered the invasion of Panama (1989) and Operation Desert Storm (1990) to liberate Kuwait from Iraqi occupation. He also helped oversee the peaceful dismantling of the Soviet Union (1991), and worked with Mikhail Gorbachev to end the arms race. A poor economy contributed to his defeat in the 1992 election; his son George W. Bush later became the nation's 43rd president.

Bush, George W., *b. New Haven, Conn., 1946.* **Forty-third U.S. president.** A former governor of Texas, George Walker Bush was the second son of a former president to ascend to the top office, winning the controversial 2000 election despite losing the popular vote to the sitting vice president, Al Gore. Bush didn't capture a majority in the Electoral College until five weeks after the election, when the U.S. Supreme Court voted 5-4 to suspend recounts in Florida, which Bush appeared to win by fewer than 1,000 votes. Despite running as a "compassionate conservative," he pushed a pro-business agenda, deep tax cuts (with resulting high deficits), and, after the terrorist attacks of 9/11, an aggressive military policy in Afghanistan and Iraq. Mounting controversies surrounding the buildup to and the aftermath of the Iraq war clouded the final days of his first term.

Bush, Vannevar, *b. Chelsea, Mass., 1890; d. 1974.* **Scientist.** A star in M.I.T.'s electrical engineering department, where he built a differential analyzer and an early analog computer, Bush convinced President Roosevelt to mobilize military research in support of U.S. forces in World War II. As director of the new federal Office of Scientific Research and Development, he institutionalized the relationship between business, government, and the scientific community. Bush's Memex concept, introduced in a groundbreaking *Atlantic Monthly* article called "As We May Think," pioneered the idea of hypertext research—a theory that shaped development of the World Wide Web.

Byrd, Richard Evelyn, *b. Winchester, Va., 1888; d. 1957.* **Aviator and polar explorer.** Byrd and Floyd Bennett made the first flights over the Greenland icecap, in 1924–25; and over the North Pole, from Spitsbergen, in 1926. Byrd led two expeditions to Antarctica (1929–30 and 1933–35), during which he made the first flight over the South Pole and wintered alone at a camp in the interior. He subsequently commanded three expeditions to Antarctica in 1939–41, 1947–48 (Operation High Jump), and 1956–57 (Operation Deep Freeze), and flew twice more over the South Pole. He also promoted peaceful international cooperation in Antarctic exploration.

Byron, George Gordon (Lord), *b. London, 1788; d. 1824.* **Poet.** Clubfooted but legendarily handsome, Byron had affairs with perhaps 200 women, including his half-sister, and several men. His notoriety led to exile in Switzerland and Italy. His great poetic gift was for narrative and satire, written with mastery of English verse forms. The first two cantos of *Childe Harold* (1812) made him famous, and subsequent poems introduced the "Byronic hero," the individualistic, iconoclastic immoralist who reappears definitively in his tragedy *Manfred* (1817). Byron's greatest poem, *Don Juan,* a comic, epic satire written 1819–24, was his last. He died in Greece while training troops for that country's war of independence.

Caesar, Julius *b. Rome, ca. 102 B.C.; d. 44 B.C.* **Roman general and statesman.** A popular orator and an accomplished military commander, Julius Caesar was considered by some a political reformer and proponent of the people, and by others a dictator seeking to destroy the Roman republic and usurp absolute power. Before leaving to fight in the Gallic wars (58-50 B.C.), Caesar joined forces with Pompey and Crassus in the First Triumvirate. The alliance fell apart during that time, and in 48 B.C. Caesar returned to wage civil war on Pompey's forces, crossing the river Rubicon and invading Rome. After a series of victories, particularly the one at Pharsalus, Caesar gained control of Rome. Believing that Caesar was trying to create a monarchy—although he refused a crown offered by Mark Antony—a group of senators murdered Caesar in the senate chamber on the Ides of March, (March 15) 44 B.C.

Cagney, James, *b. 1899, New York City; d. 1986.* **Actor.** The epitome of the Warner Brothers gangster, Cagney's performances are distinguished for their intensity and unpredictability. He started out as a song-and-dance man in vaudeville and began his Hollywood career with supporting roles in a variety of genres before getting his big break as *The Public Enemy* (1931), in which he hit Mae Clarke in the face with a grapefruit. In addition to gangsters, he played fighter pilots, G-men, boxers, and Bottom the Weaver in *A Midsummer Night's Dream* (1935). He returned to the gangster film in the classic *White Heat* (1949), in which he slugged prison guards while keening for his mother.

Calder, Alexander, *b. Philadelphia, Pa., 1898; d. 1976.* **Sculptor, painter, illustrator, printmaker, and designer.** Calder is best known for his kinetic sculptures, or mobiles—delicately balanced arrangements of conjoined hanging pieces that move in response to air currents. Calder was influenced by the surrealists' affinity for incorporating the element of chance. His constructions usually feature abstracted organic shapes, as in *Lobster Trap and Fish Tail* (1939). Other well-known works include *A Universe* (1934) and *Constellation with Red Object* (1943).

Calhoun, John Caldwell, *b. Abbeville, N.C., 1782; d. 1850.* **American politician and political theorist.** In 1817 Calhoun became secretary of war in the cabinet of President James Monroe; he later served as vice president under Andrew Jackson and secretary of state under John Tyler. As United States senator from South Carolina 1832, he championed states' rights and the institution of slavery. In 1832 he challenged a tariff with a theory of a states' right to nullification of bills they felt harmful. His essays on minority rights in majority rule and pluralism are considered important contributions to political theory.

Caligula *b. A.D. 12; d. A.D. 41.* **Roman emperor from 37 to 41.** Gaius Caesar, called Caligula from a childhood nickname meaning "little boot," succeeded Tiberius. His reign was marked by savagery and madness of a legendary nature, some true, some exaggerated, and some outright fabricated, such as the story that he appointed his horse consul. Many scholars believe that a seven-month illness shortly after he came into power left him insane, resulting in mass executions, cruelty, delusions of divinity, and a questionable relationship with his sister, Drusilla, whom he deified after her death. Having squandered a vast amount of Rome's fortune, Caligula was assassinated at the Palatine Games by conspirators in 41. His wife and daughter were also killed.

Callas, Maria, *b. New York City, 1923; d. 1977.* **Greek-American soprano.** Callas was an international opera star whose wide-ranging performances and many recordings were mainly responsible for restoring early 19th-century bel canto opera to the popular repertoire in the 1950's. Notable roles include Bellini's Norma and Donizetti's Lucia, as well as Verdi's Violetta and Giordano's Maddelena. Her fiery temperament and makeover into a svelte beauty brought jet-set celebrity at the cost of vocal problems. She made only seven Metropolitan Opera appearances.

Cavendish, Henry, *b. 1731, Nice, France; d. 1810.* **English physicist and chemist.** Reclusive and taciturn, Cavendish was one of the great scientists of his day. His most important contributions lay in his research into the chemical properties of gases, by which he isolated hydrogen and through his research on air, discovered (as did James Watt, independently) that water is a compound, not an element. Cavendish also made major contributions to electrical theory, anticipating the work of Faraday, Coulomb, and Ohm. In his seventies, he devised the Cavendish experiment to determine the gravitational constant and measure the density of the Earth.

Calvin, John, *b. 1509, Noyon, France; d. 1564.* **Protestant reformer.** A conversion experience in 1533 propelled Calvin into the cause of Protestant reform. His *Institutes of Christian Religion* (1536) followed Luther in rejecting papal authority and embracing justification by faith alone and belief in predestined salvation. He was banished from Geneva in 1538 but welcomed back in 1541; he then achieved a full reform of the city under ecclesiastical codes of law and conduct harmonious with industrial society. Calvin exceeded Luther in his diminution of Catholic sacraments, and Protestantism soon split into Lutheran and "Reformed" sects. By his death, Calvin had spread his influence from Scotland to the Netherlands.

Camus, Albert, *b. Mondovi, Algeria, 1913; d. 1960.* **Algerian-French novelist, playwright, and essayist.** Because of his view that life is absurd, Camus is linked, against his wish, with the philosophical existentialist movement. After being involved in a theater group in Algiers, he became a journalist in Paris during World War II and joined the French Resistance. In 1942 his essay "The Myth of Sisyphus" and his short, terse novel *The Stranger* expressed his theory of the absurd. Other novels are *The Plague* (1947), which dramatizes his belief that humanity can act nobly in the face of meaningless death, and *The Fall* (1956). *The Rebel* (1951) is a collection of essays. Plays include *Caligula* (1944) and *State of Siege* (1948).

Cantor, Georg, *b. 1845, d. 1918* **German mathematician.** Cantor was the first mathematician to cope directly with infinity. He determined how to compare the sizes of different infinite sets, proving that the set of rational numbers (fractions) is the same size as the set of whole numbers (1895). But both the set of real numbers (any numbers represented by decimals, including infinite decimals) and the set of points in a plane, although equal in size to each other, have more members than the whole numbers. Cantor's work solved problems concerning infinite series but also introduced paradoxes not yet completely resolved.

Capra, Frank, *b. Bisacquino, Sicily 1897, ; d. 1991.* **Film director.** Frank Capra made hugely entertaining movies in a variety of genres but always returned to the populist social comedy, in which honesty, optimism, and compassion defeat cynicism and corruption. Among his most important films are the classic screwball comedy *It Happened One Night* (1934), *Mr. Smith Goes to Washington* (1939), and the perennial Christmas favorite, *It's a Wonderful Life* (1946). He also produced and directed a series of famous wartime propaganda films, *Why We Fight*.

Caravaggio, Michelangelo Merisi da (Merisi, Michelangelo), *b. Milan or Caravaggio, Italy, 1571; d. 1610.* **Painter.** After an early career painting portraits, still lifes, and genre scenes, Caravaggio turned to religious subjects, espousing a bold style that emphasized the contrast between light and shade. Rejecting the formality of his Mannerist predecessors, he painted common people rather than idealized beauties. Caravaggio repeatedly ran into trouble with the law, culminating in a murder he committed in 1600. His paintings, which influenced later European artists such as Rubens and Velázquez, include *The Lute-Player* (ca. 1595–97) and *The Calling of St. Matthew* (1599–1602).

Carlyle, Thomas, *b. Ecclefechan, Scotland, 1795; d. 1881.* **Author.** Educated in Scotland and later resident in London (1834), he was an expert on German literature and philosophy. His *Sartor Resartus* (1833–4) is a complex spiritual autobiography. Carlyle, influenced by transcendentalism, had a religious outlook without conventional Christian belief. *The French Revolution: A History* (1837), was an acclaimed interpretation of an event that spoke to the fears and hopes of the day. In his later work he alienated former allies such as John Stuart Mill by attacking parliamentary systems and glorifying autocratic "heroes" such as Cromwell and Frederick the Great.

Carnegie, Andrew, *b. Dunfermline, Scotland, 1835; d. 1919.* **Scottish born American industrialist and philanthropist.** Carnegie's father, in search of factory work, moved his family to Pittsburgh in 1848. After working in a mill and as a telegraph operator, Carnegie became a railroad superintendant. He entered the steel business in 1864 and built up the business through mergers and acquisitions, often with his competitors. A violently supressed strike at the Homestead Plant in 1892 sullied his reputation. In 1901, unsatisfied with his life, Carnegie sold his company and began to give away his money in ways of direct benefit to society. By the time of his death he had given away nine-tenths of his enormous wealth to philanthropic causes including public libraries and New York's Carnegie Hall.

Carothers, Wallace Hume, *b. 1896, d. 1937.* **American chemist.** Carothers, working at the Du Pont chemical corporation, established by experiment the theory of how polymers, the chemical basis of plastics, form. He applied this to developing neoprene (1932), an artificial rubber that resists the degradation caused in natural rubber by heat, light, or chemicals. Carothers next turned to artificial fibers, and produced nylon in 1934. Not only has nylon replaced silk for some types of clothing and wool for durable rugs, but it is also used as a strong solid plastic.

Carter, Jimmy (James Earl), *b. Plains, Ga., 1924.* **Thirty-ninth U.S. president, 1977–81.** Carter grew up on a farm with no plumbing or electricity but realized his dream of attending the U.S. Naval Academy, after which he joined the submarine fleet and studied nuclear physics. He left the Navy in 1953 to run the family peanut business, was elected to the Georgia state senate in 1962, and became governor in 1970. Carter's, homespun style and vows of honesty struck a chord with voters after Watergate, and he defeated the incumbent, Gerald R. Ford, for the presidency in 1976. Lack of Washington connections helped his candidacy but not his presidency, as congress ignored Carter's pleas for tax reform and a long-range energy policy. When oil prices doubled, most Americans blamed Carter for runaway inflation; this, combined with the Iran hostage crisis, led to his landslide defeat in the 1980 election. In later years he became a trusted figure around the world, often monitoring contentious elections.

Cartier, Jacques, *b. Saint-Malo, France, 1491; d. 1557.* **French navigator.** Cartier may have sailed with Giovanni da Verrazano to North America and to Brazil (1524–27).

He persuaded Francis I to sponsor a search for the Northwest Passage, and in 1534 he explored Canada between Newfoundland and New Brunswick. A second expedition the next year sailed up the St. Lawrence River as far as the Huron settlement of Hochelaga (Montreal). On his third and probably last voyage (1541–42), to help establish a French colony in Canada, Cartier reached the Lachine Rapids above Hochelaga.

Cartier-Bresson, Henri, *b. Chanteloup, France, 1908; d. 2004.* **Photographer.** After studying to be a painter, Cartier-Bresson chose photography as his art form, and, using simple technique and equipment, black-and-white film, and realistic, unstaged conditions, he became the 20th century's leading photojournalist. Beginning with his creation of an underground photography unit during the World War II French resistance, he captured historic events and conditions of life around the world. He was also famous for his photographic portraits of the world's most famous people (Gandhi, Sartre, Matisse, et al.). Among several books of his collected photographs, the best-known is *The Decisive Moment* (1952), a title that expresses his artistic purpose.

Cash, Johnny, (John R.) *b. , Kingsland, Ark., 1932; d. 2003.* **Country vocalist and songwriter, also known as "The Man in Black."** Cash was one of the most respected and influential figures in modern country music. His deep baritone voice perfectly complemented his earnest compositions, most which combined the emotional honesty of folk music, the rebelliousness of rock and roll, and the world-weariness of country. Key recordings include "Folsom Prison Blues" (1956/1968), "I Walk the Line" (1956), "Ring of Fire" (1963), "Jackson" (1967), and "A Boy Named Sue" (1969).

Cassatt, Mary (Stevenson), *b. Allegheny City (now in Pittsburgh), Pa., 1844; d. 1926.* **American painter and printmaker, active in France.** In her early career, Cassatt worked primarily as a genre painter, exhibiting regularly in the U.S. and at the Paris Salon. As her style became looser and more innovative, Degas invited her to join the Impressionist circle, in which she had considerable success with her portraits of women and children. After being forced to retire in 1915 because of cataracts, she continued to advise younger artists. Her works include *Woman in a Loge* (1879) and *The Bath* (1891).

Cassini, Gian Domenico, *b. Perinaldo, Italy, 1625; d. 1712.* **Astronomer.** At Bologna he studied the sun and planets, determining the periods of rotation around their own axes of Jupiter, Mars, and Venus. At Paris, where he was director of the Royal Observatory, he discovered four satellites of Saturn and studied its ring system; he also initiated the mapping of the geographic meridian passing through Paris.

Castro, Fidel Ruz, *b. near Birán, Cuba, 1926 or 1927.* **Cuban dictator.** Castro seized power in 1959, when his army of 800 guerrillas routed Gen. Fulgencio Batista's 30,000 government troops. He began turning Cuba into the first communist state in the Western Hemisphere, cutting ties with the U.S. and opening trade and arms agreements with the Soviet Union. In 1961, the U.S.-led Bay of Pigs invasion failed to overthrow Castro. Cuba remained communist even after the fall of the Soviet Union, but in the 1990's, Castro began permitting Cubans to leave the country; thousands fled to the United States.

Cather, Willa, *b. Winchester, Va., 1873; d. 1947.* **Novelist.** The child of a pioneer family, Cather grew up in frontier Nebraska and went on to become a magazine editor in New York before turning to the writing of fiction. Cather's best-known novels, of which *O Pioneers!* (1913) and *My Antonia* (1918) are considered her finest, depict the life of the pioneer as a celebration of spirit and courage. Other novels include *One of Ours* (1922), which won the Pulitzer Prize, and *Obscure Destinies* (1932).

Catherine the Great (Sophie Fredericke Auguste von Anhalt-Zerbst), *b. Stettin, Prussia (now Szczecin, Poland), 1729; d. 1796.* As empress for more than 30 years, she molded Russia into a modern European superpower. Months after her husband Peter took the throne in 1762, Catherine had him deposed and murdered. Under her reign, Russia seized vast new territories and was swiftly modernized and westernized (often at the expense of the serfs). A patron of the arts, she founded the Hermitage Museum and many academies and libraries. Though her sexual escapades have been exaggerated, she did take many lovers, including state advisors.

Cato (the Younger) **Marcus Porcius Cato,** *b. 95 B.C.; d. 46 B.C.* **Roman statesman, born , and great-grandson of Cato the Elder (Cato the Censor).** A longtime opponent of Julius Caesar and a conservative supporter of the principles of the Roman republic and senatorial rule, Cato was eulogized by Cicero and other Roman thinkers as the model of political conviction and moral virtue. When the first triumvirate— Caesar, Pompey, and Marcus

Licinius Crassus— fell apart, Cato and his party, the Optimates, supported Pompey in the civil war against Caesar. After a series of defeats, Cato committed suicide in Utica, northern Africa.

Catullus *b. Verona, Italy, ?84 B.C.; d. ?54 B.C.* **Roman lyric poet.** A contemporary of Caesar, Cicero, and Pompey, Catullus is considered one of the finest lyric poets. He arrived in Rome around 62 B.C. and established himself as an aristocrat and prominent figure. His poems, 116 of which survive, were often short, sometimes satirical, and always skillful. His most famous works are passionate poems addressing Lesbia, the pseudonym for his mistress, probably Clodia, the sister of a well-known Roman statesman.

Cervantes (Saavedra), Miguel de, *b. 1547, Alcala de Henares, Spain; d. 1616.* **Novelist, poet, playwright.** He was wounded at the battle of Lepanto in 1571, enslaved by Barbary pirates, impoverished, and briefly imprisoned. Cervantes took up writing poetry, stories, and plays, and in 1605 he produced the first part of the most internationally popular work of Spanish literature, *Don Quixote* (Part II, 1615), a long burlesque of chivalric romance, featuring an aging, gaunt, self-proclaimed knight who sets out, in the company of his round, earthy squire, on a series adventures to impose his idealism on Spanish society. It has often been called the world's first novel. Cervantes continued to publish—stories, stage-pieces, and a romance—until his death.

Cézanne, Paul, *b. Aix-en-Provence, France, 1839; d. 1906.* **Painter.** His early work featured dark, fantastical subjects, but Cézanne later adopted the Impressionists' colorful, rhythmic brushstrokes and love of nature. Departing from the Impressionists' ambition to capture fleeting moments, however, Cézanne aspired to portray permanence and solidity in his images, and is therefore considered a Postimpressionist. His still lifes, landscapes, and portraits are seen as precursors to important developments in 20th-century artwork, particularly Cubism. Not fully recognized during his lifetime, Cézanne has become famous for images such as *Still Life with Apples* (1879–82) and *Mont Sainte-Victoire* (ca. 1885–87).

Chamberlain, Wilt, *b. Philadelphia, Pa., 1936; d. 1999.* **The dominate basketball player of his generation.** Chamberlain compiled 31,419 points and 23,924 rebounds in a storied N.B.A. career (1959–73). He ranks third on the all-time N.B.A. list in scoring and first in rebounding. Chamberlain's records also include single-season scoring average (50.4 in 1962) and most points in one game (100). Known as "Wilt the Stilt," the 7'1" center was named M.V.P. four times (1960, 1966–68) and won championships in 1967 with the Philadelphia '76ers and in 1972 with the Los Angeles Lakers.

Chaplin, Charlie (Charles Spencer Chaplin) *b. London, England, 1889; d. 1977.* **Silent film comedian and director.** His Dickensian childhood inspired his screen character, the Little Tramp, who embodied the dreams and disappointments of the lower social classes. Chaplin was a superb pantomimist; his forte was his graceful handling of props to define character and reveal emotions. The Little Tramp emerged in the short *Kid Auto Races at Venice* (1914) and was fully formed by *The Tramp* (1915). Chaplin, who directed himself, moved to feature-length films with the *The Kid* (1921) and *The Gold Rush* (1925), his masterpiece. Other classics include *Modern Times* (1931) and *The Great Dictator* (1940). He won special-achievement Oscars in 1929 and 1972.

Charlemagne (Carolus Magnus, Charles the Great), *b. ca. 742; d. 814.* **King and emperor.** As king of the Franks in 768, Charlemagne fought successful military campaigns throughout Western Europe, extending Frankish possessions in modern France to include much of Germany, Italy, and Spain. In 800, Pope Leo III crowned him emperor of a restored western Roman Empire which later became the Holy Roman Empire. At his court in Aachen Charlemagne sponsored a revival of the arts and learning known as the Carolingian renaissance.

Charles, Ray (Ray Charles Robinson), *b. Albany, Ga., 1930; d. 2004.* **Blues and soul vocalist, pianist, and composer.** Charles merged 1950's R&B, gospel-powered vocals, and hints of jazz, blues, and pop to create the genre known as soul music. Blind since the age of six (from glaucoma), he helped to popularize black music to an integrated audience; he even incorporated country music in his 1962 album, *Modern Sounds in Country and Western* Music. Key recordings include "What'd I Say" (1959), "Georgia" (1960), "Hit the Road Jack" (1961), "Unchain My Heart" (1961), "One Mint Julep" (1961), "I Can't Stop Loving You" (1962), and "Busted" (1963).

Chaucer, Geoffrey, *b. London, ca. 1343; d. 1400.* **Narrative poet.** The first great, and greatest medieval,

English poet, spent most of his life around the English court in government service. Being both commoner and aristocrat, he understood people of every station. After he completed an elegy, *The Book of the Duchess,* in 1370, diplomatic travels to Italy acquainted him with the writing of Boccaccio, which influenced Chaucer's greatest works, *Troilus and Criseide,* (ca. 1385) and *The Canterbury Tales* begun about 1386 and never completed.

Chekhov, Anton (Pavlovich), *b. Taganrog, Ukraine, 1860; d. 1904.* **Playwright, novelist, short story writer.** Considered a master of the short-story and one of the founders of modern drama, Chekhov wrote more than 50 short stories, notably "Neighbors" (1892), "An Anonymous Story" (1893), "The Black Monk" (1894), and "Ward Number Six" (1892); some were later adapted for the stage as one-act farces. His full-length plays often show the isolation and frustrations of intellectuals living in the provinces of Russia; famous works include *The Seagull* (1898), *Uncle Vanya* (1899), *Three Sisters* (1901), and *The Cherry Orchard* (1904).

Chiang Kai-shek, (Mandarin pronunciation Jiang Jieshi), *b. Zhejiang Province, China, 1887; d. 1975;* . **Chinese nationalist leader.** Chiang received a military education under the Qing dynasty and became a follower of Sun Yat-sen after the Revolution of 1911. Chiang became party leader after Sun's death in 1925. Chiang's Northern Expedition of 1926–28, which reunified the warlord-riven country, included an "extermination campaign" designed to wipe out the Chinese Communist Party. He was later criticized for fighting communism rather than concentrating on the invading Japanese. His wartime alliance with the United States was facilitated by the diplomacy of Mme. Chiang (Soong Meiling, 1898–2003). Defeated by Mao Zedong's forces in the civil war of 1946–49, Chiang's government retreated to Taiwan, where he remained president until his death.

Chief Joseph (In-mut-too-yah-lat-lat), *b. Wallowa Valley, Ore., 1840?; d. 1904.* **American Indian chief.** After becoming chief of the Nez Perce in 1871, he resisted the takeover of his homeland by white settlers. When the U.S. government attempted to force the tribe onto an Idaho reservation, Chief Joseph led his people on a brilliantly executed 1,400-mile retreat toward Canada, winning four major battles along the way. The Nez Perce were ultimately forced to surrender, and were resettled in Oklahoma, where many died of disease. In 1885, Chief Joseph was sent to a reservation in Washington.

Child, Julia (Julia McWilliams Child), *b. Pasadena, Calif., 1912.; d. 2004.* **Chef.** After studying at the Cordon Bleu, Child introduced French cooking to the United States with the overnight best seller *Mastering the Art of French Cooking* (co-written with Simone Beck and Louisette Bertholle). The book's success gave birth to the immensely popular PBS TV series *The French Chef,* and turned Child into America's first TV celebrity chef. She appeared in half a dozen other TV cooking programs and wrote several more cookbooks, including *The Way to Cook* (1989).

Chomsky, Noam, *b. Philadelphia, Pa., 1928.* **Linguist and activist.** Chomsky was educated at the University of Pennsylvania and has been on the faculty of MIT since 1955. His theory of transformational grammer, which proposes that humans have an innate ability to learn language, has influenced generations of linguists. Since the 1960's, Chomsky has been known for his political activism in support of left-wing causes and opposition to American interventions especially in Latin America.

Churchill, John, First Duke of Marlborough, *b. Ashe, England, 1650; d. 1722.* **English military leader.** After James II's accession to the throne in 1685, Churchill was made commander in chief of the English army. His transference of allegiance to William III helped ensure that the Glorious Revolution of 1689 was largely bloodless. On her accession, Queen Anne appointed him commander of the British army again. Among his major victories were Blenheim (1704) and Ramillies (1706). In return for his services, he was created a duke, and a palace was built for him, named after his victory at Bleinheim. He lost Anne's favor and withdrew from public life in 1710.

Churchill, Winston Leonard Spencer, *b. Blenheim Palace, Oxfordshire, Britain, 1874; d. 1965.* **English statesman and man of letters.** Son of the Tory statesman Randolph Churchill, Winston saw war in India and Africa as an officer and journalist. In 1900 he was elected to the House of Commons, where he remained until 1964 except for two years. He served as home secretary (1910–11) and first lord of the Admiralty (1911–15), a tenure that ended after the disastrous defeat at Gallipoli. He rejoined the army and between the world wars, served in several more cabinet posts. His greatest achievements began when he became prime minister in 1940 at the beginning of World War II. His inspiring oratory, his alliance with the United States, and his understanding of geopolitics helped to guide England through its most challenging era. His prodigious literary output included *The Second World War* (six volumes) and *The History of the English Speaking Peoples* (four volumes). He was awarded the Nobel Prize in Literature in 1953.

Cicero, (Marcus Tullius Cicero) *b. 106 B.C.; d. 43 B.C.* **Roman orator and statesman.** More of Cicero's writings survive than those of any other Roman of his time, most notably the Phillipics, a series of attacks on Mark Antony. Cicero held the positions of aedile, praetor, and consul during his long and contentious political career. He was responsible for prosecuting Catiline in 61 B.C. and was exiled for having five of Catiline's supporters illegally executed. He returned in 57 B.C. and remained in public life, supporting Pompey in the civil war against Julius Caesar. His opposition to Mark Antony was at the root of his undoing. After Caesar's assassination and the formation of the second triumvirate—Octavian, Lepidus, and Mark Antony—Cicero was executed in 43 B.C.

Clarke, Arthur C., *b. Somerset, England, 1917.* **Novelist and essayist.** As a young writer, Clarke developed a vision of the future that proved, from the start, to be startlingly prescient—in 1945 he predicted a satellite system that in fact came into use two decades later. Author of more than 70 books, Clarke began publishing science-fiction novels in 1953, when *Childhood's End* appeared, followed by *The City and the Stars* (1956). His novels *Rendezvous with Rama* (1973) and *The Fountains of Paradise* (1979) both won the Nebula and the Hugo awards. The 1968 film *2001: A Space Odyssey* is based on Clarke's work.

Claudius *b. 10 B.C.; d. A.D. 54* **Roman emperor.** Kept out of public life largely by his grandfather, Augustus, because of his physical disabilities and unattractiveness, Claudius studied and wrote historical works until the assassination of his nephew Caligula in A.D. 41. Claudius is said to have been hiding out in the palace, fearful that he, too, would be murdered, when the Praetorian Guard discovered him and proclaimed him emperor. His reign saw expansion to Britain, Mauritania, and Thrace, although Claudius is historically considered a pawn of the army and other influences. He was poisoned and killed in A.D. 54, probably by his fourth wife, Agrippina, who had persuaded Claudius to make her son, Nero, successor.

Clay, Henry *b. Hanover County., Va., 1777; d. 1852.* **American statesman.** Called the Great Pacificator and the Great Compromiser, Clay began as a highly successful Kentucky lawyer. He served as a Jeffersonian Republican, in the state legislature and U.S. House of Representatives where he worked to precipitate the war of 1812 and pass the Missouri Compromise in 1820. He became a leader of the Whig Party, and opposed war with Mexico, which cost him the presidency in 1844. He was U.S. secretary of state (1825–29) and served several senate terms. There he was instrumental in the passage of several important treaties and compromises that balanced free and slave states' rights, including the compromise tariff of 1833, which resolved the nullification crisis over South Carolina's attempt to secede.

Cleisthenes, *b. ca. 570; d. ca. 507 B.C.* **Athenian statesman.** A member of an old Athenian family, Cleisthenes spent much of his life in exile owing to a combination of curses against his family and political tumult at Athens. He served as chief archon in 525–524, and led opposition to the tyrant Hippias in 512–511 B.C. In 508 he persuaded the Assembly to expand the democratizing measures instituted by Solon. He reorganized the body politic into ten tribes of ten demes (or townships), giving preference to citizenship of a place rather than membership in a tribe, and encouraging greater participation in Athenian politics.

Clemenceau, Georges, *b. Mouilleron-en-Pareds, France, 1841; d. 1929.* **French statesman and journalist.** As a senator in 1913, "Le Tigre" feared German aggression, and founded a newspaper, *L'Homme Libre* ("The Free Man"), to publicize his opinion. When World War I began a year later, he urged the United States to join the fight. Clemenceau's elevation to prime minister (1917–20) of France's Third Republic was instrumental in the Allied victory. He also was a major player in negotiating the difficult terms of the Treaty of Versailles, including the return of Alsace-Lorraine to France and the disarmament of Germany.

Cleopatra, *b. 69 B.C.; d. 30 B.C.* **Queen of Egypt.** Probably the most frequently referenced woman in the ancient world, Cleopatra VII and her brother, Ptolemy XIII, were left to rule Egypt in 51 B.C. after the death of their father. She was exiled by supporters of her brother and formed an alliance with Julius Caesar, with whom she had a son, Caesarion. After Caesar was assassinated, she returned to Egypt. Mark Antony went to her with charges of supporting his enemies, but ended up forming a romantic relationship with her instead. She bore him three children, though he married Octavian's sister, Octavia. When the alliance between Octavian and Mark Antony disintegrated, Octavian declared war on them. Mark Antony committed suicide on mistakenly hearing of Cleopatra's death after their defeat in the Battle of Actium in 31 B.C. Cleopatra committed suicide in 30 B.C. after a failed attempt to negotiate with Octavian, reportedly dying from the bite of an asp.

Cleveland, Grover, *b. Caldwell, N.J., 1837; d. 1908.* **Twenty-second and twenty-fourth president, 1885–89; 1893–97.** The only president to serve two nonconsecutive terms, Stephen Grover Cleveland showed scant interest in politics until Buffalo elected him mayor in 1881; the next year he became governor. His war on corrupt Tammany Hall made Cleveland the perfect Democratic reform candidate for president in 1884. After winning the election, he pushed for civil service reform and lower tariffs, seized 81 million acres of unused land from railroads, and signed the Interstate Commerce Act (1887). He was defeated in the 1888 election, but four years later he won a rematch with Benjamin Harrison.

Clinton, Bill, *b. Hope, Ark., 1946.* **Forty-second U.S. president, 1993–2001.** As governor of Arkansas, William Jefferson Clinton became a leading figure among so-called New Democrats, who called for welfare reform and smaller government; in 1992, he beat the incumbent president, George Bush, in a three-way race. Clinton found little support for his domestic programs, however, although the decade's economic prosperity and booming stock market generated so much tax income that the Reagan-Bush deficits turned to surpluses by 1998. During his second term, the ongoing Whitewater scandal unearthed evidence of an affair between Clinton and a young White House intern, Monica Lewinsky. His lies under oath about the relationship led the Republican-controlled House to approve two articles of impeachment, although neither article mustered enough votes to pass.

Cobb, Ty, *b. Narrows, Ga., 1886; d. 1961.* **Baseball player.** Although not the most beloved player in the annals of baseball, Cobb is one of the game's all-time greats. In 24 seasons (1905–28), most with the Detroit Tigers, the "Georgia Peach" compiled the highest career batting average (.367) and second-most hits (4,197) in major-league history. His career totals rank in the top five of virtually every offensive category except home runs. A fiercely aggressive competitor, Cobb batted over .400 three times, hit .300 or better 23 times, and won 12 American League batting titles.

Coleman, Ornette, *b. Fort Worth, Tex., 1930.* **Jazz saxophonist and composer.** A leading proponent of avant-garde jazz, Coleman burst on the scene in 1959 with a series of dynamic quartet albums. His improvisational alto sax playing dispensed almost completely with traditional harmony, and served to influence other free jazz players, including John Coltrane. Key albums include *The Shape of Jazz to Come* (1959), *Change of the Century* (1959), *This Is Our Music* (1960), and *Free Jazz* (1960).

Coleridge, Samuel Taylor, *b. Ottery St. Mary, Devonshire, England, 1772; d. 1834.* **Poet and essayist.** After Coleridge's impulsive, dreamy, scholarly youth, his poetic career took shape when he and William Wordsworth collaborated on *Lyrical Ballads* (1798), which initiated what we call English Romanticism. The collection contained Coleridge's most famous poem, *The Rime of the Ancient Mariner,* whose mysterious, supernatural qualities also flavored his "Kubla Khan" and *Christabel,* both written early but published in 1816. Coleridge also excelled in writing more sober, meditative poems such as "Frost at Midnight" (1798) and "Dejection: An Ode" (1802). His output was constricted by physical suffering and opium addiction. Later philosophical writings and very important literary criticism were collected in *Biographia Literaria* (1817).

Collins, Michael, *b. Clonakilty, Ireland, 1890; d. 1922.* **Irish Nationalist.** Collins took part in the Easter Rising of 1916 and was held in detention for several months. After the Irish Assembly voted for independence in 1918, he was responsible for numerous attacks on the police and others from 1919 to 1921. He was one of the principal negotiators of a peace that in 1921 gave Ireland self-government within the British Empire. This did not satisfy more radical leaders, like Eamon DeValera, who organized resistance to the new government. Collins took charge of crushing the insurgency in 1922. Shortly thereafter, he was ambushed and killed by insurgents.

Colt, Samuel, *b. Hartford, Conn., 1814; d. 1862.* **Inventor.** Colt devised the first remotely controlled explosive and utilized the first underwater telegraph cable, but he is best known as the inventor of the revolver that bore his name. After the U.S. military ordered a large supply of the new guns for use in the Mexican War, Colt established a manufacturing plant where he developed the concepts of interchangeable parts and a mass production line. The Colt .45 became the signature sidearm of the American West.

Coltrane, John William, *b. Hamlet, N.C., 1926; d. 1967.* **Jazz saxophonist and composer.** One of the most controversial figures in the history of jazz, Coltrane was a great hard bop player with a Herculean style who moved beyond traditional musical forms and helped develop the genre known as free jazz. His later playing employed both soprano and tenor sax in the pursuit of a radically experimental style. Important recordings include "Giant Steps" (1960), "My Favorite Things" (1961), "Chasin' the Trane" (1962), "A Love Supreme" (1965), and "Ascension" (1965).

Columbus, Christopher, *b. Genoa, 1451; d. 1506.* **Italian explorer.** Columbus commanded the first ships to cross the mid-Atlantic from Europe to the Americas. His fleet sailed from Spain to the Azores and on to the Bahamas, where the Spanish landed on October 12, 1492. They later visited Cuba and Hispaniola, where one ship was lost, and returned to Spain on March 15, 1493. Columbus made three more voyages (1493–96, 1498–1500 and 1502–04), reaching mainland South America and Central America on the third and fourth voyages. Dogged but politically inept, he died wealthy but embittered at the lack of support from his royal patrons.

Comte, Auguste, *b. Montpellier, France, 1798; d. 1857.* **Philosopher and sociologist.** Founder of the philosophical school of positivism, which holds that only scientific knowledge is valid and that metaphysical questions are unanswerable; and of the discipline of sociology, to which he gave its name. A social reformer and early collaborator of Henri de Saint-Simon, Comte held that all sciences led to and contributed to sociology, which would provide the basis for a reformed and harmonious society. His detailed plans for such a society, however, were attacked as hierarchical and undemocratic.

Confucius, *b. Shandong Province, China, ca. 551 B.C.; d. ca. 479 B.C.;* **Chinese philosopher. He was** born to the minor aristocracy at a time of intense socio–political change in ancient China. Confucius is a latinized form of Kongfuzi, "great master Kong." He aspired to high office in his native state of Lu so that he could put into practice his theory of government by a natural elite of the virtuous. Thwarted, he gathered disciples to whom he taught his principles of hierarchy and filial piety (the state modeled on the patriarchal family), harmony, and personal self-cultivation; his teachings are preseved in the *Lunyu* ("Analects of Confucius"). His view of the ideal society and how to achieve it dominated Chinese political philosophy for over two thousand years.

Conrad, Joseph, (Jozef Konrad Korzeniowski) *b. Poland, 1857; d. 1924.* **English novelist.** Conrad learned English at sea and became one of the great English novelists and prose stylists. Many of his works are set at sea, among them *The Nigger of the Narcissus* (1897); *Lord Jim* (1900), which introduces his innovative technique of an intermediate narrator and tells the story from multiple points of view; and several superb novellas, including *Heart of Darkness* (1902) and *The Secret Sharer* (1909). Other major works. such as *Nostromo* (1904), *The Secret Agent* (1907), and *Under Western Eyes* (1911), have political contexts. His characters confront moral isolation, corruption and the complexity of human interaction.

Constantine I (The Great), *b. Naissus, Moesia, ?280; d. 337.* **First Christian emperor of Rome.** Constantine was hailed caesar after the death of his father, Constantius, in A.D. 306. Ruling only in Gaul at that time, Constantine invaded Italy and defeated Maxentius at the Milvian Bridge in 312, taking control of the western empire. Attributing his victory to the christian God, Constantine granted christians freedom to practice their religion in the Edict of Milan in 313. After he gained control of the whole empire, the major events in his reign were the Nicene Creed of 325, which proclaimed the basic doctrine of Christianity that persists to this day, and the move of the seat of power in 330 from Rome to the eastern city of Byzantium, thereafter known as Constantinople until the 20th century.

Cook, James, *b. Marton-in-Cleveland, England, 1728; d. 1779.* **English explorer.** A self-taught navigator, Captain Cook entered the Royal Navy at 27 and was quickly recognized for his abilities. His survey of the St. Lawrence River in 1759–60 helped ensure the British victory at Quebec, and in 1763–66 he charted Newfoundland. He led three circumnavigations of the world (1768–71, 1772–75, and 1776–80), during which he sailed around Antarctica; charted Australia, New Zealand, and many Pacific and Southern Ocean islands; and visited the Pacific Northwest, Alaska, Siberia, and Hawaii, where on his second visit he was killed in a skirmish on the beach.

Coolidge, Calvin, *b. Plymouth, Vt., 1872; d. 1933.* **Thirtieth U.S. president, 1923–29.** Coolidge entered Republican politics in 1899, rose through a succession of state offices, and was elected governor of Massachusetts in 1918. He was the Republican vice presidential nominee in 1920 and assumed office after Warren G. Harding's death. "Silent Cal" was the butt of jokes for his laconic utterances, but his minimalist approach to government restored respectability to a White House tainted by Harding's corrupt appointees. Pronouncing that the "business of America is business," he ushered in the heady years of "Coolidge prosperity" as the stock market soared higher and higher.

Cooper, Gary, (Frank James Cooper) *b. Helena Montana, 1901; d. 1961.* **American movie actor.** More than any other star, Cooper came to represent the image Americans wished to project to the world. *The Virginian* (1929) established him as a western star, but thanks to a childhood spent moving between Montana and England, Cooper could be just as convincing in a business suit as in a cowboy hat. He was Lou Gehrig in *Pride of the Yankees* (1942), Mr. Deeds and John Doe for Frank Capra, and the upright sheriff in *High Noon* (1952). His career spanned 35 years during which he appeared in more than 100 films.

Copernicus, Nicolas, *b. Torun, Poland 1473; d. 1543.* **Astronomer.** He studied astronomy and other subjects in Poland and Italy, and became canon of the cathedral in Frauenburg, East Prussia (1512). His great work *On the Revolutions of the Heavenly Spheres* (completed, in Latin, about 1530, published 1543) described a heliocentric system of sun and planets, where for the first time the sun rather than the earth was placed at the center. However, his belief that the planetary orbits are circular necessitated complex adjustments called epicycles. His work paved the way for Kepler's laws of planetary motion.

Coppola, Francis Ford, *b. 1939, Detroit, Mich.* **Director.** One of the most successful directors to emerge from the "film school" generation of the 1970's, Coppola started out working for Roger Corman's B-movie factory and earning a degree in film studies from UCLA. After a number of apprentice works, he struck critical and commercial gold with *The Godfather* (1971), which was followed by two sequels, *The Godfather II* (1974) and *The Godfather III* (1990). His Vietnam epic, *Apocalypse Now* (1979), became a legend. Like many of his film-school peers, Coppola has been at least as influential a close-up producer as director, backing films by George Lucas, and Paul Schrader, among others.

Cortés, Hernán (Hernando), *b. Medellin, Spain, 1485; d. 1547.* **Spanish conquistador.** Cortés was an experienced soldier when he reached the Americas in 1504. He took part in the conquest of Cuba in 1511, and in 1518 he commanded an expedition to explore the Yucatán Peninsula. Burning his fleet at Veracruz in August 1519, he led his 500 men and their Indian allies inland to Tenochtitlán, capital of Montezuma's Aztec empire (now Mexico City). Overcoming numerous obstacles, including other Spaniards, Cortés (and smallpox) defeated the Aztecs in 1521. He served as captain-general of New Spain (1521–28) and retired to Spain in 1540.

Coubertin, Baron Pierre de, *b. Paris, 1863; d. 1937.* **Father of the modern Olympic movement.** Inspired by excavations at Olympia, Greece, the nobleman and educator Baron Pierre de Coubertin successfully promoted the idea of reviving the ancient Games at an international athletic congress in 1894. The first modern Olympics were held two years later in Athens. Coubertin was president of the International Olympic Committee (I.O.C.) from 1896 to 1925; he remained a member of I.O.C. until his death.

Coulomb, Charles *b. Angoulême, France 1736; d. 1806.* **French physicist.** Coulomb made critical discoveries about the nature of magnetism and electricity after retiring as a military engineer in 1789. His inventions of the magnetometer, magnetoscope and torsion balance led to his formulation of Coulomb's law which stated that the force between two electric charges could be measured from the product of the charges and the distance between them. This clarified knowledge of attraction and repulsion between unlike and like charges, as well as the bonds that hold atoms and molecules together. The coulomb, or unit of electric charge (one ampere enduring for one second), is named for him.

Coward, Noel, *b. Teddington, England, 1899; d. 1973.* **Playwright, actor, and composer.** Coward began appearing on the stage at the age of twelve. His successful plays, the drama *The Vortex* (1924) and the comedy *Hay Fever* (1925), established him as one of the most popular playwrights of twentieth century. Coward's comedies (among them *Private Lives*, 1930; *Design for Living*, 1933; and *Blithe Spirit*, 1941), witty and sophisticated, capture the speech and manners of the post–World War I British upper class. Coward also wrote musicals and short stories. He produced, directed, and performed in many of his works.

Crawford, Joan (Lucille le Sueur), *b. San Antonio, Tex., 1908; d. 1977.* **American movie actress.** Her early years working as a department store clerk and a Broadway chorine set the pattern for many of her early roles; *Our Dancing Daughters* (1928) made her a star. After notable dramatic roles in *Grand Hotel* (1932) and *The Women* (1939), she won an Oscar for *Mildred Pierce* (1945). *Johnny Guitar* (1954) and *What Ever Happened to Baby Jane?* (1962) have become cult favorites. After her fourth husband's death in 1959, she took over his director's position with Pepsi-Cola.

Crazy Horse (Ta-sunko-witko or Tashunca-Uitco), *b. Rapid Creek, Lakota Nation (S.D.), 1842?; d. 1877.* **American Indian chief.** Celebrated for his ferocity and his vision, Crazy Horse was determined to preserve his Oglala Lakota people's way of life. He scored his most memorable triumph in 1876, when he joined forces with Sitting Bull and Chief Gall to massacre General George Armstrong Custer's Seventh Cavalry at Little Bighorn. After his fighters were forced to surrender to U.S. authorities in 1877, he was killed by a soldier's bayonet while resisting arrest.

Crick, Francis Harry Compton, *b. Northampton, Britain, 1916; d. 2004.* **English molecular biologist.** Crick and James Dewey Watson at Cambridge University discovered the structure of deoxyribonucleic acid, DNA, that carries genetic information in living organisms. Their paper of 1953 described the double-helix structure of DNA and the coding system within it. Crick and Watson, together with Maurice Wilkins, were awarded the Nobel Prize in Physiology or Medicine in 1962.

Cromwell, Oliver , *b. Huntingdon, England, 1599; d. 1658.* **English soldier and political leader.** A fiery Puritan in his youth, Cromwell led the parliamentary forces in the English Civil War in overthrowing the Stuart monarchy of King Charles I. But his reign (1653–58) as lord protector of the republican Commonwealth of England was marked by religious tolerance. He restored England to a position of power in Europe not seen since the death of Queen Elizabeth I. He refused an offer to become king, but was also unable to share power with Parliament, which he twice dismissed. After Cromwell's death and the restoration of the monarchy (in 1660), his body was disinterred and his head impaled on a pole atop Westminster Hall, where it stayed for more than 20 years.

Crosby, Bing (Harry Lillis Crosby), *b. 1905, Tacoma, Wash.; d. 1977.* **Actor, singer.** A fixture of Hollywood musicals throughout the 1930's, Bing Crosby had an easygoing manner and mellow voice made him America's best-loved crooner. Among jazz critics he is considered one of the great performers. In 1940 he appeared in *The Road to Singapore* with Bob Hope and Dorothy Lamour, inaugurated a series of equally popular *Road* movies throughout the 1940's. Crosby won an Oscar for his dramatic performance as a Catholic priest in *Going My Way* (1944).

Cummings, E. E. (Edward Estlin), *b. Cambridge, Mass., 1894; d. 1962.* **Poet.** One of the most popular American poets of his time, Cummings is best recognized for the idiosyncratic shaping of his verse and his elimination of uppercase letters, even in his own name. In 15 volumes he wrote, often with humor, sometimes in poems without beginnings or ends, or with quirky phrasing ("pity this monster, manunkind," "all ignorance toboggans into know") of joy and sadness, of love, and (rather explicitly) of sex. He was also an accomplished painter and wrote a successful memoir of his imprisonment during World War I, *The Enormous Room* (1922).

Cunningham, Merce (Mercier Philip Cunningham), *b. Centralia, Wash., 1919.* **Innovative modern dance choreographer.** While in California Cunningham met composer John Cage, who became his longtime companion and artistic collaborator. Cunningham danced with the Martha Graham Company in 1939–45, giving his first independent concert in 1942; he danced his own works as a soloist 1945–53, then formed his company. Notable works include *Suite by Chance* (1952), *Summerspace* (1958), and *Rainforest* (with sets by Andy Warhol, 1968). He began choreographing with the computer in the later 1980's, in works such as *Trackers* (1991), and continued performing until the early 1990's, when arthritis ended his career.

Curie, Marie, *b. Warsaw, Poland, 1867; d. 1934.* **Chemist/physicist.** Marie Curie and her husband Pierre expanded scientific understanding of uranium rays and coined the term "radioactivity." They shared the 1903 Nobel Prize for Physics with, fellow researcher, Henri Becquerel. After Pierre's death in 1906, Marie assumed his professorship, becoming the first woman to teach at the Sorbonne. In 1911, she won an unprecedented second Nobel Prize, this time in chemistry. Working with her daughter Irène (a future Nobel Prize winner), she created x-ray vans at the French front lines during World War I. Her research paved the way for advanced nuclear physics and cancer therapies.

Custer, George Armstrong, *b. New Rumley, Ohio, 1839; d. 1876.* **American military leader.** Custer graduated from the U.S. Military Academy at West Point in 1861 and entered the Civil War. A bold cavalry officer, he became a brigadier general at the age of 23, the youngest general in the Union Army, and continued to distinguish himself throughout the war. After the war he fought in the Indian wars; and in the battle of the Little Bighorn in Montana on June 25, 1876, he and his troops were vastly outnumbered, defeated, and killed by Sioux warriors.

Cyrus II (The Great) *b. Media (now in Iran), ?590-580 B.C.; d. ca. 529 B.C.* **King and founder of the ancient Achaemenian Persian empire.** Most of what is know of Cyrus' life and reign comes from Greek historian Herodotus and later Xenophon in more legendary form. He was portrayed as a model ruler with a perfect balance of might and mercy. The son of Cambyses and a Medean princess, Cyrus overthrew his maternal grandfather, Astyages, ca. 550 B.C., taking control of the empire of the Medes. He went on to overthrow Croesus, king of Lydia (ca. 546 B.C.) and then Nabonidus in Babylonia (538 B.C.). A great conciliator, Cyrus was credited in the Bible with sending the captive Jews in Babylonia back to their homelands and blending Achaemenian culture with that of the people he conquered.

Dalai Lama (Lhamo Dhondrub), *b. Tsinghai province, China, 1935.* **Religious leader.** Born to a peasant family, the 14th Dalai Lama was declared by Buddhist leaders at the age of two as the latest reincarnation of the Bodhisattva of Compassion. He assumed a role as head of the Tibetan government when Chinese forces invaded Tibet in 1950. After a full-fledged uprising was crushed by the Chinese in 1959, the Dalai Lama fled to India, where he set up a government-in-exile. Revered worldwide for his spiritual teachings, he won the 1989 Nobel Peace Prize for his advocacy of nonviolent means to end the Chinese occupation.

Dalí, Salvador, *b. Figueres, Spain, 1904; d. 1989.* **Painter, draftsman, illustrator, sculptor, writer and filmmaker.** One of the most famous of the surrealist group, and a prolific artist, Dalí created imaginary worlds in which reality is grotesquely distorted. His fantastic, often nightmarish landscapes and monsterlike figures are rendered in a smooth, detailed, almost photographic style. His best-known works include *Accommodations of Desire* (1929), *The Persistence of Memory* (1931), and *Soft Construction with Boiled Beans: Premonitions of Civil War* (1936).

Dante Alighieri, *b. Florence, 1265; d. 1321.* **Poet.** Dante, the greatest Italian poet, was a nobleman intimately involved in the tumultuous politics of Florence. After the death of his beloved Beatrice, he celebrated her, and ideal love, in *The New Life* (1292). In 1302 he was banished from Florence; afterward, it is believed, he composed *The Divine Comedy*, one of the greatest works of world literature. Intricately rhymed in the Tuscan dialect, it is a three-book account of the poet's tour, guided by Virgil and Beatrice, of hell, purgatory, and paradise—a vivid, symbolic, meditative investigation of a medieval Christian's understanding of God.

Danton, Georges-Jacques, *b. Arcis-sur-Aube, France, 1759; d. 1794.* **French Revolutionary leader.** Although his role in the overthrow of the French monarchy was unclear, he nonetheless took credit for it. His opportunism resulted in his election to the Legislative Assembly, where his oratorical skills and decisiveness allowed him to shape the First French Republic. As president of the First Committee of Public Safety (1793), he led the moderate opposition, which tried, unsuccessfully, to pursue a path of negotiation and compromise. His disapproval of Robespierre's Reign of Terror led first to his withdrawal from politics, and later to his own death at the guillotine.

David, *b. Bethlehem, Judah, d. 926 B.C.* **Second Israelite king (ca. 1000–962 B.C.).** A popular warrior for his legendary slaying of the giant Goliath, David was anointed by the prophet Samuel to be the future king. He united the tribes of Israel and extended his dominion to Jerusalem (the "city of David"). He brought the ark of the Covenant (holder of the Ten Commandments) to Jerusalem, which he made the capital of his empire. Author of many of the biblical psalms, David was said to be chosen by God to be a great king of Israel; his reign was considered ancient Israel's golden age.

David, Jacques-Louis, *b. Paris, 1748; d. 1825.* **Painter.** David developed a neoclassical style influenced by the painter Poussin and the principles of the Enlightenment, rejecting the luxuriant rococo aesthetic popular in his time. Having participated in the French Revolution, David painted *The Death of Marat* (1793), documenting the murder of a revolutionary political leader who was attacked in his bathtub. Another well-known work is the *Coronation of Napoleon in Notre-Dame* (1805–07). Although David's technique was groundbreaking during his lifetime, his style became so influential that it was later considered rigid and conservative.

Davis, Bette (Ruth Elizabeth Davis), *b. Lowell, Mass., 1908; d. 1989.* **American movie actress.** Her magnetic eyes and bearing made an indelible mark on the screen for more than 50 years. Her early Oscars were for *Dangerous* (1935) and *Jezebel* (1938). She was a top star in the 1940's playing spirited women, then experienced a decline in popularity but turned it around with an iconic performance as an aging stage star, Margo Channing, in *All About Eve* (1950). Later roles included a blowsy housewife in *The Catered Affair* (1956) and a grotesque silent film fossil in *What Ever Happened to Baby Jane?* (1962).

Davis, Jefferson, *b. Fairview, Ky., 1808; d. 1889.* **President of the Confederate States of America.** As senator from Mississippi (1847–51; 1857–61), and secretary of war (1853-57), Davis vocally defended slavery, but opposed secession. When seven states seceded, however, he quit the Senate and was elected Confederate president (1862). A lack of supplies, money, and international allies spelled the Confederacy's doom. After Robert E. Lee surrendered, Davis fled Richmond in April 1865 and was captured six weeks later. He was indicted for treason, but was never tried; he was released in 1867.

Davis, Miles (Miles Dewey Davis III) *b., Alton, Ill., 1926; d. 1991.* **Jazz trumpeter and composer.** A brilliant musician, he drove jazz through a staggering variety of styles, from cool to hard bop to modal to fusion. Davis's trumpet playing was in turns lyrical and introspective; he often employed a Harmon mute for a more intimate sound. His bands frequently included sidemen (including Bill Evans, Herbie Hancock, Freddie Hubbard, and Tony Williams) who went on to stellar solo careers. Influential albums include *Birth of the Cool* (1949), *Round About Midnight* (1955), *Miles Ahead* (1958), *Kind of Blue* (1959), *Sketches of Spain* (1960), *In a Silent Way* (1969), and *Bitches Brew* (1970).

Davy, Sir Humphry, *b. Penzance, Cornwall, 1778; d. 1829.* **English chemist.** Davy was one of the foremost scientists of his day. His first discovery was on the effects of inhaling nitrous oxide. He subsequently published a work on the physiological effects of different gases and went on to devise the means of isolating by electrolysis chemical elements including potassium, sodium, and calcium. His work for the Society for Preventing Accidents in Coal Mines led to his invention of the miner's lamp.

De Beauvoir, Simone Lucie-Ernestine-Marie-Bertrand, *b. Paris, 1908; d. 1986.* **French feminist writer.** Her best-known work, *The Second Sex* (1949), is a landmark in feminist literature, arguing for the emancipation of women from their subjugation by men. She was a close companion of fellow existentialist writer, Jean-Paul Sartre, for more than 60 years; together, they founded and edited the monthly journal *Le Temps Modernes.* Her novel *The Mandarins* (1954), which tells the story of sheltered intellectuals turning to political activism, won the *Prix Goncourt*.

De Gaulle, Charles André Joseph Marie, *b. Lille, France, 1890; d. 1970.* **French soldier and statesman.** After the German victory over France in 1940, De Gaulle led the government-in-exile in London. He served as president of France's provisional government (1944–46) after liberation. He resigned when he realized that the constitution for the Fourth Republic severely curtailed the president's powers. By 1958, France's failures in Indochina and Algiers led to a popular outcry for De Gaulle's return, entreaties he refused until he was allowed to draft a new constitution. His Fifth Republic pursued independence from both the U.S. and the Soviet Union. Instead, he sought an alliance with Germany that helped to create the European Union.

de Kooning, Willem, *b. Rotterdam, Netherlands, 1904; d. 1997.* **Painter and sculptor.** A leading figure in the abstract expressionist movement in post–World War II New York, de Kooning is known for his painterly, semi-abstract images, many of them featuring women. In his painting *Woman I* (1950–52) the figure barely emerges from the background, and is shaped with wild, energetic brushstrokes that have been characterized as both violent and erotic. De Kooning gradually shifted his interests to include semiabstracted landscape. Other well-known works include *Woman and Bicycle* (1952–53) and *Two Figures in a Landscape* (1967).

Debs, Eugene Victor, *b. Terre Haute, Ind., 1855; d. 1926.* **American labor leader and Socialist.** Debs organized and became president of the American Railway Union in 1893 and in 1894 won a strike against the Great Northern Railway. The same year, after shutting down the western railroads, he was arrested and jailed because the action interrupted the mails. In jail he read books on socialism and in 1898 he organized the Social Democratic Party, running unsuccessfully for president several times. He was sentenced to ten years in prison during World War I for pacifist beliefs, but his sentence was commuted in 1921.

Defoe, Daniel, *b. London, England, 1660; d. 1731.* **Novelist.** As a young man Defoe was a merchant, but went bankrupt and later took up journalism, a field in which he was an important innovator, working feverishly for many outlets and publishing his own *Review* of international affairs. Not until late in life did he publish the books for which he is most famous, *Robinson Crusoe* (1719) and *Moll Flanders* (1722), realistic and episodic tales that are often considered the first English novels. Other important works are *Colonel Jack*, another work of fiction, and *A Journal of the Plague Year*, an account of 1665 London.

Degas, Edgar, *b. Paris, 1834; d. 1917.* **Painter, sculptor, photographer, and collector.** A founding member of the Impressionist movement, considered a realist within the group, Degas was trained classically and believed in the importance of drawing. He wanted to document modern life and had a preference for artificial light and urban subjects, particularly female workers and ballerinas. His works include *The Star* (*Dancer on a Stage*, ca. 1878) and *The Glass of Absinthe* (1876). After 1886 Degas rarely showed his work.

DeMille, Cecil. B., *b. Ashfield, Mass., 1881; d. 1959.* **Film producer and director.** A master showman, DeMille became famous for elaborate films with luxurious settings, colorful costumes, and large casts. In 1913 he formed a partnership with Jesse Lasky, resulting in one of the first films shot in Hollywood, *Squaw Man* (1914). Their company became Paramount, where DeMille spent his entire career. His major films, including *The Ten Commandments* (1923) and *Sign of the Cross* (1932), carefully balanced the depiction of explicit sin with traditional morals. His last film was a remake of his own *Ten Commandments* (1956).

Dempsey, Jack, *b. Manassa, Colo., 1895; d. 1983.* **Boxer.** Nicknamed the "Manassa mauler," Dempsey was one of the best and most popular heavyweight fighters of the 20th century. He became champion in 1919 by knocking out Jess Willard but lost the title to Gene Tunney in 1926. Their controversial rematch in 1927 remains one of the most famous fights in history. Dempsey knocked down Tunney in the seventh round but since he failed to immediately return to a neutral corner, the referee delayed the count. The "long count" enabled Tunney to come back and win. Dempsey never fought again and retired with a record of 64 wins, 6 losses, and 9 draws.

Deng Xiaoping *b. Sichuan Province, China, 1904; d. 1997.* **Chinese political leader.** In 1924 Deng joined the Chinese Communist Party while studying in France. An early supporter of Mao Zedong, Deng benefited from Mao's rise to the party chairmanship during the Long March (1934–35). After long service as an army political commissar, he became general secretary of the party in 1956. Although he was purged in 1969 during the Cultural Revolution, and again in 1976 after the death of his patron Zhou Enlai, Deng returned to power in 1977 and became China's de facto supreme leader until his death. Deng crushed the Tiananmen Square democracy movement (1989), but his economic reform policies ("the Four Modernizations," 1978) set the stage for China's emergence as a world economic power.

Descartes, René, *b. La Haye, France, 1596; d. 1650.* **Philosopher, mathematician, and scientist.** His many mathematical contributions include the development of Cartesian coordinates and analytic geometry. He is regarded as a founder of modern philosophy; his ideas are set out in *Discourse on Method* (1637) and *Meditations* (1641). He began with the undoubted knowledge of self (*cogito, ergo sum*: I think, therefore I am), and went on to expand knowledge, including knowledge of God. He regarded the physical world as mechanistic and entirely divorced from the mind, a position called dualism; the two realms are connected only by the intervention of God.

Dewey, John, *b. 1859, Burlington, Vt., d. 1952.* **Educator and philosopher.** One of the leading educators of his day, Dewey opposed authoritarian methods of teaching and was influential in progressive education based on experiment and practice. His approach was instrumentalism. Forms of human activity are instruments to solve social and personal problems; and since problems change, the instruments to confront them must also change. Democracy is a fundamental value, and truth is seen as not transcendental but evolving, accessible to all who inquire. Dewey was also active in social and political reform, including women's suffrage. His many books include *The School and Society* (1899), *Experience and Nature* (1925), and *Freedom and Culture* (1939).

Dickens, Charles, *b. Portsmouth, England, 1812; d. 1870.* **Novelist.** Dickens is unsurpassed as a creator of vivid, idiosyncratic, often comic, characters. His rich descriptions of poverty and suffering were informed by an impoverished childhood. His first books were collections, *Sketches by Boz* (1836) and *Pickwick Papers* (1837), which brought him fame; and the novel *Oliver Twist* (1838). His famous short novel, *A Christmas Carol*, was published in 1843. Dickens wrote long books quickly in installments for magazines, and even the best could lack finish. These best include *Dombey and Son* (1848), *David Copperfield* (1850), *Bleak House* (1853), *Hard Times* (1854), *Great Expectations* (1861), and *Our Mutual Friend* (1865). Dickens was a father of 10; his marriage was complicated by close friendships with his wife's sisters.

Dickinson, Emily, *b. 1830, Amherst, Mass.; d. 1886.* **Poet.** Daughter of a onetime congressman, Dickinson seems to have lived a normal life until her late twenties, when she began to withdraw into a lifelong reclusiveness in her Amherst home. There she developed into one of the greatest and most influential American poets, unrecognized until, after her death, her sister discovered more than 1,500 of her poems. These poems, plain in diction but original in imagery, meter, and their irregular rhyming, revealed a quietly passionate woman sensitive to nature, in love with an unnamed man, and troubled by the specter of death and uncertainty about faith and immortality.

Diderot, Denis, *b. 1713, Langres, France; d. 1784.* **Philosopher and encyclopedist.** One of the foremost figures of the European Enlightenment, Diderot made a meager living as a hack writer, essayist, novelist, playwright, and translator. Approached for a translation of the British *Chambers' Cyclopaedia*, he expanded on that assignment to edit and publish the magisterial *Encyclopédie* (1751–72; 17 volumes of text and 11 of plates), a work of sublime erudition and revolutionary opinions. It contributors included his partner, the mathematician Jean Le Rond d'Alembert; and the philosophers Jean-Jacques Rousseau and Voltaire.

Dietrich, Marlene (Maria Magdalene Dietrich), *b. Berlin, Germany, 1901; d. 1992.* **Film actress.** An exotic glamour queen who sometimes dressed in men's clothing, Dietrich was a uniquely erotic addition to Hollywood during the 1930's. She was discovered in Germany by Josef von Sternberg, who constructed her image as the mysterious femme fatale for *The Blue Angel* (1930). They made six more films together in Hollywood, including *Shanghai Express* (1932) and *The Devil Is a Woman* (1935). Though her film career faltered in the 1950's, she reinvented herself as a nightclub performer.

Diocletian *b. Salonae, Dalmatia (now Solin, Croatia), 245; d. 316.* **Roman emperor (284–305).** Known for restoring order to the Roman Empire and waging a persecution of the Christians later in his reign, Diocletian came into power through his military service and the death of Numerian, brother of the emperor Carinus. After his soldiers hailed him emperor in 284 and Carinus was killed by his own soldiers, Diocletian rendered the senate and other remnants of the republic virtually powerless. He divided the empire with Maximian, who ruled the western half, in 286. In 293 he further divided the empire, naming four caesars to govern. He abdicated in 305, leaving the empire in disarray until Constantine I took power.

Disney, Walt, (Walter Elias Disney) *b. Chicago, Illinois, 1901; d. 1966.* **Animator, producer.** The world's most successful producer of children's entertainment, Walt Disney trained and worked as a commercial artist in Kansas City and then, in 1923, moved to Hollywood, where he created Mickey Mouse and Donald Duck. He made *Steamboat Willie* (1928), the first animated cartoon to use synchronized sound; and *Snow White and the Seven Dwarfs* (1937), the first feature-length cartoon. In the 1950's, Disney expanded into live-action features, television series, and a theme park, Disneyland, that has become one of America's most popular tourist attractions.

Disraeli, Benjamin, first Earl of Beaconsfield, *b. London, 1804; d. 1881.* **English statesman and man of letters.** Disraeli was elected to the House of Commons in 1837; after a brief term as prime minister in 1868 he regained the post from 1874 to 1880. As prime minister he guided legislation to aid the working class, borrowed money to gain controlling interest in the Suez Canal, and gave Queen Victoria the title empress of India. He also wrote novels that reflected his experience in the workings of politics.

Djerassi, Carl, *b. Vienna, Austria, 1923.* **Chemist.** Djerassi invented the first oral contraceptive for women (the Pill). His honors include the National Medal of Science, the National Medal of Technology, and the Priestley Medal. Turning to writing later in life, Djerassi published his first novel, *Cantor's Dilemma*, in 1991. He is the author of several plays, novels, and works of autobiography including *The Pill, Pygmy Chimps, and Degas' Horse* (1992).

Donatello (Donato di Niccolo di Betto Bardi), *b. Florence, 1386 or 1387; d. 1466.* **Sculptor.** Donatello worked under Ghiberti and became the most innovative and versatile sculptor of the early Renaissance. Moving away from the conventions of the late Gothic period, he sought inspiration from the classical sculptors of antiquity. His remarkably lifelike statues include *David* (ca. 1425–30), depicted as a nearly nude adolescent, and the armored *St. George* (ca. 1415–17); his bronze work includes *The Feast of Herod* (ca. 1425), on the baptismal font in Siena Cathedral. Donatello invented the shallow *schiacciato* method of relief. He was patronized and supported by Cosimo de'Medici, who had Donatello buried beside him in the family vault.

Donne, John, *b. 1572, London, d. 1631,* **Poet.** Donne, the first "metaphysical" poet, introduced a new poetic style—witty, colloquial, almost perverse in its leaps of thought and imagery—that strongly influenced poets of the 20th century. Donne left the Catholic Church, joined military expeditions, became a courtier, and pursued ladies; then in 1615 he became an Anglican priest. He is at once a great poet of physical love ("The Ecstasy," "The Canonization") and religious devotion. Keenly conscious of death, he composed several elegies, as well as satires and celebrated prose sermons. Nearly all of Donne's poetry was published posthumously.

Dos Passos, John, *b. Chicago, 1896; d. 1970.* **Novelist.** Dos Passos traveled as a newspaper correspondent in Europe after World War I before settling in the United States to write novels that addressed the social and economic conditions of the day. His naturalistic novels, sometimes called documentary novels, are characterized by strict realism and the accumulation of material, such as newspaper headlines and popular songs, taken from the real world. These novels include the *U.S.A.* trilogy: (*The 42nd Parallel* (1930), *1919* (1932), and *The Big Money* (1936).

Dostoyevsky, Fyodor, *b. 1821, Moscow; d. 1881.* **Novelist.** Dostoyevsky's father was killed by his own serfs; this event informed the psychological searching, violence, and examination of guilt in the son's novels. Dostoyevsky's own time in a penal colony for socialist activities left him with epilepsy and a deep Russian Orthodox faith, which influenced his development into the greatest of all religious novelists in his most important works: *Crime and Punishment* (1866), a tale of violent sin and redemption; *The Idiot* (1868), a portrait of a Christlike figure; *The Possessed* (1872), a rejection of socialist revolutionary ideas; and *The Brothers Karamazov* (1880), his investigation of evil and faith.

Douglass, Frederick (Frederick Augustus Washington Bailey), *b. Tuckahoe, Md., 1818; d. 1895.* **Abolitionist.** Born to a slave mother and a white father, he spent his childhood in slavery but secretly learned to read. As a teenager, he was hired out to a brutal overseer before escaping to the North. Douglass became a powerful orator and a leading voice in the struggle against slavery. In 1845, his autobiography was published to great acclaim, and during the Civil War he served as a consultant to President Lincoln. He was U.S. minister to Haiti from 1889 to 1891.

Doyle, Sir Arthur Conan, *b. Edinburgh, Scotland, 1859; d. 1930.* **Author.** Trained as a medical student and fascinated by forensic diagnosis, Conan Doyle became famous as a fiction writer when he created one of the world's most memorable literary characters, the fastidious and eminently logical detective Sherlock Holmes. Conan Doyle turned out dozens of wildly popular Sherlock Holmes short stories, which gave birth to hundreds of radio, television, and movie dramatizations. He also produced historical novels and military chronicles; he devoted much of his later life to essays and nonfiction expounding on his deep belief in spiritualism.

Drake, Sir Francis, *b. Tavistock, England, 1540; d. 1596.* **English privateer and navigator.** In 1569–70, Drake sailed with his cousin to trade illegally in the Spanish Caribbean, where their ships were ambushed by the Spanish. In 1577–80, he commanded the *Golden Hind* on the first English circumnavigation of the globe, for which accomplishment he was knighted by Elizabeth I. In 1586, he rescued survivors of Sir Walter Raleigh's failed Roanoke colony. Drake played a leading role in England's struggle with Spain, and he sailed as vice admiral during the defeat of the Spanish Armada (1588). He died of dysentery while privateering in the Caribbean.

Du Bois, W. E. B. (William Edward Burghardt), *b. Great Barrington, Mass.; 1868; d. 1963.* **Author and civil rights leader.** A Ph.D. from Harvard (1895), Du Bois conducted pioneering empirical studies of black society. He advocated full black political and civil rights and was an early leader in the Pan-African movement and in cultural nationalism. He helped found the National Association for the Advancement of Colored People (NAACP), where he was research director and editor (1910–1934) of *The Crisis*. Disillusioned with the U.S., he late in life joined the Communist Party (1961), moved to Ghana, and renounced American citizenship.

Duchamp (Henri-Robert-) Marcel, *b. Blainville, France, 1887; d. 1968.* **Painter, sculptor, writer.** A groundbreaking and extremely influential artist, Duchamp became involved with the Dadaist movement (1915–22), which explored irrationality, chance, and the unconscious, as well as with Dada's successor, Surrealism, which was influenced by psychoanalytic theory. In the wake of these movements Duchamp invented the ready-made or found object sculpture; his piece *Bicycle Wheel* (1913), a single wheel mounted on a household stool, is a famous example of this playful yet highly theoretical genre. Other works include *Nude Descending a Staircase No. 2* (1912) and *Fountain* (1917).

Dulles, John Foster, *b. Washington, D.C., 1888; d. 1959.* **American statesman.** After serving as a U.S. adviser to the founding of the United Nations in 1945, and negotiating the peace treaty with Japan (1951), Dulles was appointed secretary of state by President Eisenhower in 1953. Pursuing a strong anticommunist strategy, he negotiated mutual defense treaties in Southeast Asia and the Middle East, and promoted the European Defense Community. His announced threat of "massive retaliation" with nuclear weapons against communist aggression was widely criticized as "brinkmanship."

Dumas, Alexandre, *b. 1802, Villers-Cotteret, France; d. 1870.* **Novelist.** The illegitimate son of an aristocratic father and a Haitian slave, Dumas, with little education, became an extraordinarily popular and wealthy Romantic novelist. He began as a playwright, first achieving success with *Henri III* in 1829. Turning to novels, he worked with collaborators and did not succeed until *The Three Musketeers* (1844), followed by two sequels, as well as *The Count of Monte Cristo* (1845) and *The Black Tulip* (1850).

Duncan, Isadora (Dora Angelica Duncan), *b. San Francisco, Calif., 1877; d. 1927.* **Legendary modern dancer and choreographer.** Largely self-educated in dance, Duncan began performing as a child, managed by her mother, who took her to New York in the mid-1890's. Isadora began giving solo recitals for wealthy New Yorkers, making a sensation with her barefoot, free-flowing performances, given in a loose-fitting tunic. In 1900, she traveled to London, where she was an immediate sensation, and a trip to Greece inspired her to begin "recreating" its ancient dances. She toured Europe and in 1921 she opened a school in Russia. A final U.S. tour was a failure, and she moved to Paris in 1925; two years later, she died in a freak automobile accident.

Dürer, Albrecht, *b. Nuremberg, Germany, 1471; d. 1528.* **Painter, printmaker, and writer.** Considered one of the greatest German artists, Dürer traveled to Italy early in his life, where he studied the work Renaissance masters. He made major contributions to the development of printmaking, and his most important works include a series of 15 woodcuts on the Book of Revelation, *The Apocalypse* (1496–98). His best-known pieces include *Death and the Devil* (1513), *Melencolia I* (1514) and *Four Apostles* (1526). Dürer was interested in the mathematical principles of images, and his writings include a treatise on proportion

Dvorák, Antonín, *b. Nelahozeves, Bohemia, 1841; d. 1904.* **Czechoslovakian (Bohemian) composer of the late Romantic era.** One of the great nationalist European composers of the 19th century, Dvorák was a natural melodist; many of his works evoke Bohemian and American folk songs. Notable works include Romance for Violin and Orchestra, Op. 11 (1873-7); Serenade in E Major for Strings, Op. 22 (1875); *Slavonic Dances*, Op. 46 (1878); Symphony No. 7 in D Minor (1884-5) Op. 70; Symphony No. 9 in E minor (*From the New World*) (1893) Op. 95; String Quartet No. 12 in F Major ("American"), Op. 96 (1893); and Cello Concerto in B Minor, Op. 104 (1894-5).

Dylan, Bob (Robert Allen Zimmerman), *b. Duluth, Minn., 1941.* **Folk and rock songwriter and vocalist.** One of the most influential songwriter of the 1960's., Dylan pioneered several different schools of songwriting, including the confessional singer-songwriter and stream-of-consciousness narrative styles. Throughout his career he embraced and popularized several styles, from the folk revival of the early 1960's through electric folk-rock and country rock. Important compositions include "Blowin' in the Wind" (1963), "The Times They Are A-Changin'" (1964), "Mr. Tambourine Man" (1964), and "Like a Rolling Stone" (1965); albums include *Highway 61 Revisited* (1965), *Blonde on Blonde* (1966), *Nashville Skyline* (1969), and *Blood on the Tracks* (1975).

Earhart, Amelia, *b. Atchison, Kan., 1897; disappeared 1937.* **Aviator.** Earhart initially made an impression in 1928 as the first woman to fly across the Atlantic Ocean as a passenger. Determined to win fame for her own achievements, she set out to cross the Atlantic again as a solo pilot, completing the journey in just under 15 hours. In 1935, she made an even longer solo flight from Hawaii to California, marking the first time anyone, male or female, had safely navigated this route. She set off on a round-the-world flight in 1937 but vanished mysteriously over the Pacific.

Earp, Wyatt, *b. Monmouth, Ill., 1848; d. 1929.* **Lawman.** An icon of the American West, Earp was an itinerant gambler and gunslinger, noted as a tough lawman during his stint as marshal of Dodge City, Kan. After Wyatt drifted to Tombstone, Ariz., where his brother Virgil was marshal, the Earps developed a bitter feud with the Clanton gang, culminating in 1881 in a famous shootout at the O.K. Corral. In 1882, after his brother Morgan was murdered, Earp was accused of killing two suspects. Fleeing a murder charge, he drifted through the West, eventually settling in California to make a living in real estate, mining, and gambling.

Eastman, George, *b. Waterville, N.Y., 1854; d. 1932.* **Inventor and industrialist.** Eastman's many innovations included a dry-plate photographic process, roll film, the Kodak camera (1888), and, late in his life, a color film (1928). He successfully incorporated his inventions into a well-organized, efficient manufacturing process for photographic equipment, and as a result was instrumental in transforming photography from a complex, expensive enterprise to a mass pursuit. He was active as a philanthropist in Rochester, where his production facilities were located, and elsewhere.

Eastwood, Clint, *b. San Francisco, 1930.* **American movie actor and director.** He began acting in B pictures and in *Rawhide* on televison (1959–66) and became a star in Italian westerns such as *The Good, the Bad, and the Ugly* (1966). With *Dirty Harry* (1971) he went on to play a string of taciturn action heroes, then turned to directing. He won an Oscar for best director for *Unforgiven* (1992).

Edison, Thomas Alva, *b. Milan, Ohio, 1847; d. 1931.* **American inventor and entrepreneur.** Edison devoted his life to developing practical inventions that could be commercialized. Beginning in 1876 he produced a stream of inventions that included improvements in the telegraph system, the phonograph, the incandescent electric light, electric dynamos, a motion picture camera, a storage battery, and a multitude of other devices he commercialized. He pioneered the organized invention process itself that has become the standard in most industries today.

Edwards, Jonathan, *b. East Windsor, Conn., 1703; d. 1758.* **American preacher and religious philosopher.** In 1729 Edwards became pastor in Northampton, Mass. The position provided a forum for his eloquent sermons and influential writings in support of a rigorous Calvinism. Together with other preachers, he brought about the Great Awakening, a religious revival in the American colonies. But his censorious views and actions in Northampton resulted in his being dismissed from the church in 1750. Until his death he continued to preach and write on questions of free will and determinism in Christian faith.

Einstein, Albert, *b. Ulm, Germany, 1879; d. 1955.* **German-American theoretical physicist.** Einstein was educated and began teaching in Zurich. In 1905 he published three papers that changed the history of physical science, introducing revolutionary concepts regarding the nature of light-particles (photons), the existence and nature of molecules (and Brownian motion), and the electrodynamics of moving bodies (special theory of relativity). In 1914 he accepted a professorship at Berlin's Kaiser Wilhelm Institute and in 1921 was awarded the Nobel Prize in Physics. In 1934, when the Nazi regime stripped the Jewish Einstein of citizenship and property, he moved to a post at Princeton University, soon to become an American citizen. A pacifist and humanitarian, he nonetheless encouraged President Roosevelt to pursue development of an atomic bomb, to preempt the Germans. One of the greatest synthesizers of scientific thought, Einstein helped develop quantum physics, but never accepted it as a unifying theory, and never realized his quest to find one.

Eisenhower, Dwight D., *b. Denison, Tex., 1890; d. 1969.* **Thirty-fourth U.S. president, 1953–61.** After graduating from West Point Dwight David Eisenhower spent World War I as a tank-training instructor, and in World War II he rose rapidly through the ranks, becoming commander of U.S. forces in Europe in 1942 and the country's first five-star general. Famous for his role in planning D-Day he served as army chief of staff until 1948, was named commander of NATO forces in 1950, and accepted the Republican nomination for president in 1952. "Ike" became one of the most popular presidents in U.S. history, though many questioned his lax work habits and detached management style. He ended the Korean War but aggressively pursued a strong military response to Soviet and communist expansion.

Eisenstein, Sergei, *b. Riga, Latvia, 1898; d. 1948.* **Film director and theoretician.** His experiments with the manipulative powers of editing expanded the perimeters of Russian montage and influenced filmmakers around the world. Eisenstein theorized that editing together two unrelated shots could result in an abstract idea or metaphor, a technique now called intellectual montage. Though evident in his first film, *Strike* (1925), Eisenstein's ideas took full shape in the groundbreaking *Battleship Potemkin* (1925). Denounced by Stalin for being too formalistic, he made few films in his later years; those included *Alexander Nevsky* (1938) and *Ivan the Terrible, I and II* (1944–46).

Eleanor of Aquitaine, *b. Fontevrault, France, c. 1122; d. 1204.* **Queen of both France (1137–52) and England (1152–1204).** Eleanor was considered the most influential woman in Europe in the 12th century. She inherited from her father, more French land than possessed was by the French king, Louis VII, whom she married in 1137. She retook possession of Aquitaine when the marriage was annulled in 1152, and then married Henry Plantagenet, heir to the British throne. When he acceded, as Henry II, he ruled England, Normandy, and western France. She was mother of Richard I (Richard the Lion-Heart) John I.

Eliot, George (pseudonym of Mary Ann Evans), *b. 1819, Warwickshire, England; d. 1880.* **Novelist.** Mary Ann (or Marian) Evans grew up in a devout evangelical home but renounced religion and lived with a married man, G. H. Lewes. Her first novel was *Adam Bede* (1859), followed by *The Mill on the Floss* (1860), and her best-known, *Silas Marner* (1861). Writing mainly of rural life, she keenly observed society and was deeply concerned with moral responsibility. Other novels are *Romola*, a historical romance (1863); *Felix Holt* (1866); *Middlemarch*, her masterpiece (1872);, and *Daniel Deronda* (1876).

Eliot, T. S. (Thomas Stearns), *b. St. Louis, 1888; d. 1965.* **American-English poet, dramatist, and critic.** Eliot moved permanently to England in 1914 and soon published an entirely new kind of poetry for the 20th century, beginning with the ironic, anxiously edged, uneven-lined monologue, "The Love Song of J. Alfred Prufrock" in 1915. With *The Waste Land* (1922), a long, allusive, diverse poem, he established himself as a great poet who had found the voice and prosody to capture the barren and broken condition of Western civilization after World War I. He later expressed Christian faith in poems such as "Ash Wednesday" (1930) and the *Four Quartets* (1943). Eliot was a particularly astute critic of Elizabethan and Jacobean poetry and drama. After his historical drama, *Murder in the Cathedral* (1935), he wrote plays with contemporary settings, including *The Cocktail Party* (1950).

Elizabeth I, *b. Greenwich, England, 1533; d. 1603.* **Queen of England (1558–1603).** The 45-year reign of the "Virgin Queen" was known as the Elizabethan age, an era in which England became a major power in European politics and the arts. The daughter of Henry VIII and Anne Boleyn, she succeeded her half-sister Mary I, who had reinstated Catholicism as the law of the land. Elizabeth's coronation was publicly and prominently celebrated as the return of Protestant Reformation. In 1588, the queen's navy stunned the mighty Spanish Armada, catapulting England to the rank of world power. Elizabeth never married and died without heirs.

Ellington, Duke (Edward Kennedy Ellington), *b. Washington, D.C., 1899; d. 1974.* **Jazz composer, arranger, pianist, and bandleader.** Ellington was one of the most important composer in the history of jazz, and the leader of one of its longest-lasting and most influential big bands. He used his band as a laboratory for his new compositions, and often shaped his writing to showcase the talents of individual band members. Important songs include "East St. Louis Toodle-Oo" (1926), "Black and Tan Fantasy" (1928), "Mood Indigo" (1931), "It Don't Mean a Thing (If It Ain't Got That Swing)" (1932), "Sophisticated Lady" (1933), "Caravan" (1937), "Take the 'A' Train" (1941), "I Got It Bad (And That Ain't Good)" (1941), and "Don't Get Around Much Anymore" (1943).

Emerson, Ralph Waldo, *b. Boston, 1803; d. 1882.* **Poet and essayist.** Emerson, like his father, was a Unitarian minister, but his unorthodox views led to an early end to his clerical career and ostracism by Harvard Divinity School. He took up a literary (and lecturing) career and expressed, beginning with the essay "Nature" in 1836, a philosophy to be known as "Transcendentalism" that became an important literary movement. It held that God was immanent in man and nature, and emphasized individual freedom. His lecture "American Scholar" (1837) was a historic call for cultural independence from Europe. *Essays* (1841) contained the famous "Self-Reliance"; his other books include *Representative Men* (1850) and *The Conduct of Life* (1860). Noted poems are "The Rhodora" (1834), "Concord Hymn" (1837), and "Threnody" (1846).

Engels, Friedrich, *b. Barmen, Germany, 1820, d. 1895.* **Revolutionary and social philosopher.** He managed a factory in Manchester, England, and wrote *The Condition of the Working Class in England* (1845). In 1844, he met Karl Marx and began a close lifelong collaboration. They published the *Communist Manifesto* (1848), predicting the overthrow of capitalism and the triumph of communism. After the failure of the revolutions in 1848 in Europe, Engels moved back to England, where, as a successful businessman, he supported Marx's work on *Das Kapital.* He edited the second and third volumes after Marx's death.

Erasmus, Desiderius, *b. Rotterdam, c.1466; d.1536.* **Humanist, scholar, and Roman Catholic priest.** He was one of the leading figures of the Renaissance, widely known for his editions of Greek and Latin classics and the church fathers, his translation of the New Testament into Latin from the original Greek, and his personal humor and tolerance. His own writings were mainly critical and satirical works, the latter including *In Praise of Folly* (1509). Although he had attacked clerical abuses and favored Church reform, he opposed the Reformation and became a bitter enemy of Martin Luther.

Ericsson, Leif ("the Lucky"), *b. Iceland, ca. 970; d. ca. 1020.* **Norse-Icelandic explorer.** Ericsson and his father, Eric "the Red" Thorvaldsson, settled in Greenland ca. 985. While returning from a visit to Norway ca. 1001, he was blown off course and apparently sailed as far west as Labrador or Newfoundland, previously visited by Bjarni Herjulfsson in the 980's. Around 1001, Ericsson sailed for lands he called Helluland, Markland, and Vinland, possibly Baffin Island, Labrador, or Newfoundland. Around 1005 his brother attempted to colonize Vinland, possibly at L'Anse aux Meadows, Newfoundland, but the colony was abandoned after he was killed.

Euclid, *b. birthplace unknown, Greece, fl. ca. 300 B.C.* Working in Alexandria, Euclid organized what was known about mathematics in his time into a complete axiomatic system in a work called *Elements*. His selection of axioms and postulates, although criticized for a few unstated assumptions, shows great sophistication. Many theorems in *Elements* are thought to be original, especially those in number theory.

Euler, Leonhard, *b. Basel, Switzerland, 1707; d. 1783.* **Swiss mathematician.** Euler created much of the calculus that is taught in colleges today, including many specific sequences and series; advanced trigonometry; and much of standard notation, such as $f(x)$ for a function. More than a dozen well-known results bear his name and *e*, the base of the natural logarithms, is called Euler's number. Euler contributed to all branches of mathematics, including number theory and geometry. It is calculated that Euler averaged about 800 pages of new mathematics each year from the time he was 16 until the day of his death.

Euripides, *b. Athens, 484 B.C.; d. 406 B.C.* **Playwright.** One of the three great tragic playwrights of ancient Greece, Euripides created psychological but realistic dramas in which complex characters are responsible for their fate. Of a total of 92 plays, only 19 still exist. Among them are *Medea* (431 B.C.), *The Trojan Women* (415 B.C.), and *The Bacchae* (c. 406 BC).

Evert, Chris (Chris Evert Lloyd), *b. Fort Lauderdale, Fla., 1954.* **Tennis player.** Noted for her poise on the court, her strong two-handed backhand, and her nearly flawless baseline game, she won at least one Grand Slam title every year from 1974 to 1986. She won seven French Open titles (1974–75, 1979–80, 1983, 1985–86), six U.S. Open titles (1975–78, 1980, 1982), three Wimbledon titles (1974, 1976, 1981), and two Australian Open titles (1982, 1984).

Eyck, Jan van, *b. ?Maaseick, Netherlands, ca. 1395; d. 1441.* **Painter.** Beginning his career as an illuminator, van Eyck perfected the fine technique and small scale that characterize his paintings. One of the first artists in northern Europe to promote oil painting, he is known for vibrant colors and a polished finish. Van Eyck worked for John III, count of Holland; and was court painter to Philip the Good. His works, which include *Man in a Red Chaperon* (1433) and *Giovanni Arnolfini* and *Giovanna Cenami* (1434), influenced later artists in Italy and northern Europe.

Fairbanks, Douglas, Sr., (Douglas Elton Ulman) *b. Denver, Colo., 1883; d. 1939.* **Silent film actor.** In the silent era, he created the icon of the American film hero—attractive, morally courageous, and action-oriented. Fairbanks's physical agility and devil-may-care attitude made him a top star in such stunt-filled adventures as *The Mark of Zorro* (1920), *The Thief of Bagdad* (1924), and *The Black Pirate* (1926). To combat the increasing power of the big studios, Fairbanks, Mary Pickford, Charlie Chaplin, and D. W. Griffith formed United Artists in 1919 to distribute their films. Fairbanks and Pickford married the following year, enhancing their star power.

Faraday, Michael, *b. Newington, England, 1791; d. 1867.* **Physicist and chemist.** The discoverer of electromagnetic induction, Faraday was fascinated with electricity from a young age. His first scientific achievements were in chemistry. In 1825 he isolated benzene. He later turned to physics, inventing the first electric motor and dynamo, and developing laws of electrochemistry.

Farragut, David Glasgow, *b. Campbell's Station, Tenn., 1801; d. 1870.* **U.S. Navy officer.** Adopted son a of U.S. Navy captain, David Porter, Farragut joined the navy at age nine and served in the War of 1812 and the Mexican War. At the start of the Civil War, Farragut commanded the West Gulf Blockading Squadron, with which he seized New Orleans on April 25, 1862. On July 4, 1863, Farragut's riverine fleet helped capture Vicksburg, Miss., and in August 1864 his ships captured the approaches to Mobile, Ala. To honor Farragutís accomplishments, Congress created the ranks of rear admiral, vice admiral, and admiral.

Faulkner, William, *b. New Albany, Miss., 1897; d. 1962.* **Novelist.** Faulkner is regarded as the greatest southern writer. His four most important novels were written in a short span: *The Sound and the Fury* (1929), *As I Lay Dying* (1930), *Light in August* (1932), and *Absalom, Absalom!* (1936). In them he created an imaginary Mississippi county, Yoknapatawpha, with recurring characters, in which the traditional southern family and society are racked by intense psychological and historical strain. In content they are vividly emotional, graphic, and often violent. Faulkner later focused three novels— *The Hamlet* (1940), *The Town* (1957), and *The Mansion* (1959)—on the Snopeses, a family of ascendent "poor whites." *Intruder in the Dust* (1948), which deals harshly with racism, led to his winning the Nobel Prize in Literature in 1949.

Fellini, Federico, *b. Rimini, Italy, 1920; d. 1974.* **Film director.** Mixing autobiography and neorealism, Fellini fashioned a style that was personal in content but universal in theme. He began as a screenwriter for the neorealist director Roberto Rossellini; and his first films—*Variety Lights* (1951), *The White Sheik* (1952), and *I Vitelloni* (1953)—had neorealist characteristics. With *La Strada* (1954), starring his wife and muse Guilietta Masina, he embraced a more personal style, reaching his peak with *La Dolce Vita* (1960) and *8 1/2* (1963). Four of Fellini's films won Oscars as best foreign film: *La Strada*, *The Nights of Cabiria* (1957), *8 1/2*, and *Amarcord* (1973).

Fermat, Pierre de *b. Beaumont de Lomagne, France, 1601; d. 1665.* **French mathematician.** Fermat was a lawyer by profession but discovered analytic geometry a year before Descartes and employed some of the main ideas of calculus before either Newton or Leibniz. His main fame today, however, comes from many discoveries about number relationships. Fermat's "last theorem," that for natural numbers there is no number n greater than 2 for which $xn + yn = zn$ is true, is especially well known. Fermat claimed a proof of this theorem, but did not reveal it. It was finally proved in 1995.

Fermi, Enrico, *b. Rome, Italy, 1901 d. 1954.* **Italian-American physicist.** Fermi is the only physicist of the 20th century whose experimental work and theoretical work are equally valuable. In the 1920's he developed the first mathematical treatment of how electrons and similar particles of matter—now called fermions—interact physically. This work with electrons became the basis of the modern theory of conductivity. Fermi also showed experimentally that slow-moving neutrons can change one element or isotope into another. In 1942 Fermi was the chief designer of the first working nuclear reactor, based on using slow neutrons and techniques that he had developed to control nuclear fission in uranium.

Feynman, Richard, *b. Far Rockaway, N.Y., 1918; d. 1988.* **American physicist.** Feynman was one of the leading developers of quantum physics, the theory of sub-atomic particle behavior that expanded Einstein's theory of relativity—and, specifically, of quantum electrodynamics, for which work he was a co-winner of a 1965 Nobel Prize. He was also a lucid explicator, known for the Feynman diagram (1949), which depicted the paths and interactions of particles in space and time. Feynman was one of the youngest of the major participants in the Manhattan Project that developed the atomic bomb, and four decades later identified the cause—faulty "O-rings"—of the *Challenger* spaceship disaster.

Fielding, Henry, *b. Somerset, England, 1707; d. 1754.* **Novelist and playwright.** Fielding is considered, with Samuel Richardson, to be a founder of the English novel. His first novel, *Shamela* (1741), is a parody of Richardson's *Pamela* (1740). Although other of his novels also began as parodies, Fielding quickly found in the novel a form for social criticism. His most famous work, *Tom Jones* (1749), is masterful in its social commentary and established the novel as a literary form.

Fields, W. C. (William Claude Dukinfield) *b. Philadelphia, 1879; d. 1946.* **Comic actor.** Starting out in vaudeville, he became a Ziegfeld star with his juggling and monologues, then went on to make many silent movies in the 1920's. His gnarled face and matching voice made his screen nastiness uproarious in later films such as *It's a Gift* and *The Man on the Flying Trapeze* (both 1934); a sole dramatic success came with *David Copperfield* (1935) in which he played Mr. Micawber. His movie with Mae West, *My Little Chickadee*, (1939) had brought him long-lasting fame. Fields wrote many of the stories for his comic movies.

Fillmore, Millard, *b. Locke Township, N.Y., 1800; d. 1874.* **Thirteenth U.S. president, 1850–53.** The son of a poor farmer, Fillmore entered politics as an Anti-Mason and was a four-term congressman when the Whigs made him Zachary Taylor's vice president in 1848. Dignified good looks were Fillmore's main political asset; he was quite unprepared for the presidency when Taylor died suddenly in 1850. Fillmore delayed civil war another decade by signing the Compromise of 1850, but he lost the nomination in 1852 when the Whigs turned to Gen. Winfield Scott, yet another genial war hero and the party's last candidate.

Fischer, Bobby, *b. Chicago, Ill., 1943.* The only American ever to become world chess champion, the quixotic Fischer was 15 when he became the world's youngest grandmaster. He won an unprecedented 20 straight matches in the Interzonal and Candidates' matches of 1970 and 1971 to win the right to challenge the champion, Boris Spassky. After overwhelming Spassky in 1972, Fischer refused to play another match in public, and forfeited his world title in 1975.

Fitzgerald, F. Scott, *b. St. Paul, Minn., 1896; d. 1940.* **Novelist.** Fitzgerald left Princeton without graduating, joined the army, and then wrote his first novel, *This Side of Paradise* (1920), about college life, which was an immediate success; he followed it with *The Beautiful and the Damned* (1922). He married an Alabama belle, Zelda Sayre, and they lived prodigally in New York City. *The Great Gatsby* (1925), set in the "jazz age" of that time and place, is his most famous novel. *Tender Is the Night* (1934), is set among American expatriates in France, a life he and Zelda also lived. The romance of his own life was scuttled by alcoholism and Zelda's mental illness. Dead at 44 of a heart attack, he left an unfinished novel, *The Last Tycoon.*

Flaubert, Gustave, *b. Rouen, France, 1821; d. 1880.* **Novelist.** A surgeon's son, Flaubert was a master of realism who wrote of French middle-class life with controlled, if scornful, objectivity and legendary stylistic precision. His first and best-known novel, *Madame Bovary* (1857), describes the adulterous adventures of an unhappy provincial woman, and led to his trial for immorality, of which he was acquitted. Of equal merit is *Sentimental Education* (1870), in which romance and other aspirations are swallowed by mercenary conditions of French society. Flaubert suffered from epilepsy and lived mostly with his mother. Other works are the novels *Salammbô* (1863) and *The Temptation of St. Anthony* (1874).

Fleming, Sir Alexander, *b. 1881, Lochfield, Ayr, Scotland; d. 1955.* **Bacteriologist.** A researcher and university professor, Fleming discovered the antibiotic properties of the *Penicillium notatum* mold while studying *Staphylococcus* bacteria in 1928, and published his work on penicillin the following year. In its raw form, penicillin is unstable, and Fleming dropped his research. In 1940, the Oxford scientists Howard Florey and Ernst Chain isolated and purified penicillin and devised means for its mass production. The three shared the 1945 Nobel Prize for Physiology or Medicine "for the discovery of penicillin and its curative effect in various infectious diseases."

Fonda, Henry, *b. 1905, Grand Island, Neb.; d. 1982.* **Actor.** Tall, slim, slow, and steady, Henry Fonda started out doing Community Theater in Omaha, before moving east to join the Cape Cod University Players, where he was soon joined by James Stewart. His film career began with a series of honest country-boy roles in the late 1930's. For John Ford, he starred in *Young Mr. Lincoln* (1939) and *The Grapes of Wrath* (1940), and he played the legendary Wyatt Earp in *My Darling Clementine* (1946). His greatest stage success was 1948's *Mister Roberts*, and he split his career between Broadway and Hollywood from the 1950's on. He won the Oscar for Best Actor for his last film, *On Golden Pond* (1982). His other important films include *The Lady Eve* (1941), *The Oxbow Incident* (1943), *The Wrong Man* (1957), and *12 Angry Men* (1952).

Fonda, Jane, *b. 1937, New York City.* **Actress.** The daughter of actor Henry Fonda, Jane was an art student and model before beginning studies at the Actors Studio in 1958. In 1965, she married the French director Roger Vadim for whom she made the sci-fi live-action comic strip movie *Barbarella* (1968). She graduated from sexpot to serious actress with *They Shoot Horses, Don't They* (1969), and won Best Actress Oscars for *Klute* (1971) and *Coming Home,* (1978). Her antiwar activities, including a trip to North Vietnam in 1972, earned her the nickname "Hanoi Jane."

Fonteyn, Margot (Peggy Hookham), *b. Reigate, England, 1919; d. 1991.* **Ballet dancer.** Fonteyn joined the Vic-Wells Ballet in London at age 14. She was a favorite of the choreographer Fredrick Ashton, who created many of his classic dances for her, including *Façade* (1939) and *Scènes de Ballets* (1948). Fonteyn made her U.S. debut in 1949, and her successes continued through the 1950's. In 1961, while touring Russia, she saw the young dancer Rudolf Nureyev perform, and a year later she arranged for him to costar with her in a production of *Giselle*. The two became famous partners, with the young Russian revitalizing Fonteyn's career in the 1960's.

Ford, Gerald R., *b. Omaha, Neb., 1913.* **Thirty-eighth U.S. president, 1974–77.** The only vice president and president never elected to either office, Ford served in Congress from 1949 until he was appointed to the vice presidency in December 1973, replacing Spiro T. Agnew under the 25th Amendment. From 1965 to 1973 he was Republican minority leader. Richard Nixon's resignation made Ford the new president on August 9, 1974. Ford announced that "our long national nightmare is over," but a month later he shocked the nation by giving Nixon a blanket pardon. He sought reelection in 1976 but lost to Jimmy Carter in the first defeat of an incumbent president since Herbert Hoover's.

Ford, Henry, *b. Springwells Township, Mich., 1863; d. 1947.* **American industrialist and automotive pioneer.** In 1903 Ford founded the Ford Motor Company to build the first mass-produced car for a mass market. He adopted the assembly line to lower the cost of production and allow him to price his cars low, and the company became the world's largest auto producer. The first Model T was shipped in 1908 and revolutionized transportation. In 1914 Ford began paying his workers the extraordinary wage of $5 for an eight-hour day, and offered them a share of the profits. By 1927 more than 15 million Model T's had been sold, but after that he lost his domination of the market to General Motors. His reputation was tarnished by anti-Semitic writings in his *Dearburn Independent* and by his anti-union policies.

Ford, John, (Sean Aloysius O'Fearna or O'Feeney) *b. Cape Elizabeth, Me., 1895; d. 1973.* **Film director.** Ford's personal vision was remarkably consistent during his 50-year career. His deceptively simple narratives embodied larger American experiences, and his protagonists represented the pioneer spirit of individualism. He went to Hollywood in 1917 and directed his first major silent film, *The Iron Horse* in 1924. His first successful "talkie" ws the *The Informer* (1935), set in revolutionary Ireland. He made John Wayne a star with *Stagecoach* (1939), beginning an association that yielded such western classics as *The Searchers* (1956) and *The Man Who Shot Liberty Valance* (1962). Though acclaimed for westerns, Ford won directing Oscars for his other work: *The Informer* (1935), *The Grapes of Wrath* (1940), *How Green Was My Valley* (1941), and *The Quiet Man* (1952).

Foreman, George, *b. Marshall, Tex., 1948.* **Heavyweight boxer.** A gold medalist at the Olympics of 1968. Foreman won his first 34 pro fights to earn a title shot in 1973 against Joe Frazier, whom he knocked down six times in two rounds. His first loss came in 1974 in Zaire to Muhammad Ali. Foreman retired in 1977 and was ordained as a minister, but he began a comeback in 1987 at age 39. In 1994, he became the oldest champion in any weight division by defeating Michael Moorer.

Forster, E. M. (Edward Morgan), *b. London, 1879; d. 1970.* **Novelist.** A traditional novelist but technically and stylistically superb, Forster published all his novels between 1905 and 1924. They include *A Room with a View* (1908), *Howards End* (1910); and *Maurice*, finished in 1914 but not published until 1971 because the relationships it explores are homosexual. In *A Passage to India* (1924), Forster's last novel, the relationships concern British colonials and native residents. Forster's major theme is the difficulty of forming meaningful human relationships, in society and in love. His *Aspects of the Novel* (1927) is an important work of literary criticism.

Francis I (Francis of Angoulême), *b. Cognac, France, 1494; d. 1547.* **King of France** (1515–47). Crowned at age 20, Francis I immediately waged a war to recapture the duchy of Milan (1515–16); he had himself knighted after the bloody victory. But the accession of Charles V as Holy Roman Emperor marked the end of Francis's power. Already king of Spain, Charles now surrounded France and had his sights on all of Europe. The enmity between the two kings set off a war that lasted more than two decades (1521–44). Captured at the Battle of Pavia (1525), Francis never again wielded influence in Europe.

Francis of Assisi, (Francesco di Pietro di Bernardone) *b. Giovanni Bernardone, Assisi, Italy, 1181–82?; d. 1226.* **Roman Catholic saint, founder of the Franciscan monastic order.** He was the son of a wealthy merchant. As a young soldier, Francis was imprisoned, then stricken ill, and experienced a sudden conversion during an expedition, about 1205. He embraced absolute poverty and became a hermit but was inspired to travel and preach. He attracted a small band of followers, which grew into an order of several thousand mendicant friars during his lifetime. His devotee, St. Clare, founded an order of nuns. Francis endured his hardships joyfully, loving all God's creation and, famously, preaching to animals and birds. He traveled to France, Spain, and Palestine, winning concessions for Christians from the sultan of Egypt. During his last years, Francis yielded active leadership of his order and is said to have received the wounds of Christ's crucifixion, or the stigmata.

Francis Xavier (Saint), *b. Xavier Castle, Navarre, Spain, 1506; d. 1552.* **Jesuit missionary, patron saint of Roman Catholic missions.** Francis Xavier, a nobleman and knight, was one of the first Jesuit priests, an associate of the order's founder, St. Ignatius of Loyola. After working with Ignatius in Rome, he went to Lisbon; from there, in 1541, he embarked on a Portuguese mission to Goa—and a career that would earn him the sobriquet "apostle to the Indies." A noted preacher, skilled in relating to people within their own cultures, he traveled to India, Ceylon, Malacca, the Moluccas, and Japan, and is estimated to have converted about 30,000 to Christianity. He died while sailing to China.

Franklin, Benjamin, *b. Boston, 1706; d. 1790.* **Printer and publisher, writer, inventor and scientist, statesman.** Franklin was a man of many talents and experiences. Among his best-known published works is *Poor Richard's Almanack* (1732–57). His inventions included the efficient Franklin (wood) stove and bifocal glasses. The lightning rod was a result of his famous experiments into the nature of electricity. Franklin's ideas for community resources included a library, fire department, insurance company, police, hospital, and an academy, that later became the University of Pennsylvania. Franklin was deputy postmaster general for the northern colonies (1753–74); Pennsylvania delegate to the Albany Congress; London (Parliament) agent for Pennsylvania, Georgia, New Jersey, and Massachusetts; delegate to the Second Continental Congress (helping draft the Declaration of Independence); and commissioner to France, securing military and economic aid for the American Revolution. Franklin was a member of the Constitutional Convention of 1787, which wrote the United States Constitution.

Frazier, Joe, *b. Beaufort S.C., 1944.* **Boxer.** Nicknamed "Smokin' Joe" for his relentless punching style, Frazier was a 1964 Olympic gold medalist and heavyweight champion from 1970 to 1973. But many in boxing did not consider him the champ until 1971, when he defeated Muhammad Ali, who had been stripped of his title in 1967. Frazier lost the title two years later in a stunning second-round knockout by George Foreman. Frazier later lost two wildly hyped bouts to Ali, including a 14th-round knockout in 1975 in the "Thrilla in Manila," one of the greatest fights of all time.

Frederick the Great (Frederick II), *b. Berlin, 1712: d. 1786.* **King of Prussia.** Soon after Frederick became king in 1740, he seized Silesia (now in southwestern Poland), which Austria ceded to him in 1745. Austria remained unrecounciled to its loss. In 1756, Frederick launched a preemptive war, which ended in 1763 with Frederick still in control of Silesia. Frederick's greatest diplomatic triumph was to persuade Austria and Russia to join him in the first partition of Poland in 1772. Frederick was a domestic reformer and a patron of the arts and letters, who, like many of his contemporary rulers, believed in "enlightened despotism."

Freud, Sigmund, *b. Freiburg, Moravia, 1856; d. 1939.* **Physician, founder of psychoanalysis.** Freud moved to Vienna at age four, and would live and work there nearly all his life. He studied medicine, which was one of the few professions open to Jews. Influenced by Josef Breuer, Freud became interested in using hypnosis to treat hysteria; then, working with J. M. Charcot in Paris, he moved toward a theoretical understanding of psychopathology, with emphasis on sexual causes. Hypnosis gave way to his technique of "free association," by which patients revealed repressed feelings believed to be the sources of neurotic symptoms. Freud developed a complex dynamic theory of the mind, dividing it into the unconscious id, containing irrational (including sexual) impulses; and the civilizing ego and conscientious superego. He published his groundbreaking first book, *The Interpretation of Dreams,* in 1900, followed by *The Psychopathology of Everyday Life* (1904). Other important works are *Totem and Taboo* (1913), *Beyond the Pleasure Principle* (1919), *The Ego and the Id* (1923), and, on religion, *The Future of an Illusion* (1927). After the Nazi annexation of Austria, Freud spent his last year in London.

Friedman, Milton, *b. New York City, 1912.* **American economist.** From 1946 to 1976, Friedman taught at the University of Chicago, where he was the leading voice of the Chicago school of monetary economics, arguing that the Federal Reserve should regulate the supply of money to achieve economic stability during business cycles. He strongly advocated a free market system with emphasis on individual freedom. Among his important books are *A Theory of the Consumption Function* (1957), *Capitalism and Freedom* (1962), *A Monetary History of the United States, 1867–1960* (1963) with Anna Schwartz, *A Theoretical Framework for Monetary Analysis* (1971), and *Free to Choose* (1980), with his wife, Rose Friedman. He was awarded the Nobel Prize in Economic Science in 1976.

Frost, Robert Lee, *b. San Francisco, 1874; d. 1963.* **Poet.** Frost moved to Lawrence, Mass., at age 10, and is considered the quintessential 20th-century New England poet. After withdrawing from Harvard, he lived meanly as a New Hampshire farmer, then moved to England and published his first books of poetry, *A Boy's Will* (1913) and *North of Boston* (1914). Their success brought him back home, where he became America's most famous poet. His use of traditional verse patterns, colloquial diction, and natural settings in lyrical poems like "Mending Wall," "After Apple Picking" (both 1914), and "Stopping by Woods on a Snowy Evening" (1923), make them appealing, yet closer reading reveals inklings of mystery and danger. Important narrative poems include "The Death of the Hired Man," "Home Burial" (both 1914), and "Two Tramps in Mud Time" (1936). His style was consistent throughout many volumes of poems, for which he won four Pulitzer Prizes.

Gable, Clark, *b. Cadiz, Ohio, 1901; d. 1960.* **American movie actor.** "The King" with his knowing grin that signaled rugged force made more than 65 films, many with the beautiful stars of succeeding generations: Joan Crawford, Jean Harlow, Hedy Lamarr, Lana Turner, Grace Kelly, and Marilyn Monroe. He won an Oscar for a comic performance in *It Happened One Night* (1934) and is best known as Rhett Butler in *Gone With the Wind* (1939). In *The Misfits* (1960)—his last film, made shortly after his death—he played a tough, aging cowboy.

Galen (Galenos), *b. Pergamum, Mysia, Anatolia [now Bergama, Turkey) 129; d. ca. 216.* **Greek physician, writer, and philosopher.** Galen spent most of his career in Rome. A prolific author and unabashed promoter of his theories, he was an early advocate of dissection, which he used to expand knowledge of the nervous system and demonstrate that arteries carry blood, rather than air, as had been thought for centuries. But because he could work only with animals (human dissection was forbidden), he often mistook animal anatomy for human. Although his conclusions were often wrong, his methods of observation and investigation, described in copius writings, were sound, and his influence on medicine lasted for centuries.

Galileo (Galileo Galilei), *b. 1564, d. 1642* **Italian astronomer, physicist, inventor, mathematician.** Galileo taught at the University in Pisa and Padua and worked in Florence as a Medici patron. After developing the first astronomical telescopes, Galileo discovered the moons of Jupiter, the phases of Venus, the mountains and plains of the Moon, sunspots, and the individual stars of the Milky Way. In physics his experiments showed that all bodies would fall at the same distance in the same amount of time in a vacuum and that objects in motion continue to move in a straight line unless a force acts against them. He also contributed to the study of mathematical infinity and invented the first way to measure temperature. Galileo promoted Copernican views as early as 1604 and did not stop when in 1616 the church declared such ideas to be heresy. Galileo, who had enjoyed close relations with Church officials was put before the Inquisition and informed that he must recant or be tortured; he recanted, but spent the last years of his life under house arrest.

Gandhi, Indira, *b. Allahabad, India, 1917; d. 1984.* **Prime minister of India.** Daughter of Jawaharlal Nehru, India's first prime minister, she herself became India's head of state in 1966. She made strides in modernizing India but never quelled its political turmoil. In 1971, Gandhi provided military support for the secession of East Bengal from Pakistan, creating Bangladesh. She won the election of 1972 in a landslide, but courts later upheld charges of election fraud in 1975. Gandhi responded by jailing her opponents and suspending civil liberties. In 1977, she was toppled from power, later regaining her post as prime minister in 1980. After quashing a Sikh uprising in 1984 she was assassinated by her Sikh bodyguards. Her son Rajiv succeeded her, and he, too, was assassinated in 1991.

Gandhi, Mahatma (Mohandas Karamchand Gandhi), *b. Porbandar, India 1869; d. 1948.* **Indian revolutionary.** Gandhi studied law in London and practiced in South Africa, where his spirituality deepened and he first exercised nonviolent resistance. He returned to India in 1915 and became involved in national affairs. Considered the father of modern India—Mahatma means "Great Soul"—Mohandas Gandhi used the tactics of nonviolent protest to throw off British rule and establish an independent India in 1947. His invention of *satyagraha*, or devotion to truth, encompassed civil disobedience, sit-ins, fasting, and other forms of nonviolent resistance. Weeks after fostering a truce between rioting Hindus and Muslims in Delhi, Gandhi was assassinated by Nathuram Godse, a Hindu fanatic.

Garbo, Greta,(Greta Louisa Gustafsson) *b. Stockholm, Sweden, 1905; d. 1990.* **Film actress.** Garbo became one of Hollywood's enduring legends when she created her star image as an enigmatic woman of mystery. Discovered by the Swedish director Mauritz Stiller, she came to Hollywood during the silent era to make *The Torrent* (1926) for MGM. She successfully survived the coming of sound with *Anna Christie* (1930), then moved on to such classic dramas as *Anna Karenina* (1935) and *Camille* (1937), generally playing an aloof, remote woman pained by love . She retired in 1941 and received a career Oscar in 1954.

Garcia Marquez, Gabriel, *b. 1928, Aracataca, Colombia.* **Novelist, short-story writer.** Garcia Marquez worked as a journalist before publishing his first book of fiction, *Leafstorm and Other Stories*, in 1955. In that, a subsequent collection, and an internationally popular novel, *One Hundred Years of Solitude*, he developed into the best-known practitioner of Latin-American "magical realism," which combines realistic narrative with myth and fantasy. Although he has lived largely in Mexico and Spain, his writing focuses on Colombia, and deals with the tension between solitude and love. Other novels are *Autumn of the Patriarch* (1975), *Love in the Time of Cholera* (1985), and *The General in His Labyrinth* (1989).

Garfield, James A., *b. Orange, Ohio, 1831; d. 1881.* **Twentieth U.S. president, 1881.** Garfield was a classics professor, president of Hiram College, a lawyer, and at age 30 the youngest Union general in the Civil War. He left the battlefield in 1864 to enter Congress, where he remained until the Republicans nominated him for president in 1880. Garfield won the fall election, but after only four months in office was shot in a Washington, D.C., railroad station by Charles J. Guiteau, a disappointed office-seeker. He died 80 days later.

Garibaldi, Giuseppe, *b. Nice, France, 1807, ; d. 1882.* **Italian patriot.** A merchant seaman by trade, Garibaldi was a radical advocate of Italian unification, women's rights, workers, and racial equality. In exile from Italy (1836–48) he fought for Brazilian and Uruguayan independence movements. In 1860, he helped usher in the kingdom of Italy with his invasion of Sicily and Naples. Governments kept him at arm's length, but he led the campaign of 1866 that took Venice from Austria. An attack on Rome failed owing to French resistance, but he fought for the French in the Franco-Prussian War (1870–71) before retiring to Caprera Island.

Garland, Judy (Frances Ethel Gumm), *b. 1922, Grand Rapids, Minn.; d. 1969.* **Singer and movie actress.** Raised in vaudeville, she became a star as Dorothy in *The Wizard of Oz* (1939), singing her signature "Over the Rainbow." After several spirited "let's put on a show" pictures with Mickey Rooney, she grew into adult roles in such notable musicals as *Meet Me in St. Louis* (1944), *The Harvey Girls* (1945), and *Easter Parade* (1948). Fired by MGM in 1950, she made a glamorous comeback in *A Star Is Born* (1954), then went on to successful worldwide concerts and a turbulent year on television.

Garrison, William Lloyd, *b. Newburyport, Mass., 1805; d. 1879.* **Abolitionist.** Publisher of *The Liberator* (beginning in 1831), a newspaper famous for its searing moral attacks on the institution of slavery, Garrison advocated immediate and complete abolition. His self-righteous tone and demand for overnight reform alienated many. He advocated secession of the North from the Union because the

Constitution permitted slavery, and he opposed the Civil War until Lincoln issued the Emancipation Proclamation. Garrison served as president of the American Anti-Slavery Society for more than two decades.

Garvey, Marcus, *b. Saint Ann's Bay, Jamaica, 1887; d. 1940.* **Black nationalist leader.** Garvey's experience as a printer in Jamaica inspired him to lead blacks into better economic conditions and give them pride in their African heritage. In 1914 he founded the Universal Negro Improvement Association, moving to New York City in 1916. He espoused a "Back to Africa" movement and founded the Black Star Line in 1919 to transport blacks to Africa. But mismanagement doomed the enterprise, and he was charged with mail fraud in 1922, convicted, and jailed in 1925. His sentence was commuted in 1927, and he was deported to Jamaica, where he was unable to rebuild the U.N.I.A.

Gates, Bill (William Henry Gates III), *b. Seattle, Wash., 1955.* **Businessman.** At age 19, Gates and his childhood friend Paul Allen founded the Microsoft Company. In 1980 they began producing MS-DOS, the operating system for IBM's first personal computer. DOS and subsequent programs, including Windows, made Microsoft the world's largest software producer. Aggressive marketing earned Microsoft billions in profits (and persistent accusations of antitrust violations). Often proclaimed the world's richest man, Gates also founded Corbis, a massive digital archive of art and photography; and he endowed a $24 billion philanthropic foundation to tackle global health and education issues.

Gauguin, Paul, *b. Paris, France, 1848; d. 1903.* **Painter, printmaker, sculptor, ceramicist.** After a successful stint as a stockbroker, Gaugin left his wife and five children to pursue a life devoted to art. Inspired by Impressionism, Gauguin developed a unique style of Symbolism that incorporated elements from primitive Polynesian culture, and spent several years in Tahiti, developing an "untamed" aesthetic. With the artist Emile Bernard, Gauguin invented a method of rendering pictoral space that uses large patches of flat color and thick line; these techniques influenced early 20th-century artists. Gauguin's works include *Vision after the Sermon: Jacob Wrestling with the Angel* (1888), *Mahana no atua (Day of the God)* (1814), and *Savage Tales* (1902).

Gauss, Carl Friedrich *b. Brunswick, Germany, 1777, d. 1855* **German mathematician and physical scientist.** Between the ages of 19 and 28 Gauss discovered the first major new geometric construction since Greek times (1796) and developed the first proof that all polynomial equations have a solution, the fundamental theorem of algebra (1799); completely restructured number theory (1801); and invented a way to calculate the path of a planet from a few observations (1809). Later he created the theory that mathematically describes properties of surfaces (1827) and also became the first to establish a non-Euclidean geometry. Gauss also studied Earth's magnetic field and with a collaborator built one of the first working telegraphs (1833).

Gehry, Frank Owen, *b. Toronto, 1929.* **Architect.** His early houses included the Davis Studio and Residence (1968–72) in Malibu and his own house in Santa Monica (1977–78, and 1991–2002) and exhibit his imaginative use of industrial materials in incongruous settings. The Guggenheim Museum (1991–97) in Bilbao, Spain, with its billowing titanium exterior walls, gained him world attention and put the city of Bilbao on the tourist map. Gehry demonstrated his inventiveness with the DG Bank building (1995–2001) in Berlin. The exterior of the Walt Disney Concert Hall (1987–2003) in Los Angeles, is a variation in stainless steel of the sweeping curves of the Bilbao Guggenheim.

Gell-Mann, Murray, *b. New York City, 1929* **American physicist.** In 1963 Gell-Mann showed that some short-lived subatomic particles do not decay as fast as predicted, because of a quality Gell-Mann named "strangeness". Gell-Mann developed a theory called the eightfold way that enabled him to predict the properties of a previously unknown particle, later discovered and named the omega-minus. In 1964 Gell-Mann proposed that mesons, protons, and other heavy subatomic particles are constructed from smaller particles called quarks, an idea now generally accepted as proved by experiment.

Genghis Khan (Chinggis, Jenghiz), *b. Mongolia, ca. 1162; d. 1227.* **World conquerer.** The orphan Temujin assembled a band of comrades to kill his father's murderers. A natural leader, he then set about assembling larger and larger coalitions of Mongol tribes for raiding and conquest. He was confirmed as great leader of all the tribes at an assembly in 1206, and took the name Genghis Khan ("oceanlike ruler"). In an unending cycle of conquest marked by both strategic genius and great brutality, his armies subdued a vast territory from northern China across Central Asia to west of the Caspian Sea and into south-central Russia. He died from injuries from a riding accident while on campaign; his secret tomb has never been found.

George III, *b. London, 1738; d. 1820.* **King of Great Britain and Ireland, elector of Hanover and king of Hanover.** George succeeded to the throne in 1760 and was determined to be an active ruler. But his policies helped to provoke the American Revolution, and the English defeat nearly forced him to abdicate. A mental condition, possibly porphyria, caused a progressive dementia, and in 1811 it had become so severe that his son, later George IV, was appointed regent until his death.

Geronimo (Goyathlay), *b. present-day site of Clifton, Ariz., 1829; d. 1909.* **American Indian warrior.** Renowned as a great medicine man and spiritual leader, Geronimo was one of the last holdouts against the inexorable white settlement of North America. His elite band of Apache warriors raided white settlements in what is now Arizona and New Mexico before being captured and forced onto a reservation in 1876. Geronimo escaped and eluded U.S. troops for a decade. Forced to surrender in 1886, he was shipped to Florida for imprisonment. Geronimo was ultimately settled in Oklahoma and never saw his homeland again.

Gershwin, George (Jacob Gershvin) *b. New York City, 1898; d. 1937.* **Popular composer.** Gershwin was both a talented songwriter in the Tin Pan Alley tradition (usually collaborating with his lyricist brother Ira) and a composer of serious classical music. Noteworthy compositions include the popular songs "Swanee" (1919), "Someone to Watch Over Me" (1926), "I Got Rhythm" (1927), "But Not for Me" (1927), "Embraceable You" (1927), "They Can't Take That Away from Me" (1937), and "Let's Call the Whole Thing Off" (1937); the classical compositions "Rhapsody in Blue" (1924) and "American in Paris" (1928); and the opera *Porgy and Bess* (1935).

Gibson, Bob, *b. Omaha, Neb., 1935.* **Baseball player.** Playing for the St. Louis Cardinals (1959–75), Gibson was baseball's best pitcher from 1964 to 1970, intimidating hitters with inside pitches. His 1.12 earned true average in 1968 is the lowest seasonal mark in National League history. He led the league in victories, strikeouts, and ERA only once, but he won 20 games five times and routinely struck out 200 batters per season. His World Series record is 9-2 (including two victories in game 7), 1.89 ERA, and 92 strikeouts in 81 innings. Gibson was elected to the Hall of Fame in 1981.

Gillespie, Dizzy, (John Birks Gillespie) *b. Cheraw, S.C., 1917; d. 1993.* **Jazz trumpeter and composer.** Dizzy was one of the most complex jazz trumpeters of all time. Along with the saxophonist Charlie Parker, he defined and popularized the bebop style; he also helped to popularize Afro-Cuban (Latin) jazz. With his puffed-out cheeks, bent trumpet, and easy wit, Dizzy was a particularly popular performer. Recordings include "Salt Peanuts" (1944), "Shaw Nuff" (1945), "A Night in Tunisia" (1946), and "Manteca" (1948).

Gingrich, Newton Leroy, "Newt," *b. Harrisburg, Pa., 1943.* **American politician.** Elected to the U.S. House of Representatives as a Republican from Georgia in 1978, Gingrich pursued conservative policies that he subsequently summarized in the "Contract with America," a platform that helped Republicans—for the first time in 40 years—regain the House and Senate in 1994. He became speaker of the House in 1995 but resigned his seat in 1999 amid charges of unethical conduct.

Ginsberg, Allen, *b. Newark, N. J., 1926; d. 1997.* **Poet.** A member of the Beat movement and one of the most famous American poets of the late 20th century, Ginsberg rose to prominence in the 1950's with the publication of his epic poem *Howl* (1956). Deeply influenced by Buddhism, Ginsberg's poems show a concern with ordinary language and natural speech patterns. Among his collections are *Kaddish and Other Poems* (1961), and *The Fall of America: Poems of These States, 1965–1971* (1972), which won the National Book Award.

Giotto (di Bondone), *b. Vespignano (?), Italy, 1267–75; d. 1337.* **Painter and designer.** Regarded as the first artist in the Gothic tradition to have depicted nature in a convincingly realistic manner, Giotto represents a crucial turning point in the progression of western art toward the illusionism of the Renaissance. To his contemporaries, Giotto's, lifelike paintings were considered revolutionary. He is best known for his frescoes in the Arena Chapel in Padua, which include *The Lamentation* (1305–6), as well as for small panel paintings such as *Madonna* (ca. 1310). In 1334 Giotto was appointed head of the Florence Cathedral workshop.

Gish, Lillian, *b. Springfield, Ohio, 1896; d. 1993.* **Actress.** The "first lady of the silver screen," Gish was part of D. W. Griffith's stock company of film actors, who developed a credible style of screen acting less exaggerated than stage performance. She and her sister, Dorothy, began working for Griffith in 1912 on *An Unseen Enemy*. She became his favorite actress, starring in his major feature films such as *The Birth of a Nation* (1915) and *Broken Blossoms* (1919). She also acted in films by other directors, before returning to the stage in the 1930's. She received a career achievement Oscar in 1970 and made her last screen appearance in *The Whales of August* (1987).

Gladstone, William Ewart, *b. Liverpool, England, 1809; d. 1898.* **Statesman and man of letters.** As a young Tory in Parliament, Gladstone served in several national posts under Robert Peel and became an advocate for free trade; he ultimately joined and led the Liberal Party. During the first of his four terms as prime minister (1868–74), Gladstone passed a series of reform bills on education, the judiciary, and civil service. During his later terms (1880–1885, 1886, and 1892–94), he continued to press measures for social reform. Throughout his life he wrote about political issues and contributed literary criticism to reviews and magazines. Long a supporter of Irish causes, he fought within his own party for Irish home rule. Though greatly controversial in his time, he is considered by many the moral conscience of Victorian Britain.

Glenn, John Herschel, Jr. *b. Cambridge, Ohio, 1921.* **Astronaut, senator.** A Marine pilot during World War II and the Korean War, Glenn was recruited as one of the first seven astronauts for Project Mercury, and became the first man to orbit the Earth on February 20, 1962, in the Friendship 7 space capsule. In 1964 Glenn retired from the space program, and in 1978 he was elected U.S. senator from Ohio, serving four terms. He returned to space aboard the Discovery in 1998, at age 77, the oldest person ever to do so, as part of research into weightlessness and the aging process.

Godard, Jean-Luc, *b. Paris, 1930.* **Film Director.** The most controversial member of the French New Wave, Godard is known for the radical form and political content of his films. Beginning with his first feature, *Breathless* (1959), he broke away from filmmaking norms, preferring the roughness of jump cuts and handheld camera to established techniques. Later, attempting to use film as a political instrument, he stripped down his narrative structures and cast aside dramatic form, as in *Masculine Feminine* (1966), *Weekend* (1968), and *Wind from the East* (1969). During the 1980's, he returned to conventional filmmaking but remained controversial (*Hail Mary*, 1985).

Goddard, Robert Hutchings, *b. Worcester Mass., 1882; d. 1945* **Physicist and rocket pioneer.** He designed and built early high-altitude rockets, including the first liquid-fueled rocket (1926). His inventions included an automatic rocket–steering system and many other rocket devices. He developed a general theory of rocket action and demonstrated rocket propulsion in a vacuum. Goddard was a professor of physics at Clark University.

Gödel, Kurt, *b. Brunn, Austrian Empire. 1906, d. 1978* **Austrian-American logician.** Gödel's first major work demonstrated that every statement in the most basic form of logic can either be proved or disproved (1930). His proof in 1931 that any system that contains the arithmetic of whole numbers is either not complete or not consistent—known as Gödel's incompleteness theorem—is his most famous result. In the 1940's and 1950's, Gödel and Albert Einstein became friends, leading Gödel to formulate a mathematical framework for Einstein's theories.

Goebbels, Paul Joseph, *b. 1897, Rheydt, Germany; d. 1945.* **German politician.** The premier propagandist for Adolf Hitler and the Nazi Party, with which he was associated from 1924, Goebbels held a doctorate in philosophy from Heidelberg University. Under the Nazis, he headed the National Ministry for Public Enlightenment and Propaganda, the Ministry of Culture, and, in 1944, the Reich Plenipotentiary for the Total War Effort, among other positions. He killed himself, his wife, and their six children in Hitler's bunker the day after succeeding Hitler as chancellor of the Reich upon the latter's suicide.

Goethe, Johann Wolfgang von, *b. Frankfurt, 1749; d. 1832.* **Poet, dramatist, and novelist.** Goethe began writing as part of the romantic *Sturm und Drang* movement, to which he contributed the popular novel *The Sorrows of Young Werther* (1774). More classical writings followed: the dramas *Iphigenie in Tauris* (1787) and *Egmont* (1788) and the epic poem *Hermann and Dorothea* (1797). His novel *The Apprenticeship of Wilhelm Meister* (1796) is the first bildungsroman, or novel of a young man's development. Goethe's masterwork is the poetic drama *Faust,* published in two parts in 1808 and 1832. Based on the legend of a learned man's bargain with the devil, it is a profound investigation of the human condition and the soul's struggle for salvation.

Goldwater, Barry Morris, *b. Phoenix, Ariz., 1909; d. 1998.* **American politician.** After service in World War II, Goldwater entered politics as a Republican and was elected to the U.S. Senate in 1952. He advocated conservative policies of states' rights, free enterprise, and anti-communism. In 1964 he became the Republican candidate for president and although he was defeated decisively by Lyndon. B. Johnson that campaign is considered the beginning of the conservative "revolution" in American politics. He returned to the Senate and served intermittedly until in 1986.

Goldwyn, Samuel (Schmuel Gelbfisz, later Samuel Goldfish) *b. Warsaw, Poland, 1882; d. 1974.* **Film producer.** Known for his cantankerous nature and quotable malapropisms ("Include me out"), Goldwyn was one of Hollywood's most successful independent producers during the studio era. He was a glove salesman before going into the film business with his brother-in-law, Jesse L. Lasky, in 1913, and founded Samuel Goldwyn Productions in 1923. It merged with Metro Pictures and Louis B. Mayer 's company to become Goldwyn-Mayer (MGM) in 1925. As an independent producer, his most important films were directed by William Wyler, including *The Best Years of Our Lives,* which won the Oscar for Best Picture in 1946.

Gompers, Samuel, *b. London, 1850; d. 1924.* **American labor leader.** Gompers moved with his family to the United States in 1863 and became active in the labor movement. He worked to organize a national federation of unions, which in 1886 became the American Federation of Labor, and he became its president. He advocated moderate policies rather than strikes and resisted militant unions in the A.F.L. He used the power of the A.F.L. to influence legislation favorable to workers. After World War I he traveled abroad to internationalize the policies of the A.F.L.

Goodall, Jane, *b. London, 1934.* **British Naturalist.** Mentored by the renowned paleontologist and anthropologist Louis Leakey, Goodall, at age 26, began years of lonely work monitoring wild chimpanzees on the shores of Africa's Lake Tanganyika. Her observations, based on years of painstaking observation, transformed human knowledge of chimpanzee behavior and raised fascinating questions about the evolution of humans. Her decades of fieldwork, frequently profiled by *National Geographic,* shaped all future studies of primates. A prolific author, Goodall is an international spokesperson for conservation.

Goodman, Benny (Benjamin David Goodman) *b. Chicago, Ill., 1909; d. 1986.* **Jazz clarinetist and bandleader.** Dubbed "the king of swing," Goodman was the most celebrated bandleader of the swing era. His distinctive clarinet playing gave an identity both to his popular big band and to the smaller groups he led. Goodman also showcased black performers to white audiences, in particular two band members, Lionel Hampton and Teddy Wilson. His recordings include "Moon Glow" (1934), "Stompin' at the Savoy" (1935), "Sing, Sing, Sing" (1935), "Avalon" (1938), "One O'Clock Jump" (1938), and "And the Angels Sing" (1939).

Goodyear, Charles, *b. New Haven, Conn., 1800; d. 1860.* **American inventor.** Goodyear began working on the problems of converting rubber into useful goods in the early 1830's. It was soft when heated and brittle when cold. After many experiments, in 1838 he accidentally discovered that when combined with sulfur and heated to a high temperature rubber remained flexible when hot or cold. The process was named "vulcanization." But he was never able to successfully commercialize his discovery and spent years fighting patent infringement suits. Periodically in debtors' prison, he died in poverty.

Gorbachev, Mikhail, *b. 1931, Privolnoye, U.S.S.R.* **Russian politician.** Born to a peasant family, Gorbachev joined the Communist Party in 1952 and later received a law degree. Rising through the ranks, he was general secretary (head) of the Communist Party (1985–92). In an effort to revive the Soviet Union's enervated economy, he endorsed policies of *glastnost* (openness), *perestroika* (reform) and democratization. Partial reform proved impossible, and he oversaw the transformation of the Soviet Union into the Commonwealth of Independent States in 1991. He received the 1990 Nobel Peace Prize for his efforts to end the cold war and the Soviet intervention in Afghanistan.

Goya, Francisco, *b. Fuendetodos, Spain, 1746; d. 1828.* **Painter.** Considered one of the greatest painters of the emotionally expressive Romantic movement, Goya was a highly esteemed court painter, despite the fact that he produced mercilessly unflattering portraits such as *The Family of Charles IV* (1800). Goya's gruesome *The Third of May, 1808* (1814–15) portrays the execution of Madrid citizens by Napoleon's Army. Toward the end of his life, having lived through turbulent political times, Goya grew more reclusive, and his work grew darker. Eighty-two prints, called *Disasters of War* (1810–20), recall moments during the Peninsular War (1808–1814), and the nightmarish painting *Saturn* (1820–23) depicts the devouring of a human figure. In 1824 Goya left Spain for Paris, and eventually Bordeaux.

Graham, Martha, *b. Allegheny, Pa., 1894; d. 1991.* **Innovative modern dancer and choreographer.** Graham studied with the dancer-choreographers Ruth St. Denis and Ted Shawn from 1916–23 and also danced in New York revues. She founded her company in 1926, and gained attention for her innovative choreography and magnetic dancing. Among her best-known solos was *Lamentation* (1930); well-known group dances included *Primitive Mysteries* (1931) and *Appalachian Spring* (1944). From the 1950's through the end of her career, Graham turned to Greek myth and biblical stories for inspiration. She won numerous awards, including a Kennedy Center Honor in 1979.

Grange, Red (Harold Edward), *b. Forksville, Pa., 1903; d. 1991.* **Football player.** Credited with making professional football a major spectator sport, the "Galloping Ghost" was a thrilling and elusive broken-field runner. He won All-America honors three times (1923–25) at the University of Illinois and set off a major controversy by turning pro before graduation. A 17-game barnstorming tour attracted large crowds at every stop. Grange played for the New York Yankees of the American Football League and the Chicago Bears of the National Football League until 1934.

Grant, Cary (Archibald Alexander Leach) *b. Bristol, England, 1904; d. 1986.* **Actor.** Witty and debonair without ever being effete, Grant owed his impeccable comic timing to his early training as an acrobat and juggler. He ran away from home at age 13 to join Bob Pender's traveling show, and was appearing in Broadway musicals by the 1920's. His first big screen role was *She Done Him Wrong* (1933) with Mae West. His best films were directed by Howard Hawks (*Bringing Up Baby*, 1938; *His Girl Friday*, 1940), George Cukor (*The Philadelphia Story*, 1940), and Alfred Hitchcock (*Notorious*, 1946; *North by Northwest*, 1959). He retired from movies in 1966.

Grant, Ulysses S., *b. Point Pleasant, Ohio, 1822; d. 1885.* **Eighteenth U.S. president, 1869–77.** A graduate of West Point he fought in the Mexican War under Gen. Zachary Taylor. During the Civil War Grant rose rapidly to brigadier general during and acquired the nickname "Unconditional Surrender" for his string of western victories, notably at Vicksburg and Chattanooga. Once Lincoln made him supreme commander in 1864, Grant opened a relentless offensive that quickly ended the war; he personally accepted Gen. Robert E. Lee's surrender at Appomattox in 1865. Elected president in 1868, he pressed radical Reconstruction in the South to mixed results. His presidency was marred by corruption, notably the Jay Gould (1869), Crèdit Mobilier (1872), and Whiskey Ring (1875) scandals. His memoirs are considered among the finest writing about war.

Grass, Günter, *b. Danzig (now Gdansk), Poland, 1927.* **Novelist and playwright.** With the publication of his first novel, *The Tin Drum* (1956), Grass quickly rose to prominence as the voice of the German postwar generation. His work, overtly political, addressing topics such as the rise of Naziism, the threat of nuclear war, the destruction of the environment, and German reunification, includes *Cat and Mouse* (1961), *Dog Years* (1963), *The Rat* (1986), and *My Century* (1999). He received the Nobel Prize for Literature in 1999.

Greco, El (Doménikos Theotokópoulos), *b. Candia, now Herakleion, Greece, ca. 1541; d. 1614.* **Greek painter, active in Italy and Spain.** After living in Crete, painting in a Byzantine style, El Greco went to Venice, Rome, and eventually Toledo, becoming one of the most original artists in Europe. It was in Italy, where he lived from 1567 to 1577, that he was first called "Il Greco." He absorbed the use of rich color and light typical of the Venetian school, but rejected some of the Western norms of perspective and proportion. His dramatic compositions include the portrait of Cardinal Fernando Niño de Guevura (ca. 1600) and *Burial of the Count of Orgaz* (1586–88).

Greene, Graham, *b. Berkhamsted, England, 1904; d. 1991.* **Novelist, short-story writer, journalist, and playwright.** Deeply inspired by his Catholic faith, Greene separated his more serious literary novels from novels that he labelled "entertainments," which are thrillers, such as *This Gun for Hire* (1936), spy stories such as *The Quiet American*

(1955), and comic novels such as *Our Man In Havana* (1958), and *Travels With My Aunt* (1969). His most important novels have religious themes, presenting characters in often sordid, morally decayed settings caught between grace and damnation. These include *Brighton Rock* (1938) *The Power and the Glory* (1940), and *The Heart of the Matter*, (1948). Greene wrote much journalism, short fiction, several plays, and film scripts including *The Third Man* (1950).

Gregory I (Saint) (Gregory the Great), *b. ca. 540, Rome; d. 604.* **Pope, doctor of the church.** A wealthy Roman prefect, Gregory donated his property for the building of monasteries, joined the Benedictine order, and reluctantly answered calls to be an abbot, deacon of Rome, church ambassador, papal advisor, and, in 590, pope. Yet he established the institution of the medieval papacy, opposing the Donatist heresy, reinforcing papal supremacy, and centralizing church administration. By defending Rome against a Lombard invasion and negotiating for peace, he enhanced the temporal authority of the papacy. He conformed and improved liturgical practice and his name was given to "Gregorian chant." Gregory wrote books on scripture, church leadership, and a life of St. Benedict.

Gretzky, Wayne, *b. Brantford, Ontario, Canada, 1961.* **Hockey player.** Wayne Gretzky is widely regarded as the greatest player in the history of ice hockey. In a 20-year NHL career (1979–99), he set all-time records for goals (894), assists (1,963), and total points (2,857). Known as "the great one," the smooth-skating center topped the league in scoring 10 times, won M.V.P. honors nine times, and led the Edmonton Oilers to four Stanley Cups. His single-season records include most goals (92 in 1982), assists (163 in 1986), and points (215 in 1986).

Griffith, D. W., (David Lewelyn Wark Griffith) *b. LaGrange, Ky., 1875; d. 1948.* **Director.** Griffith pioneered many techniques still used by filmmakers today. His innovations in editing formed the basis of Hollywood continuity editing, and his developments in lighting and camera movement influenced others to expand further. He developed his craft at American Biograph from 1908 to 1913, beginning with the one-reel *Adventures of Dollie* and ending with the four-reel *Judith of Bethulia*. His mastery over filmmaking techniques is evident in the epic *The Birth of a Nation* (1915) but its racist content forever marred his reputation. Later features include *Intolerance* (1916) and *Broken Blossoms* (1919).

Griffith-Joyner, Florence, *b. Los Angeles, Calif., 1959; d. 1998.* **Runner.** Viewers on television immediately identified "Flo-Jo" by her long flowing hair, brightly colored outfits, and dazzlingly painted long fingernails, but her competition rarely saw anything but her back. At the 1988 U.S. Olympic trials, she set a world record for the 100-meters dash and a U.S. record for the 200-meters, and went on to win both events easily at the Seoul Olympiad. She also won a gold medal on the 4x100-m relay team and a silver on the 4 x 400-m relay team.

Grimm, Jacob *(1785–1863)* and **Wilhelm** *(1786–1859), b. Hanau, Germany.* **Linguists and folklorists.** Wilhelm was the virtual founder of philology, the comparative study of languages, and conceived "Grimm's law," governing the shifts of consonants in Indo-European languages. As a related interest, the brothers collected the folktales told by German country people, and, with the help of Dorothea, Wilhelm's wife, published them, often in edited form, as *Household and Nursery Tales* in three volumes (1812, 1815, 1822). The stories, translated into more than 70 languages, include "Cinderella," Sleeping Beauty," "Snow White," "Hansel and Gretel," "Little Red Riding Hood" and "Rumpelstilskin." The brothers also began the work on the definitive German dictionary.

Gropius, Georg Walter Adolf, *b. Berlin, 1883; d. 1969.* **German-born American architect and educator.** Gropius's early fame rests on his role in founding the Bauhaus in Weimar, Germany, in 1919; this was a school that combined craftsmanship with design and brought together artisans, painters, sculptors, and architects. In 1926 Gropius moved the Bauhaus to Dessau, into a radical new building complex he had designed and that was an icon of what came to be called the International Style. He came to America and in 1938 became chairman of the department of architecture at Harvard University. He continued to design works including the Bauhaus-like Harvard Graduate Center (1949).

Guevara, Che (Ernesto Guevara de la Serna), *b. Rosario, Argentina, 1928; d. 1967.* **Revolutionary and author.** Guevara left Argentina to foment socialist reform throughout Latin America. In 1954, he joined forces in Mexico with Fidel Castro, who was plotting to overthrow the Cuban dictator Fulgencio Batista. An initial defeat left their forces decimated, but made Guevara one of Castro's closest confidants. After the Communist victory, Guevara was a key figure in the new government. He chronicled the revolution in *Reminiscences of the Cuban Revolutionary War* (1963) and the fledgling Communist nation in *Man and Socialism in Cuba* (1965). He was executed by government troops in Bolivia, where he led a guerilla uprising.

Gustavus II (Gustavus Adolphus), *b. Stockholm, Sweden, 1594; d. 1632.* **King of Sweden.** Gustav became king in 1611. Under his rule, Sweden became a major European power. Assisted by his chancellor, Oxenstierna, he also transformed the Swedish state by instituting a variety of reforms. Supported by French subsidies, he invaded Germany during the Thirty Years' War on behalf of the beleaguered Protestants, who were being pressed by the Hapsburgs and their Catholic allies. He won major victories in 1632 at Breitenfeld and Luetzen but was killed at the height of his power.

Gutenberg, Johannes, *b. ca. 1395, d. 1468.* Around 1450 the German goldsmith Guttenberg became the first European to mass-produce books and documents. His method was based on movable type, a smudge-resistant ink he had developed, paper (the first German paper mill was about 50 years old), and a wine press used as a printing press. Although movable type had been invented earlier in China, Gutenberg is credited with developing techniques for manufacturing hundreds of identical letters and aligning them so that they produced a flat surface for printing. His 42-line Bible, so called for the length of its columns, is still considered one of printing's masterpieces.

Halsey, William F., Jr. (Bull), *b. Elizabeth, N.J., 1882; d. 1959.* **Naval commander.** Halsey was an early advocate of air power and became an aviator in 1935, when he was over 40. After Pearl Harbor, his carrier group was virtually the only operational unit in the Pacific available for combat. In early 1942, his group launched the planes that participated in Doolittle's air raid on Tokyo. Halsey showed a unique ability to coordinate naval and air support of land operations at Guadalcanal, at Okinawa, and elsewhere.

Hamilton, Alexander, *b. Nevis, West Indies, 1755; d. 1804.* **American statesman and political theorist.** Hamilton attended King's College (Columbia) in New York (1773–74), then served in the Revolution as an artillery captain and Washington's aide-de-camp. Back in New York he was a successful trial-lawyer and delegate to the Continental Congress, (1782–83). At the Constitutional Convention in 1787 he was a leading advocate for a strong central government and for the ratification of the Constitution as drafted. He was a principal contributor to the Federalist Papers and a central figure in the Federalist party. As the nation's first treasury secretary, (1789–95), he created the national bank. In 1800, when the popular election resulted in a tie between Thomas Jefferson and Aaron Burr, Hamilton influenced Congress to elect Jefferson president. His again blocking Burr from becoming New York governor led to a pistol duel between them, at which Hamilton was mortally wounded.

Hammerstein, Oscar, II *b. New York City, 1895; d. 1960.* **Lyricist.** Working with the composer Richard Rodgers, Hammerstein helped to redefine the Broadway musical by integrating songs into the plot. Before teaming up with Rodgers, he wrote lyrics for the musicals *Show Boat* (1928) and *Sweet Adeline* (1929), and collaborated with other notable composers, including George Gershwin and Jerome Kern. His best-known songs include "Ol' Man River" (1928), "Lover, Come Back to Me" (1928), "All the Things You Are" (1939), "People Will Say We're in Love" (1943), "Some Enchanted Evening" (1949), and "Getting to Know You" (1951).

Handel, George Frideric, *b. Halle, Germany, 1685; d. 1759.* **German-born composer and organist of the Baroque period.** Handel spent most of his life in England, where he was acknowledged as one of the greatest composers of his age. He contributed to every musical genre of his time, with operas dominating his early career; he spent his later years focusing on large-scale vocal works, such as the English oratorio, which he invented. Handel's most famous composition is the oratorio *The Messiah* (1741). He wrote more than 20 oratorios, along with nearly 50 operas and a large number of concerti grossi and orchestral pieces. Notable works include *Water Music* (ca. 1717), the *Coronation Anthems* (1727), Trio Sonatas op. 2 (1722–33) and op. 5 (1739), Concerto Grosso op. 6 (1739), and *Music for Royal Fireworks* (1749).

Hannibal *b. 247 B.C.; d. ?182 B.C.* **Carthaginian general.** Son of the general Hamilcar Barca, Hannibal was a sworn enemy of Rome from childhood. He set out to avenge Carthage's losses in the First Punic War, first taking over Spain and then mounting his famous invasion of Italy after trekking over the Pyrenees with thousands of soldiers, cavalry, and elephants in the Second Punic War (218–202). He lost thousands at the Alps but invaded northern Italy with success until he was eventually forced to retreat. He was finally defeated by Scipio Africanus in

Carthage at Zama in 202 B.C. He went on to reform his own government while paying tribute to Rome until forced into exile where he poisoned himself.

Harding, Warren Gamaliel, *b. Blooming Grove, Ohio, 1865; d. 1923.* **Twenty-ninth U.S. president, 1921–23.** Harding taught, studied law, and sold insurance before following his father into the newspaper business. He was a staunch Republican whose pro-business editorials for the *Marion Star* got him elected state senator, lieutenant governor, and U.S. senator. Elected to the presidency by an unprecedented 61 percent majority, Harding promised a return to "normalcy" for Americans tired of war and Woodrow Wilson. His administration featured higher tariffs, lower taxes, and immigration restriction—but also pervasive corruption and incompetence by Harding's crooked appointees. Harding died suddenly of an embolism on August 2, 1923; scandals involving secret love affairs, official graft, and the vast Teapot Dome swindle erupted soon thereafter.

Hardy, Thomas, *b. Upper Bockhampton, Dorset, England, 1840, d. 1928.* **Novelist and poet.** Hardy's pessimistic fiction is set in his native Dorsetshire, renamed Wessex, and concerns the strivings of provincial people for happiness against the forbidding forces of nature and cosmic fate. Important novels include *Return of the Native* (1878), *Tess of the D'Urbervilles* (1891), and *Jude the Obscure* (1896). After the last was criticized as immoral, he treated the same themes in poetry of plain language but stark power. He wrote mostly lyrics, including the somber "The Darkling Thrush" to usher in the 20th century, but also an "epic-drama" of the Napoleonic Wars, *The Dynasts* (1908).

Harrison, Benjamin, *b. North Bend, Ohio, 1833; d. 1901.* **Twenty-third president, 1889–93.** The grandson of the ninth president, William Henry Harrison, Benjamin Harrison was a prominent Republican in Indiana, where he was elected senator in 1881. A colorless compromise candidate for president, Harrison won the 1888 election despite receiving fewer popular votes than Grover Cleveland. The McKinley Tariff, the Sherman Anti-Trust Act, the Sherman Silver Purchase Act (all 1890), and Secretary of State James G. Blaine's vigorous foreign policy were hallmarks of Harrison's administration, which oversaw the admission of six new states.

Harrison, George, *b. Liverpool, England, 1943; d. 2001.* **Rock-pop vocalist, guitarist, and songwriter.** As the Beatles' lead guitarist, Harrison had a sparse but lyrical style of playing. As a songwriter, he made infrequent memorable contributions ("Something," "While My Guitar Gently Weeps," "Here Comes the Sun"). Post-Beatles, Harrison embraced social causes and Indian music; he organized the Concert for Bangladesh (1971),, one of the first all-star charity concerts. His post-Beatles recordings include "My Sweet Lord" (1970), "Isn't It a Pity?" (1970), "Give Me Love (Give Me Peace on Earth)" (1973), "All Those Years Ago" (1981), and the triple album *All Things Must Pass* (1970).

Harrison, John, *b. 1693, Foulby, England; d. 1776.* **English clockmaker.** In 1714, the British Parliament established the Board of Longitude and offered £20,000 for a timepiece accurate enough to enable navigators to determine longitude (one's position east or west of a given point) to within half a degree after a voyage to the West Indies. Harrison built his first chronometer, weighing 72 pounds, in 1735. The accuracy of his fourth, a pocket watch called H4 completed in 1759, exceeded the requirement. Parliament balked at awarding the prize—even after Captain James Cook praised it—and did so only slowly.

Harrison, William Henry, *b. Charles City County, Va., 1773; d. 1841.* **Ninth U.S. president, 1841.** Son of a signatory of the Declaration of Independence, Harrison had an illustrious military career and served in both the house (1816–19) and the Senate (1825–28). He received the Whig nomination for president in 1840; in the first election full of hoopla and hype, the slogan "Tippecanoe and Tyler Too" linked Harrison's most famous military victory with his obscure running mate. Harrison caught a cold at his inauguration from which he never recovered, and succumbed to pneumonia 31 days later. His grandson, Benjamin Harrison, was the 23rd president.

Harvey, William, *b. Folkestone, Kent, England, 1578; d. 1657.* **Physician.** A graduate of Cambridge University and the University of Padua in Italy, Harvey served as physician extraordinary to James I and was later personal physician to Charles I. He is best remembered for his groundbreaking research into the circulation of the blood, first widely articulated in his *On the Motion of the Heart and Blood in Animals* (1628), which explained the function of heart valves, arteries, veins, and pulmonary circulation,

Hatshepsut Maatkare, *r. ca. 1479/1473–1458/57 B.C.* **Egyptian pharaoh.** One of the most powerful women known from antiquity, Hatshepsut was the daughter of

Thutmose I and wife of her half-brother, Thutmose II. After her husband's death, she took the unusual step for a woman of ruling as a pharaoh during the minority of her nephew and stepson, Thutmose III. She is best remembered for her temple at Deir el-Bahri (Luxor). After her death, Thutmose III had virtually all references to her name obliterated.

Hawking, Stephen, *b. Oxford, England, 1942.* **English physicist.** In 1974 Hawking calculated that black holes emit a form of energy now known as Hawking radiation. Since then he has analyzed the shape and fate of the universe in technical studies and popular books. Although Hawking has been afflicted with severe progressive muscle degeneration since the early 1960's, he manages with the use of a speech synthesizer to continue as Lucasian Professor of Mathematics at Cambridge University (since 1979), the chair once held by Isaac Newton.

Hawks, Howard, *b. Goshen, Ind., 1896; d. 1977.* **Film director.** Hawks excelled at crafting tightly structured stories in almost any genre. He began as a prop master during the silent era, then worked his way up to film cutter, assistant director, and story editor. He directed his first film, *The Road to Glory*, in 1925. After the coming of sound, Hawks made his best films, *Scarface* (1932), *Bringing Up Baby* (1938), *The Big Sleep* (1946), *Red River* (1948), and *Gentlemen Prefer Blondes* (1953). He received a career Oscar in 1975.

Hawthorne, Nathaniel, *b. 1804, Salem, Mass.; d. 1864.* **Novelist, short-story writer.** Hawthorne was a secluded child who became a secluded writer. His first novel, *Fanshawe* (1829), was unsuccessful, but *Twice-Told Tales* (1837, 1842) gained recognition. Of Puritan stock, Hawthorne searched into human darkness, examining moral issues through the lens of symbolism. His greatest novel, *The Scarlet Letter* (1850), a tale of adultery, guilt, and revenge, is set in 17th-century Puritan Salem. It was followed by *The House of the Seven Gables* (1851) and *The Blithedale Romance* (1852). He served as a port official in Salem and a consul in England. Living in Italy influenced his last novel, *The Marble Faun* (1860).

Haydn, Franz Joseph, *b. Rohrau, Austria, 1732; d. 1809.* **Composer.** The most celebrated composer of his time, Haydn is known as the "father of the symphony," having composed 104 symphonic works; he also helped to develop the string quartet and contributed to the development of the sonata and to sonata form. Notable works include the opera *Orfeo ed Euridice* (1791), Symphony No. 94 in G (*Surprise*) (1791), Symphony No. 100 in G (*Military*) (1794), Symphony No. 101 in D (*Clock*) (1794), Symphony No. 104 in D (*London*) (1795), Concerto in E flat for Trumpet and Orchestra (1796), *Die Schöpfung* (*The Creation*) (1797–8), and *Die Jahreszeiten* (*The Seasons*) (1798–1801).

Hayes, Rutherford B., *b. Delaware, Ohio, 1822; d. 1893.* **Ninteenth U.S. president, 1877–81.** A decorated Civil War veteran, Hayes founded the Ohio Republicans, served as governor of Ohio, and was nominated as a scandal-free presidential candidate in 1876. Although he lost the election to the Democrat Samuel Tilden, congressional Republicans disputed enough state vote totals to put "Rutherfraud" in office. Hayes never overcame the resulting stigma of political bargain, even though he effectively ended Reconstruction in the South by removing federal troops; he also put the nation back on the gold standard, put down railroad strikes, and reformed the civil service. He kept his promise to serve only one term.

Heaney, Seamus, *b. Derry, Ireland, 1939.* **Poet.** A Nobel laureate in 1995, Heaney is regarded as the finest Irish poet since Yeats. His early books of poetry, *Death of a Naturalist* (1966), *Door into the Dark* (1969) and *Wintering Out* (1972), focused on rural Ireland, but with *North* (1975) he began to address his country's political and religious "troubles." In *Station Island* (1984), he incorporates his own experience as an Ulster native into his country's bitter history. Technically brilliant, musical, and poignant, Heaney's poetic volumes include *Field Work* (1979), *The Haw Lantern* (1987), *Seeing Things* (1991), *The Spirit Level* (1996), and a translation of *Beowulf* (2000).

Hearst, William Randolph, *b. San Francisco, 1863; d. 1951.* **American publisher, and politician.** In 1887 when Hearst was 23 his father put him in charge of the *San Francisco Examiner;* thereafter he helped to reshape a large segment of American newspapers into vehicles of sensationalism called "yellow journalism." He acquired many other papers and magazines, and he controlled a newsreel and a movie company. His grandiose political ambitions resulted in only two terms in Congress.

Hegel, Georg Wilhelm Friedrich, *b. Stuttgart, Germany, 1770; d. 1831.* **Philosopher.** A clerk's son, Hegel was an undistinguished theology student who persevered to become a teacher at the University of Jena—and, ultimately, one of the greatest systematic philosophers. His first great work, *The Phenomenology of Mind* (1807), established him as an idealist, for whom all reality was spiritual, a manifestation of the "Absolute," or infinite God. His system for understanding all reality, all history, was the "dialectic," a progressive, rational process in which each thesis incorporates its antithesis to develop a synthesis. Hegel's later career was spent at the University of Berlin. His most comprehensive work is *Encyclopedia of the Philosophical Sciences* (1817); *Philosophy of Right* (1821) sums up his whole philosophy.

Heidegger, Martin, *b. Messkirch, Germany, 1889; d. 1976.* **Philosopher.** Generally regarded as a founder of existentialism, he disliked the attribution. He was influenced by the phenomenology of Edmund Husserl. His major work is *Being and Time* (1927). His concern was with the problem of being; he investigated aspects of human existence and the individual's relationship to death; he attributed the difficulties of society to individuals' awareness of their own temporality. He was a supporter of Hitler during the latter's early years in power, and as a result was banned from teaching after World War II.

Heine, Heinrich, *b. Dusseldorf, Prussia, 1797; d. 1856.* **Poet.** The best-known poet of Germany's Romantic movement, Heine was born into a Jewish family but later reluctantly converted to Protestantism. Heine rose to prominence in 1827 with the publication of *The Book of Songs* (1827), a series of poems, often set to music, that explore the schism between the artistic sensibility and reality. Heine's late collection, *Romanzero* (1851), contains some of his most powerful work.

Heisenberg, Werner Karl, *b. Wurzburg, Germany, 1901; d. 1976.* **Physicist.** At the age of 23, Heisenberg published his theory of quantum mechanics, which showed that the position, velocity, and other mechanical quantities of atomic particles can be described only by abstract mathematical "matrices" and not by ordinary numbers. For this he received the 1932 Nobel Prize in Physics. In 1927, Heisenberg defined his principle of uncertainty, which states that it is impossible to measure exactly the position and velocity of any object, particularly at the atomic and subatomic level.

Hemingway, Ernest, *b. 1899, Oak Park, Ill.; d. 1961.* **Novelist and short-story writer.** Hemingway was wounded in World War I, then settled in Paris and wrote a book of stories, *In Our Time* (1925), and two very successful novels, *The Sun Also Rises* (1926) and *A Farewell to Arms* (1929). These introduced a new American prose style, terse and rhythmically repetitious, and a writer whose literature overlapped with a life of confronting danger and proving manhood. His stories, in volumes such as *Men Without Women* (1927) and *The Snows of Kilimanjaro* (1936), and the novel *For Whom the Bell Tolls* (1940), are much admired. The novella *The Old Man and the Sea* (1952) led to the Nobel Prize in Literature. Hemingway killed himself in 1961.

Henie, Sonja, *b. Oslo, Norway, 1912; d. 1969.* **Figure skater.** Sonja Henie won a record three straight Olympic gold medals in women's singles competition beginning at the games in 1928 in St. Moritz, Switzerland, when she was only 15. She also won 10 consecutive world titles (1927–36) and six European championships (1931–36). Her innovative ballet moves and whirling style revolutionized the sport and raised it to new levels of popularity. Henie turned professional after the 1936 Olympics, expanding her international celebrity in skating revues and Hollywood films.

Henry II (Henry Plantagenet, Henry of Anjou, Henry Curtmantle), *b. LeMans, England, 1133; d. 1189.* **King of England (1154–89).** His marriage to Eleanor of Aquitaine (1152) greatly expanded his kingdom to Normandy and western France. But his public dispute with Thomas à Becket, archbishop of Canterbury, concerning the power of church courts over royal authority (which culminated in Becket's murder) made him enemies in Rome. His quarrels with his wife and his sons ultimately put his own life in jeopardy. These squabbles obscured his great accomplishment: trial by judge and jury, a practice that was in existence at the time, but not routinely used.

Henry V, *b. Monmouth, Wales, 1387; d. 1422.* **King of England (1413–22).** His victory over the French at Agincourt (1415) during the Hundred Years' War made England one of the most influential European powers. It also allowed him to join forces with the Holy Roman emperor Sigismund to end the papal schism with the election of Pope Martin V (1417). His marriage (1420) to Catherine of Valois made him heir to the French throne as well, but he died of camp fever during the sieges of Melun and Meaux before he had the chance to accede.

Henry VIII, *b. Greenwich, England, 1491; d. 1547.* **King of England (1509–47).** Henry's long reign influenced English history for centuries. His first wife, Catherine of Aragon, failed to provide him with a male heir, so he sought an annulment from Pope Clement VII. But when the pope refused, the king instead divorced the English

Church from Rome, and declared himself its leader on Earth. He married Anne Boleyn, then annulled the marriage to Catherine, earning himself an excommunication from the pope. The breach with Rome marked the beginning of the English Reformation. Though he married six times, he only produced one male heir. He ordered the beheading of two of his wives and of the advisor, Thomas Cromwell, who arranged one of his marriages.

Henry, Patrick, *b. Studley, Va., 1736; d. 1799.* **Orator, statesman.** A self-taught lawyer, Henry excelled in criminal law. As a member of the Virginia colonial legislature, he fiercely and eloquently opposed the British Stamp Act, and went on to become a delegate to the Continental Congresses of 1774 and 1775, where he delivered his most famous line "[G]ive me liberty or give me death." Henry served as the Virginia's first governor and as a member of the state legislature. He strongly opposed ratification of the U.S. Constitution, believing it neglected state and individual rights, but he was a central figure in the development of the Bill of Rights.

Herzl, Theodor, *b. Budapest, Hungary, 1860; d. 1904.* **Founder of political Zionism.** Herzl was not the first to advocate a Jewish state—Napoleon suggested it as early as 1799—but his pamphlet *The Jewish State* (1896) gave the idea strength by suggesting that it was a political question to be determined by an international council. A tireless organizer, Herzl created the World Zionist Organization and was its first president. He died 40 years before the creation of Israel, but he believed he had created the political movement and laid the groundwork that would eventually lead to a Jewish homeland.

Hepburn, Katharine, *b. Hartford, Conn., 1907; d. 2003.* **Movie actress.** One of the last of Hollywood's golden age, she played strong, independent women on stage and screen for 60 years, winning an early Oscar for *Morning Glory* (1933) and going on to win a record four with *Guess Who's Coming to Dinner* (1967), *The Lion in Winter* (1968), and *On Golden Pond* (1981). In Spencer Tracy she found her perfect foil (and real-life love) in the nine films they made together. *The Philadelphia Story*, which she commissioned for the stage, was also the film (1940) that brought her renewed popularity.

Herodotus *b. Halicarnassus, Asia Minor, ca. 484 B.C.; d. ca. 425 B.C.* **Greek historian.** Herodotus is known as the father of history, and his work serves as the precursor to studies of history, anthropology, and geography. Herodotus spent his life traveling and writing about the people and places he saw and the cultures, histories, and legends of those regions.

Himmler, Heinrich, *b. 1900, Munich, Germany; d. 1945.* **German politician.** Close associate of Adolf Hitler's from the time of the Munich Putsch in 1923, Himmler was head of the SS (*Schutzstaffel*, "Protective Corps," Hitler's bodyguard). After Hitler was elected chancellor, Himmler became second in command of the Gestapo (secret police). He was the primary architect for the "final solution" to annihilate European Jewry, and he oversaw the death camps of Eastern Europe. Hitler ordered his arrest for negotiating secretly with the Allies in April 1945. Later caught by the Allies, Himmler killed himself before he could be brought to trial.

Hippocrates, *b. ca. 460 B.C., Cos, Greece; d. 377 B.C.* **Physician; the "father of medicine."** Hippocrates was a physician and teacher renowned for his writings on various diseases, including *Epidemics*, *The Sacred Disease* (epilepsy), *Prognostics*, and *Aphorisms*. In antiquity, his writings—and many written around his time but probably not by him—were compiled into the *Hippocratic Collection* (*Corpus Hippocraticum*). The so-called Hippocratic oath, attributed to him, establishes the reciprocal obligations of students and teachers, and enjoins practitioners among other things to prescribe beneficial treatments, discourage abortion and assisted suicide, and respect patients confidentiality.

Hitchcock, Alfred, *b. London, England, 1899; d. 1980.* **Film Director.** The master of suspense, Hitchcock elevated the mystery thriller to the level of art by infusing his films with universal themes of guilt and moral consequence. He began as an intertitle designer, then worked as a screenwriter, assistant director, and art director. In 1925 he directed his first feature, *The Pleasure Garden*, but *The Lodger* was his first thriller (1926) followed by *The Thirty-nine Steps* (1935). In 1939, he moved to Hollywood to direct *Rebecca* (1940). Among the highlights of his remarkably consistent career are *Notorious* (1946), *Strangers on a Train* (1951), *Rear Window* (1954), *Vertigo* (1958), *North by Northwest* (1959), *Psycho* (1960), *The Birds* (1963), and *Frenzy* (1972).

Hitler, Adolf, *b. 1889, Braunau, Austria; d. 1945.* **German dictator.** Originally an artist, Hitler moved to

Germany in 1913. After serving in the army in World War I, he joined the National Socialist (Nazi) Party in 1919, articulating virulent anti-Semitism and calling for a revival of German militarism and revenge for the penalties imposed on Germany at the end of World War I. Elected chancellor in 1933, he became Fuhrer (leader) the next year. His invasion of Poland in 1939 started World War II. German success was compromised by Hitler's inept strategic choices, including the invasion of Russia and declaring war on the United States. He killed himself in Berlin in April 1945.

Ho Chi Minh (born Nguyen That Thanh), *b. Hoang Tru, Vietnam, 1890; d. 1969.* **Vietnamese political leader.** He left Vietnam when he was only 21 years old and lived in the U.S., England, and France where he joined the French Communist Party. He lived in Moscow and China and returned to Vietnam in 1941, changing his name to Ho Chi Minh ("he who enlightens") and the revolutionary movement's to Viet Minh. In 1945, with the help of the U.S., he expelled Japanese forces from Vietnam and declared independence. As president (1945–69) of the Democratic Republic of Vietnam, he battled first France and then the United States to maintain his country's freedom from colonialism.

Hobbes, Thomas, *b. Westport, England, 1588; d. 1679.* **Philosopher.** His materialistic, pessimistic philosophy is evident in *Leviathan* (1651) in which he paints a dismal picture of the state of nature, where life is "nasty, brutish, and short." Hobbes argued that people give up their natural rights, in fear of the violence of the state of nature, in exchange for protection from an absolute ruler; once the subjects contract to trade their rights, the ruler's power is absolute. Later writers such as Rousseau (and, in the 20th century, John Rawls) had a broader, less authoritarian view of the social contract.

Hoffa, James Riddle, *b. Brazil, Ind., 1913; d. 1975?.* **American labor leader.** In 1934 "Jimmy" Hoffa took the local union he had organized in 1930 in Detroit into the International Brotherhood of Teamsters. Thereafter he worked to conclude a national contract for all teamsters that would give the union enormous power over the trucking industry. He succeeded in 1964. But he was dogged by charges of corruption and ties to organized crime. He was convicted of jury tampering, fraud, and conspiracy in 1964 and sentenced to a federal penitentiary. Pardoned in 1971, he disappeared on July 30, 1975. His disappearance was never satisfactorily explained, though it is widely believed that he was assassinated by organized crime.

Hogan, Ben, *b. Dublin, Tex., 1912; d. 1997.* **American golfer.** Hogan dominated professional golf during the 1940's and 1950's. Hogan ranks third on the list of career PGA Tour victories, with 63. Known for his precise, controlled play, the 5'7" Texan won the U.S. Open four times, the Masters and PGA championship twice, and the British Open once. He was named PGA Player of the Year four times (1948, 1950–51, 1953). Hogan suffered a near-fatal automobile accident in 1949 but overcame permanent leg injuries to play his best golf after returning the following year.

Holbein (the Younger), Hans, *b. Augsburg, Germany, 1497–98; d. 1543.* **Painter, and designer.** Active in Switzerland and England, Holbein began his career in Basel, creating altarpieces and woodcuts. He went on to become the most important portrait painter in England during the Reformation, working mainly under the patronage of King Henry VIII and his courtiers. Holbein's most famous paintings include *The Ambassadors* (1533) and *Henry VIII* (1540).

Homer, Winslow, *b. Boson, Mass., 1836; d. 1910.* **Painter, illustrator.** One of the most admired late 19th-century American artists, Homer was a landscape painter who shared many of the attitudes of the Hudson River school. Known for bold, fluid brushwork and strong compositions, he worked extensively in watercolor, helping to popularize the medium in paintings such as *Adirondack Guide* (1894). Homer depicted unsentimental images of the relationship between man and nature. Important works include *The Morning Bell* (1870) and *Snap the Whip* (1872).

Hoover, Herbert Clark, *b. West Branch, Iowa, 1874; d. 1964.* **Thirty-first U.S. president, 1929–33.** Hoover became a world-famous mining engineer and a multimillionaire by age 40. In World War I he helped rescue Americans stranded in Europe, distributed food supplies to occupied Belgium, and persuaded the nation to save food ("Hooverize") for the war effort. Hoover was Woodrow Wilson's economic adviser at Versailles, and earned prominence as the secretary of commerce in the 1920's. He was elected president on the promise of a "chicken in every pot," but the Wall Street crash brought on the Great Depression. Paralyzed by his conservative instincts, Hoover could not halt the spread of bank failures, bankruptcy, and unemployment; shantytowns across the country were dubbed Hoovervilles. Massively defeated by Franklin D. Roosevelt in 1932, Hoover was blamed for decades for the depression but salvaged his reputation with more relief work after World War II. Hoover later chaired two bipartisan commissions on government reorganization, issuing many important recommendations for federal reform.

Hoover, J. (John) Edgar *b. Washington, D.C., 1895; d. 1972.* **Director of the F.B.I.** Hoover first made his name in the Justice Department by compiling an enormous list of suspected communists and anarchists, 10,000 of whom were arrested in 1919 in the Palmer Raids. In 1924, Hoover assumed the helm at the Federal Bureau of Investigation, building the bureau's storied image by taking on gangsters such as John Dillinger and Machine Gun Kelly. But in later years, Hoover avoiding fighting the Mafia, instead using surveillance techniques to harass anyone he considered politically radical including Martin Luther King, Jr. Paranoid and vengeful, he kept secret files on hundreds of left-leaning celebrities, politicians, and journalists.

Hope, Bob (Leslie Townes Hope), *b. Eltham, England, 1903; d. 2003.* **Actor and comedian.** Famous for his ski-slope nose and rapid-fire comic delivery, Bob Hope was already a big radio star when he made his movie debut singing "Thanks for the Memory" on *The Big Broadcast* of 1938. He made more than 30 movies , the most successful of which were the six *Road* movies (starting with *Road to Singapore*) that he made with Bing Crosby and Dorothy Lamour between 1940 and 1952. He entertained American troops with his USO shows during every major conflict from World War II to the first Gulf War, starred in numerous television specials, and frequently hosted the Academy Awards in the 1950's and 1960's.

Hopkins, Gerard Manley, *b. Stratford, Essex, England, 1844, d. 1889.* **Poet.** One of the most original English poets, Hopkins introduced diction, syntax, and rhythm embraced in the 20th century. He converted to Catholicism in 1866 and was ordained a Jesuit priest in 1877. After burning his early poems, he resumed writing with "The Wreck of the Deutschland" (1876), a meditational narrative concerning the drowning of five nuns. Many of his poems are devotional sonnets and other lyrics that praise the God revealed in nature, such as "God's Grandeur," "The Windhover," and "Pied Beauty," each written in 1877 but like all his work not published until 1918. In other sonnets, such as "Carrion Comfort" and "No Worst, There Is None" (both 1885), he struggles with spiritual despair.

Hopper, Edward, *b. Nyack, N.Y., 1882; d. 1967.* **Painter, and illustrator.** In a plain, realist style, Hopper's paintings depict scenes of urban isolation, featuring quiet, solitary figures and documenting an everyday American life of movie theaters, storefronts, and city streets. A pupil of the painter Robert Henri, Hopper was profoundly influenced by several trips to Europe. His most famous images include *Night Shadow* (1924) *Early Sunday Morning* (1930), *Gas* (1940), *Nighthawks* (1942), and *Second-Story Sunlight* (1960).

Horace (Quintus Horatius Faccus) *b. Venusia, Italy, 65 B.C.; d. 8 B.C.* **Roman poet.** Horace is considered the greatest Roman lyric poet of his time. Having been written under the patronage of Virgil and Maecenas, much of Horace's work is in praise of the emperor Augustus and the state. His great works are *Satires*, *Epodes*, *Odes*, *Epistles* (including the famous *Ars Poetica*), and *Secular Hymn*.

Housman, A. E. (Alfred Edward), *b. Fockbury, England, 1859; d. 1936.* **Poet.** In pessimistic though romantic and occasionally ironical verse, Housman demonstrated a mastery of alliteration, parallelism, and mood. In Houseman's first collection, *A Shropshire Lad* (1896), he assumed the persona of a farm laborer. His most popular poems include "When I was One-and-Twenty" and "To an Athelete Dying Young," from *A Shropshire Lad*. Housman was equally renowned as a scholar and translator of Latin texts.

Howe, Gordie, *b. Floral, Saskatchewan, Canada, 1928.* **Hockey player.** Gordie Howe, known as "Mr. Hockey," was the NHL's all-time leading scorer with 801 goals until Wayne Gretzky passed him in 1994. The brilliant right wing joined the Detroit Red Wings in 1946 and played professional hockey through the 1979–80 season (though he retired for two seasons in the 1970's before returning to play with his sons in the World Hockey Association). Howe won the Hart Trophy, annually awarded to hockey's best player, six times. His teams won the Stanley Cup five times.

Hudson, Henry, *b. England, ca. 1550; d. 1611.* **Explorer.** Of obscure origin, Hudson made his first known voyages in command of Muscovy Company expeditions to find the Northeast Passage; he discovered Jan Mayen Island (1607) and explored Novaya Zemlya (1608). The Dutch East India Company hired Hudson to find the Northeast

Passage in 1609. Frustrated by the ice, he turned west and ascended the Hudson River as far as Albany. While the Dutch established New Amsterdam the next year, Hudson sailed north for the English Northwest Company and discovered Hudson Strait and Hudson Bay, where his mutinous crew marooned him.

Hughes, Howard, *b. Humble, Tex., 1905; d. 1976.* **Businessman and aviator.** Heir to an oil industry fortune, Hughes spent his life and money in a variety of pursuits. As a pilot, he set numerous speed records in the 1930's; and his firm, Hughes Aircraft Company, produced several models through the years, none more famous than the *Spruce Goose*, a cargo aircraft made from birch. (It was flown only once.) He also directed movies, including *Hell's Angels* and the original *Scarface*. Later in life, Hughes, one of the world's richest men, withdrew completely from the public eye.

Hughes, Langston, *b. Joplin, Mo., 1902; d. 1967.* **Poet, short story writer, and translator.** A member of the Harlem Renaissance group of writers that included Zora Neale Hurston and Jean Toomer, Hughes wrote of the black experience in America. He achieved critical success early on—his poem "The Negro Speaks of Rivers" was published in 1921, when he was only 19. His books include *The Weary Blues* (1926), *Fine Clothes to the Jew* (1927), and the short-story collection *The Ways of White Folks* (1934).

Hugo, Victor, *b. 1802, Besancon, France; d. 1885.* **Poet, novelist, dramatist.** Hugo was already a well-known Romantic poet when his play *Hernani* (1830) introduced Romanticism into drama and stirred a riot in the theater. Other plays are *Le Roi s'amuse* (1832), and *Ruy Blas* (1838). His best-known novels, are *Notre Dame de Paris* (*The Hunchback of Notre Dame*) (1832); and *Les Miserábles* (1862). Hugo's opposition to Napoleon III caused his banishment from 1851 to 1870. He returned to France a hero and was elected to the Senate.

Hull, Cordell, *b. Overton County (now Picket County), Tenn., 1871; d. 1955.* **American statesman.** A U.S. congressman (1907–21, 1923–31) and senator (1930–33), he was appointed secretary of state in 1933 by President Franklin Roosevelt. He negotiated important economic and defense treaties with other nations and during World War II he represented the U.S. in meetings with the Allies and strongly advocated the establishment of the United Nations. In 1945 he was awarded the Nobel Peace Prize.

Hurston, Zora Neale, *b. Notasulga, Ala., 1891; d. 1960.* **Folklorist and novelist.** A member, with Langston Hughes, of the Harlem Renaissance. Hurston's work wasconcentrated primarily on preserving the folklore of African Americans in the South. After dropping out of school at age 13, Hurston went on to graduate from Howard University and Barnard University, and to pursue graduate studies in anthropology at Columbia University. Her first novel, *Jonah's Gourd Vine*, was published in 1934; her most famous novel, *Their Eyes Were Watching God*, was published in 1937.

Huston, John, *b. Nevada, Mo., 1906; d. 1987.* **Screenwriter and director.** Huston specialized in directing tales of social misfits and rebels, who were brought to life through well-crafted dialogue. He began as a screenwriter and directed his first film, *The Maltese Falcon*, in 1941. His collaboration with the star Humphrey Bogart resulted in their best work, including *Treasure of the Sierra Madre* (1948), *Key Largo* (1948), and *The African Queen* (1951). Later films include *Fat City* (1973) and *The Man Who Would Be King* (1975). An Oscar winner for both writing and directing, John was the son of the actor Walter Huston and father of the actress Anjelica Huston.

Ibsen, Henrik, *b. Skien, Norway, 1828; d. 1906.* **Playwright.** Ibsen is one of the great social dramatists and Norway's most internationally famous writer. Ibsen's early plays are drawing room dramas; some look to Norwegian folklore (*Peer Gynt*, 1867) for inspiration. His later works, beginning with the revolutionary *A Doll's House* (1879), which is thought to have ushered in modern drama, focus on psychology and social issues. Other works include *Ghosts* (1881), *The Wild Duck* (1884), and *Hedda Gabler* (1890).

Ignatius of Loyola (Saint), *b. Azpeitia, Guipuzcoa, Spain, 1491; d. 1556.* **Religious leader, founder of the Jesuits.** Ignatius was a nobleman and soldier who experienced a conversion while reading a life of Christ after being wounded. He wrote *Spiritual Exercises* which became the basic text of his followers. In 1534 at the University of Paris, he formed the Society of Jesus (the Jesuits), confirmed by the pope as a religious order in 1538. Ignatius spent the rest of his life establishing schools and universities all over the world. The Jesuit emphasis on education, contemplation, and purity reinvigorated the Catholic Church during the Counter-Reformation. He was canonized in 1622.

Imhotep, *fl. 27th century B.C.* **Egyptian architect.** Imhotep designed the tomb complex and pyramid of the pharaoh Zozer, for whom he was chancellor, at Saqqara ca. 2680 B.C. The size and scope of the complex are unprecedented for its time in Egypt, and the monumental stepped pyramid marks the beginning of the pyramid form in the tombs of later pharaohs. Imhotep's name is cut into the stone of the pyramid, where he is called "first after the king of Upper and Lower Egypt." Later he was deified as one of a trinity with Horus and Isis.

Ingres, Jean-Auguste-Dominique, *b. Montauban, France, 1780; d. 1867.* **Painter.** A French neoclassicist and pupil of the painter David, Ingres lived in Italy for 18 years and championed history painting. He was an accomplished draftsman and portrait painter, able to combine psychological insight with perfectionist physical accuracy. Highly interested in myths about the Orient, Ingres is famous for such polished, sensuous images as *Turkish Bath* (1863) and *Odalisque* (1814).

Innocent III (Lothair of Segni), *b. Campagna di Roma, Papal States, 1160; d. 1216.* **Pope (1198–1216).** His Fourth Lateran Council (1215) brought the medieval papacy's influence and prestige to their zenith. It required confession at least annually, and communion every Easter. He endorsed the vows of poverty and itinerant preaching favored by St. Dominic and St. Francis of Assisi. He disapproved of the Fourth Crusade (1202–04) on Constantinople, but agreed to it in hopes of reuniting the Eastern and Western churches. The bloody Albigensian Crusade (1209), to convert heretics in southern France, bore his approval.

Ivan the Terrible (Ivan IV; Ivan Vasilyevich; Ivan Grozny), *b. Kolomenskoye, Russia, 1530; d. 1584.* **First czar of Russia (1547–84) and grand prince of Moscow (1533–84).** After proclaiming himself czar Ivan worked to limit the power of the greatest nobles ("boyars"); he established a general council (1566) that included merchants and the lower ranks of nobility. Ivan's dream of bringing Russia closer to Europe by obtaining access to the Baltic encouraged him to wage brutal, costly wars against Sweden and Poland that nearly bankrupted Russia. His vision of a vast Russian empire with Moscow at its center and non-Slav states surrounding it was more successful, though it necessitated a reign of terror against the nobility of his own country.

Ives, Charles, *b. Danbury, Conn., 1874; d. 1954.* **American composer.** Ives was an influential figure in the history of music, his work foreshadowing the innovations of younger avant-garde composers. He was fascinated with clashing rhythms and tonalities, as exemplified by two bands playing different tunes or different sections of the orchestra playing in different keys. Notable works include *Variations on a National Hymn, "America"* (1891), Psalm 67 (1893), *Song for Harvest Season* (1893), Symphony No. 3 (*The Camp Meeting*) (1904-11), *New England Holidays* (1904–13), *The Unanswered Question* (1906, rev. ca. 1932), Orchestral Set No. 1 (*Three Places in New England*) (1908–14), Sonata No. 2 (*Concord, Mass., 1840–1860*) (1911–1915).

Jackson, Andrew, *b. Waxhaw, S.C., 1767; d. 1845.* **Seventh U.S. president, 1829–37.** The first first-generation American to become president, Jackson was elected to Congress in 1796 but soon resigned, disgusted with Washington politics. In Tennessee, Jackson became a respected judge and honorary major general of the militia, and in the War of 1812 he led troops to victory at the Battle of New Orleans (1815). Now a national icon, "Old Hickory" reentered the Senate in 1823 and unsuccessfully ran for president in 1824; he won the 1828 election as the "people's choice" reform candidate. As president, Jackson aggrandized the power of his office by expanding suffrage, rotating officeholders (the "spoils system"), and economizing in government by vetoing federal road-building and blocking the renewal of the charter of the Bank of the United States.

Jackson, Michael Joseph, *b. Gary, Ind., 1958.* **Pop-rock vocalist and songwriter.** As a child, Jackson was the lead singer in a successful Motown group the Jackson 5; he grew up to become the biggest pop star of the 1980's. Jackson's style combined elements of soul, rock, and dance music; his album *Thriller* in 1982 became the biggest-selling album of all time, and he was the first black artist to find stardom on MTV. His solo recordings include "Got to Be There" (1971), "Rock with You" (1979), "Thriller" (1982), "Billie Jean" (1982), "Beat It" (1982), "Bad" (1987), and "Black or White" (1991).

Jackson, Thomas , "Stonewall," *b. Clarksburg, now W.Va., 1824; d. 1863.* **American general of the Confederacy.** A graduate of West Point he served bravely in the Mexican War. Jackson joined the Confederate army in 1861 and rose quickly to become brigadier general and the most trusted commander under General Robert E. Lee. Getting his nickname at the first battle of Bull Run (1861), he helped win the seven days battle of Richmond (1862), the second battle of Bull Run (1862), and the battle of Fredricksburg (1862). His role was decisive in the victory at Chancellorsville (1863), but he was accidentally shot and killed by one of his own men.

James I, *b. Edinburgh, Scotland, 1566; d. 1625.* **King of Scotland (James IV) and first Stuart king of England and Ireland.** The only son of Mary Stuart, (Queen of Scots), James became king of Scotland on her abdication in 1567. After an alliance with Queen Elizabeth I of England, he became king of England on her death in 1603. Convinced that kings rule by divine right, he feuded with parliament for power. He initiated a new translation of the Bible that came to be called the King James Version, or the Authorized Version in Great Britain.

James II, *b. London, 1633; d. 1701.* **Stuart king of England, Ireland, and Scotland.** Son of King Charles I, James became king on the death of his older brother Charles II in 1685. His Catholic beliefs provoked wide opposition and in the bloodless Glorious Revolution of 1688–89 he was deposed and replaced by William III, called William of Orange who was married to James' daughter, Mary. The revolution established the constitutional monarchy, giving parliament greater power. James died in exile in France.

James, Henry, *b. 1843, New York City; d. 1916.* **American-English novelist and critic.** James, brother of the philosopher-psychologist William, settled in England in 1876. In the novels of his first period, such as *The Portrait of a Lady* (1881), he examined the tensions between American innocence and European tradition. He turned then to social and political themes in *The Princess Casamassima* (1886) and other novels, and, after a failed trial as a playwright, wrote short drama-like novels, including *The Turn of the Screw* (1898). The fiction of his last and greatest period (*The Ambassadors*, 1903; *The Golden Bowl*, 1904) again took up the international theme, with psychological intricacy in a dense style.

James, William, *b. New York City, 1842; d. 1910.* **Philosopher and psychologist.** Trained as a doctor, he taught at Harvard first in physiology and then in psychology and philosophy. In his groundbreaking *Principles of Psychology* (1890) he shaped the modern discipline of psychology, placing it among the laboratory sciences based on experimental method. In his influential philosophical works, James developed and expounded pragmatism, according to which the truth of ideas is found only in their correspondence with experiential consequences. William James was the brother of the novelist Henry James.

Jay, John, *b. New York City, 1745; d. 1829.* **American statesman and jurist.** Elected to the Continental Congress in 1774 and 1775, Jay advocated a strong national central government and with James Madison and Alexander Hamilton he wrote *The Federalist* papers. George Washington appointed him the first chief justice of the United States Supreme Court in 1789, and in 1794 he concluded Jay's Treaty settled territorial and commercial differences with England. In 1795 he resigned from the court to serve two terms as governor of New York.

Jefferson, Thomas, *b. Albemarle County, Va., 1743; d. 1826.* **Third U.S. president, 1801–09.** Jefferson joined the Virginia House of Burgesses in 1769; as a delegate to the Continental Congress in 1776, he drafted the Declaration of Independence. Congress sent him to Europe in 1784 as minister to France; he later served under Washington as secretary of state, and under Adams as vice president, after losing the 1796 election. Chosen president by the House of Representatives in 1800 (after a tie in the electoral vote with Aaron Burr), Jefferson slashed the budget, lowered taxes, reduced the national debt, and sent marines to fight Barbary pirates. His greatest feat as president was the Louisiana Purchase from France in 1803; which doubled the size of the United States. Retiring to Monticello in 1809, Jefferson busied himself with inventions and designing the University of Virginia; his broad interests spanned music, science, architecture, agronomy, and the classics. Jefferson was an early opponent of the slave trade but was himself a slaveholder and allegedly fathered several children with the slave Sally Hemings.

Jenner, Edward, *b. Berkeley, Gloucestershire, England, 1749; d. 1823.* **Physician; inventor of smallpox vaccination.** Apprenticed to a surgeon at the age of 13, Jenner is best known for his discovery that matter from cowpox—a relatively benign disease that humans could contract from contact with infected cows—could be used to inoculate people to render them immune from smallpox. This procedure, which takes its name from *vacca*, Latin for "cow," has since been adopted for developing numerous vaccines against other diseases.

Jerome, *b. Stridon, Dalmatia, 347; d. 420.* **Saint, theologian, translator, and father and doctor of the church.** A contemporary of St. Augustine, Jerome renounced secular scholarship after converting to christianity and retired to the desert to devote himself to scriptural and linguistic studies. He later was secretary to Pope

Damasus I. A great scholar, he is best known for preparing the Vulgate, the Latin translation of the Old and New Testaments. He also translated Origen and wrote biographies, histories, biblical commentaries, letters, and tracts against heresy.

Jesus (Jesus Christ; Jesus of Nazareth), *b. Bethlehem, ca. 4 B.C.; d. ca. 30 A.D.* **Jewish teacher and prophet, founder of Christianity.** The main sources for his life are the four Gospels, based on earlier traditions, written A.D. 70–95. He was born the son of Mary of the tribe of Judah and of Joseph, a carpenter. Little is known of his life until he was about 30, when after baptism by John he began his ministry. He preached the coming of God's kingdom and the need to love God and one's neighbor, attacked the priestly elite, and healed the sick. In the third year of his ministry he was betrayed by Judas, one of his disciples, in Jerusalem and crucified by the Romans. In Christian belief he rose from the dead and ascended into heaven. In Christianity (*Christ* = anointed), he is the Son of God.

Jinnah, Mohammed Ali, *b. Gujarat, India, 1876; d. 1948.* **Indo-Pakistani politician; founder of Pakistan.** Educated in law in England, Jinnah entered Indian politics in 1906. Interested in greater Indian nationhood and Hindu-Muslim unity, he joined the All-India Muslim League in 1913. He withdrew from politics in response to Gandhi's "Non-Cooperation Movement" in 1920, and in 1930 over differences within the Muslim League. After Muslims fared poorly in India's elections in 1937, Jinnah called for a separate Muslim state, an idea rejected by Gandhi, Nehru, and the British authorities, but realized in the partition of 1947. Jinnah was first governor-general of independent Pakistan.

Joan of Arc, *b. Domremy, Champagne, France, 1412; d. 1431.* **French saint and military heroine.** As a girl, Joan of Arc heard the voices of St. Michael, St. Catherine, and St. Margaret, who directed her to assist the dauphin of France in his attempt to claim his throne against the English. Her military victories at Orléans and Patay brought him to power as Charles VII. When taken by the English and tried by a papal court, Joan eventually admitted heresy, then recanted, and was burned at the stake. Decades later, she was exonerated by a court under Charles.

Jobs, Steve, *b. San Francisco, 1955.* **One of the founders of the personal computer industry.** Jobs and Stephen Wozniak helped launch the personal computer revolution by introducing the Apple computer in 1976. Jobs successfully established Apple's Macintosh as an elegant, innovative, and user-friendly alternative to traditional PCs. He was forced out of Apple in 1985 in a corporate power struggle. In 1986, he cofounded Pixar, an animation studio that has produced some of the most successful animated films in Hollywood history. In 1997, Jobs returned as C.E.O. of Apple, where he helped to pioneer a new business model for downloading music.

Joffre, Joseph-Jacques-Cesaire, *b. Rivesaltes, France, 1852: d. 1931.* **Soldier.** In 1911, Joffre was appointed chief of the French general staff; he was responsible for drafting a disastrous war plan that almost led to defeat in the early days of World War I. Once he realized the mistaken assumptions of the original plan, he improvised a new strategy that drove the Germans back at the first battle of the Marne in 1914. Mounting losses and a perception that he had failed to anticipate the German attack on Verdun forced him to retire in 1916.

John XXIII (Angelo Giuseppe Roncalli), *b. Sotto il Monte, Italy, 1881; d. 1963.* **Pope** (1958–63). A compromise candidate expected to serve only as interim pontiff, he became one of the most popular popes ever because of the Second Vatican Council (1962–65), which brought the Roman Catholic Church into the modern era. Vatican II, as it was known, permitted vernacular, rather than Latin, in the celebration of the mass. It suggested that lay members could find God even outside the church, and permitted opportunities for them to do so, such as Bible study groups and social justice organizations. John was beatified in 2000.

John, Elton (Reginald Dwight) *b. Middlesex, England, 1947.* **Pop-rock vocalist, pianist, and songwriter.** Elton John was the pop superstar of the early 1970's, known for his melodic songwriting (often with the lyricist Bernie Taupin) and his outlandish stage performances. His albums *Madman Across the Water*, *Don't Shoot Me I'm Only the Piano Player*, and *Goodbye Yellow Brick Road* helped to define album-oriented FM radio of the era. His recordings include "Your Song" (1970), "Tiny Dancer" (1971), "Levon" (1971), "Rocket Man" (1972), and "Daniel" (1973); his song "Candle in the Wind" (1973) became the fastest-selling single of all time following his performance of the tune at Princess Diana's funeral in 1997.

John Paul II (Karol Józef Wojtyla), *b. Wadowice, Poland, 1920.* **Pope** (1978–). The first pope from a Slavic country and the first pope of the global age, he has worked to broaden the Roman Catholic Church's reach with more than 90 papal visits to countries around the world. He supported the Polish Solidarity movement and pressured the Soviet Union on human rights issues. In 2000, he made a historic trip to the Holy Land in an effort to find common ground among the world's major religions. He staunchly opposed such reforms as the ordination of women and allowing priests to marry.

John the Baptist, *d. ca. 30.* **Saint.** Said to be a cousin of Jesus Christ, John acts in the Gospels as Jesus's prophet and forerunner. He baptized many people in the Jordan River, calling them to repent and prepare for the coming of the Messiah. Recognizing Jesus as the savior and "Lamb of God," John baptized him, and Scripture reports that God the Father appeared in the sky to bless the event. When John denounced King Herod's marriage to his brother's wife Herodias, Herod imprisoned him. At the request of Herodias's daughter Salome, John was beheaded, and his head was served on a platter.

Johns, Jasper, *b. Augusta, Ga., 1930.* **Painter, sculptor, printmaker.** A key figure in the Pop Art movement, Johns became famous for painting images of well-known objects such as targets and the American flag. He worked closely with the painter Robert Rauschenberg, and both artists were able to combine figurative imagery with some of the painting techniques developed by the Abstract Expressionists. Influenced by Duchamp's ready-mades, Johns created sculptures that replicated everyday objects such as lightbulbs, raising questions about the role of the artist and the process of creation. His works include *Target with Four Faces* (1955) and *Three Flags* (1958).

Johnson, Andrew, *b. Raleigh, N.C., 1808; d. 1875.* **Seventeenth U.S. president, 1865–69.** The first president to be impeached, Johnson served as a state legislator, congressman, governor, and senator. Alone among 22 southern senators, Johnson stayed loyal to the Union in 1861, and he was nominated for vice president on the "National Union" ticket in 1864. Suddenly made president by Lincoln's assassination, Johnson vowed to carry on Lincoln's policy of leniency toward the South, but radical Republican opposition and his own coarse ineptitude led to serious clashes with Congress. Impeached in the House for defying the Tenure of Office Act, Johnson was tried in the Senate—and acquitted by a single vote.

Johnson, Lyndon B., *b. Stonewall, Texas, 1908; d. 1973.* **Thirty-sixth U.S. president, 1963–69.** A powerful and persuasive politician, Lyndon Baines Johnson was elected to Congress in 1937, and to the Senate in 1948 where he was majority leader from 1955 unil he accepted John F. Kennedy's offer of the vice presidency in 1960. He was made president after Kennedy was assassinated. Johnson vowed to continue Kennedy's programs, pushing them through Congress with surprising ease—most notably the Civil Rights Act and the Equal Opportunity Act. After his reelection in 1964, Johnson unveiled plans for a "Great Society" free from poverty and discrimination, but his presidency unraveled as American losses in Vietnam mounted, antiwar protests grew strident, and race riots exploded in inner cities across the nation.

Johnson, Magic (Earvin, Jr.), *b. Lansing, Mich., 1959.* **Basketball player.** An all-time N.B.A. great, Johnson first came to national prominence when he led Michigan State to the N.C.A.A. title over Larry Bird's Indiana State team. As a member of the Los Angeles Lakers, Magic appeared in the N.B.A. finals nine times and won five championships. He was named league M.V.P. three times. After testing positive for HIV in 1991, he retired. He returned to win a gold medal on the 1992 U.S. Olympic Dream Team and later to briefly coach and play for the Lakers. He retired in 1996.

Johnson, Philip Cortelyou, *b. Cleveland, Ohio, 1906.* **Architect.** Johnson's first important work was his own Glass House (1949) in New Canaan, Conn., inspired by Ludwig Mies van der Rohe's Farnsworth House. He collaborated with Mies on the Seagram Building (1954–58) in New York, and went on to produce a number of buildings in variations of the modernist idiom; but he responded creatively when modernism began to go out of style. He readily adapted to the postmodern movement in his AT&T Building (1979) in New York with its Chippendale top, and in many later works.

Johnson, Samuel, *b. 1709, Lichfield, England; d. 1784.* **Essayist, critic, and poet.** Dr. Johnson was his century's leading literary scholar and one of England's greatest critics and literary personalities. He struggled as a magazine writer, poet ("The Vanity of Human Wishes," 1749), and dramatist (*Irene,* 1749), until he completed his groundbreaking *Dictionary of the English Language* in 1755. He published essays in his own periodicals, *The Rambler,* (1750–52) and *Idler,* (1758–60), and criticism in his edition of *Shakespeare* (1765) and *Lives of the Poets* (1779, 1781). In the prose romance *Rasselas* (1759) he expressed a pessimistic view of humanity, but his decency, openness, faith, and legendary wit were recorded in James Boswell's enduring contemporary biography.

Johnson, Walter, *b. Humboldt. Kan., 1887; d. 1946.* **Baseball player.** In a long career with the Washington Senators, Johnson amassed one of the most impressive pitching records in major-league history. Possessed of a legendary fastball, the "Big Train" won 417 games (second only to Cy Young's 511). The right-hander notched a record 110 shutouts and won 20 or more games 10 years in a row. He led the American League in strikeouts 12 times and earned run average five times. His lifetime record was 417-279, with a 2.17 E.R.A. and 3,508 strikeouts.

Jones, Bobby, *b. Atlanta, Ga., 1902; d. 1971.* **Golfer.** Though he competed for only eight years (1923–30) and remained an amateur throughout his career, Jones is considered one of the greatest golfers of all time. He won the U.S. Open at age 21, going on to capture 13 of the 27 majors he entered, including three U.S. Opens, four U.S. Amateurs, and one British Open. After sweeping the U.S. Open, the British Open, the U.S. Amateur, and the British Amateur in 1930, Jones retired at age 28 to practice law.

Jones, John Paul, *b. 1747, Kirkcudbright, Scotland; d. 1792.* **American naval officer.** A founding father of the U.S. Navy, Jones sailed in merchant ships for 15 years before being commissioned a lieutenant in the Continental Navy (1775). His most celebrated victory was fought in the French-built *Bonhomme Richard*, which sank after fighting HMS *Serapis* in September 1779. After the Revolution, Jones served as an admiral in the Russian navy of Catherine the Great (1788–90). He died and was buried in Paris. In 1906, President Theodore Roosevelt ordered his remains exhumed for interment at the U.S. Naval Academy in Annapolis, Maryland.

Jones, Inigo, *b. London, 1573; d. 1652.* **Architect and stage designer of the Renaissance.** From 1605 to 1640 he designed sets for more than 50 dramatic presentations. During a trip to Italy in 1613–14 he carefully studied ancient buildings, often with a copy of the *Four Books on Architecture* by Palladio at hand; this experience shaped his subsequent career as an architect. He brought the Renaissance ideals of classical architecture to England together with the teachings of Palladio and changed the course of English architecture. His Banqueting House in London (1619–21) and the Queen's House in Greenwich (1616–35) were entirely new to England in their restrained classicism and exquisite proportioning.

Jonson, Ben, *b. London, 1572; d., 1637.* **Playwright and poet.** Jonson is considered by many to be, the second-greatest playwright of the Elizabethan and Jacobean periods. His plays are characterized by vibrant characters, by one overarching side of their personality; witty dialogue and careful plotting. Jonson's plays include *Volpone* (1606), *The Alchemist* (1610), and *Bartholomew Fair* (1614).

Jordan, Michael, *b. Brooklyn, N.Y., 1963.* Basketball player. Widely regarded as the greatest basketball player of all time, Michael Jordan led the N.B.A. in scoring a record 10 times (1987–93, 1996–98), earned the M.V.P. award five times (1988, 1991–92, 1996, 1998), and won six championships with the Chicago Bulls (1991-93, 1996-98). Dubbed "Air Jordan" for his remarkable leaping ability, Jordan thrilled spectators with his acrobatic dunks and game-winning shots. Off the court, Jordan became a celebrity and one of the most sought-after commercial spokesmen in the world.

Joyce, James, *b. Dublin, 1882; d. 1941.* **Novelist.** Joyce is one of the towering figures of modern literature. His four major works, set in Dublin, which he left in his early twenties, are progressively innovative. *Dubliners* (1915), a volume of stories, was succeeded by *A Portrait of the Artist as a Young Man* (1916), a powerful autobiographical novel that takes expressionistic leaps in style. *Ulysses* (1922), composed with stream-of-consciousness technique that merges interior life and external context, is an account, modeled on Homer's *Odyssey*, of one day in Dublin, June 16, 1904. The dense, multilingual wordplay and character transformations in *Finnegans Wake* (1939) make it a seldom-read masterpiece.

Jung, Carl Gustav, *b. 1875, Kresswil, Switzerland; d. 1961.* **Psychoanalytic theorist.** As a young psychiatrist in Switzerland, Jung published *The Psychology of Dementia Praecox* (schizophrenia) in 1906, which led to an association with Sigmund Freud. But *Psychology of the Unconscious* (1911–12) began a break with Freud by challenging the exclusively sexual character of the libido drive. Jung's "analytic psychology" incorporated mythology and religion. He believed that individuals have both a personal and a collective unconscious, that each psyche contains an "archetype" of the opposite sex, and that the goal of analysis is "individuation," a wholeness harmonizing the conscious and unconscious. Jung also introduced the theory of introverted and extroverted personality types. His other books include *Psychology and Religion* (1937).

Justinian I (Flavius Justinianus; Petrus Sabbatius), *b. Tauresium, Dardania (now probably Serbia), 483; d. 565.* **Roman Emperor of Byzantium (527–65).** Justinian and his ambitious wife Theodora set out to reclaim much of Rome's western empire for Constantinople, succeeding in reestablishing dominion over Spain, North Africa, and much of Italy. His greatest legacies are the *Codex Justinianus* (534), a codification of the Roman laws, which had immeasurable influence on succeeding legal systems; and the church of Hagia Sophia in Constantinople, the crown jewel of his extensive building program, still extant in Istanbul.

Kafka, Franz, *b. Prague, 1883; d. 1924.* **Novelist, short-story writer.** A middle-class Jew, Kafka earned a law degree and worked for years in the insurance business. He wrote in German and published little while he was alive. *The Metamorphosis* (1916), a story in which a man wakes up one morning as an insect is his most famous work. Kafka's surrealistically isolated characters, described in clear, straightforward prose, strongly influenced 20th-century literature. His own life was pained by romantic disappointment and the tuberculosis that brought early death. His novels were all published posthumously: *The Trial* (1925), *The Castle* (1926), and *Amerika* (1927).

Kahlo, Frida, *b. Mexico City, Mexico, 1907; d. 1954.* **Painter.** Kahlo began painting while recovering from an accident that crippled her. She is known for riveting self-portraits that use fantasy and a semi-primitive style to explore her physical and psychological circumstances. She drew on popular Mexican art and often pointedly clothed herself in Mexican rather than European or American garments. Kahlo was married to the artist Diego Rivera. Her works include *Frida and Diego Rivera* (1931), *Henry Ford Hospital* (1932), and *The Two Fridas* (1939).

Kant, Immanuel, *b. Konigsberg (Kaliningrad), 1724; d. 1804.* **Philosopher.** One of the great figures of metaphysics, Kant held that only phenomena, objects of experience, can be known; things beyond experience, noumena, cannot be known or scientifically demonstrated. In his *Critique of Pure Reason* (1781), he argued that God, immortality and freedom are unknowable by scientific thought, but he also held that belief in them is required by morality. Kant's famous moral imperative is: act only according to that rule which you can at the same time will to become a universal law.

Keaton, Buster, (Joseph Francis Keaton) *b. Piqua, Kans., 1895; d. 1966.* **Silent film comedian.** Keaton created a screen persona dubbed the "Great Stone Face" because of his deadpan expression despite all adversity. Keaton's youth as a part of his family's vaudeville act served as his training ground in acrobatics and physical comedy, which became the basis of the large-scale stunts in his films. His first film role was in *The Butcher Boy* (1917). Keaton starred in and directed his best work during the 1920's, including *Sherlock Jr.* (1924) and his masterpiece, *The General* (1927).

Keats, John, *b. 1795, London; d. 1821.* **Poet.** Keats produced more great writing in a comparably brief period than any other English poet. Important early poems included "On First Looking into Chapman's Homer" and *Endymion.* Then, in 1819, poor, sickly, and unhappily in love, he wrote an astonishing series of superior poems, including his six great odes, published in *Lamia, Isabella, The Eve of St. Agnes and Other Poems.* He also composed some of the finest English sonnets and two aborted but celebrated "epics," *Hyperion* and *The Fall of Hyperion*. In melodious, exquisitely sensuous, beautifully phrased verse, Keats expressed the tension between the richness and sadness of physical and emotional experience.

Kennedy, John Fitzgerald, *b. Brookline, Mass., 1917; d. 1963.* **Thirty-fifth U.S. president, 1961–63.** The youngest man elected president, the only Roman Catholic, and the first born in the 20th century, Kennedy served three undistinguished terms in Congress before he was elected to the Senate in 1952. In 1960, he won the presidency over vice president Richard M. Nixon by just 118,000 votes out of 69 million cast. Just after taking office, Kennedy approved the disastrous Bay of Pigs invasion, and a year later, he confronted the Soviets over the presence of their nuclear missiles in Cuba. As racial unrest spread in the turbulent early 1960's, Kennedy cautiously supported the civil rights movement, introducing sweeping legislation that would not pass in his lifetime—nor would his plans for aid to education and medical care for the elderly reach fruition before his death. In a motorcade in Dallas, Tex. on November 22, 1963, Kennedy was fatally shot by Lee Harvey Oswald, a left-wing ex-marine who was in turn murdered by Jack Ruby two days later.

Kennedy, Joseph P., *b. East Boston, Mass., 1888; d. 1969.* **American businessman and diplomat.** Father of President John F. Kennedy, and senators Robert F. Kennedy and Edward M. Kennedy, he amassed a fortune during Prohibition and the Depression, in businesses ranging from banking to shipbuilding to motion picture distribution. The patriarch of the Kennedy clan used his power and influence to secure political office for his sons. As ambassador to Great Britain (1937–40), he supported Chamberlain's policy of appeasement. Persistent rumors of links with organized crime surrounded him but were never proved.

Kennedy, Robert F. (Bobby), *b. Brookline, Mass., 1925; d. 1968.* **U.S. politician.** Younger brother of President John F. Kennedy, Bobby served as the most trusted advisor of his brother's administration. As U.S. attorney general, he attacked organized crime and staunchly supported civil rights. During the Cuban missile crisis, he advocated a naval blockade, rather than a military response. After his brother's assassination, he resigned from Lyndon Johnson's cabinet and won a Senate seat from New York (1964). In 1968, he made his own bid for the presidency, but he was slain by Sirhan Sirhan in Los Angeles, hours after winning California's Democratic primary.

Kepler, Johannes, b. Weil der Stadt, Germany, 1571; d. 1630. **Astronomer.** Kepler, influenced by Copernicus' teachings, became Tyco Brahe's assistant in 1600. He published (1609) Brahe's calculations of the orbit of Mars, adding the first two of his own laws: that planetary orbits are elliptical, not circular, and that a planet's speed increases as its distance from the sun decreases. His third law relates the average distance of a planet from the sun and the time it takes to complete its orbit. Kepler's work was instrumental in Newton's development of the laws of motion and gravity.

Keynes, John Maynard, *b. Cambridge, England, 1883; d. 1946.* **Economist.** Keynes gained prominence with *The Economic Consequences of the Peace* (1919), which predicted accurately that the onerous reparations levied against Germany after World War I would drive it into dangerous economic nationalism and militarism. During the Great Depression he published *The General Theory of Employment, Interest and Money* (1936), a vastly influential book expounding a revolutionary view that prolonged recessions are not self-correcting but require government spending to stimulate economic growth. Its thesis became known as Keynsian economics and shaped government policies in a number of countries. In 1944 at the Bretton Woods Conference he helped to establish the postwar system of exchange rates, the International Monetary Fund, and the International Bank for Reconstruction and Development (World Bank).

Khrushchev, Nikita, *b. Kalinovka, Kursk Province, Russia, 1894; d. 1971.* **Premier of the Soviet Union (1958–64).** Born a peasant, Khrushchev rapidly rose through Communist Party ranks and, with Nikolai Bulganin, seized power after Stalin's death in 1953. In 1956, he denounced the worst excesses of Stalin's regime (omitting his own role). Although he released thousands of political prisioners, he crushed budding independence movements in Hungary and Poland. In 1958, Khrushchev became prime minister and assumed control over both state and party. Despite his attempted reforms, the Soviet economy soured and individual liberties remained limited. Even as he pursued the arms race, he acknowledged the dangers of the cold war and called for "peaceful coexistence." Khrushchev was ousted in 1964 after the Cuban missile crisis and a bitter ideological split with China.

Kierkegaard, Søren , *b. Copenhagen, Denmark, 1813; d. 1855.* **Philosopher and religious writer.** He was a precursor of the existentialists and a major influence on Protestant theology. He argued that advancing through the three stages of the aesthetic, the ethical and the religious by means of an "existential dialectic" brings the individual closer to God. A leap of faith is required; reason is not a help. But awareness of the relationship to God leads to despair as the individual contrasts temporality with eternal truth. His major works include *Either/Or* (1843) and *Fear and Trembling* (1843).

Killy, Jean-Claude, *b. Saint-Cloud, France, 1943.* French skier. Killy became a national hero and earned a place in Olympic history by sweeping the men's Alpine events—downhill, slalom, and giant slalom—at the 1968 Winter Games in Grenoble, France. In a stellar career, Killy also won the World Championship combined title twice (1965–66) and the World Cup overall championship twice (1967–68).

King, Martin Luther Jr., *b. Atlanta, 1929; d. 1968.* **Minister and social activist.** The foremost leader of the civil rights movement of the 1960's, King employed nonviolence to end legal segregation of blacks in the United States, especially in the South. His leadership during the Montgomery bus boycott (1955-56) drew national attention, and persuaded him to start the Southern Christian Leadership Conference. From this pulpit, he organized sit-ins and protest marches against segregation, notably the 1963 March on Washington, at which he delivered his famous "I have a dream" speech. His words moved the nation and led to the passage of the Civil Rights Act of 1964, the same year he was awarded the Nobel Peace Prize. King's march on Selma, Alabama, led to the Voting Rights Act of 1965. He was assassinated by a sniper, James Earl Ray, at a motel in Memphis on April 4, 1968.

Kinsey, Alfred, *b. Hoboken, N.J., 1894; d. 1956.* **Biologist.** A professor of zoology and botany, Kinsey shocked the United States in 1948 with his publication of *Sexual Behavior in the Human Male*, the first academic inquiry into people's sexual habits. Based on more than 18,000 interviews, Kinsey's report revealed levels of bisexuality and masturbation that were much higher than previously thought. Although his *Sexual Behavior in the Human Female* (1953) was less controversial and less successful, Kinsey's research changed public perception of sexuality, contributing to the sexual revolution of the 1960's.

Kipling, Rudyard, *b. Bombay, India, 1865; d. 1936.* **Poet, novelist, and short-story writer.** Forever associated with the spirit of imperialism that existed before World War I, Kipling's works drew from his experience in the colonies of the British Empire. His *Barrack-Room Ballads* (1892) — which included "Gunga Din" — proved a popular edition of poetry, and he followed it with the children's favorite, *The Jungle Book* (1894). Kipling collected several short children's tales in *Just-So Stories* (1902), and he published a critically acclaimed novel, *Kim* (1902). He won the Nobel Prize for Literature in 1907.

Kissinger, Henry Alfred, *b. Fürth, Germany, 1923.* **German-born American statesman and scholar.** Emigrating from Germany in 1938, Kissinger taught government at Harvard University from 1954 to 1969 when President Richard Nixon appointed him national security advisor. In this post, and after 1973 as secretary of state, he arranged President Nixon's trip to mainland China and the Soviet Union in 1972, negotiated a cease-fire in the Vietnam War in 1973, and helped arrange a cease-fire in the Arab-Israeli war of 1973. He shared the Nobel Peace Prize with Le Duc Tho of North Vietnam in 1973. His critics accuse him of being involved in the suppression of socialist revolutions in Latin America and elsewhere.

Klee, Paul, *b. Münchenbuchsee, near Berne, Switzerland, 1879; d. 1940.* **Painter, printmaker.** While his work is highly theoretical (he drew inspiration from music, poetry, and color theory), Klee strove to achieve qualities found in the art of the untrained, children, and the insane. He developed unique methods of picture-making, including such oil transfer drawings as his *Twittering Machine* (1922), in which simplified forms mock modern machinery. Klee was revered by the surrealists and the abstract expressionists and was targeted by the Nazi regime. Well-known works include *Around the Fish* (1926) and *Park Near Lu(cerne)* (1938).

Kublai Khan, *b. 1215, d. 1294.* **Mongol leader.** Kublai, the grandson of Genghis Khan, was chosen as leader of the Mongols in 1260. From the beginning, Kublai evinced an interest in China, and he proclaimed his own dynasty, in the Chinese style, the Yuan. Kublai finally defeated the ruling Chinese dynasty, the Sung, in 1279, reuniting China, which had been divided between north and south since the end of the Tang dynasty. Kublai fought a number of wars with neighboring kingdoms, including Burma and Japan, with mixed success.

Kubrick, Stanley, *b. Bronx, New York, 1928; d. 1999.* **Film director.** A filmmaker known for his visual boldness, black humor, and pessimistic outlook, his acclaimed indictment of military justice, *Paths of Glory* (1956), led to an invitation to complete the wide-screen epic *Spartacus* (1961). Unhappy with Hollywood, he moved to England, where he made the films that polarized his fans and critics: *Dr. Strangelove* (1964), *2001: A Space Odyssey* (1968), and *A Clockwork Orange* (1971). His work continued to be controversial up until his final film, *Eyes Wide Shut* (1999).

Kurosawa, Akira, *b. Tokyo, Japan, 1910; d. 1998.* **Film director.** The first Japanese director to become famous in the West, Kurosawa astounded audiences with both historical films about honor among the samurai (*Seven Samurai*, 1954) and modern tales of great humanism (*Ikiru*, 1952). His directed his first film, *Judo Saga*, in 1943, but it was *Drunken Angel* (1948) that announced him as a serious talent and *Rashomon* (1951) that secured his reputation. *Drunken Angel* began a lifelong collaboration with the star Toshiro Mifune. Among his best films are *Throne of Blood* (1957) based on *Macbeth*; *Yojimbo*, (1961) a Japanese western; and *Ran* (1985), based on *King Lear*.

La Follette, Robert M. (Sr.), *b. Primrose, Wis., 1855; d. 1925.* **Politician.** In a long career that included stints as a

U.S. senator and representative as well as governor of his native Wisconsin, La Follette earned the nickname "Fighting Bob" for his ceaseless campaigns against corruption and his support for public causes. His reforms advanced such issues as open primary elections, unemployment compensation, and progressive income taxation. When criticized for his vote against the United States' entry into World War I in 1917, he defended the right to free speech in wartime. Although he was a Republican for most of his career, La Follette ran for president on the Progressive ticket in the election of 1924.

Lamarck, Jean-Baptiste Pierre Antoine de Monet, Chevalier de, *b. Bazantin, France, 1744; d. 1829.* **Naturalist.** Lamarck studied and classified invertebrates, worked in botany, and developed invertebrate paleontology. He is known today for his idea that life-forms have changed over geologic time as a result of needs created by the environment. This evolutionary approach was a forerunner of Darwin's, but Lamarck's proposed mechanism of change, the inheritance of acquired characteristics, was rejected as the principles of heredity were developed.

Lancaster, Burt, *b. New York City, 1913; d. 1994.* **Movie actor.** Trained as a circus acrobat, he defined swashbuckling, whether playing the title role in *The Crimson Pirate* (1952) or an obstinately romantic old man in *Atlantic City* (1980). He is remembered for his debut in *The Killers* (1946) and a career of more than 65 films, notably *From Here to Eternity* (1953), *Sweet Smell of Success* (1957), and *Birdman of Alcatraz* (1962).

Lang, Fritz, *b. Vienna, Austria, 1890; d. 1976.* **Film director.** A legendary German Expressionist filmmaker, Lang excelled at using composition, set design, and lighting to convey his themes of fate and destiny. Though trained as an architect, he preferred writing screenplays for the busy German film industry after World War I. He directed his first film, *Halbblut*, in 1919; it was followed by several critical successes, including *Metropolis* (1927) and *M* (1931). He emigrated to America in the 1930's, directing his first Hollywood film, *Fury*, in 1936. His best Hollywood films include *You Only Live Once* (1937), *Scarlet Street* (1945), and *The Big Heat* (1953).

Laozi *(dates unknown).* **Chinese philosopher.** The historical reality of an individual known as Laozi ("Old Master") is doubtful; the conventional identification of Laozi with Lao Dan, a figure of the sixth century B.C. is almost certainly wrong. *The Book of Laozi* (also known as the *Daodejing*, "The Way and Its Power"), a fundamental text of Daoist philosophy and religion, was compiled from earlier materials ca. 300 B.C. Envisioning a primitive agrarian society ruled by a sage-king empowered by his possession of the dao (the "Way"), it poses a radical challenge to Confucian social theory and imperial-bureaucratic government. Laozi was later regarded as an immortal and as one of the high gods of religious Daoism.

Lavoisier, Antoine Laurent, *b. Paris, 1743; d. 1794.* **Chemist and physicist.** Lavoisier was a founder of modern chemistry. He introduced effective quantitative methods in chemistry, explained combustion, elucidated the role of oxygen in respiration, and established the composition of water and many other compounds. In his classification of substances he suggested the modern distinction between chemical elements and compounds. His famous textbook, called in English *Elements of Chemistry*, was published in 1789. Active as a government expert and official, he was executed during the revolution in France.

Lawrence, D. H. (David Herbert), *b. Eastwood, Nottinghamshire, England, 1885; d. 1930.* **English novelist and poet.** Lawrence's largely autobiographical first major novel, *Sons and Lovers* (1913), introduced his themes of the unhealthy separation of man from nature, and the stifling effects of social convention, and intellectualism. With *The Rainbow* (1915) and *Women in Love* (1921), he achieved his highest art and received much criticism for their sexually explicit content. After World War I, his notoriety and that of his previously married German wife, Frieda, caused them to leave England and live in the southwestern United States, Mexico, Australia, and other places. His most famous novel, *Lady Chatterley's Lover,* (1928), was banned in the U.S. and U.K. because of sexual content. His short-stories (including "Rocking Horse" and "Odor of Chyrysanthemums,") are highly regarded and his poetry, including "Snake," "Figs," and "Blue Gentians" increasingly appreciated.

Le Corbusier (Charles-Edouard Jeanneret-Gris), *b. La Chaux-de-Fonds, Switzerland, 1887; d. 1965.* **Architect, painter, and theorist.** Considered by many the most influential architect of the 20th century, he designed one of the great works of modern architecture, the Villa Savoye in Poissy, France (1928–30). In a seminal book, *Toward a New Architecture* (1923), he delivered his famous dictum, "The house is a machine for living in";

but his houses were elegant, with hints of classicism. He produced work of astonishing diversity, including the Unite d'Habitation (1946–52), an apartment building in Marseilles, France; the pilgrimage church of Notre-Dame-du-Haut (1950–55) in Ronchamp, France; and the principal public buildings for the capital of Punjab in Chandigarh (1951–65), India.

Lee, Robert Edward, *b. Stratford, Va., 1807; d. 1870.* **American general of the Confederacy.** The son of a Revolutionary War hero, Lee attended West Point and later served in the Mexican War. He became superintendant at West Point, and later led the troops who captured John Brown at Harpers Ferry. In 1862, Lee was given command of the Army of Northern Virginia. Thereafter he led the Confederate forces brilliantly in historic Civil War battles, including the second Bull Run, Antietam, Chancellorsville, and Fredericksburg; but at Gettysburg he suffered the defeat that spelled the beginning of the end of the Civil War. He surrendered to General Ulysses S. Grant at Appomattox courthouse on April 9, 1865.

Leibniz, Gottfried Wilhelm, Baron von, *b. Leipzig, 1646; d. 1716.* **German philosopher and mathematician.** An impressive scientist and scholar who also held diplomatic posts under various German princes, his main contributions are now regarded as those in mathematics and logic. He invented the calculus at the same time as, but independently of, Newton, and he was one of the founders of symbolic logic. His philosophy was an optimistic, consistent rationalism. He held that the universe was made up of monads, infinite in number, nonmaterial, and hierarchically arranged, and that divine guidance made the existing world the best of possible worlds.

Lemieux, Mario, *b. Montreal, Canada, 1965.* **Hockey player.** Lemieux burst onto the scene with the Pittsburgh Penguins in 1984, scoring 100 points and winning the Calder trophy for outstanding rookie. He won the MVP award in 1988 and led the Penguins to back-to-back Stanley Cup championships in 1991 and 1992. In 1993, he was diagnosed with Hodgkin's disease, and after missing 20 games for treatment, "Super Mario" returned, scored 160 points in just 60 games, and won his second M.V.P. Lemieux has been the league's leading scorer six times; he reentered the NHL in 2000 after a three-year retirement.

Lenin (Vladimir Ilyich Ulyanov), *b. Simbirsk, Russia, 1870; d. 1924.* **Russian political leader.** Inspired by the writings of Karl Marx, Lenin founded Russia's Communist Party and orchestrated the Bolshevik revolution (1917). When it succeeded, he became the first leader of the new Soviet state (1917–24). Under his leadership, the Bolsheviks withdrew from World War I, distributed land to the peasants, and granted independence to Finland, Poland, and the Baltic republics. The promise of Soviet Communism ended even before Lenin's death, as the state began brutally quashing dissent and civil war ravaged the country.

Lennon, John Winston, *b. Liverpool, England, 1940; d. 1980.* **Rock-pop vocalist, guitarist, and songwriter; member of the Beatles.** As half of the Lennon-McCartney songwriting team, he wrote or cowrote many of the great popular songs of the 1960's, most notably "Norwegian Wood," "Revolution," "In My Life," "Strawberry Fields Forever," and "A Day in the Life." Post-Beatles, Lennon's success was spreading. He was shot and killed outside his New York apartment building on December 8, 1980, by Mark David Chapman. Lennon's solo recordings include "Give Peace a Chance" (1969), "Cold Turkey" (1969), "Instant Karma" (1970), "Imagine" (1971), and "(Just Like) Starting Over" (1980).

Leo I (Saint) (Leo the Great), *b. ca 400, Tuscany?; d. 461.* **Pope (440-61), Doctor of the Church.** Leo was one of the most important figures in the establishment of the bishop of Rome as pope and supreme leader of the Christian church, specifically by securing an edict from Emperor Valentinian III that recognized the pope's authority over other bishops. Leo also effectively battled the Manichaean and Nestorian heresies; and in his *Tome of Leo* and at the Council of Chalcedon (451), he led the condemnation of Eutyches's doctrine that Christ has one divine nature. His successful negotiation with Attila the Hun to prevent an attack on Rome in 452 was a critical event in the development of the papacy's temporal rule.

Leonardo da Vinci, *b. Anchiano, Italy, 1452; d. 1519.* **Painter, sculptor, architect, designer, theorist, engineer, scientist.** Founder of the High Renaissance movement, and painter of the *Mona Lisa* (1503–5), arguably the most famous and influential image in Western art. Other well-known works include *The Last Supper* (1495–98). Leonardo's radical technical and conceptual innovations established an unprecedented standard of realism in painting. He developed a method of modeling figures using light and shade called *chiaroscuro*, and his paintings have a luminous, hazy quality referred to as *sfumato*. Committed to a study of nature, Leonardo left behind hundreds of drawings and notes; he developed the technique of modern scientific illustration, and his many inventions include machinery and military engineering.

Lewis, Carl, *b. Birmingham, Ala., 1961.* **U.S. track-and-field star.** Lewis won a record-tying nine gold medals and one silver medal in appearances at the 1984, 1988, 1992, and 1996 Olympic Games. A sprinter and long jumper, he equaled Jesse Owens's feat of 1936 by taking gold in the 100 m, 200 m, long jump, and 4 x 100-m relay at the 1984 Olympics in Los Angeles.

Lichtenstein, Roy, *b. New York, N.Y., 1923; d. 1997.* **Painter, sculptor, printmaker, decorative artist.** A central figure in the Pop Art movement, Lichtenstein is famous for paintings that mimic comic books. Using simplified color schemes and black outlines, and representing tonal variation with tiny dots, he invites the viewer to examine everyday aspects of American culture. In his later career Lichtenstein put his comic book technique to use in renderings of such famous painting styles as Cubism and Abstract Expressionism. Well-known works include *Whaam!* (1963), *Hopeless* (1963), and *Brushstrokes in Flight* (1984).

Lincoln, Abraham, *b. Hodgenville, Ky., 1809; d. 1865.* **Sixteenth U.S. president, 1861–65.** Lincoln was born in a log cabin and accumulated barely a year's total education while growing up. Family moves took him to Indiana and then to Illinois by the time he was 21; a failed storekeeper, Lincoln worked at odd jobs while he taught himself law, sometimes walking 20 miles to borrow books. He was elected to the Illinois state legislature (as a Whig) in 1834 and to Congress in 1846, and unsuccessfully ran for the Senate in 1858, drawing national attention in debates with Stephen A. Douglas, the nation's leading Democrat. He was rewarded with the Republican party's nomination for president in 1860, and defeated three opponents to win the general election. As southern states left the Union, Lincoln preached conciliation, although he vowed to crush secession and forced the issue at Fort Sumter. After early reverses in the Civil War, Lincoln decided that slavery had to be abolished altogether to restore the Union, and he issued the Emancipation Proclamation (1862). Five days after the war's end, Lincoln was shot and killed by John Wilkes Booth, an arch-Confederate. Lincoln's prestige has grown with time, until many have come to regard him as the nation's greatest president.

Lindbergh, Charles A., *b. Detroit, 1902; d. 1974.* **American aviator.** On May 20–21, 1927, he made the first nonstop solo flight across the Atlantic in a small plane, "The Spirit of St. Louis." After completing the journey from New York to Paris in 33.5 hours, Lindbergh immediately became an international hero. In 1929, he married the writer Anne Morrow. Their infant son was kidnapped and murdered in 1932 in a crime that received worldwide attention. His support of fascist governments caused him to lose his heroic stature but his 1953 account of his flight, *The Spirit of St. Louis*, won a Pulitzer Prize.

Linnaeus, Carolus, *b. Råshult, Sweden, 1707; d. 1778.* **Botanist and taxonomist.** Linnaeus originated the system of classification of animals and plants, in which organisms are placed on the basis of natural characteristics into a hierarchy of groups. From the broadest to narrowest these are kingdom, phylum (in botany, division), class, order, family, genus, and species. Linnaeus also developed the binomial naming system. For each organism the genus is given first and then the species, e.g. lion: *panthera leo*. Modified by the influence of evolutionary theory and new scientific discoveries, Linnaeus's work remains the basis of modern taxonomy.

Lloyd George, David, *b, Manchester, England, 1863; d. 1945.* **British politician.** First elected to parliament in 1890 as a Liberal, he served as a minister in several governments. He rose to prominence when he introduced the National Insurance Act of 1911, which established health and unemployment insurance for English workers and marked the beginning of the modern welfare state. He was immensely popular as prime minister (1916–22), especially during World War I, when he devised a solution to the food shortages caused by German submarine attacks. At the negotiations for the Treaty of Versailles, he lobbied for a peace that was less punitive to Germany than the one sought by France's Georges Clemenceau.

Locke, John, *b. Wrington, England, 1632; d. 1704.* **Philosopher.** Considered the founder of British empiricism, his two main works, *Essay Concerning Human Understanding* (1690) and *Two Treatises on Civil Government* (1690), made him the leading philosopher of freedom. Against Hobbes, he held that the state of nature was happy, and that all humans were equal and free to pursue "life, health, liberty and possessions." The social contract forms the state, which is guided by natural law and guarantees inalienable rights. Locke also developed the idea of checks and balances found in the U.S. Constitution.

Longfellow, Henry Wadsworth, *b. Portland, Me., 1807; d. 1882.* **Poet.** Longfellow published his first book of verse, *Voices of the Night*, and a prose romance, *Hyperion*, in 1839. Highly popular in both America and England during his lifetime, he composed some of America's best-known poems, both short and long. Among the former are "The Village Blacksmith" and "The Wreck of the Hesperus" (both 1841). *Poems on Slavery*, revealing abolitionist sentiment, was published in 1842. His long narrative poems, set in his country's past and written in intricate, "antique" rhythms, include *Evangeline* (1847), *The Song of Hiawatha* (1855), *The Courtship of Miles Standish* (1858), and *Paul Revere's Ride* (1861).

Lorca, Federico García, *b. Fuente Vaqueros, Spain, 1898; d. 1936.* **Poet and playwright.** Responsible for revitalizing the drama and literature of Spain in the early 20th century, Lorca was strongly influenced by the folk traditions and social conditions of his native Andalusia as well as by surrealism and expressionism. His poems look back to the Gypsy ballads and romances of classical Spain, and his plays, among them *Blood Wedding* (1933) and *The House of Bernarda Alba* (1936), explore the search for love within a restrictive society. Lorca, a revolutionary during the Spanish Civil War, was arrested and executed in 1936.

Louis IX (St. Louis) *b. Poissy, France, 1214; d. 1270.* **King of France (1226–70)** The only French king to be canonized by the Roman Catholic Church (1297), Louis IX was an immensely popular king who led the Seventh Crusade into the Holy Land, which had fallen under Muslim control. Though the military operation failed, Louis negotiated several important alliances that made the endeavor a success. He also achieved a lasting peace with England (1258) and sponsored the first great encyclopedia. He died on a crusade to Tunisia.

Louis XIV (Louis the Great), *b. Saint-Germain-en-Laye, France, 1638; d. 1715.* **King of France (1643–1715).** One of the great monarchs of European history, the "Sun King" attempted to rule through divine right. He built lavish palaces for himself, including the one that still stands at Versailles, where he moved the seat of government in 1682. He greatly expanded his domain into the Netherlands (1667–78) and parts of the Hapsburg empire on France's eastern border. But he earned the enmity of Protestants when he revoked (1685) the Edict of Nantes, which had guaranteed their freedom of worship.

Louis XV (Louis the Well-Beloved), b. Versailles, France, 1710; d. 1774. **King of France (1715–74).** He ascended to the throne at age five because both his parents and his brother had died three years earlier. He took little interest in politics, causing the monarchy's authority to wane. In the Seven Years' War (1756–63), Louis allied France with Austria against England and Prussia, resulting in the loss of almost all French colonial possessions in India and North America.

Louis XVI, *b. Versailles, 1754; d. 1793.* **King of France, 1774-92.** Louis, the last Bourbon king, came to the throne in a time of fiscal crisis and popular ferment. He appointed capable ministers to stabilize government and economy, but failed to gain the cooperation of the aristocracy, who refused to be taxed and prevailed on him to summon the long-dormant Estates General in 1789. Louis stifled the influence of the third, or popular, estate, which then declared itself the National Assembly. Rumors of suppression of this body were a cause of the storming of Bastille prison on July 14, 1789, the focal date of the French Revolution. Louis and his queen were confined to the Tuileries palace, and his attempt to escape, his refusal to implement the Constitution of 1791 and his alliances with foreign armies against the revolution led to his conviction for treason and his beheading.

Louis, Joe (Joseph Louis Barrow), *b. Lafayette, Ala., 1914; d. 1981.* **Boxer.** The longest-reigning heavyweight champion in history the "Brown Bomber" won the title in 1937 and successfully defended it 25 times before retiring in 1949. His most famous bout was a first-round knockout of the German heavyweight Max Schmeling (Hitler's symbol of Aryan racial supremacy) in 1938. During the height of his career, Louis enlisted in the army, a move that helped in desegregating U.S. armed services. Louis won 68 of 71 career fights, 54 by knockout. Generous to a fault, Louis fell deep into debt, eventually owing the I.R.S. more than $1 million.

Lucas, George, *b. Modesto, Calif., 1944.* **Screenwriter, director, and founder of Industrial Light and Magic (ILM).** As creator of *Star Wars*, one of the most successful film series of all time, Lucas helped push the Hollywood industry toward action-driven genres. He directed his first film, *THX 1138*, in 1971, and the financial success of his second feature, *American Graffiti* (1973), made *Star Wars* (1977) possible. *The Empire Strikes Back* (1980) and *The Return of the Jedi* (1983) completed the first *Star Wars* trilogy, which combined old-fashioned Hollywood storytelling with ideas from mythology.

Ludendorff, Erich, *b. near Poznan, Poland, 1865; d. 1937.* **German military leader.** Prior to World War I, he was attached to the German general staff and was responsible for revisions to the Schlieffen Plan. At the start of the war, he was assigned to Paul von Hindenburg in the east, where they won a great victory at Tannenberg in 1914. In 1916, the team was given supreme military command and assumed a virtual dictatorship over the German state. Fearing American involvement in the war, Ludendorff launched a series of offenses in the west in 1918 that came close to succeeding but ultimately failed. After the war, he did much to undermine the Weimar Republic and for a time was an associate of Adolf Hitler.

Luther, Martin, *b. 1483, Eisleben, Saxony; d. 1546.* **Protestant reformer.** A Catholic monk and theology professor, Luther became discontented with the church about 1510, when he observed in Rome the widespread sale of indulgences, which reduced the spiritual penalties for sins. Luther believed salvation was God's free gift, and when a papal indulgence was offered in Saxony in 1517, he nailed 95 theses of objection to the Wittenberg church door. He soon published writings rejecting the authority of the pope, and in 1521 he was excommunicated and condemned at the imperial diet (assembly) at Worms. The articles of faith of his Lutheran Church were established in the Augsburg Confession of 1530. Luther translated the Bible into German and for the rest of his life was a central figure of the Reformation.

MacArthur, Douglas, *b. Little Rock, Ark., 1880: d. 1964.* **Military leader.** MacArthur became U.S. Army chief of staff in 1930 and was military adviser to the Philippines from 1935 to 1941. He fought a delaying action in the Philippines after World War II broke out. Recalled to Australia, he was made commander of the southwest Pacific theater in 1942. As Allied governor of Japan from 1945 to 1951, he radically reformed Japanese society. He was chosen to command United Nations forces in Korea when war began there in 1950, but was relieved of command by President Truman for insubordination in 1951.

Machiavelli, Niccolo, *b. Florence, Italy, 1469; d. 1527.* **Political philosopher, statesman, and author.** A senior official of the Florentine Republic, he undertook vital diplomatic missions to France, the Vatican, and Germany, and replaced mercenaries with a citizens' militia. He lost his office with the return of Medici rule (1512). Machiavelli's most famous work, *The Prince* (1532), describes the ways, amoral and calculating, in which a prince may maintain power, but his *Discourses* (1531) displays his republican principles; he also wrote poems, plays, and histories.

Macmillan, Harold, *b. London, 1894; d. 1986.* **English statesman.** Elected to Parliament in 1924, Macmillan served, with a break (1929–1931), to 1963. He held posts in the wartime cabinet of Winston Churchill and later in other cabinets. He became prime minister in 1957 and signed the the Nuclear Test Ban Treaty with the United States and the Soviet Union in 1963. However, he failed to have England admitted into the European Economic Community, and he resigned in 1963 amid a scandal involving his war secretary, John Profumo.

Madison, James, *b. Port Conway, Va., 1751; d. 1836.* **Fourth U.S. president, 1809–17.** A graduate of Princeton, Madison was the youngest member of the Continental Congress in 1780, when he led the movement to revise the Articles of Confederation. At the Constitutional Convention in Philadelphia in 1787, Madison's Virginia Plan became the pivot of discussion; he (with John Jay and Alexander Hamilton) was a coauthor of *The Federalist* papers, drafted the Bill of Rights, and cofounded the Democratic-Republican party. After ascending to the presidency, Madison successfully led the country in the fight against the British in the War of 1812.

Magellan, Ferdinand, *b. Oporto, Portugal, 1480; d. 1521.* **Navigator.** Magellan spent six years in Portuguese Asia, voyaging to India, Malacca, and perhaps the Spice Islands. He approached Spain's Charles I with a plan to sail from South America to the Spice Islands. His were the first ships to transit the Strait of Magellan (1519) and to cross the Pacific, taking fourteen weeks to reach the Mariana Islands (1520). Magellan was killed in 1521, in the Philippines. Under Juan Sebastian de Elcano, the first circumnavigation of the world was completed on September 6, 1522.

Magritte, René, *b. Lessines, Hainaut, Belgium, 1898; d. 1967.* **Painter, sculptor, photographer, filmmaker.** Magritte was one of the founding members in 1926 of the Belgian Surrealist group, which developed independently from the French surrealists. Not wanting the style of his paintings to detract from the subject, he created a straightforward, unembellished visual language, which he used to depict scenes in which reality is pointedly skewed. His painting *Red Model* (1935), for example, shows a pair of shoes with human toes. Other important works include *Threatened Assassin* (1927), *Treachery of Images* (1929), and *Empire of Light* (1950).

Mahler, Gustav, *b. Kalist, Bohemia, 1860; d. 1911.* **Austrian composer, conductor, and pianist.** Educated in Vienna, Mahler conducted several orchestras in Europe and the New York Philharmonic (1909–11) and Metropolitan Opera (1908–10). Mahler's music combined romantic eloquence with subtle chromaticism and polyphony, anticipating the coming avant-garde movement. Notable works include Symphonies No. 1 in D Major (1884-88), No. 2 in C Minor (*Resurrection*) (1888–94), No. 4 in G Major (1899–1900), No. 5 in C# Minor (1901–02), No. 6 in A Minor (1903–05), and No. 9 in D Major (1909–10); *Das Lied von der Erde* (*The Song of the Earth*) (1907–09); and the song cycles *Lieder eines Fahrenden Gesellen* (*Songs of a Wayfarer*) (1884) and *Des Knaben Wunderhorn* (*The Youth's Magic Horn*) (1888–99).

Mailer, Norman, *b. Long Branch, N.J., 1923.* **Non-fiction writer, and novelist.** Mailer, an uncommonly gifted and prolific writer, has published nonfiction books, novels, essays, articles, poems, plays, and more. An early practicioner of the New Journalism of the 1960's, Mailer had already gained fame for *The Naked and the Dead* (1948), a novel recounting his experience in World War II. Other well-known non-fiction works include *Miami and the Siege of Chicago* (1968), *Of a Fire on the Moon* (1971), and *Marilyn* (1973). He won two Pulitzer prizes, one in nonfiction for *The Armies of the Night* (1968) and one in fiction for *The Executioner's Song* (1979).

Maki, Fumihiko, *b. Tokyo, 1929.* **Japanese architect.** Maki calls himself a modernist, but his buildings, in their human scale and use of diverse materials, do not reflect a strict modernist style. His vast Makuhari Messe Exhibition Center (1986–89) in Tokyo and Kirishima International Concert Hall (1994) make use of modern industrial materials softened by a plastic approach to form. The Center for the Arts, Yerba Buena Gardens (1991–93), in San Francisco is an important work in the United States. Maki was a winner of the 1993 Pritzker prize.

Malthus, Thomas Robert, *b. near Guilford, Britain, 1766; d. 1834.* **English economist.** Malthus is best known for his theory of population in his *Essay on Population,* first published in 1798 and revised in several subsequent editions. He argued that population increases geometrically while the food supply increases arithmetically. Population growth is limited by famine, disease, and war when it outstrips the food supply, but these undesirable forces can be mitigated by abstinence and birth control. The thesis was influential and came to be known as Malthusianism.

Mandela, Nelson, *b. Qunu, Transkei region, South Africa, 1918.* **Political leader.** After South Africa's white government banned the African National Congress resistance movement in 1961, its leader, Nelson Mandela, continued his political activities underground. He was eventually arrested and imprisoned for 27 years. During his captivity, his fame spread abroad, and "free Nelson Mandela" became an international rallying cry. In 1990, President F. W. de Klerk lifted the ban on the A.N.C. and released Mandela. Mandela and de Klerk shared the 1993 Nobel Peace Prize. In 1994, Mandela was elected South Africa's first black president.

Manet, Edouard, *b. Paris, 1832; d. 1883.* **Painter.** A realist who influenced and was influenced by the Impressionists of the 1870's, in his lifetime Manet's avant-gardism was often ill–received. Images such as *Déjeuner sur l'herbe* (1863) and *Olympia* (1863) were thought to bring a vulgar modernity to classical subjects. Influenced by Velázquez and Japanese woodblock prints, Manet's paintings are characterized by flatly applied tones. *Boating* (1874) demonstrates the high color value and broken brushwork also typical of the Impressionists. Manet sought to document contemporary Parisian life, as he did in *Bar at the Folies-Bergère* (1882).

Mann, Thomas, *b. Lubeck, Germany, 1875; d. 1955.* **Novelist and essayist.** Mann explored several themes in his fiction, including the clash between the rational and the irrational and between liberal and conservative values, and above all the place of the artist in a rapidly changing society. His first novel *Buddenbrooks* (1901) described the decay and fall of a prominent family; *Death in Venice* (1912) depicted the conflict between death and art. Other notable works are *The Magic Mountain* (1924) and the tetralogy *Joseph and His Brethren* (1933–43). Mann received the Nobel Prize for Literature in 1929. Also a distinguished political and literary essayist, he left Nazi Germany in 1933 and lived 14 years in the U.S.

Mantle, Mickey (Charles) *b. Spavinaw, Okla., 1931; d. 1995.* **Baseball player.** The switch-hitting New York Yankees center fielder possessed a rare combination of speed and power that made him one of the game's most exciting players. He was the American League M.V.P. three times. Though slowed by various injuries throughout his 18-year career, Mantle ended up with 536 career home runs. He added a record 18 career World Series home runs. Mantle played for seven World Series winning teams and was elected to the National Baseball Hall of Fame in 1974.

Mao Zedong, *b. Hunan Province, China, 1893; d. 1976.* **Chinese Communist leader.** Mao was born to a prosperous peasant family and moved to Beijing in 1918, where he studied Marxism. A revolutionary activist and founding member of the Chinese Communist Party (Shanghai, 1921), Mao had unorthodox ideas about peasant-based revolution that marginalized him within the party. During the Long March (1934–35) Mao was elected party chairman. Vindicated, he used the party base at Yan'an as a laboratory of Maoist ideology in action. After victory over the Nationalists in the Civil War (1946–49), Mao quickly solidified Communist control, quashing all opposition. Despite the catastrophic Great Leap Forward (1958–60) and the disruptive Cultural Revolution (1966–76), Mao remained chairman until his death, which was followed by an era of post-Mao economic and social reform.

Marciano, Rocky (Rocco Marchegiano), *b. Brockton, Mass., 1923; d. 1969.* **World heavyweight boxing champion, 1952–56.** Marciano began to box in the army during World War II and did not turn professional until age 23 in 1947. His impressive knockout record raised him through the heavyweight ranks and he became the leading title contender when he knocked out former longtime champion Joe Louis in 1951. He took the title with a 13th-round knockout of Jersey Joe Walcott on Sept. 23, 1952, and defended it successfully six times before retiring in 1956. Marciano won all 49 of his professional fights, 43 of them by knockout. He was killed in a plane crash in Iowa.

Marconi, Guglielmo, *b. 1874, d. 1937.* **Italian inventor.** Marconi learned in 1894 that Heinrich Hertz (b. 1857, d. 1894) had produced invisible waves that travel through space. Marconi thought such waves could be used to send wireless communications similar to the dot-and-dash messages sent by telegraph. Within a year he was sending and detecting signals over distances of more than a mile (1.6 km). On December 12, 1901, Marconi showed that he could decipher signals sent across the Atlantic Ocean. Marconi was awarded the 1909 Nobel Prize in Physics for his invention of wireless telegraphy ("wireless"), the first form of radio.

Marcus Aurelius *b. 121; d. 180.* **Roman emperor.** The adopted son of emperor Antonius Pius, Marcus Aurelius took power after his father's death in 161. He made his adoptive brother, Lucius Verus, co-emperor. Marcus largely overshadowed his brother and is regarded as one of Rome's most wise and just emperors, respected for instituting political and social reforms, as well as writing *Meditations*, a work of Stoic philosophy. His reign was marred by ongoing wars, and he left his son Commodus, a notoriously brutal leader, as successor.

Marie Antoinette, *b. 1755, Vienna; d. 1793.* **Queen of France.** The daughter of the Austrian emperor of the Holy Roman Empire, Marie married the French dauphin in 1770. Indecisive and unprepared to rule, he ascended to the French throne in 1774 as Louis XVI. While discontent was percolating throughout France, Marie's extravagant lifestyle infuriated the public. As the French Revolution exploded in 1789, a mob descended on the lavish palace at Versailles, demanding that Marie and Louis move to Paris, where they became virtual prisoners in the Tuileries. In 1792, the royal family was arrested for treason. Marie followed her husband to the guillotine in 1793.

Marlowe, Christopher, *b. Canterbury, England (?), 1564; d. 1593.* **Poet and playwright.** Considered to be the finest English playwright before Shakespeare, he was a great innovator in the development of blank verse, in which unrhymed iambic pentameter is used to dramatic effect, Marlowe exerted a lasting influence on, among others, Shakespeare and Milton. His plays include *Tamburlaine the Great* (1587), *Edward II* (1594), *Doctor Faustus* (1604), and *The Jew of Malta* (1633). He was killed in a barroom fight perhaps because he had been acting as an agent of Queen Elizabeth. His unfinished poem *Hero and Leander* was published in 1598.

Marshall, George C., *b. Uniontown, Pa., 1880; d. 1959.* **American military leader and statesman.** A career army officer, he graduated from Virginia Military Institute, served in World War I, and rose to the rank of five-star general (1944) and chief of staff of the U.S. Army during World War II. But he is best remembered for the European Recovery Program—better known as the Marshall Plan (1947)—which brought U.S. aid to a war-ravaged Europe. As secretary of state (1947–49) and secretary of defense (1950–51), he laid the groundwork for the formation of NATO. In 1953, he became the first professional soldier to win the Nobel Peace Prize.

Marshall, John, *b. near Germantown, Va., 1755; d. 1835.* **American statesman and jurist.** After the American Revolution, Marshall practiced law in Richmond, Va., and served in the Virginia Assembly, the U.S., House of Representatives, and as secretary of state in President John Adams's cabinet. In 1801 he was appointed the fourth chief justice of the Supreme Court, where he had a profound impact on constitutional law. In *Marbury v. Madison* (1803) the court asserted a power to overrule legislation it deemed unconstitutional. Other decisions further increased the power of the Supreme Court, including decisions in conflicts between the states and the federal government.

Marx, Groucho (Julius Henry Marx) *New York City, 1890; d. 1977.* **Comedian.** His greasepaint mustache and funny walk brought ironic reality to the madcap antics of his brothers Harpo and Chico, first in their Broadway successes *The Cocoanuts* and *Animal Crackers*, then in Hollywood in such notable movies as *Duck Soup* (1933) and *A Night at the Opera* (1935). The Marx Brothers continued making movies into the 1950's; Groucho went on to fame on TV as the wacky host of the quiz show *You Bet Your Life*.

Marx, Karl, *b. Trier (Treves), Prussia, 1818; d. 1883.* **German political and economic theorist and philosopher.** Trained in law and a doctor of philosophy, Marx, along with his longtime collaborator and patron, Friedrich Engels, employed Hegel's dialectical system to develop his theory of dialectical materialism, an economic view of history that saw the triumph of the working class over capitalist control as inevitable. Committed to action as well as theory—to the cause of class struggle—the two men enunciated their beliefs in the concise *Communist Manifesto* ("Workers of the world, unite!") in 1848, the same year as the failed revolutions in Europe. He then worked as a journalist in Cologne but when the paper was suppressed, he settled permanently with his family in London in 1849, where he was a correspondent for the *New York Tribune*. Here he wrote his magnum opus, *Das Kapital*, published, with the help of Engels, especially after Marx's death, in three volumes from 1867 to 1894. Marx was a founder and leader of the International Workingmen's Association (the First International, 1864-72).

Mary, Queen of Scots (Mary Stuart), *b. Linlithgow, Scotland, 1542; d. 1587.* **Queen of Scotland.** Daughter of James V, king of Scotland, Mary became queen as an infant. She married the dauphin of France in 1559 but his death in 1560 brought her back to Scotland in 1561 as queen. But she was a Catholic ruling a Protestant government and her marriages to Lord Darnley and the Earl of Bothwell increased opposition to her rule. Her armies were defeated by Scottish nobles in 1567 and 1568. and she fled to the English court of Elizabeth I. She was beheaded after being involved in Catholic plots to assassinate Elizabeth.

Masaccio (Tommaso di Ser Giovanni di Mone Cassai), *b. San Giovanni Val d'Arno, Italy, 1401; d. 1428.* **Painter.** Regarded as the founder of Italian Renaissance painting, Masaccio was the first painter of his time to employ Brunelleschi's system of linear perspective. Also inspired by Giotto, Masaccio created mathematically proportioned spaces, fully three-dimensional figures, and a realistic depiction of light, all of which were significant developments for his time. His fresco *Trinity* (ca. 1425–27) was groundbreaking for placing the crucifixion scene in an illusionistic architectural setting. Other well-known works include *The Tribute Money* (ca. 1427), a fresco in the Brancacci Chapel.

Matisse, Henri, *b. Le Cateau-Cambrésis, France, 1869; d. 1954.* **Painter, sculptor.** Matisse came to painting late in life, having earned a degree as a lawyer. He became a leading figure in the Fauvist movement and one of the most influential artists of the 20th century. The Fauvists, or "wild beasts," produced paintings radical in their simplicity, with bold distortions and a primitive use of colors in high value. Matisse's best-known work is perhaps *Joy of Life* (1905–06), a modern interpretation of a classical Bacchanalian scene; other important work includes *The Red Studio* (1911).

Maxwell, James Clerk, *b. Edinburgh, 1831; d. 1879.* **Scottish physicist.** In 1857 he showed that Saturn's rings must consist of small particles. Three years later, he determined the statistical distribution of moving molecules in gases, explaining diffusion and conduction of heat. Maxwell was the first to show that the primary colors of light are red, green, and blue, and in 1861 he demonstrated the first color photograph based on this idea. From 1856 through 1873 he developed laws showing that light is a form of electromagnetic wave and predicted the rest of the electromagnetic spectrum.

Mayer, Louis (Eliezar Mayer) B., *b. Minsk, Russia 1885; d. 1957.* **Film producer.** One of the most powerful moguls of the Hollywood studio system, he was in the scrap-iron business when he bought his first movie theater in Haverhill, Mass., in 1907. He soon branched out into film distribution and production and moved to Hollywood in 1918. Mayer was the studio head at Metro-Goldwyn-Mayer (MGM) from its formation in 1924 until he was forced out in 1951. During this time, MGM films became known for their glamorous stars, high production values, and wholesome subject matter.

Mays, Willie, *b. Westfield, Ala.; 1931.* **Baseball player.** After his major league debut at age 19, Mays quickly emerged as one of baseball's most exciting and talented players. In 22 seasons, most with the New York and San Francisco Giants, the "Say Hey Kid" hit 660 home runs, fourth on the all-time list. He also ranks among the top 10 in career hits, runs, runs batted in, and total bases. A superb center fielder, Mays won a Gold Glove in each of the first 12 seasons it was awarded. He was twice named National League M.V.P. (1954, 1965) and played in a record-tying 24 All-Star Games.

McCarthy, Joseph Raymond, *b. near Appleton, Wis., 1908; d. 1957.* **American politician.** Elected to the U.S. Senate in 1946, McCarthy began an anti-communist campaign that defined his career as a senator. He claimed in 1950 to have a list of 205 communists who worked in the State Department – though he never produced the list. In 1952 he accused Secretary of Defense George C. Marshall of being a traitor and Secretary of State Dean Acheson of Communist sympathies. But his investigation of the army was his undoing in 1953 and the Senate censured him in 1954. The term "McCarthyism" became synonymous with witch-hunting.

McCartney, Paul (James Paul), *b., Liverpool, England, 1942.* **Rock-pop vocalist, bassist, guitarist, and songwriter; member of the Beatles.** Along with bandmate John Lennon, he wrote or cowrote most of the group's hit songs, including "All My Loving," "Yesterday," "Eleanor Rigby," "Here, There, and Everywhere," "Penny Lane," "Let It Be," and "The Long and Winding Road." His post-Beatles career includes both solo recordings and stints with the group Wings. Recordings include "Maybe I'm Amazed" (1970), "Another Day" (1971), "Band on the Run" (1973), and "Silly Love Songs" (1976).

McKinley, William, *b. Niles, Ohio, 1843; d. 1901.* **Twenty-fifth president 1897–1901.** The last Civil War veteran to become president, William McKinley was elected to Congress in 1876, where he wrote the record-high McKinley Tariff of 1890. He then served two terms as governor; he won the presidency in 1896. Strongly pro-business, McKinley raised the tariff still higher and reluctantly led the country into the Spanish-American War (1898). By acquiring the Philippines and other islands, America became a world power, and McKinley went on to proclaim the open-door policy in China. He was enjoying great popularity when the anarchist Leon Czolgosz shot and killed him in Buffalo, N.Y.

McLuhan, Marshall (Herbert Marshall McLuhan), *b. Edmonton, Canada, 1911; d. 1980.* **Communications theorist.** A communication professor at the University of Toronto and elsewhere in Canada and the U.S., McLuhan predicted the enormous impact of the electronic age in his book *Understanding Media: The Extensions of Man*, (1964). He proclaimed that "the medium is the message" and predicted the death of the printed page. Regarded by many as the "high priest of pop culture," he coined the terms "media" and "global village." As one of the first media critics, McLuhan was concerned with how technology influenced social interactions, warning that "we become what we behold."

McNamara, Robert Strange, *b. San Francisco, 1916.* **Business executive; U.S. secretary of defense.** After serving in the Pentagon during World War II, and rising to president of the Ford Motor Company, McNamara was appointed secretary of defense by President Kennedy in 1961. He brought his analytic skills to the management of the Pentagon but is best remembered for his role in the U.S. involvement in the Vietnam War. Initially in favor of the war, he came to believe that it was wrong but obeyed President Johnson's orders to send 500,000 U.S. troops and expand the war. He resigned in 1968 to become president of the World Bank (1968–81).

Mead, Margaret, *b. Philadelphia, Pa. 1901; d. 1978.* **Anthropologist.** Her first and most important book, *Coming of Age in Samoa* (1928), became a perennial best-seller and made her a celebrity. Based on her observations of natives in American Samoa, the book promotes the theory of cultural determinism, or the idea that cultural demands can influence an individual's development. It caused controversy for intimating that the so-called civilized world might learn something from more primitive societies. Among her other books are *Sex and Temperament in Three Primative Societies* (1935) and *Male and Female* (1949) Awarded the Presidential Medal of Freedom in 1979, Mead was an outspoken advocate for women's rights, population control, and environmental causes.

Meany, George, *b. New York, 1894; d. 1980.* **Labor leader.** As president of the American Federation of Labor from 1948 to 1979, he oversaw the organization through its complicated merger with the Congress of Industrial Organizations (in 1955). Under his powerful leadership, the combined AFL-CIO used lobbying and arbitration, rather than the traditional tools of strikes and marches, to achieve its goals. Meany's support for civil rights in the workplace was instrumental in the passage of the 1964 Civil Rights Act. He was awarded the Presidential Medal of Freedom in 1977.

Meier, Richard Alan, *b. Newark, N.J. 1934.* **Architect.** Early in his career he established a vocabulary of impeccably white buildings, composed mostly of abstract rectilinear forms, such as the Smith House (1965) on Long Island, N.Y. Acknowledging a debt to Le Corbusier, Frank Lloyd Wright, and Mies van der Rohe. Meier has been a prolific designer of a wide variety of buildings that reflect his sensitivity to the play of light and shadow on white surfaces and in clearly articulated spaces. Among his larger works are the High Museum in Atlanta (1980–83); the city hall and Central Library (1986–95), The Hague, Netherlands; and the Getty Center complex (1989–97) in Los Angeles. He won the Pritzker Prize in 1984.

Melville, Herman, *b. 1819, New York City; d. 1891.* **Novelist, and poet.** As a young seaman, he was captured in the South Pacific by cannibals and imprisoned for mutiny; these experiences provided material for a series of dramatic and profitable romances, beginning with *Typee* (1846). Though not popular, *Moby-Dick* (1851) was his masterpiece — a long, profound, intricate, symbolic tale of a captain's vengeful quest for the whale that had taken his leg. Its failure, and that of *Pierre* (1852) and *The Confidence Man* (1857), required him to work as a customs inspector in New York. An important novella, *Billy Budd*, was completed in his last year but not published until 1924. Poems include *Battle-Pieces* (1866) and a long narrative, *Clarel* (1876).

Mencken, H. L. (Henry Louis) *b. Baltimore, 1880; d. 1956.* **Journalist and social critic.** Mencken was a writer for the *Baltimore Sun* for much of his life. He and George Jean Nathan coedited the influential literary magazine *The Smart Set* (1914–23), and cofounded (in 1924) *The American Mercury*. No subject was safe from Mencken's barbs: women, religion, the South, the middle class, Prohibition, even democracy itself. His most famous quotes include "No one ever went broke underestimating the taste of the American public," and "Freedom of the press is limited to those who own one."

Mendel, Gregor Johann, *b. Hyncice, Czech Republic, 1822; d. 1884.* **Roman Catholic monk and experimental geneticist.** He was the first to develop, through careful pollination techniques and statistical analysis, a clear analysis of heredity. He showed that inherited characteristics are determined by a combination of genes from both parents, and that genes can be either dominant or recessive. He carried out his experiments on garden peas and other plants at the Augustinian monastery at Brno.His work, published in 1866, was ignored in his lifetime but rediscovered independently by three researchers in 1900.

Mendelssohn, Felix, *b. Hamburg, 1809; d. 1847.* **German composer, pianist, organist, and conductor.** Mendelssohn's father, Abraham, son of the Jewish intellectual Moses Mendelssohn, converted to Christianity. Felix was a child prodigy who began composing seriously at 17. Mendelssohn's music bridged the Classical and Romantic periods, serving as a "lovely interlude" (Nietzsche, 1886) between Beethoven and Wagner in German music. Notable works include *A Midsummer Night's Dream*, Op. 21 (1826); *Hebrides Overture (Fingal's Cave)*, Op. 26 (1830); Symphony No. 3 in A Minor, Op. 56 (*Scotch*) (1830–42); Symphony No. 5 in D Minor, Op. 107 (*Reformation*) (1830–2); Concerto No. 1 in G Minor for Piano and Orchestra, Op. 25 (1832); Symphony No. 4 in A, Op. 90 (*Italian*) (1833); Violin Concerto in E Minor, Op. 64 (1844); and the oratorio *Elijah*, Op. 70 (1846).

Messier, Mark, *b. Edmonton, Alberta, Canada, 1961.* **Hockey player.** Famous for his leadership, Messier is also one of the most prolific goal scorers in NHL history. He figured prominently in six Stanley Cup winning teams. He was drafted by the Edmonton Oilers in 1979 and won five Stanley Cups in Edmonton, four alongside Wayne Gretzky. In 1994, he led the New York Rangers to their first Cup in 54 years. He retired in 2004 with 1,756 games played, second only to Gordie Howe; and 1,887 points, second only to his old teammate Gretzky.

Metternich, Klemens, Furst von, *b. 1773, Koblenz, Germany; d. 1859.* **Austrian diplomat and statesman.** The son of an Austrian envoy, Metternich studied diplomacy, although his studies were interrupted by the advance of French revolutionary armies. As minister to France and later minister of foreign affairs (1809–48), Metternich sought to minimize Austrian exposure during the Napoleonic Wars. He was chief architect of the Congress of Vienna (1814–15), where he sought a balance of power in Europe that helped prevent a major war for 100 years, but his policies were repressive and led to the revolutions of 1848.

Michelangelo Buonarroti (Michelagnolo di Lodovico Buonarroti Simoni), *b. Caprese, Italy, 1475; d. 1564.* **Sculptor, painter, draftsman, architect.** A chief figure in the Roman High Renaissance, prolific in all his endeavors, Michelangelo thought of himself primarily as a sculptor. His monumental marble sculptures include the placid yet powerful *David* (1501–04) and the figure of *Moses* (ca. 1513–15) from the unfinished tomb of Julius II. Michelangelo's masterpiece is thought to be the series of frescoes on the Sistine Chapel Ceiling (1508–12) in the Vatican, which depict scenes from the book of Genesis. For the last 18 years of his life (1546–64) he served as the chief architect for St. Peter's in Rome.

Mies van der Rohe, Ludwig, *b. Aachen,Germany, 1886; d. 1969.* **Architect.** Mies intensely studied new building materials, their aesthetic potential, and the plasticity of architectural space. His Tugendhat House (1928–30) in Brno, Czech Republic, and the German Pavilion (1929) at the Barcelona International Exposition were the culmination of his European work. Mies emigrated to America and in 1938 became director of the architectural department at Illinois Institute of Technology, where he planned the campus and designed the major buildings (1938–56). There he worked out the simplification of architectural elements that he summed up in his famous phrase, "Less is more." Later buildings were the glass-walled concrete-and-steel Farnsworth House (1945–50) and the bronze Seagram Building (1954–58), New York, with Philip Cortelyou Johnson.

Mill, John Stuart, *b. London, 1806; d. 1873.* **English philosopher and economist.** Mill learned the theory of utilitarianism from his father, John Mill (1773–1836); and from Jeremy Bentham. His *Utilitarianism* (1863) systematically founded knowledge on empirical experience and reason. He is probably best known for his essay "On Liberty" (1859), which argued the paramount importance of individual liberty to oppose political and social tyranny. In later years he softened his utilitarian views and advocated women's equality, proportional voting representation, and labor unions. Other important books were *System of Logic* (1843), *Principles of Political Economy* (1848), and his *Autobiography* (1873).

Miller, Arthur, *b. New York City, 1915.* **Playwright.** Miller is considered one of America's greatest modern playwrights. His plays of the 1940's and 1950's were meditations on issues of social justice. In works such as *All My Sons* (1947) and *Death of a Salesman* (1949, winner of the Pulitzer Prize) Miller explored the ravages of society on the individual. *The Crucible* (1953), an even more overtly political play, used the Salem witch trials as an allegory for McCarthyism.

Milton, John, *b. London, 1608; d. 1674.* **Poet.** One of the greatest English poets, Milton was also a political and religious activist and tract writer. He served as foreign secretary in Cromwell's Puritan government. Blind after 1651, he wrote some of the finest English sonnets, but his towering stature rests on the long, biblically-based poems of his later years: the epics *Paradise Lost* (1667) and *Paradise Regained* (1671), and the "closet" drama *Samson Agonistes* (1671). *Paradise Lost* dramatizes the rebellion and defeat of Satan and the fall of Adam and Eve. *Paradise Regained* presents Christ's contrasting triumph over Satan in the wilderness.

Modigliani, Franco, *b. Rome, 1918; d. 2003.* **Italian-born American economist.** Modigliani was strongly influenced by the ideas of John Maynard Keynes, and his early study of savings rates demonstrated the "life-cycle" theory that individuals save most when they are earning the most—usually during their middle years—and then consume savings in later years. The theory influenced pension plans and the Social Security system. With Merton Miller he argued that investors value companies not by the amount of their debt-to-equity ratio but by their anticipated earnings, and his technique for calculating a company's future earnings became a standard tool in corporate finance. He was awarded the Nobel Prize in Economic Science in 1985.

Molière (Jean-Baptiste Poquelin), *baptized Paris, 1622; d. 1673.* **Playwright.** Considered France's greatest comic playwright, Molière was well educated, but left the life of the court to become a traveling actor and playwright. His comedies, exuberant farces that skewer the behavior of irrational characters, include *Tartuffe* (1664), *The Misanthrope* (1666), *The Miser* (1668), and *The Imaginary Invalid* (1673). Molière's acting company, Theatre Illustre, exists today as the Comedie Francaise.

Mondrian, Piet, *b. Amersfoort, Netherlands, 1872; d. 1944.* **Painter.** Regarded as one of the founders of abstract art, Mondrian is best known for works that feature geometric patterns, often involving a grid of horizontal and vertical lines with a limited palette. Mondrian hoped his paintings would convey the vitality that he saw in modern cities and in modern jazz. He was influenced by the Cubist movement. His best-known works include *Composition with Red, Blue, and Yellow* (1930) and *Broadway Boogie-Woogie* (1942–43).

Monet, Claude, *b. Paris, 1840; d. 1926.* **Painter.** Monet's paintings epitomize the Impressionist style, which when first introduced was criticized as sloppy and unfinished but has grown to enjoy great popularity. Influenced by Manet's concept of the color patch, Monet devoted his life to exploring the shifting qualities of light and atmosphere and is thought of as the leader of the Impressionist group. He painted landscapes *en plein air,* and in the 1890's he began producing series paintings, working at one time on a number of canvases that depicted the same site. His most famous works include *Gare St-Lazare* (1877), *Rouen Cathedral: The Portal (In Sun)* (1894), and *Water Lillies, Giverny* (1907).

Monroe, James, *b. Westmoreland County, Va., 1758; d. 1831.* **Fifth U.S. president, 1817–25.** The last Revolutionary hero and member of the "Virginia Dynasty" to become president, Monroe learned law as an aide to Thomas Jefferson. He served as minister to France in 1794 and governor of Virginia from 1799 to 1802; he later negotiated the Louisiana Purchase and served as both secretary of state and secretary of war under James Madison. As president, Monroe presided over the "era of good feelings," a period marked by minimal sectional or partisan discord. In 1823 he proclaimed American opposition to European encroachment in the Western Hemisphere; his policy became known as the Monroe Doctrine.

Monroe, Marilyn (Norma Jean Baker), *b. Los Angeles, 1926; d. 1962.* **Movie actress.** Her seductive figure and breathy voice made her the outstanding sex symbol of the 1950's, but she always felt unfulfilled as an actress. Brief roles in *The Asphalt Jungle* and *All About Eve* (both 1950) led to stardom in many films, notably *The Seven-Year Itch* (1955) and *Some Like It Hot* (1959). She married the baseball legend Joe DiMaggio and later the playwright Arthur Miller, who wrote her last film, *The Misfits* (1960).

Montana, Joe, *b. Monongahela, Pa., 1956.* **Football player.** Montana led the San Francisco 49ers to four Super Bowl championships (after the 1981, 1984, 1988, and 1989 seasons) and was M.V.P. in three of them. He ended his career (1979–94) among the top five quarterbacks in most major passing categories; Montana completed a remarkable 63 percent of his passes and threw nearly two touchdowns for every interception. He was elected to seven Pro Bowls. In 1993 he was traded to the Kansas City Chiefs, where he played two more years before retiring.

Montezuma II, *b. 1466; d. 1520.* **Aztec emperor.** The ninth Aztec emperor, Montezuma ascended the throne of an empire that extended from Mexico to Nicaragua in 1502. His reign was one of almost incessant warfare against subject tribes, which made them willing to support Hernando Cortez in 1519. Montezuma believed Cortez to be the god Quetzacóatl, but failed to appease him. Cortez took Montezuma hostage at Tenochtitlán and attempted to rule the Aztecs through him. He was killed in 1520—by the Spanish according to Aztec accounts, by the Aztecs according to the Spanish.

More, Thomas, *b. 1478, London; d. 1535.* **Statesman, author, and Catholic saint.** A distinguished lawyer, More was drafted into diplomatic service by King Henry VIII, knighted, and appointed lord chancellor in 1529. A devout Catholic, he disapproved of the king's first divorce, and when he refused to swear to the Act of Succession and Supremacy naming Henry head of the church in England, he was imprisoned and executed. More, a humanist, was the author of the brilliant satirical tale *Utopia* (1516), a description of a mythical, totally rational, propertyless realm, which introduced a new literary genre. More also wrote biographies, including *A History of Richard III*, poetry, and devotional works.

Morgan, John Pierpont, *b. Hartford., Conn., 1837; d. 1913.* **American financier.** Morgan worked three years in New York before joining his father's London-based bank. Soon he was a partner in his own bank and invested in railroads, including railroad mergers that stifled competition. This became J.P. Morgan and Co. in 1895. Other investments included Thomas Edison's incandescent light and generation plants, and in 1892 the creation of General Electric. In 1901 he combined a number of steel companies into the United Steel Corporation, the largest industrial company in the world. He stopped the U.S. gold crisis of 1894–95 and led the rescue of the banking system in 1907.

Morrison, Toni, *b. Lorain, Ohio, 1931.* **Novelist and essayist.** Morrison won the Nobel Prize for Literature in 1993. She began publishing fiction in 1970 with her novel *The Bluest Eye*. From the start her work, which chronicles the African-American experience, has been characterized by poetic language, dazzling intellect, and innovative storytelling. Other novels include *Sula* (1973), *Song of Solomon* (1977), *Tar Baby* (1981), *Beloved* (1987, winner of the Pulitzer Prize), and *Paradise* (1998). *Playing in the Dark: Whiteness and the Literary Imagination* was published in 1992.

Morse, Samuel Finley Breese, *b. Charlestown, Mass., 1791; d. 1872.* **American inventor.** Morse was an accomplished artist, known especially as a portrait painter, before becoming invovled with electricity. In 1844 he successfully tested his device to send electrical impulses through a wire that drove another device to inscribe a series of dots and dashes on a moving strip of paper at the other end. He also devised a code for the letters of the alphabet, the Morse Code. The telegraph came to dominate long-distance telegraphic communications in a wide range of applications.

Moses, Grandma (Anna Mary Robertson), *b. Greenwich, N.Y., 1860; d. 1961.* **Painter.** In her seventies, after a life of farming in Virginia and upstate New York, and with no formal training, Grandma Moses began to paint rural scenes, such as *Wash Day* (1945) and *Hoosick Falls, N.Y. in Winter* (1944). Her treatment of figures and buildings is considered primitive yet charming; details are often borrowed from Currier & Ives prints and magazines. She was discovered when a collector found some of her pictures at the Women's Exchange of a drugstore in Hoosick Falls.

Mozart, Wolfgang Amadeus, *b. Salzburg, 1756; d. 1791.* **Austrian composer, keyboard player, violinist, violist, and conductor.** A child prodigy, he was taught the harpsichord, violin, and organ by his father, who when the boy was six began to present him in concerts before the royalty of Europe. By the time Mozart was 13 he had written symphonies, concertos, and sonatas, and was known throughout the world of music. By the time of his death at age 35 he had produced more than 600 works—symphonies, operas, concertos, quartets, cantatas—almost all of them of the most astonishing quality. He is regarded by many as the world's greatest natural musical genius; his mature compositions are distinguished by their melodic beauty, formal elegance, and richness of harmony and texture. Notable works include Piano Concerto No. 21 in C (K. 467, 1785), Serenade No. 13 in G for Strings (*Eine kleine Nachtmusik*, K. 525, 1787), Symphony No. 40 in G Minor (K. 550, 1788), Symphony No. 41 in C (*Jupiter*, K. 551, 1788), and the operas *Le Nozze de Figaro* (*The Marriage of Figaro*, 1785–86); *Don Giovanni* (1787); *Cosi fan tutti* (1790); and *Die Zauberflöte* (*The Magic Flute*) (K. 620, 1790-1).

Muhammad, *b. c. 570, Mecca; d. 632.* **Prophet of Islam.** Muhammed was employed by the widow Khadijah (whom he later married) to take caravans to Syria, where he met Christians and Jews. He struggled with ideas of monotheism in contrast to the polytheism of Mecca. Finally he concluded that there is but one God, whose prophet he was; in a visitation, he was told to recite, words ultimately collected in the Koran. With the hejira (flight) to Yathrib (now Medina) in 622 (the Muslim calendar's first year) he established his theocratic state, later conquering Mecca and purifying it of idols.

Muir, John, *b. Dunbar, Scotland, 1838; d. 1914.* **U.S. naturalist.** Muir was instrumental in the creation of the National Park System. His writings about nature and his friendship with President Theodore Roosevelt led to federal protection for Yosemite (1890), Sequoia (1890), Mount Rainier (1899), Petrified Forest (1906), and Grand Canyon (1908) National Parks. In 1892, he led a group of naturalists in forming the Sierra Club, and he served as the group's first president until his death. Muir's camping trip with Roosevelt at Yosemite persuaded the president to set aside more than 148 million acres of additional national forest.

Mussolini, Benito, *b. Predappio, Italy, 1883; d. 1945.* **Italian dictator.** Mussolini began his career as a journalist and socialist labor agitator with a penchant for violence. During World War I, he became a fierce nationalist, and in 1919 he founded the Fasci di Combattimento—Europe's first fascist party. He became prime minister in 1922 and instituted a program of salutary public works. His foreign policy proved disastrous, from the widely condemned invasion of Abyssinia (Ethiopia) to his support of Nazi Germany. Arrested in 1943, he was rescued by German paratroopers, only to be killed attempting to flee Italy in disguise.

Nabokov, Vladimir, *b. St. Petersburg, Russia, 1899; d. 1977.* **Russian-American novelist.** Nabokov left Russia after the revolution of 1917, studied in England, and settled in the United States in 1940. His early novels were in Russian, and he began writing in English in 1938. *Bend Sinister* (1947) was followed by one of the most famous—and infamous—books of the century, *Lolita* (1955). An ironic, comic-serious, self-reflectively artistic account of an earnest madman's love for a 12-year old girl, it was banned in America for three years. Nabokov is considered one of the geniuses of 20th-century fiction—an erudite, allusive, verbally adroit weaver of meanings. Other novels include *Pnin* (1957), *Pale Fire* (1957), and *Ada* (1969).

Namath, Joe, *b. Beaver Falls, Pa., 1943.* **Football player.** Namath burst onto the scene with the New York Jets, earning AFL rookie of the year honors in 1965 and leading the league in passing in 1966 and 1967. His high-flying lifestyle and cocksure attitude earned him the nickname "Broadway Joe" and made him a celebrity. In 1969, he guaranteed that his Jets of the upstart AFL would upset the heavily favored Baltimore Colts in Super Bowl III, and he won the M.V.P. award in New York's 16-7 win. Knee and shoulder injuries limited Namath in later years, and he retired in 1977. He was elected to the Hall of Fame in 1985.

Napoléon I (Napoléon Bonaparte; Napoleon), *b. 1769, Ajaccio, Corsica; 1821.* **French emperor.** A brilliant soldier, Napoleon distinguished himself in the French Revolutionary Wars and was a general by 24. Though defeated in Egypt and Syria in 1798–99, in the latter year he became supreme ruler in France and proclaimed himself emperor in 1804. His important and long-lasting reforms in education, civil law, and military organization were offset by his aggressive expansionism. His brilliant victories over a coalition of European powers at Austerlitz (1805), Jena (1806), and Borodino (1812) gave him an aura of invincibility. His invasion of Russia (1812) proved his undoing, and in 1814 he was exiled to Elba. He returned in 1815, but was defeated at the Battle of Waterloo and exiled to remote St. Helena.

Napoléon III (Louis-Napoléon), *b. 1808, Paris; d. 1873.* **French emperor.** Nephew of Napoléon I, Louis Napoléon was raised in exile but developed a keen interest in politics and military affairs. Attempts to usurp power in France ended in exile in the U.S. and England before he became president (1848) and emperor (1852). He promoted social welfare and industrialization domestically, sought rapprochement with England and promoted the Suez Canal. France's humiliating defeat in the Franco-Prussian War forced him into exile in England.

Nasser, Gamal Abdel, *b. 1918, Alexandria; d. 1970.* **Egyptian president.** One of the most important figures in modern Arab history, Nasser foughtin the 1948 Arab-Israeli War. After leading two coups in 1952 and 1954, he was elected president in 1956. His nationalization of the Suez Canal succeeded when the U.S. failed to support Britain and France. Nasser's effort to create a pan-Arab state, the United Arab Republic (1958–61)was a failure. The 1967 Six-Day War ended in Egypt's defeat and the loss of the Sinai Peninsula. Nasser also promoted the Soviet funded AswanHigh Dam on the Nile River (1960–70).

Nebuchadnezzar, *b. ca. 630, Babylon; d. 562 B.C.* **Chaldaean king.** Second ruler of the Chaldaean Empire founded by his father, he was an able military commander who succeeded his father in 605. He campaigned extensively in Syria, Palestine, and northern Arabia and against Egypt, and he became a major figure in the diplomacy of the Near East generally. In 586 he captured Jerusalem and took many of its leading citizens in captivity to Babylon—a city he had done much to improve—though he is viewed in a generally positive light by the authors of the Hebrew Bible.

Nehru, Jawaharlal, *b. 1889, Allahabad, India; d. 1964.* **Indian politician.** The English-educated Nehru joined the Indian National Congress in 1919, serving as general secretary (1923–25, 1927–29) and president (from 1929). During World War II, Nehru favored support for Britain but sided with Gandhi; both were jailed, Nehru for the ninth time. He split with Gandhi over the idea of partition with Pakistan, and he became India's first prime minister in 1947. An advocate of Democrat Socialism, he favored non-alignment in foreign policy. His daughter Indira Gandhi and grandson Rajiv Gandhi also served as prime minister.

Nelson, Horatio (Viscount Nelson), *b. Burnham Thorpe, England, 1758; d. 1805.* **Naval commander.** Nelson was knighted for his imaginative tactics at the battle of Cape St. Vincent in 1797. In 1798, at the battle of the Nile, he annihilated the French fleet that had transported Napoleon to Egypt. In 1801, he destroyed the Danish fleet at the battle of Copenhagen. In 1805, he had his greatest triumph, defeating a combined French and Spanish fleet at the battle of Trafalgar, where he was killed.

Nero (Lucius Domitus Ahenobarbus) *b. 37 A.D.; d. 68.* **Roman emperor (54–68).** Nero owed his rise to power to his mother Agrippina, sister of Caligula and great-granddaughter of Augustus. She urged her new husband, the emperor Claudius, to make her son his successor and then murdered Claudius. Under the tutelage of Seneca the Younger, Nero began his reign with political and social reforms. His reputation as a mad tyrant arose after he had his mother killed, in 59, and later his wife. At this point, he began to dwell on obscure religious pursuits, and developed delusions of artistic greatness. During this period a great fire destroyed half of Rome (64) and Nero blamed the Christians, whom he subsequently persecuted. He killed himself in 68, having been abandoned by his army and political supporters.

Neruda, Pablo, *b. Parral, Chile, 1904; d. 1973.* **Poet.** Neruda, awarded the Nobel Prize for Literature in 1971, stands as one of the great poets of the 20th century. He published one of his best-known works, *Twenty Love Poems and a Song of Despair* (1924) at a young age, and he traveled the world as a diplomat for his native Chile. A political activist, Neruda sided with the Republicans in the Spanish Civil War and returned to Chile as an elected member of the Communist Party. His other works include *Spain in the Heart* (1937) and *Canto General* (1950).

Newman, Paul, *b. Cleveland, Ohio, 1925.* **Actor.** Coming from Broadway and TV, he made his mark playing cocky outsiders in such films as *The Hustler* (1961) and *Hud* (1963), and craven heroes in Tennessee Williams's *Cat on a Hot Tin Roof* (1958) and *Sweet Bird of Youth* (1962). Later films revealed his versatility Butch Cassidy and *The Sundance Kid* (1969), *The Sting* (1973), *The Verdict* (1982), and *The Color of Money* (1986), for which he finally won an Oscar. He founded Newman's Own, a line of food products, and he donates the profits to charity.

Newton, Sir Isaac, *b. Lincolnshire, England, 42. d. 1727* **English physicist and mathematician.** Newton was a student at Cambridge University when a plague epidemic caused Cambridge to close during 1665–66. During this period, he first developed new methods in mathematics—extending the binomial theorem, finding a useful method for approximating solutions to equations, and inventing the calculus. He also experimented with light, finding that white light is a mixture of all colors, and began to think about gravity. Instead of publishing his work, however, he circulated manuscripts to friends. After he built the first reflecting telescopes, the Royal Society elected him a fellow. He began to communicate some of his discoveries more widely. He was urged to publish his theory explaining the motions of planets, and Newton's *Principia* (1687) contained his laws of motion and gravity as well as such topics as artificial satellites. He wrote a full account of his study of light, called *Opticks* (1704). Although Newton devoted a major portion of his life to alchemy, the predecessor of chemistry, he did not publish any results.

Nicklaus, Jack, *b. Columbus, Ohio, 1940.* **Golfer.** The "Golden Bear" compiled one of the most impressive record in the annals of golf. With his mammoth drives and clutch shot-making, he claimed a record 18 victories in major PGA events—six Masters, five PGA Championships, four U.S. Opens, and three British Opens. Nicklaus won more than 100 tournaments in all, including 70 on the PGA Tour (second only to Sam Snead). He was named Player of the Year five times and was the tour's leading money winner eight times.

Nicholson, Jack, *b. Neptune, N.J., 1937.* **Movie actor.** After 10 years in B movies, he became a star in *Easy Rider* (1969). Since then his bad-boy grin and devilish eyebrows have lit up comedies and dramas. He has won Oscars for *One Flew Over the Cuckoo's Nest* (1975), *Terms of Endearment* (1983), and *As Good as It Gets* (1997). Other notable films include *Chinatown* (1974) and *Batman* (1989).

Nietszche, Friedrich Wilhelm, *b. Roecken, Prussia, 1844; d. 1900,* **Philosopher.** Originally a professor of classical languages, Nietzche wrote his philosophical works over 20 years, before suffering a mental breakdown in 1889. He argued for a new, heroic mentality that would reject the "slave morality" of Christianity, part of the bourgeois Western civilization that he rejected with passion. A group of "supermen," with a will to power, would lead the mass of inferior humanity. His main works are *Thus Spake Zarathustra* (1883–91) and *Beyond Good and Evil* (1886). His doctrines were later used to justify Nazi racial and national ideology, but most scholars regard this as a perversion of Nietzsche's own thought.

Nijinsky, Vaslav, *b. Kiev, Russia, 1889; d. 1950.* **Dancer-choreographer.** Nijinsky studied in St. Petersburg at the Imperial Theatre from 1898–1907, making his professional debut a year before his graduation. He joined the Maryinsky Theatre Ballet from 1907–1911, and from 1909 danced with Diaghilev's Ballet Russes. Diaghilev encouraged him to choreograph, and Nijinsky created his famous *L'Après Midi d'un faune* in 1912 and *Le Sacre du Printemps*, with a score by Igor Stravinsky, a year later; *Sacre* caused riots on its Paris premiere. He left the company in 1913, beginning to show the effects of his coming mental illness; he last performed in 1919, and he spent the rest of his life primarily in institutions for treatment of his schizophrenia.

Nimitz, Chester W., *b. Fredericksburg, Tex., 1885; d. 1966.* **Naval commander.** After Pearl Harbor, Nimitz became commander of the U.S. Pacific fleet and eventually the supreme Allied commander for the Pacific. Under his direction, the outnumbered U.S. Navy won major victories over the Japanese navy at the battles of the Coral Sea and Midway in 1942. He was also in charge of the amphibious operation in the Pacific that culminated in the capture of Iwo Jima and Okinawa in 1945. He ended his career as chief of Naval Operations.

Nixon, Richard M., *b. Yorba Linda, Calif., 1913; d. 1994.* **Thirty-seventh U.S. president, 1969–74.** The only president to resign from office, Richard Milhous Nixon rode into Congress on the Republican wave of 1946, and gained fame in the anticommunist trial of Alger Hiss. He entered the Senate in 1950 and was chosen as Eisenhower's running mate in 1952. After losing the 1960 presidential election to John F. Kennedy, Nixon staged a comeback and won the presidency in 1968. Seeking "peace with honor" in Vietnam, Nixon built up the South Vietnamese army and withdrew U.S. troops—while massively escalating bombing of North Vietnam. During his reelection campaign in 1972, five burglars were arrested in the Democratic Party headquarters, and the ensuing "Watergate" scandal exposed the Nixon administration's rampant corruption, obstruction of justice, and abuse of power. The House began impeachment proceedings, and on August 9, 1974, Nixon resigned the presidency.

Nurmi, Paavo, *b. Finland, 1897; d. 1973.* **Track star.** Nurmi established his reputation as the greatest distance runner in the history of the modern Olympics by winning nine gold and three silver medals at the games of 1920, 1924, and 1928. Known as the "Flying Finn," he won six individual golds in 1,500m, 5,000m, 10,000m, and cross-country events. He was barred from the 1932 Olympics for accepting expense money while on tour.

O'Keeffe, Georgia, *b. San Prairie, Wisc., 1887; d. 1986.* **Painter.** A highly influential figure in American art, O'Keeffe developed a unique style that borrowed from naturalism, realism, symbolism, abstraction, and photography. She was married to the photographer Alfred Stieglitz. O'Keeffe is best known for semiabstracted large close-up flower paintings, such as *Black Iris* (1926). Other works include *Cow's Skull with Calico Roses* (1931). She is also known for her cityscapes and images from New Mexico, where she moved in 1949. After going blind in 1971, she learned to be a hand-potter.

O'Higgins, Bernardo, *b. 1776, Chillán, Chile; d. 1842.* **South American revolutionary leader and first Chilean head of state.** O'Higgins commanded the military forces that won independence from Spain. As general in chief of Chile's defensive forces, he fought unsuccessfully against the invading Peruvian army and was forced into exile. In 1817, O'Higgins helped to reconquer Chile from the Spanish, and he served as the country's supreme director for the next six years. O'Higgins was associated with an Argentine-sponsored scheme of continental independence, and in 1823 he was forced to resign in the face of growing Chilean nationalism.

Olivier, Laurence, *b. Dorking, England, 1907; d. 1989.* **Actor, director, and producer.** He made his stage debut in Shakespearean repertory at Stratford-on-Avon in 1922 and made his first film in 1930. His refined looks, magnetic voice, and athletic versatility made him a Renaissance man of stage and screen, notably in major Shakespearean roles at London's Old Vic and then at the National Theatre. He was appointed as first director of the National Theatre in 1962. He also directed and performed in three Shakespeare films: *Henry V* (1945), the Oscar-winning *Hamlet* (1948), and *Richard III* (1955). Always changing—from his dashing Heathcliff in *Wuthering Heights* (1939) to his seedy Archie Rice in *The Entertainer* (1960) to the dying Lord Marchmain in TV's *Brideshead Revisited* (1981)— yet always Olivier.

O'Neal, Shaquille, *b. Newark, N.J., 1972.* **Basketball player.** Beginning in 1992, the 7'1" O'Neal used all of his 300 pounds to dominate the low post, and helped transform the Orlando Magic from a mediocre expansion team to a playoff contender. O'Neal was an even more dominating presence off the court as a marketing giant who capitalized on his amiable personality to capture the attention of a new generation of teenagers. After joining the Los Angeles Lakers, he was named M.V.P. of the N.B.A. finals three times in a row while leading the team to consecutive championships (2000–02).

O'Neill, Eugene, *b. New York City, 1888; d. 1953.* **Playwright.** O'Neill was a four-time Pulitzer Prize winner and winner of the Nobel Prize in Literature in 1936, His most famous plays were often intensely personal, drawing on the combative relationship of his parents, his brother's alcoholism, and his own depression. O'Neill was a master of many different styles, employing the techniques of expressionism, symbolism, and realism to explore psychology. His major works include *The Emperor Jones* (1920), *The Hairy Ape* (1922), *Mourning Becomes Electra* (1931), *The Iceman Cometh* (1939), and *Long Day's Journey Into Night* (1943).

O'Connor, Flannery, *b. Savannah, Ga., 1925; d. 1964.* **Short-story writer, novelist.** O'Connor's literary works are few but her contributions are significant. After being diagnosed with lupus while in her twenties, O'Connor returned to her family's home in Milledgeville, Ga., where she lived for the remainder of her life. She was a devout Catholic and her short stories are remarkable for their moral, ironic, and comic qualities. Her works include two short-story collections, *A Good Man Is Hard to Find* (1955) and *Everything That Rises Must Converge* (1964); along with two novels, *Wise Blood* (1952) and *The Violent Bear It Away* (1960).

Onassis, Jacqueline Bouvier, *b. Southampton, N.Y., 1929; d. 1994.* **American first lady and socialite.** Wife of John Fitzgerald Kennedy, she entered the White House with him in 1961 on his election as president. She became known for her stylish fashions and redecoration of the White House. After President Kennedy's assassination, she retired to private life, and later married the Greek shipping magnate Aristotle Onassis in 1968. One of her most memorable personal achievements was the preservation of Grand Central Station in New York.

Orr, Bobby, *b. Parry Sound, Ont., Canada, 1947.* **Hockey player.** The first hockey defenseman to take an active role on offense, he revolutionized the game. He joined the Boston Bruins in 1966 as an 18-year-old, signing a two-year contract for $75,000, an unheard-of amount for a rookie. Orr became the only defenseman to win the scoring title (1970 and 1975) and the first player to record more than 100 assists in a season (1971). He led the Bruins to Stanley Cup championships in 1970 and 1972 and was the NHL's M.V.P. three straight years (1970–72) before injuries forced his retirement at age 30 in 1978.

Orwell, George (Eric A. Blair), *b. Bengal, India, 1903; d. 1950.* **English essayist and novelist.** At 19 Orwell became a policeman in Burma, the setting for his first novel, *Burmese Days* (1934), and one of his best essays, "Shooting an Elephant" (1936), both indictments of British imperialism. He embraced socialism and joined the Republican forces in the Spanish Civil War, where he recognized the tyranny of Soviet communism, described in *Homage to Catalonia* (1938). His two most famous books extended this view: *Animal Farm* (1945), a fable exposing the corruption of the Soviet system; and *Nineteen Eighty-Four* (1949), a novel depicting a nightmarish world under an enslaving dictatorship. Orwell's lucid prose is a modern English model.

Otto, Nikolaus August, *b. 1832, d. 1891.* **German inventor.** Otto learned in the early 1860's that a balky internal combustion engine running on coal gas had been introduced in France by Jean-Joseph Lenoir. Otto developed a more improved version, which he exhibited at the Paris World's Fair in 1867. While manufacturing and selling that engine, he designed a much improved four-stroke internal combustion engine (1876), which remains the basis of the most common type of engine today. Variations on Otto's engines were used in the first motorbikes and automobiles.

Owens, Jesse, *b. Danville, Ala., 1913; d. 1980.* **Track-and-field star.** The son of sharecroppers, Jesse Owens turned in the most memorable performance in the history of the Olympics by winning four gold medals—in the 100 m, 200 m, long jump, and 4 x 100-m relay—at the 1936 games in Berlin. The stunning performance by an African American embarrassed Adolf Hitler, who had declared the Berlin Games a showcase for Aryan supremacy. The previous year, at Ohio State University, Owens tied the world record for the 100-yard dash and set new marks in the 220-yard dash, 220-yard hurdles, and long jump—all one day.

Ovid (Pulius Ovidius Naso) *b. Sulmona, Italy, 43 B.C.; d. ?17 A.D.* **Roman poet.** Although his father urged him to study law, Ovid was a natural poet. Even his earliest works, the *Amores*, notably *The Art of Love*, display extraordinary skill with meter and verse. Emperor Augustus morally objected to Ovid's subject matter and exiled him just after he completed what most consider his masterpiece, *Metamorphoses*, an epic containing 15 books of mythology. In exile, Ovid completed many works, including *Fasti* concerning the Roman calendar.

Paine, Thomas *b. Thetford, Norfolk, England, 1737; d. 1809.* **English-American writer.** Born in England, Paine moved to America in 1774; there he published political articles against slavery and in support of American independence. "Common Sense" (1776) greatly influenced the Declaration of Independence. Paine argued for "a continental constitution" that would lay out a strong central government for the independent colonies. In 1787 he went to Europe where he wrote *Rights of Man* (1791) in support of the French Revolution. His arguments against monarchy and for social welfare gained him a indictment of treason in England. In France, he was jailed by Robespierre's repressive regime for his criticism of its terror tactics. Paine became (inaccurately) known as an atheist after publishing *The Age of Reason* (1794).

Palestrina, Giovanni Pierluigi da, *b. Palestrina, ca. 1525; d. 1594.* **Composer.** Prolific Italian composer of masses (104), motets (more than 300), and madrigals (more than 140). He was one of the primary musical figures of the late 16th century, and one of the few Italian musicians of that era who assimilated the polyphonic techniques of their French and Flemish predecessors. Notable works include *Missa Papae Marcelli* (c. 1562), *Missa Brevis* (1570), *Jesu Rex Admirabilis*, *Litaniae de Beata Virgine Maria*, *Magnificat*, *Missa Tu Es Petrus*, and *Stabat Mater*.

Palmer, Arnold, *b. Latrobe, Pa., 1929.* **Golfer.** Palmer's popularity is widely credited for the explosive growth of golf during the 1960's. His personal charisma and exciting style of play attracted throngs of followers, referred to as "Arnie's army," wherever he played and brought golf to the masses through the new medium of television. Palmer won a total of 61 PGA events, including seven majors (four Masters, two British Opens, and one U.S. Open), from 1955 to 1973. He was named Player of the Year in 1960 and 1962.

Parker, Charlie, (Charles Christopher Parker, Jr.) *b. Kansas City, Kan., 1920; d. 1955.* **Jazz saxophonist, also known as "Bird."** Perhaps the greatest jazz saxophonist of all time and (along with the trumpeter Dizzy Gillespie and pianist Bud Powell) the founder of the modern bebop style. Parker could play remarkably fast lines on his alto sax, employing intricate extended harmonies, but every note made sense in relation to the song's chord structure. He suffered from heroin addiction, and died at age 34. His recordings include "Ornithology" (1945), "Ko Ko" (1945), "Yardbird Suite" (1945), "Parker's Mood" (1948), and "Scrapple from the Apple" (1949).

Parnell, Charles Stewart, *b. Avondale, Ireland, 1846; d. 1891.* **Irish statesman and nationalist.** Elected to Parliament in 1875, Parnell was a strong proponent of home rule for Ireland. He supported the Liberal prime minister William Gladstone in the election of 1880 but broke with him over the Land Act. He was jailed in 1881–82 for advocating disobedience to the act and was released by Gladstone when he renounced these policies. His political career was shattered in 1890 by the revelation of an illicit affair with Katherine O'Shea, wife of one of his lieutenants.

Pascal, Blaise, *b. Clermont-Ferrand, France 1623; d. 1662.* **Mathematician, physicist, and philosopher.** Pascal extended the principles of hydrostatics (1648), creating the theory behind the hydraulic press. In mathematics he helped found probability theory (1654) and analyzed infinite series and the geometry of curves. Pascal invented the first mechanical calculator, a machine that used gears. The first working model of his adding machine, the pascaline, appeared for sale in 1642. He is considered a major French philosopher and author for his books *Provincial Letters* (1656) and *Pensées* (1670), a classic work of Christian apologetics in which he argued that mankind can achieve glory only through Jesus Christ.

Pasteur, Louis, *b. Dole, France, 1822; d. 1895.* **French chemist.** Leading a scientific life of rigorous experimentation, Pasteur made fundamental contributions to the study of organic and mineral molecules, bacterial contamination and its elimination ("pasteurization"), the germ theory of diseases, sanitary practices, and vaccines. Pasteur's breakthroughs, derived from his studies of fermentation were critical to the success of beer and dairy industries, and because his research on silkworm diseases, the silk industry. The vaccines developed to fight anthrax and rabies changed the way that medicine is practiced.

Patrick (Saint), *b. Britain, ca. 387; d. 461.* **Patron saint of Ireland.** Patrick's family were Christians and Roman citizens. At 16, he was kidnapped by Irish marauders and taken to Ireland to work as a herder for six years. In his own account, the *Confessio*, he described a dream that allowed him to escape to Gaul, and another dream—after he had entered a monastery and returned to Britain—in which he was instructed to Christianize Ireland. In 432, after years of study under Bishop Germanus of Auxerre, he was sent to Ireland, accommodating his message to tribal structures and laws, was extraordinarily successful, converting nearly the entire nation by the time of his death.

Patton, George S., *b. San Gabriel, Calif., 1885; d. 1945.* **American military leader.** Early on Patton appreciated the potential of tank warfare. Given command of an armored division in 1940, he saw action in North Africa and Sicily. He was relieved of command for striking a hospitalized soldier but was eventually given command of the Third Army, which raced across northern France in 1944 following the invasion of Normandy. That army helped relieve Americans surrounded at Bastogne during the battle of the Bulge. Patton, whose nickname was "Old Blood and Guts," died in a car crash in Heidelberg after the war's end.

Paul (Saint), *b. Tarsus, Asia Minor; d. ca. 64–67.* **Christian missionary and writer.** Paul, originally Saul, was a Jewish rabbi who persecuted early Christians. About the year 35, riding on the road to Damascus, he was reportedly knocked from his horse, heard God's voice, and converted to Christianity. After retiring to the desert for many years to study and meditate, he became the most important figure in early Christianity. Reaching out to non-Jews, he was the church's greatest missionary and its first, and most important, theologian. He set up communities throughout Greece and Asia Minor, and wrote them his Epistles, which explicated such fundamental Christian doctrines as grace and resurrection.

Pavarotti, Luciano, *b. Modena, Italy, 1935.* **Tenor.** After his debuts in Italy (1961) and in the United States (1967), the "king of the high C's" became a worldwide favorite in such notable roles as Donizetti's Nemorino, Puccini's Rodolfo and Cavarodossi, and Verdi's Riccardo, often performing at the Metropolitan Opera. He has made numerous concert recordings with great sopranos and was one of the "Three Tenors"—a venture that brought him mounting fame and fortune.

Paz, Octavio, *b. 1914, Mexico City; d. 1998.* **Poet and essayist.** After publishing poems as a university student (*Forest Moon* 1933) Paz visited his father's native Spain and wrote a successful book of poems reflecting that country's revolution: *Beneath Your Clear Shadow and Other Poems* (1937). Paz was Mexico's leading literary figure of the 20th century, and a Nobel laureate. His poetry approached politics (from a liberal-leftist direction), religion (he was influenced by Hinduism and Buddhism) and physical love. Volumes include *The Sun Stone* (1957), *The Violent Condition,* (1958) *East Slope* (1971), and *A Tree Within* (1987). Paz was Mexico's ambassador to India from 1962 to 1968.

Peary, Robert Edwin, *b. Cresson, Pa., 1856; d. 1920.* **American polar explorer.** Peary made four expeditions to Greenland between 1886 and 1900. In 1902, he attempted to reach the North Pole with his African-American valet Matthew Henson, and an Inuit guide, but drifting ice pushed them from their goal. They made a second attempt (1905–06) in the steamer *Roosevelt*, which was damaged by ice 200 miles from the pole. On a third attempt, Peary claimed that he, Henson, and the Inuit Egingwah, Seeglo, Ootah, and Ooqueah reached the North Pole on April 6, 1908, an assertion that is widely considered suspect.

Pei, Ioeh Ming, *b. Canton, China, 1917.* **American architect.** An early work was the Mile High Center (1952–56) in Denver, which brought him to prominance. With his partners he designed the sharply angular East Building (1968–78) of the National Gallery of Art in Washington D.C.; the Morton Myerson Symphony Center (1981–89), in Dallas; and the extension of the Musée du Louvre (1983–93) with its glass pyramid in the courtyard, below which he rationalized the circulation patterns that lead into different sections of a complex museum.

Pelé (Edson Arantes do Nascimento), *b. Brazil, 1940.* **Soccer player.** Brazilian soccer player who is widely acknowledged as the greatest player in the history of the sport. A professional by age 15, he became the only player to participate in four World Cups and to win three (1958, 1962, 1970). He scored a total of 1,281 goals in his career, most of it spent with Brazil's Santos club. He played his last three seasons (1975–77) with the New York Cosmos of the North American Soccer League.

Penn, William, *b. London, 1644; d. 1718.* **English Quaker and founder of Pennsylvania.** Penn became a Quaker in 1667 and thereafter served several short terms in prison in England for his beliefs. Hoping to found a society in America that guaranteed freedom of conscience to believers in God, and to free himself of debt, he received a charter to Pennsylvania in 1681 from King Charles II. He established a legislature and sold land for farms, but he fell further into debt, and his dream of an ideal society was dashed by boundary disputes and conflicts within the colony.

Pericles *b. Athens, ca. 495 B.C.; d. 429 B.C.* **Athenian statesman.** From 454 B.C. for about 30 years, Pericles was elected and reelected *strategos*, or "general," by the Athenian people. Pericles oversaw the Delian League's power and the prosperity, influence, and military dominance that this grouping of Greek city-states enjoyed. He was responsible for promoting the arts in Athens, the building of the Parthenon, and various political reforms, including salaries for all government officials, and making dual Athenian parentage required for citizenship. Near to the end of his life, war broke out between Athens and Sparta, the glory of Athens flagged, and Pericles was deposed. Thucydides reported Pericles' most famous oration appealing to Athenian pride. He was soon reinstated but died of the plague shortly afterward.

Peter (Saint) *b. Bethsaida, Galilee; d. ca. 64.* **Apostle of Jesus.** According to the Gospels, Peter, originally Simon, was a fisherman called by Jesus. When Simon recognized Jesus as Messiah, Jesus renamed him Cephas ("Peter" in Greek), signifying the "rock" upon which he would build his church. Despite Peter's primacy among the apostles, Jesus predicted, with apparent accuracy, that Peter would deny him. After his master's death, Peter was a church leader at Antioch and a missionary in Asia Minor. He is believed to have to have become the first bishop of Rome – to Roman Catholics, the first pope – and to have been martyred there under Emperor Nero.

Peter I, the Great, *b. 1672, Moscow, Russia; d. 1725.* **Russian czar and emperor.** Peter ruled in a co-regency with his half-brother, Ivan V (1682–96), and thereafter alone. A man of wide practical interests, Peter traveled extensively in western Europe (1697–98) to learn first-hand ways of modernizing Russian industry and government. His reforms strengthened the monarchy and weakened the church and nobility. Peter also founded the Russian navy and expanded Russia's access to ice-free ports on the Black Sea and Baltic, through war with Ottoman Turkey (1696–99) and the Great Northern War with Sweden (1700–21). He became emperor in 1721.

Petrarch (Francesco Petrarca), *b. Arezzo, Tuscany, Italy, 1304; d. 1374.* **Poet.** Petrarch's poetry was a bridge from the Middle Ages to the Renaissance and an important factor in the development of vernacular literature. He spent much of his life in France but returned to Italy for his last two decades. A classicist and the original humanist, he discovered Roman manuscripts and linked Greek and Roman tradition to Christian culture. He was the first great writer of sonnets; his were addressed to a woman named Laura. His ode *Italia Mia* expresses his advocacy of Italian unity. His Latin poems include the epic *Africa*, about the Second Punic War, and *Eclogues*.

Philip II, *b. 1527, Valladolid, Spain; d. 1598.* **Spanish king.** When he became King of Spain in 1556, Philip inherited one of Europe's most extensive empires from his father the Hapsburg emperor Charles V, with holdings in Italy, the Netherlands, France, and the Spanish Americas. This legacy, coupled with his four marriages (including one to England's Mary I), embroiled him in European pol itics of the day. A leader of the Counter-Reformation, he sought to suppress the Dutch independence movement (1568–1609) and to undermine its English allies, against whom he launched the disastrous Spanish Armada (1588). He also fought the Ottoman Empire, and upon the death of his heirless nephew, Sebastian, became king of Portugal in 1580.

Piaget, Jean, *b. Neuchâtel, Switzerland, 1896; d. 1980.* **Child psychologist.** A pioneer in developmental psychology, Piaget devised the first systematic study of the way children reason and acquire understanding. According to Piaget's theory of "genetic epistemology," children's minds evolve as they grow older. Because their mental growth is inextricably linked with their physical development, Piaget believed that children cannot develop certain thought processes until they reach the proper age.

Piano, Renzo, *b. Genoa, Italy 1937.* **Architect.** Piano's first major work was the influential Pompidou Center (1971–77) art museum in Paris with the English architect Richard Rogers; they exposed the viscera of the building—trusses, pipes, ducts, exhaust vents —as its primary aesthetic experience. Later work exhibits great diversity in building types and includes the Menil Collection Exhibition Building (1981–86) in Houston; the football stadium (1987–90) in Bari, Italy; and the Kansai air terminal (1988–94), built on an artificial island in Osaka Bay. Piano won a Pritzker Prize in 1998.

Picasso, Pablo, *b. Málaga, Spain, 1881; d. 1973.* **Painter, sculptor, printmaker, decorative artist, writer.** One of the most influential figures in 20th-century art, Picasso produced works in an astonishing range of styles, from neoclassical portraits to aggressively inventive abstracted images. Together with the artist Georges Braque, he is credited with developing Cubism, a style of painting that breaks the picture plane into collagelike fragments. Picasso lived much of his life in Paris and other parts of France, and was influenced by the Postimpressionists as well as by African and Oceanic art. Among his many famous works are *Gertrude Stein* (1906), *Les Demoiselles d'Avignon* (1907), and *Guernica* (1937).

Pickford, Mary (Gladys Smith) *b. Toronto, Canada, 1893; d. 1979.* **Silent film actress.** Dubbed "America's Sweetheart", Pickford's screen image as an innocent, energetic adolescent made her an international star. She began as a child performer on the stage but turned to movies in 1909. She starred in several shorts for D. W. Griffith, including *The Lonely Villa*. One of the first major movie stars, she moved from studio to studio, increasing her salary each time. Her popular feature films included *The Foundling* (1916), *Pollyanna* (1920), and *My Best Girl* (1927). In 1919 Pickford joined her husband Douglas Fairbanks, Griffith, and Charlie Chaplin to form the studio United Artists.

Pierce, Franklin, *b. Hillsboro, N.H., 1804; d. 1869.* **Fourteenth U.S. president, 1853–57.** A leader of Jacksonian Democrats in Congress in the 1830's, Pierce had been absent from national politics for a decade when the deadlocked Democratic convention nominated him for president in 1852. A dark horse candidate, Pierce won enough southern votes to become the youngest president as of that date. He greatly hastened the coming of the Civil War by signing the Kansas-Nebraska Act (1854), which repealed the Missouri Compromise and reopened the dangerous issue of expanding slavery. In 1856 Pierce became the only elected president to be denied his own party's renomination.

Pincay, Laffit, Jr., *b. Panama City, Panama, 1946.* **American Jockey.** Despite being plagued by weight problems throughout his career, Laffit Pincay became the winningest jockey of all time on December 10, 1999, when he surpassed Bill Shoemaker's 8,833 victories. He retired because of injury at age 56 in 2003, with 9,531 winners overall. Pincay won the Eclipse Award for the nation's best jockey five times. He won the Belmont Stakes three times and captured the Kentucky Derby in 1984 aboard Swale.

Pinter, Harold, *b. London, England, 1930.* **Playwright and screenwriter.** Born into a working class family, Pinter became an actor before turning to playwriting. With the production of his first full-length play, *The Birthday Party*, in 1958, Pinter revealed the characteristics of his work: psychological exploration taking precedence over plot; dialogue that relies on silence and subtext; and characters disrupted in their behavioral patterns by the arrival of a stranger. Other plays of note are *The Caretaker* (1960), *The Homecoming* (1965), and *Betrayal* (1978).

Pissarro, Camille, *b. Charlotte Amalie, St. Thomas, Danish Virgin Islands, 1830; d. 1903.* **Painter and printmaker.** Sometimes cited as the father of the Impressionist movement, Pissarro was the only artist to show in all of the Impressionist exhibitions. By the early 1870's he was using a bright palette in patches of unmixed color; after meeting Signac and Seurat in 1885, he began to paint in a method similar to pointillism, which he ultimately found constricting. He then returned to a purer Impressionist style. His well-known works include *Versailles Road at Louveciennes* (1870) and *Wooded Landscape at l'Hermitage, Pontoise* (1878).

Pitt, William, First Earl of Chatham ("Pitt the Elder"), *b. Westminster, 1708; d. 1778.* **Statesman.** Pitt came from a family that had become wealthy in India. As a young and contentious member of Parliament, he was an enemy of King George II, but his eloquence and popularity led to his becoming secretary of state in 1756, effectively prime minister at the time. He attacked the French empire, winning Canada, a section of America, and the French West Indies, and later expelling French power from India. In 1761 he resigned, but in 1766 he formed a new government that ended in failure in 1768.

Pitt, William ("Pitt the Younger"), *b. Hayes, 1759; d 1806.* **English statesman.** Second son of William Pitt, he became the youngest prime minister ever at the age of 24, remaining in office for 18 years. He restored England's economy and pride after defeat in the American Revolution, but resigned in 1801 over King George III's opposition to Catholic emancipation in Ireland. He was brought back in 1804 and died in office in 1806.

Pius IX (Pio Nono), *b. 1792, Senigallia, Italy; d. 1878.* **Pope (1846–78).** Pius IX's tenure, the longest in church history, was roiled by international events that transformed him from a reformer to a political and theological reactionary. Opposing a nationalist takeover of Rome, he fled the city in 1848. Backed by France, he returned in 1850, but could not prevent—or accept—his ultimate loss of temporal authority and control of the papal states. In 1854 Pius declared the doctrine of the Immaculate Conception of the Virgin Mary, and in 1869 he summoned the Vatican council, at which the pope was declared infallible when speaking *ex cathedra* on faith and morals.

Pizarro, Francisco, *b. Trujillo, Spain, 1476; d. 1541.* **Conquistador.** Pizarro arrived in the Americas in 1509 and took part in Balboa's expedition of 1513 to the Pacific. After Balboa's execution (in which he conspired) in 1519, Pizarro explored the Pacific coast between Panama and Peru until 1528. Returning to Spain, he persuaded Charles I to sponsor his expedition of 1531 against the Incas; during this expedition he marched inland from the coast of Ecuador, captured the cities of Cajamarca and Cuzco, and seized and executed the emperor Atahualpa in 1533. Two years later he founded Lima, Peru, where he was assassinated.

Plath, Sylvia, *b. Boston, 1932; d. 1963.* **Poet, novelist.** Plath wrote poems characterized by turbulent imagery, acute sensitivity, and pain, in seeming contrast to her bourgeois New England upbringing and academic success. She published one edition of poems during her lifetime, *The Colossus* (1960). In her subsequent novel, *The Bell Jar* (1963), she described a nervous breakdown suffered while studying at Smith College. A month after its publication, Plath committed suicide at the age of 30. Her other volumes of poems include *Ariel* (1965), *Crossing the Water* (1971), and *The Collected Poems* (1981), edited by her husband, the English poet Ted Hughes.

Plato, *b. ca. 427 B.C.; d. 347 B.C.* **Philosopher.** Plato was a pupil and friend of Socrates; his early dialogues have Socrates in conversations that illustrate the unity of virtue and knowledge and virtue and happiness. In the *Republic* and other writings, Plato explains his ideas on the relationships between the individual, the state (to be ruled by the philosopher-king), and the cosmos.

Poe, Edgar Allan, *b. Boston, 1809; d. 1849.* **Poet, short-story writer, critic.** Poe's parents died before he was three, and he was raised by an uncle and aunt. He published *Tamerlane and Other Poems* at 18, then became a magazine editor and writer in several eastern cities, contributing poems, stories, and literary criticism. His vivid, surrealistic, often macabre tales, such as "The Tell-Tale Heart," "The Fall of the House of Usher," and "The Cask of Amontillado," were complemented by detective stories ("Murders in the Rue Morgue," "The Purloined Letter"), a genre he invented. His poem "The Raven" (1845) made him famous. He died after a drinking spree in Baltimore while en route to his second wedding.

Polk, James Knox, *b. Mecklenburg County, N.C., 1795; d. 1849.* **Eleventh U.S. president, 1845–49.** A star orator in Tennessee politics, Polk was Speaker of the House and governor of Tennessee before he won the presidency in 1844 as a dark horse candidate. From his inaugural address onward he pursued expansion in the West. When Mexico attacked U.S. troops in disputed Texas territory, Polk called it an invasion, and the ensuing Mexican War (1846–48) won California and the Southwest for the United States. Polk declined a second term, having fulfilled the nation's "Manifest Destiny" to span the continent.

Pollock, (Paul) Jackson, *b. Cody, Wyo., 1912; d. 1956.* **Painter.** A pioneer in the Abstract Expressionist movement, which flourished in New York after World War II, Pollock is often called an "action painter." His earlier work is based on figurative images, but he began producing his famous abstract poured paintings in 1947. With sticks and other tools, he threw drips of paint onto large canvases in loose, energetic patterns. Well-known works include *Autumn Rhythm: Number 30* (1950) and *Male and Female* (1942). Pollock was married to the artist Lee Krasner. He suffered from alcoholism and was killed in a car accident.

Polo, Marco, *b. 1254, Venice (?); d. 1324.* **Venetian merchant and explorer.** Marco Polo joined his father and uncle on their second journey to China in 1271. Traveling from Palestine through Asia Minor, Iran, and Afghanistan and along the Silk Road to China, they reached the court of Kublai Khan around 1274. They remained in the Orient for about seventeen years and returned by sea as escorts of a Mongol princess betrothed to a Persian khan. Polo later dictated his memoirs while in a Genoese prison after being captured in a naval battle. His *Travels* have enjoyed immense popularity ever since.

Pompey (The Great; Gnaeus Pompeius), *b. Rome, 106 B.C.; d. 48 B.C.* **Roman general and statesman.** After an illustrious military performance in the civil war, siding with the victor Sulla against Gaius Marius, Pompey was elected consul in 70 B.C. and then went on to military service in the Mediterranean. In 59 B.C. Pompey, Julius

Caesar, and Marcus Crassus formed the First Triumvirate and took control of Rome. After Crassus died the political bonds began to dissolve. Caesar returned from Gaul in 49 B.C. and crossed the river Rubicon to fight Pompey's forces. Pompey was finally defeated at Pharsalus and fled to Egypt, where he was killed by Ptolemy.

Pope, Alexander, *b.1688, London; d. 1744.* **English poet.** A tubercular child, Pope grew to be just 4 feet 6 inches. Denied educational and economic advantages because of his Catholicism, he became wealthy from his translations of Homer. Pope was a brilliant wit, master of the rhyming heroic couplet, and the greatest English verse satirist. Important works include: *An Essay on Criticism* (1711); *The Rape of the Lock* (1714), a nonpareil mock-epic satirizing high society; *The Dunciad* (1728), which attacked his mostly inferior literary enemies; the philosophical *An Essay on Man* (1734); and *Epistle to Dr.Arbuthnot* (1735).

Porter, Cole, *b. Peru, Ind, 1891; d. 1964.* **Popular composer.** Along with George Gershwin and Irving Berlin, Porter was one of America's great songwriters. He wrote both music and lyrics; and his songs were featured in numerous Broadway and Hollywood musicals and have become true standards. Important compositions include "Love for Sale" (1930), "Night and Day" (1932), "Anything Goes" (1934), "I Get a Kick Out of You" (1934), "You're the Top" (1934), "Begin the Beguine" (1935), "I've Got You Under My Skin" (1936), "I Love Paris" (1952), and "All of You" (1954).

Pound, Ezra, *b. Hailey, Idaho, 1885; d. 1972.* **Poet.** Pound moved to Europe in 1908. He was one of the most influential modern poets, but his aesthetic theories were bound up with antidemocratic political and economic views that drove him, ultimately, to Mussolini's Italy, which he supported. His poetry, rooted in spare "imagism," expanded into longer poems such as *Hugh Selwyn Mauberly* (1920), which were fragmented to express the dissolution of civilization. Thereafter he composed only his *Cantos*, 116 in all, which he saw as one long poem merging his life, his mind, and history. Pound was arrested for treason in 1945 and committed to a sanatorium in Washington for 13 years.

Presley, Elvis Aaron, *b. Tupelo, Miss., 1935; d. 1977.* **Rock 'n' roll vocalist.** Arguably the most important figure in 20th-century popular music, Elvis was the musician most responsible for popularizing rock 'n' roll on an international level. He was the first performer to fuse country and blues music into the style known as rockabilly, and the first white vocalist to sing in a "black" style. His recordings include "Heartbreak Hotel" (1956), "Hound Dog" (1956), "Love Me Tender" (1956), "All Shook Up" (1957), "Little Sister" (1961), "Suspicious Minds" (1969), "In the Ghetto" (1969), "Kentucky Rain" (1970), and "Burning Love" (1972).

Proust, Marcel, *b. Auteuil, outside Paris, 1871; d. 1922.* **French Novelist.** Proust was weakened from childhood by asthma. Although as a young man he moved amid Parisian society and joined the army, he became a recluse after his mother's death in 1905. After publishing an unsuccessful collection of short pieces in 1896, Proust turned to his magisterial work, *Remembrance of Things Past*, a seven-novel sequence, beginning with *Swann's Way* (1913). This cycle, much of it published posthumously, is one of the greatest and most influential works of modern fiction — a semiautobiographical, profound, sensuous monologue that explores the meaning of human experience as lived and remembered in time.

Puccini, Giacomo, *b. Lucca, 1858; d. 1924.* **Italian opera composer.** Puccini's first opera (*Edgar*, commissioned in 1889) was a failure, but his second (*Manon Lescaut*) was a triumph, and led to further successes. His operas are marvels of characterization, sentiment, and craftsmanship; and his mastery of melody and genius for orchestration have made his works among the most popular and beloved in the repertoire. His later works included influences from contemporaries such as Debussy and Schoenberg. Notable works include *Manon Lescaut* (1890–92), *La Bohème* (1894–95), *Tosca* (1898–99), *Madama Butterfly* (1901–1903), *La rondine* (The Swallow) (1914–16), and *Turandot* (1920–26).

Pushkin, Aleksandr, *b. 1799, Moscow; d. 1837.* **Poet.** Most celebrated of Russian poets, Pushkin had a brief career marked by political and romantic strife. His early satires on the upper class and his "Ode to Liberty" led to exile in southern Russia, and another freedom-embracing poem, *The Gypsies*, brought further confinement. He is best known for narrative poetry, including *The Bronze Horseman* (1833), in praise of Peter the Great; *Eugene Onegin*, (1831) a "verse novel" dealing with contemporary society; and the tragic historical drama *Boris Godunov* (published 1831). Pushkin was killed in a duel by a Frenchman accused of being the lover of the poet's wife.

Putin, Vladimir, *b. 1952, Leningrad (St. Petersburg).* **Russian politician.** Putin graduated with a law degree from Leningrad State University and subsequently worked with the Foreign Intelligence Service and on the Leningrad–St. Petersburg City Council. In 1994–96, he was first deputy chairman of the city government and chairman of the committee for external relations. He joined Boris Yeltsin's staff and served as deputy chief of staff and, from 1998, director of the Federal Security Service and secretary of the Security Council. In 1999 he was appointed acting prime minister. He won election as president of the Russian Federation in 2000 and 2004.

Pynchon, Thomas, *b. Glen Cove, N. Y., 1937.* **Novelist and short-story writer.** Pynchon first rose to prominence in 1963 with the publication of his absurdist first novel, *V*. In novels characterized by a fanciful, satirical, postmodern worldview such as *The Crying of Lot 49* (1966), *Gravity's Rainbow* (1973), and *Vineland* (1990). Pynchon has continually pushed the boundaries of the literary novel, exploring such genres as science fiction and magical realism.

Qin Shihuangdi, *b. Shaanxi Province, China, 258 B.C.; d. 210 B.C.* **Chinese emperor.** Prince Zheng came to the throne of the ancient Chinese state of Qin in 245 B.C., at a time of incessant warfare among the independent royal states of the time. Assisted by able advisers, he transformed Qin into a highly mobilized military-agrarian state that defeated and absorbed all rivals by 221. As self-proclaimed Qin Shihuangdi ("First Emperor of Qin"), he built the Great Wall, promulgated a code of laws, standardized weights and measures, and instituted administrative reforms. Repressive and despotic, his regime provoked popular unrest; the Qin dynasty was overthrown in 206, four years after the First Emperor's death. His tomb near Xi'an, guarded by some 7,000 life-sized terra-cotta soldiers, is one of the archaeological wonders of the world.

Rabin, Yitzhak, *b. Jerusalem, 1922; d. 1995.* **Israeli prime minister.** During the 1967 Six-Day War, Rabin led Israel to victory over Egypt, Syria, and Jordan, tripling Israel's territory. He became prime minister in 1974, achieving an agreement with Egypt that led to the Camp David Accords. Ousted as prime minister in 1977, he was reelected in 1992. He negotiated with Yasir Arafat, offering Palestinian self-rule in the Gaza Strip, Jericho, and the West Bank. Rabin, Shimon Peres, and Yasir Arafat shared the 1994 Nobel Peace Prize. Rabin also negotiated a full peace treaty with Jordan. In 1995, Rabin was assassinated by a right-wing Jewish student.

Racine, Jean, *baptized, La Ferté-Milon, France, 1639; d. 1699.* **Playwright and poet.** Considered the master of the French neoclassical tragedy, Racine is noted for fusing the metaphysical concerns of 17th-century France with the style and structure of Greek tragedy. Notable works include *Andromaque* (1667), *Britannicus* (1669), and *Berenice* (1670). Throughout his life Racine struggled to reconcile his interest in theater with his religious beliefs, and he gave up writing secular drama altogether after the premiere of his masterpiece, *Phèdre*, in 1677. During the last 20 years of his life, Racine wrote only religious poetry and drama.

Raphael (Santi, Raffaello; Sanzio, Raffaello), *b. Urbino, Italy, 1483; d. 1520.* **Painter, architect.** Although he was not the most inventive artist of his period, Raphael was able to synthesize all of its developments in highly illusionistic representation, resulting in what is thought of as the definitive High Renaissance style. Raphael produced devotional paintings, altarpieces, and portraits. Some of his well-known works are *Madonna of the Meadow* (1505); *The School of Athens* (1510–12), which depicts Greek philosophers gathered around Plato and Aristotle in a grand architectural setting; and *Galatea* (1513).

Rayburn, Samuel "Sam," *b. Roane County, Tenn., 1882; d. 1961.* **American politician.** First elected to the U.S. House of Representatives as a Democrat from Texas in 1912, Rayburn served 25 consecutive terms. He became speaker of the house in 1940 and remained speaker for a total of 17 years (1940–47, 1949–53, and 1955–61) the longest tenure ever. He was one of the most effective New Deal legislators and a close ally of Senator Lyndon B. Johnson in the 1950's.

Reagan, Ronald, *b. Tampico, Ill., 1911; d. 2004.* **Fortieth U.S. president, 1981–89.** Ronald Wilson Reagan was a B-movie actor who, despite his lack of experience, was elected governor of California in 1966. His good humor and optimistic outlook charmed voters, and he won the presidency in a landslide in 1980. His "Reaganomics" resulted in massive tax cuts that caused a meteoric rise in the national debt; he called the Soviet Union an "evil empire" and applied military pressure to end decades of communist rule. In 1987 his invincible popularity finally succumbed to the Iran-Contra scandal: White House staffers had secretly sold arms to Iran and used the profits to illegally fund Contra fighters in Nicaragua.

Redford, Robert, *b. Santa Monica, Calif., 1937.* **Actor and director.** A cautious actor who sometimes seems at odds with his movie-star good looks, he became a real star with *Butch Cassidy and the Sundance Kid* (1969) and *The Sting* (1973). Other notable films include *All the President's Men* (1976) and *The Natural* (1984). He won an Oscar as best director for *Ordinary People* (1980). In 1981 he founded the Sundance Institute, with its annual festival featuring the work of young and independent filmmakers.

Rembrandt (Harmenszoon) van Rijn, *b. Leiden, Netherlands, 1606; d. 1669.* **Painter.** At the center of what is thought to be the Dutch golden age, Rembrandt painted landscapes, figures, animals, history, and mythology, particularly Old Testament subjects such as *The Blinding of Samson* (1636) and *The Blessing of Jacob* (1656). He was also a sought-after portraitist and executed many self-portraits. His works are characterized by Baroque sumptuousness and a fascination with glowing light. Famous images include a group portrait of a military company known as *The Night Watch* (1642), *Aristotle Contemplating the Bust of Homer* (1653), and *The Jewish Bride* (ca. 1665).

Renoir, Pierre Auguste, *b. Limoges, France, 1841; d. 1919.* **Painter, printmaker, sculptor.** One of the founders of the Impressionist movement, Renoir produced some of the group's best-known images, which often focus on leisure activities. His painting *Ball at the Moulin de la Galette* (1876) is an ambitious rendering of the crowd at an outdoor dance hall, depicting the complex effects of dappled light and shade. Other well-known works include *Two Young Girls at the Piano* (1892). Renoir departed from the Impressionist circle in 1878, adopted a more classical style, and became a society painter.

Renoir, Jean, *b. Paris, France, 1894; d. 1979.* **Film director.** Son of the Impressionist painter Auguste Renoir, Jean used money inherited from his father to set up a film production company. Self-taught, he directed his first feature, *La Fille d'Eau*, in 1925. Social consciousness became his primary focus in the 1930's, as in *Boudu Saved from Drowning* (1932), *The Crime of Monsieur Lange* (1936), *Grand Illusion* (1937), and his masterpiece *Rules of the Game* (1939). During World War II, he directed several films in Hollywood, including *The Southerner* (1945). After returning to Europe, Renoir became eclectic in style and in subject, experimenting with color and form.

Reuther, Walter, *b. Wheeling W. Va. 1907; d. 1970.* **Labor leader.** As president of the United Automobile Workers (U.A.W.) from 1946 until his death in 1970, Reuther effectively used strikes and collective bargaining to win higher wages and fewer hours for his union. He increased membership to more than 1.5 million and made the U.A.W. one of the country's strongest unions. He became president of the Congress of Industrial Organizations in 1952; he immediately began negotiations with George Meany, president of the American Federation of Labor, for a merger between the two organizations, completed in 1955.

Rhodes, Cecil (John), *b. Hertfordshire, England, 1853; d. 1902.* **British financier, statesman, and effective founder of Rhodesia (now Zimbabwe).** The son of a vicar, Rhodes traveled to South Africa as a young man, for his health. He enhanced his wealth mining the Kimberley diamond mines, and in 1888 he formed his own company, De Beers Consolidated Mines. Rhodes became prime minister of the Cape Colony in 1890, but resigned in 1896 amid controversy over raids into neighboring Transvaal by a colleague. His will established the Rhodes Scholarships, which enable foreign nationals to study at Oxford.

Ricardo, David, *b. London, 1772; d. 1823.* **English economist.** Influenced by the work of Adam Smith, Ricardo held that the economy follows scientific laws, and he systematized classical economics with his theories of value, rent, and international trade. His major work was *The Principles of Political Economy and Taxation* (1817), in which he argued that the value of a good is determined by the amount of labor required to produce it, a theory that influenced Karl Marx. He also formulated the law of diminishing returns, a major contribution to economic thought.

Rice, Jerry, *b. Starkville, Miss., 1962.* **Football player.** The greatest wide receiver in history, Rice combined speed and agility with rare durability over two decades with the San Francisco 49ers and Oakland Raiders. The all-time leader in receptions, receiving yards, and touchdowns. He was NFL player of the year in 1987 and 1990, logging over 1,000 yards receiving each year, he was the M.V.P. of Super Bowl XXIII (after the 1988 season) and also excelled in the 49ers' Super Bowl victories in 1990 and 1995.

Richard III, *b. Fotheringhay Castle, 1452; d. 1485.* **Last of the Plantagenet kings of England.** Richard became king in 1483 after his brother, King Edward IV, died and Parliament declared on dubious grounds that Edward's young son, Edward V, was illegitimate. Richard's reign of two years was cut short when he was defeated and killed at the battle of Bosworth Field fighting against Henry Tudor, later Henry VII, the first Tudor king. Richard's villainous portrayal in Shakespeare's *Richard III* is generally considered to be exaggerated.

Richelieu, Cardinal (Armand-Jean du Plessis), *b. 1585, Richelieu, Poitou; d. 1642.* **French cardinal and politician.** Known as the "Red Eminence," Richelieu entered the priesthood at 22. Politically adept, he was appointed secretary of state at 31, and by 1614 was chief minister to Louis XIII. Among his primary aims was to check Spanish Hapsburg power in Europe and to quell Huguenot opposition to the crown in France; this policy led to French involvement in the Thirty Years' War. At home, he supported French trading companies and industries, laid the foundation for the French navy, and founded the French Academy.

Riefenstahl, Leni (Berta Helene Amalie Riefenstahl) *b. Berlin, 1902; d. 2003.* **Actress, film director, photographer.** She was a ballet dancer before she began acting in a series of melodramatic "mountain films" in the late 1920's. On the strength of *The Blue Light*, which she wrote and directed in 1932, Hitler commissioned her to record the 1934 Nuremburg rally (*Triumph of the Will*, 1935) and the 1936 Berlin Olympics (*Olympiad*, 1938). Blacklisted from filmmaking after the war, she continued to depict physical and natural beauty, without political overtones, in her photographic studies of African tribesmen and of undersea life.

Riemann, Bernhard *b. Breselenz, Germanay 1826; d. 1866.* **German mathematician.** Riemann's work made mathematics more general or abstract and put the integral calculus on a firmer basis. He invented a new way to show functions of complex numbers on a plane (1851) and developed the mathematics to handle such representations. He rethought the foundations of geometry in spaces of *n* dimensions (1854), suggesting new non-Euclidean geometries. The truth of his conjecture about a complex function called the zeta function (1859) remains among the main unresolved issues of mathematics.

Rilke, Rainer Maria, *b. Prague, 1875; d. 1926.* **Czech-German poet.** Rilke was a an unhappy child and had a restless life. Married only briefly, often ill, he moved frequently around Europe and Russia and sought stability and meaning in his art. Considered the best German lyric poet of the 20th century, he wrote poems that are strongly imagistic, often erotic; and his search for meaning led him to explore God, mysticism, and death. In *New Poems* (1907–08), he introduced the "object-poem," which sought to reach the core reality of physical things. Other volumes are *Sonnets to Orpheus* (1921) and his most optimistic work, *Duino Elegies* (1922).

Rimbaud, Arthur, *b. Charleville, France, 1854; d. 1891.* **Poet.** An important French Symbolist, Rimbaud was an original poet who wrote most or all of his poems before he was 20. At 16 he began an amorous relationship with the poet Paul Verlaine that ended when Verlaine shot and wounded Rimbaud. Rimbaud's poetry is dreamlike, rushing headlong from image to image and dipping into the subconscious. A successful effort to match poetic form with visionary content is "The Drunken Boat." Somewhat more restrained are the personal poems in *Last Verses*. *Illuminations* contains 40 innovative prose-poems, and *A Season in Hell* (1873) is a confessional renunciation, in prose and verse, of his wicked life

Robbins, Jerome (Jerome Rabinowitz), *b. New York City, 1918; d. 1998.* **Broadway and ballet choreographer.** Robbins was educated at N.Y.U. (1935–38), danced on Broadway from 1938–40, and joined Ballet Theatre in 1940–44. His first major ballet, *Fancy Free*, inspired the musical *On the Town*, which he also choreographed. From 1949 to 1959, Robbins was a member of the New York City Ballet, but continued to work on Broadway, choreographing a series of major hits: *The King and I* (1951), the classic *West Side Story* (1957), *Gypsy* (1959),and *Fiddler on the Roof* (1964). Robbins returned to New York City Ballet in 1969, and created several of the company's signature works including "Dances at a Gathering" (1969) and "The Goldberg Variations" (1971).

Robertson, Oscar, *b. Charlotte, Tenn., 1938.* **Basketball player.** The "Big O" was a star at the University of Cincinnati before becoming the prototypical NBA guard, paving the way for the likes of Magic Johnson and Michael Jordan. Robertson starred for the Cincinnati Royals and the Milwaukee Bucks during a career that spanned the years 1960 through 1974. He scored 26,710 points and held the NBA record for assists with 9,887 until Johnson and later John Stockton passed him. He won a gold medal in the 1960 Olympics, was named Rookie of the Year in 1961, and was named the league M.V.P. in 1964.

Robert the Bruce (Robert I), *b. 1274; d. 1329.* **King of Scotland.** Crowned king in 1306, Robert fought throughout his reign to free Scotland from English rule. In 1314, he won a decisive victory over the English at Bannockburn. The English finally agreed to Scottish independence in 1328.

Robespierre, Maximilien (Francois-Marie-Isidore de), *b. Arras, 1758; d. 1794.* **French revolutionary leader.** A lawyer by training, Robespierre was appointed to the Estates General and joined the Jacobins in 1789. In 1792 he was elected to the National Assembly (successor to the Estates General), where he called for Louis XVI's execution. A member of the extremist Montagnards, in 1793 he joined the Committee of Public Safety. Although he abetted the Reign of Terror, he deplored its most extreme abuses. Perceived both as a dictator and as a moderate, he was indicted by the Legislative Assembly and executed together with more than 100 supporters.

Robinson, Jackie, *b. Cairo, Ga., 1919; d. 1972.* **Baseball player.** Robinson was a star athelete at UCLA before he changed the face of society when he was signed by the Brooklyn Dodgers and became the first African American to play modern major-league baseball. Although harassed and threatened by fans and opposing players in his debut season of 1947, the infielder batted .297, won Rookie of the Year honors, and became a symbol of personal courage. Known for his daring on the base paths—he stole home 19 times—Robinson led the Dodgers to the National League pennant in six of his 10 years. He was named M.V.P. in 1949, leading the league in batting (.342) and stolen bases (37), while knocking in 124 runs.

Rockefeller, John Davison, *b. Richford, N.Y., 1839; d. 1937.* **Industrialist and philanthropist.** Starting out in Cleveland, Rockefeller and his partners built an oil refinery in 1863 and set up business in the Pennsylvania oil patch. In 1870 Rockefeller organized the Standard Oil Company to end the volatility in the industry by buying up smaller companies and combining them into a company large enough to control the market. By 1879 the company controlled 90 percent of America's refining capacity. In 1911 the Supreme Court dissolved the Standard Oil Trust and reorganized it into 38 companies. Rockefeller withdrew from the company in 1896 and devoted the rest of his life to philanthropy.

Rockne, Knute, *b. Voss, Norway, 1888; d. 1931.* **Football player and coach.** A legendary figure in American football, he is best known as the coach of the University of Notre Dame from 1918 to 1930. Sparked by his inspirational halftime speeches—his "Win one for the Gipper" speech was immortalized in the 1940 film *Knute Rockne,-AllAmerican*—the "Fighting Irish" enjoyed five undefeated seasons and compiled a record of 105-12-5 during the Rockne era. As players, in 1913, "Rock" and Notre Dame quarterback Gus Dorais first established the forward pass as an effective offensive weapon.

Rockwell, Norman, *b. New York City, 1984; d. 1978.* **Illustrator and painter.** Best known for his magazine illustrations, Rockwell contributed to publications such as *The Saturday Evening Post*, *Boy's Life*, and *Look*. He was a realist, influenced by the narrative genre style of artists, and he documented optimistic images of American life. His works include *Freedom from Want* (1943) and *Rosie the Riveter* (1943), the wartime working woman. Rockwell's work of the 1960's reflects the changes and conflicts of the time—pictures of the desegregation of schools, astronauts, and Peace Corps volunteers.

Rodgers, Richard, *b. Hammels Station, NY, 1902; d. 1979.* **Popular composer.** Arguably the most successful composer for the Broadway theater he collaborated with the lyricists Lorenz Hart and Oscar Hammerstein II. His later works redefined the musical form by using music to advance the plot, instead of as stand-alone vignettes. His musicals include *Babes in Arms* (1937), *Pal Joey* (1940), *Oklahoma!* (1943), *Carousel* (1945), *South Pacific* (1949), *The King and I* (1951), *Flower Drum Song* (1958), and *The Sound of Music* (1959); important songs include "Isn't It Romantic?" (1932), "Blue Moon" (1934), "My Romance" (1935), "The Lady Is a Tramp" (1937), "My Funny Valentine" (1937), "You'll Never Walk Alone" (1945), "Some Enchanted Evening" (1949) and "My Favorite Things" (1959).

Rodin, Auguste, *b. Paris, 1840; d. 1917.* **Sculptor.** Regarded as one of the greatest sculptors of the modern age, Rodin came from a working-class background and for 20 years labored as a craftsman and ornamenter. He relied on models for inspiration, and becaused he encouraged the reproduction of his work in bronze and marble editions, he is well represented in collections all over the world. His most famous works include *The Thinker* and *The Kiss*.

Roosevelt, Eleanor, *b. New York City, 1884; d. 1962.* **First lady and social activist.** Born to a socially prominent family, she married her fifth cousin, Franklin Delano Roosevelt. When he became president in 1933, Eleanor expanded the role of first lady beyond its ceremonial duties, holding weekly press conferences with female reporters, writing a syndicated newspaper column, broadcasting her own radio program, and visiting U.S. troops worldwide. Uncompromising on civil rights, she publicly ignored segregation laws and resigned from the Daughters of the American Revolution when the organization barred the black singer Marian Anderson from performing in its hall. After Franklin Roosevelt's death in 1945, she continued a life of public service and Democratic party politics. Appointed to the U.S. delegation to the U.N., she chaired the U.N. Commission on Human Rights and helped to draft the U.N. Declaration of Human Rights.

Roosevelt, Franklin Delano, *b. Hyde Park, N.Y., 1882; d. 1945.* **Thirty-second U.S. president, (1933–45).** The cousin of Theodore Roosevelt, Franklin Delano Roosevelt was paralyzed by polio in 1921. His success as governor of New York helped him win the 1932 presidential election by a landslide, assuring Americans they had "nothing to fear but fear itself." His first 100 days saw the enactment of the New Deal, which established the federal government's responsibility for protecting farmers, workers, and the unemployed while actively regulating the economy to prevent another crash. Roosevelt won an unprecedented third term in 1940 and, as war loomed in Europe, used his mastery of public opinion to lead Americans away from isolation. After Pearl Harbor, World War II occupied his full attention as he orchestrated the mammoth war effort, and he won his fourth election in 1944. Just after the Yalta Conference of 1945, Roosevelt died suddenly of a cerebral hemorrhage, days before the war ended in Europe.

Roosevelt, Theodore, *b. New York City, 1858; d. 1919.* **Twenty-sixth U.S. president, (1901–09).** During the Spanish-American War, Roosevelt left a job at the Navy Department to lead the Rough Riders volunteer regiment in Cuba, achieving glory at the battle of San Juan Hill. After serving as governor of New York, Roosevelt was named William McKinley's running mate in 1900, and assumed the presidency after McKinley's assassination. The youngest president at 42, "T.R." promised a Square Deal to close the gap between capital and labor, and signed progressive laws to regulate railroads and inspect food and drugs. He became the first American to win the Nobel Peace Prize, for helping to end the Russo-Japanese War, although he considered beginning the Panama Canal his greatest achievement. Roosevelt kept his pledge not to seek a third term in 1908—but in 1912 he ran against his chosen successor, William Howard Taft, who had leanings toward big business. Denied his party's nomination, Roosevelt won more than 4 million votes as the Progressive, or Bull Moose, candidate, which threw the election to Democrat Woodrow Wilson.

Rossetti, Dante Gabriel, *b. London, England, 1828; d. 1882.* **Painter and poet.** He was the most famous member of the Pre-Raphaelite Brotherhood, whose work was championed by Ruskin; Rossetti urged an adherence to nature found in Italian artwork before Raphael. Rossetti's own art was characterized by symbolism and often illustrated scenes from literature. In his later life he published translations of Dante and several collections of his own poetry.

Roth, Philip, *b. Newark, N.J., 1933.* **Novelist, and short- story writer.** After extensive study and work as a college teacher, Roth looked to his Jewish roots for inspiration in his early fiction. He won the National Book Award for his debut, *Goodbye, Columbus* (1959), a collection of the titular novella and five short stories. *Portnoy's Complaint* (1969) was a funny and sometimes shocking story of a young Jewish man's sexual education. The prolific writer later captured the Pulitzer Prize for Fiction with *American Pastoral* (1997) and followed that with *The Human Stain* (2000).

Rothko, Mark (Marcus Rothkowitz), *b. Dvinsk, Russia (now Daugavpils, Latvia), 1903; d. 1970.* **American painter.** A major figure in the Abstract Expressionist movement who is also considered a color - field painter, Rothko migrated to the U.S. in 1913. His most famous paintings feature blurred rectangles of color resting on an abstract ground; they include *White and Greens in Blue* (1957) and *Ochre* and *Red on Red* (1954). Toward the final years of his career, his palette grew darker, and his life ended in suicide.

Rousseau, Jean-Jacques, *b. Geneva, 1712; d. 1778.* **Philosopher and political theorist.** After a desultory early life Rousseau met an older woman who became his patron and moving with her to Paris, began to write for Diderot's *Encyclopédie*. Rousseau was one of the Enlightenment figures who most profoundly affected French Revolutionary thought, Romanticism, and philosophy to the present day. In the *Discourse on the Inequalities of Men* (1754) and the *Social Contract* (1762), he argued that men were good and equal in the state of nature, but were corrupted by the rise of property, agriculture, commerce, and science. They entered into a "social contract" to create government to correct the inequities of civilization. He also wrote on education (*Emile*, 1762), and his autobiography (*Confessions*, 1781).

Rubens, Peter Paul, *b. Siegen, Flanders, 1577; d. 1640.* **Painter and diplomat.** Rubens developed his extremely influential Baroque style after visiting Italy, where he studied ancient sculpture, the High Renaissance, and the paintings of Caravaggio. Images like *The Raising of the Cross* (1609–10), *Rape of the Daughters of Leucippus* (1617), *Venus and Adonis* (ca. 1635) and *The Garden of Love* (ca. 1638) combine a southern European approach to color, brushwork, and light with a typically Flemish attention to meticulous, realistic detail. His paintings are characterized by swirling compositions, rosy coloring, and sensuous, fleshy figures.

Rushdie, Salman, *b. Bombay, 1947.* **Indian-English novelist.** A middle-class Muslim, Rushdie was educated in England, and settled there. He attracted notice with the novel *Midnight's Children* in 1981, a dreamlike allegory, set in India, that placed him in the magical realist movement. It was followed by *Shame* (1983), set in Pakistan, and *Satanic Verses* (1988), another allegorical and adventure novel whose treatment of the Prophet Muhammad aroused a call for Rushdie's death by Iran's Ayatollah Khomeini. Forced into hiding, Rushdie continued to write essays, stories, and a novel. After the death sentence was lifted in 1998, he published the novel *The Ground Beneath Her Feet* in 1999.

Rusk, (David) Dean, *b. Cherokee County, Ga., 1909; d. 1994.* **Statesman.** From 1946 to 1952 Rusk served in a number of posts in the State Department, and in 1952, became president of the Rockefeller Foundation. He was appointed secretary of state in 1961 by President Kennedy. After Kennedy's assassination, he continued under President Lyndon Baines Johnson and played a leading role in the escalation of U.S. involvement in the Vietnam War.

Ruskin, John, *b. London, 1819; d. 1900.* **Critic.** In sharp, energetic prose, Ruskin advanced the art of criticism by turning his eye initially to the works of Turner and later to art of the Middle Ages and then the work of the Pre-Raphaelites. His works on architecture include *The Seven Lamps of Architecture* (1849) and *The Stones of Venice* (1851 and 1853). His works of cultural criticism include *The Work of Iron in Nature, Art, and Policy* (1859).

Russell, Bertrand, *b. Trelleck, Wales, 1872; d. 1970.* **Philosopher, mathematician, and social reformer.** His most important works are *Principles of Mathematics* (1903) and, with Alfred North Whitehead, *Principia Mathematica* (3 vol., 1910-13). In these works he attempted to illustrate how the laws of mathematics can be deduced from the fundamental axioms of logic. He was an ardent realist, convinced of the dependence of knowledge on the data of experience. A social activist, he was imprisoned for being a pacifist in World War I and vigorously opposed nuclear weapons and U.S. involvement in Vietnam. He won the Nobel Prize for Literature in 1950. Other influential books include *History of Western Philosophy* (1945), *Human Knowledge: Its Scope and Limits* (1948), and his *Autobiography* (1967–69).

Ruth, Babe (George Herman Ruth), *b. Baltimore, Md., 1895; d. 1948.* **Baseball player.** Though some of his records have been eclipsed, Babe Ruth remains the greatest player in baseball history. As a pitcher for Boston (1914–19), the "Bambino" compiled a record of 89-46 and twice led the majors in homers. The Red Sox traded the slugging pitcher to the then-hapless New York Yankees (1920–35), who made Ruth an everyday player. His prodigious clouts ended baseball's "dead-ball era" and revived the game after the Black Sox scandal of 1919. The "Sultan of Swat" led the Bronx Bombers to seven pennants and four World Series championships. Ruth's single-season record of 60 homers, set in 1927, stood for 34 years; his career total of 714 went unsurpassed until 1974.

Rutherford, Ernest, *b. 1871 d. 1937.* **New Zealander-Canadian-English physicist.** Early in the 20th century, Rutherford showed that radioactivity consists of alpha particles (helium nuclei), beta radiation (electrons), and gamma rays (high-energy electromagnetic waves). Rutherford and coworkers established that radioactive elements change into other elements. They showed that the atom has a positive nucleus surrounded by negative electrons (1911); this finding resulted in Rutherford's discovery of the proton. In the 1920's Rutherford was the first to "smash" atoms, breaking up light atoms with alpha particles. In the 1930's he demonstrated fusion of atoms of heavy hydrogen (deuterium) into tritium (hydrogen with two neutrons).

Ryan, Nolan, *b. Refugio, Tex., 1947.* **Baseball player.** Baseball's all-time strikeout leader (5,712), Ryan was the only pitcher to throw seven no-hitters. He struck out more than 300 batters five times (1972, 1973, 1974, 1976, and 1977) over a 28-year career (1966–93). Even in his best strikeout seasons, Ryan sometimes lost more games than he won. But his winning percentage increased as he aged, and he continued to puzzle hitters well into his 40's.

Sadat, Anwar, *b. Mit Abul Kom, Egypt, 1918; d. 1981.* **President of Egypt.** Sadat joined Gamal Abdel Nasser to depose King Farouk in 1952, and became president when Nasser died in 1970. An economy ruined by war and discontent among the poor persuaded Sadat to seek peace with Israel. But in 1973, after Israel rejected Sadat's peace proposal, he attacked Israeli forces in the Sinai, recapturing land lost during the Six-Day War of 1967. In 1977, he made history with a visit to Israel that led to the Camp David Accords in 1979. He and Prime Minister Menachem Begin of Israel shared the 1978 Nobel Peace Prize. Sadat was assassinated in 1981 by Muslim extremists who opposed his peace initiatives.

Saladin (in Arabic, Salah Ad-din Yusuf Ibn Ayyub) *b. Tikrit, Mesopotamia, ca. 1137–38; d. 1193.* **Muslim sultan of Egypt, Syria, Yemen, and Palestine.** Saladin founded the Ayyubid dynasty and is the most famous of Muslim heroes. He was born into a prominent Kurdish family, and at the age of 31 was appointed vizier and commander of the Syrian troops in Egypt. Inspired by the notion of jihad, Saladin fought to unite the Muslim territories of Syria, northern Mesopotamia, Palestine, and Egypt. In 1187 his armies defended his lands against the Christian armies of the Third Crusade and took the kingdom of Jerusalem.

Samuelson, Paul Anthony, *b. Gary, Ind., 1915.* **Economist.** In his seminal book *Foundations of Economic Analysis* (1947), Samuelson used mathematical analysis to describe equilibrium and dynamics in new and innovative ways and ushered in the modern era of using sophisticated mathematics to study economics. His pioneering work explored a broad range of topics in microeconomics and macroeconomics in which he made groundbreaking contributions. His best-selling textbook, *Economics*, first published in 1948 and revised many times, was based on the theories of John Maynard Keynes. He was the first American awarded the Nobel Prize in Economic Science, in 1970.

Sanger, Margaret (Margaret Louisa Higgins), *b. Corning, N.Y., 1879; d. 1966.* **Founder of the U.S. birth control movement.** As an obstetrical nurse, Sanger saw countless deaths from childbirth and botched abortions; this experience persuaded her to dedicate her life to birth control, a term she coined. Her birth-control clinic, the first of its kind, led to her arrest in 1917 for creating a "public nuisance," but it swayed public opinion in favor of birth control. In 1921 she founded the American Birth Control League, which evolved into Planned Parenthood Federation of America; Sanger was its first honorary chairman.

Sappho *b. Lesbos, Asia Minor, ca. 610 B.C.; d. ?580 B.C.* **Greek lyric poet.** Little is known of Sappho's life, and only fragments of her work survive. She was probably married to an aristocrat with whom she had a daughter, but spent most of her adult life as a poet and teacher to an association of women in Mytilene on the island of Lesbos. These associations were common for young, unmarried aristocratic women at the time, but Sappho's group was thought to be superior. Her work is of a very personal nature, often expressing passionate emotions toward other women, but whether or not she was actually homosexual is unknown. Her work was extolled by her contemporaries and later poets and thinkers in the ancient world.

Sargent, John Singer, *b. Florence, Italy, 1856; d. 1925.* **American painter active in England.** Sargent was influenced by the Impressionists and the Barbizon school, and became the most sought-after portrait painter in both England and the United States. His best-known works include the dramatic *Madame Gautreau* ("Madame X") (1884), and *Carnation, Lily, Lily, Rose* (1885–86). In 1894 Sargent accepted a commission to create a series of murals for the Boston Public Library; this and another commission at the Boston Museum of Fine Arts occupied much of his energy for the rest of his career.

Sartre, Jean-Paul, *b. Paris, 1905; d. 1980.* **Philosopher and author.** Sartre was a leading philosopher of existentialism whose work achieved popular success after World War II. His works include his definitive philosophical book *Being and Nothingness* (1943), plays, such as *No Exit* (1944), and several novels. He portrays the individual adrift in a meaningless universe, possessed of a frightening freedom of choice. He declined to accept the 1964 Nobel Prize in Literature. With Bertrand Russell, he opposed U.S. involvement in Vietnam.

Schiller, Friedrich, *b. Marbach, Germany, 1759; d. 1805.* **Playwright and poet.** Along with Goethe, his friend and contemporary, Schiller figured prominently in the German Romantic period. Through his plays and poems, Schiller displayed a revolutionary mind; he also wrote a history of the revolt of the Netherlands. Schiller's plays include *The Robbers* (1781), the *Wallenstein* trilogy (1796–99), and *William Tell* (1804). His most famous poem, "Ode to Joy," provided the words sung in the fourth movement of Beethoven's Ninth Symphony.

Schoenberg, Arnold, *b. Vienna, 1874; d. 1951.* **Composer, conductor, and teacher.** One of the most influential figures in the history of music, Schoenberg developed the revolutionary 12-tone system of composition, in which each of the 12 notes in an octave are played in a set order, resulting in a rigid atonality. Notable works include *Pelleas und Melisande*, Op. 5 (1902–03); *3 Pieces for Pianoforte*, Op. 11 (1909); *Das Buch der Hängenden Gärten*, Op. 15 (1908–09); *Five Orchestral Pieces*, Op. 16 (1909); *Pierrot Lunaire*, Op. 21 (1912); *Five Piano Pieces*, Op. 23 (1920–23), *Serenade*, Op. 24 (1920–23); and *Suite for piano*, Op. 25 (1921).

Schopenhauer, Arthur, *b. Danzig, Prussia, 1788; d. 1860.* **Philosopher.** He taught at the University of Berlin but failed to gain a following, in part because of his surly temperament. After 1831 he lived reclusively in Frankfurt am Main. His emphasis on the primacy of the will, enunciated in *The World as Will and Representation* (1819), places him in opposition to Hegel and German idealism and as a significant influence on Wagner, Nietzsche, Tolstoy, and Freud. To him the will was greater than reason or spirit, but because the individual will cannot be satisfied and comes into conflict with others, the will must be negated. Relief from its frustrations can be found in art.

Schrödinger, Erwin, *b. Vienna, 1887; d. 1961.* **Physicist.** Schrödinger is known primarily as the creator in 1926 of the wave equation for quantum mechanics, a year after Werner Heisenberg's development of quantum mechanics. Schrödinger's equation allows physicists to compute energy levels for electrons and remains an important tool in particle physics. After World War II, Schrödinger considered fundamental problems in biology, expressing his views in the philosophical book *What Is Life?* (1944).

Schubert, Franz, *b. Vienna, 1797; d. 1828.* **Composer of the early Romantic era.** Schubert is best known for his contributions in chamber music, piano music, and German lieder. Notable works include Quintet in A Major (*Trout*) for Piano and Strings (1819); *Fantasia* in C (*Wanderer*) (1822); Symphony No. 8 in B Minor (*Unfinished*) (1822); the song cycle *Die Schöne Müllerin* (1823); String Quartet No. 14 in D Minor (*Death and the Maiden*) (1824); Symphony No. 9 in C Major (*Great*) (1825); Piano Trio No. 1 (*lieder*) in B^{b} (1827); and more than 500 individual songs.

Schumann, Robert, *b. Zwickau, 1810; d. 1856.* **German composer, pianist, conductor, and critic of the Romantic era.** Husband of the composer and pianist Clara Schumann (1819–96), his duel interest in literature and music led him to develop historically informed music criticism, as well as a musical style deeply indebted to literary models. Notable works include *Carnaval: Scènes Mignonnes sur 4 notes*, Op. 9 (1834–4); *Fantasy in C*, Op. 17 (1836); *Kinderscenen*, Op. 15 (1838); the song cycle *Dichterliebe*, Op. 48 (1840); Symphony No. 4 in D Minor (1841), Op. 120; and Piano Concerto in A Minor, Op. 54 (1841-5).

Schumpeter, Joseph Alois, *b. Triesch, now the Czech Republic, 1883; d. 1950.* **Economist.** Schumpeter first worked in Austria and later in the U.S. He is best known for his theory of entrepreneurship, first articulated in *Theory of Economic Development* (1911). In it he argued that economic growth depends on individual entrepreneurs who innovate in pursuit of profit. Later books, including *Business Cycles* (1939) and *Capitalism, Socialism, and Democracy* (1942), concluded that capitalism was doomed to be destroyed by government, leading to socialism. His *History of Economic Thought* (1954) was published posthumously.

Scott, Walter, *b. Edinburgh, 1771; d. 1832.* **Poet and novelist.** Scott was a very popular and extraordinarily productive writer. He wrote short lyrical poems and ballads (e.g., "Lochinvar,") and long narrative poems influenced by medieval romance (*The Lay of the Last Minstrel*, 1805; *The Lady of the Lake*, 1810) and was an originator of the regional and the historical novel. His first fictional efforts were the "Waverley novels," a series of colorful, well-plotted narratives set in Scotland, including *Waverley* (1814), *Rob Roy,* and *The Heart of Midlothian* (both 1818). *Ivanhoe* (1820), set in 12th-century England, was his first historical novel, followed by *Kenilworth* (1821) and several others.

Selznick, David O., *b. Pittsburgh, Pa., 1902; d. 1965.* **Film producer.** The most successful independent producer of the golden age of Hollywood, Selznick worked for

MGM, Paramount, and RKO before forming Selznick International in 1936. He brought Ingrid Bergman and Alfred Hitchcock to America, and he produced the first major films of George Cukor and Katharine Hepburn. In 1939, he guided *Gone with the Wind* through three directors and fifteen screenwriters; one of the most expensive productions of its time, it became one of the most profitable films in history.

Seton, Elizabeth Ann, *b. New York City, 1774; d. 1821.* **Saint.** In 1974 Elizabeth Ann Seton became the first native-born American saint. Born Episcopalian, the daughter of a medical doctor, she married a well-off merchant who died in 1803 and left her with five children. She converted to Catholicism in 1805 and pioneered the parochial school system when she founded, in Emmitsburg, Md., the first Catholic free school in the United States. Taking vows as Mother Seton, she founded the Sisters of Charity in 1809; this was the first American Catholic religious community of women.

Seuss, Dr. (Geisel, Theodore Seuss), *b. Springfield, Mass., 1904; d. 1991.* **Children's writer and illustrator.** Geisel was originally an illustrator for magazines such as *Life* and *Vanity Fair*, and later worked in advertising. He became an immensely popular writer and illustrator of children's books. Among his most popular books are *How the Grinch Stole Christmas* (1957), *The Cat in the Hat* (1957), and *Green Eggs and Ham* (1960). Geisel's work is characterized by an enormous vocabulary of nonsense words and by the introduction of chaos to ordered life.

Seward, William, *b. Florida, N.Y., 1801; d. 1872.* **Politician.** As governor (1839–43) and senator from New York (1849–61), Seward led the antislavery arm of the Whig Party. He joined the Republicans in 1855 as the Whigs' influence waned. Seward lost the Republican presidential nomination in 1860, then campaigned hard for Abraham Lincoln, who appointed him secretary of state. He was stabbed the same night Lincoln was assassinated, but survived and returned to his position, holding the government together during a national crisis. In 1867, he negotiated the purchase of Alaska from Russia for $7.2 million.

Shaka, *b. ca. 1787; d. 1828.* **Zulu leader.** An outcast at birth, Shaka proved himself a brilliant warrior and became head of the Zulus in 1816. Under his leadership, the foundations of a Zulu empire in southern Africa were laid, based on strict discipline and standardized tactics and weapons. After his mother died in 1827, he became increasingly erratic and was murdered.

Shakespeare, William. *b. Stratford-on-Avon, 1564; d. 1616.* **Playwright and poet.** Considered the greatest of all English playwrights, Shakespeare was the author of 38 plays—13 comedies, 10 histories, 10 tragedies, and five romances—dramatic poems, and a sequence of 154 sonnets. (see pp. 377–79 for a full discussion of his life.)

Shaw, George Bernard, *b. Dublin, 1856; d. 1950.* **Playwright and critic.** Shaw settled in London in 1816 and became England's leading social critic, art critic, and one of the great modern playwrights. A socialist, he wrote plays with a broad range of historical and social settings but specialized in witty comedies that satirized English middle-class pretension and convention. An early play, *Mrs. Warren's Profession* (1893), dealt humorously with prostitution. *Candida* (1896) presented the first of Shaw's great heroines, a type that took fullest form with *Saint Joan* (1923). Other plays are *The Devil's Disciple* (1897), *Caesar and Cleopatra* (1899), *Man and Superman* (1904), *Major Barbara* (1905), *Pygmalion* (1913), and his melancholy World War I play, *Heartbreak House* (1917).

Shelley, Percy Bysshe, *b. Horsham, Sussex, England, 1792; d. 1822.* **Poet.** Born to wealth, Shelley was attracted to nonconformity and radical causes. His first significant poem, *Queen Mab*, advocated the toppling of established institutions. With Mary Wollstonecraft Godwin, the novelist, he fled to France, then Italy, where he created his finest works before drowning at age 30. These include his masterpiece, the verse drama *Prometheus Unbound*; a tragedy, *The Cenci* (both 1819); *Epipsychidion* (1821); and *Adonais* (1821), his elegy for John Keats. Famous shorter poems are the ironic "Ozymandias" and the lyric "Ode to the West Wind." Shelley was a moral and philosophical poet who hoped for human redemption through the power of love.

Sherman, William Tecumseh, *b. Lancaster, Ohio, 1820; d. 1891.* **Civil War general.** An 1840 West Point graduate, Sherman served in the Mexican War. A strong supporter of the Union, Sherman was a reluctant military leader who was promoted to major general after several successes, especially at the battle of Shiloh. His famous capture of Atlanta and subsequent "march to the sea" introduced a "total warfare," or the complete destruction of the general infrastructure and countryside through which he marched, thus reducing the Confederacy's ability to wage war. In 1869 he became commanding general of the army and used his position to enact a policy of forcing Indian tribes onto separate reservations, again using his tactic of economic destruction. Reported to have said, "War is hell."

Shockley, William Bradford, *b. London, 1910; d. 1989.* **American physicist.** With his collaborators John Bardeen (1908–91) and Walter H. Brittain, Shockey developed the first transistor, which eventually replaced larger vacuum tubes that consumed more power in electronic applications for consumer products, a crucial development in the emerging computer industry. The three received the Nobel Prize in Physics in 1956. In his later years Shockley was accused of racism for his views on eugenics and inherited intelligence.

Sinatra, Frank (Francis Albert Sinatra) *b. Hoboken, N.J. 1915; d. 1998.* **American singer and actor.** The "chairman of the board" started out in the 1940's as a big band crooner who sent teenage girls into shrieking hysterics at Times Square's Paramount; his smooth style and sophisticated way with lyrics in many recordings made him an enduring star. His early films were musicals, notably *On the Town* (1949); then he was reborn as a dramatic actor, winning an Oscar for *From Here to Eternity* (1953). Later films include *The Manchurian Candidate* (1962) and *The Detective* (1968).

Sitting Bull (Tatanka Iyotaka), *b. Grand River, Lakota Nation (S. D.), ca. 1831; d. 1890.* **American Indian chief.** Known for his resistance to U.S. power and promises, Sitting Bull became head chief of the Lakota nation around 1868. After joining with Chief Gall and Crazy Horse to massacre General George Armstrong Custer's Seventh Cavalry at Little Bighorn (1876), Sitting Bull fled to Canada. The near-extinction of buffalo in Canada forced him to surrender to U.S. authorities in 1881. In 1885, he joined Buffalo Bill's Wild West Show. In 1890, he was arrested by Lakota police and was killed during a gunfight when his acolytes tried to rescue him.

Smith, Adam, *b. Kirkcaldy, Scotland, 1723; d. 1790.* **Economist and philosopher.** With the publication of *An Inquiry into the Nature* and *Causes of the Wealth of Nations* (1776), Smith laid the foundations of classical economics. He rejected the prevailing policy of mercantilism and argued instead that if individuals are left to pursue their self-interest without government interference they will act, in Smith's famous words, as if "led by an invisible hand" to benefit society as a whole. He also explored the concepts of the division of labor, specialization, free trade, the determination of price and value, the distribution of income, and the accumulation of capital.

Smith, Emmitt, *b. Pensacola, Fla., 1969.* **Football player.** In 2002–03, his 13th season in the NFL, running back Emmitt Smith broke Walter Payton's all-time rushing record of 16,726 yards. Already the career leader in rushing touchdowns, Smith reached the landmark 150th of his career later that season. Despite his small stature (5'9"), the quick, powerful running back was an All-America at the University of Florida in 1989. As a pro, he won four rushing titles, three Super Bowls, and one Player of the Year award (1993) with the Cowboys. He is considered a certain member of the Pro Football Hall of Fame.

Socrates, *b. Athens, 469 B.C.; d. 399 B.C.* **Philosopher.** One of the greatest philosophers, he is known from the works of his pupil Plato and those of Xenophon. Socrates eagerly discussed justice, piety, and virtue with his fellow citizens, seeking wisdom about correct conduct to help guide the affairs of Athens. He used the dialectic (or Socratic) method, posing questions and examining the implications of responses. Socrates looked upon the soul as the seat of consciousness and character, equating virtue with the knowledge of true self. His trial and death with the cup of poison hemlock are described by Plato.

Solon, *b. ca. 630 B.C.; d. ca. 560 B.C.* **Athenian statesman; one of the seven wise men of Greece.** Solon ended exclusive aristocratic control of the government, substituted control by the wealthy, and introduced a more humane code of law. His reforms included forbidding mortgages on bodies; repealing the laws of Dracon, which punished even small offenses with death; creating a supreme court; and forming the council of 400, with 100 members each from the four tribes in Athens. Solon was also a noted poet, using poetry to forward his ideas to the populace.

Solzhenitsyn, Aleksandr, *b. Kislovodsk, Russia, 1918.* **Novelist and historian.** In 1945 Solzhenitsyn was sent to a labor camp for eight years for criticizing Stalin. His novel about the camps, *One Day in the Life of Ivan Denisovich*, was published with the blessing of Premier Khrushchev in 1962. Later critical novels, *The First Circle* and *The Cancer Ward* (both 1968), led to restrictions of his freedom, and *The Gulag Archipelago* (1973), about the Stalinist prison system, led to his expulsion from the Soviet Union in 1974.

After living in Vermont, he returned to Russia in 1994. Other books are the novel *August 1914* and the nonfiction *The Oak and the Calf* and *The Mortal Danger* (both 1980).

Sophocles, *b. Colonus, Greece, ca. 496 B.C., d. 406* B.C. **Playwright.** Sophocles is thought to have written 123 plays, of which only seven survive. As exemplified in his masterpieces, *Oedipus Rex*, *Antigone*, *Electra*, *Philoctetes*, and *Ajax*, his plays demonstrate an economy of events and characters and a sense of inexorable movement toward a tragic fate. Chief among his innovations in theater were introducing a third actor to the stage and increasing the size of the chorus from 12 to 15 members.

Soyinka, Wole (Akinwande Oluwole), *b. Obeokuta, Nigeria, 1934.* **Dramatist, novelist, essayist.** Soyinka, the first black African to win the Nobel Prize in Literature, writes in English. After founding theater companies, he was imprisoned in the 1960's for his support of Biafran secession. He wrote *Poems from Prison* and a prose account, *The Man Died* (1972), about the experience. Some of his plays, such as the early *Dance of the Forest* (1960), are comically satirical; others are more seriously critical of Nigerian society and government. These include *Kongi's Harvest* (1965), *Death and the King's Horseman* (1975), and *From Zia with Love* (1992). He has written literary essays, an autobiography, *Ake* (1981); and novels, including *The Interpreters* (1965).

Spenser, Edmund, *b. London, 1552/3; d. 1599.* **Poet.** Spenser is deemed the leading nondramatic Elizabethan poet and was a great originator of verse patterns. His first important work, *The Shepheardes Calendar* (1579), was a series of Virgilian pastoral eclogues. In 1580 he became secretary to the lord deputy of Ireland and there composed his greatest, though unfinished, work, *The Faerie Queene* (1590–96), an allegorical and fiercely anti-Catholic epic-romance, structured in beautiful nine-line "Spenserian stanzas." Other works include his sonnet sequence, *Amoretti*; a marriage poem, *Epithalamion*, and *Astrophel*, his elegy for Sir Philip Sidney, all published in 1595.

Spielberg, Steven, *b. Cincinnati, Ohio, 1947.* **Film director and producer.** A skilled craftsman and storyteller, Spielberg specializes in genre action-driven films which he imbues with universal themes and emotional resonance. Crowd-pleasers such as *Raiders of the Lost Ark* (1981), *E.T.* (1982), and *Jurassic Park* (1992) have shattered worldwide box-office records; and his more thoughtful films have become cultural touchstones, as with *Schindler's List* (1993) and *Saving Private Ryan* (1998). In 1994 Spielberg formed a studio, Dreamworks SKG, in partnership with two other industry heavyweights.

Spinoza, Baruch, *b. Amsterdam, 1632; d. 1677.* **Philosopher.** Spinoza was a member of the Amsterdam's Sephardic Jewish community, from which he was expelled for heresy. He was by trade a lens grinder but achieved great philosophical fame in his own day. The major work published in his lifetime is *A Treatise on Religious and Political Philosophy* (1670). For Spinoza, truth (like geometry) follows from first principles; ideas and physical things are the aspects of a single substance, God and Nature, where God is Nature in its fullness. A virtuous person acts out of understanding, and his ambition is the intellectual love of God.

Spitz, Mark, *b. Modesto, Calif., 1950.* **Swimmer.** Spitz won an unprecedented seven gold medals—four in individual events and three in relays, all in world-record time—at the 1972 Olympics in Munich. It was the most dominant performance by any swimmer in the history of the games. Combined with his haul in 1968, Spitz won a total of 11 Olympic medals (9 gold, 1 silver, 1 bronze). Spitz swam for four national collegiate championship teams at Indiana University. He set a total of 33 world records and 38 U.S. records during his career.

Spock, Benjamin McLane (Dr. Spock), *b. New Haven, Conn., 1903; d. 1998.* **Pediatrician and author.** *Dr. Spock's Common Sense Book of Baby and Child Care* (1946) has been the bible of new parents since its publication, which coincided with the start of the U.S. baby boom. It has sold nearly 50 million copies and has been translated into dozens of languages. While most pediatricians of his era stressed rigid feeding schedules and discouraged parents from publicly showing affection for their children, Spock urged permissiveness and flexibility. He was convicted for counseling draft evaders during the Vietnam War but the conviction was later overturned.

Springsteen, Bruce Frederick, *b. Freehold, N.J., 1949.* **Rock-pop vocalist, guitarist, and songwriter.** Springsteen was hailed by critics of the mid-1970's as the "savior of rock and roll." His music embodies all the best aspects of rock, combining driving rhythms, majestic "wall of sound" production values, and thoughtful lyrics. His roots-oriented rock has enjoyed enormous popularity through three decades, with his concerts with the E Street Band approaching the fervor of religious revivals. His albums include *Born to Run* (1975), *Darkness on the Edge of Town* (1978), *The River* (1980), *Nebraska* (1982), *Born in the U.S.A.* (1984), and *The Rising* (2002).

Stalin, Joseph (Josif Vissarionovich Dzhugashvili), *b. Gori, Georgia, 1879; d. 1953.* **Soviet dictator.** A Bolshevik from 1903, Stalin outmaneuvered his rivals to assume Lenin's mantle as leader of the Soviet Union in 1924. His implementation of successive agricultural and industrial five-year plans proved economically ruinous, and his extreme paranoia led to the execution of millions suspected of being bourgeois, counterrevolutionary, or otherwise a threat to his power. His nonaggression pact with Hitler proved short-lived, and Germany's invasion in 1940 resulted in catastrophic losses. Nonetheless, Stalin managed to build a powerful military that was instrumental in defeating Germany. After the war he brought Eastern Europe into the Soviet sphere and developed atomic weapons thereby precipitating the 50-year-long cold war.

Stanton, Elizabeth Cady, *b. Johnstown, N.Y., 1815; d. 1902.* **Feminist social reformer.** In 1848 she helped to organize the first women's rights convention in the U.S. and she was a driving force in the women's movement for 50 years. She and Susan B. Anthony formed the National Woman Suffrage Association, with Stanton as president. Stanton published *Revolution*, a feminist newspaper; was coauthor of the first three volumes of the *History of Woman Suffrage* (1881–86); and produced the *Women's Bible*, which recast many biblical passages that Stanton found derogatory to women.

Starr, Ringo (Richard Starkey), *b. Liverpool, England, 1940.* **Rock-pop drummer and vocalist; member of the Beatles.** While not a technically complex player, Ringo Starr was arguably the most influential drummer of the rock era. When the Beatles appeared on Ed Sullivan's television program in 1964, tens of thousands of young boys rushed to purchase four-piece Ludwig drum kits like the one Ringo played. His playing style was simple but complementary to the song, and helped to define pop/rock drumming in the 1960's. He was an occasional solo singer and wrote two Beatles songs "Don't Pass We By" and "Octopus's Garden." Post-Beatles, he had a modest solo career; in recent years he has toured with other artists of the 1960's and 1970's in his All-Starr Band.

Stein, Gertrude, *b. Allegheny, Pa., 1874; d. 1946.* **Novelist and poet.** Stein was a key figure of the artistic world of the early 20th century, not so much for her own works as through her association with numerous authors and painters. Her flat in Paris served as a salon for such people as Picasso, F. Scott Fitzgerald, and Ernest Hemingway. In her own writing, she experimented with techniques such as the cubist styles seen in the poems of *Tender Buttons* (1914), or in perspective, as evidenced in the *Autobiography of Alice B. Toklas* (1933), the story of her own life as seen through the eyes of her longtime companion.

Steinbeck, John, *b. Salinas, Calif., 1902; d. 1968.* **Novelist and short-story writer.** Winner of the Nobel Prize for Literature in 1962, Steinbeck was a writer of formidable talent who created novels, plays, short stories, and nonfiction. His particular cause was the plight of the common worker. His novel *The Grapes of Wrath* (1939) focused on the exploitation of migrant laborers and remains the literary symbol of the Great Depression. Among Steinbeck's many other novels are *Tortilla Flat* (1935), *Of Mice and Men* (1937), *The Pearl* (1945), and *East of Eden* (1952).

Steinem, Gloria, *b. Toledo, Ohio, 1934.* **Feminist writer.** Steinem began her career as a journalist with an attention-grabbing article called "I Was a Playboy Bunny" (1963), recounting her experience as a waitress at Hugh Hefner's Playboy Club. In 1971, she helped found the National Women's Political Caucus, she also launched *Ms.* magazine, which covered current events from a feminist viewpoint. She is the author of *Outrageous Acts and Everyday Rebellions* (1983), a collection of essays; and *Revolution from Within* (1992), a nonfiction work on women's self-esteem.

Stendhal (Marie-Henri Beyle), *b. Grenoble, France, 1783; d. 1842.* **Novelist.** Stendhal, a self-proclaimed egotist, called this same trait in his characters "Beylism," after himself. At odds with his father and the Catholic Church, he joined Napoleon's army and began writing in Milan after the emperor's final defeat in 1814. Following the unsuccessful novel *Armance* (1827), he published his most famous novel, *The Red and the Black*, in 1831, about a young, ambitious priest who engages in a tempestuous adulterous affair. His other great novel is *The Charterhouse of Parma* (1839), featuring a quintessential passionate egotist. In the 1830's Stendhal served as French consul at Trieste and Civitavecchia.

Stephen, *d. ca. 36.* **Saint and first Christian martyr.** As reported in Acts of the Apostles, Stephen, a Greek-speaking Jew, was one of the original seven Christian deacons and preached to his own Hellenistic community, whose members accused him of blasphemy. Brought before the

Sanhedrin, the high rabbinical court in Jerusalem, he presented a defense in which, while expressing his reverence for Judaism, he disparaged the Temple and the narrowness of the "Temple cult." His angered accusers then seized him, dragged him out of Jerusalem, and stoned him to death. His feast day is the day after Christmas.

Stevens, Wallace, *b. Reading, Pa., 1879; d. 1955.* Poet. The imaginative variety in Stevens's poetry is remarkable, considering that for much of his life he was an executive at an insurance company in Hartford, Conn., and maintained little contact with the literary world. Neverthless, Stevens stands as a major poet of the early 20th century. His most famous poems, "Sunday Morning" and "Thirteen Ways of Looking at a Blackbird," exhibit his characteristic symbolism and love for the imagination. His editions include *Harmonium* (1923), *Notes Towards a Supreme Fiction* (1942), and *Collected Poems* (1954) which won the Pulitzer Prize.

Stewart, James, *b. Indiana, Pa., 1908; d. 1997.* **American movie actor.** His likable persona moved easily from stage to screen and gave us the drawling innocent guy he personified in *Mr. Smith Goes to Washington* (1939), *The Shop Around the Corner* (1940)and the Capra classic *It's a Wonderful Life* (1946). He won an Oscar for *The Philadelphia Story* (1940). Darker roles and a newfound intensity replaced the shy charm in several westerns, such as *The Naked Spur* (1953), *The Man Who Shot Liberty Valence* (1962), *Rear Window* (1954), and *Vertigo* (1958).

Stieglitz, Alfred, *b. Hoboken, N.J., 1864; d. 1946.* **Photographer.** One of America's most influential photographers, Stieglitz promoted photography as art and was a great supporter of modern art in the United States. Stieglitz founded and led a succession of photography groups, publications, and galleries, including Photo-Secession, *Camera Work*, and the "291" gallery. His most notable works include *Sun's Rays—Paula, Berlin* (1889), *Steerage* (1907), and a series of his wife, the painter Georgia O'Keeffe. His *Equivalents* series, composed mainly of cloud and sky photographs, was revolutionary in conveying emotion through form instead of subject.

Stirling, James Frazer, *b. Glasgow, 1926; d. 1992.* **Scots architect.** Stirling's early work in collaboration with James Gowan included the Engineering Building (1959–63) at the University of Leicester, which brought him to prominence. Later, in collaboration with Michael Wilford, he designed the Music School and Theater Academy (1977–84) in Stuttgart, Germany, which combines the materials and planning of a prior 18th-century museum into a new configuration of geometric forms in harmony with its site; and the Performing Arts Center (1983–88) at Cornell University.

Stowe, Harriet Beecher, *b. Litchfield, Conn., 1811; d. 1896.* **Author/abolitionist.** Sister of the famous preacher and abolitionist Henry Ward Beecher, she is best known as the author of *Uncle Tom's Cabin* (1852), an abolitionist novel that ignited a storm of controversy. Its vivid depiction of the brutality of slavery was dismissed by critics as propaganda, but the novel galvanized the national debate. Abraham Lincoln referred to her as "the little lady who made this big war."

Strauss, Richard, *b. Munich, 1864; d. 1949.* **German composer, conductor, and pianist.** Equally adept at conducting and composing, Strauss was a master of several musical forms, most notably operas and orchestral tone poems; his richly melodic work embraced a fading romanticism in stark contrast to the increasingly atonal musical environment of the 20th century. Notable works include the tone poems *Tod und Verklärung* (1888–89); *Till Eulenspiegels Lustige Streiche* (1894–95); *Also sprach Zarathustra* (1896); and *Don Juan* (1898); the operas *Salome* (1903–05); *Elektra* (1906–08); and *Der Rosenkavalier* (1909–10); and the symphonic works *Metamorphosen* (1945); and *Vier Letzte Lieder* (*Four Last Songs*) (1947–48).

Stravinsky, Igor, *b. Oranienbaum, Russia 1882; d. 1971.* **Russian-born composer, conductor, pianist, and writer.** One of the most widely performed and influential composers of the 20th century, Stravinsky explored a variety of musical styles over the course of his career. His most notorious composition, the ballet *The Rite of Spring* (1911–3), shocked audiences with its abrasive harmonies and jagged rhythms. Notable works include *The Firebird* (1909–10); *Petrushka* (1910–11); *Les Noces* (1914–17); *L'histoire du soldat* (*The Soldier's Tale*) (1918); *Symphonies of Wind Instruments* (1918–20); *Oedipus Rex* (1926–7); *Symphony of Psalms* (1930); *Symphony in C* (1938–40); *Symphony in Three Movements* (1942–5); and *Orpheus* (1947).

Streep, Meryl, *b. Summit, N.J., 1949.* **Movie actress.** After Yale Drama School and some Broadway and TV roles, she made her mark in films with prodigious skill at accents and a presence at once cool and intense. Notable films include *Silkwood* (1983) and *A Cry in the Dark* (1988).

She had Oscar-winning roles in *Kramer vs. Kramer* (1979) and *Sophie's Choice* (1982), and performed in *Angels in America* (2004).

Streisand, Barbra, *b. Brooklyn, N.Y., 1942.* **Singer and actress.** After early nightclub stints, she won wider attention on Broadway in *I Can Get for You Wholesale* (1962) and became a star playing Fanny Brice in *Funny Girl* onstage and winning an Oscar for the film (1968). Numerous recordings "Evergreen", "People" and "Don't Rain on My Parade", and "The Way We Were"—have given her dynamic voice wide popularity, as has her resolute self-importance in such films as *The Way We Were (1973),A Star Is Born* (1976)—and *Yentl* (1983), which she also directed.

Strindberg, August (Johan), *b. Stockholm, Sweden,1849; d. 1912.* **Playwright, novelist, short-story writer.** Strindberg's early work, characterized by naturalistic dialogue, fascination with psychology, and starkness of setting as exemplified in the play *Miss Julie* (1888), turned a radical, critical eye on Swedish society, exploring issues of social class and relations between the sexes. His later work, such as *A Dream Play* (1902) and *The Ghost Sonata* (1907), rely on symbols rather than realistic depiction of events to explore the internal world.

Sulayman the Magnificent (Süleyman I), *b. ca. 1495; d. 1566.* Becoming sultan of the Ottoman Empire in 1520, he undertook campaigns that led to its naval dominance in the eastern Mediterranean and extended its military power into central Europe. Süleyman also undertook campaigns in the east that succeeded in bringing Iraq under Ottoman control, but he failed to conquer Persia. In 1551, he conquered Tripoli, in modern Libya. Süleyman was a noted patron of architecture and the arts in general.

Suharto, Thojib N J, *b. Java, Dutch East Indies (now Indonesia), 1921.* **President of Indonesia, 1967–98.** Suharto had a successful military career, rising through the ranks of the Indonesian army following the country's independence to become a major general in 1962. In 1965 he helped crush a left-wing coup. He took control of the Indonesian government in 1966 and was appointed president the following year. Three decades of uninterrupted rule followed, giving Indonesia much-needed political stability and sustained economic growth. In 1998, Suharto's authoritarian regime fell victim to an economic downturn and its own internal corruption.

Sukarno, *b. Java, Dutch East Indies (now Indonesia), 1901; d. 1970.* **Leader of the Indonesian independence movement and the country's first president (1945–67).** Sukarno spent two years in a Dutch jail and eight years in exile for challenging colonialism. In 1945 he defined the *pantjasila* ("five principles") of nationalism, internationalism, democracy, social prosperity, and belief in God, which became the state doctrine. That same year, Sukarno declared Indonesia's independence and became president of the new republic, eventually suppressing the country's original parliamentary system in favor of an authoritarian "guided democracy." He was deposed in 1966 by Suharto's coup d'état.

Sulla, Lucius Cornelius, *b. 138 B.C.; d. 78 B.C.* **Roman general and politician.** Sulla was dictator of Rome from 82 to 79 B.C. He began his career under Gaius Marius; after fighting several victorious wars abroad, Sulla returned to Rome and was declared a public enemy by Marius's ruling party. Sulla's march on Rome launched the empire's first civil war, which ended with his victory at Colline Gate in 82. As the new dictator, he chose the name Felix. During his rule he reorganized the senate and judiciary and strengthened the Roman Empire.

Sullivan, Louis Henri , *b. Boston, 1856; d 1924.* **American architect.** With his partner, Dankmar Adler (1844–1900), Sullivan realized that the skyscraper, made desirable by rising real estate prices and made possible by modern building materials, required a new aesthetic celebrating verticality. His Wainright Building in St. Louis (1890–1991) epitomizes his famous statement that a tall building "must be every inch a proud and soaring thing." Other important works included the Guaranty Building (1894–96), Buffalo, and the Schlesinger-Mayer department Store (1898–1904, now the Carson-Pirie-Scott store), Chicago. The maxim "form follows function"—that is, the look of a building must be subordinate to its purpose—is also attributed to Sullivan and was later taken up by other 20th-century architects.

Sun Yat-sen, *b. Guangdong Province, China, 1866; d. 1925.* **Chinese Revolutionary Leader.** Sun's name is the Cantonese Yixian pronunication of Mandarin Yixian; he is usually known in China by his nom de guerre Sun Zhongshan. Of peasant background, the future "father of the chinese revolution" earned a medical degree in Hong Kong, but abandoned medicine for revolutionary politics in the 1890's. Sun traveled extensively overseas, visiting

Chinese communities, raising funds, and plotting to overthrow the Qing dynasty. When the Revolution of 1911 broke out, he returned to China and briefly became provisional president; soon ousted, he repudiated the republic's corrupt and undemocratic government. Thereafter he led the Nationalist Party's opposition regime in Canton and formulated its core doctrine, the "three principles of the people" (nationalism, socialism, democracy).

Swift, Jonathan, *b. Dublin, 1667; d. 1745.* **Poet and satirist.** Swift lived in both England and Ireland and served his last three decades as Anglican dean of St. Patrick's Cathedral, Dublin. He wrote witty poems and love poems but became England's supreme prose satirist, beginning with *A Tale of a Tub* and *The Battle of the Books* (both published 1704). He wrote powerfully against English policy toward Ireland; his "Drapier Letters" (1724), opposing the debasement of currency, and his ironic classic, "A Modest Proposal" (1729), made him a permanent Irish hero. *Gulliver's Travels* (1726), an account of a journey to four fanciful lands, is regarded as the greatest (and fiercest) English satire.

Tacitus (Cornelius Tacitus), *b. A.D. 56; d. ca. 120.* **Roman historian.** Little is known about the life of Tacitus, author of the *Annals*, which cover the lives of emperors Tiberius, Claudius, and Nero. He was a friend of Pliny the Younger and consul for a time. Other works include *Agricola*, a biography of his father-in-law; and *De Origine et Situ Germanorum* (also called *Germania*), which discusses German tribal customs.

Taft, William Howard, *b. Cincinnati, Ohio, 1857; d. 1930.* **Twenty-seventh U.S. president, (1909–13).** Taft tried to carry on Theodore Roosevelt's policies, but he wrecked the Republican party by alienating progressives over tariff and conservation issues. Although he initiated the income tax and pursued antitrust suits against big business, Taft generally sided with wealthy interests. In 1921, Taft was appointed chief justice of the United States; he served with distinction, alternating liberal nationalism in economic affairs with political and social conservatism.

Talbot, William Henry Fox, *b. Dorset, England, 1800, d.1877.* **English inventor.** Fox Talbot has the best claim among several pioneers of having invented photography, which he first thought of in October 1833. After several years of experiments creating images with silver nitrate on paper, he described his invention to the Royal Society on January 31, 1839. Later that year he developed the first form of photographic negatives, patenting the process early in 1841. Fox Talbot's early photographs of scenes and people around Lacock Abbey in England are still effective and are often reprinted.

Talleyrand(-Périgord), Charles-Maurice de (Prince de Bénévent), *b. 1754, Paris; d. 1838.* **French statesman.** A master of political survival, Talleyrand held important offices during the French Revolution, under Napoleon, and during the Bourbon Restoration. Elected to the National Assembly in 1789, he was soon denounced and fled to England and then the U.S. He served as foreign minister for the Directory (1797) and Napoleon, who appointed him grand chamberlain. Having abandoned Napoleon by 1808, he was the restored Louis XVIII's foreign minister at the Congress of Vienna, though royalists secured his removal. Under Louis-Philippe, he served as ambassador to Britain (1830–34).

Taylor, Elizabeth, *b. 1932, London, England.* **Actress.** Famous for her eight marriages, two to Richard Burton, Taylor made the difficult leap from child star (*National Velvet*, 1944; *Little Women*, 1948) to romantic lead (*Father of the Bride*, 1950; *A Place in the Sun*, 1951), before solidifying her reputation with two adaptations of plays by Tennessee Williams, *Cat on a Hot Tin Roof* (1958) and *Suddenly, Last Summer* (1959). Her tempestuous relationship with Burton began on the set of *Cleopatra* (1963). Together, they made *Who's Afraid of Virginia Woolf?* (1966), for which she won her second Oscar (the first had been for *Butterfield 8*, 1960).

Taylor, Zachary, *b. Montebello, Va., 1784; d. 1850.* **Twelfth U.S. president, 1849–50.** Taylor was the first president to have no previous political experience. He served as a professional soldier for nearly 40 years; his finest hour came during the Mexican War, when he captured Monterrey and smashed General Santa Ana's much larger army at the battle of Buena Vista (1847). "Old Rough and Ready" was the last Whig to be elected president, in 1848. Taylor died suddenly of acute indigestion after a long, hot Fourth of July ceremony at the Washington Monument.

Tchaikovsky, Pyotr, *b. Votkinksk, 1840; d. 1893.* **Russian composer and conductor of the Romantic era.** Tchaikovsky was the first composer to assimilate the traditions of Western European symphonic music into the Russian national style, in the process ushering in a new age of serious music composed specifically for dramatic dance. Notable works include *Romeo and Juliet*

(1869); *Capriccio*, Op. 8 (1870); *Swan Lake*, Op. 20 (1875-6); Violin Concerto in D, Op. 35 (1878); *1812, Ceremonial Overture,* Op. 49 (1880); *The Sleeping Beauty*, Op. 66 (1888–9); *The Nutcracker*, Op. 71 (1891–2); and Symphony No. 6 in B Minor, Op. 74 (*Pathétique*) (1893). He wrote 11 operas including *Eugene Onegin* (1879), and *The Queen of Spades* (1890).

Tecumseh, *b. (modern) Clark Co., Ohio, 1768; d. 1813.* **Shawnee chief.** Tecumseh was a great orator and won fame by calling for an end to the torture of whites. He was chosen as leader of his band, and in 1795 he rejected the Treaty of Greenville for giving away land, which he believed to be a communal right. Tecumseh then served as the Indians' spokesman at the Ohio great councils. Turning to action, he helped the Shawnee fight against the U.S., and he joined with the British in the War of 1812, organizing a massive Indian force to enable the taking of Detroit. He was killed in battle when William Henry Harrison led troops into Canada.

Tennyson, Alfred (Lord), *b. Lincolnshire, England, 1809; d. 1892.* **Poet.** The most popular Victorian poet, he had composed fine poems, such as "The Lotos-Eaters," by 1833, when the death of his friend Arthur Hallam deepened his poetic sensibility. His pessimism about 19th-century progress and the quest for religious faith are evident in *Poems* (1842), which includes "Ulysses," and in *Morte d'Arthur* (poems characteristically based on literature of the past). His long, contemplative elegy for Hallam, *In Memoriam A.H.H.*, was published in 1850, the year he was appointed poet laureate. In poems widely varied in length, meter, and setting, Tennyson sustained throughout his long career an uncommon ability to enchant the ear.

Tesla, Nikola, *b. Smiljan, Croatia, 1856; d. 1943.* **Physicist and inventor.** After building the first alternating-current electric motor in 1883, Tesla migrated to the United States and worked for Thomas Edison whose fledgling electric power plants were based on direct current (DC). In 1887 Tesla established his own company which produced patents in alternating-current (AC) technology. George Westinghouse bought many of his patents and brought them to commercial fruition and AC became the global standard. Tesla designed the first hydroelectric powerplant at Niagara Falls (1895). Tesla's difficult personality created problems with those he worked with, and helped to delay recognition of the technology that revolutionized electric power. After about 1913 he lived in seclusion in New York City. He held over 700 patents.

Thackeray, William Makepeace, *b. Calcutta, 1811; d. 1863.* **English novelist.** Like his contemporary, Dickens, Thackeray wrote novels serially in magazines. He was a satirist who attacked hypocrisy and burlesqued other novelists. His greatest and most famous novel, *Vanity Fair* (1848), is a masterly satire of the English upper class, featuring Becky Sharp, a clever, crooked, successful schemer who is one of the major figures in English fiction. It was followed by the partly biographical *Pendennis* (1850) and the historical novels *Henry Esmond* (1852) and *The Virginians* (1857–59). Thackeray worked feverishly to support his family after his wife went insane around 1840, and he lectured widely in Britain and America.

Thatcher, Margaret, *b. Grantham, England, 1925.* **British prime minister.** A grocer's daughter, Maggie Thatcher won a seat in Parliament at age 34, and quickly climbed the ranks of Britain's Conservative Party. She assumed the party leadership in 1975, and in 1979 she was elected Britain's first female prime minister. She promptly dismantled many social welfare programs, cut taxes for the wealthy, reduced government spending, battled trade unions, and privatized nationalized industries. Thatcher was a major foreign-policy partner of Ronald Reagan. Her introduction of a poll tax eroded her support, and she resigned in 1990. In 1992, she became a baroness, and entered the House of Lords.

Thomas, Dylan, *b. Swansea, Wales, 1914; d. 1953.* **Poet and playwright.** In many ways, Thomas was a Romantic poet born a century too late. His flamboyant personality and notorious drinking brought him public attention, and like Byron and Keats, he died at a relatively young age. In his most famous poems, "Do Not Go Gentle into That Good Night" and "Fern Hill," Thomas displays a fierce love of life and a sense of nostalgia. His works include *18 Poems* (1934), *Collected Poems* (1952), and the play *Under Milk Wood* (published posthumously in 1954).

Thomson, J. J. (Joseph John), *b. Manchester, England, 1856; d. 1940* **English physicist.** In 1897 Thomson discovered the electron. He later showed that the electron's mass is much smaller than that of any atom and that atoms contain electrons. Thomson also invented the first version of a mass spectrometer (a device that separates ions by mass) and used it to discover two different-mass atoms of neon, the first physical proof that isotopes (different forms of the same element) exist.

Thoreau, Henry David, *b. Concord, Mass., 1817; d. 1862.* **Author and poet.** Thoreau was Ralph Waldo Emerson's protegé and a main figure in the Transcendental movement. An advocate of individualism and antimaterialism and a keen observer of nature, he lived alone for two years in a cabin on Walden Pond near Concord, and recorded his natural and philosophical observations in the classic *Walden* (1854). Other books include *A Week on the Concord and Merrimac Rivers* (1849) and *The Maine Woods*, published posthumously. His essay "Civil Disobedience," (1849) written after he was jailed for not paying a poll tax to support the Mexican War, has had an international influence on civil rights movements.

Thorpe, Jim, *b. Prague, Okla., 1888; d. 1953.* **Athlete.** Thorpe was voted the greatest male athlete of the first half of the 20th century by the Associated Press. A Native American, he won All-America honors in football in 1911 and 1912 at the Carlisle (Pa.) Indian School, also competing in baseball, track, and lacrosse. At the 1912 Olympics in Stockholm, Thorpe won gold medals in both the pentathlon and the decathlon. He was stripped of the medals in 1913 for violating the rules of amateurism—he had played professional football and baseball—but they were restored posthumously in 1982.

Thucydides, *b. ca. 460 B.C.; d. ca. 404 B.C.* **Greek historian of the Peloponnesian War (431–404 B.C.).** Thucydides was not only a pivotal figure for the study of history but possibly the first journalist in the modern sense. His firsthand account of the Peloponnesian War covers everything from military details to profiles of the participants. Little is known of his life, but he was a general in exile for a military failure during much of the writing of his account, leaving it somewhat biased. He is thought to have returned to Athens after its defeat in 404 B.C. His account was never completed and ends in 411 B.C.

Thutmose III Menkheperre, *r. ca. 1479–25 B.C.* **Egyptian pharaoh.** Assuming the throne as a minor, Thutmose reigned jointly with his aunt, Hatshepsut (probably Egypt's most powerful woman), until her death in 1457. Shortly thereafter, Thutmose led his army into Palestine and won a major victory at Megiddo, the first battle in history recorded in detail, on a wall at Karnak in Thebes. It was the first of Thutmose's 17 campaigns, which brought Egypt to the height of its imperial reach in Palestine, Syria, and Nubia (Sudan). During his reign, Egypt also received tribute from Minoan Crete, the Hittites, and Mesopotamia.

Tiberius (Tiberius Claudius Nero Caesar), *b. 42 B.C.; d. A.D. 37.* **Roman emperor.** Tiberius was the stepson and successor of Augustus, taking power after his death in A.D. 14 at age 54. He spent his early life as a prominent figure in Roman politics and then became disillusioned and retired for a period. He returned to Rome in 6 B.C. after the death of Augustus' other heirs and regained power. The early part of his 23-year reign was marked by peace, prosperity, and social reform. However, after the death of his son Drussus in 23 A.D, Tiberius became infamous for executions, brutality, and torture. He died on Capri, probably killed by the head of his praetorian guard, leaving Caligula as his successor.

Timur (also known as Tamerlane, Tamburlaine, or Timur Lenk), *b. Kesh, Transoxania (now in Uzbekistan), 1336; d. 1405.* **Turkic conqueror.** Timur is remembered for the barbarity of his conquests. He established dominion over the Transoxania lands by 1366, and for the next 10 years fought against the khans of Jatah and Khorezm. His troops occupied Moscow, defeated the Lithuanians near Poltava, conquered Persia (1383), and invaded India (1398). The poverty, bloodshed, and desolation caused by his campaigns gave rise to many legends, which in turn inspired such works as Christopher Marlowe's *Tamburlaine the Great*.

Titian (Tiziano Vecellio or Vecelli,), *b. Pieve di Cadore, Italy, ca. 1488/90; d. 1576.* **Painter.** A chief figure in the High Renaissance, thought of as the greatest artist of the Venetian school, Titian painted scenes from history and mythology, religious subjects, and allegories, as well as portraits. He helped to establish the 16th-century style, with its looser brushwork and subtler colors. His well-known works include a scene of pagan revelry, *Bacchanal of the Andrians* (mid-1520's), *Venus of Urbino* (1538), and *Pietà* (1573–76).

Tolstoy, Leo, *b. near Tula, Russia, 1828; d. 1910.* **Novelist and philosopher.** Count Tolstoy grew up on an estate and was orphaned at nine. He lived aimlessly before joining the army at 23. His army service contributed to a successful collection of stories, *Sevastapol Sketches* (1855–56); a short novel, *The Cossacks* (1863) and his long epic of the Napoleonic Wars, *War and Peace* (1865–69), one of the greatest narrative achievements in literature. Another great novel, *Anna Karenina* (1874–77), tells the parallel stories of an adulterous love between a passionate woman and a military officer, and of an introspective estate owner. After converting to what has been called Christian anarchy, Tolstoy lived a life of pacifism, poverty, and moral searching. Other fictional works include the novellas *The Death of Ivan Ilych* (1886) and *The Kreutzer Sonata* (1889).

Trotsky, Leon (Lev Davidovitch Bronstein), *b. Yanovka, Ukraine, 1879; d. 1940.* **Russian politician.** A first- generation Russian Communist leader, Trotsky was twice exiled to Siberia by the czarist government (1898 and 1905). He collaborated with Lenin as early as 1902. Instrumental in the Bolsheviks' rise to power during the October Revolution (1917), he subsequently served as commissar of war in the final months of World War I. Losing to Stalin in a struggle to head the Communist Party after Lenin's death in 1924, he was eventually stripped of his party membership. He was murdered in Mexico on Stalin's orders.

Truffaut, François, *b. Paris, 1932; d. 1984.* **Screenwriter and director.** Truffaut's humanist films made him the most popular director of the French New Wave. He had been mentored by the film theorist André Bazin, who hired him to write for the magazine *Cahiers du cinéma*. One of his articles was the basis for the auteur theory. Truffaut's first feature was *The Four Hundred Blows* (1959), the first of a cycle of autobiographical films, which include *Love at 20* (1962) and *Stolen Kisses* (1968). Other films by Truffaut films are *Jules and Jim* (1961), *Wild Child* (1970), and *Day for Night* (1972).

Truman, Harry S, *b. Lamar, Mo., 1884; d. 1972.* **Thirty-third U.S. president (1945–53).** A plain-spoken midwesterner who was a World War I artilleryman, Harry S Truman (the S does not stand for a middle name) entered politics as a Democrat in the 1920's after his Kansas City haberdashery failed. The local Pendergast machine arranged his election to the Senate as a New Dealer in 1934, and he was chosen for the vice presidency in 1944. After only a few weeks in office, Truman had the presidency thrust upon him by Roosevelt's sudden death; utterly unprepared, he vowed to carry on Roosevelt's policies—and proved to be a remarkably capable chief executive. In his first four months, Truman approved the United Nations, accepted the German surrender, met with Allied leaders at Potsdam, and ordered atomic bombs dropped on Japan. In 1947 he proclaimed the Truman Doctrine, promising U.S. aid to threatened countries, and the Marshall Plan to aid European recovery. He also committed the country to the NATO alliance and sent troops to South Korea when Communist armies invaded in 1950.

Tubman, Harriet (Araminta Ross), *b. Dorchester county, Md., c. 1820; d. 1913.* **Escaped slave, abolitionist, and "conductor" on the Underground Railroad.** A slave from birth, she married John Tubman, a free black, in 1844. But when she heard she was to be sold, she fled to Philadelphia. In 1850, she returned to Baltimore to help her mother and two sisters escape slavery. She made 18 additional trips into Maryland to guide more than 300 fugitive slaves along the Underground Railroad into Canada. Abolitionists deemed her the "Moses of her people," while slaveholders offered $40,000 in rewards for her capture.

Turgenev, Ivan, *b. Orel, Russia, 1818; d. 1883.* **Novelist, short-story writer, playwright.** Born to landed wealth, Turgenev advocated westernization for Russia, wrote a book of stories, *A Sportsman's Sketches* (1852), that influenced the end of serfdom; and, after being banished to his estate in the 1850's, lived mainly in Paris. His greatest novel, *Fathers and Sons* (1862), was controversial for its sympathetic characterization of a nihilist (a term he invented) who opposes the Russian upper class. Other novels include *Rudin* (1855), *A Nest of Gentlefolk* (1859), and *Virgin Soil* (1877). His plays include *A Month in the Country* (1850), and among his highly esteemed stories is "First Love" (1870).

Turner, J. M. W. (Joseph Mallord William), *b. Chelsea (now in London), England, 1775; d. 1851.* **Painter and printmaker.** Turner dominated the field of landscape painting in the first half of the 19th century. Interested in history and the sublime, he saw himself as a modern master in the tradition of Claude and Poussin, although some of his later studies of light have led to comparisons with the Impressionists. In 1804 he opened a gallery to show his paintings. His best-known works include *The Slave Ship* (1840) and *The Decline of the Carthaginian Empire* (1817).

Turner, Nat, *b. Southampton County, Va., 1800; d. 1831.* **American slave leader.** Turner, born into slavery in Virginia, believed he had been selected by God to lead his fellow slaves to freedom. In the uprising of 1831, Turner and his followers killed several dozen slave owners before being defeated by government forces. Many of the participants were summarily executed, and Turner was subsequently captured, tried, and sentenced to death for his role. His life served as the inspiration for *The Confessions of Nat Turner*, a work of historical fiction by William Styron that won the Pulitzer Prize in 1968.

Tutankhamen Nebkheperre, *r. ca. 1333–23 B.C.* **Egyptian pharaoh.** Originally named Tutankhaten, "Living image of the Aten," Tutankhamen changed his name as part of a repudiation of the monotheistic Aten-worship of his father-in-law, Akhenaton. He also moved his capital and encouraged worship of the old gods. Tutankhamen died aged about 18. Memory of his reign was obliterated in the 19th dynasty, and his small burial tomb in the Valley of the Kings was unknown to grave robbers until 1922, when its elaborate contents were revealed to the world by Howard Carter. Tutankhamen's fame today depends entirely on his obscurity in antiquity.

Twain, Mark (Samuel Langhorne Clemens) *b. Florida, Mo., 1835; d. 1910.* **Author, novelist.** Twain is regarded as the greatest American humorist. His experience as a Mississippi River pilot provided his pseudonym (slang for "two fathoms of water"). His first book, *The Innocents Abroad* (1869), recounted a trip around the Mediterranean. His most famous books are novels based on his Missouri boyhood, *The Adventures of Tom Sawyer* (1876) and *Adventures of Huckleberry Finn* (1884). After his marriage in 1870, Twain settled in Hartford, Conn. Bad investments plummeted him into debt, and in the 1890's he lectured around the world. Other books are *Life on the Mississippi* (1883), and the novel *A Connecticut Yankee in King Arthur's Court* (1889).

Tyler, John, *b. Charles City County, Va.; d. 1862.* **Tenth U.S. president, (1841–45).** Tyler was the first vice president to become president by succession. He had been a Virginia legislator, congressman, senator, and governor before the Whigs chose him as William Henry Harrison's running mate in 1840. As president after Harrison's death, "His Accidency" earned the Whig party's ire by changing parties. In 1842 his cabinet resigned, his party expelled him, and outraged members of Congress called for his impeachment. This was the first time impeachment proceedings were introduced in Congress, although the proposal was eventually defeated.

Unitas, Johnny, *b. Pittsburgh, Pa., 1933; d. 2002.* **Football player.** He was the premier quarterback of his era, who over 18 seasons (1956–73)—all except one with the Baltimore Colts—led his team to four NFL championships and earned league Player of the Year honors three times (1959, 1964, 1967). By the time he retired, "Johnny U" had appeared in 10 Pro Bowls and set career records (all since surpassed) in virtually every major passing category.

Updike, John, *b. Shillington, Pa., 1932.* **Novelist, essayist, and short story writer.** A prominent figure in contemporary American letters, Updike has had a varied career and has written novels, short stories, poetry, and many articles and book reviews for *The New Yorker*. He won Pulitzer Prizes in fiction for *Rabbit is Rich* (1981) and *Rabbit at Rest* (1991), two in a series of four novels that track the life of Rabbit Angstrom, a former high school basketball star who finds little glory as an adult. In these novels and others, (*The Poorhouse Fair*, 1959; *Couples*, 1968) Updike examines the moral foibles of modern American society especially its middle class.

Valentino, Rudolph (Rodolfo Alfonzo Raffaele Pierre Philibert Guglielmi), *b. Castellaneta, Italy, 1895; d. 1926.* **Silent film actor.** Darkly handsome, passionate, and graceful, Valentino epitomized the exotic lover so popular in the silent era's adventure fantasies. He began as a dancer in nightclubs and dance halls before landing work as a Hollywood extra. The screenwriter June Mathis discovered him and cast him in *Four Horsemen of the Apocalypse* (1921), which skyrocketed him to stardom. He followed with starring roles in *The Sheik* (1921) and *Blood and Sand* (1922). His premature death drove fans into a mass frenzy, which reflected the star worship of the era.

Van Buren, Martin, *b. Kinderhook, N.Y., 1782; d. 1862.* **Eighth U.S. president, 1837–41.** Van Buren's staunch party loyalty elevated him to the Senate in 1821; his brief service as governor of New York ended when Andrew Jackson appointed him secretary of state in 1829. He helped build the Democratic Party, and Jackson made him vice president in 1832. He ascended to the presidency in 1836, but two months after he took office the Panic of 1837 launched a severe economic depression and he was limited to one term. In 1844 Van Buren lost the Democratic nomination, then guaranteed a Democratic defeat by founding the Free Soil party, which split the decisive New York vote.

Van Gogh, Vincent (Willem), *b. Zundert, Netherlands, 1853; d. 1890.* **Painter.** Van Gogh was unrecognized during his lifetime, but his life and work have become legendary. He was inspired to paint peasants in the style of Millet, as demonstrated in his early work *The Potato-Eaters* (1885), but later he abandoned the dark tones of that piece for vibrant colors and thick, textured layers of busy brushwork. Van Gogh is thought of as Postimpressionist, and he was influenced Japanese woodcuts. Tormented by mental illness, epilepsy, and he famously cut off part of his ear late in life. He was supported by his brother Theo, and left behind prolific correspondence before committing suicide. His most famous works include *The Night Café* (1888), *Starry Night* (1889), and *Crows in a Wheat-Field* (1890).

Velázquez, Diego (Rodríguez de Silva y), *b. Seville, Spain, 1599; d. 1660.* **Painter.** After early successes such as *The Water Carrier of Seville* (ca. 1619), Velázquez was appointed court painter in Madrid in 1623; he spent most of his life producing portraits of the royal family. As well as the famous *Pope Innocent X* (1650). His masterpiece is *Las Meninas* (1656), one of the best-known works of the Baroque period; a group portrait that includes the young Princess Margarita, it is considered a superb study of light, color, and space.

Venturi, Robert, *b. Philadelphia, Pa. 1925.* **Architect, theorist, and educator.** Venturi rejected the "modernist" idiom. His influence derives from both his designs and his writings. His books, *Complexity and Contradiction in Architecture* (1966, 2nd edition 1977) and *Learning from Las Vegas* (1972, 2nd edition 1977) written with his wife, Denise Scott Brown, set forth his critique of modern architecture. His designs, include his early Guild House (1960–63) in Philadelphia and the Vanna Venturi House (1963) in Chestnut Hill, Pa., and the later Seattle Art Museum (1984–91). He won the Pritzker Prize in 1991.

Verdi, Guiseppe, *b. Le Roncole, near Busseto, Parma, 1813; d. 1901.* **Composer of the Romantic era.** Born into an ordinary family, Verdi composed some of the most popular and critically acclaimed operas of all time. Because of his technical mastery of the operatic form and his unsurpassed powers of characterization his work remains extremely popular today. He wrote 30 operas, including *Macbeth* (1846–7), *Rigoletto* (1850–1), *Il trovatore* (1851–2), *La traviata* (1852-3), *Don Carlos* (1867), *Aida* (1870), *Otello* (1884–6), and *Falstaff* (1889–92); his *Requiem* mass (1874) is highly regarded.

Verlaine, Paul, *b. Metz, France, 1844; d. 1896.* **Poet.** After publishing two volumes of lyric poetry as a young bohemian in Paris, Verlaine, with the publication of *Songs Without Words* (1874), joined the Symbolist movement, which advocated freedom from conventional poetic form. A younger Symbolist, Arthur Rimbaud, became his lover, and Verlaine was imprisoned for shooting and wounding him. After prison, he wrote religious poetry in the volume *Sagesse* (1881). He was later associated with the end-of-the-century decadent poets, as his life became more dissipated. Verlaine's poetry is highly regarded for its sensuality and musicality. His later volumes include *Jadis et Naguère* (1884) and *Parallèlement* (1889).

Vermeer, Johannes (Jan), *b. Delft, Netherlands, 1632; d. 1675.* **Painter.** Best known for portraits of women engaged in domestic, often solitary activities, Vermeer was fascinated by the quality of light in interior spaces. Works such as *Woman with a Water Jug* (1662–25) and *Head of a Girl with a Pearl Earring* (ca. 1665) depict a tranquil beauty in everyday life. The solemn, nonnarrative qualities in his compositions set him apart from other Dutch genre painters in the Baroque period. Because his working process was painstaking, his output was limited, and only 35 of his paintings survive.

Victoria (Alexandrina Victoria), *b. Kensington Palace, England, 1819; d. 1901.* **Queen of Great Britain, 1837–1901.** She gave her name to an era, the Victorian age. Alexandrina Victoria was the only child of the fourth son of King George III; when her uncle William IV died childless in 1837, she became queen of England. She married her cousin, Prince Consort Albert of Saxe-Coburg-Gotha, in 1840; they had nine children, through whose marriages were descended many of the royal families of Europe. During Victoria's reign, the longest of any English monarch, the monarchy took on its modern ceremonial character.

Villa, Pancho (Doroteo Arango), *b. San Juan del Rio, Mexico, 1878; d. 1923.* **Revolutionary and guerrilla leader.** Villa, joined Francisco Madero's uprising against the dictator Porfirio Diaz in 1909. He was imprisoned by General Victoriano Huerta in 1912 but escaped and formed a band of several thousand men, known as the División del Norte. Revolting against Huerta's dictatorship, he joined with Venustiano Carranza and defeated Huerta in June 1914. He then broke with Carranza and engaged in banditry and various guerrilla activities, receiving an official pardon only after the overthrow of Carranza's government in 1920.

Virgil (Publius Vergilius Maro), *b. Andes (near Mantua), Italy, b. 70 B.C.; d. 19 B.C.* **Roman poet.** Virgil is considered by many to be the greatest Roman poet. Educated in Rome, he was befriended and patronized by Maecenas, Augustus' chief imperial minister. Virgil's major works include the *Eclogues* and *Georgics*, books of pastoral poems; but by far his most lauded and important work is the*Aeneid*. Considered one of the great epics of all time, the*Aeneid*, published posthumously and unfinished, tells of the adventures of the Trojan Aeneas and how he went on to found Rome after the Trojan War.

Vivaldi, Antonio, *b. Venice, 1678; d. 1741.* **Composer and violinist of the Baroque period.** The son of a violinist, Vivaldi was ordained as a priest (1703) but his love of life and music brought him into conflict with church leaders so he frequently traveled throughout Europe. A contemporary of J. S. Bach, he was known primarily for his string concertos, but recent scholarship shows he wrote over 45 operas, (16 survive) 73 sonatas, 33 cantatas—nearly 800 works in all. Notable works include Op. 3, *L'Estro Armonico*, 12 concertos for various instruments (1711); Op. 4, *La Stravaganza*, 12 violin concertos (1714); Op. 8, *Il cimento dell'Armonia e Dell'inventione*, 12 violin concertos, the first four (E, G minor, F, and F minor) known as *The Four Seasons* (1725); Op. 10, six flute concertos (1728); and *Gloria* in D.

Volta, Alessandro, *b. Como, Italy, 1745; d. 1827.* **Physicist.** Volta is remembered for his invention in 1799 of the electric battery, which used a chemical reaction to produce the first electric current—previously only static electricity had been known. About 25 years earlier, Volta had also perfected the electrophorus, a device still used today for creating a large amounts of static electricity. In 1778 he became the first to recognize methane, the gas released from marshes. The "volt" measure of electric potential is named for him.

Voltaire, (Francois Marie Arouet de), *b. Paris, 1694; d. 1778.* **Philosopher and author.** Voltaire was one of the leading figures of the Enlightenment. He began writing in earnest while in prison in 1717 for remarks about the regent actually made by someone else. Once more unjustly imprisoned and he was banished to England in 1726, where he learned to admire English liberalism and in *Letters Concerning the English Nation* (1733) helped bring English philosophy and science to the French Enlightenment. A stay at the court of Frederick II in Prussia (1749–53) was discordant, and he returned to live near Geneva. He wrote *Philosophical Dictionary* (1764) and many plays and histories and polemical writings. His most widely read work today is his satirical novel *Candide* (1759).

Wagner, Richard, *b. Leipzig, 1813; d. 1883.* **Composer, conductor, poet, and author.** He is one of the key figures in the history of music particularly in opera which he elevated to epic proportions through the use of larger orchestras, more prominent instrumental passages, "endless melody"—eliminating arias—and organically conceived, through-composed structures. Later composers, including Richard Strauss and Gustav Mahler, regarded his music as the source of their own. His writings on music and drama have remained influential while his virulent anti-semitic screeds have permanently damaged him. Notable musical works include *Der fliegende Holländer* (The Flying Dutchman) (1841); *Tannhauser* (1844) *Tristan und Isolde* (1857–9); *Die Meistersinger von Nürnberg* (The Mastersingers of Nuremberg) (1862–7); *Siegfried Idyll* (1870); *Parsifal* (1878–82); and the fifteen-hour opera cycle *Der Ring des Nibelungen* (The Nibelung's Ring): *Das Rheingold* (The Rhine Gold) (1853–4), *Die Walküre* (The Valkyrie) (1854–6), *Siegfried* (1856–7), and *Götterdämmerung* (Twilight of the Gods) (1869–74).

Walcott, Derek, *b. St. Lucia, 1930.* **Poet and playwright.** Although his poetry focuses on themes from his native Caribbean, Walcott's body of work surpasses the merely regional and has earned worldwide acclaim, including the Nobel Prize for Literature in 1992. His volumes include *In a Green Night* (1962) and *Omeros* (1990), an epic poem that melds Homeric legend and Caribbean folklore. A background and lifelong interest in painting also influenced his poetry. In addition, he has written a number of plays.

Walesa, Lech, *b. Popowo, Poland, 1943.* **Trade union activist and president of Poland.** An electrician in the Gdansk shipyards, Walesa was fired in 1976 for antigovernment union activities. But in 1980, as massive strikes paralyzed Poland, Walesa returned to lead the protests and form Solidarity, a coalition of workers' groups. The communist government outlawed Solidarity and imposed martial law in 1981. Walesa was harrassed by Poland's secret police for years, even after winning the 1983 Nobel Peace Prize. In 1989, the Communist Party allowed parliamentary elections; Solidarity candidates triumphed and Walesa became Poland's first non-communist president. He was defeated in a reelection bid in 1995.

Warhol, Andy (Andrew Warhola), *b. Pittsburgh, Pa., 1928; d. 1987.* **Painter, sculptor, illustrator.** After a career as a commercial artist, Warhol began painting symbols and scenes borrowed from popular culture and became a main figure in the Pop Art movement. His images of consumer goods, ads, newspaper headlines, and famous faces are among the best-known pieces of American art. Such works include *Gold Marilyn Monroe* (1962) and *Campbell's Soup Cans* (1962). Warhol made himself a prominent public persona, enlisting the help of a studio of assistants known as the Factory.

Warren, Earl, *b. Los Angeles, 1891; d. 1974.* **Politician and jurist.** As attorney general of California (1938–1942) and as governor (1942–1953) Warren championed clean government but also supported the internment of Japanese-Americans after the attack on Pearl Harbor. In 1953 President Dwight D. Eisenhower appointed him chief justice of the Supreme Court; during his tenure the court rendered decisions of far-reaching importance, including *Brown v. Board of Education of Topeka* (1954), which outlawed segregated schools. Other decisions upheld the rights of the accused, legislative apportionment, voting rights, and freedom of the press. He headed the commission on the assassination of President John F. Kennedy (1963) and retired in 1969.

Warren, Robert Penn, *b. Guthrie, Ky., 1905; d. 1989.* **Novelist and poet.** Warren distinguished himself as a novelist, poet, and critic in a career largely spent in academia. During his teaching career, he cowrote two influential textbooks, *Understanding Poetry* (1938) and *Understanding Fiction* (1943). Warren won the Pulitzer prize in fiction for *All the King's Men* (1947), a work loosely based on the life of Louisiana's governor Huey Long. Later, he captured two Pulitzer Prizes in poetry for *Promises* (1958) and *Now and Then* (1979).

Washington, Booker T., *b. Franklin County, Va., 1856; d. 1915.* **Educator and leader.** Born into slavery, Washington was a prominent figure in black America until his death. He is best known for his administration of the Tuskegee Institute in Tuskegee, Ala., where he developed an educational system for blacks that focused on the development of practical industrial skills. Washington served as an adviser on African-American issues to two presidents, and his autobiography, *Up from Slavery* (1901), was a best seller.

Washington, George, *b. Westmoreland County, Va., 1732; d. 1799.* **First U.S. president, 1789–97.** Washington first joined the Virginia militia in 1753 and fought in the French and Indian War; in 1775 he was appointed by the Continental Congress to command the Continental Army, and he prevailed over the British. Washington retired to his Mount Vernon estate but later presided over the Constitutional Convention in Philadelphia in 1787, which framed the presidency with him in mind. His first act as president was to urge adoption of the Bill of Rights; other notable achievements included quelling the Whiskey Rebellion, bolstering the treasury with a national bank, settling Jay's Treaty of commerce with Britain, and maintaining neutrality in the French Revolution.

Watson, James Dewey, *b. Chicago, 1928.* **American molecular biologist.** Watson and Francis Harry Compton Crick at Cambridge University discovered the structure of deoxyribonucleic acid, DNA, which carries genetic information in living organisms. Their paper of 1953 described the double-helix structure of DNA and the coding system within it. Crick and Watson, together with Maurice Wilkins, were awarded the Nobel Prize in Physiology or Medicine in 1962. Watson published his personal memoir, *The Double Helix*, in 1968.

Watt, James, *b. Greenock, Scotland, 1736; d. 1819.* **Scottish inventor.** Working on a model of Thomas Newcomen's steam engine, Watt produced a series of inventions that vastly improved the efficiency and range of applications of the steam engine. In 1781 he patented a rotary engine that could power factories and ships, and the critical new mode of transportation, the railroad. Watt's design for the steam engine was major factor in the transformation of industry in the Industrial Revolution.

Waugh, Evelyn, *b. Hampstead, England, 1903; d. 1966.* **Novelist.** During his early career, Waugh, a professed reactionary and a convert to Catholicism, specialized in tearing apart contemporary society with razor-sharp comic wit, clever use of irony, and stylish prose. His novels include *Decline and Fall* (1928), *A Handful of Dust* (1934), *Brideshead Revisited* (1945), *The Loved One* (1948) and a World War II trilogy, *Men at Arms* (1952), *Officers and Gentlemen* (1955), and *Unconditional Surrender* (1961). Waugh also wrote travel books, two biographies; and his own autobiography, *A Little Learning* (1964).

Wayne, John (Marion Michael Morrison), *b. 1907, Winterset, Iowa; d. 1979.* **Movie actor.** "The Duke" projected an enduring image of tough survival from westerns of the 1930's to the Vietnam era and beyond. His many roles as cowboys and soldiers—notably in such films as *Stagecoach* (1939), *Fort Apache,* and *Red River* (both 1948), and *The Searchers* (1956)—set his swaggering image. Criticized by some, praised by others for his right-wing politics, he won sympathy fighting cancer and finally won an Oscar for *True Grit* (1969).

Weber, Max, *b. Erfurt, Germany, 1864; d. 1930.* **Economist and social historian.** Weber rejected the rigid economic determinism of Karl Marx in his famous book *The Protestant Ethic and the Spirit of Capitalism* (1904–05), and argued for the importance of religious values, ethical principles, and charismatic leaders in shaping society. He maintained that the Protestant work ethic played a major role in the rise of Western capitalism. By contrast, in the three volumes of his series *Religions of the East* (1920–21), he sought to show that capitalism failed to develop in Eastern societies because of their religious and philosophical beliefs.

Webster, Daniel *b. Salisbury, N.H., 1782; d. 1852.* **Lawyer, orator, politician.** In 1812 Webster was elected to the House of Representatives from New Hampshire. He won fame as a lawyer in several important cases including *McCulloch v. Maryland*. In 1827 he became a senator from Massachusetts and later served as secretary of state under William Harrison and John Tyler. He was famous as an orator and for his rejoinder in a debate with a southerner advocating secession "Liberty and Union, now and forever, one and inseparable!"

Webster, Noah, *b. West Hartford, Conn., 1758; d. 1843.* **Lexicographer.** His *American Dictionary of the English Language* (1828) gave American English an equal footing with its British counterpart. He believed that rules of spelling, grammar, and punctuation should evolve as the spoken language changes, rather than hew to prescribed rules, and his books reflect that belief. His *American Spelling Book* (1783), known as the "Blue-Backed Speller," has never been out of print; its sales, estimated by some at more than 100 million, made Webster a rich man.

Weissmuller, Johnny, *b. Freidorf, Hungary (now Romania), 1904; d. 1984.* **American swimmer and actor.** Raised in Chicago, he was the first Olympic swimmer to win five gold medals, taking three at the 1924 games and two at the 1928 games, all in the freestyle. He also won 52 U.S. national championships and set 67 world records in 10 years of high-level competition. Weissmuller's career as an actor was highlighted by the title role in 12 *Tarzan* movies from 1932 to 1948.

Welles, Orson (George), *b. Kenosha, Wis., 1915; d. 1985.* **Actor, screenwriter, director.** Originally a stage actor and director, he gained notoriety with a radio broadcast of "War of the Worlds" in 1938 that frightened many listeners. Welles signed with RKO Studios in 1940, creating his first feature film, *Citizen Kane* (1941) which stretched the boundaries of the classic narrative style with his inventive narrative structure and deep-focus photography. The box-office failure of *Kane* and *The Magnificent Ambersons* (1942) resulted in his dismissal from RKO. Though stylish and inventive, his subsequent films suffered from studio interference, as with *The Lady from Shanghai* (1948) and *Touch of Evil* (1959); or from lack of sufficient funds, as with *Othello* (1952).

Wellesley, Arthur, First Duke of Wellington, *b. Dublin, Ireland, 1769: d. 1852.* **British army commander and politician.** Nicknamed the "Iron Duke," Wellington first earned a military reputation in India. In 1808, he was sent to Portugal. He fought the French throughout the Iberian Peninsula until 1814. Among his most important victories were Talavera in 1809 and Salamanca in 1812. In 1815, he defeated Napoleon at Waterloo, in modern Belgium. He entered politics, serving as prime minister from 1828 to 1830. Although a Tory, he pragmatically supported both Catholic emancipation (1829) and parliamentary reform (1832).

Wells, H. G., *b. Bromley, England, 1866; d. 1946.* **Novelist and historian.** One of the fathers of science fiction, Wells popularized the genre with such works as *The Time Machine* (1895), *The Invisible Man* (1897), and *The War of the Worlds* (1898). In other books, he described how humans might travel to the moon and predicted the calamitous possibilities of the airplane. Later in his career, Wells turned to social criticism—particularly of the

Victorian era—and nonfiction, including *The Outline of History* (1920) and *The Science of Life* (1929).

Welty, Eudora, *b. Jackson, Miss., 1909; d. 2001.* **Novelist and short-story writer.** A photographer for the WPA before turning to fiction, Welty is one of the great Southern regional writers. Her work focused on Mississippi, where she spent almost her entire life. Among her short-story collections is *A Curtain of Green* (1941), which includes, "Why I Live at the PO." Her novels include *Delta Wedding* (1946) and *The Optimist's Daughter* (1972), which won the Pulitzer Prize.

West, Mae, *b. Brooklyn, N.Y., 1892; d. 1980.* **Stage and movie star.** Like tiny Shirley Temple, buxom, 40-year-old Mae West sashayed into movies and helped save her studio in the financially challenged 1930's. She grew up in vaudeville and went on to the theater as the author and star of *Sex* and *Diamond Lil* in the 1920's. Hollywood called and she answered with comic innuendo, tilted smiles, and her trademark swinging gait, making America laugh at sex. Notable films include *She Done Him Wrong* (1933) with Cary Grant, *Klondike Annie* (1936), and *My Little Chickadee* (*1939*) with W.C. Fields.

Wharton, Edith, *b. New York City, New York, 1862; d. 1937.* **Novelist and short-story writer.** Born into a well-to-do family of the leisure class, Wharton turned her penetrating eye toward high society in two of her best-known works, *The House of Mirth* (1905) and *The Age of Innocence* (1920), for which she won the Pulitzer Prize. Her popular novel *Ethan Frome* appeared in 1911. A prolific writer of novels and short stories, Wharton was widely honored during her lifetime, and she now stands as one of the foremost novelists in American literature.

Whistler, James (Abbot) McNeill, *b. Lowell, Mass., 1834; d. 1903.* **American painter, printmaker, designer, and active in England and France.** Inspired by the realism of Courbet and Manet, and by Japonisme, Whistler became a member of the Aesthetic Movement. He used musical terms such as *symphony* in the titles of his work, emphasizing the abstract features of their compositions rather than their subjects. His most famous painting is *Arrangement in Grey* and *Black No. 1: Portrait of the Artist's Mother* (1872). When the critic John Ruskin insulted his work in 1877, Whistler famously sued him for libel.

Whitman, Walt, *b. West Hills, Long Island, N.Y., 1819; d. 1892.* **Poet.** Whitman is widely considered the greatest American poet. He grew up in Brooklyn, where he worked for several newspapers as a reporter and editor, and where he published *Leaves of Grass* (1855). In theme (the poet as the embodiment of common humanity), form ("free verse," without rhyme or fixed meter), and content (vivid scenes, depicting nudity and evoking sexuality), it broke new ground, and it became one of American literature's most influential works. Whitman continually expanded it, publishing eight more editions through 1892. His *Drum-Taps* and *Sequel to Drum-Taps* (1865) reflect his service as a Civil War army nurse. His final book of poetry was *November Boughs* (1888), his principal prose works are *Democratic Vistas* (1871) and *Specimen Days* (1881).

Whitney, Eli, *b. Westboro, Mass., 1765; d. 1825.* **Inventor and manufacturer.** Whitney is famous for his invention of the cotton gin (1793), a hand-cranked engine (or "gin") that separates cotton fibers from seeds, increasing the output of a worker 50-fold. His introduction of special machines and interchangeable parts for his musket factory (1798), however, was as important to American industry as the cotton gin. He also developed the milling machine, a modified lathe that turns out irregularly shaped parts.

Wilde, Oscar, *b. Dublin, 1854; d. 1900.* **Playwright, poet, novelist.** Known in London as a great dandy and wit, Wilde published a book of poems in 1881 and, in 1891, the novel *The Picture of Dorian Gray*, concerning a young man whose pursuit of beauty leads to corruption. His most successful achievements were his plays, including *Salome* (1893), *Lady Windemere's Fan* (1892), *An Ideal Husband* (1895), and the enormously witty comedy of manners *The Importance of Being Earnest* (1895). He lost a libel suit he had filed in response to a charge of homosexual behavior, and served two years in prison. Out of this experience he wrote the poem *Ballad of Reading Gaol* (1898) and the posthumously published memoir-apology *De Profundis*.

Wilder, Billy (Samuel Wilder), *b. Vienna, Austria, 1906; d. 2002.* **Screenwriter, director, producer.** Famous for his cynical wit, Wilder was a master at creating morally flawed characters who spoke in literate dialogue. He began as a screenwriter, partnering with Charles Brackett in 1938. Their collaboration resulted in such hits as *Ninotchka* (1939) and *Ball of Fire* (1942). In 1942 he directed his first film, *The Major and the Minor*, which was followed by *Double Indemnity* (1944) and *The Lost Weekend*

(1945). The 1950's proved to be Wilder's most productive period; among his films were *Sunset Boulevard* (1950), *The Seven Year Itch* (1955), and *Some Like It Hot* (1959).

Wilder, Thornton, *b. Madison, Wis., 1897; d. 1975.* **Playwright, and novelist.** A writer of diverse talents, Wilder won three Pulitzer prizes, one for his novel *The Bridge of San Luis Rey* (1927), and two in drama, for *Our Town* (1938) and *The Skin of Our Teeth* (1942). In *Our Town,* Wilder depicted the lives of the citizens of Grover's Corners, New Hampshire, a fictional town represented onstage by a minimalist set. The play, still a popular production, focuses on the theme that we should savor each moment of our lives.

William III, (William of Orange) *b. The Hague, Holland, 1650; d. 1702.* **King of England and stadtholder of the Netherlands.** Son of William II, prince of Orange and stadtholder (chief magistrate) of the Netherlands, William married Mary, eldest daughter of the future King James II of England, in 1677. Fearful of the growth of Roman Catholic power under James II, his opponents secretly invited William to invade England in 1688, leading to the bloodless Glorious Revolution, and William's proclamation by Parliament to the monarchy together with his wife in 1689. In 1690 he defeated Irish supporters of James; thereafter he opposed the territorial ambitions of Louis XIV of France.

William the Conqueror (William I), *b. Falaise, France, ca. 1028; d. 1087.* In 1035, William became duke of Normandy. Edward the Confessor, king of England and William's cousin, died childless in 1066, and William sailed for England, claiming that Edward had named him as heir. At the battle of Hastings in the same year, William defeated the Anglo-Saxons under Harold Godwineson and was crowned king. The rest of his life involved a series of campaigns both in England and on the continent to bolster his rule. His most famous administrative accomplishment was the compilation of an economic census of England known as the Domesday Book.

Williams, Ted (Theodore), *b. San Diego, Calif., 1918; d. 2002.* **Baseball player.** Nicknamed the "Splendid Splinter" and "The Kid," Ted Williams was baseball's most feared hitter during his 19-year career with the Boston Red Sox. Despite losing nearly five seasons of his prime to military service, which he performed with distinction as a Marine fighter pilot, Williams earned six American League batting titles, two M.V.P. awards (1946, 1949), and two Triple Crowns (1942, 1947). He compiled a .344 lifetime batting average, .483 on-base percentage (the highest ever), and 521 home runs. He is the last player to bat .400 for a full season, finishing at .406 in 1941.

Williams, Tennessee (Thomas Lanier), *b. Columbus, Miss., 1911; d. 1983.* **Playwright.** In plays that explore the clash of a deluded, romantic vision of the world with the world's harsh reality and show broken characters yearning for their former grandeur, Williams created a vision of the American South as a place fraught with an undercurrent of sex and violence, of a once genteel society now in a state of ruin. Williams's first commercial success was *The Glass Menagerie* (1944); *Summer and Smoke* (1948), *The Rose Tatoo* (1950), and *Camino Real* (1953) are other well-known works. He later won the Pulitzer Prize for *A Streetcar Named Desire* (1947), and *Cat on a Hot Tin Roof* (1955).

Williams, William Carlos, *b. Rutherford, N. J., 1883; d. 1963.* **Poet.** A poet who also practiced medicine throughout his adult life, Williams is known for extreme simplicity and naturalism of style, particularly in his early work, exemplified by the poem "Red Wheelbarrow" (1923) and "This is Just to Say" (1934). In his later career, Williams used his poetry to critique the world. *Paterson* (5 vols., 1946–58), the great poem of his later years, looks at the complexity of the city as a metaphor for the complexity of man.

Wilson, Woodrow, *b. Staunton, Va., 1856; d. 1924.* **Twenty-eighth U.S. president, 1913–21.** Thomas Woodrow Wilson attracted the attention of Democratic bosses after he was elected president of Princeton in 1902, and they persuaded him to run for governor of New Jersey in 1910. A strong progressive, Wilson won easily—and then turned on party bosses by sponsoring antimachine reforms. He won the presidency for the Democrats in 1912, after Taft and Roosevelt split the Republican vote. Wilson remained neutral on the war in Europe until Germany spurned his attempts at mediation and resumed attacks on Allied shipping. In April 1917, Congress declared war at Wilson's behest; after the armistice in November 1918, Wilson became the first president to visit Europe when he attended the Paris peace conference that produced the Versailles Treaty. Wilson's dream of "peace without vengeance" was frustrated at Versailles, where he compromised away his Fourteen Points to obtain the League of Nations for collective security. In October 1919 he suffered a paralytic stroke; Wilson's second wife, Edith

Bolling Galt, shielded the disabled president from the press and politicians until the end of his term in 1921.

Winthrop, John, *b. Edwardstone, England, 1588; d. 1649.* **Historian and first governor of Massachusetts.** In 1629 the Massachusetts Bay Company appointed Winthrop governor to settle the colony. He governed under the patent granted to the company, but disputes arose frequently over powers he claimed for himself and a small inner circle and those claimed by the settlers. He served four terms (1629–34, 1637–40, 1642–44, 1646–49) and is generally credited with creating the institutions that ensured the colony's survival. His journal, published as *History of New England 1630–49* (1825–26), is an important document of Puritanism in early America.

Wittgenstein, Ludwig, *b. Vienna, 1889; d. 1951.* **Philosopher.** He argued in *Tractatus Logico-Philosophicus* (1921) that language and thought act as pictures of the real world, and that to understand any sentence one must understand the relationship of its components to each other and to the real. There are, however, things beyond language, the unsayable, and here Wittgenstein allowed for the possibility of a metaphysics, unlike the *logical positivism* movement. His later work in Cambridge, England, influenced "ordinary-language" philosophy, which holds that philosophical questions arise from the ambiguities of language.

Woods, Tiger (Eldrick Woods), *b. Cypress, Calif., 1975.* **Golfer.** Tiger Woods established himself as the game's top player and one of the all-time greats while still in his twenties. A child prodigy, Woods was the first golfer to win three consecutive U.S. Amateur titles (1994–96). After attending Stanford, he turned pro in 1996 and the following year became the youngest player ever to win the Masters. Tiger claimed 34 P.G.A. victories—including eight majors—through 2002. That year he also won his unprecedented fourth straight P.G.A. Player of the Year award.

Woolf, Virginia, *b. London, 1882, d. 1941.* **Novelist.** The daughter of the critic and philosopher Leslie Stephen, Virginia Woolf and her husband, Leonard, were the hosts of the Bloomsbury Group of writers and artists. Like James Joyce, she developed the stream-of-consciousness technique, taking it in a more lyrical direction, and emphasizing neither plot nor character but experience. From *Jacob's Room* (1922) through *Mrs. Dalloway*, (1925), *To the Lighthouse* (1927), and *The Waves* (1931), this style became freer and more experimental as she examined time and change pressing upon personal development and human relationships. A victim of recurring mental traumas, Woolf drowned herself at age 59.

Wordsworth, William, *b. Cockermouth, Cumberland, England, 1770; d. 1850.* **Poet.** Wordsworth grew up in the English Lake District, the beauty of which inspired his poetic career. A trip to France in 1790 fired him with democratic sentiment and helped influence a radically new direction in English poetry, charted with Samuel Taylor Coleridge in *Lyrical Ballads* (1798). With simple diction, Wordsworth described humble people and celebrated nature. It included his great picturesque and meditative poem "Tintern Abbey." Within a decade Wordsworth had done most of his best work, including the extended *The Ruined Cottage* (1799) and *Michael* (1800), "Ode: Intimations of Immortality" (1807), and many well-known lyrics and sonnets. His 14-book autobiographical poem, *The Prelude*, considered his masterpiece, was completed by 1805 but not published until after his death.

Wren, Christopher, *b. East Knoyle, England, 1632; d. 1723.* **Architect and scientist of the Renaissance.** His early scientific studies were admired by Isaac Newton but his fame rests on his later prolific work as an architect. The great fire of London in 1666 gave him the opportunity to create ingeniously differing designs for many parish churches as well as Saint Paul's cathedral (1675–1710), with its monumental western facade, splendid dome, and vaulted interior. His important works include the Naval Hospital in Greenwich (1682–89); the Library at Trinity College (1676–84), Cambridge; and Marlborough House (1709–11), London.

Wright, Frank Lloyd , *b. Richland Center, Wisc., 1867; d. 1959.* **American architect.** Considered by many the greatest architect of the 20th century, Wright's works have had a profound influence on its architecture. After serving an apprenticeship with Louis Sullivan, he began developing his distinctive "prairie houses" with their open plans arranged around large central fireplaces; they included the Robie House (1906–10) in Chicago. Wright also produced two major large works: Unity Temple (1904) in Oak Park, and the Larkin Company Administration Building (1903–06, since demolished) in Buffalo. He lived almost to 92 and designed some of his greatest works after age

60, including Fallingwater (1936–38) in Mill Run, Pennsylvania; and the Johnson Wax Building (1936–37) in Racine, Wisconsin. But his Usonian houses, designed in the 1930's as affordable for middle-class owners, were perhaps his most important achievement.

Wright, Richard, *b. Natchez, Miss., 1908; d. 1960.* **American novelist and short-story writer.** The grandson of slaves, Wright was born into poverty in rural Mississippi. His first collection of short stories, *Uncle Tom's Children* (1938), addressed the impossibility of living in a racist world. *Native Son* (1940), his greatest work, follows the life of a young African-American man, Bigger Thomas, who, after the accidental killing of a white girl, must flee through a hostile world. Among Wright's other works are the existential novel *The Outsider* (1953) and the memoir *Black Boy* (1945). A member of the Communist Party from 1932 to 1944, Wright lived as an expatriate in Paris from the end of World War II until his death.

Wright, Wilbur, *b. Millville, Ind., 1867; d. 1912,* and **Orville Wright,** *b. Dayton, Ohio, 1871; d. 1948.* **American inventors and aviation pioneers.** The Wrights were bicycle mechanics who used the tools and materials in their Dayton shop for their early aeronautic constructions. They began the study of aeronautics in 1886 and experimented with gliders at Kitty Hawk, N.C., in 1900, 1901, and 1902. On December 17, 1903, at Kitty Hawk they flew four times in an engine-powered craft and became the first ever to develop and fly an airplane in sustained and controlled flight. They continued to advance their inventions, developing biplanes and forming a company that, after Wilbur's death, Orville sold in 1915.

Yeats, William Butler, *b. Dublin, 1865; d. 1939.* **Poet and playwright.** Yeats is regarded as the 20th century's greatest English-language poet. His early poetry—e.g., "The Stolen Child" (1889), and "The Lake Isle of Innisfree" (1893)—has a dreamy, musical quality derived partly from Irish folklore. In midlife he embraced the Irish nationalist cause in "Easter 1916" (1921), and "Meditations in Time of Civil War" (1928) and helped establish the Irish National Theater. Yeats incorporated a complex symbolic spiritual system into his mature poetry—as in "The Tower" (1928) and "Byzantium" (1933)—yet his work is almost always approachable, rooted in vivid imagery and physical reality, and phrased with startling beauty.

Xerxes I (The Great) *b. ca. 519 B.C.; d. 465 B.C.* **King of Persia (486–465 B.C.).** Xerxes was the Son of Darius I and maternal grandson of Cyrus the Great. His most famous exploit was his invasion of Greece in the Persian wars by building a bridge of ships over the Hellespont. In 480 B.C. Xerxes's forces defeated the famous Spartan Leonidas and his 300 legendary soldiers at Thermopylae, and went on to invade Athens. When his naval fleet was defeated at Salamis, Xerxes retired and was subsequently killed by his own men.

Yeltsin, Boris, *b. 1931, Sverdlovsk, Russia.* **Russian politician.** Yeltsin joined the Communist Party in 1960 and worked his way through the ranks to become first secretary of the Communist Party in Moscow in 1985. Ousted in 1987 for criticizing the slow pace of Gorbachev's reforms, in 1989 he was elected to the Supreme Soviet. When the Russian Soviet Federated Socialist Republic became independent, he was elected president in June 1991. Two months later, he gained worldwide acclaim for facing down an attempted coup by the army. His tenure as president was less inspired, and he resigned his post in 1999.

Young, Brigham, *b. Whitingham, Vt., 1801; d. 1877.* **American religious leader.** In 1832 Young converted to the Church of Jesus Christ of Latter-Day Saints (Mormons), founded by Joseph Smith. To escape religious persecution, he moved with Smith and their followers from Ohio first to Missouri and later to Illinois. After Smith was imprisoned and murdered in 1844, Young organized a migration west and settled in the Salt Lake Valley in Utah in 1847. From then until his death he worked to build a society based on Mormon principles that succeeded in spite of hostility from the federal government and others.

Young, Cy (Denton True Young), *b. Gilmore, Ohio., 1867; d. 1955.* **Baseball player.** Professional baseball's first major star, Cy Young remains the all-time statistical leader in several major pitching categories: wins (511), losses (316), complete games (749), and innings (7,356). In a 22-year career (1890–1911), the right-hander topped 30 wins five times and 20 wins 15 times. He pitched three no-hitters, one of them a perfect game. In 1903, Young won two games for Boston in the first modern World Series. Today, the annual award given to the most outstanding pitcher in each league is named in his honor.

Zapata, Emiliano, *b. Anenecuilco, Mexico, 1879; d. 1919.* **Mexican revolutionary and national hero.** Zapata campaigned for the restoration of village lands confiscated by *hacendados*, with the slogan "Tierra y libertad." In 1910, he played an important role in the fight against the dictator Porfirio Diaz; after the revolution, Zapata became disillusioned with Francisco Madero's land reforms and continued his guerrilla fight for land and liberty. His Plan of Ayala called for seizure of foreign-owned land and confiscation of one-third of all land held by "friendly" *hacendados*. In 1919, he was killed in a trap perpetrated by one of Venustiano Carranza's generals.

Zátopek, Emil, *b. Koprivinice, Czechoslovakia, 1922; d. 2000.* **Runner.** The Czech long-distance runner accomplished one of the most remarkable feats in Olympic history by winning the 5,000 m, 10,000 m, and marathon at the 1952 games in Helsinki. In his Olympic debut four years earlier, he won a gold medal in the 10,000 and a silver medal in the 5,000. Before ending his career in 1956, Zátopek had set 18 world records at nine different distances, including five in the 10,000.

Zhou Enlai, *b. Jiangsu Province, China, 1898; d. 1976.* **Statesman.** Zhou was born into a scholar-official family and had a privileged upbringing. He studied abroad in Japan and Europe, joining the Chinese Communist Party in France in 1922. His political, administrative, and diplomatic skills propelled his rapid rise in party ranks; he was careful always to be an ally, not a rival, of Mao Zedong. Zhou was elected to the Politburo in 1927, served as China's premier from the founding of the People's Republic in 1949 until his death, and was never demoted or purged. His was the reasonable face that Chinese communism showed to the outside world, so he played a large role in President Nixon's rapprochement with China in the early 1970's.

Zola, Emile, *b. Paris, 1840; d. 1902.* **Novelist.** Zola was the premier French writer in the naturalist movement, which presented life with scientific realism, focusing on mean physical, social, and psychological conditions. His first novel in this manner was *Therese Raquin* (1867). From 1871 to 1893 he composed a series of novels known as the "Rougon-Macquart Cycle," investigating lower-class and laboring-class conditions and revealing the effects of heredity as well as environment. The best-known of these is *Nana* (1880). In 1898 Zola famously wrote a public letter, known as "J'accuse" ("I accuse"), in which he indicted the French army leadership for anti-semitism in the Dreyfus affair.

Zoroaster (Persian: Zarathushtra), *b. Persia, ca. 628 B.C.; d. ca. 551 B.C.* **Religious teacher and prophet.** Founder of Zorastrianism, a religion with holy writings (*Avesta* = law) in old Iranian, akin to Vedic Sanskrit. Little is known of Zoroaster's life. He divided traditional Persian deities into the good (led by Ahura Mazdah), who will ultimately prevail, and the evil (led by Ahriman); individuals by their conduct help one or the other side and go to the realm of light or perdition accordingly.

INDEX

A

Aaron, Henry, 955
abacus, invention of, 390
Abbasid Dynasty, 222, 224
abbreviations, 793–95
Abdul-Jabbar, Kareem, 687, 690, 955
Abelard, Pierre, 955
Aborigine, 243
Abraham, 214
Abstract Expressionism, 101
Academy Awards, 883–89
  for Cinematography, 888–89
  for Foreign Language Film, 888
  origins of, 25
Achaeans, 214
Acheson, Dean Gooderham, 955
Achilles, 471
Acmeists (in poetry), 343
acronyms, 794
Acropolis, 4
actinium, 581
Adam, James, 8
Adam, Robert, 9
Adams, Ansel, 114,955
Adams, Harriet Stratemeyer, 371
Adams, Henry, 955
Adams, John, 51, 276, 955–56
Adams, John Quincy, 955
Adams, Samuel, 956
Addams, Jane, 956
Addison's disease, 446
Addison, Thomas, 439
adjectives, 769–70
  overuse, 782
  using correctly, 781–84
Adonis, 471
Adventist Churches, 501
adverbs, 770
  modifiers, misplaced, 782
  overuse, 782
  participles, dangling, 782
  placing correctly, 783–84
  using correctly, 781–84
advertising, history of, 151–54
Aegir, 481
Aegisthus, 471
Aeneas, 471
Aeneid, the, 339
Aeolus, 471
Aeschylus, 375, 956
aesthetics, 484
Afghanistan, 252, 813
Africa, 174–76, 210, 220, 222, 224–25, 232, 237, 241–42
  climate, 174–75
  economy, 175–76
  languages, 802
  people, 175
  physical features, 174
African-American Composers, 61
African Literature, 347–48
Africanus, Scipio, 254
Agamemnon, 471
Agave, 471
Agincourt, Battle of, 255
Aguinaldo, Emilio, 285
Aguirre, the Wrath of God, 32
AIDS, 443–45
air conditioning, development of, 642
aircraft, development of, 639
Ajax, 471
Akbar, 230, 956
Akhenaten, 213, 956
Akkadian Empire, 212
Aksumite, 220
Al-Khwarizmi, Muhammad, 390
Al-Qaeda, 252
Ala-ud-din, 224
Alabama (U.S. State), 861
Alamo, 278
Alaska (U.S. State), 861
Alatai, 231
Albania, 813
Albee, Edward, 383, 956
Albertus Magnus, 956
Albinoni, Tomaso, 46
Albuquerque, New Mexico (U.S. City), 876
Alcibiades, 253
Alcott, Louisa May, 361
Alderotti, V, 437
Aldiss, Brian, 374
Aldrin, Buzz, 957
Alexander II, 261
Alexander the Great, 217, 470, 957
Alfred the Great, 222
algebra, 392
Algeria, 813
Ali, Muhammad, 748, 757, 957
Alien and Sedition Acts, 276
Allbutt, Thomas, 439
allemande, 55
Allen, Ethan, 258
Allen, Woody, 28, 957
allergies, 444–45
Altdorfer, Albrecht, 93
Altman, Robert, 28
aluminum, 581
Alzheimer's disease, 445
Ambrose (Saint), 957
Amel, Dominique, 438
Amenhotep IV, 213
American Anti-Slavery Society, 278
American Bandstand, 74
American Literature, 358–68
American Revolution, 236, 258–60
American Society for the Promotion of Temperance, 278
American Stock Exchange, establishment of, 164
American System of manufacturing, 141
americium, 581
Amiens, 268
Amiens cathedral, 7
Amis, Kingsley, 358
Amis, Martin, 358
amniocentesis, 462
Amon, 480
amphitrite, 471
Amundsen, Roald, 957
amyotrophic lateral sclerosis (ALS), 445
An, 479
An Lushan, 223
Anabaptist Churches, 501
analytic geometry, 392
anatomy, comparative, 566
Anawrahta, 225
Anaxagoras, 485
Anaximander, 485
Anaximenes, 485
Anchises, 471
Andersen, Hans Christian, 957
Anderson, Marian, 957–58
Anderson, Sherwood, 363, 958
Andorra, 813–14
Andromeda, 471
Angelico, Fra, 92, 958
Angelou, Maya, 365, 958
Angiography, 462
angles, 218
Angola, 814
Angry Young Men, 32, 382
animal foods, 936–37
Annam, 223, 231, 239, 243
anorexia nervosa, 629
Anschluss, 245
Anselm of Canterbury, Saint, 489
Antarctica, 176–77
  climate, 176
  people, 176–77
  physical features, 176
anthem, 53
Anthemios of Tralles, 6
Anthony, Susan B., 958
anthrax, 445
anthropic principle, 623
antianxiety drugs, 632
antiatoms, 618
antidepressant drugs, 632
Antietam, Battle of, 262
Antigone, 472
Antigonus, 217
Antigua, 814
antimanic drugs, 632
antimony, 581
Antiope, 472
antiparticles, 617
Antonioni, Michelangelo, 34
Anubis, 480
anxiety, 628
anxiety disorders, 458
Aphrodite, 470
Apis, 480
Apollo, 470
Apollo Program, 252
apostrophes, 787
Apple Computing, development of, 652
apples, 926
Appomattox Courthouse, 265
Apsu, 479
aqueducts, Roman, 5
Aquinas, Thomas, 489, 958–59

Arabic (language), 804
Arachne, 472
Arafat, Yasir, 959
Archaean Eon, 596
Archilochus, 215
Archimedes, 959
architectural orders, 4
architecture, 2–16
  18th- and 19th- Century, 8–9
  African, 13
  American (Indigenous), 13–16
  Baroque, 8
  Buddhist, 12–13
  Christian and Byzantine, 5–6
  East Asian, 12
  Egyptian, 3
  glossary of terms, 14–16
  Gothic, 6–7
  Greek, 3–4
  history of, 2–12
  Islamic, 13
  Modern, 9–11
  Neolithic, 2
  Non-Western, 12–14
  Paleolithic, 2
  Renaissance, 7–8
  Roman, 4–5
  Romanesque, 6
  South Asian, 12
  Western Asian, 2–3
Arden, John, 382
Arecibo (telescope), 534
Ares, 470
Argentina, 814
Argon, 581
Argonne Forest, 268
Argus, 472
aria, 54
Ariadne, 472
arietta, 54
Ariosto, Ludovico, 376
Aristarchus, 530
Aristophanes, 375, 959
Aristotle, 40, 375, 487, 530, 548, 605–06
Arizona (U.S. State), 861–62
Arkansas (U.S. State), 862
Arledge, Roone, 419
Armenia, 814
Armstrong, Lance, 959
Armstrong, Louis, 69, 959
Armstrong, Neil, 252, 959
Army of the Potomac, 262
Arnaz, Desi, 413
Arnold, Benedict, 258, 260, 959
Arnold, Matthew, 352, 959–60
Arp, Hans (Jean), 100
Arrow War, 242
arsenic, 581
Art
  ancient, 88–91
  ancient Greek, 88–89
  ancient Mesopotamian, 88
  Baroque, 94–95
  Byzantine, 90
  Celtic, 90
  Egyptian, 88
  Etruscan, 89
  Gothic, 91–92
  history of, 88–103
  Impressionism, 98
  Islamic, 91
  Mannerism, 93
  Minimalism, 102
  Modernism, 99–101
  Neoclassicism, 95–97
  Orientalism, 96
  Pointillism, 98
  Post-Impressionism, 98
  Postmodernism, 102–03
  Realism, 97
  Renaissance, 92–93
  Rococo, 95
  Roman, 89–90
  Romanticism, 95–97
  Symbolism, 98–99
Artaud, Antonin, 382
Artemis, 470
arteries, 557
arthritis, 445
Arthur, Chester A., 960
Arts Theater Guild, 36
Aryans, 215
Arzner, Dorothy, 26
Asclepius, 472
Ashbery, John, 368
Ashcan School, 100
Asia, 177–79, 218, 224–25
  climate, 178
  economy, 178–79
  people, 178
  physical features, 177–78
Asia Minor, 213
Asimov, Isaac, 373
Asoka, 218
Asperger's disorder, 628
Assyrian Empire, 214
Assyrians, 214
Astaire, Fred, 960
astatine, 581
asteroids, 541
astronomical unit, 531
Astronomy
  ancient, 530
  glossary of terms, 545–46
  history of, 530–32
  in the Middle Ages, 530
  in Renaissance, 530–31
  in 17th and 18th Centuries, 531–32
  techniques of, 532–34
astrophysics, 611
Atalanta, 472
Atari 2600, 667
Ataturk, Kemal, 244, 960
Aten, 480
Athena, 470
Athens, 215, 253
atherosclerosis, 450–51
Atkins diet, 951
Atlanta, Georgia (U.S. City), 876
Atlantic Charter, 269
Atlas, 472
atmosphere, 595
atomic bomb, 246, 270
atomic clocks, 636
atomic structure, 579
attention deficit hyperactivity disorder (ADHD), 628
Attila, 960
Atum, 480
Aubrey, James T., 418
Auden, W.H., 354, 960
Auenbrugger, Leopold, 438
Augustine of Hippo, Saint, 489, 958
Augustus, 217, 960–61
Aurangzeb, 238
Aurelius, Emperor Marcus, 488
Aurelius, Marcus, 218
Austen, Jane, 355, 961
Austin, Stephen, 961
Austin, Texas (U.S. city), 876
Australia, 179–80, 243, 815
  climate, 179–80
  economy, 180, 815–17
  geography, 815–17
  government, 815–17
  people, 180, 815–17
  physical features, 179
Austria, 815
autism, 458
autistic disorder, 628
Auto Racing, 763–65
  Formula One, 763–65
  Indianapolis 500 winners, 766
  Indy Car, 764–65
  Le Mans, 765
  NASCAR, 763–65
  notable NASCAR drivers, 764–65
autoimmune diseases, 446
Averroës, 489
Avicenna, 489
avocado, 929
Awards and Prizes, 883–920
Azerbaijan, 815
Aztec Empire, 228

B

Babbage, Charles, 439
Babur, 226, 230
Babylonia
  Astronomy in, 530
Babylonian Empire, 212, 214
Bach, Johann Sebastian, 44, 46, 961
Bacon's Rebellion, 273
Bacon, Francis, 102, 490, 961
Baez, Joan, 68
Baha'i, 513
Bahamas, The, 815
Bahrain, 815–16
Baker v. Carr, 306
Baker, James Addison, 961
Balanchine, George, 18, 21, 961
Balboa, Vasco Núñez de, 961
Balder, 481
Baldwin, James, 365, 962
Balfour Declaration, 247
Balkans, 244
Ball, Lucille, 413, 962
Ballard, J.G., 374
ballet (dance), 17–18
ballet (music), 58–59
Ballinger-Pinchot controversy, 286
balloons, hot air, development of, 638
Baltimore, David, 962
Baltimore, Maryland, 876
Balzac, Honoré de, 341, 962
Bambaaataa, Afrika, 65
bananas, 927
Bang, Liu, 219
Bangladesh, 247, 816
Bank of the United States, 278
Banting, Frederick, 440
Baptist Churches, 501
Baraka, Amiri, 962
Barbados, 816
Barbuda, 814
Bardeen, John, 962
barium, 581–82
Barker, George, 354

barley, 925
Barnard, Christian, 962
Barnum, Phineas Taylor, 962
Barry, Capt. John, 259
Barrymore, Ethel, 963
Barrymore, Lionel, 23, 963
Bartók, Béla, 52
Barton, Clara, 963
Baruch, Bernard, 963
Baryshnikov, Mikhail, 963
Baseball, 672–85
  early scandals, 672–73
  glossary of terms, 684–85
  Hall of Fame, 676–83
  history of, 672–75
  rules of, 675
Basketball, 686–92
  college (men's), 687–88
  college (women's), 688–89
  glossary of terms, 691–92
  Hall of Fame, 693–96
  history of, 687–91
  professional, 689–91
  rules of, 686–87
baskets and cloth, development of, 633
Basquiat, Jean-Michel, 102
Bastet, 480
Bataan Death March, 269
Batista, Fulgencio, 249
Battle of the Bulge, 270
Battleship Potemkin, 33
Batu, 226
Baudelaire, Charles Pierre, 341, 963
Bauhaus, 10
Bay of Pigs, 249
Bayeux Tapestry, 91
beans, 929–30
Beard, James, 963
Beardsley, Aubrey, 963
Beaumont, Francis, 379
Beaumont, William, 439
Becket,Thomas á, 963–64
Beckett, Samuel, 342, 382, 964
Bede (the Venerable), 964
beef, 936–37
Beethoven, Ludwig van, 47–48, 964
beets, 930
Beg, Ulugh, 226
Begin, Menachem, 964
behavioral therapy, 632
behaviorism, 627
Behn, Aphra, 372
Beijerinck, Martinus, 439
Beijing Film Academy, 35
Belarus, 816
Belgium, 240, 816
Bell Telephone Company, 142
Bell, Alexander Graham, 142, 964
Bell, Charles, 439
Bellamy, Edward, 373, 964
Bellerophon, 472
Bellini, Giovanni, 92
Bellona, 472
Bellow, Saul, 964–65
Bely, Andrei, 343
Benedict (Saint), 221, 965
Benegal, Shyam, 35
Bengali, 803
Benin, 816–17
Benny, Jack, 965
Benso di Cavour, Camillo, 240
Bentham, Jeremy, 965
Benton, Thomas Hart, 965
Benz, Karl, 965
Beowulf, 348
Berg, Alban, 965
Bergman, Ingmar, 35, 965
Bergman, Ingrid, 965–66
Bergson, Henri, 493
Berkeley, George, 491
berkelium, 582
Berle, Milton, 413
Berlin Airlift, 248
Berlin Wall, 248, 251
Berlin, Irving, 62, 966
Berlioz, Hector, 49
Bernard, Claude, 439
Berners-Lee, Sir Tim, 654, 966
Bernini, Gianlorenzo, 94
Bernini, Giovanni, 8, 966
Bernstein, Elmer, 51
Bernstein, Leonard, 51, 63
Berra, Yogi, 966
Berry, Chuck, 74, 966
Bertolucci, Bernardo, 34
beryllium, 582
Betjeman, John, 354
Bettleheim, Bruno, 966
Bevin, Ernest, 966
Bhutan, 817
Bibles
  Books of, 520–28
  Hebrew, 519
  New Testament, 519
  Old Testament, 519
  Septuagint, 519
Bierstadt, Albert, 97
Big Bang, 545, 607
Bill of Rights, U.S., 327–31
Billy the Kid, 966
binge eating, 630
biochemistry, 566-67, 576
biodiversity, 571–76
biogeography, 567
Biology, 548–76
  cell, 552–56
  disciplines in, 548
  evolution, 565–67
  genetics, 567–70
  history of, 548–49
  human body, 556–65
biomes, 570
biophysics, 613
biopsy, 462–63
bipolar disorder, 458, 630
Bird, Larry, 690, 966–67
Birdseye, Clarence, 967
Birth of Venus, 92
Birth of a Nation, 23
Bismarck, Otto von, 240, 243, 265, 967
bismuth, 582
Bitzer, Billy, 23
Black Death, 228
Black Panthers, 250
Black, Hugo, 967
Blackstone, William, 296, 967
Blair, Anthony (Tony), 967
Blake, William, 96, 351, 967
Blakey, Art, 72
blank verse, 349
blood cells, red, 556–57
blood cells, white, 557, 558
blood tests, 463, 465–66
blood vessels, 557
blood, human, 556–57
blueberries, 927
bluegrass, 66–67
blues (music), 63–64
Board of Trade, 273
boats and ships, development of, 634–35
Boccaccio, Giovanni, 228, 339, 967
Boccioni, Umberto, 100
body mass index, 952
Boer War, 242
Bogart, Humphrey, 26, 967
Bogdanovich, Peter, 28
Bohr, Niels, 610, 968
bohrium, 582
Boleyn, Anne, 968
Bolivar, Simon, 241
Bolivia, 817
Böll, Heinrich, 342
Bollywood, 35
Bolsheviks, 244, 267
Bonaparte, Joseph, 241
Bonaparte, Napoleon, 236, 1035
Bonapartism, 240
bond funds, 167
Bonds, Barry, 674, 675, 968
bone density tests, 463
bone scan, 463
bones, human, 560
Boniface VIII, 226
Bonnard, Pierre, 99, 968
Bonnie and Clyde, 28
Book of Kells, 90
Boone, Daniel, 968
Boone, Pat, 74
Booth, John Wilkes, 968
Borden, Lizzie Andrew, 968
Borges, Jorge Luis, 968–69
Boromini, Francesco, 8
boron, 582
Bosch, Hieronymous, 969
Bosnia and Herzegovina, 817
bosons, 617
Boston Massacre, 275
Boston Tea Party, 275
Boston, Massachusetts, 876–77
Boswell, James, 969
Botswana, 817
Botticelli, Sandro, 92, 228, 969
Bougainville, Louis-Antoine, Comte de, 969
Bourke-White, Margaret, 969
bow and arrow, development of, 634
Boxer Rebellion, 243
boxing, 756–59
  history of, 756–57
  notable champions, 757–58
  olympic, 758–59
Boyle, Robert, 969
Boyle, T.C., 368
brackets (punctuation), 790–91
Brackett, Charles, 27
Bradbury, Ray, 374, 969
Bradford, William, 358
Bradstreet, Anne, 358, 969–70
Bragi, 481
Brahe, Tycho, 234, 531, 969–70
Brahm, Otto, 381
Brahmanas, 215
Brahms, Johannes, 49, 970
brain, human, 561, 562
Braine, John, 358
Bramante, Donato, 7
Brancusi, Constantin, 101, 970
Brandeis, Louis, 970
Brando, Marlon, 970
Braque, Georges, 100

Brazil, 37, 818
Brecht, Bertolt, 382, 970
Breen, Joseph, 25
Brennan, William, Jr., 970
Breton, André, 970
Bretton Woods Conference, 246
British Invasion, 75
Britten, Benjamin, 50
Broadway musicals, 62–63
Broca, Paul, 439
Bromine, 582
Brontë, Charlotte, 355, 970-71
Brontë, Emily, 355, 970-71
Bronze Age, 212, 213–16
Bronzino, Agnolo, 93
Brooke, Rupert, 353
Brooks, Gwendolyn, 971
Brooks, Mel, 28, 971
Brown v. Board of Education of Topeka, 289, 306
Brown, Charles Brockden, 359
Brown, James, 65
Brown, Jim, 971
Brown, John, 281, 971
Browning, Elizabeth Barrett, 352, 971
Browning, Robert, 352, 971
Brubeck, Dave, 72, 971
Bruckner, Anton, 49
Bruegel I, Pieter, 93, 971–72
Brunei, 818
Brunelleschi, Filippo, 92
Bryan, William Jennings, 284, 972
Bryant, William Cullen, 972
bubonic plague, 228
Buchanan, James, 972
Buck, Pearl, 972
Buddha, 218, 972
Buddhism, 219, 511–13
 belief and practice, 511
 history, 512–13
 Mahayana, 512
 schools and sects, 511–12
 scripture, 511
 Theravada, 511–12
 Vajrayana, 512
Budge, Don, 726
Buffalo Bill (William F. Cody), 972
Bulgaria, 818
Bulge, Battle of the, 270
bulimia nervosa, 629
Bull Moose Party, 286
Bull Run, Battle of, 262
Bunche, Ralph Johnson, 972
Bunraku, 239
Bunshaft, Gordon, 973
Buñuel, Luis, 34
Burger, Warren Earl, 973
Burgess, Anthony, 973
Burgoyne, General, 259
Burke, Edmund, 973
Burkina Faso, 818
Burma, 239, 247
Burns, Robert, 973
Burnside, Ambrose E., 263
Burr, Aaron, 973
Burroughs, Edgar Rice, 373, 973
Burroughs, William S., 365
Burstyn v. Wilson, 28
Burton, Richard, 973
Burundi, 818–19
Bush v. Gore, 308
Bush, George H. W., 291, 973–74
Bush, George W, 292, 974
Bush, Vannevar, 974
Business, 138–57
 brief history of, 138–54
 factory system, 139
 glossary of terms, 154–57
 industrialization in Europe, 139
 industrialization in U.S., 139–43
 marketing, birth of, 143–44
Butler, Samuel, 350
Butter, 938
Byrd, Richard, 974
Byrne, David, 78
Byron, George Gordon (Lord), 351, 974

C

cabbage, 930
Cabeza de Vaca, Alvar Núñez, 358
The Cabinet of Dr. Caligari, 31
Cabot, John, 232, 272
caccia, 54
cadmium, 582
Cadmus, 472
Caesar, Julius, 217, 339
Caesar, Sid, 413
Cage, John, 51
Cagney, James, 26, 974–75
Cahiers du cinema, 31
calcium, 582
calculus, 391–92
 and astronomy, 531
Calder, Alexander, 975
Calhoun, John Caldwell, 278, 280, 975
California (U.S. state), 862
californium, 582
Caligula, 975
Callas, Maria, 975
calories, time to burn off, 950
calotype, 105
Calvin, John, 233, 975
Calvino, Italo, 342
Calydonian boar, 472
Calypso, 472
Cambodia, 819
Cambrian period, 596
camera obscura, 104
Cameroon, 819
Camp David accords, 251
Campbell, Jr., John W., 373
Campin, Robert, 91
Camus, Albert, 342, 975
Canada, 819
Canals and locks, development of, 635
Cancer, 446–51
Cannes International Film festival, 35
Canova, Antonio, 95
cantata, 54
Canterbury cathedral, 7
Canterbury Tales, 349
Canton system, 242
Cantor, Georg, 975–76
canzona, 54
Cao Dai, 516
Cape Verde, 819–20
Capetian Dynasty, 222
capillaries, 557
capital letters, using, 799–800
capitalism, 120, 135
Capra, Frank, 26, 976
Caravaggio, Michelangelo Merisi da, 94, 976
carbohydrates, 576, 946
carbon, 582–83
Carboniferous period, 596
cardiovascular disease, 450–51
Carlyle, Thomas, 976
Carne, Marcel, 30
Carnegie, Andrew, 142, 976
Carolina, 273
Carolingian Empire, 221
Carothers, Wallace Hume, 976
Carracci, Annibale, 94
carrots, 930
Carter, Jimmy, 251, 291, 976
Carthage, 217
Cartier, Jacques, 976
Cartier-Bresson, Henri, 977
Carver, Raymond, 368
Cash, Johnny, 74, 977
Cassandra, 472
Cassatt, Mary (Stevenson), 98, 977
Cassini, Gian Domenico, 531, 977
Cassiopeia, 472
Castor, 472
Castro, Fidel, 249, 977
categorical imperative, 492
Cather, Willa, 977
Catherine II "the Great", 237, 977
cathode-ray tube, development of, 644–46
Catholicism
 Eastern, 499–500
 Roman Catholic Church, 499
 Roman Rite Churches, 500
Cato (the Younger), 977–78
Catullus, 339, 978
Cavalier Poets, 349–50
Cavendish, Henry, 975
cells (biology), 552–56
 division, 556
 homeostasis and enzymes, 555
 meiosis, 556
 mitosis, 556
 specialized structures, 555
 transport, 555–56
 types of, 556
Cenozoic era, 596
Centaur, 472
Central African Republic, 820
Cephalus, 472
ceramics and glass, development of, 633
Cerberus, 472
cereals and grains, 925–26
cerebellum, 561
cerebral palsy, 451
cerebrum, 561
cerium, 583
Cervantes (Saavedra), Miguel de, 978
Cervantes, Miguel de, 234, 340
cesium, 583
Cézanne, Paul, 98, 978
chaconne, 55
Chad, 820
chamber music, 55
Chamberlain, Neville, 268
Chamberlain, Wilt, 687, 690, 978
Champlain, Samuel de, 232
Chancellorsville, Battle of, 263
Chandler, Raymond, 371
Chandra X-ray Observatory, 534

Chandragupta Maurya, 218
chanson, 54
Chaos, 472
Chaplin, Charlie, 24, 978
Chapman, Ray, 673
Charge of the Light Brigade, 261
charge-coupled device (CCD)
  in astronomy, 534
Charlemagne (Carolus Magnus, Charles the Great), 221–22, 978
Charles I, 234, 257
Charles II, 257
Charles River Bridge v. Warren Bridge, 303–04
Charles V, 233
Charles VI, 257
Charles, Jacques, 638
Charles, Ray, 64, 978
Charlotte, North Carolina, 877
Charon, 472
Chartres cathedral, 7
Charybdis, 472
Chateau Thierry, 268
Chaucer, Geoffrey, 349, 978–79
Cheese, 938
Cheever, John , 368
Chekhov, Anton, 343, 381, 979
chemicals, top 20 industrial produced in U.S., 579
chemistry, 577–92
  applications of, 578–79
  glossary of terms, 591–92
  history of, 577–79
  and industrialization, 578
  modern, 578
Cheng, 215
cherries, 927
Chesnutt, Charles , 365
Chesterton, G. K., 372
Chiang Kai-shek, 979
Chicago, Illinois, 877
Chicago, Judy, 103
Chichimecs, 228
chicken, 936
Chief Joseph, 979
Chikamatsu Monzaemon, 239
Child, Julia, 979
Children's Crusade, 255
Chile, 820
chili peppers, 930
Chimera, 472
China, 211, 213, 215–16, 219, 223, 229, 231–32, 239, 242–43, 248, 251, 820–21
  and ancient astronomy, 530
Chinese Exclusion Act, 284
Chinese (language), 803
Chinese Literature, 344–45
Chinese folk religions, 515–16
Chinese Revolution, 243
Chiron, 473
Chlorine, 583
Chloris, 473
chocolate, 938–39
cholera, 451–53
cholesterol levels, 948
Chomsky, Noam, 627, 979
Chopin, Kate , 363
choral symphony, 55
chorale, 53
chorale prelude, 55–56
Choson, 229
Christ, Churches of, 502
Christ, Jesus, 1016
Christian Scientists, 502
Christianity, 498–506
  afterlife, 499
  belief and practice, 498–99
  geography and numbers, 506
  history, 505–06
  sacraments, 499
  schools and sects, 499–505
  scripture, 498
Christie, Agatha , 370
Christo (Christo Javacheff), 103
Christy Minstrels, 61
chromium, 583
Chrysippus, 488
Chrysler Building, 11
Chrysler Corporation, 145
Chrysler, Walter P., 145
Church, Frederick Edwin, 97
Churchill, John, First Duke of Marlborough, 257, 979
Churchill, Winston, 246, 247, 266, 268, 979–80
Chytilova, Vera, 34
Cicero, 339, 980
Cimino, Michael , 29
Cinecittà, 34
Cinematheque Français, 31
cinématographe, 22
Circe, 473
circulatory system, human, 556–57
Cissé, Souleymane, 37
cities, U.S. (largest), 875–82
Citizen Kane, 26
City Lights, 25
Civil Rights Act of 1957, 289
Civil Rights Cases, 304
Civil Rights movement, 250
Civil War, American, 261–65
Civil Wars, English, 234, 257
Clark, George Rogers, 260
Clark, William , 276
Clarke, Arthur C., 373, 980
Clarke, Kenny, 72
Claudel, Camille, 99
Claudius, 980
clauses (grammar), 773–74
Clay, Cassius, 957
Clay, Henry, 279, 980
Clayton Antitrust Act, 286
Cleisthenes, 980
Clemenceau, Georges, 980
Cleopatra, 980–81
Cleophon, 253
Cleveland, Grover, 981
Cleveland, Ohio, 877
climate, 172
Clinton, William J., 292, 981
Clive, Robert, 238, 258
clocks, development of, 636
Clough, Arthur Hugh , 352
Clytemnestra, 473
CNN, 421
cobalt, 583
Cobb, Ty, 672, 981
Coca, Imogene , 413
Coca-Cola, 144
Cocteau, Jean , 30, 382
cod, 935
Coen Brothers, 30
Coercive Acts, 275
coffee, 939
cognitive therapy, 632
Cohens v. Virginia, 303
cold, common, 453
cold war, 247–48
Cole, Thomas, 96
Colecovision, 667
Coleman, Ornette, 72, 981
Coleridge, Samuel Taylor, 351, 981
Collins, Michael, 981
Collins, Wilkie , 369
collodion process, 105–07
Colombia, 821
colonoscopy and sigmoidoscopy, 463
colons (punctuation), 790
color, 28
Colorado (U.S. State), 862–63
Colorado Springs, Colorado, 877
Colt, Samuel, 981–82
Coltrane, John, 72, 982
Columbia, 26
Columbia Pictures, 29
Columbus, Christopher, 228, 272, 358, 982
Columbus, Ohio, 877
comets, 541
Comiskey, Charles, 673
commas (punctuation), 784–86
commedia dell'arte, 376
Communist Manifesto, 121
Communist Party, 244
Comoros, 821
Compton Gamma Ray Observatory, *534*
computer tomography (CT), 463
Computers
  e-mail spam, 656
  in early 20th century, 647
  glossary of terms, 659–66
  history of, 646–59
  hobby, 650
  IBM PC, development of, 651–52
  supercomputing, 658
  viruses, 655
Comte, Auguste, 982
conceptual art, 102–03
concert aria, 54
Concert of Europe, 240
concertino, 56
concerto, 56
conditioning, classical, 627
conduct disorder, 628
conductus, 53
Confucianism, 513–14
Confucius, 215, 982
congenital problems, 453
Congo, Democratic Republic of the, 821
Congo, Republic of the, 821
Congress of Berlin, 242
Congress of Vienna, 237, 240
Congress Party, Hindu, 247
Congreve, William , 380
conjunctions, 771
Connecticut (U.S. State), 863
Conrad III, 254
Conrad, Joseph, 356, 982
conservation laws, 614–15
Constable, John, 96
Constantine, 218
Constantine I (The Great), 982
Constitution, U.S., 313–27
  amendments to, 327–36
Constitutional Convention, 276, 281, 313
Consumer Price Index, 135
Continental Army, 259
Continental Congress, 258–59, 275
Continental System, 261
continents, 174–85

Convention on International Trade in Endangered Species, 251
conversion disorder, 631
Cook, James, 982
Cooke, Sam, 64
Cool Hand Luke, 29
Coolidge, Calvin, 287, 983
Cooper, Gary, 983
Cooper, James Fenimore, 360
Copernicus, Nicolas, 234, 530-31, 983
Copland, Aaron, 51
copper, 583
Coppola, Francis Ford, 28, 983
Coptic Church, 500
Coral Sea, Battle of the, 269
Corea, Chick, 73
Corinthian order (architecture), 4
Corn Laws, 240
Corneille, Pierre, 379
Cornwell, Patricia, 371
Corot, Camille, 96
Correll, Charles, 409
Cortés, Hernán (Hernando), 232, 983
Costa Rica, 822
Costello, Elvis, 78
Cote d'Ivoire, 822
Cotton, John, 359
Coubertin, Baron Pierre de, 983
Coulomb, Charles, 608, 983
Council of Chalcedon, 218
Council of Clermont, 254
Council of Trent, 233
Count Basie, 71
Counter-Reformation, 233
Country music, 66–68
Country-Rock, 76
courante, 56
Courbet, Gustave, 97
Coward, Noel, 983
Cowley, Abraham, 349
Cranach, Lucas the Elder, 93
cranberries, 927
Crashaw, Richard, 349
Crawford, Joan, 984
Crazy Horse, 984
Creon, 473
Cretaceous period, 596
Crete, 213
Crick, Francis, 567, 984
Crimean War, 261
Croatia, 822
Crohn's disease, 446
Cromwell, Oliver, 235, 257, 984
Cronus, 473
Crosby, Bing, 71, 984
crossword puzzles, 805–12
  concise dictionary, 806–12
  how to solve, 805
Crusades, 227, 254–55
Cuba, 37, 249, 822
Cuban missile crisis, 249
Cubism, 100
Cullen, Countee, 365
Cultural Revolution, 250
culture, 463
Cumaean, 473
Cummings, E(dward) E(stlin), 984
Cunningham, Merce, 18, 19, 984
Curie, Marie, 984–85
curium, 583
Currency Act, 274
Custer, Gen. George A., 284, 985
Cyclopes, 473
cyclothymic disorder, 630
Cyprus, 823
Cyrus II (The Great), 214, 985
Czech Republic, 823

D

D-Day, 270
Dadaism, 100
Daedalus, 473
Daguerre, Louis Jacques Mandé, 104–05
daguerreotypes, 113
dairy foods, 937–38
Dalai Lama, 985
Dali, Salvador, 100, 985
Dallas, Texas, 877
Dalton, John, 610
Daly, Carroll John, 370
Danae, 473
Dance, 17–21
  break dancing, 20
  Latin, 20
  modern, 18–19
  post-World War II, 20
  social, 19–20
  swing, 20
Dante Alighieri, 339, 985
Danton, Georges-Jacques, 236, 985
Daphne, 473
Darius I, 214, 253
Darius III, 217
dark energy, 547
Dartmouth College v. Woodward, 303
Darwin, Charles, 549, 565, 625
Das Kapital, 121
dashes (punctuation), 789
dates, 927
Daumier, Honoré, 97
David (King), 214, 985
David, Jacques-Louis, 95, 985–86
Davie, Donald, 354
Davis, Bette, 986
Davis, Jefferson, 986
Davis, Miles, 73, 986
Davy, Sir Humphry, 986
Dawes Act, 284
Dawes, Williams, 258
Dawud, Askia, 232
De Beauvoir, Simone, 986
De Gaulle, Charles, 986
De Stijl, 101
Debs, Eugene Victor, 286, 986–87
Debussy, Claude, 51
decadent school (poetry), 341
decadent school (literature), 353
Decameron, The, 339
Declaration of Independence, 235, 259
The Defiant Ones, 27
Defoe, Daniel, 355, 987
Degas, Edgar, 98, 987
Deianeira, 473
Delacroix, Eugéne, 96
Delaware (U.S. State), 863
DeLillo, Don, 366, 368
delirium, 629
Delium, 253
demand curve, 122
dementia, 629
Demeter, 470
DeMille, Cecil. B., 24, 987
Democritus, 486, 605
Demosthenes, 338
Dempsey, Jack, 757, 987
Deng Xiaoping, 987
Dengue fever, 453
Denmark, 34, 823
Dennis v. United States, 306
Denver,Colorado, 877
DePalma, Brian, 28
depersonalization disorder, 629
depression, 458, 630
deregulation (economics), 123
Descartes, René, 391, 490, 625, 987
deserts, 173–74
Després, Josquin, 42
Detroit, Michigan, 877–78
development economics, 130–32
  balance of trade, 134
  exchange rates, 132–34
  free trade, 134
  global movement of capital, 132–34
  tariffs and quotas, 134
Devonian period, 596
Dewey, John, 493, 987
Dewey, Thomas E., 288
diabetes, 453
Diaghilev, Sergei, 18
diagnostic tests (medical), 462–66
diaphragm (respiration), 558
Dick, Philip K., 374
Dickens, Charles, 355, 987–88
Dickinson, Emily, 361, 988
Dickson, W.K.L., 24
Diderot, Denis, 988
Dido, 473
Didrikson, Mildred "Babe", 747
Dienbienphu, 248
diet and dieting, 947–52
Dietrich, Marlene, 988
Difference Engine (in computing), 646
digestive process, 559
digestive system, human, 558–59
DiMaggio, Joe, 673
dinosaurs, 603
Diocletian, 218, 988
Diodochi, 217
Dionysus, 471
Diophantus, 390
Diphtheria, 453
disco, 77
disease, 442–62
Disney Company, 29
Disney, Walt, 988
disorders
  childhood, 628–29
  cognitive, 629
  eating, 629–30
  factitious, 630
  mental, 628
  mood, 630
  personality, 630
  psychotic, 631
  somatoform, 631
  substance-related, 631
disposable razors, 144
Disraeli, Benjamin, 988
dissociative amnesia, 629

dissociative disorders, 458, 629
dissociative fugue, 629
dissociative identity disorder, 629
District of Columbia, 863
divertimento, 56
Divine Comedy, The, 339
Dixon, Thomas, 23
Djerassi, Carl, 988
Djibouti, 823
DNA, 550, 567
Domagk, Gerhard, 441
Dome of the Rock, 13
Dominica, 823–24
Dominican Republic, 824
Dominicans, 227
Domino, Fats, 74
Don Quixote de la Mancha, 340
Donatello, 92, 228, 989
Donne, John, 349, 989
Doolittle, James, 269
Doppler, Christian, 620
Dorian invasions, 215
Doric order (architecture), 4
Dos Passos, John, 364, 989
Dostoyevsky, Fyodor, 343, 989
Douglas, Kirk, 27
Douglas, Stephen A., 280
Douglass, Frederick, 362, 989
Dovzhenko, Alexander, 33
Dow Jones industrial average, 165
Dowson, Ernest, 353
Doyle, Sir Arthur Conan, 369, 989
Drabble, Margaret, 358
Drake, Sir Francis, 233, 989
Drama
- ancient Greek, 374–75
- ancient Roman, 375
- in 18th century, 380
- Elizabethan and Jacobean, 376–79
- French Neoclassical, 379–80
- in Italian Renaissance, 376
- Medieval, 375–76
- Modern, in Europe, 381–82
- in 19th century, 381
- in Restoration, 380
- Western, history of, 374–83
- world, 384

Dreamcast, 670
Dred Scott v. Sanford, 304
Dreiser, Theodore, 362
drugs
- antianxiety, 632
- antidepressant, 632
- antimanic, 632
- antipsychotic, 632

Druze Community, 514
Dryden, John, 350, 380
Du Bois, W. E. B., 365, 989–90
Dubnium, 583
Dubuffet, Jean, 102
Duccio, 91
Duchamp, Marcel, 100, 101, 990
duke of Wellington, 236, 261
Dulles, John Foster, 990
Dumas, Alexandre, 341, 990
Dumbarton Oaks Conference, 246
Dumuzi, 479
Duncan, Isadora, 18, 990
Dunstable, John, 42
Durand, Asher, 96
Duras, Marguerite, 342
Dürer, Albrecht, 93, 990
Dutch West India Company, 273
Dvorák, Antonín, 49, 990
DVRs, 429
Dwan, Allan, 24
Dylan, Bob, 68, 990
dysprosium, 583
dysthymic disorder, 630

E

Eakins, Thomas, 97
Ealing Studios, 32
Earhart, Amelia, 990–91
Earnhardt, Dale, 764
Earp, Wyatt, 991
Earth
- features and composition, 536–37, 594–95
- formation of, 594
- in upheaval, 600–02

earthquakes, 600–01
East India Company, 238
East Timor, 824
Eastern Catholicism, 499–500
Eastern Orthodox Church, 500
Eastman, George, 108, 109, 991
Eastwood, Clint, 991
ebola, 455
Echidna, 473
Echo, 473
ecology, 570–71
economic development, institutions for, 131
economic man, 122
Economics, 120–37
- development economics, 130–32
- glossary of terms, 135–37
- history of, 120–21
- international, 132–35
- macroeconomics, 124–30
- microeconomics, 121–24

ecosystems, 570
Ecuador, 824
Edict of Nantes, 235
Edict of Restitution, 256
Edison, Thomas, 22, 141, 639, 991
Edo Period, 231
Edward I, 255
Edward III, 255
Edward IV, 256
Edward the Black Prince, 255
Edwards, Jonathan, 274, 359, 991
eggplant, 930
Egypt, 824–25
- in ancient history, 212–14
- astronomy in ancient, 530

Ehrlich, Paul, 441
Einstein, Albert, 607, 608, 609, 991
Einsteinium, 583
Eisenhower, Dwight, 270, 289, 991–92
Eisenstein, Sergei, 33, 992
El Boom (in Latin American literature), 344
El Greco, 93
El Niño, 173
El Paso, Texas, 878
El Salvador, 825
Eleanor of Aquitaine, 992
Electra, 473
electric power, development of, 639
electricity, laws of, 616
electrocardiogram, 463
electromagnetism, 606–08
electromyogram, 463
electron, 617
elements, 579–91
Eliot, George, 356, 992
Eliot, T. S., 353, 364, 992
Elizabeth I, 376–78, 992
Ellington, Duke, 71, 992
ellipses (punctuation), 791
Ellis Island, 284
Ellroy, James, 371
Emancipation Proclamation, 263
embryology, comparative, 566
Emerson, Ralph Waldo, 360, 992–93
Emmy Awards, 890–92
Empedocles, 485
Emphysema, 454
Empire State Building, 11
empiricism, 490
employment cost index, 135
encephalitis, 454
endocrine System, 561
- glands and secretions, 564

endoscopy, 463–64
energy, conservation of, 615
Engels, Friedrich, 121, 993
engine, internal combustion, development of, 641–42
England, 235–36, 238–39
English (language), 803
English Civil Wars, 234, 257
ENIAC, 648
Enki, 479
Enkidu, 479
Enlil, 479
Environment
- challenges, 572–74
- trends, 575

Enyo, 473
Eocene epoch, 596
Eos, 473
Epic Theater (of Brecht), 382
Epictetus, 488
epicureanism, 488
Epicurus of Samos, 488
Episcopal Churches, 502
epistemology, 484
Equal Rights Amendment, 291
Equatorial Guinea, 825
Equiano, Olaudah, 359
Erasmus, Desiderius, 93, 233, 340, 993
Eratosthenes, 530
Erbium, 583
Ereshkigal, 479
Ericson, Leif, 272, 993
Erie Railroad Co. v. Tompkins, 306
Erinyes, 473
Eris, 473
Eritrea, 825
Eros, 474
Erving, Julius "Dr. J", 690
essayists, American, 360
Estates General, 236
Estes, Richard, 102
Estonia, 825–26
Ethical Culture Society, 516
ethics, 484
Ethiopia, 826

Ethiopian Orthodox Church, 500–01
ethnic cleansing, 252
Euclid, 605, 993
Euclid of Alexandria, 390
Eugene of Savoy, 257
Euler, Leonhard, 993
Eumenides, 473
Euripides, 375, 993
Europa, 474
Europe, 180–81, 210, 220–22, 226–28, 234–35, 240–41
  climate, 181
  economy, 181–82
  people, 181
  physical features, 180–81
European Economic Cooperation, 247
Europium, 583–84
Eurydice, 474
Eustachio, Bartolomeo, 437
Evert, Chris, 726, 993
evolution, 565–67
  evidence of, 566–67
Ex Parte Milligan, 304
exchange rates (currency), 133
exclamation point (punctuation), 784
excretory system, human, 559
existentialism, 494
Expressionism (in art), 99–100
Expressionism (in drama), 382

F

Fabricius, Hieronymus, 437
Fairbanks, Douglas, Sr., 993–94
Fair Oaks, Battle of, 262
Fallingwater, 9
Falloppio, Gabriele, 437
Falun Gong, 516
Famicon, 667
FAMU, 34
fantasia, 56
Faraday, Michael, 611, 639, 994
Farnsworth, Philo T., 411
Farragut, David G., 262, 994
Fates, 474
fats, 946–947
Faulkner, William, 364, 994
faults (geology), 599
fecal occult blood test, 464
Federal Communications Commission (F.C.C.), 407, 415–16
federal funds rate, 129
Federal Immigration Act, 284
Federal Reserve, 161–62
Federal Reserve Act, 286
Federal Trade Commission, 286
Federation of Malaysia, 247
Fellini, Federico, 34, 994
Fenrir, 481
Ferdinand VII, 241
Fermat, Pierre de, 391, 994
Fermi, Enrico, 994–95
fermions, 617
fermium, 584
Fessenden, Reginald, 640
feudalism, 221
Feynman, Richard, 646, 994–95
Fielding, Henry, 355, 995
Fields, W. C., 995
Fifth Generation, 35
figs, 927
Fiji, 826
file sharing, 429
Fillmore, Millard, 280, 995
Film, 22–39
  coming of sound, 25–26
  in Eastern Europe, 33–34
  in France, 30–31
  in Germany, 31–32
  glossary of terms, 37–39
  Golden Age of Hollywood, 26–27
  in Great Britain, 32
  history of, 22–39
  international, 30–39
  in Italy, 34
  rise of the american film industry, 23–25
  in Soviet Union, 32–33
film music, 59
finance, 158–70
  glossary of terms, 168–70
  history of, 158–63
  in American Revolution, 160–63
  in Renaissance, 159–60
  and stock markets, 163–66
Finland, 826
Fiorentino, Rosso, 93
fire, development of, 633
Fischer, Bobby, 995
fish, 934–36
Fitzgerald, Edward, 352
Fitzgerald, Ella, 71
Fitzgerald, F. Scott, 364, 995
Flaubert, Gustave, 341, 995
Fleming, Alexander, 441, 995
Fletcher v. Peck, 303
Fletcher, John, 379
flight, development of, 638–39
Florida (U.S. State), 863–64
Flourens, Jean Pierre, 439
Floyer, John, 438
fluorine, 584
folds (geology), 598
Folk Religions, 515–16
Folk Rock, 75
Fonda, Henry, 995–96
Fonda, Jane, 996
Fonteyn, Margot, 996
food-borne illnesses, 454
Food, Dictionary of, 925–39
Football, 697–709
  college, history of, 698–701
  glossary of terms, 708–09
  Hall of Fame, 704–06
  positions, 697–98
  professional, history of, 701–04
  rules of, 697–98
  Super Bowl results, 707
Forbidden City, 12
Ford, Gerald R., 291, 996
Ford, Henry, 996
Ford, John, 26, 379, 996
Foreman, George, 757, 758, 996
Forman, Milos, 34
Forseti, 481
Forster, E. M., 356, 996
Forsyth, Alexander, 637
Fort Sumter, 261
Fort Ticonderoga, 258
Fort Worth, Texas, 878
forums, Roman, 4–5
fossil record, 566
fossils, 603–04
Foster, Hannah Webster, 359
Foster, Stephen, 61
Fowler, Mark, 423
Fracastoro, Girolamo, 438
France, 240, 826–27
  drama in, 379–80
  wine, 940–41
Francis I, 257, 997
Francis of Assisi, 997
Francis Xavier (Saint), 997
Franciscans, 227
francium, 584
Franco-Prussian War, 240, 265
Franklin, Aretha, 65
Franklin, Benjamin, 359, 606, 997
Franks, 218
Franz Ferdinand, Archduke, 244
Frazier, Joe, 757, 997
Frederick I, 254
Frederick the Great (Frederick II), 235, 255, 257-258, 997
Frederick V, 256
Frederick William "the Great Elector", 235
Fredericksburg, Battle of, 263
Free Cinema, 32
Freed, Arthur, 26
Freedmen's Bureau, 282
French (language), 804
French and Indian War, 235, 274
French Revolution, Wars of the, 236, 260–61
Fresno, California, 878
Freud, Sigmund, 626, 997–98
Freyja, 481
Freyr, 481
Friedman, Milton, 129, 998
Friends, Society of (Quakers), 502
Frigg, 481
frontier, American, 360
Frost, Robert Lee, 998
fruit, 926–29
Fugitive Slave Act, 280
fugue, 56
fungi, 933–34
funk music, 65
Funk, Casimir, 440

G

G.I. Bill, 288
Gabin, Jean, 30
Gable, Clark, 998
Gabon, 827
gadolinium, 584
Gaea, 474
Gage, General Thomas, 258
Galaxies, 544
Galen, 436, 998
Galileo Galilei, 234, 531, 606, 998
Gallipoli, 266, 979
gallium, 584
Galvani, Luigi, 438, 608, 639
Gambia, The, 827
GameCube, 670
gamma radiation, 533–34
Gandhi, Indira, 998–99
Gandhi, Mahatma, 243, 999
Gang of Four, 251
gangsta rap, 66
Garbo, Greta, 999
Garcia Marquez, Gabriel, 999
Gardner, Erle Stanley, 371
Garfield, James A., 999

Garibaldi, Giuseppe, 240, 999
Garland, Hamlin, 363
Garland, Judy, 999
Garlic, 931
Garrick, David, 380
Garrison, William Lloyd, 278, 999–1000
Garvey, Marcus, 1000
Gates, Bill, 651, 1000
Gates, Horatio, 259, 260
GATT, 250
Gauguin, Paul, 98, 1000
Gauss, Karl Friedrich, 1000
gavotte, 56
Gaza Strip, 251
Geb, 480
Gehrig, Lou, 673
Gehry, Frank Owen, 1000
Gell-Mann, Murray, 618, 1000
General Agreement on Tariffs and Trade, 250
General Electric, 141
General Motors, 146, 148
General Thomas Gage, 275
Genet, Jean, 382
genetic code, 567–69
genetic diseases, 454–55
Genetics, 567–70
  engineering, 569
  mutations, 569
  patterns of inheritance, 569–70
  principle of dominance, 569
  principle of segregation, 569
Genghis Khan, 1000–01
genomes, 569
Genroku Period, 239
Gentileschi, Artemesia, 94
Geography, 172–208
  glossary of terms, 207–08
  islands and archipelagos, 198–204
  major seas, gulfs, and straits, 190–94
  mountain ranges, 204–06
  oceans, 190
  physical, 172–74
  rivers and canals, 194–98
  rivers of the world, by length, 199–200
Geology, 593–604
  continental drift, 597
  earthquakes, 600–01
  historical, 594–97
  history of, 593–94
  physical, 597–98
  plate tectonics, 596–98
  seafloor spreading, 597
  structural, 598–600
  time scale, 595, 596
  volcanoes, 601–02
Geometry, 392–93
Geophysics, 611–13
George II, 257
George III, 258, 1001
Georgia (U.S. State), 273, 827, 864
Gerd, 482
Gericault, Théodore, 96
germanium, 584
German (language), 804
German surrender, 269
Germantown, Battle of, 259
Germany, 240, 45, 827–28
Gernsback, Hugo, 373
Geronimo, 284, 1001
Gershwin, George, 52, 62, 1001
Gershwin, Ira, 62
Ghana, 828
Ghiberti, Lorenzo, 92, 228
Ghirlandaio, Domenico, 92
Gibbons v. Ogden, 303
Gibson, Bob, 1001
Gibson, William, 374
Gide, André, 342
Gideon v. Wainwright, 306–07
Gilgamesh, 338, 479
Gillespie, Dizzy, 72, 1001
Gingrich, Newt, 292, 1001
Ginsberg, Allen, 365, 1001
Giorgione, 93
Giotto, 91, 1001
Gish, Dorothy, 23
Gish, Lillian, 23, 1002
glaciers, 599–600
Gladstone, William Ewart, 1002
Glam-Rock, 77
Glass, Philip, 51, 52
Gleason, Jackie, 413
Glenn, John Herschel, Jr., 1002
gliders, development of, 638
globalization, 252
Glorious Revolution, 235
Gluck, Christoph Willibald von, 48
gluons, 618
goat, 937
Godard, Jean-Luc, 1002
Goddard, Robert Hutchings, 1002
Gödel, Kurt, 1002
Godfrey of Bouillon, 254
Godwinson, Harold, 227
Goebbels, Paul Joseph, 1002
Goethe, Johann Wolfgang von, 340, 1002–03
Gogol, Nikolai, 343
Golan Heights, 251
gold, 584
gold standard, 161
Goldenson, Leonard, 414
Golding, William, 357
Goldsmith, Oliver, 380
Goldwater, Barry, 1003
Goldwyn, Samuel, 1003
Golf, 717–21
  British Open winners, 723
  glossary of terms, 719–21
  history of, 717–18
  Masters winners, 721
  PGA Championship winners, 722
  rules of, 718–19
  U.S. Open winners, 722
  Women's Grand Slam Champions, 724
  Women's Open champions, U.S., 724
Gompers, Samuel, 1003
Goodall, Jane, 1003
Goodman, Benny, 71, 1003
Goodyear, Charles, 1003
Gorbachev, Mikahil, 251, 1003
Gore, Albert, 292
Göring, Hermann, 269
Gorky, Maxim, 343
Gosden, Freeman, 409
Gounod, Charles-François, 49
Goya, Francisco, 96, 1003-1004
Graaf, Regnier de, 438
Graces, 474
The Graduate, 28
Graeco-Indian kingdom, 218
Graf, Steffi, 727
Grafton, Sue, 371
Graham, Martha, 19, 1004
grammar. see Writer's Guide
Grammy Awards, 898–900
grand motet, 53
Grand Ole Opry, 66
grand unified theories, 611, 617
Grandmaster Flash, 65
Grange, Harold "Red", 699, 702, 1004
Grant, Cary, 1004
Grant, Ulysses S., 262, 1004
grapefruit, 927–28
grapes, 928
graph theory, 393
Grass, Günter, 342, 1004
Graves' disease, 446
Graves, Robert, 353
graviton, 618–24
gravity, law of, 613–14
Great Awakening, 274
Great Depression, 165, 287
  causes of, 162
The Great Dictator, 25
Great Leap Forward, 250
Great Mutiny, 243
Great Northern War, 237
Great Proletarian Cultural Revolution, 250
Great Pyramid of Cheops, 212
Great Schism, 228
The Great Train Robbery, 23
Great Trek, 241
Great Wall, 219
Greco-Persian Wars, 253
Greece, 214–17, 828
  astronomy in ancient, 530
  Olympics, 745–46, 752
Green Revolution, 250
Green, Anna Katherine, 371
Greene, Graham, 357, 1004–05
Gregorian chant, 41, 54
Gregory I, Pope (Saint), 220, 1005
Gregory VII, Pope, 226
Gregory VIII, Pope, 254
Grenada, 828
Gretzky, Wayne, 711, 1005
Grierson, John, 32
Griffith, D.W., 23, 1005
Griffith-Joyner, Florence, 1005
Grimm, Jacob, 1005
Grimm, Wilhelm, 1005
Grissi, Carlotta, 17
Griswold v. Connecticut, 307
Gropius, Georg Walter Adolf, 10, 1005
Gros, Jean-Antoine, 96
Gross Domestic Product (G.D.P.), definition, 136
Gross National Product (G.N.P.), definition, 136
Group Theatre, 383
group therapy, 632
Grünewald (Matthais Gothardt Neithardt), 93
grunge, 78
Grupo Cine Liberacion, 37
Guatemala, 828–29
Guevara, Che, 1005–06
Guggenheim Museum, 9
guilds, 227
Guinea, 829
Guinea worms, 461–62

Guinea-Bissau, 829
Gulf and Western, 28
Gulf of Tonkin Resolution, 290
Gulf War, 252
Gunn, Thom, 354
Gunpowder, development of, 637
guns, development of, 637
Gupta Empire, 218
Gupta India, 222
Gustavus II (Gustavus Adolphus), 234, 256, 1006
Gutenberg, Johannes, 637, 1006
Guthrie, Woody, 68
Gutierrez Alea, Tomas, 37
Guyana, 829

H

habitats, 570
Habsburg Empire, 228, 235, 237, 257
Hadean eon, 596
Hades, 474
hafnium, 584
Hagia Sophia, 6, 960
Haiti, 241, 829
Haley, Bill, 74
Hals, Frans, 94
Halsey, William F., Jr. (Bull), 1006
Halsted, William, 439
Hamilton, Alexander, 276, 1006
Hammerstein II, Oscar, 63, 1006
Hammett, Dashiell, 371
Hammons, David, 103
Hammurabi, 212
  Code of, 294
Han Dynasty, 219
Hancock, Herbie, 73
Hancock, John, 258
Handel, George Frideric, 44, 1006
Hannibal, 217, 253, 254, 1006
Hansen, Joseph, 371
Hansen's Disease (leprosy), 456
Hanson, Duane, 102
Hapi, 480
Harappa, 213
Harding, Warren G., 287, 1007
Hardy, Thomas, 352, 356, 1007
Hari Krishnas, 516
Harlem Renaissance, 365
Harlow, Jean, 26
harmonia, 474
Harpies, 474
Harrison, Benjamin, 1007
Harrison, George, 1007
Harrison, John, 636, 1007
Harrison, William Henry, 277, 1007
Hart, Sir Robert, 242
Hart, William S., 24
Hartford Convention, 277
Harvey, William, 437, 1007
hassium, 584
Haswell, Susanna Rowson, 372
Hathor, 480
Hatshepsut Maatkare, 213, 1007–08
  tomb of, 3
Hawaii (U.S. State), 864
Hawking, Stephen, 607, 1008
Hawks, Howard, 26, 1008
Hawthorne, Nathaniel, 361, 1008
Haydn, Franz Joseph, 46–47, 1008
Hayes, Rutherford B., 1008
Hays, Will H., 24
Haywood, Eliza, 372
HDTV, 429
Heade, Martin Johnson, 97
Heaney, Seamus, 354, 1008
Hearst, William Randolph, 1008
Heart of Atlanta Motel, Inc. v. United States, 307
heart, human, 557
  heart attack, 451
  heart failure, 451
heat (physics), 608–10
heavy metal, 76
Hebe, 474
Hebrew Bible, 496
Hecate, 474
Hector, 474
Hecuba, 474
Hegel, Georg Wilhelm, 492, 1008–09
Heidegger, Martin, 494, 1009
Heimdall, 482
Heine, Heinrich, 341, 1009
Heinlein, Robert, 373
Heisenberg, Werner, 610, 616, 617, 1009
Hel, 482
Helen, 474
helicopter, development of, 639
Helios, 474
helium, 584
Hellenic League, 217
Helmholtz, Herman, 439
Hemingway, Ernest, 364, 1009
hemorrhagic fevers, 455
Henie, Sonja, 1009
Henri, Robert, 100
Henry II, 1009
Henry V, 255, 1009
Henry VI, 256
Henry VII, 256
Henry VIII, 233, 1009–10
Henry Hudson, 233
Henry the Fowler, 222
Henry "the Navigator," 228
Henry, Patrick, 258, 1010
hepatitis, 455–56
Hepburn, Katharine, 26, 1010
Hephaestus, 471
Hera, 471
Heracles, 474
Heraclitus, 485
Herbert, George, 349
herbs, 933
Hermaphroditus, 474
Hermes, 471
Herodotus, 338, 1010
Heron of Alexandria, 638
Herophilus, 436
Herrick, Robert, 350
Herrman, Bernard, 51
Hertz, Heinrich, 608, 640
Herzl, Theodor, 1010
Hesiod, 338
Hess, Rudolf, 269
Hesse, Hermann, 342
Hestia, 471
Heyer, Georgette, 372
Hibbert, Eleanor, 372
Hideyoshi, 232
Hillerman, Tony, 371
Himes, Chester, 371
Himmler, Heinrich, 1010
Hindenburg, Paul von, 266
Hindi, 803
Hinduism, 215, 218, 508–10
  belief and practice, 508–10
  caste system, 509
  deities, 509–11
  geography and numbers, 510–11
  history, 510
  holidays, 510
  schools and sects, 510
  scripture, 508
  yoga, 509
Hippocrates, 436, 1010
Hippolytus, 474
Hirohito, 245
Hiroshima, 270
historical materialism, 493
History, American, 272–92
History, World, 210–52
Hitchcock, Alfred, 26, 1010
Hitler, Adolf, 245, 270, 1010–11
Hittites, 213
Ho Chi Minh, 248, 290, 1011
Hobbes, Thomas, 490, 625, 1011
hockey, ice, 710–14
  equipment, rules, and field of play, 711–12
  glossary of terms, 712–14
  Hart Trophy winners, 715
  history of, 710–11
  Stanley Cup champions, 714
  Vezina Trophy winners, 716
Hodgkin, Thomas, 439
Hodur, 482
Hoffa, James Riddle, 1011
Hoffmann, Felix, 440
Hogan, Ben, 1011
Hohenzollern, 235
Holbein (the Younger), Hans, 93, 1011
Holiday, Billie, 71
Holiness Churches, 503
Holland, Agnieszka, 33
Holly, Buddy, 74
holmium, 584
Holocaust, 246, 247
Holocene epoch, 596
Holy League, 230
Holy Roman Emperor, 233
Holy Roman Empire, 226, 233, 235, 256
Holy See (Vatican City), 829–30
Holy Sepulcher, 254
Home Shopping Network (HSN), 421
Homer, 338
Homer, Winslow, 97, 1011
Homestead Act, 281
Honduras, 830
Hong Kong, 35
honky-tonk music, 67
Honolulu, Hawaii, 878
Honorius III, 255
Hooke, Robert, 438, 636
Hooker, Joseph, 263
hookworms, 461–62
Hoover, Herbert, 287, 1011–12
Hoover, J. Edgar, 1012
Hope, Bob, 1012
Hopkins, Gerard Manley, 353, 1012
Hopper, Edward, 101, 1012
Horace (Quintus Horatius Faccus), 339, 1012
Horae, 474

hormones, 576
Horner, William George, 22
hornet, 269
Horney, Karen, 626
Horse Racing, 739–43
  betting, 740
  breeding, 739
  glossary of terms, 742–43
  history of, 740–42
  Kentucky Derby winners, 744
  origins of, 739
  Triple Crown, 742
  types of races, 739
Horus, 480
Houdon, Jean Antoine, 95
House of Burgesses, 258, 272
Housman, A.E., 352, 1012
Houston, Texas, 878
Howard, Henry, 349
Howe, General William , 259
Howe, Gordie, 710, 1012
Howells, William Dean , 363
Howlin' Wolf (Chester Arthur Burnett), 64
Hoxha, Enver, 247
Hsiao-hsien, Hou, 36
Huayna Capac, 229
Hubble Space telescope, 533
Hudson River School, 96–97
Hudson, Henry, 1012
Hugh Capet, 222
Hughes, Howard, 1013
Hughes, Langston, 365, 1013
Hughes, Ted , 354
Hugo, Victor, 341, 1013
Huguenots, 235
Hull, Cordell, 1013
Human Body, 556–65
humanism, 490
humanistic and existential therapy, 632
humanists, 228
Humbaba, 479
Hume, David , 491
Humphrey, Doris, 19
Hundred Years War, 228, 255–56
Hungary, 830
Hunt, Leigh , 352
Hunt, William Holman, 98
Hunter, Evan , 371
Hunter, Jim "Catfish", 674
Hurston, Zora Neale, 365, 1013
Hussein, Saddam, 251, 292
Husserl, Edmund , 494
Huston, John, 1013
Hutchinson, Anne, 273, 359
Huygens, Christiaan, 608, 636
hybrid funds, 167
Hydra, 475
hydrogen, 584–85
hydrosphere, 595
Hyksos, 213, 214
hypertension, 451, 452
hyphens, 791–93
Hypnos, 475
hypochondriasis, 631
hypothalamus, 564

I

I.B.M. (International Business Machines), birth of, 647
I.B.M. PC, development of, 651–52
Ibsen, Henrik, 381, 1013
Icarus, 475
Ice Age, 211–12
Iceland, 830
Idaho (U.S. State), 864–65
Idealism, 493
Idun, 482
Ieyasu, Tokugawa, 231
Iger, Robert , 425
Ignatius of Loyola, 1013
igneous rocks, 597–98
Il-sung, Kim, 248
Iliad, The, 338
Illinois (U.S. State), 865
imaging, 464
Imhotep, 3, 1013
Immigration and Naturalization Service v. Chadha, 308
immune system, human, 557–58
immunization, 468
Inanna, 479
Inca Empire, 229, 232
Ince, Thomas, 24
index funds, 167
India, 215, 218, 222–23, 230–31, 243, 830–31
India Act, 238
Indian Literature, 346–47
Indian National Congress, 243
Indiana (U.S. State), 865
Indianapolis, Indiana, 878
indium, 585
Indochina, 242
Indonesia, 831
Indonesian (language), 803
Industrial Revolution, 235
infinitives (grammar), 778
influenza, 456
Information Age, 252
infrared radiation, 533
Ingres, Jean-Auguste-Dominique, 95, 1014
Innocent III, Pope, 254, 255, 1014
Innocent IV, Pope, 255
Ino, 475
intelligence, artificial, 645
Intellivision, 667
interjections, 771
intermedio, 59
intermezzo, 56
International Bank for Reconstruction and Development, 246
International Economics, 132–35
International Labor Organization, 250
International Monetary Fund, 246
International Society for Krishna Consciousness, 516
International Style (architecture), 10
Internet, 252
Internet, development of, 653–55
Interstate Commerce Act, 283
intifada, 251
Intolerable Acts, 275
Io, 475
iodine, 585
Ionesco, Eugène , 382
Ionic order (architecture), 4
Iowa (U.S. State), 865
Iphigeneia, 475
Iran, 831
Iraq, 831
Iraqi invasion of Kuwait, 252
Ireland, 831–32
iridium, 585
Iris, 475
iron, 585
Iron Age, 213–16
Irving, John Winslow , 365
Irving, Washington , 360
Isidoros of Miletus, 6
Isis, 480
Islam, 221, 222–23, 225–26, 251, 506–08
  and ancient astronomy, 530
  belief and practice, 506–07
  Five Pillars of, 506–07
  geography and numbers, 508
  history, 507–08
  holidays, 508
  pilgrimage to Mecca (Hajj), 507
  prayer, 506
  schools and sects, 507
  scripture, 506
  Shiite, 507
  Sufism, 507–09
  Sunni, 507
Israel, 214, 247–48, 832
Italian Risorgimento, 240
italics, 788–89
Italy, 832
  wines of, 941–42
Ivan III "the Great," 227
Ivan IV "the Terrible," 234, 1014
Ives, Charles, 1014
Ivory Coast. see Cote d'Ivoire.

J

Jackson, "Shoeless" Joe, 673
Jackson, Andrew, 277, 1014
Jackson, Michael, 1014
Jackson, Thomas "Stonewall," 262, 1014–15
Jacksonville, Florida, 878
Jacobs, Harriet Ann , 362
Jacquard, J. M. , 139
Jadwiga, 227
Jagellonian dynasty, 234
Jainism, 514
Jamaica, 832
James I, 257, 349, 379, 1015
James II, 235, 717, 1015
James, Henry, 356, 363, 1015
James, William, 626, 1015
Jamestown, 272
Janáçek, Leos, 52
Janequin, Clément, 43
Janus, 475
Japan, 219–20, 223–24, 231–32, 239, 242–43, 245, 832–33
Japanese (language), 804
Japanese literature, 345–46
Jarry, Alfred , 382
Jason, 475
Jaspers, Karl , 494
Java Man, 210
Jay Treaty, 276
Jay, John, 1015
Jazz, 69–73
  bebop, 71–72
  big band, 69–71
  cool, 72
  free, 72
  fusion, 72–73
  hard bop, 72
  New Orleans/Dixieland, 69
  post bop, 73
  smooth, 73
  soul, 72
  swing, 69–71

The Jazz Singer, 25
Jefferson, Thomas, 276, 359, 1015
Jehovah's Witnesses, 503
Jenner, Edward, 438, 1015
Jericho, architecture of, 3
Jerome, 1015
Jesus, 218, 1016
jet engines, development of, 637
Jim Crow laws, 285
Jinnah, Mohammed Ali, 1016
Joan of Arc, 255, 1016
Jobs, Steve, 1016
Jocasta, 475
Joffre, Joseph, 267, 1016
John I, 227
John II, 255
John of Austria, 255
John the Baptist, 1017
John XXIII, 1016
John, Elton, 1016
Johns, Jasper, 102, 1017
Johnson Wax Building, 9
Johnson, Andrew, 282, 1017
Johnson, Lyndon B, 290, 1017
Johnson, Magic, 688, 1017
Johnson, Philip Cortelyou, 1017
Johnson, Samuel, 351, 1017–18
Johnson, Walter, 1018
joints (geology), 598–99
Jolson, Al, 25
Jones, Bobby, 718, 1018
Jones, Inigo, 8, 1018
Jones, John Paul, 260, 1018
Jonson, Ben, 349–50, 377, 1018
Joplin, Scott, 61
Jordan, 833
Jordan, Louis, 64
Jordan, Michael, 691, 1018
Jormurgandr, 482
Joseph II, 235
Joyce, James, 357, 1018
Judaism, 496–98
  belief and practice, 496–97
  Conservative, 497
  dietary restrictions, 496–97
  geography and numbers, 498
  Hebrew Bible, 496
  history of, 497–98
  holidays, 498
  Kabbalah, 496
  Orthodox, 497
  prayer and worship, 496–97
  Reform, 497
  rites of passage, 497
  schools and sects, 497
  scripture, 496
  Talmud, 496
Judd, Donald, 102
Jung, Carl, 626, 1018–19
Jupiter, features and composition, 538–39
Jurassic period, 596
Justinian I, 220, 1019
Jutes, 218
Jutland, Battle of, 266

K

Kabbalah, 496
Kabuki theater, 239, 384
Kafka, Franz, 342, 1019
Kahlo, Frida, 1019
Kai-shek, Chiang, 245
Kandinsky, Vasily, 101
Kangxi Emperor, 239
Kansas (U.S. State), 280, 866
Kansas City, Missouri, 878–79
Kansas-Nebraska Act of 1854, 280
Kant, Immanuel, 492, 1019
Karnak, temple of, 3
Kashmir, 247
Kassites, 214
Kaurismaki, Aki, 35
Kazakhstan, 833
Keaton, Buster, 24, 1019
Keats, John, 352, 1019
Keck I (telescope), 534
Kellogg, Willie Keith, 143–44
Kelly, Ellsworth, 101
Kelly, Gene, 26
Kennedy, John F., 249, 289, 1019
Kennedy, Joseph, 1020
Kennedy, Robert F., 290, 1020
Kensett, John Frederick, 96
Kentucky, Commonwealth of (U.S. State), 866
Kenya, 833
Kepler, Johannes, 234, 531, 606, 1020
  Laws of Planetary Motion, 531
Kerensky, Alexander, 244, 267
Kerouac, Jack, 365
Keynes, John Maynard, 1020
Khan, Altan, 231
Khan, Genghis, 226
Khan, Kublai, 226
Khnum, 480
Khrushchev, Nikita, 1020
Ki, 479
Kierkegaard, Søren, 493, 1020
Kieslowski, Krysztof, 33
Killy, Jean-Claude, 1020
Kincaid, Jamaica, 365
kinetograph, 22
kinetoscope, 22
King George's War, 257
King Jr., Rev. Martin Luther, 290
King Sejong, 229
King, B.B. (Riley B.), 64
King, Billie Jean, 726
King, Martin Luther Jr., 250, 290, 1020–21
King, Stephen, 373
Kingsolver, Barbara, 368
Kingston, Maxine Hong, 365
Kingu, 479
Kinsey, Alfred, 1021
Kintner, Robert, 417
Kipling, Rudyard, 353, 1021
Kirchner, Ernst Ludwig, 100
Kiribati, 833–34
Kirstein, Lincoln, 18
Kissinger, Henry Alfred, 1021
Klee, Paul, 1021
Klimt, Gustav, 100
Knights of Labor, 283
Knossos, 213
Know Nothings, 280
Koch, Robert, 439
Kooning, Willem de, 101, 986
Koons, Jeff, 102
Koran, 222
Korea, 248
Korea, North, 834
Korea, South, 834
Korean War, 248
Korematsu v. United States, 306
Koryo Dynasty, 223, 229
Kosovo, 252
Kozintsev, Grigori, 33
Kramer, Stanley, 27
krypton, 585
Ku Klux Klan, 23, 287
Kublai Khan, 255, 1021
Kubrick, Stanley, 1021
Kuleshov, Lev, 33
Kuomintang, 245
Kurosawa, Akira, 36, 1021
Kushan Empire, 218
Kuwait, 834
Kyrgyzstan, 834–35

L

La Follette, Robert M., 1021
La Niña, 173
Laënnec, René, 438, 439
Laertes, 475
Laius, 475
Lamarck, Jean-Baptiste Pierre Antoine de Monet, 1022
lamb and mutton, 937
Lancaster, Burt, 27, 1022
Land Area, world, by selected region, 173
Landis, Kenesaw Mountain, 673
Landor, Walter Savage, 352
Lang, Fritz, 31, 1022
Languages, 801–04
  isolates, pidgins, and creoles, 803
  language families, 801-03
  major languages of the world, 803–04
lanthanides, 585
lanthanum, 585
Laos, 835
Laozi, 1022
Lares, 475
Larkin, Philip, 354
Larsen, Nella, 365
Las Vegas, Nevada, 879
Lascaux cave, 2
lasers, development of, 644–46
Lassa fever, 455
Latin America, 245
Latin-American Literature, 343–44
Latvia, 835
lauda, 53
Lavoisier, Antoine Laurent, 438, 1022
Law, 294–336
  American Constitutional system, 297–99
  Anglo-American, 295–96
  brief history of, 294–97
  canon, 302
  civil, 299–300, 300–01
  common law, history of, 295–98
  contract, 299
  court system, U.S., 300
  criminal, 299, 301–02
  in Enlightenment era, 296–97
  family, 299–300
  glossary of terms, 308–12
  in ancient Greece, 294
  in ancient Rome, 294–95
  international, 302–03
  Medieval, 295
  property, 299
  shariah, 302
  tort, 299

Laws of Planetary Motion, 531
Lawrence v. Texas, 308
Lawrence, D. H., 353, 356, 1022
Lawrence, Florence, 24
lawrencium, 585
Le Corbusier, 10, 1022–23
lead, 585–86
Lead Belly (Huddie Ledbetter), 68
League of Nations, 268, 287
Lebanon, 835
Leda, 475
Lee, Manfred B., 370
Lee, Robert Edward, 262, 1023
Lee, Spike, 30
Leeuwenhoek, Antoni van, 438
LeGuin, Ursula K., 374
Leibniz, Gottfried Wilhelm, Baron von, 234, 391, 491, 638, 1023
Leighton, Frederick, 97
Lemieux, Mario, 711, 1023
lemon, 928
Lend-Lease Act, 269, 288
Lenin, Vladimir I., 244, 1023
Lennon, John, 1023
Leo I, 1023
Leonardo da Vinci, 92, 228, 1023–24
leprosy (Hansen's disease), 456
Lesotho, 835
Lessing, Doris, 357
Leto, 475
lettuces, 931
Leucippus, 486
Lever Brothers, 144
Lewis, C. Day, 354
Lewis, Carl, 1024
Lewis, Lennox, 758
Lewis, Merriwether, 276
Lewton, Val, 26
Lexington and Concord, Battles of, 275
Leyte Gulf, Battle of, 270
Liberia, 835–36
Libya, 836
Lichtenstein, Roy, 1024
Liechtenstein, 836
lieder, 54–55
Life of an American Fireman, 23
life processes, basic, 551–52
light (physics), 608
  laws of, 616
lime, 928
Limón, José, 19
Lincoln, Abraham, 261, 281, 1024
Lind, James, 438
Lindbergh, Charles A., 1024
Lindy Hop, 20
linguistic analysis, 494
Linnaeus,Carolus, 551, 1024
linotype, 637
lipids, 576
Lippershey, Hans, 531
Lister, Joseph, 439
Liston, Sonny, 757
Liszt, Franz, 49
Literature, 338–88
  African, 347–48
  American, 358–68
  in American colonies, 358–59
  in ancient Western world, 338–39
  Chinese, 344–45
  in 18th-century Europe, 340–41
  in 18th-century America, 359
  essayists, American, 360
  fantasy, 373–74
  glossary of terms, 384–88
  Indian, 346–47
  Japanese, 345–46
  Latin American, 343–44
  in Medieval Europe, 339
  mystery, 369–72
  in 19th-Century Europe, 341
  in 19th Century America, 359–60
  popular, 368–74
  in Renaissance Europe, 339–40
  romance, 372–73
  Russian, 342–43
  science fiction, 373–74
  in 17th-Century Europe, 340
  women's domestic fiction, 361–62
  world, 338–48
lithium, 586
Lithuania, 836
Little Big Horn, Battle of, 284
Little Richard, 74
liver, human, 559
Lloyd George, David, 1024
Locarno Treaties, 245
Lochner v. New York, 304
Locke, John, 625, 1024–25
logic, 484
logical positivism, 494
Loki, 482
Lomonosov, Mikhail, 342
London, Jack, 363
Long Beach, California, 879
Long March, 245
Long, Crawford, 439
Long, Gia, 239
Longfellow, Henry Wadsworth, 361, 1025
Lorca, Federico García, 342, 1025
Lord Baltimore, 273
Lord Cornwallis, 260
Lorenzetti, Ambrogio, 91
Los Angeles, California, 879
Lothair, 221
Louis IV, 257
Louis IX, 255, 1025
Louis VII, 254
Louis XI, 256
Louis XIV, 235, 1025
Louis XV, 1025
Louis XVI, 236, 260, 1025
Louis, Joe, 757, 1025
Louis, Murray, 19
Louisiana (U.S. State), 866
Louisiana Purchase, 276
Lovecraft, H. P., 373
Lovelace, Richard, 350
Loving v. Virginia, 307
Loyola, Ignatius, 233, 1013
Lucas, George, 28, 29, 1025–26
Ludendorff, Erich, 266, 1026
Luftwaffe, 269
Lully, Jean Baptiste, 17, 44
Lumet, Sidney, 28
Lumière brothers (Auguste and Louis), 22
lungs, 558
lupus, 446
Lutetium, 586
Luther, Martin, 233, 1026
Lutheran Churches, 503
Luxembourg, 836–37
Lyman FUSE (telescope), *534*
lymphatic system, 558
Lysander, 253

M

Ma'at, 480
MacArthur, Douglas, 269, 289, 1026
MacDiarmid, Hugh, 354
Macedon, 217
Macedonia, The Former Yugoslav Republic of, 217, 837
Machiavelli, Niccolo, 340, 376, 490, 1026
Machu Picchu, architecture of, 14
Mack, Connie, 673
Macmillan, Harold, 1026
MacNeice, Louis, 354
Macroeconomics, 124–30
  challenges in new world economy, 129–30
  common issues, 125–28
  development of, 124
  disposable Income, 128
  fiscal policy, 128
  forecasts and business cycles, 126
  Gross Domestic Product, 124
  international trade, 126–28
  labor force, 125–26
  monetary policy, 128–29
  multipliers and accelerators, 128
  national income, 124–25
  output and employment, 125
  prices and inflation, 126
Madagascar, 837
Madame Bovary, 341
Madison, James, 276, 277, 1026
Madison, James, 276
madrigal, 55
Maeterlinck, Maurice, 382
Magadha, 218
Magazines, history of, 433–34
Magellan, Ferdinand, 232, 1026
magical realism (in literature), 344
Magna Carta, 227
magnesium, 586
Magritte, René, 100, 1026–27
Magyars, 221
Mahabharata, 346
Mahavishnu Orchestra, 73
Mahayana, 219
Mahler, Gustav, 50, 1027
Mahmud of Ghazni, 224
Mailer, Norman, 368, 1027
Maillol, Aristide, 99
Maine (U.S. State), 866–67
maize, 925
Major League Baseball. see Baseball
Maki, Fumihiko, 1027
Malamud, Bernard, 365
Malaria, 456
Malawi, 837
Malay, 803
Malaya, 247
Malaysia, 837–38
Maldives, 838
Mali, 225, 838
Malone, Moses, 690
Malpighi, Marcello, 437

Malraux, André, 342
Malta, 838
Malthus, Thomas Robert, 130, 1027
Malus, Etienne, 608
Mamet, David, 383
mammogram, 464
Manchu, 239
Mandate of Heaven, 216
Mandela, Nelson, 1027
Manet, Edouard, 97, 1027
Manganese, 586
manic-depressive illness, 630
Manila Bay, Battle of, 285
Mankiewicz, Herman J., 26
Manley, Mary de la Rivière, 372
Mann, Thomas, 342, 1027–28
manned spaceflight, 252
Mannerism, 93
Mantle, Mickey, 673, 1028
Manzikert, Battle of, 225
Mao Zedong, 1028
Maori, 243
Marathon, 216, 253
Marbury v. Madison, 276, 303
March to the Sea, 264
Marciano, Rocky, 757
Marconi, Guglielmo, 640, 1028
Marcus Aurelius, 1028
Marduk, 479
Marey, Etienne-Jules, 439
Margaret of Anjou, 256
Maria Theresa, 257
Marie Antoinette, 236, 1028
marine chronometer, development of, 636
Maris, Roger, 674
marketing, birth of, 143–44
Marlowe, Christopher, 349, 377, 1028
Marne, Battle of the (Second), 268
Mars, features and composition, 537–38
Marshall Islands, 838–39
Marshall Plan, 247, 289
Marshall, Alfred, 122
Marshall, George C., 1028–29
Marshall, John, 1029
Marvell, Andrew, 350
Marx, Groucho, 1029
Marx, Karl, 121, 493, 1029
Marxism, 136
Mary, Queen of Scots, 1029
Maryinsky Ballet, 17–18
Maryland (U.S. State), 273, 867
Masaccio, 92, 1029
Maslow, Abraham, 627
masque, 59
Mass, Catholic (music), 53
mass, conservation of, 615
mass-energy, conservation of, 615
Massachusetts Bay Colony, 273
Massachusetts, Commonwealth of (U.S. State), 867
Master of Flémalle, 91
Masters, Edgar Lee, 363
Mathematics, 390–402
  branches of, 392–93
  early arithmetic, 390
  formulas, 393–96
  glossary of terms, 398–402
  history of, 390–92
Mather, Cotton, 359
Mathewson, Christy, 672
Matisse, Henri, 99, 1029
Matsuo Basho, 239
matter, condensed, 611
Maupassant, Guy de, 341
Mauritania, 839
Mauritius, 839
Mauryan Empire, 218
Maximus, Fabius, 254
Maxwell, James Clerk, 109–10, 608, 1029–30
Maya, 216
Mayer, Louis, 1030
Mayflower Compact, 272
Mays, Carl, 673
Mays, Willie, 673, 1030
Mazzini, Giuseppe, 240
MCA, 28
McAuliffe, Anthony, 270
McBride, Mary Margaret, 408
McCarthy, Joseph, 248, 289, 1030
McCartney, Paul, 1030
McClellan, George B., 262
McCulloch v. Maryland, 303
McEnroe, John, 726
McEwan, Ian, 358
McGwire, Mark, 674
McKay, Claude, 365
McKinley, William, 285–86, 1030
McLuhan, Marshall, 1030
McNamara, Robert Strange, 1030
Mead, Margaret, 1031
Meade, George C., 263
Meany, George, 1031
measles (rubeola), 456–58
measurement (mathematics), 393
Meat Inspection Act, 286
mechanics, grammar, 793–95
Medea, 475
Medes, 214
Media, 404–34
  electronic, 404–29
  print, 430–34
medications, 466–68
Medicine, 435–68
  alternative therapies, 441–43
  in antiquity, 436–37
  during Dark Ages, 437
  history of, 436–42
  in 19th century, 438–40
  Renaissance, 437–38
  in 20th century, 440–43
medulla oblongata, 561
Medusa, 475
Meier, Richard Alan, 1031
Meiji Constitution, 243
Meiji Restoration, 243
meiosis, 556
Meitnerium, 586
Méliès, Georges, 22
melons, 931
Melville, Herman, 361, 1031
Memphis, Tennessee, 879
Menander, 375
Mencken, H.L., 1031
Mendel, Gregor Johann, 440, 549, 1031
Mendelevium, 586
Mendelssohn, Felix, 49, 1031
Menelaus, 475
Ménendez de Avilés, Pedro, 272
Menes, 212
meningitis, 457–58
Menshevik, 244
menstrual cycle, 565
mental illness, 458
Mentuhotep, tomb of, 3
Menzel, Jiri, 34
mercury, 586
Mercury (planet), features and composition, 535
Meredith, George, 352
Merode Altarpiece, 91
Merrill Lynch, establishment of, 165–66
Mesa Verde cliff dwellings, 14
Mesa, Arizona, 879
Mesmer, Franz Anton, 625
Mesoamerican civilization, 216
Mesopotamia, 212, 214
Mesozoic era, 596
Messier, Mark, 1031–32
metals, development of, 634
metamorphic rocks, 598
Metaphysical Poets, 349
metaphysics, 484
Method Acting, 383
Methodist Churches, 503
Metis, 475
Metropolis, 31
Metternich, Klemens, Furst von, 240, 1032
Mexico, 236, 839
MGM, 26
Miami,Florida, 879
Michelangelo Buonarroti, 7, 92, 1032
Michelson, Albert, 609
Michigan (U.S. State), 867–68
Microeconomics, 121–24
  consumers, 122
  markets, pricing, and the allocation of resources, 122
  natural monopolies, 122–23
  producers, 122
Micronesia, Federated States of, 839
microwave ovens, development of, 643–44
Midas, 475
Middle Kingdom, 212
Midway, Battle of 269
Mies van der Rohe, Ludwig, 10, 1032
Mifune, Toshiro, 36
milk, 938
Milky Way Galaxy, 543–44
Mill, John Stuart, 1032
Miller, Arthur, 383, 1032
Millet, François, 96, 97
Milton, John, 350, 1032
Milwaukee, Wisconsin, 879
minerals, 598, 947
Ming Dynasty, 229, 231
minimum wage, poverty and, 127
Minneapolis, Minnesota, 879–80
Minnesota (U.S. State), 868
Minoans, 215
Minos, 213, 475
Minotaur, 475
Minow, Newton, 416
minstrel music, 61
minstrel shows, 381
minuet, 57
Miocene epoch, 596
Miranda v. Arizona, 307
Mississippi (U.S. State), 868
Missouri (U.S. State), 868–69
Missouri Compromise, 277
Mitchell, Joan, 101
mitosis, 556

Mizoguchi, Kenji, 36
Modern Times, 25
Modernism (in art), 99–101
Modernism (in literature), 364–69
Modigliani, Amedeo, 99
Modigliani, Franco, 1032–33
Mohacs, Battle of, 229, 238
Mohammed II, Askia, 232
Mohenjo-Daro, 213
Moldova, 839–40
Molière, 1033
Moltke, Marshall von, 265
molybdenum, 586
Mona Lisa, 92
Monaco, 840
Mondrian, Piet, 101, 1033
Monet, Claude, 98, 1033
monetarism, 129
money market funds, 167
money supply, 129
money, development of, 158–59
Mongol Empire, 226
Mongolia, 840
Monk, Meredith, 19
Monk, Thelonious, 72
Monmouth, Battle of, 260
Monroe Doctrine, 241, 277
Monroe, Bill, 67
Monroe, James, 277, 1033
Monroe, Marilyn, 27, 1033
Montana (U.S. State), 869
Montana, Joe, 1033
Monteverdi, Claudio, 44
Montezuma I, 228
Montezuma II, 1033
Montgomery, Bernard, 269
Montgomery, General Richard, 258
Moody, Helen Wills, 725, 726
Moonves, Les, 426
Moorcock, Michael, 374
Moore's Law, 649
Moore, Douglas, 50
Moore, G. E., 494
Moore, Henry, 101
Moore, Sir Thomas, 233, 352
More, Thomas, 1033
Morels, 934
Morgagni, Giovanni, 438
Morgan, Daniel, 260
Morgan, John Pierpont, 142, 1034
Morgan, Thomas Hunt, 440
Morisot, Berthe, 98
Morley, Edward, 609
Morley, Thomas, 43
Mormon Church, 504–05
Morocco, 840
Morrill Act, 281
Morrison, Toni, 365, 1034
Morse, Samuel Finley Breese, 141, 639, 1034
Morton, Jelly Roll, 69, 70
Moses, 214
Moses, Grandma, 1034
Mosley, Walter, 371
Mossadegh, Mohammad, 251
motet, 53
Motion Picture Patents Company, 23
Motion Picture Producers and Distributors of America, 24
Motion Picture Production Code, 25
Motown, 65
mountains of the world, 599
Mozambique, 840–41
Mozart, Wolfgang Amadeus, 47, 48, 1034
MRI, 464
MTV, 77–78, 421
Muddy Waters, 64
Mughal Empire, 230, 238
Muhammad, 222, 1034
Muir, Edwin, 353
Muir, John, 1034
Muldoon, Paul, 354
multi-infarct dementia, 629
multiple sclerosis, 446
Munn v. Illinois, 304
muon, 618
Murdoch, Iris, 357
Murdoch, Rupert, 423
Murfreesboro, Battle of, 263
Murrow, Edward R., 408
Musa, Mansa, 225
muscles, 560
musculoskeletal system, human, 560
Muses, 476
mushrooms, 933–34
Music, 40–88
  African, 78
  American popular, 61–78
  in ancient Greece and Rome, 40–41
  Caribbean, 78
  Celtic, 78–79
  church, 53–54
  in Classical period, 46–48
  Classical, history of, 40–53
  country, 66–68
  dramatic, 58–61
  Eastern European, 79
  folk, 68–69
  forms, 53–60
  glossary, 81–84
  in Baroque period, 43–46
  Indian, 79
  instrumental, 55–58
  Jazz, 69–73
  Latin, 79
  in the Middle Ages, 41–42
  Middle Eastern, 79
  minstrel, 61
  publishing industry, 61–62
  in the Renaissance, 42–43
  in the Romantic period, 48–50
  symbols and notation, 84–87
  vocal, 54–55
  world, 78–79
musical instruments, 79–81
  brass, 80
  electronic, 80–81
  keyboard, 80
  percussion, 80
  string, 79–80
  woodwind, 80
musical theater, 59
Muslim League, 247
Mussolini, Benito, 245, 269, 270, 1034–35
Mut, 480
Mutsuhito, 243
mutual funds, 166–67
  key terms for, 167
  kinds of, 167–70
Muybridge, Eadweard, 22, 108
Myanmar, 841
myasthenia gravis, 446
Mycenae, 215
myelogram, 464

N

Nabokov, Vladimir, 365, 1035
NAFTA, 137
Nagasaki, 270
Naismith, James, 686
Namath, Joe, 702, 1035
Namibia, 841
Nanakh, Guru, 238
Nanna, 482
nanotechnology, development of, 646
Napier, John, 638
Napoleon, 27, 261, 1035
Napoleon III, 240, 1035
Napoleonic Wars, 237, 260, 261
Narcissus, 476
narrowcasting, 427–29
Nashville, Tennessee, 880
Nasser, Gamal Abdel, 248, 1035
National Assembly, 236
National Bank Acts, 281
National Basketball Association. see Basketball
National Hockey League. see Ice Hockey
National Labor Relations Board v. Jones & Laughlin Steel Corp., 306
National Origins Act, 287
National Recovery Administration, 288
National Socialism, 245
naturalism (in literature), 362–63
Nauru, 841
Navigation Acts, 273
Navratilova, Martina, 726
Nazi, 245
Neanderthals, 210
Nebraska (U.S. State), 869
Nebuchadnezzar II, 214, 1035
Nehru, Motilal, 1035–36
Nelson, Horatio, 261, 1036
Nemesis, 476
Neo-Paganism, 516–17
Neoclassical Period (in literature), 350
Neoclassicism (in art), 95
neodymium, 586
Neogene period, 596
Neolithic, 211
Neolithic Revolution, 211–12
neon, 586
Neoplatonism, 489
Nepal, 239, 841–42
Nephthys, 480
Neptune, features and composition, 540
neptunium, 586
Nereids, 476
Nereus, 476
Nero, 1036
Neruda, Pablo, 1036
nervous system, human, 560–61
Nestor, 476
Nestorian Church, 501
Netherlands, 842
network theory, 393
neurons, 560
neurotransmitters, 576
Neutrality Act of 1939, 288
neutrinos, 618
neutron, 618
Nevada (U.S. State), 869
New Deal, The, 162, 287–88
New Hampshire (U.S. State), 869
New Jersey (U.S. State), 870
New Kingdom, 213

New Mexico (U.S. State), 870
New Model Army, 257
New Netherland, 273
New Orleans, Louisiana, 880
New Spain, 236
New Wave (music), 78
New World Folk Religions, 516
New York (U.S. State), 870–71
New York City, New York, 880
New York Stock Exchange, establishment of, 164
New York Times Co. v. Sullivan, 307
New York Times Co. v. United States, 307
New Zealand, 842
Newcomen engine, 638
Newcomen, Thomas, 138, 638
Newman, Paul, 1036
Newspapers, history of, 430–33
Newton, Sir Isaac, 234, 391, 491, 531, 606, 1036
Nibelungenlied, 339
Nicaragua, 842
Nicholas Brothers, 20
Nicholas I, Czar, 261
Nicholas II, 244
Nichols, Mike, 28
Nicholson, Jack, 1036
nickel, 586–87
Nickelodeons, 22–23
Nicklaus, Jack, 1036
Niépce, Joseph Nicéphore, 104
Nietszche, Friedrich Wilhelm, 1036–37
Niger, 842–43
Nigeria, 843
Nightingale, Florence, 261
Nijinsky, Vaslav, 18, 51, 1037
Nike, 476
Nikolais, Alwin, 19
Nimitz, Chester W., 1037
Nintendo 64, 670
Nintendo Entertainment System, 667
Niobe, 476
Niobium, 587
Nitrogen, 587
Nixon, Richard M., 248, 290, 1037
Njord, 482
Nobel Prizes, 911–20
  for Peace, 911–12
  in Chemistry, 915–17
  in Economic Sciences, 915
  in Literature, 919–20
  in Physics, 917–19
  in Physiology or Medicine, 912–15
nobelium, 587
Noble, Edward J., 407
Nobunaga, Oda, 231
Nolde, Emile, 100
nominalism, 490
Normans, 225
Norns, 482
Norris, Frank, 362
North America, 182–84, 211, 216, 220, 228–29, 232–33
  climate, 183
  economy, 183–84
  people, 183–84
  physical features, 182–83
North American Free Trade Agreement, 292
North American Free Trade Agreement (NAFTA), 137
North Atlantic Treaty Organization, 248, 289
North Carolina (U.S. State), 871
North Dakota (U.S. State), 871
Northern Expedition, 245
Northwest Passage, 232
Norway, 843
Notre Dame cathedral, 7
nouns, 768
Novel, English, 354–58
  early Modern, 356–57
  in Edwardian age, 356
  late Victorian, 356
  in 19th century, 355–56
  psychological, 356
  romantic, 355
  satirical, 355–56
  in 20th century, 356–58
Nuclear Physics, 610–11
nuclear power, development of, 643
numbers
  grammatical usage, 793
  systems, 396–98
  theory, 393
Nurhachi, 231
Nurkse, Ragnar, 130
Nurmi, Paavo, 1037
Nut, 480
Nutrition, 946–52
nuts, 939
Nyx, 476

O

O'Brien, Tim, 368
O'Connor, Flannery, 364, 1038
O'Higgins, Bernardo, 1037
O'Keeffe, Georgia, 101, 1037
O'Neal, Shaquille, 691, 1037–38
O'Neill, Eugene, 364, 383, 1038
Oakland, California, 880
Oates, Joyce Carol, 368
oats, 925
obsessive-compulsive disorder, 628
oceanids, 476
Oceans, 190
Ockham's razor, 489–90
October Revolution, 244
ode (music), 55
Odets, Clifford, 383
Odin, 482
Odysseus, 476
Odyssey, The, 338
Oedipus, 476
Oersted, Christian, 608
Offenbach, Jacques, 50
Oglethorpe, William, 273
Ögödei Khan, 226
Ohio (U.S. State), 871–72
Oklahoma (U.S. State), 872
Oklahoma City, Oklahoma, 880
Old Kingdom (Egypt), 212
Oldenburg, Claes, 102
Oligocene epoch, 596
olives, 931
Olivier, Laurence, 1037
Olmec, 216
Olympic games, 745–51
  history of, 745–46, 752
  summer games, 1896–2008, 746–49
  summer program, 751
  winter games, 1924–2006, 749–51
  winter program, 751
Omaha, Nebraska, 880
Oman, 843
Onassis, Jacqueline, 1038
onions, 931
Open City, 34
Open Source software, 653
Opera, 59–60
  in Baroque period, 44–46
  in Classical period, 48
  in Romantic period, 49–50
Operation Market-Garden, 270
Operation Overlord, 270
operetta, 60
Opium War, 242
Oppositional defiant disorder, 629
oral diseases, 458–59
oranges, 928
oratorio, 53–54
Ordovician period, 596
Oregon (U.S. State), 872
Orestes, 476
organisms, classification of, 551
Organization for Economic Cooperation and Development, 247
Orientalism (in art), 96
Orion, 476
Ornish Diet, 952
Orpheus, 476
Orr, Bobby, 1036
Orthodox Christianity, 221
Orton, Joe, 383
Orwell, George, 357, 1036
Osborne, John, 382
Osiris, 480
Oslo Agreement, 251
osmium, 587
osteoporosis, 459
Otto I, 222
Otto, Nikolaus August, 1036
Ottoman Empire, 225, 229–30, 241, 244, 266
Ouedraogo, Idrissa, 37
ovaries, 564
overture, 57
Ovid, 339, 1036
Owen, Wilfred, 353
Owens, Jesse, 747, 1036–39
oxygen, 587
Ozu, Yasujiro, 36

P

packaged foods, innovation in, 143–44
Pahlavi, Mohammad Reza, 251
Paik, Nam June, 103
Paine, Thomas, 259, 359, 1039
Pakistan, 843–44
  creation of, 247
Palaeogene period, 596
Palau, 844
Paleocene epoch, 596
Paleolithic, 210
paleontology, 602–04
Palestinian Authority, 251
Palestrina, Giovanni Pierluigi da, 43, 1039
Paley, William S., 407
Palladio, Andrea, 7, 958
palladium, 587
Palmer, Arnold, 718, 1039
Pan, 476
Panama, 844
pancreas, 564
Pandora, 476

panic disorder, 628
Panic of 1907, 161
pantheism, 491
pap smear, 464
papaya, 928
paper, development of, 635–36
Papua New Guinea, 844
Paracelsus, 438
Paradise Lost, 350
Paradjanov, Sergei , 33
Paraguay, 845
Paramount, 26, 28
parentheses, 790
Paretsky, Sara , 371
Pargeter, Edith Mary , 371
Parker, Charlie, 72, 1039
Parkinson's disease, 459
Parkinson, James, 439
Parmenides, 485
Parmigianino, 93
Parnell, Charles Stewart, 1039
Parsiism, 514
Parthenon, 4
particle physics, 610, 612
particles, J/psi, 618
particles, strange, 618
particles, W and Z, 618
Pascal, Blaise, 340, 391, 638, 1039
Pasiphae, 476
Passchendaele, 267
Passer, Ivan, 34
Pasteur, Louis, 439, 1039
Pastorius, Jaco, 73
Patrick (Saint), 1039
Patroclus, 477
Patton, George S., 1040
Pauli, Wolfgang, 610
Pavlov, Ivan, 627
Pax Britannica, 239
Pax Romana, 217
Paxton, Joseph, 9
Paz, Octavio, 1040
Peace of Paris, 236
Peace of Prague, 256
Peace of Utrecht, 257
Peace of Westphalia, 256
peaches, 928–29
pear, 929
Pearl Harbor, 245
Peary, Robert Edwin, 1040
peas, 931–32
Pegasus, 477
Pei, Ioeh Ming, 11, 1040
Peking Man, 210
Pelé, 737–38, 1040
Peleus, 477
Peloponnesian War, 216, 253
Penates, 477
Penderecki, Krzysztof, 50–51
Penelope, 477
Penn, Arthur, 28
Penn, William, 273, 1040–41
Pennsylvania, Commonwealth of (U.S. State), 273, 872
Pentagon Papers, 291
Pentecostal Churches, 503–04
People's Republic of China, 35, 247
Peoples Party, 284
Pepin III, 221
Pericles, 216, 253, 1041
period (punctuation), 784
Periodic Table, 580–81
Perkins, Carl, 74
Permanent Neutrality Bill, 268
Permian period, 596
Perry, Matthew, 243
Perry, Oliver, 277
Persephone, 477
Perseus, 477
Persian Empire, 214, 216
Persian (language), 804
Persian Wars, 216
Peru, 845
Petain, Philippe, 267
Peter (Saint), 1041
Peter I, the Great, 1041
Peter III, 258
Peter the Great, 237
Peter the Hermit, 254
Petrarch, 228, 1041
Petronas Towers, 11
Phaedra, 477
Phaethon, 477
Phanerozoic eon, 596
phenomenology, 494
Philadelphia, Pennsylvania, 880
Philip I, 217
Philip II, 233, 254, 1041
Philip V, 257
Philip VI, 255
Philippines, 236, 845
Philippine Sea, Battle of, 270
Phillips, Irna , 409
Philosophy, history of, 484–94
  19th century, 492–93
  20th century, 493–94
  in ancient Greece, 484–86
  branches of, 484
  Continental, 494
  early Modern, 490–91
  in the Enlightenment, 491–92
  Hellenistic, 488
  Medieval, 488–90
  Roman, 488
Phineus, 477
phobias, 628
Phoenix, Arizona, 881
phosphorus, 587
Photography, 104–18
  art history of, 113–16
  color, 109–10
  conceptualism, 115
  digital, 111–12
  documentary, 115
  early printing, 107–08
  glossary of terms, 116–18
  in the 20th century, 110
  invention of, 104–07
  Modern Realism in, 115
  photojournalism, 115
  portraiture, 113
  technical history of, 104–11
photometry, *534*
photon, 617
Physics, 605–24
  astrophysics, 611
  basic laws of, 613–17
  biophysics, 613
  geophysics, 611–13
  history of, 605–13
  nuclear, 610–11
  particle, 610
Piaget, Jean, 627, 1041
Piano, Renzo, 1041
Picasso, Pablo, 99, 1042
Pickett's Charge, 263
Pickett, George , 263
Pickford, Mary, 23, 1042
Pierce, Franklin, 1042
Pierce, Fred , 418
Piero della Francisco, 92
Pincay, Laffit, Jr., 1042
Pineapple, 929
Pinkerton, Allan , 369
Pinter, Harold, 383, 1042
Pinworms, 461–62
pion, 618
Pirandello, Luigi , 382
Pisa Cathedral, 6
Pissarro, Camille, 98, 1042
Pitt, William (the Elder), 1042
Pitt, William (the Younger), 1042
pituitary gland, 564
Pius IX, Pope, 1042–43
Pizarro, Francisco, 232, 1043
plainchant, 54
Plains of Abraham, Battle of the, 235
plainsong, 54
Planck, Max, 610
Planets
  details of, 535–40
  direct sampling of, 532–33
  extrasolar, 541
Plangman, Mary Patricia , 371
plastics, 642
plate tectonics, 596–98
Plateau, Joseph, 22
Plath, Sylvia, 1043
platinum, 587
Plato, 487, 530, 1043
Plautus, 375
Player, Gary, 718
Playstation, 670
Pleistocene epoch, 596
Plessy v. Ferguson, 285, 304
Pliocene epoch, 596
Plotinus, 489
plum, 929
Pluto (deity), 474
Pluto (planet), features and composition, 540–41
plutonium, 587
Plymouth, 272
pneumonia, 459
Poe, Edgar Allan, 361, 1043
Poetry
  after World War I, 353–54
  and American Renaissance, 360–62
  Elizabethan, 349
  English, 348–58
  in Restoration, 350–51
  in 17th century, 349–50
  Irish, contemporary, 354–58
  late Victorian, 352–53
  Middle English, 348–49
  nature poetry, 351
  old English, 348
  pre-Raphaelite, 352
  Romantic, 351–52
  in Tudor period, 349
  in Victorian age, 352
Poitier, Sidney, 27
Poland, 33, 227, 234, 237, 845
poliomyelitis, 459
Polk, James Knox, 279, 1043
Pollio, Marcus Vitruvius, 4
pollock (fish), 935
Pollock, Jackson, 101, 1043
Pollux, 477
Polo, Marco, 227, 1043
polonium, 587
Polynices, 477
Polyphemus, 477
Pompey (The Great; Gnaeus Pompeius), 1043
Ponce de León, Juan, 272
PONG, 666
Pont du Garde aqueduct, 5

pop art, 102
pop music, 74–75
Pope, Alexander, 351, 1044
popular song, American, 62–63
population, world, 173, 188–90
pork, 937–38
Porter, Cole, 63, 1044
Porter, Edwin S., 23
Porter, Katherine Anne , 364
Portland,Oregon, 881
Portugal, 845–46
Poseidon, 471
positivism, 982
post-traumatic stress disorder (PTSD), 628
Postmodernism
  in art, 102–03
  in literature, 368
potassium, 588
potato, 932
Potsdam Conference, 246
Pound, Ezra, 364, 1044
Powell, Anthony , 357
Power, Lionel, 42
Poznan uprising, 33
praeseodymium, 588
Pragmatism, 493
Pre-Romantics (in poetry), 351
predation, 571
prelude, 57
prepositions, 771
Presbyterian Church, 504
Presley, Elvis, 74, 1044
Prevert, Jacques , 30
Priam, 477
Priapus, 477
price incentives, 123–24
Principia (of Isaac Newton), 531
printing, development of, 637
prion diseases, 459–60
probability (mathematics), 393
Proclamation Act of 1763, 274
Proclamation of Amnesty and Reconstruction, 281
Procris, 477
Procter and Gamble, 144
Production Code Administration, 25, 28
programme music, 57
Progressive Rock, 77
Prokofiev, Sergei, 50
Prometheus, 477
promethium, 588
pronouns, 769
  correct usage, 778–81
  without references, 780
protactinium, 588
Protagoras, 486
protein synthesis, 567–69
proteins, 576, 946
Proterozoic eon, 596
Protestant Churches, 501–06
proton, 617
Proust, Marcel, 342, 1044
Prusiner, Stanley , 440
PSA test, 464
psoriasis, 446
Psyche, 477
Psychedelic Rock, 75–76
psychodynamic therapy, 632
Psychology, 625–32
  areas of research, 625
  biopsychology, 625
  clinical, 625
  cognitive, 625, 627–28
  common treatments, 631–32
  developmental, 625
  history of, 625–27
  humanistic, 627
  social, 625
Ptah, 480
Ptolemy, 530, 605
public goods, 123
Public Works Administration, 288
Puccini, Giacomo, 50, 1044
Pudovkin, Vsevolod I., 33
Pulitzer Prizes, 901–11
  for Biography/ Autobiography, 907–08
  for Drama, 905
  for Fiction, 904
  for General Nonfiction, 909–10
  for History, 906–07
  for International Reporting, 903
  for Music, 910
  for National Reporting, 902
  for Poetry, 908–09
  for Public Service in Newspaper Journalism, 901–02
Pulmonary function tests, 464
punctuation, 784–93
  apostrophes, 787
  brackets, 790–91
  colons, 790
  commas, 984–86
  dashes, 789
  end marks, 784
  exclamation point, 784
  hyphens, 791–93
  italics, 788–89
  parentheses, 790
  period, 784
  question mark, 784
  quotation marks, 787–88
  semicolons, 786–87
  slashes, 7891
Punic Wars, 217, 253–54
Punk rock, 77
Purcell, Henry, 44, 53
Pure Food and Drug Act, 286
Pushkin, Aleksandr, 343, 1044
Putin, Vladimir, 1045
Pygmalion, 477
Pynchon, Thomas, 1045
pyramids, 3
Pyramus, 477
Pyrrho of Elis, 488
Pythagoras, 40, 485, 530

Q

Qatar, 846
Qianlong Emperor, 239
Qin Dynasty, 219
Qin Shihuangdi, 1045
Qing Dynasty, 231, 239
quantum mechanics, 617
quantum theory, 610
  laws of, 616–17
quarks, 618
Queen Anne's War, 257
Queen Elizabeth, 233
Queen, Ellery , 370
question mark (punctuation), 784
quotation marks, 787–88

R

R&B, 63–66
Ra, 480
Rabelais, Francois, 340
Rabin, Yitzhak, 1045
Racine, Jean, 340, 379, 1045
radar, development of, 643
Radcliffe, Ann , 372
radiation
  bands of, 533
  telescopes and, *534*
radio radiation, *533*
radio, development of, 640
Radio, history of, 404–11
  broadcast news, 408
  creation of RCA, 404–05
  daytime, 408–13
  early uses of, 404
  entertainment and advertising, 408
  and Federal Communications Commission, 407–08
  need for regulation, 406
  network programming, 408–11
  prime time, 409–13
radium, 588
radon, 588
Ragtime, 61
railroads, development of, 640–41
Rainer, Yvonne, 19
Rajputana, 222
Raleigh, Sir Walter , 272
Ramayana, 346
Ran, 482
Rap music, 63–66
Raphael (Raffaello Sanzio), 93, 1045
rare-earth elements, 588
raspberries, 929
Rastafarianism, 517
Ravel, Maurice, 51
Ray, Satyajit, 35
Rayburn, Samuel, 1045
Razi, 437
Reagan, Ronald, 251, 291, 699, 1045
Realism (in art), 100–02
Realism (in literature), 363
recycling in U.S., 575
Red Scare, 287
Redford, Robert, 30, 1046
Redon, Odilon, 99
Reed, Walter , 440
Reform Acts, 240
Reformation, Age of, 233–34
Reformed Churches, 504
refrigeration, development of, 642
Regulation (economics), 123
Reich, Steve, 52
Reign of Terror, 236
relativity (physics), 609–10
  general theory of, 607
  special theory of, 609
Religion, 496–28
  glossary of terms, 518
Rembrandt van Rijn, 94, 1046
Remus, 477
Renoir, Auguste, 98, 1046
Renoir, Jean, 30, 1046
reproductive system, human, 561–66
  female, 565
  male, 561–65
Republican Party, 281
respiratory system, human, 558
Reuther, Walter, 1046
Revere, Paul, 258
Rhea, 477

Rhee, Syngman, 248
Rheims cathedral, 7
rhenium, 588
rheumatoid arthritis, 446
Rhode Island and Providence Plantations (U.S. State), 873
Rhodes, Cecil (John), 1046
rhodium, 588
Rhys, Jean , 358
Ricardo, David, 130, 1046
Ricci, Matteo, 231
rice, 925–26
Rice, Jerry, 1046
Rice, T. D. , 381
ricercare, 57
Richard I of England, 254
Richard III, 256, 1046–47
Richardson, Samuel, 355, 372
Richelieu, Cardinal, 234, 1047
Riefenstahl, Leni, 1047
Riemann, Bernhard, 1047
Riis, Jacob A., 114, 285
Rilke, Rainer Maria, 342, 1047
Rimbaud, Arthur, 341, 1047
Rivers of the World, 194–200
Rivers, Larry, 101
RKO, 26
RNA, 550, 567
Roach, Max, 72
Roanoke Island, 272
Robbins, Jerome, 1047
Robert the Bruce (Robert I), 1047
Robert, Nivelle, 267
Robertson, Oscar, 1047–48
Robespierre, Maximilien, 236, 1048
Robinson, Bill "Bojangles", 20
Robinson, Jackie, 687, 1048
robotics, development of, 644
Rock 'n' Roll, 74–79
rockabilly music, 74
Rockefeller Center, 11
Rockefeller, John Davison, 142, 1048
rockets, development of, 637
Rockne, Knute, 1048
Rockwell, Norman, 1048
Rodgers, Jimmie, 66
Rodgers, Richard, 63, 1048
Rodin, Auguste, 99, 1048
Rodríguez Cabrillo, Juan, 272
Roe v. Wade, 291, 307
Roebuck, Alvah Curtis, 143
Roger Williams, 273
Rollins, Sonny, 72
Roman Catholic Church, 499
Roman Empire, 217–18, 220–21
Roman Rite Churches, 500
Romania, 846
Romanov, Michael, 234
Romanticism (in American literature), 360–62
Romanticism (in art), 96
Romanticism (in poetry), 351–52
Rommel, Erwin, 269
Romulus, 477
Roosevelt, Eleanor, 1048–49
Roosevelt, Franklin D., 246, 268, 287, 1049
Roosevelt, Theodore, 285, 286, 1049
Rorschach, Hermann, 626
Rosenberg, Isaac , 353
Rosenberg, Stuart, 29
Rossellini, Roberto, 34
Rossetti, Christina , 352
Rossetti, Dante Gabriel, 98, 1049
Rossini, Antonio, 49–50
Roth, Philip, 365, 1049
Rothko, Mark, 101, 1049
Rouault, Georges, 100
Rousseau, Henri, 99
Rousseau, Jean Jacques, 340, 491, 1049–50
Rousseau, Théodore, 96
Rowlandson, Mary White , 358
Rowson, Susanna Haswell , 359
Rubber, development of, 640–41
rubella, 460
Rubens, Peter Paul, 94, 1050
rubidium, 588
Run D.M.C., 65–66
Rushdie, Salman, 358, 1050
Rusk, Dean, 1050
Ruskin, John, 1050
Russell, Bertrand, 494, 1050
Russia, 226, 234, 237–38, 244–45, 247, 846
Russian Literature, 342–43
Ruth, Babe, 673, 1050
ruthenium, 588
Rutherford, Ernest, 610, 1050
rutherfordium, 588
Rwanda, 252, 846–47
Ryan, Nolan, 1050–51
rye, 926

S

Saarinen, Eero, 10
Sabines, 478
Sacramento, California, 881
sacraments, 499
Sadat, Anwar, 1051
Safavid Dynasty, 230
Sailendra, 223
Saint Kitts and Nevis, 847
Saint Lucia, 847
Saint Vincent and the Grenadines, 847
Saladin (in Arabic, Salah Ad-din Yusuf Ibn Ayyub), 254, 1051
Salamis, 216
salt, 933
Salvation Army, 504
samarium, 588
Samoa, 847
Sampras, Pete, 727
Samuelson, Paul Anthony, 1051
San Antonio, Texas, 881
San Diego, California, 881
San Francisco Conference, 246
San Francisco, California, 881
San Jacinto, Battle of, 278
San Jose, California, 881
San Juan Hill, Battle of, 285
San Marino, 847–48
San Martín, José de , 241
Sand, George, 341
Sandburg, Carl , 363
Sanger, Margaret, 1051
sanskrit, 218
Santa Ana, 278, 279
Sao Tome and Principe, 848
Sappho, 215, 338, 1051
sarabande, 57
Sargent, John Singer, 1051
Sargon II, 214
Sarnoff, David , 404, 411
Sartre, Jean-Paul, 342, 494, 1051
Sassoon, Siegfried , 353
satire (in literature), 350–51
Saturday Night Fever, 20
Saturn, features and composition, 539–40
Satyr, 478
Saud, 238
Saudi Arabia, 848
Saul, 214
Sayers, Dorothy L. , 370
Sayles, John , 30
Scandinavian, 222
scandium, 588
Scarlatti, Alessandro, 44
Scarlatti, Domenico, 44
Schelling, Friedrich , 493
Schenk v. United States, 306
Schiele, Egon, 100
Schiller, Friedrich, 341, 1051–52
schizophrenia, 458, 631
Schoenberg, Arnold, 51, 1052
Scholasticism, 489
Schonlein, Johann , 439
Schopenhauer, Arthur , 493, 1052
Schrader, Paul , 28
Schrödinger, Erwin, 1052
Schubert, Franz, 49, 1052
Schuller, Gunther, 52
Schumann, Robert, 49, 1052
Schumpter, Joseph Alois, 1052
Schütz, Heinrich, 44
Schwann, Theodor, 549
Scientific Revolution, 234, 606–13
Scorsese, Martin, 28
Scott, Walter, 352, 355, 1052
Scott, Winfield, 279
scratch tests, 464
Scudéry, Madeleine de , 372
Scylla, 478
seaborgium, 588
seafloor spreading, 597
Seagram Building, 10
Sears, Richard Warren, 143
Sears, Roebuck and Company, 143
Seattle, Washington, 881
Second Coalition, 261
Second Empire, 240
Second Republic, 240
Securities and Exchange Commission, 288
Sedan, Battle of, 265
sedimentary rocks, 598
Sega Genesis, 670
Sega Master System, 667
Sega Saturn, 670
Segovia aqueduct, 5
Sekhmet, 481
Sekigahara, Battle of, 231
Selene, 478
selenium, 588
Seleucus, 217
Selim I the Grim, 229
Selim II "the Sot", 230
Selim III, 237
Selznick, David O., 1052–53
Sembene, Ousmane , 37
Semele, 478
semicolons, 786–87
Seminole Indians, 277
Semmelweiss, Ignaz , 439
Sen, Mrinal, 35
Seneca, 375, 488
Senegal, 848
Sennett, Mack, 24

sentences, 772–84
  classification, 774
  grammar, 772–84
  structure, 772–72
  types of, 774–75
separation anxiety, 629
September 11, 2001 (9-11), 252, 292
Serbia and Montenegro, 848
serenata, 55
serial comma, 785
Sermisy, Claude de, 43
set theory, 393
Seth, 481
Seton, Elizabeth Ann, 1053
Seurat, Georges, 98
Seuss, Dr. (Geisel, Theodore Seuss), 1053
Seven Arts, 28
Seven Years War, 235, 238, 258, 274
The Seventh Seal, 35
Seward, William, 280, 1053
sexigesimal (base-60) counting system, 530
sexually transmitted diseases (STDs), 460
Seychelles, 848–49
sfumato, 92
Shah Abbas I "the Great", 230
Shah Jahan, 230
Shah Tahmasp, 230
Shah, Nadir, 238
Shaka, 1053
Shakespeare, William, 234, 349, 377–78, 1053
Shang, 215
Shang Dynasty, 213
shared psychotic disorder, 631
Shaw, George Bernard, 381, 1053
Shaw, Joseph T. "Cap", 370
Shay's Rebellion, 275
Shelley, Mary, 373
Shelley, Percy Bysshe, 351, 1053
shellfish, 935–36
Shepard, Sam, 383
Sheridan, Philip, 264
Sherman Antitrust Act, 142, 283, 286
Sherman, Maude, 688
Sherman, William Tecumseh, 264, 1053–54
Shi'a, 222
Shiite, 507
Shikai, Yuan, 243
Shimabara Uprising, 232
Shintoism, 514–15
Shockley, William Bradford, 1054
Shorter, Wayne, 73
Shostakovich, Dmitry, 50
Shu, 481
Siam, 225
Sibelius, Jean, 50
Siddhartha Gautama, 218
Sidney, Philip, 349
Siduri, 479
Siena cathedral, 7
Sierra Leone, 849
Siger de Brabant, 489
Sigismund II, 234
Signac, Paul, 98
Sigurd, 482
Sikhism, 515
Sikhs, 238
silicon, 589
Silk Route, 227
Silla, 219, 223
Sillitoe, Alan, 358
Silurian period, 596
silver, 589
Silver, Horace, 72
Silverman, Fred, 418
Simenon, Georges, 371
Simpson, James Young, 439
Simpson, O.J., 700
Sina, Ibn, 437
Sinatra, Frank, 71, 1054
Sinclair, Upton, 285
Singapore, 849
single lens reflex cameras, development of, 109
Sino-Japanese War, 242
Sirens, 478
SIRTF (Space Infrared Telescope Facility), *534*
Sisley, Alfred, 98
Sistine Chapel, 92–93
Sisyphus, 478
Sitting Bull, 1054
Sivadi, Raja, 238
Skadi, 482
Skepticism, 488
skin, human, 559
Skinner, B.F., 627
skyscrapers, development of, 641
slashes (punctuation), 791
Slaughter-House Cases, 304
slave narrative, in American literature, 362
slavery, 273, 281
Slovakia, 849
smallpox, 460
Smith, Adam, 121, 1054
Smith, E. E. "Doc", 373
Smith, Emmitt, 1054
Smith, John, 272
Smithson, Robert, 103
Smollett, Tobias, 355
Snow, C. P., 357
Snow, John, 438
Soccer, 734–37
  club, 734–35
  glossary of terms, 735–37
  history of, 734
  rules of, 734
  World Cup champions, men, 737–38
  World Cup champions, women, 737
Social Security Act of 1935, 288
Socialist Party, 286
Socrates, 486, 1054
Soderbergh, Steven, 30
sodium, 589
SOFIA (Stratospheric Observatory for Infrared Astronomy), 534
Soka Gakkai, 517
solar power, development of, 642–43
solar system, 534–45
  direct sampling of, 532–33
Solomon, 214
Solomon Islands, 849–50
Solon, 215, 1054
Solzhenitsyn, Aleksandr, 343, 1054–55
Somalia, 252, 850
somatization disorder, 631
Somme, Battle of the, 267
sonata, 57
Sondheim, Stephen, 51, 63
Song Dynasty, 223
Songgye, Yi, 229
Songhay, Kingdom of, 225
sonnet, development of, 349
Sons of Liberty, 275
Sony Corporation, 29
Sophists, 486–88
Sophocles, 375, 1055
Soto, Hernando de, 272
soul music, 65
sound recording, development of, 641–42
Sousa, John Philip, 61
South Africa, 850
South America, 184–85, 216, 220, 228–29, 232–33, 241
  climate, 184
  economy, 185
  people, 185
  physical features, 184
South Carolina (U.S. State), 873
South Carolina v. Katzenbach, 307
South Dakota (U.S. State), 873
South Sea Bubble, 164
Southern Christian Leadership Council, 250
Southey, Robert, 352
Soviet Union, 33, 244, 246–48, 251, 269
Soyinka, Akinwande Oluwole, 348, 1055
spacecraft, direct sampling of planets by, 532–33
Spain, 236–37, 850–51
  wines of, 942
Spanish (language), 803
Spark, Muriel, 357
Sparta, 215, 253
Spector, Phil, 74
spectroscopy, *534*
speech, parts of, 768–72
spelling, 795–97
  words most frequently misspelled, 796
Spender, Stephen, 354
Spenser, Edmund, 349, 1055
spices, 933
Spielberg, Steven, 28, 29, 1055
spinach, 932
spinal cord, 561
spinal tap, 464
Spinoza, Baruch, 491, 1055
Spitz, Mark, 762, 1055
Spock, Benjamin, 1055
Springsteen, Bruce, 78, 1055–56
squash, 932
Sri Lanka, 851
St. Denis, Ruth, 18–19
St. John de Crèvecoeur, J. Hector, 359
St. Louis,Missouri, 882
St. Mihiel, 268
stagflation, 162
Stalin, Joseph, 33, 244, 246, 1056
Stalingrad, Battle of, 269
Stamp Act, 275
Standard Oil, 146
Standard Oil Co. of New Jersey v. United States, 304
Stanford-Binet intelligence test, 626
Stanislavski, Constantin, 381
Stanley Cup Champions, 714
Stanton, Elizabeth Cady, 1056
Stark, Brigadier General John, 259

Starr, Ringo, 1056
stars
  death of, 542–43
  interstellar medium and star formation, 541–42
  life cycles of, 541
  main sequence, 542
States, U.S., 862–75
statistics, 393
steam engines, development of, 638
Steffens, Lincoln , 285
Stegner, Wallace , 364
Stein, Gertrude, 364, 1056
Steinbeck, John, 365, 1056
Steinbrenner, George, 674
Steinem, Gloria, 1056
Steiner, Max, 51
Stendhal, 341, 1056
Stephen, 1056
stereo (music), 28
Sternberg, Joseph von, 26
Sterne, Laurence , 355
Stevens, Wallace, 1057
Stewart, James, 26, 1057
Stieglitz, Alfred, 114, 1057
Stirling, James Frazer, 1057
stock funds, 167
stock markets, 163–66
Stockhausen, Karlheinz, 50–51
Stoicism, 488
Stonehenge, 2, 530
Stoppard, Tom , 383
Stout, Rex , 370
Stowe, Harriet Beecher, 280, 362, 1057
Stratemeyer, Edward L. , 371
Strauss, Johann, 50
Strauss, Richard, 49, 1057
Stravinsky, Igor, 51, 1057
Streep, Meryl, 1057
Streisand, Barbra, 1058
stress, acute, 628
Strindberg, August, 381, 1058
string quartet, 57
string theory, 613
Stroheim, Erich von, 24
stroke, 451
strontium, 589
Strutt, Jedediah, 141
Stuart Dynasty, 233
Student National Coordinating Council, 250
Sturgeon, Theodore , 373
Sturges, Preston , 26
subatomic particles, 617–18
Suckling, John , 350
Sudan, 851
Suez Canal, 242, 248
Sufism, 507
Sugar Act, 274
Sugarhill Gang, 65
Suharto, 1058
Sui Dynasty, 223
suite, 57–58
Sukarno, 1058
Sulayman the Magnificent (Sueleyman I), 229, 1058
sulfur, 589
Sulla, Lucius Cornelius, 294, 1058
Sullivan, Louis Henri, 9
Sumarokov, Aleksandr, 342
Sumeria, Astronomy in, 530
Summa Theologiae, 489
Sun Yat-sen, 1058–59
Sundance Institute, 30
Sunni Muslims, 222, 507
Super Bowl results, 707–08
Super NES, 670
supersymmetry, 613
Supreme Court, U.S., important decisions, 303–08
Suriname, 851
Surrealism, 100
Sutton, Walter , 440
Swan, Joseph, 639
Swaziland, 851–52
Sweden, 852
sweet potato, 932
Swift, Jonathan, 350, 1059
Swimming, 760–62
  basic strokes, 760–61
  history of, 760
  in the Olympics, 761–62
Swinburne, Algernon Charles, 352
Switzerland, 852
Symbiosis, 571–76
Symbolism (in drama), 382
Symbolists, 341
symphonic poem, 58
symphony, 58
Syria, 852
Syria-Palestine, 213
systemic lupus erythematosus (lupus), 446

T

Tacitus (Cornelius Tacitus), 1059
Taft, William Howard, 286, 1059
Taft-Hartley Act, 288
Taiping Rebellion, 242
Taiwan, 35, 239, 852–53
Taj Mahal, 230
Tajikistan, 853
Takamine, Jokichi , 440
Takauji, Ashikaga , 229
Talbot, William Henry Fox, 105, 106, 1059
Taliban, 252
Talleyrand, Charles-Maurice de, 1059
Tally, Thomas H., 22
Talmud, 496
Tamerlane. see Timur
Tan, Amy , 365
Tang Dynasty, 220, 223
Tang the Victorious, 213
tantalum, 589
Tantalus, 478
Tanzania, 853
Taoism, 515
Tarantino, Quentin , 30
Tarbell, Ida , 285
Tarkovsky, Andrei , 33
Taro, 932
Tartarus, 478
Tartikoff, Brandon , 424
Tate, Allen , 363
Tax Policy, 128–29
Taxonomy, 551
Taylor, 279
Taylor, Cecil, 72
Taylor, Edward , 359
Taylor, Elizabeth, 1059
Taylor, Zachary, 279, 1059
Tchaikovsky, Pyotr, 56, 1059–60
tea, 939–40
Tea Act, 275
Teapot Dome Scandal, 287
technetium, 589
technology, 633–70
  significant technologies, history of, 633–46
Tecumseh, 277, 1060
Tefnut, 481
Teive, Diogo de, 272
telegraph, development of, 141, 639–40
Telemachus, 478
telephone, development of, 141–42, 639–40
telescope
  invention of reflecting, 531
  uses in astronomy, 533–34
Television
  and VCRs, 422
  cable television, beginnings of, 420
  deregulation, 422–24
  early programming, 413
  history of, 411–29
  and home video, 422
  in the digital era, 426–29
  invention of, 411–12, 640
  miniseries, 419
  network news, 416
  prime time soaps, 419–20
  programming in the network era, 417–19
  public broadcasting, 416
  rise of commercial, 412–15
  three major networks today, 424–26
tellurium, 589
temples, Roman, 5
Temujin, 226
Tennessee (U.S. State), 873–74
Tennis, 725–29
  glossary of terms, 728–29
  Grand Slam champions, men, 730–31
  Grand Slam champions, women, 732–33
  history of, 725–27
  rules of, 727–28
Tennyson, Alfred (Lord), 261, 352, 1060
Tenochtitlán, 228
Tenrikyo, 517
Teotihuacán, 13, 220
terbium, 589
Terence, 375
Terminus, 478
Terra Amata, 2
Tesla, Nikola, 639, 1060
testes, 564
Tet offensive, 249, 290
Tethys, 478
Texas (U.S. State), 874
Thackeray, William Makepeace, 1060
Thailand, 853–54
Thalberg, Irving, 26
Thales of Miletus, 485
thallium, 589
Thanatos, 478
Tharp, Twyla, 19
Thatcher, Margaret, 1060
Theater. See Drama
Théatre Robert-Houdin, 22
Themis, 478
Theophrastus, 548
Theosophy, 517
thermodynamics, laws of, 615–16
Thermopylae, 253
Theseus, 478
Thetis, 478
Third Coalition, 261
Third Intermediate Period, 214
Third Republic, 241
Thirty Years War, 234, 256

Thisbe, 478
Thomas, Dylan, 354, 1060
Thompson, Benjamin, 608
Thomson, J. J., 1060–61
Thomson, Virgil, 50–51
Thor, 482
Thoreau, Henry David, 360, 1061
thorium, 589
Thorpe, Jim, 699, 754, 1061
Thoth, 481
3-D films, 28
Three Kingdoms Period, 219
Thucydides, 216, 338, 1061
Thulium, 589–90
Thutmose I, 213
Thutmose II, 213
Thutmose III Menkheperre, 213, 1061
thyroid gland, 564
Tiamat, 479
Tiananmen Square, 251
Tiberius (Tiberius Claudius Nero Caesar), 1061
Tiepolo, Giambattista, 94
Timur (also known as Tamerlane, Tamburlaine, or Timur Lenk), 226, 1061
tin, 590
Tin Pan Alley, 62
Tinker, Grant, 424
Tintoretto, 93
tintypes, 107
Tiomkin, Dmitri, 51
Tiresias, 478
Tisch, Lawrence, 426
titanium, 590
Titans, 478
Titchener, Edward Bradford, 626
Titian, 93, 1061
Tito, Josip Broz, 247
toccata, 58
Togo, 854
Tojo, Hideki, 269
Tokugawa shogunate, 231, 239
Toland, Gregg, 26
Tolkien, J.R.R., 373
Tolstoy, Leo, 343, 1061–62
Toltec, 224
tomato, 932
Tonga, 854
Tonkin, 243
Tony Awards, 893–97
Toomer, Jean, 365
Toulouse-Lautrec, Henri, 98
Tourette syndrome, 629
Townshend Acts, 275
Track and Field, 753–55
trade, free, 134
Trafalgar, 261
Traherne, Thomas, 349
Trail of Tears, 278
Transcendental Meditation, 517
Transcendentalism (in literature), 360–62
transfermium elements, 590
transistor, invention of, 638
Treaty of Aix-la-Chapelle, 257
Treaty of Amiens, 261
Treaty of Frankfurt, 265
Treaty of Guadelupe Hidalgo, 279
Treaty of Hubertusburg, 258
Treaty on the International Law of the Sea, 251
Treaty of Kuchuk Kainarji, 237, 238
Treaty of Nanking, 242
Treaty of Paris, 238, 258, 261, 274, 285
Treaty of Tientsin, 242
Treaty of Tordesillas, 232
Treaty of Versailles, 268
Trevor, William, 358
Triassic period, 596
triglycerides, 948
Trinidad and Tobago, 854
A Trip to the Moon, 22
Triple Alliance, 244
Tripolitan War, 242
Triton, 478
Trotsky, Leon, 1062
Truffaut, François, 1062
truffles, 934
Truman Doctrine, 247
Truman, Harry S, 270, 1062
tuberculosis (TB), 460–61
Tubman, Harriet, 1062
Tucson, Arizona, 882
Tudor dynasty, 256
Tudors, 228
Tula, 228
Tulipmania, 164
Tulsa, Oklahoma, 882
tuna, 935
tungsten, 590
Tunisia, 854
Turgenev, Ivan, 343, 1062
Turing Machine, 647–48
Turkey, 854–55, 936
Turkish (language), 804
Turkmenistan, 855
Turner, J.M.W., 96, 1062
Turner, Nathaniel, 278, 1062
Turner, Ted, 420
turnips, 932–34
Tutankhamen Nebkheperre, 214, 1063
Tuvalu, 855
Twain, Mark, 363, 1063
Twentieth Century Fox, 26
Tyche, 478
Tyler, John, 1063
Typhoid, 461
Tyr, 482
Tyson, Mike, 758

U

Uganda, 855
Ukraine, 855–56
Ullr, 482
ultrasound, 464
ultraviolet radiation, *533*
Ulysses, 357
Umayyad Dynasty, 222
Un Chien Andalou, 34
Uncle Tom's Cabin, 280
Unification Church, 517
Unitarian Universalist Association, 504
Unitas, Johnny, 1063
United Arab Emirates, 856
United Artists, 26, 29
United Kingdom, 856
United Nations, 246
United States, 856–57
  cities, 876–82
  Civil War, 261–65
  climate, 183
  Constitution of, 313–27
  geographic distribution of population, 186
  geographic divisions, 185–86
  geography of, 185–88,
  physiographic regions of, 186–87
  history of, 272–92
  regional populations and percentages, 186
  states, 861–76
  urban areas and urbanization, 186
  wines of, 943
United States v. E.C. Knight Co., 304
United States v. Lopez, 308
United States v. Nixon, 307
United Steel Corp., 142
Unity Temple, 9
UNIVAC, 648
universe, contents of, 534–45
University of California Regents v. Bakke, 307–08
ununbiium, 590
ununhexium, 590
ununnilium, 590
ununquadium, 590
unununium, 590
Upanishads, 215
Updike, John, 368, 1063
upper GI series, 464–66
uranium, 590
Uranus, 478
Uranus, features and composition, 540
Urban II (Pope), 254
urbanization, world, 189–90
urinary system, human, 559
Urshanabi, 479
Uruguay, 857
usage. See Writer's Guide
Utah (U.S. State), 874
Utu, 479
Uzbekistan, 857

V

V-E Day, 270
V-J Day, 270
Valenti, Jack, 29
Valentino, Rudolph, 1063
Valéry, Paul, 342
Vali, 482
Valkyries, 482
Valley Forge, 260
Valois, 228
Van Buren, Martin, 1063
van Eyck, Jan, 92
vanadium, 590
Vandals, 218
Van Gogh, Vincent, 98
Vanuatu, 857
Vasco da Gama, 230
Vásquez de Coronado, Francisco, 272
Vásquez, Pedro, 272
Vaudeville, 381
Vaughan, Henry, 349
veal, 936–37
Vedas, 215
vegetables, 929–32
veins, 557
Velázquez, Diego, 94, 1064
Venezuela, 857
Venturi, Robert, 11, 1064
Venus, features and composition, 535–36
verbs, 768–69
  common errors, 779
  correct usage, 775–78
  irregular, 776
  mood, 777–78
  tense, 775–77
  voice, 778
Verdi, Guiseppe, 50, 1064
Verdun, 267
Verlaine, Paul, 341, 1064

Vermeer, Johannes, 94, 1064
Vermont (U.S. State), 874
Verne, Jules, 373
Verrazano, Giovanni de, 272
Vertov, Dziga, 32
Very Large Telescope (VLT), 534
Very Long Baseline Array (telescope), 534
Vesalius, Andreas, 234, 437
Vicksburg, 263
Victor Emmanuel II, 240
Victoria (Alexandrina Victoria), 1064
Vidar, 482
video games, history of, 666–70
Vidocq, François Eugène, 369
Vidor, King, 24
Viet Cong, 249, 290
Vietminh, 249
Vietnam, 248, 858
Vietnam War, 249–50
Vietnamization, 249
Vikings, 272
Villa, Pancho, 1064
Virgil, 339, 1065
Virginia Beach, Virginia, 882
Virginia, Commonwealth of (U.S. State), 874–75
viruses, 548
Visconti, Luchino, 34
visible radiation, 533
Visigothic, 218
vitamin-related diseases, 461
vitamins, 947
  value of, 948–50
Vitruvius, 636
Vivaldi, Antonio, 44, 1065
Vogt, A.E. van, 373
volcanoes, 601–02
Volkswagen, 148
Volta, Alessandro, 608, 639, 1065
Voltaire, Francois Marie Arouet de, 340, 1065
voluntary (music), 54
Vonnegut, Kurt, 368
Voting Rights Act, 290
Voyager (space probe), 533
Vsesoyuznyi Gosudarstvenyi Institut Kinematografia, 33
Vuillard, Edouard, 99

W

Wagner, Richard, 50, 1065
Wahhabi, 238
Wain, John, 358
Wajda, Andrzej, 33
Walcott, Derek, 1065
Walesa, Lech, 1065–66
Walker, Alice, 365
Wallace, Alfred Russel, 565
Waller, Edmund, 350
Walter the Penniless, 254
Walthall, Henry B., 23
War on Terror, 252
War of the Austrian Succession, 238, 257–58
War of the Spanish Succession, 257
War on Poverty, 290
Ward, Aaron Montgomery, 143
Warhol, Andy, 102, 1066
Warner Brothers, 25, 26, 28
Warner, Susan, 361
Warren, Earl, 1066
Warren, Robert Penn, 363, 1066
Warring States Period, 215, 231
Wars, Major, 253–70
Wars of Religion, 233
Wars of the Roses, 228, 256
Washington (U.S. State), 875
Washington, D.C., 882
Washington, George, 258, 276, 1066
Waterloo, 236, 261
Watson, James Dewey, 567, 1066
Watson, John, 627
Watt, James, 138, 638, 1066–67
Waugh, Evelyn, 357, 1066–67
Wayne, John, 26, 1067
weather, 173
Weaver, Sylvester "Pat," 414
Weber, Max, 1067
Webster, Daniel, 279, 1067
Webster, John, 379
Webster, Noah, 360, 1067
Wedekind, Franz, 382
Weight Watchers, 951–52
weights and measures, 921–24
  area, 921
  dry volume, 922
  electrical measure, 924
  fluid volume, 922
  force, work/energy, power, 923–24
  length or distance, 921
  mass and weight, 922–23
  temperature, 923
  time, 923
Weill, Kurt, 382
Weimar Republic, 244
Weissmuller, Johnny, 761, 1067
Welch, Jack, 424
Welfare Reform Act, 292
Welles, Orson, 26, 1067
Wellesley, Arthur, First Duke of Wellington, 1067
Wells, H.G., 373, 1067–68
Wells, Horace, 439
Welty, Eudora, 364, 1068
Wesker, Arnold, 382
West Bank, 251
West Virginia (U.S. State), 875
West Virginia Board of Education v. Barnette, 306
West, Benjamin, 95
West, Mae, 1068
Western Swing, 66–67
Westminster Abbey, 7
Wharton, Edith, 363, 1068
Wharton, Thomas, 438
wheat, 926–27
Wheatley, Phillis, 359
wheels, development of, 635–36
Whiskey Rebellion, 276
Whistler, James McNeill, 97, 1068
Whitehead, Alfred North, 493
Whitman, Walt, 361, 1068
Whitney, Eli, 141, 1068
Wichita, Kansas, 882
wide-screen, 28
Wigman, Mary, 18
Wild Strawberries, 35
Wilde, Oscar, 353, 1068
Wilder, Billy, 27, 1068–69
Wilder, Thornton, 383, 1069
Wilderness, Battle of the, 264
Wilhelm II, Kaiser, 244
William I of Prussia, 265
William III, 1069
William III of Orange, 235
William of Normandy, 227
William of Ockham, 489
William of Orange, 1069
William the Conqueror (William I), 255, 1069
Williams, Hank, 67
Williams, Ralph Vaughan, 52
Williams, Roger, 273
Williams, Ted, 1069
Williams, Tennessee, 383, 1069
Williams, William Carlos, 364, 1069
Willis, Thomas, 438
Wilson, Angus, 358
Wilson, Barbara, 371
Wilson, Brian, 75
Wilson, Harriet, 362
Wilson, Woodrow, 268, 286
windmills, development of, 636
winds, 172–73
Wine
  and food, 944–47
  Argentinian, 944
  Australian, 943–44
  Chilean, 944
  European, 942–43
  French, 940–41
  glossary of, 945–47
  history of, 940
  Italian, 941–42
  regions, 940–44
  South African, 944
  South American, 944
  Spanish, 942
  made in United States, 943
Winthrop, John, 358, 1070
Wisconsin (U.S. State), 875–76
Withering, William, 438
Wittgenstein, Ludwig, 494, 1070
Wladislaw II, 227
Wolf, Hugo, 49
Women's Rights Convention, 279
Wood, Grant, 100
Wood, Robert, 418
Woods, Tiger, 718, 1070
Woolf, Virginia, 356, 1070
Woolworth, Frank Winfield, 143
words, commonly confused, 798–99
Wordsworth, William, 351, 1070
World
  births, deaths, and population growth, 188
  islands and archipelagos, 198–204
  languages, 801–04
  largest countries, by population, 188
  largest urban areas, 1950-2015, 189
  mountain ranges, 204–06
  oceans, 190
  population, 188–90
  rivers and canals, 194–98
  rivers, by length, 199–200
  seas, gulfs, and straits, 190–94
  oceans, 190
World Bank, 131, 246
World Trade Center, 252
World Trade Organization, 250

World War I, 265–68
World War II, 247, 268–70, 288
worms and disease, 461–62
Worms Cathedral, 6
Wounded Knee, 284
Wren, Christopher, 8, 1070
Wright brothers, 638, 1071
Wright, Frank Lloyd, 9–10, 1070
Wright, Richard, 365
Wright, Wilbur, 1071
Writer's Guide
  abbreviations, 793
  acronyms, 794
  adjectives, definition, 769–70
  adjective usage, 781–84
  adverbs, definition, 770
  adverb usage, 781–84
  apostrophes, 787
  brackets, 790–91
  capitalization, 799–800
  clauses, 773–74
  colons, 790
  commas, 784–86
  commonly confused words, 798
  compound words, 768, 792, 797
  conjunctions, 771
  dashes, 789
  degree, in adjectives and adverbs, 781–82, 783
  dialogue and quotations, 800
  ellipses, 791
  exclamation point, 784
  foreign terms, 789
  homophones, 797
  hyphens, 791–93
  infinitives, 778
  interjections, definition, 771
  italics, 788–89
  mechanics, 793–95
  mood, in verbs, 777–78
  nouns, definition, 768
  numbers, 793
  parentheses, 790
  participles, dangling, 782
  parts of speech, 768–71
  period, 784
  phrases, 772–73
  plurals, 796–97
  possession, 787
  prefixes, 793, 796
  prepositional phrases, 782–83
  prepositions, definition, 771
  pronouns, definition, 769
  pronoun usage, 778–81
  proper nouns, 799–800
  punctuation, 784–93
  question mark, 784
  quotation marks, 787–88
  semicolons, 786–87
  sentence classification, 774
  sentence grammar, 772–84
  sentence structure, 772–74
  sentence types, 774–75
  slashes, 791
  spelling, 795–99
  suffixes, 795–96
  tense, in verbs, 775–77
  titles, 794
  verb errors, common, 779
  verbs, definition, 768–69
  verbs, irregular, 776
  verb tense, 775–77
  verb usage, 775–78
  voice, in verbs, 778
Wu (Emperor), 219
Wunderlich, Carl, 439
Wundt, Wilhelm, 625
Wyatt, Thomas, 349
Wyoming (U.S. State), 876

X

X radiation, *533*
Xavier, Francis, 232
Xbox, 670
Xenon, 590–91
Xerxes I (The Great), 253, 1071
Xia Dynasty, 213
Xiaoping, Deng, 251
Xiuquan, Hong, 242
XYZ Affair, 276

Y

Yalta Conference, 246
Yamasaki, Minoru, 11
Yat-sen, Sun, 243, 245
Yayoi civilization, 219
Yeats, William Butler, 353, 1071
yellow fever, 462
Yeltsin, Boris, 1071
Yemen, 858
Yimou, Zhang, 35
yoga, 509
yogurt, 938
Yoritomo, Minamoto no, 229
Yorktown, 260
Young, Brigham, 1071
Young, Cy, 672, 1071
Young, Thomas, 608
Youngstown Sheet and Tube Co. v. Sawyer, 306
Ypres, Third Battle of, 267
ytterbium, 591
yttrium, 591
Yuan Dynasty, 226, 229

Z

Zaharias, Babe Didrikson, 718
Zama, 254
Zambia, 858
Zanussi, Krysztof, 33
Zapata, Emiliano, 1072
Zapotec, 216
Zátopek, Emil, 747, 754, 1072
Zedong, Mao, 245, 248, 250, 251
Zeno of Citium, 488
Zeno of Elea, 485
Zenta, Battle of, 238
Zeus, 471
Zheng, He, 229
Zhou Enlai, 215, 1072
Zhu Yuanzhang, 229
Zhukovsky, Vasily, 343
Zimbabwe, 858
Zimmerman Telegram, 287
zinc, 591
Zionist movement, 247
zirconium, 591
Ziusudra, 479
zoetrope, 22
Zola, Emile, 341, 1072
Zone diet, 952
Zoroaster, 214, 1072
Zulu, 237
Zworykin, Vladimir, 411